COMBINED INDEX TO THE NEW BOOK OF KNOWLEDGE

The index pages reprinted here also appear,
letter by letter, at the end of each volume.

This extra guide is prepared especially for school and library use.

ISBN 0-7172-0504-5
Library of Congress Catalog Card Number: 72-91051

HOW TO USE THE INDEX

When a traveler visits a large city, he uses a map or a guide to help him find his way about. When you want to find information in an encyclopedia, you need a guide too. The Index is your guide to the information in all 20 volumes of THE NEW BOOK OF KNOWLEDGE.

When you start to look something up in this encyclopedia, it is important always to refer to the Index first. It will tell you where you can find what you want to know; and sometimes, if you need just one key fact, it will tell you all you want to know.

The Index is designed to bring together all the references to information about a particular subject. It tells you where in this set that subject, and every subject related to it, is discussed. In most cases when you use the Index to look up a topic you will find along with it a short definition or identifying phrase. This brief definition explains a term that may be unfamiliar to you, and helps you make sure you have found the topic you are looking for. Because it includes these definitions, the Index is called a Dictionary Index. You will also find throughout the Index more than 5,000 brief biographies and summaries of subjects not included in the main articles.

HOW THE INDEX IS ARRANGED

Each volume of THE NEW BOOK OF KNOWLEDGE contains the corresponding alphabetical division of the Index.

Suppose the subject you want to find out about is anthropology. If you look it up in the Index, this is what you will see:

Anthropology (an-thro-POL-ogy), study of man   **A** 300–09
  archeology related to   **A** 349, 364
  blood groups studied   **B** 258
  prehistoric man   **P** 442–46
  races of man   **R** 29–32
  research methods   **R** 182
  See also Ancient civilizations; Prehistoric art

The subject you are looking up, **Anthropology**, is called the **heading** and is in boldface type. In parentheses next to the heading there is a

pronunciation guide (an-thro-POL-ogy). This is provided for all heading words that may be difficult to pronounce. (The pronunciation guide is described on pages 579, 580, and 581 of this volume.)

Next to the pronunciation guide are a few words that identify the topic—"study of man." These words are called the **identification**. A volume letter (in boldface type) and page numbers follow the identification—**A** 300-09. **A** tells you in which volume the article on **Anthropology** is and 300-09 tells you on which pages of the A volume you will find the main article on Anthropology. The heading, its identification, and its volume and page numbers together make up the **entry**.

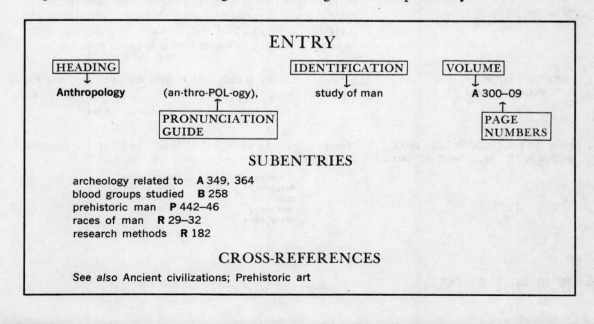

ENTRY

HEADING — Anthropology

(an-thro-POL-ogy), — PRONUNCIATION GUIDE

IDENTIFICATION — study of man

VOLUME — A 300–09 — PAGE NUMBERS

SUBENTRIES

archeology related to   A 349, 364
blood groups studied   B 258
prehistoric man   P 442–46
races of man   R 29–32
research methods   R 182

CROSS-REFERENCES

See *also* Ancient civilizations; Prehistoric art

Beneath the entry there is a list of additional references to your subject. These references are called **subentries**. They are indented and arranged in alphabetical order. The subentries refer to all the important information about your subject throughout the set. Unless you look in the Index you may not think of all the points about your subject that have been covered in the encyclopedia. (Subentries, in turn, may appear as main entries in other parts of the Index under their own initial letters.)

In the case of **Anthropology** there are only a few subentries. But sometimes, if you look up a broad topic, such as **Vocations** or **Sports**, you will find dozens of subentries. Subentries are really a kind of listing that is helpful if you want to review the whole of a particular field.

Finally, in the last line of the **Anthropology** listing, you come to the words *"See also,"* followed by two Index headings. The *"See also"* listings are called **cross-references**. They tell you where to look to find more information related to your subject. Cross-references are guides to Index entries, not to article titles.

Pictures are noted in the Index only if they fall on a page that is different from the main entry, or if they are to be found in a different article.

Bluebirds, junior group of Camp Fire Girls **G** 37; pictures **G** 38, 39

Bridges B 395–401
Tower Bridge, London, picture **E** 305

Maps are not noted in the Index. If you look up a country, state, or province article, you will find at least one map, often with its own index, included within the pages of the article.

Parentheses, besides being used to enclose pronunciation guides, are also used to enclose initials, alternative forms of names, and dates.

Initials: Air Route Traffic Control (ARTC)

Alternative forms of names:

> **Aaron, Hank** (Henry Louis Aaron)
> **Austro-Prussian War** (Seven Years War)

Dates: Life dates of persons are given in parentheses when there is a brief biographical sketch of the person.

Adamic, Louis (1899-1951), American author, b. Blato, Dalmatia (now Yugoslavia). He came to United States (1913) and was naturalized (1918). Many of his stories and books are about immigrants in United States. He was first recognized for *The Native's Return*, about life in Yugoslavia. His other works include *Laughing in the Jungle* and *My America*.

Dates are also used to distinguish between persons of the same name:

Adams, Charles Francis (1807–1886), American diplomat
Adams, Charles Francis (1866–1954), American lawyer

Dates are also given for historical events which are summarized briefly in the Index.

Atlantic Charter (August, 1941)

WHAT SHALL I LOOK FOR?

Think of the specific word about which you need information and look for that. Go directly to the name you usually use for the thing you want. (It will most often be the plural form.) If you want to find out about ants, turn directly to **Ants** in the Index. You do not have to hunt first under **Insects**, although you would find ants listed there too.

HOW DO I LOOK UP A PERSON'S NAME?

Look for the last name, just as you do when you use the telephone book.

Blake, William, English poet and artist **E** 259

HOW DO I LOOK UP NAMES THAT BEGIN WITH "M'," "Mc" OR "Mac"?

Names beginning with "M'," "Mac," and "Mc" are placed in alphabetical order just as they are spelled.

MacArthur, Douglas	Maze
Macbeth	Mba, Leon
Mac Cool	McBurney
Machinery	McKinley
Macy, Anne	

WHAT IF THE PERSON IS KNOWN BY MORE THAN ONE NAME?

Some persons are known by more than one name. Such entries are listed by their best-known names: **Buffalo Bill**; **Twain, Mark**; **Napoleon**. However, if you should look under the person's official name, a cross-reference will tell you the right place to look:

Bonaparte, Napoleon see Napoleon I
Clemens, Samuel Langhorne see Twain, Mark
Cody, William Frederick see Buffalo Bill

HOW DO I LOOK UP NAMES BEGINNING WITH "SAINT" OR "ST."?

Saint is always spelled out. Place names beginning with Saint are listed under **Saint**.

Saint Louis, Missouri

But the names of saints are listed according to the name. "Saint" is placed after the name.

Paul, Saint

WHAT IF THERE IS MORE THAN ONE SPELLING FOR MY TOPIC?

If you use a different (but correct) spelling from the Index, you will also find a *"see"* reference.

Archaeology see Archeology

HOW ARE THE HEADINGS IN THE INDEX ARRANGED?

Because this is a Dictionary Index, it is arranged like a dictionary, letter by letter.

Mink
Minneapolis
Minnesingers
Minnesota

WHAT IF A HEADING IS MADE UP OF MORE THAN ONE WORD?

Even when headings are made up of more than one word, they are still arranged alphabetically, letter by letter.

New Amsterdam
Newark
Newberry
New Castle

When there is a comma in the heading, the letter-by-letter arrangement goes through to the comma only—so that all the same names will be brought together.

Black, color
Black, Hugo
Black, Joseph
Blackball
Black Hills
Black market
Black widow spiders

WHAT ABOUT WORDS IN PARENTHESES, TITLES, AND ROMAN NUMERALS?

The alphabetical arrangement of headings is not affected by words in parentheses, titles, or Roman numerals. Just look up the heading as if it did not contain these added words or symbols.

Adler (AHD-ler), Alfred
Adler (ADD-ler), Felix
• • •
Gregory, Lady Augusta
Gregory, Dick
Gregory, Saint
• • •

John I, II, and III, books of the Bible, New Testament
John, king of England
John II, king of France
John XXIII, pope
John, Saint, one of the Twelve Apostles

HOW DO I LOOK UP A HEADING THAT BEGINS WITH A NUMBER?

If a number is the first word in a heading, the number is spelled out and put in its alphabetical place.

Seven Cities of Cibola
Seven seas
Seven Sisters
Seventeenth Amendment to the United States Constitution
Seven wonders of the ancient world

If a number appears in any other place in a heading, the rule is simple: numbers come before letters.

Carbon
Carbon 14
Carbon black

DO I LOOK UP "A," "AN," AND "THE"?

"A," "an," and "the" are not used in alphabetizing. If any one of these words is part of the title of a book or play, the word is put at the end of the title.

Big Wave, The
Midsummer Night's Dream, A

HOW ARE INITIALS INDEXED?

You will find initials in their proper alphabetical order. A *"see"* reference along with them will lead you to the heading for which the initials stand.

CIA see Central Intelligence Agency

HOW DO I LOOK UP THE ABBREVIATION "MT."?

Mount is always spelled out and is placed after the name.

Everest, Mount

The word "lake," too, as a geographical term, is placed after the name.

Michigan, Lake

But you can look up the names of forts, towns, and rivers just as you would say them.

Fort Dearborn   **Mount Vernon**
Lake Placid   **Mississippi River**

HOW DO I LOOK UP A POEM?

Poems are listed individually by name, and also by their authors.

To Autumn, poem by John Keats   **K 201**

Keats, John
  "To Autumn"   **K 201**

HOW DO I LOOK UP A STORY?

If the story you are looking for has been included in its complete form, you will find it listed under the heading **Stories, told in full**. If the story you want is part of a longer work, you will find it listed individually by its name.

Oliver Twist, book by Charles Dickens, excerpt

Other listings similar to **Stories, told in full** are **Experiments and projects**; **Hobbies**; **How to**.

NEW BOOK OF KNOWLEDGE
PRONUNCIATION GUIDE

The pronunciation guide used in THE NEW BOOK OF KNOWLEDGE was designed to make the pronunciation of a word immediately recognizable, while making as few changes as possible in the original spelling. Known as the Minimal Change System, it was developed for this encyclopedia by Allana Cummings-Elovson of Columbia University and Jeanne Chall of Harvard University, after extensive research with children in elementary schools.

The system is based on the simplest and most direct way of presenting visually the pronunciation of a word. The words are broken down into letter groups that do not necessarily follow the rules of syllable division. Wherever possible, these letter groups are familiar short words or units. Consequently, the student is not required to learn something new or different from something previously learned. The system avoids the use of special marks, symbols, or extensive phonetic respellings.

It was conclusively demonstrated that students using the Minimal Change System, in comparison with students using other pronunciation systems, (1) make fewer mistakes in pronouncing unfamiliar and difficult words, (2) make fewer mistakes in pronouncing the words when next seen without pronunciation guides, (3) make fewer spelling mistakes in the words after the pronunciation is learned.

USING THE PRONUNCIATION GUIDE

There are only a few basic rules that anyone using this pronunciation guide needs to be familiar with. These rules will apply only when the familiar spelling of a letter group cannot properly identify a sound. In most cases, natural responses to the letter groups will follow previously learned phonetic rules.

Stressed or Accented Syllables

The stressed or accented syllable is indicated by capital letters:

Achilles (ack-ILL-ese)
Adobe (ad-O-be)
Affenpinscher (AF-fen-pin-sher)
Airedale (AIR-dale)

Hard and Soft Consonant Sounds

The sound of c before o, a, and u is regularly hard, like the c in "collar," "card," and "cut." The sound of c before e, i, and y is always soft, like the c in "cent," "city," "fancy."

Canis (CAY-nis) hard c
Ceres (CE-rese) soft c

The sound of g is generally hard before a, o, and u, as in "game," "golf," and "gum." The sound of g is generally soft before i, e, and y, as in "ginger," "gem," and "gymnasium."

Gabriel (GAY-bri-el) hard g
Genetics (gen-ET-ics) soft g

However, there are exceptions to this rule, as illustrated by comparing "ginger" and "girl," "gem" and "get." When the *g* is to retain the hard sound in spite of the vowel that follows it, the letter *h* will appear after the *g*.

Gezo (GHE-zo)
Gibbons (GHIB-ons)

Vowel Sounds

When the vowels *a, e, i, o,* and *u* are followed by a consonant (except for *r* and *l*) in a letter group, the vowel is usually pronounced with the short sound like the *a* in "bat," the *e* in "bet," the *i* in "bit," the *o* in "cot," the *u* in "but." The *r* and *l* sounds often modify the sound of the vowel, as in "tar," "err," "Irish," "cold," "pull."

A final *e* in a letter group gives the previous vowel its alphabetical, or long letter, sound, as illustrated by the vowel sound in "make," "cede," "like," "toe," "mute."

Galen (GALE-en)
Matisse (ma-TECE)

The Vowel A

The *a* sound as in "gate" will appear in different ways, depending upon the word. When the *a* falls at the end of a letter group, *y* or *e* might be added.

Babel (BAY-bel)
Calais (cal-AY)
Cambridge (CAME-bridge)

The *a* followed by a consonant in a letter group is pronounced like the *a* in "cat."

Cabochon (CAB-osh-on)
capacity (ca-PAS-ity)

The *a* pronounced as in "all" will be identified in the spelling.

Galsworthy (GALLS-worthy)
Raleigh (RALL-e)

The Vowel E

E at the end of a letter group is pronounced as in "beat."

Bidault (be-DO)
Cereus (CE-re-us)

When *e* is followed by a consonant in a letter group, it is pronounced as in "bet."

basenji (ba-SEN-ji)
cerebellum (cer-eb-ELL-um)
Chekhov (CHEK-off)

The Vowel I

I followed by a consonant in a letter group is pronounced as in "bit."

Cicero (CIS-er-o)
coalition (co-al-ISH-on)
reciprocal (re-CIP-ro-cal)

The *i* sound as in "bite" may be spelled with a *y* or given other identifiable spelling.

Bayous (BY-os)
benign (be-NINE)
butadiene (bu-ta-DIE-ene)
Goliath (go-LY-ath)

The *i* at the end of a letter group takes the *e* sound of "see."

Gobi (GO-bi)
Pico Turquino (PI-co tur-KI-no)
Rialto (ri-AL-to)
Richelieu (RI-shel-lu)

The Vowel O

O followed by a consonant in a letter group is pronounced like the *o* in "cot."

bibliography (bib-li-OG-raphy)
Biloxi (bil-OX-i)
mosques (MOSKS)

When *o* appears at the end of a letter group, it is pronounced as in "old."

Goliath (go-LY-ath)
Maggiore (ma-JO-ray)

The *oo* combination is pronounced as in "boot."

Baruch (bar-OOK)
Bernoulli (bair-NOOL-li)

The Vowel U

U in a letter group by itself is pronounced like "you."

Uganda (u-GAN-da)
Ukraine (U-kraine)
ukulele (u-ke-LAY-le)

The "you" sound for *u* may also be demonstrated in the spelling, as in:

Ljubljana (l'YOO-bel-ya-na)
Milluni (mi-YU-ni)

or when there is an *e* at the end of the letter group, as in:

Butte (BUTE)

When *u* is followed by a consonant in a letter group, it is pronounced as in "but."

borough (BUR-o)
medulla (me-DUL-la)

When it appears as the last letter in a letter group, it is usually pronounced as in "mood."

Buddha (BU-dha)
Rubaiyat (RU-by-ot)
ruminants (RU-min-ants)

Vowel Combinations

The *ow* combination is pronounced as in "howl."

Maui (MOW-i)
Mauna Kea (MOW-na KAY-a)

The *au* combination is pronounced as in "saw."

Laurier (LAU-ri-ay)
Maugham (MAUM)
Monaural (mon-AUR-al)

Non-English Words and Names

The pronunciations of these are indicated by the closest equivalent sounds in English.

Blois (BLWA)
Böttger (BERT-ker)
Ramazzini (ra-ma-TZI-ni)

A, first letter of the English alphabet **A** 1
See also Alphabet
A-1, term meaning "first-class" **A** 1
AA see Alcoholics Anonymous
Aa (AH-ah), lava **V** 378; picture **V** 379
AAA see Agricultural Adjustment Administration
AAA see American Automobile Association

Aachen (AH-ken) (pop. over 177,000), city in West Germany in state of North Rhine-Westphalia, about 40 miles SW of Cologne, near Belgian and Dutch borders. It is known as Aix-la-Chapelle to the French. An industrial and commercial city, located in a coal-mining region, it produces steel, textiles, electrical machinery, and other manufactures. The city is also noted for its baths, established by the Romans. Charlemagne made the city his northern capital and built its cathedral, which contains his tomb. Until the 16th century it was the coronation city of the Holy Roman emperors. During World War II, Aachen was the first important German city to be captured by the Allies (1944).

Aachen, Treaties of see Aix-la-Chapelle, Treaties of

Aalto (AHL-to), **Alvar Henrik** (1898–   ), Finnish architect and designer, b. Kuortane. He was a leader in the use of functional design in architecture and furniture. His buildings include a theater and sanatorium in Finland, the Finnish Pavilion at the 1939 New York World's Fair, and a dormitory at M. I. T.
modern architecture **A** 387

AAM, air-to-air missiles **M** 347
A & P see Atlantic and Pacific Tea Company, Great
Aardvark, African, mammal **M** 66; picture **M** 69
Aardwolf, hyenalike animal **H** 308

Aaron (A-ron), in Old Testament, brother of Moses and first Jewish high priest, said to have lived sometime between 16th and 13th centuries B.C. He revolted against Moses and built a golden calf, an idol, which Moses destroyed.
Moses and Aaron **M** 468
See also Golden Calf

Aaron, Hank (Henry Louis Aaron) (1934–), American baseball player, Negro, b. Mobile, Ala. He was signed by the Milwaukee (now Atlanta) Braves, 1952. He was National League batting champion, 1956, 1959, chosen the league's Most Valuable Player, 1957, led the league in home runs, 1966 and 1967. He has over 700 home runs. Picture **B** 76.

Aar River, Switzerland, picture **S** 498
AAU see Amateur Athletic Union of the United States
Abaca (ab-a-CA), plant fiber **R** 332
Abacus (AB-a-cus), device for counting **A** 2–3; **N** 392
an early office machine **O** 55
first computing machine **C** 449–50; pictures **C** 451
Japanese soroban **J** 27

Abadan (ah-bah-DAHN) (pop. over 300,000), city in southwest Iran on Abadan Island near Iraq border. Abadan is a port city, situated on the Shatt al-Arab River about 30 miles from the Persian Gulf, and one of the world's largest petroleum-refining centers. The refineries are connected with Iran's rich oil fields by pipelines. The first refinery was established by the British in 1909.

Abalone (ab-al-O-ne), also called ear shell, a mollusk found along coastline in many parts of the world. It has beautiful red, green, or black shell, used to make mother-of-pearl buttons or ornaments.
gastropods **O** 276; shell, picture **S** 148

Abbai (ob-I), name for Blue Nile in Ethiopia **E** 299
Abbate, Niccolo dell', Italian painter **R** 171

Abbe (AB-be), **Cleveland** (1838–1916), American meteorologist, b. New York, N.Y. He issued first daily weather reports in United States. Their popularity led to formation of U.S. Weather Bureau, which he organized. He was responsible for adoption of U.S. standard time.

Abbey Theatre, Dublin, Ireland **D** 298; **I** 394
theater of the west **T** 161
Yeats, William Butler **Y** 344

Abbott, Douglas Charles (1899–   ), Canadian Supreme Court judge, b. Lennoxville, Quebec. He was elected to the House of Commons (1940) and served as minister of national defense (1945) and finance (1946–54). He was appointed to the Supreme Court in 1954.

Abbott, Jacob, American writer **C** 238

Abbott, Sir John Joseph Caldwell (1821–1893), Canadian statesman, b. St. Andrews, Quebec. He was dean of the Faculty of Law at McGill University (1855–80) and a leading authority on commercial law. He served in the Legislative Assembly of Canada and the House of Commons (1859–74, 1881–87) and was appointed to the Senate (1887). He was mayor of Montreal (1887–89), Conservative Party leader, and prime minister (1891–92).

Abbott, Sir John Joseph Caldwell (1821–1893), Canadian lisher, Negro, b. St. Simons Island, Ga. He founded (1905) and edited Chicago *Defender,* a weekly newspaper devoted to interests of the Negro. The paper's strong editorials greatly encouraged migration of southern Negroes to northern industrial centers.
NAACP, history of **N** 96

Abbreviations **A** 4–6
amateur radio **R** 63
how filed in libraries **L** 186
knitting and crocheting **K** 278
shorthand systems based upon **S** 164
states see state articles
used as slang **S** 194
See also individual letters of the alphabet
ABCD see Accelerated Business Collection-Delivery, mail service

ABC Powers, term derived from initials of Argentina, Brazil, and Chile. These nations were closely allied before World War I and formed board (1914) to settle differences between United States and Mexico.

Abdomen, part of the body
doctor's examination of **M** 208h
insects **I** 262, 263
Abdul-Hamid II (OB-dul ha-MEED), sultan of Turkey **T** 329
Abdullah ibn Hussein (ab-dul-LAH ibn huss-INE), king of Jordan **J** 139
Abdul Rahman, Tunku see Rahman, Tunku Abdul
Abel see Cain and Abel

Abel (A-bel), **John Jacob** (1857–1938), American physician and chemist, b. Cleveland, Ohio. He is noted for his studies on chemical composition of animal glands, tissues, and fluids. In the course of research he discovered crystalline form of insulin, essential in treating diabetes, and adrenaline (epinephrine), a substance that raises blood pressure.

Abel (OB-el), **Niels Henrik** (1802–1829), Norwegian mathematician, b. Findoe. His proofs and theorems of algebraic equations have caused him to be known (with K. G. Jacobi) as creator of higher trigonometry.

Abelard (AB-el-ard), **Peter** (1079–1142), French philosopher and theologian, b. near Nantes. His fame as lecturer and teacher attracted students from many countries, but his philosophy offended the Church and he was condemned for heresy (1140). His marriage to Héloïse displeased her uncle Fulbert, who was responsible for a physical attack upon Abelard. After the attack Abelard withdrew to a monastery and Héloïse became a nun. Their letters and love story have become famous.

Aberdeen, Scotland **S** 87
Aberdeen, South Dakota **S** 324
Aberdeen, University of, Scotland **S** 87
Aberdeen Angus, breed of beef cattle **C** 147

Aberhart, William (1878–1943), Canadian political leader, b. Seaforth, Ontario. He formed Social Credit Party of Alberta and was premier of Alberta (1935–43). He supported program of social credit advocating return of government profits to consumers in form of dividends.

Abernathy, Ralph David, Rev. (1926–), American minister and civil rights leader, Negro, b. Linden, Ala. He succeeded Martin Luther King as leader of the Southern Christian Leadership Conference, April, 1968, and in May led the Poor People's Campaign on Washington, D.C. He has been jailed many times in his efforts to bring attention to poverty and discrimination.
continuing struggle in Negro history **N** 104b
See also Poor People's March; Southern Christian Leadership Conference

Aberrations, faults
defects of lenses **L** 148–49
Abhorrers, British political party **P** 378
Abiata, Lake, Ethiopia **E** 300
Abidjan (ab-id-JON), capital of Ivory Coast **I** 489; pictures **D** 119; **I** 491, 492

Abigail, in Old Testament (I Samuel), wife of Nabal and, after Nabal's death, wife of David. Story relates that when David was marching with his armies against Nabal, Abigail met him with a supply of provisions and thus subdued his anger and prevented the fight.

Ability
as measured by intelligence tests **P** 489; **T** 117–18
counseling tests in guidance **G** 399
individual differences in learning abilities **L** 106
learning ability among animals **L** 104
Ability grouping, of students **E** 79
Ablation, removal, as by evaporation, or vaporization
ice loss from glaciers **I** 7
Able seamen **U** 183
ABM see Safeguard anti-ballistic missile
Abolitionist movement, in Negro history **N** 94–95
Adams, John Quincy **A** 15
Brown, John **B** 411–12
Civil War issue **C** 320, 321, 324
Douglass, Frederick **D** 288
Dred Scott case **D** 310, 311
political party opposed to slavery **P** 380
Underground Railroad **U** 11–12
women, role of **W** 212b

Abomey (ah-BO-may), Dahomey **D** 4
Abominable Snowman **H** 129
Aborigines (ab-or-IJ-in-ese)
Australia **A** 499, 501
desert nomads **D** 127–28
school boys, picture **E** 83
Stone Age culture **P** 442

Abracadabra, supposedly magical word used to invoke aid of good spirits in preventing or curing disease or misfortune. When inscribed on an amulet worn around the neck, it was supposed to ward off evil spirits. Word was first used by Sammonicus, a 2nd-century physician.

Abraham, father of the Jews **A** 7; **J** 102
Bible, Old Testament **B** 154
Dome of the Rock mosque in Jerusalem **J** 78–79
Isaac, son of **I** 413
Islam **I** 414–16
Muslim traditions **M** 196
Abraham, Plains of, Quebec **F** 462
battle a part of global war **Q** 16
site of battle of Quebec, picture **F** 461
Abraham Lincoln Birthplace National Historic Site, Kentucky **K** 220
Abrahams, Peter, South African novelist **A** 76b
Abraham's Sacrifice, etching by Rembrandt **D** 358
Abramovich (ab-RA-mo-vich), or **Abramowitz, Shalom Jacob,** Hebrew and Yiddish author **H** 103; **Y** 350
Abrasives (a-BRAI-sives), materials used for grinding and polishing **G** 387–89
grinding machines **T** 219
optical glass grinding **O** 174–75

Abruzzi (a-BRU-tzi), **Duke of the** (Luigi Amedeo Giuseppe Maria Ferdinando Francesco, Prince of Savoy Aosta) (1873–1933), Italian explorer, mountaineer, and naval officer, b. Madrid, Spain. He led North Pole expedition aboard ship Stella Polare, attaining farthest northern latitude (86° 33′ N) of any explorer up to that time (1899–1900). He made first ascent of Mt. Elias, Alaska (1897), commanded Italian Navy in Adriatic during World War I, and developed colonization programs for Italian Somaliland.

Absalom, in Old Testament (II Samuel 13–19), son of King David of Israel. He rebelled against his father and was slain by Joab, David's captain. John Dryden's satirical poem "Absalom and Achitophel" makes use of the story of Absalom.

Absaroka (ab-SA-ro-ka) **Range,** Rocky Mountains, picture **W** 333
Absentee ballots, for voting in elections **E** 113
Absolute magnitude, of stars **S** 406
Absolute zero **H** 90; **M** 177
Absolution, forgiveness **P** 435
Absorbent papers **P** 53

Absorption, process by which one substance takes in (absorbs) another. Liquids, gases, sound, light, and heat are absorbed by porous solids, liquids, and gases. It is also the process by which digested food passes into the bloodstream.

Absorption refrigerating system **R** 137
Abstinence syndrome, in narcotic withdrawal **N** 13
Abstract art, modern art movement **M** 397
African sculpture **A** 76; pictures **A** 74, 75
art of the artist **A** 438g
collage **C** 376–77

Abstract art (continued)
Dutch **D** 362
France **F** 432
Germany's The Blue Rider group **G** 171
Kandinsky, Wassily **K** 166
Abstract expressionism, art movement **P** 31, 32; **U** 122
modern art **M** 397
Abstract words **S** 118

Abu Dhabi, largest of the seven formerly British-protected sheikhdoms that make up the United Arab Emirates along Persian Gulf. The traditional economy, centered around fishing and pearling, is being supplanted by oil production (since 1962). The principal town, Abu Dhabi, located on the coast, becomes an island during high tide.

Abundant numbers **N** 379–80
Abu Simbel, temples of ancient Egypt **D** 21; **E** 100; pictures **E** 91, 101
Abyssal (a-BISS-al) **plain,** flat area of ocean floor **O** 28–29
deep-sea vessels and underwater exploration **U** 17
Abyssinia see Ethiopia
Abyssinian cats **C** 142; picture **C** 144
Abyssinian wild ass **H** 244
A.C. see Alternating current
Acacia (ac-A-sha), tree
ant dwellings **A** 328
bull-horn acacia, home of ants **P** 283
Academic dress **U** 205–06

Academic freedom, principle advocating freedom to teach or learn whatever is thought to lead to truth, without fear of coercion. It protects teachers and scholars from loss of position or other persecution because of ideas they may express.

Academy, school in Athens, started by Plato **P** 332

Academy of Motion Picture Arts and Sciences (AMPAS), honorary organization composed of people in motion picture industry. It annually presents Academy Awards ("Oscars") to those who have made outstanding contributions to the industry in such areas as acting, writing, and directing. It was founded in 1927, has headquarters in Los Angeles, Calif., and publishes *Credits Bulletin.*

Academy of Science, Canberra, Australia, picture **C** 87

Acadia (a-CAY-dia), French name for area now Nova Scotia and New Brunswick, Canada. It was fought over by French and English from 1610 to 1713, when a treaty granted England possession. In 1755 English expelled all French settlers (Acadians) who would not take oath of allegiance to England. Deported Acadians, many of whom settled in Louisiana, are immortalized in Henry Wadsworth Longfellow's poem *Evangeline.*
Canada, early history of **C** 70

Acadia National Park, Maine **M** 41
Acadians, original French habitants of New France, now Canada **C** 48, 69, 70; **N** 138, 344a, 344h
going into exile, picture **C** 70
Maine settlers **M** 38
See also Cajuns

Acanthus, prickly plant found in tropics and southern Europe. Some varieties have white or rose-colored thorny flowers, while others have no flowers. Plant usually grows to about 3 ft. Its graceful design was copied by ancient Greeks in their architecture (Corinthian columns).
Picture **F** 505

A cappella (oc-ap-PEL-la), **musical form**
choral music **C** 277
Acapulco (oc-a-POOL-co), Mexico, picture **M** 246
Accelerated Business Collection-Delivery, mail service for businessmen **P** 410
Acceleration, change in speed of an object **M** 470–71
gravity and gravitation **G** 322–23
human body, effects on **S** 340j
law of falling bodies **F** 34
Accelerators, in chemistry
plastics **P** 327
Accelerators, particle see Particle accelerators
Accelerometer (ac-cel-er-OM-et-er), instrument to show changes in speed **N** 68; **S** 340g
Accents, in poetry **P** 353–54
Accents, marks of stress in pronunciation **P** 478
Accessories, things added to give style
interior decorating **I** 301–02
Accident insurance see Insurance, accident
Accidents
first-aid treatment for **F** 157–63
National Traffic and Motor Vehicle Safety Act, 1966 **A** 550
occupational health and safety **O** 15–16
safety **S** 2–7
Accordion, folk music instrument **F** 329–30; **K** 240; picture **K** 239
Accounting and bookkeeping **B** 311–14
insurance **I** 297
See also Calculators; Computers
Accra (AC-cra), capital of Ghana **G** 196; picture **G** 194
AC–DC, or universal, **motors** **E** 139
Ace, hole in one, in golf **G** 255
Aces, fighter pilots in World War I **U** 159
Acetate (AS-e-tate) **fibers,** man-made **N** 424
Acetic (a-CE-tic) **acid,** in vinegar **F** 348
Acetone (AS-e-tone), flammable chemical formed by fermentation **F** 90
Acetylene (a-CET-il-ene), gas **G** 62
automobile headlights **L** 285
fuel **F** 490

Achaeans (a-KEE-ans), a people of ancient Greece. They originally migrated into northern Greece and settled in Thessaly. About the 13th century B.C. they moved southward into the Peloponnesus, which they dominated until displaced by other Greek-speaking tribes, particularly the Dorians. In Homer's *Iliad* the Greeks who fought in the Trojan War are usually refered to as Achaeans. Their region in Greece was called Achaea.
Trojan War **T** 293–94

Achard (OC-hart) **Franz Carl,** German chemist **S** 456
Achebe, Chinua, Nigerian novelist **A** 76c

Acheson, Dean Gooderham (1893–1971), American lawyer and statesman, b. Middletown, Conn. He was undersecretary of treasury (1933), assistant secretary of state (1941–45), and secretary of state (1949–53) under Truman. He played an important role in founding NATO, and received Presidential Medal of Freedom (1964). His book, *Present at the Creation: My Years in the State Department,* won the Pulitzer Prize (1970) for autobiography.

Acheson, Edward Goodrich (1856–1931), American inventor, b. Washington, Pa. He was Thomas A. Edison's assistant (1880–81). He discovered a process for producing artificial graphite and founded Acheson Graphite Co. (1899).
carborundum **G** 388–89

Achievement tests T 117, 120
  counseling tests in guidance G 399
  examinations for college entrance E 348–49
Achievers, of Junior Achievement, Inc. J 157–58
Achilles (ack-ILL-ese), in Greek mythology G 366
  Iliad I 69
Acid dyes D 371
Acids C 216
  canning of food F 346
  fatty acids O 76, 77
  tests for (experiments) C 217
  See also names of acids

Aclinic line, or **magnetic equator,** imaginary line on earth's surface, lying close to geographical equator. At any point along this line attraction between North and South magnetic poles is balanced, and a magnetic needle will show no dip.

ACLU *see* American Civil Liberties Union
Acne D 190
Aconcagua (oc-on-CA-gua), highest peak in Andes
  A 253, 391; picture S 275
  mountain systems of the world M 499
Aconite, or monkshood, plant P 322
Acorns, fruit of oak trees
  Acorn Area Indians of North America I 174–75
Acoustics (a-COO-stics), science of the behavior of sound
  S 260–61
  How do musical instruments make sounds? M 544
  noise control N 270
Acquired characteristics, in biology
  Lamarck's theory of evolution E 344
Acre, measure of land A 96; W 111
Acropolis (a-CROP-o-lis), highest area of a Greek city
  A 374
Acrostics (a-CROST-ics), word games W 236
Acrylic (a-CRIL-ic) **fibers,** man-made N 424

Actaeon (ac-TE-on), in Greek mythology, hunter who happened upon Artemis (goddess of the hunt) bathing in a river. Angered and offended, Artemis changed him into a deer, and he was hunted down and eaten by his own hounds.

ACTH, stands for adrenocorticotrophic hormone, a chemical substance produced in man's brain by anterior pituitary gland. It is taken from the same gland in cattle, mainly for use in treatment of rheumatoid arthritis. It stimulates the adrenal gland to produce cortisone.

Acting T 156
  charades C 188
  how to put on a play P 335–41
  importance to Oriental dance D 292, 293
  pantomimes with the dance D 35
Acting president, duties of the vice-president V 325
Actinide (AC-tin-ide) **series,** of rare earth elements
  E 159
Actinium (ac-TIN-ium), element E 154, 159
Action and reaction, Newton's third law of motion M 471
Action painting, a technique
  Pollock, Jackson P 387
Actium, battle of, 31 B.C. M 100
Activating enzymes B 296
Act of Settlement, 1701, England E 225
Act of Union *see* Acts of Union
Actors and actresses P 336
  Barrymore family B 67–68
  circus performers, pictures C 300, 302
  motion picture industry M 472–88
  Shakespeare, William S 130–33

  star system in motion pictures M 473
  theater T 156–57

Actors' Equity Association, labor union of actors, dancers, chorus members, and other performers in the legitimate theater. It was the first union to include a clause in its contracts providing for arbitration of all disputes. It was founded by 112 actors in 1913 and has its headquarters in New York, N.Y.

Acts of the Apostles, The, Bible, New Testament B 160;
  C 279–80
Acts of Trade and Navigation, British U 129
Acts of Union
  England and Ireland, 1801 E 228; I 391; P 265
  England and Scotland, 1707 E 225; S 86, 89
  Upper and Lower Canada united, 1841 C 73; Q 16
  Wales and England, 1536 W 4
Actuaries, insurance I 297

Acupuncture (AK-u-punk-chur), medical treatment developed by Chinese around 2700 B.C. Needles of varying lengths are used to puncture precise areas of the body in order to relieve or cure illness. In this century it has also been used to replace anesthetics.
  medicine, history of M 208a, 208b

Acute angles, in geometry G 124; diagram G 125
ADA *see* Americans for Democratic Action
Adam, James and **Robert,** Scottish architects and furniture designers E 240; F 507
  Drury Lane Theatre, London, design for, by Robert
  Adam, picture E 240

Adam and Eve, in the Old Testament (Genesis), first man and woman and parents of human race. Adam (from Hebrew word for "life") was created by God in His image out of dust. Eve (from Hebrew word for "mother of all living") was made by God from one of Adam's ribs. They were placed in Garden of Eden but were expelled for eating forbidden fruit of the tree of knowledge of good and evil. They had three sons: Cain, Abel, and Seth.
  earliest palindrome W 236

Adam and Eve, sculpture by Brancusi S 104
Adamawa Highlands, Nigeria N 254
Adam de la Halle (ad-ON d'la OLL), French poet-musician F 443
Adams, Abigail Smith, wife of John Adams A 8; F 165
  mother of John Quincy Adams A 12

Adams, Adrienne (1906–), American illustrator of children's books, b. Fort Smith, Ark. Among books she illustrated are *Thumbelina, The Shoemaker and the Elves, Snow White, Rose Red, The Littlest Witch, Mouse House,* and *The Ugly Duckling.*

Adams, Brooks, American historian A 18
Adams, Charles Francis (1807–1886), American diplomat
  A 18
Adams, Charles Francis (1866–1954), American lawyer
  A 18
Adams, Charles Francis, Jr. (1835–1915), American economist A 18
Adams, Henry, first of the Adams line A 18

Adams, Henry Brooks (1838–1918), American historian, b. Boston, Mass. A grandson of John Quincy Adams, he was secretary to his father, Charles Francis Adams, during his term as U.S. minister to Great Britain (1861–68). He taught history at Harvard University (1870–77), where he instituted the seminar method of

Adams (continued)
study and edited the *North American Review*. His writings include *History of the United States* in 9 volumes, on the Jefferson and Madison administrations, *Mont-Saint-Michel and Chartres*, and *The Education of Henry Adams*.

American literature, place in **A** 207

Adams, James Truslow (1878–1949), American historian, b. Brooklyn, N.Y. He won the Pulitzer prize for history (1921) for *The Founding of New England*, part of a trilogy with *Revolutionary New England, 1691–1776* and *New England in the Republic, 1776–1850*. He was also editor of the *Dictionary of American History* and *Atlas of American History*.

Adams, John, 2nd president of United States **A** 8–11
as Vice-president, picture **V** 325
Adams family **A** 18
casting vote of vice-presidents **V** 327
favored Independence Day celebrations **I** 112

Adams, John Couch, English astronomer **P** 277
astronomy, history of **A** 475

Adams, John Quincy, 6th president of United States **A** 12–15
Adams family **A** 18
Clay, Henry **C** 335

Adams, Léonie Fuller (1899–   ), American poet and educator, b. Brooklyn, N.Y. She was a lecturer at Columbia University (1947–68) and was poetry consultant to Library of Congress (1948–49). In 1969 she received the Brandeis medal for poetic achievement. Her works include *Those Not Elect, High Falcon,* and *This Measure.*

Adams, Louisa Johnson, wife of John Quincy Adams **A** 13; **F** 166–67

Adams, Maude (Maude Kiskadden) (1872–1953), American actress, b. Salt Lake City, Utah. She is noted for her roles in J. M. Barrie's plays, especially *Peter Pan,* and for her role as Juliet in Shakespeare's *Romeo and Juliet.* She retired (1918), returned briefly to the stage, and later taught dramatics at Stephens College, Columbia, Mo.
Utah, famous people from **U** 253

Adams, Samuel, American Revolutionary patriot and statesman **A** 16–17
Adams family **A** 18
Committees of Correspondence **R** 196

Adams, Samuel Hopkins (1871–1958), American magazine writer and novelist, b. Boston, Mass. He was a reporter on New York *Sun* (1891–1900) and was on staff of *McClure's Magazine* (1903–05). He wrote a famous serial exposing quackery in patent medicine (1905). This serial was in part responsible for passage of first Pure Food and Drug Act. His works include *It Happened One Night* (filmed in 1934), and *The Incredible Era.*

Adam's apple, bulge in front part of throat. Part of the larynx, it is especially prominent in men. Name comes from legend that part of the apple became stuck in Adam's throat when he ate the forbidden fruit.
speaking mechanism **S** 377

Adams family, of Massachusetts **A** 17–18
Adams National Historic Site, Quincy, Mass. **M** 144
famous people from Massachusetts **M** 147
Adams National Historic Site, Quincy, Massachusetts **M** 144

Adamson Act, 1916 **W** 179
Adams-Onís Treaty (Transcontinental Treaty of 1819) **T** 109, 272
diplomatic triumph for Adams **A** 13
No-Transfer Principle in Monroe Doctrine **M** 427
Adana (a-DA-na), Turkey **T** 326
Adaptability
behavior of animals **A** 286–87
Adaptation, in biology **L** 214–27
anthropological findings **A** 306–07
birds **B** 209–10, 221–23
cactus **C** 3–4
camels **C** 34
camouflage of fishes **F** 193; pictures **F** 192
evolution theory **E** 346
home areas of plants **P** 304
insects **I** 274–76
lizards **L** 319–20
mammals **M** 63–64
pinnipeds **W** 5–8
whales **W** 151
See *also* Ecology; Estivation; Hibernation; Life; Plant defenses; Protective coloration
Adaptive radiation, in biology
birds **B** 209–10
Addams, Charles, American cartoonist **C** 127, 128
Addams, Jane, American social worker **A** 19
peace movements **P** 105
Addends, in arithmetic **A** 398
Addiction, to drugs **D** 329–30
smoking labeled habituation, not addiction **S** 203
the life of addicts **N** 13–14
See *also* Alcoholism
Adding machines **C** 450
office machines **O** 56
Addis Ababa, capital of Ethiopia **E** 300, 301; pictures **E** 296, 298, 301; **A** 68, 69
Addison, Joseph, English essayist **E** 258, 292
magazine publisher **M** 14
Addition, in mathematics **A** 398–99
abacus **A** 2–3
algebra **A** 158–59
decimal fractions **F** 401
fractions **F** 399
OR computer circuits **C** 454
use of binary numeration system for computers **C** 456
using base-4 system **N** 400
Additives, chemicals
food regulations and laws **F** 350–52
for lubricants **L** 371
gasoline **G** 63
Address, forms of, in speaking and writing **A** 19–21
See *also* Letter writing
Addressing machines **O** 58

Ade, George (1866–1944), American journalist, playwright, and humorist, b. Kentland, Ind. He worked on newspapers in Indiana and Chicago (1887–1900). He was known for his wit and the plain, slang-talking people in his books. His best-known work is *Fables in Slang.* Other books of his include *The Old-Time Saloon* and *The Girl Proposition.* Ade's plays include *Father and the Boys* and *The College Widow,* and he wrote several movie scenarios.
satire **H** 280

Adelaide, capital of South Australia **A** 512, 514
Adelie (ad-A-le) **penguins** **P** 121–24
Antarctic regions, picture **P** 370
migration, picture **H** 185
through the year with birds **B** 212, 213
Adelita, Mexican song **N** 27

Aden (A-den), city of Yemen (Aden)   **Y** 347
   Middle East   **M** 301

Adenauer (OD-en-our), **Konrad** (1876–1967), German statesman, b. Cologne. He was chief mayor of Cologne and a member of Prussian Upper House (1917–33) and president of Prussian Council of State (1920–33). He was a member of Provincial Diet and Provincial Committee of Rhine Province (1917–33) but was removed from office by Nazis and imprisoned twice. Reinstated as chief mayor of Cologne in 1945, he was one of founders and leaders of Christian Democratic Union. Adenauer was chancellor of German Federal Republic (1949–63). Pictures   **E** 111; **P** 456a.

Adenoids, lymph tissue in nasal passages   **D** 210
Adenosine (ad-EN-os-ene) **triphosphate,** or ATP
   B 296–97
   photosynthesis forms this compound   **P** 222
Adeste Fideles (ad-EST-ay fid-AY-les), or "O Come, All Ye Faithful"   **C** 122
Adhesion, in physics   **L** 310; **P** 233
Adhesives   **G** 242–43
   hot-press bonding of plywood   **F** 503–04
   See also Glue
Ad hoc committees, of organizations   **P** 80
Adiabatic cooling, of air   **C** 358
Adirondack (ad-ir-ON-dack) **Mountains**   **N** 213; picture   **N** 215
Adjectives, words that modify nouns   **P** 91
Adjectival clauses, in sentences   **P** 91

Adler (OD-ler), **Alfred** (1870–1937), Austrian psychiatrist, b. Penzing-Vienna. Originally a close associate of Sigmund Freud, he later disagreed with basic Freudian ideas and developed theory that inferiority complex is root of most psychological problems. He spent much time in United States (after 1925) and finally settled in New York City (1935). He lectured and taught at several medical schools and founded School of Individual Psychology, Vienna. He started *Journal of Individual Psychology* and was author of numerous works, including *The Science of Living* and *The Pattern of Life.*

Adler (AD-ler), **Felix** (1851–1933), American scholar, lecturer, and founder (1876) of Society for Ethical Culture, b. Alzey, Germany. He came to United States in 1857. He taught Hebrew and Oriental literature at Cornell University (1874–76) and was professor of ethics at Columbia University (1902–33). Adler started first free kindergarten in New York, N.Y., and was active in movements to create better housing and to eliminate child labor.

Adler, Mortimer Jerome (1902–), American author and educator, b. New York, N.Y. He was associate professor (1930–42) and professor (1942–52) of philosophy of law at University of Chicago. Co-editor of *Great Books of the Western World* (since 1945), Adler became director of Institute for Philosophical Research, San Francisco (1952). His books include *How to Read a Book, The Difference of Man and the Difference it Makes,* and *Time of Our Lives.*

Adler, Ruth (1915–68), American author and illustrator of children's books, b. Sullivan County, N.Y. She has illustrated books, including *Electronics* and *Magic House of Numbers* (written by her husband). She collaborated with her husband, **Irving Adler** (1913–), on such books as "Reason Why" series, *The Earths' Crust,* and *Oceans.* Both are known particularly for works on science and mathematics.

Adler (AD-ler) **Planetarium and Astronomical Museum,** Chicago, Illinois   **M** 513
Administrator, or **administratrix,** of a will   **W** 174
Admiralty Court, Canada   **C** 78
Admiralty Islands, Australia   **I** 425
Admiralty law see Maritime law
Adobe (ad-O-be), sun-dried bricks   **B** 391
   houses   **H** 173
   pueblo, picture   **A** 302
Adolescence (ad-ol-ES-cence)   **A** 22–24
   acne   **D** 190
   drug abuse   **D** 329, 331, 332
   juvenile delinquency   **J** 162–64
   See also Family

Adonis (ad-ON-is), in Greek mythology, handsome youth loved by Aphrodite and Persephone and ordered by Zeus to spend half the year with each goddess. He was killed by a boar while hunting.

Adoption   **A** 25–26
   social work, practice of   **S** 225
Adoration, prayer of   **P** 434
Adoration of the Magi, painting by Botticelli   **N** 41
Adoration of the Magi, painting by Gentile da Fabriano   **U** 2
Adoration of the Magi, painting by Rubens   **D** 356
Adoula (ad-OO-la), **Cyrille,** prime minister of Congo (Leopoldville), now Congo (Zaïre)   **Z** 366d
Adrar des Iforas (od-RAR days e-fo-RA), mountains in North Africa
   Mali   **M** 58
Adrenal (ad-RE-nal) **glands**   **B** 279–80
   epinephrine (adrenaline) released by   **B** 297
Adrenocorticotropic hormone see ACTH
Adrian IV, pope   **H** 163
Adriatic Sea   **O** 45

Adsorption, process by which a solid or liquid substance holds on its surface (adsorbs) another substance. In gas masks activated charcoal, an adsorbent, holds poison gas molecules, allowing wearer to breathe in pure air. Adsorption is often confused with absorption, in which one substance takes in another.

Adularescence (ad-u-la-RES-cence), in gemstones   **G** 70
Adult education
   Denmark   **D** 107, 109
   recreation for older citizens   **O** 100
   Togo, picture   **E** 84
Adulteration, of food   **F** 351
   drugs, quality control of   **D** 325
Ad valorem (ad va-LO-rem) **tariff**   **T** 25
Advection fog   **F** 288–89
Advent, religious holidays   **R** 155
   start of Roman Catholic Church year   **R** 290

Adventist, member of a religious group believing that hope of world lies in second coming of Christ. Advent movement was founded by William Miller (1782–1849), a New England Baptist who predicted that the world would come to an end in 1843, at which time Christ would appear. Many Adventist churches with differing views were organized in the 19th century, and some, such as the Seventh-Day Adventist Church, are still in existence.

Adventure stories
   early rogue, or picaresque, novels   **N** 345–46
Adverbs, words that modify verbs, adjectives, or another adverb   **P** 91–92
Advertising   **A** 27–34
   book publishing   **B** 331, 334

Advertising (continued)
  commercial art **C** 424–27
  communication **C** 441
  consumer education **C** 494, 494a
  department stores **D** 120
  difference between it and public relations **P** 507
  how radio broadcasting is financed **R** 56
  illustration and illustrators **I** 92, 95–96
  mail order **M** 31
  modeling, fashion **M** 384–85
  newspaper circulation **N** 197
  photography **P** 205
  posters **P** 404
  radio programs **R** 60
  smoking ads banned on radio and TV **S** 203
  television **T** 70, 70b, 71
  trade and commerce **T** 243
  trademarks **T** 244–45
  See also Opinion surveys
Advocates *see* Lawyers
Adze, tool, pictures **T** 210b
AE *see* Russell, George William
AEC *see* Atomic Energy Commission
Aegean (e-GE-an) **civilization** **P** 15–16; **S** 94
  art as a record **A** 438b
Aegean Sea **O** 45
Aegina (e-JY-na), Greece, picture **G** 336
Aeneas (an-E-as), hero of Vergil's *Aeneid* **A** 35
Aeneid (an-E-id), epic poem by Vergil **A** 35
  Trojan War **T** 293–94
  Vergil's plan of the *Aeneid* **V** 304–05

Aeolus (EE-ol-us), in Greek mythology, the ruler of the winds. He lived in the Aeolian Islands, where the winds were kept. In the *Odyssey*, Aeolus gives a bag of wind to Odysseus (Ulysses) to help speed his ship home after the Trojan War. There was another Aeolus who was king of Thessaly and the legendary ancestor of the Aeolians, a people of ancient Greece.

Aeration
  water purification **W** 68
Aerial acts, in a circus **C** 304; picture **C** 300
Aerial Lift Bridge, Duluth, Minn., picture **B** 401
Aerial perspective **P** 158
Aerial photography **P** 206
Aerial roots, of plants, picture **P** 291
Aeries, eagle's nests **E** 2
Aerodynamics, science of air in motion **A** 36–41
  airplane design **A** 558–59
  birds, flight of **B** 204–05
  glider flight **G** 238–39
  helicopters, how they fly **H** 105–06
  hydrofoil boats **H** 304–05
  supersonic flight **S** 469–73
  What keeps a plane up in the air? **A** 38
Aeromedicine, part of man-in-space program **H** 248
Aeronautical engineering **E** 205–06
Aeronautics *see* Aviation
Aeronauts, operators or travelers in airships or balloons
  parachute-jumping **P** 59–61
Aerosol containers
  Freon gas used in **G** 62
  household pest control **H** 260–63
  insecticide bombs **I** 258
Aerospace Defense Command, of U.S. Air Force **U** 161
Aerospace industry **A** 564–65
  photography **P** 208
Aerospaceplanes, future space vehicles **R** 262
Aerotrain, new development in transportation **T** 267
Aeschylus (ESC-il-us), Greek dramatist **G** 351
  ancient Greek drama **D** 294

Aesculapius (es-cu-LAPE-ius), legendary Greek doctor **M** 203
  serpent wand of, picture **M** 208c
Aesop (E-sop), Greek author of fables **F** 2–3; **H** 280
  "Ant and the Grasshopper, The" **F** 5
  "Four Oxen and the Lion, The" **F** 5
  "Lion and the Mouse, The" **F** 4
Aesthetics (es-THET-ics), or **esthetics,** the branch of philosophy that studies beauty **P** 192
Aetna, Mount *see* Etna, Mount
Afar-Issa Territory, formerly French Somaliland **S** 255
  France, overseas possessions **F** 415
Afaworq, Gabra Iyasus, Ethiopian writer **A** 76b
Affenpinscher (AF-fen-pin-sher), dog, picture **D** 260
Affinity, chemical
  in the dyeing process **D** 370
Afghan hound, dog, picture **D** 254
Afghanistan (af-GHAN-ist-an) **A** 42–45
  flag **F** 237
AFL-CIO *see* American Federation of Labor–Congress of Industrial Organizations
Africa **A** 46–69
  art *see* African art
  birds of **B** 226
  Congo River **C** 465
  education **E** 84; **T** 43
  flags of African countries **F** 235–36
  food specialty, couscous **F** 335; picture **F** 337
  homes, the old and the new, pictures **H** 174
  immigration **I** 103
  life, plant and animal communities **L** 258
  literature *see* African literature
  mountain peaks, highest in Africa **M** 494
  music *see* African music
  Negro history **N** 89–91
  Nile River **N** 260–61
  poverty **P** 424–424b
  prairies **P** 430–33
  proverbs **P** 487
  Sahara, desert **S** 8
  Spanish overseas territories **S** 356–57
  Stanley and Livingstone, explorers of **S** 400
  teachers **T** 43
  waterfalls, selected list **W** 57
  World Wars I and II **W** 275, 290
  See also names of countries
Africa Hall, Addis Ababa, Ethiopia **E** 301; picture **E** 298
African Americans *see* Black Americans
African art **A** 70–76
  decorative designs on homes, picture **A** 60
  use by Modigliani **M** 403
African kingdoms, early **N** 90–91
  Africa, history of **A** 66–67
  Benin **N** 256
  Fulani-Hausa **N** 256
  Kimbundu in the Dongo region, Angola **A** 261
  Mali **M** 59
  Yoruba empire of Oyo **N** 256
  Zimbabwe, Rhodesia, ruins of, picture **R** 230
African literature **A** 76a–76d
  A Story, A Story, folktale, picture from **C** 245
African music **A** 77–79; **N** 253–54
African violet, plant **H** 268–69
African warthogs, wild pigs **H** 209; **P** 248–49
Afrikaans (af-rik-AHNS), language spoken by South African people of Dutch descent **A** 56; **B** 299; **S** 268
Afrikaners, South Africans of Dutch descent **S** 268
Afro-American history **N** 89–105
Afro-Americans *see* Black Americans
Afterburners, in turbofan engines **J** 86
Agades, Niger **N** 251

Aga Khan (OG-a kahn), spiritual leader of ismaili Muslim sect. He claims descent and spiritual authority from Mohammed through his daughter Fatima. Shah Karim Khan (1936–) became Aga Khan IV upon the death of his grandfather Aga Khan III in 1957. He married Sarah Croker Poole (1969), making her Begum Aga Khan.

Agam, Vaacov, Israeli painter
    Double Metamorphosis II, painting   **P** 31, 32
Agamemnon (ag-a-MEM-non), drama by Aeschylus
    D 294
Agamemnon, in Greek mythology   **G** 365–66;   **T** 293

Aganippe (ag-an-IP-pe), in Greek and Roman mythology, fountain of the Muses (nine goddesses of the arts) at foot of Mt. Helicon in Boeotia, Greece. It was said to inspire those who drank from it.

Agar-agar (OG-ar-OG-ar), a gum obtained from algae
    A 157;   **R** 185
Agassiz (AG-as-se), **Elizabeth Cary,** wife of Jean Louis
    Rodolphe Agassiz   **A** 80
Agassiz, Jean Louis Rodolphe, Swiss-born American geologist and naturalist   **A** 80;   **G** 115
    ice age findings   **I** 19
Agassiz, Lake, ancient glacial lake   **M** 324–25;   **N** 324
    agricultural land in Manitoba   **M** 76
Agate, chalcedony quartz   **Q** 7
Agate Fossil Beds National Monument, Nebraska   **N** 81
Age see Aging
Aged, the see Old age
Agee (AGE-e), **James,** American novelist   **A** 213
Agents, or brokers, in wholesale selling   **S** 116–17
Agents provocateurs (oj-ONT prov-oc-a-TER), spies   **S** 389
Age of Exploration and Discovery   **E** 372–73, 385–87
    geographical expeditions   **G** 98
Age of Fishes, Devonian period in geology   **F** 181–82
Age of Kings, 17th and 18th centuries in Europe
    A 438f–438g
Age of Mammals   **F** 388–89
Age of Reason   **H** 136
    American literature   **A** 197–98
Age of Reptiles   **F** 383, 387
    dinosaurs   **D** 172, 181; chart   **D** 174
Ageratums (a-GER-a-tums), flowers   **G** 46;   picture **G** 50
Aggregation, a form of group behavior
    fishes   **F** 201–02
Agincourt (AJ-in-court), **battle of,** 1415   **H** 282
Aging   **A** 81–87
    age of fish   **F** 185–86
    a life process   **L** 210–11
    cell aging and division   **C** 159
    clam shell showing stages of growth, picture   **S** 149
    horses' teeth   **H** 243
    How long do insects live?   **I** 265–66
    old age   **O** 96–101
    percentages of older people in populations   **P** 397
    stroke, brain damage   **D** 208
    trees   **T** 274

Agnes, Saint, Christian martyr and patron saint of young girls, lived during 3rd century. She is thought to have been executed when only 12 or 13 years old. According to legend, a young girl could learn whom she would marry by following certain rituals on St. Agnes' Eve (January 20). The legend was used by Keats in his poem "The Eve of St. Agnes."

Agnew, Spiro T., American public official   **M** 126;
    pictures   **N** 262d, **V** 331
Agnon, Shmuel Yosef (Samuel Joseph Czaczkes), Hebrew
    novelist   **H** 103

Agora, marketplace in ancient Athens, picture   **A** 229
    main open spaces of Greek cities   **A** 375
Agoutis (a-GOO-tis), rodents   **R** 280
Agra, India   **I** 122
    Taj Mahal   **T** 14

Agricola (ag-RIC-o-la), **Georgius** (Georg Bauer) (1494–1555), German mineralogist, b. Glauchau, Saxony. Called the father of mineralogy, he was first to write about minerals and mining from own observations. He followed custom of the time and wrote in Latin, signing his name Agricola, Latin word for "farmer" (*bauer* is German for "farmer"). His most famous work is 12-volume *De Re Metallica* ("About Metals"), correlating all then known about metals and the mining and refining of ores.
    early geologists   **G** 110–11

Agricultural Adjustment Administration (AAA)   **R** 322
Agricultural engineering   **E** 206
Agricultural experiment stations   **A** 95
Agricultural fairs   **F** 12; picture **F** 13
Agricultural geography   **G** 107
Agricultural Index   **I** 115
Agricultural machinery see Farm machinery
Agricultural pests
    boll weevil   **C** 523
    boll weevil, monument to   **A** 119
    control by U.S. Department of Agriculture   **A** 94
    locusts   **C** 507
    weeds   **W** 104–06
Agricultural Revolution, early discoveries in agriculture
    A 100
Agriculture   **A** 88–100
    agricultural engineers   **E** 206
    antibiotics, uses for   **A** 314–15
    Asia, pictures   **A** 464
    Balance Agriculture with Industry (BAWI) program,
        Mississippi   **M** 363
    "breadbasket" of South America   **S** 291
    Burbank's experimental farm   **B** 453
    Carver, George W., new uses of plants   **C** 128–29
    child labor   **C** 235
    communes of Communist China   **C** 267
    corn belt a basic concern of Soviet Union   **U** 37;
        picture   **E** 306
    county and state fairs   **F** 12
    dairy farming   **D** 7–10
    desert farming   **D** 127
    farmers' co-operatives   **C** 499–500
    farming the sea see Sea farms
    farm life   **F** 48–54
    farm machinery   **F** 55–62
    fertilizers   **F** 95–98
    feudal system   **F** 99–103
    food plants, history of   **P** 305
    forest management   **F** 372–73
    4-H clubs   **F** 46, 47
    fur farming   **F** 513–14
    Future Farmers of America   **F** 45, 46
    grasses   **G** 314–19
    Indian farmers   **I** 183
    industrial value of   **I** 246
    insecticides   **I** 258
    intensive land use in Europe   **E** 324
    irrigation   **I** 408–10
    livestock   **C** 145–52
    migratory, or slash and burn   **J** 155–56;   **Z** 367
    milpa agriculture   **Z** 366a
    open-field system in early England   **E** 216
    poultry farming   **P** 420–23
    poverty caused by crop failure   **P** 424a
    prairie farming   **P** 431–32

Agriculture (continued)
  prehistoric man **P** 445–46
  rain forest farmers **R** 100
  slash and burn, or migratory **J** 155–56; **Z** 367
  Stone Age man becomes a food producer
    F 332
  United States began as a farming society
    U 128
  women, role of **W** 212
  world crop regions **W** 263–64
  See also domestic animals and livestock by name;
    agriculture section of continent, country, province,
    and state articles; headings beginning with the words
    Agricultural and Farm
Agriculture, United States Department of **A** 94
  conservation bureaus **C** 484, 485, 488
  consumer protection agencies **C** 494a
  Forest Service **N** 34
  4-H clubs, Federal Extension Service **F** 47
  Meat Inspection Service **M** 195

Agrippa, Marcus Vipsanius (63–12 B.C.), Roman general
and statesman. Son-in-law and personal adviser to
Emperor Augustus, he crushed a rebellion in Gaul (38
B.C.). Elected consul (37 B.C.), he defeated Mark Antony's
fleet at battle of Actium (31 B.C.). He became chief
counselor to Augustus (23 B.C.).

Agrippina (ag-rip-PY-na), Roman empress, mother of
    Nero **N** 114
Agronomy see Agriculture

Aguinaldo (og-e-NOLD-o), **Emilio** (1869–1964), Philippine
leader and hero in struggle for Philippine independence,
b. Luzon. He led an unsuccessful revolt against Spain
(1896). After Americans defeated Spanish (1898), he proclaimed Philippine independence and took office as first
president (1899). When America's colonial intentions became evident, he again headed a revolt (1899–1901) until
captured. He pledged his loyalty to United States but
wore a black mourning bow tie until the Philippines
finally achieved independence (1946). He ran for president (1935) but was defeated by Manuel Quezon. During
later years he served on Philippines Council of State.
  Philippines, history of **P** 190

Aguiyi-Ironsi, Johnson, military leader of Ibos in Nigeria-
    Biafra civil war **N** 258
Ahab (A-hab), king of Israel **E** 176; **J** 104
Ahad Ha-am (AH-od ha-OM), born Asher Ginzberg, He-
    brew writer **H** 103
Ahasuerus (a-has-u-E-rus), king of Persia **P** 540
Ahimsa (a-HIM-sa), or nonviolence, Hindu belief **H** 130
    also a teaching of Jainism **R** 147
Ahura Mazda, Zoroastrian god of fire **Z** 380
Ahvenanmaa see Aland Islands
Aïda (ah-E-da), opera by Verdi **O** 139; picture **O** 141
    Suez Canal opening commemorated **S** 452

Aiken, Conrad Potter (1889–1973), American poet and
novelist, b. Savannah, Ga. Awarded Pulitzer prize for
Selected Poems (1930) and National Book Award for
Collected Poems (1954), he was appointed to Chair of
Poetry in the Library of Congress (1950–52). His novels
include *Blue Voyage* and *Great Circle.*

Aiken, George David (1892–   ), U.S. senator from
Vermont; b. Dummerston, Vt. He served in the Vermont
legislature and as lieutenant governor and governor
(1937–41) of Vermont. He was elected to the Senate
in 1940. He is a member of the Foreign Relations
Committee and liberal Republican leader in the Senate.

Ailerons (AIL-er-ons), of airplanes **A** 554, 556
Ainu (I-nu), a people of Japan **J** 24, 42
    Kurile Islands and Sakhalin **I** 434, 436
Air **A** 479–82
  aerodynamics **A** 36–41
  air conditioning **A** 101–03
  balloons inflated with hot air **B** 30
  Boyle's law **B** 354; **C** 209–10
  chemical formulas of its chief gases **C** 198
  chemistry, history of, first theories **C** 206
  cloud formation **C** 358–59
  compressed air **W** 71
  demonstrate "lift" **A** 38
  deodorizers **D** 117
  dust **D** 346–48
  gases **G** 58–59
  International Geophysical Year, findings **I** 317
  jet streams **J** 88–91
  matter, states of **M** 171
  pollution **A** 108–11; **E** 272f–272g
  pressure see Air pressure
  resistance to falling bodies **F** 33
  Why does air move?" **W** 184
  winds **W** 184–87
Air, compressed see Compressed air
Air, liquid see Liquid air
Air-age maps, in North Pole-centered azimuthal
    projection **M** 93
Air base, Greenland, picture **G** 371
Airbrakes **R** 88
Air conditioning **A** 101–03
  heat pumps **H** 99
  air conditioners **E** 119
  air cycle system of refrigeration **R** 137, 138
  spacecraft and space suits **S** 338, 340a, 340L
Aircraft see Airplanes; Balloons and ballooning; Gliders;
    Helicopters; Satellites, man-made
Aircraft carriers
  United States Navy capital ships **U** 192
Air-cushioned vehicles **T** 267–68
  being tested on the Arctic Slope, Alaska **A** 138
Airedale (AIR-dale) **terrier,** dog, picture **D** 255
Airfields see Airports
Air Force, Canada see Royal Canadian Air Force
Air Force, United States see United States Air Force
Air Force Cross, American award, picture **M** 199
Air Force Reserves (AFRes) **U** 165
Air guns **G** 424; **P** 348
Airlift, Berlin, Germany **B** 144; **G** 164
Airline hostesses and stewardesses **A** 566; **S** 125
  women, role of **W** 213
Airlines **A** 566
  See also transportation section of country, province,
    and state articles
Airline stewardesses see Airline hostesses and
    stewardesses
Airmail **P** 407
  first airmail, milestones of aviation **A** 574
Airman's Medal, American award, picture **M** 199
Air mass **W** 76
Air National Guard, United States **N** 43; **U** 165
Airplane models **A** 104–07
Airplanes **A** 553–74
  aerodynamics, theory of flight **A** 36–41
  gliders compared to **G** 238
  hydraulic systems **H** 303
  inventions in air transportation **I** 338
  jet liners, pictures **A** 573, **I** 230
  models **A** 104–07
  "otter aircraft," in Far North, picture **C** 60
rocket-powered **S** 472–73; pictures **A** 571, **R** 262,
    S 471

supersonic flight **S** 469–73
use as farming tool **F** 59
Air plants, or epiphytes **P** 318
Air pollution A 108–11; **F** 289; pictures **E** 272a, 272c, 272f
  automobiles, search for a low-pollutant engine **A** 552
  cancer **C** 92
  deodorizers **D** 117
  disease, prevention of **D** 221
  environment, problems of **E** 272f–272g
  lead in gasoline **G** 63
  smog **F** 289
  See also Dust; Fallout
Airports A 562–63; **H** 37
  Cairo, picture **E** 90f
  circular airport of the future **T** 268
  harbor and port facilities in port cities **H** 37
  holding patterns, diagram **A** 565
  plane loading, picture **I** 249
  Tokyo, Japan, picture **A** 467
  See also transportation section of country, province, and state articles
Air pressure A 479; demonstration **A** 482
  barometer **B** 54
  deep-sea diving hazard **D** 81, 82
  how a tornado causes damage **H** 297–98
  pumps, action of **P** 528
  tornadoes, how they cause damage **H** 297–98
  tunnels, underwater **T** 318
  vacuum formed by **V** 263
  Venturi effect in aerodynamics **A** 37–39, 40
Air Route Traffic Control (ARTC) **A** 564
Air sacs, or alveoli, of the lungs **B** 277; **D** 203–04
Airships
  hydrogen used in **H** 305–06
  inventions in air transportation **I** 338
Air space
  international control of radio frequencies **R** 54
Airspeed indicator, in airplanes **A** 560
Air terminals see Airports
Air traffic control A 563–64
Aitken, William Maxwell see Beaverbrook, Lord
Aiún, capital of Spanish Sahara **S** 356
Aix-la-Chapelle see Aachen, West Germany

Aix-la-Chapelle (EX-la-shap-ELL), **Treaties of,** three pacts signed by European powers in Aix-la-Chapelle (French name for German city of Aachen). The first (1668) ended War of Devolution between France and Spain. The second (1748) ended War of Austrian Succession, during which Prussia, Spain, Sardinia, Bavaria, Saxony, Poland, and France had tried to seize the Austrian Empire. The third (1818) was an attempt to solve problems that had arisen as a result of French defeat in Napoleonic Wars.

Ajax (A-jax), name of two legendary Greek heroes of the Trojan War. Ajax the Greater was renowned for his strength and size, and as a warrior was considered second only to Achilles. Ajax and Odysseus (Ulysses) both claimed the armor of the dead Achilles. When Odysseus won the armor, Ajax, insane with rage, slaughtered a flock of sheep and then, in shame, killed himself. He is the subject of a play, Ajax, by Sophocles. Ajax the Lesser was punished by the sea god Poseidon (Neptune) for having violated the prophetess Cassandra after the fall of Troy. He was shipwrecked and drowned.

Ajolotes, lizards **L** 320

Akbar (Jalal-ud-Din Muhammad) (1542–1605), third emperor of Mogul dynasty of India, b. Umarkot. Called Akbar the Great, he came to throne (1556) and extended empire to include much of India, Kashmir, Afghanistan, and Baluchistan. He practiced religious and political tolerance and evolved new religion, Din Ilahi, combining parts of Islam, Christianity, and Hinduism.
  India **I** 133

Akeley, Carl Ethan (1864–1926), American taxidermist, sculptor, inventor, and explorer, b. Clarendon, N.Y. He headed expeditions to Africa to explore and collect specimens of wildlife for museums. Several of his sculptures and exhibits are in American Museum of Natural History in New York, N.Y. He invented the Akeley cement gun and a motion picture camera used to photograph wildlife. His books include In Brightest Africa.

Akhnaton or **Akhenaten** (Amenhotep IV), king of ancient Egypt **A** 223; **E** 91
  Egyptian art and architecture **E** 100–01, 102

Akiba (a-KI-ba) **ben Joseph** (50?–132), Jewish scholar, b. Lydda, Palestine. He taught at rabbinical school near Jaffa, Palestine, and developed a method of interpreting Bible in which every word and sign has particular significance. His collection of Jewish oral law was basis of Mishnah (first part of Talmud, book of Jewish civil and religious law). He supported Bar Cocheba in revolt against Roman Emperor Hadrian (132) and was executed for disobeying a Roman law that prohibited teaching of Jewish law. He is one of 10 martyrs mentioned in Jewish prayer of repentance.
  Talmudic scholars **T** 15

Akihito (ah-ki-HE-to), Crown Prince of Japan
  J 48

Akins (A-kins), **Zoë** (1886–1958), American playwright, b. Humansville, Mo. Her first success was Déclassée (1919). Her other plays include The Greeks Had a Word for It and an adaptation of Edith Wharton's The Old Maid, for which she won a Pulitzer prize (1935). She also wrote screenplays, poetry, and a novel, Forever Young.

Akita, dog, picture **D** 260
Akron, Ohio **O** 72
Aksum, Ethiopia **E** 301, 302
  early written literature **A** 76b
Akureyri (ok-u-RAY-ri), Iceland **I** 43
Al- in Arabic names see main part of name, as Azhar, University of al-
ALA see American Library Association
Alabama A 112–27
  holiday, Fraternal (Columbus) Day **H** 149
  places of interest in Negro histroy **N** 94
Alabama, University of A 121
Alabama Claims G 296
Alabama River A 115, 120
Alabama State Capitol, picture **A** 124

Alabaster, name given to two mineral substances. Modern alabaster, a form of gypsum, is relatively soft and usually white and is used in statues and ornamental carvings. Large deposits of it are found in Italy. Oriental alabaster is a kind of marble and was used in ancient times for making statues.

Aladdin and the Wonderful Lamp, story from Arabian Nights **A** 345–46
Alakaluf (a-la-ka-LOOF), Indians of South America
  A 306–07
Alamein, El, battle of, 1942 **W** 295
Alamo, battle of the, 1836 **M** 238; **T** 122, 137

Alamo, battle of the (continued)
Bowie, James, hero of **B** 344
Crockett, Davy, hero of **C** 533
flag **F** 228
Alamogordo (al-a-mo-GOR-do), New Mexico
Trinity Site, first atomic bomb test **N** 191

Alanbrooke, 1st Viscount (Alan Francis Brooke) (1883–1963), British general; b. Bagneres-de-Bigore, France. He commanded British 2nd Corps in France at beginning of World War II and played an important role in the evacuation of Dunkirk (1940). He was chief of Imperial General Staff (1941–46). He was made a field marshal (1944) and created 1st Viscount Alanbrooke of Brookeborough (1946).

Aland (OL-and) **Islands**, Finland **I** 425–26

Alarcón (ol-ar-CONE), **Hernando de**, Spanish explorer and navigator who lived during 16th century. He assisted Coronado in expedition into what is now southwestern United States, and he explored Gulf of California and Colorado River (1540–41).

Alarcón, Juan Ruiz de, Mexican-born Spanish playwright **L** 71
golden age of Spanish literature **S** 369
Alarcón, Pedro Antonio de, Spanish writer **S** 370

Alaric (AL-a-ric) (370?–410), king of the Visigoths; b. Peuce, an island at the mouth of the Danube River. For a time Alaric commanded Gothic troops serving in the Roman army. Elected king of the Visigoths (395), he led them in an invasion of Greece. The Romans made peace by appointing him military governor in the colony of Illyricum (now in Yugoslavia). In 401 he invaded Italy, and after several sieges captured Rome (410). The city was plundered, but its religious shrines were spared. Alaric planned to establish a kingdom in northern Africa, but his fleet was wrecked by a storm and he died soon after.

Alarm clocks **W** 49
Alas, Leopoldo, Spanish writer **S** 371
Alaska **A** 128–43; **T** 112
Dawes Glacier, picture **G** 224
discovery by Vitus Bering **B** 142
Eskimo food **F** 339–40
Eskimo life **E** 284–91
glacier with terminal moraine, picture **I** 18
gold discoveries **G** 253
holiday, William Henry Seward's Day **H** 148
Katmai National Monument **A** 140; picture **N** 54
land areas of the United States **U** 92–93
Mount McKinley National Park, pictures **A** 134, **N** 51
origin of Alaskan flag **A** 128
pioneers **P** 262
purchase cartoon **T** 107
taiga, picture **C** 343
tundra, picture **C** 344
Alaska, Gulf of **A** 130, 134
Alaska, University of **A** 139
Alaska Highway, United States and Canada **A** 138, 143
British Columbia **B** 406d; **C** 61
famous highways **R** 253
part of the Pan American system **P** 50
Yukon Territory **Y** 365
Alaska Methodist University **A** 139
Alaskan, or northern, fur seals **W** 6–7
Alaskan brown bears **B** 106, 107
Alaskan fur seals, migration **H** 190–91
Alaska Peninsula **A** 130

Alaska Range **A** 130, 132; picture **A** 134
Al Azhar University see Azhar, University of al-
Alba, Fernando Alvarez de Toledo, duke of see Alva, Fernando Alvarez de Toledo
Albacore, fish
habitat, feeding habits, uses **F** 215

Albanel, Charles (1616–1696), French explorer and Jesuit missionary who spent many years at Tadoussac, Canada. He was a member of first French expedition from Quebec to Hudson Bay (1670–71). On his second trip there (1674) he was captured by English and taken to England. He returned to Canada (1676), and continued missionary work until his death.

Albania (al-BAY-nia) **A** 144–46
created by Balkan wars **B** 19
flag **F** 239
Albanian Workers' Party (Communist) **A** 144, 146
Albany, capital of New York **N** 222

Albany Plan of Union, first formal plan for unification of American colonies. It was proposed by Benjamin Franklin and adopted in 1754 by Albany Congress, a convention of delegates from the colonies and representatives of Iroquois Indians who met to discuss Indian problems and colonial defense. The plan called for a grand council, with representatives from each colony, which would deal with problems of taxation, defense, and trade. It was rejected by both Great Britain and the colonies but served as a basis for later plans of unification.
Franklin's plan used in forming the Articles of Confederation **F** 454

Albany Regency, New York political group **V** 273
Albatrosses, birds **B** 228
locomotion in air, picture **A** 295
principles of flight **B** 205
Albee, Edward, American playwright **A** 216; **D** 300
Albéniz (al-BAY-neez), **Isaac**, Spanish composer **S** 373
Albers (OLB-ers), **Josef**, German-born American painter **D** 143
Bauhaus **B** 105
Homage to a Square: Silent Hall, picture **D** 142
Albert I, king of Belgium **B** 131; **W** 271–72; picture **W** 270
Albert I, prince of Monaco **M** 406, 407
Albert, prince of Saxe-Coburg-Gotha, consort of Queen Victoria **E** 226–27; **V** 332
designed table centerpiece **D** 78
first Christmas tree in England **C** 291

Albert, Carl Bert (1908–), American lawyer and legislator, b. McAlester, Oklahoma. Albert practiced law in Oklahoma (1936–40), and served in the Army during World War II. He was elected to the House of Representatives in 1947 and became Speaker of the House in 1971.

Albert, Lake, east central Africa **L** 26
Alberta, Canada **A** 146a–h–147
Banff National Park **B** 42–43
Jasper National Park **J** 54–55
Alberta, University of **A** 146d
Alberti (ol-BER-ti), **Leon Battista**, Italian architect **A** 380; **I** 467, 477
Renaissance architecture **R** 164–65
Albert Lasker awards see Lasker Foundation, Inc.

Albertus Magnus, Saint (Albert, Count von Bollstadt) (1206?–1280), German philosopher, theologian, scientist, and writer, b. Lauingen, Swabia. Called Albert the Great or Universal Doctor, he became a Dominican monk (1223). He was teacher of Thomas Aquinas at Cologne (1248–54) and Bishop of Ratisbon (1260–62). Recognized by contemporaries as one of the foremost scholars of his time, he was noted for work on Aristotle and for his scientific investigations. He wrote *Summa de Creaturis.* He was beatified in 1622 and canonized in 1932.

Albigensian (al-bi-JEN-sian) **heresy** R 292

Albino (al-BY-no), human being or other animal born without normal color (pigment) in skin, hair, and eyes. An albino's hair is white, and eyes and skin are pink. Condition called albinism is hereditary. Plants also may be albinos.

Aldrich, Thomas Bailey (1836–1907), American author and editor, b. Portsmouth, N.H. He served as editor of *Every Saturday* (1865–74), and of *Atlantic Monthly* (1881–90). Although he is remembered chiefly for his novel *The Story of a Bad Boy* and short story "Marjorie Daw," other works include poems "Fredericksburg" and "Elmwood," novels *Prudence Palfrey* and *Stillwater Tragedy,* and nonfiction *Ponkapog Papers.*
  children's literature, place in C 240

Aldridge, Ira Frederick (1805?–1867), American actor, b. New York, N.Y. Called the African Roscius, he made his debut in London (1826) in title role of Shakespeare's *Othello.* One of the first Negroes to achieve stage fame, he is noted for interpretations of title roles in Shakespearian tragedies *Othello, Macbeth,* and *King Lear.*

Aldrin, Edwin E., Jr. ("Buzz") (1930–   ), American astronaut, b. Montclair, N. J. A fighter pilot in the Korean War, he worked with experiments in the Gemini-Titan flights before appointment as astronaut (1964). As lunar module pilot of Apollo 11 moon expedition in July, 1969, Col. Aldrin became the second man to walk on the moon. Pictures M 452, S 340h.
  first men on the moon S 399–340a
  space flight data S 344, 345, 346

Alexander, Chief (Wamsutta) (?–1662?), American Indian chief of Wampanoag Tribe of New England. He was brother of Chief Metacomet, known as King Philip. According to Indian legend, he was poisoned by English during Indian uprisings that ended in King Philip's War (1675–76).

Alexander I (1777–1825), czar of Russia (1801–25); b. St. Petersburg (Leningrad). He became czar after the assassination of his father, Czar Paul I. At the beginning of his reign Alexander promised social reforms, including emancipation of the serfs and a constitution, but these were never realized. His great struggle with Napoleon led to the invasion of Russia and the burning of Moscow (1812). Alexander took part in the Congress of Vienna (1815) following Napoleon's defeat, and formed the Holy Alliance with Austria and Prussia. During his reign Poland and Finland came under Russian rule.
  architecture in the Empire style U 54

Alexander II (1818–81), czar of Russia (1855–81), b. Moscow. He succeeded his father, Czar Nicholas I, during the Crimean War (1854–56). Alexander's greatest achievement was the emancipation of the serfs (1861), which won him the name Czar Liberator. He also initiated reforms in the Army, the government administration, and the courts, and introduced local self-government in provinces and cities. During his reign Russia gained territory in Central Asia and the Caucasus. The Czar's moderate reforms, however, failed to satisfy the radicals, and in 1881 Alexander was assassinated by revolutionaries.

Alexander III (1845–94), czar of Russia (1881–94), b.

Alexander III (continued)

Tsarskoye Selo (now Pushkin). He came to the throne after the assassination of his father, Czar Alexander II. Alexander III's rule was marked by his reaction against his father's moderate reforms. A strong nationalist, he tried to Russianize the subject peoples of Poland, Finland, and the Baltic countries, and he persecuted the Jews severely. The harsh conditions of the Russian peasants were alleviated somewhat during his reign, and industrial expansion was encouraged.

Alexander, Grover Cleveland (1887–1950), American baseball player; b. St. Paul, Nebr. He was one of baseball's greatest pitchers. During his 20-year career (1911–30) in the National League (with Philadelphia, Chicago, and St. Louis) he won 373 games, a league record he shares with Christy Mathewson. In 1916 he pitched 16 shutouts, a major league record. He was elected to the Baseball Hall of Fame in 1938.

Alexander, Harold Rupert Leofric George, 1st earl Alexander of Tunis (1891–1969), British field marshal, b. Tyrone, Ireland. During World War II he was in charge of evacuation of Dunkirk (1940) and commander in chief in Middle East (1942). As deputy allied commander in chief in North Africa, he directed invasions of Sicily and Italy (1943). Made field marshal and supreme allied commander of Mediterranean area (1944), he was also governor-general of Canada (1946–52) and British minister of defense (1952–54).
 World War II in North Africa **W** 295

Alexander III, king of Macedonia see Alexander the Great

Alexander I (Obrenovich) (1876–1903), king of Serbia (1889–1903), b. Belgrade. The last of the Obrenovich dynasty, he suspended (1894) liberal constitution of 1888 and annulled a series of laws passed by the radical government. He became more unpopular with his marriage to a commoner, Madame Draga Mashin. Both were finally assassinated by a group of military officers.

Alexander VI, pope
 Papal Line of Demarcation, of the New World
  E 378
Alexander Archipelago, island group, Alaska **I** 427
 Alaska's Panhandle **A** 130
Alexander Graham Bell Association for the Deaf **D** 53

Alexander Nevski (1220?–1263), Russian national hero and saint of Russian Orthodox Church, b. Vladimir. He defended Russia against invasions from west and in 1240 defeated Swedes at Neva River, thus earning surname Nevski. He became grand duke of Kiev and Novgorod (1246) and of Vladimir (1252).

Alexander the Great, king of Macedonia **A** 151–53;
  S 388
 Aristotle and Alexander **A** 397
 Greek civilization extended by **A** 230
 Soviet Central Asia **U** 46
 submarine experiment **S** 444
Alexandria, Louisiana **L** 360
Alexandria, Museum of **M** 510
Alexandria, Egypt **E** 90f; picture **E** 90b
 Alexander the Great founds **A** 152
 Pharos, lighthouse, wonder of ancient world **W** 216
 scientists of Alexandria **S** 63–64
Alexandria, Virginia **V** 357
Alexandrian Library, ancient Egypt **L** 194
 higher education in the ancient world **E** 65
Alexandrite (al-ex-AN-drite), gemstone **G** 75

Alexius I Comnenus (com-NE-nus) (1048–1118), Byzantine emperor (1081–1118), b. Constantinople. Usurping the throne from Nicephorus III, he strengthened the military forces, reinforced the treasury, and through war and diplomacy resisted foreign enemies, including Scythians, Turks, and Normans. He improved relations with the papacy, and the First Crusade (1196–99) took place during his reign. His life is recorded in the *Alexiad,* by his daughter Anna Comnena.
 Crusades **C** 538, 539

Aleykhem (a-LAI-kem), or **Aleichem, Sholem** (Solomon J. Rabinovich) (1859–1916), Jewish writer and humorist, b. Kiev, Russia. Considered one of classic modern Yiddish writers, he is remembered for his witty and satiric stories, written in rich idiomatic style, of Jewish life in Russia and America. Aleykhem inherited a large fortune but soon lost it in a publishing venture to encourage young Yiddish writers. He left Russia (1905) and settled in New York. His books include *Adventures of Mottel, The Great Fair,* and *The Writings of a Traveling Salesman.*
 Yiddish literature **Y** 350–51

Alfalfa, plant of the pea family, cultivated extensively as food for cattle and horses. Distinguished by its small purple flower, it was originally native to Asia and was probably introduced into Europe by invading armies before birth of Christ. Brought to New World by Spaniards, it is now widely cultivated in western plains of United States. A hardy plant, alfalfa is adaptable to most climatic and soil conditions. It is considered a soil-building crop, since it returns nitrogen to the soil. It may also deplete the soil of certain other elements. Picture **I** 409.

Alfaro (ol-FAR-o), **Eloy,** Ecuadorian political reformer
  E 58
Alfheim (OLF-heim), Norse fairyland **N** 279
Alfieri (al-fi-AIR-i), **Vittorio,** Italian poet **I** 479
Alfonso XIII, king of Spain **S** 358
Alfonso X, the Wise, king of Castile **S** 366–67
 gave Castilian Spanish a phonetic spelling **S** 366
Alfred the Great, king of England **A** 154–55; **E** 216–17
 English literature flourished under **E** 246–47
Algae (AL-ge), flowerless plants **A** 155–57; **M** 280
 eutrophication of water sources **W** 59
 experiments on use in spaceships **E** 352
 fertilizers stimulate growth and cause pollution
  E 272d, 272e
 food and oxygen for space travel **S** 349
 food use in future **P** 223, 310
 fossil, picture **F** 382
 lichens **F** 94
 plankton **P** 279–80
Algebra, branch of mathematics **A** 157–59; **M** 156
 Hamilton's algebra **M** 159–60
 new math ideas and subjects **M** 163
 See also Arithmetic
Alger, Horatio, American writer **C** 240
Algeria **A** 160–63
 Algerian family, picture **F** 42
 flag **F** 235
Algiers, capital of Algeria **A** 162
Algol, star **S** 409
 study of variable stars **A** 475–76
Algonkin, Indians of North America **I** 170–71
 present-day life in Quebec **Q** 10a
Alhambra (al-HAM-bra) **palace,** Spain **I** 421; **S** 350
 Court of the Lions, picture **S** 363
 Spanish art and architecture **S** 360
Alhazen (ol-ha-ZEN), Arab mathematician and optical scientist **O** 166; **S** 65

Ali, Muhammad (Cassius Marcellus Clay, Jr.) (1942–), American boxer, Negro, b. Louisville, Ky. In 1964 he took world heavyweight title and held it until 1967, when it was taken from him for refusing induction into the armed forces. In 1970 he was exonerated by the courts and returned to boxing. He met Joe Frazier for the title in 1971 but was defeated.
  boxing **B** 353

Ali Baba, hero of story "The Forty Thieves" from Arabian Nights **A** 346
Alice in Wonderland, book by Lewis Carroll **A** 164–65; **C** 123; excerpt **A** 164
Alice Springs, Australia **A** 503
Alien and Sedition Acts, United States **A** 10–11
  Alien Act and Alien Enemies Act, 1798 **A** 166
Alien Contract Labor Law, 1885 **I** 99–100
Aliens A 166
  citizenship and aliens **C** 311
  immigration and emigration **I** 98, 102
  naturalization **N** 58
  See also Citizenship; Immigration and emigration; Naturalization
Alimony, in divorce **D** 234
Alkalies, chemical bases **C** 216
  soaps contain **D** 145
Alkali metals C 216, 218; **E** 158
  electron shells, diagram **C** 203
Alkaline earth metals E 158
Alkyd (AL-kid) **resins,** types of liquid plastics
  paints **P** 32
  varnishes made from **V** 279
Allagash (AL-la-gash) **Wilderness Waterway,** Maine **M** 41
Allah (OL-lah), Arabic name for God of Islam **M** 404
Allahabad (al-la-ha-BAD), India
  religious bathing center **G** 25
All-American Canal, California **C** 19
All-American Soap Box Derby see Soap Box Derby
All Around the Kitchen, folk song **F** 324
Allegheny (AL-le-gainy) **Front,** escarpment
  a wall blocking overland trails **O** 254
Allegheny Mountains, North America
  canals **C** 86
Allegheny Plateau, eastern North America **M** 116–17; **N** 213; **P** 130–31; **W** 128
Allegheny River, picture **P** 130
Allegory, story to explain or teach something **F** 111
  early English literature **E** 248
  early French literature **F** 436
  Everyman, greatest morality play **E** 250
  Pilgrim's Progress **E** 256
Allegri, Antonio see Correggio, Antonio Allegri da
Allen, Ethan, American Revolutionary War hero **A** 166–67; **V** 319–20
  Revolutionary War **R** 199
Allen, Frederick Lewis, American writer **A** 214
Allen, Hervey, American novelist **A** 213
Allen, Horatio, American engineer **R** 88–89
Allen, Joseph P., IV, American astronaut **S** 346

Allen, Richard (1760–1831), American clergyman, b. Philadelphia, Pa. A slave who was freed by his master, he became a wandering minister and organized first church for Negroes (1787). He was first Negro minister in Methodist Episcopal Church (1799) and helped organize African Methodist Episcopal Church (1816), serving as its first bishop until his death.

Allende (ah-YEN-day), **Salvador** (Salvador Allende Gossens) (1908–), Chilean statesman, b. Valparaiso. A political activist at medical school, he was jailed for opposition to the government. He was elected a national deputy in 1937. With Socialist and Communist support, he ran unsuccessfully for the presidency in 1952, 1958, and 1964. In 1970 he became the first Marxist-Socialist ever elected president of a Western democracy.
  Chile, history of **C** 255

Allentown, Pennsylvania P 142
Allergy D 190–92
  streptococcal infections cause allergies **D** 207
All Hallows' Day H 15
Alliance for Labor Action (A.L.A.) **L** 7

Alliance for Progress (Alianza para el Progreso), a program of social and economic development for Latin America. It was first proposed by President John F. Kennedy and formally adopted by the U.S. and 19 Latin American countries under the Charter of Punta del Este in Uruguay in 1961. The Alliance's goals include tax and land reform; industrial and agricultural development; and improved education, housing, and transportation. The program is administered within the framework of the Organization of American States (OAS). The Latin American countries provide 80 percent of its funds, while the U.S. supplies 20 percent.
  OAS, aims and work of the **O** 211

Alliances, of nations **I** 322
Allied Control Council, over Germany after World War II **G** 163–64

Allied Youth, Inc., organization that sponsors educational programs for high school students. Programs are directed against the dangers of alcohol and narcotics. Founded in 1931, the organization has headquarters in Arlington, Va., and publishes The Allied Youth.

Allies, among nations **I** 322
Allies, in World War I **W** 272, 282
Alligators C 533–35; **R** 181
  leather from endangered species now little used **L** 107
  See also Reptiles

Alliluyeva, Svetlana Stalina (1926–), daughter of Soviet dictator, Joseph Stalin, b. Moscow, U.S.S.R. She came to the United States in 1967 from Moscow, where she had been a teacher of Soviet literature and English. She is the author of Twenty Letters To A Friend and Only One Year. In 1970 she married William W. Peters, chief architect of the Frank Lloyd Wright Foundation.

Alliteration, repetition of the same first sounds in a group of words **P** 353
  Beowulf **B** 141
All Men are Brothers see Water Margin, The, Chinese novel
Allotropes, different forms of a chemical element **C** 218

Allouez (ol-WAY), **Claude Jean** (1622–1689), French Jesuit missionary to North America, b. Saint-Didier, Haute Loire. He explored parts of Mississippi valley and Lake Superior region, where he founded missions.

Alloys A 168–69
  aluminum **A** 177
  amalgam **C** 218
  bronze and brass **B** 408–10
  cast iron **I** 405
  chemistry, history of **C** 205
  chromium alloys **C** 296
  copper **C** 502–03
  gold alloyed with other metals **G** 248
  kinds of steel **I** 396

Alloys (continued)
  magnesium alloys **M** 22
  magnets **M** 29
  nickel **N** 249–50
  properties of metals changed **M** 232
  silver **S** 182
  soldering and brazing, used in **S** 249–50
  standard jewelry alloys of gold **G** 248
  tin used in **T** 195
  tungsten and steel alloys **T** 308
  type metal **T** 343–44
    See also Brass; Brazing; Bronze; Metals and metallurgy; Soldering; Welding
Alloy steels **A** 168; **I** 396
All Saints' Day **H** 15
  Feast of All Saints **R** 154, 290
All Souls' Day, religious holiday **R** 154, 290
Allspice **S** 382
All-star games, in baseball **B** 78
All-star games, in football **F** 365
All's Well That Ends Well, play by Shakespeare **S** 133
All the Friendly Beasts, Christmas folk song **F** 325
Alluvial (al-LU-vial) **deposits** **R** 239
  gold found in **G** 248
Alluvial Floodplain, area of Louisiana **L** 350–51
Alluvial soils **S** 234
Alluvium (al-LU-vium), river deposits **R** 239
Almagro (ol-MA-gro), **Diego de**, Spanish soldier **P** 266
Almanacs, type of reference book **R** 130–31
  Poor Richard's Almanack **F** 452
Almandite (AL-mand-ite), garnet gemstone **G** 71
Almonds **N** 420–21
Almoravids (al-MO-ra-vids), Berber dynasty
  Moroccan empire founded by **M** 461
Alnico, alloy **M** 29
Alnilam, star **S** 407
Aloha (a-LO-ha) **State**, nickname of Hawaii **H** 56
Alouette (ol-oo-ETT), folk song **F** 322
Alpacas (al-PAC-as), hoofed mammals **H** 210; picture
  H 213
  native to the Andes **A** 253
Alpha-amylase (al-pha-AM-il-ace), digestive enzyme
  B 294
Alphabet **A** 170–73; **W** 318
  Arabic **M** 305
  Arabic letters used in Islamic art **I** 417
  Braille **B** 252–53
  communication advanced by **C** 431
  Communists introduce alphabet for Chinese **C** 258
  Danish has 29 letters **D** 106
  development of languages **L** 38
  encyclopedias in unit and split-lettered alphabetical
    systems **E** 197
  flags for the letters (International Code), pictures
    F 245
  forming letters in handwriting **H** 31–32
  Hebrew **H** 100
  Hindi, picture **I** 119
  indexes, learning to use **I** 115
  Initial Teaching Alphabet **I** 254
  Japanese language has none **J** 28
  Latin language **L** 76
  letter-by-letter arrangement in an index **I** 115
  letters, capitals and lower case, in manuscript and
    cursive writing, picture **H** 32
  letters in several type styles, picture **T** 343
  most used letter **E** 1
  pronunciation **P** 478
  Russian **U** 57
  sampler, picture **E** 187
  Should it be taught to a preschool child? **R** 108
  Welsh alphabet **W** 3

  word-by-word arrangement in an index **I** 115
    See also Writing; individual letters of the alphabet
Alpha Centauri, star **S** 405
  how distances between stars are measured **A** 475
Alpha particles, of radioactive atoms **A** 488; **R** 67
  ions and ionization **I** 353
Alpha rays, streams of alpha particles of radioactive
    elements **R** 67
  radioactive radiation **R** 45
  radiations emitted by nuclei **N** 359
Alpine glaciers **G** 223; **I** 19–20
  flow of ice, diagrams **I** 7, 8
Alpine plants
  wild flowers **W** 171
Alpine skiing **S** 184b, 185, 187
Alps, mountains of Europe **A** 174–75
  Alpine regions of Austria **A** 521–22; picture **A** 519
  branches named and located **E** 309
  cable cars, picture **G** 103
  great mountain systems of the world **M** 499
  landforms of Italy **I** 451
  Liechtenstein **L** 206–07
  Switzerland **S** 499–500
Al-Razi, Arab physician see Rhazes

Alsace (AL-sass) **and Lorraine**, historic region of eastern
France, a bone of contention between France and Germany through the Thirty Years War, the Franco-Prussian
War, and World Wars I and II. The chief cities are
Strasbourg, Metz, and Nancy. It is an agricultural area,
noted for its wines. Lorraine has rich iron ore deposits.
  France, history of **F** 418

Al-Salal, Abdullah *see* Salal, Abdullah al-
Alsted (OL-shtet), **Johann**, German encyclopedist **E** 197

Alston, Charles Henry (1907–   ), American artist, Negro,
b. Charlotte, N.C. began career in commercial art but
turned to depiction of Negro life in portraits and murals.
He has taught at Art Students League of New York (since
1950). His paintings include *Painting* and *The Family*.

Altaic (al-TAI-ic), or Turkic, **languages** **L** 40
Altair (al-TIRE), star **C** 493
Altamira Cave, Spain
  cave paintings **P** 14, 440
Alternating current (A.C.), in electricity **E** 134
  electric generators **E** 121–22
  electric motors **E** 137, 138–39
  rectified by diodes (electron tubes) **E** 146
  transformers **T** 249
Althing, Iceland's legislature **I** 44; **V** 339
Altimeter, measures altitude **A** 560; **B** 54
Altiplano regions, of South America **S** 276
  Bolivia **B** 303–04
Altitude
  climate and altitudes **C** 346
  climate control factor **W** 88–89
  cloud formation **C** 358
  in geometry **G** 125
  vertical life zones **Z** 372–73
  Yosemite's trails, range in altitude of **Y** 353
Alto, female voice **C** 277
Alto-cumulus clouds **C** 360; picture **C** 361
Altoona, Pennsylvania **P** 142
Alto-stratus clouds (AL-to-STRAIT-us) **C** 360; picture
  C 361
Altricial (al-TRI-cial) **birds** **B** 215

Alum, a white solid chemical compound. The most
common form contains potassium, aluminum, sulfur,
and oxygen. It is widely used in purifying water, dyeing

cloth, and making paper and also, in styptic-pencil form, to stop bleeding from small cuts.
    used as a mordant in dyeing **D** 369

Alumina, aluminum oxide **A** 176
    abrasive for grinding and polishing **G** 388
Aluminum, or **aluminium** **A** 176–77; **E** 154, 159
    atomic structure **A** 486
    canoes made of **C** 100
    five-ton ingot, picture **M** 231
    metals, chart of some ores, location, properties, uses **M** 227
    non-ferrous alloys **A** 168, 169
    world distribution, diagram **W** 260
Aluminum bronze, alloy **B** 409
Aluminum foil
    reflective insulation **I** 291
Aluminum oxide, or alumina **A** 176
    abrasive for grinding and polishing **G** 388
Alva, Fernando Alvarez de Toledo, duke of, Spanish statesman **N** 120

Alvarado (ol-va-RA-tho), **Pedro de** (1495?–1541), Spanish soldier, b. Badajoz. A companion of Cortez in conquest of Mexico (1519–21), he held command of Mexico City in Cortez' absence (1520). In Mexican rebellion he is said to have escaped death by jumping across a large gap in the causeway now known as Alvarado's Leap. He was an important figure in siege of Mexico City (1527), and he was governor of Guatemala (1530–32).

Alvarez (OL-va-raith), **Luis Walter,** (1911–), American physicist, b. San Francisco, Calif. A professor of physics at University of California (since 1945), he developed ground-controlled (radar) approach system for landing aircraft and did atomic research at Los Alamos (1944–45). In 1968 he received the Nobel Prize for contributions to physics of subatomic particles.

Alveoli (al-VE-ol-i), or air sacs, of the lungs **B** 277; **D** 203–04
Always Prepared, motto of U. S. Coast Guard **U** 175
Alyssum, sweet, flowers, pictures **G** 27, 28
A.M., ante meridiem, or before noon **T** 189–90
AM, radio see Amplitude Modulation

Amado (a-MA-do), **Jorge** (1912–), Brazilian novelist, b. Ilheos. His novels are noted for their portrayal of Brazilian life and social problems. Among his best-known works are *Terras do sem fim* (*The Violent Land*), *Cacáu* ("Cacao"), *Mar Morto* ("Sea of the Dead"), and *Shepherds of the Night.*

Amahl and the Night Visitors, opera by Gian-Carlo Menotti **O** 139–40; picture **O** 141

Amalekites (a-MAL-ek-ites), fierce nomadic tribe of Biblical times. They were traditional enemies of Israelites, who first encountered them during exodus from Egypt and thereafter fought them many times under Joshua, Saul, and David.

Amalgam (a-MAL-gam), alloy **C** 218
    gold and mercury **G** 247
    silver-mercury alloys **S** 182
Amalgamated Clothing Workers of America **C** 354
Amalgamation (a-mal-ga-MAY-tion), of ores **M** 228
    gold-extracting process **G** 249
Amana (am-AN-a) **colonies,** Iowa **I** 367
Amanitas (am-a-NI-tas), poisonous fungi **F** 499; pictures **F** 500
    destroying angel mushroom **M** 521

Amateur athletics
    Olympic Games **O** 108

Amateur Athletic Union of the United States (AAU), federation of amateur athletic clubs that serves as the governing body of all competitive amateur sports. It awards U.S. amateur championships, provides uniform rules, and keeps a bureau of records. Founded in 1888, it has headquarters in New York, N.Y., and publishes rule books for various sports and a monthly, *Amateur Athlete.*

Amateur Bicycle League of America **B** 171
Amateur Hockey Association **I** 35
Amateur radio see Radio, amateur

Amateur Softball Association of America (ASA), governing body for amateur softball in the United States. It provides standardized rules of play. Founded in 1933, ASA has headquarters in Oklahoma City, Okla., and publishes *Balls and Strikes,* a monthly.

Amateur Telescope Makers (ATM's) **T** 64
Amateur theatricals **T** 156
    putting on a play **P** 335–41
Amati (a-MA-ti) **family,** Italian violin makers **V** 342
Amazing Stories, science-fiction magazine **S** 84
Amazon ants **A** 324–25
Amazonite (AM-az-on-ite), gemstone **G** 76
Amazon River, South America **A** 178–79
    Amazon and Orinoco river systems **S** 277
    Brazil **B** 380–81
    How did the Amazon River get its name? **A** 179
    tidal bores **T** 185

Amazons, in Greek mythology, race of women warriors who lived around the Caucasus, allowing no men among them. Their children were fathered by men from neighboring nations, and sons were either killed or sent back to fathers. Their queen supposedly was killed by Achilles during Trojan war. They were a favorite subject in Grecian art and poetry.
    how the Amazon River got its name **A** 179

Ambassadors, highest-ranking officers in Foreign Service **F** 370
Ambassadors, The, painting by Holbein **N** 38
Amber, fossil resin **R** 184
    discovery of static electricity **E** 123
    "display case" for insects **E** 340; picture **E** 341
    organic gems **G** 76

Ambergris, waxy, grayish-black substance formed in digestive tract of sperm whales. It is usually obtained from slaughtered whales but is sometimes found floating in the sea. It is used to make perfume and is extremely valuable.
    fixatives in perfumes **P** 155
    whale products **W** 147, 152

Ambler, Eric (1909–), English author of mystery novels and films, b. London. His works are often based on international spying. He served in British Army in North Africa and Italy in World War II. His books include *A Coffin for Dimitrios, Journey into Fear,* and *Dirty Story.*
    spy-adventure stories **M** 556

Ambon, Indonesian Moluccas **I** 221
Ambrogini, Angelo see Poliziano
Ambrose, Saint **C** 283; **R** 289
    converted Saint Augustine **A** 494
    hymn composer **H** 311

Ambrosia, in mythology, food of the gods. Ambrosia supposedly gave immortality to those who ate it. In modern usage, it is anything pleasing to the taste.

Ambrosia beetles **P** 285
Ambulances (AM-bu-lan-ces)
 flag **F** 246
 stretcher being transferred, picture **H** 248
Amen, god *see* Amon-Re
Amendments to the United States Constitution **U** 155–58
 civil rights amendments in the Bill of Rights **C** 314
 Eleventh Amendment **J** 56
 First 10, Bill of Rights **B** 179
 Fourteenth Amendment **J** 125
 freedom of religion, speech and press in 1st amendment **F** 457
 how U.S. Constitution has been changed **U** 147–48
 See also Bill of Rights, American
Amenemhet I (om-en-EM-het), king of ancient Egypt **E** 98
Amenhotep III (om-en-HO-tep), king of ancient Egypt **E** 100; **N** 90
Amenhotep IV *see* Akhnaton
America
 American colonies **A** 180–94
 exploration and discovery of **E** 376–78, 382–84
 first shown on world map, picture **E** 376
 Vespucci, Amerigo, continents named for him **V** 323
 Viking discovery of **V** 339–40
 See also Central America; Latin America; North America; South America; names of countries
America, ocean liner **O** 22
America, song by Samuel Francis Smith **N** 24

American Academy of Arts and Letters (AAAL), honorary institution for advancement of creative work in literature, music, and art. Founded in 1904 by National Institute of Arts and Letters, it is composed of 50 members chosen from parent body on basis of their achievements. It awards grants and medals for distinguished work. Headquarters is in New York, N.Y.

American architecture *see* United States, architecture of
American art *see* United States, art of the

American Association for the Advancement of Science (AAAS), largest scientific society in United States. Members represent all fields of science. AAAS was founded in 1848. Most of its members reside in United States and Canada. The society maintains headquarters in Washington, D.C., and publishes the weekly *Science.*

American Association of School Librarians **L** 200
American Automobile Association (AAA) **V** 259

American Badminton Association (ABA), governing body for badminton in United States. The association aids in development of new clubs, maintains rules and determines status of players, and directs tournaments. It was founded in 1937 and has headquarters in San Diego.

American Bar Association (ABA), organization of attorneys who are admitted to practice law before state bars. The ABA seeks higher standards of legal education, sound federal and state legislation, uniform laws throughout states, and better administration of justice. Founded in 1878, it maintains headquarters in Chicago, Ill., and publishes *American Bar News* and *American Bar Association Journal.*

American Basketball Association **B** 90
American beech, tree, picture **T** 278

American Bible Society, nonprofit organization devoted to the circulation of the Bible throughout the world. It translates and distributes copies of the Bible in all languages and prepares a list of daily Bible readings annually. Founded in 1816, it has international headquarters in New York, N.Y., and publishes *Bible Society Record.*

American Bill of Rights **B** 177–80
American Bowling Congress (ABC) **B** 348, 349
American Boy, magazine **M** 16
American buffalo *see* Bison

American Camping Association (ACA), organization of camp owners, directors, counselors, camps, businesses, and others interested in organized camping. The association has committees on standards, health and safety, and agency and private camping, and it conducts the Campcraft Certification program. It was founded in 1910, has headquarters in Martinsville, Ind., and publishes *American Camping Magazine.*

American Cancer Society **C** 92
American Canoe Association **C** 101
American Checker Federation **C** 191

American Civil Liberties Union (ACLU), organization that seeks to protect the rights of all people, regardless of color, race, national origin, sex, creed, or political belief, as stated in the Declaration of Independence and the Constitution. It supports court test cases and protests repressive legislation and infringement of rights. It was founded in 1920, has headquarters in New York, N.Y., and publishes *Civil Liberties.*
 civil rights, protection of **C** 315

American Civil War *see* Civil War, United States
American College Testing (ACT) **E** 348
American colonies **A** 180–94
 architecture **A** 383–84
 cattle and other livestock **C** 146
 colonial life in America **C** 385–99
 communication **C** 435–36
 Declaration of Independence, events preceding **D** 59
 education and early schools in America **E** 69–70
 flags, historic **F** 228
 French and Indian Wars **F** 458–62
 homes **H** 180–82
 Jamestown, Virginia **J** 20–21
 Lafayette's role in American Revolution **L** 22
 literature **A** 195–96
 Oglethorpe founded Georgia **O** 59
 Penn, William **P** 127
 Pitt, William, Earl of Chatham **P** 265
 Plymouth Colony **P** 343–46
 police **P** 373
 political parties **P** 379
 population **U** 131–32
 postal service **P** 407
 prisons and criminals **P** 468
 Raleigh established Roanoke Island **R** 101
 Revolutionary War, events leading to **R** 194–98
 slavery, development of **S** 197–98
 taxation **T** 26
 territorial expansion **T** 105, 108
 thirteen stripes in the flag **F** 248
 United States began as a farming society **U** 128
 westward movement **W** 142–46
 Zenger, John Peter, wins fight for free press **Z** 369
American Colonization Society **N** 94
 Liberia **L** 167

American Conference, National Football League F 365
American crawl, swimming S 490–91
American Dental Association D 115
American drama D 299–300
   American literature, place of drama in A 215–16
American Dream #1, painting by Robert Indiana U 120
American eagles see Bald eagles
American Educational Theater Association T 162–63
American elk, or wapiti H 219
American elm, tree, picture T 276
   leaf, diagram L 115
   state tree of Massachusetts, Nebraska, North Dakota
     M 134; N 72, 323
American English W 240
   slang S 194
American Expeditionary Force (A.E.F.) W 279–80
   Pershing, commander in chief P 157

American Farm Bureau Federation (AFBF), federation of
50 state co-operative groups made up of farm and ranch
families. It promotes educational and legislative programs of benefit to farmers and conducts research in
agriculture, marketing, and transportation. Founded in
1919, in Chicago, it publishes *Nation's Agriculture*.

American Federation for the Blind B 254

American Federation of Arts (AFA), organization of art
institutions and individuals interested in fostering art
appreciation in the United States. It originates and
sponsors traveling art exhibitions, in the United States
and abroad, representing all the visual arts. It was
founded in 1909 and has its headquarters in New York,
N.Y. The federation publishes *Who's Who in American
Art*.

American Federation of Labor (AFL) L 4
   child labor laws, supporter of C 235
   Gompers, Samuel G 263
American Federation of Labor–Congress of Industrial
   Organizations (AFL-CIO) L 7
American Field Service V 259
American flag F 229
   flag code F 231, 234
   flying over the South Pole, picture P 370
   pledge to see Pledge of Allegiance
American folklore see Folklore, American
American Folklore Society F 314
American Football League F 365
American Foundation for Overseas Blind B 254

American Friends Service Committee (AFSC), relief organization sponsored by the Religious Society of Friends
(Quakers). Supported and staffed by members of all
denominations, it aims to relieve suffering and promote
peace; helps victims of war, poverty, and disaster
through relief and rehabilitation; and is also concerned
with race relations, housing, unemployment, and other
community problems. Founded in 1917, it has headquarters in Philadelphia, Pa. It shared the 1947 Nobel
peace prize with the Friends Service Council of Great
Britain.
   Quakers today Q 3

American Friends Society see Quakers
American Fur Company, of John Jacob Astor F 523

American Gold Star Mothers, patriotic organization of
mothers whose sons or daughters were killed in World
Wars I and II, the Korean conflict, and the Vietnam
War. Founded in 1928, it has headquarters in Washington, D. C., and publishes *Gold Star Mother*.

American Gothic, painting by Grant Wood W 221
American Guild of English Handbell Ringers B 136
American Hall of Fame see Hall of Fame for Great
   Americans
American Heart Association see Heart Association,
   American (AHA)
American Hero, The, song by Nathaniel Niles N 23
American history see America, exploration and discovery
   of; American colonies; United States, history of the
American holly
   state tree of Delaware D 87
   See also Holly
American Home Economics Association H 166

American Humane Association (AHA), organization of
societies and persons desiring to prevent cruelty to
children and animals. It was founded in 1877 and has
headquarters at Denver, Colo. Its publications include
National Humane Review, and *Shelter Shoptalk*.

American Indians see Indians of North America; Indians
   of South America

American Institute of Architects (AIA), professional society of architects. In collaboration with professional
schools, it offers educational programs for practicing
architects, interns, and students, and it conducts research, along with government and technical organizations, to help develop standards and codes in the
architectural field. It was founded in 1857 and has
headquarters in Washington, D.C. It publishes *AIA Journal*
monthly.

American Institute of Graphic Arts B 326
American Instructors of the Deaf D 53
Americanisms W 240

American Jewish Committee, a national organization of
American Jews, founded in 1906. Its aims are to fight
prejudice, to protect civil and religious liberties, and to
promote understanding through education and human
relations. Its publications (issued bi-monthly) include
the *Committee Reporter, Human Relations*, and a newsletter. It also publishes the monthly *Commentary*, an
independent magazine of opinion and criticism. The
Committee's headquarters are in New York City.

American Jewish Congress (AJC), organization of American Jews dedicated to preserving democracy, justice,
and the fundamental freedoms of the Constitution for all
groups. It works on behalf of civil rights by supporting
antidiscrimination laws and bringing court action against
violators of Constitutional freedoms. Founded in 1918 by
Louis Brandeis and other American Jews, it has
headquarters in New York, N.Y., and publishes *Congress
and Judaism*.

American Junior Rodeo Association (A.J.R.A.)
   R 282
American Kennel Club D 252, 259
   dog shows D 261
American Labor Party L 8
American Lawn Bowling Association B 349
American League, baseball B 75, 77

American Legion, organization of men and women veterans of World Wars I and II, the Korean conflict, and
the Vietnam War. It supports patriotism, national defense, and education in good citizenship and also works
for veteran benefits. Founded in 1919 by World War I
veterans, it has headquarters in Indianapolis, Ind., and
publishes *American Legion Magazine*.

American Library Association L 191
  book awards B 309–10b
American literature A 195–216
  contributions to art of the novel N 348–49
  place in the history of the drama D 299–300
  See also Canadian literature; Children's literature:
    Drama; Folklore, American; Humor; Latin-American
    literature; Literary criticism; Magazines; Short
    stories; names of writers

American Medical Association (AMA), national association of physicians. It provides professional information
to its members, assists in setting and maintaining
standards for medical schools and hospitals, and
promotes medicine and public health. Founded in 1847,
it has headquarters in Chicago, Ill., and publishes the
Journal of the American Medical Association.

American Museum of Natural History, New York City
  M 512; picture M 515
American music see United States, music of the; Folk
  music; Jazz; Negro spirituals
American National Red Cross see Red Cross

American National Theater and Academy (ANTA), organization of persons and groups in the professional, or
amateur theater. It aids in civic, industrial, charity, and
university productions and acts abroad as U.S. agency
for performing arts, exchange programs, and copyrights.
Founded in 1935, it has headquarters in New York, N.Y.
  stimulates appreciation for the theater T 162

American Newspaper Guild N 205
American Newspaper Publishers Association
  N 204–05
American Numismatic (nu-mis-MAT-ic) **Association** C 375

American Nurses Association (ANA), professional society
of registered nurses. The association sponsors research
in all fields of nursing, maintains a library, and gives
awards in special areas of nursing. It was founded in
1896 and has its headquarters in New York, N.Y. It
publishes *American Journal of Nursing* monthly.
  nursing organizations N 413

American painting see United States, art of the
American Party, or Know Nothing Party F 125; P 380
American Peace Society P 104
American Pharmaceutical (phar-ma-CEU-tic-al) **Associa-
tion** D 322
American Philosophical Society P 183
  founded by Franklin F 453
  scientific societies, growth of S 69–70
American Popular Revolutionary Alliance (APRA), Peru-
  vian political party P 166
American Printing House for the Blind B 253
American Professional Football Association F 365

American Public Health Association (APHA), professional
organization of public and industrial health officials and
workers to promote and protect personal and public
health. It conducts research in public health, publishes
information on the causes of communicable disease, and
explores worth of various medical care plans. Founded in
1872, it has headquarters in New York, N.Y., and
publishes *American Journal of Public Health.*

American Public Welfare Association (APWA), organization of public welfare agencies, professional staff
members, and others interested in public welfare. It was
founded in 1930 and has its headquarters in Chicago, Ill.
The association publishes *Public Welfare* quarterly.

American Radio Relay League (ARRL) R 63
American Red Cross see Red Cross
American Regionalist, art style
  Wood, Grant W 221
American Revolution see Revolutionary War
American Samoa S 25–27
  Pacific coaling stations for United States T 114

Americans for Democratic Action (ADA), organization of
politicians, businessmen, students, and other citizens
interested in liberal political ideas. It seeks to "formulate liberal domestic and foreign policies, based on the
realities and changing needs of American democracy"
and to obtain public support of such policies. The ADA
tries to realize its ideas through the major American
political parties. Founded in 1947, it has headquarters in
Washington, D.C., and publishes *ADA World* monthly.

American Shakespeare Festival Theater, Stratford, Conn.,
  picture C 479
**American Society for the Prevention of Cruelty to Ani-
mals** see Society for the Prevention of Cruelty to
Animals, American

American Society of Composers, Authors, and Publishers
(ASCAP), association of music writers and publishers. It
protects copyrights of members by licensing commercial
users of music (radio and TV stations and hotels),
tabulates the number of public performances of a member's work, and distributes royalties. ASCAP was founded
in 1914 by Victor Herbert, George Maxwell, Nathan
Burkan, and others. Its headquarters is in New York.

American Society of Newspaper Editors N 205
American Stock Exchange S 432–33
American upland, class of cotton C 523

American Veterans Committee (AVC), organization of
men and women who served in World Wars I and II, the
Korean conflict, and Vietnam. Its purpose is "to achieve a
more democratic and prosperous America and a more
stable world." Founded in 1943, it has headquarters in
Washington, D.C., and publishes the *AVC Bulletin.*

American Veterans of World War II and Korea see
  AMVETS
American War of Independence see Revolutionary War
American White Water Affiliation C 101
American Youth Hostels, Inc. H 253

America's Cup, yacht-racing trophy (originally called
Hundred Guinea Cup). It was won by U.S. schooner
America (1851) and presented to New York Yacht
Club (1857) to be used as an international challenge
trophy. Since 1870 it has been sought by numerous
challengers, mostly British, but has thus far been kept
by American yachts.

America the Beautiful, song by Katherine Bates
  N 25
Americium (am-er-IS-ium), element E 154, 159
Amerigo Vespucci see Vespucci

Ames, Lee Judah (1921–), American author and
illustrator of children's books, b. New York, N.Y.
Animator of Walt Disney and Terrytoon cartoons and
illustrator of comic books, magazines, and advertisements, he wrote *Draw, Draw, Draw* and (with his wife,
Jocelyn Ames) *City Street Games.*

Amethyst (AM-eth-ist), quartz gemstone G 75; Q 7;
  picture G 73

legend that the stone keeps its wearer from drunkenness **G** 74

Amharic (am-HARR-ic), official language of Ethiopia. It is the native language of the Amharas, who are descended from Semitic-speaking people from Arabia and are concentrated in central plateau region of Ethiopia. The Amharas are Christian.
    Ethiopian literature **A** 76b
    ruling group of Ethiopia **E** 296

Amicable numbers **N** 380
Amiens, Treaty of, 1802 **N** 10
    British win control of Trinidad **T** 292
Amin, Idi, Uganda president **U** 7
Amine, chemical **V** 370b
Amino (a-MI-no) **acids,** in body chemistry **B** 290–91, 295–96
    biochemists' study of **B** 184
    chain of molecules, picture **V** 363
    genetics **G** 84–85
    proteins in nutrition **N** 416
    structure of antibodies **I** 106
Amir, Arabic title see Emir
Amish (OM-ish), religious group, branch of Mennonite Church **P** 128; **F** 290
Amistad Revolt see Cinque, Joseph
Amman (OM-mon), capital of Jordan **J** 138
Ammeters (AM-met-ers), devices to measure electric current **E** 133
Ammonia (am-MO-nia), gas **G** 59; **N** 262
    absorption refrigerating systems **R** 137
    structural formula **C** 200
Ammonites, creatures with coiled shells **P** 437
Ammunition **G** 414–26
    explosives **E** 388–94
    lead **L** 94
Amnesty and Reconstruction, Proclamation of, 1863 **R** 117
Amoebas (a-ME-bas), one-celled animals **M** 277–78
    a giant amoeba **A** 265
    feeding habits **A** 274
    invertebrates, picture **A** 264
    reproduction **G** 77
Amoebic dysentery, disease **M** 278
Amon-Re (om-on-RAY), ancient Egyptian sun-god **A** 221
Amon-Re, Great Temple of, Karnak, Egypt **A** 371–72; **E** 100
Amortization, of a debt **R** 112
Amos (A-mos), book of Bible, Old Testament **B** 155
Amos, Hebrew prophet **J** 105
Amoskeag (AM-os-keg) **Mills,** New Hampshire **N** 153
Amperage (AM-per-age), of electricity **E** 122, 133
Ampère (ON-pare), **André Marie** **E** 129, 133; **T** 51
    electric motors, history of **E** 140
    experiments in magnetism **M** 28
Amperes (AM-peres), units of measure in electricity **E** 133; **T** 250
Amphetamines (am-PHET-a-means), drugs
    drugs as stimulants **D** 330
Amphibians (am-PHIB-ians), aircraft **A** 557
Amphibians, land-water animals **F** 470–78
    evolution of fishes **F** 182–83
    prehistoric animals, development of **P** 437
    three-chambered heart **M** 72
Amphibious ships
    United States Navy **U** 192
Amphibious warfare
    United States Marine Corps **U** 178
Amphitheaters (AM-phi-theaters), outdoor theaters **T** 156
    Epidaurus, Greece, picture **G** 335
    Greek drama, picture **D** 294

Amphitrite (am-PHIT-ri-tee), in Greek mythology, goddess of the sea. The wife of sea god, Poseidon, she cared for ocean creatures and controlled the waves.

Amphoras, ancient Greek vases, pictures **A** 364; **D** 69
Amplification, of electric currents
    triodes (electron tubes) **E** 146
Amplification, of sound
    electronic music **E** 142h
Amplifiers
    transistors **T** 254
Amplitude, in physics
    noise, in decibels of sound **N** 269–70
    sound waves **S** 258–59
    strength of waves **T** 253
Amplitude modulation (AM)
    radio **R** 57
Amsterdam, capital of the Netherlands **N** 116, 118; picture **N** 115
    canal bridge, picture **H** 170
    early stock exchanges **S** 429
Amsterdam Island, in Indian Ocean, picture **I** 423

Amtrak, quasi-governmental corporation created by Congress to take over responsibility of maintaining railroad passenger service between 300 American cities went into operation, May 1, 1971.
    railroads, history of **R** 80

Amu Darya (om-U DAR-ya), river, formerly Oxus, in western Asia **A** 43, 44
Amulets (AM-u-lets), ornaments to ward off evil **G** 74
Amundsen, Roald, Norwegian explorer
    first Northwest Passage by sea **N** 338; **P** 364, 365
    first to reach South Pole **P** 366

Amundsen (OM-un-sen) **Sea,** body of water in South Pacific off coast of Antarctica (east of Ross Sea, between Thurston Peninsula and Cape Dart). It was explored by a Norwegian, Nils Larsen, who named it (1929) after Raold Amundsen, discoverer of South Pole.
    Antarctic Ocean, arms of **O** 45

Amur (om-OOR) **River,** Asia **R** 242
    beach at Khabarovsk, Siberia, picture **U** 47
Amusements see Recreation

AMVETS (American Veterans of World War II and Korea), veterans' organization that aims to promote peace, protect the American way of life, and improve the welfare of veterans. It was founded in 1944.

An, Babylonian god see Anu
Anableps, four-eyed fish, picture **F** 191
Anaconda (an-a-CON-da) **Company** **M** 443
Anacondas, snakes **A** 263; **S** 207
Anacortes (an-a-COR-tese), Washington, picture **W** 21
Anadolu, Asian Turkey **T** 324
Anadromous (a-NAD-ro-mous) **fish**
    habitat, feeding habits, uses **F** 215
Anaerobic bacteria **B** 11
    hyperbaric chambers, use against **M** 210
Anagrams, word games **W** 236
Analgesics, substances that relieve pain **N** 13
Analysis, in chemistry **C** 196, 218
Analytical method, of philosophy **P** 191
Analytic geometry **M** 157
Anansi (Spider), hero of African folktales **A** 76a
Anapests, metrical feet in poetry **P** 354
Anarchism (AN-arc-ism), theory that all government is evil **G** 276

Anasazi (ah-na-SA-zi), cliff dwellers **C** 415
Anatolia (an-a-TO-lia), Asia Minor, now Anadolu, Turkey **A** 238; **T** 324
  See also Asia Minor
Anatomy (a-NAT-omy), **comparative**
  body plan of animals **B** 269–70
Anatomy, human, structure of human body **B** 267–83
  father of, Andreas Vesalius **B** 189
Anaximander (an-ax-i-MAN-der), Greek philosopher **S** 62
Ancestor worship **R** 145
  African art reflects **A** 72
  art of the Pacific islands **P** 9
  China **C** 260
Anchises (an-KY-sese), father of Aeneas **A** 35
Anchorage (ANC-or-age), Alaska **A** 141
Anchors Aweigh, song by Miles and Lovell **N** 25
Anchovies (AN-cho-vies), fishes **P** 163
Ancient civilizations **A** 217–32
  African kingdoms, early **A** 66–67; **N** 90–91
  aqueducts **A** 344
  art as a record **A** 438b
  art see Ancient world, art of the
  Asia **A** 466
  Aztec Indians of North America **I** 195, 197
  bread and baking **B** 385
  early history of Greece **G** 338
  education systems **E** 61–62
  Egypt, ancient **E** 91–92
  European civilization, development of **E** 330
  fairs and expositions **F** 9
  food in ancient times **F** 333
  grain crops **G** 281
  historical writings **H** 134
  homes **H** 177–78
  Incas, Indians of South America **I** 203–07
  masonry of brick and stone **B** 393–94
  Maya Indians of North America **I** 197–99
  Mediterranean Sea regions **M** 214
  Middle East called the cradle of civilization **M** 306
  music see Ancient world, music of the
  mythology **M** 557–64
  science, advances in **S** 60
  slavery **S** 195
  technology **T** 45–46
  Zimbabwe, picture of stone ruins **R** 230
  See also Archeology; names of ancient races and peoples; names of countries of ancient times
Ancient history see Ancient civilizations
Ancient world, art of the **A** 233–43
  art as a record **A** 438b
  Egyptian art and architecture **E** 93–103
  furniture design **F** 505
  Indian art of North and South America **I** 152–57
  See also Ancient civilizations; Archeology; Architecture; Prehistoric art; Sculpture; Wonders of the world; names of ancient countries
Ancient world, music of the **A** 243–47
  See also Musical instruments
Ancohuma (on-co-OO-ma), mountain in Bolivia **B** 303–04
Ancón (an-CONE), Ecuador **E** 55
Andalusia (an-da-lu-SI-a), Spain **S** 357
  folk music **S** 372, 373
Andalusian dialect, of Spain **D** 152
Andaman (AN-da-man) Islands, India **I** 427
Andaman Sea **O** 45
AND circuits, of computers **C** 454; picture **C** 455
Anders, William A., American astronaut **S** 344, 345, 346
Andersen, Hans Christian, Danish writer of fairy tales **A** 247–49; **F** 21
  Andersen Medal, book award **B** 310
  children's literature **C** 238
  "Emperor's New Clothes, The" **A** 249–51

place in Scandinavian literature **S** 52
  "Princess on the Pea" **F** 26
Anderson, Carl, American cartoonist **C** 128

Anderson, Dame Judith (1898–   ), actress, b. Adelaide, Australia. She has lived primarily in United States. Noted for performances of tragic roles in such plays as Eugene O'Neill's *Mourning Becomes Electra* and Robinson Jeffers' *Medea*, she is also famous as a Shakespearean actress, especially for roles in *Hamlet* and *Macbeth*.

Anderson, Marian, American singer **A** 251; **N** 98, 107
Anderson, Maxwell, American playwright **A** 216
Anderson, Orvil A., American military balloonist **B** 32

Anderson, Robert (1805–1871), American army officer, b. Louisville, Ky. He was graduated from U.S. Military Academy at West Point (1825) and served in Black Hawk, Seminole, and Mexican wars. He was in command at Fort Sumter during Confederate attack that marked start of Civil War (1861).

Anderson, Sherwood, American writer **A** 207; **S** 167
Anderson, South Carolina **S** 308
Andersonville National Cemetery, Georgia **G** 142
Andes (AN-dese), mountains of South America **A** 252–53; **M** 499
  ancient Indian civilizations **I** 201–07
  Argentina **A** 391; picture **A** 392
  Bolivian **B** 303–04
  Chile **C** 252, 253
  in Peru, picture **M** 498
  landforms of South America **S** 276
  railroad pass, picture **G** 102
  Venezuela **V** 297

Andes, Army of the, carried out one of the great feats in military history by crossing the Andes in January, 1817. Recruited and trained by the Argentinian liberator José de San Martín, the army of some 5,000 men left Mendoza, Argentina, and traveled through passes at average altitudes of some 12,000 feet to Chacubuco, Chile. The crossing was dangerous and costly; most of the men survived, but more than half of the 9,000 mules and nearly one third of the 1,600 horses did not. The army's victory at Chacabuco marked the first decisive battle for South American independence from Spain.
  Chile, history of **C** 254
  flag **F** 239
  San Martín, José de **S** 36

Andesite (AN-dese-ite), a volcanic rock **S** 433
Andorra (an-DOR-ra) **A** 254–55
  flag **F** 239
Andorra la Vella, capital of Andorra **A** 254, 255
Andover, New Hampshire, picture **N** 153
Andradite (an-DRA-dite), gem mineral **G** 75
André, Brother, Canadian churchman **Q** 13
André (ON-dray), Major John, English spy **R** 207
  Arnold and André **A** 436
  famous spies **S** 388
  Purple Hearts awarded to André's captors **M** 198
Andreä (on-DRAY-a), Johann Valentin, German Lutheran minister **U** 255
Andrea Chénier (shain-YAY), opera by Giordano **O** 140
Andrea del Sarto see Sarto, Andrea del
Andrea Doria, ocean liner **O** 24
Andrew, Saint, one of the 12 Apostles **A** 332–33
  Scottish feast of St. Andrew **H** 156
Andrews, Roy Chapman, American zoologist, explorer, and writer **W** 206

Andrews, Texas
an open-plan school, picture **S** 57
Andreyev (on-DRAY-ef), **Leonid,** Russian author **U** 61
Andric (AN-dreech), **Ivo,** Yugoslav writer **Y** 355

Androcles (AND-roc-lese), or **Androclus,** Roman slave who lived sometime during 1st century A.D. According to legend, after escaping from his master he befriended a wounded lion. He was later saved from death when the lion chosen to kill him in the arena turned out to be his old friend. George Bernard Shaw's *Androcles and the Lion* was based on this story.

Andromeda (an-DROM-e-da), constellation **C** 493
spiral galaxy in, diagram **U** 197
Andromeda, in Greek mythology **G** 362
Andronicus, Lucius Livius see Livius Andronicus, Lucius
Andros, Sir Edmund, English governor **C** 466, 480
And Wonder, sonnet by Merrill Moore **S** 256
Anegada, one of the Virgin Islands, British **C** 118
See also Virgin Islands, British
Anemia (a-NE-mia) **D** 192–93
dietetics and study of anemia **B** 182–83
pernicious anemia **V** 370d
transfusion used in treatment **T** 251
sickle-cell anemia, crescent-shaped red blood cells of, picture **D** 192
Anemometers (an-em-OM-et-ers), instruments to measure winds **W** 84
Anemones (a-NEM-o-nes), **sea,** polyps **J** 74
pictures **J** 72
damselfish immune to poison, picture **F** 204
Aneroid (AN-er-oid) **barometer B** 54; **W** 82–83
Anesthesia (an-es-THE-sia) **A** 256–59
acupuncture **M** 208b
drugs **D** 326
progress in modern surgery **M** 208a
See also Drugs; Medicine, history of
Anesthetics (an-es-THET-ics) **A** 258; **P** 314
Angel, painting by Fra Angelico **R** 166
Angel Falls, Venezuela **S** 277; **V** 298; **W** 56b
Angelfish, picture **F** 192
Angelico (on-GEL-ic-o), **Fra,** Italian painter **A** 259; **P** 20
Renaissance art **R** 166

Angelus, Roman Catholic prayer that may be recited at the sound of the Angelus bell three times daily, morning, noon, and evening; name comes from first line of prayer *Angelus Domini nuntiavit Mariae* ("The Angel of the Lord declared unto Mary").

Anger, feeling of, psychology **M** 220–21
divorce, attitudes toward **D** 235
Angerstein (ANG-er-stine), **John Julius,** English merchant and art patron **N** 39
Angiospermae, division of the plant kingdom **P** 292
Angkor, ruins of ancient empire in Cambodia **C** 31
Angkor Thom, capital of the Khmer Empire **S** 334
ruins of the ancient city in Cambodia **C** 33
Angkor Wat (Vat) temple in Cambodia **S** 334; picture **C** 33
picture on Cambodian flag **C** 31
Angle of incidence, in physics of light, diagram **L** 261
Angle of reflection, in physics of light, diagram **L** 261
Angles, Germanic people, invaders of Britain **E** 216
Angles, in geometry **G** 124; diagrams **G** 125
Angleworms see Earthworms
Anglican Church, or Protestant Episcopal Church **P** 483–84
Reformation **R** 134–35
See also England, Church of
Angling see Fishing

Anglo-Egyptian Sudan see Sudan
Anglo-Irish Trade Agreement, 1965 I 389
Anglo-Norman French language F 433
Anglo Romanies, gypsies **G** 433
Anglo-Saxon Chronicle E 246
Alfred the Great **A** 155
Anglo-Saxon language E 243
compared with Anglo-Norman French **F** 433
names **N** 4
Anglo-Saxon (Old English) **literature E** 245–47
Beowulf **B** 141–42
Anglo-Saxons, Teutonic peoples who settled in England **E** 216
Celtic and Anglo-Saxon art **E** 233–34
conversion to Christianity **C** 284

Anglund, Joan Walsh (?–), American author and illustrator of children's books, b. Hinsdale, Ill. She is noted for her small, uniquely illustrated books, which often rhyme. Her works include *A Friend is Someone Who Likes You* and *Love Is a Special Way of Feeling.*
A Friend is Someone Who Likes You, picture from **C** 245

Angola (an-GO-la) **A** 260–61; **P** 402
Angora (an-GO-ra), now Ankara, capital of Turkey **T** 326
Angora goats C 151, 152
Angostura, Venezuela see Ciudad Bolivar

Angström (ONG-strem), **Anders Jonas** (1814–1874), Swedish physicist, b. Lödgö. He was a founder of spectroscopy—science dealing with light separated into its various colors or wavelengths. His studies of wavelengths of light led to his discovery (1862) of hydrogen in the atmosphere. Angstrom unit (A), used in measuring wavelengths of light, is named in his honor.
units of measure of light wavelengths **E** 24

Anguilla (an-GWIL-ah), one of the Leeward Islands in the West Indies, formerly a British colony. The island has an area of 34 square miles. It was affiliated with islands of St. Kitts and Nevis in February, 1967, to form associate self-governing state within the Commonwealth of Nations.
Caribbean Sea and islands **C** 116–19

Animal behavior see Animals: Intelligence and behavior
Animal defenses
adaptations for self protection **L** 219
butterflies and moths **B** 470
frogs, toads, and other amphibians **F** 477–78
insects **I** 274–76
lizards' protective behavior **L** 320–21
mammals **M** 66–67
Animal diseases
vectors **V** 283
veterinarians and what they do **V** 324
Animal gods M 560
Animal intelligence see Animals: Intelligence and behavior
Animal kingdom K 249–59
classes of animals **A** 262, 264
eggs and embryos **E** 88–90a
how classification works **T** 30
Animal locomotion see Animals: Locomotion
Animal plankton P 280–81
Animals A 262–74
Africa **A** 50; pictures **A** 51
agents for dispersal of seeds **F** 281–82
ages of, how to tell, pictures **A** 86
amphibians **F** 470–78
Asia's wildlife **A** 451

Annapolis Valley, Nova Scotia, Canada **N** 344b; picture **N** 344e

Annapurna, mountain peak in Nepal, picture **N** 112

Ann Arbor, Michigan
music festival **M** 522

Annatto (an-NOT-to), yellow dye **D** 369

Anne, Princess (Anne Elizabeth Alice Louise) (1950–), second child of Queen Elizabeth II of England and Philip, Duke of Edinburgh, b. London. She is fourth in line to throne of England, after older brother, Prince Charles, and younger brothers, princes Andrew and Edward.

Anne, queen of Great Britain and Ireland **E** 224–25

Anne, Saint, mother of Virgin Mary and wife of Joachim. She is often pictured wearing a veil. One of many shrines dedicated to her is Ste. Anne de Beaupré near Quebec City, Canada. She is believed by many to have the power to effect miraculous cures. She is the patron saint of Quebec. Feast day is July 26th.

Annealing, heating-cooling process **M** 232
bronze and brass **B** 410
glass **G** 232
steel **I** 403
wire **W** 190a

Anne Boleyn see Boleyn, Anne

Anne in White, painting by Bellows **U** 118

Annelids (AN-nel-ids), worms **W** 309–10

Anne of Cleves, 4th wife of Henry VIII of England **H** 109

Annobón, island area of Equatorial Guinea **E** 273, 274

Annotations, for books
library catalog cards **L** 187

Annual rings, of tree growth **T** 286–87

Annuals, plants **P** 303
cultivated grasses **G** 317
gardens and gardening **G** 29–30, 46

Annuities, insurance **I** 295

Annular eclipses **E** 46

Annulment of marriage **D** 234

Annunciation Day, religious holiday **R** 154

Annunciation of the Virgin, in New Testament (Luke), announcement by archangel Gabriel to the Virgin Mary that she would bear a son, to be called Jesus. Feast day is celebrated March 25.

Annuu see Samoa

Anoles (a-NO-les), lizards **L** 319; picture **L** 318

Anopheles (a-NOPH-el-ese) **mosquito** **H** 260
insects harmful to man **I** 283

Anouilh (on-NUI), **Jean,** French playwright **F** 441

Anselm, English archbishop **C** 236

Ant and the Grasshopper, The, fable by Aesop **F** 5

Antarctic, south polar region **P** 363, 366–71
American claims by exploration **T** 115
birds of **B** 226, 228
Ewing-Donn theory of Ice Ages **I** 24
frigid, or polar zones **Z** 372
icebergs **I** 27
ice sheet and ice islands **I** 11–12
International Geophysical Year **I** 319–20
penguins, where they live, map-diagram **P** 121

Antarctica (ant-ARC-tic-a), hub of the Antarctic region **P** 366; picture **C** 344
Argentina claims in **A** 390
exploration by Byrd **B** 481
mountain peaks, highest in Antarctica **M** 494

Antarctic Ocean **O** 45

Antarctic Treaty, 1959 **P** 363, 371

Antares (an-TAR-ese), star **C** 493

Anteater civets, or falanoucs, animals **G** 93

Anteaters, mammals **M** 66
Australian wildlife **A** 504

Anteaters, spiny **P** 333–34

Antelopes, hoofed mammals **H** 221
antelope family, pictures **H** 217

Antennae (an-TENN-e), of animals
butterflies and moths **B** 468
crustacea **S** 169–70
"feelers," of insects **I** 262–63, 266–69
fire ant, picture **A** 323

Antennas, of radar and radio **R** 35, 51
Apollo tracking antennas **S** 340g
communications satellites **E** 142e, 142f
radio-astronomy observatories **O** 10
radio telescopes **R** 70–72

Anthem, musical form **M** 535

Anthemius of Tralles (anth-E-mius of TRAL-les), Byzantine architect **B** 485

Anthems, national see National anthems and patriotic songs

Anthers, of flowers **F** 277; **P** 295; picture **F** 276

Anthocyanins (an-tho-CY-an-ins), plant pigments **T** 282

Anthony, Susan Brownell (1820–1906), American woman suffragist and reformer, b. Adams, Mass. Born into a Quaker home, she was first a schoolteacher, then an active worker for temperance, abolition, and women's rights. She lectured across the United States for equal rights for women, was one of the organizers, with Elizabeth Cady Stanton, of the National Woman Suffrage Association (1869), and was president of the National American Woman Suffrage Association (1892–1900).
woman suffrage movement **W** 212b

Anthony of Padua, Saint (1195–1231), Franciscan monk and theologian, b. Lisbon, Portugal. He taught theology and preached in France and Italy. According to legend, once when he could not get people to listen to him, he turned and preached to a school of fish. who miraculously gave him their attention. He was canonized in 1232 and is patron saint of Portugal and Padua.

Anthracite, hard coal **C** 362, 363; **F** 487

Anthrax, disease **I** 287; **M** 208
disease, conquest of **D** 215
Koch discovers microbes causing **K** 293
Pasteur, Louis **P** 96–97

Anthropology (an-thro-POL-ogy), study of man **A** 300–09
archeology related to **A** 349, 364
blood groups studied **B** 258
Mexico City's National Museum of Anthropology **M** 251, 253
prehistoric man **P** 442–46
races of man **R** 29–32
research methods **R** 182
See also Ancient civilizations; Prehistoric art

Anti-aircraft guns **G** 426

Anti-aircraft missiles, or SAM—surface-to-air missiles **M** 347

Antibiotics **A** 310–16; **M** 208a
disease, conquest of **D** 217
drug industry **D** 323
Fleming's work **F** 249
genetic strains of microbes produce antibiotics **G** 88
only drugs that kill microbes directly **D** 327

Antibodies **A** 317; **V** 260
acquired immunity **I** 104–05; **M** 209
Behring's research **D** 215–16
control of parasite diseases **D** 188
rejection of organ transplants **M** 211
structure and source **I** 106–07

Anticline, rock formation, with oil deposit, diagram **P** 170

Anti-Comintern Pact, 1936 **W** 286

Anticorrosives see Corrosion

Anticosti Island, Quebec **I** 427

Anticyclones, or highs, in meteorology **W** 75, 187

Antidotes, remedies for effects of poisons **P** 356
  first aid for oral poisoning **F** 158

Antietam (an-TEE-tam) (Sharpsburg), **battle of,** 1862, Civil War **C** 324

Antietam National Battlefield Site, in Maryland **M** 123

Antifouling paints **P** 33

Antifreeze, chemical **I** 4

Antigens **A** 317
  acquired immunity **I** 105

Antigonish, poem by Hughes Mearns **N** 274

Antigua (an-TI-gwa), Guatemala **G** 391; picture **G** 393

Antigua (an-TI-ga), a member of West Indies Associated States, and self-governing within the Commonwealth of Nations, is located in the Lesser Antilles island group in the Caribbean, with the capital at St. Johns. It administers the Barbuda and Redonda islands. Its economy is based on sugar, cotton, and rum distilling. Discovered by Columbus (1493), the island of Antigua was settled by the British in 1632.
  Caribbean Sea and islands **C** 116–19

Antihistamines, drugs for allergic diseases **D** 192

Anti-Lebanon Mountains, Syria **S** 507

Antilles (an-TILL-es), island group dividing Caribbean Sea from Atlantic Ocean **C** 116–19

Antilles Current **G** 411

Antilles, Greater see Greater Antilles

Antilles, Lesser see Lesser Antilles

Antimasque, comic dance preceding masque **D** 25

Antimissile missiles **M** 347

Antimony (AN-tim-ony), element **E** 154, 159
  metals, chart of some ores, location, properties, uses **M** 227

Antioch (AN-ti-ock), ancient city, now Antakya, Turkey
  center of Apostles' missions to Gentiles **R** 288

Antioch College, Yellow Springs, Ohio
  Horace Mann, president **M** 83

Antiochus Epiphanes (an-TY-o-chus e-PIPH-an-ese), Syrian king **H** 35

Antioxidants (an-ti-OX-id-ants), additives to lubricants **I** 371
  vitamin E **V** 371

Antiparticles, subatomic particles **N** 370

Anti-perspirants (an-ty-PER-spir-ants)
  deodorizers **D** 117

Antiprotons, subatomic particles **N** 370

Antiques (an-TEEKS) **and antique collecting** **A** 318–21
  furniture design **F** 505–10
  interior decorating **I** 302–03

Antiquities (an-TI-quit-ies), **popular** **F** 302

Anti-Semitism, hostility toward Jews and Judaism **J** 110

Antiseptics **D** 222; **M** 202
  Lister, Joseph **L** 311
  See also Disinfectants

Antiserums, used to acquire passive immunity **I** 106; **V** 261
  contain antibodies **A** 317

Antisubmarine weapons **S** 446

Antitoxins, a kind of antibody **V** 260

Antitrust laws **T** 305–06

Antlers
  deer **D** 83; **H** 219
  mammals **M** 67

Antoinette Perry Memorial Award see Tony Award

Antonescu (on-to-NES-cu), **Ion,** Rumanian general **R** 359–60

Antonioni, Michelangelo, Italian motion-picture director **M** 488

Antony, Mark, Roman general **M** 100; **R** 303
  Cicero's opposition to **C** 298

Antony and Cleopatra, play by Shakespeare **S** 133

Antonyms and synonyms **S** 504

Antrodemus, dinosaur **D** 174

Ants **A** 322–31
  animal maze tests **A** 283; picture **A** 284
  aphids, "ant cows," picture **P** 286
  bull-horn acacia, home of ants **P** 283
  household pests **H** 261
  how to build an ant observation nest **A** 330
  strength of **I** 273–74

Ant's cows see Aphids

Antwerp, Belgium
  trade, early development of **S** 428

Anu, Babylonian god **M** 557

Anubis (a-NU-bis), in Egyptian legend and religion, god of the dead, who ruled over graves and supervised burial. He was the son of Osiris, chief Egyptian god and symbol of regeneration, fertility, and life. Picture **M** 560

Anvil, bone in the ear, diagram **B** 285

Anvil-topped cumulo-nimbus cloud, picture **C** 361

Anzacs, nickname given to Australian and New Zealand soldiers. The name is formed from initials of Australian-New Zealand Army Corps. The term originally referred only to those who took part in Gallipoli landings (1915) but applied in World War II to all New Zealand and Australian troops.

Anzio, Italy
  beachhead battle, World War II **W** 298

Anzus Council, or **Pacific Council,** organization comprised of Australia, New Zealand, and U.S., from whose initials the name is derived. It was established by Tripartite Security Treaty (1951), a pact to provide for mutual defense of the 3 nations and of their possessions in the Pacific.

Aorta (a-OR-ta), artery carrying blood from heart **B** 276
  heart action **H** 86a

Aoudad (OWD-ad), a kind of wild sheep **S** 145

AP see Associated Press

Apache (ap-ACH-e), Indians of North America **I** 193–95
  Arizona **A** 413
  beadwork, pictures **I** 194
  Geronimo **G** 189
  Indian Wars **I** 214
  New Mexico **N** 187
  See also Cochise

Apartheid (a-PART-ate), racial segregation in Republic of South Africa. The term is Afrikaans for "separateness." Apartheid is a continuation of economic, political, and social discrimination and segregation that existed from the 17th century. It became a political issue when incorporated into Nationalist Party platform (1948). Aim of the white group is establishment of separate residential districts for nonwhites. This policy has been condemned by UN General Assembly.
  South Africa **S** 268
  South West Africa **S** 336

Apartment houses **H** 182–84

ancient Rome **H** 178
Borneo, picture **B** 338
New York City, picture **N** 232
Stockholm, picture **S** 484
Tel Aviv, Israel, picture **A** 468
See also Condominium
Apennines (AP-en-nines), mountain range of Italy **I** 451
San Marino **S** 35–36
Apéritifs (a-per-i-TEEFS), or appetizer wines **W** 188
Apes **M** 418
ancestors of apes **E** 347
animal communication **A** 280, 281
ape family, pictures **M** 419
feet and hands **F** 83
Aphelion (a-PHE-li-on), point in comet's or planet's orbit
farthest from the sun **S** 241
Mars **M** 105
Mercury's orbit, picture **R** 144
Aphids, plant lice **P** 285–86, 288
ant food **A** 329; picture **A** 322
vectors of plant diseases **V** 284
Aphrodite (aph-rod-ITE-e), Greek goddess **G** 361
Apia (a-PI-a), capital of Western Samoa **S** 23
Apiary (APE-i-ary), colony of bees **H** 202
Apis (A-pis), sacred bull of Egypt **C** 145
Aplodontia (ap-lo-DON-tia), or mountain beaver **R** 277;
picture **R** 278
store hay **M** 66
Apocalypse (a-POC-a-lips), Biblical book of Revelation
B 162
Apocrypha (a-POC-riph-a) **B** 152, 156–57, 159
Apodes (AP-o-dese), order of fishes **E** 85
Apogee, point of a satellite's orbit farthest from earth
S 40
moon's orbit **M** 446
Apollo, or Phoebus Apollo, Greek and Roman god **G** 360
Temple in Corinth, ruins, picture **G** 340
Apollo, Project, name of U.S. project to put man on the
moon, landing areas map **M** 449
Apollo 8 and 10, around the moon **S** 339, 342
Apollo 11, moon landing **E** 368; **M** 450; **S** 339–340a,
340h–340i; pictures **S** 340b–340c, 340h
Apollo 12, moon landing **S** 344, 345
Apollo 13, first in-flight failure **S** 341, 345
Apollo 14, moon landing **S** 344, 345
Apollo 15, moon landing **S** 344, 345
Apollo 15 team with Nixon, picture **N** 262e
Apollo 16, moon landing **S** 345
Apollo 17 **S** 345
Lunar Rover, picture **S** 340g
navigation **N** 68, 69; **S** 340f–340g
observatories **O** 14
space suit, life-support system, diagrams **S** 388, 340L
tracking network **S** 340g
Apollodorus of Damascus, Greek engineer **E** 208
Apollo-Saturn spacecraft, diagrams **S** 340a, 340h
Apoplexy *see* Stroke
A posteriori (ay-pos-tir-i-OR-i) (from later on) **U** 194
Apostles, The, 12 disciples of Jesus Christ **A** 332–33;
C 279–80, 281
chosen by Jesus **J** 83
New Testament of the Bible **B** 160
Peter, Saint **P** 167
Roman Catholic Church, history of **R** 287
Apostles' Creed **R** 295
Apostle spoons **K** 285
Apostolic (ap-os-TOL-ic) **succession** **O** 228
Apostrophes (a-POS-tro-phese), punctuation marks
P 532

Appalachia (ap-a-LAY-chi-a), name given disadvantaged
region in the Appalachian Mountains in eastern United

States. The region consists of parts of 11 states from
northern Pennsylvania to north central Alabama.
poverty in the United States **P** 424a–424b

Appalachian Highway system **W** 134
Appalachian Mountains, North America **M** 496: **N** 285
Canada **C** 50; **Q** 10a
formation of **E** 11
overland trails **O** 254
United States **U** 89
westward movement **W** 142–45
Appalachian Trail **M** 116
Appaloosas (ap-pa-LOO-sas), horses, picture **H** 238
Nez Percé Indians breed **I** 176
Apparent magnitude, of stars **S** 406
Appeals, in law **C** 530
Appellate courts **C** 530
state courts (the judiciary) **S** 415
Appendages, organs or parts hung on some animals
crustacea **S** 169–70
Appendicitis (ap-pen-di-CY-tis) **D** 193
Appendix **D** 193; diagrams **B** 274, **D** 202
Appert (ap-PARE), **Nicholas,** French chef **F** 345; **I** 346
Appian Way, Roman road **E** 208; **T** 259
Apple **A** 333–37
Arkansas, state flower of **A** 418
drying process **D** 317
golden apples of Hesperides, myth **G** 363
harvest in New York, picture **U** 105
Johnny Appleseed, excerpt from story of **F** 315–16
Michigan, state flower of **M** 259
Newton discovers law of gravitation **N** 206
seeds and fruit, pictures **P** 298, 309
trees and their leaves, pictures **T** 277
Apple of Discord, legend **G** 365
Appleseed, Johnny, American folk hero **F** 311–12
Appleton, Wisconsin **W** 205
Applied art *see* Commercial art; Industrial arts
Applied research **R** 183
Appomattox (app-o-MAT-tox) **Court House,** Virginia **C** 327
Lee, Robert E., surrenders to Grant **L** 126
Appomattox Court House National Historical Park **V** 353
Apprentices, persons learning a trade **G** 403
colonial America **C** 388
slaves set free to become apprentices **S** 197, 199
Approach Control, of airplanes **A** 564
Approximations, successive, method of, in psychology
P 498
Apricot **P** 107–09
April, 4th month of year **A** 338–39
April Fool's Day **A** 338; **H** 154–55
A priori (ay-pri-OR-i) (from beforehand)
languages **U** 194
Apron, of the stage **T** 155
Apse, part of a church **A** 376; picture **A** 370
cathedrals **C** 131
Apsu, Babylonian god **M** 557
Aptitude tests **T** 117–18
counseling tests in guidance **G** 399
examinations for college entrance **E** 348–49
Aqaba (OC-a-ba), **Gulf of,** extension of the Red Sea **E** 90d;
J 137
Arab-Israeli wars **I** 445
Nasser closed gulf to Israeli ships **N** 15
Aqaba, Jordan's seaport **J** 138
Aqualung, breathing apparatus for underwater swim-
ming **S** 189–90
oceanography, use in **O** 42
underwater exploration **U** 14
Aquamarines, gemstones **G** 71; picture **G** 73
Aquanauts, underwater explorers **U** 19–20
United States Navy **U** 193

Aquaplaning see Water-skiing

Aqua regia (RE-gia), hydrochloric and nitric acids
G 247

Aquariums A 340–43
  water pets P 181

Aquarius, constellation C 491; sign of, picture S 244

Aquatic animals
  animal plankton P 280–81
  dolphins or porpoises D 270–79
  walruses, sea lions, and seals W 5–8
  whales W 147–51

Aquatic plants
  algae A 155–57
  aquarium plants A 341
  plant plankton P 279–80

Aquatic sports see Water sports

Aquatint, etching process E 294–95; G 307

Aquavit, a distilled beverage W 159

Aqueducts A 344
  ancient Roman A 231; picture A 232
  Pont du Gard, near Nîmes, France, picture B 395
  Rome's water supply a contribution to public health
    and the advancement of medicine M 204
  water supply W 65

Aquidneck Island, or Rhode Island R 223

Aquifers, water-bearing layers of permeable rocks G 96;
  W 122

Aquila, constellation C 493

Aquinas (a-KWY-nas), **Saint Thomas,** Italian monk and
    philosopher A 344; C 285
  Roman Catholic Church, history of R 292
  philosophical system P 192

Arab Emirates, United, formerly Trucial States
    (Trucial Oman) M 301

Arabesques (ar-a-BESKS), pattern designs
  furniture F 508; picture F 509
  Islamic art I 417, 422
  ornamentation of tapestry T 22
  Spanish art S 360

Arabia (a-RAY-bia), or **Arabian Peninsula,** southwestern
    Asia, the Middle East M 301
  Kuwait K 305–08
  Saudi Arabia S 44–49
  Yemen (Aden) Y 347
  Yemen (Sana) Y 348–49
  See also Arabs

Arabia Felix, Roman name for an area usually restricted
    to Yemen (Sana) Y 348

Arabian camels C 34; H 210; picture H 213

Arabian coffee plant C 372

Arabian Desert, in Africa, east of the Nile, Egypt E 90d

Arabian horses H 237

Arabian Nights A 345–47
  early history of the short story S 165

Arabian Peninsula see Arabia

Arabian Sea O 45

Arabic-Hindu (ARR-a-bic-HIN-du) **numerals** N 391–92

Arabic language L 39
  common language of early science S 64
  Islam, language of I 416
  Middle East M 305
  North African literature A 76d
  northern Africa A 55; M 458

Arab-Israeli wars I 444–45; J 81, 113
  Egypt E 92
  Jordan J 139
  Nasser, Gamal Abdel N 15

Arab League, league of sovereign states founded in 1945
to promote the political, cultural, and economic unity of
the Arab community. This covenant, based on the Alexandria Protocol, was signed by Egypt (later United Arab
Republic), Iraq, Saudi Arabia, Syria, Lebanon, Jordan,
and Yemen, with Libya joining in 1953, the Sudan in 1956,
Tunisia and Morocco in 1958, Kuwait in 1961, and Algeria
in 1962. The league is made up of a council in which
each country has one vote, a permanent secretariat in
Cairo, and several special committees.

Arable land G 96

Arab Republics, federation of Egypt, Libya, and Syria
  E 92; S 508

Arabs A 55
  alchemists C 207–08
  drugs, early use of D 322
  Morocco M 458–61
  Saudi Arabia S 44–49
  smoking waterpipes, picture M 304
  Soviet Central Asia U 46
  Syria S 505

Arachne (ar-ACK-ne), in Greek mythology, proud peasant
girl, a skilled weaver, who dared challenge goddess
Athena to a spinning contest. When Arachne wove
scenes showing disrespect for gods, Athena destroyed
her work and turned her into a spider, to remind men
not to compete with the gods. All spiders were believed
by ancient Greeks to be descended from Arachne.
  spiders a class of animals called arachnids S 383

Arachnids (a-RAC-nids), a class of animals I 283–84
  spiders S 383–88

Arafura (ar-a-FU-ra) **Sea,** part of the Pacific Ocean that
lies between New Guinea and Australia, containing Aru
Islands which were Japanese air base in World War II.

Arago (a-RA-go), **François** (Dominique F. J.), French
    scientist E 129
  electric motors, history of E 140

Aragon, ancient kingdom in Spain
  Ferdinand II, king F 87

Aragon, Louis, French poet F 442

Aral Sea, central Asia L 26; U 33

Aramaic (ar-a-MAI-ic) **language** H 100
  Dead Sea Scrolls D 48–49
  in the Bible B 152, 153

Aramis (a-ra-MECE), one of *The Three Musketeers*
  D 342–43

Arana Osorio, Carlos, Guatamalan leader G 394

Aransas National Wildlife Refuge, Texas T 126

Arapaho, Indians of North America I 164

Ararat, Mount, in Asian Turkey T 324

Araucanians (ar-auc-ON-ians), Indians of South America
  I 210
  Chile C 249

Arawak (AR-a-wak), Indians of South America I 207–09
  Puerto Rico P 516

Arbeau (ar-BO), **Thoinot,** French priest D 27

Arbela (ar-BE-la), **battle of,** 331 B.C. B 100
  Alexander's defeat of the Persians A 152

Arbitration
  labor-management relations L 16
  provided for in treaties T 273

Arbor Day, or Arbor and Bird Day H 152–53
  Jewish Arbor Day in Israel R 154
  origin in Nebraska N 72

Arboretums (ar-bo-RE-tums), plantings of trees and
    shrubs Z 379

Arbutus, trailing, also called Mayflower
  state flower of Massachusetts M 134

Arc, of a circle G 127

Arcadia (ar-CAY-dia), province of southern Greece. Mythical mountain home of the god Pan, it was almost inaccessible in olden times. Poets have praised the peaceful life of Arcadian shepherds, and so "Arcadian" is often used to describe simple, pastoral living.

Arcadian poetry I 479

Arcaro, Eddie (Edward Arcaro) (1916–   ), American jockey, b. Cincinnati, Ohio. He rode over 4,000 winners (since 1932), making him one of the richest jockeys in racing history, with total purses estimated at over $20,000,000. He was a five-time winner of the Kentucky Derby and only man to ride two Triple Crown winners.

Arc de Triomphe, Paris see Arch of Triumph
Arcetri (ar-CHAY-tri) **Observatory,** Italy S 466
Arch, in architecture see Arches
Archaeology see Archeology
Archaeopteryx (arc-e-OP-ter-ix), first known bird B 207
Archaic Period, of Greek art G 344–45; S 94–95
Archangel (ARC-angel), Union of Soviet Socialist Republics U 33
   main port on the White Sea O 49
Arch bridges B 395, 397; pictures B 399
Archeology (arc-e-OL-ogy), study of things of the past A 348–65
   aerial photography P 206
   anthropology related to A 300, 307–08
   cave dwellers and their art P 439–41
   ceramics, a source of information C 172
   Israel, discoveries in I 444
   Pompeii P 390
   pre-Columbian collection in Mexico's national museum M 253
   prehistoric man P 442–46
   research methods R 182
   Schliemann, Heinrich S 53–54
   scuba divers recover Roman marble, picture S 190
   tree-ring calendars T 287
   Troy rediscovered T 293–94
   underwater archeology U 20; picture U 14
Archer, constellation see Sagittarius
Archery A 366–68
   longbows at battle of Crécy H 281–82
Arches, in architecture
   flying buttresses A 378; G 265; pictures A 379, G 266
   Gothic pointed G 265
   Roman A 376; R 285
Archimedes (arc-i-ME-dese), Greek inventor and mathematician A 369
Archimedes' principle, physics law A 369; F 252
Archipelago, a group of islands
   Alexander Archipelago, Alaska I 427
   Philippines P 186
Architectural (arc-i-TECT-ural) **engineering** E 205
Architecture (ARC-i-tec-ture) A 370–87
   ancient A 235–37, 238, 240, 242
   architectural engineering E 205
   banks in modern style, pictures B 44d, 45
   baroque period B 55–62
   bricks and masonry B 390–94
   building construction B 431
   Byzantine B 483–90
   Canberra, Australia, design for a city C 88
   castles F 375
   cathedrals C 130–33
   colonial American C 388–89
   Egyptian E 93–103
   English E 233–42
   Gothic architecture G 264–72
   Greek architecture G 346–48

   homes of the past and of today H 168–84
   Islamic I 417–22
   library floor plan, picture L 182
   Louvre, Paris, France L 366–68
   mechanical drawing M 197
   Michelangelo M 257
   Middle Ages M 296–97
   oriental architecture O 212–19
   Renaissance architecture R 163–71
   rococo decoration, pictures G 170
   school buildings S 58; pictures S 56, 57
   South America, modern, pictures S 284
   Tudor houses, Stratford, picture S 130
   United States U 122–25
   See also Ancient world, art of; Building construction; Building materials; Homes
Architecture, modern A 385–87; picture A 438g
   art of the artist A 438g
   Bauhaus school, Germany B 103–05
   Frank Lloyd Wright's "organic" architecture W 314–15
   geodesic dome of Buckminster Fuller I 232
   Sullivan, Louis S 457
   trends in hospital planning H 251

Archives (ARC-ives), place in which public or private records and documents of historical value are preserved. National Archives, established by Congress in 1934, is located in Washington, D.C., and holds such notable documents as Declaration of Independence, Constitution, and Bill of Rights. Public Archives of Canada, founded in 1872, is located in Ottawa.

Arch of Titus (TY-tus), Rome, Italy J 106
Arch of Triumph, Paris P 74; pictures E 304; P 71
   designed as a Roman triumphal arch F 432
   France's tomb for an unknown soldier U 225
Arc-jet rocket engines S 348
Arc lamps I 334
Arc lighting L 285; picture L 283
Arctic, north polar region P 363, 364–66, 367
   Alaska's Arctic slope and Point Barrow A 133, 140
   Bering Strait, discovery of B 142
   Canada's Yukon and Northwest Territories Y 360–65
   cold deserts D 124
   Eskimo life E 284–91
   frigid, or polar zones Z 372
   Greenland ice sheet I 9–11
   icebergs I 25–27
   International Polar Years (IPY-1 and 2) I 310–11
   Lapland L 44–45
   North Asia A 450
   Northwest Passage N 338
   Peary, Robert E. P 116
   taiga, forests T 10–11
   See also Northeast Passage
Arctic Archipelago see Arctic Islands
Arctic Basin, Canada C 52
Arctic Current see Labrador Current
Arctic foxes D 249–50; F 397
Arctic hares R 23–24
Arctic Islands, or Arctic Archipelago, landform region of Canada C 51; Y 361
Arctic Ocean O 45; P 364
   Ewing-Donn Theory of Ice Ages I 24
Arctic Slope, Alaska A 133, 135, 138
Arctic tern, bird
   migration H 186
Arctic wolf, picture D 245
Arcturus (arc-TU-rus), star C 492
Arc welding W 118–19
Ardennes, battle of the see Bulge, battle of the

Ardizzone (ar-dit-ZO-ne), **Edward** (1900–), English author and illustrator of children's books, b. Haiphong, Indochina (now North Vietnam). His first reputation was as an artist, but he is best-known for his series of books about Tim and his sea adventures, including *Little Tim and the Brave Sea Captain*, and *Tim All Alone*, which won Britain's Kate Greenaway Medal (1956).

Area (AIR-e-a) **codes,** for telephoning **T** 59
Area plan, for libraries **L** 173
Areas, in geometry **G** 129
Arecibo Observatory, Puerto Rico, picture **R** 73
Arenas (a-RE-nas), places used for public entertainment
    bullfighting **B** 449
    Roman ruins at Arles, France, picture **F** 417
Arena stage, or theater in the round **T** 155–56
Areopagitica (ar-e-o-pa-JIT-ic-a), pamphlet by John
    Milton **E** 255; **M** 311
Arequipa (ar-ae-KI-pa), Peru, picture **P** 164
Ares (AIR-ese), Greek god **G** 361
Argali (AR-ga-li), a kind of wild sheep **S** 145; picture
    H 218

Argall, Sir Samuel (?–1626), English adventurer. He was the first to sail the northern route directly from England to Virginia (1609). Accompanying Lord Delaware to Virginia (1610), he helped replenish the colony's food supplies; kidnapped Pocahontas, thus securing the release of English captives (1612); and overthrew French colonies in Maine and Nova Scotia (1613). He was deputy governor of Virginia (1617–19).

Argand oil lamps **L** 282
Argentina (ar-gen-TI-na) **A** 388–96
    Buenos Aires **B** 426–28
    cattle raising, picture **S** 289
    fascism in **F** 64
    flag **F** 242
    Islas Malvinas (Falkland Islands) **I** 430; **S** 278
    life in Latin America **L** 47–61
    national anthem **N** 20–21
    Pampa, The, picture **G** 314
    San Martín, José de, early fighter for freedom **S** 36
    sheep ranch in Patagonia, picture **P** 433
Argol see Tartar
Argon, element **E** 154, 159; **G** 59
    industrial uses **G** 62
    Langmuir's use in light bulbs **L** 35
    one of the noble gases **N** 109
    use in welding, picture **G** 60
Argonauts (AR-go-nauts), in Greek mythology **G** 364
Argumentation see Debates and debating
Aria (AR-ia), accompanied song for the single voice
    M 535; **O** 131–32
    popular form in baroque period **B** 65
Ariadne (arri-AD-ne), in Greek mythology **G** 365
    in story from *Tanglewood Tales* **H** 75–76
Arianism (AR-i-an-ism), heresy of Arius condemned by
    church council **C** 283
Arias, Arnulfo, president of Panama **P** 46
Arica (a-RI-ca), Chile
    rainfall least in world **R** 94
Aries, constellation **C** 490; sign of, picture **S** 244
Arif (a-REEF), **Abdul Salam,** president of Iraq **I** 383
Arif, Rahman, president of Iraq **I** 383
Arikara (a-RIK-a-ra), Indians of North America
    South Dakota **S** 326
Ariosto (ar-i-OS-to), **Lodovico,** Italian poet **I** 478
Aristarchus (ar-is-TARC-us) **of Samos** **S** 63–64
Aristocracy (ar-i-STOC-racy), government **G** 274
Aristophanes (ar-is-TOPH-an-ese), Greek dramatist **G** 353
    ancient Greek comedy **D** 294

Aristotle, Greek philosopher **A** 396–97; **P** 191–92
    air theory **E** 351
    Alexander the Great and Aristotle **A** 151
    ancient civilizations **A** 230
    biologist of the ancient world **B** 187
    contributions to science, summary **S** 63
    earth theory **C** 206
    encyclopedia, father of the **E** 193
    government systems **G** 274
    Greek literature **G** 355
    his library **L** 194
    literary criticism **L** 312
    medical advances **M** 203
    memory, law of association **P** 493
    oratory and rhetoric **O** 180
Aristotle Contemplating the Bust of Homer, painting
    by Rembrandt **G** 354
Arithmetic **A** 398–401
    abacus **A** 2–3
    binary numeration system **C** 453, 456
    computer circuits **C** 454
    fractions **F** 397–402
    graphs **G** 309–13
    interest **P** 149–50
    new math teaches why computations work **M** 163
    numbers and number systems **N** 384–88
    numerals and numeration systems **N** 389–401
    percent **P** 148–49
    sets **S** 126–27
    textbooks, old and new, pictures **E** 78
    See also Calculators; Computers
Arithmetic mean, or mean, a kind of average of a set of
    numbers **S** 417
Arius (a-RY-us), Greek theologian **R** 289
    rise of the great heresies of Christianity **C** 283
Arizona **A** 402–17
    Grand Canyon **G** 290–92
    Hopi Indians descendents of cliff dwellers **I** 190–91
    irrigated desert regions, pictures **D** 126
    modern church architecture, picture **C** 288
Arizona, University of, at Tucson, picture **A** 410
Arizona Highways, magazine **A** 410
Arkansas (ARK-an-saw) **A** 418–32
Arkansas River, United States **A** 422, 426, 429; **O** 83
    Fryingpan–Arkansas River Project **C** 405
Arkansas Toothpick, or Bowie knife **B** 344

Ark of the Covenant, sacred chest containing agreement between God and Israel made on Mt. Sinai. It was kept by Israelites during years of wandering in desert. After they settled in Promised Land, it was placed in King Solomon's temple in Jerusalem. Today the term refers to a holy chest holding the scroll of the Torah, or law of Moses, which is placed along the eastern wall of every synagogue as a symbol of the original.

Arkwright, Richard, British inventor and early industrialist **I** 236, 238; **T** 140–41
Arlandes (ar-LOND), **Marquis d',** French balloonist **B** 30
Arles, France
    Roman ruins, picture **F** 417
Arlington National Cemetery, Virginia **N** 28–30; **V** 353
    amphitheatre, picture **H** 224
    Unknown Soldier **U** 225
    Washington, D.C. **W** 32
Arm, bones of the **F** 79
Armada (ar-MA-da), **Spanish,** 1588 **B** 101; **E** 222
    Drake defeats King Philip's fleet **D** 290–91
    first naval battle fought entirely under sail **S** 159
    race for overseas empires created conflicts **E** 386
Armadillos (ar-ma-DIL-los), mammals **M** 66–67; picture
    M 69

Armageddon (ar-ma-GEDD-on), in the Bible, the place of the final battle between powers of good and evil on judgment day (Revelation 16:16). In modern usage, the term refers to any great battle.

Armagh, Northern Ireland **U** 73
Armature, framework used in clay modeling **C** 336
Armatures, in electric motors **E** 137–38
  electric generators **E** 121, 122
Armed Forces, U. S. see United States Armed Forces
Armed Forces Day **H** 150
Armenian (ar-ME-nian) **Soviet Socialist Republic** **U** 44
  languages of the U.S.S.R. **U** 28
  popular foods **F** 335
Armies
  Alexander the Great **A** 151–153
  Canadian armed forces **C** 79–82
  United States **U** 166–75

Armistead, James, American patriot, Negro slave, b. New Kent County, Va., dates unknown. He collected valuable information concerning British forces at Portsmouth, Va., for Lafayette during American Revolution. For this he was granted freedom, by the Virginia State Legislature (1786).

Armistice, an agreement to halt hostilities in a war. A partial armistice or truce usually affects only a single battlefield or other limited area, while a general armistice, which must be agreed to by the heads of the governments involved, suspends all fighting and is often a beginning of peace negotiations.
  New York celebration, Armistice, 1918, picture **W** 280

Armistice Day see Veterans' Day
Armitage, Kenneth, English painter **E** 242
Armonica (ar-MON-ic-a), invented by Franklin **F** 453; picture **F** 452
Armor **A** 433–35
  coats of arms **H** 115–18
  combat arms of United States Army **U** 168
  early decorations **D** 75
  knights, knighthood, and chivalry **K** 272–73
  Metropolitan Museum of Art display, picture **M** 237
  Roman soldiers, picture **R** 305
Armored tanks see Tanks, armored
Armory Show, New York art show, 1913 **P** 30; **U** 122
  modern art in the United States **M** 397
Arms races, reasons for disarmament **D** 186
  between the World Wars **W** 282–85
Armstrong, Edwin, American engineer, picture **E** 147
Armstrong, Louis, American jazz musician **J** 58–59; **N** 101

Armstrong, Neil Alden (1930–   ), American astronaut, b. Wapakoneta, Ohio. A combat pilot in Korea and test pilot before joining the astronaut program, he was command pilot of Gemini 8 (1966). On July 20, 1969, as only civilian member of Apollo 11 crew, he became the first man to walk on the moon's surface.
  first men on the moon, "One small step," modern exploration **E** 368; **S** 339–340a
  space flights and space flight data **S** 344, 345, 346

Army, Canadian see Canadian Armed Forces
Army, United States Department of the **U** 166–67
  conservation projects of Corps of Engineers **C** 488
Army Air Corps Song, by Robert Crawford **N** 26
Army ants **A** 331
Army National Guard, United States **U** 175
Army of the Andes see Andes, Army of
Army of the Potomac see Potomac, Army of the
Army worms **P** 289; picture **P** 288

Arnarsson, Ingólfur, Norwegian Viking **I** 44
Arne, Thomas, English composer **N** 27
Arnold, Benedict, American soldier and traitor **A** 436
  Revolutionary War **R** 199, 204, 206–07
Arnold, Matthew, English author **E** 262
Arnolfo di Cambio, Italian architect **I** 463
Arno River, Italy **I** 452
Aromatic plants see Herbs; Spices and condiments
Aron Kodesh (a-RONE KO-desh), in Judaism **J** 119
Aroostook (a-ROOS-took) **River,** Maine **M** 36
  bloodless war, boundary dispute **M** 47; **N** 138g
Arosemena (a-ro-say-MAY-nia) **Monroy, Carlos Julio,** president of Ecuador **E** 58
Arouet, Francois Marie see Voltaire

Arp, Hans (Jean) (1888–1966), French artist, b. Strasbourg, Alsace (then part of Germany but now part of France). He was a founder of the Dada movement in Zurich, Switzerland (1916), and after 1925 a member of a group of surrealist painters in Paris. During the 1920's he did many abstract reliefs on wood but after 1930 devoted himself mainly to sculpture. He has published a collection of poems and essays, *On My Way.*
  surrealism in modern art **M** 395; **S** 105

Árpád (AR-pod), (?–907), Hungarian national hero. Leader of the Magyar tribe, he was elected prince of all seven Hungarian tribes, and he led nomadic tribes (896?) into region of Danube basin in what is now Hungary. He established the Árpád dynasty (890?–1301), of which Saint Stephen was the first crowned king and King Andrew was the last.

Arrack, alcoholic beverage from coconut palm **C** 369
Arraignment, in law **C** 527
Arrest, for breaking the law **C** 527
  steps in law enforcement **L** 88, 89
Arretine (ARR-a-tene) **ware,** pottery **R** 306
Arrhenius (ar-RAE-nius), **S. A.,** Swedish chemist **C** 215
Arrow and the Song, The, poem by Longfellow **L** 343
Arrow plant, source of Mexican jumping beans **J** 150
Arrowrock Dam, Idaho, picture **I** 58

Arrowroot, edible starch produced from rootlike stems of several tropical plants, particularly arrowroot (*Maranta arundinacea*), grown in the West Indies. It is a light and tasteless whitish powder, easily digested and often used for cookies, puddings, and crackers.

Arrows, in archery **A** 366–68
Arrowworms, or glassworms, sea animals **P** 281
Arroyos, dry river beds **R** 239
Arsenal, building for storing weapons
  Harper's Ferry National Historical Park, West Virginia **W** 135
Arsenic, element **E** 154, 159
  insecticides **I** 258
Arson **F** 153–54
Art **A** 437–438g
  African art **A** 70–76
  American see United States, art of the
  ancient **A** 233–43
  color in art **D** 141, 143
  decorative arts **D** 66–78
  graphic arts **G** 302–08
  modern **M** 386–98
  museums **M** 514–20
  painting **P** 14–32
  prehistoric art **P** 439–41
  religious see Religious art
  sculpture **S** 90–105
  See also names of individual artists, such as Rem-

Art (continued)

brandt; of specific countries, as Italian art; of art periods, as Baroque art; and of art forms, as Painting or Industrial design

Art, ancient see Ancient world, art of

Art, commercial see Commercial art

Art directors
motion pictures **M** 479, 481
plays **P** 336

Artemis (AR-te-mis), Greek goddess **G** 360

Arteries, blood vessels **B** 275—76
cholesterol in body chemistry **B** 293
hardening of **D** 196—97
heart **H** 86—86a
pulse and pulse rates **M** 208f

Arterioles, arteries branching from large arteries **B** 279
heart action **H** 86a

Arteriosclerosis (ar-te-rio-scle-RO-sis), hardening of the arteries, disease **D** 196—97

Artesian (ar-TE-sian) **wells W** 123

Art galleries see Art Museums

Arthritis D 193

Arthropods, animals **P** 436

Arthur, Chester Alan, 21st president of United States **A** 438h—441
as Vice-President, picture **V** 328
civil service, beginnings of **C** 317

Arthur, King legendary hero of Britain **A** 442—45; **L** 129
English literature, legends based on **E** 247—48
last Romano-British leader **E** 216
story of the sword, a fragmentary myth **M** 560
Welsh folklore **W** 3

Artichokes, vegetable **V** 289
flowers we eat **P** 308; picture **P** 309

Articles of Confederation, 1781 **R** 203
Albany Plan of Franklin **F** 454
attacked by *The Federalist* **F** 78
first government for United States **U** 134—35, 145
need to regulate trade between states **I** 331
Northwest Ordinance, 1787, its greatest achievement **W** 143
Ohio established as Northwest Territory **O** 74
weaknesses **U** 135, 145

Articulated diving bell D 81

Artifacts, things used in past eras **A** 348—49, 351, 358
means of dating **A** 360—62

Artificial languages L 40

Artificial limbs, for handicapped persons **H** 28

Artificial pearls P 114

Artificial respiration F 159—61

Artificial satellites see Satellites, man-made

Artigas (ar-TI-gos), José G., Uruguayan leader **U** 239

Artillery, weaponry **G** 424—26
United States Army **U** 168

Art Institute of Chicago, Illinois **I** 80

Artiodactyla (ar-ti-o-DACT-il-a), order of even-toed hoofed mammals **H** 207—08; **M** 62, 68

Artist in His Studio, painting by Jan Vermeer **D** 360

Artists' materials
drawing tools and materials **D** 301, 303
sculpture **S** 90—91

Art museums M 514—20
See *also* names of museums

Art nouveau, new art movement
decorative art of Henry Van de Velde **D** 78

Arts see Art

Arts and crafts see Decorative arts; Handicrafts

Art song, or lied **C** 333; **M** 538
styles of singing **V** 376

Aruba (a-RU-ba), island of the Netherlands Antilles off the coast of Venezuela. The island is self-governing and sends members to the Antilles legislature which meets in Curaçao. The chief town is Oranjestad. Although the economy depends on refining and shipping of Venezuelan oil, there is a growing tourist industry.
Caribbean Sea and islands **C** 116—19

Arusha, Tanzania **T** 19

Aryans (AR-i-ans)
cultural life of India **I** 116

Asbestos (as-BEST-os), name of the fibrous form of several different minerals. This material is extremely important for fireproofing and electrical and heat insulation. Its fibers can be used as a woolly filling material or spun and woven into a fabric.
floor coverings **V** 341
North American production **N** 295
Quebec, Canada, world's largest producer **Q** 12

Ascanius (as-CAY-nius), son of Aeneas **A** 35

ASCAP see American Society of Composers, Authors, and Publishers

Ascension Day, or Ear of Wheat Thursday, religious holiday **R** 153—54, 290

Ascension Island, South Atlantic **I** 427

Ascham (ASC-am), **Roger,** English writer and scholar **E** 250

Asclepius see Aesculapius

Ascorbic acid, or vitamin c **V** 370d

Asen (OS-en), **John I and II,** rulers of Bulgaria **B** 444

Asen, Peter, ruler of Bulgaria **B** 444

Asexual reproduction R 177—78

Asgard, home of the Norse gods **N** 277, 278

Ash, tree of the olive family
leaf, diagram **L** 114
uses of the wood and its grain, picture **W** 223
white ash, picture **T** 277

Ashanti, a people of Africa **G** 194, 198
carved gold weights **A** 72; pictures **A** 70, 73
funeral customs **F** 494

Ashanti Crater, in Africa **C** 421

Ashcan school, American painting **U** 122

Ashdod, Israel, picture **G** 106

Ashe, Arthur, Jr. (1943—   ), American tennis champion, Negro, b. Richmond, Va. He took National Collegiate Athletic Association singles and doubles titles (1966) while at UCLA. In 1968 he led winning U.S. Davis Cup team, became first American to win U.S. Amateur singles title since 1955 and won first annual U.S. Open Tennis Championship. He was the Davis Cup singles winner in 1969. In 1970 he signed a professional contract.

Asheville, North Carolina **N** 318

Ash flows, volcanic eruptions **V** 382

Ashikaga, ancient ruling clan of Japan **J** 43

Ashkenazic (osh-ken-OZ-ic) **ritual,** in Judaism **J** 118, 119

Ashley, William Henry (1788?—1838), American pioneer and politician, b. Powhatan Co., Va. He explored and trapped furs along the Missouri River as far as the Yellowstone River (1822—23), traveled from Nebraska across the eastern Rockies to Wyoming (1824—25), and served in Congress (1831—37).
Rocky Mountain Fur Company and mountain men **F** 523

Ashmole, Elias, English antiquarian **M** 511

Ashmolean Museum, Oxford, England **M** 511

Ashoka see Asoka

Asia Minor (known also as Anatolia) peninsula forming western extremity of Asia, including major portion of Turkey. It is bordered on the north by Black Sea, on the south by Mediterranean Sea, on the west by Aegean Sea. It was the first settlement of kingdom of Hittites (about 1900–1200 B.C.) and a principal crossroads of Eastern and Western civilizations in ancient times.

Asimov (AZ-i-mof), **Isaac** (1920–   ), American writer, educator, b. Russia. He and his family came to the United States in 1923. He attended Columbia University, where he took his B.S., M.A., and Ph. D. in chemistry. He taught biochemistry at Boston University Medical School but left in 1958 to devote full time to writing. A prolific writer with some hundred books to his credit, he is able to explain complex scientific processes in terms easily understandable to the layman. His books range from science fiction and science fact for adults and young people to textbooks and major historical works.

Asquith, Herbert Henry, 1st Earl of Oxford and Asquith (1852–1928), British statesman, b. Morley, Yorkshire. Educated at Oxford University, he became a barrister (trial lawyer) before entering Parliament in 1886 as a Liberal. He served as home secretary (1892–95), chancellor of the exchequer (1905–08), and prime minister (1908–16). Among the measures adopted by his government was the Parliament Act (1911), which ended the veto power over bills by the House of Lords.

Assassins, secret Muslim sect, founded in the 11th century, that believed in the murder of its enemies as a religious duty. Its name comes from Arabic word *hashshāshīn,* meaning "hashish eaters," because the members were thought to be under the influence of that drug when they went on their murderous missions. The sect flourished in Syria and Persia and spread over much of the Near East until subdued by Mongols and Mamelukes during 13th century. Today the word "assassin" is applied to any murderer, especially one who kills a political figure.

Assemblage, modern art form in which the artist assembles objects not necessarily intended for artistic use. Such things as scraps of paper, cloth, wood, and metal are used. Assemblages may be either two- or three-dimensional. The French artist César (1921–   ) creates assemblages by welding pieces of metal, as in *Motor 4,* and by compressing parts of automobiles, as in *The Yellow Buick.* Collage is an assemblage in two dimensions.

Assemblies of God, Protestant denomination. This pentecostal sect, which does mainly evangelical and missionary work, was founded in 1914. Members believe in second coming of Christ and divine healing.

Assumption of the Virgin, painting by Correggio I 472
Assurbanipal see Ashurbanipal
Assyria (a-SIR-ia), ancient empire of Asia A 225–26
  aqueducts A 344
  architecture A 373
  art A 239–41
  conquest of kingdom of Israel J 104
  sculpture S 93

Astaire, Fred (Fred Austerlitz) (1899–   ), American dancer and actor, b. Omaha, Nebr. He is noted for his singing and dancing in such musical films as *Top Hat*, *The Gay Divorce*, *Easter Parade*, and *Finian's Rainbow*. He had a nonmusical part in the film *On The Beach*.

Astatine (AST-a-tene), element E 154, 159
  one of the halogens I 349
Aster, pattern of cell division C 164
Asterism, star effect in gemstones G 70
Asteroids, or planetoids, small planets S 239–40, 243
  astronomers study the planets A 475
  planet-like objects P 273–74
Asters, flowers G 51; picture W 170
Asthma, allergy disease D 192
Astigmatism (a-STIG-ma-tism), eye defect L 150, 265
Astley, Philip, English circus performer C 301
Astor, John Jacob, German-born American merchant and fur trader F 523; O 256
  Oregon, history of O 207
  real estate fortune R 112

Astor, Lady (Nancy Witcher Langhorne Astor, Viscountess Astor) (1879–1964), first woman member of British Parliament, b. Greenwood, Va., U.S.A. She succeeded her husband, Waldorf Astor, as Conservative member in House of Commons (1919–45) when he became a peer, and she campaigned for women's rights, temperance, and child welfare.

Astoria, Oregon, picture O 202
  Fort Astoria F 523
Astrida see Butare, Rwanda
Astrodome, Houston, Texas H 270
Astrolabes (AST-rol-abes), navigation instruments N 64
  exploration stimulated E 372
Astrology (a-STROL-ogy), once the study of stars and planets, now a method of fortune telling by stars A 470
Astronauts and cosmonauts S 344–45, 346–47
  food and meals F 342
  manned satellites of the future S 43
  navigation in space N 69
  using camera, picture P 209
Astronomical (ast-ro-NOM-ic-al) photography, or astrophotography P 207–08
Astronomical telescopes O 167

Astronomical unit (A.U.), the mean distance from the earth to the sun—about 93,000,000 miles. The unit is sometimes used in astronomy to express large distances.

Astronomy (a-STRON-omy) A 469, 470–77
  comets C 418–19
  constellations C 490–93
  eclipses E 46–47
  experiments, demonstrations and projects E 361
  history see Astronomy, history of
  Mars M 104–11
  measuring the distance of galaxies U 202–03
  meteors and meteorites C 419–21
  observatories O 8–15
  planets P 269–78

  quasars and pulsars Q 7–8
  radio and radar astronomy R 69–76
  Rudolphine tables of fixed stars B 361
  seasons S 108–12
  solar system S 239–49
  stars S 405–11
  sun S 458–67
  tektites C 421
  telescopes T 60–64
  universe U 196–204
  See also Comets; Constellations; Earth; Eclipses; Meteors and meteorites; Moon; Planets; Radar astronomy; Radio astronomy; Satellites; Solar system; Space exploration and travel; Stars; Sun; Telescopes; Tides; Universe; names of planets
Astronomy, history of A 470–77; S 77, 79
  Brahe, Tycho, works of B 361
  Copernicus, father of modern astronomy C 501
  Galileo's discoveries G 6, 7
  Kepler, Johannes K 234
Astrophotography (ast-ro-pho-TOG-raphy), or astronomical photography P 207–08
Astrophysics P 238
  astrophysical observatories O 9
Asunción (a-soon-ci-OHN), capital of Paraguay P 65; picture P 62

Asuncion (formerly Assumption) Island, island located in northern part of Marianas island group in western Pacific. This U.S. trusteeship is an uninhabited volcanic island about 2 miles in diameter.

Asvagosha, Indian writer O 220e
Aswan (os-WON), Egypt E 90f
Aswan High Dam, Egypt D 21; E 90e; picture E 91
  Egyptian art, concern for E 93
  man-made lake engulfs historical sites of Sudan S 449
Asymmetrical (a-sim-MET-ric-al) balance, in design D 133
Asymmetry, lack of proportion
  What makes modern music different and unpredictable? M 399
As You Like It, play by Shakespeare S 133–34
Atabrine, synthetic drug that acts like quinine P 313
Atacama (at-a-CA-ma) Desert, Chile C 251–52; pictures D 126; G 106
  landforms of South America S 276
Atahualpa (ata-HUAL-pa), Inca ruler P 165, 266
  end of the Inca Empire I 207
  methods used to control Incas E 386

Atalanta, in Greek mythology, young girl known for her beauty, speed, and ability as a huntress. She wounded the Calydonian boar when men failed. She consented to marry the man who could beat her in a footrace and was outwitted by Hippomenes (or Melanion) with help of Aphrodite (goddess of love). During the race Hippomenes dropped three golden apples and Atalanta paused to pick them up. Aphrodite, angered because she received no thanks for her aid, changed the couple into lions.

Atatürk, Mustafa Kemal, president of Turkey T 326, 329

Atbara (OT-ba-ra) River, tributary of the Nile N 260
Atchison, Topeka, and Santa Fe Railroad N 195
Aten (OT-en), or Aton, ancient Egyptian god A 223; E 100
Athabasca (ath-a-BAS-ca) Glacier, Canada, picture G 223
Athabasca Lake, Canada L 26; S 38c
  Arctic Basin of Canada C 52

Athabasca River, Canada, picture **J** 54

Athanasius (ath-a-NAY-shus), **Saint,** Bishop of Alexandria **C** 283; **R** 289

Athapascan (ath-a-PASC-an) **language family,** of North American Indians **A** 136

Athena (a-THE-na), Greek goddess **G** 361
  Parthenon, her temple on the Acropolis, in Athens, pictures **A** 375, **E** 322, **G** 335

Athenaeum (ath-en-E-um), literary or scientific association or club. Term is derived from Greek "Athenaion" (Temple of Athena), where poets read their works. Name was also given to school for study of arts built in Rome (2nd century A.D.) by Emperor Hadrian.

Athens, capital of Greece **G** 331; pictures **G** 335; **C** 306
  ancient civilization in Athens **A** 228
  early form of democracy **D** 104
  education in early Athens **E** 62–63
  oratory **O** 180
  Parthenon **A** 374, picture **A** 375
  Pericles, its greatest statesman **P** 156
  Solon, founder of democracy in ancient Athens **S** 252

Atherosclerosis (ath-er-o-scler-O-sis), hardening of the arteries **B** 293

Athlete's foot D 193

Athletics see Gymnastics; Olympic Games; Physical education; Sports

Athlone, 1st earl of (Alexander Augustus Frederick William Alfred George Cambridge) (1874–1957), British army officer and governor-general, b. London. An uncle of the future King George VI, he fought in the Boer War and in World War I. He was governor-general of the Union of South Africa (1923–31) and of Canada (1940–46).

Athos, Mount, religious state in Greece **G** 332

Athos, one of *The Three Musketeers* **D** 342–43

Athus (ot-URS), Belgium
  steelworkers, picture **B** 128

Atkins, Tommy, traditional nickname for British soldier, comparable to American "GI Joe." Name originated in British War Office in 19th century as demonstration name used in filling out forms and was made popular through poems of Rudyard Kipling.

Atlanta, capital of Georgia **G** 143–44
  Civil War **C** 326–27
  Memorial Arts Center **G** 139
  Sherman captured the city **S** 151

Atlantic, battle of the, 1940–41 **W** 291

Atlantic and Pacific Tea Company, Great (A & P) **S** 468

Atlantic Basin, Canada **C** 51–52

Atlantic Charter (August, 1941), declaration of common principles and war aims by President Franklin D. Roosevelt and Prime Minister Winston Churchill. Charter was signed aboard battleship U.S.S. *Augusta* off coast of Newfoundland. It expressed hope that all men "may live out their lives in freedom from fear and want" and called for general disarmament and the establishment of a permanent peace-keeping structure. Its provisions were endorsed by 15 anti-Axis nations and were later incorporated into United Nations Declaration (1942).

Atlantic City, New Jersey **N** 166

Atlantic Coastal Plain, United States **U** 89

Atlantic Monthly, magazine
  Holmes's essays **H** 160

Atlantic Ocean A 478

cables, submarine **T** 52–53, 54
earthquake belt **E** 34
Gulf Stream **G** 411
history of, diagram **E** 11
hurricanes, months when they occur **H** 293
icebergs in the North Atlantic **I** 25–26
mid-ocean ridge explored by geologists **G** 114
ocean currents **O** 32–33; diagram **L** 232
ocean floor **O** 28–29
ocean liner crossings **O** 17, 19
tide schedule, typical **T** 180

Atlantic Provinces of Canada see New Brunswick; Newfoundland; Nova Scotia; Prince Edward Island

Atlantides, in mythology, water nymphs **A** 478

Atlantis, legendary island in Atlantic Ocean, described by Plato as having an ideal state and a highly developed civilization. According to tradition it was destroyed by an earthquake and sank beneath the sea.
  how Atlantic Ocean was named **A** 478

Atlantis II, ship, floating oceanographic laboratory, picture **O** 25

Atlas, in Greek mythology **G** 363; **W** 243

Atlas, rocket, picture **R** 255

Atlases, bound volumes of maps **M** 93
  reference books **R** 129
  research methods **R** 183

Atlas Mountains, northern Africa **A** 46, 160; **M** 460; picture **A** 162

Atman, or Brahman, Hindu spiritual principle **O** 220d

Atmosphere, gases enveloping our earth **A** 479–82
  air pollution **A** 109, 110; **E** 272f–272g
  clouds **C** 358–61
  comets **C** 418–19
  cosmic rays **C** 511–13
  earth's shield **E** 24–25
  formation of earth's atmosphere **E** 19
  how earth's atmosphere is held **E** 23
  International Geophysical Year findings **I** 316–17
  layers **E** 16–17
  Mars **M** 108, 110
  meteors, meteorites **C** 419–21
  moon lacks **M** 453
  ozone layer **O** 269
  planets **P** 269–78
  research with ballooning **B** 31–32
  solar radiation **S** 235
  space dust **D** 347
  sun's atmosphere **S** 460–62
  twinkling layer of air **S** 409
  weather of the atmospheric layers **W** 71–72
  See *also* Air; Meteorology

Atmospheric pressure A 479; **W** 72
  boiling point affected by **H** 93–94
  freezing point affected by **H** 94
  pumps, action of **P** 528
  See *also* Air pressure

Atolls, coral islands **P** 2
  corals **C** 504

Atomic bomb N 362–63
  Einstein's work on **E** 105–06
  Hiroshima and Nagasaki, Japan **J** 48
  man-made radiation belts **R** 49
  Truman, Harry S, and bombing Japan **T** 300
  underwater explosion at Bikini, 1946, picture **N** 353
  United States Air Force **U** 160
  World War II **W** 308

Atomic energy see Nuclear energy

Atomic Energy Commission, five-man commission created by Atomic Energy Act of 1946 to provide civilian

Atomic Energy Commission (continued)
administration of U.S. atomic energy program. The commission is solely responsible for development of atomic energy for military purposes. Since 1954 it has shared with private industry the responsibility for development of peacetime uses.

Atomic numbers A 486–87; C 201, 218
  elements E 153–59
  nuclear energy N 355
  See also Periodic table
Atomic physics *see* Nuclear physics
Atomic power *see* Nuclear energy
Atomic weight A 484, 487; C 218
  Dalton's theory D 15
  elements E 153–54
  experimental measurements C 212
  isotopes C 203–05
  nuclear energy N 356, 357–58
Atomium, symbol of Brussels World's Fair F 16
Atoms A 483–89; C 218
  alloy structures A 168, 169
  ancient "elements" C 206–07
  atomic shower, International Geophysical Year findings
    I 312–13
  carbon chains and rings C 106
  chemical structure C 201, 216, 196
  chemistry, history of, theories C 206–07, 212–13
  cosmic rays C 511–13
  crystals C 541–42
  Dalton's theory C 212; D 15
  electricity E 123, 126, 128
  electronics E 143–44
  elements, chemical E 153–59
  ions and ionization I 350–55
  magnetism M 28
  nuclear energy N 352–71
  radiation R 40
  radioactive dating R 64–66
  radioactive elements R 67
  Rutherford's theory R 361
Atoms for Peace Plan, 1953 D 184
Atom smashing, process for studying atoms A 489
Aton *see* Aten
Atonality, in music M 400
Atonement, Day of, Jewish holy day J 120
ATP, adenosine triphosphate B 296–97
  photosynthesis forms this compound P 222
Atrium, center hall of a Roman house, picture R 306
Atriums, chambers of the heart B 276; D 197; diagrams
    B 276, D 198
  coronary circulation of the heart H 86a–86b
Atropine (AT-ro-pene), drug P 314, 321
Atta, or leaf-cutting, **ants** A 326
Attachés (at-ta-SHAYS), representatives of the armed
    forces in the Foreign Service F 370
Attar of roses
  Bulgaria, major producer of B 441
Attassi, Nureddin el-, president of Syria S 508
Attica, region around Athens
  Attic dialect becomes common language of Greece
    G 349
  Attic vases G 343

Attila (AT-til-a) (406?–453), king of the Huns. He became king in 433, ruling jointly with his brother Bleda until the latter's death (444?). The Huns, an Asian people, had migrated into eastern Europe in the 4th century. Under Attila they conquered most of eastern and central Europe and invaded the eastern Roman Empire, advancing to the gates of the capital, Constantinople (now Istanbul). The destruction wrought by Attila earned him

the name Scourge of God. In 451 he invaded Gaul (modern France), but his westward expansion was checked by Roman and Gothic troops at the battle of Chalôns—one of the great battles of history. In 452 he invaded northern Italy. According to legend, Attila is said to have spared Rome at the entreaty of Pope Leo I. After Attila's death the Hunnish empire quickly disintegrated.
  Chalons, battle of, 451 B 100
  Nibelungenlied and Volsung Saga, legends
    L 130
  See also Huns

Attlee, Clement Richard (1883–1967), Earl Attlee, English statesman, b. London. He was elected to Parliament as Labour member (1922) and became leader of Labour Party (1935–55). He held various posts in Winston Churchill's coalition government during World War II, was British delegate to UN conference in San Francisco (1945), and served as prime minister (1945–51), during which time he helped to bring various industries under state ownership and to institute extensive health and welfare services. He was made a peer in 1955.

Attorney General, member of the cabinet of the U.S. president, and head of U.S. Justice Department P 448
Attorneys *see* Lawyers

Attucks (AT-uks), **Crispus** (1723?–1770), American revolutionary patriot, Negro, killed in the Boston Massacre. Almost nothing is definitely known of Attucks' life up to the time of his death, but he is thought to have been born a slave (possibly in Massachusetts) and to have escaped and worked as a seaman. Attucks was in Boston at a time when strong local feeling had been aroused by the presence of British troops. A number of fights had already broken out between troops and colonists. On the evening of March 5, 1770, a crowd of Boston men, including Attucks, confronted a small party of British soldiers. A barrage of sticks and stones was met by the soldiers' gunfire. Attucks and four others were killed. A memorial to the five men stands today on Boston Common.
  Boston Massacre R 196
  Negro in American history N 91

Attu Island, Alaska A 128

Atwater, Richard T. (1892–1948), American author of children's books, b. Chicago, Ill. He wrote *Mr. Popper's Penguins* with his wife, **Florence,** inspired by film on Admiral Byrd's first Antarctic expedition. He also wrote *Captain Cook* and *Troubles with a Penguin.*

A. U. *see* Astronomical unit
Auburn, Maine M 44
Auburn system, of punishment P 468–69
Auckland, New Zealand N 241
Auctions
  tobacco T 201
Auden, W. H., English-born American poet E 266
Audible sounds S 259–60
Audiologists (aud-i-OL-o-gists), test hearing D 50
Audiometer, device to test hearing, picture H 84
Audio signal, television T 66, 68
Audio-visual aids
  education E 77–78
  special services of libraries
    L 171–72
Audit, in bookkeeping B 311
  insurance auditors I 297

Audubon (AUD-u-bon), **John James,** American naturalist and painter **A** 490–91; **K** 216
 Audubon Memorial State Park, Louisiana **L** 358–59
 birdbanding started in North America **B** 229
 United States, art of **U** 117, 120
 Wild Turkey, painting **U** 118

Audubon Society, National, organization devoted to the preservation of wildlife (birds, animals, plants) and the conservation of their habitats. Society is named after John J. Audubon, famous painter of birds. Founded in 1905, its headquarters is in New York, N.Y. Its publications include the *Audubon Magazine.*

Aue, Hartmann von see Hartmann von Aue
Augean (au-GE-an) **stables,** in Greek mythology **G** 363
Auger (AUG-er) **bits,** tools **T** 214; **W** 230
 auger mining of coal **C** 365
Augmented Roman Alphabet **I** 254
Augsburg Confession, 1530 **P** 483
August, 8th month of year **A** 492–93
Augusta (au-GUST-a), capital of Maine **M** 43–44
Augusta, Georgia **G** 145
Augustin I see Iturbide, Augustin de
Augustine, Saint (354–430), early Christian leader and Bishop of Hippo **A** 494: **C** 283–84; picture **C** 282
 father of Latin theology **R** 289
 philosophical system **P** 192
Augustine, Saint (?–604), archbishop of Canterbury **R** 290
 Anglo-Saxons converted to Christianity **E** 216
Augustus, emperor of Rome **R** 303; statue **R** 286, **S** 95
 Aeneid written in honor of Augustus **A** 35
 heir of Julius Caesar **C** 6
 Latin literature, golden age of **L** 79–80
 second triumvirate with Mark Antony and Lepidus **M** 100

Auks, seabirds, related to gulls and terns, of colder regions of the Northern Hemisphere. Auks are black-and-white birds with short tails, webbed feet, and small wings that they use in swimming.
 great auk, extinct **B** 231

Aulaire (O-laire), **Ingri** (1904–) and **Edgar Parin** (1898–) **d',** American authors and illustrators of children's books. As husband-and-wife team, they illustrate books about children of other lands and figures from history. Their works include *Ola, Don't Count Your Chicks,* and *Abraham Lincoln* (Caldecott winner, 1940).

Auld Lang Syne, song by Robert Burns **B** 460
Aulos, double oboe of ancient Greece **A** 247
Aurangzeb (AUR-ang-zeb), emperor of Mogul dynasty of India **I** 133
Aureomycin (aur-e-o-MY-cin), antibiotic **A** 312

Auriol, Jacqueline (1917–), French aviatrix, b. Challans. Considered France's leading woman flyer and one of France's top test pilots, she is unofficially known as world's speediest woman. She was the second woman to break the sound barrier (1955), flying at 715 mph.

Auriol, Vincent (1884–1966), French politician, b. Revel Haute-Garonne. He was Socialist member of the Chamber of Deputies (1914–40) and general secretary of Socialist group in Parliament (1919–36). Imprisoned after German conquest of France (1940), he escaped (1943) and joined French underground, later being active in De Gaulle's Free French movement and becoming first president (1947–53) of Fourth Republic.

Aurochs (AUR-ocks), extinct wild cattle **H** 221

Aurora (uh-ROR-a), in Roman mythology, the goddess of the dawn. In Greek myth she is known as Eos, the daughter of the Titan Hyperion and the sister of Helios (the sun god) and Selene (the moon goddess). She is supposed to have ushered in each new day by driving a chariot, drawn by two white horses, across the morning sky.

Aurora australis (aus-TRAY-lis), south polar lights **I** 310, 353
Aurora borealis (bo-re-AL-is), or northern lights **I** 310, 353
Auroras, polar lights **I** 310, 353
 International Geophysical Year findings **I** 313–15
 radiation belts **R** 49
 shown in the ionosphere, diagram **E** 16
 solar flares **E** 27
Austen, Jane, English novelist **A** 494
 place in English literature **E** 261
 style and themes of her novels **N** 346
Austerlitz, battle of, 1805 **N** 11
Austin, capital of Texas **T** 133
Austin, Moses, American pioneer miner **M** 366
Austin, Stephen F., American pioneer **M** 366–67; **T** 135
Austin, Warren R., American statesman **V** 320
Australia (aus-TRAY-lia) **A** 495–517
 Canberra, capital of Australia **C** 87–88
 dependencies **C** 428
 favorite foods **F** 335, 339
 flag **F** 240
 football **F** 366
 gold discoveries **G** 253; **M** 320
 immigration **I** 103
 kangaroos and other pouched mammals **K** 167–75
 Melbourne **M** 215
 mountain peaks, highest in Australia **M** 494
 national anthem **N** 21
 Papua, New Guinea, a trust territory of **N** 147
 prairies **P** 430–32
 rabbit plague **R** 24
 rodeos, as in United States and Canada **R** 281–82
 Sydney **S** 503–04
 western desert area, picture **D** 125
 winter season, picture **S** 111
 Wollomombi waterfall **W** 57
Australian Alps **A** 502–03
Australian ballot **E** 115
Australian Capital Territory **A** 514; **C** 87
Australian crawl, swimming **S** 490
Australian Elizabethan Theatre Trust **T** 163
Australian region, land region of animal life **L** 234–35
Australian Rules, football, Melbourne home of **M** 215

Austral Islands, or **Tubuai Islands,** chain of Pacific islands in French Polynesia, south of the Society Islands. There are four volcanic islands and one uninhabited atoll. The islands produce vanilla, arrowroot, and copra.

Australoids, Australia's aborigines (people) **A** 499, 501
 Stone Age culture **P** 442
Australopithecus, early manlike creature **P** 442; pictures **A** 305, **P** 444
Austria **A** 518–25
 flag **F** 239
 German and Austrian literature **G** 174–81
 German and Austrian music **G** 183–89
 German language **G** 172–73
 handicrafts, picture **E** 318
 national anthem **N** 21
 World War II, annexed by Hitler, 1938 **W** 286

Autonomy (au-TON-omy), in general, quality or state of
being independent, free, and self-governing. In government, it is degree of self-determination or political
control possessed by a minority group, territorial
division, or political unit in relation to state or
community of which it is a part, ranging from local self-
government to full independence.

Avant-garde (ov-on-GARD), French term meaning "before
the rest." It describes those people who through experimentation and innovation lead their field in original
designs, ideas, or techniques during any given period. It
also means people who are ahead of their time and are
therefore considered unconventional.

Aventurine (av-ENT-ur-ene), quartz Q 7
Avenue, The, Middelharnis, painting by Hobbema D 361
Averages, values of sets of numbers S 416

Averill, Esther (1902–), American author and publisher
of children's books, b. Bridgeport, Conn. She published
children's literature and worked in graphic arts in Paris
(1925–35). Her books include *Daniel Boone, Flash,* and
The Voyages of Jacques Cartier.

Avery, Milton (1883–1965), American painter, b. Altmar,
N.Y. He studied at the Connecticut League of Art Students but was primarily self-taught. During the Depression
years he worked for the Works Progress Administration.
His subjects are mostly figures and coastal landscapes
that have a quality of stillness and serenity.

Avery (AVE-ery) Island, Louisiana L 359
Aves (A-vese), class name for birds B 199
Avesta (av-ES-ta), holy book of Zoroastrianism
  Z 380
Aviation A 553–74
  aeronautical charts and maps, picture M 91
  air transport T 266–67
  balloons and ballooning B 30–34
  Berlin airlift B 144; G 164
  gliders G 238–40
  helicopters H 105–06
  jet propulsion J 85–87
  Lindbergh's New York-Paris flight L 300;
    M 374–75
  naval aviation, first flight U 186
  navigation, air N 67
  parachutes P 59–61
  polar exploration P 365
  supersonic flight S 469–73
  United States Air Force U 159–66
  United States air transportation U 110
  United States Navy U 193
  What keeps a plane up in the air? A 38
  World War I W 276
  Wright, Wilbur and Orville W 316–17
  See also Civil Aeronautics Board
Avicenna, Persian philosopher S 64
Avignon (ov-ene-YON), France
  seat of papacy for 70 years R 293
Ávila, Pedro Arias de see Pedrarias Dávila
Ávila, Spain S 356
  Romanesque wall, picture E 330
Ávila Camacho (OB-i-la ca-MA-cho), Manuel, Mexican
  president M 250
Avilés, Pedro Menéndez de see Menéndez
Avocado, fruit
  showing seed, picture P 298
Avocations see Hobbies
Avodire, tree
  uses of the wood and its grain, picture
    W 223

Avogadro (ov-o-GA-dro), Count Amedeo (1776–1856),
Italian scientist, b. Turin. He discovered a basic law of
chemistry, Avogadro's law, which states that equal
amounts of different gases under equal conditions will
have the same number of molecules.

Avoirdupois (av-er-du-POIS), weight W 113, 115
Awards, literary
  book awards for children's literature B 309–10b
  Nobel prizes N 266
  Pulitzer prizes P 524–28
Awls, tools for piercing holes N 89; S 162

AWOL, U.S. Army term meaning "absent without leave."
It is a serious offense for anyone in the armed services
to be absent from his duty or station without official
permission or authorization.

Axenfeld, Israel, Yiddish author Y 350
Axiomatic method, in mathematics M 159
Axioms, mathematical assumptions M 159
  geometry G 123
Axis, a central line
  lenses L 143–44

Axis, of celestial bodies
  earth's E 4, 24; G 96
  Mars M 106
  moon's M 447
  planets, diagram P 277

Axis Powers (Rome-Berlin-Tokyo Axis), alliance of Italy,
Germany, and Japan, which opposed Allied Powers during
World War II. It originated in formal pact between
Germany and Italy, pledging economic and military co-
operation (1936). Japan allied with Germany in Anti-
Comintern pact (1936), agreeing to combine efforts in
combatting Communism. They were joined by Italy
(1937). Axis was solidified in "Pact of Steel" (1939)
(Germany and Italy) and in Tripartite pact (1940).
  chief antagonists in World War II W 282

Axles, of wheels W 157
Axminster carpets R 353
Axons, of brain cell bodies B 364
Axum see Aksum, Ethiopia
Aycock, Charles Brantley, American statesman N 319
Aye-ayes (EYE-eyes), lemurs M 418
Ayer's Directory of Newspapers and Periodicals M 15
Ayllón (ile-YONE), Lucas Vázquez de, Spanish explorer
  S 309
Aymará (eye-ma-RA), Indians of South America I 203, 207
  Bolivia B 302
  Peru P 160
Ayolas (a-YO-los), Juan de, Spanish explorer P 65
Ayres, songs R 173
Ayrshire, breed of dairy cattle C 147; D 8; picture D 5
Ayub Khan (a-YUBE KAHN), Field Marshal Mohammad,
  Pakistani political leader P 41
Azalea (a-ZALE-ya), shrub, pictures G 28, 36, N 314
Azalea Trail, Mobile, Alabama A 122
Azerbaijan (a-zer-by-JON) Soviet Socialist Republic U 45
  languages of the U.S.S.R. U 28
Azhar, University of al-, Cairo, Egypt C 8; E 90d

Azikiwe (oz-i-KI-way), Nnamdi (1904–   ), Nigerian political leader, b. Zungeri. He was prime minister of
Eastern Nigeria (1954–59), president of Federation of
Nigeria Senate (1960), president of National Council
of Nigeria and the Cameroons, and governor-general
and commander in chief of Federation of Nigeria
(1960–63). He was president of Federal Republic of
Nigeria (1963–66) until a military coup toppled the
government.

Azimuthal (az-i-MUTH-al) projections, of maps M 93
Azizia (a-zi-ZI-a), Libya, record high temperature A 50
Azores (a-ZORES), islands off Portugal I 427; P 401;
  picture I 431
Azorin see Martínez Ruiz, José
Azov (A-zof), Sea of O 45
Aztec calendar stone, pictures I 195, W 220
Aztecs, Indians of North America I 195, 197
  arts, development of I 155
  cacao beans and chocolate originally used by C 274
  calendar stone, a wonder of the world I 195; W 220
  Cortes, conqueror of C 508
  dance L 68
  factors important in helping Cortes conquer Mexico
    M 247–48
  mythology M 561–62

ILLUSTRATION CREDITS

The following list credits, by page, the sources of illustrations used in Volume A of THE NEW BOOK OF KNOWLEDGE. Credits are listed illustration by illustration—left to right, top to bottom. Wherever appropriate, the name of the photographer or artist has been listed with the source, the two being separated by a dash. When two or more illustrations appear on one page, their credits are separated by semicolons.

2　Lee J. Ames
3　Lee J. Ames
8　James F. Cooper
10　Bettmann Archive
11　Courtesy of the Sons of the Revolution
12　James F. Cooper
14　The Metropolitan Museum of Art, Gift of I. N. Phelps Stokes, Edward S. Hawes, Alice Mary Hawes, Marion Augusta Hawes, 1937; Bettmann Archive.
15　Bettmann Archive
16　Jack Hearne
27　Warshaw Collection of Business Americana; Doyle, Dane, Bernbach, Inc.
31　Carl Perutz; Carl Perutz; J. Walter Thompson Co.
32　Kenyon & Eckhardt; Doyle, Dane, Bernbach, Inc.; Allen & Reynolds, Inc.; Doyle, Dane, Bernbach, Inc.
34　The Advertising Council
36–　Lee J. Ames
40
41　The Ryan Aeronautical Co.; UPI; The Boeing Co.
43　George Buctel; Marc Riboud—Magnum.
44　Marc Riboud—Magnum; Aloys Michel; Stephanie Dinkins; Marc Riboud—Magnum.
47　John Lewis Stage—Lensgroup; Harrison Forman; John & Bini Moss—Photo Researchers; Carl Frank; George Rodger—Magnum.
48　Jere Donovan
51　M. S. Klein—Shostal; George Rodger—Magnum; Hilda Harrison—C. P. Cushing; M. S. Klein—Shostal; George Rodger—Magnum.
53　George Buctel
54　E. Kollmar—Shostal; Marc & Evelyne Bernheim—Rapho Guillumette; Carl Frank; H. Street—Shostal; Tom Larson—American Museum of Natural History; Marc & Evelyne Bernheim—Rapho Guillumette; Carl Frank.
57　Jeppesen & Company
59　George Rodger—Magnum; E. Kollmar—Shostal; Brian Brake—Magnum; E. Kollmar—Shostal.
60　Louis Renault—Photo Researchers; Pete Turner—FPG; George Rodger—Magnum; Marc Riboud—Magnum.
63　Marc Riboud—Magnum; Marc Riboud—Magnum; Duncan Edward—FPG; Carl Frank; W. R. Donagho—Shostal.
64　Hal Linker—Shostal
66　Inge Morath—Magnum
68　Carl Frank; Carl Frank; Marc Riboud—Magnum; Kryn Taconis—Magnum; Carl Frank.
69　Carl Frank
70　W. Bruggmann—E. Leucinger Collection; Lee Bolton.
71　Charles Uht—Museum of Primitive Art
73　W. Bruggmann—Ethnological Collection, Zurich; Lee Bolton—Museum of Primitive Art, New York; W. Bruggmann—In the Possession of the Oni of Ife; Charles Uht—Museum of Primitive Art; Lee Bolton; W. Bruggman—Rietberg Museum, Zurich.
74　W. Bruggmann—Rietberg Museum, Zurich; W. Bruggmann—Rietberg Museum,
Zurich, Von Der Heydt Collection; W. Bruggmann—Rietberg Museum, Zurich; Frank Newens—Pitt Rivers Museum, Oxford University; J. A. Lavaud—Musée de l'Homme, Paris.
75　W. Bruggmann—Ethnological Collection, Zurich; W. Bruggmann—Rietberg Museum, Zurich, Von Der Heydt Collection; I. Zafrir—Israel Dubiner Collection, Tel Aviv; University Museum, Philadelphia; Charles Uht—Museum of Primitive Art; University Museum, Philadelphia; University Museum, Philadelphia.
76　Charles Uht—The Museum of Primitive Art
77　Peter Larson—FPG; Robert S. Kane.
79　Ken Heyman—Rapho Guillumette
80　Archives, Museum of Comparative Zoology Library, Harvard University
81　George Sottung
82　Don Spaulding
85　Courtesy of Professor V. N. Nikitin—University of Kharkov
86　F. E. Nichy—U.S. Bureau of Commercial Fisheries; By permission, British Museum (Natural History); Smithsonian Institution; Walter Dawn; Reprinted from *Seals, Sea Lions, and Walruses* by Victor B. Scheffer, with permission of the publishers, Stanford University Press, © 1958 by the Board of Trustees of the Leland Stanford Junior University.
89　W. T. Mars
90　Shostal; Shostal; Ray Manley—Shostal.
91　Allis Chalmers; H. Armstrong Roberts; Courtesy of Atlee Burpee.
97　Ed Drews—Photo Researchers; Dan Budnik—Magnum; John Lewis Stage—Photo Researchers; Eric Lessing—Magnum.
98　Birnback; Eric Lessing—Magnum; Ned Haines—Rapho Guillumette.
99　Birnback; Stephanie Dinkins; Henri Cartier-Bresson—Magnum; Tom Hollyman—Photo Researchers.
101　Bettmann Archive
102　Weimer Pursell
103　Weimer Pursell
104　Willy Ronis
106　The Blankfort Group
107　Cioffero—Fundamental Photographs
108　The New York *Times*; Lee J. Ames.
109　Frank Bauer—C. P. Cushing; Henry Genn.
110　Courtesy of Bethlehem Steel Co.
111　Los Angeles County Air Pollution Control District; St. Louis *Post Dispatch*—Black Star.
113　S. A. Grimes; Mem Tierce; Rutherford Platt; Color Illustration, Inc.
114　Douglas Faulkner; Diversified Map Corp.
115　Diversified Map Corp.
116　Diversified Map Corp.
119　Douglas Faulkner
123　Ray Atkeson; Douglas Faulkner; George Buctel.
124　Douglas Faulkner
125　Diversified Map Corp.
129　John J. Koranda; George W. Merriman; Steve McCutcheon; Color Illustration, Inc.; Diversified Map Corp.
131　Diversified Map Corp.
132　Diversified Map Corp.
133　Steve McCutcheon; Bob & Ira Spring.
134　C. J. Ott—Shostal
137　C. W. Sorensen
138　Diversified Map Corp.
139　C. W. Sorensen
140　George Buctel
141　Ward Wells—Shostal
144　George Buctel
146　European Picture Service; Gunther Reitz—Pix.
146b　Malak; George Hunter; Annan Photo Features.
146e　Diversified Map Corp.
146f　Gene Ahrens—Shostal
146g　George Hunter—Shostal; Malak.
150　George Sottung
152　Robert E. Conlan
153　Robert E. Conlan
154　George Sottung
155　George Sottung
156　Walter Dawn; Bruce Hunter—American Museum of Natural History; Walter Dawn; Walter Dawn; Dr. George A. Llano—Courtesy of *Scientific American*.
161　George Buctel
162　Michel Hetier—Rapho Guillumette; Shostal; G. Mangin—Rapho Guillumette.
164　Sir John Tenniel
165　Sir John Tenniel
167　Don Spaulding
169　Revere Copper & Brass, Inc.
172　Lee J. Ames
174　Bob & Ira Spring
175　Ray Manley—Shostal; Bob & Ira Spring; Swiss National Tourist Office.
177　Jack Hearne
178　J. David Bowen; Rene Burri—Magnum.
179　George Holton—Photo Researchers; Davis Pratt—Rapho Guillumette; Davis Pratt—Rapho Guillumette.
180　Howard Koslow
182　Jack Hearne
183　Jack Hearne
188　Jack Hearne
187　Jack Hearne
190　Jack Hearne
191　Jack Hearne
193　Jack Hearne
194　Jack Hearne
197　Robert Frankenberg
198　Bettmann Archive
199　Robert Frankenberg
201　Robert Frankenberg
203　Robert Frankenberg
204　Robert Frankenberg
205　Robert Frankenberg
207　Robert Frankenberg
208　Robert Frankenberg
210　Tom Hollyman—Photo Researchers
212　Robert Frankenberg
215　Harper & Bros.
216　Artcraft Lithography Printing Co.; New York Public Library
217　Robert Frankenberg; Hirmer Fotoarchiv.
218　Robert Frankenberg
219　Editions Tel; Hirmer Fotoarchiv.
221　From *The March of Archaeology* by C. W. Ceram, published by Alfred A. Knopf; Robert Frankenberg.
222　Egyptian Collection, Staatlichen Museum, Berlin—Art Reference Bureau; Ancient

Egyptian Paintings, Oriental Institute, University of Chicago.
223 Robert Frankenberg
224 Courtesy of Museum of Fine Arts, Boston; Robert Frankenberg.
225 Archaeological Survey of India—Art Reference Bureau, Inc.
226 Robert Frankenberg
227 Alison Frantz—Art Reference Bureau
228 The Metropolitan Museum of Art, Fletcher Fund, 1931
229 Robert Frankenberg
230 Courtesy, Museum of Fine Arts, Boston; Courtesy, Museum of Fine Arts, Boston; Lee Boltin—The Metropolitan Museum of Art, Rogers Fund, 1952; Courtesy, Museum of Fine Arts, Boston.
231 Robert Frankenberg
232 American Numismatic Society; Chase Manhattan Bank, Money Museum; Bill Froelich; Alinari—Art Reference Bureau.
233 By permission of the trustees of the British Museum—Art Reference Bureau
234 Oriental Institute, University of Chicago
235 Hirmer; Editions Tel.
236 John Baker—Shostal; Raymond V. Schoder.
237 Alison Frantz—Art Reference Bureau
239 Hirmer; Josephine Powell.
240 © British Museum—Art Reference Bureau
241 Courtesy of the Trustees of the British Museum; Louvre—Editions Tel.
242 William G. Froelich; Art Reference Bureau.
243 Staatlichen Museum, Berlin
244 Art Reference Bureau; Courtesy of the Trustees of the British Museum; Tomb of the Leopards, Tarquinia—Art Reference Bureau.
246 Metropolitan Museum of Art, Fletcher Fund, 1956
249 W. T. Mars
252 Cornell Capa—Magnum; John Meyer—Shostal; Tom Hollyman—Photo Researchers; C. W. Close—Shostal.
255 George Buctel; Tom Hollyman—Photo Researchers; Peter Wichman—Birnback.
256 Boston Medical Library, Massachusetts Medical Society
257 New York Hospital; Gorman-Rupp Industries, Inc.
261 George Buctel; Harrison Forman.
262– Don Spaulding
264
267– Don Spaulding
274
275 Ylla—Rapho Guillumette
276 David Corson—Shostal; Courtesy of Bell Telephone Laboratories, Inc.
277 Allan D. Cruickshank—National Audubon Society; Lynwood Chace.
279 Robert Meyerriecks; Lawrence E. Perkins; Lawrence E. Perkins; Henry C. Johnson.
280 Kitchen Kinne—National Audubon Society
281 William Bartlett
282 FPG; George Bakacs
283 Roy De Carava
284 Al Bassy—Three Lions; Dr. Ross E. Hutchins.
285 George Bakacs; The Times, London—Pictorial Parade.
286 George Bakacs
287 Professor Harry F. Harlow—Primate Laboratory, University of Wisconsin
288 Lilo Hess—Three Lions
289– Alex Ebel
293
294 Ylla—Rapho Guillumette; Alex Ebel.
295 Lyn—Annan; Karl W. Kenyon—National Audubon Society; Allan D. Cruickshank—National Audubon Society.

296 Frederic Webster & Donald Griffin; Alex Ebel.
297 © MCMLV, Walt Disney Productions, World Rights Reserved.
298 © MCMLXII Walt Disney Productions, World Rights Reserved; © Walt Disney Productions, World Rights Reserved.
299 Lee J. Ames
300 Constance Stuart—Black Star; Richard Harrington—Three Lions; Olin's Winchester Western.
301 John Hiney—Photo Researchers; Shostal; Tom Hollyman—Photo Researchers.
302 Shostal; Shostal; Rapho; Shostal.
303 South African Tourist Corp.; Courtesy of American Museum of Natural History; National Film Board of Canada; Marc & Evelyne Bernheim—Rapho.
304 H. Armstrong Roberts; Harold Schultz; Wide World; Swedish National Travel.
305 James Cooper
306 Camera Press-Pix; Carleton S. Coon for Alfred A. Knopf, Origin of the Races.
307 William W. Bacon III—Rapho Guillumette; Irish Tourist Office; D. Forbert—Shostal; FPG; Bill Brindle—Photo Researchers; Sabine Weiss—Rapho Guillumette; John Moss—Photo Researchers; Marc & Evelyne Bernheim—Rapho Guillumette; Ernest Kleinberg—Rapho Guillumette.
309 © by Chicago Natural History Museum
311 Chas. Pfizer & Co.
313 Weimer Pursell
314 Chas. Pfizer & Co.
315 New York Academy of Medicine; Chas. Pfizer & Co.; Chas. Pfizer & Co.; Eugene H. Kone—Rockefeller Institute; Wide World.
316 George Bakacs
317 Lee J. Ames
318 National Gallery of Art, Index of American Design; Lee Boltin—Courtesy, Cooper Union Museum; Lee Boltin—Courtesy, Cooper Union Museum.
319 Lee Boltin—Courtesy, Cooper Union Museum; Sandak; Corning Museum of Glass; New York State Historical Association, Cooperstown, N.Y.; Antique Coin Bank Collection of the Seaman's Bank for Savings, New York City.
321 Metropolitan Museum of Art, Gift of William R. Stewart, 1926; Metropolitan Museum of Art, Bequest of A. T. Clearwater, 1933; Metropolitan Museum of Art, Gift of Mrs. Abraham Lansing, 1901; Metropolitan Museum of Art, Bequest of A. T. Clearwater, 1933.
322 Gaetano Di Palma; Dr. Ross E. Hutchins.
323 Dr. Ross E. Hutchins
324 M. W. F. Tweedie—National Audubon Society
325– Dr. Ross E. Hutchins
328
329 Gaetano Di Palma
330 Gaetano Di Palma
331 Rudolf Freund—Nettie King Associates
332 Roberto Hoesch
335 R. Bagby—FPG; Grant Heilman.
336 FPG; FPG; FPG; FPG; FPG; Fundamental Photos; FPG; FPG; Fundamental Photos; FPG; Fundamental Photos; Fundamental Photos
337 A. Upitis—FPG
341 Dr. Herbert R. Axelrod
342 Dr. Herbert R. Axelrod; Dr. Herbert R. Axelrod; Dr. Herbert R. Axelrod; Dr. Herbert R. Axelrod; Dr. Herbert R. Axelrod; Treat Davidson—National Audubon Society; Dr. Herbert R. Axelrod.
345 James Caraway
346 James Caraway

347 James Caraway
348 Lee Boltin; The Metropolitan Museum of Art—Courtesy of Chanticleer Press; Lee Boltin; Josephine Powell—Dawn of Civilization, published by Thames & Hudson, London and McGraw-Hill, New York; British Museum—Art Reference Bureau; Lee Boltin—University Museum, Philadelphia; Art Reference Bureau.
350 Courtesy of the Oriental Institute, University of Chicago
351 Chicago Natural History Museum
352 Lee Boltin
353 Kathleen M. Kenyon—Archaeology in the Holy Land, published by Ernest Benn Ltd., London; Ace William—Shostal; American Museum of Natural History.
354 Charles Perry Weimer; Lee Boltin; Art Reference Bureau.
355 Stockpile; Fritz Henle—Photo Researchers.
356 Mississippi River Comm., U.S. Army
357 Courtesy of the Oriental Institute, University of Chicago, Prehistoric Project
358 Lee Ames; Courtesy, Oriental Institute, U. of Chicago, Prehistoric Project
359 Chicago Natural History Museum
360 Courtesy of the Smithsonian Institution, Freer Gallery of Art, Washington, D.C.; The Metropolitan Museum of Art.
361 Courtesy of the Oriental Institute, University of Chicago, Prehistoric Project
362 Danish National Travel Office
363 Birnback Publishing Company; Courtesy of the Oriental Institute, University of Chicago; Hildegard Geisler-Baker.
364 John Cochran
365 Courtesy of the Oriental Institute, University of Chicago
366– Jack Hearne
368
369 Weimer Pursell
370 Raymond V. Schroder
372 The Metropolitan Museum of Art, Purchase, 1890, Levi Hale Willard Bequest
373 E. F. Schmidt—Courtesy of the Oriental Institute, University of Chicago
374 Lawrence Cherney—Birnback
375 J. Allan Cash—Rapho Guillumette
376 Don Spaulding
379 Gunther Reitz—Pix; Don Spaulding.
380 Ray Manley—Shostal
382 G. E. Kidder Smith
383 Alinari—Art Reference Bureau
384 ANI; Ray Manley—Shostal.
385 Sandak
386 Ezra Stoller Associates
387 Alinari—Art Reference Bureau; Ezra Stoller Associates; Lewis P. Watson.
389 George Buctel
391 Dieter Grabitsky; Art D'Arazien—Shostal.
392 Jerry Cooke
395 Dieter Grabitsky
397 Alinari—Art Reference Bureau
402 Color Illustration Inc.; Harry L. & Ruth Crockette; George T. Renner.
404– Diversified Map Corp.
406
409 Chuck Abbott—Rapho Guillumette; Ray Manley—Shostal.
410 Ray Manley—Shostal; Josef Muench.
412 George Buctel
413 Debs Metzong—Davon Photos
414 Esther Henderson—Rapho Guillumette
415 Diversified Map Corp.
418 Color Illustration Inc.; Walter Singer—Shostal; S. A. Grimes; J. Horace McFarland.
420– Diversified Map Corp.
422
423 H. Armstrong Roberts; J. R. Bull—Shostal

424 Reynolds Metals Co.
428 George Buctel
429 Art D'Arazien—Shostal; Harold Phelps —Arkansas Publicity & Parks Comm.
430 Diversified Map Corp.
433 Bettmann Archive; The Metropolitan Museum of Art; The Metropolitan Museum of Art.
434 Metropolitan Museum of Art, Bashford Dean Memorial Collection, Gift of Helen Fahnestock Hubbard, 1929, in memory of her father, Harris C. Fahnestock; Metropolitan Museum of Art, Rogers Fund, 1904; A.N.I.; A.N.I.; Metropolitan Museum of Art, Dick Fund, 1939; Metropolitan Museum of Art, the Bashford Dean Memorial Collection, Bequest of Bashford Dean, 1929; Metropolitan Museum of Art, Bashford Dean Memorial Collection, Gift of Helen Fahnestock Hubbard, 1929, in memory of her father, Harris C. Fahnestock; A.N.I.
435 A.N.I.; The Metropolitan Museum of Art, Gift of Bashford Dean, 1914; The New York Public Library; British Museum; A.N.I.; A.N.I.
436 Jack Hearne
437 From *Egyptian Painting* pub. by Skira
438 James Cooper
438a Metropolitan Museum of Art—The Cloisters Collection Purchase, 1954; Metropolitan Museum of Art—Anonymous gift, 1932.
438c Metropolitan Museum of Art, Bequest of Mrs. H. O. Hevemeyer, 1929; Metropolitan Museum of Art, Robers Fund, 1952.
438d Metropolitan Museum of Art, Bequest of William Church Osborn, 1951; The Museum of Modern Art—Sandak.
438e Collection of Mr. & Mrs. Austin Bruggs
438g Eugene Luttenberg—Editorial Photocolor Archives
439 Bettmann Archive
440 Bettmann Archive
442 W. T. Mars
443 W. T. Mars
446 Ewing Krainin—Stockpile, Harrison Forman; Aramco.
447 Ed Lettan—Shostal; William G. Froelich; P. P. Karan.
453 George Buctel

454– Jeppesen & Company
455
456– Jere Donovan
457
458 Nat & Yanna Brandt—Photo Researchers; Indrajit Nalawalla—Shostal; Ergy Landau—Rapho Guillumette; Harrison Forman—Shostal; Fujihira—Monkmeyer.
459 Stephanie Dinkins—Photo Researchers; Sammy Abboud—FPG; C. W. Sorensen; Fujihira—Monkmeyer; C. W. Sorensen; Ewing Krainin—Stockpile
461 *Der Stern*—PIP
463 Ace Williams—Shostal; Stephanie Dinkins—Photo Researchers; William G. Froelich; Henri Cartier-Bresson—Magnum.
464 Ewing Krainin—Stockpile; Fujihira—Monkmeyer; Harvey Hurtt—Shostal; Tom Tucker—Photo Researchers.
467 Van Bucher—Photo Researchers; Frances Mortimer—Rapho Guillumette; John Taylor—Rapho Guillumette; Ewing Krainin—Stockpile; M. Williams—Shostal; Birnback.
468 Van Bucher—Photo Researchers; A. L. Goldman—Rapho Guillumette.
470 Lee J. Ames; Art Reference Bureau.
471 Lee J. Ames
472 Lee J. Ames
473 George N. Sottung
474 Lee J. Ames
475 Lee J. Ames
477 Mount Palomar and Mount Wilson Observatories; Lee J. Ames.
479 Lee J. Ames
480 Lee J. Ames
481 Cioffero—Fundamental Photographs
482 Cioffero—Fundamental Photographs
483 Lee J. Ames
484 Cenco Instruments Corp.; Lee J. Ames.
485 Lee J. Ames
486 Lee J. Ames
487 Lee J. Ames
488 Lee J. Ames
489 Lee J. Ames
490 National Audubon Society; George Porter—National Audubon Society.
491 National Audubon Society; New York Historical Society.
495 George Buctel

496 Stockpile
497 George Buctel
498 Australian News & Information Bureau
499 G. R. Roberts—Photo Researchers
500 Jeppesen & Company
504 Birnback; Australian News & Information Bureau; George Buctel.
505 George Buctel
506 Australian News & Information Bureau; J. Nisbett—Shostal.
509 Australian News & Information Bureau; Stockpile; Stockpile; Stockpile.
511 Jere Donovan
512 Jerry Cooke—Photo Researchers
515c G. R. Roberts; Photographic Library of Australia.
516 Australian National Travel Association
519 Toni Angermayer—Photo Researchers; Eric Lessing—Magnum; Ewing Galloway.
521 George Buctel
522 Shostal
529 George Bakacs
531 Consulate General of Japan
533 Bernard G. Silverstein—Rapho Guillumette; Whitin Machine Works.
534 Wide World
535 Revell, Incorporated; The Blankfort group; The Blankfort group
536 Courtesy of Revell, Inc.
537 Aurora Plastics Corp.
538 Al Bochroch
539 Al Bochroch
540 Firestone Tire & Rubber Co.; Pierre Perrin Assoc.
543– Dan Todd
547
549 American Motors Corp.; General Motors, Buick Division.
550 Volkswagen of America, Inc.
552 Dan Todd
553 Dan Todd
555 Dan Todd
556 Dan Todd
559 Sperry Gyroscope Co.
561– Dan Todd
565
568 Jack Hearne
569 Jack Hearne
570 Jack Hearne
571 Jack Hearne
573 British Aircraft Corp. Ltd.

B, second letter of the English alphabet   **B** 1
   See also Alphabet
Baa, Baa, Black Sheep, nursery rhyme   **N** 407
Baal (BAY-al), pagan god   **E** 176
Baal and the Dragon, apocryphal book of Bible
   B 159
Baalbek (BA-al-beck), Lebanon
   Temple of Bacchus, picture   **L** 124

Baal Shem-Tov (BOL SHEM-tove) (Israel ben Eliezer) (1700?–1760), Jewish teacher and founder of Chasidism in Poland, b. Ukraine, Russia. He appealed to common people as well as scholars in his belief that God exists in all things and is approachable through joyous and sincere prayer rather than merely through intellect.

Baarle-Hertog (BAR-L'HER-tok), Belgium   **B** 129
Babcock, Alpheus, American piano builder   **P** 242

Babcock, Stephen Moulton (1843–1931), American agricultural chemist, b. Bridgewater, N.Y.: developed the Babcock test for determining amount of butterfat in milk (1890). He was professor of agricultural chemistry at University of Wisconsin (1887–1913), chief chemist (1887–1913) and assistant director (1901–13) of Wisconsin Agricultural Experiment Station.
   Babcock test   **B** 467;   **W** 199

Babcock test, determined amount of butterfat in milk
   B 467
Babe, blue ox of Paul Bunyan   **F** 312

Babel (BAY-bel), **Tower of,** in old Testament (Genesis 11, 1–9), a tower in the plain of Shinar, or Babylonia, in ancient Mesopotamia, built by descendants of Noah, who wished to build a tower reaching to heaven. This angered God, and He brought it to pass that the builders of the tower could no longer understand each other's speech. Unable to continue their work, they scattered over the earth in small groups, each speaking a tongue alien to its neighbor. According to Scripture, this is reason for diversity of races and languages.
   ziggurats of the Chaldeans   **A** 241

Babelthuap (BA-bel-tu-op), fertile, forested island in western Pacific, the principal island of the Palau group, in Caroline Islands. The chief export is bauxite.

Baber, Mogul emperor of India   **I** 133
Babirusa (bab-i-RU-sa), wild pig   **P** 249
   hoofed mammals   **H** 209; picture   **H** 212
Baboons   **M** 420; pictures   **L** 224;   **M** 421
   social organization   **A** 280–81
Babur ("Tiger") *see* Baber, Mogul emperor of India
Baby   **B** 2–4
   child development   **C** 231–34
   Eskimo, picture   **A** 304
   in a hospital nursery, picture   **H** 249
   locomotion, picture   **A** 292
   origins of family life   **F** 37
   tests for hearing   **D** 50–51
   zoo babies   **Z** 375–76
Babylonia (bab-il-O-nia), ancient empire, now Iraq
   ancient civilizations   **A** 218–20
   ancient music of Sumerians and Babylonians
      A 245
   art   **A** 236–37, 241–42; pictures   **A** 235
   building methods   **B** 435
   creation myths   **M** 557
   Jewish community of exile   **J** 104, 107
   mail service   **P** 406
   medical writings   **M** 203

   numeration system   **N** 394–96, 391
   science, advances in   **S** 60
   sculpture   **S** 93
   tunnels, earliest built   **T** 314

Baby's breath, decorative plant native to Europe and northern Asia, introduced into North America. Two to three ft. tall, it has numerous small white flowers. It is used by florists in trimming bouquets.

Baby teeth   **T** 47
Bacchus (BACC-us), Greek and Roman god   **G** 360;   **W** 188
Bacchus, Temple of, Baalbek, Lebanon, picture   **L** 124
Bach (BOCK), **Johann Sebastian,** German musician and composer   **B** 4–5;   **G** 182–83
   baroque period   **B** 66
   chorales   **H** 312
   choral music   **C** 278, 279
   electronic arrangements of his works   **E** 142h
   Mendelssohn revived music of   **M** 219
   organ music   **O** 209
Bach, Karl Philipp Emanuel, German composer   **C** 330;   **G** 183–84
Bachelor's degrees *see* Degrees, university and college
Bach Festival, Bethlehem, Pennsylvania   **M** 552
Bacillus (ba-CILL-us), a rod-shaped bacteria   **B** 10

Back, Sir George (1796–1878), English explorer, b. Stockport. He explored Spitsbergen seas with Sir John Franklin. While searching for Captain Ross in Arctic, he discovered Great Fish River. He wrote *Narrative of an Expedition in H.M.'s Ship Terror, in the Years 1836–7.*
   Northwest Passage   **N** 338

Backbone, or spine, of animals   **K** 251
   animals with and without backbones   **A** 264
   birds   **B** 201
   body's skeleton   **B** 270–71
   snakes have long backbones and short tails
      S 204
Backer, Americus, London musical-instrument maker
   P 242
Backgammon   **B** 5–6
Backhand, tennis stroke   **T** 91, 93
Backpack, space suit   **S** 340L–341; diagrams   **S** 388, 340L
Backpacker, camping   **C** 40, 41
Back saws, tools   **T** 212
Backstaffs, navigation instruments   **N** 65
Backstage, space behind the stage in a theater   **T** 156
Backstage crews, of plays   **T** 158
Back stitches, in sewing   **S** 129
Backstroke, in swimming   **S** 492; picture   **S** 490
Back to normalcy with Harding, campaign slogan   **H** 39
Backwoodsmen, frontier inhabitants   **W** 142–43
Bacon, Francis, English philosopher and essayist   **B** 7;   **E** 253–54, 292, 293
   contributions of his method to science   **S** 67–68
   heat theory   **H** 86d
   New Atlantis, The   **U** 256
   quotation from   **Q** 19
Bacon, Francis, Irish painter   **E** 242
Bacon, Nathaniel, English colonist in Virginia   **V** 359
   leader of Bacon's Rebellion   **B** 8–9

Bacon, Peggy (1895–   ), American artist and writer, b. Ridgefield, Conn. Known for her caricatures of American society, she wrote and illustrated books for children, such as the *Lion-Hearted Kitten and Other Stories* and *Mercy and the Mouse.* Her works are exhibited in permanent collections of Metropolitan Museum of Art and Whitney Museum of American Art.

Bacon, Roger, English scientist and author **B** 7; **E** 389
  writings on the science of optics **O** 166
Bacon's Rebellion, 1676 **B** 8–9; **V** 359
Bacteria B 9–13; **M** 208, 280–82
  aid digestion **B** 275
  antibiotics **A** 310
  bacteriostatic antiseptics **D** 222
  fermentation **F** 90
  food spoilage **F** 344, 352–54
  meteorite yields unknown bacteria **C** 421
  place in the food chain **L** 242–43
  plant enemies **P** 287
  possible fourth kingdom of living things **K** 251
  soils, microorganisms in **S** 232
  vitamin K produced by **V** 371
  See also Antiseptics; Disinfectants; Microbiology
Bacterial diseases D 187
  gonorrhea **D** 196
  Koch discovers microbes causing anthrax **K** 293
  lockjaw **D** 200–01
  pneumonia **D** 203–04
  streptococcal sore throats **D** 207–08
  tonsillitis **D** 210
  trench mouth **D** 210
  tuberculosis **D** 211–12
Bacterial viruses, or bacteriophages **V** 364

Bacteriological warfare (also called germ, or biological, warfare), warfare in which living organisms are used to transmit disease to enemy. Bacteria of such diseases as diphtheria, typhus, and smallpox are introduced into air or drinking water of enemy. Infected animals also can be used to transmit disease. Although techniques are available for such warfare, it has rarely been used.
  Soviet Union and U. S. resolution, 1971, to prohibit **D** 185

Bacteriology (bac-ter-i-OL-ogy), science that deals with bacteria
  Koch, Robert **K** 293
  medical laboratory tests **M** 201, 209
Bacteriophages (bac-TER-i-o-phages), or bacterial viruses **V** 364; picture **V** 361
Bactrian camels C 34; **H** 210; picture **H** 213
Baden-Powell (BADE-en PO-well), **Agnes,** English founder of Girl Guides **G** 213
Baden-Powell, Robert, English soldier, founder of scouting movement **B** 356–57
  Girl Guides **G** 213
Badgers O 242
Badger State, nickname for Wisconsin **W** 197
Badges, in heraldry **H** 118
Badges of honor see Medals
Badlands, area in Great Plains region, North America
  Alberta, Canada **A** 146a; picture **A** 146b
  Montana, in Makoshika State Park **M** 431, 439
  North Dakota **N** 325; picture **N** 333
  South Dakota **S** 315; picture **S** 314
Badlands National Monument, South Dakota **S** 322; picture **S** 314
Badminton B 13–15
Badr, battle of, 624 **M** 405

Baedeker (BAY-dek-er), **Karl** (1801–1859), German publisher of travelers' guidebooks, b. Essen. He started his book business in Coblenz (1827) and wrote guidebook about that city (1829). Later he moved to Leipzig and published a series of world-famous guidebooks in German, English, and French about European countries, the Orient, and parts of North America. The name "Baedeker" is identified with the most authentic travel information.

Baekeland (BAKE-land), **Leo Hendrik** (1863–1944), American chemist and inventor, b. Ghent, Belgium. He went to United States (1889) and became a citizen (1893). Baekeland invented an improved method of manufacturing photographic paper. He is noted especially for his discovery of synthetic resin Bakelite (announced 1909), a substitute for hard rubber and amber that has been important in development of plastics industry.
  plastics, history of **P** 324

Baer (BARE), **Karl Ernst von** (1792–1876), German biologist, b. Estonia. This pioneer in embryology (the study of animal development in its early stages before birth) was first to see the human egg. Von Baer's law states that each animal in its early development goes through stages similar to those gone through in its evolutionary history.

Baez (BA-ez), **Joan** (1941–), American folk singer, b. N.Y. She has performed on concert tours, at colleges, and on TV, singing and accompanying herself on the guitar. Her recordings include *Joan Baez* and *Joan Baez in Concert*. She has also taken part in a number of civil rights and anti-war demonstrations.

Baffin, William, English navigator
  Northwest Passage **N** 338

Baffin Bay, part of the North Atlantic Ocean between Greenland and the Canadian Northwest Territories. The bay is partially ice-free during summer months. The bay was discovered by the English explorer William Baffin during his search for a northwest passage (1616).

Baffin Island, Arctic Ocean **I** 427
  Arctic Archipelago in Canada's Northwest Territories **C** 51; **Y** 361
  Northwest Territories, Canada **Y** 361
Bagasse (ba-GASS), fibrous part of sugarcane **S** 454
  sweet grasses **G** 319
Bagatelle, musical form **M** 535
Baggataway (bag-GAT-a-way), Canadian Indian game **C** 67
  lacrosse, a national sport of Canada **L** 20–21
Baghdad, capital of Iraq **I** 382
  Kadhimain, a suburb, picture **M** 302

Baghdad Pact, mutual defense pact signed by Turkey and Iraq and later joined by Iran, Pakistan, and the United Kingdom (1955). Also known as the Middle East Treaty Organization (METO), it was formed mainly for military purposes but works for economic development as well. When Iraq withdrew in 1959, headquarters was switched from Baghdad to Ankara and the name was changed to Central Treaty Organization (CENTO).

Bagpipe F 329; pictures **F** 330, **W** 182
Baguios (BOG-yos), hurricanes in Philippine Islands **H** 292

Baha'i (BA-ha-i) **Faith,** or the Faith of Baha'u'llah, was founded (1844) in Persia (now Iran) by Ali Mohammed of Shiraz, called the Báb ("the Gate"), who announced the coming of a new prophet. In 1863 Mirza Husayn Ali proclaimed himself the awaited Messiah. He took the name Baha'u'llah ("Splendor of God"), and it is on his teachings that the religion is based. World headquarters is in Haifa, Israel, and the Universal House of Justice is the international governing body. Members believe in one God, one evolving religion, one mankind, and strive to eliminate all forms of prejudice.
  hybrid religions **R** 152

Bahamas (ba-HA-mas) **B** 16–17
Bahia, city in Brazil see Salvador, Brazil
Bahia Hona Bridge, Key West, Florida, picture **I** 424
Bahrain (bah-RAIN), sheikhdom in Persian Gulf **M** 301
    flag **F** 237
Bahutu see Hutu
Baikal (by-KALL), **Lake,** southeastern Siberia, U.S.S.R.
    L 26
Bail, in law **C** 527

Bailey, Carolyn Sherwin (1875–1961), American author,
b. Hoosick Falls, N.Y. She is known for children's books,
such as *Children of the Handcrafts, Pioneer Art in
America,* and *Miss Hickory,* which was awarded the
Newbery medal (1947).

Bailey, of a castle **F** 375
Bailey, Donald, English bridge designer **B** 400

Bailey, Pearl (1918–), American entertainer, Negro, b.
Newport News, Va. Known for her distinctive singing
style, in which she half sings, half talks, and frequently
ad-libs, she has appeared on Broadway (*St. Louis
Woman, Hello, Dolly*), in movies (*Carmen Jones, That
Certain Feeling*), in nightclubs, and on TV.

Baird, John Logie (1888–1946), Scottish inventor, b.
Helensburgh. A pioneer in the development of television,
he gave the first public demonstration of true television
in London in 1926. He also pioneered in transatlantic and
color television and invented the Noctovisor, a device for
seeing in the dark.

Baird, Spencer Fullerton (1823–1887), American zoologist, b. Reading, Pa. As secretary of Smithsonian
Institution, he greatly increased collections, improved
cataloging methods, and founded the National Museum.
As first head of U.S. Fish Commission, he founded
Woods Hole Marine Biology Station and promoted use of
hatcheries and laws against overfishing to protect fish
resources. One of America's greatest naturalists, Baird
wrote *Catalogue of North American Birds* and *Catalogue
of North American Mammals.*

Bait, for fishing **F** 206
Bait casting, fishing **F** 208–09
    tackle **F** 206
Baja (BA-ha) **California,** Mexico **M** 242
Bajans, or Barbadians, name for people of Barbados **B** 53
Baji, l'Masoudi al-, Tunisian writer **A** 76d
Baji, Muhammad al-, Tunisian writer **A** 76d
Baked Bean State, nickname for Massachusetts **M** 135
Bakelite (BAKE-el-ite), a plastic **P** 324
Baker, Dorsey S., American railroad builder **W** 27
Baker, Elwood T., American inventor of gin rummy **C** 115
Baker, George Pierce, American educator and teacher of
    playwriting **D** 300

Baker, Josephine (1906–), American entertainer, Ne-
gro, b. St. Louis, Mo. She spent most of her adult life in
Europe, where she developed an international reputation.
During World War II, Josephine Baker served in the Air
Auxiliary of the Free French Forces and was awarded the
French Legion of Honor medal. She adopted 12 orphans
of different races and nationalities, and she sponsors a
children's village at Les Milandes in France.

Baker Island see Howland and Baker Islands
Bakewell, Robert, English agriculturalist **A** 100
Baking and bakery products **B** 385–89
    recipes for cookies and cupcakes **R** 116
    See also Flour and flour milling

Baking powder **B** 389

Baking soda, sodium bicarbonate ($NaHCO_3$). Baking soda
is used in cooking to make baked goods rise, and it is
often found as one of the ingredients in baking powder.

Bakota, a people of Gabon **G** 2
Bakr, Ahmad Hassan al-, president of Iraq **I** 383
Baku, Union of Soviet Socialist Republics **E** 323; **U** 36
    Azerbaijan, capital **U** 45
Balaguer, Joaquin, Dominican Republic president
    D 283

Balakirev (ba-LA-kir-ef), **Mily Alekseevich** (1837–1910),
Russian composer, b. Nizhni Novgorod (now Gorki).
Balakirev was the leader of "The Mighty Five," a group of
Russian composers, including Mussorgsky, Rimsky-Korsakov, Borodin, and Cui, who developed a distinctive Russian
style of music. He was also director of the Imperial
Capella in St. Petersburg (1883–94). He is best known for
his orchestral works *Russia* and *Tamara* and for his
arrangements of Russian folk songs.
    Russian music **U** 63

Balaklava (bal-ok-LA-va), **battle of,** Crimean War battle
in which a British cavalry unit was nearly wiped out by
Russians as the result of a misunderstood command.
The disaster inspired Lord Tennyson's poem *The Charge
of the Light Brigade,* which glorifies obedience of soldiers.

Balance, in design **D** 133
Balance, sense of **B** 287–88
    animals: locomotion **A** 291–93
Balance of nature **L** 258–59
    cat family important in **C** 135
    communities of living things affect each other **K** 259
    dog family **D** 243
    environment, a balance of resources **E** 272b, 272f
    food chain broken **L** 242
    insecticides **I** 258
Balance of payments, of trade **I** 329
Balance of power, among nations **I** 322
Balance scales, for weighing **W** 112
Balance sheet, in bookkeeping **B** 312, 313
Balance wheels
    watches and clocks **W** 45
Balanchine (BAL-an-chene), **George,** Russian-born Amer-
    ican choreographer **D** 26
    ballet in America **B** 28
Balata (ba-LA-ta), a gum **R** 185
Balaton (BALL-a-ton), **Lake,** Hungary **L** 26
    Hungary's largest body of water **H** 285
Balboa (bol-BO-a), Panama Canal Zone **P** 48
Balboa, Vasco Núñez de, Spanish explorer **B** 18;
    E 382–83

Balchen (BOL-ken), **Bernt** (1899–), American aviator,
b. Topdal, Norway. Balchen went to the United States
(1926) and became a citizen (1931). As chief pilot of
Byrd's Antarctic Expedition (1928–30), he piloted first
flight over South Pole. Active in Norwegian underground
during World War II, he entered U.S. Army Air Corps in
1941, rising to rank of colonel. Balchen wrote *The Next
Fifty Years of Flight* and *Come North with Me.*

Balcones (bal-CO-nes) **Escarpment,** Texas **T** 124
Balcony, second floor of a theater **T** 156
Bald cypress, tree, picture **T** 276
    See also Cypress
Bald eagles **E** 2
    on front Great Seal of the United States **G** 330
    threatened species **B** 232; picture **B** 230

Balder, Norse god **N** 279
Baldness, loss of hair **H** 2–3
Baldwin, Abraham, American statesman **G** 145

Baldwin I (1058–1118), French crusader and king of Jerusalem. With his brother Godfrey of Bouillon, he was one of original leaders of First Crusade. He succeeded Godfrey as ruler of Jerusalem (1100). Jerusalem became the most important Latin state in the East.

    Crusades, history of **C** 539

Baldwin I (1171–1205?), French crusader and emperor of Constantinople. As Baldwin IX of Flanders, he joined Fourth Crusade and was elected first Latin emperor of Constantinople when the city was captured (1204). He was defeated at battle of Adrianople (1205).

Baldwin, James (1924–), American writer, b. New York, N.Y. A prominent leader and spokesman in the civil rights movement, Baldwin gives insight into what it means to be a Negro today. His novels include *Go Tell It on the Mountain* and *Another Country;* his books of essays include *Notes of a Native Son* and *The Fire Next Time;* and his plays include *Blues for Mr. Charlie,* first produced on Broadway in 1964.

    Negro in American literature **A** 213; **N** 102

Baldwin, Matthias William (1795–1866), American industrialist and philanthropist, b. Elizabethtown, N.J. Baldwin was the first U.S. manufacturer of bookbinders' tools and calico printers' rolls. He built "Old Ironsides," one of the first American locomotives; founded M. W. Baldwin Co. (now Baldwin Locomotive Works); established a school for Negro children; and helped found Franklin Institute.

Baldwin, Robert, Canadian statesman **O** 125
    Canada, history of **C** 73

Baldwin, Stanley, 1st Earl Baldwin of Bewdley (1867–1947), English statesman, b. Bewdley. Baldwin was elected Conservative member of Parliament (1908). As chancellor of the exchequer (1922–23), he negotiated settlement of Britain's war debt to United States. He served three terms as prime minister (1923–24, 1924–29, 1935–37) and also was lord president of the council (1931–35).

Balearic (bal-e-ARR-ic) **Islands,** east of Spain **I** 427; **S** 356; picture **I** 431
Baleen (ba-LEEN), or whalebone **W** 147, 152
Baleen whales, or mysticetes **W** 149
    special food adaptations of mammals **M** 66
    whaling **W** 152
Balers, farm machinery **F** 60; pictures **F** 61

Balewa (ba-lay-WA), **Alhaji Sir Abubakar Tafawa** (1912–1966), Nigerian political leader, b. Bauchi. He was elected to the House of Assembly of the Northern Region of Nigeria (1946) and served as representative of the Northern Provinces in the Legislative Council (1947–51). A founder (1951) of the Northern Peoples Congress (NPC) Party, he was elected to the federal House of Representatives. He held several ministerial posts (1952–57), becoming prime minister of the Federation of Nigeria (1957–63) and of the Federal Republic of Nigeria (1963–66). He was killed in a military coup in 1966.

Balfour, Arthur James, 1st Earl of Balfour and Viscount Traprain (1848–1930), English statesman, b. Whitinghame, East Lothian. Balfour served as Conservative member of Parliament (1886–1911) and head of his party for over 20 years (after 1891) and as prime minister

(1902–05). He retired (1911) but resumed office in coalition government of 1915 as first Lord of the Admiralty and later as foreign secretary (1916–19). He wrote Balfour Declaration, stating that British Government favored establishment of a Jewish state in Palestine (1917). He was also representative to the League of Nations (1920). Writings include *Foundations of Belief* and *Theism and Thought.*

Balfour Declaration, 1917 **J** 112
    support for Zionism **Z** 371
    Weizmann, Chaim **W** 118
Bali (BA-li), Indonesia **I** 219–20
    dancing an ancient art **D** 31–32
    funeral ceremony, cremation, picture **F** 495
    Hindu ceremony, picture **H** 131
Balkans **B** 19
    Albania **A** 145
    architecture, late Byzantine churches **B** 490
    Bulgaria **B** 439–44
    Rumania **R** 355–60
    World War I **W** 275
    World War II **W** 290
    Yugoslavia **Y** 354–59
Balkan Wars **B** 19, 444
Balkhash (bol-KASH), **Lake,** Kazakh Republic of U.S.S.R. **L** 26
Ball **B** 20–21
    antique baseball started museum **B** 80
    bowling ball **B** 345, 346
    dodge ball, game **G** 14
    golf **G** 254, 262
    official baseball **B** 70
    official basketball **B** 82
    softball **S** 229
    volleyball **V** 387
    See also names of individual ball games, as Baseball

Ball, George Wildman (1909–), U.S. lawyer and public official, b. Des Moines, Iowa. He began his career as a government lawyer (1933–35), practiced law in Chicago (1935–42), and was associate general counsel for the Lend-Lease Administration (1942–44). He directed the U.S. Strategic Bombing Survey in London (1944–45). Ball was under secretary of state for economic affairs, then under secretary of state (1961–66). He served as U.S. representative at the United Nations, 1968.

Ball, Lucille (1911–), American actress, b. Jamestown, N.Y. She appeared in numerous films during the 1930's and 1940's, but she is perhaps best-known as one of television's top comediennes. Her shows *I Love Lucy, The Lucy Show,* and *Here's Lucy* have been consistently top-rated. In 1967–68 she won an Emmy Award for *The Lucy Show.* She is president of Desilu Productions (1962–).

Balla (BA-la), **Giacomo,** Italian futurist painter **M** 391
    Dog on a Leash, painting **M** 390
Ballade (bal-LOD), a musical form **M** 535
Ballade, a poetic form **P** 353
Ballads (BAL-lads) **B** 22–23; **M** 535
    American folk ballads **F** 310–11
    folklore **F** 303
    folk music **F** 318
    narrative poems suitable for singing **P** 354
    sagas and Scandinavian literature **S** 51
    See also Folk music
Ballast, for railroad roadbeds **R** 77, 78

Ball bearing, circular part of a machine containing small steel balls that roll on a track. The ball bearing is fitted into moving parts of a machine for smooth running and less friction. It is used in bicycles, for example, to make wheels turn easily. This is also the name of the ball used in such a bearing.

Ball clay C 174
Ballet (BAL-lay) B 23–29
  Canada C 63
  dance music development D 36–37
  dance spectacles D 25–26
  festivals M 551
  Leningrad Ballet School, picture U 40
  Midsummer Night's Dream, A, picture D 25
  musical comedy, first use as part of plot M 543
  New York City Ballet's home, Lincoln Center L 298
  Petrouchka U 64
  Serenade, picture D 22
  Stravinsky's ballet music S 437
Ballets Russes de Monte Carlo B 28; M 406
Ballinger, Richard A., American politican T 8
Ballistic Missile Early Warning System (BMEWS) U 161
Ballistic missiles M 344
Ball lightning F 286
Balloonfish, picture F 183
Balloons and ballooning B 30–34
  aerodynamics of A 40
  aviation history A 567
  hydrogen used in H 305–06
  IGY use for weather studies I 317; picture I 316
  Missouri's role in ballooning history M 374–75
  mistaken for flying saucers F 285
  observatories send up telescopes O 13–14
  Piccard, Auguste P 244
  races, first international balloon M 374
  solar research with E 29
  Why do balloons float? F 251–52
Ballot (BAL-lot) E 114–15
  origin of the word B 21
Ball-point pens P 146–47
  ink I 255
Ballroom dancing, or social dancing D 26–28
Ball's Bluff, Virginia, site of Civil War battle C 322
Ball valves, diagram V 269
Balmaceda (bal-ma-SADE-a), **José Manuel,** president of Chile C 255
Balsa (BALL-sa), tree
  lightest wood in commercial use W 228
  wood used for airplane models A 104
Balsam fir, tree
  leaves, needlelike, pictures L 119
Balsas, fishing boats P 163; pictures A 252, B 304, L 30, 50
Balta (BOL-ta), **José,** president of Peru P 166
Baltic (BALL-tic) **languages**
  Union of Soviet Socialist Republics U 27
Baltic Sea O 45

Baltic States, countries of Lithuania, Estonia, and Latvia, situated on the Baltic Sea. Formerly part of the Russian Empire, they became independent in 1918, but were reannexed by the Soviet Union in 1940. They are now republics of the Soviet Union.
  constituent republics of the U.S.S.R. U 43–44
  World War II W 287–88

Baltimore, Lord see Calvert, George
Baltimore, Maryland B 35; M 120, 125
  Star-Spangled Banner Flag House F 248
Baltimore and Ohio Railroad R 89
  first electric locomotive L 331
  first in U.S. to provide public transportation T 264
  Maryland section M 121–22

Baltimore orioles, birds B 219–20; picture B 233
  Maryland, state bird of M 115
  nest, picture B 213
Balto-Slavic languages L 39; U 27
Baluba (ba-LU-ba), a people of Africa A 76
Balustrades
  escalators E 174–75
Balzac, Honoré de, French novelist B 36; F 441
  great European novelists N 348
  Rodin's *Monument to Balzac*, picture M 387
Bamako (BAM-ak-o), capital of Mali M 59
Bambara (bom-BAR-a), a people of central West Africa
  African sculpture A 70, 72, 76
  Mali M 58
Bamboo, giant grass G 318
  jungle growth J 154
Bamboo Curtain, imaginary barrier between Communist Asia and the West I 323
Banana B 36–38; F 484
  Costa Rican export, picture C 514
  Ecuador, world's largest producer E 56; picture L 59
  flower, picture F 276
  Guatemalan crop, picture G 394
  Honduras export H 196
  Puerto Rican crop, picture P 520
Banaras, India G 25
Bancroft, George, American historian H 137
  historical writing in American literature A 202
Band, The, American rock music group R 262d

Banda (BON-da), **Hastings Kamuzu** (1906–), 1st president of Malawi, b. Kasungu District, Nyasaland. He was prime minister of Nyasaland (1963–64) and remained prime minister when Nyasaland became the Commonwealth nation of Malawi (1964). When Malawi became a republic (1966), Dr. Banda was elected its 1st president.
  Malawi, history of M 51

Bandages and bandaging
  tourniquets, splints, use of, pictures F 157, 162
Bandai-san, volcano, Japan V 382

Bandaranaike (bon-da-ra-NY-kee), **Solomon West Ridgeway Dias** (1899–1959), Ceylonese statesman, b. Colombo. He was a leader of Buddhist revivalism, formed Sri Lanka Freedom Party, and was prime minister of Ceylon from 1956 until his assassination in 1959. He was succeeded in office by his wife, **Sirimavo Rawatte Dias Bandaranaike** (1916–), who served as prime minister until 1965. She was re-elected in 1970. Picture W 212b.
  Ceylon, history of C 180
  women, role of W 213

Banda (BON-da) **Sea,** part of the Pacific Ocean encircled by the Indonesian islands. The sea contains the Banda Islands, noted for spices since their discovery by the Portuguese in the 16th century.

Bandeira (bon-DAI-ra), **Manuel** (1886–1968), Brazilian writer, b. Pernambuco. Bandeira was director of Sociedade Brasileira de Música de Câmara. He won literary prize (1946) of Brazilian Institute of Education and Culture. His works include *Poesia e Prosa*, *Biografia de Gonçalves Dias*, and *Pasásgala*, his memoirs.

Banderillos (bon-dai-RI-lyos), in bullfighting B 449–51
Bandicoots, marsupials K 174
Bandjermasin, Indonesian Borneo I 221
Bands and band music B 38–41
  circus music C 301

Bands and band music (continued)
drum D 333–36
how bands differ from orchestras O 182, 183
jazz bands J 60
military marches of Elgar E 176, 271
percussion instruments P 151–53
rock music R 262a–262b, 262d
The President's Own, U.S. Marine Corps Band
U 182
wind instruments W 182–83
See also Orchestra; Percussion instruments; Wind instruments
Band saws, tools T 218

Bandung (bon-DOONG) **Conference,** meeting in Bandung, Indonesia (April, 1955), of 29 Asian and African nations to discuss common problems. The conference, the first of its kind ever held, symbolized the desire of Asian and African peoples for a voice in world affairs. The participants discussed economic and cultural co-operation, world peace, human rights, and colonialism.

Banff National Park, Alberta, Canada B 42–43
Valley of the Ten Peaks, picture A 146f
Banff School of Fine Arts B 43
Bangaway of Sirrah Crest, champion boxer dog D 261
Bangkok, capital of Thailand T 151; pictures C 308,
S 332; T 147, 148
Buddha's statue, picture B 423
permanent headquarters of SEATO S 335
Bangladesh (BANG-la-desh), formerly East Pakistan
B 44–44c; N 262f; P 41
Bangor, Maine M 44
Bang's disease, of cattle C 149
Bangui (bon-GHE), capital of Central African Republic
C 169
Banjermasin (bon-jer-MA-sin), Indonesia B 337
Banjo F 329; picture F 330
Banjul, formerly Bathurst, capital of Gambia G 9
Bankhead, William Brockman, American statesman A 125
Bank holidays, in Great Britain H 152
Banking Act, 1933 B 48
Bank notes, issuing of B 47
Bank of England B 47
London institution L 335
nationalized in 1946 U 79
Bank of North America B 47
Bank of the United States B 47
Andrew Jackson opposes J 7
Tyler, John T 341
Banks, of the continental shelf F 218
Banks and banking B 44d–51
automation employed in A 531–32
depressions and recessions D 122
inflation and deflation, control of I 253
installment buying, rates on loans for I 289
interest P 149–50
international trade operates through I 329
Jackson's pet banks J 7
Roosevelt institutes deposit insurance R 321
Rothschild family R 337
See also Inflation and deflation; Money

Banks Islands, South Pacific volcanic island group. A part of the New Hebrides chain, they are administered jointly by Great Britain and France. The islands were discovered (1793) by English naval officer William Bligh.

Bannack, Montana M 442
Banneker, Benjamin, American mathematician N 93
Banners, flags F 225
heraldry H 115, 117

Bannister, Roger Gilbert, English champion miler B 51
Bannockburn, battle of, 1314 S 88
wins sovereignty for Robert Bruce B 414
Banquets
food in ancient times F 333

Banshee, or **banshie,** in Celtic folklore, supernatural being or spirit whose appearance or wailing foretells the death of some person. The word comes from the Gaelic *bean,* meaning "woman," and *sith,* meaning "fairy." The banshee is portrayed in Irish folklore as either a lovely weeping maiden or an ugly old hag.

Bantam chickens P 420
Bantamweight, in boxing B 352
Banting, Sir Frederick Grant, Canadian doctor and scientist B 52; D 217; picture D 216

Bantu, aboriginal inhabitants of central and southern Africa. Numerically and geographically they are the most important ethnolinguistic group in Africa. The various Bantu tribes share no particular racial or cultural characteristic other than language. The Bantu language family includes over 200 languages and dialects, among them Zulu and Swahili.
African literature in Bantu languages A 76b
Congo C 462
South West Africa S 336
Zaïre Z 366a

Bantustans, or homelands for Bantus of South Africa
S 268–69
Banyan trees G 203; picture G 202
aerial roots of trees T 279
Great Banyan Tree, in Calcutta C 11
Baobab trees, or bottle trees P 283
famous trees in the Sudan S 448
Bao Dai, emperor of South Vietnam V 335
Baptism E 41
Jesus Christ J 83
sacrament of Roman Catholic Church R 301
Baptist Church P 484
Baptistery of Florence Cathedral, Ghiberti's doors I 467;
R 163–64; picture R 165
Bar, or measure, in musical notation M 531

Barabbas (bar-AB-as), in New Testament (Matthew 27: 16–21), criminal released by Pontius Pilate upon the request of the people of Judea at the time that Jesus was condemned. Pilate, the Roman governor, customarily permitted the people of Judea to choose one prisoner who should go free each year during Passover.

Barada River, Syria, picture S 505

Barak (ba-ROK) (from Hebrew, meaning "lightning"), in the Old Testament (Judges 4–5), the son of Abinoam of the tribe of Naphtali. Under the direction of Israelite judge Deborah he commanded a force of 10,000 men from Zebulun and Naphtali against Canaanite forces under Sisera at the Plain of Esdraelon. He conquered Sisera, relieving Israel of Canaanite oppression.

Baranof (ba-RA-nof), **Alexander,** first Russian governor of Alaska A 142, 143
Barataria (bar-a-TAR-ia) **Bay,** Louisiana
Laffite's headquarters L 23
Barb, a type of horse H 237
Barbados (bar-BAY-doze) B 53
Caribbean Sea and islands C 116–19
flag F 241
Barbara Fritchie, poem by Whittier M 125

Barbarian tribes, in Europe during Middle Ages **M** 296
　art as a record **A** 438b, 438c, 438e
　Italian art of early Middle Ages **I** 458
　sculpture **S** 96

Barbarossa ("Redbeard"), name of two Barbary pirates. **Barbarossa I** (Horush, or Arouj) (1473?–1518) was head of a band of pirates who raided Spanish and North African coasts. After his death, his brother **Barbarossa II** (Khizr, or Khair ed-Din) (1466?–1546) became head of pirates and formed alliances with several Turkish sultans. He was appointed admiral of Turkish fleet (1533) and captured Tunis for Turkey (1534).

Barbarossa, Frederick see Frederick I, or Frederick Barbarossa
Barbary corsairs, pirates **P** 263
　early history of U.S. Marines **U** 177
Barbary States, North Africa
　piracy **P** 263
Barbecueing **O** 247
Barbed wire
　World War I **W** 274
Barbells, weights used for exercise **W** 107
Barbels, feelers of fish **F** 193
Barber, Samuel, American composer **O** 139
Barber of Seville, The, opera by Rossini **O** 140
Barberry, plant
　wheat rust, host of **F** 498
Barbers
　early doctors and surgeons **M** 205
Barbieri, Francisco Asenjo, Spanish composer **S** 373

Barbirolli (bar-bir-O-li) **Sir John** (1899–1970), English symphony and opera conductor, b. London. Barbirolli began his career as a cellist (1911). He formed Barbirolli Chamber Orchestra (1925) and was conductor of New York Philharmonic Orchestra (1936–42). Knighted in 1949, he was conductor in chief of the Hallé Orchestra, Manchester, and conductor emeritus of Houston Symphony.

Barbiturates (bar-BIT-u-rates), drugs **D** 326
　abuse of **D** 330
Barbizon School, of French painting **F** 426; **P** 29
　modern art **M** 387

Barbosa (ber-BORJ-a), **Ruy** (1849–1923), Brazilian statesman, jurist, and writer, b. São Salvador. An advocate of individual freedom, Barbosa was active in establishing Brazilian republic (1889). He was representative to The Hague Peace Conference (1907) and member of Permanent Court of International Justice (1921–23).
　Brazil, history of **B** 384

Barbuda, Caribbean island (Lesser Antilles group),
　administered by Antigua **C** 118
Barca, Pedro Calderón de la see Calderón de la Barca, Pedro
Barcarolle, a musical form **M** 535
Barcelona (bar-cel-O-na), Spain **S** 355–56; pictures **S** 350, 354, 365

Bardeen, John (1908–), American physicist, b. Madison, Wis. In 1948, together with W. H. Brattain and W. Shockley, he invented the transistor—device that acts as an electron tube but is much smaller and less fragile, uses less current, and does not require warm-up period. In 1956 the three scientists received Nobel prize in physics for work on semiconductors, materials from which transistors are made. Picture **E** 147

Bards, wandering poet-singers of British Isles and Gaul, chiefly during early Middle Ages. They composed and recited verses about heroic deeds and important people while accompanying themselves on the harp.
　Africa's bards or minstrels **A** 76a
　early Irish literature **I** 392

Barefoot skiing **W** 63

Barenboim, Daniel (1942–), Israeli pianist and conductor, b. Buenos Aires. He made his first public appearance in Buenos Aires at the age of 7. His family settled in Israel in 1952. Barenboim has played and conducted with the Israel Philharmonic Orchestra, the English Chamber Orchestra, and many other leading orchestras.

Barents (BAR-ents), **Willem,** Dutch navigator **E** 384
Barents Sea **O** 45–46
Bar examinations, for lawyers **L** 92
Bargain basements, in department stores **D** 119
Barges, boats
　dump scows for dredging **D** 309
Bar graphs **G** 309–11
Barite, mineral **G** 138
　Arkansas, leading producer **A** 426
Baritone, male voice **C** 277
　voice training **V** 375
Barium (BARR-ium), element **E** 154, 159
　barium sulphate, use for X ray pictures **M** 208h
Bark, of trees **T** 280
　cork oak tree **C** 505
　defense against weather **P** 283
　wood and wood products **W** 225
Barkley, Alben W., American statesman **T** 301; **V** 331; picture **V** 330
Barley, grain **G** 284, 287
　Colombian farm, picture **C** 381
　grasses **G** 318
　seeds and ear, pictures **G** 283
Barlow, Joel, American poet and diplomat **A** 198
　quoted on patriotic songs **N** 15
Bar magnets
　demonstrating magnetic lines of force **E** 129–30, 132
Bar Mitzvah, ceremony in Judaism **J** 118, 119
Barnacles, a kind of crustacean **S** 171

Barnard, Christiaan Neethling (1922–), South African surgeon, b. Beaufort West, S.A. He performed the first successful human heart transplant at Cape Town in December, 1967. The patient lived 18 days. Dr. Barnard, who received a Ph.D. at the U. of Minnesota Medical School, had his most notable success with transplant patient Dr. Philip Blaiberg, who lived for 19 months with his new heart. Dr. Barnard is the creator of the Barnard valve, used in open-heart surgery.

Barnard, Henry, American educator **C** 475

Barnburners, progressive reform faction of New York State Democratic Party during 1840's. The nickname (from Dutch story of farmer who burned his barn to eliminate rats) was coined by opponents who felt the group's proposed plans would destroy institutions they were trying to save. Barnburners nominated Martin Van Buren for president (1848) and then united with Free Soil Party. Many joined Republican Party when it was formed (1854).
　Van Buren, Martin **V** 275

Barn dances see Square dances
Barnegat (BAR-ne-gat) **Lighthouse,** New Jersey, picture **N** 174

Barns, for farm animals
stanchions versus loose housing **D** 8–9; picture **D** 6
Barn swallows, birds **B** 219; picture **B** 218

Barnum, Phineas Taylor (1810–91), American showman, b. Bethel, Conn. As a boy, he worked in his father's grocery store. An ardent abolitionist, he published a Danbury newspaper, the *Herald of Freedom*. In 1834 he entered show business. An imaginative promoter, he won fame by sponsoring such attractions as Tom Thumb and Jenny Lind. In 1881 he and John Bailey produced the famous circus now run by Ringling Bros.
exhibited Jumbo, the elephant **E** 171
was mayor of Bridgeport, Conn. **C** 477

Barographs, weather instruments **W** 83
Baroja (ba-RO-ha), **Pío,** Spanish writer **S** 371
Barometer (ba-ROM-et-er) **B** 54
make a barometer **E** 366
pressure observations of weather **W** 82–83
Torricelli's barometer **E** 351
use of vacuum principle **V** 263
Barons, members of the nobility, feudal lords
England, power struggle with king **E** 217–19, 220
Magna Carta and King John **M** 22
Baroque (ba-ROKE) **architecture B** 55–62
architecture, history of **A** 383
City Hall, Brussels, picture **B** 131
Latin America **L** 64
Russian architecture **U** 53
Spain **S** 363
Baroque art B 55–62
Bernini, Giovanni Lorenzo **B** 148
decorative arts **D** 77
French Academy combats **F** 437
furniture design **F** 508
Italian art and architecture **I** 472
Latin America **L** 63
painting **P** 23
Rubens, Peter Paul **R** 348
sculpture **S** 101
Spanish art influenced by Caravaggio **S** 361–62
Baroque music B 62–66
German composers **G** 182–83
opera, development of the aria **O** 131–32
sonata, before classical age **C** 331
sonatas **M** 539
Baroque pearl B 55
Barracudas (barr-a-CU-das), fish **F** 188; picture **F** 183
swimming speed **A** 290
Barranquilla (bar-ron-KI-ya), Colombia **C** 383
Barre (BAR), for ballet practice, picture **B** 24
Barre (BARRIE), Vermont **V** 318
Barred galaxies U 198
Barrel cacti C 4
Barrels, of guns **G** 425
Barrels, wooden **D** 89
Barren Grounds, Northwest Territories, Canada **Y** 363
Barren Ground caribou **H** 219
See also Tundra
Barrie, Sir James Matthew, Scottish writer **B** 67
dressed his realism in fantasy and humor **D** 298
children's literature **C** 241
English literature, place in **E** 267–68
Peter Pan, excerpt **P** 167–68
Barrientos Ortuño, René, president of Bolivia **B** 306
Barrier beaches
Atlantic City, N.J. on Absecon Beach **N** 166
New York's Fire Island **N** 215
Barrier reefs
coral **C** 504
Great Barrier Reef, Australia **A** 503

Barristers, lawyers **L** 93
courts **C** 529
Barro Colorado, island, Panama Canal Zone **P** 44
Barrow, Alaska **A** 140

Barrow, Errol Walton (1920–   ), political leader, Negro, b. Barbados, West Indies. He was elected premier (1961). At his re-election (1966), he became the first prime minister of the newly independent Barbados.

Barry, Charles, English architect **E** 241

Barry, John (1745–1803), American naval officer, b. County Wexford, Ireland. Barry went to America (1760) and was one of first to be commissioned captain (1776) in Revolutionary War. As commander of the *Lexington*, he captured the *Edward*, first British ship taken by Americans. He was commissioned senior captain (1794), then the navy's highest rank, and supervised construction of frigate *United States*, which he later commanded.
Revolutionary War, at sea **R** 205

Barry, Philip, American playwright **A** 216
Barrymore family, Ethel, Lionel, and John, American actors **B** 67–68
Bar soaps, manufacturing process **D** 148
Barter, system of economics
trade without using money **T** 242
use of money replaces barter **M** 409–10
William Penn trades tools for land, picture **A** 191
Bartered Bride, The, opera by Bedřich Smetana **O** 140
Barter Theater, Abingdon, Virginia **V** 353

Barth, Karl (1886–1968), Swiss Protestant theologian, b. Basel, Switzerland. Professor of theology at the University of Basel, Barth stressed that man could not know God through the power of reason, but only through the Bible and through Christ.

Barthé (bar-TAY), **Richmond** (1901–   ), American sculptor, Negro, b. Bay St. Louis, Miss. Barthé executed a bust of Booker T. Washington for Hall of Fame and various coins for Republic of Haiti. His other works, which have been viewed in most major U.S. museums, include *African Boy Dancing* and *Negro Mother*.

Bartholdi (bart-ol-DI), **Frédéric Auguste,** French sculptor **L** 168
Bartholomew (bar-THOL-o-mew), **Saint,** one of the 12 Apostles **A** 333
Bartholomew Fair, England **F** 10

Bartlett, Captain Bob (Robert Abram Bartlett) (1875–1946), American Arctic explorer, b. Brigus, Newfoundland, Canada. Bartlett commanded *Roosevelt* on Arctic voyage (1905–09) and also made expeditions to Arctic, Ellesmere Land, Siberia, and Labrador (between 1917 and 1945). He wrote *Last Voyage of the Karluk* and *Sails over Ice*.

Bartlett, Josiah, American physician and Revolutionary War patriot **N** 161
Bartlett pear P 112
Bartók (BAR-toke), **Béla,** Hungarian composer **B** 68; **H** 283
modern music **M** 401

Bartolommeo (bart-o-lo-MAY-o), **Fra** (Bartolommeo di Pagolo del Fattorini) (1475–1517), Italian painter, b. Savignano, Tuscany. He was also called Baccio della Porta. An important figure in Florentine school in High Renaissance, he excelled in painting drapery and in coloring. Most of his works are found today in Pitti Palace, Florence, including his masterpiece, St. *Mark.*

Barton, Clara, founder of American Red Cross **B** 68
  Red Cross **R** 127
Barton, Otis, American scientist **U** 16
Barton, William, co-designer of Great Seal of the United States **G** 329

Bartram, John (1699–1777), American botanist, b. Chester County, Pa. Known as father of American botany, he founded country's first botanical garden near Philadelphia, Pa.

Bartram, William, American writer **A** 198
Baruch (BAY-rook), apocryphal book of Bible **B** 159
Baruch (bar-OOK), **Bernard Mannes,** American economist and financier **S** 308–09
  coined phrase "cold war" in international relations **I** 325
Baruch Plan, 1946, for control of nuclear weapons **D** 184
Barundi, people of Burundi **B** 463
Barye (ba-RE), **Antoine Louis,** French sculptor **S** 102
  Jaguar Devouring a Hare, sculpture **S** 102
Baryons, a group of subatomic particles **N** 370

Barzun, Jacques (1907–), American historian and educator, b. Paris, France. He came to United States (1919) and became citizen (1933). He is a member of Columbia University faculty (since 1927), and was dean of faculties and provost (1958–67). His works include *Teacher in America* and *The American University.*

Basal metabolism, the minimum amount of energy needed by an animal or plant to carry out basic processes such as breathing. It is measured in terms of the rate (basal metabolic rate) at which oxygen is taken in by the organism when at rest.

Basal readers **R** 109
Basalt (ba-SALT), a lava rock **R** 264; picture **R** 265
  earth's crust **E** 10, 19; **G** 113
  used for monuments and statues **S** 433
  volcanic action **V** 379
Basant, or Holi, religious holiday **R** 154
Bascule bridges **B** 400
Base, in algebra **A** 159
Base-4 system, of numeration **N** 399
Base-10 system, or decimal system, of numeration **N** 393
Base-12 system, or duodecimal system, of numeration **N** 396, 398
Baseball **B** 69–81
  Little League Baseball **L** 315–17
  National Hall of Fame and Museum **B** 80–81
  Ring Lardner's short stories **S** 166
  Robinson, Jackie **R** 254
  Ruth, George Herman ("Babe") **R** 361
  softball **S** 229
  Where did baseball begin? **B** 69
  World Series records **B** 79–80
  See also Little League Baseball; Softball
Baseball Writers' Association of America **B** 81
Base-burners, stoves **H** 97–98
Basedow (ba-zed-O), **Johann,** German educator **P** 225
Basel (BA-zel), Switzerland **S** 498
Basel, University of **S** 496
Base line, of a graph **G** 309
Basenji (ba-SEN-ji), barkless dog **D** 261; picture **D** 254
Bases, in chemistry **C** 218
  tests for (experiments) **C** 217

Bashō, Matsuo, Japanese haiku poet **J** 28; **O** 220b

Basic English, system using 850 normal English words, designed by British scholar C. K. Ogden about 1925. It was devised for use in international communication and is used to teach English and to clarify and simplify writings in English. Six hundred words refer to things, 150 describe qualities, and 100 are action words.
  universal languages **U** 195

Basic oxygen process, in steelmaking **I** 398
Basie, William ("Count"), American jazz musician **J** 60; picture **J** 61
Basil (BAZ-il), an herb **S** 382; picture **S** 381
Basil II, Byzantine emperor
  "Bulgar killer," conqueror of Bulgaria **B** 444

Basilica (ba-SIL-ica) (from Greek word *basilikos,* meaning "royal"), a long rectangular building with interior colonnades and at least one apse (semicircular projection). Basilicas were originally Greek and Roman justice or assembly halls. Their architectural plan was widely used for churches.
  early church architecture **A** 376; **I** 458; diagram and pictures **A** 379; **I** 459

Basil (BAZ-il) **the Great, Saint** (330?–379), doctor of the Christian Church, b. Caesarea, Cappadocia. He founded first monastery in Asia Minor at Pontus (about 360) and became known as the Patriarch of Eastern Monasticism. He was ordained a priest (about 365), and later became bishop of Caesarea (370). Basil tried to stamp out heresies within the Church, especially Arianism, which denied the divinity of Christ. His feast is celebrated on June 14 in the Western Church and on January 1 in the Eastern.
  Christianity, history of **C** 283
  Christmas patron for Greek children **C** 292

Basin and Range Region, United States **U** 91
Basins, of lakes **L** 25
Baskerville, John, English type designer **T** 345
Basketball **B** 82–90
  girls' basketball **B** 89
  Olympic game, picture **O** 114
Basketmakers, primitive Indians of North America **I** 164
Baskets, hanging, for flowers, picture **G** 38
Basket weaving
  Pomo Indian art **I** 156, 174; picture **I** 157
  Tonga, picture **T** 210

Baskin, Leonard (1922–), American sculptor and graphic artist, b. New Brunswick, N.J. Baskin began teaching at Smith College in 1953. He sculpts simple, massive human forms out of stone or wood. His works include *The Great Dead Man* and *Walking Man.*

Basking sharks **S** 140
Bas Mitzvah *see* Bat Mitzvah
Basotho, a people of Lesotho **L** 156

Basov (ba-SOV), **Nikolai** (1922–) Soviet radiophysicist. He has been Deputy Science Director, Lebedev Physics Institute, since 1958. In 1964 he won the Nobel prize in physics for discovering how to produce high-intensity beams of radiation through use of masers and lasers.

Basque (BASK) **language** **L** 40
  Pyrenees section of Spain **S** 366
Basques, people of western Pyrenees section of France and Spain **S** 352
  folk dancers, picture **F** 298

Basques (continued)
Idaho, immigrants to **I** 59
jai alai players **J** 10
Basra (BOS-ra), Iraq **I** 382
Bas-relief (BA rel-IEF), in sculpture **S** 90
Bass, fish, pictures **F** 210
baits and lures **F** 206
sea bass **F** 214
Bass, George, English explorer and doctor **A** 516
Bass (BASE), male voice **C** 277
voice training **V** 375
Bass clef, or F clef, in musical notation **M** 525-26
Bass drum D 334
Basset horn, picture **W** 183
Basset hound, dog **D** 261
Bassett, Charles A., II, American astronaut **S** 346

Bassett, Richard (1745-1815), American statesman, b. Cecil County, Md. Active in Delaware politics, he represented this state at the Annapolis Convention (1786) and at the Constitutional Convention (1787). He was also presidential elector (1797) and governor of Delaware (1799-1801).

Bassoon (bas-SOON), musical instrument **M** 549; picture **W** 183
orchestra seating plan **O** 186
Bass viol, or **viola de gamba,** musical instrument, picture **S** 439
in concert, picture **I** 482
Basswood, tree
uses of the wood and its grain, picture **W** 223
Bast fibers F 106
Bastille, fall of the, 1789 **F** 464-65; picture **F** 463
Place de la Bastille, Paris **P** 74
Bastille Day, July 14 **H** 152
importance to French history **F** 406
July holidays **J** 148
Basting stitches, in sewing **S** 129
Bastions, of forts **F** 375, 377
Basutoland (ba-SU-to-land), now Lesotho **L** 156-156a
Bat, baseball **B** 70
Bat, The (*Die Fledermaus*), operetta by Johann Strauss, Jr. **O** 156, 157-58; **S** 437
Bata, Equatorial Guinea **E** 274
Bataan (ba-TAN), Philippines
World War II **W** 294
Batavia (bat-A-via), former name of Djakarta **D** 236, 237
Bat-eared foxes D 250
Batéké Plateau, Congo (Brazzaville) **C** 461, 462
Batékés, Congo people **C** 462, 464

Bates, Katherine Lee (1859-1929), American educator and author, b. Falmouth, Mass. She was professor of English at Wellesley College (1891-1925) and wrote books for children, scholarly works on literature, and collections of poems. She is best known for lyrics of "America the Beautiful." **N** 25

Batfish, name given to certain types of saltwater fish up to a foot long. It lives on bottom in tropical oceans, where it "walks," using four fins. Its front fins, sticking out from bulge on each side of body, give it a batlike appearance. Certain anglerfish are also called batfish.

Bath, North Carolina **N** 317
Baths and bathing B 91
Ganges River, India, religious bathing **G** 25
Japan **J** 26
knights of the bath **K** 276-77

Bathsheba (bath-SHE-ba), in Old Testament (II Samuel), wife of Uriah and Hittite. She fell in love with David, King of Israel, and became his second wife after the death of Uriah. Bathsheba was the mother of Solomon.

Bathurst, *see* Banjul
Bathurst, New Brunswick, Canada **N** 138c
Bathyscaphe (BATHI-scaph), underwater ship **P** 244
deep-sea exploration **D** 82
oceanographic research **O** 44
underwater exploration **U** 16-17
Bathysphere, sphere for deep-sea study **D** 81-82
underwater exploration **U** 16
Batik (ba-TEEK), method of hand-printing textiles **M** 54
dyeing the cloth, picture **D** 368
folk art **F** 296
Indonesian industry **I** 217; picture **I** 219

Batista y Zaldivar (ba-TI-sta e sol-DI-var), **Fulgencio** (1901-73), Cuban dictator, b. Banes. He was active in military overthrow of dictatorship of Gerado Machado (1931-33) and became dictatorial chief of staff of Cuban Army (1933-39). He was president of Cuba (1940-44) and authoritarian president (1952) after overthrowing President Prio. He was deposed (1959) by rebel group under Fidel Castro and fled into exile. He died in Spain.
Castro and Cuba **C** 129, 550, 551

Batlle y Ordóñez (BAH-zhay e or-DONE-yes), **José** (1856-1929), Uruguayan statesman and journalist, b. Montevideo. He established newspaper *El Día* (1886), through which he publicized his political proposals later incorporated into Constitution of 1918. He led liberal Colorado Party and was president of Uruguay (1903-07, 1911-15), introducing executive council based on Swiss system. His leadership led to universal suffrage and increased governmental roles in business, welfare, and labor reform.
Uruguay, history of **U** 239

Bat Mitzvah, ceremony in Judaism **J** 119
Batoche National Historic Park and Museum, Saskatchewan **S** 38f
Baton Rouge, capital of Louisiana **L** 360
Bats B 92-97
body changes in hibernation **H** 123
cave dwellers **C** 152-53
guano **C** 153
hand pattern changed for flying **F** 84
How do bats find their way in the dark? **B** 96
locomotion **A** 295-96
mammals, food adaptations **M** 66; picture **M** 69
nectar-feeding bat, picture **F** 279
Battalion, army troop unit **U** 172
Battambang (BAT-tam-bang), Cambodia **C** 33
Batteries B 97-99
automobiles operated on batteries **A** 542, 552
bacterial fermentation produces electricity **F** 91
Davy's experiments **E** 129
direct current **E** 134
ionization, principle of **I** 355
solar batteries **S** 238
Batteries, electric *see* Electric batteries
Battersea, Celtic shield of, picture **E** 234
Battery, artillery troop unit **U** 172
Battle, trial by M 291
jury replaces **J** 159
Battle above the Clouds, 1863, Civil War **C** 326
Battle Creek, Michigan **M** 270
Battle Cry of Freedom, The, song **N** 25
Battledore, children's book **C** 237
Battledore and shuttlecock *see* Badminton
Battle Hymn of the Republic, The, by Julia Ward Howe **N** 25

Battle of Constantine, The, painting by Piero della Francesca **R** 167
Battles **B** 100–02
    Alexander the Great **A** 151–53
    National Battlefields, parks, and sites, lists **N** 49, 50
    See also names of battles
Battleships *see* Warships
Battuta, or **Batuta,** Ibn *see* Ibn Battuta
Batutsi *see* Tutsi
Batwa *see* Twa, a people of Rwanda
Baucis *see* Philemon and Baucis
Baudelaire (bode-LAIRE), **Charles,** French poet **F** 440
Baudot (bo-DO), **J. M. E.,** French inventor **T** 53

Baudouin (BO-dwan) (1930–), king of the Belgians, b. Brussels. Baudouin became Prince Royal (1950) when his father, Leopold III, transferred royal constitutional powers to him because of postwar political unrest. He was crowned king when his father abdicated (1951).

Bauer, Georg *see* Agricola, Georgius
Bauhaus (BOU-house), former German art school
    B 103–05
    architecture, history of **A** 385
    furniture design **F** 510
    industrial design **I** 231
    influence on decorative arts **D** 78
    Kandinsky, Wassily **K** 166
    modern German art **G** 171

Baum (BOHM), **L. Frank** (Lyman Frank Baum) (1856–1919), American journalist and author of children's stories, b. Chittenango, N.Y. He is best known for series of fantasies for children about the land of Oz, beginning with *The Wonderful Wizard of Oz.* That book and 13 other Oz stories that followed were an attempt to create a distinctly American fairyland. The first Oz book was made into a movie in 1939.

Bauxite (BOK-site), ore of aluminum **A** 176; picture **R** 272
    Arkansas first in U.S. production **A** 424, 425, 426
    bauxite-producing regions of North America **N** 294
    Jamaica **J** 16
Bavaria (ba-VAIR-ia), Germany **G** 158
    costumes, traditional, picture **C** 349
    Thompson, Benjamin, service in government **T** 166
Bavarian Alps, in Austria and Germany **A** 174; **G** 153
Bay, geographic term *see* by name, as Fundy, Bay of
Bayard, James Asheton, American statesman **D** 99
Bayard, Thomas F., American statesman **D** 99

Bayberry, shrub of eastern coastal North America. It has dark-green leaves about 3 inches long, small flowers, and round, waxy, grayish-white berries. Wax myrtles of southeastern and western coastal North America are similar, belonging to same genus (*Myrica*). The berries yield tallow, used to make candles and soap.
    candles, how to make **C** 97, 399

Bay Bridge, San Francisco, picture **S** 31
Bayeux (ba-YER) **tapestry,** medieval embroidery **E** 187
Bay leaves, spice **S** 382; picture **S** 381

Baylor, Elgin (1936–), American basketball player, Negro, b. Washington, D.C. All-American player from Seattle University, he played for Los Angeles Lakers of the National Basketball Association. He was among the league's all-time leading scorers and was frequently named to the NBA All-Star team.

Bay lynxes, or bobcats **C** 139

Bay of Pigs Invasion *see* Pigs, Bay of
Bayous (BY-os), marshy creeks
    Louisiana's bayous **L** 348; picture **L** 353
Bayou State, nickname for Louisiana **L** 349

Bay Psalm (SALM) **Book** (correct title, *The Whole Book of Psalms Faithfully Translated into English Metre*), book of psalms adapted by several Puritan ministers in Massachusetts Bay Colony for use with familiar hymn tunes. It is famous as the first book in English printed in the New World (1640).
    hymns in America **H** 313

Bayreuth (by-ROIT), Germany, Federal Republic of
    Festival of Wagner's operas **M** 550; **W** 2
Bay State, nickname for Massachusetts **M** 135
Bazaars, pictures **C** 8; **I** 381
Bazán, Emilia Pardo *see* Pardo Bazán, Emilia
BB gun, or air rifle **G** 424
BCG, vaccine against tuberculosis **D** 212
B-complex vitamins **V** 370c–370d
Beaches
    Australia's Manly Beach, picture **A** 496
    Bahamas' Eleuthera Island, picture **B** 16
    barrier beaches of Louisiana **L** 351
    Brazil's Copacabana, picture **B** 372
    left by ice ages **I** 17
    New York City, picture **U** 101
    oil pollution, picture **E** 272d
    Tossa del Mar, Spain, picture **S** 353
Beaconsfield, Earl of *see* Disraeli
Beads, jewelry
    early glass articles **G** 226
    Indian beadwork **I** 157–59
Beagle, dog, picture **D** 254
Beagle, H.M.S., British ship **D** 40
    Darwin's voyage **E** 344–45
Beaks, or bills, of birds **B** 221
    eagles **E** 2
Beal, Frank Peer, American clergyman
    inventor of paddle tennis **P** 11
Bean, Alan L. American astronaut **S** 340i, 344, 345, 346
Beans **V** 289
    biological rhythms in life **L** 248–49; picture **L** 247
    classification **T** 30
    seed, structure of, picture **F** 283
    See also Soybeans
Bear cats, mammals related to mongooses **G** 89, 91

Beard, Charles Austin (1874–1948), American historian, writer, and educator, b. near Knightstown, Ind. Beard was professor of politics, Columbia University (1915–17) and helped found New School for Social Research. Books written with his wife, **Mary Ritter Beard** (1876–1958), include *A Basic History of the United States* and *The Rise of American Civilization.*

Beard, Daniel Carter, a founder of Boy Scouts of America **B** 357

Beardsley, Aubrey Vincent (1872–1898), English book illustrator, b. Brighton. Beardsley is known for his stylized, decorative line drawings in black and white. His works include illustrations for Ben Jonson's *Volpone,* Oscar Wilde's *Salomé,* and the English periodical *Yellow Book.*

Bear Festival, of the Ainu **J** 42
Bear Flag Revolt, California **T** 112
Bearings, machinery
    made of diamonds **D** 155
    watches and clocks **W** 48

Bearing walls, of buildings **B** 434
  bricks and masonry **B** 392–93
Bear Mountain Bridge, New York, picture **N** 215
Bear Run, Pennsylvania
  Falling Water, house, picture **A** 385
Bears B 106–08
  bear cub, picture **A** 294
  circus act, picture **C** 300
  dancing bear, picture **G** 433
  foot bones, diagram **F** 81
  partial hibernation of **H** 122
  polar bears, picture **P** 363
  tracks, picture **A** 271
  Yellowstone National Park **Y** 346
Bears and bulls, in stock exchanges **S** 432
Beast, bird, or fish, group game **I** 226
Beast epics F 4
Beasts of burden
  early means of transportation **T** 257
Beasts of prey
  cats **C** 134–41
Beat, in music **S** 262–63
  orchestra conducting **O** 188
Beater goes round, circle game **G** 14

Beatification (be-at-if-ic-A-tion), in Roman Catholic Church, papal act by which a virtuous or holy person is declared blessed after his death. Often this is the first step to canonization. To become beatified, a person must have led a life of heroic virtue and have performed at least two miracles.

Beatles, The, popular English rock group. John Lennon, Paul McCartney, Ringo Starr, and George Harrison began singing together in Liverpool, England (1962), and became known the world over for their originality and versatility as musicians and composers as well as for their singing. They made several movies including *A Hard Day's Night.* They received the Order of the British Empire in 1965. The Beatles officially broke up in 1971 to pursue their individual musical careers. Picture **R** 262b.
  rock music **R** 262c, 262d

Beaton, Cecil Walter Hardy (1904–), English photographer, writer, and designer, b. London. His work became known through magazines in England and America. He is noted especially for his photographs of beautiful women and is official photographer of British royal family (since 1939). He wrote *Air of Glory* and other books while working for the British Ministry of Information during World War II. His other books include *The Book of Beauty* and *Cecil Beaton's New York.*

Beatrice, Dante's ideal and inspiration **D** 38;
  I 476
Beats, sections of a city
  assignments of newspaper reporters **N** 201
  covered by patrolmen **P** 375

Beatty (BEAT-ty), **David,** 1st Earl Beatty of the North Sea and of Brooksby (1871–1936), British naval officer, b. Nantwich, Cheshire. Beatty commanded battle cruiser fleet, which led the attack against German fleet at battle of Jutland (1916) in World War I. He was commander in chief of British Grand Fleet (1917–18) and accepted surrender of German Navy (1918). He was admiral of the fleet (1919) and first sea lord (1919–27).

Beauchamp (bo-SHON), **Charles Pierre,** French ballet dancer and choreographer **B** 24, 29
  history of the dance **D** 25

Beaucourt (bo-COOR), **François Malepart de** (1740–1794), Canadian painter, b. Lapraisie, Quebec. The earliest known of native Canadian artists, he specialized in portraits and religious works. His best-known, *Portrait of a Negro Slave,* hangs in National Gallery, Ottawa.

Beaufort (BO-fort) **Sea,** part of the Arctic Ocean lying between Alaska and the Arctic Archipelago. It was partially explored (1915) by Vilhjalmur Stefansson (1879–1962) of Canada.

Beaufort wind scale W 84
Beauharnois (bo-HARN-wa), Quebec, Canada **C** 57
Beaujoyeulx (bo-jwa-YER), **Balthazar de,** Italian-born French choreographer **B** 24
Beaumarchais, Pierre, French writer **F** 439

Beaumont (BO-mont), **Francis** (1584–1616), English dramatist, b. Leicestershire. Although he wrote some plays on his own, his best-known works were collaborations with John Fletcher. Beaumont and Fletcher co-authored more than 50 plays, of which the best-known are *The Knight of the Burning Pestle, Philaster,* and *The Maid's Tragedy.*
  drama, history of **D** 296

Beaumont, William, American frontier surgeon **B** 109
  contribution to medicine **M** 207

Beauregard (BO-re-gard), **Pierre Gustave Toutant de** (1818–1893), American Confederate general, b. near New Orleans, La. Beauregard ordered firing on Fort Sumter, which began Civil War (1861). He led South to victory at Bull Run (1861), defended Charleston (1862–64), and together with General Bushrod Johnson surrendered to General Sherman (1865). His writings include *Principles and Maxims of the Art of War.*
  Civil War, history of **C** 318, 322

Beauty culture B 110–11
  See also Cosmetics; Perfumes
Beaver, Indians of North America **I** 164

Beaverbrook, Lord (William Maxwell Aitken, 1st baron of Beaverbrook) (1879–1964), English newspaper publisher and politician, b. Maple, Ontario, Canada. He made his fortune in cement industry and moved to England to enter politics. A Conservative member of Parliament (1910–16), he was raised to peerage (1917). He held various government positions during both world wars and was publisher of three of London's leading newspapers: *Daily Express, Evening Standard,* and *Pall Mall Gazette.* He was known for his strongly conservative views. His works include *Canada in Flanders* and *Men and Power.*
  New Brunswick, people associated with **N** 138c

Beaver Island, in Lake Michigan **M** 268
Beavers B 112–14
  aplodontia, or mountain beaver **R** 277; picture **R** 278
  fur **F** 517
  hats **F** 511
  homes of **M** 67
  Indian hunting beaver, picture **C** 68
  tracks, picture **A** 272
Beaver State, nickname for Oregon **O** 193
Bebop, early name for modern jazz **J** 60
Becharof Lake, Alaska **A** 133
Becharre (bish-AR-re), Lebanon, picture **L** 123
Bechet (besh-AY), **Sidney,** jazz musician **J** 58
Bechuanaland *see* Botswana

Beck, Sir Adam (1857–1925), Canadian financier, b. Baden, Ont. He served as mayor of London, Ont. (1902–04); Conservative member of the Ontario Legislative Assembly (1902–19, 1923–25); and as a provincial cabinet minister without portfolio (1905–14, 1923–25). He led a commission investigating development and distribution of power from Niagara Falls (1903), and introduced the bill creating the Hydro-Electric Power Commission (1906), of which he was chairman until his death.

Becket, Saint Thomas à, English churchman **B** 115
    kings versus clergy in English history **E** 219

Beckett, Samuel (1906–), Irish writer, b. Dublin. He settled permanently in France in 1937 and has written in French since 1945. He has translated several of his own works into English. His best-known play is *Waiting for Godot.* In 1969 he received the Nobel prize.

Beckmann (BECK-monn), **Max** (1884–1950), German expressionist painter, b. Leipzig. His pictures, many taken from incidents during World War I, portray brutality of human nature. His works include *Christ in Limbo* and triptychs *The Actors, Blindman's Buff,* and *Departure.*
    Departure, painting **G** 168

Becknell, William, American pioneer, father of Santa Fe trail **O** 257

Beckwourth, James Pierson (1798–1867), American fur trapper, b. Virginia. He accompanied fur-trading expeditions to West. Influential among Crow Indians, he joined expeditions to Missouri, Colorado, and California and fought in Cheyenne War (1864).

Bécquer (BAKER), **Gustavo Adolfo,** Spanish poet **S** 370

Becquerel (BECK-rel), **Antoine Henri** (1852–1908), French physicist, b. Paris. Known for his discovery (1896) of radioactivity, he shared Nobel prize in physics (1903) with Pierre and Marie Curie for work on radioactivity. His physicist father, **Alexandre Edmond** (1820–1891), is known for work on light and its chemical effects. His grandfather **Antoine César** (1788–1878), also a physicist, is considered one of the founders of electrochemistry.

Bedbugs, insects **H** 262; picture **H** 263
Bede, the Venerable, English historian-monk **E** 246–47
    children's books **C** 236
    Christianity, history of **C** 284

Bedford, Gunning, Jr. (1747–1812), American statesman and lawyer, b. Philadelphia, Pa. Prominent in Delaware politics, he served as delegate to the Continental Congress (1785–86) and the Annapolis Convention (1786). At the Constitutional Convention (1787) he strongly supported states' rights and equality in voting.

Bed in Summer, poem by Robert Louis Stevenson **S** 424
Bedivere, knight of King Arthur's court **A** 442

Bedlam, hospital of Saint Mary of Bethlehem in London (name became slurred in popular usage: "Bethlem" and then "Bedlam"). It was built as a monastery (1247) and was later used as a lunatic asylum. Hence the term also refers to a madhouse or any place of noise and confusion.

Bedloe's Island (now Liberty Island), Upper New York Bay **L** 168
Bedouins (BED-du-ins), nomadic Arabic tribes **D** 128; picture **J** 138

    Egypt **E** 90c
    Saudi Arabia **S** 45
    Syria **S** 506
Beds
    canopy bed, picture **C** 389
    Chinese, picture **D** 73

Beebe (BEE-be), **William** (Charles William Beebe) (1877–1962), American naturalist, explorer, and author, b. Brooklyn, N.Y. He was director of New York Zoological Society Department of Tropical Research (1900–52) and curator of birds at New York Zoological Park (Bronx Zoo). He led many wildlife expeditions to South America and elsewhere. With O. Barton, he was first to explore ocean region of perpetual darkness in record dive (3,028 ft.) with his bathysphere, reported in his book *Half Mile Down.* Other notable books of his are *Jungle Peace* and *The Bird.*
    Beebe and the bathysphere **O** 44; **U** 16

Beech, tree
    uses of the wood and its grain, picture **W** 223

Beecham, Sir Thomas (1879–1961), English symphony and opera conductor and impresario, b. St. Helens, Lancashire. He used his personal fortune to back several orchestras and opera companies, including Covent Garden Opera Company, London Philharmonic Orchestra, and Royal Philharmonic Orchestra. He introduced many operas to English audiences and toured extensively. Beecham was knighted (1915). He wrote his autobiography, *A Mingled Chime.*

Beecher, Henry Ward, American clergyman **B** 115
    "Beecher's Bibles" shipped to Kansas **C** 320

Beecher, Lyman (1775–1863), Presbyterian clergyman; b. New Haven, Conn. He served as pastor of churches in East Hampton, N.Y., Litchfield, Conn., and Boston, and was first president (1832–50) of Lane Theological Seminary in Cincinnati, Ohio. A controversial figure, Beecher won fame for his revivalist preaching, but his views were attacked by more conservative clergymen. He was the father of Henry Ward Beecher and Harriet Beecher Stowe.

Beechey, Frederick William (1796–1856), English explorer. He commanded ship *Blossom* on Arctic expedition (1825–29). He wrote an account of earlier Arctic expedition (1818) on which he accompanied Sir John Franklin.
    Northwest Passage **N** 338

Beef, meat of cattle **M** 192; cuts of, picture **M** 193
    baby beef **C** 148
    cow beef **C** 148–49; **D** 8
    what you eat depends on where you live **F** 332
Beef cattle **C** 147–49
Beefeaters see Yeomen of the Guard
Beehive State, nickname for Utah **U** 241, 254
Beekeeping **H** 202

Beelzebub (be-EL-ze-bub) (from Hebrew *Baal-zebub,* meaning "Lord of Flies"), Philistine god worshiped at Ekron. Considered a false god by Jews in Old Testament (II Kings 1: 3,6), he is mentioned in New Testament (Matthew, Mark, and Luke) as prince of devils. He appears in Milton's *Paradise Lost* as a fallen angel ranking second only to Satan.

Beer, Jakob Liebmann see Meyerbeer, Giacomo
Beer and brewing **B** 116–17
    malt extract from barley **G** 286
Beerbohm (BEER-bome), **Sir Max,** English writer **E** 268

Bees B 117–24
  adaptations to other organisms L 220–21
  biological rhythms L 248
  clock-compass H 193
  homing, meaning of H 185
  honey H 201–02
  How do honeybees make honey? H 201
  strength of I 273
  See also Honey
Beeswax W 70
  candles made of C 97, 399
  storing of honey H 202
Beethoven (BATE-ho-ven), **Ludwig van,** German composer B 124–25
  chamber music C 186
  choral music C 278
  classical age, compositions of C 330, 332, 333
  Fidelio, his only opera O 134, 144
  German music G 185
  symphonies M 541
Beetles, insects, pictures I 272, 281
  boll weevil C 523
  carpet beetles H 262
  freshwater creatures, pictures L 257
  ground beetle, picture I 262
  leg, diagram I 273
  luminescent tracks, picture B 197
  plant enemies and pests P 284–85, 288–89
  strength of I 273–74
  used as biological control for weeds W 106
Beets V 289
  roots we eat, picture P 306
  sugar beets S 456–57
Beet sugar S 456
B.E.F. see British Expeditionary Force
Befana (bay-FA-na), **La,** Italian Santa Claus C 292

Begbie, Sir Matthew Baillie (1819–1894), British colonial judge, b. Edinburgh, Scotland. He was appointed a judge in colony of British Columbia (1858), where he was instrumental in maintaining law and order during gold rush. He was chief justice of mainland of British Columbia (1869) and of whole province (1870–94).

Beggar's Opera, by John Gay E 257
  parody on Italian opera O 132
  satire H 280
Begonia (be-GO-nia), plant H 269
  festival in Belgium, picture B 128
  tuberous begonia centerpiece, picture J 51
Béhanzin (bay-HON-zin), king of Dahomey D 4
Behavior
  brain function B 363, 369
  impulses to take drugs N 13–14
  learning L 98–106
  sociology, study of S 226–27
Behaviorism, psychology P 496–97

Behring (BEAR-ing), **Emil von** (1854–1917), German bacteriologist, b. Hansdorf. Known for his work on diphtheria and tetanus, he discovered that blood serum of an animal infected with one of these diseases, when injected into a healthy animal, provided immunity against that disease. He was first to apply word "antitoxin" to these substances and was awarded first Nobel prize in medicine and physiology (1901).
  serum and antibodies D 215

Behring, Vitus see Bering, Vitus

Behrman (BEAR-man), **S. N.** (Samuel Nathaniel Behrman) (1893–   ), American playwright known for his comedies, b. Worcester, Mass. His works include *The Second Man, No Time for Comedy,* and *Fanny* (with Joshua Logan). He also wrote motion picture scenarios.

Beida, Libya L 204
Beiderbecke, Leon ("Bix"), American jazz musician J 59
Beijerinck (BAY-jer-ink), **M. W.,** Dutch scientist V 362
Beirut (bay-ROOT), capital of Lebanon L 122; picture L 123
Bel see Baal, pagan god

Belafonte (bel-af-ON-te), **Harry** (Harold George Belafonte, Jr.) (1927–   ), American folk singer and actor, Negro, b. New York, N.Y. He popularized calypso music. He appeared on Broadway in *Three for Tonight* and on the screen in *Carmen Jones, Island in the Sun,* and *The Angel Levine.* He has also made many concert, nightclub, and TV appearances. His best-selling records include "Matilda," "Scarlet Ribbons," and "Try to Remember." He has been active in civil rights work. Picture N 102.

Belasco, David (1854–1931), American theatrical producer and playwright, b. San Francisco, Calif. He was stage manager of various New York theaters before he opened first of his own theaters (1902). His success is attributed to careful attention to stage detail, and he was first to conceal footlights from the audience. He was author and collaborator of many plays, including *The Return of Peter Grimm* and *The Girl of the Golden West.*
  American drama D 299

Belaúnde (bay-la-ON-day) **Terry, Fernando,** president of Peru P 166
Belém (bel-EM), Brazil B 381; pictures A 179; B 382

Belep Islands, coral group in southwestern Pacific. A dependency of New Caledonia, the islands are administered by France.

Belfast, capital of Northern Ireland U 73
Belgian Congo B 131
  See also Zaïre
Belgian horse, picture H 240
Belgium B 126–31
  flag F 239
  Flemish and Dutch art D 349–62
  Industrial Revolution I 241
  invasion by Hitler, 1940 W 288–89
  invasion in World War I W 271–72
  national anthem N 21
  Zaïre Z 366a
Belgrade, capital of Yugoslavia Y 357

Belial (BE-li-al), (from Hebrew, meaning "worthless" or "wicked") in Old Testament, word used to describe an evil person. In New Testament, it is a personification of spirit of evil, also called the Devil or Satan.

Belize see Honduras, British (Belize)
Bell, Alexander Graham, Scottish-born American inventor and scientist B 132–33
  airplane research A 572
  Alexander Graham Bell Museum, Nova Scotia N 344d
  Bell Homestead, place of interest in Ontario O 125
  communication and the telephone C 438–39
  dictation machine O 57
  telephone T 56
Bell, Charles, Scottish-born British physician B 287
Bell, Chichester, American pioneer in phonograph development P 197
Bell, Currer, Ellis, and **Acton** see Brontë family
Bell, Eric Temple, American mathematician M 161

Bell, James Madison (1826–1902), American poet, Negro, b. Gallipolis, Ohio. He was elected delegate from Ohio to Republican National Convention in Philadelphia (1872). A close associate of abolitionist John Brown, he was a noted antislavery orator. His poetry, collected in *Poetical Works*, includes "The Dawn of Freedom," "The Day and the War," and "The Triumph of Liberty."

Bell, John, American statesman **T** 86
Bell, Joseph, English doctor, model for Sherlock Holmes **D** 288

Bell, Margaret Elizabeth (1898–   ), American author of children's books, b. Prince of Wales Island, Alaska. She is best known for novels set in Alaska, including *Watch for a Tall White Sail* and *The Totem Casts a Shadow.*

Belladonna, drug, from the plant, the deadly nightshade **D** 323; **P** 322
   plants, medicinal **P** 314; picture **P** 315
Bellamy, Edward, American novelist **A** 206
   Looking Backward **U** 256
Bellay (bel-LAY), **Joachim du,** French poet **F** 434, 436
Belle Isle, Strait of, north of Newfoundland, Canada **N** 141
   Cartier's explorations **C** 124
Bellerophon (bell-ER-o-phon), hero in Greek myth **G** 364
Belleville Breviary, illuminated manuscript, picture **B** 319
Bellevue, Nebraska **N** 82

Bellingshausen (BELL-ings-how-zen) **Sea,** part of the South Pacific off Antarctic, between Palmer Peninsula to the east and Thurston Peninsula to the west. It was named for Fabian Gottlieb von Bellingshausen, the leader of a Russian Antarctic expedition (1819–21).
   arm of the Antarctic Ocean **O** 45

Bellingrath Gardens, Alabama, picture **A** 123
Bellini (bel-LI-ni), **Giovanni,** Venetian painter **P** 21
   Bellini family **B** 134
   Renaissance art **R** 169
   Titian, pupil of Bellini **T** 199

Bellini, Vincenzo (1801–1835), Italian composer, b. Catania, Sicily. Known chiefly for his operas, he is noted for elegance of his melodic style, which has been compared to Chopin's. His best-known operas are *I Puritani, La Sonnambula,* and *Norma.*
   Italian styles in opera **O** 135
   Norma, opera **O** 149

Bellini family, Jacopo, Gentile, and Giovanni, Italian painters **B** 134
Bell Island, Newfoundland, Canada
   iron mines at Wabana **N** 143
Bellman, Carl Michael, Swedish poet **S** 52

Bello (BAY-o), **Andrés** (1781–1865), South American educator, statesman, and author, b. Caracas, Venezuela. He accompanied Simón Bolívar to London and served on Colombian, Venezuelan, and Chilean legations (1810–29). As Chilean secretary of state (1834), he wrote Chilean code of civil law. His works include *Silva a la agricultura de la zona tórrida.*
   Chile, history of **C** 255

Belloc, Hilaire (Joseph Hilary Pierre Belloc) (1870–1953), English writer, b. St. Cloud, France. He was a Liberal member of Parliament (1906–10). With G. K. Chesterton and C. Chesterton he founded *New Witness,* a review designed to attack political abuses (1912). He was leader

of intellectual Catholicism in England. Among Belloc's numerous works are *The Bad Child's Book of Beasts,* a four-volume *History of England,* and a travel journal, *The Path to Rome.*
   The Yak, nonsense rhyme **N** 274

Bell of Freedom, Berlin **B** 143
Bellow, Saul, American novelist **A** 213
Bellows, for making fires hotter **F** 143
Bellows, George Wesley, American artist **U** 122
   Anne in White, painting **U** 118
Bells **B** 134–37
   bronze **B** 409
   Christmas customs **C** 290
   communication, use in **C** 437
   Liberty Bell **L** 169
   orchestra, use in **P** 153
Bell-shaped curve, or **normal curve,** in probability **P** 472

Bell-Smith, Frederic Marlett (1846–1923), Canadian painter, b. London, England. Noted for landscapes and street scenes, he was one of the founders of Society of Canadian Artists (1867). Works include *Lights of a City Street* and *Tower Bridge, London.*

Bell Telephone Company
   library in Holmdel, New Jersey, picture **L** 178
   public utilities **P** 513
Bell towers see Campaniles
Belmont Stakes, horse race **H** 232
Belmopán, capital of British Honduras **H** 100, 200
Belorussia (byel-o-RU-sia) (Belorussian Soviet Socialist Republic) **B** 138–39; **U** 27, 37
   flag **F** 239

Belshazzar (bel-SHAZZ-ar), in Old Testament (Daniel 5), son of Nabonidus, last Chaldean king of Babylonia. During a feast at which he allowed his court to drink from vessels taken from temple, mysterious handwriting appeared on wall. Daniel interpreted it as end of Chaldean kingdom, and that night Belshazzar was killed and Babylonia conquered (539 B.C.). The phrase "handwriting on the wall" now refers to impending calamity.

Belt conveyors **H** 145
Belt loaders, construction equipment **B** 446
Beltsville Small White, turkeys **P** 423
Beltways, or **ringroads,** around cities
   Baltimore and Washington, D.C. **M** 121
   Boston **M** 141
Belugas, whales **W** 147; picture **W** 149

Belyayev, Pavel I. (1925–70), Russian cosmonaut, b. Chelishchevo. A fighter pilot during World War II, he later served in the Far East and Black Sea areas before joining the cosmonaut program (1960). He commanded space craft Voskhod II (1965) when Aleksei Leonov made first walk in space. Both are heroes in the Soviet Union.
   space flight data **S** 344, 345

Bemelmans (BEM-el-mans), **Ludwig** (1898–1962), American author and illustrator, b. Merano, Austria (now in Italy). He went to United States (1914) and became a citizen (1918). He wrote and illustrated books for children and adults. He is known for his humor and whimsical charm of his stories and paintings. His books for children include *Parsley, Quito Express,* and *Madeline's Rescue,* which won Caldecott Medal in 1954. Some of his adult books are *How to Travel Incognito* and *Best of Times.*
   Madeline's Rescue, picture from **B** 309
   picture books for children **C** 243

Ben, meaning in names **N** 5

Benares, India see Banaras

Benavente (bay-na-VEN-tay), **Jacinto,** Spanish writer **S** 371

Ben Bella, Ahmed (1919–), former premier of Algeria, b. Marnia. One of the "nine fathers of Algerian independence," he helped found Secret Organization (1947) and took part in other nationalist activities; he was captured and jailed by the French (1956–61). He was named vice-premier in provisional government (1958), and premier when Algeria won independence (1962). He was president of the Republic of Algeria (1963–65) until ousted by a military coup.

Algeria, history of **A** 163

Benchley, Robert Charles (1889–1945), American humorist, writer, and actor, b. Worcester, Mass. He was drama critic for *Life* (1920–29) and *The New Yorker* (1929–40). He wrote, directed, and acted in many screen shorts. He appeared in supporting roles in several motion pictures and participated in many radio programs. His books include *The Early Worm,* and *Inside Benchley.*

Bendick, Jeanne (1919–), American author and illustrator of children's books, b. New York City. She writes non-fiction books for elementary school-age children and has written about 60 and illustrated over 100. Among her books are *The Human Senses* (1968) and *The First Book of Names, Sets, and Numbers* (1971).

Books: From Author to Library **B** 329–34

Bends, knots **K** 291

Bends, the, or caisson disease **U** 15

deep-sea divers victims of **D** 81, 82

helium mixture helps prevent **H** 108

problem for oceanographic research **O** 42

tunnels **T** 318

Benedict XV (Giacomo della Chiesa) (1854–1922), Italian pope (1914–22), b. Pelgi, near Genoa. He became archbishop of Bologna (1907), then cardinal (1914), and he succeeded Pius X as pope. He made repeated statements advocating world peace. The *Code of Canon Law* was issued (1918) during his reign.

Roman Catholic Church, history of **R** 298

Benedict, Ruth Fulton (1887–1948), American anthropologist, b. New York, N.Y. She taught at Columbia University (1923–48). While with the U.S. Office of War Information (1943–46), she studied contemporary cultures. Her book about Japan, *The Chrysanthemum and the Sword,* was helpful in shaping U.S. policy there. She believed anthropologists should participate in solving social problems. In *Race: Science and Politics* she tried to disprove theories of racial superiority. She was author of *Patterns of Culture.*

Benedict of Nursia, Saint (480?–543?), Italian monk, called Patriarch of Western Monasticism, b. Nursia, Umbria. He was educated in Rome, where he became disillusioned by the corrupt life around him. He retreated to a cave in Subiaco (500?), and a community of monks grew up around him. He established a monastery (529?) on Monte Cassino that became center of Benedictine Order. He wrote *Regula Monachorum,* a set of strict rules that govern monks of this order.

Benedictines, or Rule of Saint Benedict, religious order

Christianity and the monasteries **C** 283; **M** 294; **R** 291

Benefice (BEN-e-fis) **system,** in Catholic Church **R** 293

Beneficiaries (ben-e-FI-ci-aries), persons receiving money from insurance, wills, or trusts **I** 295

Benelux, economic union of Belgium, the Netherlands, and Luxembourg. The original agreement, signed in 1944, was put into effect in 1948. Its primary goal of removing tariff barriers was achieved (1950), but other aims, such as uniform taxes, wages, and prices, have yet to be realized. An example of prosperity through cooperation, it was a precursor of European Common Market.

Beneš (BEN-esh), **Eduard** (1884–1948), Czechoslovakian statesman, b. Kožlany, Bohemia. He worked with Tomáš Masaryk for a Czechoslovak national state (formed 1918). A delegate to Versailles peace conference (1919–20) and to League of Nations (1923–27), he was elected Czechoslovak president (1935). He resigned when Germans invaded (1938) and became head of Czech government-in-exile (1939–45). He was re-elected president after war (1946) but resigned (1948) rather than co-operate with Communists in the government. His writings include *My War Memories* and *Democracy: Today and Tomorrow.*

Benét (ben-AY), **Laura** (1884?–), American poet and author of books for children, b. Fort Hamilton, N.Y. The sister of William Rose and Stephen Vincent Benét, she has written biographies, such as *The Boy Shelley* and *Enchanting Jenny Lind,* and novels *The Hidden Valley* and *Goods and Chattels.*

Benét, Stephen Vincent, American poet **A** 210

Benét, William Rose (1886–1950), American writer, b. Fort Hamilton, N.Y. Brother of Stephen Vincent Benét, he was on staff of *Century Magazine* (1911–18), N.Y. *Evening Post Literary Review* (1920–24), and *Saturday Review of Literature* (from 1924). His volumes of poetry include *Merchants from Cathay* and *The Falconer of God.* He wrote an autobiography in verse, *The Dust Which Is God,* for which he was awarded the Pulitzer prize (1942). His novels include *The First Person Singular.*

Benevolent and Protective Order of Elks see Elks, Benevolent and Protective Order of (BPOE)

Bengal, Bay of, arm of the Indian Ocean **O** 47

Bengali, language **B** 44c

Bengalis, people of Bangladesh **B** 44, 44c; picture **B** 44a

Bengal tigers **T** 186

cat family **C** 136

Benghazi (ben-GHA-zi), Libya, dual capital with Tripoli **L** 203–04

Benguela (beng-EL-a), Angola **A** 260

Ben-Gurion (ben-GU-ri-on), **David,** first prime minister of Israel **B** 140; picture **P** 456a

Ben Hur, a Story of the Christ, motion picture **M** 474

Benign tumors, of the body **C** 89; **D** 194

Benin (ben-ENE), ancient kingdom in Africa **N** 256

early art achievements **A** 71–72

ivory carvings, pictures **A** 73, **I** 488

Benin City, Nigeria **N** 255

Benjamin, in Old Testament (Genesis 35:16–18), founder of tribe of Benjamin, one of 12 tribes of Israel, and youngest son of Jacob and Rachel. His tribe occupied an area in center of Palestine between Judah on the south and Ephraim on the north.

Joseph and Benjamin **J** 140

Benjamin, Judah Philip, British-born American lawyer and statesman **L** 361

Ben Khedda, Ben Youssef, Algerian leader **A** 163

Bennett, Arnold, English novelist **E** 266

Bennett, Floyd (1890–1928), American aviator, b. Warrensburg, N.Y. Aide to Admiral R. E. Byrd, he accompanied him on expedition to Greenland (1925) and on flight over North Pole (1926). He was awarded Congressional Medal of Honor for first polar flight.

  Byrd and Bennett **B** 481

Bennett, James Gordon (1795–1872), American newspaper publisher, b. Keith, Banffshire, Scotland. He emigrated to Halifax, Nova Scotia, and then to United States (1819). He became Washington correspondent of New York *Enquirer* (1826), and when that paper merged with *Morning Courier* (1829), he served as associate editor (until 1832). He started New York *Herald* (1835), which acquired a tremendous circulation because of Bennett's innovations: accurate, detailed, and often sensational reporting of news events; personal interviews; use of the telegraph in reporting; and distribution by carriers.

Bennett, John, American writer **C** 241

Bennett, Lerone, Jr. (1928–   ), American author and lecturer, Negro, b. Clarksdale, Miss. A staff member of the Johnson Publishing Company, Inc. (since 1953), he was associate editor of *Jet* magazine and has been senior editor of *Ebony* magazine (since 1960). In addition to short stories and articles for periodicals, he has written *Before the Mayflower: A History of the Negro in America 1619–1964,* and *Black Power, USA.*

Bennett, Richard Bedford, Viscount Bennett (1870–1947), Canadian statesman, b. Hopewell Hill, New Brunswick. Conservative member of Canadian House of Commons (1911–17, 1925–39), he was minister of justice and attorney general (1921), minister of finance (1926), leader of Conservative Party (1927–38), and prime minister (1930–35). During his administration Bank of Canada and Canadian Broadcasting Commission were established. He retired to England (1938) and was made viscount (1941).

  New Brunswick, people associated with **N** 138c

Ben Nevis, highest mountain in Great Britain **S** 86
Bennington flag, 1777 **F** 229

Benny, Jack (Benjamin Kubelsky) (1894–   ), American comedian, b. Waukegan, Ill. He started his career as violinist in 1912. The Jack Benny Show, first heard on radio in 1932, has been seen on TV since 1950. Benny, perpetually 39, was given a special award (1957) by the National Academy of Television Arts and Sciences for the best continued performance by a male entertainer. Pictures **R** 58, **T** 301.

Benson, Benny, designed Alaska's flag **A** 128
Benteen, Frederick, American army officer **I** 214

Bentham, Jeremy (1748–1832), English reformer and philosopher, b. London. He was a leading advocate of utilitarianism, a system of ethics defining highest good as "greatest good for the greatest number." He gave up his law practice in order to devote himself entirely to social criticism and reform. His works include *Introduction to the Principles of Morals and Legislation.*

Bentley, E. C., English author of detective stories **M** 555
Benton, Thomas Hart (1782–1858), American statesman
  M 379
Benton, Thomas Hart (1889–   ), American artist
  M 379
  teacher of Jackson Pollock **P** 387

Bent's Fort, Colorado **C** 410
  famous trading posts and forts **F** 376
Benue (BEN-oo-ay) **River,** west Africa **N** 255
Benz, automobile **A** 545

Benz (BENTS), **Karl** (1844–1929), German engineer and automobile manufacturer, b. Karlsruhe. He is often credited with constructing first practical motorcar (1885), essentially a three-wheeled carriage propelled by a gasoline engine. He established a firm in Mannheim, Germany, for manufacture of motorcars, which merged (1926) with firm of engineer Gottlieb Daimler to manufacture the Mercedes-Benz auto.

Benzene (C_6H_6), a colorless, highly inflammable liquid made by distilling coal tar, also obtainable from petroleum. It has the structure of a six-sided ring with a carbon atom at each corner. Discovered (1825) by Michael Faraday, it is a basic raw material in manufacture of many important chemicals. It is also used as a solvent for paints and varnishes, and in aircraft and auto fuels. It is classed scientifically as an aromatic hydrocarbon.

  Faraday's discoveries **F** 44

Benzine, commercial name for a highly volatile and inflammable mixture of carbon-hydrogen compounds derived from petroleum. It is also referred to as petroleum ether and cleaner's naphtha, since it is used as a solvent. It is not to be confused with the single substance benzene.

Ben-Zvi (ben-tz-VE), **Isaac,** or **Itzhak** (1884–1963), Israeli statesman, b. Poltava, Russia. He organized Zionist movement in Russia. He fled to Palestine (1907) and helped organize Jewish army that later became rebel underground Haganah. As head of governing Council of Palestine, he was spokesman for Israeli independence under British mandate. As head of Mapai (Labor) Party, he was elected second president of Israel (1952). A noted Oriental scholar, he wrote on archeology, ethnology, and history of Near East. His works include *Eretz Israel in Past and Present,* written with former Israeli prime minister David Ben-Gurion.

Beograd, Yugoslavia see Belgrade
Beowulf (BAY-o-wulf), epic poem **B** 141–42
  Old English literature **E** 245
Be Prepared, Scout motto **B** 360
Berbera, Somalia **S** 254

Berbers, peoples of the Berber Hamitic language group of Libya, Tunisia, Algeria, and Morocco. Majority are farmers or herdsmen and reside in self-governing villages loosely united in confederations. The Tuareg Berbers are nomadic camel herdsmen organized into clans, which are united into groups, each headed by a chief. They profess Islam. Berber culture is depicted on tomb paintings of ancient Egypt.

Berceo, Gonzalo de see Gonzalo de Berceo
Berceuse, a musical form **M** 535
Berea (ber-E-a) **College,** Berea, Kentucky **K** 220

Berenson, Bernard (1865–1959), American art critic, collector, and writer, b. Vilna, Lithuania. He was an authority on Italian Renaissance art. His works include *The Venetian Painters of the Renaissance.*

Berg (BAIRK), **Alban** (1885–1935), Austrian composer, b. Vienna. He was one of leading composers of early 20th century. A pupil and disciple of Arnold Schoenberg, he

Berg, Alban (continued)
wrote songs, chamber music, and orchestral works, but he is chiefly known for his operas *Wozzeck* and *Lulu* (incomplete) and his Violin Concerto.
  Wozzeck, opera **O** 155

Berg (BERG), **Patty** (Patricia Jane Berg) (1918–), American golfer, b. Minneapolis, Minn. She won most major golf tournaments, both amateur and professional, including U.S. Women's Amateur (1938) and U.S. Women's Titleholders (seven times between 1937 and 1957). She was chosen three times as outstanding woman athlete of the year by Associated Press.

Bergelson, David, Yiddish author **Y** 351
Bergen, Edgar, American ventriloquist **V** 301
Bergen, Norway **N** 344
Bergerac, Cyrano de see Cyrano de Bergerac

Bergh, Henry (1811–1888), American philanthropist, b. New York, N.Y. Son of New York shipping magnate Christian Bergh, he was founder (1866) and first president of American Society for the Prevention of Cruelty to Animals (ASPCA). He helped found Society for the Prevention of Cruelty to Children (1875).

Bergman, Ingmar, Swedish motion–picture director **M** 488

Bergman, Ingrid (1915–), Swedish stage and screen actress, b. Stockholm. She gained international fame from her first American film, *Intermezzo*, with Leslie Howard (1939). She won Antoinette Perry (Tony) award for Broadway performance of *Joan of Lorraine* (1947) and Academy Awards for *Gaslight* (1944) and *Anastasia* (1956). Her other films include *For Whom the Bell Tolls*, *The Inn of the Sixth Happiness*, *Cactus Flower*, and *A Walk in the Spring Rain*.

Beriberi, disease caused by lack of thiamine, or vitamin B_1. It can be prevented by diet containing whole grains. It is most common in parts of Far East where main food is rice from which thiamine-rich outside coating is removed. It affects nerves, especially those that control muscles.
  vitamins, discovery of **V** 370a, 370c–370d
  vitamins in control of disease **D** 216

Bering (BARING), **Vitus,** Danish explorer **B** 142
Bering Sea **O** 46
  early Eskimo called Bering Sea people **E** 284
Bering Strait, separating Asia and North America **B** 142
  Alaska's distance from Asia **A** 128
  connects Bering Sea with Arctic Ocean **O** 46
Berkeley, Sir William, English colonial governor **B** 8–9
Berkelium (BER-kli-um), element **E** 154, 159
Berkner, Lloyd, American physicist **I** 310–11
Berkshire Hills, Massachusetts **M** 137; picture **M** 140

Berkshire Music Festival, series of outdoor summer concerts begun by Henry K. Hadley at Interlaken, Mass. (1934). Series is located (since 1936) at Tanglewood in Lenox, Mass., where the Boston Symphony Orchestra performs a 6-week concert series in July and August.
  music festivals in the United States **M** 551

Berlanga (ber-LON-ga), **Tomás de,** discovered Galápagos Islands **E** 56

Berlin, Congress of (1878), assembly in Berlin of delegates from Germany, Austria-Hungary, France, Britain, Italy, Russia, and Turkey. It met in response to Britain's and Austria-Hungary's disapproval of the Treaty of San Stefano (1878), signed by Russia and Turkey, which increased Russian influence in the Middle East. Congress resulted in Treaty of Berlin, which granted independence to Montenegro, Serbia, and Rumania and divided Bulgaria into three parts. It also defined spheres of influence in Middle East of Great Britain, Austria-Hungary, and Russia.
  Bismarck, Otto von **B** 250
  Cyprus, transfer of **C** 558

Berlin, Germany **B** 143–45; **G** 157
  "Cold War," start of, between East and West **G** 164
  Hansa quarter, picture **E** 332
  made an enclave at end of World War II **W** 306
  main street in East Berlin, picture **G** 163
  main street in West Berlin, picture **G** 164
  Truman orders Berlin airlift **T** 302

Berlin, Irving (Israel Baline) (1888–), American songwriter, b. Temum, Russia. He went to United States in 1893. He wrote scores for such shows as *Annie Get Your Gun* and *Call Me Madam* and such movies as *Top Hat* and *Blue Skies*. His approximately 1,000 show tunes and songs include "Alexander's Ragtime Band," "Easter Parade," and "White Christmas." He was awarded special gold medal by Congress (1954) for "his services in composing many popular songs, including 'God Bless America.' "

Berlin airlift **I** 325
  United States Air Force, role in **U** 160

Berliner, Emile (1851–1929), American inventor, b. Hanover, Germany. He went to United States in 1870. He invented microphone and Gramophone, forerunner of modern phonograph, which first used discs instead of cylinders like those of Edison's machine. He invented method of reproducing discs in quantity and worked to improve telephone.
  records or discs for the phonograph **P** 197; **R** 123

Berliner Ensemble, theater, East Berlin **T** 160
Berlin-to-Baghdad Railroad **I** 381
Berlioz (BAIR-li-ose), **Hector,** French composer **B** 145
  band music **B** 39
  choral music **C** 279
  French music **F** 445
  La Damnation de Faust **F** 73
  opera **O** 137
  romantic orchestral music **R** 311
Bermuda (ber-MU-da), British crown colony of islands in the Atlantic Ocean **B** 146–48
  limestone quarry, picture **Q** 5
Bermuda chub, fish, picture **A** 280
Bermuda grass **G** 317
Bermuda onions **O** 118
Bermúdez (ber-MU-deth), **Juan de,** Spanish navigator **B** 148
Bern, capital of Switzerland **S** 498

Bernadette of Lourdes (Maria Bernarde Soubirous), **Saint** (1844–1879), French peasant girl said to have had visions of Virgin Mary at Lourdes (1858), b. Lourdes, Hautes-Pyrénées. Through her, waters at Lourdes with miraculous healing power were made known. She joined Sisters of Charity at Nevers (1866). She was canonized in 1933.

Bernadotte (BER-na-dot), **Count Folke** (1895–1948), Swedish diplomat and humanitarian, b. Stockholm. A member of Swedish royal family, he was vice-chairman of Swedish Red Cross during World War II. He helped speed exchange of war prisoners and acted as peace emissary at end of war. He was assassinated in Palestine by terrorists while trying, on behalf of United Nations, to stop fighting between Arabs and Jews. He wrote *The Curtain Falls, Instead of Arms,* and *People I Have Met.*

distinguished Swedish statesmen **S** 487

Bernadotte, Jean Baptiste *see* Charles XIV John, king of Sweden and Norway

Bernard (bair-NAR), **Claude,** French psysiologist **D** 325; **M** 207

studies of the animal body **B** 195

Berne Convention, 1886 **T** 245

Bernese Alps, Switzerland **A** 174; picture **S** 497

Bernhardt, Sarah (Henriette Rosine Bernard) (1844–1923), French actress, b. Paris. Called Divine Sarah, she was known for her *voix d'or* ("golden voice"). She performed with Comédie Française (1874–80), touring Europe and United States with great success. She was noted for her performances in plays by Hugo, Sardou, Rostand, and Racine. Despite a leg amputation (1915), she continued her acting career. She wrote a volume of memoirs and several plays. She was made member of Legion of Honor (1914).

Bernini (ber-NI-ni), **Giovanni Lorenzo,** Italian sculptor, painter, and architect **B** 148

baroque architecture **B** 57, 59

Italian architecture **I** 472

place in the history of sculpture **S** 101

statue of David **D** 44; **S** 100

Vision of Saint Theresa, picture **B** 56

Bernoulli (bair-NOOL-li), **Daniel,** Swiss scientist and mathematician **A** 36

Bernoulli's principle, law in physics **A** 36, 40

Bernstein, Leonard (1918–   ), American conductor, pianist, and composer, b. Lawrence, Mass. Associated with New York Philharmonic from 1943 and musical director 1958–69, he was the first man born and trained in the United States to hold that position. His compositions, ranging from classical to popular, include symphonies *The Age of Anxiety* and *Jeremiah,* a ballet, *Fancy Free,* the theatrical rock *Mass,* and scores of several musical shows, such as *Wonderful Town* and *West Side Story.*

musical comedy, history of **M** 543

Berra, Yogi (Lawrence Peter Berra) (1925–   ), American baseball player, b. St. Louis, Mo. He was catcher for New York Yankees (1947–63) and was chosen to play in the All-Star game 14 times. He was the American League's Most Valuable Player (1951, 1954, 1955). Berra was field manager for the Yankees (1964). He was a coach for the New York Mets and manager since 1972.

Berries

garden fruits **G** 52

poisonous plants **P** 322–23

Berrigan, Daniel J. (1921–   ), American Jesuit priest, writer and peace activist, b. Virginia, Minn. He became active in the peace movement and was a member of a peace group that went to North Vietnam (1968) to arrange the release of 3 captured U.S. airmen. He and his brother, **Philip F.** (1923–   ), also a Jesuit priest, became nationally known when they destroyed draft files in Catonsville, Md. (1968). Tried and convicted for this act, they served sentences in federal prisons. Books by Daniel Berrigan include *False Gods, Real Men; Trial of the*

Catonsville Nine. Philip Berrigan has written *Prison Journals of a Priest Revolutionary.*

Berruguete (bair-ru-GAY-tay), **Alonso,** Spanish artist **S** 364

Berry, Chuck, American rock music performer **R** 262c

Berry, Martha McChesney (1866–1942), American educator and philanthropist, b. near Rome, Ga. She was founder (1902) of Berry schools for underprivileged children from the mountain areas of Georgia. This self-supporting school system now includes three schools and a college at Mt. Berry, Ga. She was awarded Roosevelt Memorial Medal for service to the nation (1925) and in a national poll (1931) was voted one of 12 greatest American women.

Bertelli (ber-TEL-li), **Luigi,** Italian writer **I** 480

Bertha, or **Berthrada,** mother of Charlemagne **C** 189

believed to be original Mother Goose **N** 402

Berthon, George Theodore (1806–1892), Canadian painter, b. Vienna, Austria. Known for his portraits, he was an honorary life member of Ontario Society of Artists. A portrait of Sir John Beverly Robinson, considered his masterpiece, hangs in Osgoode Hall, Toronto.

Berthrada *see* Bertha

Beryl, gem mineral **G** 71

Beryllium (ber-ILL-ium), element **E** 154, 159–60

used in space ships and nuclear equipment **M** 313

Berzelius (ber-ZE-lius), **Jöns,** Swedish chemist **C** 212–13

Beschady (be-yesh-CHA-dy) **Mountains,** Europe **P** 359

Bessarabia (bess-a-RAY-bia), Union of Soviet Socialist Republics **R** 358

the Moldavian Republic **U** 44

Bessemer (BESS-em-er), **Sir Henry,** English Inventor of Bessemer steel process **B** 149

Bessemer process, for producing steel **B** 149

iron and steel **I** 398

Bessette, Alfred *see* André, Brother

Best, Charles H., Canadian physiologist **B** 52; picture **D** 216

Best Dog in Show, award **D** 261

Best Friend of Charleston, locomotive **L** 328

early transportation in South Carolina **S** 301–02

railroads, early history **R** 89

Best of Breed, dog show award **D** 261

Betancourt (bate-an-COOR), **Rómulo,** Venezuelan statesman **V** 300

Beta (BAY-ta) **particles,** of radioactive atoms **A** 488; **R** 67

ions and ionization **I** 353

radioactive radiation **R** 45

Beta rays, streams of beta particles of radioactive elements **R** 67

radiations emitted by nuclei **N** 359

Betelgeuse (BET-el-geuse), star **S** 407

constellations **C** 491

Bethesda, in New Testament (John 5:2–9), pool in Jerusalem possessed of miraculous healing powers. It is the place where Jesus is said to have cured a man who had been an invalid for 38 years.

Christian shrines in Old City of Jerusalem **J** 80

Bethlehem, Jordan **J** 139

birthplace of Jesus Christ **J** 82

Israeli occupation, 1967 **J** 139

Bethune, Mary McLeod, American educator **B** 149

Negro political leaders **N** 100

Beti, Mongo, Cameroonian novelist **A** 76c

Betsy Ross flag F 244; picture F 229
Betsy Ross House, Philadelphia P 182

Better Business bureaus, nonprofit agencies in United States and Canada that protect both public and business from misleading or fraudulent business practices.

Bev, unit of energy in nuclear physics *see* Electron volt
Bevel gears G 66
Beverages
  beer B 116–17
  coffee C 371, 374
  grain products G 286
  tea T 37–40
  what you drink depends on where you live F 332–33
  whiskey and other distilled beverages W 159
  wine W 188–89

Beveridge, William Henry, 1st Baron Beveridge of Tuggal (1879–1963), British statesman and economist, b. Rangpur, India. He was director of London School of Economics and Political Science (1919–37) and head of Unemployment Insurance Statutory Committee (1934–44). He is known for his proposal for lifetime social security plan for all British citizens, which he helped enact (1946).

Bevin, Ernest (1881–1951), British labor leader and statesman, b. Somersetshire. He was national organizer of Dockers' Union (1910–21). He organized national Transport and General Workers' Union (1922) and served as general secretary (until 1940). He was member (1925–40) and chairman (1936–37) of general council of Trades Union Congress, Labour member of Parliament (after 1940), minister of labour and national services (1940–45), and foreign secretary (1945–51).

Bey, a Turkish ruler
  Tunisia under the Turks T 312
Beyle, Marie Henri *see* Stendhal
Bhagavad Gita (BHA-ga-vad GHE-ta), Hindu literature H 132
  Indian literature O 220d
B'Hai *see* Bahaism
Bharal (BUR-al), a kind of wild sheep S 145
Bharat *see* India
Bhasa, Indian playwright O 220e
Bhotias (BO-di-as), people of Sikkim S 176
Bhutan (bu-TON), kingdom in Himalayas B 150–51
  flag F 237
Bhutto, Zulfikar Ali, Pakistani president B 44c; P 41
Biafra, eastern region of Nigeria N 258
Biafra, Bight of, west coast of Africa E 273
Bialik (BIA-lik), **Hayyim (Chaim) Nahman,** Hebrew poet H 103
Bialowieza (b'ya-wov-YEJ-a) **National Park,** Poland P 359
Biathlon event, in Winter Olympics O 109
Bibb, William Wyatt, first governor of Alabama A 125
Bible B 152–62
  Abraham A 7
  Apostles, The A 332–33
  Bible stories in the Koran K 295
  Biblical dance D 23
  Biblical names N 8
  Biblical origins of the Jewish people J 102
  Book of Kells K 202–03
  cattle and other livestock C 145
  civil liberties, historical origins C 313–14
  Dead Sea Scrolls, commentaries on D 48–49
  early French picture Bible G 271
  Esther, Book of, the Purim story P 540
  Evangelists, The E 335

  gospels of Matthew and Mark, excerpts J 83, 84
  Gutenberg Bible G 427
  Hebrew literature H 101
  illuminated manuscripts, pages from I 87, 88
  Isaac I 413
  Isaiah I 413
  Jeremiah J 77
  Joshua, leader of Israelites J 141
  Luther's translation C 286; R 134
  miracle plays M 339–40
  Moses M 468
  Negro spirituals, Biblical sources N 105
  Paul quoted on women's role W 211
  prayers P 434–35
  Protestantism P 482–86
  proverbs, traditional sayings P 487; Q 19
  Renaissance studies by the humanists R 160
  Roman Catholic Church R 287
  Solomon S 252
  Ten Commandments T 72–73
  See also Prophets; names of Biblical characters
Bible stories B 163–69
  Boy Jesus B 168–69
  Daniel in the Lion's Den B 167–68
  David and Goliath B 164–65
  Jonah B 166–67
  Noah's Ark B 163–64
Biblical names N 8
Bibliography (bib-li-OG-raphy) B 170
  as a reference tool R 130
  library research project L 187–88
  national: Cumulative Book Index I 115
  parts of a book L 182
  reports R 176
  select list of children's books C 245–48b
Bibliothèque National (bi-bli-o-TEK na-si-o-NAL), Paris L 196–97
Bicameral legislature L 135–36
Bickell, J. P., Foundation F 392
Bicorne, two-cornered hat, picture H 55
Bicuspids (by-CUS-pids), or premolars, teeth T 48
Bicycle racing B 171, 173
  many kinds of racing R 33
  race in Majorca, picture E 314
Bicycles and bicycling B 171–73
  Africa A 65; picture A 68
  Bermuda, picture B 147
  hosteling H 254
  important means of transportation T 265
  Indonesia, picture I 216
  pump, a pneumatic device P 347
  rubber tires, first use of T 196
  Wright brothers W 316

Bidault (be-DO), **Georges** (1899–   ), French statesman, b. Moulins, Allier. A leader in French underground during World War II, he was president of National Council of the Resistance (CNR) (1943–44). He was twice premier and several times foreign minister (between 1944 and 1954). He split with Charles de Gaulle over Algeria and lived in exile 1962–68.

Bidding, in game of bridge C 107

Biddle, Francis (1886–1968), American lawyer, jurist, and cabinet member, b. Paris, France. Private secretary to Supreme Court Justice Oliver Wendell Holmes (1911–12), he was also special assistant U.S. attorney (1922–26), U.S. Circuit Court of Appeals judge (1939–40), U.S. attorney general (1941–45), and U.S. representative to Nuremburg war-crimes trials (1945–46). He was appointed by President Truman to Permanent Court of

Arbitration at The Hague (1951). His writings include *Mr. Justice Holmes* and *The Fear of Freedom*.

Biddle, Nicholas, American financier **J** 7
Biddy basketball **B** 90
Bidpai (BID-pie), **Fables of** **F** 4, 6
Bidwell, John, American pioneer and rancher **O** 263–64
Biennials (by-EN-ni-als), plants **P** 303
  gardens and gardening **G** 29–30, 46
Bienville (bi-EN-vill), **Jean Baptiste Lemoyne, Sieur de,** French founder of New Orleans, Louisiana **L** 361, 362
Bierce, Ambrose, American writer and journalist **H** 280
Bifocal glasses **O** 166
Bifrost, bridge to Asgard, home of the Norse gods **N** 277
Big bang theory, of the universe **U** 204
Big Bear, constellation *see* Ursa Major
Big Ben, clock bell, London **L** 335; pictures **L** 338, **U** 70
  bells and carillons **B** 137
Big Bend National Park, Texas **T** 133
Big Bertha, giant German cannon **G** 425
Big Black River, Mississippi **M** 352
Big business, in United States **U** 130–31
Big Dipper, star group **C** 491, 492
  direction finder **D** 183
Big Dog, constellation *see* Canis Major
Big Ear, the National Radio Astronomy Observatory, West Virginia **W** 137; picture **R** 69
Bigelow (BIG-elow), **Erastus,** American inventor **R** 352
Bigelow Papers, The, by James Russell Lowell **L** 369

Big Four, term originally designating Great Britain, France, Italy, and United States, or their leaders at Paris Peace Conference (1919). Since World War II, Soviet Union has replaced Italy in their conferences.

Big-game hunting **H** 290–91
Big Hole National Battlefield, Montana **M** 438
Bighorn Mountains, Wyoming **W** 325
Bighorns, or Rocky Mountain sheep **S** 145; picture **H** 218
  hoofed mammals **H** 221
Big Muddy, Missouri River **M** 383
Big Sky Country, name given to Montana **M** 428
Big stick, foreign policy of Theodore Roosevelt **R** 329
Big Thompson River, Colorado **C** 405
Big top, circus tent **C** 302
Big Trees, sequoias **P** 316
  giants of nature **G** 200, 202–03
  Yosemite National Park **Y** 352
Big Wave, The, book by Pearl Buck, excerpt **B** 421–22
Bikila, Abebe, Ethiopian athlete **E** 299

Bikini, coral atoll in west central Pacific, Marshall Islands. The inhabitants were relocated because of U.S. nuclear testing (1946–58). Inhabitants were allowed to return (1968). Since 1947 the islands have been part of U.S. Trust Territory of the Pacific Islands.

Bilateral (by-LAT-er-al) **agreements,** between two nations **I** 323
Bilateral treaties **T** 270–71
Bile, secretion of the liver as aid to digestion **B** 275
Bilingual World, The, or Monde Bilingue, Le, French movement for joint use of French and English **U** 195
Billboards, used for outdoor advertising **A** 28–29
  Ogden Nash, poem against **H** 280
  See also Signs and billboards
Bill Haley and the Comets, American rock music group **R** 262c

Billiard balls **P** 324
Billiards **B** 174–76
Billings, Montana **M** 440
Billings, John Shaw, American surgeon and librarian **L** 188–89
Billings, Josh *see* Shaw, Henry Wheeler
Billings, William, American hymn composer **H** 313
  songs of the Revolutionary War **N** 23
Billingsgate, London **L** 339

Bill of lading, a contract between a shipper and a carrier in which carrier acknowledges receipt of goods to be shipped and promises to deliver them at a certain time.

Bill of Rights, American **B** 177–80
  civil rights, historical origins **C** 314
  freedom of religion, speech, and press **F** 457
  The Federalist, position of **F** 78
  jury, trial by **J** 159–60
  Madison, principal author **M** 8
  ten original amendments to the U.S. Constitution **U** 146, 155
  See also Civil liberties and civil rights; United States Constitution
Bill of Rights, Canadian **B** 180; **C** 78
Bill of Rights, English **B** 180
  civil rights, historical origins **C** 314
  England, 1689 **E** 224; **J** 159
  English Bill of Rights and taxation **T** 26
Bill of Rights, French
  French Declaration of the Rights of Man **B** 180; **C** 314
Bill of Rights, Universal
  Universal Declaration of Human Rights **B** 180; **C** 314
Bill of Rights Day **B** 180

Bill of sale, written agreement by which one person transfers his right to, or interest in, goods or personal property to another. Such a paper is signed when one individual buys a house from another.

Bills, suggested laws **U** 140–41
Billy goats **G** 244

Billy the Kid (William H. Bonney) (1859–1881), American outlaw, b. New York, N.Y. He worked for cattleman in Pecos Valley (1877) until employer's death at outbreak of Lincoln County cattle conflict (1878). The Kid became leader of a war faction in 1878. A notorious outlaw, he became heavily involved in cattle theft. Captured by sheriff Pat Garrett in 1880, he escaped but was later fatally shot by Garrett. He killed a total of 21 persons.

Biloxi (bil-OX-i), Mississippi **M** 360
  shrimp boats, picture **M** 357
Bimetallism (by-MET-al-lism), monetary system **M** 409
Bimini Islands, Bahamas **B** 17
  Ponce de León's search for Fountain of Youth **P** 391
Binary form, a basic design used in writing music **M** 535
Binary (BY-nary) **stars** **S** 409
  study of revolving stars **A** 475
Binary numeration system **N** 401
  automation **A** 530
  computers **C** 453, 456
Binchois, Gilles, Flemish composer **D** 363; **F** 443
  Renaissance music **R** 172
Binding knots **K** 290
Binding of books *see* Bookbinding
Bindweed **W** 104

Binet (bi-NAY), **Alfred** (1857–1911), French psychologist, b. Nice. He was director of the laboratory of physiologi-

Binet, Alfred (continued)
cal psychology at the Sorbonne in Paris and began
(1895) the journal *L'Année psychologique* ("Psychology
Yearbook"). Together with Theodore Simon he developed Binet-Simon test for measuring intelligence.
He is the author of *Introduction to Psychology*.
   tests and testing **T** 117

Bing, Rudolf (1902–), Austrian-English opera impre-
sario, b. Vienna, Austria. He became a naturalized
British subject in 1946. He has been associated with
several concert agencies and opera houses in Austria
and Germany (1922–33) and helped found Glyndebourne
Opera (1934) and Edinburgh International Festival of
Music and Drama (1947). He was general manager of the
New York Metropolitan Opera (1950–72).

Bingham, Hiram, American missionary in Hawaii **H** 70
Binoculars **O** 167
   prism binoculars **L** 147, 265; diagram **L** 264
Binocular (two-eyed) **vision** **P** 490–91
Bionominal, name of two terms to show genus and spe-
   cies **K** 252
Binomial (by-NO-mial) **theorem,** mathematical formula
   worked out by Newton **N** 206
Binturongs, mammals related to mongooses **G** 89, 91
Bío-Bío River, Chile **C** 254
Biocells, batteries **B** 99
   bacterial fermentation produces electricity **F** 91
Biochemistry, study of the composition of living things
   B 181–84; **C** 214
   advances in, as branch of biology **B** 195
   body chemistry **B** 289–97
   medical laboratory tests **M** 201, 209
   Pasteur, Louis **P** 95
   viruses **V** 361–70a
   See also Body chemistry; Genetics; Photosynthesis
Biodegradable materials
   problems for water supplies **W** 59
Biogenesis (by-o-GEN-e-sis), **Pasteur's theory of** **B** 194
Biogeography (by-o-ge-OG-raphy), study of geography of
   plants and animals **G** 107–08
   life, distribution of plant and animal **L** 233
Biographical (by-o-GRAPH-ic-al) **dictionaries** **R** 129–30
Biographical novel **B** 186
Biography (by-OG-raphy), author's account of a person's
   life **B** 185–86
   American literature **A** 196, 214–15
   Boswell's *Life of Samuel Johnson* **E** 258
   creative writing **W** 321
   library arrangement **L** 183
   list of books of, for children **C** 248a
   Pulitzer prizes **P** 526–27
Biological clocks **L** 247–50
Biologicals (by-o-LOJ-ic-als), drugs **D** 326–27
Biological warfare see Bacteriological warfare
Biology (by-OL-ogy) **B** 187–96
   biochemistry **B** 181–84
   genetics **G** 77–88
   life, rhythms and clocks **L** 243–50
   medicine, history of **M** 203–208c
   Mendel's experiments in genetics **M** 219
   science, advances in **S** 76
   science and society **S** 79
   taxonomy **T** 28–32
   See also Evolution
Bioluminescence (by-o-lu-min-ES-cence), light emitted by
   living organisms **B** 197–98
   centipedes and millipedes **C** 168
   natural sources of light **L** 288

Biome, in ecology, a major grouping of plants and animals as, for example, tundra. It is based chiefly on climate factors. The word comes from Greek words meaning "life" and "group."

Biometrics, or **biometry,** use of statistical methods in
biology. By testing only a small part, one can estimate
the results that one can obtain in testing the whole.

Biophysics **P** 238
Biopsy, examination of a living tissue **M** 209
Biosatellite, picture **S** 42

Biosphere, the entire realm of living organisms on earth,
as well as the air, soil, and water in which they live. The
biosphere does not include those parts of the earth that
are not inhabited by living things.

Biotic patterns, in geography **G** 99
Biotin, a B-complex vitamin **V** 370d
Biplanes, early types of airplanes **A** 572
Birch, tree
   a dicot, picture **P** 292
   shapes of leaves, picture **L** 116
   state tree of New Hampshire **N** 149
   uses of the wood and its grain, picture **W** 223
Birdbanding **B** 229
   migrating ducks, picture **H** 187
Bird Came Down the Walk, A, poem by Emily Dickinson,
   D 164
Bird Day see Arbor Day
Birdhouses **B** 248–49
   how to attract birds **B** 243
Birdie, golf score **G** 255
Bird in Space, sculpture by Brancusi, picture **F** 431
   Brancusi's style **B** 370

Bird of paradise, member of a family of birds in which
the males are brilliantly colored and decorated. The females are somewhat drab, but the males are among the
most beautiful of birds—most have long, silky feathers
that can be spread out like a fan over the bird's body.
The birds are found chiefly in the forests of Australia,
New Guinea, and neighboring islands.
   birds of the equatorial rain forests **B** 225

Birds **B** 199–249
   adaptations to other organisms **L** 221
   adaptive radiation **B** 209–10, 221
   aging process **A** 83
   animal communication **A** 276–77, 278–80
   animal problem-box tests **A** 284–85
   Audubon's paintings **A** 490–491
   banding **B** 229
   beaks, or bills **B** 221, 222, 223
   biological clocks and compasses **L** 249–50
   birdbaths **B** 243
   birdhouses, how to build **B** 248–49
   bird watching **B** 233–44
   caring for the young **B** 215–16
   carry diseases **I** 286
   courtship and mating **B** 212
   devices to attract birds **B** 243
   distribution by vegetation belts **B** 223, 224
   egg and embryo, diagram **E** 89
   eggs and incubation **B** 213–14
   evolution of **B** 206–10
   extinct and threatened species **B** 229–32
   feeders and food **B** 243
   feeding their young **B** 215–16
   feet **F** 83–84
   finches showing adaptations supporting Darwin's the-
      ory of natural selection, picture **E** 345

flash patterns of color **B** 237
flight patterns **B** 237
flyways of North America, map-diagram **B** 217
fossil **B** 206–07, 209–10
four-chambered heart **M** 72
giants of nature **G** 200, 204
habitats and haunts **B** 219–28, 237, 243
history and evolution of **B** 206–10
homing and migration **H** 186–88
identifying **B** 233, 237
largest **A** 263
life lists, records of bird watching **B** 244
locomotion **A** 294–96
migration **B** 211, 216–17; **H** 186–88
myths about **M** 559–60
nest building **B** 212–13
nest identification **B** 244
nests, where located **B** 220; pictures **B** 218
New Zealand birdlife **N** 239–40
of prey **B** 222
pets **B** 245–49; **P** 180–81
pollination of flowers **F** 279
poultry **P** 420–23
prehistoric animals, development of **P** 438
protection of birds **B** 232
protective coloration **B** 200, 225
provincial see Canadian province articles
refuges, pictures **B** 211, 230
songs and other sounds **B** 212, 237
state **U** 90–93; for pictures see state articles
"talking" birds **P** 83–86
territory songs **A** 278; picture **A** 279
through the year with birds **B** 211–17
wading birds **B** 223
warm-blooded **B** 259
web-footed **B** 223
where birds live **B** 218–28, 238
Birds, fossil **B** 206–07, 209–10
Birds as pets **B** 245–49; **P** 180–81
Birdseye, Clarence, American inventor **I** 346–47
food preservation and processing **F** 346
Bird's Eye View of the Mandan Village, A, painting by
Catlin **U** 119
Birds fly, line game **G** 23
Bird snakes **S** 207
Bird's-nest fungi **F** 500
Birds of prey **B** 222
eagles **E** 2
Birdsongs **B** 212, 237
Bird watching **B** 233–44
Bird Woman see Sacajawea
Biremes (BY-remes), ships **T** 261
Birmingham, Alabama **A** 112–13, 122, 124
Birmingham, England **U** 71
Birney (BER-ni), **Alice McLellan,** American educator
P 67
Birney, James G., American abolitionist **N** 94; **P** 385
Birr Castle, Ireland, gardens, picture **G** 32
Birth control see Family planning
Birthday cards, how to make **G** 374
Birthday parties **P** 87–89
Birthdays, of famous people
arranged by the month see articles on individual
months
holidays honoring **H** 147–50
Birthday stones see Birthstones
Birth defects
causes of mental retardation **R** 190–91
Birthmark, The, story by Nathaniel Hawthorne **S** 166
Birth of a Nation, The, motion picture **M** 472
Birth of Venus, painting by Botticelli **I** 466
Birthrate, number of births per thousand persons **P** 394

Birthstones **G** 72
See also names of stones and articles on individual
months
Biscuits, manufacture and packaging of **B** 389
Bishop, Barry C., American scientist **E** 337

Bishop, Billy (William Avery Bishop) (1894–1956), Canadian aviator, b. Owen Sound, Ontario. He is credited with
shooting down 72 enemy aircraft during World War I and
was awarded many medals, including Victoria Cross
(1917), Britain's highest award for bravery. As member
of British Air Ministry, he established separate Canadian
Air Force (1918). He was co-founder of one of the first
commercial aviation companies in Canada. He was honorary air vice-marshal and director of air force recruiting.
Canadian Air Force, history of **C** 82

Bishop, Charles Reed, American banker in Hawaii **H** 70

Bishop, Claire Huchet (?–   ), American author, b.
Brittany, France. She headed first French public library
for children (1924), L'Heure Joyeuse, begun by Americans in Paris. Her books for children include *Pancakes-
Paris, Augustus,* and *The Five Chinese Brothers.*

Bishops, of the church **C** 281
cathedral, principal church of a bishopric **C** 131
conflicts between bishops of east and west led to
break in the church **R** 289
Bishops' schools, or Cathedral schools **M** 295
Bishop's University, Lennoxville, Quebec **Q** 10b
Bismarck, capital of North Dakota **N** 334
Bismarck, Otto von, the "Iron Chancellor", German
statesman **B** 250; pictures **B** 250, **P** 456a
Germany, history of **G** 161
Bismarck Archipelago, Pacific Islands **P** 5
Bismarck Sea **O** 46
Bismuth, element **E** 154, 160
metals, chart of ores, properties, uses **M** 227
Bison (BY-son) hoofed mammals **B** 250a; pictures
B 250a, **H** 216
Bison Area Indians of North America **I** 164–69
National Bison Range, Montana **M** 439
Old Bison Hunters, Indians of North America **I** 163
slaughter in Kansas **K** 176
Wood Buffalo National Park, Alberta, Canada **C** 57
Bisque (BISK), unglazed china
dolls made of **D** 265
Bissell, George, American lawyer **P** 177
Bisymmetrical (by-sim-MET-ric-al) **balance,** in design
D 133
Bitonality, in music **M** 400–01
Bitter, a sense of taste **B** 286

Bittern, small to medium-size bird of the heron family.
Bitterns live in swamps and marshy ponds, where their
yellowish-brown coloring blends with the reeds and
grasses. They have long legs, long necks, and long,
sharp bills with which they spear fish. When alarmed,
bitterns remain motionless, their bills pointing upward.
The American bittern is known for its croaking call.
nest, picture **B** 244

Bitterroot, flower
state flower of Montana **M** 428

Bittersweet, vine or shrub that grows in most of North
America. Up to 30 ft. long, it bears clusters of small
green flowers. Its yellow fruit shows red seeds. "Bittersweet" is also a popular name for nightshade, a woody
climbing shrub with purple flowers and poisonous red
berries, found in North America, Europe, and Asia.

Bituminous (bit-TU-min-ous) **coal,** soft coal **C** 362, 363
fuels **F** 487
Bivalves, mollusks with two shells **O** 271–74; **S** 148
Bizerte (bi-ZERT), Tunisia **T** 310

Bizet (bi-ZAY), **Georges** (Alexandre César Léopold Bizet) (1838–1875), French composer, b. Paris. He is best known for opera *Carmen.* Bizet greatly influenced French dramatic music. Besides *Carmen,* his operas include *The Pearl-Fishers* and *The Fair Maid of Perth.* He also wrote incidental music for the play *L'Arlesienne,* the suite *Children's Games,* and a symphony in C.
Carmen, opera **O** 142
French music of the 19th century **F** 446

Bjerknes (BYURK-nes), **Jakob Aall Bonnevie** (1897–   ), Norwegian-American meteorologist, b. Stockholm, Sweden. His applications of theories of his father, Vilhelm Bjerknes, are now used in weather forecasting. He has proposed the theory that cyclonic storms are created when cold polar air moves in under warm air masses. He won the National Medal of Science in 1966.

Bjørnson (BYERN-son), **Bjørnstjerne,** Norwegian author **S** 51
Blab schools
Lincoln's schooling **L** 292
Black, color **D** 139
funeral custom **F** 494

Black, Hugo La Fayette (1886–1971), American jurist, b. Harlan, Ala. Black received his law degree from the University of Alabama (1906). During World War I he served as an artillery officer. He practiced law in Birmingham and was active in local Democratic politics. In 1926, and again in 1932, he was elected U.S. Senator. He was a strong supporter of President Franklin D. Roosevelt's New Deal policies, and in 1937 Roosevelt appointed him to fill a vacancy as Associate Justice of the U.S. Supreme Court. Black was a strong advocate of individual liberties and civil rights. He retired in 1971.

Black, Joseph, Scottish scientist **M** 23; **S** 70–71, 72

Black, Shirley Temple (Mrs. Charles Black) (1928–   ), American movie star and political figure, b. Santa Monica, Cal. Her movie career began when she was 3½, and she starred in such films as *The Littlest Rebel* and *Rebecca of Sunnybrook Farm.* She entered politics in California, running unsuccessfully for Congress (1967). She was a member of U.S. delegation to United Nations in 1969. Picture **M** 475.

Black Americans **N** 89–105
Abolitionist movement **N** 94–95
civil rights movements **C** 316
Civil War, United States **C** 318, 320–21, 327–28
Confederate States **C** 458, 459
Dred Scott Decision **D** 310–11
Emancipation Proclamation **E** 185–86; **N** 95
Hall of Fame for baseball **B** 81
literature **A** 213; **N** 101
Negro hymns and spirituals **H** 313; **N** 105–07
Reconstruction Period **R** 117–20
rock music **R** 262a, 262b, 262d
segregation **S** 113–15
slavery **S** 197–20
Uncle Tom's Cabin by Harriet Beecher Stowe **S** 436
Underground Railroad **U** 11–12
United States · **U** 132–33
United States Constitution, Amendments **U** 155–58
Black Angus cattle, picture **C** 149

Blackball, to vote against **B** 21

Blackbeard (Edward Teach, or Thatch) (?–1718), British pirate. He was privateer for British in West Indies during War of Spanish Succession (1701–13) and then turned to piracy, plundering coasts of North Carolina and Virginia (1713–18). He is believed to have been under protection of corrupt governor of North Carolina. He was killed during attack by ships sent out by planters and governor of Virginia.
piracy and buried treasure off the Outer Banks of North Carolina **N** 308; **P** 264

Black bears **B** 106; picture **B** 107
Black Belt, or Black Prairie, landform in southern United States
Alabama **A** 115
Mississippi **M** 352
Blackberries **G** 298, 301

Blackbirds, any of several varieties of birds mostly black in color and feeding mainly on seeds, grains, and insects. North American blackbirds belong to a family that includes the orioles, cowbirds, and grackles. Perhaps best known is the red-winged blackbird. Males are black with a flash of red at the upper part of each wing. Females are brownish and lack shoulder markings. The European blackbird, found in Europe and Asia, belongs to the thrush family and is not related to the North American. The male is black with an orange bill; the female brownish with a dark bill. Pictures **B** 216, 240.

Black cats **S** 475
Black Codes, laws passed by Southern states just after Civil War **R** 117
Johnson, Andrew **J** 125
Negro history **N** 95
Black death see Bubonic plague
Blackett, Patrick M. S., English physicist **G** 121
Black-eyed Susans, flowers, picture **W** 170
Maryland, state flower of **M** 115
Black-figure pottery, ancient Greece **P** 414
Blackfoot, Indians of North America **I** 166; picture **I** 167
Black Forest, Germany **G** 153; picture **G** 105
Blackfriars, London theater **S** 132
Black Hawk, Indian chief **I** 84

Black Hawk War, war between United States and faction of Fox and Sauk (Sac) Indians led by Chief Black Hawk. War was caused by Black Hawk's refusal to recognize cession of 50,000,000 acres of land in Illinois, Wisconsin, and Missouri to U.S. Government by representative of the two tribes in 1804. When squatters laid claim to Black Hawk's village near Rock Island, Ill. (1831), Black Hawk began the war, which ended with his defeat (1832) at Bad Axe River in Wisconsin.
Indian wars against westward expansion of settlement **I** 213; **W** 207

Blackheads **D** 190
Black Hills, South Dakota, Wyoming **S** 312, 315; **W** 323; picture **S** 319
Black Hills National Forest, South Dakota, picture **N** 35

Black Hole of Calcutta, dungeon in Fort William, 18th-century British fort in Calcutta, India. When the fort was taken by the Nawab (governor) of Bengal (1756), 146 British were imprisoned in the poorly ventilated dungeon, 18 feet by 15 feet. All but 23 of the prisoners suffocated.

Blackjack oak, tree
leaves, shapes of, picture **L** 116

Black Kettle (1803?–1868), Cheyenne Indian chief, b. in what is now S. Dak. He offered peace and friendship to U.S. troops in Colorado but was refused. He obeyed orders to move his village to Sand Creek but was betrayed and attacked by militia (1864). In spite of treaty and reparations made to the Indians, their new village in Washita Valley was attacked by General Custer's troops, and Black Kettle was killed.

Black lady, card game **C** 112
Black letter, typeface design **T** 345

Black market, illegal market where goods are bought and sold in violation of government regulations. Black markets may develop where and when commodities are scarce and people are willing to pay higher prices. Term may also apply to trading of currency.

Blackmun, Harry Andrew (1908–   ), American jurist b. Nashville, Ill. Graduated from Harvard Law School, he was in private practice in Minneapolis (1934–50), and was resident counsel at Mayo Clinic (1950–59). He was appointed to U.S. Court of Appeals by President Eisenhower (1959). Blackmun was unanimously confirmed by the Senate as 99th Justice of the U.S. Supreme Court (1970) following its refusal to confirm two Southern nominees.

Black Muslims (Nation of Islam) **N** 104a–104b
   somè national Negro organizations **N** 98
   See also Elijah Muhammad

Blackout, covering or putting out of all lights to hide an area or object as protective measure against air attack. Blackouts were used especially as defense against Nazi air attacks during World War II. Unplanned blackouts sometimes occur due to electrical power failures.

Black Panthers (Black Panther Party) **N** 105
   some national Negro organizations **N** 98
Black Peter, servant of Sinter Klaas, picture **C** 293
Black powder, or gunpowder, explosive **E** 389–90, 391
   guns and ammunition **G** 414

Black Power, slogan, first popularized in 1966, that has come to represent a political and economic movement on the part of Negroes to become independent of the white community. It expresses also the desire of many Negroes to relate to their African background and to be known as Blacks. Many define the term as the power of Black peoples to control their own destiny. Some militants see Black Power as a dream of a separate state. The term was used by Stokely Carmichael in a call for removal of whites from leadership and policy-making positions in civil rights organizations. By 1968 Black Power in its non-separatist sense had been accepted by less militant leaders, such as Whitney Young of the Urban League.
   continuing struggle in Negro history **N** 104b

Black racer, snake, picture **S** 205
Black Renaissance (ren-nais-SONCE) **N** 98
Blacks **N** 89–105
   See also Black Americans; Negroes; names of African countries, Negro leaders and organizations
Black Sea **O** 46

Black September Organization, a Palestinian guerrilla group that takes its name from the month in 1970 when the government of Jordan opened its campaign to crush Arab terrorist groups. The organization, which deals in occasional random terrorism directed against the State

of Israel, was responsible for the murder of eleven Israeli athletes at the 1972 Olympic Games in Munich, Germany.

Blackshirts, fascist parties
   British **F** 64
   Italian fascists and Mussolini **F** 63; **M** 552
Black snake, picture **S** 205
Black Stone of Mecca see Kaaba
Blackstrap molasses **S** 453
Black Tea **T** 38
Blacktop, asphalt for roads **R** 252
Black walnuts **N** 423
Black Warrior River, Alabama **A** 115, 120
Blackwater River, Ireland **I** 388

Blackwell, Elizabeth (1821–1910), first woman physician in United States, b. Bristol, England. She went to United States in 1832. After graduating from medical school, she found that because she was a woman, no hospital would permit her to practice, so she opened New York Infirmary for Indigent Women and Children (1854), and first women's medical college (1868). She helped found London School of Medicine for Women (1869).

Black widow spiders **I** 284; **S** 388; pictures **I** 282, **S** 387
Bladder **B** 278
Blades, of airplane propellers **A** 558
Blades, of broad leaves **L** 114
Blade tools, prehistoric man **P** 444
Blaeu (BLA-u), **William,** Dutch geographer **M** 94
Blaiberg, Philip see Barnard, Christiaan
Blaine, James Gillespie, American statesman **M** 45
   Garfield and Blaine **G** 55
Blair, Eric see Orwell, George

Blair House, historic mansion in Washington, D.C. Built in 1824 by Joseph Lovell, first surgeon general of the U.S. Army, and bought in 1836 by Francis Preston Blair, Sr., a member of Andrew Jackson's "kitchen cabinet," it has been owned by the U.S. Government since 1942 and is used to house distinguished guests. It is joined to Lee Mansion and sometimes called Blair-Lee House.

Blake, Nicholas see Lewis, Cecil Day
Blake, William, English poet and artist **B** 250b
   children's literature **C** 237
   English literature **E** 259
   God Creates the World, drawing **E** 259
   illustration of books **I** 90
   water-color painting **E** 240
Blanc (BLON), **Mont,** France **A** 174; pictures **A** 175, **F** 409, **G** 94
   first successful ascent **M** 489
   Mer de Glace, glacier, picture **G** 224

Blanchard, Doc (Felix Anthony Blanchard) (1924–), American football star, b. McColl, S.C. He was an outstanding fullback for U.S. Military Academy (1944–46) and winner of over 20 national football awards.

Blanchard (blon-SHAR), **Jean-Pierre François** (1753–1809), French balloonist, b. Les Andelys. He made his first balloon ascent in 1784. With American physician Dr. John Jeffries, he piloted first air trip across English Channel (1785). Blanchard made numerous first ascents in Europe and United States (1785–96).
   balloon and parachute experiments **B** 31; **P** 59–60

Bland, James Allen (1854–1911), American self-trained songwriter and minstrel performer, b. Flushing, N.Y. He

Bland, James Allen (continued)
wrote Virginia's official state song, "Carry Me Back to Old Virginia," in addition to "Oh Dem Golden Slippers," "In the Evening by the Moonlight," and "Climbing up the Golden Stairs."

Bland Bill, 1877 **H** 81
Blankets, electric **E** 118
Blanket stitch, in embroidery **E** 188
Blank verse, unrhymed verse **P** 353
  selected quotations from Shakespeare's plays
    S 133–37
Blantyre, Malawi **M** 51

Blarney stone, an inscribed stone supposed to impart gift of words, especially of flattery, persuasion, or deception, to any one who kisses it. It is located in 15th-century Blarney Castle in County Cork, Ireland, where tourists or pilgrims lean over backward to reach it.

Blasco-Ibáñez (BLAS-co-e-BON-yeth), **Vicente,** Spanish author **S** 371
Blast furnaces **I** 397; pictures **M** 319
  refining of metals **M** 228
Blasting, in mining, pictures **M** 315–16, 434
  quarrying method **Q** 5
Blasting caps **E** 392; picture **E** 391
Blasting gelatin, picture **E** 390
Blaze, horse marking, picture **H** 238
Blazoning, describing arms in heraldry **H** 117–18;
  pictures **H** 115
Bleaching
  beauty culture of the hair **B** 111
  chlorine **I** 349
  furniture **F** 504
  of fats and oils **O** 77
  paper making **P** 52
Bledsoe, Jules, American singer **N** 107
Bleeding
  first aid **F** 157–58
Bleeding Kansas **K** 191, 192
Blegen (BLAIG-en), **Carl W.,** American archeologist **T** 293
Blenheim (BLEN-im), **battle of,** 1704 **B** 101
Blenheim Palace, Oxfordshire, England, picture **U** 69
Blennerhassett Island, West Virginia **W** 136

Blennies (name means "slimy"), large group of small, slender, slimy fish with few or no scales. This group includes rock eel, Molly Miller, and rock skipper. Most live in shallow waters of Atlantic and Pacific, but some live in deep waters of these oceans and in Arctic Ocean.

Blessings, prayers **P** 434–35
Blériot (blay-ri-O), **Louis,** French engineer **A** 572
Blessed Virgin Mary see Mary, Virgin

Bligh (BLY), **William** (1754–1817), English naval officer, b. Tynten, Cornwall. Captain of the ship *Bounty,* he was set adrift in an open boat with 18 of his men by a mutinous crew and finally reached the East Indies after a 4,000-mile voyage (1789). (*Mutiny on the Bounty,* by James Norman Hall and Charles B. Nordhoff, is based on this incident.) He later became governor of New South Wales, Australia (1805–08), where his soldiers mutinied and imprisoned him (1808–10). He returned to England in 1810 and was made a vice-admiral (1814).
  breadfruit introduced to Jamaica **J** 18

Blight, general name for many plant diseases and symptoms such as spots, wilting, and death of plant or its parts, when these are caused by fungi or bacteria.

Blind **B** 251–54
  Keller, Helen **K** 201
  library service **L** 172
  public assistance **W** 120
Blindfish **C** 157; picture **C** 158
Blind Man's Buff, painting by Goya **G** 279
Blind Men and the Elephant, The, fable by John Godfrey Saxe **F** 7
Blindness **B** 251–52
  electric eels injure their own eyes **E** 86–87
  night blindness **V** 370b
Blindness of Tobit, The, etching by Rembrandt **G** 304
Blind salamanders **C** 157; picture **C** 158
Blind snakes **S** 207
Bliss, Mary Elizabeth ("Betty") Taylor, acting first lady in Taylor's administration **F** 170; picture **F** 171
Blitz, bombing of England, 1940 **W** 290
  London raids **L** 340

Blitzkrieg (BLITZ-kreeg) (German for "lightning war"), sudden military attack launched by combined air and ground forces with overwhelming speed and force, designed to cause an enemy's rapid surrender. It was first used by Germans during invasion of Poland (1939).

Blixen, Baroness Karen see Dinesen, Isak

Bloch (BLOCK), **Ernest** (1880–1959), American composer, b. Geneva, Switzerland. He went to United States (1916) and became citizen (1926). He was director of Cleveland Institute of Music (1920–25) and San Francisco Conservatory (1925–30). Much of his music, such as *Trois Poèmes Juifs, Schelomo,* and *Suite hebraique,* was the result of his Jewish heritage. He also wrote an opera, *Macbeth,* and a rhapsody, *America.*

Block, Adriaen, Dutch explorer of North America. He made voyages up Hudson River (1610 and 1614); navigated Long Island Sound, Connecticut River, and Buzzards' and Nahant bays in Massachusetts; and discovered Block Island, R.I., which bears his name. He provided valuable information for first detailed map (1616) of southern New England coast.

Block, Conrad (Konrad Bloch) (1912–), American biochemist, b. Neisse, Germany. Higgins professor of biochemistry at Harvard University (since 1954), he won Nobel prize in physiology and medicine (1964) for studies that showed how cholesterol is made and used.

Blockade, blocking of a coastline or harbor by enemy warships, or of a frontier by enemy troops, to prevent anyone or anything from entering or leaving. A blockade is an act of war intended to isolate an enemy by cutting off his means of trade, supplies, and communications.

Blockhouses, forts **F** 377
Block Island, Rhode Island **R** 220
Block mountains **M** 496
Block printing
  Chinese, ancient **C** 433; picture **C** 432
  history of printing **P** 457
  woodcut printing **W** 228–29
Block-signal system, of railroads **R** 85
Bloemfontein (BLOOM-fon-tain), judicial capital of South Africa **S** 271
Blois (BLWA), France
  château, Renaissance style **F** 421; picture **F** 422
Blood **B** 255–59
  anemia **D** 192–93
  blood counts in blood tests **B** 257; **M** 201, 209
  blood derivatives, medical techniques with **M** 211

cells, picture **C** 160
circulation, studies of **B** 188, 189; **M** 205–06
circulatory system of human body **B** 275–77
genes determine types **G** 87
Harvey's contribution to studies of circulation
H 52
heart **H** 86–86c
hemophilia **D** 188
insect's blood system **I** 271
stain removal **L** 84
transfusion **T** 251
vitamin K aids clotting **V** 371
warm- and cold-blooded animals **B** 259
Blood, diseases of
anemia **D** 192–93
leukemia **D** 200
Blood, Sweat and Tears, American rock music group
R 262d
Blood banks M 201, 211
blood transfusions **T** 251
Blood counts B 257; **M** 201, 209
Blood groups or blood types **B** 257–58
reactions to blood transfusions **T** 251
study of races of man **R** 29
Bloodhound, tracking dog **D** 262
Blood pressure M 208f–208g
high blood pressure **D** 198–99
smoking, effects of **S** 203
Blood tests B 257; **M** 201, 209
Blood transfusion T 251
blood groups **B** 258
medicine, techniques of **M** 210–11
Blood vessels B 275–76
heart, function of **H** 86–86c
Bloodworms W 310
Bloody Mary see Mary I, queen of England

Bloomer, Amelia Jenks (1818–1894), American reformer,
b. Homer, N.Y. She wrote and lectured on temperance
and women's rights and popularized new style in
women's dress designed by Elizabeth Smith Miller. Consisting of a short-skirted dress over trousers, it became
known as bloomer costume, and pants as bloomers.
bicycle changed women's fashions **B** 173

Blooms, rapid growth of algae **P** 279–80

Blount, Winton Malcolm (1921–   ), American businessman and administrator, b. Union Springs, Ala. He was
founder and president of a large construction firm,
and served as president of U.S. Chamber of Commerce.
He was postmaster general (1969–71).

Blow, Henry Taylor (1817–1875), American businessman
and politician, b. South Hampton Co., Va. He played an
important role in industrial development of St. Louis, Mo.
A strong opponent of spread of slavery, he joined the Free-
Soil Party, and helped establish the state Republican Party.
He served in U.S. House of Representatives (1863–67).
Dred Scott case **D** 310

Blow, Susan, American educator **K** 244
Blowflies, picture **I** 282
Blowfish see Puffer
Blowguns G 424; pictures **A** 301
Blowouts, or gushers, oil wells **P** 172–73
Blowpipes, glassmaking **G** 226, 230; picture **G** 231
bottle making **B** 341
Blowtorch, oxacetylene **G** 60–61
Blubber, fatty tissue **W** 151
Eskimo food **E** 290
extracting whale oil **W** 153

Blue babies, children born with defective hearts
H 86b
Blue-Backed Speller, by Noah Webster **P** 193–94
early textbooks **T** 138
spelling words from **S** 379
Blueberries G 301; picture **G** 299
Bluebirds B 220; picture **B** 239
Idaho, mountain bluebird state bird of **I** 54
Missouri, state bird of **M** 367
Nevada, mountain bluebird state bird of **N** 123
New York, state bird of **N** 210
Bluebirds, Camp Fire Girls **C** 37; pictures **C** 38, 39
Bluebonnet, state flower of Texas **T** 123
Bluebottle flies, pictures **I** 276
Blue Boy, The, painting by Thomas Gainsborough **G** 4
Blue cheese D 13
Blue-collar workers L 8
Bluefin, fish
habitat, feeding habits, uses **F** 215
Bluefish F 188
Bluegill, fish, picture **F** 209
Bluegrass Basin, of Kentucky **K** 215
Bluegrass State, nickname for Kentucky **K** 212
Blue Grotto, Capri, Italy **C** 156; **I** 428
Blueground, or kimberlite, diamond-bearing rock **G** 70
Blue hen chicken
state bird of Delaware **D** 87
Blue Hen State, nickname for Delaware **D** 86, 87
Blue jays, birds, pictures **B** 245, 247

Blue laws, legislation that seeks to regulate matters of
individual conscience or conduct, such as laws prohibiting drinking or Sunday labor. The term originated during
colonial days in New Haven, Conn., where such laws
were bound in blue paper.

Blue Nile River, Africa **N** 260; **E** 299
Blue ox, Babe, belonging to Paul Bunyan **F** 312
Blue Plate, Legend of the L 133

Blueprint, photographic print on bright-blue background,
made by process invented (1842) by Sir John Herschel.
Process is used mainly for copying architects' plans and
mechanical drawings. The name has come to be used for
any plan or design.
airplane models, top secret **A** 105–06
plumbing systems **P** 343

Blue Riband, award for Atlantic crossing **O** 17
Blue Rider, The, modern art group in Germany **M** 391
German art **G** 171
Kandisky, Wassily **K** 166
Klee, Paul **K** 271
Blue Ridge mountain range, eastern United states
G 135
Maryland **M** 116
North Carolina **N** 309
South Carolina **S** 298
Tennessee **T** 76
Virginia **V** 346; picture **V** 355
Blue Ridge National Parkway N 315–16; picture **N** 308
Blues, the, music **J** 57–58
folk songs **F** 304
gospel song **N** 106
Handy, W. C., father of the blues **H** 34
Negro folklore **F** 313
Blue spruce, tree
Colorado, state tree of **C** 401
Utah, state tree of **U** 241

Bluestocking, term used to mock literary or pedantic
woman, often implying that she has only affected or

Bluestocking (continued)
superficial interest in intellectual matters. Term derived from women's literary discussion group in 18th-century London, called Bluestocking Club because of informal blue stockings worn by a guest.

Blue whales **W** 149
  giants of nature **G** 202
  largest mammal **M** 61
  ocean life **O** 40–41
Blum (BLOOM), **Léon**, French statesman **F** 419
Blunderbuss, smooth-bore gun **G** 420
Blunger (BLUN-ger), a clay-mixing machine, used in ceramics **C** 174
Blurb, form of advertising on book jacket **B** 317

Bly, Nellie (Elizabeth Cochrane Seaman) (1867–1922), American journalist, b. Cochran Mills, Pa. She wrote for Pittsburgh *Dispatch*, New York *World*, and New York *Journal*. She pretended insanity to get into mental ward at Blackwell's Island, New York, in order to write about conditions there. She made round-the-world trip (1889) to beat fictional record in Jules Verne's *Around the World in 80 Days*. Traveling by ship, train, and horse, she completed trip in 72 days, 6 hours, 11 minutes, then a record time. She wrote *10 Days in a Madhouse*, *Around the World in 72 days*, and *Nellie Bly's Book*.

Blytheville, Arkansas **A** 430
BMEWS (Ballistic Missile Early Warning System) **U** 161

B'nai B'rith, Independent Order of (from Hebrew, meaning "sons of the covenant"), Jewish fraternal organization founded in 1843 to promote charity and brotherly love by uniting Jews in cultural, social, civic, and philanthropic activities. There are over 2,500 lodges in 33 countries, whose activities include Hillel chapters on college campuses, the B'nai B'rith Youth Organization, Anti-Defamation League, UN Liaison Office, and vocational and armed services programs. The organization publishes the *National Jewish Monthly* and *Jewish Heritage*.

B'nai B'rith Youth Organization (BBYO), international Jewish youth organization, founded (1924) to give Jewish youth an understanding of their religious heritage through cultural, religious, social, and athletic programs. It has headquarters in Washington, D.C.

Bo, Sierra Leone **S** 175

Board of trade, organization for development and protection of business interests. Term also refers to organization of merchants and manufacturers of a city, working to promote civic enterprises of a community.

Boars, male pigs **H** 209; **P** 248
  wild boar, picture **H** 212
Boar's Head, The, English carol **C** 122
Boas, snakes **S** 206; picture **S** 212
Boat racing **B** 264
  rowing competition **R** 338–39
Boats and boating **B** 260–64
  ancient water craft **S** 155
  balsas, pictures **A** 252, **L** 50
  Bangladesh **B** 44; picture **B** 44b
  canal boats **E** 278–80
  canoes and canoeing **C** 99–101
  catamaran, picture **T** 262
  Chinese dwellings **C** 263
  early transportation **T** 257
  felucca, on the Nile, pictures **N** 260, **R** 240

  gondolas on the canals, Venice, pictures **B** 55, **H** 179, **I** 456
  houseboats **H** 176–77
  hydrofoils **H** 304–05
  iceboating **I** 28–29
  inventions in water transportation **I** 337
  johnboats for float fishing **M** 366
  junks, picture **R** 249
  kayaks **C** 99; **E** 289; picture **G** 370
  Mississippi riverboats, pictures **I** 358, **M** 352
  murkab on the Nile, picture **S** 449
  rowing **R** 338–39
  safety measures **S** 6
  sailboats, types of, pictures **S** 9
  sailing **S** 9–15
  sightseeing on Lake Xochimilco, picture **L** 30
  weather warning flags **F** 246
  Why do boats float? **F** 251
  See also Canoes and canoeing; Rowing; Sailing; Water sports
Bobber, for pole and line fishing **F** 205
Bobbies, English policemen **P** 373; picture **P** 372
  London **L** 338
Bobbin, spool for holding thread **I** 234
  cotton yarn on spools **C** 525
Bobbin lace **L** 19
Bobcats **C** 139; picture **C** 140
Bobko, Karol J., American astronaut **S** 347
Bobo Dioulasso (BO-bo diu-LA-so), Upper Volta **U** 228
Bobolinks, birds **B** 220; picture **B** 233
Bobsledding **B** 264–66
  Olympic event **O** 109
Bobwhites, or quail, birds **B** 220; picture **B** 233
  See also Quail
Bocachee see Tomochichi
Boccaccio (bo-CA-chi-o), **Giovanni**, Italian writer **I** 476–77
  short stories **S** 165
Boccherini (bo-car-E-ni), **Luigi**, Italian composer **C** 186; **I** 485
Boccioni (bo-CHO-ni), **Umberto**, Italian painter **I** 473
  modern art **M** 391
  space shapes in sculpture **S** 105
Bock beer **B** 117
Böcklin (BUK-lene), **Arnold**, Swiss artist **G** 171
Bode (BO-da), **Johannes**, German astronomer **S** 242–43
Bode's law **S** 242
Bodhisattvas (bo-dis-AT-vas), Buddhist deities **B** 424
Bodleian (bod-LE-ian) **Library**, Oxford University **L** 197
Bodmer, Johann, Swiss professor **G** 175
Bodoni (bo-DO-ni), **Giambattista**, Italian printer **T** 345
Body, human **B** 267–83
  adolescence, changes during **A** 22
  aging **A** 81
  air pollution, effect on **A** 108–09, 110
  anthropological studies **A** 306–07
  antibodies and antigens **A** 317
  blood **B** 255–59
  body's senses **B** 283–88
  brain **B** 363–69
  cancer and cancer research **C** 89–95
  cells **C** 159–64
  chemistry see Body chemistry
  control of parasite diseases **D** 188
  dreaming, effects of **D** 306
  drugs affect **D** 326–27
  energy, source of **E** 201
  feet and hands, basic pattern of **F** 79–80, 83
  G-forces and weightlessness **S** 340j–340 L
  hair **H** 2–3
  health **H** 82–85
  heart **H** 86–86c
  immunology **I** 104–07

mental health **M** 220–22
osmosis **O** 234–35
physical examination by a doctor **M** 208e–208h
senses, guards on the alert **B** 280–82, 283–88
smoking, effects of **S** 203
teeth **T** 47–49
voice apparatus **V** 375
water percentage in **W** 51
Body chemistry **B** 289–97
biochemistry **B** 183–84
body catalysts **C** 199
cancer research **C** 94–95
drugs supply hormones **D** 326
food chain processes **L** 239–40
living matter, chemical makeup of **L** 211–12
viruses, chemical makeup of **V** 363
Body-drop, automobile assembling **A** 550
Body lice **I** 283–84
Body's senses **B** 283–88
guards on the alert **B** 280–82
nervous system, biological studies of **B** 195
Body temperature **B** 279
anesthesia produced by lowering **A** 259
hibernation **H** 122–24
how a nurse takes temperature **N** 414
medical examination, techniques of **M** 208e
sleep lowers **S** 200
studies of Alakaluf Indians **A** 306–07
Boerhaave (BOOR-ha-va), **Hermann,** Dutch doctor **M** 206
Boers, Dutch settlers in South Africa **S** 273
Africa, history of **A** 68
Boer War **B** 298
Boer War, 1899–1902 **B** 298–99
Africa, struggle for **A** 68
in English history **E** 228
in history of South Africa **S** 273

Bogart, Humphrey DeForest (1899–1957), American actor, b. New York, N.Y. His portrayals of hardened and cynical characters, starting with stage and screen versions of *The Petrified Forest* (1935–36), made him one of Hollywood's greatest box-office attractions. Appearing in over 50 motion pictures, he won the 1951 Academy Award for best actor for his performance in *The African Queen*.

Bogalusa, Louisiana **L** 361
Bogey (BOAG-y), golf score **G** 255
Bog iron **I** 406
New Jersey's Pine Barrens **N** 171
Bogotá (bo-go-TA), capital of Colombia **C** 383; pictures **C** 379, 383
University of the Andes, picture **S** 285
Bogs
cranberry bog, picture **G** 300
Okefenokee Swamp, Georgia **G** 132; picture **G** 143
Bohème (bo-EM), **La,** opera by Giacomo Puccini **O** 140

Bohemia (bo-HE-mia), territory of Czechoslovakia bounded by the countries of Austria, Germany, and Poland and the regions of Moravia and Silesia. Rich in mineral, agricultural, and industrial resources, it is especially famous for its hops and glass and ceramics industry. Principal cities are Prague and Pilsen, and noted resorts include Carlsbad and Marienbad. Attaining the height of its political power during the Luxemburg dynasty (1310–1437), it became part of Austrian Empire (1526–1918). Incorporated as a province of Czechoslovakia (1918), it now is linked with Moravia and Silesia to form a state (since 1949). Picture **C** 563.

Böhl de Faber (BURL dav FA-ber), **Cecilia,** Spanish writer **S** 370

Bohr, Niels, Danish atomic physicist **B** 300; **C** 216; picture **C** 215
contributions to physics **P** 232
Boiardo (bo-YAR-do), **Matteo Maria,** Italian poet **I** 477
Boileau-Despréaux (bwa-LO-day-pray-O), **Nicholas,** French poet **F** 438
Boilers
heating systems **H** 98–99
steam engines **S** 421
Boiling point **H** 92–93
liquids, properties of **L** 310
water **W** 54
why a geyser plays **G** 193
Boise (BOI-se), capital of Idaho **I** 65–66
Boise National Forest, Idaho **I** 64
Boise River, Idaho **I** 57; picture **I** 58
Bok, Edward, Netherlands-born American writer **A** 215
Bokassa, Jean, Central African Republic leader **C** 170
Bok Singing Tower, Florida **F** 269
Bolas, hunting devices **I** 211
Bolas spiders **S** 386
Boleyn (BULL-in), **Anne,** 2nd queen of Henry VIII of England **E** 220; **H** 109
Reformation in England **C** 286
Bolívar (bo-LI-var), **Simón,** South American liberator and patriot **B** 301, 306
Colombian independence leader **C** 384
flags **F** 227
present Organization of American States outgrowth of his ideal **O** 210
San Martín, José de, meeting with **S** 36
signature reproduced **A** 527
Simón Bolívar's birthday holiday **H** 149
Bolivia (bo-LIV-ia) **B** 302–06
corn harvest, picture **S** 290
flag **F** 242
life in Latin America **L** 47–61
national anthem **N** 21
Peace Corps member, picture **P** 102
Bollée (bo-LAY), **Amédée,** French inventor **A** 544
Boll weevil **C** 523
Alabama's monument to cotton pest **A** 119
Bolmarcich, Francisco Orlich see Orlich, Francisco Bolmarcich

Bologna (bol-ON-yah), **Giovanni da** (Jean Bologne) (1529?–1608), Flemish sculptor, b. Douai, France. He became court sculptor to Medici family in Italy (1558). His statues include Fountain of Neptune in Bologna and equestrian statue of Cosimo I de' Medici.

Bolsheviks, Communist supporters of Lenin **L** 138
Stalin, an organizer for **S** 395
Bolshoi State Theater of Opera and Ballet, Minsk, picture **B** 138
Bolt, Robert, English playwright **E** 268
Bolt-action, of guns and rifles **G** 418–19
Bolton, Guy, English-born American dramatist **M** 542

Bolton, Sarah Knowles (1841–1916), American author and reformer, b. Farmington, Conn. She wrote such biographies as *Poor Boys Who Became Famous, Girls Who Became Famous,* and *Famous Men of Science.*

Bolts, fasteners **N** 3
Bolyai, Johann, Hungarian mathematician **M** 159

Bomarc, U.S. Air Force surface-to-air missile armed with a nuclear warhead. The Bomarc finds its target by means of radar signals. It has two sections, or stages. The upper stage is powered by ramjet engines. The lower stage is a solid-fuel booster rocket (some Bomarcs still

Bomarc (continued)
have liquid-fuel boosters, however).
  Canadian bases **C** 82

Bombardier, Joseph-Armand, Canadian inventor of the
  snowmobile **S** 215
Bombay, India **B** 307–08
  commercial center of India **I** 122; pictures **I** 124
  nuclear power plant, picture **P** 427
  one of the great cities of the world, picture **C** 310
Bombs
  atomic **N** 362–63
  hydrogen **H** 306; **N** 364–65

Bonaire (bo-NAIRE), or **Buen Aire,** or **Buen Ayre,** tropical
island of the Netherlands Antilles in the Caribbean Sea.
Its main products—sisal, divi-divi, and goat manure—
are exported from Kralendijk, the chief city.
  Caribbean Sea and islands **C** 116–19

Bonanza farms, large wheat farms **N** 328
Bonaparte, Napoleon see Napoleon I

Bonaparte family (Buonaparte in Italian), Corsican
family of Italian descent, brought to prominence in
Europe by French emperor **Napoleon I** (1769–1821).
Joseph (1768–1844), brother of Napoleon I, was king of
Naples (1806–08) and king of Spain (1808–13). **Louis**
(1778–1846), brother of Napoleon I, was king of the
Netherlands (1806–10). **Jérôme** (1784–1860), brother of
Napoleon I, was king of Westphalia (1807–13). **François
Charles Joseph,** or **Napoleon II** (1811–32), son of Napo-
leon I, was titular king of Rome. **Charles Louis Napoleon,**
or **Napoleon III** (1808–73), son of Louis and nephew of
Napoleon I, was emperor of France (1852–70).

Bonar Law, Andrew see Law, Andrew Bonar

Bond, Carrie Jacobs (1862–1946), American songwriter,
b. Janesville, Wis. Her most famous and popular songs
were "A Perfect Day" and "I Love You Truly."

Bond, George, American naval officer **U** 19

Bond, Julian (1940–), American politician and civil
rights leader, Negro, b. Nashville, Tenn. Elected a member
of the Georgia House of Representatives (1965), he was
barred from taking his seat because of his anti-Vietnam
War stand, but the U.S. Supreme Court ruled (1966) his
constitutional rights had been violated. He was the first
Negro nominated for vice-president (1968 Democratic
convention)—a symbolic nomination, since he was not
old enough to serve. Picture **N** 104a

Bond, Shadrach, American statesman and pioneer **I** 84
Bonding, of adhesives **G** 242
Bondmen, peasants bound to the land **S** 197
Bondone, Giotto di see Giotto di Bondone
Bonds, certificates of loans **S** 428
Bonds, chemical C 200, 218
Bône, Algeria see Annaba
Bone china, ceramic work **C** 173
  English porcelain **P** 418
Bones, of animals
  birds **B** 199, 200–01
  body, human **B** 270; diagram **B** 271
  feet **F** 80–82
  hands **F** 83
  marrow of **B** 273
  What is a backbone? **K** 251
Bongo drums D 336
Bongos, hoofed mammals **H** 221; picture **H** 217

Bonheur (bon-ER), **Rosa** (Marie Rosalie Bonheur)
(1822–1899), French painter, b. Bordeaux. She is known
for spirited animal paintings, as *Horse Fair.*

Bonhoeffer, Dietrich (1906–45), German Protestant theologian and pastor, b. Breslau, Germany. Barred from
teaching because of his early opposition to Nazism, he
was active in international activities of his church. He
joined in underground German resistance to Hitler, was
arrested in 1943, and hanged in 1945. In *Letters and
Papers from Prison* published in 1951, he stressed the
need for religion to involve itself in worldly activities.
He is an important voice in Protestant radical theology.

Bonhomme Richard, ship commanded by John Paul
  Jones **J** 134
  battle scene **R** 206
Boniface (BON-i-face) **VIII,** pope
  dispute with King Philip The Fair of France
  R 293
Boniface, Saint, English missionary **C** 284; **R** 290

Bonin Islands, volcanic islands in the Pacific Ocean. The
three main groups are the Bailey Islands, the Beechey
Islands, and the Parry Islands.
  Pacific Ocean and islands **P** 5

Bonito (bon-E-to), fish **F** 188
Bon Marché (bon mar-SHAY), Paris, first department
  store **D** 118
Bonn, capital of West Germany **G** 158
  Christmas in, picture **C** 291
Bonneville (BON-nev-ille), **Benjamin L. E. de,** French-born
  American explorer **O** 260
Bonneville, Lake, Utah **L** 31
  prehistoric geological formation **U** 244
Bonneville Dam, Oregon and Washington **D** 19–20
Bonneville Salt Flats, Utah **U** 243
  automobile racing **A** 540; **S** 22
Bonney, William H. see Billy the Kid
Bonspiel, curling tournament **C** 555

Bontemps (BON-tomp), **Arna Wendell** (1902–73), American author, b. Alexandria, La. He was a distinguished
member of a group of black writers and poets known
as the Harlem Renaissance group. His books include
The Story of the Negro and *Black Thunder.*

Booby, seabird with long pointed wings, wedge-shaped
tail, and straight beak. They dive for their food with
great force, and sleep on the water's surface. The bird
was named "booby" (which means "fool" or "dunce")
because it does not attempt to escape or defend itself
when in danger.

Book, Shrine of the, Jerusalem **J** 81
  picture **M** 513
Book awards
  children's literature, awards for **B** 309–10b
  influence on children's literature **C** 242
  Nobel prizes **N** 266
  Pulitzer prizes **P** 524–28
  See also National Book Awards
Bookbinding B 327–29
  how medieval books were made **B** 320–21, 322
Book catalogs, in libraries **L** 185
Book clubs P 514
  paperbacks for young people **P** 58a
Book design B 323–26, 331
  choice of typefaces **T** 345–46
  medieval books **B** 319–21
Booker T. Washington National Monument V 353

Boothe, Clare see Luce, Clare Boothe

Booth family, English family of evangelists associated with Salvation Army. Salvation Army was started by **General William** (1829–1912) as Christian Mission in Whitechapel district of London (1865). It later became Salvation Army (1878), with chapters around the world; **William Bramwell** (1856–1929) succeeded his father as general, and another son, **Ballington** (1859–1940), withdrew to found Volunteers of America; other descendants have continued in Salvation Army affairs.

Boothia Peninsula, in Arctic Circle, picture **C** 53
Bootleggers, in the Roaring Twenties **C** 496
Boots and shoes see Shoes
Bora (BO-ra), wind of Adriatic region **M** 213
  Albania **A** 145
Borah, William Edgar, American statesman **I** 67
Borax, mineral **C** 22
Bordeaux, France **F** 406
Borden, P. E. I., Canada **P** 456b, 456e

Borden, Gail (1801–1874), American inventor and surveyor, b. Norwich, N.Y. He invented meat biscuit, condensed milk, and method of concentrating juices. He opened first condensing plant in Wassaic, N.Y. (1861), and introduced dairy sanitation methods that are now compulsory. Borden took charge of survey of Texas and made first topographical map of Republic of Texas.

Borden, Sir Robert Laird (1854–1937), Canadian lawyer and statesman, b. Grand Pré, Nova Scotia. He was elected to Canadian House of Commons (1896), where he became leader of Conservative Party (1901). As prime minister (1911–20) he led Canada through World War I and afterward served as delegate to Paris Peace Conference and as representative to League of Nations. He was knighted in 1914.
  Canada, history of **C** 75, 81

Border states, American Civil War **C** 458
Borecole see Kale
Borers, insects **P** 289
Bores, of guns **G** 414–15
Bores, tidal waves **T** 185
  Amazon River **A** 179
  Bay of Fundy, Canada **N** 138
Borescopes, optical instruments **O** 168

Borges (BOR-hace), **Jorge Luis** (1899–   ), Argentine author and university professor, b. Buenos Aires. A member of Argentine Academy of Letters, he is a writer of essays, poems, and novels, including *El Idioma de los Argentinos* and *Ficciones.*

Borghese Gallery, Rome, picture **M** 510

Borgia (BOR-ja) **family,** noble Italian family of Spanish origin, powerful during 15th and 16th centuries. **Alfonso** (1378–1458) became Pope Calixtus III (1455), and **Rodrigo** (1431?–1503) became Pope Alexander VI (1492). Rodrigo's son **Cesare** (1475?–1507) was a cardinal who left his office and tried to conquer a kingdom in central Italy. Cesare was known for his cruelty and treachery. His methods are praised in Machiavelli's *Il Principe.* Rodrigo's daughter **Lucrezia** (1480–1519) was a great patron of the arts. She was reputed to have been cruel and villainous, but probably did not commit many of the crimes of which she has been accused.

Borglum, Gutzon (John Gutzon de la Mothe Borglum) (1871–1941), American sculptor, b. Idaho. He is best

known for national memorial at Mt. Rushmore, S.D., with its heads of Washington, Jefferson, Lincoln, and Theodore Roosevelt. His other works include large head of Lincoln at the Capitol in Washington, D.C., and *The Mares of Diomedes,* in the Metropolitan Museum of Art.

Borgo Maggiore (ma-JO-ray), San Marino **S** 35
Boris I (BO-ris), czar of Bulgaria **B** 444
Boris III, king of Bulgaria **B** 444
Boris Godunov (BOR-is goo-du-NOF), dramatic poem by Pushkin **D** 298
Boris Godunov, opera by Mussorgsky **O** 140–41
Borlaug, Norman, American agronomist **F** 343
Borman, Frank, American astronaut **S** 344, 345, 346

Bormann (BOR-monn), **Martin Ludwig** (1900–   ), German Nazi leader, b. Halberstadt. Chief of staff of Nazi Party (1933–41), he was appointed Hitler's third deputy (1941). He was sentenced in absentia at Nuremberg Trials (1946) to die as war criminal, but it is not known whether he is dead or alive and in hiding.

Borneo **B** 336–38; **I** 218–19
  See also Malaysia
Bornholm (BORN-holm) **Island,** Denmark **D** 108
Bornou (BOR-nu), ancient African empire **C** 183
Borodin (BO-ro-din), **Alexander,** Russian scientist and composer **U** 63
  opera **O** 136
Boron, element **E** 154, 160
  control rods for nuclear reactors **N** 363
Borough (BUR-o), unit of municipal government **M** 503
Borromini, Francesco, Italian architect **I** 472
Bosch, Hieronymus, Flemish painter **P** 23
  Dutch and Flemish art **D** 352
  Temptation of Saint Anthony, painting **D** 355

Bosch (BOSH), **Juan** (1909–   ), Dominican statesman and writer, b. La Vega. He founded Dominican Revolutionary Party (1939). During his political exile (1942–61) he traveled in Latin America. Elected president of Dominican Republic in first free general elections (1962), he served until overthrown and exiled (1963). An attempt in 1965 to restore him to power failed because of American intervention, and he lost his bid for re-election in 1966.
  Dominican Republic, history of **D** 283

Bosnia and Herzegovina (HER-tze-go-vi-na), Yugoslav state **Y** 358
Bosporus, strait, Turkey **T** 324
Boston, capital of Massachusetts **B** 339–40; **M** 141
  Boston Metropolitan Area **M** 146
  first high school, 1820 **E** 72
  Hub of the Universe, origin of the term **M** 134
  museums and libraries **M** 143–44
  police strike, Coolidge's stand **C** 495–96
  skyline view, picture **M** 139
  urban landscape of New England **N** 138h

Boston, Lucy (1892–   ), English author. She served in a French hospital during World War I and traveled widely in France, Italy, Austria, and Hungary. Her children's books include *The Children of Green Knowe, Treasure of Green Knowe,* and *The River at Green Knowe.*

Boston, Ralph (1939–   ), American long jumper, Negro, b. Laurel, Miss. He won long jump at 1960 Olympic Games. In 1961 he became first man to jump more than 27 feet, leaping 27 feet, 3¼ inches, to break Jesse Owens' 25-year-old record.

Boston Light, Boston Harbor, Massachusetts **L** 278

Boston Massacre, 1770 R 196
  Adams, John **A** 8
  Adams, Samuel, protests **A** 17
  events leading to Declaration of Independence **D** 60
Boston Mountains, Arkansas **A** 421
Boston Port Bill, 1774 **R** 197
Boston Public Latin School **B** 339
  colonial education **C** 394
Boston's City Hall **A** 387; picture **B** 340
Boston Symphony Orchestra
  Berkshire Festival **M** 551
Boston Tea Party, 1773 **R** 196
  Adams, Samuel, organizes **A** 17
  described in *Johnny Tremain* **R** 209–10
  events leading to Declaration of Independence **D** 60
  Revere, Paul, participates in **R** 192–93
Boston terrier, dog **D** 261; picture **D** 256
Boswell, James, Scottish biographer **E** 258–59
  Samuel Johnson's Club **J** 131
Botanical (bo-TAN-ic-al) **gardens** **Z** 379; pictures **Z** 378
Botany (BOT-any), study of plants **B** 340; **P** 290–304
  archeological studies **A** 359–60
  biology, branch of **B** 190
  Carver, George W., new uses of plants **C** 128–29
  cell structure **C** 159–64
  classification of plants (taxonomy) **T** 28–32
  experiments and projects **E** 356–59
  food plants **P** 305–10
  fossils **F** 378
  fruit defined **F** 280
  genetics **G** 77–88
  kingdoms of living things **K** 249–59
  leaves **L** 114–20
  life **L** 208–14
  Linnaeus invented classification system **L** 304
  medicinal plants **P** 310–15
  Mendel's experiments **G** 80–82; **M** 219
  odd and interesting plants **P** 316–20
  photosynthesis **P** 221–23
  poisonous plants **P** 321–23
  reproduction **R** 176–80
  taxonomy **T** 28–32
  See also Plants
Botany Bay, Australia **A** 516
Botha (BO-ta), **Louis,** Afrikaner leader **S** 273
Bothnia, Gulf of, an arm of the Baltic Sea **O** 45
Bothwell, James Hepburn, 4th earl of, husband of Mary
  Queen of Scots **M** 130
Bo Tree, sacred to Buddhists **B** 423

Botsford, Amos (1744–1812), Canadian statesman, b.
Newtown, Conn. He fought for British in American
Revolution and represented British Government in settling Loyalists in Nova Scotia (1782). He was the first
speaker of New Brunswick's House of Assembly.

Botswana (bot-SWA-na) **B** 340a
  children, picture **A** 54
  flag **F** 235
  poetry of the Tswana **A** 76a
Botswana, Lesotho, and Swaziland, University of, at
  Roma, Lesotho **S** 481
Böttger (BERT-ker), **Johann,** German potter, first porce-
  lain maker in Europe **C** 172–73
Botticelli (bo-ti-CHEL-li), **Sandro,** Italian painter **B** 340b;
  I 469
  Adoration of the Magi, painting **N** 41
  Birth of Venus, painting **I** 466
  Florentine painting **P** 20
  Primavera, painting **B** 340b
  Renaissance art **R** 162, 166
  Saint Augustine of Hippo, painting **C** 282

Bottled gas **F** 489
Bottlenose dolphins **D** 270–73, **274, 276**
Bottlenose whales **W** 147, 149
Bottles and bottling **B** 341–43
  antique bottles **A** 320
  vacuum, or thermos, bottles **V** 265
Bottle trees, or baobab trees **P** 283
  famous trees in the Sudan **S** 448
Botulism (BOT-ul-ism), poisoning **F** 354

Boucher (bu-SHAY), **François** (1703–70), French painter,
b. Paris. He was appointed first court painter to Louis XV
(1765) and director of the Royal Academy of Painting
and Sculpture (1765). A protégé of Madame de Pompadour (from 1745), he painted portraits, genre pictures,
landscapes, and designs for tapestries in decorative,
rococo style. His works include *Diana and Callisto.*
  French art, history of **F** 425
  rococo style in painting **P** 24

Boudinot (BU-din-o), **Elias** (1740–1821), American political leader, b. Philadelphia, Pa. He joined Committee of
Correspondence in New Jersey (1774) and was then
elected to the Continental Congress (1777). As president
of Congress, he signed peace treaty with Great Britain
(1782) ending Revolutionary War. He was elected to
House of Representatives (1789–95) and served as
director of U.S. Mint in Philadelphia (1795–1805). He
organized (1816) and was first president (1816–21) of
American Bible Society.

Bouffant (bou-FONT), shape in fashion design **F** 65

Bougainville (BOU-gan-vil), volcanic island in southwestern Pacific, largest of the Solomon Islands and part
of Australia's New Guinea trusteeship. Bougainville
contains two densely forested mountain ranges and rich
volcanic soil. It was the last major Japanese stronghold
in Solomon Islands during World War II.

Bought Me a Cat, folk song **F** 322
Boulder, Colorado **C** 414
Boulder caves **C** 156–57
Boulder clay, soil deposited by glaciers **S** 234
Boulle (BOOL), **André,** French cabinetmaker **D** 77
  furniture design **F** 508

Boulton (BOLT-on), **Matthew** (1728–1809), English manufacturer and engineer, b. Birmingham. He became a
partner of James Watt (1775) and supplied capital,
factory, and know-how for producing Watt's steam
engines. He also invented a steam-powered press for
making coins, used in Britain until 1882. He was
prominent in British scientific circles and was a friend of
Benjamin Franklin, Priestley, and Darwin.
  Industrial Revolution **I** 239

Boumedienne, Houari, Algerian military leader **A** 163
Boundaries
  defined by rivers **R** 241
  territorial expansion of the United States **T** 105–15
Bounties
  government aid to agriculture **A** 94
  military service encouraged by bounties **D** 289
  See also Subsidies
Bounty, Mutiny on the *see* Bligh, William
Bourassa (BOO-ras-sa), **Henri,** Canadian journalist **Q** 13

Bourbon, House of, French royal family descended from
9th-century baron Aimar (or Adhemar), whose seat was
Castle of Bourbon. The dynasty, founded (1589) in
France by Henry IV, lasted until 1793 and continued dur-

Bourbon, House of (continued)

ing restoration (1814–30) under Louis XVIII and Charles X and under Louis Philippe (1830–48) of Bourbon-Orléans line. The grandson of Louis XIV, Duke of Anjou, founded Bourbon royal line in Spain (1700–1931) as Philip V of Spain. Philip's son Charles founded royal family (1735–1861) in Naples and Sicily. The house is remembered for extravagances of Louis XIV and Louis XV of France.

France, history of **F** 415–16

Bourgeoisie (BOORJ-wah-zi), people of the middle class power and economic influence increased by Age of Exploration **E** 387
Bourguiba (boor-GHE-ba), **Habib,** president of Tunisia **T** 312
Bournonville, Auguste, father of Danish ballet **B** 28
Bourse, a money exchange **S** 428
Bouts, Dierik, Dutch painter **D** 351
Last Supper, painting **D** 354
Bovidae (BO-vi-de), cattle family **C** 147
hoofed mammals **H** 220
Bovines (BO-vines), cattlelike hoofed mammals **H** 220; pictures **H** 216
Bow and arrow see Bows and arrows

Bowditch (BOWD-itch), **Nathaniel** (1773–1838), American mathematician and astronomer, b. Salem, Mass. A self-educated man, he went to sea in 1795 as a clerk and became a ship's master in 1802. His revision of J. H. Moore's *The Practical Navigator,* which appeared as *The New American Practical Navigator* in 1802, was made the standard authority of the United States Navy Department. Bowditch worked on astronomical problems in his leisure time and wrote articles on the subject.

Bowdoin (BO-din), **James** (1726–1790), American statesman, b. Boston, Mass. He was a member of Massachusetts General Court (1753–56) and Council (1757–69) and of the Constitutional Convention (1779). As governor of state (1785–87) he put down Shays' Rebellion. He was a delegate to national constitutional convention and first president of American Academy of Arts and Sciences (1780–90). Bowdoin College in Maine is named for him.

Bowdoin College, Maine **M** 40
Bow drill, tool **T** 210b–211
Bowed instruments M 545–46
Bowell (BO-well), **Sir Mackenzie,** Canadian statesman **O** 125
Bowen, Elizabeth, English writer **E** 267
Bowerbirds, picture **A** 273
Bowes-Lyon, Elizabeth see Elizabeth, queen consort of George VI
Bowhunters, archers **A** 366
Bowie (BOO-ie), **James,** American soldier and frontiersman **B** 344
Travis succeeds him as commander of Alamo **T** 135
Bowie knife, origin of **B** 344
Bow kite K 270
Bowknots K 290
Bowler hats, picture **L** 335

Bowles, Chester Bliss (1901–), American diplomat, b. Springfield, Mass. He established advertising firm of Benton and Bowles (1929) and was special assistant to secretary-general of UN (1946–48), governor of Connecticut (1949–51), ambassador to India and Nepal (1951–53), congressman (1959–60), undersecretary of state (1961), and president's special advisor on African, Asian, and Latin-American affairs (1961 to 1963). He was again ambassador to India (1963 to 1969). He is author of

several books, including *Ambassador's Report* and *The Conscience of a Liberal.*

Bowl games, in football **F** 365
Bowlines, knots **K** 290
Bowling B 345–49
See also Cricket
Bowling, pitching in cricket **C** 531–32
Bowl of Plums, painting by Chardin **F** 424
Bowls, or lawn bowling **B** 349

Bowne, John (1627?–1695), American Quaker leader, b. Matlock, England. He arrived in Boston in 1649 and settled in Flushing in 1653. In his home Bowne held Quaker meetings, for which he was imprisoned and later banished. Harsh treatment of him helped bring religious freedom to citizens of New Netherland in 1663.

Bows and arrows A 366–68
famous inventions **I** 335
Bow-steerers, iceboats **I** 29; picture **I** 30
Box cameras P 202–03
photography as a hobby **P** 215
Boxcars, of railroads **R** 82
Boxer, dog, picture **D** 254
Boxer Rebellion, 1900, revolt in China against foreigners **B** 350; **C** 272
Open-Door policy **M** 189–90
Peking's Legation Quarter **P** 118
Boxing B 351–53
related to fencing **F** 84
Olympic Games, combative sports **O** 109
Boxing Day H 152
Box kites K 268–69
invention of **K** 267
Box office, where theater tickets are sold **T** 156
Box turtles T 332
pets **P** 181
Box wrenches, tools **T** 215
Boy Blue, nursery rhyme **N** 406
Boyce, William D., American publisher, organized Boy Scouts of America **B** 357

Boycott, refusal of business or social group to deal with an individual, organization, or country to show disapproval or to force acceptance of demands. Boycotts are used by organized labor against employers whom they consider to be unfair and sometimes by nations for political purposes. Term originated in Ireland when Captain Charles Cunningham Boycott (1832–97) treated tenants on his estate so unjustly that it resulted in their refusal to deal with him.
Martin Luther King's bus boycott **K** 248

Boyd, Belle, American Civil War spy **S** 389
Boyden, Seth, American inventor and manufacturer **N** 178
Boyer, Jean Pierre, Haiti president **H** 10
Boy Jesus, Bible story **B** 168–69
Boyle, Robert, English scientist **B** 354
chemistry, history of **C** 209
Boyle's law B 354
chemistry, history of **C** 209
gases **G** 57
Boyne, battle of the, 1690 **I** 390; **U** 73
Boyne River, Ireland **I** 388
Boy Prisoners in the Tower, legend **P** 470
England, history of **E** 220
Boys' camps see Camping, organized
Boys' clubs
Junior Achievement, Inc., a student business **J** 157–58

Boys' Clubs of America B 355
Boy Scouts B 356–60
  bugle, use of B 429
  Burmese, picture A 459
  sending messages with signal flags, picture
    F 247
Boy Scouts of Canada B 357, 360
Boysenberries G 301
Boy's Life, magazine M 16

Boys' State, convention, sponsored by American Legion, of high school boys, usually juniors, chosen for leadership, character, scholarship, and service. It has been held annually (since 1935), usually at a college or university. Its object is to show members how government operates. Headquarters is in Indianapolis, Ind.

Boys Town, Nebraska N 82
Boz, pen name used by Charles Dickens D 158–63

Bozeman Trail, frontier trail to Montana goldfields. It ran from Julesburg, Colorado, to Virginia City, Montana, and was named for John M. Bozeman (1835–67), who opened it (1863). The trail ran through Sioux hunting territory and was scene of many Indian attacks during next decade until all posts were finally abandoned.
  Wyoming W 330, 337

BPOE see Elks, Benevolent and Protective Order of
Brace-and-bit, tool T 214
Bracelets, jewelry J 99, 100
  Danish, picture D 71
Brachiosaurs (BRAC-ki-o-saurs), dinosaurs D 177
  giants of nature G 200
Brackenbridge, Hugh Henry, American novelist
    A 198
Bracket fungi F 500
Bracts, of plants P 295
Braddock, General Edward, British soldier F 460
  Washington, George, on his staff W 37
Bradford, William, governor of Plymouth Colony
    P 346
  American colonies, history of A 187
  American literature A 195

Bradley, Omar Nelson (1893–   ), American army officer, b. Clark, Mo. During World War II he led U.S. First Army in Normandy invasion on D Day (June 6, 1944). As commander of Twelfth Army Group (1945) he commanded largest American force ever to serve under one field leader. He became general in 1945 and was promoted to general of the Army in 1950. He served as head of Veterans Administration (1945–48), chief of staff of the Army (1948–49), first chairman of Joint Chiefs of Staff (1949–53), and chairman of military committee of NATO (1949–53). He has been chairman of the board of Bulova Watch Co. since 1958.

Bradley, Thomas (1917–   ), American politician, b. Calvert, Texas. A former police officer, he was elected to the Los Angeles City Council in 1963. In 1973 he won election as the first black mayor of Los Angeles.

Bradstreet, Anne, American poet A 196

Brady, Diamond Jim (James Buchanan Brady) (1856–1917), American financier, b. New York, N.Y. A longtime employee of New York Central Railroad, he made his fortune as promoter and executive for companies manufacturing railroad equipment. His nickname comes from his love of valuable jewels. He used part of his money for producing Broadway shows and for charity.

Brady, Mathew B. American photographer C 434
Braga (BRA-ga), Portugal P 401
Bragg, Braxton, American Civil War general C 326
  Mexican War M 239
Bragi (BROG-i), Norse god N 280
Brahe (BRA), **Tycho,** Danish astronomer B 361
  astronomy, history of A 472
Brahman see Atman, Hindu spiritual principle
Brahmans, a caste in Hindu society H 130
  education of ancient times E 62
Brahmaputra (brah-ma-PU-tra) **River,** Asia R 242
  joins the Ganges G 25
  rivers of India I 125
Brahms, Johannes, German composer B 362; pictures
    B 362, G 188
  choral music C 279
  First Symphony O 189
  German music G 188
  symphonies M 541
Braille (BRAIL), alphabet of the blind B 252–53
  Braille typewriter, picture T 347
Braille, Louis, French teacher and musician B 252–53
Brain B 363–69
  birds B 203
  body controls and guards B 280, 282–83
  body's senses B 283–88
  damage caused by a stroke D 208
  Does a larger brain mean greater intelligence? B 366
  dreaming experiments D 305–06
  electroencephalograms show "brain waves"
    M 208h–209
  epilepsy D 196
  hypnosis H 314–16
  in fishes, size of regions related to senses F 190
  insects I 269
  learning L 98–106
  mammals M 61
  medical and surgical techniques M 208h, 209, 210
  operations in hyperbaric chambers M 210
  primates M 418
  psychology P 488–501
  ultrasonoscope, to detect abnormal conditions M 209
Brain coral, picture J 74

Brain drain, migration of specialists and technicians from one country to another. The term was originally used with special reference to the immigration of British engineers, doctors, and scientists to the United States and to countries of the Commonwealth. However, the brain drain is now becoming an international problem. It is particularly serious when underdeveloped countries lose their highly-trained people. In 1967 the United Nations was asked to undertake a study of the international migration of talent and skills.

Brainstorming, method used to solve problems through unstructured group discussion. Method is based on idea that more effective solutions can be reached through interplay of several minds than by one individual alone.

Brainteasers, puzzles T 289
Braintree (now Quincy), Massachusetts, home of Adams family A 8, 12

Braithwaite, William Stanley Beaumont (1878–1962), American poet and anthologist, Negro, b. Boston, Mass. He published annually (1913–29) *Anthology of Magazine Verse and Year Book of American Poetry.* His writings include *The House of Falling Leaves,* anthologies *The Book of Elizabethan Verse* and *The Book of Modern British Verse,* and autobiography *The House Under Arcturus.* He was recipient of Spingarn medal (1918).

Brakemen, on trains R 86
Brakes
  airbrake, invention of the R 88
  hydraulic H 303
  Westinghouse, George, and air brakes W 125
Bramah (BRA-mah), **Joseph,** English engineer L 324
Bramante (brom-ON-tay), **Donato,** Italian architect
  I 467
  Renaissance architecture R 167
  Tempietto of San Pietro Church, Rome, picture I 464
Bran, of grain G 282
  flour and flour milling F 275
Branca (BRON-ca), **Giovanni,** Italian architect
  E 209
  showed principle of steam turbine T 320
Brancusi, Constantin, Rumanian-French sculptor B 370
  Adam and Eve, sculpture S 104
  Bird in Space F 431
  French school of art F 432
  place in the history of sculpture S 104
Brand, Hennig, German alchemist
  phosphorus discovered by C 212; M 152
Brand, Vance D., American astronaut S 346
Brandeis (BRAND-ice), **Louis,** American jurist B 370
Brandeis University, Waltham, Massachusetts B 370
Brandenburg Gate, East Berlin, Germany, map G 151
Branding, of cattle R 104–05
Brand names see Trademarks

Brando, Marlon (1924–), American actor, b. Omaha,
Neb. He appeared on Broadway in *I Remember Mama,
Candida,* and *A Streetcar Named Desire.* Hollywood introduced him to the film public in 1950 in *The Men.* He then
did the film version of *A Streetcar Named Desire* and
followed it with memorable performances in *On the Waterfront* (for which he won an Academy Award in 1954), *The
Young Lions, Burn,* and *The Godfather.* He directed and
starred in *One-Eyed Jacks.*

Brandon, Manitoba, Canada M 81

Brandt (BRONT), **Willy** (Herbert Frahm) (1913–),
German political leader, b. Lübeck. A member of the Social Democratic Party, he fled Germany when Nazis
gained power. He was a journalist in Norway and Sweden
(1933–45) and correspondent for Scandinavian newspapers in Berlin, Germany (1945–47). He returned to Germany and regained German citizenship in 1948. He was
member of Bundestag (1949–57), president of Berlin
House of Representatives (1955–57), and governing
mayor of West Berlin (1957–66). He was vice-chancellor
and foreign minister of West Germany (1966–69), and
chancellor (1969–). He was awarded the Nobel peace
prize (1971).

Brandy, a distilled beverage W 159
Branford Trolley Museum, East Haven, Conn. C 476

Branley, Franklyn M. (1915–), American science writer,
b. New Rochelle, N.Y. A graduate of New York and
Columbia Universities, he has taught high school science
and has written about 50 books on all phases of science
for young people from beginning readers up. Among his
books are *Air Is All Around You, The Big Dipper,* and *Man
in Space to the Moon.*

Brant, Joseph (Thayendanegea), Mohawk Indian B 371
  hostilities during Revolutionary War R 205
  Indian Wars I 212
Braque (BROC), **Georges,** French painter B 371; P 30
  Clarinet, collage, picture C 376
  modern art M 390

Picasso and Braque P 243
  Still Life: The Table, painting B 371
Brasília (bra-ZI-lia), capital of Brazil B 380; picture
  C 308
  president's palace, picture S 295
Brass B 410
  alloys A 168
  antiques A 321
  major Connecticut industry C 473
  zinc Z 370
Brass band B 38
Brass instruments M 549; pictures M 547
  bugle B 429
  orchestra O 183; picture O 187
  orchestra seating plan O 186
  wind instruments W 182–83
Bratislava (BRA-ti-sla-va), Czechoslovakia C 562
Bratsk (BROTSK), U.S.S.R.
  hydroelectric power plant, picture P 425
Brattain, Walter H., American physicist T 252; picture
  E 147
Braun, Wernher von see Von Braun, Wernher

Braxton, Carter (1736–1797), American statesman, b.
Newington, Va. He was a member of the Virginia House
of Burgesses between 1761 and 1775 and served at
the Continental Congress (1775–76, 1777–83, 1785),
where he signed the Declaration of Independence.

Brazil B 372–84
  Amazon River A 178–79
  coffee C 371–72
  coffee beans drying, picture S 289
  flag F 242
  landforms of South America S 276
  Latin-American art and architecture L 64
  Latin-American politics L 52
  life in Latin America L 47–61
  literature L 72–73
  national anthem N 21
  origin of name D 369
  Portugal, history of P 403
  Rio de Janeiro R 236–37
  roads near Santos, picture G 102
  rubber trees R 342
  São Paulo S 37–38
Brazil Current, of Atlantic Ocean A 478; S 279
Brazilein (bra-ZIL-le-in), dye D 369
Brazil nuts N 421
Brazilwood B 372
Brazing and soldering S 249–50
Brazos (BRA-zos) **River,** Texas T 125

Brazza (BRA-tza), **Count Pierre Paul François Camille
Savorgnan de** (1852–1905), French explorer of Africa, b.
Rio de Janeiro, Brazil. A brother of explorer Giacomo de
Brazza, he made several expeditions to West Africa,
where he founded Franceville and Brazzaville and
claimed the territory for France (1879). He was governor
of French Congo (later French Equatorial Africa) from
1886 to 1897. C 464

Brazzaville, capital of the Congo C 461–464;
  picture C 462, 464
Bread B 385–89
  ancient millstones for grinding flour, picture A 355
  black or rye bread R 364
  bread wheats W 154, 156
  Cyprus, ancient baking methods, picture C 558
  Egyptian statuette, bread making, picture A 350
  experiments: growing bread molds A 316; E 351
  flour from different kinds of wheat F 274

food regulations and laws **F** 350
mold **F** 496, 497
unleavened and leavened compared **F** 88
wheat **W** 154, 156
See also Flour and flour milling
Bread-and-butter notes L 158–59
Breadfruit, a tropical fruit **M** 74
introduced into Jamaica by Captain Bligh **J** 18
Bread Loaf Mountain, Vermont
Bread Loaf School of English, Middlebury College
V 316
Bread mold F 496, 497
experiments **A** 316; **E** 351
fungi division of plant kingdom, picture **P** 292
Breakbone fever *see* Dengue
Breakers, giant waves
surfing **S** 478
Breakers, hard-coal preparation plants **C** 367
Breakfast cereals G 285
Breaking a mirror, superstition **S** 475
Breaking a wishbone, superstition **S** 475

Breakwater, a structure built out into the sea or a lake to break the force of the waves and so protect the harbor or beach; differs from jetty which has the function of directing the course of water to make it carry sediment farther out.

Breast cancer C 92
Breastplates
armor, picture **A** 434
diving equipment **D** 79
Breaststroke, in swimming **S** 492; picture **S** 489
Breastworks, field fortifications **F** 377
Breathing B 277–78
artificial respiration **F** 159–61
birds **B** 203
crocodilian adaptations for staying underwater
C 535
dolphins and porpoises **D** 273
emphysema (disease) affects **D** 196
first aid for stoppage of breathing **F** 159–61
narcotics cause interruption of breathing and death
results **N** 13
oxygen and oxidation **O** 269
plants, respiration of **P** 294
respiratory system of fishes **F** 186–87
ventriloquism **V** 301–03
voice training and singing **V** 375–76

Brébeuf (bray-BUF), **Jean de, Saint** (1593–1649), French Jesuit missionary, b. Bayeux. He went to Canada (1625) and worked among the Huron Indians. He established first mission on Georgian Bay (1626) and translated catechism into Huron language. He was captured and killed by Iroquois. He was canonized in 1930.

Brecht (BRECKT), **Bertolt,** German playwright **G** 179
Breckinridge, John Cabell, vice-president, United States
K 225; **V** 331; picture **V** 327
Confederate general in Civil War **C** 321
Breech-loaders, guns **G** 418
Breeder reactors, for producing plutonium **U** 231
Breeds, of animals
cats, pedigreed **C** 141
cattle **C** 147
dairy cattle **D** 7–8; pictures **D** 5
dogs **D** 252–62
fur colors, by mutation **F** 514
horses, pictures **H** 239–240
pigs **C** 151
Breed's Hill, Boston, near Bunker Hill **R** 199–200

Breezes, sea *see* Sea breezes
Breitinger, Johann, Swiss professor **G** 175
Bremen (BREM-en), Germany **G** 158

Brendan, or **Brenainn, Saint** (484–577), Irish saint, b. Tralee, County Kerry. He is the hero of medieval legend *The Navigation of St. Brendan,* which tells of his journey in search of the "isles of the blessed." The legend has become exaggerated but is probably based on two short voyages that he did make. He founded several monasteries in Ireland, including Clonfert (559), of which he was abbot. His feast day is celebrated May 16th in Ireland.

Brennan, William Joseph (1906–), American jurist, b. Newark, N.J. After graduation from the University of Pennsylvania (1928), he earned his law degree from Harvard (1931). He practiced law in Newark until 1949 (except for military service during World War II). From 1949 to 1956 he served successively as judge of the New Jersey Supreme Court, Appelate Division; and the State Supreme Court. In 1956 Eisenhower appointed Brennan associate justice of the U.S. Supreme Court. Justice Brennan has been identified with the more liberal element in his opinions dealing with civil rights.

Brenner Pass, through the Alps **A** 174
Breslau, now Wroclaw, Poland **P** 361

Brest-Litovsk, Treaty of, peace agreement between Russia and the Central Powers, signed (Mar., 1918) during World War I. Bolsheviks took control of Russian government (Nov., 1917), surrendered to Germany (Dec., 1917). Russia lost Poland, Lithuania, and southern Latvia to Germany, and parts of Transcaucasia to Turkey. Finland, Estonia, northern Latvia, and the Ukraine became independent after defeat of Central Powers. Russia declared treaty invalid (Nov., 1918).

Breton, André, French poet and surrealist **F** 442;
M 394
Bretons, people of Brittany, France **F** 403
Brett, John, English engineer **T** 52
Bretton Woods, New Hampshire **N** 160
Bretton Woods Conference, 1944 **B** 50–51
Breuer (BROI-er), **Marcel,** Hungarian furniture designer
and architect **F** 510
use of concrete in architecture **A** 386
Brewis, colonial American dish **C** 390

Brewster, Sir David (1781–1868), Scottish physicist, b. Jedburgh. He made important studies of light and lenses, discovering law, named for him, that deals with reflected light. His theories led him to invent such instruments as the kaleidoscope and a lens used in lighthouses.

Brewster, William, Pilgrim father **P** 344

Brezhnev (BRAYGE-nef), **Leonid Ilyich** (1906–), Soviet political leader, b. Dneprodzerzhinsk, Ukraine. A member of the Communist Party since 1931, he was a political commissar in the Army (1941–45) and a party leader in the Ukraine, Moldavia, and Kazakhstan. He became a member of the Central Committee of the Communist Party (1952) and the Presidium (1957). He has been chairman of the Presidium (1960–64) and first secretary of the Central Committee (since 1964). He shares leadership of the U.S.S.R. with Premier Kosygin. **U** 51
Communism **C** 443

Brian Boru, king of Ireland **I** 390
Briand (bri-ON), **Aristide,** French statesman **P** 105
Briand-Kellogg Pact, 1928 *see* Kellogg-Briand Pact, 1928

Bricklaying B 391–93
  building a house, picture **B 437**
Bricks B 390–94
  building construction **B 430**
  houses H 174–75
Bridal rings J 98
Bridal Veil, waterfall N 243
Bridal veils W 100
Bride-price, or lobola S 268
Bridewell, a prison P 469
Bridge, card game C 107–12
Bridge, The, modern art group in Germany M 391
Bridgeport, Connecticut C 476–77
Bridger, Jim, American scout and mountain man F 523
  overland trails O 260
  Wyoming, settlement of W 335
  Yellowstone National Park Y 346
Bridges B 395–401
  Chesapeake Bay Bridge-Tunnel B 399; M 117; T 318
  Galata Bridge, Golden Horn, Turkey, picture T 327
  Jefferson Street Bridge, Indiana I 147
  Kaibab Suspension Bridge, picture G 292
  New York City N 230
  reinforced concrete used in C 166; picture C 165
  swinging bridge, picture J 155
  Tower Bridge, London, picture E 305
  twin bridge, Delaware Memorial, picture D 94
  Verrazano-Narrows Bridge, New York City, picture W 220
  See also Covered bridges
Bridges, of ships O 23
Bridges, Robert, English poet E 265
Bridgetown, capital of Barbados B 53; picture C 117

Bridgman, Laura (1829–1889), American teacher of the handicapped, b. Hanover, N.H. Blind, deaf, and mute, she was educated by means of a newly devised raised letter alphabet. Her achievements led to modern methods of teaching the disabled.

Brigade system, for fur trading F 524
Briggs, Austin, American illustrator I 95
Brigham Young University, Provo, Utah U 249
Bright, Charles, English engineer T 52
Brightness, or magnitude, of stars S 406–07
Brighton, England, picture U 68
Bright's disease D 201–02
Brimstone see Sulfur
Brine, salt and water solution S 20; W 56
  leather process for preserving hides L 108
  processing of fish F 212, 222
  use in preserving food F 347
Brine shrimp S 171

Brink, Carol Ryrie (1895–   ), American writer of children's books, b. Moscow, Idaho. Her most popular book, *Caddie Woodlawn,* based on incidents out of her grandmother's frontier childhood, won the Newbery Medal in 1936. Other titles include *All Over Town* and *Anything Can Happen on the River.*

Brisbane, capital of Queensland, Australia A 514

Briscoe, Robert (1894–1969), Irish statesman, b. Dublin. As a member of Sinn Fein movement and the Irish Republican Army, he worked for Ireland's independence from Britain (1922). He served in the Irish parliament (1927–65) and was twice lord mayor of Dublin (1956–57; 1961–62), the first Jew to hold the post.

Bristlecone pine, tree T 274
  oldest living things on earth P 317

Bristle worms, or polychaetes W 310
Bristol Clock Museum, Bristol, Conn. C 476
Britain, ancient name of England, Scotland, Wales
  early history of England E 214–17
  Hadrian's Wall, picture A 353
Britain, battle of, 1940 W 289–90
Britannia metal K 288
British Columbia, Canada B 402–07
  Canada's Cordillera C 51
  Salmon Area Indians I 180
  taiga region, agriculture in T 11
  valley formed by a glacier, picture I 16
  Vancouver V 276
British Columbia, University of B 405
British Commonwealth of Nations see Commonwealth of Nations
British East India Company E 43
  early monopoly of trade T 305
  Ganges valley controlled by I 133
British Empire E 225–32
  extent of, 1939 E 229
  United Kingdom of Great Britain and Northern Ireland U 65, 66
  See also Commonwealth of Nations
British Expeditionary Force (B.E.F.)
  World War I W 273
  World War II W 288
British Guiana see Guyana
British Honduras (Belize) H 199–200

British Indian Ocean Territory, British dependency consisting of Chagos Archipelago (former dependency of Mauritius), and Aldabra, Des Roches, and Farquhar islands (former dependencies of Seychelles). The territory was formed in 1965 by agreement with Mauritius and Seychelles.

British International (Harmsworth) **Cup Race,** boating B 264
British Isles, group that includes Great Britain, Ireland, and many smaller islands E 212; U 66
  geographic makeup (land areas) of the United Kingdom U 68
British Museum, London M 511, 514; picture M 515
  library L 177, 197–98; picture L 179
British North America Act, 1867 M 3
  Canada C 73
  Quebec Q 16
British Patent Office P 97
British Society for the Promotion of Permanent and Universal Peace P 104
British Solomon Islands Protectorate
  Guadalcanal P 6
British Somaliland, now Somalia S 254
British South Africa Company Z 368
British thermal units, or Btu's, measure of heat H 91
British Togoland see Togo
British Union, historic flag F 227
Britons, early people of England E 214–15
Brittany, region of France, pictures F 410, 413
Britten, Benjamin, English composer E 271
  opera O 138
  Peter Grimes, opera O 151
Brno (BER-no), Czechoslovakia C 562
Broadcast, a way of sowing seed F 58
  early agriculture A 96
Broadcasting, radio and television R 53–58; T 70–71
Broadheads, tips of archery arrows A 367
Broad jump, now called Long jump, field event T 240
Broadsides, newssheets
  ballads B 22
  political songs N 22

Broadtail, fur **F** 518
Broadway theater district, New York City **T** 161
   theaters in New York City **N** 233–34
Broadwood, John, English piano builder **P** 242
Broccoli, vegetable **V** 289
   flowers we eat **P** 307–08; picture **P** 309
Broch, Hermann, German writer **G** 180
Brock, Sir Isaac, British soldier **O** 125
   Canadian forces in War of 1812 **W** 11
Broilers, chickens **P** 420
Brokers, or agents, negotiators of sales and purchases
   S 116–17
   real estate **R** 113
   stocks and bonds, dealers in **S** 431
Bromine (BRO-mene), element **E** 154, 160
   iodine and other halogens **I** 349
Bronchial (BRONC-ial) **tubes,** respiratory system **B** 277
Bronchitis (bron-KY-tis), inflammation of bronchial tubes
   D 193–94
   smoking, effects of **S** 203
Bronchoscopes (BRONC-ho-scopes), optical instruments
   O 168

Bronck, or **Bronk, Jonas** (?–1643?), Danish pioneer in
America. He was the first settler (1639) in area of New
York above the Harlem River, now lower Westchester
County and the Bronx, which is named after him.

Broncos, untamed horses
   rodeo riding **R** 281
   See also Mustangs
Brontë (BRON-te), **Anne,** English novelist **B** 408; **E** 261
Brontë, Branwell, English writer **B** 408
Brontë, Charlotte, English novelist **B** 408; **E** 261
   themes of her novels **N** 346
Brontë, Emily, English novelist **B** 408; **E** 261
   themes of her novels **N** 346
Brontë family B 408
Brontosaurs, dinosaurs **D** 176–77
   giants of nature **G** 200
   prehistoric animals **P** 436–38
Bronx, New York City **N** 228–29
   Bronx campus of New York University, picture **N** 234
Bronx Zoo, New York City, picture **Z** 375
Bronze B 408–10
   alloys **A** 168
   ancient art **A** 236
   armor **A** 433
   bell casting **B** 135
   chemistry, history of **C** 205
   China's early use of **C** 268–69
   decorative arts **D** 68, 75
   tin **T** 195
Bronze Age B 408–09
   metals and metallurgy **M** 233
   prehistoric man **P** 446
   time of the Trojan War **T** 294
Bronze Star, American award, picture **M** 199
Brooches (BROACH-es), jewelry **J** 99
Brooke, Alan Francis see Alanbrooke, 1st Viscount

Brooke, Edward William (1919–), U.S. senator from
Massachusetts, Negro, b. Washington, D.C. He headed
the Boston finance commission (1961–62) and served as
attorney general of Massachusetts (1962–66). He was
elected to the U.S. Senate in 1966. Picture **N** 101.

Brooke, Sir James, British ruler (White Rajah) of
   Sarawak **M** 56
Brooke, Rupert, English poet **E** 265
Brook Farm, utopian community, Massachusetts **U** 256
   in American literature **A** 202

Brooklyn, New York City **N** 228
Brooklyn Botanical Garden, New York, picture **Z** 375
Brooklyn Bridge, New York City **B** 398; **N** 230

Brooks, Angie Elizabeth (Mrs. Isaac Randolph) (1928–
   ), b. Virginia, Liberia. Liberian assistant secretary
of state, she has been a delegate to the U.N. since
1954 and was 2nd woman president of the General Assembly (1969–70).

Brooks, Gwendolyn (1917–), American poet, b. Topeka,
Kans. She was the first Negro woman to win a Pulitzer
prize (1950), which was given to her for her collection of
poems *Annie Allen.* Her other collections include *A Street
in Bronzeville* and *Bean Eaters.*
   Negro artists and writers **N** 102

Brooks, Phillips, American Episcopal bishop, author of
   "O Little Town of Bethlehem" **C** 122
Brooks, Van Wyck, American writer **A** 214
Brooks Range, Alaska **A** 132, 135
Brook trout, fish, picture **F** 210
Broomcorn, a sorghum **K** 182
Brooms, poem by Dorothy Aldis **F** 120

Brotherhood Week, observance dedicated to increasing understanding among people of different ethnic and
religious backgrounds. Established in 1946 by the National Conference of Christians and Jews, it is celebrated during the week of Washington's birthday.

Brothers Karamazov, The, novel by Dostoevski **D** 287
Brothers of the Bridge, early order of bridge builders
   B 395
Brotherton, now Indian Mills, New Jersey
   first Indian reservation in United States **N** 178
Brotulids (bro-TU-lids), deep-sea fishes **F** 197
Broughton, Jack, English boxing champion **B** 353

Browder, Earl Russell (1891–), American Communist
Party leader, b. Wichita, Kans. He was general secretary
of the American Communist Party (1930–45) and Communist candidate for president (1936, 1940). He was
removed from post (1945) and expelled from party
(1946) for advocating co-operation with capitalism, then
officially vindicated by party (1956).

Brown, Charles Brockden, American novelist **A** 198

Brown, Claude (1937–), American author, Negro, b.
New York, N.Y. His autobiography, *Manchild in the Promised Land* (1965), is a description of life in the ghetto.

Brown, Father, fictional character created by Gilbert
   Keith Chesterton **M** 555
Brown, Ford Madox, English artist **E** 241
Brown, George, Canadian statesman **B** 411
   Brown and Macdonald **M** 3
Brown, H. Rap, American black power advocate **N** 104b
Brown, James, American singer **R** 262d

Brown, Jimmy (James Nathaniel Brown) (1936–),
American football player, Negro, b. St. Simons Island, Ga.
After starring at Syracuse University, he played pro
football as a fullback with the Cleveland Browns
(1957–66). He set several records and was named National Football League Player of the Year (1958, 1963)
and Athlete of the Year (1965). After retiring from football
he became a movie actor.

Brown, John, American abolitionist **B** 411–12
   abolitionist movement in Negro history **N** 94

Brown, John (continued)
events leading to Civil War **C** 320, 321
John Brown Memorial Park, Osawatomie, Kansas
K 187

Brown, Joseph Rogers (1810–1876), American inventor and manufacturer, b. Warren, R.I. After working in his father's clock-manufacturing business, he became interested in the development of machine tools. He invented an automatic machine for graduating rules, more precise calipers, a gear-cutting machine, and a universal milling machine. His most important invention was the universal grinder, with which hardened steel objects could be ground to shape.

Brown, Marcia (1918–   ), American author and artist, b. Rochester, N.Y. She illustrates books for children. Her translation and illustration of *Cinderella* won the Caldecott medal (1955). Her other books include *Dick Whittington and His Cat* and *Once a Mouse.*

Brown, Margaret Wise (1910–1952), author and editor of children's books, b. New York, N.Y. Under pen name of Golden MacDonald and under her own name she wrote over 60 books. Her books include *Little Lost Lamb,* the Noisy books, and *Little Island* (Caldecott medal, 1947).

Brown, Nicholas (1729–1791), American merchant, b. Providence, R.I. He headed a leading trading firm, Nicholas Brown & Co. (from 1762), which extended its activities to Europe and the West Indies and built and transported military arms and clothes for American soldiers during the Revolutionary War. The Browns, four brothers, were largely responsible for the location of Rhode Island College (later named Brown University) in Providence, R.I.

Brown, Robert, English botanist **S** 73

Brown, Sterling Allan (1901–   ), American poet, author, and professor, b. Washington, D.C. He incorporates Negro folk themes and exact dialect into his poetry. He was editor of the Federal Writer's Project (1936–39) and staff member of the Carnegie-Myrdal Study (1939). He became first Negro professor at Vassar (1945). He wrote *Southern Road* and edited *The Negro Caravan.*

Brown, William Hill, American novelist **A** 198

Brown, William Wells (1816?–1884), American reformer, historian, and writer, b. Lexington, Ky. A Negro slave, he escaped to Ohio and adopted the name Wells Brown from a Quaker who had helped him. He worked as steward on Lake Erie steamboat and helped many Negroes to freedom (1843–49). He lectured before abolitionist societies in New York and Massachusetts and was also interested in temperance movement, women's suffrage, and prison reform. His works include *Narrative of William W. Brown: A Fugitive Slave,* and *The Black Man: His Antecedents, His Genius and His Achievements.*

Brown creeper, bird, picture **B** 222
Browne, Charles Farrar, American humorist **A** 206
Browne, Frances, Irish writer
history of the fairy tale **F** 21
Browne, Sir Thomas, English author **E** 254
Brown family, American manufacturers and philanthropists **R** 224–25

Brownian movement, zigzag motion of small particles suspended in liquid or gas. This motion is explained by assumption that molecules of liquid or gas are in constant motion. These molecules collide with and bounce off small suspended particles. Thus bombarded, particles move off in different directions. This movement is named after English botanist Robert Brown (1773–1858), one of the first to observe it.

Brownie camera **E** 44
Brownie Girl Scouts **G** 216, 217; pictures **G** 214
Browning, Elizabeth Barrett, English poet **B** 412–13
"How do I love thee?" sonnet **B** 413

Browning, John Moses (1855–1926), American inventor of firearms, b. Ogden, Utah. He received first rifle patent (1879) and devised automatic pistols, repeating rifles, and machine guns. He manufactured arms with his brother, **Jonathan Edmund Browning** (1859–1939). Browning machine guns and automatic rifles (known as the BAR) were used extensively by the United States in World War II and in the Korean War.
memorial in Belgium for Utah inventor **U** 253

Browning, John M., Memorial **U** 253
Browning, Robert, English poet **B** 412–13; **E** 263
collection of works at Baylor University, Texas **T** 131
"Pied Piper of Hamelin, The," excerpt **B** 413–14
quotation from *Pippa Passes* **Q** 19

Brownout, a popular term used to describe a reduction in electrical voltage. At times during the early 1970's more power was needed than could be produced, especially on hot days, with many air conditioners running. Reduction of voltage prevented the complete loss of electrical power (blackouts) in some areas.

Brown rats **R** 278
Brown rice **G** 282; **R** 232
Brown Shirts, Nazi storm troopers **N** 71
Fascism **F** 64
Brownstone, a kind of sandstone **S** 433
Brown sugar **S** 453
Brown Swiss, cattle **C** 147; **D** 8; picture **D** 5
Brown thrashers, birds **B** 220
state bird of Georgia **G** 133
Brown University, Providence, Rhode Island **R** 218; picture **R** 219
Broz, Josip see Tito

Brubeck, Dave (David Warren Brubeck) (1920–   ), American jazz musician, b. Concord, Calif. He began his career with small dance bands in San Francisco. He formed Dave Brubeck Trio (1950) and then Quartet (1951), in which he plays piano, and toured Europe and Middle East for U.S. State Dept. (1958). His recordings of modern jazz include *Jazz Goes to College.*

Bruce, Blanche Kelso (1841–1898), American politician, b. Farmville, Va. He held several local and state offices, then served (1875–81) as one of the two Negro senators from Mississippi during Reconstruction period. He was recorder of deeds in Washington, D.C. (1889–95).

Bruce, James, Scottish explorer **A** 67
Bruce, Robert see Robert I, king of Scotland
Brucellosis (bru-cel-LO-sis), disease, or **undulant fever** **C** 149; **D** 220
Bruckner (BROOK-ner), **Anton,** Austrian composer and organist **G** 188
choral music **C** 279
Mahler influenced by **M** 30
symphonies **M** 541
Brueghel (BRUR-ghel), **Pieter, The Elder,** Flemish painter **B** 414–15

Dutch and Flemish art   **D** 352
Children's Games, painting   **D** 354
Harvesters, The, painting   **R** 170
Wedding Dance, The, painting   **B** 415
Bruges (BRUGE), old Flemish town in Belgium   **S** 428
Brulé (bru-LAY), **Étienne,** French explorer   **G** 326, 329;
   M 272

Brumel, Valery (1942–   ), Russian athlete, b. Tolbuzino,
Siberia. He jumped 7 feet 5¾ inches, setting new world
high-jump record in Moscow (1963). He was named
Master of Sport of U.S.S.R., highest honor awarded to
athlete by Soviet Union, in 1961. He won a gold medal
in 1964 Olympics. A motorcycle accident the next year
ended his career. Picture   **O** 114.

Brumidi (bru-MI-di), **Constantino,** Italian artist   **W** 30

Brummell, Beau (George Byron Brummell) (1778–1840),
English dandy, b. London. A close friend of Prince of
Wales, later George IV, who made him an officer in
King's regiment (1794), he became noted for excellent
taste in dress, and established standards of fashion.
After losing his fortune by gambling, he fled to Calais,
France, to escape creditors (1816). He was British consul
in Caen (1830–32) and died in insane asylum in Caen.

Brunei (BRUNE-i), **sultanate of,** British protectorate on
   Borneo   **B** 336, 338
   flag   **F** 237
   Malaysia   **M** 56
   Southeast Asia   **S** 328
Brunel (bru-NEL), **Isambard,** English engineer   **O** 24
Brunelleschi (bru-nel-LESC-i), **Filippo,** Italian architect
   A 380–81
   Florence Cathedral, Italy, picture   **I** 462
   Foundling Hospital, Florence   **R** 163; picture   **R** 165
   Italian architecture   **I** 465
   perspective rules established   **P** 158
   Renaissance architecture   **R** 161, 163

Brunhoff, Jean de (1899–1937), French author and
illustrator of children's books, b. Paris. He exhibited with
group of artists at Galérie Champigny in Paris. His
stories about an elephant who leaves the jungle to lead
life in Paris were based on bedtime stories told to his
children. His books include *The Story of Babar, the Little
Elephant* and *The Travels of Babar.*
   Babar, the King, picture from   **C** 246

Brünnhilde *see* Brynhild
Brushes
   paintbrushes, how to care for   **P** 34
Brushes, of electric generators and motors   **E** 121, 131
   electric motors   **E** 137
Brusilov (bru-SI-lof), **Aleksei,** Russian general   **W** 278
Brussels, capital of Belgium   **B** 129
   City Hall, picture   **B** 131
   German troops, 1914, picture   **W** 272
Brussels sprouts, vegetable related to cabbage   **V** 287
   leaves we eat   **P** 307; picture   **P** 306
Brussels Universal and International Exhibition, 1958
   F 17
Brutus, Marcus Junius, Roman statesman   **C** 6
Bryan, John Neely, first settler in Dallas, Texas   **D** 14
Bryan, William Jennings, American statesman   **B** 415–16
   famous Nebraskan   **N** 84
   McKinley and Bryan   **M** 188
   oratory   **O** 181
Bryant, William Cullen, American poet and editor   **B** 416
   American literature   **A** 200
Bryce Canyon National Park, Utah   **U** 249; picture **U** 106

Bryde's whales   **W** 149–50
Brynhild (BRURN-hilt), in Norse mythology   **N** 281
   in Wagner's operas called Brünnhilde   **O** 152
Bryophyllum, or **life plant,** picture   **P** 300
   leaves, special kinds of, picture   **L** 120
Btu's *see* British thermal units
Buada, main center of Nauru   **N** 61
Bubble chambers
   ions and ionization   **I** 353
Bubble sextants, instruments for air navigation   **N** 67

Buber (BU-ber), **Martin** (1878–1965), Jewish religious
philosopher, b. Vienna, Austria. A professor of comparative religion at the University of Frankfurt (1923–33), he
was forced by Nazis to leave Germany. He went to Israel
and became professor of social philosophy at Hebrew
University in Jerusalem (1938–51). He played an important role in Zionist movement and in reviving literature and culture of Chasidic sect.

Bubi, a people of Africa   **E** 273
Bubonic plague, disease   **I** 287
   disaster at the end of the Middle Ages   **M** 295
   medieval England   **E** 219
   Norway   **N** 344
   Roman Catholic Church damaged by   **R** 293
Buccaneers (buc-ca-NEERS), pirates of the Spanish
   Main   **P** 263
   Henry Morgan, lieutenant governor of Jamaica   **J** 18
Bucephalus (bue-CEPH-a-lus), favorite horse of Alexander
   the Great   **A** 151, 153
Buchanan, James, 15th president of United States
   B 417–20
   pre-Civil War days   **C** 321, 322
Bucharest (bu-ca-REST), capital of Rumania   **R** 357; pic-
   tures **R** 358, 359

Bucher, Lloyd (1927–   ), American naval officer, b. Pocatello, Idaho. He commanded the U.S.S. *Pueblo,* an
electronic intelligence ship that was seized by North
Korea in the Sea of Japan on January 23, 1968. Bucher
and his crew were held as spies for nearly a year. After
lengthy negotiations and a United States government
apology, the North Koreans released Bucher and his men.
A U.S. Navy court of inquiry later recommended that
Bucher be court-martialed for failing to defend his ship
properly, but the Secretary of the Navy set aside the
court's ruling.

Buchmanism (BOOK-man-ism) (also called the Oxford
Group Movement), international program organized
(1921) at Oxford University by American evangelist **Frank
Nathan Daniel Buchman** (1878–1961). Its program of
spiritual restoration advocated "world-changing through
life-changing." It held that path to ideal society lay in
character improvement, especially development of such
traits as honesty and selflessness. The movement spread
to 60 countries and was later called Moral Re-Armament.

Buck, Pearl, American author   **B** 421
   American literature   **A** 212
   Big Wave, The, excerpt   **B** 421–22
Bucket brigades, for fire fighting   **F** 146
Buckeye, tree
   state tree of Ohio   **O** 61
Buckeye State, nickname for Ohio   **O** 61, 64
Buckingham, James, English traveler and author   **U** 256
Buckingham Palace, of Britain's royal family   **L** 336
Buckskin, leather from deer   **L** 107
Buckwheat, grain   **G** 285
   seeds, pictures   **G** 284
Bucolic (bue-COL-ic) **poetry,** about country life   **E** 151

Bucrania (bu-CRAY-nia), sculptured ornament **D** 70
Budapest (BU-da-pest), capital of Hungary **H** 286; picture **H** 287
  bookmobile, picture **L** 199
Buddha (BU-dha), **Prince Siddhartha Gautama,** founder of Buddhism **B** 422–25
  statue in Kamakura, Japan, picture **R** 147
Buddhism, religion founded by Buddha **B** 423–25
  Asia, chief religions of **A** 460
  Burma **B** 454
  China **C** 261
  fables and folk tales **F** 3
  first five commandments **L** 41
  food taboos **F** 334
  funeral customs **F** 492
  Great Buddha of Kamakura, Japan, picture **J** 47
  Indian literature **O** 220e
  Japan **J** 24–25, 31, 46
  Lamaism in Tibet **T** 175
  marriage rites **W** 102–03
  oriental sculpture **O** 212–13, 216
  originated in India **I** 131
  religions of the world **R** 147
  religious holidays **R** 154
  Southeast Asia **S** 330
  Thai monks, picture **A** 447
Budding, a type of reproduction **R** 177
  hydra **J** 73
Budding, plant propagation by grafting **N** 420
  apple trees **A** 335, 337
  orange trees **O** 178

Budge, Don (John Donald Budge) (1915–), American tennis player, b. Oakland, Calif. He was first to achieve tennis "Grand Slam," winning U.S., British, Australian, and French singles championships in same year (1938). He became professional player (1939) and thereafter won several professional championships. He wrote *How Lawn Tennis Is Played* and *Budge on Tennis.*

Budgerigars (BUDGE-eri-gars), "talking" birds **P** 83; pictures **P** 84
  budgies as pets **B** 245
Budget, United States Bureau of the
  fiscal policy **I** 253
Budgets, family **B** 425–26
  installment buying **I** 288–89
  See also Consumer education
Budgies see Budgerigars
Buds, of plants
  trees **T** 282–83
Bud scales, of plants **P** 295
Buen Aire see Bonaire, island
Buena Vista (BUANE-a VE-sta), **battle of,** 1847 **M** 239
  Taylor, Zachary **T** 35

Bueno (bu-A-no), **María Esther** (1940–), Brazilian tennis player, b. Rio de Janeiro. She won Brazilian National Championship (1954), U.S. Women's Singles Championship (1959, 1963, 1964, 1966), British Women's Singles (Wimbledon) (1959, 1960, 1964).

Buenos Aires (BUANE-os I-res), capital of Argentina **B** 426–28
  cities of Argentina **A** 394, 395
  Plaza de Mayo, picture **A** 391
  port, picture **S** 293

Buff, Conrad (1886–), American artist and author, b. Speichen, Switzerland, is noted for lithographs (in the Metropolitan and British museums) as well as for murals. His wife, **Mary Buff** (1890–), has been an art teacher, critic, and assistant art curator of Los Angeles Museum. They have written and illustrated books for children, including *Dancing Cloud,* and *Forest Folk.*

Buffalo, American see Bison
Buffalo, hoofed mammals **B** 250a; pictures **B** 250a, **H** 216
  Asian work animal **A** 451
  plowing a rice paddy, picture **B** 456
Buffalo, New York **N** 222–23
Buffalo Bill (William F. Cody), American scout **B** 428
  Pony Express rider **P** 392
Buffalo Gap National Grassland, South Dakota **S** 318

Buffer state, small independent country situated between larger rival powers and serving, it is hoped, to reduce conflict between them or absorb military clashes. Belgium and Luxembourg were buffer states between France and Germany before World War II.

Buffet (buf-FAY) meals **T** 2–3
Bugaku, Japanese drama **T** 164
Buganda (bu-GAN-da), former kingdom, now a region in Uganda **U** 6, 7

Bugging, or electronic eavesdropping, is the practice of using supersensitive listening devices for the purpose of intercepting private conversations. The propriety of government use of these devices for law enforcement became a controversial topic during the late 1960's.

Bugle, musical instrument **B** 429; **M** 549
  See also Trumpet
Bugle calls **B** 429
Bug River, Europe **P** 359
Bugs see Insects
Buhlwork, decorative art **D** 77
Building construction **B** 430–38
  air conditioning **A** 101–03
  bricks and masonry **B** 390–94
  bridges **B** 395–401
  bulldozers and other equipment **B** 445–48
  construction engineers **E** 205, 207
  elevators and escalators **E** 172–75
  explosives in construction **E** 394
  fireproofing **B** 438
  heating **H** 96–99
  hoisting and loading machinery **H** 143–45
  insulation and insulating materials **I** 290–92
  Invention of tools for **I** 348
  lighting **L** 279–90
  masonry **B** 391–94
  mechanical drawing **M** 197
  plumbing **P** 341–43
  stone masonry **B** 392–94
  Why don't tall buildings blow down in a strong wind? **B** 438
Building materials **B** 430–31
  adobe houses **H** 173
  bricks and brick masonry **B** 390–94
  cement and concrete **C** 165–66
  fireproofing **B** 438
  glass, as a structural material **G** 237
  homes **H** 171–77
  influenced architecture **A** 384, 385, 386, 387
  insulating materials **I** 290–92
  iron and steel **I** 396–408
  lumber and lumbering **L** 372–77
  stone **S** 433
  stone masonry **B** 393–94
  wood and wood products **W** 222–28

Bujumbura, capital of Burundi **B** 463, 464
Bukavu, Zaire, formerly Costermansville, map
Z 366a
Bukovina (bu-ko-VI-na), Rumania **R** 355–56
Bulawayo, Rhodesia **R** 229
Bulbs, underground stems **P** 300
 gardens and gardening **G** 40; picture **G** 41
 garden selection **G** 29
 leaves, special kinds **L** 120

Bulganin (bull-GAN-yin), **Nikolay Aleksandrovich**
(1895–), Russian political leader, b. Nizhni-Novgo-
rod (now Gorki). He joined Communist Party in 1917 and
served with secret police (1918–22). He held various Party
offices, including membership on Central Committee
(1939–61), Politburo (1948–52), and Party Presidium
(1952–59). He was minister of defense (1953–55), member of Supreme Soviet (1937–58), and premier (chairman
of Council of Ministers) of Soviet Union (1955–58) until removed from office on charge of conspiring against Party.

Bulgaria (bul-GAIR-ia) **B** 439–44
 Balkan wars **B** 19
 flag **F** 239
 World War I **W** 275, 281
Bulge, battle of the, 1944–45 **W** 304
 Belgium **B** 131
 Eisenhower, Dwight D. **E** 109–10
Bulkheads, protecting partitions **T** 318
Bull, constellation see Taurus
Bull, John, English composer **N** 16
Bull, Ole, Norwegian violinist **G** 376
 founded Norwegian Theater, Bergen **I** 2
Bullboats, made of buffalo hide **M** 383; **N** 329
Bull dancing, of ancient Crete **B** 449
Bulldog, picture **D** 256
Bulldozers B 445–46
 clear land for farming **F** 57
 roads and highways **R** 251
 shaping a yard, picture **B** 437
 See also Hoisting and loading machinery
Bulletproof vests, of fiber glass **A** 435
Bullets, ammunition for guns **G** 414, 417
Bullfighting B 449–51
 arenas, pictures **A** 212, **E** 304
 How did bullfighting begin? **B** 449
 Mexico **M** 241
 South America, picture **S** 285
 Spain **S** 352; picture **S** 350
Bullfrogs F 470, 472, 473
Bullheads, fish
 baits and lures **F** 206
 habitat, feeding habits, uses **F** 216
Bull-horn acacia, tree **A** 328; **P** 283
Bull in the ring, circle game **G** 13
Bullion, gold bars **G** 247
 money **M** 409
Bull-leaping, sport of ancient Crete **A** 227
Bull Moose Party, or **Progressive Party,** United States
 P 381
 Roosevelt, Theodore **R** 330
 symbol **P** 379
 Taft, William Howard **T** 9
Bull Run, battles of, 1861, 1862, Civil War **C** 322, 323
 Jackson, Thomas J., gets nickname "Stonewall" **J** 8
Bulls
 Apis, sacred bull of Egypt **C** 145
 Assyrian art **A** 240; picture **A** 241
 dairy cattle **D** 8
 elephants **E** 167
 moose, picture **H** 215
 rodeo riding **R** 281

Bulls and bears, in stock exchanges **S** 432
Bully, starting play in field hockey **F** 115
Bulnes (BOOL-nase), **Manuel,** president of Chile **C** 255
Bulwer-Lytton, Edward see Lytton, E.G.E.L. Bulwer-
Bumblebees B 124; pictures **B** 123, 124

Bumbry, Grace (1937–), American soprano, b. St.
Louis, Mo. She sang with the State Opera in Basel,
Switzerland (1960–63), and was the first Negro to sing at
the Bayreuth Festival in Germany. Her Metropolitan
Opera debut (1965) was as Princess Eboli in *Don Carlos*.

Bumppo, Natty, hero of Cooper's Leatherstocking
 Tales **C** 498
 American literature, classics in **A** 200
Bunche, Ralph, American educator and United Nations
 mediator **B** 452
 Negro educators and public officials **N** 99

Bund (from German, meaning "league" or "union"), pro-
Nazi organization formed in United States (1930's)
mainly by German-Americans who supported Adolf
Hitler. It pursued a policy of anti-Semitism and was
headed by Fritz Kuhn, who was jailed in 1941. It was
disbanded after United States entered World War II.

Bund, The, avenue in Shanghai, China **S** 138
Bundestag, West German parliament, lower house **G** 158
Bunin (BOON-yin) **Ivan,** Russian author **U** 61
Bunker Hill, battle of, 1775 **R** 199
Bunker Hill flag F 244; picture **F** 229
Bunker Hill Monument, site of battle **A** 12

Bunsen burner, gas burner used in laboratories to
provide a very hot, clean flame. It was named for Robert
Bunsen, German chemist.

Bunt, in baseball **B** 72
Buntline, Ned see Judson, Edward
Buntline Special, Colt revolver **G** 422
Buñuel, Luis, Spanish motion-picture director **M** 488a
Bunyan, John, English writer and preacher **E** 256
Bunyan, Paul, American folk hero **F** 312
 children's literature **C** 236
 statue in Bangor, Maine **M** 44
Bunyoro (bun-YO-ro), former kingdom, Uganda **U** 6
Buonaparte see Bonaparte
Buonarroti, Michelangelo see Michelangelo
Buoninsegna, Duccio de see Duccio de Buoninsegna
Buoyancy (BOY-an-cy), upward push on a floating ob-
 ject **F** 250
 giants of nature **G** 204
Buoys
 ocean currents measured with **O** 32–33
Burbage, James, English actor **D** 295
Burbage, Richard, English actor **S** 131
Burbank, Luther, American plant breeder and horticul-
 turalist **B** 453
Burdock, weed, picture **W** 105

Bureaucracy, a term generally used to refer to the administrative machinery of a government. It is sometimes applied to any large organization divided into
many departments or bureaus with a hierarchy of employees each responsible to a superior. It is often used
as a term of disparagement.
 See also Civil service

Bureaus, of the United States Government see by name,
 as Customs, United States Bureau of

Burger, Warren Earl (1907–), American lawyer and

Burger, Warren Earl (continued)
jurist, b. St. Paul, Minn. He entered private practice after graduating from law school (1931) and was later named (1955) a judge on the U.S. Court of Appeals for the District of Columbia, where he became known for his strong stand on law and order. He was named (1969) by Nixon to succeed Warren as chief justice of the U.S. Supreme Court.

Burgess, Gelett (Frank Gelett Burgess) (1866–1951), American humorist, writer, and illustrator, b. Boston, Mass. Known for writing nonsense jingles, such as "The Purple Cow," he also coined many new words—such as "blurb," meaning the writing on a book jacket. He illustrated many of his own books, including *Why Men Hate Women* and *Look 11 Years Younger*.
  "I Wish That My Room Had a Floor," nonsense rhyme **N** 274

Burgess, Thornton Waldo (1874–1965), American writer, b. Sandwich, Mass. Associate editor of *Good Housekeeping* (1904–11), he is best known for nature and animal stories written for children, including Old Mother West Wind series, *Burgess Bedtime Stories*, and *Burgess Bird Book for Children*.

Burgesses, House of, Virginia **V** 358
  Jefferson, Thomas **J** 64
Burghers of Calais, statues by Rodin **S** 103
Burghley, Lord *see* Cecil, William
Burgoyne, John, English military commander **R** 203–04
  Washington and Burgoyne **W** 40
Burgundian (bur-GUN-dian) **period,** in Dutch and Flemish music **D** 363
Burgundy wine W 189
Buri, Norse god **N** 277
Burial customs *see* Funeral and burial customs
Buried treasure P 264
Burins, cutting tools **D** 75
  engraving and graphic arts **E** 272; **G** 303
  woodworking **W** 229
Burke, Edmund, English statesman **E** 259; **O** 181
Burke, John, American statesman **N** 335
Burkitt's tumor, type of cancer **C** 93–94

Burleigh (BUR-li), **Henry Thacker** (1866–1949), American singer and composer, Negro. b. Erie, Pa. He introduced Negro spirituals on concert stage in United States and abroad, and he preserved, in writing, folk songs of the Negro race, which were previously handed down orally. Burleigh sang command performances before King Edward VII of England and other heads of state. His best-known works include songs "Little Mother of Mine," "Deep River," and "Just You."
  Negro spirituals **N** 107

Burlesque, a form of humor **H** 280
Burlington, Vermont **V** 318
Burma B 454–59
  Boy Scout, picture **A** 459
  bride and groom, picture **F** 41
  Buddhism, official religion **B** 425
  dance **D** 31
  flag **F** 237
  gemstones found in **G** 70
  monks at mealtime, picture **F** 339
  Thant, U **T** 154
  World War II **W** 294, 302, 306
Burma Road B 459
Burmese cats C 142; picture **C** 143

Burne-Jones, Sir Edward Coley (1833–1898), English painter, b. Birmingham. He was associated with pre-Raphaelite artists Dante Gabriel Rossetti and William Morris. His paintings are characterized by dreamlike, romantic idealism. They include *The Golden Stairs, The Depths of the Sea,* and *King Cophetua and the Beggar Maid.* He also designed tapestries and stained-glass windows for firm of William Morris.
  Praising Angels, tapestry **T** 23

Burnett, Frances Hodgson, American novelist
  children's literature **C** 240
Burnett, Peter H., American pioneer **O** 261
Burney, Charles, English music scholar **G** 183; **M** 524

Burnford, Sheila (1918–), Canadian author, b. Scotland. She was author of popular animal story *The Incredible Journey* and *Field of Noon,* as well as articles for *Punch,* the Glasgow *Herald,* and *Canadian Poetry.*

Burnham, Forbes (1923–), (Linden Forbes Burnham), prime minister of Guyana (formerly British Guiana). The son of a village schoolmaster, Burnham was a brilliant student. He completed his education in England, where he earned his law degree. He entered politics on his return to British Guiana, and at the age of 36 was elected mayor of Georgetown, the capital city. In 1964 he was elected prime minister. He continued to hold that post when the colony became independent Guyana in 1966. Burnham holds moderate political views in a country where political and racial tension between East Indian and Negro populations is a problem.

Burning, combustion **F** 137
Burnoose, Arab dress **C** 351

Burns, E. L. M. (Eedson Louis Millard Burns) (1897–), Canadian general, b. Westmount, Quebec. He held various commands during World Wars I and II and was chief of staff of UN Truce Supervision Organization in Palestine (1954–56) and commander of UN Emergency Force in Middle East (1956–59). He was Canadian representative to disarmament conferences in Geneva (1960, 1962–67); and was adviser to Canadian government on disarmament (1960–68).

Burns, John Horne, American novelist **A** 213
Burns, Robert, Scottish poet **B** 460; **E** 259
  quotation from "To a Louse" **Q** 20
  "Red, Red Rose, A" **B** 460
  Robert Burns's Birthday, holiday **H** 147
  "Sweet Afton" **B** 460

Burns, Tommy (Noah Bursso) (1881–1955), Canadian boxer, b. Hanover, Ontario. He won heavyweight title (1906) in 20-round decision over Marvin Hart but lost title (1908) to Jack Johnson in a fight so brutal police had to stop it in 14th round.

Burns and scalds
  first aid **F** 162
  safety measures **S** 3
Burnside, Ambrose, American soldier and statesman **R** 225
  Civil War campaigns **C** 325
Bur oak
  state tree of Illinois **I** 70
Burr, Aaron, American political leader **B** 461–62
  as vice-president, picture **V** 325
  Blennerhassett Island, West Virginia **W** 136
  duels and dueling **D** 341
  Hamilton and Burr **H** 20
  Jefferson and Burr **J** 68

Burritt, Elihu, American advocate of peace **P** 104
Burros, or donkeys **H** 235
   Colorado miners' work animal, monument **C** 400
Burroughs, Edgar Rice, American author
   science fiction **S** 84

Burroughs (BURR-ose), **John** (1837–1921), American naturalist and writer, b. near Roxbury, N.Y. His interest in birds can be seen in books *Wake-Robin* and *Birds and Poets.* He built (1895) secluded cabin, "Slabsides," on farm near Esopus, N.Y., where he spent much time writing nature essays for *Atlantic Monthly* and *New York Leader.*

Burroughs, William Seward (1855–1898), American inventor, b. Rochester, N.Y. He worked on machines for solving arithmetic problems and organized American Arithmometer Co. to manufacture them (1885). He was granted patent for first practicable calculating machine (1888).

Burrowing bees **B** 123
Burrows, of animals
   prairie dog "town," picture **A** 281
Burt, William Austin, American inventor
   made first American typewriter **C** 433

Burton, Richard (1925–   ), British actor, b. Pontrhydfen, Wales. His first stage appearance (1943) was in *Druid's Rest* in Liverpool. He acted in various Shakespearean plays, such as *The Tempest, Henry V,* and *Hamlet,* and also in films *Look Back in Anger, The Night of the Iguana, The Spy Who Came in from the Cold, Who's Afraid of Virginia Woolf?,* and *Anne of the Thousand Days.*

Burton, Robert, English author **E** 254

Burton, Virginia Lee (1909–68), American illustrator and author of children's books, b. Newton Centre, Mass. She was awarded Caldecott medal (1943) for *The Little House.* Her other books include *Katy and the Big Snow* and *Mike Mulligan and His Steam Shovel.*

Burundi (bur-UN-di) **B** 463–64
   flag **F** 235
   special-issue stamp, picture **S** 399
   See *also* Rwanda
Buses and bus travel **B** 465–66; **T** 265
   bus segregation case **S** 115
   double deckers in London, picture **L** 337
   New York City **N** 230
   pedicab, in China, picture **C** 258
Bush babies, or galagos, primates **M** 422
Bushbucks, game animals, picture **C** 488
Bush dog, of South America **D** 251

Bushido (from Japanese, meaning "the way of the warrior"), Japanese system of ethical conduct developed from code of samurai (warrior class). It includes loyalty to overlord, honor in family and social relationships, and courage in all conflicts, extending to the duty of hara-kiri, or ritual suicide. It influences Japanese life, although formal code no longer applies.
   code of the knight, a merger of three religions **J** 45–46; **R** 149

Bushmen, tribal people, numbering over 50,000, living in Botswana and South West Africa. Of slight build and thought to be related to Pygmies, they live in small nomadic bands, each led by headman. Nearly all their daily life is concerned with search for water and food. Many have left desert bands to become serfs of Bantu groups in Botswana.

   hunting to make a living **A** 62; picture **A** 300
   South West Africa **S** 336

Bushnell, David, American inventor **S** 445
Bushongo, a people of Africa **A** 76
Bush pilots, of airplanes **A** 572
Bushwhackers, proslavery men of pre-Civil War days **C** 320
Bushy Run, battle of, 1763 **P** 145
Business
   advertising **A** 27–34
   bookkeeping and accounting **B** 311–14
   co-operatives **C** 499–500
   depressions and recessions **D** 121
   fairs and expositions **F** 9–18
   international trade **I** 326–30
   Junior Achievement, Inc., student business **J** 157
   mail order **M** 31
   public relations **P** 507–08
   ranching **R** 103–04
   selling **S** 116–17
   stocks and bonds **S** 427–33
   tariff influences buyers **T** 25
   taxation **T** 26–27
   trademarks and copyright **T** 244–45
   trusts and monopolies **T** 303–06
   unemployment **U** 25–26
Business cycles, recurring series of good times and bad
   depressions and recessions **D** 121
   inflation and deflation **I** 252–53
   unemployment **U** 25
Business letters **L** 160
Business machines see Office machines
Business managers
   plays **P** 336
Busing, of students **N** 105, 262f
Busnois (bu-NWA), **Antoine,** French musician **D** 363
Busoga, Uganda **U** 6
Bustards, birds **A** 265
Bust of Ptolemy, carving, picture **G** 166
Butadiene (bu-ta-DIE-ene), gas **R** 346
Butane (BU-tane), gas
   fuel **F** 489
Butare, Rwanda **R** 363
Butcher bird see Shrike
Butler, John, American Loyalist **R** 205
Butler, Nicholas Murray, American educator **P** 105
Butler, Reg, English sculptor **E** 241
Butler, Samuel, English satirist **E** 264
Butte (BUTE), Montana **M** 440
Butter **B** 467
   dairy products **D** 12
   ghee, clarified butter **F** 340
   oils and fats **O** 79
   tests for keeping qualities, picture **F** 354
Buttercups, flowers, picture **W** 168
Butterfield Overland Stage **C** 436
Butterflies **B** 468–75
   collecting **B** 476–78
   How can you tell a butterfly from a moth? **B** 468
   how insects protect themselves, pictures **I** 275
   legend for symbol of successful love **J** 9
   locomotion **A** 296
   metamorphosis **M** 235
   migration **H** 188–89
   scales on the wings, picture **I** 272
   sucking tube, diagram **I** 270
   See *also* Metamorphosis
Butterfly collecting **B** 476–78
Butterfly fish, picture **F** 183

Butterfly stroke, swimming S 492–93
Butterfly valves, diagram V 269
Buttermilk, liquid left over from making butter B 467
   dairy products D 12
Butterwort, plant, picture P 316
Butting, contest among Eskimo E 289
Button, Sir Thomas, British explorer-trader in Canada
   M 82
Buttonholes, how to make E 188
Buttons and button collecting B 478–80
   abacus made of buttons, picture A 2
Buttonwood Tree Agreement, 1792 S 430
Buttress, in architecture A 378
   Gothic flying buttress G 265
   Middle Ages, architecture of the M 296–97
Butyl (BU-til), synthetic rubber R 346
Butyl alcohol F 90
Buxtehude (boox-teh-HU-de), Dietrich, German com-
   poser B 64
Buyers, for stores F 70
Buying on margin, a stock purchase in which only a
   part of price is paid S 432
Buys Ballot's law, of winds and pressure W 186

Buzzards, soaring hawks, worldwide in distribution.
Closely related to eagles, buzzards have hooked bills
and broad, rounded wings. They feed on a variety of
small mammals and reptiles. In America these birds
are commonly called hawks.

Buzzards Bay, Massachusetts
   light tower, picture L 277
Byblos (BIB-los), site of ancient Phoenician city, Lebanon, picture L 124
   invention of alphabet A 170
Byelorussia see Belorussia

Bykovsky, Valery Fyodorvich (1934–70), Russian cosmonaut, b. Pavlovo-Pasad. He orbited earth (June, 1963)
simultaneously with Valentina Vladimirovna Tereshkova
(first woman astronaut), although in different space capsule. He orbited 81 times and covered 2,046,000 miles
in 4 days, 23 hours, and 6 minutes—setting new records.
   space flight data S 344, 345

Bylaws, laws or rules by which a city, corporation, or
other organization governs its affairs and members. In
the case of a municipality a bylaw has the force of law,
whereas in other organizations it is merely an agreement among members. Term also refers to a secondary
rule subordinate to a constitution.
   parliamentary procedure P 79

Bypass engines J 86
Byrd, Harry F., U.S. senator V 360
Byrd (BIRD), Richard Evelyn, American explorer B 481
   polar exploration by air P 365
   polar regions P 368
Byrd, William, English composer E 269
   chamber music C 185
   Renaissance music R 173
Byrd, William, II, Virginia diarist A 196–97
Byrnes, James Francis, American statesman S 309
Byron, George Gordon, Lord, English poet B 481–82
   place in English literature E 260–61
   Childe Harold's Pilgrimage, excerpt B 482
   Prisoner of Chillon, The, excerpt B 482
Byssus (BISS-us), filaments of mussels O 272
Byzantine (BIZ-an-tene) architecture B 483–90
   art as a record A 438b
   cathedrals C 131
   early architecture A 377
   Russian architecture U 52
Byzantine art B 483–90
   art as a record A 438b
   early Christian art in Italy I 458
   enameling E 191; picture E 192
   Harbaville Triptych, picture S 97
   illuminated manuscripts I 87–88
   influence on medieval art M 296, 297
   jewelry designs J 94
   mosaics, painting P 17–18; picture P 16
Byzantine Empire, or Eastern Roman Empire B 491–92
   art and architecture B 483–90
   Constantine the Great C 489
   Crusades C 538–40
   decline of the Roman Empire in the west R 308
   decorative arts D 70
   Turkey, history of T 327
Byzantium (bi-ZAN-tium), later Constantinople (now Istanbul), Turkey B 491; T 326
   one of the world's great cities C 305

ILLUSTRATION CREDITS

The following list credits, by page, the sources of illustrations used in Volume B of THE NEW BOOK OF KNOWLEDGE. Credits are listed illustration by illustration—left to right, top to bottom. Wherever appropriate, the name of the photographer or artist has been listed with the source, the two being separated by a dash. When two or more illustrations appear on one page, their credits are separated by semicolons.

234 Harry & Ruth Crockett; John H. Gerard; courtesy picture; John H. Gerard; John H. Gerard.
235 Karl Maslowski—Photo Researchers; Camera Clix; Arthur A. Allan—Bird Photographs; National Audubon Society; Karl Maslowski—Photo Researchers.
236 Camera Clix; John H. Gerard; Arthur A. Allan—Bird Photographs; courtesy picture; courtesy picture.
238 Gaetano Di Palma
239 Leonard Lee Rue—Annan; John H. Gerard; courtesy picture; John H. Gerard; Karl Maslowski—Photo Researchers.
240 George Systrand—Annan; Bird Photographs; John H. Gerard; Photo Researchers; Bird Photographs; Louis Ruhe & David Roth—National Audubon Society.
241 John Markham—Annan; John H. Gerard; John H. Gerard; N. D. Searcy; John H. Gerard.
242 John H. Gerard; Karl Maslowski—Photo Researchers; S. A. Grimes; Hal H. Harrison—Camera Clix.
243 Gaetano Di Palma
244 Gaetano Di Palma
245 Charles E. Mohr—National Audubon Society
246 Bradley Smith—Photo Researchers
247 FPG; John H. Gerard; H. V. Lacey—Annan.
249 George Bakacs
249a Culver Pictures
250 Rae McIntyre—Annan; Bern Keating—Black Star.
252 The Lighthouse, New York Association for the Blind
253 American Foundation for the Blind, Inc.
255 Donald Johnson and Caspar Henselmann
256 Donald Johnson and Caspar Henselmann
257 Chas. Pfizer & Co., Inc.; Dr. Keith R. Porter—Biological Laboratories, Harvard University.
258 Donald Johnson and Caspar Henselmann
259 Donald Johnson and Caspar Henselmann
260 DPI; Horst Schafer—Photo Trends.
261– George Bakacs
263
265 Myles Adler
267– Donald Johnson and Caspar Henselmann
285
286 Donald Johnson and Caspar Henselmann; Nancy Grossman.
289– Donald Johnson and Caspar Henselmann
292
294 Donald Johnson and Caspar Henselmann
295 Donald Johnson and Caspar Henselmann
298 George Buctel
300 I. Fat—Black Star
301 Robert Conlan
303 George Buctel
304 Tom Hollyman—Photo Researchers
305 Charles Perry Wiemer; Foto Linares.
307 George Buctel; Government of India.
308 E. Boubat—Réalités; Joseph Breitenbach.
309 Copyright 1953 by Ludwig Bemelmans, permission of the Viking Press
310 Copyright 1952, 1953 by Mary Norton, permission of Harcourt Brace
310a From Up the Road Slowly by Irene Hunt, Follett Publishing Co., 1966; Copyright 1970 by Maurice Sendak. Harper & Row, Publishers.
310b Copyright 1962 by Brian Wildsmith—Permission of Franklin Watts, Inc.
311 Ezra Stoller Associates

318 Courtesy of Oriental Institute, University of Chicago; Howard Koslow
319 Bibliothèque Nationale
320 The Pierpont Morgan Library
321 From A History of Book Illustration by David Bland, published by Harcourt, Brace & World.
323 Reprinted with permission of the publisher from Ronnie and the Chief's Son by Elizabeth Coatsworth, illustrated by Stefan Martin, Copyright 1962 by The Macmillan Co.
324 From Gunnar's Daughter by Sigrid Undset, reprinted with permission of Alfred A. Knopf, Inc.
328 James Caraway
330 Robert Bendick
333 Gerald McConnell
334 Suzanne Szasz
335 Robert Frankenberg
336 Christa Armstrong—Nancy Palmer
337 George Buctel
338 Lowber Tiers—Monkmeyer; Horace Bristol, Jr.—Photo Researchers; Lowber Tiers—Monkmeyer; UPI.
339 George Buctel
340 Elliot Erwitt—Magnum
340a George Buctel
341 Glass Container Manufacturers Institute Inc.
343 Ewing Galloway
344 Robert Frankenberg
345 Edward Vebell; Edward Vebell; George Bakacs.
346 Edward Vebell; George Bakacs.
347 George Bakacs
351 Marvin E. Newman
354 The National Portrait Gallery, London
355 Boys' Clubs of America
356 William Hillcourt—Boy Scouts of America
358 Don Spaulding
359 Boy Scouts of America; William Hillcourt—Boy Scouts of America; Greater New York Councils, Boy Scouts of America.
361 Culver
362 Bettmann Archive
363 Donald Johnson and Caspar Henselmann
364 Donald Johnson and Caspar Henselmann
367 Caspar Henselmann
368 Donald Johnson and Caspar Henselmann
371 National Gallery of Art, Washington, D.C., Chester Dale Collection
372 Martin Swithinbank—PIP
373 George Buctel
374 Jerry Frank—Alpha
376 Dan Page—Photo Researchers
377 Harrison Forman
379 Ed Drews—Photo Researchers; Scheier—Monkmeyer.
380 Joe Barnell—Shostal
381 David Pratt—Rapho Guillumette; Dan Page—Photo Researchers.
382 Raymond Nania—Photo Researchers; John Moss—Photo Researchers.
385 David Sousa
386 George Sottung
387 George Sottung
390 Marc & Evelyne Bernheim-Rapho
392 Herbert Lanks—A. Devaney; George Bakacs.
394 Scofield—Ewing Galloway; James Sawders—Cushing.
395 Sabine Weiss—Rapho Guillumette
396 Charles Rotkin—PFI
397 Howard Koslow
398 Fred Lyon—Rapho Guillumette

399 Manugian Studio—Cyr Agency; Ben Feder; Camera Press Ltd.—Illustration Research Service.
400 Barnaby's Picture Library—Illustration Research Service
401 Allen J. Herman—Alpha
403 George Hunter—Shostal
404 George Hunter; Bob & Ira Spring.
405 George Buctel
406 Esther Henderson—Rapho Guillumette; Bob & Ira Spring; George Hunter.
406b British Columbia Government Photo
406c Diversified Map Corp.
406d Annan Photo Features
409 Olin Mathieson Chemical Corp.
413 W. T. Mars
415 The Detroit Institute of Arts
417 James Cooper
418 Mercersberg Academy; The James Buchanan Foundation for the Preservation of Wheatland, Lancaster, Pa.
419 Bettmann Archive
420 Bettmann Archive
423 William Froelich
424 Henri Cartier-Bresson—Magnum; Lawrence L. Smith—Photo Researchers.
426 George Buctel
427 Jerry Cooke; Totino; Ed Drews—Photo Researchers.
428 Robert Frankenberg
429 Shostal
432 Chase Manhattan Bank; Chase Manhattan Bank; Chase Manhattan Bank.
433 Henry Brennan; Chase Manhattan Bank; J. Alex Langley—Pan American.
436 A. Devaney; A. Devaney; National Association of Home Builders; National Association of Home Builders; Henry Brennan; A. Devaney.
437 National Association of Home Builders; Ray Jacobs' Studio; Henry Brennan.
439 George Buctel
440 Camera Press Ltd.—Pix
441 PIP; Shostal.
442 Peter Schmid—Pix
443 Dennis Stock—Magnum
445 ANI
446 Caterpillar Tractor Co.; Alpha.
447 ANI; Ted Speigel—Rapho Guillumette.
451 Vincent J-R Kehoe
452 United Nations
453 UPI
455 George Buctel
456 Pictorial Parade; United Nations.
457 Stockpile
458 Fujihira—Monkmeyer; Harrison Forman.
461 Robert Conlan
463 George Buctel
464 Black Star
465 Greyhound Corp.
467 USDA Photo
468 Annan; Hugh Spencer; Lynwood M. Chace.
469 Gaetano Di Palma
470 Ross E. Hutchins
471 T. Shaw—Annan
472– Gaetano Di Palma
475
476 George Bakacs
478 Robert Crandall Associates
484 Scala; Shostal.
485 Hirmer; George R. Hann.
486 Hirmer
487 Art Reference Bureau
488 Jane Latta—Photo Researchers
489 Hirmer; Josephine Powell.
490 Hirmer
491 W. T. Mars

C, third letter of the English alphabet **C** 1
See also Alphabet
C-14 see Carbon-14

Cabala (CAB-al-a), or **Kabbalah** or **Cabbala,** mystical tradition in Judaism, attributing mystical significance to each word, letter, and number found in Scriptures. It was popular in many medieval Jewish communities, especially during 12th to 16th centuries. The tradition was subscribed to by Christians, who believed they could substantiate divinity of Christ and other Christian beliefs in the Cabala. The Zohar (Book of Splendor) is the most sacred book of Cabalists.

Caballero, Fernán see Böhl de Faber, Cecilia
Cabaret, musical **M** 543
Cabbage, vegetable **V** 290
   Alaska produces, picture **A** 137
   leaves we eat **P** 307; picture **P** 306
Cabbage palmetto (Sabal palmetto), tree
   state tree of Florida, South Carolina **F** 259; **S** 296

Cabell (CAB-ell), **James Branch** (1879–1958), American author, b. Richmond, Va. He wrote a series of romantic novels set in fictional country of Poictesme. In this collection, known as the Biography of Manuel, characters often trace ancestry to historic Virginia. Cabell's best-known works are *Jurgen, Smire,* and *Let Me Lie.*

Cabeza de Vaca (ca-BAY-tha day BA-ca), **Alvar Núñez** (1490?–1557?), Spanish explorer and public official, b. Jerez de la Frontera. He was one of four survivors on the ill-fated Spanish expedition to Florida (1528) that ended on an island off Texas. After 8 years spent wandering and in captivity of Indians, he reached a Spanish settlement in Mexico. Returning to Spain (1537), he was appointed colonial governor of Paraguay (1540). But the colonists revolted, and Cabeza de Vaca was sent back to Spain and then banished to Africa (1545). He was later recalled to be supreme court judge of Seville.

Cabinda (ca-BIN-da), enclave province of Angola **A** 260
Cabinet, of the United States **P** 447–48
   flags **F** 230
   Harding's cabinet, picture **H** 40
Cabinetmaking **W** 230
   furniture **F** 504
Cabinets, in government **P** 81
   United States, presidential advisers **P** 447–48
Cable, George Washington, American novelist **A** 205
Cable cars
   Bavarian Alps, picture **G** 103
   San Francisco **S** 31
Cable logging **L** 374; **R** 331, 332
Cables, submarine **T** 54; picture **E** 142e
   communication, history of **C** 438
   electronic communication, history of **E** 142d–142e
   Field, Cyrus, promoted first underwater transatlantic cable **F** 113
   first transatlantic cable **T** 52
   telephone **T** 59–60
   underwater telephone network **C** 439
Cable tool drilling, for petroleum **P** 172
Cable TV, device in electronic communication **E** 142c
   television, new industry in **T** 67, 70b–70c, 71
Cabochon (CAB-osh-on), cut of gemstones **G** 71
Cabooses (ca-BOO-ses), of freight trains **R** 83
Cabot, John, Italian explorer for England **C** 2; **E** 382
   English claim to Canada **C** 68
   flag he carried **F** 228
Cabot, Sebastian, Italian explorer for England **C** 2
   how Argentina was named **A** 388

Cabot family, of Massachusetts **M** 147
Cabral (ca-BROL), **Pedro Alvares,** Portuguese navigator **E** 382; **P** 403

Cabrillo (cab-RI-yo), **Juan Rodríguez** (?–1543), Portuguese navigator. He sailed to Mexico (1520) with Pánfilo de Narváez under Spanish flag and was with Hernando Cortés at capture of Mexico City (1521). He explored California coast (1542).
   California, history of **C** 28

Cabrini (cob-RI-ni), **Saint Frances Xavier** (Mother Cabrini) (1850–1917), first U.S. citizen to be canonized, b. Sant'Angelo Lodigiano, Italy. She founded Missionary Sisters of the Sacred Heart in Codogno, Italy, and was then sent to United States (1889) to work among Italian immigrants. She became American citizen (1909) and traveled throughout United States, South America, and Europe establishing convents, schools, and hospitals. She was canonized (1946) by Pope Pius XII, who later named her patron saint of emigrants (1950).

Cabriole leg, of furniture **F** 507; picture **F** 508
Cacao (ca-CA-o), tree yielding chocolate and cocoa **C** 274–75
   cocoa butter **O** 79
Cachalots (CASH-a-lots), or sperm whales **W** 147
Cachí (ca-CHI), Costa Rica, picture **C** 517
CACM see Central American Common Market
Cacomistles (CAC-o-mistles), animals related to racoons **R** 26–27
Cactus, plant **C** 3–4
   adaptations of plants to surroundings, pictures **L** 215
   Burbank's spineless cactus, picture **B** 453
   desert plants, pictures **D** 125, 126
   desert terrarium, how to make **T** 104
   organ pipe cactus, Arizona **A** 414
   saguaro cactus, state flower of Arizona **A** 402, 414
   source of peyote **C** 4
Cactus wrens, birds, pictures **B** 234
   state bird of Arizona **A** 402
Caddies, carriers of golf clubs **G** 260
   how to become a good golfer **G** 255–56
Caddis flies, insects **I** 279
Cadets, students at United States Military Academy, picture **U** 167
Cadette (ca-DETT) **Girl Scouts** **G** 216, 218; pictures **G** 215, 217

Cadillac, Sieur Antoine de la Mothe (1656?–1730), French soldier and official in America, b. Gascony. He went to America (1683) and was given command of post at Mackinac (1694). He conceived plan to fortify Detroit River, protecting French fur trade in region from English and established settlement (1701) later called Detroit. He was governor of Louisiana (1713–16).

Cadman, Charles Wakefield (1881–1946), American composer and organist, b. Johnstown, Pa. His interest in music of American Indians is reflected in such works as operas *The Land of the Misty Water* and *Shanewis* and song "From the Land of the Sky-Blue Water."

Cadmium, element **E** 154, 160
Cadmus, legendary Phoenician prince **A** 172
Caduceus (ca-DU-ce-us), symbol of the doctor, picture **M** 208c
Caecilians (ce-CIL-ians), land-water animals **F** 476–77
Caedmon (CAD-mon), English poet **E** 246
Caesar (CE-zer), **Gaius Julius,** Roman general and statesman **C** 5–6
   Cicero's opposition to **C** 298

Caesar, Gaius Julius (continued)
ciphers used in secret messages **C** 369, 370
dictator of Roman Republic **R** 303
England invaded by **E** 215
Julius Caesar, play by Shakespeare **S** 135
Mark Antony delivered his funeral oration **M** 100
place in Latin literature **L** 78–79
quoted **B** 130; **Q** 20
Roman calendar **C** 12
Why were the Roman emperors called Caesars? **C** 6

Caesar (CE-zar), **Sid** (1922–), American comedian, b. Yonkers, N.Y. Known as a master of pantomime, his TV shows include *Your Show of Shows* with Imogene Coca and Carl Reiner, *Caesar's Hour*, and *The Sid Caesar Show*. He appeared on Broadway in *Little Me* (1962–63) and *Four on a Garden* (1971).

Caesar Augustus see Augustus
Caesarea, Israel **I** 444
Caetano (cay-TAHN-o), **Marcello,** premier of Portugal **P** 403
Cafeterias (ca-fet-ERE-i-as), restaurants **R** 186
Caffeine (ca-FENE), substance in coffee and tea **C** 374
drugs as stimulants **D** 329–330
Cagayan (ca-ga-YON) **River,** Philippines **P** 187
Cagliavi, Paolo see Veronese, Paolo
Cagniard de la Tour (can-YAR d'la TOUR), **Charles,** French doctor **F** 88
Cahaba (ca-HA-ba), Alabama **A** 127
CAI (computer-assisted instruction) **C** 457; **P** 477

Caiaphas (CAI-af-as) or **Caiphas, Joseph,** Jewish high priest (about A.D. 18–35). According to Bible (Matthew 26), he presided at council before which Christ was arraigned. Later he was present at trial of John and Peter when they were forbidden to preach (Acts 4).

Caiman, or cayman, a kind of crocodile, picture **C** 534
kinds of reptiles **R** 180–81

Cain and Abel, in the Old Testament (Genesis 4), sons of Adam and Eve. Abel was a sheep herder, Cain a tiller of the ground. Cain killed his brother when God favored Abel's offering. For his sin Cain was condemned by God to a life of wandering.

Cairo (KIRE-O), capital of Egypt, The Arab Republic of **C** 7–8; **E** 92f
Nile River, at Cairo, picture **E** 90b
tomb-mosque of Sultan Hasan, picture **I** 417
Caisson disease see Bends, the
Caissons, watertight chambers for construction work **D** 81
building construction **B** 401, 434
Caisson Song, by Edmund L. Gruber **N** 25
Cajuns (CAY-juns), French Canadian settlers in Louisiana **L** 349, 353
Cakewalk, dance, musical forerunner of jazz **J** 57
Calais (cal-AY) **Lighthouse,** France, picture **L** 278
Calamine (CAL-a-mine), ore **Z** 370

Calamity Jane (Martha Jane Burke) (1852?–1903), American frontier personality, b. near Princeton, Mo. She grew up in Montana mining camps, where she became expert marksman and rider. She dressed and acted like a man. Her nickname came from legend that calamity followed her constantly. She often rode with frontiersman Wild Bill Hickok during her days in Deadwood, S.D.

Calamus root, or sweet flag, plant
plant remedy **P** 314; picture **P** 315

Calcars, spurs, of bats, picture **B** 92
Calcite, form of calcium carbonate **R** 267; picture **R** 265
Calcium, element **E** 154, 160
coral polyp content **C** 503; picture **C** 504
lime needed for plant growth **F** 96
nutrition, use in **N** 416
strontium chemically similar to calcium **E** 156
water desalting **W** 56a
Calculators, office machines **O** 55–56
automation **A** 532–33
See also Computers
Calculus (CAL-cu-lus), branch of mathematics **M** 157
Newton, Isaac **N** 206
Calcutta (cal-CUT-ta), India **C** 9–11; **I** 122; picture **I** 128
branch of a New York bank, picture **B** 51

Caldecott (CALL-de-cott), **Randolph** (1846–86), English artist and illustrator, b. Chester, England. Still honored by the award that bears his name, given each year to the artist of the most distinguished American picture book, Caldecott pursued an art career throughout his life. His sketches appeared in England and the United States. He also modeled in clay and worked in oil. Hoping to improve his delicate health and, at the same time, to sketch the American scene, he went to Florida in 1886. There he died of tuberculosis at the height of a distinguished career. Among the many books he illustrated are *The Diverting Story of John Gilpin* and *The Three Jovial Huntsmen*.
"John Gilpin's Ride," picture **C** 239

Caldecott medal, book award **B** 309; **C** 242
Calder (CALL-der), **Alexander,** American sculptor **U** 116
sculpture of forms in motion **S** 105
Lobster Trap and Fish Tail **M** 398
mobile, picture **D** 137
modern art **M** 397
Seven-Footed Beastie, sculpture, picture **A** 438e
Steel Fish, mobile **S** 104
Caldera, caved-in summits of ancient volcanos
Crater Lake, Oregon **O** 192
Valles Caldera, New Mexico **N** 183
Caldera, Rafael, Venezuelan president **V** 300
Calderón de la Barca (cal-der-ON day la BAR-ca), **Pedro,** Spanish dramatist **D** 296
Spanish literature and music **S** 369, 372–73
Calendar Islands, Maine **M** 44
Calendars **C** 11–13
ancient Egyptian **A** 222
Aztec calendar stone, pictures **I** 195; **W** 220
biological calendars of plants and animals **L** 247–50
Caesar, Julius **C** 6
Easter, how the date falls **E** 41
folklore of calendar customs **F** 305
international date line **I** 309–10
measuring time by moon and sun **T** 193–94
moon's phases shown on July, 1969, calendar **M** 447
New Year's Day around the world **N** 208
religious holidays by different calendars **R** 153
timing of migration **H** 191–92
tree-ring calendars **T** 286–87
Calendar clocks or watches **W** 50
Calenders, machines with heavy rollers
calendered paper **P** 53
plastics and rubber **P** 330; **R** 348
use in textile manufacturing, picture **T** 142
Calfskin leather **L** 107
Calgary (CAL-ga-ry), Alberta, Canada **A** 146f; **C** 67
Calgary Exhibition and Stampede, Canadian rodeo, **R** 281; picture **A** 146g
Calhoun (cal-HOON), **John C.,** American statesman **C** 13
as vice-president, picture **V** 326

Compromise of 1850 opposed by **C** 448
Jackson opposes his states' rights theories **J** 6
Cali (CA-li), Colombia **C** 383
Calibers (CAL-ib-ers), diameters of gun bores **G** 419;
R 233
Calico, cloth, how named **E** 385
Calico scallop, mollusk
shell, picture **S** 147
California **C** 14–30
Apollo tracking antenna at Goldstone **S** 340g
Bear Flag, 1846 **F** 228
Big Trees in Sequoia National Park, picture **N** 47
Compromise of 1850 **C** 448
earth's crust of moving plates produces faults
G 117
gold discoveries **G** 250–51
Joshua Tree National Monument, picture **N** 54
lemon growing **L** 137
local color in American literature **A** 205
Los Angeles **L** 344–47
Los Padres National Forest, picture **N** 36
Mexican War **M** 239
olive trees **O** 101
San Francisco **S** 30–31
Shasta Dam, picture **D** 17
Yosemite National Park **Y** 352–53
California, University of **C** 23
campus at Los Angeles, picture **U** 102
California Aqueduct **C** 19
California gold rush **M** 320
California gulls, state bird of Utah **U** 241
California laurel, tree, picture **T** 278
California poppies, flowers, picture **W** 170
California sea lions **W** 6
California State College **C** 23
California Test of Personality, sample **T** 119
California Trail **O** 263–65
Pony Express **P** 392
Californium (cal-i-FOR-ni-um), element **E** 154, 160

Caligula (ca-LIG-u-la) (12–41), (Gaius Caesar) Roman emperor, b. probably Antium, Italy. He was a son of Germanicus and Agrippina. Raised in army camps, he gained the nickname Caligula, or "Little Boots." He succeeded Emperor Tiberius in 37, beginning his reign with acts of generosity and justice. Following recovery from an illness that possibly affected his mind, he became increasingly cruel and capricious and demanded to be worshiped. Assassinated by Praetorian Guards, he was succeeded by his uncle Claudius.

Caliper, instrument for measuring distance between two points, such as thickness or diameter of pipes. It consists of two thin metal legs that can be opened or closed by turning screw joining them. Pictures **T** 216.

Caliphs, Age of
Moorish poets **A** 76d
Calisthenics (cal-is-THEN-ics), floor exercises **G** 428–29
rhythmical activities in physical education **P** 226–29

Caliver, Ambrose (1894–1962), American educator, Negro, b. Saltville, Va. After serving as head of the manual arts department (1918–25), he became assistant dean (1925–27), and then dean (1927–30) of Fisk University, Nashville, Tenn. He was appointed education specialist (1930) and Negro higher education specialist (1946) in the U.S. Office of Education in Washington, D.C. He became assistant to the Commissioner of Education, Federal Security Agency (1950). Instrumental in establishing Adult Education section of Office of Education, he was appointed head at its formation (1955).

Callas (CA-las), **Maria Meneghini** (1923–), operatic soprano, b. New York, N.Y. She is known for tempestuous nature and fine acting ability. Of Greek background, she studied in Athens and made her debut (1938) with National Opera of Greece in *Cavalleria Rusticana*. She gave her first American performance (1954) in *Norma* in Chicago. She has sung leading roles at La Scala in Milan and Metropolitan Opera House in New York.

Callers, for square dancing **F** 299
Calley, William, American army officer **W** 10

Callicrates (cal-LIC-ra-tese), Athenian architect and sculptor who lived during 5th century B.C. He was designer, with Ictinus, of Parthenon and temple of Athena Nike, both on Acropolis in Athens.

Callières Bonnevue (cal-YARE bon-VUE), **Louis Hector de** (1646–1703), French army officer and colonial governor in French Canada, b. Cherbourg. Appointed governor of Montreal (1684), he attempted unsuccessfully to obtain support from French King in launching offensive against English in New York. He led reinforcements from Montreal to defend Quebec from attack by English (1690). He was appointed governor of Canada (1699) at death of Frontenac, and he concluded peace treaty with Iroquois Indians (1701).

Calligraphy (cal-LIG-raphy), art of beautiful writing
H 33; pictures **W** 320, 321
Chinese art **A** 461; **O** 215
Chinese books **B** 318
Chinese literature **O** 220a
illuminated manuscripts of Islam **I** 88
illustration of scrolls and manuscripts **I** 88, 90
Islamic art **I** 417
Japan **J** 28; picture **J** 29
monks in Middle Ages **M** 297
Callimachus (cal-LIM-ac-us), Greek scholar and librarian
G 355
Calling of Saint Matthew, painting by Caravaggio
I 472

Calliope (ca-LY-o-pi), goddess of epic poetry in Greek mythology. She and her eight sisters, the daughters of Zeus and Mnemosyne, were the muses, or patrons of the arts and sciences. She was the wife of Apollo and the mother of Orpheus. Her name was given to the musical instrument whose gay sound is often heard at fairs and circuses. Operated by forcing steam through a series of whistles on a keyboard, the calliope is sometimes called a steam organ or steam piano.
See also Muses

Callisto (ca-LIST-o), satellite of Jupiter **P** 275
Call letters, of radio stations **R** 54
Call number, of books **L** 184–85
Call of the Wild, The, book by Jack London **A** 209;
picture **A** 208
Callot (cal-LO), **Jacques,** French artist
etching, *Two Clowns* **G** 304

Calloway, Cab (Cabell Calloway) (1907–), American bandleader and singer, known as the "Hi-de-ho man," b. Rochester, N.Y. His orchestra played alternately with Duke Ellington's at Cotton Club in New York (1929–39). Songs "Minnie the Moocher" and "St. James Infirmary Blues" became his trademarks. He played in all-Negro casts of film *Stormy Weather* and play *Hello, Dolly!*

Calonne (cal-LONNE), **Charles de,** French statesman
F 464

Caloric (ca-LOR-ic) **theory,** of heat **H** 86d—87
Calories (CAL-o-ries), heat units **E** 199; **H** 91
  nutrition **N** 415—16
Calorimeter (cal-or-IM-et-er), instrument for measuring specific heats **H** 91
Calotype, a photographic process **P** 212
Calpurnia (cal-PUR-nia), wife of Julius Caesar **C** 6
Calumet, land area, Indiana **I** 140; picture **I** 141
Calumet, peace pipe **I** 196
  used by Bison and Wild Rice area Indians **I** 167, 178
Calusas (ca-LU-sas), Indians native to Florida **F** 272
Calvary, or Golgotha, place of Jesus Christ's crucifixion **J** 84
Calvert, Cecil, 2nd Lord Baltimore **M** 127
  named American colony Maryland **A** 192
Calvert, George, 1st Lord Baltimore **A** 192; **M** 127
Calvert, Leonard, first governor of Maryland colony **A** 192; **M** 126, 128
Calves, young cattle **C** 148
  dairying **D** 8
  roped at rodeos **R** 281—82
  young of moose, elk, and caribou called calves **D** 83
Calvin, John, French theologian and Reformation leader **C** 30, 286; picture **R** 133
  English psalter, of hymns **H** 312
  Protestantism **P** 482—83
  Reformation **R** 134

Calvin, Melvin (1911—), American chemist, b. Saint Paul, Minn. He was awarded Nobel prize (1961) in chemistry for finding number and order of chemical reactions in photosynthesis (process by which plants make sugar from water and carbon dioxide). The plants used in his research were one-celled algae. Radioactive atoms helped trace path of chemical elements involved.

Calving (CAV-ing), detachment of icebergs from glaciers **I** 7, 25
Calvinism, religious belief **C** 286; **P** 483—84
Calvino, Italo, Italian writer **I** 481
Calypso (ca-LIP-so), Greek goddess **O** 53
Calypso music **F** 321
Cam, Diogo see Cão, Diogo
Camargo (ca-MAR-go), **Marie,** Belgian-born French ballerina **B** 24; **D** 25
Camas, plant
  Camas Area Indians of North America **I** 175—77
Cambio, Arnolfo di see Arnolfo di Cambio
Cambium layer, of plant growth **P** 290—91
  how tree rings are formed **T** 286
  trunks of trees **T** 280; **W** 225
Cambodia (The Khmer Republic) **C** 31—34
  Buddhist wedding, picture **W** 103
  dancing an ancient art **D** 31
  flag **F** 237
Cambrian period, in geology **F** 383, 384; picture **F** 385
Cambridge, Alexander A.F.W.A.G. see Athlone, 1st earl of
Cambridge (CAME-bridge) **University,** England **U** 67
Camellia (cam-E-lia), flower
  state flower of Alabama **A** 113
Camelot (CAM-el-ot), court of King Arthur **A** 442, 444
Camelot, musical play
  source of the story **E** 248
Camels **C** 34
  Africa uses for transportation **A** 65
  Arizona's trial use for transportation **A** 402
  Asian work animals **A** 451
  camel family, pictures **H** 213
  camel market, picture **E** 90b
  desert transportation, pictures **D** 126, 129
  hoofed mammals **H** 210
  in Bedouin villages, picture **S** 506

  Kuwait, picture **M** 308
  land bridges aided distribution **L** 237
  mail service, picture **P** 408
  plowing, picture **A** 99
  western Sudan, picture **S** 449
  Yemen (Aden), picture **A** 467
  yurts (tents) being loaded on camels, picture **M** 415
Camembert (CAM-em-bair) **cheese** **D** 13
Cameos (CAM-e-os), carved gemstones **J** 93; picture **J** 95
  ancient Greek art **G** 348
Camera hunting **H** 290
Camera obscura, a dark room or box with small opening for light **P** 210
Cameras **P** 201—13
  camera terms used in motion-picture production **M** 487
  communication advanced by **C** 434
  Eastman, George **E** 44
  kinds for various uses **P** 215
  lamp lens-card experiment to illustrate principle of the camera **L** 264
  lenses used in **L** 144—45
  movie cameras **P** 219
  pinhole camera, how to make **E** 364
  telescope-cameras **O** 11
  television cameras **T** 65—70
  underwater, pictures **O** 41, 43
  use in astronomy **A** 474
Camera-telescopes **T** 63
Cameroon (cam-er-OON) **C** 35—36
  flag **F** 235
Cameroon, Northern see Nigeria
Cameroon Mountains, western Africa **A** 49
Camille (ca-MELE), play by Alexandre Dumas *fils* **D** 342
Camino Real (ca-ME-no ray-OL), **El,** "The Royal Highway," historic trail in California **C** 23
Camões (Camoëns), **Luis Vaz de,** Portuguese poet **E** 387
Camouflage (CAM-o-flodge) **L** 219—20
  demonstration of camouflage **L** 220
  fishes **F** 193; pictures **F** 192
  insects use for protection **I** 274
  snakes, diamond-back rattler, picture **S** 210
  See also Protective coloration

Camp, Walter Chauncey (1859—1925), "The Father of American Football," b. New Britain, Conn. An outstanding undergraduate athlete at Yale, where he became athletic director (1888), he helped alter English rugby to approximate form of today's American football by decreasing number of players from 15 to 11, initiating position of quarterback, and putting ball in play under control of single player by means of scrimmage. He began choosing All-American football team (1889) and developed exercises known as "daily dozen."

Campanella, Roy (1921—), American baseball player, b. Homestead, Pa. As catcher for the Brooklyn Dodgers (1948—57), he was three times voted Most Valuable Player of the National League. His career was ended by serious automobile accident (1958). He was one of first Negroes in organized baseball, and was elected to Baseball Hall of Fame in 1969.

Campanella, Tommaso, Italian philosopher
  City of the Sun, book **U** 256
Campaniles (cam-pa-NE-lese), bell towers **I** 460

Campbell, Sir Alexander (1822—1892), Canadian statesman, b. Yorkshire, England. He was elected Liberal-Conservative member of Legislative Council of Canada

(1858) and was leader of Conservative opposition party in senate (1873–78). He served as postmaster general (1867–73, 1879–80, 1880–81, 1885–87), minister of justice (1881–85), and lieutenant governor of Ontario (1887–92).

Campbell, Alexander, Irish-born American founder of the Disciples of Christ **W** 138
    Protestantism, history of **P** 484
Campbell, Donald, English speedboat racing champion **B** 264

Campbell, John Archibald (1811–88), American jurist and Confederate official, b. Washington, Ga. As a U.S. Supreme Court justice (1853–61) and a loyal Southerner, he tried to avert the Civil War by mediation. He became assistant secretary of war in the Confederacy (1862–65).

Campbell, John W., Jr., author and editor **S** 85
Campbell, Sir Malcolm, English automobile racer **A** 540

Campbell, Mrs. Patrick (Beatrice Stella Tanner) (1867–1940), English actress, b. London. She is noted primarily for her roles in relatively modern dramas. She played in Henrik Ibsen's *Little Eyolf* and *Hedda Gabler* and is identified with title roles in *Magda* and *The Second Mrs. Tanqueray*. She originated the role of Eliza Doolittle in George Bernard Shaw's *Pygmalion,* which he wrote expressly for her.

Campbell, Robert (1808–1894), Canadian fur trader and explorer, b. Glenlyon, Scotland. As agent for Hudson's Bay Company (1832–71), he explored Mackenzie River district of northwest Canada. He discovered Pelly River (1840) and its source, the Yukon River, and later helped to map the region.
    first trading post in Yukon **Y** 365

Campbellton, New Brunswick, Canada **N** 138c
Camp Fire Girls **C** 37–39
Campfires, how to build **C** 43–44

Camphor ($C_{10}H_{16}O$), white resin of *Cinnamomum camphora,* evergreen tree native to Formosa. It is also made synthetically. Camphor is used in manufacture of plastics, drugs, disinfectants, explosives, and chemicals.

Campin, Robert see Flémalle, Master of
Campiña, Enrique Granados see Granados, Enrique
Camping **C** 40–46
    Camp Fire Girls **C** 37–39
    equipment to be carried in boats **B** 263
    Girls Clubs of America **G** 220
    Girl Scouts **G** 219; picture **G** 213
    National Park System **N** 55
    Olympic Mountains, picture **W** 25
    organized see Camping, organized
    vacations and travel **V** 258
Camping, organized **C** 47
    boys' camp, picture **U** 101
    for diabetic children, picture **D** 195
    vacations **V** 258
Campion, Thomas, English poet and composer **E** 270
Camp meetings, for religious services **H** 313
Campobello (cam-po-BEL-lo) **Island,** New Brunswick **M** 43
    Roosevelt Campobello International Park **N** 138d–138e
Cámpora, Hector, Argentine president **A** 396
Camps see Camping; Camping, organized
Camus, Albert, French author **F** 442
Canaan (CANE-an), ancient region corresponding to Palestine, now Jordan and Israel **I** 444
    the Promised Land **A** 7; **B** 154; **M** 468

Canada **C** 48–67
    agriculture **A** 88–92, 93–95, 100
    art **C** 63–64
    automobiles **A** 551
    ballet **C** 63
    Banff National Park **B** 42–43
    Consumer and Corporate Affairs, Department of **C** 494a
    Dominion Day **H** 152
    education **C** 62
    favorite foods **F** 342
    flag **F** 241
    football **F** 366
    foundations **F** 392
    fur trade in North America **F** 520–24
    gold discoveries **G** 253
    government see Canadian government
    history see Canadian history
    holidays **H** 147, 150, 152
    ice hockey originated **I** 35
    immigration **I** 102
    Indian dwellers of Caribou Area **I** 169–72
    Jasper National Park **J** 54–55
    literature see Canadian literature
    music **C** 63
    muskegs in the taiga belt **T** 11
    Niagara River, Horseshoe Falls **N** 243–44; picture **O** 120b
    Ottawa, capital of Canada **C** 76; **O** 124, 237–39
    paper industry **P** 56
    patriotic songs **N** 27
    police **P** 374–75
    religion **C** 289
    Saint Lawrence River and Seaway **S** 15–17
    territorial settlements with United States **T** 105, 108
    theater **C** 62–63
    United States, military co-operation with **C** 82
    See also names of provinces and territories, and principal cities

Canada, United Church of, union of Methodist, Congregationalist, and some Presbyterian churches formed by United Church of Canada Act (1924). The membership makes up approximately 20 percent of total Canadian population.
    Protestantism in Canada **C** 289; **P** 484

Canada Council, government foundation **F** 392
    cultural activities in Canada **C** 62
    Massey Commission **M** 150
Canada lynxes (LINX-es) **C** 139; picture **C** 140
Canada thistle, picture **W** 105
Canadian Armed Forces **C** 79–82
Canadian Association of Children's Librarians
    book awards **B** 309
Canadian Broadcasting Corporation (CBC) **C** 61; **O** 122
Canadian Confederation **C** 73; **P** 456e, 456h
Canadian Department of Transport **B** 262
Canadian government **C** 76–78
    civil service **C** 317
    history **C** 72–73
Canadian Group of Painters **C** 64
Canadian Guards (Governor General's Foot Guard) **Band,** picture **B** 41
Canadian history **C** 68–75
    Bill of Rights **B** 180
    boundary and territorial settlements with United States **T** 105, 108
    Cartier, Jacques **C** 124
    confederation fathered by George Brown **B** 411
    Diefenbaker, John George **D** 165
    King, William Lyon Mackenzie **K** 248
    Laurier, Sir Wilfrid **L** 85

Canadian history (continued)
 Macdonald, Sir John A.   M 3–4
 Mackenzie, Sir Alexander   M 5
 Mackenzie, William Lyon   M 5
 Massey, Vincent   M 150
 Pearson, Lester   P 115
 Revolutionary War, American   R 201
 Saint Lawrence River   S 15–16
 Seven Years War (French and Indian War)   F 458–62
 War of 1812   W 10–13
 See *also* history section of province articles
Canadian Labour Congress (C.L.C.)   L 10
Canadian Library Association (Association Canadienne des Bibliothèques), joint committees with American Library Association   L 191, 192
Canadian literature   C 63–64
 Book of the Year for Children Medal   B 309
Canadian National Railways (CNR)   C 58; picture   C 60
 Macdonald's National Policy helps build   M 4
Canadian Rockies   N 284
Canadian Shield, North America   N 285, 288
 Canada, landforms and mineral resources of   C 50, 56
 Labrador   N 140
 Michigan, Upper Peninsula of   M 260
 Ontario section   O 120
 Prairie Provinces section   A 146a; M 76, 81; S 38a
 Quebec section   Q 10, 11
 Yukon and Northwest Territories section   Y 361
Canadian Wildlife Service
 birdbanding   B 229
Canal (ca-NAL) **boats**   E 278–80
Canal du Midi (Languedoc Canal), France   E 208
Canaletto, Antonio, Italian painter   I 473
Canals   C 83–86
 Amsterdam, the Netherlands   N 118
 Bruges, Belgium, picture   B 127
 Canada   O 121–22
 canal fever in Indiana   I 142–43
 Djakarta, Indonesia   D 237
 Erie Canal   E 276–80
 Florida's system   F 262
 Grand Canal, Venice, picture   E 304
 Griboyedov Canal, Leningrad, picture   L 140
 Mars, none shown on   M 104; P 273
 new sea-level canal route considered for between North and South America   P 49
 Nicaragua considered for canal   N 246
 Ohio   O 66
 Panama Canal   P 46–49
 Saint Lawrence Seaway   S 16–17
 Saulte Sainte Marie Canals   M 266
 Suez Canal   S 450–52
 Thailand klong, picture   T 148
 transportation, importance to   T 261
 tunnels   T 314
 United States   U 110
 Which canal took its boats over a mountain by rail?   C 86
Canals, of ear   B 287–88; diagram   B 285
Canal Zone see Panama Canal Zone
Canaries, birds   B 245–46; picture   B 247
 animal learning, picture   A 284
 pets   P 181
Canaries Current   G 411
Canary Islands, off northwest Africa   I 427–28; S 356
Canasta (can-AS-ta), card game   C 113–14
Canaveral, Cape see Kennedy, Cape, Florida
Canberra (CAN-ber-ra), capital of Australia   C 87–88
 aerial view   A 499
 Apollo tracking antenna   S 340g
 Australia's cities   A 514

Cancer, constellation   C 491
 sign of, picture   S 245
Cancer, Tropic of see Tropic of Cancer
Cancer and cancer research   C 89–95
 cytocidal viruses   V 367
 diseases, research problems in   D 194, 218
 fund established by Mildred Zaharias   Z 366
 leukemia, disease   D 200
 Public Health Service testing programs   P 504
 smoking and lung cancer   S 203
 virus study   V 370–70a
Cancer epidemiology, study of the occurrence of cancer in different groups of people   C 92
Candelilla (cand-el-LI-ya), plant
 wax obtained from   W 69
Candide (con-DEDE), book by Voltaire   V 388
 European novels   N 348
 satire   H 280
Candid pictures   P 216
Candlefish torch, picture   L 280
Candlemas Day   H 159; R 155
 known as a Witches' Sabbath   W 208
Candlenut tree
 state tree of Hawaii   H 56
 torch, picture   L 280
Candlepins, a bowling game   B 349
Candles   C 96–97
 Austrian handicraft, picture   E 318
 Easter symbol   E 41
 lighting   L 280–81
 light intensity (brightness) measured in foot-candles   L 267
 made by American colonists   C 399
 riddle "Little Nanny Etticoat"   J 132
 smoke candles for search parties   F 156
Candlewood, Lake, Connecticut   C 470
Candling, egg see Egg candling
Candy and candymaking   C 98–99
 chocolate   C 274, 275
 recipes   R 115, 116
Canes, walking sticks
 symbol of furrier trade   F 515
 technique of use by the blind   B 254
Cane sugar   S 454
 sugarcane   G 319; picture   G 318
Canidae (CAN-id-e), dog family   D 243
Canis (CAY-nis), dog genus   D 243
Canis Major ("Big Dog"), constellation   C 492
Canis Minor ("Little Dog"), constellation   C 492
Cankerworms   P 289; picture   P 288
Cannae (CAN-ne), **battle of,** 216 B.C.   H 34
Cannas, flowers   G 41
Canned foods
 grades, and can sizes   M 101
Canneries
 first successful cannery in United States   F 346
 floating canneries of Japan   A 462
Cannibalism (CAN-ni-bal-ism), practice of eating one's own kind
 animals' eating habits   A 266
 early custom of Fijians   F 122
 former custom of Carib Indians   I 210

Canning, George (1770–1828), English statesman, b. London. He entered Parliament (1794) as supporter of Prime Minister William Pitt. He was undersecretary for foreign affairs (1796–99) and foreign secretary (1807–09) and leader of House of Commons (1822), and he succeeded Liverpool as prime minister (1827). Canning is noted for acknowledging independence of Spanish colonies in New World, promoting nonintervention policy, encouraging liberal and nationalist movements in

Europe, and advocating emancipation of Roman Catholics in England. He established Great Britain's independence of Holy Alliance.

Canning and preserving F 345–46
  baked goods, canned B 388–89
  botulism, poisoning, how to guard against F 354
  developed by Nicholas Appert F 345

Cannon, Annie Jump (1863–1941), American astronomer, b. Dover, Del. A long-time curator at Harvard Observatory, she was in charge of photographs of stars and other celestial bodies. She introduced best modern method of classifying stars according to surface temperatures, as shown by kind of light they give off. Miss Cannon discovered five new stars and was first to show changes in brightness for 300 other stars.

Cannonball express, railroad train T 74
Cannon bone, of the feet of animals F 81, 82; diagram F 80
Cannon Mountain or **Profile Mountain,** New Hampshire N 148, 157
Cannons G 414–26
  man shot from cannon, picture C 303
Canoes (ca-NOOS) **and canoeing** C 99–101; S 155
  birch-bark canoe, picture F 521
  earliest type of ships S 155
  hosteling H 254–55
  Indian braves building a canoe, picture I 179
  Indian workmanship, pictures I 171, 179, 182, 186
Canon, a musical form M 535
Canon, books accepted as Holy Scriptures B 152

Canonicus (ca-NON-ic-us) (1565?–1647), American Indian chief of Narragansett tribe. He ceded to Roger Williams land on which state of Rhode Island was founded (1636). Through Williams' influence, he remained friendly with English and signed a treaty acknowledging their sovereignty (1644).

Canonization, final process whereby a deceased person is declared by pope to be a saint. This occurs when at least two miracles are declared to have been brought about by intercession of person already beatified, or blessed.

Canon law L 87
Canopy bed, picture C 389
Canova (ca-NO-va), **Antonio,** Italian sculptor I 473
  neoclassic sculpture S 101–02
  Tomb of Countess Maria Christina, sculpture S 102
Cantabrian Mountains, Spain S 352
Cantaloupes (CAN-ta-lopes), melons M 216, 217
Cantata (can-TA-ta), musical form B 64–65; M 535
  choral music C 277–78
Canter, gait of a horse, picture H 230

Canterbury, Archbishop of, Primate of All England, bishop of diocese, or region, of Canterbury, and spiritual and symbolic authority of Anglican Communion. He presides at Lambeth Conferences of Anglican (Episcopal) bishops throughout the world. Augustine was consecrated first archbishop of Canterbury (597) by Pope Gregory. British Reformation Parliament (1529–36) under King Henry VIII severed all ties with Catholic Church in Rome, and British monarch replaced pope as secular head of Church of England, with archbishop of Canterbury as spiritual head. Arthur Michael Ramsey became archbishop of Canterbury in 1961.

Canterbury Cathedral, England E 235; picture E 234

Canterbury Tales, by Geoffrey Chaucer C 190; E 249; picture E 248
Cantilever (CAN-til-e-ver) **bridges** B 399
Canton (cant-ON), China C 262, 263
Canton (CANT-on), of a flag F 243
Canton, Ohio O 72

Canton and Enderbury islands, coral atolls south of the equator in central Pacific, part of the Phoenix Islands chain. They have been administered jointly by United States and Great Britain since 1939. Canton, largest of the Phoenix group, was used as transpacific airline base and satellite tracking station. Both islands were formerly worked for guano, but are now uninhabited.
  outlying areas of the United States U 100

Cantor, leader of musical services in synagogues J 119
  choral music C 276

Canute (994?–1035), king of Denmark and first Danish king of England. He invaded England and became king in 1016. He then returned to Denmark to strengthen his hold there and reigned from 1020 to 1035. Legend relates that to discourage belief in his limitless power, he took his courtiers to edge of sea and ordered waters to halt; his limitations were proved when the tide continued to come in.
  Danish Vikings' invasion of England E 217; V 340

Canvas-back duck, picture B 222
Canyonlands, Utah U 242
Canyonlands National Park, Utah U 249
Canyons, or deep valleys M 493, 495
  Mars M 109
Cão (CAUN), **Diogo,** Portuguese navigator C 465
  Angola A 261
Capacitance (ca-PAS-it-ance), in electricity E 126
Capacitors (ca-PAS-it-ers), devices for storing electric energy E 126–27
Capacity (ca-PAS-ity), volume
  metric units of W 115
Cape, for the geographic feature see name of cape as Kennedy, Cape
Cape Breton Island, Nova Scotia I 428; N 344a, 344b
Cape buffalo, of Africa B 250a
Cape Coast, University College of, Ghana G 195
Cape Cod, Massachusetts M 136–37
Cape Cod Bay, Massachusetts M 138
Cape Cod Girls, folk song F 323
Cape Cod National Seashore, Massachusetts M 144
Cape Coloreds, or **Coloureds** see Coloreds, or Coloureds, a people of mixed race in Africa
Cape Hatteras National Seashore N 316
Cape hunting dogs D 250; picture D 251
Capek (CHA-pek), **Karel,** Czech playwright D 298
Capella (ca-PEL-la), **Martianus,** Latin scholar T 138
Cape of Good Hope Province, South Africa C 102
Capetian (ca-PE-tian) **kings,** of France F 415
Cape Town, legislative capital of South Africa C 102–03; S 271; picture S 272
Cape Verde (VERD) **Islands,** off African coast I 428; P 401–02
Cap-Haïtien (cape HAI-shen), Haiti H 9
Capillaries, tiny blood vessels H 86
  digestive function B 276–77
Capillary action L 310
Capistrano, swallows of see San Juan Capistrano
Capital
  capital goods, productive factor in trade T 242
  cattle, early form of money M 410
  economic factor of production E 48

Capital (continued)
    labor and capital **L** 2–3
    stocks and bonds **S** 427–33
Capitalism **C** 104–05; **S** 220
    economic systems **E** 48–49
    poverty, cures for **P** 424b
    trust and monopoly regulation **T** 305
    See also Socialism
Capitalization (cap-it-al-i-ZAY-tion) **P** 532–33
Capitals, letters of the alphabet **A** 173
    punctuation **P** 532–33
Capitals, of columns
    three Greek orders **G** 346, 348; pictures **G** 347
Capitol, Washington, D.C. **W** 30; picture **W** 33
    American classical architecture **U** 123
Capitol Pages, messengers for Congress and the
    Supreme Court **W** 31
Capone (ca-PONE), **Al** **C** 497
Capote (cap-O-te), **Truman,** American novelist **A** 213

Capp, Al (Alfred Gerald Caplin) (1909–), American
cartoonist, b. New Haven, Conn. Best-known for his
comic strip *Li'l Abner,* begun in 1934 for United Features
Syndicate, he was columnist for New York *Herald
Tribune.* He wrote and illustrated *Return of the Shmoo*
and several books based on *Li'l Abner.*

Cappadocia (cap-pa-DO-shi-a) **region,** Turkey, picture
    T 328
Capri (CA-pri), island at entrance to Bay of Naples
    I 428; picture **I** 432
Capricorn, constellation **C** 491
    sign of, picture **S** 244
Capricorn, Tropic of *see* Tropic of Capricorn
Caprification (cap-ri-fi-CAY-tion), pollination of fig tree
    flowers **F** 117
Capri figs **F** 117
Capsule, of a spacecraft *see* Command module
Captains of industry, United States **U** 131

Capulets, 13th-century Italian political group. The name
adopted by Luigi da Porto in story of feud between
Capulet and Montague families of Verona (Capelletti and
Montecchi), which in a later version is basis of
Shakespeare's *Romeo and Juliet.*

Capybara (capy-BA-ra), rodent of South America **R** 280
Carabiner (car-a-BI-ner), snap link used in mountain
    climbing **M** 490
Carabiniere (ca-ra-bin-IER-e), Italian police **P** 374;
    picture **P** 373
Caracalla, Baths of
    model for Pennsylvania Station **U** 123
Caracals, lynxlike wild cats **C** 139
Caracas (ca-RA-cos), capital of Venezuela **V** 299; pic-
    ture **V** 298
    Simón Bolívar Center, picture **S** 284
Caracci (ca-RA-chi), **Annibale,** Italian painter **P** 23
Caramels, candy **C** 98
Carapace, shell on the back of some animals
    turtles **T** 331
Carats, units for measuring gemstones **J** 92, 93
    See also Karats
Caravaggio (ca-ra-VA-jo), **Michelangelo Merisi da,** Italian
    painter **C** 105; **I** 473
    art of the artist **A** 438f
    baroque art **B** 56–57
    Calling of St. Matthew, painting **I** 472
    Conversion of Saint Paul, The, picture **B** 57
    Musicians, The, painting **A** 438c
    nature copied faithfully **P** 23
Caravans, companies of travelers, picture **S** 8

Caravans, houses on wheels **H** 175, 177
Caravel (CA-ra-vel), sailing vessel **E** 372–73

Caraway, Hattie Wyatt (1878–1950), first woman elected
to the U.S. Senate, b. Bakerville, Tenn. After being
elected (1932) to fill the seat of her late husband, Thaddeus H. Caraway, she was re-elected senator from
Arkansas (1933–44). She was appointed by President
Roosevelt to the U.S. Employees Compensation Commission (1945).

Caraway seed **S** 382
Carbines, guns **G** 423; picture **G** 418
Carbohydrates (car-bo-HY-drates)
    body chemistry of **B** 289–90
    nutrition, needs in **N** 416
    starch **S** 401
    sugar **S** 453
Carbon, element **C** 105–06; **E** 153–54, 160
    alloys **A** 168
    atomic structure, model **A** 487
    atomic symbol, picture **D** 15
    batteries **B** 97
    coal, chief ingredient of **C** 363
    diamonds **D** 153
    importance to fuels, especially coal **F** 487
    lamp filaments **L** 284
    rings and chains, structural formulas **C** 200
Carbon-14, radioactive variety of carbon
    dating by use of radioactive carbon **R** 65–66
    for ice age dating **I** 22–23
    use in archeology **A** 362
Carbon arc lamps **L** 285
Carbon black **R** 348
Carbon cycle, a fusion reaction **S** 463–64
Carbon dioxide (dy-OX-ide) **C** 105
    action to keep air warm **I** 24
    atmosphere contains **A** 479
    blood carries **B** 256, 275, 277
    chemical reaction, how to show, picture **C** 197
    fermentation **F** 88–89
    fire extinguishers, use in **F** 136, 137
    first studies by Helmont **C** 210
    formation of earth's atmosphere **E** 19
    gases **G** 59
    Mars **M** 108, 110
    photosynthesis **P** 222–23
    wells in New Mexico **N** 187
    See also Dry ice
Carbon disulfide (dy-SUL-fide) **C** 196
Carbonic (car-BON-ic) **acid**
    cave formations **C** 153–54
Carboniferous (car-bon-IF-er-ous) **period,** geology **G** 116
    fossils **F** 384; picture **F** 386
Carbon monoxide (mon-OX-ide), poisonous gas **G** 59
    hyperbaric chambers, use in cases of poisoning **M** 210
    low-pollution automobiles being developed **E** 272g
    poisoning **P** 357
    Priestley's discovery **P** 456

Carbon paper, thin paper coated on one side with a waxy
ink. Pressure from uncoated side results in reproduction
of impression on paper placed under the carbon paper.

Carbon tetrachloride (CCl_4), colorless, nonflammable
heavy liquid used as a fire extinguisher, insect extermi-
nator, spot remover, or dry-cleaning solvent. It is made
from carbon disulfide and chlorine in the presence of a
catalyst.

Carbon tissue, transfer material **P** 467
Carborundum (car-bor-UN-dum), abrasive **G** 388–89

Carburetors (CAR-bu-raters), of internal-combustion engines **I** 306
  use principle of the venturi tube **A** 37
Carcassonne (car-cas-SONN), France, pictures **M** 289; **W** 219
Carcinogens (car-CIN-o-gens), cancer-causing agents **C** 91, 93
Carcinomas (car-ci-NO-mas), cancers **C** 89–90
Cardamom seed, spice **S** 382; picture **S** 381
  chief export of Sikkim **S** 177
Cardano (car-DA-no), **Girolamo**, or Geronimo, Italian mathematician **M** 156
  codes and ciphers **C** 369
Cardboard **P** 53
  book matches cut from **M** 153
Card catalogs, in libraries **L** 185–86
Cárdenas (CAR-they-nos), **García López de**, Spanish explorer, first European to see Grand Canyon **G** 292

Cárdenas (CAR-thay-nos), **Lázaro** (1895–1970), Mexican political leader and president, b. Jiquilpán de Juárez, Michoacán. He supported Mexico's revolutionary movements between 1915 and 1929 and served as governor of his native Michoacán (1928–32) and as president of the country (1934–40). His term was marked by a 6-year reform plan including redistribution of land to peasants, development of rural education, and expropriation of foreign-owned oil properties.
  Mexico, history of **M** 250

Card games **C** 106–15
Cardiac (heart) **patients** **H** 86c
Cardiff, capital of Wales **W** 4
Cardiff giant, famous hoax **I** 360
Cardinal Albert of Brandenburg as St. Jerome in His Study, painting by Lucas Cranach **G** 167
Cardinals, birds **B** 220; picture **B** 234
  Illinois, state bird of **I** 70
  Indiana, state bird of **I** 136
  Kentucky, state bird of **K** 213
  North Carolina, state bird of **N** 307
  Ohio, state bird of **O** 61
  Virginia, state bird of **V** 344
  West Virginia, state bird of **W** 127

Cardinals, Sacred College of, advisory body of Roman Catholic cardinals appointed by pope as his cabinet. College directs Curia Romana, or papal administration, and has sole responsibility for election of pope. It was formed under Alexander III (12th cent.). The red hat (galero) that was associated with the office was eliminated by Pope Paul VI (1969) to simplify dress.

Cardinal virtues, chief virtues considered by the Roman Catholic church as the main types of all possible excellences. The early Christians borrowed four—prudence, fortitude, temperance, and justice—from Greek philosophy and added three—faith, hope, and love.
  beliefs of the Roman Catholic Church **R** 301

Carding, of fibers
  cotton **C** 525
  wool **W** 235

Cardozo (card-O-zo), **Benjamin Nathan** (1870–1938), American jurist, b. New York, N.Y. He was admitted to New York bar (1891) and elected to New York State Supreme Court (1913), but shortly thereafter he was appointed to New York State Court of Appeals, of which he later became chief justice (1927). He was appointed by President Hoover to U.S. Supreme Court (1932), where he played an important role during Roosevelt era with his liberal interpretations of the Constitution. His works include *The Nature of the Judicial Process.*

Card tricks **M** 19–20
  pick a card, trick **T** 288
Carducci (car-DU-chi), **Giosuè**, Italian poet **I** 480
CARE see Cooperative for American Relief Everywhere
Careers see Vocations

Carey, James Barron (1911–), American labor leader, b. Philadelphia, Pa. He was president of United Electrical, Radio, and Machine Workers (UE) (1936–41) but lost position because of his stand barring Communists from holding union offices. When UE was expelled from CIO on charges of Communist domination, he became president (1950–65) of newly formed International Union of Electrical, Radio, and Machine Workers (IUE). He was elected a vice-president of AFL-CIO in 1955.

Cargo cults, Pacific islands **M** 564
Cargo ships, or freight ships **S** 158
Carib (CARR-ib), Indians of South America **I** 209
  Caribbean Islands **C** 116, 118
  Puerto Rico **P** 516
Caribbean (ca-ribb-E-an) **Sea and islands** **C** 116–19
  cruise ships **O** 22
  Cuba **C** 547
  dances **D** 30
  Dominican Republic **D** 280–83
  Haiti **H** 7–11
  Indian tribes **I** 207–08, 209
  Jamaica **J** 14–18
  life in Latin America **L** 47–61
  outlying areas of the United States **U** 100
  Trinidad and Tobago **T** 290–92
Cariboo Road, British Columbia, Canada **B** 406d
Caribou (CARR-i-boo), hoofed mammals **H** 219; pictures **H** 186, 215
  Alaska **A** 135; picture **A** 134
  Eskimo's uses of **E** 290
  Indians of the Caribou Area, northern Canada **I** 169–72
Caricatures (CARR-i-ca-tures), drawings that exaggerate and make ridiculous **C** 125
  Daumier, Honoré **D** 43
Caries (CARRIES), disease of the teeth **T** 48
Carillons (CA-rill-ons), sets of bells for ringing tunes **B** 136–37
  Bok Sing Tower, Florida **F** 269
  keyboard instruments **K** 240
  tower at University of Wisconsin, picture **W** 203
Carissimi (ca-RI-si-mi), **Giacomo**, Italian composer **I** 484
  baroque music **B** 64
Carleton, Sir Guy, British army officer and colonial governor **Q** 13
  Canada, history of **C** 71
Carlisle, Anthony, English scientist **E** 129

Carlota (kar-LO-ta) (1840–1927), empress of Mexico (1864–67), b. Laeken, Belgium. Only daughter of Leopold I of Belgium, she married (1857) Maximilian, Archduke of Austria, and accompanied him to Mexico (1864) when he was made emperor of Mexico by Napoleon III of France. After Maximilian was deposed, Carlota, having returned to Europe, became insane, and was confined in a castle near Brussels (1879–1927).
  Mexico, history of **M** 249

Carlsbad, health spa in Czechoslovakia **C** 562
Carlsbad Caverns, New Mexico **C** 153–55
Carlsbad Caverns National Park, New Mexico **N** 189

Carlson, Natalie Savage (1906–), American author of children's books, b. Winchester, Va. Her numerous books include *Alphonse, That Bearded One, The Talking Cat and Other Stories of French Canada, The Happy Orpheline,* and *Sashes Red and Blue.*

Carlyle, Thomas, Scottish historian, critic, and philosopher **E** 262

Carman, Bliss (William Bliss Carmens) (1861–1929), Canadian poet and journalist, b. Fredericton, New Brunswick. He wrote primarily romantic poems and ballads describing nature. He was literary editor of New York *Independent* (1890–92) and held editorial position on *Atlantic Monthly* magazine. He served as editor of *Oxford Book of American Verse* (1927) and was poet laureate of Canada (1928). Collections of his poems include *Low Tide on Grand Pré* and *Sappho.*

Carmel Mission, California, picture **M** 348
Carmen, opera by Georges Bizet **O** 142

Carmichael, Hoagy (Hoagland Howard Carmichael) (1899–), American songwriter and pianist, b. Bloomington, Ind. He abandoned a law career to compose popular songs, such as "Stardust," "Lazybones," "Georgia on My Mind," and "In the Cool, Cool, Cool of the Evening" (won Oscar award for 1951). He has had his own radio and TV programs and has played in motion pictures.

Carmichael, Stokely (1941–), American civil rights leader, Negro, b. Port of Spain, Trinidad. He came to the U.S. at the age of 11 and attended public schools in New York. After graduating from Howard University (1965), he joined the civil rights movement, taking part in freedom rides and voter registration drives among Negroes in the South. He was chairman of the Student Nonviolent Coordinating Committee (SNCC) (1966–67) and popularized slogan "Black Power." His wife is Miriam Makeba.
continuing struggle in Negro history **N** 104b

Carmona (car-MO-na), **Antonio Oscar de Fragoso,** president of Portugal **P** 404
Carnation, flower
Mother's Day flower, how worn **H** 158
state flower of Ohio **O** 61
Carnauba (car-na-U-ba), wax palm tree of Brazil **B** 378
wax **W** 70
Carné, Marcel, French motion-picture director **M** 487
Carnegie, Andrew, Scottish-born American industrialist and philanthropist **C** 119
foundations **F** 391
libraries **L** 200
peace movements **P** 105

Carnegie, Dale (1888–1955), American author and lecturer, b. Maryville, Mo. He began giving courses in public speaking (1912) and later broadened these to include study of success in all aspects of life. His book *How to Win Friends and Influence People* was followed by a series of radio lectures of same name. He also wrote *How to Stop Worrying and Start Living.*

Carnegie Endowment for International Peace **P** 105

Carnegie Foundation for the Advancement of Teaching, organization established (1905) by Andrew Carnegie with a gift of $10,000,000, to provide retirement pensions for professors in field of higher education in United States and Canada. It provides research funds for educational problems and consulting services on higher education.

Carnegie Hero Fund Commission, organization endowed (1904) by Andrew Carnegie with $5,000,000, to recognize civil heroes otherwise little appreciated. It awards the Carnegie medal to persons performing heroic deeds in saving or attempting to save human lives and gives financial aid to injured heroes or their survivors.

Carnegie Institute, Pittsburgh, Pennsylvania **C** 119
Carnegie Library School, Pittsburgh, Pa.
first to train children's librarians **C** 242
Carnegie medal, book award **B** 310
Carnegie Peace Palace, The Hague **P** 105
Carnelian (car-NE-lian), chalcedony quartz **Q** 7
Carnival of the Animals, The, music **F** 446
Carnivals **C** 120–21
Latin-American celebrations **L** 58
Carnivores, meat-eating animals **M** 65–66
balance of nature **L** 258–59
bears **B** 106
cats **C** 134–41
communities of living things **K** 258–59
dog family **D** 242–51
mammals, orders of **M** 62, 69
pinnipeds **W** 5–8
snakes **S** 212
teeth **M** 65–66
Carnivorous (car-NIV-or-ous) **plants** **P** 317–18; pictures **P** 316

Carnot (car-NO), **Sadi** (Nicolas Léonard Sadi Carnot) (1796–1832), French physicist, b. Paris. The most important of his ideas led to science of thermodynamics (study of relation of heat to energy of motion—for example, a steam engine or any engine can work only if heat is passed from a warmer to a colder body).

Carob (CARR-ob) **tree** **C** 557
Carol I, king of Rumania **R** 358
Carol II, king of Rumania **R** 358–59
Carolina, colony of **A** 193
Carolina Bay lakes **N** 309; **S** 298
Carolina cuckoo, bird
bill, picture **B** 223
Carolina jessamine, flower
state flower of South Carolina **S** 296
Carolina parakeets, extinct birds **B** 232
Carolina parrot, bird
bill, picture **B** 223
Carolina wren, bird
state bird of South Carolina **S** 296
Caroline Islands, Pacific Ocean **P** 5
Carolingian kings of France **F** 415
Carols, songs **C** 122
Christmas customs **C** 290
folk carols **F** 303
folk songs **F** 325
hymns for special occasions **H** 312
Carom billiards **B** 176
Carotene, substance convertible to vitamin A **V** 370c
leaves **T** 282
milk **M** 310
Carothers, Wallace H., American scientist **N** 428
fibers, man-made **F** 108
Carp, fish **F** 187
baits **F** 206
habitat, feeding habits, uses **F** 216

Carpaccio (car-PARCH-o), **Vittore** (1455?–1523?), Italian Renaissance artist, b. Venice. He is noted for historical and sacred works painted for Venetian religious orders. His paintings include a series of pictures entitled *History of St. Ursula* and *Life of St. George.*

Carpathian (car-PATHE-ian) Mountains, Europe P 359
  Czechoslovakia C 560
  Rumania R 356
Carpatho-Ukraine, or Ruthenia, U.S.S.R. C 564

Carpentaria, Gulf of, large inlet of the Arafura Sea along the northern Australian coast. It contains Sir Edward Pellew Islands, Groote Eylandt, and Wellesley Island. Explored by the Dutch seaman Abel Tasman (1644), it was probably named for Dutch official Pieter Carpentier.

Carpenter, John Alden, American composer M 402

Carpenter, Malcolm Scott (1925–), American astronaut, b. Boulder, Colo. He was one of seven pilots chosen (1959) for Project Mercury, manned satellite program. Carpenter became second American and fourth person in the world to orbit the earth (May 24, 1962). He left the program (1967) to work in oceanographic research.
  space flight data S 344, 345

Carpenter ants A 329; pictures A 328; I 281
  biting jaws, diagram I 270
Carpenter bees B 123
Carpenters' Hall, Philadelphia P 182
Carpentry W 230
  building construction, pictures B 436
Carpetbaggers, Northerners in the South after the Civil War R 120
Carpetbag rule see Reconstruction Period
Carpet beetles, insects H 262; pictures H 263
Carpets see Rugs and carpets
Carpi, Ugo da, Italian artist
  woodcut, Diogenes G 304
Carr, Emily, Canadian artist B 404–05; C 64
Carr, Gerald P., American astronaut S 346
Carr, Mary Jane, American writer O 206
Carranza (car-RON-za), Venustiano, Mexican statesman M 250
Carré (car-RAY), Ferdinand, French inventor R 137

Carrel (car-REL), Alexis (1873–1944), French zoologist and surgeon, b. Sainte-Foy-lès-Lyon. He was awarded Nobel prize (1912) in physiology and medicine for method of repairing broken blood vessels and for techniques in keeping tissues alive outside the body. He was first to keep whole organs, such as heart and kidney, alive outside the body.

Carreño, Maria Terese, Venezuelan pianist R 123
Carrera (car-RAY-ra), José Miguel de, Chilean leader C 254
Carriages and coaches T 260

Carrier, Willis Haviland (1876–1950), American inventor, b. Angola, N.Y. He developed first scientific air-conditioning system (1902). Air conditioning was used mainly in industry until the early 1920's, when Carrier produced a machine using a safe cooling material. Machine was introduced into theaters and railroad cars. He founded Carrier Engineering Corp., later Carrier Corp., (1915).
  called Father of airconditioning A 102

Carriers of disease see Vectors
Carrier transmission
  electronic communication, history of E 142, 142d
  telegraph T 53–54
  telephone T 59–60
Carrol, Diahann, American Negro singer and actress, picture N 104b
Carroll, Charles, American Revolutionary War leader M 126

Carroll, Daniel (1730–1796), American statesman, b. Upper Marlboro, Md. He was a member of Continental Congress (1780–84), a delegate to Constitutional Convention (1787), a representative from Maryland to first U.S. Congress (1789–91), and commissioner of District of Columbia (1791–95).
  Founding fathers F 395

Carroll, John (1735–1815), American Roman Catholic prelate, b. Upper Marlboro, Md. Carroll was ordained a Jesuit priest in France, but, in 1774, after the suppression of the Jesuit order in that country, he returned to the United States. In 1789, Carroll, named first bishop of Baltimore by Pope Pius VI, became the first Roman Catholic bishop in the United States. As bishop and later (1808) archbishop of Baltimore, he founded many Catholic educational institutions in Maryland.

Carroll, Lewis, pen name of Charles Lutwidge Dodgson, English mathematics professor and writer C 123
  Alice's Adventures in Wonderland, book, excerpt A 164–65
  children's literature C 239
  English literature E 265
  "Jabberwocky," poem N 272–73
  Through the Looking-Glass, book, excerpt A 165
Carrots V 290
  roots we eat P 307; picture P 306
Carryl (CARR-il), Charles E., American author
  The Walloping Window-Blind N 275
Cars, motor see Automobiles
Cars, of railroad trains R 80–81
Carson, Kit (Christopher), American frontiersman C 123; N 193
  Indian wars in New Mexico N 195
  Navajo moved to Fort Sumner I 193
Carson, Rachel, American writer A 214
  quoted on the environment E 272h
Carson City, capital of Nevada N 133
Cartagena (car-ta-GE-na), Colombia C 383
  Palace of the Inquisition, picture C 382
Cartagena, Spain S 351
Cartago (car-TA-go), Costa Rica C 515; picture C 514
Carte, Richard D'Oyly see D'Oyly Carte, Richard
Cartels (car-TELS), international monopolies T 306

Carteret, Sir George (1610?–1680), English naval officer, b. island of Jersey. Appointed lieutenant governor of Jersey (1643), he gave military assistance to Royalists and granted asylum to Royalist exiles during the English civil war. After surrendering to the Commonwealth (1651), he received a commission in the French Navy. After the Restoration he served as treasurer of the navy (1661–67) but was banished from House of Commons for mismanaging funds (1669). A Carolina proprietor, he and Berkeley received land, named New Jersey in his honor.

Carteret, Philip (1639–1682), English colonial governor, b. Jersey, Channel Islands. The first governor of New Jersey, he was appointed by English Lords Proprietors of colony. He became involved in dispute with New York over customs jurisdiction.

Cartesianism (car-TE-sian-ism), philosophy of Descartes D 123
  philosophical systems P 192

Carthage, ancient city on northwestern coast of Africa in modern Tunisia, was founded in 9th century B.C. (according to legend, by Dido, Queen of Carthage). Its location on Mediterranean made it a powerful commercial center controlling Sardinia, Corsica, and Malta during its height

Carthage (continued)

(410–264 B.C.). The city was conquered and destroyed by Romans during Punic Wars of 3rd and 2nd centuries B.C. It is now a residential suburb of Tunis.

Hannibal and the Punic Wars **H** 34; **P** 533

Phoenician settlements in Spain and Tunisia **S** 351; **T** 311

Carthusians (car-THU-sians), monks **C** 284

Cartier (car-ti-AY), **Sir George Etienne,** Canadian statesman **Q** 13

Cartier, Jacques, French explorer **C** 124

discovers cure for scurvy **P** 310

early history of Canada **C** 68

exploration of the New World **E** 383

Quebec **Q** 14

Saint Lawrence River, discoverer of **S** 15

Cartier-Bresson (car-ti-AY bre-SON), **Henri** (1908–), French photographer, b. Chanteloup, France. First trained as a painter, he turned to photography in 1930. After World War II, in which he served in the French underground following his escape from the Nazis, he used his camera increasingly to secure candid photographs of dramatic events. He is the author of *The Decisive Moment.* His work has been exhibited in the Museum of Modern Art, New York, and in the Louvre, Paris.

Cartilage (CAR-ti-lage), tough animal tissue **S** 140

Cartography (car-TOG-raphy), map making **M** 88–95

branch of geography **G** 108

photogrammetry used in map making **O** 171–72

surveying, use in **S** 479

Cartoon, drawing guide **D** 301

designs for tapestries **T** 23

Cartoons **C** 125–28

animated **A** 297–99

Thurber cartoon, picture **A** 215

See also Comic books

Cartoons, animated see Animated cartoons

Cartoons, political **C** 126–27

Arthur, Chester Alan, cartoons **A** 439, 440

Cleveland, Grover, cartoon **C** 342

Daumier, Honoré **D** 43

Garfield and Crédit Mobilier scandal, cartoon **G** 55

Harrison, Benjamin, cartoon **H** 46

Jackson, Andrew, cartoon **J** 5

McKinley tariff bill, cartoon **M** 188

Nast, Thomas **C** 126

Pulitzer prize for editorial cartooning **P** 524

Roosevelt, Theodore, cartoon **R** 329

Tilden-Hayes election, cartoon by Nast **H** 80

Cartridges, ammunition for guns **G** 417, 418, 419

Cartridges, tape recorders **T** 21

Cartridge television see Video cassettes

Carts **W** 157–58

Costa Rica's ox carts **C** 515; picture **C** 517

Cartwright, Alexander J., American promoter of baseball **B** 69–70

Cartwright, Edmund, English inventor **I** 235

Cartwright, John Robert (1895–), Canadian judge, b. Toronto. He served in the Army during World War I (1914–19). After practicing law in Toronto, he was appointed (1949) justice of the Canadian Supreme Court. He was Chief Justice from 1967 to 1970.

Caruso, Enrico (1873–1921), Italian tenor, b. Naples. His unusual vocal power and control made him a legendary figure even during his lifetime. He sang at opera houses throughout the world and was leading tenor with Metropolitan Opera Company (1903–21). Caruso sang over 40 leading roles, those in *Rigoletto, Tosca,* and *I Pagliacci* being among the most famous.

as the Duke in *Rigoletto,* picture **O** 135

recording for the phonograph, history of **R** 123

Caruthers (car-OTHERS), **William Alexander,** American novelist **A** 200

Carver, George Washington, American botanist and educator **C** 128–29

peanuts, research on **P** 110

research at Tuskegee Institute, Alabama **A** 125

statue, as a boy **M** 377

Carver, John, governor of Plymouth Colony **P** 344

Carver, Jonathan (1710–1780), American explorer, b. Weymouth, Mass. He explored parts of Wisconsin and Minnesota and shores of Lake Superior (1766–68) in attempt to find northwest passage. He wrote *Three Years Travels Through the Interior Parts of North America.*

his book a best seller in Europe **M** 336

Carving, in sculpture **S** 90

soap sculpture **S** 216–17

Carving, meat

cuts of beef, pork, and veal, pictures **M** 193–94

Carving, wood see Wood carving

Cary, Phoebe and **Alice,** American poets **C** 237

Cary's Rebellion (1711), colonial uprising in North Carolina. Quakers, angered by discriminating restrictions barring them from voting or holding office and by naming Church of England official church, had deputy governor Thomas Cary removed from office. Cary then led an unsuccessful revolt against the new governor.

Casaba (ca-SA-ba) **melons** **M** 216, 217

Casablanca (ca-sa-BLON-ca), Morocco **M** 458, 461

Allied conference, 1943 **W** 297

Casablanca Conference, World War II meeting of President Roosevelt, Prime Minister Churchill, and leaders of Free French. Held at Casablanca, Morocco (Jan. 14–24, 1943) to co-ordinate British and American war policy, the conference resulted in decision to demand "unconditional surrender" of Axis Powers. It also appointed General Eisenhower supreme commander of Allied forces.

World War II **W** 297

Casals (ca-SOLS), **Pablo** (1876–1973), Spanish cellist, conductor, and composer, b. Vendrell. He lived in self-imposed exile in France and later in Puerto Rico in protest against Franco's regime. Considered a master of the cello, he organized annual music festivals at Prades, France (1950) and Puerto Rico (1957).

Casals Festivals **M** 551

Sardana melodies for folk dancing **F** 299

Casamance (ca-za-MONCE), region of Senegal **S** 120

Casanova, Giovanni (Giovanni Jacopo Casanova de Seingalt) (1725–1798), Italian adventurer of dubious repute, b. Venice. He excelled as gambler, violinist, preacher, dramatist, spy, and rogue. While in exile in Bohemia (1785–98), he wrote his famous *Mémoires,* highly colored account of his romantic and adventurous life. His name has come to describe person who uses his charms to unscrupulous ends.

duels in literature **D** 341

Casbah

Morocco, old quarter, picture **M** 459

Muslim section of Algiers **A** 160, 163

Cascade, a small fall of water W 56b
Cascades, mountain range, North America U 92; W 14, 15
 climate C 346–47; picture C 343
 Crater Lake, picture L 29
 Oregon O 194, 196
Cascara, drug P 314
Casein (case-EEN), a protein of milk M 310–11
 glue G 243
Case Western Reserve University, Cleveland, Ohio C 338
Cash, Johnny, American singer R 262d; picture R 262c
Cash crops A 88
Cashews, nuts N 421
Cash registers O 58
Casimir II, Polish king P 361
Casing, glass process G 229
Casing, pipe that lines wells P 177
 water wells W 123
Casino (ca-SI-no), at Monte Carlo, Monaco M 406
Caslon (CAS-lon), **William,** English type designer T 345
Casper, Wyoming W 335

Casper, Billy (William Earl Casper, Jr.) (1931–), American professional golfer, b. San Diego, Calif. Noted as an excellent putter, he won U.S. Open (1959, 1966), Masters (1970), and played on several U.S. Ryder Cup teams.

Caspian Sea L 27
Cass, Lewis, American lawyer and statesman M 270–71
 Taylor and Cass T 35

Cassandra (Alexandra), in Greek mythology, a daughter of King Priam and Queen Hecuba of Troy. She received the gift of prophecy from Apollo, who later cursed her so that no one would place faith in her prophecies. She foretold the destruction of Troy at the hands of Greeks. Enslaved by Agamemnon, she predicted his death and subsequent revenge by his son Orestes. The name today signifies anyone who continually predicts disaster.

Cassatt, Mary (1845–1926), American artist, b. Allegheny City, Pa. She lived primarily in France and painted in the impressionist style, generally using women and children as her subjects. She exhibited with impressionist school in France (1879–86). Her paintings include *The Bath*.

Cassava (cas-SA-va), or manioc, plant from which tapioca is made
 African dish *gari* prepared from A 61
 Brazil B 376
 starch used for making adhesives G 243
Cassegrain, N., French scientist T 62
Cassettes, tape recorders T 21
Cassian (CASH-ian), **John,** monk, promoted monasticism in southern France C 283
Cassia plant, or senna (legume) P 314
 seeds, picture P 298

Cassini (ca-SI-ni) **family,** French astronomers for four generations, each of whom became director of Paris Observatory. **Jean Dominique** (1625–1712) first accurately measured distance of sun from earth. He discovered four moons of Saturn and large gap in Saturn's ring. **Jacques** (1677–1756) studied shape of earth. **César François** (1714–1784) made first accurate map of a region of earth (most of France). **Jacques Dominique,** Count de Cassini (1748–1845), completed father's map of France and wrote history of family (1810).
 map making history of M 94
 Cassini's division in rings of Saturn P 276

Cassiodorus (cas-si-o-DOR-us), **Flavius Magnus Aurelius,** Roman nobleman and librarian L 195–96
 scriptoria, writing rooms B 319
Cassiopeia (cas-si-o-PE-a), polar constellation C 491
Cassiterite (cas-SIT-or-ite), mineral T 195
Cassoni (ca-SO-ni), wooden chests D 77

Cassowary (CAS-uh-weri), flightless bird of Australia, New Guinea, and nearby islands. Cassowaries live in dense jungles. They have black, bristlelike feathers and a bony head crest. Folds of pink skin hang from the neck. Both head and neck are brightly colored and bare of feathers. Cassowaries are powerful birds. They stand about 5 feet high, weigh about 74 pounds, and have sturdy feet ending in long, sharp claws. Cassowaries are strong enough to kill a full-grown man. They do this by leaping at a victim, feet first, and slashing with their claws.

Castagno (cast-ON-yo), **Andrea del** (1421?–1457), Florentine painter, b. Castagno. Noted primarily for frescoes characterized by spontaneity and monumentality of style, he influenced 15th-century Florentine, Venetian, and Paduan painters through effects of foreshortening and precise draftsmanship. His works include frescoes *Last Supper* and *Famous Men and Women*.

Castanets (cas-ta-NETS), musical instruments P 152–53
Casteau, Belgium, European headquarters of SHAPE B 131

Castelo-Branco, Camillo, Visconde de Correia Botelho (1826–90), Portuguese writer, b. Lisbon. A prolific author, he wrote poetry, plays, and criticism but was most famous for his novels. Castelo-Branco's best-known novels, written in a romantic, ornate, and poetic style, include *Amor de Perdição*, *Amor de Salvação*, and *Os Misterios de Lisboa*.

Castes, system of social division I 120
 ants A 322–23
 Hinduism H 130
 poverty in India and Pakistan P 424a
 segregation in India S 114
Castiglione (ca-stil-YO-nay), **Baldassare,** Italian writer
 Renaissance man R 162
Castile (cas-TELE), former kingdom in Spain S 352, 356
 Ferdinand and Isabella F 87
 Spanish language and literature S 366
Castilian (cas-TIL-ian) **Spanish,** official language of Spain S 366
 dialect of Castile D 152; S 352
Castilla (ca-STI-ya), **Ramón,** president of Peru P 166
Casting, in fly fishing F 211
Casting, shaping of substances
 ceramics C 175
 continuous casting, steel process I 407
 jewelry making J 100
 metallurgy M 230
 sculpture S 91–92
Cast iron I 405
 building material B 435, 438
Castle, Vernon and Irene, American dancers D 27
Castles F 375; picture F 99
 Alcazar, in Segovia, Spain, picture S 359
 architecture A 379–80
 built by Crusaders in Syria, picture S 506
 Carcassonne, France, picture B 394
 Conway Castle, Wales, picture W 4
 English architecture E 234
 homes, types of H 178–79
 Kronborg, the Elsinore of *Hamlet*, picture D 107

Henry V of England (1420) and bore him Henry VI (1421). After the death of Henry V she retired from public life, marrying a Welshman, Owen Tudor. She bore Tudor a son, Edmund, who was made Earl of Richmond (1453) by his half brother Henry VI, father of Henry VII.

Catherine the Great, empress of Russia **U** 49
  architecture, neoclassical **U** 53
  Hermitage Museum **H** 119
  Jewish repression **J** 110

Cathode, metallic rod or plate that acts as source of electrons (small particles with negative electric charge). In a battery the cathode (also called negative electrode) is the source of electric current. In an X-ray tube a stream of electrons given off by heated cathodes strikes a metal surface and causes it to give off X rays. In radio tubes, fluorescent light bulbs, and electron microscopes, such streams of electrons have other effects.

Cathode rays **X** 339–40
Cathode-ray tubes, electron tubes **E** 148
Catholic Association, Ireland **O** 49
Catholic Church see Roman Catholic Church
Catholic Library Association **L** 192
Catiline, Roman politician
  Cicero's denunciation of **C** 298
Catkins, of trees **T** 284
Catlin, George, American artist **U** 120–21
  Bird's Eye View of the Mandan Village, A, painting **U** 119
Cato (CAY-to), **Marcus Porcius,** Roman statesman and writer **L** 77
Catoctin (ca-TOC-tin) **Mountain Park,** Maryland **M** 123–24
Cats **C** 134–41
  domestic see Cats, domestic
  leopards **L** 155
  lions **L** 307
  tigers **T** 186
  tracks, picture **A** 271
Cats, domestic **C** 141–44
  animal problem-box test **A** 284
  dominance orders **A** 280
  fleas **H** 260
  pets **P** 179
  scratch fever **I** 286
  superstitions about **S** 475
Cats'-eyes, gemstones **G** 69–70, 75
Catskill Mountains **N** 211, 213
Cat's paw, knot **K** 292
Catt, Carrie Chapman, American woman suffragist **W** 212b
Cattle **C** 145–49, 151
  Africa **A** 62, 64; picture **C** 148
  African songs about **A** 78
  anthrax **I** 287
  Argentina **A** 395–96
  Bernese Alps, pictures **S** 497
  dairy see Dairy cattle
  dolphins and porpoises related to **D** 272, 273
  Hawaii's famous ranch **H** 64
  herds, pictures **A** 90, **M** 434
  hides, source of leather **L** 107
  hoofed mammals **H** 220–21
  Kirghiz crossbreed **U** 45
  marketing cattle **M** 191–92
  meat packing **M** 191–96
  Paraguay, Chaco region, picture **P** 65
  ranch life **R** 102–05
  roundups, pictures **A** 409, **N** 186
  ruminants, or cud-chewing animals **H** 208

  sacred in India, picture **C** 10
  stomach of cud-chewing animals **H** 208
  Texas **T** 122
  whales related to cattle **W** 150
  wild cattle **H** 221
  world distribution, diagram **W** 265
Cattle drives **C** 146–47
  Goodnight-Loving Trail in New Mexico **N** 188
  Wyoming **W** 329
Cattle wars
  Wyoming **W** 337
Catton, Bruce, American writer **A** 214
Catullus (ca-TULL-us), **Gaius Valerius,** Roman poet **L** 78
CATV see Cable TV
Cauca (CA-uca) **River,** Colombia **C** 381

Caucus, a meeting of leaders of a group to discuss internal affairs. The term, possibly from the Algonkian Indian *caucauasu,* meaning "adviser," was used in colonial Boston to denote factional political meetings. Congressional caucuses were used to select presidential candidates (1796–1824). Today caucuses are held locally to select candidates for offices or elect convention delegates. In Congress they are called to choose candidates for Senate and House positions, to assign members to committees, and to draft party policy.
  organization in U.S. Congress **U** 144

Caucasian languages **L** 40
Caucasoid (CAU-ca-soid) **race**
  Africa **A** 55
  proper meaning of race **R** 31
Caucasus (CAU-ca-sus), mountain range in Soviet Europe **E** 309
  the Transcaucasian Republics **U** 44–45

Caudill, Rebecca (1899–   ), American author of children's books, b. Harlan County, Ky. She lived in woods of Kentucky, from which she derived much of material for her books, including *Happy Little Family* and *Schoolhouse in the Woods.* Her books for younger children include *Barrie and Daughter* and *Tree of Freedom.*

Cauliflower, vegetable **V** 290
  flowers we eat **P** 307–08; picture **P** 309
Causeways, roads raised over water
  Lake Pontchartrain, Louisiana **L** 33
Cauto (CA-ut-o), major river in Cuba **C** 548
Cavalier of the Rose, The, opera by Richard Strauss **O** 153
Cavalier poets, in English literature **E** 254
Cavaliers, royalists in English Civil War **C** 536
Cavalleria Rusticana, opera by Pietro Mascagni **O** 142
  based on story by Verga **I** 480

Cavanna (ca-VAN-na), **Betty** (Elizabeth Allen Cavanna) (1909–), American author, b. Camden, N.J. Her stories deal chiefly with the lives and problems of teen-agers. Among her many books are *Angel on Skis, Going on Sixteen, Paintbox Summer,* and *Spurs for Suzanna.*

Cave, Edward (Sylvanus Urban), English printer and publisher **M** 14
Caveat emptor, Latin for "let the buyer beware" **C** 494
Cave bears
  fire repelled **F** 139
Cave drawings **P** 14–15
  art as a record **A** 438
  communication method of Stone Age **C** 430
  prehistoric art **P** 439–41

Cave dwellers C 157–58
  art as a record A 438, 438b
  fire and early man F 139
  Neanderthal man P 443
  painting, earliest artists P 14–15
  prehistoric art P 439–41
Cave flowers C 155
Cavelier, Robert *see* La Salle, Robert Cavelier, Sieur de

Cavell (CAV-ell), **Edith Louisa** (1865–1915), English nurse, b. Swardeston, Norfolk. She ran a hospital in Belgium (1914–15) for wounded soldiers in World War I. She helped Allied soldiers return to battlefields and aided Belgian men in escaping from the Germans. She was captured by the Germans (1915) and tried and executed, despite intervention of Allied governments on her behalf. There is a monument to her in London.

Cave men *see* Cave dwellers
Cavendish, Henry, British chemist C 210; E 7; S 72; picture C 211
  developed idea of resistance in electricity E 127

Cavendish, or Candish, Thomas (1560?–1592), English navigator and privateer, b. Suffolk. The third navigator to circle globe (1586–88), he returned home by way of Cape of Good Hope, after looting Spanish towns on western coast of South America.

Caves and caverns C 152–58
  art as a record A 438
  Ash Cave entrance, Ohio, picture O 71
  bats B 93; picture B 95
  homes of the past H 177
  ice cave, picture I 12
  Lascaux Caves, France, picture W 217
  Lewis and Clark Cavern, picture M 439
  painting, earliest artists P 14–15
  paintings found in France, picture A 354
  prehistoric art P 439–41
  spelunking S 380

Caviar, roe (eggs) of sturgeon and other large fish, such as tunney and mullet, that has been processed and salted. It is served as an hors d'oeuvre.

Cavies (CAVE-ies), rodents R 280
  See also Guinea pigs
Cavill, Richard, Australian swimmer S 490
Cavities, or tooth decay T 48
Cavour (ca-VOOR), **Camillo di,** Italian leader I 457
Caxton, William, English printer P 457
  early ads A 34
  first printing of children's books C 236
  printed *Morte Darthur* A 445
Cayenne (ca-YEN), capital of French Guiana G 397

Cayley, Arthur (1821–1895), English mathematician, b. Richmond, Surrey. He originated many new fields of mathematics, some important in work on theory of relativity and quantum theory.

Cayley, Sir George, English inventor A 567

Cayman Islands, island group of the West Indies made up of Grand Cayman, Little Cayman, and Cayman Brac. Discovered by Columbus (1503) and first colonized in the 18th century by the English, they were a dependency of Jamaica (until 1962) but are now administered by the British Colonial Office. The capital of the islands is Georgetown, Grand Cayman. Principal industries include turtle and shark fishing, ropemaking, and tourism.

Caymans, reptiles C 533–35
Cayuga (cay-U-ga), Indians of North America I 184
Cayuga, Lake, New York L 28
CBC *see* Canadian Broadcasting Corporation
CBI *see* Cumulative Book Index
CBS Building, New York City U 125
CCC *see* Civilian Conservation Corps
C clef, in musical notation M 526
Cebu-City (say-BU-city), **Philippines** P 189
Cebus (CE-bus) **monkeys,** picture A 287

Cecil (CES-il), **Robert,** 1st earl of Salisbury and 1st Viscount Cranborne ("the crooked-backed earl") (1563?–1612), English statesman, b. probably Westminster, London. The son of William Cecil, he was appointed secretary of state under Queen Elizabeth I (1596). Aiding James VI of Scotland to succeed to the English throne as James I (1603), he continued as secretary of state until appointed lord treasurer (1608).

Cecil, William, 1st Baron Burghley (1520–1598), English statesman, b. Bourn. He served as secretary to the protector Somerset (1548–50) and as secretary of state (1550–53). As chief secretary of state (1558–72) and lord high treasurer (1572–98) to Queen Elizabeth I, he held great power. To counteract possible plots against the throne, he formed a network of informers (1570), and he had Mary Queen of Scots executed (1587).
  England, history of E 178

Cecilia, Saint (2nd or 3rd century), one of most venerated martyrs of early Christian Church. She converted to Christianity her pagan husband, Valerian, and his brother Tiburtius, who were martyred before her. Patroness of music, she is usually portrayed with musical instrument. Her feast day is November 22.

Cecropia (ce-CRO-pia) **moth**
  cocoon, picture I 265
  metamorphosis, picture M 235
Cedar Rapids, Iowa I 369
Cedar trees, conifers T 284
  of Lebanon L 122
  uses of the wood and its grain, picture W 223
Cedar waxwings, birds B 216; picture B 234
Ceiba (SAI-ba), or silk-cotton tree, yields kapok fibers K 193
Cela (SAY-la), **Camilo José,** Spanish author S 372
Celebes (CEL-eb-ese) (Sulawesi), island in Indonesia I 219

Celebes Sea, branch of the Pacific Ocean bounded by Borneo on the west, the Philippines on the north, and Celebes on the south. The major port is Menado, founded (1657) by the Dutch on the island of Celebes.

Celery, vegetable V 290
  leaf stalks we eat P 307; picture P 306
Celery seed, spice S 382; picture S 381
Celesta (ce-LES-ta), keyboard instrument K 240; M 550
  orchestra seating plan O 186
Celestial navigation, of airplanes A 562
Celestial poles, of the celestial sphere S 109
Celestial sphere S 109
Cell, voltaic *see* Voltaic cell
Cella, inner chamber of Greek temple A 374
Cellini (chell-E-ni), **Benvenuto,** Italian sculptor I 472
  autobiography I 478
  decorative saltcellar D 77; picture D 74
  Perseus, statue I 469
Cello, musical instrument, picture M 545
  orchestra seating plan O 186
Cellophane, a transparent material P 331

Cells, basic units of life   **C** 159–64
 aging   **A** 84
 animal and plant cells, compared, diagram   **K** 250
 blood corpuscles   **B** 256–57
 body chemistry, composition of cells   **B** 289–97
 cancer and cancer research   **C** 89–95
 cell-killing viruses   **V** 367
 cell membrane in body chemistry   **B** 269, 293
 cell theory, in biology   **B** 193;   **S** 73
 cork cells   **C** 505
 egg cell division to become an embryo   **E** 90
 functions in the human body   **B** 267
 fungi   **F** 496
 genetics   **G** 77–78
 living matter, composition of   **L** 211
 nerve cells of the brain   **B** 363–65
 nutrition   **N** 415
 one-celled organisms   **M** 277
 osmosis   **O** 234–35
 reproduction   **R** 177
 steps in division, diagram   **B** 267
 unit structure of living things, picture   **K** 250
 See also Eggs; Embryos
Cells, electric see Electric batteries
Celluloid, a plastic material   **P** 324
 early example of applied research   **R** 183
 substitute for ivory   **I** 488
Cellulose
 cellophane   **P** 331
 crystalline material   **C** 541
 nutrition, use in   **N** 417
 paper making   **P** 51
Celsius, Anders, Swedish scientist   **H** 89
Celsius, or centigrade, scale of thermometers   **T** 165
 heat   **H** 89
 measurement systems   **W** 117
Celsus, Roman writer   **M** 204
Celtic art and architecture
 crosses   **E** 233–34
 Stonehenge   **E** 233

Celts, or **Kelts,** tribes that occupied France, Spain, northern Italy, western Germany, and British Isles, reaching height of their power in 5th and 4th centuries B.C. A fair-haired, warlike people, noted for courage and skill in use of iron weapons, they gradually mixed with other races or were destroyed by Romans. Their religion was primarily Druidism. Surviving branches of Celtic language are Irish, Scots-Gaelic, Manx (on Isle of Man), Welsh, and Breton.

Cement   **C** 165–66
 adhesives   **G** 242
 masonry   **B** 391–93
Cementum, bonelike material of teeth   **T** 48
Cemeteries
 national cemeteries of the United States   **N** 28–31
 See also Funeral and burial customs
Cenaculum see Coenaculum, site of Jesus' Last Supper
Cenerentola (chay-nay-RAIN-to-la), **La,** opera by
  Gioacchino Rossini   **O** 142
Cenozoic era, in geology   **F** 383, 389
 prehistoric animals, development of   **P** 438

Censorship (from Latin *censere,* meaning "assess" or "tax"), restriction or denial of freedom of speech or press by government inspection of mail and regulation of books, newspapers, radio and TV, and other means of communication. In democracies it is used only to preserve military secrets and control obscene or subversive literature. It achieves maximum jurisdiction in wartime.
 civil liberties and censorship   **C** 316

 motion picture industry   **M** 488a, 488c
 television production   **T** 70b, 70c, 70d–71

Census, official count of people and property   **P** 397
 automation used for data   **A** 532
 Doomsday Book   **W** 173
 How many different censuses are taken?   **P** 396
Census, Bureau of the, see United States Bureau of the Census
Centenary International Philatelic Exhibition, 1947   **F** 12
Centennial State, nickname for Colorado   **C** 401
Centigrade, or Celsius, scale of thermometers   **T** 165
 heat   **H** 89
 measurement systems   **W** 117
Centimeter, measure of length   **W** 114–15
Centimeter-gram-second, system of measurement   **W** 117
Centipedes, many-legged animals   **C** 167–68
 compared to insects, picture   **I** 263
Central African Republic   **C** 169–70
 flag   **F** 235
Central America   **C** 171
 agriculture   **N** 299
 Caribbean Sea and islands   **C** 116–19
 flags   **F** 241
 Indian art   **I** 152–57
 Inter-American Highway   **P** 50
 life in Latin America   **L** 47–61
 Monroe Doctrine and Roosevelt Corollary   **M** 425, 426–27;   **R** 329
 Organization of American States   **O** 210–11
 Panama Canal and Zone   **P** 46–49
 See also names of individual countries

Central American Common Market (CACM), economic group originally made up of Costa Rica, El Salvador, Guatemala, Honduras, and Nicaragua. Established (1960) through a series of treaties beginning in 1951, its purposes are to remove tariffs and customs duties on products of member nations and to establish a common tariff on goods of non-member nations. The Common Market promotes development of industries that, to function efficiently, require markets larger than any one Central American country can offer.

Central American University, Nicaragua   **N** 249
Central Falls, Rhode Island   **R** 224
Central heating   **H** 98–99

Central Intelligence Agency (CIA), U.S. Government agency established (1947) under National Security Act in order to co-ordinate intelligence activities of several government agencies and departments. The agency advises and makes recommendations to National Security Council. Its headquarters are in Washington, D.C.
 espionage (spying) agencies   **S** 390

Central Lowlands, North America   **U** 90
Central nervous system   **B** 282–83; diagram   **B** 281
Central Park, New York City   **N** 234; pictures   **N** 232, **P** 76
 Olmsted's design   **P** 77
Central Park Carrousel, collage-sculpture   **U** 116

Central Powers, nations that fought against Allied Powers during World War I. These countries were Austria-Hungary, Bulgaria, Germany, and Turkey.
 World War I   **W** 274, 276

Central Treaty Organization (CENTO), name given to defense alliance of Iran, Pakistan, Turkey, and United Kingdom (1959), based on Baghdad Pact (1955). The United States is an associate member.

Centrifugal (cen-TRIF-u-gal) **casting,** of metals **M** 231
Centrifugal force E 5–6
earth's spin acts against gravity **G** 323
Centrifugal pumps P 530
Centrifuge, picture **V** 367
Centrioles (CENT-ri-oles), of cell **C** 163; picture **C** 164
Century Dictionary and Cyclopedia D 165
Century plant, Mexican agave **I** 194
Cephalopods (CEPH-al-o-pods), mollusks **O** 274–75
Cephalothorax (ceph-a-lo-THO-rax), head-chest section of crustacea and arachnids **S** 169, 383
Cepheid (CE-phe-id) **variables,** stars **A** 476; **S** 408
Ceramics C 172–76
bowl, Persian, picture **D** 68
folk art **F** 295–96
Islamic art **I** 422; picture **I** 418
pottery, ceramic vessels **P** 413–19
Ceratopsia (cer-a-TOP-sia), dinosaurs **D** 181
Ceratosaurs (cer-AT-o-saurs), dinosaurs **D** 175
Cerberus (CER-ber-us), watchdog in Greek mythology **G** 357, 363–64
Cerci (CER-ci), feelers of some insects **I** 263
Cereal grasses G 317
Cereals, grain **G** 280–87
cereal grasses **G** 317
corn **C** 506–07
food production of high yielding cereals and population growth **F** 343
living standards judged by cereal consumption **F** 332
nutrition, need in **N** 417
oats **O** 4
rye **R** 364
wheat **W** 154–56
See also Grain and grain products
Cereals, prepared G 285
Cerebellum (cer-eb-ELL-um), part of the brain **B** 366
function in body control **B** 282
Cerebral (ce-RE-bral) **cortex,** of the brain **B** 366

Cerebral palsy (CER-eb-ral POL-sy), disorder of nervous system affecting person's ability to control muscles. It is caused by injury to brain before or at birth.

Cerebrum (cer-E-brum), part of the brain **B** 366; picture **B** 364
function in body control **B** 282
Ceres (CE-rese), asteroid **A** 475
small planets **P** 273
solar system **S** 243
Ceres, Roman goddess **G** 359–60
origin of word "cereal" **F** 332; **G** 281
Cereus (CE-re-us), night-blooming cactus **C** 4

Cerf, Bennett (1898–1971), American publisher and editor, b. New York, N.Y. He was president (from 1925) of Modern Library. He founded (1927) Random House, Inc., of which he was chairman of the board. He appeared on TV and edited several books of humor.

Cerium, element **E** 154, 160
Cernan, Eugene, American astronaut **S** 344, 345, 346
Certification, of teachers **T** 42
Certified Public Accountant (C.P.A.) B 314
Certosino (chair-to-SI-no), ivory inlay **D** 77
Cervantes (cer-VON-tes) **Saavedra, Miguel de,** Spanish writer **C** 176
Don Quixote, excerpt **D** 285–86
Don Quixote, quotation from **Q** 20
duels in literature **D** 341
golden age of Spanish literature **S** 368–69
monument in Madrid, pictures **M** 12, **S** 354
satire **H** 280

Cervera y Topete (thair-VAIR-a e to-PAY-tay), **Pascual,** Spanish admiral **S** 375
Cesium (CE-zi-um), element **E** 154, 160
ion-drive for spaceships **I** 351
Cesta, basket to catch the ball in the sport jai alai **J** 11
Cestus, boxing glove **B** 352
Cetaceans (cet-A-tians), marine mammals
dolphins and porpoises **D** 270, 272–73
mammals, orders of **M** 62, 64, 68
whales **W** 147–51
Cetology (ce-TOL-ogy), study of whales **D** 272
Ceuta (ce-U-ta), Spanish city, enclave in Morocco **S** 357
Ceylon (ce-LON), or Sri Lanka **C** 177–80
Buddhism **B** 425
dance **D** 31
flag **F** 237
folk dancers, picture **F** 298
gemstones found in **G** 70
Cézanne (sai-ZANNE), **Paul,** French painter **C** 181
French art **F** 431
Kitchen Table, painting **P** 28
modern art **M** 388
Mount Sainte-Victoire with Tall Pine, painting **C** 181
Picasso and Cézanne **P** 243
Pines and Rocks, painting **F** 429
Rocky Landscape, painting **M** 389
style of his still-life painting **P** 29
Cgs system see Centimeter-gram-second
Chacabuco (cha-ca-BU-co), **battle of,** 1817 **S** 36
Chaco (CHA-co), region of South America **S** 277, 280
Argentina **A** 391–92
Paraguay **P** 62, 64
Chaconne, a musical form **M** 535
Chad C 182–83
children, pictures **A** 54, **U** 87
flag **F** 235
Chad, Lake, north central Africa **L** 27
Africa, lakes of **A** 50
Chad **C** 182, 183
Chadwick, Edwin, English reformer **M** 208

Chadwick, Florence (1918–), American long-distance swimmer, b. San Diego, Calif. She set women's record when she swam English Channel from France to England in 13 hours, 20 minutes (1950). The first woman to swim Channel from England to France (1951), she has also swum Dardanelles, Bosporus, and Strait of Gibraltar.

Chadwick, French Ensor, American naval officer **W** 138

Chadwick, Sir James (1891–), English physicist, b. Manchester. He was awarded Nobel prize in physics (1935) for discovery of the neutron, one of two types of particles in nucleus of atom.

Chaff, of grain **F** 60
Chaffee, Roger B., American astronaut **S** 346
Chagall (sha-GOL), **Marc,** Russian painter **C** 184
I and the Village, painting **C** 184
Over Vitebsk, painting **U** 57
stained-glass windows for synagogue, picture **S** 394
Chagga (CHA-ga), a people of Africa **T** 16
Chagres River (CHA-grace), Panama Canal Zone **P** 47
Chaillot, Palais de, Paris **P** 71
Chain, Ernst, English scientist **A** 312; picture **A** 315
Chain dance D 28
Chained books, in early libraries **L** 196; picture **L** 195
Chain lightning T 172
Chain mail, armor **A** 433
Chain newspapers N 200
Chain reactions, of atoms **N** 360–63
What is "atom smashing"? **A** 489

Chain stores S 468
  retail stores **R** 188
Chairs
  colonial, pictures **C** 389
  frames being joined, picture **F** 501
  Mies van der Rohe's Barcelona chair, picture **D** 73
  mountain "settin' chair" **T** 74
  upholstery **U** 227
Chaitanya, Indian poet **O** 220e
Chalcedony (cal-CED-ony), quartz **Q** 7
  gemstones **G** 75
Chalcocite, a copper ore, known as copper glance **C** 502
Chalcopyrite (cal-co-PY-rite), mineral **G** 249
  copper, ore of **C** 502
Chaldean (cal-DE-an), or Neo-Babylonian, **Empire,** of
    Mesopotamia **A** 241
  ancient art **A** 241–42; picture **A** 243
Chalets (sha-LAYS), houses **H** 169
  Gsteig, Switzerland, picture **E** 314

Chaliapin (shol-YA-pin), or **Shalyapin, Feodor Ivanovich**
(1873–1938), Russian operatic bass, b. Kazan. Known for
his character acting as well as his great voice, he toured
Russia and United States (1898–1915). He was a leading
singer at New York's Metropolitan Opera (1921–35),
becoming famous for title roles in *Boris Godunov, Ivan
the Terrible, Mefistofele,* and *Don Quichotte.*
  as Boris Godunov, picture **O** 137

Chalice, cup used at a Communion service, picture
    G 227
Chalk, form of limestone **R** 267
  drawing materials **D** 301, 303
  white cliffs of Dover, England **E** 213

Challenger expedition, scientific expedition on H.M.S.
Challenger (1872–76) sponsored by British Royal Society
under direction of Scottish naturalist Charles Thomson.
Members traveled around the world investigating aspects
of the seas, including temperature and composition of
water, currents, depth, and marine life. Findings were
published in 50-volume *Challenger Report.*

Châlons (shol-ON), **battle of,** 451 **B** 100
Chama foxes D 250
Chambered, or pearly, **nautilus,** mollusk **O** 275; **S** 149

Chamberlain, Joseph (1836–1914), English statesman, b.
London. He was father of statesmen Neville and Sir
Austen Chamberlain. As mayor of Birmingham
(1873–76), he advocated slum-clearance plans and
educational reforms. As colonial secretary (1895), he
worked for closer union of Britain with its self-governing
colonies. He gained passage of Workmen's Compensation
Act (1897) and Commonwealth of Australia Bill (1900)
and was first chancellor of Birmingham University
(1901).

Chamberlain, Joshua Lawrence (1828–1914), American
soldier and educator, b. Brewer, Maine. He served in
20th Maine Infantry (1862–66) in Civil War. He was
awarded Medal of Honor at Gettysburg and made
brigadier general on the field for gallantry by General
Grant (1864). Chamberlain was governor of Maine
(1866–70) and president of Bowdoin College, Maine
(1871–83), and he wrote *Maine: Her Place in History.*

Chamberlain, Neville (Arthur Neville Chamberlain) (1869–
1940), British statesman, b. Birmingham. As prime minister (1937–40), he negotiated treaty recognizing Italy's
Ethiopian conquest (1938) and signed Munich Pact with
Italy, France, and Germany (1938), giving Hitler part of

Czechoslovakia to "keep peace in our time." He declared
war on Germany when Hitler invaded Poland (1939) but
resigned post as prime minister largely because of
criticism of his war policies.
  Churchill opposes appeasement policies in events lead-
    ing to World War II **C** 297–98; **W** 286

Chamberlain, Owen (1920–   ), American nuclear physicist, b. San Francisco, Calif. He worked on development
of atomic bomb (1942–46). With physicist Emilio Segrè
he discovered the antiproton. They shared the Nobel
prize in physics (1959) for this discovery.

Chamberlain, Wilt (Wilton Norman Chamberlain)
(1936–   ), American basketball player, b. East Philadelphia, Pa. Nicknamed Wilt the Stilt (he is 7 ft. 1 in.) he
played for University of Kansas (1955–58) and Harlem
Globetrotters (1958–59). Joining National Basketball Association's Philadelphia (now San Francisco) Warriors, he
was named the league's Rookie of the Year and Most
Valuable Player (MVP) in 1960. He also played for
Philadelphia 76ers, and is now with the Los Angeles
Lakers. He holds almost every scoring record and was
named MVP three consecutive years (1966–68).

Chamberlain's Men, an acting company **S** 131

Chamberland (cham-ber-LAN), **Charles Edouard** (1851–
1908), French bacteriologist, b. Chilly-le-Vignoble, France.
He is best known for his filter of unglazed porcelain,
which permits liquids but not bacteria to pass through.
With Pasteur and Roux he made studies of the cause of
rabies and was first to use preparations of weakened
bacteria in the treatment of disease.

Chamberlin, Thomas Chrowder (1843–1928), American
geologist, b. Mattoon, Ill. He was professor of geology
and director of Walker Museum at University of Chicago
(1892–1928). His significant contributions to science
include research on glacial phenomena and investigations of climates during geological periods. He formulated "planetesimal," or spiral-nebula, hypothesis, which
advanced theory that our solar system resulted from
near collision of sun with passing star, drawing off
masses of gas, which then orbited sun. Chamberlin's
writings include *The Origin of the Earth* and *The Two
Solar Families.*
  planetesimal theory **S** 247

Chamber music C 184–86
  basic record library **R** 125
  chamber orchestras **O** 182
  English music for viols **E** 270
  festival in Marlboro, Vermont **M** 552
  musical forms, definitions of **M** 535–38

Chamber of commerce, association of businessmen—on
community, state, or national level—whose purpose is to
promote commercial and industrial interests.

Chamber orchestra O 182
  chamber music **C** 184–86
Chameleons (ca-ME-le-ons), lizards **L** 318–19

Chamizal (CHA-mi-zal), **El,** a tract of 437 acres of land
involved for over a century in a Mexican–U.S. border dispute. It was named *El Chamizal* after the Spanish word
for the thickets that cover the land. The dispute came
about because of an 1848 treaty that fixed the Rio
Grande River as the boundary between the U.S. and
Mexico. However, the river changed its course, transferring hundreds of acres of land to the U.S. side. In

Chamizal, El (continued)
1963 the U.S. Government agreed to hand El Chamizal back to Mexico. The ceremonies marking the formal transfer of the land were held in 1967.

Chamois (SHA-mi), brownish, mountain-dwelling animal with short, hollow horns that are hooked at the end and are carried by both sexes. Found in Europe and Asia, it feeds on herbs, flowers, and pine shoots. It is related to sheep and goats. Picture **H** 218.

Champagne (sham-PANE) **W** 189
Why are ships christened with champagne? **S** 160
Champions, in sports
characteristics of **B** 15
Champlain (sham-PLAIN), **Lake,** northeastern United States **L** 27
Champlain, Samuel de, French explorer **C** 187
Canada **C** 68–69, 79
exploration of the New World **E** 384
Quebec **Q** 14
Saint Lawrence River, settlements near **S** 15
Champlain Valley, Vermont **V** 308
Champlevé (shon-lev-AY), enameling technique **E** 191; picture **E** 192
decorative arts **D** 70

Champollion (shon-pall-YON), **Jean François** (1790–1832), French archeologist, b. Figeac. One of founders of science of Egyptology, he used Rosetta stone to find solution to translation of Egyptian hieroglyphics. He is most famous for book about his discoveries, *Précis du Système Hiéroglyphique des Anciens Egyptiens.*

Champs-Elysées (shons-ay-le-ZAY), **Avenue des,** Paris, picture **P** 71
Chance, science of see Probability

Chancellor, Richard (?–1556), English navigator. He reached Moscow (1553) while on expedition to find northeast passage to India, and obtained trade concessions from Russian emperor Ivan IV, leading to formation of Muscovy Company (1554). He was shipwrecked and lost returning from second voyage to Russia (1555–56).

Chancellorsville, battle of, 1863, Civil War **C** 325
Jackson, Thomas J. ("Stonewall") **J** 8
Chan-Chan, city of ancient Peru **P** 165
Chandidas, Indian poet **O** 220e
Chandni Chowk, or Street of Silver, Delhi, India **D** 101–02
Chandragupta Maurya (chan-dra-GUP-ta MA-ur-ya), king of Magadha (modern Bihar), India **I** 131

Chandrasekhar (chun-dra-SHAY-khar), **Subrahmanyan** (1910–), American astronomer, b. Lahore, India (now Pakistan). He developed many equations and theories regarding, among other things, the densities of stars and the relation of their color to their temperature.

Chanel (shan-ELL), **Gabrielle** ("Coco") (1883–1971), fashion designer and creator of Chanel No. 5 perfume, b. Auvergne, France. In 1919 she introduced her "poor-girl look" in Paris. This youthful style emphasized comfort and was characterized by shorter skirts, straight-lined cardigans, and long pearl necklaces worn with jersey dresses. A musical comedy, "Coco," based on her life, opened on Broadway in 1969.
Chanel suit, picture **F** 69

Chang, John, Korean statesman **K** 302
Changan, China see Sian

Change, adaptations to **L** 216–17
Change ringing, of bells **B** 135–36
Channel Islands, Great Britain **I** 428
Channels, television **T** 66–67
Chansons (shon-SON), French songs **F** 444; **M** 538
Chantilly (shan-TILLY) **lace L** 19
Chants, in church music
choral music **C** 276
Chanukah see Hanukkah
Chanute, Octave, American engineer **G** 239–40

Chao Phraya (CHOW pra-YA) **River** (also called the Menam), Thailand's main river. It drains the northern and central regions of the country, flowing approximately 160 miles before it empties into the Gulf of Siam. The river irrigates one of Asia's most important rice-producing areas.

Chaos (CAY-os), in Greek mythology **G** 356
Chaparral (chap-par-AL) **birds,** or roadrunners
state bird of New Mexico **N** 180
Chapbooks, early paperbacks **P** 58
ballads **B** 22
children's literature **C** 237

Chaplin, Charlie (Charles Spencer Chaplin) (1889–   ), English film actor, producer, and director, b. London. He emigrated to United States in 1910 and became an exile in Switzerland in 1952. He is famous as the sad-faced tramp he portrayed in many silent films and is also a master of pantomime. His movies include *The Circus, The Gold Rush, Modern Times,* and *The Great Dictator.*
as the Little Tramp, picture **M** 473

Chapman, Frank Michler (1864–1945), American ornithologist, b. Englewood, N.J. He was curator of ornithology at the American Museum of Natural History, New York, N.Y. (1908–42), where he introduced exhibits of bird groups in their natural environments. He conducted zoological expeditions in the American temperate and tropical zones. Among his numerous works on bird life are *Handbook of Birds of Eastern North America.*

Chapman, George (1559?–1634), English poet and dramatist, b. near Hitchin, Hertfordshire. He is famous for his translations of Homer's *Iliad* and *Odyssey.* The latter inspired John Keats's famous sonnet *On First Looking into Chapman's Homer.* Chapman also wrote poem "The Shadow of Night" and plays, including *The Blind Beggar of Alexandria* and *All Fools.*

Chapman, John see Appleseed, Johnny
Chapman, Philip K., American astronaut **S** 346
Chapman, Sydney, English scientist **I** 310–11
Chapultepec (cha-POOL-tep-ec), **battle of,** 1847 **M** 239
Chapultepec Park, Mexico City **M** 251
Characters, literary
heroes of fiction **F** 109–12
in novels **N** 345
short stories **S** 166
Characters of Chinese words see Chinese writing
Character witnesses, in law cases **J** 159
Charades (sha-RADES) **C** 188
Charbonneau, Toussaint, interpreter for Lewis and Clark expedition **I** 66
Charcoal C 105
deodorizing property **D** 117
drawing material **D** 301
fuel **F** 487
outdoor cooking uses **O** 247
used for C-14 dating **A** 362

Charcot (shar-CO), **Jean Baptiste Etienne Auguste** (1867–1936), French physician and explorer, b. Neuilly-sur-Seine. He headed Clinic of the Faculty of Medicine at University of Paris (1896–98) and led Antarctic expeditions (1903–05, 1908–10), on which he mapped Graham Land and its islands and discovered Charcot Land.

Charcot, **Jean Martin** (1825–1893), French physician, b. Paris. He organized the study of nervous diseases and was first to describe many nervous ailments. His studies of hypnosis influenced Freud's theories on treating the mentally ill.
   Freud and Charcot **F** 469

Chardin (shar-DAN), **Jean Baptiste Simeon,** French painter **F** 425; **P** 24
   Bowl of Plums, painting **F** 424
Chardonnet (shar-don-NAY), **Hilaire, count de,** French inventor **N** 427
   man-made fibers, history of **F** 108
   textiles **T** 142
Chares (CARE-ese) **of Lindos,** Greek craftsman **W** 216
Charge accounts **I** 289
   department stores allow **D** 119
Charges, electric see Electric charges
Charging, of storage cells in batteries **B** 99
Charioteer, statue **G** 345
Chariot races
   women drivers, picture **O** 105
Chariots, ancient wheeled vehicles **W** 157
Chari River, central Africa **C** 170, 183
Charities
   foundations (endowments) **F** 390
Charlemagne (SHAR-l'mane), **Charles I** or **Charles the Great,** ruler of the Franks **C** 189–90
   architecture **A** 377; **M** 296
   art as a record **A** 438e
   Austria's founder **A** 518
   Christianity, history of **C** 284
   education furthered by **E** 66
   founded Germany's First Reich **G** 159
   Holy Roman Empire **H** 161–63
   jury system **J** 159
   legends based on actual deeds **L** 129–30
   Middle Ages (Dark Ages) not so dark **M** 290
   religious reform by force **R** 291
   signature reproduced **A** 527

Charles I (1226–1285), count of Anjou and Provence. He was the son of Louis VIII of France. After defeating Manfred (1266), king of Naples and Conradin (1268), contender for the throne of Naples, he reigned as king of Two Sicilies (1266–85). He influenced the election of French pope Martin IV (1281).

Charles II, **Holy Roman Emperor** (Charles I, king of France, called Charles the Bald) **F** 99
Charles V, **Holy Roman Emperor** (Charles I, king of Spain) **H** 164
   keeps Reformation from Italy **I** 456
Charles VI, **Holy Roman Emperor A** 525
Charles, **Jacques,** French balloonist **B** 30; **G** 57
   aviation history **A** 567
Charles I, **king of England C** 536
   clashes with the Puritans **E** 222–23

Charles II, **king of England E** 224
   beginning of Whigs and Tories (political parties) in Great Britain **P** 378

Charles VII (Charles the Victorious) (1403–1461), king of France (1422–61), b. Paris. When he succeeded his

father, Charles VI, to throne, northern and part of southwestern France was under English rule. Aided by Joan of Arc, he captured Orleans (1429) and was crowned at Reims (1429). He concluded a treaty with Duke of Burgundy (1435) and entered Paris (1436). During his reign he effected a tax reform, formed the first standing army of France, and declared the Pragmatic Sanction of Bourges (1438) to restrict papal power over French Church.
   Joan of Arc and Charles VII **J** 121

Charles X (before accession, Charles Philippe, comte d'Artois) (1757–1836), king of France (1824–30), b. Versailles. After the outbreak of the French Revolution, he joined royalist exodus to England (1789). At the Restoration (1815) he returned to France and led the ultraroyalist faction. He succeeded his brother Louis XVIII (1824) and tried to establish an absolute monarchy. Faced with mounting opposition, he dismissed Chamber of Deputies (1830) and issued "July ordinances" curbing freedom of press and declaring new election methods. He was forced by the July Revolution (1830) to abdicate.

Charles II (1661–1700), king of Spain (1665–1700). He succeeded his father, Philip IV, to throne under regency (until 1675) of queen mother Mariana de Austria. His reign was marked by weakness and corruption. He joined a coalition that declared war against French king Louis XIV, resulting in Peace of Ryswick (1697). Charles had no children and was forced to choose Philip of Anjou, grandson of Louis XIV, as successor. His death sparked War of the Spanish Succession.

Charles IV (1748–1819), king of Spain (1788–1808), b. Naples, Italy. He succeeded his father, Charles III, to the throne (1788). He yielded Louisiana to France (1800) and joined Napoleonic France in war against England, resulting in destruction of Spanish fleet by England at Trafalgar (1805). A weak monarch, he was dominated by his wife, Maria Louisa, and his incompetent prime minister, Manuel Godoy. Following French invasion of Spain, he abdicated (1808) in favor of his son Ferdinand, who was supplanted by Joseph Bonaparte.

Charles XII, **king of Sweden S** 486
Charles III, **prince of Monaco M** 407

Charles, **prince of Wales** (Charles Philip Arthur George), son of Queen Elizabeth II and heir to British throne, b. 1948, Buckingham Palace. He was educated at schools in England, Scotland, and Australia and entered Cambridge University in 1967. He became heir to the throne in 1952 and prince of Wales in 1958. He was invested as prince of Wales (1969) in colorful ceremonies at Caernarvon Castle, Wales.
   Elizabeth II **E** 179

Charles XIV John, **king of Sweden and Norway S** 487
Charles' law, on gases **G** 57
Charles Martel ("Charles the Hammer") (689?–741), grandfather of Charlemagne. His historic defeat of Arabs at battle of Tours (Poitiers) (732) stopped Islamic advance into western Europe. His son, Pepin the Short, became first Carolingian king of the Franks.
   Carolingian kings of France and the Roman Catholic Church **F** 415; **R** 290–91

Charles River, **Massachusetts,** picture **M** 139
Charles the Bald see Charles II, Holy Roman Emperor (Charles I, king of France)
Charles the Bold, **duke of Burgundy D** 363
   Switzerland, attempt to conquer **S** 502

Charles the Great see Charlemagne
Charles the Simple, king of France **V** 339
Charleston, capital of West Virginia **W** 137; picture
   W 139
Charleston, dance **D** 27
Charleston, South Carolina **S** 307
   colonial life **C** 397–98
Charles Town, West Virginia **W** 136
Charles University, Czechoslovakia **C** 562, 563

Charlevoix (sharl-ev-WA), **Pierre François Xavier de**
(1682–1761), French Jesuit historian, b. St. Quentin. He
taught in missions of Quebec, Canada (1705–09), and
traveled (1720–22) through French colonies and down
Mississippi to New Orleans in search of "Western Sea."
He was author of a history of New France.

Charlie Is My Darling, folk song **F** 327

Charlot (shar-LO), **Jean** (1898–   ), American artist and
writer, b. Paris, France. He emigrated to United States
(1929). He lived and worked in Mexico, bringing the
influence of massive figures of Mexican art to many of
the murals and color lithographs for which he is famous.
His art works include *Mother and Child* and *Landscape,
Milpa Alta.* He wrote *Art from the Mayans to Disney*
and *Artist on Art: Collected Essays of Jean Charlot.*

Charlotte, North Carolina **N** 318
Charlottesville, Virginia **V** 357
Charlotte's Web, book by E. B. White, excerpt **W** 160–61
Charlottetown, capital of Prince Edward Island, Canada
   P 456e, 456h; picture **P** 456c
Charm bracelets, jewelry **J** 99
Charnock, Job, English founder of Calcutta **C** 11
Charon (CARE-on), boatman in Greek mythology **G** 357
Charpentier, Marc Antoine, French composer **F** 445
Charrúa (char-RU-a), Indian tribe of South America
   U 235
Charter airlines **A** 566
Charter Oak, historic landmark in Hartford, Conn.
   C 466
Charters, laws of municipal government **M** 503
Chartres (SHART-ra), **Cathedral of,** France, picture
   G 268

Charybdis (ca-RIB-dis), in Greek mythology **O** 54

Chase, Mary Ellen (1887–1973), American author and
educator, b. Blue Hill, Maine. She was professor of
English Literature at Smith College (1926–55) and
professor emeritus since 1955. A prolific writer, she
was best known for her novels set along the Maine
seacoast. They include *Mary Peters* and *Windswept.*

Chase, or frame, for printing type **P** 461–62

Chase, Richard (1904–   ), American folklorist and author
of children's books, b. Huntsville, Ala. He compiled and
edited works such as *The Jack Tales, Grandfather Tales,*
and *Hullabaloo.*

Chase, Samuel (1741–1811), American Revolutionary
leader and Supreme Court justice, b. Somerset County,
Md. He signed Declaration of Independence but opposed
ratification of Constitution. Appointed Supreme Court
justice (1796) by President Washington, he was impeached
(1804) for disregard of law, but was acquitted (1805).
   impeachment not a weapon for removing political
      enemies **I** 108

Chasing, art of ornamenting metal surfaces **D** 75
Chassis (SHAS-sy), of automobiles **A** 543, 550

Chateaubriand (sha-to-bri-ON), **François René, vicomte
de,** French novelist **F** 439
Château Frontenac, Quebec City **Q** 16; picture **Q** 17
Château-Thierry (sha-TO-ti-AER-ry), **battle of,** 1918 **W** 280
Châteaus, or chateaux, large country houses **F** 407
   Blois, France **F** 421; picture **F** 422
   Renaissance architecture **A** 381
   Chenonceaux, picture **F** 414
Chatham, New Brunswick, Canada **N** 138c
Chatham Islands, New Zealand **N** 237
Chatoyancy (sha-TOY-ancy), cat's-eye effect in gemstones
   G 69–70
Chattahoochee National Forest, Georgia **G** 139
Chattahoochee River, United States **A** 115, 120
Chattanooga, Tennessee **T** 85–86; picture **T** 82
   Civil War campaigns **C** 326
Chatterton, Thomas, English poet **E** 259
Chaucer, Geoffrey, English poet **C** 190
   beginnings of English literature **E** 249
   Middle English, the language of Chaucer **E** 244
Chaulmoogra, tree **P** 313; picture **P** 312

Chaumonot (sho-mon-O), **Pierre Joseph Marie** (1611–
1693), French Jesuit missionary, b. Burgundy. He worked
among Huron Indians in Canada and Iroquois in New
York (1639–92) and wrote grammar of Huron language.

Chautauqua (sha-TAU-qua) **Institution,** New York **N** 221
   music festival **M** 552
Chávez (CHA-base), **Carlos,** Mexican composer **L** 75

Chavez, Cesar Estrada (1927–   ), American labor organizer, b. Yuma, Ariz. Son of a migrant worker, Chavez
has devoted himself to bettering working conditions of
Mexican-American farm laborers. In 1965 his association
joined others in striking California grape growers. His
group became affiliated with AFL-CIO. The workers' plight
gained much sympathy and support and the growers
began signing labor contracts with the unions in 1970.

Chavez (SHA-vez), **Dennis,** American statesman **N** 193
Chavin (cha-VEEN), early civilization of Andes **I** 155

Chavis, John (1763?–1838), American educator and
preacher, a free Negro. A classics scholar, he instructed
white boys of prominent families, including several who
became senators and statesmen.

Chayefsky (cha-YEF-ski), **Paddy** (Sidney Chayefsky)
(1923–   ), American playwright, b. New York, N.Y. He
introduced new realism into drama of 1950's. His film
Marty, adapted from early TV drama, won an Academy
Award and New York Film Critics' award (1956).

Checkers, a game **C** 191–92
   How old is the game of checkers? **C** 191
   See also Chess
Checking accounts, at banks **B** 46
Checkmate, chess term **C** 224
Checkoff, of labor union dues **L** 9, 16
Checks, at banks **B** 46, 49
Checks and balances, system of government
   division of power of U.S. government **U** 139
   United States Congress **U** 142
Check valves **V** 270
Cheddar cheese **D** 13
Cheese **C** 192–93
   Edam cheese, picture **N** 117
   how cheese is made **D** 12–13
   legend of its origin **F** 333
   outdoor snack **O** 248
Cheetahs, wild cats **C** 139; **M** 63; picture **C** 138

Cheever, John (1912–), American writer, b. Quincy, Mass. He is a member of the National Institute of Arts and Letters. His works include *The Wapshot Chronicle* (National Book award, 1958), *The Way Some People Live*, *The Wapshot Scandal*, and *Bullet Park*.

Chehalis, Indians of North America **I** 180
Chekhov (CHEK-off), **Anton,** Russian writer **S** 165
  poetic realism in the drama **D** 298
  Russian literature **U** 61
Chemical bonding, adhesive process **G** 242
Chemical carcinogens (car-CIN-o-gens), cancer-causing agents **C** 91
Chemical coatings **P** 33
Chemical elements see Elements, chemical
Chemical energy **E** 199, 202; **P** 234–35
  nuclear energy **N** 352–71
Chemical engineering **E** 205–06
Chemical fertilizers **F** 97
Chemical industry **C** 193–95
  Delaware **D** 87, 93
  hydrogen gas used in **G** 61
  industrial importance **I** 247
  New Jersey **N** 169
  salt, uses in **S** 21
  synthetic dyes **D** 369–71
  wood products **W** 227
Chemical oceanography **O** 33–34
Chemicals, products of the chemical industry **C** 193–95
  drug industry **D** 323
  Ehrlich's 606, treatment for syphilis **D** 216
  food contamination **F** 355
Chemical symbols, of elements **E** 155, 156–57; **C** 220
  alphabetical table of elements **C** 197–98
  periodic table **C** 213

Chemical warfare, warfare in which chemicals other than explosives, such as gases that irritate, burn, or kill, are used.

Chemise (shem-ESE), or sack dress **F** 65
Chemistry **C** 196–205
  applied to agriculture **A** 100
  atoms **A** 483–89; **C** 196
  batteries **B** 97–99
  biochemistry **B** 181–84
  body chemistry **B** 289–97
  branches of **C** 205
  catalysts **C** 199
  compounds **C** 196
  computers used for research **C** 449
  crystals **C** 541–46
  dyes and dyeing **D** 366–72
  electrolysis **E** 129
  elements **E** 153–65
  equations, balanced **C** 198–99
  experiments and projects in chemistry and physics **E** 362–67
  explosives **E** 388–94
  fermentation **F** 87–91
  fine and heavy chemicals **C** 194–95
  fire and combustion **F** 136–37
  formulas **C** 197–200
  history see Chemistry, history of
  inorganic see Chemistry, inorganic
  iodines and other halogens **I** 349
  ions and ionization **I** 354–55
  matter, chemical changes in **M** 176–77
  Nobel prizes **N** 268a–269
  oils and fats **O** 76–79
  organic see Chemistry, organic
  origin of the word **C** 207

  oxygen and oxidation **O** 268–70
  periodic table, of chemical elements **C** 202
  petrochemistry, chemistry of petroleum **P** 176–77
  physics and chemistry compared **C** 196
  reactions (changes) **C** 196–97, 199, 201
  spectro-chemical analysis **L** 269
  symbols, chemical **C** 220; **E** 155, 156–57; Dalton's chart of atomic symbols **C** 213
  terms of **C** 216–20
  valence **C** 199–200
  See also Atoms; Biochemistry; Chemical industry; Chemurgy; Crystals; Ions and ionization; Micro-chemistry; Nuclear energy; and names of elements and chief compounds
Chemistry, history of **C** 205–16
  chemical revolution in the history of science **S** 71–72
  Curie, Marie and Pierre **C** 552–53
  Faraday, Michael **F** 44
  Lavoisier's contributions **L** 86
  radioactive elements **R** 67–68
Chemistry, inorganic
  chemical industry **C** 194
  how chemistry led to biochemistry **B** 181–82
Chemistry, organic **C** 214
  chemical industry **C** 194
  contributions to biology **B** 193–94
  new branch of chemistry **S** 74
  origins of biochemistry **B** 181–82
  plastics **P** 324–31
Chemistry, physiological see Body chemistry
Chemotherapy (kem-o-THER-apy), treatment of diseases with chemicals **B** 182
  cancer treatment **C** 95

Chemurgy, branch of applied chemistry that adapts agricultural products for industrial use. Examples of these products include soybean oil, used in the production of paint and plastics, and oat hulls, used to make furfural, an important industrial chemical.

Chengtu (cheng-DU), China **C** 262

Chennault (shen-NOLT), **Claire Lee** (1890–1958), American aviator, b. Commerce, Tex. He pioneered in use of paratroops and in parachute landing of supplies. Chennault became air adviser to Chinese commander Chiang Kai-shek (1937) and organized American Volunteer Group ("The Flying Tigers") to aid China against Japanese aggression (1941–42). He was chief of U.S. air operations in China (1942). He wrote *The Role of Defensive Pursuit.* See also Flying Tigers

Cheops (KE-ops), king of ancient Egypt **W** 214
  Great Pyramid of **A** 221; **E** 96; picture **W** 215
Chephren (KEPH-ren), king of ancient Egypt **E** 96
  Great Sphinx and pyramid of, picture **E** 93
Cherokee, Indians of North America **I** 213
  Georgia's Cherokee nation **G** 147
  Indians of the Southeastern Maize Area **I** 187–88
  removed from Alabama **A** 127
  Sequoya **S** 124
  Unto These Hills, outdoor drama **N** 315
  Why was Sam Houston called the Raven? **H** 271
Cherokee Outlet, Oklahoma **O** 84
Cherokee rose, flower
  state flower of Georgia **G** 133
Cherrapunji (churra-POON-ji), India
  Asia's rainfall **A** 452
  rainfall heaviest in the world **R** 94
Cherry **P** 107–09
Cherry blossom festivals
  Japanese celebration **J** 31

Cheshire cat, fictional cat with a wide grin, said to have been created by Lewis Carroll in *Alice's Adventures in Wonderland.* The cat was able to vanish, leaving only his smile. Carroll's character may have been inspired by pictures of lions rampant on signs above many inns in Cheshire, England.

Chesnutt, Charles Waddell (1858–1932), American Negro author, b. Cleveland, Ohio. He was principal of Fayetteville, N.C., state normal school and was subsequently admitted to the bar (1887). He is famous for *The Conjure Woman,* series of humorous stories related by fictional Uncle Julius. Many of his novels depict struggles of American Negro as he knew them growing up in North Carolina.

Chesterfield, 4th earl of (Philip Dormer Stanhope) (1694–1773), British politician and man of letters, b. London. He was ambassador to The Hague, the Netherlands (1728–32, 1744). Lord high steward but dismissed for opposing bill favored by Sir Robert Walpole (1733), he attacked government of George II in letters signed "Geffery Broadbottom" (1743). He was lord lieutenant of Ireland (1745–46) and secretary of state (1746–48). His name became a synonym for gallant manners and worldliness. Chesterfield is best-known for *Letters to His Son* and *Letters to His Godson.*

Chesterfield Islands, uninhabited coral islands in the southwestern Pacific. A dependency of New Caledonia, they are administered by France. The islands were formerly worked for guano.

Chiang Kai-shek, Madame (Mei-ling, or Mayling, Soong) (1898-   ), wife of Generalissimo Chiang Kai-shek, b. Shanghai. She was educated in United States and worked as interpreter and aid to her husband. Her books include *China in Peace and War* and *This Is Our China.*

Chicano, an American of Mexican descent. The term probably developed as a short form of *Mexicano,* the Spanish word for Mexican. In the 1960's, young militant Mexican Americans gave the term a new meaning that suggested racial and cultural pride.

Chichester, Sir Francis (1901–72), British pilot and yachtsman, b. North Devon, England. An aviator before turning to sailing he won first singlehanded Transatlantic Yacht Race (1960), and set record (1962) for solo east-west Atlantic crossing. In 1966–67 he solo circumnavigated the globe in his boat, *Gypsy Moth IV.* He wrote *The Lonely Sea and the Sky,* and *Gypsy Moth Circles the World.* He was knighted in 1967. In 1971 he sailed solo across the Atlantic in 22 days.

society teaches girls and boys their roles **W** 211
television programs **T** 71
women, role of **W** 211
See also Adolescence
Childe Harold's Pilgrimage, by Lord Byron **E** 260; excerpt **B** 482
Child is father of the man, quotation from Wordsworth **C** 231
Child labor **C** 235
early factories of the Industrial Revolution **I** 238
government regulation **L** 14
Child Labor Act, 1916 **W** 179
Child Protection and Toy Safety Acts, 1966, 1969 **F** 352
Child psychology see Child development
Children
adoption **A** 25–26
Australia, school by radio **A** 499; picture **A** 498
baby **B** 2–4
Christmas patrons around the world **C** 292
colonial America **C** 390–92
development see Child development
divorce, problems involving **D** 234–35
educating the blind **B** 252
family responsibility **F** 37–43
fashion modeling **M** 385
first aid **F** 157–63
foster-family care **O** 227
games **G** 10–24
handicapped, rehabilitation of the **H** 27–30
hearing, tests for, picture **D** 51
indoor activities for rainy days **I** 223–26
juvenile delinquency **J** 162–64
kindergarten and nursery schools **K** 242–47
libraries **L** 170, 175–76
literature for children **C** 236–48b
museums for **M** 520
orphanages and foster-family care **O** 227
percentage in populations **P** 397
pioneer life **P** 256; pictures **P** 257
playgrounds **P** 77–78
poverty, chance to break cycle of **P** 424b
public assistance **W** 120–21
reform schools **P** 470
retardation, mental **R** 190–91
safety **S** 2–7
society teaches girls and boys their roles **W** 211
storytelling **S** 434–36
toys **T** 230–35
women, role of **W** 211
See also Child labor

Children's Book Council (CBC), nonprofit organization that aims to encourage children to read better books. It sponsors National Children's Book Week, updates booklist and award information, and maintains a library. It was founded in 1945, has its headquarters in New York, N.Y., and publishes *Children's Book Council Calendar.*

Children's Crusade **C** 540
Children's Day **H** 158
Japan **H** 159; **K** 266
Children's Games, painting by Pieter Brueghel **D** 354
Children's literature **C** 236–248b
Alcott, Louisa May **A** 149
book awards and medals **B** 309–10b
Field, Eugene **F** 113–14
figures of speech **F** 119–20
German forerunners of comic strips **G** 178
illustration of children's books **I** 97
libraries, children's services **L** 170, 180–88

magazines **M** 16
Newbery, John **N** 137
nursery rhymes **N** 402–08
poetry **P** 349–55
See also Fables; Fairy tales; Folklore; Nursery rhymes; Storytelling; names of individual authors
Children's zoos **Z** 379

Childs Cup, trophy awarded for victory in Childs Cup rowing race. Established by George W. Childs (1879), publisher of Philadelphia *Public Ledger,* for competition among Columbia, Princeton, and Pennsylvania, it is oldest trophy for sprint, or short-distance, racing.

Child's Garden of Verses, A, by Robert Louis Stevenson, poems from **S** 424
Child welfare **W** 120–21
adoption **A** 25–26
orphanages and foster-family care **O** 227
social work with child welfare agencies **S** 225
Chile (CHIL-e) **C** 249–55
flag **F** 242
life in Latin America **L** 47–61; picture **S** 289
national anthem **N** 21
nitrate fertilizers **F** 98
O'Higgins, Bernardo **O** 59
San Martín, José de, early fighter for freedom **S** 36
special stamp, picture **S** 399
Chili powder, blend of spices **S** 382
Chilkat, Indians of North America **I** 180

Chilkat Pass, route from Haines, Alaska, to the Yukon, located 50 miles west-northwest of Skagway. Used during the Klondike gold rush of the 1890's, it is now crossed by the Alaska Highway.

Chilkoot Pass, pass through Coast Mts. on border between Alaska and British Columbia, Canada. It was used by Indians, fur traders, and particularly prospectors during gold rush in Klondike (1896) as shortest way to Yukon Territory. It stretches 29 miles, from former village of Dyea, Alaska, to Lake Bennett, Canada, at approximate elevation of 3,500 ft., much of it being dangerous canyons and perpendicular walls. Travel lessened through pass after Yukon Railroad was built through White Pass (1900).

Chill, coldness of body **D** 206
Chimborazo (chim-bo-RA-zo), inactive volcano in Ecuador **E** 54
Chime clocks **W** 50
Chimera (kim-ER-a), monster in Greek mythology **G** 364
age chimera **A** 87
Chimes, sets of bells **B** 136, 137; picture **M** 548
jade stones make musical chimes **J** 9–10
Chimney Rock, landmark on Oregon Trail **N** 81; picture **N** 83
Chimney swifts, birds **B** 220
Chimpanzees **M** 419
animal intelligence tests **A** 287–88; pictures **A** 285, 288
learning experiments, picture **L** 101
Chimp-O-Mat tests, chimpanzees trained to operate **A** 288
Chimu (CHI-mu), ancient Indian empire in Peru **I** 207
crafts, pictures **I** 203, 205
China **C** 256–73
acupuncture **M** 208a, 208b
art see Chinese art
Asia dominated by **A** 448–49
Asia's population, concentration **A** 452–53
Boxer Rebellion **B** 350

China (continued)
bridges, admired by Marco Polo **B** 397–98
Buddhism and Confucianism **B** 425
canal system **C** 83, 84
ceramic work, or porcelain, developed in **C** 172, 173
Confucius **C** 460
decorative arts **D** 68–69
dialects **D** 152
drama **D** 292
dynasties **C** 270–71; chart of dates **C** 269
education in the Orient **E** 62
fans **F** 43
fireworks **F** 156
flags, origin of those made of cloth **F** 225
food, typical meals **F** 339
funeral and burial customs **F** 492; picture **F** 493
Great Wall, picture **W** 219
holidays **H** 150, 152, 154, 158
ideographic writing **C** 431, 433
India ink first made in **I** 256
jade carvings **J** 9–10
Kites' Day **K** 266
largest encyclopedia **E** 193
literature **O** 220–220b
Manchuria **C** 262, 265
Marco Polo's travels in **E** 371; **P** 389–90
marriage rites **W** 103
missiles invented by Chinese in 13th century **M** 343
Mongolia **M** 416
music **O** 220d–221
Open-Door policy **M** 189–90
paper **C** 432; **P** 56
paper for accordion-folded books **B** 318
porcelain **P** 414, 415, 417
rice eaten mainly in south China **G** 282
San Men dam foundations, picture **D** 18
silk **S** 178–79
Sun Yat-sen **S** 467
theater **T** 163
Truman, Harry S, policy toward **T** 303
Yangtze River **Y** 343
See also names of major cities
China, People's Republic of (Communist) **C** 268, 272–73
Chiang Kai-shek's struggle against **C** 227
differences with Soviet Union **C** 445
education **E** 82
flag **F** 237
international relations **I** 323
Kashmir **K** 199
Korean War **K** 304
Mao Tse-tung **M** 86
modern factory, picture **A** 463
national anthem **N** 21
Peking **P** 117–19
relations with India **I** 135
relations with U.S. **I** 325
Shanghai **S** 138–39
Shenyang **S** 150
Tibet, autonomous territory of China **T** 175–78
Tientsin **T** 185
China, Republic of (Nationalist) **C** 257, 273
Chiang Kai-shek, first president **C** 227
flag **F** 237
national anthem **N** 21
Taiwan **T** 12–13
China Sea **O** 46–47
Chinatown, San Francisco, California **S** 31
Chinaware
antique **A** 320; pictures **A** 318, 319
dolls made of **D** 265
Chinchillas (chin-CHIL-las), rodents **R** 280; **F** 518
native to the Andes **A** 253

Chinchona see Cinchona, tree
Chincoteague (CHINC-o-teag) **National Wildlife Refuge**
V 348
Chincoteague ponies **V** 344
Ch'in dynasty, ancient rule of China **C** 270
Chinese art **O** 215–17; pictures **O** 214, 220
art as a record **A** 438f
porcelain **P** 414, 417
vase, Shang dynasty, picture **A** 360
woodcut from the *Diamond Sutra* **G** 302
Chinese chestnuts, picture **P** 298
Chinese crested dog **D** 261; picture **D** 260
Chinese drama **D** 292
Chinese Exclusion Act, 1882 **I** 99
policies of the Arthur administration **A** 441
Chinese insect wax **W** 70
Chinese language **O** 220
Chinese literature **O** 220–220b
Chinese music **O** 220d–221
Chinese National Holiday **H** 152
Chinese theater **T** 163
dance **D** 33
Chinese water deer **H** 220; picture **H** 214
Chinese writing **C** 258–59, 269
communication by ideographs **C** 431, 433
writing, development of **W** 318

Ch'ing (Manchu) dynasty (1644–1912), last Chinese imperial dynasty. Its rulers, the Manchus, invaded China from Manchuria. They governed through Chinese officials and brought a period of peace and prosperity. (More books were published in China during this time than in all the rest of the world.) Powerful rulers, they extended the Chinese empire into Tibet, Mongolia, Nepal, and Korea, up to founding of Chinese Republic (1912).
China and Mongolia, history of **C** 271; **M** 416
Shenyang (Mukden), capital **S** 150

Chinoiserie (she-nua-zer-E), Chinese influence on decorative arts **D** 78
Chinook (shin-OOK), warm, dry wind **G** 96
a "snow-eater" **R** 95
Colorado **C** 406
Prairie Provinces **A** 146c; **C** 55
Wyoming **W** 327–28
See also Foehn
Chinstrap penguins **P** 124
Chipewyan, Indians of North America **I** 164, 170
Chipmunks **L** 252–53
each organism has its own niche **L** 222
pets **P** 180
rodents **R** 276; pictures **R** 275, 277
why small animals hibernate **H** 124
Chippendale, Thomas, English furniture designer
F 507
antiques **A** 318
Chippewa, Indians of North America **I** 178–79
See also Ojibway
Chipping sparrows, birds **B** 219
Chiricahuas (chi-ri-CA-huas), Indians of North America
G 189
Chirico (KE-ri-co), Giorgio di, Italian surrealist painter
I 473; **M** 395
Melancholy and Mystery of a Street, painting **I** 472

Chiropody (kir-OP-ody) (from combination of Greek words *cheir*, "hand," and *pous*, "foot"), branch of medicine dealing with the care and treatment of the human foot. It is also called podiatry.

Chiropractic (KY-ro-prac-tic) (from Greek *cheir*, meaning "hand," and *praktikos*, meaning "efficient," "practical," or "operative"), system of healing based on premise that irregularity in the nervous system causes disease. Treatment involves manipulation of the body structures, especially of spinal column, by hand.

Chiroptera, order of mammals **B** 92; **M** 62, 69
Chisels, tools **T** 213
  woodworking **W** 230

Chisholm, Shirley (1925–   ), American legislator, b. Brooklyn, N.Y. A former teacher, she became interested in politics and served in the New York state legislature. In 1968 she was elected the nation's first black congresswoman.

Chisholm Trail O 266
  Oklahoma **O** 86
  Wichita, Kansas, early trading post **K** 188
Chitarrone (ki-tar-RO-nay), musical instrument, picture **S** 438
Chitons (KI-tons), mollusks **O** 276; **S** 149
Chittagong, Bangladesh **B** 44a
Chivalry (SHIV-al-ry), knight's code of behavior **K** 274–75, 277
  early French literature **F** 435
  King Arthur, legends of **A** 442–45
  medals and decorations **M** 198
Chives, plants of onion family **O** 118
Chlorella, alga, food source **A** 157
Chlorine (CLOR-ine), element **G** 59
  action of catalysts **C** 199
  elements, some facts about **E** 154, 160
  iodine and other halogens **I** 349
  ions and isotopes **C** 203; diagrams **C** 204, 205
  water desalting **W** 56a
Chloroform, used as anesthetic **A** 257, 258
Chlorophyll (CLOR-o-phyll), in plants **P** 221–22
  algae **A** 155
  cell functions **C** 162
  fungi lack **F** 496
  in food chain, exchange of forms of energy **E** 202
  leaves of odd and interesting plants **P** 318
  leaves of trees and their function **T** 281
  magnesium in **M** 23
  plant plankton **P** 279–80
  term adopted by Liebig **B** 194
Chlorophyta, division of plant kingdom **P** 292
Chloroplasts, in plant cells **P** 294; picture **B** 183
  cell structure **C** 162
  photosynthesis **P** 221
Chloroprene (CLOR-o-prene), chemical **C** 195
Chmielnicki (hm-yel-NEET-ski), **Bogdan,** Cossack hero **U** 9

Choate (CHOAT), **Rufus** (1799–1859), American lawyer, b. Hog Island, Mass. He served in the U.S. House of Representatives (1831–34) and Senate (1841–45). An organizer of the Massachusetts Whigs, he opposed the emergence of the Republican Party.

Chocolate C 274–75
  candymaking **C** 99
  Hershey, Pennsylvania, the Chocolate Capital **P** 142
  stain removal **L** 84
Choctaw, Indians of North America **A** 126; **I** 187
Choibalsan (CHOI-bol-son), Mongolia **M** 415
Choirs (KWIRES), music
  ancient Hebrew **A** 246
  choristers singing carols, picture **C** 290
  hymns, advanced, for professional choirs **H** 309
  training in Flemish and French schools **D** 363
  See also Choral music; Choruses (music)

Choke, valve on a carburetor **I** 306
Choking on foreign bodies
  first aid **F** 163
Cholera (COL-er-a), **Asiatic,** disease caused by certain bacteria that enter digestive system. It causes loss of body fluids through vomiting and diarrhea and is treated by replacement of fluids. It occurs in epidemic form where water supply is contaminated by bacteria, chiefly in Far East. Vaccination prevents it for short time.

Cholesterol (co-LES-ter-ol), chemical found in all animal tissues and fluids. Necessary for life, though its role is not well understood, it can be changed by body into other chemicals needed for proper functioning—for example, vitamin D in humans. It is of recent interest as clue to cause of heart disease.
  body chemistry, lipids in **B** 293
  special diets **N** 418
  vitamin D **V** 370d–371

Cholla (CHOLE-ya), cactus, picture **C** 3
Cholon (cho-LUN), South Vietnam **V** 334b
Choltitz, Dietrich von, German general **P** 75
Chomedey, Paul de see Maisonneuve, Paul de Chomedey
Chomolungma (cho-mo-LUNG-ma), Tibetan name for Mount Everest **E** 336
Chopin (SHO-pan), **Frédéric,** Polish pianist and composer **C** 276
  French music **F** 446
  nocturnes **R** 311
Chops, meat, outdoor cooking **O** 247
Chop suey, food **F** 339
Chorale, a musical form **M** 535
Chorales (co-RALS), German hymns **H** 311–12
  religious music in Germany **G** 182
Choral (COR-al) **music C** 276–79
  ancient Hebrew **A** 246
  basic record library **R** 125
  English **E** 269, 271
  festivals **M** 551
  German **G** 182
  hymns **H** 309–13
  Mass as musical form **D** 363
Choral Symphony, or Ninth Symphony, by Beethoven **C** 278; **G** 185
Chord (CORD), of airplane wing **A** 554
Chords, in music **M** 529
  for guitar **G** 410
Chords, of circles **G** 127
Choreography (cor-e-OG-raphy), arrangement of dances **D** 22
  avant-garde dancers **D** 34
  ballet **B** 24–29
  dance music development **D** 37
Choreomanias (cor-e-o-MANE-ias), dance manias of Middle Ages **D** 24
Chores
  for pioneer children, pictures **P** 257
  on the farm **F** 52–53
Choruses, music
  ancient Greece **A** 247
  See also Choirs (music)
Choson ("Land of Morning Calm") (Korean), or **Chosen** (Japanese), name for Korea **K** 296
Chotts, or shotts, salt lakes **A** 160; **T** 309
Chouart, Médart see Groseilliers, Médart Chouart

Chou (JO) **Dynasty,** third and longest ruling house in Chinese history (about 1028–256 B.C.). Begun by Wu Wang (rulers took title *Wang,* meaning "King"), it controlled most of China north of Yellow River during

Chou Dynasty (continued)
Western Chou period, but was forced to flee from
barbarians later and moved eastward during the Eastern
Chou period. It was characterized by advanced knowledge and craftsmanship. The three most important
Chinese philosophers, Lao-tzu, Confucius, and Mencius,
wrote during this period and laid foundation of Chinese
thought.

transportation advances **T** 258

Chou En-lai (JO en-LIE) (1898?–   ), Chinese Communist leader, b. Hwaiyin, Kiangsu. He served under Chiang
Kai-shek, leader of Kuomintang (Nationalist Party),
during First United Front, a period of co-operation with
Chinese Communists (1924–27). He was Political Commissar of First Army (1926). After Chiang Kai-shek's
purge of Communists from Kuomintang (1927), Chou
joined with Chu Teh, head of Red Army. During Second
United Front (1937–45), when China and Japan were at
war, he acted as adviser to Chiang Kai-shek's government. With proclamation (1949) of People's Republic of
China, he became foreign minister (until 1958) and has
continued as premier under Mao Tse-tung.

Chouteau (shoot-O), **René Auguste**, American fur trader
M 379
Saint Louis, Missouri **S** 17
Chouteau family, fur dynasty **F** 522–23
Chouteau Trading Post Marker, Oklahoma **O** 91
Chow mein, food **F** 339
Chraibi, Driss, Moroccan writer **A** 76d
Chrétien de Troyes (cret-YEN d'TRWA), French poet
F 436
Arthurian legends **A** 445
Christ see Jesus Christ
Christchurch, New Zealand **N** 241
Christ Church, Philadelphia **P** 182
Christi, John, English organ manufacturer **M** 550
Christian art and symbolism S 96

Christian Brothers, or **Brothers of the Christian Schools,**
order of Roman Catholic Brothers who devote their lives
to educating young. The order was founded (1680) in
France by Jean Baptiste de la Salle. Their innovations in
child education helped bring about general primary
education in Europe. They have about 1,500 schools and
colleges throughout the world. There are approximately
18,000 Brothers.

Christian Church, or Disciples of Christ **P** 484

Christian Endeavor, International Society of (ISCE),
Christian organization for young people in the United
States, Canada, and Mexico. The society aims to
promote Christian life among its members and to train
them for church work. It sponsors citizenship projects
and contests and Youth Week. It was founded in 1881
and has headquarters in Columbus, Ohio. It publishes
Christian Endeavor World.

Christiania, Norway see Oslo, Norway
Christianity C 279–89
Abraham honored by **A** 7
Africa **A** 56, 58
Anglo-Saxon England becomes Christian **E** 216
Apostles, The **A** 332–33
Armenia **U** 44
art as a record **A** 438b
Asia, chief religions of **A** 460
Augustine, Saint **A** 494
Bible **B** 152–62
Byzantine art and architecture **B** 483–90

Byzantine church **B** 492
Christmas customs **C** 289–94
Constantine the Great, first Christian ruler **C** 489
Coptic church **A** 56, 58; **E** 296, 303
Crusades **C** 538–40; **E** 370
dance a part of worship in the early church **D** 24
divorce **D** 234
early Christian art **I** 458
Easter **E** 41–42
funeral customs **F** 494, 495
historical writings **H** 134–35
hymns **H** 309–13
Japan **J** 44, 46
Jerusalem **J** 78–81
Jesus Christ **J** 82–84
Middle Ages **M** 293–95
missions and missionaries **M** 348–49
Orthodox Eastern churches **O** 228–30
Patrick, Saint **P** 98
persecutions of Christians by Nero **N** 114
Peter, Saint **P** 167
Protestantism **P** 482–86
Reformation **R** 132–35
religions of the world **R** 149–50
religious holidays **R** 153–55
Roman Catholic Church **R** 287–302
Roman Empire **R** 307–08
sculpture of early Christians **S** 96
Southeast Asia **S** 330
Ten Commandments **T** 72–73
wedding customs **W** 100–02
See also names of saints, popes, Christian leaders
Christian names N 7
Christians and Jews, National Conference of see National
Conference of Christians and Jews
Christian Science Monitor, newspaper **N** 200
Christian Scientists, or Church of Christ, Scientist **P** 484

Christie, Agatha (Agatha Mary Clarissa Miller Christie
Mallowan) (1891–   ), English mystery-story writer, b.
Torquay. Creator of fictional Belgian detective Hercule
Poirot, she writes novels and plays.

Christmas C 289–95
Australia and Vermont, pictures **S** 111
Advent **R** 155, 290
A Visit from St. Nicholas, by Moore **C** 295
carols **C** 122
crib, or manger, scene begun by St. Francis **F** 449
folk music **F** 325
holy month of December **D** 56
Latin America **L** 61
mistletoe **P** 318
toys **T** 233
Yuletide and Yule log, pagan Norse customs **N** 277
Christmas cards C 292; 294
greeting cards **G** 372–74
Christmas carols C 289–90
Christmas Island, Indian Ocean **A** 496

Christmas Island, largest coral atoll in the Pacific. One
of the Line Islands, it is administered by British as part
of Gilbert and Ellice Islands. The island was discovered
by Captain Cook on Christmas Eve, 1777. It was used as
World War II base for Allied troops, and after the war,
for nuclear experiments by Great Britain (1956, 1958)
and United States (1962).

Christmas trees C 291; picture **C** 294
Montana grows many **M** 436
Christmas trees, collections of valves and controls on
oil derricks **P** 173–74

Christophe (chris-TOPHE), **Henri** (1767–1820), king of Haiti, b. Grenada, British West Indies. He participated in first Negro revolt (1791) against French in Santo Domingo and joined second uprising (1803–04) of Jean Jacques Dessalines, upon whose death in ambush (1806) he made himself King Henri I of northern Haiti. His rule became oppressive and caused rebellion (1818–20) and his suicide. He built palace of Sans Souci and fortress of the Citadelle.

Christopher, Saint, early Christian martyr who probably lived during the 3rd century. He is believed to have been from Syria. According to legend, he had gigantic strength and once unknowingly carried Christ child across stream on his back. He is patron saint of travelers.

Christophers, The, three kings of Denmark. **Christopher I** (1219–1259) reigned (1252–59) through period of conflict with archbishop of Lund. **Christopher II** (1276–1332) was considered incompetent ruler, and Denmark was divided during his reign (1320–26, 1330–32). **Christopher III** (1418–1448), known as "Christopher of Bavaria," king of Denmark and Sweden (1440–48) and Norway (1442–48), made Copenhagen official royal residence (1443).

Chrysler, Walter Percy (1875–1940), American automobile manufacturer, founder and president of the Chrysler Corporation, b. Wamego, Kan. He was assistant manager of the American Locomotive Company (1910) and president and general manager of the Buick Motor Company (1916–19). In 1919 he became a vice-president of General Motors and later executive vice-president of the Willys-Overland Company (1920–22). He founded the Chrysler Corporation in 1924 and was responsible for the construction of Chrysler Building in New York, N.Y.

Churches of the Nazarene, union of several small church groups as part of Holiness Movement started after Civil War. It follows doctrines of holiness and sanctification as taught by 18th-century evangelist John Wesley. Union was founded 1908 in Pilot Point, Tex.

Churchill, Sir Winston (continued)
coined phrase "Iron Curtain" **I** 323
oratory **O** 181
Teheran Conference, 1943, picture **W** 298
visits Coventry Cathedral, picture **E** 230
with Stalin and Roosevelt at Yalta, picture **R** 324
Churchill Downs, race track in Louisville, Kentucky
H 232–33; picture **K** 220
Churchill Falls (Grand Falls), Newfoundland **N** 143
Churchill River (Hamilton River), Labrador **N** 143
Churchill River, western Canada **M** 76; **S** 38c
Church music
ars antiqua of French music **F** 443
baroque period **B** 64; picture **B** 65
choral music **C** 276–79
Dutch and Flemish music **D** 363–64
early use of plainsong in Italy **I** 482
hymns **H** 309–13
Middle Ages **M** 298–99
Palestrina **P** 41
Church of Christ, Scientist, or Christian Scientists
P 484
Church of England see England, Church of

Church of God, name used by many small Protestant
denominations in United States. Sects were organized in
1903 by Bishop A. J. Tomlinson.

Church of Jesus Christ of Latter-day Saints see Mormons
Churn, vessel for making butter **B** 467
Churriguera (chu-ri-GAY-ra), **José,** Spanish architect
S 363
decorative arts **D** 77
Churrigueresque (chu-rig-er-ESK), baroque style of art
and architecture **D** 77
Latin-American architecture **L** 63
Spanish architecture **S** 363

Chute, Marchette (1909–   ), American author, b. Waycata,
Minn. She is noted for biographies and literary histories,
such as *Shakespeare of London, Ben Jonson of Westminster,* and *Geoffrey Chaucer of England.* Her books of
poetry include *Rhymes About the Country.* She also wrote
First Liberty: A History of the Right to Vote in America.

Ch'ü Yüan, Chinese poet **O** 220a
CIA see Central Intelligence Agency

Ciardi (CHAR-di), **John** (1916–   ), American poet, author,
and literary critic, b. Boston, Mass. English professor at
Harvard University (1946–48) and at Rutgers University
(1953–61), he is noted for his English verse translation
of Dante's *Inferno.* He is poetry editor of the *Saturday
Review.* His works include *How Does a Poem Mean?*
"The Reason for the Pelican," nonsense rhyme **N** 274

Cíbola (CI-bo-la), **Seven Cities of,** seven fabled Zuni
(Pueblo Indian) towns in northern Mexico, purported to
be cities of gold. Riches were found to be only legendary
by Spanish explorer Francisco Vásquez de Coronado
(1540) on the expedition during which he discovered the
Grand Canyon.
Zuni Indians **I** 192

Cicadas (ci-CAY-das), insects **I** 268; picture **I** 281
animal homes, pictures **A** 273
sucking insects **P** 285
Cicero (CIS-er-o), **Marcus Tullius,** Roman orator and
statesman **C** 298
disapproved of dancing **D** 23
oratory **O** 180–81
place in Latin literature **L** 78

Cichlids (CICK-lids), common aquarium fishes **F** 201
Cicutoxin (cic-u-TOX-in), plant poison **P** 321
Cid, El, Spanish national hero **L** 130
beginnings of Spanish literature **S** 366–67
bullfighting **B** 449
Cid, Le, play by Pierre Corneille **D** 296
Cider, apple beverage **A** 333
Cierna, Czechoslovakia
conference of Soviet leaders, 1968 **C** 564
Cierva (ce-AIR-va), **Juan de la,** Spanish aeronautical en-
gineer **H** 105
Cigarettes
bronchitis and emphysema **D** 194, 196; **S** 203
cancer research **C** 91–92
smoking and cancer **S** 203
tobacco **T** 200–01
Cigar-store Indian, sculpture **U** 117
Cilia (CIL-ia), hairlike threads on some cells **M** 276
animal movement in water **A** 266
Ciliates (CIL-i-ates), micro-organisms **M** 276
Cimabue (chi-ma-BU-ay), **Giovanni,** Florentine painter
P 18
humanism of the late Middle Ages **I** 463
Cimarron (CIM-a-rone) **River,** United States **O** 83
Cimarron Cutoff, part of Santa Fe Trail **O** 257
Cinchona (cin-CO-na), tree **P** 313; pictures **D** 327,
P 312
bark a source of quinine **D** 323
Cincinnati, Ohio **O** 71; picture **O** 72

Cincinnati, Society of the, American fraternal and patriotic
organization founded in 1783 by Revolutionary War
officers, and later including their male descendants and
kinsmen. The organization was named after the Roman
statesman Lucius Quinctius Cincinnatus. Its first president was George Washington. Until 1792 it had a branch
in France. Headquarters are in Washington, D.C.

Cincinnati Turngemeinde see Turnverein

Cincinnatus of the West, Lord Byron's epithet for George
Washington in *Ode to Napoleon Buonaparte.* The term
was probably taken from legendary Roman statesman
Lucius Quinctius Cincinnatus, whose name came to
represent simplicity, ability, and virtue.

Cinder cones, of volcanos, picture **V** 383
Cinderella, most loved folktale **F** 302–03
Perrault's version of the story **F** 305–08
La Cenerentola, opera by Rossini **O** 142
scene from animated movie **A** 298
Cinema see Motion picture industry
Cinemascope, motion picture projection system **M** 478
The Robe, first Cinemascope film **M** 487
Cinerama, motion picture projection system **M** 477–78
Cinnabar, mercury ore, picture **R** 272
Cinnamon, spice **S** 382; picture **S** 381

Cinque, Joseph (1811–52), b. Africa, leader of Amistad
Revolt. Sold into slavery in Havana, Cuba, he was purchased by Spaniards who put him with 38 other slaves
on the schooner *Amistad* to be shipped to Principe Island, off coast of Africa. Cinque led the slaves in revolt.
The ship landed in Connecticut, where the slaves were
imprisoned. New England Abolitionists defended them,
and finally the U.S. Supreme Court freed them and
allowed them to return to Africa.

CIO see Congress of Industrial Organizations
Ciphers (CY-phers), method of secret writing **C** 369–71
Circassians (cir-CAS-sians), non-Arab Muslim people
of Jordan **J** 136

Circle dances D 28; F 297, 299
  Middle Ages, picture D 24
Circle games, or ring games G 13–16
Circle graphs, or pie charts G 313
Circle of Fire, or Ring of Fire, volcanoes M 499
Circles, in geometry G 127
Circle strideball, circle game C 15
Circuit riders P 259
Circuits, electronic, of computers C 453–54
Circular saws, tools T 218
Circular waveguide, device in electronic communication
  E 142f; picture E 142d
Circulation (circ-u-LAY-tion), of blood B 275–77
  heart, function of H 86–86c
Circulation, of newspapers N 200
Circulatory (CIR-cu-la-tory) system, of blood
  body, human B 275–77
  fish, amphibian, bird, diagrams B 202, F 186
  heart, function of H 86–86c
Circum-Caribbean (cir-cum-ca-ribb-E-an) Indians I 207–08
  Puerto Rico P 516
Circumcision, Feast of R 290
Circumference, of a circle G 127
Circus C 299–304
  circus building in Bulgaria, picture B 441
  Circus World Museum, Baraboo, Wisconsin W 201
  elephants E 171
  toy circus, picture T 235
  See also Carnivals
Circus, The, poem by Elizabeth Madox Roberts
  P 352
Circus Maximus, in ancient Rome C 299–300
Cire perdue process, of casting bronze D 75
Cirques (CIRKS), formed by glaciers, picture I 16
Cirro-cumulus (cirro-CU-mu-lus) clouds C 360; picture
  C 361
Cirro-stratus clouds C 360; picture C 361
Cirrus clouds C 360; picture C 361
Cistercians (cis-TER-cians), religious order C 284;
  R 292
Citadel, fortress in Quebec City, Canada Q 16
Citadel, Haiti, pictures H 11, W 217
Cithara (CITH-a-ra), or kithara, ancient musical instru-
  ment A 247, picture A 246
Cities C 305–10
  air pollution A 108–11; E 272f–272g
  ancient civilizations A 218–19, 223–24, 225
  Asia, chief cities in A 452
  cement "hives" keep fire from spreading F 148
  city-states of Italy I 455
  environment, problems of E 272a–272h
  Europe E 319, 322–23
  family F 39
  growth with Industrial Revolution I 239–40
  homes in the city H 182–84
  island cities I 425
  juvenile delinquency J 163
  Latin America L 56–57
  libraries for urban centers L 172
  Metro, union of Toronto and suburbs T 227
  Middle Ages sees their growth M 292–93
  moon, future cities on M 455
  municipal government M 503–08
  North America N 298
  Oklahoma City, "built in a day" O 91–92
  parks and playgrounds P 76–78
  police force P 372–77
  population shifts from rural to urban areas P 397
  port cities H 37
  poverty P 424, 424a
  public utilities P 510–13
  refuse disposal S 33–34

  Roman Empire, city life in R 306
  sanitation S 32–34
  state governments and cities S 415
  traffic control T 247–48
  transportation T 264
  urban landscape in New England N 138h
  urban planning U 232–34
  water supply W 65–68
  zoning plans to control floods F 257
  See also Federal cities; Urban planning; country,
    province, and state articles; and names of cities
Citizen King, Louis Philippe of France F 417
Citizens' action groups
  television, influence of T 70d
Citizens Band Radio, type of amateur radio E 142c
Citizenship C 311–13
  American Indians granted citizenship I 215
  Commonwealth Immigrants Act, 1968 I 103
  conservation, a part of good citizenship C 483
  democracy D 104–05
  education for S 223
  geography for G 99, 107
  income tax obligations I 111
  jury duty J 159–60
  naturalization N 58
  preferences for immigrants I 102
  qualification for voting E 113
  See also Aliens; Naturalization
Citizenship Day H 152
Citrine, quartz gemstone G 71, 75; Q 7
Citron, citrus fruit L 138

Citronella oil, yellowish-green oil with sharp odor, used as
an insect repellent and as perfume in soap. The source
of the oil is citronella grass, which grows in Ceylon,
India, the Malay peninsula, and Java.

Citrus fruits
  citron L 138
  lemon and lime L 136–38
  orange and grapefruit O 176–79
  orange groves, Florida, pictures F 260, 265
  subtropical fruits F 481, 484
  vitamins, discovery of V 370a
City editors, on newspapers N 202
City of Brotherly Love, name for Philadelphia P 182
City of Light, Paris P 69
City of Refuge National Historical Park, Hawaii H 66
City of Roses, Portland, Oregon P 398
City planning see Urban planning
City-states C 305
  ancient Greece G 338
  Italy during the Renaissance R 157
Ciudad Bolívar, Venezuela V 300
Civets, catlike animals G 89, 90, 93
Civic Repertory Theater, New York City T 161
Civics, study of government and laws S 224

Civil Aeronautics Board (CAB), federal agency that
supervises civilian aviation. Its five members are
appointed by the president and approved by the Senate
for 6-year terms. Located in Washington, D.C., it
regulates tariffs, fares and mail rates.
  interstate regulatory agencies I 332

Civil Air Patrol (CAP), a civilian auxiliary of the U.S. Air
Force, with membership comprised of high school cadets
and adults. The CAP participates in search and rescue
missions, operates nationwide radio network, provides
educational services, books, films, and workshops. Many
members are licensed pilots. It was founded in 1941, and
has headquarters at Maxwell Air Force Base, Alabama.

Civil defense, refers to federal, state, and local programs for protecting life and property against enemy attack or natural disaster. The United States Office of Civil Defense operates a vast communications system, offers emergency financial aid to state and local governments, and provides medical aid for survivors of a disaster. Interest in civil defense reached its height in the 1950's and early 1960's, when there was widespread fear of atomic attack. More recently, interest has declined.

Civil disobedience
  Gandhi leads India's movement for self-rule
    G 24
  Indian national movement **I** 133
  Martin Luther King's philosophy **K** 248
Civil Disobedience, essay by Henry David Thoreau
  A 201
Civil engineering E 204–05
  canals **C** 83–86
  dams **D** 16–21
  road building **R** 251–52
  tunnels **T** 313–18
Civilian Conservation Corps (CCC), relief program
  R 322
  conservation of natural resources **C** 486
Civilizations, ancient *see* Ancient civilizations
Civil law
  courts **C** 526–30
  jury trials **J** 159, 160
Civil liberties and civil rights C 315–16
  beliefs of the Founding Fathers **F** 396
  Canada **C** 78
  censorship in wartime *see* Censorship
  Civil Rights Acts, 1964, 1968 **N** 102, 104b–105
  courts **C** 526–30
  Declaration of Independence **D** 61, 63
  democratic privileges **D** 105
  Four Freedoms of Franklin Roosevelt **R** 324
  Fourteenth Amendment **J** 125
  freedom of religion, speech, and press **F** 457
  Human Rights, Universal Declaration of **U** 84, 88
  Johnson, Andrew, and Reconstruction **J** 125
  jury, trial by **J** 159–60
  King, Martin Luther **K** 248
  Magna Carta **M** 22
  Negro history **N** 95–98, 104b–105
  Plessy v. *Ferguson,* Supreme Court ruling on separate
    but equal facilities **N** 96
  Reconstruction in the South **R** 118
  segregation waning in United States **S** 115
  women, role of **W** 212a–213
  See also Freedom of assembly; Freedom of petition;
    Freedom of religion; Freedom of speech; Freedom
    of the press; Habeas corpus
Civil rights *see* Civil liberties and civil rights
Civil Rights Acts, 1964, 1968 **N** 102, 104b–105
Civil service C 317
  council-manager form, municipal government
    M 506
  Pendleton Act, 1883 **A** 441; **C** 317
  Roman Empire **R** 304
  state governments **S** 414–15
  See also Spoils system

Civil Service Commission, federal personnel organization established by the Pendleton Act of 1883. To appoint civil servants on the basis of their ability rather than of religious or political association, a bipartisan board of three members was formed and a system of examinations devised for selection of government employees. Further legislation has increased efficiency in recruiting, selecting, and promoting civil servants.

Civil War, English, 1642–49 **E** 223
  Cromwell, Oliver **C** 536
  English literature, effect on **E** 255
  Milton given post in Cromwell's government **M** 311
  Puritan Revolution **P** 343–44
Civil war, in China **C** 272–73
Civil War, Spanish, 1936–39 **S** 358
Civil War, United States, 1861–65 **C** 318–28
  Alabama location of formation of Confederate States
    of America **A** 127
  American literature **A** 204
  Barton, Clara **B** 68
  Brady's photography **C** 434
  Brown, John **B** 411–12
  Buchanan, could he have prevented it? **B** 420
  clothing industry stimulated **C** 353
  Compromise of 1850 **C** 448
  Confederate States **C** 458–60
  Davis, Jefferson **D** 45
  draft and conscription laws **D** 289
  Dred Scott decision **D** 310–11
  Emancipation Proclamation **E** 185–86
  Grant, Ulysses S. **G** 294–95
  Indian loyalties divided during **I** 213–14
  industrial expansion, result of the war **U** 130
  Jackson, "Stonewall," Confederate general **J** 8
  Kansas-Nebraska Act **K** 192
  Lee's campaigns **L** 125–26
  Lincoln, Abraham **L** 295–97
  Medal of Honor established **M** 198
  Missouri Compromise **M** 382
  Negro history **N** 91–105
  New Mexico **N** 195
  northernmost action, St. Albans, Vermont **V** 321
  Reconstruction Period **R** 117–20
  Sherman, William Tecumseh, Union general **S** 151
  slavery **S** 199
  songs **N** 24–25
  submarine made first successful attack **S** 445
  Trent Affair, 1861 **C** 322
  United States Navy **U** 186
  Unknown soldiers, inscription on grave in Arlington,
    quoted **N** 29
  women spies **S** 388–89
  See also Reconstruction Period; Slavery; names of individual leaders

Civitan International, a service organization of business and professional men interested in promoting effective citizenship on local, national, and international levels. It sponsors essay contest and awards scholarships to winners. It was founded in 1920.

Claiborne (CLAI-borne), **William** (1587?–1677?), Virginia colonist, b. Westmorland, England. In 1621 he emigrated to Virginia, where he served as secretary of state (1625). A trading post he set up on Kent Island in Chesapeake Bay became the subject of a bitter ownership dispute between Virginia and Maryland and was finally settled in favor of Maryland (1638).

Claiborne, William Charles Coles, American lawyer **L** 361
Claims adjusters, for insurance **I** 297
Clair, René, French motion picture director **M** 484
Clams, mollusks **O** 272–73
  bioluminescence experiment **B** 197
  giant clam of the tropics **A** 265; **G** 200
  nervous system, diagram **B** 363
  shells **S** 148; pictures **S** 149
Clans and clan system A 303
  Africa **A** 58
  Chippewa Indians **I** 179

Creek Indians **I** 188–89
Hopi Indians **I** 191
Japan **J** 43
totem poles **I** 156; pictures **I** 182, 183
Zuni Indians **I** 192
See also Family
Clapboard (CLAB-ard) **houses H** 169
Clapperton, Hugh, Scottish explorer of Africa **S** 8

Clare, or **Clara, of Assisi, Saint** (1194–1253), Italian nun, b. Assisi. After hearing Saint Francis of Assisi preach, she founded (1212) order of Franciscan nuns that became known as Order of Poor Ladies or Poor Clares. Living strictly by rule of poverty, she served as their abbess until her death. She was canonized in 1255.

Clarín see Alas, Leopoldo
Clarinet, musical instrument **C** 329; **M** 549
  ancient instrument **A** 245
  orchestra seating plan **O** 186

Clark, Abraham ("Congress Abraham") (1726–1794), American political leader, b. Elizabethtown, N.J. An early supporter of the Revolution, he joined the New Jersey Committee of Safety (1774) and was a member of the New Jersey Provincial Congress (1775). He sat in the Continental Congress (1776–78, 1779–83), signed the Declaration of Independence (1776), and served in the U.S. House of Representatives (1791–94).

Clark, Ann Nolan (1898–   ), American author and educator, b. Las Vegas, N.Mex. She worked in U.S. Indian Service, concerned with education of American Indians. She was U.S. delegate to UNESCO Conference, Brazil. Her works include *Secret of the Andes,* which won Newbery medal (1952).

Clark, Champ, American statesman **M** 380
Clark, Charles Badger, American poet **S** 325
Clark, George Rogers, American Revolutionary War
    leader and explorer **K** 225
  Clark and his Long Knives win Illinois territory from
    British **I** 85–86
  Revolutionary War **R** 205

Clark, Jimmy (James) (1936–1968), Scottish automobile racer, b. Fife Co., Scotland. He began driving junior cars in the 1950's. He won the Grand Prix Championship (1963, 1965), as well as the Indianapolis 500 (1965). He died in a crash at Hockenheim, W. Germany.

Clark, John Pepper, Nigerian poet and playwright **A** 76c

Clark, Kenneth Bancroft (1914–   ), American educator and psychologist, Negro, b. Panama Canal Zone. A professor at the College of the City of New York, he was a founder of the Northside Center for Child Development and of Harlem Youth Opportunities Unlimited (HARYOU). His book *Desegregation: An Appraisal of the Evidence,* about the effects of racial discrimination upon Negro and white children, was cited by the United States Supreme Court in its 1954 school desegregation ruling. He was director of HARYOU (1962–64). In 1966 he became the first black on the New York State Board of Regents.
  Negro history, years of change in **N** 103

Clark, Mark Wayne (1896–   ), U.S. Army officer, b. Madison Barracks, N.Y. He commanded 5th Army Group, including all Allied fighting forces in Italy (1944–45). He was commander in chief, U.S. Occupation Forces in Austria (1945–47) and UN commander in Korea (1952–53), succeeding General Matthew B. Ridgway. He signed

Korean peace treaty (1953). He was president of The Citadel (the Military College of South Carolina) (1954–65), and has written *Calculated Risk* and *From the Danube to the Yalu.*

Clark, Ramsey (1927–   ), American lawyer, b. Dallas, Texas. The son of former Supreme Court Justice Tom Clark, Ramsey Clark graduated from the University of Texas and received his law degree from the University of Chicago. He practiced law in Texas until his appointment as assistant U.S. attorney general in 1961. He served as U.S. attorney general (1967–69), and then returned to law practice.

Clark, Thomas Campbell (1899–   ), American jurist, b. Dallas, Tex. He was co-ordinator of alien enemy control in Western Defense Command during World War II and U.S. attorney general (1945–49). He was associate justice of U.S. Supreme Court (1949–67), until his son, **Ramsey Clark** (1927–), became U.S. attorney general.

Clark, William, American explorer **L** 162
  Idaho **I** 54
  Missouri **M** 379

Clarke, Arthur Charles (1917–   ), English astronomer and science-fiction writer, b. Minehead. He was one of the first to suggest the use of man-made satellites for international communications (1945). With his partner Mike Wilson he has been conducting undersea explorations off the Australian coast and Great Barrier Reef since 1954. His numerous books include nonfiction (*The Exploration of Space* and *Profiles of the Future*) and fiction (*The Sands of Mars* and *Tales of Ten Worlds*).

Clarke, Charles Cowden, English scholar **K** 200
Class distinction
  clothing **C** 351–52
  France before the Revolution **F** 462
Classes, divisions of biological classification **T** 29
Classical Age, in Greek art **G** 345–46
  art as a record **A** 438b
Classical age in music C 330–33
  German composers **G** 184–85
  Mozart **M** 502
  orchestra **O** 184
  sonatas **M** 539
  See also Romantic age in music
Classical art see Greek art; Roman art
Classical conditioning, in learning **L** 99
Classical literature see Greek literature; Latin literature
Classical mathematics M 156
Classicism (CLASS-i-cism)
  French literature **F** 437–38
Classics in literature C 334
  children's literature **C** 238–39
  paperback editions **P** 58a
  types of literature **L** 313–14
Classification (class-i-fi-CAY-tion), in biology **B** 191
  insects, orders of, chart **I** 280
  kingdoms of living things **K** 249–52
  Linnaeus, Carolus **L** 304
  mammals, orders of, chart **M** 62
  races of man **R** 29–32
  See also Taxonomy
Class numbers, of books in libraries **L** 184
Classrooms
  kindergarten and nursery schools **K** 245
  schools **S** 55–58
Class struggle
  Communism, ideas of **C** 442–45

Claudel (clo-DEL), **Paul**, French dramatist F 441
Claude Lorrain (CLODE lo-RAN) (Claude Gellée), French
 painter B 60; F 422, 425
 Landscape with the Flight into Egypt, painting
 B 58
 View of Harbor, painting F 423
Claudius I, Roman emperor R 304
 conquest of Britain E 215
Claudius, **Appius**, Roman official E 208

Clausius (CLOW-ze-us), **Rudolf Julius Emanuel** (1822–
1888), German physicist, b. Köslin, Germany (now
Poland). Best-known for work on the different ways gas
molecules can move, he founded science of thermodynamics (relation of the energy of motion to heat energy)
and was first to state second law of thermodynamics,
that heat cannot pass by itself from a colder to a hotter
body. He was first also to present a way to calculate
entropy (amount of energy no longer available for work
in physical systems, such as steam engines).
 physics, history of P 234

Clavichord (CLAV-i-cord), keyboard instrument K 237–
 38; M 547
Clavichord, **The Well-tempered**, by Bach B 5

Clavilux (from Latin words *clavis*, meaning "key," and
lux, meaning "light"), instrument exhibited (1922) by
Thomas Wilfred for creating art form called lumia, or
color music. A complex keyboard controls form, color,
and motion of light, which is projected on screen in
moving patterns. Compositions are sometimes performed
to musical accompaniment.

Clavius (CLA-vi-us), **Christopher**, Bavarian astronomer
 C 12; M 450
Claws
 bats B 92
 cats C 134
 crustacea S 170
Clay S 231
 aluminum A 176
 ancient cities built with clay A 219
 bricks B 390–93, 430
 ceramics C 172–76
 clay modeling C 336–37
 eroded clay cliffs, Utah, picture N 133
 pottery clay P 413
 sculptors' material S 90–91
 tablets for writing A 219; C 172
Clay, **Cassius Marcellus, Jr.** *see* Ali, Muhammad
Clay, **Henry**, American orator and statesman C 335
 Adams, John Quincy, and Clay A 14
 Compromise of 1850 C 448
 Missouri Compromise M 382
 nullification crisis J 7
 opposes statehood for Texas P 384–85
 personal and political feud with Tyler T 339, 341
 slavery question S 199

Clay, **Lucius DuBignon** (1897–), American military
engineer and army officer, b. Marietta, Ga. He was
military governor of American Zone and commander of
U.S. Occupation Forces in Germany (1947–49) and
commander in chief, European Command (1947). Instrumental in organizing airlift to counteract Soviet blockade
of Berlin (1948–49), he helped draft constitution of
Federal Republic of Germany (1949). He was sent as
President John F. Kennedy's personal representative in
Berlin to give assurance of continuing U.S. support
against Soviet pressure (1961–62); he wrote *Decision in
Germany*.

Clay modeling C 336–37
 in nursery school, picture K 243
 See also Ceramics; Pottery
Clay pigeons, for trapshooting T 268
Clay tablets A 219; C 172
 libraries L 192–93
Clayton Antitrust Act, 1914 T 306
 Wilson's domestic policies W 179
Clayton-Bulwer Treaty, 1850 T 36
Clean Air Acts, 1963, 1967 A 111
Cleanliness
 baths and bathing B 91
 hair H 3, 84–85
 health H 82–85
Clean rooms, atmosphere-controlled areas for atomic
 technology D 339
Clearcutting, of timber L 373
Clearinghouse, for checks in banking, diagram B 46
Clearing of land, by pioneers P 252
Clearstory, in architecture *see* Clerestory
Cleavage, cell division E 90
Cleavage, of minerals R 270
Cleaveland, **Moses**, American pioneer, founded Cleve-
 land, Ohio C 338

Cleaver, **Eldridge** (1935–), American black militant
and author, b. near Little Rock, Ark. He wrote *Soul
on Ice* while serving a prison term for assault. Paroled
in 1966, he joined the Black Panther movement (1967),
and served as its minister of information. In 1968, he
was the presidential candidate of the Peace and Freedom
Party. His parole was revoked when a new charge of
assault was made. He fled to Algeria when he faced
possible imprisonment.
 Black Panther Party N 105

Clefs, in musical notation M 524, 525
Cleft palate (PAL-at), a mouth deformity H 27, 28
Clemenceau (CLAI-mon-so), **Georges**, French publisher
 and statesman C 337; pictures P 456a; W 180, 270
 France in World War I F 419
 Paris Peace Conference, 1919 W 282
Clemens, **Samuel Langhorne** *see* Twain, Mark
Clement V (CLEM-ent), pope R 293
 France held the papacy under Clement F 415

Clement VII (Giulio de' Medici) (1478–1534), pope
(1523–34), b. Florence, Italy. An Avignon pope, he joined
the Holy League of Cognac (1526) with France, Venice,
and Milan against Charles V, but he crowned Charles
emperor in 1530. He refused (1534) to sanction the
divorce of Henry VIII of England, causing a split between
the Church of England and Rome.
 Christianity, history of C 286

Clement, **Rene**, French motion-picture director M 488

Clement I, **Saint** (Clement of Rome), pope (90?–99?),
third successor to Saint Peter as bishop of Rome. He is
believed perhaps to have been the Clement cited by Paul
in Philippians (4:3). The only work definitely known as his
is the first Epistle to the Corinthians.

Clemente, **Roberto** (1934–72), American baseball player,
b. Puerto Rico. A star outfielder with Pittsburgh Pirates,
he was one of 11 players in baseball history to get 3,000
hits. Regarded as a national hero, he was killed in an
airplane crash while carrying supplies to aid victims of
an earthquake in Nicaragua. He was admitted to Baseball's Hall of Fame in 1973. B 81

Clementi, **Muzio**, Italian composer I 485

Clements Mountain, Glacier National Park, Montana, picture **G** 222

Cleopatra (cle-o-PAT-ra) (69–30 B.C.), last Macedonian queen of Egypt, b. Alexandria. She ruled with Ptolemy XII, her brother and husband, and later with Ptolemy XIII, another brother whom she married. Cleopatra became favorite of Julius Caesar and Mark Antony, with whom she met defeat at Actium (31 B.C.). Rather than submit to victorious Octavian, she killed herself (according to legend, with an asp). She is heroine of Shakespeare's *Antony and Cleopatra*.
    Caesar and Mark Antony **C** 6; **M** 100
    cosmetics and perfumes **C** 510; **P** 154
    Ptolemaic rulers of Egypt **E** 92
    scenes from motion pictures about **M** 477

Cleopatra makeup, picture **P** 340
Cleopatra's Needle, ancient Egyptian obelisk **O** 6
    Egyptian art **E** 96
    in London **L** 337
Clepsydras, or water clocks **W** 45; picture **W** 44
Clerestory (CLERE-story), a part of a church **A** 376; **E** 234
Clergy, persons ordained for religious service
    kings versus clergy in English history **E** 219
Clermont, first steamboat **F** 491
Clervaux (clair-VO), Luxembourg, picture **L** 379
Cleveland, Frances Folsom, wife of Grover Cleveland **F** 175; pictures **C** 340, **F** 174
Cleveland, Grover, 22nd and 24th president of the United States **C** 339–42
Cleveland, Mount, highest peak in Glacier National Park, Montana **G** 222
Cleveland, Ohio C 338
    leading city of Ohio **O** 71; picture **O** 72
Cleveland, Rose, acting first lady in Cleveland's administration **F** 175

Cliburn (CLY-burn), **Van** (Harvey Lavan Cliburn, Jr.) (1934–), American pianist, b. Shreveport, La. In 1948 he made his debut at Carnegie Hall and won National Music Festival award. He gained world fame by winning International Tchaikovsky Piano Competition, Moscow (1958). He makes many concert tours.

Click beetles P 284–85
Cliff dwellers, ancestors of Pueblo Indians **C** 415
    Indian Cliff Palace, Mesa Verde, pictures **A** 353, **C** 413

Clifford, Clark McAdams (1906–), U.S. lawyer and statesman, b. Fort Scott, Kans. After serving as a naval aide (1946) and as Special Counsel (1946–50) to President Truman, Clifford went into private law practice in Washington, D.C. (1951–61). In 1962 President Kennedy appointed him chairman of the Foreign Intelligence Advisory Board. Clifford was President Johnson's secretary of defense (1968–69).

Climate C 343–48; **W** 89–90
    altitude creates zones of climate **Y** 353; **Z** 372–73
    atmosphere **A** 479–82
    climatic barriers to spread of life **L** 235
    climatology, study of world climate **G** 108
    clothing and climate **C** 351
    earth's changes studied by geologists **G** 110
    earth's history **E** 21
    effects of dust from volcanic eruptions **D** 347–48
    equator areas **E** 272h
    fruitgrowing **F** 481–82
    gardening to suit climates **G** 30, 52
    homes adapted to **H** 168–70
    how shown on maps **W** 77–79; picture **M** 92
    ice ages **I** 13–24
    man-made in botanical gardens **Z** 379
    modified by lakes **L** 26
    mountains influence climate **M** 497
    ocean currents **O** 32–33; **W** 88
    polar regions **P** 363–71
    prairies **P** 430
    rain forests **R** 99–100
    seasons **S** 108–12
    soils, effect on **S** 233
    taiga **T** 10–11
    trade winds **T** 246
    tropics **T** 294–95
    vegetables, cool- and warm-season crops **V** 287–88
    weather and climate **W** 71, 87–89
    weather control **W** 91–96
    winds and weather **W** 184–87
    world climates and vegetation patterns, diagram **W** 256
    world rainfall **R** 94–95
    zones, a simple classification of climate **Z** 372–73
    See also Weather; continent, country, province, and state articles
Climate maps W 77–79
Climatology (cli-ma-TOL-ogy), study of world climates **G** 108
Climatron, The, botanical garden, picture **Z** 378
Climax, Colorado **C** 414
    observatory **O** 9
Climbing
    animals: locomotion **A** 294
    snakes, concertina climbing **S** 211
Clingstone peach P 106
Clinical microscopy (my-CROSC-opy), division of a medical laboratory **M** 201
Clinics, medical, groups of doctors
    medical laboratory tests **M** 201–02
    speech and hearing, picture **D** 50
Clinton, De Witt, American statesman **N** 223
    Erie Canal promoted by **E** 276–77
Clinton, George, vice-president, United States **N** 223; **V** 331; picture **V** 325
Clinton, Sir Henry, English military commander **R** 204; **W** 40
    correspondence with Benedict Arnold **A** 436

Clio (CLY-o), goddess in Greek mythology. She was the daughter of Zeus and Mnemosyne, and the muse of history. Led by Apollo, she and her sisters were the nine muses, or patrons of the arts and sciences. Her symbols were the laurel wreath and the scroll.
    See also Muses

Clip, containers for cartridges **G** 422
Clipper ships, or Yankee clippers, sailing ships **S** 159–60; pictures **S** 156, **T** 263
    importance to transportation **T** 261
    United States Merchant Marine **U** 183

Clipperton Island, uninhabited coral atoll west of Panama, part of French Polynesia. The island was named for John Clipperton, an English pirate who used it as a hideout. Its location made it important at opening of Panama Canal. Ownership dispute between Mexico and France was settled in favor of France (1930).

Clips, as jewelry **J** 99
Clitellum (clit-EL-lum), section of a worm **W** 309

Clive, Robert, Baron Clive of Plassey (1725–1774), British soldier and colonial administrator, b. Styche, Shropshire.

Clive, Robert (continued)
He went to Madras, India (1743), as writer for East India Company and distinguished himself in Britain's struggle for domination of India. Clive established British supremacy in Bengal in victory at Plassey (1757) over superior forces of nawab of Bengal and French auxiliaries. As governor and commander in chief of Bengal (1764–67), he instituted many reforms and strengthened British rule in India. He was politically attacked for corrupt practices upon his return to England and finally committed suicide.

Clymer, George (1739–1813), American merchant and politician, b. Philadelphia, Pa. An active revolutionist, he sat in the Continental Congress, serving on war and treasury boards (1776–78, 1780–83), and signed the Declaration of Independence (1776) and U.S. Constitution (1788). He was a member of the U.S. House of Representatives (1789–91).

Clytie, in Greek mythology, a water nymph who loved Apollo, sun god, in vain and daily watched his chariot cross sky. Gods took pity on her and changed her into sunflower that constantly turns toward sun.

Cnossus see Knossos
Coaches, in sports
   famous college football coaches   **F** 364
Coaches and carriages   **T** 260
   Concord, N.H. coaches   **N** 148
Coagulants (co-AG-u-lants)
   water purification   **W** 68
Coahuiltecs (co-a-hu-EEL-tecs), Indians of North America   **I** 177
Coal and coal mining   **C** 362–68
   atomic energy released in burning   **A** 489
   blasting, picture   **E** 391
   China's anthracite deposits   **A** 450
   coal barges, picture   **G** 154
   coal-producing regions of North America   **N** 295
   English coal-mining town of 19th century, picture **E** 226
   Europe's resources   **E** 311
   fuel   **F** 487
   Germany's major resource   **G** 155
   heating with stoves   **H** 97
   importance to Industrial Revolution   **I** 236–37
   poverty in Appalachia   **P** 424a–424b
   United Kingdom   **U** 70
   world distribution, diagram   **W** 261
   world distribution of coal an evidence of continental drift   **G** 111
Coalescence (co-a-LES-cence), a drawing together, a process of growth
   causes of precipitation   **W** 76
Coal gas   **F** 488–89
Coaling stations
   Pacific islands   **T** 114
Coalition (co-al-ISH-on) **governments**   **P** 382
   prime ministers   **P** 456
Coal oil see Kerosene
Coal tar, sticky black liquid left from distillation of coal
   cancer-causing agent   **C** 91
   dyes made from   **D** 369
Coastal Plain, North America   **U** 89
Coaster car race see Soap Box Derby
Coast Guard see United States Coast Guard
Coast Guard Academy, New London, Connecticut
   U 176
Coast Guard Auxiliary   **U** 176
Coast Mountains
   Alaska   **A** 130–31
   Canada   **C** 51
Coast Ranges, North America
   California   **C** 16, 18
Coated abrasives   **G** 387, 389
Coated steels   **I** 402–03
Coatings, chemical
   plastics   **P** 330–31
Coatis (co-OT-is), animals related to raccoons   **R** 27
Coat of many colors, given to Joseph   **J** 140
Coats of arms   **H** 115–18
   knights, knighthood, and chivalry   **K** 272
   Washington's   **F** 243

Coatsworth, Elizabeth (Elizabeth Coatsworth Beston) (1893–   ), American author of children's books, b. Buffalo, N.Y. Awarded Newbery medal (1931) for *The Cat Who Went to Heaven,* story reflecting her interest in life and legends of Buddha, she also wrote *Here I Stay.*

Coaxial (co-AX-ial) **cables**   **T** 59; picture   **E** 142d
   cable TV   **E** 142c
   television   **T** 67
Cobalt (CO-balt), element   **E** 154, 160
   metals, chart of ores, location, properties, uses   **M** 227
   radioactive cobalt in cancer treatment   **C** 91
   steel   **I** 396

Cobb, Irvin Shrewsbury (1876–1944), American author and humorist, b. Paducah, Ky. As journalist, he worked on New York *World* (1905–11), *Saturday Evening Post* (1911–22), and *Cosmopolitan Magazine* (1922–32). He also acted in films and was noted after-dinner speaker. Cobb won first O. Henry short-story award (1922).

Cobb, Ty, American baseball player, picture   **B** 81
Cobblers see Shoemakers

Coblentz, Catherine Cate (1897–1951), American author of children's books, b. Vermont. Her published works include *Beggars' Penny, Martin, Abraham Lincoln,* and *The Blue Cat of Castle Town.*

COBOL, language in computer programing   **C** 457
Cobras (CO-bras), snakes   **S** 207–08; picture   **S** 206
   kinds of reptiles, pictures   **R** 181
   mongooses kill and eat   **G** 92; picture   **G** 91
   with snake charmer, picture   **A** 275
Coca (CO-ca), shrub, leaves yielding cocaine   **B** 303; picture   **D** 327
   Peruvian Indians use   **P** 161
Cocaine, drug
   a local anesthetic   **A** 258
   drugs as stimulants   **D** 330
   plants, medicinal   **P** 314
Coccus, one of the ball-shaped bacteria   **B** 10; picture **B** 11
Cochabamba (co-cha-BOM-ba), Bolivia   **B** 306
Cochineal (COCH-in-eal), dye made from insects' bodies **D** 369
   cochineal insect, picture   **D** 367

Cochise (?–1874), American Indian, chief of Chiricahua Apaches of southwestern United States. After he and other chiefs were captured while under flag of truce and tortured by U.S. Army officer, he campaigned to drive white men from territory. At end of Civil War (1865), Army waged a war of extermination against Apaches, and Cochise finally surrendered (1871) and lived on Chiricahua reservation established (1872) in Arizona.
   Apache Indians   **I** 195

Cochlea (COC-le-a), inner ear   **B** 285, 288

Cochran (COCK-ran), **Jacqueline** (Jacqueline Cochran Odlum) (1910?–   ), American aviatrix, b. Pensacola, Fla. Commissioned lieutenant colonel in Air Force Reserves (1948), she was first woman to fly faster than speed of sound (1953) and to fly at "Mach 2," twice speed of sound (1960).

Cockatoo, bird, picture   **P** 84
Cockerels, young roosters, picture   **P** 421
Cocker spaniel, sporting dog, picture   **D** 253
Cockfighting
   Cuba   **C** 547

Cockle, mollusk
shell, picture S 147
Cockneys, Londoners L 333–34
Cockroaches, insects H 262; picture H 263
ant colony dwellers A 325
conditioned responses A 283
Cocks, a kind of valve V 269
Cocks-of-the-rock see Cotingas
Cocktail Party, The, verse play by T. S. Eliot E 177
Coco see Chanel, Gabrielle
Cocoa C 274–75
Ghana produces G 195
stain removal L 84
Cocoa butter C 274, 275
oils and fats O 79
Coconut, fruit of the coconut palm C 368–69
seed, cut section, picture P 298
seed dispersal F 281
Coconut oil O 79
Coconut palm, tree, pictures L 234, T 276
copra C 369; P 5
Philippines, called tree of life in P 188
Cocoons (coc-OONS), of insects I 264–65, 279
ants A 323
bees B 123
butterflies and moths B 469
how made by silkworms S 179
Cocos Islands, Indian Ocean A 496
Cocteau (coc-TO), Jean, French dramatist F 441
Cod, fish F 222–23
egg laying of E 89
fishing the Grand Banks C 57, 68
habitat, feeding habits, uses F 213
Coda, or final section, in a sonata cycle M 539

Coddington, William (1601–1678), American colonial
leader, b. Boston, England. He arrived in Massachusetts
Bay colony (1630) and moved to Aquidneck (R.I.) (1638)
after dispute with Massachusetts authorities regarding
colony's lack of religious freedom. He founded Pocasset
(Portsmouth) and then Newport, which later united
under Roger Williams' Providence Plantations.

Codeine (CO-dene), narcotic drug N 12
Code Napoléon see Napoleonic code
Code of Terpsichore (terp-SIC-or-e), by Carlo Blasis
D 25
Codes, of honor
knight's code K 274–75, 277
Codes, of law
canon law L 87
Hammurabi A 220; L 87; picture A 219
Louisiana's legal system based on Napoleonic Code
L 348–49
Napoleonic Code N 10
See also Justinian's Code
Codes, radio and telegraphic
International Morse Code R 63
Codes, secret writing C 369–71
coded legend used with the Ten Commandments
E 1
spirituals, meanings in singing of N 105
Codex (CO-dex), early Roman book B 319; L 194;
picture B 218
Codicils (COD-i-cils), additions to wills W 175
Codling moths A 335
C.O.D. mail delivery service P 410
Cody (CO-dy), William F. (Buffalo Bill), American
frontier scout B 428
Pony Express rider P 392
Co-education
universities and colleges U 205–24

Coelacanths (CE-la-canths), lobe-finned fishes F 183; pic-
ture F 182
Coelenterates (ce-LEN-ter-ates), jellyfishes J 70–75
coral polyps C 503–04
Coelophysis (ce-LO-phis-is), genus of dinosaurs D 174
Coelostats (CE-lo-stats), for observing the sun S 466
Coenaculum (ce-NAC-u-lum), site of Jesus' Last Supper
J 81
Coenzyme (co-EN-zyme), in body chemistry B 294
Coeur d'Alene (cur-d'al-ANE) Lake, Idaho, picture I 57

Coexistence, living together or at the same time. Word
usually refers to nations that, in spite of widely differing
beliefs and apparently incompatible policies, manage to
maintain diplomatic and trade relations and to refrain
from outright conflict.

Coffee C 371–74
Brazil's production and exports B 379, 382
Central American export crop C 171
Colombian farms C 380, 382; picture C 372
Costa Rican plantation workers, picture A 97
El Salvador's major export E 182
fruits we eat P 308; picture P 309
Guatemala G 392; pictures G 394, L 59
world distribution, diagram W 266
Coffeehouses C 371
Austria A 520
established in England R 186
Coffeepot, antique, picture A 318
Coffeepot, guessing game I 226
Coffee rust, disease of coffee plants C 371, 373
Cofferdams, temporary structures D 18
Coffin, Levi, American abolitionist U 12
abolitionist movement in Negro history N 94

Coffin, Robert Peter Tristram (1892–1955), American
writer, b. Brunswick, Maine. He wrote mainly about his
native state. He was English professor at Wells College
(1921–34) and Bowdoin College (1934–55). His books of
verse include Strange Holiness, for which he was
awarded a Pulitzer prize (1935), and Primer for America.

Cog railroad, picture R 78
Cohan, George M., American actor–songwriter R 225
national anthems and patriotic songs N 26
musical comedy M 542
Cohen, Isidore, American violinist, picture C 185
Coherent (co-HE-rent) light P 239
lasers M 133
Cohesion (co-HE-sion), in physics L 310
discoveries of the properties of liquids P 233
Coils, induction E 131–32
electric generators E 121
Coimbra (co-EEM-bra), Portugal P 401
Coin bank, picture A 319
Coin laundries L 84
Coin-operated machines see Vending machines
Coins and coin collecting C 374–75
ancient Roman, pictures A 232
history of coins M 411
nickel N 249–50
silver S 181–82
stamped out by coining dies D 166, 167
United States Mint M 338
Coin shift, trick T 288
Coir, fiber of coconut husk C 369
kinds of fibers F 106
Coke C 364
carbon structure C 105
fuel F 488
use in processing of iron and steel I 404

Coke (COOK), **Sir Edward** (called Lord Coke) (1552–1634), English jurist, b. Mileham, Norfolk. He was chief justice of the Court of Common Pleas (1606) and chief justice of the King's Bench (1613). His conflict with James I and Francis Bacon over royal prerogative resulted in his suspension from council and loss of his right to exercise judicial duties (1616). He is famous in legal history for having upheld supremacy of law over royal power, thus laying the foundation for the principle of constitutional supremacy in democratic government.

Coker, David R., American plant specialist **S** 297

Colbert (col-BARE), **Jean Baptiste** (1619–1683), French statesman, b. Rheims. Financial minister (1661–83) to Louis XIV, he worked for France's economic independence by encouraging industry, regulating tariffs, diminishing trade barriers within France, and developing strong navy. He became unpopular when forced to increase taxes to finance Louis XIV's extravagances and wars. Colbert was a patron of the arts and sciences and founded several academies, including the Académie des Inscriptions and Académie des Sciences (1666).
   set up state-owned Gobelins rug and tapestry work shops **R** 351–52; **T** 24

Cold, common see Common cold
Cold, meaning "having little heat" **H** 86d
   anthropological study of Alakaluf Indians **A** 306–07
   body's sense of **B** 287
   high-altitude climates **C** 346
   refrigeration **R** 136–38
Cold-blooded animals B 259
   fishes, temperature of **F** 187
   hibernation **H** 123
   reptiles **R** 180–81
   snakes **S** 204–14
   turtles **T** 334
Cold chisels, tools **T** 213
Cold cream, cosmetics **C** 509, 510
   invention of **B** 111
Cold drawing, steel process **I** 401
Cold front, in meteorology **W** 76; diagram **W** 77
Cold light see Bioluminescence
Cold-rolling, of metals
   bronze and brass **B** 410
   steel processing **I** 402
Cold storage of food see Cool storage of food
Cold type composition, in printing **P** 465
Cold War, in international relations **I** 325
   disagreements over division of Germany **G** 164
   Stalin's seizure of lands in Eastern Europe **S** 395
Cold-water suits, for skin diving **S** 190

Cole, Cozy (William R. Cole) (1909–), American jazz drummer, Negro, b. East Orange, N.J. He has played with Cab Calloway (1939) and Louis Armstrong (1949–53), and with numerous bands. He opened a drum school with Gene Krupa (1954) and has been featured in such motion pictures as *The Glenn Miller Story.* Cole's recordings include *Crescendo in Drums.*

Cole, Nat "King" (Nathaniel Adams Coles) (1919–1965), American singer and pianist, Negro, b. Montgomery, Ala. He began his career with King Cole Trio (1937–48) and specialized in soft ballads. His records include *Mona Lisa* and *Nature Boy.* He played roles in such films as *Istanbul* and *Autumn Leaves.*

Cole, Thomas, American painter **U** 121

Colechurch, Peter, English clergyman **B** 395
Coleman, Ann, fiancée of James Buchanan, picture **B** 418
Coleman, Ornette, American jazz musician **J** 61–62
Coleridge, Samuel Taylor, English poet **E** 260
   odes **O** 52
   quotation from *The Rime of the Ancient Mariner* **Q** 20
   William and Mary Wordsworth **W** 242
Coleridge-Taylor, Samuel, English composer **N** 107

Colette, Sidonie Gabrielle Claudine (1873–1954), French author, b. Saint-Sauveur-en-Puisaye. Considered France's leading woman writer during her lifetime, she published at least one novel a year. Her works, largely autobiographical in nature, include *Chéri,* and *Gigi.*

Coleus (CO-le-us), house plant, picture **H** 269

Colfax, Schuyler (1823–1885), American politician, b. New York, N.Y. A resident of Indiana, he was elected to the U.S. House of Representatives (1855–69) and became speaker of the House (1863–69). He served one term as U.S. vice-president (1869–73). Picture **V** 327.

Collage (col-LODGE), in art **C** 376–77
   Braque, Georges **B** 371
   Central Park Carrousel, by Cornell **U** 116
   Grandmother, by Arthur Dove, picture **D** 142
   Le Courrier, by Braque, picture **D** 136
   modern art **M** 390–91
   Picasso **P** 243
   used by some 20th century painters **P** 30
   See also Assemblage
Collar cells, of sponges **S** 392
Collators (CO-lay-tors), office machines **O** 58
Collective bargaining W 253
   labor's position **L** 8, 12
   management's position **L** 12, 14, 15
Collective farms
   Albania and Bulgaria **A** 144; **B** 439
   Czechoslovakia **C** 562; picture **C** 563
   Union of Soviet Socialist Republics **U** 36–37
Collective security, principle of international relations **L** 96
   United States **U** 138–39
Collections, of dresses **F** 70
Collectors and collecting
   antiques **A** 318–21
   autographs **A** 526–27
   automobile models **A** 535–37
   butterfly collecting **B** 476–78
   buttons **B** 479–80
   coin collecting **C** 374–75
   dolls **D** 263–69
   leaves **L** 117
   phonograph record collecting **R** 123–25
   photography of other hobby interests **P** 218
   plankton **P** 280
   prints **G** 308
   rock and mineral collecting **R** 273
   shells **S** 147–49
   slime mold sporangia **F** 497–98
   stamp collecting **S** 396–400
College Board examinations E 348–49
College Entrance Examination Board E 348
College Handbook, The E 348
College of Pistors, society of bakers of ancient Rome **B** 386
Colleges see Universities and colleges; education section of country, state, province, and city articles
Collegium (col-LE-gi-um), group of college professors of Middle Ages **E** 67

Coloreds, or **Coloureds,** people of mixed races in Africa
  A 55
  South Africa **S** 268
  South West Africa **S** 336
Color engraving **P** 458
Color filters **L** 268
Colorimeters (color-IM-et-ers), optical instruments
  O 174
Color photography **P** 204
Color television **T** 68–70
Color wheel **D** 139; picture **D** 138
Colosseum (col-os-SE-um), Roman arena **A** 231–32;
  R 313; pictures **R** 285, 312; **W** 217
  gladiators fighting, pictures **R** 305, **S** 196
Colossians (co-LOS-sians), book of the Bible **B** 161
Colossi of Memnon, statues, picture **E** 99
Colossus of Rhodes **W** 216; picture **W** 215
Coloureds see Coloreds, people of mixed races
Colt, Samuel, American inventor of guns **G** 421–22

Colter, John (1775?–1813), American explorer, b. near
Staunton, Va. He joined the Lewis and Clark expedition
to explore U.S. territory to the Pacific coast (1803) and
became the first white man to explore the Yellowstone
National Park region. He fought with Crow and Flathead
Indians against the Blackfeet (1808 and 1809).
  exploration of Wyoming **N** 44; **W** 335

Colter's Hell, early name for Yellowstone **W** 335

Coltrane, John (1926–67), American jazz musician, Negro; b. Hamlet, N.C. A saxophonist, he played with various top jazz bands and eventually formed his own quartet. His jazz style, developed in the 1950's, has been
described as "sheets of sounds" and as having the "effect of an aural battering ram." In 1965 he was named
Jazzman of the Year by *Down Beat* magazine.

Colts, young horses **H** 243
Colubrids, family of snakes **S** 204
Colugos, gliding mammals **M** 64; picture **M** 69
Columbanus (col-um-BAY-nus) **Saint,** Irish monk **R** 290
Columbia, capital of South Carolina **S** 307
Columbia, Cape, northernmost tip of Canada **C** 51
Columbia, the Gem of the Ocean, song **N** 24
Columbia Plateau, Idaho **I** 57
  Oregon **O** 194–95
  Washington **W** 16
Columbia Presbyterian Medical Center, New York
  City, picture **H** 247
Columbia River, North America **R** 242
  picture **R** 239
  flood stage, picture **E** 283
  Lewis and Clark expedition **L** 162–63
  Washington **W** 17, 20
  waterway system in Oregon **O** 195, 199
Columbia River Basin, Washington **D** 19

Columbia Scholastic Press Association (CSPA), an organization to promote student writing by encouraging school
publications. The association holds annual conferences
for scholastic yearbook, magazine, and newspaper staffs.
It was founded in 1925, has headquarters in New York,
N.Y., and publishes *School Press Review.*

Columbia School of Journalism **P** 524
Columbia University, New York, N.Y. **N** 219; picture
  N 234

Columbine, traditional character in Italian theater
(*commedia dell'arte*), usually daughter of Pantaloon and
wife or sweetheart of Harlequin. Columbine is also found

in French comic opera and English pantomime and is a
forerunner of characters in today's light comedies.

Columbines, flowers, pictures **G** 49, **W** 168
  state flower of Colorado **C** 401
Columbium see Niobium
Columbus, capital of Ohio **O** 70–71
Columbus, Georgia **G** 145
Columbus, Bartolomé, Italian explorer, brother of
    Christopher Columbus **D** 282
  founded Santo Domingo, Dominican Republic **D** 282
Columbus, Christopher, discoverer of America **C** 416–17
  Caribbean Sea and islands **C** 118
  corn introduced to Europe **C** 506–07
  Costa Rica **C** 515
  exploration of the New World **E** 375–76, 378
  Ferdinand and Isabella **F** 87
  flag of Spain, 1492 **F** 228
  holiday honoring **H** 149
  Jamaica given to his family **J** 14
  monument in Mexico City, picture **M** 252
  Nicaragua, discovery of **N** 248
  tomb in Santo Domingo, Dominican Republic **D** 283
  towns and cities named for **E** 386
Columbus Circle, New York City, picture **N** 233
Columbus Day **H** 149
Columbus Theater (Teatro Colón), Buenos Aires **A** 390;
  B 428
Columns, in architecture **A** 375; diagram **A** 376
  ancient Greek stone masonry **B** 394
  Greek orders **G** 346, 348; pictures **G** 347
Colville River, Alaska **A** 133
Coma (CO-ma), cloudlike head of the comet **C** 418–19
Comanche (co-MAN-che), cavalry horse, lone survivor of
  Custer's last stand **K** 176
Comanche, Indians of North America **I** 164

Comanduras, Peter Diacoumis (1908–   ), American physician, b. Lowell, Mass. He was particularly concerned
with international medicine and founded the Medical
International Cooperation Organization (MEDICO) (1958)
with Thomas Dooley. Comanduras was also assistant
executive director of CARE (1962–63).

Combat, trial by **M** 291
Combat arms, of United States Army **U** 168
Combat Arms Regimental System **U** 172
Combative sports, in the Olympics **O** 109
Combination locks **L** 326
Combination square, measuring tool **T** 216
Combines, farm machinery **F** 60; **W** 155; picture **F** 61
  harvesting wheat, picture **A** 90–91
  in North Dakota, picture **N** 327
Comb jellies, ctenophores **J** 75; picture **J** 74
Combustion, burning **F** 137
  chemical reaction **C** 218
  explosives **E** 388
  Lavoisier's explanation **L** 86
  rapid oxidation **O** 268
  See also Fuels; Heat
COMECON see Council for Mutual Economic Assistance

Comédie-Française, national theater of France. It performs past masterpieces and highly selective contemporary works. In 1680 Louis XIV consolidated the Comé-
diens du Roi and the combined troupes of the Théâtre du
Marais and the company of Molière into what became
known as the Comédie-Française.
  Paris theater center **P** 71; **T** 160

Comedy, form of drama **D** 293–94
  English **E** 256–57, 268

Comedy (continued)
  Greek **G** 353
  origin of the word **D** 293–94
  slapstick and farce **H** 278
Comedy of Errors, The, play by Shakespeare **S** 134
Comedy of Manners
  English **E** 256–57, 268
  Molière **M** 405
Comenius (co-ME-nius), **John Amos,** Czech educator and theologian **E** 68
  first picture book for children **C** 236
  kindergarten, origin of **K** 243
Comets **C** 418–19
  radar astronomy studies **R** 74
  solar system **S** 245–46

Comfort, Mildred H. (1886–   ), American author of children's books, b. Winona, Minn. Her books include *Winter on the Johnny Smoker*, about life on a boat frozen in a cove, and its sequel, *Treasure on the Johnny Smoker*.

Comic books **C** 422–23
Comic opera see Opéra bouffe
Comics Magazine Association of America, The **C** 422, 423
Comic strips **C** 127, 128
  animated cartoons compared to **A** 297
  German forerunners **G** 178
  made into comic books **C** 422
Comintern, later Cominform see Third International

Commager, Henry Steele (1902–   ), American historian and educator b. Pittsburgh, Pa. History professor at Columbia U. (1938–56) and at Amherst College (since 1956), he has written a large number of historical books, most of them supporting his theory that absence of thought is the world's greatest threat. His works include *Documents of American History* (editor) and *Freedom, Loyalty, Dissent.*

Commander-in-chief, presidential powers **P** 452
Command module (CM), section of Apollo spacecraft **S** 339, 340e, 340j; pictures **M** 454; **S** 340b, 340c

Commandos, small bands of men organized to pursue native cattle raiders during the early days of white settlement in South Africa. The name was later applied to Boer fighters in the Boer Wars (1881, 1889–1902) and British shock troops, trained for man-to-man combat and other special operations, who carried out important missions in World War II. U. S. Army's Special Forces employ commando-like units.

Command-service module, section of Apollo spacecraft **S** 339, 340, 340a; pictures **M** 454, **S** 340b, 340c
Commas, punctuation marks **P** 531
Commedia dell'arte (com-MAY-dia dell AR-tay), Italian company of character actors **D** 295
Commemorative stamps **P** 409
Commentators, news service of radio broadcasting **R** 58
Commerce see International trade; Trade and commerce
Commerce, United States Department of **P** 448
  National Bureau of Standards **W** 110
  Patent Office **P** 98
Commercial art **C** 424–27
  illustration and illustrators **I** 92, 95
  industrial design **I** 229–32
  mechanical drawing **M** 197
  posters **P** 404
  See also Advertising; Posters
Commercials, in advertising **A** 33
  television **T** 70b, 71
Commission, form of municipal government **M** 505

Commissioned officers, United States Army **U** 167
Commissions, fees, for real estate brokers **R** 113
Committee of Public Safety, French Revolution **F** 467–68
Committees, of the United States Congress **U** 141, 144
Committees of Correspondence **A** 17
  communication in American colonies **C** 436
  events leading to Revolutionary War **R** 196
  political parties in colonial America **P** 379
Common cold, virus disease **D** 194–95
Common Cormorant, The, nonsense rhyme **N** 272
Common law **L** 88
  origin in medieval England **E** 218
Common Market see European Economic Community
Common Market, Central American **C** 171
Common nouns **P** 90
Commons, House of, British Parliament **E** 219, 222–23; **U** 78–79
  growth of the parliamentary system **P** 81
Commons, House of, Canada **C** 76–77
Commons, or village greens **P** 77
  New England, picture **N** 138h
Common schools **E** 70–71
Common Sense, pamphlet by Thomas Paine **P** 13
  how Declaration of Independence was adopted **D** 61
  literature of the American colonies **A** 198
Common stocks, shares in a company **S** 428
Commonwealth, English
  Cromwell, head of **C** 538
Commonwealth Air Force Memorial, picture **O** 239

Commonwealth Fund, trust fund established (1918) by Mrs. Stephen V. Harkness to promote health through grants for medical education and health services.

Commonwealth Immigrants Act, 1968 **I** 103
Commonwealth of Nations **C** 428; **E** 232; **U** 79
  Commonwealth Day **H** 150
  Singapore, Republic of, a member as of 1966 **S** 184a
  See also United Kingdom of Great Britain and Northern Ireland; names of individual member nations
Commonwealths
  four states of the United States **P** 142
  Puerto Rico's status **P** 522–23; **U** 103
Commonwealth Trans-Antarctic Expedition **P** 370

Commune, a collective settlement of people who are not related but choose to live as a family unit. They share living quarters, work, food, child care, and finances. In the late 1960's young people in the United States began to establish communes as an alternative life pattern. The Israeli kibbutz is a form of communal living.
  group care for children **F** 40

Communes, China's government-run farms **C** 267
Communicable diseases, or infectious diseases **D** 186
Communication **C** 429–41
  advertising media **A** 27–34
  alphabet, origin of **A** 170–73
  animals **A** 275–80
  braille for the blind **B** 251–54
  cables **T** 52, 54
  civil and human rights ideas spread by modern communication **C** 316
  communications satellites **C** 440; **S** 43; **T** 59, 60, 67
  data communication **T** 54–55
  deaf, communication with **D** 51
  geographical knowledge **G** 95
  handwriting **H** 31–33
  "hot line" between governments **D** 185
  inventions advance **I** 338, 345–46
  journalism **J** 142–45
  language arts **L** 36

Community chest, or **United Fund,** general fund collected from individual contributions and used for the community's health, welfare, and recreation needs. This combined charitable fund-raising and budgeting drive is thought to have been given the name "Community Chest" in Rochester, N.Y., in 1913. The **United Community Funds and Councils of America** (UCFC), founded in 1918, with headquarters in New York, N.Y., is the national association. It publishes the magazine *Community.*

Composed upon Westminster Bridge, sonnet by William
Wordsworth **S** 255
Composers
chart of names, dates, pictures **M** 522–23
Composing rooms, of newspapers **N** 203
Composing machine, for typesetting **P** 457
Composing stick, to hold type **P** 463
Composite numbers N 379
Composite volcanoes V 384
Composition, in printing **P** 465
Composition, music **M** 522–41
baroque period **B** 65
electronic music **E** 142g–142h
Composition, painting by Piet Mondrian **D** 362
Composition III, painting by Kandinsky **M** 391
Compositions, in writing and speaking **C** 446–47
bibliography **B** 170
book reviews as compositions **B** 317
creative writing **W** 317–21
essays **E** 292–93
outlines **O** 250–51
proofreading **P** 479
report writing **R** 175–76
Composition sketch, preparatory drawing **D** 301
Compositors, typesetters for printing **P** 463
Compost, fertilizer heap **G** 30
refuse disposal **S** 34
Compound, or open, **fractures,** broken bones
first aid **F** 162
Compound interest P 150
Compound microscopes M 283, 288; picture **M** 286
lenses **L** 147–48
Compounds, chemical C 196, 218
atomic combinations **A** 485
body chemistry, composition of cells **B** 289
structure of matter **M** 175
Compressed air G 59
atmospheric pressure compared to compressed air
W 71–72
deep-sea diving equipment **D** 79
pneumatic devices **P** 347–48
Compressibility, property of a gas **P** 233
Compression ratio, of engines
diesel engines **D** 171
fuel-air mixture of internal-combustion engines
I 305
Compression refrigerating system R 136; diagram
R 137
Compression waves, of sound **S** 257
Compressors, for gases
engines **E** 211
Compromise of 1850 C 448
abolitionists and debate over slavery **N** 95; **S** 199
achievement of Fillmore's administration **F** 125
Calhoun's protest **C** 13
Clay, Henry **C** 335
Webster, Daniel, one of the Famous Five senators
W 99
Zachary Taylor's opposition **T** 35–36

Compton, Arthur H. (1892–1962), American physicist, b.
Wooster, Ohio. He is known for his work on first nuclear
chain reaction and also for his discovery that X rays
striking a surface at an angle have a longer wavelength
on rebounding than they had on striking. For this
discovery, called the Compton effect, he was awarded a
Nobel prize (1927). He was chancellor of Washington University, St. Louis (1945–53).

Compulsory education E 69
Compurgation, in law **J** 159, 160
Computer-assisted instruction (CAI) C 457; **P** 477

Computers C 449–57
abacus **A** 2
automation **A** 530, 531–33; picture **A** 534
aviation **A** 562
binary number system **C** 456; **N** 401
designed by electronics engineers, picture **E** 204
documentation in libraries **L** 177
earthquake location **E** 34
election results based on probability theories,
picture **P** 474
first electronic computer, picture **E** 147
guidance systems of rockets **R** 261
library use for information storage and retrieval
L 174
meteorological uses **W** 85
navigation, uses in **N** 69
need for more mathematics **M** 162
observatories, use in **O** 12
ocean liners, use in **O** 18
office machines **O** 58; picture **O** 56
paper for cards, bleached bristols **P** 53
police make use of **P** 376
spacecraft guidance **S** 340e, 340f
teaching machines **P** 477
telephone and the computer **E** 142b
traffic control system **T** 248
typewriters, an essential part **T** 348
See also Calculators
Comstock Lode, mining discovery in Nevada **N** 129
fifty-niners gold rush **G** 251
Comte (CONT), Auguste, French philosopher **S** 227

Comus (CO-mus) (from Greek *kōmos,* meaning "a revel"),
in late Roman mythology, the god of gaiety, feasting, and
drunken revelry. A companion of Dionysus, he and
Momus were in charge of entertainment for the Olym-
pians. Comus is represented as a youth dressed in
white and wearing a crown of roses. He holds a lighted
torch in his hand.

Comyn (COME-in), John, Scottish chieftain **B** 414
CONAD (Continental Air Defense Command) **U** 161
Conakry (CON-ak-ry), capital of Guinea **G** 405–06

Conant (CO-nant), James Bryant (1893–   ), American
educator, b. Dorchester, Mass. President of Harvard
University (1933–53) and U.S. ambassador to Germany
(1955–57), he conducted studies on American public high
schools and on education of American teachers that
resulted in his best-known books, *Slums and Suburbs: A
Commentary on Schools in Metropolitan Areas* and *The
Education of American Teachers.*

Concave lenses T 61, 62
Concave mirrors L 262
Concentration, in psychology **S** 440
Concentration, of ores **M** 227–28

Concentration camps, prison camps often used for
confinement of prisoners of war, political prisoners, or
refugees. One of the first camps to which term was
applied, in which Boer civilians of South Africa were
"concentrated" to prevent their aiding Boer guerrillas
(1900–02), was under English general Kitchener. Term
also refers to Spanish general Weyler's camps during
Cuba's war of independence (1896–97). Most infamous
were concentration camps of Nazis, first established at
Oranienburg and Dachau, Germany (1933), and gradually
set up throughout occupied Europe, in which approximately 7,000,000 people were killed because of their
"political unreliability" or Jewish extraction.
memorial to victims of Nazism, picture **N** 71

Concepción (cone-cep-ci-OHN), Chile **C** 254
Concept books **C** 243–44
Concertina (con-cer-TI-na) **F** 330
Concertos (con-CHERT-ose), in music **M** 535–36
  baroque period **B** 66
  basic record library **R** 125
Concerto grosso, a kind of orchestral composition **O** 184
Conching, chocolate-making process **C** 275
Conchobar (con-CO-bar), legendary king of Ulster **I** 392
Conchology see Shells and shell collecting
Conchs, shell-bearing mollusks, gastropods **O** 276;
  S 148
Conciergerie (con-ci-airge-REE), La, Paris **P** 73
Concord, capital of New Hampshire **N** 159
Concord, Massachusetts **M** 144–45
  Alcott, Louisa May, home in **A** 149
  home of eminent American writers **A** 201
  Revolutionary War begins **R** 198
Concordat (con-CORD-at), a kind of treaty
  Concordat of 1801 **F** 416, 418; **N** 10
  Concordat of Worms, 1122 **R** 291; **T** 272
Concorde, supersonic passenger plane **S** 472
Concorde, Place de la, Paris **P** 70; picture **F** 420
  obelisks brought from Egypt **O** 5–6
Concord grapes **G** 297
Concord Hymn, poem by Emerson **E** 190
Concrete **C** 165–66
  advantages of, as bridge material **B** 401
  architectural possibilities **A** 386–87
  building material **B** 430–31; pictures **B** 433
  dams **D** 16–21
  highway surfaces **R** 252
  homes **H** 175
  masonry **B** 393–94
  Roman architecture used **R** 285–86
  termite-proof house, picture **A** 302
Concrete arch dams **D** 16
Concurrent powers, in government **U** 139
Condensation **H** 93
  action of geysers **G** 193
  cloud formation **C** 359
  dew **F** 289
  distillation process **D** 224–25
  fog **F** 288–89
  insulation prevents **I** 290
  rain **R** 93–95
  water cycles **W** 51
  water desalting **W** 56
Condensed milk **D** 11–12
Condensers, devices for accumulating and holding
    electrical energy **E** 127
Condensers, steam
  distilling equipment **D** 224
  Watt's invention **S** 420
Condiments see Spices and condiments
Conditioned reflexes, psychology **P** 496
  impulses to take drugs **N** 13
  learning **L** 99
  of animals **A** 282–83
  Pavlov, Ivan **P** 100
Conditioning exercises see Exercise, conditioning

Condominium, joint control by two or more powers over
politically dependent territory. Example is principality of
Andorra, ruled by France and Spanish bishops of Urgel
(since 1278). In current use, joint ownership of property,
or property so owned, such as an apartment complex with
each unit bought and sold, without the approval of other
owners. Common facilities are maintained by a service fee.

Condon, Edward Uhler (1902–   ), American physicist, b.
Alamogordo, N.Mex. He worked in the research project
responsible for the development of the atomic bomb. He
has since been a strong advocate of international atom
bomb control. He has held high positions in the
government and in scientific research projects. Condon
is co-author of Quantum Mechanics.
  study of UFO sightings **F** 287

Condors, birds **B** 205, 226, 232
Conducting, of music **O** 188–91
  ancient music **A** 245
Conduction, movement of heat through matter **H** 94,
  96
Conductors, electric see Electric conductors
Conductors, on trains **R** 86
Conduits, pipes or tubes
  early plumbing systems **P** 342
Cone-bearing trees see Conifers
Cones, in geometry **G** 129, 131
Cones, of retina of the eye **B** 284–85
  birds **B** 204
Cone shell, picture **S** 147
Conestoga (con-es-TO-ga) wagons **C** 458; pictures
  A 199; **I** 80; **O** 257; **P** 253; **T** 258
  designed to transport freight **T** 260
  Santa Fe Trail **O** 257–59
  originated in Pennsylvania **P** 136
  pioneer life **P** 253
Coney Island, New York City, picture **N** 232
Coneys, or pikas, animals of the rabbit family **R** 24
Confectioners' sugar **S** 453
Confections **C** 98–99
Confederated Unions of America **L** 7
Confederate Memorial Day **H** 151
Confederate States of America **C** 458–60
  Benjamin, Judah P. **L** 361
  Civil War **C** 318–28
  Davis, Jefferson **D** 45
  flags **F** 248; pictures **F** 228
  Lee, Robert E. **L** 125–26
  Lincoln, Abraham **L** 295–97
  map **C** 319
  Museum of the Confederacy, Richmond **V** 353
  Tyler, a representative of Confederate Provisional
    Congress **T** 342

Confederate Veterans, Sons of, benevolent organization
of descendants of Confederate Civil War veterans. It
preserves historical relics and maintains a library of
Confederate books. It was founded in 1896 and has its
headquarters in Hattiesburg, Miss.

Confederation
  early government of United States **U** 134–35
  See also Articles of Confederation
Confederation of Canada **C** 73
  "Birthplace of Canada," Prince Edward Island **P** 456e,
  456h
Confederation of National Trade Unions (C.N.T.U.) **L** 10
Confession, the "I'm sorry" prayer **P** 434–35
Confessions, branches of Christianity **O** 228
Confessions of Saint Augustine **A** 494
Confirmation, sacrament of Roman Catholic Church
  R 301
Confucianism **C** 460; **R** 147–48
  Chinese literature **O** 220a
  compared with religions of Asia **A** 460
  Southeast Asia **S** 330
Confucius, Chinese philosopher **C** 460; **R** 147–48
  Chinese literature **O** 220a
  ideas on government **C** 268, 269
  national sage of China **C** 260, 261
Conga, or tambora, drum **D** 336

Congeners (CON-gen-ers), impurities in distilled beverages W 159
Congenital diseases D 188
  deafness D 50
  heart disease present at birth D 197; H 86b
  syphilis D 208–09, 216
Congenital handicaps H 27
  blue babies H 86b
Conger eels E 85
Conglomerate (con-GLOM-er-ate), rock R 266; picture R 267
Congo (Kinshasa) see Zaïre, Republic of
Congo, People's Republic of the (Brazzaville) C 461–464
  flag F 235
Congo eels, land-water animals F 475–76
Congo River C 465
  Africa, rivers of A 49
  fishing, picture A 301
  picture C 463
Congregational Church, Groton, Massachusetts, picture P 484
Congress, United States see United States Congress
Congressional districts U 142–43
Congressional Medal of Honor see Medal of Honor

Congressional Record, The, published account of proceedings of U.S. Senate and House of Representatives, published daily (since 1873). Similar records under different names had been published previously (since 1789).

Congress of Industrial Organizations (CIO) L 6
  Lewis, John L. L 161
Congress of Racial Equality (CORE) N 98, 103
Congress of Vienna see Vienna, Congress of
Congress Party, of India I 133; P 380
Congreve (CON-greve), William (1772–1828), English designer of rockets M 343
Congreve, William (1670–1729), English dramatist D 297
Conic projection, of maps M 92–93

Conic section, any one of several curves obtained when a cone is cut through by a plane. Kind of curve depends on angle at which plane cuts through cone. Curves resulting are circle, hyperbola, parabola, and ellipse. All are useful in designing bridges and, in astronomy, for describing paths of planets and certain comets.

Conifers, trees T 284
  forests F 371
  gymnospermnae, picture P 292
  history of plants on land P 304
Conjugations, in Latin grammar L 76
Conjunctions, words that join words, phrases, or clauses P 92
  grammar G 289
Conkling, Roscoe, American politician A 439
  Hayes and Conkling H 81

Connally, John Bowden (1917–), American lawyer and politician, b. Floresville, Texas. He helped to organize a radio station in Austin, Texas, and served as its attorney, president, and general manager (1946–49). Connally served as Secretary of the Navy (1961–62) and governor of Texas (1963–69). He was seriously wounded by the assassin who killed President John F. Kennedy in 1963. President Richard Nixon appointed Connally Secretary of the Treasury (1971–72).
  famous Texans T 135

Connecticut C 466–81
  American colonies A 189
  colonial life in America C 385–99
  Danbury Fair, picture F 13
  Founding fathers of the United States F 395
Connecticut, University of, at Storrs, Conn., formerly Storrs Agricultural School C 475, 480
Connecticut River C 470
  Massachusetts M 137
  New Hampshire N 151

Connelly, Marc (Marcus Cook Connelly) (1890–   ), American playwright, b. McKeesport, Pa. Author, with George S. Kaufman, of Beggar on Horseback, he is best-known for Pulitzer Prize winning play (1930), The Green Pastures, which shows Old Testament from point of view of Southern Negroes.

Connolly, James, American athlete O 110
Connolly, James, Irish patriot I 391

Connolly, Maureen Catherine ("Little Mo") (1934–1969), American tennis player, b. San Diego, Calif. She won U.S. women's singles championship at age 16 (1951) and was first woman to win a "grand slam"—all four major championships (U.S., French, English, and Australian) in one year (1953).

Connotation, of a word S 118
Conquian (CON-ki-an), Spanish card game C 112
Conrad, Charles, Jr., American astronaut S 340i, 344, 345, 346
Conrad Joseph, Polish-born English writer C 482; E 266
  themes of his novels N 347

Conscientious (con-shi-EN-tious) objector, one who is opposed to participation in military service. U.S. Supreme Court ruled in 1970 that the draft law exempts "all those whose consciences, spurred by deeply held moral, ethical, or religious beliefs, would give them no rest or peace if they allowed themselves to become a part of an instrument of war."
  draft exemptions and regulations with classifications D 289, 290; P 105

Conscription see Draft, or conscription
Conservation C 482–89
  Arizona's soil and water control A 407
  balance of nature can be upset by insecticides I 258
  beavers' role in B 114
  communities of living things K 259
  dams, benefits of D 18–19
  erosion, practices to halt E 281–82
  fishing industry F 217, 223–24
  forests, protection of F 372–74
  hunting, rules of sportsmanship in H 289–90
  irrigation I 408–10
  National Forests, United States, history of N 34
  National Park System, of the United States N 51
  petroleum P 178
  public lands P 507
  Roosevelt, Theodore, resources program R 329
  soils S 234
  tree-farming in Mississippi's forests M 355
  water pollution W 58–59
  water storage to control floods F 257
  Why should topsoil be conserved? S 233
  wild flowers W 171
  See also Environment; Natural resources; country, province, and state articles
Conservation of energy, first law of thermodynamics E 200–01; M 174

definition of work **W** 245
in nuclear reactions **N** 370
studies in physics **P** 238
Conservation of matter **P** 237–38
laws of **M** 172–73
Conservative Judaism **J** 118–19
Conservative Party, Canada **C** 77
Conservatives, British political party **P** 379
Conservatories, music schools **M** 524
Conshelf, or Continental Shelf Station, underwater station
U 17–18
Consolidated schools **E** 75
Consolidations and mergers, business
newspapers **N** 199–200
Consonants, speech sounds
alphabet **A** 170, 173
closed sound of letter B **B** 1
double consonants in Welsh words **W** 3
evolution of letter J from vowel **J** 1
how named **D** 1
Latin language **L** 76
pronunciation **P** 478
speech **S** 377–78
Constable, John, English painter **P** 27; **E** 240
Hay Wain, The, painting **N** 38
Constables, police officers **P** 372
Constans, son of Constantine the Great **C** 489
Constanta (cone-STON-tsa), Rumania **R** 357
Constantine, Algeria **A** 163
Constantine I, king of Greece **G** 339

Constantine II (1940–), king of Greece, b. Athens. He
succeeded his father, King Paul I, a descendant of Denmark's royal house of Glücksburg. Constantine won an
Olympic gold medal in yachting (Rome, 1960). He married Princess Anne-Marie of Denmark in 1964. In 1968 he
fled Greece after his failure to overthrow a military
junta, which had taken over Greek government (1967).
Greece, history of **G** 339

Constantine II, son of Constantine the Great **C** 489
Constantine the Great, Roman emperor **C** 489
art as a record **A** 438b
Byzantine art and architecture **B** 483
Byzantine Empire **B** 491
Christianity made state religion of Roman empire
C 282; **R** 308
ended persecution of Christians **R** 288–89
Constantinople, or Byzantium (now Istanbul), Turkey
B 491, 492; **C** 489; **R** 308
art as a record **A** 438b
Byzantine art and architecture **B** 483–85, 490
captured by Crusaders, 1204 **C** 540
Russian Vikings attack **V** 339
See also Istanbul
Constantinople, Council of, 381 **R** 289
Constantius I, Roman emperor, father of Constantine the
Great **C** 489
Constantius II, son of Constantine the Great **C** 489

Constellation, U.S. frigate built to subdue Barbary
pirates, launched in 1797. In hostilities between United
States and France (1798–1801) it captured French ships
Insurgente (1799) and *Vengeance* (1800), becoming first
U.S. Navy ship to capture a foreign warship. Frigate is
now a national shrine at Fort McHenry, Baltimore, Md.
believed to be oldest ship afloat **B** 35

Constellations **C** 490–93
ancient sky map **A** 470
Corvus, the crow, picture **R** 70
galaxy clusters **U** 200

how to make a planetarium to study stars **E** 361
planetarium **P** 267–68
twelve constellations of the zodiac **S** 243–45
See also Stars
Constitution, American naval vessel **W** 12
saved by Holmes's poem "Old Ironsides" **A** 203; **H** 160

Constitution, system of rules of nation, state, or body
politic that defines form of government, limits of
governmental power, people's rights, and means of exer-
cising governmental authority. It may be written, like
U.S. Constitution, or unwritten, like the British.
state constitutions **S** 412

Constitution, United States see United States Constitution
Constitutional Convention, 1787 **U** 145–46
delegates become the Founding Fathers of the United
States of America **F** 395
Washington, George, chosen its president **W** 41
Constitutional democracy, government by the many
G 274
Constitutional monarchies **G** 276
government of the United Kingdom **U** 77–78
Constitutional-Union Party, United States **P** 380
Constitution Day, Japan **H** 150
Constitution Plaza, Hartford, Conn., pictures **C** 481,
U 233
Constitution State, nickname for Connecticut **C** 474
Construction see Architecture; Building construction;
Engineering
Construction engineering **E** 205; picture **E** 207
Constructivism, in art **M** 391, 392
sculpture **S** 105
Consular service **F** 369
Consulates, headquarters of consular service **F** 369
Consumer buying **C** 494, 494a
budgets, family **B** 425–26
buying through co-operatives **C** 499–500
consumer demand **T** 243
"consumer propositions" in advertising **A** 30
economics **E** 50, 51
food regulations and laws **F** 350–52
installment buying **I** 288–89
marketing **M** 100–03
Consumer co-ops **C** 499
Consumer education **C** 494–494a
new consumer demands **T** 243
opinion surveys **O** 160
See also Food regulations and laws
Consumerism see Consumer education
Consumer Reports, magazine for testing agencies of
Consumers Union **C** 494a
Consumer Services, United States Office of **C** 494a
Consumers League, National see National Consumers
League
Consumers Unions, International Organization of
C 494a
Contact lenses **L** 151
Contagious (cont-A-gious) **diseases** **D** 187
early studies of **M** 208
quarantine to prevent spread of disease **D** 221
smallpox **D** 207
whooping cough **D** 212
Containerboard **P** 53
Containers, paper **P** 51
Containment, a policy in international relations
I 325
Contamination of food see Food spoilage and
contamination

Contempt of court, term used in law courts to refer to an
act that embarrasses, hinders, or obstructs court

Contempt of Court (continued)
proceedings or lessens dignity or authority of court. Term also refers to failure to comply with court order.

Conway, Thomas (1735–1800?), Irish soldier of fortune. He went to America (1777) and served in Continental Army. He is remembered for his part in conspiracy, "Conway Cabal," designed to have General Horatio Gates replace George Washington as commander in chief of Continental Army (1778). Conway resigned when conspiracy was discovered and left America to serve with French Army (1779–87). He was governor general of French possessions in India (1787).

Conway Castle, Wales, picture W 4

Conyers, John, Jr. (1929–), U.S. congressman, b. Detroit, Michigan. In 1963 he was appointed by President John F. Kennedy to the national Lawyers' Committee for Civil Rights Under Law. Elected to Congress from Michigan in 1964, 1966, 1968, and 1970, he was the first Negro to serve on the House Judiciary Committee.

Cook, Captain James (1728–1779), English navigator, b. Marton, Yorkshire. He led expedition to Tahiti (1768–71). Cook journeyed to New Zealand and New Hebrides, and discovered New Caledonia (1772–75) in attempt to locate great Southern Continent then believed to exist. He enforced strict hygienic rules on his voyages and thus conquered fever and scurvy, winning Copley gold medal. Cook also charted Pacific coast of North America as far as Bering Strait.

Cook, Mount, New Zealand N 237; picture M 498
Cook Depth Trench E 15
Cooke, Hope, American married to maharajah of Sikkim S 177
Cooke, John Esten, American novelist A 200

Cooke, Terence James, Cardinal (1921–), American Roman Catholic churchman, b. New York. Cooke was ordained in 1945 and taught social science at Fordham University. In 1968 he succeeded Francis, Cardinal Spellman as archbishop of New York. Pope Paul VI named him cardinal in March, 1969.

Cooke, William F., English inventor and engineer **T** 51
Cookies, manufacture and packaging of **B** 389
   recipes **R** 115, 116
Cooking
   appliances **E** 118
   bread and baking **B** 385–89
   camp meals **C** 44–45
   candy and candymaking **C** 98–99
   cheesemaking **D** 12–13
   flour, kinds of **F** 274–75
   food spoilage **F** 354–55
   French **F** 404–05
   nutrition and balanced meals **N** 417
   origin of, through use of fire **F** 140–41
   outdoor cooking and picnics **O** 247–48
   recipes **R** 114–16
   recipes originating from limited food supply **F** 332
   restaurant specialties **R** 187
   terms **R** 114
   See also Marketing
Cooking appliances E 118
Cook Islands, Pacific Ocean **P** 6
Cookworthy, William, English porcelain maker **P** 418
Coolant, fluid cooling agent
   helium **H** 107–08
Cooley, Charles H., American sociologist **S** 227

Cooley, Denton Arthur (1920–), American surgeon, b. Houston, Tex. As an intern at Johns Hopkins Hospital in 1944 he assisted in the first "blue baby" operation. A specialist in cardio-vascular surgery, he has since performed numerous heart transplants, including the first operation that utilized an artificial heart.

Coolidge, Calvin, 30th president of United States
   C 494b–497
   as Vice-President, picture **V** 329
   Harding cabinet member, picture **H** 40
Coolidge, Grace Goodhue, wife of Calvin Coolidge
   F 177–78; pictures **C** 495, 496

Coolidge, Olivia E. (1908–), American teacher and author of children's books, b. Buckinghamshire, England. A gifted storyteller from childhood, she has written such books as Greek Myths and Legends of the North.

Coolidge, William David, American physicist **I** 334
Coolidge Homestead, Vermont, picture **V** 320
Cooling
   air conditioning principle **A** 101–03
   Why does an unglazed ceramic jug keep liquids cool?
   C 175
Cool storage, of food **F** 346–47
   apples require **A** 337
   refrigeration **R** 138

Cooney, Barbara (Barbara Cooney Porter) (1917–), American writer and illustrator of children's books, b. Brooklyn, N.Y. She wrote and illustrated King of Wreck Island and Captain Pottle's House and illustrated Chanticleer and the Fox, for which she received Caldecott medal (1959), and The Little Juggler.

Coonskin Library, Amesville, Ohio **O** 68

Cooper, Gary (Frank James Cooper) (1901–1961), American film actor, b. Helena, Mont. He won Academy Award

for Sergeant York (1941) and High Noon (1952). He was given a special Academy Award (1961).

Cooper, James Fenimore, American novelist **C** 498
   American literature **A** 200
   children's literature **C** 238
Cooper, L. Gordon, Jr., American astronaut **S** 344, 345, 346
Cooper, Peter, American industrialist and philanthropist
   C 498
   designed and raced the Tom Thumb, locomotive **L** 330
Co-operation, international see International co-operation
Co-operative apartments H 183
Co-operative communities
   Rochdale Society, England **C** 500
   Zoar Village, Ohio **O** 70
   See also Utopias
Co-operative Extension Service A 94
   4-H club work **F** 47

Cooperative for American Relief Everywhere (CARE), nonprofit agency for the international assistance of needy people on a voluntary, personal basis. CARE provides food and clothing, as well as educational, vocational, and agricultural equipment. Through MEDICO (Medical International Cooperation Organization) it provides medical treatment and training. Founded in 1945, it is sponsored by 26 American voluntary organizations.

Co-operatives C 499–500
   Central Bank for Co-operatives **B** 50
   Costa Rica **C** 518
   Czechoslovakia **C** 560, 562
   Danish farms **D** 109, 110
   Eskimo, in Canada **Y** 364
   Israel **I** 443
   Korea **K** 301
   Rumania **R** 356–57
   Saskatchewan Wheat Pool **S** 38d
   Shakespeare's acting company, Chamberlain's Men
   S 131
Cooperstown, New York, "Home of Baseball" **B** 80–81
Cooper Union, New York, N.Y. **C** 498
   Lincoln's speech in 1860 **L** 295
Coosa River, Alabama **A** 115
Copacabana (co-pa-ca-BA-na) **Beach,** Rio de Janeiro, Brazil, picture **B** 372
Copán (co-PON), Honduras **H** 198
Copenhagen (co-pen-HAIG-en), capital of Denmark
   D 106, 107, 112
Copepods (CO-pe-pods), very small crustaceans **S** 168; picture **L** 230
   animal plankton **P** 280–81
   insecticides, effect on **E** 272e
   ocean life **O** 37
Copernican (co-PER-nic-an) **system,** of astronomy
   Galileo developed **G** 6, 7
   science, advances in **S** 66–67
Copernicus (co-PER-nic-us), **Nicolaus,** Polish astronomer
   C 501
   modern astronomy begins **A** 472
   Renaissance humanist **R** 160–61
Coping saws, tools **T** 213; picture **T** 212

Copland (COPE-land), **Aaron** (1900–), American composer, b. Brooklyn, N.Y. A developer of contemporary music, he is noted for musical re-creations of American scenes. Copland has been assistant director of the Berkshire Music Festival since 1945. His compositions include Appalachian Spring (Pulitzer prize, 1945), A Lincoln Portrait, and the ballet Billy the Kid.
   modern music, history of **M** 402

Copley, John Singleton, American painter **U** 116–17
  Paul Revere, painting **U** 118
Copper C 502–03; **E** 154, 160
  alchemy **C** 207
  alloys **A** 168, 169
  antiques **A** 321
  beginnings of the history of chemistry **C** 205
  bronze and brass **B** 408–10
  cooking utensils, picture **M** 232
  copper-producing regions of North America **N** 293
  metals, chart of ores, location, properties, uses **M** 227
  open-pit mines, pictures **C** 252, **M** 319, **N** 59, 186, 293, **S** 275, **U** 97
  ore, picture **R** 272
  pyrite, "fool's gold," picture **R** 271
  silver found in copper ores **S** 181
  smelter, picture **A** 409
  wire **W** 190a
  world distribution, diagram **W** 260
Copper-eyed Persian cats, picture **C** 143
Copper glance, chalcocite, a copper ore **C** 502

Copperheads, Northern Democrats who, while not necessarily in sympathy with the Southern cause, opposed the Civil War in favor of negotiated peace. The name was taken from the copperhead snake, which strikes its victim without warning, and signified a surprise blow dealt Northerners from within their own ranks.

Copperheads, snakes **S** 209
  animals harmful to man **I** 284
Copper River, Alaska **A** 133
Copra (CO-pra), dried meat of coconuts **C** 369
  important cash crop of Pacific islands **P** 5; picture **P** 4
Cops, or **coppers,** name for American policemen **P** 373–74; picture **P** 372
Coptic Church
  Africa **A** 56, 58
  Ethiopian Coptic (Orthodox) Church **E** 296, 303
Copy editors B 331
  rim men, of newspapers **N** 202
Copying machines O 57; pictures **O** 56
Copyright T 244–45
  copyright page of a book **B** 331
  date of a book **L** 181
  encyclopedias use continuous revision to insure a current copyright date **E** 197
  Webster, Noah, efforts to promote **W** 99
Copy writers, in advertising
  book promotions **B** 334
Coquina (co-KI-na), type of limestone **R** 267
Coracle, a small boat, picture **T** 262
Coracoid (COR-a-coid) **bone**
  strongest in a bird's skeleton **B** 201
Coral Gables, part of Greater Miami, Florida **M** 254
Corals, marine animals or polyps **C** 503–04
  ocean life **O** 38–39
  organic gems **G** 76
  polyps related to jellyfishes and other coelenterates **J** 74–75
Coral Sea O 47
Coral Sea, battle of, 1942 **W** 294
Coral snakes S 208–09
  Arizona coral king snake, picture **S** 205
  harmful to man **I** 284, 285; picture **I** 282
Corbett, James John, American boxer **B** 353
Corbusier, Le see Le Corbusier
Cordgrasses, builders of land **G** 319
Cordilleras (cor-dil-AIR-as), groups of mountain systems **M** 499

  Andes **A** 252–53
  Canada's westernmost landform **C** 51
  North American **N** 282, 284
  See also systems by name
Córdoba (CORD-o-ba), Argentina **A** 394
Córdoba, Spain **S** 352, 356
Cordobés, El, Spanish bullfighter **B** 450
Cordovan (CORD-o-van) **leather L** 110
Cordwainers, workers in cordovan leather **L** 110
CORE see Congress of Racial Equality
Core, of the earth **G** 119
  earthquakes tell about **E** 39–40
  how the earth formed **E** 19
Corelli (cor-EL-li), **Arcangelo,** Italian violinist and composer **V** 342–43
  baroque music **B** 66
  Italian music **I** 483
Corfu, island west of Greece **I** 428; picture **I** 433
Corgi, Welsh, breed of dog (Pembroke and Cardigan) pictures **D** 254
Coriander, a spice product **S** 382
Corinth, ancient Greek city-state, ruins, picture **G** 340

Corinth (co-RINT), **Lovis** (1858–1925), German painter b. Tapaiu, East Prussia. Corinth combined the delicate characteristics of impressionism with bold strokes of clear natural color. His works include the landscape *Walchensee,* the religious picture *Ecce Homo,* and the portrait *Meier-Graefe.*

Corinth Canal, Greece, picture **G** 101
Corinth Canal bridge, Greece, picture **B** 399
Corinthian (co-RIN-thi-an) **order,** Greek architecture **A** 375; **G** 348; pictures **A** 376, **G** 347
Corinthians I and II, books of Bible **B** 161
Coriolanus (cor-i-o-LAY-nus), play by Shakespeare **S** 134
Coriolis (cori-O-lis) **force,** deflection due to earth's rotation **E** 7
  trade winds **T** 246
  What makes atmosphere move? **W** 73
  why the winds blow east and west **W** 186–87
Corisco, island area of Equatorial Guinea **E** 273
Cork, bark of cork oak tree **C** 505
  insulating material **I** 290
Cork, Ireland **I** 385; picture **I** 387
Cork tiles, floor covering **V** 341

Cormorants (COR-mor-ants), water birds found throughout the world. The adult is a dark-colored bird from 1½ to 3 feet long, with a slender hooked bill, short, strong legs, and webbed toes. The throat-pouch and face parts are usually bare of feathers and may be brightly colored. Cormorants live in groups and fish for food, chiefly in salt water.

  Japanese use for fishing **J** 38
  nonsense rhyme about **N** 272

Corms, underground stems **P** 300
  gardens and gardening **G** 40–41
  garden selection **G** 29
Corn C 506–07
  canning of **F** 346
  cereal grasses **G** 317
  chromosomes, diagram **G** 83
  corn belt a basic concern of Soviet Union **U** 37; picture **E** 306
  corn bins, in Rumania, picture **R** 357
  corn oil **O** 79
  early dolls fashioned from husks **D** 265–66
  effect of fertilizer, picture **F** 96
  farmlands in Iowa, picture **I** 361

fields, pictures **G** 280, **I** 79, 361
flower, picture **F** 276
food plants **P** 308
food producer for a pyramid of living material **L** 240
furfural, industrial liquid made from grain **G** 286
grain and grain products **G** 284, 286
harvesting in Illinois, picture **I** 79
hybrid corn **G** 287; picture **G** 88
Indians of North America, maize-growing areas
  I 183, 189
seeds and ear, pictures **G** 283
shelled corn, picture **U** 105
starch, source of **S** 401
vegetable **V** 290
What makes popcorn pop? **C** 506
world distribution **W** 264, 265
Corn Belt, United States **C** 507
pig production center **C** 151
Corn borers, European, larvae of moths **C** 507; picture
  P 288
plant enemies **P** 284
Cornea, of the eye **B** 284
contact lenses **L** 151
Corn earworm, larva of moth **C** 507
plant enemies **P** 284
Corneille (cor-NAY), **Pierre,** French dramatist **D** 296
golden age of French literature **F** 437
Cornelia (cor-NE-lia), first wife of Julius Caesar **C** 5

Cornelia (lived about 150 B.C.), Roman matron, paragon
of virtue. She was the daughter of Scipio Africanus,
wife of Tiberius Sempronius Gracchus, and mother of
the Gracchi, champions of democratic reforms. She refused to remarry after her husband's death, and devoted
herself to the care and education of her sons. Legend
says that she once shamed a foolish woman who was
inordinately fond of jewels by pointing to her own children and saying, "These are my jewels."

Cornell, Ezra (1807–1874), American businessman and
philanthropist, b. Westchester Landing, N.Y. Assisting
Samuel Morse in construction of the Washington-Balti-
more telegraphic line, he developed a method of
insulating telegraph wire supported by poles. He established numerous lines, including ones in New York,
Vermont, Quebec, and the Middle West. He merged his
company with others, forming the Western Union
Telegraph Company. He served as a director of this
company (1855–74). He sat in New York State Assembly
(1861–63) and Senate (1863–67) and with Andrew
Dickson White founded Cornell University (1865).

Cornell, Joseph, American sculptor **U** 116

Cornell, Katherine (1898–   ), American actress, b.
Berlin, Germany. She is well-known for her roles in *The
Barretts of Wimpole Street, Candida,* and *Romeo and
Juliet* and is the author of an autobiography, *I Wanted to
Be an Actress.*

Corner Brook, Newfoundland, Canada **N** 144

Cornering the market, stock-market term for buying all
or most of the stock in a commodity in order to be able
to control its price. Today it is an infrequent manipulation. Some of the most famous corners occurred in late
19th and early 20th centuries. In the United States
cornering was prohibited by the Securities Exchange Act
of 1934, which prevents deception in sale of stocks. The
term also refers to a virtual monopoly in any area.

Corner spry, line game **G** 23

Cornford, Frances, English poet
  "Country Bedroom, The," poem **P** 355
Cornhusker State, name for Nebraska **N** 72
Corn Islands, outlying area of the United States **U** 100
Corn oil O 79
Corn Palace, Mitchell, South Dakota **S** 323
Corn picker, picture **F** 61
Corn silks C 506

Cornstalk (1720?–1777), Shawnee Indian chief who allied
himself with French traders and led raid against English
settlers in Virginia (1759). He raided settlements in
western Virginia during Pontiac's War (1763) and formed
a treaty with the governor of Virginia, Lord Dunmore,
after his defeat (1774) at Point Pleasant. After 3 years of
peace (1777) Cornstalk went to warn white settlers that
the Shawnee, incited by the British, were about to attack
them. He was held as hostage and was murdered.

Cornucopia, horn of plenty, picture **T** 153
Cornwallis (corn-WA-lis), **Charles, Lord,** British general
  R 201
Washington and Cornwallis **W** 40
Cornwallis, Edward, English founder of Halifax **N** 344h
Cornwell, Dean, American illustrator and painter **I** 92
Coroebus, Greek athlete, first Olympic Games winner
  O 104
Corona (co-RO-na), luminous halo around the sun
  S 462; picture **E** 29
studied by means of radio astronomy **E** 30
Coronado (cor-o-NA-do), **Francisco Vásquez de,** Spanish
explorer in America **E** 384
Coronagraphs (co-RO-na-graphs), special kind of tele-
scope **S** 466–67
Coronary circulation of blood, in the heart **H** 86a
heart disease **D** 197, 198

Coronation (from Latin *coronare,* meaning "to wreathe" or
"to crown"), act or ceremony of crowning a king, queen,
or sovereign's consort.

Coronation of the Virgin, painting by Fra Angelico **P** 20
Corot (cor-O), **Jean Baptiste,** French painter **F** 426;
  P 29
Corporal punishment P 468

Corporate state, system of government in which workers
and employers in each industry are organized into
corporations that assume jurisdiction over particular
areas of the state's economic life. An attempt was made
to form a corporate state in Italy (1925–39) under
Mussolini, but the system was maintained only by
dictatorship and police power.

Corporation for Public Broadcasting (CPB) **T** 70b
Corporations, in business and industry
companies in industry **I** 242–51
foundations store funds for **F** 391
income tax on profits **I** 110–11
Junior Achievement, Inc., miniature corporations
  J 157–58
labor and management represented **L** 11
stocks and bonds **S** 427–33
trusts and monopolies **T** 303–06
Corps, army combat unit **U** 173
Corpus Christi ("Body of Christ"), **Feast of C** 284
religious holiday **R** 154, 290
Corpuscles (COR-puscles), blood **B** 256–57
Correggio (cor-REJ-o), **Antonio Allegri da,** Italian artist
  I 472
Corregidor, Philippines
World War II **W** 293

Correlative conjunctions, in sentences P 92
Correspondence *see* Letter writing
Corridos (cor-RI-dose), Latin-American folk music L 74
Corrosion
  aluminum resists A 177
  anticorrosive paints P 32
  See also Rust
Corrugated paper P 53
Corsac foxes D 250
Corsairs, Barbary, pirates P 263
Corsica, island south of Genoa I 428–29
  birthplace of Napoleon I N 9
  French places of interest F 408
Cortes (COR-tes), **Hernando,** Spanish conqueror of
    Mexico C 508
  cacao beans (chocolate) introduced to Spain C 274
  exploration of the New World E 383
  factors important in helping Cortes conquer Mexico
    M 247–48
  myths of Aztecs helped Spanish conquest M 561–62
Cortex, of the brain B 366
Cortisone, drug P 313

Cortot (cort-O), **Alfred Denis** (1877–1962), French pianist
and conductor, b. Nyon, Switzerland. He is noted for
interpretations of Richard Wagner's music. He formed a
trio with violinist Jacques Thibaud and cellist Pablo
Casals (1905) and founded (1919) and directed the École
Normale de Musique in Paris.

Corundum (cor-UN-dum), aluminum oxide, gem mineral
    G 71
  abrasive for grinding and polishing G 387
Corvinus, Matthias *see* Matthias Corvinus
Corvus, constellation
  located by radio waves, picture R 70
Corydon, former capital of Indiana I 151
Cos, Greek island, home of Hippocrates M 203

Cosa (CO-sa), **Juan de la** (1460?–1510), Spanish navigator. He accompanied Christopher Columbus on his first
voyage to America (1492) and in his exploration of Cuba
(1498). Cosa also made voyages to the coast of South
America and made the oldest known map of the New
World (1500).

Cosby, Bill (1938–), American comedian and actor, b.
Philadelphia, Pa. A high school dropout, he joined the
U.S. Navy and later attended Temple University on an
athletic scholarship. He writes his own material, based
mainly on his childhood experiences. He has played in
numerous nightclubs, and his comedy albums have sold
millions of copies. He is the first Negro entertainer
to co-star in a weekly dramatic television series. He
received the Emmy Award for 2 years (1966–67) for
the role of Scotty, undercover agent in the TV series
I Spy. He later starred in his own TV series. Picture
N 104b

Cosby, William, American colonial governor Z 369

Cosgrave, William Thomas (1880–1965), Irish statesman
b. Dublin. He was a member of the Sinn Fein movement
for Irish independence and was elected to the Dail
Eireann (Assembly of Ireland) (1917). He was president
(1922–32) of the Executive Council of the Irish Free State
and leader (1932–44) of the opposition party in the government of Eamon de Valera.

Così fan tutte (co-SI fon TU-tay), opera by Mozart O 143
Cosmetics C 509–10
  deodorants D 117

  makeup, theatrical P 341; T 156
  perfumes P 154–55
  Where did pioneer women get their cosmetics?
    C 510
  See also Beauty culture; Perfumes
Cosmic rays C 511–13
  cloud chambers to detect radioactivity A 489
  interact with earth's magnetic field E 27
  ions and ionization I 353
  radiation belts R 46–49
  radioactive dating R 65
  solar energy S 236
  subatomic particles and nuclear energy N 354–56
Cosmology (cos-MOL-ogy), the branch of metaphysics
    that studies the structure of the universe P 192
  relativity R 139–44
Cosmonauts, U.S.S.R. space explorers S 340
  space flights and flight data S 344, 345
  See also Astronauts
Cosmos, flowers G 46
Cosmos, term used for universe U 196–204

Cossacks (from Turkish for "freeman" or "adventurer"),
wild, warring tribes of czarist Russia. The Cossacks were
runaways, discontents, and adventurers who formed
settlements (16th century) on the Ukrainian frontier.
They gained a reputation as daring horsemen and served
in the czar's security police (19th century) in return for
land.
  trench charge, World War I, picture W 275
  Ukraine, history of U 9

Costa Brava ("Rugged Coast"), Spain, picture S 353
Cost accountants B 314
Costagini, Filippo, Italian artist W 30

Costain, Thomas Bertram (1885–1965), American editor
and author, b. Brantford, Ontario, Canada. He was an
editor with *Saturday Evening Post* (1920–34) and Doubleday and Company (1939–45) but is best-known for his
novels, *The Silver Chalice* and *The Black Rose.*

Costa Rica C 514–19
  agriculture, picture A 97
  banana crop, picture B 37
  flag F 241
  life in Latin America L 47–61
  national anthem N 21
Coster, Charles de, Belgian writer B 129
Costermansville, Zaïre *see* Bukavu
Cost of living *see* Standard of living
Costume
  dolls of the world, pictures D 263–69
  fashions through the centuries, pictures
    F 66–69
  folk dancing F 300
  hats from different parts of the world and from
    history, pictures H 53, 55
  national costumes, traditional, pictures C 349, 350
  Pilgrim boy and girl T 152
  plays P 341; pictures P 339, 340
  shoes, historical survey of, pictures S 163
  See also Academic dress; Clothing; Uniforms; and
    people section of country articles
Costume designers, of plays T 158
  motion pictures M 481
Costume jewelry J 92, 101
Coterie (CO-ter-rie), social unit, for animals A 281

Cotingas, birds of the Western Hemisphere, chiefly of
tropical forests. All cotingas are alike in structure of
the vocal organs, legs, and feet. But they vary widely

in appearance. Some are drab, while others are brightly colored and ornamented by crests, beards, or feathered tassels. Cotingas include the brilliantly colored Cock-of-the rock, which has a fanlike crest running from the top of its head to the tip of its bill. Another unusual cotinga is the Umbrella bird. Hanging from its throat is a feathered extension that it can inflate, and on its head is a crest of feathers it can expand like an umbrella.

Cotman, John Sell, English painter **E** 241
Cotonou (co-ton-NU), Dahomey **D** 3, 4
Cotopaxi (co-to-PAX-i), active volcano in the Andes
    E 54; picture **A** 252
Cottage cheese D 13
Cottage industries, supplanted by the Industrial Revolution **I** 233–34
    English thatched cottage, picture **A** 302
Cottage system, of reformatories **P** 470
Cotton C 519–25
    bales ready for shipment, picture **U** 105
    boll weevils **P** 285
    Confederate States of America **C** 459
    cotton gin in Georgia **G** 132–33
    fibers **F** 106
    first grown in India **A** 224
    flame cultivators **F** 59
    guncotton, explosive **E** 392
    harvesting, picture **N** 310
    Industrial Revolution, America's contribution of the cotton gin **I** 238–39
    King Cotton economy, Alabama **A** 119–20, 127
    rope **R** 333
    stripping cotton, picture **N** 303
    textile industry **T** 141
    Whitney, Eli **W** 166
Cotton belt, cotton-growing area of United States **C** 523
Cotton bolls C 519, 524; picture **C** 520
Cotton-boll weevils P 285
Cotton Bowl, Dallas, Texas, New Year's Day football game **D** 14; **F** 365
Cotton Bowl Stadium, Dallas, Texas **D** 14
Cotton gin C 521, 523
    early textile industry in America **T** 141
    Whitney, Eli **W** 166
Cotton Kingdom, term applied to the southern United States **S** 198
    Industrial Revolution in America **I** 239
Cottonmouths, or water moccasins, snakes **S** 209; **I** 284
    pictures **L** 218, **S** 210
Cotton picker C 524; picture **C** 522
Cottonseed oil O 79
Cottonseed products C 525
    margarine and shortenings **O** 77, 79
Cotton stripper C 524
Cottontail rabbits R 22, 23
Cottonwood, tree, pictures **T** 276
    bud scales and leaf scar, picture **L** 119
    Kansas, state tree of **K** 177
    male and female flowers, picture **P** 297
    Wyoming, state tree of **W** 322
Cotyledons (cot-i-LE-dons), of seeds **F** 283
    inside the seed, starch for developing plants **P** 299
Coubertin (coo-ber-TAN), **Pierre de,** French businessman and sportsman **O** 103, 107

Coué (coo-A), **Émile** (1857–1926), French psychologist, b. Troyes. He developed program of treating mental illness In which patient makes suggestions to himself, such as, "Day by day, in every way, I am getting better and better." His method was applied at his clinic in Nancy, France, and became popular in England and United States in the 1920's.

Cougars (COO-gars), mountain lions **C** 138
Coulees (COO-lees), small valleys **A** 146a; **M** 325; **W** 14

Coulomb (coo-LOM), **Charles Augustin de** (1736–1806), French physicist, b. Angoulême. He invented the torsion balance and used it to discover the law named for him. This law states that the attraction or repulsion of two electrical charges or two magnetic poles is inversely proportional to the square of the distance between them. The coulomb, electrical unit, was also named for him.

Council for Mutual Economic Assistance (COMECON), organization of Soviet satellites founded by Soviet Union (1949) to co-ordinate development within Soviet bloc.
    trade in Eastern Europe **E** 330; **U** 39

Council Grove, Kansas **K** 186
Council-manager, form of municipal government **M** 506
Council of Europe E 333
Council of Economic Advisers, U.S. E 51

Council of Foreign Ministers, organization for supervision and preparation of peace settlements after World War II and for discussion of other postwar European problems. Established in 1945 at Potsdam meeting of Great Britain, Soviet Union, and United States, it drafted peace treaties for Italy, Finland, Rumania, and Hungary.

Council of Jerusalem, A.D. 50 **R** 288
Council of Ministers, Union of Soviet Socialist Republics **U** 42
Council of Nicaea see Nicaea, Council of, 325
Council of the Entente, Africa
    Dahomey **D** 3–4
Council of Trent see Trent, Council of
Councils, church see Church councils
Councils, ecumenical see Ecumenical councils
Counseling see Guidance; Social work; Vocational guidance and counseling
Counselors at law see Lawyers
Countercurrents, of the ocean **E** 16; **O** 33
    IGY findings **I** 319
Counterespionage (counter-ES-pi-o-nodge) **S** 388
Counterpoint, in music **M** 299, 533
    Bach's *Art of the Fugue* **B** 5; **M** 536
Counter Reformation, of Roman Catholic Church **C** 287
Counterspies S 389
Counties, major divisions of states **M** 503–04
    See also county maps for each state
Counting, or natural, **numbers N** 384
Count of Monte Cristo, The, novel by Dumas *père* **D** 342
Country-and-western music R 262a–262d
    Tennessee **T** 83
Country Bedroom, The, poem by Frances Cornford **P** 355
Country dances D 29
Country life see Farm life
County agent, adviser on agriculture **A** 94, 95

Coup d'etat (coo d'et-TA) (from French, meaning literally "stroke of state"), sudden overthrow of existing government by unconstitutional and sometimes violent means. It differs from outright revolution in that there is no popular uprising and no prolonged fighting. Louis Napoleon produced a "coup d'etat" (1851) when he dismissed the popular assembly and had himself declared emperor of France.

Couperin (coo-PRAN), **François,** French composer
    F 444–45
Couple dances F 299

Couplet (CUP-let), in poetry **P** 353
  Dryden's use of heroic couplet **E** 256
Coups (KOOZ), successful blows against an Indian enemy **I** 167, 168, 196
Courbet (coor-BAY), **Gustave,** French painter **F** 426
  modern art **M** 386–87
  realism in painting **P** 29
  Sleeping Spinner, painting **F** 427
Coureurs de bois (COUR-er d'BWA), French-Canadian fur traders **F** 520; picture **F** 521

Courlander, Harold (1908–   ), American folklorist, journalist, and novelist, b. Indianapolis, Ind. He is leading specialist in African and Afro-American cultures. His works include *The King's Drum and Other African Stories,* and collections of U. S. Negro folk tales, *Terrapin's Pot of Sense.*

Courses of study
  programs in the social studies **S** 224
Coursing, racing after live game **R** 33
Court, contempt of see Contempt of court
Courtly love
  French literature **F** 436

Court-martial, military court comprised of commissioned officers responsible for trial of members of armed forces or those civilians who commit offenses against military or naval law in time of war or during military operations.

Courts, of law **C** 526–30
  adoption laws **A** 26
  Are British and American courts different? **C** 529
  Canada **C** 77–78
  civil rights and civil liberties protected **C** 316
  common law, origin of, in England **E** 218
  divorce **D** 234–35
  International Court of Justice (World Court) **I** 321
  jury **J** 159–60
  juvenile courts **J** 164
  lawyer's work **L** 92
  president of the United States, judicial powers **P** 454
  probate proceedings for wills **W** 175
  state courts (the judiciary) **S** 415
  Supreme Court of the United States **S** 476–77
  See also Law and law enforcement; Lawyers; Prisons
Courtship
  Latin America **L** 56
  See also Dating, a social custom
Courtship, of animals
  birds **B** 212
  fishes **F** 200
  snakes **S** 213–14
Court tennis **T** 100
  See also Tennis
Couturiers (coo-TU-ri-ers), designers of high fashion **F** 70
Cousteau (coo-STO), **Jacques-Yves,** French inventor of the Aqualung **S** 189–90
  oceanographic research **O** 42
  underwater exploration **U** 14
Covalent (co-VALE-ent) **bond,** in chemistry **C** 218
Covent (CUV-ent) **Garden,** London, England **L** 337
Coventry, England
  cathedral, modern **C** 133
Cover crops **A** 93
  soil conservation **S** 232

Coverdale, Miles (1488?–1569), English ecclesiastic and reformer, b. Yorkshire. Coverdale made first English translation of entire Bible (1535). He superintended new English edition of Great Bible and second edition, called Cranmer's Bible (1540). He left England (1540) after

execution of Protestant reformer Thomas Cromwell and became Lutheran minister in Germany. In 1548 he returned to England as chaplain to Edward VI, and became bishop of Exeter in 1551. His religious views again forced him to leave England (1553) when Mary I became queen. He returned in 1559 when Elizabeth I came to throne and Protestantism became free from danger in England.
  Bible in English, history of **B** 153

Covered bridges **B** 400
  Cornwall Bridge, Connecticut **C** 477
  longest in the world, Hartland, New Brunswick, picture **N** 138b
Covered wagons see Conestoga wagons
Coveys, of quail see Quail
Covington, Kentucky **K** 224
Coward, Noel, English actor and playwright **D** 298
Cow beef **C** 148–49; **D** 8
Cowbirds, picture **B** 235
Cowboys **C** 146–47
  Argentina's gauchos **A** 388–89; picture **A** 391
  Arizona, picture **A** 413
  Chile **C** 250
  Costa Rican **C** 516
  folk songs **F** 311
  "Git Along, Little Dogies," folk song **F** 320
  llaneros of Venezuela **V** 296
  National Cowboy Hall of Fame and Western Heritage Center **O** 88
  Pecos Bill, cowboy hero **F** 316–17
  ranch life **R** 102–03; picture **R** 105
  rodeos **R** 281–82
  roping **R** 333–35
  stockmen of Australian outback **A** 499
  work songs **F** 304
Cowcatcher, device to remove animals from railroad tracks **L** 330

Cowell, Henry Dixon (1897–1965), American composer, b. Menlo Park, Calif. He developed tone clusters by hitting keyboard with forearm, elbow, or fist; invented, with Leon Theremin, the Rhythmicon, device for mechanically producing rhythms and cross-rhythms; and founded *New Music Quarterly* (1927) for publication of ultramodern music. His compositions include *Dynamic Motion,* hymns and fuguing tunes, and the opera *O'Higgins of Chile.*

Cowish, an herb with edible roots
  a food of Camas area Indians of North America **I** 175, 176
Cowley, Abraham, English poet **O** 52
Cowling, protective covering
  bobsleds **B** 264
Cow pea, name for annual plants native to tropical areas of the Old and the New World. It has leaves in groups of three and seeds in long, thin pods. It is grown in the United States primarily as food for livestock.

Cowpens, battle of, 1781 **R** 208
Cowpens National Battlefield Site, South Carolina **S** 303
Cowper (COO-per), **William,** English poet **E** 258
Cowpox, virus disease **D** 214
  Jenner's studies **J** 76
  19th century medical contributions **M** 207
Cowries, shell-bearing mollusks, gastropods **O** 276
Cows
  dairy farming **D** 7–10
  India, sacred animals **C** 145
  milk **M** 310
  spectrograms of animal sounds, pictures **A** 276

Cowslip, common name of many different kinds of plants. In the United States name refers to the Virginia cowslip, with trumpet-shaped, bluish flowers in clusters, and to the marsh marigold, with bright-yellow flowers. Cowslip mentioned by Shakespeare is a yellow-flowered plant native to England.

Cow towns, Kansas **K** 186, 188
Cox, David, English painter **E** 241

Coxey's Army, group of persons unemployed following Panic of 1893, led by Jacob Sechler Coxey in march to Washington, D.C. (1894). They presented petition to Congress urging allotment of funds to build new roads and make other public improvements that would give work to many of the unemployed. Known as the Commonweal of Christ, they were later joined by industrial groups from the Pacific coast.
    labor unrest in Ohio **O** 75

Coxswain (COX-in), steersman of racing boat **R** 338–39
Coyotes (KY-otes) **D** 246–47
Coyote State, nickname for South Dakota **S** 313
Coypus, or nutrias, South American rodents **R** 280
Cozzens (CUZZ-ens), **James Gould,** American novelist **A** 213
C.P.A. see Certified Public Accountants
CPB see Corporation for Public Broadcasting
Crab, constellation see Cancer
Crab apples A 333
    seedling, picture **G** 40
Crabgrass, picture **W** 105
Crab Nebula, supernova **S** 409; picture **A** 477
    pulsars **Q** 8
Crabs, crustaceans **S** 168–71
    Chesapeake Bay fisheries, picture **M** 121
    fiddler crabs measure time **L** 246–47
    horseshoe crab, related to crabs **H** 245
Crab's-eye bean, picture **P** 298
Crab spiders S 387
Crackers, manufacture and packaging of **B** 389
Cracking, extracting gasoline from petroleum **G** 63
Cracow (CRA-cow), Poland **P** 360–61
Cradle, device for washing gold from sand **G** 251; picture **G** 252
Cradle, harvesting tool **F** 60
Cradleboards, for Indian babies **I** 167, 196
Cradlesongs F 303–04
Craft guilds G 401–03
Crafts see Handicrafts
Crafts (trades) see Vocations
Craft unions L 8–9
Craig, James, city planner of Edinburgh, Scotland **U** 233
Craigie House, Longfellow's home in Cambridge, Mass. **L** 342
Crampons, sharp spikes to fit on boots for mountain climbing **M** 491

Cranach (CRA-nock), or **Kranach,** or **Kronach** (KRO-nock), **Lucas,** the Elder (1472–1553), German artist b. Kronach. Noted primarily for religious pictures, portraits, and classical subjects, he also engraved both wood and copper and was court painter at Wittenburg (1504). His paintings include *Crucifixion* and *Bathsheba at the Bath.*
    Cardinal Albert of Brandenburg as St. Jerome in His Study, painting **G** 167

Cranberries G 301; picture **G** 300
Cranberry bog, picture **G** 300
Crane, Hart, American poet **A** 210
Crane, Ichabod, character in *Legend of Sleepy Hollow, The* **A** 199–200

Crane, Stephen, American novelist **A** 206, 209; **N** 178

Cranes, any one of a family of large, long-legged, migrating birds that inhabit marshes and prairies of all continents except South America. All have a long neck, head partly bare of feathers, and a loud, distinctive call. They feed on grain, fruits, some insects, and a few fish. The famous whooping crane of North America is the tallest of American birds. Picture **B** 230.

Cranes, machines **H** 143–44
    shipbuilding, picture **S** 161
Crankshaft, of internal-combustion engine **I** 304
Cranmer, Thomas, archbishop of Canterbury **E** 221
    annulled marriage of Henry VIII and Catherine of Aragon **H** 109
    Protestantism in England **P** 484
    the Reformation in England **C** 286
Crannogs, island refuges in lakes see Lake dwellers
Cranston, Rhode Island **R** 223–24
Crappie, fish, picture **F** 209
Crassus, Marcus Licinius, Roman statesman
    Caesar and Crassus **C** 5
Crater Lake, Oregon **L** 28; pictures **L** 29; **O** 202
    volcanic origin **O** 192
Crater Lake National Park, Oregon **O** 203; picture **N** 50
Craters, cup-shaped holes
    Mars **M** 107, 109; **P** 273
    meteors and meteorites **C** 420–21
    moon **M** 450–51
    volcanoes **V** 383
Craters of the Moon National Monument, Idaho **I** 64
Crawford, Robert, American teacher and poet **N** 26
Crawl, swimming stroke **S** 490; picture **S** 492
Crawler tractor, construction machine **B** 446
    "cat" train, picture **M** 80
    farm machinery **F** 55
Crayfish, crustaceans **S** 168
    blood system, diagram **B** 259
    fresh water creatures, pictures **L** 257
    nervous system, diagram **B** 363
Crayons, drawing materials **D** 303

Crazy Horse (1849?–1877), chief of Oglala Sioux Indians. He led part of Sitting Bull's forces in battle of Little Big Horn (1876), where Colonel George Armstrong Custer made his famous "last stand." He surrendered (1877) at Red Cloud agency in Nebraska. He was arrested when army officers feared a planned uprising and was mortally wounded as he tried to escape.
    Indian Wars **I** 169, 214; **N** 82

Crazy Horse Memorial, South Dakota **S** 312
Cream, fat content of milk **B** 467; **M** 310
    Babcock invented mechanical separator **B** 467
Cream cheese D 13
Cream of tartar see Tartar
Creams, cosmetics **C** 509, 510
Creasy, Edward, English historian
    list of important battles **B** 100–02
Creation of Adam, painting by Michelangelo **M** 255
Creation of the world
    in Greek mythology **G** 356
    in Norse mythology **N** 277
    mythology **M** 557–64
Creative writing see Writing (authorship)
Crèche (CRESH), French word for crib, Christmas Nativity **C** 289; picture **C** 294
Crèche, name used for a group of penguin chicks **P** 123
Crécy (crai-CY), **battle of,** 1346 **H** 281–82
    knights made warfare pay **K** 274

Credit
department store charge accounts   **D** 119
in bookkeeping   **B** 312
installment buying   **I** 288–89

Credit card, an identifying card authorizing a person or organization to charge goods or services and be billed at a later date. Issued by banks, petroleum companies, hotels, department stores, or other large companies, they have become very widely used.

Crédit Mobilier (cray-DI mo-bi-li-AY) **of America,** company involved in bribe scandal   **G** 55

Credit union, co-operative association formed to finance small, short-term loans of members at low interest rates, the funds being raised by the members' buying shares in the union. These nonprofit organizations are chartered by either the states or the federal government, and their profits are returned to members through dividends.
co-operative movement, growth of   **C** 499, 500
installment plans, loans, and costs   **I** 289

Credle, Ellis (Mrs. Charles deKay Townsend) (1902–   ), American author and illustrator of children's books, b. North Carolina. She began her career by drawing for American Museum of Natural History and for Brooklyn Children's Museum. Her books include *Down, Down the Mountain* and *Johnny and His Mule.*

Cree, Indians of North America   **I** 170
Creedence Clearwater Revival, American rock music group   **R** 262d
Creek, Indians of North America   **I** 188–89
Alabama   **A** 112, 126–27
Horseshoe Bend, battle of, 1814   **J** 4
impact of Europeans and Americans on   **I** 199
settled in Florida and since known as Seminoles   **F** 273

Creepers, slender, small birds of forest regions throughout the cooler parts of the Northern Hemisphere. Of speckled and spotted bownish color, the creeper has a stiffened tail that it uses as a brace when climbing trees in search of insects. (Several birds of the nuthatch family are also called creepers but these birds do not use their tails as braces when climbing.) The brown creeper has the widest range of all the creepers. It is found from Alaska to Nicaragua in the New World and from Siberia to Japan in the Old World. Picture **B** 222.

Creeping
animals: locomotion   **A** 294
Creighton (CRIGH-ton), **Helen,** Canadian folk music collector   **C** 63
Cremation, of the dead   **F** 493
Crenshaw melons   **M** 216, 217
Creole, language of Haiti   **H** 7
Creoles, descendants of original French settlers of Louisiana   **L** 353
Creole State, nickname for Louisiana   **L** 349

Creosote, dark-brown to yellowish oily liquid with a smoky odor. It is made by distilling coal or wood tar and is used to preserve wood and as a disinfectant.

Creosote bush, a plant   **N** 123
Crepe (CRAPE) **rubber**   **R** 345
Crerar (CRE-rar), **Henry Duncan Graham,** Canadian soldier   **C** 80
Crescent moon   **M** 447

Crespi (CRAIS-pi), **Juan** (1721–1782), Spanish Franciscan missionary in America. He went to America in 1749 and became missionary to Sierra Gorda, Mexico. He joined Gaspar de Portola's expedition (1769) to occupy San Diego and Monterey and continued north up California coast with Portola, with whom he discovered San Francisco Bay (1772) and went on Juan Perez' expedition to Alaska (1774). The diaries he kept during explorations are important as historical sources.

Cress Delahanty, novel by Jessamyn West   **H** 278

Cressida, in mythology, daughter of Trojan priest Calchas. Cressida broke vows to her Trojan lover, Troilus, and transferred her affections to Greek hero Diomede. Chaucer and Shakespeare wrote versions of the legend.

Cresting, painted bands on arrows   **A** 367
Crests, in heraldry   **H** 118
Cretaceous (cret-A-cious) **period,** in geology   **F** 387
dinosaurs   **D** 172, 174, 175, 181; reconstruction   **D** 178
fossil birds   **B** 207, 209
water and land areas, diagram   **E** 342
Crete, island southeast of Greece   **I** 429
ancient civilization   **A** 227
bull dancing in ancient Crete   **B** 449
clay calendar, picture   **C** 12
Greece, landforms of   **G** 333
Minoan architecture   **A** 373–74
Minoan art   **A** 237–38
painting at Knossos   **P** 15–16
ruins at Knossos, picture   **A** 355
water and drainage system   **P** 342–43
World War II   **W** 290
Crevasses (cre-VASS-es), cracks
glaciers   **I** 7–8
Crèvecoeur (crev-CUR), **St. John de,** French-born American writer   **A** 198

Crichlow, Ernest (1914–   ), American painter, Negro, b. New York, N.Y. His work is known for its portrayals of the touching simplicity of children. He has also illustrated a number of children's books.

Crichton (CRY-ton), **James** (1560–1582), Scottish scholar, b. probably Eliock, Dumfriesshire. Called the Admirable Crichton, he is said to have mastered 12 languages. He was famous for his knowledge and his ability to debate in all fields of learning and also for his skill in dueling.

Crick, Francis H. C. (1916–   ), English biochemist, b. Northampton. Known for work on the large molecules making up all living things, he was awarded Nobel prize (1962) in medicine (with J. D. Watson and M. H. F. Wilkins) for showing the coiled structure of nucleic acids —the molecules that control heredity.

Cricket, game   **C** 531–32
favorite sport in the United Kingdom   **U** 68
Marylebone Cricket Club, England   **T** 90
Crickets, insects
ant colony dwellers   **A** 325
ears, diagram   **I** 267
leg, diagram   **I** 273
Crime and criminals
arson   **F** 153–54
courts   **C** 526–30
Federal Bureau of Investigation   **F** 76–77
fingerprinting   **F** 129
jury   **J** 159–60

law and law enforcement **L** 89
narcotics addicts **N** 13–14
police **P** 372–77
prisons **P** 468–70
Crime and Punishment, novel by Dostoevski **D** 287

Crimean (cri-ME-an) **War** (1854–1856), armed conflict in which Russia was defeated by the combined armies of England, France, Sardinia, and Turkey. It was caused by Russia's effort to obtain control of Black Sea and eventual partition of Turkey. It was named after Crimean peninsula, where the war was fought, and was ended by the Treaty of Paris (1856).
Nightingale, Florence **N** 259

Crime stories *see* Mystery, detective, and suspense stories
Criminal law
courts **C** 526–30
jury **J** 160
lawyers' work on criminal cases **L** 92
Criollos (cri-OLE-yos), Latin Americans of European descent **L** 50
early Spanish settlers in Peru **P** 160, 161
Crippen, Robert L., American astronaut **S** 346

Crippled Children, Association for the Aid of (AACC), foundation financing research on the causes, effects, and prevention of conditions leading to crippling in children. The organization was founded in 1900 and maintains headquarters in New York, N.Y.

Crisscross, or christcross, mark used in hornbooks **C** 236
Cristobal (cris-TO-bol), Panama Canal Zone **P** 48
adjoined to Colon **P** 45
Cristofori (cris-TOF-o-ri), **Bartolommeo,** Italian inventor of the piano **P** 241
Italian music **I** 484
keyboard instruments **K** 239
Critical size, in a chain reaction **N** 361–62
Criticism, literary *see* Literary criticism
Critics, literary L 312–13

Crivelli (cri-VEL-li), **Carlo** (1430?–1494?), Italian Renaissance artist, b. Venice. Associated with Venetian school of art, he painted mostly madonnas. He was skilled in use of tempera colors. His works include *Madonna della Candeletta* and *Coronation of the Virgin.*

Crizzling, of antique glass **A** 319

Croaker, any one of several long, flat fishes that produce rumbling sound, which gives fish its name. Atlantic croaker is found in warm, shallow waters of the Atlantic. Brassy in color, with dark spots, it is one of the main food fishes of the middle Atlantic states.

Croatia (cro-A-sha), Yugoslav state **Y** 358
Croatoan Island, North Carolina **A** 181
Croce (CRO-chay) **Benedetto,** Italian philosopher and critic **I** 480
Crocheting (cro-SHAY-ing) **K** 281–84
Crockery, unglazed ceramic work **C** 175
Crockett, Davy, American frontiersman **C** 533
folk hero tales **F** 311
Crocodiles C 533–35; **R** 180–81
Crocodilians (croc-o-DIL-ians), groups of reptiles **C** 533–35
Crocoite (CRO-co-ite), mineral **C** 296
Crocuses, flowers
garden planting **G** 42; picture **G** 44

Crofton, Sir Walter, Irish prison reformer **P** 469
Crofts, Freeman Wills, Irish writer **M** 555
Croix de Guerre (crwa d'GAIR), French award, picture **M** 200
Cro-Magnon man, picture **A** 305
Crome, John, English painter **E** 240

Crompton (CRUMP-ton), **Samuel** (1753–1827), English inventor, b. Firwood, near Bolton. He invented the spinning mule (1779), which, with modifications, is used in nearly all textile mills today. This machine produced finer, smoother cloth by drawing, twisting, and winding cotton in one operation.

Cromwell, Oliver, Lord Protector of England **C** 536; **E** 223–24
Irish crushed **I** 390
Milton accepts post in his government **M** 311
Cromwell, Richard, Lord Protector of England, son of Oliver Cromwell **C** 536

Cronin (CRO-nin), **Archibald Joseph** (1896–), English novelist and physician, b. Dumbartonshire, Scotland. He left the medical profession in 1930 to devote his time to writing. His works include the novels *The Citadel* and *The Keys of the Kingdom.*

Cronkite, Walter (1916–), American journalist and commentator, b. St. Joseph, Mo. He was war correspondent for United Press (1942–45) and chief correspondent at the Nuremberg war crimes trials. Cronkite joined the news staff of the Columbia Broadcasting System (1950–) and is managing editor of CBS Evening News with Walter Cronkite. He was the recipient of the George Foster Peabody award in 1962 for his regular news program.

Cronstadt (CROON-stet), **Axel,** Swedish scientist **N** 249
Cronus (CRO-nus), Greek god **G** 356

Crook, George (1829–1890), American soldier, b. near Dayton, Ohio. Before the Civil War he served in Army as Indian fighter and explorer of Northwest. As member of Union Army, he fought in battles of South Mountain and Antietam (1862) and in Chickamauga campaign (1863). He commanded Union forces in West Virginia and led infantry corps during General Sheridan's Shenandoah Valley campaign (1864). After the war he played an important part in Indian wars, especially against Apache chief Geronimo (1885). He is known for fairness to Indians at a time when they were often persecuted by white soldiers and settlers.
Indian Wars **I** 214

Crookes, Sir William (1832–1919), English scientist, b. London. He discovered element thallium (1861), distinguished different forms of uranium, and invented Crookes tube and radiometer for studies of electric discharges in gases.
cathode rays **X** 339

Crop, food storage chamber of birds' gullets **B** 202, 221
Crops, farm A 88–89, 93, 96
main crops of United States **U** 105, 108
world distribution **W** 263–64
Croquet (cro-KAY), game **C** 536–37
See *also* Billiards

Crosby, Bing (Harry Lillis Crosby) (1904–), American singer and movie actor, b. Tacoma, Wash. He began singing career with Paul Whiteman's trio (1927) and starred in many films, among them *Going My Way,* for

Crosby, Bing (continued)
which he received an Academy Award as best actor (1944), and *White Christmas.*

Crosby, David, American rock music composer and performer **R** 262d
Crosby, Stills, Nash, & Young, American rock music group **R** 262d
Cross, Mary Ann Evans see Eliot, George

Cross, Wilbur Lucius (1862–1948), American scholar, dean, and governor of Connecticut, b. Mansfield, Conn. He joined the faculty of Yale University in 1902 and was dean of the graduate school from 1916 to 1930. He was governor of Connecticut (1931–39), and there is a Connecticut parkway named for him. He edited several English classics, such as Macbeth, and wrote *History of Henry Fielding* and *Connecticut Yankee, an Autobiography.*

Crossbar switching, in telephony **T** 58
Crossbills, birds **B** 209
Crossbreeding
  cattle **C** 147–48; **D** 7–8
  domestic dog, origin of the **D** 248
Cross-country and road running, track events **T** 238
Cross-country skiing S 184b
Crosscut saws, tools **T** 212
Cross examination, in law **C** 530
Crossing guards, for schools **S** 5
Crossing your fingers, superstition **S** 474
Cross of Gold, speech by William Jennings Bryan **B** 415–16
  oratory **O** 181
Cross-pollination, of flowers **F** 277–80
  fruitgrowing **F** 483
  Mendel's study of heredity **G** 88–89
Crpss-references, in indexes and in library catalogs **I** 114–15; **L** 186
Crossroads of America, motto of Indiana **I** 142
Crossroads of the East, or Southeast Asia **S** 328
Cross staff, or forestaff, navigation instrument **N** 64
Cross the T's, saying **T** 1
Crossword puzzles W 237
Cross your heart, superstition **S** 474
Crotal, bell-like rattle **B** 134–35
Croup (CROOP), acute form of laryngitis **D** 195
Crow, constellation see Corvus
Crow, Indians of North America I 168
Crown, glassmaking process **G** 229
Crown, of teeth **T** 48
Crown gall tumor, in plants **C** 90

Crown jewels, emblems or insignia, often including crowns, scepters, and swords, inherited by monarch when he ascends throne. English crown jewels are kept in Wakefield Tower, Tower of London.
  famous diamonds **D** 156

Crowns, royalty
  French crown, picture **J** 97
  head coverings, pictures **H** 53, 55
  Kohinoor diamond **D** 156
Crown slips, pineapple **P** 249
Crows, birds **B** 220; picture **B** 235
  pets **P** 181
  talking birds **P** 86; picture **P** 84
Crows and cranes, line game **G** 24
Crozat (craw-ZA), **Antoine,** French merchant **L** 362
Crucifixion, of Jesus Christ **J** 84

Byzantine art depicting B 488–89
  detail from German carving depicting, picture **G** 166
Crude oil P 169–70
  petroleum before being refined **F** 488
Cruelty, grounds for divorce **D** 234
Crufts dog show D 261
Cruikshank (CROOK-shank), **George,** English artist
  etching from *Oliver Twist* **I** 91
Cruisers, United States Navy U 192
Cruise ships O 17, 19
Crunden, John, English architect **E** 240
Crusades C 538–40
  building methods, effect on **A** 380
  Byzantine Empire weakened **B** 492
  castle built by Crusaders, picture **S** 506
  clothing, new types introduced to Europe **C** 351
  cosmetics brought to Europe **C** 510
  Constantinople captured, 1204 **B** 492
  exploration encouraged **E** 370–71
  Jews persecuted in Europe during **J** 108
  kettledrums used in battle **D** 336
  medals used to identify knights **M** 198
  Muslims versus Christians **I** 414
  Roman Catholic Church **R** 292
  Venetians destroy Byzantine art **B** 490
Crusoe, Robinson, hero of Defoe's *Robinson Crusoe,*
  picture **F** 111
  See also Selkirk, Alexander
Crust, of the earth **E** 8, 9–10, 18–19
  earthquakes **E** 31–32, 34–35, 39–40
  ocean site chosen for Project Mohole, picture **G** 120
  theory of crust's balance **G** 114
Crustaceans (crust-A-ce-ans), a large class of mostly aquatic animals **S** 168–71
  animal plankton **P** 280–81
Crustal plates see Plates, of the earth crust
Crutchers, soap mixing machines **D** 147
Crux Australis (aus-TRAY-lis), Southern Cross, constellation **C** 491
Cruz (CROOSE), **Juana Inés de la,** Mexican poet **L** 71
Cruz, Ramón Ernesto, president of Honduras **H** 199
Cruzen, Richard, American naval officer **P** 368
Crwth (KRUTHE), musical instrument, picture **M** 548
Cryogenics (cry-o-GEN-ics), science of low temperatures **H** 90
  liquid oxygen and other liquid gases **L** 308
Cryolite (CRY-o-lite), mineral
  aluminum refining **A** 176
  Greenland, major source of **G** 369
Cryptography (cryp-TOG-raphy), secret writing using codes and ciphers **C** 369–71
Crystal glass G 230; picture **G** 237
  cut crystal goblets, picture **G** 236
Crystalline lens, of the eye **L** 149–50
Crystallography, study of crystals
  ways of identifying minerals **R** 272
Crystal Palace, International Exposition, 1851 **F** 13
Crystals C 541–46
  alloys **A** 168, 169
  diamond **D** 153
  gemstones **G** 69
  how solids form **S** 251
  ice crystal clouds **C** 359, 360
  maser action, picture **M** 132
  piezoelectricity, a characteristic of quartz crystals **Q** 6
  polarized light **L** 273–74
  polarizing microscopes used to study **M** 283, 288
  quartz **Q** 6–7
  rocks and minerals **R** 264, 272
  snowflakes **R** 95–96
Ctenophora (TEN-o-phora), jellyfishlike animals **J** 75

Ctesibius (te-SIB-ius), Greek physicist and inventor who lived in Alexandria during the 2nd century B.C. He is credited with many mechanical inventions, including water clock and force pump.
  gear wheels **G** 65–66

Cuauhtémoc (cwow-TAY-moc), nephew and successor to Montezuma II, and last Aztec emperor **M** 248
Cuba **C** 547–51
  Caribbean Sea and islands **C** 116–19
  Castro, Fidel **C** 129
  Columbus' discovery **C** 417
  flag **F** 241
  issue of imperialism for McKinley **M** 189
  Kennedy, John F., administration policies **K** 210
  life in Latin America **L** 47–61
  Monroe Doctrine, why it was not invoked in 1960 **M** 427
  national anthem **N** 21
  Ostend Manifesto, U.S. attempt to buy Cuba **B** 419; **P** 247
  Spanish-American War, 1898 **S** 374–76
  territorial expansion of the United States **T** 113–14
Cube, geometric figure
  crystals **C** 544
Cubes, of numbers
  metric system **W** 116
Cubic measure, of volume **W** 111, 116
  matter measured by space occupied **M** 170
Cubism, modern art movement **F** 431–32
  art of the artist **A** 438g
  Braque and les fauves **B** 371
  Cézanne's influence **C** 181
  modern art **M** 390
  Mondrian, Piet **M** 408
  painting in the 20th century **P** 30
  Picasso **P** 243
  planes, flat surfaces in design **D** 136
  sculpture of the 20th century **S** 104
Cubits, measures of length **W** 109
Cub Scouts **B** 357, 358, 359
  Wolf Cubs of Canada **B** 360
Cuchulain (cu-HUL-in), Irish hero **I** 392
Cuckoo clocks **W** 50; picture **W** 48

Cuckoo (CU-koo), small, long-tailed, brownish bird with short bill curved downward. Cuckoos are found in most parts of world in forest areas. The name comes from mating call of male. Some species lay eggs in nests of other birds for care and feeding. Picture **B** 233.
  adaptations in process of natural selection **L** 217

Cucumbers **V** 291
Cucurbit (cu-CUR-bit), gourd family
  melons **M** 216–17
Cud-chewers, animals **H** 208
Cue, billiards **B** 174
Cuestas (cu-ES-tas), landforms **W** 323

Cuffe, Paul (1759–1817), American merchant and philanthropist, Negro, b. Cuttyhunk Island, Mass. He worked to improve position of Negroes in America and was influential in passing Massachusetts law (1783) that gave Negroes equal legal rights and privileges, including right to vote. He advocated settlement of Negroes in Africa and financed voyages to Sierra Leone.
  Negro history **N** 94

Cugnot (coon-YO), **Nicholas,** French engineer **A** 541; **T** 264
  Cugnot's horseless carriage, picture **A** 543
Cukor (CU-kor), **George,** American motion picture director, picture **M** 479

Culbertson, Ely (1893–1955), American writer and contract bridge expert, b. Poyana de Vervilao, Rumania. He was editor of *Bridge World Magazine,* captain of American team in international bridge tournaments, founder and president of The World Federation, Inc., chairman of Citizens Committee for United Nations Reform, and author of *Contract Bridge Blue Book.*

Cullen, Countee (1903–1946), American poet, Negro, b. New York, N.Y. He wrote lyrical poetry describing life of the Negroes. Cullen was assistant editor of *Opportunity: Journal of Negro Life* (1926–28). His works include *On These I Stand* and *Ballad of the Brown Girl.*
  Negro Renaissance **N** 98

Cullen, Michael, American supermarket owner **S** 468
Cullinan, diamond, history of **D** 156
Culottes (cu-LOTTS), French knee breeches **C** 352
Culpepper Minutemen, flag, 1775 **F** 229
Cultivators and cultivation, of the soil **F** 58–59
  vegetable gardening **V** 288
Cultural anthropology **A** 300–05, 309
  artifacts from past cultures compared **A** 360
Cultural patterns, in geography **G** 99
Cultural Revolution, 1966–69, China **C** 273
  Mao Tse-tung and Chiang Ching **M** 86
Cultured milk products **D** 11
Cultured pearls **P** 114–15
Culture heroes **M** 560–61
Cultures, of bacteria **B** 11
  medical laboratory tests **M** 201, 209
  studies in microbiology **M** 275
Culverts, drainpipes **R** 251
Cumaná (cu-ma-NA), Venezuela **V** 300
Cumberland, Maryland **M** 125
Cumberland Gap, eastern United States **K** 214
  Wilderness Road **O** 255
Cumberland Gap National Historical Park
  Kentucky **K** 221
  Tennessee **T** 83–84
  Virginia **V** 353
Cumberland House, fur-trading post **F** 521
Cumberland Narrows, natural gorge, picture **M** 116
Cumberland National Forest, Kentucky **K** 220
Cumberland River **T** 77
Cumberland Road, or National Road **P** 260
  first made by Braddock **O** 255, 267
  how transportation affects interstate commerce **I** 331
  Maryland **M** 121
  Ohio **O** 66
  West Virginia **W** 133–34
Cumin, a spice product **S** 382
Cummings, Edward Estlin, (e e cummings) American poet and painter **A** 210
Cumulative (CU-mu-la-tive) **Book Index** **I** 115
Cumulative stories and songs **F** 303, 322–23
Cumulonimbus (cum-mu-lo-NIM-bus) clouds **C** 360; picture **C** 361
  hail-producing **R** 98
Cumulus clouds **C** 360; picture **C** 361
Cuneiform (CU-ne-if-orm), ancient writing system
  alphabet **A** 170
  ancient civilizations **A** 219, 225
  how numbers were written **N** 395; picture **N** 397
  libraries on clay tablets **L** 192–93
Cunha (COON-ya), **Euclides da,** Brazilian writer **B** 377
Cunningham, R. Walter, American astronaut **S** 344, 345, 346
Cup fungi **F** 498
Cupid (CU-pid), Roman god **G** 361
  Valentines **V** 266
  See also Eros

Cup plates, antique glass receptacles **A** 319
Cupronickel, copper and nickel alloy **A** 169
Cups and Balls, magic trick **M** 18

Curaçao (cu-ra-SA-o), the largest island of the Netherlands Antilles off the coast of Venezuela. Discovered (1499) by Alonso de Ojeda and Amerigo Vespucci and colonized by the Spanish (1527), it has been Dutch since 1634 except for British occupation during the Napoleonic Wars. The principal industry, refining and shipping Venezuelan oil, is centered at the capital, Willemstad. Picture **E** 82.
    Caribbean Sea and islands **C** 116–19
    Netherlands, history of **N** 121

Curare (cu-RA-re, poison used as drug **D** 325
    plants, medicinal **P** 314; picture **P** 315
Curds, of milk **D** 12–13
    used in making cheese **C** 193

Curfew, an order setting a specific time in the evening when certain rules apply, such as that no one may be outside. Taken from the French, meaning "cover the fire," the curfew in medieval Europe signaled the time when fires should be put out.

Curie (cu-RIE), **Eve,** French musician and author **C** 553
Curie, Irène Joliot see Joliot-Curie, Jean-Frédéric and Irène
Curie, Jacques, French physicist **C** 552
Curie, Marie, Polish-born French physicist **C** 552–53
    chemistry, history of **C** 216
Curie, Pierre, French physicist **C** 552–53
Curie's Law **C** 552
Curing, preserving of food
    cheese **D** 13
    meat **M** 192
Curitiba (cu-ri-TI-ba), capital of Paraná, Brazil **B** 380
Curium (CU-ri-um), element **E** 154, 160
Curling, game **C** 554–55
    a favorite sport in Canada **C** 67

Curran, Joseph Edwin (1906–), American labor leader, b. New York, N.Y. He began career as merchant seaman (1922). He has been president of National Maritime Union (NMU) (since 1937) and vice-president of CIO (1940). A member of executive committee of AFL-CIO, he writes column and articles for NMU paper *Pilot.*

Currants, berries **G** 52
Currency, money as a medium of exchange **M** 411
    coins and coin collecting **C** 374–75
    monetary units of countries see country articles
Current electricity **E** 123
Current-measuring buoys **O** 32–33
Current River, Missouri **M** 366; picture **M** 368
Currents, ocean see Ocean currents
Curriculum (cur-RIC-u-lum), course of study **E** 76–77

Currier & Ives, American lithographers whose prints, popular in the 19th century, included political cartoons, landscapes, and scenes that captured spirit of growing young nation. Nathaniel Currier (1813–88) went into lithography business (1834) and took artist James Merritt Ives (1824–95) into partnership (1857).
    popular art distinguished from folk art **F** 292

Curry, Jabez Lamar Monroe (1825–1903), American educator and statesman, b. Lincoln County, Ga. He was member of U.S. House of Representatives (1857–61). During Civil War he was member of Confederate Congress (1861–63, 1864) and Confederate Army (1864–65). After war, Curry was president of Howard University in Alabama (1865–68) and U.S. minister to Spain (1885–88, 1902). As agent for Peabody and Slater Funds and supervising director of Southern Education Board, he worked in South to establish schools for both Negroes and whites.

Curry, John Steuart (1897–1946), American painter, b. Dunavant, Kans. Famous for scenes of rough life, violent weather, and calm landscapes in Kansas farm country, such as *Line Storm, Baptism in Kansas,* and *Tornado over Kansas,* he also painted circus scenes, including *The Flying Codonas.*

Curry powder, blend of spices **S** 382
Cursive writing **H** 31–33
Curtains
    styles and fabrics **I** 302
Curtain walls, of buildings **B** 434; picture **B** 433
Curtis, Charles, American statesman **K** 189; **V** 331; pictures **C** 496, **V** 330

Curtis, Cyrus Hermann Kotzschmar (1850–1933), American publisher and philanthropist, b. Portland, Maine. He founded the Curtis Publishing Co. (1890), which acquired and published various newspapers and magazines, including *Ladies' Home Journal* (established by Curtis), *The Saturday Evening Post, Country Gentleman,* and the Philadelphia *Inquirer.* Generous with his wealth, he made donations to colleges, hospitals, and charities.

Curtis Cup, trophy awarded to winners of match between women's amateur golf teams of United States and Great Britain. It was donated by Harriot and Margaret Curtis and is awarded every other year (since 1930).

Curtiss, Glen Hammond (1878–1930), American inventor and pioneer aviator, b. Hammondsport, N.Y. He designed the airplane June Bug and piloted it for 1 km. in first public flight in United States (1908). During World War I his factories produced military planes for the Allies. His most important contribution was the invention of the aileron, a movable wing part that provides lateral control.

Curved mirrors **L** 261–62
Curves, geometric **G** 124

Curwood, James Oliver (1878–1927), American novelist, b. Owosso, Mich. He worked as reporter and editor for the Detroit *News-Tribune* (1900–07). His 2 years of writing for the Canadian Government in the northwest was a main source for his 26 novels about rugged people, wild animals, and outdoor life. His works include *The Grizzly King, The Valley of Silent Men,* and *Nomads of the North.*
    Mount Curwood, Michigan **M** 261

Cuscuses (CUS-cus-es), marsupials **K** 175

Cushing (COO-shing), **Harvey Williams** (1869–1939), American surgeon, b. Cleveland, Ohio. Cushing reduced death toll in brain operations through his techniques of controlling bleeding, cutting out tumors, and avoiding shock. He introduced continuous taking of blood pressure during surgery, a valuable method of detecting shock. Cushing first described the disease bearing his name, which he found to be associated with pituitary-gland tumor. He wrote several classics on brain structure and disease, including *Pituitary Body and Its Disorders* and Pulitzer-prize-winning biography of physician Sir William Osler.

Cushing, Richard, Cardinal (1895–1970), Roman Catholic churchman, b. Boston, Mass. Ordained a priest in 1921, he served as pastor in Archdiocese of Boston (1921–39). He was active in Society for the Propagation of the Faith and became its director (1929). Archbishop of Boston (1944–70) and cardinal after 1958, he wrote many articles on social and ecclesiastical problems.

Cushions
  furniture, uses in **U** 226, 227

Cushites, in Old Testament, the descendants of Cush, the son of Ham. The name generally refers to the inhabitants of the land of Cush, or Ethiopia. First dominated by Egypt (approximately 1991–1786 B.C.), they later established an Ethiopian, or Cushite, line of kings over Egypt (715–656 B.C.) but were forced by Assyria to return to their own land.

Cushitic (cush-IT-ic) **languages** **L** 39
  spoken in Africa **A** 55

Cushman, Charlotte Saunders (1816–1876), American actress, b. Boston, Mass. After playing in New York and Philadelphia theaters (1837–44), she won wide acclaim in England (1845–49) and successfully toured the United States (1849–52). Though her most celebrated roles included Meg Merriles in *Guy Mannering* and Nancy Sykes in *Oliver Twist*, she also appeared in such male roles as Romeo and Hamlet.

Cusimanses (cu-si-man-ses), animals related to mongooses **G** 93; picture **G** 92
Cuspids, teeth **T** 47
Custer, George Armstrong, American army officer **I** 214
  coming of the white man **I** 168–69
Custer Battlefield National Monument, Montana **M** 438
Custer's Last Stand **I** 214; picture **I** 215
  Teton Sioux Indians **I** 168–69
Custer State Park, South Dakota **S** 322–23
Custis-Lee Mansion, Virginia **N** 29
  places of interest in Virginia **V** 353
Custody, of children in divorce **D** 234
Custom-made, production of goods **M** 151
  "customizing" model cars **A** 536–37
  glove making **G** 240–41
Customs (tariff) see Tariffs
Customs, United States Bureau of
  Customs Agency Service **F** 76
Customs, social see People, how they live and work sections of continent, country, province, and state articles
Cut-and-cover tunnels **T** 314–15
Cut glass **G** 230, 232
Cutin (CU-tin), waxy substance of leaves **L** 120
Cutler, Manasseh, American clergyman **W** 143
Cutlery, knives, forks, and spoons **K** 285–88
Cutter, Charles Ammi, American librarian **L** 189
Cutting, of gemstones **G** 71
Cuttings, from plants **H** 268–69
Cuttlefishes, mollusks **O** 275; picture **L** 230
  ink made from ink sac **C** 432
Cutworms, caterpillars **P** 289
Cuvier (cu-vi-AY), **Georges**, French naturalist **F** 381
  Cuvier and the correlation of parts **B** 191
  early work in geology **G** 112
Cuza (CU-za), **Alexandru Ioan**, prince of Rumania **R** 358
Cuzco (CU-zco), Peru, capital of Inca Empire **I** 206
  ancient Inca road **P** 165; picture **P** 160
Cyangugu, Rwanda **R** 363
Cyanide method, gold extracting process **G** 249
Cyanocobalamin, vitamin B$_{12}$ **V** 370d

Cybernetics, comparative study of learning in animals and machines, including study of the way information is received and stored and the way problems are solved on basis of past experience. It was first treated as separate science in Norbert Wiener's book *Cybernetics* (1948).

Cycad trees, ancient tropical plants **D** 178
Cyclades (CIC-la-dese) **Islands**, southeast of Greece **I** 429; picture **I** 432

Cyclamate, an artificial sweetener used in various food products to replace sugar. In 1969, U. S. Secretary of Health, Education, and Welfare Robert H. Finch banned use of cyclamates in soft drinks and other foodstuffs. Ban was due to laboratory tests indicating a possibility that cyclamates might be a cause of some forms of cancer.
  chemicals that cause cancer **C** 91
  FDA tests and ban on **F** 351

Cyclamen (CIC-la-men), house plant, picture **H** 268
Cycles, miracle plays **M** 339
Cycling see Bicycles and bicycling
Cyclones, low-pressure areas accompanying hurricanes and tornadoes **H** 293
  highs and lows affecting weather **W** 74
  Pecos Bill ropes a cyclone, story **F** 316–17
  wind patterns **W** 187
Cyclopropane (cy-clo-PRO-pane), an anesthetic **A** 258
Cyclopes (cy-CLO-peze), in Greek mythology
  cyclopean masonry **B** 394
  Odyssey **O** 53
Cyclotrons (CY-clo-trons), atom smashers **A** 489
  nuclear energy **N** 366
Cygnus (CIG-nus), constellation **C** 492
  astronomy, discoveries in **A** 477
Cylinder, geometric figure **G** 129
Cylinder (CIL-in-der) **presses**, for printing **P** 461–62
Cylinder recordings, for the early phonograph **R** 123
Cylinders, of engines
  automobiles **A** 543
  hydraulic machines **H** 301
  internal-combustion engines **I** 304, 305
  steam engines **S** 419
Cymbala, bell chime **B** 136
Cymbals, musical instruments **M** 550; picture **M** 548
  ancient music **A** 246
  bronze **B** 409
  percussion instruments **P** 152

Cymbeline, drama by William Shakespeare. The title is the name of an English king who ruled Britain from about A.D. 5 to 40, and the plot is based on a story about him from the collection *Decameron* by the Italian writer Giovanni Boccaccio. The tale involves a bet made by Iachimo that Imogen, Cymbeline's daughter, will not remain true to her husband, Posthumus. Iachimo steals a bracelet from Imogen as she sleeps and convinces Posthumus of her infidelity. Iachimo's treachery is finally revealed, and the couple is reunited.

Cynewulf (KIN-e-wolf), early English poet **E** 246

Cynics, members of philosophical school founded by Greek philosopher Antisthenes (445?–365? B.C.). Cynics believed in "the natural life," free from vanity and hypocrisy of social conventions, as means of achieving virtue. Most famous Cynic was Diogenes (412?–323 B.C.), who supposedly lived in a tub and carried a lantern in search for "an honest man." Cynics' contempt for civilized people and customs gave rise to their Greek name, *kynikós*, meaning "doglike," and to modern

Cynics (continued)
meaning of "cynic," someone who has no faith in human goodness or sincerity.

Cypress, evergreen tree found throughout the world. It has small, rounded cones and scalelike leaves. The wood, often fragrant, is used in making pencils, shingles, and boats. Unrelated trees called cypress include the bald cypress of the southern United States. This tree is large at the base, tapering toward the top. Its wood is used in making railroad ties and posts.

Cyprian, Saint (Thascius Caecilius Cyprianus) (200?–258), Christian martyr, b. Carthage. Converted to Christianity about 248, he labored for unity of Church and re-admission of Christians who had renounced their religion under persecution. He was beheaded during Christian persecution under Emperor Valerian.

Cyrano de Bergerac (ce-ra-NO d'bear-jer-OC), **Savinien de** (1619–1655), French poet and soldier, b. Périgord. He served in army (1637–40) and established reputation as poet and duelist. Forced to retire as result of wounds, he devoted rest of life to writing. Cyrano was immortalized in Edmond Rostand's play *Cyrano de Bergerac,* although plot actually has little basis in fact.

Cyrus the Younger (424?–401 B.C.), Persian prince, son of Darius Nothus. He plotted against his brother Artaxerxes II (401 B.C.) but was pardoned and restored as prince of Asia Minor. In command of Asiatic forces, he met Artaxerxes at Cunaxa in Babylonia, was defeated and killed. The subsequent Greek retreat (401–399 B.C.) was recorded in the *Anabasis* by Xenophon.

Cystic fibrosis, inherited disease affecting exocrine glands—those producing mucus, sweat, saliva. Disease results in improper functioning of many organs, including lungs, pancreas, and sometimes liver.

Czaczkes, Samuel Joseph see Agnon, Shmuel Yosef

Czerny (CHER-ni), **Carl** (1791–1857), Austrian piano teacher and composer, b. Vienna. He studied with Beethoven, and he taught piano to Liszt. Czerny is best known for his piano exercises, *The School of Fingering.*

ILLUSTRATION CREDITS

The following list credits, by page, the sources of illustrations used in Volume C of THE NEW BOOK OF KNOWLEDGE. Credits are listed illustration by illustration—left to right, top to bottom. Wherever appropriate, the name of the photographer or artist has been listed with the source, the two being separated by a dash. When two or more illustrations appear on one page, their credits are separated by semicolons.

308a Walter R. Aguiar; Audrey Topping.
308b V. Lefteroff
309 J. Allan Cash—Rapho Guillumette; Inger Abrahamsen—Rapho Guillumette.
310 George Daniell—Photo Researchers
314 J. Cron—Monkmeyer Press Photo Service
318 Culver
319 Harry Scott
321 Rare Book Division, The New York Public Library
323- Edward Vebell
325
327 Edward Vebell
329 Popsie
330 Robert Conlan
335 Bettmann Archive
336 Arline Strong; Harold M. Lebow; Lois Lord.
338 George Buctel; Hastings-Willinger & Associates.
339 James Cooper
340 Bettmann Archive
342 Bettmann Archive
343 John Lewis Stage—Photo Researchers; Ralph Anderson—Shostal; Ray Manley—Shostal.
344 Chuck Abbott—Rapho Guillumette; John Lewis Stage—Photo Researchers; Gene Klebe; Carlos Elmer—Shostal.
345 Harrison Forman; Josef Muench; Harrison Forman.
349 W. T. Mars
350 W. T. Mars
355 W. T. Mars
356 Cal Bernstein—Black Star
357 Cal Bernstein—Black Star; Louis Goldman—Rapho Guillumette.
358 George Bakacs
361 Anthony Sas, Madison College
362 Howard Koslow
363 Howard Koslow
365 Howard Koslow
366 Howard Koslow
370 George Bakacs
372 Standard Oil Co. of New Jersey; Standard Oil Co. of New Jersey; Bob Yeargin—Mandrel Industries, Inc.
374 Chase Manhattan Bank, Money Museum; The American Numismatic Society; The American Numismatic Society.
376 Sandak, Copyright, The Museum of Modern Art, New York, 1962; Sandak; Lois Lord.
377 Hella Hammid
379 George Buctel; Dietar F. Grabitzky.
380 Lillian Tonnaire—Taylor
381 Shostal
382 Columbia National Tourist Board
383 Mike Andrews—Camera Press-Pix
385 George Sottung
386 George Sottung
388 George Sottung
389 George Sottung
391- George Sottung
393
395- George Sottung
399
401 Color Illustration Inc.; Rutherford Platt; Colorado Department of Public Relations; Colorado Department of Public Relations.
402 Josef Muench; Diversified Map Corp.
403 Diversified Map Corp.
404 Diversified Map Corp.

407 Ray Manley—Shostal
408 Margaret Durrance—Rapho Guillumette
410 George Buctel
411 Josef Muench
412 Josef Muench; Shostal.
413 Winston Pote—Shostal; Diversified Map Corp.; Lawrence S. Williams—Rapho.
417 Tyyne/Hakdla
418 Yerkes Observatory, U. of Chicago
419 Miller Pope
420 Royal Canadian Air Force; Fairchild Aerial Surveys; Dr. Virgil E. Barnes.
421 American Museum of Natural History
422 National Periodicals Publications, Inc.
423 National Periodicals Publications, Inc.
424 Courtesy of RCA Victor Co., R. M. Jones, Art Director, Jan Balet, Artist; W. S. Eberle, Zurich-Eastman Kodak Co.; Photos from National Biscuit Co. through Kenyon-Eckhart Advertising Agency.
425 Coca-Cola Co.; Volkswagon of America, Inc.; Westinghouse Electric Corp.; Bovril Ltd.; Distributed in America by Red Line Commercial Co.
426 New York City Department of Traffic; David Stone Martin.
427 Courtesy of The New York Times, BBDO Advertising Co.; Container Corp. of America; Hartwall Co.; The Times Publishing Company, Ltd.
429- Howard Koslow
432
433 The New York Public Library
435 Howard Koslow
437 Howard Koslow
438 From Communication through the Ages by Alfred Still, published by Murray Hill Books, Inc.
439 Howard Koslow
440 Courtesy of Bell Telephone Laboratories
442 Sovfoto
445 Marc Riboud—Magnum
449 The General Electric Computer Dept.
450 The General Electric Computer Dept.
451 Attilio Sinagra; International Business Machine Corp.
452 Courtesy of the Computation Laboratory of Harvard University
454 The General Electric Computer Dept.
457 The General Electric Computer Dept.
461 George Buctel
462 Harrison Forman
463 Naud—De Wys, Inc.
464 Naud—De Wys, Inc.
465 W. D. Friedman—PIP
466 Color Illustration Inc.; J. Horace McFarland; Allan D. Cruickshank—National Audubon Society; J. Horace McFarland.
468 Diversified Map Corporation
469 Diversified Map Corporation
470 Diversified Map Corporation
471 Arthur Griffin; Peter Roll—Photo Researchers.
473 Jerry Cooke
474 Robert Tschirky—Annan
476 Diversified Map Corp.
477 George Buctel
479 Robert Tschirky—Annan
481 Phoenix Mutual Life Insurance
483 USDA Photo
484 Monkmeyer
485 A. Devaney
486 Annan; Josef Muench.

487 Tom Hollyman—Photo Researchers; Josef Muench; Marshall Lockman, Life Magazine © 1961 Time Inc., all rights reserved.
488 Ronald D. K. Hadden—PIP; Tomas D. W. Friedman—PIP.
490 George Bakacs
492 George Bakacs
493 George Bakacs
494 James Cooper
495 Wide World Photos; Brown Brothers.
496 Bettmann Archive; Brown Brothers; Wide World Photos.
499 The Consumers Co-operative Association
501 Don Spaulding
504 George Bakacs
505 C. W. Sorenson
506 Alpha
507 George Bakacs
508 W. T. Mars
511 Miller Pope; Fordham University News Office.
512 Miller Pope; Brookhaven National Institute.
513 Miller Pope
514 Douglas Faulkner
515 George Buctel
516 Jane Latta
517 Jane Latta
518 Douglas Faulkner
520 National Cotton Council
521 The New York Public Library; National Cotton Council.
522 Cletis Reaves—Alpha; C. W. Sorensen; Shostal.
526 Robert Frankenberg
528 Robert Frankenberg
529 Robert Frankenberg
531 Edward Vebell
532 Edward Vebell
534 Gaetano Di Palma
535 Ralph Krubner—Black Star
537 Robert Frankenberg
538 W. T. Mars
540 W. T. Mars
541 Walter Dawn
542 M. Pope; Professor Ralph W. G. Wyckof.
543 Miller Pope
544 Miller Pope
545 Miller Pope
546 Courtesy of the American Museum of Natural History; Courtesy of the American Museum of Natural History; Miller Pope; Miller Pope.
547 Rene Burri—Magnum
548 George Buctel
549 Cyr Agency
550 Shostal
551 Rene Burri—Magnum
552 Brown Brothers
553 Culver
554 Rapho Guillumette
555 Robert Frankenberg
556 Robert Davis—Photo Researchers
557 George Buctel
558 Emil Brunner—Pix; Robert Davis—Photo Researchers.
559 Embassy of the Czechoslovak Socialist Republic
560 George Buctel
561 Lomeo Bullaty—Nancy Palmer
562 Jerry Cooke; Martin Swithinbank—PIP.
563 Eastfoto

D, fourth letter of the English alphabet **D** 1
See also Alphabet

Dablon (da-BLON), **Claude** (1619?–1697), French Jesuit missionary, b. Dieppe. He went to French Canada in 1655 and worked among Indians in New York and in Hudson Bay area (1655–70). As Superior of Canadian missions (1671–80, 1686–93) he directed expansion of Jesuit missionary and exploration work.

Dacca, capital of Bangladesh **B** 44a, 44c; picture **B** 44b
Dachau (DA-cow), Germany
　monument to Nazi war crimes victims, picture **N** 71
Dachshund (DOCKS-hoont), dog **D** 261; picture **D** 254
Dacia (DAY-cia), Roman province in southeastern Europe
　R 358
　Rumanians descendants of Dacians **R** 355
Dacko, David, Central African political leader **C** 170
Dacron, trade name of a polyester fiber
　rope **R** 332–33
Dactyls (DAC-tils), metrical feet in poetry **P** 354
Dadaism, modern art movement **M** 393, 398; **S** 104–05
　See also Assemblage
Daddy longlegs, spider, picture **S** 384
Dadié, Bernard, Ivory Coast poet and novelist **A** 76c
Daedalus (DED-a-lus), in Greek mythology **A** 36
　legendary flight **A** 567

Daffodil, flowering plant grown from bulbs. A single yellow or white trumpet-shaped flower grows at the end of a 12-inch stalk. Flat, sword-shaped leaves about 12 in. long grow from the bulb and surround the stalk. The flowers bloom early in spring. The **jonquil** is similar to the daffodil, but its flowers have cup-shaped centers and the leaves are narrower. Picture **G** 43.

Daffodils, poem by William Wordsworth **W** 242
Dafne, first opera **B** 63
Dafoe, Allan Roy, Canadian doctor see Dionne quintuplets
Dafydd ap Gwilym, Welsh poet **W** 3
Da Gama, Vasco see Gama, Vasco da
Dag Hammarskjöld (DOG HA-mar-sherld) **Library,** United
　Nations, picture **L** 178
Daguerre (da-GAIR), **Louis,** French photographer **D** 2
　beginnings of photography **P** 211
Daguerreotypes (da-GAIR-e-o-types), first permanent
　photographs **D** 2
　beginnings of photography **P** 211–12
　importance to communication **C** 434
Dahlias, flowers **G** 51
Dahomey (da-HOME-y) **D** 3–4
　doctor working with schoolchildren, picture **D** 241
　flag **F** 235

Daibutsu (die-BU-tsu) (Great Buddha), giant images of Buddha found in Japan. The daibutsu in Nara, which stands 55.77 feet high including the base, is considered the representative daibutsu in Japan. Another famous daibutsu, 44.4 feet high, is in Kamakura.

Dailey, Ulysses Grant (1885–1961), American surgeon, b. Donaldsonville, La. One of the first Negroes to gain recognition in medicine, he received his M.D. from Northwestern University (1906). He established Dailey Hospital and Sanitarium (1926) and was senior attending surgeon at Provident Hospital, Chicago, Ill. (1933–52). He undertook State Department assignments in India, Ceylon, Africa (1952–53). He was a fellow of International College of Surgeons and of National Medical Association (president 1915–16).

Daily Courant, early English newspaper **J** 142

Daimler, automobile **A** 543
Daimler (DIME-ler), **Gottlieb,** German inventor **A** 543
　built first practical motorcycle **M** 488b

Daimyo (DIME-yo), or **daimio,** Japanese feudal land-holders and military lords. They were often recipients of estates given to some members of emperor's court. Daimyo became powerful under centralized feudal system during 17th century, declined by 19th century, and lost all feudal privileges when system was abolished.

Dairy bacteriology
　cheese **D** 13
　processing of milk **D** 10–12
Dairy cattle **D** 5–10
　breeds of cattle **C** 147, 148–49
Dairying and dairy products **D** 5–13
　Canada **C** 58
　dairying unlike beef cattle production **C** 149
　Germany, picture **A** 98
　Vermont pasture, picture **V** 310
　Wisconsin **W** 199; pictures **W** 200
　See also Butter; Cheese; Ice cream; Milk

Daisy, any of more than a hundred species of flowering plant. It is native to Europe but now spread through most of North America. The white, or ox-eye, daisy blooms in summer and has flower 1 to 2 inches wide with a bright yellow center and 20 to 30 long slender white rays. Other species include the yellow daisy, or black-eyed Susan, with black center and yellow rays, and daisies with yellow centers and blue or pink rays.

Dakar (da-KAR), capital of Senegal **S** 120

Daladier (da-lod-YAY), **Édouard** (1884–1970), French statesman, b. Carpentras, Vaucluse. He served in World War I (1914–18) and was member of Chamber of Deputies (1919–40), president of Radical Socialist Party (1934), and premier of France (1933, 1934 for 11 days, and 1938–40). He signed Munich Pact (1938) and declaration of war against Germany (1939). He resigned the premiership (1940) when France surrendered to Germany and was arrested by Vichy government (1940) and imprisoned (1941–45). He served in National Assembly (1946–58).
　Munich Conference, 1938 **F** 419; **W** 286

Dalai Lama (DA-LIE LA-ma), name given former ruler and chief monk of Tibet. Lamaism, a form of Buddhism, established the title of Dalai Lama in 1640. Lamaists believe that the Dalai Lama is the reincarnation of a revered Buddhist deity, and that upon his death, his spirit passes into the body of a baby just born. Priests use magic rites to find the proper baby, who is then carefully trained to his great responsibility. The Chinese Communists suppressed Lamaism in Tibet in 1950. An unsuccessful revolt against the Communist forces by the Tibetans in 1959 forced the present Dalai Lama and his followers into exile in India.
　Tibet, history of **T** 175, 178

Dalcroze, E. J. see Jaques-Dalcroze, Emile
Dale, Chester, American banker and art patron **N** 40–41
Dale, Sir Thomas, English governor of Jamestown colony
　J 21

Daley, Richard J. (1902–　　), American politician, b. Chicago, Ill. After serving in the Illinois state legislature (1936–46) and in various positions in state government, he became chairman of his country's Democratic Party. He was elected mayor of Chicago (1955) and is currently

Daley, Richard (continued)
serving his fourth consecutive term governing the second largest city in the United States.

Dalgliesh, Alice (1893–   ), American author, b. Trinidad. She has been professor of children's literature at Teachers College of Columbia University, and was children's book editor for Charles Scribner's Sons (1934–60). Her books for children include *The Silver Pencil, A Book for Jennifer,* and *Along Janet's Road.*

Dalhousie (dal-HOW-zie), **9th earl of** (George Ramsay) (1770–1838), British general and colonial official, b. Dalhousie Castle, Scotland. One of Wellington's generals in France and Spain during Napoleonic Wars, he was Lieutenant Governor of Nova Scotia (1816), governor in chief of Canadian colonies (1819–28), and commander in chief in India (1829–32).

Dalhousie, New Brunswick, Canada **N** 138c
Dalhousie University, at Halifax, Nova Scotia **N** 344d

Dali (DA-li), **Salvador** (1904–   ); Spanish artist, b. Figueras, Catalonia. Using a surrealistic style, he was associated with various modern schools of painting. Interest in dream symbolism and abnormal psychology is reflected in his art. He is noted for his paintings *The Persistence of Memory* and *Christ of St. John of the Cross.* He published *Secret Life of Salvador Dali* and collaborated with Luis Buñuel in his film called *Le Chien Andalou.*
   surrealism in modern art **M** 395
   The Persistence of Memory, painting **M** 396a

Dallaire, Jean, Canadian painter **C** 64

Dallas, George Mifflin (1792–1864), American politician, b. Philadelphia, Pa. His early career included diplomatic service abroad and a return to local politics in Philadelphia. He filled a vacancy in the United States Senate (1831–33), followed by a term (1833–35) as Pennsylvania's attorney general. After 2 years (1837–39) as minister to Russia, Dallas was Democratic vice-president under Polk (1845–49) and United States minister to Great Britain (1856–61). Picture **V** 326.

Dallas, Texas **D** 14
Dall sheep **S** 145; picture **H** 218
   hoofed mammals **H** 221
Dalmatian, dog, picture **D** 256
Dalmation coast, of the Adriatic, Yugoslavia **Y** 356; picture **Y** 354
Dalton, John, English chemist and physicist, father of atomic theory **D** 15
   atomic theory in history of chemistry **C** 212–13
   atomic theory in history of physics **P** 231
   sciences, advances in **S** 74
Daly, Augustin, American playwright **D** 299
Daly, Marcus, Irish-born American financier **M** 441
Damages, in civil law cases **C** 527, 530
Damão (da-MA-o), India **P** 402, 404
Damariscotta (dam-ar-is-COT-ta) **Lake,** Maine, picture **M** 43
Damascening (dam-a-SCENE-ing), art of decorating metals **D** 75
Damascus (da-MAS-cus), capital of Syria **S** 508; picture **S** 505
Damascus steel swords **T** 308
   early use of steel **I** 405
   former industry of Damascus, Syria **S** 508
D'Amboise (d'on-BWOZ), **Jacques,** American ballet dancer, picture **B** 27

Dame, British title **K** 277
Dame schools **E** 68
Damien (dom-YAN), **Father** (Joseph Damien de Veuster), Belgian priest and missionary in Hawaii **H** 70
Dammam, Saudi Arabia **S** 47

Damocles (DAM-oc-lese), **sword of,** symbol of precarious nature of power. The term is derived from anecdote of Greek courtier Damocles of Syracuse, who greatly admired wealth and power of royalty. To cure him of this admiration, the tyrant Dionysius invited Damocles to a banquet. When Damocles looked up, a sword suspended by a single horsehair dangled above his head.

Damon (DAY-mon) and **Pythias,** or **Phintias,** philosophers of Syracuse, Greek city in ancient Sicily. They are remembered as models of devoted friendship. When the tyrant Dionysius condemned Pythias to death, Damon offered to take Pythias' place in prison until he settled his affairs. Pythias returned just as Damon was to be killed. Impressed by their friendship, Dionysius pardoned them.

Dampers, of chimneys **H** 97

Damrosch (DAM-rosh), **Walter Johannes** (1862–1950), American musician, b. Breslau, Silesia (now part of Poland). The son of Leopold Damrosch, a noted musician, Walter was director of the Newark (N.J.) Harmonic Society when he was nineteen. During his distinguished musical career, he conducted and directed at the Metropolitan Opera House, served as director of the N.Y. Symphony and Oratorio societies (1885), organized and toured with the Damrosch Opera Company (1894–99), served as director of the N.Y. Symphony Society (1903–27), and inaugurated the weekly Music Appreciation Hour over NBC (1928–42), a program popular with millions of schoolchildren. He composed choral music, operas, and songs. His autobiography, *My Musical Life* was published in 1923 (revised 1930).

Damrosch Park, Lincoln Center for the Performing Arts **L** 298
Dams **D** 16–21
   Arkansas, Norfolk Lake formed by, picture **A** 423
   Arrowrock dam, Idaho, picture **I** 58
   artificial lakes **L** 25
   beaver dams **B** 112–14
   canals **C** 84
   Columbia River, Washington **W** 20
   conservation and irrigation, picture **C** 485
   construction in China, picture **C** 266
   Douglas Dam, Tennessee, picture **T** 76
   fish ladders **F** 224; **O** 197
   floods and flood control **F** 254–57
   Garrison Dam, North Dakota, picture **N** 324
   Hirakud Dam, India, picture **W** 220
   Hungry Horse Dam, Montana **M** 428; picture **M** 431
   irrigation **I** 408–10
   Kentucky Dam on Tennessee River, picture **K** 214
   Parker Dam, Colorado River, picture **R** 243
   rivers used for power and irrigation **R** 241–42
   waterpower **P** 425
   water supply **W** 66
   Why don't we get all our electric power from water? **W** 62
   world power sources **W** 257
Damselfish **F** 204

Damson plums, a sweet variety of small, oval plums, dark purple in color. They were introduced into Europe from Asia Minor, and are used in jelly and jam.

Dan, in Old Testament, son of Jacob and Bilhah. He founded Tribe of Dan, one of 12 tribes of Israel. The Danites moved north of their assigned territory and seized control of town of Laish near headwaters of Jordan, renaming town Dan.

Dana (DAY-na), **Charles Anderson** (1819–1897), American newspaperman, b. Hinsdale, N.H. He was managing editor, New York *Tribune* (1847–62), assistant secretary of war (1864–65), owner and editor of New York *Sun* (1868–97), where he was noted for developing human interest stories. His books include *The Art of Newspaper Making.*

Dana, John Cotton, American librarian L 188
Dana, Richard Henry, American writer A 202

Danaides (da-NAY-id-ese), in Greek mythology, 50 daughters of Danaus who were forced to marry their cousins, 50 sons of Aegyptus. At wedding feast Danaus gave each of the girls a dagger with command to murder their husbands on their wedding night. All obeyed but Hypermnestra who helped husband, Lynceus, escape. They were punished in Hades by having to draw water from a deep well with sieves. Hence phrase "Danaid's work" means an endless, fruitless task.

Danang, Republic of Vietnam (South Vietnam) V 334b
Danbury, Connecticut C 473
Danbury Fair, Connecticut, picture F 13
Dance D 22–34
African music A 77
American Indian dances, pictures I 161
ballet B 23–29
bee "dances" B 120
Bolivian Indian feasts and fairs B 303
folk dancing F 297–301
Latin-American dancing L 68–69
minuet, picture C 392
music see Dance music
Peruvian Indians, picture S 285
poetry, beginnings of P 349
rhythmical activities in physical education P 226
singing games G 11–13
theater of India T 163
Dance music D 35–37
Latin-American folk music for the dance L 74
play-party tunes of folk music F 323–24
Spain S 372
Strauss, Johann, Jr. S 437
Dancer on the Stage, drawing by Degas F 430
Dance suite, form of musical composition D 36; M 538
baroque period B 66
Dancing Siva, Hindu god, picture O 213
Dandelions W 168, 171; picture W 105
"Dandelions," poem by Frances M. Frost F 119
seed, dispersal of F 280; pictures F 281, L 233
Danegeld (DANE-gheld), tribute of gold or silver V 338
Danelaw (DANE-law), eastern section of England V 339
Danes, Teutonic Norsemen and Vikings
Alfred the Great and the Danes A 154–55
Danish rulers of England, chart U 77
English language influenced by E 243
invasions of England E 216–17

Danforth Foundation, corporation founded (1927) by Mr. and Mrs. William H. Danforth to serve education. It instituted Danforth Foundation award for college teachers (1963) to stress need for emphasizing personal elements in education and to honor outstanding teachers. Its headquarters is in St. Louis, Mo.

Daniel, book of Bible, Old Testament B 156

Daniel, Saint Anthony (1601–1648), French Jesuit missionary, b. Dieppe, Normandy. He worked in Indian missions in Canada (1633–48) and was among a group of Jesuits killed by Indians. He was canonized in 1930.

Daniel Deronda, novel by George Eliot E 17
Daniel in the Lion's Den, Bible story B 167–68

Daniell, John Frederic (1790–1845), English physicist and chemist, b. London. He was known for work in meteorology. He invented (1820?) hygrometer, an instrument for measuring moisture in the air, developed plan of weather reporting followed later by Greenwich Observatory, and also invented constant output battery (Daniell cell). Daniell wrote *Meteorological Essays* to explain atmosphere by physical laws and *Introduction to Chemical Philosophy.*

Daniels, Josephus, American journalist and diplomat N 319
Danilova (da-NI-lo-va), **Alexandra,** Russian-born American ballerina B 28
Danish furniture F 510
Danish literature S 50–53
Dannay, Frederic see Queen, Ellery
D'Annunzio (d'a-NOONTZ-io), **Gabriele,** Italian writer and poet I 480
Dan Patch, famous racing horse H 234
Dante (DON-tay) **Alighieri,** Italian poet D 38
Holy Roman Empire, concern for peace under H 164
Italian literature, place in I 475–76
peace movements P 104
Danton (don-TON), **Georges Jacques,** French revolutionary leader F 466, 467, 468
Danube River, Europe R 242
Austria A 522
Czechoslovakia C 560
Hungary H 284–85
Rumania's major waterway R 356
Danville, Virginia V 348–49
Danzig (DON-zig), now Gdansk, Poland P 362; W 286

Daphne (DAPH-ne), in Greek mythology, a nymph whom the god Apollo tried to woo. Daphne fled from Apollo and prayed to her father, the river god Peneus, for protection. Zeus, at Gaea's request, turned Daphne into a laurel tree, which from that time on was Apollo's favorite tree. Wreaths of laurel leaves came to be used to crown winners of certain contests.

Daphni, church of, near Athens, Greece
Byzantine mosaics in B 488–89
DAR see Daughters of the American Revolution
Darby, Abraham, English inventor I 237

Darby and Joan, English couple said to have lived during 18th century in Yorkshire, England, known for their virtuous and happy married life. Their names came to signify any old, happily married couple.

Darby Ram, folk song F 323
Dardanelles (dar-da-NELLS), **Strait of the,** Turkey T 324
Dardanelles Campaign, World War I W 274
Dare, Virginia, first English child born in America A 181
Fort Raleigh National Historic Site, birthplace N 316
Dar es Salaam (dar es sa-LOM), capital of Tanzania T 19; picture T 16
Darien (DARE-i-en), Connecticut
school auditorium, picture S 55
Darien (dare-i-EN), region between Panama and Colombia C 381
Balboa's name for Panama B 18

Darién Range, mountains of Panama   P 44
Darin, Bobby, American singer   R 262c
Darío (da-RI-o), **Rubén,** Nicaraguan poet   L 71
Darius I, king of Persia see Darius the Great
Darius III, king of Persia
   defeated by Alexander the Great   A 152

Darius the Great (da-RY-us) (Darius I, Darius Hystaspis) (558? B.C.–486 B.C.), Persian king. He was crowned 521 B.C. He was the first Oriental conqueror to extend his empire into Europe. He made Persia the first great naval power of Asia. He introduced such innovations as uniformity of coinage, regular taxation, system of roads, and postal system.
   coming of the Persians   A 226

Darjeeling (dar-JEE-ling), India   I 125
Dark Ages see Middle Ages
Dark and Bloody Ground, Kentucky   K 212
   Boone's Wilderness Road, migration route   O 255
Dark continent, Africa   A 46
Dark Hills, The, poem by Edwin Arlington Robinson
   P 355

Dark horse, term signifying racehorse whose ability and chances of winning are generally unknown. The term has come to mean a political candidate who wins unexpectedly.
   Polk was first such little-known candidate to become president   P 383

Dark Lady of the Sonnets, woman to whom Shakespeare addressed many of his later sonnets. Her actual identity is uncertain and widely disputed. The name was used as title of comedy by George Bernard Shaw.

Darkrooms, in photography   P 217
Darlan (dar-LON), **Jean,** Vichy French leader   W 296
Darling River, Australia   A 503
Darnley, Henry Stuart, Lord, husband of Mary Queen of Scots   M 130

Darrow, Clarence Seward (1857–1938), American lawyer, b. Kinsman, Ohio. He won national repute as labor lawyer. He was counsel to Eugene V. Debs, indicted (1894) for conspiracy in Railway Union strike case. He obtained sentence of life imprisonment, rather than execution, for Leopold and Loeb in their trial for murder (1924). He is noted for defending right of John T. Scopes to teach evolution in Tennessee public schools (1925). His books include *Crime, Its Cause and Treatment, The Story of My Life,* and *Farmington.*
   defended miners in Idaho   I 68

Darrow, Frank E., American doll maker   D 267
Dart, Raymond, anthropologist   P 442
D'Artagnan (d'ar-tan-YON), friend of *The Three Musketeers*   D 342–43
Dartmouth, Nova Scotia, Canada   N 344d
Dartmouth College, Hanover, New Hampshire   N 157
   ice sculpture at Winter Carnival, picture   N 159
Darts, game   D 38–39
Darwin, capital of Northern Territory, Australia   A 513
Darwin, Charles Robert, English naturalist   D 39–41
   coral reef formation, theory of   C 504
   evolution, theory of   E 344–45
   Huxley, Thomas H., supporter of   H 300
   influence on study of biology   B 192
   Lyell's theories in geology, interest in   G 113
   place in history of science   S 73–74
Darwin, Erasmus, English naturalist, grandfather of Charles Darwin   E 344

Darwin, Sir Francis, English botanist, son of Charles Darwin   D 41
Dashes, punctuation marks   P 531
Das Kapital, book by Karl Marx   M 113
   source of Communistic ideas   C 442–43
Data, facts   S 416
Data banks, automated storage and retrieval systems   A 531
Data communication   T 54–55
   data sets   E 142b
Data processing, or punch card systems   O 58
   use in libraries   L 177
Data transmission see Data communication
Date, fruit   D 41–42
   Iraq world's largest producer   I 381
Date line, International see International date line
Dating, a social custom
   "going steady," in adolescence   A 23
   See also Courtship
Dating, radioactive see Radioactive dating
Daudet (do-DAY), **Alphonse,** French novelist   F 441
Daud Khan, Mohammed, president of Afghanistan   A 45
Daugherty, Harry M., American politician   H 40, 41
   scandals of the Harding and Coolidge era   C 496

Daugherty (DAW-her-ty), **James Henry** (1889–   ), American illustrator, mural painter, and writer, b. Asheville, N.C. He is one of the best-known illustrators of children's books. He illustrated Washington Irving's *Knickerbocker's History of New York* and Carl Sandburg's *Abe Lincoln Grows Up,* and wrote and illustrated *Daniel Boone.*

Daughters of the American Revolution (DAR), organization of female descendants of American Revolutionary War veterans. Established in 1890, with headquarters in Washington, D.C., it publishes *DAR Manual for Citizenship.*

Daughters of the Confederacy, United, society of women descendants of persons who gave service to Confederate cause during Civil War. The society maintains museum and library at headquarters in Richmond, Va.

Daughters of the Union, National Society of, organization of women descendants of Union veterans of Civil War, or of women whose service to North was recognized by government. It grants scholarships to students at Lincoln Memorial University in Harrogate, Tenn. It was founded in 1912.

D'Aulaire, Ingri M. and Edgar Parin see Aulaire, Ingri M. and Edgar Parin
Daumier (do-mi-AY), **Honoré,** French cartoonist and painter   D 43
   French art, realism in   F 426
   hero of lithography   G 308
   political cartoonist   C 125–26
   realism in illustrations   I 91
Dauphin, Manitoba   M 81
Dauphin, title of eldest son of a French king   J 121
Davenant (DAV-en-ant), **Sir William,** English poet and dramatist   O 132

Davenport, Marcia Gluck (1903–   ), American novelist and music critic, b. New York, N.Y. On staff of *The New Yorker* magazine (1928–31), she was also music critic for *Stage* magazine (1934–39). Her books include *The Valley of Decision* and *Too Strong for Fantasy.*

David, Sir Edgeworth (Tannatt William Edgeworth) (1858–1934), Australian geologist and explorer, b. Cardiff, Wales. He was professor of geology at Sydney University (1891–1924) and a member of Shackleton expedition to Antarctic (1907–09). With Sir Douglas Mawson he reached and recorded South Magnetic Pole (1909).

David (DA-veet), **Gerard,** Dutch painter **D** 352
The Nativity, painting **C** 280
David (da-VEED), **Jacques Louis,** French painter **F** 425
classicism in French painting **P** 27, 29
Fragonard and David **F** 402
Madame Julie Récamier, painting **P** 26, 29
Oath of the Horatii, painting **F** 424
David (DAY-vid), king of Israel **D** 44
David and Goliath, Bible story **B** 164–65
Psalms, first hymns **H** 309, 312
role in Jewish history **J** 103
statues **M** 257; pictures **D** 44, **I** 468, **S** 100
tomb in Jerusalem **J** 81
Twenty-Third Psalm **P** 435

David (DAY-vid), **Saint** (6th century), patron saint of Wales. He preached against heresies. On one occasion, the ground on which he stood is supposed to have risen and become a hill so that all might see and hear him preach. He founded 12 monasteries in Wales that followed strict rules. On March 1, his feast day, Welshmen wear a leek in their caps in memory of a battle against Saxons, when, on David's advice, they wore leeks to distinguish themselves from the enemy.

David, statue by Bernini **B** 148; pictures **D** 44, **S** 100
David, statue by Michelangelo **I** 468
poor piece of marble made into most popular work of art **M** 257
David and Goliath, Bible story **B** 164–65
David Copperfield, book by Charles Dickens, excerpt **D** 160–61
David Kalakaua see Kalakaua I, king of Hawaii

Davidson, Jo (1883–1952), American sculptor, b. New York, N.Y. He was internationally famous for portrait busts of notable figures and for this reason was called biographer in bronze. His subjects included Woodrow Wilson, Anatole France, David Lloyd George, and Tagore.

Davies, Sir Louis Henry (1845–1924), Canadian lawyer and politician, b. Charlottetown, Prince Edward Island. He was prime minister and attorney general of Prince Edward Island province (1876–79). Elected (1882) to Canadian House of Commons, he was later chief justice of Supreme Court of Canada (1918–24).

Dávila (de Ávila), **Gil Gonzáles,** Spanish explorer **N** 248
Dávila, Pedrarias see Pedrarias Dávila
Da Vinci, Leonardo see Leonardo da Vinci
Davis, Angela, American Negro leader, picture **N** 104a

Davis, Benjamin O. (1877–1970), American army officer, Negro, b. Washington, D.C. He was commanding general of 4th Cavalry Brigade during World War II, having been made first Negro brigadier general in U.S. Army.

Davis, Benjamin O, Jr. (1912–), American air force officer, b. Washington, D.C. After graduating from U.S. Military Academy, he entered Air Force and flew during World War II. After serving in Europe and Korea, he was promoted to lieutenant general (1965), the first Negro to reach that rank. In 1967 he was made commander of 13th Air Force. Retired (1970), he was briefly Director of Public Safety, Cleveland, Ohio. Picture **N** 99.
Negro forces in World War II **N** 100–01

Davis, Bette (Ruth Elizabeth Davis) (1908–), b. Lowell, Mass. She won a scholarship to drama school and later joined a stock company. From 1931 to 1952 she made over 70 films among them Jezebel, The Little Foxes, Dark Victory, and Watch on the Rhine. She is the winner of two Academy Awards. In 1952 she appeared in a Broadway revue, Two's Company. She has also made numerous radio and television appearances. She has a daughter by one of her four marriages, as well as two adopted children.

Davis, Floyd, American illustrator **I** 92

Davis, Glen Woodward (1924–), American football star, b. Claremont, Calif. He won national fame with Felix Blanchard as outstanding player on West Point's football team (1944–46). He is noted for running speed. He played professionally with Los Angeles Rams (1950–51).

Davis, Henry C., American officer **N** 26
Davis, Jefferson, president of the Confederate States of America **D** 45; **C** 458, 459
Civil War, United States, role in **C** 318, 321
Davis family in Mississippi **M** 361
home at Beauvoir, near Biloxi, Miss. **M** 359
Kentucky shrine **K** 225
Montgomery, Ala., home **A** 122
Davis, John, American navigator **P** 366
Davis (Davys), **John** (1550?–1605), English explorer **N** 338
Davis, John W., American lawyer and politician **C** 496
Davis, Miles, American jazz musician **J** 62

Davis, Ossie (1921–), American playwright and actor, Negro, b. Cogdell, Ga. He is noted as author and star of play Purlie Victorious, comedy about Negro life. He also wrote the book of the musical, Purlie, based on his play, and has been a film director.
Negroes in the arts **N** 102

Davis, Richard Harding (1864–1916), American journalist and author, b. Philadelphia, Pa. He was a war correspondent during six wars, including Spanish-American War, Boer War, and World War I. He was also managing editor of Harper's Weekly (1890). His writings include Soldiers of Fortune and The Bar Sinister.

Davis, Sammy, Jr. (1925–), American entertainer, Negro, b. New York, N.Y. He was a member of Will Mastin Trio, which played in nightclubs (1930–48). He appeared in Broadway musicals Mr. Wonderful (1956) and Golden Boy (1964) and in film Porgy and Bess, and wrote autobiography Yes I Can.
Negroes in the arts **N** 102

Davis, Stuart, American artist **U** 122
Visa, painting **U** 120
Davis Cup, in tennis **T** 98
Davis Dam, Arizona **A** 407

Davis Strait, strait between southwestern Greenland and southeastern Baffin Island (a part of Canada's Northwest Territories). Discovered in 1587 by English explorer John Davis, the strait connects Baffin Bay with the Atlantic.

Davy, Sir Humphry, English chemist **D** 46
anesthesia **A** 256; **M** 208a
carbon monoxide **P** 357
discoveries of new elements **C** 213
electric arc light **E** 129; **I** 334
Faraday, his protégé **F** 44
invented miner's safety lamp **C** 364
leather tanning discoveries **L** 111
magnesium, work with **M** 23
predicts existence of aluminum **A** 176

Davy Jones, in sailor's slang, evil spirit of sea. The phrase "Davy Jones's Locker" refers to ocean bottom, where drowned bodies remain.

Davys (Davis), John (1550?–1605), English explorer   **N** 338

Dawes, Charles Gates (1865–1951), American statesman and financier, b. Marietta, Ohio. He received international acclaim as the author of the Dawes plan (1924), a method by which Germany reorganized its fiscal policy and made war reparations. This won him the Nobel Peace Prize (1925), which he shared with Sir Austen Chamberlain. His distinguished career included important government appointments by presidents McKinley, Harding, and Hoover. He served as vice-president of the United States under Coolidge (1925–29) and ambassador to Great Britain (1929–32). Picture   **V** 329.

Dawes, William (1745–1799), American patriot, b. Boston, Mass. He rode with Paul Revere from Lexington to Concord, alerting countryside to British attack.
   Paul Revere's ride   **R** 193, 198

Dawes Act (General Allotment Act), 1887   **I** 200
Dawes Glacier, Alaska, pictures   **A** 133, **G** 224
Dawn horse, or Eohippus, ancestor of the horse   **H** 236; picture   **E** 343

Dawson, Simon James (1820–1902), Canadian civil engineer and member of parliament, b. Redhaven, Banffshire, Scotland. He explored northwestern Canada and reported possibility of settling there. He was a member of Canadian House of Commons (1878–91).

Dawson, William Levi (1898–   ), American composer, Negro, b. Anniston, Ala. His works include *Negro Folk Symphony* and several choral works.
   work influenced by Negro spiritual   **N** 107

Dawson, Yukon Territory, Canada   **Y** 364; pictures **Y** 360, 362
Day, measure of time   **W** 112
   daylight saving time   **T** 190
   earth's period of rotation   **E** 4
   how to make a sundial   **T** 192–93
   international date line   **I** 309–10
   length of, during the seasons   **S** 108
   migration determined by length of day   **H** 191–92
Day, Benjamin H., American newspaper publisher **N** 198
   first penny newspaper in New York City   **J** 142

Day, Clarence Shepard (1874–1935), American humorist, b. New York, N.Y. He was famous for book *Life with Father*, a satire, based on his own childhood, of upper-class Victorian family. He also illustrated his own books, including *Thoughts without Words* and *Scenes from the Mesozoic.*

Dayaks (DY-aks), a people of Borneo   **B** 337–38

Dayan, Moshe (1915–   ), Israeli government official, b. Degania, Palestine. He became a soldier when he was 14 and gained experience in World War II fighting for the British and in Israel's war for independence (1948–49). In 1956 and 1967 he led Israel's forces to lightning victories over the Arabs. He has served as army chief of staff (1953–58), minister of agriculture (1959–64), and minister of defense (1967–   ).

Day and night, by the clock-calendar of the earth **T** 187–88

demonstration of earth's rotation   **E** 4–5
   equinoxes and the equator   **E** 272h
Day camps   **C** 47
Day care centers, development from infant schools **F** 37;   **K** 242
   women, role of   **W** 213
Day-Lewis, Cecil see Lewis, Cecil Day

Daylight saving time (DST), 1 hour, occasionally 2 hours, later than standard time. In areas where it is used, the clock is advanced during late spring, summer, and early fall, to provide more daylight hours for work and recreation.
   extra hour of daylight   **T** 190

Day nurseries, development from infant schools   **K** 242
Day of Doom, poem by Michael Wigglesworth   **A** 196
Day of the Race, Latin-American holiday   **H** 150

Days of grace, in law, number of days (usually 3) beyond originally allotted time allowed as favor to person who must perform some act or make some payment.

Days of the week   **D** 47
   in French   **F** 434
   in Hebrew   **H** 102
   in Italian   **I** 478
   in Spanish   **S** 368
   international date line   **I** 309–10
   names honor Norse gods   **N** 277
   origin of, for the calendar   **C** 11–12
   Sunday, or sabbath for different religions   **R** 153

Dayton, Jonathan (1760–1824), American soldier and politician, b. Elizabethtown (now Elizabeth), N.J. Dayton was a soldier in the Revolutionary War, a member of the Continental Congress (1787–89), a New Jersey representative to the House of Representatives (1791–99), speaker of the House (1795–99), and senator from New Jersey (1799–1805). He was arrested for his part in Aaron Burr conspiracy but never tried. Dayton, Ohio, is named for him.

Dayton, Ohio   **O** 72
Daytona Beach, Florida
   stock-car race   **A** 539
DC see Direct Current
D.C. see District of Columbia
DC-3, passenger airplane   **A** 573; picture   **A** 570
D Day, World War II   **W** 299
   how named   **D** 1
   Eisenhower's broadcast, excerpt from Anne Frank's Diary   **D** 157
   Eisenhower's historic decision   **E** 109
DDT (dichloro-diphenyltrichloro-ethane), insecticide **I** 258
   environment, effect on   **E** 272e–272f
Deaconesses, early church workers concerned with nursing   **N** 409
Deacons, of the church   **C** 281
Deadlines, for newspaper editions   **N** 203
Deadly amanitas, poisonous fungi   **F** 499;   **M** 521
   causes death by cell destruction   **P** 322
Deadly nightshade, or belladonna, plant   **P** 314; picture **P** 315
   poisonous plants   **P** 322
   uses in the drug industry   **D** 323
Dead mail, or dead letters   **P** 409
Dead reckoning, a method of navigation   **N** 67
   airplanes   **A** 560
Dead Sea, between Israel and Jordan   **L** 28
   Israel   **I** 442

Dead Sea Scrolls D 48–49
  Apocrypha **B** 156–57, 159
  Shrine of the Book, picture **M** 513
  skins replace papyrus for bookmaking **B** 319
Dead Souls, novel by Gogol **N** 347
Deadwood, South Dakota **S** 323–24

Deadwood Dick, hero of light adventure novels written mainly by Edward L. Wheeler. The character was probably modeled on life of Richard W. Clarke (1845–1930), English-born frontiersman noted as Indian fighter and express guard of Black Hills gold shipments.

Deaf, education of the D 50–53
  Bell, Alexander G., teacher **B** 132
  children sensing vibrations of the piano, picture **E** 75
  Keller, Helen **K** 201
  nursery school, picture **K** 247
Deaf mute, deaf, non-speaking person **D** 53
Deafness D 50
  Beethoven **B** 125
  Edison, Thomas A. **E** 59
  See also Ear; Hearing
Deaf Woman's Courtship, folk song **F** 321

Dean, Dizzy (Jerome H. Dean) (1911–), American baseball player and sports commentator, b. Lucas, Ark. A pitcher for the St. Louis Cardinals (1930–38), he had one of the highest strike-out totals in baseball history. He became a TV sports commentator in 1950, and is famous for his showmanship and his habit of coining words. He was elected to Baseball Hall of Fame (1953).

Dean, H. Trendley, American dentist **F** 284

De Angeli, Marguerite (1889–), American author and illustrator of children's books, b. Lapeer, Mich. She is noted for her stories about persons from foreign lands and their experiences in the United States. Her books include *The Door in the Wall* (Newbery medal, 1950), *Elin's Amerika,* and *Bright April.*

Death
  funeral and burial customs **F** 492–95
  hibernation close to a living death **H** 122
  how caused by narcotics **N** 13
Death camas, plant **P** 282
Death rate, number of deaths per thousand persons **P** 394
Death Valley, California **D** 131
  landforms of California **C** 16; picture **C** 17
  least rainfall in United States **R** 94
  lowest point in North America **N** 285; picture **N** 284
  mirage on, picture **M** 341
Death Valley National Monument, California **C** 25

DeBakey, Michael Ellis (1908–), American surgeon, b. Lake Charles, La. He implanted the first artificial heart in man in 1966. He was chairman of the President's Committee on Heart Disease, Cancer, and Stroke and is the recipient of many awards and honorary degrees for his outstanding contributions to medicine. He now serves as consultant surgeon to many hospitals in Texas.

Debates and debating D 54–55
  debating the motion, in parliamentary procedure **P** 80
  Lincoln-Douglas debates **L** 299
  television debates between Kennedy and Nixon **K** 209
  What is the difference between a debate and a discussion? **D** 54
  See also Parliamentary procedure; Public speaking

Debit, in bookkeeping **B** 312

Deborah, in Old Testament, only woman judge of Israel. She was considered a prophetess, or "inspired woman." She delivered her people from the oppression of Jabin, King of Hazor. The "Song of Deborah" (or, more accurately, "Song to Deborah"), the oldest piece of Hebrew literature in existence, was sung in celebration of the Israelite victory over Sisera and the kings of Canaan.

Debrecen (DEB-ret-cen), Hungary **H** 286; picture **H** 288
Debs, Eugene V., American labor leader **L** 5, 8; picture **L** 4
Debt (DET)
  true interest rates of installment plans **I** 289
Debussy (d'BU-sy), **Claude,** French composer **D** 55
  chamber music **C** 186
  French music **F** 447
  musical impressionism **M** 401
  opera **O** 138
  Pelléas et Mélisande, opera **O** 150–51

Debye (deb-BYE), **Peter Joseph William** (1884–1966), American chemist and physicist, b. Maastricht, the Netherlands. He won a Nobel prize in chemistry (1936) for his work on the use of X rays and electrons to study molecules. He was the first to show that some solids are made up of ions (atoms with electric charge) and developed an important theory (with E. Huckel) about the kinds of solutions that conduct electricity. Debye also developed a method for bringing substances to the lowest temperatures known to science today.

Decalogue see Ten Commandments
Decameron (de-CAM-er-on), book of short stories by Boccaccio **I** 476–77
  development of the short story **S** 165
Decathlon (de-CATH-lon), ten events, in the Olympic Games **O** 112
  track and field events **T** 241

Decatur (de-CATE-ur), **Stephen** (1779–1820), American naval officer, b. Sinepuxent, Md. He was promoted to captain during Tripolitan war for heroism in the burning of American frigate *Philadelphia* (1804), which had been captured by Barbary pirates. In War of 1812 he commanded frigate *United States,* which defeated British ship *Macedonian.* He is remembered for a toast delivered at banquet: "Our country! . . . may she always be in the right; but our country, right or wrong."

Decay, of plants and animals **E** 272b; **L** 242–43
  bacteria cause **B** 11–12
Decay, radioactive see Radioactive decay
Decay, tooth **T** 48
Deccan plateau, India **I** 125
Deceleration, loss of speed
  human body, effects on **S** 340k, 341
December, 12th month of year **D** 56–57
  Christmas **C** 289, 292

Decemvirs (de-CEM-virs) (from Latin *decem* meaning "ten," and *viri,* meaning "men"), in ancient Rome, two groups of 10 magistrates (*decemviri*) appointed (551 and 450 B.C.) to draw up laws for Twelve Tables and entrusted with supreme government of Rome. "Decemvirs" refers to any council or ruling body of 10, and a member of such a body is called a decemvir.

Decibels, units measuring sound **S** 259
  noise units **N** 270
  terminology for the deaf **D** 53

Deciduous (de-CID-u-ous) **trees** **T** 281–82
  forests, kinds of trees in **F** 371
  leaves of deciduous plants **L** 119
Decimal classification, of books **L** 183–84
Decimals **F** 401–02
  percent **P** 148–49
  probability **P** 473
  changing measurements of the metric system **W** 115
Decimal system, or base-10 system, of numerals **N** 393
  computers **C** 453, 456
Decius (DE-shius), Roman emperor **C** 281
Decker, Thomas see Dekker
Deck tennis **D** 58
Declaration of Human Rights see Universal Declaration
  of Human Rights
Declaration of Independence **D** 59–65
  Adams, Samuel, signer **A** 17
  American literature, place in **A** 198
  civil liberties and civil rights **C** 314
  defended by John Adams **A** 9
  Founding Fathers create **F** 394
  gives new dignity to American cause **R** 202
  Independence Day commemorates **I** 112
  Jefferson, Thomas, author of **J** 64
  Liberty Bell rang to celebrate **L** 169
  Locke's political ideas **L** 321
  North Carolina, an earlier declaration **N** 321
  Rhode Island's declaration on May 4, 1776 **R** 226
  right of Englishman to trial by jury of his peers **J** 159
  Seneca Falls Woman's Rights document parallels
    W 212b
  signatures prized by autograph collectors **A** 526
  signed in Independence Hall **I** 113
Declaration of the Rights of Man and of the Citizen,
  French **B** 180; **C** 314
  French Revolution **F** 466
Declensions, in Latin grammar **L** 76
Decomposition, or decay, of plants and animals **L** 242–43
Decompression chamber **D** 81
  workers in tunnels **T** 318
Decompression sickness see Bends, the
Decoration Day see Memorial Day
Decorations, of honor see Medals
Decorative arts **D** 66–78
  ancient Greece **G** 348
  Byzantine **B** 483–90
  enameling **E** 191–92
  folk art **F** 290–96
  interior decoration, accessories **I** 300–02
  Islamic art **I** 417, 422
  leathercraft **L** 112–13
  mosaics **M** 463
  papier-mâché **P** 58b–59
  pottery **P** 413
  Spanish architecture **S** 363–64
  stained-glass windows **S** 393–95
  tapestry **T** 22–24
  wood carving **W** 228
  See also Industrial arts
De Cosmos, Amor, Canadian journalist and premier **B** 404
De Coster, Charles see Coster, Charles de
De Dion Bonton, automobile **A** 544–45
Deed, or title, document of land ownership **R** 113
Deep Bay Crater, in Canada, picture **C** 420
Deep River, Negro spiritual, excerpt **N** 106
Deep-sea diving **D** 79–82
  aids for oceanographers **O** 41–42
  compared to skin diving **S** 188
  Piccard, Auguste **P** 244
  underwater exploration **U** 13–24
  See also Scuba diving; Skin diving; Underwater ex-
    ploration

Deep-sea fishes **F** 197; pictures **F** 198
  bioluminescence **B** 198
Deer, hoofed mammals **D** 83
  balance of nature **L** 258–59
  Catskill Game Farm, picture **Z** 377
  deer family, pictures **H** 214–15
  "follow the leader," social organization **A** 281
  hoofed mammals **H** 219–20
  hunting of **H** 290
  leg and hoof, diagram **F** 80
  pets **P** 180
  tracks, picture **A** 271
Deere, John, American industrialist **I** 84
Deer in the Garden, painting by Franz Marc **G** 168
Deer mice ·**R** 279
Deeter, Jasper, American theatrical director **T** 161
De facto segregation **S** 113
De Falla, Manuel see Falla, Manuel de
Defendant, in law **C** 527
Defense, United States Department of
  United States Air Force **U** 159–66
  United States Army **U** 166–75
  United States Navy **U** 189

Defense Intelligence Agency, agency of the U.S. Department of Defense that directs, manages, and controls the
intelligence resources of the department. This agency was
established in 1961.

Defense program, North America
  Canadian bases **C** 82
Deferments, for the draft **D** 290
Deficiency diseases **D** 189
  conquest of **D** 216
  food taboos **F** 334–35
Deficient numbers **N** 379–80
Deflation see Inflation and deflation
Defoe, Daniel, English journalist and novelist **E** 259–60
  children's literature **C** 236
  published first magazine, *The Review* **M** 14
  Robinson Crusoe, important to development of modern
    fiction **F** 111
  style and themes of his novels **N** 346
Defoliant (de-FO-li-ant), spray to remove leaves **C** 524

De Forest, Lee (1873–1961), American inventor, b. Council
Bluffs, Iowa. He invented the three-element electronic
tube, now called the triode, which is used as an amplifier
or transmitting tube and is basic to such electronic
instruments as radio and television. He also invented
the modern process for moving-picture sound tracks.
Picture **E** 147.
  inventions basic to radio and television **I** 345; **R** 53;
    T 70

Deformation, in topology **T** 220
Degania (de-ga-ni-YA), Israel **L** 28
Degas (d'GA), **Edgar,** French painter **D** 84
  Dancer on the Stage, drawing in pastels **F** 430
  French impressionist painting **F** 431
  modern art **M** 388
De Gasperi (de GA-spay-ri), **Alcide,** Italian statesman
  I 457
De Gaulle (d'GOLLE), **Charles,** French general and states-
  man **D** 84–85
  Free French forces organized **F** 419
  Gaullist party symbol **P** 381
  resignation, 1969 **F** 420
  with President Truman, picture **T** 300
Degenerate matter **M** 178
Degenerative diseases **D** 189
Degree days, for heating **W** 87

Degrees, units of measure
in geometry, measurement of angles **G** 124
latitude and longitude **L** 82, 83
measurement of time zones **T** 190–91
temperature scales **H** 88–90
Degrees, university and college **U** 205–06
Dehydration
dried fruits **D** 316–17
drying and freeze-drying of food **F** 348, 349; **S** 341
milk **D** 12
Deimos (DIE-mos), satellite of Mars **M** 107, 108
orbits of planets **P** 272–73

Deiphobus (de-IPH-o-bus), in Greek mythology, Trojan war leader and hero. The son of Priam and Hecuba and brother of Hector and Paris, he forced Helen to marry him after death of Paris. Deiphobus was killed by Odysseus, Menelaus, or Helen during sack of Troy.

Deirdre (DIR-dre), heroine of Irish legend. The prophecy that her beauty would bring banishment and death to heroes caused King Conchobar to hide her until she could marry him. She saw accidently and fell in love with Naoise, who took her to Scotland with his two brothers. The warrior Fergus was sent by Conchobar to bring them back. The brothers were killed, and Deirdre later died of grief.
Irish literature **I** 392

Deir el-Bahri (DAIR el-BAH-ri), Egyptian temple **E** 100;
picture **E** 103
Deism (DE-ism), system of thought **R** 294–95

De Jong (de YONG), **Meindert** (1909–), American author of children's books, b. Friesland, the Netherlands. He emigrated to United States in 1917. His works include *The Tower by the Sea* and *Smoke above the Lane. Journey from Peppermint Street* won the 1969 National Book Committee award.

De jure (de-JU-re) segregation **S** 113
Dek, numeral **N** 396
dekagram, unit of measure **W** 115
De Kalb, Baron see Kalb, Johann

Dekker, or **Decker, Thomas** (1570–1641?), English dramatist, b. London. He was the author of pamphlets, including *The Gull's Hornbook,* realistically describing London street life. With writer Ben Jonson and others, he collaborated on plays, including the comedy *The Shoemaker's Holiday.*
drama, history of **D** 296

De Kooning (de-KOO-ing), **Willem** (1904–), American painter, b. Rotterdam, the Netherlands. He moved to United States in 1926, later becoming associated with a group of abstract artists in New York City. He is considered a leader in American abstract expressionism, having gained recognition with his first one-man show, at the Egan Gallery in New York City (1948). He is particularly well-known for paintings of women in which he used abstract-expressionist techniques. His most notable works include *The Attic* and *Woman* series.
abstract expressionism in modern art **M** 397;
  U 122
Tree Grows in Naples, A, painting **M** 396

De Koven (d'KO-ven), **Reginald** (Henry Louis Reginald De Koven) (1859–1920), American composer, b. Middletown, Conn. Music critic for *Harper's Weekly,* New York *World* and New York *Herald,* he founded and conducted Philharmonic Orchestra in Washington, D.C. (1902–05).

His compositions include operettas *Robin Hood* and *The Begum,* operas *The Canterbury Pilgrims* and *Rip Van Winkle,* 400 songs, and incidental music.
operetta in the United States **O** 157

De Kruif (dek-RIFE), **Paul Henry** (1890–1971), American bacteriologist and writer, b. Zeeland, Mich. A bacteriologist at the University of Michigan (1912–17) and at the Rockefeller Institute (1920–22), he is best-known for his books and articles popularizing medical science. His books include *Our Medicine Men,* and *Microbe Hunters.*

Delacroix (del-la-CRWA), **Ferdinand Victor Eugène,**
French painter **D** 85; **P** 29
French painting **F** 425–26
illustration, his art as **I** 91
Orphan Girl at the Cemetery, painting **P** 27
romanticism in painting **P** 29
De la Mare, Walter, English poet
children's literature **C** 241
"Little Red Riding-Hood" **F** 29–32
"Silver" **F** 119

Delany, Martin Robinson (1812–1885), American Negro leader, physician, and army officer, b. Charles Town, Va. (now W.Va.). He attended Harvard Medical School. Delany worked to aid the Negro people and favored their return to Africa and formed the National Emigration Convention (1854). He served with Union Army in Civil War, during which he was the first Negro to attain rank of major in the U.S. Army. He wrote *The Condition, Elevation, Emigration, and Destiny of the Colored People of the United States, Politically Considered.*

De la Roche (d'la ROSH), **Mazo** (1885–1961), Canadian author, b. Toronto, Ontario. For over 30 years she wrote novels and short stories about the Whiteoak family in Ontario. The first, *Jalna,* was published in 1927. Her autobiography, *Ringing the Changes,* appeared in 1957.

Delaroche, Paul (Hippolyte Paul Delaroche) (1797–1856), French painter, b. Paris. He is noted for portraits and historical paintings, including *Death of Queen Elizabeth, Princes in the Tower,* and *Execution of Lady Jane Grey.* He is best-known for series of paintings in École des Beaux-Arts in Paris (1837–41).

DeLaval, Carl Gustaf see Laval, Carl Gustaf de
Delaware **D** 86–100
American colonies **A** 192
colonial life in America **C** 385–99
early Lenni-Lenape Indian settlements **I** 185
flag of New Sweden **F** 228
Founding Fathers of the United States **F** 395

Delaware, Lord (Thomas West, also known as Baron De La Warr) (1577–1618), English administrator, b. Hampshire. He served in Parliament and fought in the Low Countries and Ireland before becoming a council member of the Virginia Company. Appointed first governor and captain general of the Colony of Virginia, he sailed to Virginia in 1610 with 150 colonists, arriving in time to save the settlement from collapse. He returned to England in 1611 and worked to gain aid for the Virginia colony.

Delaware, University of **D** 95
Delaware Aqueduct, for New York City **A** 344
Delaware Memorial Bridge, picture **D** 94
Delaware River, United States **R** 243
river system in Delaware **D** 88
Washington crossing **R** 202

Delaware Swedish Colonial Society   D 86
Delaware Water Gap, New Jersey, Pennsylvania   N 166;
P 141
Delayed-reaction tests
animal intelligence, measures of   A 286
Deledda, Grazia, Italian novelist   I 480

De Leeuw (d'LAY-oo), **Adèle Louise** (1899–   ), American
writer, b. Hamilton, Ohio. Author of more than 30 books
(many of them for children), Adèle de Leeuw has often
collaborated with her sister, **Cateau de Leeuw** (1903–   ),
an artist and writer. Some of their books done jointly are
The Caboose Club, Apron Strings, and *Love Is the
Beginning.*

Delegated powers, in government   U 139
De Lesseps, Ferdinand, Vicomte *see* Lesseps, Ferdinand,
Vicomte de
Delft, the Netherlands   N 118
Delftware, pottery   P 417; picture   P 416
Delgado (del-GA-do), **José Matías,** Roman Catholic
priest, El Salvador liberator   E 184
Delhi, India   D 101–03
twin cities of Delhi and New Delhi   I 122

Delhi Sultanate, former Muslim state in northern India.
It encompassed much of northern India and was ruled
by six dynasties of slave kings (1206–1526). It was
begun by Aibak Kutb-ud-din, who assumed title of
sultan of Delhi (1206), but it was reduced to area of
Jumna Valley after invasion and desolation by Tamerlane (1398). The state was dissolved (1526) with establishment of Mogul empire under Babur.

Delian (DE-li-an) **League,** early confederacy of Greek
city-states   G 338

Delibes (del-EBE), **Léo** (Clément-Philibert-Léo) (1836–
1891), French composer, b. St. Germain-du-Val. He was
professor of composition at the Paris Conservatory
(1881–91) and is noted for his ballets *Coppelia* and *Sylvia*
and for such operas as *Le Roi l'a Dit* and *Lakmé.*

Delicatessen, origin of the term   F 340
food in a delicatessen, picture   B 385

Delilah (de-LILE-ah), in Old Testament (Judges 16), a
Philistine woman from the valley of Sorek who was loved
by Samson of Israel. She found that the secret of
Samson's great strength lay in his long hair, so she had
it cut off and betrayed him to the Philistines, who were
then able to capture him.

Delirium, state of   M 223
Delius, (DE-li-us), **Frederick,** English composer   E 271;
N 107
Della Porta, Giambattista *see* Porta, Giambattista della
Della Robbia, Luca *see* Robbia, Luca della

Della Robbia (RO-bia) **family,** Italian sculptors and ceram-
ists, b. Florence. **Luca** (1400?–82) experimented with the
technique of covering terra-cotta sculpture with enamel
glaze, founded the Della Robbia workshop, and established the name of Robbia ware. One of his more important sculptures is the cantoria ("singing gallery")
in the museum of the Florentine cathedral. **Andrea**
(1437–1525), Luca's nephew, adapted the polychrome
glaze technique to large, decorative reliefs and is known
for the roundels in the Florentine foundlings' work.
Giovanni (1469?–1529?), Andrea's son, sculpted coarser
works than his father or his younger brother, **Girolamo**
(1488–1556), who executed terra-cotta decoration for

royal buildings in France.
Renaissance art   R 163

Dello Joio (DEL-lo JOI-o), **Norman** (1913–   ), American composer, organist, pianist, and teacher, b. New
York, N.Y. Descended from Italian musical family, his
compositions include opera *Triumph of St. Joan,
Magnificat* for orchestra, ballet *Wilderness Stair,* choral
work *Western Star.* He won Pulitzer Prize (1957) for
Meditations on Ecclesiastes.

Dells of the Wisconsin River   W 203; picture   W 194
Delmarva Peninsula, United States   D 88;   V 346

Del Monaco (del MON-a-co), **Mario** (1915–   ), Italian
opera singer, b. Florence. He began career in Europe
and then became prominent member of Metropolitan
Opera company (1951). He is noted for roles in *Otello,
Manon Lescaut, Lucia di Lammermoor,* and *Andrea
Chénier.*

Delmonico's, restaurant in New York City   R 186
Delos (DE-los), Greece   I 429
Delphi, Greece   G 338
Oracle, in Greek mythology   G 361
Delphinidae, or delphinids, mammal family of dolphins
and whales   W 147; picture   D 271
Delphiniums *see* Larkspur
Delta Cephei (CE-phie), variable star   S 408
discoveries of pulsating stars   A 475
Delta Plan, the Netherlands   N 118
Deltas, earth deposits at river mouths   R 238
floodplain, Louisiana   L 350–51; picture   E 283
Ganges-Brahmaputra rivers of India   G 25
Mississippi River   M 365
Nile River   N 261
origin of the name   D 1
Delvaux, Paul, Belgian painter   B 128
Demand deposits, banking   B 46
Demantoid, gemstone   G 75
Demarcation, Line of *see* Tordesillas, Treaty of
Demerol *see* Meperidine
Demersal eggs, of fishes   F 195
Demeter (de-ME-ter), Greek goddess   G 359–60
Demetz, Frédéric Auguste, French prison reformer   P 470
Demilitarized Zone (DMZ), in Vietnam   V 335

De Mille, Agnes George (1905?–   ), American dancer and
choreographer, b. New York, N.Y. She made her debut as
a ballet dancer in 1928. She is famous for the
choreography of *Rodeo,* a ballet set in the Old West, and
was choreographer for *Oklahoma!, Brigadoon,* and
Carousel. She is credited with bringing ballet to musical
comedies. She has written several books.

De Mille, Cecil B., American motion-picture producer
M 474; picture   M 477
De Mille, James, Canadian writer
Maiden of Passamaquoddy, excerpt   N 273
Democracy   D 104–05
ancient Athens   A 228
Aristotle's idea of   G 275
Bill of Rights   B 177–80
education in early Athens a preparation for   E 62–63
Fascism contrasted with   F 63
first democratic parliament, Iceland's Althing   I 44
freedom of religion, speech, and press   F 457
government, forms of   G 273–78
Homestead Act, 1862, free land   P 506
initiative, referendum, and recall   O 205
Jacksonian   J 5–6
journalism, duties of   J 143

Mayflower Compact   **A** 186;   **M** 185;   **P** 344
parliamentary procedure   **P** 79–80
pioneer experience in America   **P** 262
political parties   **P** 378–82
propaganda   **P** 481
Solon, founder of Athenian democracy   **S** 252
town meetings in American colonies   **A** 188
Democratic Party, United States   P 380–81
Bryan, William Jennings   **B** 415–16
symbols   **C** 126;   **P** 382
Who were the Barnburners?   **V** 275
Democrat-Republican Party, United States   P 380
symbol   **P** 379

Democritus (de-MOC-rit-us) (Abderite) (460?–370? B.C.),
Greek philosopher, b. Abdera, Thrace. He developed
atomic theory of Leucippus, which taught that matter
consists of tiny particles called atoms. He believed that,
since form of atoms determines material qualities, soul
consists of finest and most agile atoms. He also
developed an ethical system that urged tempering
pleasure with avoidance of excess. He was known as the
Laughing Philosopher because of his optimism.
atomic theory in the history of science   **C** 206–07;
P 230;   **S** 62

Demography (dem-OG-raphy), statistical study of popula-
tion   **P** 397
what sociologists study   **S** 227
Demoiselles d'Avignon, Les, by Picasso   **M** 390
Demonstrations
battle against segregation   **N** 104b, 105;   **S** 115
Demonstrative pronouns   P 90
Demosthenes (de-MOS-the-nese), Greek orator   **O** 180
Greek language and literature   **G** 355

Dempsey, Jack (William Harrison Dempsey) (1895–   ),
American boxer, b. Manassa, Col. His first fights were
in western mining camps. He won heavyweight title from
Jess Willard in 1919. Nicknamed the Manassa Mauler,
he defended his title until 1926, when he lost to Gene
Tunney. In 1927 he lost rematch with Tunney, who
benefited from famous "long count" after being knocked
down.
the "Manassa Mauler" of boxing   **B** 353;   **C** 415

Denarius (de-NAR-ius), Roman coin   **M** 411
Denatured alcohol   A 147
Denby, Edwin, American politician
Teapot Dome scandal   **C** 496
Dendrites, of brain cell bodies   **B** 364
Dendrochronology (den-dro-cro-NOL-ogy), dating past
events by tree rings   **T** 287
Deneb, star   **S** 407
constellations   **C** 492
Dengue (DENG-e), disease   **I** 283
Denham, Dixon, British explorer of Africa   **S** 8

Denim, a durable cloth made of coarse cotton. Originally
called "serge de Nîmes" after the French city where sails
of the cloth were made in the 15th century, it has become
a popular material for informal clothing. In the familiar
indigo-blue color, it is used for making dungarees and
jackets for men and women.

Denis (DEN-iss), or **Denys, Saint,** martyred priest who
lived during 3rd century A.D., b. Italy. A patron saint of
France, he was sent on mission to Gaul, where Church
was persecuted. He was beheaded in Paris in 275 (?).
His feast day is celebrated on October 9.

Denishawn, school for dancers   **D** 33

Denmark   D 106–13
chinaware factory, picture   **C** 174
English literature, early influence   **E** 245–46
favorite foods   **F** 342
flag   **F** 243; picture **F** 239
furniture design   **F** 510
Greenland   **G** 367–71
Iceland   **I** 45
invasion by Hitler, 1940   **W** 288
national anthem   **N** 21
national dances   **D** 30
old age assistance plans   **O** 98
Scandinavia, origin of the word   **S** 49
Scandinavian literature   **S** 50–53
Denner, Johann, German flute and clarinet maker
C 329
Denominations, or sects, in religion
Protestantism   **P** 483–85
Christianity, history of   **C** 288–89
Denominator, of a fraction   **F** 398

Denonville (de-NON-veel), **Jacques René de Brisay,
Marquis de** (1642?–1710), French official in Canada. He
replaced La Barre as governor of Canada (1685–89) and
tried to check Iroquois by building fort at Niagara but
was unable to crush remaining Iroquois tribes, who
massacred inhabitants of village of Lachine (1689).

Denotation, of a word   **S** 118
Density, in physics   **M** 171–172
gravity of planet Jupiter   **P** 275–76
liquids   **L** 309–10
metals   **M** 226
specific gravity   **F** 253;   **M** 172
why some bodies sink and others float
F 250–51, 253
Density, population   P 394–95; diagram **P** 396
See also country, province, and state articles
Dental caries (CARRIES), disease of the teeth   **T** 48
care of the teeth   **H** 85
fluoridation   **F** 283
Dental hygienist (hy-GE-nist)   **D** 114, 115
Dental pulp, soft substance of teeth   **T** 48
Dent corn   C 506
Dentin, hard substance of teeth   **T** 48
Dentists   D 114–15
care of the teeth   **H** 85
gold used by   **G** 248
silver amalgams used by   **S** 182
teeth   **T** 47–49

D'Entrecasteaux (d'on-tre-ca-STO) **Islands,** island group
in the Pacific, off the southeastern coast of New Guinea.
The island group is made up of three main mountainous
islands—Goodenough, Fergusson, and Normanby—and
many islets and atolls. The islands are part of the
Territory of Papua, which is administered by Australia.

Denver, capital of Colorado   **D** 116
trade and transportation center   **C** 412–13
United States Mint   **M** 338
Denver, James, governor of Kansas Territory   **D** 116
Deodorants (de-O-der-ants), body deodorizers   **D** 117
Deodorizers   D 117
Deoxyribonucleic acid see DNA
Deoxyribonucleotides (de-oxy-ribe-o-NU-cleo-tides),   nu-
cleic acid chains   **B** 291
Deoxyribose (de-oxy-RIBE-ose), body sugar   **B** 291

De Palma, Ralph (1883?–1956), American automobile
racer, b. Italy. He reportedly won 2,557 of 2,889 races

De Palma, Ralph (continued)
(1908–34)—allegedly more than won by any other driver up to his death. De Palma was elected to the Racing Hall of Fame.

Department stores D 117–20
    advertising **A** 27–34
    retail stores **R** 188, 189
    selling **S** 116–17,
    See *also* Supermarkets

Deportation, banishment. In law, deportation means removal from a country of an alien whose presence is illegal or considered dangerous.

Deposits, bank **B** 46
Depressants, drugs **D** 326
    abuse of .**D** 330–31
Depression of the 1930's **D** 121, 122; **E** 51; **U** 26
    American literature during **A** 212
Depressions and recessions
        D 121–22
    bank failures and financial panic **B** 47–48
    economic stability **E** 50, 51
    Federal Reserve System **B** 48, 50; **I** 253
    Hoover's administration **H** 224
    inflation and deflation **I** 252, 253
    Panic of 1837 **V** 271, 274
    panics due to stock speculation **S** 429
    Roosevelt's New Deal program **R** 321
    unemployment insurance **U** 26
    See *also* Inflation and deflation
DePriest, Oscar, American congressman **N** 99
Depth charges, antisubmarine weapons **S** 446
Depth perception, stereoscopic vision **P** 490–91
De Quincey, Thomas, English essayist **E** 262
    quoted on nonsense rhymes **N** 272

Derain (der-AN), **André** (1880–1954), French painter, b. Chatou. He was a leader, with artists Maurice de Vlaminck and Henri Matisse, of fauvist art movement. His most noted painting from this period is *London Bridge.* Later he turned to a more realistic style. His works include *The Fruit Bowl* and *Window on the Park.*
    fauvism in modern art **M** 388, 390

Derby (DAR-be), English horse race **H** 231
Derby (DER-bi), hat, picture **H** 55
Deringer (DERR-in-ger), **Henry, Jr.,** American gunsmith **G** 421
Dermatologist, skin specialist **D** 239
Dermoptera (der-MOP-ter-a), order of mammals **M** 62, 69
De Rochemont, Louis, American motion-picture producer **M** 477
Derricks, hoisting machines **H** 144–45
    oil-drilling derrick **P** 171–72; pictures **P** 169, 172
Derringers, small guns **G** 421
Derry see Londonderry

Dervish (from Persian word for "mendicant" or "beggar"). Term refers to members of certain Muslim orders known for devotional exercises that use religious chants accompanied by increasingly rapid physical movement, such as whirling or dancing.

Desalting (desalinization) see Water desalting
Descartes (day-CART), **René,** French mathematician and philosopher **D** 123
    analytic geometry **M** 157
    Cartesian dualism **P** 192
    father of modern psychology **P** 493

"I think, therefore I am," foundation of modern philosophy **F** 438
    universal language, plan for **U** 194
Descent from the Cross, The, painting by Giotto **P** 19
Descent from the Cross, The, painting by Rogier van der Weyden **D** 353
Desdemona (des-de-MON-a), character in Shakespeare's *Othello* **O** 236
Desegregation
    United States Supreme Court ruling, 1954 **S** 115
Deseret (des-er-ET), Utah, name of early Mormon settlement **S** 22
    provisional government set up by Mormons in Utah **U** 254
    Young, Brigham **Y** 353
Desert animals **D** 124; pictures **A** 270
    birds of **B** 226
    camels **C** 34
    kangaroo rats **R** 277; picture **K** 257
    lizards **L** 319–20
Desert Fox see Rommel, Erwin
Desertion and non-support, in divorce **D** 235
Desert plants **D** 124
    cacti **C** 3–4
    defenses **P** 283
    leaves **P** 295
    wild flowers **W** 171
Deserts **D** 123–31
    Africa **A** 46
    climates, effects of **C** 345; pictures **C** 344
    Death Valley, California **D** 131
    deserts can be made to serve man, pictures **G** 106
    irrigation **I** 408–10
    make a desert terrarium **T** 104
    nomadic life **N** 271
    oases **O** 2–3
    oil well in Libya, picture **L** 202
    Rub' al-khali, desert in Saudi Arabia, picture **A** 446
    Sahara **S** 8
    soils **S** 233
    Sudan, northeast central Africa **S** 447–48
    tropics **T** 294–95

De Seversky, Alexander Procofieff (1894–   ), American aviator and aircraft engineer, b. Tiflis, Russia. He invented various airplane devices, such as automatic bombsight and landing gear for use on land, water, or ice.

Design **D** 132–37
    airplane **A** 558–59
    automobiles **A** 548, 552
    book design **B** 323–36, 331
    bottles **B** 341
    collage **C** 376–77
    Byzantine patterns **B** 486–87
    clothing industry **C** 354
    commercial art **C** 425
    drawing **D** 303, 305
    dyes used in textile printing **D** 372
    fans **F** 43
    fashion designer **F** 66, 70
    first playing cards **C** 107
    folk art **F** 290–96
    furniture design **F** 505–10
    glass **G** 229
    graphic arts, Japanese prints **G** 303
    illuminated manuscripts **I** 87–88
    Index of American Design **N** 41
    Indian beadwork **I** 158
    industrial **I** 229–32
    interior decorators **I** 303

Islamic art I 417, 422; picture I 418
jewelry J 92–101
kaleidoscope, use of K 166
lace patterns L 19
mechanical drawing M 197
mechanical engineers design engines E 205
medieval books, how made B 319–21
modelmaking M 385
posters P 404
sculpture S 90–105
See also Decorative arts
De Smet (d'SMET), Pierre, Belgian-born missionary
Idaho I 68
Montana M 441
Des Moines (d'MOIN), capital of Iowa I 368–69
Des Moines River, Iowa, picture I 369
De Soto, Hernando, Spanish explorer D 144
Alabama A 126
Arkansas A 431
exploration of the New World E 383–84
Florida F 272
Georgia G 146
Mississippi M 362
Des Prez, Josquin see Josquin des Prez

Dessalines (day-sa-LENE), Jean Jacques (1758–1806), Haitian revolutionary and emperor (1804–06), b. Grande-Rivière-du-Nord. With British aid, he drove French from Haiti (1803), proclaimed Haitian independence, established republic (1804), and abolished slavery, making Haiti first free nation in Latin America. As a result of his growing despotism, he was assassinated in rebel ambush (1806).
history of Haiti H 10; N 93

Dessau (DESS-ow), Germany
Dessau Bauhaus B 104–05
Desserts
baked goods B 388–89
ice cream I 31–34
party refreshments P 89
recipes R 115, 116
Dessert wines W 189
De Stijl (da STILE), Dutch art movement
Mondrian, Piet M 408
Destroyers
United States Navy U 192
Destroying angel amanitas (am-a-NY-tas), poisonous mushrooms M 521
causes death by cell destruction P 322
fungi F 499
Destructive distillation D 225
Detectives
city police P 376
Federal Bureau of Investigation F 76–77
Postal Inspection Service P 410
Scotland Yard L 337; P 373
Detective stories see Mystery, detective, and suspense stories

Détente (day-TONT), a relaxing, or easing off. It refers particularly to the relaxing, or lessening, of strained relations and tensions between nations.

Detergents D 145–49
additives to lubricants L 371
dry cleaning D 337–38
environment, pollution of E 272d–272e
water conservation problem, picture C 483
water pollution W 58–59
Detergent tablets D 149
Determiners, in grammar G 289

Detonation (det-o-NATION), explosion E 389
Detonator (DET-o-nator), explosive charge E 391
Detritus (de-TRY-tus), loose particles, products of disintegration
plant and animal debris in ocean L 231
Detroit, Michigan D 150–51; M 270; pictures D 150, M 263
automobile industry, history of A 547–49

Dett, Robert Nathaniel (1882–1943), American composer, Negro, b. Drummondville, Quebec, Canada. He used folk music of Negro race in his classical themes. His works include oratorio *The Ordering of Moses* and symphony *An American Sampler.*
Negro spirituals N 107

Deucalion (deu-CAY-lion), in Greek mythology, son of Prometheus. When Zeus sent the Deluge, Deucalion with his wife, Pyrrha, escaped in wooden chest and sailed for 9 days and nights, finally resting on summit of Mount Parnassus. He was told by an oracle to cast his mother's bones behind him, and he interpreted this as meaning stones of mother earth. His stones became men, Pyrrha's became women. Deucalion was the Greek Noah.

Deus ex machina (DAY-us ex MAC-in-a), term in literature, and drama D 294
Deuterium (deu-TE-ri-um), hydrogen isotope A 487; diagrams E 153
nuclear energy N 356
Deuteronomy (deu-ter-ON-omy), book of Bible B 154

Deutsch (DOITCH), Babette (1895–), American poet and novelist, b. New York, N.Y. She translated extensively from Russian and German with her husband, Avrahm Yarmolinsky. Her books of verse include *Banners, Fire for the Night,* and *One Part Love.* She is author of a number of books on criticism and co-author of children's book *More Tales from Faraway Folk.*

Deutsches Museum, Munich, Germany M 513
Deutschland-Lied, national anthem of Federal Republic of Germany (West Germany) N 18
De Valera (de va-LARE-a), Eamon, president of Ireland I 391; picture P 456a

De Valois (d' val-WA), Dame Ninette (1898–), British choreographer, b. Baltiboys, Ireland. She was permanent member of Diaghilev Ballet company from 1923 to 1925 and founded Sadler's Wells Ballet and Sadler's Wells Theatre Ballet (1931), which were granted title of Royal Ballet by Queen Elizabeth II (1957). De Valois choreographed a number of ballets, including *Job, Checkmate,* and *The Rake's Progress.*
ballet in England B 26

Developable Column, sculpture by Pevsner, picture M 393
Developing, in photography P 217
Developing countries and areas
anthropologists aid A 305
consumer education and government protection of the consumer C 494a
foreign aid programs F 368
natural resources N 59–60
Peace Corps P 101–03
poverty P 424–424b
tropics T 294–95
United Nations interest in U 88
Developments, housing, picture R 112

Devi (DAY-vi), in Hinduism, great mother goddess. She is

Devi (continued)

daughter of Himalaya mountains and wife and female energy of Shiva, destroyer god. In her gentle aspect, she assumes form of Guari (yellow), Parvati (mountaineer), Uma (light), and Jaganmata (mother of the world). She is more frequently worshiped in her terrible aspect as Durga (inaccessible), Kali (the black one), Chandi (fierce).

Devil (from Greek *diabolos*, meaning "slanderer"), in Christian tradition, angel who rebelled against God and as a consequence was expelled from heaven into hell. Ruler of hell and tempter of mankind, he is represented as serpent, dragon, leviathan, or flash of lightning. Devil is known also as Satan, Lucifer, or Beelzebub.

Devilfish see Manta rays

Devil's advocate, popular name for Promoter of the Faith, official of the Congregation of Rites in Roman Catholic Church. He examines evidence of alleged miracles and virtues of a candidate for beatification or canonization. Term also means one who supports losing cause for sake of argument.

Devils Island, French Guiana **G** 397
Dreyfus, Alfred **D** 316
prison colony **P** 468
Devils Tower National Monument, Wyoming **W** 332; picture **W** 333
first national monument **N** 49

Devil worshipers, or **Yezidis** (from modern Persian, meaning "worshiper of God"), religious sect found primarily near Mosul, Iraq, and also in Caucasus and Armenia. They worship devil as a redeemed angel and an active agent of supreme god. The devil is represented by peacock. Devil worshipers consider themselves descendants of Adam alone and thus isolate themselves from mankind.

Devlin, (Josephine) **Bernadette** (1947–   ), civil rights leader in Northern Ireland, b. County Tyrone. While a university student, she rose to prominence as a leader of the People's Democracy, a radical group that was formed following civil rights demonstrations in Northern Ireland late in 1968. Elected to the Parliament of the United Kingdom from Mid-Ulster in 1969 and 1970, she is an active leader of Ulster Catholics.
Northern Ireland and Ireland **U** 73

Devolution, War of (1667–68), attempt by Louis XIV of France to gain Spanish (Belgian) Netherlands through death of his father-in-law, Philip IV of Spain. The attempt was blocked by triple alliance of England, Holland, and Sweden. The word "devolution" is derived from a custom in the Netherlands for survivor of married couple to be entitled to use of property, while title is passed to children.

Devonian (de-VO-nian) **period,** in geology **F** 384; picture **F** 386
Age of fishes **F** 181–82
Dévote (day-VOTE), **Sainte,** patron saint of Monaco **M** 406
De Voto (de VO-to), **Bernard,** American writer **A** 214

De Vries (de VREES), **Hugo** (1848–1935), Dutch botanist, b. Haarlem. He was first to present theory that new kinds of living things are produced as a result of mutations, or sudden and inheritable changes, in plants or animals, and one of three men who, working separately, rediscovered (1900) Mendel's laws of heredity.

Dew **F** 289
humidity indicators, hygrometers **W** 80–81

Dewar, Sir James (1842–1923), Scottish physicist and chemist, b. Kincardine-on-Forth. He is noted for studies on specific heat and properties of matter at low temperatures. In course of research he invented Dewar flask (forerunner of vacuum flask, or thermos bottle), discovered liquid and solid hydrogen, and invented cordite (smokeless gunpowder pressed into cordlike shapes).

Dewberries **G** 301
Dewclaws, toes **H** 208
Dewey, George, American admiral **S** 375
Manila Bay, battle of **P** 190
Dewey, John, American philosopher and educator **D** 151
education, influence on **E** 76
development of kindergarten **K** 243
Dewey, Melvil, American librarian **L** 188

Dewey, Thomas E. (1902–71), American lawyer and politician, b. Owosso, Michigan. He won national recognition as prosecutor in investigation of organized crime in New York City (1935–37). Dewey was later district attorney for New York County (1937–38), governor of New York (1942–54), and Republican presidential candidate (1944 and 1948).
elections of 1944 and 1948 **R** 324; **T** 301

Dewey Decimal System, of book classification **L** 183–84

De Witt Clinton, first steam locomotive to be operated in New York State (1831). The train ran with three coaches on Mohawk and Hudson Railroad between Albany and Schenectady and was named for promoter of Erie Canal.

DEW line see Distant Early Warning line
Dew point, or saturation temperature **F** 288
cloud formation **C** 358
hygrometer **W** 80–81
Dextrose, or glucose, kind of sugar **B** 290; **S** 453
Dhole (DOLE), wild dog of Asia **D** 250
Dhows (DOWS), sailing vessels, pictures **L** 29, **M** 303
Diabetes (dya-BE-tese), disease **D** 195–96
biochemists learned how to make hormones **B** 183
conquest of **D** 217
discovery of insulin by Banting **B** 52
metabolic deseases **D** 189
saccharin, use of **S** 455
Diacritical (dy-a-CRIT-ic-al) **marks,** to show pronunciation **P** 478
phonics **P** 194–95
Diadem, headband, picture **D** 71
Diaghilev (d'YA-ghi-lif), **Sergei,** Russian ballet producer **B** 26
kept ballet a vital art **D** 26
Prokofiev, Sergei, friend of **P** 477
Diagnoses (dy-ag-NO-sese), of illnesses **D** 238
examining the heart **H** 86b
medicine, tools, tests, techniques **M** 201–02, 208d–211
X rays **X** 339–41
Dialects **D** 152
Castilian Spanish **S** 352, 366
Chinese language **C** 258–59
descriptive linguistics **L** 301
French **F** 433
German **G** 172
Italian language, development of **I** 474
mimicked by humorists **H** 279
pronunciation **P** 478

Dialogues of Plato, The, conversations between Socrates and his students **P** 332
    Greek literature **G** 353–54
Diameter (di-AM-et-er), of a circle **G** 127
Diamondback terrapins T 332
Diamond Head, volcanic crater in Honolulu, Hawaii **H** 69; picture **H** 72
Diamond Jubilee, of Queen Victoria **V** 332
Diamonds D 153–56
    abrasive for grinding and polishing **G** 387
    beliefs about **G** 74
    carbon form **C** 106
    crystals **C** 542, 544, 546
    deposits in Arkansas **A** 418
    discovery by a Boer farmer **S** 273
    France's necklace scandal **J** 99–100
    gemstones **G** 69, 71
    jewelry trade in precious gems **J** 93
    mining **M** 320
    Mohs' scale of relative hardness of gemstones **G** 69
Diamond State, nickname for Delaware **D** 86
Diamond Sutra, Buddhist book, woodcut from **G** 302
Diana, Roman goddess **G** 360
    story of the Dog Star, Sirius **D** 47
    temple of Diana **W** 214–15
Diaper laundries L 84
Diaphone, fog signal **L** 277
Diaphram (DY-a-phram), muscle **B** 278; diagram **B** 277
    voice training **V** 375
Diaphragm, of a camera **P** 202
Diaphragm, of a telephone transmitter **T** 55
Diaries D 157–58
    Adams, John Quincy **A** 12
    American literature **A** 196
    English diarists **E** 254
    ships' logs or logbooks, official records of data of a voyage **C** 417
Diary of Anne Frank, excerpts **D** 157, 158
Dias, Bartholomeu, Portuguese explorer **E** 374; **P** 403
Dias, Diogo, Portuguese sea captain
    Madagascar discovered by **M** 49
Diaspora (dy-ASP-o-ra), scattering, or dispersion, of people
    destruction and dispersion of Jewish State **J** 105–06
    Orthodox Eastern Churches **O** 228
Diastole, action of the heart **H** 86
Diastolic (dy-as-TOL-ic) **pressure,** of blood **D** 199; **M** 208f, 208g

Diathermy (from Greek words *dia,* meaning "through," and *therme,* meaning "heat"), medical or surgical treatment that creates heat in body tissues by means of high-frequency electric currents. It is used to relieve pain; or with higher temperatures, to destroy tumors.

Diatoms, algae **A** 157; **M** 280; pictures **A** 156, **M** 281
    life, distribution of **L** 229
    ocean life **O** 37
    plankton **P** 279–80
Díaz, Porfirio, Mexican president **M** 249–50
Díaz de Bivar, Rodrigo, see Cid, El
Díaz de Guzmán, Ruy, Argentine author **A** 390
Díaz del Castillo, Bernal, Spanish explorer **L** 70
Díaz de Solís, Juan see Solís, Juan Díaz de
Díaz Ordaz, Gustavo, Mexican president **M** 250
Dice
    dominoes related to **D** 284
    probability theories **P** 473
Dichloro-diphenyltrichloro-ethane see DDT
Dick, Ayzik Meir, Yiddish publisher **Y** 350
Dick Act, 1903 **N** 43
Dickens, Charles, English writer **D** 158–60

David Copperfield, excerpt **D** 160–61
    modern fiction **F** 110–11
    Oliver Twist, excerpt **D** 161–63
    place in English literature **E** 264
    themes of his novels **N** 346
Dickinson, Emily, American poet **D** 163–64
    American literature **A** 206
    "Bird Came Down the Walk, A" **D** 164
    "I'll Tell You How the Sun Rose" **D** 164
Dickinson, John, American statesman and writer **D** 99
    American literature **A** 198
    author of early patriotic song **N** 22

Dick test, test for susceptibility to scarlet fever. The test was named for physicians George and Gladys Dick, who invented it (1924). An injection into skin of diluted filtrate of streptococcus, which causes scarlet fever, produces small area of redness within 12 hours in those who are susceptible to the disease.

Dicotyledons (dy-cot-il-E-dons), or dicots, seed plants **P** 299
    plant kingdom, main divisions of the **P** 292
Dictaphone, pictures **I** 232, **O** 56
Dictation machines O 57
Dictatorship
    Fascism **F** 63–64
    Hitler, Adolf **H** 139–40
    Mussolini, Benito **M** 552
    Nazism **N** 70–71
    propaganda **P** 481
    rise of dictators before World War II **W** 284–86
Dictionaries D 164–65
    building a vocabulary **V** 372
    reading instruction **R** 109
    reference books **R** 129
    research methods **R** 183
    scientific names **T** 32
    spelling, use in **S** 378
    Webster, Noah **W** 99
Didactic poems, poems that teach **P** 354
Diddley, Bo, American rock music performer **R** 262c
Diderot (di-DRO), **Denis,** French philosopher **F** 439
    edited famous encyclopedia **E** 197
Dido (DIDE-o), queen of Carthage
    Aeneas and Dido **A** 35
Dido and Aeneas (e-NE-as), opera by Purcell **E** 270
Didrikson, Babe see Zaharias, Mildred
Didymus see Thomas, Saint
Die casting, type of molding **D** 166, 167
    of metals **M** 230–31
Diefenbaker (DE-fen-baker), **John George,** Canadian statesman **D** 165

Die is cast, the, expression meaning a step has been taken from which it is impossible to retreat, supposedly said by Julius Caesar as he crossed Rubicon river to invade Italy.

Diem, Ngo Dinh see Ngo Dinh Diem
Dienbienphu (d'yen-b'yen-PHU), Democratic Republic of Vietnam (North Vietnam) **V** 334c, 334d
Diencephalon (dy-en-CEPH-a-lon), of the brain **B** 366
Dieppe (di-EPP) **Raid,** 1942 **W** 296
Dies, for shaping and cutting materials **D** 166–67
    bronze and brass, forging of **B** 410
    die casting of metal **M** 230–31
    jewelry stamping **J** 100–01
    steel wire **I** 401
    plastics **P** 329–30
    wire **W** 190a
Diesel (DE-zel), **Rudolf,** German inventor **D** 168–69

Diesel engines D 168–71; **E** 211
  bulldozers and other construction equipment
    B 446–48
  internal-combustion engines **I** 307–08
  locomotives **L** 328, 332; picture **L** 331
  railroads **R** 79
  ships **S** 161
  submarines **S** 443
Diesel locomotives L 328, 332; picture **L** 331
  railroads **R** 79
Diet H 82
  aging effected by **A** 85
  food around the world **F** 331–43
  sick person's diet **N** 414–15
  wise food planning **N** 417–19
  See also Nutrition

Diet, a legislative assembly. Word is used for parliaments
in some countries—among them Denmark, Germany and
Japan—and for councillors' assemblies of Holy Roman
Empire, as in Worms, Diet of (1521).
  Japanese National Diet **J** 40

Dietary laws F 334
  Jewish **J** 116
Dietetics (diet-ET-ics), study of how body uses foods
    B 182–83

Dietrich (DE-trick), **Marlene** (Maria Magdalena Dietrich)
(1904–), American actress, b. Berlin, Germany. She
achieved international recognition for German film *The
Blue Angel.* She went to the United States (1930). Her
many pictures include *Destry Rides Again* and *Witness
for the Prosecution.* She made her debut on Broadway in
1967 in a one-woman concert. This performance won her a
Tony Award from the League of New York Theaters.

Differential gears, in automobiles **A** 544
Diffraction, of light **L** 271–72
Diffraction gratings, for measuring light wavelengths
    L 272
  spectroscopes **S** 464
Diffusion, in physics **G** 58
  osmosis **O** 233–35
  principle use in dyeing process **D** 370
  processes in animal cells **C** 163
Digestion B 274–75; diagram **D** 202
  bacteria aid **B** 12
  Beaumont's studies of **B** 109
  birds **B** 202, 221
  chemistry of **B** 294–95
  early studies **M** 207
  health **H** 82–85
  insects **I** 270–71
  stomachs of ruminants, or cud-chewing animals
    H 208
Digestive system, of the body, diagram **D** 202
Digital computers C 450; **T** 54–55
Digitalis (digit-AL-is), drug **D** 323
  drugs that act on particular organs **D** 326
  heart disease, used for **D** 198; **H** 86c
  poisonous plants used as medicine **P** 321
Digraphs, letters joined to make a single sound **I** 254
Dihedral (dy-HE-dral) **tilting,** of airplane wings **A** 554
Dikes, embankments **D** 16
  "Leak in the Dike," poem by Phoebe Cary **C** 237
  protect from floods, picture **F** 256
  reclaimed land in the Netherlands **N** 118
  See also Levees

Dillon, Douglas (Clarence Douglas Dillon) (1909–),
American banker and diplomat, b. Geneva, Switzerland.

After a successful career as a banker and in naval
service during World War II, Dillon became active in
Republican politics. He has served as ambassador to
France (1953–57), undersecretary of state for economic
affairs (1958–59), undersecretary of state (1959–60), and
secretary of the treasury (1960–65). He became president
of the Metropolitan Museum of Art (1970).

Dillon, George (1906–68), American poet, b. Jacksonville,
Fla. Except during military leave in World War II, Dillon
edited *Poetry* magazine from 1937 to 1950. Earlier he
had written two volumes of poems—*The Flowering
Stone,* which won the Pulitzer prize (1931), and *Boy in
the Wind.* With Edna St. Vincent Millay he made an
English translation of Baudelaire's *Fleurs du Mal.*

Dill seed, spice **S** 382; picture **S** 381

Di Maggio (di MAJ-io), **Joe** (Joseph Paul Di Maggio)
(1914–), American baseball player, b. Martinez, Calif.
Outfielder with N.Y. Yankees (1936–43, 1946–51), he was
Most Valuable Player in American League (1939, 1941,
1947) and•set record for hitting safely in 56 consecutive
games. His lifetime batting average is .325. He was
elected to Baseball Hall of Fame (1955). Picture **B** 76.

Dime novels, early paperback books **P** 58
Dime stores see Variety Stores
Dimethyl (di-METH-il) **ether**
  structural formula **C** 200

Diminishing returns, law of, economic principle stating
that every factor in production is liable to decreasing
productivity. For example, if capital remains the same,
increasing number of workers beyond a certain point will
inevitably result in a steadily declining productivity.
Similarly, increasing capital while maintaining same
number of workers will show a like effect.

Dimitrov (di-ME-truf), **Georgi Mikhailov** (1882–1949),
Bulgarian political leader, b. Kovachevtski. He led attempt
to overthrow Bulgarian Government (1923). Dimitrov was
accused by Nazis of participating in Reichstag fire (1933).
He was acquitted and made Soviet citizen through intervention of Soviet Union. He was then secretary general of Comintern (Communist International) (1934–43)
and prime· minister of Bulgaria (1946–49).
  Bulgaria, history of **B** 444

Dinanderie (di-non-DRE), type of metalwork **D** 70
Dinaric (din-AR-ic) **Alps E** 309

Dinesen (DI-nuh-sun), **Isak** (pseudonym of Baroness
Karen Blixen) (1885–1962), Danish novelist, b. Rungsted-
lund. She was a master storyteller, noted for her
skillfully written, sometimes mystical, tales. Most of her
books were written in English and translated into
Danish. She married her cousin, a Swedish nobleman
(1914), and lived with him on a coffee plantation in
Kenya. She returned to Denmark in 1931. Her book, *Out
of Africa* (1937), is based on her experiences in Africa.
Among other books are *Seven Gothic Tales* (1934), and
Winter's Tales (1943). *The Angelic Avengers* (1947) was
written under the pseudonym Pierre Andrézel.

Dingoes, wild dogs of Australia **D** 247
  Australian wildlife **A** 505
Dining cars, of railroads **R** 80–81
Dinners and dining
  family mealtime, pictures **F** 42
  mealtime around the world, pictures **F** 336–39
  table settings **T** 2–3

Dinoflagellates (dy-no-FLADGE-el-lates), a kind of alga P 279–80
  life, distribution of L 229
  microorganisms, groups of M 279
Dinosaur National Monument, Utah-Colorado U 250;
    picture N 51
  special museum built around dinosaur bones D 172
Dinosaurs D 172–81
  bird life during age of dinosaurs B 207, 209
  eggs and footprints, pictures F 379
  extinction, possible reasons for L 225
  giants of nature G 200, 202, 204
  largest extinct animals A 263
  mammals, the rise of M 63
  See also Fossils

Dinwiddie, Robert (1693–1770), British colonial officer, b. Germiston, Scotland. He was appointed lieutenant governor of Virginia in 1751 and in 1753 sent George Washington to warn French to withdraw from Ohio region, claimed by Great Britain. Dinwiddie failed in attempts to establish co-operation between American colonies but precipitated collapse of New France.
  Washington and Dinwiddie W 36

Diocese (DY-o-cese) (from Greek *dioikesis*, meaning "administration"), originally referred to management of household. Word came to mean administration or government in general, but usually refers to territory or churches under jurisdiction of bishop.
  cathedrals, principal churches C 131

Diocletian (dy-o-CLE-tian), Roman emperor R 308
  Christianity, history of C 281
  war of extermination of Christians R 288
Diodes (DY-odes), electron tubes E 146

Diogenes (di-OJ-en-ese) (the Cynic) (412?–323 B.C.), Greek philosopher, b. Sinope in Asia Minor. He was member of Cynic school of philosophy, which advocated asceticism as means of attaining virtue. According to some legends, in practicing this philosophy he gave up all possessions and lived in a tub. Diogenes was known for his sarcasm and gloomy temperament.
  See also Cynics

Diogenes, woodcut by Carpi G 304
Diomede (DY-o-mede) **Islands,** in Bering Strait A 128
Diomedes (dy-o-ME-dese), in Greek legend I 69
Dion and the Belmonts, American rock music group
    R 262c

Dionne (di-ON) **Quintuplets,** five daughters born to Mr. and Mrs. Oliva Dionne, near Callender, Ontario, Canada (1934). Cécile, Yvonne, Emilie (died 1954), Annette, and Marie (died 1970) were the first set in medical history known to have survived childhood. Their birth attracted worldwide attention, and their welfare was considered a state concern. In 1935 the Ontario Government made them wards of the province. Their physician, Dr. Allan Roy Dafoe, also gained international prominence.

Dionysius (dy-o-NISH-ius), Russian artist U 54

Dionysius (di-o-NISH-ius) **the Elder** (430?–367? B.C.), tyrant of Syracuse. After having himself appointed (405 B.C.) general of the Greek army fighting Carthage, Dionysius took over the government and then strengthened his position by a political marriage. He fought several other wars against Carthage between 398 and 368 B.C. and waged campaigns in Italy. He also encouraged learning and was himself a playwright.

Dionysus (dy-o-NY-sus), Greek god G 360
  god of wine W 188
Diop, David, Senegalese poet A 76c
Diophantus (dy-o-PHAN-tus), Greek mathematician M 156

Dior, Christian (1905–57), French fashion designer, b. Granville. He designed for fashion houses in Paris (1938, 1942–46) and opened his own house (1947). Dior became famous when he designed controversial, long-skirted "new look" (1947). After his death, the Dior name was carried on by Yves St. Laurent and Marc Bohan.

Diorama (di-or-AM-a) (from Greek words *dia*, meaning "through," and *horama*, meaning "a sight"), partly transparent painting viewed from distance through an opening. It was invented by Louis Daguerre and Charles Bouton and first exhibited in London (1832). Word also means a representative scene using small three-dimensional figures.
  airplane models A 106
  book exhibits B 316
  Daguerre, Louis D 2
  showing prehistoric man, picture A 309

Diphtheria (diph-THER-ia), disease
  booster shots V 261
  conquered by Behring D 215–16
Diphthongs (DIPH-thongs), two vowels sounded together
    O 1
  pronunciation P 478
Diplodocus (di-PLOD-oc-us), genus of dinosaurs D 177
Diplomacy (dip-LO-ma-cy), practice of achieving national goals by peaceful means I 323
  duties of a diplomat F 369
  Foreign Service of the United States, part of Department of State F 369
  Franklin's career F 454–55
  Vienna, Congress of, 1815 I 324
Diplomatic service F 369
Dipole antennae (DY-pole an-TEN-ne), of radio telescopes
    R 71–72
Dipper see Big Dipper; Little Dipper
Dipper dredge, picture D 309

Dipping needle, instrument consisting of a magnetic needle fixed so that it swings vertically instead of horizontally, as does a compass. The needle indicates the "dip," or inclination, of the earth's magnetic field— the direction of the field at the place on the earth's surface where the instrument is being held. A dipping needle can be used to locate underground magnetic objects.

Direct current (DC), in electricity E 134
  AC changed to DC by rectifiers E 146
  electric generators E 122
  electric motors E 137–38
  electroplating E 150
  transformers T 249
Direct-distance dialing, telephone T 59
Direct dyes D 371
Directed election, system enforced by autocratic governments G 276, 278
Direction D 182–83
  dead reckoning N 67
  gyroscope G 435–36
  navigation by stars N 63
  navigation instruments N 64–67
  navigation of birds H 192–93
  optical instruments used in navigation O 171
  orienting maps and globes M 90–91
  radar techniques of finding R 35

Direction (continued)
why winds blow east and west **W** 186–87
wind observations **W** 83–84
windward and lee, points of sailing **S** 13
Direct-mail advertising A 29
Directories, type of reference book **R** 129–30
Directors, of plays **T** 157
how to give plays **P** 335
Directory, French government just after the Revolution **F** 468
Direct primary system, of elections **E** 115
Oregon system **O** 205
Direct reduction, of iron ore into iron **I** 407
Direct taxes T 26
Dirigibles, airships
aerodynamics of **A** 40
hydrogen used in **H** 305–06

Dirksen, Everett McKinley (1896–1969), American political leader, b. Pekin, Ill. He was elected to House of Representatives (1932–48) and to Senate (1950), where he was Senate minority leader (1959–69).
known as an orator **I** 85

Disabled American Veterans, association founded (1921) for veterans with disabilities or ailments connected with service in Armed Forces. Main activity is producing and selling "identotags," small copies of automobile license plates for keychains.

Disappointment River, Mackenzie's name for what is now the Mackenzie River, Canada **F** 522
Disarmament D 184–86
basic aim of peace movements **P** 104
Hague conferences **P** 104
Kellogg-Briand Pact, 1928 **C** 497; **W** 284
League of Nations **L** 96–97
peace organizations **P** 104–05
Rush-Bagot Agreement, 1817 **C** 81
United Nations, Disarmament Commission **U** 81
Washington Armament Conference, 1920–21 **W** 283
See also Geneva Summit Conferences, 1955; International relations
Disasters
National Guard called to help **N** 43
Disbarment, of lawyers **L** 93
Discharge method, of printing textiles **D** 372
Disciples, Twelve see Apostles, The
Disciples (dis-CY-pels) **of Christ,** or Christian Church **P** 484
Discipline, of children
guidance **G** 397–400
See also Child development
Disc jockeys, of radio **R** 61
first heard on early recordings **R** 123
See also Disk jockeys
Discordia, Roman goddess **G** 365

Discotheque (DIS-co-tek), a place for dancing to rock-and-roll music. The music is usually recorded, though there are live groups in some discotheques.

Discount houses, retail stores **R** 188

Discoverer, name for a series of satellites put into orbit by the United States Air Force to gather information about outer space.

Discoveries, in geography see Exploration and discovery; articles on individual countries, states, and provinces

Discovery, ship, carried colonists to America **A** 183
Jamestown **J** 20
Discrimination S 113
civil liberties and civil rights **C** 315–16
Negro history **N** 100–05
segregation **S** 113–15
women, role of **W** 211–213
Discrimination, problem in radar **R** 37
Discs see Records, phonograph
Discussions, by panels of speakers **D** 54–55
What is the difference between a debate and a discussion? **D** 54
See also Parliamentary procedure
Discus throw, field event **T** 241
Discus-Thrower, statue by Myron **G** 345
Disease, conquest of D 213–18
locating disease-causing organisms, pictures **M** 275
vaccination and inoculation **V** 260–61
vectors **V** 282–85
Disease, prevention of D 219–21; **M** 208d
antitoxins **D** 206, 219; **V** 260
health **H** 82–85
immunology **I** 104–07
Public Health Service, United States **P** 504
Diseases D 186–90; selected list described **D** 190–212
animal diseases see Diseases, of animals
animals harmful to man **I** 283–87
antibiotics **A** 310–16
bacteria as cause **B** 11
cancer and cancer research **C** 89–95
carriers **V** 282–85
conquest of **D** 213–18
doctors **D** 238–41
drug industry research **D** 324
dyes used for revealing **D** 372
insects harmful to man **I** 282–83
medical laboratory tests **M** 201–02, 209
medical terms, selected list **D** 206
medicinal plants **P** 310–315
medicine, history of **M** 203–208c
"notifiable" diseases **P** 503
occupational diseases **D** 189
of plants **P** 286–87
parasitic fungi **F** 496, 498
prevention of see Disease, prevention of
public health **P** 502–06
"quarantinable" diseases **P** 504
sanitation **S** 32–33
vaccination and inoculation **V** 260–61
vectors, disease carriers **V** 282–85
viruses **V** 361–70a
vitamin deficiency diseases **V** 370b–371
water pollution **W** 58
what diseases are caused by viruses? **V** 370
See also Medicine; names of diseases
Diseases, mental see Mental illness
Diseases, of animals
anthrax **D** 215; **K** 293
cattle **C** 149, 151
foot-and-mouth disease **C** 151
treating sick animals in zoos **Z** 377
veterinarians and what they do **V** 324
See also Distemper
Disinfectants D 222
deodorizers **D** 117
halogens, iodine and chlorine **I** 349
See also Antiseptics
Disjoint sets, in mathematics **S** 127
Disk harrows F 58; picture **F** 56
Disk jockey, also **disc jockey,** a person who conducts and announces a radio or television program of musical recordings **R** 262b

Disk plows F 58
Dismal Swamp, Virginia V 346
Disney, Walt (Walter Elias Disney), American motion
    picture producer **C 28**
  animated cartoons in motion picture history **A** 298;
    M 475
Disneyland, at Anaheim, California **C** 26; picture **C** 24
  attractions at **L** 346
Dispersion, of light **L** 267–68
Displaced persons see Refugees
Displaced Persons Act, 1948 **I** 101
Display, courtship behavior of birds **B** 212
  penguins **P** 122
Disputation, a formal debate **E** 67
Disraeli (dis-RAE-li), **Benjamin,** 1st earl of Beaconsfield,
    English statesman and novelist **D** 223; **E** 227, 230;
    pictures **D** 223, **E** 230, **P** 456a
  Gladstone, political opponent of **G** 225
Dissection, of laboratory specimens **O** 37
Dissenters, or Non-conformists, religious group outside
    Church of England **E** 224
  Bunyan, John **E** 256
  Puritans in New England **A** 187–88
  schools **E** 70
Dissertation upon Roast Pig, essay by Lamb **E** 293
Dissonance, in music **M** 399
Distance Measuring Equipment (DME), navigation de-
    vice in airplanes **A** 561
Distant Early Warning line (DEW) **C** 82
Distemper, artist's paint **P** 30

Distemper, virus disease of dogs and other animals. It
is contagious, and marked by fever and cough.

Distillation D 224–26
  chemical term **C** 218
  fractional distillation of petroleum **P** 174–75
  Kuwait's plant largest in the world **K** 305
  liquid gases **L** 308
  metals, refining of **M** 229
  perfumes **P** 155
  solar stills **S** 239
  water desalting **W** 56, 56a, 67, 68
  water for ocean liners **O** 18
  whiskey and other distilled beverages **W** 159
  wood yields chemicals **W** 227
Distinguished Flying Cross, American award, picture
    M 199
Distinguished Service Cross, American award, picture
    M 199
Distinguished Service Medal, American award, picture
    M 199
Distinguished Service Order (DSO), British award, picture
    M 200
Distortion, of space **R** 143
  map projections **M** 90–92
Distributive properties, of numbers **N** 388
  in the new mathematics **M** 165
Distributors, of motion pictures **M** 482
District attorney, prosecutor, in law **C** 527
District of Columbia, United States **W** 30–35
  emancipation in **L** 294
  home rule city council plan **W** 35
  places of interest in Negro history **N** 94
  slavery abolished **C** 324
  slave trade abolished by Compromise of 1850 **C** 448
  Smithsonian Institution **S** 202
  White House **W** 162–65
  See also Washington, D.C.
Ditch-digging machines B 448
Dithyramb (DITH-ir-am), Greek poetry honoring Dionysus
    D 294

Diu, India **P** 402, 404
Diuretics (dy-u-RET-ics), drugs **D** 198
  use in heart conditions **H** 86c
Diurnal temperature range W 87
Divan Japonias, lithograph by Toulouse-Lautrec
    G 306
Diverging lenses L 145–46
  refraction of light **L** 263
Divertimento, or serenade, a musical form **M** 536, 540
Divide, Continental see Continental Divide
Dividend, in arithmetic **A** 400–01
Dividends, share in a company's profits **S** 427–28
  returns on investments in industry **I** 244
Dividers, measuring tools **T** 216
  use with geometric figures **G** 130

Divine, "Father" (M. J. Devine) (George Baker) (1882–
1965), founder of American religious cult, Negro, b.
near Savannah, Ga. He started movement known as
Father Divine's Peace Mission, which seeks to establish
creedless, classless society. Father Divine achieved
notoriety through claims of miracles and frequent court
judgments regarding source of wealth.

Divine Comedy, by Dante Alighieri **D** 38; **I** 476

Divine right of kings, doctrine sanctioning absolute
power of monarch, based on belief that king's right to
rule came directly from God rather than from subjects.
King could do no wrong and subject had no right of
appeal. Doctrine was expanded primarily during 17th-
century reign of Stuarts in England and reached height
during reign of Louis XIV of France (1643–1715).
  French Revolution put an end to the doctrine **F** 462,
    468

Diving D 226–33
  swimming **S** 488–94
  See also Skin diving
Diving, deep-sea see Deep-sea diving
Diving, scuba see Scuba diving
Diving, skin see Skin diving
Diving, submarine see Deep-sea diving; Skin diving
Diving bells D 79, 81
Diving Saucer, undersea craft **U** 18

Divining rod, forked instrument, usually of witch hazel
wood, with which persons have claimed they can detect
presence of water or minerals. It allegedly dips sharply
downward when held over underground source of water
or minerals.
  used in locating petroleum **P** 170

Division
  abacus **A** 2
  algebra **A** 159
  arithmetic **A** 400–01
  decimal fractions **F** 402
  fractions **F** 400
  NOR computer circuits **C** 454
  slide rule **M** 167
Division, army combat unit **U** 172–73
Divisionism, in art **P** 27
Division of powers, in government **U** 139
Divisor, in arithmetic **A** 400–01
Divorce D 234–35
  family **F** 40
Divot, piece of turf of golf course **G** 260
Dix, Dorothea, American social reformer **D** 235
Dixie, origin of word as name for South **A** 112
Dixie, song by Dan Emmett **N** 24–25
Dixie County, Utah **U** 244

Dixiecrats, popular name for States' Rights Democrats, U.S. political party formed (1948) by southern Democrats who opposed strong civil rights program of national Democratic Party. They nominated Governor J. Strom Thurmond of South Carolina for president and carried four states in 1948 election, after which party disbanded almost entirely.

third parties in the United States **P** 381;
T 301

Dixieland, New Orleans jazz **J** 58

Dixon, Dean (Charles Dean Dixon) (1915–), American conductor, b. New York, N.Y. He appeared with the NBC Symphony Orchestra (1941) and was the first Negro to conduct the New York Philharmonic-Symphony Orchestra (1941). He formed the American Youth Orchestra, which gave concerts from 1944 to 1949. Since conducting the Berlin Philharmonic Orchestra (1949), he has introduced many American works to European audiences.

Dixon, Jeremiah, English surveyor **M** 133
Djabali, Leila, Algerian poet **A** 76d
Djakarta (ja-KAR-ta), capital of Indonesia **D** 236–37
Indonesia's principal city **I** 221
Djebar, Assia, Algerian novelist **A** 76d
Djibouti (ji-BOO-ti), capital of Afar-Issa Territory (formerly French Somaliland) **S** 255
DME see Distance Measuring Equipment
DMZ see Demilitarized Zone, in Vietnam.
DNA (deoxyribonucleic acid), in body cells **B** 293, 295–96; diagrams **B** 292, **G** 85
cancer and cancer research **C** 94–95
chemical makeup of viruses **V** 363, 370
genetics **G** 84
in cell nucleus **C** 161
Dnieper (NE-per) **River,** Europe **R** 243
Union of Soviet Socialist Republics **U** 33

Dniester (NE-ster) **River,** river in western European Soviet Union that rises in the Carpathian Mountains in western Ukraine, flows through Moldavia, and empties into the Black Sea. Its total length is 875 miles. It freezes over from December to March. When navigable, its lower course is used for transporting lumber and grain.

Do a Good Turn Daily, Scout slogan **B** 360

Dobbs, Mattiwilda (1925–), American soprano, b. Atlanta, Ga. She was first Negro to sing principal role at New York Metropolitan Opera and at La Scala in Milan.

Dobell, William, Australian painter **A** 502

Döbereiner (DER-ber-rine-er), **Johann Wolfgang** (1780–1849), German chemist, b. Hof. He showed that in certain groups of three elements one element has an atomic weight equal to half the combined weight of the other two elements. This discovery led to development of periodic table, which shows weights and properties of all elements. Döbereiner discovered furfural, a chemical widely used as weed killer and in plastics.

Doberman pinscher, dog, picture **D** 255

Dobie, James Frank (1888–1964), American educator and writer, b. Live Oak County, Tex. Best-known as an authority on Southwestern American folklore, he was a teacher at University of Texas (1925–47) and visiting professor at Cambridge University, England (1943–44). His books include *Coronado's Children* and *The Longhorns.*

Dobler International List of Periodicals for Boys and Girls, The **M** 16

Dobrynin (do-BRE-neen), **Anatoly Fedorovich** (1919–), Russian diplomat, b. probably Ukraine. He served with Secretariat of UN (1957–60) and was counselor for Soviet delegation at Big Four Conference at Paris (1960). He headed American department of Soviet Ministry of Foreign Affairs (1960–61). He is now Ambassador to United States (since 1962).

Dobson, William, English painter **E** 237
Dobsonflies, pictures **I** 277
d'Ockeghem, Jean see Ockeghem, Jean d'
Docking, of a spacecraft see Rendezvous and docking
Dock Street Theater, Charleston, South Carolina **S** 307
Doctor, form of address for Doctor of Medicine, M.D., or Doctor of Philosophy, Ph.D. **A** 19
Doctors **D** 238–41
astronauts, care of **S** 340a, 340g, 340j
Australia's flying service **A** 499
medicine, tools and techniques of **M** 208d–211
number of hospitals and doctors in various countries compared **H** 252
regular checkups for good health **H** 85
test drugs for the industry **D** 324
vaccination, in Pakistan, picture **D** 219
Doctor Zhivago, novel by Boris Pasternak **U** 61
Doctrine, body of defined truth of the Roman Catholic Church **R** 289, 299, 301
Doctrine of the Faith, Congregation for the, formerly Holy Office, Congregation of the, Roman Catholic Church **I** 257
See also Index librorum prohibitorum
Documentary motion pictures **M** 475–77
television production **T** 70a, 70b, 70d–71
Documentation, techniques of arranging, coding, and storing information in mechanical devices, such as computers, for rapid access and retrieval **L** 177
Dodders, plants **P** 318; picture **P** 319
weeds **W** 104
Dodds, Johnny, American jazz musician **J** 58
Dodecanese (do-DEC-an-ese), islands in the Aegean **I** 429

Dodge, Mary Mapes (Mary Elizabeth Dodge) (1831–1905), American writer and editor, b. New York, N.Y. She was known for years as foremost American author of children's books. Her greatest success was with classic tale of Dutch children *Hans Brinker; or the Silver Skates,* which was honored by French Academy and translated into many languages. She was first editor of children's magazine *St. Nicholas* (1873–1905), drawing to it many of noted authors of the time, including Twain and Kipling. Her prose works include *Donald and Dorothy.*
American children's magazines **C** 240; **M** 16

Dodge ball, circle game **G** 14
Dodge City, Kansas **K** 186; picture **K** 187
on the Chisholm Trail for cattle drives **O** 266–67
Dodgson, Charles Lutwidge see Carroll, Lewis
Dodoma, Tanzania **T** 19
Dodos, extinct birds **B** 229; **M** 181
Doe, John see John Doe

Doenitz (DERN-itz), **Karl** (1891–), German admiral, b. Grünau. He planned and commanded submarine fleet constructed (1930's) in violation of Versailles treaty. He was grand admiral and commander in chief of German Navy (1943). As Hitler's successor, he surrendered to Allied forces at end of World War II in Europe (1945) and was sentenced to 10 years imprisonment for war crimes

(1946). Doenitz published his *Memoirs* (1959).
  World War II **W** 307

Doesburg (DOOS-burk), **Theo van,** Dutch artist
  M 393
Dog days, hot summer days   **D** 47
  August   **A** 492

Doge (from Latin word meaning "leader"), principal official of republics of Venice (697–1797) and Genoa (1339–1797, 1802–05).

Doge's Palace, Venice, picture   **I** 460
Dog family   **D** 242–51
  foxes   **F** 396–97
  wolves   **W** 210

Dogfish, any of several small sharks found in all oceans of the world. Named for its doglike habit of forming packs to hunt food, the spiny dogfish is much used in classrooms and laboratories for teaching animal dissection. Gray with small white spots, it may measure up to 4 feet and weigh about 15 pounds. Spiny dogfish has poisonous spine in front of each dorsal (back) fin.
  sharks, kinds of   **S** 143; pictures **S** 142

Dogger Bank, in the North Sea
  fishing industry   **F** 218
Doggett's Coat and Badge, boat race   **R** 339
Dog handling, in shows   **D** 262
Dogon (DO-gohn), a people of the Sudan
  African sculpture   **A** 76
Dog on a Leash, painting by Balla   **M** 390
Dog racing   **R** 33
Dog-Rib, Indians of North America   **I** 164, 170
Dogs   **D** 252–62
  animal intelligence tests   **A** 284, picture **A** 286
  classification of the domestic dog   **T** 31
  Collie puppies, picture   **G** 79
  dog family   **D** 242–51
  dog-guides for the blind   **B** 253–54
  dog sledding for mail service   **P** 407
  Eskimo huskies, pictures   **E** 285
  fleas   **H** 260
  foot bones, diagram   **F** 81
  Pavlov's conditioning experiment in learning   **L** 99; **P** 496
  pets   **P** 179
  rabies   **I** 286–87
  spectrogram of a dog's bark, picture   **A** 276
  state dog of Maryland   **M** 114
  tracks, picture   **A** 271
  ultrasonic sound heard by   **S** 267
  See *also* names of dogs and of species of the dog family
Dog shows   **D** 261–62
Dogsledding
  Eskimo dog team, picture   **E** 285
  mail routes   **P** 407
Dog star see Sirius

Dog tag, U.S. Army term for the identification tag that a soldier wears around his neck. The tag, bearing the soldier's name, serial number, religion, and blood type, is worn at all times.

Dogwood, tree, picture   **T** 275
  leaves, special kinds of, pictures   **L** 120
  Missouri, state tree of   **M** 367
  North Carolina, state flower of   **N** 307
  Virginia, state flower of   **V** 344
Doha, capital of Qatar   **M** 301

Dohnányi (DO-non-yi), **Ernst von** (1877–1960), Hungarian composer, pianist, and conductor, b. Pressburg (now Bratislava, Czechoslovakia). He was professor of piano at Berlin Conservatory (1908–15) and director of Conservatory in Budapest (1919–44), serving as president (1918–44) and conductor of Philharmonic there. He emigrated to United States (1949). He composed chamber music and operas. Works include *Variations on a Nursery Song* and four rhapsodies for piano.

Doldrums, almost windless area near equator   **W** 186
  horse latitudes   **T** 246;   **W** 73
  patterns, or belts of weather and climate   **W** 73
  region where trade winds come together   **T** 246
Dole, James D., American pioneer in Hawaii's pineapple industry   **H** 70
Dole, Sanford Ballard, American lawyer and political leader in Hawaii   **H** 70, 71
Dolgoruki, Yuri see Yuri Dolgoruki
Dollar, a basic monetary unit   **M** 410
  Great Seal of the United States   **G** 329–30

Dollar-a-year man, one who serves government in a special capacity, receiving only token salary.

Dollar diplomacy, a government's use of economic influence to enhance business interests of its private citizens in other countries. A derogatory term, it originally applied to an aspect of U.S. foreign policy during Taft administration (1909–13). It also refers to overseas investments by American financiers originally intended to promote U.S. business interests abroad and maintain balance of power in China. In general, it refers to area of U.S. foreign policy influenced by U.S. financial interests abroad.

Dollar sign   **M** 410
Dollfus, Audouin, French astronomer, picture   **O** 14
Dollfuss, Engelbert, Austrian statesman
  Hitler's annexation of Austria   **W** 286
Dolls   **D** 263–69
  African decorative arts, picture   **D** 76
  favorite toys, pictures   **T** 232, 234, 235
  Feast of Dolls, Japan   **H** 158;   **J** 31
  Inca doll, picture   **I** 154
  See *also* Puppets and marionettes
Dolls, Feast of, or Girls' Day, Japan   **H** 158;   **J** 31
Doll's House, A, play by Henrik Ibsen   **I** 2
Dolmetsch, Arnold, French musical authority   **R** 121
Dolomite (DOL-o-mite), a kind of limestone   **S** 433
Dolomites, Alps range in Italy   **A** 174
Dolphins, or porpoises   **D** 270–79
  animal intelligence   **A** 288
  dolphin design in furniture, picture   **F** 507
  learning experiments, picture   **L** 100
  locomotion   **A** 290
  Tuffy delivers mail, picture   **U** 22
Domagk (DO-mok), **Gerhard,** German chemist   **D** 217
Domed mountains   **M** 496

Dome of the Rock, Muslim shrine in Jerusalem built over Sacred Rock. Erected (691) by Caliph Abd-al-Malik, it remains as earliest surviving Muslim architectural monument. It was built at site of holy Rock of Sacrifice, where Abraham prepared to offer his son to God. Located within courts of temples of kings Solomon and Herod, where Jesus taught, it is said to be place from which Mohammed rose to heaven.
  eastern part of Jerusalem   **J** 79, 138

Domes, in architecture   **A** 377
  Byzantine, use and meaning of   **B** 486, 487

Domes (continued)
  concrete **A** 386; pictures **A** 387
  geodesic dome of Buckminster Fuller **I** 232
  Islamic arcitecture **I** 419
  Roman architecture **A** 376
  Saint Peter's **A** 381; picture **A** 382
  Taj Mahal **T** 14

Domesday (DOOMS-day), or **Doomsday, Book,** results of a census in England ordered by William the Conqueror and completed in 1086. It was a survey of population, value, extent, and ownership of lands at that time. Written in Latin in two volumes of over 800 pages, it is now kept in Public Record Office, London, England.
  William the Conqueror **W** 173

Domestic animals
  agriculture, history of **A** 96, 100
  buffalo of Asia **B** 250a
  camels **C** 34
  cattle **C** 147–51; **D** 7–9
  cats, domestic **C** 141–44
  dogs, origin and breeds **D** 248, 259, 261
  goats **C** 151–52
  hoofed mammals **H** 206–21
  horses and their relatives **H** 235–44
  livestock **C** 151–52
  pigs **C** 151
  prehistoric man domesticated animals **P** 445–46
  sheep **S** 145
  transportation **T** 257
  See also names of domestic animals
Domestic science see Home economics
Domestic service occupations **S** 124
Domestic Shorthair cats **C** 142; picture **C** 144
Dominance orders, among animals **A** 280–81
Dominant traits, in genetics **G** 80
Dominic, Saint, Spanish Roman Catholic priest **C** 284–85

Dominica (dom-i-NI-ca), one of the Windward Islands in the Caribbean, discovered by Columbus in 1493, and noted for mountainous scenery. Its capital is Roseau. As a member of the West Indies Associated States, Dominica is self-governing within the Commonwealth of Nations.
  Caribbean Sea and islands **C** 116–19

Dominican (do-MIN-i-can) **Republic** **D** 280–83
  Caribbean Sea and islands **C** 116–19
  flag **F** 241
  life in Latin America **L** 47–61
  national anthem **N** 21
  United States Marine Corps action **U** 178
  See also Haiti
Dominicans, religious order **R** 292
Dominion Day, Canada **H** 152
Dominoes **D** 284
Donalda, Pauline, Canadian singer **C** 63
Donald Duck, cartoon character **A** 299
Donatello (don-a-TELL-o), Italian sculptor **D** 285; **I** 46
  David, statue **S** 100
  Gattamelata, statue **I** 465
  Renaissance art **R** 164
  Renaissance sculpture **S** 99
Don Baltasar Carlos in Hunting Costume, painting by Velázquez **S** 361
Don Carlos, opera by Giuseppe Verdi **O** 143
Donelson, Emily, an acting first lady in Jackson's administration **F** 168
Donets (don-YETS) **Basin,** Ukraine, Union of Soviet Socialist Republics **U** 8–9
Don Giovanni (gi-o-VA-ni), opera by Mozart **O** 143
Doniphan, Alexander, American officer **M** 239

Donizetti, Gaetano (1797–1848), Italian composer, b. Bergamo. He composed nearly 70 operas, the earliest showing influence of Gioacchino Rossini. His best-known operas include *Lucia di Lammermoor, Don Pasquale, L'elisir d'amore,* and *Lucrezia Borgia.*
  Italian opera **O** 135
  Lucia di Lammermoor, opera **O** 145–46

Don Juan (don JU-an), by Lord Byron **E** 260
Don Juan (don WAN), character in literature **S** 369
  duels in literature **D** 341 ·
Donkey engines **B** 445
Donkeys, or burros **H** 235
  cartoon symbol **C** 126
  transportation in Jamaica, picture **J** 16
Donne (DUNN), **John,** English poet **E** 254
Donner party, of pioneers on the California Trail **O** 264–65
Donner Pass, California **C** 16
Donovan, British rock music composer and performer **R** 262d
Don Quixote (don ki-HO-te), novel by Cervantes **C** 176; excerpt **D** 285–86
  classic satire **H** 280
  first full-fledged novel, themes of **N** 345
  golden age of Spanish literature **S** 369
  landmark in development of fiction **F** 110–11
  statues with monument to Cervantes, Madrid, Spain **M** 12; **S** 354
Don River, Union of Soviet Socialist Republics **R** 243
  Union of Soviet Socialist Republics **U** 33
Don't give up the ship, slogan, spoken by James Lawrence **N** 178
  Perry's battle flag **P** 157
Don't shoot until you see the whites of their eyes, order of American commander William Prescott **R** 199
Doodlebug, unscientific device used to locate petroleum or water **P** 170

Dooley, Dr. Tom (Thomas Anthony Dooley) 1927–1961), American physician and author, b. St. Louis, Mo. As Navy medical officer, he established camps for Indo-Chinese refugees from North Vietnam (1954) and organized and led medical missionary team in Laos (1956). His books include *Deliver Us from Evil.*

Doolittle, Hilda (H.D.), American poet **A** 209

Doolittle, James Harold (1896–   ), American aviator and army officer, b. Alameda, Calif. He led first bombing raid over Tokyo, Japan, during World War II, for which he received Medal of Honor. He commanded U.S. air forces in North African invasion and was appointed lieutenant general of Army (1944). He retired from Army (1946) and served as chairman of National Advisory Committee for Aeronautics (1956–58).
  World War II **W** 294

Dooms, laws of Anglo-Saxon England **E** 216
Doomsday Book see Domesday Book
Door-to-door selling **S** 116
Doppler, Christian, Austrian scientist **S** 263
Doppler effect, law of physics **L** 269
  navigation **N** 67
  sound **S** 263
Dorantes, Esteban, Spanish explorer see Estevanico

Dorati (do-RA-ti), **Antal** (1906–   ), American conductor, b. Budapest, Hungary. He has been conductor of several symphony orchestras, and in 1970 became music director of Washington National Symphony. Dorati has composed orchestral music and arranged ballet *Graduation Ball.*

Dorcas (Tabitha), in New Testament (Acts 9:36), Christian woman of Joppa (Joffa, Israel) known for good works. She made garments for poor. She was raised from dead by Saint Peter. Name is now applied to women's church groups engaged in sewing clothing for poor.

Dorchester Heights National Historic Site, Boston, Massachusetts **M** 144

Doré (dor-AY), **Gustave** (Paul Gustave Doré) (1833–1883), French artist, b. Strasbourg. His sketches were first shown in *Journal pour Rire* (1848). Best-known for illustrations of classic works—among them the Bible, Dante's *Divine Comedy,* and Cervantes' *Don Quixote*—he also produced paintings and sculptures, including a monument to Alexandre Dumas *père* in Paris.
  illustration of the miracle of the loaves and fishes **B** 160

Dorian mode, seven-note musical scale **A** 247
Dorians, a people of ancient Greece
  invasions end Mycenaean Age **G** 343
Doric order, Greek architecture **A** 375; **G** 346; pictures **A** 376; **G** 347
Dormancy
  hibernation **H** 121–24
  seeds **F** 283
Dormouse (plural dormice), rodent **H** 121
  surface area compared to rabbit's, diagram **H** 124

Dorne, Albert (1904–65), American artist and writer, b. New York, N.Y. He was founder and president (1930–34) of the Kent Studios and founder and president (1947–65) of Famous Artists School of Westport, Conn. He received first New York Art Directors gold medal award for distinguished career (1953).
  Six Greedy Loafers, illustration **I** 94

Dörpfeld (DERP-felt), **Wilhelm,** German archeologist **T** 293

Dorr's Rebellion, popular movement, led by Thomas W. Dorr, to extend suffrage in Rhode Island state constitution. In 1841 state constitution of Rhode Island, still operating under charter of 1663, limited vote to landholders. Dorr and supporters attempted to gain control of state legislature (1842) to introduce new constitution providing suffrage for adult men, but they were blocked by Governor King, who sent state militia to suppress the revolt. The reforms were adopted (1843).
  Rhode Island's constitution revised **R** 226–27

Dorset, England
  farm animals, picture **C** 150
Dos Passos, John, American novelist **A** 211
Dostoevski (dos-to-YEV-ski), **Fëdor,** Russian novelist **D** 286–87
  Russian literature **U** 61
  themes of his novels **N** 348
Dothan, Alabama **A** 124
Dotted notes, in musical notation **M** 530–31
Douala (du-AL-a), Cameroon **C** 35, 36
Douay (doo-AY) **Bible,** English version of Vulgate **B** 153
Double bass, stringed instrument **O** 183; picture **M** 545
  orchestra seating plan **O** 186
Double bogey, golf score **G** 255
Doubleday, Abner, American army officer
  "invention" of baseball **B** 69, 80
Double entry, bookkeeping system **B** 312
Double Metamorphosis II, painting by Vaacov Agam **P** 31, 32
Double planetary system, earth and moon **M** 446

Double Tenth, or Chinese National Holiday **H** 152
Doubt, River of, Brazil (later Roosevelt River) **R** 330
Dough, bread **B** 385
  fermentation **F** 88

Douglas, Sir James (1803–1877), Canadian fur trader and colonial official, b. Demerara, British Guiana. He served Hudson's Bay Company (1821–58) and established a company post on Vancouver Island (1843), serving as its governor (1851–64). He was governor of colony of British Columbia (1858–64).
  Father of British Columbia **B** 403–04

Douglas, Stephen A., American statesman **D** 287
  events leading to Civil War **C** 321
  Kansas-Nebraska Act, 1854 **K** 192
  Lincoln-Douglas debates **L** 299
  Lincoln's campaign against **L** 294–95
  slavery, the great debate **S** 199

Douglas, Thomas Clement (1904–), Canadian statesman, b. Falkirk, Scotland. He served in House of Commons (1935–44) and was then elected to Saskatchewan Legislature (1944), serving as premier and president of Executive Council (1944–61). Douglas has been national leader of New Democratc Party since 1961.

Douglas, William O. (William Orville Douglas) (1898–), American associate justice, U.S. Supreme Court (since 1959), b. Maine, Minn. After serving on law faculties of Columbia University (1925–28) and Yale University (1928–34), he was appointed to Supreme Court (1939) by President Franklin D. Roosevelt. An enthusiastic hiker and outdoorsman, he has written *My Wilderness* and *Of Men and Mountains.* He also wrote *Points of Rebellion.*

Douglas Dam, Tennessee, picture **T** 76
Douglas fir, tree, picture **T** 277
  state tree of Oregon **O** 193
  uses of the wood and its grain, picture **W** 223
Douglas-Home see Home, Sir Alexander Frederick Douglas
Douglass, Andrew E., American astronomer **T** 286
Douglass, Frederick, American journalist and anti-slavery leader **D** 288
  Negro history **N** 94
Doukhobors (DOO-ko-bors), Russian religious sect **S** 38g
  under Verigin, in Canada's Prairie Provinces **B** 405

Douro (DO-roo) **River,** among the longest rivers in the Iberian Peninsula (about 475 miles). It originates in the mountains of Old Castile (Spain), flows through Portugal, and empties into the Atlantic Ocean. Filled with rapids and gorges, it is difficult to navigate at its upper and lower courses. The river forms part of the Spanish-Portuguese border, and is a source for irrigation and hydroelectric power.

Dover, capital of Delaware **D** 97, 98
Dover, England **E** 213

Doves, birds found throughout the world except for polar regions. They are generally drab, although some tropical birds are brightly colored. Doves have small heads, short necks, and pointed wings. The birds have a mournful, somewhat monotonous call. The dove is unique among birds in being able to drink by sucking up water rather than by tilting the head and letting water flow into the throat. Doves are included in a large family of birds many of which are called pigeons. In general, "pigeon" refers to larger, heavier birds; "dove" to smaller, more

Doves (continued)

delicate species. The dove has played a central role in many legends and has long been known as a symbol of peace.

See also Pigeons

Dowager, widow having property or title from her late husband. The term is often added to a title to distinguish her from the wife of the heir, and it can also refer to an elderly woman of imposing appearance, dominating personality, or prominent position.

Dow Jones averages, daily average of stock prices, representing price fluctuations of stock market as a whole. It is based on averages of 30 industrial, 20 railroad, and 10 utility stocks.

Dowland, John, English composer **E** 270

Downes, Olin (Edwin Olin Downes) (1886–1955), American music critic, b. Evanston, Ill. He was music critic for Boston *Post* (1906–24) and New York *Times* (1924–55) and music lecturer at Boston University, Metropolitan Opera Guild, and Berkshire Music Festival. His writings include *The Lure of Music.*

Downing Street, No. 10, London **L** 335
Down in Yon Forest, English carol **C** 122
Downs, in football **F** 360
Down's syndrome, or **mongolism** **R** 190

Down under, nickname for Australia and New Zealand. It derives from popular belief that part of earth diametrically opposed to where one is standing lies beneath one's feet. Hence, if one is in Greenwich, England, antipode is "down under" in Australia or New Zealand.

Downy mildew, fungi **F** 498
Dow process, for magnesium extraction **M** 23

Dowry, the gift that a woman brings to her husband at the time of their marriage. Less frequently, the husband presents his bride with a dowry. The gift can be in the form of money, cattle, jewels, or any other symbol of wealth. The custom of dowry giving is an ancient one and has been abandoned in many countries. The term "dower rights" refers to the legal rights of a wife to a portion of her deceased husband's estate.

cattle as a dowry **K** 228

Dowson, Ernest Christopher (1867–1900), English poet and short-story writer, b. Kent. Associated with Aesthetic movement of late 19th-century English literature, he is most famous for poem "Non Sum Qualis Eram" (known as "Cynara").

Doyle, Sir Arthur Conan, English doctor and detective-story writer **D** 288
mystery, detective, and suspense stories **M** 554
D'Oyly Carte, Richard, English impresario and stage manager **G** 209
Dozens, rhyming game **F** 313
D. P.'s (displaced persons) see Refugees
Drachma (DRAC-ma), Greek coin **M** 411
Dracones, flexible containers for transportation of liquids **P** 175
Draft, or conscription **D** 289–90
National Guard duty **N** 42–43
New York City Draft Riots during Civil War **C** 326
United States Army soldier **U** 167
Draft horses see Workhorses

Drafting see Mechanical drawing
Drag, air resistance to moving objects
aerodynamics theory **A** 38, 39
problem in aircraft design **A** 559; diagram **A** 553
supersonic flight **S** 470
Dragline excavators **B** 446–47

Dragon, mythical creature appearing in folklore of almost all peoples. It is usually represented as monstrous snake or crocodile with scaly body, four legs with huge claws, and head of either lion, eagle, or hawk. It generally has wings and breathes out fire and usually dwells in lakes or caves. Dragon must be appeased by human sacrifice. Although symbol of Satan in Christian tradition, it is benevolent creature in Chinese folklore.

Dragon Boat Festival, China **H** 155–56
Dragonet, fish, picture **F** 201

Dragonfly, any of a group of more than 1,500 kinds of insects found throughout the world but especially in tropics. It has long, slender body, four long, narrow wings, enormous eyes, strong jaws, and legs suited for grasping food. It may reach a length of 5 inches and has wingspread of 6 inches. Wings are always spread even when at rest. Its flying has been timed at 60 miles per hour. Dragonfly helps control mosquitoes and flies. Damsel flies are similar, but have thinner bodies, fly more slowly, and fold their wings when at rest. Pictures **G** 199; **I** 269, 272, 281.

Drag racing, hot-rod cars **A** 539
Drainage, of land **A** 93
Drainage basins, of rivers **R** 238
Drais (DRICE), **Baron Karl von,** German inventor of draisine, early bicycle **B** 173
Drake, Edwin L., American petroleum worker **P** 177
Drake, Sir Francis, English sailor and explorer **D** 290–91
American colonies **A** 181
California **C** 14
exploration of the New World **E** 384
signature reproduced **A** 527

Drake, Frank Donald (1930–), American astronomer, b. Chicago, Ill. By studying radio waves coming from outer space, he discovered many new stars (called radio stars). He also determined a powerful belt of radiation circling planet Jupiter and temperature of surface of planet Venus and headed U.S. efforts to detect messages from intelligent beings on other worlds.

Drakensberg (DRA-kens-berg) **Mountains,** southern Africa **A** 49
South Africa **S** 270
Drama **D** 292–300
African dramatists **A** 76c
American literature **A** 215–16
creative writing **W** 320
English see English drama
French literature **F** 437, 438, 439, 441
German literature **G** 175, 179
Greek tragedy **G** 351
Indian literature in Sanskrit **O** 220e
Irish National Theatre (Abbey Theatre) **I** 394
Japanese literature **O** 220d
literature, types of **L** 314
Menora, puppet shadow play of Malaysia **M** 53
miracle plays **M** 339–40
motion-picture industry **M** 472–88
musical comedy **M** 542–43
opera **O** 130–55
Othello, by Shakespeare, criticized by Rymer **O** 236

pageants **P** 12
plays **P** 335–41
Pulitzer prizes **P** 527
puppets and marionettes **P** 534–39
Scandinavian literature **S** 51–52
theater **T** 155–64
See also names of well-known dramatists
Dramatic Art *see* Acting
Dramatic monologue, in poetry **E** 263
Dramatic voice V 375
Dramatists, or playwrights, writers of plays **T** 156–57
Drapeau, Jean, Canadian public official **Q** 13

Draper, John William (1811–1882), American scientist and historian, b. St. Helenes, England. Best-known for studies on chemical reactions caused by light and on the nature of light given off by glowing solids, he was pioneer in photography and first to take a photograph of a celestial object (the moon) and of an object under a microscope.
use of the camera in astronomy **A** 474

Draughts (DRAFTS), English game of checkers **C** 191–92
Draughtsmanship *see* Mechanical drawing
Dravidian (dra-VID-ian), language group of Asia **A** 460
Indian literature **O** 220e
language families **L** 40
spoken in southern India **I** 119
Dravidians, a people of India **I** 116
Bangladesh **B** 44
Drawbridges B 400
fortification of a castle **F** 375
Drawing D 301–05
animated cartoons **A** 297–99
cartoons **C** 125–28
engraving **E** 272
Gothic architects' plans of buildings **G** 272
mechanical drawing **M** 197
optical illusions **O** 161–65
perspective **P** 158–59
techniques and uses of the graphic arts **G** 302–08
See also Cartoons; Design; Etching
Drawing, of metals **M** 231
Drawing frame, textile processing machine **C** 525
Drawing room comedies E 256–57, 268
Draw looms, weaving **R** 352
Drawn work, kind of embroidery **E** 187
Drayton, Michael, English poet **E** 251
Dreamers, Northwest Indian society **M** 563
Dreaming D 305–07
extrasensory perception **E** 394–95
sleep **S** 201
Dredges D 308–10
fishing equipment **F** 218
Louisiana waterways, picture **L** 351
Dred Scott Decision D 310–11
Buchanan upheld the decision **B** 419–20
events leading to Civil War **C** 320
Lincoln-Douglas debates **L** 299
Supreme Court **S** 476
Dreiser (DRY-ser), **Theodore,** American novelist **A** 207
Dresden, Germany **G** 157
Dresden Art Gallery, Dresden, Germany **M** 514
Dresden diamond G 71
Dresden dolls D 265
Dresden porcelain P 418
Dress *see* Clothing
Dresser, Paul, American songwriter **I** 136
Dressmaking D 311–15
sewing **S** 128–29
See also Clothing industry

Drew, Charles Richard (1904–1950), American physician, Negro, b. Washington, D.C. Best-known for work on methods of preparing and storing supplies of human blood needed for transfusions, in World War II he headed efforts to send blood plasma to Allies.
Negro scholars and scientists **N** 98

Dreyfus (DRAY-fus), **Alfred,** French army officer **D** 316
Devils Island **P** 468
Dreyfus case in French history **F** 418
Jews, history of **J** 110
Zola helped in Dreyfus' release **Z** 371
Dribble, in basketball **B** 83, 85
Dried fruits D 316–17
dates **D** 41–42
fig **F** 117
peaches, prunes, and apricots **P** 106–07
seedless grapes **G** 297
Dried milk D 12
Drift, of airplanes **A** 560
Drifters, American rock music group **R** 262c
Drifters, documentary motion picture **M** 476

Drift ice, ice that has floated from place where it was formed. The term also refers to any floating ice except icebergs or other ice that has formed on land.

Drift meter, airplane instrument **A** 560
Drift mining, of coal **C** 365
Drift Prairie
North Dakota **N** 324
Drill bits, tools **W** 230
Drilling, a way of sowing seed **F** 58
Drilling and boring
mining **M** 314
quarrying **Q** 4
wells **W** 122–24
Drill press, machine tool, picture **T** 218
Drills, baboons *see* Mandrills
Drills, tools **T** 210b–211; pictures **T** 214, 216
Drinking *see* Alcoholism
Drinking water, for camping **C** 46

Drinkwater, John (1882–1937), English dramatist and poet, b. Leytonstone, Essex. He co-founded Pilgrim Players, amateur dramatic group, and his work influenced revival of serious drama.

Dripstone, cave formations **C** 155
Drive, or tee shot, in golf, pictures **G** 257
Drive-in restaurants R 186
Driver, William, American sea captain **F** 248
Driver ants A 331
Driver education D 318–21
safety **S** 6
traffic signs and signals **T** 248
See also Traffic control
Drogues, or drags
parachutes slow down spacecrafts **S** 340j; picture **S** 340c
Dromedaries (DROM-ed-aries), one-humped camels **C** 34; pictures **H** 213
hoofed mammals **H** 210
Drone, continuous low note in music **A** 245
of the bagpipe **F** 329
Drones, male bees **B** 118, 122–23
Drop forging, of metals **M** 229
Droplet infection, spread of disease germs **D** 206
Drosophila *see* Fruit flies
Droughts (DROUTS) **C** 486
caused by high-pressure areas **W** 75
environment of prairies **P** 430

Drowning
artificial respiration and first aid **F** 159–61
preventive measures **S** 6
Dr. Seuss see Seuss, Dr.
Drug abuse see Drugs, abuse of
Drug addiction **D** 328; **N** 12–14
Drug dependence **N** 12, 13
Drug Enforcement Administration, United States **F** 76
Drug industry **D** 321–25
Drugs **D** 325–28
anesthetics **A** 258
antibiotics **A** 310–16
antidotes for poisons **P** 356–57
antiseptics and disinfectants **D** 222
cancer treatment **C** 95
drug industry **D** 321–25
Federal Food, Drug, and Cosmetic Act, 1938 **F** 350
first aid for poisons **F** 158
hallucinogenic drugs and vapors **D** 331
medicinal plants **P** 310–15
medicine, history of **M** 208a–208b
narcotics **N** 12–14
Paracelus one of first to use drugs scientifically **M** 205
poisonous plants **P** 321
poisons, antidotes for **P** 356–57
Drugs, abuse of **D** 329–32
narcotic antagonists to block effects of narcotics **N** 14
Drugstores
bazaars selling medicinal plants, first drugstores **P** 311
Druids, priests of ancient Gaul and Britain
Halloween customs taken from **H** 15
mistletoe tradition **C** 291
Drum, musical instrument **D** 333–36
African drums **A** 78–79; picture **A** 77
communication method of primitive peoples **C** 437
message system **T** 50
musical instruments, types of **M** 549–50
Negro Latin-American dancing **L** 69
orchestra **O** 183–84
percussion instruments **P** 151–52
Drum elevators **E** 172
Drumlins, hills formed by glacial deposits **M** 136, 137; picture **I** 14
Wisconsin **W** 194
Drummer boy, Civil War, U.S., picture **C** 327
Medals of Honor awarded to two drummer boys **M** 198

Drummond, William Henry (1854–1907), Canadian poet, b. County Leitrim, Ireland. He emigrated to Canada (1865) and dialectally portrayed life of habitants, French-Canadian farming class. His books include *The Habitant, Johnny Courteau, The Voyageur,* and *The Great Fight.*

Drunkenness see Alcoholism
Drupes, fruit with stones (hard seeds)
peach, plum, and cherry **P** 106–09
Drury Lane Theatre, London, design for, by Robert Adam, picture **E** 240

Druzes, or **Druses,** members of Syrian religious sect inhabiting Central Syria and Lebanon. Sect was founded by Darazi and Hamzah, who claimed that al-Hakim, Caliph of Egypt (996–1021), was incarnation of God. Religious beliefs include aspects of Muslim, Jewish, Christian, and Sufi (Muslim mysticism). Druses call themselves Unitarians because of belief in one God, who can be known only through incarnations.
communities in Israel and Lebanon **I** 439; **L** 121

Dryad (from Greek word meaning "tree" or "oak"), in Greek and Roman mythology, nymph who lived within a tree and died at same moment as tree. She is also called Hamadryad.

Dry cells, in batteries **B** 97, 99; picture **B** 98
Dry cereals **G** 285
Dry cleaning **D** 337–39
See also Laundry
Dryden, John, English poet **E** 255–56; **O** 52
Dry distillation **D** 225
Dry farming
Canada **C** 58

Dry ice, common name for frozen carbon dioxide. It is so called because, unlike ordinary ice, no liquid residue is left on melting. Dry ice is used as refrigerant, especially in transporting foods.
polar caps of Mars **M** 110
use in weather control by cloud seeding **W** 91–93

Drying, of foods **F** 347–48
Drying oils **O** 77, 79
Dry measure **W** 113, 115
Drypoint, engraving technique **G** 305
Drysdale, Russell, Australian painter **A** 502
Dry Tortugas (tor-TU-gas), islands in Gulf of Mexico, Fort Jefferson National Monument, Florida **F** 268
Dry wines **W** 189
DSO see Distinguished Service Order
DST see Daylight Saving Time
Dual Alliance, France and Russia **W** 270
Dual citizenship **C** 312
Duars plain, region of Bhutan **B** 150

Du Barry, Marie Jeanne Bécu, Countess (1746?–1793), French courtier, b. Champagne. She was court favorite of Louis XV. Aided by confidant, Duc d'Aiguillon, she ruled king and court (1769–74) until Louis's death. Arrested by Robespierre (1793) and tried by Revolutionary tribunal, she was condemned and guillotined.

Dubček (DOOB-check), **Alexander** (1921–   ), Czechoslovak political leader, b. Uhrovec, western Slovakia. He succeeded Antonin Novotný (1968) as first secretary of Communist Party, the first Slovak to lead it. He started a process of liberalization that was ended by invasion by USSR and some of Warsaw Treaty Organization members in August, 1968. He was replaced as first secretary (1969).
Czechoslovakia, history of **C** 564

Dubinsky, David (David Dobnievski) (1892–   ), American labor union official, b. Brest-Litovsk, Poland (now U.S.S.R.). After emigrating to United States (1911), he became member of International Ladies Garment Workers Union (1911) and was its president (1932–66). He was founder of Americans for Democratic Action (1947).

Dublin, capital of Ireland **I** 385
O'Connell Street, picture **I** 384
Dublin, University of, or Trinity College, Ireland **I** 385
Dublin Gate Theatre **T** 161
Dubois, Pierre, French jurist **P** 104

Du Bois (du-BOIS), **William Edward Burghardt** (1868–1963), American editor and author, Negro, b. Great Barrington, Mass. He was one of founders of National Association for the Advancement of Colored People (1909), director of publicity and research and editor of magazine *Crisis* (1910–32), and consultant to United Nations (1945). He joined Communist Party in 1961 and became Ghanaian citizen in 1963. Du Bois wrote 19 books, including *Suppression of the African Slave Trade.*

NAACP, history of **N** 96

Du Bois (du-BWA), **William Pène** (1916–   ), American author and illustrator of children's books, b. Nutley, N.J. His works include *The Twenty-one Balloons*, which won Newbery prize (1947), and the "Otto" series.

Dubos (du-BOSE), **René**, French-born American scientist **A** 312; picture **A** 315

Dubrovnik (DU-brov-nik), Yugoslavia, picture **Y** 359

Dubuffet (du-bu-FAY), **Jean** (1901–   ), French painter, b. Le Havre. His collages and paintings are characterized by childlike style, use of rich color and thick paint, and sense of humor. His works include *Snack for Two* and *The Butterfly Man.*

Dubuque (dub-UKE), Iowa
lock on the Mississippi, picture **I** 358

Dubuque, Julien, French-Canadian settler in Iowa **I** 356

Dubuque, University of, Dubuque, Iowa **I** 366

Duccio di Buoninsegna (DU-cho di bwon-een-SAYN-yah) (1255?–1319?), Italian painter. A prominent member of Sienese school, which combined Byzantine and Italian traditions, he is noted for development of characterization in his paintings. He portrayed figures having weight and solidity and anticipated later Renaissance style. Works include *Maesta*, located in Cathedral Museum at Siena, Italy.

altarpiece, picture **I** 461

Christ Choosing Two Disciples, painting **C** 282

humanism in Italian painting **I** 463

Duce (DU-chay), **Il,** popular name for Benito Mussolini **M** 552

Duchamp (du-SHON), **Marcel** (1887–1968), French painter, b. Blainville. Brother of artist Ramon Duchamp-Villon and Jacques Villon, he was a member of the cubist and dadaist art schools. He is best-known for his controversial painting *Nude Descending a Staircase.* He has been called the father of pop art.

Dada exhibited as sculpture **M** 393; **S** 105

Duchamp-Villon (du-SHOM-vi-ON), **Raymond** (1876–1918), French sculptor, b. Damville. A brother of artists Marcel and Gaston Duchamp, he was influenced by sculptor Auguste Rodin but later identified with cubists. Works include *The Horse, The Lovers,* and *Song.*

Duchesse (du-SHESS) **lace L** 19

Duckbills or platypuses, egg-laying mammals **M** 71; **P** 333–34

Australian wildlife **A** 504

Duck-billed dinosaurs D 179

Ducking stool, picture **C** 393

Duckpins, a bowling game **B** 349

Ducks, waterfowl with short legs, webbed front toes, and short, straight bills. These birds have a dense body covering, with down underlying the feathers. They dress their plumage with oil from a gland at the base of the tail. This helps waterproof the body. They shed their wing quills after breeding and at these times the birds are flightless. The birds travel in flocks and find their food under water. Dipping ducks, such as the common mallard, live in fresh water and feed by bobbing their head and neck into the water. Diving ducks feed by diving headfirst into the water.

animal communication **A** 277

Audubon painting of hawks and wild duck **A** 490

canvas-back duck, picture **B** 222

diving birds, special adaptations of **B** 223; picture **B** 222

flight feathers **B** 200

migration of, picture **H** 187

poultry **P** 423; picture **P** 422

tracks, picture **A** 272

Ductility, property of metals **M** 226
wire **W** 190a

Ductless glands B 279–80

Dude ranch, ranch resort for tourists or vacationers. Dude ranches often combine horseback riding and other ranch activities with comforts of a hotel.

Dudevant, Madame see Sand, George

Dudingston Curling Society, Edinburgh, Scotland **C** 555

Dudley, Edward R. (1911–   ), American public official and judge, Negro, b. South Boston, Va. He was assistant attorney general of New York State, U.S. ambassador to Liberia (1948–53), justice of the New York City Domestic Relations Court, and president of the Borough of Manhattan (1961–65). He was appointed to the New York State Supreme Court in 1965.

Dudley, Robert, earl of Leicester, English courtier, favored by Elizabeth I **E** 178

Dudok van Heel (DU-dok von HALE), **W. H.,** Dutch scientist **D** 276

Duels and dueling D 339–41

fencing **F** 84–86

flintlock pistols used **G** 416

Three Musketeers, The, excerpt **D** 342–43

See also Fencing

Du Fay, Charles, French chemist **P** 235

discoveries in electricity **E** 124, 125

Dufay, Guillaume (1400?–1474), Flemish composer, b. Hainault. He was a member of the Papal Choir in Rome (1428–33 and 1436–37), canon in cathedrals of Cambrai and Mons (1445–74), leader of Burgundian school, and greatest composer of his time. He wrote both religious and secular music, including masses, motets, Magnificats, and French chansons.

Burgundian Period in music **D** 363

choral music **C** 277

Renaissance music in France **F** 443–44; **R** 172

Dufek, George, American naval officer **P** 370

Duff, Sir Lyman Poore (1865–1955), Canadian jurist, b. Meaford, Ontario. He was a Canadian Supreme Court justice (1906) and chief justice (1933–44), and main author of report of Royal Commission on Transportation, known also as Duff Commission, set up to investigate Canada's railway problems.

Dufourspitze (der-FOUR-shpit-se), mountain, Switzerland **S** 500

Dufy (du-FE), **Raoul Ernest Joseph** (1877–1953), French painter, b. Le Havre. He was a member of controversial fauvist art movement in France. He later turned to textile, ceramic, and tapestry design. His paintings include *Sailboat at Sainte-Adresse, Honfleur Harbor,* and *The Paddock.*

Fishing, woodcut print **W** 229

Duggar, Benjamin Minge (1872–1956), American botanist, b. Gallion, Ala. He discovered aureomycin, a drug that is obtained from fungi and is effective against a wide range of bacterial diseases and some virus diseases. He also developed and introduced scientific methods into mushroom-growing industry.

Dugongs (DU-gongs), aquatic mammals **S** 106–07
  wildlife of Asia **A** 451
Dugouts, canoelike boats **C** 99; picture **H** 200
  early transportation **T** 257
Duich (DU-ick), **Lake,** Scotland, picture **S** 88
Duikers (DY-kers), hoofed mammals **H** 221

Du Jardin, Rosamund (1902–1963), American writer, b. Fairland, Ill. After publishing numerous stories and novels for adults, Rosamund du Jardin began writing for and about teen-agers. *Practically Seventeen* was the first of her books for younger readers, and later titles include *Showboat Summer* and *The Real Thing.*

Dukas (du-KA), **Paul Abraham** (1865–1935), French composer, b. Paris. A winner of the Prix de Rome (1888), he taught at Paris Conservatory (1910–35). His works include opera *Ariane et Barbe-Bleue,* ballet *La Péri,* and orchestral work *The Sorcerer's Apprentice.*
  musical impressionism in France **F** 447

Duke, Charles M., Jr., American astronaut **S** 345, 346
Duke Endowment F 391
Dukenfield, William Claude see Fields, W. C.
Duke University, Durham, North Carolina
  Rhine's research in extrasensory perception **E** 395–96
Dukhobors see Doukhobors
Dulcimer, musical instrument, picture **S** 439

Dulles, Allen Welsh (1893–1969), American administrator, b. Watertown, N.Y. He entered diplomatic service in 1916, later serving as chief of State Department's Division of Near Eastern Affairs (1922–26). He was chief of Office of Strategic Services in Switzerland (1942) after V-E Day, heading OSS mission to Germany. He was also director of Central Intelligence Agency (1953–61), member of Warren Commission (1963–64) reporting on assassination of President Kennedy, and author of *The Craft of Intelligence* and *The Secret Surrender.* He was awarded National Security medal in 1961.

Dulles, John Foster (1888–1959), American lawyer and statesman, b. Washington, D.C. He was a delegate to San Francisco Conference to organize United Nations (1945) and U.S. delegate to United Nations (1946–48, 1950). He was appointed interim U.S. senator from New York (1949) and secretary of state during Eisenhower administration (1953–59). His books include *War, Peace and Change* and *War or Peace.*

Duluth (dul-OOTH), Minnesota **M** 334
  Aerial Lift Bridge, picture **B** 401
Duluth (Dulhut), **Sieur** (Daniel Greysolon), French explorer **M** 336
Dumas (du-MA), **Alexandre,** *fils,* French novelist and playwright **D** 342; **F** 441
Dumas, Alexandre, *père,* French novelist and playwright **D** 342; **F** 441
  romanticism in French drama **D** 297
  Three Musketeers, The, excerpt **D** 342–43

Du Maurier, George Louis Palmella Busson (1834–1896), English novelist and illustrator, b. Paris, France. The grandfather of author Daphne Du Maurier, he is noted for illustrations in *Punch.* His books include *Peter Ibbet-*

sen and *Trilby,* the latter of which created the well-known character Svengali, the hypnotist.

Dumbarton Oaks Conference (1944), meeting to prepare proposals for international organization. At this conference the basis for United Nations charter (1945) was made. It was attended by representatives of United States, Great Britain, Soviet Union, and later China at Dumbarton Oaks mansion in Washington, D.C.
  United Nations, beginnings of **U** 80

Dumbbells, weights used for exercise **W** 107
Dumbfish, colonial American dish **C** 390
Dummy, in printing
  bookmaking **B** 330, 332
  magazines **M** 16
  newspapers **N** 202
Dummy, in ventriloquism **V** 302–03
Dumping, trade policy **I** 328
Dumps, refuse disposal spots **S** 34
Dump trucks B 447; **T** 297

Dun and Bradstreet, Inc., mercantile agency that compiles and distributes credit information on firms and persons in all types of business concerns. The findings, based on capital and credit, are published in *Reports* and *The Reference Book.* The firm was established (1933) by union of two credit information agencies.

Dunant (du-NON), **Henri,** Swiss philanthropist and founder of the Red Cross **R** 126; **S** 499
Dunbar, Paul Laurence, American poet **D** 344
  "Promise," poem from *Lyrics of Lowly Life* **D** 344
Duncan, Isadora, American dancer **D** 33
Duncan I, king of Scotland **S** 88

Duncan, Robert Todd (1903–   ), American singer and teacher, Negro, b. Danville, Ky. He has taught at Howard University, Washington, D.C., since 1931. Duncan's stage career includes the creation of the role of Porgy in Gershwin's *Porgy and Bess* (1935). He returned to Broadway in *Cabin in the Sky* (1940) and in a 1942 revival of *Porgy and Bess.* He has given concerts in the United States and Europe and has continued teaching.
  Negro artists and musicians **N** 102

Duncan Phyfe furniture F 509
Duncan technique, modern dance form **D** 33
Dunciad, The, by Alexander Pope **P** 393
Dundee, Scotland **S** 87
Dunedin (dun-E-din), New Zealand **N** 241
Dunes
  fences against erosion, picture **E** 281
  Michigan, Sleeping Bear Dunes National Lakeshore **M** 268
  national monument areas, pictures **C** 411; **I** 147

Dunham, Bertha Mabel (1881–1957), Canadian author and librarian, b. Harriston, Ontario. A winner of Canadian Library Association's medal (1948) for *Kristli's Trees,* her works for adults include *Toward Sodom, The Trail of the King's Men, Grand River,* and *Trail of the Conestoga.*

Dunham, Katherine (1910–   ), American dancer, choreographer, and ethnologist, Negro, b. Chicago, Ill. She is best-known for her repertoire of dances based on anthropological research in ritual, dance, and folklore of Caribbean and South America. She appeared in Broadway musical *Cabin in the Sky* and films *Carnival of Rhythm* and *Stormy Weather.*
  Negroes in the arts **N** 102

Dunkers, or **Tunkers,** or **Dunkards** (from German *eintunken*, meaning "to dip"), popular name for German Baptists. This religious sect was founded in 1708 at Schwarzenau, Germany, by Alexander Mack. It is characterized by close adherence to teachings of New Testament, simplicity in living, opposition to military service, advocacy of nonresistance, and practice of triple immersion of candidate for church membership (hence the name). Dunkers emigrated to Pennsylvania (1719–29) to seek religious asylum. Since 1728 schism, a number of branches have appeared.

Dunkirk, or **Dunkerque,** seaport and fortress of northern France, on the English Channel, about 10 miles from the Belgian border. Dunkirk was the destination of the fighting retreat of the British and French troops in May, 1940.
World War II **W** 289

Dunlap, William, American playwright **D** 299
first professional playwright in American literature **A** 215
Dunlop, John Boyd, Scottish inventor **T** 196
bicycles with rubber tires improve transportation **T** 265

Dunmore, 4th earl of (John Murray) (1732–1809), British colonial governor, b. Scotland. He was appointed governor of New York (1770) and then of Virginia (1771). Accused of inciting war known as Lord Dunmore's War (1774) with Ohio Indians to distract Virginia colonists from grievances against England, he was routed by colonists and returned (1776) to England.

Dunmore's War, 1774 **W** 140

Dunning, John Ray (1907–), American physicist, b. Shelby, Nebr. He headed scientific team that produced first atomic fission reaction in United States. His work was vital in development of atomic bomb and included constructing atom smashers and showing importance of uranium 235.

Dunninger, Joseph, American magician and mind reader **M** 19

Duns Scotus (DUNS SCO-tus), **John** (Doctor Subtilis) (1265?–1308?), Scottish theologian, b. probably Duns. He was the founder of Scotism, system of thought that contended with scholastic system of St. Thomas Aquinas. He is believed to have won title of Doctor Subtilis by his oratorical skill in defending doctrine of Immaculate Conception. His works include philosophic grammar and commentaries on the Bible and Aristotle. Ridicule of his work and followers in 16th century gave rise to use of term "dunce" for a pedant or blockhead.

Dunstable, John, English composer **E** 268
Duodecimal system, or base-12 system, of numeration **N** 396, 398
Dupin, Amandine *see* Sand, George
Duplessis, Maurice LeNoblet, Canadian statesman **Q** 13
Duplicating machines **O** 57; pictures **O** 56
copying inks **I** 256
photocopy machines in libraries **L** 174–75
Du Pont, Eleuthere Irénée, French-born American industrialist **D** 99
Du Pont, Lammot, American chemist and inventor **E** 390
Du Pont, Pierre S., American industrialist **D** 99
Du Pont Laboratories, near Wilmington, Delaware, picture **D** 92

du Pré, Jacqueline (1945–), British cellist, b. Oxford, England. She made her concert hall debut in London at the age of 16. Soloist with various leading orchestras, she has also appeared in many of her later concerts with her husband, Daniel Barenboim, a pianist-conductor.

Dupré (du-PRAY), **Marcel** (1886–1971), French organist and composer, b. Rouen. Organist at Notre Dame Cathedral and St. Sulpice church (both in Paris), he was known for his original improvisations. His compositions include *Symphonie-Passion*, *Le Chemin de la Croix*, and a cantata, *Psyché*.

Dupuy de Lôme (der-PWE d'LOM), **Enrique,** Spanish ambassador **S** 374
Duquesne (du-KANE), **University of,** Pittsburgh, Pa. **P** 137
Durand, Peter, English inventor of tin cans **F** 345–46
Durango, Colorado **C** 414
Durant, Will, American writer **A** 215
Durante (dur-AN-te), **Jimmy,** American actor, pictures **J** 58, **R** 59
Durazzo (du-RA-tzo), Albania **A** 146
Durban, South Africa **S** 271
Dürer (DUR-er), **Albrecht,** German artist and engraver **D** 345
German art **G** 169
graphic arts **G** 303, 305; **I** 89
Holy Family, The, engraving **B** 161
Knight, Death, and the Devil, engraving **G** 303
magic square **N** 382, 383
medieval illustrations, picture **I** 89
Penitent, The, woodcut **G** 169
Renaissance art **R** 171
Self Portrait, painting **R** 170
woodcut printing **W** 228
Durham, North Carolina **N** 318
Durham Cathedral, England **G** 266; picture **E** 235
Durham report, recommending self-government for Canada **C** 73
Durkheim, Émile, French sociologist **S** 227
Dürrenmatt, Friedrich, Swiss writer **G** 179
Durum Triangle, North Dakota, wheat-raising section **N** 328–29
Durum wheats **W** 154, 156
Duryea (DUR-yay), automobile **A** 545; picture **A** 543

Duryea, Charles Edgar (1861–1938), American inventor and manufacturer, b. near Canton, Ill. Considered a "father of the automobile," he sold first American-built automobile (1896). He invented the spray carburetor (1892) and was first to use pneumatic (air-inflated) tires on automobiles (1893).
automobile manufacturing, history of **A** 547

Du Sable, Jean Baptiste Pointe, Haitian trader **N** 91

Duse (du-ZAY), **Eleonora** (1859–1924), Italian actress, b. railway carriage near Venice. Considered one of the greatest Italian actresses, she popularized plays of Gabriele D'Annunzio with her interpretations of title roles in *La Gioconda* and *Francesca da Rimini*. She also appeared in plays by Ibsen and Dumas.

Düsseldorf, Germany **G** 158
Dust **D** 346–48
air pollution **A** 109
atmosphere contains **A** 479
cloud formation and dust **C** 358–60
comets **C** 418–19
diamond dust for grinding and polishing **D** 155; **G** 387

ILLUSTRATION CREDITS

The following list credits, by page, the sources of illustrations used in Volume D of THE NEW BOOK OF KNOWLEDGE. Credits are listed illustration by illustration—left to right, top to bottom. Wherever appropriate, the name of the photographer or artist has been listed with the source, the two being separated by a dash. When two or more illustrations appear on one page, their credits are separated by semicolons.

E, fifth letter of the English alphabet **E** 1
  See also Alphabet
Ea (AY-a), Babylonian god **M** 557

Eads, James Buchanan (1820–1887), American engineer and inventor, b. Lawrenceburg, Ind. He built seven ironclad ships in 65 days (1861) for Union defense of Mississippi River. He constructed (1867–74) Eads Bridge across Mississippi at St. Louis and opened a mouth of the river (1874–79) by channeling river deposits.
  first steel deck-arch bridge **B** 398

Eagle, constellation *see* Aquila
Eagle, golf score **G** 255
Eagle, Brooklyn, newspaper edited by Walt Whitman **W** 165
Eagle, The, poem by Alfred, Lord Tennyson **T** 101
Eagles, birds **E** 2; pictures **B** 230; **E** 2
  emblem, national **G** 329–30
  figures on Roman standards **F** 225
  Is the bald eagle really bald? **E** 2
  nests **B** 213
  Old Abe, eagle mascot **W** 192
  threatened species **B** 232
  where birds live **B** 226
Eaglets, baby eagles **E** 2
Eakins (A-kins), **Thomas,** American painter **U** 121
Eames, Charles, American designer **F** 510
Ear **B** 285
  body's senses are guards on the alert **B** 280–81
  brain, sensory systems **B** 365
  care of **H** 85
  deafness **D** 50–53
  ear examination **M** 208h
  fishes, hearing organs of **F** 191–92
  noise, how ear and hearing are affected by
    N 269–70
  of insects **I** 267–68
  sound, how we hear **S** 259
Eardrum, membrane in the ear **B** 285

Earhart (AIR-hart), **Amelia** (Amelia Earhart Putnam) (1898–1937), American aviatrix, b. Atchison, Kan. She was first woman to cross Atlantic in plane (1928) and to make solo transatlantic flight (1932) and solo transpacific flight, from Hawaii to California (1935). She was lost over Pacific on flight around the world.

Earls, English nobility **E** 216

Early, Jubal Anderson (1816–1894), American officer in Confederate Army, b. Franklin County, Va. He opposed secession but joined Confederate Army when Virginia seceded (1861), and he commanded attack on Washington through Shenandoah Valley (1864–65). Defeated by Commander Sheridan at Waynesboro, Va., and relieved of command, Early fled to Mexico and took ship to Canada (1866). He returned to Virginia (1869), but refused to take oath of allegiance to United States.

Early Bird, communication satellite **C** 440; **S** 43; picture **S** 42
Ear of Wheat Thursday, religious holiday **R** 153–54

Earp (ERP), **Wyatt** (Berry Stapp Earp) (1848–1929), American frontiersman, b. Monmouth, Ill. He was chief deputy marshal of Dodge City (1876), guard for Wells Fargo and Co., and sheriff of Tombstone, Ariz. (1879). With his brothers and a friend he won a 60-second gunfight in O.K. Corral, restoring order in Tombstone. The question of whether he should be considered a heroic frontiersman or ruthless killer is still disputed.
  Dodge City, Kansas **K** 186

Earrings, jewelry **J** 99
Ear shells, mollusks *see* Abalones
Earth **E** 3–17
  age of **E** 21
  area, percentages of water and land areas **E** 3
  atmosphere **A** 479–82; **E** 23
  axis **E** 4, 24
  caves and caverns **C** 152–58
  chemical theories of "ancient elements" **C** 206
  climate **C** 343–48; **W** 87–90
  clock-calendar of earth **T** 187–88
  clouds **C** 358–61
  core **E** 8, 19, 39–40
  cosmic rays **C** 511–13
  crust **E** 8, 9–10, 18–19, 31–32, 39–40; balance of,
    diagram **G** 114
  direction, how to tell **D** 182–83
  distance from sun **E** 3, 22
  dust **D** 346–48
  earth and its sun **E** 22–30
  earthquakes **E** 31–40
  earth tides **M** 449
  eclipses **E** 46–47
  environment **E** 272a–272h
  equator **E** 272h
  equinoxes **E** 272h **S** 109
  erosion **E** 13
  evolution and age of the earth **E** 338
  Ewing-Donn theory of Ice Ages **I** 24
  fossils show geologic ages of earth **F** 383
  geography **G** 94–108
  geology **G** 109–21
  geophysicists study earth's interior **G** 119
  geysers and hot springs **G** 192–93
  glaciers **G** 223–25
  gravity and gravitation **G** 320–25
  ground water **W** 53
  history of **E** 18–21
  ice, area covered by **I** 3
  inner heat, a possible source of energy **E** 203
  International Geophysical Year (IGY) **I** 310–20
  islands, formation of **I** 423
  jet streams **J** 88–91
  landforms see by name, as Deserts, Lakes, etc.
  latitude and longitude **L** 81–83
  Magellan's voyage around **E** 380–81; **M** 17
  magnetic field **M** 26
  magnetism causes radiation belts **R** 47–48
  mantle **E** 8, 19, 39–40
  maps and globes **M** 88–95
  Mars and earth compared, diagram **M** 105, 106
  mass **E** 7
  meteors and meteorites **C** 419–21
  Moho boundary between crust and mantle **E** 8, 39–40
  moon, planetary system of earth and moon
    M 446–47; **P** 272
  mountain building **M** 492–99
  ocean currents, diagram **L** 232
  ocean floor **E** 14; **G** 119–20
  orbit of **E** 22–23
  origin and history **E** 18–21
  origins, mythological **G** 356–57; **M** 557–59
  planetary system of earth and moon **P** 272
  population **P** 394–97
  Pythagorean theory **A** 471
  radiation of earth's crust **F** 35–36
  rain, snow, sleet and hail **R** 93–98
  rotation gives us our clock-calendar **T** 187–88
  seasons **S** 108–12
  shape of **E** 5
  soils **S** 230–34
  solar system **S** 239–49

Earth (continued)
  sunspot disturbances **A** 476; **S** 458–60
  tides **T** 179–85
  universe, beginning and end, theories **U** 196–204
  Venus and earth compared **P** 270–71
  volcanoes **V** 377–86
  water cycle **W** 51–53
  water regulates earth's temperature **W** 54
  Why is ocean water salty? **E** 16
  winds affected by earth's rotation **W** 186
  world, as seen from a space ship **W** 254
  zones **Z** 372–73
  See also World

Earth Day, April 22, 1970, was first day declared for action against environmental pollution in United States. Millions throughout the country celebrated earth's "birthday" by cleaning up neighborhoods or marching down streets free of traffic. In Washington D.C., legislation was proposed to curb pollution of natural resources.
  environment **E** 272a–272h

Earthenware, pottery **P** 413
  ceramic work **C** 173
Earth pig see Aardvark
Earthquakes **E** 31–40
  Alaska **A** 132, 141
  California **C** 28; **L** 347
  Chile **C** 253
  earth's interior **E** 8–9, 13
  geological study of earth's interior **G** 112
  geophysical findings with seismograph **G** 118–19
  Iceland, located over great rift in the earth **I** 42
  IGY studies **I** 315–16
  Japan, 1923 **J** 33; **T** 204
  man-made, to study earth's interior **E** 40
  man-made vibrations used to locate minerals **M** 314
  mountain building **M** 493
  ocean floor movements **O** 35
  San Francisco earthquake and fire, 1906 **S** 31
  tidal waves see Tsunamis, seismic sea waves
  Tokyo earthquake, 1923 **T** 204
  Wright's earthquake-proof buildings **W** 315
Earth sciences
  experiments-weather, geology, oceanography **E** 359–61
Earthshine, on the moon **M** 448
Earthworks, of forts **F** 377
Earthworms **W** 309–11
  animal movement on land **A** 265
  blood system, diagram **B** 259
  helpful to the soil **S** 232
  nervous system, diagram **B** 363
Earwigs, insects, picture **P** 288
East Africa, Portuguese see Mozambique
East Africa Protectorate, now Kenya and Uganda **K** 228–33; **U** 7
East Asia, or Far East **A** 448–49
East Berlin, capital of East Germany **B** 145
  Alexandra Platz, picture **B** 144
East China Sea **O** 46
East Corinth, Vermont, picture **V** 308
East End, district of London, England **L** 338–39
Easter **E** 41–42
  festival in a nonreligious form in U.S.S.R. **U** 29
  how to make an Easter card **G** 374
  religious holidays fixed by Easter **R** 153–54
  toys **T** 233
Easter eggs
  Fabergé's jeweled egg **J** 100; picture **J** 97
  pagan Norse custom, origin **N** 277
Easter Island, Chile **I** 429; picture **I** 433
  art of the Pacific islands **P** 10

Chile's island possessions **C** 251
  stone heads, wonders of the world, picture **W** 217
Easterlies, winds **W** 186–87
Easter lilies
  Bermuda Easter lilies **B** 146
Eastern, or Uniate, **Catholics** see Uniats
Eastern Desert, Egypt see Arabian Desert
Eastern goldfinches, birds, picture **B** 235
  Iowa, state bird of **I** 357
  New Jersey, state bird of **N** 164
Eastern hemlock, tree, picture **T** 275
  state tree of Pennsylvania **P** 129
Eastern Ice Yachting Association **I** 29
Eastern Michigan University **M** 267
Eastern music see Oriental music
Eastern Orthodox churches see Orthodox Eastern churches
Eastern Penitentiary, Cherry Hill, Pennsylvania **P** 468
Eastern phoebe, bird, picture **B** 235
  See also Flycatchers
Eastern Region, Nigeria (Biafra) **N** 256, 258
Eastern Roman Empire see Byzantine Empire
Eastern Schism see Great Schism
Eastern Shore, of Maryland **M** 116

Eastern Star, Order of the, charitable and social organization of Master Masons and their female relatives. The order was introduced into colonies by French general Lafayette during Revolutionary War. Chapters were started throughout United States and Scotland (1868) by Robert Macoy, who wrote the ritual.

Eastern Townships, Quebec, Canada **Q** 10a
Eastern white pine, tree
  Maine's state flower and tree **M** 32
  state tree of Michigan **M** 259

Easter Rebellion (1916), Irish attempt to gain independence at a time when England was fighting World War I. Led by P. H. Pearse of the Republican National Brotherhood and James Connolly of the Sinn Fein ("Ourselves Alone") Party, the uprising in Dublin failed when German arms and aid from Irish Volunteers did not materialize. Casement and 14 other leaders were captured and executed, and hundreds were imprisoned.

East Germany see German Democratic Republic
East Greenland Current **I** 43
East India companies **E** 43
East India Company, British **E** 43
  Ganges valley controlled by **I** 133
  trading monopolies **T** 305
East Indies see Indonesia; Southeast Asia
East Lynne (LINN), novel by Mrs. Henry Wood **D** 299
Eastman, George, American inventor **E** 44
  George Eastman House, a museum **N** 222
  photography, history of **P** 212
  photography's role in communication **C** 434
Eastman Kodak Company **P** 212
Eastman School of Music, Rochester, New York **E** 44
Easton flag, 1776 **F** 229
East Pakistan see Bangladesh
East Providence, Rhode Island **R** 224
East River, New York City **N** 228

East Siberian Sea, part of the Arctic Ocean along the Russian coast between New Siberian Islands and Wrangle Island. A shallow sea, it is navigable only during ice-free months of August and September. The principal port is Ambarchik, Soviet Union.

Easy-to-read books **C** 243

Eaton, Anna Thaxter (1881–1971), American editor and author of children's books. She compiled poetry books, including *Poet's Craft*, *Animals' Christmas*, and *Welcome Christmas*. She wrote *Reading with Children*.

Eaton, Jeanette (1886?–1968), American author, b. Columbus, Ohio. She was noted for her biographies written for teen-age readers. She graduated from Vassar College, received a master's degree from Ohio State University, and did post-graduate work at the Sorbonne. Among her books were *Gandhi: Fighter Without a Sword*; *The Story of Eleanor Roosevelt*; *Washington, the Nation's First Hero*; *Young Lafayette*; *Trumpeter's Tale, the Story of Young Louis Armstrong*; and *America's Own Mark Twain*.

Eaton, Margaret ("Peggy") **O'Neill,** wife of Jackson's Secretary of War   **J** 6
Eaves, of roofs   **H** 170

Eban (E-ban), **Abba Solomon** (1915–   ), Israeli statesman, b. Capetown, South Africa. He worked for independent Jewish state and presented the case to UN (1947). With formation of independent Israel, he became minister to UN (1949–59), where he was known for eloquent debating in six languages. As ambassador to United States (1950–59), he helped negotiate settlement of Suez crisis. Eban has been minister of education (1960–63), deputy prime minister (1963–66), and minister of foreign affairs (since 1966).

Ebbinghaus (EBB-ing-house), **Hermann,** German psychologist   **P** 493–94

Ebb tide, an outgoing tide. It is the opposite of flood tide.

Ebenezer (eb-en-NE-zer) (from Hebrew words meaning "the stone of help"), in Old Testament (Samuel 4:1, 5:1), site of battle in which Israelites were defeated by Philistines and sacred Ark of the Covenant was stolen. Ebenezer also refers to the stone erected by Samuel to commemorate God's help in victory over Philistines.

Ebert (A-bert), **Friedrich,** German statesman   **G** 162
  end of World War I   **W** 281
Ebro (A-bro) **River,** Spain   **R** 243
EB virus   **C** 93–94

Ecce Homo (ECH-e HO-mo) (Latin, meaning "Behold the Man!"), in New Testament (John 19:3), words spoken by Pilate when presenting Christ to Jews before crucifixion. It was title of controversial essay on Christ's life and teachings by Sir John Seeley. In art the term refers to portrayal of Christ wearing crown of thorns.

Ecclesiastes (ec-cle-si-AST-ese), book of Bible,   **B** 156
Ecclesiasticus (ec-cle-si-AST-ic-us), apocryphal book of Bible   **B** 159
Echandi Jiménez, Mario, president of Costa Rica   **C** 519
Echeverria Alvarez, Luis, Mexican president   **M** 250
Echidnas (e-KID-nas), or "spiny anteaters"   **P** 333–34
  mammals   **M** 71
Echinoderms (ec-KY-no-derms), spiny-skinned sea animals
  sea urchins and their relatives   **S** 404
  starfishes   **S** 402–03
Echo (EC-ho)   **E** 45
  behavior of sound   **S** 260–61
  echolocation of bats   **B** 97
  ghost echoes, or ocean's deep scattering layer   **O** 37
  radio detection and ranging   **R** 34
  whispering galleries, ellipse-shaped domes   **G** 129

Echo I and II, balloon-satellites   **B** 34; picture   **H** 107
  antenna to receive signals, picture   **R** 72

Echo, In Greek and Roman mythology, an oread, or nymph. She distracted Hera from Zeus's philanderings and thenceforward was permitted to speak only after someone else had spoken and then only to repeat what had been said. She is supposed to have wasted away to a voice while pining for Narcissus.

Echolocation (ec-ho-lo-CAY-tion), process of locating objects by sound waves
  bats   **B** 97
  dolphins and porpoises   **D** 274, 275
  echo   **E** 45
Echo sounder, device used in oceanography   **O** 27

Eckener, Hugo (1868–1954), German airship constructor and commander, b. Flensburg. President of Zeppelin Airship Co., he made a transatlantic airship flight (1924) in ZR-3 (later named Los Angeles). He commanded first global airship flight (1929) in *Graf Zeppelin* and designed many airships, including ill-fated *Hindenburg.*

Eclecticism (ec-LEC-ti-cism) (from Greek *eklektikos*, meaning "selective"), in art, practice of selecting best aspects of various old styles and combining them to produce new works of superior merit. Term also refers to any philosophy that borrows from different schools of thought in an attempt to resolve philosophical problems.
  architecture since the Victorian Age   **E** 241

Eclipses   **E** 46–47
  astrologers' early records   **A** 470
  confirmation of general relativity theory, picture   **R** 144
  double shadow of the moon   **L** 260
  how to make a "sun camera" for looking at an eclipse   **E** 361
  moon and sun, eclipses demonstrated   **M** 448
  myths of Korea   **M** 558–59
Eclipsing binary stars   **S** 409
Ecliptic, of the sun   **S** 109
Ecology (e-COL-ogy)   **E** 272a; **L** 250–59
  adaptations, each organism its own niche   **L** 222–23
  life in the forest   **F** 371–72
  life zones by altitude   **Y** 352–53; **Z** 372–73
  living things living together   **K** 257, 259
  world vegetation and climate patterns   **W** 254–55

Econometrics, a mathematical expression of economic theory. The system measures the relationships between different forms of economic activity and may predict the result of different economic policies.

Economic Advisers, Council of, advisory body established by Employment Act of 1946. Consisting of three members appointed by president with advice and consent of Senate, it assists in preparing presidential economic reports for Congress, appraises national economy, and recommends economic policies.
  executive office of the president   **P** 452
  Truman's administration   **T** 301

Economic and Social Council, United Nations   **U** 84
Economic assistance see Foreign aid programs
Economics   **E** 48–51
  automobile, impact on   **A** 551
  banks and banking   **B** 44d–51
  budgets, family   **B** 425–26
  capitalism   **C** 104–05

Economics (continued)
causes of population growth **P** 395
Communist system **C** 442–45
co-operatives **C** 499–500
depressions and recessions **D** 121–22
France's concerted economy **F** 411
inflation and deflation **I** 252–53
international trade **I** 326–30
Marx, Karl **M** 113
mass production **M** 151
money **M** 409–12
Nobel prize see **Nobel Prize in Economic Science**
poverty **P** 424–424b
socialism **S** 220
social studies **S** 223
stock market **S** 427–33
tariff **T** 25
taxation **T** 26–27
trade and commerce **T** 242–43
trusts and monopolies **T** 303–06
unemployment insurance helps control recessions
    U 26
work, world of **W** 251–53
world distribution of economic activities, diagram
    W 267
Economic sanctions see Sanctions, International

Economy (from Greek *oikos*, meaning "house," and *nomos*, meaning "manager"), art of managing a household. Word also refers to the orderly management of a community's or nation's resources for development of productivity. It has developed into science, with laws regulating production and distribution of wealth.

ECSC see European Coal and Steel Community
Ector, foster father of King Arthur **A** 443
Ecuador (EC-wa-dor) **E** 52–58
    flag **F** 242
    life in Latin America **L** 47–61
    national anthem **N** 21
Ecumenical (ec-u-MEN-ic-al), or unity, **movement,** among
    churches **P** 486
Ecumenical councils, of Roman Catholic Church **R** 294
    early Christian Church **O** 228
    movement toward greater unity **R** 135
    Nicaea, Council of, A.D. 325 **R** 289
    Pope John XXIII **J** 122; **P** 99
    Trent, Council of, 1545–63 **G** 375; **R** 294
    Vatican Council II **R** 298–99
Eczema (EC-ze-ma), allergy disease **D** 192
Edam (E-dam) **cheese** **D** 13
Eddas, Icelandic books of songs and legends, basis of
    Norse mythology **N** 277
    Icelandic literature **I** 42
    Scandinavian literature **S** 50
Eddy, Mary Baker, American founder of Church of Christ,
    Scientist **N** 161
    Protestant denominations **P** 484
Eddy, William A., American meteorologist **K** 267
Eddystone Light, folk song **F** 323
Eddystone Light, Plymouth, England **L** 275, 276

Eden, Anthony (Sir Robert Anthony Eden, Earl of Avon)
(1897–   ), British statesman, b. Ferry Hill, Durham. He
has been Conservative member of Parliament (1923–57),
secretary of state for foreign affairs (1935–38, 1940–45,
1951–55), secretary of state for war (1940), leader,
House of Commons (1942–45), deputy prime minister
(1951–55), and prime minister (1955–57).

Eden, Garden of
    Was the "apple" really an apple? **A** 334

Edentata, order of mammals **M** 62, 69
Ederle (A-der-le), **Gertrude,** American swimmer **E** 58
Edict, decree or order see by name, as Milan, Edict of
Edinburgh (ED-in-bur-a), capital of Scotland **S** 87; **U** 72
    planned expansion **U** 233
Edinburgh, Duke of, see Philip, Prince
Edinburgh Castle, Scotland, picture **U** 72
Edinburgh Festival, Scotland **M** 551
Edirne (ed-IR-ne), Turkey, picture **T** 327

Edison, Charles (1890–1969), American businessman and
public official, b. West Orange, N.J. The son of Thomas
Alva Edison, he served as assistant secretary (1937–39)
and secretary (1939–40) of the Navy and as governor of
New Jersey (1941–44).

Edison, Thomas Alva, American inventor **E** 59–60
    communication advanced by inventions **C** 434
    incandescent lamp **L** 284
    invented singing doll **D** 268
    phonograph **P** 196
    quoted on genius **Q** 20
    several inventors worked on incandescent lamp **I** 334
Edison National Historic Site, West Orange, New Jersey
    E 60; **N** 174
Edith Cavell, Mount, Alberta, Canada **J** 55
Edith Macy Training Center, for Girl Scouts, Pleasant-
    ville, New York **G** 219
Edition, in engraving and printing **E** 272
Editorials, essays giving opinions of editors or publishers
    N 201
    cartoons **C** 125–28
Editors and editing
    book publishing **B** 330, 331; **L** 181; **P** 513–15
    communication **C** 441
    magazines **M** 15
    magnetic tape for records **H** 125
    motion pictures **M** 484
    newspapers **N** 201, 202
Edmonds, Walter D., American novelist **A** 213
Edmonton, capital of Alberta **A** 146f; picture **A** 146g
    cities of Canada **C** 67
Edmontonia (ed-mon-TO-nia), dinosaur **D** 180
Edmundston, New Brunswick, Canada **N** 138c
Edo, Japan see Tokyo, capital of Japan
Edom see Esau
Educable (ED-u-ca-ble), mildly retarded children **R** 191
Education **E** 61–84
    ability grouping **E** 79
    adult see Adult education
    audio-visual education **E** 77–78
    blind, education of the **B** 251–54
    child development **C** 231–34
    children's literature, new theories in development of
        C 237
    colleges and universities **U** 205–24
    colonial America **C** 392, 394; picture **C** 391
    computer-assisted instruction (CAI) **C** 457
    consumer education **C** 494–494a
    deaf, special classes for **D** 51–53
    Dewey, John **D** 151; **E** 76
    driver education **D** 318–21
    economics **E** 48
    examinations for college entrance **E** 348–49
    French system **F** 404
    Froebel, Friedrich **E** 71; **K** 243
    grant money from foundations **F** 392
    guidance counseling **G** 397–400
    handicapped, rehabilitation of the **H** 27–30
    health education **H** 82–85
    Huxley, Thomas, promoted science teaching **H** 300
    industrial arts **I** 227–28

Edward the Confessor, Saint (1002?–1066), king of England (1042–66), b. Oxfordshire. He spent early part of life in Normandy, France. He was called to throne (1042) to succeed half-brother, Harthacnut. Despite intrigues by members of his court, his reign was one of nearly unbroken peace. He ordered construction of Westminster Abbey. Edward was canonized in 1161. His feast day is Oct. 13.

Effervescent (ef-fer-VES-cent) **salt,** mixture of a carbonate, usually sodium bicarbonate, and a solid organic acid, such as citric or tartaric acid. When dissolved in water, the acid reacts with the carbonate to release carbon dioxide gas, as can be seen from the resulting bubbles in such products as headache tablets and fruit drinks.

Egghead, term for an intellectual, often used in a belittling manner. It became widely popular during presidential campaign of 1952 as expression to describe Democratic candidate Adlai Stevenson and his followers.

Eggs (continued)
  grades for marketing M 102–03
  nutrition in food substances N 416
Egg tempera, artist's paint P 30
Egley, William, English artist, early designer of Christ-
    mas cards C 294

Egret, slender-bodied wading bird with long legs and
neck found throughout the world. Snowy egret is white
with black legs and yellow feet. Up to 18 inches tall, this
bird develops many plumes on its back during breeding
season. Killed for these plumes, snowy egret is now
greatly reduced in numbers. Picture B 238

Egypt (The Arab Republic of Egypt) E 90b–92
  Aswan High Dam D 21
  Cairo C 7–8
  Egyptian mourners at pyramids of Giza, picture F 495
  flag F 236
  homes, picture H 173
  joint military command with Iraq I 383
  literature A 76d
  movie theater, near the pyramids, picture M 485
  Nasser, Gamal Abdel N 15
  national athem N 22
  Nile River N 260–61
  Suez Canal S 450–52
  Syria S 508
  UNESCO teacher training center T 43
  waterwheel for irrigation, picture A 63
  See also Egypt, ancient
Egypt, ancient A 217, 220–23
  alchemy C 207
  animal gods M 560
  architecture of see Egyptian architecture
  art of see Egyptian art
  astronomy, origins of A 470–71
  ball games as religious ceremonies B 20–21
  beauty culture B 110
  bread making B 385–86
  building construction B 435
  burial customs E 95–102
  calendar A 222
  canal system C 83
  candles, use of C 96
  cat, sacred animal of C 141, 142
  communication, hieroglyphic writing C 431
  dance accompanies rites of worship D 23
  decorative arts D 67–68
  development of cities U 232
  engineering projects E 207
  funeral customs F 492
  geometry G 122–23
  homes H 177–78
  jewelry styles J 93; picture J 95
  Jewish settlement in 1st century J 106–07
  libraries L 193–94
  lighthouse, Pharos, a wonder of the ancient world
    L 275; W 216
  locks and keys L 322–23
  masonry, history of B 393–94
  medical treatments M 203
  music A 245–46
  mythology M 560
  Negro rulers N 89–90
  Nile River N 261
  numerals N 390
  papyrus "paper" scrolls B 318
  science, advances in S 60–61
  ships and shipbuilding S 155
  slavery S 195
  timekeeping W 44

wonders of the ancient world W 214, 216
writing, early systems W 318
writing inks I 256
Egyptian architecture E 93–103
  art as a record A 438b
  obelisks O 5–6
  tombs and temples to last forever A 371–72
Egyptian art E 93–103
  art as a record A 438b
  fresco from tomb, picture A 361
  furniture design F 505
  painted carving, picture A 437
  painting P 15
  pottery P 414
  sculpture S 92–93
  statues and statuettes, pictures A 348, 350, D 134
  temple to Ramses II, picture A 363
Egyptian cotton C 524
Egyptian Museum, Cairo, picture M 510

Ehrenburg (ERE-en-bork), Ilya Grigorievich (1891–1967),
Russian writer, b. Kiev. He joined Bolshevik Party (1906),
was arrested (1908), but escaped to Paris (1909–17). He
was a famous Soviet journalist during World War II. His
novels include The Extraordinary Adventures of Julio
Jurenito, Out of Chaos, and The Thaw.

Ehrlich (EHR-lick), Paul, German bacteriologist D 216
  first drug to be created in the laboratory D 327

Eichmann (IKE-monn), Adolf (1906–1962), German lieutenant colonel in Hitler's National Socialist (Nazi) elite
corps (SS), b. Solingen. He was head of Gestapo's "Jewish affairs" (1939–45), in charge of location, deportation,
and extermination of Jews in Germany, other Axis
countries, and occupied areas. Arrested in Argentina
(1960) by Israeli agents and taken to Israel for trial, he
was convicted (1961) of war crimes and crimes against
humanity. Eichmann was hanged in first civil execution
to be carried out in Israel.

Eiderdown, fine, soft down from eider duck, used in
    quilts and upholstery B 200; U 227
Eielson (A-el-sen), Carl Ben, American aviator A 142
  first flight to Antarctica P 368

Eiffel (I-fel), Alexandre Gustave (1832–1923), French
engineer, b. Dijon. He constructed framework for Bartholdi's Statue of Liberty, designed locks for Panama
Canal, and is famous for construction (1887–89) of 984-
foot Eiffel Tower in Paris.

Eiffel Tower, Paris P 70; picture F 403
  built for French International Exposition, 1889 F 16
Eight, The, art group P 30
Eighteenth Amendment, to the U.S. Constitution U 157
  See also Prohibition; Volstead Act
Eijkman (IKE-mon), Christiaan, Dutch doctor D 216
  vitamins, discovery of V 370a
Einhard (INE-hart), monk and historian of Charlemagne's
    reign C 189
Einkorn, a kind of wheat W 154
Einstein (INE-stine), Albert, German-born American scien-
    tist E 104–06
  gravitation and acceleration theory G 325
  nuclear energy N 353
  physics, advances in P 238
  relativity R 139–44
  science, advances in S 76
  theory of matter and energy M 173
Einsteinium, element E 154, 161
Eire (AIR-uh), Gaelic name for Ireland I 386

Eisele, Donn F., American astronaut **S** 344, 345, 346
Eisenhower, Dwight D., 34th president of United States
   E 107–11
   Abilene, Kansas family home **K** 190
   connection with football **F** 356
   D Day broadcast, excerpt from Anne Frank's Diary
     D 157
   Eisenhower Center, Abilene, Kansas **K** 183, 184
   Eisenhower dollars minted **C** 375
   Eisenhower National Historic Site, Gettysburg,
     Pennsylvania **P** 138
   with Richard Nixon, picture **N** 262c
Eisenhower, Mamie Doud, wife of Dwight D. Eisenhower
   E 108; **F** 179; pictures **E** 108, **F** 178
Eisenhower Doctrine **E** 111
Eisenhower Tunnel, Colorado **C** 415
Eisenstein, Sergei, Russian motion picture director
   M 484, 487
Eisteddfod, Welsh national festival **W** 3
Eklutna (ek-LU-tna), Alaska **A** 140
Ekwensi, Cyprian, Nigerian novelist **A** 76c
El, numeral **N** 396
El, except for entries below see second part of name,
   as Alamein, El
Elands (E-lands), antelopes **H** 221
Elapids, cobra snakes **S** 207–08; pictures **S** 206

Elastic Clause, last clause of Article I, Section VIII of
U.S. Constitution, which gives Congress power to make
all laws "necessary and proper" for executing powers
specifically granted to government. It grants Congress
"implied powers" whose exact nature has been subject
of controversy since Constitution was passed (1788).

Elasticity (e-las-TIS-ity) **P** 233
El Azhar University see Azhar, University of al-
Elba, island off western coast of Italy **I** 429
   Napoleon I **N** 12
Elbe River, Europe **R** 243–44
   rises in Bohemia, Czechoslovakia **C** 560
Elbert, Mount, Colorado **C** 402
Elbrus, Mount, Caucasus Mountains, Europe **E** 309
Elburz (el-BOORZ) **Mountains,** Iran **T** 49; picture **I** 374
El Camino Real see Camino Real, El
El Cordobés, Spanish bullfighter **B** 450
Eldee Foundation **F** 392
Elder Edda, Icelandic book of songs and legends, basis
   of Norse mythology **N** 277
El Djem, Tunisia, picture **A** 66
El Dorado, Arkansas **A** 430

El Dorado (Spanish phrase meaning "the Gilded One"),
legendary ruler and his kingdom in South America. The
chief was ceremonially covered with oil and gold dust,
which led people to search for this legendary land of
fabulous wealth. Quest resulted in numerous discoveries
and conquests during 16th and 17th centuries, notably
of Guiana (1595) by Sir Walter Raleigh. El Dorado is
referred to by Voltaire in his novel *Candide*. Term is now
used figuratively to refer to a place of great wealth.
   man's long search for the "Gilded One" and for gold
     C 382; **G** 250

Eldridge, Roy (David Roy Eldridge) (1911–   ), American
jazz musician, Negro, b. Pittsburgh, Pa. One of the top
jazzmen of the 1940's, Eldridge first gained fame as
trumpeter and singer with Gene Krupa's band (1941–43).
He was later on the CBS radio music staff (1943–44) and
with Artie Shaw's band (1944–45). In the 1950's he
toured Europe with Benny Goodman's jazz sextet. He often
appeared in the annual "Jazz at the Philharmonic" shows.
   jazz of the 1930's and 40's **J** 60

Elect, The, doctrine of **C** 30
Election Day, United States **H** 154
Elections **E** 112–15
   Canada **C** 77
   computers, using probability theories, calculate re-
     sults **P** 474
   democratic process of government **G** 276
   democratic voting rights **D** 105
   dyeing the voter's thumb **D** 366
   Electoral College **E** 116
   Hayes-Tilden election, 1876 **H** 79–80
   initiative, referendum and recall, the Oregon system
     O 205
   national nominating convention originated in Jackson's
     administration **J** 6
   opinion polls **O** 160
   parliaments **P** 82
   political parties **P** 382
   women, role of **W** 212b–213; picture **W** 212
   See also facts and figures table of country, province,
     and state articles
Electoral College, United States **E** 116
   Burr, Aaron, vice-president and tragedy **B** 462;
     J 67–68
   duty of the Congress to witness count of electoral
     votes **U** 144
   Harrison, Benjamin, and election of 1888 **H** 47
   Hayes election by an Electoral Commission **H** 78, 80
   Jefferson's election in 1800 **J** 67–68
   Lincoln's election **L** 295
Electorate, people who have the vote **E** 112

Electra, in Greek mythology, the daughter of Agamemnon
and Clytemnestra. When Aegisthus and Clytemnestra
killed her father, she sent her young brother Orestes to
safety in Phocis. Aeschylus' *Libation Bearers*, Sophocles'
Electra, and Euripides' *Electra* tell how she helped Orestes kill the murderers.

Electrical engineering **E** 206
   putting topology to work **T** 226
Electrical industry **I** 247–48
Electrical recordings, for the phonograph **R** 124
Electric appliances **E** 117–20
   AC-DC, or universal motors most efficient in small sizes
     E 139
   insulation used for **I** 292
   uses of batteries **B** 99
Electric arc **E** 129
Electric automobiles **A** 542, 552
Electric batteries **B** 97–99
   electric motors **E** 139, 140
   chemical elements found by use of **C** 213
Electric charges **E** 123–27, 129–30
Electric circuits **E** 133
Electric conductors **E** 125–28
   electronics, use in **E** 144
Electric currents **E** 127–35
   electron emission **E** 143–45
   magnetism, causes of **M** 28–30
   Ohm's law **E** 132–33
   photoelectricity **P** 199
   Steinmetz' work **S** 422
   telephone, use in **T** 55–56
   transformers **T** 249–50
Electric drill, picture **T** 216
Electric eels **E** 86–87
   fishes and electricity **F** 202
Electric energy **E** 198, 199, 203
   research on electric energy **P** 235–36
Electric eye see Photoelectric cell
Electric fans see Fans, electric

Electric fishes
electric and torpedo rays **S** 143; pictures **S** 142
electric eels **E** 86–87
fishes and electricity **F** 202
Electric generators **E** 121–22
Edison designed and made practical **E** 60
Faraday, principle discovered by **F** 44
Gramme dynamo powers early electric motors
E 140–41
how mechanical energy is converted into electricity
E 132
power plants **P** 425–26
See also Electric motors
Electric guitar **G** 409
rock music **R** 262d
Electric heating **H** 99
Electric irons **E** 118
Electricity **E** 123–35
advances in experimental science **S** 71
aluminum a good conductor **A** 176
atmospheric **T** 170–73
atoms **A** 486, 488
batteries **B** 97–99
chemical reactions caused by **C** 199, 213–15
communication advanced by **C** 438
computers, how they work **C** 451–52; picture **C** 450
crystals, piezoelectricity from **C** 552; **Q** 6
electrical energy, in physics **P** 235–36
electric motors **E** 136–41
electronics **E** 143–48
Faraday's experiments in generating current **F** 44
farm machinery **F** 57
fire prevention **F** 154; **S** 4
fishes and electricity **F** 202
Franklin's experiments and contributions **F** 453–54
generators **E** 121–22
house wiring, diagram **B** 437
how to put out electrical fires **F** 136, 149
industrial growth **I** 245
insulation **I** 292
inventions introduced new sources of energy **I** 336
law of electrical charges **E** 124
lightning **T** 170–73
magnetism **M** 28–30
make a nerve-steadiness tester **E** 363
meters, picture **P** 511
nuclear power plant, diagram **N** 363
photoelectricity **P** 199–200
piezoelectricity **C** 552; **Q** 6
population and need for more electricity
E 272b, 272g
power plants **P** 425–27
public utility **P** 511
quartz for electrical uses **Q** 6
rocket propulsion **R** 261
safety **E** 135; **S** 4
solar energy can generate electricity **S** 237
thermoelectricity **P** 426–27
thunder and lightning **T** 170–73
transformers **T** 249–50
transistors **T** 252–54
Why were electric irons invented? **E** 118
See also Lightning; Magnets and magnetism; Radio;
Telegraph; Telephone; Television; X rays; headings
beginning with Electric and Electro
Electric lamps
development of electric light bulbs **I** 333–34
Edison's invention of practical filament and bulb **E** 60
Langmuir's improvement of **L** 35
light bulbs made by machine, picture **G** 235
lighting, electric **L** 284
vacuum in a light bulb **V** 265

Electric lighting **L** 284
electric meter, picture **P** 511
fire prevention **F** 154; **S** 4
Electric lines
telegraph **T** 52
telephone **T** 57
Electric locomotives **L** 328; picture **L** 331
railroads, history of **R** 79
Electric meters, picture **P** 511
Electric motors **E** 136–41
appliances **E** 119
automobiles **A** 542
Faraday put electromagnetism to work **E** 131
locomotives **L** 328; picture **L** 331
motors that tell time **E** 120
ocean liners **O** 23
submarines **S** 443
Electric power **E** 134
batteries **B** 97–99
nuclear energy can supply **P** 511
power plants **P** 425–27
public utility **P** 511
transformers **T** 249–50
Why don't we get all our electric power from
water? **W** 62
Electric resistance **E** 127–28, 133
heating elements of electric appliances **E** 117
Electric shock **S** 4
first aid rescues **F** 162–63
mentally ill, electroshock treatment for **M** 225
Electric slot racing, of model cars **A** 537
Electric switchgear
telegraph **T** 54
telephone **T** 57
Electric typewriters **O** 57; **T** 348; pictures **C** 452,
O 56
Electric watches and clocks **W** 48–49
Electric waves **L** 271
Electric wiring
safety measures **S** 4
system in a house, diagram **B** 437

Electrocardiograph, machine that records the electric
current produced by each heartbeat. The machine
photographs or traces with a stylus on graph paper the
pattern of the electric current. The visual record is an
electrocardiogram, from which a doctor can detect
certain types of heart disease. The electrocardiograph
was invented in 1903 by Willem Einthoven (1860–1927).
electrocardiograms transmitted by Dataphone **E** 142b
examing the heart **H** 86b
medicine, tools and techniques of **M** 209

Electrochemistry, study of effects of electric current on
chemical substances, usually solutions. Research methods often involve passing current through a solution
from one metal plate to another. By doing this, chemists
can study such things as ability of solution to conduct
current, way particles of solution break up, and
deposition of dissolved substances on plates that
conduct current. Many industrial processes, such as
electroplating, depend on this science.
ions and ionization **I** 355
science, history of **S** 71

Electrocution, method of executing criminals by passing
electric current through the body. New York was the first
state to adopt it (1888).

Electrodes, in dry-cell batteries, picture **B** 98
ions and ionization **I** 355
ore detection uses **M** 314

Electrodialysis, in water desalting **W** 56a
Electroencephalograph (e-lec-tro-en-CEPH-a-lo-graph), machine that measures brain impulses **M** 208h–209
   dreaming **D** 305–06, 307
Electroforming, type of electroplating **E** 150
Electroluminescent (el-ec-tro-lu-mi-NES-cent) **light** **L** 287
Electrolysis **E** 129
   chlorine obtained by **I** 349
   how to clean silver by **I** 354
   laws discovered by Faraday **F** 44
   metallurgy, uses in **M** 228
   method of separating ions **I** 355
Electrolyte, substance that can carry an electric current **C** 218
   ions and ionization **I** 355
Electrolytic (e-lec-tro-LIT-ic) **refining,** of metals
   gold **G** 249
Electromagnetic radiation see Electromagnetism
Electromagnetic spectrum **L** 271; diagrams **L** 270, **R** 43
Electromagnetic waves **V** 265
Electromagnetism **E** 129–32
   electric generators **E** 121–22
   electric motors **E** 136–41
   electromagnetic radiation **R** 40–41
   Faraday's experiments **F** 44
   light waves **L** 266
   physics, advances in **S** 75
   plasma and fusion, to power space ship **I** 351–52
   radiation **R** 40–45
   sunspots **E** 26
   transformers **T** 249–50
Electromagnets **M** 29
   Morse's use in telegraph invention **M** 462
   telegraph, uses in **T** 50–51
   telephone, use in **T** 56
Electron beam welding **W** 119
Electronic appliances **E** 120
Electronic circuits see Circuits, electronic, of computers
Electronic communication **E** 142–142f
   cable TV and video cassettes **T** 70c, 71
   television **T** 65–70
Electronic computers see Computers
Electronic digital computer **O** 58
Electronic evesdropping see Bugging
Electronic instruments, in music **M** 544
Electronic music **E** 142g–142h
   electronic carillon bells **B** 137
   modern music **M** 402
   "performance" of a work by tape recorder **M** 532
   rock music **R** 262d
Electronic Numerical Integrator and Computer (ENIAC) **O** 58
   automation **A** 533
Electronic organ **K** 240; **O** 208; picture **K** 237
Electronics, science dealing with flow of electrons **E** 143–48
   automation, applications in **A** 530
   electronics engineers **E** 206
   electron microscope **M** 288
   elevator call button **E** 174
   hi-fi and stereo **H** 125–26
   inventions in communication **I** 345–46
   ions and ionization **I** 350–55
   masers and lasers **M** 131–33
   medicine, tools and techniques **M** 208h–209
   microscope **M** 288
   music **E** 142g–142h
   photoelectricity **P** 199–200
   railroads' use of **R** 84
   space suit, applications in, diagram **S** 338
   tape and wire recorders **T** 20–21
   teaching machines **P** 477

television **T** 65–70
transistors **T** 252–54
Electronic synthesizer **E** 142g
Electronic watches **W** 49
Electron jump **R** 40–41; diagrams **R** 40, 42
Electron microscopes **M** 288
   biology, use in **B** 196
   photomicrography, use in **P** 205
Electron microscopy, a technique of medical laboratories **M** 202
Electrons, atomic particles **A** 485, 486, 487
   chemical structure **C** 201, 218
   cosmic rays **C** 511
   electronics, science of **E** 143–48
   elements **E** 153–59
   International Geophysical Year findings **I** 312–13
   ions and ionization **I** 350–55
   magnetism, causes of **M** 28
   negative charges of electricity **E** 123–27, 132–33
   nuclear energy **N** 355
   photoelectricity **P** 199
   physics, advances in **P** 232
   radiation **R** 40–41
   shells **C** 202; pictures **C** 203
   static electricity **E** 170–71
Electron tubes **E** 145–48
   how we use a vacuum **V** 265
   television **T** 70
   transistors **T** 252

Electron volt (ev), a unit of energy in nuclear and cosmic ray physics. One electron volt is equal to the energy gained by an electron when it passes through an electric field that has a potential difference of one volt. In describing particle accelerators, the terms Mev (million electron volts) and Bev (billion electron volts) are used.

Electrophorus (e-lec-TROPH-or-us), apparatus for producing and transporting static electricity needed for various experimental purposes. Electrophorus was invented (1775) by Alessandro Volta.

Electroplating **E** 149–50
   chromium plating **C** 296
   gold, electroplated, in electronic devices **G** 248
   ions and ionization **I** 355
   knives, forks, and spoons **K** 287–88
   silver **S** 182
Electropolishing, electroplating in reverse **E** 150
Electrorefining, of metals **M** 229
Electroscope, instrument to detect static electricity, experiment **E** 364
Electroshock, treatment for mentally ill **M** 225
Electrotypes, in printing **P** 467
   use of electroforming in printing **E** 150
Electrovalent bond **C** 218–19
Elegies, poems in memory of the dead **E** 151–52; **P** 354
Elegy Written in a Country Churchyard, by Thomas Gray, excerpt **E** 151–52
Elementary and Secondary Education Act, 1965
   aid to school libraries **L** 175
Elementary schools **E** 69–71
   Frankfurt, West Germany, picture **G** 150
   guidance **G** 397–400
   language arts **L** 36
   libraries **L** 175–76
   new math **M** 161–68
   physical education **P** 224–29
   reading **R** 107–11
   schools and school buildings **S** 58
Elements, chemical **E** 153–65
   alphabetical table of elements with their symbols,

Elements, chemical (continued)
    numbers, weights, discoverers, **year** discovered
    E 154–55
    alphabetical table of symbols for the elements **C** 197
    ancient "elements" **C** 206–07
    atoms **A** 484–85
    chemical structures **C** 196–97, 219
    Curies' discoveries **C** 553
    defined by Boyle **C** 210
    fertilizer elements **F** 95–97
    gold **G** 247–49
    helium **H** 107–08
    iodine and other halogens **I** 349
    ions and ionization **I** 350–55
    magnesium **M** 22–23
    matter **M** 174–75
    nitrogen **N** 262
    nuclear energy **N** 354
    oxygen **O** 268–70
    periodic table **C** 202; **E** 156–57
    radioactive elements, discovery of **C** 216
    radioactive isotopes, man-made **R** 68
    silver **S** 181–82
    spectroscopic analysis **O** 173
    table of 20 most common elements **A** 484
    See *also* Periodic table
Elephant bird, picture **G** 204
Elephants **E** 166–71
    Africa, picture **A** 51
    aging **A** 84
    brain size **B** 366
    Burma, work in lumber industry, picture **B** 458
    cartoon symbol **C** 126
    circus act, picture **C** 299
    distribution changed by Ice Ages **L** 237–38
    fossil collections in University of Nebraska State
      Museum **N** 79
    giants of nature **G** 203
    Hannibal used elephants **H** 34
    ivory **I** 487–88
    largest land animals **A** 263
    mother and baby, picture **S** 271
    Mysore, India, picture **A** 467
    workers in lumber industry, picture **L** 376
    zoos, Munich Zoo, picture **Z** 377
Elephant's Child, The, story by Kipling **K** 262–65
Elephant seals, or sea elephants, animals **W** 8
Elephant shrews, animals of insectivore group **I** 261
Eletelephony, poem by Laura E. Richards **N** 274
Eleuthera (e-LEUTH-er-a) **Island,** Bahamas **B** 17; picture
    B 16
Elevation, in mechanical drawing **M** 197
Elevation, or altitude of an area
    climate control factor **W** 89
Elevators **E** 172–74
    hydraulic systems **H** 303
    importance to building construction **B** 438
Elevators, for storing grain **W** 155
Elevators, of airplanes **A** 556
Eleventh Amendment, to the U.S. Constitution **U** 155
Elfreth's Alley, Philadelphia **P** 182; picture **P** 183
Elgar, Sir Edward, English composer **E** 176
    English music **E** 271

Elgin (EL-ghin) **Marbles,** pieces of ornamental sculpture from Parthenon and other Greek temples, considered among finest examples of ancient Greek art. They were collected by Thomas Bruce, 7th earl of Elgin and 11th earl of Kincardine, and brought to England (1803–12). Removal of sculpture from Athens was debated, notably in Lord Byron's poem "The Curse of Minerva."
    British Museum **M** 514

El Greco *see* Greco, El

Eli (E-lie), in Old Testament (Samuel), Hebrew judge and high priest at Shiloh, teacher of prophet Samuel. His line came to an end because his wicked sons, Hophni and Phinehas, took the sacred Ark of the Covenant with them into battle against the Philistines and Israel was defeated and the Ark lost.

Elia (E-lia), pen name of Charles Lamb, for *Essays of Elia* **L** 34
    famous essay "Dissertation Upon Roast Pig" **E** 293
Elijah (e-LY-jah), a prophet **E** 176
    Passover **P** 94

Elijah Muhammad (Elijah Poole) (1897–   ), leader of American Negro organization known as Black Muslims, b. Sandersville, Ga. The son of a Baptist minister, he joined the movement in 1931 and assumed leadership (1934) with title "Messenger of Allah." The group, which has its headquarters in Chicago and may number as many as 250,000, advocates separation from whites and development of Negro economic independence.
    Black Muslims **N** 104a

Eliot, George, pseudonym of Marian, or Mary Ann, Evans, English novelist **E** 177
    English literature **E** 264
    themes of her novels **N** 346

Eliot, John (1604–1690), American missionary, b. Probably Widford, England. Called Apostle of the Indians, he devoted most of his life to converting Indians in Massachusetts. He also translated Bible into Algonkian language and established self-governing communities among Indians.
    Praying Towns in Massachusetts **M** 149

Eliot, T. S. (Thomas Stearns), American-born English poet and critic **E** 177
    American literature **A** 209–10
    English literature **E** 265, 268

Elisha (e-LIE-sha), in Old Testament (Kings I and II), Hebrew prophet and priest. He was found by Elijah, who chose him as successor by casting his mantle upon him. As chief prophet, he was known for care of unfortunate and for miracles.
    Elisha and Elijah **E** 176

Elixir, in Middle Ages, substance thought to be capable of turning metals into gold. "Elixir of life" was believed to give eternal life to those who drank it. In pharmacy elixir is an aromatic and sweet-tasting preparation very often used to flavor drugs as well as for medicinal purposes.

Elizabeth I, empress of Russia
    westernization of architecture **U** 53
Elizabeth, mother of John the Baptist **J** 122
Elizabeth (Bowes-Lyon), queen consort of George VI of Great Britain **E** 179
Elizabeth I, queen of England **E** 178–79, 221–22
    American colony, Virginia **A** 180, 181
    clothing, laws governing **C** 352
    cosmetics, use of **C** 510
    Drake, Sir Francis **D** 290–91
    jewelry **J** 96
    Mary Queen of Scots **M** 130
    musical ability **E** 269
    portrait **E** 251

Raleigh, Sir Walter **R** 101
Elizabeth II, queen of Great Britain and Northern Ireland **E** 179, 232
Canada, queen of **C** 76
Commonwealth of Nations head **C** 428
opening Parliament, picture **G** 274
state procession, picture **E** 231

Elizabeth, Saint, mother of John the Baptist and cousin of the Virgin Mary. According to the Gospel of St. Luke, the angel Gabriel appeared to Elizabeth and her husband Zacharias. The angel predicted that Elizabeth, although old, would give birth to a son called John. Mary visited Elizabeth before the birth of Jesus, and this vigil is known as the "Visitation." The feast day of Saint Elizabeth is November 5.

Elizabeth, Saint (1207–1231), princess of Hungary, b. Pressburg. She was devoted to life of piety and charity. Her husband, Louis IV, died while on a crusade, and she was driven from her lands by Henry Raspe (1227). She lived in Bamberg and Marburg. She joined the Franciscan order and is believed to have performed miracles. She was canonized in 1235. Her feast day is celebrated Nov. 19.

Elizabethan (el-iz-a-BEETH-an) **Age,** England **E** 222
art and architecture **E** 236
English literature **E** 250–53
music **E** 268–70
Elizabethan style
furniture design **F** 506
Elizabethan theater
Renaissance drama **D** 295–96
Elk, hoofed mammals **H** 219; picture **H** 214
locomotion of animals, picture **A** 293
Elkhart, Indiana **I** 148
Elk Island National Park, Alberta, Canada **A** 146d

Elks, Benevolent and Protective Order of (BPOE), fraternal organization known for its charitable and patriotic activities, founded in 1868. There are approximately 2,000 lodges in United States. BPOE has headquarters in Chicago, Ill. and publishes *Elks Magazine.*

Ellery, William (1727–1820), American patriot, b. Newport, R.I. As Rhode Island's delegate to the Continental Congress (1776–81, 1783–86), he signed the Declaration of Independence. He was chief justice of Rhode Island in 1785.

Ellesmere (ELLS-mere) **Island,** northwest of Greenland **I** 429–30; picture **I** 424
Arctic islands, land areas of Canada **C** 51
Yukon and Northwest Territories **Y** 361

Ellington, Duke (Edward Kennedy Ellington) (1899–   ), jazz musician, Negro, b. Washington, D.C. Internationally known as a pianist, composer, and orchestra conductor. Duke Ellington has given jazz concerts at Carnegie Hall in New York, the Chicago Opera House, and the San Francisco Philharmonic Hall. He has made many recordings and has appeared in films and on TV. Among the almost 1,000 tunes that he wrote are *Mood Indigo* and *Sophisticated Lady.* In 1967 he received an honorary doctorate from Yale. Picture **J** 61.
Negro artists and musicians **J** 60; **N** 102

Ellipse (e-LIPS), in geometry **G** 127, 129
Mars, moon, orbits of **M** 105, 446
shape of a satellite's orbit **S** 40
See also Conic section

Elliptical galaxies **U** 198–99
Ellis, Griffin Ogden, American publisher **M** 16

Ellis, Havelock (Henry Havelock Ellis) (1859–1939), English author and anthropologist, b. Croydon, Surrey. He began career as physician and later wrote first serious English treatise on sex, seven-volume *Studies in the Psychology of Sex* (1897–1928).

Ellis, Jimmy, American boxer **B** 353
Ellis, Joel, American doll maker **D** 265
Ellison, Ralph, American novelist **A** 213; **N** 102
Ells, measures of length **W** 109
Ellsworth, Lincoln, American polar explorer **P** 365

Ellsworth, Oliver (1745–1807), American statesman, b. Windsor, Conn. He was delegate to Continental Congress (1777–83) and to Constitutional Convention (1787–88), U.S. senator from Connecticut (1789–96), and chief justice of United States (1796–99).

Elm, tree, picture **T** 276
American elm, state tree of Massachusetts, Nebraska, North Dakota **M** 134; **N** 72, 323
Dutch elm disease **V** 284
leaves and flowers **T** 283; picture **L** 115
uses of the wood and its grain, picture **W** 223
Elmira (el-MY-ra) **system,** of reforming criminals **P** 469
El Morro, fortress in Puerto Rico, picture **P** 519
Elobey Islands, Equatorial Guinea **E** 273

Elodea (el-O-de-a), underwater plant bearing many small leaves and tiny flowers that float on surface. The plant is found in streams, ponds, and springs of tropical and temperate regions. It grows easily and quickly and is often used in aquariums.

Elohim (el-O-him) (Hebrew word meaning "gods" or "God"), used in Old Testament to refer to heathen gods and idols. The word usually refers to God of Israel.

El Paso, Texas **T** 134
El Salvador **E** 180–84
flag **F** 241
life in Latin America **L** 47–61
national anthem **N** 21
Elsie Dinsmore books **C** 240
Elsinore *see* Kronborg Castle
Eluard, Paul, French poet **F** 442
Elvers, or glass eels **E** 86; **F** 199

Elves, in Teutonic mythology, small supernatural beings able to cause diseases and nightmares in addition to performing good deeds. Elves include dwarfs, pixies, and mermaids.

Elves, The Shoemaker and the, fairy tale by Grimm brothers **G** 377–78
Elysian (e-LIZ-ian) **Fields,** in mythology **G** 357
El Zerqa, Jordan *see* Zerqa, El
Emancipation, or manumission, of slaves **S** 195
England's Act of 1833 **S** 197
Emancipation Proclamation **E** 185–86
Civil War, United States **C** 324, 459
Lincoln, Abraham **L** 296
Negro history **N** 95
slavery **S** 199
Embalming, preservation of the dead **F** 492
Embankment dams, made of earth and rock **D** 16

Embargo (from Spanish *embargar,* meaning "to arrest"), order prohibiting foreign ships from entering or leaving

Embargo (continued)
the ports of a country. Embargoes are often imposed to forbid export of goods needed for war. They are also used as punitive measures, as in trade embargo placed on Cuba (1962) by Organization of American States.

Embargo Act, 1807
Jefferson uses to combat impressment **J** 68–69
Embarkation for Cythera, painting by Jean Antoine Watteau **P** 25
Embassies, headquarters of diplomatic service **F** 369
Ember Days, religious holidays **R** 153
Emblems
flags **F** 225–48
Roman fasces **F** 63
See also signs and symbols
Embolism
air embolism fatal to divers **S** 191
Embossing
leathercraft **L** 113
Embroidery E 187–89
folk art, pictures **F** 296
Paracas Indian, picture **I** 154
Embryophyta, division of plant kingdom **P** 292
Embryos, first stages of development in plants or animals **E** 90–90a
baby **B** 2
baby marsupials **K** 168–69; picture **K** 167
seeds, structure of **F** 282–83
See also Cells; Eggs
Emerald Isle, name for Ireland **I** 384
Emeralds, gemstones **G** 71
Colombia **C** 382

Emeritus (from Latin *emerere*, meaning "to obtain by service"), honorary title held after retirement from active service, as in "professor emeritus."

Emerson, Ralph Waldo, American writer and teacher **E** 190–91
American literature **A** 201
"Concord Hymn," poem **E** 190
essays **E** 293
prayer **P** 434
quotations **Q** 19, 20

Emery, Anne (1907–), American writer, b. Fargo, N. Dak. She is noted for books for teen-age girls, including *Mountain Laurel* and *Sorority Girl*.

Emery, form of corundum **G** 387
Emigration see Immigration and Emigration
Emil and the Detectives, book by Kästner **G** 181; picture **G** 180
Émile (a-MEEL), novel by Rousseau **E** 68

Eminent domain, power of state to take over private property for public use, giving reasonable compensation. It is exercised in time of war for national safety or in peace for building roads and communication systems.

Emir (im-EER), Arabic title
Kuwait **K** 307
Emmanuel see Immanuel
Emma Willard School, Troy, New York **W** 172
Emmer, a kind of wheat **W** 154
Emmerich (EM-mer-ick), **Rudolf,** German doctor **A** 310; picture **A** 315
Emmett, Dan, American composer **N** 24
Emmet, Robert, Irish patriot **I** 391

Emmy, annual award (since 1949) for outstanding

achievement in TV industry. It is presented by National Academy of Television Arts and Sciences to individuals in fields of acting, directing, writing, and other areas of television.

Emotions, feelings
adolescence **A** 22–24
connotations of words **S** 118
divorce, attitudes toward **D** 235
handicapped, emotional problems of the **H** 30
mental health **M** 220–22
mental illness **M** 222–25
old-age problems **O** 97
peptic ulcer, causes of **D** 202
Empedocles (em-PED-o-clese), Greek philosopher
earth theory **C** 206
science, advances in **S** 62
Emperor penguins P 124–25
Emperor's New Clothes, The, story by Hans Christian Andersen **A** 249–51
Emperor's Top, shell, picture **S** 148
Emphysema (em-phi-SE-ma), lung disease **D** 196; **S** 203
Empire Day, Great Britain **H** 150
Empire State Building, New York City **N** 231; pictures **U** 107, **W** 218
Empire State, nickname for New York **N** 210
Empire style
furniture design **F** 508–09
Empire (om-PEER) **waistline F** 65
Empirical probability P 473
Empiricism, a philosophy
Locke, John **L** 321
Employer's liability see Workmen's compensation
Empty set, in the new mathematics **M** 164
sets **S** 126–27
Ems, spaces between words in printing **T** 344

Emulsion, mixture of one liquid with very tiny droplets of another liquid. Salad dressing is an example. (Although oil is thoroughly mixed with vinegar, oil does not dissolve in it. Oil and vinegar separate, but do so extremely slowly.) Milk containing cream is another example.

Emus (E-muse), large Australian birds, over 5 feet tall and second in size only to ostriches. Thick black or brown plumage of slender, drooping feathers covers tiny wings. Although the emu is unable to fly, it has strong legs and can run at speeds of over 25 miles an hour. It lives in dry plains. The eggs are hatched by the father, who also cares for the young. Picture **B** 227.
Australian wildlife **A** 505
flightless, owing to giant size **G** 204

Enamel, of teeth **T** 48
Enameling E 191–92
decorative arts **D** 70
jewelry **J** 92–93
pottery **P** 414
Enamels, paints **P** 32
Encarnación (en-car-na-ci-OHN), Paraguay **P** 65
Encaustic (en-CAU-stic), method of painting **G** 344; **P** 30
ancient Greece and Rome **P** 17
Encephalitis (en-ceph-a-LY-tis), disease **I** 283
Enchanted Princess, old German fairy tale **F** 23–25
Encina (enth-E-na), **Juan del,** Spanish dramatist **S** 367
Encircling, commercial fishing method **F** 217
Enciso (en-CI-so), **Martín Fernández de,** Spanish colonizer **B** 18

Enclave, small area of land that is surrounded by foreign territory. Portuguese Goa has been cited as the classic example, and Brunei, Borneo, and Cabinda, Africa, are enclaves that exist today. The term "enclave" can also refer to a cultural island of people distinct in race, language, or customs.

Endive, leafy plant related to chicory, sometimes broad-leaved, sometimes curly-leaved. The frilled lower leaves and the inner crisp, whitish leaves are used in salads.

Endor, Witch of, in Old Testament (I Samuel 28:7–25), old witch who lived in Endor, small village in Palestine. The witch was consulted by Saul, King of Israel, on eve of fateful battle of Gilboa, in which he was to die.

Endymion (end-IM-ion), in Greek mythology, beautiful youth loved by moon goddess, Selene. According to some legends he was given an eternal life of sleep by Zeus so that Selene could always visit him.

Engels, Friedrich (1820–1895), German Socialist leader and author, b. Barmen. He co-founded Communism with Karl Marx and collaborated with him in writing much of its literature, notably *Communist Manifesto*. He organized underground revolutionary movements in France, Germany, and Belgium (1845–50); participated in revolutionary movement in Baden, Germany (1848–49); and played a major role in Communist First (1864) **and** Second (1889) Internationals. He edited second and third volumes of Marx's *Das Kapital*. His other works include *The Origin of the Family, Landmarks of Scientific Socialism,* and *Private Property and the State*.

Eniwetok (en-i-WE-tok), coral atoll in west central Pacific,
part of the Ralik group of the Marshall Islands. Taken by
United States during World War II, Eniwetok has been
part of the United States Trust Territory of the Pacific
Islands since 1947. The inhabitants were relocated
(1948) because of U.S. nuclear testing.

Enlightenment, Age of F 394
  education E 68–69
  Jewish life, influence on Y 350
Ennius, Quintus, Roman poet L 77

Enoch (E-nock), son of Cain, who named city after him (Genesis 4:17). In another account (Genesis 5:18–24), he was descendant of Seth and father of Methuselah and was carried to heaven without dying because he pleased God. Christians have interpreted this as proof of immortality (Hebrews 11:5). In apocalyptic books he is a revered teacher and prophet.

Enoch Pratt Free Library, Baltimore M 123
En passant (on pa-SON), in chess C 225
Enriched bread B 387

Enrico Fermi award, award presented annually by the Atomic Energy Commission to persons who have made a valuable contribution to the development, use, and control of nuclear energy. The award was established in 1956 in honor of the late atomic scientist Enrico Fermi. It consists of a medal, a citation, and a sum of money up to $50,000. It may be given to one person or divided among several people.

Enright, Elizabeth (1909–68), American author and illustrator, known for children's books, b. Chicago, Ill. She wrote and illustrated *Thimble Summer,* which won Newbery medal (1939). Her other books include *The Saturdays* and *Then There Were Five.*

Enrober, candymaking machine C 99
Ensembles, in music C 186
Ensilage *see* Silage
Ensor, James, Belgian painter D 358
Entac, SSM, antitank missile M 347
Entamoebas, micro-organisms M 278
Entanglement, a commercial fishing method F 218

Entente Cordial (on-TONT cor-DIAHL) (French for "cordial understanding"), mutual-support agreement between France and England (1904) against the threat of German power. The agreement became the Triple Entente when Russia joined (1907). The three countries formed the nucleus of the Allies in World War I.
  background of World War I F 418; W 270–71

Entertaining *see* Parties
Entomologists (en-to-MOL-o-gists), scientists who study insects I 280
Entrapment, commercial fishing method F 217
Entrepreneur (on-tre-pre-NUR), businessman E 48, 49
Entries, of indexes I 114
Entropy (EN-tro-py), of energy, second law of thermodynamics E 201
Enugu (en-NU-gu), Nigeria N 255
Enumerators, census takers P 397
Envelopes V 268
Environment E 272a–272h
  adaptations to surroundings in world of life L 214–15
  child development and environment C 231
  environmental engineers E 205
  food contamination F 355
  individual differences C 232
  learning process L 98–106
  life, rhythms and clocks in plant and animal L 243–50
  life distributed in three main environments L 227–28
  man changes environment L 226, 238
  pollution of air and water A 108–11, E 272a–272h; W 58–59
  prairies P 430–33

response to, characteristic of living things K 255–56
  sanitation S 32–34
  See also Ecology; Conservation; Pollution and pollutants
Environmental science, study of the improvement of natural resources N 60
Environmental Science Services Administration, U.S. W 96
Enzymes (EN-zymes) B 293–96
  biochemists' study of enzymes B 184
  body catalysts C 199
  body chemistry B 296
  digestion in human body B 274–75
  "ferments" of the body F 90
  food spoilage F 344, 352
  genetics G 84–85
  honeybees H 202
  in metabolism K 253–54
  metabolic diseases result from lack of D 189
  vitamins, building blocks for V 370b
  yeast F 90
Eocene epoch, of the Anozoic era, in geology F 388
Eohippus (eo-HIP-pus), or Dawn horse, ancestor of the horse H 236; picture E 343

Eos (E-os) (from Greek word meaning "dawn"), in Greek mythology, goddess of dawn. She is often pictured driving horse-drawn chariot across the sky, ushering in dawn. She corresponds to Roman goddess Aurora.

Épées (a-PAYS), fencing swords F 86; pictures F 85
Ephesians (eph-E-sians), book of the Bible B 161
  Paul quoted on woman's role W 211
Ephesus, Turkey
  Temple of Diana, one of the Seven Wonders of the Ancient World W 214–15

Ephraim (E-phrai-im) (Hebrew, meaning "fruitful"), in Old Testament, Egyptian-born son of Joseph. He was the founder of tribe of Ephraim, one of tribes of Israel.

Epics, long poems dealing with heroic action P 354
  Aeneid, by Vergil A 35
  Africa's heroic, or epic, poetry A 76a–76b
  Beowulf B 141–42
  early form of fiction F 110
  Iliad, by Homer I 69
  India's dance-drama T 163
  Odyssey, by Homer O 53–54

Epicurus (ep-ic-U-rus) (341?–270 B.C.), Greek philosopher, b. Samos. He founded a philosophical school in Athens (306). His philosophy, called Epicureanism, taught that pleasure is supreme good, but unlike many other hedonist philosophies, it advocated prudence and virtue.

Epicycles (EP-i-cycles), astronomical system A 471, 472
Epidaurus (ep-i-DAUR-us), Greece
  Greek theater, picture G 335
Epidemic (ep-i-DEM-ic) **diseases** D 188; P 503
  influenza, 1918 D 200
  Reed's findings on yellow fever R 128
  sanitation S 32
Epidermis, outer layer of skin, or surface tissue of plants
  hair H 2
  leaves L 120; picture P 294
  plants P 294
  skin, diagram B 268
Epigrams, short clever sayings
  essays and poems contain E 293; P 354
  quotations, selected Q 20
Epilepsy (EP-i-lep-sy), disease D 196

Epilogue (EP-ilog) (from Greek words *epi*, meaning "upon," and *logos*, meaning "speech"), concluding part of literary work or speech or short poem addressed to audience at end of play. It is also called the afterword.

Epimetheus (epi-ME-theus), Greek god **G** 357

Epinephrine (epi-NEPH-rin) (adrenaline), hormone released by adrenal glands **B** 297

Epiphany, or Twelfth Night, religious holiday **R** 155, 290
  carnival time begins **C** 120
  celebrations in Italy **I** 448

Epiphytes (EP-i-phytes), or air plants **P** 318

Episcopal Church
  Cranmer's prayer books **E** 221

Epistemology (ep-ist-em-OL-ogy), study of the problems of defining knowledge **P** 192

Epistles, or Letters, books of Bible **B** 161

Epistles of Saint Paul see Pauline Epistles

Epistolary (e-PIST-ol-ary) **novels E** 260
  Richardson's *Pamela* and *Clarissa Harlowe* **N** 346

Epitaphs, lines written about a dead person, or inscriptions on gravestones **E** 151–52
  Stevenson's *Requiem* **S** 424
  Wren's epitaph "If you seek a monument" **W** 313
  Yeats, William Butler **Y** 344

Epithelium, type of body tissue **V** 370b

E Pluribus Unum, former motto of the United States, replaced in 1956 by "In God We Trust" **G** 330

Epoxy resin adhesive, a thermosetting synthetic adhesive, permanently hardened when heated, and insoluable after curing. It is useful for metals, glass, and ceramics.

Eppes, Maria Jefferson, acting first lady in Jefferson's administration **F** 165–66

Epsom salts M 22

Epstein (EP-stine), **Sir Jacob** (1880–1959), English sculptor, b. New York, N.Y. He is known for architectural sculpture, large-scale figures, and portraits in stone and bronze. His works include *Rima* in Hyde Park, London, tomb of Oscar Wilde, and *Night and Day.*
  modern English sculpture **E** 242
  Risen Christ, The **E** 242

Epstein, Samuel (1909–), b. Boston, Mass., and **Beryl** (1910–), b. Columbus, Ohio, American writers of children's books. This husband-and-wife team has written many non-fiction books on a variety of topics. Titles include *Medicine from Microbes, European Folk Festivals,* and *Real Book About Spies.*

Epstein-Barr virus see EB virus

Epworth League (called Methodist Youth Fellowship since 1939 unification of Methodist churches), organization for young people that encourages study, worship, and service, in addition to vocations in ministry and mission fields. It was founded (1889) in Cleveland, Ohio.

Equal Employment Opportunity, President's Committee on
  vice-president, chairman **V** 332

Equalitarian farmily F 40

Equality State, nickname for Wyoming **W** 335

Equal Time Ruling, political broadcasting **P** 382

Equations
  algebra **A** 157–58
  chemical **C** 198–99, 219

Equator E 272h
  climate **C** 345
  earth's shape **E** 5–6
  latitude zero degrees **L** 81, 82
  rainfall **R** 94
  season always summer **S** 108–09
  torrid zone, hours of day and night **Z** 372

Equatorial Guinea E 273–74
  flag **F** 235

Equestrian (e-QUEST-rian) **portraits**
  Velazquez's portrait of Prince Balthasar **V** 294

Equestrian sports see Horsebackriding

Equestrian statues, monuments
  Bernini's statue of Louis XIV **B** 148
  Marcus Aurelius, Roman emperor, picture **S** 95
  Sherman Monument in New York's Central Park **U** 115

Equidae (EK-wid-e), horse family **H** 235

Equilateral triangle, diagram **G** 125

Equilibrium, in general, state in which all forces acting in a situation or on a thing are balanced by equal and opposite forces. The term is used in many sciences. For example, in chemistry "equilibrium" is used when rate at which new substances form in chemical reaction is equal to rate at which they break down.

Equinoxes, "equal nights," position of the sun **E** 272h
  procession through a celestial sphere **S** 109

Equisetineae, division of plant kingdom **P** 292

Equivalents, in topology **T** 220

Equivalent sets, in mathematics **S** 127

Era of Good Feeling, Monroe's administration **M** 425

Erard (a-RAR), **Sébastien,** French harp maker **H** 44

Eras, geologic F 384–88
  geological time scale **G** 113
  prehistoric animals, development of **P** 436–38

Erasistratus (er-a-SIST-ra-tus), Greek doctor **M** 203–04

Erasmus (e-RAS-mus), **Desiderius,** Dutch scholar **E** 274
  German literature **G** 175
  humanistic thought leading to Reformation **C** 285
  peace movements **P** 104
  Renaissance humanist **R** 160

Erato (ER-uh-to), goddess in Greek mythology. She and her eight sisters, daughters of Zeus and Mnemosyne, were the muses, or patrons of the arts and sciences. Erato was the muse of lyric poetry, and her favor was often sought by young lovers. Her symbol was the lyre. *See also* Muses

Eratosthenes (era-TOS-then-ese), Greek geographer and astronomer **G** 98; **S** 64
  the Sieve of Eratosthenes, for prime numbers **N** 379

Erbium, element **E** 154, 161

Ercilla y Zúñiga (er-CIL-ya y ZU-nyi-ga), **Alonso de,** Spanish soldier-poet **L** 70

Erebus (ER-e-bus), in Greek mythology **G** 356

Erechtheum (e-REC-the-um), temple on the Athens Acropolis **G** 346; picture **G** 347

Erewhon (ER-e-whon), by Samuel Butler **E** 264

Ergot, rye fungus **R** 364

Ergs, kind of sand dunes **S** 8
  in northern Africa **A** 160

Ergs, units of force **W** 117

Erhard (AIR-hart), **Ludwig** (1897–), German economist and political leader, b. Fürth, Bavaria. He was dismissed (1942) from government-supported research bureau because of anti-Nazi beliefs and founded his own market research bureau (1942–45). He was chosen (1945) by Allies to take charge of post-war industrial reorganization in Nuremberg-Fürth area. He was minister of economics of Federal Republic of Germany (West Germany), vice-chancellor (1957–63), and chancellor (1963–66).

Erickson, Carl, American illustrator **I** 92

Ericson, Leif, Norse sailor and explorer **E** 275
  exploration and discovery of the New World **E** 369
  Leif Ericson Day, October 8 **H** 149
  Vikings **V** 339

Ericsson, John (1803–1889), American engineer, b. Varmland, Sweden. Best-known as the designer of the Civil War ironclad fighting ship *Monitor,* Ericsson also designed the fire engine and a steam locomotive.

Eric the Red (lived during 10th century), Norse chieftain. He left Norway for Iceland, sailed west, and explored island that he named Greenland to attract settlers. He returned to Iceland to lead colonizers to Greenland and established colony (986). He vainly resisted attempts of his son, Leif Ericsson, to Christianize Greenland.
  Leif the Lucky and Greenland **E** 275; **G** 370–71
  Vikings **V** 339

Erie, Lake, battle of, 1813 **P** 157
Erie, Lake, one of Great Lakes **G** 328, 329
  industry in Cleveland, Ohio **C** 338
Erie, Pennsylvania P 141–42
Erie Canal E 276–80
  canal building in the United States **C** 84
  important to interstate commerce **I** 331
  labor-saving construction equipment **B** 445
  New York **N** 226
  setting for film about, picture **M** 483

Erinyes (e-RIN-i-ese), in Greek mythology, goddesses whose duty was to pursue the guilty and punish crimes not punishable by human justice. They are usually represented as three—Alecto, Megaera, and Tisiphone. Frightening in appearance, with serpents for hair and eyes that wept tears of blood, they were called Furies by Romans.

Eris (E-ris), Greek goddess of discord **G** 365
Eritrea (eri-TRE-a), Ethiopia **E** 299, 301
Erivan, capital of Armenia (Armenian Soviet Socialist Republic) **U** 44

Erl-King (from German Erl-König), in German mythology, goblin who haunts forests and lures people, especially little children, to destruction. This goblin was the subject of a poem by Johann von Goethe, "Der Erl-König."

Erl King, The, song by Franz Schubert **G** 186
Ermines, weasels
  fur **F** 518; **O** 242; picture **O** 243
Ernst, Max, German painter **M** 394
  Little Tear Gland That Says Tic-Tac, The, picture **M** 395

Eros, in Greek mythology, god of love, called "Cupid" by Romans; in early legends, described as beautiful youth who gives gifts to men; later appears as mischievous little winged boy with bow and arrows, son of Aphrodite and Ares; often pictured blindfolded to show that love is blind.
  Aphrodite and Cupid **G** 361

Erosion E 281–83
  caves and caverns, formation by **C** 153–56
  conservation way of life **C** 482–89
  earth's changes studied by geologists **G** 110
  ever-changing earth **E** 13
  experiment to show effects of **E** 359
  grasses and soil **G** 319
  ice ages, glacial erosion **I** 15–16
  land management in agriculture **A** 92–93

mountains worn down by **M** 493, 495
  rivers, work of **R** 239
  soils formed by **S** 230
  See *also* Dust; Soil conservation
Erratics, or wanderers, rocks transported by ice, pictures **G** 115; **I** 17

Ersatz (ER-zotz), German word meaning "substitute" or "replacement," as in "ersatz coffee," an artificial product. The term usually refers to synthetic replacement of natural product.

Erskine, Robert, American geographer **M** 94

Esau (E-sau), or **Edom,** in Old Testament, son of Isaac and Rebekah and rival of twin brother, Jacob. He was forced into selling his birthright to Jacob for bowl of soup and cheated out of blind father's blessing through Jacob's skillful contriving.

Escalation, a term often used to describe the fighting in Vietnam when, like an ascending escalator, each side increases its military efforts to match the other.
  Vietnam War, 1958– **V** 336

Escalators E 174–75
Escapements, devices in timepieces **W** 45
Escape velocity, of a spacecraft **S** 340d, 340g
  Mars **M** 106
Escarpment, rock formation
  Allegheny Scarpment **O** 254
  Brazil **B** 372
  Niagara Escarpment **O** 121
Esch-sur-Alzette, Luxembourg **L** 380
Escorial (es-CO-rial), palace, near Madrid, Spain **S** 363; picture **S** 360
Escorts, small destroyers, U.S. Navy **U** 192
Escrow, a legal agreement, real estate term **R** 112
Esdras I and II, apocryphal books of Bible **B** 156–57
Esenin (yis-YAY-nin), **Sergei,** Russian poet **U** 62

Eshkol (ESH-kol), **Levi** (Levi Shkolnik) (1895–1969), Israeli statesman, b. Oratov, Russia. He emigrated to Palestine (1913) and was a founder of *kibbutz* Degani B. He organized transfer of Jewish immigrants from Nazi Germany to Palestine (1933–36) and was first director general of Israeli Ministry of Defense (1948). He was minister of agriculture (1951–52), minister of finance (1952–63), minister of defense (1963–67), and prime minister (1963 until his death).

Eskers, formed by glaciers, picture **I** 14
Eskimo E 284–91
  Alaska **A** 136
  Arctic regions **P** 365
  Canadian population **C** 49–50; **Y** 364
  costumes, traditional, picture **C** 349
  education of, Canada **C** 62
  Eskimo ice cream, recipe **F** 340
  favorite foods **E** 290; **F** 339–40
  fishing, picture **A** 300
  folk art **C** 64
  girl and huskies, picture **F** 517
  Greenland **G** 367–71
  houses **H** 172–73
  igloo, picture **A** 303
  kayaks **C** 99
  Nain, Labrador, northernmost community **N** 143
  races of man, geographical, pictures **R** 30
  trapper with furs, picture **F** 511
Esmeralda, heroine of the *Hunchback of Notre Dame,* picture **F** 112

Esmeraldas (es-may-ROL-dos), river in Ecuador   E 55
Esophagus (e-SOPH-a-gus), or gullet, food passage tube
  B 274–75
  birds   B 202
ESP see Extrasensory perception

Espejo (es-PAY-ho), **Antonio de** (lived during late 16th
century), Spanish merchant and explorer. He explored
Pueblo Indian region of New Mexico (1582–83).

Esperanto, universal language   U 194
  language families   L 40
Espionage see Spies and spying
Espronceda (esp-ronth-A-tha), **José,** Spanish poet
  S 370
Essay on Man, by Alexander Pope   P 393
Essays   E 292–93
  American literature   A 201, 215
  compositions   C 446–47
  creative writing   W 321
  English literature   E 253–54, 258
  Japanese literature   O 220c
  magazines   M 14–16
Essays of Elia, by Charles Lamb   E 293

Essenes, ascetic Jewish sect that lived (200 B.C.–A.D. 100)
near Dead Sea. They worshiped in the direction of the
sun and lived an austere, communal life. The Essenes are
described in writings of Jewish historians Flavius Josephus and Philo Judaeus.

Essential oils   O 76
  perfumes   P 154

Estate, in law, property or possessions that a person
owns. For example, one says, "He has an estate worth
$1,000,000." Land and buildings are referred to as real
estate because they are relatively immovable.

Estates General, former French legislative body   F 462,
  464
  France on the edge of the French Revolution   F 416
  political parties in France   P 379

Este (ES-tay), **House of,** ancient Italian noble family. The
name was adopted by **Alberto Azzo II** (996–1097) after
Emperor Henry VII gave him Este and other Italian fiefs.
Azzo VI (1170–1212) led Guelph Party in Italy and ruled
Ferrara. **Ippolito II** (1509–72) became Cardinal d'Este
and archbishop of Milan and built Villa d'Este in Tivoli.
The line ended with **Ercole III Rinaldo** (1727–1803).

Esterbrook, Richard, American pen manufacturer   C 432
Esterhazy (es-ter-ha-ZY), **Major Ferdinand,** French army
  officer   D 316
Esterházy (ES-ter-ha-zy), **Miklós, Prince,** Hungarian noble-
  man
  Haydn's patron   H 77
Esters, chemicals
  lubricants   L 371

Estes, Eleanor (1906–), American author of children's
books, b. West Haven, Conn. She is best-known for books
about Moffat and Pye families. She received the Newbery
medal (1952) for *Ginger Pye.* She also wrote *The
Hundred Dresses* and *The Sleeping Giant and Other
Stories.*

Estevanico, or **Estabanico,** or **Estevan** (lived during 16th
century), Moorish explorer, b. Azamor, Morocco. He was
a survivor of unsuccessful expedition (1528) of Pánfilo
de Narváez, who sought to subject country between

Florida and Rio de las Palmas, Mexico, to Spanish rule.
He explored Texas, New Mexico, and Arizona (1528–36).
  Negro explorers   N 91

Esther, book of Bible, Old Testament   B 156
  apocryphal additions   B 157
  Purim   P 540
Esther, Feast of see Purim
Esther, Queen, wife of King Ahasuerus, king of Persia
  P 540
Esthetics, or aesthetics, the branch of philosophy that
  studies beauty   P 192
Estivation, summer sleep, or resting state of animals
  H 121
  crocodilians   C 535
Estonia (Estonian Soviet Socialist Republic)   U 43;
  W 281, 288
  languages of the U.S.S.R.   U 27
Estuaries, of rivers   R 238
  harbors and ports located on   H 37
Etah, Greenland   E 287
Etching   E 293–95
  Abraham's Sacrifice by Rembrandt   D 358
  cartoons   C 125
  glass   G 232
  illustration of books   I 90
  Rembrandt's work   D 357
  techniques of the graphic arts   G 303, 305, 307
  Whistler, James Abbott McNeill   W 160
  See also Engraving
Eternal City, Rome, Italy   R 313
Eternal frost, climate type   W 90
Ethelred, king of England, called the Unready or Redeless
  E 217
  Viking Era in England   V 340
Ether (E-ther), a general anesthetic   A 257, 258
  early use, picture   M 208a
Ether, luminiferous, early theory of light   R 140
  early studies of wave theory of light   S 75
Etherege, Sir George, English dramatist   E 257
Etherophone see Theremin

Ethical Culture, movement begun in New York, N.Y., with
founding of Society for Ethical Culture by Felix Adler
(1876). It was established to cultivate a morality based
on ethical principles and to apply it to all aspects of
personal, social, national, and international life. Nonsec-
tarian, with supporters of all major faiths, it spread
throughout United States and Europe. It has been
involved in progressive education, settlement house
work, and various social reform causes.

Ethics, or moral philosophy, branch of philosophy
dealing with principles men live by. It was developed
when men questioned reasons for and results of their
deeds. Since it is concerned with good and bad and with
duty and obligation, it is often based on religion.
  branches of philosophy   P 192
  Chinese literature   O 220

Ethiopia (e-thi-O-pia)   E 296–303
  Ethiopian scholar, picture   A 54
  flag   F 235
  legislature, picture   A 68
  literature   A 76b
  Mussolini attacks, 1935   W 285
Ethiopian Coptic (Orthodox) Church   E 296
Ethiopian Region, land region of animal life   L 234;
  diagram   L 235

Ethnic group (from Greek *ethnikos,* meaning "foreign" or
"national"), persons bound together and readily identifi-

able by common racial, linguistic, and cultural traits. They often live within alien community but remain separate. Such groups as Irish and Italians are ethnic groups when living outside their native homes.

ethnic groups in Europe, Saskatchewan **E** 316; **S** 38d

Ethnology (eth-NOL-ogy), cultural study of man
cultural anthropology **A** 300, 305, 309
races of man **R** 29–32
Ethos (E-thos), statue in Canberra, Australia, picture **C** 88
Ethrog, a citron fruit **L** 138
Ethyl (ETH-il) (tetraethyl lead)
reduces engine knock **G** 63
Ethyl alcohol A 147
structural formula **C** 200
Ethyl chloride, chemical used for anesthesia **A** 259
Etinger (et-ing-ER), **Solomon,** Yiddish author **Y** 350
Etiquette (ET-i-kett)
address, forms of **A** 19–21
flag, how to display **F** 231–34
letter writing **L** 157–60
parties **P** 87–89
table settings **T** 2–3
Etna, Mount, Sicily **I** 451
Etruscan art and architecture R 285; **S** 95
jewelry **J** 94

Etruscans, inhabitants of ancient Italy who lived in region of Etruria (now Tuscany and part of Umbria) from 8th to 1st century B.C. Their origin is unknown, although they may have emigrated from Lydia in Asia Minor. They probably were not native to Italy, as their language and culture are entirely different from earlier Italian cultures. Noted mariners, they traded extensively with the East. They were skilled in pottery and bronze, with Greek influence evident. Their cities became disunited because of attack by Gauls from the north and Romans from the south.

ETS see Educational Testing Service

Ets, Marie Hall (1895–   ), American author and illustrator of children's books, b. near Milwaukee, Wis. She began her career by sketching and drawing for stories. Later she wrote and illustrated her own books, which include *Mr. Oley: The Sea Monster* and *In the Forest.*
picture books for children **C** 243

Et tu, Brute! (et tu bru-TE), Caesar's last words **C** 6
Etymology (ety-MOL-ogy), study of words **W** 238

Eucalyptus, any of several tall, fragrant trees growing up to 300 feet. Also called the gum tree, it has reddish-brown stringy bark. Its petals join to form lid on flower and drop off as flower grows. It is native to Australian regions but also grows in semitropical and warm temperate regions. Its pale, hard wood is used for floors and furniture. Oil from the leaves is used as medicine.

Eucharist (EU-ca-rist), or Holy Communion **C** 281, 284
Orthodox Eastern Churches **O** 229
Roman Catholic Church **R** 288, 301

Eucharistic Congress, international gathering of Roman Catholic churchmen and laymen where Holy Eucharist is celebrated and glorified to increase devotion to the sacrament. The first Eucharistic Congress was held in Lille, France (1881). These gatherings are presided over by a papal legate.
Pope Paul VI attends, at Bogota, Colombia **P** 99

Euclid (EU-clid), Greek mathematician **G** 123; **M** 154–55
Greek civilization at Alexandria **A** 230
musical scale **A** 247
Euclidean (eu-CLID-e-an) **geometry G** 123–24
contrasted with non-Euclidean geometries **M** 158–59
mathematics, history of **M** 154–55
Eugene, Oregon **O** 205
Eugene Onegin (eu-GENE on-YEG-in), opera by Peter Ilyich Tchaikovsky **O** 143

Eugenics (from Greek *eugenēs,* meaning "wellborn"), science of biological improvement of man based on principles of human heredity through control of human reproduction. The science was founded in 19th century by Sir Francis Galton. Modern eugenics is directed at discouraging propagation on part of mentally and physically unfit.

Eugénie (eu-JANE-e), **Empress** (Eugénie Marie de Montijo de Guzmán) (1826–1920), French empress (1853–71), b. Granada, Spain. The wife of Emperor Napoleon III, she advocated strong support of Church and suppression of liberalism and democracy. She acted as regent in absence of Emperor (1859, 1865, 1870). She was a leader in European fashions, adding much to brilliance of French court.

Eugénie Grandet (eu-JANE-e gron-DE), novel by Balzac **B** 36
Euglena (eu-GLE-na), microscopic organism, a protist **K** 250
flagellates **M** 279; picture **M** 278

Eulenspiegel (OIL-en-SHPEEG-el), **Till** (Dyl Ulenspiegel), 14th-century German folk hero, b. probably Kneitlingen, Brunswick. He is the subject of many tall tales about a mischievous and clever peasant who roams country playing wicked pranks to make townsmen look foolish. The first book of these stories appeared in Germany about 1500. He is also hero of novels and poems throughout Europe and inspired musical tone poem *Till Eulenspiegel's Merry Pranks,* by Richard Strauss.
German literature **G** 174
statue of Till Eulenspiegel, picture **G** 175

Euler (OIL-er), **Leonhard,** Swiss mathematician **T** 221
Euler's theorem T 222–23

Eulogy (from Greek *eulogia,* meaning "praise") a discourse, usually a prepared speech in praise of someone or something, such as commendation of work and character of a deceased person. More generally, the term means "high praise."

Euphemism, substitution of mild, inoffensive, or less explicit term to express something unpleasant or offensive. For example, one says "he passed away" in place of "he died."

Euphrates (eu-PHRATE-ese) **River,** Asia **R** 248
Iraq **I** 379
Syria **S** 507
Euphues (EU-phu-ese), novel by John Lyly **E** 250
Euphuism (EU-phu-ism), style of writing, origin of term **E** 250
Eurasia, Europe and Asia considered as one continent **A** 447–48; **E** 304
taiga belt **T** 10–11
Euratom, European Atomic Community **E** 335
Eureka (eu-RE-ka) ("I have found it"), expression attributed to Archimedes **A** 369
Euridice (a-oo-RI-di-chay), opera by Jacopo Peri **O** 131

Euripides (eu-RIP-id-ese), Greek dramatist **G** 352–53
  the unities of action, time, place **D** 294

Europa, in Greek mythology, daughter of King Agenor who was abducted from Phoenicia across the sea to Crete by Zeus disguised as a bull. She gave birth to Minos, Rhadamanthus, and possibly Sarpedon, and married king of Crete, who then adopted her children.

Europe **E** 304–33
  agriculture **A** 92, 96–98
  Alps **A** 174–75
  countries **E** 307; list **E** 308
  dairying, history of **D** 10
  education, history of **E** 66
  European Community (Common Market) **E** 334–35
  flags **F** 239–40
  immigration **I** 103
  international relations **I** 323–24
  language families **L** 38–39
  maps before and after World War I **W** 278, 279, 283
  mountain peaks, highest in Europe **M** 494
  national dances **D** 29–30
  prairies **P** 430; picture **P** 433
  teachers and education **T** 42–43
  waterfalls, selected list **W** 57
European Atomic Community, or Euratom **E** 335
European brown bear and cubs, picture **B** 108
European Coal and Steel Community (ECSC) **E** 334
European Commission on Human Rights **C** 315
European community **E** 334–35
European corn borers, moth larvae **C** 507; picture **P** 288
European Economic Community, or Common Market **E** 333, 334–35
  Brussels, Belgium, headquarters **B** 131
  reduction in trade barriers **I** 329
  tariff **T** 25
  United Kingdom **U** 79
  West Germany **G** 164
European Free Trade Association (EFTA) **E** 333, 335; **T** 25
European great horse **H** 237
European Recovery Program, or Marshall Plan **M** 111
European Russia **U** 32
European starlings, birds **B** 219
European War (1914–18) see World War I
Europium (eu-RO-pi-um), element **E** 154, 161
Europoort, the Netherlands **N** 121
Eurovision, television network of western Europe **T** 71

Eurydice (eur-ID-is-se), in Greek mythology, wife of Orpheus, who followed her to Hades when she died. By charming gods with his lyre and singing, Orpheus persuaded them to give Eurydice back to him on condition that he not look back at her on their way up from underworld. But just as they were about to reach upper world, Orpheus turned around to make sure Eurydice was still behind him, and she vanished forever into world of dead.

Eustachian tube, of the ear, diagram **B** 285

Euthanasia (u-tha-NA-sia), mercy-killing, putting to death by painless methods persons with incurable diseases; not a recognized ethical practice.

Euterpe (u-TER-pi), goddess in Greek mythology. She was the daughter of Zeus and Mnemesyne, and the consort of Bacchus. She and her eight sisters were the muses, or patrons of the arts and sciences. Euterpe presided over lyric poetry, and her symbol was the flute.
  See also Muses

Eutrophication, a process in nature
  detergents, environmental problems of **D** 149
  water pollution **W** 59
EV see Electron volt
Evangeline, poem by Longfellow **L** 342
  Grand Pré National Historic Park **N** 344d
Evangelists, The, authors of the Gospels, Matthew, Mark, Luke, and John **E** 335
  Kells, Book of, symbols of, picture **K** 202
  New Testament, of the Bible **B** 159–62
Evans, John, American governor **C** 414
Evans, Marian, or **Mary Ann** see Eliot, George
Evans, Oliver, American inventor **D** 99
  beginnings of the automobile **A** 541
  first automatic flour mill **F** 274
  steam engines **S** 421
Evans, Ronald E., American astronaut **S** 345, 346
Evaporated milk **D** 11–12
Evaporation **H** 93
  air conditioning **A** 101–03
  effect on amount of salt in lakes **L** 25
  hydrologic, or water, cycles **W** 52
  loss is low from liquid gases **L** 308
  rain **R** 93–95
  refrigeration process **R** 136
  water cycle and climate **C** 347
  water desalting **W** 56
  water supply and evaporation control **W** 67
  Why does an unglazed ceramic jug keep liquids cool? **C** 175
Eve see Adam and Eve
Evelyn (EVE-lin), **John,** English diarist **D** 157; **E** 254
Even-toed mammals **F** 81–82; **H** 206, 207–08; pictures **H** 212–18
Everest, George, English military surveyor **E** 336
Everest, Mount **E** 336–37; **M** 489–90
Everglades, swamp in Florida **F** 261
Everglades National Park **F** 268
Evergreens **T** 282
  Christmas customs **C** 291
  leaves **L** 119
  lemon and lime **L** 136–38
  taiga **T** 11; picture **T** 10
Evergreen State, nickname for Washington **W** 14, 15

Evers, Medgar (1926–63), American civil rights leader, b. Decatur, Miss. As Mississippi field secretary for NAACP (1954–63) he organized civil rights rallies, marches, and economic boycotts. He was assassinated in Mississippi and buried in Arlington National Cemetery. **Charles Evers** (James Charles Evers) (1923–) assumed his brother's NAACP position. He was elected mayor of Fayette, Miss. (1969), the first Negro mayor in a biracial Mississippi community since Reconstruction. Picture **N** 104a

Every Good Boy Deserves Fun, saying to help in memorizing musical notes **M** 526
Everyman, 15th-century morality play **E** 250
Everyone Sang, poem by Siegfried Sasoon **F** 120
Evesdropping see Bugging
Evidence, in law courts **C** 529

Evil eye (also called overlooking), look or glance believed to cause disease, suffering, and misfortune. Belief in evil eye has been widespread in all civilizations, and many formulas and charms have been developed to ward off its dangers.
  folklore, superstition, and witchcraft **F** 310; **S** 473; **W** 209

Evolution **E** 338–47
  adaptive radiation **B** 209–10

animals without blood to those with **B** 258–59
anthropological studies **A** 306
basic adaptations **B** 210
birds **B** 207, 209
Darwin, Charles Robert **D** 39–41
earth's history **E** 18–21; **G** 116–17
evidence from fossils **F** 382–83
fishes **F** 181–82
genetics and heredity **G** 87–88
horses and their relatives **H** 235–44
Huxley, Thomas H., supported Darwin **H** 300
life, adaptation to change **L** 216
mammals **M** 61–73
marsupials **K** 167–75
plants, history of **P** 304
protective coloration **L** 219–20
science, history of **S** 73–74
Scopes "monkey" trial **B** 416
theory of, in biology **B** 192
Evzones, Greek soldiers (the Royal Guards), costumes, picture **G** 336
Ewe (A-way), a people of Africa **T** 202
Ewes (USE), female sheep **S** 145
Ewing-Donn theory, of Ice Ages **I** 24
Ewry, Ray, American athlete **O** 110
Examinations
college entrance examinations **E** 348–49
National Teacher Examination **T** 42
See also Tests and testing
Excalibur (ex-CAL-i-bur), sword of King Arthur **A** 444
Excavation, in engineering
dredges used in **D** 308, 309
foundations for building, pictures **B** 432, 433, 436
giant bucket excavator, picture **M** 318
mining **M** 316
Excavations, archeological
digging sites **A** 350–51, 353, 355–57
Schliemann, Heinrich **S** 53–54

Excelsior (Latin word meaning "higher"), exhortation to strive always for better and greater things. This motto, accompanied by image of rising sun, is seal for New York State. The motto is also the title and refrain of famous poem by H. W. Longfellow.

Exchange, trade and commerce **T** 242–43
Exchequer Court, Canada **C** 78
Excise taxes **T** 26
Exclamation points, punctuation **P** 531
Excommunication, from the Catholic Church
Luther, Martin **R** 134
Michael Caerularius, 1054, results in east-west church schism **R** 291
Executive Office of the President **P** 447; table of offices **P** 452
Executive power
presidency of the United States **P** 451
Executor or **executrix,** of a will **W** 174

Exegesis (ex-e-GE-sis) (from the Greek, meaning "to explain" or "to interpret"), in theology, explanation and interpretation of Biblical texts.

Exercise, conditioning **P** 226–29
health **H** 82–83
Kata, training for judo **J** 147
weight lifting **W** 107
See also Gymnastics; Physical education; Sports
Exhaust gas, from internal combustion engines
carbon monoxide poisoning **P** 357
Exhaust systems, of engines **I** 307

Exhibits in law courts **C** 528
Exilarch, Jewish king without a kingdom **J** 107

Exile (from Latin *exsilium*, meaning "banishment"), forced removal, or banishment, of someone from his native country. Word also means voluntary absence or separation from one's country, and in Old Testament, period of "the Captivity," when King Nebuchadnezzar authorized deportations of Jews.

Existentialism, philosophy **F** 442
See also Kierkegaard, Søren Aabye
Exodus, book of Bible, Old Testament **B** 154
Exodus, in the Bible, delivery of Hebrews from Egypt **P** 93
Exoskeleton, an outside skeleton found on some animals
crustacea **S** 170
Exosphere, highest layer of earth's atmosphere **W** 72
Expanding universe theory **U** 201
Expansion, in physics
heat **H** 94
Expatriation, or giving up citizenship **C** 313
Expeditions, scientific
anthropological teams **A** 305
archeological **A** 357–59
Experiment, in research see Research, scientific
Experimental probability **P** 473
Experimental psychology **P** 492–98
Experiment in International Living, educational organization **V** 316
Experiments and projects **E** 350–67
abacus, how to make and use **A** 2
acids or bases, tests for **C** 217
air, expansion of **B** 30
air resistance **F** 33
ant observation nest **A** 330
aquarium, set up for the home **A** 340
Archimedes' principle **F** 252
barometer, how to make **E** 366
birdhouses **B** 248–49
bird watching, finding and attracting birds **B** 233–44
bread mold **A** 316; **E** 351
butterfly collecting **B** 476
camera, pinhole, how to make **E** 364
camouflage and protective coloring **L** 219–20
cats, how to care for **C** 141–42
chemical reactions **C** 196, 197
cloud formation, how to show **E** 360
codes, send messages in **C** 370
color wheel **D** 139
compass, magnetic how to make **M** 24
Coriolis force, demonstration of **W** 187
crystals, growing your own **C** 545
direction, how to find **D** 182–93
dogs, how to select, care for, and train **D** 252–59
earth's motions, how to show **E** 4, 5
earthworm farm, how to make **W** 311
echo used to estimate speed of sound (Newton's study) **E** 45
eclipses, how to show **M** 448
electricity **E** 123, 124, 127, 128, 129
electric steadiness tester **E** 363
electrolysis, clean silver by **I** 354
electroscope, how to make **E** 364
ellipse, how to make, to study "whispering gallery" effect **G** 127, 129
erosion, how to demonstrate **E** 359
fire, test that oxygen is needed for **F** 136
flower arrangement **J** 52
fossil imprints, show how formed **G** 110
geometric shapes, how to make from paper **G** 128
graphs and pictographs **G** 309–13

Experiments and projects (continued)
gyroscope, properties of **G** 435
haiku, game verses, how to write **J** 28
heat conduction **E** 365
ice-skating, show the physics of **I** 4
Indian beadwork **I** 159
inertia, how to demonstrate **E** 37
jewelry made from wire **J** 100
latitude, how to find by the stars **N** 63
leaf collections and prints **L** 117, 118
leathercraft **L** 112–13
lens puzzle **L** 148
letter writing to pen pals **L** 159–60
library research project **L** 186–88
Locke's experiment for measuring temperature
H 87–88
magnets and magnetism **M** 24–28
matter, properties of **M** 173–78
mice, training of **E** 353–54
microscope, water-drop, how to make **E** 363
microscopes, things to look at **M** 284–85
Möbius strip, how to make **T** 222
mushrooms, spore prints **F** 498–99
musical glasses **S** 266
musical sounds, how to show the working principles
M 544
Newton's laws of motion, how to show **M** 469–71
number games and puzzles **N** 372–77
optical illusions **O** 163, 164
osmosis **E** 367; **O** 235
paper chromatography **E** 366
penicillin molds, how to grow **A** 316
photograph star "trails" **E** 362
phototropism shown by plants **E** 357
planetarium, how to make **E** 361
plankton collecting **P** 280
plant hormones **E** 352
plants **P** 302, 303
plays, putting on **P** 335–41
polarimeter, how to make **E** 365
prime numbers, how to find **N** 379
probability demonstrations **P** 471–73
protective coloring and camouflage **L** 219–20
psychology **P** 489, 492, 493, 500a
psychrometer (humidity indicator), how to make **W** 81
rock and mineral collecting **R** 273
rocks, how broken up to form soil **S** 230, 231
science, 100+ ideas **E** 356–67
scientific methods **S** 80–82
seasons, show how they change **S** 110, 112
seismic waves of earthquakes, how to show **E** 32–33
shell collecting **S** 149
ship models **S** 151–54
short circuits, how to demonstrate **E** 133
simple machines, lever, pulley, inclined plane **W** 246–50
slide rule, how to make **M** 166–67
soils **E** 360; **S** 230, 231, 233, 234
solar eclipses, how to watch **E** 46, 361
sound **S** 266
specific gravity **F** 253
spore prints of mushrooms **F** 498–99
summer, show why it is hotter **S** 109
sundial, how to make **T** 192–93
taste map of the tongue, how to make **B** 286
telegraph system **T** 53
temperature observations **W** 79–80
terrarium **T** 103
thinking and remembering, tests for **P** 492
tools of early man, how to make **A** 365
topology **T** 220–26
triangle numbers, how to find **N** 380–81
weaving **W** 97–98

wind observations **W** 83–84
woodworking **W** 231–33
word games **W** 237–38
Exploration and discovery **E** 368–88
Australia **A** 515–17
Bering Strait, discovery of **B** 142
Byrd in the Antarctic **B** 481
Cabot, John and Sebastian **C** 2
Caribbean islands **C** 116–19
Cortes' conquest of Aztec Empire **C** 508
Drake, Sir Francis **D** 290–91
early geographical expeditions **G** 98
Ericson's route to America **E** 275
food exchange between New and Old Worlds **F** 334
Lewis and Clark Expedition **L** 162–63
missions and missionaries **M** 348–49
Mississippi River **D** 144; **L** 46; **M** 103
moon exploration **E** 368; **M** 454–56; **S** 339–44
Northeast Passage **P** 364
Northwest Passage **N** 338
Piccard's deep-sea descents **P** 244
polar regions **P** 364–71
routes of major voyages **E** 377
space exploration and travel **S** 338–49
spice trade **S** 380–81
underwater exploration **U** 13–24
United States Navy **U** 186
Vikings **V** 338–40
What did New World explorers bring back? **E** 380
See also names of individual explorers and history
section of country, province, and state articles
Explorer I, III, and IV, artificial satellites **R** 46–47
radar telescope for tracking, picture **R** 73
Explorer Post groups, division of Scouting **B** 360
Explosives **E** 388–94
ammunition for guns **G** 414–26
blasting mats, picture **B** 432
coal mining **C** 366
fire and combustion **F** 137
nitrogen **N** 262
Nobel, Alfred **N** 263
solid rocket fuels **F** 490
TNT weight compared to atomic bomb, diagram **N** 354
Expo 67, World's Fair, Montreal, Canada **F** 18
Expo '70, World's Fair, Japan **F** 18, **J** 40; picture **F** 9
Exponents, in algebra **A** 159
Exports **T** 243
international trade **I** 326–27, 330
See also country, province, and state articles
Expositions *see* Fairs and expositions
Ex post facto laws **W** 9
Exposure meters
photography, use in **P** 199, 200
Express highways *see* Roads and highways
Expressionism, in art
abstract expressionism **M** 397
"Bridge, The," group of painters **G** 171
modern German movement **M** 391
painting, modern period of Dutch art **D** 358
Expressionism, in literature
dramatic form **D** 297
German writers **G** 179
Expulsion from Paradise, The, painting by Masaccio
R 166
Extemporaneous speech delivery **P** 510
Extended family **F** 37
Extension Service, U.S. Department of Agriculture
see Federal Extension Service
Extensive agriculture **A** 89
External-combustion engines **E** 210
steam engines **S** 419–21
steam turbines **T** 320–21

ILLUSTRATION CREDITS

The following list credits, by page, the sources of illustrations used in Volume E of THE NEW BOOK OF KNOWLEDGE. Credits are listed illustration by illustration —left to right, top to bottom. Wherever appropriate, the name of the photographer or artist has been listed with the source, the two being separated by a dash. When two or more illustrations appear on one page, their credits are separated by semicolons.

F, sixth letter of the English alphabet **F** 1
See also Alphabet
FAA see Federal Aviation Agency
Faber (FAY-ber), **Johann Lothar von,** German manufacturer of pencils **P** 148
Fabergé (fa-ber-JAY), **Peter Carl,** Russian jewelry designer **J** 97, 100
Fabian, pope, Christian martyr **C** 281

Fabian (FABE-ian) **Society,** socialist group founded (1884) in England by middle-class intellectuals. Named for Roman general Quintus Fabius, they advocated gradual rather than revolutionary establishment of socialism. They proposed improved labor conditions and universal suffrage, and won renown with publication (1889) of *Fabian Essays.* Members included George Bernard Shaw, H. G. Wells, and Sidney and Beatrice Webb. The society is now a research and publicity agency.
    Shaw's interest in social reforms **S** 144

Fables **F** 2–8
    early form of fiction **F** 110
    See also Folklore; Legends

Fabre (FABR), **Jean Henri** (1823–1915), French zoologist, b. Saint-Leons, Aveyron. His studies of habits and instincts of insects and related animals are classics in field of animal behavior and psychology. He wrote many books on natural history for young readers, such as *Insect Adventures.*

Fabriano, Gentile da see Gentile da Fabriano
Fabricius of Acquapendente (fab-RI-cius of aqua-pen-DEN-te), Italian surgeon and teacher **M** 205
    biology during the Renaissance **B** 188
    Harvey one of his pupils **H** 52
Fabrics **T** 140–45
    clothing industry **C** 352
    dressmaking **D** 311, 312
    dry cleaning **D** 337–39
    dyes and dyeing **D** 366–68, 370–72
    early designs with woodcuts **G** 303
    fashion **F** 65–66
    silk **S** 178–80
    weaving **W** 97–98
    See also Textiles
Fabulists, writers of fables **F** 2–4

Façade (fa-SOD), in architecture, exterior face of building, usually front, often containing principal entrance.

Face plate, or **face mask,** diving aid **O** 41; **S** 188
Face powder **C** 509
    beauty culture **B** 110
Facets (FAS-ets), cuts of gemstones **G** 71
Face veneer, for furniture **F** 503
Facsimile (fac-SIM-i-le) **transmission** **T** 54
    electronic communication, history of **E** 142
Factories, trading posts **E** 43
Factories and factory system
    automation **A** 528–34
    beginnings of socialism **S** 220
    child labor **C** 235
    China, picture **A** 463
    clothing **C** 354; picture **C** 357
    deodorizing methods **D** 117
    industrial design, methods of production **I** 231
    Industrial Revolution **I** 236
    mass production **M** 151
    programed instruction **P** 475
    women, role of **W** 212, 212a
Factory ships **W** 153

Faculae (FAC-u-le), bright areas in sun's photosphere **S** 460; picture **S** 458
FAD (flavin adenine dinucleotide), coenzyme **B** 294
Fadeev (fod-YAY-if), **Aleksandr,** Russian author **U** 62
Faerie Queene, The, poem by Edmund Spenser **E** 251
Faeroe Islands see Faroe Islands, Denmark
Fafnir (FAF-nir), dragon in Norse mythology **N** 281
Fagatogo (fon-go-TONE-go), seat of government of American Samoa **S** 26

Fahrenheit (FARR-en-hite), **Gabriel Daniel** (1686–1736), German physicist, b. Danzig (now Gdansk), Poland. Because of his carefully constructed glass tubes and his improved method of purifying mercury, he was able to produce first accurate thermometer. Fahrenheit invented temperature scale, named after him, that marks freezing point of water as 32 degrees and its boiling point as 212 degrees.
    first accurate thermometers **H** 89

Fahrenheit scale, of thermometers **T** 165
    heat **H** 89
    range of temperatures, diagram **H** 86d
    weights and measures **W** 117
Faidherbe (fay-DAIRB), **Louis Léon César,** French governor of Senegal **S** 120
Faience (fai-ONTS), pottery **P** 417
    game board and pieces, picture **D** 76
Fainting
    first aid **F** 163
Fairbanks, Alaska **A** 141

Fairbanks, Charles Warren (1852–1918), United States senator and vice-president, b. near Unionville Center, Ohio. After gaining wealth and success as a railway lawyer in Indiana, he became a leader in the Republican Party. He served as senator from Indiana (1897–1905) and then as vice-president under Theodore Roosevelt (1905–09). Picture **V** 329.

Fairbanks, Douglas (1883–1939), American actor, b. Denver, Colo. Noted for daring feats and physical agility in such films as *The Mark of Zorro, The Three Musketeers, Robin Hood, The Thief of Bagdad,* and *The Iron Mask,* he also appeared on stage in *Frenzied Finance, A Gentleman from Mississippi,* and other plays. Picture **M** 474.
    star system in silent films **M** 473

Fairbanks, Richard, postmaster of Massachusetts Bay Colony **C** 435

Fairbanks, Thaddeus (1796–1886), American inventor and manufacturer, b. Brimfield, Mass. Best-known for devising first platform scale, which he later manufactured, he also obtained patents on improved plow, parlor stove, and flax and hemp dressing machine.
    manufacturing in Vermont **V** 315

Fairbanks House, Dedham, Massachusetts **U** 123
Fair catch, in football **F** 361
Fair Deal administrative program of President Truman **T** 301

Fairies, in folklore, small supernatural beings who possess magical powers, such as the ability to become invisible, to fly, or to cast spells. They include brownies, pixies, Irish leprechauns, Germanic and Scandinavian dwarfs and trolls, and Arabian genies. The tiny creatures became popular in English literature in 16th century and play a large part in Shakespeare's *A Midsummer Night's Dream* (1595?). Before this, fairies were generally thought

Fairies (continued)
of as almost human in size and appearance, and were considered unfriendly and even dangerous to man. The helpful "fairy godmother" first appeared in 17th century French tales. Some fairies are believed to dwell in "fairyland"; others may be associated with nature (dryads, nymphs, undines) or with particular occupations (shoemaking, tailoring).
Midsummer Night's Dream, A **M** 309

Fair trade, agreement between manufacturers and retailers setting minimum price of trademarked, or brand-name, articles. Fair trade acts permit manufacturer to fix price of his goods.

Faith healing, method of treating bodily or mental sickness through faith in a supernatural being or force. The belief that faith can cure disease is centuries old. The ancient Greeks practiced faith healing, and the Bible contains descriptions of it. In modern times, a number of religious groups practice faith healing. The largest of these groups is the Christian Science church.

Fakir (fa-KEER) (from Arabic *faqir,* meaning "poor"), wandering Muslim beggar. Designation arose from a saying attributed to Mohammed, "Poverty is my pride." Fakirs are believed to possess miraculous powers. The word is also applied by Westerners to Hindu monks.

Falange ("Phalanx"), Spanish fascist party founded (1933) by José Antonio Primo de Rivera but taken over by General Franco in his struggle against Republic. It was combined (1934) with other right-wing groups into Spanish Phalanx of Traditionalism and the Offensive Nationalist-Socialist Committees (known as JONS). A member of this party, which still exists though is not as powerful as previously, is referred to as Falangist.
    Spain, history of **S** 358
    symbol **P** 381

Falashas (fa-LA-shas) (from Ethiopian, meaning "stranger" or "immigrant"), dark-skinned Ethiopian tribe of Jewish faith numbering about 35,000. Some claim descent from servants of Solomon and Queen of Sheba. Their religious practices are similar to those of early Judaism, yet include many distinctive features. The Falashas are traditionally ignorant of Hebrew and the Talmud. They speak the dialects of the places they inhabit. Their beliefs emphasize high moral standards. Each village contains its own synagogue and priest.
    Ethiopia, a people of **E** 296

Falconet (fol-co-NAY), **Étienne,** French sculptor **S** 101

Falconry, art of employing falcons and hawks in hunt, often termed "hawking." Thought to have originated in China about 2000 B.C., it was once confined by law to kings and nobility. In Europe, where the sport was popular from 9th to 17th century, game, or quarry, consisted of pheasant, ducks, and rabbits. Training involves experience and skill in observing temperament and constitution of birds. Falconry is prohibited in many states of United States.

Falcons, any one of several kinds of hunting birds found throughout world except in arctic regions. They are usually grayish in color with black heads and flight feathers, and short-necked with long, pointed wings, legs covered with feathers. Falcons feed on insects, birds, rodents and were once widely trained to hunt game birds for man.
    hunting with falcons, picture **E** 218
    special adaptations in birds **B** 222

Falla (FA-ya), **Manuel de** (1876–1946), Spanish composer, b. Cadiz. Having studied under Pedrell, founder of modern national Spanish school, he was awarded prize for best national opera, *La Vida Breve.* He then spent 7 years in Paris and evolved less exclusively national style. Falla won international fame with ballets *The Three-Cornered Hat* and *El Amor Brujo,* and he wrote marionette-play *Master Peter's Puppet Show.*
    Spanish music **O** 137; **S** 373

Fallout shelter, area or specially built structure (with at least 12 sq. ft. of floor space per person) designed for survival during nuclear attack, particularly in the first 2 or 3 days, when level of radiation is highest. It uses materials (such as concrete) heavy enough to afford protection by absorbing radiation, and is most effective when constructed underground.

Fallow, idle land **A** 96
Fallow deer, picture **H** 214
Falls, accidents **S** 2–3
False alarms, for fire **F** 153–54
False Face Society, of Iroquois Indians **I** 187
False trumpets, snails **S** 148
Falstaff, opera by Giuseppe Verdi **O** 144; picture **O** 147
Famagusta (fa-ma-GU-sta), Cyprus **C** 557; picture **C** 556
Families, divisions of biological classification **T** 29
Family **F** 37–43
   adolescent relations with **A** 24
   anthropological studies **A** 302–03
   Asia's way of life **A** 453, 459
   basic unit in the westward movement **W** 144
   bathing together **B** 91
   budgets **B** 425–26
   child development **C** 231–34
   circus people **C** 304
   coat of arms, use of the **H** 118
   colonial life in America **C** 385–99
   Confucius' way to an orderly world **C** 460
   divorce **D** 234–35
   environment and family planning **E** 272c
   family allowances of social security programs **S** 222
   foster-family care **O** 227
   guidance **G** 397–400
   holidays for members of the family **H** 156, 158–59
   home economics training **H** 165–66
   Japanese family dinner, picture **J** 27
   joint family life in India **I** 119–20
   life insurance **I** 295–96
   life underwater on a sea farm **U** 23–24
   old age, problems of **O** 96
   public-assistance programs **W** 120–21
   social organization of animals **A** 281
   songs of family life **F** 326
   space exploration, families needed **S** 349
   wedding customs **W** 100–03
   women, role of **W** 211
   See also Adoption; Foster-family care; and way of life section of country articles
Family Compact, political group of Upper Canada **M** 5
Family Group, painting by Jan Miense Molenaer **D** 365
Family Group, sculpture by Henry Moore **E** 242
Family names **N** 4
Family planning
   food and population **F** 343
   poverty, cures for **P** 424b

Family Service Association of America, organization established to improve methods of casework and family counseling. Founded in 1911, it has headquarters in New York, N.Y., and publishes monthly *Social Casework* and *Family Service Highlights.*

Family trees
   coats of arms and the science of heraldry **H** 115–18
Famine
   food and population **F** 343
   potato famine in Ireland, 1845–48 **I** 391, 393

Faneuil (FAN-el), **Peter** (1700–1743), American merchant, b. New Rochelle, N.Y. He built Faneuil Hall and presented it to city of Boston (1742). Hall, known as Cradle of Liberty because of the fiery speeches made there in Revolutionary meetings, contains a marketplace, a town meeting hall, and an artillery collection.

Fanfani (fon-FA-ni), **Amintore** (1908–), Italian economist and political leader, b. near Arezzo. He was associated after World War II with liberal Roman Catholic intellectuals as leader of Christian Democratic Party. He has been professor of economics at University of Rome intermittently since 1954) and has supported European Economic Community. He has held various cabinet posts, as minister of labor, agriculture, and foreign affairs. He was premier of Italy (1958–59, 1960–63), and was president of the United Nations General Assembly (1965–66). He became president of the Italian Senate in 1968.

Fang, a people of Africa
   Equatorial Guinea **E** 273
   Gabon **G** 2

Fangio, Juan Manuel (1912–), Argentine automobile racer. Son of an Italian immigrant, he began full-time racing at 38 and won world driving championship five times before retiring at 47 (1958).

Fangs, of animals
   snakes **S** 207
   spiders and other arachnids **S** 383

Fanning Island, coral atoll in central Pacific, one of the Line Islands. Part of British Gilbert and Ellice Islands, it is owned by Fanning Island Plantations, Ltd. It was important as a link in the British Pacific cable between Canada and Fiji. There is no native population, and Gilbertese labor is imported to produce copra.

Fanon, Frantz (1925–61), psychiatrist and writer, b. Martinique, France. Educated in France, he served at a psychiatric post in a French hospital in Algeria, until he felt impelled to join the Algerian rebels in their battle for liberation from French rule. Author of *Black Skin, White Masks* and *The Wretched of the Earth,* he had a profound influence on blacks and the New Left by his writings against all aspects of colonialism.
   African literature **A** 76d

Fans **F** 43
   fan design in furniture **F** 507; picture **F** 508
Fans, electric
   invention **F** 43
Fantasia, a musical form **M** 535, 536
Fantasy
   how it differs from science fiction **S** 83–84
   list of books of, for children **C** 248–49
   short stories **S** 167

Fantin-Latour (fon-TAN-la-TOUR), **Henri** (Ignace Henri Joseph Théodore Fantin-Latour) (1836–1904), French artist, b. Grenoble. He is noted for paintings of flowers, done while he lived in England; for portrait groups of contemporary artists and musicians, l'Hommage a Delacroix and l'Atelier à Batignolles.

FAO see Food and Agriculture Organization
Farad, Wali D., founder of The Black Muslims **N** 104a
Faraday, Michael, English scientist **F** 44; **P** 237; pictures **P** 236; **S** 75
   discovery of electric generator **E** 121
   electric and magnetic lines of force **E** 129–30
   electric motors **E** 131, 140
   invented transformer **E** 134
   magnesium, work with **M** 23

Faraday, Michael (continued)
    magnetic force theory **M** 25
    magnetic induction **E** 132
    rubber, chemistry of **R** 345
Farce, form of humor **H** 278
Farces, comical plays **E** 250
Far East, or East Asia **A** 448—49
Farel (fa-REL), **Guillaume,** French religious reformer, picture **P** 482
Farewell to Arms, A, novel by Ernest Hemingway **A** 212
Fargo, North Dakota **N** 334—35

Fargo, William George (1818—1881), American pioneer in transportation, b. Pompey, N.Y. He organized Wells, Fargo and Company (1852) to conduct express business on Pacific coast and between New York and San Francisco, Calif., by way of Isthmus of Panama. He was mayor of Buffalo, N.Y., and president of American Express Company (1868—81).

Farjeon (FAR-jon), **Eleanor** (1881—1965), English author of children's books, b. London. At 16 she wrote the book for her brother's opera, performed by Royal Academy of Music. She was awarded Carnegie medal (1955), Hans Andersen medal (1956), and Regina medal (1959) for work with children. Among her 80 works are *Nursery Rhymes of London Town* and *The Glass Slipper*.

Farley, James Aloysius (1888—   ), American politician, b. Grassey Point, N.Y. Credited with insuring Democratic Party's support of Franklin D. Roosevelt (1932, 1936), he was postmaster general (1933—40) and chairman of Democratic National Committee (1932—40). Farley is director and chairman of board of Coca-Cola Export Corporation (since 1949). He is author of *Behind the Ballots*.

Farley, Walter (1915—   ), American author, b. Syracuse, N.Y. Interested in horses since childhood, he published (1941) his first horse story, *The Black Stallion*, when still a student at Columbia. He lives on a farm in Pennsylvania, where he raises horses. His other children's books include *Black Stallion Mystery* and *Man O'War*.

Farm agent see County agent

Farman, Henri (1874—1958), French aviator and aircraft manufacturer, b. Paris. He set world's endurance and speed records (1909). His characteristic pusher biplane (1914 model) was used extensively for artillery observation and reconnaissance in World War I, and his *Goliath* was first long-distance passenger airliner, beginning regular Paris-London flights (1919). He developed ailerons and wheeled landing gear.

Farm bloc, bipartisan organization of legislators representing farming interests in both houses of U.S Congress. Founded in 1921, it has headquarters in Washington, D.C.

Farm Bureau Federation, American, federation of state and county farm bureaus that studies such agricultural problems as marketing and transportation and promotes education and social welfare among farmers and ranchers. Founded in 1919, it has headquarters in Chicago, Ill., and publishes *Nation's Agriculture.*

Farm clubs **F** 45—47
    country and state fairs **F** 12

Farmer, Fannie Merritt (1857—1915), American cooking teacher, b. Boston, Mass. As "Mother of Level Measurements," she introduced accurate measurements in cooking. She started Miss Farmer's School of Cookery (1902), where courses were designed to train housewives. The victim of a paralytic stroke in high school, she gave a course in invalid cookery at Harvard Medical School and edited *The Boston Cooking School Cook Book.*

Farmer, James Leonard (1920—   ), American civil rights leader, Negro, b. Marshall, Tex. He was a founder of Congress of Racial Equality (CORE) at University of Chicago (1942), serving as its first national chairman (1943) and national director (1961—65). He advocates nonviolent means of achieving racial integration through demonstrations. He was appointed (1969) assistant secretary of health, education, and welfare, but resigned from the post in 1970. Picture **N** 104.

Farmer, Moses Gerrish (1820—1893), American teacher, pioneer electrician, and inventor, b. Boscawen, N.H. He was superintendent in Boston (1851—53) of first American electric fire-alarm system. He accomplished electrical deposition of aluminum. His inventions include incandescent electric lamp, duplex and quadruplex telegraphs, and "self-exiting" dynamo. He advanced torpedo warfare of U.S. Navy.

Farmer Cooperative Service, U.S. Government organization, within Department of Agriculture, for research and service assistance to farmers' co-operatives. It also administers (since 1953) Cooperative Marketing Act (1926), designed to promote knowledge of co-operative principles and practices in conjunction with educational and marketing agencies.

Farmer Labor Party **P** 381
Farmers, Indians of North America **I** 183—99

Farmer's Alliance, name used by many organizations that grew out of rural discontent in 1870's and 1880's. These are primarily trade organizations, established to promote farmer's co-operatives and stabilize farm prices in United States. They joined Grangers and others in 1890's to form Populist Party.

Farmer's Almanac, guide published annually in New England since 1792. Originally a guide, based on astronomical calculations, for planting and harvesting crops, it now contains popular riddles, folk cures, superstitions, plant and animal lore, recipes, customs, and proverbs of historical interest. It predicts weather and gives tables of tides, sunrise and sunset, and eclipses.

Farmers Organization, National, association established (1955) as a bargaining agent for the sellers of farm commodities. The organization attempts to organize farmers over a large area in order to be able to set fair prices and withhold their products from the market when the price is not met. The organization's headquarters is in Corning, Iowa; its publication is the *NFO Reporter.*

Farmers Union (Farmers Educational and Cooperative Union of America), organization devoted to promoting interests of, and co-operation among, small farmers and landless workers. It is the only farm organization to support family-type farming, proposed in Brannan plan (1949). It tends to follow labor in legislative programs.

Farm implements see Farm machinery
Farming see Agriculture; agriculture section of country, province, and state articles

Farm life   F 48–54
  colonial America   **C** 387
  dairy farms   **D** 5–13
  family   **F** 40
  juvenile delinquency   **J** 164
  rural poverty and the farmer's ability to live off
    the land   **P** 424, 424a–424b
  See also Farm clubs; Ranch life; Tenant farmers; agri-
    cultural section of country and state articles
Farm machinery   **F** 55–62
  Bohemia, Czechoslovakia, picture   **C** 563
  fertilizer application machine, picture   **F** 98
  McCormick, Cyrus   **M** 186
  mechanization in agriculture   **A** 88, 89
  milking machines and equipment   **D** 9; pictures **D** 6, 11
  planting vegetables,   **V** 288
Farm produce *see* agriculture section of country, province,
    and state articles; names of products and crops, and
    kinds of farming
Farmstead machines   **F** 62
Farm teams, in baseball   **B** 77
Far North
  Eskimo life   **E** 284–91
Faroe (FARR-oe) **Islands**, Denmark   **D** 112; **I** 430
Farouk (fa-ROOK), king of Egypt   **E** 92

Farquhar (FAR-quar), **George** (1678–1707), English dramatist, b. Londonderry, Ireland. He wrote of Ireland and
military life, using conventional tricks of Restoration
comedy (such as unraveling every plot by disguises) but
placing new emphasis on social problems. He represents
transition between Restoration comedy of manners and
early English novel (which he influenced). His last play,
considered his best, is *The Beaux' Stratagem.*

Farquharson, Martha, pen name of Martha F. Finley,
  American author of Elsie Dinsmore books   **C** 240
Farragut, David Glasgow, American naval hero   **F** 62
  capture of New Orleans in the Civil War   **C** 323

Farrar (far-RAR), **Geraldine** (1882–1967), American so-
prano, b. Melrose, Mass. She made her operatic debut as
Marguerite in *Faust* at Berlin opera (1901), giving her
most notable performances as Madame Butterfly and
Carmen at Metropolitan Opera (1906–22) in New York,
N.Y. Picture   **O** 137.

Farrell, Eileen (1920–   ), American soprano, b. Williman-
tic, Conn. She is a member of Metropolitan Opera
Company. Her operatic roles include parts in *Il Trovatore, Medea,* and *La Gioconda.* She made her radio debut
in 1941 and sang on radio for 6 years. Her European
career began (1959) in Spoleto, Italy, and she has sung
throughout Europe and United States.

Farrell, James T., American novelist   **A** 212
Farsightedness, eye defect   **L** 150, 265
Fasces (FAS-cese), Roman symbol of authority   **F** 63
Fascism (FASH-ism)   **F** 63–64
  Franco, Francisco   **F** 450
  Italy   **I** 457
  Mussolini, Benito   **M** 552
  Nazism, a Fascist movement   **N** 69–71
  Spanish Civil War, 1936–39   **W** 285–86
Fashion   **F** 65–71; illustration   **I** 95, 96
  clothing, history of   **C** 351
  dressmaking class, picture   **I** 228
  early dolls displayed dress styles ·   **D** 267
  furs   **F** 511
  gloves   **G** 240–41
  hairdressing, styles in, pictures   **H** 4–5
  hats and hatmaking   **H** 53–55

  modeling, fashion   **M** 384–85
  shoes   **S** 162–63
  See also Clothing industry
Fashion Institute of Technology, New York, N.Y.   **C** 356
Fashion modeling *see* Modeling, fashion

Fast, Howard Melvin (1914–   ), American novelist, b.
New York, N.Y. As a member of Communist Party
(1944–57), he won Stalin International Peace Prize
(1953). He wrote of his disillusionment with Communism
in *The Naked God.* His best-known historical novels are
Spartacus and *Citizen Tom Paine.*

Fast color, in dyeing   **D** 370
Fasting, one of Gandhi's methods of nonco-operation to
  gain self-rule for India   **G** 24
Fasts and feasts *see* Festivals; Religious holidays

Fates, in Greek and Roman mythology, three goddesses
who spun the thread of fate and thus controlled men's
lives. According to the Greeks, they were named Clotho,
Lachesis, and Atropos. Clotho wrapped the thread around
a spindle; Lachesis determined the length of the thread;
and Atropos cut the thread when a man was to die.
In Roman mythology, the three were named Noma,
Decuma, and Morta. The Norns—three similar figures
in Scandinavian mythology—are named Urth, Verthand,
and Skuld.
  Greek and Norse mythologies   **G** 357;   **N** 277

Father Brown, detective in Chesterton's novels   **E** 266
Father Christmas   **C** 292; picture **C** 293
Father Frost, Polish Santa Claus   **C** 292

Father of airconditioning, Willis Carrier.
Father of algebra, Diophantus.
Father of American botany, John Bartram.
Father of American football, Walter Camp.
Father of angling, Izaak Walton.
Father of British Columbia, Sir James Douglas.
Father of comedy, Aristophanes.
Father of English history, the Venerable Bede.
Father of epic poetry, Homer.
Father of geometry, Euclid.
Father of Greek tragedy, Aeschylus.
Father of history, Herodotus.
Father of medicine, Hippocrates.
Father of scouting, Robert Baden-Powell.
Father of the American Navy, John Barry.
Father of the American Revolution, Samuel Adams.
Father of the Constitution, James Madison.
Father of the United Nations, Cordell Hull.

Father of Waters, or Mississippi River   **M** 364–65
Fathers and Sons, novel by Turgenev   **N** 347
Father's Day   **H** 158;   **J** 152

Fathers of Canadian Confederation, 33 representatives
who planned federal union of Canadian provinces at
Quebec Conference of October, 1864. They submitted
Quebec Resolutions to Imperial Parliament, which
passed them as British North America Act (effective July
1, 1867), uniting Canada, Nova Scotia, and New
Brunswick into Dominion of Canada. Sir John A. Macdonald was the Dominion of Canada's first prime minister.

Fathers of Confederation Memorial Centre, Charlottetown,
  P.E.I., Canada, picture   **P** 456h
Fathers of the Church   **C** 282–83

Fathom, measure of length equal to 6 ft. It was first used
in reference to land as the Anglo-Saxon word for out-

Fathom (continued)

stretched arms, and is now used chiefly in measuring depth of water by sounding (line or plummet).

    sounding the ocean depths **O** 26

Fathometer (fa-THOM-et-er), type of sonar system to measure depth of ocean **R** 37; **S** 267

Fatigue, metal see Metal fatigue

Fatima, Our Lady of, apparition of Virgin Mary that is said to have appeared (May, 1917) during World War I to three children in Fatima, Portugal. Apparition urged them to pray and do penance to avert another, more terrible, war. The miracle is recognized by authorities of Roman Catholic Church.

Fats **O** 76–79

    butter **B** 467
    cocoa butter **C** 275
    cosmetics made of **C** 509
    detergents and soaps **D** 145, 147
    digestion of **B** 275
    lanolin from wool **W** 235
    lipids in body chemistry **B** 293
    milk **M** 310
    nutrition, needs in **N** 416
    See also Oils

Fattori (fa-TO-ri), **Giovanni,** Italian painter **I** 473

Fatty acids, body compounds **B** 293

    oils and fats **O** 76, 77

Faucets, water, diagram **P** 341

    how to change a washer **P** 342

Faulkner, Nancy (Anne Irvin Faulkner) (1906–), American author, b. Lynchburg, Va. Most of her books for young people are historical fiction. They include *Tomahawk Shadow, Knights Besieged, Sword of the Winds, Traitor Queen,* and *Great Reckoning.*

Faulkner, William, American novelist **F** 71; **A** 211

    Mississippi, scene of his novels **M** 361
    themes of his novels **N** 349

Faults, geological **M** 493

    earthquakes cause **E** 32
    lake basins **L** 25
    Mars **M** 109

Fault scarp, face of a block mountain **M** 496

Fauna see Flora and fauna

Fauntleroy, Little Lord, main character in novel of same name by Frances Hodgson Burnett. A 7-year-old American boy who goes to England as heir to earldom, he wins affection of cranky grandfather for himself and for his poverty-stricken mother in America. The long curls and lace-collared velvet suit he wore now symbolize the too-good-to-be-true child.

Faunus, Roman god see Pan

Fauré (faur-AY), **Gabriel-Urbain** (1845–1924), French composer, organist, and teacher, b. Pamiers. He was director of Paris Conservatory (1905–20). His music is distinguished for its great refinement, formal clarity, and harmonic originality. Known chiefly for his numerous songs and the *Requiem,* he also wrote many piano pieces, chamber works, and orchestral pieces, as well as incidental music for the stage and two operas.

Fauset (FAU-set), **Jessie Redmon** (1884?–), American novelist, Negro, b. Philadelphia, Pa. Her books, such as *The Chinaberry Tree* and *Comedy, American Style,* are about Negroes whose lives are hurt by race prejudice.

Faust (FOWST), drama by Goethe **G** 246

Faust, opera by Charles Gounod **O** 144

Faust in His Study, Watching a Magic Disk, painting by Rembrandt **F** 73

Faust legends **F** 72–73

    Witches' Sabbath, picture **G** 176

Fauteux, Joseph Honoré Gerald (1900–), Canadian Supreme Court Judge, b. St. Hyacinthe, Quebec. He practiced law in Montreal and served successively as Crown attorney, chief Crown counsel, and judge of the Superior Court before his appointment in 1949 as judge of the Supreme Court of Canada. When the Royal Commission undertook an investigation into spying activities in Canada, Fauteux acted as legal advisor.

Fauvism (FO-vism), French school of painting **F** 431

    Braque, Georges **B** 371
    Matisse, Henri **M** 169
    modern art **M** 388, 390

Favors, for parties **P** 88

Fawcett, Millicent, British woman suffrage leader **W** 213

Fawkes, Guy, English soldier, and leader of "Gunpowder Plot" of 1605 **H** 150

Fawns, young deer **D** 83

    hoofed mammals **H** 219

Fayetteville, Arkansas **A** 429–30

Fayetteville, North Carolina **N** 318

FBI see Federal Bureau of Investigation

FCC see Federal Communications Commission

F clef, or bass clef, in musical notation **M** 525–26

FDA see Food and Drug Administration, United States

F'Dérik, formerly Fort Gouraud, Mauritania **M** 180; picture **M** 179

FDIC see Federal Deposit Insurance Corporation

Fealty, loyalty owed to a feudal lord **F** 101

Fear

    Freud's theories **F** 470

Feast in the House of Levi, painting by Veronese **J** 82

Feast of Lights see Hanukkah

Feast of Lots, or Purim **P** 540

Feast of the Dead, Huron Indian celebration **I** 185

Feast of Weeks, religious holiday **R** 154

Feasts and fasts see Festivals; Religious holidays

Featherbedding, a labor-management issue **L** 17–18

Feather-duster worms **W** 310

Feathers **B** 199–200

    feather cape, picture **A** 348
    feather collections **B** 244

Featherweight, in boxing **B** 352

Feature articles, in newspapers **N** 201

Feboldson (FE-bold-son), **Febold,** American mythical hero —a product of local tradition and newspaper humor of Great Plains area, particularly Nebraska. A Swedish pioneer of tremendous strength, he cut through fog and tied tornadoes into knots as they swept across plains.

February, second month of year **F** 74–75

Federal aid to libraries **L** 173

Federal Arts Projects, United States, program of grants to artists during the Depression

    Pollock, Jackson **P** 387

Federal Aviation Agency (FAA) **A** 564

    promotes interstate commerce **I** 332

Federal Bureau of Investigation **F** 76–77

    federal police system of law enforcement **L** 89
    fingerprinting **F** 129
    intelligence agency for the federal government **S** 390
    police, assistance to **P** 375, 377

Federal cities
Brasília, Brazil **B** 380; picture **C** 308
Canberra, Australia **C** 87–88
city planning of capitals **U** 233
Madrid, Spain **M** 11–13
New Delhi, India **D** 101
Ottawa, Canada, federal district of **O** 124
Washington, D.C. **W** 30–35
Federal Communications Commission (FCC) **I** 332
consumer protection agencies **C** 494a
radio programs **R** 60
radio supervision **R** 55–56
rock music, development of **R** 262b
television **T** 70a, 70b
Federal Convention, 1787 *see* Constitutional Convention, 1787
Federal Deposit Insurance Corporation (FDIC) **D** 122
banks and banking **B** 48
Roosevelt's administration **R** 321

Federal district, area set aside as seat of the national government. In United States, term refers to District of Columbia, originally consisting of 100 square miles ceded by Maryland and Virginia. This area was reduced to 70 square miles by return of Virginia's portion (1846).

Federal Employee's Compensation Act, 1916 **W** 253

Federal Extension Service, agency of U.S. Department of Agriculture. Extension agents give latest scientific findings, economic facts, and practical advice to people in rural communities. They work with young people through 4-H Clubs.
4-H Club leadership **F** 47

Federal Farm Loan Act, 1916 **W** 179
Federal Food and Drug Act, 1906 **F** 350
Federal Food, Drug, and Cosmetic Act, 1938, 1958
F 350, 351
drug industry **D** 324
Federal government
states work with U.S. government, diagram **S** 413
United States **U** 139–42
Federal Highway Administration
protects interstate commerce **I** 332

Federal Housing Administration (FHA), U.S. government agency organized (1934) to insure mortgage loans used to finance purchase or improvement of residential property. The FHA provides protection to banks, which in turn grant to homeowners long-term loans of up to 97 percent of property value.
urban planning **U** 234

Federal Institute of Technology, Zurich, Switzerland
S 496

Federal Intermediate Credit Bank, one in a system of 12 banks designed to facilitate loans for crop financing in farm credit districts. The banks were established under the Agricultural Credit Acts (1923) and make loans to banks and lending companies but not to individuals.

Federal Investigative Agencies F 76
Federalism, government that divides power between central authority and its divisions
Trudeau's *Federalism and the French Canadians* **Q** 13
United States Constitution **U** 147
Federalist, The, papers supporting the United States Constitution **F** 78
Hamilton's writings under the name of Publius
H 19

Jay, John **J** 56
Madison, James **M** 7–8
ratification of the Constitution **U** 147
Federalist Party, American political party **P** 380
Adams, John **A** 10
Adams, John Quincy **A** 13
Federal Maritime Commission I 332

Federal Mediation and Conciliation Service, organization established by Labor Management Relations Act (1947) to prevent disruption of interstate commerce resulting from labor-management disputes. It attempts to resolve differences over new contract terms or over grievances arising under existing contracts and makes recommendations but cannot legally enforce them.

Federal Power Commission, commission that regulates interstate features of the electric power and natural gas industries. It issues and administers permits and licenses for the planning, construction, and operation of nonfederal hydroelectric power projects on waters or lands subject to federal jurisdiction and controls the rates of interstate gas commerce. It publishes information on the entire electric power industry and on natural gas companies under its jurisdiction.
regulatory agencies in interstate commerce **I** 332.

Federal Railroad Administration
protects interstate commerce **I** 332
Federal Republic of Germany *see* Germany, Federal Republic of (West Germany)
Federal Reserve Act, 1913 **W** 179
Federal Reserve Board B 47, 48
Federal Reserve notes, picture **M** 412
Federal Reserve System, of banking **B** 48, 50
inflation and deflation, control of **I** 253
Federal style
furniture design **F** 509
Federal Theater Project T 161
Federal Trade Commission I 332
consumer protection agencies **C** 494a
Federal Trade Commission Act, 1914 **T** 306; **W** 179
regulation of food advertising **F** 352

Federation Cup, championship matches (established 1963) for women's tennis teams of all nations.

Fédération Internationale de l'Automobile (F.I.A.)
A 539, 540
Fédération Internationale des Échecs (FIDE), international organization of chess players **C** 222
Federation of— see under main part of name, as South Arabia, Federation of
Fedor III (f'YO-dur), Russian ruler **P** 168
Feeble-mindedness see Retardation, mental
Feedback, control system
automation **A** 528–29
Feeding and feeds
barley and oats **G** 284, 285
dairy cattle **D** 7, 8
pasture grasses and hay **G** 317
salt in **S** 21
zoo animals **Z** 376–77
See also Soybeans
Feeding frenzy, of sharks **S** 143
scavengers of the seas **O** 38
Feeling, sense of see Touch, sense of
Feelings see Emotions
Feet, or measures, in poetry **P** 353–54
Feet, parts of the body **F** 79–84
Alakaluf Indians, special adaptations **A** 306
animal tracks, pictures **A** 271, 272

Feet (continued)
bats **B** 92
birds **B** 221
footprints, identification **F** 129
hoofed mammals **H** 206
horses **H** 236
locomotion on land **A** 291–94
man's body plan **B** 269–70
primates **M** 417
skeleton, diagram **B** 271
tube feet of starfishes **S** 403
See also Claws

Fehling (FAIL-ing) **solution,** blue solution used to test for sugars and other substances that are similar chemically. The solution is put into test tube containing an unknown substance. If the solution turns yellow, and if yellow particles at the bottom of the tube turn red after heating, the unknown is a sugar. Fehling solution is used in medicine to test for the presence of sugar in blood and in urine, particularly when diabetes is suspected.

Feininger (FY-ning-er), **Lyonel Charles Adrian** (1871–1956), American painter and graphic artist, b. New York, N.Y. He lived in Germany from 1887 to 1937, and was a leader of the nonrepresentational movement in German painting while professor at the Bauhaus (1919–33). An architectural spirit is prominent in many of his works, including *Marine* and *Last Voyage.*

Feldspar, most abundant group of minerals in the earth's crust, chemically composed of the elements aluminum, silicon, and oxygen, and either potassium, sodium, or calcium. Many varieties exist in different colors (white, gray, salmon, pink, brown, yellow, green). When crushed, feldspar is an important raw material for strengthening and coloring glass and pottery. Picture **R** 265.
ceramics **C** 174
gemstone **G** 76

Felines, animals of the cat family **C** 134–44
Felis lybica (FE-lis LY-bi-ca), ancestor of house cat **C** 141
Fellahin (fel-la-HEEN), country people or peasants of Egypt **E** 90c

Feller, Bob (Robert William Andrew Feller) (1918–), American baseball player, b. Van Meter, Iowa. Feller pitched for the Cleveland Indians (1936–42 and 1945–56) and won the most games of any Indian pitcher (266). He pitched three no-hit games and was named to Baseball Hall of Fame in 1962. His pitch was once clocked at 98.6 miles per hour.

Fellini (fel-LI-ni), **Federico,** Italian motion picture director **M** 488

Fellowship, grant of money for special study at graduate level. Fellowships are supplied by public and private funds, including private foundations and industry. The Institute of International Education supervises many fellowships and issues reports on those available.

Felony, in law **C** 527
jury trials **J** 159

Fels Fund, Samuel S., foundation that supports charitable, educational, and scientific projects and grants fellowships in the humanities and sciences. It was incorporated (1935) in Philadelphia, Pa., to be terminated 30 or 40 years after death of donor Samuel Fels.

Felsite, lava rock **R** 264; picture **R** 265
Felspar see Feldspar
Felt, wool fiber **F** 107
hats **H** 53; pictures **H** 54
textiles **T** 144
Felting needles N 89
Feltre, Vittorino da see Vittorino da Feltre
Feluccas (fel-LU-cas), boats, picture **N** 260
Femur (FE-mur), the thighbone, extending from the hip to the knee, diagram **B** 271
Fencing F 84–86
dueling as a sport **D** 341
Olympic match, picture **O** 113

Fenians (FE-ni-ans), or **Fianna,** warriors of Old Irish folklore who guarded Ireland's high kings during 2nd and 3rd centuries. The most famous were the chieftain Finn Mac Cool and his son Ossian, who have prominent roles in the legends known as the Fenian Cycle. The Fenian legends are said to have been composed by Ossian.
Fenian Cycle in early Irish literature **I** 392

Fennec foxes F 397; picture **D** 245
dog family, foxes branch **D** 250

Fennel, two- to three-foot-tall heavily scented plant bearing small yellow flowers in clusters. Fennel is related to parsley, and its dried leaves and seeds are used to flavor foods. It is native to Europe but is grown elsewhere. Hog fennel, a short-stemmed plant with white, yellow, or purple flowers, is found on the U.S. Pacific coast.
popular spice products **S** 382

Fenner, Phyllis Reid (1899–), American author of children's books, b. Almond, N.Y. Her works include *Ghosts, Ghosts, Ghosts, There Was a Horse* (folktales), and *No Time for Glory.*

Fenrir, in Old Norse mythology, gigantic wolf whose open jaws reached from earth to heavens. He was offspring of evil giant (or deity) Loki and giantess Angurboda. Fenrir was bound by gods with magic cord but freed himself and swallowed supreme god, Odin. He was then killed by Odin's son, Vidar.

Fens, salt marshes
Hackensack Meadows, New Jersey **N** 166
Fenugreek (FEN-u-greek), a spice product **S** 382

Feoktistov, Konstantin Petrovich (1926–), Soviet astronaut, b. Voronezh. With Vladimir Komarov and Boris Yegorov he took part in the flight of Voskhod 1 on Oct. 12–13, 1964, the first multi-manned space flight, remaining aloft 24 hours and 17 minutes and completing 16 orbits of the earth. Feoktistov was the first nonmember of the Communist Party to become a Soviet cosmonaut.
space flight data **S** 344, 345

Feral animals
wild dogs **D** 242–43, 248
wild horses **H** 235
Feraoun, Mouloud, Algerian writer **A** 76d

Ferber, Edna (1887–1968), American novelist and playwright, b. Kalamazoo, Mich. She won a Pulitzer prize (1925) for her novel *So Big.* Other novels of hers, including *Show Boat, Cimarron,* and *Giant,* have been made into films.

Ferdinand II, king of Aragon, patron of Columbus **F** 87
Caribbean islands, colonization of **C** 118

Columbus and Ferdinand **C** 417
Spanish Inquisition **I** 257
Ferdinand V, king of Castile and Leon *see* **Ferdinand II,**
king of Aragon
Ferdinand VII, king of Spain
Prado **P** 429
Ferdinand, prince of Saxe-Coburg-Gotha, czar of Bulgaria
B 444
Ferlo Desert, Senegal **S** 120
Fermat (fer-MA), **Pierre de,** French mathematician **M** 156
probability **P** 471
Fermentation F 87–91
bacteria cause **B** 12
beer and brewing **B** 116
bread **B** 385
cacao bean (chocolate) processing **C** 275
food preservation **F** 348
Pasteur discovers cause of **B** 194; **P** 96
whiskey and other distilled beverages **W** 159
wine **W** 188
yeast **F** 496, 498
Fermi (FER-mi), **Enrico,** Italian-born American nuclear
physicist **F** 91–92
contributions to physics **P** 237

Fermi, Laura (1907–   ), American author, b. Rome, Italy,
widow of Dr. Enrico Fermi, Nobel prize-winning physicist.
She came to the United States with her husband and
family (1939) and became citizen (1944). Mrs. Fermi is
particularly concerned with clear scientific writing for
use in high schools and authored *The Story of Atomic
Energy* and *Atoms in the Family.*
Fermi, Enrico, and Mrs. Fermi **F** 91–92

Fermium, element **E** 154, 161
Fernández de Encisco, Martin *see* Encisco, Martin Fernández de
Fernando Po, Equatorial Guinea **E** 273–74; **S** 357
Fernow (FER-no), **Bernhard E.,** German-born American
scientist **C** 485
Ferns F 92–93
adaptations in the world of life, picture **L** 215
fossils, picture **F** 379
make a woodland terrarium **T** 102–04
reproduction by means of spores **F** 497; **R** 177–78
wild flower garden, picture **W** 171
Ferré, Luis A., governor of Puerto Rico **P** 523

Ferrelo (fer-RAY-lo), **Bartolomeo,** Spanish navigator who
accompanied Juan Rodriguez Cabrillo's expedition to the
western coast of North America (1542–43). The voyage
established Spain's right to the coast.
early exploration of the Orgeon coast **O** 206

Ferrets, type of weasels **O** 243
pets **P** 180
Ferries
Alaska's system **A** 138–39
ferry boat, pictures **C** 396, **T** 263
used as ice-breakers, P.E.I., Canada **P** 456g
Ferrosilicon, alloy **M** 23
Ferrotypes, or tintypes, kind of photograph **P** 212
Ferrous alloys A 168
Ferrous sulfide C 196, 198
Ferry, Elisha P., American lawyer and statesman **W** 27
Fertile Crescent, region in the Middle East **M** 302
southwest Asia **A** 450
Fertility, Sea of, on the moon **S** 348
landing area sites, map **M** 449
Fertilization, union of genes **G** 78
eggs and embryos **E** 90
flowers **F** 277

mosses **F** 93
plants **P** 296–97
reproduction **R** 178
Fertilizers F 95–98
apple trees require **A** 335
chemical fertilizers, discovery of **A** 100
environment, pollution of **E** 272d, 272e
fruitgrowing **F** 482–83
garbage and refuse disposal **S** 34
gardens and gardening **G** 30
lawn care **L** 90–91
nitrogen **N** 262
pellets for house plants, picture **H** 267
soil management in agriculture **A** 93, 100
See also Guano
Fessenden, Reginald A., American physicist **C** 439; **R** 53
Festival of Two Worlds, Spoleto, Italy **M** 551
Festivals
Brazil's Carnival, picture **B** 374
Buddhist Festival of Lights, Burma **B** 455
Christmas customs around the world **C** 289–95
Easter **E** 41–42
holidays around the world **H** 154–56
India **I** 120
Indian fiestas in Peru **P** 161
Japan **J** 31
music festivals **M** 550–52
rock music festivals **R** 262d
Shakespearean *see* **Shakespeare Memorial theaters**
Thanksgiving Day **T** 152–54
theater **T** 159
valentines **V** 266–68
See also Carnivals; Harvest festivals; Holidays; Re-
ligious holidays; country and state articles
Fetch, of a wave **O** 34
Fetishes, objects believed to have magical powers **P** 9
Fetus (FE-tus), an unborn or unhatched mammal **E** 90
baby **B** 2

Feuchtwanger (FOICT-vong-er), **Lion** (1884–1958), German
novelist and dramatist, b. Munich. He collaborated with
Bertolt Brecht on numerous plays. Because of his
Jewish parentage and revolutionary ideas, Feuchtwanger
fled Nazi Germany, finally settling in Hollywood, Calif.
(1940–58). His historical novels include *The Ugly
Duchess, Power,* and *This Is the Hour.*

Feudalism F 99–103
Albania, clan system **A** 144
Charlemagne's empire and rule by feudal lords **M** 290
citizenship and loyalty to feudal lord **C** 311
feudal law **L** 87
Japan **J** 43, 45–46
knights, knighthood, and chivalry **K** 272–77
land ownership of Middle Ages **R** 112
Roman Catholic Church **R** 291
tolls for crossing a lord's bridge, picture **M** 293
See also Chivalry; Knights and knighthood; Middle
Ages
Feuds L 88
The Hatfields and the McCoys, drama, an annual event
in West Virginia **W** 137

Fever, condition in which body temperature is raised
above normal range of 98 to 99 degrees Fahrenheit, as
measured by oral thermometer. Fever accompanies
many diseases and other body conditions, such as loss
of water. It is thought to be of value in fighting disease,
but its role and the process by which a fever is brought
about are not yet clearly understood.
use of a fever thermometer **M** 208e, 208f; **N** 414
See also names of fevers, as Scarlet fever

Few, William (1748–1824), American statesman, b. near Baltimore, Md. He was a member of the General Assembly and executive council of Georgia and a delegate to the Philadelphia Convention (1787), which drafted the United States Constitution. He then served (1789–93) as a senator from Georgia. After moving to New York City (1799), he served for 4 years in the New York General Assembly.

Feynman (FINE-man), **Richard P.** (1918–), American physicist, b. New York, N.Y. He is noted for his work in quantum electrodynamics. Feynman shared the 1965 Nobel prize in physics with Sin-itiro Tomonaga and Julian S. Schwinger for work in this field.

Fez, Treaty of, 1912 **M** 461
FFA see Future Farmers of America
FHA see Federal Housing Administration
Fianarantsoa, Malagasy Republic **M** 49
Fianna, band of Irish warriors **I** 392

Fiat (from Latin, meaning "let it be done"), official sanction or permission, also an order or command. *Fiat lux,* means "let there be light."

Fiberboard, material made by compressing felted wood or other vegetable fibers (often cornstalks or waste paper) into thick, stiff sheets or boards. Fiberboard is used for paneling where moderate strength is required.
    composition boards **W** 227

Fiber glass G 237
    archery equipment made of **A** 366–67
    boats in shipyards at Lunenburg, Nova Scotia, picture **N** 344e
    insulating material **I** 290–91
    synthetic fibers made of minerals **F** 107–08; **N** 425
Fiber reactive dyes D 371
Fibers F 104–08
    cotton **C** 519–25
    dyes and dyeing **D** 370–72
    extruded filaments of thermoplastics **P** 329; picture **P** 326
    How are man-made fibers named? **N** 425
    jute **J** 161–62
    kapok **K** 193
    nylon and other man-made fibers **N** 424–28
    optical instruments made of fibers **O** 168–69
    paper **P** 51–57
    rope **R** 331–33
    rugs and carpets **R** 354
    silk **S** 178–80
    textiles **T** 140–45
    weaving **W** 97–98
    wool **W** 234–35
    See also Cotton; Paper; Silk; Wool

Fibonacci (fi-bo-NOT-chi), **Leonardo** (also Leonardo of Pisa) (1180?–1250?), Italian mathematician, b. Pisa. His Book of the Abacus introduced into Western civilization the Arabic system of writing numbers. He also made innovations in other areas of mathematics, such as in use of algebra in geometry.

Fibrin (FY-brin), formed from fribinogen, in blood **B** 257; **M** 211
Fibula (FIB-u-la), the outer and smaller of the two bones of the leg, diagram **B** 271
Fiction F 109–12
    art of writing **W** 319–20
    historical fiction for children, list **C** 248a
    library arrangement **L** 182–83

    literature, types of **L** 313–14
    mystery, detective, and suspense stories **M** 553–56
    novels **N** 345–49
    Pulitzer prizes **P** 524–25
    science fiction **S** 83–85
    short stories **S** 165–67
Fiddle, folk music instrument **F** 329
    See also Violin
Fiddleheads, of ferns **F** 92–93
Fiddler crabs L 243, 249
    measure time, diagram **L** 246–47
    tidal feeding rhythm, picture **L** 245
Fiddler on the Roof, musical **M** 543
Fidelio (fi-DAY-li-o), opera by Beethoven **O** 144

Fiedler (FEED-ler), **Arthur** (1894–), American orchestra conductor, b. Boston, Mass. He founded (1929) the free open-air Boston Esplanade Concerts and is conductor of the Boston Pops Concerts (since 1930). Young soloists are often featured at his children's concerts.

Fiedler, Leslie Aaron (1917–), American author, b. Newark, N.J. Known best as an essayist, he has also written stories, novels, and poems. Among his books are *The Art of the Essay, Love and Death in the American Novel, The Second Stone, A Love Story,* and *Waiting for the End.*

Fiefs (FEEFS), land grants by a feudal king **F** 100
Field, Cyrus, American financier **F** 113
    Atlantic cable **T** 52
    communication advanced by **C** 438
Field, Eugene, American poet and journalist **F** 113–14
    children's poetry **C** 241
    "Dutch Lullaby, A" **F** 114

Field, John (1782–1837), Irish composer and pianist, b. Dublin. He studied with Clementi, whom he followed to Paris (1802) and St. Petersburg (1803), where remained as a teacher and performer. On his concert tours in Russia and Europe he played many of his own works. His piano nocturnes, the first ever written, influenced other composers, particularly Chopin.

Field, Marshall (1834–1906), American merchant, b. near Conway, Mass. When he was 22, Field went to Chicago as a clerk. In 8 years he was head of his own store, and in 1881 the firm became Marshall Field & Co. The department store takes up a whole city block. His most notable gift to Chicago is the chief endowment of the Field Museum of Natural History (1893). **R** 112

Field, or ground, of a flag **F** 243; picture **F** 234

Field, Rachel Lyman (1894–1942), American author and illustrator of children's books, b. New York, N.Y. She wrote and illustrated *An Alphabet for Boys and Girls* and *Polly Patchwork* and is author of *Hitty* and *Calico Bush,* set on coast of Maine, and the frequently produced play *Three Pills in a Bottle.* Her best-known novel for adults is *All This and Heaven Too.*
    "The Little Rose Tree," poem **F** 120

Field army, combat unit **U** 173
Field commands, United States Army **U** 173–74

Field Foundation, Inc., foundation established for broad charitable purposes. Founded in 1940 by Marshall Field III (1893–1956), its interests are child welfare, intercultural and interracial relations. Headquarters are in New York, N.Y.

Field goal, in football   F 361
Field hockey   F 115–16

Field Hockey Association of America (FHAA), governing body for men's amateur field hockey in the United States. Established in 1930, it arranges game schedules and sponsors national and international tournaments.

Fielding, Henry, English novelist   E 260
  novels of humorous adventure   N 346
Field magnets   E 137
Field mice, or voles   R 278
Field Museum, Chicago, picture   C 230
Field of Yellow Corn, painting by Van Gogh   P 28
Field pelleters, farm machinery   F 60

Fields, W. C. (William Claude Dukenfield) (1880–1946), American actor, b. Philadelphia, Pa. A juggler in circus and vaudeville, he gained fame in Ziegfeld Follies (1915–21) with comedy routines about tramps and drunks, and appeared in such films as *The Bank Dick* and *My Little Chickadee.*

Field sports see Track and field
Field tractors   F 55
Field trials, in dog shows   D 262
Fiesole, Giovanni Angelico da see Angelico, Fra
Fiestas see Carnivals; Festivals; Holidays; Religious holidays
Fife
  fife and drum band, picture   B 38
Fifer, The, painting by Manet   F 429
Fifteen-stripe flag   F 248; picture   F 229
Fifteenth amendment, to the U. S. Constitution   U 157
  author, William M. Stewart   N 135
  Negro history   N 95

Fifth column, group working within a country in an attempt to undermine government in power. The expression was coined by General Mola during the Spanish Civil War (1936–39), when four columns of General Franco's Nationalist Army were aided in an attack on Madrid (1936) by a "fifth column" of Nationalist sympathizers within the city.
  secret fighters within enemy lines   U 10

Fifth Republic, France   F 420
  governmental structure of France   F 412
Fifty-four forty or fight, political slogan   P 385
  territorial expansion of United States   T 110
Fifty-niners, silver prospectors in Nevada   G 251
Fig   F 117
  dried fruits   D 316–17
F.I.G. see International Gymnastics Federation
Figg, James, English boxing champion   B 352
Fight for the Water Hole, painting by Remington   U 119
Fighting see Battles; War
Figueres (fi-GARE-es), **José,** president of Costa Rica   C 519
Figure, sculpture by Lipchitz   S 104
Figured bass, in music   B 65
Figure-eight knots   K 290

Figurehead, ornamental carving on bow of sailing ship, often a patriotic symbol or portrayal of a mythological character. The term has been applied to a leader who is only the nominal, not the effective, head of a group or organization. A collection of wooden figureheads in the Mariners Museum, Newport News, Va., represents American sculpture of late 18th and early 19th centuries.

Figure in the Carpet, ballet, picture   B 27

Figure skating   I 48–50
  artistic form of roller-skating   R 284
  Olympic event   O 109
Figures of speech   F 118–20
Figure studies, drawings of people   D 301
Fiji   F 121–22
  drying copra, picture   P 4
  flag   F 240
Fikri, Abdel Qader, Algerian novelist   A 76d
Filament, anther-bearing stalks of a stamen, in a flower   F 276
Filament lamps   L 284
Filaments, long fibers   F 105
  incandescent light, or electric light bulb, development of the invention   I 334
  in electric lighting   L 284
  nylon and other man-made fibers   N 426

Filaria (fi-LAR-ia), small roundworm, from 1 to 4 in. long, found in tropical and subtropical countries. The adult worms live within the human lymph glands, causing a disease (elephantiasis) in which the surrounding area becomes swollen and greatly enlarged.

Filberts, or hazelnuts   N 421
Filchner Ice Shelf, Antarctica   I 12
Files, tools   T 213

Filibuster (from Spanish *flibote,* meaning "pirate"), attempt to delay or prevent legislation, usually by long speeches. A filibuster can be limited by cloture (closure), as when U.S. Senate curbed debate (June, 1964) on a civil rights bill to 1 hour per senator.
  debate in Congress   U 142

Filicineae, division of plant kingdom   P 292
Filigree, design in gold or silver wire   D 69–70
Filing systems
  encyclopedias   E 193–97
  indexes   I 114–15
  libraries   L 186
Filipinos (fil-i-PEEN-os), people of Philippines   P 184
Fillers, in plastics   P 327
Fillies, young female horses   H 232
Filling, or weft, crosswise strands on a loom   T 140
Fillmore, Abigail Powers, wife of Millard Fillmore   F 170; picture   F 171
Fillmore, Millard, 13th president of United States   F 123–25
  as Vice-president, picture   V 326

Fillmore, Parker Hoysted (1878–1944), American author of children's books, b. Cincinnati, Ohio. He wrote stories based on his teaching experience in the Philippine Islands. His stories about children include *The Rosie World* and *The Young Idea.* He is also the author of *Czechoslovak Fairy Tales* and of *The Wizard of the North,* retold stories from the Finnish epic *Kalevala.*

Films, in photography   P 204
  designed for different types of pictures   P 214
  film positives used in offset printing, picture   P 466
  moviemaking at home   P 220
  television, recording for   T 70a
  X rays, how film is affected by, diagram   X 341
Filters
  air conditioning, filter in   A 103
  filtration, for purification of water supply   W 68
Filters, in photography
  absorption of light waves   L 268
  moviemaking at home   P 220

Filtration, for water purification and storage **W** 67
Finance (fin-ANCE)
   banks and banking **B** 44d–51
   budgets, family **B** 425–26
   installment-buying interest rates **I** 288–89
   interest **P** 149–50
   stocks and bonds **S** 427–33
   taxation **T** 26–27
Financial statements see Bookkeeping and accounting

Finch, Robert Hutchison (1925–), American politician, b. Tempe, Ariz. He served as lieutenant governor of California (1967); President Nixon's secretary of health, education, and welfare (1969–70); and presidential counselor (1970–72).

Finches, birds
   evolution or adaptive radiation in birds **B** 209; pictures **E** 345
   purple finch, state bird of New Hampshire **N** 149
Findlay, Jane Irwin, acting first lady in Harrison's administration **F** 169; picture **F** 168

Fine arts, those arts that are valued for their aesthetic quality (music, dancing, painting, literature, sculpture) rather than for any practical purpose. Architecture, usually regarded as a fine art, would be an exception, as it includes practical aspects of design.
   art **A** 437–438g

Fines, type of law enforcement **L** 88–89
Fin-footed mammals, or pinnipeds **W** 5–7

Fingal, semi-mythical hero of poems by James Macpherson (1736–96), who claimed they were translations of Gaelic poems by 3rd-century poet Ossian, Fingal's son. The authenticity of the poems was challenged, and the "translations" were discovered to be traditional legends edited by Macpherson.

Fingal's Cave, Scottish Hebrides **C** 156

Finger, Charles Joseph (1869–1941), American writer of children's books, b. Sussex, England. His books include *Tales from Silver Lands,* which won Newbery medal (1925), and *Courageous Companions.*

Finger Lakes, west central New York **L** 28; **N** 213, 215
Fingerlings, little fish up to one year of age
   salmon led around dams **F** 224
Finger nails see Nails
Finger painting **F** 126–28
   in nursery school, picture **K** 243

Finger play, use of finger movements to dramatize or interpret poems for children.

Fingerprinting **F** 129
   aliens **A** 166
   FBI Identification Division **F** 77
Finger puppets **P** 535
Fingers, of the hand **F** 79
   counting device of early man, picture **C** 451
Finger spelling, of the deaf **D** 52
Finger-style guitar **G** 409
Finishing, of wood
   furniture-making **F** 504
Finite sets, in mathematics **S** 126
Fink, Mike, American folk hero **F** 311
Finland **F** 130–35
   favorite foods **F** 341

   flag **F** 239
   Lapps **L** 44; picture **L** 45
   national anthem **N** 21
   sauna baths **B** 91
   Scandinavia **S** 49
Finland, Gulf of, an arm of the Baltic Sea **O** 45
Finlandia, symphonic poem by Sibelius **S** 172
Finlay, Carlos J., Cuban physician **S** 376
Finley, John, American trail guide and trader **O** 255
Finley, Martha F. see Farquharson, Martha
Finnish music
   Sibelius, Jean **S** 172
Finn Mac Cool, legendary Irish hero **I** 392
Fins, of fishes **F** 184
   eels **E** 85
   fin whales **W** 149
   locomotion in water **A** 290; pictures **A** 289
   sharks, skates, and rays **S** 140

Finsen, Niels Ryberg (1860–1904), Danish physician, b. Thorshavn, Faroe Is. He was interested in the influence of light on living organisms and established the first light institute (1895) in Copenhagen. He won the Nobel prize in medicine and physiology (1903) for his work on the treatment of diseases with concentrated light rays.

Fin whales, or rorquals **W** 149; picture **W** 148
Fioravanti (fi-o-ra-FON-ti), **Rodolpho,** Italian architect **U** 52
Fiordland National Park, New Zealand, picture **N** 237
Fiords, long, narrow bays **G** 96
   Alaska **A** 132; picture **A** 133
   Canada, Admiralty Inlet, Arctic Archipelago **Y** 361
   Canada, off Inside Passage **C** 51
   Chile, southern coastline **S** 276
   Greenland, Umanak Fjord, picture **G** 367
   Norway **N** 341
   Norway, Geiranger Fjord, picture **E** 306
Fir, tree
   Douglas fir, state tree of Oregon **O** 193
   leaves, needlelike, pictures **L** 119
   uses of the wood and its grain, picture **W** 223
Fire **F** 136
   arson **F** 153–54
   camping, how to build a campfire **C** 43–44
   combustion, or burning, kinds of **F** 137
   energy, source of **E** 202
   explosives **E** 388–94
   fire and early man **F** 138–45; **P** 444
   fireproof buildings **B** 438
   first man-made fires **F** 140
   fuels **F** 486–90
   great fires see Fires
   Greek fire **B** 491; **E** 389
   heating methods **H** 97–99
   magnesium as burning element **M** 22–23
   matches and ways of making fire **M** 151–53
   prevention rules **F** 154–55
   Prometheus, Greek god who gave fire to man **G** 357–58
   sacred fire **F** 144
   spontaneous combustion **F** 137
   Vulcan or Hephaestus, god of fire **G** 358
   ways to put out a fire **F** 136–37
   what to do if fire breaks out **F** 149
   See also Combustion; Fires; Fuels; Heat
Fire alarms **F** 150
Fire ants **A** 329, 331; pictures **A** 323, 329
Firearms see Guns
Fireballs
   lightning mistaken for flying saucers **F** 286
   meteors **C** 420

Fire blight, plant disease **P** 112
Fireboats **F** 151
Firebrick **B** 390
Firebug, criminal who commits arson **F** 153–54
Fire clay **C** 174
Firecrackers **E** 388–89

Firedamp, an explosive mixture of methane gas and air that occurs naturally in coal mines and is a constant danger to miners because it may form unnoticed.

Fire drill, device for making fires **F** 140
Fire drills and escape plans **F** 149–50
  safety at school **S** 5

Fire-eaters, Northern designation for Southern extremists who wanted to secede from the Union before the American Civil War (comparing them to fire-eating jugglers). "Fire-eaters" now refers to quarrelsome people.

Fire engines, pictures **F** 147
Fire extinguishers **F** 136, 149
Fire fighting and prevention **F** 146–55
  fire-retardant paints **P** 34
  forests, picture **C** 484
  safety measures **S** 4
  Smokey the Bear, picture **A** 34
Fireflies
  bioluminescence **B** 197
  "Firefly," poem by Elizabeth Madox Roberts **P** 351
  light signals **A** 278
  natural lighting **L** 288
Fire inspectors **F** 153
Fire insurance see Insurance, fire
Fire Island National Seashore, New York **N** 220
Firemen, of railroad locomotives **R** 86
Fire on the mountain, circle game **G** 13
Fireplaces **H** 97
  log cabins **P** 253; picture **P** 255
Fireproofing
  building construction **B** 438
  fire-retardant paints **P** 34
Fires
  Chicago Fire, 1871 **C** 228
  London, great fire of, 1666 **L** 334–35
  Moscow destroyed, 1812, to defeat Napoleon **M** 467
  Rome, great fire of A.D. 64 **R** 304
  San Francisco earthquake and fire, 1906 **S** 31
Fireside chats, Roosevelt's radio talks to the public, picture **R** 322

Firestone, Harvey Samuel (1868–1938), American industrialist, b. Columbiana County, Ohio. He organized the Firestone Tire and Rubber Co. (1900) and was its president (1903–32) and chairman of the board (1932–38). Firestone played an important role in investigating and developing rubber growing in Liberia and was the author of *Rubber, Its History and Development.*

Fire-tube boilers **S** 421

Fire walking, ancient ordeal or ceremony of walking barefoot through flames or over embers or hot stones in order to exhibit supernatural power. It was sometimes considered a test of truth, chastity, or holiness. It dates back to about 1200 B.C. in India, where it is still practiced. It is not known how performers escape injury. In recent times fire walking has been reported in New Zealand, Japan, China, Spain, and Bulgaria.

Fireworks **F** 156
  display, picture **E** 199

Independence Day displays **I** 112
  speeds of explosion **E** 388–89
Firing, of clay
  sculpture **S** 91
Firn, packed snow **I** 6, 7
First aid **F** 157–63
  antiseptics **D** 222
  camping, supplies for **C** 46
  disinfectants **D** 222
  medical supplies in the home **M** 202
  occupational health and safety programs **O** 16
  poisons and antidotes **P** 356–57
First Book of Time, The, by Jeanne Bendick **B** 329–34
First in war, first in peace, and first in the hearts of his countrymen, spoken of George Washington **W** 36
First ladies **F** 164–180
  White House **W** 162–65
First Noel, The, carol **C** 122
  folk music **F** 325
First Republic, France **F** 416
Firsts, historical, arranged by date of month *see* articles on individual months
First State, nickname for Delaware **D** 86, 87
Fiscal authority, for municipal governments **M** 504
Fiscal policy, of a government **I** 253

Fischer, (FISH-er), **Bobby** (Robert James Fischer) (1943–), American chess champion, b. Chicago, Ill. He was the youngest winner of the national junior chess championship (1956), and international grandmaster of chess in 1958. He has won the U. S. championship several times and in 1972 won the world championship.
  chess, a war game **C** 221

Fischer, Emil (1852–1919), German chemist, b. Euskirchen. He did pioneer research on the structures of sugar molecules; by studying the way a sugar crystal bent a beam of light passed through it, he was able to plot the position of each atom in a molecule of that crystal. He also solved the mystery of why some sugar crystals bend light to the right and others to the left. He also synthesized purines, a group of substances that are vital to the chemistry of living cells. Later he studied the structures of proteins and in 1907 became the first to create a protein molecule in the laboratory. For his studies of sugars and purines, he received the 1902 Nobel prize in chemistry.

Fish *see* Fishes
Fish, constellation *see* Pisces
Fish, electric *see* Electric fishes

Fish, Hamilton (1808–1893), American statesman, b. New York, N.Y. He served as governor of New York (1849–50) and as secretary of state (1869–77). He was "the voice of moderation" in President Grant's administrations and was responsible for the Treaty of Washington (1871), which provided arbitration with Great Britain for settlement of the *Alabama* Claims.

Fish, tropical *see* Tropical fishes

Fish and Wildlife Service, United States, organization created (1956) under Department of Interior to preserve and study fish and wildlife. It replenishes fish hatcheries and owns approximately 321 national wildlife refuges. The service makes studies to improve methods of wildlife, fish, and shellfish culture and investigates pollution and disease among fish and other wildlife.
  birdbanding **B** 229

Fish as food *see* Seafood

Fisher, Dorothy Canfield (1879–1958), American author, b. Lawrence, Kans. She wrote primarily about New England life. Her novels include *Understood Betsy,* about a city child on a Vermont farm, and *Gunhild,* about a Norwegian girl born in Kansas.

Fisher, Sir Ronald Aylmer (1890–1962), English mathematician and geneticist, b. East Finchley. He worked out the theory and formulas by which statistics could be used in biology. He showed that Darwin's theory of evolution does not contradict Mendel's laws of heredity.

Fisk Jubilee Singers, group of Fisk University students who toured the United States and Europe during the 1870's to acquaint audiences with the Negro spiritual and raise money for Fisk.
  Negro spirituals **N** 107

Fisk University Choir **T** 83
Fission, a division into parts
  bacteria, reproduction of **B** 10
Fission, nuclear *see* Nuclear fission
Fissure eruptions, of volcanoes **V** 383

Fitch, John (1743–1798), American inventor, b. Windsor, Conn. He pioneered in the development of the steamboat, operating his first steamboat on Delaware River in 1787. He carried passengers from Philadelphia, Pa., to Burlington, N.J., in a steam-powered paddlewheel boat in 1788, two decades before the launching of Robert Fulton's *Clermont.* The inventions were financial failures.
  transportation, history of **T** 262

Fitz, meaning in names **N** 5
FitzGerald, Edward, English poet **E** 263

Fitzgerald, Ella (1918–), American singer, Negro, b. Newport News, Va. She is a versatile performer of jazz, calypso, and popular ballads and appears in nightclubs and on TV. Known as the First Lady of Song, she became famous with her recording of "A-Tisket, A-Tasket" (1938).

Fitzgerald, F. Scott, American writer **A** 211
  novel in the 20th century **N** 349
Fitzpatrick, Thomas, American trail guide **F** 523–24;
  O 264

Fitzsimmons, Robert Prometheus (called Fighting Bob and The Village Blacksmith) (1862–1917), American prizefighter, b. Helston, Cornwall, England. He won the world's middleweight championship (1891) from "nonpareil" Jack Dempsey (not the Jack Dempsey of a later time) and the world's heavyweight championship from James J. Corbett (1897). Fitzsimmons lost the heavyweight title to James J. Jeffries in 1899.

Fitzsimmons, Thomas (1741–1811), American congressman and financier, b. Ireland. He helped establish Bank of North America (1781), the first bank in the United States. He was elected to the new Congress (1782) established by Articles of Confederation, and was a member of Constitutional Convention (1787). A strong nationalist, he supported program of Federalist Party.

Five Civilized Tribes, phrase used to describe the Choctaw, Creek, Chickasaw, Cherokee, and Seminole Indians, who had their own government and written laws. They were removed from their original homes in the southeastern United States to Indian Territory in Oklahoma (1830–40) and became citizens when Oklahoma was admitted as a state (1907).
    Oklahoma, history of **O** 80, 84, 95

Five Nations (later Six Nations), confederacy of Iroquois Indian tribes **C** 69–70
Fivepins, a bowling game **B** 349
Five-Year plans
    Union of Soviet Socialist Republics **U** 51
Fixatives, substances that stabilize perfumes **P** 154
Fixing, in photography **P** 211

Fizeau (fi-ZO), **Armand Hippolyte Louis** (1819–1896), French physicist, b. Paris. He is noted for research in light and optics. Fizeau was the first to measure the speed of light fairly accurately. He explained the Doppler effect. This is a change in frequency of light and sound waves when a source of light or sound moves toward or away from a receiver or when a receiver moves toward or away from a source.
    speed of light **L** 266

Fjords see Fiords

Flack, Marjorie (1897–1958), American author and illustrator of children's books, b. Greenport, N.Y. She wrote animal stories, including *Angus and the Ducks, Walter, the Lazy Mouse, The Restless Robin,* and *The Story About Ping,* about a small duck on Yangtze River. She was wife of poet William Rose Benét.

Flag Day, June 14 **J** 152
    patriotic holidays **H** 152
Flagella (fla-GELL-a), whiplike appendages of many organisms **S** 392; picture **B** 10

Flagellants (from Latin *flagellum,* meaning "a scourge"), religious enthusiasts who believe that sins of world can be forgiven only by self-inflicted scourging and flogging. They are heirs to the ancient practice of extreme asceticism, dating from early 13th-century Italy. The practice eventually spread across Europe during plague of black death, believed by some to be a punishment inflicted by God. Flagellants still exist in some isolated locations.

Flagellates (FLAJ-el-lates), micro-organisms **M** 279
    single-celled organisms **L** 213; picture **L** 212

Flagg, James Montgomery (1877–1960), American commercial artist and author, b. Pelham Manor, N.Y. Illustrator for various magazines and travel books, he wrote screenplays and satirical comedies. During World Wars I and II he did patriotic posters. His caricatures appear in collected drawings published as a book, *The Well-Knowns as Seen by James Montgomery Flagg.*

Flagler, Henry, American businessman **F** 271–72
    Miami **M** 254
Flag of truce **F** 246
Flags **F** 225–48
    banners with heraldic devices **H** 118
    how to display the American flag **F** 231–34
    Olympic Games symbol **O** 108; picture **O** 109

    parts of a flag, diagram **F** 234
    pirate **P** 263
    political campaign flag, picture **H** 50
    Ross, Betsy, maker of first American flag **R** 335
    state flags see state articles
    storm warnings **B** 262

Flagstad (FLOG-sta), **Kirsten Marie** (1895–1963), Norwegian soprano, b. Hamar. She made her debut in New York City as Sieglinde in Wagner's *Die Walküre* (1935). A member of Metropolitan Opera Company before and after World War II, she also specialized in lieder singing. Her interpretations of Wagnerian roles were particularly notable. Picture **O** 136.

Flagstaff, Arizona **A** 412
Flaherty, Robert, American motion picture producer **M** 475
Flake tools, prehistoric man **P** 444
Flame cultivators **F** 59
Flamenco (fla-MEN-co), dance of Spain **D** 29–30
    Manuela Vargas, picture **S** 373
Flamingos, birds **B** 232; picture **B** 230
Flaminian (fla-MIN-ian) **Way,** Roman road **E** 208
Flaminius, Gaius, Roman official **E** 208
Flanagan, Edward Joseph, Irish-born American Roman Catholic monsignor, founder of Boys Town **N** 82
Flanders, northern region of Belgium and France **B** 126
    Flemish art **D** 349
    Flemish and Dutch music **D** 363–65
Flange, a projecting rim
    role in early history of railroads **R** 87
    wheels **W** 158
Flares, fireworks **F** 156
Flares, solar see Solar flares
Flashbulbs, in photography **P** 217
    cameras **P** 203
Flashlights **B** 97, 99; pictures **B** 98, **L** 289
Flash point of a fuel **F** 136
Flasks, containers
    antique portrait flasks, picture **A** 319
Flatboats
    pioneer life **P** 260
Flatcars, of railroads **R** 82–83
Flatfish
    habitat, feeding habits, uses **F** 213
Flatirons, for pressing clothes **E** 118
Flat paints **P** 32
Flat-plate collectors, of solar energy **S** 237–38
Flats, scenery for plays **P** 339; pictures **P** 337, 338
Flatware, knives, forks, and spoons **K** 285–88
Flatworms **W** 312
Flaubert (flo-BAIR), **Gustave,** French writer **S** 165
    French literature, place in **F** 441
Flavorings
    for ice cream **I** 33
Flax
    drying near Courtrai, Belgium, picture **B** 128
    linseed oil obtained from **O** 79
    rope **R** 333
Flea beetles
    vectors of plant diseases **V** 284
Fleas, insects **I** 274
    household pests **H** 260; picture **H** 263
    spread plague disease of rats to man **D** 221
Fledermaus (FLAY-der-maus), **Die,** (Bat, The), operetta by Johann Strauss, Jr. **O** 156, 157–58; **S** 437
Fleece, or wool coat of sheep **W** 234–35
Fleet Marine Forces, United States Marine Corps **U** 176, 179
Fleet Street, London **L** 334

Fleischmann (FLY-shmann) **Foundation of Nevada,** foundation interested mainly in educational buildings and equipment, scholarships, museums, and research in medical and biological sciences. Established in 1952 by Max C. Fleischmann, it has headquarters in Reno.

Flémalle (flai-MOLLE), **Master of,** Flemish painter **D** 351
  Nativity, painting **D** 353
Fleming, Sir Alexander, Scottish bacteriologist **F** 249
  antibiotic research **A** 311, 312; picture **A** 315
  conquest of disease by penicillin **D** 217
  contributions to medicine **M** 208a

Fleming, Ian Lancaster (1908–1964), British author, b. London. Following careers as a journalist in Moscow (1929–33), a banker and stockbroker in London (1933–39), an officer in British Naval Intelligence during World War II, and foreign manager of the London *Sunday Times* until 1959, he began (1953) writing the spy thrillers that made him famous. Built around the fictitious character of James Bond, Agent 007 of Her Majesty's Secret Service, they include *From Russia, With Love* and *Goldfinger.* His *Chitty Chitty Bang Bang* (1965) relates the adventures of the Potts family and their flying, floating car.
  James Bond films **M** 488a

Fleming, Sir John Ambrose (1849–1945), English electrical engineer, b. Lancaster. Noted for his work on the practical applications of electricity, he aided in development of telephone, wireless telegraph, and electric lamp.
  early history of radio **R** 52

Fleming, Sir Sandford, Canadian engineer **O** 125
Flemings, Flemish-speaking people of Belgium **B** 126
Flemish, Germanic language of northern Belgium and France **B** 126
Flemish art **D** 349–62
  baroque period **B** 60–61
  Bosch, Hieronymus **P** 23
  Brueghel, Pieter **B** 414–15
  furniture design **F** 506
  lace **L** 19
  painting in Flanders **P** 23, 24
  Renaissance paintings **R** 171; picture **A** 438a
  Rubens, Peter Paul **R** 348
  Spanish art, influence on **S** 361
  Van Dyck, Anthony **V** 277
  See also Dutch art
Flemish music *see* Dutch and Flemish music

Fletcher, John (1579–1625), English dramatist, b. Sussex. He collaborated with dramatist Francis Beaumont. Noted for his comedies and dialogue in blank verse, he is believed to have written part of *The Two Noble Kinsmen* and *Henry VIII* (both attributed to Shakespeare). He also wrote pastoral play *The Faithful Shepherdess.*
  drama, history of **D** 296

Fletching, feathers attached to an arrow **A** 367

Fleur-de-lis (fler-de-LE) ("flower of lily"), emblem of France. A heraldic charge of unknown origin, it is believed to have been used by Charlemagne and was represented (from 1179) in coat of arms of kings of France. The emblem was appropriated (1340) by Edward III of England when he claimed French throne and was used by his successors (until 1801).
  "lily" pattern on furniture **F** 505; picture **F** 506

Flexner, Abraham (1866–1959), American educational reformer, administrator, and author, b. Louisville, Ky. He criticized educational systems in *The American College*

and *Medical Education in the United States and Canada.* He founded and directed Institute for Advanced Study at Princeton, N.J. (1930–39).

Flexner, Simon (1863–1946), American physician, bacteriologist, and pathologist, b. Louisville, Ky. He contributed research on meningitis and infantile paralysis. He was professor at Johns Hopkins University; visiting and Eastman professor at Oxford University; first director of laboratories of Rockefellar Institute for Medical Research (1903–35); and chairman of Research Fellowship Board National Research Council (1919–37).

Flickers, birds of the woodpecker family. Brownish in color, the flicker has a red (or black) "moustache" on either side of its bill. Unlike most woodpeckers, the flicker spends much of its time on the ground, searching for ants and other insects. Flickers range from Alaska through Canada to the Gulf states. Pictures **B** 208, 242.
  state bird of Alabama **A** 113

Flickers, name for early movies **M** 472
Flickertail State, nickname for North Dakota **N** 323
Fliegende Holländer (FLEEG-en-der HOLL-en-der), **Der,**
  opera by Richard Wagner **O** 144
Flies, household pests **H** 260
  acrobats of the insect world **A** 296
  mouth parts, diagram **I** 270
  pupa, pictures **I** 265
Flies, in theaters where scenery can be stored **T** 156
Flies, lures for fishing **F** 211; pictures **F** 207
Flight
  aerodynamics **A** 36–41
  airplane models **A** 104, 105
  animals that fly **A** 265–66
  animals: locomotion **A** 294–96
  birds **B** 199, 204–05
  giant birds unable to fly **G** 204
  gliders **G** 238
  How does a helicopter fly? **H** 105
  why a kite flies **K** 271
  Why can't people use artificial wings and fly like birds? **A** 558
Flight into Egypt, of the Holy Family **M** 113
Flight into Egypt, painting by Giotto de Bondone **I** 461

Flinders bar, rod of unmagnetized iron on a ship to keep its compass accurate. The bar is magnetized by earth's magnetic field, as are other iron parts of the ship. Bar is placed so that its magnetism cancels out magnetism of rest of ship, leaving compass unaffected.

Flin Flon, Manitoba **M** 81
Flint, form of quartz **G** 388; **Q** 6
  fire making **F** 140
  implements studied by archeologists **A** 360; picture **A** 361
Flint, Michigan **M** 270
Flint corn **C** 506
Flintlock muskets, early guns **G** 416; picture **G** 414
Flint tools, prehistoric man **P** 444
Flip cards, for illustrating optical illusions **O** 164
Flippers, or swim fins, for skin diving **S** 189
Flittermice, bats, picture **B** 93
Float fishing **M** 366; picture **M** 368
Floating **F** 250–53
  bar soaps that float **D** 148
  in swimming **S** 491–92
Floating bridges **B** 399–400
Floating gardens
  Aztecs built farm lands **I** 195, 197
  Lake Xochimilco **L** 34; **M** 253; picture **L** 30

Floating mountains E 13
Flocculi, gases in the sun's chromosphere S 461
Flodden Field, battle of, 1513 S 88
Flonzaley (flon-ZAY-ley) **Quartet,** chamber music ensemble C 186
Flood eruptions, of volcanoes V 383
Floodlights, picture L 289
Floods and flood control F 254–57
  Calcutta, picture W 185
  China C 262
  dams D 18, 19; picture C 485
  erosion caused by E 282
  Florence, Italy I 450
  hurricane damage H 295
  irrigation, natural and man-made I 408
  Johnstown, Pennsylvania P 139
  Mississippi waterways experiment stations M 350, 359–60
  Missouri River M 383
  Nile River N 260–61
  rivers, work of R 239
  See also Dams

Flood tide, an incoming, or rising, tide. It is the opposite of ebb tide.

Floor coverings
  interior decorating I 299
  rugs and carpets R 350–54
  vinyl and other floor coverings V 340–41

Flora and fauna, term that refers in general to plant (flora) and animal (fauna) life of a particular geographical area or period of time in earth's history.

Florence, Italy I 450
  birthplace of Dante D 38
  bookmaking, art of B 321–22
  Botticelli, Renaissance painter B 340b
  Florentine language becomes standard Italian I 474
  Foundling Hospital A 438e–438f; picture R 165
  Giotto di Bondone G 211
  Italian art and architecture I 464–65, 467, 468–69
  May Festival M 551
  Medici family B 45; I 477
  Michelangelo M 255–56
  opera's beginning O 130–31
  Palazzo Vecchio, picture A 380
  political parties, Guelfs and Ghibellines P 378
  Ponte Vecchio, picture B 399
  Renaissance, growth of city-states R 157
  Renaissance, in art and architecture R 163–66
  Renaissance painting P 20–21
  Uffizi Gallery U 2–3
Florence Cathedral (Santa Maria del Fiore) I 450; picture I 462
Florence, South Carolina S 308
Florentine Camerata, composers of baroque music B 63
Flores (FLO-rais) **Juan José,** Ecuadorian general, first president of Ecuador E 58

Flores (FLO-res) **Sea,** part of the Pacific Ocean encircled by the Indonesian islands. It contains many small islands. Its northern arm, the Gulf of Bone, forms a deep inlet on southern Celebes coast.

Florey (FLO-rey), **Howard,** English scientist A 312; picture A 315
Floribunda (flo-ri-BUN-da) **roses,** flowers, picture G 27
Floriculture see Gardens and gardening
Florida F 258–73
  boundary settlements T 105, 108

Gulf Stream, map-diagram O 33
  lemon growing L 137
  Miami M 254
  orange industry O 177
  places of interest in Negro history N 94
  Ponce de León P 391
  Vehicle Assembly Building, picture W 220
Florida, University of F 267
Florida Current G 411
Florida Key deer H 219; picture H 215
Florida Keys F 261; picture F 260
  Bahia Hona Bridge, picture I 424
Florida Plateau F 260
Florio (FLO-ri-o), **John,** English author E 292
Flotation process, in ore milling M 227–28, 318

Flotow (FLO-to), **Friedrich von** (1812–1883), German opera composer, b. Teutendorf, Mecklenburg-Schwerin. Born into the nobility and educated as a diplomat, he wrote operas in French, Italian, and German. His German operas include *Alessandro Stradella* and *Martha,* his most popular work.
  Martha, opera O 148

Flotsam, jetsam, and lagan, or ligan, classification of ship's goods at sea. Flotsam (from French *flotter,* "to float") refers to goods washed overboard and floating on sea. Jetsam (from French *jeter,* "to throw") is cargo thrown overboard to lighten ship in distress. Lagan (perhaps cognate of "lie") refers to goods attached to buoy for identification, which, if found, must be returned to owner according to law of salvage.

Flounder, fish F 194; pictures F 183, 194
  adaptations with camouflage E 347; L 219
  habitats, feeding habits, uses F 213
Flour and flour milling F 274–75
  flour from sardines M 460
  grain and grain products G 282
  oat flour O 4
  rye compared to wheat R 364
  wheat W 156
  See also Baking and bakery products; Bread
Flour corn C 506
Flower animals, polyps J 74
Flower arrangement J 49–53
Flower gardens G 26
Flowering dogwood
  Missouri's state tree M 367
  state flower of Virginia V 344
Flowering plants P 290
Flower in the Crannied Wall, poem by Tennyson T 101
Flowerless plants A 155
Flowers F 276–80
  adaptations to insects L 221
  begonia festival in Belgium, picture B 128
  fig F 117
  flowers we eat P 307
  functions for plants P 295–96
  gardens and gardening G 26–52
  Japanese and Western arranging J 49–53
  months see month articles
  perfumes P 154–55
  poisonous garden flowers P 323
  province see province articles
  reproductive parts, diagram R 179
  state flowers U 90–93; for pictures see state articles
  trees T 283–84
  wild flowers W 168–71
  See also Seeds; names of flowers
Flox, fluoridizer-oxidizer, for rocket fuels R 258

Floyd, William (1734–1821), American politician, b. Brookhaven, N.Y. He was a signer of the Declaration of Independence and served in the Continental Congress (1774–77, 1778–83) and at the first session of the Congress of the United States (1789–91).

Flu see Influenza
Fluids, substances without fixed shape L 310
   density F 250–51
   See also Liquids
Fluke, fish
   habitats, feeding habits, uses F 213
Flukes, fins of dolphins D 271–72
Flukes, worms W 312

Fluorescence (flur-ES-cence), giving off of light by some substances when subjected to ultraviolet rays or certain other forms of radiation. In a fluorescent electric light a fluorescent material lines the inside of a glass tube containing mercury vapor. Electric current causes the vapor to give off ultraviolet rays. The lining, in turn, gives off light as long as the radiation continues.

Fluorescence microscopes M 283
Fluorescent brightening dyes D 371
Fluorescent light L 270
   lamps L 286; diagram L 287
Fluorescent paints P 34
Fluoridation (flur-i-DAY-tion) F 283–84
   community helps in prevention of disease D 220
   teeth, care of T 49
Fluoride, mineral N 417
Fluorine, element E 154, 161
   iodine and other halogens I 349
Fluorocarbons, fluorine compounds I 349

Fluoroscope, instrument used by doctors to observe the interior of the body in action. The patient is placed between an X-ray machine and a chemical-coated screen. X rays passing through his body cause the chemicals on the screen to glow. Bones and organs, blocking the passage of X rays, appear on the screen as shadows. The fluoroscope also has industrial uses, such as the detection of flaws in metals. Picture D 211.
   examining the heart H 86b
   use in physical examinations M 208h

Fluorspar, fluorite, mineral N 143

Flushing Remonstrance (1657), early document of American democracy written by Tobias Feake, sheriff of Flushing, N.Y., denouncing persecution of English Quakers. It was a statement of principles of freedom of conscience, for which Feake was dismissed from office and fined by Peter Stuyvesant.

Flute, musical instrument M 547
   ancient instrument A 245, 246
   orchestra seating plan O 186
Fluting, ornamental design F 505; picture F 506
Fluxes, substances used to help other substances melt
   together I 349
   glass G 226
   soldering and brazing S 249–50
   steelmaking I 404
   welding W 119
Fly see Flies
Fly agaric, poisonous mushroom
   affects nervous system P 322

Fly ash, small solid particles of burned and unburned matter driven into the air from furnaces and incinerators. These and other particles must be removed by screens or water spray or settled out by gravity in order to prevent air pollution. Some types of fly ash are collected and used in manufacture of phonograph records, cement, and bricks.

Flycasting, fishing F 209; picture F 208
Flycatchers, birds of the woods and fields B 220
   eastern phoebe, picture B 235
   scissortailed flycatcher, picture B 240
Flyer, Wright brothers' airplane A 568; picture A 569
Flying see Flight
Flying buttress, in architecture A 378; G 265; pictures
   A 379, G 266
   Middle Ages, architectural skills of Gothic art M 297
Flying chair, early lifting device E 172

Flying Dutchman, legendary full-rigged phantom ship seen by sailors rounding Cape of Good Hope in a storm. The ship is said to be doomed to sail forever because of pact with devil or by captain's rash oath or cruelty. Captain and crew appear like dead men, not answering when hailed. Believed to be a bad omen, it is the subject of Richard Wagner's opera *Der Fliegende Holländer.*
   Flying Dutchman, The, opera by Wagner O 144

Flying Farmers, International (IFF) association of farm families in the United States and Canada in which at least one member holds a pilot's license. Its purpose is to promote the use of the airplane in agriculture. It encourages soil and water conservation through state air tours and sponsors goodwill tours in North America and Mexico. Founded in 1944, with headquarters in Wichita, Kansas, it publishes the *International Flying Farmer.*

Flying fishes, any of several fishes able to glide over surface of water for short periods of time. They are usually found in open oceans in tropical areas.
   large pectoral fins F 189

Flying foxes, bats B 93
Flying lemurs, gliding mammals B 96; M 64; picture
   M 69
Flying saucers F 285–87
Flying shuttle I 234
Flying squirrels M 64
   rodents R 276; picture R 277

Flying Tigers, popular name for the American Volunteer Group (AVG), a corps of volunteer pilots under the command of General Claire Chennault, which aided the Nationalist Chinese against the Japanese early in World War II (1941–42). In 1942, after the United States' entry into the war, the Flying Tigers were incorporated into the U.S. 14th Air Force.

Flypaper plants P 317
Flyways, bird migration routes B 217
Flyweight, in boxing B 352

Flywheel, heavy-rimmed wheel attached to drive shaft of an engine or other machine. It maintains constant speed of machine to which it is fixed by storing energy, which is used at short intervals when extra energy is needed. It absorbs bursts of excess energy from engine.
   special types of wheels W 158

FM see Frequency modulation
Foals, young horses H 243
Foam, insulation I 291
Foam, of detergents D 149
   problem with water W 59; picture C 483

Foam rubber R 345
FOBS see Fractional Orbiting Bombing System
Focal distance, of a lens L 143–44
    refraction of light L 263–64
Foch, Ferdinand, French general W 280
Focus
    principal focus of a lens L 143–44
Foehn (FERN), warm, dry wind G 96
    Austrian Alps A 523
    causes avalanches in the Alps S 500
    See also Chinook
Fog, cloud formation at ground level F 288–89
    air pollution from smog A 110
    London's "pea-soup" fogs cleared L 340
    Los Angeles, California L 344–47
    seeding with dry ice, pictures W 94
    sound guideposts from lighthouses L 277
Fog, poem by Carl Sandburg S 29
Fogazzaro, Antonio, Italian novelist I 480
Fogg Art Museum, Cambridge, Massachusetts M 144
Fog signals see Signals and signaling

Foil, metal, a very thin sheet metal (between 0.00059
and 0.00024 in. in thickness), used as insulation,
moistureproof covering, and decorative wrapping. It is
usually made of lead, copper, aluminum, tin, or gold.

Foils, weapons in fencing F 84–85
Fokine (fo-KENE), Michel, Russian-born American dancer
    and choreographer B 26; D 26
Folacin, or Folic Acid, a B-complex vitamin V 370d
Fold mountains M 496

Folger (FOLE-ger), Henry Clay (1857–1930), American
lawyer and bibliophile, b. New York, N.Y. He was
president (1911–23) of Standard Oil Co. of New York.
He endowed Folger Library in Washington, D.C., and
donated his library to it, including his collection of
Shakespearean quartos and folios. Folger Shakespeare
Memorial, which he founded (1930), is largest and most
complete Shakespearean collection in world.

Foliage patterns, in furniture design F 505; picture
    F 506
Foliar (FO-li-ar), or leaf, feeding, of plants
    fertilizing fruit trees F 482
    pineapple leaves absorb fertilizer P 250
Folk art F 290–96
    arts and crafts, folklore of demonstrated tradition
        F 304, 309
    Canada C 64
    museums M 513
    wood carving W 228
Folk dancing F 297–301
    basic national dance forms D 28
    dance music D 35
    Greek dancers, picture G 336
    Latin-American dancing L 68–69
    play party songs F 323–24
Folk high schools, Denmark D 107, 109
Folklore F 302–17
    African A 76a
    American see Folklore, American
    Arabian Nights, The A 345–47
    books of folklore for children, list C 248a–248b
    Christmas customs around the world C 289–95
    distinguished from fables F 3
    distinguished from fairy tales F 19
    early form of fiction F 109
    Faust folktales and legends F 72–73
    folktales defined F 320
    Grimm, Jacob and Wilhelm G 376–77

    Japanese legend of the Sun Goddess J 42
    jokes and riddles J 132
    nursery rhymes N 402–08
    proverbs P 487
    literature of storytelling S 434
    mythology M 557–64
    superstition S 473–75
    See also Mythology
Folklore, American F 309–17
    Arkansas Traveler A 427
    first myth-heroes in American literature A 199–200
    James, Jesse J 19
Folk music F 318–28
    African A 77–79
    ballads B 22–23
    Bartók's use of Hungarian folk music B 68
    Canada C 63
    guitar and guitar music G 409–10
    Hungarian H 283–84
    hymns H 309
    instruments see Folk music instruments
    Latin-American L 74
    recorder, music for R 122
    Spain S 372
Folk music instruments F 329–30
    guitar G 409–10
    instruments for folk dancing F 301
Folk proverbs F 304
Folk-rock, a type of rock music R 262d
Folk songs F 303
    American F 310–11
    Negro spirituals N 105–07
    types of song M 538
    See also Folk music
Folk tales see Folklore
Folkways, behavior patterns of social groups L 87
    shown in restorations of American villages F 305
Follicle, of hair H 2
Folsom (FOLE-som) man, primitive human being
    Folsom State Monument, New Mexico, site of archeo-
        logical discovery N 191
    Old Bison Hunters, North America I 163
Fomalhaut (FO-mal-ho), star C 493
Fondant, candy C 98

Fong, Hiram L. (Yau Leong Fong) (1907–), United
States senator, b. Honolulu, Hawaii. Fong has been a
lawyer, a businessman, a member of the Hawaiian
legislature (1940–54) and vice-president of the Territorial
Constitutional Convention (1950). Since 1959, when
Hawaii became a state, he has been Hawaii's senior
senator. He is the first U.S. senator of Chinese descent.

Font, a set of type T 344
Fontaine, Jean de la see La Fontaine, Jean de
Fontainebleau (fon-tain-BLO), School of, France R 171

Fontana (fon-TA-na), Domenico (1543–1607), Italian
architect, b. near Lake Como. He collaborated on St.
Peter's Basilica, helping to complete dome (1590). He
built Lateran Palace and Vatican Library.
    moving an obelisk O 5–6

Fontana (fon-TAN-a) Dam, North Carolina, picture F 257

Fonteyn (font-AYN), Dame Margot (1919–), English
prima ballerina, b. Reigate. She acquired fame as
Aurora in The Sleeping Beauty (1946). Prima ballerina of
Royal Ballet of Great Britain and president of Royal
Academy of Dancing (since 1954), she has performed in
many classical and modern ballets.
    as Odette in Swan Lake, picture B 25

Footnote, notation at bottom of printed page or added to
main text of book (or any printed work) in separate list.
It usually consists of definition of a word or source of
information for material appearing in text.

Foot-pound, a unit of energy or work   **E** 198;   **W** 244
Footprints, identification for babies   **F** 129
Foot-setter, glass craftsman   **G** 232
Forage crops   **F** 60
  dairying   **D** 8
  oats, a stock feed   **O** 4
  pasture grasses   **G** 317
  soybeans   **S** 337
Foraminifera (fo-ram-in-IF-er-a), or **forams,** one-celled water animals
  shells show temperatures in the past   **I** 21–22

Forbes, Esther (1894?–1967), American novelist and historian, b. Westborough, Mass. Considered one of the most knowledgeable authors on the American Revolutionary era, her books have been translated into 10 languages. *Paul Revere and the World He Lived In* won the Pulitzer prize in history (1942). *Johnny Tremain: A Novel for Young and Old,* a Newbery award winner (1944), is a juvenile classic. Miss Forbes received honorary doctorates in law and literature, as well as many other honors. Among her books are *The Running of the Tide* and *Paradise.*
  Johnny Tremain, excerpt   **R** 209–10

Forbes Road, overland trail   **O** 255

Forbidden City, or **Purple City,** walled compound in center of Peking containing imperial palaces of China. It is surrounded by 2-mile moat enclosing immense cobbled courtyards and pillared halls rising from terraces of white marble. It was opened as museum (1924) and is considered masterpiece of Chinese art and architecture.
  Palace Museum in Peking   **M** 511;   **P** 118

Force, in physics   **W** 243–44
  gravitational   **G** 321–22
  hydraulic systems   **H** 302–03
  lines of, electric and magnetic   **E** 129–32, 134;   **M** 25
  magnetism   **M** 24–25
  motion, laws of   **M** 470
  units of measure   **W** 117
Force of mortality, in insurance rates   **A** 81
Ford, Henry, American automobile manufacturer
  F 367;   **T** 264
  mass producer of automobiles   **A** 547–48
  Henry Ford Museum   **D** 151
Ford, John, English dramatist   **D** 296
Ford, Whitey, American baseball player   **B** 80

Ford Foundation, world's wealthiest philanthropic organization (assets over $3,000,000,000). It was endowed (1936) by Henry and Edsel Ford to promote peace, democratic principles, education, and better economic conditions worldwide. Its headquarters are located in New York.
  what foundations do   **F** 392

Ford Motor Company
  assembly line method of manufacture   **M** 85

Ford's Theatre, Washington, D.C., scene of assassination of President Lincoln by John Wilkes Booth (April 14, 1865). The theater was later used by War Department for records and housed the Lincoln Museum. It was restored (1968) for the production of plays.

Fore, courtesy term used by golfers   **G** 260
Forehand, tennis stroke   **T** 90–91
Foreign affairs see International relations

Foreign Agricultural Service, agency within the Department of Agriculture to promote the export of United States agricultural products. Its functions include operating a global reporting and analysis network covering world agricultural production, trade competition, and policy situations that affect American agriculture; implementing the Food for Peace program; and supplying information to United States consumers on imported foreign farm products.

Foreign aid programs   **F** 368
  Truman, Harry S, and the Marshall Plan   **T** 302
  See *also* names of programs, as Alliance for Progress
Foreigners see Aliens
Foreign exchange, of money   **I** 327–28

Foreign legion, military force of foreign volunteers. French Foreign Legion was inaugurated (1831) by King Louis Philippe. Legions have often consisted of adventurers and refugees, leading to reputation of mystery and romance often associated with them. French Foreign Legion is best known, but legions have also served other countries, such as Spain.

Foreign missions see Missions and missionaries
Foreign policy, of nations   **I** 322–23
  powers of U.S. president   **P** 454

Foreign Policy Association, educational organization to promote understanding of and participation in U.S. foreign policy. Founded in 1918, its headquarters is in New York, N.Y. It publishes *Intercom* and *Headline Series,* both periodicals on international affairs.

Foreign population see Immigration and emigration
Foreign relations see International relations
Foreign service   **F** 369–70;   **P** 94
Foreign trade see International trade
Foreign trade zones see Free ports
Foreign Trade Zones Act, 1934   **I** 330;   **P** 522

Foreign Wars of United States, Military Order of, organization for commissioned officers of U.S. armed forces and their direct male descendants. Organization was founded in 1894 and has its headquarters in Lansing, Michigan.

Foreman, of a jury   **J** 160
Foreman, George, American boxer   **B** 353
Forensic oratory, suitable to law courts   **O** 180

Foreshortening, in art, refers to perspective applied to single object giving depth and illusion of reality (for example, a hand is made larger than other parts of picture in order to seem nearer to viewer). It was first used about 500 B.C. by Greek vase painters but was perfected by Renaissance artists.

Forestaff, or cross staff, navigation instrument   **N** 64

Forester, C. S. (Cecil Scott Forester) (1899–1966), English newspaperman and novelist, b. Cairo, Egypt. He wrote biographies of Napoleon, Horatio Nelson, and others, but he is especially known for Horatio Hornblower stories about Royal Navy. His murder novel *Payment Deferred,* when adapted for stage and screen, helped establish Charles Laughton's reputation as an actor.

Foresters, orders of, fraternal and benevolent organizations in Canada, United States, and Great Britain. The original order (founded in 1813), known as the Royal Order of Foresters, was subdivided several times. Members hold annual celebrations and revivals of ancient English archery shows at London's Crystal Palace.

Forest fire, relay race **G** 18
Forest fires **F** 148, 152
  air pollution **A** 109
  destruction of Douglas fir, picture **F** 373
  how to build a safe campfire **C** 43–44
  lookout towers, picture **F** 374
  Smokey the Bear, symbol of forest fire prevention **N** 180
Forest rangers, United States **F** 374
  National Forests **N** 32
Forest reserves see National Forests, United States
Forests and forestry **F** 371–74
  Africa's plants, animals, and products **A** 50–51, 64
  animals of the forest, pictures **A** 267
  Asia's resources **A** 450–51
  Canada **C** 56
  climate, marine west coast, effect of, picture **C** 345
  conservation **C** 484–85; pictures **G** 104, 105
  fires and firefighting **F** 148; 152; picture **C** 484
  flowers, woodland **W** 168, 171
  food consumer levels of life **L** 240
  gallery forests **J** 154; **P** 430
  importance to American colonies **A** 194
  importance to industry **I** 246
  jungles **J** 154–56
  lumber and lumbering **L** 372–77
  Maine, conservation practices in **M** 37
  Mediterranean scrub forest, or maquis **A** 145
  Mississippi a leading tree-farm state **M** 355
  mountain resources **M** 498
  National Forests, United States **N** 31–37
  North America, vegetation and animal life **N** 292
  petrified forests **A** 414; **F** 380
  primitive forest, picture **T** 285
  rain forest **R** 99–100
  South America **S** 280, 292
  state forests see individual state articles
  taiga **T** 10–11
  trees **T** 274–85
  wood and wood products **W** 222–28
  world distribution of vegetation **W** 254
  See also Lumber and lumbering; Trees; Wood; country, province, and state articles
Forest Service, United States **F** 374
  conservation **C** 485
  National Forests **N** 31, 32, 34
Forewords, of books **L** 181
Forge, The, painting by Goya **S** 362
Forgery
  handwriting experts can detect **H** 31

Forget-me-nots, slender plants with tiny five-petaled flowers growing in clusters. Flowers are usually bluish, but may be white, yellow, or pink. The plant grows in shady, damp places. It is native to Europe but is found in many parts of northern Asia and North America. Picture **W** 168.
  state flower of Alaska **A** 129

Forgetting, psychology **P** 493
  in the learning process **L** 105
Forge welding **W** 118
Forging, of metals **M** 229
  bronze and brass **B** 410
  forging dies **D** 166
Forklift trucks, hoisting machines **H** 145
Forks **K** 285–88
  decorative art objects, picture **D** 66
  table settings **T** 2–3

Formaldehyde (for-MAL-de-hyde), strong-smelling chemical highly irritating to skin. Its chemical formula is CH_2O. It is gaseous at room temperature. When mixed with water and alcohol, it makes a colorless solution called formalin, which is used to preserve animals for anatomical study; to produce synthetic resins, such as Formica; and in many other materials and processes.
  gases in industry **G** 61

Formal gardens, pictures **G** 27, 31
Forman, Milos, Czech motion-picture director **M** 488a
Form follows function, principle in design **I** 231
  Bauhaus, former art school **B** 103
  Louis Sullivan's famous rule for architecture **S** 457
Formicidae (for-MIS-id-e), ant family **A** 322
Formigny (for-meen-YE), **battle of,** 1450 **H** 282
Formosa see Taiwan
Formosa Strait, picture **A** 464
Forms, in art **A** 438g
Forms of address see Address, forms of
Formula, baby's food **B** 3
Formulas
  algebraic equations **A** 157–59
  chemical **C** 197–200, 219

Forrest, Nathan Bedford (1821–1877), American Civil War Confederate general, b. Bedford County, Tenn. He is noted particularly for leading raids behind Union lines (1862–64). He is often quoted as having said, "I git thar fustest with the mostest men." He is thought to have been grand wizard of original Ku Klux Klan.

Forster, E. M. (Edward Morgan Forster) (1879–1970), English writer, b. London. A distinguished man of letters, Forster received the Order of Merit on his 90th birthday. Among Forster's novels is *A Room with a View* (1908). After his last novel, *A Passage to India* (1924), he wrote criticism, beginning with *Aspects of the Novel* (1927).
  English fiction **E** 266

Forsyte Saga, by Galsworthy **E** 266
Forsyth, Alexander, Scottish minister **G** 416

Forsythia (for-SITH-ia), ornamental shrub originally grown in Europe and Asia. It is now grown widely in the United States. It is named for William Forsyth (1737–1804), a Scot, who was superintendent of the Royal Gardens of Kensington Palace. The shrub has great masses of yellow bell-shaped flowers. Forsythia is one of the earliest shrubs to bloom in the spring. Picture **G** 36.

Fortas, Abe (1910–   ), American lawyer, b. Memphis, Tenn. He served as counsel to various government agencies, and director of the Division of Power of the Department of the Interior (1942–46). He was appointed Supreme Court justice (1965), and retired (1969) to resume private law practice.

Fort-Archambault (FOR-ar-shom-BO), Chad **C** 182
Fort Astoria, Oregon, trading post **O** 207
Fort Atkinson, Nebraska **N** 87
Fort Benning, Georgia **G** 145
Fort Boise (BOI-se), trading post **F** 376
Fort Bragg, North Carolina **N** 318
Fort Bridger, trading post **F** 376
Fort Bridger Historical Preserve **W** 333
Fort Crèvecoeur (crev-CUR), trading post
  built by La Salle **L** 46
Fort Dearborn, military post **F** 376
  early history of Chicago **C** 228
Fort Donelson National Military Park, near Dover, Tennessee, site of siege **T** 84
  Grant coins phrase "unconditional surrender" **C** 322

Fort Duquesne (du-KANE), military post **F** 376
  French and Indian War **F** 460

Forten, James (1766–1842), American sailmaker and philanthropist, b. Philadelphia, Pa. He was one of Negroes who fought in American Revolution. Active in social work among Negroes in Philadelphia, he worked with William Lloyd Garrison and led conventions of free Negroes in northern states against movement to resettle Negroes abroad.

Fort Frontenac (fraunt-NOC), trading post **F** 376
  built by La Salle **L** 46
Fort Garry, near Winnipeg, Manitoba **M** 79, 82; **W** 190
Fort Gouraud, Mauritania see F'Dérik
Fort Hall, trading post **F** 376
Fort Knox, Kentucky, gold depository **K** 227; picture
  K 226
Fort-Lamy (for-la-ME), capital of Chad **C** 182
Fort Langley National Historic Park, British Columbia
  B 406a
Fort Laramie, trading post **F** 376
  Oregon Trail, supply stop, picture **O** 263
Fort Laramie National Historic Site, Wyoming **W** 332–33
Fort Larned, Kansas **K** 186
Fort Lisa, Nebraska **N** 86
Fort Loudoun, Tennessee **T** 88
Fort Louisburg, military post **F** 376
Fort Mandan, North Dakota **N** 336
Fort McHenry, Baltimore harbor, Maryland **F** 376;
  M 129; picture **M** 127
Fort McHenry National Monument and Historic Shrine,
  Maryland **M** 124; picture **M** 127
Fort Moultrie (MOLE-trie), South Carolina **S** 304, 306;
  beginnings of the Civil War **C** 322
Fort Moultrie flag, 1776 **F** 229
Fort Necessity, military post **F** 376, 460
Fort Niagara, trading post **F** 376
Fort Orange, trading post **F** 376
Fort Peck Dam, Montana **M** 431
Fort Pensacola, military post **F** 376
Fort Pulaski National Monument, Georgia **G** 141; pic-
  ture **G** 143
FORTRAN, language in computer programing **C** 457
Fortresses see Forts and fortification
Fort Riley, Kansas **K** 186
Fort Rodd Hill National Historic Park, British Columbia
  B 406a
Forts and fortification **F** 375–77
  Citadel, Haiti, pictures **H** 11, **W** 217
  Gibraltar, British military base **G** 205
Fort Scott, Kansas **K** 186–87
Fort Sill Military Reservation, Oklahoma **O** 91
Fort Smith, Arkansas **A** 430
Fort Smith, Northwest Territories, Canada **Y** 360
Fort Snelling, Minneapolis, Minnesota **M** 333
  Twin Cities grew from army post **M** 321
Fort Stanwix, military post **F** 376
Fort Sumter, Charleston, South Carolina **F** 376; **S** 303
  Civil War **C** 318, 322
Fort Ticonderoga (ty-con-der-O-ga), military post **F** 376;
  N 222
  capture by Ethan Allen's Green Mountain Boys **A** 167
  French and Indian War **F** 461
  Revolutionary War **R** 199

Fortunatus' (for-tu-NAY-tus) **purse,** gift from Fortune to destitute folk hero Fortunatus who chose to have riches over any other gift. The purse could never be emptied but proved to be Fortunatus' ruin. The story appeared in German *Volksbuch* in Augsburg (1509). The purse is now synonymous with good luck.

Fortune, Amos (?–1801), American slave, b. Africa. As a young prince, he was captured in Africa and taken to the United States in a slave ship. Eventually he was able to buy his own and his wife's freedom. His gravestone in Jaffrey, N.H., tells that he "was born free in Africa, a slave in America, he purchased liberty, professed Christianity, lived reputably, and died hopefully."

Fortune, business magazine **M** 15
Fortune-telling, by gypsies **G** 434
Fort Vancouver (van-COO-ver), trading post **F** 376
Fort Vincennes (vin-CENNS), military post **F** 376
Fort Wayne, Indiana **I** 148
  military post **F** 376
Fort Wayne, Treaty of, 1809 **H** 50
Fort Worth, Texas **T** 134

Forty and Eight, secret organization of members of the American Legion, founded (1920) with headquarters in Indianapolis, Ind. It was named for the *40 hommes-8 chevaux* ("40 men-8 horses") boxcars used in France during World War I. Originally a subsidiary of the American Legion, it was expelled (1959) for having a racially restrictive membership.

Forty-niners, gold prospectors in California **G** 250; pic-
  ture **G** 252
Forty Thieves, The, story from Arabian Nights **A** 346–47
Forum, public square in Roman cities **A** 375; **U** 232
Forward pass, in football **F** 359–60
Forza del Destino (FORT-za del des-TI-no), **La,** opera by
  Giuseppe Verdi **O** 144–45
Fosbury, Dick, American Olympic star, picture **O** 116
Foscolo (FO-sco-lo), **Ugo,** Italian writer and poet **I** 479

Fosdick, Harry Emerson (1878–1969), American Protestant clergyman, b. Buffalo, N.Y. A spokesman for "modernists" in United States, urging the acceptance of scientific theory, he was pastor of Riverside Church, New York, N.Y. (1926–46). He was the author of numerous works, including *A Guide to Understanding the Bible.*

Fossas, catlike animals related to civets **G** 93; picture
  G 92
Fossil resins **R** 184
Fossils **F** 378–89
  amphibians, early history of **F** 471
  Archaeoceti, or ancient whales **W** 150
  bats **B** 94, 96
  beginnings of paleontology, study of fossils **G** 112
  biologists' studies of **B** 191
  birds **B** 206–07, 209–10
  coal formation **C** 362
  Darwin's theories of evolution **D** 40
  demonstrate how fossil imprints were formed **G** 110
  dinosaurs **D** 172–81
  earth's history **E** 20–21
  elephants **E** 170
  evolution, clues to **E** 340, 342
  failures to adapt **L** 224–25
  fishes **F** 181–82
  fossil fuels **F** 487
  fossil magnets **G** 121
  living fossils **E** 347
  petrified forests **A** 414; **F** 380
  petroleum formation **P** 169, 171
  prehistoric animals **P** 436–38
  prehistoric man **P** 442–46
  rocks contain **R** 268
  sea animals found on mountains **E** 10
  shells show climate changes of the past **I** 21–22
  See also Dinosaurs; Evolution

Foster, Genevieve (1893–   ), American author and illustrator of children's history books, b. Oswego, N.Y. Her works include *George Washington's World*, *Abraham Lincoln's World*, and *Augustus Caesar's World*. Her books have been translated into many languages.

Foster, Hanna, American novelist **A** 198
Foster, Stephen Collins, American composer and songwriter **F** 389
Foster-family care **O** 227
  social work, practice of **S** 225
  See also Adoption
Foucault (foo-CO), Léon, French scientist **L** 266

Foucault pendulum, metal ball hanging by long cord that is free to swing in any direction. If ball is set swinging in one direction, it will eventually swing through all directions of the compass, returning to its original direction. This movement results from rotation of earth. Speed of pendulum's rotation depends upon latitude. The pendulum was first used as evidence of earth's rotation by Léon Foucault in 1851. There is one in the Smithsonian Institution, Washington, D.C.

Fouday, France, picture **F** 410
Fouling, clogging of gun barrels **G** 415
Foundation Center, New York **F** 391–92
Foundations (endowments) **F** 390–93
  See also names of foundations or endowments
Foundations, building **B** 434
  bridges **B** 401
  coated concrete used **C** 166
Founding Fathers of the United States **F** 393–96
  some opposed universal suffrage **E** 112–13
  United States Constitution, written and signed by **U** 146
Foundling Hospital, in Florence, Italy **A** 438e–438f; picture **R** 165
Fountain of Youth, legend **A** 84
  Florida, history of **F** 272
  Ponce de Leon **P** 391, picture **A** 81
Fountain pens **P** 146
  communication advanced by **C** 433
  ink **I** 255
Fouquet (foo-KAY), Jean, French artist **F** 421
Four, magic number of American Indian **F** 313
Four bits, money, picture **M** 410
Four-color map, topological problem **T** 222; picture **T** 223
Four Corners, United States
  Arizona **A** 403, 404, 408
  Colorado **C** 415
  New Mexico **N** 181
  Utah **U** 241–42
Fourdrinier (fur-DRIN-ier), Henry and Sealy, English paper manufacturers **P** 57
Fourdrinier machines, for making paper **P** 52–53
Four-eyed fish **F** 191

Four freedoms, freedom of speech and religion and freedom from want and fear. These were the goals of democratic nations as formulated by President Roosevelt in his State of the Union speech (1941) during World War II.
  Roosevelt's plans for the future **R** 324

Four-H (4-H) clubs **F** 46, 47
  county and state fairs **F** 12
Four-H (4-H) Center, National, Washington, D.C. **F** 47
Four-horned antelope, hoofed mammal, picture **H** 217

Four Horsemen of the Apocalypse, in New Testament (Revelations 6:1–8), men representing evils of conquest, slaughter, famine, and death. Conquest (sometimes interpreted as Christ) rides white horse, Slaughter (or War) a red horse, Famine a black horse, and Death a pale horse. The New Testament story inspired a series of woodcuts by Albrecht Dürer and a novel, *Four Horsemen of the Apocalypse*, by Vincente Blasco Ibáñez.

Four Hundred, The, originally synonymous with top of New York City society but now refers to any exclusive social set. The phrase was coined (1888) by Ward McAllister, who remarked, "There are really only four hundred people in New York that one really knows."

Fourier (foo-ri-AY), François Marie Charles (1772–1837), French social philosopher, b. Besançon. He published a plan for organization of society into economically and socially independent associations of families living in communal buildings. An experimental colony (established in 1838) failed to achieve harmony envisioned in basically agricultural utopia of Fourierism.
  Utopian socialism **S** 220

Fourier, Jean Baptiste Joseph (1768–1830), French mathematician and physicist, b. Auxerre. He is noted for his studies on the theory of heat and of numerical equations. In the course of his research on heat conduction he developed his mathematical series, known as Fourier's series. This is a mathematical technique used to break up complicated mathematical expressions into a series of simple expressions, which can then be studied more easily than the original.

Fourneyron (foor-nay-RON), Benoit, French engineer and inventor **T** 319
  first turbine for production of water power **W** 62

Four-o'-clock, plant 1 to 3 feet high with long, trumpet-shaped flowers, white, reddish, or yellow in color and often striped. It is native to tropical America but also grows in temperate climates. The flowers open in cloudy weather or in late afternoon.

Four Oxen and the Lion, The, fable **F** 5
Fourteeners, mountains in Colorado **C** 402
Fourteen Points, President Wilson's peace program **W** 181, 280
Fourteenth amendment, to the U.S. Constitution **U** 156
  application of the Bill of Rights **B** 179–80
  citizenship **C** 312
  Johnson, Andrew, advises against **J** 125
  Negro history **N** 95
  Reconstruction **R** 118

Fourth estate, daily press and newspapermen. The phrase "Estates of the Realm" (classes or ranks in Great Britain) included Lords Spiritual (clergy), Lords Temporal (nobility), and Commons, to which British statesman Edmund Burke is said to have added the press, which he referred to as fourth and most powerful estate.

Fourth of July see Independence Day
Fourth Republic, France **F** 419–20
  overseas possessions **F** 412–13
Fourth state of matter, plasma **M** 178
Four-wheel drive, of a truck **T** 296
Fowl see Poultry

Fowler, Henry Hamill (1908–   ), American politician, b. Roanoke, Va. After graduating from Yale Law School, in 1933, Fowler was a lawyer with the Tennessee Valley Authority (1934–38) and, later, TVA assistant general counsel (1939). During World War II and the Korean War,

Fowler served in various government agencies, including the Office of Production Management and the War Production Board. He was assistant secretary of the treasury (1961–64), and secretary of the treasury (1965–69).

Fowling pieces, hunting guns **G** 415

Fox, Charles James (1749–1806), English statesman and orator, b. Westminster. A great debater, he came into disfavor because of his sympathy for French Revolution. He was removed from privy council (1798) for proposing toast to "Our Sovereign, the people." He advocated repeal of tea tax on American colonies and abolition of slave trade. He was a member of Parliament (1780–1806).

Fox, George, English religious leader and founder of the
  Quakers **Q** 2
Fox, Gilbert, American singer **N** 23

Fox, John, Jr. (John William Fox) (1863–1919), American novelist, b. Stony Point, Ky. He was a Rough Rider in Spanish-American War and correspondent for *Harper's Weekly*. Best-sellers about Kentucky, West Virginia, and Tennessee mountaineers include *The Little Shepherd of Kingdom Come* and *The Trail of the Lonesome Pine*.

Foxes **F** 396–97
  diet, chart **L** 252
  dog family **D** 248–50
  fox fur mutations **F** 514
  fur **F** 518
  fur farms **F** 513
  mammal hair, picture **M** 64
  tracks, picture **A** 271
Fox fire fungus
  bioluminescence **B** 197
Foxgloves, plants **P** 314; pictures **P** 315, 321
  conquest of heart disease **D** 214
  flowers, picture **G** 46
  source of digitalis **D** 323
Foxholes, field fortifications **F** 377
Fox hunting **D** 249
Fox squirrels **R** 276
Fox terrier, dog, picture **D** 255

Foxx, Jimmy (James Emory Foxx) (1907–67), American baseball player, b. Sudlersville, Md. First baseman and hitter (534 home runs) for Philadelphia Athletics, Boston Red Sox, Chicago Cubs, and Philadelphia Phillies, he was elected (1951) to Baseball Hall of Fame.

Fra Angelico *see* Angelico, Fra
Fractional distillation, a method of separating hydrocar-
  bons **D** 225, 226
  kerosene **K** 235
  noble gases **N** 110
  petroleum **P** 174–75
Fractional Orbiting Bombing System **M** 347
Fractions **F** 397–402
  arithmetic **A** 398
  musical notes **M** 530
  number systems **N** 385
  percent **P** 148–49
  probability ratios **P** 471
  ratios, or fractions, called rational numbers **M** 155
Fractures, broken bones
  first aid **F** 162
Fractur style, in writing **F** 293
Fra Filippo Lippi *see* Lippi, Fra Filippo
Fragonard (fra-gon-AR), **Jean Honoré,** French painter
  F 402
  French rococo painting **F** 425; **P** 24

Frame houses, development of **B** 434
Frame of reference, point of view
  development of Einstein's theory of relativity **R** 141
Frames, steps in programed instruction **P** 475, 477
  picture **P** 476
France **F** 403–20
  Andorra, between France and Spain **A** 254–55
  architecture *see* French architecture
  art *see* French art
  cave paintings at Lascaux, picture **A** 354
  cooking arts, haute cuisine **F** 340
  flag **F** 239
  flag, royal standard **F** 227
  food specialties, picture **F** 337
  French Bill of Rights **B** 180
  French family, picture **F** 38
  history *see* France, history of
  history 1789–99 *see* French Revolution
  holidays **H** 148, 152, 155, 156, 158
  language *see* French language
  literature *see* French literature
  Liberty, Statue of, gift to United States **L** 168
  Monteynard dam, picture **D** 18
  municipal government system **M** 507–08
  music *see* French music
  national anthem **N** 17–18
  Paris **P** 68–75
  postman, picture **P** 406
  theater **T** 160

France (FRONCE), **Anatole** (Jacques-Anatole-François Thibault) (1844–1924), French novelist, critic, and historian, b. Paris. He was elected to French Academy (1896) and awarded Nobel prize for literature (1921). A socialist, he supported Émile Zola in defense of Alfred Dreyfus. Among his relatively unorthodox works are *Penguin Island*, *Pierre,* and *The Human Tragedy*.

France, history of **F** 415–20
  Algeria **A** 160, 163
  American independence recognized and alliance
    formed **R** 204
  Bill of Rights, French **B** 180
  Canada (New France) **C** 68–70, 124
  Cardinal Richelieu **R** 233
  Charlemagne **C** 189–90
  Clemenceau, Georges **C** 337
  Congo (Brazzaville), formerly part of French Equa-
    torial Africa **C** 461, 464
  De Gaulle, president of the Fifth Republic **D** 85
  Dreyfus, Alfred **D** 316
  East India Company **E** 43
  feudalism in Europe **F** 99–103
  French and Indian War **F** 458–62
  Hundred Years War **H** 281–82
  Joan of Arc **J** 121
  Marie Antoinette **M** 99
  Middle Ages **M** 291
  Napoleon I **N** 9–12
  political parties **P** 379
  Revolution *see* French Revolution
  Seven Years War, 1756–63, in North America **C** 70
  Suez Canal **S** 450–51
  Tunisia **T** 312
  Vietnam **V** 334c, 334d
  Vikings **V** 339
  World War I **W** 273–81
  World War II **W** 288, 300–01, 304
France, S.S., ocean liner **O** 18; pictures **O** 20, 22
Francesca (fron-CHES-ca), **Piero della,** Italian painter
  F 448; **I** 469
  Battle of Constantine, The, painting **R** 167

Francesca, Piero della (continued)
Renaissance art **R** 166
Resurrection, The, painting **E** 41

Francescatti (fran-ces-CA-ti), **Zino** (1905–), French violinist, b. Marseilles. He began violin lessons at age 3, making first public appearance at 5. He entertained wounded soldiers in Marseilles hospitals while still a young child. He has made many records and toured extensively in Europe and America.

Franchise, right to vote see Suffrage
Franchises
government sponsored monopolies **T** 304
public utilities **P** 510
Francia (FRON-cia), **José Gaspar Rodríguez de,** Paraguayan dictator **P** 66
Francis, James B., English-born American engineer **T** 319
Francis I, king of France
Louvre art collection started by **L** 367
Renaissance brought to France **R** 171
Franciscans, religious order **R** 292
missions to American Indians **I** 177

Francis de Sales, Saint (1567–1622), French churchman, b. Sales, near Annecy. Bishop of Geneva (from 1602), his holiness and culture advanced Counter-Reformation. He converted Protestants of Chablais from Calvinism to Catholicism and stated his beliefs in *Introduction to the Devout Life.* His feast day is January 29.

Francis Ferdinand (Franz Ferdinand) (1863–1914), archduke of Austria (1875–1914), b. Graz. He was heir apparent to Austrian empire and kingdom of Hungary after death of his father (1896). His assassination (June, 1914), with his wife, Sophie Chotek, by a Serbian nationalist at Sarajevo, Bosnia (now Yugoslavia), was immediate cause of World War I.
Sarajevo, capital of Bosnia, Yugoslavia **Y** 358

Francis Joseph I (Franz Josef) (1830–1916), Austrian emperor (1848–1916) and king of Hungary (1867–1916), b. Schönbrunn. He was an absolute ruler unsympathetic to modern parliamentary government and growing nationalism. He was defeated in Austro-Prussian War (1866) but joined Germany (1879) in what later became Triple Alliance. He held empire together until his death, after Austria entered World War I. Picture **W** 270.

Francis of Assisi (os-SI-zi), **Saint F** 449
Christianity, history of during Middle Ages **C** 284
founded order of the Friars Minor **R** 292
Italian literature **I** 475
prayer **P** 434
set up one of the first Nativity scenes **C** 289

Francis of Paola (PA-o-la), **Saint** (1416–1507), Italian monk, b. Paola, Cosenza. He founded order of Minims (1436), whose chief virtue was humility. Known for his austerity, he helped the dying Louis XI of France. His feast day is April 2.

Francistown, Botswana **B** 340a
Francis Xavier, Saint see Xavier, Saint Francis
Francium, element **E** 154, 161
Franck (FRONCK), **César,** Belgian-born French composer and organist **F** 449
most popular symphony by a Frenchman **F** 446
Franco, Francisco, Spanish head of state **F** 450
Fascism **F** 64
Spain, history of **S** 358

Franco-Flemish period, of music **D** 364
François, André, French illustrator
illustration for *Roland* **C** 243

Françoise (fron-SWOZ) (Françoise Seignobosc) (1897–1961), French author and illustrator, b. Lodève. She is known for her children's books, particularly those about Jeanne-Marie, such as *Jeanne-Marie at the Fair.*

Franconia (fran-CO-nia) **Notch,** White Mountains, New Hampshire **N** 157; picture **N** 159
Great Stone Face, rock formation **N** 148

Franco-Prussian War (1870–71), war between France, under Napoleon III, and Prussia, chief state of North German Confederation. France's defeat marked downfall of Napoleon III's Second Empire and beginning of German imperialism, with William (Wilhelm) I, king of Prussia, as German emperor. According to treaty of Frankfurt (1871), Germany acquired province of Alsace and part of Lorraine with the city of Metz, and France paid indemnity of $1,000,000,000.
background to World War I **W** 270
Napoleon III in French history **F** 418
Paris **P** 75

Frank, Anne, German-Dutch diarist **D** 157–58
excerpt from her diary on D-day broadcast **D** 157

Frankenstein, hero of horror tale *Frankenstein, or the Modern Prometheus,* by Mary W. Shelley, wife of the English poet. A German student who creates an evil monster by galvanizing a corpse is destroyed by it as retribution for presuming to create a human being. The name now usually refers to monster rather than to its creator.

Frankfort, capital of Kentucky **K** 223–24; picture **K** 225
Frankfurt (on the Oder), East Germany **G** 157
Frankfurt, West Germany **G** 158
Frankfurt Book Fair, Frankfurt, West Germany **P** 515

Frankfurter, Felix (1882–1965), American jurist and law professor, b. Vienna, Austria. He was professor at Harvard Law School (1914–39) and associate justice of U.S. Supreme Court (1939–62). He argued for release of convicted murderers Sacco and Vanzetti (1921) and wrote *The Case of Sacco and Vanzetti.* He received Presidential Medal of Freedom (1961).

Frankfurters, meat **M** 195
outdoor cooking **O** 247
Frankie and Johnny, folk song **F** 321

Frankincense, or **olibanum,** gum resin from tree growing chiefly in East Africa. It is used in incense for religious purpose and was one of gifts of Magi to Christ Child in New Testament.
resins, kinds of **R** 184

Franking privilege (from "frank," meaning "open" or "free of charge or other conditions"), right to send mail free of postage, indicated by use of a signature instead of a stamp. In the United States the privilege is extended to presidents, congressmen, various members of the executive branch of the federal government, and during wartime to members of the Armed Forces.

Frankland, Edward, English chemist **C** 214

Franklin, Aretha (1942–), American popular music singer b. Memphis, Tenn. As a young girl she sang with her father's church choir, and she made her first record at the age of 12. Throughout the 1960's and early 1970's she made many recordings, most of which sold over 1,000,000 copies. She writes many of her own songs and also does the arrangements. The major trade magazines of the music business named her the top female vocalist of 1967. Picture **R** 262c

rock music **R** 262d

Franklin, Benjamin, American diplomat, statesman, and scientist **F** 450–56
academy founded by **E** 70
agriculture, interest in **A** 100
American literature **A** 197–98
Declaration of Independence **D** 61
demonstration of value of lime fertilizer **F** 98
electricity, theory of **P** 235
family life in colonial America **C** 385–86
flag with red, white, and blue stripes **F** 248
fund set up to assist young craftsmen **F** 390
Gulf Stream, first accurate chart of **G** 411
invented bifocal spectacles **O** 166
kite experiment **K** 267; **T** 170
letter to a friend **L** 156b
libraries **L** 198; **P** 137
"Lighthouse Tragedy, The," ballad about the Boston Light **L** 278
lightning and kite experiment **E** 127; **T** 170
magazine publisher **M** 14
Poor Richard's Almanack, selections **F** 452
postal service **P** 407
postmaster of American colonies **C** 435
quoted on taxes **Q** 20
quoted on the importance of a nail **N** 3
science, advances in **S** 71
Who were the Founding Fathers of the United States? **F** 393–94

Franklin, John, English Arctic explorer **N** 338

Franklin, John Hope (1915–), American historian, Negro, b. Rentiesville, Okla. He was chairman of the history department at Brooklyn College, N.Y. (1956–64). He has been professor of American history at University of Chicago (since 1964) and head of the history department (since 1967). His books include *From Slavery to Freedom: A History of American Negroes, Reconstruction After the Civil War,* and *The Emancipation Proclamation.* Picture **N** 102.

Franklin, State of, early name of Tennessee **T** 88–89
Franklin D. Roosevelt National Historic Site, Hyde Park, N.Y. **N** 220

Franklin stove F 453
Franks, Germanic tribe **F** 415
Charlemagne, ruler of **C** 189–90
early German art **G** 165
Germany, early history of **G** 158–59
See also Charles Martel; Pepin III, the Short
Franz, German form of Francis see Francis
Frasch process, of sulfur mining **L** 356

Fraser, Dawn (1937–), Australian swimmer, b. Sydney. She held four world freestyle swimming records and was winner of 10 gold medals and six silver medals in Olympic Games and British Empire Games. In the 1964 Olympic Games she broke her own record (set in 1956) for 100 meters.

Fraser, James Earle (1876–1953), American sculptor, b. Winona, Minn. He was designer of the buffalo nickel and is noted for his monuments depicting pioneer life. His works include a bust of Theodore Roosevelt, a statue of an Indian on horseback, *The End of the Trail,* and figures of Lewis and Clark. He was awarded a gold medal for sculpture by the National Institute of Arts and Letters (1950) and by the American Academy of Arts and Letters (1951).

Fraser, Simon, Vermont-born Canadian fur trader and partner in the North West Company **C** 72
explored British Columbia, 1808 **B** 404, 407
Fraser River, Canada **B** 404; **C** 52
Fraternal societies see by name, as Freemasons, etc.
Fraternal twins G 86

Fraunces (FRAWN-ces), **Samuel** (1722?–95), American innkeeper, b. West Indies. In 1763 he opened a tavern at Broad and Pearl Streets in New York City. Later known simply as Fraunces Tavern, it became highly popular, and Fraunces soon made a reputation as New York's best innkeeper. The tavern was the site of George Washington's Farewell Address (1783). When Washington was elected president, he made Fraunces his household steward in New York, the nation's first capital, and in Philadelphia, its second.

Fraunhofer (FROWN-ho-fer), **Josef von,** Bavarian optician **A** 474
Fray Bentos (FRY BEN-toce), Uruguay **U** 238

Frazier, E. Franklin (Edward Franklin Frazier) (1894–1962), American sociology professor, Negro, b. Baltimore, Md. An authority on the problems of the Negro race, he was chosen chairman of UNESCO committee of experts on race (Paris, 1949). He received John Anisfield Award (1940) for book *The Negro Family in the United States.* He was head of department of sociology at Howard University, Washington, D.C., from 1934 to 1959.
Negro Renaissance **N** 98

Frazier, Joe (1944–) American boxer, Negro, b. Beaufort, S.C. He was acknowledged as world heavyweight champion after defeating Jimmy Ellis in 1970. In 1971 he defeated ex-champion Muhammad Ali in a widely-heralded bout. Frazier lost his title to George Foreman in 1973.
boxing **B** 353

Freckles, light-brown or yellowish spots on the skin, usually produced by exposure to sunlight.

Frederick II (1194–1250), emperor of the Holy Roman Empire, b. Jesi, Italy. The son of Henry VI of Germany and Constance, he was orphaned (1198) and brought up as a ward of the pope. He inherited the title of king of Sicily as Frederick I (1198) and was crowned king of Germany (1215) and emperor of the Holy Roman Empire (1220). During his reign he supported the union of Germany and Italy in spite of papal opposition. After leading a crusade to the Holy Land (1228), he had himself crowned king of Jerusalem (1229).

Frederick I, king of Prussia **G** 160
Frederick I, or Frederick Barbarossa, king of the Germans and Holy Roman emperor **H** 163
Germany, early history of **G** 159
related to both Guelph and Ghibelline parties in Italy **I** 455
Frederick II, or Frederick the Great, king of Prussia **F** 456
rise of Prussia **G** 160
regulated composition of military bands **B** 39
Frederick, Maryland **M** 125

Frederick C. Robie House, picture **U** 124
Frederick Douglass' Paper, first Negro magazine in
    United States **M** 14
Fredericksburg, Virginia
    Civil War battle site **C** 325
Frederick the Great, king of Prussia see Frederick II, or
    Frederick the Great
Frederick William, the "Great Elector" of Brandenburg
    and duke of Prussia **G** 160
    Berlin **B** 143
Fredericton, capital of New Brunswick, Canada **N** 138c;
    picture **N** 138d
Free, or private, **enterprise system I** 251
    capitalism and democratic privilege **C** 105; **D** 105

Free city, city, together with its adjoining areas, that is
partly self-governing but under authority of an international organization. The term also refers to self-governing cities or city-states, usually having supreme power,
such as the 11th-century Italian city-states.

Freed, Alan, American disk jockey **R** 262a
Freedmen's Bureau N 95
    Johnson, Andrew, opposes **J** 125
    Reconstruction Period **R** 118
Freedom, academic see Academic freedom
Freedom Fighters, Hungarian H 288
Freedom March, 1963 K 248
Freedom of assembly, in First Amendment to the United
    States Constitution **B** 179
    civil liberties **C** 313
    democratic privilege **D** 105
Freedom of petition, in First Amendment to the United
    States Constitution **B** 179
Freedom of religion F 457
    American colonies **A** 182–83, 185–86, 187–88, 191
    Bill of Rights **B** 179
    democratic privilege **D** 105
    Jefferson introduces Virginia law **J** 64
    Maccabees, revolt of against Syria **H** 35
    Maryland act **M** 128
    Pilgrims **P** 343
    Quakers **Q** 2–3
    Reformation **R** 132–35
    Spain **S** 352
    Rhode Island founded on principle **R** 212; **W** 172
    Union of Soviet Socialist Republics **U** 28
Freedom of speech F 457
    Alien and Sedition Acts, United States **A** 10–11, 166
    Bill of Rights **B** 179
    civil liberties **C** 313
    Declaration of the Rights of Man **F** 466
    democratic privilege **D** 104–05
    government by democratic system **G** 275
    Speakers' Corner, Hyde Park, London, picture **C** 314
Freedom of the press F 457
    Alien and Sedition Acts, United States **A** 10–11, 166
    Bill of Rights **B** 179
    communication advanced by **C** 441
    democratic privilege **D** 104–05
    journalism **J** 143
    Milton's *Areopagitica* **E** 255
    newspaper honesty and integrity **N** 205
    Supreme Court ruling on confidential Vietnam War
        documents (Pentagon Papers) **C** 316; **S** 477
    Zenger, John Peter **Z** 369

Freedom Pledge, pledge concerned with preservation and
propagation of ideals and principles of U.S. Constitution.

Freedom riders, groups of white and Negro integration-
ists who traveled (May 4–17, 1961) from Washington,
D.C., to New Orleans, La., to test racial discrimination in
interstate travel terminals. Several of the groups met
violence and arrest before an Interstate Commerce
Commission order (effective Nov. 1, 1961) banned
segregation in terminal facilities.
    travel, segregation in **N** 104

Freedom's Journal, Negro newspaper **N** 94

Freedom Train, a seven-car red, white, and blue train
that toured 48 states (1947–49), exhibiting U.S. historic
documents to remind American citizens of democratic
ideals. Among the displays were a letter written by
Columbus, the Mayflower Compact, Jefferson's draft of
the Declaration of Independence, the original Bill of
Rights, Lincoln's handwritten Gettysburg Address, and
the UN Charter. The project was sponsored by the
American Heritage Foundation.

Free enterprise I 251
    capitalism **C** 105
    democratic privilege **D** 105
    poverty, cures for **P** 424b
Free fall, in sky-diving **S** 193
Free French, forces and government-in-exile **F** 419
    De Gaulle **D** 85
    World War II and the Vichy government **W** 289

Freeholder, one who owns land for an indefinite period
of time, usually having the right to pass title on through
inheritance. Freeholders were the only citizens privileged
to vote or hold office in seven of the original American
colonies. The term "freehold" was used in land-grant
policies established by colonial charters in America.

Freeman, Daniel (1826–1908), American homesteader
and Union soldier, b. Preble County, Ohio. He claimed
and received the first free land grant under the
Homestead Act (1862). His quarter section, or 160 acres,
near Beatrice, Nebr., became part of Homestead National
Monument of America (1929).

Freeman, Douglas Southall, American writer **A** 215
Freeman, Mary E. Wilkins, American writer **A** 205

Freeman, Orville Lothrop (1918–), American politician,
b. Minneapolis, Minn. A Minneapolis lawyer, Freeman
was governor of Minnesota (1955–61), and secretary of
agriculture (1961–69).

Freeman, R. Austin, English author **M** 554–55
Freeman, Theodore C., American astronaut **S** 346
Freeman's Farm, battles of R 204

Freemasons, secret fraternal societies that originated in
England (17th century) and since have spread throughout most of the world. They preserve secrets concerning
signs and rituals of traveling stonemasons of the Middle
Ages, who had to identify themselves as "Free and
Accepted Masons" before being employed. George Washington was among the early American members.

Free Methodist Church of North America, founded (1860)
by B. T. Roberts to correct alleged general laxness in
Methodism. Its policies go back to early teachings of
John Wesley, emphasizing perfection as goal of Christian
life. Members are fundamentalists, who stress revivals
and testimonies of religious experience. In church conferences laymen are equal to ministers.

Free ports I 330
    Colon's Free Zone **P** 45

Mayaguez, Puerto Rico **P** 522
Shannon Free Airport, Ireland **I** 389
Shannon Free Airport Industrial Estate **I** 389
Free Soil Party, United States **P** 380
Polk's administration **P** 387
Van Buren, a presidential candidate **V** 275
Free speech see Freedom of Speech
Free State, nickname for Maryland **M** 115
Freestone peach **P** 106

Freethinker, one who believes that all men can arrive at the same conclusions about religion and morality by natural reason, unaided by outside authority. Freethinkers were connected with 18th-century deists in England, and in France with Voltaire, who renounced Christianity. Among early American freethinkers were George Washington and Ethan Allen of Vermont.

Freetown, capital of Sierra Leone **S** 175
Free trade
Colón, Panama, Free Trade Zone **P** 45
free ports **I** 330
GATT **I** 329; **T** 25
Free verse, unrhymed, unmetrical verse **P** 353
Freeze, of wages and prices **N** 262f
Freeze-drying, of foods **F** 349
meat **M** 195
space crews, food for **S** 341
Freezers, refrigerating machinery **R** 138
Freezing **I** 3–4
liquids **L** 310
methods of, to preserve food **F** 347
supercooled water **I** 4
water desalting **W** 56a
Freezing point **H** 92
Freiburg (FRY-boorg), Germany, picture **C** 131
Freight
trucks and trucking **T** 295–97
Freight cars, of railroads **R** 82; pictures **R** 85
Freight service, of railroads **R** 81
Freight ships, or cargo ships **S** 158
Freight yards, of railroads **R** 83
Frei Montalva, Eduardo, Chilean president **C** 255
Frémont (FRE-mont), **John Charles,** American explorer and soldier **F** 458
explored Utah **U** 243
Kit Carson and Frémont **C** 123
tried to free slaves in Missouri **C** 324

French, Allen (1870–1946), American author of books for boys, b. Boston, Mass. He wrote about New England in *The Runaway* and *Pelham and His Friend Tim* and about Iceland in *The Story of Rolf and Viking's Bow.* His book *The Golden Eagle* is about sailing, and he adapted legends of King Arthur's court in *Sir Marrok.*

French, Daniel Chester, American sculptor **U** 115
French, Sir John, British field marshal **W** 273
French Academy **F** 435
influence on French literature **F** 437
French Afar Territories, Africa see Afar-Issa Territory
French and Indian Wars, 1689–1763 **F** 458–62
change in British policies toward American colonists leads to Revolutionary War **R** 194
fur country changes hands **F** 521
Iroquois almost destroy New France **C** 69–70, 79
Ottawas and Pontiac **P** 391
Pennsylvania's Fort Pitt **P** 145
Pitt, William, Earl of Chatham **P** 265
Plains of Abraham battle, part of global war **Q** 16
Seven Years War, 1756–63, in North America **C** 70
Washington, George **W** 37

French architecture **F** 421–32
baroque period, Versailles created in **B** 62
Gothic **G** 269–70
Renaissance **A** 381–82
Romanesque **R** 309
French art **F** 421–32
baroque period **B** 62
furniture design **F** 508; pictures **F** 509
jewelry **J** 97
modern art **M** 386–91
painting **P** 24, 27, 29–30; picture **A** 438d
Renaissance **R** 171
sculpture **S** 101–03
Sèvres porcelain **P** 418
tapestry weaving **T** 24
French Canadians **C** 48–49
Maritime Provinces **N** 138c, 344d; **P** 456e
Montreal **M** 443–45
New Hampshire **N** 152
Quebec **Q** 9, 10a
theater **C** 63

French chalk, soft white variety of the mineral talc, or steatite. It is used for marking cloth, as in garment manufacturing.

French Community, association of states (seven overseas territories, four overseas departments, seven self-governing African republics, and Metropolitan France) established (1958) by the Fifth French Republic to replace the French Union (term used to describe French colonial holdings). It is led by the president of the Republic and an executive council, which meets several times a year in various capitals and deals with such matters as foreign policy, communication, and defense.
overseas possessions in France's government and history **F** 413, 415

French Congo see Congo (Brazzaville); French Equatorial Africa
French cookery **F** 340, 404–05
French curve, mechanical drawing tool **M** 197

French Equatorial Africa, region in central Africa formerly under French control (1910–58) and at one time known as the French Congo (1891–1910). The area now consists of four independent states—Chad, Central African Republic, Gabon, and People's Republic of the Congo (Brazzaville).

French Guiana (gui-AN-a) **G** 395, 397
Devils Island **P** 468
life in Latin America **L** 47–61
French Guinea see Guinea
French horn, musical instrument **M** 549; picture **M** 547
orchestra seating plan **O** 186
French Indochina, name for former French colonies in Southeast Asia **V** 334c
French Indochinese Union **C** 34
French knots, in embroidery **E** 188
French language **F** 433–35
African literature in French **A** 76c–76d
Canada **C** 48–49
English influenced by **E** 244
Switzerland **S** 495
Walloons of Belgium **B** 126
French Lick, health resort, Indiana **I** 147
French literature **F** 435–42
contributions to art of the novel **N** 348
drama **D** 296, 297, 298
fables of La Fontaine **F** 3

French literature (continued)
   fairy tales **F** 22
   legends and romances **L** 128
   Roland, legend of **L** 130–33
   See also names of chief writers
French music **F** 443–48
   choral music **C** 277
   French opera **O** 132, 134, 137, 138
   opera develops from early pageants **O** 132
   See also names of composers and musicians
French Polynesia **P** 7
French Radio and Television, House of, Paris **P** 71
French Revolution **F** 462–68
   abolition of slavery **S** 199
   advances interest in historical writing **H** 136–37
   changes effect status of Jews **J** 109
   clothing, style change **C** 352
   flag **F** 243
   France, history of **F** 416
   Lafayette's role in **L** 22–23
   Marie Antoinette **M** 99
   Marseillaise, La, French national anthem **N** 17–18
   Napoleon I **N** 10
   Paine, Thomas **P** 13
   Paris **P** 74
   Roman Catholic Church suppressed **R** 295
   Rousseau **R** 337
   underground movements **U** 10
   Voltaire **V** 388
   XYZ Affair in United States **A** 9–10
French Somaliland, now Afar-Issa Territory **S** 255
   France, overseas possessions **F** 415
French Sudan *see* Mali

French West Africa, region of western Africa formerly administered by France (1895–1958). The area now consists of eight independent states—Guinea, Dahomey, Ivory Coast, the Islamic Republic of Mauritania, Niger, Mali, Senegal, and Upper Volta.

Freneau (fray-NO), **Philip,** American poet **A** 198
Freon, man-made gas **G** 61–62
   used as refrigerants **F** 347; **R** 136–37
Frequency, in physics
   noise, in decibels of sound **N** 270
   radiation measurement **R** 42
   radio waves **R** 56
   sound waves **S** 258, 261, 263
   television **T** 66–67
   wave characteristics **T** 254
Frequency modulation (FM)
   radio **R** 57
   See also Hi-fi; Stereo
Frescobaldi, Girolamo, Italian composer **B** 65
Frescoes, paintings on plaster **P** 30
   Egyptian tomb, picture **A** 361
   Francesca, Piero della **F** 448
   Giotto di Bondone **G** 211
   Islamic art **I** 421
   Lérida Cathedral, Spain, picture **G** 271
   Michelangelo **M** 255, 257
   Romanesque churches **M** 297
   Tribute Money, The, fresco by Masaccio **P** 20
Freshwater life
   fish, habitat, feeding habits, uses **F** 216
   freshwater environment contrasted with salt water **L** 228
   pond creatures, pictures **L** 257
Fresneau (fray-NO), **François,** French scientist **R** 341

Fresnel (fray-NEL), **Augustin Jean** (1788–1827), French physicist, b. Broglie. He provided the mathematical basis for the wave theory of light. He did many experiments in the study of light. He designed a lens (also designed separately by D. Brewster) that is used in most lighthouses today.
   science, history of **S** 75

Fresnel lens, for lighthouses **L** 276
Frets, metal strips on a stringed instrument **G** 409
Frets, ornamental designs or patterns **F** 505
Freud (FROID), **Sigmund,** Austrian psychologist **F** 469–70
   contributions to medicine **M** 208
Frey (FRAY), Norse god **N** 279
Freya (FRAY-a), Norse goddess **N** 279–80

Freyre (FRAY-re), **Gilberto de Mello** (1900–), Brazilian sociologist and writer, b. Recife. After completing his education in Brazil, he went to the United States for further studies. He traveled extensively in Europe and taught at universities there and in the United States, as well as in his native country. Among his best-known works is *The Masters and the Slaves,* a sociological history of the people of Brazil.
   Brazilian literature **B** 377

Friars, male members of certain religious orders **C** 284
   missions **M** 348
Friar Tuck, member of Robin Hood's band **R** 253
Frick, Ford C., American baseball executive **B** 81

Frick, Henry Clay (1849–1919), American industrialist, b. West Overton, Pa. He founded Frick and Co., which built and operated coke ovens in Pennsylvania. He served as chairman of Carnegie Steel Corp. (1889–1900) and played an important part in the formation of the United States Steel Corp. (1901), later becoming a director. He left his home in New York for use as a museum.

Friction **M** 470
   friction matches **M** 152
   heat of friction at supersonic flight **S** 471
   lubrication and lubricants **L** 370–71
   work, power, and machines **W** 243
Friday, character in Defoe's *Robinson Crusoe,* picture **F** 111
Friday, origin of name **D** 47

Friedan, Betty (1921–), American feminist, b. Peoria, Ill. She is the founder of the National Organization for Women (NOW), which she headed from 1966 to 1970. As an active participant in the Women's Liberation movement, she has devoted her efforts to achieving career opportunities, higher education, and political rights for women. Her book *The Feminine Mystique,* published in 1963, contributed much toward popularizing the ideas and philosophy of the modern feminist movement. In 1971 she became one of the founders of the National Women's Political Caucus, an organization endeavoring to bring women into all levels of American political life.

Friedrich, Caspar David, German painter **G** 171
Friendly Islands *see* Tonga
Friends, Society of *see* Quakers
Friendship
   popularity important to the adolescent **A** 23
Friendship dolls **D** 268
Friendship International Airport **M** 122
Friends Service Council of England **Q** 3

Fries (FREES), **John** (1750?–1818), American insurgent, b. Montgomery County, Pa. He led an armed band of Pennsylvania Germans that freed prisoners in Bethlehem who were being held for opposing the direct property tax, levied in anticipation of war with France (1799). He was twice sentenced to death for treason but finally was pardoned by President John Adams.

Frigate birds B 226; picture B 227
Frigates, ships S 159
   name for large naval destroyers U 192
   War of 1812 W 11–12
Frigga, Norse goddess N 279
Frigid zones, or polar regions Z 372
Friml, Rudolf, Czech-born American composer O 157
   Rose Marie, operetta O 158
   Vagabond King, The, operetta O 158
Fringe benefits, elements of wage settlements between
   labor and management L 17
   benefits for teachers T 44
Frisch, Karl von, Austrian zoologist F 278; H 193
   studies of bees B 120; picture B 119
Frisch, Max, Swiss writer G 179
Frisian (FRI-sian), language of Friesland, the Netherlands
   N 115

Fritchie, Barbara (1766–1862), American woman who supposedly hoisted the Union flag as Confederate general Stonewall Jackson marched through Frederick, Md., during Civil War. She was immortalized in the poem "Barbara Frietchie," by John Greenleaf Whittier, the most famous lines of which are, " 'Shoot, if you must, this old gray head,/But spare your country's flag,' she said."

Frobisher (FRO-bish-er), **Joseph** (1740–1810), Canadian fur trader, b. Halifax, England. He went into the trading business with his brothers, Benjamin and Thomas, and became an original member (1779) of the North West Company, organized to finance transcontinental traffic. He represented Montreal (1792–96) in the Legislative Assembly of Lower Canada.

Frobisher, Martin, English mariner E 384; I 427
   Northwest Passage N 338
Froebel (FRER-bel), **Friedrich,** German educator, founder
   of kindergarten system E 71
   kindergarten and nursery schools K 243
Froggie Went A-Courting, folk song F 318–19

Frogmen, members of U.S. Navy underwater demolition team during World War II. They swam in rubber suits with foot paddles like frogs' feet and planted explosives by night in enemy ships and installations in enemy harbors. Frogmen are now used in salvage operations.
   spies and spying S 389

Frogs F 470–73, 477–78
   animal communication A 278; picture A 279
   animal maze test, picture A 285
   egg laying E 89; pictures E 88, L 211
   electricity, Galvani's experiments with E 128
   forelimb, picture F 80
   freshwater creatures, picture L 257
   goliath frog, of Cameroon C 36
   metamorphosis M 234–35
   second-level consumer, picture L 239
   spectrograms of animal sounds, pictures A 276

Frohman, Charles (1860–1915) and **Daniel** (1851–1940), American theater managers. Charles helped to found Theatrical Syndicate (1896) and guided many stars, such as Ethel Barrymore, to fame. Charles's most successful productions include *The Girl I Left Behind Me, The Little Minister,* and *Peter Pan.*

Froissart, Jean, French poet and historian F 436
From ghoulies and ghosties, ancient Scottish prayer
   P 435

Fromm (FROME), **Erich** (1900–), American psychoanalyst and social philosopher, b. Frankfurt, Germany. He came to the United States in 1933 after finishing his psychoanalytic training. He is the author of *Escape from Freedom, The Sane Society, The Art of Loving,* and other books. Concerned with man's social and cultural problem, Fromm proposes love as the only productive and sane solution for man's alienation in today's society.

From the Halls of Montezuma, song by Henry C. Davis
   N 26
   "The Marines' Hymn" U 178

Frondizi (fron-DI-tzi), **Arturo** (1908–), former president of Argentina, b. Paso de los Libres, Corrientes province. Frondizi opposed the regime of President Juan Perón, while supporting his programs of social security, better schools, and housing. As president of Argentina (1958–62) and head of the Intransigent Radical Party, he attempted to stabilize the economy but was deposed.
   Argentina, history of A 396

Fronds, leaves of ferns F 92–93
Front, in meteorology W 76

Frontenac, Louis de Buade, Comte de (1622–1698), French colonial governor, b. Paris. He was governor of New France, Canada (1672–82 and 1689–98), advocating an expansionist policy there. He was recalled to France (1682) by King Louis XIV because of his independent ideas, but was sent back to Canada as governor in 1689. He revived trade, defended Quebec against the British, and suppressed the Iroquois Indians.
   La Salle and Frontenac L 46

Frontier and pioneer life see Pioneer life
Frontiersmen, in westward movement W 143–44
Frontinus (fron-TY-nus), **Sextus,** Roman writer E 208
Front matter, of a book B 331
   parts of a book, for teaching how to use a library
     L 180–81
Front of National Liberation (FLN), Algeria A 163
Front organizations, Communist C 443
Front Ranges, of the Rocky Mountains N 284
Frost F 289
   apple orchards, protection against A 335
   Jack Frost doesn't paint the leaves T 281–82

Frost, Frances Mary (1905–1959), American novelist and poet, b. St. Albans, Vt. She is known especially for poems about country life in New England, collected in *Mid-Century, These Acres,* and *Christmas in the Woods.* She also wrote *American Caravan,* a children's story in rhyme, and series of childrens' books, including *Windy Foot at the County Fair* and *Sleigh Bells for Windy Foot.*

Frost, Robert, American poet F 479–80; N 161; pictures
   F 479, A 210
   American literature, place in A 209
   "Last Word of a Bluebird, The" F 480
   "Pasture, The" F 480
   quoted on the fine arts U 115
   "Road not Taken, The" F 480
   "Runaway, The" P 355
   "Stopping by Woods on a Snowy Evening" F 480

Frostbite, injury to parts of the body caused by extreme cold, especially moist cold. People with circulatory dis-

Frostbite (continued)
ease are the most vulnerable. In moderate to severe cases, blisters and superficial or deep gangrene may result.

Frost giants, in Norse mythology **N** 277
Frottage (fro-TODGE), art technique of texture rubbings **M** 394
Frozen foods see Foods, frozen
Fructose, or **levulose,** fruit sugar **S** 453
Fruit
    berries **G** 298–301
    dried or dehydrated fruits **D** 316–17
    garden fruits **G** 52
    grapes, most grown fruit **G** 297–98
    marketing for the home **M** 102, 103
    melons **M** 216–17
    nutrition, use in **N** 417
    nuts, fruits of trees **N** 419–24
    olive **O** 101–03
    peach, plum, and cherry, stone fruits **P** 106–07
    plants that have fruits we eat **P** 308; pictures **P** 309
    seeds, dispersal of **F** 280–82
    seeds of plants **P** 296–97; pictures **P** 298
    stain removal **L** 84
    tropical **M** 74
    Was the "apple" in the Garden of Eden really an apple? **A** 334
    See also names of fruits, as Apple, Orange
Fruit flies (*Drosophila*), pictures **G** 83, 84
    use in breeding experiments **B** 196
Fruitgrowing **F** 481–85
    apple orchards **A** 334–35, 337
    dates **D** 41–42
    fig **F** 117
    garden fruits **G** 52
    grapes and berries **G** 297–301
    insecticides **I** 258
    lemon and lime **L** 137–38
    melons **M** 216–17; **V** 291
    orange and grapefruit **O** 177–79
    pear **P** 112
    stone fruits, peach, plum, cherry, and apricots **P** 107–08
    training of trees **T** 283
    See also names of fruits
Fruitlands, co-operative community in Massachusetts **U** 256
Frum cult, New Hebrides **M** 564
Frunze, capital of Kirghizia (Kirghiz Soviet Socialist Republic) **U** 45
Fry, Christopher, English dramatist **E** 268

Fry, Elizabeth Gurney (1780–1845), English philanthropist and prison reformer, b, Norfolk. As a young girl she became interested in improving prison conditions, especially for women and children. She gained fame throughout Europe and Russia for promoting reforms and founding homes for homeless in England and New South Wales. A Quaker minister, she wrote about her work in *Observations on . . . Female Prisoners.*

Fryingpan-Arkansas River Project, in Colorado **C** 405
Fuad (fu-OD) **I,** king of Egypt **E** 92

Fuca (FU-ca), **Juan de** (Apostolos Valerianos) (?–1602), Greek navigator who sailed with Spanish Navy. He claimed to have discovered (1592) the strait believed by 16th-century geographers to be the northwest passage to India. The claim was never authenticated, but the strait, which lies between Vancouver Island and Washington (in Bering Sea), is now named for him.

Fuchs, Bernie, American illustrator **I** 94, 95

Fuchs (FOOKS), **Klaus Emil Julius** (1911–), British atomic scientist, b. Rüsselsheim, Germany. He confessed to giving secret information to Russia and was sentenced to 14 years' imprisonment for espionage (1950). After he was released, having been deprived of British citizenship, he became a citizen of East Germany.

Fuchs, Sir Vivian, British explorer **P** 370–71

Fuchsias (FU-shias), group of flowering shrubs and small trees, named after Leonard Fuchs, a 16th-century German botanist. Originally native to tropical Latin America and New Zealand, fuchsias today are cultivated in gardens in many parts of the world. The plant has conspicuous red, purple, or white flowers.

Fuel cells, electricity generating device **B** 99
    electricity generated from burning gases **G** 61
    ions in action **I** 351
    power plants **P** 427
    spacecraft, uses in **S** 341
Fuels **F** 486–90
    air pollution **A** 110; **E** 272f–272g
    coal **C** 364
    diesel engines **D** 171
    fire and combustion **F** 136
    gasoline **G** 63
    heating degree days **W** 87
    heating systems **H** 97–99
    kerosene **K** 235
    liquid gases **L** 308–09
    mineral fuels, world distribution **W** 260–61
    missiles **M** 345
    natural gas **N** 56–57
    petroleum **P** 169–78
    population and the fuel supply **E** 272b, 272f–272g
    power plants **P** 425–26, 511–12
    rockets **R** 257–58
Fugitive Slave Law, 1850 **S** 199
    Compromise of 1850 **C** 448
    Dred Scott Decision **D** 310–11
    Fillmore, Millard **F** 125
    Negro history **N** 95
    Underground Railroad **U** 12
Fugue, in music **M** 536
Fuji (FU-ji), or **Fujiyama, Mount,** Japan **J** 34; **T** 204; pictures **J** 24; **M** 498; **V** 384
Fujiwara, ancient ruling family of Japan **J** 43
Fujiwara period, of Japanese art **O** 217

Fulani (fu-LA-ni), a people, numbering about 6,000,000, dwelling primarily in west African countries of Cameroon, Dahomey, Guinea, Mali, Niger, Nigeria, Senegal, and Upper Volta. Some live in small nomadic bands and work as dairy cattlemen. The others, primarily farmers, live in large settlements. The nomads are pagan or Muslim; the settled Fulani are primarily Muslim.

Fulbright, James William, American statesman **A** 431
Fulcrum, of levers **W** 248

Fuller, Margaret, Marchioness Ossoli (Sarah Margaret Fuller) (1810–1850), American author and social reformer, b. Cambridgeport, Mass. She advocated higher education and equal rights for women. She was editor of the transcendentalist magazine *Dial* (1840–44) and literary critic for the N.Y. *Tribune* (1844–46).

Fuller, Melville Weston (1833–1910), American jurist, b. Augusta, Maine. He was chief justice of the United

States (1888–1910) and upheld the rights of person and property against the trend toward government regulation, favoring strict control of governmental powers through specific grants. He served as a member of the Permanent Court of Arbitration, The Hague (1900–10).

Fuller, R. Buckminster (1895–   ), American engineer, inventor, and author, b. Milton, Mass. Fuller, whose work extends into many fields, from philosophy to city planning, is best-known for his invention of the geodesic dome. This multipurpose structure, which combines lightweight structural units so that the whole is stronger than the sum of its parts, exemplifies Fuller's theory of "doing more with less" to improve the quality of human life. His books include *Operating Manual for Spaceship Earth.*
  industrial design **I** 232

Fuller's earth, naturally occurring claylike substance, ranging from white to brown in color. It is used for decolorizing and refining oils and fats and for cleaning cloth and is mined in many parts of the United States.
  bleaching fats and oils **O** 77

Fullerton, Charles G., American astronaut **S** 346
Fulminates, explosives
  gun primers **G** 416–17
Fulton, Robert, American inventor **F** 491
  steamboat, in the history of transportation **T** 262
Fumaroles (FU-ma-roles), or volcanic gas vents **V** 382
Fumes see Vapor
Fumigants, gases **I** 258
Functional diseases **D** 190
Functionalism, in design
  building construction **B** 430
  homes **H** 184
  industrial design **I** 230–31
  Sullivan, Louis **S** 457
  United States architecture **U** 123
  Wright, Frank Lloyd **W** 315
Function words, parts of speech **P** 92
  grammar **G** 289
Fundamental Orders of Connecticut **C** 474, 478, 480
Fundamentals, in music **S** 264–65

Fund for the Advancement of Education, fund that makes grants to nonprofit organizations for study of curricula and teaching resources and improvement of educational personnel. A supporter of educational TV, it was established in 1951 by the Ford Foundation. Its headquarters is in New York, N.Y.

Fund for the Republic, fund set up to conduct and promote study of principles of Declaration of Independence, Constitution, and Bill of Rights. Its Basic Issues Program is concerned with political parties, race relations, and international power relationships. It was founded in 1952, and its headquarters is located in Santa Barbara, Calif., where it established (1959) the Center for the Study of Democratic Institutions.

Fundy, Bay of, Canada **N** 138
  Reversing Falls, St. John, New Brunswick **C** 52
  tidal bore, picture **T** 184
  tidal power project on Passamaquoddy inlet **M** 37
Fundy National Park, New Brunswick, Canada **C** 67
Funeral and burial customs **F** 492–95
  Egypt, ancient, preservation of decorative art **D** 67;
    E 95–102
  elegies and epitaphs **E** 151–52
  mourning rings **J** 99
  national cemeteries of the United States **N** 28–31
  Shivah, mourning period in Judaism **J** 120

Mexican practices **L** 55
  mourning, or keening, songs **F** 326
  Sacrament of the Sick, last rites of the Roman
    Catholic Church **R** 301
Fungi **F** 496–500
  algae, partnership with **A** 156
  ant food **A** 325, 326
  bioluminescence of toadstools, picture **B** 197
  borderline between plants and animals **L** 213
  corn smut **C** 507
  lichens **F** 94
  microscopic fungi **M** 280; picture **M** 281
  mushrooms, as food **M** 521
  nematode control **P** 286; picture **P** 287
  plant enemies **P** 286–87

Fungicides (FUN-jis-ides), chemical substances used to destroy or stop the growth of fungi. Compounds of sulfur, copper, and mercury control such fungus diseases of plants as blights and rusts. Fungicides also prevent the rotting of wood and mildewing of fabrics and cure certain fungus diseases of man. The commonest of these diseases are ringworm and athlete's foot.

Fungus diseases **D** 187
  athlete's foot **D** 193
  ringworm **D** 205
Funiculars, cable railways **S** 497

Funk, Casimir (1884–1967), American biochemist, b. Warsaw, Poland. He is known for giving the name vitamines (now spelled "vitamins") to the substances that prevent such diseases as beri-beri and scurvy. He did a great deal of research on vitamins. His work stimulated further research in the field of vitamins.
  vitamins, discovery of **V** 370b

Funnel, of a tornado **H** 297
Fur farms, or ranches **F** 513–14; **C** 57
Furfural, industrial liquid produced from grain **G** 286
  See also Döbereiner, Johann Wolfgang
Furies, goddesses see Erinyes

Furlong, Charles Wellington (1874–1967), American explorer and painter, b. Cambridge, Mass. He led expeditions to Africa, Asia, Central America, and South America (Tierra del Fuego and Patagonia). His life drawings of the now extinct Ona and Yahgen Indian tribes of Tierra del Fuego are in the Smithsonian Institution.

Furnaces
  blast furnaces **I** 397
  central heating systems **H** 98–99
  thermostats for automatic control **A** 528; picture
    A 529

Furness, Betty (Elizabeth Mary Furness) (1916–   ), American entertainer and consumer affairs expert, b. New York, N.Y. A former movie actress and radio personality, Miss Furness became best-known for her television appearances. She worked on the U.S. anti-poverty program and served as special assistant for consumer affairs to President Johnson (1967–69). She was appointed Commissioner for Consumer Affairs for New York City in 1973.

Furniture **F** 501–04
  antique **A** 318
  colonial, pictures **C** 389
  Danish modern **D** 111
  decorative arts **D** 77; pictures **D** 72, 73

Furniture (continued)
design **F** 505—10
interior decorating **I** 298—303
pioneer crafts **P** 255
plywood **W** 226—27
upholstery **U** 226—27
veneer **W** 227
woods and their chief uses **W** 223—24
woodworking and cabinet making **W** 229—34
Furs F 511—19
beavers **B** 112—14
farms **C** 57
fox **D** 249
hat felts of **H** 53—54
mammals **M** 65
mink **O** 244
otters and their kin **O** 240, 241, 244
Soviet Union, picture **U** 35
taxidermy **T** 27
See also names of fur-bearing animals
Fur seals W 6—7
migration **H** 190—91
Fur trade in North America F 520—24
Alaska **A** 138, 143
beaver trade in Plymouth Colony **P** 346
Canada **C** 68, 71, 72
La Salle combines with exploration **L** 46
Mackenzie, Sir Alexander **M** 5
modern age in the fur trade **F** 511—12
Montana **M** 442
New France (Canada) **C** 68—70
Nicolet, Jean **N** 250
Northwest Passage **N** 338
Oregon **O** 207
overland trails **O** 254
Prairie Provinces, Canada **A** 146h; **M** 82; **S** 38h
rendezvous system **W** 322
Saint Lawrence River, route of **S** 16
South Dakota **S** 326
Washington **W** 28
West Virginia **W** 140
Wyoming **W** 336
See also names of principal fur-bearing animals, as Beavers
Fuselage (FUSE-e-lodge), of airplane **A** 554; diagram **A** 555
Fuses
electricity in the home, safety measures **S** 4
in artillery shells **G** 426
miner's safety fuse **E** 390
Fushimi Castle, Kyoto, Japan, picture **O** 219
Fusiliers, riflemen
Royal Welsh Fusiliers, picture **H** 200
Fusion, nuclear see Nuclear fusion
Fust (FOOST), **Johann,** German who loaned money to Gutenberg **G** 427
Fustic, wood, yields yellow dye **D** 369

Future Business Leaders of America, organization sponsored by National Business Education Association, to encourage high school and college students preparing for careers in business or business education. Founded in 1942, its headquarters is in Washington, D.C. It publishes the quarterly *Future Business Leader Forum.*

Future Farmers of America F 45, 46
county and state fairs **F** 12
Future Farmers of America Foundation, Inc. F 46

Future Homemakers of America, organization of high school students of home economics in the 50 states of the United States, Puerto Rico, and the Virgin Islands. Founded in 1945, its headquarters is in Washington, D.C.

Future Scientists of America, organization sponsored by National Science Teachers Association. It presents annual science achievement awards, to encourage high school students with scientific aptitude. Founded in 1960, its headquarters is in Washington, D.C. It publishes *Vistas in Science* and *Centrifuge.*

Future Teachers of America, organization to encourage students interested in teaching profession. Founded in 1937, it has its headquarters in Washington, D.C. It publishes the semiannual *FTA Newsletter.*
Is teaching the career for you? **T** 41—42

Futurism, modern art movement
Italian art **I** 473; **M** 391
sculpture **S** 105

Fyleman, Rose (1877—1957), English writer, b. Nottingham. Her books of whimsical verse for children include *Fairies and Chimneys, The Fairy Flute, The Fairy Green,* and *Fairies and Friends.* Her stories include *Forty Good Morning Tales,* and *The Rainbow Cat.*

ILLUSTRATION CREDITS

The following list credits, by page, the sources of illustrations used in Volume F of THE NEW BOOK OF KNOWLEDGE. Credits are listed illustration by illustration —left to right, top to bottom. Wherever appropriate, the name of the photographer or artist has been listed with the source, the two being separated by a dash. When two or more illustrations appear on one page, their credits are separated by semicolons.

66– Don Spaulding
69
73 Pierpont Morgan Library
77 FBI
79– Donald Johnson and Caspar Henselmann
81
82 George Sottung
84 Donald Johnson and Caspar Henselmann
85 Edward Vebell
86 Edward Vebell
88 Miller Pope
89 Miller Pope
90 Lee J. Ames
91 Miller Pope
93 Hugh Spencer; Miller Pope; Hugh Spencer; John H. Gerard from Missouri Botanical Garden.
94 Roche Photography; H. Spencer; M. Pope.
95 Jack Dermid
96 The American Agricultural Chemical Co.
97 Jane Latta
98 The American Agricultural Chemical Co.
99– W. T. Mars
101
103 W. T. Mars
104 George Bakacs
107 George Bakacs; Courtesy of American Craftsman's Council; Courtesy of American Craftsman's Council.
109 Carl Perutz—Courtesy of Doubleday
110– Robert Frankenberg
112
114 Gregori—Gelb
115 Les Mahon—Monkmeyer Press
116 Edward Vebell
117 Gottscho—Schleisner
119 Kenneth Longtemps
120 Kenneth Longtemps
121 George Buctel
122 Rob Wright, Suva, Fiji Islands
123 James Cooper
124 Library of Congress
127 Dr. Henry Ray—Courtesy of Victoria Beddford Betts
128 Courtesy of Murial Ray, Emerson Jr.-Sr. High School; Courtesy of Murial Ray, Emerson Jr.-Sr. High School; Binney & Smith Inc.
129 FBI
130 Mort Beebe—Photo Trends; Sabine Weiss—Rapho Guillumette.
131 George Buctel
132 Suomen Kuvapalvelu—PIP
135 Ed Drews—Photo Researchers; Fritz Henle—Photo Researchers.
136 George Bakacs
137 George Bakacs
138– Herman B. Vestal
143
145 Herman B. Vestal
146 UPI
147 Dan Todd
149 Howard Mellen
151 New York Fire Department
154 Howard Mellen
155 Howard Mellen
156 John MacFie—DPI
157 George Bakacs
159 George Bakacs
161 George Bakacs
162 George Bakacs
165 George Sottung
167 George Sottung
168 George Sottung
171– George Sottung
174
177– George Sottung
180
181 Florida Silver Springs; Gaetano Di Palma.
182 Gaetano Di Palma; New York Zoological Society; Courtesy of American Museum of Natural History.

183– Gaetano Di Palma
191
192 Russ Kinne—Photo Researchers; John H. Tashjian; Stan Wayman—Rapho Guillumette; Russ Kinne—Photo Researchers.
193 Gaetano Di Palma
194 Courtesy of A. M. Winchester
195 Russ Kinne—Photo Researchers
196 Courtesy of American Museum of Natural History
198 Gaetano Di Palma
199 Vancouver Public Aquarium
201 Douglas P. Wilson
202 H. W. Kitchen—National Audubon Society; Douglas Faulkner; John H. Tashjian.
203 Gaetano Di Palma; Douglas Faulkner—Photo Researchers.
204 Marineland of Florida; Douglas Faulkner.
205 Annan
207 Ron Perkins, Courtesy, Garcia Corp.
208 Dennis Fritz
209 Leonard Cole
210 Leonard Cole
213– Leonard Cole
216
219 George Bakacs
222 Jack Berns—PFI
225– Ron Perkins
230
231– Miller Pope
234
235– Ron Perkins
242
245 Ron Perkins
246 Ron Perkins
247 Gerry Turner—Creative Associates; R. I. Nesmith—FPG.
249 Keystone; Chas. Pfizer & Co., Inc.
250– Miller Pope
253
255 Birnback; Billy Davis—Courier-Journal, Louisville, Kentucky.
256 J. P. Brouwer—Photo Researchers; Carl Frank—Photo Researchers.
257 Tennessee Valley Authority; Department of the Army, Office of the Chief of Engineers.
259 Color Illustration Inc.; Harriet Arnold and Nancy Palmer; Samuel Grimes; Charles J. Balden.
260 Diversified Map Corp.; Carroll Seghers—Alpha; Anderson—FPG; R. T. Tuffin—Photo Trends.
261 Diversified Map Corp.
263 Diversified Map Corp.
265 Donato Leo
266 Shostal; Florida Development Commission.
269 Graphic Arts International
270 Diversified Map Corp.
271 Florida Development Commission; Miami Beach News Bureau.
274 Howard Koslow
275 Howard Koslow
276 George Bakacs
279 George Bakacs
280 Ron Perkins
281– George Bakacs
283
285 Josef Scaylea—The Seattle Times Co.
286 The Astrophysical Laboratory, Smithsonian Institution; Dr. John C. Jensen—Nebraska Wesleyan University.
287 Shell Oil Co.
288 Aerofilms—Annan
289 Miller Pope
290 Shelbourne Museum, Shelbourne, Vermont; Shelbourne Museum, Shelbourne, Vermont; from Folk Art in Pictures, Spring Books, London; Whaling Museum, New Bedford, Massachusetts.

291 Alfred Schiller—from Hungarian Peasant Art, Corvina, Budapest; Ron Perkins—Courtesy of Marjorie Munsterberg; from collections of the Mercer Museum, Bucks County Historical Society, Doylestown, Pennsylvania; Ron Perkins—Courtesy of Swedish National Travel Office.
292 Ron Perkins—Courtesy of Marjorie Munsterberg; used by permission of Gerd Doerner from Mexican Folk Art, published by Wilhelm Andermann, Verlag, Munich, © 1962; Ron Perkins—Courtesy of Swedish National Travel Office.
293 Courtesy of Abby Aldrich Rockefeller Folk Art Collection, Williamsburg, Virginia; Art Reference Bureau; A. J. Wyatt—Philadelphia Museum of Art.
294 Alfred Schiller—from Hungarian Peasant Art, Corvina, Budapest; Courtesy of American Antiquarian Society; Taylor Museum, Colorado Springs Fine Arts Center.
295 Courtesy of Abby Aldrich Rockefeller Folk Art Collection, Williamsburg, Virginia; Art Reference Bureau; Art Reference Bureau.
296 Ron Perkins—from Peasant Art of Europe and Asia, H. T. Bassert, Verlag Ernst Wasmuth, Tübingen, Germany; Ron Perkins—from Ornamente der Volkunst, H. T. Bassert, Verlag Ernst Wasmuth, Tübingen, Germany.
297 Sabine Weiss—Rapho Guillumette; Ace Williams—Shostal; Serraillier—Rapho Guillumette.
298 Stephanie Dinkins; Harrison Forman; Lawrence Smith; Sabine Weiss—Rapho Guillumette.
303 Jack Hearne
306 Jack Hearne
308 Jack Hearne
311 Jack Hearne
312 Jack Hearne
314 Jack Hearne
316 Jack Hearne
317 Jack Hearne
330 Wayne Dunham
336 Eliot Elisofon—Life Magazine, © Time Inc., all rights reserved; Eliot Elisofon—Life Magazine, © Time Inc., all rights reserved; Swiss Cheese Co.
337 Jane Latta; Eliot Elisofon—Life Magazine, © Time Inc., all rights reserved; Eliot Elisofon—Life Magazine, © Time Inc., all rights reserved; Fritz Henle—Photo Researchers; Jane Latta.
338 Eliot Elisofon—Life Magazine, © Time Inc., all rights reserved; John Lewis Stage—Photo Rsearchers; John Lewis Stage—Photo Researchers.
339 Rene Burri—Magnum; Henri Cartier-Bresson—Magnum.
344 Ron Perkins
345 Ron Perkins
351 FDA
352 FDA
354 Miller Pope
355 U.S. Department of Agriculture
357– Edward Vebell
364
372– American Forest Products Industries, Inc.
373
374 U.S. Forest Service
375 Keith de Folo—Photo Researchers
378 Sovfoto
379 Peabody—Museum of Natural History, Yale University; Roland T. Bird—Courtesy of American Museum of Natural History; Courtesy of American Museum of Natural History; Martin F. Glaessner; Stephen J. Chan.
380 Stephen J. Chan; Wide World.
381 U.S. Department of the Interior, Na-

tional Park Service; Smithsonian Institution.

382 Smithsonian Institution; Robert Hermes—Annan; New York State Museum and Science Service; Lynwood M. Chace.
384– Stephen J. Chan
388
389 Foster Hall Collection, Pittsburgh, Pa.
394 Gerald McConnell
396 Leonard Lee Rue III
403 Robert Doisneau—Rapho Guillumette
404 A. L. Goldman—Rapho Guillumette; Gerry Cranham—Rapho Guillumette.
405 George Buctel
407 French Government Tourist Office
409 Ray Manley—Shostal; R. Hanlin—Shostal.
410 Henri Cartier-Bresson—Magnum; Howard Friedman—Photo Researchers.
413 Henri Cartier-Bresson—Magnum
414 Ray Manley—Shostal
417 Spirale—Rapho Guillumette
420 Susan McCartney—Photo Researchers
422 Louis H. Frohman; Louvre, Paris—Art Reference Bureau.
423 Louvre, Paris—Art Reference Bureau
424 Louvre, Paris—Art Reference Bureau; Metropolitan Museum of Art, Munsey Fund, 1954; Henry B. Belville—Phillips Collection, Washington.
426 Metropolitan Museum of Art
427 Louvre, Paris—Art Reference Bureau; Art Reference Bureau.
428 Collection, Museum of Modern Art, New York, Mrs. Simon Guggenheim Fund; Louvre, Paris—Art Reference Bureau.
429 Louvre, Paris—Art Reference Bureau; Art Institute of Chicago, Mr. and Mrs. Lewis L. Coburn Memorial Collection; Museum of Modern Art, New York, Lillie P. Bliss Collection.
430 Elton Schnellbacher—Carnegie Institute, Museum of Art; Louvre, Paris—Art Reference Bureau; National Gallery, Washington, Chester Dale Collection.
431 Museum of Modern Art, New York
432 Lucien Hervé
437 Avery Peters
440 Avery Peters
442 Karsh, Ottawa—Rapho Guillumette
445– Tom Funk
447
451 W. T. Mars
452 Bettmann Archive
453 W. T. Mars
454 W. T. Mars
459 Robert Frankenberg
460 Robert Frankenberg
461 Quebec Government General Agency
463 Fred Mason
465– Fred Mason
468
469 Illustration Research Service
470 John H. Gerard; Edward R. Degginger.
471 Ross E. Hutchins
472 Arabelle Wheatley; Karl Maslowski—National Audubon Society.
473 J. L. Stone—National Audubon Society; Albert Pozzi—Alpha.
474 John H. Gerard; Karl Maslowski—Photo Researchers; Leonard Lee Rue III—Monkmeyer.
475 New York Zoological Society; New York Zoological Society; Albert Pozzi—Alpha.
476 Arabelle Wheatley
478 Walker Van Riper—Courtesy of University of Colorado Museum
479 Jacob Lofman—PIX
483 FPG
484 Alpha
485 Alpha
486 Brian Seed, from Ireland, Life World Library, © 1964 by Time Inc.; Tom Hollyman—Photo Researchers.
489 Courtesy of Cities Service Company
490 U.S. Navy
491 Howard Koslow
493 Marc & Evelyne Bernheim—Rapho Guillumette; Ewing Kranin—Stockpile.
495 George Holton—Photo Researchers; Ewing Kranin—Stockpile; Ewing Kranin—Stockpile.
496 Walter Dawn; Lynwood M. Chace; Chas. Pfizer & Co., Inc.; Hugh Spencer; Ross E. Hutchins.
497 Arabelle Wheatley
499 Arabelle Wheatley; Hugh Spencer; Arabelle Wheatley.
500 John Markham; John Markham; Walter H. Hodge; Rutherford Platt.
501– Martin Helfer—Harvey Probber, Inc.
504
505 Paul Granger
506 Paul Granger; photograph from Council of Industrial Design, Courtesy of Norwich Museum Committee, as seen in Decoration, Volume II, published by French & European Publications, Inc.
507 Paul Granger; Courtesy of Bloomingdale's, New York.
508 Paul Granger; Louis H. Frohman—Rapho Guillumette.
509 Paul Granger; Courtesy of Henry Francis du Pont Winterthur Museum.
510 Louis Reens—as seen in Decoration, Volume II, published by French & European Publications, Inc.
511 Harrington—Hudson's Bay Company
513 UPI
514 Fur Information & Fashion Council
516 Fur Information & Fashion Council
517 Ace Williams—Photo Researchers
519 Photo Trends
520 Robert Frankenberg
521 Robert Frankenberg
522 Robert Frankenberg
523 Robert Frankenberg
524 Robert Frankenberg

G, seventh letter of the English alphabet **G** 1
See also Alphabet
G, slang for $1,000 **G** 1
Gaberones (ga-ber-O-nes), capital of Botswana **B** 340a
Gabirol, Solomon ibn *see* Ibn-Gabirol, Solomon
Gable, Clark, American actor, picture **M** 475

Gable, in architecture, a triangular wall formed by two sloping roof lines meeting at the end of a ridged roof. The forms vary from the gambrels (gabled roofs with double slope) of Warner House in Portsmouth, N. H., to the peaked gables of steep roofs in medieval German villages, Gables occur on Greek temples as "pediments" —low gables decorated with sculpture.

Gabo (GA-bo), **Naum,** Russian sculptor **M** 393; **S** 105
Gabon (ga-BON) **G** 2–3
flag **F** 235
Gaboon, snake, picture **S** 209
Gaboriau (ga-bor-YO), **Émile,** French author **M** 554
Gaborone (ga-bor-ON), capital of Botswana **B** 340a

Gabriel (GAY-bri-el), one of the seven archangels of Judeo-Christian tradition, second in rank to Michael. Gabriel served as God's messenger and interpreter to Daniel in the Old Testament and to Zacharias and Mary in the New Testament. He was the angel of mercy who, however, in Talmud, destroyed wicked host of Sodom and Sennacherib. He is credited with revelations to Mohammed in Koran and is believed to blow a horn heralding judgment day.

Gabrieli (ga-bri-AY-li), **Giovanni,** Italian composer **M** 540
baroque music **B** 65
Renaissance music **R** 174

Gad, in Old Testament, Jacob's seventh son, his first by his wife Leah's handmaid, Zilpah. Gad became the patriarch of one of the 12 tribes of Israel, to which he gave his name. Gad's tribe defended David against Saul.

Gaddi (GA-di), **Taddeo** (1300?–1366), Italian painter and architect, b. Florence. A student of Giotto, he continued Giotto's work on the campanile in Florence. Gaddi painted frescoes in the church of Santa Croce and designed Ponte Vecchio, the oldest bridge in Florence.

Gadolinium (gad-ol-IN-ium), element **E** 154, 161
Gadsden, Alabama **A** 124
Gadsden, Christopher, American Revolutionary leader **S** 308
Gadsden, James, American statesman **S** 308
speech at Stamp Act Congress 1765, proclaimed colonial unity **R** 195
Gadsden Purchase, 1853 **T** 112
Arizona **A** 417
New Mexico **N** 194
Pierce, Franklin **P** 247
Gaelic (GAE-lic), language of Ireland and Scotland **I** 384
Irish literature **I** 392
Gaelic Celts, a people of ancient Ireland **I** 390
Gaelic League **I** 394
Gaff cutter, sailboat, picture **S** 9
Gafsa, Tunisia, picture **O** 3

Gág (GOG), **Wanda** (1893–1946), American author and illustrator, b. New Ulm, Minn. She translated and illustrated *Tales from Grimm* and *Snow White and the Seven Dwarfs,* and she wrote and illustrated *Millions of Cats* and *The Funny Thing.*
Millions of Cats, illustration from **I** 97
Grimm's *Tales,* illustration **G** 377, 378, 380–386

Gagarin, Yuri Alexeyevich (1934–68), Russian cosmonaut, b. Gzhatsk, Smolensk. First man to travel in space, he circled earth for 89.1 minutes (April 12, 1961) in spaceship Vostok. Author of *The Road to the Cosmos,* he died in a jet training flight plane crash.
space flight data **S** 344, 345

Gage, Thomas, British general **R** 196, 197, 198, 199
Gagnan, Émile, French inventor of the Aqua-Lung **S** 189–90

Gag Resolution, rule preventing discussion of abolitionist proposals in U.S. House of Representatives (adopted 1836). Silencing of antislavery petitioners meant Congress would have no power over slavery in slaveholding states. Rule was repealed when Northern Democratic support was withdrawn in 1844.

Gaillard (GAIL-lard) **Cut,** Panama Canal **P** 47
Gainer, former name for reverse dive **D** 231
Gainsborough, Thomas, English painter **G** 4
distinct school of portrait painters in England **P** 24
English art **E** 238
Full Length Study of a Lady, drawing **G** 4
The Market Cart, painting **E** 239
Gaitán (guy-TON), **Jorge,** Colombian political leader **C** 384
Gaius Julius Caesar *see* Caesar, Gaius Julius
Galagos (ga-LAY-gos), or bush babies, primates **M** 422
Galahad, knight of King Arthur's court **A** 442
Galambos, Robert, American scientist **B** 96–97
Galápagos (ga-LA-pag-os) **Islands,** Ecuador **E** 55, 56;
picture **I** 424
Darwin's observations **B** 192–93; **E** 344–45
giant tortoises **T** 332; picture **T** 333
lizards and tortoises, island-hopping **L** 236
Galata Bridge, Istanbul, Turkey, picture **E** 319

Galatea (ga-la-TE-a), in Greek mythology, sea nymph loved by the Cyclops Polyphemus, whom she spurned for Acis, a Sicilian shepherd. When Acis was killed by Polyphemus, she turned Acis' blood into a stream. Galatea is also the name of a statue said to have been brought to life by Aphrodite in answer to Pygmalion's prayer.

Galatians (ga-LAY-tians), book of Bible **B** 161
Galaxies, vast islands of stars **U** 196–204
discoveries in astronomy **A** 476
Milky Way **U** 196–98; photograph and drawing **O** 11
NGC 4038 and 4039, picture **R** 70
quasars and pulsars **Q** 7–8
radio astronomy explores Milky Way **R** 75–76

Galbraith, John Kenneth (1908–), American economist, diplomat, and author. He is noted as an economist and has been a professor of economics at Harvard University since 1949. President John F. Kennedy appointed him United States Ambassador to India (1961–63). He has held other government posts and served two terms as national chairman of the Americans for Democratic Action (ADA). He is the author of several books, including *The Affluent Society, The New Industrial State, Ambassador's Journal,* and *Economics, Peace and Laughter.*

Galdós, Benito Pérez *see* Pérez Galdós, Benito
Gale, Zona, American writer **A** 208
Galen (GALE-en), **Claudius,** Greek scientist **B** 187–88
conquest of disease **D** 213
early history of medicine **M** 204
science, advances in **S** 64

Galena (ga-LE-na), mineral ore source of lead **L** 95
ores, types of **R** 270; pictures **R** 271
Galilee, Sea of, or Lake Tiberias, now called Lake Kinneret, northern Israel **I** 441, 444; **L** 28
Galileo (ga-li-LAY-o), Italian astronomer **G** 5–7
air theory **E** 351
beginning of modern research **R** 182
chemistry, role in history of **C** 209
falling bodies, law of **F** 34
invented the idea of using telescope **I** 346
Italian literature, place in **I** 479
lenses for a telescope **L** 142
light, speed of, experiment to measure **L** 266
modern astronomy begins **A** 472
moon, studies of **M** 449
new outlook affects history of medicine **M** 205
physics, forerunner in **P** 230
science, advances in **S** 68
sunspots studied by **E** 26
telescope, use of **T** 61, 63
thermometer **H** 88

Gall (1840?–1894), American Sioux Indian chief, b. in what is now S. Dakota. With Crazy Horse he defeated General Custer at battle of Little Big Horn (1876). He surrendered (1881) and settled on reservation, serving as judge (1889–94) at Court of Indian Offenses.

Galla, a people of Ethiopia **E** 296
Galland (gal-LON), **Antoine,** French writer **A** 345

Gallatin (GAL-la-tin), **Albert** (Abraham Alfonse Albert Gallatin) (1761–1849), American statesman, diplomat, and financier, b. Geneva, Switzerland. A member of U.S. House of Representatives (1795–1801) and secretary of treasury (1801–14), he led peace negotiations with Great Britain after War of 1812 and was U.S. minister to France (1816–23) and to Great Britain (1826–27).

Gallaudet (ga-lau-DET), **Thomas Hopkins,** American teacher of the deaf **D** 51
Gallaudet College, Washington, D.C. **W** 34
Gall bladder, diagram **B** 274
Galle (GOLL-e), **Johann,** German astronomer **A** 475
Gallegos (ga-YAY-goce), **Romulo,** Venezuelan novelist and statesman **V** 300
Galleons, sailing ships of the 15th century **P** 264
Gallery forests
prairie trees along streams **P** 430
riverbank jungles **J** 154
Galleys, in printing **P** 463; picture **B** 332
proofreading **P** 479
Galleys, ships **S** 155
rowing **R** 338
transportation, history of **T** 260–61
Galliard, dance
Byrd's lighter music **R** 173

Gallico, Paul (1897–   ), American sportswriter and author, b. New York, N.Y. He established (1927) annual Golden Gloves amateur boxing tournament. His children's books include *Thomasina,* and he also wrote *Mrs. 'Arris Goes to Paris* and *The Snow Goose.*

Galli-Curci (GA-li-COOR-chi), **Amelita** (1882–1963), Italian soprano, b. Milan. She performed in Italy and South America before making U.S. debut as Gilda (in *Rigoletto*) with Chicago Opera Company (1916). She was a member of Metropolitan Opera Company (1920–30).

Gallipoli (gal-LIP-o-li) **Campaign,** World War I **W** 274–75
Gallium (GAL-lium), element **E** 154, 161

Gallon, measure of volume **W** 111
Gallop, gait of a horse, picture **H** 230
Galls, plant tissue growths **P** 286; picture **P** 287
crown gall tumor **C** 90
insect larvae **I** 278–79

Gallup Poll, measurement of public opinion by questioning cross-section of people. Initiated (1935) by George Gallup. it is used particularly to gauge American and British political trends.

Galsworthy (GALLS-worthy), **John,** English novelist **E** 266
popular realistic drama **D** 298

Galt, Sir Alexander Tilloch (1817–1893), Canadian statesman, b. London, England. As minister of finance (1858–62) and Canadian high commissioner in England (1880–83), he represented English-speaking minority in French Canada. He was a delegate to Charlottetown and Quebec conferences, which led to formation of Dominion of Canada (1867). He wrote *Canada from 1849 to 1859.*

Galton, Sir Francis, English scientist, devised system for classifying fingerprints **F** 129
Galvani (gol-VA-ni), **Luigi,** Italian physician **M** 206
discoveries in electricity **E** 128; **S** 71
Galvanism **E** 128
Galvanized iron **Z** 370
Galvanized steel **I** 403
Galvanometers (gal-va-NOM-eters), devices for measuring electric current **E** 131
mirror galvanometer **T** 52
recording earthquakes **E** 38

Gálvez, Bernardo de (1746?–1786), Spanish colonial administrator, b. Macharaviaya, Málaga. He was governor of Louisiana (1777). He acquired Florida for Spain in a peace settlement (1783) after war with Great Britain and was appointed captain general of Louisiana, Florida, and Cuba (1784). He succeeded (1785) his father as viceroy of New Spain.
Louisiana, history of **L** 363

Galway, Ireland **I** 385
Gama (GA-ma), **Vasco da,** Portuguese explorer **G** 7; **P** 403
Africa **A** 67
voyage to India opens trade in spices **E** 379

Gamaliel I (ga-MAY-li-el) (1st century), Jewish pharisee and teacher of the Law. A member of Sanhedrin (Supreme Court and Legislature), he advocated tolerance and leniency toward the apostles. According to New Testament, he was the teacher of apostle Paul.

Gambia, The **G** 8–9
flag **F** 235

Gambier Islands, four main islands and several uninhabited islets in the Pacific, part of French Polynesia. The principal products are copra, coffee, and mother-of-pearl. The largest and most important island is Mangareva.

Gambling
probability, use in **P** 471
Game birds **H** 291
mallard ducks, picture **B** 239
prairie chickens, near-extinct birds **B** 232
ptarmigans **B** 225; picture **B** 224
See also Grouse; Quail
Game fish, pictures **F** 209, 210
Game hunting see Hunting

Gamow (GAME-ov), **George** (1904–68), American physicist and author, b. Odessa, Russia. His mathematical explanation of radioactive alpha-particle emission indicated which particles would most effectively split atomic nuclei. His books, which explain scientific subjects in simple terms, include *Mr. Tompkins in Wonderland, One, Two, Three . . . Infinity,* and *A Star Called the Sun.*

Gandhi (GON-di), **Indira** (1917–), prime minister of India, b. Allahabad. Daughter of Prime Minister Jawaharlal Nehru, she worked (1947) for Mahatma Gandhi in Hindu-Muslim riot areas. She was president of All-India National Congress Party (1959–60) and a cabinet minister in the Shastri government (1964–66). She became India's first woman prime minister in 1966. Pictures **P** 456a; **W** 212b.

Gangrene (GANG-rene), death of tissue in a part of the body because of lack of blood circulation to that part. Among the causes are direct injury; diseases that cause changes in blood vessels, thereby interfering with circulation of blood to a part of the body; and infections. Treatment usually consists of the use of antibiotic drugs and surgery.

Gannet, large white sea bird found in temperate regions. Bird is grayish on throat, with gray bill and patch of light brown on back of head. It has large black feathers on wings. It dives for fish, which are eaten whole.

Gannett, Ruth Chrisman (1896–), American illustrator, b. Santa Ana, Calif. After illustrating John Steinbeck's *Tortilla Flat,* she turned to children's books. She illustrated *Miss Hickory* (Newbery medal, 1947) and *My Father's Dragon.*

Ganymede, in Greek mythology, beautiful mortal youth who became cupbearer of Zeus, supplanting Hebe. He was believed to be the spirit of water. He is represented among stars by constellation Aquarius and is sometimes pictured sitting on back of flying eagle. Name was assumed by Rosalind masquerading as a man in Shakespeare's *As You Like It.*

Ganz (GONTZ), **Rudolph** (1877–), American pianist and conductor, b. Zurich, Switzerland. He conducted the St. Louis Symphony Orchestra (1921–27) and the New York Philharmonic and San Francisco Young People's Concerts (1938–49). He was president of the Chicago Musical College (1929–54). His compositions include orchestral and piano works and many songs.

Gar, a freshwater fish found west of the Rocky Mountains from southern Canada to Costa Rica and Cuba. Gars have long, narrow bodies and jaws, sharp teeth, and tough scales. They prey almost entirely on smaller fish. The largest species, the alligator gar, is greenish in color. These fish may grow to 14 ft. in length and weigh over 100 lbs.

G.A.R. see Grand Army of the Republic

Garakonthie ("Moving Sun"), **Daniel** (1600?–1676), American Indian chief of Onondaga tribe, b. present-day New York State. Called Father of the French for rescuing over 60 white captives from hostile Indian tribes, he was a respected orator and mediator and was probably head councillor of Iroquois Confederacy. He was converted to Christianity and named Daniel.

Garamond (GARR-a-mond), **Claude**, French type designer **T** 345

Garand, John Cantius (1888–   ), American inventor, b. St. Remi, Canada. He designed light machine gun and invented gas-operated semi-automatic (M-1, or Garand) rifle, which was adopted (1936) as official U.S. Army shoulder gun. It was replaced (1960) by the M-14 rifle.

Garbage disposal see Refuse and refuse disposal

Garbo, Greta (Greta Gustaffson) (1905–   ), Swedish film star, b. Stockholm. She is noted for serious roles in *Mata Hari, Camille, Anna Karenina,* and *Grand Hotel.* She retired in 1941 and has remained a legendary figure.

Garcia (gar-CI-a), **Carlos Polestico** (1896–1971), Philippine statesman, b. Talibon, Bohol. He was a member of Philippine delegation to U.N. Conference on International Organization at San Francisco (1945). He served as vice-president of Philippines and succeeded to presidency upon the death of President Magsaysay (1957). He was later elected to a full term as president (1957–61).

García Íñiguez, Calixto (1836?–1898), Cuban lawyer and revolutionary, b. Holguín, Santiago. A revolutionary general during Spanish-American War (1898), he represented Cuba in negotiations with United States for Cuban independence (1898). He became a legendary figure through Elbert Hubbard's essay "A Message to García."

García Gutiérrez (gar-CI-a goot-YAIR-es), **Antonio,** Spanish dramatist **S** 370
García Lorca, Federico, Spanish writer **S** 372
Garcilaso de la Vega (gar-ci-LA-so day la VAY-ga), Spanish poet **S** 368
  history of the Incas **L** 70
Garda, Lake, north central Italy **L** 28
Garden, Alexander, Scottish naturalist and physician **S** 296

Garden, Mary (1874?–1967), American opera singer, b. Aberdeen, Scotland. Brought to America in 1883, she went to Paris to study singing in 1895. There she got a chance to sing the lead in *Louise* and was an immediate success. Returning to America, she became one of the great stars of the Chicago Opera Co. (1910–30). In 1921 and 1922 she was its director.

Garden Club of America, association of amateur gardening enthusiasts. It is concerned with promoting conservation, civic planting, and interest in gardening. Founded in 1913, with headquarters in New York, N.Y., it publishes the bimonthly *Bulletin.*

Gardenia (gar-DE-nia), any of several shrubs or small trees native to subtropical regions of the world. Its glossy leaves grow in groups of three or opposite each other along a branch. Its large, usually fragrant flowers, which may be yellow or white, are used in corsages.

Garden in Sochi, painting by Gorky **U** 119

Garden of Eden see Eden, Garden of
Garden of Gethsemane see Gethsemane, Garden of
Garden of the Gods, Colorado Springs, Colorado, picture **C** 411
Garden of the Gulf, P.E.I., Canada **P** 456b
Gardens and gardening **G** 26–52
  Aztec floating gardens **I** 195, 197; **L** 34; **M** 253; picture **L** 30
  Bellingrath Gardens, Alabama, picture **A** 123
  botanical gardens **Z** 379
  childhood gardens in Kenya **K** 228
  experiments with plants **E** 352, 356–58
  fertilizer **F** 95–98
  garden fruits **G** 297–301
  insecticides **I** 258
  lawns **L** 90–91
  Mexico City, floating gardens **I** 195, 197; **M** 253
  Netherlands **N** 119; picture **N** 117
  oriental garden, Brooklyn Botanical Garden, picture **Z** 375
  parks **P** 76
  plant pests **P** 288–89
  South Carolina gardens of interest **S** 304, 306
  terrariums **T** 102–04
  tractors **F** 57
  vegetables **V** 286–94
  weeds **W** 104–06
  wild-flower garden, picture **W** 171
  window garden, picture **H** 266
  See also Flowers; Lawns; Soils
Garden spiders **S** 385–86
Garden State, nickname for New Jersey **N** 164

Gardner, Erle Stanley (1889–1970), American lawyer and writer of detective stories, b. Malden, Mass. His detective novels featuring detective-lawyer Perry Mason include *The Case of the Borrowed Brunette* and *The Case of the Dangerous Dowager.*

Gardner, John William (1912–   ), American educator and government official, b. Los Angeles, Calif. President of the Carnegie Corporation of New York and the Carnegie Foundation for the Advancement of Teaching (since 1955), Gardner was appointed secretary of health, education, and welfare (1965). He resigned from the Cabinet in 1968 and returned to the Carnegie Foundation. Gardner received the Presidential Freedom Award in education (1964) and is the author of *Excellence: Can We Be Equal and Excellent Too?*

Garfield, James A., 20th president of United States **G** 53–56
Garfield, Lucretia Rudolph, wife of James A. Garfield **F** 173–74; picture **G** 54
Gargantua (gar-GAN-tu-a), circus gorilla **C** 304
Gargantua and Pantagruel, book by Rabelais, scene from **F** 437

Gargoyle (from French, meaning "throat"), an ornamental waterspout carved in grotesque human or animal form. In medieval architecture, it served to direct water from roof away from walls of building.

Garibaldi (gar-i-BALD-i), **Giuseppe,** Italian patriot and soldier **G** 57
  Italian unification **I** 457

Garibaldi, saltwater fish found along rocky shores of southern California and the Baja California peninsula. Adults are bright orange in color. The young fish, which are less than 4 in. long, are orange with iridescent blue spots and streaks.

Garland, Augustus H., American stateman   **A** 431
Garland, Hamlin, American writer   **W** 205–06
   local color in American literature   **A** 205

Garland, Judy (Frances Ethel Gumm) (1922–1969), American actress, b. Grand Rapids, Minn. She made her stage debut at 2½ and later became a child movie actress. Fame and an Academy Award rewarded her playing of Dorothy in *The Wizard of Oz* (1939), in which she sang "Over the Rainbow," later her theme song. She made many movies, concert and nightclub appearances.

Garlic, plant of onion family   **O** 118
   supposed medicinal powers   **F** 335
Garment industry see Clothing industry

Garner, Erroll (1921–   ), American jazz pianist and composer, Negro, b. Pittsburgh, Pa. Garner began as a nightclub pianist when he was 23. In the 1950's his concert tours and recordings brought him wide popularity. "Misty" is the best known of his many compositions.

Garner, John Nance, American statesman   **T** 135
   vice-president, United States   **V** 331; picture **V** 330
Garnerin (gar-ner-AN), **André Jacques,** French aeronaut   **B** 31; **P** 61

Garnet, Henry Highland (1815–1882), American clergyman and Negro abolitionist leader, b. Kent County, Md. Called "Thomas Paine of the abolitionist movement," he called on Negro slaves to go on strike collectively against their masters. He was made U.S. minister to Liberia (1881).

Garnets, gemstones   **G** 71; picture **G** 73
   abrasive for grinding and polishing   **G** 388
Garonne (ga-RONE) **River,** France   **R** 244
   river systems in France   **F** 408

Garrett, Pat (Patrick Floyd Garrett) (1850–1908), American lawman, b. Alabama. As sheriff of Lincoln County, N.Mex., he shot and killed his former friend Billy the Kid (1881). He wrote *The Authentic Life of Billy the Kid.*

Garrett, Robert, American athlete   **O** 110
Garrick, David, English actor and playwright   **E** 257
Garriott, Owen K., American astronaut   **S** 346
Garrison, William Lloyd, American abolitionist   **N** 94
Garrison Dam, North Dakota   **N** 325; picture **N** 324

Garter, Order of the, England's highest order of knighthood. Founded by King Edward III (about 1350), it was originally limited to 25 knights and the king. Later enlarged, it now includes the queen and other women. The insignias are a dark blue ribbon edged with gold, bearing the motto *Honi soit qui mal y pense* ("Shame to him who evil thinks"), and an emblem of St. George, the patron saint of the order. Knights of the Garter may use the abbreviated title K.G. after their names.

Garter snakes, pictures   **L** 239, 257; **S** 205
Garter stitch, in knitting   **K** 279

Garvey, Marcus (1887–1940), American leader of Negro nationalists, b. Jamaica, British West Indies. He founded Universal Negro Improvement Association (UNIA) in Jamaica (1914). He came to New York and published *Negro World* (1918–23) and established UNIA branches. He was deported to Jamaica for mail fraud (1927).

Gary, Indiana   **I** 148
Gas, fuel   **P** 511–12
   natural gas   **N** 56–57

Gas detectors, electric, for use in mines   **C** 364
Gaseous diffusion process, for separation of uranium isotopes   **U** 231
Gases   **G** 57–59
   air pollution   **A** 108–11
   atmosphere contains   **A** 479
   balloons and ballooning   **B** 30–34
   Boyle's law   **B** 354
   contrasted with crystalline solids   **C** 544
   earth's history   **E** 18
   Faraday's work   **F** 44
   fuels   **F** 488–89
   helium   **H** 107–08
   how heat changes matter   **H** 93
   liquid gases   **L** 308–09, 310
   matter, one of the states of   **M** 171, 174
   meters   **P** 511
   mining dangers   **M** 317
   natural gas   **N** 56–57
   noble gases   **N** 109–10
   origin of word for all airlike vapors   **C** 210
   oxygen   **O** 268–70
   poison gas in World War I   **W** 276–77
   public utility   **P** 511–12
   rocket fuels   **R** 257–58
   safety measures   **S** 3–4
   specific gravity   **F** 253
Gases in industry   **G** 59–62
   helium   **H** 107–08
   lighting   **L** 283
   liquid gases   **L** 308–09
   natural gas   **N** 56–57
   noble gases   **N** 109–10
   public utility   **P** 511–12
Gas lasers, devices projecting light beams   **G** 62
Gas masks
   charcoal filters in   **C** 106
Gas meters   **P** 512; picture **P** 511
Gasoline   **G** 63
   fuels   **F** 488
   internal-combustion engine process   **I** 304
   petroleum refining   **P** 174
   What is octane?   **G** 63
Gasoline engines   **E** 210–11

Gaspar, José (Gasparilla) (1756–1821), Spanish pirate. He stole a ship from the Spanish Navy and set up a base on Gasparilla Island, Fla. According to his diary, he and his gang robbed and sank 36 ships in 11 years. When Americans captured his ship, he jumped overboard and drowned. Tampa holds an annual Gasparilla Pirate Invasion Celebration.

Gaspée (gas-PAY), ship, incident leading to Revolutionary War   **R** 196
   Providence, R.I. residents in rebellion against the Stamp Act   **R** 226
Gaspé Peninsula, Quebec, Canada   **Q** 10a; picture **Q** 9
Gasperi, Alcide de see De Gasperi, Alcide
Gas pressure, a physical property of all gases   **P** 233
Gastric juice
   Beaumont's discovery of   **B** 109
Gastro-intestinal examination, of the body   **M** 208h
Gastropods, mollusks   **O** 276
Gas turbines   **T** 321–22
   engines, types of   **E** 211
   internal-combustion engines   **I** 308
   locomotives   **L** 328
   structure of the jet engine   **J** 85
Gas welding   **W** 119

Gates, Doris (1901–   ), American author of children's

Gates, Doris (continued)
books, b. Mountain View, Calif. She wrote *Blue Willow*, a story about desire of child in migrant camp for permanent home. Other books of hers are *Cat and Mrs. Cary, Sarah's Idea, Sensible Kate,* and *Trouble for Jerry.*

Gates, Horatio, American military leader   **R** 204
   Purple Heart awarded to   **M** 198
   rival of Washington   **W** 40
Gates of Paradise, doors   **R** 164; picture   **R** 165
Gate valves   V 270
Gateway Arch, memorial in St. Louis, designed by
   Saarinen   **S** 18
Gather, of glass   **G** 226, 230
Gatherers, Indian tribes of North America   **I** 172–80
Gathering, in bookbinding   **B** 327

Gatling, Richard Jordan (1818–1903), American inventor, b. Hertford County, N.C. He made numerous innovations in farm machinery, including a rice-sowing machine and motor-driven plow. During the Civil War he invented a marine steam ram and a rapid-fire (Gatling) gun that was officially adopted (1866) by U.S. Army.

Gatling guns, early machine guns   **G** 423; picture   **G** 424
GATT see General Agreement on Tariffs and Trade
Gattamelata, equestrian statue by Donatello   **I** 465
Gatún (ga-TOON) **Lake,** Panama Canal Zone   **P** 47
Gauchos, cowboys of South America   **R** 103
   Argentina   **A** 388–89; picture   **A** 391
   dances   **L** 69
   in Latin-American literature   **L** 71
   Uruguay   **U** 237

Gaudí (gau-DI), **Antonio** (Antoni Gaudí y Cornet) 1852–1926), Spanish architect, b. Reus, Tarragona. He used color and unconventional materials in such structures as *Casa Batlló* and *Casa Milá* in Barcelona. He is considered an unconventional Gothic revivalist and is noted for the fantastic and dramatic effects he used for the church of the Sagrada Familia in Barcelona.
   modern Spanish art   **S** 365

Gaugamela, battle of see Arbela, battle of
Gauge (GAGE), width of railroad tracks   **R** 77, 86
   importance to transportation   **T** 264
Gauguin (go-GAN), **Paul,** French painter   **G** 64
   modern art   **M** 388
   postimpressionism in France   **F** 431
   reaction against impressionism   **P** 29
   White Horse, The, painting   **G** 64
Gaul, Roman name for France and parts of bordering
   countries   **F** 403, 415
   Caesar's conquest of   **C** 6
   Charlemagne, ruler of   **C** 189
   early migrations of Gauls to England   **E** 215
Gauntlets, gloves, picture   **G** 240

Gauss (GOWSS), **Karl Friedrich** (1777–1855), German mathematician and astronomer, b. Brunswick. He is noted for his development of mathematical theories in algebra, analytical geometry, and electricity, and for his calculation of the orbits of the asteroids Ceres and Pallas. He also discovered that a circle can be divided into 17 equal arcs.
   non-Euclidean geometries   **M** 159

Gauss, unit of measure of a magnetic field   **M** 26
   sunspots and the earth   **E** 26
Gautama Buddha, Prince Siddhartha see Buddha
Gautier (go-ti-AY), **Théophile,** French poet
   ballet, *Giselle*   **B** 25

Gavarnie (ga-var-NIE), waterfall, France   **W** 56b
Gavials, reptiles   **C** 533–35;   **R** 181
Gavotte, dance   **D** 29
Gawaine, knight of King Arthur's court   **A** 442
   Arthurian legends in English literature   **E** 247–48
Gay, John, English playwright   **E** 257
   satire   **H** 280
   writer of fables   **F** 4

Gayarré (ga-yar-RAY), **Charles Etienne Arthur** (1805–1895), American historian, b. New Orleans, La. In 1830 he published his first work on Louisiana history and was elected to the state legislature. Elected to the U.S. Senate in 1835, he was forced by illness to resign. He wrote a four-volume *History of Louisiana.*

Gay-Lussac (gay-lu-SOC), **Joseph Louis** (1778–1850), French chemist and physicist, b. St. Leonard. He is noted for his work on the way gases combine to form a new substance. He developed the first method fo obtaining the elements potassium and boron and also made the first balloon flight for scientific purposes.

Gay nineties, the American term for the 1890's, the last decade of the 19th century. In England this period is called the naughty nineties.

Gaza Strip, United Arab Republic
   leads down to Negev region of Israel   **I** 441, 445
Gazelles (ga-ZELLS), hoofed mammals   **H** 221; picture
   H 217
Gazetteers (gaz-et-TEERS), type of reference book   **R** 129
Gazettes, newspapers or official governmental publications
   early colonial newspapers often called gazettes   **N** 198
G clef, or treble clef, in musical notation   **M** 525
GCS system see Gram-centimeter-second
Gdansk (g'DONSK), formerly Danzig, Poland   **P** 360, 361, 362
   World War II   **W** 286
Gear pumps   P 530
Gears, toothed wheels that pass along motion and power
   G 65–66
   differential gears   **A** 544
   planetary gears   **T** 256
   pumps   **P** 530
   toothed wheels in watches and clocks   **W** 45
   transmissions   **T** 255–56
   wheels   **W** 158
Gebal see Byblos, Lebanon
Geber (GHE-ber), or Jābir ibn-Hayyān, Arabian alchemist
   C 207
Geckos, lizards, pictures   **L** 318, 320

Geddes (GED-des), **Norman Bel** (1893–1958), American designer and architect, b. Adrian, Mich. He designed stage sets for the Metropolitan Opera (after 1918) and for theater productions, including *The Miracle* and *Hamlet.* He also designed furniture, introduced streamlining to automobiles, railroad cars, ocean liners, and airline interiors, and created a city plan for Toledo, Ohio (1945).
   industrial design   **I** 232

Geertgen tot Sint Jans (GAIRT-gen tot sint YONS), Dutch
   painter ·   **D** 352
   painting, *Saint John the Baptist in the Wilderness*
   D 354
Geese
   animal communication   **A** 275
   diving birds have adaptations to habitats   **B** 223
   flight feathers   **B** 200
   migration   **H** 187

poultry **P** 423
  snow geese, picture **L** 248
  young Canada geese, picture **B** 214
Ge'ez, ancient Semitic language **E** 296
  Ethiopian literature **A** 76b
Gefion (GEV-yon), heroine of Norse legend **D** 106
Gegs, people of Albania **A** 144

Gehrig, Lou (Henry Louis Gehrig) (1903–1941), American baseball player, b. New York, N.Y. Called the Iron Man, he set record for appearance in consecutive games (2,130). He set numerous batting records as first baseman of New York Yankees (1925–39). He was made a member of Baseball's Hall of Fame (1939).

Geiger (GUY-ger), **Hans**, German scientist **G** 67
Geiger counter **G** 67–68
  air pollution check, picture **A** 111
  atoms detected by **A** 488
  carbon-14 dating **R** 65–66
  cosmic rays studied by **C** 512
  ions detect radioactivity **I** 353
  mines and mining **M** 314
  uranium **U** 231
Geisel, Theodor Seuss see Seuss, Dr.

Geishas (GAI-shas), Japanese girls trained from childhood as professional hostesses. Geishas are skilled in conversation and in singing, dancing, and playing the samisen. Geishas have been a Japanese institution since the 18th century, but their number is declining.
  Japanese dance **J** 32; picture **D** 32

Geissler (GUY-sler) **tube**, glass tube containing thin gas that produces light when electricity is passed through it. It was designed (1858) by Heinrich Geissler, a German inventor. Fluorescent tubes and neon lights are among the direct outgrowths of this invention.

Gelatin, protein substance obtained from bones, skin, and connective tissue of animal bodies. Gelatin is brittle, yellowish white, tasteless, and odorless. Dissolved in hot water, it cools to form a gel that holds other substances in suspension. It is used in the manufacture of certain foods, such as ice cream and candy. Easily digested, gelatin has a number of medical and scientific uses.
  photography, use in **P** 212

Gelatin dynamite, explosive **E** 392
Gélinas, Gratien, French-Canadian actor-producer **C** 63
Gellée, Claude see Claude Lorrain
Gellert, Christian, German writer **G** 175
Gemara (ghem-AR-a), Jewish Oral Law **J** 116, 119
  Talmud **T** 15
Gemini, constellation **C** 492
  sign of, picture **S** 244
Gemini, series of manned U.S. space flights in capsules designed to carry two astronauts
  space flight data **S** 344
Geminiani (jay-meen-YA-ni), **Francesco**, Italian violinist and composer **V** 343
Geminid, meteor shower **C** 420
Gemology, science of gems **G** 71
Gem State, nickname for Idaho **I** 54, 55
Gemstones **G** 68–76
  ancient Greek art **G** 348
  Ceylon, gem mines of **C** 179; picture **C** 178
  crystals especially cut for gemstones **C** 542
  diamonds **D** 153–56
  gem quartz **Q** 7
  jade **J** 9–10
  jewelry **J** 92–94; pictures **J** 97, 98

pearls **P** 113–15
  Where are gemstones found? **G** 70
  See also Precious stones
Gendarmes (JON-darmes), French police **P** 374; picture **P** 373
Genealogical (ge-ne-a-LOJ-ic-al) **Society Library**, Salt Lake City, Utah **U** 249

Genealogy (ge-ne-OL-ogy), history of the descent of a person, family, or group, arrived at by tracing ancestors and descendants in natural line of succession.

Genera, divisions of biological classification **T** 29
General, The, aquatint and collage by Kohn **G** 306
General Agreement on Tariffs and Trade (GATT) **I** 329
  international tariff co-operation **T** 25; **U** 86
General Allotment Act (Dawes Act), 1887 **I** 200
General Assembly, United Nations **U** 82–83
General delivery, mail service **P** 410

General Education Board (GEB), an organization founded by John D. Rockefeller, Sr., to promote education among all persons in the United States, regardless of race, sex, or religion. It functioned from 1902 to 1965.

General Mining Laws, 1872 **C** 485
General Motors Corporation
  Soap Box Derby, sponsors of **S** 215
General practitioners, doctors **D** 239
General Revision Act, 1891 **P** 507

General staff, Army, group of specially trained military officers who assist their commanders in such areas as logistics (details of transport, quartering, etc., of troops), operations, and personnel. The U.S. general staff was established in 1903.

General theory of relativity **R** 143–44
Generation of 1898, Spanish literature **S** 371
Generators, electric see Electric generators
Genes, molecules determining heredity **G** 77
Genesis (GEN-e-sis), first book of the Bible **B** 154
  commentaries among Dead Sea Scrolls **D** 48

Genêt (jen-AY), **Citizen** (Edmond Charles Édouard Genêt) (1763–1834), French diplomat, b. Versailles. Genêt, first French minister to United States, tried to draw the United States into France's war with England and Spain by arousing public sympathy and arming U.S. privateers. He was replaced (1794) at request of President Washington.
  Jefferson and Genêt **J** 67

Genetics (gen-ET-ics) **G** 77–88
  adaptation results from genetic differences **L** 216
  cancer research **C** 94–95
  DNA molecular theory of heredity **B** 293
  evolutionary change **E** 346
  Mendel's studies in heredity **B** 196; **M** 219
  mutation theory in biology **C** 94–95; **E** 346
  studies in biochemistry **B** 184
  transduction process **V** 365; diagram **V** 366
Genets, catlike animals **G** 89–90
Geneva (gen-E-va), **Lake**, between France and Switzerland **L** 28
Geneva, Switzerland **S** 498–99
  center of Protestantism under Calvin **C** 30
  headquarters of the League of Nations **L** 96
  memorial to Protestant Reformation, pictures **C** 287; **P** 482
Geneva Bible **B** 153
Geneva Conventions, Red Cross treaties **R** 126; **S** 499
  flags **F** 226

Geneva Summit Conference, meeting (July, 1955) of leaders of East and West to discuss disarmament, European security, cultural and economic interchange, and German reunification on basis of free elections. Talks were inconclusive but led to long series of disarmament conferences.

Genghis Khan (GEN-ghis KAHN), Mongol warrior and empire builder **G** 93
  conquests in China **C** 270; **M** 416
  Mongolia **M** 416
  Soviet Central Asia **U** 46

Genie (GE-nie), English form of word "jinni," the name for a supernatural spirit or demon of Arabic and Islamic folklore. Genies were generally evil but were sometimes useful. They usually took the form of an animal, such as goat or snake, but were often thought to be humans which could change shape and size. Genies have been immortalized in such stories as "Aladdin."
  "Alladin and the Wonderful Lamp," excerpt **A** 345–46

Genius, person having highly developed intellectual and creative capacities. In Roman religion, a genius was a guardian spirit, assigned to every man at birth, that determined his character and future. A man with extraordinary intelligence or creativeness was referred to as a genius, since it was believed that he was under special control of his guiding spirit, or genius.

Genoa, Italy **I** 450; picture **E** 329
Genocide, attempt to destroy an entire people because of their race or religion **C** 316

Genre (JON-ra) **art,** painting that uses scenes of everyday life for its subject matter. The tradition of genre art was established in 16th-century Flanders by Bosch, Breughel and others. It is represented in work of impressionists such as Manet and Renoir and in modern social realism.
  Breughel and Bosch **B** 414–15; **D** 352; **P** 23
  Dutch and Flemish art **D** 357; **P** 23

Gentians, group of flowering plants, usually growing wild. They are native to Europe, Asia, and North America. They generally grow in high mountain pastures and meadows. Most varieties are blue, but some varieties, which grow in the Alps, are bright yellow. The roots are used as medicine. Two common varieties are the bottle, or closed, gentian and the fringed gentian.

Gentian violet, purple dye used as medicine **D** 370
Gentile da Fabriano, Italian artist
  Adoration of the Magi, painting **U** 2

Gentiles (from Latin *gens,* meaning "race"), in Old and New Testaments, foreigners or non-Jewish people, particularly Christians.

Gentleman, man of noble birth **K** 275, 277
Gentleman's Magazine, The **M** 14

Gentlemen's agreement, an agreement in which parties are bound only by their honor.
  applications in restrictions on immigration **I** 100

Genus (GE-nus) (plural genera), a division of biological classification **T** 29
Genus of a surface, in topology **T** 225–26

Geocentric theory, theory developed from earlier theories around A.D. 150 by Ptolemy, astronomer of Alexandria, Egypt. It states that the earth is the center of the universe and that the planets, the sun, and the stars revolve around it. This theory was accepted for hundreds of years. In the 16th century Copernicus' heliocentric theory, which says that the earth and planets revolve around the sun, began to replace it.

Geochemistry, chemistry of earth's crust
  ore location method **M** 313–14
Geodesic dome, of Buckminster Fuller **I** 232
Geodesy (ge-OD-esy), branch of mathematics which determines the exact position of geographical points
  satellites locate points on earth's surface **S** 43
  surveying, use in **S** 479
  twentieth-century cartography **M** 94–95
Geodetic (geo-DET-ic) **surveying** **S** 479
Geoffrey (GEF-frey) **of Monmouth,** Welsh historian **A** 445
  source of the Arthurian legends **E** 247
Geography **G** 94–108
  atlases **M** 93; **R** 129
  climate, types of **C** 343–48
  deserts **D** 123–31
  dinosaur extinction result of changes in **D** 181
  direction, how to tell **D** 182–83
  equator **E** 272h
  exploration and discovery **E** 368–88
  food habits depend on where you live **F** 332–33
  gazetteers **R** 129
  geographical barriers to spread of life **L** 235
  geographical races of man **R** 32
  glaciers **G** 223–25
  globes, grid lines on **M** 90
  Greenwich Observatory's prime meridian **G** 372
  islands and island groups **I** 423–37
  lakes **L** 25–34
  maps and globes **M** 88–95
  mountains **M** 492–99
  oceans and seas **O** 45–49
  Polar regions **P** 363–71
  races of man, geographical differences **R** 29–32
  rivers **R** 237–49
  seasons **S** 108–12
  social studies **S** 223
  surveying **S** 479–80
  taiga **T** 10–11
  tropics **T** 294–95
  waterfalls **W** 56b–57
  world **W** 254–69
Geological Survey, United States **C** 485
  map making by the Topographic Branch **M** 94
  provides maps of possible fossil-bearing rock areas **F** 380
Geological time scale, of geologic eras **F** 384–88; **G** 113
  prehistoric animals **P** 436–38
Geology **G** 109–21
  archeological studies **A** 360
  caves and caverns **C** 152–58
  coal formation **C** 362–63
  earthquakes **E** 31–40
  earth's interior **E** 8
  geologic analysis in search for minerals **M** 313–14
  geysers and hot springs **G** 192–93
  glaciers **G** 223–25
  ice ages **I** 13–24
  landforms, of Massachusetts **M** 136
  mountains **M** 493
  ocean floor **E** 14; **G** 119–20
  petroleum geology **P** 169–71
  radioactive dating **R** 64–66
  rocks, minerals, and ores **R** 263–73
  soils **S** 230–34

time scales, fossils **F** 383, 384, 387, 388
underwater research by aquanauts **U** 21
volcanoes **V** 377–86
See also Geophysics
Geometry and geometric forms **G** 122–31
branch of mathematics **M** 154–55
Descartes' analytic geometry **D** 123
geometry in the new math **M** 168
surveying **S** 479–80
topology **T** 220–26
Geomorphology (geo-mor-PHOL-ogy), study of landforms **G** 108
Geophones, instruments that receive reflected shock waves **P** 171
Geophysics **G** 118–21
earth's interior **E** 8
IGY studies **I** 315–16
research by physicists **P** 238

George, Henry (1839–1897), American economist, b. Philadelphia, Pa. He originated the single-tax theory—a tax on land values only—formulated in his most famous book, *Progress and Poverty.*

George, Jean Craighead (1919–   ), American author and illustrator of children's books, b. Washington, D.C. She is remembered for books about animals, often written in collaboration with her former husband, **John L.** (1916–   ), who directed conservation programs and contributed numerous scientific articles to magazines and journals. Their books include *Vision, the Mink.*

George I, king of Great Britain **E** 225
George II, king of Great Britain **E** 225
William Pitt, Earl of Chatham, opposes the king **P** 265
George III, king of Great Britain **D** 59, 61
American Revolutionary War **R** 196
Pitt, William, the Younger **P** 265
George V, king of Great Britain **E** 179, 230; picture **W** 270
George VI, king of Great Britain **E** 179

George, Saint (?–303?), legendary historic Christian martyr, b. probably Cappadocia. He is patron saint of England. The most famous legend about him tells of his killing a dragon and rescuing the king's daughter, Sabra (representing the triumph of Church over Devil).

George Cross, Great Britain's award to civilians
Malta awarded **M** 60

George Junior Republic, a self-governing community for young people (16–21 years). Located in Freeville, N.Y., it consists of a community farm and industries. It was founded in 1895 by William Reuben George.

Georgetown, capital of Guyana **G** 396
Georgetown, P.E.I., Canada **P** 456e
Georgetown University, Washington, D.C. **W** 34
George Washington, portrait by Gilbert Stuart **U** 118, **W** 37
George Washington Birthplace National Monument **V** 354
George Washington Carver Foundation **C** 129
Georgia **G** 132–47
American colonies **A** 193–94
colonial life in America **C** 385–99
Founding fathers of the United States **F** 395
Oglethorpe, James, founded state **O** 59
places of interest in Negro history **N** 94
Georgia, University of **G** 139
Georgiana Seymour, painting by Reynolds **E** 239

Georgian Bay, arm of Lake Huron **G** 327
Georgian Soviet Socialist Republic (Georgia) **U** 45
languages of the U.S.S.R. **U** 28
Mtskheta, former capital, picture **U** 47
Stalin, Joseph **S** 395
Georgian style, in art and architecture **E** 240
antique furniture **A** 318
furniture design **F** 507

Georgia Warm Springs Foundation, foundation that operates hospital at Warm Springs, Ga., to train personnel and rehabilitate victims of infantile paralysis and other neuromuscular diseases.

Georgie Porgie, nursery rhyme **N** 403
Geosynclines (geo-SIN-clines), geological formations
earth's crust **E** 10, 11
mountains **M** 493
Geotropism (ge-OT-rop-ism), plant movements **P** 301
Geraniums (ge-RAY-niums), flowers, pictures **G** 38, 48

Gerbil (JER-bil), a small, brownish rodent native to dry, sandy areas of Africa and southwestern Asia. A gerbil usually measures some 3 to 5 inches in length and has an equally long tail. Gerbils eat seeds and leaves and need little water. They breed rapidly—a female can produce a litter (usually 4 gerbils) once a month. Gerbils are clean and playful and make wonderful pets.

Geriatrics (ge-ri-AT-rics), branch of medicine dealing with diseases of old age **O** 98
aging **A** 81–87
today's problem diseases **D** 218
Géricault (jay-ri-CO), **Théodore,** French painter **F** 426; **P** 29
Raft of the Medusa, painting **F** 427
Gerlache (ger-LOSH), **Adrion de,** Belgian explorer **P** 366
German art and architecture **G** 165–71
Dresden porcelain **P** 418
etching **E** 293
modern art **M** 391
painting in the Renaissance **R** 171
16th-century painting **P** 23
German Democratic Republic (East Germany) **G** 148, 157, 158, 164
Berlin **B** 143–45
English language **E** 243–45
flag **F** 239
Germanic, or Teutonic, **languages** **L** 39
Europe **E** 317
Germanic, or Teutonic, **tribes**
invasion of Roman Empire at beginning of the Middle Ages **M** 289–90
Germanium (ger-MAY-ni-um), element **E** 154, 161
German language **G** 172–73
German and Norse names in Norse myths **N** 280
Switzerland **S** 495
German literature **G** 174–81
contributions to art of the novel **N** 347
drama **D** 297, 298
fairy and folk tales **F** 20–21
fairytale, *The Enchanted Princess* **F** 23–25
Faust legends **F** 72–73
Grimm brothers' fairy and folktales **G** 376–86
See also names of chief writers, as Goethe, Johann
German measles, or rubella, virus disease **D** 196
mental retardation caused by **R** 190
German music **G** 181–89
chorales, German hymns **G** 182; **H** 311–12
opera begins with early *Singspiel* **O** 133
See also names of German composers

German shepherd dog, picture **D** 255
German silver *see* Nickel silver
Germans in America **A** 192
Germantown, battle of, 1777 **R** 203
Germany **G** 148–64
  Berlin **B** 143–45
  Bismarck, Otto von **B** 250
  Christmas tree custom started in **C** 291
  costumes, traditional Bavarian, picture **C** 349
  dairy cattle, picture **A** 98
  favorite foods **F** 340
  flags to 1945 **F** 227
  history *see* Germany, history of
  national dances **D** 30
  Nazism **N** 69–71
  Reformation **C** 285–86
  synthetic dyes **D** 370
  toy making, center of **T** 231
Germany, Democratic Republic of *see* German Democratic Republic
Germany, East *see* German Democratic Republic
Germany, Federal Republic of (West Germany) **G** 148, 156, 157–58, 164
  Berlin **B** 143–45
  flag **F** 239
  national anthem **N** 18
  theater **T** 160
Germany, history of **G** 158–64
  Charlemagne **C** 189–90
  Frederick the Great **F** 456
  Hilter, Adolf **H** 139–40
  Holy Roman Empire **H** 161–64
  Nazism **N** 69–71
  war crimes trials **W** 9–10
  World War I, 1914–18 **W** 270–81
  World War II, 1939–45 **W** 282–308
Germany, West *see* Germany, Federal Republic of
Germicides, chemicals that kill germs **D** 222
Germination, of plants **P** 299
  sprouting stages of seeds **F** 283
Germs, microorganisms **M** 274
  antibiotics, germ-killing **A** 310–16
  antiseptics **D** 222
  detergents and soaps destroy **D** 146
  disinfectants **D** 222
  germ theory of disease **D** 214–15; **P** 96
  medical laboratory tests **M** 201, 209
  sanitation to check spread of germs **S** 32–34
  types of disease caused by **D** 186
  See also Bacteria
Germ warfare *see* Bacteriological warfare
Gernsback, Hugo, author and publisher **S** 84–85
Geronimo (ge-RON-im-o), Indian leader **G** 189; **I** 195
Gerontology (ger-on-TOL-ogy), study of aging **A** 84–87
  old age **O** 96–100
  today's problem diseases **D** 218

Gerry, Elbridge (1744–1814), American statesman, b. Marblehead, Mass. The word **gerrymander**, meaning unfair division of voting districts, comes from his name. While governor of Massachusetts (1810–12), he won passage of a bill to redistrict the state that gave advantage to Republicans. Earlier he was a signer of the Declaration of Independence and a member of the Continental Congress (1776–81, 1782–85) and the Constitutional Convention (1787). In 1797 and 1798 he served on the XYZ mission to France. He was elected vice-president in 1812. Picture **V** 325.

Gershwin, George, American composer **G** 190
  musical comedy **M** 542
  Porgy and Bess, opera **O** 151

Gershwin, Ira, American lyricist **G** 190
  musical comedy **M** 542
Gersoppa (gher-SOP-pa) Falls, India **W** 56b

Gesell (g'ZELL), Arnold Lucius (1880–1961), American psychologist and pediatrician, b. Alma, Wis. He founded (1911) the Yale Clinic of Child Development. He is the author of many books and co-author of *The First Five Years* and *The Child from Five to Ten*.

Gesner (GHES-ner), Abraham, Canadian doctor **K** 235
Gesso (JESSO), paste of chalk and glue **A** 238
  use on Roman book or codex **B** 319
Gestapo (ghes-TA-po), Nazi German police **P** 374

Gestation period, period (in mammals) from fertilization of an egg cell to birth of the young. The length of the gestation period varies according to species.
  pregnancy and birth of mammals **M** 71–73

Gestido, Oscar, Uruguayan political leader **U** 239
Gethsemane (geth-SEM-an-e), Garden of, Jerusalem **J** 80
  Jesus Christ **J** 84
Gettysburg, battle of, 1863 **B** 102; **C** 325–26, 460
  Lee, Robert E., suffers defeat **L** 126
Gettysburg Address, by Abraham Lincoln **G** 191; **L** 297
Gettysburg National Military Park, Pennsylvania **P** 138; picture **P** 139
  Cemetery Hill **N** 30
Geyserite (GUY-ser-ite), mineral **G** 193
Geysers (GUY-sers) **G** 192–93
  Nevada's area near Beowawe **N** 132
  Old Faithful, picture **Y** 345
Geysir, great hot spring, Iceland **I** 42
Gezo (GHE-zo), king of Dahomey **D** 4
G-force, of gravity **G** 324–25
  effect on the body **S** 340j–340k
Ghalib, Indian poet **O** 220e
Ghana (GHA-na) **G** 194–98
  early western African empires **A** 66–67; **N** 90
  flag **F** 235
  industries, pictures **A** 63
  Nkrumah, Kwame **N** 262f
  Peace Corps teacher, picture **P** 103
Ghana, University of **G** 195; picture **G** 196
Ghardaïa (ghar-DA-ya), Algeria, picture **A** 162
Ghebers (GHE-bers), Zoroastrians in Iran **Z** 380
Ghee, clarified butter **F** 340
  dairy product of India **D** 12
Ghent, Belgium
  guildhalls, picture **G** 401
Ghent, Treaty of, 1814 **J** 5
  Adams, John Quincy signs **A** 13
  Clay, signer of **C** 335
  end of War of 1812 **W** 13
Ghettos, restricted city areas **J** 108
  ghetto riots **N** 104b
  poverty in the United States **P** 424a
  segregation **S** 114
  Warsaw, 1943 uprising **P** 362
Ghibellines *see* Guelphs and Ghibellines
Ghiberti (ghi-BAIR-ti), Lorenzo, Italian sculptor **I** 467–68; **S** 99
  Gates of Paradise, doors, picture **R** 165
  Renaissance art **R** 163–64

Ghirlandaio (ghere-lon-DA-yo), Domenico (Domenico di Tommaso Bigordi) (1449–1494), Italian painter and mosaicist, b. Florence. A teacher of Michelangelo, he helped decorate Sistine Chapel in Rome. His paintings include *An Old Man and His Grandson*.

Ghist, Christopher see Gist, Christopher
Ghor, Jordan River Valley J 137
Ghost crabs S 168; picture S 169
Ghost Dance, of the Plains Indians I 169; pictures
  I 161, 169
  Indian music of religious ceremonies I 160
  Messiah War, 1890, in South Dakota S 327
  modern myth M 563
Ghosts, play by Henrik Ibsen I 2
Ghosts, word game W 238
Ghost towns, abandoned towns
  places of interest in Nevada N 132
Ghostweed see Snow-on-the-mountain
Ghostwriting, writing for someone else who gets credit as
  author W 318–19
  autobiographies B 186

GI, U.S. Army term for American soldier. The abbreviation comes from the description of army equipment as
"government issue."

Giacobini's (gia-co-BI-ni's) comet, picture
  R 74

Giacometti (gi-oc-o-MAY-ti), Alberto (1901–66), Swiss
sculptor and painter, b. Stampa. Early in his career he
was associated with cubism. His later sculptures were
surrealistic. His interest in movement and space was
expressed in sculptures of elongated human figures,
designed to express modern pessimism. His works include Walking Man, Man Pointing, and City Square.
  modern sculpture M 395; S 105

Giant clams A 265; G 200
Giant pandas
  in Peking Zoo, picture Z 376
  wildlife in Asia A 451

Giants, in Greek mythology, a race of monsters who
sprang from the blood of Uranus. Subsequently they
stormed heaven but were defeated by the gods and were
buried under various volcanic mountains in Italy.

Giants, of nature G 199–204
  giraffes, special adaptations G 212
  largest animals A 262–63
Giant stars S 407
Giap, Vo Nguyen see Vo Nguyen Giap, Vietnamese leader

Giauque (gi-OKE), William Francis (1895–   ), American chemist, b. Niagara Falls, Canada. He is noted for
his discovery of the isotopes (different forms) of oxygen
and for his method of producing and maintaining
extremely low temperatures. He received the 1949 Nobel
prize in chemistry, mainly for his research on the
behavior of substances at extremely low temperatures.

Gibberellins (jib-ber-ELL-ins), group of substances, including gibberelic acid, that stimulate plant growth.
They are used to increase the size and extend the growing season of many crops.

Gibbon (GHIB-bon), Edward (1737–1794), English historian, b. Putney. He is best-known for his accurate and
authoritative work The Decline and Fall of the Roman
Empire, which viewed the Roman Empire as continuing
until the fall of Constantinople (1453). He described history as "little more than the register of the crimes, follies,
and misfortunes of mankind."

Gibbons, Grinling, English wood carver W 228
  decorative wood pieces for Charles II E 237

Gibbons, Orlando, English composer C 185
Gibbons, primates M 419
  social organization A 281
Gibbons v. Ogden, case in constitutional law M 112
Gibbous (JIB-us) moon M 447
Gibbs (GHIBBS), Josiah W., American scientist C 215

GI Bill of Rights, U.S. government-sponsored program for
veterans of military service. It provides for loans for
businesses and homes, vocational training and education,
and medical and other benefits. The original GI Bill, the
Servicemen's Readjustment Act of 1944, was passed by
Congress for veterans of World War II. Similar bills were
passed by Congress in 1952 and in 1967.

Gibraltar G 205

Gibran (ji-BRON), Kahlil (1883–1931), Lebanese-Ameri-
can poet and artist, b. Baherri, Lebanon. While still in
his teens he was known throughout the Middle East for
his plays and prose poems in Arabic. He later settled
in New York, N.Y., where he wrote in English. His most
famous book is The Prophet (1923), a series of prose
poems on topics such as good and evil, love, and religion.

Gibson, Althea, American tennis champion G 206

Gibson, Bob (Robert) (1935–   ), American baseball player,
Negro, b. Omaha, Neb. He overcame delicate health in
childhood to become a great athlete. He was all-state basketball player, and shortstop and pitcher while at Creighton
University in Omaha. He played with the Harlem Globetrotters before joining the St. Louis Cardinals. Gibson
pitched the Cardinals to world championships in the World
Series of 1964 and 1967. In 1968 he set a new World
Series record when he struck out 17 batters in one game.

Gibson, Charles Dana (1867–1944), American illustrator,
b. Roxbury, Mass. Well-known for society cartoons, he
created the "Gibson Girl," representing fashionable lady
of the 1890's.
  "Gibson girl," illustration I 92

Gibson, Edward G., American astronaut S 346
Gibson, Kenneth A., American mayor N 101; picture
  N 104a
Gide (GEDE), André, French novelist F 442

Gideon, in Old Testament (Book of Judges). As judge, he
raised army and saved Israelites by defeating Midianites.
Gideon was offered kingship by his people but refused it.

Gideons International (GI), Christian organization that
places Bibles in hotels, hospitals, schools, prisons, and
military camps. It was founded in 1899, and its
headquarters is in Nashville, Tenn. It publishes The
Gideon.

Gielgud (GIL-good), Sir John (Arthur John Gielgud)
(1904–   ), English stage and screen actor, b. London. He
produced and acted in Shakespeare's plays at Stratford-
on-Avon and has played Hamlet more than 500 times.

Gieseking (GHE-se-king), Walter Wilhelm (1895–1956),
German pianist, b. Lyons, France. He was noted
interpreter of both classical and modern composers, but
particularly French impressionists.

Gifford Pinchot (GHIF-ford PIN-cho) National Forest,
  Washington, picture N 37
Gift, The (Le Cadeau), dada sculpture by Man Ray
  M 393; picture M 394

Gift of the Magi, The, short story by O. Henry **H** 110–13
Gifts
Christmas **C** 291–92
gift wrapping **G** 206–09
New Year customs **N** 208–09
Gift wrapping G 206–09
making your own gift-wrapping paper **I** 224
Gila (HE-la) **monsters,** lizards **L** 320
Gila River, Arizona **A** 404
Gila Trail O 259
Gilbert, Henry F., American composer **U** 126

Gilbert, Sir Humphrey (1539?–1583), English soldier and navigator, b. Compton. Half brother of Sir Walter Raleigh, he wrote *Discourse of a Discovery for a New Passage to Cataia,* urging discovery of a northwest passage. In 1583 he established first English colony in North America at St. Johns, Newfoundland.
early exploration of America **A** 180; **C** 68

Gilbert, William, English physicist **G** 119
contributions to physics **P** 235
electricity discoveries **E** 123
new experimental approach to science **S** 67
theory of earth's magnetic field **M** 26
Gilbert, Sir William S., English playwright and librettist **G** 209–11
Gilbert and Ellice Islands, Pacific Ocean **P** 6
Gilbert and Sullivan operettas G 209–11
delightfully English music **E** 271
"pirated" **T** 245
Gilded One, legendary ruler *see* El Dorado

Gilels (GHE-lels), **Emil Grigoryevich** (1916–), Soviet pianist, b. Odessa. He won first prize at International Competition for Pianists at Brussels (1918) and has taught at Moscow Conservatory for many years.

Gill, Eric, English sculptor **E** 241

Gillette, William (1855–1937), American actor and playwright, b. Hartford, Conn. During his long career he played both in classics and in his own original plays, such as *Secret Service.* He is most famous as the star of his own adaptation of *Sherlock Holmes* (1899).

Gill (GHILL) **fungi F** 498–500
Gills, of fishes **F** 186
horseshoe crabs **H** 245
sharks, skates, and rays **S** 140, 142
Gills, of mushrooms **F** 498; **M** 521
Gilmore, Patrick S., Irish-American band leader **B** 40

Gilpin, Charles Sidney (1878–1930), American actor, Negro, b. Richmond, Va. Gilpin was manager of the first all-Negro stock company in New York City (1916). His most famous role was the lead in Eugene O'Neill's *Emperor Jones* (1920). He received the Spingarn medal (1921).

Gilpin, Joshua and Thomas, Delaware paper manufacturers **D** 93
Gimbals
used to steer rockets **R** 260
Gin, a distilled beverage **W** 159
Gin, cotton *see* Cotton gin

Ginastera (he-na-STAIR-a), **Alberto Evaristo** (1916–), Argentine composer, b. Buenos Aires. His most widely known work is the opera *Bomarzo.* Prolific and versatile, he has also written chamber music, choral works, dances, and symphonies.

Ginevra de' Benci, painting by Leonardo da Vinci **R** 168
Ginger, spice **S** 382; picture **S** 381
Gingerbread boy, picture **F** 303
Gingerbread House, "Hansel and Gretel," picture **G** 383
Gingko (GHINK-go), tree, picture **T** 275
living fossil **E** 347
Gin rummy, card game **C** 115

Ginsberg, Allen (1926–), American poet, b. Newark, N.J. With the publication of his volume *Howl and Other Poems* in 1955, Ginsberg was recognized as a spokesman for the "beat" movement in American literature and as a unique critic of contemporary society. In the 1960's he became increasingly involved in peace movements and in Eastern religious and ethical thought. His poetry includes *Reality Sandwiches* (1963) and *TV Baby Poems* (1968).

Ginseng (GIN-seng), plant **P** 314
Ginza, street in Tokyo, Japan **T** 206–07; pictures **J** 39, **T** 206
major cities of Japan **J** 40
Ginzberg, Asher *see* Ahad Ha-am
Gioconda, La *see* Mona Lisa
Giordano (gior-DA-no), **Umberto,** Italian composer
Andrea Chenier, opera **O** 140

Giorgione (jor-JO-nay) (Zorzi da Castelfranco) (1478?–1510), Italian painter, b. Castelfranco Veneto. A student of Giovanni Bellini, Giorgione became one of the leading Venetian painters. Among his works are *The Three Philosophers* and *The Sleeping Venus.* Giorgione's luminous style influenced a number of Venetian artists, particularly Titian.
Renaissance painting in Venice **I** 469, 470; **R** 169; **T** 199

Giotto di Bondone (gi-OT-to di bon-DO-nay), Italian painter **G** 211
Descent from the Cross, The, painting **P** 19
Flight into Egypt, painting **I** 461
Joachim and the Shepherds, painting **G** 211
Meeting at the Golden Gate, painting **R** 164
naturalism in Italian art **I** 463–64
Renaissance art **R** 163
tempera painting **P** 18
Giraffes G 212; picture **C** 488
Africa, picture **A** 51
giants of nature **G** 199–200
hoofed mammals **H** 220
Lamarck's theory of long necks **E** 344
life, adaptation to other adaptations **L** 217
Girard (gi-RARD), **Stephen,** French-born American merchant **P** 143

Giraudoux (gi-ro-DOO), **Jean** (Hippolyte Jean Giraudoux) (1882–1944), French playwright, novelist, and diplomat, b. Bellac. He is famous for such plays as *La Guerre de Troie N'Aura Pas Lieu* (*Tiger at the Gates*), *La Folle de Chaillot* (*The Madwoman of Chaillot*), *Ondine,* and *Electre.* Many of his plays are based on Greek myths.
French literature, history of **F** 441

Girl Guides Association G 213–15
See also Girl Scouts
Girls' camps *see* Camping, organized
Girls Clubs of America G 220
Girl Scouts of the United States of America G 213, 215–19
badges for roller-skating **R** 284
See also Girl Guides Association

Girls' Day, or **Feast of Dolls,** Japan **H** 158; **J** 31

Girls State, leadership program sponsored by state auxiliaries of National American Legion Auxiliary. It enables girls of high school age to participate in mock state government. Sessions are held annually. Two representatives from each Girls State session are chosen to attend Girls Nation in Washington, D.C.

Girl with a Bowl of Fruit (Lavinia), painting by Titian **I** 471
Girl with a Watering Can, painting by Renoir **N** 41
Gironde estuary, of the Garonne River, France **F** 408; **R** 244
Girtin (GHIR-tin), **Thomas,** English painter **E** 241

Girty (GUR-ty), **Simon** ("The Great Renegade") (1741–1818), American Revolutionary War soldier, b. near Harrisburg, Pa. He was Indian interpreter for Continental Congress (1776). After desertion to British (1778), he sided with Indian tribes in Ohio country who opposed peace with Americans.

Giselle (ge-ZELL), ballet **B** 25

Gish, Lillian (1896–), American actress, b. Springfield, Ohio. Called First Lady of Silent Screen, she is noted for film roles in *Birth of a Nation* and *The Scarlet Letter.* Her sister **Dorothy** (1898–1968) also appeared on stage and in films.

Gissing, George Robert (1857–1903), English writer, b. Wakefield. Novelist, critic, and essayist, Gissing did his best work in novels, such as *New Grub Street,* about the English middleclass and the effects of poverty on people.

Gist (Ghist), **Christopher** (1706?–59), American explorer and soldier, b. Maryland. In 1750 Gist explored the Ohio River valley. He thus became (18 years earlier than Daniel Boone) the first white man to explore and map the area. While accompanying George Washington to Fort Duquesne (1753–54), Gist twice saved Washington's life.
   overland trails **O** 255

Gist, George see Sequoya
Gist's Trace, overland trail **O** 255
Git Along, Little Dogies, cowboy song **F** 320
Give me liberty, or give me death!, Patrick Henry **H** 114; **R** 198
Given names N 7
   boys' **N** 6–7
   girls' **N** 6
Givens, Edward A., Jr., American astronaut **S** 346
Giza (GHE-za), Egypt
   Great Pyramids **E** 96; **W** 214; picture **W** 215
   Sphinx **E** 96
Gizzard (GHIZ-zard), second part of bird's stomach **B** 202, 221
Glacial epochs see Ice Ages
Glacial geology G 115
Glacial till I 14–15
Glaciation (glay-ci-A-tion), action of glaciers on rock surfaces **G** 115
Glacier Bay National Monument, Alaska **A** 140
Glacier National Park, British Columbia **B** 406a
Glacier National Park, Montana **G** 221–22
   Going-to-the-Sun Road **M** 436
   highway tunnel, picture **G** 103
   Saint Mary Lake, picture **M** 439
Glaciers G 223–25
   Agassiz's study of **A** 80
   Alps **A** 174

   Antarctic region **P** 366; picture **P** 370
   caves **C** 156; picture **C** 157
   Denmark's landform **D** 107–08
   erosion caused by **E** 282–83
   erosion in mountains **M** 495
   Finland **F** 132
   glacial geology, studies in **G** 115
   Glacier National Park in Montana **G** 221–22
   Greenland ice cap **G** 368
   Himalayas, picture **H** 128
   ice, rivers of **I** 6–8
   ice ages **I** 13–24
   icebergs **I** 25–27
   lake basins **L** 25
   Massachusetts, geologic past **M** 136
   moraines, glacial deposits **I** 19; pictures **I** 18
   sea level variations, due to glaciers **W** 51–52
   See also Ice Ages
Glacis (GLACE-is), of a fort **F** 377

Glackens, William James (1870–1938), American painter and illustrator, b. Philadelphia, Pa. He was one of "the Eight," a group of American painters whose exhibit (1908) symbolized beginning of realistic movement in U.S. art.

Gladiator (from Latin *gladius,* meaning "sword"), in ancient Rome, armed warriors who engaged in fights for public entertainment. These spectacles took place in huge amphitheaters such as Colosseum.
   slaves in Rome served as gladiators **R** 305; **S** 196

Gladioli (glad-i-O-li), flowers **G** 40–41, 51
   corms, picture **P** 300
Gladstone, William Ewart, English statesman **G** 225; picture **P** 456a
   supported home rule for Ireland **E** 228
Glands B 279–80
   adolescence, changes during **A** 22
   animals, insulin produced from **M** 196
   mumps affect **D** 201
   scent glands of skunks **O** 241

Glaser, Donald A. (1926–), American physicist, b. Cleveland, Ohio. He invented bubble chamber, a sensitive device for detecting and making visible paths of nuclear particles. He received Nobel prize in physics (1960).

Glasgow (GLAS-go), **Ellen,** American novelist **A** 208
   regional novels **N** 349
Glasgow, Scotland **S** 87
   United Kingdom, cities of **U** 72, 74

Glaspell, Susan (1882–1948), American novelist and playwright, b. Davenport, Iowa. She won Pulitzer prize (1931) for *Alison's House,* play based on poet Emily Dickinson's life.

Glass G 226–37
   antique **A** 318–20
   bottles, history of **B** 341
   electric charges in **E** 123–24
   enameling, use of powdered glass **E** 191–92
   fire makes glass **F** 144
   glass foam, insulating material **I** 291
   glassmaking in West Virginia **W** 126, 132; picture **W** 133
   heat, effect on glasses, diagram **H** 95
   kaleidoscope **K** 166
   lenses **L** 141–51
   noncrystalline solids contrasted with crystal **C** 544
   obsidian, natural glass **G** 226; **R** 264; **V** 378; picture **V** 379

Glass (continued)
optical glass **O** 174
quartz lenses **Q** 6
stained-glass windows **S** 393–95
Venetian glassblowers **T** 305

Glassboro, town in southern New Jersey, pop. over 12,-
000. Site of summit meetings (1967) between U.S. President Lyndon Johnson and Soviet Premier Aleksei Kosygin.
Talks were held at Hollybush, the campus residence of the
president of Glassboro State College. Discussions centered on the June Middle East crisis, the Vietnam War,
and nonproliferation of nuclear arms.
Johnson and Kosygin, picture **J** 130

Glass eels, or elvers **E** 86
Glasses for the eyes see Eyeglasses
Glass fibers see Fiber glass
Glassworms, or arrowworms, sea animals **P** 281
Glaucoma (glau-CO-ma), eye condition **B** 251
Glaucus, in Greek legend **I** 69
Glazes, glass coating, or finish
ceramics **C** 176
pottery **P** 413
Glazing, of furs **F** 517
Glazunov (gla-zu-NOV), **Alexander,** Russian composer
U 64
Glen Canyon Dam, Arizona **D** 16
Glendale, Arizona **A** 413
Glendower (GLEN-dur), **Owen,** Welsh chief **W** 4

Glenn, John Herschel, Jr. (1921–   ), American astronaut,
b. Cambridge, Ohio. Glenn became the first American to
orbit the earth when, on February 20, 1962, his Mercury
capsule Friendship 7 circled the earth three times. After
his war service with the Marines, which included flying
jets, Glenn became a test pilot. In 1957 he made the
first supersonic transcontinental flight. He retired from
the space program in 1964.
space flights and flight data **S** 344, 345, 346

Glickel of Hameln, Yiddish writer **Y** 350
Gliders, engineless aircraft **G** 238–40
aerodynamics **A** 40–41
aviation history **A** 567; picture **A** 568
Wright brothers' early experiments **W** 316
Gliding
animals: locomotion **A** 295
birds **B** 205

Glière (gli-ER), **Reinhold Moritzovich** (1875–1956), Russian composer, b. Kiev. His ballet *Red Poppy* was first
Soviet melodrama. He won Stalin prize (1950) for
ballet *The Bronze Horseman*.

Glima (GLI-ma), Icelandic wrestling, picture **I** 42
Glinka (GLEEN-ka), **Mikhail,** Russian composer **U** 63
Globe and Mail, The, Canadian newspaper **O** 122
Globe-Democrat, St. Louis, Missouri newspaper **M** 375
Globes, representations of the earth **M** 91; pictures
M 89
grid lines **M** 90
help work out time zones **T** 190–92
important social studies tool, picture **S** 223
Globe Theater, Elizabethan theater in London **E** 251
American Shakespeare Festival Theater, Stratford,
Conn., modeled on the Globe, picture **C** 479
Shakespeare, William **S** 131
Globe valves **V** 270
Globulins (GLOB-u-lins), proteins
antibody formation **I** 106; picture **I** 107
use in immunization **M** 209–10

Glockenspiel, musical instrument **M** 550; picture **M** 548
percussion instruments **P** 153
Glomar Challenger, ship for geological drilling project
G 114, 115
Glomeruli (GLOM-er-u-li), of the kidneys, diagram
D 201–02
Glorieta, battle of, 1862 **N** 195
Glorious Revolution, 1688, in England **E** 224
Glory holes, furnaces **G** 230
Glory lily, picture **P** 323
Gloss paints **P** 32
Gloucester (GLOS-ter) **Cathedral,** England, picture **G** 269

Glover (GLOVE-er), **John** (1732–1797), American Revolutionary War officer, b. Salem, Mass. He led the advance
on Trenton (1776), and campaigned against General Burgoyne (1777). He was a member of the court sentencing
British spy André (1780) and a member of the Massachusetts convention to ratify the Federal Constitution (1788).

Gloves **G** 240–41
boxing **B** 351
glove or hand puppets **P** 535–36
Glowworms
bioluminescence **B** 197
Gluck (GLOOK), **Christoph Willibald,** German composer
G 241
classical age, operas of **C** 332
German and Austrian music **G** 184
opera **O** 133–34
opera "war" in Paris **F** 445
Orfeo ed Euridice, opera **O** 149
Glucose, or dextrose, a kind of sugar **S** 453
body sugar **B** 290
photosynthesis **P** 222–23
Glue **G** 242–43
edge gluing of lumber for furniture **F** 502
hot-press bonding of plywood **F** 503–04
See also Adhesives
Glue prints, how to make **G** 308
Gluten, a protein in wheat **W** 154
bread **B** 385
flour and flour milling **F** 274

Glycerol (GLIS-er-ol), or **glycerin,** colorless sweet-tasting
liquid that can be obtained from all animal and vegetable fats and oils. It is used in manufacture of many products, such as antifreeze, lubricants, skin creams. **D** 147

Glycogen (GLY-co-gen), storage form of glucose **B** 290,
297
body, human **B** 275
Glyndebourne Festival, England **M** 550–51
Glyphs (GLIPHS), symbols and signs **U** 195
Gnats, insects **H** 260; picture **H** 263
G-men, of Federal Bureau of Investigation **F** 76
Gneiss (NICE), metamorphic rock **R** 269; picture **R** 268

Gnomes (NOMES), in legend, ageless, often deformed
dwarfs who live in center of earth and guard its treasures.
They were popularized by German-Swiss physician
Paracelsus in *De Nymphis* (1658).

Gnomon (NO-mon), or hand of a sundial **T** 192
Gnomon numbers **N** 383
Gnossus see Knossos

Gnosticism (NOST-i-cism) (from Greek *gnosis,* meaning
"knowledge"), mystical beliefs prevalent primarily during 2nd century. It taught existence of higher knowledge,
attainable by a select few. It was derived from Oriental
beliefs and elements of Judaism, combined with Christian

teachings. It emphasized deliverance of soul from evil material world through spiritual enlightenment.

G.N.P. see Gross national product
Gnu, hoofed mammal, picture **H** 217
Goa, India **I** 133
  former Portuguese overseas territories **P** 402, 404
  Magellan helps conquer **M** 17
Goalies, goalkeepers in sports
  ice hockey **I** 37
  soccer **S** 218–19
Goat, constellation see Capricorn
Goat cheese C 193
Goats G 244
  cloven-hoofed **F** 82
  distinguished from sheep **S** 145
  hoofed mammals **H** 221
  livestock **C** 151–52; picture **C** 150
  milk **M** 310
  Rocky Mountain goat, picture **H** 218
  wild goats and sheep, pictures **H** 218
  Yemen (Aden), picture **M** 303

Gobbi, Tito (1915–), Italian baritone, b. Bassano del Grappo. He made his opera debut in Rome in 1938. Noted for acting ability that enables him to play different roles, he has sung in films and produced operas himself.

Gobelins (GOB-el-ins) **tapestries T** 24; picture **T** 23
  carpet and tapestry workshops **R** 351–52
Gobi (GO-bi) **Desert,** central Asia **M** 414
  landform of China **C** 257
  pastoral nomadic dwellers **D** 128
Goblets, drinking glasses, picture **G** 228
  how made, pictures **G** 231

Goblins, ugly household spirits, sometimes evil but more often playfully mischievous, moving furniture and breaking dishes. They are prevalent in French folklore.

God
  prayer **P** 434–35
  See also Philosophy; Religions; names of religions, denominations, and sects
Godard, Jean-Luc, French motion-picture director **M** 488a
God Bless America, song by Irving Berlin **N** 26

Goddard, Henry Herbert (1866–1957), American professor, and psychologist, b. Vassalboro, Maine. Author of *The Kallikak Family,* a book about feeble-mindedness, Goddard started (1906) a school for retarded children.

Goddard, Robert Hutchings, American physicist **G** 244–46
  with first liquid fuel rocket, picture **R** 257

Godey (GO-dy), **Louis Antoine** (1804–1878), American publisher, b. New York, N.Y. In 1830 Godey co-founded *Godey's Lady's Book,* published until 1898. It was the most important early woman's magazine, reaching a record-breaking circulation of 150,000 in the 1850's. The magazine was most famous for its elegant colored fashion plates, collectors' items today.

Godey's Lady's Book, magazine **M** 14
Godfrey, Sir Daniel, English bandmaster **B** 39
Godfrey, Thomas, American inventor **N** 65

Godiva (go-DY-va), or **Godgifu, Lady** (lived about 1040), wife of Leofric, Earl of Mercia. She begged her husband to relieve the citizens of Coventry, England, of their heavy taxes. He agreed to if she would ride naked through the marketplace. She did, covered only by her long hair. The term "peeping Tom" is derived from the name of a townsman who became blind for disobeying the command to refrain from looking at her.

Go Down, Moses, religious folk song **F** 324; excerpt **N** 106
Godoy, Lucila see Mistral, Gabriela
Gods and goddesses, in mythology **M** 557–64
  Greek and Roman mythology **G** 356–66
  Hawaii, ancient **H** 56, 62
  Hindu **H** 130–31
  Norse **N** 277–81
God Save the Queen, national anthem of the United Kingdom **N** 16–17
Godthaab (GAWT-hawp), capital of Greenland **G** 367

Godunov (god-u-NOF), **Boris Fёdorovich** (1551?–1605), czar of Russia. Godunov freed Russia from patriarchate of Constantinople, regained some Baltic areas, conquered the Cossacks, and recolonized Siberia. He was offered throne (1598) but insisted upon being elected by an assembly. To strengthen power, he took land and slaves from boyars and exempted Church from taxes. His death was followed by period of disorder and foreign invasion. Godunov is subject of poem by Pushkin and opera by Mussorgsky.

Godwin Austen, or **K 2,** mountain in Kashmir **K** 198

Goebbels (GURB-bels), **Joseph Paul** (1897–1945), German Nazi politician and propagandist, b. Rheydt. Goebbels joined Nazis (1922). He became member of Reichstag (1930), and as president of Kulturkammer, censored and regimented German culture. He killed self and family after Allied victory. Comments and actions of Nazi Party leaders are recorded in his *Diaries.*

Goering (GUR-ing), **Hermann Wilhelm** (1893–1946), German Nazi politician, b. Rosenheim. Made member (1928) and then president (1932) of Reichstag, he organized Gestapo and first concentration camps and commanded air attacks on Poland and England. Hitler named him his successor but later expelled him from party for treason. After war he was sentenced to death but committed suicide at Nuremberg (October, 1946).
  plan for air attack on England **W** 290

Goes (GOOS), **Hugo van der,** Flemish painter **D** 351; **R** 171

Goethals (GO-thals), **George Washington** (1858–1928), American engineer, b. Brooklyn, N.Y. He was appointed first chief engineer of Panama Canal Commission (1907). He was governor of Canal Zone (1914–16) and was made major general in the United States Army by special act of Congress for his accomplishment.
  Panama Canal, history of **P** 49

Goethe (GER-ta), **Johann Wolfgang von,** German poet, novelist, and dramatist **G** 246
  Faust **F** 72–73
  German literature, place in **G** 176
  German romantic drama **D** 297
  novel, contributions to the art of **N** 347

Gog and Magog, in Old Testament, leader (Gog) of a people (Magog) destined to invade Israel and be defeated. They symbolize enemies of God. In British folklore, they are the last of a race of giants. There are two 9-foot

Gog and Magog (continued)
carved statues of them in Guildhall, London, destroyed and reconstructed twice since they were sculpted during the reign of Henry V. Picture **B** 137

Goggles, for the eyes
   first underwater goggles **U** 13
Gogh, Vincent van see Van Gogh, Vincent
Gogol (GOR-gol), **Nikolai,** Russian author **U** 60
   drama **D** 298
   novels **N** 347
   short stories **S** 165–66
Going steady, relationship in adolescence **A** 23
Golan Heights, Syria **I** 445; **S** 508
Golconda (gol-CON-da), India **D** 153
Gold **G** 247–49
   Africa **A** 52, 64
   African art **A** 72
   alchemy **C** 207
   Archimedes and the golden crown, legend **A** 369
   art works of ancient Greece **G** 341
   coins and coin collecting **C** 374–75
   crystals, picture **R** 272
   decorative arts, uses in **D** 67
   dolls made of **D** 267
   dredging, picture **Y** 362
   "El Dorado" Indian legend, Colombia **C** 382
   elements, some facts about **E** 154, 161
   Fort Knox, Kentucky, depository, picture **K** 226
   gold-producing regions of North America **N** 293
   jewelry **J** 92
   metals, and ores, location, properties, uses **M** 227
   mining, chief centers for **M** 313
   Montana **M** 442
   Nevada mines **N** 129
   silver found with gold ores **S** 181
   South Dakota leading producer **S** 320–21
   world distribution **W** 261; diagram **W** 264
Gold, discoveries of **G** 250–53
   Alaskan strikes **A** 129, 143
   Brazil's gold rush **B** 378
   California **C** 29
   Canadian gold rush in 1896 **Y** 364
   Colorado gold rush **C** 416
   Georgia **G** 138
   mines and mining **M** 320
   San Francisco and the gold rush of 1848 **S** 31
   South Africa **S** 270
   South Dakota **S** 327
Goldbach, Christian, German mathematician **N** 379

Goldberg, Arthur J. (1908–), American lawyer and statesman, b. Chicago. During World War II he did intelligence work for the O.S.S. He had an active career as a labor counsel and arbitrator. President Kennedy appointed him secretary of labor (1960), and he was associate justice of the United States Supreme Court 1962–65). He succeeded Adlai E. Stevenson as U.S. Representative to the United Nations (1965), but retired in 1968 to return to private law practice. In 1970 he ran as Democratic candidate for governor of New York.

Goldberger, Joseph (1874–1929), American medical scientist, b. Austria. He served in the United States Public Health Service and the Hygienic Laboratory in Washington. He discovered the nature of and treatment for pellagra, a deficiency disease.

Gold Bug, story by Poe, picture **F** 112
Gold Coast, former name of Ghana **G** 194, 198
   gold weights **A** 72
   Nkrumah prime minister **N** 262f

Gold Cup Race, boating **B** 264
Gold dust **G** 251

Golden, Harry Lewis (Harry Lewis Goldenhurst) (1902–), American writer and publisher, b. New York, N.Y. He worked for New York newspapers *Post* and *Mirror* and established monthly newspaper, *Carolina Israelite* (1942). He won fame with best-selling books *Only in America* and *For 2¢ Plain,* which are collections of witty essays.

Golden Age of Athens **G** 338
Golden apples of the Hesperides, in Greek mythology **G** 363

Golden Calf, in Old Testament (Exodus 32), idol made by Aaron, at urging of Israelites, while Moses was on Mt. Sinai. Idol was destroyed when Moses returned with Ten Commandments and saw people worshiping the idol as their means of deliverance from Egypt.
   Moses and the Children of Israel **M** 468

Golden conure, bird, picture **P** 84
Golden door, in Emma Lazarus' poem engraved on the Statue of Liberty **I** 98; **L** 168
Golden eagles **E** 2
Golden Fleece, in Greek mythology **G** 364, 365
   primitive mining device **M** 320
Golden Gate Bridge, San Francisco, California **B** 398; pictures **B** 398, **S** 30, **U** 106
Golden Gate International Exposition, 1939 **F** 17
Golden Gloves Association **B** 352
Golden Hind, ship of Sir Francis Drake **D** 291
Golden Horn, inlet of Bosporus, Turkey **T** 326; picture **T** 327
Golden Lotus, The, Chinese novel **O** 220b
Golden Mean, in philosophy
   Aristotle's middle way **A** 397; **G** 355
Golden moles, animals of insectivore group **I** 261
Golden poppy, flower
   state flower of California, picture **C** 14
Goldenrod, flower, picture **W** 168
   Kentucky, state flower of **K** 213
   Nebraska, state flower of **N** 72

Golden Rule, axiom of good conduct expressed by Jesus in The Sermon on the Mount (Matthew 7:12): "all things whatsoever ye would that men should do to you, do ye even so to them."
   other versions of the Golden Rule **C** 460; **Z** 380

Golden Spike National Historic Site, Utah **U** 250
   picture of the ceremony **A** 204
Golden State, nickname for California **C** 14
Goldfaden, Abraham, Yiddish playwright and producer **Y** 351
Gold-filled articles **G** 248

Goldfinches, any of several small birds of finch family. American goldfinch, about 5 inches long, is the most common type in Americas. Male is yellow, with black wings, tail, and forehead, and female is olive-brown. It may be identified in air by its rising and falling flight. It nests later than most birds, laying three to six pale-blue eggs in July and August. Picture **B** 235.
   Eastern goldfinch, state bird of Iowa, New Jersey **I** 357; **N** 164
   willow goldfinch, state bird of Washington **W** 15

Goldfish
   aquariums, varieties for, pictures **A** 342
   experiment showed preferred temperature **F** 187
   pets **P** 181

Golding, William, English novelist **E** 267

Goldman, Edwin Franko (1878–1956), American conductor, b. Louisville, Ky. Conductor (1911–56) of Goldman Band, he started Goldman Band free outdoor concerts (1918). These have been held in Central Park, New York (since 1922), and in Prospect Park, Brooklyn (since 1934). Goldman composed over 75 marches. His son, **Richard Goldman** (1910–   ) succeeded him as conductor (1956).
    bands in the United States **B** 41

Goldmark, Karl (1830–1915), Hungarian composer, b. Kiszthely. He studied in Vienna, where he lived most of his life, composing, teaching, and writing music criticism. His works include six operas, chamber music, songs, two violin concertos, and *Rustic Wedding Symphony.*

Gold Museum, Bogotá, Colombia **M** 514
Goldoni (gol-DO-ni), **Carlo,** Italian playwright **I** 479
Goldrush see Gold, discoveries of
Goldsmith, Oliver, English playwright and novelist **E** 257
    established as writer by John Newbery **N** 137
    Irish literature **I** 393
    Restoration drama **D** 297
Goldsmiths
    Central African Republic, picture **C** 170
    decorative arts **D** 75, 77
Gold standard, measures currency values **M** 409
    Bryan's Cross of Gold speech **B** 415–16
    United States goes off the gold standard, 1933 **R** 322
    uses of gold **G** 247

Gold Star Mothers, American, society of mothers of servicemen killed in war. Founded 1928, the society has its headquarters in Washington, D.C.

Gold Star Wives of America, society of servicemen's widows who serve as volunteers in veteran and civilian hospitals. Founded in 1945, the society has headquarters in Avondale Estates, Georgia.

Goldwater, Barry Morris (1909–   ), American politician, b. Phoenix, Ariz. After serving in the U.S. Senate (1953–64), he was the unsuccessful Republican Party candidate for president in 1964. He represents the most conservative branch of his party.
    U.S. political parties, history of **P** 381

Golf G 254–62
    Jones, Bobby, makes "grand slam" **J** 135
    in Jasper National Park, picture **J** 54
    Zaharias, Mildred "Babe" Didrikson **Z** 366
Golfito (gole-FI-to), Costa Rica **C** 516

Golgi (GOL-ji), **Camillo** (1844–1926), Italian medical scientist, b. Corteno. He is noted for his work on nervous tissues and their cell structure. He discovered dark spots in the cytoplasm of certain cells, which are called Golgi bodies in his honor. He shared the 1906 Nobel prize in medicine and physiology with S. Ramón y Cajal.
    Golgi bodies, of plant cells, diagram **C** 162

Golgotha (GOL-go-tha), or Calvary, place of Jesus Christ's crucifixion **J** 84
    Via Dolorosa, Way of the Cross **J** 80
Goliath (go-LY-ath), Philistine giant slain by David **D** 44
    Bible story of David and Goliath **B** 164–65
Goliath frog, of Cameroon **C** 36
Gombu, Nawang, Sherpa guide and mountaineer **E** 337
Gomes (GO-mese), **António Carlos,** Brazilian composer **B** 377

Gómez (GO-mez), **Estevan** (1470?–1530?), Portuguese navigator. Gómez was a pilot of one of Magellan's ships, the *San Antonio.* During the struggle to sail through the Straits of Magellan, Gómez, discouraged, led a mutiny. He took over the ship and fled back to Spain with most of the provisions while the rest of the expedition continued on their voyage around the world.

Gómez, Juan Vicente, president of Venezuela **V** 300
Gomorrah see Sodom and Gomorrah
Gompers, Samuel, American labor leader **G** 262–63; **L** 4
Gomulka (go-MAUL-ka), **Wladyslaw** (1905–   ), Polish statesman, b. Krosno. He was active in defense of Warsaw (1939) and was secretary (1943) of outlawed Polish Communist Party and vice-premier (1944) of Warsaw government. He was relieved of posts for "nonappreciation of the decisive role of the Soviet Union" and arrested (1951). He was released (1956) and served as first secretary of Polish Central Committee until a government crisis forced him to resign in 1970. **C** 444

Goncharov (gon-char-OFF), **Ivan,** Russian author **U** 60
Gondar, Ethiopia **E** 296
Gondola, of a balloon **B** 31; pictures **B** 33
Gondola cars, of railroads **R** 82
Gondolas, boats
    on the canals, Venice, pictures **B** 55; **E** 304; **H** 179; **I** 456
Gondoliers (gon-dol-IERS), **The,** operetta by Gilbert and Sullivan **G** 210
Gone With the Wind, novel by Margaret Mitchell **A** 213
    motion picture **M** 475
Góngora (GON-go-ra), **Luis de,** Spanish poet **S** 369
    imitated in Latin-American literature **L** 70
Gonorrhea (gon-or-RE-a), venereal disease **D** 196

Gonzales (gon-ZA-les), **Pancho** (Richard Alonzo Gonzales) (1928–   ), American tennis player, b. Los Angeles, Calif. He won U.S. Singles Championship (1948, 1949), Wimbledon Doubles Championship with Frank A. Parker (1949), and was a member of victorious U.S. Davis Cup Team (1949). He turned professional in 1949. His autobiography is called *Man With a Racket.*

González, Dávila Gill see Dávila, Gil González
González (gon-THA-leth), **Julio,** Spanish sculptor **S** 105
González Prada (PRA-tha), **Manuel,** Peruvian author **P** 166
Gonzalo de Berceo (gon-THA-lo day berth-A-o), Spanish poet **S** 366
Goobers see Peanuts
Good Earth, The, novel by Pearl Buck **B** 421
Good Feeling, Era of, Monroe's administration **M** 425
Good Friday E 41
    holy days of the church **R** 290
Good Hope, Cape of C 102
    Dias first called it Cape of Storms **E** 374
Good King Wenceslaus, Christmas carol **C** 563

Goodman, Benny (Benjamin David Goodman) (1909–   ), American clarinetist and jazz band leader, b. Chicago, Ill. Goodman organized a swing jazz band (1934). He was first American jazz musician to play in Soviet Union (1962). He has written an autobiography, *Kingdom of Swing.* Picture **C** 329.

Good Neighbor Policy, foreign policy, relative to Latin America, proclaimed (1933) by President Roosevelt. It advocated noninterference in affairs of another state (repudiation of former U.S. policies in Latin America), and it meant co-operative enforcement of Monroe Doctrine by

Good Neighbor Policy (continued)
all American states, renouncement by United States of Platt amendment, which allowed interference in Cuba, and evacuation of U.S. troops from Haiti.
  Monroe Doctrine extended **M** 427; **P** 46

Goodnight-Loving Trail, New Mexico **N** 188
Goodrich, Samuel Griswold see Parley, Peter
Goodricke, John, English astronomer **A** 475–76
Goodspeed, ship, carried colonists to America **A** 183
  Jamestown settlement **J** 20

Goodwill Industries of America, association of 140 agencies established for rehabilitation and employment of the disabled and handicapped. Founded in 1902, it has its headquarters in Washington, D.C.

Goodyear, Charles, American inventor **G** 263
  Connecticut, famous people from **C** 478
  rubber, vulcanizing of **R** 341

Goodyear, Miles (1817–1849), American pioneer settler in Utah. He built (1845) Ft. Buenaventura where Ogden, Utah, now stands. A small part of the fort remains.

Goofy, cartoon character, picture **A** 297

Googol, name for the number 10¹⁰⁰ (1 followed by 100 zeros). The term was introduced by the American mathematician Edward Kasner (1878–1955).

Goolagong, Evonne (1951–), Australian tennis player, b. Barellan, New South Wales. An aborigine, she came to the attention of Australian tennis experts who helped make her the first tennis star of her race. In 1971 she won Wimbledon singles title and the French crown.

Goose see Geese
Goose Bay, Labrador, Canada **N** 144

Gooseberry, shrub with prickly stems and small flowers found in temperate and cold regions of world. Its many-seeded berries are used as food. Barbados gooseberry, unrelated to gooseberry, is a cactus.

GOP see Grand Old Party
Gophers, rodents **R** 277
  pocket gopher, picture **R** 277
Gopher State, nickname for Minnesota **M** 322
Gopher tortoises **T** 334

Gordian knot, in Greek legend, complicated knot of bark tied by peasant Gordius on his wagon to signify his leaving his old life when he was made King of Phrygia. An oracle decreed that whoever untied it would conquer Asia. Alexander the Great cut it and then fulfilled prophecy. Term now refers to difficult task or problem.
  Alexander, king of Asia **A** 152

Gordimer, Nadine, South African writer **A** 76b

Gordon, Charles George (called "Chinese" Gordon and Gordon Pasha) (1883–1885), English general, b. Woolwich. He served in the Crimean War and later commanded Chinese irregular forces which put down Taiping rebellion (1863–64). Governor of the Egyptian Sudan and equatorial provinces, he brought law and order to the area and suppressed slave trade (1877–80). He was killed by native rebels after the fall of Khartoum.

Gordon, George Hamilton see Aberdeen, 4th earl of

Gordon, John Campbell see Aberdeen, Lord
Gordon, Richard F. Jr., American astronaut **S** 344, 345 346
Gordone, Charles, American playwright **D** 300
Gore, Leslie, American rock music performer **R** 262c

Goren, Charles H. (1901–), American card games expert, b. Philadelphia. Trained as a lawyer, he enjoyed greatest success as bridge player, originating point-count system of bidding, and was long world's outstanding player. He was author of many books and articles and wrote syndicated newspaper column and regular articles for *Sports Illustrated* on bridge.
  bidding system in contract bridge **C** 107–08

Gorgas, Josiah, American educator **A** 125
Gorgas, William Crawford, American doctor **P** 49
  Panama and Panama Canal **P** 45
Gorges, Sir Ferdinando, English promoter of settlement in Maine **M** 45, 46–47
  American colonies **A** 189
  trading monopolies in the New World **T** 305
Gorgias (GOR-gi-as), Greek orator and sophist **O** 180
Gorgonian coral, picture **J** 74
Gorgons, monsters in Greek mythology **G** 362
Gorgosaurs (GOR-go-saurs), dinosaurs **D** 175

Gorham, Nathaniel (1738–1796), American statesman, b. Charlestown, Mass. Before the Revolutionary War he was a colonial official. He became a member of the Continental Congress (1782–83, 1785–87), serving as its president in 1786. After representing Massachusetts at the Constitutional Convention in 1787 and signing the Constitution, he returned to participate in the state convention that ratified the Constitution the next year.

Gorillas **M** 418
  feet **F** 83
  in Bronx Zoo, picture **Z** 375
  placental mammals **M** 71
Gorkha, or **Gurkha,** Nepal **N** 113
Gorki, Union of Soviet Socialist Republics **E** 323; **U** 36
Gorky, Arshile, American artist **M** 397
  Garden in Sochi, painting **U** 119
Gorky, Maxim, Russian author **U** 61
Gorman, Lawrence ("Larry"), Canadian folk singer **C** 63

Gorrie, John (1803–1955), American inventor, b. Charleston, S.C. As physician, he was interested in cooling air of hospital rooms artificially and took out first U.S. patent (1851) for mechanical refrigeration.
  refrigeration, invention of **I** 346; **R** 136

Gorton, Samuel (1592?–1677), American colonist and religious leader, b. Lancashire, England. Expelled (1638) from Massachusetts colony for heresy, he settled in Rhode Island, where he served in representative government (1649–66) and established the Gortonian sect.

Gosnold, Bartholomew (?–1607), English navigator, b. probably Suffolk. He discovered and named Cape Cod and Martha's Vineyard, Mass., in 1602. He commanded ship *Goodspeed,* which carried first settlers (1607) to Jamestown, Va.
  Massachusetts, history of **M** 148

Gospel, "good news," of Jesus Christ **C** 279, 281
Gospel hymns (white spirituals) see Gospel songs
Gospels, books of Bible, New Testament **B** 160–61
  Apostles' teachings **R** 288
  Evangelists, The **E** 335
  Kells, Book of **K** 202–03

Gospel songs H 313
  Negro spirituals **N** 106
  rock music, development of **R** 262a, 262d
Gossec, François, French bandmaster **B** 39
Goteborg (yer-te-BORG), Sweden **S** 484–85
Gothic, type face design **T** 345
Gothic architecture **G** 264–72
  art as a record **A** 438e
  cathedrals **C** 132; pictures **C** 131, 132
  decorative arts **D** 75
  England **E** 234–35
  France, development in **F** 421
  French technique **A** 378
  German cathedrals **G** 166
  Italian architecture influenced by **I** 463; picture **I** 460
  Latin America's modified version **L** 62
  sculpture in Gothic cathedrals **S** 98
  stained-glass windows **S** 393–95
Gothic art **G** 264–72
  art as a record **A** 438e
  England **E** 235
  furniture design **F** 505
  German sculpture **G** 166
  golden age of tapestries **T** 22
  Middle Ages, art of **M** 297
  painting mostly book illustration **P** 18
  sculpture **S** 98; picture **S** 99
  stained-glass windows **S** 393–95
Gothic novels **E** 260
Gothic stories, dealing with the supernatural **S** 165

Goths, ancient Germanic people said to have migrated from Sweden and settled north of Black Sea. They split during 3rd century to form Visigoths (West Goths) and Ostrogoths (East Goths). The Visigoths, pressured by attack of Huns, fled across Danube to Roman territory. Harshly treated, they rebelled and began western movement (400). They sacked Rome (410), withdrew (412), and set up kingdoms first in southern France (until 507) and then in Spain (until 711). They were overcome by Arabs in 711. Ostrogoths remained east of Danube and were dominated by Huns until death of Attila (453), when they joined Roman Empire. They ruled Italy (493–553) under Theodoric the Great.

Gotland, Sweden **S** 484
Götterdämmerung (gert-ter-DEM-mer-ung), **Die,** opera by Richard Wagner **O** 152–53

Gottschalk (GOTT-shalk), **Louis Moreau** (1829–1869), American pianist and composer, b. New Orleans, La. He made his European debut at 15, returned to United States the most celebrated American pianist of his day, and featured his own compositions in all his concerts.

Gottsched, Johann, German writer **G** 175
Gouache (GWASH), paint **I** 87; **P** 30
Goudimel (goo-di-MEL), **Claude,** French composer **F** 444
Goudy, Frederic W., American printer and type designer **B** 326
Gougane Barra (GOO-gawn barra), **Lake,** Ireland, picture **I** 387
Gouges (GOW-ges), tools **T** 213
  woodcut printing **W** 229
  use for relief printing in the graphic arts **G** 302
Gough (GOFF), **John,** English philosopher **D** 15
Goujon, Jean, French sculptor **R** 171
Goulart (goo-LAR), **João,** president of Brazil **B** 384
Goulash, stew of meat and vegetables, favorite in Hungary **H** 284
Gould, Chester, American cartoonist, creator of *Dick Tracy* **C** 128

Gould (GOOLD), **Glenn Herbert** (1932–), Canadian pianist and composer, b. Toronto. He made his debut at age 14 with Toronto Symphony Orchestra.

Gould, Lawrence McKinley (1896–), American geologist, b. Lacota, Mich. He was deputy commander of Byrd antarctic expedition (1928–30), director of United States antarctic program for International Geophysical Year.

Gould, Morton (1913–), American composer, b. Richmond Hill, N.Y. He is noted for compositions on American themes, such as *Cowboy Rhapsody, Harvest, Minstrel Show, American Concertette,* and *Spirituals.*

Gounod (goo-NO), **Charles François** (1818–1893), French composer, b. Paris. He is famous for opera *Faust.* His other operas include *Sapho, Romeo and Juliet,* and an adaptation of Molière comedy *Le Médecin malgré lui.* He composed much sacred music, including *Messe de Sainte Cécile,* and the well-known *Ave Maria.*
  Faust, opera **F** 73; **O** 144

Gourdan Cave, France
  carvings of prehistoric man **P** 441

Gourds, any one of several climbing vines, such as cucumbers, melons, squash, and pumpkin. They are mostly native to tropical regions but are grown elsewhere. Gourds have broad leaves and trumpet-shaped flowers. Their fruits have thick rinds and many seeds.
  vegetables **V** 287

Government, forms of **G** 273–78
  constitutions, as plans of government **U** 145–46
  democracy **D** 104–05
  division of powers of U.S. Government **U** 139
  elections **E** 112–15
  feudalism **F** 102–03
  impeachment, a safeguard against bad government **I** 108
  imperialism **I** 109
  initiative, referendum and recall **O** 205
  international law **I** 320–21
  law and law enforcement **L** 87–89
  Madison's ideas on government **M** 7–8
  municipal government **M** 503–08
  parliaments **P** 81–82
  political parties **P** 378–82
  prime minister **P** 456–456a
  propaganda **P** 481
  responsible government, Canada **C** 77
  socialism **S** 220
  social studies programs of instruction **S** 223–24
  state governments **S** 412–15
  taxation **T** 26–27
  What is anarchism? **G** 276
  What is oligarchy? **G** 278
  See also Communism; Democracy; Fascism; government section of continent, country, province, and state articles
Government ownership
  public utilities **P** 510–13
  socialism **S** 220
  Sweden, "The Middle Way" **S** 486

Government Printing Office, United States, located in Washington, D.C., authorized (since 1860) to handle government printing and binding. **W** 34

Government regulation, of business and industry **I** 251
  economics **E** 50, 51
  public utilities **P** 510–13

Government reports
How many different censuses are taken? **P** 396
Governor, machine control device **A** 532
Governor general, in Canadian government **C** 76
Governors, of states **S** 413–14
terms of see state articles
Governors Island, part of New York City, picture **I** 426
Gower, John, English poet **E** 248–49
Go West, young man, Horace Greeley's advice **N** 161
Gowon, Yakubu, military leader in Nigeria **N** 258
Goya, Francisco, Spanish painter **G** 279
art of the artist **A** 438g
Blind Man's Buff, painting **G** 279
leading graphic artist of 19th century **G** 307–08
place in Spanish art **P** 27; **S** 362–63
Prado **P** 428–29
Self-portrait, painting **P** 27
The Forge, painting **S** 362
Goyathlay, see Geronimo, Apache Indian leader
GPO see Government Printing Office

Grace, prayer asking blessing on food before meal or giving thanks to God after meal. It is part of rabbinical tradition required by Old Testament (Deuteronomy 8:10). The custom was adopted by early Christians.

Grace, princess of Monaco (1929–), former American actress Grace Kelly, b. Philadelphia, Pa. Her first important film role was in *High Noon* (1952). She married Prince Rainier III of Monaco (1956).
Monaco, history of **M** 407

Graces, Three, in Roman mythology, the Gratiae, personifications of grace, charm, and beauty; in Greek mythology and religion, the Charities, Aglaia, Euphrosyne, and Thalia (symbols of splendor, mirth, and abundance respectively).

Gracián (groth-YON), **Baltasar,** Spanish poet **S** 369
Grackles, birds, picture **B** 234
Grade, degree of slope, of railroad tracks **R** 78
Graduate schools **U** 205
Grady, Henry W., American editor **G** 146, 147

Graffiti (gra-FI-ti) (from Italian *graffio,* scratch; Greek, *graphein,* to write), words or phrases scratched or written on sidewalks or the walls of buildings.

Grafting, process of transferring and attaching parts of one plant to another. The plant that receives a graft is the stock; the grafted portion is the scion. Scions are usually inserted into cuts made in the stock. Grafting has been practiced since ancient times, to heal plant wounds, to grow new strains, and to propagate seedless plants.
apple trees **A** 335, 337
nut trees **N** 420

Grafting, transplant of body tissue
aging experiments **A** 87
Grafton, West Virginia
Mother's Day observation **H** 156; **W** 139

Graham, Billy (William Franklin Graham) (1918–), American Baptist minister and evangelist, b. Charlotte, N.C. He is noted for nationwide evangelical campaigns (since 1946), and he broadcasts radio and TV show Weekly Hour of Decision. He conducted first of President Nixon's White House Sunday services.

Graham, Martha, American dancer **D** 33

Graham, Thomas (1805–1869), Scottish chemist, b. Glasgow. He first formulated the law, named for him, concerning the way gases diffuse: the heavier their molecular weight, the more slowly they diffuse. He first distinguished colloids as chemical substances that do not pass through such membranes as parchment. This was later shown to be due to the large size of colloidal molecules, of which proteins are an example.

Grahame, Kenneth (1859–1932), English author, b. Edinburgh, Scotland. He wrote novels about his childhood in English countryside, including *The Golden Age* and *Dream Days.* His famous *The Wind in the Willows,* written for children, is enjoyed by adults as well.
quoted on boats **B** 264; **C** 241

Graham's Magazine **M** 15
Graiae (GRAI-e), sisters in Greek mythology **G** 362
Grain, measure of weight **W** 112
Grain, of wood, pictures **W** 223–24
veneered furniture **F** 501, 503–04
Grain and grain products **G** 280–87
beer and brewing **B** 116–17
Canada **C** 58
cereal grains, food plants **P** 308–10
cereal grasses **G** 317–18
corn **C** 506–07
fired pottery for storage of **F** 143
flour and flour milling **F** 274–75
oats **O** 3–4
products listed for several types of grain **G** 283–84
rice **R** 231–32
rye **R** 364
wheat **W** 154–56

Grain elevator, tall bin equipped to lift, store, and discharge grain. It enables rapid handling and preserves surplus crops. A grain elevator has a capacity of from 500,000 to 5,000,000 bushels. Pictures **K** 178, **U** 106.
wheat storage **W** 155

Grainger, Percy Aldridge (1882–1961), Australian pianist and composer, b. Melbourne. He emigrated to United States (1914). Grainger helped revive English folk songs. Many of his works incorporate folk music.

Gram, measure of volume **W** 116

Gramatky (gra-MAT-ke), **Hardie** (1907–), American artist, illustrator, and author of children's books, b. Dallas, Tex. He wrote and illustrated *Sparky, Bolivar, Homer and the Circus Train, Little Toot.*
picture books for children **C** 243

Gram-centimeter-second, system of measurement **W** 117
Grammar **G** 288–90
anthropological studies **A** 308
descriptive linguistics **L** 302
dialects **D** 152
English language **E** 244
inflections **E** 244
languages show relationship by grammatical structure **L** 37, 38
Latin language **L** 76
learning rules **P** 499
parts of speech **P** 90–92
punctuation **P** 530–33
rules for word order differ for different languages **L** 37
syntax **E** 244
young readers identify new words by structural units **R** 109
Grammar in a Nutshell, poem **G** 290

Grammar schools   E 64

Gramme (GROMM), Zénobe, Belgian inventor   I 334
  developed electric generator   E 140

Grampian Mountains, Scotland   S 86

Granada (gra-NA-dtha), Nicaragua   N 247

Granadilla (gran-a-DIL-la), wood used in clarinets   C 329

Granados (gra-NA-dthos), Enrique, Spanish composer
  S 373

Gran Chaco (gron CHA-co), South America   S 277
  plant life in South America   S 280

Gran Colombia ("Great" Colombia), former republic of
  Colombia, Ecuador, and Venezuela   B 301
  Colombia   C 384
  Ecuador   E 58
  Venezuela   V 300

Grand Alliance, or Quadruple Alliance, 1815   I 324

Grand Army of the Republic (G.A.R.), national society of
Union army and navy veterans of the Civil War. It
fostered brotherliness and patriotism and aided needy
families of veterans. It was founded 1866 and inaugurated celebration of Memorial Day (May 30).

Grand Bahama Island   B 17

Grand Banks, off Newfoundland, Canada   C 57, 68
  fishing industry   F 218
  meeting of Labrador Current and Gulf Stream   G 411
  Newfoundland   N 143

Grand Canal, China   C 83, 84
  Peking   P 117

Grand Canal, Venice, picture   E 304

Grand Canyon, gorge cut by Colorado River   G 290–92
  Arizona   A 404, 414
  rock formations, picture   G 109

Grand Canyon National Park, Arizona   A 414
  muleback party, picture   C 486

Grand Central Station, New York City
  Grand Central Tower, picture   A 438g

Grand Coulee (COO-lee) Dam, Washington   D 16, 19;
  W 17, 20; pictures   G 101,   U 108,   W 21

Grand Dixence Dam, Switzerland   D 20–21

Grandes Bergeronnes (grond ber-jer-ONN), Quebec,
  picture   Q 11

Grand Falls, New Brunswick, Canada   W 56b; picture
  N 138b

Grandfather clause, clause in constitutions of some
southern states after Civil War that stated that persons
who could vote on Jan. 1, 1867, were exempt from the
difficult financial, literacy, and property ownership
requirements others had to meet in order to vote, and
that their direct descendants were also exempt. This
clause resulted in Negroes being deprived of their right
to vote and was declared unconstitutional (1915).

Grandfather clock, pictures   C 389, W 48

Grand Forks, North Dakota   N 335

Grand jury   J 159
  courts   C 527

Grand master keys   L 325

Grand National Steeplechase, horserace, Aintree, England   H 231

Grand Old Party, nickname for Republican Party coined
by campaigners (1880). Title was shortened to GOP.

Grand opera   O 135–55
  Italian   I 486

Grand piano, pictures   K 239,   P 240

Grand Portage National Monument, Minnesota   M 332

Grand Prix (gron PRE), international auto racing   A 538;
  picture   A 539

Grand Rapids, Michigan   M 270

Grand Teton (te-TON) National Park, Wyoming   W 332;
  picture   N 47

Grand Trunk Railway, Canada   C 73

Grand Union flag   F 243; picture   F 229

Grandview State Park, West Virginia   W 136; picture
  W 128

Grange, farm organization   M 337
  See also National Grange of the Patrons of Husbandry

Grange, Red (Harold E. Grange) (1903–   ), American
football player, b. Forksville, Pa. He was halfback at
University of Illinois (1923–25) and played professionally
for Chicago Bears (1925–34), earning title "the Galloping
Ghost."

Granger, Lester Blackwell (1896–   ), American educator and community relations expert, Negro, b. Newport News, Va. Granger was executive secretary of the
National Urban League (1941–61). As consultant to Secretary of the Navy James Forrestal (1945), he influenced
revision of the Navy's racial policy. He has been president (1961) and honorary president (1964) of the International Conference of Social Workers.

Granite, rock   R 264, 266
  building stone   Q 6; S 433
  earth's crust   E 10, 19

Granite State, nickname for New Hampshire   N 149, 150

Grant, Julia Dent, wife of Ulysses S. Grant   F 173;
  G 294; picture   F 172

Grant, Ulysses S., 18th president of United States
  G 293–96
  Civil War   C 322, 326, 327, 459, 460
  Lee and Grant   L 126
  Lincoln promotes   L 297

Grants, gifts and subsidies
  foundations   F 392

Grant's Tomb, New York City, picture   G 296

Granulated sugar   S 453

Granules, of detergents and soaps   D 148–49

Granville-Barker, Harley, English critic and playwright
  S 144

Grapefruit   O 179; pictures   F 484,   O 176

Grapes   G 297–98; pictures   G 299, 300
  dried to make raisins   D 316, 317
  garden fruits   G 52
  harvest in Spain, picture   A 98
  labor problems see Chavez, Cesar
  wine   W 188–89

Grapes of Wrath, The, novel by John Steinbeck   S 422
  migrants from Oklahoma   O 95

Grape sugar   S 453

Graphic arts   G 302–08
  book design   B 326
  drawing   D 301–05
  engraving   E 272
  etching   E 293–95
  linoleum-block printing   L 304–06
  lithography   L 314–15
  photography   P 201–13
  printing   P 457–67
  Rosenwald collection in National Gallery of Art   N 41
  silk-screen printing   S 180
  type faces   T 345–46
  woodcut printing   W 228–29
  See also Painting

Graphite, form of carbon   C 106; D 154
  development of writing tools   C 433
  "lead" in pencils   L 95
  lubricants   L 371
  pencils   P 147–48

Graphs G 309–13
Grass (GROS), **Günter,** German writer G 181
   The Tin Drum, cover design for G 180
Grasse (GROS), **Comte de,** French admiral W 40
   victory in Chesapeake Bay R 208
Grasses G 314–19
   Are all grasses alike? G 316
   corn plant C 506
   grain and grain products G 280–87
   houses of H 172
   lawns L 90–91
   life, plant and animal communities L 258
   National Grasslands, United States N 31–32
   oats belong to grass family O 3
   pollination of flowers F 277
   prairies, expanses of grassland P 430
   ranchers grow for cattle feed R 103–04
   rice R 231
   rye R 364
   savannas of Africa A 50
   stain removal L 84
   wheat W 154–56
Grasshopper and the Ant, The, or The Ant and the Grasshopper, fable F 5
Grasshopper Glacier, Montana M 439
Grasshoppers, insects I 263; pictures I 262, 281
   ears, diagram I 267
   first-level consumer, picture L 239
   leg, diagram I 273
   Nebraska invaded by N 87
   sound-making apparatus, diagram I 268
   vectors of plant diseases V 284
Grassland P 430–33
Grass spiders S 385
Grateau (gra-TO), **Marcel,** French barber, created Marcel
   wave B 111
Grateful Dead, The, American rock music group R 262d
Graveline, Duane B., American astronaut S 346

Gravely, Samuel L. (1922–   ), Rear Admiral, United States
Navy, b. Richmond, Va. He enlisted in the Naval Reserve
in 1942 and was the first Negro to be graduated from
midshipman's school. In 1944 he was commissioned as
an ensign, and he advanced in rank to captain in 1967. He
is the first Negro to become a Rear Admiral. His selection
was approved by President Nixon on April 27, 1971.

Graves, Robert Ranke (1895–   ), English poet and
writer, b. London. He evolved theory of "non-literary"
poetry and reconstructed ancient Rome in novels *I, Claudius* and *Claudius the God.* As a classical scholar, he
translated Homer's *Iliad* and wrote *The Greek Myths.* His
volumes of poetry include *Mock Beggar Hall, The Penny
Fiddle,* and *Poems for Children.*

Graveyard of the Atlantic, Outer Banks of North Carolina
   N 308
Gravimeter (grav-IM-et-er), instrument for measuring
   gravity G 323; picture G 322
Gravity and gravitation G 320–25
   airplane lift offsets A 38; diagram of forces A 553
   comets, meteors, meteorites and tektites C 418–21
   earth's history E 18
   falling bodies F 32–34
   locomotion of animals, effect on A 289, 291
   mass and weight of matter M 171
   moon's pull and its origin M 449, 456
   Newton and his famous book the *Principia* N 207
   planets P 269–78
   relativity, general theory of R 143–44
   resistance, natural force of W 244
   satellites S 39

   sense of balance B 287–88
   shape of the earth E 5–6
   solar system, planetary orbits and gravitation in
      S 241–42
   spacecraft launching, g-forces S 340d, 340j
   sun's gravity S 464
   tides T 179–85
Gravity concentration, of ores M 228
Gravity dams, made of concrete D 16; picture D 17
Gravity meters, instruments to measure differences in
   earth's magnetism P 171
Gravure (grav-URE), or intaglio printing P 460, 467
Gravure plates, for printing P 467

Gray, Asa (1810–1888), American botanist, b. Sauguoit,
N.Y. With Dr. Torrey he wrote *Flora of North America.* An
advocate of Darwinism, he was author of *Darwiniana,*
and also wrote a study of Japanese botany and its relation to that in North America. Gray was professor (1842–
88) of natural history at Harvard University.

Gray, Elisha (1835–1901), American inventor, b. Barnes-
ville, Ohio. Gray made various refinements on the
telegraph. He filed a report for invention of telephone to
U.S. Patent Office a few hours after Alexander Graham
Bell filed his patent, resulting in long conflict over
patent rights, which were finally awarded to Bell.

Gray, Elizabeth Janet see Vining, Mrs. Elizabeth Gray
Gray, Hawthorne, American military balloonist B 32
Gray, Robert, American explorer and trader R 225
   Oregon O 192, 207
   Washington W 28
Gray, Thomas, English poet E 151
   "Elegy Written in a Country Churchyard," excerpt
      E 151–52
   quotation Q 20
Gray foxes D 250; F 397; picture D 251

Gray Ladies, volunteer group of American National Red
Cross concerned with recuperation of convalescents in
civilian and military hospitals. The group, founded in
1918, was named for gray uniforms.
   Red Cross groups R 127

Gray matter, of the nervous system B 367
Gray's Inn see Inns of Court
Gray whales W 150; picture W 148
Gray-Wolf see Hofsinde, Robert
Gray wolves W 210
   dog family D 243–44

Graz (GROTS) (pop. about 250,000), city in southeast
Austria. The second largest city in the country, Graz, on
the Mur River, has a hydroelectric plant, steel works,
and mills. Home of the state university, fine museums,
an opera house, and churches, it is also a cultural center.
Founded in the 12th century, it is built around a castle
fortress topped by a famous clock tower.

Grazing lands see Pastures
Greasepaint, theatrical makeup P 341
Greases, lubricating L 371
   stain removal L 84
Greasewood see Creosote bush
Great Atlantic and Pacific Tea Company see Atlantic and
   Pacific Tea Company, Great
Great auk, extinct bird B 231
Great Banyan Tree, in Calcutta C 11
Great Barrier Reef, Australia A 503
Great Basin region, Nevada-Utah N 124; U 242–43
   Indians of North America, the Gatherers I 172

Great Bear, constellation *see* Ursa Major
Great Bear Lake, northwest Canada L 31; Y 361
Great blue heron, pictures B 208, 222

Great Books Program, course of study instituted (1937) at St. John's College, Annapolis, Md., by Stringfellow Barr and Scott Buchanan. Program focused on selected list of classics, or "great books," of Western tradition. Term also refers to any adult education program that encourages group discussions of classics.

Great Britain, largest island of the British Isles and part of the United Kingdom of Great Britain and Northern Ireland U 66
Great Britain and Northern Ireland, United Kingdom of *see* United Kingdom of Great Britain and Northern Ireland
Great Central Plain, North America N 285
Great-circle route G 96
Great Colombia *see* Gran Colombia
Great Compromiser, The, Henry Clay C 335; M 382
Great Dane, dog, picture D 255
Great Depression *see* Depression of the 1930's
Great Design, plan for peace P 104
Great Dissenter, The, Oliver Wendell Holmes, Jr. H 161
Great Eastern, steamship O 23–24
    laying the cable T 52
Great Emancipator, The, Abraham Lincoln E 186
Greater Antilles (an-TILL-ese), Caribbean island group C 116, 118
    Cuba C 547–51
    Hispaniola D 280–83; H 7–11
    Jamaica J 14–18
    Puerto Rico P 517
Greater Sunda (SOON-da) Islands, Indonesia I 218–19
Great Falls, Montana M 440
Great Gatsby, The, novel by F. Scott Fitzgerald A 211
Great Lakes, North America G 326–29
    Canada C 68
    industry in Cleveland, Ohio C 338
    Michigan M 258, 261, 266
    Saint Lawrence River and Seaway S 15–17
    War of 1812 W 12
Great Lakes Plain, North America N 211–12
Great Lakes–St. Lawrence Lowlands, landform region of Canada C 50, 64; O 120
Great Lakes–St. Lawrence waterways G 326; S 15–17
    Ontario O 121–22
Great London Fire, 1666 L 334
Great Plains, North America U 90
    Canada C 51
    overland trails O 251–67
    pioneer life P 254
    prairies P 430
    westward movement W 145–46
Great Proletarian Cultural Revolution *see* Cultural Revolution, 1966–69, China
Great Pyramid of Cheops (KE-ops), at Giza, Egypt W 214; picture W 215
    Egyptian art and architecture E 96
    Egyptian civilization A 221
    oldest engineering project in the world E 207
Great Quillow, The, by James Thurber, excerpt T 174
Great Rift Valley, Africa A 49, 50
    Ethiopia E 299
    Kenya K 231–32
    Malawi M 50
    Tanzania T 17
    Uganda U 5
Great Saint Bernard (ber-NARD), early inn and hospice in Swiss Alps H 256–57
Great Salt Lake, Utah L 31; U 243–44; picture U 242

Great Schism (SISM), division of the Christian Church
    Orthodox Eastern churches O 228
    Patriarch of Constantinople excommunicated R 291
Great Seal of the United States G 329–30
Great Slave Lake, northwest Canada L 31; Y 361
Great Slave Railway, Alberta, Canada A 146h
Great Smoky Mountains, eastern United States T 76
Great Smoky Mountains National Park N 315; T 83
Great Society, program of President Johnson J 131
    20th century Utopias U 256
Great South Bay Scooter, iceboat racing I 29
Great Square of Pegasus C 493
Great Stone Face, New Hampshire rock formation N 148; picture N 150
    Hawthorne's famous story, how written H 73
Great Train Robbery, The, early motion picture M 472; P 218
Great Trek, 1836–38, of Boers in South Africa S 273; picture B 298
    Dutch settlements in Africa A 68
Great Valley, Virginia V 346–47

Great Wall of China, wall extending about 1,500 miles east and west across China from sea at Shanhaikuan northeast of Peking to northern frontier of Kansu province. Construction was started (214 B.C.) under first emperor of China, Shih Huang Ti, to protect country from invasions of northern tribes. It was built of stone and brick and stands between 20 and 30 feet high with 42-foot sentry towers at 200-yard intervals. Today much of it is still in excellent condition. Pictures C 256, W 219.
    China, history of C 270
    forts and fortification F 375
    Shih Huang Ti C 269–70
    U. S. table tennis team at the Wall, picture N 262f

Great Western Schism (1378–1431), within the Roman Catholic Church R 293
    two popes F 415

Grebe, any of a family of water birds with short legs, a pointed bill, and lobed toes, related to the loons. Awkward in flight and on land, grebes often escape danger by diving. Most are found in temperate zones.

Grechaninov (grech-on-YE-nof), Alexander Tikhonovich (1864–1956), Russian composer, b. Moscow. Noted chiefly for his sacred music, he was influenced by Tchaikovsky and Rimsky-Korsakov. He also composed operas, six symphonies, and many songs. Grechaninov lived in United States after 1939.

Greco, El, Spanish painter, born Crete G 330
    place in Spanish art P 23–24; S 362
    The Assumption, painting S 361
    View of Toledo, painting P 22

Greco, José (1918–), American dancer and choreographer, b. Montorio nei Frentani, Italy. He was partner (1943–45) of celebrated Spanish dancer Argentinita and organized company of Spanish dancers (1948), which toured Europe, United States, and South America. His best-known dances include *Cana y Farruca* and *El Cortjo*.

Gredos, Sierra de, Spain S 354
Greece G 331–39
    Balkan wars B 19
    Cyprus C 556–58
    favorite foods F 340
    flag F 239
    folk dancers, picture F 297

Green, Paul Eliot (1894–   ), American playwright, b. Lillington, N.C. Green is known for dramas on historical subjects for outdoor production, including *The Common Glory* and *Faith of Our Fathers.* He won Pulitzer prize (1927) for *In Abraham's Bosom.*

Greenaway, Kate (Catherine Greenaway) (1846–1901), English illustrator and watercolorist, b. London. Noted for her children and country-folk characters, she painted an Empire style of dress that became known in England as the Kate Greenaway style. Her works include *Under the Window* and *Kate Greenaway's Birthday Book.*

Greenbacks, popular name for U.S. notes, also known as legal tender, which were printed on the back with green ink. The first paper currency issued (1862) by U.S. government, it was intended primarily to finance the Civil War. Controversy over legal status of greenbacks gave rise to "Greenback movement," which supported national issuance of the notes. In 1878 Congress declared over $346 million worth of greenbacks in permanent circulation.

Greenberg, Hank (Henry Benjamin Greenberg) (1911–   ), American baseball player, b. New York, N.Y. As first-baseman for Detroit Tigers (1933–46), he hit total of 331 home runs and twice won American League's Most Valuable Player award. He was elected to Baseball's Hall of Fame (1956).

Greene, Graham (1904–   ), English novelist and jour-

nalist, b. Berkhampstead, Herfordshire. A convert to Roman Catholicism, his stories often are concerned with religion. His works include *The Power and The Glory*, *The Heart of the Matter*, and *Our Man in Havana*.
  English literature, history of **E** 267

Greene, Nathanael, American Revolutionary War officer **R** 225
  campaigns of the Revolutionary War **R** 199, 207–08
  Greensboro, N.C. named for him **N** 318
Greene, Robert, English writer **E** 253
Greeneville, Tennessee, home of Andrew Johnson **J** 123–24
Greenfield Village, Dearborn, Michigan **D** 151; **M** 268
  museums **M** 514
  store front, picture **B** 137

Greenhouse, glass structure for cultivation and protection of tender or out-of-season plants. Inside temperature, humidity, and ventilation are regulated. Picture **Z** 378.

Greenland G 367–71
  aerial view of glacier **I** 16
  Denmark, overseas possessions **D** 112–13
  Ericson, Leif **E** 275
  Eric the Red **V** 339
  Eskimo life **E** 284–91
  glaciers **G** 223
  icebergs **I** 25–26
  ice sheet depths **I** 9–10
  Peary, Robert E. **P** 116
Greenland Current I 25, 43

Greenland Sea, southern part of Arctic Ocean off the northeastern coast of Greenland, bordered by Iceland on the southwest and the Spitsbergen archipelago on the northeast. It is sometimes considered part of the Norwegian Sea.

Greenleaf, Ralph (1899–1950), American pocket-billiard player, b. Monmouth, Ill. Considered one of greatest pocket-billiard players, he won world championship 13 times (between 1919 and 1937).

Green manure F 96; **S** 232
Green Mountain Boys, local militia in colonial times **V** 320–21
  Allen, Ethan, leader **A** 167
  Revolutionary War **R** 199
Green Mountain National Forest, Vermont
  ski area **V** 316; picture **V** 310
Green Mountains, Vermont **V** 309
Green Mountain State, nickname for Vermont **V** 307
Green revolution, development of high-yielding cereal grains **F** 343
Green River, North America **W** 326
Greensboro, North Carolina **N** 318
Green Still Life, painting by Pablo Picasso **P** 31
Green tea T 38
Green turtles T 335; picture **T** 331
Greenville, South Carolina **S** 307
Greenwich (GREN-ich) **meridian,** or prime meridian **T** 190
Greenwich Observatory, Royal G 372
  prime meridian **L** 83
Green wood, preparation of, for furniture-making **F** 501–02
Greeting cards G 372–74
  Christmas **C** 292, 294
  New Year good wishes **N** 209
  valentines **V** 266–68

Gregg, John Robert (1867–1948), Irish-American inventor of Gregg shorthand system, b. Rockcorry, Ireland. He gained fame with the development of his shorthand system (1888). He moved to U.S. (1893), where his *Gregg Shorthand Manual* became standard shorthand text.
  shorthand systems **S** 164

Gregorian (gre-GO-rian) **calendar C** 12–13
  Gregory XIII **G** 375
  religious holidays **R** 153
  time by the solar calendar **T** 194
Gregorian chants C 276
  development of musical notation **M** 524
  German music **G** 182
  hymns **H** 311
  Italian music **I** 483
  Middle Ages **M** 298
Gregory IX, pope
  established Papal Inquisition **I** 257
  Jewish persecution **J** 108
Gregory XIII, pope **G** 375
  calendar **C** 12–13
Gregory, Saint (Gregory I, pope) ("Gregory the Great") **C** 283
  Gregorian chant named for **C** 276
  Middle Ages, music of **M** 298
Gregory, Saint (Gregory VII, pope, real name Hildebrand)
  church reforms **R** 291
  Holy Roman Empire **H** 163
Gregory, Lady Augusta, Irish playwright **D** 298
  Yeats and Lady Gregory **Y** 344

Gregory, Dick (1932–), American entertainer and civil rights leader, b. St. Louis, Mo. His comedy routines often contained quips about civil rights. He produced a documentary series for television, *Walk in My Shoes*. His books include *From the Back of the Bus* (1964); an autobiography, *Nigger* (1964); and *What's Happening* (1965). In the late 1960's he became a civil rights leader. In 1968 he was a candidate for president.

Gregory of Nazianzus, Saint C 283
Gregory of Nyssa, Saint C 283
Gregory the Great see Gregory, Saint (Gregory I, pope)

Gregory the Great, Order of Saint, order established (1831) by Pope Gregory XVI to honor subjects of the Papal States. Today the pope confers the honor on Roman Catholics in any country for distinguished service.

Greiner (GRINE-er)**, Ludwig,** German-born American doll maker **D** 265

Grenada (gren-ADE-a), one of the Windward Islands group in the Caribbean, a member of the West Indies Associated States and self-governing within the Commonwealth of Nations. Its capital is St. George's. Colonized by France in 1650, the island was taken over by Britain (1762).
  Caribbean Sea and islands **C** 116–19

Grendel, monster in epic poem *Beowulf* **B** 141
  Old English literature **E** 245

Grenfell, Sir Wilfred Thomason (1865–1940), English physician, medical missionary, and writer, b. Cheshire. He sailed to Labrador (1892), where he founded hospitals, orphanages, and co-operative stores. He established (1912) King George V Seamen's Institute in St. John's, Newfoundland. Grenfell wrote *Adrift on an Ice Pan*.

Grenoble (gren-O-bel), France, picture **F** 407
  glovemaking **G** 241

Grenville, George (1712–1770), English statesman, b. Buckinghamshire. Prime minister (1763–65), he is noted for his administration's passage of the Stamp Act (1765).

Grenville, or **Greynville, Sir Richard** (1541?–1591), English naval officer. He led fleet, sent by Sir Walter Raleigh, which carried colonists to Virginia (1585). He was mortally wounded and his ship, the *Revenge,* captured after a heroic battle with a Spanish fleet (1591). His exploit is commemorated in Tennyson's *The Revenge.*

American colonies, history of **A** 180, 181

Gresham's Law, in economics, the principle that bad money tends to drive good money out of circulation. For example, if two coins have the same face value but different metallic content, the one with less intrinsic value will be circulated, while the more precious coin will be hoarded. The law was named for the English financier **Sir Thomas Gresham** (1519?–79).

Grethel, Gammer, Grimm brothers' storyteller **F** 21

Greuze (GRERZE), **Jean Baptiste** (1725–1805), French artist, b. Tournus. Noted for his portraits and genre scenes, he painted numerous moralistic works, including *Village Betrothal* and *Paralytic Cared for by His Children.* He is known also for his graceful studies of girls, *The Broken Pitcher* and *Girl with Doves.*

Grey, Lady Jane (Lady Jane Dudley) (1537–1554), English pretender to crown, b. Bradgate, Leicestershire. She was a niece of Henry VIII and married Lord Guildford Dudley to aid plot to change succession to throne from Tudors to Dudleys. In accordance with young King Edward VI's will, she was proclaimed queen (July 9, 1553) and reigned for 9 days. Mary I, daughter of Henry VIII, was supported in her claim as lawful successor and was proclaimed queen. Lady Jane Grey was executed (1554) after she refused to deny Protestantism and after her father participated in Wyatt's Rebellion against Queen Mary's marriage to Catholic Spanish King Philip II.

England, history of **E** 221

Grey, Zane (1875–1939), American novelist, b. Zanesville, Ohio. Grey is noted for Western adventure stories. Among his 54 novels are *The Lone Star Ranger, West of the Pecos,* and *Riders of the Purple Sage.*

Greyfell, horse, faithful steed of Sigurd, in Norse mythology **N** 281
Greyhound, dog, picture **D** 254
dog racing **R** 33
Greylag geese, ancestors of domesticated geese **P** 423
Gridiron, a football field **F** 357
Gridley, Charles V., American naval captain **S** 375
Grids, in electron tubes **E** 146
Grids, of maps **M** 90
Grieg (GREEG), **Edvard,** Norwegian composer **G** 376
Grierson, John, English motion picture producer **M** 475
Grievance procedure, in labor-management relations **L** 16; picture **L** 17

Griffin (from Latin *gryphus,* meaning "with hooked nose"), in ancient and medieval mythology, a fabulous creature having body of lion and head and wings of eagle. In Eastern legend, these creatures are supposed to have guarded gold of North from Arimaspians in Rhipaean mountains.

Griffin, Donald R., American scientist **B** 96–97
Griffin, Walter Burley, American architect **C** 88

Griffith, D. W. (David Lewelyn Wark Griffith) (1875–1948), American motion picture director and producer, b. La-Grange, Ky. His first important film was *The Birth of a Nation* (1914), the first American spectacular. He pioneered use of the fade-out, flashback, close-up, crowd scene, and other techniques. Among his major works are *Intolerance, Way Down East,* and *Broken Blossoms.* Picture **M** 473.

motion pictures, history of **M** 472

Griffith, John see London, Jack
Griffith, Sam, American boat racer **B** 264
Grimaldi (gri-MOL-di), **Francesco,** Italian scientist **L** 271
Grimaldi family, rulers of Monaco **M** 407
Grimké, Angelina Emily and **Sarah Moore** (sisters), American abolitionists and women's rights advocates **S** 309

Grimke, Archibald Henry (1849–1930), American lawyer and writer, Negro, b. near Charleston, S.C. As a leader of NAACP and editor of the *Hub* (1883–85), he crusaded for Negro rights. He wrote biographies of abolitionists Charles Sumner and William Lloyd Garrison, served as U.S. consul to Santo Domingo (1894–98), and was awarded the Spingarn medal (1919).

Grimké, John Faucheraud, family **S** 309
Grimm, Jacob and Wilhelm, German philologists and writers of fairy tales **G** 376–86
children's literature **C** 238
"Hansel and Gretel" **G** 380–86
history of the fairy tale **F** 20
Märchen (folklore) collections **F** 302
"Rapunzel" **G** 378–80
"Shoemaker and the Elves, The" **G** 377–78
short stories **S** 165
storytelling **S** 434–35
Grimmelshausen, Haus von, German writer **G** 175
Grinding and polishing **G** 387–89
diamonds and diamond dust **D** 155
optical glass **O** 174
tools **T** 219

Grinnell (grin-NELL), **Henry** (1799–1874), American merchant and financier, b. New Bedford, Mass. He financed expeditions (1850 and 1853) primarily to locate English arctic explorer Sir John Franklin and to complete the Northwest Passage. Grinnell Land in Northwest Territories of Canada is named for him.

Grippe see Influenza

Gris (GREECE), **Juan** (José Vittoriano González) (1887–1927), Spanish painter and lithographer, b. Madrid. A leader and theoretician of cubist school of painting, Gris designed settings for Diaghilev's ballet *Temptation of a Shepherd.* His works include *Still Life with Dice.*

Spanish art **S** 365

Grisi (GRE-zi), **Carlotta,** Italian ballerina **B** 25

Grissom, Virgil Ivan ("Gus") (1926–67), American astronaut, b. Mitchell, Ind. He was chosen (1959) to be one of the seven original Project Mercury astronauts. He made the second Project Mercury space flight (1961) and became first man to make two space flights when he and Young made the Gemini 3 spaceshot (1965). Grissom, with fellow astronauts Roger Chaffee and Edward White, died during test runthrough of Apollo launching.

space flight data **S** 344, 345, 346

Grit numbers, of sandpaper **G** 387

Grizzly bears B 106–07

Grofé (gro-FAY), **Ferde** (Ferdinand Rudolph von Grofé) (1892–1972), American composer, pianist and arranger, b. New York, N.Y. He composed *Grand Canyon* Suite and other works describing American scene and orchestrated George Gershwin's *Rhapsody in Blue*. Grofé was pianist and arranger for Paul Whiteman's orchestra.

Grolier de Servières (gro-li-AY d'sair-vi-AIR), **Jean,** Vicomte d'Aiguis (1479–1565), French bibliophile, b. Lyons. He gained a reputation for his love of finely bound and printed books (collected 3,000 volumes). He served as ambassador to the Vatican and treasurer under Francis I. The Grolier Club, a book club, and Grolier Incorporated, publisher of *The New Book of Knowledge* and other educational volumes, are named for him.
noted book collectors B 322

Gromyko (gro-ME-ko), **Andrei Andreyevich** (1909–), Soviet foreign minister, b. Gromyki, Byelorussia. After graduating from Moscow's Institute of Economics (1936) he taught economics at the Academy of Sciences and in 1939 entered the Soviet diplomatic service. His first foreign post was as counsellor to the Soviet embassy in Washington (1939–43). From 1943 to 1946 he was ambassador to the United States. During 1946 he represented the U.S.S.R. in the UN Security Council. He was ambassador to Great Britain (1952–53). He became deputy foreign minister in 1953 and since 1957 has served as foreign minister.

Groningen, the Netherlands N 118

Gronouski, John Austin (1919–), U.S. government official, b. Dunbar, Wisc. After service in the Air Force, he taught public finance at the University of Maine (1948–50). Expert also in tax administration and statistics, he held several research and administrative posts. In 1960 he was Wisconsin Commissioner of Taxation. He was postmaster general (1963–65).

Grooming, care of a horse, pictures H 228

Gropius (GRO-pi-us), **Walter** (1883–1969), American architect, b. Berlin, Germany. He was founder and director (1919–28) of Bauhaus school of architecture (teaching unity of art, science, and technology; functionalism in architecture; and use of abstract art) and chairman of School of Architecture at Harvard University (1938–52). He designed buildings in Germany, England, and United States.
Bauhaus B 103–04
United States, architecture of A 385; U 125

Groseillers (gro-zer-YAY), **Médart Chouart, Sieur de** (1625?–1697?), French explorer, b. Charly-sur-Marne. Between 1658 and 1663 he and his brother-in-law Pierre Radisson explored the upper Mississippi, Lake Superior, and Hudson Bay. Their British-backed expedition to Hudson Bay in 1668 resulted in the founding of Hudson's Bay Co. (1670).
fur trading and exploration F 520–21; S 16

Gross, Chaim (1904–), American sculptor, b. Carpathian mountains, Austria. He came to the United States in 1921. His work *Alaska Snowshoe Mail Carrier* was chosen in national competition and placed in Post Office Building in Washington, D.C.

Grossglockner (GROSS-glock-ner), highest mountain in Austria A 521

Gross national product (G.N.P.) E 51; G 96
Grossularite (GROS-su-la-rite), gem mineral G 75

Grosz (GROSS), **George** (1893–1959), German artist, b. Berlin. His satirical drawings, such as *The Entrée* and *Ecce Homo,* were suppressed by the Nazis. He came to United States (1932) to teach at the Art Students League of New York.

Grotesquerie, Italian Renaissance furniture designs F 505; picture F 506
Grotius (GRO-shi-us), **Hugo,** Dutch scholar I 320
peace movements P 104
Groton (GRO-ton), Connecticut C 473; picture C 471
Grotzen, line of fur on a pelt F 517
Ground, or field, of a flag F 243; picture F 234
Ground, acid-resisting substance used in etching and engraving E 293; G 305
Ground beetle, picture I 262
Ground-controlled approach, or GCA, radar technique in aviation R 36
Ground effect machines see Air-cushioned vehicles
Groundfish F 220
habitat, feeding habits, uses F 213–14
Groundhog Day F 74; H 159
Groundhogs, or woodchucks, rodents R 276, pictures R 275, 277
Grounding, in electricity E 125
Ground nuts see Peanuts
Grounds, for divorce D 234
Ground squirrels R 276; pictures R 275, 277
body changes in hibernation H 123
why small animals hibernate H 123–24
Groundwater W 53
climate and water cycle build groundwater C 347
lake basins formed by L 25
mines require constant pumping M 317
Nebraska soils store water N 75–76
water supply W 66–67
wells W 122
Groundwood papers P 53
Group counseling G 400
Grouper, fish, picture F 195
Group life insurance see Insurance, group
Group of seven, Canadian painters C 64
Group personality tests T 118
Group therapy, for the mentally ill M 225
nursing activities in psychiatric institutions N 410

Grouse, any of several medium-to-large game birds found in all northern regions. They resemble chickens, except that legs and nostrils are covered with feathers. Their feathers are dull brown, red, or gray. Grouse live and build nests on ground. Their short, broad wings whir loudly when they rise. Males court females with lively dances: they ruffle feathers and cackle, and some can make booming sounds with wings or air sacs. Scientists include prairie chickens with this group. Picture B 208.

Grout, thin mortar, used in making mosaic M 463

Grove, Lefty (Robert Moses Grove) (1900–), American baseball player, b. Lonaconing, Md. Primarily a fast-ball pitcher, Grove won 300 games and lost 141, and struck out over 2,000 men. He played for the Philadelphia Athletics (1925–33) and Boston Red Sox (1934–41). He was elected to Baseball Hall of Fame in 1947.

Growing seasons
forest growth F 371
length of summer days offsets short growing season, Alaska, North Dakota A 134; N 326

Growing seasons (continued)
vegetables **V** 286–94
See also agriculture section of country, province, and state articles
Growth
a life process **L** 210–11
child development **C** 231–34
plant growth patterns **P** 302–03
Growth rings, of trees
wood and wood products **W** 225
Gruber, Edmund L., American officer **N** 25–26
Gruber, Franz, Austrian organist, composer of "Silent Night, Holy Night" **C** 122
Grubs, larvae
plant pests **P** 289; picture **P** 288

Gruenberg, Louis (1884–1964), American pianist and composer, b. Brest-Litovsk, Russia. He is best known for opera scores *Jack and the Beanstalk, Green Mansions,* and *The Emperor Jones* and for his violin concerto, in which he evokes Negro and rural-American music.

Gruenther, Alfred Maximilian (1899–   ), American general, b. Platte Center, Nebr. He was chief of staff of NATO (1951), supreme commander of Allied Powers in Europe (1953). After retiring from the army (1956), he was president of American Red Cross (1957–64). After 1965 he was appointed to various government advisory committees.

Grundtvig (GROONT-veeg), **N.F.S.,** Danish educator **D** 109

Grundy, Mrs., symbol of British propriety. A character who never actually appears but is constantly referred to in Thomas Morton's 18th-century play *Speed the Plough.*

Grünewald (GRURN-ev-alt), **Matthias,** German painter **G** 169
Isenheim altarpiece, painting **G** 167
Grunions, fish **L** 244–45; pictures **L** 246
Grunts, fish, picture **F** 202
Grunwald (GROON-valt), **battle of,** 1410 **P** 361
Gryphius, Andreas, German dramatist **G** 175
Guadalajara (gua-da-la-HA-ra), Mexico **M** 247
Guadalcanal, Pacific island **P** 6
battle of, 1942 **W** 295
Guadalquivir (gua-dol-ki-BEER) **River,** Spain **R** 244; **S** 354
Guadalupe (gua-da-LU-pay), **Day of Our Lady of,** religious holiday **R** 155
pilgrims at Basilica of the Virgin of Guadalupe, picture **M** 247
Guadalupe fur seals W 6
Guadalupe Hidalgo, Treaty of, 1848 **M** 239
Arizona **A** 417
Mexican cession of territory to United States **T** 112
New Mexico **N** 194
Polk, James K. **P** 386
Guadalupe Mountains, New Mexico-Texas **T** 124
Carlsbad Caverns, discovery of **C** 152
Guadarrama, Sierra de, Spain **S** 354
skiing in **M** 11

Guadeloupe (GWA-de-loop), Caribbean islands (Grande-Terre and Basse-Terre) in the Leeward group. An overseas department of the French Republic, its population is mainly Negro and mulatto. Its chief products are sugar, vanilla, coffee, and cacao. Discovered by Columbus, it was settled by the French in 1635.
Caribbean Sea and islands **C** 116–19

Guaira (gwy-RA) **Falls,** Brazil and Paraguay **W** 56b

Guam (GUOM) **P** 6; **T** 114
Guanabara (gua-na-BA-ra) **Bay,** Rio de Janeiro, Brazil, picture **B** 379
Guanacos (gua-NA-cos), hoofed mammals **H** 210; picture **H** 213
Guano (GUA-no), fertilizer **P** 163
found in caves **C** 153
Guantánamo (gu-on-TA-na-mo), Cuba
United States Naval Base **C** 550
Guarani (gua-ra-NI), Indians of South America **I** 210
Paraguay **P** 62
Guaranty (GARR-an-ty) **Building,** Buffalo, New York **U** 124
Guard cells, of leaves **L** 120
Guard hair, of furs **F** 516
Guardi, Francesco, Italian painter **I** 473
Guardia (GUAR-dia), **Tomás,** Costa Rican dictator **C** 519
Guardian, The, Negro newspaper **N** 96

Guarneri (guar-NAIR-i) **family,** violin-makers of Cremona, Italy, in 17th and 18th centuries. The first craftsman was **Andrea** (1625?–98). The most noted was **Giuseppe Bartolomeo** (1698–1744), whose violins, distinguished by rich tone and bold modeling, were made famous by Nicolò Paganini. The secret of their fine tone is believed to be a special kind of varnish.
violin making, history of **V** 342

Guast, Pierre du see Monts, Pierre du Guast
Guatemala (gua-te-MA-la) **G** 390–94
flag **F** 241
life in Latin America **L** 47–61
national anthem **N** 21
Pan American Highway **P** 50
religious procession, picture **L** 54
special stamp, picture **S** 399
Guatemala City, capital of Guatemala **G** 391; picture **G** 394
Guatemoc see Cuauhtémoc, last Aztec emperor
Guava (GUAV-a), a tropical fruit **M** 74
Guayana (gua-YA-na), **The,** or Guiana Highlands, South America **S** 276; **V** 297–98
Guayaquil (gua-ya-KEEL), Ecuador **E** 57; picture **E** 54
Guayas-Daule (GWY-os-DOW-lay), river system in Ecuador **E** 55
Gudea (gu-DAY-a), king of Sumer **A** 234; statue, picture **A** 235
Gudrun (GOOD-roon), or **Gutrune,** in Norse mythology **N** 281
Guelphs and Ghibellines (GWELFS and GHIB-el-lenes), Italian political parties **P** 378
Holy Roman Empire **H** 163
Guerezas (ghe-REZ-as), monkeys **M** 418
Guericke (GAY-rick-a), **Otto von,** German physicist **S** 71; **V** 263–64
Guernica (gher-NI-ca), mural by Picasso **P** 243
Guernsey, breed of dairy cattle **C** 147; **D** 8; pictures **D** 5, 6
Guernsey, one of the Channel Islands, Great Britain **I** 428; picture **I** 425
Guerrero (gher-RAY-ro), **Lorenzo,** Nicaraguan political leader **N** 249
Guerrero, Manuel, president of Panama **P** 46
Guerrero, Vicente, Mexican patriot **M** 248
Guerrilla warfare, undercover fighting **U** 10
American tactics during Revolutionary War **R** 207
Special Forces of United States Army **U** 173
Vietnam War, 1958– **V** 334d, 336
Guess, George see Sequoya
Guessing games I 226
charades **C** 188

Guest, Edgar Albert (1881–1959), American poet, b. Birmingham, England. He wrote popular verse about everyday things, and his books include *Just Folks, All That Matters, The Light of Faith,* and *A Heap of Livin'.*

Guettard, Étienne, French geologist **G** 112

Guevara, Ernesto (Che) (1928–67), revolutionary leader, b. Buenos Aires, Argentina. He joined Fidel Castro in the overthrow of Batista in Cuba, and later held important posts in the Cuban government. He was killed by an army patrol while leading a guerrilla band in Bolivia. His books include *Guerrilla Warfare* and *Memoirs of the Sierra Maestra.*

Guggenheim, or Categories, a word game **W** 238

Guggenheim (GU-gen-hime) **family,** American family descended from **Meyer Guggenheim** (1828–1905), b. Switzerland, who founded and developed Guggenheim copper mining and smelting properties in Colorado. His son **Solomon R.** (1861–1949) was an art patron and established the Solomon R. Guggenheim Foundation. His son **Simon** (1867–1941) was U.S. senator from Colorado (1907–13).

Guggenheim (Solomon R.) **Foundation,** an organization that promotes understanding and appreciation of art and makes awards to international artists. Solomon R. Guggenheim Museum in New York, N.Y., features exhibitions of nonobjective painting. The organization, founded in 1937, has headquarters in New York, N.Y.
Solomon R. Guggenheim Museum **M** 518

Guggenheim (John Simon) **Memorial Foundation,** a philanthropic organization that subsidizes artists and musicians and grants fellowships for advanced study in all fields of knowledge. Founded in 1925, it has headquarters in New York, N.Y.

Gugs, Ethiopian sport **E** 299
Guiana (ghi-AN-a) **Highlands S** 276
Guianas, The G 395–97
life in Latin America **L** 47–61
Guidance G 397–400
adolescence **A** 22–24
advice and help for the elderly **O** 100
child development **C** 231–34
divorce, counseling services for **D** 235
juvenile delinquency, control and prevention **J** 164
meanings of test scores **T** 119–20
vocational guidance and counseling **V** 373–74
Guided missiles M 344–45
Guide Dogs for the Blind, school **D** 259
Guidi, Tommaso see Masaccio
Guido (GHE-do), **José María,** Argentine political leader **A** 396
Guido d'Arezzo (GUI-do d'a-RETZ-o), Italian monk **M** 525
Guildhalls G 401
Guilds G 401–03
artisans and tradesmen as musicians **G** 181
bakers **B** 386
dyers **D** 369
established monopolies **T** 304–05
jewelry crafts **J** 94
labor movement, beginnings of **L** 2
leathermaking centers in England **L** 110
Middle Ages, industry in **M** 293
Middle English drama **E** 249–50
miracle plays **M** 339
rise of middle class German literature **G** 174
students' guilds of Middle Ages **E** 67

Guilford, Connecticut, pictures **C** 479
Guilford, Sir Henry, painting by Hans Holbein the Younger **H** 146
Guilford Courthouse, battle of, 1781 **N** 321
Guilford Courthouse National Military Park **N** 316
Guillaume de Machaut (ghi-YOME de ma-SHO), French poet and composer **F** 443
choral music **C** 277
Middle Ages, music of the **M** 299

Guillot (ghe-YO), **René** (1900–), French author of children's books, b. Courcoury. Best-known for animal stories based on folk tales and legends he collected in Africa, he spent many years in Africa, traveling and teaching at Lycée of Dakar in Senegal. His books include *Elephant Road* and *Grishka and the Bear.*

Guillotine (GHIL-lo-tene), device for cutting off heads **F** 467–68
Guilt, feeling of, psychology **M** 220–21
divorce, attitudes toward **D** 235
Guinea (GHIN-e) **G** 404–06
African art **A** 76
flag **F** 235
special-issue stamp, picture **S** 399
Guinea, Gulf of, western coast of Africa
Dahomey located on **D** 3, 4
Guinea highlands, western Africa **A** 49
Guinea pigs, or cavies, rodents **G** 407–08; **R** 280
pets **P** 179
Guinevere (gu-IN-e-vere), **Queen,** wife of King Arthur **A** 442, 444
Guinizelli (gui-ni-TZEL-li), **Guido,** Italian poet **I** 475

Guinness, Sir Alec (1914–), British actor, b. Marylebone, London. He played Hamlet in modern dress (1938) at the Old Vic in London, but is most famous for character roles in films. Guinness starred in *Oliver Twist, The Lavender Hill Mob,* and *Lawrence of Arabia* and won Oscar (1958) for *The Bridge on the River Kwai.*
British motion pictures **M** 487

Guion (GUY-on), **David Wendell Fentress** (1895–), American composer, Negro, b. Ballinger, Tex. He emphasizes national folk music, and is famous for setting of "Home on the Range." Among his cowboy compositions is *Western Ballet.*

Guitar G 409–10
folk music instruments **F** 329; picture **F** 330
quiterna, early guitar, picture **S** 438
rock music **R** 262d
Segovia, guitar virtuoso, picture **S** 373
stall in Bolivia, picture **L** 53
Guiteau (ghit-O), **Charles J.,** American assassin of President Garfield **G** 56; **M** 225

Guiterman (GIT-er-man), **Arthur** (1871–1943), American poet, b. Vienna, Austria, of American parents. He wrote about urban America. His volumes of poetry include *Ballads of Old New York,* and *Brave Laughter.*
"Habits of the Hippopotamus," nonsense poem **N** 274

Gulbenkian (gool-BEN-ki-an), **Calouste,** Armenian oilman **M** 520
Gulf, geographic term see name of gulf, as Mexico, Gulf of
Gulf of Tonkin Resolution see Tonkin Resolution
Gulf Plain, bordering Gulf of Mexico **N** 285
Gulf Stream, current of Atlantic Ocean **G** 411
climate and the Gulf Stream **C** 346
currents in the Atlantic Ocean **A** 478

Gulf Stream (continued)
    icebergs I 26
    measuring ocean currents O 32–33
    rotation of the earth E 16

Gulick (GU-lick), **Luther Halsey** (1892–   ), American educator and government administrator, b. Osaka, Japan. He taught at Columbia University (1931–42) and was a member of U.S. reparations mission to Japan (1945–46). Chairman of The Board of Trustees of Institute of Public Administration (since 1961), he wrote *Modern Management for the City of New York.*
    founded Camp Fire Girls C 37

Gullet, or **esophagus**, food passage tube B 274–75
    birds B 202
Gulliver's Travels, book by Jonathan Swift, excerpt
      G 412–13
    place in English literature E 258
    satire H 280
    Swift, Jonathan S 488

Gulls, any of several seabirds found throughout the world. Gulls are whitish in color, being darker on the back and wings. They have squarish tails and bills that curve downward into a sharp hook. Gulls are experts at gliding and soaring on their long, pointed wings. Some gulls are fishers, but many are scavengers, feeding on a variety of animal and vegetable food. Gulls breed in large colonies, usually on small coastal islands. Pictures B 236, 238.
    animal communication A 277, 278
    sea gulls saved crops for the Mormons U 240

GUM, state department store, Moscow, Union of Soviet Socialist Republics, pictures M 466, U 34
Gum arabic R 185
Gumbo see Okra
Gumbotil, glacial deposit I 20
Gumdrops C 98
Gums, juices from plants R 185

Gumwoods, or **gums**, varieties of gum, tupelo, and eucalyptus trees, growing in many parts of the world.
    shapes of leaves, picture L 116
    uses of the wood and its grain, picture W 223

Gun-cotton; explosive E 392
Gunnar (GU-nar), or **Gunther**, in Norse mythology N 281
Gunpowder, or black powder, explosive E 389–90, 391
    guns and ammunition G 414
    Goddard's rocket experiments with G 244–45
Gunpowder Gypsies, of Yugoslavia G 433–34
Gunpowder Plot, 1605
    Guy Fawkes Day commemorates H 150
Guns G 414–26
    communication method of pioneers C 437
    first mass-produced by Eli Whitney C 473; W 166
    hunting rifles H 291
    museum at Berryville, Arkansas A 427
    safety measures S 4
    What is a blunderbuss? G 420
Guntersville Lake, Alabama A 115
Gunther (GOON-ter), or **Gunnar**, in Norse mythology N 281
Gunther (GOON-ter), **Fritz**, German scientist D 148
Gunther (GUN-ther), **John**, American writer A 214
Guppies, fishes P 181
    aquariums A 343
Gupta dynasty, India I 131
    oriental art and architecture O 212–13, 215
Gurkha (GOORK-ha), or **Gorkha**, Nepal N 113

Gurkhas, soldiers of Nepal N 111, 114
Gurney system, shorthand S 164
Guru, teacher see Sikhs
Gushers, or blowouts, oil wells P 172–73
Gustavus I, king of Sweden S 486
Gustavus Adolphus, king of Sweden S 486
Gutenberg (GU-ten-berg), **Johann**, German inventor of movable type for printing G 427
    communication advanced by printing press C 433–34
    history of printing P 457
    history of the book B 321
Gutenberg Bible P 457; pictures B 320, C 433
    earliest printed books B 321
    Gutenberg, Johann G 427
    illuminated page, picture B 157
Guthrie, Tyrone, English producer-director C 62–63

Guthrie, Woody (Woodrow Wilson Guthrie), (1912–67), American folk singer and composer, b. Okemah, Okla. Accompanying himself on the guitar, Guthrie sang of the beauty of the American countryside, and of the social and economic ills of life in the United States. Among his most famous songs are "This Land is Your Land" and "So Long, It's Been Good To Know You." He had a great influence on later folk singers. His son, **Arlo** (1947–   ), is known for composing the song "Alice's Restaurant", and for starring in the movie of the same name.

Guthrum (GOOTH-room), Danish king of East Anglia A 154–55
    England invasion E 217
Gutiérrez, Antonio, García see García Guttlérrez, Antonio
Gutiérrez, René Schick see Schick, René Gutiérrez
Gutrune (gu-TRU-ne), or **Gudrun**, in Norse mythology N 281

Gutta percha, nonelastic substance obtained from sap of certain trees grown in Malaya and parts of East Indies. It is easily shaped when heated and hardens when cooled. It is used as temporary filling for cavities and permanent filling for pulp canals of dead teeth. A good insulator and more resistant to water than rubber, it is used as covering for underwater cables.
    covering of golf ball G 262
    resins, types of R 185

Guyana (ghi-AN-a), formerly British Guiana G 395, 396
    flag F 242
    life in Latin America L 47–61
    sugar plantation, picture S 275
Guy de Lusignan, French king of Cyprus C 558
Guy Fawkes Day H 150
Guyots (GHE-yots), flat-topped seamounts M 492
Guzmán Blanco, Antonio, president of Venezuela V 300
Gwelo, Rhodesia R 229
Gwilym, Dafydd ap see Dafydd ap Gwilym
Gwin, William M., American statesman P 392

Gwinnett, Button (1735?–1777), American politician, b. Gloucestershire, England. His trading interest in Georgia drew him to settle there before 1765. As one of Georgia's delegates to the Continental Congress (1776–77), he signed the Declaration of Independence. He served briefly in 1777 as president of the State of Georgia and died in a duel brought on by a political quarrel.
    rare signatures and autographs A 526

Gwyn, Nell (Eleanor Gwyn) (1650–1687), English actress, b. probably Hereford. She was a popular comic actress and dancer at Theatre Royal (1665–82) and a favorite of Charles II.

ILLUSTRATION CREDITS

The following list credits, by page, the sources of illustrations used in Volume G of THE NEW BOOK OF KNOWLEDGE. Credits are listed illustration by illustration— left to right, top to bottom. Wherever appropriate, the name of the photographer or artist has been listed with the source, the two being separated by a dash. When two or more illustrations appear on one page, their credits are separated by semicolons.

H, eighth letter of the English alphabet **H** 1
   See also Alphabet
Haakon VII (HAW-kon), king of Norway **N** 344
Haarlem, the Netherlands **N** 118
Habakkuk (ha-BAK-kuk), book of the Bible **B** 155
Habana *see* Havana
Habanera (ha-ba-NAY-ra), from the opera *Carmen,* beginning of **O** 142

Habeas corpus (HAY-be-as COR-pus) (Latin for "you have the body"), in law, a writ issued by a judge ordering an official to show cause for detaining someone. It originated in early English law to prevent illegal imprisonment and is considered a cornerstone of civil liberty. According to U.S. Constitution, it cannot be denied unless, in cases of rebellion or invasion, public safety is at stake.

Habit
   brain habits **P** 500a
   food preferences **F** 334
   smoking **S** 203
   study, how to **S** 440–42
   See also Instinct; Psychology
Habitants, farmers in New France, early Canada **C** 69; **Q** 9
Habitat groups, in museums **M** 512
Habits of the Hippopotamus, poem by Arthur Guiterman **N** 274

Habsburg, or **Hapsburg, House of,** German royal family (from 11th century), named after castle of Habsburg in Switzerland. They were sovereigns of the Holy Roman Empire, Austria, and Spain. **Count Rudolph** (1218–91) became Holy Roman Emperor, a position held by his descendants (1298–1308, 1438–1740, 1745–1806). **Charles V** (1500–58) was Holy Roman Emperor (1519–56) and King Charles I of Spain (1516–56), where his descendants reigned (until 1700). His brother **Ferdinand** (1503–64) and his descendants continued the Holy Roman imperial line (1556–1740, 1765–1806) until the dissolution of the empire, and thereafter the Austrian imperial line (to 1918).
   Austria and the Holy Roman Empire **A** 524–25; **H** 164

Haciendas (ha-ci-EN-das), large estates
   Peru **P** 161
Hackney horse, picture **H** 239
Hacksaw, tool **T** 213; picture **T** 212
Hack writing, professional work, usually for hire **W** 318

Hadassah (ha-DA-sah), Women's Zionist Organization of America, group that supports medical and social welfare projects in Israel. In the United States it provides educational and charitable services and a program for Jewish youth. Founded in 1912, it maintains headquarters in New York, N.Y.

Hadassah-Hebrew University Medical Center, Jerusalem
   Chagall stained-glass window, picture **S** 394
Haddad, Malek, Algerian poet **A** 76d
Hadden, Briton, American editor and publisher **M** 15

Haddock, ocean-dwelling fish found in northern Atlantic. It is distinguished by black lateral (side) line and large black spot behind gill. Like its relative the cod, haddock has three dorsal (back) fins, feeds on such creatures as mollusks, crustaceans, and worms. Important food fish, those caught weigh 1 to 4 lbs.
   habitats, feeding habits, uses **F** 213

Hader, Elmer (1889–   ), American author and illustrator. Collaborating with wife, **Berta,** he wrote *Mr. Billy's Gun, Jamaica Johnny, The Big Snow* (Caldecott medal, 1949), *Spunky, Farmer in the Dell, Two Funny Clowns, Green and Gold,* and *The Little Stone House.*

Hades (HADE-ese), Greek god **G** 357, 362
Had I But Known, a kind of mystery story **M** 554
Hadley, John, English mathematician and inventor **N** 65
Hadrian (HAY-drian), Roman emperor **R** 304
   Why were the Roman emperors called Caesars? **C** 6
Hadrian's Wall, in Britain, picture **A** 353
Hadrosaurs (HAD-ro-saurs), dinosaurs **D** 179
Hafnium, element **E** 154, 161
Haganah, Jewish resistance group, now Israeli army **U** 11
Hagar (HAY-gar), mother of Ishmael **A** 7

Hagen, Walter C. (1892–1969), American golf champion, b. Rochester, N.Y. First American to win British Open Championship (1922), he also won French, Australian, and American opens. He led American team to victory for Ryder Cup (1927) and won Professional Golfers Association and Western Open titles (each five times).

Hagerstown, Maryland **M** 125
Hagfish **F** 182
Haggai (HAG-gai-i), book of the Bible **B** 155–56

Haggard, Sir Henry Rider (1856–1925), English author, b. Norfolk. He is remembered for his exotic tales of adventure in Africa, including *Ayesha, Swallow,* and *Allan Quatermain.* His best-known romantic novels, set in African background, are *King Solomon's Mines* and *She.*

Hagia (HA-ja) **Sophia,** Byzantine church, now a museum **B** 485, 486, 490
   early architecture **A** 377
Hague (HAIG), **The,** seat of government of the Netherlands **N** 118
Hague Conventions, 1899, 1907 **I** 321
   basis of war crimes trials **W** 10
   peace movements **P** 104

Hahn (HON), **Otto** (1879–1968), German chemist and physicist, b. Frankfurt. He was noted for his work on radioactive substances. In the course of his research he discovered five elements, including protactinium (with Lisa Meitner). He received Nobel prize (1944) in chemistry for his discovery of nuclear fission in uranium.
   splitting the uranium atom **N** 360; **U** 230

Hahnium, radioactive element **E** 154, 161; **R** 68
Haida, Indians of North America **I** 182
   Alaska **A** 136
Haifa (HY-fa), Israel **I** 444; picture **I** 445
Haig, Sir Douglas, British general **W** 278
Haiku (HY-ku), Japanese verse form **J** 28; **O** 220b
   Japanese literature **O** 220b
Hail **R** 97–98
   control of hailstorms **W** 95
Hail Columbia, song, by Joseph Hopkinson **N** 23

Haile Selassie I (HY-le sel-LAS-sie) (title of Ras Tafari Makonnen) (1892–   ), emperor of Ethiopia, b. Harar. Crowned king of Ethiopia (1928) and emperor (since 1930), he defended Ethiopia against Italian invasion (1935) but was forced to flee country. He was restored to throne (1941) during World War II when the Italians were defeated.
   Ethiopia, history of **E** 303

Hainan (ha-i-NON), island off coast of China **C** 262
Haiphong (hi-PHONG), Democratic Republic of Vietnam (North Vietnam) **V** 334b

Hair, rock musical **M** 543; **R** 262d
Hair, animal
  furs **F** 511–16
  mammals **M** 65; pictures **M** 64
  wool compared with hair **W** 234
Hair and hairdressing **H** 2–6
  beauty culture **B** 111
  care of, for health **H** 84–85
  cosmetics **C** 509
  jeweled ornaments **J** 99
  Tibetan women, picture **T** 178
  What makes hair curly? **H** 2
  Why doesn't it hurt to cut your hair? **H** 6
Hair cells, of the body **B** 285
Haircuts **H** 3–4, 6
Hair seals, animals
  fur **F** 519
Hairsprings, in watches and clocks **W** 46
Haise, Fred W. Jr., American astronaut **S** 344, 345, 346
Haiti **H** 7–11
  abolition of slavery **S** 199
  Caribbean Sea and islands **C** 116–19
  flag **F** 241
  life in Latin America **L** 47–61
  national anthem **N** 21
  Toussaint L'Ouverture **T** 229
  United States Marine Corps action **U** 178

Hake, any of about 10 species of ocean fish related to cod. Several are choice food fish. All are slender with two soft-spined dorsal (back) fins. Most important commercially in North America is squirrel hake, abundant in Atlantic from southern Canada to Virginia. Hake is found down to 1,000 feet, is usually reddish brown in color, and is distinguished by long spine projecting from front dorsal fin. The hake generally weighs up to 3 pounds and reaches a length of 30 in.
  habitats, feeding habits, uses **F** 213

Hakim Tawfiq al- see Tawfiq al-Hakim
Hakirya (ha-KEER-ya), government center, Jerusalem **J** 80

Hakluyt (HAK-loot), **Richard** (1552?–1616), English geographer, b. Herefordshire. He was archdeacon of Westminster (1603) and member of Virginia Co. of London, organized to colonize Virginia. He is known for compilation *Principall Navigations, Voiages, and Discoveries of the English Nation.*

Halas, George Stanley (1895–   ), American football player and coach, b. Chicago, Ill. He played end at University of Illinois and coached Decatur Staleys, which he moved to Chicago and renamed Bears (1922). He is a charter member of National Professional Football Hall of Fame (1963).

Hale, Edward Everett (1822–1909), American author and minister, b. Boston, Mass. He is best-known for patriotic tale *The Man Without a Country* and is also noted for scholarly work *Franklin in France.*

Hale, George Ellery (1868–1938), American astronomer, b. Chicago, Ill. He planned and directed Yerkes Observatory, Chicago, Ill. (1895–1905), and Mt. Wilson Observatory, Mt. Wilson, Calif. (1904–1923). A pioneer in solar research, he invented the spectroheliograph—an instrument that can photograph the sun using light of a single wavelength. Through his observations of magnetic fields in sunspots he discovered magnetism outside of the earth.
  astronomy, history of **A** 474

Hale, Lucretia, American writer of children's books **C** 240
Hale, Nathan, American Revolutionary War hero **H** 12
  Nathan Hale Schoolhouse, East Haddam, Conn. **C** 478
  Revolutionary War campaign in New York **R** 201
  spies and spying **S** 388

Hale, Sarah Josepha Buell (1788–1879), American writer and editor, b. Newport, N.H. She was editor of *Ladies' Magazine* (1828–37) and *Godey's Lady's Book* (1837–77). She wrote "Mary Had a Little Lamb," which was published in *Poems for Our Children,* compiled and published *Letters of Madame de Sevigne to Her Daughter and Friends.*
  magazines, history of **M** 14
  Thanksgiving Day **T** 154

Haleakala (ha-lay-o-ka-LA) **National Park,** Maui, Hawaiian Islands **H** 66; picture **N** 47
Halevi, Judah see Judah Halevi
Half-Breeds, political group, faction of Republican Party **A** 440
  Blaine and his group supported Garfield **G** 55
Half-face camps, of pioneers **P** 252
Half hitches, knots **K** 291
Half-life, of radioactive elements **R** 67–68
  fallout **F** 35
  radioactive dating **R** 64
Half Moon, ship of Henry Hudson **H** 273
Half steps, in music **M** 527
Half-timbered houses **H** 168–69, 179
  building construction **B** 435
  Tudor architecture feature **E** 235–36; picture **E** 233
Halftone engraving, in printing **P** 459

Halibut, any of four ocean fish, largest members of the flatfish family. It is brown with strong teeth on both sides of jaw. Fish move to increasingly deeper water as they grow older—oldest found at depths of 3,000 feet. Two types, the Pacific and Atlantic halibuts, live in northern seas, grow to 9 feet and weigh 500 pounds or more. The other two types are smaller.
  aging process **A** 83–84
  important commercial groundfish, habitat, feeding habits, uses **F** 213

Halicarnassus (hal-i-car-NASS-us), Mausoleum at **W** 216; picture **W** 215
Halifax, capital of Nova Scotia, Canada **N** 344d; picture **N** 344f

Halifax, Earl of (Edward Frederick Lindley Wood) (1881–1959), British statesman, b. near Exeter, Devonshire. He began his career in 1910 as a member of Parliament and served in various posts, including that of governor-general of India (1926–31). As foreign secretary (1938–40), he played a part in negotiating the Munich Pact. He served as ambassador to the United States (1941–46).

Halifax Citadel National Historic Park **N** 344d; picture **N** 344f
Halifax Resolves, 1776 **N** 321
Halite, native salt from salt domes **S** 20
Hall, Asaph, American astronomer **M** 107

Hall, Charles Martin (1863–1914), American chemist, b. Thompson, Ohio. In 1886 he invented a method of producing aluminum by dissolving alumina (aluminum oxide) in molten cryolite and passing an electric current through the mixture. This made possible the cheap, large-scale production of aluminum. A Frenchman, Paul Héroult (1863–1914), independently invented the process in the same year. For this reason the process is generally called the Hall-Héroult process.

Hall-Héroult process **A** 176

Hall, Emmett Matthew (1898–), Canadian judge, b. St. Columban, Quebec. He was appointed chief justice of Saskatchewan (1957) and of the Court of Appeal (1961). He became justice of the Supreme Court of Canada (1962).

Hall, Esther Greenacre (1904–), American author of books for girls, b. Greeley, Colo. Her books include *Up Creek and Down Creek, Back to Buckeye,* and *The Here-to-Yonder Girl.*

Hall, Granville Stanley (1846–1924), American psychologist, b. Ashfield, Mass. President of Clark University (1889–1919), he founded *American Journal of Psychology,* first in its field in America, as well as journal of child-study movement, *Pedagogical Seminary.* His books include *Adolescence* and *Educational Problems.*

Hall, James Norman (1887–1951), American writer, b. Colfax, Iowa. Together with Charles Nordhoff, wrote *Mutiny on the Bounty* (which was made into movie), *Men Against the Sea,* and *Pitcairn's Island.* Having long lived in Tahiti, he called his autobiography *My Island Home.*

Hall, Prince (1735–1807), American Freemason, Negro, b. Barbados, W.I. He organized the first Masonic Lodge for Negroes in the U.S. After serving in the Revolutionary War, he obtained a charter from England for the first African Lodge No. 459 (1787). He also championed Negro rights, campaigning for schools for Negro children in Boston.

Hall, Samuel Read, American educator **V** 316
Hallam, Arthur, English writer **T** 100, 101
Halle, Adam de la see Adam de la Halle

Halleck (HAL-leck), **Henry Wagner** (1815–1872), American general, b. Westernville, N.Y. He was commissioned major-general in Union Army at outbreak of Civil War and commanded departments of Missouri (1861) and the Mississippi (1862). He was general-in-chief (1862–64) and chief of staff (1864–65).

Civil War, United States, campaigns of **C** 323

Halley (HAL-ley), **Edmund** (1656–1742), English astronomer and mathematician, b. London. Noted for his calculations of the orbit of comets, he predicted return of great comet of 1682, since known as Halley's comet. He also discovered pattern of motion of stars and made first catalog of southern stars.

Halley's (HAL-ley's) **comet** **C** 418, 419
  birth and death dates of Mark Twain **T** 336
  objects in the solar system **S** 246
Halley's insurance tables, of life expectancies **I** 296
Hall-Héroult (HALL ay-ROO) **process,** of aluminum refining **A** 176

Halliburton (HAL-lib-urt-on), **Richard** (1900–1939), American adventurer, b. Brownsville, Tenn. He scaled many mountains, including Matterhorn (1921), Fujiyama (1923), and Olympus (1925). He swam Panama Canal (1928) and Sea of Galilee (1931), and traced travels of Ulysses, Cortes, Balboa, Alexander the Great, and Hannibal. His books include *The Royal Road to Romance.*

Hallmark, official stamp on articles to attest to their purity **A** 320
Hall of Fame, National Lawn Tennis **T** 99–100

Hall of Fame for Great Americans **H** 12–14
Halloween **H** 15–17
  known as a Witches' Sabbath **W** 208
  October celebration **O** 50
Hallstatt, Austria **A** 524

Hallucination (hal-lu-cin-A-tion), seeing or hearing things when there is no basis outside the mind for such perceptions. A person hearing voices in a completely silent room is said to be suffering from hallucinations. Hallucination often results from nervous disorders.
  hallucinogenic drugs and vapors **D** 331
  images in the psychology of thinking **P** 500
  lack of sleep **S** 200
  psychoses in mental illness **M** 224

Hallucinogenic drugs **D** 331

Halo (HAY-lo), ring of light, or sometimes arching bands or spots of light. A halo may be seen around sun or moon when light from these bodies passes through a region of atmosphere containing ice particles. The word also refers to golden disk surrounding representations of head of Christ or other saintly persons.

Halogens (HAL-o-gens), chemical elements **I** 349
  chemical terms defined **C** 219
  electron shells, diagram **C** 203
  periodic table, place on **E** 158
Halpern, M. L., Yiddish author **Y** 351
Hals (HOLS), **Frans,** Dutch portrait painter **H** 18
  Dutch art **D** 357
  importance to baroque period **B** 60
  Laughing Cavalier, painting **H** 18
  Malle Bobbe, picture **B** 57
  Portrait of a Married Couple, painting **D** 361

Halsey (HALL-sey), **William Frederick, Jr.** (1882–1959), American naval officer, b. Elizabeth, N.J. He commanded (1942–44) Allied naval forces in South Pacific during World War II. He was appointed rear admiral (1938) and vice admiral (1940), led naval raids on Japanese in Gilbert and Marshall Islands (1942), stopped a Japanese attack on Guadalcanal by sinking 23 Japanese ships off Solomon Islands (1942), and commanded U.S. Third Fleet in Pacific (1944–45). He retired in 1947.

Halteres, wing parts of flies, pictures **A** 296, **I** 272
Halyards, on sailboats **S** 10

Ham, in Old Testament, one of Noah's three sons and father of Canaan.

Hama (HA-ma), Syria **S** 508
Haman (HAY-man), Persian prime minister **P** 540
Hambletonian, famous trotting horse **H** 234
Hamburg, Germany **G** 158; picture **R** 240
Hamburgers, origin of **F** 340
  outdoor cooking **O** 247
Hamilcar Barca, Carthaginian general, father of Hannibal **H** 34
  founded Barcelona, Spain **S** 356
Hamilton, Alexander, American statesman **H** 18–20
  duels and dueling **D** 341
  fatal duel with Burr **B** 462; picture **B** 461
  Federalist, The **F** 78
  Jefferson and Hamilton **J** 67
  opposed to universal suffrage **E** 112–13
  political parties **P** 379–80
Hamilton, Andrew, Scottish-born American lawyer
  defended Zenger and freedom of the press **Z** 369
  Independence Hall designed by **I** 113

Hamilton, capital of Bermuda **B** 146–48
Hamilton, Lady Emma, wife of Sir William Hamilton, British ambassador
Lord Nelson and Lady Hamilton **N** 108
Hamilton, Ontario **O** 124–25

Hamilton, William Rowan (1805–1865), Irish mathematician and astronomer, b. Dublin. He developed a three-dimensional algebra called quaternions, which has many uses in geometry, and he discovered a mathematical theory that is important in study of light.

Hamilton's algebra **M** 159–60
Hamishah Asar B'Shevat, religious holiday **R** 154
Hamitic languages **L** 39–40
Hamlet, play by William Shakespeare **H** 20–21; **S** 132
outline of the plot **S** 134
Hamlin, Hannibal, American statesman **M** 45; **V** 331;
picture **V** 327
Hammadas (ha-MA-das), desert uplands **S** 8
Algeria **A** 160
Hammarskjöld (HA-mar-sherld), Dag, Swedish diplomat, United Nations secretary-general **H** 21
Dag Hammarskjöld Library, United Nations, picture **L** 178
Hammer, bone in the ear, diagram **B** 285
Hammer and sickle, Soviet symbol **P** 381
Hammerhead sharks **S** 140
Hammerstein (HAM-mer-stine), Oscar, 2nd, American dramatist **M** 542
Hammers, tools **T** 211; pictures **T** 212
woodworking **W** 230
Hammer throw, field event **T** 241

Hammett, Dashiell (Samuel Dashiell Hammett) (1894–1961), American author of detective novels, b. St. Mary's County, Md. He is credited with creating new form of detective fiction through use of tough, realistic underworld characters. Many of his novels are based on experiences as a private detective. His books, several of which were made into movies, include *The Maltese Falcon, The Thin Man,* and *The Glass Key.*
mystery-detective fiction **M** 555

Hammocks
Indian invention **I** 209

Hammond, John Hays (1855–1936), American mining engineer, b. San Francisco, Calif. Chief consulting engineer for Cecil Rhodes, one of leaders in development of South African resources, he was convicted of treason (1896) for his part in reform movement against South African statesman Paul Kruger.

Hammurabi (ha-mu-RA-bi), king of Babylon **A** 236
Hammurabi, Code of **A** 220; picture **A** 219
treatment of slaves **S** 195
Hampton Court Palace, England **A** 382
maze of hedges, the model for studies of learning **P** 495
Hampton Institute, Virginia **N** 95, 96
Negro spirituals popularized **N** 107
Washington, Booker T., student at **W** 29
Hampton Roads, channel and port, Virginia **V** 350, 357
Merrimac-Monitor battle, 1862, Civil War **C** 323
Hams, amateur radio operators **R** 62–63
electronic communication, uses of **E** 142c
studies made with a radio telescope **R** 70
Hamsters, rodents **G** 407–08
body changes in hibernation **H** 123
pets **P** 179
rodents and their relatives **R** 279

Hamsun (HOM-sun), Knut, Norwegian author **S** 53
Hamtramck, Polish settlement in Detroit **M** 262
Ha-nagid, Shmuel, Hebrew poet **H** 102
Hancock, John, American Revolutionary War leader and statesman **H** 22
Declaration of Independence signature **D** 59, 62
Hancock, Thomas, English inventor **R** 341

Hancock, Winfield Scott (1824–1886), American general and political leader, b. Montgomery Square, Pa. He served as brigadier general and major general during Civil War and captured 4,000 prisoners at Spottsylvania Court House (1864). He was Democratic presidential candidate in 1880 but was defeated by James Garfield.

Handball **H** 22–25
Handbells **B** 136
Handbooks and manuals, types of reference books **R** 130–31
Hand drills, tools **T** 214
Handel, George Frederick, German-born English composer **H** 26
baroque period **B** 66
choral music **C** 278
opera **O** 133
oratorios **G** 183
Handicapped, rehabilitation of the **H** 27–30
blind, education of the **B** 251–54
deaf, education of the **D** 51
sight switch developed by space research **S** 349
Handicapping, to give an equal chance
golf **G** 255
sailing **S** 14
Handicrafts, decorative arts **D** 66, 78
African art **A** 72, 76
basketmaking, in Tonga, picture **T** 210
embroidery **E** 187–89
Eskimo **E** 287, 289
folklore of demonstrated tradition **F** 305
Indian beadwork **I** 157–59
indoor activities, things to make **I** 224
leathercraft **L** 112–13
mosaics **M** 463
papier-mâché **P** 58b–59
rug and carpet making **R** 354
Switzerland **S** 500–01
weaving **W** 97–98
wood carving **W** 228
Zaire, picture **Z** 366c
See also Hobbies; How to
Handicrafts Capital, of the United States, Gatlinburg, Tenn. **T** 74
Hand lotions **C** 509
Hand puppets **P** 535; pictures **P** 534
Hands, parts of the body **F** 79–84
bats **B** 92
folk dancing, importance in **F** 300
left-handedness **H** 33
Leonardo da Vinci drawing **D** 301
man's body plan **B** 270
monkeys' feet used as hands **M** 417–18
raccoon manipulates paws as hands **A** 285
Handwriting **H** 31–33
English round hand, picture **W** 320
importance to compositions **C** 447
Handwriting on the wall see Belshazzar
Handy, William Christopher, American jazz musician and composer **H** 34; **N** 98
famous blues **J** 57–58

Han (HON) Dynasty, Chinese dynasty divided into two periods: Western Han (202? B.C.–A.D. 9), founded by Liu

Pang with its capital at Changan, and Eastern Han (A.D. 25–220), with its capital at Loyang. The Han Dynasty conquered northern Korea and southern Manchuria, subjugated Annam and Hainan in south, established contact with Japan and Roman Empire, and set up civil service examination favoring scholars.

China, history of **C** 270
Oriental art **O** 217

Hangars, shelters for airplanes **A** 562
Hanging baskets, of flowers, picture **G** 38
Hanging Gardens of Babylon W 214; picture **W** 215
ancient art **A** 241
parks and playgrounds **P** 76
Hangman, a word game **W** 238
Hang together or . . . hang separately, remark made by Benjamin Franklin **F** 455
Hanifs (han-eefs), people of Mecca **M** 404
Hankow, China **C** 262
Hanna, Marcus Alonzo, American politician **M** 188
Hannibal, Carthaginian general **H** 34
Punic Wars **P** 533
Hannibal, Missouri
Twain, Mark **T** 336
Hannibal and St. Joseph Railroad M 374
Hanoi (ha-NOI), capital of Democratic Republic of Vietnam (North Vietnam) **V** 334b, 334d, 336
Hanover, House of, English royal family **E** 225; **U** 77

Hansberry, Lorraine (1930–1965), American playwright, b. Chicago, Ill. First Negro woman to write play produced on Broadway, she achieved fame with *A Raisin in the Sun*, dealing with transition in life of modern Negro family (New York Drama Critics' Circle Award for best American play, 1959).

years of change in Negro history **N** 102

Hans Christian Andersen Medal, book award **B** 310
Hanseatic (han-se-AT-ic) **League,** trade organization of north European cities in Middle Ages **G** 159
controlled herring fishing industry **F** 212
flag **F** 227
fur trade **F** 511
spread of the German language **G** 172
Hansel and Gretel, by Grimm brothers **G** 380–86
opera by Engelbert Humperdinck **O** 145
Hansen, Niels, Dannish American plant specialist **S** 325
Hansen's disease see Leprosy
Hanukkah (HA-nu-kah), Jewish religious festival **H** 35
celebrates Jewish victory over Greeks **J** 106
holiday toys **T** 233

Happening, an event, which may be announced in advance, but which unfolds spontaneously, often involving the audience, which responds naturally.

Hapsburg see Habsburg

Hara-kiri (from colloquial Japanese, meaning "belly cut"), Japanese ritual suicide. The ceremony was performed with dagger by feudal warriors, or samurai, as an alternative to execution, which was considered dishonorable. It became the honorable last resort of those who suffered misfortune, and was preferred to surrender by some Japanese soldiers captured during World War II. The preferred expression is *seppuku*.

Harappa (ha-RA-pa), site of chief city (from about 2500 to 1500 B.C.) of Indus valley civilization, now West Pakistan. Geometrical planning indicates effective central government. The city left steatite seals not yet decoded.

ancient Indus civilization **A** 223

Harar, Ethiopia **E** 302
Harbin, China **C** 265
Harbors and ports H 35–37
artificial harbors **W** 298, 300; picture **W** 299
Baltimore **B** 35
Bombay, India **B** 307–08
Buenos Aires, port, pictures **B** 427; **S** 293
colonial seaport, picture **C** 386
Europe **E** 326, 329
free ports **I** 330
Genoa, Italy, picture **E** 329
Gibraltar **G** 205
Hampton Roads, Virginia **V** 350, 357
Helsinki, Finland, picture **F** 130
Hong Kong **H** 203–05
Houston, Texas **H** 270
inland port, Montreal **M** 444
London, England **L** 339
marinas, boat basins or docks **B** 260
Mombasa, Kenya, picture **K** 232
Montreal **M** 444
New Orleans **N** 196
New York **N** 227–28, 230; picture **G** 101
oceans and seas with their chief ports **O** 45–49
Philadelphia **P** 183
Saint Lawrence Seaway, Great Lakes ports **S** 16–17
San Francisco **S** 30–31
Singapore **S** 184a
Sydney, Australia **S** 503–04; pictures **A** 515; **S** 503
Toronto, Canada **T** 227–28
United Kingdom **U** 76–77
Yokohama, Japan, picture **J** 41
Harbor seals, animals **W** 8
Hard coal see Anthracite, hard coal
Hardening of the arteries, disease **D** 196–97
Hardenpont, Nicolas, Belgian priest **P** 112

Hardin, Clifford Morris (1915–   ), American educator, b. Knightstown, Ind. After teaching at the University of Wisconsin and Michigan State College, Hardin became chancellor of the University of Nebraska (1954). He held membership on the President's Committee to Strengthen the Security of the Free World (1963) and National Science Board (1966). In 1969 he succeeded Orville Freeman as U.S. secretary of agriculture.

Harding, Florence Kling, wife of Warren G. Harding **F** 176–77; **H** 38–41; picture **F** 177
Harding, Warren G., 29th president of United States **H** 38–41
Coolidge and Harding **C** 496
Hard money, specie **B** 47
Hardness, in physics
abrasives for grinding and polishing **G** 387–89
annealing and tempering of metals **I** 403; **M** 232
diamonds **D** 154–55
gemstones, Mohs' scale **G** 69
minerals **R** 270
rock scratch tests **R** 270
Hardtack, bread **B** 389

Hardware, metalware such as tools, locks, hinges, parts of machines and appliances, metal building equipment, weapons, and other combat equipment. In computer technology the term **hardware** refers to any electronic or mechanical equipment used in data processing, in contrast to **software,** the written programs or charts.

Hardwoods, trees
forests **F** 371, 373–74
furniture veneers **F** 503
wood and wood products **W** 225

Hardy, Thomas, English poet and novelist **H** 41; **E** 265
  themes of his novels **N** 346
Harebells, flowers, picture **W** 169

Hare Krishna (HAR-i KRISH-na), a sect related to Hinduism, which grew up in Western countries in the 1960's. Members wearing light orange robes chant, dance, and ring bells on city streets. Male members have shaved heads, except for a topknot of hair. All live simply in city communes and are vegetarians.

Harelip, deformity from birth in which upper lip is divided. Often combined with cleft palate, it can be corrected by surgery at an early age.

Harem (HARE-em) (from Arabic *Harīm,* meaning "forbidden"), secluded quarters of Muslim women, out of bounds to all men except head of family.

Hares **R** 22–24
  mammal order, Lagomorpha, picture **M** 69
  What is the difference between a rabbit and a hare?
  R 23

Hare system (named after Thomas Hare, English political reformer), method of proportional representation in voting. When quota of votes needed to elect a candidate is reached, the rest of his votes are transferred from him to next choice indicated by voters.

Hargrave, Lawrence, Australian inventor **K** 267
Hargraves, Edward H., Australian prospector **M** 320
Hargreaves, James, English inventor **I** 235

Harkness family, family of philanthropists. **Anna M.** (1838?–1926) established (1916) Commonwealth Fund, and donated Harkness Memorial Quadrangle to Yale University. Her son **Edward Stephen** (1874–1940) continued the family's philanthropy, eventually donating more than $100,000,000 to various institutions, including Yale, Harvard, and Columbia universities. His wife **Mary** (1875–1950) donated the Gutenburg Bible to Yale. **William Hale** (1900–54) endowed (1950) the Harkness Foundation, Inc.

Harlan, John Marshall (1833–1911), American jurist, b. Boyle County, Ky. After serving as a Union colonel in the Civil War (1861–63), he was attorney general of Kentucky (1863–67). As associate justice on the U.S. Supreme Court (1877–1911), he supported civil rights and opposed legislation that would limit constitutional guarantees.

Harlan, John Marshall (1899–   ), American jurist, b. Chicago, Ill., grandson of **John Marshall Harlan** (1833–1911). He served as assistant U.S. attorney (1925–27), assistant attorney-general of New York (1928–30), and chief counsel for the New York State Crime Commission (1951–53). He was appointed to the U.S. Supreme Court by President Eisenhower in 1954. Harlan was considered a conservative in the liberal Warren Court of the 1950's and 1960's. He retired in 1971.

Harlem Globetrotters, basketball team **B** 90
Harlem Renaissance **N** 98
Harlem River **N** 228

Harlequin, servant character in *commedia dell'arte* of Italian theater or pantomime (16th to 18th century). A childish, amorous clown and wit, he was equipped with mask, parti-colored costume, and wooden sword. Harlequin is associated with love for Columbine.
  See also Columbine

Harmattan (har-mat-TAN) dry trade winds of West
  Africa **E** 281
  Ghana **G** 196
  Nigeria **N** 255

Harmon, Tommy (Thomas D. Harmon) (1919–   ), American football player, b. Rensselaer, Ind. As halfback for University of Michigan (1938–40) he was named All-American and elected to Football Hall of Fame. He played professionally for Los Angeles Rams (1946–47).

Harmonica, a musical instrument **H** 42–43
  folk music instruments **F** 330
Harmonics, or overtones, of sound **S** 264–65
Harmonic telegraph, early communications device **T** 56
Harmonium (har-MO-ni-um), keyboard instrument **K** 240
  reed organs **O** 208
Harmony, in music **M** 522
  African music **A** 78
  Bach's *Art of the Fugue* **B** 5; **M** 536
  baroque forms **B** 65
  counterpoint **M** 299, 533
  Debussy's impressionist form **D** 55
  jazz improvisation on chord structures **J** 62
  modern music **M** 399
  polyphony **G** 182; **I** 482–83
Harmony, of color in art **D** 143
Harnesses, for horses and oxen, invention of **I** 335
Harness racing **H** 233–34
  standardbred horse, picture **H** 239

Harnett, William Michael (1848–1892), American painter, b. County Cork, Ireland. He is particularly noted for his still lifes. His works include *Emblems of Peace.*

Harold II, king of England **E** 217
  Hastings, battle of **B** 100–01; **W** 173
  Viking Era in England **V** 340
Harold Hardrada, king of Norway **V** 340
Harold the Fair-haired, king of Norway **N** 344
Harp, a musical instrument **H** 43–44; **M** 544
  ancient instrument **A** 245; pictures **A** 244, 348
  orchestra **O** 183
  orchestra seating plan **O** 186
  stringed instruments, pictures **S** 439
Harp, constellation see Lyra
Harp, or saddleback, **seals** **W** 8
Harpers Ferry, West Virginia **W** 126; picture **W** 134
  Civil War **C** 321
  John Brown's raid **B** 411–12
Harpers Ferry National Historical Park, West Virginia
  W 135
Harper's Weekly, American magazine
  Nast cartoons **C** 126
  Winslow Homer illustration **I** 91

Harpies, in Greek mythology, Aello, Ocypete, Celaeno, and Podarge, winged creatures with faces of women. They are ravenous creatures who carry off the souls of the dead and ruin the food of the living. Probably they are personifications of storm winds.

Harpoons
  fishing **F** 218
  whaling **W** 152
Harpsichord, keyboard instrument **K** 238–39;
  M 546–47; pictures **B** 64; **K** 238
Harpy eagles **B** 226; picture **B** 224
Harridge, William, American baseball executive **B** 81

Harriman, Averell (William Averell Harriman), (1891–   ), American diplomat, b. New York, N.Y. Son of railroad magnate **Edward Henry Harriman** (1838–1909), he was ambassador to U.S.S.R. (1943–46) and Great Britain (1946), U.S. secretary of commerce (1946–48), and governor of New York (1955–58). He was an undersecretary of state for political affairs (1963–65), ambassador-at-large (1965–68) and U.S. representative at the Paris peace talks (1968–69).

Harris, Joel Chandler, American writer **A** 205
  African source of "Bre'r Rabbit" tales **A** 76a
  children's literature **C** 240
  fables **F** 4
  Uncle Remus stories, folklore of animal tales **F** 313
Harris, John, English scientist and encyclopedist **E** 197

Harris, Julie (Julia Ann Harris) (1925–), American actress, b. Grosse Pointe, Mich. She was named best actress in 1952 (New York Drama Critics Circle) and has played in both the stage and film versions of *I Am a Camera* and *Member of the Wedding.* She also starred in play *The Lark* (Antoinette Perry award, 1956), TV program *Victoria Regina* (Emmy, 1961), and *Forty Carats* (Antoinette Perry award, 1969). Picture **T** 156.

Harris, Patricia Roberts (1924–), American lawyer and diplomat, b. Mattoon, Ill. Appointed ambassador to Luxembourg (1965), she was the first Negro woman to serve as a U.S. ambassador. A professor of law at Howard University, she served as attorney in the appeals and research section of the Justice Department's Criminal Division (1960–61) and co-chairman of the National Women's Committee for Civil Rights (1963). In 1967 she was appointed alternate representative of the United States to UN General Assembly. She is now on the boards of directors of several large corporations. Picture **N** 100.
  years of change in Negro history **N** 101

Harris, Robert, Canadian artist
  Robert Harris Memorial Art Gallery, Charlottetown, P.E.I. **P** 456e
Harrisburg, capital of Pennsylvania **P** 141; picture **P** 140
Harrison, Anna Symmes, wife of William Henry Harrison and grandmother of Benjamin Harrison **F** 169; **H** 49
Harrison, Benjamin, 23rd president of the United States **H** 45–48
Harrison, Caroline Lavinia Scott, wife of Benjamin Harrison **F** 175; **H** 45; picture **F** 174
Harrison, Jane Irwin, acting first lady in Harrison's administration **F** 169
Harrison, John, English inventor **I** 346
  chronometers, truly reliable clocks **W** 46
  importance of the chronometer to navigation **N** 66

Harrison, Rex (Reginald Carey Harrison) (1908–), English stage and screen actor, b. Huyton. He performed in *Major Barbara, My Fair Lady* and *Cleopatra.*

Harrison, Wallace Kirkman (1895–), American architect, b. Worcester, Mass. He served as co-architect for Rockefeller Center, architect in charge of Lincoln Center, and director of planning for the United Nations.

Harrison, William Henry, 9th president of the United
  States **H** 49–51
  Tecumseh **T** 47
  War of 1812 **W** 12
Harrison Act, 1914 **N** 14

Harrison Land Act (1800) (named for William Henry Harrison, delegate from Northwest Territory), law that discouraged land speculation on U.S. frontier and encouraged purchase of farmlands by settlers through easy credit and smaller tracts. It set foundation of federal government's democratic policy with regard to public lands.
  pioneer life **P** 260–61
  public lands, history of **P** 506

Harrows, farm machinery **F** 58; picture **F** 56
  early use in agriculture **A** 96
Harry S Truman Library, Independence, Missouri **M** 376
Harsha, Hindu king **I** 131

Hart, John (1711?–1779), American patriot, b. Stonington, Conn. An advocate of colonial independence and popular rights, he served as New Jersey delegate to the Continental Congress (1776), where he signed the Declaration of Independence. He was elected to New Jersey Assembly and served as house speaker (1776) and member of Council of Safety (1777–78).

Hart, Lorenz, American lyricist **M** 542
Hart, Moss, American playwright **A** 216; **M** 543
Harte Bret, American writer **A** 205
  local-color stories, writer of **S** 167
Hartebeest (HAR-te-beest), African antelope **H** 221; picture **H** 217
Hartford, capital of Connecticut **C** 476
  Constitution Plaza, pictures **C** 481; **U** 233

Hartford Convention, secret meeting in Hartford, Conn., (Dec. 1814–Jan. 1815) of 26 New England conservative Federalists who opposed War of 1812 and President Madison's policies in general, and discussed secession from Union. Its resolutions, placing states' rights above national interest in time of crisis, were rendered null by Treaty of Ghent and end of war.
  War of 1812, history of **W** 12

Hartford Foundation, Inc., John A., privately supported organization granting awards to various charitable and scientific projects. Recently it has stressed contributions to medical research. The foundation was established in 1929 and incorporated in 1942. Headquarters is in New York, N.Y.

Hartigan, Grace (1922–), American artist, b. Newark, N.J. She was influenced by school of abstract expressionism. Her works include *Persian Jacket* and illustration of James Schuyler's "Salute" in *Silk Screen Paints for Four Volume Poetry.*

Hartland Covered Bridge, New Brunswick, Canada **N** 138d; picture **N** 138b

Hartley, Marsden (1877–1943), American artist and poet, b. Lewiston, Maine. He was one of the earliest abstract painters in United States. His paintings include *Portrait of a German Officer, The Wave,* and *Smelt Brook Falls.*

Hartline, H. K., Canadian doctor
  studies of the senses **B** 288
Hartmann von Aue, German poet **G** 174
Hartridge, H., English scientist **B** 96
Hartsfield, Henry W., Jr., American astronaut **S** 346
Harunobu (ha-ru-NO-bu), Suzuki, Japanese artist
  woodcut, *Osen of Kasamori* **G** 305

Harvard, John (1607–1638), English clergyman, b. London. He went to New England (1637) and settled in Charlestown, Mass. He left half of his estate and a

Harvard, John (continued)
library of about 400 volumes to a newly founded institution that was later named Harvard College in his honor.

Harvard University, Cambridge, Mass. **U** 205, 213;
    pictures **E** 73; **M** 146
    New England schools in colonial America **C** 394
Harvester ants A 322, 326–27; picture **A** 325
    animal maze test, picture **A** 284
Harvesters, The, painting by Brueghel **R** 170
Harvest festivals
    August "harvest home" **A** 492
    Japan **J** 31
    Thanksgiving Day **T** 152–54
Harvesting, of crops
    apples **A** 337
    fruit **F** 484
    garden vegetables **G** 42
    vegetable gardening **V** 288
    wheat **W** 155
Harvesting machines F 59–60
Harvey, E. Newton, American scientist **B** 198
Harvey, George, American editor **W** 178
Harvey, William, English physician and scientist
    H 52
    advances in biology **B** 188, 189
    medicine, history of **M** 205
    physiology, advances in science of **S** 69
Harz (HARTS) **Mountains,** Germany **G** 152
Hasan, Mahammad, Somali poet **A** 76a
Hasdrubal (HAS-drub-al), Carthaginian general, brother
    of Hannibal **H** 34
Hashemite Kingdom of Jordan see Jordan
Hashish, concentrated form of marijuana **D** 331
Hasidism, Jewish religious movement **Y** 350
Haskell, Charles Nathaniel, American statesman **O** 93
Haskell Institute, Lawrence, Kansas **K** 183
Hasmoneans see Maccabees

Hassan II (HA-san) (Moulay Hassan) (1929–), king of
Morocco, b. Rabat. As crown prince, he participated in
negotiations at Paris for Moroccan independence (1955–
56). He served as commander in chief of the army
(1957), minister of defense (1960–61), and vice-premier
(1960–61). As prime minister (1961–63) and king (since
1961), he has followed a foreign policy of neutrality.
    Morocco, history of **M** 461

Hassan, Mohammad Abdullah see Mohammad Abdullah
    Hassan
Hasse (HA-sa), **Johann,** German composer **O** 133
Hassler, Hans Leo, German composer **G** 182
Hastie, William H., American jurist **N** 99
Hastings, battle of, 1066 **B** 100–01
    Bayeux tapestry depicts **E** 187
    England, history of **E** 217
    Vikings **V** 340
    William the Conqueror **W** 173

Hastings (HASTE-ings), **Warren** (1732–1818), British colonial administrator, b. Churchill, Oxfordshire. He helped
Robert Clive recapture Calcutta but resigned from
council there and returned to England (1764). As
governor of Bengal (1772–73), he reformed revenue and
judicial systems. As first British governor general of
India (1774–85), he seized French possessions in India
and fought native insurrections. He was charged with
high crimes but acquitted.

Hastings Cutoff, on the California Trail **O** 264
Hasty pudding, colonial American dish **C** 390
Hatch, Carl A., American statesman **N** 193

Hatch Act restricts political activities of most federal
office holders, their participation in campaigns, solicit-
ing funds, or using their offices to influence elections.
Introduced (1939) by Senator Hatch of New Mexico, act
was extended (1940) to cover many state and local employees and to limit candidate's campaign expenditures.

Hatcher, Richard G., American political leader **N** 101
Hatch Experiment Station Act, 1887 **C** 485
Hatching process, in incubation of eggs **B** 215
Hat dance L 69
    folk dancing **F** 301
Hats and hatmaking H 53–55
    Chinese bride's hat, picture **J** 96
    fur trade for beaver hats **F** 520
    Panama hats, picture **L** 53
Hatshepsut (hat-SHEP-suit), queen of ancient Egypt
    A 222
    Egyptian art **E** 98, 100
    temple of, picture **E** 103
Hatteras, Cape, North Carolina **N** 308
    lighthouse, pictures **L** 277; **N** 317
Hattusas (ha-tu-SHASH), capital of Hittite Empire **A** 238
Hatuey (ot-WAY), Indian chieftain of Cuba **C** 550
Hauberk (HAU-berk), armor **K** 272
Hauptmann (HOWPT-monn), **Gerhart,** German poet and
    dramatist **D** 298
    German literature **G** 179

Hausa (HOW-sa), a term referring to both a Negroid
people of Niger and northern Nigeria and a Hamitic
language. Established as a strong political power during
the Middle Ages, the alliance of Hausa states was
conquered by the Fulani during the early 19th century.
United primarily by language and the Muslim religion,
the Hausa are governed by Islamic law, involving a
system of small villages ruled by separate chiefs united
in centralized community.

Haussmann (O-smonn), **Baron George Eugène** (1809–
1891), French magistrate and town planner, b. Paris. As
prefect of the Seine (1853–70) at a time when city
growth necessitated replanning, he instituted improvements in sanitation and landscape in Paris. He widened
and connected streets for traffic; built parks, fountains,
and bridges; and improved the sewer and water systems.
    Paris, history of **P** 74

Haute couture (ote coo-TURE), high fashion **F** 70–71
Haüy (ah-ur-E), **Valentin,** French educator **B** 252
Havana, capital of Cuba **C** 549, 550
Havasupai (ha-va-SU-pa-i), Indians of North America
    A 413–14
Hawaii (ha-WA-i) **H** 56–72
    annexation to United States **T** 113
    favorite foods **F** 340
    flag, 1845 **F** 228
    Hawaiian Girl Scout, picture **G** 219
    Haleaka Crater, picture **N** 47
    Kamehameha Day, holiday **H** 149
    land areas of the United States **U** 93
    sugar plantation, picture **S** 455
    surfing, popular sport **S** 478
    territorial acquisition ceremony, 1898, picture **T** 107
Hawaii, University of H 65
Hawaiian goose, or **nene,** bird
    state bird of Hawaii **H** 56, 61
Hawaiian language H 63
Hawaii Volcanoes National Park H 66

Hawes (HAWS), **Charles Boardman** (1889–1923), American
author, b. Clifton Springs, N.Y. He was noted particularly

for adventure and sea stories. His works include *The Dark Frigate*, which won Newbery award (1923).

Hawkeye State, nickname for Iowa **I** 357
Hawking see Falconry

Hawkins, Sir John (1532–1595), English naval officer, b. Plymouth. An English slave trader, he violated Spanish law by transporting Negro slaves from Africa and marketing them in the West Indies and northern South America. He was appointed treasurer of the English Navy (1573) and was knighted after serving as rear admiral during the Spanish Armada defeat (1588).
  slave trade in Africa **G** 197; **S** 197

Hawks, any one of several birds of prey found throughout the world, except in Arctic regions. Hawks have sharp, hooked bills and long claws used in grasping prey. Hawks are among the most keen-eyed of birds. They pursue prey with strong, swift flight.
  Audubon painting **A** 490
  nest, picture **B** 244
  special adaptations in birds **B** 222

Hawksbill turtles **T** 331; picture **T** 334

Hawley-Smoot Tariff, act passed by Congress (1930) that raised protective tariffs on many agricultural goods and some manufactured items to their highest level in U.S. history. It was supported by agricultural, labor, and manufacturing interests but was strongly opposed by leading economists and exporters as an obstacle to world trade. Many foreign countries raised tariffs, and international trade declined. The act was modified by the Reciprocal Trade Agreements Act of 1934.
  Hoover's administration **H** 224

Hawser, heavy rope **R** 331
Hawthorn, shrub
  Missouri's state flower **M** 367
Hawthorne, Nathaniel, American novelist **H** 73
  American literature **A** 201–02
  children's literature **C** 238
  House of the Seven Gables, The, excerpt **H** 73–74
  short stories **S** 166
  style and themes of his novels **N** 348–49
  Tanglewood Tales, excerpt **H** 74–76
  Wonder Book, The, cover of, picture **I** 93
Hay, dried pasture grasses **G** 317; picture **G** 316
  animals that store hay **M** 66
Hay, John, American statesman
  Open-Door policy **M** 189–90
Haya de la Torre (AH-ya day la TOR-ray), **Víctor Raúl,** Peruvian political leader **P** 166
Hay-Bunau-Varilla (bu-NOW-va-RI-ya) **Treaty,** 1903
  Panama **P** 46
Hayden, Carl Trumbull, American statesman **A** 416
Hayden, Melissa, Canadian ballerina, picture **B** 27

Hayden Foundation, Charles, an association that assists boys' and young men's organizations. It gives funds for equipment and physical facilities to organizations such as boys' clubs, camps, and the Boy Scouts. Founded in 1937, it has headquarters in New York, N.Y.

Hayden Planetarium, Department of Astronomy of American Museum of Natural History, New York, N.Y. Movements of celestial bodies on 75-foot hemispherical dome are demonstrated by means of 12-foot Zeiss projector. The planetarium offers courses in astronomy and sponsors astronomical research programs. It was opened (1935) on endowment of Charles Hayden.

Haydn (HY-den), **Franz Joseph,** Austrian composer **H** 77;
  pictures **G** 184, **H** 77
  chamber music **C** 186
  choral music **C** 278
  classical age, compositions of **C** 330, 333
  Mozart and Haydn **M** 502
  "Song of Germany" composed by **N** 18
  string quartets and symphonies **G** 184
  symphonies **M** 540

Hayes, Helen (1900–), American actress, b. Washington, D.C. She is known as First Lady of the American Stage. Helen Hayes Theatre in New York was named for her. Her notable performances include *What Every Woman Knows, Victoria Regina, Mary of Scotland, Touch of the Poet,* and the 1970 revival of *Harvey.* She has also appeared in films, winning an Academy Award as best actress in 1932 for *Sin of Madelon Claudet,* and as best supporting actress in 1970 for *Airport.* Picture **T** 157.

Hayes, Lucy Webb, wife of Rutherford B. Hayes **F** 173;
  H 79; picture **F** 172

Hayes, Roland (1887–), American tenor, b. Curryville, Ga. Noted for singing of Negro spirituals, he gave concert tours throughout United States and sang at Buckingham Palace, England. He was winner of Spingarn medal (1925), given for outstanding achievement among Negroes.
  Negro Renaissance **N** 98
  Negro spirituals **N** 107

Hayes, Rutherford B., 19th president of United States **H** 78–81
  services to fugitive slaves **U** 12
Hay fever, allergy disease **D** 192
Haymarket Square riot, labor problem **L** 4
Hayne, Paul Hamilton, American poet **A** 204

Haynes, Elwood (1857–1925), American inventor, b. Portland, Ind. A metallurgist and petroleum engineer, he developed a number of alloys, including tungsten chrome steel (1881), chromium and nickel (1897), cobalt and chromium (1900), and stainless steel (1911), which he patented in 1919. He designed and built a horseless carriage (1893–94), supposedly the oldest American automobile, now exhibited at the Smithsonian Institution.

Hay-Pauncefote Treaty (Nov. 18, 1901), pact between Britain and the United States providing for American construction and management of the Panama Canal and supervision of its neutrality. It was named for Secretary of State John Hay and British Ambassador Lord Pauncefote. It superseded the Clayton-Bulwer Treaty of 1850.

Haystacks, picture **A** 97
Hayter, Stanley William, English engraver **G** 308
  Tarantelle, engraving **G** 306
Hay Wain, The, painting by John Constable **N** 38; **P** 27
Hayward, Nathaniel M., American inventor **R** 341
Hazaras (ha-ZAR-as), people of Afghanistan **A** 42

Hazel, nut-bearing shrub or small tree found throughout Northern Hemisphere. Its flowers hang down in long clusters. The nut, enclosed in a husk, is usually at end of branches and is eaten raw or used in cooking.

Hazelnuts, or filberts **N** 421

Hazing, nautical term referring to bullying of sailors by ship's officers, especially by heavy assignment of hard work. In U.S. colleges, it refers to initiation of new

Hazing (continued)
students or fraternity pledges by exacting unpleasant or difficult tasks or exposing them to ridicule.

Hazlitt, William, English writer **E** 261
H-Bomb see Hydrogen bomb
Head, sculpture by Modigliani, picture **M** 403
Headings, of index entries **I** 114
Headless horseman, in "Legend of Sleepy Hollow," picture **A** 199
Head of a Woman, sculpture by Picasso **S** 104
Head of a Young Girl, painting by Vermeer **B** 58
Head of Youth, drawing by Raphael **R** 106
Headphones **T** 57
Heads, human
    differences in physical traits, pictures **A** 307
    races of man, pictures **R** 30, 31
Headsails, for sailboats **S** 10
Health **H** 82–85
    air pollution menace **A** 111; **E** 272f–272g
    baths and bathing **B** 91
    camping precautions **C** 45–46
    concern of dentists **D** 114
    disease, prevention of **D** 219–21
    disinfectants and antiseptics **D** 222
    drugs, abuse of **D** 330
    exercise, conditioning **P** 226–29
    grant money from foundations **F** 392
    gymnastics **G** 428–32
    importance to a singer **V** 375
    insurance see Insurance, health
    medicine, tools and techniques of **M** 208d–211
    mental health **M** 220–22
    narcotics, effects of addiction **N** 12–14
    National Health Service, United Kingdom **U** 78
    noise and noise control **N** 269–70
    nutrition needs **N** 415–19
    old age **O** 97
    old-age insurance plans **O** 99
    physical education and physical fitness **P** 224–29
    public health **P** 502–06
    sleep **S** 200–01
    smoking, a health hazard **S** 203
    soap and health **D** 146
    teeth **T** 47–49
    weight **P** 229
    See also Mental health; Safety
Health, Education, and Welfare, U.S. Dept. of **E** 75; **P** 502
    air pollution control **A** 111
    consumer protection agencies **C** 494a
    Food and Drug Administration **F** 350, 351, 352
    Social and Rehabilitation Services **H** 29
    water pollution control **W** 59
Health insurance see Insurance, health
Hearing **B** 285
    bats **B** 96
    body's senses, guards on the alert **B** 280–81
    deaf, education of the **D** 50–53
    noise and noise control **N** 269–70
    See also Sound

Hearn, Lafcadio (Yakumo Koizumi) (1850–1904), American writer, b. Santa Maura, Greece. He worked as journalist in the United States before going to Japan, where he became a citizen. He taught English literature at Imperial University of Tokyo and translated stories of Théophile Gautier in *One of Cleopatra's Nights.*

Hearne, Samuel (1745–1792), English explorer, b. London. After joining the Hudson's Bay Company (1763), he made expeditions into British northwest America (1768–72), becoming the first white man to arrive at the Arctic Ocean by land from Hudson Bay (1771–72). He established the trading post, Cumberland House (1774).
    fur trading and exploration **S** 38h; **Y** 365
    Northwest Passage **N** 338

Hearst, Phoebe Apperson, founder of PTA **P** 67
Hearst, William Randolph, American newspaper publisher **N** 200
    Hearst San Simeon State Historical Monument **C** 25
Heart **H** 86–86c
    diseases **D** 197–98, 218
    drug quinidine for regulating heartbeat **D** 326
    four-chambered, of birds and mammals **B** 202; **M** 72
    Harvey's studies **B** 188, 189
    medicine, tools and techniques of **M** 209
    pulse and pulse rates **M** 208f

Heart Association, American (AHA), organization devoted to the prevention and treatment of heart and circulatory diseases. With a membership of physicians, scientists, and laymen, the organization promotes research, education, and community programs aimed at lowering illness and death resulting from these diseases. Founded in 1924, it is financed by public contributions.

Heart disease **D** 197–98, 218
    heart attacks and heart failure **H** 86c
    smoking **S** 203
Heart-lung machines **M** 211
    hospital services **H** 248
Heart of Dixie, nickname for Alabama **A** 113
Hearts, card game **C** 112

Heart transplant, a surgical operation in which a living person's diseased heart is removed and replaced with a healthy heart taken from a person who has just died. The operation was first performed by Dr. Christaan Barnard in Capetown, South Africa (1967).
    heart surgery **H** 86c
    medicine, life-saving techniques **M** 211
    See also Barnard, Christiaan

Heartwood, of trees **T** 281
    What is wood? **W** 222–23
    woody stems of plants **P** 290
Heat **H** 86d–95
    advances in experimental science **S** 70–71
    air conditioning **A** 103
    aluminum a good conductor and insulator **A** 176–77
    atmosphere **A** 481, 482
    body's sense of **B** 287
    climates **C** 346
    clouds retain, as a blanket **C** 359
    demonstrate conduction of heat through metal **E** 365
    diamonds, effect on **D** 154
    earth's surface heat **E** 6–7, 18
    electric appliances **E** 117–20, 128
    gases **G** 57–59
    heat energy **E** 198, 199–203
    How hot is the sun? **E** 22
    hydrogen bonding **W** 55
    infrared radiation, a kind of solar energy **S** 235
    insulation **I** 290–92
    kindling temperature or flash point of fuel **F** 136
    lubricants to reduce friction **L** 370
    matter, changes in volume of **M** 172
    melting point of ice **I** 3
    physics, studies in **P** 233–34
    pollution see Thermal pollution
    radiation **R** 40–41

refrigeration process **R** 136
symbol for in a chemical equation **C** 198
thermometer **T** 165
Thompson, Benjamin, studies of **T** 166
See also Combustion; Fire; Heating
Heat engines **E** 209
diesel engines **D** 168–71
internal-combustion engines **I** 303–08
steam engines **S** 419–21

Heath, Edward Richard George (1916–   ), British prime minister, b. Broadstairs, Kent. Elected to Parliament in 1952, he became Chief Conservative Party Whip in 1955. He also served as Minister of Labour, president of the Board of Trade, and Lord Privy Seal. He defeated Labour prime minister Harold Wilson in an upset victory, 1970.

Heathenism *see* Paganism
Heath hens, extinct birds **B** 232
Heating **H** 96–99
degree days **W** 87
fuels **F** 486–90
hot springs used for **G** 192
insulation and insulating materials **I** 290–92
petroleum **P** 176
system in a house, diagram **B** 437
thermostat, picture **A** 529
See also Air conditioning
Heat pollution *see* Thermal pollution
Heat pumps **H** 99
Heat sense, of snakes **S** 213
Heat shield, of spacecraft **S** 340a, 340j
Heavy hydrogen, or deuterium **N** 356
Heavyweight, in boxing **B** 352
Hebbel, Friedrich, German writer **G** 178
Hebraic faith *see* Judaism
Hebrew language **H** 100–01
acrostics in the Bible **W** 236
alphabet **C** 431
Bible **B** 152–59
Dead Sea Scrolls **D** 48–49
Hebrew typewriter, picture **T** 347
Israel's official language **I** 438–39
language families **L** 39
Talmud **T** 15
See also Yiddish language and literature
Hebrew literature **H** 101–03
Bible **B** 152–59
Talmud **T** 15
See also Yiddish language and literature
Hebrew music
ancient music **A** 246
choral music **C** 276
hymns **H** 309, 310
Hebrews *see* Jews
Hebrews, book of Bible, New Testament **B** 162
Hebrew University, Jerusalem, Israel **I** 439; **J** 80;
picture **I** 440
Hebrides (HEB-rid-ese), islands off west coast of Scotland **I** 430
Hebron, Jordan **J** 139
Abraham's burial place **A** 7

Hecatomb (HEC-a-tome) (from Greek *hekaton,* meaning "hundred"), large public sacrifice. In ancient Greece and Rome, a hecatomb applied to sacrifice of 100 oxen or cattle but later referred to sacrifice of any large number of victims—persons or animals.

Hecht (HECT), **Ben** (1894–1964), American playwright, author, and producer, b. New York, N.Y. He wrote play *A Flag Is Born,* advocating establishment of an inde-

pendent Jewish state, and *The Front Page* (with Charles MacArthur). He also wrote and produced, with Alfred Hitchcock, films *Spellbound* and *Notorious.*

Heckscher (HECK-sher), **August** (1913–   ), American author, journalist, and public official, b. Huntington, N.Y. He was chief editorial writer for New York *Herald Tribune* (1952–56), president of Woodrow Wilson Foundation, editor of *The Politics of Woodrow Wilson,* and author of *A Pattern of Politics.* He became New York City Commissioner of Parks in 1967.

Hector, in Greek mythology **G** 366
Iliad **I** 69
Heddle, part of a loom **T** 140
Hedgehog cacti **C** 4
Hedgehogs, animals of insectivore group **I** 260; picture **I** 261
Hedgerow Theater, Moylan-Rose Valley, Pennsylvania **T** 161

Hedonism (HE-don-ism) (from Greek *hedone,* meaning "pleasure"), in philosophy, belief that pleasure is man's highest good. It was the doctrine of the school of Aristippus and Cyrenaics, which sought satisfaction of sensual desire, while that of Epicurus found pleasure in the absence of pain and in self-control. In modern British philosophy, especially utilitarianism of Jeremy Bentham and John Stuart Mill, the term refers to the greatest happiness of the greatest possible number.

Hegel (HEY-gel), **Georg Wilhelm Friedrich,** German philosopher **P** 192
Hegira (he-JY-ra), year of Mohammed's flight from Mecca **I** 414; **M** 405
Heidelberg (HIDE-el-berg), Germany **G** 158; picture **G** 149
Heifers (HEF-ers), female calves **D** 8

Heifetz (HY-fetz), **Jascha** (1901–   ), American violinist, b. Vilna, Russia. Noted for his phenomenal technique, he was a child prodigy at age of 3. He has played in concerts throughout world and has arranged works of Bach and Vivaldi for violin and has commissioned modern composers to write concertos for him.

Height, Dorothy, American political leader, picture **N** 104
Heimdall (HAIM-dol), Norse Watchman of the Gods **N** 278
Heimskringla (HAIM-skring-la): **sagas of the Norwegian kings,** by Snorri Sturluson **S** 50
Heine (HI-na), **Heinrich,** German poet **H** 104
German romanticists **G** 177

Heinlein, Robert Anson (1907–   ), American author, b. Butler, Mo. He specializes in science fiction for children and adults. He wrote a story, "Blowups Happen," about uranium bomb 2 years before the first nuclear chain reaction in a laboratory. His books include *The Green Hills of Earth, The Star Beast, The Puppet Masters,* and *Rocket Ship Galileo.*

Heisenberg (HI-zen-berk), **Werner Karl** (1901–   ), German physicist, b. Duisburg. He developed a new system of quantum mechanics, a branch of mathematics that deals with the behavior of subatomic particles, such as electrons and protons. This system of mathematics helped scientists studying the atom and led to the discovery that ordinary hydrogen actually has two different forms. For his work Heisenberg received the 1932 Nobel prize in physics. He is also known for his

Heisenberg, Werner Karl (continued)
uncertainty principle, which states that it is impossible to measure accurately certain pairs of quantities at the same time.

Heisman, John, American football coach **F** 364

Heisman Memorial Trophy, annual award made (since 1935) by Downtown Athletic Club of New York, N.Y., to most valuable college football player. It was named in honor of John W. Heisman, player and coach.

Hekla, volcano in Iceland **I** 42
Helena, capital of Montana **M** 440

Helena (hel-E-na), **Saint** (250?–330?), Greek saint of Christian Church, b. Nicomedia, Bithynia, Asia Minor. She used her influence as mother of Emperor Constantine the Great to propagate Christianity. She made a pilgrimage to Jerusalem (225?), where she built Church of the Holy Sepulcher and Church of the Nativity, and, according to tradition, discovered holy sepulcher and authentic cross.

Helen of Troy, in Greek mythology **H** 104
Iliad **I** 69
stories from Greek myths **G** 365
Trojan War **T** 293
Helgoland, island in North Sea **I** 430
Helical (HEL-ic-al) **gears** **G** 66
Helicopters **H** 105–06
at Ellesmere Island, Canada, picture **I** 424
aerodynamics **A** 41
aviation development **A** 573–74; picture **A** 570
fight forest fires **F** 152
Leonardo da Vinci's design, picture **L** 154
polar ice cap landing, picture **C** 344
spraying insecticides, picture **E** 272f
surveying, use in **S** 480
transportation, new methods of **T** 267; picture **T** 265
Helictites (hel-IC-tites), cave formations **C** 155

Heliocentric (he-li-o-CEN-tric) **theory,** theory published by Copernicus in 1543, claiming that the sun (Greek, *helios*) was center of the solar system and that the planets revolved around it. This theory has replaced the geocentric, or earth-centered, theory.

Heliograph (HE-li-o-graph) **signaling** **C** 438; **T** 50
Helios (HE-lios), god of the sun
Colossus of Rhodes **W** 216

Heliotrope (HE-li-o-trope), fragrant flowering plant found in temperate areas. Plant bears small white, lilac, or blue flowers in clusters at end of stems or along sides.

Helium (HE-lium), element **H** 107–08
atom, structure of the, diagrams **N** 355
balloons inflated with **B** 30
effect on voice sounds in underwater houses **U** 19
elements, some facts about **E** 154, 161
gases **G** 59
helium 4, or alpha rays **N** 359
hydrogen fusion produces helium **H** 306
industrial and scientific uses **G** 62
Kansas, first discovery in U.S.A. **K** 180, 182
liquid helium, at absolute zero, diagram **H** 90
noble gases **N** 109
nuclear-fusion reactions in sun's interior **S** 463
spacecraft fuels **S** 348
Helix (HE-liks), something spiral in form
DNA and RNA molecules, picture **B** 292

Hellbenders, land-water animals **F** 475; picture **F** 474

Hellen, in Greek mythology, son of Deucalion and Pyrrha, the only survivors of a flood. He founded Hellenes, or Greek race, and he was father of Aeolus, Dorus, and Xuthus, who established Aeolian, Dorian, Ionian, and Achaeon branches of the race. In modern Greece the monarch is still designated "king of the Hellenes."

Hellenistic (hel-len-IST-ic) **Age of Greece,** from use of the word "Hellas" for Greece **G** 338
Greek literature **G** 355
Greek sculpture of **G** 346; **S** 95
Hellespont, see Dardanelles
Hellman, Lillian, American playwright **A** 216
Hellstrom Chronicle, motion picture, picture **M** 488c
Helmets
armor **A** 433; pictures **A** 435
decorated, picture **D** 67
diving equipment **D** 79
Roman officer's, picture **H** 55

Helmholtz, Hermann Ludwig Ferdinand von (1821–1894), German scientist, b. Potsdam. He made outstanding contributions in several fields, including medicine, physics, physiology, and mathematics. Among his most important achievements were the first mathematical statement of the principle of conservation of energy; the first measurement of the speed of nerve impulses; the development of a theory of color vision; and the invention of the ophthalmoscope.
science, history of **S** 76

Helmont, Jan Baptista van, Belgian alchemist **C** 210
Héloïse see Abelard, Peter
Helots, Spartan slaves **S** 196
Helsinki, capital of Finland **F** 133, 134; picture **F** 130
Hematite, iron ore **I** 404; picture **R** 265
Hematology (he-ma-TOL-ogy), study of the blood **M** 201
medicine, tools and techniques of **M** 209
Hemingway, Ernest, American writer **H** 108–09
American literature, place in **A** 211–12
novels **N** 349
short stories **S** 167
Hemispheres, of the earth **E** 272h
jet streams in Northern Hemisphere **J** 89–90
Hemlock, tree, picture **T** 275
Eastern hemlock, state tree of Pennsylvania **P** 129
Western hemlock, state tree of Washington **W** 15
Hemlock, water, poisonous plant **P** 323
medicinal in small doses **P** 314
root contains poison, cicutoxin **P** 282, 321, 322
Hemming, in dressmaking **D** 315
Hemming stitches, in sewing **S** 129
Hemoglobin (HE-mo-glo-bin), in blood **B** 256, 259, 290
oxygen carrier, diagram **O** 268
Hemolytic streptococci (he-mo-LIT-ic strep-to-cocc-i), bacteria **D** 207
Hemophilia (he-mo-PHIL-ia), disease **D** 188
Hemp, plant **R** 332
marijuana and hashish **D** 331
Hen dance, of Denmark **D** 30
Henday, Anthony, fur trader in Canada **A** 146h; **S** 38h
Henderson, Fletcher, American jazz musician **J** 59–60
Henderson, Marge, American cartoonist **C** 128
Hendricks, Thomas A., vice-president, United States **V** 331; picture **V** 328
Henequen (HEN-ek-en), plant fiber **R** 332
Hengelo, the Netherlands **N** 118
Hengist and Horsa, German tribal chieftains who invaded Britain **E** 243
See also Jutes

Henie, Sonja (1913–69), American skater, b. Oslo, Norway. She won women's figure-skating championship in Olympic Games (1928, 1932, 1936). The first ballerina on ice, she produced and starred in ice revues and movies. Her autobiography is *Wings on My Feet*. Picture **O** 111.

Henize, Karl G., American astronaut **S** 346
Henlein (HEN-line), **Peter,** German locksmith **W** 46
  studies of mechanical energy **P** 233
Henley, William Ernest, English poet **Q** 20
Henley Royal Regatta, English rowing race **R** 339
Henna, hair dye **B** 111

Hennepin, Father Louis (1640?–1701), French missionary and explorer in America, b. Flanders. In 1675 Hennepin went to Canada as a missionary. In 1680 the Sieur de La Salle sent him to explore the Upper Mississippi River. Hennepin was taken prisoner by the Sioux and later released. He returned to France and wrote three books about his adventures and explorations. His claim to have discovered the mouth of the Mississippi before La Salle was proven false. **M** 336, 364; **N** 243

Henry IV (1050–1106), Holy Roman Emperor and king of Germany (1056–1105). He struggled for the empire with the papacy by investing the bishop of Milan in opposition to Pope Gregory VII. Threatened with deposition, he sought absolution at Canossa (1077). When the Pope recognized Rudolf of Swabia as king of Germany, Henry brought about election (1080) of the antipope Clement III, who crowned him emperor (1084).
  Henry and Pope Gregory VII **G** 375; **H** 163; **R** 291

Henry II, king of England **E** 218; **M** 291
  Becket's martyrdom **B** 115
  invasion of Ireland **I** 390
  jury system **J** 159

Henry IV (Henry of Bolingbroke) (1367–1413), king of England (1399–1413), created duke of Hereford (1397). Exiled for many years, he was banished forever at the death of his father, John of Gaunt, by his cousin King Richard II. He invaded England, defeated Richard II, was acclaimed king by Parliament (1399), and established rule of House of Lancaster. His reign was troubled by uprisings of Richard's supporters, especially by the Percy family at the famous Hotspur Revolt in 1403.

Henry V, king of England **E** 219
Henry VI, king of England **E** 219–20
Henry VII, king of England, or Henry Tudor **E** 220
Henry VIII, king of England **H** 109
  Elizabeth I, daughter **E** 178–79
  England, Tudor era of **E** 220–21
  heads Church of England **C** 286
  hunted in London's St. James's Park **L** 335
  jewelry worn by **J** 94, 99
  More, Sir Thomas, relations with **M** 456
  painting by Hans Holbein the Younger **E** 236

Henry IV (1553–1610), king of France (1589–1610) and of Navarre (as Henry III) (1572–1610). As chief of Huguenots, he fought the Catholic League, which refused to recognize him as heir to throne. He later converted to Catholicism to become the first Bourbon king of France. He settled religious question by Edict of Nantes (1598). Henry was preparing for war against Spanish and Austrian Hapsburgs when he was assassinated.
  Bourbon kings of France **F** 416
  Great Design, plan for peace **P** 104
  weavers established as a monopoly **T** 305

Henry, Andrew, American trapper and explorer **F** 523
Henry, John, American folk hero **F** 314–15

Henry, Joseph (1797–1878), American physicist, b. Albany, N.Y. Noted for his research on electric currents in coil of wire, he constructed the first electromagnetic motor and an electromagnetic telegraph and developed a system for weather reporting.

Henry, Marguerite (1902–), American author of children's books, b. Milwaukee, Wis. Her works include illustrated geography books for third and fourth graders, as well as story books. She is best-known for *Justin Morgan Had a Horse, The Little Fellow, Benjamin West and His Cat Grimalkin, King of the Wind, Brighty of the Grand Canyon,* and *Misty.*

Henry, O., pen name of William Sydney Porter, American writer **H** 110
  American literature **A** 208–09
  "Gift of the Magi, The," story **H** 110–13
  short stories **S** 167
Henry, Patrick, American Revolutionary War patriot and orator **H** 113–14
Henry IV, play by Shakespeare **S** 134
Henry V, play by Shakespeare **S** 134

Henry VI, play by Shakespeare (thought by some to have been written in collaboration with Marlowe, Kyd, Lodge, Peele, or Greene), based on chronicle of Hall and Holinshed. First part involves early reign of Henry VI and his wars with France. Second part tells of Henry's marriage to Margaret of Anjou and the beginning of the War of the Roses between House of Lancaster and House of York. Third part covers King Henry's surrender of the crown to Duke of York and murder of Henry by Richard, Duke of Gloucester (1471).

Henry VIII, play by Shakespeare involving Henry's divorce of Catherine of Aragon and his subsequent marriage to Anne Boleyn and the christening of Princess Elizabeth. The burning of the Globe Theatre in 1613 is supposed to have been caused by a cannon firing at the end of Act I.

Henry Ford Museum, Dearborn, Michigan **D** 151; **M** 514
Henry Francis du Pont Winterthur Museum, Delaware **D** 96
Henry of Navarre see Henry IV, king of France
Henry the Navigator, Portuguese prince **P** 403
  discoverer of discoverers **E** 374
Hens see Poultry

Henson, Matthew (1866–1955), American explorer, Negro, b. Charles County, Md. As a member of Commander Robert E. Peary's expedition, he was the first man to reach the North Pole, where he planted an American flag on April 6, 1909. This achievement was the goal that Peary and Henson had tried to accomplish on seven previous explorations. Henson was the author of *A Negro Explorer at the North Pole.* In 1945 Congress awarded him a medal for "outstanding service to the Government of the United States in the field of science." Ten years later he was honored by President Eisenhower at the White House.
  Peary's expedition to the North Pole **P** 116

Henze, Hans Werner, German composer **G** 189; **O** 138
Hepaticae, division of plant kingdom **P** 292
Hepaticas (he-PAT-ic-as), flowers, picture **W** 170

Hepatitis (hep-a-TY-tis), virus disease **D** 198
 drug abuse may lead to **D** 330
Hepburn, Audrey, American actress, picture **M** 479

Hepburn, Katherine (1909–   ), American actress, b. Hartford, Conn. Daughter of a doctor and a suffragist, she attended private schools before entering Bryn Mawr College. After a stint in summer stock, she made her Broadway debut in *Night Hostess.* Her first success, *The Warrior's Husband,* brought Hollywood offers. Among her best films were *Bill of Divorcement, African Queen,* and *Guess Who's Coming to Dinner.* Later Broadway successes included *As You Like It, The Philadelphia Story,* and *Coco.* She is the winner of three Academy Awards.

Hephaestus (heph-ES-tus), Greek god **G** 358

Hepplewhite, George (?–1786), English furniture designer. He worked in London, where he probably designed winged easy chair and shield-back chair. His name became synonymous with the curved, delicate style—prevalent in England during reign (1760–1820) of George III—that replaced more massive Chippendale furniture.
 antiques and antique collecting **A** 318
 furniture design **F** 507

Hepworth, Barbara, English sculptor **E** 241
Hera, Greek goddess **G** 357
Heracles (HER-ac-lese), hero in Greek mythology
 G 362–63
Heraldry, science of genealogies, crests, and coats of arms **H** 115–18
 banners displayed in Metropolitan Museum, picture **M** 237
 flags **F** 225, 243
 heraldic motifs on furniture **F** 506; picture **F** 507
 knights, knighthood, and chivalry **K** 272–77
Heralds, court messengers and announcers in the Middle Ages **H** 117
Herat (her-OT), Afghanistan **A** 42
Herbaceous (her-BAY-ceous) (non-woody) plants **P** 293, 303
 garden flowers, picture **G** 49
 vegetables **V** 286–94
Herbals, books about medicinal plants **P** 311
Herbariums, collections of dried plants **Z** 379

Herbart, Johann Friederich (1776–1841), German philosopher, b. Oldenburg. He devised an educational system, based on psychology and philosophy (then considered the same), intended to develop moral character. He also devised a new method of teaching literature.

Herbert, Victor, American composer **O** 157
 musical comedy **M** 542
 Naughty Marietta, operetta **O** 158
 Red Mill, operetta **O** 158
Herbert Hoover Library-Museum, West Branch, Iowa
 I 366
Herb gardens **G** 26
Herbicides, chemical agents for weed killing **A** 100;
 C 524; **F** 59
Herbivores, plant-eating animals **M** 65

Herblock (Herbert Block) (1909–   ), American editorial cartoonist, b. Chicago, Ill. He is on staff of Washington *Post* (since 1946). His cartoons, which characterize current events or trends, twice won Pulitzer prize (1942 and 1954).

Herbs **S** 380; picture **H** 265
 botanical gardens **Z** 379

 early use as drugs **D** 322
 grown in flower gardens **G** 26
 herb farmers, Lepchas, of Sikkim **S** 177
 pioneer medicine **P** 256
Herculaneum (her-cu-LANE-eum), Italy **P** 390
Hercules (HER-cu-lese), hero in Roman mythology
 G 362–63
Herd Book Society, dairy cattle breeders **D** 8
Herder, Johann, German writer **G** 175–76
Herding, of animals
 Africa **A** 62
Herdsman, constellation see Boötes
Hereditary rule, or royal autocracy, government rule by royal birth **G** 275–76
Heredity, traits determined by genes **G** 77–88
 biology and genetics, history of **B** 194, 196
 cancer research **C** 93
 child development, individual differences in
 C 231–32
 congenital diseases **D** 188
 cross-pollination of flowers **F** 277
 Mendel's experiments **M** 219
Hereford, breed of beef cattle **C** 147; pictures **C** 149;
 S 319
Heresy, departure from accepted beliefs **R** 289
 Albigensian heresy **R** 292
 Christianity, history of **C** 283
 Ferdinand and Isabella revive Inquisition **F** 87
Heretics, dissenters from church dogma **I** 257
 Reformation, forerunners of **R** 132
Here we go gathering nuts in May, singing game **G** 13
Herman's Hermits, English rock music group **R** 262c
Hermes (HER-mese), asteroid **P** 274
Hermes, Greek god **G** 360
Hermitage, home of Andrew Jackson **J** 4; picture **J** 7
Hermitage Museum, Leningrad, Union of Soviet Socialist Republics **H** 119–20; **M** 511; picture **M** 509
Hermit crabs **S** 168; picture **S** 169
Hermit thrushes, birds, pictures **B** 236
 bill, picture **B** 223
 state bird of Vermont **V** 307
Hermod (HER-mode), messenger of Norse gods **N** 280
Hermon, Mount, Syria **S** 507
Hernández, José, Argentine poet **A** 390
Hernández Martínez (air-NON-dez mar-TI-nez), **Maximiliano,** former dictator of El Salvador **E** 184
Herndon, William H., American lawyer, partner of Abraham Lincoln **L** 292–93
Herne, James A., American playwright **A** 215

Hero and Leander (le-AN-der), in Greek mythology, a priestess of Aphrodite and her lover. Leander lived across the Hellespont, which he swam every night to see her. One stormy night Hero's guiding torch was extinguished, and Leander was drowned. When she found his body, Hero cast herself into sea. They are subjects of many well-known literary works, including the poem *Hero and Leander* by Christopher Marlowe and George Chapman.

Herod I (Herod the Great) (73? B.C.–4 B.C.), king of Judea (37 B.C.–4 B.C.). His reign was marked by violence and intrigue. He executed one of his 10 wives and three of his sons, and according to Matthew's gospel (2:16), all male children 2 and under in Bethlehem. He rebuilt some cities, giving them imperial names. Under Augustus, his authority was extended.
 Mary and Joseph, flight to Egypt with the infant, Jesus **M** 113

Herod Antipas, ruler of Judea
 John the Baptist **J** 122

Herodotus (he-ROD-o-tus), (480? B.C.–425? B.C.), Greek historian, b. Halicarnassus, Asia Minor. Sometimes called the father of history, he wrote an account of Persian Wars (500 B.C.–479? B.C.) with Greece. He is read for his entertaining, though not strictly accurate, anecdotes.
  Greek prose writers **G** 98, 350–51; **H** 134

Heroes
  culture heroes **M** 560–61
  folk heroes **F** 311–13
  Greek mythology **G** 361–65
  See also Carnegie Hero Fund Commission
Heroic couplet, in poetry **E** 256
Heroin, narcotic drug **D** 330; **N** 12–14

Herons, any of several wading birds with long necks and long, thin legs. Many have plumes on their heads. Herons usually have long, straight bills, used for spearing or grasping fish, their chief food. They have long, broad wings. In flight, the heron's neck outlines an S shape. Pictures **A** 272; **B** 208, 222
  adaptive radiation in birds **B** 209
  green heron, picture **A** 279

Hero of Alexandria, Greek scientist **E** 209
  toys made by **T** 231
Héroult (a-ROO), **Paul,** French scientist **A** 176
  See also Hall, Charles Martin
Herpetology, study of reptiles, see Reptiles
Herrera (er-RAY-ra), **Fernando de,** Spanish poet **S** 368

Herrera, Francisco de (called El Viejo, "The Elder") (1590?–1656), Spanish artist, b. Seville. A painter in the so-called tenebrist style, his notable works include Last Judgment, St. Peter, and Temptation of St. Jerome. His son **Francisco de Herrera** (El Mozo, "The Younger") (1622–85) was a painter-architect noted for still lifes.

Herrera, José, president of Mexico **P** 386
Herrera, Juan de, Spanish architect
  Herreran style **S** 363
Herrera, Omar Torrijos see Torrijos Herrera, Omar
Herrera, Tomás, Panamanian leader **P** 46
Herreran style, of architecture **L** 63; **S** 363

Herrick, Robert (1591–1674), English lyric poet, b. London. Considered one of the best of the Cavalier poets, he modeled epigrams on ancient Greek epigramists and Latin poets. He celebrated old English country life in such pastorals as "Corinna's Going a-Maying." He also published 1,200 secular and religious lyrics in Hesperides, or the Works both Human and Divine of Robert Herrick, Esq.

Herring, large family of fish, almost all ocean-dwelling. The group includes herrings, sardines, shad, menhaden, and alewives. All have flat bodies with sharply forked tails. The most common species is the herring, found in most of northern Atlantic and in the Pacific Ocean. It swims in very large schools. Herrings usually weigh up to 1 lb., although weight of annual catch exceeds that of any other Atlantic food fish. They are more numerous than any other backboned animal.
  habitat, feeding habits, uses **F** 187, 214, 220
  Norwegian sardine industry **N** 343
  scales, types of, picture **F** 185

Herringbone, milking method **D** 9
Herringbone gears **G** 66
Herring gulls, birds, picture **B** 236
Herschel (HER-shel), **Sir William,** German-born English
  astronomer **T** 63–64

amateur astronomer's discovery **A** 475; picture **A** 474
asteroids **P** 273
infrared radiation and radiant energy **L** 269; **P** 236
Uranus, planet **P** 277

Herschel family, English family of astronomers. **Sir William** (1738–1822) discovered planet Uranus and the two satellites of Saturn and built new kind of reflecting telescope. **Caroline Lucretia** (1750–1848), his sister and assistant, discovered eight comets. **Sir John Frederick William** (1792–1871), his son, is noted for his classification of heavenly bodies and his work in photography of the heavens. He invented sensitized paper for use in developing photographs.

Hersey, John, American novelist **A** 213

Hershey, Milton Snavely (1857–1945), American businessman and philanthropist, b. Dauphin County, Pa. He began manufacturing chocolate (1893) in Lancaster, Pa., and became chairman of the board of Hershey Chocolate Corporation in Hershey, Pa. He founded (1905) and endowed Hershey Industrial School for orphaned boys.

Hershey, Pennsylvania **P** 142

Herter, Christian (1895–1966), American politician, b. Paris, France. He was U.S. secretary of state (1959–61), governor of Massachusetts (1953–57), and co-chairman of U.S. Citizens Commission on NATO (1961–62).

Herty, Charles H., American chemist **G** 133
Hertz, Heinrich, German scientist **P** 237
  Marconi inspired by **M** 98
  radio waves demonstrated by him **R** 52; **T** 54
Hertzsprung-Russell star chart **A** 477
Herzegovina see Bosnia and Herzegovina
Herzl (HERTZ-el), **Theodor,** Hungarian Zionist **Z** 371
  Jews and Judaism **J** 112
  shrine to, in Jerusalem **J** 81
Hesiod (HE-siod), Greek poet **G** 350
  fables **F** 3

Hesper, or **Hesperus,** in Greek mythology, brother of Atlas, who was changed into evening star. It was also the Greek name for Venus as the evening star. In this use its Latin counterpart is Vesper. Pythagoras was first to identify Hesper, the evening star, with Phosphorus, the morning star.

Hesperides (hes-PER-id-ese), in Greek mythology **G** 363
Hesperornis (hes-per-OR-nis), prehistoric bird **B** 207, 209

Hess, Dame Myra (1890–1965), English pianist, b. London. An immediate success at her first public appearance (1907), she toured Europe and North America. During World War II she arranged daily midday concerts at National Gallery in London, earning knighthood (1941).

Hess, Rudolf (Walther Richard Rudolf) (1894–   ), German politician, b. Alexandria, Egypt. He was third deputy of Hitler, second in succession to German dictatorship. On eve of German attack on Russia (1941), he made a solo flight to Scotland, hoping to arrange an Anglo-German peace settlement. He was sentenced to life imprisonment at the Nuremberg Trials (1946).

Hess, Victor, Austrian scientist **C** 511
Hesse (HESS-a), **Hermann,** German-Swiss writer **G** 180
Hessians, German mercenary soldiers hired by King George III to fight for England **R** 201, 202

Hestia, Greek goddess **G** 357
Hetep, Egyptian nobleman, statue of, picture **E** 99
Heure espagnole, L', opera by Maurice Ravel **O** 145

Heuss (HOIS), Theodor (1884–1963), German statesman, b. Brackenheim, Württemberg. Newspaper editor, publisher, author, and educator, Heuss was also a member of the Reichstag (1924–28; 1930–33) until the Nazis forced him out of government. Returning to public life after World War II, he became first chairman of the Free Democratic Party and a member of the Parliamentary Council that framed the West German constitution (1948–49). He was elected first president of the German Federal Republic in 1949, serving two 5-year terms before his retirement.

Hexagon, six-sided geometric figure, pictures **G** 131
Hexameter, meter in poetry **P** 354
Hey Diddle, Diddle, nursery rhyme **N** 404

Heyerdahl (HY-er-dahl), Thor (1914–   ), Norwegian ethnologist and author, b. Larvik. He sailed (1947) balsa raft, *Kon Tiki*, from Peru to Tuamotu Island, South Pacific, to prove theory that ancient Peruvians could have settled in Polynesia and recorded his adventures in book *Kon-Tiki*. A later book, *Aku-Aku*, recounts expedition to Easter Island. He sailed (1970) papyrus raft, Ra II, from Africa to Barbados to prove Egyptians could have reached Caribbean 4,000 to 5,000 years ago.
   distribution of life with the Peru Current **L** 232–33

Heyward (HAY-ward), DuBose (1885–1940), American author, b. Charleston, S.C. Descended from the American revolutionary Thomas Heyward, he wrote about Gullah Negroes of South Carolina and Sea Islands. He is most famous for Pulitzer prize winning play (1927) *Porgy*, which he dramatized from his novel *Porgy*.
   musical comedy of the 1930's **M** 542

Heyward, Thomas (1746–1809), American revolutionary, b. St. Helena's Parish (now St. Luke's Parish), S.C. He signed Declaration of Independence and served as delegate from South Carolina to Second Continental Congress (until 1778).

Heywood, John, English dramatist **D** 295
   quotation **Q** 20

Hezekiah (hez-e-KY-ah) (lived about 700 B.C.), king of Judah (720? B.C.–692 B.C.). He rose up against Assyria (712 B.C.) but was defeated by Sennacherib. He withstood Sennacherib's subsequent invasion (according to Old Testament, because a plague broke out in the Assyrian army). He is said to have been encouraged by prophet Isaiah to restore theocratic spirit and abolish idolatry.

Hialeah, port of Greater Miami, Florida **M** 254

Hiawatha (hi-a-WA-tha) (from Indian, meaning "Maker of Rivers"), North American Indian of Mohawk tribe who united (about 1570) five tribes into league of Iroquois, pledging to abolish war and maintain law and order. The name became title of hereditary chiefs of Mohawks. Later, Hiawatha became confused with mythical Iroquois deity of same name, and resulting legends were celebrated by Longfellow in *The Song of Hiawatha*. Picture **F** 110.

Hiawatha, Song of, poem by Longfellow, setting in
   Michigan **M** 258
   parody "Song of Milkanwatha" **N** 272
Hibachis, oriental cookers **O** 247

Hibbing, Minnesota **M** 330
Hibernation, sleep or resting state of animals **H** 121–24
   bats **B** 94
   bears **B** 106
   crocodilians **C** 535
   mammals **M** 70
   turtles **T** 334–35
   yearly rhythms in plant and animal life **L** 244
Hibiscus (hi-BIS-cus), red, Hawaii state flower **H** 56

Hiccup, or hiccough, an involuntary spasmodic contraction of the diaphragm. Indrawing of air is stopped by sudden closing of the glottis, producing a sound similar to that of word "hiccup."

Hickel, Walter Joseph (1919–   ), American businessman and politician, b. Ellinwood, Kan. After arriving penniless in Alaska, Hickel made his fortune in the construction business. Turning to politics, he became the first elected Republican governor of Alaska (1967). In 1969 he accepted an appointment as President Nixon's secretary of the interior. He held this post until 1970.

Hickman, Henry Hill, English doctor **A** 256

Hickok, Wild Bill (James Butler Hickok) (1837–1876), American lawman, b. Troy Grove, Ill. He served as Indian scout with generals Custer, Hancock, and Sheridan and for Union Army during Civil War. As deputy U.S. marshall at Fort Riley (1866–67), Hays City (1869–71), and Abilene (1871), he maintained law and order in wild Kansas border towns. He toured the East with Buffalo Bill Cody (1872–73). Hickok was killed during a poker game by Jack McCall.

Hickory, Dickory, Dock, nursery rhyme **N** 406
Hidalgo, asteroid **P** 274
Hidalgo y Costilla (e-DAL-go e co-STI-ya), Miguel, Mexican priest and patriot **M** 248
Hides and skins
   leather **L** 107–11
Hieroglyphics (hi-er-o-GLIPH-ics), picture writing of ancient Egypt **W** 318
   alphabet not applicable to **A** 170
   communication, ancient method **C** 431, 432
Hieronymus see Jerome, Saint
Hi-fi, sound reproduction **H** 125–26
   phonographs **P** 198
   realistic quality, or "presence" of sound **T** 21
   record collecting **R** 124–25
Higgins Flat, New Mexico, archeological site, picture **A** 351
Higginson, Francis, American writer **A** 195
Highball, railroad signal **R** 84
High blood pressure **D** 198–99
   heart, disorders of **H** 86c

Highet, Gilbert Arthur (1906–   ), American classics scholar and educator, b. Glasgow, Scotland. Considered authority on Greek and Latin literature, comparative literature, and teaching methods, he is Anthon professor of Latin language and literature at Columbia University (since 1950). He translated the poems in *Oxford Book of Greek Verse* and is author of *The Classical Tradition*.

High-fidelity sound reproduction see Hi-fi
High German, dialect of southern Germany **G** 172, 173
High jumping, field event **T** 238; picture **O** 114
Highlands, Scotland **S** 86
High-level languages, in computer programing **C** 457
High Point, North Carolina **N** 318
High relief, in sculpture **S** 90

High riggers, lumbermen **L** 374
Highs, or anticyclones, in meteorology **W** 74–75
  winds and weather **W** 186
High schools **E** 72, 80, 82
  driver education **D** 318–21
  examinations for college entrance **E** 348–49
  libraries **L** 176
  physical education programs **P** 226
  school systems **S** 58
High-speed trains **R** 90
  Osaka-Tokyo **O** 232
High Tatra, mountains, Europe see Tatra Mountains
High Veld, grasslands of South Africa **P** 430, 432; **S** 270
Highways see Roads and highways
Highway safety
  driver education **D** 318–21
Highway Safety Act, 1966 see National Traffic and
  Motor Vehicle Safety Act
High Wycombe (WIC-om), Buckinghamshire, England,
  picture **E** 213

Hijacking, stealing goods from a truck, train, or ship
in transit. During the 1960's plane hijacking (or skyjacking), forcing the pilot to fly to an unscheduled destination, became increasingly frequent.

Hikes, iceboat racing technique **I** 30; picture **I** 28
Hiking
  hostels and hosteling **H** 253–56
  how to keep from getting lost **C** 46
  Long Trail, in the Green Mountains, Vermont **V** 316
Hildebrand see Gregory, Saint (Gregory VII, pope)
Hildebrandt, Johann Lukas von, Austrian artist
  G 169–70

Hill, Graham (1929–), English sports-car racer, b.
Hampstead. The world champion Grand Prix racer, he
won his fourth Grand Prix de Monaco in 1968. He also
won the United States Grand Prix and the Rheims
(France) international sports-car race with Joachim Bon-
nier of Sweden (both 1964). He took first place in the
Indianapolis 500 in 1966.

Hill, James Jerome, Canadian-born American railroad
  executive and financier **M** 334–35
Hill, Sir Rowland, English postal authority **S** 396
Hillary, Sir Edmund P., New Zealand mountain climber
  E 337
  Commonwealth Trans-Antarctic Expedition, 1957–58
  P 371
  Himalayas **H** 129
  mountain climbing **M** 489–90
Hill City, South Dakota **S** 324

Hillel (surnamed the Elder) (?–A.D. 9?), Jewish scholar
and teacher. Reputedly descended from houses of David
and Benjamin, he set forth the principles of Talmudic
Judaism and founded a dynasty of patriarchs who led
Jews until 5th century. He was president of the
Sanhedrin (Jewish council), where he introduced seven
of the traditional rules for scriptural study. He summed
up teaching of the Torah in a form of the Golden Rule.
  Talmud **T** 15

Hiller, Raphael, American violist, picture **C** 185
Hilliard, Nicholas, English painter
  Queen Elizabeth I **E** 251

Hillman, Sidney (1887–1946), American labor leader, b.
Zagare, Lithuania. In his career as a moderate union
official, he promoted union-management co-operation. He
was president of Amalgamated Clothing Workers of

America (1915–46) and vice-president of Congress of
Industrial Organizations (1935–40). He was chairman of
the CIO Political Action Committee (1943–46).

Hill stations, mountain resorts, India **I** 125

Hillyer, Robert Silliman (1895–1961), American poet, b.
East Orange, N.J. He taught English literature at Harvard
(1919–26, 1928–45), Trinity College (1926–28), and the
University of Delaware (1952–61), published many volumes of poetry, and received the Pulitzer prize for
poetry in 1934 for *Collected Verse.*

Hilo, Hawaii **H** 69

Hilton, Conrad N. (1887–), American hotel executive,
b. San Antonio, N. Mex. As president and chairman of
Hilton Hotels Corporation and president of Hilton Hotels
International and the Hotel Waldorf-Astoria Corporation,
he owns and operates hotels in major cities throughout
the world. He is the author of *Be My Guest.*

Hilton, James (1900–1954), English novelist, b. Leigh,
Lancashire. Many of his popular, romantic novels have
been filmed, including *We Are Not Alone, Knight Without Armour, Lost Horizon,* and *Good-bye Mr. Chips.*

Himalayan (HIM-a-lay-an) **black bears** **B** 108
Himalayan cats **C** 142; picture **C** 144
Himalayas (him-MOL-yas), mountain range, central Asia
  H 128–29; **M** 499
  Bhutan **B** 150–51
  central Asia **A** 448
  Everest, Mount **E** 336–37
  India **I** 123, 125
  Indian village, picture **I** 124
  Is there really an Abominable Snowman? **H** 129
  Kanchenjunga Mountain, picture **A** 447
  Kashmir **K** 197–98; picture **M** 497
  Sikkim **S** 176–77

Himes, Chester (1909–), American author, Negro, b.
Jefferson City, Mo. As a member of the Works Progress
Administration's Federal Writers' Project (1938–41), he
wrote a history of Cleveland, Ohio. He then worked in a
shipyard (1941–44) and began publishing novels. His first
was *If He Hollers, Let Him Go.* Others include *The Third
Generation, The Primitive,* and *Cotton Comes to Harlem.*

Himmler, Heinrich (1900–1945), German Nazi official, b.
Munich. He was leader of SS (1929–45) and chief of
Gestapo (1936–45). He also served as minister of Interior
(1943) and chief of troops stationed in Germany
(1944–45). As Gestapo commander, he initiated use of
concentration camps and gas chambers for imprisonment, torture, and extermination of Jews and other
minority groups. He committed suicide before he could
be brought to trial for war crimes.

Hinayana (hi-na-YA-na), teachings of Buddha **B** 424

Hindemith (HIN-dem-it), **Paul** (1895–1963), German composer, b. Hanau. After performance of his works was
banned in Nazi Germany, he went to United States,
joining faculty of Yale University (1940–53). Best-known
for symphony *Mathis der Maler,* music taken from his
opera of same title, he also wrote children's opera *Wir
bauen eine Stadt.* Other operas include *Cardillac* and
Die Harmonie der Welt. He also wrote much piano music,
chamber music, several ballets, and many songs (including song cycle *Das Marienleben*) and orchestral pieces.
  new kinds of chamber music **C** 186; **G** 189

Hindenburg, airship **H** 306

Hindenburg, Paul Ludwig Hans Anton von Beneckendorff und von (1847–1934), German general and last president of Weimar Republic, b. Posen.. During World War I he became (1916) supreme commander of Central Powers and established so-called Hindenburg line of defense across northeastern France. He defeated Hitler for presidency of Reich (1932). As president (1925–34), he remained a conservative Prussian monarchist.

Germany, World War I, and Hitler's rise to power **G** 162; **W** 274, 285

Hindi, official language of India **I** 117
Hindu-Arabic numerals **N** 391–92
Hindu drama **D** 293
Hinduism **H** 130–32; **R** 146
Africa **A** 58
Bangladesh **B** 44, 44c
dance combined with India's religion **D** 31
food taboos **F** 334
funeral customs **F** 493
Ganges River, India, part of Hinduism **G** 25
Hindu at prayer, picture **R** 146
Indian literature **O** 220d–220e
marriage rites **W** 103
pilgrims at Amarnath, picture **H** 128
pilgrims at the Ganges, pictures **A** 447, **I** 124
religious holidays **R** 154
Southeast Asia **S** 330
women, role of **W** 211
Hindu Kush, mountain range in central Asia
Afghanistan **A** 43

Hindustan (hin-du-STAN), vague designation applied at various times in the history of India to whole Indian subcontinent. The term is usually applied to Ganges Plain (where Hindi is spoken) between Himalayas and Deccan Plateau.

Hines, Earl "Fatha," American jazz musician **J** 59

Hipparchus (hip-PARC-hus) (lived during 2nd century B.C.), Greek astronomer, b. Nicaea, Bithynia (now Iznik, Turkey). His major discovery was precession of the equinoxes—a movement of the earth that puts it at slightly different angle to stars, on a given day, from year to year. The greatest astronomer of his time, he charted almost 1,000 stars and influenced Ptolemy's theory of universe. He was founder of trigonometry.

science, history of **S** 64

Hippies, young people who reject the values and mores of conventional society and who may take hallucinogenic drugs. The term comes from "hip," a slang word meaning familiarity with the latest ideas, styles, etc. The hippies usually come from middle and upper socio-economic backgrounds. They preach love, non-violence, honesty, joy, personal freedom, and mysticism. They usually dress unconventionally, scorn money, do not work for a living, and, in general, "drop out" of society.

Hippo, North Africa
Saint Augustine bishop of **A** 494
Hippocrates (hip-POC-ra-tese), Greek physician
  D 213
Greek and Roman medicine **M** 203
humoral theory in Greek medicine **S** 62
Hippocratic (hip-poc-RAT-ic) **Oath** **M** 208b

Hippodrome (from Greek *hippos,* meaning "horse," and *dromos,* meaning "racecourse"), stadium, oval in shape,

for horse and chariot races in ancient times. The earliest was at Olympia, Greece, and the largest and most splendid was at Constantinople (now Istanbul). The hippodrome was usually placed on the slope of a hill. The Circus Maximus in Rome was a famous hippodrome.

horseracing at first Olympic Games **H** 231; **O** 105

Hippolyta (hip-POL-it-a), in Greek mythology **G** 363
Hippopotamuses (hip-po-POT-a-mus-es) **H** 133
Africa, picture **A** 51
circus act, picture **C** 303
hoofed mammals **H** 209; picture **H** 212
"The Habits of the Hippopotamus", nonsense poem
  N 274
Hirakud Dam, India, picture **W** 220
Hire-purchase plan see Installment buying

Hirohito (he-ro-HE-toe) (1901–), Japanese emperor (since 1926), b. Tokyo. After being regent (1921–26), he succeeded to throne as 124th descendant of the legendary first emperor, Jimmu. Following World War II, he surrendered Japan (1945) to Allies under command of General MacArthur. He renounced power and divinity and drew up a democratic constitution for Japan (1946).

Japan, history of **J** 42, 48

Hiroshige (hi-ro-SHI-ghe), **Ando** (1797–1858), Japanese artist, b. Edo (now Tokyo). He is noted for his woodblock prints and delicately colored landscapes.

Hiroshima (hi-ro-SHI-ma), Japan **J** 48
first atomic bomb **W** 308

Hirsch, Baron Moritz (also Maurice de Hirsch) (1831–1896), German businessman and philanthropist, b. Munich. He and his wife, Clara, contributed millions of dollars for the education and relief of Jews. They financed the Jewish Colonization Association to assist Jewish refugees in many parts of the world. They also founded the Baron de Hirsch Fund (incorporated 1891) to help Jewish immigrants in the United States.

His Master's Voice, Victor trademark **P** 198
Hispania, ancient name for Spain **S** 351

Hispanic Society of America (HSA), society founded for the purpose of establishing a reference library and museum for the representation of the culture of Hispanic peoples. Founded in New York, N.Y., in 1904, it has a membership distinguished in Hispanic art and literature.

Hispaniola (hisp-an-i-O-la), island of West Indies, comprising Dominican Republic and Haiti **D** 280–83;
  H 7–11
Caribbean Sea and islands **C** 116–19
Columbus' discovery **C** 417
Ponce de Léon **P** 391
Toussaint L'Ouverture **T** 229

Hiss, Alger (1904–), American diplomat, b. Baltimore, Md. Among his various State Department assignments (1936–47), he served as principal adviser to the U.S. delegation to the General Assembly (1946). Accused by Whittaker Chambers (1948) of betraying government secrets to Soviet Russia, he was convicted (1950) of perjury and imprisoned (1951–54).

Histadrut (the General Federation of Jewish Labor), organized by Ben-Gurion **B** 140

Histamine, chemical found in the tissues of plants and animals. It causes stretching of the smallest blood vessels and stimulates the making of stomach juices. It is thought that allergic reactions are caused by the release of histamine from the cells. Drugs called antihistamines oppose the effects of histamine release.

Histology (hist-OL-ogy), study of plant and animal tissues **B** 190
Historical events, arranged by date of month *see* articles on individual months
Historical fiction
  children's literature **C** 241
  list of, for children **C** 248a
  novels, styles of **N** 346
  Scott, Sir Walter **S** 89
Historical firsts, arranged by date of month *see* articles on individual months
Historical geography G 108
Historical geology G 113
Historic places *see* places of interest section of country, province, and state articles
Historic Sites Act, 1935 **N** 51
History H 134–38
  American literature **A** 202, 214, 215
  ancient civilizations **A** 217–32
  archeology an aid to study of history **A** 348
  Herodotus, father of history **G** 351
  legends often have basis in history **L** 128
  Livy's history of Rome **L** 317
  Middle Ages, how dated by historians **M** 289
  museums **M** 513, 518
  Pulitzer prizes **P** 526
  research methods **R** 182
  social studies **S** 223
  Turner's theory of the frontier in American history **W** 206
  See also History in country, province, and state articles
History, ancient *see* Ancient civilizations

Hitchcock, Alfred Joseph (1899–   ), English film producer and director, b. London. He is noted for highly suspenseful film dramas, including *The 39 Steps, Suspicion, To Catch a Thief, Psycho,* and *Rebecca,* which won Academy Award for best picture (1940). He has been director, narrator, and host of TV program *Alfred Hitchcock Presents* (1955–60) and the *Alfred Hitchcock Hour* (1961–65). Picture **M** 484.
  motion pictures, history of **M** 485

Hitches, knots **K** 291
Hitler, Adolf, Austrian-born German chancellor and dictator **H** 139–40; picture **N** 69
  civil and human rights in conflict with idea of racial superiority **C** 316
  Jewish persecution **J** 111
  Nazism **N** 70
  plot against, 1944 **W** 302–03
  rise and fall of Germany's Third Reich **G** 162–63
  rise of dictators before World War II **W** 284, 285
  World War II **W** 282–308
Hitomaro, Kakinomoto, Japanese poet **O** 220b

Hitotsubashi (he-to-tsu-BA-shi) (Chinese, Keiki) (1837–1902), adopted member of Hitotsubashi house and last Japanese shogun (1867–68). His resignation marked the conclusion of a shogunate dictatorship that had existed for almost 700 years, restitution of political power to the emperor, and the beginning of Japanese modernization.

Hittites, Indo-European people who settled in small city-states in Asia Minor about 2nd millennium B.C. Alluded to in Old Testament as people in region of Canaan, they reached their cultural and political height in Hittite Empire (1450? B.C.–1200 B.C.), especially under reign of Suppiluliumas I (1375 B.C.–1335 B.C.). They were noted for advanced techniques in metallurgy, particularly iron smelting. After clashes with migrating tribes, the empire collapsed.
  ancient world, art of **A** 238–39
  language, history of **L** 303

Hives, allergy disease **D** 192
Hives, of bees **B** 118; **H** 202; picture **B** 119

Hi-Y Clubs, groups of high school students sponsored by YMCA who promote Christian values according to their program of "clean speech, clean scholarship, clean sportsmanship, and clean living." They participate in community and world service projects and promote good citizenship through annual youth and government program, which sets up a model legislature in each state.

H.M.S. Pinafore, operetta by Gilbert and Sullivan **G** 210
Hoban, James, Irish-born American architect **W** 162
Hobart, capital of Tasmania, Australia **A** 514
Hobart, Garret A., vice-president, United States **V** 331; picture **V** 328

Hobbema (HOB-em-a), **Meindert,** or **Meyndert** (1638–1709), Dutch landscape painter. He studied with the Dutch painter Jacob van Ruisdael, who strongly influenced his works in effects of light and atmosphere. He painted primarily quiet Dutch landscapes, water mills, and country roads—for example, *The Avenue, Middelharnis, The Hermitage, St. Petersburg,* and *The Water Mill.*
  landscape painting in Dutch art **D** 357
  The Avenue, Middelharnis, painting **D** 361

Hobbes, Thomas, English philosopher **P** 192
Hobbies H 140–42
  airplane models **A** 104–07
  antiques **A** 318–21
  aquariums **A** 340–43; **P** 181
  autograph collecting **A** 526–27
  automobile models **A** 535–37
  bird watching **B** 233–44
  butterfly collecting **B** 476–77
  button collecting **B** 478–80
  camping **C** 40–46
  clay modeling **C** 336–37
  coin collecting **C** 374–75
  cooking **O** 247–48; **R** 114–16
  doll collecting **D** 265, 267
  drawing **D** 301–05
  dressmaking **D** 311–15
  embroidery **E** 187–89
  finger painting **F** 126–28
  fishing **F** 205–11
  flower arranging **J** 49–53
  folk dancing **F** 297–301
  gardens and gardening **G** 26–52; **V** 286–94
  houseplants **H** 265–69
  Indian beadwork **I** 157–59
  jewelry making **J** 100
  karting **K** 195–96
  kites **K** 266–71
  knitting and crocheting **K** 277–84
  knot tying **K** 289–92
  leaf prints **L** 118
  leathercraft **L** 112–13
  letter writing by pen pals **L** 159–60
  linoleum block printing **L** 304–06
  magic **M** 18–21

Hobson, Laura Keane Zametkin (1900–   ), American author, b. New York, N.Y. Her novel *Gentleman's Agreement* studies aspects of anti-Semitism in America. She was on staff of *Time, Fortune,* and *Life* magazines (1934–40).

Hobson's choice, phrase implying that one actually has no choice at all. The phrase alludes to practice of Tobias Hobson, a liveryman in 16th- and 17th-century England who had large supply of horses for hire but made customers take horse nearest stable door.

Hochhuth, Rolf (1931–   ), German dramatist, b. Eschwege. He is the author of two controversial plays: *The Deputy* (1963), which accused Pope Pius XII of refraining from intervening with Hitler on behalf of the Jews; and *Soldiers* (1967), which accused Winston Churchill of terror bombing in World War II.

Ho Chi Minh (HO CHE MIN) (Nguyen That Thank) (1890–1969) Vietnamese political leader, b. Northern Province. He began his political activity in Paris, where he preached revolution to Vietnamese, founded and edited anti-imperialist *Le Paria,* and joined French Socialist Party. Returning to Indochina (1930), he organized an independence party, Viet Minh, to resist Japanese aggression during World War II. He declared Vietnam a democratic republic (1945) and conducted guerrilla campaign against French (1945–54). He was president of North Vietnam (1954–69).
  Vietnam, history of V 334c, 334d, 336

Hodgkin (HODGE-kin), **Alan Lloyd** (1914–   ), English physiologist, b. Danbury. He is the chief contributor to the currently accepted theory of nervous conduction, the sodium theory, which is based on the movement of sodium ions and other ions across nerve-cell membranes. For this and other major contributions to neurophysiology he received the Nobel prize for medicine and physiology (1963) with A. F. Huxley and J. C. Eccles.

Hoffer, Eric (1902–   ), American philosopher, b. New York, N.Y. Blind for 8 years as a child, he was a migrant worker (1920–43) before becoming a longshoreman (1943) in California. He began writing in 1938 and is the author of such books as *Working and Thinking on the Waterfront, Eric Hoffer: An American Odyssey,* and *The True Believer.*

Hoffman, Dustin (1937–   ), American actor, b. Los Angeles, Calif. His first important stage role was in the off-Broadway production of *The Journey of the Fifth Horse.* For his performance as a middle-aged Russian clerk, Hoffman won the Obie Award as the best off-Broadway actor of the 1965–66 theater season. Hoffman appeared on Broadway in *Jimmy Shine* (1968–69). His films, for which he has won great critical acclaim, include *The Graduate, Midnight Cowboy,* and *Little Big Man.*

Hoffman, Malvina (1887–1966), American sculptor, b. New York, N.Y. She studied sculpture with Gutzon Borglum and Herbert Adams in New York and Auguste Rodin in Paris. Her works are in many museums, including the Metropolitan Museum of Art and the American Museum of Natural History in New York and the Chicago Natural History Museum. The sculptor of many portraits of prominent persons, she also did the American Battle Monument at Epinal, France, and the stone reliefs on the Joslin Clinic in Boston.

Hofmann (HOFE-monn), **Hans** (1880–1966), German-American painter, b. Weissenburg. A leading exponent of abstract expressionism, he founded the School of Modern Art in Munich, Germany (1915), and later established schools in New York, N.Y., and Provincetown.

Hofsinde, Robert (?–   ), American author-illustrator, b. Denmark. He came to the United States as a youth and lived in Minnesota. His interest in Indian culture began when he saved the life of a Chippewa Indian boy and was made a blood brother of the tribe. He was given the name of Gray-Wolf. His titles include *Indian Games and Crafts, Indian Sign Language, Indian Medicine Man,* and *Indian Arts.*

Hogan (HO-gan), **Ben** (William Benjamin Hogan) (1912–   ), American golf player, b. Dublin, Tex. He made a notable success before suffering severe injuries in an automobile crash (1949). He returned to competitive golf (1950) and won National Open Championship in 1950, 1951, and 1953, as he had in 1948. He won Masters (1951 and 1953) and British Open Championship titles (1953). Picture **G** 261.

Hogans, homes of the Navajo Indians **I** 192, 196
Hogarth (HO-garth), **William,** English painter **E** 238
  illustration of books **I** 90
  father of the modern cartoon **C** 125
  The Shrimp Girl **E** 239
Hogg, James S., American statesman **T** 135
Hogmanay (hog-ma-NAY), December 31, holiday in Scotland **H** 156
Hog-nosed skunks S 192
Hogs see Pigs
Hohenzollerns (HO-en-zol-lerns), rulers of Prussia and Germany **G** 160
Hohokam, prehistoric culture of Arizona **A** 416
Hoisting and loading machinery H 143–45
  elevators and escalators **E** 172–75
  hydraulic systems **H** 303–04
  pulleys, principle of **W** 248–49
Hoists, machines for raising and lowering heavy loads **H** 143
Hokkaido (ho-KY-do), island of Japan **J** 34, 37

Hokusai (HO-ku-sa-i), **Katsushika** (1760–1849), Japanese artist, b. Edo (now Tokyo). He was a famous master of woodcuts and landscape prints. Hokusai works include *Ono Waterfall* and *Hundred Views of Mount Fuji*; sketches published in 12-volume *Mangwa* (Random Sketches).

Holarctic (hol-ARC-tic), land region of animal life **L** 234; diagram **L** 235
Holbein (HOL-bine), **Hans, the Younger,** German painter **H** 146
  Ambassadors, The, painting **N** 38
  court painter and most important artistic figure in Tudor England **E** 236
  Henry VIII, painting **E** 236
  Sir Henry Guilford, painting **H** 146
Holberg, Ludvig, Danish author **S** 51

Holding company, a "parent" corporation that buys or exchanges stock in order to control and derive income from one or more other companies, called subsidiaries. Authorized by state corporation law and controlled by antitrust legislation, the arrangement is frequently found in public utilities.

Holding patterns, airports **A** 564; diagrams **A** 561, 565
Holdorf, Willi, German athlete, picture **O** 115
Hole in one, golf score **G** 255
Holger Nielsen method of artificial respiration **F** 160–61
Holi, or Basant, religious holiday **R** 154
Holidays H 147–59
  August, entire month a holiday **A** 492
  carnivals **C** 120–21
  February, many holidays **F** 74
  greeting cards **G** 372–74
  Independence Day, July 4 **I** 112
  national holidays around the world, by nation **H** 157
  New Year's Day around the world **N** 208–09
  pageants **P** 12
  parades **P** 61
  potlatch of the Salmon Area Indians **I** 181–82
  religious see Religious holidays
  Thanksgiving Day **T** 152–54
  toys **T** 233

Valentine's Day **V** 266
  See also holidays by the month in the month articles; names of holidays; annual events section of state articles and people section of country articles.
Holidays, Religious see Religious holidays
Holinshed (HOL-ins-hed), **Raphael,** English chronicler **M** 2–3
Holland see Netherlands

Holland, Clifford Milburn (1883–1924), American civil engineer, b. Somerset, Mass. He directed design and construction of Holland Tunnel (1919–24), named for him. The tunnel, first of its kind, was built under Hudson River, connecting New Jersey and New York.

Holland, John, Irish-American inventor **S** 446
Holland, Michigan **M** 262; picture **M** 271
Holland Music Festival M 551
Holland Tunnel, New York, N.Y. **T** 314
Hollerith, Herman, American statistician **C** 450; **O** 58

Holling, Holling Clancy (1900–), American author and illustrator of children's books, b. Henriette, Mich. He uses material collected from his interest in primitive tools, from observations of wild animal behavior, and from outdoor living. His books include *Paddle to the Sea, Tree in the Trail, Seabird, Minn of the Mississippi,* and *Pagoo.*

Holly
  American holly, state tree of Delaware **D** 87
Hollyhocks, flowers **G** 46
Hollywood, Los Angeles, California **L** 344, 347
  center of motion picture production **M** 473
  television industry **T** 70c
Hollywood Bowl, Los Angeles, picture **L** 346
  Easter sunrise service, picture **E** 42
Hollywood gin, card game **C** 115
Holmes, Arthur, English geologist **G** 117–18
Holmes, David, first governor of Mississippi **M** 361
Holmes, Oliver Wendell, American doctor and author **H** 160
  American literature **A** 203
  anesthesia, origin of term **A** 257
Holmes, Oliver Wendell, Jr., American jurist **H** 160–61
Holmes, Sherlock, master detective created by Arthur Conan Doyle **D** 288
  mystery, detective and suspense stories **M** 554
Holmium (HOLE-mi-um), element **E** 154, 161
Holmquest, Donald L., American astronaut **S** 347
Holograms, laser-beam photographs, pictures **P** 208
Holographic wills W 174
Holst, Gustave, English composer **E** 271
Holstein-Friesian (HOL-stine-FRE-sian), breed of dairy cattle **D** 8; picture **D** 5
  livestock **C** 147

Holt, Harold Edward (1908–67), Australian statesman, b. Sydney. He studied law at the University of Melbourne and received his first cabinet appointment (Minister Without Portfolio) at the age of 31. A founder of the Liberal Party, he was leader of the House of Representatives. He was named minister of Labor and National Service (1940) and minister of the Treasury (1958). He succeeded Robert Menzies as prime minister (1966) but his career came to a premature end when he drowned near his country home in Portsea.

Holy Alliance, 1815 **I** 324
Holy Communion, or Eucharist **C** 281, 284
  Orthodox Eastern churches **O** 229
  Roman Catholic Church **R** 288, 301
  See also Last Supper

Holy days of obligation, for Roman Catholics   R 290
Holy Eucharist see Holy Communion
Holy Experiment, William Penn's system of government
    P 144;   Q 2
Holy Family, picture   B 489
Holy Family, The, engraving by Dürer   B 161
Holy God, We Praise Thy Name, hymn, words and music
    H 310
Holy Grail   A 442
Holy Land, in present-day Israel and Jordan   I 441–44;
    J 138–39
    Crusades   C 538–40
    Jerusalem   J 78–81
Holy Liturgy
    Orthodox Eastern Churches   O 229

Holy Name Society, society of Roman Catholic men who
encourage reverence for and devotion to name of Jesus.
The society, founded in 1274, has its U.S. headquarters
(since 1878) in New York, N.Y., and publishes monthly
Holy Name Journal.

Holy Office, Congregation of the (now Doctrine of the
    Faith, Congregation for the)   I 257
Holy Orders, sacrament of Roman Catholic Church
    R 301
Holy Roman and Universal Inquisition   I 257
Holy Roman Empire   H 161–64
    Charlemagne   C 189–90
    flag   F 227
    Germany's First Reich   G 159
    Gregory VII, Saint, pope   G 375
    Inquisition   I 257
    Italy   I 454–55
    Middle Ages, power of the church   M 293–94
    Roman Catholic Church   R 291
Holy See see Popes, Roman Catholic Church
Holy Sepulcher (SEP-ul-ker), Church of the, Jerusalem
    J 80, 138
Holy Thursday or Maundy Thursday   E 41
Holy water   R 301
Holy Week   E 41
Holy Wisdom, Church of see Hagia Sophia
Homage, to a feudal lord   F 101; picture   F 100

Home (HUME), Sir Alexander Frederick Douglas- (1903–
), British statesman, b. London. He has been a
member of Parliament from South Lanark (1931–45),
secretary of state for Commonwealth relations (1955–
60), lord president of council (1957, 1959–60), prime
minister of Great Britain (1963–64), and leader of the
Conservative Party (1964–65). In 1970 he became secretary of state for foreign and Commonwealth affairs.

Home and school associations   P 66–67
Home canning
    botulism, poisoning, how to guard against   F 354
Home economics   H 165–66
    budgets, family   B 425–26
    child development   C 231–34
    clothing   C 348–57
    cooking   O 247–48;   R 114–16
    domestic service occupations   S 124–25
    dressmaking   D 311–15
    interior decorating   I 298–303
    marketing   M 100–03
    nursing, home   N 413–15
    parties and entertaining   P 87–89
    safety   S 2–7
    sanitation in the home   S 33
    sewing   S 128–29
    table settings   T 2–3

women, role of   W 211, 212
Home Economics, Institute of, U.S. Department of
    Agriculture   C 494a
Home medicine chest, with supplies, picture   M 202
Home missions see Missions and missionaries
Home nursing   N 413–15
Home on the Range, song by Brewster Higley
    K 176

Homeopathy (ho-me-OP-athy) (from Greek words meaning
"like" and "suffering"), treatment of disease by administration of small doses of drugs that have an effect on a
healthy body similar to that of the disease itself. This
curative method was developed and expounded (1796) by
Hahnemann.

Homer, Greek poet   H 167
    Aeneid compared to works of Homer   A 35
    dancing described in Iliad   D 23
    Greek literature, beginnings of   G 350
    Iliad   I 69
    Odyssey   O 53–54
    Trojan War   T 293–94
Homer, Winslow, American painter   H 167
    illustration in magazines   I 91
    Snap the Whip   U 119
    United States, art of the   U 121
Homeric hymns (ho-MER-ic hims), by Greek poets
    G 350
Home Rule, for Ireland   I 391
    O'Connell, Daniel   O 49
Home rule, for municipal governments   M 503
Home run, in baseball   B 71
Homes   H 168–84
    Africa, pictures   A 60
    American Indian homes, picture   I 200a
    ancient architecture   A 235
    ancient bridge dwellings   B 396
    animal homes, pictures   A 273
    anthropologists study family and homes
        A 302–03
    Asia   A 459
    building methods   B 434; pictures   B 436, 437
    China's boat dwellings   C 263
    climate and homes   C 347
    colonial American   C 388–89
    co-operatives   C 499
    English architecture   A 382
    English coal-mining town, picture   E 226
    English manor houses   E 235, 236
    Eskimo   E 286, 290; pictures   E 287, 291
    farm life   F 48–54
    Fiji   F 121
    furniture shown in rooms, pictures   F 506, 507, 508,
        509, 510
    gable-roofed dwellings of the Haida Indians   I 182
    Ghanaian village, picture   G 196
    heating systems   H 96–99
    India   I 120–21
    insulation and insulating materials   I 290–92
    interior decorating   I 298–302
    Ivory Coast village, picture   I 490
    Kenya, pictures   K 229, 230
    Korea, picture   K 298
    lighting in panels, picture   L 290
    log cabins   P 252–53
    mammal homes   M 67
    nomadic life   N 271
    on stilts, pictures   B 381,   J 156,   V 334b
    pioneer life   P 251–62
    plumbing   P 341–43
    ranch life   R 102–06

sampans, Hong Kong, picture **H** 204
sod houses **P** 254–55
20th-century architecture **A** 385
See also Urban planning; people section of continent, country, province, and state articles
Homestead Act, 1862, in U.S. history **P** 506
Homestead National Monument, Beatrice, Nebraska **N** 81
importance to pioneer life **P** 261
Nebraska rush for land **N** 87
Homesteading, Canada M 82; **S** 38d, 38h
displays in Western Development Museum **S** 38f
Homing and migration H 185–93
bats **B** 94
birdbanding records by licensed banders **B** 229
birds **B** 211, 216–17
butterflies and moths **B** 470
eels **E** 85–86; **F** 198–99
fishes **F** 198
fish ladders built at dams **D** 20
flyways for birds of North America, map-diagram **B** 217
hibernation substitutes for migration **H** 122
lemmings **R** 278–79
mammals **M** 67, 70
salmon **F** 199–200
turtle's "compass sense" **T** 335
yearly rhythms in plant and animal life **L** 244, 249
Homing pigeons, picture **H** 193
Homochitto River, Mississippi **M** 352
Homogenization (ho-moj-en-i-ZAY-tion), of milk **D** 11
Homonyms (HOM-o-nims), words having similar sound or spelling, but different meaning **H** 194
semantics **S** 117
Homophones see Homonyms
Homophony (ho-MOPH-ony), in music **I** 483
Homo sapiens, scientific name for the human species **R** 29
prehistoric man **P** 442
Homs, Syria **S** 508
Hondas, knots **K** 290
roping and rope spinning **R** 334
Honduras H 195–99
flag **F** 241
life in Latin America **L** 47–61
national anthem **N** 21
Honduras, British (Belize) H 199–200
Honegger (HO-negg-er), **Arthur,** French composer **F** 448
Honey H 201–02
How do honey bees make honey? **H** 201
nectar changed to honey **B** 118
Honey badgers, or ratels **O** 246
Honeybees B 117–23; **H** 201–02
adaptations for getting nectar, diagram **L** 221
Honeycombs, of bees **B** 118; **H** 202; picture **B** 119
Honeydew melons M 216, 217
Honey locust, tree
plant defenses, porcupine plants **P** 282
Honeymoons W 100
Honey possum, or noolbenger, marsupial **K** 175
Hong Kong H 203–05; pictures **A** 458; **C** 309
British colony **C** 263, 272
flag **F** 237
housing project, picture **H** 183
police, picture **P** 375
World War II **W** 293
Honnecourt (on-COOR), **Villard de,** French architect
drawing from sketchbook **D** 302
Honolulu, capital of Hawaii **H** 69
Honshu, island of Japan **J** 34
Hooch (HOKE), **Pieter de,** Dutch artist **D** 357
Hood, Mount, Oregon, pictures **O** 198, 202; **P** 398

Hoods
head coverings, pictures **H** 55
part of academic dress **U** 206
Hoofed mammals, or ungulates **H** 206–21
bison and buffalo **B** 250a
camels **C** 34
cattle **C** 145–50
deer **D** 83
giraffes **G** 212
goats **G** 244
hippopotamuses **H** 133
horses and their relatives **H** 235–44
livestock **C** 145–52
locomotion **A** 291–94
odd-toed and even-toed **F** 81–82
pigs **P** 248–49
rhinoceroses **R** 211
sheep **S** 145
See also names of hoofed mammals
Hoofs, or **hooves,** of animals **F** 81–82; pictures **F** 80
Hooghly (HOOG-ly) **River,** India **C** 9

Hooke, Robert (1635–1703), English scientist, b. Freshwater, Isle of Wight. He was the first to state the law, named for him, that elastic bodies are stretched or bent by amounts proportional to the force applied to them. The greatest inventor of his age, he developed spring-regulated weighing scales and invented the spiral spring for watches. He built the first compound microscope and was the first to describe cells.
his drawing of cells seen under a microscope **C** 159
was assistant to Robert Boyle **B** 354

Hooked rugs, picture **R** 353
Hooker, Joseph, American Union general **C** 325
Hooker, Thomas, English clergyman **C** 478
American colonies, early history of **A** 189
Hookworm, parasitic disease **D** 186; **W** 312; picture **D** 187
Hookworms W 312

Hooper, William (1742–1790), American patriot, b. Boston, Mass. After being admitted to the bar, he moved to Wilmington, N.C. (1764). Elected (1773) to the North Carolina Assembly, he was on the Committee of Correspondence. He served in the Continental Congress until he resigned (1777) and was a signer of the Declaration of Independence.

Hoosic River, Massachusetts **M** 137
Hoosier state, nickname for Indiana **I** 136
Hoover, Herbert Clark, 31st president of United States **H** 222–25
connection with football **F** 356
Harding cabinet member, picture **H** 40
Library-Museum, West Branch, Iowa **I** 366

Hoover, John Edgar (1895–1972), American government official, b. Washington, D.C. He was a staff member of Department of Justice (1917) and director of Federal Bureau of Investigation (1924–1972). He was awarded Medal of Merit (1946) and President's Award for Distinguished Federal Civilian Service (1958). He wrote *Persons in Hiding* and *Masters of Deceit.*

Hoover, Lou Henry, wife of Herbert Hoover **F** 178
Hoover Commission, on reorganization of executive branch of government **H** 225
Hoover Dam, formerly Boulder, near Arizona-Nevada border **D** 20; pictures **D** 17; **N** 133
Arizona **A** 407
Nevada **N** 132

Hoover Institute and Library on War, Revolution, and Peace C 23
Hooves, of animals F 81–82; pictures F 80
Hop, step, and jump, field event T 240–41

Hope, Bob (Leslie Towne Hope) (1903–), American comedian, b. London, England. He appeared in musicals *Roberta* and *Ziegfeld Follies*. He has made numerous films, including "Road" pictures with Bing Crosby, such as *Road to Singapore.* He performed for U.S. troops during World War II, in Korea, and in Vietnam. He was awarded a Congressional gold medal in 1963 for his services. His books include *I Owe Russia $1200.*

Hope diamond D 156
  famous gemstones G 71
Hopewell Cape, New Brunswick, Canada N 138d; picture N 138a
Hopi (HO-pi), Indians of North America I 190–91
  Arizona A 413
  family F 40, 41
Hopkins, Gerard Manley, English poet E 263
Hopkins, Mark, American educator H 226

Hopkins, Stephen (1707–1785), American politician, b. Providence, R.I. He often served in the Rhode Island General Assembly between 1732 and 1777 and was an assistant justice (1747–49) of the Rhode Island superior court, becoming chief justice in 1751. Nine times elected governor of Rhode Island between 1755 and 1767, he was also the first chancellor (1764) of Rhode Island College (later Brown). An active member of the Continental Congress (1774–76), he signed the Declaration of Independence.

Hopkinson, Francis, American writer A 198
Hopkinson, Joseph, American jurist and poet N 23

Hoppe (HOP-pe), **Willie** (William Frederick Hoppe) (1887–1959), American billiards player, b. Cornwall-on-the-Hudson, N.Y. He won 51 world titles in both balk-line and three-cushion billiards (1906–52). He wrote *Thirty Years of Billiards* and *Billiards as It Should Be Played.*

Hopper, Edward (1882–1967), American artist, b. Nyack, N.Y. He painted and etched scenes of American life. His well-known works include *House by the Railroad, Corner Saloon,* and *Night Hawks.*
  Night Hawks, painting U 120

Hopper cars, of railroads R 83

Hops, flowering vines related either to the mulberry or to the Indian hemp. One species, the common hop, is used widely in brewing beer. Only the female flowers produce the cone-shaped hops used in this process. The stems of hop plants are used to make fiber. The plant heads may be eaten and are used in making some kinds of perfumes and medicines.
  beer and brewing B 116

Hopscotch, an old game played by children. The rules vary regionally, but they always involve a small court, rectangular or curved, marked off in sections—often 10. In one version, the first player throws a small weight or stone called a *puck* or *potsy,* into number 1 section. He hops on one foot into the adjoining section, picks up the stone, and hops back to starting place. He repeats this in each of the successive sections. If he loses his balance or steps on a line, he loses his turn to the next player. The player who first reaches the last section and returns to starting position wins.

Hoptoads
  calling sounds F 473
Hora (HO-ra), dance of Israel D 31
Horace, Roman poet H 226
  literary versatility L 79
  odes O 52
Horatian ode O 52

Horatii (ho-RAY-shi-y), in Roman legend, three brothers, who slew the Curiatii, three brothers from Alba, during the reign of Tullus Hostilius (7th century B.C.). The only surviving brother also slew his sister Horatia for mourning the death of one of the Curiatii, her lover. He was delivered up to justice by his father but was reprieved by the people of Rome. The story is the subject of Corneille's tragedy *Horace.*

Horehound, plant, 1 to 3 ft. high, of mint family, native of Europe, northern Africa, and parts of Asia, but grown elsewhere. It has oval-shaped leaves covered with fine hairs, and small whitish flowers clustering at points where leaves join stems. It is used as flavoring for candy and for cough medicines.

Horizon, point where our vision ends P 158
  artificial, for airplanes A 560
Horizon Club, of Camp Fire Girls C 37, 38; picture C 39
Horizontal bar, use in gymnastics, pictures G 432
Horizontal wheels, a kind of waterwheel W 62
Hormones, secretions of ductless glands B 279
  body chemistry B 297
  endocrinology, study of hormones B 183
  experiment with plant hormones E 352
  hormone diseases D 217
  insulin as a drug D 326
  tumors in plants C 90
Horn, musical instrument
  ancient music A 246
  bugle B 429
  types of wind instruments M 549
  wind instruments, pictures W 182, 183
Hornbein, Thomas F., American mountain climber E 337
Horn Book Magazine, The C 242
Hornbooks, early primers for children T 138
  children's books C 236
  early texts and tools in education E 69

Horne, Lena (1918–), American entertainer, b. Brooklyn, N.Y. The first Negro woman to sign a long-term film contract, she has appeared in several motion pictures, among them *Cabin in the Sky, Stormy Weather,* and *Death of a Gunfighter.* She is perhaps best known for her numerous recordings, and nightclub and television appearances.

Horned toads, lizards L 319
Hornet fly, insect I 275
Hornets, insects H 261; picture H 263
  nests exterior and interior, pictures I 278
Horn of Africa, northeastern Africa
  Somalia S 253
Horns, of mammals M 67
  age shown in sheep's horn, picture A 86

Hornsby, Rogers (1896–1963), American baseball player, b. Winters, Tex. Considered one of the greatest right-handed hitters, with .358 average, he played with St. Louis Cardinals (1915–26). He was manager of various teams (1925–33) and was chosen most valuable player in National League (1925 and 1929). Hornsby was elected to National Baseball Hall of Fame (1942).

Hornung, E. W., English author   M 554
Hornworms, caterpillars   P 284

Horowitz, Vladimir (1904–   ), American pianist, b. Kiev, Russia. He made his U.S. debut with the New York Philharmonic and has since made many concert tours, gaining worldwide reputation as a virtuoso.

Horsa see Hengist and Horsa
Horseback riding   H 227
   American saddle horse, picture   H 239
   Olympic event   O 109
   rodeos   R 281–82
Horse chestnut, tree
   leaves, diagram   L 115
Horse collars   T 260
Horse conchs, snails   S 148–49
Horse latitudes, belts of calm weather   T 246
   weather and climate   W 73
   winds and weather   W 185
Horseless carriages, early name for automobiles   T 264
   carriage design followed   A 544
Horsemanship see Horseback riding
Horsepower, a unit of power   W 250
   measure of capacity of steam engine   S 420
Horse racing   H 231–34
   Churchill Downs, picture   K 220
   famous tracks near Paris   F 406
   thoroughbred stallion, picture   H 239
   See also Hippodrome
Horse reins, kind of knitting   I 225
Horses   H 235–44; parts of a horse, diagram   H 227
   animal intelligence tests   A 285–86
   armor, picture   A 433
   city named for Alexander the Great's favorite horse   A 153
   evolution of   E 343–44;   H 236
   Greyfell, in Norse mythology   N 281
   horseback riding   H 227
   horse farms in Kentucky   K 218; picture   K 219
   horse ranches   R 105
   importance to Indians   I 166, 176
   knights' horses   K 272; picture   A 433
   leather made from hides   L 107
   leg and hoof, diagram   F 80
   odd-toed mammals   F 82;   H 206–07
   Pegasus, in Greek mythology   G 364
   racing see Horse racing
   rodeos   R 281–82
   Tennessee walking horse   T 74; picture   T 81
Horseshoe, or Canadian, Falls   N 243; picture   O 120b
Horseshoe Bend, battle of, 1814   J 4
   Alabama, history of   A 127
Horseshoe Bend National Military Park, Alabama   A 121
Horseshoe crab   H 245
   successful life adaptation   L 224
Horseshoe pitching   H 246
Horseshoes
   invention of   I 335
Horsetails, plants   P 304
   equisetineae, picture   P 292
Horseweed, picture   W 105
Horsley, John Calcott, English painter   G 373
   designed first Christmas card   C 292
Horthy (HOR-ty), Miklós, Hungarian ruler   H 288
Horticulture see Fruitgrowing; Gardens and gardening

Horus (HO-rus), in Egyptian mythology, combination of the sun-god Horus the Elder, often indistinguishable from Ra, and Horus the Child, who was the son of Osiris and Isis and was known as the god of silence.
   animal gods of Egypt   M 560

Hosea (ho-ZE-a), book of Bible, Old Testament   B 155
Hosea, Hebrew prophet   J 105
Hospice of San Michele, Rome, Italy   P 470
Hospital insurance   H 251;   I 295
Hospitals   H 247–52
   disinfecting an operating room, picture   D 222
   Dix, Dorothea, pioneered for mentally ill   D 235
   doctors   D 241
   Greenland, picture   G 368
   hyperbaric chambers, medical techniques   M 210
   insurance   H 251;   I 295
   intensive care unit, picture   E 142
   medical laboratories   M 201–02, 209
   mental, or psychiatric, hospitals   M 222–23
   narcotics addicts   N 13
   Nightingale, Florence   N 259
   North Africa, picture   A 68
   nurses and nursing   N 409–13
   planning agencies of states   P 504
Host, animal or plant on which a parasite lives   M 279
   barberry plant, host of wheat rust   F 498
   vectors   V 282

Hostage, person given as pledge to guarantee fulfillment of agreement, request, or treaty. Hostages were often taken in ancient times in occupied countries to discourage or punish rebellious acts.

Hostels and hosteling   H 253–56
   travel opportunities for teen-agers   V 259
Hostesses, airline   A 566;   S 125

Hostos (OSS-toss), Eugenio María de (1839–1903), journalist, educator, and writer, born in Mayaguez, Puerto Rico. He was educated in Spain, where he published his first works, principally a novel in the form of the hero's diary, The Pilgrimage of Bayoan (1863). Bayoan's dream, the independence of Cuba, Santo Domingo, Haiti, and Puerto Rico, became the chief lesson of Hostos' own life and work. This is also the reason all these countries honor him as a great teacher.

Hot-air turbines   T 322
Hot dogs, term for frankfurters   W 241
Hôtel des Invalides (o-TEL days an-va-LEDE), Paris   P 70
Hotels   H 256–58
   Beirut, Lebanon, picture   L 123
   Djakarta, Indonesia, picture   D 237
   Jamaica, picture   J 16
   ocean liners, floating hotels   O 17–24
   See also Hostels and hosteling; Motels; Restaurants
Hot line, direct communications link between governments   D 185
Hot potato, circle game   G 15;   I 226

Hot Rod Association, National (NHRA), organization for people interested in automobiles that have been rebuilt for high speed. It sets standards for competitions and construction, sponsors drag races, and certifies records. Founded in 1951, it has its headquarters in Los Angeles, Calif. It publishes the National Dragster and safety and educational pamphlets.

Hot rodders, automobile racers   A 539
Hot springs   G 192
   Banff National Park   B 43
   Iceland's Geysir   I 42
   Lava Hot Springs, Idaho   I 65
   New Zealand   N 239; picture   N 238
   Yellowstone's Emerald Pool, picture   Y 345
Hot Springs, Arkansas   A 429;   G 192
Hot Springs National Park, Arkansas   A 429

Hottentot, one of a South African race, basically akin to Bushmen. Numbering about 15,000, they herd sheep and cattle and hunt (Bushmen only hunt). The first natives to make contact with Dutch settlers on Cape of Good Hope (mid-17th century), they were forced to the interior as Dutch took coastal land for farming.

Houdin (oo-DAN), **Robert,** French magician **M** 18

Houdini (hoo-DEE-ni), **Harry** (Ehrich Weiss) (1874–1926), American magician, b. Appleton, Wis. An escape artist who could free himself from handcuffs and locked containers, he took his name from Houdin, a French magician, and from the subject of his book *The Unmasking of Robert Houdin.*

Houdon (oo-DON), **Jean Antoine,** French sculptor **S** 101
Hough (HUFF), **Benjamin Franklin,** American pioneer in forestry conservation **C** 484

Hough (HUFF), **Emerson** (1857–1923), American journalist and novelist, b. Newton, Iowa. He campaigned for conservation and preservation of national parks as writer for *Saturday Evening Post.* Hough specialized in well-documented historical fiction about early American West, such as *The Law of the Land, Fifty-Four Forty or Fight,* and *The Covered Wagon,* which was made into a movie.

House Internal Security Committee *see* Un-American Activities, House Committee on
House of Commons *see* Commons, House of

House of David, religious community founded in Benton Harbor, Mich. (1903) by Benjamin Purnell. Its members believe they are descendants of the 12 lost tribes of Israel and will become rulers and judges of the kingdom of God. They are vegetarians, and the men have long hair and do not shave. Their communal colony runs businesses, including farms and touring baseball teams.

House of Lords *see* Lords, House of
House of Representatives, United States *see* United States House of Representatives

Houses *see* Homes
Houses of correction, or workhouses, for criminals **P** 468

Houssay (OW-sy), **Bernardo Alberto** (1887–   ), Argentine physiologist, b. Buenos Aires. His work on the relationship between the pituitary gland and diabetes made him the first South American scientist to win a Nobel prize (medicine and physiology, 1947). He helped found (1944) the Institute of Biology and Experimental Medicine in Buenos Aires and has directed it ever since.

Houston (HU-ston), **Samuel,** American soldier and statesman **H** 270–71; **T** 135
Howard, Catherine, fifth wife of Henry VIII **H** 109

Howard, Elston Gene (1929–   ), American baseball player, b. St. Louis, Mo. He was first Negro to play for New York Yankees (1955–67), and then played for Boston Red Sox. He was given Babe Ruth Award in World Series (1958) and Most Valuable Player Award for American League (1963).

Howard, Henry, Earl of Surrey, English poet **S** 255–56
Howard, John, English prison reformer **P** 468

Howard, Oliver Otis (1830–1909), American Army general, b. Leeds, Maine. In Union army (1864), he led the right wing of army in march to sea. He was commissioner of Freedman's Bureau and founder and first president (1860–74) of Howard University, named in his honor.

Howard, Sir Ebenezer, English reformer **U** 233
Howard University, Washington, D.C. **N** 95; **W** 34
How do I love thee?, sonnet by Elizabeth Browning **B** 413
How do you like to go up in a swing, from *The Swing* by Robert Louis Stevenson **S** 424
Howe, Elias, American inventor **H** 271–72
clothing industry **C** 353

Howe, Gordie (1928–   ), Canadian hockey player, b. Floral, Saskatchewan. He joined Detroit Red Wings of National Hockey League (1946); went on to score more goals than any other player in NHL history. He won Most Valuable Player award five times.

Howe, Joseph, Canadian political leader **N** 344h

Howe, Julia Ward (1819–1910), American author, b. New York, N.Y. She was a dedicated worker for woman suffrage, prison reform, and international peace. With her husband, Samuel Gridley Howe, she edited abolitionist paper Boston *Commonwealth.* She wrote lyrics of song "The Battle Hymn of the Republic." Her books include *Is Polite Society Polite?*
    patriotic songs **N** 25

Howe, Samuel Gridley (1801–1876), American humanitarian and physician, b. Boston, Mass. He served as soldier and surgeon in Greek war for independence from Turkey (1824–30). He was appointed to open and head a school for the blind in Boston, Mass. (1832), later called the Perkins Institution. He interested himself in the antislavery movement. He was co-editor of the *Commonwealth* with his wife, Julia Ward Howe.

Howe, Sir William, English general **R** 199, 202, 203
    campaigns against Washington **W** 39
Howe Caverns, New York **C** 158
Howells, William Dean, American novelist **A** 206
    themes of his novels **N** 349
Howitzers, guns **G** 426

Howland and **Baker islands,** uninhabited coral atolls 40 miles apart in the central Pacific, just north of the equator. Administered by United States, they were unimportant until Howland became an air base on Hawaii-Australia route in the 1930's and Baker became a World War II naval base. Baker was taken (1942) by Japan, then recaptured (1944) by United States.

Howler monkeys **M** 422
How many miles to London town?, game **G** 20
Howrah Bridge, Calcutta **C** 9
How to
    abacus, make and use **A** 2
    ant observation nest **A** 330
    birdhouse **B** 248–49
    birds, attracting **B** 243
    cats, care of **C** 141–42, 144
    clay modeling **C** 336–37
    crochet **K** 281–84
    dogs, care of **D** 252, 257–58
    earthworm farm **W** 311
    eclipses, how to watch **E** 46, 361
    faucets, changing washers **P** 342
    flower arrangements and containers **J** 50–53
    glue prints **G** 308
    greeting cards **G** 374
    guitar **G** 409–10
    harmonica **H** 42–43
    index of this encyclopedia, how to use **A** 575–81
    Indian beadwork **I** 159
    information, how to locate **R** 131
    interior decorating **I** 298
    invisible ink **I** 256
    jewelry, make from wire **J** 100
    knit **K** 277–81
    leaf collections and prints **L** 117, 118
    leathercraft **L** 112–13
    library, how to use **L** 180–88
    linoleum-block printing **L** 304–06
    microscope, care of **M** 284
    mosaic, how to make **M** 463
    origami, art of paper folding **O** 223–26
    pets, care of **P** 181
    pinhole camera **E** 364
    psychrometer (humidity indicator) **W** 81
    puppets and marionettes, how to make **P** 536–39
    radio operator, amateur (ham) **R** 63
    recorder **R** 121–22
    ship models **S** 152–54
    silver cleaned by electrolysis **I** 354
    slide rule **M** 166–67
    soap sculpture **S** 216–17
    stamps, how identified **S** 398–400
    storytelling **S** 435–36
    study **S** 440–42
    table setting **T** 2–3
    tea, how to make **T** 38
    tests, preparing for and taking **T** 120–21
    valentines **V** 266
    weaving **W** 97–98
    See also Experiments and projects; Games; Hobbies; Indoor activities; Sports
Hoyle, Edmond, English writer on card games **C** 107

Hoyle, Fred (1915–), English astronomer and writer, b. Bingley. He developed the steady-state theory, which says that the universe has no beginning or end and that matter is being created continuously. Hoyle became Director of the Institute of Theoretical Astronomy at Cambridge in 1967. His books include *The Nature of the Universe* and *Frontiers of Astronomy.* He has also written *The Black Cloud* and other science-fiction works.
    quasars **Q** 8

Hruodland, legendary figure **C** 189; **L** 129
Hsi-Ling-Shih (Lei-tsu), Chinese empress **S** 178
Huascarán (hua-sca-RON) **Valley,** Peru, picture **S** 290
Huaso, cowboy of Chile **C** 250

Hubbard, Cal (Robert Calvin Hubbard) (1900–), American football player and baseball umpire, b. Keytesville, Mo. He played tackle with New York Giants (1927–28, 1936) and helped Green Bay Packers win three titles (1929–35). American Baseball League umpire (1936–51, 1954–58), he was appointed supervisor of umpires of American Baseball League (1958). He was elected to Helms Athletic Foundation Pro Hall of Fame in 1959 and the Professional Football Hall of Fame in 1962.

Hubbard, Kin (Frank McKinney Hubbard) (1868–1930), American humorist, b. Bellefontaine, Ohio. His series of drawings and sayings about a rustic character named Abe Martin, which began in the Indianapolis *News* (1904), was syndicated and made into a series of books.
    memorial in Brown Co. State Park, Indiana **I** 146

Hubbell, Carl Owen (1903–), American baseball player, b. Carthage, Mo. This southpaw was known for his screwball. In All Star Game (1934) he struck out in succession Babe Ruth, Lou Gehrig, Jimmy Foxx, Al Simmons, and Joe Cronin. He won 253 games.

Hub of the Universe see Boston
Huckleberries **G** 301
Huckleberry Finn, The Adventures of, novel by Mark Twain **N** 349
Hudson, Henry, English navigator and explorer **H** 272–73
    America, exploration and colonization of **A** 189; . **E** 384
    Dutch East India flag **F** 228
Hudson, William Henry, English author **C** 241
Hudson Bay, Canada **C** 52, 70
    rise in bay floor level **I** 17
Hudson Bay Basin, Canada **C** 52
Hudson River, New York **R** 244
    "Marriage of the Waters," excerpt from Carmer's *The Hudson* **E** 279
    New York City **N** 228

Hudson River (continued)
New York state, importance to **N** 215
tunnels, Holland and Lincoln **T** 314
Hudson's Bay Company, fur traders **F** 520–21
Canada **C** 70, 72
controlled Rupert's Land, now Prairie Provinces, Canada **M** 82
Cumberland House, Saskatchewan **S** 38h
Eskimo trading post, picture **E** 286
post at Spence Bay, Boothia Peninsula, picture **C** 53
Yukon Territory controlled by **Y** 365
Hue (hu-AY), Republic of Vietnam (South Vietnam) **V** 334b

Hue and cry, outcries of alarm and protest made by criminal pursuers. Formerly a call issued by sheriff, or offended party, to alert people of community, it is also a written proclamation for capture of criminal or recovery of stolen goods.

Huerta (HUER-ta), **Victoriano,** Mexican general **M** 250

Huggins, Miller James (1879–1929), American baseball player-manager, b. Cincinnati, Ohio. He played second base for the Cincinnati Reds (1904–08) and the St. Louis Cardinals (1909–17) and was the Cardinals' manager (1913–17). Under his management (1918–29) the New York Yankees, who had never won a pennant, won three World's Series and six American League pennants.

Hughes, Charles Evans, American jurist **H** 273–74
Harding Cabinet member, picture **H** 40

Hughes, Howard Robard (1905–), American aviator, airplane manufacturer, and motion picture producer, b. Houston, Tex. He designed his own planes. Flying one, he established a world land flying speed record of 352 mph (1935). Hughes designed, built, and flew the world's largest seaplane (1947). He produced motion pictures including *Hell's Angels, Scarface,* and *Front Page.*

Hughes, Langston, American writer **H** 274; **N** 98; picture **N** 99
"Refugee in America," poem **H** 274

Hughes, Thomas (1822–1896), English author, b. Uffington, Berkshire. Remembered for his novels *Tom Brown's School Days* and *Tom Brown at Oxford,* depicting life in English public schools, he was associated with Christian Socialist movement, active in improving condition of poor. Hughes helped establish Working Men's College in London (1854) and acted as its principal (1872–83). He founded Rugby Colony, unsuccessful co-operative community in Tennessee (1879).
stories of school life in children's literature **C** 238

Hugin, raven of Odin, Norse god **N** 278
Hugo (HU-go), **Victor,** French poet and novelist **H** 275
French literature **F** 440
Miserables, Les, excerpt **H** 275–77
romantic drama **D** 297
themes of his novels **N** 348

Huguenots (HU-ghen-ots), name given French Protestants during the 16th and 17th centuries, when they opposed French Catholics. The Edict of Nantes (1598) gave them religious freedom and helped them gain power. They lost political power after a war (1625–28) in which Cardinal Richelieu sought to destroy them. When Louis XIV took away their religious freedom (1685), many Huguenots left France. They regained freedom under Louis XVI (1787).
France, history of **F** 416
Maine settlers **M** 38

Richelieu crushes **R** 233
South Carolina **S** 310
temporary colony in Florida **F** 273
textile industry spread through Europe **T** 140

Huks, Communist-influenced rebels, Philippines **P** 190
Hula (HU-la), Hawaiian dance **H** 65

Hull, Bobby (Robert Marvin Hull) (1939–), Canadian hockey player, b. Point Anne, Ontario. He joined Chicago Black Hawks in 1957 and became one of the game's greatest offensive players, winning scoring titles in National Hockey League and becoming first man to score more than 50 goals in a season; named to all-star team numerous times and twice (1955, '56) winner of Most Valuable Player award.

Hull, Cordell, American statesman **T** 86–87
beginnings of the United Nations **U** 80
Hull, Quebec, Canada **Q** 13
Hull House, Chicago settlement house **A** 19
Hulls, of ships **S** 160
Hulls, part of nuts **N** 419
Human body see Body, Human
Human Comedy, The (*La Comédie humaine*), series of novels by Balzac **B** 36
Humane societies see Society for the Prevention of Cruelty to Animals, American; Society for the Prevention of Cruelty to Children
Human heredity G 85–88
Humanism, revival of secular culture and learning during the Renaissance **R** 159–60, 163
art as a record **A** 438e–438f
Erasmus **E** 274
Germany's Renaissance period **G** 166, 169
Italian art **I** 463
Italian Renaissance literature **I** 477
Humanities, branches of learning, cultural in character grant money from foundations **F** 393
Human race see Anthropology; Man; Races of man
Human rights see Civil liberties and civil rights; Universal Declaration of Human Rights
Human Rights, International Year for see International Year for Human Rights
Human Rights, Universal Declaration of see Universal Declaration of Human Rights
Human Things, poem by Howard Nemerov **P** 355
Humason, Milton, American astronomer **U** 201
Humboldt, Baron Alexander von, German geographer and biologist **G** 98
Humbolt Current, or Peru Current **P** 162
climate of South America affected **S** 279
earth's rotation and ocean currents **E** 16
marine life enriched by its salts **L** 232
Humbolt River, Nevada **N** 124
California Trail **O** 263
Humboldt University, East Berlin, Germany **B** 145
Humerus (HU-mer-us), bone in upper part of arm extending from shoulder to elbow, diagram **B** 271
Humidity, moisture content of atmosphere **W** 75–76, 80–81
air conditioning **A** 101, 102
rainfall areas of the United States by types, map **W** 89
Hummingbirds B 220; pictures **B** 208, 218; **F** 279
principles of its flight **B** 205
locomotion **A** 295
Humor H 277–81
advertising, pictures **A** 32
American folk humor **F** 313
American literature **A** 195, 203, 205–06
children's literature **C** 238, 240
Franklin, Benjamin **F** 455
jokes and riddles **J** 132–33

limericks N 275–76
nonsense rhymes N 272–76
poetry P 354
prayer for a sense of humor P 434
tricks and puzzles T 288–89
Twain, Mark T 336–38
See also Cartoons; Comic books
Hump, mountains between China and India, World
    War II W 302
Hump, of camel C 34; H 210
**Humpback whales W 150; picture W 148
Humperdinck, Engelbert, German composer
    Hansel and Gretel, opera O 145
Humphrey, Doris, American dancer D 34

Humphrey, Hubert H. (1911–   ), American public official, b. Wallace, S.Dak. He was elected mayor of Minneapolis in 1945. In the same period, he became one
of the founders of the liberal political organization,
Americans for Democratic Action. He was elected to the
U.S. Senate as Democratic senator from Minnesota in
1948, beginning a 16-year Senate career. In 1964, he and
Lyndon Johnson were elected vice-president and president
respectively. Humphrey was Democratic nominee for the
presidency in 1968. In 1970, he was returned to the
Senate. Picture V 331.
    Minnesota, career in M 335

Humphreys, Joshua, American shipbuilder W 11–12
Humphreys Peak, Arizona A 404
Humpty Dumpty, nursery rhyme N 408
Humus (HU-mus), decaying organic matter S 231
    gardens thrive on G 26
Hunchback of Notre Dame, picture F 112
Hundred Days, of Napoleon I N 12
Hundredweights, measures of weight W 113–14
Hundred Years War, 1337–1453 H 281–82
    France, history of F 415
    Joan of Arc J 121
    Middle Ages M 292, 295
**Hungarian music H 283–84
    Bartók, Béla B 68
Hungarian revolution, 1956 H 288
    national Communism in Hungary C 444
Hungary (HUNG-gary) H 283–88
    emigration to Canada C 49
    favorite foods F 340
    flag F 239
    national anthem N 21
    "national Communism" C 444
    national dances D 30
    wheat harvest, picture E 325
    See also Austria-Hungary
Hunger
    population and food supply E 272b
    See also Famine
**Hung jury C 530; J 160
Hungry Horse Dam, Montana M 428; picture M 431
Hunkers, New York conservative Democrats V 275
Hunley, Confederate submarine S 445

Huns, a fierce, nomadic people who originally came from
Asia. About the 4th century A.D. they migrated into
southeastern and central Europe, defeating the Gothic
tribes that lived there. The Huns reached the height
of their power under their king Attila (406?–453), who
led them in conquests as far west as modern France and
into Italy to the gates of Rome. The Huns were a threat
to both the eastern and western Roman empires until
Attila's death, when the empire of the Huns fell apart.

Hunt, George W. P., American political leader A 416

Hunt, John, English mountain climber E 336; M 489

Hunt, Leigh (James Henry Leigh Hunt) (1784–1859),
English author and critic, b. Southgate, Middlesex. He
established (1808) and edited (1808–23) a liberal newspaper, The Examiner, and was imprisoned (1813–15) for
including derogatory article on Prince Regent. He was
associated with poet Lord Byron, with whom he published in Italy an unsuccessful magazine, The Liberal
(1822–23). His works include controversial book Lord
Byron and Some of His Contemporaries.

Hunt, Richard Morris (1827–1895), American architect, b.
Brattleboro, Vt. After studying in Geneva (1844) and
Paris (1845–54), he opened a studio in New York (1858).
His works include the Tribune Building, many Newport,
R.I., residences and New York town houses, the main
portion of the Metropolitan Museum, the base of the
Statue of Liberty, and the National Observatory in
Washington. He was one of the founders, the first
secretary (1857–60), and third president (1888–91) of the
American Institute of Architects.

Hunt, Wilson, American fur trader and explorer F 523
Hunter, constellation see Orion
Hunter, John, English surgeon and anatomist
    Jenner, Edward, pupil of J 76
Hunters, Indian tribes of North America I 164
**Hunting H 289–91; pictures A 300, 301
    Africa A 62
    archery A 366
    cheetahs, hunting animals C 139
    colonial America C 390
    different ways of hunting, pictures A 300, 301
    dog family, food hunting methods D 242
    early man aided by fire F 141
    Eskimo E 285–86
    North Dakota's hunting of deer and other large game
        N 327
    shotguns used for G 424
Hunting and gathering stage, of primitive society
    fire and early man F 138–45
    food F 331
    Indians of North America I 162–64
    prehistoric man P 442–43
    present state of food-getting from the sea U 22
Hunting dogs, classed as sporting dogs D 259, 262;
    pictures D 253

Huntington, Henry Edwards (1850–1927), American railway executive, b. Oneonta, N.Y. Nephew of the railroad
magnate Collis P. Huntington, he developed urban and
interurban traffic systems in California. After selling his
Southern Pacific Railroad lines (1910), he began developing electric power. He built a library, botanical gardens,
and an art gallery in San Marino, Calif.

Huntington, Samuel (1731–1796), American politician, b.
Windham, Conn. Active in legislative and judicial affairs
in Connecticut, he was a member (1776–84) and
president (1779–81, 1783) of the Continental Congress
and a signer of the Declaration of Independence. He was
lieutenant governor (1785) and governor (1786–96) of
Connecticut.

Huntington, West Virginia W 137
Huntington Library and Art Gallery, California C 23
Hunt of the Unicorn: The Unicorn in Captivity, tapestry
    T 23
Huntsville, Alabama A 113, 124
Hunyadi (HOON-ya-di), **János,** Hungarian national hero
    H 287

Huon Islands, uninhabited coral group in South Pacific. A dependency of New Caledonia, 170 miles away, they are administered by France.

Hurston, Zora Neale (1901–60), American author and anthropologist, b. Eatonville, Fla. A noted Negro folklorist, she studied voodoo rites in Haiti. Her works include *Jonah's Guard Vine*, *From Sun to Sun* (play), and an autobiography, *Dust Tracks on a Road.*

Hussein I (hu-SANE) (Hussein ibn Talal ibn Abdullah el Hashim) (1935–), king of Jordan, b. Amman. He succeeded (1952) to the throne when the Jordanian parliament declared his father mentally incompetent to rule. With Faisal II of Iraq, he created the Arab Union, which was dissolved the same year (1958) by a military coup in Iraq. He discussed unity with Nasser of UAR (1964).

Hutchinson, Anne Marbury (1591–1643), American pioneer and religious liberal, b. Alford, England. She emigrated to America in 1634 and was banished from Massachusetts Bay Colony in 1638 for preaching a religion in which the individual intuitively finds God's love and grace instead of following a code of church and state law. She was murdered by Indians in 1643.

Hutson, Donald (1913–), American football player, b. Pine Bluff, Ark. As an end for the Green Bay Packers (1935–45), he established National Football League records for passes caught, yards gained catching passes, and touchdown passes received. He was elected to the National Professional Football Hall of Fame (1963).

Hutterian Brethren (Hutterites), descendants of Moravian Anabaptists who were followers of Jacob Hutter. After Hutter was burned at the stake (1536) in Innsbruck, Austria, they were driven eastward into Russia. They went to North America (about 1874) with Russian Mennonites and settled in Minnesota, Montana, and South Dakota in the United States and in Manitoba, Canada. The Hutterites practice common ownership.

Hutton, James (1726–1797), Scottish geologist, b. Edinburgh. He advanced theory of uniformitarianism, concerning changes in earth's surface.

Hutu, or **Bahutu,** a Bantu Negroid people comprising about 85 per cent of the populations of Rwanda and Burundi. They earn a livelihood by farming and cattle-breeding and were dominated by the Watusi tribe for about 300 years, until a revolution (1959) in Rwanda.

Huxley, Andrew Fielding (1917–), English physiologist, b. London. With A. L. Hodgkin and J. C. Eccles he was awarded the Nobel prize in medicine in 1963 for explaining the transmission of nerve impulses. He is also noted for his studies of muscle contraction.

Huxley, Sir Julian Sorell (1887–), English biologist and writer, b. London. He wrote essays on science and ethics. As first director-general of UNESCO (1946–48) he campaigned for eugenics and a single world culture. His books include *Man in the Modern World.*

ILLUSTRATION CREDITS

The following list credits, by page, the sources of illustrations used in Volume H of
THE NEW BOOK OF KNOWLEDGE. Credits are listed illustration by illustration
—left to right, top to bottom. Wherever appropriate, the name of the photographer
or artist has been listed with the source, the two being separated by a dash. When two
or more illustrations appear on one page, their credits are separated by semicolons.

I, ninth letter of the English alphabet **I** 1
　　See also Alphabet
Iago, character in Shakespeare's *Othello* **O** 236
Iambic (i-AM-bic), a metrical foot in poetry **P** 354
Iambic pentameter (pen-TAM-et-er), meter in poetry **P** 354
I and the Village, by Chagall, painting **C** 184
IATA see International Air Transport Association
Ibadan (i-BA-don), Nigeria **N** 255
Ibadan, University of, picture **N** 253
Ibáñez, Vicente Blasco see Blasco Ibáñez, Vicente
I-beams, for building construction, picture **I** 407

Iberian (i-BER-ian) **peninsula,** southwestern peninsula of Europe whose area of about 228,000 square miles includes Spain and Portugal. It is bounded by Atlantic Ocean on west and north, by Mediterranean on east and southwest, by Pyrenees on northeast, and by Strait of Gibraltar on south.

Iberians, ancient people of western Europe
　　Spain **S** 350
　　Spanish art and architecture **S** 360

Ibert (e-BARE), **Jacques** (1890–1962), French composer, b. Paris. He won the Prix de Rome in 1919. His popular symphonic suite *Escales* ("Ports of Call") was inspired by a Mediterranean cruise while he was serving in the French Navy during World War I. He was director of the French Academy in Rome (1937–55) and of the Paris Opéra and Opéra-Comique (1955–57). His compositions include operas, ballets, orchestral works, and vocal, chamber, and piano music.

Iberville (e-ber-VEEL), **Pierre Lemoyne, Sieur d'** (1661–1706), French-Canadian naval commander and explorer, b. Montreal. After serving in the French Royal Navy (1675–85), he participated (1686–97) in French attempts to expel the British from North America by attacks on English forts and Hudson's Bay Company fur-trading posts. When the French and English war ended (1697), he was commissioned (1698) by the French Government to found a colony in Louisiana. He established a colony at Biloxi Bay (1699) and was made governor of Louisiana (1704).

Ibex (I-bex), grayish-brown wild goat found high in the mountains of temperate Europe and Asia. The ibex has a short tail and a beard hanging from the middle of its lower jaw. Its horns curve upward, backward, and to the sides. Picture **H** 218.
　　wild goats and hoofed mammals of the bovine family **G** 244; **H** 221

Ibis (I-bis), any of several wading birds found along shores and in marshes of temperate and tropical regions. Ibises are long-legged and have a long, thin bill that curves downward. In many the face (or entire head and neck) is bare of feathers, revealing black or brightly colored skin.

IBM see International Business Machines
Ibn, meaning in names **N** 5
　　See also for those not listed below, first part of name, as Abdullah ibn Hussein
Ibn-Batuta, Moroccan writer **A** 76d
Ibn Ezra, Moses, Hebrew poet **H** 102–03
Ibn-Gabirol (ib'n-ga-BI-rol) **Solomon,** Hebrew poet **H** 102–03
Ibn-Khaldun, Tunisian writer **A** 76d

Ibn Saud (IB'n sa-OOD) (Abdul Aziz ibn Saud) (1880–1953), first king of Saudi Arabia (1932–53), b. Riyadh. He won control of most of Arabian peninsula and founded the kingdom of Saudi Arabia (1932). He established a considerable measure of law and order in a previously lawless land. **S** 49

Ibn Sina see Avicenna
Ibo (E-bo), a people of Nigeria **N** 253, 258
　　proverbs quoted **A** 76a
Ibsen, Henrik, Norwegian poet and playwright **I** 2
　　Grieg suites for *Peer Gynt* **G** 376
　　realistic drama **D** 297
　　Scandinavian literature **S** 51
I came, I saw, I conquered, Caesar's victory message **C** 6
Icarus (IC-a-rus), asteroid **P** 274

Icarus, in Greek mythology, youth imprisoned by King Minos with his father, Daedalus, who contrived wings for them to escape. When Icarus flew too near sun, the wax holding his wings together melted and he fell into Icarian Sea (named for him). According to legend, Hercules buried his body, which had been washed ashore on island since called Icaria.
　　legendary flight of Icarus **A** 36, 567; picture **A** 568

ICBM's see Intercontinental ballistic missiles
ICC see Interstate Commerce Commission
Ice **I** 3–12
　　glacial caves **C** 156; picture **C** 157
　　glaciers **G** 223–25
　　How does an ice skate glide on ice? **I** 4
　　how heat changes matter **H** 92
　　iceboating **I** 28–31
　　ice crystals formed into snowflakes **R** 95–96
　　ice-particle theory of electricity in clouds **T** 172–73
　　IGY studies in Antarctica **I** 319–20
　　moon, theories about **M** 451
　　physics of ice skating **I** 4
　　polar regions **P** 366
　　sculpture, picture **N** 159
　　sublimation of clouds **C** 359, 360
　　water cycle **W** 51, 53
　　water desalting **W** 56a
　　See also Dry Ice; Icebergs
Ice ages **I** 13–24
　　Agassiz's findings **A** 80
　　Canadian Shield, Canada **Q** 10
　　caves, formation of **C** 156
　　distribution of animal life **L** 237
　　earth's history **E** 9, 21
　　glacial geology, studies in **G** 115
　　Glacier National Park **G** 222
　　ice sheets of the earth **I** 8–12
　　prehistoric art **P** 439–41
　　prehistoric man **P** 442–46
Icebergs **I** 25–27
　　ablation processes (calving), in glaciers **I** 6–7
　　Antarctic regions **P** 366
　　Greenland, picture **G** 370
　　looming mirage, picture **M** 342
　　Titanic disaster **O** 24
　　why they float **I** 5
Iceboating **I** 28–31
Ice boxes see Refrigeration

Icebreaker, ship with special hull designed to force path through ice. Such ships are used in Arctic and Antarctic exploration. First nuclear-powered icebreaker was built (1959) by Soviet Union.
　　IGY studies, use of an icebreaker in, picture **I** 316

Ice cream **I** 31–34
　　Dr. Coles Trust Fund **F** 390

Ice Cream (continued)
   introduced to U.S. by Thomas Jefferson **F** 340
   stain removal **L** 84
   sundae, origin **F** 335
Ice crystal clouds **C** 359, 360
Iced tea **T** 38
Ice-glass, Venetian glassmaking process **G** 229
Ice hockey **I** 35–40
   Canada **C** 67
   Olympic Games **O** 109; picture **O** 113
   See also Field hockey; Stanley Cup
Iceland **I** 41–45; **S** 49
   center of mid-ocean rift **E** 15
   Ericson, Leif **E** 275
   flag **F** 239
   geysers and hot springs **G** 192
   Icelandic literature **S** 50–51
   pagan Norse culture kept alive **N** 277
   Viking migrations to **V** 339
Icelanders, immigrants to Manitoba **M** 77
Icelandic literature **S** 50–51
Iceland moss **F** 95
Iceland spar, mineral **R** 271–72
Ice milk, frozen dessert **I** 34
Ices, frozen desserts **I** 34
Ice sheets **I** 8–12
Ice skating **I** 46–53
   high standard required for ice hockey **I** 37
   How does an ice skate glide on ice? **I** 4
   physics of **I** 4
   racing in the Netherlands **N** 116
   See also Ice hockey; Roller-skating
Ichabod Crane, character in *Legend of Sleepy Hollow, The* **A** 199–200
Ichthyology (ic-thi-OL-ogy), study of fishes **F** 181
Ichthyornis (ic-thi-OR-nis), prehistoric bird **B** 207, 209
Ickelsamer (ick-el-ZA-mer), **Valentin,** German teacher **P** 193

Ickes (ICK-es), **Harold L.** (1874–1952), American politician, b. Frankstown Township, Pa. After active participation in Chicago political reform movements, he became one of the principal New Dealers under Franklin D. Roosevelt. While secretary of interior (1933–46), he was administrator of public works (1933–39), co-ordinator of fisheries (1942–46), and hard-fuels administrator (1943–46).

Iconoclasts (i-CON-o-clasts) (from Greek word meaning "image-breaking"), originally, group in 8th- and 9th-century Byzantine Empire who opposed use of images in religious worship on grounds that this practice led to idolatry. The movement was outlawed by ecumenical council of Nicaea (787), which advocated veneration, but not adoration, of statues and pictures in churches. Term is now used to refer to anyone who departs from traditionally accepted views.
   Byzantine art, period of iconoclasm in **B** 487

Iconostastis (i-con-OS-ta-sis), screen in churches **U** 54
Icons (I-cons), religious images and holy pictures **O** 229
   Byzantine art form, pictures **B** 485, 490
   Russian art **U** 55; pictures **U** 56
Icterus see Jaundice

Ictinus (ict-I-nus) (mid-5th century B.C.), Greek architect. He was the chief designer of the Parthenon (construction begun 447 B.C.) and designed the Temple of Demeter and Persephone at Eleusis and the Temple of Apollo at Bassae.

Idaho **I** 54–68
   Sawtooth National Forest, picture **N** 36
Idaho, University of **I** 63
Idaho Falls, Idaho **I** 66
Id-Al-Adha, religious holiday **R** 154
Id-al-Fitr, religious holiday **R** 155
Ideal states see Utopias
Identical twins **G** 86; picture **G** 78
Identification
   by fingerprints **F** 129
   by laundry marks **L** 85
Identification bracelets **J** 99
Identification cards, carried by aliens **A** 166
Identity element for addition, or zero **N** 388
Identity element for multiplication, or one **N** 388
Ideographs (I-de-o-graphs), characters in Chinese writing **C** 431
   writing, development of **W** 317

Ides, in Roman calendar, 15th day of March, May, July, and October and 13th day of any other month. It was used by Romans as fixed point (along with calends and nones) from which to designate the days of the months. It is referred to in Shakespeare's *Julius Caesar*—"Beware the ides of March."
   Caesar's assassination **C** 6

Idler, The, essays by Samuel Johnson **E** 293
Idlewild Airport see John F. Kennedy International Airport
Idols, images representing gods **R** 145–46
Idris I (id-REES), king of Libya **L** 205
Idris, Moroccan ruler **M** 461
Idun (E-dun), Norse goddess **N** 280
Idylls of the King, by Tennyson **E** 262; **T** 101
Iemitsu (e-ye-MI-tsu), Japanese shogun **J** 46
Ieyasu (e-AY-a-su), Japanese statesman and shogun **J** 45, 46
If, poem by Rudyard Kipling **K** 261
Ifé (E-fe), ancient kingdom in Africa
   early art achievements **A** 71–72; picture **A** 73
Ifé, Nigeria **N** 258

Ifni (IF-ni), small area on southwestern coast of Morocco having dry land and climate. It was occupied by Spain in 1934 and remained a Spanish overseas territory after Moroccan independence (1956). It was ceded to Morocco (1969) after 11 years of negotiation. Its principal city is Sidi Ifni.
   Morocco and Spain **M** 461; **S** 356

IFR see Instrument Flight Rules
Igloos, Eskimo homes and shelters **E** 290; picture **E** 287
   anthropologists study family and homes **A** 302–03
   houses of snow **H** 172–73

Ignatius (ig-NAI-tius) (50?–107?), third bishop of Syrian Antioch, Christian martyr, and saint, b. Syria. He is believed to be disciple of St. John the Evangelist. While en route to Rome, where he was martyred, he wrote seven letters now included in book *Apostolic Fathers.*

Ignatius of Loyola, Saint see Loyola, Saint Ignatius
Igneous (IG-ne-ous) **rock** **R** 263–66
   mountain building **M** 493
   studies by early geologists **G** 111
Ignimbrite, rock **V** 382

Igorots (ig-o-ROTS), several ethnic groups inhabiting parts of the Philippine Islands. The Igorots are now engaged in agricultural pursuits, mainly rice-growing. Most of them live in villages on the island of Luzon.

Iguanas (i-GUA-nas), kind of lizard
  Galápagos Islands, Ecuador **E** 56
  marine iguana **L** 319
Iguanodon (i-GUA-no-don), dinosaur **D** 172, 177–79
Iguazú (i-gua-SU) **Falls,** or **Iguaçu** (Iguassu) **Falls,** South
  America **A** 392, 393; picture **S** 274
  famous waterfalls **W** 56b
IGY see International Geophysical Year
I Had a Dove, poem by John Keats **K** 200
I have a little shadow that goes in and out with me, from
  My Shadow by Robert Louis Stevenson **S** 424
I have not yet begun to fight, words of John Paul Jones
  J 135
Ijsselmeer (I-sel-mare), lake in the Netherlands **L** 31;
  N 118
Ikebana, Japanese flower arranging **J** 49

Ikeda (e-KED-a), **Hayato** (1899–1965), Japanese political
leader, b. Yamaguchi Prefecture. He began government
service as an administration officer in Ministry of Finance
(1925) and served as vice-minister of finance (1947–48),
minister of finance (1949–52, 1956–57), minister of international trade and industry (1959–60), and prime minister
of Japan (1960–64). During the occupation (1945–52) he
worked with American authorities on anti-inflationary
policies that guided Japan to new prosperity.

Ikhnaton see Akhnaton
I Know Where I'm Going, folk song **F** 320
Ile de la Cité, (ELE d'la ci-TAY), Paris **P** 73
Ile Saint Jean (san JON), now Prince Edward Island,
  Canada **P** 456b–456h
Ile Saint-Louis, Paris **P** 69
Iliad (IL-i-ad), epic poem by Homer **I** 69
  Aeneid compared with **A** 35
  dancing described **D** 23
  early form of fiction **F** 110
  early Greek literature **G** 350
  Homer **H** 167
  Trojan War **T** 293–94
Iliamna Lake, Alaska **A** 133
Ilium, or **Ilion,** Greek name for Troy **T** 293

Illampú (ee-yam-PU), mountain of the Cordillera Real
range of the Bolivian Andes. Glacier-covered and perpetually snow-capped, it rises to a height of 21,275 feet—
about 200 feet less than its twin peak, Ancohuma. It is
often given the name Sorata, after the village located
high on its slopes.

Illia (EEL-ya), **Arturo,** Argentine political leader **A** 396

Illimani (ee-yee-MA-nee), volcanic mountain in the central
Andes. Situated in Bolivia southeast of La Paz, the mountain rises to a height of more than 21,000 feet, making it
one of the highest peaks in the country. Its perpetual
snow line begins at about 15,000 feet.

Illinois (ill-in-OI) **I** 70–86
  Chicago **C** 227–30
  modern public library in Skokie, picture **L** 200
  places of interest in Negro history **N** 94
Illinois, University of **I** 79; picture **I** 74
Illiteracy see Literacy
I'll Tell You How the Sun Rose, poem by Emily Dickinson **D** 164
Illuminated (il-LU-min-ated) **manuscripts** **I** 87–88
  art, the meanings of **A** 438
  Berthold Missal, picture **G** 167
  how medieval books were made **B** 320
  illustration of books **I** 89–90
  important art form for early Germany **G** 165–66

  Islamic art **I** 417
  Kells, Book of **K** 202–03
  Limburg brothers **D** 349
  medieval painting **P** 17–18; picture **P** 19
  Middle Ages, art of **M** 297
Illuminating Engineering Society of America
  L 289
Illumination see Lighting
Illusions, incorrect perceptions **P** 488–91
  magic tricks **M** 18
Illustration and illustrators **I** 89–97
  art departments of magazines **M** 15–16
  book illustration **B** 330
  Caldecott medal for children's books **B** 309–10
  children's books **C** 242–43
  comic books **C** 422–23
  commercial art **C** 424–27
  early bookmaking **B** 321
  Islamic books **I** 421; picture **I** 418
  mechanical drawing **M** 197
  photography **P** 205
  See also Illuminated manuscripts

Illustrators, Society of, association to advance the art of
illustration. It conducts classes, grants scholarships, and
holds exhibits of the year's best illustrations. Founded
in 1901, it maintains headquarters in New York, N.Y.,
and publishes an annual entitled *Illustrators.*

ILO see International Labour Organisation
Il Penseroso (il-pen-ser-O-so), poem by Milton
  M 311
Imagemaker, or variable image reflector, a criminal
  identification tool **P** 376
Imagery, in writing
  Beowulf **B** 141
Images, in psychology **P** 500–500a
Images, optical
  light reflection **L** 261
  real and virtual of lenses **L** 144–46
Imaginary numbers, as the square root of a negative
  number **N** 386
Imagination
  use of images in thinking **P** 500–500a
Imagists, group of poets **A** 209
Imam (e-MOM), Muslim leader **I** 416
  Yemen (Sana) ruler **Y** 348
Imhotep (im-HO-tep), ancient Egyptian counselor to King
  Zoser **E** 95
  tombs and temples in ancient Egypt **A** 221

Immaculate Conception, Roman Catholic doctrine that
states that the Virgin Mary, although born of human
parents, was conceived free from original sin. Catholics
believe that all other human persons, from the very
beginning of life, inherit a human nature that has a
strong inclination to sin. Mary was especially privileged
to be conceived immaculate because she was to be the
mother of Christ. The doctrine of the Immaculate Conception should not be confused with that of the Virgin
Birth—the belief that Jesus Christ was born of a virgin
mother.

Immaculate Conception, Feast of the, religious holiday
  R 155, 290

Immanuel, or **Emmanuel** (Hebrew word meaning "God is
with us"), in Old Testament (Isaiah 7:14) symbolic name
of son who Isaiah said would be a sign that God was
with his people, protecting them against Syria and
Ephraim. This passage is often interpreted as promise of
a messiah by Christians.

Immigration and emigration I 98–103
  Addams, Jane, aided immigrants A 19
  aliens and registration of aliens A 166
  American Museum of Immigration with Statue of Liberty L 168
  Australia A 499
  Brazil B 372–74
  Canada C 49
  Chinese restricted, Hayes administration H 81
  folklore of immigrant groups F 309–10
  immigrant visas P 95
  Jews to Palestine and later to Israel J 112–13
  Liberty, Statue of L 168
  population and census taking P 394
  segregation S 114
  United States U 133
  Westward movement in U.S. history W 142–46
  See also Citizenship; Naturalization, and people section of state and province articles
Immigration and Nationality Act of 1952, or McCarren-Walter Act, 1952 I 101
  citizenship C 312, 313
Immigration and Naturalization Service, U.S. I 102; N 58
  Investigations Division F 76

Immortality, endless or perpetual life. Belief in immortality of the soul is common in many religions, such as Islam and Christianity.

Immune responses, in immunology I 104
Immunization, medical techniques of M 209–10
Immunology (im-mu-NOL-ogy) I 104–07
  active and passive immunity A 317
  antibiotics A 310–16
  disease, prevention of D 219–21
  Pasteur, Louis P 97
  vaccination and inoculation V 260–61
  vectors V 282–85
Impalas (im-PA-las), Africa's antelopes, picture A 51
Impeachment, legal action against a public official I 108
  Johnson, Andrew J 125–26; R 119
  limitation on presidential pardoning power P 454
  recall O 205
Imperfect flowers P 296
Imperial City, Peking, China P 118
Imperial gallons, liquid measures W 114
Imperial Hotel, Tokyo, Japan
  designed by Frank Lloyd Wright W 315
Imperialism I 109
  British in Asia and Africa E 227–28
  McKinley administration in United States M 189–90
  policy of increasing power of a nation over other nations I 322–23
Imperial Valley, California C 19; picture G 106
  a vast oasis O 3
Impetigo (im-pe-TY-go), skin disease D 199
Implements see Farm machinery; Tools
Imports T 243
  international trade I 326–27, 330
  tariff discourages imports T 25
  See also country, province, and state articles
Imposition, arrangement of pages of a book for printing B 327; pictures B 328, 333
Impressionism, in art P 29
  art of the artist A 438g
  Degas, Edgar D 84
  France F 426, 431, 447
  Manet, Édouard M 73
  modern art M 387–88
  Monet, Claude M 408
  See also Pissarro, Camille

Impression: Sunrise, painting by Monet M 386
Impressment, of seamen
  Jefferson and the embargo J 68–69
  War of 1812 W 10–11
Imprint, of a book L 181
Imprints, fossil F 110
Impromptu, a musical form M 536
Impromptu speech delivery P 510
Improper fractions F 398
Improvisation (im-pro-vi-ZAY-tion), composition on the spur of the moment
  acting T 160
  African and American folk music A 78
  jazz J 57, 62
  music M 402
  Negro spirituals N 106
  Oriental music O 220d
Impulse engines E 209
Impulses, nerve B 283, 288
Impulse turbines E 210
Inauguration, of a United States president P 447
  Eisenhower's inaugural parade, picture E 110
  Polk's, in the rain, picture P 385
  oath of office P 447
  Twentieth Amendment to the U.S. Constitution U 157
Incandescence (in-can-DES-cence), emission of light from intense heat I 333–34
  cold light, or bioluminescence B 197
Incandescent filament lamps L 284–85
Incas, Indians of South America I 203–07
  development of arts I 155–56
  earliest roads in the Americas T 259
  Ecuador E 52, 57
  exploration, methods of the conquerors E 386
  influence on Latin-American art and architecture L 64
  knotted ropes as records K 289; picture C 451
  Machu Picchu ruins, pictures A 354; W 219
  Peru P 165
  Pizarro, Francisco P 266
  pre-Columbian dance L 68
  quipu (knotted rope), counting device, picture C 451
  South America unified over a huge area S 293
Incense P 154
  resins used for incense R 184
  Somalia, leading exporter of S 253
Inch, measure of length W 111
Inchon, Korea K 303
Incinerators (in-CIN-er-ators), to burn refuse S 34
Incisors (in-CY-sors), teeth T 47
Inclined planes, simple machines W 246–47
  first inventions I 335
Income E 51
  budgets, family B 425–26
  consumer education C 494, 494a
  how to divide between labor and management L 11
  per capita income I 327
  poverty, assured annual income as cure for P 424b
Income tax I 110–11
  principle of a good tax T 26, 27
Incubation, hatching of eggs E 90–90a
  birds B 214–15
Incubators (IN-cu-bators), for chicks, picture P 421
Incunabula (inc-u-NAB-u-la), term used for earliest printed books B 321
Indefinite pronouns P 91

Indemnity (from Latin in plus damnum, meaning "hurt"), an assurance of compensation in case of loss or damage.

Indentured servants, in colonial America C 386–87
  Negro history N 91

Independence Day F 156; I 112
 July holidays J 148
Independence Hall, Philadelphia, Pennsylvania I 113
 Liberty Bell L 169
 places of interest in Philadelphia P 182
 signing of Declaration of Independence D 59
Independence National Historical Park, Philadelphia
  P 182
Independent Man, statue dedicated to Rhode Island
  R 212; picture R 223
Independent Treasury Act, 1846 P 385

Index librorum prohibitorum (Latin for "index of forbidden books"), catalog of books judged dangerous to
faith or morals by Roman Catholic Church. Members of
the Church are forbidden to read any of these books
except with special permission. The Index, as it is popularly called, includes very few books in English. The list
was first published in 1559 during the pontificate of
Pope Paul IV and has been revised periodically since
then. In 1966, The Congregation for the Doctrine of the
Faith declared that there would be no more editions of
the Index.

Indexes, periodical I 115
Indexes and indexing I 114–15
 encyclopedias E 197
 how to use the index of this encyclopedia A 575–81
 maps, use of grids M 90
 parts of books L 182
 reference books R 130
 research methods R 183
Index fossils, used to trace strata of rock G 113
India I 116–35
 Alexander the Great invades A 152–53
 art and architecture O 212–13, 215
 art as a record A 438f
 Asia's population, concentration of A 453
 Bangladesh B 44–44c; N 262f; P 41
 Bombay B 307–08
 Calcutta C 9–11
 civil and human rights conflicts C 316
 costumes, traditional, pictures C 350; D 264
 cotton, early use of C 519
 dance combined with religion D 31
 Delhi D 101–03
 dyed cloth drying, picture D 368
 early Hindu drama D 293
 East India companies E 43
 fables F 3
 favorite foods F 340
 flag F 237
 funeral customs F 493
 Gama, Vasco da, opens trade with Europe E 379;
  G 7
 Gandhi, Mohandas Karamchand G 24
 Ganges River G 25
 Girls High School, picture E 81
 Himalayas H 128–29
 Hinduism H 130–32
 holidays H 155, 158
 jute preparation, picture A 464
 Kashmir dispute K 198–99
 legend "The Mallard That Asked for Too Much" L 135
 literature O 200d–220e
 Madras, capital of Tamil Nadu M 10
 music O 221; picture O 220d
 national anthem N 21
 Nehru, Jawaharlal N 107
 New Delhi D 101–03
 poverty P 424a, 424b
 Sikkim, a protectorate of India S 177

 Taj Mahal T 14
 Tamil Nadu, formerly Madras state M 10
 theater T 163
 Victoria made empress of India E 227
 voting, picture E 115
 Zoroastrianism Z 380
India ink I 256
Indiamen, trading vessels of East India Company E 43
Indian, or Bengal, tigers T 186
Indiana I 136–51
 holiday, Discovery Day H 149
Indiana, Robert, American artist
 American Dream #1, painting U 120

Indian Affairs, Bureau of, agency of U.S. Department of
War until creation of Department of Interior (1849). It
works toward giving full citizenship to American Indians
and natives of Alaska through better education and
economic independence. It was founded in 1824. Its
headquarters is in Washington, D.C.

Indianapolis (indian-AP-o-lis), capital of Indiana I 147–48
 automobile racing A 539
Indianapolis Children's Museum, Indiana I 145
Indianapolis Motor Speedway, Indiana I 147
Indian art, of North and South America I 152–57
Indiana University I 143; picture I 142
Indian beadwork I 157–59
 Chimu collar, picture I 203
Indian brave makeup, picture P 340
Indian Chief, group game I 226
Indian City, U.S.A., Oklahoma O 88
Indian Cliff Palace, Mesa Verde, Colorado, picture A 353
Indian corn see Corn
Indian music, of India O 221; picture O 220d
 rock music R 262d
Indian music, of North America I 160–61
Indian music, of South America L 73–74
 Ecuador E 52–53
Indian Mutiny see Sepoy Mutiny, 1857
Indian National Congress, political party N 107
Indian Ocean O 47
 ocean floor explored by geologists G 115
Indian paintbrush, plant
 state flower of Wyoming W 322
Indian Reorganization Act, 1934 I 200
Indian reservations I 176–77, 196
 Arizona A 413–14
 boarding school cafeteria, picture I 200b
 first one at Brotherton, New Jersey I 199
 North Dakota N 327–28
 Sioux of the present day I 169
 South Dakota S 323
Indian rice, or wild rice M 329
Indians of North America I 162–200b
 arts, development of I 156
 Arizona's population largest in United States A 408
 Athapascans, in Canada Y 364
 Brant, Joseph B 371
 Buffalo Bill, Indian fighter and scout B 428
 Canadian folk art C 64
 Canadian population C 49
 canoes C 99–100
 cave paintings C 158
 communication by smoke signals C 437
 corn C 506; I 183, 189
 first Americans U 131
 Five Civilized Tribes O 80, 84, 95
 folklore F 313–14
 French and Indian War F 458–62
 funeral customs F 494
 fur trade F 520

Indians of North America (continued)
　Geronimo, Apache leader **G** 189
　Haskell Institute, Lawrence, Kansas **K** 183
　hieroglyphic writing **C** 431
　horses **H** 241
　Hurons **C** 69
　Indian Cliff Palace, Mesa Verde, picture **A** 353
　Indian Wars **I** 212–15
　Iroquois **C** 69–70
　Jackson's resettlement program **J** 6
　lacrosse **L** 20–21
　leather tanners **L** 110–11
　"Legend of the White Deer" **L** 134
　missionary work in early Massachusetts **M** 149
　myth of origin of potlatch **M** 559–60
　Oklahoma, former Indian capitals in **O** 92–93
　paintings of George Catlin **U** 120–21
　Plymouth Colony **P** 345
　Pontiac **P** 391
　potlatch custom **I** 181; **M** 559–60
　pueblos, pictures **A** 302; **N** 186
　Quebec, present-day life in **Q** 10a
　reservations see Indian reservations
　Sequoya **S** 124
　Sun Dance religion of Plains tribes **M** 563–64
　sweet potatoes discovered by **P** 307
　Tecumseh **T** 47
　wampum **C** 374; **M** 411
　See also history section of province, and state articles;
　　names of families and tribes
Indians of South America **I** 201–11; **S** 293
　arts, development of **I** 155–56
　Alakaluf studied by anthropologists **A** 306–07
　Bolivia, most Indian South American nation **B** 302
　corn **C** 506
　farmers market in Bogotá, picture **C** 379
　folklore **F** 313–14
　Latin-American languages **L** 49
　life in Latin America **L** 50–51
　Peru **P** 161
　pre-Columbian dance **L** 68
　See also country articles; names of tribes
Indian summer **H** 159
Indian Territory, Oklahoma **O** 80, 94–95
Indian wars **I** 212–15
　Apache leader Geronimo **G** 189
　Champlain helps defeat Iroquois **C** 187
　French and Indian War **F** 458–62
　garrison houses for places of refuge **N** 163
　gold discoveries led to war **G** 253
　Pontiac **P** 391
　Tecumseh **T** 47
　War of 1877 **I** 176
　westward movement **W** 142–44
Indictment (in-DITE-ment), in law **C** 527
Indies, Council of the, colonial Latin America **L** 52
Indigo, plant
　dyestuff, source of **D** 367
　dying cloth, Nigeria, picture **N** 257
　early commercial crop in South Carolina **S** 296
Indigo snake, picture **S** 212
Indirect taxes **T** 26
Indium, element **E** 154, 161
Individual differences **C** 232
　family life influences **F** 43
Individualized instruction see Programed instruction
Indo-America, Indian culture in Latin America **L** 51
Indo-Aryan, language group of Asia **A** 460
　Bangladesh **B** 44
　India **I** 117, 119
Indochina, former name for area of Southeast Asia
　comprising Vietnam, Cambodia, and Laos **S** 328

Indochina War, 1946–54 **V** 334d
Indochina War, Second see Vietnam War, 1958–
Indo-European languages **L** 38–39
　anthropological studies **A** 308
　in historical linguistic studies **L** 303
Indo-Iranian (i-RAY-nian) **languages** **L** 39
Indonesia (in-do-NE-sia) **I** 216–22
　batik cloth, hand-dyed, picture **D** 368
　Djakarta **D** 236–37
　flag **F** 237
　orchestral music **O** 221; picture **O** 220d
　picking tea, picture **T** 40
　typical meal, the rice-table **F** 341
　West Irian in New Guinea **N** 147
Indoor activities **I** 223–26
　airplane models **A** 104–07
　automobile models **A** 535–37
　card games **C** 106–15
　charades **C** 188
　checkers **C** 191–92
　chess **C** 221–26
　clay modeling **C** 336–37
　darts **D** 38–39
　dolls **D** 263–69
　dominoes **D** 284
　dressmaking **D** 311–15
　finger painting **F** 126–28
　gift wrapping **G** 206–09
　Indian beadwork **I** 157–59
　jewelry making **J** 100
　jokes and riddles **J** 132–33
　leathercraft **L** 112–13
　linoleum-block printing **L** 304–06
　magic **M** 18–21
　mosaic, how to make **M** 463
　number games and puzzles **N** 372–77
　origami **O** 222–26
　papier-mâché, how to make **P** 58b–59
　parties **P** 87–89
　puppets and marionettes **P** 534–39
　putting on plays **P** 335–41
　railroading, model **R** 91–92
　soap sculpture **S** 216–17
　tops **T** 226
　toys, how to make **T** 230–35
　tricks and puzzles **T** 288–89
　valentines, how to make **V** 266–68
　ventriloquism **V** 301–03
　weaving **W** 97–98
　word games **W** 236–38
　See also Games; Hobbies
Indoor games see Games
Induced tolerance, type of immunization **I** 107
Induction, magnetic see Magnetic induction
Induction motors, electric **E** 139
Indulgences (in-DUL-gen-ces), papal grants **C** 285;
　R 133, 294
　Luther's theses against **L** 378
Indus River, Asia **R** 244
　ancient civilization **A** 223–25; **I** 116
　land of India, north Indian alluvial plains **I** 125
　Tarbela Dam **D** 21
Industrial alcohol **A** 147; **G** 286
Industrial arts **I** 227–28
　machine-made decorative arts **D** 78
　printing **P** 457–67
　woodworking **W** 229–34
Industrial design **I** 229–32
　Bauhaus school, Germany **B** 103–05
　commercial art **C** 424–27
Industrial diseases see Occupational diseases
Industrial geography **G** 108

Industrial painting see Painting, industrial
Industrial Revolution I 233–41
  advertising begins **A** 34
  building construction, effect on **B** 435
  capitalism became a great force **C** 104
  chemical industry **C** 194
  cities, greatest growth during **C** 307–08
  England **E** 226; **U** 65
  farm machinery **F** 55
  industrial growth **I** 244–45
  inventions, selected list **I** 339–45
  labor movement, history of **L** 2
  machine-made decorative arts **D** 78
  manufacturing **M** 83–84
  mining expanded rapidly **M** 320
  socialism, history of **S** 220
  technology, development of **T** 46
  unemployment for first time **U** 25
  wheels, part played by **W** 158
Industrial spies **S** 389
Industrial unions **L** 8–9
Industrial wastes
  water pollution **E** 272e; **W** 58, 59; picture **E** 272d
Industrial Workers of the World (I.W.W.) **L** 6
Industry I 242–51
  air pollution **A** 108–11; **E** 272f–272g
  agriculture a business enterprise **A** 92, 100
  automation **A** 528–34
  big business in United States **U** 130–31
  captains of industry **U** 131
  control and development of natural resources **N** 60
  detergents and soaps, uses in **D** 146
  environment, problems of **E** 272a–272h
  factories changed by electric motors **E** 141
  growth affects labor-management relations **L** 11–12
  how shown on maps, picture **M** 90
  Industrial Revolution **I** 233–41
  international trade **I** 326–30
  Japan's rapid industrial development **J** 35, 37
  jewelry **J** 101
  manufacturing **M** 83–85
  mass production **M** 151
  monopolies permitted to encourage industry **T** 305
  museums **M** 513
  New Jersey, concentration in **N** 169
  noise, protection from **N** 270
  nursing in industry **N** 410
  public relations **P** 507–08
  retailing second largest business in U.S. **R** 188
  rivers, uses of **R** 242
  safety measures **S** 7
  Soviet method of locating heavy industry **U** 38
  special libraries for industry **L** 176–79
  steel industry, importance of **I** 407–08
  tariff adopted to protect home industry **T** 25
  technology **T** 45–46
  unemployment **U** 25–26
  UN Industrial Development Organization **U** 86
  waste, a conservation problem **C** 483
  women, role of **W** 212
  woodworking industries **W** 229
  work methods, changes in **W** 251
  world industrial areas **W** 266–67
  X-ray photography **P** 206
  See also country, province, and state articles, and
  names of industries
Indy (an-DI), **Vincent d'**, French composer **F** 446
Inequalities, in mathematics **M** 165–66
Inert, chemical term **C** 219
Inert gases see Noble gases
Inertia (in-ER-sha), (physics) **M** 171; demonstration **E** 37
  motion, Newton's laws of **M** 469

  satellites **S** 39
  seismograph **E** 37–38
Inertial guidance, navigation system **N** 68, 69
  gyroscope **G** 435–36
  missiles **M** 344
  rockets **R** 261
  space navigation **S** 340f

Infallibility, Roman Catholic doctrine that states that the pope, or the bishops acting jointly, cannot err when they define a doctrine concerning faith or morals. Such a definition, however, may later require refinement or clarification.

Infantile paralysis see Poliomyelitis
Infantry
  United States Army **U** 168
Infants see Baby
Infant schools **K** 242
Infectious diseases, or communicable diseases **D** 186
  early studies of **M** 208
  number of hospitals in various countries compared **H** 252
  Public Health Service in checking epidemics **P** 503
  vectors, carriers of disease **V** 282–85
Infectious mononucleosis (mon-o-nu-cle-O-sis), disease **D** 199

Inferiority complex, in psychology, term used by Alfred Adler to describe an individual's sense of real or fancied inferiority. He believed that striving for superiority is the strongest human impulse and, if thwarted, results in feeling of inferiority. An individual reacts, according to Adler, either by withdrawing from society or by overcompensating (as in achievements of genius).

Infielder, in baseball **B** 74
Infinite sets, in mathematics **S** 126
Infinity **M** 160
  mathematical symbol for **M** 154
Inflation and deflation, of prices **I** 252–53
  economic cycles **E** 50, 51
  financial panic and bank failures **B** 47–48
  Nixon's wage-price freeze **N** 262f
  problems of old age insurance **O** 97
  See also Banks and banking
Inflections, in language **E** 244
  Latin declensions **L** 76
In-flight motion pictures, picture **M** 486

Inflorescence, natural arrangement of flowers on a plant. The flowers or flower clusters are supported by a part of the plant called the floral axis, which is a part of a branch or of a stem. Inflorescences take on a great variety of forms and structures. They are very important in the classification of plants.

Influenza, virus disease **D** 200
  vaccination **V** 261
  virus, picture **V** 361
Information storage and retrieval systems
  computers **C** 449–57
  punched-card machines and computers **O** 58
  use in libraries **L** 174, 177
Infrared microscopes (in-fra-RED MY-cro-scopes) **M** 283
Infrared radiation **R** 44
  light, spectrum analysis of **L** 269–70
  missile guidance **M** 345
  photography **P** 207
  solar energy **S** 235
Infusorians (in-fu-SO-rians), microscopic organisms **B** 193

Inge, William (1913–73), American playwright, b. Independence, Kans. Plays of his that have been made into movies include *Bus Stop, Picnic* (Pulitzer prize, 1953), *The Dark at the Top of the Stairs,* and *Come Back, Little Sheba.*

Ingersoll (ING-er-soll), **Jared** (1749–1822), American lawyer, b. New Haven, Conn. One of the most distinguished lawyers in Philadelphia, he was a delegate to the Continental Congress (1780 and 1781) and to the Constitutional Convention (1787). He was also city solicitor (1798–1801), attorney general of Pennsylvania (1790–99, 1811–17), Federalist candidate for vice-president (1812), and presiding judge of the district court of the county and city of Philadelphia (1821–22).

Ingersoll, Robert Green (1833–1899), American orator, b. Dresden, N.Y. He is celebrated for his speech nominating James G. Blaine for Republican presidential candidate (1876). Called the great agnostic, he was a popular speaker and published his lectures in *The Gods* and *Some Mistakes of Moses.*

In God We Trust, motto on United States coins
  M 338
Ingots
  steel **I** 399; picture **I** 405

Ingres (ANGR-ra), **Jean Auguste Dominique** (1780–1867), French artist, b. Montauban. A student of David, he was a noted classicist and conservative member of French Academy. He shows attention to line in works such as *The Turkish Bath* and *Odalisque.* His other paintings include *The Painter Granet, Madame Rivière,* and *Madame de Senonnes.*
  neoclassical style in French art **F** 425; **P** 29

Ingstad (ING-stad), **Helge,** Norwegian explorer
  V 339–40
Inherited characteristics **G** 85–88
Inherited diseases **D** 188
Inhibitors, in chemistry
  plastics **P** 327
Initials, commonly used as abbreviations **A** 4–6
Initial Teaching Alphabet **I** 254
  reading aid **R** 109
Initiative, referendum, and recall, legislative processes in government, the Oregon system **O** 205

Injunction, written court order either prohibiting a person or group from performing, or requiring them to perform, a certain act. Injunctions are often used in labor disputes and in instances of restraint of trade. Excessive use of the injunction against strikers led to the Norris-LaGuardia Act of 1932.

Injuries see First Aid
Ink **I** 255–56
  ball-point pens **P** 147
  communication advanced by **C** 432
  drawing inks **D** 303
  Gutenberg discovers an ink for metal type **P** 457
  magnetic ink for computer input **C** 452
Ink-blot tests **T** 118
Inland Sea, Japan **J** 34; picture **J** 47
Inland seas, lakes **L** 25
Inland waterways
  Great Lakes-St. Lawrence system **G** 326; **S** 15, 16–17
  Ontario **O** 121–22
  section at Fort Lauderdale, Florida, picture **U** 107
Inlaying, or marquetry, of furniture **D** 77; **F** 508

Inman, Henry (1801–46), American painter, b. Yorkville, New York. Well-known during his lifetime as a portrait painter, he included among his subjects such celebrities as Martin Van Buren and William Wordsworth. He also painted landscapes and familiar scenes of everyday life. Many of his works, including *The Young Fisherman* and *Picnic in the Catskills,* hang in American museums.

Inner Asia **A** 449, 452
Inner Mongolia, a region of China **M** 413
Inner Six, of the European Economic Community (Common Market) **E** 334–35
Inner Temple see Inns of Court

Inness (INN-ess), **George** (1825–94), American artist, b. Newburgh, N.Y. In his youth he was apprenticed to an engraver and showed considerable artistic talent. After painting in Rome and in Paris, he opened a studio in New York City and became well known for his landscapes, several of which hang in American museums. He died in Scotland. His son, **George Inness, Jr.,** (1854–1926), gained a wide reputation as a painter of landscapes and animals.
  landscape painting in the United States **U** 121

Innings, in baseball **B** 70

Innis, Roy (1935–), American civil rights leader, b. St. Croix, Virgin Islands. He is National Director of the Congress of Racial Equality (CORE). He drafted for introduction to the United States Congress a bill called the Community Self-Determination Act of 1968, which proposed the establishment of community development corporations in which the members of poor black and white communities could purchase shares. In October, 1970, he submitted a brief to the United States Supreme Court concerning community-controlled schools and the busing of pupils.

Innisfallen (IN-nish-FALL-en), island in Loch Leane, Ireland **L** 31

Innisfree (IN-nish-FREE), a tiny, picturesque island in Lough Gill, County Sligo, Ireland. Many visitors have been captivated by its tranquil beauty. The Irish poet William Butler Yeats described the island in his famous poem "The Lake Isle of Innisfree."

Innisfree, Lake Isle of, poem by Yeats
  Y 344
Innocent III, pope **M** 294
  abolished trial by ordeal **J** 159
  Albigensian heresy stamped out **R** 292
  Jews persecuted by **J** 108
  world domination of papacy **R** 292

Inn River, tributary of the Danube in central Europe. Rising in Switzerland, the river flows for over 300 miles through Austria and Germany before emptying into the Danube. Part of its length forms the Austro-German border.

Inns see Hotels; Motels

Innsbruck (INNS-brook), Austrian city. Situated on the Inn River in the Austrian Alps, it is a popular winter and summer resort. Among its tourist attractions are a botanical garden that houses a large variety of Alpine plants, a 15th-century castle, and a 16th-century church. Innsbruck, the fifth largest city and the capital of the province of Tyrol, has a population of approximately 100,000.

Inns of Court, name given to the group of buildings that house London's four legal societies. These societies— Gray's Inn, the Inner Temple, Lincoln's Inn, and the Middle Temple—were founded in the late 13th and early 14th centuries. The buildings were the original homes and schools of young legal apprentices. Today the societies exercise complete control over permission to practice law in England.

Innuit see Eskimo

Ino (I-no), Greek goddess, daughter of Harmonia and Cadmus. The second wife of Athamas, she was the mother of Learchus and Melicertes. When Athamas went mad and tried to kill her, she plunged into the sea and was transformed into the sea goddess Leucothoe.

Inoculation see Vaccination and inoculation

Inonu (ee-no-NU), **Ismet** (1884–   ), Turkish statesman. He fought in World War I and played an active role in Turkey's struggle for independence from Greece. In 1923 he became prime minister of the new republic and served as its president (1938–1950). Since then he has been a leading figure in the political life of Turkey, heading two unsuccessful coalition cabinets.

Inorganic chemistry see Chemistry, inorganic
Inorganic fertilizers F 97
Inorganic substances C 219

Inouye (in-o-OO-yeh), **Daniel Ken** (1924–   ), American politician, b. Honolulu, Hawaii. He has been majority leader of the Territorial House of Representatives (1954– 58), member of the Territorial Senate (1958–59), member of the U.S. House of Representatives (1959–62), and U.S. senator from Hawaii (since 1963).

Input and output units, of computers C 450, 451–52

Inquest, in law, a judicial inquiry, by a jury, especially one conducted by coroner into a cause of death. The term also refers to the findings of such a jury. A grand jury investigation is sometimes called a grand inquest.

Institute for Advanced Study, organization founded (1930) at Princeton, N.J., for postdoctoral research in the humanities, mathematics, mathematical physics, and historical studies. It publishes (with Princeton University) *Annals of Mathematics.*

and *muralis*, "of a wall"), competitive sports between teams representing different schools.

Internal-combustion engines I 303–08
  automobiles **A** 542–43
  aviation **A** 557, 568
  construction equipment **B** 446
  diesel engines **D** 168–71
  diesel locomotives **L** 328
  engines, types of **E** 210–11
  ethyl gasoline reduces engine knock **G** 63
  fuels **F** 486
  gas turbines **T** 321–22
  industrial growth **I** 245
  invention replaces steam engine **I** 336
  mechanical energy **E** 203
  Wankel engine **I** 303, 308, 309
Internal energy, in physics **H** 87
Internal Revenue Code, United States I 110
Internal Revenue Service, United States I 110
  Alcohol and Tobacco Tax Division **F** 76
  Intelligence Division **F** 76

International, The, federation of working-class parties organized to change capitalist societies into socialist commonwealths and unify them in a world federation. The First International, or International Workingmen's Association (1864–74), founded in London, was led by Karl Marx. The Second International (1889–1914), founded in Paris, urged prevention of war. The Third International (1919–43) (Communist International, or Comintern), founded in Berne, Switzerland, to promote world revolution against capitalism, was reorganized as the Cominform (1947).

International, The, original anthem of Soviet Russia **N** 19

International Air Transport Association (IATA), organization of most international airlines. Founded in 1945, it regulates fares and appoints travel agents. Its headquarters is in Montreal.
  Canada's airways **C** 61

International Amateur Athletic Federation (IAAF), body that governs international track-and-field events. It was founded in 1913. The Marquis of Exeter is its president.

International Association of Automotive Modelers A 537
International Atomic Energy Agency (IAEA) **U** 85
  disarmament **D** 184
International Badminton Federation B 13
International Bank for Reconstruction and Development (World Bank) **U** 86
  international banks **B** 51
International Bobsleigh and Tobogganing Federation
  B 266

International Boundary and Water Commission, United States and Mexico, commission that deals with boundary and water matters between United States and Mexico. It constructs and operates international storage dams and power plants on the Rio Grande and supervises Rio Grande Rectification and Canalization Projects and Lower Rio Grande flood control project. It was founded in 1889 and has headquarters in El Paso, Tex., and Ciudad Juárez, Mexico.

International Boundary Commission, United States and Canada, commission in charge of demarcation of boundary line between United States and Canada. Founded (1906) by treaty with Great Britain, it has headquarters in Washington, D.C.

International Brotherhood of Teamsters (I.B.T.) **L 7**
International Bureau of Expositions F 16

International Bureau of Weights and Measures, scientific organization, of approximately 31 countries, that has established international standards for metric system and for measurement of units of electricity; it was founded in 1875 and has headquarters at Sèvres, France.

International Business Machines Corporation (IBM)
  laboratories at Poughkeepsie, picture **N** 216
International Canoe Federation C 101
International Civil Aviation Organization (ICAO)
  U 86
  Canada **C** 61
International Code
  signal flags **F** 245
International Committee of the Red Cross
  R 126
International Confederation of Free Trade Unions
  (I.C.F.T.U.) **L** 10
International co-operation
  Antarctic regions **P** 368, 370–71
  postal service **P** 405–10
  Red Cross **R** 126–27
  United Nations **U** 80–88
International Cooperative Alliance C 500

International Council of Scientific Unions (ICSU), federation of scientific unions formed to promote and coordinate activities in the fields of natural and exact sciences. It was formed (1931) to succeed the International Research Council. It directed International Geophysical Year activities (1957–58). Headquarters is in London, England.
  International Geophysical Year **I** 310–20

International Council of Women (ICW), union of women's organizations of all races and creeds. Founded in Washington, D.C. (1888), it aims to promote the welfare of all peoples and to support international peace and the establishment of equal rights for women. Headquarters is in Zurich, Switzerland. Its publications include the *Bulletin.*

International Court of Justice, The Hague **U** 85
  Coolidge favored **C** 497
  international relations **I** 321

International Criminal Police Organization (Interpol), association of police forces from 90 countries working in a co-operative effort to prevent crime. Founded in 1923, headquarters is in Paris, France. It publishes *International Criminal Police Review.*
  duties of Interpol and its organization **P** 377

International date line I 309–10
  Alaska **A** 128
  180th meridian **L** 83
  where time begins **T** 190–92
International Development Association (IDA) **U** 86
  international banks **B** 51
International Exhibition, 1862, London, picture **F** 14
International Exposition of 1851, London **F** 13
International Federation of Trade Unions (I.F.T.U.) **L** 10
International Fencing Federation F 86
International Finance Corporation (IFC) **U** 86
  international banks **B** 51
International Geophysical Year (IGY) **I** 310–20
  jet streams studied **J** 91
  polar regions **P** 368, 370

International Gymnastics Federation (F.I.G.) G 431–32
International Ice Hockey Federation I 35
International Ice Patrol I 27
    United States Coast Guard duties U 176

International Joint Commission (IJC), council of six U.S. and Canadian delegates who settle cases involving boundary waters and common frontier between United States and Canada. Organized in 1911, it has headquarters at Washington, D.C., and Ottawa, Canada.

International Kennel Club D 261
International Labor Day see May Day
International Labour Organisation (ILO) L 10
    a specialized agency of the United Nations U 85
International Ladies' Garment Workers' Union C 354
International Languages see Universal languages
International law I 320–21
    aliens A 166
    codes developed by peace congresses P 104
    copyright T 245
    naturalization N 58
    passports and visas P 94–95
    patent owners, rights of P 98
    treaties T 270–73
    war crimes trials W 9–10
    World Court an umpire in international relations I 325
International Lawn Tennis Federation (ILTF) T 90
International Livestock Exhibition, Chicago C 230
International Missionary Council P 486
International Monetary Fund (IMF) U 86
    international banking B 50–51
International Morse Code see Morse Code, International
International News Service N 201
International Olympic Committee (I.O.C.) O 107–08
International Organization of Consumers Unions (IOCU)
    C 494a
International Peace Bridge see Peace Bridge International
International Peace Garden, North Dakota–Manitoba
    M 79; N 333
International Periodicals Directory M 15

International Phonetic Alphabet (IPA), series of symbols designed by International Phonetic Association (1888) to represent speech sounds of languages. In transcription of speech, each symbol denotes one sound.
    alphabetic systems of writing, problems of speech
    sounds L 38

International Polar Years (IPY-1 and 2) I 310–11
    polar regions P 368
International Quiet Sun Year (IQSY) I 320

International Reading Association (IRA), association of reading teachers interested in research and study of reading problems. Founded (1956) when International Council for the Improvement of Reading Instruction merged with National Association for Remedial Teaching, it has headquarters in Newark, Del.

International Red Cross see Red Cross

International Refugee Organization (IRO), temporary specialized UN agency organized in 1948 (discontinued 1951) to aid, protect, and resettle refugees and displaced persons. Its headquarters was at Geneva, Switzerland.

International relations I 322–25
    between the world wars W 282–87
    Bismarck's unification of Germany B 250
    disarmament D 184–86
    foreign aid programs F 368

foreign service F 369–70
grant money from foundations F 393
imperialism I 109
international law I 320–21
international trade I 326–30
League of Nations L 96–97
Monroe Doctrine M 425, 426–27
narcotics traffic N 14
Open Door Policy for China M 189–90
Organization of American States O 210–11
patent owners, rights of P 98
Peace Corps P 101–03
peace movements P 104–05
powers in foreign affairs of U.S. president P 454
treaties T 270–73
United States U 136–37
Washington, George, administration of W 43
What is the Bamboo Curtain? I 323
What is the Iron Curtain? I 323
International Rice Research Institute, Philippines R 231
International road signs, picture D 320
International Skeeter Association I 29
International Society for Contemporary Music M 550
International Telecommunications Satellite Consortium
    see Intelsat
International Telecommunications Union (ITU) U 86
    control of air space and broadcasting rights R 54
International trade I 326–30
    cartels, international monopolies T 306
    Europe and the Common Market E 329–30, 334–35
    free ports I 330
    selling S 116–17
    ships and shipping S 155–61
    tariff T 25
    trade and commerce, history of T 242–43
    triangular trade, New England, West Indies, Africa
    S 198
    United States U 109
    What is a free port? I 330
International Typographical Union N 205
International Whaling Commission W 151

International Year for Human Rights (1968), observance marking the 20th anniversary of the adoption, by the United Nations, of the Universal Declaration of Human Rights. The president of the General Assembly officially opened the year-long celebration on January 1. The theme was "greater recognition and full enjoyment of the fundamental freedoms of the individual and of human rights everywhere."

International Youth Hostel Federation H 253
Internist, physician D 239

Internment, in international law, the confining of property, enemy aliens, or suspicious persons within prescribed limits. It was used, for example, by United States during World War II to detain Japanese aliens and their native-born children. A 166

Interns, in hospitals D 241; H 250
    dental interns D 115
Internuncios, ambassadors of the popes V 281
    Pius XII, service to Bavaria P 266
Inter-Parliamentary (in-ter-par-li-MENT-ry) Union, representatives of national legislative bodies P 82
Interplanetary space see Space, outer
Interpol see International Criminal Police Organization
Interrogative pronouns P 90
Interrupted projections M 93; picture M 94
Interstate commerce I 331–32
    Marshall's ruling for federal government M 112

Interstate Commerce Act, 1887 I 332
Interstate Commerce Commission (ICC) I 332
Inter-Testament, apocryphal books of the Bible
    B 152
Intertidal areas
    life, plant and animal adaptations L 222–23
Intertype, slug-casting machine in printing P 465
    type casting T 344–45

Interventionists, persons favoring interference by force
or threat of force, in affairs of another state, usually to
further political ends or to protect life or property.

Interviewing
    opinion surveys O 159
    tools of research R 182–83
Intervision, television network of eastern European
        countries T 71
Intestate, one who dies without a will W 174
Intestinal cancer C 92, 95
Intestines
    digestive function in human body B 275; diagram
        B 274
In the pond, line game G 23
Intolerable Acts, 1774, British reprisals against American
        colonies D 60
    events leading to Revolutionary War R 196–97
    Quebec Act listed with them C 71
Intoxication see Alcoholism
Intracoastal Waterway, eastern and Gulf coasts, United
        States N 313–14
    Florida section F 267
    South Carolina S 302
    Texas T 125

Intramural games (from Latin intra, meaning "within"
and muralis, "of a wall"), athletics in which competition
is confined to teams within an individual school.

Intransitive verbs P 91
    grammar G 289
Invalides see Hôtel des Invalides
Invalids
    home nursing N 413–15
    nurses and nursing N 409–13
Invariants, in topology T 220
Inventions I 333–48
    agricultural tools A 96
    aided growth of industry I 245
    air conditioning A 102
    alphabet A 170–73
    Archimedes A 369
    automobiles A 541–42
    aviation A 567–574
    Bessemer's steel process and other inventions B 149
    cotton gin C 521, 523
    diving equipment D 79
    Edison, Thomas A. E 59–60
    farm machinery F 55–62
    Franklin's F 453–54
    Industrial Revolution I 234–39
    Langmuir, Irving L 35
    Leonardo da Vinci L 152–55
    McCormick's reaper M 186
    patents I 347; P 97–98
    printing P 457–58
    spinning jenny I 235
    technology and inventions T 45–46
    telephone T 56
    Watt, James W 68–69
    wax paper W 70
    weaving loom I 235

Westinghouse, George W 125
What is a patent? I 347
What is the difference between an invention and a
        discovery? I 336
What president of the United States was also an in-
        ventor? I 335
Why has no one invented a perpetual-motion machine?
        I 333
Why were electric irons invented? E 118
writing W 317–18
See also Farm machinery; Patents; Technology; and
        inventions and inventors by name

Inverness (in-ver-NESS), capital of Inverness county,
Scotland. A seaport on the Ness River, its population
numbers about 30,000. Inverness castle, built in 1835,
is said to be on the site where Macbeth murdered
Duncan.

Inverse-square law, rule of electric forces between two
        particles N 367
Inversion, temperature F 289
    air pollution A 109; E 272g
Invertebrates (in-VER-teb-rates), animals without back-
        bones A 264
    jellyfishes and other coelenterates J 70–75
    kingdoms of living things K 251
    learning ability L 104
    prehistoric animals, development of P 437
    starfishes S 402–03
Investment banks B 49–50
Investments, economic activities
    depressions and recessions D 122
    insurance I 297
    investment banks B 49–50
    real estate R 112–13
    stocks and bonds S 427–33
Investment trusts, in which property or money is held
        for safekeeping T 303
Investors, people who buy securities S 427
Invincible Armada see Armada, Spanish
Invisible inks I 255–56
Invitations, letters L 159
    for parties P 87–88
    to Halloween parties H 15
Invocation, a calling prayer P 434
Involuntary muscles, diagram B 272
Involute curve, picture G 131
In winter I get up at night, from Bed in Summer by
        Robert Louis Stevenson S 424

Io, in Greek mythology, a mortal whom Zeus loved and
turned into a white heifer to protect her from Hera's
jealousy. In some versions it was Hera who transformed
Io, torturing her with gadfly until she jumped into sea
(named Ionian after her), swam to Egypt, was restored
to human form, and became mother of Epaphus.

Iodine, element I 349
    elements, some facts about E 154, 161
    nutrition, use in N 417
    tincture of M 202
Iodized salt S 21
Iolani Palace, Honolulu, Hawaii H 66, 69
Iolanthe (i-o-LANTH-e), operetta by Gilbert and Sullivan
        G 210

Ionesco (yon-ES-ko), Eugene (1912–), French playwright, b. Bucharest, Rumania. He is a controversial,
avant-garde playwright whose characters are often considered eccentric and grotesque. He writes about hope-
lessness of human communication in Rhinoceros.

Ionian (i-O-nian) Islands, west of Greece I 430, 434
  landforms of Greece G 333
Ionian School, of Greek philosophers S 61–62
Ionian Sea O 47
Ionic (i-ON-ic), Greek style of architecture G 346; picture G 347
  architectural orders A 375; picture A 376
I only regret that I have but one life to lose for my country, last words of Nathan Hale H 12
Ionosphere (i-ON-o-sphere), upper layer of earth's atmosphere A 481; E 17
  effect of solar radiation S 235–36
  ions and ionization I 352
  magnetic storms in E 27
  radio R 52
  weather in the ionosphere W 72
  Why can you hear radio stations from farther away at night? R 50
Ion propulsion, for rockets R 261
Ions and ionization C 219; I 350–55
  chemistry of ions C 202
  crystals C 542
  electron emission E 144–45
  electroplating E 149–50
  International Geophysical Year findings I 317
  ion-exchange resins to purify water R 185
  lightning T 170–71
  physical chemistry, development of C 215
  water desalting W 56a

I.O.U. (IOU), colloquial term for "I owe you"; a piece of paper with the letters IOU, a signature admitting the debt, and the amount of money owed; an informal promissory note.

Iowa (I-o-wa) I 356–71
Iowa University of I 364; picture I 367
Iowa, State University of Science and Technology, at Ames I 364, 366
Iowa City, former capital of Iowa I 367
Iowa Test of Basic Skills, sample T 118
Iowa Wesleyan (WES-le-yan) College I 366
Ipecac (IP-e-cac), plant P 314
Iphigenia (iph-i-ge-NY-a), in Greek mythology G 365
IPY-1 and 2 see International Polar Years
IQ see Intelligence Quotient
Iqbal, Indian poet O 220e
IQSY see International Quiet Sun Year
Iquitos (ee-KI-tose), Peru P 164
I.R.A. see Irish Republican Army
Iran (ir-AN) I 372–77
  archeological site at Tepe Sarab, picture A 357
  Azerbaijan U 45
  flag F 237
  rug weaving industry, Persian rugs R 354
  Teheran T 49–50
  See also Persia
Iraq (ir-OK) I 378–83
  archeological site at Jarmo, picture A 357
  flag F 237
Irazú (ir-a-ZU), volcano in Costa Rica C 516
Irbid, Jordan J 139
Ireland I 384–91
  agriculture, picture A 97
  ancient Irish blessing P 435
  Christianity, history of C 283, 284
  England, history of E 222, 228, 232
  flag F 239
  Gaelic football F 366
  gardens, pictures G 32
  Gladstone's reform programs G 225
  harp playing H 43

holiday, Saint Patrick's Day H 148
literature see Irish literature
national anthem N 21
Northern Ireland U 73
O'Connell, Daniel O 51
Patrick, Saint P 98
peat used for fuel, picture F 486
potato famine, 1845, 1846 P 411
Roman Catholic Church R 290
theater T 161
Viking era V 338
Yeats, William Butler, a senator Y 345
Ireland, National University of U 207
Ireland, Northern U 73
  Belfast U 73
  England, history of E 232
Irene, Goodnight, folk song F 321
Iriarte see Yriarte, Tomas de
Iridium (i-RID-ium), element E 154, 161
  alloyed with platinum J 92
  metals, chart of ores, location, properties, uses M 227

Iris (I-ris), Greek goddess of the rainbow. A handmaiden of Zeus and Hera, she served as messenger for the gods. The familiar colorful garden flower is named for her.

Iris, of the eye B 284; M 208g
Irises, flowers G 41; picture T 206
  Japanese Iris Festival J 31
  state flower of Tennessee T 75
Irish harp, picture H 44
Irish literature I 392–95
  arts in Ireland I 386
  drama D 298–99
  Irish Renaissance in English literature E 266
  Kells, Book of K 202–03
  Yeats, William Butler Y 344
Irish moss, a seaweed N 344b
  in ice cream I 33
Irish potatoes P 411–12
Irish Republican Army (I.R.A.) I 391; U 73
Irish Sea O 47
Irish setter, dog, picture D 253
Irish system, of reforming criminals P 469
Irish Volunteer movement, of nationalists I 391
Irish wolfhound, dog, pictures D 250, 254

Irkutsk (ir-KUTSK), industrial city of Siberia. Situated on the Angara and Irkut rivers near Lake Baikal, this busy port is the site of a hydroelectric plant. Known also as a cultural center, the city is the home of a leading university and several colleges. A major port on the Trans-Siberian Railroad, Irkutsk has a population of about 400,000 people.

Irminger Current, North Atlantic, diagram G 411
IRO see International Refugee Organization
Iron I 396–408
  antique ironwork A 321
  armor, chain mail A 433
  Assyrians used for weapons A 225
  building material B 438
  carbon added to make steel C 106
  chemical symbol from its Latin name C 198
  decorative arts D 77
  elements, some facts about E 154, 161–62
  ferrous alloys A 168
  filings used to show magnetic lines of force E 130; M 25–26
  galvanized iron Z 370
  how radiation changes form R 41

importance to Industrial Revolution **I** 236–37
Lapland's deposits **L** 45
magnetic qualities **M** 26–28
Mesabi Range in Minnesota **M** 329–30, 337
metals, chart of ores, location, properties, uses
M 227
mordant in dyeing **D** 369
nutrition, use in **N** 416–17
ore formations in Labrador **N** 141
Quebec, Canada, a leading producer **Q** 11
rusting, slow oxidation **O** 268
wrought iron and cast iron plows **F** 57
See also Steel
Iron age **P** 446
metallurgy **M** 233
tools, Roman **T** 211
Iron Chancellor, nickname for Otto von Bismarck **B** 250
Ironclads, Confederate and Union warships
Civil War **C** 323
Iron Cross, German award, picture **M** 200
Iron Curtain, imaginary barrier dividing Eastern Europe
from the West **I** 323
origin of the phrase **C** 298; **M** 375
Iron Duke, nickname of the Duke of Wellington **W** 122
Iron filings, how to make and use for experiments
E 130; **M** 25–26
Iron industry and trade **I** 404–05
Ironing, laundry **L** 85

Iron lung, metal tank used as an apparatus of artificial
respiration. Patient's head protrudes from the tank, and
a rubber collar around neck prevents leakage of air. Air
pressure in tank, electrically controlled, decreases and
increases, resulting in expansion and contraction of
chest. The lung is used for those paralyzed by polio,
poisoning, or asphyxia. It is also called a Drinker Res-
pirator, after its designer, Philip Drinker (1928).

Iron Mask, Man in the (?–1703), an unidentified French
prisoner of state, said to have worn a velvet mask, who
died in Bastille and was buried under name of Marchioli
in St. Paul Cemetery, Paris. Title was given to him by
Voltaire, who described him as wearing an iron mask.
He was subject of much speculation and romantic literature, including novel of same name by Alexandre Dumas,
who characterized prisoner as twin brother of Louis XIV.

Iron metals **E** 158
Iron Mountain, Michigan
ski area, picture **M** 271
Iron ore **I** 403–04
Europe **E** 315
Mesabi Range, Minnesota **M** 329–30, 337
North America world's greatest source **N** 292–93
Sweden **S** 485
world distribution, diagram **W** 261
Iron pyrites, mineral nicknamed "fool's gold" **G** 249
Irons, for pressing clothes **E** 118
Why were electric irons invented? **E** 118
Irons, golf clubs, picture **G** 254
how to use, pictures **G** 258
Ironsi, Johnson Aguiyi- see Aguiyi-Ironsi, Johnson
Iron Triangle, Korea **K** 304
Ironwood, Michigan **M** 270
Ironwork
Spain **S** 364
welding **W** 118–19
wrought iron **I** 405
Irony (I-ro-ny), a form of humor **H** 281
Iroquois (IR-o-quoi), Indians of North America **I** 186–87
carved masks **I** 156
Champlain makes bitter enemies of **C** 187

early conflicts with Algonkians in New York **N** 224
family life **A** 302–03
Indian wars **I** 212
League of Six Nations **I** 184
New France almost destroyed by **C** 69–70
present-day life in Quebec **Q** 10a
Irradiation
meat preservation process **M** 195
Irrational numbers, those that cannot be expressed as
quotient of two integers **N** 385
Irrawaddy (ir-ra-WA-dy) **River,** southeast Asia **R** 244
largest river in Burma **B** 456
Irregular verbs, principal parts **P** 91
Irrigation **I** 408–10
Arizona desert, picture **D** 126
California projects **C** 19
care of cotton crop **C** 524
dams **D** 16
deserts, future of **D** 129, 130
ditches, picture **F** 256
how rivers provide water **R** 241–42
India, picture **I** 123
Middle East **M** 302–03
Nebraska's Platte River **N** 76–77
oases **O** 2–3
orchards **F** 482
prairie farming **P** 432
Reclamation Act, 1902 **C** 485
soil management in agriculture **A** 93
sugar beet field, picture **U** 108
vegetable gardening **V** 288
water power **W** 61
waterwheel, picture **A** 63
See also Dams

Irving, Sir Henry (John Henry Brodribb) (1838–1905),
English actor, b. Keinton Mandeville. With Ellen Terry as
his leading lady, he formed (1878) his own company in
his own theater, the Lyceum. In 1883 he made the first
of eight tours in America. One of his greatest triumphs,
Tennyson's Becket (1893), was performed by command
before Queen Victoria at Windsor Castle. Hamlet was his
finest Shakespearean role. The first actor to be knighted
(1895), he was buried in Westminster Abbey.

Irving, Washington, American writer **I** 410–11
American literature **A** 199–200
children's literature **C** 238
essays **E** 293
"Rip Van Winkle," excerpt **I** 411–12
short stories **S** 166
Irwin, James B., American astronaut **S** 344, 345, 347

Irwin (ER-win), **Will** (William Henry Irwin), (1873–1948),
American journalist and author, b. Oneida, New York.
He first gained prominence for his report in The Sun
of the San Francisco earthquake and fire in 1906. This
story was later published in book form as The City
That Was. During World War I he was a correspondent
for the London Daily Mail and several American publications. He also wrote poetry, biographies, and collaborated
on two plays, The Thirteenth Chair and Lute Song.

Isaac (I-zac), Hebrew patriarch **I** 413
Abraham's sacrifice **A** 7
Isaac (E-zoc), **Heinrich,** Flemish composer **D** 364
Renaissance music **R** 172–73
Isaacs (E-socs), **Jorge,** Colombian writer **C** 380
Isabella I, Spanish queen, aided Columbus **F** 87
art, patron of **S** 361
Caribbean islands, colonization of **C** 118
Columbus and Isabella **C** 417

Isabelline, Spanish art style **S** 361

Isafjordur (E-sof-yur-dur), Iceland, picture **I** 41

Isaiah (i-SAI-ah), book of the Bible **B** 154, 155

Isaiah, Hebrew prophet **I** 413
  history of the Jews **J** 105
  Michelangelo painting **B** 158

Ise (E-say), Japan, site of shrine to sun goddess **J** 42

Isenheim altarpiece, painted by Grünewald **G** 167, 169

Isfahan (is-fa-HON), Iran **I** 376
  mosque, picture **I** 372

I shall find a way or make one, words of Robert E. Peary **P** 116

I shall return, words of Douglas MacArthur **M** 2

Ishmael (ISH-may-el), in Old Testament, son of Abraham and Hagar. Ishmael was exiled with Hagar from Abraham's house and was miraculously found in the wilderness and saved. He married an Egyptian and according to tradition founded the Arab race. His name is now used to denote an outcast or misfit.
  Abraham's son **A** 7
  Muslim traditions **I** 414–16; **M** 196

Ishmaelites (ISH-may-el-ites), nomadic peoples, descended from Ishmael, who pitched their tents in northern Arabia and traded with Egypt. They are mentioned in several places in the Bible.

Ishtar Gate, picture **A** 243

Isis (I-sis), chief goddess of the early Egyptians, sister-wife of Osiris and mother of Horus. Isis ruled over all matters concerning fertility and motherhood. Her worship began around Memphis centuries before the birth of Christ.

Islam, religion of Muslims **I** 414–16
  Africa **A** 56
  Arabic language **L** 39
  art and architecture *see* Islamic art and architecture
  Asia, chief religions of **A** 460
  Azerbaijan **U** 45
  Bangladesh **B** 44, 44b
  customs being revised by civil law in Tunisia **T** 309
  divorce **D** 234
  funeral customs **F** 493
  holy war against Christian world **R** 290–91
  Judaism and founding of Islam **J** 107
  Koran **K** 294–95
  lunar calendar **T** 194
  marriage rites **W** 102
  Mauritania **M** 179
  Mecca, holy city of **M** 196
  Mohammed **M** 404–05
  Muslims at prayer, picture **R** 150
  prayer from the Koran **P** 435
  religion of the Middle East **M** 305
  religious holidays **R** 154
  Saudi Arabia, site of the holy cities **S** 48
  science, advances in **S** 64
  Southeast Asia **S** 330
  Soviet Central Asia **U** 46
  two sects, the Sunnites and the Shi'ites **R** 150–51

Islamabad (is-LA-ma-bod), capital of Pakistan **P** 40

Islamic art and architecture **I** 417–22
  Blue Mosque, Istanbul, picture **T** 323
  Court of the Lions, Alhambra, picture **S** 363
  illuminated manuscripts **I** 88
  in Spain **S** 360–61
  Taj Mahal **T** 14
  tapestry **T** 22

Islands **I** 423–37
  Caribbean **C** 116–19
  how coral islands were formed **O** 39
  Indonesia's major groups **I** 218–20
  life, distribution of animals and plants **L** 236
  Mediterranean Sea **M** 213
  mid-Atlantic ridge, islands of **A** 478
  New York, a city of islands **N** 227–28
  North American continent, those islands considered part of **N** 282
  Pacific Ocean and islands **P** 2–10
  Southeast Asia **S** 328–35
  See also islands by name, as Liberty Island

Islas Malvinas (Falkland Islands) **I** 430; **S** 278

Isle of Man, in the Irish Sea **I** 435

Isle of Pines, mountainous, densely forested island in the South Pacific, a dependency of New Caledonia, administered by France. A former penal colony, the island is now a tourist resort.

Isle of Wight, in English Channel **I** 437

Isle Royale National Park, Lake Superior, Michigan **M** 268
  a few surviving wolves live in the park **D** 245

Ismay, Thomas H., English ship owner **O** 24

Isobars (I-so-bars), lines of weather maps indicating equal barometric pressures **W** 78–79

Isocrates (i-SOC-ra-tese) (436–338 B.C.), Athenian educator. A great speech writer and teacher, he opened a school where he taught politics and the art of speech-making. Although he himself never made speeches, he wrote many for Athenian statesmen to deliver. He was a strong believer in the unification of the Greek city-states under the leadership of Athens.

Isodorus of Miletus (is-o-DOR-us of mi-LE-tus), Byzantine architect **B** 485

Isolationism, a policy in international relations **I** 322
  American colonies and later **U** 136
  Jefferson's policies **J** 67

Isomers (I-so-mers), in chemistry **C** 200, 219

Isometrics (i-so-MET-rics) (from Greek *isos*, meaning "equal," and *metron*, meaning "measure"), system of exercises based on the action of muscles against strong resistance. This results in muscular contraction with little shortening of the muscle fibers. Isometric exercises increase muscle tone.

Isoniazid (i-so-NY-a-zid), drug, used for tuberculosis **D** 212

Isoprene (I-so-prene), liquid hydrocarbon **R** 345–46

Isosceles (i-SOS-cel-ese) **trapezoids**, geometric forms **G** 126

Isosceles triangles, diagram **G** 125

Isostasy (i-SOS-ta-sy), theory of the balance of earth's crust **G** 114–15

Isotherms (I-so-therms), diagram **Z** 373

Isotopes (I-so-topes), of chemical elements **E** 153–54
  atomic weight **A** 487–88
  cancer treatment **C** 91, 95
  chemistry of isotopes **C** 203–05
  defined **C** 219
  nuclear energy **N** 356
  radioactive elements and isotopes **R** 67–68
  uranium 235 and 238 **U** 231

Isotype, picture symbol representing a fixed number or quantity of the thing symbolized, such as a stick figure of a man to represent 10,000 people. Isotypes are used for statistical charts and in visual education.

Israel (IS-ray-el) **I** 438–45
 aqueduct **A** 344
 Arbor Day, Hamishah Asar B'Shevat **R** 154
 Ben-Gurion, David, first prime minister **B** 140
 Biblical history of **B** 155
 co-operative movement **C** 500
 David **D** 44
 Dead Sea Scrolls **D** 48–49
 draft, or conscription of women **D** 289
 flag **F** 237
 history of the kingdom of Israel **J** 104
 homeland regained **J** 112
 immigrants **I** 103; picture **I** 102
 Jerusalem, New City **J** 80–81
 kibbutzim **F** 42
 Kosher style of cooking of favorite foods **F** 341
 Mapai party, symbol **P** 380
 modern Hebrew language **H** 101
 national anthem **N** 22
 national dances **D** 31; pictures **D** 266
 Solomon **S** 252
 special-issue stamp, picture **S** 399
 Weizmann, Chaim, first president **W** 118
 Zionism **Z** 371
Israel ben Eliezer see Baal Shem-Tov
Israeli-Arab wars see Arab-Israeli wars
Israelites, descendants of Hebrew patriarch Jacob **B** 154
Israel Museum J 80
 Shrine of the Book, picture **M** 513

Israëls (E-sra-els), **Jozef** (1824–1911), Dutch painter, b. Groningen. When ill health forced him to live in the fishing village of Zandvoort, near Haarlem, he turned from portrait paintings to the paintings of Dutch fisherfolk and peasants that made him a leader of The Hague school of genre painting (flourished 1870–90). His gray-brown, almost monochrome paintings express great compassion for the inhabitants of Dutch fishing villages and of the Jewish quarter of Amsterdam.

Israfil, or **Israfeel** (ees-ra-FEEL) (probably from Hebrew *Serāfim,* the highest order of angels), Muslim angel of music. According to the Koran, Israfil, Gabriel, and Michael were the angels who warned Abraham of Sodom's destruction. Israfil was Mohammed's companion for 3 years until Gabriel replaced him. Israfil is enormous, has four wings, and is covered with hair, mouths, and tongues. Called Lord of the Trumpet, he will blow the trumpet on Judgment Day.

Issa, Kobayashi, Japanese poet **O** 220b
Issas, a people of Afar-Issa Territory **S** 255
Istanbul (is-tan-BOOL) (formerly Constantinople), Turkey **T** 326; picture **G** 100
 Blue Mosque, picture **T** 323
 Galata Bridge, picture **E** 319
 See also Constantinople
Isthmus, geographical term **G** 96
 See also isthmuses by name, as Panama, Isthmus of

Istria (IS-tree-a), peninsula in the Adriatic Sea. Often a source of conflict among Yugoslavia, Italy, and Austria, most of the area was ceded to Yugoslavia in 1947. The population is mostly Yugoslav and Italian; the chief city is Pola. The peninsula covers about 2,000 square miles.

István see Stephen, Saint, of Hungary
I.T.A. see Initial Teaching Alphabet
Italian architecture I 458–73
 baroque period **B** 56–57, 59
 Foundling Hospital, Florence **A** 438e–438f; picture **R** 165

 Palladian style **A** 383–84
 Renaissance **A** 380–81; **R** 161–62, 163–64
Italian art I 458–73
 art, the meanings of **A** 438
 baroque period **B** 55–59
 Bellini family **B** 134
 Dutch and Flemish art influenced by **D** 352
 futurism, modern art movement **M** 391
 humanism in Renaissance art **A** 438e–438f
 painting **P** 18, 20–21, 23; pictures **A** 438a, 438c
 Renaissance **R** 161–62, 163–70
 sculpture **S** 98–99
 Uffizi gallery **U** 2–3
 Venetian glass **B** 341–42; **G** 229
 See also names of artists
Italian language I 474
 Switzerland **S** 495
Italian literature I 474–81
 Dante **D** 38
 novelists **N** 347
 Renaissance period **R** 159–60
Italian music I 482–86
 opera's beginning **O** 130–31
 See also names of Italian musicians
Italian Somaliland now Somalia **S** 254
Italics, or underlining, punctuation **P** 532
 book arts **B** 322
Italic type T 345
Italy I 446–57
 beehive houses, picture **H** 175
 favorite foods **F** 341; picture **F** 336
 flag **F** 239
 gardens, pictures **G** 32, 33
 holidays **H** 150, 152
 national anthem **N** 20
 Rome **R** 312–17
 San Marino, a republic within Italy **S** 35–36
 theater **T** 160
 Vatican City **V** 280–82
Italy, history of I 454–57
 ancient Roman civilization **A** 231–32; **R** 303
 Ethiopia **E** 303
 Fascism comes to power **F** 63
 Garibaldi **G** 57
 Mazzini, Giuseppe **M** 186
 Mussolini, Benito **M** 552
 political parties **P** 378
 Renaissance **R** 157–62
 World War I **W** 275–81
 World War II **W** 284, 297
 See also Punic Wars; Roman Empire; Rome, ancient
Itasca (i-TAS-ca) **State Park,** Minnesota
 source of the Mississippi River **M** 333
I think, therefore I am, philosophical reasoning of Descartes **F** 438

Iturbi, (e-TOUR-be), **José** (1895–   ), Spanish pianist and conductor, b. Valencia. He graduated (1912) from the Paris Conservatory with honors and began his career as a virtuoso after teaching in the Geneva Conservatory (1919–23). He went to the United States (1938) and was conductor of the Rochester Philharmonic Orchestra (1936–44). He has been guest conductor with major world orchestras and has appeared in movies.

Iturbide (i-toor-BI-day), **Agustín de,** Mexican emperor **M** 248
Ivan I (iv-ON), Russian grand prince **M** 466
Ivan III, the Great, Russian grand prince **M** 467; **U** 48
 architecture he promoted **U** 53

Ivan the Terrible (Ivan IV Vasilievich) (1530–1584), czar

Ivan the Terrible (continued)
of Russia (1533–84). He succeeded his father, Basil III (1533), and at age 17 was crowned czar of All the Russias—the first to use the title officially. During his reign he introduced a new code of law and established diplomatic and commercial relations with England. But after 1560 he developed a deep distrust of all with whom he came in contact. He created a special royal domain that eventually included half the territory of the state, with a special police force that committed great cruelties in order to prevent treason. He used his immense powers, unlimited by any form of control, to torture and execute a vast number of people. He even murdered his son and heir, Ivan, in a fit of anger (1581).
Moscow, the state, in Russian history **M** 467; **U** 48

Ivan V, Russian ruler **P** 168

Ives, Burl (Burl Icle Ivanhoe Ives) (1909–   ), American folk singer, b. Hunt, Ill. He has made many world tours, singing American folk songs. He has published collected folk music in *Burl Ives Song Book* and also recorded series *Historical America in Song* for Encyclopædia Britannica. He starred in movies *So Dear to My Heart* and *The Big Country* (won 1959 Oscar).

Ives, Charles, American composer **I** 487; **U** 126
modern music **M** 401

Ives, Joseph Christmas (1828–1868), American soldier and explorer, b. New York, N.Y. He was put in command of an expedition to explore the Colorado River (1857–58), and his detailed report added greatly to the knowledge of that little-known region. He was also engineer and architect of the Washington national monument (1859–60), astronomer and surveyor for a commission surveying the California boundary (1860–61), and an engineering officer in the Confederate Army during Civil War.

Ivoiriens, Ivory Coast citizens **I** 489
Ivory **I** 487–88
Byzantine carvings **B** 486–87, 489–90
decorative arts **D** 68, 70
elephant tusks **E** 169
Ivory-billed woodpeckers, birds **B** 232; picture **B** 230
Ivory Coast **I** 489–92
flag **F** 235
thatched houses, pictures **A** 303, **I** 490

Ivy League, term referring to a group of colleges and universities located in the northeastern part of the United States, and to the athletic league in which these schools compete. The schools include Harvard, Yale, Columbia, Princeton, Brown, Cornell, Dartmouth, and Pennsylvania. The term "Ivy League" connotes such characteristics as high scholastic achievement, prestige, and sophistication.

Iwanowski, Dmitri, Russian scientist **V** 362
I Wish That My Room Had a Floor, poem by Gelett Burgess **N** 274

Iwo Jima (E-wo JI-ma), an island in northwestern Pacific, largest of the Volcano group. Formerly under Japanese rule, it was occupied by United States Marines during World War II. Administered by the United States 1945–68, it was then returned to Japan.
Volcano Islands **P** 8

Iwo Jima, battle of (1945), important engagement for United States forces before the occupation of Japan. Iwo Jima, a volcanic island heavily fortified by the Japanese, was bombarded from sea and air before it was assaulted by U.S. Marines (Feb. 19, 1945). A famous photograph shows a group of Marines, after fierce fighting and heavy losses, raising the U.S. flag on Mt. Suribachi.
World War II **W** 305

I.W.W. see Industrial Workers of the World

Ixion (IX-e-on), in Greek mythology, King of the Lapiths, and father of the centaur monsters. For daring to love Hera, queen of the gods and wife of Zeus, he was banished to Tartarus to burn forever on a fiery, revolving wheel.

Ixtacihuatl (i-sta-CI-hua-tel), extinct volcano, Mexico **M** 242

Izaak Walton League of America, private conservation organization with nationwide membership. It was founded (1922) for preservation of wildlife and soil and water resources. It has headquarters in Glenview, Ill., and publishes *The Izaak Walton Magazine.*

Izalco (i-ZOL-co), volcano in El Salvador **E** 181
Izmir (eez-MERE), formerly Smyrna, Turkey **T** 326
Izvestia (eez-v'YEST-ya) Soviet newspaper **U** 41

ILLUSTRATION CREDITS

The following list credits, by page, the sources of illustrations used in Volume I of THE NEW BOOK OF KNOWLEDGE. Credits are listed illustration by illustration —left to right, top to bottom. Wherever appropriate, the name of the photographer or artist has been listed with the source, the two being separated by a dash. When two or more illustrations appear on one page, their credits are separated by semicolons.

J, 10th letter of English alphabet **J** 1
  See also Alphabet
  a type of humor **H** 279

Jabbar, Kareem Abdul (Lew Alcindor) (1947–), American basketball player, Negro, b. New York City. Over 7 feet tall, he led UCLA to three national titles as college player and won All-American honors each year (1967–69). He then played for Milwaukee Bucks of National Basketball Association, winning Rookie of the Year award (1970) and leading Bucks to NBA title in 1971, when he was named Most Valuable Player. A Muslim, he changed his name from Alcindor in 1971.

Jābir ibn-Hayyān (JA-bir ibn-hy-YAIN) or Geber, Arabian alchemist **C** 207
J'Accuse, Zola's letter **Z** 371
Jabberwocky, nonsense poem by Lewis Carroll **N** 272–73
Jack, a kind of naval flag **F** 243
  United States **F** 230
Jackals, wild dogs **D** 247; picture **D** 246
Jack and Jill, nursery rhyme **N** 404
Jackass penguin, local name for African, or black-footed, penguin **P** 126
Jackdaws, birds, picture **P** 84
  nest, picture **B** 213

Jack Frost, an imaginary creature personifying cold and frosty weather. He is thought to be a busy little elf who nips people's noses and makes them red and paints windows and bare tree branches with silvery crystals.
  Jack Frost does not paint the leaves **T** 282

Jack Horner, nursery rhyme **N** 408
Jack-in-the-pulpits, flowers, picture **W** 168
Jack-knife dive **D** 231
Jackling, Daniel Cowan, American engineer **U** 253

Jack-o'-lantern (also jack-with-a-lantern), Halloween emblem possibly symbolizing a nightwatchman or a man carrying a lantern. It is a hollowed-out pumpkin or turnip with holes cut for the face and a light inside.

Jack plane, tool, picture **T** 213
Jackrabbits **R** 23
Jacks, in electricity **T** 57–58
Jacks, or jackstones, game **J** 2
Jacks, hydraulic **H** 303
Jackscrew, picture **W** 250
Jackson, Andrew, 7th president of United States **J** 3–7
  Adams, John Quincy, political opponent **A** 14–15
  defeats Creek Indians in Alabama **A** 112
  opposed central banking system **B** 47
  Polk's relations with Jackson **P** 383
  presidential leadership **P** 449–50
  spoils system **C** 317
  War of 1812 **W** 12
Jackson, capital of Mississippi **M** 360; picture **M** 361

Jackson, Helen Hunt (Helen Maria Fiske Hunt Jackson) (1830–1885), American writer, b. Amherst, Mass. She wrote *A Century of Dishonor,* report on the treatment of American Indians, and was appointed a U.S. special commissioner to study the problems of the Mission Indians (1882). She is best-known for her novels *Mercy Philbrick's Choice* and *Ramona.*
  literature especially to appeal to older girls **C** 240

Jackson, Henry Martin (1912–), American legislator, b. Everett, Washington. He was elected to Congress (1940) and to the United States Senate (1953). Jackson is chairman of the Interior and Insular Affairs Committee.

Jackson, Mahalia (1911–72), American gospel singer, Negro, b. New Orleans, La. A contralto, she was a concert performer in the United States and Europe and a popular recording artist.
  gospel songs **N** 102, 106

Jackson, Rachel Donelson Robards, wife of Andrew Jackson **F** 167–68; **J** 4, 6
Jackson, Sarah Yorke, acting first lady in Jackson's administration **F** 168–69
Jackson, Sheldon, American educator **A** 142
Jackson, Thomas Jonathan ("Stonewall"), American Confederate general **J** 8
  Civil War campaigns **C** 323, 325
  Jackson's Mill, West Virginia restoration **W** 138
  Lee and Jackson **L** 125, 126
Jacksonian Democracy, Era of **J** 3, 5–6
Jacksonville, Florida **F** 270
Jack Sprat, nursery rhyme **N** 403

Jacob (JAY-cob), son of Isaac and Rebekah. According to Old Testament (Gen. 25:19–50:15), he was father of twelve sons who founded Twelve Tribes of Israel.
  Esau and Jacob, sons of Isaac **I** 413

Jacobean (jac-o-BE-an) **period,** in England
  English literature **E** 253
Jacobins (JAC-o-bins), extremists in French Revolution **F** 467
  political parties in France **P** 379

Jacobites (JA-co-bites) (from Latin *Jacobus,* James), name given to the supporters of the exiled Stuart king, James II, and his descendants. The movement was organized in 1688 after the Glorious Revolution, when William and Mary became England's rulers.

Jacobs (JAY-cobs), **Helen Hull** (1908–), American tennis champion, b. Globe, Ariz. She was the first player to win the national women's singles crown at Forest Hills, N.Y., for 4 consecutive years (1932–35). She won Wimbledon title (1936). Among her books are an autobiography *Beyond the Game;* and *Famous American Women Athletes.*

Jacobs, Joseph, Australian fabulist **F** 4
  collections of stories for storytelling **S** 435

Jacob's ladder, a flexible ladder of rope and chain used on ships. The name comes from the Old Testament (Gen. 28:12). According to the Biblical story the patriarch Jacob dreamed that he saw angels of God going up and down a ladder that extended from heaven to earth.

Jacobson's organs, specialized nerve cells
  lizards **L** 319
  snakes **S** 213
Jacob's Well, Sychar, Jordan **W** 66
Jacquard (ja-CAR), **Joseph Marie,** French weaver and inventor **A** 532
  rugs and carpets **R** 352
  textiles **T** 141
Jacquards, figured textile weaves **T** 141
Jade, a gemstone **J** 9–10
  China, decorative carvings **D** 69
  oriental art **O** 217; picture **O** 214
  types of gemstones **G** 75
Jadeite (JADE-ite), gem mineral **G** 75; **J** 9
Jaffa, Israel **I** 443–44
Jaffna Peninsula, Ceylon **C** 179
Jagello (ya-GHEL-lo), Polish king **P** 361
Jagellonian (yag-el-LO-nian) **University,** Cracow, Poland **P** 358

Jaguar Devouring a Hare, sculpture by Barye **S** 102
Jaguars, wildcats **C** 138
    Indian (Olmec and Chavin) art symbol **I** 152, 155
Jaguarundi (jag-uar-UN-di), or otter-cats **C** 141
Jahan, Shah see Shah Jahan
Jahangir (ja-hong-EER), Mogul emperor of India **I** 133

Jahn (YAHN), **Friedrich Ludwig** (1778–1852), German teacher and patriot, b. Lanz. With the twofold purpose of strengthening German youth and unifying national resistance to Napoleonic rule, he opened the first outdoor gymnasium in Berlin. Out of this program developed the *Turnvereine,* gymnastic associations that spread throughout Germany.

Jai alai (HI-lie), sport **J** 10–13
    Cuba **C** 547
Jails, places of short-term imprisonment **P** 468
Jainism (JY-nism), religion **I** 131
    food taboos **F** 334
    religions of the world **R** 147
    temple, in Calcutta, picture **C** 10
Jaipur (JAP-oor), India **I** 132
Jakarta see Djakarta

Jalisco (hah-LEES-co) (pop. 3,350,000), state of southwest Mexico bordering Pacific Ocean. It is the second most populated state in Mexico and is rich in agricultural products, minerals, and timber. Lake Chapala, the largest freshwater lake in Mexico, is a popular tourist attraction. Jalisco's capital is Guadalajara, a major manufacturing center and Mexico's second largest city.

Jam see Jelly and jam
Jamaica **J** 14–18
    Caribbean Sea and islands **C** 116–19
    flag **F** 241
    life in Latin America **L** 47–61
Jama Masjid (ja-ma mos-JED), mosque, Delhi **D** 102–03
Jamborees
    Boy Scouts **B** 357
James, book of Bible, New Testament **B** 162
James, Henry, American novelist **J** 18; picture **N** 348
    American literature **A** 206
    themes of his novels **N** 346, 349
James, Jesse, American outlaw **J** 19
James I, king of Great Britain (James VI of Scotland) **E** 179
    American colony grants **A** 183, 185
    Bible, King James Version **B** 153–54; **E** 253
    England and Scotland had the same king **E** 222; **S** 89
    Raleigh condemned to death by **R** 101
James II, king of Great Britain **E** 224
    Ireland **I** 390
James VI, king of Scotland see James I, king of Great Britain

James, Marquis (1891–1955), American author, b. Springfield, Mo. He wrote historical biographies and books about American business institutions such as insurance companies and banks. He won Pulitzer prizes for *The Raven, a Biography of Sam Houston* (1940); and for *Andrew Jackson, Portrait of a President* (1938). *The Cherokee Strip* recalls his boyhood.

James, Saint, the Elder, one of the 12 Apostles **A** 332, 333
James, Saint, the Younger, one of the 12 Apostles **A** 333
James, Will (William Roderick James), American writer and illustrator **M** 441
James, William, American psychologist and philosopher **J** 19

James Bay, Canada **C** 52
Jameson, Leander, South African political leader **S** 273
    Rhodes, Cecil, and Jameson **R** 227
James River, Virginia **J** 20; **V** 358
Jamestown, Virginia **J** 20–21
    American colonies **A** 184–85
    Bacon's Rebellion **B** 8–9
    British colonial flag **F** 228
    colonial life in America **C** 385
    glassmaking **G** 230
    Indian wars started with massacre **I** 212
    Smith, John **S** 201
    tobacco **T** 200
Jamestown Festival Park, Virginia **V** 354; picture **V** 355
Jammu, district of Kashmir **K** 197
Jam sessions, improvisations of jazz music **J** 60
Jane Avril, poser by Toulouse-Lautrec **T** 229
Jane Eyre (AIR), novel by Charlotte Brontë **B** 408
Janequin (jon-KAN), **Clément,** French composer **F** 444; **R** 173
Janney, Eli H., American inventor **R** 90

Jansenism, position formulated by Cornelis Jansen (1585–1638), a Roman Catholic Dutch theologian, and based on his interpretation of works of Saint Augustine. His view of predestination was declared heretical. He also opposed justification by faith alone and maintained that membership in Catholic Church was necessary for salvation. Jansenism's most famous convert was Blaise Pascal (1623–62).
    Pascal's *Thoughts* (*Pensées*) **F** 438

Jansky, Karl Guthe (1905–50), American radio engineer, b. Norman, Okla. He is known as the father of radio astronomy because he was the first to recognize microwaves, the shortest radio waves.
    how radio astronomy began **R** 69; **T** 64

Janssen (YON-sen), **Hans and Zacharias,** Dutch spectacle makers **M** 283

Januarius (jan-u-AIR-ius), **Saint** (San Gennaro) (?–305?), Christian bishop martyred during reign of Diocletian. He is the patron saint of Naples, where relics believed to be his are preserved. Periodically, solidified blood contained in a flask becomes liquid when brought near a silver bust believed to contain head of Saint Januarius. This occurrence has not been explained by natural causes.

January, first month of year **J** 22–23
Janus (JAY-nus), Roman god **J** 22
    January **N** 208
Japan **J** 24–48
    art class, picture **E** 81
    automation, picture **A** 531
    baseball **B** 78
    Big Wave, The, by Pearl Buck, excerpt **B** 421–22
    Buchanan received first delegates to United States, picture **B** 420
    Buddhism and Zen Buddhism **B** 424
    costumes, traditional, picture **C** 349
    cultured pearls **P** 114–15
    dance **D** 33; picture **D** 32
    drama **D** 292–93
    earthquakes **E** 36
    Expo '70, at Osaka **F** 18; **J** 40; picture **F** 9
    fans **F** 43
    Fillmore authorizes expedition to open trade relations **F** 125
    fishing industries **A** 462
    flag **F** 237

flag in World War II F 227
flower arranging J 49–53
folk dancers, picture F 298
funeral customs F 492
garden, picture G 34
holidays H 150, 158–59; J 29–32
houses H 171
immigration to United States, restrictions I 100
Japanese family, picture F 39
judo and karate J 146–47; K 194
kite fighting, sport K 266
literature O 220b–220d
Manchuria, invasion of, 1931 W 284
marriage rites W 102
national anthem N 19–20
ocean liners and cruise ships O 19
origami O 222–26
Osaka O 231–32
pearl farm, picture P 113
Perry, Matthew C., opens trade relations P 156
protest meeting of miners, picture L 10
publishers of paperback books P 58, 58a
religions B 424; J 24; R 148–49
retail stores R 188
rice paddies, picture R 232
samurai (warrior) doll, picture D 264
Scout World Jamboree, 1971 B 357
Shintoism R 148–49
skiing and skating, pictures G 102; M 498
Stamp week stamp, picture S 399
super-speed train, picture R 89
theater T 163–64
Tokyo T 204–08
tsunami waves E 36
war crimes trials W 9–10
War in China, 1937 C 272
World War I W 272, 275
World War II W 292–95, 297–98, 307–08
Zen Buddhism B 424

Japan Current, or Kuroshio (koor-o-SHE-o), warm ocean current of the Pacific Ocean. A dark-colored current (*kuroshio* means "black stream" in Japanese), it is a branch of the North Equatorial Current. It washes the eastern shores of Formosa, flows northward toward Japan, and turns east to sweep along the coast of North America. Its warm waters affect coastal temperatures, rainfall, and fog conditions.
climate of Japan J 34
North America, effect on N 289

Japanese architecture O 219
houses of paper and wood H 171
Japanese art O 217–19'
art as a record A 438f
folk art, pictures F 291, 292
Japanese prints G 303; pictures G 305; O 218
scroll drawing, picture D 134
Japanese beetles P 284–85
plant pests P 288–89
Japanese drama D 292–93
Japanese flower arranging J 49–53
Japanese in the United States
Hawaii H 63
relocated as aliens, 1942 A 166
Japanese language L 40
Japanese typewriter, picture T 348
Oriental literature O 220
Japanese literature O 220b–220d
Japanese prints G 303; pictures G 305, O 218
Japan Sea O 48
Japan wax W 69

Jargon codes C 371
Jarmo (jar-MOO), Iraq
archeological test pits and findings, pictures A 357, 358

Jarring, Gunnar V. (1907–   ), Swedish diplomat, b. Brunnby. After serving his country as minister to India, Pakistan, and Iraq, he became its permanent representative to the United Nations (1956–58). He served on the Security Council (1957–58) and was appointed ambassador to the United States (1958–64) and then to the Soviet Union (1964–   ). He heads the special U.N. Mission to the Middle East (1967–   ).

Jarves (JAR-ves), **Deming,** American glassmaker G 234
antiques and antique collecting A 319

Jarvis, Anna (1864–1948), American founder of Mother's Day, b. Grafton, W. Va. Miss Jarvis' efforts to honor her mother, Mrs. Anna Reeves Jarvis, resulted in a Mother's Day observance in 1908 in Grafton and in Philadelphia. Miss Jarvis worked for the passage of a resolution in the U.S. Congress (1914) making the 2nd Sunday in May a national holiday to honor all mothers.
Mother's Day H 156, 158; W 139

Jason (JAY-son), hero in Greek mythology G 364, 365
Jasper, opaque quartz Q 7
Jasper, Wedgwood pottery P 419
Jasper National Park, Alberta, Canada J 54–55
Alberta, places of interest A 146a
Athabasca Glacier, picture G 223
Jassy (YA-sy), Rumania R 357
Jataka (JA-ta-ka), folk tales and fables from India F 3
Jaundice, disease D 206
Java, island of Indonesia I 218; pictures A 467, I 220
coffee C 371
Java man, or Pithecanthropus erectus P 442;
picture A 305
prehistoric period in southeast Asia I 222; S 334
tools, pictures P 444
Java Sea O 48
Javelin (JAV-el-in) **throw,** field event T 241

Javits, Jacob Koppel (1904–   ), U.S. Senator from New York, b. New York City. A leader in the liberal wing of the Republican Party, he started his career as a trial lawyer after graduating from N.Y.U. Law School. A U.S. Congressman for four terms (1947–55), Javits was elected to the U. S. Senate in 1956, 1962, and 1968.

Jawara, David Kairaba, first persident of The Gambia G 9
Jaws, framework for holding the teeth M 65; T 48
fishes F 182
snakes S 212
Jay, John, American statesman and jurist J 56
Federalist, The F 78
Jayadeva, Indian poet O 220e
JAYCEES see Junior Chamber of Commerce
Jayhawk, or Jayhawker, **State,** Kansas K 177, 191
Jayhawkers, free-state men of pre-Civil War days C 320
Jays, birds, pictures B 245, 247
crow family, "talking birds" P 86
Jay's Treaty, 1794 J 56
Jazz J 57–62
African music A 77, 78
clarinet a brilliant solo instrument C 329
dance craze in United States D 27
dance music influenced by D 37
gospel song N 106
Handy, W. C. H 34

Jazz (continued)
 Jazz Museum in New Orleans **N** 196
 pick and electric guitars **G** 409
 rock music, development of **R** 262a, 262d
Jazz Age, or the Roaring 20's, United States **C** 496
 Fitzgerald, F. Scott **A** 211
Jazz Singer, The, first talking film **M** 474
JDL see Jewish Defense League
Jealousy, feeling of, psychology **M** 220–21
Jeanne d'Arc see Joan of Arc
Jeanneret, Charles Édouard see Le Corbusier

Jeans, Sir James Hopwood (1877–1946), English physicist, b. Birkdale. He made contributions in the fields of physics, mathematics, and astronomy. He is best known for his theories on the origins of nebulae and planetary systems. His best-known books are *Through Space and Time* and *The Universe Around Us.*

Jebba, Nigeria, picture **R** 245
Jebel Druze, mountainous region of Syria **S** 507

Jeep, GI nickname for military car in use during World War II. The word was coined from the initials "G.P." of vehicle's official army name, "General Purpose Car."

Jeffers, Robinson, American poet **A** 210
 "Summer Holiday," poem **P** 355
Jefferson, Martha Wayles Skelton, wife of Thomas Jefferson **J** 64
Jefferson, Thomas, 3rd President of United States **J** 63–69
 agriculture, interest in **A** 100; **F** 58
 American literature **A** 198
 archeology, interest in **A** 350
 architectural contributions **A** 384; pictures **A** 384, **V** 356
 as Vice-president, picture **V** 325
 author of Declaration of Independence **D** 61, 63
 capital building, Richmond, Virginia, architect of, picture **V** 356
 inventions **I** 335
 Lewis and Clark expedition **L** 162
 Louisiana Purchase **L** 365
 Monroe, James, friendship with **M** 423
 presidential leadership **P** 448–49
 quoted **Q** 20
 Rotunda of the University of Virginia, picture **A** 384
 Virginia, University of, founder **J** 69; **V** 352
Jefferson Airplane, The, American rock music group **R** 262d
Jefferson City, capital of Missouri **M** 378
Jefferson Memorial, Washington, D.C. **W** 32; pictures **J** 69, **W** 34
Jefferson National Expansion Memorial, Saint Louis **S** 18
 places of interest in Missouri **M** 377
Jefferson Street Bridge, Huntington, Indiana **I** 147

Jeffries, James J. (1875–1953), American heavyweight prizefighter, b. Carroll, Ohio. He won the heavyweight title from Bob Fitzsimmons in 11 rounds (1899) and continued fighting, retaining his title, until he retired (1905). He returned to the ring to fight champion Jack Johnson, who defeated him (1910).

Jeffries, John, American physician and scientist **B** 31

Jehovah (Yahweh), personal name of God in the Bible (primarily Old Testament) formed from letters YHWH, which are transliteration of Hebrew divine proper name considered too sacred to say. The name is generally thought to have derived from verb "to be" ("he is" or "will be" or "causes to be"). The shorter form Jah (yah) is found in words such as "hallelujah."

Jehovah's Witnesses, religious group organized as The Watch Tower Bible and Tract Society by Charles T. Russell (1884). Each member is trained by group to be a minister. They believe existing social orders are soon to be destroyed by God at Armageddon and expect a new order to be established under God's kingdom. They refuse to bear arms or take part in observances of national loyalty. International headquarters is in Brooklyn, N.Y. They publish *The Watchtower* semimonthly.

Jekyll, Dr., and Hyde, Mr., characters in *The Strange Case of Dr. Jekyll and Mr. Hyde,* by Robert Louis Stevenson. Dr. Jekyll, a law-abiding physician, concocts a potion to turn himself into Mr. Hyde, a basically brutal person, and then another potion to become Dr. Jekyll again. Finally, unable to find drug to turn himself back into Dr. Jekyll, he becomes frightened of his brute nature and poisons himself. The two symbolize the conflict of good and evil in man's personality.

Jekyll Island, Georgia, picture **G** 143
Jellaba (jel-LA-ba), costume of Muslim women **M** 459; picture **M** 458

Jelly and jam, food preparations made of fruit and sugar cooked together. Jelly is made of strained, clear fruit juice; jams are thick, containing both fruit pulp and juice; preserves or conserves contain fruits in their natural shapes, not cut up or mashed.
 food preservation by means of sugar **F** 348

Jelly candies **C** 98
Jellyfishes **J** 70–75
 fossil, picture **F** 382
 harmful to man **I** 285–86
 largest **A** 265
 locomotion by type of jet propulsion **A** 291
Jena (YAY-nah), battle of **N** 11
Jena, Germany **G** 157

Jenifer, Daniel of St. Thomas (1723–90), American statesman and signer of U.S. Constitution, b. Charles County, Md. He became president of the Maryland Council of Safety (1775). He served in the state senate (1777), the Continental Congress (1778–82), as financial agent of Maryland (1782), and as delegate to the federal convention in Philadelphia (1787).

Jenner, Edward, English doctor **J** 76
 antibodies and antigens **A** 317
 disease, conquest of **D** 214
 medical contributions of the 19th century **M** 207
 vaccination and inoculation **V** 260
Jennet, horse **H** 237
Jenny, spinning see Spinning jenny

Jensen, J. Hans Daniel (1907–), German physicist, b. Hamburg. He and M. G. Mayer shared half of the Nobel prize in physics, 1963 (E. P. Wigner received the other half); each had independently developed the shell concept of atomic nuclei. This concept states that an atom's nucleus is like a series of shells, one within another. Each particle in the nucleus moves in its own definite orbit.

Jenson, (jon-SON), **Nicolas,** French-born Venetian printer **T** 345
 Jenson type **T** 346

Jephthah (JEF-thah), a judge of Israel. Called upon to lead his people against the warring Ammonites, he vowed that, if victorious, he would sacrifice the first of his household to greet him on his return. Unknowing, his little daughter welcomed him, and he was obliged to sacrifice his only child in fulfillment of the vow. The story is told in the Old Testament, Judges 11:1–12.

Jequitinhonha (jek-i-teen-YO-nia) **River,** Brazil **D** 153
Jerboas (jer-BO-as), rodents **R** 279
Jeremiah (jer-e-MY-ah), book of Bible, Old Testament **B** 154, 155
Jeremiah, Hebrew prophet **J** 77
  history of the Jews **J** 105
  Michelangelo painting **B** 158
Jeremiah, Letter of, apocryphal book of Bible **B** 159
Jerez, Spain **S** 357
Jericho (JER-ic-o) Jordan **J** 139
  Joshua captured **J** 141
  Stone Age walls, picture **A** 353
Jeritza (YER-ri-tza), **Maria,** Austrian singer, picture **O** 137
Jerky, dried meat **F** 348
  colonial American beef dish **C** 390
Jerome, Saint **J** 77
  Christianity, history of **C** 283
  quote on classics in literature **C** 334
  Vulgate, Latin version of Bible **B** 153; **R** 289
Jersey, breed of dairy cattle **C** 147; **D** 8; picture **D** 5
Jersey, one of the Channel Islands, Great Britain **I** 428
Jersey City, New Jersey **N** 177
Jerstad, Luther G., American mountain climber **E** 337
Jerusalem (je-RU-sa-lem) **J** 78–81
  Biblical origins of the Jews and Judaism **J** 103
  capital city of Israel **I** 443
  Christianity after fall of Jerusalem **C** 279, 281
  Crusaders attack **C** 539, 540; picture **C** 538
  David conquered **D** 44
  eastern part of Jerusalem **J** 138
  Jesus Christ **J** 84
  Latin Kingdom established **R** 292
  museum, Shrine of the Book, picture **M** 513
  Temple built by Solomon **S** 252
Jerusalem, Council of A.D. 50 **R** 288
Jerusalem artichokes, underground stems **G** 41
Jessamine see Jasmine
Jesselton, now Kota Kinabalu, capital of Sabah, Malaysia **M** 55
Jesters, or fools **J** 133
  jester makeup, picture **P** 340
Jesuits, or Society of Jesus, religious order **R** 294
  Canada, missionaries to **O** 128
  Christianity, history of, rise of monastic orders **C** 287
  Loyola, Saint Ignatius, founder **L** 369
  Martyrs' Shrine, near Midland, Ontario **O** 125
  Micmac Indians of Nova Scotia **I** 171
  missions and missionaries **M** 348
  Paraguay **P** 65–66
Jesus Christ **J** 82–84
  Bible **B** 152, 159–62
  Boy Jesus, Bible story **B** 168–69
  Byzantine art depicting **B** 484, 488, 489
  Christ Choosing Two Disciples, by Duccio di Buoninsegna, painting **C** 280
  Christmas **C** 289–94
  Easter **E** 41
  John the Baptist **J** 122
  Last Supper, The, painting by Leonardo da Vinci **A** 332
  Mary, Virgin **M** 113
  Nativity The, painting by Gerard David **C** 280
  Roman Catholic Church **R** 287
  The Nativity, painting by David **C** 280
  See also Apostles, The; Christianity

Jesus Christ, Superstar, rock opera **M** 543; **R** 262d; picture **R** 262c
Jet, mineral **G** 76
Jet airplanes **A** 557–58, 573, 574; pictures **A** 573, **I** 230
  environment, effect on **E** 272c–272d
  jet engines **J** 85–87
Jet engines **J** 85–87
  missiles **M** 345
  reaction engines **E** 211
  space exploration, engines for **S** 348
  supersonic planes, use in **S** 471–72
Jethro, priest of Midian **M** 468
Jet propulsion **J** 85–87
  airplane models use gas-jet cartridges **A** 105
  airplanes **A** 557–58, 573, 574
  engines compared **E** 211
  gas turbine engine **I** 308
  Goddard's work **G** 246
  kerosene as a fuel **K** 235
  locomotion in water of certain animals **A** 266, 291
  turbine combined with a propeller **T** 322
Jetsam see Flotsam, jetsam, and lagan, or ligan
Jet streams, of air, at high altitudes **J** 88–91; **A** 480
  weather and climate **W** 85
Jetty see Breakwater
Jeunesses Musicales du Canada (juh-NESS mu-si-CAL du ca-na-DA), Les **C** 63
Jeux (JUH), ballet, by Claude Debussy **M** 401
Jewel bearings, of watches and clocks **W** 48
Jewelry **J** 92–101
  African art **A** 72
  birthstones **G** 72–73
  decorative arts through the ages, pictures **D** 71
  diamonds **D** 153, 156
  gemstones **G** 68–76
  gold, standard alloys of **G** 248
  how to make with shells or macaroni **I** 224
  jade **J** 9–10
  pearls **P** 113–15
  silver **S** 181
  What is a carat? **J** 92
  wire **W** 190b
Jewels, Spanish game **C** 547
Jewelweeds, flowers, picture **W** 168
Jewett, Sarah Orne, American writer **A** 204
  children's literature **C** 240

Jewish Defense League (JDL), group organized in 1968. Its purpose was to act as a neighborhood anti-crime patrol. More recently the League has been involved in a series of militant demonstrations, most of them calling attention to the plight of Soviet Jews. The group claims 10,000 members in New York and other U.S. cities. Controversial director, Rabbi Meir Kahane, has been arrested for disorderly conduct and manufacturing explosives.

Jewish Theological Seminary of America, academic center of conservative Judaism. Located in New York, it has a co-educational undergraduate college, a graduate school for advanced Jewish studies, a rabbinical department, and a cantors' institute. Its branch, the University of Judaism in Los Angeles, consists of an undergraduate school and a limited graduate school.

Jewish War Veterans of the U.S.A. (JWV), organization of American Jewish veterans who served in U.S. wars.

Jewish Welfare Board, National (JWB), federation of national organizations founded (1917) to provide for religious and social welfare of Jews in the armed forces. It merged (1921) with Council of Young Men's Hebrew Association (YMHA). It has its headquarters in New York,

Jewish Welfare Board (continued)
N.Y., and publishes periodicals *Jewish Community Center Program Aids* and *JWB Circle*.

Jewish Women, National Council of, organization that provides programs for social action and related community service, as well as sponsoring overseas projects. It was founded in 1893 and has its headquarters in New York, N.Y.

Jew's harp, small musical instrument. It consists of a lyre-shaped metal frame to which one end of a flexible metal tongue is attached. The other end of the metal tongue is bent at right angles. The player's jaws grasp the frame so that the metal tongue, when plucked with the finger, vibrates between the teeth. Variations of tone are made by changing the size and shape of the mouth cavity. There is doubt about the origin of the name. Some historians believe it to be a corruption of "Jaw's harp"; others think it came from the Dutch *Jeudgtromp,* meaning "child's trumpet."

Jingoism, term applied to any extreme patriotism in support of war. The term originated from popular song "By Jingo," often sung by supporters of British intervention in Russo-Turkish War (1877–78).

Jinnah, Mohammad Ali (1876–1948), Muslim statesman and lawyer of India, b. Karachi (now in Pakistan). He was president of All-India Muslim League (between 1916 and 1948). After 1938 he advocated a separate Muslim state, and when Dominion of Pakistan was established (1947), he became its first governor-general.
  Pakistan, history of P 40

Joel, minor prophet, son of Pethuel. He lived in Judah and prophesied in Jerusalem, but nothing more is known about him. The book of Joel is one of the 12 minor prophetical books of the Old Testament.

Joffre (JOFFR), **Joseph Jacques Césaire** (1852–1931), French army officer, b. Rivesaltes. As commander in chief of French armies (1914–16) and head of allied armies in France, he was responsible for victory of the Marne (1914), which prevented German entry into Paris. He became a marshal of France (1917).
  World War I W 272

John, Augustus Edwin (1879–1961), British artist, b. Tenby, Wales. His famous portraits include those of James Joyce, Dylan Thomas, George Bernard Shaw, Lloyd George, and Queen Elizabeth II. Other works in oils are *Seraphita*, and *The Orange Jacket*.
    English tradition of portraiture **E** 242

John, I, II, and III, books of the Bible, New Testament **B** 162
    Evangelists, The **E** 335
John, king of England **E** 218
    kings and lords in the Middle Ages **M** 291
    Magna Carta **M** 22
John II, king of France **K** 273
John XXIII, pope **J** 122
    summoned second Vatican Council **R** 298
John, Saint, one of the Twelve Apostles **A** 333
    Christianity, history of **C** 279–80
    Evangelists, The **E** 335
    Gospel of **B** 161
John Asen I and II *see* Asen

John Birch Society, an arch-conservative organization named for a Baptist missionary killed in China. It exists primarily to combat Communism in United States, but it also opposes the UN, NATO, foreign aid, social security, and graduated income tax. It supported presidential candidacy of Barry Goldwater (1964). It was founded in 1958, has its headquarters in Belmont, Mass., and publishes the monthly *American Opinion*.

Johnboats, for float fishing **M** 366
John Brown's Body, song **N** 25

John Bull, name personifying England or a typical Englishman. The British counterpart of United States' Uncle Sam, John Bull was first given a personality in a series of political pamphlets called *A History of John Bull* (1712), by Scottish writer John Arbuthnot. John Bull is frequently depicted as a stocky, dignified gentleman in 18th-century costume, wearing a waistcoat fashioned from a British flag.

John Doe and **Richard Roe** (also called Goodtitle and Troublesome), fictitious plaintiff and defendant in old legal actions of ejectment. The names are now used for argument's sake or for an example, to indicate a person whose name is not known.

John F. Kennedy Center for the Performing Arts, Washington, D.C. **S** 202; **W** 34
John F. Kennedy International Airport, New York City
    holding patterns **A** 565
    immigrants, picture **I** 98
John Henry, American folk hero story, excerpt **F** 314–15
John Newbery medal, book award **B** 310, 310b
Johnny Appleseed, American folk hero story, excerpt **F** 315–16

Johnny Reb (Johnny Rebel), name coined by Union soldiers for Confederates during American Civil War.

Johnny Tremain, novel by Esther Forbes, excerpt **R** 209–10

John of Gaunt (1340–99), English statesman and soldier, b. Ghent, Belgium. The fourth son of King Edward III of England, he became one of the richest and most influential nobles in England. His marriage to Blanche of Lancaster brought him the dukedom of Lancaster (1362). After Blanche's death, he married Constance of Castile, gaining claim to the Castilian throne. He was the power behind the throne during much of the reign of his nephew, Richard II. John's son, Henry Bolingbroke, became King Henry IV, the first of the royal line of Lancaster.

Johns, Jasper, American artist **M** 398; **P** 31
    Numbers in Color **M** 396
Johns Hopkins University, Baltimore, Maryland, picture **M** 122
John III Sobieski (so-bi-ES-ki), Polish king **P** 362
Johnson, Andrew, 17th President of United States **J** 123–26
    as Vice-President, picture **V** 327
    blocks Congress' efforts for Reconstruction **R** 117–19
    impeachment, not to be a weapon for removing political enemies **I** 108
    "not guilty" vote by Edmund Ross **K** 189
    vice-presidents who became presidents **P** 450

Johnson, Charles Spurgeon (1893–1956), American sociologist and educator, b. Bristol, Va. A specialist in race relations in America, he was a faculty member of Fisk University (1928–56) and its second Negro president (1946–56), as well as co-editor of *Race and Culture*.
    Negro Renaissance **N** 98

Johnson, Claudia Alta Taylor, wife of Lyndon B. Johnson **F** 179–80; **J** 131
Johnson, Edward, American writer **A** 195
Johnson, Eldridge, American pioneer in phonograph recording **P** 197
Johnson, Eliza McCardie, wife of Andrew Johnson **F** 172; **J** 123
Johnson, Harriet Lane (Mrs. Henry Elliot Johnson), acting first lady in Buchanan's administration **B** 419; **F** 170–71

Johnson, Jack (John Arthur Johnson) (1878–1946), American boxer, b. Galveston, Tex. He became the first Negro heavyweight champion when he knocked out Tommy Burns at Sydney, Australia (1908), and he held the title until Jess Willard knocked him out at Havana (1915).
    boxing, history of **B** 353

Johnson, James P., American jazz musician **J** 59
Johnson, James Weldon, American author and educator **J** 126; **N** 98

Johnson, John Harold (1918–), American editor and publisher, Negro b. Arkansas City, Ark. He is founder, president, publisher, and editor of Johnson Publishing Co. (founded 1942), which publishes magazines *Ebony*, *Jet*, *Negro Digest*, and *Tan*. Picture **N** 103.
    years of change in Negro history **N** 101

Johnson, "Lady Bird" *see* Johnson, Claudia Alta Taylor
Johnson, Lyndon Baines, 36th president of United States **J** 127–31
    as Vice-President, picture **V** 331
    at the Kennedy inauguration, picture **K** 208
    Great Society program **J** 131; **U** 256
    Lyndon B. Johnson Library **T** 131
    message on plight of American Indians **I** 200a–200b
    Vietnam War, first peace negotiations **V** 337

Johnson, Martin Elmer (1884–1937), American explorer-photographer, b. Rockford, Ill. With his wife, **Osa** (1894–1953), he made photographic explorations of South Sea Islands, Australia, Borneo, and Africa. They filmed vanishing jungle life of Africa for the American Museum of Na-

Johnson, Martin Elmer (continued)
tural History (1924–29). The Johnsons produced 15 motion picture features and a number of books.

Johnson, Mordecai Wyatt (1890–   ), American educator and Baptist clergyman, b. Paris, Tenn. He was the first Negro president of Howard University (1926–60) and transformed the university into a nationally approved institution. He was awarded the Spingarn medal (1929).

Johnson, Philip Cortelyou (1906–   ), American architect b. Cleveland, Ohio. A prominent figure in the field of modern design, he was chairman of department of architecture at New York Museum of Modern Art. Among his works are the Seagram Building in New York (with Mies van der Rohe), the New York State Theater in Lincoln Center (1964), the Sculpture Garden in east wing of N.Y. Museum of Modern Art (1964), and the Kline Biology Science Tower (with Richard Foster) at Yale University (1966). He is co-author of book, *The International Style*.
architecture today **A** 386

Johnson, Rafer (1935–   ), American track and field star, Negro, b. Hillsboro, Texas. He attended the University of California, at Los Angeles, where he was president of the student body. After shattering world records for individual scoring in 1955 and in 1958, he won the decathlon gold medal at the 1960 Olympics and the title of "the greatest all-around athlete in the world."

Johnson, Richard M., vice-president, United States **V** 331; picture **V** 326
Johnson, Samuel, English author **J** 131
English literature, place in **E** 258–59
essays **E** 292–93
first English dictionary **D** 164
oats, definition in dictionary **O** 4
quoted on London **L** 340
Johnson, Walter, American baseball pitcher **B** 78; picture **B** 81
Johnson County Cattle War, 1892, Wyoming **W** 337

Johnston, Joseph Eggleston (1807–91), American Army officer, b. Cherry Grove, Va., He served in Mexican War (1846–48), joined Confederate Army (1861) and commanded all Mississippi forces, including army that lost to Grant at Vicksburg (1863). He was given command of Tennessee forces (1863, 1865) and surrendered to Sherman (1865). He was a member of the House of Representatives (1879–81) and was U.S. commissioner of railroads (1885–91).
Civil War, United States, campaigns of **C** 323, 326

Johnston Island, atoll in the North Pacific, southwest of Hawaii, discovered in 1807, and following World War II used as a nuclear testing site.

Johnstown, Pennsylvania, flood of 1889 **P** 139
disasters to dams **D** 21
John the Baptist, Saint **J** 122
baptizes Jesus **J** 83
John the Evangelist see John, Saint
John the Priest see Prester John
Johore, Straight of, Asia **S** 184
Joining, or constructing, in sculpture **S** 90
Joint Chiefs of Staff, United States **U** 173
U.S. Navy membership **U** 189
Joint FAO/WHO Expert Committee on Food Additives, United Nations **F** 352
Joints, in brick masonry **B** 392
Joints, in the skeleton
body, human **B** 270; diagrams **B** 271

Jokes **J** 132–33
cycles of folk humor **F** 313

Joliot-Curie (jaw-li-O-cu-RE), **Jean-Frédéric** (1900–1958) and **Irène** (1897–1956), French physicists, b. Paris. When Jean-Frédéric Joliot, laboratory assistant to the famous Marie Curie, married Madame Curie's daughter Irène, he added the name Curie to his own to keep it from dying out (the Curies had no sons). Frédéric and Irène worked as a team investigating radioactivity. Their experiments contributed to the discovery of the neutron by the English physicist James Chadwick (1932). In 1934 they created the first artificial radioactivity. For this work they received the Nobel prize in chemistry (1935). Their studies of the heavy elements—particularly uranium—were an important step in achieving nuclear fission.
Marie Curie's daughters **C** 553

Jolliet (jol-li-ET), **Louis,** Canadian explorer **M** 103
discovers and maps Lake Erie **G** 328
exploration of the New World **E** 384
Jolly Miller, The, singing game **G** 12
Jolly Roger, pirate flag **P** 263

Jolson (JOLE-son), **Al** (Asa Yoelson) (1886–1950), American entertainer, b. St. Petersburg (now Leningrad), Russia. He first became known for his distinctive singing style as a blackface minstrel. The songs "Swanee" and "Mammy" became his trademarks. He went on to win even greater popularity in Broadway musical comedies, radio, and motion pictures. *The Jazz Singer*, in which he starred, was the first film to employ sequences with sound (1927).

Jonah (JO-nah), Bible story **B** 166–67
Jonah, book of Bible, Old Testament **B** 155
Jonah, Hebrew prophet **J** 106
Michelangelo painting **B** 158
Jonah and the whale, illustration by Stas Pyke **I** 96

Jonathan (Jonathan Maccabeus) (?–143 B.C.), in the Old Testament, Jewish patriot. He fought under brother Judas for Jewish independence from the Syrians, took over leadership of Judea (160–143 B.C.), became Hasonaean high priest (152 B.C.), and devoted himself to freeing Judea from Syrian domination. He was killed by Tryphon, a Syrian.

Jonathan, son of Saul and friend of David **D** 44
Jonathan, Leabu, Lesotho political leader **L** 156a

Jones, Casey (John Luther Jones) (1864–1900), American railroad engineer, b. Jordan, Ky. His brave deed, which caused his death in a railroad accident, was immortalized in a ballad originally written by Wallace Saunders, a Negro roundhouse worker. According to one version of the event, Casey was driving an Illinois Central train, the Cannonball Express, from Memphis, Tenn., to Canton, Mississippi. Suddenly a stationary freight train loomed into sight ahead of the speeding train. Casey, after ordering his fireman to jump, stayed on the train to apply the brakes. This eased the unavoidable collision and saved the passengers. A bronze tablet was dedicated to his memory in 1938 in Cayce, Ky., where he had lived during his youth and from where he got his nickname, Casey.
burial place and memorial in Tennessee **T** 74

Jones, Inigo, English architect **A** 382
designed masques with Ben Jonson **D** 25
English art and architecture **E** 237
Jones, James, American novelist **A** 213

Jones, James Earl (1931–), American actor, b. Arkabutla, Miss. He learned his craft in Shakespearean repertory, the off-Broadway theater, and television. Jones rose to the status of a celebrated Broadway star when he appeared as Jack Jefferson in *The Great White Hope* (1968–69), based on the career of the first black heavyweight champion, Jack Johnson (1878–1946). Jones won the Antoinette Perry Award for his performance in the play. He repeated his role in the film version.

Jones, John Paul, American naval officer **J** 134–35
  early days of U.S. Navy **U** 185
  John Paul Jones House, New Hampshire **N** 158
  John Paul Jones Memorial, Maine **M** 43
  Revolutionary War **R** 205–06

Jones, LeRoi (Ameer Baraka) (1934–), American novelist, poet, dramatist, and black militant, b. Newark, N.J. A graduate of Howard University, Jones taught at Columbia University and The New School for Social Research. He received a Guggenheim fellowship (1965–66) and a Whitney fellowship (1960–61). Among his published works is *Dutchman and The Slave* (1964).

Jones, Robert Tyre ("Bobby"), American golfer **J** 135;
  picture **G** 261
  golf championships **G** 262
  good sportsmanship in golf **G** 260
Jones, Rufus M., American Quaker leader **Q** 3
Jones, Tom, Welsh singer **R** 262d
Jonesboro, Arkansas **A** 430
Jonker (YON-ker) **diamond D** 156
Jonquils, flowers **G** 42
  See also Daffodil
Jonson, Ben, English playwright and poet **E** 253; picture **E** 252
  designed masques **D** 25
  Elizabethan period in English drama **D** 296
Joplin, Scott, American composer of ragtime music **J** 57
Jordan J 136–39
  desert patrol, picture **P** 376
  flag **F** 237
  Jerusalem, Old City **J** 78–80
  national anthem **N** 22
  Stone Age walls of Jericho, picture **A** 353
Jordan, Camille, French mathematician **T** 224

Jordan, Vernon (1935–), American civil rights leader, b. Atlanta, Georgia. Before assuming the position of Executive Director of the National Urban League in 1971, he was Executive Director of the United Negro College Fund. From 1964 to 1968 he was Director of the Voter Educational Project for the Southern Regional Council.

Jordan River, Israel, Jordan **I** 441–42; **J** 137
Jordan River, Utah **U** 243
Jordan theorem, in topology **T** 224
Jos, Nigeria **N** 254
Joselito, Spanish bullfighter **B** 450
Joseph, chief of Nez Percé Indians **I** 67
  Big Hole National Battlefield, Montana **M** 438
  last battles of the Indian Wars **I** 215
  War of 1877 **I** 176–77
Joseph, Hebrew patriarch (Bible, Old Testament) **J** 140
Joseph II, Holy Roman emperor **A** 525

Joseph, Saint, in New Testament (especially Gospels of Matthew and Luke), carpenter at Nazareth who became husband of Mary and foster father of Jesus. He is said to have lived a singularly humble life and is known as patron saint of workingmen. His feast day is March 19.
  Jesus, and Mary and Joseph **J** 83; **M** 113

Joseph Andrews, novel by Henry Fielding **N** 346
Josephine de Beauharnais (jo-zeph-ENE d'boh-ar-NAY), empress of the French **J** 141
  Napoleon I **N** 10, 11
Josephine Lake, Glacier National Park, Montana, picture **G** 222
Joseph's Well, Cairo **W** 66

Josephus (jo-SEE-fus), **Flavius** (A.D. 37?–100?), Jewish scholar and historian, b. Jerusalem. As governor of Galilee, he took an active part in the Jewish revolt against the Romans (A.D. 66) but he was obliged to surrender to the Roman general Vespasian, who later became emperor. Josephus remained under the new emperor's patronage and adopted Vespasian's family name, Flavius. His best-known books are *History of the Jewish War* and *The Antiquities of the Jews*, both considered essential historical documents to a study of the Jewish people.
  described communities like those referred to in the Dead Sea Scrolls **D** 48
  Greco-Roman period of Greek literature **G** 355

Joshua, book of Bible, Old Testament **B** 154
Joshua, military leader in the Old Testament **J** 141
Joshua tree, pictures **N** 124, **T** 278
Joshua Tree National Monument, California **C** 25;
  picture **N** 54
Josquin des Prez (jo-SCAN day PRAY), Flemish composer **D** 364; **F** 444
  choral music, influence on **C** 277
  Renaissance music **R** 172
Joule (JOOL), **James P.,** English physicist **P** 234; **S** 76
Joules (JOOLS), units of energy **W** 117
Journalism J 142–45
  cartoons, history of **C** 125–28
  freedom of the press **F** 457
  magazines **M** 14–16
  newspapers **N** 197–205
  Pulitzer, Joseph, and Pulitzer prizes **P** 524–28
  University of Missouri, first to grant degree in **M** 375
  Zenger, John Peter **Z** 369
Journals, in bookkeeping **B** 312
Journeymen, of craft guilds **G** 403
Jousting, knightly combat in tournaments **K** 274; picture **A** 443
  now the state sport of Maryland **M** 114
Jove, see Jupiter, Roman god
Joyce, James, Irish writer **I** 395
  themes of his novels **N** 347
  20th century English literature **E** 266–67
Joyce Kilmer Memorial Forest, North Carolina **N** 315

Juan Carlos of Bourbon, Prince (1938–), Spanish nobleman, b. Rome, Italy. Educated at Spain's three military academies, with graduate work at U. of Madrid, Juan Carlos is grandson of Alfonso XIII (1886–1941), king of Spain, who fled when Spain became a republic (1931); and the son of Don Juan (1913–), Count of Barcelona, whom Alfonso named as heir in 1941. In 1969, Franco, Spain's head of state, designated Juan Carlos to succeed him as head of state and to become future king. Don Juan, who lives in Portugal, maintains that he is legitimate heir to the throne.
  Spain, government of **S** 358

Juan de Fuca Strait (HWON de FOO-ca), a body of water separating Vancouver Island, British Columbia, Canada, from the state of Washington. It is 100 miles long, between 11 and 17 miles wide, and connects the Pacific Ocean with Puget Sound on the south and the Strait of Georgia on the north. It was named for a Greek sailor who, legend said, discovered the Strait for Spain in the

Juan de Fuca Strait (continued)
16th century. This was subsequently proven false, but the name was kept.
  western coastal waters of Canada **C** 52

Juan Fernández (fer-NAN-dez) **Islands,** two volcanic islands and one islet about 400 miles west of Valparaiso, Chile. The islands have a moderate climate, and the chief occupation is giant-lobster fishing. Administered by Chile, they also are called Robinson Crusoe Islands because the story of a marooned seaman's 4-year stay there was the inspiration for Daniel Defoe's novel *Robinson Crusoe.*
  Chile, off-shore holdings of **C** 251; **S** 278

Juan Manuel (hu-ON ma-nu-EL), **Don,** Spanish writer **S** 367
Juárez, Benito, Mexican statesman **J** 145; **M** 249
Juba (JU-ba), Sudan **S** 448

Jubilee (JU-bi-lee) (from Hebrew *yobel,* meaning "ram's horn," used as trumpet to proclaim year of jubilee), in Old Testament, a sabbatical year (year of rest) occuring every 50, and occasionally every 7, years. Once characterized by freeing of slaves and forgiveness of debts, it now refers to an anniversary, usually the 50th.

Jubilee Singers of Fisk University **N** 107

Judah (JU-dah), fourth son of Jacob and Leah, b. Haran (northwest of Mesopotamia). In the Old Testament (Genesis), he is said to have advised the selling of his brother Joseph into Egypt as a slave to prevent Joseph's being killed by his jealous brothers. Judah received Jacob's blessing as a ruler of what was later to become the tribe of Judah—one of the 12 tribes of Israel. This was the tribe from which it is said that Jesus was descended.
  Judah, Benjamin, and Joseph **J** 140

Judah, kingdom of **J** 104, 139
Judah, or **Judas, Maccabee,** famous Jewish leader **H** 35
  history of the Jews **J** 105–06
Judah Halevi (ha-LE-vi), Hebrew poet **H** 103
Judaism (JU-da-ism) **J** 114–20
  Abraham, founder of **A** 7
  Apocrypha **B** 156–57, 159
  Bible, Old Testament **B** 152–59
  Dead Sea Scrolls **D** 48–49
  divorce **D** 234
  Ezra **E** 396
  forms of address for the rabbi **A** 21
  funeral customs **F** 494
  Hanukkah **H** 35
  Hasidism **Y** 350
  Hebrew language and literature **H** 100–03
  Israel, religions in **I** 439
  marriage rites **W** 101–02
  moon-sun calendar **T** 194
  moral codes **C** 281
  Passover **P** 93–94
  prayer from the Jewish liturgy **P** 434
  Purim **P** 540
  religions of the world **R** 149
  religious holidays **R** 154
  Talmud **T** 15
  Ten Commandments **T** 72–73
  See also Hillel; Jews
Judaism, University of *see* Jewish Theological Seminary of America
Judas (JU-das) (Thaddaeus), or **Jude, Saint,** one of the Twelve Apostles **A** 333

Judas Iscariot (is-CAR-i-ot), one of the Twelve Apostles **A** 333; **J** 84
Jude, book of Bible, New Testament **B** 162
Jude, Saint or **Judas** (Thaddaeus), one cf the Twelve Apostles **A** 333

Judea (ju-DE-a), southernmost of three areas, including Galilee and Samaria, into which Palestine was divided in Christ's time. In Biblical terms, Judea was also referred to as Kingdom of Judah. Today it is southwestern Israel and western Jordan. The chief cities are Jerusalem and Bethlehem. Judea has both farming and grazing lands.

Judge, in law **J** 159, 160
  courts **C** 528, 530

Judge Advocate General, one of three appointed military officers from each of the armed forces who is attorney and legal adviser to his respective military service. He supervises system of military justice and is responsible for records pertaining to military matters.

Judges, book of Bible, Old Testament **B** 154
Judgment, in law **C** 530
Judicial review, power of the Supreme Court to establish fundamental law **S** 476
  Marshall establishes **M** 112
Judiciary *see* Courts
Judy *see* Punch and Judy
Judith, apocryphal book of Bible **B** 157
Judo **J** 146–47
  Japanese art of self-defense **J** 33
  See also Wrestling

Judson, Clara Ingram (1879–1960) American author of children's books, b. Logansport, Ind. Her books include "They Came From" series, about lives and contributions of immigrants to United States. She wrote biographies, *Abraham Lincoln, friend of the people, Andrew Carnegie, Benjamin Franklin, Mr. Justice Holmes.* She won the Laura Ingalls Wilder Book Award (1960).

Judson, Edward, American writer **G** 422

Judson, Wilfred (1902–), Canadian judge, b. England. A member of the bar of Ontario (1932), he was appointed to Supreme Court of Ontario (1951). He has been a justice of the Supreme Court of Canada since 1958.

Juggernaut (popular form of "Jagannath," meaning "lord of the world"), in Hindu mythology and religion, a form of the deity Krishna and an incarnation of the deity Vishnu. A statue of the Juggernaut is located at Puri, in Orissa, India, and is drawn in procession in an annual festival. The expression "beneath the wheels of the Juggernaut" has come to refer to a powerful force that tends to crush anything in its path.

Jugglers, or **jongleurs,** French entertainers **F** 443
Jugs
  Why does an unglazed ceramic jug keep liquids cool? **C** 175

Jugular (JUG-u-ler) **veins** (from Latin *jugulus,* meaning "collarbone"), veins located on each side of the neck. There are two on each side—the external, or superficial, and the internal, or deeper. The greater part of the blood that has circulated in the head, neck, and face returns to the heart through these veins. The internal veins are much larger than the external. Lacerating an internal jugular vein can be dangerous to life because of rapid blood loss.

Juilliard (JU-li-ard) **Musical Foundation,** organization founded (1920) by Augustus D. Juilliard (headquarters, New York, N.Y.). It aids worthy students of music in securing a complete and adequate musical education; arranges for and gives, without profit to the foundation, musical entertainments, concerts, and recitals; aids the Metropolitan Opera Company; and maintains the Juilliard School of Music.

Juilliard School of Music L 298
Juilliard String Quartet, picture **C** 185
Jujitsu, forerunner of modern judo **J** 146

Jukes, The, the name given to a family that intermarried and produced many criminals, degenerates, and mentally ill in period of over 130 years. A study undertaken (1875) by Richard L. Dugdale suggested that these characteristics were inherited—a conclusion later disputed. This was followed up by Eastabrook (1915), who substantiated Dugdale's findings. The Jukes are similar to the Kallikak family described by H. H. Goddard.

Julian (Flavius Claudius Julianus) (331–363), Roman emperor, known as Julian the Apostate, b. Constantinople. He was brought up as a Christian, but after studying in Athens, he became a pagan and opposed Christianity. As governor of Gaul, Spain, and Britain, he repelled barbarian invaders of Gaul, defeating them in a great battle near what is now Strasbourg (357). He became emperor upon Constantinius' death (361). Julian was an able ruler and did away with many abuses.
   Christianity, history of **C** 283

Julian, Percy Lavon (1899–   ), American chemist, Negro, b. Montgomery, Ala. He derived valuable ingredients for production of Cortisone and other synthetic drugs from natural sources, as soy bean and yam roots. Professor and head of the chemistry department at Howard University (1931–32), he also was president and research director of Julian Laboratories, which he established. He received the Spingarn medal (1947) for his work in chemical research. Picture **N** 99.
   Negro Renaissance **N** 98

Juliana (JOO-li-AN-uh) (Juliana Louise Emma Marie Wilhelmina (1909–   ), queen of the Netherlands, b. The Hague. She married Prince Bernhard of Lippe-Biesterfeld (1937) and has 4 daughters, the princesses Beatrix, Irene, Margarit, and Maria. Juliana and her daughters lived in England and Canada during the World War II German occupation of their country (1940–45). Juliana succeeded to the throne when her mother, Queen Wilhelmina, abdicated (1948). Queen Juliana's reign has been noted for her support of efforts at international co-operation.

Julian calendar C 12
   religious holidays **R** 153
   time by the solar calendar **T** 194
Julian the Apostate see Julian (Flavius Claudius Julianus), Roman emperor
Juliet, heroine of *Romeo and Juliet,* play by Shakespeare **R** 317–18
Juliette Gordon Low Birthplace, National Program Center for Girl Scouts, Savannah, Georgia **G** 219

Julius, name of three popes. **Saint Julius I** (?–352) during his reign (337–352) upheld controversial Athanasius, who was opposed by Arians. **Julius II** (Giuliano della Rovere) during his reign (1503–13), noted for advancement in the arts, arranged League of Cambrai against Venice (1508), formed Holy League against France (1511), and began reconstruction of St. Peter's in Rome (1506). **Julius III**

(Giammaria Ciocchi del Monte) (1487–1555), as pope (1550–55), presided over Council of Trent (1545), attempted religious reform, and advocated papal neutrality in European power struggle.
   Julius II and Michelangelo **M** 257

Julius Caesar see Caesar, Gaius Julius
Julius Caesar, play by Shakespeare **S** 135
Jultomte (YURL-tom-te), Swedish Santa Claus **C** 292
July, seventh month of year **J** 148–49
   July, 1969, calendar, picture **M** 447
   named for Julius Caesar **C** 6
July Fourth see Independence Day
Jumbo, famous circus elephant **E** 171
   circus acts **C** 304
Jumna River, India
   Taj Mahal **T** 14
Jumping, field events **T** 238, 240
Jumping, in skiing **S** 184b
Jumping beans, Mexican **J** 150–51
Jumping mice R 279
Juncos, birds **H** 191; picture **B** 241
June, sixth month of year **J** 152–53
Juneau (JU-no), capital of Alaska **A** 141, 143
Juneau, Solomon, pioneer settler in Wisconsin **M** 312

Jung (YOONG), **Carl Gustav** (1875–1961), Swiss psychologist, b. Basel. He extended theories of his colleague Sigmund Freud (1913) and founded school of analytical psychology. In book *Psychological Types,* Jung originated theory that individuals tend to be either introverted or extroverted. He emphasized the role of myth and the collective unconscious, with its inherited ways of thinking. His other works include *Psychology of the Unconscious.*

Jünger (YOONG-er), **Ernst,** German writer **G** 180
Jungfrau (YOONG-frow), mountain, Switzerland **S** 500
   Alps **A** 174; pictures **A** 175; **M** 492
Jungle Books, by Rudyard Kipling **K** 260
Jungles J 154–56
   tropics **T** 294
   See also Forests and forestry; Rain forest
Junior Achievement, Inc. J 157–58

Junior Chamber of Commerce, United States (JAYCEES), national organization for young men between the ages of 21 and 36 that provides leadership training through civic programs. Founded in 1920, it has headquarters in Tulsa, Oklahoma. It publishes *Future Magazine.*

Junior colleges U 205
   first public junior college **E** 73

Junior Engineering Technical Society (JETS), organization with an international membership of high school and junior college students who have an interest in the engineering sciences. Local groups, with volunteer supervision by scientists, carry out technical and scientific projects. Founded in 1950, the organization has headquarters in New York, N.Y., and publishes *Jets Journal.*

Junior Girl Scouts G 216, 217
Junior Hi Camp Fire Girls C 37; pictures **C** 38, 39
Junior high schools S 58
   education, history of **E** 73–74

Junior Leagues of America, Association of the, women's social welfare organization with branches in United

Junior Leagues of America (continued)
States, Canada, and Mexico. It has more than 96,000 members belonging to 209 local Junior Leagues. Its members, between the ages of 18 and 40, are trained for community volunteer service. They work in programs to stimulate public concern with community affairs in health, education, welfare, art, and culture. Founded in 1921, its headquarters is in New York City.

Junior Red Cross R 127
Junior rodeos R 282
Junior Showmanship, dog handling competition **D** 262

Junk, usually trading or fishing vessel found on the rivers and seas of China and surrounding Southeast Asia. A wooden boat with a high stern and bow, small, if any keel, and from one to five pole masts with cotton sails, it is known for its versatility and hardiness. The word generally refers to any wooden Chinese boat.
Pictures **H** 203, **R** 249

Junkers, Prussian landowning class **B** 250
Juno, Roman goddess **G** 357

Junta (HOON-ta), group of persons organized usually for political or governmental purposes, especially after revolutionary power seizure or in times of government crisis; In Spain and Italy the word refers to an administrative council.

Junto, club organized by Franklin **F** 452
Jupiter, character in Poe's Gold Bug, picture **F** 112
Jupiter, planet **P** 274–76
  comets **C** 418
  Galileo discovers moons revolve around **G** 6
  radio signals **A** 477
  space probes **O** 15; **S** 348–49
Jupiter, Roman god **G** 356

Jura (JOO-ra) **Mountains,** mountain range forming part of Swiss-French border. The mountains extend in parallel ridges from the Rhone River gorge northward to the Rhine near Basel, rising about 5,500 ft.
  landforms of Europe **E** 309; **S** 499

Jurassic (ju-RAS-sic) **period,** in geology **F** 387
  dinosaurs **D** 174; reconstruction showing **D** 177
Jurors **J** 160
Jury **J** 159–60
  courts **C** 528–30
  Magna Carta guaranteed jury trials **M** 22
  trial by jury begins **M** 291
Jus sanguinis, law of the blood, citizenship rule
  C 311–12
Jus soli, law of the soil, citizenship rule **C** 312

Just, Ernest Everett (1883–1941), American biologist, b. Charleston, S.C. He was the first winner of the Spingarn medal, awarded annually to an outstanding American Negro. He received the medal for his researches in biology. He was professor of zoology at Howard University (1912–41), and author of many books on biology.

Justice, administration of
  courts **C** 526–30
  International Court of Justice, the Hague **U** 85
  jury **J** 159–60
  law and law enforcement **L** 87–89
  lawyer's code of ethics **L** 93
  Supreme Court of the United States **S** 476–77
Justice, United States Department of
  Attorney General, head of the department and cabinet

  member **P** 448
  Bureau of Narcotics and Dangerous Drugs **N** 14
  Federal Bureau of Investigation **F** 76–77

Justice of the peace, an official of a town, county, or precinct, with limited judicial and administrative powers. The office may be elective or appointive. Powers and duties differ in different states. A justice of the peace may preside at the trials of small civil suits and crimes involving minor offenses. Among other duties, he may also perform marriage ceremonies. The office, which has existed in United States since colonial times, began in 13th-century England, when the official was known as the keeper, or conservator, of the peace.

Justices, of courts
  Supreme Court **S** 476–77
Justify, to even up lines in printing **P** 463; **T** 344

Justinian I (jus-TIN-i-an) (Flavius Petrus Sabbatius Justinianus) (483–565), called Justinian the Great, Byzantine emperor (527–565) b. Taurisium, Illyricum. He became emperor of the eastern Roman empire upon the death of his uncle Justin I, with whom he had shared power. During his reign he restored to the Roman empire some of its former possessions in Italy and North Africa. His best known work is the collection of Roman laws known as the Justinian Code.
  art as a record **A** 438b
  Byzantine art **B** 483–85
  silk brought out of China **S** 178

Justinian's Code, compilation of early Roman laws and legal principles. Concerned with the law, Justinian I commissioned a group of scholars to draw up a new code clarifying the laws of that time. This was done between A.D. 528 and 534. The code was known as *Corpus Juris Civilis*, which means "body of civil law." It consists of four parts—*Codex*, or *Code*, a collection of statutes and principles; *Pandects*, or *Digest*, writings and decisions of noted Roman jurists; *Institutes*, a text for students and lawyers; and *Novellae*, new laws proposed by Justinian. This code is the basis for much European law today.

Just So Stories, by Rudyard Kipling **K** 261; excerpt **K** 262–65
Jute, fiber **J** 161–62
  soaked in water, India, picture **A** 464
  types of fibers **F** 106

Jutes (JOOTS), early Germanic tribe that shared in the occupation and conquest of England in the 5th century. Little is known of the tribe except that it came from an area near the Rhine River and settled in Kent and on the Isle of Wight. Jutland (now Denmark) may have gotten its name from the Jutes. According to the *Anglo-Saxon Chronicle* (English historical records from about 892–1154), Hengist and Horsa were the leaders of the tribe in the invasion of Britain, but some historians believe these names to be mythical.
  invaders of England and the beginnings of the English language **E** 216, 243

Jutland, battle of, 1916 **W** 276
Jutland Peninsula, Denmark **D** 108
Juvara, Filippo, Italian painter **I** 473
Juvenal, Roman satirist **L** 80
Juvenile delinquency **J** 162–64
  mental illness **M** 223–24
  social work **S** 225
Juveniles, children's books **P** 513

K, eleventh letter of the English alphabet **K** 165
  See also Alphabet
K 2, or Godwin Austen, mountain peak in Kashmir **K** 198
Kaaba (KA-ba), sacred shrine of Islam, in Mecca **M** 196;
  S 48; pictures **I** 415, **M** 196, 307, **S** 44
  Islam **I** 415
  Koran **K** 294
  Mohammed **M** 404, 405
Kabaka (ka-BA-ka), title of former king of Buganda **U** 4, 6
Kabbalah see Cabala
Kabinda see Cabinda
Kabuki (ka-BU-ki), Japanese drama **D** 33, 292–93
  No and Kabuki **J** 32
  theater in Japan **T** 164
Kabul (KA-bul), capital of Afghanistan **A** 42
Kachina dolls, of the Hopi Indians **I** 196
Kadar, Jan, Czech motion-picture director **M** 488a
Kadhimain, Bagdad, Iraq, picture **M** 302
Kadmus see Cadmus
Kaduna, Nigeria **N** 255
Kaédi (KAH-edi), Mauritania **M** 180
Kaffa, province in Ethiopia
  first coffee plants grown in **C** 371

Kaffir (KAF-ur), or **Kafir** (from Arabic, meaning "unbe-
liever"), Bantu-speaking Negro people of South Africa.
The Muslims originally used the word to mean all non-
Islamic people, but later the Europeans adopted it as a
name for the Bantus and their language. The Kaffirs are
divided into several tribes. Their occupations are chiefly
agricultural and hunting.

Kaffir cats **C** 141

Kafka (KOF-ka), **Franz** (1883–1924), Austrian author, b.
Prague, Czechoslovakia (then Austria-Hungary). He received a doctorate in law (1906) and unenthusiastically
held a civil service post most of his adult life. Few of
his works appeared during his lifetime. His friend Max
Brod published posthumously three incomplete novels
—*The Trial* (*Der Prozess*), *The Castle* (*Das Schloss*), and
Amerika. Throughout Kafka's writings run the themes
of man's inability to comprehend God and the absurdity
of human existence.
  themes of his novels **G** 180; **N** 347

Kahanamoku, Duke (1890–1968), American freestyle swimmer, b. Honolulu, Hawaii. He introduced widespread use
of the crawl stroke among American swimmers and won
Olympic gold medals (100-meter race) in 1912 and 1920.
  development of the crawl stroke in swimming **S** 491

Kahl, Virginia (1919–), American author and illustrator
of children's books, b. Milwaukee, Wis. She spent several
years as a librarian in Austria and wrote and illustrated
Away Went Wolfgang, The Duchess Bakes a Cake, and
The Habits of Rabbits. She is co-author (with Edith
Vacheron) of *Voici Henri!* (*Here is Henri!*) and *Encore
Henri!* (*More About Henri!*)
  picture books for children **C** 243

Kahoolawe (ka-hoo-LA-we), one of the Hawaiian Islands
  H 58
Kaibab National Forest **A** 414
Kaibab Suspension Bridge, Grand Canyon, picture **G** 292
Kairouan (kare-WAHN), Tunisia
  Great Mosque, picture **I** 420
Kaiser (KY-zer), **Georg,** German playwright **D** 298

Kaiser, Henry John (1882–1967), U.S. industrialist, b.
Canajoharie, N.Y. Among the more than 70 major construction and industrial projects in which he was active
were the Hoover Dam and the Grand Coulee Dam. During World War II he became the world's largest and
swiftest producer of ships by using assembly-line techniques. He shared in establishing the Kaiser-Frazer Corporation, an automobile manufacturing concern (1945–
55). His last years were spent in developing resort and
community facilities in continental United States and
Hawaii.

Kaiser, title of German rulers **C** 6
  Bismarck made William I kaiser (emperor) of Germany
  B 250
  derived from "Caesar" **C** 6
Kaiser Max see Maximilian I, Holy Roman emperor
Kalahari (ka-la-HA-ri) **Desert,** in southern Africa **B** 340a;
  picture **D** 130
Kalakaua I (ka-la-KOW-a), or **David Kalakaua,** king of
  Hawaii **H** 70
Kalamazoo, Michigan **M** 270

Kalamazoo case (1874), court case involving school
authorities and citizens. The authorities planned to tax
residents for support of high school and hiring of
administrative superintendent, but the residents protested. The state supreme court ruled that the taxes
were legal, setting an important precedent by confirming
state's right to establish schools from elementary level
through university.

Kalambo (ka-LOM-bo) **Falls,** border of Malawi and Tan-
  zania **W** 56b
Kalaupapa (ka-la-u-PA-pa) **leper colony,** now Kalawao
  County, Molokai, Hawaii **H** 59

Kalb, Johann (Baron de Kalb) (1721–1780), German
general in American Revolution, b. Huttendorf. He went
to the United States as a secret agent for France (1768),
joined the Continental Army with Lafayette (1777), and
served at Valley Forge. He was killed in the battle of
Camden, S.C.
  Revolutionary War, campaigns of **R** 202–03

Kale, a hardy cabbagelike vegetable with food value in
large curled leaves that do not form heads.

Kaleidoscope (ka-LIE-do-scope) **K** 166
Kaler, James Otis see Otis, James
Kalevala (KA-lev-a-la), Finnish epic **S** 51
Kalgoorlie, Australia **A** 503, 513
  gold discoveries at the famous Golden Mile **G** 253
Kalidasa (KA-li-da-sa), Indian playwright and poet **D** 293;
  O 220e
Kalikata (ka-li-KA-ta), now Calcutta, India **C** 11
Kalimantan (ka-lim-MON-tan), formerly Dutch Borneo,
  and now a part of Indonesia **B** 336, 338; **I** 218
Kalmar (KOL-mar) **Union,** 1397 **S** 486

Kalmucks (KAL-muks), or Kalmuks, people of Asia, descendants of Mongols who migrated from western China
to Russia (about 1636). Mostly Buddhists, they were
fine fighting men and horsemen and became an important part of the Russian Army. Under Soviet rule
they were granted autonomy (1920), and in 1935 the
Kalmuck Autonomous Soviet Socialist Republic was
formed. Because the Kalmucks were accused of collaborating with the Germans during World War II, the
republic was dissolved (1943). They were exiled to Soviet Central Asia, but they were granted minority rights
in 1957 and permitted to return to their homes.

Kamakura (ka-ma-ku-ra) **period,** of Japanese art **O** 217,
  219

Kamehameha I (ka-may-ha-MAY-ha), king of Hawaiian Islands **H** 70, 71
holiday honoring **H** 149

Kamehameha III, or **Kauikeaouli** (1813–54), Hawaiian king (1825–54). He proclaimed the first Constitution of the Kingdom of Hawaii (1840), which created a supreme court and guaranteed religious freedom. He obtained from the United States (1842) and from Great Britain and France (1843) recognition of the independence of Hawaii. His order of 1848 gave the common people ownership of land for the first time.

Kamehameha IV, or **Alexander Liholiho** (1834–63), Hawaiian king (1854–63). Concerned about the health of his subjects, he asked the legislature to pass a law (1859) setting up a hospital on the main islands. He introduced the use of English in Hawaiian schools and translated into Hawaiian the Episcopal Book of Common Prayer.

Kamehameha Schools, Honolulu, Hawaii **H** 65
Kames, cone-shaped hills **W** 194; picture **I** 14

Kamikaze (ka-mi-KA-ze) (from Japanese, meaning "divine wind"). Japanese legend tells that typhoons sent by the Sun Goddess defeated the Mongol Kublai Khan's attempted invasions of Japan in 1274 and 1281. During World War II, *Kamikaze* referred to members of Japanese suicide air corps assigned to destroy a target (usually a ship) by a crash dive.
Kamikaze Corps in World War II **W** 305

Kamloops, British Columbia **B** 406d
Kampala (kom-PA-la), capital of Uganda **U** 6; picture **U** 4
Kanagawa, Treaty of, 1854 **J** 46; **P** 156
Japan opened to trade **P** 248
Kanchenjunga (kan-chen-JUN-ga), mountain in Himalayas, picture **A** 447
Kand, ancient Persian sweets **C** 98
Kandahar (kon-da-HAR), Afghanistan **A** 42
bazaar, picture **A** 44
Kandinsky (kond-YEEN-ski), **Wassily,** Russian painter **K** 166
Bauhaus school in Germany **B** 103; **G** 171
Composition III, painting **M** 391
modern art **M** 392

Kane, Paul (1810–71), Canadian painter, b. Mallow, county Cork, Ireland. He studied art in the United States, France, and Italy and observed the life of Indians of North West Canada as he traveled by canoe, horseback, and snowshoe to reach them. He produced paintings now in the Royal Ontario Museum at Toronto and Parliament Buildings at Ottawa.

Kanem (KA-nem), ancient African empire **C** 183

Kangaroo court, court in which legal principles are ignored or perverted. The term usually refers to a prison court organized by and for the inmates to punish newcomers and those who do not conform to their rules or "code." The title is often applied to courts without legal standing set up in frontier territories. The phrase possibly originated in Australia, the kangaroo habitat, when it served as a British penal colony.

Kangaroo rats **R** 277; picture **K** 257
Kangaroos **K** 167–75
Australia's marsupials **A** 505
leather made from hides **L** 107

K'ang-hsi (KONG-SHI) (1654–1722), Manchu emperor (1662–1722) of China. He added three northern provinces to China; reorganized Khalkha states of Mongolia (1691); and conquered Yunnan (1681), Formosa (1683), and Tibet (1720). He sent the Jesuit Jean-François Gerbillon to negotiate Treaty of Nerchinsk (1689), establishing Sino-Russian boundaries, and issued a Jesuit toleration edict (1693). He maintained internal peace and fostered art and scholarship.

Kaniksu National Forest, Idaho **I** 64
Kano (KA-no), Nigeria **N** 255
Kansas **K** 176–91
"bleeding Kansas" and John Brown **B** 411
Civil War: pre-war incidents **C** 320
Kansas, University of **K** 183
Kansas City, Kansas **K** 188
Kansas City, Missouri **M** 378; picture **M** 379
Kansas-Nebraska Act, 1854 **K** 192
Civil War, events leading to **C** 320; **S** 199
Douglas, Stephen A. **D** 287
Kansas, early history of **K** 180–81
Lincoln-Douglas debates **L** 299
Lincoln leader of movement opposing **L** 294
Missouri Compromise repealed **M** 382
Nebraska, early history of **N** 87
Negro history **N** 95
Pierce, Franklin **P** 247
Kansas River, or **Kaw River** **K** 179
Kansas State University of Agriculture and Applied Science **K** 183
Kant (KONT), **Immanuel,** German philosopher **K** 192
peace movements **P** 104
philosophical systems **P** 192

Kantor, MacKinlay (1904–   ), American journalist and novelist, b. Webster City, Iowa. He has been a newspaperman (1921–27) and movie script writer (since 1934). A diversified author, he writes novels about the Civil War as well as about modern lower-class America. Some of his best-known novels are *Long Remember, The Voice of Bugle Ann,* and *Andersonville,* for which he received the Pulitzer prize (1956).

Kanuri (ka-NU-ri) **language,** spoken in eastern Africa **A** 55
Kaohiung (gou-shy-OONG), or **Kaohsiung,** Taiwan **T** 13
Kaolack (KA-o-lack), Senegal **S** 120
Kaolin (KAY-o-lin), china clay **C** 173
Kapital, Das see Das Kapital

Kapitza (KA-pi-tza), **Peter Leonidovich** (1894–   ), Soviet physicist, b. Kronstadt. He is best known for his studies of extreme low-temperature phenomena and of magnetism. He discovered superfluidity—the ability, found only in helium at very low temperature, to flow almost without friction.

Kaplan, Joseph (1902–   ), American physicist, b. Tapolca, Hungary. He is noted for identification of spectral lines emitted by atoms and molecules in the upper atmosphere. He co-ordinated the United States effort for the International Geophysical year (1957–58). In 1946 he founded the Institute of Geophysics, Los Angeles, Calif., and was its director (1946–47).

Kaplan, Victor, Austrian engineer **T** 319–20
Kapok (KAY-pok) **K** 193
types of fibers **F** 106

Kapteyn (kop-TINE), **Jacobus Cornelius** (1851–1922), Dutch astronomer, b. Groningen. A pioneer of modern statistical astronomy, he worked out (1905) a method for estimating the size and structure of the Milky Way by observing stars in certain selected areas. He discovered from these data (1908) that the stars in the Milky Way appear to be moving in two distinct streams in opposite directions, thus indicating orderly motion.

Karachi (ka-RA-chi), Pakistan **P** 40
relations with Afghanistan **A** 45

Karajan (KA-ra-yon), **Herbert von** (1908–), Austrian conductor, b. Salzburg. He was conductor of the Berlin Opera (1937–41), musical director of the Berlin Philharmonic (1954–56), and has been head of the Vienna State Opera since 1956. He has toured the United States and Europe with, among others, the Vienna Symphony Orchestra and the Philharmonia Orchestra of London. He has conducted at various music festivals.

Karakoram (ka-ra-KO-rom) **Mountains,** central Asia
K 198
India **I** 123
Tibet **T** 176
Karakul sheep **A** 45
Kara Sea **O** 48
Karate (ka-RA-te) **K** 194
Japanese art of self-defense **J** 33
judo compared **J** 146
Karats, units for measuring gold **G** 247–48
gold jewelry **J** 92
See also Carats
Kariba (ka-RI-ba) **Dam,** Zambezi River, Rhodesia-Zambia
R 229; picture **D** 17
Karlsbad see Carlsbad
Karl Schwarzschild Observatory **T** 63
Karma, spiritual law in Hinduism **H** 131; **R** 146
Karnak, Temples of
Egyptian architecture **E** 100
Great Temple of Amon-Re **A** 221, 371–72
Karting **K** 195–96
Karyotyping, analyzing and counting chromosomes, a medical laboratory test **M** 202

Kasavubu (ka-sa-VU-bu), **Joseph** (1910?–1969), Congolese politician, b. probably Tshela. He was a civil servant and teacher (1939–49), and he served as president of Abako (Association of Lower Congo) (1955), mayor of Dendale (1958–59), and president of the Congo Republic (now Zaïre) (1960–65).
Zaïre **Z** 366d

Kashmir **K** 197–99
Baltoro Glacier in the Himalayas, picture **H** 128
boat people, picture **H** 176
India-Pakistan dispute **I** 135; **P** 40
Kasner, Edward see Googol
Kassala (KASS-a-la), Sudan, picture **S** 450
Kassim (ka-SEEM), or **Kassem, Abdul Karim,** military ruler of Iraq **I** 383
Kassites, barbarian conquerers of Babylon **A** 237
Kästner (KEST-ner), **Erich,** German writer **G** 181
Kastrioti, Gjergj, called Skënderbeg, Albanian leader
A 146
Kat, woody shrub **Y** 349
Katanga (ka-TAN-ga), province of Zaïre **Z** 366c, 366d
Kate Greenaway Medal, book award **B** 310b
Katmai (KAT-my) **National Monument,** Alaska **A** 140; picture **N** 54
Katmandu (kot-mon-DU), capital of Nepal **N** 113; picture **N** 111
U.S. Information Agency Library, picture **L** 178
Katydids, insects **I** 268

Katzenbach (KATZ-en-back), **Nicholas** (Nicholas deBelleville Katzenbach) (1922–), American lawyer, b. Philadelphia, Pa. He was professor of law at the University of Chicago (1956–60) and was made assistant attorney general in 1961. A major force behind the Civil Rights Act (1964) and the voting rights bill of 1965, he was appointed U.S. attorney general (1965). He later served as U.S. undersecretary of state (1966–68).

Kauai (kow-I), one of the Hawaiian Islands **H** 59
Kaufman (KAUF-man), **George S.,** American playwright
A 216; **M** 542
Kauikeaouli see Kamehameha III

Kaunda (KOWN-da), **Kenneth David** (1924–), Zambian politician, b. near Chinsali, Northern Rhodesia. As president of United National Independence Party (since 1960), he was chosen prime minister when Northern Rhodesia was declared a British protectorate (January, 1964) and became its first president when it became the independent republic of Zambia (October, 1964).

Kawabata, Yasunari, Japanese novelist **O** 220c–220d
Kaw River, or **Kansas River** **K** 179
Kay see Key, a low island
Kay, son of Sir Ector, in legends of King Arthur **A** 443
Kay, John, English inventor **I** 234
Kayaks (KA-yaks), boats **C** 99
Eskimo **E** 289
Greenland, picture **G** 370

Kaye, Danny (David Daniel Kominski) (1913–), American comedian and actor, b. Brooklyn, N. Y. A portrayer of numerous types of roles, he has acted in Hans Christian Andersen, The Secret Life of Walter Mitty, and The Court Jester, among other films. His Broadway shows include the musical, Two by Two. His entertaining on behalf of UNICEF earned him the title of ambassador-at-large.

Kayes (KY-es), Mali **M** 59
Kazakh (ka-ZAHK) **Soviet Socialist Republic** (Kazakhstan)
U 45
languages of the U.S.S.R. **U** 28
Kazakhs, a Turkic Muslim people of Mongolia **M** 413
Kazakhstan **U** 45

Kazan (ka-ZAN), **Elia** (Elia Kazanjoglous) (1909–), American actor and director, b. Constantinople (now Istanbul), Turkey. He is winner of direction awards for stage productions The Skin of Our Teeth, A Streetcar Named Desire, Death of a Salesman, and films Gentleman's Agreement and On the Waterfront. He co-founded the Actor's Studio (1947) and has written books America America, and The Arrangement.

Kazantzakis (ka-zont-ZA-kis), **Nikos** (1885–1957), Greek author, b. Candia, Crete. He gained international recognition for long epic poem The Odyssey: A Modern Sequel, a continuation of Odysseus' adventures. He directed the Greek Ministry of Public Welfare (1919–27), served as minister of state (1945), and supervised the bureau of translations of the classics for UNESCO (1947–48). His other works include novels Report to Greco, Zorba the Greek, and The Greek Passion.

Kazin, Alfred, American writer and critic **A** 215

Kazoo (ka-ZOO), toy musical instrument usually made of a plastic or wooden tube open at one end, with a membrane-covered side hole through which one sings. It produces amusing, caricaturist vocal sounds. Of uncertain origin, it is known as a mirliton in France and a

Kazoo (continued)
Tommy talker in Britain. The name "kazoo" probably comes from the sound the instrument produces.

KDKA, first radio broadcasting station   **R** 54

Kean, Edmund (1787–1833), English actor, b. London. He was the outstanding tragedian of his day. He worked as a roving actor, achieving his first success as Shylock at the Drury Lane theater (1814). His subsequent Shakespearean roles included Richard III, Othello, King Lear, Hamlet, and Iago.

Kearny (KAR-ny), **Stephen,** American general   **M** 239
   first description of Iowa's prairies   **I** 370–71

Keaton Buster (1896–1966), b. Pickway, Kansas. At the age of 3 he was performing with his parents in an acrobatic act. He started his film career in the Keystone Kop comedies, and turned to full-length features in the 1920's. Of his more than 30 silent films, 3 are considered classics: *The Navigator* (1925), *The General* (1927), and *The Cameraman* (1928). After 1950 he achieved new fame in television and as a motion picture director. His famous deadpan pantomime style of comedy was seen in such later films as *A Funny Thing Happened on the Way to the Forum* and *When Comedy Was King.*

Keats, Ezra Jack (1916–), American author and illustrator of children's books, b. Brooklyn, N.Y. He was awarded the Caldecott medal (1963) for *The Snowy Day.* He also wrote and illustrated *John Henry,* co-authored *My Dog is Lost,* and illustrated *The Naughty Boy, Zoo Where Are You,* and *In the Night.*
   illustration from *The Snowy Day*   **C** 248b

Keats, John, English poet   **K** 200–01
   English literature, place in   **E** 261
   epitaph   **E** 152
   "I Had a Dove"   **K** 200
   "Ode to a Nightingale," excerpt   **O** 52
   "On the Grasshopper and Cricket"   **K** 200
   "To Autumn"   **K** 200
Keb *see* Geb, Egyptian god
Keddah, elephant corral   **E** 171
Keelboats, kind of riverboat   **M** 383; picture   **P** 261
Keelung, Taiwan   **T** 13
Keening, or mourning, **songs**   **F** 326
Keep, or donjon, of a castle   **F** 375
Keep Cool with Coolidge, campaign slogan   **C** 496
Kefauver (ke-FO-ver), **Carey Estes,** American statesman   **T** 87
Keflavik (KEP-la-veek), Iceland   **I** 43
Keijo (kai-jo), Japanese name for Seoul   **S** 121
Keino (KAY-no), **Kipchoge,** Olympic star, picture   **O** 116

Keita (KAI-ta), **Modibo** (1915–), Mali nationalist politician, b. Bamako, French Sudan. President of Mali from its independence in 1960 to 1968, he was also leader of the sole political party, the Union Soudanaise-Rassemblement Democratique African (US-RDA), and minister of defense. He won the Lenin peace prize (1962) and is author of an autobiography, *I Shall Be Free.*
   Mali, government of   **M** 59

Keitel (KITE-el), **Wilhelm** (1882–1946), German general, b. Helmscherode. Chief of the administration department in the Ministry of War (1935–38), he became chief of the High Command of the Armed Forces in 1938. In 1940 he was made field marshal by Adolf Hitler, and the act of military surrender was signed by him in May, 1945. He was later tried and hanged as a war criminal.

Keith (KEETH), **Sir Arthur** (1866–1955), Scottish anthropologist, b. Aberdeen. An authority on the fossil remains of man and a theorist on the evolution of man and race origins, he wrote a number of books. They include *Nationality and Race* and *Essays on Human Evolution.*

Keith, Harold Verne (1903–), American author and sports writer, b. Lambert, Okla. He has been director of sports publicity at the University of Oklahoma since 1930. He is considered an authority on Oklahoma history. His books include *Boys' Life of Will Rogers* and *Oklahoma Kickoff.* He received the Newbery award (1958) for *Rifles for Watie.*

Keith, Minor C., American railroad builder in Costa Rica   **C** 517

Kekulé von Stradonitz, (KAY-ku-lay fon SHTRA-do-nitz), **Friedrich August** (1829–1896), German chemist, b. Darmstadt. He specialized in the study of carbon and its compounds and originated the concept of linkages between carbon atoms. He is best-known for his discovery of the benzene ring, a six-sided arrangement of carbon atoms that is a basic building block of many substances. Kekulé's work made possible many later discoveries of tremendous importance.
   chemistry, history of   **C** 214

Kellar, Harry, American magician   **M** 18
Keller, Gottfried, Swiss writer   **G** 178
Keller, Helen, American educator of the blind   **K** 201
   home in Alabama   **A** 125
   See also Blind
Kelley, Oliver Hudson, American organizer of farm groups   **M** 337

Kellogg, Frank Billings (1856–1937), American statesman, b. Potsdam, N.Y. He was a corporation lawyer before serving as senator from Minnesota (1917–23), ambassador to Great Britain (1924–25), and United States secretary of state (1925–29). With Aristide Briand he developed and negotiated the Kellogg-Briand Pact to outlaw war, which was later signed by more than 60 nations. He received the 1929 Nobel peace prize.

Kellogg, Winthrop N., American scientist   **D** 274, 275
Kellogg-Briand Pact, 1928   **P** 105
   basis for war crimes trials   **W** 10
   Coolidge favored   **C** 497
   efforts toward peace between two wars   **W** 284
   Stimson Doctrine regarding treaties   **T** 271
Kells, Book of   **K** 202–03
   at Trinity College, Dublin, Ireland   **I** 386
   survival of ancient thought   **R** 290

Kelly, Colin P., Jr. (1915–1941), American army captain, b. near Madison, Fla. After the Pearl Harbor attack during World War II, he flew a bomber, which demolished a Japanese battleship. He commanded crew to jump from the impaired plane but was himself killed when it crashed. The Distinguished Service Cross was presented to him posthumously.

Kelly, Ellsworth, American artist   **P** 32

Kelly, Eric Philbrook (1884–1960), American author, b. Amesbury, Mass. A professor of journalism (1929–54), he is noted for his children's books. His works include *Don Pedro's Christmas* and *In Clean Hay.* He was presented the Newbery award (1929) for *The Trumpeter of Krakow.*

Kelly, Grace *see* Grace, Princess of Monaco

Kelly, Luther Sage ("Yellowstone Kelly") **(1849–1928),** American army scout, b. Geneva, N.Y. A trapper in the Yellowstone region, he acted as a chief army scout and as a guide for exploring expeditions in Alaska (1898, 1899). He later became an Indian agent in Arizona (1904–08).

Kelly, Walt, American cartoonist, creator of Pogo **C** 128

Kelly, William (1811–1888) American inventor, b. Pittsburgh, Pa. He was a Kentucky ironmaker who independently developed the "air-boiling process" for making steel (patent issued 1857), later called the Bessemer process (named after Henry Bessemer, English engineer who developed same process).
the Bessemer process **I** 398

Kelmscott Press, founded by English artist, William Morris **B** 322
Kelp, seaweeds **A** 156, 157
in ice cream **I** 33
life, distribution of **L** 229
Kelsey, Henry, British fur trader **M** 82; **S** 38h
Kelts *see* Celts
Kelut, volcano, Indonesia **V** 382
Kelvin, William Thomson, 1st Baron, English scientist **H** 90
Atlantic cable **T** 52
Kelvin scale, based on absolute zero temperature **H** 90
compared with Fahrenheit, and Celsius, diagram **H** 89
Kemal Ataturk *see* Ataturk, Mustafa Kemal

Kemble, Fanny (Frances Anne Kemble) (1809–1893), English actress and writer, b. London. She came from a famous English family of actors, and though an acclaimed actress, she left the vocation in 1844, returning in 1851. She gave highly successful readings from Shakespeare and wrote accounts of her life in the United States, poetry, plays, and essays. Her writings include *Journal of a Residence in America.*

Kempis, Thomas à (Thomas Hamerken or Hammerlein) (1380?–1471), German mystic and religious writer, b. Kempen, Prussia. He entered an Augustinian monastery in the Netherlands (1407), and was appointed a subprior (1425?–1447). His writings are devotional, stressing piety and meditation, and despite some controversy, he is generally accepted as the author of the classic *The Imitation of Christ.* He also wrote tracts, sermons, and biographies of the founders of the Brethren of the Common Life, a communal religious group.
quotation from **Q** 20

Kendall, Edward Calvin (1886–   ), American biochemist, b. South Norwalk, Conn. He isolated thyroxin, the thyroid hormone, important in the normal functioning of the body. He played a major role in the isolation and synthesis of cortisone, a hormone used to treat arthritis. For this work he shared the 1950 Nobel prize in physiology and medicine with P. Hench and T. Reichstein.

Kenko, Yoshida, Japanese essayist **O** 220c
Kennebec (KEN-eh-beck) **River,** Maine **M** 36
Kennebunkport (KEN-ne-bunk-port), Maine, picture **M** 44
Kennedy, Avenue du President, Paris **P** 71
Kennedy, Cape, Florida **F** 258, 272; picture **F** 266

Kennedy, David Matthew (1905–   ), American banker and finance expert, b. Randolph, Utah. He worked for the Federal Reserve Board (1930–46) and in the Treasury Department (1953–54). During the Johnson administration Kennedy headed a commission on the federal budget. He was secretary of the treasury (1969–70), then became ambassador at large dealing with international economic problems.

Kennedy, Edward M., United States senator **K** 211
Kennedy, Jacqueline Lee Bouvier, wife of John F. Kennedy **F** 179; **K** 207, 211; picture **F** 180
campaign picture **K** 208
Kennedy, John F., 35th president of the United States **K** 204–11
Arlington National Cemetery, right of military burial **N** 29
football, connection with **F** 356; **K** 211
Kennedy Round of tariff negotiations **T** 25
message on physical fitness **P** 224
Peace Corps **P** 101–03
quotation from Inaugural Address **Q** 20
with Herbert Hoover, picture **H** 225
Kennedy, John Pendleton, American novelist **A** 200
Kennedy, Joseph Patrick, American businessman and diplomat **M** 147
Kennedy, Robert F., American public official **K** 211
Kennedy family, of Massachusetts **M** 147; picture **K** 206
only family in history to have 3 sons in U.S. Senate **K** 211
Kennedy International Airport *see* John F. Kennedy International Airport
Kennel Club, American *see* American Kennel Club
Kennels, shelters for dogs **D** 253
Kennesaw (KEN-nes-aw) **Mountain National Battlefield Park,** Georgia **G** 141

Kenny, Sister Elizabeth (1886–1952), Australian nurse, b. Warrialda. She developed a treatment for infantile paralysis based on stimulation and "re-education" of muscles through heat treatments and massages. Her method, revolutionary at the time, was later accepted by Australian hospitals. She went to the United States (1940), where she established the Elizabeth Kenny Institute in Minneapolis. She wrote (with Martha Ostenso) an autobiography *And They Shall Walk.*

Kenosha (ke-NO-sha), Wisconsin **W** 204
Kensington, borough of London, England **L** 336
Kensington, P.E.I., Canada **P** 456e
Kensington Rune Stone, said to have been left by Norsemen in Minnesota **M** 336
displayed in Alexandria, Minn. **M** 333
exploration of the New World **E** 369

Kent, Louise Andrews (1886–1969), American author, b. Brookline, Mass. She was a columnist for the Boston *Traveler* (1911) under pseudonym Teresa Tempest and editorial writer for the Boston *Herald* (1928–31). She was author of *He Went with Christopher Columbus,* and *He Went with Marco Polo.*

Kent, Rockwell (1882–1971), American artist and author, b. Tarrytown Heights, N.Y. known for his decorative illustrations and wood engravings, he exhibited widely. His earlier works include many landscapes and figure paintings. He illustrated numerous books, including the works of Shakespeare. Among his works are *Maine Winter* and *Lone Woman.* He wrote an autobiography, *This is My Own.*
illustration of Captain Ahab from *Moby Dick* **I** 92

Kente cloth, hand-woven in Ghana **G** 194

Kenton, Simon (1755–1836), American pioneer and Indian fighter, b. probably Fauquier County, Va. Appointed a scout by Daniel Boone in 1775, he took part in the local encounters with the Indians. In 1805 he was made head of Ohio militia, and served in War of 1812.

Kentucky K 212–27
  Boone, Daniel, first settler **B** 335
  folk dancing **F** 299
  overland trails pioneered by Boone **O** 255
  poverty in Appalachia **P** 424a–424b
  tobacco field, picture **T** 200
Kentucky, University of K 220; picture **K** 219

Kentucky and Virginia Resolutions (1798, 1799), resolutions passed by Kentucky and Virginia declaring the Alien and Sedition Acts unconstitutional (1798). The Kentucky Resolutions were written by Thomas Jefferson and the Virginia Resolutions were formulated by James Madison. They held that the states could decide whether federal laws were constitutional and could, if necessary, nullify such laws. In the 19th century they were invoked in arguments over states' rights and nullification.

Kentucky Derby, American horse race **H** 232–33
  annual event in Kentucky **K** 223
  Churchill Downs, picture **K** 220
Kentucky rifle, picture **G** 416
Kenya (KEEN-ya) **K** 228–33
  Asians, exodus of **I** 103
  boys' school, picture **E** 81
  flag **F** 235
  Kenya Polytechnic, picture **A** 68
  public health measures, picture **P** 505
  sisal industry, picture **A** 63
Kenya, Mount K 231

Kenyatta, Jomo (1889?–   ), African political leader, b. Kikuyu, village near present-day Nairobi, Kenya. He has been active in movements to improve housing, wages, and land distribution since 1922. He has served as president of Kenya African Union (1947) and was imprisoned (1953–59) and exiled (1959–61) for involvement in the Mau Mau movement. Kenyatta was elected prime minister (1963) after Kenya achieved independence, and was elected president in 1964.
  Kenya, history of **K** 233

Kenyatta Avenue, Nairobi, Kenya, picture **K** 228

Keokuk (KE-o-kuk) (Watchful Fox) (1780?–1848), American Indian chief, b. near present site of Rock Island, Ill. At the time of the Black Hawk War (1832), he aided the Americans and became the leader of the Sauk tribe. As spokesman for the Sauk and Foxes, he helped arrange peace in Washington, D.C., between these tribes and the Sioux (1837) after a land-claim dispute.

Kepler, Johannes, German astronomer **K** 234
  Brahe and Kepler **B** 361
  Mars, study of **M** 107
  motions of planets, laws of **A** 472
  science, advances in **S** 68
  solar system **S** 241–42
Kepler's Laws, of planetary motion **K** 234; **S** 241–42
Keppard, Freddy, American jazz musician **J** 58
Kerala (KAY-ra-la), India, picture **I** 129
Keratin, body protein **B** 290
  hair cells contain **H** 2

Kerensky (ker-EN-ski), **Alexander Feodorovich** (1881–1970), Russian revolutionary leader, b. Simbirsk. He joined the politically moderate Labor Party and became a representative to the fourth Duma, or Russian parliament (1912). During the revolutionary period (1917), he held various government posts, was removed from power by the Bolsheviks (November, 1917), and became editor, lecturer, and author in Europe and United States (after 1918). His books include *The Prelude to Bolshevism* and *The Catastrophe.*

Kerguélen-Trémarec (ker-gay-LEN-tray-ma-REC), **Yves Joseph de** (1734?–1797), French explorer, b. Quimper. He discovered a group of islands in the Indian Ocean (1772). Known as the Kerguelen Islands, they have since been used as whaling bases and seal-hunting grounds.

Kerkyra (KER-key-ra), or **Corfu,** island west of Greece **I** 428; picture **I** 433
Kermes (KER-mese), dye extracted from insects' bodies **D** 367, 369
Kern, Jerome, American composer **M** 542
Kernels, inner part of nuts **N** 419–20
Kerogen (KER-o-gen), bituminous material in oil shales **P** 178
Kerosene K 235
  fuel for space rockets **S** 348
  fuel of early steam automobiles **A** 542
  fuels **F** 488
Kerosene lamps L 281–82
Kerouac (KER-oo-ac), **Jack,** American novelist **A** 213

Kerr, Walter Francis (1913–   ), American drama critic and writer, b. Evanston, Ill. He taught drama at Catholic University, Washington, D.C. (1938–49), and has been drama critic for *The Commonweal* (1949–51), the New York *Herald Tribune* (1951–66), and the New York *Times* (since 1966). He has written shows, including *Touch and Go,* with his wife, Jean. His books include *Criticism and Censorship* and *The Decline of Pleasure.*

Kerr Dam, Montana, picture **C** 485
Kerwin, Joseph P., American astronaut **S** 345, 347

Kerwin, Patrick (1889–1963), Canadian chief justice, b. Sarnia, Ontario. He became judge of the Supreme Court of Ontario in 1932 and joined the Supreme Court of Canada in 1935, serving as chief justice (1954–63).

Ketch, sailing vessel, picture **S** 9

Ketchel, Stanley (Stanislaus Kiecal) (1887–1910), Polish-American middleweight world boxing champion (1908–10), b. Grand Rapids, Mich. He fought 61 bouts, scored 44 knockouts, and lost only four times. He was elected to Boxing Hall of Fame (1954).

Kettering, Charles, American engineer and inventor **K** 236
  automobile headlights **L** 286
Kettledrum, or timpani **D** 335–36; picture **M** 548
  percussion instruments **P** 151–52
Kettles, depressions in glaciated land areas **W** 194; picture **I** 14
  landforms in Massachusetts **M** 136
Keukenhof (kur-KEN-hof) **Gardens,** the Netherlands, picture **G** 43
Kew Gardens, near London, England, picture **Z** 378
Key (music) **M** 528–29
  modern music **M** 399

Key, or **kay** (influenced by Spanish *cayo,* meaning "reef"), low island or reef, particularly one of coral islands off tip of Florida coast (Florida Keys). Pictures **F** 261, **I** 424.

Key, Francis Scott, American lawyer, author of "The Star-Spangled Banner" **N** 16
  flag, history of **F** 248
  Fort McHenry, Maryland, battle site, inspiration of the anthem **M** 126
Key, Ted, American cartoonist, creator of Hazel **C** 125, 128
Keyboard instruments K 236–40
  classical age in music **C** 331
  organ **O** 208–09
  piano **P** 240–42
  types of musical instruments **M** 544, 546–47
Keyhole saw, tool, picture **T** 212
Keys see Locks and keys
Key signatures, in musical notation **M** 528–29
Keystone, emblem of Boys' Clubs **B** 355
Keystone Province, Ontario, Canada **O** 119–29
Keystone State, nickname for Pennsylvania **P** 128–29
Key words
  composition outlines **C** 446
  headings and entries in indexes **I** 114
  how to look up quotations **Q** 19
  note-taking for reports **R** 175
  reference books, all about anything **R** 130
  research projects, finding topics in library catalogs **L** 186–87
  taxonomic keys **T** 31–32
K.G., title see Garter, Order of the
Khadijah (ka-DI-ja), first wife of Mohammed **M** 404
Khafre see Chephren
Khalkhas (KAL-kas), a people of Mongolia **M** 413
Kham (KOM), eastern part of Tibet **T** 177
Khamsin (kam-SEEN), wind **J** 137
  hot desert wind, Egypt **E** 90e
  Syria **S** 507
Kharieh Djami church, Constantinople
  Byzantine wall paintings of **B** 490
Kharkov (KAR-kof), Ukraine, Union of Soviet Socialist Republics **U** 8, 36
  cities of Europe **E** 323
Khartoum (kar-TOOM), capital of Sudan **S** 448
Khartoum, University of S 448
Khatchaturian (ka-tcha-TOUR-ian), **Aram Ilich,** Armenian composer **U** 64
Khayyam, Omar see Omar Khayyam
Khmer (KMER) **Empire,** Cambodia **C** 31, 34
  Southeast Asia, early history of **S** 334
Khmer Republic see Cambodia
Khorsabad (kor-sa-BOD), city in ancient Assyria **A** 240
Khrushchev (kroosh-CHOFF), **Nikita,** Soviet political leader **K** 240–41
  Communism **C** 443
  with Vice-President Nixon, picture **N** 262c
Khufu see Cheops
Khuzistan, plain in Iran **I** 375
Khwarazm (kwa-RAZ-em) (now Aral) **Sea L** 26
Khyber Pass, links Afghanistan with West Pakistan **A** 43; **P** 36
  road, picture **A** 467
Kiang, wild horse of Tibet, picture **H** 243
Kibbutz (kib-BOOTZ), a collective settlement in Israel **I** 443; picture **I** 442
  one type of family organization **F** 41, 42
Kickapoos, Indians of North America
  prayer sticks **C** 431
Kick the stick, game **G** 18–19
Kidd, Captain William, British pirate **K** 241
  pirates and piracy **P** 264
Kidnapped, by Robert Louis Stevenson, excerpt **S** 426–27
Kidneys B 278
  drugs regulate function of **D** 326
  interior view, diagram **D** 201

nephritis, disease **D** 201–02
  organ transplants **M** 211
Kids, young goats **G** 244
Kidskin leather L 107

Kieft (KEEFT), **Willem** (1597–1647), Dutch colonial governor, b. Amsterdam. As governor of the Dutch colony of New Netherland (1638–45) he was held responsible for the Indian attacks (1643–45) brought on by his brutal policy. He instigated the massacre of about 80 Indian men, women, and children in a surprise attack (1643).

Kiel (KEEL), **Peace of,** treaty signed (1814) at Kiel (then in Denmark) by which Denmark gave Helgoland to Great Britain and Norway to Sweden and received Swedish Pomerania and Rügen from Sweden.

Kier, Samuel M., American businessman **P** 177

Kierkegaard (KIER-keg-or), **Søren Aabye** (1813–55), Danish philosopher and Protestant theologian, b. Copenhagen. His philosophy is considered the precursor of existentialism. Kierkegaard believed that the individual's unique experience, both social and spiritual, determines the individual's concept of truth. His writings include *Fear and Trembling* (1843), *Stages on Life's Way* (1845), and *Practice in Christianity* (1849).
  See also Existentialism

Kiesinger (KI-singer), **Kurt Georg** (1904–   ) West German political leader, b. Ebingen. After serving (1949–58) in the Bundestag (the lower house of Parliament), he was elected (1958) minister-president of the state of Baden-Württemberg and president (1962) of the Bundesrat (the upper house of Parliament). The Christian Democratic party named him chancellor to succeed Ludwig Erhard, and he served (1966–69).

Kiev (KI-ef), capital of Ukraine, U.S.S.R. **U** 9, 36
  church architecture **U** 52
Kigali (ki-GA-li), capital of Rwanda **R** 363

Kikuyu (ki-KU-yu), negroid tribe, of the Bantu language group, that occupies agricultural and grazing lands in central Kenya and numbers approximately 1,026,300. Its members govern themselves through patriarchal clans and democratic councils of older men. Kikuyu political groups, such as the Kenya Africa Union (founded 1944), were formed in response to conflicts with Europeans over land and labor relations. This racial unrest led to the Mau Mau disturbances (1950's).
  Kenya, history of **K** 233
  See also Mau Mau

Kilauea (ki-la-WAY-a), volcano, Hawaii **V** 382; picture **H** 59
Kilimanjaro (kil-i-mon-JAR-o), **Mount,** Tanzania **T** 17; pictures **A** 47, **M** 498
Killarney, Lakes of, Ireland **L** 31–32
Killer whales W 147; picture **W** 149

Killy, Jean Claude (1943–   ), French skier, b. St. Cloud. He began skiing after moving to Alps as child and by 1966 was world's foremost skier. In 1966–67 and 1967–68 seasons, he led French team to world championships and won World Cup for himself. In 1968 Winter Olympics he became second man in Olympic history to sweep downhill, slalom, and giant slalom races. He then turned professional. Picture **O** 116.

Kilmer, Joyce (Alfred Joyce Kilmer) (1886–1918), American poet and critic, b. New Brunswick, N.J. He is

Kilmer, Joyce (continued)
primarily remembered for his poem "Trees." Killed during World War I, he was posthumously awarded the Croix de Guerre. His works include *Summer of Love.*

Kilns, furnaces or ovens **C** 175–76; **F** 143; picture **C** 174
   brick making **B** 391
   dry kilns for lumber **L** 376
   wood, kiln-dried **W** 226
Kilocalories (KIL-o-ca-lo-ries). heat units **H** 91
   how energy is measured **E** 199

Kilocycle (KC), or **kilohertz** (KHz), term usually used to indicate the frequency of a radio signal. When so used, it is an abbreviation for kilocycles per second—the number of thousands of radio waves, or cycles, per second. ("Kilo-" is a prefix meaning "thousand." Thus, 1 kilocycle means 1,000 cycles.)
   measurement of high frequency waves **R** 56, 58

Kilogram-meter-second, system of measurement **W** 117
Kilometer (kil-OM-et-er), measure of length **W** 114–15

Kilowatt (KIL-o-watt), unit of measure of electric power. One kilowatt means 1,000 watts. (One watt is 1 ampere of current under the pressure of 1 volt.) One kilowatt equals about 1⅓ horsepower.

Kilpatrick, William H., American educator **E** 76
Kilt, Scottish skirt **C** 352; picture **C** 350
Kimberley, British Columbia **B** 406d
Kimberley, South Africa **S** 270
   first diamond discovery **D** 153
Kimberlite, or blueground, diamond-bearing rock **G** 70
Kimigayo (ki-mi-GA-yo), Japanese national anthem **N** 19–20

Kim Il Sung (1912?–), Korean politician, b. Man Gin-dyu. He organized a guerilla force, known as the Korean People's Revolutionary Army, which fought against Japan during World War II. He has been an active participant in the Korean Communist Party since 1945, and prime minister of North Korea since 1948. **K** 301, 302

Kimonos (ki-MO-nos), Japanese robes **C** 352; **J** 26; picture **J** 41
Kin, family relationships **F** 38–43
Kinabatangan (kin-uh-but-ANG-un) **River,** Malaysia **M** 54
Kindergarten K 242–47
   children dancing, picture **C** 234
   class in Peking, China, picture **A** 461
   education, history of **E** 71
   first in the United States in Wisconsin **W** 201
   Lomé, Togo, picture **T** 202
Kindling temperature, of a fuel **F** 136
Kinetic (ki-NET-ic) **energy E** 198–203
Kinetic theory, of heat **T** 166
Kinetograph (kin-E-to-graph), motion picture camera **P** 213

King, Billie Jean (1943–), American tennis player, b. Long Beach, Calif. She is five time Wimbledon champion, winning her first title in 1966. She won the U.S. Open two times, and in 1971 became the first professional woman athlete to win over $100,000. In 1973 she beat Bobby Riggs in a much publicized match held in Houston, Texas, that was billed as "the battle of the sexes."

King, Martin Luther, Jr., American pastor and civil rights leader **K** 248; picture **N** 104
   Negro history, continuing struggle in **N** 104b–105

segregation **S** 115
with Dr. James Nabrit, Jr., picture **N** 104

King, Rufus (1755–1827), American Federalist statesman, b. Scarboro, Mass. (now Maine). He was representative to Congress under the Confederation (1784–86), supporting a firm central government at the Constitutional Convention (1787). He contributed part of the Ordinance of 1787, prohibiting slaveholding in the Northwest Territory, and was elected U.S. Senator from New York (1789, 1795, 1813, and 1820). King served as minister to Great Britain (1796–1803) and was the Federalist candidate for president but lost to James Monroe (1816).

King, Ruth Ann, American ballerina, picture **B** 29
King, William Lyon Mackenzie, Canadian statesman **K** 248
   intensified development of Canada **C** 75
King, William R., vice-president, United States **V** 331; picture **V** 327
King Arthur see Arthur, King
King crab see Horseshoe crab
Kingbirds B 220
Kingdoms of living things K 249–59
   animal kingdom **A** 262
   differences between plant and animal life **L** 212–13
   life, adaptations **L** 214–27
   life, distribution of plant and animal **L** 227–39
   life, food chains in **L** 239–43
   life, webs of **L** 250–59
   plants **P** 290–304
   See also Taxonomy

Kingfishers, any of several birds with short necks and large heads, sometimes crested. Most are brightly colored. Found in many parts of the world, kingfishers usually live near freshwater streams and lakes. There are two main groups of kingfishers. The fishing kingfishers have a long, straight, pointed bill, breed in holes in riverbanks, and feed on a variety of water-dwelling creatures. The forest kingfishers have wider, flatter bills, breed in tree holes, and eat a variety of small animals, including insects and lizards. Picture **B** 218
   where birds live **B** 220

King George's War (1744–48), one of the French and Indian Wars fought by England and the American colonies against France, the French colonists, and their Indian allies. It was the colonial counterpart of conflict between England and France in the War of the Austrian Succession (1740–48). Raids carried out by colonists of both countries resulted in no conclusive victory for either side. It ended with the signing of the Peace of Aix-la-Chapelle (1748).
   flag, ancestor of Grand Union flag **F** 244
   French and Indian War, campaigns of **F** 459

King James Version, of the Bible **B** 153–54
   Christianity, history of **C** 287
   place in English literature **E** 253

King John, historical play by Shakespeare based on the anonymous play *The Troublesome Raigne of King John.* The play covers entire reign of King John (1199–1216), is concerned primarily with the tragedy of young Arthur, and ends with death of John at Swinstead Abbey.

King Lear, play by Shakespeare **S** 135
   nonrealistic set design, picture **T** 158

Kingman, Dong (Dong Moy Shu Kingman) (1911–), Chinese-American artist, b. Oakland, Calif. He studied in

Hong Kong and taught at Columbia University (1946–58) and Hunter College in New York, N.Y. (1948–53). He made a world lecture tour for the U.S. Department of State cultural exchange program in 1954. Best-known for his watercolor techniques, he painted for film *Flower Drum Song* (1961) and has done covers for national magazines, including *Life* and *Fortune*.

Kingman Reef, small reef at the northern end of the Line Islands in the central Pacific Ocean. It is triangular in shape and encloses a deep lagoon. Discovered in 1798, it was named for Captain W. E. Kingman, who described it in 1853. Annexed by the United States (1922), it is now under the control of the Department of the Navy.
King of beasts, the lion **C** 135–36; **L** 307
King penguins **P** 125

King Philip's War (1675–76), massive Indian attack led by King Philip (Metacomet), chief of the Wampanoags, against English colonists in Maine, New Hampshire, Massachusetts, and Rhode Island. Early Indian success was dampened by lack of co-operation between tribes. The English forced Indians out of southern New England. Conflict subsided when Philip was shot (1676).
   Indian wars in New England **I** 212

King Ranch, Texas **T** 123
Kings I and II, books of Bible, Old Testament **B** 154
King salmon
   state fish of Alaska **A** 135
Kings Canyon National Park, California **C** 24
King's English **D** 152

Kingsford, William (1819–1898), English engineer and historian in Canada, b. London. He was employed as civil engineer in construction of Hudson River Railway, Panama Isthmus Railway, and Grand Trunk Railway and was chosen engineer in charge of the harbors of Great Lakes and St. Lawrence (1873–79). He wrote *Canadian Archaeology* and a 10-volume *History of Canada*.

Kingsley, Charles, English writer **E** 264
   children's literature **C** 241
   poem from *The Water Babies* **P** 351
Kingsley, Sidney, American playwright **A** 216
King's Men, acting company **S** 132
King snake, picture **S** 205
King's Path, United States, early highway **P** 136
Kingsport, Tennessee **T** 78
Kingston, capital of Jamaica **J** 17
Kingu, Babylonian god **M** 557
King William's War, 1690–97 **F** 459
Kinkaid, Moses Pierce, American statesman **N** 84
Kinkaid Act, 1904 **N** 87
Kinkajous (KIN-ka-joos), animals related to raccoons **R** 27; picture **R** 26
Kinkakuji (keen-ka-KU-ji) **Temple,** Kyoto, Japan, picture **J** 47

Kinnaird, Mary Jane, Lady (1816–1888), English philanthropist, b. Northamptonshire. She was one of the founders of the Young Women's Christian Association in Great Britain (1855) and was known for her interest in religious and educational works. She was active during Crimean War (1854–56) in sending aid to the wounded.

Kinneret (ki-NAIR-et), **Lake,** Israel **I** 441, 444
   Galilee, Sea of, or Lake Tiberias, now Lake Kinneret **L** 28

Kino (KE-no), or **Chini, Eusebio Francisco** (1645?–1711), Italian missionary, b. Segni. His explorations in

Lower California (1682) showed that area to be a peninsula, and a map he drew became widely known in Europe. Working among the Indians of the northern Mexico and southern Arizona areas (1687–1711), he founded many missions that later became towns.
   Arizona, history of **A** 416

Kinsale, battle of, 1601 **I** 390; **U** 73
Kinshasa (kin-SHA-sa), formerly Leopoldville, capital of Zaïre **Z** 366d; picture **Z** 366d
Kinship, in the family **F** 38, 39

Kinzie, John (1763–1828), Canadian fur trader, b. Quebec. He traded with the Indians on Maumee River, Ohio, and settled near Fort Dearborn (1804), the present site of Chicago. After the Indian massacre of Fort Dearborn troops in 1812, he was forced to abandon his settlement. He helped make a treaty with Indians (1821).

Kiowa, Indians of North America **I** 164
Kipling, Rudyard, English writer and poet **K** 260–61
   children's literature **C** 241
   "Elephant's Child, The," story **K** 262–65
   English literature, place in **E** 265
   "If," poem **K** 261
   "Mowgli's Song Against People," poem **K** 261–62

Kirchhoff, (KIR-coff), **Gustav Robert** (1824–1887), German physicist, b. Königsberg, Prussia (now Kaliningrad, Soviet Union). Together with Robert W. Bunsen he invented the spectroscope and founded the science of spectroscopy. The two men discovered the elements cesium (1860) and rubidium (1861). Kirchhoff also used spectroscopy to study the chemical makeup of the stars.
   chemistry, history of **C** 214

Kirchner (KIRSH-ner), **Ernst,** German painter **M** 391
Kirghiz (kir-GHEEZ) **Soviet Socialist Republic** (Kirghizia) **U** 45–46
   languages of the U.S.S.R. **U** 28

Kirsten, Dorothy (1917–), American soprano, b. Montclair, N.J. She made her opera debut with the Chicago Opera Company in 1940, and 2 years later, in *La Bohème,* she made her first New York opera appearance. She joined the Metropolitan Opera Company in 1945. She has sung the title roles in *Tosca, Louise,* and *Madama Butterfly.*

Kiruna, Sweden **S** 485
Kisangani (ki-san-GA-ni), Zaïre, formerly Stanleyville **C** 465; **S** 400
Kisatchie National Forest, Louisiana **L** 358

Kish, ancient city of Mesopotamia in what is now central Iraq. Kish flourished under Sumerians (5000–3000 B.C.) and is believed to be the world's oldest city, having endured from protoliterate times. The city was excavated by Oxford University (1922), revealing important temple and palace constructed about 3000 B.C.

Kishi, Nobusuke (1896–), Japanese political leader, b. Yamaguchi prefecture. A member of Premier Hideki Tojo's wartime government (1941–44), he was imprisoned (1945–48) as war criminal but was allowed to re-enter politics in 1952. Kishi served as prime minister and as president of Liberal Democratic Party (1957–60).

Kishinev, capital of Moldavian Soviet Socialist Republic **U** 44
Kismayu (kis-MAY-u), Somalia **S** 254

Kissinger, Henry Alfred (1923–   ), American professor, author, and advisor to President Nixon, b. Fuerth, Germany. He came to the United States in 1938 and became a naturalized citizen in 1943. He was associated with Harvard University (1951–69) and is the author of many books. Kissinger served as advisor to the government and Special Assistant to the President for National Security Affairs before becoming Secretary of State in 1973.

Kisumu (ki-SU-mu), Kenya   K 233
Kitakyushu (ki-TA-kyoo-shu), Japan   J 39
Kitchen, or vegetable, **gardens**   G 26, 51–52;   V 288–94;
   picture   G 28

Kitchen Cabinet, unofficial and informal group of advisers to President Andrew Jackson, more influential than regular cabinet. It included Blair, Donelson, Eaton, Kendall, Lewis, and Van Buren. The term is now generally applied to any such group who unofficially advise president or governor.

Kitchener, Horatio Herbert (1st Earl Kitchener of Khartoum and Broom) (1850–1916), British general, b. County Kerry, Ireland. As commander in chief of Egyptian army, he attempted reconquest of Sudan from controlling Dervishes (1896–99). He played an important role in combating Boer resistance during Boer War In South Africa (1900–02) and became commander in chief in India (1902–09). Kitchener served as British agent and consul general in Egypt (1911–14), and he organized British forces as secretary of war during World War I.
   the Boar War   B 299

Kitchen middens, prehistoric refuse mounds marking site of primitive dwellings. They contain remains of meals, tools, bones, and shells. They first were discovered on the coast of Denmark, in which country there are several hundred known mounds. Since then they have been found in the British Isles, North America, and elsewhere. The earliest remains were dated to the Old Stone Age.
   Turtle Mound, New Smyrna, Fla.   F 268

Kitchen Table, painting by Paul Cézanne   P 28

Kite, bird of prey found throughout the world except in polar regions. There are several kinds of kites. Most are grayish or brownish birds and have a sharp, down-curved bill. Many have long, pointed wings and a forked tail. Their diet includes insects, lizards, and sometimes small birds and snakes. Excellent fliers, kites may pick up prey in their sharp claws and eat while still in flight.

Kitega, Burundi, marketplace, picture   B 464
Kites   K 266–71
   Franklin's experiment with electricity   F 453–54
   kite flying a New Years sport in Japan   J 31
   Why does a kite fly?   K 271
Kit foxes   D 250;   F 397; picture   D 251
Kithara see Cithara
Kitimat, British Columbia, Canada   C 56, 57
Kitō (ki-TO), **Takai**, Japanese Haiku poet   J 28

Kitt, Eartha (1928–   ), American singer, Negro, b. North, S.C. Early in her career she sang in Paris nightclubs, where she became an instant success. Returning to the United States, she filled many nightclub engagements and won wide praise for the number "Monotonous" in the revue New Faces of 1952. She has made numerous popular recordings and TV appearances.

Kittatinny Mountains, New Jersey   N 166

Kittinger, Joseph W., Jr., American aeronaut   P 61
Kitt Peak, Arizona
   solar observatory, a sunscope, pictures   E 28,   O 10

Kittson, Norman Wolfred (1814–1888), Canadian fur trader, b. Chambly. He was a trading agent with the American Fur Company in upper Minnesota and Red River Valleys, trading with Indians in competition with Hudson's Bay Company until forced out of the area. He left the fur-trading business in 1854 and later (1871) became a founder and head of Red River Transportation Company (with James J. Hill).

Kitty Hawk, North Carolina   N 316
   aviation history   A 568
   Wright brothers   W 316
Kivas (KI-vas), Indian ceremonial rooms   I 192, 196
Kivu (KI-vu), Lake, Rwanda   R 362
   market, picture   R 363

Kiwanis (ki-WA-nis) **International**, service club, founded in Detroit (1915), for business and professional men. It supports activities for boys and girls, including agricultural and conservation groups, church groups, Key Club International for high school boys, Circle K International for college men, and vocational guidance services. Its headquarters is in Chicago, Ill., and its publications include The Kiwanis Magazine.

Kiwis, birds   B 226;   N 240; picture   B 227

Kjelgaard (KEL-gard), **James Arthur** (1910–1959), American author of children's stories, b. New York, N.Y. His boyhood was spent in Pennsylvania mountains, where outdoor life became the basis for many of his later stories. His works include Forest Patrol, Big Red, and Irish Red, Son of Big Red.

Klamath, Indians of North America   I 180
Klamath Mountains, California   C 16, 18
Klamath weed, or Saint-John's-wort   W 106
   poisonous plants   P 323
Klaproth (KLA-prote), **Martin**, German chemist, discovered
   chromium   C 296
   named uranium   U 230
Klee (KLAY), **Paul**, Swiss artist   K 271
   Bauhaus school in Germany   B 103;   G 171
   modern art   M 392
   Twittering Machine, painting   M 392

Klem, Bill (William J. Klem) (1874–1951) American baseball umpire, b. Rochester, N.Y. He umpired in National League (1905–41). His first experience as umpire in World Series (1908) led to his appearance in 18 World Series. Given a plaque (1939) for dedicated service by New York chapter of Baseball Writers Association, he was named posthumously to the Baseball Hall of Fame in 1953.

Klemperer, Otto (1885–1973), German conductor, b. Breslau. He began his career with an appointment as conductor at the German National Theater, Prague (1907), going on to important conducting posts at opera houses in various cities in Europe. He became first conductor at the Berlin State Opera in 1927. He was conductor of the Los Angeles Philharmonic (1933–39). He conducted at the Budapest Opera (1947–50) and has been principal conductor of the Philharmonia Orchestra in England since 1959.

Kline, Franz, American artist   M 397
   Black Reflections, painting   M 396b

Klondike gold rush G 253; M 320
Yukon and Northwest Territories Y 364, 365
Klopstock, Friedrich, German poet G 175
Klos, Elmer, Czech motion-picture director M 488a
Klotz family, Bavarian violin makers V 342
Kms system see Kilogram-meter-second

Knauer, Virginia Harrington Wright (1915–), American consumer expert, b. Philadelphia, Pa. While on the Philadelphia City Council (1960–67) she became interested in consumer problems. She was director of Pennsylvania Bureau of Consumer Protection (1968–69) and in 1969 became Nixon's special assistant for consumer affairs.

Kneecap (patella), bone of the leg, diagram F 79
Kneller, Sir Godfrey, English painter E 238
Knesset, Israeli parliament J 80
Knickerbocker, Father, myth-hero of Irving's *History of New York* A 199
Knickerbocker, The, early literary magazine M 14
Knife see Knives

Knight, Eric Mowbray (1897–1943), American novelist, b. Menston, England. He served in Canadian Army during World War I and in United States Army during World War II. He was killed on an official mission. Known for his children's book, *Lassie Come Home,* Knight's works include *The Happy Land,* and *This Above All.*

Knight, Death, and the Devil, engraving by Dürer G 303
Knighthood, title of honor in Great Britain K 277
Knights and knighthood K 272–77
armor A 433–35
Arthur, King A 442–45
fighting men supplied to a feudal lord F 100
heraldry H 115–18
Japanese samurai J 45–46
knight as poet-composers G 181
medals and decorations M 198
Knights Hospitalers (HOSP-it-al-ers), or **Knights of Malta,** a crusading order M 60
flag, Grand Master, Order of Malta F 227

Knights of Columbus (K of C), fraternal and philanthropic society of Roman Catholic men 18 years of age and over. Established (1882) to promote charity and vocational education, it also provides insurance for members. Its headquarters is in New Haven, Conn. It publishes *Columbia* and *Knights of Columbus News.*

Knights of Labor L 3–4
child labor laws passed by C 235
Knights of Malta see Knights Hospitalers, a crusading order

Knights of Pythias (PITH-ias) (KP), international fraternal order based on principles of friendship, charity, and benevolence. The name is taken from the legend of the devotion of Damon and Pythias to each other. Founded in 1864, KP has headquarters in Stockton, Calif. It publishes the *Pythian International.*

Knights of St. Gregory the Great, pontifical order of knighthood that rewards distinguished service, by Catholic laymen, to the Church. Founded (1831) by Pope Gregory XVI and named after St. Gregory the Great, the order has headquarters in Rome, Italy.

Knights of the Round Table, of King Arthur A 442, 444

Knights of the White Camelia, secret society that arose in New Orleans in 1867 during the Reconstruction era

and spread to other areas. Organized to maintain the supremacy of the white race, it frightened Negroes from voting and acted as a vigilance committee, punishing and controlling the conduct of unruly Negroes. Often guilty of lawlessness, it was disbanded in 1870.

Knit fabrics T 144
Knitting K 277–81, 284
carpetmaking process R 354
how to make horse reins I 225
machines, picture I 235
skill in colonial America C 391–92
Knitting needles N 89
Knives K 285–88
Bowie knife B 344
decorative art objects, pictures D 66, 67
penknife P 146
table settings T 2–3
Knock, a sound in an engine
how to reduce G 63
Knocking on wood, superstition S 474
Knossos, city of ancient Crete A 227, 373
ruins of Minoan civilization A 354; picture A 355

Knot, wading bird of the sandpiper family. The largest of the sandpipers, the knot measures about 10 or 11 inches in length. Brownish above, it has speckled brownish white on the underparts. A bird of the far north, the knot migrates south to New Zealand, Australia, South Africa, and South America.

Knots K 289–92
quipus, knotted ropes, record keeping of Inca Indians, picture C 451
Knots, measurement of speed in nautical miles per hour N 65
Knowledge, theory of S 77
Knowlton's Rangers, in Revolutionary War H 12
Know-Nothing Party F 125
movement fails to become a leading political party P 380
Know thyself, Socrates' motto P 191

Knox, Henry (1750–1806), American general, b. Boston, Mass. He was active in most of the important engagements of the Revolutionary War and became a close friend and adviser to General Washington. Under his direction, Washington's troops crossed the Delaware River (1776). He became a major general in 1781 and was placed in command of West Point in 1782. In 1783 Knox founded the Society of Cincinnati. He served as United States secretary of war (1785–94).
Revolutionary War, campaigns of R 201

Knox, John, Scottish reformer R 134; picture R 133
Protestantism P 482–83
Knoxville, Tennessee T 86
KO, knockout, in boxing B 352
Koalas (ko-AL-as), pouched animals K 175; pictures A 504; K 174
Australian wild life A 505
Kobe (KO-be), Japan J 40

Koch (KAWCK), **Johan Peter** (1870–1928), Danish explorer, b. Destenskov. He was a member of the Danish expedition (1906–08) that explored the northeastern coast of Greenland. Later he made a successful crossing of the country (1912–13).

Koch (KAWCK), **Robert,** German doctor and pioneer bacteriologist K 293
contributions to medicine M 208

Koch, Robert (continued)
  germ theory of disease, work in   **D** 215
  microbe cultures, preparation for microscope
    M 274–75
Kodachrome, color film   **P** 204–05
Kodak, a camera   **P** 212
  Eastman, George   **E** 44
Kodiak (KO-di-ak) **Island,** Alaska   **A** 130

Kodály (KO-da-ye), **Zoltán** (1882–1967), Hungarian composer, b. Kecskemet. In association with Béla Bartók he collected over 3,500 Hungarian folk songs. He was associated with Budapest Academy of Music (1907–19). He composed the opera *Háry János* and orchestral works *Summer Evening, Dances of Galanta,* and *Psalmus Hungaricus,* as well as chamber music and songs.
  Hungarian music   **H** 283

Koestler (KEST-ler), **Arthur** (1905–), Hungarian writer, b. Budapest. A correspondent for the German Ullstein newspaper chain (1926–31), he was also special correspondent for London *News Chronicle* (1936–38). He was condemned to death as anti-Fascist but released. He later wrote *Reflections on Hanging,* opposing capital punishment. He was once a member of the Communist Party, whose beliefs he later renounced. His best-known novels include *The Gladiators* and *Darkness at Noon.*
  Hungarian literature   **H** 284

Kofa Mountains, Arizona, picture   **G** 94
K of C see Knights of Columbus
Kohinoor (koh-i-NOOR), diamond, history of   **D** 156

Kohlrabi (kohl-RAB-i), type of cabbage developed in Europe in the 16th century from the marrow cabbage. The stem is thickened and looks somewhat like a turnip. Kohlrabi was introduced into the United States about 1906, but it is used more commonly in Europe.

Kohn, Misch, American artist
  aquatint and collage, *The Géneral*   **G** 306

Kokoschka (kó-KOSH-ka), **Oskar** (1886–), Austrian writer and painter of German expressionist school, b. Pochlarn. He lived in Germany from 1908 until he was opposed by Hitler as one of the "degenerate artists." He taught at Dresden Academy of Art (1919–24). He was founder of International Summer Academy of Fine Arts in Salzburg, where he has been an instructor since 1953. His best-known paintings include "psychoanalytic" portraits of his friends, *Elbe at Dresden,* and *Self-Portrait.*

Kolinskies, yellow weasels   **O** 244

Kollwitz (KOLE-vits), **Käthe Schmidt** (1867–1945), German artist, b. Königsberg, East Prussia. She was the first woman accepted by the Berlin Academy (1919), but was ousted when Hitler came to power. She is noted for her woodcuts, lithographs, and etchings, often depicting the anguish of war and poverty. Her works include woodcuts *War and Proletariat,* and lithographs on *Death.*
  Mother with child, etching   **G** 171

Kolyma (ko-LE-ma), river in Russia rising in Cherski Range and flowing 1,335 miles to its delta at the East Siberian Sea. The river passes through the Kolyma gold-mining area. It can be navigated (June to October).

Komachi, Ono no, Japanese poet   **O** 220b

Komarov, Vladimir Mikhailovitch (1927–67), Soviet astronaut, b. Moscow. He commanded the flight of Voskhod 1 (Oct. 12–13, 1964), in which Boris Yegorov and Konstantin Foektisov participated. It was the first multimanned space flight, the first flight in which the astronauts wore ordinary clothing instead of space suits, and it was the first time that Soviet astronauts came down with the capsule. Col. Komarov died on his second mission into space in Soyuz 1, when his craft's re-entry parachute became snarled and his ship fell to earth.
  space flight data   **S** 344, 345

Komodo (ko-MO-do) **monitors,** lizards   **L** 319; picture
  L 318
Kompong Som, formerly Sihanoukville, Cambodia   **C** 22, 33

Konev (KON-yif), **Ivan Stepanovich** (1897–), Russian marshal, b. Lodeyno. A distinguished soldier, he was named marshal of the Soviet Union in 1944 and later commander in chief of the Soviet Army (1946–50). The Warsaw conference placed the unified armed forces of the European Communist countries under his command (1955–60), and he then headed the Soviet forces in East Germany (1961–62). Since 1962 he has been a general inspector at the Ministry of Defense.

Konig, line game   **G** 22
Königsberg (KUR-nics-berk) **bridges,** topological problem
  T 220–21
Konkouré River, West Africa   **G** 404
Kon Tiki, balsa raft of Thor Heyerdahl   **L** 232

Koo, Vi Kyuin Wellington (Ku Wei-chūn) (1888?–), Chinese diplomat and judge, b. Shanghai. A delegate at many international conferences, he also has been ambassador to France, Great Britain, and the United States. He was judge at the International Court of Justice (1957–66).

Koontz, Elizabeth Duncan (1919–), American educator, b. Salisbury, N.C. She was the first Negro elected (1968) president of the National Education Association (NEA). She was appointed (1969) director of Women's Bureau of the labor department.

Kootenay (KOO-ten-ay) **National Park,** British Columbia
  B 406a
Kootenay River District, British Columbia, Canada   **C** 56
Korab (KOR-op), **Mount,** Albania   **A** 145
Koran (ko-RON) (Arabic: Qu'ran), holy book of
  Islam   **K** 294–95
  Islamic illumination   **I** 417, 419; picture   **I** 418
  Islamic prayer   **P** 435
  Mohammed   **M** 404
  Moroccan children learn the Koran   **M** 459
  teachings of Islam   **I** 414
Korda, Sir Alexander, Hungarian-born English motion
  picture director   **H** 283
Kore, figure in Greek sculpture   **S** 94
Korea (kor-E-a)   **K** 296–302
  astronomical myths   **M** 558–59
  students playing the kaya-ko, picture   **O** 220d
Korea, Democratic People's Republic of (North Korea)
  K 296, 298–99, 301–02
  Korean War   **K** 303–04
  flag   **F** 237
Korea, Republic of (South Korea)   **K** 296, 299, 301–02
  Korean War   **K** 303–04
  flag   **F** 238
  Seoul   **S** 121
Korean language   **L** 40
Korean War, 1950–53   **K** 303–04
  Eisenhower, Dwight D.   **E** 110
  MacArthur, Douglas   **M** 2

Seoul **S** 121
Truman, Harry S **T** 303
United States Marine Corps **U** 179
Korista, Albania **A** 144, 145

Kornberg, Arthur (1918–), American biochemist, b. Brooklyn, N.Y. In 1955 he succeeded in synthesizing DNA (deoxyribonucleic acid), one of the building blocks of the nuclei of living cells. For this achievement Kornberg shared the 1959 Nobel prize in physiology and medicine with Severo Ochoa.

Koror Island, island of volcanic origin. It is a major island of the Palau group in the Western Carolines, in the western Pacific, east of the Philippines, and the headquarters of Palau District in the United States Trust Territory of the Pacific Islands.

Korzeniowski, Teodor Jósef Konrad see Conrad, Joseph
Kos, island in the Aegean Sea **I** 429
Kosciusko (kos-ci-US-ko), **Mount,** Australia **A** 502
Kosciusko, Thaddeus, Polish general, volunteer aid to Americans **R** 203
  led Polish revolt, 1794 against Russia **P** 362
Koshare (ko-SHA-ray) **Indian dancers,** Colorado **C** 409
Kosher, food selected and prepared according to Jewish ritual laws **J** 119
  favorite foods of Israel **F** 341

Kossuth (KO-shoot), **Lajos** (1802–1894), Hungarian national leader and orator, b. Monok, Zemplin. A deputy member of the Diet, he was imprisoned (1837–40) for arousing public opinion in his *Parliamentary Reports* against Austrian rule. He edited (1841–44) the influential nationalistic newspaper *Pesti Hirlap.* He was elected to the Diet (1847), where his brilliant speeches (1848) led to the Hungarian revolution of 1848–49. He was elected governor of the independent Hungarian republic (1849) but was forced to flee to Turkey (1849). He continued his efforts to liberate Hungary while in exile.
  Hungary, history of **H** 288

Kosygin (ko-SEEG-in), **Aleksei Nikolayevich** (1904–), Soviet statesman, b. Leningrad. He joined the Red Army (1919–22), worked in various co-operatives and textile plants in Siberia and Leningrad (1924–38), and became mayor of Leningrad (1938–39). He criticized industrial lag and gained notice of Stalin, who appointed him minister of finance (1948). He was chosen minister of light industry (1948–53) and of consumer goods production (1953–54), and he held various posts as member of Communist Party (1946–60). Kosygin served as first deputy premier (1960–64) and is now premier (since 1964). Picture **J** 130.
  Communism **C** 443

Kota Bharu (KO-ta BAH-roo), Malaysia **M** 54
Kota Kinabalu, formerly Jesselton, capital of Sabah, Malaysia **M** 55
  apartment houses, picture **B** 338

Koufax (KO-fax), **Sanford** ("Sandy") (1935–), American baseball player, b. N.Y. Left-handed pitcher for the Dodgers (1955–66), his major league records include 4 no-hit games and most strikeouts in one season (382). Picture **B** 76.

Kouros (KOO-ros), figure in Greek sculpture **S** 94

Koussevitzky (koo-sev-ITS-ki), **Serge Alexandrovitch** (1874–1951), Russian-American conductor, b. Vichny-Volotchok. A noted master of double bass, he founded

and conducted (1909–18) his own symphony orchestra in Russia. He organized and conducted summer "Concerts Koussevitzky" in Paris (1921–28) and was conductor of Boston Symphony Orchestra (1924–49). He initiated Berkshire Music Center at Tanglewood, Mass., and organized Berkshire Music School (1940).
  Berkshire Festival **M** 551

Koven, Reginald de see De Koven, Reginald

Kovalevski (kov-al-YEF-ski), **Sonya** (1850–1891), Russian mathematician, b. Moscow. She studied in Germany, meeting many difficulties because of being a woman, but received her degree in 1874. She has been called the greatest woman mathematician of the 19th century.

Kowloon, peninsula in Hong Kong **H** 203–05; **U** 79

KP, U.S. Army term for "kitchen police." This refers to tasks, other than cooking, connected with preparing meals or cleaning up after meals. KP duty is sometimes used as a punishment for minor infractions.

Kraals, South African villages **S** 269
  cattle enclosures **A** 62
Krakatau (Krakatoa), volcanic island, Indonesia **V** 381–82
  dust resulting from 1883 eruption **D** 347, 348
  in Sunda Strait, separating Java from Sumatra **I** 218
  landforms of Southeast Asia **S** 328, 329
Krak des Chevaliers, Crusader castle, picture **S** 506
Kramer, Gustav, German scientist **H** 192–93
Kramer, Max O., German scientist **D** 272–73
Kranach see Cranach, Lucas

Krebs, Sir Hans Adolf (1900–), German-British biochemist, b. Hildesheim, Germany. He left Nazi Germany in 1935 and went to England, where he specialized in investigating metabolism. He soon had enough evidence to map out the citric-acid cycle (often called the Krebs cycle after him), one of the chief ways in which the body burns fats and carbohydrates. He shared the 1953 Nobel prize in physiology and medicine with F. A. Lipmann.

Kreisler (KRY-sler), **Fritz** (1875–1962), Austrian-American violinist, b. Vienna. He displayed talent at early age, making his American debut in New York (1888). He interrupted his musical career with studies in art and medicine but re-appeared as violinist in Berlin (1899). He toured United States and Europe after serving in Austrian Army during World War I. His compositions include violin concertos, *Caprice Viennois, Tambourin Chinois,* and operettas *Apple Blossoms* and *Sissy.*

Kremlin, Moscow, Union of Soviet Socialist Republics **M** 465–67; pictures **M** 464, **U** 55, **W** 220
  Cathedral of the Dormition, picture **U** 55
Kremlin, or fortress in Russian towns **U** 52

Krenek (KREN-ek), **Ernst** (1900–), Austrian-American composer, b. Vienna. Identified with Arnold Schoenberg's 12-tone technique, he was opera coach at Kassel, Germany (1925–27), professor of music at Vassar College (1939–42), and dean of fine arts at Hamline University, Saint Paul (1942–47). His compositions include a popular jazz opera, *Jonny Spielt Auf,* the opera *Orpheus und Eurydike,* orchestral works, choral music, chamber music, and songs. He is also a writer on music.
  twentieth-century music **C** 279; **G** 189

Kresge (KRES-ke) **Foundation,** philanthropic organization whose grants support educational, medical, social wel-

Kresge Foundation (continued)
fare, and research programs. Currently grants are given only to institutions in United States and Canada. Founded by Sebastian S. Kresge (1924), the foundation has its headquarters in Detroit, Mich.

Kress, Samuel Henry (1863–1955), American business executive and art collector, b. Cherryville, Pa. He was owner and founder of the S. H. Kress and Company 5-, 10-, and 25-cent store chain. He established (1929) the Samuel H. Kress Foundation to make art donations to American museums and grants to medical institutions. He became president of National Gallery of Art (1945). His famous donations include painting and sculpture from the Italian Renaissance and Medieval periods.
    National Gallery of Art (Washington, D.C.) **N** 40

Kress Collection, of art **N** 40
Kreutzer (KROIT-zer), **Rodolphe,** French violinist **V** 343
Krewes, carnival organizations, New Orleans **C** 120
Krill, small crustaceans **P** 280–81
    food of baleen whales **M** 66
    food of penguins **P** 121
    life, food chains in **L** 241
Krimml Falls, Austria **W** 56b
Krio, language of Sierra Leone **S** 174

Krips, Josef (1902–), Austrian conductor, b. Vienna. Conductor at Vienna State Opera (1933–38) and professor at Vienna Academy of Music (1935–38), he conducted again in Vienna (1945–47), gaining a wide reputation. He was appointed conductor of London Symphony Orchestra (1950) and later of Buffalo Philharmonic Orchestra (1952). He has been musical director of San Francisco Symphony Orchestra since 1963.

Krishna Menon, Vengalil Krishnan (1897–), Indian statesman and lawyer, b. Calicut. Secretary of the India League (1929–47), group dedicated to Indian independence, he later served in London as high commissioner for India (1947–52). He was Indian representative to UN General Assembly (1952–61), and member of Indian Parliament (1953–57), and minister of defense under Nehru (1957–62). He was also editor of Twentieth Century Library and a founding editor of Pelican Books (1930's). In 1969 he was re-elected to Parliament.

Kriss Kringle, German Santa Claus **C** 292

Kroll, Leon (1884–), American artist, b. New York, N.Y. He has done landscapes, genre paintings, and murals. His later works show the influence of Poussin, Cézanne, and Renoir. *The Road from the Cove* won the top award at the Carnegie International Exhibition in 1936. His figures have been described as being as smooth and still as statues. The Department of Justice building in Washington, D.C., is decorated with his murals.

Kronach see Cranach, Lucas
Kronborg Castle, the Elsinore of *Hamlet,* picture **D** 107

Kruger (KROOG-er), **Paul** (1825–1904), South African statesman, b. Colesberg, Cape Colony. Of German origin, he was one of the founders of the province of Transvaal and was its president (1883–1900). He was a leader of the Boer rebellion (1880) and declared war against the British (1899) to prevent their taking over the Transvaal. Too old to fight in the war, he went to Europe and sought aid there, dying in Switzerland.
    South Africa, history of **S** 273

Kruger National Park, South Africa **S** 270
Kruif, Paul de see De Kruif, Paul

Krumgold, Joseph Quincy (1908–), American writer and motion picture producer, b. Jersey City, N.J. He was a motion picture writer and producer for Paramount, Columbia, Republic, and RKO companies. He emigrated to Israel, where he produced documentary films (1947–51). He is now president of Krumgold Productions Co. (since 1950). He is the author of *Thanks to Murder* and recipient of two Newbery awards for the children's books *And Now Miguel* (1954) and *Onion John* (1960).

Krupp family, German industrialists. **Friedrich** (1787–1826), an ironmaster, founded the Krupp Works at Essen around 1810, and his son **Alfred** (1812–87) expanded the business through technical improvements and the use of the Bessemer steel process. Alfred's son **Friedrich Alfred** (1854–1902) further enlarged the firm and manufactured machinery, also a staple under the regime of **Gustav Krupp von Bohlen und Holbach** (1870–1950), who produced armaments for Hitler. The last head of the Krupp empire was **Alfred** (1907–67), convicted as a war criminal in 1948 and released in 1951.

Krutch (KROOTCH), **Joseph Wood,** American writer **A** 214
Krutt, cheese made from camel's milk **C** 192
Krylov (kril-OFF), **Ivan Andreevich,** Russian fabulist **F** 4
Krypton (KRIP-ton), element **E** 154, 162
    atmosphere, gases in **A** 479
    gases in industry **G** 62
    noble gases **N** 109–10
    standard measurement, uses in **W** 111, 114; picture **W** 110
Kshatriyas (K'SHUT-ri-yas), a caste in Hindu society **H** 130
Kuala Lumpur (KUA-la LUM-pure), capital of Malaysia **M** 55; pictures **M** 55, 56
    government buildings, picture **A** 468

Kuan-yin, or **Kwan-yin,** Chinese form of Buddhist deity Avalokitesvara, goddess of mercy and fertility. Pictured on lotus flower, cloud, or wave, she wears a crown adorned with Amitabha Buddha's likeness and often holds a child. In Japan the goddess is known as Kwannon.

Kubelik (KU-bel-ik), **Rafael** (Jeronym Rafael Kubelik) (1914–), Czech conductor and composer, b. Bychory, Bohemia (now part of Czechoslovakia). Son of the famous violinist Jan Kubelik, he conducted Czech Philharmonic Orchestra (1936–39) and served as head conductor (1942–48). Major conductor with Chicago Symphony Orchestra (1950–53), he also directed London's Covent Garden Opera (1955–58). He is head conductor of Bayrischer Rundfunk in Munich, Germany (since 1961). His compositions include opera *Veronika,* a violin concerto, and two symphonies. He was named music director of Metropolitan Opera to begin conducting in the 1973–74 season.

Kubitschek (KU-bit-chek) **de Oliveira, Juscelino,** president of Brazil **B** 380, 384
Kubla Khan, poem by Coleridge **E** 260
Kublai Khan (KU-bly kahn), Mongol ruler of China **M** 416
    China, history of **C** 270
    grandson of Genghis Khan **G** 93
    Japanese conquest averted **J** 43
    Lamaism adopted as state religion **T** 178
    Marco Polo **E** 371; **P** 389–90
    Peking **P** 117

Kubrick, Stanley, American motion-picture director
M 488

Kuching (KU-ching), capital of Sarawak, Malaysia   M 55

Kuhn (KUNE), **Walt** (1880–1949), American artist, b. New York, N.Y. A painter of realistic portraits and still lifes, he often did paintings of circus and vaudeville performers. He began his career as a cartoonist in San Francisco (1899–1900). In New York he became an art instructor and was a co-organizer of the 1913 Armory Show. In his later period he was especially influenced by Matisse and Picasso, among other modernists. His works include *Blue Clown, Apples in the Hay,* and *Juggler.*

Kühne (KOO-neh), **Wilhelm** (1837–1900), German physiologist, b. Hamburg. He is known especially for his studies on the chemistry of digestion and the physiology of muscles and nerves.

   first to identify and use the name "enzyme" F 90

Kuiper (KY-per), **Gerard,** American astronomer **P** 277, 278

Ku Klux Klan, secret society   R 120
   Negro history N 96

Kukui (ku-KU-i), or candlenut tree
   state tree of Hawaii H 56

Kumasi (ku-MA-si), Ghana **G** 196, 198; picture **G** 197

Kumasi University College of Science and Technology, Ghana **G** 195

Kumquat, a citrus fruit **O** 179; picture **O** 176

Kun (KOON), **Béla** (1885–1937?), Hungarian Jewish Communist leader, b. Transylvania. He joined the Bolshevik Party in Russia (1918) and returned to Hungary that same year, when revolution broke out. There he founded and edited the Communist daily *Red News* (1918–19). A leader in the establishment of the Hungarian Communist Government (1919), he became premier. His administration was defeated in a counter-revolution later that year, and he fled finally to Russia.

K'ung Fu-tzu see Confucius

Kuniyoshi (ku-ni-YO-shi), **Yasuo** (1893–1953), American painter, b. Okayama, Japan. He taught at the Art Students League and New School for Social Research and established Artists Equity Association, becoming its first president (1947). He was primarily a stylist, and his work is a fusion of French and Oriental influences. His paintings include *Cemetery, Pie in the Sky,* and *Girl Thinking.*

Kunlun, mountains in Tibet **T** 176
Kuntaur, The Gambia **G** 9

Kuomintang (guo-min-TONG) (Chinese for "National People's Party"), nationalist party of China founded by Sun Yat-sen (1912) to establish a central democratic government. Following Sun Yat-sen's death (1925), Chiang Kaishek gained party control and excluded Chinese Communists from membership. The party held power until ousted from the mainland by the Communist forces (1949). It is now the dominant party of Taiwan under Chiang Kai-shek.
   Chiang Kai-shek **C** 227
   China, history of **C** 272
   Mao Tse-tung **M** 86
   Sun Yat-sen **S** 467

Kupang, Indonesian Timor **I** 221
Kurds, Indo-Aryan people of the Middle East **I** 378
Kurile (ku-REEL) **Islands,** north of Japan **I** 434
Kurosawa, Akira, Japanese motion-picture director
   M 488
Kuroshio see Japan Current

Kusch, Polykarp (1911–   ), German-American physicist, b. Blankenburg, Germany. His most important work, determining the magnetic moment of the electron, threw new light on the structure of the atom. He shared the 1955 Nobel prize in physics with Willis E. Lamb. In 1969 he was named vice-president of Columbia University, where he had joined the faculty in 1937.

Kush, Land of, now Sudan, Africa **S** 448
Kuskokwim (KUS-ko-kwin) **River,** Alaska **A** 133
Kutenai, Indians of North America **I** 175
Kuwait (ku-WA-it) **K** 305–08
   Arab, picture **A** 459
   camels and oil wells, picture **M** 308
   flag **F** 238
   Middle East **M** 301; picture **M** 308
Kuwait, capital of Kuwait **K** 307
KVD, Committee for State Safety, spy network of the Soviet Union **S** 390
Kwakiutl (kwa-ki-U-tel) **Indians,** of North America **I** 181
Kwan-yin see Kuan-yin

Ky, Nguyen Cao (KI, nwin KOW) (1930–   ), Vietnamese military and political leader, b. Son Tay. A French-trained combat pilot, he became commander of the South Vietnamese Air Force after the overthrow of President Ngo Dinh Diem in 1963. Ky became premier of South Vietnam under a military junta in 1965. In 1967 he was elected vice-president, with General Nguyen Van Thieu as president. He resigned in 1971.
   Vietnam, history of **V** 334c

Kyaks see Kayaks
Kyd (KID) **Thomas,** English dramatist **D** 296; **E** 253
Kyoto (ki-YO-to), Japan **J** 40; **T** 204; pictures **J** 41, 47
   Fushimi Castle, picture **O** 219
Kyrenia (ky-RE-nia) **Mountains,** Cyprus **C** 557
Kyushu (ki-YU-shu), island of Japan **J** 34

ILLUSTRATION CREDITS

The following list credits, by page, the sources of illustrations used in Volume J-K of THE NEW BOOK OF KNOWLEDGE. Credits are listed illustration by illustration—left to right, top to bottom. Wherever appropriate, the name of the photographer or artist has been listed with the source, the two being separated by a dash. When two or more illustrations appear on one page, their credits are separated by semicolons.

L, twelfth letter of the English alphabet **L 1**
See also Alphabet

Laban (LAY-ban), father of Leah and Rachel. According to the Old Testament story, he was a crafty man who cheated Jacob into working for him for 14 years. As a reward for 7 years' labor, Jacob was to receive Rachel as his wife. Laban gave him Leah instead, and Jacob had to work another 7 years for Rachel. When Laban tried to detain Jacob further, the two quarreled. Finally agreeing to make peace, they set up a mound of stones to separate their two regions. The story is considered by some to be an allegory of Syrian-Israeli relationship.

Labels, on food containers
government-required information **F 350**
Labor **L 2–10**
agriculture **A** 89, 92, 96
automation **A** 528–34
child labor **C** 235
contract and wage agreements **L** 12
discrimination in employment prohibited **N** 104
economic factor of production **E** 48
government regulation **L** 14
guilds **G** 401–03
Industrial Revolution **I** 238–41
International Labour Organisation (ILO) **U** 85
iron and steel employment statistics **I** 408
labor and management **L** 11–18
Labor Day **H** 154
labor reserve schools of Soviet Union **U** 30
May Day, or International Labor Day **H** 153
occupational health and safety **O** 15–16
rotos, Chilean workers **C** 250
serfs under feudalism **F** 102
service industries and occupations **S** 124–25
slave labor **S** 195–200
sweat shops in early clothing industry **C** 353–54
trade, productive factor in **T** 242
unemployment and unemployment insurance **U** 25–26
work, the world of **W** 251–53
working conditions in Industrial Revolution **I** 238–41
workmen's compensation **W** 253
work songs of occupations **F** 304, 319
Labor, U.S. Department of, established 1913 **L** 5
handicapped persons helped by **H** 29
Laboratories (LAB-or-a-tories)
floating laboratory for oceanographic research **O** 26
high school chemistry laboratory, picture **E** 72
IBM laboratories, picture **N** 216
language laboratories **E** 78; picture **E** 79
medical laboratory tests **M** 201–02, 209
Skylab, in space **S** 343
underwater laboratory, Sealab I **U** 19–20
Labor camps, for criminals **P** 468
Labor contracts **L** 15; picture **L** 16
Labor Day **H** 154
See also May Day, International Labor Day
Labor-Management Relations Act (Taft-Hartley Act), 1947 **L** 6, 15
Truman, Harry S **T** 301
Labor-Management Reporting and Disclosure Act (Landrum-Griffin Act), 1959 **L** 15
Labor mediators **L** 18
Labors of Heracles (HER-a-clese), in Greek mythology **G** 363
Labor unions **L** 2–10
capitalism modified by **C** 104
changes in the world of work **W** 252–53
clothing industry **C** 354
folk song, words and music, "Solidarity" **F** 320
Gompers, Samuel **G** 263

guilds **G** 401–03
Industrial Revolution **I** 241
Lewis, John L. **L** 161
newspapers **N** 205
work, changes in the world of **W** 252–53
See also National Labor Relations Act (Wagner Act), 1935; Railway brotherhoods; Railway Labor Act
Labour Party, Great Britain **P** 379
socialism and labor **S** 220
Labrador, Newfoundland, Canada **N** 140–45
Labrador Current, of Atlantic Ocean **A** 478
foggy conditions **C** 55
Gulf Stream, meeting with **G** 411
icebergs **I** 26
Labradorite (LAB-ra-dor-ite), gemstone **G** 76
Labrador retriever, sporting dog, picture **D** 253
La Brea (la-BRAY-a) **Pits,** Los Angeles, California **L** 345
La Bruyère (la bru-YARE), **Jean de,** French social critic **F** 438

Laburnums, shrubs or small trees related to the bean, cultivated as ornamental plants in many parts of the world. Laburnums have glossy leaves and an abundance of yellow flowers, growing in clusters. The plants, especially the seeds, are poisonous if eaten by people but harmless to most animals. Laburnum wood is tough. It is used in cabinetwork and for musical instruments.

Labyrinth (LAB-ir-inth), in Greek mythology **G** 365
Labyrinth, inner ear
of fishes **F** 191; picture **F** 193
Lac, a resin **R** 184
Lace **L** 19
Belgian lacemaking, picture **B** 127
La Ceiba, Honduras **H** 197
Lacertas (la-CER-tas), lizards, picture **L** 321
Lacewood, tree
uses of the wood and its grain, picture **W** 223
Lachaise (la-SHEZ), **Gaston,** French-born American sculptor **U** 116
20th century sculpture **S** 103–04
Laclède (la-CLED), **Pierre,** French fur trader **F** 522–23
early settlement of St. Louis **S** 17

Lacombe (la-COM), **Albert** (1827–1916), Canadian missionary, b. St. Sulpice. He was ordained a priest (1849) and ministered to Indians in Northwest territory. He helped draw up treaty with Indians (1898), and he wrote a dictionary and grammar of Cree language.

La Condamine (la con-da-MENE), **Charles de,** French scientist **R** 340
Lacquers (LAC-ers) **V** 280
Japanese box, picture **D** 74
lacquered wood statue, picture **O** 218
Lac resin **V** 279
Lacrosse **L** 20–21
Canada **C** 67
Indians playing lacrosse, picture **I** 188
La Crosse, Wisconsin **W** 205
Lactose, or milk sugar **M** 311; **S** 453
Lactic acid, in sour milk **M** 311
Ladd, Edwin Fremont, American chemist **N** 335
Ladd, William, American worker for peace **P** 104
Ladder-back chair, picture **C** 389
Ladder ditchers, machines **B** 448
Ladder division, in arithmetic **A** 401
Ladders
on fire engines, pictures **F** 146, 147
superstitions about **S** 474
Ladies' Home Journal, The, magazine **M** 14
Ladies Professional Golfers' Association **G** 262

Ladino (la-DI-no), popular name for Judeo-Spanish language spoken by descendants of Jews who were expelled from Spain in 15th century and who settled along the Mediterranean. Ladino is basically 15th-century Spanish, with many words borrowed from Turkish, Greek, and Hebrew. It is written with modified Hebrew alphabet. The term also refers to a Spanish-speaking Latin American of mixed Spanish, Indian, or Negro blood.

Ladoga (LA-do-ga), Lake, northwestern European U.S.S.R. **L** 32
Lady, British title **K** 277
Lady and Tramp, cartoon characters, picture **A** 297
Ladybird beetles, or lady bugs, pictures **I** 269, 276
Lady Day, or Annunciation Day, religious holiday **R** 154
Lady of Shalott, poem by Alfred, Lord Tennyson **T** 101
Lady's slipper, flower, picture **W** 170
  state flower of Minnesota **M** 323
Laënnec (laen-NEC), **René,** French doctor **M** 206–07
La Farge, John, American painter and glassmaker **S** 395

La Farge, Oliver Hazard Perry ("Oliver II") (1901–1963), American novelist and anthropologist, b. New York, N.Y. He is noted for his special interest in American Indians and for his efforts to improve their living conditions. He served on archeological expeditions to Arizona, Mexico, and Guatemala. He was president of Association on American Indian Affairs (1937–42, 1948–63) and was awarded the Pulitzer prize (1929) for novel about Indians, *Laughing Boy.*

Lafayette, Louisiana **L** 360–61
La Fayette (la-fay-ETT), **Marie, Comtesse de,** French novelist **F** 438; **N** 348
Lafayette, Marquis de, French soldier **L** 22–23
  feted in Independence Hall **I** 113
  in American Hall of Fame **H** 14
  National Guard so named to honor Lafayette **N** 42
  Revolutionary War **R** 202
Lafayette, U.S. nuclear submarine, picture **S** 442
Laffite (la-FEET), **Jean,** French-born American pirate and adventurer **L** 23
  Louisiana, early history of **L** 361
La Follette (la FOLL-ett), **Philip F.,** American statesman **W** 205, 208
La Follette, Robert, American statesman and political reformer **L** 24
  Wisconsin Idea, progressive government **W** 208
La Follette, Robert, Jr., American legislator **L** 24
La Fontaine (la fon-TAIN), **Jean de,** French writer of fables **F** 3, 438
Laforet (la-for-EH), **Carmen,** Spanish writer **S** 372
LAFTA see Latin American Free Trade Association
Lagan see Flotsam, jetsam, and lagan, or ligan
Lagash (LAY-gash), city of Babylonia **A** 217
Lager (LOG-er) **beer B** 116–17
Lagerkvist (LOG-er-kvist), **Pär,** Swedish author **S** 51–52 53
Lagerlöf (LOG-er-lerv), **Selma,** Swedish author **S** 53
Lagomorpha (lag-o-MORPH-a), order of mammals **M** 62, 69; **R** 22

Lagoon, area of water protected from the open sea by a sandbar or coral reef. Biscayne Bay between Miami Beach and Miami, Fla., and Great South Bay between Fire Island and Long Island, N.Y., are lagoons. Venice, Italy, is built in a shallow lagoon. The circular body of water enclosed by an atoll is also a lagoon.

Lagos (LAY-gos), capital of Nigeria **N** 255; pictures **A** 60, 68
Lag screws N 3; picture **N** 2

La Guardia (la gu-AR-dia), **Fiorello,** American lawyer and political leader **L** 24
La Guma, Alex, South African novelist **A** 76b
Lahaf (LA-haf), robe of Libyan women, picture **L** 201
Lahaina (la-HA-i-na), Maui, Hawaiian Islands **H** 66
Lahontan (la-HON-tan), Lake, Nevada **N** 124–25
Lahore (la-HORE), Pakistan **P** 40
  Badshahi mosque, picture **P** 37
  dyed fabric, picture **A** 463

Laird, Melvin Robert (1922–   ), American politician, b. Marshfield, Wis. He served in the Wisconsin state senate (1946–52), the U.S. House of Representatives (1953–69), and as secretary of defense (1969–73). In 1973 he became chief domestic adviser to President Nixon.

Laissez-faire (les-say-FAIR) (French, meaning "let do" or "let things alone"), principle of allowing problems to work themselves out without interference or regulation. As an economic doctrine opposes state interference in economic affairs. It originated among 18th-century French economists and was later expanded by English economist Adam Smith. The concept is based on belief in a natural order, in which individual interests are in harmony with economic progress.

Lake, chemical compound used in dyeing **D** 371
Lake Charles, Louisiana **L** 360
Lake District, in northwestern England **E** 212

Lake dwellers, people who live in houses built on piles in water. In ancient times, farmers in alpine areas of Europe built dwellings along the margins of lakes in order to save land for agriculture and pasturage. Irish, Scottish, and English people of olden times built dwellings on man-made islands called crannogs.
  homes of the past **H** 177

Lake Isle of Innisfree, The, poem by Yeats **Y** 344
Lake of the Woods, Minnesota-Ontario **M** 325; **O** 120a
  territorial boundaries, Northwest Angle **T** 108, 109
Lake Placid, New York, Van Hoevenberg bobrun **B** 265

Lake poets (Lake school), term applied to the romantic poets Wordsworth, Coleridge, and Southey, who lived in the Lake District of Cumberland and Westmorland in England. They gained inspiration from nature and viewed poetry as a means of emotional expression. The title originated as a term of contempt in the *Edinburgh Review* but later lost its scornful connotation.

Lakes L 25–34
  dams create man-made lakes **D** 19
  Glacier National Park, Montana, pictures **G** 221, 222
  Indiana Dunes National Lakeshore **I** 146; picture **I** 147
  Kashmir, picture **K** 199
  national lakeshores, list **N** 52
  North America has largest number **N** 288–89
  See *also* land section of country, province, and state articles; lakes by name, as Erie, Lake
Lakeshores, National, list **N** 52
  Wisconsin's Apostle Islands National Lakeshore **W** 203
Laki (LA-ki), volcano, in Iceland **I** 45
La Libertad (la li-ber-TOD), El Salvador, picture **E** 182
Lalique (la-LEEK), **René,** French jeweler **J** 97
L'Allegro, poem by John Milton **M** 311
Lalo (la-LO) **Edouard,** French composer **F** 446
Lamaism (LA-ma-ism), religion
  Bhutan **B** 150
  Mongolia **M** 413

Land-grant colleges A 95; U 205
in the history of education E 73
Morrill, J. S., sponsor of land-grant act V 316

Land grants, government land allotted for construction of roads, railroads, and public works or for establishment of agricultural or technical colleges. Term also refers to public lands distributed to private citizens for settlement. In United States, land-grant legislation includes the Pacific Railway Acts (1862–64), the Morrill Act (1862) for state agricultural colleges, and the Homestead Act (1862) for private settlement.
railroads, history of R 90

Landing, moon E 368; S 339–340a, 340g–340i
Landing gear, of airplane A 556–57
Landini (lon-DI-ni), **Francesco,** Italian composer I 483
Middle Ages, music of the M 299
Landis, Kenesaw Mountain, American baseball commissioner B 81
Land of Enchantment, nickname for New Mexico N 180
Land of Haunted Castles (Luxembourg) L 379
Land of Lincoln, official nickname for Illinois I 70

Land of Nod, in Old Testament, the land, east of Eden, where Cain took refuge after killing his brother Abel (Genesis 4:16). The term is thought to be derived from the Hebrew word meaning "wanderer," and it signifies a condition of sleep.

Land of Sky-blue Waters, a nickname for Minnesota M 323
Land of Steady Habits, nickname for Connecticut C 467, 481
Land of 10,000 Lakes, a nickname for Minnesota M 322
Land of the Dakotas, nickname for North Dakota N 323
Land of the Midnight Sun, Arctic region P 364
Eskimo life E 284
nickname for Alaska A 129
Land of the Pagodas (Burma) B 454
Land of the Shining Mountains, Indian name for Montana M 428
Landon, Alfred Mossman, American statesman K 190
anagrams on his name W 236

Landowska (lon-DOF-ska), **Wanda** (1879–1959), Polish harpsichordist and pianist, b. Warsaw. She taught harpsichord, upon invitation, in Berlin (1912–19) and founded and taught at Saint-Leu-la-Forêt, near Paris, a school for the study of baroque and classical music (1925–40). She made numerous concert tours in Europe, North and South America, and Africa, and she composed songs, music for string orchestra, and pieces for piano. She wrote (with her husband) *La musique ancienne* on the music of the 17th and 18th centuries.

Landrum-Griffin Act see Labor-Management Reporting and Disclosure Act
Landscape gardening G 26, 29
Landscape painting
American wilderness painters U 121
Dutch and Flemish art D 357
English E 238, 240
Sung dynasty of China O 216
Turner, Joseph Mallord William T 329
Landscape with the Flight into Egypt, painting by Claude Lorrain B 58, 60

Landseer, Sir Edwin Henry (1802–1873), English painter, b. London. Noted for his paintings of animals, he modeled the lions at base of Nelson Monument in Trafalgar Square, London. His paintings include *Stag at Bay,*

Dignity and Impudence, and *Cat's Paw.* Some paintings were engraved by his elder brother Thomas.

Land's End, England E 213
Land snails, mollusks O 276
Landsteiner (LAND-sty-ner), **Karl,** Austrian physician, classified blood types B 257
blood transfusions T 251
Land use
studied in agricultural geography G 107

Landy, John (1930–), Australian track star, b. Melbourne. He ran the mile in a record 3 min. 58 sec. in Turku, Finland (1954), surpassing Roger Bannister's record of 3 min. 59.4 sec. He lost to Roger Bannister in British Empire Games in British Columbia (1954) and retired in 1957.

Lane, Harriet, acting first lady in Buchanan's administration *see* Johnson, Harriet Lane
Lane, Ralph, English seaman A 181
Lang, Andrew, Scottish writer S 435
Langer, William, American political leader N 335
Langland, William, English poet E 248
Langley, Samuel, American astronomer and aeronautical pioneer A 568
Langmuir, Irving, American scientist and engineer L 35
cloud-seeding experiment for weather control W 92
filament lamps L 284
Langrenus, Belgian astronomer M 449

Langston, John Mercer (1829–97), American educator and diplomat, Negro, b. Louisa County, Va. Orphan son of a plantation owner and a freed slave, he was raised by a family friend. After graduating from the theology department of Oberlin College, he read law and was admitted to the bar. Chosen clerk of Brownhelm township, Ohio (1855), he was probably the first Negro to win an elective office. He later served as dean of Howard Law School, minister to Haiti, and chargé d'affaires in Santo Domingo. He won a Republican Congressional election (1888), but the election was contested and he was not seated for 2 years. His autobiography is entitled *From the Virginia Plantation to the National Capital.*

Langton, Stephen, English theologian E 218
Magna Carta, an author of M 22
Language and languages L 37–40
Africa A 55–56
African tone languages A 79
alphabet A 170–73
Anglo-Saxon (Old English) in *Beowulf* B 141
animal signals A 275–76
anthropological studies A 300, 308
Asia A 459–60
Bible translations B 152–54
child development C 232–33
Chinese C 258–59
communication by speech C 429–30
computer programing languages C 457
days of the week in five languages D 47
dialects D 152
dictionaries D 164–65
Europe E 317
French official language of many countries F 433–35
grammar, the way a language works G 288–90
Grimm brothers, first scientific study of German grammar G 376
Hawaiian H 63
India's regional languages I 119
international trade problems I 328
Japanese J 27–28

laboratories in schools **E** 78; picture **E** 79
Latin once a world language **L** 76
linguistics **L** 301–03; **R** 182
North America **N** 297
phonics **P** 193–96
population geography studies distribution of languages
 G 108
pronunciation **P** 478
Romany, or gypsy **G** 434
semantics **S** 117–18
slang **S** 194
South America **S** 282, 288
speech **S** 376–78
spelling **S** 378–79
taxonomy, a kind of universal language **T** 29
television production **T** 70a
treaties **T** 272
universal languages **U** 194–95
word origins **W** 238–41
writing **W** 317–21
See also Alphabet; Dialects; Grammar; Linguistics;
 Semantics; Speech; Universal languages; Writing;
 articles on individual countries; names of principal
 languages and language groups
Language arts L 36
handwriting **H** 31–33
punctuation **P** 530–33
reading **R** 107–11
speech **S** 376–78
spelling **S** 378–79
vocabulary **V** 371–72
See also Compositions; Grammar; Handwriting; Letter
 writing; Reading; Reports; Spelling
Languages, universal see Universal languages
Languedoc Canal see Canal du Midi
Langweiser Viaduct, Switzerland, picture **E** 328
Lanier (la-NIER), **Sidney,** American poet **A** 204;
 G 146
was prisoner in Maryland in Civil War **M** 128
Lanolin, fat from wool **W** 235
use in cosmetics **C** 510
wool wax **W** 69
L'Anse aux Meadows, Newfoundland **N** 143
Lansing, capital of Michigan **M** 269–70
Lanston, Tolbert, American lawyer **P** 465
Lantern Festival, China **H** 154

Lanternfish, any member of a family of small, club-
shaped fish found in the deep waters of the Atlantic
Ocean and the Mediterranean Sea. Lanternfish live at
depths of about 2,500 feet, often surfacing at night. All
have large eyes and wide mouths, and most are from 3
to 6 inches long. Luminous dots are found along the side
of the body, and in one species the front of the head
also gives off light.

Lanterns, Feast of, Japan **J** 31
Lanterns, outer casings for lights **L** 281–83
Lanthanide (LANTH-an-ide) **series,** of rare earth elements
 E 159
Lanthanum, element **E** 154, 162

Laocoön (la-OC-o-on), in Greek mythology, Trojan priest
who warned citizens of Troy to be on guard against
wooden horse presented by Greeks as gift to Athena.
According to one story, for his distrust of the gift horse
Athena sent two serpents to crush him and his two sons.
His death was taken by the citizens of Troy to mean that
his warnings were false and that the horse was indeed
sacred. Ancient sculpture depicting his death (discovered
1506) is now displayed in the Vatican.
Trojan War **T** 293

Laos (LAY-os) or (LOUS) **L** 41–43
flag **F** 238

Lao-tzu (LA-o-DZU), or **Lao-tse,** or **Lao-tsze,** Chinese
philosopher and reputed founder of Taoism. Traditionally
believed to have been born in Nonan province during 7th
century B.C., he served as librarian in Chou court. As
reputed author of *Tao Tê Ching (The Way and Its Virtue)*,
he advocated doctrine of naturalness and spontaneity,
by which man achieves ideal or oneness with universe
by renouncing artificiality—forms and ceremonies.
Chinese literature **O** 220a
religions of China **C** 260–61
Taoism, a great mystic faith **R** 148

La Paz (la POS), capital of Bolivia **B** 302, 306; pictures
 B 305; **L** 47; **S** 274

Lapchick, Joseph (1900–1970), American basketball player
and coach, b. Yonkers, N.Y. He played with N.Y. Celtics
(1922–27) and later helped organize and played with
the Original Celtics (until 1936). He coached the St.
John's University's Redmen (1936–47, 1955–65) and
participated in National Invitation Tournament, winning
the 1943, 1944, 1959, and 1965 championships. He
coached the New York Knickerbockers (1947–55). He was
elected to Basketball Hall of Fame (1961).

La Peltrie, Marie Madeleine de (1603–1671), French nun,
b. Alençon. She founded Ursuline convent for French and
Indian girls at Quebec (1639) and accompanied a group
of colonists who founded Montreal (1642). She returned
to Quebec (1643), becoming an Ursuline novice.

Lapis lazuli (LAP-is LAZ-u-li), or lazurite, gemstone **G** 76
Laplace (le-PLOS), **Pierre, Marquis de,** French mathemati-
cian and astronomer **S** 247
Laplace theory, of origin of solar system **S** 247
La Plata, Rio de see Plata, Rio de la
Lapland L 44–45
children playing with lassos, picture **A** 304
Lapland family, picture **F** 39
taiga **T** 11
Laps, rolls of raw cotton **C** 525
Lapstone, shoemakers' stone used in leatherworking
 S 162
Laptev (LOPT-yef) **Sea O** 48
Laramie, Wyoming **W** 335
Larboard, port or left side of a ship **S** 155

Larcom, Lucy (1824–1893), American poet and story
writer, b. Beverly Farms, Mass. She compiled and edited
Roadside Poems and *Hillside and Seaside in Poetry* and
collaborated with Whittier on editing anthologies. Her
works include *Similitudes from Ocean and Prairies,
Ships in the Mist, Poems,* and an autobiography, *A New
England Girlhood.* She was a teacher at Wheaton College,
Mass. (1854–62), and an editor of magazine *Our Young
Folks.*

Lard, fat obtained from hogs **O** 79
Larderello (lar-der-EL-lo), Italy
natural steam runs generators, picture **E** 203
Lardner, Ringgold Wilmer ("Ring"), American writer
 M 272
short stories **S** 167

Lares (LAY-rese) **and penates** (pe-NAY-tese), in ancient
Rome, protective household gods (each family had a *lar*
and several *penates*). *Lares* were usually deified spirits
of ancestors, and *penates* were gods and guardians of
hearth and storehouses. They were also deities of the

Lares and penates (continued)
state and were therefore worshiped publicly as well as privately. The term has come to mean one's most valuable personal and household possessions.

Lariats R 333
  honda knots used for K 290
  roping R 334

Lark, any of several small brown- or gray-streaked birds noted for their songs, which are especially beautiful when the birds are in flight. Larks live in fairly open country and usually nest on the ground. They walk or run, but they never hop. Larks are found chiefly in the Old World, from tundra areas south.

Lark buntings, birds, picture B 236
  state bird of Colorado C 401
Larkin Building, Buffalo, New York W 315
Lark in the Morning, folk song F 320

Larkspur, or **delphinium,** flowering plant of the Northern Hemisphere that has long been a favorite with gardeners. It grows to a height of 3 to 4 feet and has a spirelike cluster of flowers. The flowers are usually blue, but some varieties bear white, pink, lavender, or purple blossoms. Plant's sap is poisonous. Pictures G 27, 49.

La Rochefoucauld (la rosh-foo-CO), **François, duc de,** French writer F 438
Larra, Mariano José de, Spanish writer S 370
Larsen, Don, American baseball pitcher B 80
Larsen, Henry A., Royal Canadian Mounted Police officer commands trip through Northwest Passage N 338
Larvae (LAR-ve), early forms of animals that must undergo metamorphosis M 234
  ants A 323, 331
  bees B 122–23
  butterflies and moths B 469
  clothes moths H 261
  eels E 86
  eggs and embryos E 89
  frogs, toads, and other amphibians F 470–78
  insects I 264–65; pictures I 276, 277
  plant enemies P 284–87
  plankton, animal P 281
Laryngitis (la-rin-JITE-is), inflammation of the larynx D 195
Larynx (LARR-inx), voice box V 375
  speech S 377
La Salle, Robert Cavelier, Sieur de, French explorer L 46
  Canada C 69
  exploration of the New World E 384
  Saint Lawrence River S 16
La Scala (la SCA-la), opera house, Milan I 486
Lascaux (la-SCO) **Caves,** France, pictures P 440, W 217
  laser mirror on moon S 340a, 340i; diagram S 340i
Lasers (LAZE-ers), devices for amplifying light waves M 131–33
  electronic communication E 142f
  gas lasers, for projecting light beams G 62
  holograms, pictures P 208
  laser mirror on moon S 340a, 340i; diagram S 340i
  new discoveries in physics P 239
  telephone, uses in T 60
  welding W 119

Lasker Foundation, Inc., Albert and Mary, organization that donates funds for medical research. It encourages research in the areas of cancer, heart disease, and mental illness. The organization presents Lasker awards yearly for important contributions in medical research

and writing, as well as in public health administration. Founded in 1942, its headquarters are in New York, N.Y.

Lassen Peak, California V 380
  only active volcano in the first 48 mainland states C 16
Lassen Volcanic National Park, California C 24
Lassoing, roping R 333–35
  children playing with lassos, picture A 304
  honda knots used for K 290
Lassus, Roland de, Belgian composer D 365; F 444
  Renaissance music R 173–74
Last, block used in shoemaking S 162–63
Last Frontier, nickname for Alaska A 129
Last Judgment, fresco by Michelangelo M 257; picture M 256
Last of the Mohicans, The, novel by Cooper C 498
Last Supper, of Jesus Christ J 84
  Holy Thursday commemorates events leading to Easter E 41
  See also Holy Communion
Last Supper, painting by Tintoretto I 470, 471
Last Supper, The, painting by Dierik Bouts D 354
Last Supper, The, painting by Leonardo da Vinci A 332
Last Word of a Bluebird, The, poem by Robert Frost F 480
Las Vegas (los VAY-gas), Nevada N 133–34
Latakia (lat-a-KI-a), Syria S 508
Lateen (la-TEEN) **sails** T 261
Latent (LATE-ent) **heat** I 4
Lateral moraines I 19; picture I 18
Lateral pass, in football F 360
Lateran Councils, of the Roman Catholic Church R 292, 294
Lateran Treaty, 1929 V 280
Latexes (LAY-tex-es)
  rubber R 340, 343–45
  synthetic latexes, paints P 32

Latham (LAY-tham), **Jean Lee** (1902–   ), American author and playwright, b. Buckhannon, W.Va. She was editor in chief of Dramatic Publishing Company (1930–36) and worked as a free-lance writer (1936–41 and since 1945). Her career was interrupted during World War II, when she trained women inspectors for the Signal Corps, U.S. War Department (1943–45). She is best-known for fictionalized biographies of prominent Americans, including *Carry on, Mr. Bowditch,* which won the Newbery award (1956), *The Story of Eli Whitney, Medals for Morse,* and *Trail Blazer of the Seas.*

Lathes, machine tools T 217; picture T 218

Lathrop (LAY-throp), **Dorothy Pulis** (1891–   ), American illustrator and author of children's books, b. Albany, N.Y. She wrote and illustrated *The Fairy Circus* and the first book to win a Caldecott medal (1938), *Animals of the Bible.*

Latimer, Hugh (1485?–1555), English prelate and reformer, b. Thurcaston, Leicestershire. An ardent defender of reformed Anglican doctrine, he was periodically out of favor at court during reigns of Henry VIII and Edward VI. He was consecrated bishop of Worcester (1535) but resigned (1539) when he could not sanction the Act of the Six Articles. He was accused of heresy under Mary Tudor, an ardent Catholic. Convicted, he was burned to death at Oxford.

Latimer, Lewis Howard (1848–1928), American inventor, Negro, b. Chelsea, Mass. He was employed by Alexander Graham Bell to make patent drawings for the first telephone. He invented (1881) the first incandescent electric bulb with a carbon filament. As an engineer for the Edison Company, he supervised the installation of light systems in New York, Philadelphia, Montreal, and London.

Lattimore, Eleanor Frances (1904–), American author of children's books, b. Shanghai, China. She is known for books about Chinese children, including *Little Pear* and *The Chinese Daughter.*

Laubach, Frank Charles (1884–1970), American missionary and educator, b. Benton, Pa. He was a missionary in the Philippines (1915–40), where he developed a system for teaching illiterates to read using phonetic symbols and pictures. Students became teachers according to his motto, "Each one teach one." Laubach directed the Maranaw Folk Schools in the Philippines (1929–40) and wrote *Toward a Literate World* among other books.

Laugh-In, a television comedy show. Introduced in 1968, this program offered a totally different format from the usual TV fare. The comedy team of **Dan Rowan** (1922–) and **Dick Martin** (1922–) head a cast that specializes in poking fun at the American way of life by means of rapid-fire jokes and comedy sketches.

Laurel and Hardy, American film comedy team. Stan Laurel (Arthur Stanley Jefferson) (1890–1965), b. Ulverson, England, and Oliver Norvell Hardy (1892–1957), b. Atlanta, Ga., were both vaudeville performers before their paths crossed in 1926. In over 100 feature films, among them *Pardon Us, Pack Up Your Troubles, Blockheads,* and *Babes in Toyland,* timid Laurel suffered the insults of Hardy, the blustering bully. A short, *The Music Box,* won an Academy Award.

Lausanne, University of   S 496
Lauth, Bernard, Alsatian-born American inventor of a method of cold-rolling steel   I 406
Lava, volcanic molten rock   R 264;   V 378; picture R 265;   V 379
  caves   C 156
  diamonds formed in   D 153
  earth formations of   E 13–14
  intrusion and extrusion of, diagram   G 111
Lava Beds National Monument, California   C 25
Lava Hot Springs, Idaho   I 65
Laval (la-VOL), Carl Gustav de, Swedish engineer   T 320
  cream separator inventor   M 310
Laval, François, French bishop   Q 17

Laval (la-VOL), Pierre (1883–1945), French politician and lawyer, b. Chateldon. He shifted his political sentiments from socialist to republican and finally to fascist. He served as France's prime minister and minister of foreign affairs (1931–32, 1935–36), minister of labor (1932), and minister of foreign affairs (1934–35). He became premier (1942–45) of the Vichy government and after the war was executed as a Nazi collaborator.
  Vichy government   W 289

La Valette, Jean de, French knight of Malta   M 60
Lavalleja, Juan, Uruguayan patriot   U 239

Laval-Montmorency (la-VOL MON-mo-RON-cy), François Xavier de (1623–1708), first Bishop of Quebec, b. Montigny-sur-Avre, France. He came to Canada as vicar apostolic (1659) and later was appointed Bishop of Quebec (1674–88). The seminary he founded (1663) was the core of Laval University, founded later.

Laval University, Quebec City, Canada   C 62;   Q 10b, 17
Lava River Caves, Oregon, picture   C 156

Laver, Rod (Rodney George Laver) (1938–   ), Australian left-handed tennis player, b. Rockhampton. He won the Australian, French, British (Wimbledon), and United States championships in 1 year (1962), to make the second "grand slam" in history (first made by Don Budge, 1938). He was a member of the Australian Davis Cup team (1959–62), and then turned professional. In 1969 he became first man to capture a second "grand slam."

La Vérendrye (la vai-ron-DRE), Pierre Gaultier de Varennes, Sieur de (1685–1749), French explorer, b. Three Rivers, Canada. In search of the Western Sea, he explored the area west of Lake Superior. Besides establishing five forts, he explored Manitoba and the northwest territories of Canada.

Lavinia, painting see Girl with a Bowl of Fruit
Lavoisier (la-vwa-si-AY), Antoine Laurent, French chemist L 86; picture   C 211
  chemistry of breathing   M 206
  law of conservation of matter   C 212
  phlogiston theory disproved   C 210–12
  the new chemistry in the history of science   S 72
Law, Andrew Bonar, Canadian-born British statesman N 138c
Law and law enforcement   L 87–89
  adoption laws   A 26
  Anglo-Saxon basis of English law   E 216, 217–18
  Bill of Rights   B 177–80
  Canadian courts   C 77–78
  child labor laws   C 235
  civil rights and civil liberties protected   C 316
  codes see Codes, of law
  corporation law and trusts and monopolies   T 304

  courts   C 526–30
  divorce   D 234–35
  FBI training of officers   F 77
  fishing laws   F 223–24
  food regulations and laws   F 350–52
  French civil law in Quebec, Canada   C 71
  Holmes, Oliver Wendell, Jr., the "Great Dissenter" H 160–61
  immigration, legislation on   I 99–102
  income tax   I 111
  insurance   I 296
  international law   I 320–21
  interstate commerce   I 331–32
  jury   J 159–60
  lawyers   L 92–93
  legislation   U 140–41
  legislatures   L 135–36
  Magna Carta   E 218;   M 22
  marriage laws   W 101
  Marshall, John   M 112
  mentally ill, problem of the   M 224–25
  municipal government   M 503
  narcotics, legal measures to control use of   N 14
  "no conflict" principle, layers of law   S 412, 414
  oldest written laws   A 220; picture A 219
  pioneer life   P 260
  police   P 372–77
  president's executive ordinances   P 453
  prisons   P 468–70
  Roman law   A 232
  Supreme Court   S 476–77
  trademarks and copyright   T 244–45
  United States Constitution   U 145–58
  What is meant by "Possession is nine points of the law"?   L 93
  wills   W 174–75
  women, role of   W 211, 212a–213
  See also Civil liberties and civil rights; Lawyers
Law Courts, London, picture   E 241

Law Day, U.S.A., national observance to foster respect for and understanding of U.S. democratic rule of law—in contrast to law under a Communist system. It is sponsored by the American Bar Association and is proclaimed annually by the president of the United States. It began in 1958 and occurs on May 1.

Lawless, Theodore Kenneth (1892–   ), American dermatologist, Negro, b. Thibodeaux, La. A distinguished dermatologist and syphilologist in Chicago, he is a member of the Chicago Board of Health and of the Chicago Civil Liberties Committee. He has received a number of awards for outstanding work in medicine.

Lawman see Layamon, English priest
Lawn bowling, or bowls   B 349
Lawn games
  badminton   B 13–15
  bowls or lawn bowling   B 349
  croquet   C 536–37
  lawn tennis   T 90–99
Lawns   L 90–91
  lawn and garden tractors   F 57
Lawn sprinklers
  show reaction principle of jet propulsion J 85
Lawn tennis see Tennis
Law of see inverted form as Moses, Law of
Lawrence, Andrea Mead, American athlete   O 113; picture O 112
Lawrence, D. H., English novelist   E 267
  themes of his novels   N 347

Lawrence, Ernest Orlando (1901–58), American physicist, b. Canton, S. Dak. A pioneer in nuclear research, he invented the cyclotron in 1930 and in 1932 turned lithium into hydrogen by bombardment with a high-energy proton beam. In World War II he adapted the cyclotron for use in extracting uranium-235 for the first atomic bomb. For his invention and development of the cyclotron he received the Nobel prize in physics in 1939. The man-made element lawrencium is named for him.
  particle accelerators N 366

Lawrence, Jacob (1917–), American painter, Negro, b. Atlantic City, N.J. His works have appeared in many exhibitions and are included in the collections of major museums. From 1958 to 1965 he taught at the Pratt Institute art school. He was represented in an exchange exhibit with the Soviet Union in 1959. In 1965 he was artist in residence at Brandeis University.
  Negro Renaissance N 98

Lawrence, James, American naval officer N 178, 179

Lawrence, Robert (1936–67), American astronaut, Negro, b. Chicago, Ill. A major in the Air Force, he was a flight instructor and a service research scientist at the Air Force Weapons Laboratory. He was one of the final four chosen from sixteen prospective astronauts for the Defense Department's Manned Orbiting Laboratory program. Lawrence was killed in a crash of an F-104 Starfighter jet as it landed after a routine training flight. He held a doctorate in physical chemistry from Ohio State University.

Lawrence, Thomas Edward ("Lawrence of Arabia") (also wrote under pseudonym T. E. Shaw) (1888–1935), British archeologist, soldier, writer, and diplomat, b. Tremadoc, North Wales. He was associated with the British Museum in excavation expeditions (1910–14), was a member of the intelligence service in Egypt during World War I (1914–16), and made intensive studies of feasibility of Arab revolt against the Turks. He organized and led Arabs to victory over Turks at Damascus in 1918. Lawrence was a member of the Arab delegation at the Paris Peace Conference (1919) and adviser on Arab affairs, Middle East division of the British Colonial Office (1921–22). An enigmatic personality, he joined Royal Air Force and Royal Tank Corps under assumed names. His best-known book is Seven Pillars of Wisdom.
  World War I in Syria S 508

Lawrence-Haverhill Metropolitan Area, Massachusetts M 147
Lawrencium (law-REN-ci-um), element E 154, 162
  atomic number A 487
Laws see Law and law enforcement
Lawson, Harry J., English builder of first safety bicycle B 173

Lawson, Robert (1892–1957), American author and illustrator, b. New York, N.Y. He worked as stage designer for the Washington Square Players and as a magazine illustrator (1914–17) before devoting his time to children's books. He illustrated the classic The Story of Ferdinand, by Munro Leaf, in addition to his own works for children, including Ben and Me, They Were Strong and Good (Caldecott medal, 1941), and Rabbit Hill (Newbery medal, 1945).

Lawton, Oklahoma O 92
Lawyers L 92–93
  complaints and pleadings for court cases C 527

  divorce D 234
  insurance I 297
  jury trials J 160
  patent lawyers I 347
  patron saint of Catholic lawyers, Sir Thomas More M 456
  See also American Bar Association; Law and law enforcement
Laxatives, from medicinal plants P 314
Lay, short epic poem
  related to ballads B 23
Layamon (LAY-a-mon), English priest A 445
  Middle English literature E 247
Layard, Sir Austen Henry, British archeologist and diplomat L 192
Laye, Camara, Guinean novelist A 76c
Lay investiture, in Roman Catholic Church R 291
Layouts, in bookmaking B 322, 324; picture B 325
  commercial art C 425
  magazines M 15–16
  planning a layout, picture P 464

Lazarus (from Hebrew name Eleazar, meaning "God has helped"), brother of Mary and Martha at whose house in Bethany Jesus was a guest. Lazarus fell sick and died while Jesus was elsewhere, but 4 days after his death Jesus resurrected him (John 11:1–44). The miracle resulted in heightening Jesus' fame among the populace while provoking anger of the Sadducees and Pharisees. Only other mention of Lazarus in the Bible states that he attended a supper with Jesus (John 12:1–2).

Lazarus, Emma (1849–87), American poet and essayist, b. New York, N.Y. Her concern over the unjust treatment of the Jewish people is reflected in her later writing. Author of the sonnet inscribed on the base of the Statue of Liberty, she wrote Admetus and Other Poems for her close friend Emerson and Songs of a Semite, containing the celebrated poem "The Dance to Death." Other works include By the Waters of Babylon and a translation, Poems and Ballads of Heinrich Heine.
  poem for plaque on the Statue of Liberty, excerpt L 168

Lazurite, or lapis lazuli, gemstone G 76
Lazy daisy stitch, in embroidery E 188
Lazy stitch, in beadwork I 158
LCD see Lowest common denominator
Leaching, of ores M 228
Leacock, Stephen, Canadian economist and humorist O 127
  Canadian literature C 64
Lead L 94–95
  atom A 488
  elements, some facts about E 154, 162
  galena, ore, cleavage of R 270; picture R 271
  glass, used in making G 226
  Missouri deposits M 370
  lead-free gasolines G 63
  lead-producing regions of North America N 293
  metals, chart of ores, location, properties, uses M 227
  pencils P 147–48
  poisoning P 356
  radioactive elements break down to form lead R 64
  Roman plumbing systems of lead pipes P 343
  tetraethyl lead added to gasoline G 63
  white lead a pigment in paints P 32
Lead (LEED), South Dakota S 320–21
Lead (LED) crystal, glass G 230
Lead pencils P 147–48
  development of writing tools C 433
  What is the "lead" in a lead pencil? L 95

Leaf, Munro (1905–), American author and illustrator, b. Hamilton, Md. His best-known children's books are *Grammar Can Be Fun, Manners Can Be Fun,* and *The Story of Ferdinand.* He is also noted for the book *You and Psychiatry* (written in collaboration with William C. Menninger) and for an army manual on malaria.

League of Women Voters of the United States (LWVUS), nonpartisan women's organization formed as successor to National American Woman's Suffrage Association. Its purpose is to guide women in using voting privilege. It also attempts to cultivate citizen interest in voting. The organization was founded in 1920, has its headquarters in Washington, D.C., and publishes the *National Voter.*

Leah (LE-ah) (Hebrew, meaning "mistress"), elder daughter of Laban, older sister of Rachel, and Jacob's first wife through trickery of Laban (Genesis 29). She was the mother of his sons Rueben, Simeon, Levi, Judah, Issachar, and Zebulun and his daughter Dinah. She died prior to Jacob's departure for Egypt.

Leahy (LAY-he), **Frank** (1908–), American football coach, b. O'Neill, Nebr. A graduate (1931) of Notre Dame University, where he played under Knute Rockne, he became Notre Dame's head coach (1941–54) and built up a record that was second only to Rockne's. His team won 87 games, lost 11, and tied 9.

Leap year, 366-day year that, according to legend, was so named because during each such year February has one extra day, the 29th, causing each date following to skip, or "leap over," the day upon which it would otherwise have fallen. In Scotland a law is said to have been passed in 1288 granting women the right during leap year to propose marriage to the man of their choice. The man could not refuse unless he was willing to pay a sum of money or could prove himself bound to someone else. The custom has since been adopted in many countries.

Lebanon (LEB-an-on) **L** 121–24
  coastline, picture **E** 12
  flag **F** 238
  Middle East region **M** 300–01
Le Bris (l' BRI), **Jean-Marie,** French inventor **G** 239
Le Brun (L'BRURN), **Charles,** French baroque artist
    B 62; **F** 425
  tapestry **T** 24

Le Corbusier (L'cor-boor-si-AY) (pseudonym of Charles
Edouard Jeanneret) (1887–1965), French architect and
city planner, b. La Chaux de Fonds, Switzerland. He
headed the international committee that designed United
Nations Headquarters, N.Y. (1947–50), and designed
urban projects in Antwerp and Stockholm, the city of
Chandigarh in India, and the Ronchamp chapel, Haute
Saone. He is author of *The City of Tomorrow.*
  apartment with nursery school, picture **S** 56
  modern architecture **A** 386–87; **F** 432
  Monastery of La Tourette, picture **F** 432

Leda (LE-da), in Greek mythology, mother of Helen of
Troy, Clytemnestra, and Castor and Pollux. Helen was
the daughter of Leda and Zeus, and Clytemnestra the
daughter of Leda and Tyndareus, King of Sparta. According to one account Castor and Pollux sprang from
an egg as offspring of Leda and the swan, the form in
which Zeus appeared to her. A conflicting story states
that Pollux is the son of Zeus and Castor the offspring
of Tyndareus and Leda.

Lederberg, Joshua (1925–), American geneticist, b.
Montclair, N.J. Together with E. L. Tatum he found that
bacteria can reproduce sexually and thus recombine
their genetic material in ways biologists had not believed
possible. Later he found that certain viruses could transfer
genetic material from one bacterium to another. Lederberg
shared the 1958 Nobel prize in physiology and medicine
with Tatum and G. W. Beadle.

Ledger lines, in musical notation **M** 526
Ledgers, in bookkeeping **B** 312

Ledyard (LED-yard), **John** (1751–89), American explorer,
b. Groton, Conn. He sailed with Captain Cook's third
voyage to Pacific (1776–80). After the American Revolution, he failed to gain American aid to open fur trade
with China. He next attempted to cross Russia and
Siberia on foot. He reached Irkutsk, where he was
arrested and ordered from the country (1788). Ledyard
died on an expedition to explore the source of the Niger
River in Africa. He wrote *A Journal of Captain Cook's
Last Voyage to the Pacific Ocean.*

Lee, Canada (Leonard Lionel Cornelius Canegata) (1907–
1952), American actor, Negro, b. New York, N.Y. He was
a jockey and a boxer before he organized a dance band
that played in theaters, where he became interested in
acting. His most notable roles were as Bigger Thomas in
Native Son (1941), Caliban in Margaret Webster's
production of *The Tempest* (1945), and in whiteface,
opposite Elizabeth Bergner in *The Duchess of Malfi.*
  Negro Renaissance **N** 98

Lee, Charles, American soldier **R** 204

Lee, Doris (1905–), American painter, b. Aledo, Ill. She
is best known for paintings of rural scenes. Her works
include the mural *Rural Postal Delivery* in Washington,
D.C., post office, paintings *Thanksgiving Dinner* and
Country Wedding. She illustrated James Thurber's *The
Great Quillow.*

Lee, Francis Lightfoot (1734–1797), American statesman,
b. Westmoreland County, Va. He served in Virginia's
House of Burgesses (1758–76) and was a member of
the Virginia convention (1775), in which the Virginia
revolution is said to have begun. He was an influential
member of the Continental Congress (1775–79) and a
signer of the Declaration of Independence.

Lee, (Nelle) **Harper** (1926–), American novelist, b. Mon-
roeville, Ala. She won fame with her first novel, *To Kill a
Mockingbird,* about a contemporary southern town. She
was awarded a Pulitzer prize for fiction (1961). The book
was made into a motion picture (1963).

Lee, Henry ("Light Horse" Harry Lee), American officer
    originated the "First in war, first in peace" description
    of George Washington **W** 36
Lee, Jason, Canadian-born American pioneer **O** 205
  missionaries followed the overland trails **O** 260
Lee, Manfred, see Queen, Ellery
Lee, Richard Henry, American Revolutionary War leader
    and statesman **A** 9
  Declaration of Independence **D** 61
Lee, Robert E., American military leader **L** 125–26
  Civil War **C** 321, 324–27, 460
  Grant and Lee **G** 295
  holiday on his birthday **H** 147
  North Carolina nickname (Tarheels) first used by
    N 306

Lee, Tsung-Dao (1926–), Chinese-American physicist,
b. Shanghai, China. In 1957 Lee and a colleague, C. N.
Yang, challenged the principle of the conservation of
parity, a complex theory dealing with the behavior of
subatomic particles. For their work Lee and Yang shared
the 1957 Nobel prize in physics.

Leeches, worms **W** 310, 312

Leek, plant closely related to the onion but with a milder
flavor. It has broad, thick leaves and a long, narrow
bulb. The upper parts of the leaves are used to spice
soups and stews. The bulb is eaten, cooked or raw, as a
vegetable. The leek is native to the eastern Mediterranean region and has been used as food and medicine
since prehistoric times. It is the national emblem of
Wales. Picture **O** 118.

Lee Kuan Yew (Lee Kwan Yew) (1923–), Singapore
statesman, b. Singapore. He helped found the People's
Action Party (1954), which demanded self-government
from Britain, and helped negotiate self-rule agreements
with Great Britain (1957, 1958). Elected first prime
minister of Singapore (1959), he helped bring about the
merger of Malaya, Sarawak, North Borneo, and Singapore into Great Malayasia Union (1963), from which
Singapore has since withdrawn (1965). **S** 184a

Lee Mansion, in Virginia **N** 28–29
Leeuwenhoek (LAY-ven-hook), **Anton van,** Dutch naturalist
    L 127; **M** 206
  advances in biology **B** 190
  lenses, histoy of **L** 141
  microbiology, a new world **M** 274
Leeward, away from the wind **S** 13
Leeward Islands, Caribbean island group **C** 118
Leeward Islands, of the Society Islands group, Pacific
    Ocean **P** 8
Left, political term, origin of **P** 379
Left Bank, of the Seine, Paris **P** 73–74
Left-handedness
  how to write easily **H** 33

Left wing, political groups or branch of a political group whose views are more radical than, or in advance of, the general level of political action and thought. The term originated in France after the Revolution, when conservative members of the legislature were seated to the right of the speaker, and more radical ones to the left. Today the left wing is often identified with socialism or communism.

Legal holidays, United States   **H** 147

Le Gallienne (l'GAL-yenn), **Eva** (1899–   ), American actress, b. London, England. She is noted for interpretations of Henrik Ibsen's plays. Founder and director of the Civic Repertory Theater in New York (1926–32), she helped found the American Repertory Theater (1946). She has appeared in *Hedda Gabler, The Cherry Orchard, Liliom,* and *Peter Pan.* She has written two autobiographies, *At 33* and *With a Quiet Heart.*
   theater in the United States   **T** 161

Legal profession see Lawyers
Legal tender see Paper money
Legato, or slurred notes, in musical notation   **M** 531
Legazpe, Miguel López de see López de Legazpe, Miguel
Legend of the Blue Plate, The   **L** 133
Legend of the White Deer   **L** 134
Legends   **L** 128–35
   Alfred and the cakes   **A** 154
   Arthur, King   **A** 442–45
   Boy Prisoners in the Tower   **E** 220;   **P** 470
   early form of fiction   **F** 109–10
   Faust   **F** 72–73
   folklore of place and personal names   **F** 310
   glassmaking, origin of   **F** 144;   **G** 226
   Groundhog Day in February   **F** 74
   Holy Grail in early French literature   **F** 436
   Japanese legend of the Sun Goddess   **J** 42
   "Pied Piper of Hamelin, The," poem by Browning, excerpt   **B** 413–14
   Prometheus stole fire   **F** 144
   Robin Hood   **R** 253
   Song of Roland   **C** 189
   writing, how it began   **W** 317
   See also Folklore; Mythology
Legends, on maps   **M** 88
Legge (LEG), **Robert T.,** American doctor   **O** 16

Legion, body of soldiers making up chief unit of the Roman army. A legion originally consisted of cavalry and 3,000 footsoldiers. Under Roman consul Gaius Marius (155–86 B.C.) the number of footsoldiers was increased to 6,000.

Legionary ants   **A** 331
Legion of Honor, French award, picture   **M** 200
Legion of Merit, American award, picture   **M** 199
Legislation, lawmaking   **L** 87–88
   direct see Initiative, referendum, and recall
   how legislatures function   **L** 135–36
   presidential leadership   **P** 453–54
   United States   **U** 140–41
Legislatures   **L** 135–36
   Ethiopia's, picture   **A** 68
   Kansas' Legislative Council   **K** 188–89
   Nebraska's unicameral state legislature   **N** 85
   single national legislative bodies   **K** 233;   **U** 6
   state legislatures   **S** 415
   See also country and state articles for detailed information on national and state legislatures
Legs, of animals
   bones of the human leg, diagram   **F** 79

   insects   **C** 167;   **I** 262–63, 273
   locomotion   **A** 291–92, 293
Leguía (leg GHE-a), **Augusto,** president of Peru   **P** 166
Legumes, plants of the pea and bean family
   fertilizers   **F** 96
Lehár (LAY-har), **Franz,** Hungarian composer   **O** 156
   Merry Widow, The, operetta   **O** 158
Lehman (LEE-man), **Herbert H.,** American statesman   **L** 136
Lehman Caves, Nevada, picture   **C** 155

Lehmann (LAY-monn), **Lotte** (1888–   ), German-American soprano, b. Perleberg, Germany. She was one of the finest Wagnerian singers of her day. When she was with the Vienna Opera (1914–38), Richard Strauss selected her to sing the Young Composer for the premier of *Ariadne auf Naxos* and Barak's wife for the premier of *Die Frau ohne Schatten.* He wrote *Arabella* for her and invited her to create the role of Christine in *Intermezzo.* She sang Octavian and then the Marschallin in *Der Rosenkavalier.* Her first appearance (1934) with the Metropolitan Opera Company was as Sieglinde in Wagner's *Die Walküre,* and as a member of the company (1934–45) she sang chiefly Wagnerian roles.

Lehmbruck (LAIM-broock), **Wilhelm,** German sculptor   **S** 103
Lehr (LEER), cooling oven for glass   **G** 232
Leib (LAIB), **Mani,** Yiddish author   **Y** 351

Leibniz (LIPE-nits), **Gottfried Wilhelm** (1646–1716), German philosopher and mathematician, b. Leipzig. He developed a system of infinitesimal calculus independently of Newton and at about the same time. (Followers of the two men later stirred up a bitter rivalry between them over who had been first.) Leibniz also invented an ingenious calculating machine. In philosophy his theory of monads (tiny particles that make up all matter) was a forerunner of modern atomic theory. He has been ranked with Newton as one of the two greatest thinkers of the 17th century.
   calculus created   **M** 157

Leicester, earl of see Dudley, Robert
Leiden (Ly-den), Dutch colony on Staten Island, flag of   **F** 228
Leiden, the Netherlands   **N** 118
   Separatists settlements form the Plymouth colony   **P** 344
Leif Ericson, or Leif the Lucky see Ericson, Leif
Leigh (LE), **Vivien,** English actress, picture   **M** 475

Leinsdorf (LINES-dorf), **Erich** (1912–), American conductor, b. Vienna, Austria. He went to United States (1938), where he was chief conductor of Rochester Philharmonic Orchestra (1947–56) and Metropolitan Opera (1957–62). He was conductor and musical director of Boston Symphony Orchestra (1962–69).

Leipzig (LIPE-tzig), Germany   **G** 157
   book and fur fairs   **F** 11
Leisure activities see Hobbies; How to; Sports
Leitmotivs (LITE-mo-teefs), melodic themes in music drama   **G** 187–88
   in opera and musical drama   **O** 136
Lei-tsu see Hsi-Ling-Shih
Leixões, Portugal   **P** 401
Lely (LE-ly), **Sir Peter,** English painter   **E** 237
Le Mans (l'MON), France, sports-car race   **A** 539; picture   **F** 404
Lemmings, rodents   **R** 278–79

Lemnitzer, Lyman Louis (1899–   ), American army officer, b. Honesdale, Pa. He served as assistant chief of staff to General Eisenhower (1942), directed foreign military assistance in Department of Defense (1948–50), and commanded forces in Korean War (1951–52). After serving as Army chief of staff (1959–60) and chairman of Joint Chiefs of Staff (1960–62), he was appointed commander in chief of European command (1962) and supreme allied commander in Europe (1963). He held both posts until 1969.

Lemnos, Greek island in the Aegean **G** 333
Lemon, citrus fruit **L** 136–38
Lemon sharks **S** 143
Lemoyne, Jean Baptiste *see* Bienville, Jean Baptiste Lemoyne, Sieur de
Lempa, major river in El Salvador **E** 181
Lemus, José María, former president of El Salvador **E** 184
Lemurs (LE-murs), animals related to monkeys
    flying lemurs, gliding animals **B** 96
    have four hands **F** 83
    primates, true lemurs **M** 418, 422

Le Nain (l'NAN) **brothers,** family of French painters, b. Laon. All were elected to Royal Academy of Painting and Sculpture (1648). **Antoine** (1588?–1648) primarily painted miniatures on copper and wood, including *The Annunciation.* **Louis** (1593?–1648) is remembered for paintings of peasant families, such as *The Peasant Supper* and *The Dairyman's Family.* **Mathius** (1607?–77) is associated with paintings of historical and religious subjects, such as *The Guard.*

Lena River, Union of Soviet Socialist Republics **R** 244

Lend-Lease Act, act prepared by President Roosevelt and passed by Congress (1941) to render any aid, except troops, to Allied forces. The act resulted from heightened German aggression and Britain's inability to pay for American defense materials. It provoked heated opposition of isolationist faction in Congress. Lend-Lease allowed the President to order manufacture of arms and defense materials to be sold or loaned to nations in combat with Axis powers. Its chief beneficiaries were Britain and Soviet Union. Aid was terminated (1945) by President Truman.
    Roosevelt's provision for aid to the Allies **R** 324

L'Enfant (L'on-FON), **Pierre Charles** (1754–1825), French army officer, engineer, and architect, b. Paris. He joined the American forces (1777) and rose to rank of major (1783). After redesigning a New York City site for federal government headquarters (1789), he was commissioned by Washington to lay out plans for the new capital city (1791). The city of Washington developed in the 19th century partly in accord with his concepts. His plan was later fully acknowledged by the Washington Park Commission (1901) as a guide for urban renewal.
    Washington, D.C., history of **W** 35
    White House (President's House) included in the plan **W** 162

L'Engle, Madeleine (1918–   ), American author, b. New York, N.Y. She acted in New York theater (1940's). Her books include *Ilsa, A Winter's Love, Meet the Austins, The Moon by Night,* and *A Wrinkle in Time,* which was awarded the Newbery medal (1963).

Lenglen (lon-GLEN), **Suzanne** (1899–1938), French lawn-tennis player, b. Compiègne. French champion (1920–23, 1925–26), she was women's world champion in singles (1919–23), doubles (1925), and mixed doubles (1920, 1922, 1925).

Length, measurement **W** 108, 115
    wave length of light, a modern standard, picture **W** 110
Lenin, Vladimir I., Russian leader **L** 138
    birthday U.S.S.R. holiday **H** 148
    communism **C** 442–43
    Leningrad, U.S.S.R., named for **L** 139
    Russian Revolution and Civil War, 1917–21 **U** 50
    Stalin, warnings about **S** 395
    stamp with his portrait **S** 399
Leningrad, Union of Soviet Socialist Republics **L** 139–40
    formerly St. Petersburg, capital of Russia **U** 35–36
    Hermitage Museum **H** 119–20
    siege in World War II, 1941–44 **W** 291, 299
Lenin State Library, Moscow, picture **L** 199
Lenin (formerly Skoda) **Works,** in Czechoslovakia, picture **C** 561
Lenni-Lenape (len-ni-le-NA-pe), Indians of North America **I** 185–86
    called Delaware Indians **D** 92
    New Jersey **N** 178
Lennon, John, English rock music composer and performer **R** 262d
Leno weave, of fabrics **T** 144
Lenoir (l'NWAR), **Jean Joseph Étienne,** French inventor **A** 542
    gas engines, invention of **I** 308
Lenoir, William B., American astronaut **S** 347
Lenormand (len-or-MON), **Louis Sébastian,** French chemist **P** 59

Lenox, Walter Scott (1859–1920), American potter, b. Trenton, N.J. He served as a potter's apprentice before forming a partnership with Jonathan Cox in the Ceramic Art Co. (1889). Afflicted with blindness (1895), he nevertheless continued in his efforts to manufacture a ware similar to Irish Belleek. He organized the Lenox Co. (1906) and employed two potters who had worked at Castle Caldwell in Ireland. He succeeded in producing the creamy, richly glazed china that bears his name.

Lenses **L** 141–51
    cameras **P** 201, 203
    contact lenses **L** 151
    eye **B** 284
    lens openings and shutter speeds in cameras **P** 201–03, 215
    light **L** 263–64
    lighthouses **L** 276
    manufacture **O** 175
    microscopes **M** 283
    optical instruments **O** 166–75
    quartz crystals **Q** 6
    telescopes **T** 60–61

Lenski, Lois (1893–   ), American artist and author, b. Springfield, Ohio. She studied painting at Art Students League, New York. Author of children's books—including historical studies such as *Indian Captive* and regional books *Bayou Suzette* and *Strawberry Girl,* which won Newbery medal (1946)—she also wrote "Mr. Small" series, including *The Little Train* and *The Little Airplane.*
    picture books for children **C** 242–43

Lens puzzle **L** 148
Lent
    Mardi Gras, carnival **C** 120
    pre-Easter period **E** 41
    religious holidays connected with Lent **R** 153–54

Lentil, plant of the pea family with small, round, flattened seeds, which are used as food. Lentils were first cultivated in ancient Asian countries and in the Mediterranean regions. They are used more often in Europe and the Middle East than in North America. They are eaten as a vegetable, used in soups and stews, and ground into flour for bread.

Leo, constellation **C** 492; sign of, picture **S** 245
Leo III, pope
   Charlemagne **C** 284
Leo IX, pope
   church reforms **R** 291

Leo X (Giovanni de' Medici) (1475–1521), pope, b. Florence. The second son of Lorenzo the Magnificent, he was educated by the finest scholars and elected pope in 1513. He did much to promote literature, science, and art, but he created a huge financial debt and neglected the needs of his people. The Reformation began (1517) during his reign, and he excommunicated (1521) Luther.
   Luther's presentation of the 95 theses **R** 134

Leo XIII, pope **L** 152
   encyclicals **R** 297–98

Leo I, Saint (the Great) (390?–461), pope (440–61), b. probably Rome. One of only three popes called Great, he sustained the unity of the Catholic Church at a time of great disorder in the world, combating heresies and maintaining strict church discipline.

León (lay-OHN), **Fray Luis de,** Spanish writer **S** 368
León, Nicaragua **N** 247
León, Ponce de see Ponce de León

Leonard, Benny (Benjamin Leiner) (1896–1947), American boxer, b. New York, N.Y. He turned professional at 16, won the lightweight title in 1917, and held it for 7 years. A great scientific boxer, he was elected to the Boxing Hall of Fame in 1955.

Leonardo da Vinci (lay-o-NARD-o da VEEN-chi), Italian painter, architect and inventor **L** 152–55
   air conditioning principle **A** 102
   auto-type vehicle, plan for **A** 541
   aviation, history of **A** 567
   biology during Renaissance **B** 188
   canals, miter gate of, invented by **C** 84
   diving equipment, idea for **D** 79
   drawings of human skeleton **B** 188
   first to understand what fossils are **G** 112
   Ginevra de Benci, painting **R** 168
   helicopter, idea for a **H** 105
   Last Supper, The, painting **A** 332
   Madonna of the Rocks, painting **P** 21
   medicine and anatomy, interest in **M** 204
   Mona Lisa, painting **L** 367
   painting, history of **P** 21
   parachute, idea for **P** 59
   Renaissance man **R** 162, 167
   scenery for court masques **D** 25
   Self Portrait **L** 153
   Virgin and Child with St. Anne and the Infant St. John **L** 153
   Virgin, Jesus and St. Anne, The, painting **I** 466, 469
Leoncavallo (lay-ohn-ca-VA-lo), **Ruggiero,** Italian operatic composer **I** 486
   Pagliacci, I, opera **O** 150
Leoni (lay-O-ni), **Raúl,** president of Venezuela **V** 300
Leonid (LE-o-nid) **storm,** meteor shower, 1833 **C** 420; picture **S** 246

Leonov, Aleksei Arkhipovich (1934–), Soviet astronaut, b. Listvyanka, Siberia. On March 18–19, 1965, he took part in the flight of the spacecraft Voskhod 2, with Pavel Belyayev commanding. The craft remained aloft 26 hours, completing 17 orbits. While in orbit, Leonov left the capsule and floated in space at the end of a 16-foot lifeline, the first man to leave a spacecraft in space. This feat was seen on television in Communist countries.
   space flight data **S** 344, 345

Leopard, The, book by Lampedusa **I** 481
Leopardi (lay-o-PAR-di), **Giacomo,** Italian poet **I** 480
Leopards **L** 155
   cat family **C** 137–38
   furs **F** 519
Leopard seals, or sea leopards, animals **W** 8
Leopold I, king of the Belgians **B** 131
Leopold II, king of the Belgians **B** 131
   royal claim to Congo **Z** 366d
Leopoldville, capital of Zaïre see Kinshasa
Lepanto (le-PON-to), **battle of,** 1571 **S** 159
Lepchas, people of Sikkim **S** 176
Leper see Leprosy
Lepidoptera (lep-i-DOP-ter-a), scaly-winged insects **B** 468
Lepidus, Marcus Aemilius, Roman general **M** 100
Le Play (l'PLEH), **Frédéric,** French economist **S** 227

Leprechauns (LEP-re-cauns) (from the Gaelic *liepreachan,* meaning "little body"), mythical Irish dwarfs generally thought of as shoemakers. According to legend, leprechauns possess secret treasure. If they are caught, they can be forced to reveal where the treasure is buried. However, if leprechauns can escape by tricking their human captors into looking away, the hiding place of the treasure remains a secret.

Leprosy (LEP-ro-se) (also called Hansen's disease, after discoverer of causal bacterium), disease, recognized in ancient times, that attacks the skin, mucous membranes, and nerves. In general, its characteristics include skin ulceration, loss of feeling, and, in some cases, deformity of fingers and toes and paralysis. It progresses slowly and is not highly contagious. Treatment includes prolonged use of sulfone drugs. The disease may be cured, in most cases, if treated in early stages. Leprosy's highest prevalence is in tropical areas.
   chaulmoogra treatment **P** 313
   Hawaii's Kalawao County **H** 59

Leptis Magna, Libya, Roman theater, picture **L** 204
Leptons, a group of subatomic particles **N** 370
Lermontov, Mikhail, Russian poet **U** 60
Leroux (ler-OO), **Gaston,** French writer **M** 555
Lesage, Alain René, French novelist **F** 439
Lesbos, Greek island in Aegean Sea **G** 333
Lesotho **L** 156–156a
   flag **F** 235
Lesseps (LESS-eps), **Ferdinand, Vicomte de,** French diplomat and engineer **L** 156a
   Panama Canal attempt **P** 48
   Suez Canal **S** 450–51
Lesser Antilles (an-TILL-ese), Caribbean island group **C** 118
   Barbados **B** 53
Lesser Sunda Islands, Indonesia **I** 219–20
Lessing, Doris, Rhodesian-born English novelist **A** 76b
Lessing, Gotthold, German critic and fabulist **F** 4
   German drama **D** 297; **G** 175
Lesson books, for children **C** 236
Lester, Harry, American ventriloquist **V** 301
Let, in tennis **T** 97

Lethbridge, Alberta, Canada **A** 146f–146g

Lethe (LE-the), in Greek mythology, mythical river of forgetfulness that flows in Hades. Souls entering Hades, and those preparing for return to mortal world, drink from river to forget former life.

Leto (LE-to), Greek goddess **G** 360
Lettering, in commercial art **C** 426

Letter of credit, order from a bank addressed to one or more foreign banks instructing them to make payment up to a certain amount to the holder of the letter upon proper identification. The traveler deposits a sum of money with the bank or arranges a loan before receiving credit. Each payment is noted on the letter to show how much of the total credit remains.

Letterpress printing **P** 459–60

Letters of marque (MARK) (letters of marque and reprisal), in international law, written permission given by a government to a private person or group to appropriate the property of a foreign government or of citizens of a foreign government. Such seizure is a retaliatory action for injuries inflicted by the foreign state or its citizens. The term generally applies to private armed ships delegated by the government to retaliate against foreign ships. Congress has constitutional authority to grant letters of marque.

Letters of the alphabet see Alphabet; individual letters
Letters patent, rights granted by a government **P** 97
Letter writing **L** 156b–160
   address, forms of **A** 19–21
   autographs **A** 527
   Committees of Correspondence in American colonies
    C 436
   epistolary novels (novels in form of letters) **E** 260;
    N 346
Lettish, language of Latvia **U** 43
Lettuce **V** 291
Let us cross over the river, and rest in the shade of the
   trees, last words of Stonewall Jackson **J** 8
Leucippus (leu-CIP-pus), Greek philosopher **S** 62
Leukemias (leu-KE-mias), cancers **C** 90; **D** 200
Levant (lev-ANT), region bordering the eastern Mediter-
   ranean **M** 300
Levassor (ler-va-SUR), **Émile,** French engineer and auto-
   mobile racer **A** 538
   automobiles, history of **A** 543
Levees (LEV-ees), to control floods **F** 256; picture **F** 257
   embankment dams **D** 16
   Louisiana **L** 351
   Mississippi **M** 353
   natural levees of rivers **R** 239
Level, measuring tool, picture **T** 216
   surveyor's level **S** 479
Leverrier (lev-er-i-AY), **Urbain,** French astronomer
   A 475
   made calculations leading to discovery of Neptune
   P 277–78
Levers, simple machines **W** 247–48
   inventions of mechanical devices **I** 335
Lever tumblers, in locks **L** 324

Levi (LE-vi) (Hebrew for "joined"), third son of Jacob and Leah. He and Simeon led attack on the Shechemites to avenge the rape of their sister Dinah. Levi's sons were Gershon, Kohath, and Merari, patriarchs of three houses. The tribe of Levi's descendants, known as Levites, produced the priests of the nation of Israel.

Leviathan (lev-Y-ath-an), in Old Testament, a crocodile (Job 41) or a sea monster resembling a dragon or serpent (Psalms 74:14–17). It was a symbol of wickedness, to be destroyed by God. In creation myths of the Phoenicians, it was a sea monster with seven heads that was slain by Baal.

Leviathan, ocean liner **O** 24
   first commercial ship-to-shore radiotelephone service
   E 142a
Leviticus (lev-IT-ic-us), book of Bible **B** 154
Levitski (lev-IT-ski), **Dimitri,** Russian painter **U** 55
   portrait of Princess Dashkova **U** 55
Levita (le-VY-ta), **Elias,** Yiddish author **Y** 350
Levulose (LEV-u-loce), or fructose, fruit sugar **S** 453

Levy, Asser (Asser Levy van Swellem) (?–1681), colonial American merchant. One of the first Jews to settle in America, Levy arrived in New York with 23 immigrants from Brazil, who comprised the first Jewish community in the North American colonies (1654). He circulated a petition (1655), asking equal opportunity for Jews to have guard duty and exemption from tax imposed on them in place of guard duty. He was known as an ardent defender of Jewish rights in the colonies.

Lewes (LEW-es), Delaware **D** 97
Lewes, George Henry, English editor and writer **E** 177

Lewis, Cecil Day (1904–   ), British poet, b. Ballintogher, Ireland. Associated with British poets W. H. Auden and Stephen Spender of the "poetic political" school of 1930's in England, his verse includes *Overtures to Death and Other Poems.* He also writes detective stories under pseudonym of Nicholas Blake. He was named poet laureate in 1968.

Lewis, Francis (1713–1802), colonial American merchant in New York and signer of the Declaration of Independence, b. Llandaff, Wales. A delegate to Stamp Act Congress (1765) and a member of the Sons of Liberty, he was also a representative to the Continental Congress (1774–79) and a commissioner on the Board of Admiralty (1779–81).

Lewis, Gilbert N., American scientist **C** 216
Lewis, Jerry, American movie comedian, picture **M** 483
Lewis, John L., American labor leader **L** 161
   labor movement, history of **L** 6
Lewis, Meriwether, American explorer **L** 162
   monument near Hohenwald, Tennessee **T** 83
Lewis, Sinclair, American novelist **L** 161
   American literature **A** 208
   novels of the 1920's **N** 349
Lewis and Clark Centennial Exposition, 1905, Portland,
   Oregon **F** 12
Lewis and Clark expedition **L** 162–63
   assists U.S. competition for fur trade **F** 522–23
   Fort Clatsop National Memorial, site of winter en-
   campment **O** 203
   Idaho **I** 54, 66, 67
   overland trails and waterways **O** 256

Lewisohn (LEW-is-ohn), **Adolph** (1849–1938), American industrialist and philanthropist, b. Hamburg, Germany. He established a mining industry and sales agency for copper and other metals, but he withdrew from business concerns and turned his attention to philanthropy, the arts, and improvement of prison conditions. His donations included funds for establishment of Lewisohn Stadium in New York City and for a building for Columbia University's School of Mines.

Lewiston, Idaho **I** 66
Lewiston, Maine **M** 44
Lexington, Kentucky **K** 224
Lexington, Massachusetts
  Revolutionary War begins **R** 198

Ley (LAY), **Willy** (1906–69), American rocket expert and author, b. Berlin, Germany. He was a founding member in 1927 of the pioneering Society for Space Travel in Germany and was its vice-president (1928–34). He is best known for his books for the non-scientist. These books include *Conquest of Space.*

Leyden (LY-den) **jar,** simple device for storing electricity. Developed in the mid-18th century, it consists of a glass jar partly coated, inside and out, with metal foil. Separated by nonconducting glass, the two coatings form the electrodes of the device. A charge is introduced to the inner electrode through a metal rod, which passes through the stopper of the jar. An opposite charge is thus induced in the outer electrode, which is grounded. If a wire attached to the outer foil is brought close to the metal rod in contact with the inner foil, a spark is produced.
  possibility of use for communication **T** 51

Leyte (LAY-te) **Gulf, battle of,** 1944 **W** 302; picture **W** 301
Lhasa (LA-sa), capital of Tibet **T** 177; picture **T** 175
Liabilities (ly-a-BIL-it-ies), shown in bookkeeping statements **B** 312
Liability insurance *see* Insurance, liability

Libby, Willard Frank (1908–), American chemist, b. Grand Valley, Colo. He is best-known for his discovery of radioactive dating, using carbon-14, a radioactive form of carbon. He began this work in 1945 and perfected the technique by 1947. In 1960 he received the Nobel prize in chemistry for his work.

Libel (LY-bel), statement harmful to a person's reputation
  case of John Peter Zenger **Z** 369
  case of Oscar Wilde **W** 167
Liberación Nacional (li-bair-ah-si-OWN nah-si-o-NAL), social-democratic party, Costa Rica **C** 518

Liberalism (LIB-er-al-ism), social and political philosophy formulated in 18th and 19th centuries in Europe. During the Industrial Revolution, liberalism favored an end to privileges held by the aristocracy and state churches; a limit on central government; an extension of political and civil liberties for each individual; and an economic policy of laissez-faire. Today it favors a firm central government to check power of business and other private groups in order to insure individual civil liberties, and it encourages more government spending for wider health, education, and welfare facilities.

Liberal Party, British **P** 379
  Gladstone's career **G** 225
Liberal Party, Canadian **C** 77
  King, William Lyon Mackenzie **K** 248
  Laurier, Sir Wilfrid **L** 85
  Pearson, Lester **P** 115
  St. Laurent, Louis **Q** 13
Liberation Day, Italy **H** 150
Liberia (ly-BEER-ia) **L** 164–67
  colony for ex-slaves and free-born American Negroes **N** 94
  flag **F** 235
  Perry, Matthew C. **P** 156
  U.S. merchant marine flying "flags of convenience" **U** 184

Liberty, Equality, Fraternity, watchwords of French Revolution **F** 466
Liberty, Statue of **L** 168
  view from a helicopter **H** 105
Liberty Bell **L** 169
  how bells are made **B** 135
  Independence Hall **I** 113
Liberty Bell, Mexican **M** 251

Liberty cap (Phrygian cap), soft conical hat used as a symbol of freedom. In ancient Rome the cap was presented to slaves at their emancipation. The term also refers to red caps worn as emblems of liberty by French Revolutionists.
  Phrygian bonnet, picture **H** 55

Liberty Island, New York Harbor, site of Statue of Liberty **L** 168
Liberty of the press *see* Freedom of the press
Liberty Party, United States **P** 385
Liberty ships
  named for famous Negroes **N** 101
Liberty Song, by John Dickinson **N** 22
Liberty Tree flag, 1775 **F** 229
Libra (LY-bra), constellation **C** 491; sign of, picture **S** 245
Librarians and librarianship **L** 188–92
Libraries **L** 170–200
  ancient Assyrian civilization **A** 225
  book exhibits for National Library Week **B** 316
  books: from author to library **B** 329–34
  Carnegie, Andrew **C** 119
  Coonskin Library, Ohio **O** 68
  Crane Memorial, Quincy, Massachusetts **U** 124
  elementary school buildings **E** 79
  first circulating library in United States **P** 137
  first free tax-supported public library in United States **N** 157
  history of **L** 192–200
  how to use your library **L** 180–88
  importance to the school's reading program **R** 111
  influence on children's literature **C** 242
  librarians and what they do **L** 188–92
  Mexico, University of, Mexico City **M** 253
  modern library services **L** 170–79
  Nairobi, Kenya, University College in, picture **K** 231
  Oklahoma, University of, picture **O** 87
  oldest public library in Europe **U** 71
  paperback books **P** 58a
  presidential *see* Presidential libraries
  record library, basic **R** 125
  reference books **R** 129–31
  research methods **R** 182–83
  storytelling **S** 435; picture **S** 434
  talking books for the blind **B** 253
  Working Men's Institute Library, New Harmony, Ind. **I** 143
  See also Indexes and indexing; education section of country, province, and state articles

Library Association, The, founded (1877) as Library Association of the United Kingdom (renamed, 1896). Granted a royal charter (1898) to unite all persons engaged or interested in library work and promote the better administration of libraries, it was reorganized in 1962 and became fully professional. It publishes books and pamphlets, and the official *Library Association Record.* Headquarters are in London.
  admission by examination **L** 191
  book award, Carnegie Medal **B** 310

Library associations **L** 191–92

Library of Congress, Washington, D.C.   **L** 177, 200;
  picture   **L** 179
  books for the blind   **B** 253
  Copyright Office of   **T** 244–45
  points of interest in Washington, D.C.   **W** 31–32
Library Services Act, 1956   **L** 173
Library Services and Construction Act, 1964, 1966   **L** 173
Librations, motions of the moon   **M** 447
Librettos, words of an opera or other long musical composition   **O** 131
Libreville (LE-brev-ill), capital of Gabon   **G** 3
Libya (LIB-ia)   **L** 201–05
  agriculture, picture   **A** 99
  camel caravan, picture   **S** 8
  flag   **F** 235
  nomadic herdsmen, picture   **D** 129
Libya, University of   **L** 201
Libyan Desert, Africa   **E** 90d
  prospecting for oil, picture   **G** 106
Lice, insects   **H** 262; pictures **H** 263, **I** 283
  carriers of typhus   **I** 283
Licenses
  amateur radio operators (hams)   **R** 63
  hunting   **H** 291; picture **H** 290
  marriage licenses   **W** 101
  television stations   **T** 70a
  to private utility companies   **P** 510
Lichens (LY-kens),   **F** 94–95
  partnership of algae and fungi   **A** 156
Lichtenstein, Roy, American artist   **P** 31
Licinius (li-CIN-ius), Roman emperor   **C** 489

Licorice, herblike plants of the pea (legume) family.
Licorice is also a product of the roots, used in candy,
flavoring, and medicines. Native to Asia and southern
Europe, the plant is up to 3 ft. tall and has blue flowers.

Liddell, Alice, for whom Lewis Carroll wrote "Alice in
  Wonderland"   **A** 164; **C** 123
Lie (LEE), **Trygve,** Norwegian statesman   **L** 205

Liebig (LE-bik), **Baron Justus von** (1803–1873), German
chemist, b. Darmstadt. He pioneered in organic chemistry, discovering and perfecting methods of analyzing
organic substances. He did basic work on the behavior of
radicals (groups of atoms that behave as one unit in
chemical reactions). In 1831 he discovered the anesthetic
chloroform. He also devised improved methods for manufacturing chemicals. After 1840 he specialized in plant
and animal physiology. He was the first to experiment
with chemical fertilizers, and he set up an experimental
farm to demonstrate his theories. At the University of
Giessen he set up the first laboratory designed for the
use of students.
  discovery of chemical fertilizers   **A** 100; **F** 98; **S** 74
  his work a major development in biology   **B** 193–94

Liechtenstein (LEECK-ten-shtine)   **L** 206–07
  flag   **F** 239
Lied (LEED) (plural lieder), German art song   **C** 333;
  M 538
  styles of singing   **V** 376

Lie detector, apparatus that records changes in respiration, blood pressure, and pulse beat, as index of
emotional tension, in attempt to determine guilt or
innocence of person under questioning, based on
supposition that a guilty person shows greater emotional
response. The instrument has proved effective but not
always accurate. Therefore lie-detector tests are almost
never allowed in court as evidence for guilt.
  police use certain new technical inventions   **P** 376

Liège (li-EZH), Belgium   **B** 129
Lieutenant governor, in Canadian government   **C** 77
Life   **L** 208–14
  adaptations in the world of   **L** 214–27
  adaptive radiation in birdlife   **B** 209–10
  aging   **A** 81–87
  altitude, vertical life zones of   **Y** 352–53; **Z** 372–73
  bacteria in the cycle of   **B** 12
  biology, study of living things   **B** 187–96
  blood, stream of life   **B** 255
  butterflies and moths, life cycle   **B** 468–69
  cell, unit of life   **C** 159, 161
  cosmic rays, effect on   **C** 513
  cycles see **Life cycles**
  distribution of plant and animal   **L** 227–39
  eggs and embryos   **E** 88–90a
  energy and life   **E** 201
  evolution   **E** 338–47
  food chains in   **L** 239–43
  forest life   **F** 371–72
  genetics   **G** 77–88
  hibernation   **H** 121–24
  kingdoms of living things   **K** 249–59
  life belt of the sun   **E** 22; diagram   **E** 23
  living on moon or in space   **M** 455–56; **S** 340a, 340d–341
  Mars   **M** 104, 107, 111
  meteorites show signs of   **C** 421
  moon, life on   **C** 421
  prehistoric animals, early life forms   **P** 436
  reproduction   **R** 176–80
  rhythms and clocks in plant and animal   **L** 243–50
  temperatures, life range in, diagram   **H** 86d
  underwater exploration of life in the sea   **U** 21–22
  vertical life zones   **Z** 372–73
  water essential to all forms   **W** 51
  webs of   **L** 250–59
Life, adaptations in the world of   **L** 214–27
  animals living in caves   **C** 157
  dinosaurs, the end of the   **D** 181
  plant defenses   **P** 282–83
  rhythms and survival   **L** 243
Life, distribution of plant and animal   **L** 227–39
  plankton   **P** 279–81
Life, early humor magazine   **C** 127
Life, food chains in   **L** 239–43
  giants of nature   **G** 204
  photosynthesis   **P** 221
  underwater exploration of life in the sea   **U** 21–22
Life, magazine   **M** 15
Life, origin of   **L** 213–14
Life, rhythms and clocks in plant and animal   **L** 243–50
  hibernation and estivation   **H** 121–24
Life, webs of   **L** 250–59
  communities of living things   **K** 257–59
  environment, problems of   **E** 272a–272h
Lifeboats, on ocean liners   **O** 24
Life cycles
  ant, life cycle   **A** 323
  bullfrog, pictures   **F** 472
  newt, pictures   **F** 476
  wheat rust, diagram   **F** 499
Life expectancy see **Life spans**
Life insurance see **Insurance, life**
Life on other planets   **P** 271
Life plant, or bryophylium, picture   **P** 300
Lifesaving see **First aid; Safety**
Life sciences
  experiments and projects (involving animals and
  plants)   **E** 356–59
Life spans, average length, for man and animals   **A** 81–84
  birds   **B** 229
  elephants   **E** 170

Life spans (continued)
    insects I 265–66
    life expectancies (highest and lowest countries), list
        P 395
    turtles T 335
Life-support systems, for space exploration S 340a,
    340L–341; diagram S 340L
Life zones, belts of plant and animal communities, by
    altitude Z 372–73
    Yosemite National Park Y 352–53
Liffey River, Ireland R 244
    Dublin's river I 388
Lift, upward force opposing gravity
    aerodynamics theory and demonstration A 38
    animals: locomotion A 294–95
    aviation A 553
    hydrofoil boats H 304–05
Lifts see Elevators; Escalators; Hoisting and loading
    machinery
Ligaments, cords of tissue connecting bones B 270
Ligan see Flotsam, jetsam, and lagan, or ligan
Light L 260–74
    atmosphere A 482
    bioluminescence, cold light B 197–98
    cameras and light meters P 213
    chemical changes caused by C 199
    constant speed, how shown by an interferometer
        R 140
    deep-sea fishes, light organs of F 198
    dust scatters D 348
    effects in impressionistic painting F 426; M 408
    energy E 199
    experiments in effect of light on plants E 356–57
    interferometers, instruments O 172
    lasers M 131–33
    lenses L 141–51
    lighting L 279–90
    light waves, theories of R 140
    matter, light a special form of M 171
    Michelson-Morley experiment on the ether theory
        R 140–41
    mirage, cause of M 341–42
    Newton's experiments with the spectrum N 207
    phosphorescent paints P 34
    photoelectricity P 199–200
    photosynthesis P 221–23
    quasars and pulsars Q 7–8
    radiant energy, in physics P 236
    radiation R 43–44
    rainbow R 98
    signals for communication C 437, 438
    signals for fish A 280
    solar energy S 235
    spectrum, visible and invisible rays of E 24
    sun S 458–67
    wave theory, first studies S 74–75
    X rays and light rays X 341
    See also Bioluminescence; Color; Optical instruments
Lighter-than-air craft see Balloons and ballooning;
    Dirigibles
Light heavyweight, in boxing B 352
Lighthouses L 275–78
    Cape Hatteras, picture N 317
    Lake Superior, picture M 324
    Pemaquid Point, Maine, picture M 37
    Pharos, a wonder of the ancient world W 216; picture
        W 215
    Where is the Boston Light? L 278
    Where is the Eddystone Light? L 276
Lighting L 279–90
    candles C 96–97
    Edison's electric inventions E 60

interior decorating I 300
    lighthouses and lightships L 275–78
    neon and other noble gases N 109–10
    petroleum P 176
    photography P 216–17, 220
    plays, stage lighting P 339; pictures P 337
    Tungsten filament in light bulbs T 308
Lighting designers, of plays T 158
Light meters
    photography, use in P 213
Light middleweight, in boxing B 352
Lightning T 170–73
    ball lightning mistaken for flying saucers
        F 285–86
    fire and early man, picture F 138
    Franklin's rod F 453
    nitrogen in the air "fired" by lightning N 262

Lightning rods, sharp-pointed metallic rods set atop a
building or other such structure and connected to moist
ground or water. They protect structures from dangerous
effects of lightning stroke by conducting electric charges
into earth or water. Their invention (1752?) is usually
attributed to Benjamin Franklin.

Lightships L 277–78
Light-year, unit of interstellar measurement S 405
    quasars and pulsars, distances from earth Q 7
    universe, galaxies in U 196–204
Lightweight, in boxing B 352
Light welterweight, in boxing B 352
Lignin (LIG-nin), a substance in wood W 222, 227
Lignite, a soft coal C 362, 363
    fuel F 487
    North Dakota deposits burn constantly N 326
Lignum vitae (VY-te), tree
    bearings in machinery W 227
Liguest, Pierre Laclède see Laclède, Pierre
Ligurian (li-GU-rian) Sea O 48
Li Ho, Chinese poet O 220a
Liholiho, Alexander see Kamehameha IV, Hawaiian king
Lihue (LEEHOO-ay), Hawaii H 69
Lilacs, flowers, picture G 36
    state flower of New Hampshire N 149

Lilienthal (LI-li-en-thol), David Eli (1899–   ), American
business executive, b. Morton, Ill. He was chairman
(1941–46) of the Tennessee Valley Authority, chairman of
the Atomic Energy Commission (1946–50), chairman and
chief executive officer of the Development and Resources
Corp. (1955–62), and director of minerals and chemicals
for the Philipp Corp. (since 1962). His books include *TVA:
Democracy on the March.*

Lilienthal (LI-li-en-tol), Otto (1848–1896), German aeronautical pioneer, b. Anklam, Prussian Pomerania. He
studied flights of birds as preliminary to experiments
with gliders, and he built a series of gliders, which he
flew, inspiring the Wright brothers with his experiments.
    pioneer in aviation A 567; picture A 568
    early glider pilots G 239

Lilies, flowers G 46, 51; picture G 37
    leaves, special kinds of, pictures L 120
    lily, a monocot, picture P 292
Lilies of the valley, flowers G 42; picture G 44

Lilith, in Talmudic tradition, Adam's first wife, expelled
from Eden and believed to have borne evil spirits. In
medieval legends Lilith was a demon who threatened
infants unprotected by amulets; in Old Testament
(Isaiah 34:14) the name is associated with the owl.

Liliuokalani (li-li-u-o-ka-LA-ni), queen of Hawaii H 70, 71
Lille (LEEL), France F 406

Lillie, Beatrice (1898–   ), British actress, b. Toronto, Canada. Noted for performances as vaudeville comedienne, she appeared in *Big Top, Seven Lively Arts,* and *High Spirits.* She also appeared in *Ziegfeld Follies of 1957,* as well as in motion pictures and on radio and TV.

Lilliput, imaginary country in *Gulliver's Travels* G 412–13

Lilly Endowment, Inc., foundation that makes grants available for research and training in education, religion, and community services. It assists private social agencies and the United Fund in Indianapolis, Ind., and environs, and has provided funds for technical aid and literacy projects in Southeast Asia and the Near East.

Lilongwe, Malawi M 51
Lima (LI-ma), capital of Peru P 164; picture P 165
   Pizarro, Francisco founded Lima P 266

Lima, Declaration of (1930), proposal adopted at the Lima Conference in Peru to promote hemispheric unity and security. Introduced by U.S. Secretary of State Cordell Hull to thwart German Nazi influence in the Americas, it proposed to establish meeting of the American states if any of them felt threatened by foreign power.

Lima beans, vegetables V 289
   germination, pictures P 299
Limb darkening, of the sun S 460–61
Limbe (LIM-bay), Malawi M 51
Limburg brothers, Flemish painters D 349
   April, manuscript D 349
   The Belles Heures of Jean, Duke of Berry, picture from A 438a
Lime, calcium compound made from limestone R 268
   fertilizer F 98
   glass G 226
Lime, citrus fruit L 136–38
Limerick, Ireland I 385
Limericks (LIM-er-icks) N 273, 276
   form of humor H 279
Limestone R 267–68
   building stone S 433
   Carlsbad Caverns C 153–55
   cement made of C 165
   gemstones result from impurities in G 70
   marble R 269; S 433
   quarry in Bermuda, picture Q 5
   steelmaking uses I 404
   test to identify R 267
Limeys, nickname for British sailors L 137
   lemons and limes supplied needed food element F 335
   vitamins, discovery of V 370a

Limitations, Statute of, law, originated (1623) under James I of England, limiting the period of time during which a person or group may bring claims to court, defend certain rights, or bring action against criminal offenders. It prevents delaying trial of a case until the evidence needed for defense has been destroyed or witnesses have died. In criminal cases, it supports the principle that the offender or suspect cannot be subject to trial forever.
   war crimes trials W 9

Limners, artists F 293–94
Limoges (li-MOGE), France
   enameling artists of E 192

Limón (li-MONE), Costa Rica C 515, 516

Limón, José Arcadio (1908–72), American dancer and choreographer, b. Culiacan, Mexico. A dancer with the Humphrey-Weidman Co. of New York (1930–40), he also choreographed several Broadway shows. As principal male dancer in the modern dance theater, he and his company toured throughout the world. He last performed in 1969, but continued as artistic director for the José Limón Dance Company until his death.

Limonite (LIME-on-ite), iron ore I 404
Limp blimp, underwater house U 19
Limpets, shell-bearing mollusks, gastropods O 276
Limpopo River, east central Africa R 229
Lincoln, Abraham, 16th President of the United States L 291–97
   assassination, aftermath of Civil War C 327
   Civil War C 321, 324, 327, 458, 459
   Emancipation Proclamation E 185–86
   Gettysburg Address G 191
   Grant and Lincoln G 295
   holiday on his birthday H 147
   Illinois I 70–72, 81
   Johnson, Andrew, vice-president under J 124–25
   letter to Mrs. Bixby L 156b
   Lincoln-Douglas debates L 299
   Lincoln Homestead State Park, Kentucky K 223
   presidential leadership P 450
   quoted Q 20
   Reconstruction Period anticipated R 117
   Republican party, rise of P 380
   Thanksgiving Day proclamation T 154
   tomb in Springfield, picture I 83
   Whitman's poem "O Captain! My Captain" W 165–66
Lincoln, Benjamin, American military commander R 208
Lincoln, capital of Nebraska N 83–84
Lincoln, Illinois I 81
Lincoln, Mary Todd, wife of Abraham Lincoln F 171–72; L 293
Lincoln Boyhood National Memorial, Indiana I 146
Lincoln Center for the Performing Arts, New York City L 298
   plaza, picture N 235
Lincoln-Douglas debates L 299
   Douglas, Stephen A. D 287
   Lincoln opposes Kansas-Nebraska Act L 294–95
Lincoln Highway, transcontinental road W 330
   Abraham Lincoln Memorial monument W 333
Lincoln Memorial, Washington, D.C. W 32; picture W 34
Lincoln National Life Foundation, Fort Wayne, Indiana I 145
Lincoln's Inn see Inns of Court
Lincoln's New Salem State Park, Illinois I 81; picture I 80
Lincoln Trail, in Illinois I 81
Lincoln Tunnel, Hudson River, picture N 173
   construction, picture T 316
Lind, Don L., American astronaut S 347
Lind, James, English physician V 370a
Lind, Jenny, Swedish singer L 300
Lindauer, Martin, German scientist B 119

Lindbergh, Anne Spencer Morrow (1906–), American author, b. Englewood, N.J. Wife of aviator Charles A. Lindbergh, she was the first woman to be awarded the Hubbard medal (1934), given her for accompanying her husband as co-pilot and radio operator in flights covering five continents and totaling 40,000 miles. Her books include *Gift From the Sea, North to the Orient, The Wave of the Future* (criticized by some readers as antidemocratic), and *Dearly Beloved.*

Lindbergh, Charles, American aviator **L** 300
aided Goddard's rocket research **G** 246
airmail pilot **P** 407
autobiography **A** 215
aviation history **A** 573
Charles A. Lindbergh State Memorial Park, Minnesota **M** 333
Missouri's place in development of air transport **M** 374–75
only civilian Medal of Honor winner **M** 200
Linden, tree see Basswood, tree
Lindenwald, New York, home of Martin Van Buren, picture **V** 273

Lindgren, Astrid (1907–   ), Swedish author and editor of children's books, b. Vimmerby. Her works include *Rasmus and the Vagabond*, which won the Hans Christian Andersen medal (1958), *Nils Karlsson Pyssling*, and *Pippi Longstocking*.

Lindisfarne Gospels, illuminated page from, picture **I** 87

Lindsay, John Vliet (1921–   ), American politician, b. New York, N.Y. After receiving a Bachelor of Arts degree from Yale University, he entered the Navy and saw active service during World War II. He returned to Yale and earned a law degree. He became interested in Republican politics and was executive assistant to Attorney General Brownell in Washington. Elected to congress from New York in 1958, he was re-elected for the following three terms. In 1965 he was elected mayor of New York City, and again in 1969. In 1971 he joined the Democratic party.

Lindsay, Vachel, American poet **A** 209

Lindsey, Benjamin Barr (1869–1943), American jurist, b. Jackson, Tenn. A judge in juvenile court, Denver, Colo. (1900–27), and in California superior court (1934–43), he was known for his understanding of the juvenile delinquent and for his improvements and revisions of the juvenile court system. His public support of companionate marriage created much dispute. Among his published works are *Problems of the Children, The Beast and the Jungle,* and (with Wainright Evans) *The Companionate Marriage.*

Lindsey, Philip, American educator **E** 72
Line, element in design **D** 135
Linear (LIN-e-ar) **accelerators,** atom smashers **A** 489
Linear perspective P 158; diagrams **P** 159
Line engraving, in printing **P** 458–59
Line games G 22–24
Line graphs G 311–12

Line Islands, 11 small, barren atolls in the central Pacific. Formerly important as guano sources, they were divided between United States and Britain in 1930's and converted into air bases. Kingman Reef, Palmyra, and Jarvis belong to United States; Washington, Fanning, and Christmas are part of the British colony of Gilbert and Ellice Islands.

Linen F 106
Linenfold, an ornamental design or pattern **F** 505
Linen-supply laundries L 84
Line of Demarcation E 378
Line officers
United States Navy **U** 189
Lines, for fishing **F** 206, 211
Lines, geometric G 124
Lines of force, electric and magnetic **E** 129–32, 134
magnetism **M** 25

Ling, Per Henrik, Swedish gymnast **P** 225
Lingonberries G 301
Linguistics (lin-GUIS-tics), study of languages **L** 301–03
anthropological studies **A** 308
Lingula (lin-GU-la), stalked lamp shells **L** 224
Link, Edwin, American inventor **U** 19

Link Foundation, charitable fund that awards grants to nonprofit educational institutions and organizations for educational projects—especially in aerospace and oceanography. It was established (1953) by Edwin A. Link and has headquarters in New York City.

Linking verbs G 289
Linnaeus (lin-NE-us), **Carolus,** Swedish botanist **L** 303–04
biologists adopt classification scheme **B** 191
manager of Uppsala Botanical Gardens **Z** 379
science of taxonomy **T** 29
Linné, Carl von see Linnaeus, Carolus
Linocuts (LY-no-cuts), linoleum prints **L** 304–06
Linoleum V 340–41
cork used in **C** 505
Linoleum-block printing L 304–06
Linotype, typesetting machine **P** 463
lines of type, casting of **T** 344–45
newspapers use **N** 203

Lin Piao (1908–   ), Chinese government official, b. Ungkung, Hupeh Province, China. A member of the Nationalist Party (1922–27), he joined the Communist Party in 1927. He won important military victories (1945–49) in the Chinese civil war and commanded the Communist Chinese forces during the Korean War. In 1969 he was named Chairman Mao Tse-Tung's successor.

Linsangs, animals related to genets **G** 90
Linseed oil O 79
ink **I** 256
varnishes and lacquers **V** 279
Lindsey-woolsey, home-woven cloth **P** 256
Lint, cotton **C** 525
Lintel, term in architecture **A** 374
Linters, fibers of cottonseed **C** 525

Lin Yutang, or **Lin Yu-t'ang** (1895–   ), Chinese author, b. Changchow. He was head, Arts and Letters Division, UNESCO (1948). He is known for writings on Chinese culture and invented Chinese indexing method and typewriter with Chinese characters. He collaborated on official project for romanizing Chinese alphabet. His works include *My Country and My People.*

Lion, constellation see Leo
Lion and the Mouse, The, fable by Aesop **F** 4
Lioness, picture **A** 292
Lion Gate, Mycenae, Greece, pictures **A** 374, **S** 94

Lionni, Leo (1910–   ), American painter and children's author, b. Amsterdam, the Netherlands. He was named art director of the year by the National Society of Art Directors (1955). His books for children include *Little Blue and Little Yellow* and *Inch by Inch.*
Inch by Inch, page from, picture **C** 244

Lion of Judah, symbol of the Emperor of Ethiopia, picture **E** 296
Lions L 307
Africa, picture **A** 51
cat family **C** 134–39; pictures **C** 136, 137
Hittite art **A** 238; picture **A** 239
in heraldry, pictures **H** 117
mammal societies, picture **M** 70

Lions Clubs, International Association of, federation of community service clubs founded in 1917. It became an international organization in 1920 and has branches in 145 countries. It has headquarters in Chicago, Ill.

Lion's mane, jellyfish, picture **J** 70

Lipchitz, Jacques (1891–1973), American sculptor, b. Druskieniki, Lithuania. As a young man, he studied in Paris. When the Germans invaded France during World War II, he settled in the United States. One of the most celebrated exponents of cubist sculpture, he drew many of his themes from mythology and the Bible.
  modern art **M** 391
  Figure, sculpture **S** 104

Lipids, fatlike body compounds **B** 293; **V** 363
Lipizzaner horse *see* Lippizaner horse

Lipkind, William (1904–   ), American author and anthropologist, b. New York, N.Y. He spent 2 years (1938–40) in Brazil studying the Carajá and Javhé Indians. Under the names Will and Nicolas he and illustrator Nicolas Mordvinoff have produced a number of picture books, such as *Finders Keepers* (Caldecott medal, 1952), *Four-leaf Clover, The Two Reds,* and *The Little Tiny Rooster.* They also wrote and illustrated *Boy with a Harpoon, Boy of the Islands,* and *Boy and the Forest.*

Li Po, Chinese poet **O** 220a
Lippershey (LIPP-ers-hy), **Hans,** eyeglass maker **T** 60–61

Lippizaner horse, a special breed of dressage horse used in the Spanish Riding School, Vienna, Austria, and recently imported to the United States. It was named after the town of Lippiza, where the strain was first developed about 400 years ago. Black at birth, gray at maturity, and white in old age, the Lippizaner can be used as a ceremonial carriage horse.

Lippmann, Walter (1889–   ), American editor and author, b. New York, N.Y. He was editor of the New York *World* (1929–31) and then became a syndicated columnist for over 200 newspapers throughout the world. He won the Pulitzer prize for reporting (1958, 1962) and the Presidential Medal of Freedom (1964). His books include *Drift and Mastery, The Good Society,* and *The Communist World and Ours.*

Lipreading, of the deaf **D** 50, 52
Lipstick, cosmetic **C** 509
  beauty culture **B** 110
Lipton, Seymour, American sculptor **M** 397

Lipton, Sir Thomas Johnstone (1850–1931), Scottish businessman, b. Glasgow. As a young man, he worked in United States (about 1865–70) before returning to Glasgow to launch his business career by opening a food store (1871). He quickly expanded his interests in Britain and other countries, including United States and Germany, and developed large tea plantations in India. He was well known as a philanthropist and was knighted in recognition for his generous contributions to various charities. He was an accomplished yachtsman and a dedicated contender for the America's Cup.

Liquefaction (lik-we-FAC-tion) **fractional distiller, for**
  liquid gases **L** 308
Liquefied petroleum gas *see* LPG
Liquid air
  conversion from gas **G** 58
  industrial uses **G** 59

Liquid fuels **F** 488
  Goddard's rocket experiment with **G** 245
  missile fuels **M** 345
  petroleum **P** 169–78
Liquid gases **L** 308–09
  helium **H** 107–08
  hydrogen **H** 306
  rocket fuels **R** 257–58
  what happens near absolute zero **H** 90
Liquid measure **W** 113, 115
Liquid oxygen, or Lox **L** 308–09
  Goddard's rocket experiment with **G** 245
  oxidation **O** 269–70
  oxidizer for rocket fuels **F** 490; **R** 258
Liquids **L** 309–10
  buoyancy principle, discovery of **A** 369; **F** 252
  contrasted with crystalline solids **C** 544
  defined **C** 219
  density of fluids **F** 250–51
  detergents **D** 149
  distillation process **D** 224–26
  gases, liquefaction of **G** 58
  how heat changes matter **H** 91–94
  matter, states of **M** 170–71
  osmosis **O** 233–35
  Pascal's Law applied to hydraulic machinery
    H 301–03
  specific gravity **F** 253
  water **W** 51–55
  waves on the surfaces of water **O** 34–35

Lisa, Manuel (1772–1820), American trader and explorer, b. New Orleans, La. He traveled extensively on the Missouri River, building fur-trading posts, among them Fort Raymond (1808), the first post (later renamed Fort Manuel) on upper Missouri.
  fur traders and explorers **F** 522–23

Lisala (li-SA-la), Congo (Kinshasa), picture **C** 465
Lisboa (lees-BO-a), **Antônio Francisco,** known as Aleijadinho, Brazilian architect-sculptor **B** 376–77
  Christ at the Last Supper **L** 63
  church of São Francisco **L** 65
  Latin-American art and architecture **L** 64
Lisbon, capital of Portugal **P** 400–01
Li Shang-yin, Chinese poet **O** 220a
Listening, one of the language arts **L** 36
Listening posts, spies **S** 389
Lister, Joseph, English doctor **L** 311
  developed germ free surgery **M** 208
Liston, Sonny, American boxing champion **B** 353
Liszt, Franz, Hungarian composer and pianist **L** 312
  German music **G** 187
  romantic symphonic poems **R** 311
Litanies, prayers **O** 229
Liter (LI-ter), measure of volume **W** 116
Literacy
  Argentina, highest rate in Latin America **A** 390
  Iran's Literacy Corps **I** 372
  Japan's rate one of highest **J** 29
  Philippines has one of highest rates in Asia **P** 185
  tests required of immigrants **I** 100
  voting qualification in United States **E** 113
  women, role of **W** 211
Literary agents, for writers **W** 321
  publishing industry **P** 514–15
Literary awards and medals *see* Awards, literary; Book awards
Literary criticism **L** 312–13
  children's literature **C** 242
  classics in literature **C** 334
  critics in American literature **A** 211, 215

Literary Market Place, annual guide in publishing **M** 15
Literature **L** 313–14
  ballads **B** 22–23; **P** 354
  Bible, Old Testament, literary greatness of **H** 101
  biography, autobiography, and biographical novel
    B 185–86
  children's see Children's literature
  classics **C** 334
  creative writing, forms of **W** 319–21
  diaries **D** 157–58
  drama **D** 292–300
  duels in **D** 341
  essays **E** 292–93
  fables **F** 2–8
  fairy tales **F** 19–32
  fiction **F** 109–12
  folklore **F** 302–17
  growth of national literature during the Renaissance
    R 159–60
  humor **H** 277–81
  literary criticism **L** 312–13
  Nobel prizes **N** 266
  novels **N** 345–49
  oratory, spoken literature **O** 180
  poetry **P** 349–55
  Pulitzer prizes **P** 524–28
  romantic music based on novels and plays **R** 310
  science fiction **S** 85
  short stories **S** 165
  See also African literature; Oriental literature; lit-
    erature of countries, as German literature, and
    articles on individual authors, as Alcott, Louisa
    May
Literature for children see Children's literature
Lithium, element **E** 154, 162
  atom, structure of the, diagrams **N** 355
Lithography (lith-OG-raphy), printing technique **L** 314–15
  techniques and uses of the graphic arts **G** 302, 308
  use in the printing industry **P** 460–61
  posters **P** 404
Lithuania (lith-u-A-nia) (Lithuanian Soviet Socialist
    Republic) **U** 44; **W** 281, 288
  languages of the U.S.S.R. **U** 27
Litmus paper, for testing acidity or alkalinity **S** 234
Little America, Byrd's Antarctic base **B** 481; **P** 366,
    369
Little Bear, constellation see Ursa Minor
Little Bighorn, battle of, 1876 **I** 169; **M** 443
Little Bo-Peep, from Mother Goose, with Kate Greenaway
    illustration **C** 239; **I** 93
Little Brown Church in the Vale, Nashua, Iowa **I** 367
Little Dipper, star group **C** 491
Little Dog, constellation see Canis Minor
Little Giant, nickname of Stephen A. Douglas **D** 287
Little John, member of Robin Hood's band **R** 253
Little League Baseball **L** 315–17
  growing up in baseball **B** 78
Little Match Girl, The, story by Hans Christian Andersen
    A 248
Little Metropolitan Church, Athens, picture **B** 487
Little Nanny Etticoat, nursery rhyme riddle **J** 132
Little Pretty Pocket-Book, by Newbery, picture **C** 237
Little Red Riding-Hood, story, retold by Walter De La
    Mare **F** 29–32
Little red schoolhouse **E** 71
Little Rhody, nickname for Rhode Island **R** 212
Little Rock, capital of Arkansas **A** 429
Little Rose Tree, The, poem by Rachel Field **F** 120
Little Tear Gland that Says Tic-Tac, art by Max Ernst
    M 395
Little theaters, community theater groups **T** 161–62
  art theater movement in America **D** 300

Little Turtle (Michikinikwa) (1752–1812), American Indian, b. near present-day Fort Wayne, Ind. As chief of
the Miami Indians, he led the Indian forces that defeated
General Harmar (1790) and General St. Clair (1791). He
signed a treaty (1795) of continued peace after his
defeat by General Wayne's army (1795). Gilbert Stuart,
the famous painter, did a portrait of him (1797).

Little Women, by Louisa May Alcott, excerpt **A** 149–50
Liturgical drama see Religious drama
Liturgy
  hymns **H** 309
  Roman Catholic Church **R** 298; picture **R** 302

Litvinov (lit-VE-nof), **Maxim Maximovich** (Meer Moisee-
vich Vallakh) (1876–1951), Russian diplomat, b. Bialystok. As a youth, Litvinov joined the Social Democratic
Party (1898), participating in the revolution of 1905. He
was appointed Soviet representative to Great Britain
(1917) but was seized in exchange for a British agent
because Britain had not recognized the new Soviet
government. He advocated disarmament at international
conferences (1927, 1928, 1929) and negotiated nonag-
gression treaties with several European nations. He
served as ambassador to United States (1941–43) and
deputy commissar for foreign affairs (1941–46).

Liu Shao-ch'i (liu SHA-o-chi) (1898?–   ), Chinese
Communist theoretician and politician, b. Hunan. He
began his career as union organizer in southeastern
China, led student movements against Japanese
(1936–42), and was vice-chairman of provisional govern-
ment (1949), vice-president of World Federation of Trade
Unions (1949), and founder of Sino-Soviet Friendship
Association (1949). He is closely associated with Mao
Tse-tung in Chinese Communist Party and has been
chairman of republic since 1959.

Livelihood, means of subsistence **A** 301–02
Live oak, tree
  leaves, shapes of, pictures **L** 116
  state tree of Georgia **G** 133
Liver
  cancer of **C** 92
  chemistry of the liver cell **B** 293
  digestive function in human body **B** 275
  fish-liver oils **O** 79
  hepatitis, disease, affects the liver **D** 198

Livermore, Mary Ashton Rice (1820–1905), American
reformer and suffragist, b. Boston, Mass. She worked
with the U.S. Sanitary Commission during the Civil War.
Later she established (1869) and edited a newspaper
advocating woman's suffrage, the *Agitator*, which
merged with the *Woman's Journal* (1870). She was
president of the Illinois and later the Massachusetts
Woman's Suffrage Association and appeared frequently
as a public speaker on temperance, women's rights, and
education. Her works include "What Shall We Do With
Our Daughters?" and *My Story of the War.*

Liverpool, England **U** 71
Liverwort, plant
  hepaticae, picture **P** 292
Livery, clothing in family colors **H** 118
Livestock **C** 145–52
  Asia **A** 451
  Canada **C** 58
  Chicago's International Livestock Exhibition **C** 230
  corn as feed **C** 506, 507
  dairying and dairy products **D** 5–13
  herding in Africa **A** 62, 64

pasture grasses and hay **G** 317
plant poisoning of animals **P** 323
pollution danger in rural water supplies **W** 58
specialized, extensive agriculture **A** 89, 92
veterinarians **V** 324
See also Meat and meat-packing; agricultural section of continent, country, province, and state articles; names of domestic animals
Livestock Judging Pavilion, Raleigh, North Carolina, picture **A** 387
Live television T 70a
Live wires, of electricity
safety precautions **E** 135
Living fossils E 347
horseshoe crabs **H** 245
successful life adaptation **L** 223–24
tuatara of New Zealand **N** 240
Living obstacles, game **G** 19
Living standards see Standard of living
Livingston, Milton Stanley, American scientist **N** 366

Livingston, Philip (1716–1778), American merchant, b. Albany, N.Y. He was partly responsible for the founding of King's College (now Columbia University). He helped organize the New York Society Library (1754) and was active in New York State politics and a member of the Continental Congress (1774–78). He was a signer of the Declaration of Independence.

Livingston, Robert R., American patriot **N** 223–24
Louisiana Purchase **L** 365
Livingston, William, American statesman **N** 177
Livingstone, David, Scottish missionary **S** 400
African exploration **A** 68
Malawi, exploration **M** 51
Livingstone Falls, Congo River **C** 465
Livius Andronicus (LIV-ius an-DRON-ic-us), **Lucius,** Greek-born Roman poet and playwright **L** 77
Livy, Roman historian **L** 317
place in Latin literature **L** 80
studied by Renaissance historians **H** 135
Li Yu, Chinese poet **O** 220a
Lizards L 318–21
compared to snakes **S** 204
dinosaurs, "large lizards" **D** 172–81
forelimb, picture **F** 80
hibernation **H** 123; picture **H** 122
life, adaptation to surroundings **L** 214
reptiles, groups of **R** 181
Ljubljana (I'YOO-bel-ya-na), Yugoslavia **Y** 357
Llamas (LA-mas), hoofed mammals **H** 210; pictures **A** 252, **H** 213
grazing at Lake Milluni, picture **S** 274
pack-animals in Ecuador, picture **E** 54
Peru **P** 161
Llanos (YA-nos), grasslands of South America
Venezuela **V** 297
Lleras Camargo (YARE-as com-AR-go), **Alberto,** president of Colombia **C** 384
Llewellyn (lew-EL-lin), Welsh prince **W** 4
Llopango, lake in El Salvador **E** 181
Lloyd, Harold, American movie comedian, picture **M** 473
Lloyd, Selwyn, British statesman, picture **E** 111

Lloyd George, David (1863–1945) British statesman, b. Manchester. He held a seat in British House of Commons for a record 54 years (1890–1944). He was noted for his People's Budget (1909), his legislation for health and unemployment insurance (1911), and his efforts to produce armaments during World War I. As prime minister (1916–22) he set up coalition government and was instrumental in creating the Irish Free State (1921).

He received an earldom immediately after his resignation from Parliament (1944). Picture **W** 180.
World War I **W** 282

Lloyd's of London, insurance **I** 295–96; picture **I** 293
LM see Lunar Module, section of Apollo spacecraft
Loading machinery see Hoisting and loading machinery
Loam, soil **S** 231
Loans, bank B 48–49
college education **T** 44
installment buying **I** 288–89
interest: renting money **P** 149–50
Lobachevski (lob-a-CHEF-ski), **Nikolai,** Russian mathematician **G** 131
non-Euclidean geometries **M** 159
Lobatse, Botswana **B** 340a

Lobbying, organized attempts by persons not connected with government to influence opinions of legislators through personal contact. The term arose from the fact that persons with a vested interest in legislation frequented the lobby of a legislative house to speak to public officials.
lawmaking in the U.S. Congress **U** 142

Lobengula (lo-ben-GU-la), king of the Matabele people of Rhodesia **R** 229–30
negotiations with Cecil Rhodes **R** 227
Lobes, of leaves **L** 114
Lobito (lu-VI-tu), port of Angola **A** 261
Lobola (LO-bo-la), or bride-price, amount paid for a wife among certain African peoples **S** 268
Lobsterbacks, nickname for British soldiers **R** 196
Lobsters, crustaceans **S** 168–71
fishing fleet, Glace Bay, Nova Scotia, picture **N** 344a
lobster fishing industry **F** 221
traps, or pots **F** 217; pictures **F** 219, **M** 38, **P** 456b
Lobster Trap and Fish Tail, mobile by Calder, picture **M** 398
Local anesthetic (an-es-THET-ic) **A** 258
Local color, in literature
American literature **A** 204–05
short stories **S** 167
Local government see Municipal government
Locarno (lo-CAR-no) **Conference,** 1925 **W** 283
Germany signs Pact **G** 162
Location, natural settings for movies **M** 479, 480
Loch, Scottish for lake see names of lochs, as Ness, Loch

Loch (LOCK) **Ness monster,** a 40- to 50-foot sea serpent reportedly seen in Loch Ness, Scotland, whose existence is questionable but has not yet been disproved. The monster was first sighted in 1933. Subsequent reports included the noted photograph by Kenneth Wilson (1934) showing a long neck, tapering off to a small head, emerging from the water. It is thought by some to be a creature similar to a massive reptile, the *Plesiosaurus,* believed to be long extinct. Others feel reports of the monster are based on distorted views of diving otters or surfacing bubbles of marsh gas.

Locke, Alain Le Roy (1886–1954), American educator, Negro, b. Philadelphia, Pa. Locke was an authority on Negro art. He was head of the philosophy department at Howard University (1918–54) and an exchange professor in Haiti (1943). His works include *The New Negro, Race Contact and Inter-Racial Relations,* and (co-editor) *When Peoples Meet: A Study in Race and Culture Contact.*
Negro Renaissance **N** 98

Locke, David Ross, American humorist **A** 206

Locke, John, English philosopher **L** 321
　Carolina colony's government based on his plans
　　S 310
　Declaration of Independence **D** 63
　experimental science, interest in **H** 87–88
　influence on law in America **L** 87–88
Lockjaw, bacterial disease **D** 200–01
Lockout, shutting down work by management in labor
　troubles **L** 18
Locks, of canals **C** 83–84
　Erie Canal at West Troy, New York, picture **E** 276
　Panama Canal **P** 47
　Sault Sainte Marie Canals, picture **M** 266
Locks and keys L 322–26
　use in animal tests **A** 285
Locksmiths, makers of locks and keys **L** 323
Lockups, places of short-term imprisonment **P** 468
Locomotion of animals see Animals: Locomotion
Locomotives L 327–32
　Diesel locomotive and train, picture **D** 168
　early history **T** 263
　first in U.S. built by Peter Cooper **C** 498
　How did the cowcatcher get its name? **L** 330
　railroads, history of **R** 79, 87–88
　railroads, model **R** 92
　Stephenson's, picture **I** 237
Locoweed, plant **P** 323

Locust, any one of several insects found in many parts of
the world. In general, a locust has long, sturdy legs and
short, thick antennae. Locusts vary in size—the largest
are tropical locusts with a wingspread of 6 in. Certain
locusts are noted for their songs. The sound is produced
by rubbing the hind leg against the forewing. Swarms
of locusts sometimes do great damage to crops.
　insect migrants **H** 189

Locust, tree
　black locust, poisonous bark **P** 322
　honey locust, prickly defenses **P** 283
Lodes, layers of rock
　gold-bearing lodes **G** 251
Lodestar see North Star
Lodestone, magnetic rock **M** 24
　early use in telling direction **D** 182

Lodge, Henry Cabot (1850–1924), American statesman
and writer, b. Boston, Mass. He was assistant editor of
the *North American Review* (1873–76) and member of
House of Representatives (1887–93) and Senate
(1893–24). One of Theodore Roosevelt's closest consult-
ants on matters of foreign policy, he led senatorial
forces in opposition to United States involvement in the
League of Nations (1919). His books include *Alexander
Hamilton, Historical and Political Essays,* and *The Senate
and the League of Nations.*
　Wilson and Lodge **W** 181

Lodge, Henry Cabot, Jr. (1902–), American statesman,
b. Nahant, Mass. Grandson of Henry Cabot Lodge, he
was reporter and editorial writer for the New York *Herald
Tribune* (1924–36), U.S. Senator from Massachusetts
(1937–44; 1947–53), and U.S. delegate to the United
Nations and the Security Council (1953–60). Lodge has
been U.S. ambassador to the Republic of Vietnam
(1963–64; 1965–67), to West Germany (1968–69) and
(1969) chief negotiator at the Paris peace talks.

Lodge, Sir Oliver Joseph, English scientist
　radio, early history of **R** 52
Lodge, organization of Gothic architects **G** 272
Lodge family, of Massachusetts **M** 147

Lodges, of beavers **B** 113–14
Lodz, Poland P 361
Loess (LESS), sandy soil deposited by wind **S** 234
　Iowa soils **I** 360
　landform region in Mississippi **M** 352
　Nebraska deposits **N** 74, 75
Loesser (LESS-er), **Frank,** American composer **N** 26
　musical comedy **M** 543

Loewy (LOE-wy), **Raymond Fernand** (1893–), American industrial designer, b. Paris, France. He started his
own design organization (1927), Raymond Loewy Associates (1945), and the firm of Raymond Loewy-William
Snaith (1961). Scope of design has ranged from building
interiors, such as that of Lever House in New York, N.Y.,
to refrigerators, trade centers, and automobiles. He wrote
an autobiography, *Never Leave Well Enough Alone.*

Lofoten (lo-FO-ten) **Islands,** northwest of Norway **I** 434

Lofting, Hugh (1886–1947), American author of children's
books, b. Maidenhead, England. He settled in United
States in 1912. He illustrated letters to his children
during World War I. He later compiled these letters into
The Story of Doctor Dolittle. Lofting wrote the Doctor
Dolittle series and won Newbery medal (1923) for *The
Voyages of Doctor Dolittle.*

Log, apparatus to measure a ship's speed **N** 65
　logs or logbooks, official daily records of data of a
　　voyage **C** 417

Logan (LO-gan), **James** (John) (1725?–1780), American
Indian leader of the Mingo tribes, b. probably Shamokin,
Pa. He was named Tah-gah-jute but called Logan, probably after the American statesman James Logan. After
the Yellow Creek massacre (1774), in which members of
his family were slaughtered, he sought vengeance
against American colonists, siding with the British during
the Revolution.

Logan, Mount, Canada **C** 51; **Y** 361

Logan, Rayford W. (1897–), American educator and
author, Negro, b. Washington, D.C. Head of the history
department at Howard University (1942–64) he was United
Nations consultant for NAACP (1949) and a member of
U.S. Commission for U.N.E.S.C.O. (1947–50). He was
editor of *What the Negro Wants* and author of *The Negro
in American Life and Thought: The Nadir, 1877–1901* and
The Negro in the United States.

Loganberries, large reddish-purple acid berries of the
blackberry and raspberry group. They are named for J. H.
Logan of California, who first grew the berry from a cross
between raspberries and blackberries or dewberries. Loganberries are cultivated on the West Coast of the United
States.
　varieties of blackberries **G** 301

Logarithmic spiral, picture **G** 131
Log booms
　British Columbia, picture **L** 377
Log cabins P 252; pictures **P** 253, 258
　houses of wood **H** 171
　introduced to America by Swedes **C** 388
　origin in Delaware **D** 89
　similar wooden homes in Soviet Union **U** 29
Loge, or Loki, Norse god **N** 279
Loggerhead shrikes, birds
　bill, picture **B** 223
Loggers, lumbermen **L** 375

Longleaf pine, tree **A** 113
Long Parliament, English **E** 223
Long-playing records (LP's) **P** 198
   hi-fi and stereo **H** 125–27
   record collecting **R** 124
LOng RAnge Navigation see Loran
Longshoremen, men who load and unload ships **S** 161
Long tom, for washing gold from sand **G** 251; picture **G** 252
Long ton, measure of weight **W** 114; picture **W** 113
Longway sets, dance forms **D** 28
   contra dances, forms of folk dancing **F** 299
Longworth, Alice Roosevelt, daughter of Theodore Roosevelt **F** 176
Longworth, Nicholas, American statesman
   real estate fortune **R** 112
Lon Nol, Cambodian president **C** 33
Looby-Loo, singing game **G** 11
Looking Glass, chief of Nez Percé Indians **I** 176–77
Looking-glass tree
   seeds, picture **F** 281
Lookout Mountain, Colorado **C** 410
Lookout Mountain, Tennessee **T** 85–86
Lookout Mountain, battle of, 1863, Civil War **C** 326
Lookout towers, for forest fires **F** 152; picture **F** 374
Looming, kind of mirage **M** 342
Looms, for weaving textiles **T** 140–41
   cotton industry aided by British inventions **C** 520–21
   how to make your own looms **W** 97–98
   Indian beadwork weaving **I** 158
   Industrial Revolution improvements **I** 234

Loons, water birds noted for eerie cry and their skill in diving. Loons can dive deeper and for longer periods of time than any other bird. They live in colder northern regions of the world. Heavy-bodied birds, they are whitish below and dark above, with lighter stripes or spots. The legs are set so far back on the body that the birds are almost helpless on land. They are strong fliers but must take off from water by running rapidly along the surface. Their chief food is fish, which they can pursue underwater for long distances, propelled by their feet and aided by their wings in balancing and turning. Picture **B** 236.
   state bird of Minnesota **M** 323

Loop, The, in Chicago, Illinois **C** 228
Loop knots **K** 290
   roping **R** 333–35
Loose caboose, tag game **G** 18
Loose housing, cow-keeping system **D** 9; picture **D** 6
Lope de Vega see Vega Carpio, Lope Félix de
López (LO-pez), **Carlos Antonio,** Paraguayan dictator **P** 66
López, Francisco Solano, Paraguayan dictator **P** 66
López Arellano, Oswaldo, president of Honduras **H** 199
López de Legazpe, or **Legazpi** (LO-peth day lay-GOTH-pi), **Miguel,** Spanish navigator **M** 75; **P** 189
López de Villalobos (vi-ya-LO-boce), **Ruy,** Portuguese navigator **P** 189

López Mateos (LO-pace mat-A-oce), **Adolfo** (1910–69), Mexican statesman, b. Atizapán de Zaragoza. Professor and director of Toluca Scientific and Literary Institute, he headed Revolutionary Institutional Party. He was a federal senator (1946–52), minister of labor and social welfare (1952–58), and president of Mexico (1958–64).
   Mexico, history of **M** 250

Loran (LOng RAnge Navigation) **R** 38–39
   aid to aviation **A** 562
   United States Navy electronics and weapons **U** 193

Lorca, Federico García see García Lorca, Federico
Lord Dunmore's War see Dunmore's War
Lord Jim, by Joseph Conrad **C** 482
Lord of the Flies, by William Golding **E** 267
Lords, House of, British Parliament **E** 219; **U** 78
   parliaments, history and function of **P** 81

Lord's Prayer (also known as Our Father, Pater Noster, or Paternoster), most familiar Christian prayer. It was taught by Jesus to his disciples, and it is used in virtually all Christian services. It is derived primarily from Biblical Sermon on the Mount.
   opening lines in Anglo-Saxon and in English **L** 38
   opening words in Esperanto **U** 194
   rosary **R** 302

Lord's Prayer, The, Bible (Revised Standard Version) **P** 435
Lord's Supper see Holy Communion
Loreal (LO-re-al) **pits,** of snakes **S** 208

Lorelei (LO-rel-i), precipitous cliff over Rhine River south of St. Goarshausen, Germany. In German literature Lorelei is the name of a beautiful water nymph who lived on a rock, and with her haunting melodies, lured sailors to their ruin on rocks below. Her story is told in two operas, by Mendelssohn and Lochnar, and in "Die Lorelei," by Heinrich Heine.

Lorelei's Golden Rockbottom, champion golden retriever dog **D** 262

Lorentz (LO-rentz), **Hendrik Antoon** (1853–1928), Dutch physicist, b. Arnhem. He made many important contributions to physics, his greatest being on the theory of light. For his study of how a magnetic field affects the wavelength of light, he shared the 1902 Nobel prize in physics with his former pupil Pieter Zeeman. He is best known for the theory known as the Lorentz-Fitzgerald contraction, which states that a moving body contracts in the direction of motion.

Lorenzini, Carlo see Collodi, Carlo
Lorenzo the Magnificent see Medici, Lorenzo de'
Lorises, animals related to monkeys **M** 422
   animal life of Ceylon **C** 180
Lorrain, Claude see Claude Lorrain
Los Alamos, New Mexico **N** 181, 188
Los Angeles (los AN-ge-lese), California **L** 344–47
   harbor, man-made **H** 37
   network of freeways, picture **C** 27
Los Angeles County Museum of Art, picture **L** 346
Los Islands, Guinea **G** 405
Los Padres National Forest, California, picture **N** 36
Lost, poem by Carl Sandburg **S** 29

Lost Battalion, group of about 600 men of the 77th Division who were separated for 5 days from the rest of American forces while fighting in Argonne Forest, France, during World War I (1918). They were encircled by German forces but refused to surrender despite lack of food, water, and munitions. The battalion, which was rescued by American forces after about 400 men had died, was led by Major Charles W. Wittlesey, who was awarded a Medal of Honor for heroic command.
   World War I, in the last German offensive **W** 281

Lost Colony, The, pageant **P** 12
Lost Colony of Virginia **A** 181
   early settlement of North Carolina **N** 320
Lost generation, phrase attributed to Gertrude Stein **H** 109

Lost Ten Tribes of Israel see Ten Tribes, Hebrew

Lot, in Old Testament, son of Haran and nephew of Abraham, b. Ur. He traveled with Abraham to Canaan and Egypt, but they parted when disputes arose over pastureland. Lot took up residence in Sodom and the plain of Jordan. He left Sodom with his wife and two daughters just before its destruction. His wife became a pillar of salt when she stopped to look back at the city. Lot's descendants were founders of the nations of Moab and Ammon.

Lothrop, Harriet Mulford see Sidney, Margaret
Loti, Pierre, French novelist **F** 442

Lotus (LO-tus), water plant with pink, yellow, white, or blue flowers. The sacred flower of Buddhists of India, China, and Japan, it symbolizes divine creative power, purity, fertility, and the seats of the gods, including Brahma and Buddha. In Egypt it is an emblem of fertility, the sun, and resurrection. In Homeric legend the lotus is a fruit of a North African shrub or tree. It produces drowsiness and contentment.

Lotus-Eaters, according to Homeric legend, inhabitants of the northern coast of Africa who ate the fruit of lotus trees, causing them to forget past desires and become languidly satisfied. In the *Odyssey,* when Odysseus and his men visited them, those who ate lotus fruit no longer wanted to return home and had to be forced back on ship. The story is also recounted by Tennyson in "The Lotus-Eaters."

Louis V ("the Sluggard") (966?–987), king of France (986–987). He was the son of Lothair and the last Carolingian king of France. When he died after a hunting accident, Hugh Capet was chosen to succeed him.

Louis VI (the Fat) (1081–1137), king of France (1108–37). The son of Philip I, he was the first of the Capetian kings to break down power of the feudal nobles. He led his armies against pillaging lords and against Emperor Henry V and Henry I of England. He protected the property of the clergy.

Louis IX (Saint Louis) (1214–1270), king of France (1226–70), b. Poissy. Son of King Louis VIII, he succeeded to throne (1226), with his mother, Blanche of Castile, as regent during his youth. He tightened control in feudal and tax systems and court procedure, and he constructed Sainte-Chapelle in Paris (1245–48) to enshrine Crown of Thorns obtained from Emperor Baldwin of Constantinople. A crusader in Egypt and Syria (1248–54), on Second Crusade (1270) he succumbed to plague during epidemic in Tunis. He was canonized in 1297.

Louis XIII (1601–1643), king of France (1610–43), b. Fontainebleau. The son of Henry IV, he was dominated by his prime minister, Cardinal Richelieu. Richelieu guided him into a costly foreign policy, including war against Spain, to the neglect of the welfare of his people. Richelieu also destroyed the political power of the Huguenots and centralized the government in the hands of the king.

Lovejoy brothers, American abolitionists, b. Albion, Maine. **Elijah Parish** (1802–37), a clergyman, promoted abolitionist cause as editor of Alton *Observer* in Alton, Ill., and established Illinois chapter of American Anti-Slavery Society. He was fatally shot defending his printing press against destruction by a mob. **Owen** (1811–64), an abolitionist leader in Illinois and a representative to Congress (1857–64), formulated the bill to abolish slavery in all U.S. territories.

Lovelace, Richard (1618–1658), English poet, b. Kent. He was one of the Cavalier poets—17th-century lyric poets who supported Charles I and the Loyalists in the Civil War (1642–48). He was imprisoned twice (1642, 1648) by an anti-Loyalist Parliament. His poems were published after his death in a collection entitled *Lucasta: Posthume Poems.* His best-known poems are the celebrated

Lovelace, Richard (continued)
lyrics "To Althea from Prison" and "To Lucasta on Going to the Wars."

Lovell, James Arthur, Jr. (1928–), American astronaut, b. Cleveland, Ohio. A former Navy flier, Lovell became an astronaut in 1962. He made the Gemini 7 (1965), Gemini 12 (1966), Apollo 8 (1968), Apollo 13 (1970) flights.
  space flight data **S** 344, 345, 347

Love's Labour's Lost, play by Shakespeare **S** 135

Low, Juliette Gordon (1860–1927), American founder of Girl Scouts of America, b. Savannah, Ga. She moved to England (1886) and led Girl Guides troops in Scotland and England. Returning to United States, she organized the first Girl Guide company (1912), which became known as Girl Scouts (1913). She was first president of the national organization of Girl Scouts (1915).
  Girl Scouts **G** 213, 215, 219

Löw (LURV),**Oskar,** German doctor **A** 310
Lowboy, furniture, picture **C** 389

Low Countries, the densely populated countries situated on the northwestern European plain along the North Sea. Geographically the term applies specifically to the Netherlands and Belgium. As a political term it refers to the Benelux countries: Belgium, the Netherlands, and Luxembourg. This area is composed of very fertile and productive land, watered by three rivers that flow into the North Sea, the Rhine, the Maas, and the Schelde.

Lowell, Amy, American poet **A** 209
Lowell, James Russell, American author **L** 369
  American literature **A** 203
Lowell, Percival, American astronomer
  studies of Mars **M** 104
Lowell, Robert, American poet **A** 211
Lowell family, of Massachusetts **M** 147
Lowell Observatory, Arizona **A** 412–13; **T** 64
Lower California, Mexico **M** 242
Lower Canada **C** 71, 73
  Quebec **Q** 14, 16
Lower-case, or small, **letters of the alphabet** **A** 173
Lowest common denominator (LCD) **F** 399
Low German, dialect of northern Germany **G** 172, 173
Lowry, Malcolm, English novelist **B** 405
Lows, or cyclones, in meteorology **W** 74
  east-west movement of air **W** 186
Lox see Liquid oxygen
Loya Jirgeh, Great National Assembly, Afghanistan **A** 45
Loyalists, or Tories, colonial supporters of the British **R** 198
  political parties in colonial America **P** 379
Loyalists, United Empire see United Empire Loyalists

Loyalty Day, American national observance celebrated annually by Loyalty Day parade (May 1), sponsored by Veterans of Foreign Wars since 1947. The observance was proclaimed by Congress and approved by President Truman (1948) as a day of reaffirmation of loyalty to American tradition of freedom, to countervail Communist celebration of May Day (May 1).

Loyalty Islands, chain of three coral islands and many islets in southwest Pacific. A dependency of New Caledonia, they are administered by France. The principal exports are nickel and other metals and copra.

Loyola (loy-O-la), **Saint Ignatius,** founder of Society of Jesus, or Jesuits **L** 369

Counter-Reformation in the Roman Catholic Church **C** 287; **R** 294
  Roman Catholic reforms **R** 294
LPG, liquefied petroleum gas **F** 489
L.P.G.A. see Ladies Professional Golfers' Association
LP's see Long-playing records
LSD, hallucinogenic drug **D** 329, 331
Luanda, capital of Angola **A** 261
Luang Prabang (lu-ONG pra-BONG), royal capital of Laos **L** 41
Luau (LU-ow), Hawaiian "cook-out," or outdoor feast **F** 340; picture **H** 65
Lubrication and lubricants **L** 370–71
  internal-combustion engines **I** 307
  petroleum **P** 176
  plastics **P** 327
  powder metallurgy **M** 232
  tallow **O** 79
Lucan (LU-can), Roman poet **L** 80
Lucas, Robert, American statesman **I** 369
Luce, Henry R., American editor and publisher **M** 15
Lucerne (lu-CERN), **Lake of,** central Switzerland **L** 32
Lucerne, Switzerland **S** 499
Lucerne Festival, Switzerland **M** 551
Lucia di Lammermoor (lu-CHI-a di la-mer-MOOR), opera by Gaetano Donizetti **O** 145–46
Lucian (LU-cian), Greek satirical writer **G** 355

Lucifer, in Old Testament (Isaiah 14:12), name applied symbolically to a king of Babylon about to fall from high rank. In New Testament (Luke 10:18), through reference to Isaiah 14:12, the name alludes to Satan, who fell as lightning from heaven. The name also refers to the planet Venus when it appears as the morning star.

Luciferases (lu-CIF-er-ases), light-producing chemicals **B** 198
Luciferins (lu-CIF-er-ins), "glowing" chemicals **B** 197–98
Luck
  counter-magic **S** 473
Lucknow, India **I** 122
Luck of Roaring Camp, The, short story by Bret Harte, scene from, picture **S** 167
Lucretius (lu-CRE-tius), Roman philosophical poet **L** 78

Lucy, Saint (Italian, Santa Lucia) (283?–303), Italian virgin martyr, b. Syracuse, Sicily. According to tradition, she declared her belief in Christianity by distributing her wealth to the poor during Diocletian's persecutions. She was denounced by her betrothed and killed with a sword. Her feast day is December 13.
  Christmas patron saints **C** 292

Ludendorff (LU-den-dorff), **Erich Friedrich Wilhelm** (1865–1937), German general and strategist, b. Krusze-wina. He assisted Hindenberg in defeating Russians during World War I and was solely responsible for German victory over Rumania and Italy (1917). He fled to Sweden after German defeat but returned to Germany (1919) and took part in Kapp Putsch (1920) and Hitler's Beer Hall Putsch (1923). A member of the Reichstag (1924–28), he wrote almost fanatical anti-Semitic, anti-Catholic, and anti-Masonic material.
  World War I **W** 274, 280

Ludlow casting machine
  printing **P** 465
  type-casting process **T** 345
Luffing, in sailing **S** 12

Luftwaffe (LOOFT-va-fa) (from German word meaning

"air weapon"), Nazi air force during World War II. It was openly established (1935) under Hitler by Hermann Goering. The name is still used for the air force of the Federal Republic of Germany (West Germany).

World War II **W** 287, 288

Lugano (lu-GA-no), **Lake of,** Italy and Switzerland **L** 32
Lugano, Switzerland **S** 499
Lugard (lu-GARD), **Lord Frederick,** British colonial administrator **N** 258
Luge (small sled) **event,** in Winter Olympics **O** 109
Lu Hsun, Chinese novelist **O** 220b

Lujack, John (1925–), American football player, b. Connellsville, Pa. He played quarterback for Notre Dame (1943, 1946–47) and won Heisman Trophy for college football's outstanding player of the year (1947). He turned professional (1948–51) and played for the Chicago Bears. He retired in 1951 and became an analyst for national football telecasts.

Luke, Frank, Jr., American aviator **A** 416
Luke, Saint **E** 335
Christianity, history of **C** 280
writings in Bible, New Testament **B** 160–61
Lullabies **F** 303–04
folk music **F** 326
"Lullaby" (Rock-a-bye, baby) nursery rhyme **N** 405
Lully (lu-LE), **Jean-Baptiste,** French composer **F** 444
ballet music **D** 36
baroque music **B** 63
opera **O** 132
Lumber and lumbering **L** 372–77
Africa **A** 64
Alabama, picture **A** 119
building materials **B** 430
Burma, picture **B** 458
log booms, picture **G** 327
log drives, pictures **C** 59; **M** 38
National Forests, multiple use of **N** 31, 32; picture **N** 33
plywood and laminates **F** 503; **W** 226–27
preparing wood for furniture-making **F** 501–02
rain forests **R** 100
sawmill on Vancouver Island, picture **B** 404
shortage in Asia **A** 462
veneers **F** 503–04; **W** 226–27
wood products **W** 225–28
woodworking, dimensions for **W** 234
See also industries and products section of country, province, and state articles
Lumberjacks, lumbermen **L** 374, 375
Paul Bunyan stories **F** 312–13
Lumbertown, U.S.A., near Brainerd, Minnesota **M** 333
Luminous (LU-min-ous) **paints** **P** 34

Lumumba (lu-MOOM-ba), **Patrice Emergy** (1926–1961), Congolese nationalist leader, b. Katako Kombe, Kawai Province. As leader of Mouvement National Congolais, he became prime minister of Republic of Congo when it gained independence from Belgium (June, 1960). He tried to keep Congo unified, opposing Katanga Province's independence (July, 1960). He was overthrown by Colonel Mobutu's coup (September, 1960) and put under house arrest. He escaped, was recaptured, and was flown to Elisabethville, where he again escaped but was reported to have been killed by political enemies.

Zaïre, history of **Z** 366d

Luna, or **Lunik,** Soviet spacecraft, of which Luna 9 on Feb. 3, 1966 made the first soft landing on the moon. Its radio and television messages revealed the moon's surface in its vicinity is less radioactive than earth's, does not have a thick dust layer, and can support manned craft. In April, 1966, Luna 10 became the first craft to successfully orbit the moon. Moon landing sites **M** 449.

Luna 3 **S** 348
Luna 16, rock samples **S** 348
Luna 17 **S** 348
Lunik III **M** 447
Lunokhod, vehicle **S** 348

Lunalilo (lu-na-LI-lo), **William Charles** (1832–1874), Hawaiian king (1873–74), b. Honolulu. Hawaii's first elected ruler, he increased the rights of people and left his fortune to erect the Lunalilo Home for needy Hawaiians.

Lunar calendar **T** 193–94
Lunar eclipses **E** 46–47
moon's orbit **M** 448–49
Lunar landing day, July 20, 1969 **E** 368; **S** 339–340a
Lunar module (LM), of Apollo spacecraft **S** 339–340a, 340e, 340h, 340j, 341; pictures **S** 340a, 340b, 340h
navigation **N** 68, 69

Lunar orbiter, one of a series of U.S. spacecraft designed to orbit the moon and photograph the moon's surface. Its chief purpose was to locate possible landing sites for a manned craft. Orbiter I, launched in August, 1966, sent back more than 200 photographs and at its closest was 25 miles from the moon.

moon landing sites, choice of **M** 455; map **M** 449
observatories **O** 14

Lunar probes, or moon probes **M** 450, 455
Lunar Rover, vehicle used on the moon, picture **S** 340g
Lunar seas, of moon's surface **M** 451, 453; map **M** 449

Lunceford, Jimmie (James Melvin Lunceford) (1902–1947), American musician, Negro, b. Fulton, Mo. He studied music under Wilberforce J. Whiteman, father of Paul Whiteman, and began his bandleading career in 1927. His group was one of the few big jazz orchestras of the 1930's to be of lasting importance. His arrangements, mostly by Sy Oliver, had influence on other bands.

Lundy, Benjamin (1789–1839), American abolitionist and editor, b. Sussex County, N.J. A leading figure in the antislavery movement during 1820's, he formed the Union Humane Society (1815), one of first antislavery organizations. He also founded *The National Enquirer and Constitutional Advocate of Universal Liberty.* He traveled (1825–35) to Haiti, Canada, and Texas in search of places to establish free Negro settlements.

Lunenburg, Nova Scotia, Canada **N** 344d–344e

Lungfish, any one of six species of freshwater fishes found in parts of South America and Africa and in northeastern Australia. These fishes have lungs as well as gills. Except for one species that lives chiefly in lakes, they inhabit slow-moving or stagnant waters. All but the Australian lungfish burrow into the mud when there is an absence of water in the dry season. There they cover their bodies with a mucous cocoon they secrete that keeps them moist. They breathe, with their lungs, through a hole in the top of the cocoon. Picture **F** 182.

bony fishes, kinds of **F** 183
estivation of, picture **H** 121
successful life adaptation **L** 224

Lungs, organs of breathing **B** 277–78
air pollution, effect on **A** 108–09
birds **B** 203

Lungs (continued)
cancer **C** 91–92
emphysema disease **D** 196
heart action **H** 86
pneumonia, bacteria infection **D** 203–04
smoking **S** 203
Lunik III, Russian space probe **M** 447
Lunokhod, Soviet Union's unmanned vehicle for moon exploration **S** 348

Lunt, Alfred (1893–   ), American actor, b. Milwaukee, Wis. With his wife, Lynn Fontanne, he has been a leading figure in the theater. Some of his major roles have been in *Sweet Nell of Old Drury, The Guardsman, Arms and the Man, Idiot's Delight,* and *The Visit.*

Lupercalia (lu-per-CAY-lia), Roman festival
Valentine's Day, origin **V** 266
Luque, Hernando de, Spanish priest **P** 266
Lures, for fishing **F** 206–07
Lusaka (lu-SA-ka), capital of Zambia **Z** 368
Lusiads (LU-si-ads), **The,** by Camoëns, excerpt **E** 387
Lusignan, Guy de see *Guy de Lusignan*
Lusignan (lu-zeen-YON) **dynasty,** of Cyprus **C** 558
Lusitania (lu-si-TAY-nia), British ocean liner **O** 24
torpedoed in World War I **W** 276
Lusitanians, early people of Portugal **P** 399
Luster, brightness
minerals identified by **R** 270
orient of pearls **P** 113
Lusterware, ceramic pottery **I** 422
Lustre, or luster, metallic glaze for pottery **P** 417
Lute, musical instrument **M** 544–45; picture **S** 438
ancient instrument **A** 245; picture **A** 244
English composers for **E** 270
in concert, picture **I** 482
Lute Player and Woman Playing the Harp, painting by Israel van Meckenem **D** 364
Lutetia Parisiorum (lu-TE-tia pa-ris-i-OR-um), ancient city, now Paris, France **P** 73
Lutetium (lu-TE-shum), element **E** 154, 162
Luther, Martin, German leader of Protestant Reformation **L** 378; picture **R** 132
Bible, translation of **B** 153
Christianity, history of **C** 285–86
demands for religious reforms divide Germany **G** 159
hymn composer **H** 311
influenced German language **G** 173
introduced chorales into church music **G** 182
Protestantism **P** 482–83
Reformation **R** 133–34
Lutheran Church
Jerusalem Lutheran Church, India, picture **P** 486
Lutheranism, religious belief **P** 483
state religion of Sweden **S** 486

Luther League of America, formerly the official youth organization of United Lutheran Church. Established in 1895, with headquarters in Philadelphia, Pa., it published *Luther Life.* It was officially acknowledged in 1918 and merged in 1962 with several other Lutheran groups

Luthuli (LOO-tu-li), **Albert John** (1898–1967), South African liberation leader, b. Groutville Reserve, Natal, Rhodesia. Chief of the Abasemakholweni (Zulu) tribe (1935–52), he was deposed by the government for his role in the "defiance [of racial segregation] campaign" (1952). He was chosen president general of African National Congress (1952) and won the Nobel peace prize (1961) for nonviolent opposition to apartheid in South Africa. He was elected rector of Glasgow University (1962). He published an autobiography, *Let My People Go.*

Luttrellstown Castle, near Dublin, picture **I** 388
Luxembourg **L** 379–80
flag **F** 239
invasion by Hitler, 1940 **W** 288
Luxembourg, Palais du, Paris **P** 74
Luxembourg City, capital of Luxembourg **L** 379
Luxembourg Gardens, Paris, France, picture **G** 32
Luxor, Egypt **E** 90f; picture **E** 90b
site of ancient Egyptian temple **E** 100, 102
Luzon (lu-ZON), Philippines **P** 186
Manila **M** 75
rice fields, picture **A** 446
Lyceum (ly-CE-um), Athens school founded by Aristotle **A** 397
Lycopodineae, division of plant kingdom **P** 292

Lycurgus (ly-CUR-gus) (lived about 9th century B.C.), Spartan lawgiver, reputed to have remodeled constitution, transforming military and civil institutions so that Sparta could remain military leader in the Peloponnesus.

Lydgate (LID-gate), **John** (1370?–1451?), English poet, b. Lydgate, Suffolk. He was court poet during reigns of Henry IV, Henry V, and Henry VI. He is often called Chaucer's disciple. His works include *Falls of Princes, Troy Book, The Story of Thebes* (meant to be an addition to Chaucer's *Canterbury Tales*), and *The Life of Our Lady.*

Lydia, ancient country of Asia Minor. Rich in minerals, particularly gold in the River Pactolus, the kingdom was a commercial center between Greece and Mesopotamia. Sardis, the capital, was a city of great affluence. Lydians are believed to have been the first people to mint coins. The wealth of Croesus, Lydia's last king, has become legendary. The kingdom was conquered by the Persians (546 B.C.).

Lydian (LID-ian) **mode,** seven-note musical scale **A** 247
Lyell, Sir Charles, English geologist **G** 113
Darwin and Lyell **D** 40
forerunner of the theory of evolution **B** 192
Lyly (LILY), **John,** English writer **E** 250
quotation **Q** 20
Lymphatic (lim-PHAT-ic) **system,** of the human body **D** 199–200
cancer of **C** 90
Lymphocytes (LIM-pho-cytes), white cells **I** 107
Lymphomas, cancers **C** 90

Lynch, Robert Clyde (1880–1931), American physician, b. Carson City, Nev. He made many important contributions to otolaryngology, the medical specialty dealing with the ears, nose, and throat. He developed the frontal sinus operation known as the Lynch operation and was the first to make successful motion pictures of the larynx and vocal cords.

Lynch, Thomas, Jr. (1749–1779), American politician, b. Prince George's Parish, S.C. When he returned to South Carolina (1772) after education abroad, he was elected to many important civil offices. He was a member of the first state General Assembly (1776) and of the Continental Congress (1776–77) and was a signer of the Declaration of Independence.
rare signatures and autographs **A** 526

Lynching, punishment by a mob, without lawful trial, of an accused person. The term appears to stem from the name of Charles Lynch (1736–96) of Virginia, who molested Loyalists during American Revolution. Historically, it has usually referred to the hanging of an

allegedly guilty person **by a mob.**
Negro history **N 97**

Lyndon B. Johnson Library T 131, 135
Lyngenfjord (LURNG-en-fiord), Norway, **picture N 340**
Lynxes (LINX-es), wildcats **C 139**; picture **C 140**

Lyon, Mary (1797–1849), American educator, b. Buckland, Mass. She founded Mount Holyoke Seminary (now Mount Holyoke College) in South Hadley, Mass. (1837), the first permanent institution of higher learning for women only. She was president of Mount Holyoke (1837–49) and was elected to American Hall of Fame (1905).

Lyons (le-ON), France **F 406**
Lyra, constellation **C 492**
Lyre, ancient instrument **A 245, 246, 247**; picture **A 244**

Lyrebird, brownish bird of forests and scrublands of Australia. The bird is noted for its long, brightly colored tail. The lyrebird is about 37 in. long, of which some 22 in. are the tail. Males have highly ornamented tails which are colored and lacy in appearance when spread.

Lyrical voice V 375
Lyric poems, short, musical poems dealing with personal emotions **P 354**
    American literature **A 210**
    Greek **G 350**
    odes **O 52**
Lyrics of Lowly Life, book of poems by Paul Dunbar **D 344**

Lysander (ly-SAN-der) (?-395 B.C.), Spartan naval commander. He led his fleet to victory over the Athenians off Notium (407 B.C.), and finally caused their complete rout at Aegospotamos (405 B.C.) bringing about the end of the Peloponnesian War. He sought to gain control of all the Greek city-states. When the citizens of Boetia, a rival city-state rose against him, he was killed in battle at Haliartus.

Lysergic acid diethylamide *see* **LSD**

Lysippus (ly-SIP-us) (4th century B.C.), Greek sculptor. Probably the most prolific sculptor of the ancient world, he is said to have fashioned over 1,500 statues. He specialized in carvings of gods and men, and produced figures ranging in size from delicate statuettes to a 60-foot Zeus. Although none of his work survives, some statues found in Italy and Greece are said to show his influence. His work is described in the writings of Pliny and other historians.

Lysozyme, body enzyme **I 104**

Lytton, Edward George Earle Lytton Bulwer- (1803–1873), English writer and statesman, b. London. He wrote *Falkland* and other social novels, such as *Eugene Aram,* which concerns social justice. He was a member of Parliament (1831–41, 1852–66) and colonial secretary (1858–59). He turned to writing historical novels, among them *The Last Days of Pompeii* and *The Last of the Barons.* He was less well-known as a playwright, his most outstanding play being *Richelieu.*

ILLUSTRATION CREDITS

The following list credits, by page, the sources of illustrations used in Volume L of THE NEW BOOK OF KNOWLEDGE. Credits are listed illustration by illustration —left to right, top to bottom. Wherever appropriate, the name of the photographer or artist has been listed with the source, the two being separated by a dash. When two or more illustrations appear on one page, their credits are separated by semicolons.

140 Jerry Cooke
141– Wesley B. McKeown
147
148 Wesley B. McKeown—Fundamental Photos
149 Wesley B. McKeown
150 Wesley B. McKeown
153 Biblioteca Reale, Turin—IBM; Royal Academy of Arts, London—Art Reference Bureau.
154 IBM
156 George Buctel; British Information Services.
156b Culver Pictures; Bettmann Archive; Culver Pictures.
163 Harry Scott
164 Monkmeyer
165 George Buctel
166 United Nations
167 Monkmeyer
168 A. Devaney
169 Tom Hollyman—Photo Researchers
170 Casis School, Austin, Texas
171 Ann Zane Shanks
172 Ann Zane Shanks; Al Monner—Library Association of Portland.
173 Lawrence S. Williams—Free Library of Philadelphia; Stan Rice—Monkmeyer.
174 Micro Photo Division, Bell and Howell Co.; Kenneth Johnson—New York Public Library.
175 Federal Division, Victoreen Instrument Co.; Lisl Steiner—Franklin Junior and Senior High School, Somerset, N.J.
176 District of Columbia Public Library
177 Leonard Von Matt—Rapho Guillumette
178 United Nations; United States Information Agency; Bell Telephone Laboratories.
179 British Travel Association; Library of Congress.
180 Bruce Roberts—Rapho Guillumette; Gerald McConnell.
181 Gerald McConnell
182 Gerald McConnell
183 Gerald McConnell and Los Angeles County Public Library
185– Lisl Steiner—Franklin Junior and Senior
186 High School, Somerset, New Jersey
189 Herman B. Vestal
193 Herman B. Vestal
195 Herman B. Vestal
196 Herman B. Vestal
197 Bibliothèque Nationale; Ezra Stoller Associates.
199 Barbara M. Whitney—Peterborough Town Library; Sovfoto; A. Tessore—UNESCO; United Nations; United Nations.
200 Torkel Korling—Skidmore, Owings & Merrill
201 Courtesy of Standard Oil of New Jersey
202 George Buctel; Courtesy of Standard Oil of New Jersey.
204 Courtesy of Max Waldman—Caltex; George Holton—Photo Researchers
206 Fritz Henle—Photo Researchers
207 George Buctel
208 Lee Ames
209 Lee Ames
210 Grant Heilman
211 Walter Dawn; Harold Green—Annan.
212 Walter Dawn
213 Lee Ames
214 UPI
215 Russ Kinne—Photo Researchers; Russ Kinne—Photo Researchers; Marineland of Florida; Russ Kinne—Photo Researchers.
216 Lee Ames
217 Dick Wolff—Photo Researchers
218 John Moss—Photo Researchers; R. Lunt—Annan; Russ Kinne—Photo Researchers; Stephen Collins—Photo Researchers; John Markham; C. G. Hampson—Annan.
220 Lee Ames
221 Lee Ames
222 Cresskill—Photo Researchers; C. G. Hampson—Annan.
223 Russ Kinne—Photo Researchers
224 Cy La Tour—Marineland of the Pacific; Russ Kinne—Photo Researchers; John Moss—Photo Researchers.
227 Tom Hollyman—Photo Researchers; Cy La Tour.
228 Lee Ames
229 Roman Vishniac; Walter H. Hodge; Russ Kinne—Photo Researchers.
230 Douglas P. Wilson; Walter Dawn; Douglas P. Wilson; Annan; Russ Kinne—Photo Researchers; Jan Hahn—Oceanall.
232 Harry Scott
233 Russ Kinne—Photo Researchers; Walter Dawn; Henry M. Mayer—National Audubon Society.
234 Herbert Lanks—Rapho Guillumette
235 Harry Scott; Russ Kinne—Photo Researchers.
236 Lee Ames
237 Harry Scott
238 Commonwealth Scientific & Industrial Research Organization, Australia
239 Terry Shaw—Annan; Runk Schoenberger—Grant Heilman; D. Mohrhardt—National Audubon Society.
240 Lee Ames
241 Lee Ames
242 Grant Heilman; Grant Heilman; Lee Ames.
244 Fish and Wildlife Service, U.S. Department of Interior
245 Jane Latta; Jane Latta; Shelly Grossman; Shelly Grossman; Lee Ames.
246 Cy La Tour; Cy La Tour; Lee Ames.
247 Lee Ames
248 Hampson—Annan
251 Lee Ames
252 Lee Ames, from Buchsbaum's Basic Ecology, Based on Cook and Hamilton; Lee Ames; Lee Ames.
253– Lee Ames
255
257 Shaw—Annan; Jack Dermid; Jack Dermid; Photo Researchers; Lynwood M. Chace; George Porter—National Audubon Society; Lynwood M. Chace; Hugh Spencer; Laurence Perkins—Annan; Lynwood M. Chace; Lynwood M. Chace; Lynwood M. Chace.
258 Lee Ames
259 U.S. Department of Agriculture
260 Miller Pope
261 Miller Pope
262 Miller Pope; Miller Pope—Fundamental Photos.
263– Miller Pope
270
271 University Physics by Sears and Zemansky, published by Addison-Wesley
272 Miller Pope
273 Miller Pope
274 Miller Pope
275 Annan
276 U.S. Coast Guard
277 Bruce Roberts—Rapho Guillumette; U.S. Coast Guard.
278 Robert Mottar—Rapho Guillumette
280– Miller Pope
289
290 Miller Pope; Courtesy of Illuminating Engineering Research Institute.
291 James Cooper
293 The Granger Collection
296 The Granger Collection
297 The Granger Collection
298 Morris Warman—Courtesy of Lincoln Center for the Performing Arts
302 Bettmann Archive
305 Gerald McConnell
306 Gerald McConnell
307 Leonard Lee Rue III—National Audubon Society
309 George Bakacs
311 George Sottung
315 Nes Levotch
316 Gerald McConnell; Little League Baseball Headquarters; Little League Baseball Headquarters.
318 Janet L. Stone—National Audubon Society; Cy La Tour; Jane Burton—Photo Researchers (London); Billy Jones—National Audubon Society.
319 Cy La Tour
320 Verna R. Johnston—Photo Researchers; New York Zoological Society; Robert Bustard—Photo Researchers.
321 Cy La Tour—Brookfield Zoo
322 Yale & Towne Manufacturing Co.
323 Yale & Towne Manufacturing Co.
325 Gerald McConnell
327 Union Pacific Railroad
328 Charles McVicker
331 Charles McVicker
333 George Buctel
335 Mario Carbone—Pix
337 J. Allan Cash—Rapho Guillumette
338 Shostal; Fox—Rapho Guillumette; Hans Huber—Alpha.
343 Ken Longtemps
344 George Buctel; Shostal
345 Marc Riboud—Magnum
346 P. Biro—Photo Researchers; A. Devaney.
347 Josef Muench
348 Stephanie Dinkins; Robert Meyerriecks; Color Illustration Inc.
350 Diversified Map Corp.
351 Charles Rotkin—PFI
352 B. Smith—Photo Researchers
353 Kabel Art Photo—Publix Pictorial Service
355 Diversified Map Corp.
358 Graphic Arts International
359 Jack Zehort—Shostal
360 Diversified Map Corp.; Jerry Cooke—Photo Researchers.
364 Harry Scott
366 French Government Tourist Office
367 Ricard—ZFA; Art Reference Bureau.
368 French Government Tourist Office; French Government Tourist Office.
370 Gerald McConnell
373 Comet
375 Annan; Photo Researchers.
376 Annan
377 Annan
379 George Buctel; Ken Lambert—Alpha.

M, 13th letter of the English alphabet **M** 1
See also Alphabet
M-1 rifles, guns **G** 423
MA see Mechanical advantage
Maas, Nicolaes see Maes, Nicolaes

Mab, Queen (possibly from Welsh word *mab,* meaning "child"), queen of the fairies in 15th-century English and Welsh folklore, perhaps derived from Queen Maeve (or Mav), a character in old Irish legend. Shakespeare's *Romeo and Juliet* refers to her as "the fairies' midwife," able to bring dreams by driving her chariot over the heads of sleeping people. Queen Mab, mentioned in works by Michael Drayton and Ben Jonson, is the subject of a poem ("Queen Mab") by Shelley, in which she denounces the evils of the world.

Mac, Gaelic word for "son of" **N** 5
See also names beginning with Mc and Mac in alphabetical order as they are spelled
Macadam (ma-CAD-am) **roads R** 252
advances in transportation **T** 260

Macao (ma-CA-o) (pop. over 250,000), Portuguese overseas province (6 sq. mi.) located on the South China Sea at the mouth of the Canton River. It consists of the chief city of Macao and three small adjoining islands— two islands of Taipa and Coloane Island. Macao is administered by an appointed governor. It was the earliest European colony established in China (1557). China now recognizes Portuguese sovereignty (since 1887), but its boundaries still are not clearly marked. It is a resort area and center of commerce, gambling, and smuggling. Major exports include fish, cement, and fireworks.
South China coast, history of **C** 263, 271; **P** 402

Macapagal (ma-ca-pa-GOL), **Diosdado** (1910–), Philippine lawyer and statesman, b. Lubao, province of Pampanga. He was second secretary to the Philippine Embassy in Washington, D.C. (1948). A member of the Philippine Congress (1949–56), he served as vice-president of the Philippines from 1957 to 1961, during which time he was head of the Liberal Party. President of the Philippines (1961–65), his main policy was decentralization of government and industry.
Philippines, history of **P** 190

Macaques (ma-CAKS), Old World monkeys **M** 420; picture **M** 421
Macaroni (mac-a-RO-ni), food made from wheat **G** 282
jewelry-making **I** 224
kinds of wheat **W** 154
Macaroni penguins P 125
MacArthur, Douglas, American general **M** 2
Eisenhower and MacArthur **E** 108
Korean War **K** 303–04
Truman, Harry S, relations with **T** 303
World War II **W** 293
Macassar, Indonesian Celebes **I** 221
Macaulay (ma-CAUL-ey), **Thomas Babington,** English statesman and writer **E** 262
Macaws (ma-CAWS), birds, pictures **B** 246, **P** 84
Macbeth, play by Shakespeare **M** 2–3; **S** 132
background in Scottish history **S** 88
outline of the plot **S** 135
Maccabees, Jewish family **J** 105–06
Hanukkah celebrates victory over Syrians **H** 35
underground movements **U** 10
Maccabees I and II, apocryphal books of Bible **B** 159
Maccabiah Games, for Jewish sportsmen in Israel **I** 440
Mac Cool (Finn Mac Cool) see Finn Mac Cool
MacCracken, Henry M., American educator **H** 12, 14

MacDonald, George, Scottish novelist **C** 239
MacDonald, Golden see Brown, Margaret Wise

MacDonald, James Ramsay (1866–1937), English politician, b. Lossiemouth, Scotland. He was a member of Parliament (1906–18, 1922–37). He served as secretary (1900–12) and leader (1911–14, 1922–31) of the national Labour Party. He was the first Labour prime minister (Jan.–Oct., 1924, 1929–31) but left the party and subsequently became leader and prime minister for the coalition government (1931–35). Under Prime Minister Baldwin he was lord president of the council (1935–37).

Macdonald, Sir John A., Canadian statesman **M** 3–4
first prime minister of Canada **C** 73–75; picture **P** 456a
Macdonald's Brier, Canadian men's curling series **C** 555
MacDowell, Edward, American composer **M** 4
MacDowell Colony, Peterborough, New Hampshire **M** 4
Mace, spice **S** 382; picture **S** 381
See also Nutmeg
Macedonia (ma-ced-O-nia), native kingdom of Alexander the Great **A** 151
Balkan wars **B** 19
now a Yugoslav state **Y** 358
Maces, clubs used as weapons **K** 273

MacGregor, Ellen (1906–1954), American author and librarian, b. Baltimore, Md. She is remembered for her popular science-fiction books for children, which include *Miss Pickerell Goes to Mars, Miss Pickerell and the Geiger Counter,* and *Miss Pickerell Goes Undersea.*

Mach (MOCK), **Ernst,** Austrian scientist **S** 469
Machado (ma-CHA-tho), **Antonio,** Spanish writer **S** 371
Machado de Assís (ma-SHA-du day os-SEES), **Joaquim Maria,** Brazilian poet and novelist **B** 377
place in Latin-American literature **L** 72
Machado y Morales (ma-CHA-tho e mo-RA-lace), **Gerardo,** president of Cuba (1925–33) **C** 550
Machaut, Guillaume de see Guillaume de Machaut
Machiavelli (mac-i-a-VEL-li), **Niccolò,** Italian statesman and writer **I** 477–78
new principle in the writing of history **H** 135–36

Machine age, era in which human and animal labor is largely replaced by mechanical devices to produce goods. The machine age became established through the development of steam and electric power and of extensive transportation networks.

Machine guns G 423; picture **G** 424
Machine needles N 89
Machines and machinery
bulldozers **B** 445–46
construction equipment **B** 445–48
earth-moving **B** 446–48
effect on labor movement **L** 2–3
elevators and escalators **E** 172–75
engines **E** 209–11
environment changed by machines **E** 272c–272d
farm machinery **F** 55–62
gears **G** 65–66
hoisting and loading machinery **H** 143–45
hydraulic **H** 301–04
industry dependent on **I** 243
inventions **I** 333–48
locomotives **L** 327–32
lubrication **L** 370–71
manufacturing **M** 83–85
mechanical drawing **M** 197
office machines **O** 55–58
paper-making machines **P** 52–53; pictures **P** 54, 55

Machines and machinery (continued)
  patents P 97–98
  pneumatic devices P 347–48
  pumps P 528–30
  resentment against in folk songs F 310
  sewing machines C 353; picture C 357
  simple machines, the lever, the inclined plane, the
    pulley W 246–50
  wheels, a vital element W 158
  work, power and machines W 243–50
  See also Automation; Technology
Machine shorthand S 164
Machine tools T 216–19
  computers run machine tools C 449
Machmeters (MOCK-me-ters), instruments to measure
    speed of airplanes S 470
Mach (MOCK) **numbers,** measures of supersonic flight
    speed S 469–70
Machu Picchu (MA-chu PEEC-chu), Peru, remains of
    ancient Inca city, pictures A 354, P 166, W 219
Maciejowice (ma-che-yo-VI-cha), **battle of,** 1794 P 362
Macintosh, Charles, Scottish inventor and chemist R 341

Macintosh, William (1775?–1825), American Creek Indian
chief, b. Carrol County, Ga. He directed Creek allies of
Americans in the War of 1812 and was commissioned
brigadier general in the U.S. Army. He signed a treaty
(1825) giving Creek lands to white men, and therefore,
according to a tribal law prescribing death for cession of
land, was executed by a band of Indian warriors.

Mack, Connie (Cornelius McGillicuddy) American baseball
    manager B 78, 80
Mackay, John William, American miner and financier
    N 135
Mackenzie, Alexander, Canadian statesman O 127
Mackenzie, Sir Alexander, Scottish explorer in North
    America M 5; picture F 523
  Canada's early fur trade C 72
  North West Company, fur traders F 522

Mackenzie, Sir Alexander Campbell (1847–1935), British
composer and conductor, b. Edinburgh, Scotland. He
taught and served as principal at Royal Academy of
Music (1889–1924) and conducted the London Philharmonic Orchestra (1892–99). He was president of the
International Music Society (1908–12). His works, often
incorporating Scottish themes, include *Pibroch Suite* for
violin and orchestra, the oratorio *The Rose of Sharon*,
and the choral work *The Cotter's Saturday Night*.

Mackenzie, William Lyon, Scottish-born Canadian leader
    M 5
  Canada's demands for self-government C 73
Mackenzie Highway C 61
Mackenzie Mountains, Canada Y 361
Mackenzie River, Canada R 244
  Arctic Basin of Canada C 52
Mackerel, fish F 188
  habitat, feeding habits, uses F 214
  ocean life O 37
Mackerel sky, of cirro-cumulus clouds C 360; picture
    C 361
Mackinac (MACK-in-aw), **Straits of,** Great Lakes G 327;
    M 259; picture G 328
Mackinac Bridge, Michigan B 398; M 266; picture
    G 328
Mackinac Island, Michigan M 268; picture M 271
MacLeish (mac-LEESH), **Archibald,** American poet and
    dramatist A 210

Macleod, John James Rickard (1876–1935), Scottish
physiologist, b. New Clunie. With F. G. Banting he was
awarded the 1923 Nobel prize in medicine and physiology for the discovery of insulin and its value in treating
diabetes. He taught at a number of British, American,
and Canadian institutions.
  Banting and Macleod B 52

MacLoren, Archibald, English gymnast P 225

Maclure, William (1763–1840), American geologist, b.
Ayr, Scotland. Noted for his pioneer geological surveys,
he made a geological map of the United States (1809,
revised 1817) and served as president of the Academy of
Natural Sciences, Philadelphia (1817–40). An active
supporter of adult education and of Robert Owen's New
Harmony community (Indiana), he later founded the New
Harmony Working Men's Institute (1838).
  Indiana's New Harmony community I 143

MacMillan, Donald Baxter (1874–1970), American Arctic
explorer, b. Provincetown, Mass. After accompanying
Robert E. Peary on his historic North Pole expedition
(1908–09), he engaged in anthropological work among
the native peoples of northern Labrador (1910–12). He
headed numerous scientific expeditions to Arctic regions
(1913–58), including Greenland, Labrador, Baffin Land,
and Newfoundland. Among his works are *Four Years in
the White North, Etah and Beyond*, and *Kahda*.

MacMillan, Harold (Maurice Harold MacMillan) (1894–   ),
British statesman, b. London. A member of Parliament
(1924–29, 1931–64), he has also been director (1920–40)
and chairman (since 1963) of publishing company
Macmillan and Co., Ltd. He has served in various
governmental posts as minister of housing and local
government (1951–54), secretary of state for foreign
affairs (1955), chancellor of the exchequer (1955–57),
and prime minister (1957–63). His books include *The
Middle Way* and *Economic Aspects of Defense*.

MacMillan, H. R., Canadian lumber company executive
    B 405
Macmillan, Kirkpatrick, Scottish builder of early bicycle
    B 173
Maconochie (mac-ON-ock-ie), **Alexander,** British naval
    officer P 469

Macramé (MAC-ra-may), the art of tying knots with
threads or cord in a geometric pattern. With different
combinations of knots and varied numbers of threads,
interesting belts, bags, dolls, and pillows can be made.
This craft dates back several centuries, when travelers,
especially sailors, knotted ropes during their long, idle
hours at sea.

Macrobiotic diet N 418
Macromolecules (mac-ro-MOL-e-cules) giant molecules
    B 196
  huge molecules in body chemistry B 290
Macumba (ma-COOM-ba), Brazilian dance music L 74
Macuto (ma-CU-to) **Beach,** Venezuela, picture V 297
Macy, Anne Sullivan, teacher of Helen Keller K 201

Macy Foundation, Josiah, Jr., association to advance
scientific medicine and health care. It grants funds for
work in such fields as medical research and medical
education. Founded in 1930, it has headquarters in
New York, N.Y.

Madagascar see Malagasy Republic
Madama Butterfly, opera by Giacomo Puccini O 146
Madame Bovary (bo-va-RI), novel by Flaubert N 348

Madame Julie Récamier (ray-com-YAY), painting by David **P** 26, 29

Madder root, plant, used for dyeing **D** 367

Maddox, U.S.S., destroyer **V** 336

Madeira (ma-DE-ra), group of islands off northwestern coast of Africa **I** 434; **P** 401

Madeleine (MAD-el-in), La, (Church of St. Mary Magdalene), Paris **P** 74; picture **P** 72
  French architecture **F** 432

Madero (ma-DARE-o), **Francisco,** Mexican president **M** 250

Madinat al-Shaab, capital of Yemen (Aden) **Y** 347

Madison, capital of Wisconsin **W** 204

Madison, Dorothea "Dolley" Payne Todd, wife of James Madison **F** 166; **M** 9; picture **F** 167
  first to serve ice cream at White House **I** 31
  White House, history of **W** 162

Madison, James, 4th president of United States **M** 6–9
  Bill of Rights **B** 177
  Federalist, The **F** 78

Madog, or **Madoc,** in Welsh legend, a prince, son of Owain Gwynedd, king of North Wales. He is said to have gone to America (1170?) and to have founded a settlement on the southern Missouri river. Southey's poem *Madoc* recounts his exploits and experiences among the Aztecs of the newly founded Mexican empire.

Madonna (ma-DON-na), the Virgin Mary **M** 113

Madonna and Child, altarpiece by Duccio **I** 461

Madonna and Child, sculpture by Michelangelo **R** 168

Madonna and Child Enthroned, painting by Masaccio **I** 466

Madonna del Granduca, The, painting by Raphael **P** 21

Madonna of Pity, statue by Germain Pilon **F** 422

Madonna of the Rocks, painting by da Vinci **P** 21

Madonna of Vladimir, Byzantine painting **B** 489

Madonna with Saints and Members of the Pesaro Family, painting by Titian **P** 22, 23

Madonna with the Chancellor Rolin, painting by Jan van Eyck **D** 350

Madras (ma-DRAS), capital of the state of Tamil Nadu, India **M** 10

Madras, University of, picture **I** 122

Madras cloth **M** 10

Madrid (ma-DRID), capital of Spain **M** 11–13; **S** 355
  Apollo tracking antenna **S** 340g
  at mid-19th century, picture **S** 370
  bullfighting, picture **E** 304
  monument to Cervantes, picture **S** 354
  parade into bullring, picture **B** 451
  Prado **P** 428–29
  Royal Palace, picture **S** 364

Madrid, University of, Spain **M** 13

Madrigal (MAD-rig-al), in music **M** 536
  choral music **C** 277
  English madrigals **E** 269–70
  Italian Renaissance music **I** 483
  Renaissance music **R** 173
  vocal chamber music **C** 185

Madurodam, the Netherlands, picture **N** 117

Maeser (MY-ser), **Karl G.,** German-born American educator **U** 253

Maeterlinck (MAE-ter-link), **Count Maurice** (1862–1949), Belgian poet, dramatist, and essayist, b. near Ghent. His writing is marked by a sense of mysticism. Among his well-known works are the collection of poems *Hothouses;* the plays *The Princess Maleine, Pélleas and Mélisande* (transformed by Debussy into an opera), and *The Blue Bird;* and the classic nature study *The Life of the Bee.* He received the Nobel prize for literature (1911).
  drama, history of **D** 298

Magazines **M** 14–16
  advertising **A** 27, 28
  book reviewing influences children's literature **C** 242
  cartoons, history of **C** 125–27
  comics **C** 422–23
  commercial art techniques **C** 426
  illustration and illustrators **I** 91–92, 94–95
  indexes **I** 115; **R** 130
  journalism **J** 144
  libraries, professional publications for **L** 192
  mass communication media **C** 440
  photography **P** 205
  publishing **P** 513
  Readers' Guide to Periodical Literature locates information in magazines **R** 130
  short stories **S** 166–67

Magdalena (mog-da-LANE-a) **River,** Colombia **R** 244; **C** 381; picture **C** 380

Magdalen (MAUD-len) **College,** Oxford, England, picture **E** 73

Magdalen (MAG-da-len) **Islands,** Canada **I** 434

Magdeburg (MAG-de-burg) **hemispheres,** used to illustrate pressure of air **V** 264

Magellan (ma-GELL-an), **Ferdinand,** Portuguese explorer **M** 17
  voyage around the world **E** 380–81

Magellan, Strait of **E** 381

Magellanic (maj-el-LAN-ic) **Clouds,** galaxies **U** 199

Maggiore (ma-JO-ray), **Lake,** northern Italy **L** 32

Maghreb, The (Algeria, Morocco, and Tunisia)
  North African literature **A** 76d

Magi (MAY-ji) (plural of old Persian *magus,* meaning "wizard" or "sorcerer"), priests of ancient Media, northwestern Persia, who were said to have magical skills and knowledge of astrology. Beliefs of the Magi were incorporated into Zoroastrianism. In the Bible reference is made to the Babylonian Rabmag, head of the Magi under Nebuchadnezzar (Jeremiah 39:3, 13). The "wise men of the East" (Matthew 2:1–12) were Magi who, in search of a savior, came to Bethlehem bringing gifts to the child Jesus. English words "magic" and "magician" stem from this term.

Magic **M** 18–21
  African tribal religions **A** 56
  ancient drug making **D** 321
  dance patterns of the magicians **D** 22–23
  early religions **R** 145–46
  fetish figures of Pacific Islands **P** 9
  fire to drive away evil spirits **F** 145
  folk art **F** 292–93
  medicine of cavemen **M** 203
  prehistoric art **P** 441
  sculpture in prehistoric times **S** 92
  superstition **S** 473–75
  voodoo **H** 9
  witchcraft **W** 208–09

Magic Flute, The, opera by Mozart **O** 146; picture **O** 147
  work full of lovely melodies sometimes mistaken for folk songs **G** 185

Magic squares, arrangements of numbers **N** 382, 383

Maginot (MAJ-in-o) **Line,** line of fortifications constructed by the French just prior to World War II along the eastern frontier of France, from the Swiss to the Luxembourg border. The Germans skirted the northern end of the line and invaded France across the unprotected Franco-Belgian border.
  fortifications by-passed in World War II **F** 377; **W** 288, 289

Maidan Park, Calcutta **C** 11
Maidenhair ferns, picture **F** 93
Maiden of Passamaquoddy, The, nonsense poem, excerpt **N** 273
Maid Marion, in the Robin Hood legends **R** 253
   queen of the May **M** 182
Maid of Orleans, Joan of Arc **J** 121
Mail see Post office
Mail cars, of railroads **R** 81

Mailer, Norman (1923–   ), American author, b. Long Branch, N.J. He gained fame for novel *The Naked and the Dead,* drawn from World War II experiences. He has also written plays, film scripts, and poetry. His *Armies of the Night* won the Pulitzer Prize for nonfiction (1968). In 1969 he unsuccessfully sought the Democratic nomination for mayor of New York City.
   American literature, history of **A** 213

Maillol (ma-YOL), **Aristide,** French sculptor **S** 103
Mail order M 31
   selling **S** 116
Maiman, Theodore H., American scientist
   laser developed by **M** 131

Maimonides (my-MON-id-ese), **Moses** (Moses ben Maimon) (1135–1204), Jewish physician, philosopher, and rabbi, b. Cordoba, Spain. Although a respected physician, he was most prominent and influential for his commentaries in the fields of religion and philosophy. An acknowledged authority on Judaism, in 1180 he completed one of his greatest works, the *Mishnah Torah,* a codification of the Jewish law. A second remarkable work was *Moreh Nevukhim (Guide to the Perplexed),* an attempt to reconcile Jewish philosophy with that of the Greeks, particularly Aristotle.
   Jews, history of **J** 107

Maine M 32–47
   American colonies **A** 189
   boundary settlements **T** 108
Maine, University of the State of M 40–41
Maine, U.S.S., battleship **S** 374
   mast a memorial in Arlington cemetery **N** 29–30
   sinking of **M** 189
Mainsprings, in watches and clocks **W** 45, 47
Maintenance of membership, in labor contracts **L** 15–16
Maisonneuve (may-zon-nerve), **Paul de Chomedey, Sieur de,** French colonist **M** 443
Maitani, Lorenzo, Italian sculptor **I** 463
Maize see Corn
Majolica (ma-JOL-ic-a), pottery **P** 417
Majorca (ma-YOR-ca) **Island,** Spain **I** 427; picture **I** 431
Majority leaders, in Congress **U** 144
Major leagues, in baseball **B** 75, 77
Major medical insurance I 295
Major seconds, in music **M** 527
Makapuu (mä-ka-PU-u) **Point Light,** Hawaii, picture **L** 276

Makarios III (ma-KAR-i-oce), **Archbishop** (1913–   ), Greek Orthodox prelate, b. Ano Panayia, Paphos, Cyprus. He was elected Greek Orthodox bishop in 1948 and archbishop of Cyprus in 1950. A leader of Greek Cypriots fighting for union with Greece, he was exiled (1956–57) by the British Government as an agitator. He participated (1959) in forming the London Agreement, giving Cyprus independence, and took over duties as first president of the Republic of Cyprus (1960).
   Cyprus, history of **C** 558

Makeba (ma-KEE-ba), **Miriam** (1932–), singer, Xhosa tribe, b. Prospect township, Johannesburg, S. Africa. Although she has never had musical training, she has become a spokesman for the aspirations of her people through her African melodies and rhythms. She has many best-selling record albums and has made numerous appearances as a television, concert, and nightclub performer. Her first solo performance was for King George VI of England, when he visited South Africa.

Makeup see Beauty culture; Cosmetics
Makeup, for plays **P** 341; pictures **P** 340
   Peking Opera school practice, picture **D** 293
Makeup crews, for motion pictures **M** 481
Maksutov, Dmitriy, Russian scientist **T** 63
Maksutov telescope T 63
Malacañang Palace, Manila **M** 75
Malacca (ma-LAC-ca), Malaysia **M** 55
Malachi (MA-la-ky), book of Bible, Old Testament **B** 155
Malagasy (mal-a-GAS-y) **Republic M** 48–49
   African literature **A** 76c
   flag **F** 235
Malamute, Eskimo sled dog **E** 289
Malan (ma-LON), **Daniel François,** South African premier **S** 273
Malange, Angola **A** 261
Malapropisms (MAL-a-prop-isms), twisting of words, origin of the term **H** 278
Malaria (ma-LAIR-ia), protozoan disease **D** 187
   Anopheles mosquitos, insects harmful to man **H** 260; **I** 283
   pioneer life **P** 256
   public health **P** 505
Malaspina (ma-la-SPI-na) **Glacier,** Alaska **A** 132
Malawi (ma-LA-wi), formerly Nyasaland, Africa **M** 50–51
   flag **F** 235
Malawi, Lake, formerly Lake Nyasa **L** 32; **M** 51; pictures **L** 29; **M** 50
Malay (MAY-lay), language **M** 52
   Singapore **S** 184
   Southeast Asia **S** 329–30
Malaya (ma-LAY-a), **Federation of M** 56
Malayan marbled cats C 141
Malayan sun bears B 108
Malayo-Polynesian languages L 40
   languages of Asia **A** 460
Malays (MAY-lays), a people of Asia **A** 459
   Borneo **B** 337
   Indonesian population **I** 216
   Malagasy Republic **M** 48–49
   Malaysia **M** 52–56
   Singapore **S** 183
Malaysia (ma-LAY-sia) **M** 52–56
   flag **F** 238
   rubber trees, picture **A** 464
   Singapore, formerly a part **S** 184, 184a
   World War II in Malaya **W** 293
Malcolm III, king of Scotland **S** 88

Malcolm X (1925–65), American political leader, Negro, b. Omaha, Neb. When suspended from the Black Muslims, he formed his own protest organization, The Organization for Afro-American Unity (1964). He advocated pride in Negro heritage and believed that black society must become independent before there could be a workable black-white society. His book, *The Autobiography of Malcolm X,* published shortly after his death (1965), predicted his assassination, which took place on February 21, 1965. Picture **N** 104a.
   Black Muslims **N** 104a–104b

Malcolmson, Anne B. (1910–   ), American author of children's books, b. St. Louis, Mo. Her first book, *Yankee*

Malcolmson, Anne B. (continued)
Doodle's Cousins, grew from her desire to have stories about American folk heroes suitable for her students. She also wrote *The Song of Robin Hood*.

Maldives (MAL-dives) **M** 57
   flag **F** 238
Male (MA-lay), capital of Maldives **M** 57
Malecite, Indians of North America **I** 170

Malenkov (MA-len-kof), **Georgi Maximilianovich** (1902–   ), Soviet Communist Party and government official, b. Orenburg (now Chkalov). He advanced within party ranks to become Central Committee secretary (1939–53), chairman of the Soviet Union's Council of Ministers (1953–55), and Presidium member (1952–57). After taking part in an unsuccessful attempt to overthrow Khrushchev (1957), he was demoted to the directorship of a hydroelectric plant.

Malevich (ma-LAY-vich), **Kazimir**, Russian painter **M** 392
   White on White, painting **M** 392
Malherbe (ma-LAIRB), **François de**, French poet
   F 435, 437
Mali (MA-li) **M** 58–59
   African epic poetry **A** 76a
   early western African empire **A** 66; **N** 90
   flag **F** 236
Mali Federation, former union of Senegal and French Sudan **S** 120
Malignancy, in cells **V** 367
Malignant tumors, in cancer **C** 89
Maligne (ma-LENE) **Lake**, Jasper National Park, picture **J** 54

Malik, Adam (1917–   ), Indonesian statesman, b. Pematang Siantar, Sumatra. Starting in his teens, he was active in the movement to free Indonesia from Dutch colonial rule and was jailed several times by the Dutch. In 1937 he was one of several journalists who founded the Antara news agency, which later became Indonesia's national press agency. After Indonesian independence (1949), he entered politics. He was elected to the Indonesian parliament in 1956. Later he served as ambassador to the Soviet Union (1959–63) and then as minister of trade (1963–66). In 1966 he was appointed foreign minister. He was elected president of the 26th United Nations General Assembly in 1971.

Malik (MA-lik), **Jacob Alexandrovich** (1906–   ), Soviet diplomat, b. Kharkov, Ukraine. He served as war ambassador to Japan (1942–46) and deputy minister for Far Eastern affairs (1946–53). He succeeded Andrei Gromyko as permanent representative to UN Security Council (1948–53) and has been ambassador to England (1953–60) and deputy minister of foreign affairs (since 1960).

Malinke (ma-LEEN-kay), African people of the former (13th to 16th century) Mali empire of western Sudan. They now inhabit the independent republics of Guinea and Mali. Numbering over a million, they farm and raise cattle.

Malinovsky (ma-li-NOF-ski), **Rodion Yakovlevich** (1898–1967), Soviet army officer, b. Odessa, Ukraine. After serving in World War I and commanding armies in World War II, he was named commander in chief of ground forces (1956–57) and minister of defense (1957).

Mallard ducks, birds, picture **B** 239
   mother and young, picture **L** 257
Mallard That Asked for Too Much, The, legend **L** 135

Mallarmé, Stéphane, French poet **F** 440
Malleability (mal-le-a-BIL-ity), property of metals **M** 226
Mallet (mal-LAY), **Anatole**, Swiss engineer and inventor **L** 332
Mallets, large hammers **T** 211–12
   in croquet **C** 536
Mallorca see Majorca Island

Mallory, Molla Bjurstedt (1892?–1959), American tennis player, b. Norway. Beginning in 1915 she became the first woman to win the United States singles seven times. Ranked No. 1 United States woman player and a member of the Wightman Cup team (1923–28), she also won championships in United States doubles and mixed doubles. She was elected to Tennis Hall of Fame (1958).

Malmo (MOL-mer), Sweden **S** 485
Malnutrition
   blindness, causes of **B** 251
   deficiency diseases **D** 189, 216
   food taboos **F** 334–35
   See also Nutrition

Malory, Sir Thomas (lived during 15th century), English writer. While in prison (1451–71), he compiled *Morte Darthur*, a collection of the legendary tales of King Arthur and his knights. It is thought that he served in the Hundred Years War and in Parliament (1445).
   Arthur, story of **A** 443–45
   English literature, history of **E** 248

Malpighi (mol-PI-ghi), **Marcello**, Italian anatomy professor, first to study fingerprints **F** 129
   medicine during the Renaissance **M** 206

Malraux, André (1901–   ), French writer and political figure, b. Paris, France. He participated in and wrote about revolutionary movements of his day. *Man's Fate*, winner of the French Goncourt Prize (1933), told of China in 1927. *Man's Hope* had a background of the Spanish civil war in which Malraux fought. In World War II he fought with the French Resistance, was captured by the Germans, and escaped. An ardent supporter of General de Gaulle, Malraux served in his governments, the last time as minister of cultural affairs.
   place in French literature **F** 442

Malt, extract of barley grain **G** 286
   barley, kinds of **G** 284
   used in brewing beer **B** 116
   whiskey and other distilled beverages **W** 159
Malta, island nation in the Mediterranean **M** 60
   faldetta, hood and cape, picture **H** 53
   flag **F** 239
Maltese, dog, picture **D** 256
Maltese Falcon, The, detective story by Dashiell Hammett **M** 555
Maltese Islands **M** 60
Malthus, Thomas R., English economist **P** 396
   Darwin studied his writings **D** 40

Malthusian (mal-THU-sian) **theory**, belief of British economist T. R. Malthus (1766–1834) that if the population continued to increase at a rapid rate, the world's food supply would become inadequate. The industrial revolution and advanced methods of agricultural production led to attack on the theory, but the population explosion since World War II has revived interest in his ideas.
   overpopulation **P** 396

Maltose, malt sugar **S** 453
   how beer is made **B** 116

Mamaia (ma-MA-ia), Rumania, picture R 359
Mamas and the Papas, The, American rock music group
  R 262d
Mambas, snakes S 208; pictures S 211
Mameli (ma-MAE-li), Goffredo, Italian poet N 20
Mameluke (MAM-el-uke) Sword, Marine officers' sword
  U 182
Mammals, animals M 61–73
  adaptations in the world of life L 225–26
  aging A 81–87
  animal communication by scent signals A 280
  brain compared with bird's, diagram B 203
  cetaceans, marine mammals D 270; W 147–51
  cheetah, fastest C 139
  dolphins and porpoises D 270–79
  egg-laying monotremes P 333–34
  eggs and embryos E 90
  elephants E 166–71
  even-toed F 81–82
  feet F 81–82
  fossils F 388–89
  hands F 83
  hoofed H 206–21
  insectivores I 259–61
  kangaroos and other pouched mammals K 167–75
  kingdoms of living things K 249–59
  largest animals A 262–63
  milk producers M 310
  monkeys, apes, and other primates M 417–22
  odd-toed F 81–82
  organs, compared with birds' B 202
  pets P 179
  prehistoric animals, development of P 438
  reproduction R 178–80
  rodents, gnawing mammals R 275–80
  sexual reproduction R 178–80
  taxonomy supplies keys for identifying plants and
    animals T 32
  Viverridae family of genets, civets, and mongooses
    G 89–93
  whales W 147–51
  winged: bats B 92–97
  without feet F 82–83
  zoos Z 374–79
  See also Hoofed mammals; names of mammals
Mammary gland, milk-producing gland, of animals
  M 310
  mammae, milk glands of primates M 418
  What is a mammal? M 61

Mammon (from Aramaic word māmōnā, meaning
"riches"), material wealth. The term is used in the
Talmud and the New Testament (Matthew 6:24, Luke
16:9, 11, 13) in the sense of material riches on which too
great a value is put.

Mammoth Cave, Kentucky K 212, 221
  caves and caverns, how formed C 154
Mammoth Cave National Park, Kentucky K 212, 221
Mammoths, extinct mammals E 338–40; pictures E 339,
  340; F 378
  hunted by Neanderthal man, picture P 443
  prehistoric relatives of elephants E 170
Man R 29–32
  climate and man C 347–48; W 257
  creation myth of Aztecs M 561
  creation myths, Greek G 356–57
  creation myths, Norse N 277–78
  environment E 272a–272h
  evolution of E 338, 347
  genetics and heredity G 77–88
  interference with nature upsets web of life L 258–59

  in the sea O 41–44
  mammals M 63
  prehistoric see Prehistoric man
  races of man R 29–32
  women, role of and "mankind" W 211
  See also Anthropology; Archeology; Sociology; people
    section of continent and country articles
Man, Isle of, in the Irish Sea I 435
Man, prehistoric see Prehistoric man
Management, the owners and managers in industry
  L 11
Managua (ma-NA-gua), capital of Nicaragua N 247
Manama (ma-NA-ma), capital of Bahrain M 301
Manassa Mauler, nickname see Dempsey, Jack
Manassas (man-AS-sas), Virginia, site of Civil War battles
  of Bull Run C 322, 323
  Jackson, Thomas ("Stonewall") J 8
Manasseh (ma-NASS-eh), King of Judah, Prayer of B 159
Manatees, aquatic mammals S 106–07
  order Sirenia, picture M 68
Manaus (ma-NOUSE), Brazil B 381; picture A 179
Manawyddan (man-a-WUD-dan), legendary Welsh hero
  L 129
Manchester, England U 71
Manchester, New Hampshire N 159–60
Manchineel (man-chin-EEL), tree P 282
  poisonous plants P 322
Manchu (Ch'ing) dynasty, ancient rule of China C 271
  Mongolia, early history M 416
  Shenyang, Manchuria S 150
  See also Ch'ing dynasty
Manchukuo (mon-CHU-ku-o), former puppet state of
  Japan W 284
Manchuria (man-CHU-ria), northeast area of China
  C 262, 265, 272
  Shenyang S 150
Mandalay, Burma, on Irrawaddy River, map B 455
Mandan, Indians of North America, related to the Sioux
  N 336
  painting of a village by George Catlin U 119
Mandarin, a citrus fruit O 179; picture O 176
Mandarin, national language of China C 258–59

Mandated territory, territory administered by a nation
given authority to rule by the League of Nations. The
mandate system was established (1919) under the
League of Nations Covenant to provide government for
dependent territories of defeated World War I nations
and to aid these territories in attaining independence.
Some mandated territories have achieved self-government (Palestine). Others have become trust territories of
the United Nations since 1945 (Trust Territory of the
Pacific Islands under the United States).

Mandelbaum Gate, in Jerusalem J 81
Mandeville, Jamaica J 17
Mandibles, jaws of insects
  fire ant, picture A 323
Mandolin F 329; picture F 330

Mandrake, plant native to the Mediterranean area and
eastern Asia. The mandrake has bell-shaped flowers,
large leaves, and a thick root. The mandrake was once
supposed to have magical properties. Its roots are used
in some medicines. A North American plant, the
mayapple, also is called a mandrake. The mayapple has
a single white flower, two large leaves, poisonous roots,
and edible yellow fruit.

Mandrel, ceramic cone for making glass tubing G 236
Mandrills, monkeys M 420; picture M 421
Maned wolf, wild dog of South America D 251

Manet (ma-NAY), **Édouard,** French painter **M** 73
  impressionism in painting **P** 29
  Fifer, The, painting **F** 429
  French art **F** 426
  modern art **M** 387
  Woman with a Parrot, painting **M** 73
Manganese, element **E** 155, 162
  alloys **A** 168
  metals, chart of ores, location, properties, uses **M** 227
  paints used by prehistoric man **P** 15
  producing regions of North America **N** 294
  steel **I** 395
Manganese dioxide
  chemical catalyst **C** 199

Mangareva (mon-ga-RAY-va), island cluster in South Pacific, largest and most important of Gambier Islands. Administered by France, the island is rich in vegetation. Rikitea, capital of Gambier Islands, is the principal town and port.

Manger, or Nativity scene, Christmas custom **C** 289
Mangles, ironers **L** 84
Mango, a tropical fruit **M** 74
Mangosteen (MAN-go-steen), a tropical fruit **M** 74

Mangroves, group of subtropical and tropical shrubs and trees, usually found in marshes and shore areas. The one American species is common along the shores and in the swamps of Florida. The seeds usually sprout while still on the parent plant. The roots of the young plant dangle in the air. When the seed drops, the roots grow down, settle in the mud, and support the new tree above the water.
  mangrove jungles **J** 154; picture **J** 156

Manhattan (man-HATT-an), borough of New York City **N** 228, 234
Manhattan, icebreaking oil tanker **N** 338
Manhattan Island, part of New York City, picture **I** 426
  origin of name **A** 190
Manhattan Project, on atomic research **F** 92
Manic-depressive psychosis (sy-CO-sis), a form of mental illness **M** 224

Manichaeism (MAN-ic-e-ism), or **Manicheism,** religion founded in Babylonia by Manes (216?–276?). Influenced by Babylonian religion, Christianity, Zoroastrianism, and possibly Buddhism, Manichaeism conceived of mankind as composed of opposing forces of light (good) and darkness (evil). To attain virtue—separation or freeing of man's spark of light from darkness or evil—idolatry and animal killing were prohibited and the Elect abstained from meat, wine, and marriage. The movement was influential until the 13th century.

Manifest Destiny, slogan applied to expanding United States in 1840's **M** 238
  Polk's administration, events of **P** 385
Manila (ma-NIL-a), Philippines **M** 75; **P** 188; pictures **P** 188, **S** 332
Manila Bay, battle of, 1898 **P** 190
  Spanish-American War **S** 375
Manila hemp see Abaca
Manioc (MAN-i-oc), or cassava, plant from which tapioca is made **A** 61
  Brazil **B** 376
  vegetable adhesive **G** 243
Man is the measure of all things, belief of ancient Greeks **S** 94
Manito (MAN-it-o), great spirit of American Indians **I** 171

Manitoba (man-it-O-ba), Canada **M** 76–82
  Riel rebellions **C** 73
  Winnipeg **W** 190
Manitoba, Lake, southwestern Canada **L** 32; **M** 76, 81
Manitoba, University of **M** 79
Manitoba Act, 1870, Canada **M** 82
Manitoba Escarpment **M** 76
Manitoulin (man-i-TOO-lin), island in Lake Huron **O** 120a
Mankiewicz (MAN-kie-witz), **Joseph,** American motion-picture director, picture **M** 477
Manly Beach, Australia, picture **A** 496
Man-made elements see Transuranium elements
Man-made materials see Synthetic materials
Man-made satellites see Satellites, man-made
Man-monkey-crab, game **G** 19
Mann, Horace, American educator **M** 83
  battle for the common school **E** 70
Mann (MONN), **Thomas,** German-born American writer **G** 180
  Doctor Faustus, a modern Faust story **F** 73
  themes of his novels **N** 347
Manna, a kind of food **M** 468
Manned Orbiting Laboratory see MOL
Manned satellites **S** 43
Manned Spacecraft Center, Texas **T** 130

Mannerheim (MAN-ner-hime) **Line,** World War II line of fortification across the Karelian isthmus, from Lake Ladoga to the Gulf of Finland. The defenses were named for Finnish military leader Emil von Mannerheim (1867–1951), who supervised the raising of the line. The line was used by the Finns in Russian invasion of 1939–40.
  Russian Front, 1944 **W** 301

Mannerism, in art and architecture **I** 470, 472
  Renaissance art **R** 171
  sculpture **S** 101
  Tintoretto **T** 196
Manners see Etiquette
Mannheim (MONN-hime), Germany
  classical age of music in **C** 333
Man of Aran, documentary motion picture **M** 476
Man of La Mancha, musical **M** 543
Manolete, Spanish bullfighter **B** 450
Manon (ma-NON), opera by Jules Massenet **O** 146
Manors, feudal estates **F** 102
  agriculture **A** 96
  forms of local government **M** 503
Man o' War, Kentucky-bred race horse **K** 212
Manpower
  automation displaces **A** 530, 533–34

Manpower Development and Training Act (1962), congressional act providing for a 3-year program to retrain unemployed persons in new and essential industrial skills. The secretary of labor is authorized to investigate the effects of automation on employment and to create retraining programs, which are executed through the Manpower Administration, U. S. Department of Labor.

Manrique (mon-RI-kay), **Gómez,** Spanish poet **S** 367
Manrique, Jorge, Spanish poet **S** 367
Mansa Musa, Mali emperor **M** 59
  Negro history in Africa **N** 90
Mansard roof, French Renaissance design **F** 421–22

Mansart (mon-SAR), or **Mansard, Nicolas François** (1598–1666), French architect, b. Paris. He became architect to King Louis XIII (1636) and designed numerous churches and châteaus in the Paris vicinity. He frequently used a high roof with steep sides that

became known as a mansard roof. One of his famous works is the Château de Maisons Lafitte.
Renaissance design in French architecture **F** 421–22

Mansfield, Katherine, English writer **S** 167
20th-century English fiction **E** 267
Manta rays, fishes **S** 140, 142

Mantegna (mon-TAIN-ya), **Andrea** (1431–1506), early Italian Renaissance painter and engraver, b. Vicenza. Commissioned by Pope Innocent VIII, he painted frescoes for the Belvedere Chapel, Rome (1488–90). He is famous for his technique of perspective and the sculpturelike human figures of his paintings and engravings. Among his noted works are *The Triumph of Caesar, Parnassus, The Dead Christ,* and *Saint Sebastian.*
Adoration of the Shepherds, The, painting **A** 438a
art, the meanings of **A** 438
Renaissance art in northern Italy **R** 169

Mantis, insect usually called praying mantis because of the way it holds up its forelegs to grasp its insect prey. It is about 3 in. long. The mantis has a long, slim, green or brown body, four long walking legs, two forelegs, and strong wings. It is found in Europe, Asia, and the United States. It is helpful to man because it eats harmful insects.
eating habits **A** 266; **I** 269
leg, diagram **I** 273
newly hatched, picture **I** 265

Mantle, of the earth **E** 8, 9
earthquakes **E** 34–35, 39
earth's history **E** 19
geophysicists study earth's mantle **G** 119

Mantle, Mickey (Charles Mantle) (1931–), American baseball player, b. Spavinow, Okla. A "switch-hitter" for the New York Yankees (1951–68), he was voted Most Valuable Player in the American League (1956, 1957, 1962) and won the Triple Crown (1956) for leading the league in batting average, home runs, and runs batted in. Mantle hit over 500 home runs in his baseball career. Picture **B** 76.

Manu, Hindu Code of
quoted on women's role **W** 211
Manual alphabet, or sign language, of the deaf **D** 52–53
Manuals, or keyboards of the organ **K** 236–37
Manuals, type of reference book **R** 130–31
Manual training see Industrial arts
Manuel, Don Juan see Juan Manuel, Don
Manufacturing **M** 83–85
advantages of location: Ontario **O** 121
Africa **A** 64
automation of repetitive work **A** 530
automobiles **A** 547–51
bread **B** 387–88
chemical industry **C** 194
clothing industry **C** 354
consumer education and manufacturer's claims **C** 494
industrial design **I** 229–32
industrial growth **I** 248–49
Industrial Revolution **I** 233–41
industrial society created in United States **U** 129
mass production **M** 151
New England industry **N** 139
New York ranks first **N** 217
patents **P** 97–98
producing regions of North America **N** 299–303
technology, development of **T** 46
trade in U.K.'s manufactured goods **U** 75–76

trademarks **T** 244–45
See also country, province, and state articles; names of manufactured articles
Manuls (MA-nuls), or Pallas cats **C** 141
Manumission (man-u-MISSION), or emancipation, of slaves **S** 195
England's Act of 1833 **S** 197
Manure, organic fertilizer **F** 96
important to agriculture **A** 100
Manuscript books
art of writing preserved **C** 432
authors' originals prized by collectors **A** 526
books in preparation **B** 330
Dead Sea Scrolls **D** 48–49
medieval books **B** 319–21
Manuscripts, illuminated see Illuminated manuscripts
Manuscript writing **H** 31
language arts **L** 36
Manutius (ma-NU-shi-us), **Aldus,** Italian book publisher **B** 322
typeface designs **T** 345
Man Without a Country see Nolan, Philip
Manx cats **C** 142; picture **C** 143
Manx shearwaters, birds **H** 192
Manych Depression, in the Caucasus Mountains, lowest point in Europe **E** 309
Manzanares (mon-tha-NAR-ace) **River,** Spain **R** 244
Manzini (man-ZI-ni), Swaziland **S** 481
Manzoni (mon-ZO-ni), **Alessandro,** Italian novelist and poet **I** 480
Requiem of Verdi composed in his memory **C** 279
Manzú, Giacomo, Italian painter **I** 473
Maori (MA-or-i), a people of New Zealand **N** 236, 241–42, 243
art **P** 10
Mao Tse-tung (MA-o dzu-toong), leader of Communist China **M** 86
People's Republic of China **C** 268, 272, 273
Soviet Union's criticism of the "cult of personality" **C** 445
Maple, tree **M** 86–87
leaf, diagram **L** 114
male and female flowers, pictures **P** 297
Rhode Island, state tree of **R** 213
seeds, distribution, pictures **F** 281, **L** 233
sugar maple, picture **T** 277
sugar maple, state tree of New York, West Virginia, Wisconsin **N** 210; **W** 127, 193
uses of the wood and its grain, picture **W** 224
Maple Leaf, The, song by Alexander Muir **N** 27
Maple syrup and sugar **M** 86–87
American Indians, how prepared by **I** 178
tree sap **T** 280
Maps and map making **M** 88–95
advances in, at age of exploration **E** 372
aerial photography **P** 206
cartography, as a division of geography **G** 108
Champlain, early map maker **C** 187
early geographers and map makers **G** 98
globes **M** 91; pictures **M** 89
learning about the world from maps **W** 254
mapping the bottom of the ocean **O** 26–27
photogrammetry used in making **O** 171–72
plotting weather information, picture **W** 91
"radio maps" **R** 70
reference books **R** 129
research methods **R** 183
surveying, use in **S** 479
Vespucci, Amerigo **V** 323
weather maps **W** 77–79
See also continent, country, province, state, and city articles

Maquis (ma-KI), Mediterranean scrub forest
    Albania **A** 145
Maquis, French underground **U** 10–11
    French resistance in World War II **F** 419
Marabouts (MARR-a-boots), Muslim holy men **M** 18
Maracaibo (ma-ra-CA-i-bo), **Lake,** Venezuela **L** 32;
    V 297; picture **S** 278
Maracaibo, Venezuela **V** 299
Maradi, Niger **N** 252
Marais (ma-RAI), **La,** a section of Paris **P** 74
Maraschino (mar-a-SKI-no) **cherry** **P** 107

Marat (ma-RA), **Jean Paul** (1743–1793), Swiss-born physician who became a political figure of the French
Revolution, b. Boundry. He took part in the uprising from
the onset, founding and editing his revolutionary newspaper, *L'Ami du Peuple.* Elected (1792) to the National
Convention, he was a leading political opponent of the
majority Girondist Party. He was a leading advocate of
the tactics of the Reign of Terror. Marat was stabbed to
death by Charlotte Corday.

Marathon, battle of, 490 B.C. **B** 100
Marathon race, track event **T** 237
    footrace of Olympic Games **O** 108
Marble, metamorphic rock **R** 269; picture **R** 268
    building stone **S** 433
    quarries in Vermont **V** 314–15
    sculptors' material **S** 90–91

Marble, Alice (1913–), American tennis player, b.
Plumas County, Calif. In amateur championship matches
she won the U.S. singles (1936, 1938, 1939, 1940),
doubles (1937, 1938, 1939, 1940), and mixed doubles
(1936, 1938, 1939, 1940) and the British Wimbledon
singles (1939), doubles (1938, 1939), and mixed doubles
(1937, 1938, 1939). In 1940 she was a sports announcer
for radio station WNEW in New York, N.Y.

Marble Canyon National Monument, Arizona **A** 414
Marbles **M** 95
Marbury v. Madison, case in constitutional law **M** 112
    Supreme Court decision laying down rule of judicial
    review **S** 476

Marc, Franz (1880–1916), German painter, b. Munich. He
is noted particularly as a pioneer of the German
expressionist style, which was one outgrowth of cubism.
He often selected animals as subject matter. With
Kandinsky he founded (1911) the Blaue Reiter group. He
was killed in action during World War I. His paintings
include *The Tower of Blue Horses, Red Horses,* and
Resting Animals.
    Deer in the Garden, painting **G** 168
    German expressionism in modern art **M** 392

Marcasite, mineral composed of iron and sulfur. A
pyrite, it is a pale brass-yellow color, darkening when
exposed to light. It is found throughout the world. The
crystals are often used in ornamentation.

Marceau (mar-SO), **Marcel** (1923–), French pantomim-
ist, b. Strasbourg. He first attained fame as Arlequin in
the pantomime *Baptiste* but is most easily recognized as
"Bip," the character he introduced in 1947, a white-
faced individual who wears a middy, culottes, and tall,
worn hat. He first appeared in the United States in 1955.

March, 3rd month of year **M** 96–97
    Caesar's murder on the Ides of March **C** 6
Marches (band music) **B** 40
March Hare, character in "Alice in Wonderland" **A** 164

Marching Through Georgia, song by Henry Clay Work
    N 25
March of Time, The, motion-picture series **M** 476
March to the Sea, Civil War, United States **S** 151

Marciano, Rocky (Rocco Francis Marchegiano) (1923–
1969), American boxer, b. Brockton, Mass. Taking up
boxing while in the U.S. Army, he turned professional
after his release. In 1952 he knocked out Jersey Joe
Walcott in the 13th round, becoming the world heavyweight champion. When he retired as undefeated heavyweight champion in 1956, Marciano had won 49 straight
bouts.
    boxing past and recent **B** 353

Marconi (mar-CO-ni), **Guglielmo,** Italian inventor of wire-
    less telegraphy **M** 98
    communication advanced by inventions **C** 439
    first practical radio telegraph system **T** 54
    radio communication founded by him **R** 52
Marco Polo see Polo, Marco

Marcos, Ferdinand Edralin (1917–), Philippine lawyer
and political leader, b. Sarrat, Luzon. A military hero of
World War II and an outstanding lawyer, Marcos entered
politics in 1949. He served in the Philippine House of
Representatives (1950–60), Senate (1960–65), and was
a delegate to the UN. He was elected president of the
Philippines in 1965 and again in 1969.
    Philippines, history of **P** 189, 190

Marcos, Fray see Niza, Marcos de
Marcus, Siegfried, Austrian inventor **A** 542
Marcus Aurelius (MAR-cus au-RE-lius), Roman emperor
    R 305
    equestrian statue, picture **S** 95

Marcus Island, volcanic atoll in western Pacific, north of
Tropic of Cancer. Annexed (1899) and used by Japan,
first as a cable station, later as an air and naval base,
the island was administered by United States from
World War II until it was returned to Japan in 1968.

Mar del Plata (PLA-ta), Argentina, pictures **A** 395, **L** 60
Mardi Gras (mar-di GRA), or Shrove Tuesday, religious
    holiday **R** 153
    carnival **C** 120; picture **C** 121
    Latin Americans celebrate before Lent **L** 58
    Mobile, Ala., annual event **A** 122
    New Orleans **N** 196
Marduk (MAR-dook), Babylonian god **M** 557
Marengo, battle of, 1800 **N** 10
Mares' tails, cirrus clouds **C** 360
Margai (mar-GUY), **Albert,** prime minister of Sierra Leone
    S 175
Margai, Milton, prime minister of Sierra Leone **S** 175

Margaret, Princess, Countess of Snowdon (1930–),
sister of Queen Elizabeth II of England, b. Glamis Castle,
Scotland. She is the wife of Antony Armstrong-Jones,
Earl of Snowdon, and fifth in succession to the English
throne.

Margaret of Anjou (on-JOO), queen of Henry VI of Eng-
    land **E** 220
Margarine (MARGE-a-rin), butter substitute **P** 111
    oils and fats **O** 79

Margarita, island in the Caribbean, part of Nueva
Esparta, a state in the Venezuelan federation. Discovered
by Columbus on his third voyage (1498), the island
became a base for pearl fishing. Its chief industries are

magnesite mining and pearl and deep-sea fishing. The capital is La Asunción. A warm, healthy climate makes it a popular resort area and good agricultural region.

Caribbean Sea and islands **C** 116–19

Margays, wildcats **C** 141
Marggraf (MARG-grof), **Andreas Sigismond,** German chemist **S** 456
Margin, buying stocks on **S** 432
Marguerite, or **Margarete,** character in Goethe's Faust **F** 73
Marianas (ma-ri-AN-as) **Islands,** Pacific Ocean **P** 6
Magellan, discoverer of **M** 17
Marianas Trench, Pacific Ocean **M** 493
bathyscaphe descent **D** 82
ocean deep of the earth **E** 15
Philippine Sea, Pacific Ocean site of **O** 48

Maria Theresa (ma-RI-a te-RE-sa) (1717–1780), Austrian empress and daughter of Emperor Charles VI, b. Vienna. She married Francis of Lorraine (later Francis I of the Holy Roman Empire). When Charles VI died (1740), she inherited his possessions and became archduchess of Austria and queen of Hungary and Bohemia. Her claim to the throne was disputed by France, Prussia, and Spain in the War of Austrian Succession (1740–48). The only land she lost during the war was Silesia, which she tried unsuccessfully to recover in the Seven Years War (1756–63). An enlightened monarch, she introduced economic, administrative, and cultural reforms. Joseph II (who was a joint ruler, 1765–80), Leopold I, and Marie Antoinette were her children.

Austria, history of **A** 525

Marie Antoinette (ma-RIE on-twa-NETT), queen of France **M** 99
bedroom at Fontainebleau, picture **F** 508
French Revolution **F** 465, 467
pupil of Gluck **G** 241
Marie de France, French fabulist **F** 4
Marie de Médicis (d'may-de-CEES), queen of France **P** 74
Richelieu, Cardinal **R** 233
Marie de Médicis, Queen of France, Landing in Marseilles, painting by Peter Paul Rubens **P** 25
Marie Louise, empress of the French **N** 11
Marignano (marine-YA-no), **battle of,** 1515
Swiss losses **S** 502
Marigolds, flowers, picture **G** 50
Marijuana (mar-i-WAN-a), hallucinogenic drug **D** 331–32
not addictive **D** 329
Marimba, musical instrument **L** 74; pictures **L** 73, **P** 153
Marinas (ma-RI-nas), boat basins or docks **B** 260; pictures **B** 260, **M** 254
Marinating, of food **O** 247–48
Marine biology **O** 36–41
coral polyps **C** 503–04
life, distribution in oceans and seas **L** 228–33
plankton **P** 279–81
underwater exploration of life in the sea **U** 21–22
Marine Corps Development and Education Command **U** 180
Marine Corps Reserve **U** 180
Marine firemen **F** 153
Marine Hospital Service, United States **P** 502
Marine iguanas (ig-WA-nas), lizards **L** 319
Marine Infantry, Canada **C** 79
Marineland, Florida
dolphins and porpoises observed in oceanarium **D** 272, 274, 276
Marineland of the Pacific, California
dolphins' and porpoises' sonar abilities tested **D** 276

Marine paints **P** 33–34

Mariner II, U.S. planetary probe launched August 27, 1962, and directed toward the planet Venus. During its flight it detected a continuous "solar wind" of charged particles flowing from the sun. It passed Venus on December 14, 1962, at a distance of 21,594 miles, and relayed back a surface temperature reading of 800 degrees Fahrenheit. It detected no magnetic field around Venus. Radio contact with Mariner II was lost on January 3, 1963.

Mariner IV, VI, VII, and **IX,** space probes toward Mars **M** 104, 108, 109, 110; **O** 14, 15; **P** 273; **S** 348
Mariner V, information about Venus **O** 14; **P** 271
Marines, maritime soldiers **U** 176
Marines' Hymn, "From the Halls of Montezuma" **N** 26
Marinetti (ma-ri-NAET-ti), **Filippo Tommaso,** Italian futurist poet **M** 391
Marini, Marino, Italian painter **I** 473
Marino (ma-RI-no), **Giambattista,** Italian poet **I** 479
Marinus, Saint, founder of San Marino **S** 36
Marion, Francis, American Revolutionary War commander **M** 99
called the Swamp Fox **R** 207
Marionettes see Puppets and marionettes
Mariposa (ma-ri-PO-za) **Grove,** of "big trees," California **Y** 352

Maris, Roger Eugene (1934–), American baseball player, b. Hibbing, Minn. He reached major leagues in 1957 and played for Cleveland, Kansas City, and New York in American League and St. Louis in National League before retiring (1968). In 1961, while with N.Y. Yankees, he hit a record-breaking 61 home runs. He was named Most Valuable Player in American League in 1960, 1961.

Maritain (ma-ri-TAN), **Jacques** (1882–1973), French philosopher and educator, b. Paris. A convert to Catholicism, he became one of the most highly honored of contemporary religious philosophers. During World War II he and his wife went to the United States, where he taught at Columbia (1940–44) and Princeton (1948–53). He served as French ambassador to the Vatican (1945–48). His many works include *Creative Intuition in Art and Poetry,* and *Reflections on America.*

Maritime Administration, organization established in 1950 as one of the successors to U.S. Maritime Commission to aid development, promotion, and operation of an American merchant marine.

Maritime Alps, in Italy and France **A** 174

Maritime law, system of law concerning navigation and commerce. It represents agreements between nations over customs relating to shipping. Some cases to which it applies are the ownership and operation of vessels, the rights and duties of master and crew, and the transportation of goods and passengers on the high seas.

Maritime Provinces, Canadian provinces of New Brunswick, Newfoundland, Nova Scotia, and Prince Edward Island **N** 138–138g, 140–145, 344a–344h; **P** 456b–456h
self-government and confederation **C** 73
Maritsa (ma-RI-tsa) **River Valley,** Bulgaria **B** 440–41
Marivaux, Pierre Carlet de Chamblain, French writer **F** 439
Marjoram, herb **S** 382; picture **S** 381
Mark, Saint **E** 335
Gospel of **B** 160

Mark Antony, Roman general **M** 100
   Cicero's opposition to **C** 298
   Roman Empire **R** 303
Market Cart, The, painting by Gainsborough **E** 239
Market economy **E** 49
Marketing, for the home **M** 100–03
   consumer education in unit-pricing systems
      C 494–494a
   co-operatives **C** 500
   Hong Kong, picture **H** 203
   open-air market, Albania, picture **A** 146
   retail stores **R** 188–89
   supermarkets **S** 468
Marketing geography **G** 108
Market surveys **O** 159–60
   techniques of research **R** 182
   television industry **T** 70b
Market system, economics **E** 50, 51
   stock market **S** 431
Markham, Edwin, American poet **O** 206

Markle Foundation, The John and Mary R., organization supporting projects primarily in the field of medicine. Grants are made to keep young doctors on the teaching and research staffs of medical schools. Established in 1927, it has headquarters in New York, N.Y.

Markova (mar-KO-va), **Alicia,** English ballerina **B** 26
Marksmanship
   rifle marksmanship **R** 233–35
Mark Twain see Twain, Mark

Marlborough (MARL-bor-o), **1st duke of** (John Churchill) (1650–1722), English general and diplomat, b. Devonshire. After helping to crush the Monmouth rebellion (1685), he shifted his loyalty from James II to William of Orange and supported the Glorious Revolution (1688). He was made (1702) duke of Marlborough and captain general of the English troops by Queen Anne, whose favorite was Marlborough's wife, Sarah. During his absence from court to command the English and Allied armies in the War of the Spanish Succession (1701–13) his opponents worked against him, and in 1711 he was charged with embezzlement and dismissed. Later cleared, he regained his military posts under George I.
   England, history of **E** 224

Marlborough s'en va-t-en guerre, song **N** 27

Marlin, any of several game fishes found in warm ocean waters around the world. The marlin, which is related to the sailfish, has a rounded, swordlike extension of the upper jaw. The largest species in the Atlantic Ocean is the blue marlin, which weighs up to 1,000 pounds. It has a dark-blue back, pale-blue sides, and about 13 violet stripes on each side.

Marlowe, Christopher (1564–1593), English poet and dramatist, b. Canterbury. He is thought to have written parts of Shakespeare's *Titus Andronicus* and *Henry VI.* He is remembered especially for his poem "The Passionate Shepherd to his Love," beginning "Come live with me, and be my love." *The Tragical History of Dr. Faustus, The Jew of Malta,* and *Tamburlaine the Great* are among his noted plays. Marlowe was a playwright connected with the earl of Nottingham's theatrical company (1587–93).
   Dr. Faustus, Tragical History of **F** 72
   Renaissance drama in England **D** 296; **E** 252–53

Marlowe, Julia (Sarah Frances Frost) (1866–1950), American actress, b. Caldbeck, England. She is known especially for her Shakespearean roles. With her actor-husband, Edward Hugh Sothern, she appeared in Shakespearean plays at Stratford-on-Avon, England (1926).

Marmara, Sea of, Turkey **T** 324
Marmatite, ore **Z** 370

Mármol, José (1817–1871), Argentine poet, playwright, and novelist, b. Buenos Aires. His romantic, lyric poetry was often directed against despotism and especially against dictator Rosas, who imprisoned and exiled him (until 1852). His works include the poem *Rosas: El 25 de mayo de 1850,* the book of poems *Harmonies,* and the first historical novel in Argentine literature, *Amalia.*

Marmosets, monkeys **M** 420; **P** 180; picture **M** 421
Marmots, relatives of squirrels **R** 276

Marne, river in northeastern France that originates in the Plateau of Langres, flows 325 miles, and joins the Seine near Paris. The Marne was the scene of two crucial battles of World War I.

Marne (First), battle of the, 1914 **B** 102; **W** 274
   Paris **P** 75
Marne (Second), battle of the, 1918 **W** 280
Marquand (mar-QUAND), **John P.,** American novelist **A** 213
Marque, letters of see Letters of marque
Marquesas (mar-KAY-sas) **Islands,** Pacific Ocean **P** 6
Marquet, Albert, French painter **M** 388
Marquetry (MAR-ket-ri), inlaid furniture **D** 77; **F** 506
Marquette (mar-KETT), **Jacques,** French Jesuit missionary and explorer **M** 103
   exploration of the New World **E** 384
Marquette, Michigan **M** 270

Marquis, Don (Donald Robert Perry Marquis) (1878–1937), American humorist and journalist, b. Walnut, Ill. After serving as assistant editor to Joel Chandler Harris on *Uncle Remus' Magazine* (1907–09), he wrote his famous column "The Sun Dial" for the New York *Evening Sun* (1912–22), creating the immortal characters of archy (the cockroach), mehitabel (the alley cat), the Old Soak, and Hermione and Her Little Group of Serious Thinkers. His works include *archy and mehitabel, The Almost Perfect State,* and the play *The Old Soak.*

Marrakesh (mar-RA-kesh), Morocco **M** 461
Marranos (mar-RA-nos), Christianized Jews **J** 108
Marriage
   curious beliefs about gemstones **G** 74
   divorce **D** 234–35
   family relationships **F** 37
   matrimony a sacrament of Roman Catholic Church **R** 301
   women, role of **W** 211
Marriage customs see Wedding customs
Marriage of Figaro, The, opera by Mozart **O** 146–47
Marriage of the Waters, The, from *The Hudson,* by Carl Carmer, excerpt **E** 279; picture **E** 277
Marrow, of bones **B** 273
   blood corpuscles made in **B** 256–57
Mars, planet **M** 104–11
   astrophotographs **P** 207
   planets and planetary systems **P** 272–73
   Ptolemy's theory **A** 471
   space probes **O** 14, 15
   space travel problems **S** 348
Mars, Roman god **G** 361
Marseillaise (mar-say-AISE), **La,** French national anthem **N** 17–18

Marseilles (mar-SAY), France, picture **F** 409
  nursery school, picture **S** 56
Marsh, Dame Ngaio, New Zealand writer **N** 236

Marsh, Reginald (1898–1954), American artist, b. Paris, France. He was an illustrator and cartoonist for New York magazines and newspapers. His paintings, generally depicting New York City life, include *The Bowery, Coney Island Beach,* and *Memories of the Stork Club.* He also did murals for the Washington, D.C., Post Office and the New York City Customs House.

Marshal, police officer **P** 375
Marshall, George C., American statesman **M** 111
  Eisenhower and Marshall **E** 109

Marshall, James Wilson (1810–1885), American pioneer, b. Hunterdon Co., N.J. He traveled westward along the Oregon Trail (1844), arriving at present-day Sacramento in 1845. With John A. Sutter, he began operating a sawmill and discovered gold (1848), sparking the California gold rush of 1849.

Marshall, John, American jurist **M** 112
Marshall, Thomas R., vice-president, United States
  V 331; picture **V** 329

Marshall, Thurgood (1908–   ), U.S. Supreme Court justice, b. Baltimore, Md. As special counsel for the National Association for the Advancement of Colored People, he has won numerous civil rights cases before state and federal courts. He has served as federal judge, U.S. 2nd Circuit Court of Appeals (1962–65), and is the first Negro to have been appointed U.S. Solicitor General (1965–67), and the first to be named to the U.S. Supreme Court (1967). Picture **N** 99.
  years of change in Negro history **N** 101, 103

Marshall Islands, Pacific Ocean **P** 6
  World War II **W** 298
Marshall Plan, or European Recovery Program **M** 111
  policy of foreign economic aid under Truman
    T 302
  United States aid to Germany **G** 156
Marsh buggy, a motor driven vehicle with balloonlike tires **P** 170
Marshes, low, swampy land
  a typical community of living things **K** 257–59
  formed from lakes **L** 25
Marshmallows, candy **C** 98
Marsh marigolds, flowers, picture **W** 169
Marsupial (mar-SU-pial) **moles** **K** 174
Marsupials, pouched mammals **M** 70–71
  kangaroos and other pouched mammals **K** 167–75
  mammals, orders of **M** 62, 68
Martens, related to weasels **O** 244; pictures **O** 245

Martha, in the New Testament, the sister of Mary and Lazarus. When she scolded her sister Mary for listening to Jesus rather than helping with the housework (Luke 10:38–42), Jesus reprimanded her. She was present at the resurrection of Lazarus (John 11:1–39) and at a dinner that Jesus attended at Simon the Leper's 2 days before his last Passover (Matthew 26:6–13, Mark 14:3–9).

Martha, opera by Friedrich von Flotow **O** 148
Martha's Vineyard, Massachusetts **M** 145
Martí (mar-TI), **José,** Cuban statesman and poet **C** 548, 550
  Latin-American literature, turn of the century **L** 71
Martial (MAR-shal), Spanish-born Roman writer **L** 80
Martial law, during Reconstruction **R** 119

Martin, Abraham (known as L'Écossais, "the Scot") (1589–1664), French settler in Canada, b. Scotland. After arriving in Canada (1614?) he served with the French colonizing Company of One Hundred Associates, receiving from them plateau land west of Quebec. (The land is now known as The Plains of Abraham in honor of him.) Martin remained there after its surrender to the British.

Martin, Alexander (1740–1807), American politician, b. Hunterdon Co., N.J. After serving in the Revolutionary forces (1775–77), he was acting governor (1781–82) and governor (1782–84, 1789–92) of North Carolina and a delegate to the Continental Congress (1786–87) and to the Constitutional Convention (1787). As a United States senator (1793–99), he supported the controversial Alien and Sedition acts, which probably led to his failure to be re-elected (1798).

Martin, Luther (1748?–1826), American lawyer, b. near New Brunswick, N.J. He was the first attorney general of Maryland (1778–1805, 1818–22). A member of the Continental Congress (1785) and the Constitutional Convention (1787), he bitterly opposed the concept of a strong centralized government. An opponent of Thomas Jefferson, he supported Justice Samuel Chase during his impeachment trial (1804) and Aaron Burr during his trial for treason (1807).

Martin, Saint, feast day of (Martinmas) **H** 159; **R** 154–55
Martin du Gard, Roger, French writer **F** 442

Martinelli (mar-tin-ELL-i), **Giovanni** (1885–1969), American tenor, b. Montagnana, Italy. He made his opera debut in Milan (1910) and sang with the Metropolitan Opera Company, New York, N.Y. (1913–46). Noted for his large operatic repertoire, he appeared widely throughout Europe and the United States.

Martínez, Maximiliano Hernández see Hernández Martínez, Maximiliano
Martínez de Toledo (mar-TI-naith day to-LAY-tho), **Alfonso,** Spanish writer **S** 367
Martínez Ruiz, José, Spanish writer **S** 371

Martini (mar-TI-ni), **Simone** (Simone di Martino, Simone Memmi) (1283?–1344), Italian painter, b. Siena. A leading artist of the Sienese school, which predated the Renaissance, he worked at Assisi (1333–39) and for the court of Pope Benedict XII at Avignon (1339–44). His paintings reveal French Gothic influence and are noted for their color and flowing lines. Among his works are *St. Louis of Toulouse, The Annunciation,* and *The Holy Family.*

Martinique (mar-tin-EKE), Caribbean island, overseas department of the French Republic, one of the Windward Islands, in the Lesser Antilles. Sugar, rum, bananas, and pineapples are exported from Fort-de-France, the capital. The island, of volcanic origin, was discovered by Columbus and first colonized by the French in 1635. Picture **C** 117.
  Caribbean Sea and islands **C** 116–19

Martinmas, or Feast of St. Martin, religious holiday **R** 154–55
  Saint Martin's Day weather **H** 159
Martyrs, Age of the **R** 288
  Christianity, history of **C** 281
Marunouchi district, Tokyo **T** 205

Marvell, Andrew (1621–1678), English writer, b. Yorkshire. He composed some outstanding lyrics ("To His Coy Mistress," for example) and, as an active Puritan, produced political satires in both poetry and prose.

Marvell, Andrew (continued)
Marvell is considered one of the outstanding metaphysical poets.

Marver, metal plate for rolling glass **G** 230
Marx, Karl, German economist and political philosopher
M 113
ideas of Communism **C** 442–43
Lenin and Marx **L** 138
on capitalism **C** 104
socialism **S** 220

Marx Brothers, Chico (Leonard) (1891–1961), **Harpo** (Adolph or Arthur) (1893–1964), and **Groucho** (Julius Henry) (1895–   ), American comedians, b. New York, N.Y. Given to zany frolicking, they developed their stage characters in a vaudeville team, appearing at various times with their two other brothers **Gummo** (Milton) (1894–   ) and **Zeppo** (Herbert) (1901–   ), and on Broadway in *The Coconuts* and *Animal Crackers*. They also played in such films as *A Night at the Opera* and *A Day at the Races.*
motion pictures, history of **M** 475

Mary I (1516–1558), queen of England and Ireland (1553–58), b. Greenwich. Daughter of Henry VIII and Catherine of Aragon, she became England's first ruling queen upon the death of her younger brother, Edward VI. In 1554 she married Philip II, son of her cousin Charles V, Holy Roman emperor and king of Spain as Charles I. In her determination to restore Catholicism in England, she had nearly 300 Protestants burned at the stake, earning the nickname Bloody Mary.
Mary and Elizabeth I **E** 178, 221

Mary II, queen of England **E** 224
Mary, queen of Scotland see Mary Queen of Scots
Mary, Virgin, mother of Jesus Christ **M** 113
Day of Our Lady of Guadalupe, Mexican religious holiday **R** 155

Mary had a little lamb, first line of a poem by American writer and editor Sarah Josepha Hale.

Maryknoll, Catholic Foreign Missionary Society of America **M** 349
Maryland M 114–29
American colonies **A** 192
Baltimore **B** 35
colonial life in America **C** 385–99
Founding fathers of the United States **F** 395
places of interest in Negro history **N** 94
Maryland, My Maryland, song by James Randall
N 25
Maryland, University of M 123
Maryland Gazette-News, newspaper **M** 122
Maryland yellowthroats, birds **B** 220
Marylebone Cricket Club, England **T** 90

Mary Magdalene, in the New Testament, a woman whom Christ cured of evil spirits. She became a devoted follower and was present at the crucifixion. She often is thought to be the same as the sinful woman to whom Christ showed mercy. Thus the name "Magdalene" is a synonym for a reformed sinner.

Mary Queen of Scots, or Mary Stuart **M** 130
conflicts between Protestants and Catholics **S** 89
guest-prisoner in England **E** 222
Elizabeth I and Mary **E** 178–79
Mary's Lamb, nursery rhyme **N** 405
Mary Tudor see Mary I, queen of England

Masaccio (ma-ZA-cho) (Tommaso Guidi) (1401–1428), Italian artist, b. San Giovanni Valdarno. His paintings, noted for their strength and depth, completed the shift from medieval art to that of the early Renaissance. His frescoes in the Brancacci Chapel, Florence, such as *The Tribute Money*, were studied as examples by almost all later Florentine painters and had an important influence on Raphael and Michelangelo.
Expulsion from Paradise, The painting **R** 166
Italian art **I** 468; **P** 20
Madonna and Child Enthroned, painting **I** 466
Renaissance art **R** 164
Tribute Money, The, fresco **P** 20

Masai (ma-SY), Nilo-Hamitic tribal group of southern Kenya and northern Tanzania, presently numbering over 100,000. A nomadic people, they live in settlements called Kraals, which contain houses and cattle corrals, and subsist mainly on the meat, milk, and blood of their cattle. Before the arrival of Europeans the Masai warriors, famous for their fearlessness, made raids on surrounding tribes for cattle and land.

Masaryk (MA-sar-eek), **Jan Garrigue** (1886-1948), Czechoslovakian statesman, b. Prague. He was the son of the Czechoslovakian patriot Tomáš Masaryk. Under his father's presidency he held several diplomatic posts, including that of minister to Britain (1925–38). During World War II he was foreign minister (1940–48) and vice-premier (1941–45) of the Czech government-in-exile. Soon after the Communists took over Czechoslovakia (1948), he died, presumably by suicide.

Masaryk, Tomáš, co-founder and first president of Czechoslovakia **M** 130
nation of Czechoslovakia is created **C** 563
Mascagni (ma-SCON-ye), **Pietro,** Italian composer **I** 486
Cavalleria Rusticana, opera **O** 142
Mascons, on the moon **M** 453
Mascots
lucky emblems, "beasts" on coats of arms **H** 115

Masefield, John (1878–1967), English poet, dramatist, and novelist, b. Ledbury. Joining the merchant marine at 13, he became a sailor on a windjammer. His best-known short poems, such as "Cargoes" and "Sea Fever," express his love of the sea. "Sea Fever" was published in his first book, *Salt Water Ballads* (1902). His work includes plays, essays, novels, and narrative poems. He became England's poet laureate in 1930.
English poetry in the 20th century **E** 265

Masers, devices for amplifying microwaves **M** 131
use of ammonia **G** 61
Maseru (MAS-er-u), capital of Lesotho (formerly Basutoland) **L** 156
Mashona (ma-SHO-na), a people of Africa **R** 228
Mashpee, on Cape Cod, Massachusetts **M** 136
Masked Ball, The, opera by Giuseppe Verdi **O** 148–49
Masks
African art form **A** 72; pictures **A** 74, 75, 76
clay modeling **C** 337
Halloween customs **H** 15–17
Indian art **I** 156
Japanese theater **D** 292
skin diving **S** 188
Mason, A. E. W., English author **M** 555
Mason, Charles, English surveyor **M** 133

Mason, George (1725–1792), American statesman, b. Virginia. His Declaration of Rights (1776) for Virginia was used as a basis for part of the Declaration of Independence and the United States Constitution. He also wrote most of Virginia's constitution (1776) and outlined the Northwest Ordinance (1780). A member of the Constitutional Convention, he refused to sign the Constitution, principally because of its compromise on slave trade. His insistence on a Bill of Rights led to adoption of the first 10 amendments.

Mason, James Murray (1798–1871), American Confederate statesman, b. Georgetown, D.C. As a senator from Virginia (1847–61) he drafted the Fugitive Slave Law of 1850 and in 1861 headed for England with John Slidell to win British aid for the South. While aboard the British ship *Trent,* Mason and Slidell were captured (November, 1861) by Union forces (nearly causing war with Great Britain). They were freed in January, 1862. Mason went to England but failed to gain British recognition of the Confederacy.

Civil War, United States, and trouble with Britain C 322

Mason, John (1586–1635), English settler and founder of New Hampshire, b. King's Lynn. Appointed governor of Newfoundland (1615), he received a grant of New England land (1622). He became deputy governor of New Plymouth (1623) but left for England in 1624. Returning from England (1629), he organized, with Sir Ferdinando Gorges and a group of English merchants, the Laconia Company and founded an agricultural colony on Piscataqua River that became New Hampshire.

colonial history in America A 189; N 162

Mason, Stevens Thomson, first governor of Michigan M 271–72
Mason and Dixon's Line M 133
Missouri Compromise M 382
Pennsylvania P 145
Mason bees B 123
Mason jar, for canning and bottling B 342
Masonry B 391–94
cement and concrete C 165
paints for masonry P 32
Masonry dams D 16
Masons see Freemasons
Masque (MASK), poetic pageant E 253
dancing popular during the Renaissance D 25
development of the opera O 132
dramatic entertainment D 295
Mass, in music M 536
choral music C 277
Dutch and Flemish music D 363, 364
Mass, in physics M 171–72
acceleration and mass M 471
change of mass in nuclear reactions N 358
defined C 219
earth's E 7, 23
gravity pull G 324
mass numbers C 204, 219
measure of W 111–12
solar E 22
Mass, in Roman Catholic Church R 302
priest says Mass at Qumran, picture D 49
Massachusetts M 134–50
Boston B 339–40
colonial life in America C 385–99
first adoption law A 26
Founding fathers of the United States F 395
Intolerable Acts, 1774 D 60
Horace Mann and education M 83
places of interest in Negro history N 94
Plymouth Colony P 343–46
witches, persecution of W 209

Massachusetts, University of M 143
Massachusetts Bay Colony A 187–88
Plymouth Colony becomes part of Massachusetts Bay Colony P 346
Williams, Roger W 172
Massachusetts Bay Company M 148
Massachusetts Institute of Technology A 386; picture A 387
Massasoit (MASS-a-soit), American Indian chief P 345
Mass communication C 440–41
Massenet (mass-en-AY), **Jules,** French composer
Manon, opera O 146
Massey, Raymond, Canadian-born American actor and producer M 150
Massey, Vincent, Canadian statesman M 150
Massey, William, New Zealand statesman N 243
Massine (mass-ENE), **Léonide,** Russian ballet dancer B 26
Mass media, in communication C 440
advertising A 27–34
television T 70–71
Mass numbers, of atoms N 356
Mass production M 151
automation A 528–34
clothing C 353–54
decorative arts suitable for D 78
glassmaking process G 235
industrial design I 231–32
Industrial Revolution in America I 241
interchangeable parts developed by Whitney in Connecticut C 473
interchangeable parts of automobiles A 548–50
introduced by Henry Ford F 367
machine tools T 217; pictures T 218
manufacturing M 85
technology T 46
Whitney, Eli, pioneer of mass production W 166
Mass spectrograph
cosmic rays studied by C 512–13
Massys (mass-ICE), **Quentin,** Flemish painter
Moneylender and His Wife, The, painting P 19
Mastabas, tombs of ancient Egypt E 96
ancient architecture A 371
Master keys L 325
Masters, Edgar Lee, American poet A 209; I 73–74
Spoon River Anthology E 152
Masters, golf tournament G 262
Masters, of craft guilds G 403

Masterson, William Barclay ("Bat") (1853–1921), American peace officer and sports writer, b. Iroquois County, Ill. During his colorful and varied career he was a buffalo hunter, railroad contractor, army scout, peace officer in tough frontier towns, and a professional gambler. From 1902 until his death he was sports editor on the *New York Morning Telegraph.* A television series was based on his life.

Dodge City, Kansas, frontier town K 186

Mastodon, extinct animal, ancestor of the modern elephant. Mastodons had long, shaggy hair, a trunk like the elephant's, and long, curving tusks. Mastodon skeletons, bones, teeth, tusks, and hair have been found in many parts of the world. Picture E 340.

prehistoric relatives of the elephant E 170

Mastoid (MAS-toid), also called **mastoid bone,** one of the parts of the temporal bone of the skull. It is located at the side of the skull just behind the ear. The bottom of the mastoid extends downward forming the **mastoid**

Mastoid (continued)
process. It may be felt as the hard area just behind and below the ear.

Masurian (mas-UR-ian) **Lakes, battle of the,** 1914
   W 274
Mat, or matrix, of type   **P** 463, 465
Matabele (mat-a-BE-le), a people of Africa   **R** 228, 229–30
Matadors, bullfighters   **B** 449–51

Mata Hari (MA-ta HA-ri) (perhaps from Malayan, meaning "sun") (Gertrud Margarete Zelle) (1876–1917), dancer and spy for Germany during World War I, b. Java. An exotic woman, she charmed military secrets from the French officials she entertained. She was tried and executed after French intelligence agents discovered her identity as a German agent.
   notorious spies   **S** 389

Matanuska (ma-ta-NU-ska) **River** and **Valley,** Alaska
   A 133, 134, 137
   present-day pioneer life   **P** 262
Matches   **M** 151–53
   fire prevention rules   **F** 154–55
Matchlocks, early trigger guns   **G** 415; picture **G** 414
Match play, in golf   **G** 260
Matchstick puzzles   **T** 289
Maté (MA-tay), or yerba maté, herb tea of Paraguay
   P 63
   popular in Argentina   **A** 393
Mathematics   **M** 154–61
   abacus   **A** 2–3
   algebra   **A** 157–59
   arithmetic   **A** 398–401
   Descartes's analytic geometry   **D** 123
   geometry and geometric forms   **G** 122–31
   graphs   **G** 309–13
   Kepler's laws of planetary motion   **K** 234
   metric system of measurement   **W** 114–16
   new mathematics   **M** 161–68
   Newton, Isaac   **N** 206–07
   number lore   **N** 378–83
   numbers and number systems   **N** 384–88
   numerals and numeration systems   **N** 389–401
   percent   **P** 148–49
   probability   **P** 470–74
   Roman numerals   **R** 309–10
   sets   **S** 126–27
   slide rule, how to make your own   **M** 166–67
   statistics   **S** 416–18
   textbooks, new and old, pictures   **E** 78
   topology   **T** 220–26
   What is infinity?   **M** 160
   See also Calculators; Computers
Mathematics, new   **M** 161–68
Mather, Cotton, American writer   **A** 196
Mather, Stephen T., first director, National Park Service
   N 51
Mathewson, Christy, American baseball pitcher   **B** 80;
   picture **B** 81

Mathias (ma-THY-as), **Bob** (Robert Bruce Mathias) (1930–), American athlete, b. Tulare, Calif. A highly versatile athlete, he set a record by winning the Olympic decathlon twice in succession, at London (1948) and Helsinki (1952). He also won the American National Decathlon title a record four times (1948, 1949, 1950, 1952) and received the James E. Sullivan Memorial Trophy (1949). He is now a U.S. congressman.
   Olympiads, 1948, 1952   **O** 112

Matilda, folk song   **F** 321

Matisse (ma-TECE), **Henri,** French painter   **M** 169
   collage design, picture   **C** 376
   French art   **F** 431
   Hermitage Museum collection, picture   **M** 509
   modern art   **M** 388, 390
   pen-and-ink drawing   **D** 304
   Red Studio, The, painting   **M** 389
Matriarchal family   **F** 41
Matrimony
   sacrament of Roman Catholic Church   **R** 301
Matrix (MAY-trix), or mat, of type   **P** 463, 465
Matronymic (mat-ro-NIM-ic) **method,** of name giving   **N** 7
Matsu island, off China's mainland   **C** 273
Matsuo Basho see Basho
Matter   **M** 170–78
   atoms of three states compared, diagram   **A** 485
   changes in physical properties with speeds near speed
      of light   **R** 142
   gases   **G** 57–59
   gravitation, strength of, and equations for   **G** 321–22
   heat and change of state   **H** 91
   instruments for analyzing   **O** 173–74
   liquids   **L** 309–10
   nuclear energy   **N** 352–71
   properties of matter   **P** 232–33
   radiation, effect on matter   **R** 40–45
   relativity   **R** 139–44
   solids   **S** 250–51
   theories about, in the history of physics   **P** 230–33
   vacuum   **V** 262–65
   water as gas, liquid, or solid   **W** 51
Matterhorn, mountain, Switzerland   **S** 500
   Swiss Alps   **A** 174; pictures **A** 175,   **E** 305
Matthew, Saint, one of the 12 Apostles   **A** 333
   Evangelists, The   **E** 335
   Gospel of   **B** 160
Matthias (ma-THY-as), **Saint,** one of the 12 Apostles
   A 333
Matthias Corvinus (cor-VY-nus), king of Hungary
   H 287
Mattingly, Thomas K., American astronaut   **S** 347

Matzeliger, Jan (1852?–89), American inventor, Negro, b. Paramaribo, Dutch Guiana (now Surinam). He started work at age 10 in his father's machine shop. After settling in Lynn, Mass., where he learned the shoe trade, he designed and patented the lasting machine that revolutionized the American shoe industry.

Matzot (MA-tza), unleavened bread   **P** 93
Maudslay, Henry, English engineer   **T** 217
Maugham (MAUM), **W. Somerset,** English writer   **E** 266
Maui (MOW-i), one of the Hawaiian Islands   **H** 56, 58
Mauldin, William Henry "Bill," American cartoonist
   N 193

Mau Mau (MOW MOW), African movement composed mainly of Kikuyu tribemen and organized to oust Europeans from Kenya. It arose chiefly from Kikuyu discontent over European possession of former Kikuyu land, including fertile highlands of Mount Kenya. Members took secret oaths to kill white men and African opponents. During a state of emergency (1952–59) the British Government gathered Kikuyus into crowded reserves, imprisoned thousands, and finally, by military force, quelled the rebellion.
   Kenya, history of   **K** 233

Maumee (mau-MEE), **Lake,** ancient glacial lake, now
   Great Lakes plain   **O** 62
Mauna Kea (MOW-na KAY-a), volcano, Hawaii   **M** 492
Mauna Loa, volcano, Hawaii   **V** 380

Maundy Thursday E 41

Maupassant (mo-pa-SON), **Guy de,** French writer S 165
the short story in French literature F 441

Mauriac, François, French novelist F 442

Mauritania (maur-i-TAY-nia) M 179–80
flag F 236
postman, picture P 408

Mauritius (mau-RISH-us) M 181
dodo bird, how it became extinct B 229

Mauro (MOW-ro), **Fra,** Venetian cartographer E 372

Maurois (more-WAH), **André** (Emile Herzog) (1885–1967), French writer, b. Elbeuf. A member of the French Academy from 1938, Maurois was one of France's most widely read and celebrated writers. He wrote many novels, short stories, literary reviews, newspaper and magazine articles, but he is remembered chiefly for his fine biographies. Because he was a Jew, he had to leave France after it fell to the Nazis in 1940. He and his wife then spent a few years in the United States. His biographies include *Ariel: The Life of Shelley, Proust: Portrait of a Genius, Lelia: The Life of George Sand, Olympio: The Life of Victor Hugo,* and *Prometheus: The Life of Balzac,* written when Maurois was 80 years old.

Maury, Matthew Fontaine (1806–1873), American oceanographer, b. near Fredericksburg, Va. He was superintendent of the Depot of Charts and Instruments and of the U.S. Naval Observatory (1842–61). His research on ocean winds and currents led to an international system of reporting oceanographic data and to the laying of a transatlantic cable. After serving in the Confederate Navy (1861–65), he lived abroad, returning to teach at Virginia Military Institute (1868–73). He wrote first oceanography text, *The Physical Geography of the Sea,* and was elected to American Hall of Fame (1930).
oceanography, beginnings of O 25

Maurya (MOW-ur-ya) **Dynasty,** line of kings of India established about 324 B.C. by Chandragupta Maurya, the first true emperor of India. The third Maurya ruler, Asoka, was the most renowned. During his reign (274–232 B.C.), which was marked by peace, prosperity, and the spread of Buddhism, the noted Asokan pillars—containing his edicts, moral precepts, laws, and deeds—were erected. The last Maurya king was assassinated in 185 B.C.
Asia, history of early civilizations A 468

Mauser (MOWS-er) **rifle** G 419; picture G 418

Mausoleum (maus-o-LE-um) **at Halicarnassus** (hal-i-car-NASS-us) W 216; picture W 215

Mauve (MOAV), synthetic dye D 370

Mavericks, unbranded cattle on open rangeland R 104–05

Mawson, Sir Douglas, Australian explorer P 366, 368

Maxentius (max-EN-tius), Roman emperor, defeated by Constantine C 489

Maxim, Hiram Percy (1869–1936), American mechanical engineer and inventor, b. Brooklyn, N.Y. The son of Sir Hiram Stevens Maxim, inventor of the Maxim machine gun, he is well known for inventing the Maxim gun silencer. He also devised numerous improvements in the automobile field, such as the muffler to deaden motor noise. His books include *Life's Place in the Cosmos* and his autobiography, *Horseless Carriage Days.*

Maximilian (max-i-MIL-ian), emperor of Mexico M 249
defeated by Juárez J 145

Maximilian I, Holy Roman emperor ("Kaiser Max")
created Habsburg empire A 524

Maxim machine guns G 423–24

Maxwell, James Clerk, Scottish physicist P 236–37; S 75
color photography P 204
Saturn's rings P 277

May, 5th month of year M 182–83
folk music F 326

Maya (MA-ya), Indians of North America I 197–99
communication by hieroglyphics C 431
development of arts I 152
Guatemala G 390, 392
Honduras H 198
numeration system N 393–94
painting from a vase from Guatemala, picture A 348
pre-Columbian dance L 68
tomb, picture A 352

Mayagüez (ma-ya-GUACE), Puerto Rico P 522

Mayakovski (ma-ya-KOF-ski), **Vladimir,** Russian poet U 62

Mayapán (ma-ya-PON), ancient city of Yucatán I 199

Mayapple see Mandrake ·

Maybach (MY-bock), **Wilhelm,** German automobile builder A 543

May beetles P 284; picture P 285

May Day, International Labor Day H 153
celebrated in Union of Soviet Socialist Republics U 29

May Day Festival H 155
maypole dance, pictures F 298; H 155

Mayer, Julius Robert, German scientist S 76

Mayer, Maria Goeppert (1906–), American physicist, b. Kattowitz, Germany (now Katowice, Poland). Professor Mayer and J. H. D. Jensen shared half of the 1963 Nobel prize in physics (E. P. Wigner received the other half) for developing the concept of the shell structure of atomic nuclei. She was the second woman to receive the Nobel prize in physics. (Marie Curie was the first, in 1903.)

Mayflower (trailing arbutus), flower
Massachusetts, state flower of M 134

Mayflower, Pilgrims' ship M 184–85
Pilgrims' voyage to America A 186
Plymouth Colony, founding of P 344

Mayflower II, ship M 185

Mayflower Compact, 1620 P 344
American colonies begin self-government and democracy A 186
voyage of the Mayflower M 185

Mayflower Descendants, General Society of, organization composed of descendants of the colonists who landed at Plymouth, Mass., from the *Mayflower* in 1620. It was founded in 1897, has its headquarters in Plymouth, Mass., and publishes the *Mayflower.*

Mayfly, picture I 281

May Music Festival, Cincinnati, Ohio M 551

Mayne, William (James Carter) (1928–), English author of children's books, b. Kingston-upon-Hull, Yorkshire. An author who "prefers children to humans," his works include *A Glass Ball, A Grass Rope* (English Carnegie medal winner, 1957), and *A Day Without End.*

Maynor, Dorothy (1910–), American soprano, b. Norfolk, Va. At 14 she entered Hampton Institute and became a member of the school's choir. In 1933 she won a scholarship to Westminster Choir College. After receiving a B. Mus. degree (1935) she studied in New York. She was the first Negro to sing in Coolidge Auditorium in Washington, D.C., and was soloist at the inauguration of President Harry S Truman. In 1963 she founded the Harlem School of the Arts, in New York City.
Negro artists and singers N 98

Mayo, Charles and William, American doctors   **M** 208a
Mayo family, American doctors   **M** 335
Mayombe Mountains, Congo (Brazzaville)   **C** 461
Mayon (ma-YONE), **Mount,** Philippines   **V** 382–83
Mayor-council, form of municipal government   **M** 505
Maypole dance, pictures   **F** 298; **H** 155

Mays, Willie Howard (1931–   ), American baseball player, Negro, b. Fairfield, Ala. He joined New York (now San Francisco) Giants in 1951 and was chosen Rookie of the Year. An outstanding batter, outfielder, and base runner, he was voted the National League's Most Valuable Player in 1954 and 1965. In 1972 he joined New York Mets and retired at end of the '73 season. He hit 660 home runs. Pictures   **B** 76; **N** 103
   years of change in Negro history   **N** 101

Mazama (ma-ZA-ma), **Mount,** Oregon   **O** 192

Mazarin (MAZ-ar-in), **Jules, Cardinal** (1602–1661), French statesman, b. Pescina, Italy. He executed diplomatic missions for Pope Urban VIII (1629–34), entered French service under Richelieu (1639), and became cardinal (1641). He succeeded Richelieu as prime minister (1642–61), continuing Richelieu's foreign policy in order to strengthen France's position in Europe and weaken the Holy Roman Empire. Domestically, he broke the power of the nobility and gave all authority to the king.
   Palais-Mazarin, Paris, seat of French Academy   **P** 74

Maze, network of paths or passages   **P** 76
   animal behavior   **P** 495
   animal trial and error tests   **A** 283–84; pictures **A** 282, 285
   Jordan theorem in topology   **T** 224–25
   learning ability, test for   **L** 104
Mazurka (ma-ZUR-ka), dance of Poland   **D** 30
Mazzini (ma-TZI-ni), **Giuseppe,** Italian writer and patriot **M** 186
   Garibaldi and Mazzini   **G** 57
   Italian unification   **I** 457
   Risorgimento in Italian literature   **I** 479

Mba (umm-bah), **Leon** (1902–67), president of Gabon, b. Libreville. Mba was elected the first president of Gabon in 1961, after the country gained its independence from France (1960). Removed from office by a military coup in 1964, he was reinstated with the aid of French troops.

Mbabane (um-ba-BA-nay), capital of Swaziland   **S** 481
M'bochi, Congo people   **C** 462

Mboya (m-BOY-a), **Tom** (Thomas Joseph Mboya) (1930–1969), Kenyan statesman, b. Central Province. Formerly a health sanitation inspector, he was then involved in political leadership of the Kenya nationalist movement (from 1953). He served as general secretary of the Kenya Federation of Labor (1953–62), minister of labor (1962–63), minister of constitutional affairs (1963–64), and minister of economic development and planning from 1964 until his assassination. His autobiography is entitled *Freedom and After.*
   Kenya, history of   **K** 233

Mc, contraction of Mac   **N** 5
   See *also* names beginning with Mac and Mc in alphabetical order as they are spelled
McAdam, John Loudon, Scottish engineer   **T** 260
   roads and highways, history of   **R** 251, 252

McBurney, Charles (1845–1913), American surgeon, b. Roxbury, Mass. He pioneered in antiseptic surgery and was an authority on appendicitis operation. He discovered McBurney's point, a tender pressure point important in diagnosis of appendicitis, and McBurney's incision, a technique of appendectomy.

McCandless, Bruce, II, American astronaut   **S** 347

McCarran, Patrick Anthony (1876–1954), American politician, b. Reno, Nev. He was elected to the Nevada state legislature (1903) and served as associate justice (1913–17) and chief justice (1917–18) of the Nevada Supreme Court. As U.S. Senator from Nevada (1933–54), he sponsored the Internal Security Act of 1950 (known as the McCarran Act), requiring registration of members of Communist organizations with the federal government. He co-authored the McCarran-Walter Immigration Act of 1952, revising American immigration policy.

McCarren-Walter Act, 1952   **I** 101
   citizenship   **C** 313
McCarthy, Charlie, ventriloquist's dummy **V** 301

McCarthy, Eugene Joseph (1916–   ), American political leader, b. Watkins, Minn. After receiving M.A. from University of Minnesota (1938) he taught at high school and college level before entering politics in 1948. He represented Minnesota in Congress for 10 years. He was elected to the Senate in 1958. As member of Senate Foreign Relations Committee, McCarthy was troubled by U.S. involvement in Vietnam War. This prompted him to enter the presidential primaries in 1968, opposing President Johnson for the Democratic nomination. When Johnson decided not to seek renomination, McCarthy opposed Vice-President Humphrey.

McCarthy, Joseph Raymond (1909–1957), American politician, b. Grand Chute, Wis. While serving in the U.S. Senate (1947–57), he acted as chairman of the Senate Permanent Investigations Subcommittee. His televised investigations of Communism in the Army resulted in his formal censure by the Senate.
   McCarthyism and Kennedy   **K** 209

McCarthy, Joseph Vincent (1887–   ), American baseball manager, b. Philadelphia, Pa. He managed the Chicago Cubs (1926–30), winning one pennant; the New York Yankees (1931–46), winning eight pennants and seven World Series Championships; and the Boston Red Sox (1948–50). He was elected to the Baseball Hall of Fame in 1957.

McCarthy, Mary, American writer   **A** 215
McCauley, Mary see Pitcher, Molly
McCay, Clive M., American scientist   **A** 85
   control of aging   **A** 87

McClellan, George Brinton (1826–1885), American army officer and politician, b. Philadelphia, Pa. He was commissioned army major general (1861) in command of the department of Ohio when the Civil War broke out. His successful campaign of Rich Mountain led to his appointment as commander and later, general-in-chief of the Division of the Potomac (1861–62). He directed the unsuccessful Peninsula Campaign and was chosen to reorganize the army's defense of Washington. Accused of being overcautious, he was relieved of duty (1862). He was Democratic presidential candidate (1865) and governor of New Jersey (1878–81).
   Civil War, United States, campaigns of   **C** 322, 323–24, 326
   with Lincoln, picture   **L** 296

McCloskey, Robert (1914–), American illustrator and author of children's books, b. Hamilton, Ohio. He served as a sergeant in the Army during World War II, drawing training pictures. Primarily an illustrator, he creates stories in picture form and later connects them with sentences. He is author of *Make Way for Ducklings* (Caldecott medal winner, 1941), *Homer Price, Blueberries for Sal,* and other works.

McClure, Sir Robert John Le Mesurier (1807–1873), British naval officer and Arctic explorer, b. Wexford, Ireland. He accompanied Arctic expeditions under Sir George Back (1836–37) and Sir James Clark Ross (1848). In command of an expedition in search of Sir John Franklin (1850–54), he first proved the existence of the Northwest Passage. He later served in China (1856–61).
   Northwest Passage **N** 338

McCormack, John (1884–1945), American tenor, b. Athlone, Ireland. He studied in Italy. After winning the gold medal at the National Irish Festival (Dublin, 1902), he went on to a highly successful concert and opera career. He sang with opera companies in New York, Boston, and Chicago, excelling in Mozart and Verdi. He was also popular as a singer of sentimental ballads.

McCormack, John William (1891–), American politician, b. South Boston, Mass. A former member of the state House of Representatives (1920–22) and state Senate (1923–26) of Massachusetts, he served in the U.S. House of Representatives (1929–71). Closely associated with Sam Rayburn, he was House majority leader (1940–45, 1948–52, 1955–62) and minority whip (1946–47, 1953–54). He succeeded Rayburn as Speaker of the House (1962–71).

McCormick, Cyrus, American inventor **M** 186
   farm machinery **F** 60

McCormick, Patricia Keller (1930–), American diving champion, b. Seal Beach, Calif. In the Olympics, she placed first in springboard and high-diving competitions (1952) and in springboard and platform events (1956).

McCoy, Elijah (1843–1929), American inventor, Negro, b. Canada. He patented numerous lubricators between 1872 and 1926 and developed a method of oiling moving machinery, making it unnecessary to stop the machine to lubricate it. His lubricating cup was widely used on factory machines and on engines of trains and steamships. He established the Elijah McCoy Manufacturing Company in Detroit about 1920.

McCracken, Harold (1894–), American Arctic explorer and author, b. Colorado Springs, Colo. He led Ohio State University expedition to Alaska (1915–17) and the Stoll-McCracken expedition of the American Museum of Natural History (1928) to the Aleutian Islands, where Stone Age mummies were discovered. He has been director of the Buffalo Bill Historical Center and the Whitney Museum of Western Art, Cody, Wyoming (since 1958). His many books include *God's Frozen Children* and *Frederic Remington, Artist of the Old West.*

McCullers, Carson, American novelist **A** 213
McCulloch v. Maryland, case in constitutional law **M** 112
McCurdy, John Alexander Douglas, Canadian aviation pioneer **C** 82
McDivitt, James, American astronaut **S** 344, 345, 347

McDonald, David Lamar (1906–), American naval officer, b. Maysville, Ga. He served with the Navy Bureau

of Aeronautics (1947–50), directed the air warfare division of the office of Chief of Naval Operations (1955–57), and served as deputy assistant chief of staff, Supreme Headquarters, Allied Powers in Europe (SHAPE) (1957–60). Attaining the rank of full admiral in 1963, he was chief of naval operations from then until 1967.

McDowell, Irvin (1818–1885), American army officer, b. Columbus, Ohio. After serving in Army headquarters and territorial departments (1838–61), he attained rank of brigadier general (1861). Unsuccessful in field command, he was supplanted by General McClellan after he lost the first battle of Bull Run (1861) and was relieved of duty after suffering defeat in the second battle of Bull Run (1862). He served in territorial posts (after 1864) and became a major general (1872).
   Civil War, United States, campaigns of **C** 322

McElroy (MAC-el-roy), **Mary Arthur,** acting first lady in Arthur's administration **F** 174–75
McElroy, William D., American biologist **B** 198

McGill, James (1744–1813), Canadian fur trader, b. Glasgow, Scotland. He established his business headquarters in Montreal (1774?), and he served on the Legislative Assembly of Lower Canada (1792–96, 1800–04) and on the Quebec Executive Council (1793). At his death he left land and funds to found McGill University, Montreal.

McGill, Ralph (Emerson) (1898–1969), American journalist, b. Soddy, Tenn. He worked for the Nashville Banner (1922–28) before joining the Atlanta Constitution (1929–69) where he held several editorial positions before becoming publisher. An early crusader for civil rights, he won a Pulitzer Prize for editorial writing (1958) and was awarded the Presidential Medal of Freedom (1964).

McGill University, Montreal, Canada **C** 62; **M** 445; **U** 206
   Quebec, educational institutions **Q** 10b

McGillvray, Alexander (1759?–1793), Creek Indian chief. During the American Revolution he supported the British, and as a Loyalist, lost his Georgia lands at the beginning of the war. To unite southern Indians and halt American settlement in Georgia, Tennessee, and Kentucky, he concluded a treaty with Spain (1784) and directed raids against southern frontier settlements (1785–87). Though he signed a friendship pact with the United States (1790), he nullified it by signing another treaty with Spain (1792).

McGinley, Phyllis, American poet **O** 206
   Pulitzer prize winner **P** 528

McGovern, George S. (1922–), American political leader, b. Avon, S. Dak. After receiving his Ph.D. from Northwestern University in 1953, McGovern served as Executive Secretary of the South Dakota Democratic Party (1954–65). He represented South Dakota in Congress from 1957 to 1961, when President Kennedy appointed him director of the Food for Peace Program. He was elected to the U.S. Senate in 1962. In 1968 Senator McGovern declared himself a candidate for the Democratic presidential nomination. In 1972 he was the Democratic presidential candidate but lost the election to President Nixon.

McGraw, John J., American baseball player and manager **B** 71

McGuffey, William Holmes (1800–1873), American educa-

McGuffey, William Holmes (continued)
tor, b. near Claysville, Pa. President of Cincinnati College (1836–39) and of Ohio University in Athens (1839–43), he later became professor of moral philosophy, University of Virginia (1845–73). A strong supporter of public education, he is remembered for his widely circulated *Eclectic Readers* for elementary schools, known as McGuffey's Readers.

McHenry, James (1753–1816), American army officer, b. Ballymena, Ireland. After serving on medical staff of Revolutionary forces (1775–78), he became secretary to Washington (1778–80) and to Lafayette (1780–81). He was a member of the Maryland senate (1781–86, 1791–96), the Continental Congress (1783–86), and the Constitutional Convention (1787). He served as secretary of war under Washington and Adams (1796–1800). Historic Fort McHenry in Baltimore was named for him.

McIlwain, Carl, American scientist **R** 47

McIntyre, James Francis Aloysius, Cardinal (1886–   ), American Roman Catholic prelate, b. New York, N.Y. Ordained a priest (1921), he served as coadjutor archbishop of New York under Francis Cardinal Spellman (1946–48). He was archbishop of Los Angeles and San Diego (1948–1970), and he was made a cardinal in 1953.

McKay, Alexander (?–1811), Canadian fur trader. He joined Sir Alexander Mackenzie on his expedition to the Pacific Ocean (1793). After trading as a partner with North West Company (1799–1808), he became a partner in the Pacific Fur Company of John Jacob Astor (1810).

McKay, Claude (pseudonym Eli Edwards) (1890–1948), American author, Negro, b. Sunny Ville, Jamaica. Arriving in the United States (1912), he became associated with Floyd Dell and Max Eastman as an editor of *The Liberator* (1919–22). His poetry, often deploring racial injustices, includes the collections *Songs of Jamaica, Constab Ballads,* and *Harlem Shadows.* Among his other works are the novels *Home to Harlem, Banjo,* and an autobiography, *A Long Way From Home.*
Negro Renaissance **N** 98

McKay, Donald (1810–1880), American shipbuilder, b. Shelburne County, Nova Scotia, Canada. Establishing a shipyard in East Boston, Mass. (1844), he became internationally known for his rapid packet and clipper ships, including the clippers *James Baines* and *Lightning,* which hold the world speed records for sailing ships. He strongly advocated construction of iron ships for the U.S. Navy, and he built several naval vessels, (1864–65).

McKay, Douglas (1893–1959), American politician, b. Portland, Ore. He served as representative to the state senate (1935–37, 1939–41, 1945–47) and as governor of Oregon (1948–52). President Eisenhower appointed him secretary of the interior (1953–56).

McKay, Frederick, American dentist **F** 283–84
McKay, Gordon, American inventor **S** 162

McKean, Thomas (1734–1817), American statesman, b. Chester county, Pa. He represented Delaware at the Continental Congress (1774–83), serving as president of the Congress (1881). He was chief justice (1777–99) and governor of Pennsylvania (1799–1808).

McKee, Mary Harrison, acting first lady in Harrison's administration **F** 175

McKenzie, Roderick (1761?–1844), Canadian fur trader, b. Scotland. He took charge of Fort Chipewyan during the absence of his cousin, the explorer Sir Alexander Mackenzie (1789, 1792). He was a partner in a fur-trading company (1800–25), and he served in the Legislative Council of Lower Canada (1817–38). His notes on fur-trading history were used in *Bourgeois de la Compagnie du Nord-Ouest,* by Louis François Rodrigue Masson.

McKim, Mead and White, firm of architects **U** 123
McKinley, Ida Saxton, wife of William McKinley **F** 175; picture **F** 174

McKinley, John (1780–1852), American politician, b. Culpeper County, Va. A resident of Alabama, he served in the U.S. Senate (1826–31), the state legislature (1831–33, 1836–37), and the House of Representatives (1833–35). In 1837 President Van Buren appointed him to the U.S. Supreme Court.

McKinley, Mount, Alaska, pictures **A** 133,   **M** 496
highest point in North America **N** 285
McKinley, William, 25th president of United States
M 187–90
anarchists barred from United States **G** 276
Spanish-American War, background **S** 374–75
McKinley Tariff, 1890 **H** 47; **M** 187–88

McKissick, Floyd B. (1922–), Negro civil rights leader, b. Asheville, N.C. He attended Morehouse and North Carolina colleges and received his law degree from the University of North Carolina Law School. He succeeded James Farmer as National Director of the Congress of Racial Equality (CORE) (1966–68), and now heads Floyd McKissick Enterprises, Inc.

McKuen, Rod (1933–), American poet, composer, and singer, b. Oakland, Calif. He started as a late-night disk jockey on an Oakland radio station. He appeared in night clubs and had bit parts in Hollywood films, but achieved his first great success as a poet with *And Autumn Came.* This was followed by *Twelve Years of Christmas* and *Listen to the Warm,* a collection of song lyrics. He has written more than 1,000 songs and has also composed musical scores for several motion pictures.

McLeod, John (1788–1849), Canadian pioneer, b. Stornoway, Scotland. McLeod went to Canada and became a fur trader, joining Hudson's Bay Company in 1811. In 1815 the company sent him to organize the Red River settlement, near present-day Winnipeg, against attack by the North West Company, which claimed the region's fur resources. He retired from the company in 1848.

McLoughlin (mac-LOC-lin), **John,** Scottish-born Canadian fur trader **F** 524
Oregon **O** 205
Washington **W** 26–27

McLuhan, Herbert Marshall (1911–), Canadian educator and writer, b. Edmonton, Alberta. Professor of English at the University of Toronto, McLuhan wrote *The Gutenberg Galaxy* (1962), explaining his theory that the invention of movable type shaped the development of civilization for 400 years. In *Understanding Media: The Extensions of Man* (1964), he said that since 1900, man has been living in an electronic age of instant communication (telephone, movies, and especially television) and total involvement. Phrases like "the medium is the message" (meaning that the content of television programs is less important than the way in which television is changing the human environment) brought McLuhan international fame. In 1967–68 he held the Albert Schweitzer Chair in the humanities at Fordham University, N.Y. His other works include *The Mechanical Bride* and *The Medium is the Massage*.

McMahon (mac-MAY-on) **Line,** boundary line between India and Tibet   **T** 178
McMath-Hulbert Observatory, Michigan   **S** 466

McMeekin, Isabel McLennan (1895–   ), American author, b. Louisville, Ky. Many of her stories are about the Kentucky hill country. Her books for children include *The First Book of Horses, Kentucky Derby Winner,* and *Journey Cake.* Her adult books are written with Dorothy P. Clark under the pen name of Clark McMeekin.

McMillan, Margaret, English educator   **K** 244
McMurdo Sound, Antarctic region   **P** 370
McNair, Alexander, first governor of Missouri   **M** 381

McNair, Lesley James (1883–1944), American general, b. Verndale, Minn. As chief of staff of the General Headquarters (1940) he was in charge of a gigantic training program, in which he introduced new, realistic training methods. After the reorganization of the War Department General Staff (1942) he was named commanding general of all United States ground forces. He was killed during World War II in Normandy, July, 1944.

McNamara, Robert Strange (1916–   ), U.S. government official, b. San Francisco, Calif. He was an executive of Ford Motor Co. (1946–61), succeeding Henry Ford 2nd as president (1960). He served as U.S. secretary of defense (1961–68). In 1968 he became president of the International Bank for Reconstruction and Development (World Bank).

McNarney, Joseph Taggart (1893–   ), American general, b. Emporium, Pa. He succeeded (1945) Dwight D. Eisenhower as commander of U.S. forces in Europe and was chief of the occupation army in Germany. He served (1947–52) as senior member of the United Nations military staff committee.

McNary, Charles Linza (1874–1944), American politician, b. near Salem, Ore. Elected to the U.S. Senate in 1917, he served for the rest of his life. In 1940 he ran for vice-president as Wendell Willkie's running mate.

McNaughton, Andrew George Latta (1887–1966), Canadian army officer and diplomat, b. Moosomin, Sask. He served as chief of the General Staff (1929–35) and as commander of the Canadian Army in Great Britain (1942–43). He later became minister of national defense (1944), chairman of the Canadian section of the Canadian–United States joint board of defense (1945), and Canadian representative to the United Nations Atomic Energy Commission (1946) and the Security Council (1948).
  Canada, history of   **C** 80

McNeer, May Yonge (1902–   ), American author, b. Tampa, Fla. She has written numerous historical books

for children, many illustrated by her husband, Lynd Ward, including *The Alaska Gold Rush, America's Mark Twain, The American Indian Story,* and *Armed With Courage.*

McNutt, Paul Vories (1891–1955), American politician, b. Franklin, Ind. Following positions as law professor (1919–33) and dean (1925–33) of the University of Indiana, he was governor of Indiana (1933–37). He then became U.S. high commissioner to the Philippines (1937–39, 1945–46). He served as head of the Federal Security Agency (1939–45), director of Defense, Health, and Welfare Services (1941–43), and chairman of the War Manpower Commission (1942–45).

McPherson, Aimee Semple (1890–1944), American evangelist, b. near Ingersoll, Canada. She began preaching at 17 and traveled widely. After settling in Los Angeles (1918), she founded (1921) the Echo Park Evangelistic Association and built the Angelus Temple Church of the Foursquare Gospel.

McPherson, Kansas
  high school, picture   **S** 57
Mead, Lake, southwestern United States   **L** 32
  Arizona   **A** 407
  Nevada   **N** 125

Mead, Margaret (1901–   ), American anthropologist, b. Philadelphia, Pa. Her first book, *Coming of Age in Samoa,* was based on her research in the South Seas (1925–26). Other books of hers have been based on expeditions to New Guinea (1931–33) and to Bali and New Guinea (1936–39). She has been associated with the American Museum of Natural History (since 1926), and she is a professor at Columbia University (since 1954).

Meade, George Gordon (1815–1872), American Union general, b. Cádiz, Spain. His successful participation in the Civil War battles of Mechanicsville, Gaines's Mill, Glendale, Bull Run, and Antietam led to his appointment (1863) as commander of the Army of the Potomac shortly before the battle of Gettysburg. His victory at Gettysburg brought him further promotion and the thanks of Congress (1864).
  Civil War, United States, campaigns of   **C** 325

Meader, Stephen Warren (1892–   ), American author, b. Providence, R.I. His pirate story *The Black Buccaneer* was the first of over 20 primarily adventure stories he has written for boys. His books include *Red Horse Hill, Longshanks, Away to Sea,* and *Lumberjack.*

Meadowcroft, Enid La Monte (1898–1966), American author, b. New York, N.Y. She wrote many of her stories for her pupils and is noted for her histories, including *The Gift of the River, Land of the Free,* and *The First Year.* She has also written biographies.

Meadowlarks, common North American birds of the blackbird family. There are two main kinds of meadowlarks, eastern and western. Both kinds live in fields and nest in the grass. Their throats are yellow, with a black V, and their backs are mottled brown-black, hard to see in grassland. The eastern meadowlark has a whistling call. The western meadowlark has a high-pitched, flute-like song. Picture   **B** 241.
  Audubon painting   **A** 490
  See also Western meadowlarks

Meadows
  flowers   **W** 171

Meal, corn C 507
Meals
   meal planning for good nutrition N 417–18
   mealtime around the world, pictures F 336–39
   table settings T 2–3
Meals on wheels, old-age assistance O 100
Mealybugs P 289; picture P 288
Mean, or arithmetic mean, a kind of average of a set of
   numbers S 417

Means, Florence Crannell (1891–   ), American author
of children's books. b. Baldwinsville, N.Y. She visited and
wrote about the Hopi and Navajo Indians in the
Southwest. Her books include *Alicia, Moved Outers,
Reach For a Star,* and *Tolliver.*

Mean solar days T 188
Meany, George, American labor leader L 4; picture L 7

Meares, John (1756?–1809), British naval commander
and explorer. After forming a trading company to gather
furs on the northwestern coast of America, he made two
voyages (1786–87, 1788) and established a post at
Nootka Sound (1788). He occupied the coastal land
before Spaniards, who claimed the region and seized the
post. Meares's complaint to the king resulted in the
Nootka Sound controversy between Great Britain and
Spain, settled in Great Britain's favor (1790).
   Oregon, history of O 207

Mearne, Samuel, English bookbinder B 322
Mearns (MERNS), **Hughes**
   "Antigonish," nonsense rhyme N 274
Mears, Otto, Russian-born American pioneer builder in
   Colorado C 414
Measles, virus disease D 201
   German measles not related D 196
   vaccination V 261
Measure, or bar, in musical notation M 531
Measure for Measure, play by Shakespeare
   S 135
Measurement
   ancient scientific inventions for measuring
     I 346
   Boyle's law C 209–10
   by shoran R 39
   dressmaking measurements D 312
   mathematics M 154
   of energy in foot-pounds E 198
   tools for measuring T 215–16
   weights and measures W 108–17
   with optical instruments O 170
Measures see Weights and measures
Meat and meat-packing M 191–96
   beef cattle C 148
   cool storage F 347
   cuts of meat M 193, 194
   dairy cattle D 8
   grades of meat M 195–96
   marketing for the home M 101–02
   outdoor cooking O 247–48
   pemmican F 348, 520; I 166, 196
   trichinosis, illness from undercooked pork D 210–11;
     F 354
Meat inspection M 195
Mecca, holy city of Islam M 196
   Islam I 414
   Koran K 295
   major city of Saudi Arabia S 48
   Mohammed's birthplace M 404, 405
Mechanical advantage (MA) force-saving feature of simple machines W 246–47

Mechanical bonding, adhesive process G 242
Mechanical dolls D 268
Mechanical drawing M 197
Mechanical energy E 198
   basic research in physics P 233
Mechanical engineering E 205
   building construction B 431
Mechanics, a branch of physics P 233
   Archimedes A 369
   Galileo's laws of falling bodies, F 34; G 5–7
   motion, Newton's laws of M 469–71
   work, power, and machines W 243–50
Mechanics' Union of Trade Associations L 3
Meck, Nadezhda von, friend of Tchaikovsky T 36
Meckenem, Israel van, Flemish artist
   Lute Player and Woman Playing the Harp D 364
Medallions see Medals
Medal of Freedom, Presidential see Presidential Medal of
   Freedom
Medal of Honor M 198, 200; picture M 199
Medal play, in golf G 260
Medals M 198–200
   children's literature, awards for B 310
   Olympic gold medal, picture O 109
   portrait medallions on furniture, picture F 507
   Syrian and Greek medallions, pictures J 95, 96
   See also Carnegie Hero Fund Commission

Medaris (me-DAIR-is), **John Bruce** (1902–   ), United
States army officer, b. Milford, Ohio. He organized and
operated the Field Army Ordnance Service of the 1st
U.S. Army in World War II. He served as commanding
general of the Army Ballistic Missile Agency at Redstone
Arsenal in Huntsville, Ala. (1955–58), and as commanding general of the U.S. Army Ordnance Missile Command
(1958–62). He is author of *Countdown for Decision,* and
received Freedom Foundation awards (1959, 1960).

Medawar (MED-a-war), **Sir Peter Brian** (1915–   ), English
biologist, b. Rio de Janeiro, Brazil. For the theory and
proof that immunity to foreign substances in the body is
not inherited but acquired in the period before birth, he
and F. M. Burnet won the Nobel prize (1960) in medicine
and physiology. His work has made possible many types
of organ transplantation, skin grafts, and nerve repair.

Medea (me-DE-a), in Greek mythology G 364–65
Medellín (may-thel-YEEN), Colombia C 383
Medes, people of Media, ancient Persia, now Iran I 372
   ancient art A 241
Medhen, Gabre, Ethiopian poet A 76b
Media centers, school libraries L 176, 200
Median (ME-dian), an average of a set of numbers S 417
Mediation, labor see Federal Mediation and Conciliation
   Service
Medicaid, program for total medical care S 222
Medical care, prepaid
   insurance plans for old age O 99
   Medicaid and Medicare S 222; W 120, 121
   medical assistance to the aged O 98
Medical education P 504
Medical ethics, set of rules for doctors D 239
Medical history, of a patient M 208d–208e
   examining the heart H 86b

Medical International Cooperation Organization (MEDICO),
nonprofit agency associated with CARE. MEDICO was
founded (1958) by Dr. Peter D. Commanduras and Dr.
Tom Dooley.

Medical laboratory tests M 201–02, 209
Medical supplies in the home M 202

Medical terms, selected list D 206
Medicare, insurance program O 98; S 222; W 121
  health insurance, types of I 295
  hospitals H 251
  part of "Great Society" program J 131
  Saskatchewan, first Canadian province to have S 38d
Medici (MED-i-chi), **Lorenzo de',** the Magnificent, Italian
  statesman and art patron I 477
  court masques and dances D 25
  Michelangelo's patron M 255–56

Medici (MED-i-chi) **family,** powerful line of Italian
Renaissance rulers. **Giovanni** (1360–1429) took control of
Florence in 1421. His descendants created health and
welfare services for the poor, became patrons of the
arts, and broadened the influence of Tuscany province.
Lorenzo (1449–92), known as the Magnificent, made the
palace the center of Renaissance activity. After Lorenzo's
death the Vatican and foreign invaders began to strip the
family of strength. **Cosimo I** (1519–74) regained power,
but in 1737 the family was banished from Tuscany.
  Botticelli supported by B 340b
  early banking enterprises B 45
  Uffizi gallery U 2–3

Medicinal plants see Plants, medicinal
Medicine
  acupuncture M 208a, 208b
  anesthesia A 256–59
  antibiotics A 310–16
  computers, use in medicine C 457
  dentists and what they do D 114–15
  disease, types of D 186–90
  disinfectants and antiseptics D 222
  doctors D 238–41
  drugs D 325–28
  drugs, abuse of D 329–32
  Geiger counter, use in medicine, diagram G 68
  geriatrics O 98
  god of medicine, Aesculapius M 203, 208c
  health insurance I 295
  home nursing N 413–15
  hospitals H 247–52
  hypnosis H 314–16
  infrared photography P 207
  medical education, aid to P 504
  medical history of the patient M 208d–208e
  medical laboratory tests M 201–02
  medical supplies in the home M 202
  medical terms, selected list D 206
  medicinal plants P 310–15
  mental illness M 222–25
  Nobel prizes N 264–66
  nurses and nursing N 409–13
  occupational medicine, aims of O 16
  opium, early use of N 12
  public health P 502–06
  space research, knowledge gained S 349
  tools and techniques see Medicine, tools and
    techniques of
  veterinarians V 324
  women, role of W 212
  X rays, use of P 206
  See also First aid
Medicine, history of M 203–208c
  ancient Egyptian A 222
  Beaumont's research on human stomach
    B 109
  cancer and cancer research C 89–95
  conquest of disease D 213–18
  fire to drive away evil spirits of disease F 145
  humoral theory in Greek medicine S 62

  medicinal plants P 310–15
  pioneer life P 256
  teamwork on discovery of insulin B 52
  vaccination and inoculation V 260–61
Medicine, tools and techniques of M 208d–211
  Dataphones E 142b
  electronic equipment in hospital intensive care unit,
    picture E 142
  Why must a fever thermometer be shaken? M 208f
Medicine chest M 202
Medicine Hat, Alberta, Canada A 146g
Medicine Lodge, Kansas K 187
Medicine men M 203
  Africa A 56
  American Indians I 171, 179
  witch doctors D 213
Medici (MED-i-chi) **Palace,** Florence, Italy I 465; picture
  I 462
Medici porcelain P 417
Médicis, Catherine de see Catherine de Médicis
Médicis, Marie de see Marie de Médicis
MEDICO see Medical International Cooperation Organiza-
  tion
Medieval architecture see Middle Ages, architecture of
Medieval art see Middle Ages, art of the
Medieval history see Middle Ages
Medieval music see Middle Ages, music of the
Medina (med-DI-na), Saudi Arabia S 48
  Islamic religion established I 414
  Mohammed's flight to M 405
  writing of the Koran K 295
Medinet Habu (ma-DI-net-ha-BU), Egyptian temple E 100
Meditation, listening prayer P 435
Mediterranean (med-it-er-RANE-ean) **climate** E 310
  Spain S 354–55
  types of climate C 345
Mediterranean scrub forest see Maquis
Mediterranean Sea M 212–14
  climate C 345
  continental drift and moving plates of earth's crust
    G 117
  Europe's southern boundary E 307
  Gibraltar, British military fortress G 205
  Malta M 60
Medium, or vehicle, for artist's paints P 30
Medtner, Nikolai, Russian composer U 64
Medulla (me-DUL-la), part of the brain B 366
  function in body control B 282
Medusa (me-DU-sa), monster, one of the Gorgons, in
  Greek mythology G 362
Medusae (me-DU-se), forms of jellyfishes and other
  coelenterates J 70
Meerkats, animals related to mongooses G 93
Meeker, Ezra, American pioneer O 206

Meerschaum (MEER-shum) (from German, meaning "sea
foam"), soft mineral composed of hydrated magnesium
silicate, usually white, sometimes with grayish, yellowish, or blue-green color. Its name stems from its light
weight and porous texture, which enables it to float.
Found mainly in Asia Minor and Greece, it is used
chiefly for tobacco pipes and cigar and cigarette holders.

Meeting at the Golden Gate, painting by Giotto di Bon-
  done R 164
Megacycle (MC) or **megahertz** (MHz), measure of very high-
  frequency radio waves R 56, 58
Megaliths, large stones in prehistoric monuments P 446
  Stonehenge E 214; pictures E 215, W 219
Megalopolis (meg-a-LOP-o-lis), a supercity C 308
  Atlantic states, North America N 296
  Maryland area M 115

Megalosaurs (MEG-a-lo-saurs), dinosaurs **D** 172
Megapodes (MEG-a-podes), or mound builders, birds
B 225
Megaron, room in an ancient Greek palace **G** 340–41
Megatons, or millions of tons **N** 354
Mehemet Ali (ma-HEM-et OL-i), governor of Egypt **E** 92

Meigs (MEGS), **Cornelia Lynde** (1884–1973), American author of children's books, b. Rock Island, Ill. Her first book, *The Kingdom of the Winding Road*, evolved from stories she told her pupils. She also wrote a biography of Louisa May Alcott, *Invincible Louisa*, which won the Newbery medal (1934), and *Dutch Colt*.

Meiji (MAI-ji) **Shrine,** Tokyo
gardens, picture **T** 206
Mein Kampf (mine KOMPF), by Adolf Hitler **H** 139
Meiosis, in genetics, diagram **G** 78

Meir (may-EAR), **Golda** (Goldie Mabovitz Meyerson) (1898–   ), Israeli political leader, b. Kiev, Russia. After growing up in the U.S., she emigrated to Palestine in 1921. One of the signers of Israel's Proclamation of Independence (1948), she served as Israeli ambassador to the Soviet Union (1948–49), minister of labor and social security (1949–52), minister of labor (1952–56), minister of foreign affairs (1949–52), secretary-general of Mapai Labor Party (1966–68), and member of Knesset (parliament). In 1969 she became Israel's fourth prime minister. Picture **W** 212b.
women, role of **W** 213

Meissen (MY-sen), German chinaware, pictures **A** 318, **P** 416
glass tumbler, with view of the city of Meissen, picture **G** 228
Meissen, Germany **G** 157
Meistersingers (MY-ster-singers), German singers, members of guilds **G** 181
German literature, guilds in **G** 174
Meistersinger von Nürnberg, Die, opera by Richard Wagner **O** 149; picture **O** 148

Meitner (MITE-ner), **Lise** (1878–1968), Austrian physicist and mathematician, b. Vienna. With O. Hahn she carried out research in particle physics and discovered the principal isotope of the radioactive element protactinium (1917). In 1939 Miss Meitner and O. Frisch published the correct interpretation of the splitting of the uranium nucleus by bombarding it with neutrons. They showed that a fission reaction had indeed taken place. This research led to development of the atomic bomb.

Mekong (may-KONG) **River,** Asia **R** 244
Cambodia **C** 32
Laos **L** 42
Southeast Asia **S** 328
Vietnam **V** 334a
Melancholy and Mystery of a Street, painting by Giorgio di Chirico **I** 472
Melanchthon (mel-ANCK-thon), **Philipp,** German scholar and religious reformer **E** 67–68
Melanesia (mel-a-NE-sia), Pacific islands **P** 6
art **P** 10
cargo cults **M** 564
See also names of islands
Melanesians, Pacific islanders **P** 4
New Guinea **N** 146
Melanin (MEL-an-in), pigment in hair cells **H** 2

Melba, **Dame Nellie** (Helen Mitchell) (1861–1931), Australian coloratura soprano, b. near Melbourne. After a celebrated debut as Gilda in *Rigoletto* (Brussels, 1887), she won international acclaim. Possessing a voice of exceptional clarity, she excelled in such roles as Lucia in *Lucia di Lammermoor,* Violetta in *La Traviata,* and Marguerite in *Faust.* The title role of *Helene,* by Saint-Saëns, was composed for her. She wrote an autobiography, *Melodies and Memories.*

Melbourne, Australia **M** 215
capital of Victoria **A** 513–14; picture **A** 515
Melbourne, University of, picture **A** 512
Melbourne Cup, horse race **H** 232; **M** 215
Melcher, **Frederic G.,** American publisher
promotion of children's literature **C** 242

Melchior (MELK-i-or), **Lauritz Lebrecht Hommel** (1890–1973), American tenor, b. Copenhagen, Denmark. An outstanding interpreter of Wagnerian roles, he made his operatic debut in 1913, sang with the Royal Opera (1914–21), and frequently appeared at the Bayreuth Festival (1924–31). He was associated with the Metropolitan Opera, New York (1926–50), and he performed in major opera houses in Europe. He also has appeared in films and on TV and radio.

Melds, matched sets in card games **C** 112–13
Melgarejo (mel-ga-RAY-ho), **Mariano,** Bolivian general and dictator (1865–71) **B** 306
Melies (mail-YAYS), **Georges,** French motion-picture producer **M** 472
Melilla, Spanish city, enclave in Morocco **S** 357
Melisande *see* Melusina
Melle (MEL-la), early western African empire **N** 90
Mellette, **Arthur C.,** American statesman **S** 325
Mellon, **Andrew,** American banker and industrialist **P** 143
founded National Gallery of Art, Washington, D.C. **N** 40
Mellon Collection, of art **N** 40

Melloni (mel-LO-ni), **Macedonio** (1798–1854), Italian physicist, b. Parma. He is noted for his studies of infrared radiation and its effect on various substances. He showed that infrared rays are similar to light rays, in that they can be reflected, refracted, and so on. Melloni originated the term "diathermancy," which means the ability to transmit infrared radiation.

Mellorine-type frozen dessert **I** 34
Melodeon (mel-O-de-on), reed organ **O** 208
Melody, in music **M** 522
African **A** 78
ancient music **A** 246
folk music **F** 328
jazz improvisation **J** 62
modern music **M** 399
Oriental music **O** 220d
responsorial singing of American Indians **I** 160
Melons **M** 216–17
fruits we eat **P** 308; picture **P** 309
grown from seeds **G** 52
seeds, picture **P** 298
vegetable gardening **V** 291
Melos (ME-los), or **Milo,** island between Greece and Crete **I** 435

Melpomene (mel-POM-e-ni), goddess in Greek mythology. She and her eight sisters, the daughters of Zeus and Mnemosyne, were the muses, or patrons of the arts and sciences. Melpomene was the muse of tragedy. Her symbols were the tragic mask and the buskin, or high boot worn by actors in the tragedies of ancient times.
See also Muses

Melting, changing from a solid to a liquid **I** 3–4
how icebergs melt **I** 26
Melting point, or fusion **H** 91–92
metals **M** 226
of solids **S** 250–51
properties of water **W** 54
Melting pot
mixed population in United States **U** 132–33
North America **N** 296
Melting Pot of the Pacific, Hawaii **H** 56–72

Melungeons (me-LUN-geons) (probably from French *mélangé* or *mélange*, meaning "mixed" or "mixture"), people of western North Carolina and eastern Tennessee having mixed Indian, white, and possibly Negro blood. In recent years increasing numbers of them have intermarried with surrounding peoples and moved to other areas.

Mélusine (may-lu-SENE), or **Melisande,** in French medieval legend, a water fairy who is claimed to be the ancestor of the houses of Lusignan, Rohan, Luxembourg, and Sassenaye. As punishment for imprisoning her father in a mountain, every Saturday she was turned into a water fairy, half human and half serpent. Her marriage to Raymond, Count of Lusignan, dissolved when he broke his vow never to see her on Saturday. She had to leave him, fated to rove endlessly as a spirit. The legend was written down by Jean d'Arras (1387).

Melville, Herman, American novelist **M** 217–18
American literature **A** 202
Moby Dick, excerpt **M** 217–18
themes of his novels **N** 349
Membranes
body cells **B** 267, 269, 293
cell membranes **C** 163
osmosis process **O** 234–35

Memling, or **Memlinc, Hans** (1430?–1494), German-Flemish painter, b. Seligenstadt, Germany. A student of Rogier van der Weyden, he specialized in portraits and deeply religious paintings. Characteristic works include *Mystic Marriage of St. Catherine* and the portrait of Thomas Portinari and his wife.
Flemish painting, history of **D** 351–52

Memmi, Albert, Tunisian writer **A** 76d

Memnon, in Greek mythology, son of Ethiopian king Tithonus and the goddess of dawn, Aurora. A hero in the Trojan war, he led a large army to aid King Priam of Troy, slew Antilochus, son of the Greek leader Nestor, and was finally killed by Achilles. A statue dedicated to him in Egypt was said to emit a musical sound at each daybreak.

Memorial Day H 151
Memorial Day Sweepstakes A 539
Memory L 105
brain function **B** 369
Do you remember everything you perceive? **P** 493
dreams quickly forgotten **D** 306
hypnosis and posthypnotic suggestion **H** 315
memory bank of sensations **B** 288
psychology **P** 493–94
study, methods of **S** 441
Memory, or storage elements, of computers **C** 450, 452–53
Memphis, capital of ancient Egypt **E** 94
Memphis, Tennessee **T** 85; picture **T** 87
Men see Man
Menageries see Zoos

Menam River see Chao Phraya
Menander (me-NAN-der), Greek author **G** 353
Menard, John W., American political leader, picture **R** 119

Mencius (MEN-shus) (Latinized from Chinese Meng-tzu, meaning "Master Meng") (372?–289 B.C.), Chinese Confucian philosopher, b. present-day Shangtung province. He traveled to many Chinese state courts, boldly explaining Confucian principles to rulers. Believing that men were basically good, he urged princes to fulfill their moral duties by providing for the social and economic welfare of their subjects in order to attain peace. His sayings, compiled in the Book of Mencius, are part of the Confucian Four Books.
Chinese literature **O** 220a

Mencken, Henry L., American writer and critic **A** 215; **M** 126
Mendel, Gregor Johann, Austrian priest and botanist **M** 218–19
genetics and heredity **G** 79–82
start of modern biology **B** 194

Mendeleev (mend-yel-YAY-ef), **Dmitri Ivanovich** (1834–1907), Russian chemist, b. Tobolsk, Siberia. He recognized a relation between atomic weight and chemical properties and so established the periodic table of elements. With some revisions, it is still used today. Element 101, discovered in 1955, was named mendelevium in his honor.
matter and molecules **P** 231
periodic table in the history of chemistry **C** 213; **E** 156

Mendele Moykher Sforim, or **Mendele Mocher Sefarim** see Abramovich, or Abramowitz, Shalom Jacob
Mendelevium (men-del-LE-vi-um), element **E** 155, 162
Mendelian (men-DE-lian) **laws,** of genetics **M** 219
Mendelssohn (MEN-dels-sohn), **Felix,** German composer **M** 219
choral music **C** 278–79
Fingal's Cave **C** 156
Midsummer Night's Dream, A, overture **G** 187
orchestra-conducting tradition **O** 188
romantic concert overtures **R** 311
Mendelssohn, Moses, Jewish philosopher **H** 103

Mendès-France (mon-des-FRONS), **Pierre** (1907–), French lawyer, economist, and politician, b. Paris. Imprisoned by the Vichy administration (1940), he escaped (1941) to serve with the Free French Air Force. He has held many important government posts, including minister of national economy (1944–45), prime minister and minister of foreign affairs (1954–55), and minister of state without portfolio (1956). In 1967–68 he served in the National Assembly.

Mendoza (mend-O-sa), Argentina **A** 391
Menelaus (men-e-LAY-us), Spartan king, husband of Helen of Troy **H** 104
Greek mythology **G** 365
Trojan War **T** 293
Menelik (MEN-e-lik), legendary ancestor of Ethiopian kings **E** 303
Menelik II, ruler of Ethiopia **E** 303
Menena (men-AE-na), king of ancient Egypt
tomb painting, pictures **E** 94

Menéndez de Avilés (may-NEN-dathe day a-bi-LACE), **Pedro** (1519–1574), Spanish naval officer, b. Avilés. Created captain-general of the Indies fleet by Charles V

Menéndez de Avilés, Pedro (continued)
(1554), he led three journeys to America, and established Spanish colonial rule in Florida.
St. Augustine, founding of **F** 273

Menes (ME-nese), or Narmer, king of ancient Egypt, united Upper and Lower kingdoms **E** 94

Mengelberg, Willem (Josef Willem) (1871–1951), Dutch conductor, b. Utrecht. Widely known for his interpretations of Gustav Mahler and Richard Strauss, he gained greatest fame as conductor of Amsterdam Concertgebouw Orchestra. He was forced to leave Netherlands (1945) because of collaboration with Nazis and died in Switzerland.

Meng-tzu see Mencius
Menhaden (men-HAY-den), fish **F** 221
fish oil **O** 79
habitat, feeding habits, uses **F** 214
Meninas (may-NI-nas), **Las,** painting by Velázquez **P** 428

Meningitis (men-in-JY-tis), (from Greek *meninx,* meaning "membrane"), acute inflammation of the membranes (called meninges) of the brain or spinal cord. Meningitis can be caused by many types of germs and viruses. An examination of the cerebrospinal fluid will usually establish the type of infecting organism. Treatment varies according to the infecting agent. Symptoms include headache, vomiting, paralysis, and coma, with fever.

Menkure see Mycerinus
Menninger (MEN-nin-ger), **Karl Augustus,** American doctor and psychiatrist **K** 190
Mennonites, German religious sect **R** 135
Manitoba, Canada **M** 77
Paraguay's Chaco region **P** 62–63
settlements in Kansas **K** 181
Menomini (men-OM-in-i), Indians of North America **I** 178
decontrolled by the U.S. government **I** 200
Menorah (men-OR-ah), eight-branched candlestick, used for Hanukkah **H** 35
Menorca see Minorca Island
Menotti (men-OT-ti), **Gian-Carlo,** Italian-born American composer
Amahl and the Night Visitors, opera **O** 139–40
Festival of Two Worlds **M** 551
opera **O** 139
Mensuration see Measurement
Mental cruelty D 234
Mental health M 220–22
adolescence and changes affecting feelings and emotions **A** 22–24
astronauts in space exploration and travel **S** 341
divorce, problems involving **D** 235
noise and noise control **N** 269–70
See also Mental illness
Mental illness M 222–25
Dix, Dorothea, improves conditions for the insane **D** 235
Freud's theories **F** 469–70
hospital services **H** 249
hypnosis **H** 315
hysteria of witchcraft **W** 209
juvenile delinquency **J** 162–64
noise and noise control **N** 269–70
nursing the emotionally disturbed **N** 410
Pinel, Philippe, first in field of psychiatry **M** 206
psychology and mental illness **P** 488
reserpine, drug from medicinal plant **P** 313
See also Retardation, mental
Mental retardation see Retardation, mental

Mental suggestion
hypnosis **H** 314–16
Mental tests see Tests and testing

Menthol, colorless crystalline substance that has the refreshing smell and taste of mint. Chemically an alcohol, it is soluble in alcohol, ether, chloroform, and basic oils. Obtained from peppermint oil, it can also be prepared synthetically. Menthol is used in making medicine, perfume, candy, cigarettes, and liqueurs.

Mentuhotep II (men-tu-HO-tep), king of ancient Egypt **E** 98, 99

Menuhin, Yehudi (1916–   ), American violinist, b. New York, N.Y. Since the age of 7 he has played with major orchestras and in solo recitals throughout the world. He founded music festivals in Gstaad, Switzerland (1957), and Bath, England (1959).

Menus
camp meals **C** 45
dinner for four **R** 114
Halloween party menu **H** 15
outdoor cooking and picnics **O** 247–48
party refreshments **P** 89
restaurant planning **R** 187
table settings, rules for **T** 2–3

Menzies, Sir Robert Gordon (1894–   ), Australian statesman, b. Jeparit. He was attorney general of Australia (1934–39) and then prime minister and leader of the United Australian Party (1939–41). He again led the United Australian Party, at that time the opposition (1943–49), and was prime minister (1949–66).

Meperidine (Demerol), narcotic drug **N** 12
Mephistopheles (meph-is-TOPH-el-ese), devil in Faust legends **F** 72
Merapi (mer-OP-i), volcano, Japan **V** 384
Mercantile law L 87

Mercator (mer-CAY-tor), **Gerhardus** (Gerhard Kremer) (1512–1594), Flemish geographer, b. Rupelmonde, Belgium. He invented the Mercator system of map projection, in which the parallels of latitude and the meridians of longitude intersect at right angles. The name "atlas" was given to map books because a picture on the cover of his book of maps (published by his son in 1594) showed the Greek god Atlas holding up the world. Mercator was official cosmographer for the duke of Jülichand Cleves in Duisburg.
map projections **M** 92, 93

Mercator projection, of maps **M** 92
Mercenaries, hired soldiers **K** 277
Hessians, Germans who fought for England in Revolutionary War **R** 201, 202
Mercersburg Academy, Pennsylvania
birthplace of James Buchanan, picture **B** 418
Merchandising
advertising **A** 27–34
growth of department stores **D** 118
installment buying **I** 288–89
mail-order **M** 31
retail stores **R** 188–89
selling **S** 116–17
Merchant Adventurers, joint-stock company **P** 344
Merchant guilds G 401
Merchant marine
Maine Maritime Academy **M** 41
ocean liners **O** 17–24

ships and shipping S 155–61
United States Merchant Marine U 182–84
Merchant of Venice, The, play by Shakespeare S 136
Merchant ships S 161
Mercier (mair-ci-AY), **Philippe,** French painter
The Music Party, painting E 269
Mercuric (mer-CU-ric) **oxide** C 210
Mercury, element E 155, 162
absolute zero, effect on H 90
barometer B 54
battery B 99; picture B 98
fish, concentration in F 215, 224, 355
gold extracted from ores by G 249
metals, ores, location, properties, uses M 227
thermometers T 165; and their use M 208f; N 414
unusual properties as a liquid L 310
water pollution W 59
Mercury, planet P 269–70
orbit, diagram R 144
seen from earth both morning and evening S 244–45
space probes of the future S 348
Mercury, Roman god G 360
Mercury, series of manned U.S. space flights S 344, 345
Mercury barometer B 54
Mercury lamps L 287
Mercury-vapor turbines T 322
Mer de Glace (mare d'GLOSS), glacier in France, picture
G 224
Meredith, George, English novelist and poet E 264

Meredith, James H. (1933–), American lawyer, b.
Attala County, Miss. He was the first Negro to enroll
(1961), in the University of Mississippi after passage of
the school desegregation bill. He graduated in 1963, and
from Columbia Law School in 1969. He has been civil
rights leader in New York City and chairman of National
Community Improvement Association, Inc.

Meredith, Sir William Ralph (1840–1923), Canadian jurist,
b. Westminster township, upper Canada. He was a
member of the Legislative Assembly of Ontario
(1872–94), chief justice of the common pleas division of
the High Court of Justice in Ontario (1894–1912), and
chancellor of the University of Toronto (1900–23).

Merengue (mer-EN-gay), Latin-American dance L 74

Mergenthaler (MAIRG-en-ta-ler), **Ottmar** (1854–1899),
American inventor, b. Hachtel, Germany. In 1872 he
immigrated to the United States, where he invented the
linotype printing machine (1884), first used by the New
York *Tribune* (1886). The present-day machine is based on
Mergenthaler's, setting one line at a time.
linotype machines in printing I 345; P 463

Merezhkovski (mair-esh-KOF-ski), **Dmitri Sergeevich**
(1865–1941), Russian novelist and critic, b. St. Petersburg (now Leningrad). He is best-known for his trilogy of
philosophical novels, *Christ and Antichrist,* about Julian
the Apostate, Leonardo da Vinci, and Peter the Great.
Strongly religious (he founded a religion called the New
Road), he opposed the Bolsheviks and was sent to prison
in Siberia (1918). He escaped (1920) and fled to Paris,
where he died during the German occupation.

Mergers and consolidations, businesses T 306
newspapers N 199–200
Merida (MAY-ri-da), **Carlos,** Guatemalan artist
mosaic L 66
Meridian (mer-ID-ian), Mississippi M 360
Meridians, of longitude L 83
Greenwich meridian G 372

International Date Line I 309–10
time T 189–91
Mérimée (may-ri-MAY), **Prosper,** French novelist F 441

Merina (ma-RI-na), or **Hova,** a people occupying the central plateau of Madagascar (Malagasy Republic). Believed
to have migrated from Indonesia, they show a Southeast
Asian influence in language, appearance, and culture.
Primarily a well-educated people, they number about
1,500,000.

Merina Kingdom, now Malagasy Republic M 48
Merino (mer-RI-no), breed of sheep C 145–46
finest wool W 234, 235
Merisi, Michelangelo see Caravaggio
Merit system, in civil service C 317
administration of Chester A. Arthur A 440, 441
Merlin, magician in tales of King Arthur A 443
Mermaids, legendary sea creatures
sea cows mistaken by sailors for mermaids S 106

Merrill, Robert (1919–), American opera singer, b.
Brooklyn, N.Y. After winning the Metropolitan Opera's
Auditions of the Air (1945), he made his Metropolitan
Opera debut (1945) and has since become one of its
foremost baritones. His extensive activities include
concert, nightclub, radio, and TV performances. He has
written an autobiography, *Once More from the Beginning.*

Merrimac, ironclad ship C 323
Merrimack River, Massachusetts M 137
Merritt Parkway, Connecticut C 474
Merry Mount, early settlement in Massachusetts P 346
Merry Widow, The, operetta by Franz Lehár O 158
Merry Wives of Windsor, The, play by Shakespeare S 136

Merton, Thomas (Father M. Louis) (1915–1968), American
Trappist monk, poet, and religious writer, b. Prades,
France. A convert to Roman Catholicism, he entered the
Trappist monastery near Gethsemane, Ky. (1941). Through
his writings he became a famed religious and literary
figure and the object of pilgrimages. Among his writings are *The Seven Storey Mountain* (1949), a best-
selling autobiography; *No Man Is an Island* (1955); and
Mystics and Zen Masters (1967).

Mesa (MAY-sa), Arizona A 412
Mesas, small, high plateaus
Colorado C 403
Mesa Verde (VERD), Colorado C 403
Indian Cliff Palace, pictures A 353, C 413
Mescal (mesc-AL), or century plant I 194
Mescaline, drug obtained from peyote cactus C 4
Meseta (me-SAY-ta), tableland section of Spain
S 352, 354
Meseta Central, Costa Rica C 515, 516
Meshed, Iran I 376

Mesmer, Friedrich, or **Franz, Anton** (1734–1815), Austrian
physician, b. Weil, Germany. After experimenting with
the powers of the magnet for curing illness, he
developed a theory of animal magnetism, mesmerism,
the basis for modern-day hypnosis. Mesmer believed he
possessed supernatural powers. In 1788 he moved to
Paris, where he was denounced as an imposter.

Mesolithic (mes-o-LITH-ic) **age,** or Middle Stone Age
prehistoric man P 445
tools, pictures P 444
Mesons, subatomic particles A 486
cosmic rays C 511
nuclear energy N 367–68

Mesopotamia (mes-o-po-TAY-mia), now Iraq I 378, 383
    ancient art A 233–37, 240–43
    architecture A 372
    art as a record A 438b
    building construction B 435
    ceramics and mosaics P 15
    early agriculture A 95–96
    early cities U 232
    "land between rivers," Tigris and Euphrates R 248
    pottery P 414
    sculpture S 93
    See also Assyria; Babylonia; Sumerians
Mesopotamia, region of Argentina A 392
Mesoscaphe (MES-o-scaph), underwater ship P 244
Mesosphere, upper layer of stratosphere A 480
Mesozoic (mes-o-ZO-ic) Era, in geology F 383, 387
    mammals, origin M 63
    prehistoric animals, development of P 437–38
Mesquakie, Indians of North America I 361

Mesquites (MES-keets), group of thorny shrubs belonging to the pea family. Mesquite plants are found in the deserts of the southwestern United States and of Mexico. The mesquite plant grows only a few feet tall. Its pods, rich in sugar, are used as livestock feed.

Mesquite Area Indians, of North America I 177
Messiah (mes-SY-ah), oratorio by Handel C 278
    German music G 183
    Handel, George Frederick H 26
Messiah, "the anointed one" J 83
Messiah War, 1890 S 327
Messier (mess-YAY), Charles, French astronomer U 199
Mestizos (mes-TI-zos), Latin Americans of Indian and
    European ancestry L 51
    dances L 69
    South America S 282
    See also people section of Latin-American countries

Meštrović (MESH-tro-vich), Ivan (1883–1962), Yugoslav sculptor, b. Vrpolje. He studied in Vienna, then Paris, where he met and was influenced by Rodin. Among his most famous busts is one of the British conductor Sir Thomas Beecham. Meštrović had a one-man show at the Metropolitan Museum of Art in New York in 1947.
    the arts in Yugoslavia Y 355

Metabolic (met-a-BOL-ic) diseases D 189
Metabolism (met-AB-o-lism), in body chemistry B 293
    a life process L 210
    birds B 202
    characteristics of kingdoms of living things K 253–54
Metacomet, Chief see Philip, American Indian chief

Metal fatigue, weakening of metal under exposure to repeated stress. It begins at an imperfection in the metal and shows up as a sharp crack or rift.

Metallic soap O 77
Metallogenetic provinces, areas rich in metallic ores
    M 313
Metalloids, semimetals E 159; M 226
Metallurgy see Metals and metallurgy
Metalpoint pencil, early drawing tool D 303
Metals, transmutation of see Alchemy
Metals and metallurgy (MET-al-urge-y) M 226–33
    alchemy C 207–08
    alloys A 168–69
    aluminum A 176–77
    bronze, early use of B 409
    chromium in alloys C 296
    copper C 502–03

decorative arts D 70, 75
definition of a metal C 219
electric conductors E 125, 127–28
electroplating E 149–50
expansion and contraction of railroad rails, picture
    H 94
fire makes metals F 143
Geiger counters, uses, diagram G 68
gold G 247–49
heat travels through metal, demonstration of E 365
industrial uses of hydrogen gas G 61
iron and steel I 396–408
lead L 94–95
magnesium M 22–23
mines and mining M 313–20
nitrogen gas, inactivity with metals G 59–60
ores R 272–73
phlogiston, theory of C 210
photoelectric metals E 148
silver S 181–82
soldering and brazing S 249–50
tin T 195
tools T 211
welding W 118–19
Where do metals come from? M 226
zinc Z 370
See also Alloys; Mineralogy; Precious metals; Soldering; and names of metals
Metalwork
    bronze B 409
    coppersmithing C 502–03
    decorative arts D 70, 75
    dies and molds D 166–67
    electroplating E 149–50
    goldsmithing G 247–49
    iron and steel I 396–408
    Islamic art I 422
    jewelry J 92–101
    silversmithing S 181–82
    soldering and brazing S 249–50
    tinsmithing T 195
    welding W 118–19
    wire sculpture W 190b, 191
    wrought iron I 405
Metamorphic (met-a-MORPH-ic) rock R 263, 268–70
    mountain building M 493
    petrology (study of rocks), a branch of geology G 112
Metamorphoses (met-a-MORPH-o-sese), mythological narrative poem by Ovid L 80
Metamorphosis M 234–35
    butterflies and moths B 468–78
    eggs that produce larvae E 89
    frogs, toads, and other amphibians F 470–78
    how insects develop I 264–65
    jellyfishes and other coelenterates J 73
Metaphors, figures of speech F 118
    slang S 194
    use in poetry P 354
Metaphysical (met-a-PHIS-ic-al) poets, in English literature E 254–55
Metaphysics, a division of philosophy P 192
Metastases (met-AST-as-ese), cancer growths C 90
Metastasio, Pietro, Italian poet I 479
Metaurus (me-TAUR-us), battle of, 207 B.C. B 100

Metaxas (met-AX-as), Joannes (1871–1941), Greek general and dictator, b. island of Cephalonia. Pro-German, he was dismissed as army chief of staff and forced to leave the country when Greece entered World War I (1917). He returned (1921) to lead a counterrevolution but was again exiled (1923–24). The republic was overthrown (1935), and he became premier (1936). A few months later he gave himself dictatorial powers and in 1938 had himself named premier for life. He died while vigorously opposing Italy's invasion of Greece.

Metchnikoff (METCH-ni-koff), **Élie** (Ilya Illich Mechnikov) (1845–1916), Russian bacteriologist, b. Ivanovka. He discovered the basis for the theory of immunity—the ability of the white corpuscles in the blood to fight disease by destroying bacteria. He became subdirector of Pasteur Institute, Paris (1904). He shared Nobel prize for physiology and medicine (1908) with Ehrlich.

Meteor (ME-te-or), **Crater,** in Arizona C 420–21
Meteoric theory, of lunar craters M 450–51
Meteorology (me-te-or-OL-ogy) W 71–90
   atmosphere A 479–82
   climate, types of C 343–48
   clouds C 358–61
   fog and smog F 288–89
   geology and other earth sciences G 109
   hurricanes and tornadoes, studies of H 292–99
   IGY studies I 316–17
   jet streams J 88–91
   precipitation R 95
   solar energy, main cause of weather S 235
   thunder and lightning T 170–73
   weather control W 91–96
   weather instruments W 79–84
   weather maps W 77–79
   winds and weather W 184–87
Meteors and meteorites C 419–21
   age of E 21
   astronomy, studies in A 476
   Mars M 107
   micrometeoroids, danger to space craft S 342
   moon, effect on its surface M 450–51, 453
   radar astronomy studies R 74
   solar system S 246
   space dust D 347
   trails taken for flying saucers F 286
Meter, in music M 531–32
Meter, in poetry P 353–54
Meter, measure of length W 114–16
Metered postage P 409
Meter-kilogram-second, system of measurement W 117
Meters, electric and gas, diagrams P 511
Methadone, man-made drug N 14
Methane (METH-ane), gas G 59
   coal mining danger C 366–67
Methedrine, drug D 330
Methodist Church C 288, 289
   Reformation in England R 135
   Wesley, John W 125
Methodius, Saint see Cyril and Methodius, Saints

Methuselah (me-THU-ze-lah) ("man of the dart"), longest-living person in the Bible. Son of Enoch, father of Lamech, and grandfather of Noah, he is said to have lived 969 years (Genesis).

Methyl (METH-il), or wood, **alcohol** A 147
   distillation D 224–25
   made from synthesis gas G 61

Métis (may-TECE) (French for "half-caste"), Canadians of mixed Indian and European blood, often descended from French fur trappers. Many Métis settled in Red River in the Canadian Northwest after 1818. When the Northwest Territories were annexed to Canada (1869), the threat to the Métis' landholdings, their way of life, and their survival as a group led to the Red River insurrection (1869) and the Northwest Rebellion (1885). The Métis'

defeat brought about their disintegration as a separate group.
   French-Indian peoples of Canada C 73, 74
   Prairie Provinces M 77, 82; S 38h

Metonymy (me-TON-imy), figure of speech F 119
Metric system, a decimal system of measures W 114–16
Metronome, device for keeping time M 533, O 190

Metropolitan (met-ro-POL-it-an) **area,** densely populated area, including a large city (or cities) and the surrounding areas, dependent on the city for livelihood and amusement. According to the U.S. Census Bureau, which specifies that the core city must have a population of at least 50,000, there were well over 200 metropolitan areas in the United States in 1970.
   the Standard Metropolitan Statistical Area U 98

Metropolitan Museum of Art, New York City M 236–37
Metropolitan Opera House, Lincoln Center for the Performing Arts, New York City L 298; picture O 130
Metropolitan Toronto T 227; picture O 120b

Metternich (MET-ter-nick), **Prince Klemens Wenzel Nepomulk Lothar von** (1773–1859), Austrian statesman, b. Coblenz, Germany. As minister of foreign affairs (1809–48), he made Austria a first-rank European power. He was a leading figure at the Congress of Vienna (1814–15), and he also did much to bring about the Holy Alliance, formed by Austria, Russia, and Prussia to suppress revolutionary movements. However, Metternich gradually lost power as revolutionary forces grew, and he was forced to flee Austria in 1848.
   Austria, history of A 525

Meuse River, Europe R 244
Mev, unit of energy in nuclear physics see Electron volt
Mexican hairless, toy dog D 261
Mexican Liberty Bell M 251
Mexican War, 1846–48 M 238–39, 249
   boundary changes T 112
   California C 14, 29
   Carson, Kit C 123
   Grant, Ulysses S. G 294
   Perry, Matthew C. P 156
   Pierce, Franklin P 246
   Polk's administration P 386
   Taylor, Zachary T 35
   territory gained and the slavery question C 448
   United States Navy U 186
   Who were los ninos? M 239
Mexican yam, plant from which cortisone can be extracted P 313; picture P 312
Mexico M 240–50
   Aztec civilization I 195, 197
   corn meal dishes C 507
   Cortes, Hernando C 508
   dances D 30
   favorite foods F 341
   flag F 241
   high yielding cereal grain F 343
   holiday, Mother's Day H 158
   Indian art I 152–57
   Indian folk dances L 69
   Juárez, Benito J 145
   Latin-American art L 67
   life in Latin America L 47–61
   Mayan tomb at Palenque, picture A 352
   Mesquite Area Indians I 177
   Mexican War M 238–39
   Mexico City M 251–53
   national anthem N 22

Mexico (continued)
  Pan-American Highway **P** 50
  patriotic songs **N** 27
  pre-Aztec pyramid, picture **A** 354
  Pyramid of the Sun at Teotihuacán, picture **A** 363
Mexico, Gulf of **A** 113, 115
  embayment of the Mississippi River **M** 365
  mined for minerals dissolved in the water **T** 126
  oil drilling rig, picture **P** 172
  Texas shoreline **T** 125
Mexico, National Autonomous University of **M** 240, 253
Mexico City, capital of Mexico **M** 251–53; picture **L** 48
  National Museum of Anthropology, picture **M** 516
  Paseo de Reforme, picture **N** 298
  Plaza of Three Cultures, picture **M** 250
Meyer, Debbie, American swimming star, picture **O** 116
Meyer, Hannes, Swiss architect **B** 104

Meyerbeer (MY-er-bare), **Giacomo** (Jakob Liebmann Beer) (1791–1864), German opera composer, b. Berlin. He is remembered chiefly for his elaborate grand operas, which include *Robert le Diable, Les Huguenots, Le Prophète,* and *L'Africaine.* He also wrote songs, marches, and other works. His treatment of opera as a stage spectacle influenced Richard Wagner.
  foreign-born composers in France **F** 445

Meyerson, Goldie Mabovitz see Meir, Golda
Mezuzah (mez-UZ-ah), Jewish religious symbol **J** 116, 120
Mezzanine, first level above orchestra in theaters **T** 156
Mezzetin (mez-za-TAN), painting by Watteau **F** 424
Mezzo-soprano (met-zo-so-PRAN-o), female voice **C** 277
  voice training and singing **V** 375
Mezzotint (MET-zo-tint), technique of print making **G** 307
MHD generators see Magnetohydrodynamic generators
Miacis (MY-a-cis), prehistoric ancestor of carnivores **D** 243
Miami (my-AM-i), Florida **M** 254
  cities of Florida **F** 270
Miami Beach, Florida **M** 254; picture **F** 271
Miami University, Oxford, Ohio **O** 68

Miantonomo (mi-an-to-NO-mo) (?–1643), Narragansett Indian chief. Cleared in Boston of charges of hostility against the English (1636), he aided the colonists in the Pequot War (1637). He concluded a peace pact with the English and Mohegan chief Uncas (1638), and deeded island of Rhode Island to William Coddington (1638). In Narragansett war with Mohegans (1643) he was captured by Uncas and delivered to hostile English officials, who tried him and returned him to Uncas for execution.

Mica (MY-ca), mineral
  crystals, picture **R** 265
  mica schist, rock, picture **R** 268
Micah (MY-cah), book of Bible, Old Testament **B** 155
Micah, Hebrew prophet **J** 105
Mice, marsupial (pouched), picture **K** 173
Mice, rodents **R** 277–78
  aging experiment **A** 85, 87
  cancer research, use in **C** 93; pictures **C** 91, 94
  experiment set up with a control **E** 353–54
  forelimb, picture **F** 80
  household pests **H** 263–64
  "Lion and the Mouse, The," fable by Aesop **F** 4
  pets **P** 179–80
  tracks, picture **A** 271

Michael (from Hebrew, meaning "who is like God"), in the Bible, an archangel who battled Satan and other evil angels. He fought with the devil over Moses' body (Jude

9) and defended the Israelites against the spirit princes of Greece and Persia (Daniel 10:13, 20–21).

Michael (Mihai) (1921–   ), king of Rumania (1927–30, 1940–47), b. Sinaia. He ascended the throne following the death of his grandfather Ferdinand I (1927). Replaced by his father, Carol II (1930), who had previously yielded his claim (1925), Michael regained the throne (1940) when Carol II was forced to abdicate under German pressure. Michael helped overthrow the Facist dictator Ion Antonescu and declared war on Germany (1944), but he finally abdicated (1947) after the establishment of Communism.
  Rumania, history of **R** 360

Michaux (mi-SHO), **Ernest,** French builder of early bicycle **B** 173
Michel, Curtis, American astronaut **S** 347
Michelangelo (my-kel-AN-gel-o), Italian artist **M** 255–57
  art of the artist **A** 438f
  Creation of Adam, painting **M** 255
  David, statue **I** 468, **S** 100
  Italian art and architecture **I** 468, 469
  lyric poetry **I** 478
  Madonna and Child sculpture **R** 168
  monumental style of painting **P** 21
  Moses, statue **S** 100
  paintings of prophets **B** 158
  Pietà, at New York World's Fair, 1964–65 **F** 17
  Raphael influenced by Michelangelo **R** 106
  Renaissance, golden age of the arts **R** 162
  Renaissance art and architecture **R** 167, 169
  sculpture, place in the history of **S** 100–01
  work criticized by El Greco **G** 330
Michelangelo, S. S., ocean liner **O** 19; pictures **O** 18, 21

Michelozzo (mi-kel-OTZ-so) **de Bartolommeo** (1396–1472), Italian architect and sculptor, b. Florence. Associated with Ghiberti and Donatello in the development of Renaissance art, Michelozzo is chiefly remembered for his masterpiece, the Medici Palace in Florence.
  Medici Palace, Florence **I** 465; picture **I** 462
  Renaissance palaces **A** 381

Michelson (MY-kel-son), **Albert Abraham** (1852–1931), American physicist, b. Strelno, Prussia. Michelson made accurate measurements of the speed of light and developed a number of important optical devices, among them the interferometer. With this device he and E. W. Morley conducted a famous experiment (first done in 1881) to determine the earth's speed through the "ether," which was thought to fill an "absolute" space. Their work led to the abandonment of these concepts and influenced the development of the theory of relativity. Michelson received the 1907 Nobel prize in physics.
  speed of light and relativity **L** 266; **R** 140–41

Michelson-Morley experiment, on the ether concept **R** 140–41

Michener, James Albert (1907–   ), American novelist, b. New York, N.Y. As associate editor for Macmillan Company (1941–49), he wrote numerous articles on social studies education. His books include the short story collection *Tales of the South Pacific,* which received the Pulitzer prize (1948) and was adapted to the stage as *South Pacific.* He also wrote the novels *The Bridges at Toko-ri* and *Hawaii,* which have been made into films, and *The Source.*

Michener, (Daniel) Roland (1900–   ), Canadian statesman,

b. Lacombe, Alberta. An Oxford graduate (1922), Michener received an Ontario law degree in 1924. He was elected to the Ontario legislature (1945–48) and was a member of the Canadian Parliament (1953–62), where he was twice elected Speaker of the House of Commons (1957, 1958). Michener later served as Canada's High Commissioner to India (1964–65) and as ambassador to Nepal (1965–67). In 1967 he was appointed governor-general of Canada.

Michigan (MISH-i-gan) **M** 258–73
Detroit **D** 150–51
places of interest in Negro history **N** 94
Michigan, Lake, one of Great Lakes **G** 327–28; **I** 73
Chicago located on **C** 227; picture **C** 229
discovered by Jean Nicolet **N** 250
Michigan, University of, at Ann Arbor **M** 267
Michigan State University at East Lansing M 267
Mickey Mouse, cartoon character **A** 297
Micmac, Indians of North America **I** 171–72
Micombero, Michel, Burundi president **B** 464
Microbes (MY-crobes) **M** 274–75
antibiotics, microbe drugs **A** 310, 312, 315; pictures **A** 314
bacteria, micro-organisms or microbes **B** 9–13
viruses **V** 361–70a
Microbiology M 274–82
bacteria, micro-organisms or microbes **B** 9–13
drugs fight harmful microbes **D** 326–27
food chains **L** 241
Koch, Robert **K** 293
plankton **P** 279–81
viruses **V** 361–70a
Microcards, information storage technique **L** 174
uses of photography **P** 206

Microchemistry, analysis of very tiny amounts of chemical substances by means of special techniques and equipment. Microchemical methods were first developed by Austrian chemist Friedrich Emich.

Microfiches (MY-cro-fi-shes), information storage technique **L** 174
Microfilm, in photography. **P** 205–06
information storage technique for libraries **L** 174
photocopying by office machines **O** 58
Microliths, flint tools **P** 445; picture **P** 444
Micrometeoroids (my-cro-ME-te-or-oids), very small particles moving through space **S** 340i, 342

Micrometer (my-CROM-et-er), instrument designed for making very fine measurements, on the order of 1/1000 inch. Some micrometers are accurate to 1/10000 inch. A micrometer caliper is used in manufacturing to measure the thickness of objects. Micrometers are also used in microscopes and telescopes to measure the diameters of images.

Micronesia (my-cro-NE-sia), Pacific islands **P** 6
art **P** 10
Micronesians, Pacific islanders **P** 4
Microns, units of measure
dust measured by **D** 346–47
Micro-organisms (my-cro-OR-gan-isms) **M** 274–75
bacteria **B** 9
fermentation **F** 89–90
food preservation, canning process, history of **F** 345
food spoilage **F** 352–54
Pasteur's work with wine and milk **P** 96
smallest forms of plant and animal life **A** 265
soils, countless numbers in **S** 232
viruses **V** 361–70a

Microphones, used in transmitting sound **T** 56
hi-fi recording process **H** 125
phonograph recording **P** 198; pictures **P** 197
radio and radio broadcasting **R** 55
Microphotography see Microfilm, in photography
Microscopes M 283–88
development of, as aid to biologists **B** 190
Galileo perfected compound microscope **G** 6
how to make a water-drop microscope **E** 363
Leeuwenhoek's new world **L** 127; **M** 274
lenses **L** 147–48, 265
medicine, early uses in **M** 206
optical instruments **O** 166–67
science, advances in **S** 69
Microscopy see Clinical microscopy; Electron microscopy
Microtechniques, in libraries **L** 174
Microwave radio relay systems
carrier telephony **T** 59, 60
telegraph **T** 54
Microwaves
electronic communication **E** 142e
masers **M** 131
radar's use of electric waves **L** 271
television **T** 67

Midas (MY-das), in Greek mythology, king of Phrygia and son of Gordius and Cybele. In return for Midas' kindness to Dionysus' teacher Silenus, Dionysus granted Midas his request that all he touched would turn to gold. When even his food became gold, he implored Dionysus for relief and was directed to bathe in river Pactolus, which has since had golden sands. Later, when he chose Pan's music in a contest between Apollo and Pan, Apollo gave him asses' ears for his poor taste.

Mid-Atlantic Ridge, in Atlantic Ocean **A** 478
mid-ocean ridge of the ocean floor **O** 29
underseas mountains **E** 15; **M** 499
Middens see Kitchen middens
Middle Ages M 289–95
agriculture **A** 96
alchemy and beginnings of chemical industry **C** 194
architecture see Middle Ages, architecture of the
armor **A** 433–35
art see Middle Ages, art of the
bell music **B** 136
bookmaking, art of **B** 319–21
building construction **B** 435
castles **F** 375
Charlemagne **C** 189–90
Christianity, history of **C** 284–85
cities **C** 307; **U** 232
citizenship idea replaced by feudal system **C** 311
court jesters **J** 133
craft-guild labor system **G** 401–03
Crusades **C** 538–40
dance manias **D** 24
decorative arts **D** 70, 75
dueling tournaments **D** 339–40
education **E** 65–67
England **E** 217–19
European science **S** 65–66
fairs and expositions **F** 10
feudalism **F** 99–103
flags **F** 225, 243
German art and architecture **G** 165–66
guilds **G** 401–03
heraldry **H** 115–18
Holy Roman Empire **H** 161–64
homes **H** 178
Hundred Years War **H** 281–82
jewelry for religious decorations **J** 94

Middle Ages (continued)
  Jews persecuted in Europe **J** 108
  knights, knighthood, and chivalry **K** 272–77
  knives, forks and spoons **K** 286–87
  labor movement, how it began **L** 2, 3
  libraries **L** 195–96
  medical knowledge **M** 204–05
  medieval engineering **E** 208
  music *see* Middle Ages, music of the
  religious drama **D** 295
  Roman Catholic Church **R** 291
  trials by ordeal **C** 526
  writing, art of, preserved by monks
    C 431
  See also Feudalism
Middle Ages, architecture of the **M** 296–97
  art as a record **A** 438e
  castles **F** 375
  cathedrals **C** 130–33
  cities **C** 307; **U** 232
  Gothic art and architecture **G** 264–72
  Italian architecture **I** 460, 463
Middle Ages, art of the **M** 296–97
  art, the meanings of **A** 438
  art as a record **A** 438b, 438c, 438e
  France **F** 421
  furniture design **F** 505
  Giotto di Bondone **G** 211
  illuminated manuscripts **I** 87–88
  illustration of books **I** 89–90
  Italian art and architecture **I** 458, 460, 463
  Kells, Book of **K** 202
  painting **P** 17–20
  stained glass windows **S** 393–95
Middle Ages, music of the **M** 298–99
  France **F** 443

Middle America, geographical term referring to Central America, Mexico, and sometimes the Caribbean islands.

Middlebury College, Vermont **V** 316; picture **V** 314
Middle classes, of people **M** 292–93
Middlecoff, Cary, American golfer, picture **G** 261
Middle East **M** 300–08
  Arab-Israeli wars **E** 92; **I** 444–45; **J** 113, 139
  agriculture **A** 92
  southwestern region of Asia **A** 450
  music **O** 221
  World War I, term used was "Near East" **W** 275
  World War II **W** 290
  See also names of countries
Middle English, language **E** 244
  literature **E** 247–50
Middle High German, language **G** 172
Middle latitudes *see* Mid-latitudes
Middle Low German, language **G** 172
Middlemarch, novel by George Eliot **N** 346
Middlemen, in trade **T** 243
Middle names **N** 7

Middle Passage, ship route between the West African coast and the West Indies used in colonial American slave trade. On one "triangular" journey, slave traders sailed from New England to West Africa, exchanged commodities for slaves, returned via the "middle passage," and traded the slaves for goods in the West Indies. Conditions aboard ship on the passage were notoriously harsh, and numerous Africans, crammed into ship holds, succumbed to disease and death.
  Atlantic crossing of slave ships **N** 91; **S** 197

Middle schools, or intermediate schools **S** 58

Middle Stone Age, or Mesolithic age
  prehistoric man **P** 445
  tools, pictures **P** 444
Middle Temple *see* Inns of Court

Middleton, Arthur (1742–1787), American Revolutionary war leader, b. near Charleston, S.C. He served in the South Carolina House of Assembly (1764–68, 1772). Engaging in revolutionary activity (from 1772), he helped formulate the South Carolina constitution (1776), served in the Continental Congress (1776–78, 1781–83), and signed the Declaration of Independence (1776).

Middleton, Thomas (1570?–1627), English dramatist, b. probably London. He wrote plays with several partners, and *The Changeling* (written with William Rowley) is one of the most powerful tragedies of the early 17th century.

Middleton Gardens, near Charleston, South Carolina **S** 306; picture **S** 307
Middletown, U.S.A., Muncie, Indiana **I** 149
Middle Way, Swedish blend of democracy and socialism **S** 486
Middleweight, in boxing **B** 352
Middle West
  local color in American literature **A** 205, 208
Middlings, by-product of flour milling **F** 275
Midges, gnats **H** 260
Midget-auto racing **A** 539
  midget racer, model, picture **A** 535

Midianites (MID-ian-ites), in the Old Testament, a nomadic people who lived in the northwestern Arabian desert, east of the Gulf of Aqaba. They were the descendants of Midian, a son of Abraham and Keturah. Joseph was taken to Egypt by Midianite traders, and Moses married Zipporah, a daughter of Midianite leader Jethro. During the rule of the Judges, Israel was invaded by Midianites, who were finally expelled by Gideon (Judges 6–8).

Midlands Federation of Car Clubs **A** 537
Midlands region, of England **E** 213
Mid-latitudes, or temperate zones **Z** 372–73
  prairies **P** 430–33
Midnight, start of a new day **T** 188
Midnight Special, railroad song **F** 319
Midnight Sun, Land of the *see* Land of the Midnight Sun
Mid-oceanic ridges, of mountains **O** 29–30; diagram **G** 121
Mid-ocean rifts **O** 29
  underseas mountains **E** 15
Midrashim (mid-RA-shim), ancient Hebrew literature **H** 101
Midribs, of leaves **L** 114
Midshipmen, at U.S. Naval Academy **U** 191
Midsummer Night's Dream, A, play by Shakespeare **M** 309; **S** 132
  ballet, picture **D** 25
  outline of the plot **S** 136
Midway, amusement area of fairs **F** 15
Midway, battle of, 1942 **W** 294–95
Midway Islands, atolls in central Pacific Ocean **P** 6
  near Kure Island, Hawaii **H** 58
  occupied by United States **T** 113
Midway rails, extinct birds **B** 231
Midwest Inter-Library Center **L** 178
Midwest Stock Exchange **C** 230

Miers, Earl Schenck (1910–   ), American author, b. Brooklyn, N.Y. Mr. Miers is a graduate of Rutgers University, and his particular interest is history. Among his books for younger readers are *America and Its Presidents, Our Fifty States,* and *Rainbow Book of American History.*

Mies van der Rohe (ME-es von d'RO-e), **Ludwig** (1886–1969), American architect, b. Aachen, Germany. Last director of the Bauhaus, he closed the German art school in 1933 because of Nazi pressure. He went to the United States in 1937 and became a citizen in 1944. He was tremendously influential in the development of modern skyscraper architecture. His most famous building is New York's Seagram Building (1958), which he designed with his student Philip Johnson.
architecture in the 20th century **A** 386
Barcelona chair, picture **D** 73
Bauhaus **B** 104–05
modern furniture **F** 510
Seagram Building, New York City, picture **A** 386
United States, architecture of the **U** 125

Mieszko I (mi-ESH-ko), Polish ruler **P** 361

Mifflin, Thomas (1744–1800), American Revolutionary leader, b. Philadelphia, Pa. A radical political leader, he sat in the Pennsylvania provincial assembly (1772–76) and in the Continental Congress (1774–76, 1782–84), serving as its president from 1783 to 1784. The quartermaster general of American forces (1775–78), attaining the rank of major general (1777), he was implicated in a plot to supplant Washington with Horatio Gates but denied involvement and resigned from the Army (1779). He was the first governor of Pennsylvania (1790–99).

Mighty Fortress, A, hymn, words and music **H** 310, 311
Mighty Handful, Russian group of musicians **U** 63, 64

Migraine (MY-graine) (from Greek *hemikrania,* "half cranium"), severe recurrent head pain, usually on one side of the head. An attack of migraine is often preceded by blurring of the vision and an impression of flashing lights, and it may be accompanied by nausea. An attack may last minutes or days.

Migrant farm workers **F** 49
fruit harvesting **F** 484
Migration, of animals see Homing and migration
Migration, of people **P** 394
Indians of North America **I** 162–63
overland trails, United States **O** 251–67
pioneer "movers" to western United States **P** 252
See also Immigration and emigration
Migratory agriculture **J** 155–56; **Z** 367
milpa practices in the Congo **Z** 366a
rain forest **R** 100

Mihajlović (mi-HY-lo-vich), **Draža** (1893?–1946), Yugoslav general, b. Ivanitza, Shumadya, Serbia. During World War II he organized (1941) the Chetniks to fight against German and Italian armies of occupation and was appointed (1942) minister of war and head of the army by the exiled Yugoslav Government. The Chetniks and Tito's Partisans, a more active resistance force, refused to co-operate. Helped by the Allies, Tito's forces gained control and arrested (1946) Mihajlović. Accused of collaborating with the enemy, he was tried, convicted, and executed in Belgrade.
opposed Tito **T** 199
Yugoslavia, history of **Y** 358

Mikado (mi-KA-do), **The,** operetta by Gilbert and Sullivan **G** 210; picture **G** 211

Mikan (MY-kan), **George Lawrence** (1924–   ), American basketball player, b. Joliet, Ill. As a student at De Paul University (1941–46) the 6 ft. 9 in. athlete was considered the best college basketball player in the country. He played professional basketball (1946–54) and was on six championship teams, maintaining a per game average of 22.6 points. An Associated Press poll (1950) voted him the greatest basketball player of the first half of the 20th century, and he was one of the first players elected to the Basketball Hall of Fame (1960).

Mikhalkov (mi-HALL-koff), **Sergey,** Russian poet **N** 19

Mikoyan (mi-ka-YON), **Anastas Ivanovich** (1895–   ), Soviet administrator, b. Sanain, Armenia. He joined Communist Party in 1915, fought in the Russian civil war (1917–20), became an active Communist organizer, and held a number of important party offices. He was minister of foreign trade (1946–49) and became first deputy chairman of the Soviet Council of Ministers (1955). Mikoyan has been a member of the Presidium of the Supreme Soviet since 1952 and its chairman (1964–65).

Mil, unit of measurement **F** 104
Milan (mi-LON), **Edict of,** A.D. 313 **R** 289
Constantine **C** 489
Roman Catholic Church, history of **R** 308
Milan, Italy **I** 450; picture **I** 449
Renaissance, growth of city states **R** 157
Milan, Cathedral of, picture **C** 132

Milbank Memorial Fund, fund established "to improve the physical, mental, and moral condition of humanity." It concentrates its activities on public health and preventive medicine. It was founded (1905) by Elizabeth Milbank Anderson. Headquarters is in New York, N.Y.

Mildew, fungi **F** 498
Mile, measure of distance **W** 111, 113
nautical mile **W** 113, 115
Mile-High City, Denver, Colorado **D** 116
cities of Colorado **C** 412–13

Miles, Nelson Appleton (1839–1925), American army officer, b. near Westminster, Mass. After leading successful campaigns against Indian tribes in the West and receiving Medal of Honor (1892) for his services in the Civil War he was appointed (1895) commander in chief of United States Army. He organized an expedition to Cuba during Spanish-American War, dictated terms of the Spanish surrender, and led expedition to Puerto Rico. His several books include *Serving the Republic.*
Chief Joseph and General Miles **I** 67

Milford Sound, New Zealand, picture **N** 237

Milhaud (mi-YO), **Darius** (1892–   ), French composer, b. Aix-en-Provence. He has taught and conducted in the United States and France (since 1940). With French playwright Paul Claudel he wrote the opera *Christophe Colomb* and operas from Claudel's adaptation of the Aeschylus trilogy *Oresteia.* A versatile composer, known as one of Les Six, a group of French composers, his other works include ballets, symphonies, chamber works, piano, and vocal music.
French music **F** 448

Milhous, Katherine (1894–   ), American author and illustrator of children's books, b. Philadelphia, Pa. She served as staff artist on the Philadelphia *Record* (1925–29). Her travels through the Pennsylvania Dutch country and in Europe and South America furnished

Milhous, Katherine (continued)
material for many of her drawings and books, including *Lovina*, and *The First Christmas Crib*. Her book *The Egg Tree* was awarded the Caldecott medal in 1951.

Millais (mil-LAY), **Sir John Everett** (1829–1896), English painter, b. Southampton. A child prodigy, he became a fashionable portrait and historical painter and a founder of the Pre-Raphaelite movement, a group of artists who favored medieval and early Italian painting. He later became less concerned with the ideas of the movement. His works include *Christ in the House of His Parents*.
  Pre-Raphaelite Brotherhood **E** 241

Millay (mil-LAY), **Edna St. Vincent**, American poet
  A 210; **M** 45

Milles (MIL-les), **Carl** (Vilhelm Carl Emil Anderson) (1875–1955), Swedish sculptor, b. near Uppsala. He was influenced by Rodin. His dramatic figures are often set in fountains that form parts of buildings. He designed the fountain at the Metropolitan Museum of Art and sculptures at Rockefeller Center, New York, N.Y.

Millet, hardy, small-seed cereal grass. The grain is a staple food in parts of Asia and Africa. The whole plant is used to feed cattle. It is used in the United States and Europe for forage and for birdseed.
  cereal grains and grasses **G** 285, 287, 318
  seeds, pictures **G** 284

Millet (mil-LAY), **Jean François**, French painter **F** 426

Millett, Katharine Murray (Kate) (1934–), American feminist, b. St. Paul, Minn. She is considered the foremost theorist of the Women's Liberation Movement and is the author of *Sexual Politics*, a work which is credited with having given stature to the movement. She is married to Fumio Yoshimuro, a sculptor, but continues to use her maiden name.

Millibars, international unit of atmospheric pressure
  W 82

Millikan, Robert Andrews (1868–1953), American physicist, b. Morrison, Ill. He was the first to isolate the electron, to show that it carried a constant charge, and to measure this charge. For this work he was awarded the Nobel prize in physics in 1923. He also studied X rays and the high-energy rays from outer space, which he named cosmic rays. Among his books are *The Electron* and *Science and the New Civilization*.

Millimeter (MILL-i-me-ter), measure of length **W** 114–15

Millin, Sarah Gertrude Liebson (1889–1968), South African writer, b. Russia. As a child she went to South Africa, where she wrote many novels of life in that country, such as *God's Stepchildren* and *The Burning Man*. She also wrote biographies of South African statesmen Cecil Rhodes and Jan Christiaan Smuts, the history *The People of South Africa*, and war diaries.

Mills, Robert (1781–1855), American architect and engineer, b. Charleston, S.C. After designing the former State House, Harrisburg, Pa. (1810), he designed the country's first important monument to George Washington, in Baltimore. Thereafter his style became simpler, neoclassical, and less influenced by baroque architecture. At the apex of his career (1836–51) he worked in Washington, D.C., where he designed the Washington Monument and the Treasury and Post Office buildings.

Mills, Wilbur Daigh (1909–   ), American legislator, b. Kensett, Arkansas. Mills ran for the first public office in 1934, becoming the youngest county judge in Arkansas history. In 1938 he was elected to Congress, and in 1957 he assumed the chairmanship of the influential House Ways and Means Committee.

Milluni (mi-YU-ni), **Lake,** South America, picture **S 274**

Milne, A. A. (Alan Alexander Milne) (1882–1956), English author, b. London. Inspired by his young son Christopher Robin, he wrote in prose *Winnie-the-Pooh* and *The House at Pooh Corner* and in verse *Now We Are Six* and *When We Were Very Young*. Also an accomplished playwright, Milne wrote *Mr. Pim Passes By, The Dover Road,* and *The Truth About Blayds*. He was associate editor (1906–14) of *Punch* magazine.
   Shepard drawing for *Winnie-the-Pooh* **I 97**

Milo (MY-lo), Greek athlete **O 105**
Milo (MI-lo), or **Melos,** island between Greece and Crete **I 435**
Milpa agriculture see Migratory agriculture

Milstein, Nathan (1904–   ), American violinist, b. Odessa, Russia. He left the Soviet Union in 1925, gave concerts in Europe, and made his American debut in 1929. He is noted for his brilliant technique and for his interpretations of the classical violin repertory.

Milton, John, English poet **M 311**
   freedom of the press upheld in his *Areopagitica* **E 255**
   place in English literature **E 255**
   sonnets **S 256**
Milwaukee (mil-WAU-kee), Wisconsin **M 312**
   downtown Milwaukee, picture **W 204**
Milwaukee Depth, deepest area of Atlantic Ocean **A 478**
Milkweed, plant
   controls migration of butterflies **B 470**
Mime (MI-may), or **Regin,** dwarf in Norse mythology **N 280–81**
Mimeograph, a duplicating machine **O 57;** picture **O 56**
Mimicry (MIM-ic-ry)
   humor **H 279**
   insect protective device **I 275**
   "talking" birds **P 83**
Mimosa, tree
   leaves, responses to light, picture **P 301**

Min, Queen (?–1895), wife of the king of Korea. Member of a powerful family that had helped to rule Korea for generations, she fought Japanese attempts to run the Korean Government after the Sino-Japanese War (1894–95). Assassinated by the Japanese, she became a symbol of Korean opposition to Japan.

Minarets (min-a-RETS), towers of mosques **I 416**
   Islamic architecture **I 419**
   mosque of al-Madressa, picture **Y 348**
   Taj Mahal **T 14**
Mince pie, Christmas dessert **C 292**
Mind **P 491–92**
   dreaming **D 305–07**
   extrasensory perception **E 394–96**
   hypnosis **H 314–16**
   memory **L 105**
   mental health **M 220–22**

   mental illness **M 222–25**
   sleep **S 200–01**
   See *also* Brain
Mindanao (min-da-NA-o), Philippines **P 186–87**
   Mindayan hat, picture **H 53**
Mindoro, Sea of see Sulu Sea
Mind reading, a kind of estrasensory perception **E 394**
Mind-reading tricks **T 288**
   digit problem **M 21**

Mindszenty (MINT-sen-ty), **Joseph, Cardinal** (1892–   ), Hungarian Roman Catholic churchman, b. Csehimind-szent. Archbishop of Esztergom and Primate of Hungary, he was elevated to the rank of cardinal in 1946. Sentenced to life imprisonment by the Hungarian Communist regime in 1949, he was released during the short-lived anti-Communist revolution of 1956. He was then granted asylum in the U.S. Legation in Budapest until 1971, when he left Hungary.

Mine Health and Safety Act, 1969 **C 367**
Mineral collecting **R 273**
Mineral dressing, of ores **M 227–28**
Mineralogy (min-er-OL-ogy), study of minerals
   early work in geology **G 111**
Mineral oils **O 76**
   cosmetic creams made of **C 510**
Minerals and mineral resources **R 270–72**
   Africa **A 52–53**
   Asia, unexploited resources **A 450**
   Australia **A 508**
   collecting minerals **R 273**
   conservation of **C 482–83**
   definition of a mineral **C 219**
   deserts rich in **D 127**
   drugs supply to body **D 326, 327**
   Europe **E 315**
   gemstones **G 68–76**
   geological formations **G 111**
   magnesium, sources of **M 23**
   mineral fibers **N 425**
   mines and mining **M 313–20**
   mountain resources **M 498**
   North America, metallic and non-metallic minerals **N 292–94**
   nutrition, requirements for **N 416–17**
   ocean water **E 16**
   soils **S 230**
   South America **S 279**
   world distribution **W 260–61**
   See *also* natural resources section of continent, country, province, and state articles
Minerva (min-ER-va), Roman goddess **G 361**
Mines, Bureau of, United States **C 485**
Mines, explosives
   mine warfare ships of U.S. Navy **U 192–93**
Mines and mining **M 313–20**
   Africa **A 64**
   Canada **C 56**
   coal mining **C 364–68**
   diamonds **D 153–54**
   dredges used in **D 309, 310**
   explosives used in **E 393**
   General Mining Laws, 1872, aid conservation **C 485**
   gold **G 249**
   iron ore **I 404**
   miner's safety fuse **E 390**
   mining engineers **E 205**
   open-pit copper mines, pictures **C 252, N 59, 129**
   open-pit iron mine, largest **M 330**
   Pocahontas Exhibition Mine, West Virginia **W 133**
   safety lamp invented by Davy **D 46**

Mines and mining (continued)
  salt **S** 20
  silver **S** 181–82
  South America **S** 292–93
  underwater mining **U** 21
  See also names of specific types of mines and mining,
    as Coal and coal mining; country, province, and state
    articles
Minesweepers
  United States Navy **U** 192
Ming dynasty, ancient rule of China **C** 269, 270–71
Minho (MEEN-yo) **River,** Spain and Portugal **P** 400
Miniature cameras **P** 203
  wide-angle and telephoto lenses, pictures **P** 213
Miniatures, in illuminated manuscripts **I** 87
  medieval painting **P** 17–18
Minie (MIN-e) **ball,** gun bullet **G** 420
Minimum wages
  labor unions **L** 5, 18
Mining see Mines and mining
Mining Act, 1866 **P** 507
Mink, animals of mustelid family **O** 244
  furs **F** 518–19
  in cages on a fur farm, picture **F** 513
  mutations for fur colors **F** 514
Minneapolis (min-ne-AP-olis), Minnesota **M** 321; picture
    M 335
  Tyrone Guthrie Theatre, picture **T** 155
Minnehaha Falls, in Minneapolis, Minnesota **M** 333
Minnesingers (MIN-ne-singers), medieval German singers
    G 181
Minnesota (min-ne-SO-ta) **M** 322–37
  eskers, snakelike ridges left by glaciers, picture **I** 14
  Minneapolis-Saint Paul **M** 321
Minnesota, University of **M** 331
Minnesota River **M** 325
Minoan (mi-NO-an) **civilization,** of ancient Crete
    A 227
  architecture **A** 238, 373–74
  art **A** 237–38; **P** 15–16; pictures **A** 236
  art as a record **A** 438b
  sculpture **S** 94
Minorca (min-OR-ca) **Island,** Spain **I** 427
Minority groups, in the United States
  American Indians **I** 200–200b
  poverty in urban ghettos **P** 424a
Minority leaders, in Congress **U** 144
Minor leagues, in baseball **B** 77
  Little League Baseball **L** 317
Minor seconds, in music **M** 527
Minos (MY-nos), in Greek myth, king of Crete
    G 365
  in story from *Tanglewood Tales* **H** 74–76
  palace in Knossos, pictures **A** 226, 355
Minot (MY-not), North Dakota **N** 335
Minotaur (MIN-o-taur), monster in Greek myth
    G 365
  in story from *Tanglewood Tales* **H** 74–76
Minsk, capital of Belorussia **B** 138
Minstrels, or **jongleurs,** medieval entertainers.
  Africa's bards and minstrels **A** 76a
  early communication method **C** 430
  music of the Middle Ages **M** 298
  storytellers **S** 434
Mint, aromatic plant used for flavoring, picture **S** 381
  herbs and spices **S** 382
Mint, place where money is coined
  some early mints **M** 338
Mint, United States Bureau of the **M** 338
  See also United States Mint
Mint stamps, those not cancelled **S** 396
Minuend (MIN-u-end), in subtraction **A** 399

Minuet, a musical form **M** 537
Minuet, dance **D** 27; pictures **D** 26, 35
  colonial Virginia, picture **C** 392
Minuet-trio, musical form **C** 332

Minuit (MIN-u-it), **Peter** (1580–1638), Dutch official in
  America, b. Wesel, Duchy of Cleves (now the Nether-
  lands). He landed on Manhattan Island about 1626 and
  bought it from the Indians for about $24 in his capacity
  as director general of the Dutch West India Company.
  In 1637, in Sweden's employ, he landed near Delaware
  Bay, set up a colony called New Sweden, and built Fort
  Christina, site of present-day Wilmington.
    Dutch colonies in America **A** 190; **N** 234

Minute, measure of time **W** 112
Minute Man, by Daniel French, picture **U** 115
Minuteman, missile **M** 345–46
Minute Man National Historical Park, Lexington, Mass.
    M 144
Minutemen, American colonial militia **R** 198
  alerted by Paul Revere's Ride **R** 193
  "fired the shot heard round the world" **A** 201
Miocene epoch, of the Cenozoic era, in geology **F** 388
Miquelon see Saint Pierre and Miquelon, islands
Mira (MY-ra), star **S** 408
Mirabeau (mi-ra-BO), **Comte de,** French revolutionary
  leader **F** 464
Miracle drugs see Antibiotics
Miracle plays, medieval drama **M** 339–40
  Middle English drama **E** 249–50
  religious drama **D** 295
  theater in England **T** 159–60
Miracle rice **R** 231
Mirage (mir-ODGE) **M** 341–42
  light refraction **L** 263
Miranda (mi-RON-da), **Francisco de,** Venezuelan patriot
    V 300
  Bolivar and Miranda **B** 301
Miranda (mi-RAN-da), satellite of Uranus **P** 277

Miriam, in the Old Testament, Hebrew prophetess, sister
  of Moses and Aaron. The Song of Miriam (Exodus
  15:20–21) is a hymn celebrating the Israelites' deliverance from Egypt.

Miró (mi-RO), **Joan,** Spanish painter **M** 394–95
  Landscape, painting **M** 396a
  Wall of the Sun, painting **S** 362
Mirrors
  first glass mirrors made by Venetians **G** 229
  heliograph signaling **C** 438; **T** 50
  kaleidoscope **K** 166
  laser mirror left on moon **S** 340a, 340i; diagram
    S 340i
  light reflection **L** 261–62
  optical instruments **O** 170–71
  superstition about **S** 475
Mirror writing
  used by Leonardo da Vinci **L** 154
Misbranding, of food **F** 351
Misdemeanor (mis-de-MEAN-or), in law **C** 527
  jury trials **J** 159
Misdirection, art of, in magic **M** 19
Misérables (mi-zay-RA-ble), **Les,** novel by Victor Hugo,
  excerpt **H** 275–77
Mishnah, ancient Hebrew laws **H** 101
  Jewish Oral Law **J** 116, 120
  Talmud **T** 15
Miskolc (MISH-kolts), Hungary **H** 286
Missiles **M** 343–47
  displayed at the Smithsonian, picture **W** 34

jet propulsion **J** 85–87
liquid gases **L** 308
rocket power **R** 256–57
United States Air Force **U** 161
United States Navy **U** 193
Mission Control Center, Houston, Texas, picture **S** 340f
Missions and missionaries M 348–49
Africa **A** 58
Canada's St. Albert Mission in Alberta **A** 147
Christianity, history of **C** 279–80, 281
Indians of North America **I** 176
Indians of South America **I** 210
International Missionary Council **P** 486
Jesuits to North American Indians **I** 171; **O** 128
Livingstone, David **S** 400
Loyola, Saint Ignatius **L** 369
overland trails, United States **O** 260; picture **O** 261
Patrick, Saint **P** 98
Paul, Saint **P** 99
Peter, Saint **P** 167
Praying Towns of Massachusetts **M** 149
Roman Catholic Church **R** 294
Schweitzer, Albert **S** 59
Mississippi M 350–63
Mississippi, University of, University, Miss. **M** 358
Mississippi River M 364–65
Civil War **C** 325–26
discovered by De Soto **D** 144
explorations of Marquette and Jolliet **M** 103
flood-plain area in Mississippi **M** 350
head of navigation, Minneapolis, Minnesota **M** 321
La Salle **L** 46
lock at Dubuque, Iowa, picture **I** 358
Louisiana **L** 351
"old" and "young" river features **R** 241
river boat near Clarksville, Mo., picture **U** 107
silt from the Missouri **M** 383
source, near Lake Itasca **M** 322, 333
Twain, Mark, river pilot **T** 336
Mississippi River-Gulf Outlet, waterway **L** 356; picture
L 351
Miss Muffet, nursery rhyme **N** 404
Missouri M 366–81
events leading to Civil War **C** 320
Missouri Compromise **M** 382
places of interest in Negro history **N** 94
Saint Louis **S** 17–18
Missouri, University of, Columbia, Missouri **M** 375
Missouri, U.S.S., battleship
Japanese surrender, 1945, picture **W** 307
Missouri Compromise, 1820 **M** 382
Civil War, events leading to **C** 320
Clay, Henry **C** 335
Dred Scott decision **D** 310–11
Maine and Missouri receive statehood **M** 47
Negro history, abolitionist movement in **N** 95
repealed by Kansas-Nebraska Act, 1854 **K** 192
slavery issue **S** 199
Missouri Escarpment N 324
Missouri Fur Company F 522–23
Missouri Gazette, newspaper **M** 375
Missouri River M 383
Lewis and Clark expedition **L** 162–63
Missouri-Mississippi as a system **M** 364–65
source **M** 431
valley north of Kansas City, picture **M** 371
Missouri River Basin Development Program
South Dakota **S** 327
Mistletoe, plant **P** 318
Christmas tradition **C** 291
in Norse mythology **N** 279
state flower of Oklahoma **O** 81

Mistletoe cactus C 4
Mistral (mi-STROL), **Gabriela,** or Lucila Godoy de
Alcayaga, Chilean poet **C** 251
Latin-American literature **L** 72
Mistral, winter wind of Mediterranean region **M** 213
Misty of Chincoteaque, by Marguerite Henry **V** 344
M.I.T. see Massachusetts Institute of Technology

Mitchell, Arthur (1934–), dancer and choreographer,
b. New York, N.Y. One of the world's leading dancers and
the outstanding Negro classic dancer, he made his debut
with the New York City Ballet in 1956.
Negroes in the arts **N** 101

Mitchell, Billy (William Mitchell) (1879–1936), American
soldier and aviator, b. Nice, France. He rose from private
(1898) to the rank of brigadier general (1920), serving in
the Spanish-American War, in the Philippines and
Mexico, and as commander of U.S. air forces in France
(1917–18). His criticism of the War and Navy departments'
aviation policies led to Mitchell's court-martial (1925)
and resignation from the Army (1926).
United States Air Force, history of **U** 160

Mitchell, Edgar D., American astronaut **S** 344, 345, 347
Mitchell, John, American labor leader **L** 5

Mitchell, John Newton (1913–), American government
official, b. Detroit. A member of a Wall Street law firm,
a merger made him one of Richard Nixon's law partners
in 1967. After serving as Nixon's campaign manager,
he became attorney general in 1969. He resigned in
1972 to head the President's campaign for re-election.
Mitchell later resigned and rejoined his former law firm.

Mitchell, Joni, American rock music composer and performer **R** 262d
Mitchell, Margaret, American novelist **A** 213

Mitchell, Maria (1818–1889), American astronomer, b.
Nantucket, Mass. Under her father's guidance she became
a mathematician and astronomer. Among her achievements was discovery of a comet (1847). She was the first
woman elected (1848) to Academy of Arts and Sciences.
In 1922 she was elected to the Hall of Fame.

Miter gate, of canals **C** 84
Miter saws, tools **T** 212–13
Mites, relatives of spiders **P** 286
arachnids **S** 388; picture **S** 384
Mitochondria (my-to-CON-dria), of cell **C** 161–62
Mitosis (my-TO-sis), cell division **C** 163; picture
C 164
cell division of tumors and cancer **C** 89

Mitre (MI-tray), **Bartolomé** (1821–1906), Argentine military leader, statesman, historian, and journalist, b.
Buenos Aires. An exile, he returned to Buenos Aires
(1852) to help overthrow Juan Manuel de Rosas, became
active in the government, and was first president
(1862–68) of the Argentine Republic. He had founded the
newspaper *La Nación* in 1852, and later he wrote books,
among them *History of San Martín.*

Mitropoulos (mi-TROP-oo-los), **Dimitri** (1896–1960), American conductor, composer, and pianist, b. Athens,
Greece. He was conductor of Minneapolis Symphony Orchestra (1937–49) and New York Philharmonic (1950–58).

Mixed metaphor, figure of speech **F** 118
Mixed numbers, combinations of whole numbers and
fractions **F** 398

Mixtures, in chemistry M 175–76
Mizoguchi, Kenji, Japanese motion-picture director
 M 487, 488
Mjolnir (m'YERL-nir), hammer of Thor, Norse god N 279
Mks system see Meter-kilogram-second
Mlanje (MLON-jay), **Mount,** highest peak in Malawi M 50
Mnemonics (ne-MON-ics), memory-improving technique
 L 106

Moabites (MO-ab-ites), ancient Semitic people of Moab, a
land east of the Dead Sea that is now part of Jordan.
Little is known of the Moabites or Moab except for a few
Old Testament references, such as those found in the
Book of Ruth (Ruth was a Moabite woman).

Moabite stone, inscribed slab of stone erected by Mesha
of Moab in 850 B.C. to mark a victory against Israel. The
stone was discovered in 1868. Its inscription reveals that
the Moabites' language closely resembled Hebrew. The
stone is now in the Louvre in Paris.

Moana, documentary motion picture M 476
Moas (MO-as), extinct birds B 231
 giants of nature G 200, 204
Moat, of a castle F 375; H 178
Mobile (mo-BELE), Alabama A 124
Mobile Bay, Alabama A 113, 115, 126
 naval battle in Civil War C 326
Mobile (MO-bil) **classrooms,** Canada C 62
Mobile (mo-BELE) **River,** Alabama A 115

Mobiles (MO-beles), sculpture made of movable parts,
usually suspended by wire and rods and balanced to re-
spond to a gentle touch or breeze.
 Calder, Alexander S 105
 modern sculpture of the United States U 116; picture
  U 117
 three-dimensional design D 136; picture D 137
 toys T 234
 wire sculpture W 190b

Möbius (MER-bi-us) **strip,** in topology T 222
Mobs, of kangaroos, picture K 169

Mobutu (mo-BU-tu), **Sese Seko** (1930–), Congolese leader, b. Lisala, Upper Congo. He was secretary of state
for national defense after the Congo gained its independence (1960). He led a military coup (1960) to neu-
tralize the conflict between Premier Lumumba and President Kasavubu, directed the government for 3 months,
returned power to President Kasavubu, and was appointed commander in chief (1961). In Nov., 1965, Mobutu deposed Kasavubu and named himself president
for a 5-year term. In elections held in 1970, Mobutu, running unopposed, retained the presidency.
 Zaire, history of Z 366d

Moby Dick, novel by Melville N 349; excerpt M 217–18;
 picture A 203
 American literature, place in A 202
 Captain Ahab, an illustration by Rockwell Kent I 92
 whale hunting W 153
Moccasin flower see Lady's-slipper
Moccasin snakes S 209; picture S 210
Mocha (MO-ca), Yemen (Sana) Y 349
 coffee named for C 371
 goats and cattle, picture C 145
Mochica (mo-CHI-ca), ancient people of Peru P 165
 art of ancient Indian civilization I 155; pictures I 204,
 205
Mochila (mo-CHI-la), saddle cover with mail pouches
 P 392

Mock-heroic poetry E 258

Mockingbirds, American birds of the family commonly
called mimic-thrushes. They grow to a length of about 10
inches. Grayish in color, the bird has white patches on
its wings and tail. The mockingbird is found in southern
Canada, the United States, Mexico, and the West Indies.
It lives in shrubs and thickets and eats fruit, berries, and
insects. It is so named because it imitates the calls and
songs of other birds. Picture B 239.
 Arkansas, state bird of A 418
 Florida, state bird of F 259
 Mississippi, state bird of M 351
 Tennessee, state bird of T 75
 Texas, state bird of T 123

Mock suns see Sundogs
Mock-ups, design models I 231
Mode, a kind of average of a set of numbers S 417
Mode, musical scale M 533
 ancient Greek modes A 247
Model Aeronautics, Academy of, sponsors championships
 A 105
Model electric racing A 537
Modeling, fashion M 384–85
Modeling, in sculpture S 90
Modeling, term in drawing D 305
Models and model making M 385
 airplane models A 104–07
 automobile A 535–37
 railroads, model R 91–92
 ship models S 151–54
 taxidermy T 27
 Viking ship models, how to make S 152–54
Model T, automobile A 548; picture A 544
 Henry Ford's part in automobile history F 367
 importance to history of transportation T 264
Moderator, of a debate, or discussion D 55
Modern art M 386–98
 art, the meanings of A 438
 art of the artist A 438g
 Cezanne's influence C 181
 Chagall, Marc C 184
 collage C 376–77
 French art, 20th-century F 431–32
 furniture design F 510
 Germany G 171
 Modigliani, Amedeo M 403
 Mondrian, Piet M 408
 Op and Pop art P 30–32
 Picasso, Pablo P 243
 Pollock, Jackson P 387
 sculpture of the 20th century S 103–05
 tapestry T 24
 United States U 116, 122; pictures A 438d, 438e
 Utrillo, Maurice U 256
Modern dance, pioneered in America D 33

Modern Language Association of America (MLA), organization of college and university teachers of English and
modern foreign languages. Founded in 1883, MLA works
to advance all phases of literary and linguistic study. It
publishes a quarterly magazine, *PMLA,* and, among other
activities, conducts a Foreign Language Program comprised of a research center in New York, N.Y., and a
Center for Applied Linguistics in Washington, D.C.

Modern music M 399–402
 French *musique concrète* F 448
 sonatas M 540
 Stravinsky, Igor S 437
 symphonies M 541

Modern Poetry Association (MPA), organization that promotes modern poetry. Founded in 1946, with head-quarters in Chicago, Ill., MPA publishes *Poetry Magazine* monthly and sponsors lectures and readings in an effort to bring modern poetry to a larger audience.

Modern roman typefaces **T** 345
Modigliani (mo-deel-YA-ni), **Amedeo,** Italian painter and sculptor **M** 403
   Head, sculpture, picture **M** 403

Modjeska (mod-JES-ka), **Helena** (1840–1909), Polish actress, b. Cracow. She married her tutor, Gustav Modrzejewski, when she was about 17 and toured with him in a stock company. After his death she married Count Bozenta Chlapowski (1868) and sailed with him and other political refugees to America (1876). Her first American appearance was in San Francisco (1877). Noted for her portrayal of Shakespearean heroines, she starred with Edwin Booth (1889–90) and toured with Otis Skinner and Maurice Barrymore before retiring in 1905.

Modred (MO-dred), knight of King Arthur's court **A** 442
Moeritherium (mir-i-THE-ri-um), prehistoric ancestor of the elephant **E** 170
Moffat, Robert, Scottish missionary in Africa **B** 340a
Mofolo, Thomas, Lesothan novelist **A** 76b
Mogadishu (mog-a-DISH-u), capital of Somalia **S** 254

Mogul (mo-GUL), dynasty of Mongol rulers of India. Though it dates from Baber, a descendant of Tamerlane (Timur), who ruled (1526–30) over a large part of northern India, it was Baber's grandson, **Akbar** (1542–1605), who established the Mogul empire when he became king (1556). He conquered all of North India, built a sound administrative system, and promoted mutual understanding with the Hindus. When **Aurangzeb** (1658–1707) reversed Akbar's religious policy and drove non-Muslims into revolt, the Mogul rulers lost their power. The last, **Bahadur Shah II** (1768?–1862), was sentenced to prison by the British after the Sepoy Mutiny (1857). The greatness of the Mogul empire has survived in its art and architecture.
   India, history of **I** 131, 133

Mohács (MO-hotch), **battle of,** 1526 **H** 287
Mohair goats **C** 151
Mohammad Abdullah Hassan (mo-HAM-mad ob-du-LAH hass-AN), Somali leader **S** 254
Mohammed (Arabic: Muhammad), Arab prophet, founder of Islam **M** 404–05
   Arabic education spread by Muslim followers **E** 66
   Islam **I** 414–16
   Jews resented **J** 107
   Koran **K** 294–95
   Mecca **M** 196
Mohammed V, king of Morocco **M** 461
Mohammed Ali *see* Mehemet Ali, governor of Egypt
Mohammedans *see* Muslims
Mohammed Riza Pahlavi *see* Pahlavi, Mohammed Riza, Shah of Iran
Mohammed Zahir Shah, king of Afghanistan **A** 45
Mohave (mo-HA-vay), **Lake,** Arizona **A** 407
Mohave Desert *see* Mojave Desert
Mohawk, Indians of North America **I** 184
   Champlain made enemies for France **I** 186
   Chief Thayendanegea, Joseph Brant **B** 371
Mohawk Valley, New York **N** 214
   overland trail through the valley **O** 254

Mohenjo-Daro (mo-HEN-jo DA-ro) ("mound of the dead"), most important ancient city of the Indus valley in West Pakistan. Mohenjo-Daro covered more than 240 acres and was inhabited continuously from about 3000 to 2000 B.C., when it came to a sudden end, probably at the hands of invaders.
   ancient cities with sewers and plumbing **A** 223–24

Moho, boundary between earth's crust and mantle **E** 8, 39
Mohole, Project, for drilling a hole through earth's crust **G** 119–20; **U** 21

Moholy-Nagy (MO-ho-ye NODGE), **László** (1895–1946), Hungarian painter, photographer, industrial designer, and writer, b. Bacsbarsod. He taught at the Bauhaus in Germany until 1928. In 1937 he went to the United States and founded the short-lived New Bauhaus, renamed the Institute of Design, in Chicago. His books, in particular *Vision in Motion,* have had a significant influence on art education and industrial design.
   ideas of the Bauhaus survive **B** 105

Mohorovičić (mo-ho-ro-VI-chich), **Andrija,** Yugoslav geologist **E** 8, 39
   research in geophysics **G** 119
Mohorovičić discontinuity *see* Moho
Mohr, Joseph, Austrian pastor, author of "Silent Night, Holy Night" **C** 122
Mohs, Freidrich, German mineralogist **G** 69
Mohs' scale, measure for hardness **G** 69
   mineral's hardness **R** 270
Moiré (mwa-RAY), fabric **T** 144
Mojave (mo-HA-vay) **Desert,** California and Arizona **C** 16; picture **C** 344
Mokhelhe, Ntsu, Lesotho political leader **L** 156a
Molars, teeth **T** 47
Molasses **S** 453
   Sugar Act, 1764 angers American colonists **R** 194
   sugar cane, a source of molasses, picture **G** 318
Moldau River *see* Vltava River
Moldavia (mol-DAVE-ia), former principality, now a region of Rumania **R** 355
Moldavian Soviet Socialist Republic (Moldavia) **U** 44
Moldboard plow **F** 57
Molders, tools
   preparing wood for furniture making **F** 502
Molding, of plastics **P** 329
Molds, for shaping materials **D** 166–67
   candles **C** 96; picture **C** 97
Molds, fungi **F** 496, 497
   antibiotics **A** 310, 311; pictures **A** 314
   bioluminescence **B** 197
   cheeses: Roquefort and Camembert **D** 13
   experiment: growing bread mold **E** 351
   food spoilage **F** 344, 352
   sources of drugs **D** 323
Molecular (mo-LEC-ular) **biology** **B** 196
Molecular weight **C** 219
Molecules (MOL-ec-ules), combinations of atoms **A** 483, 485; **C** 196, 220
   detergents and soaps **D** 145
   gases, diffusion of particles **G** 57–58
   in the crystal of a bean virus **C** 543; picture **C** 542
   macromolecules, in body chemistry **B** 290
   matter and molecules **P** 231
   plastics **P** 324
   polymers and polymerization **P** 324
   separation with heating, picture **G** 58
   solids, particles in **S** 250–51
   water **W** 54–55
   See also Brownian movement
Molenaer (MO-len-ar), **Jan Miense,** Dutch painter
   Family Group, painting **D** 365

Moles, animals of insectivore group **I** 259–60
  bristles, a variety of mammal hair, pictures **M** 64, 69
Moles, marsupial **K** 174
Molière (mo-li-AIR), French playwright and actor **M** 405
  Danish literature, influence on **S** 51
  French drama **D** 296; **F** 438
Molina (mo-LI-na), **Arturo Armanda,** president of El Salvador **E** 184
Molina, Tirso de *see* Tirso de Molina
Mollusks, group of animals **O** 271–76
  animal plankton **P** 280–81
  pearls **P** 113
  shells **S** 147–49
Mollweide (MOL-vy-da) **projections,** of maps **M** 93
Molly Maguires, secret labor union **L** 3
Molly Pitcher *see* Pitcher, Molly

Molnar (MOL-nar), **Ferenc** (1878–1952), Hungarian playwright and novelist, b. Budapest. His most famous work was *Liliom,* a mixture of realism and fantasy. It was adapted as the musical *Carousel* by Rodgers and Hammerstein.
  twentieth century drama **D** 298; **H** 284

Molniya I, Soviet communication satellite **C** 440
Molokai (mo-LO-kye), one of the Hawaiian Islands **H** 58–59

Molotov (MOL-ot-off), **Vyacheslav Mikhailovich** (Vyacheslav Mikhailovich Skryabin) (1890–   ), Soviet politician, b. Kukarka, Vyatka. He was a member of the Political Bureau of the Communist Party (1926–57), chairman of the Council of People's Commissars (1930–41), deputy chairman of the Council of Ministers (1941–57), minister for foreign affairs (1939–49, 1953–56), and minister for state control (1956–57). He served as member of the Presidium of the Central Committee of the Communist Party until 1957, when he was charged with leading an anti-party group, removed from office, and sent as ambassador to the Mongolian People's Republic (1957–60). He represented the Soviet Union at the International Atomic Energy Conference in Vienna (1960–61) before retiring from public life (1962).

Molotov cocktail, hand grenade made of a bottle filled with a flammable liquid, such as gasoline. A wick or saturated rag is taped to the bottom and ignited when the grenade is thrown. Named for Soviet statesman Vyacheslav M. Molotov, it was used by the Russians against German armored vehicles in World War II.

Molten rock *see* Magma
Molting
  birds **B** 200, 216, 244
  crustacea **S** 170
  horseshoe crab **H** 245
  silkworms **S** 179
  snakes **S** 214

Moltke (MOLT-ka), **Count Helmuth Johannes Ludwig von** (1848–1916), German soldier, b. Gersdorf. As the nephew of Field Marshal Count Helmuth Karl Bernhard von Moltke (1800–91), he was given responsibilities beyond his abilities. He was made chief of the German general staff (1906), but when he failed to win a quick victory over France (1914), he was relieved of his post.
  World War I **W** 273

Moluccas (mo-LUCC-as), or Spice Islands, Indonesia **I** 220, 222; **N** 120
  Magellan's search for **M** 17
  spice trade **S** 380–81

Molucca (mol-UC-ca) **Sea,** part of the Pacific Ocean between Celebes Island and the northern Molucca islands. It is connected to the Pacific on the north through the Molucca Passage, and it contains the Indonesian Sula Islands.

Moly, magic plant **O** 54
Molybdenum (mo-LIB-den-um), element **E** 155, 162
  Colorado leading producer **C** 407
  flotation and smelting, pictures **M** 229
  metals, chart of ores, location, properties, uses **M** 227
  molybdenum-producing regions of North America **N** 293–94
Mombacho (mome-BA-cho), volcano, Nicaragua, picture **N** 248
Mombasa (mom-BA-sa), **Kenya** **K** 233; picture **K** 232
Moment of truth, in bullfighting **B** 450
Monaco (mo-NA-co), principality on Mediterranean coast of France **M** 406–07
  flag **F** 240
Monaco-Ville (mo-NA-co-vi), capital of Monaco **M** 406
Monadnocks (mon-AD-nocks), hills or mountains rising above eroded land surface **M** 136
  New Hampshire **N** 150
  South Carolina **S** 298
  Stone Mountain, Georgia, picture **G** 134
Mona Lisa (MO-na LI-sa), portrait painting by Leonardo da Vinci **L** 155
  hangs in the Louvre **L** 367
Monarch (MON-arc) **butterflies** **B** 470; pictures **B** 473, **H** 188
  chrysalis, picture **I** 265
  Viceroy butterfly resembles, picture **I** 275
Monarchy, government by single person **G** 274
  constitutional monarchy of the United Kingdom **U** 77–78
Monasteries **C** 283; pictures **C** 285, **M** 294
  architecture **A** 378–79
  Burma **B** 454
  centers of learning for Europe **R** 290
  Greece's Mount Athos **G** 332
  libraries **L** 196
  medieval books **B** 319–21
  See also Monks and monasticism; Religious orders
Monastic orders *see* Religious orders
Monaural (mon-AUR-al) **recorders** **T** 20, 21

Monck, Sir Charles Stanley (1819–1894), Irish statesman, b. Templemore. Appointed (1861) captain general, he became (1866) the first governor-general of the Dominion of Canada after confederation. He was privy councillor of Canada (1867–68).

Moncton, New Brunswick, Canada **N** 138c
Monday, origin of name **D** 47
Monde Bilingue (bi-LANG), **Le,** or **Bilingual World, The,** French movement for joint use of French and English **U** 195
Mondrian (MON-dri-on), **Piet,** Dutch painter **M** 408
  Composition, painting **D** 362
  Dutch art **D** 362
  modern art **M** 393
  Opposition of Lines: Red and Yellow, painting **M** 392
  Painting I, picture **D** 133
Monégasques (mon-e-GASKS), people of Monaco **M** 406
Monet (mo-NAY), **Claude,** French painter **M** 408
  Beach at Sainte-Adresse, painting **A** 438d
  French art **F** 426
  impressionism in painting **P** 29
  Impression: Sunrise, painting **E** 386
  modern art **M** 387
  Water Lilies, painting **F** 428

Moneta (mo-NAY-ta) ("the adviser" or "admonisher"), name given to the temple erected to Roman goddess Juno after she had advised the Romans during wartime. Because the Romans produced their first silver coins in the temple (269 B.C.), they called them *moneta*, to distinguish them from copper coins. The words "money," "mint," and "monetary" all come from the Latin *moneta*.

   money, history of **M** 409

Monetary policy, of a government **I** 253
Monetary units, of countries see country articles
Money M 409–12
   banks and banking **B** 44d–51
   budgets, family **B** 425–26
   coins and coin collecting **C** 374–75
   currency table of values and symbols for representative
      countries **M** 411
   economic institution **E** 50
   free silver coinage, Bryan's political issue **B** 415–16
   gold standard for official currencies **G** 247
   "hiring" money **I** 288
   inflation and deflation **I** 252–53
   international trade problems **I** 327–28
   monetary economy of trade and commerce **T** 243
   monetary units see facts and figures section of
      country articles
   shells used as money **M** 411
   silver **S** 181–82
   silver money under Cleveland **C** 342
   traveler's checks **V** 259
   United States Mint **M** 338
   wampum **C** 374; **M** 411
Moneylender and His Wife, The, painting by Massys
   P 18, 19
Money orders, issued at post offices **P** 409
Mongkut, king of Thailand **T** 151
   the king, in *Anna and the King of Siam* **S** 334–35
Mongol Empire M 416
Mongolia (mon-GO-lia) **M** 413–16
   flag **F** 238
   horses' role in history **H** 238
   nomads, pictures **A** 302, 458; **M** 415; **N** 271
Mongolian language M 413
Mongolian People's Republic M 413, 416
Mongolian wild horse H 243–44
Mongolism (MON-go-lism), or **Down's syndrome R** 190
Mongoloid race
   Asia **A** 459; **B** 44

Mongols, nomadic tribes of central Asia, united during the 13th century by Genghis Khan. They established the greatest land empire in history, including practically all of Asia and Russia. By 1368 they had lost their power and importance in China. However, they remained powerful in Russia until about 1500. The Mongols, no longer a ruling power, now live in the Mongolian People's Republic and neighboring districts of China and the Soviet Union.

   Genghis Khan **G** 93
   China, conquest of **C** 270
   Gobi Desert dwellers **D** 128; picture **D** 129
   Mongolia **M** 413–16
   Russia invaded by **U** 47–48
   yurt homes **H** 175; pictures **A** 458, **M** 415, **N** 271
   See also Tatars

Mongooses, animals **G** 89, 91–93
Monitor, ironclad ship **C** 323
   See also Ericsson, John
Monitor, receiver used in television production **T** 70a
Monitor, Christian Science see Christian Science Monitor

Monk, Thelonious, American jazz composer and pianist **J** 60–61
Monkey board, part of oil derrick **P** 173
Monkey fists, knots **K** 289
Monkeys M 419–22
   animal communication **A** 280, 281
   animal intelligence tests **A** 285, 286, 287
   pets **P** 180
Monkey wrenches, tools **T** 215
Monks and monasticism (mo-NAST-i-cism) **M** 294
   art, the meanings of **A** 438
   Buddhist **B** 424
   Christianity, history of **C** 283; picture **C** 285
   church music ceremonial, picture **M** 299
   communication advanced by manuscript copying
      C 431
   early bridge builders **B** 395
   early Christianization of Europe **R** 290
   founding of Dominicans and Franciscans **R** 292
   Jesuits **L** 369; **R** 294
   libraries **L** 195–96
   missions **M** 348
   Orthodox Eastern Churches **O** 228–29
   Thai Buddhists, picture **A** 447
   Tibet **T** 175
   See also Religious orders
Monk seals, animals **W** 8
Monkshood, or aconite, plant **P** 322
Monmouth, New Jersey
   Revolutionary War **R** 204
Monnet (mon-NAY), **Jean,** French statesman **E** 334
Monochord (MON-o-cord), ancient instrument **K** 237
Monocoque (MON-o-coke) **construction,** in airplanes
   A 554; diagram **A** 555
Monocotyledons (mon-o-cot-il-E-dons), or monocots, seed
   plants **P** 292
Monocytes, cells of the body **I** 104
Monofilament (mon-o-FIL-a-ment) **fishing lines F** 207
Monogamy, family relationship **F** 41
Monomers (MON-o-mers), or simple one-part molecules
   P 324
Monometallism (mon-o-MET-al-lism), monetary system
   M 409
Monongahela (mo-non-ga-HE-la) **National Forest,** West
   Virginia, picture **N** 37
Monongahela River, pictures **P** 130, 135
Mononucleosis, infectious see Infectious mononucleosis
Monophonic (mon-o-PHON-ic) **music C** 276
Monophonic reproduction, of sound
   high-fidelity recording **H** 126–27
Monoplacophores (mon-o-PLAC-o-phores), mollusks
   O 276
Monopolies (mo-NOP-ol-ies) **and trusts T** 303–06; **E** 50
   capitalism **C** 104
   guilds **G** 401–03
   patents **P** 97–98
   public utilities **P** 510–13
Monotheism (MON-o-the-ism), belief in one god **R** 146
   Asia **A** 460
Monotremes, a kind of mammal **P** 333
   mammals, orders of **M** 62, 69
Monotype, machine for typesetting and casting **P** 465;
   T 345
Monroe, Louisiana **L** 360
Monroe, Elizabeth Kortright, wife of James Monroe
   F 166; picture **F** 167

Monroe, Harriet (1861?–1936), American editor and poet, b. Chicago, Ill. The founder of *Poetry: A Magazine of Verse* (1912), she was more important as a critic and editor than as a poet, introducing to the public many poets (Carl Sandburg and Ezra Pound, for example).

Monroe, James, 5th president of the United States
    M 423–26
    Liberia's capital named for him **L** 164
    Louisiana Purchase **L** 365
    Monroe Doctrine **M** 425, 426–27
Monroe Doctrine, American foreign policy **M** 426–27
    Adams, John Quincy, helped write **A** 13–14
    aims of the Organization of American States **O** 211
    foreign affairs of Monroe's administration **M** 425
    isolationism in U.S. history **U** 137
    Polk Doctrine, an extension of **P** 386–87
    status quo policy in international relations **I** 322
    Roosevelt Corollary **R** 329
Monrovia, capital of Liberia **L** 164, 165, 166
Mons, battle of, 1914 **W** 273
Mons Meg, famous cannon **G** 425; picture **G** 415
Monsoons, seasonal winds **W** 184–85
    Asia **A** 452
    Ceylon **C** 179
    climate of India **I** 125–26
    Somalia **S** 253
    Southeast Asia **S** 328–29
    types of climates **C** 346
Mont, geographic term *see* mountains by name, as
    Blanc, Mont
Montage (mon-TODGE) **experts,** for motion pictures
    M 481
Montagnais, Indians of North America **I** 164, 170
Montague, P.E.I., Canada **P** 456e
Montaigne (mon-TAIN), **Michel de,** French essayist
    E 292; **F** 437
Montale, Eugenio, Italian poet **I** 481
Montana **M** 428–43
    Kerr Dam, picture **C** 485
Montana, University of **M** 437
Montana School of Mines **M** 437
Montan wax **W** 70
Montauk Point, Long Island, New York, picture **N** 221
Mont Blanc Tunnel, pictures **T** 313, **W** 221
Montcalm, Louis Joseph, Marquis de, French general
    F 460–61
    Seven Years War (French and Indian War) in Canada
    C 70
Mont Cenis (mon ce-NI) **Pass,** through the Alps **A** 174
Monte Carlo (MON-tay CAR-lo), Monaco **M** 406
Monte Cassino (MONE-tay ca-SI-no), abbey, Cassino, Italy
    World War II **W** 299

Montefiore (mon-te-fi-OR-e), **Sir Moses Haim** (1784–1885), English philanthropist, b. Leghorn, Italy. He amassed a fortune on the London Stock Exchange and retired in 1824. He devoted the rest of his life to serving the Jewish people, protecting their rights and their liberty. The spirit of unity he aroused among European Jews led to the growth of the Zionist movement.

Montego (mon-TE-go) **Bay,** Jamaica **J** 17
Montenegro, Julio C. M., president of Guatemala **G** 394
Montenegro (mon-te-NE-gro), Yugoslav state **Y** 358
    Balkan wars **B** 19
Monterrey (mon-ter-RAY), **battle of,** 1846 **M** 238–39
Monterrey, Mexico **M** 246
Montesquieu (mon-tes-KU), **Charles de Secondat, Baron de,** French philosopher **F** 463
    his book, *Spirit of the Laws, The* influenced American
    founding fathers **F** 439

Montessori (mon-tes-SOR-i), **Maria** (1870–1952), Italian educator and physician, b. near Ancona. Dr. Montessori was the first woman in Italy to obtain a medical degree. She developed methods of teaching children that emphasized the child's initiative and freedom of expres-

sion. Her methods have influenced teaching practices for 3- to 6-year-olds all over the world. English translations of her books include *The Montessori Method* and *Advanced Montessori Method.*
    kindergartens and nursery schools, growth of
    K 243

Monteux (mon-TER), **Pierre** (1875–1964), French conductor, b. Paris. He was conductor of the Diaghilev Russian Ballet (1911–14, 1916–17). He conducted at the New York Metropolitan Opera House (1917–18) and led the Boston Symphony Orchestra (1919–24). He founded (1929) and was chief conductor (1929–38) of l'Orchestre Symphonique de Paris. Conductor (1936–52) of the San Francisco Symphony Orchestra, he was an honored guest conductor in the United States and Europe.

Monteverdi (mon-tay-VARE-di), **Claudio,** Italian composer
    I 483–84
    baroque music **B** 63
    choral music **C** 278
    opera **O** 131
    pioneer in writing for the orchestra **O** 184
Montevideo (mon-te-vi-DAY-o), capital of Uruguay
    U 238; picture **U** 235
Monteynard dam, France, picture **D** 18

Montezuma I (mon-te-ZU-ma) (1390?–1464?), Aztec ruler of Mexico. Elected ruler about 1436, he extended Aztec conquests as far as the Gulf of Mexico, modified and codified Aztec law, and built many temples and pyramids. The aqueduct from Chapultepec to Tenochtitlán (Mexico City) was built during his reign.

Montezuma II (1480?–1520), Aztec ruler of Mexico. Elected ruler about 1502, he spread the Aztec realm farther than all others before him and organized justice in the land. He was ruler when the Spaniards landed in Veracruz (1517) and Cortés marched on Tenochtitlán (1519). Montezuma, believing that Cortés fulfilled the prophecy that the white god Quetzalcoatl would appear out of the east that year to rule Mexico, met Cortés with rich gifts but was taken hostage by the Spaniards in his own palace. He died from wounds suffered during an Aztec attack on the palace.
    Cortes' conquest of the Aztecs **C** 508; **I** 197

Montgolfier (mon-golf-YAY), **Jacques Étienne** (1745–1799) and **Joseph Michel** (1740–1810), French inventors, b. Vidalon. Their hot-air balloon was the first lighter-than-air craft. After the successful flight of an unmanned balloon in June, 1783, they sent up a load of animals, and in November of that year, the first manned balloon. In addition to their pioneer work in flight, the brothers developed a number of improvements in papermaking processes, and Joseph patented a hydraulic ram (1797).
    balloons in aviation history **A** 567; **B** 30
    parachutes **P** 59

Montgomery (mont-GUM-ery), **Sir Bernard Law,** 1st viscount Montgomery of Alamein (1887–   ), British general, b. Donegal, Ireland. During World War II he won fame as commander of the British 8th Army in North Africa for his decisive victory over the Germans at El Alamein (1942). He led British forces in the invasions of Sicily and Italy (1943) and was commander of Allied ground forces at the invasion of Normandy (1944). From 1945 to 1946 he was commander of the British-occupied zone of Germany. He served as chief of the imperial general staff (1946–48), and as deputy supreme commander of NATO forces (1951–58). Picture **E** 109.
    World War II in North Africa **W** 295

Montgomery, capital of Alabama **A** 122; picture **A** 123
  bus segregation case **S** 115
  first Confederate capital **C** 321
Montgomery, Lucy Maud, Canadian author **C** 63
  setting of *Anne of Green Gables* **P** 456e
Montgomery, Richard, American military commander **R** 201
Month in the Country, A, play by Ivan Turgenev **D** 298
Months, of the year
  calendars **C** 12
  hurricane months **H** 293
  in French **F** 434
  in Italian **I** 478
  in Spanish **S** 368
  rhythms in plant and animal life **L** 244
  See also names of months
Monticello (mon-ti-CHEL-lo), Virginia home of Thomas Jefferson **J** 64; pictures **J** 65, **V** 356
  American classical architecture **U** 123
Montini, Giovanni Battista *see* Paul VI, pope
Montmartre (mon-MAR-tre), Paris **P** 70; picture **P** 73
  sidewalk café, picture **P** 73
  Toulouse-Lautrec, Henri de, painter of **T** 228–29
Montpelier (mont-PEEL-yer), capital of Vermont **V** 318; picture **V** 319
Montpelier, home of James Madison, in Virginia **M** 6; picture **M** 9
Montreal (mon-tre-ALL), Quebec, Canada **M** 443–45; **Q** 13; pictures **C** 65, **N** 304, **Q** 12
  Cartier, Jacques **C** 124
  cities of Canada **C** 64
  Expo 67 **F** 18
Montréal (mon-ray-OL), **Université de,** Quebec, Canada **C** 62; **M** 445; **Q** 10b; **U** 206
Monts, Pierre du Guast, Sieur de, French colonizer **N** 344g
Mont-Saint-Michel (mon-san-mi-SHEL), abbey, France, pictures **F** 414, **W** 218

Montserrat (mont-ser-RAT), island in the British West Indies in the Leeward Islands. It was discovered (1493) by Columbus and colonized (1632) by the Irish. From its capital, Plymouth, its chief export is cotton.

Monument Rocks, Kansas **K** 187
Monuments
  art as a record **A** 438b, 438e
  monumental sculpture **U** 115–16
  Mount Rushmore, South Dakota **S** 312; picture **S** 322
  obelisks **O** 5–6
  sculpture **S** 90–105
  Washington Monument **W** 32; picture **W** 34
  See also Wonders of the world
Monuments, National, list **N** 46
  See also places of interest section of state articles
Monument Valley, in Utah, picture **U** 248

Moody, Dwight Lyman (1837–1899), American evangelist, b. Northfield, Mass. He retired from business (1860) to become a missionary, and conducted highly successful evangelistic campaigns in Great Britain and United States. He established Northfield Seminary for girls (1879), Mount Hermon School for boys (1881), and Chicago Bible Institute (1889).

Moody, William Vaughn, American poet **A** 209
Moog (MOGE), **Robert,** American composer **E** 142h
Moog synthesizer, for electronic music **E** 142h
Moon **M** 446–56
  calendar, history of **C** 12
  craters of **C** 420
  double planetary system of earth and moon **P** 272
  eclipses of **E** 46–47

first radar contact with the moon **A** 476
gravity and gravitation **G** 320–21
lunar, or moon calendar **T** 193
lunar landing **E** 368; **S** 339–340a, 340g–340i
moonquakes recorded by seismometer **S** 340a
possible observatory for astronomers **O** 14
satellites of planets called moons **P** 272
solar system, place in the **S** 245
space exploration and travel **S** 338–49; pictures **S** 340b, 340c, 340h
tides **T** 180–183
Moon, Mountains of the, name given by ancient geographers for Ruwenzori Mountains, Uganda **U** 5
Moonbow, rainbowlike arch, Cumberland Falls, Ky. **K** 221
Moon calendar **T** 193–94
Moonfish, or opah, picture **F** 183

Moonflower, sometimes called night beauty, a tropical vine related to the morning glory, with fragrant white or purple flowers, which bloom at night.

Moon jellyfishes **J** 73
Moon landing day, July 20, 1969 **E** 368; **S** 339–340a
Moonlight **M** 447

Moonlight schools, evening classes for adults in isolated regions. The schools were designed to promote literacy and improve community standards. They were opened first in Kentucky in 1911 and spread rapidly through other southern states where illiteracy was high.

Moon probes, or lunar probes **M** 450, 455
Moons, satellites of planets **P** 272
Moonstone, gemstone **G** 76

Moore, Anne Carroll (1871–1961), American author and librarian, b. Limerick, Maine. She was the first Supervisor of Work with Children in the New York Public Library (1906–41) and the author of children's books and books about children's literature. She also edited an edition of Irving's *Knickerbocker's History of New York*.
  influence of librarians on children's literature **C** 242

Moore, Clement Clarke (1779–1863), American scholar, b. New York, N.Y. Best-known as the author of "A Visit from Saint Nicholas" (" 'Twas the Night before Christmas"), which he wrote as a Christmas gift for his children (1822), he also published a lexicon of the Hebrew language (1809). He gave (1819) the land on which the General Theological Seminary in New York, N.Y., was built, and he was the seminary's professor of Biblical learning and of Oriental and Greek literature (1823–50).
  "A Visit from Saint Nicholas", poem **C** 295
  Christmas customs **C** 290

Moore, Henry, British sculptor **S** 105
  Family Group, sculpture **E** 242
  noted for design and use of space within solids **D** 136
  Rocking Chair II, sculpture **D** 137
  20th-century English art **E** 242
Moore, Marianne, American poet **A** 211
  translations of La Fontaine's fables **F** 4
Moore, Merrill, American poet **S** 256

Moore, Thomas (pseudonyms Thomas Little and Thomas Brown) (1779–1852), Irish poet and songwriter, b. Dublin. He gained fame as a ballad singer among the London aristocracy. A strong Irish nationalist, he greatly influenced the growth of Irish literature and music. Among his noted works are poetry collections set to music, including "Irish Melodies," "Sacred Songs," and "National Airs"; the poem *Lalla Rookh; The Twopenny Post*

Moore, Thomas (continued)
verses of political satire; and biographies of Sheridan and Byron.
 favorite Irish songs **I** 393

Moore's Creek Bridge, battle of, 1776 **N** 321
Moorish art and architecture see Islamic art and architecture
Moors, open waste land with soil of wet peat, of which heather is the principal plant
 location in England **E** 212

Moors, usually refers to the descendants of the Berbers and Arabs who invaded Spain from Africa in the 8th century. The Moors rose to great power during the Middle Ages, and many examples of their art and architecture still stand. The last of the Moors were expelled from Spain about 1609–10. Today the name generally is used to designate the Muslims of northern and northwestern Africa.
 Alhambra, palace of Moorish caliphs **S** 350
 Spain, history of **S** 351–52, 358, 360–61

Moose, hoofed mammal **H** 219; picture **H** 215
 tracks, picture **A** 272
Moosehead Lake, Maine **M** 36
Moose Jaw, Saskatchewan, Canada **S** 38g
Mora (MO-ra), **Juan Rafael,** president of Costa Rica
 C 518
Moraine (mo-RAIN), **Lake,** Alberta, Canada, picture **B** 42
Moraines, glacial deposits **I** 19; picture **I** 18
Morality plays, of the Middle Ages **D** 295
 English literature **E** 250
 pageants **P** 12
Moral Re-Armament see Buchmanism
Morandi, Giorgio, Italian painter **I** 473

Moratorium Day, October 15, 1969, was the first of a series planned for special protest against Vietnam War. Various meetings, church services, and marches took place across the United States. In Boston, approximately 100,000 people met on the Common to hear speeches. In Washington, D.C., almost 45,000 marched to the White House.

Morava (MOR-a-va) **River,** Czechoslovakia **C** 560
Moravia, Alberto, Italian author **I** 481
Moravia (mo-RAY-via), province of Czechoslovakia
 C 560

Moravians (mo-RAY-vians), members of a reformed church that traces its origin to Bohemia and the followers of John Huss (1369–1415) and Jerome of Prague (1360?–1416). Moravian immigrants in the United States founded the towns of Bethlehem and Nazareth, Pa. They are noted for their missionary work among primitive peoples.
 Schoenbrunn Village State Memorial, Ohio **O** 70
 Winston-Salem, N.C., the Old Salem section **N** 317

Moray eels **E** 85; picture **E** 87
Morazán, Francisco, Honduran statesman **H** 199
Mordant, substance used to fix dyes **D** 366, 369, 371, 372
Mordant dyes **D** 371
Mordecai (MOR-de-ky), character in the Bible **P** 540

Mordvinoff, Nicholas (1911–), American author and illustrator of children's books, b. St. Petersburg (now Leningrad), Russia. After studying at the University of Paris, he lived in the South Pacific for 13 years. In 1947 he settled in New York, where he met writer William Lipkind. Under the names Will and Nicholas the two

collaborated on many books, including *Russet and the Two Reds, Four-Leaf Clover,* and *The Christmas Bunny.* Their *Finders Keepers* won the Caldecott medal (1952).

More, Sir Thomas, English statesman and author **M** 456
 English literature **E** 250
 Erasmus, friend of **E** 274
 utopias **U** 255
Morelos y Pavón (mo-RAE-los e pa-BONE), **José María,** Mexican priest and patriot **M** 248
Morels (mo-RELS), mushrooms **M** 521
 types of fungi **F** 498
Moreri (mor-ay-RI), **Louis,** French priest and encyclopedist **E** 197

Morey (MOR-ey), **Samuel** (1762–1843), American inventor, b. Hebron, Conn. He began experimenting with steamboats about 1790 and later claimed that his ideas were stolen by Fulton. He took out patents for a steam-operated spit, rotary steam engine, windmill, waterwheel, steam pump, and an internal-combustion engine.

Morgagni (mor-GON-yi), **Giovanni Batista,** Italian physician **M** 206

Morgan, Charles Langbridge (1894–1958), English novelist, b. Kent. He was a drama critic for the London *Times* (1921–39) and wrote essays and novels. His novels, which are concerned with moral and aesthetic problems, include *The Voyage, Portrait in a Mirror, The Fountain,* and *The River Line.*

Morgan, Daniel, American military commander **R** 208

Morgan, Garrett A. (1875?–1963), American inventor, Negro, b. Paris, Ky. He invented the gas inhalator, forerunner of the gas mask. His automatic traffic stop sign was sold to the General Electric Company.

Morgan, Gib, American folk hero **F** 312
Morgan, Sir Henry, English buccaneer **P** 264
 Jamaica, lieutenant governor of **J** 18

Morgan, Thomas Hunt (1866–1945), American zoologist, b. Lexington, Ky. The 1933 Nobel prize in medicine and physiology was awarded to him for his demonstration of linkage—the tendency for certain genes to be inherited together. He and his students at Columbia University further showed that this occurrence was due to the lineup of genes along each chromosome; genes closer together were inherited together more frequently. His work with the fruit fly, Drosophila, did much to prove the existence of mutations—inheritable changes in living things.

Morgan family, founders of one of the world's leading banking firms. **Junius Spencer** (1813–90) was president (1864–90) of J. S. Morgan and Co., London. His son, **John Pierpont** (1837–1913), founder of J. P. Morgan and Co., New York, was a leader in government financing and international banking and controlled a huge financial and industrial empire. Most of J. P. Morgan's art collection is at the Metropolitan Museum, and his rare books and manuscripts are at the Morgan Library in New York. His son, **John Pierpont** (1867–1943), succeeded him (1913) as head of J. P. Morgan and Co.

Morgan horses **V** 306; picture **H** 239

Morgenthau (MORG-en-tow), **Henry** (1856–1946), American businessman and diplomat, b. Mannheim, Germany. He went to the United States in 1865. He practiced law in

New York, N.Y. (1879–99), and was director and president of many large corporations. He became the U.S. ambassador to Turkey (1913–16) and to Mexico (1920) and the technical expert to the Monetary and Economic Conference at London (1933). He was the Chairman of the Greek Refugee Settlement Commission (1923), which was organized by the League of Nations.

Morgenthau (MORG-en-thau), **Henry, Jr.** (1891–1967), American public official and publisher, b. New York, N.Y. Son of diplomat Henry Morgenthau, he published the *American Agriculturist* (1922–33) and served as the New York State conservation commissioner. He was U.S. secretary of the treasury (1934–45) and general chairman of the United Jewish Appeal (1947–50) and other organizations.

Morganite, beryl gemstone **G** 71
Morgan le Fay, sorceress in legends of King Arthur **A** 442
Moriah (mo-RY-ah), **Mount,** Jerusalem **J** 78–79
Morin (MO-rin), coloring matter from fustic wood **D** 369
Morison, Samuel Eliot, American writer **A** 215

Morisot (mo-ri-ZO), **Berthe** (1841–1895), French painter, b. Paris. She and Mary Cassatt were the only women to join the impressionists. Her early work shows the effect of Corot. She married Eugène Manet (1874) and had a significant influence on his older brother Édouard. After 1885 her work became bolder and brighter, revealing the influence of Renoir. Among her most famous paintings is *The Cradle.*

Morley, Christopher Darlington (1890–1957), American novelist, essayist, and poet, b. Haverford, Pa. A versatile writer, he was on the staff of several magazines, including the *Ladies' Home Journal* (1917–18) and the New York *Evening Post* (1920–24). His more than 50 books are very diverse in nature. *Parnassus on Wheels* and its sequel, *The Haunted Bookshop*, were immediate successes. He also wrote *Kitty Foyle.*

Morley, Edward W., American physicist **R** 140
Morley, Thomas, English composer **E** 269
Mormons, religious sect **M** 457
  colonization of Utah **U** 254
  Mormon Cemetery, near Omaha, Nebr. **N** 82
  Nauvoo State Park, Illinois **I** 82
  Protestantism **P** 484–85
  Salt Lake City **S** 22
  Utah's first actual settlers **U** 245
  Young, Brigham **Y** 353
Mormon Tabernacle Choir **S** 22; **U** 249
Mormon Trail **O** 265

Morning glory, flowering vines in the same group as the sweet potato. Most species are tropical in origin. The common morning glory is a garden favorite and is easy to raise from seeds. It has a climbing stem, big leaves, and funnel-shaped flowers. The blossoms may be pink, purple, blue, or white. The plant also grows wild.
  solar-day rhythm, picture **L** 245

Moro, Aldo (1916–   ), Italian statesman, b. Maglie. Entering politics as a member of the assembly that drew up Italy's constitution (1946), he was appointed to his first government post as under-secretary of state for foreign affairs (1948–50). Elected to the Chamber of Deputies every 5 years starting in 1948, he has held the posts of minister of justice (1955–57), enacting many reforms, and minister of education (1957–59). As political secretary of the Christian Democrat Party

(1959–63) he warned delegates against Communism. He was premier of Italy's four-party coalition government (1963–68).

Morocco (mo-ROC-co) **M** 458–61
  dyers' markets, pictures **A** 63, **D** 368
  flag **F** 236
  Marrakesh merchant, picture **A** 54
  Spanish enclaves of Ceuta and Melilla **S** 357
  See also Ifni
Moros (MO-ros), a people of the Philippines **P** 157
  Muslim Filipinos **P** 185

Morpheus (MOR-phe-us) (from Greek *morphe*, meaning "form"), in Greek mythology, the god of dreams and one of the sons of Hypnos (Sleep). He sends visions of human forms to those who sleep and is often called the god of sleep.

Morphine, narcotic drug **D** 326, 330
  plants, medicinal **P** 311
  term "narcotic" now limited to drugs with actions like morphine **N** 12
Morphology (morph-OL-ogy), study of structure of living organisms **B** 191
  kingdoms of living things **K** 252
Morphology, study of word formation **L** 302
Morrill, Justin Smith, American legislator **V** 316
  agricultural colleges established **A** 95
Morrill Act, 1862 **P** 507
  land-grant colleges to aid conservation **C** 485

Morris, Gouverneur (1752–1816), American statesman, b. Morrisania, N.Y. A signer of the Articles of Confederation (1775), he was a co-author of the New York constitution and a member of the Continental Congress (1778–79). He was appointed assistant minister of finance (1781–85) and 2 years later was a member of the Constitutional Convention. He was also U.S. commissioner to England (1790–91) and minister to France (1792–94). He served as U.S. senator from New York (1800–03).
  Morris' objection to universal suffrage **E** 113

Morris, Lewis (1726–1798), American statesman, b. Morrisania, N.Y. He was half-brother of Gouverneur Morris. He served as New York representative to the Continental Congress (1775–77), during which time he was a signer of the Declaration of Independence (1776). Appointed brigadier general of the Westchester county militia (1776), he also served as judge for that county (1777–78). He was frequently active as member of the state legislature (1777–90). He retired as major general at the end of the Revolutionary War.

Morris, Robert, English-born American financier and statesman **P** 142
Morris, William, English poet and artist **E** 263
  decorative arts defended against ugliness of machine crafts **D** 78
  founded Kelmscott Press **B** 322, 324
  influence on illustration **I** 91–92
  tapestry **T** 24
  type design **T** 346
  Victorian age in English art **E** 241

Morris, Wright (1910–   ), American novelist, b. Central City, Nebr. Many of his books, such as *The Inhabitants* and *The Home Place*, were influenced by his background on the plains. He has lectured at Swarthmore College and the University of Utah. He won the National Book Award (1957) for *The Field of Vision*.

Morris dances F 301
  English dances D 29

Morrison, Herbert Stanley (Baron Morrison of Lambeth) (1888–1965), English labor leader and statesman, b. Brixton. A member of Parliament periodically from 1923, he was the secretary to the London Labour Party (1915–47) and chairman of the National Labour Party (1928–29). Among the offices he held were those of minister of transport (1929–31), minister of supply (1940), deputy prime minister (1945–51), lord president of the Council and leader of the House of Commons (1945–51), and secretary of state for foreign affairs (1951).

Morristown National Historical Park, New Jersey N 174
Morro Castle, Havana, Cuba, picture C 549
Morrow, Anne see Lindbergh, Anne Morrow
Morrow, Dwight W., American diplomat C 497
Morse, Samuel F. B., American artist and inventor
   M 462
  communication advanced by telegraph C 438
  electronic communication, history of E 142
  telegraph T 51–52

Morse, Wayne Lyman (1900–) U.S. senator from Oregon, b. Madison, Wisc. He was professor of law and dean of the law school at University of Oregon before winning election to the Senate (1944). Originally a Republican, he resigned from the party in disagreement with the Republican presidential platform (1952) and became an independent. He was re-elected to the Senate as a Democrat (1956, 1962). He is noted for his independence and outspokenness.

Morse Code, International R 63; T 51
  communication advanced by C 438
  electronic communication, history of E 142
  invention by Samuel Morse M 462
Mortar, a cement mixture C 165
  brick masonry B 391–94
  grout for making mosaics M 463
Mortarboard cap, part of academic dress U 206
  graduation day, picture E 80
Mortars, guns G 426
Morte Darthur, book by Thomas Malory A 443–45
  early English collection of Arthur legends E 248
Mortgages (MOR-gages)
  held by banks B 48
  real estate R 113
  true interest rates I 289
  See also Installment buying
Mortise, a slot or notch to form a joint, in furniture
  F 502
Morton, "Jelly Roll," American jazz musician J 58; picture J 59

Morton, John (1724?–1777), American patriot, b. Ridley, Pa. Morton was a member of the Pennsylvania provincial assembly (1757–67, 1769–76), a delegate to the Stamp Act Congress (1765), and a judge (1770–74). He was a delegate to the Continental Congress (1774–77) and signed the Declaration of Independence.

Morton, Julius Sterling, American originator of Arbor Day N 84
Morton, Levi P., vice-president, United States V 331; picture V 328
Morton, Nathaniel, American writer A 195
Morton, Thomas, English adventurer P 346
  satirized Puritan life in book, New English Canaan A 196

Morton, William T. G., American doctor A 257
  early use of anesthesia in dentistry M 208a

M-O-S, U.S. Army term for "military occupation specialty." This refers to a specialized task a soldier is trained to perform.

Mosaic (mo-ZAI-ic) M 463
  ancient Greece G 344; picture G 342
  Aztec, picture I 154
  Byzantine B 484, 485, 488–89
  early Christian and Byzantine artistry P 17; picture
   P 16
  Islamic decoration of mosques I 420; picture
   I 418
  Italian art I 458
  Mérida mosaic, picture L 66
  O'Gorman's mosaic for library of University of Mexico
   L 67
  Pompeian, picture A 348

Mosbacher (MOSS-backer), Emil, Jr. ("Bus") (1922–), American yachtsman and government official, b. White Plains, N.Y. Introduced to sailing at an early age, he held the intercollegiate sailing championship for 2 years. The United States retained the America's Cup sailing trophy owing in large part to his skill as captain of the Weatherley (1962) and Intrepid (1967). In 1969 Nixon named him U.S. chief of protocol.

Mosby, John Singleton (1833–1916), American lawyer and soldier, b. Edgemont, Va. He practiced law in Virginia until the outbreak of the Civil War (1861), when he joined the Confederate Army. His cavalry unit (formed 1863), known as Mosby's Rangers, became famous for its daring raids, especially behind Union lines. After the war he served as United States consul in Hong Kong (1878–85) and as assistant attorney for the Department of Justice (1904–10).

Moscow, capital of Union of Soviet Socialist Republics
  M 464–67; U 35
  Allied Conference, 1943 W 297
  anniversary celebration of the Revolution, Red
   Square, picture U 48
  Cathedral of Dormition, picture U 55
  early state of Russia U 48
  ice cream vendor, picture E 314
  Kremlin, picture U 54
  Lenin State Library, picture L 199
  Muscovite period in architecture U 53
  Napoleon's retreat from N 12
  one of the world's great cities, picture C 309
  Peoples' Friendship Fountain, picture U 42
  Port of Five Seas H 37
  Saint Basil, Cathedral of, picture C 131
  subway, picture U 50
Moscow Art Theater T 161

Moseley (MOSE-ley), Henry Gwyn-Jeffreys (1887–1915), English physicist, b. Weymouth. He carried out important investigations in the field of radioactivity and in the study of the X-ray spectra of the elements. He calculated the exact number of elements from hydrogen through uranium (92), which showed that there were several elements lighter than uranium yet to be discovered. Moseley was killed in World War I.
  periodic table arranged according to atomic numbers
   E 156
  theory of atomic structure C 216

Moselle (mose-ELL) River, Europe, picture G 153

Moses, Anna Mary Robertson ("Grandma Moses") (1860–1961), American painter, b. Washington Co., N.Y. After retiring from farm work, she took up embroidery, but because of arthritis could not manipulate the needles, so she began painting. Although she was an untrained artist, her simple forms and gay colors, sometimes called American primitive, attracted the interest of a New York gallery owner in 1939.

Moses, Hebrew leader **M** 468
  Bible, Old Testament **B** 154
  leader and lawgiver of the Jews **J** 102
  Michelangelo's *Moses,* statue **S** 100
  Passover **P** 93
  spies to Canaan **S** 388
  Ten Commandments **T** 72
  See also Joshua
Moses, Horace A., American industrialist **J** 157
Moses, Law of **M** 468

Moses, Robert (1888–   ), American public official, b. New Haven, Conn. He was the president of the Long Island State Park Commission and chairman of the State Council of Parks (1924–63). Appointed New York City parks commissioner, he also administered the parkway system (1934–60) and was New York City construction co-ordinator (1946–60). He has been a consultant in state and municipal planning affairs throughout the United States and Brazil since 1942. In 1960 he became the president of the New York World's Fair.

Moses ben Maimon *see* Maimonides, Moses
Moses ibn Ezra *see* Ibn Ezra, Moses
Moshi, Tanzania **T** 19
Moslems *see* Muslims

Mosley, Sir Oswald Ernald (1896–   ), British fascist leader, b. London. Between 1918 and 1931 he served in Parliament, first as a Conservative, then as an Independent, and finally as a member of the Labour Party. He left the Labour Party to found (1931) the British Union of Fascists. He was imprisoned for a time in World War II.
  Fascism in England **F** 64

Mosques (MOSKS), Islamic places of worship **I** 416, 419–20
  Badshahi mosque, Lahore, picture **P** 37
  Bobo-Dioulasso, Upper Volta, picture **U** 228
  Blue mosque, Istanbul, picture **T** 323
  Cairo, picture **C** 8
  Delhi's Jama Masjid **D** 102–03
  Isfahan, Iran, picture **I** 372
  Islamic architecture **I** 419–20
  Jerusalem's Dome of the Rock **J** 79
  Kadhimain, Iraq, picture **I** 383
  Nigeria, picture **R** 150
  Sabers, Mosque of the, Kairouan, Tunisia, picture **I** 419
  Selimiye Mosque, Edirne Turkey, picture **T** 327
  Upper Volta, picture **U** 228
Mosquito Coast, Nicaragua **N** 246
Mosquitoes, insects **I** 269, 283; picture **I** 276
  disease carriers **D** 215
  eating habits of male mosquito **A** 266
  household pests **H** 260
  mouthparts, diagram **I** 270
  Reed discovers disease carrier **R** 128
  vectors, or carriers of diseases **V** 282–85
Moss, Spanish *see* Spanish Moss

Moss, Stirling (1929–   ), English auto racer, b. London. His father, a successful dentist, and his mother were both interested in racing, and Moss showed early signs of becoming an enthusiast. At 6 years of age he learned to steer a car, and at 10 he had one of his own. During his career he competed in about 466 events and won 194. In a race in 1962 he suffered severe injuries and subsequently retired from racing.

Moss agate, gem quartz **Q** 7
Mosses **F** 93–94
Most favored nation principle *see* Reciprocity
Mosul (MO-sul), Iraq **I** 382
Motels **H** 259; picture **H** 257
Motet, in music **M** 537
  Dutch and Flemish music **D** 363, 364
  Middle Ages **M** 299
Moth and the Star, The, fable by James Thurber **F** 8
Mother and Child, drawing by Renoir **D** 304
Mother Carey's chickens, tag game **G** 17
Mother Goose rhymes **N** 402–08
  children's literature **C** 237, 239
  Little Bo-peep, illustration by Kate Greenaway **I** 93
  Newbery published first collection **N** 137
  nonsense rhymes **N** 276
  Was Mother Goose a real person? **N** 402
Mothering Sunday, in England **H** 158
Mother-of-pearl, or nacre **G** 76
  inner surface of oyster shell **O** 271
  pearls made of layers of nacre **P** 113
Mother of Presidents, nickname for Virginia **V** 344
  Ohio also sent 8 citizens to the White House **O** 73
Mother of the West, Missouri **M** 366
Mother's Day **H** 156, 158
  how to make a Mother's Day greeting card **G** 374
  See also Jarvis, Anna
Mothers of Invention, The, American rock music group **R** 262d

Motherwell, Robert (1915–   ), American painter, b. Aberdeen, Wash. Educated in philosophy and archeology, Motherwell taught himself to paint. After World War II he emerged as a leading American painter working in the abstract style. His work can be seen in various American museums.
  The Voyage, painting **A** 438d

Mother with Child, etching by Käthe Kollwitz **G** 171
Moths **B** 468–75
  animal communication **A** 278
  clothes moth **H** 261; picture **H** 263
  How can you tell a butterfly from a moth? **B** 468
  how insects protect themselves, pictures **I** 275
  locomotion **A** 296
  metamorphosis **M** 235
  peppered moths, genetic changes **G** 87
  silk moth, life cycle **S** 178–79
  Yucca pollination **P** 320
  See also Metamorphosis

Mo Ti (MO di), or **Mo-tzu** (470?–396 B.C.), Chinese philosopher, b. probably Sung province. He was the founder of Mohism (Moism), which introduced logic into Chinese philosophy. His doctrine was universal love. He believed that all institutions should be judged by their ability to promote human welfare, and opposed aggressive war. Mo's philosophy, forgotten for 12 centuries, has been adopted now by many young Chinese.

Motion, in physics
  heat theory **H** 86d
  jet propulsion principle **J** 85
  kinetic energy **E** 198–203
  Newton's laws of **M** 469–71; **N** 207

Motion, in physics (continued)
principle of the seismograph **E** 37–38
reaction engine explained by Newton's third law
E 209
relativity **R** 140, 141
speed and direction of, on electric appliances **E** 120
Why has no one invented a perpetual-motion machine?
I 333
Motion, Newton's laws of **M** 469–71; **N** 207
behavior of rockets explained **R** 255–56
Motion picture cameras **P** 213, 219
communication advanced by **C** 434
Motion picture directors **M** 478, 481–82
Motion picture industry **M** 472–88d
animated cartoons **A** 297–99
audio-visual aids in education **E** 77–78
films for use in driver education, picture **D** 318
history of photography **P** 213
How can movies talk? **M** 474
television programs **T** 70–71
use of educational films in libraries **L** 171
Why do motion pictures seem to have "motion"? **M** 472
Motion picture photography **P** 205, 213
moviemaking at home **P** 218–20
Motion picture producers **M** 478
Motion pictures see Motion picture industry
Motions, parliamentary procedure **P** 80
Motivation, in psychology
learning **L** 101, 102
study, methods of **S** 440
Motivational research, advertising **A** 33

Motley, Constance Baker (1921–), American lawyer and public official, Negro, b. New Haven, Conn. As counsel for the Legal Defense and Educational Fund of the NAACP, she won many court decisions involving school segregation and other civil rights cases. She was the first Negro woman to be elected to the New York state senate (1964) and the first woman to serve (1965–66) as a borough president of New York City (Manhattan). In 1966 she was appointed a federal district judge for New York. Picture **N** 100.

Motley, John Lothrop, American historian **A** 202
types of historical writing **H** 137

Motley, Willard (1912–1965), American novelist, Negro, b. Chicago, Ill. Living in the slums of Chicago, wandering across the United States, and working at many odd jobs provided him with some ideas for his best-selling first novel, *Knock on Any Door,* a powerful story of the criminal hardening of a boy growing up in the slums.

Motokiyo, Seami, Japanese dramatist **O** 220d
Motor bicycles, picture **B** 128
Motorboats **B** 260–64
hydrofoils **H** 304–05
Motor centers, of nerves **B** 365
Motorcycles **M** 488d–489
Motors see Engines
Motors, electric see Electric motors
Motor scooters **M** 488b
assembly plant, Milan, picture **I** 453
Motor trucks see Trucks and trucking

Mott, John Raleigh (1865–1955), American religious worker, b. Livingstone Manor, N.Y. Mott was foreign secretary (1898–1915) and general secretary (1915–31) of the Y.M.C.A. International Committee. He made many trips throughout the world in the interest of the World Mission to Christianity. In 1946 he was co-recipient, with Emily G. Balch, of the Nobel peace prize.

Mott, Lucretia Coffin (1793–1880), American preacher and reformer, b. Nantucket, Mass. She spent 2 years as a teacher for the Society of Friends (Quakers) boarding school near Poughkeepsie. Moving to Pennsylvania, she became an "acknowledged minister" of the Society of Friends. Although her greatest interest was abolition of slavery, she also spoke for woman's rights, temperance, and peace. She helped organize the first Woman's Rights Convention in 1848.
women, role of **W** 212b

Mottes and baileys, early castles **A** 380
Mottoes, provincial see province articles
Mottoes, state **U** 91–93
See also state articles
Mouflon (moo-FLON), hoofed mammal, picture **H** 218

Moulton (MOLE-ton), **Forest Ray** (1872–1952), American astronomer, b. Le Roy, Mich. With T. C. Chamberlin he developed the planetesimal theory of how the solar system was formed. The theory states that a passing star caused the sun to throw off matter, which formed many tiny planets, or "planetesimals." The tiny planets slowly came together and formed the large planets of the present solar system. This is only one of several possible explanations known today.
the planetesimal theory **S** 247

Mound Builders, Indians of North America **O** 74
effigy mounds, Serpent Mound State Memorial, Ohio **O** 70; picture **O** 71
Indiana **I** 150
Indian art **I** 156
Mound builders, or Megapodes, birds **B** 225
Mount, geographic term see mountains by name, as Everest, Mount
Mountain beaver, or Aplodontia **R** 277; picture **R** 278
store hay **M** 66
Mountain bluebird
Idaho, state bird of **I** 54
Nevada, state bird of **N** 123
Mountain climbing **M** 489–91
Everest, Mount **E** 336–37
Himalayas **H** 128–29
Kanchenjunga peak in Sikkim, home of the gods respected **S** 176
spelunking, underground mountain climbing **S** 380
Switzerland, picture **S** 498
Mountaineering see Mountain climbing
Mountain laurel, shrub **P** 282; picture **G** 37
Connecticut, state flower of **C** 466
Pennsylvania, state flower of **P** 129
Mountain lions **C** 138–39; picture **C** 134
Mountain men, pioneer explorers, scouts, and fur traders **F** 523–24
California Trail **O** 263
Oregon Trail guides **O** 260, 261
trappers and traders of the westward movement **W** 146
Mountain music, Tennessee **T** 83
Mountain parks, grassy plateaus **N** 285
Mountain plants see Alpine plants
Mountain ranges **M** 492
Mountains **M** 492–99
Alps **A** 174–75
Andes **A** 252–53
ascents, first, of major peaks, chart **M** 490
barriers preventing spread of life **L** 236
birds of **B** 228
climate and mountain barriers **C** 346–47
climate control factor **W** 88–89
earth's mountain building **E** 10, 11
Everest, highest **E** 336–37

floating **E** 13
geological studies of mountain building **G** 116–17
Himalayas **H** 128–29
landforms of Europe **E** 308–09
North American Cordillera **N** 282, 284
of the moon **M** 450
rainfall **R** 95
Rocky Mountains **R** 274
undersea chains **E** 15
volcanoes **V** 377–86
See also landform sections of country, province, and state articles
Mountains of the Moon see Moon, Mountains of the
Mountain State, nickname for West Virginia **W** 126, 127
Mountain systems, groups of mountain ranges **M** 492
Mountbatten, Lord Louis, British admiral **W** 297
Mount Desert Island, Maine **M** 46
Mount Hood National Forest, Oregon, picture **G** 105
Mounties see Royal Canadian Mounted Police
Mount Maxwell Provincial Park, British Columbia, picture **B** 406
Mount McKinley National Park **A** 140; pictures **A** 134, **N** 50
Mount Palomar Observatory, California **O** 9; picture **O** 8
largest reflector telescope **A** 473
reflecting telescopes **T** 62–63
Mount Rainier (rain-IER) **National Park**, Washington **W** 24; picture **N** 48
Mount Revelstoke National Park, British Columbia **B** 406a
Mount Rushmore National Memorial, South Dakota **S** 312; pictures **N** 44, **S** 322
Mount Saint-Victoire with Tall Pine, painting by Cézanne **C** 181
Mount Vernon, Virginia **V** 354; **W** 36; pictures **V** 355, **W** 42
Mount Wilson Observatory, California **S** 466
Mourners, at funerals **F** 492–95
Mourning, or keening, **songs** **F** 326
Mourning doves see Doves
Mourning Monk, statue by Claus Sluter **D** 351
Mourning rings **J** 98, 99
Mouse see Mice
Mouse deer, or chevrotains **H** 210
Mouse opossums, or murine opossums **K** 171
Mouse River, see Souris River
Mouth organ, or harmonica **H** 42–43
folk music instruments **F** 330
Mouth-to-mouth artificial respiration **F** 159–60
Mouth-to-nose artificial respiration **F** 159–60
Mouton (MOO-ton) **lamb, fur** **F** 518
Movement, section of a musical composition
sonata form **C** 331
Movements of animals see Animals: Locomotion
Moviemaking at home **P** 218–20
Movies (moving pictures) see Motion picture industry
Mowatt, Anna Cora, American playwright **D** 299
Mowers, farm machinery **F** 60
Mowgli's Song Against People, poem by Kipling **K** 261–62

Moynihan, Daniel Patrick, (1927–), American sociologist and author, b. Tulsa, Okla. He served in the Office of the Governor of New York (1955–59). Appointed to U.S. Department of Labor (1961), Moynihan later became assistant secretary of labor. Author of a controversial report on the Negro (1965), in 1966 he headed M.I.T.-Harvard Joint Center for Urban Studies. President-elect Nixon appointed him White House assistant for urban affairs (Dec. 1968), and in 1970 he became a presidential counselor. He left the government the following year to return to Harvard. In 1973 he became ambassador to India.

Mozambique (mo-zom-BEEK) **M** 500–01
Portuguese overseas territories **P** 402
Mozarabic (mo-ZARR-a-bic), language **S** 366
Mozart (MO-tzart), **Leopold**, German-born Austrian violinist and composer, father of Wolfgang A. Mozart **C** 330; picture **M** 502
Mozart, Maria Anna, Austrian pianist, sister of Wolfgang Amadeus, picture **M** 502
Mozart, Wolfgang Amadeus, Austrian composer **M** 502
chamber music **C** 186
choral music **C** 278
clarinet a favorite instrument **C** 329
classical age in music **C** 330, 332, 333
Cosi Fan Tutte, opera **O** 143
Don Giovanni, opera **O** 143
first concert at age 7, picture **G** 185
German music **G** 185
influenced by Italian music **I** 485
Magic Flute, The, opera **O** 146
Marriage of Figaro, The, opera **O** 146–47
opera **C** 332; **O** 134
Salzburg Festival **M** 550
signature reproduced **A** 527
symphonies **M** 540–41
Mozzarella (mot-za-REL-la), Italian cheese **D** 13
Mphahlele, Ezekiel, South African writer **A** 76b
Mqhayi, Samuel, South African novelist **A** 76b
M. S., abbreviation for motor ship **O** 23
Mtskheta, Union of Soviet Socialist Republics, picture **U** 47
Much Ado About Nothing, play by Shakespeare **S** 136
Mucilage (MUCE-il-age), type of adhesive **G** 242
Muckrakers, crusading reporters **F** 350
Mucus (MU-cus), body substance **D** 206
eel's body mucus **E** 85
Mud eels, land-water animals **F** 475
Mudejar (mu-THE-har) **style**, art and architecture **S** 360
Latin-American architecture **L** 62
Mudflows, volcanic **V** 382
Mud-mill, dredging machine **D** 308
Mudpuppies, land-water animals **F** 475; picture **F** 474
Mud turtles **T** 332
Mueller, O. F., Danish zoologist **T** 30
Muezzin (mu-EZZ-in), Muslim crier, at time of daily prayers **I** 416
Mufflers, engine silencers **I** 307
Mugwumps, reform Republicans **C** 341
Muhammad (English: Mohammed), Arab prophet, founder of Islam **M** 404–05
Muhammad, Elijah see Elijah Muhammad
Muhammad Ali see Ali, Muhammad

Muhlenberg (MU-len-berg) **family**, distinguished family of Lutheran clergymen, patriots, statesmen, and educators. The founder, **Henry Melchior** (1711–87), was born in Germany and went to America (1742) and settled in Philadelphia, Pa. He created union and order in the Lutheran Church. Three of his sons, **John Peter** (1746–1807), **Frederick Augustus Conrad** (1750–1801), and **Gotthilf Henry** (1753–1815), made their mark in American political, religious, and academic life. Gotthilf's son **Henry Augustus Philip** (1782–1844) was the first minister to Austria, and Henry Augustus' son **Frederick Augustus** (1818–1901) was first president of Muhlenberg College. **William Augustus** (1796–1877), a grandson of Frederick Augustus Conrad, founded St. Luke's Hospital, New York.

Muir, Alexander, Scottish-born Canadian teacher **N** 27

Muir, John (1838–1914), American naturalist and conservationist, b. Dunbar, Scotland. He made botanical studies in the Midwest, hiked from Indianapolis to

Muir, John (continued)
California, and later wrote studies of the Yosemite Valley, urging that it become a national park. During travels in the United States, Alaska, Asia, and Australia he pressed for conservation. One of his books is *Our National Parks*.

Yosemite National Park Y 352–53

Muir Woods National Monument, California C 25
Mujibur Rahman, Sheikh, first prime minister of Bangladesh B 44c; P 41
Mukden see Shenyang
Mukden Incident, 1931 W 284

Mukerji (MU-ker-ji), **Dhan Gopal** (1890–1936), Indian writer, b. Calcutta. He went to the United States in 1910 and wrote books that would help explain India to American children. His titles include *Kari the Elephant* and the Newbery medal winner (1928) *Gay Neck*, about a carrier pigeon.

Mulatto (from Portuguese and Spanish *mulato*, meaning "mixed breed"), person with one Negro and one white parent. The word is also used to describe people with varying amounts of mixed white and Negro blood.

Mulberries, group of trees bearing purple or black edible berries. The leaves of one variety that grows in China and Japan are used as food for silkworm larvae.

silk, history of S 178, 179

Mulberries, term for artificial harbors, World War II W 298, 300; picture W 299
Mulberry Bush, singing game G 12
Mulch, materials to retain soil moisture G 41–42
dust mulches for vegetables V 288
Mule deer H 219; picture H 214
Mules H 235; picture A 293
Missouri mule, picture H 211
Muleta (mu-LAE-ta), bullfighter's cape B 450

Mullan, John (1830–1909), American army officer and road builder, b. Norfolk, Va. He spent 2 years (1853–55) exploring a planned railroad route from St. Paul to the Pacific and 5 years (1858–63) working on a military road from Montana to Washington, which helped open the Northwest to immigrants. Many travelers to the West consulted his *Miners' and Travelers' Guide*.

Muller, Hermann Joseph (1890–1967), American geneticist, b. New York, N.Y. He was awarded the 1946 Nobel prize in medicine and physiology for showing that X rays could cause mutations. With this method for producing mutations he gathered evidence that the majority of mutations are harmful.

Mullet, fish
habitats, feeding habits, uses F 213
Mullins, Priscilla, Pilgrim settler P 344
Multilateral (mul-ti-LAT-er-al) **treaties** T 271
agreements between several nations I 323
Multiple-choice tests
animal experiments A 285–86
points on test taking E 349; T 121

Multiple sclerosis (scler-O-sis), disease of the central nervous system. The disease results from damage to the myelin sheaths covering nerve fibers in the brain. The symptoms, which may disappear and then recur, range from muscle weakness and blurred vision to paralysis and blindness. The disease may progress slowly or rapidly. No cause or effective treatment is known.

Multiplex system, in telegraphy T 53
Multiplex telegraphy see Carrier transmission
Multiplicand (mul-ti-pli-CAND), in multiplication A 400
Multiplication, in mathematics
abacus A 2
algebra A 159
AND computer circuits C 454
arithmetic A 400
binary numeration system C 453, 456
decimal fraction F 401–02
fractions F 399
new mathematics explains the "grouping" property of numbers M 164
slide rule M 167
using base-4 system N 400
Multiplier, in multiplication A 400
Multipurpose dams D 19
Multistage rockets R 259–60
Goddard's plan for reaching moon G 245
Mu mesons, or **muons,** subatomic particles N 368

Mumford, Lewis (1895–   ), American writer, b. Flushing, N.Y. Although he has written a study of Melville (*Herman Melville*) and books (such as *Men Must Act*) about U.S. policies, he is best-known for his works about urban life and about city and regional planning. Books on these subjects include *Story of Utopias* and *The City in History*.

Mummers, actors playing buffoons and clowns D 295
Mummies, dead bodies preserved from decay
Egyptian E 95; F 492
mummy portraits P 17
Mumps, virus disease D 201

Munch (MOONSH), **Charles** (1891–1968), French conductor, b. Strasbourg (then Germany). He led the Société des Concerts du Conservatoire de Paris (1938–45) and made his American debut with the Boston Symphony in 1946. He succeeded Serge Koussevitzky as conductor and music director of the Boston Symphony (1949–62). He was noted particularly for his interpretations of works by modern French composers.

Munch (MOONCK), **Edvard** (1863–1944), Norwegian painter, b. Loten. He was interested in the subjects of love and death, and an exhibition of his work in Berlin in 1892 had a great effect on later German painting. Many of his paintings and powerful woodcut prints use swirling, curving lines, and they reveal drama and passion. Most of his paintings are in Oslo, but his prints may be seen in museums throughout Europe and the United States.

lithograph, *The Scream* G 307

Munchausen (MOONCK-how-sen), or **Münchhausen, Baron Karl Friedrich Hieronymus von** (1720–1797), German soldier, b. Hanover. He fought with the Russians against Turkey and supposedly made up tall tales based on his experiences. Rudolph Erich Raspe was the author of an English collection of the tales: *Baron Munchausen's Narrative of His Marvellous Travels and Campaigns in Russia*. Later editions included more tales and greater lies, and the name Munchausen came to suggest an improbable story.

Muncie, Indiana, Middletown, U.S.A. I 148–49

Muni (MU-ni), **Paul** (Paul Weisenfreund) (1895–1967), American actor, b. Lemberg, Austria. He arrived in the United States in 1902, became a citizen (1923), and appeared in Yiddish- and English-language stage productions before beginning a movie career in 1928 that brought him an Oscar for *The Life of Louis Pasteur* (1936). New York stage appearances included roles in *Counselor-at-Law* and *Inherit the Wind*.

Munich (MU-nick), capital of Bavaria, West Germany **G** 158
  Olympics, 1972 **O** 116b
Munich Pact, 1938 **W** 286
  Sudetenland, Czechoslovakia **C** 563
Municipal (mu-NIS-ip-al) **government** **M** 503–08
  city problems **C** 308–09; **U** 232–34
  civil service **C** 317
  education **E** 74
  income tax **I** 111
  local health departments **P** 502–03
  parks and playgrounds **P** 76–78
  public utilities **P** 510–13 ·
  re-apportionment of state legislatures **S** 412, 415
  taxation for levels of government **T** 26
  Tokyo **T** 205
Municipalities, governmental powers of **M** 504
Munin, raven of Odin, Norse god **N** 278

Muñoz Marín (MOON-yose ma-REEN), **Luis** (1898–   ), Puerto Rican politician and journalist, b. San Juan. He has been secretary to the Puerto Rican delegate to the U.S. Congress (1916–18), a member of the Puerto Rican Liberal Party in the 1920's, founder of the Popular Democratic Party (1938), president of the Puerto Rican Senate (1941–48), and governor of Puerto Rico (1949–64). He has edited the magazine *La Revista de Indias* and edited and published the newspaper *La Democracia*.
  Puerto Rico, history of **P** 523

Munro, Hector Hugh (pen name Saki) (1870–1916), English writer, b. Burma. Primarily a writer of short stories and satires, his only serious work was *The Rise of the Russian Empire*. He is remembered for collections such as *The Chronicles of Clovis* and *Beasts and Super-Beasts*. Saki's stories are marked by wit and brevity.

Munsel (mun-SEL), **Patrice** (1925–), American soprano, b. Spokane, Wash. She became, at 18, the youngest singer ever to receive a contract from the Metropolitan Opera Company, where she specialized in coloratura roles, winning special fame as Adele in *Die Fledermaus*. She has also starred in motion pictures (*Melba*), appeared on TV, and toured in musical comedy.

Muntjacs, deer **H** 219–20
Muons, or mu mesons, subatomic particles **N** 368
Muppets, puppets, picture **T** 70d
Murabba'at, ancient community near Dead Sea **D** 49
Mural painting
  ancient Rome **P** 17; picture **P** 16
  cave painting of early man **P** 14–15
  Egypt **P** 15
  fresco technique popular during Renaissance **P** 20
  Leonardo da Vinci's *Last Supper* damaged because of damp wall **P** 21
  Rivera, Diego, Mexican artist **L** 67
Murasaki, Lady, Japanese writer **J** 43; **O** 220b–220c

Murat (mu-RA), **Joachim** (1767?–1815), marshal of France and king of Naples, b. La Bastide, France. He gave up studies for the priesthood to fight in Egypt (1798–99) with Napoleon, whose sister Caroline he married (1800). Murat was named marshal of France (1804) and king of Naples (1808) and took part in Napoleon's Russian campaign (1812) before military and political defeats sent him into exile on Corsica. He was captured and executed upon trying to return to Italy.

Murchison Falls, on the Nile **N** 260; **U** 5
Murder in the Cathedral, verse drama by T. S. Eliot **E** 177
Murders in the Rue Morgue, The, by Edgar Allan Poe **M** 553
Murdock, William, English inventor **A** 541
Murex, sea snail
  shell, picture **S** 148
  source of purple dye, picture **D** 367
Murillo (mu-RILL-o), **Bartolomé Esteban,** Spanish artist **S** 362
Murine, or mouse, opossums **K** 171
Murmansk, Union of Soviet Socialist Republics **U** 33
Murphy, Charles ("Mile-a-Minute"), American bicycle racer **B** 173

Murphy, Isaac (1856–1896), American jockey, Negro, b. Pleasant Green Hill, Ky. An outstanding jockey, he was considered at his best from 1884 to 1890 and had one of the highest winning averages in racing history. In Saratoga (1882) he won 49 of his 51 races.

Murray, James, English governor of Quebec **C** 71

Murray, Mary Lindley (1726–1782), American patriot, b. Philadelphia, Pa. During the Revolutionary War she detained a detachment of British troops by offering them the hospitality of her home, Murray Hill (1776), and thus allowed a large company of the American Army to relocate.

Murray, Philip, American labor leader **L** 6
Murray, William ("Alfalfa Bill"), American political leader **O** 93
Murray River, Australia **R** 245
  Australia's central lowland section **A** 503
Murray Spillway, P.E.I., Canada, picture **P** 456f
Murre (MURR), birds of the auk family **B** 213–14

Murrow, Edward R. (1908–1965), American news commentator, b. Greensboro, N.C. Associated with CBS for more than 25 years (1935–61), he became well-known for his World War II news broadcasts from London. Returning from Europe, he was made a CBS vice-president (1946–47) and soon was famous for his television shows Person to Person and See It Now. A repeated winner of the Peabody Award for excellence in broadcasting, he received the Medal of Freedom (1964), the highest United States civilian honor. He also served as United States Information Agency director (1961–63).

Musangs (mu-SONGS), civet cats **G** 91
Muscat, capital of Oman **M** 301
Muscat and Oman, sultanate, now Oman **M** 301
Muscles
  animals: locomotion **A** 294
  birds **B** 200–01
  body, human **B** 273; diagrams **B** 272
  child development **C** 231–34
  curare, drug, paralyzes **D** 325
  exercise **P** 226–29
  fishes **F** 188
  microscopic views of muscle fibers, pictures **M** 287
  muscle sense **B** 287
  of insects **I** 273–74
  weight lifting **W** 107
Muscle Shoals, Alabama **A** 119
Muscovites, Russians **M** 467
Muscovy, former name of Russia **M** 467

Muscular dystrophy (DIS-trophy), disease in which fibers of muscles slowly waste away. The disease runs in

Muscular dystrophy (continued)
families. It usually starts in childhood, often developing slowly but in time causing disability. No cause or treatment has yet been found.

Museo del Prado see Prado

Muses, in Greek mythology, the nine daughters of Zeus and Mnemosyne who were the goddesses of the arts and sciences. They sang and danced at the festivities of the gods and were said to make people forget their troubles. In classical and English literature there are many appeals to the Muses. The Muses are: Calliope, Clio, Erato, Euterpe, Melpomene, Polyhymnia, Terpsichore, Thalia, and Urania.
See also names of the Muses

Musette (muse-ETT), wind instrument, picture **W 182**
Museumobile, of Illinois State Museum **I 80**
Museum of Modern Art, New York City **M 397**
Museum of Science and Industry, Chicago, Illinois **I 80; M 513;** picture **M 515**
Museums M 509–20
"Agassiz" museum at Harvard **A 80**
Atomic Energy, American Museum of, Oak Ridge, Tenn., picture **N 352**
Eisenhower Memorial, Abilene, Kansas **K 183, 184**
Field Museum, Chicago, picture **C 230**
Hermitage Museum, Leningrad **H 119–20**
Louvre, Paris, France **L 366–68**
Metropolitan Museum of Art, New York City **M 236–37**
National Gallery, London **N 38–39**
National Gallery of Art, Washington, D.C. **N 40–41**
Prado, Madrid **P 428–29**
Smithsonian Institution **S 202**
taxidermy prepares animal models **T 27**
Uffizi gallery **U 2–3**
See also Presidential libraries; education section of country, province, and state articles
Musgrave, Franklin S., American astronaut **S 347**
Mush, corn-meal dish **C 507**
Mushrooms, plants of the fungi group **M 521**
club and sac fungi **F 498–500**
growth rate, pictures **L 210**
yellow, orange, or red fly agaric, poisonous **P 322**

Musial (MU-zi-al), **Stanley Frank** ("Stan") (1920–   ), American baseball player, b. Donora, Pa. Outfielder and first baseman for St. Louis Cardinals (1941–44; 1946–63), he was 3 times voted Most Valuable Player in National League and won 7 league batting titles. He holds National League lifetime records for hits, runs, runs batted in, and games played. He became a Cardinal executive after his retirement. He was elected to the Baseball Hall of Fame in 1969.

Music M 522–41
acoustics **S 260–61**
African **A 77–79**
American Indian **I 160–61**
ancient **A 243–47**
ballads **F 310–11, 318**
bands and band music **B 38–41**
baroque period in music **B 62–66**
bell music **B 136**
Canada **C 63**
chamber music **C 184–86**
Christmas **C 289–90**
classical age **C 330–33**
dance music **D 35–37**
Dutch and Flemish **D 363–65**
electronic **E 142g–142h**

English music **E 268–71**
festivals **M 550–52**
folk music **F 318–28**
French music **F 443–48**
German and Austrian music **G 181–89**
harmonics **S 264–65**
Hebrew music **A 246; C 276; H 309**
hymns **H 309–13**
instruments see Musical instruments
Italian language suited to music **I 474**
Italian music **I 482–86**
jazz **J 57–62**
Latin-American music **L 73–75**
Middle Ages, music of the **M 298–99**
modern music **M 399–402**
musical comedy **M 542–43**
national anthems and patriotic songs **N 15–27**
Negro spiritual, influence of **N 107**
opera **O 130–55**
operetta **O 156–58**
orchestra **O 182–87**
orchestra conducting **O 188–91**
Oriental music **O 220d–221**
Renaissance music **R 172–74**
rock music **R 262a–262d**
romantic age **R 310–11**
Russian music **U 63–64**
sounds, musical **S 264–65**
Spanish music **S 372–74**
United States, music of the **U 125–27**
What is the origin of clef signs? **M 524**
Why are schools of music called conservatories? **M 524**
See also names of famous composers and musicians
Music, choral see Choral music
Music, modern see Modern music
Musical chairs, group game **I 226**
Musical comedy M 542–43
motion picture industry **M 487–88**
rock music **R 262d**
Musical composition see Composition, music
Musical forms M 535–41
baroque period **B 62–66**
classical age **C 331–32**
concert overtures **R 311**
English music **E 268–71**
operetta **O 156–58**
symphonic poems and program music **R 311**
Musical glasses, for a demonstration of sound **S 266**
Musical instruments M 544–50
African music **A 78–79**
ancient music **A 245–47;** pictures **A 244**
bands and band music **B 38–41**
bells and carillons **B 134–37**
classical age, new groups of the **C 331**
dance **D 35**
drum **D 333–36**
electronic music **E 142g–142h**
folk music instruments **F 301, 329–30**
forced vibrations to amplify sound **S 262**
glasses to demonstrate musical sounds **S 266**
harmonics **S 264–65**
Italian music **I 483;** picture **I 482**
jazz bands **J 60**
keyboard instruments **K 236–40**
Latin-American instruments **L 70, 74;** pictures **L 73**
Middle Ages **M 299**
orchestra **O 182–87**
Oriental, pictures **O 220d, 221**
percussion instruments **P 151–53**
stringed instruments **S 438–39**
wind instruments **W 182–83**
See also Folk music instruments; Keyboard instru-

ments; Percussion instruments; Stringed instruments; Wind instruments; names of instruments, as Bugle
Musical notation **M** 522–32
  ancient music **A** 246
  figured bass in baroque music **B** 65
Musical plays **M** 542
Musical terms **M** 532–34
Music boxes
  clocks with music box, picture **W** 48
Music drama, a kind of opera **O** 136
  operatic forms in German music **G** 187
  Wagner, Richard **W** 2
Music education see Musicology; Music schools
Music festivals **M** 550–52
  rock music festivals **R** 262d

Music hath charms to soothe the savage breast, first line of *The Mourning Bride,* by English dramatist William Congreve (1670–1729).

Musicians
  chart of names, dates, pictures **M** 522–23
Music industry, American **R** 262a–262b

Musicology, scholarly and systematic study of music, involving research into the history of music and performance practices, music theory and esthetics, acoustics, and the development of musical instruments. The comparative study of the indigenous and folk music of different cultures is called ethnomusicology. Musicology as a separate branch of study in the field of music originated in Germany during the second half of the 19th century and is today an important part of the musical curriculum in many universities in Europe and America.

Music Party, The, painting by Philippe Mercier **E** 269
Music schools (conservatories) **M** 524

Musil, Robert (1880–1942), Austrian novelist, b. Klagenfurt. At the age of 26 he published his first novel, which dealt with the conflicts of adolescence. His most important work was *The Man without Qualities,* about the life and history of prewar Austria.
  Austrian literature **G** 180

Musique concrète (mu-ZEEK con-CRET) **E** 142g
Musk, substance from special glands of animals **G** 90
  fixative for perfume **P** 155
  skunks **S** 191–92
  turtles **T** 332, 333
Musk deer **H** 219–20; picture **H** 215
Muskegs, or swamps
  North America **N** 288
  taiga **T** 11
Muskellunge, fish, picture **F** 210
Muskets, guns **G** 415

Muskie, Edmund Sixtus (1914–), American political leader, b. Rumford, Me. A graduate of Bates College, Me. (1936), and Cornell University Law School (1939), Muskie entered politics in 1946. He served for 6 years in the Maine House of Representatives and for 2 years as Democratic National Committeeman from Maine (1952–54). In 1954 he became Maine's first Democratic governor in 20 years, and in 1958, the first Democrat elected to the U.S. Senate in Maine's history. Senator Muskie was Democratic vice-presidential nominee, 1968.

Muskmelons, or summer melons **M** 216, 217

Musk-ox, large mammal found in Arctic regions of North America. The long, shaggy hair is deep brown or black in color. The horns are somewhat curved. Musk-oxen feed on low-growing vegetation. Picture **H** 216

Muskrats, rodents **R** 279; picture **A** 272; **K** 257
Muslims, followers of Islam **I** 414–16
  Abraham honored by **A** 7
  Africa **A** 56; picture **A** 47
  art see Islamic art and architecture
  Bangladesh **B** 44
  Crusades against **C** 538–40
  early education spread by **E** 66
  Egyptian invasion **E** 92
  Ethiopia **E** 296, 303
  European invasion **M** 290–91
  family **F** 41
  funeral customs **F** 493
  holiday celebration, picture **I** 118
  horses' role in history **H** 237
  Islam in Libya **L** 201
  Jerusalem **J** 78, 81
  Koran **K** 294–95
  marriage rites **W** 102
  Mecca **M** 196
  Mohammed's followers **M** 404–05
  Morocco **M** 458
  Pakistan **P** 35
  Portugal **P** 399
  science, advances in **S** 64
  slave trade in Africa **C** 170
  Turkey **T** 323–24
  Yemen (Sana) **Y** 348
  See also Arabs; Moors
Mussels, mollusks **O** 272; picture **S** 148
Musset (mu-SAY), **Alfred de,** French writer **F** 440
Mussolini (mu-so-LI-ni), **Benito,** Italian premier **M** 552
  fall of **W** 297
  Fascism in Italy **F** 63, 64; **I** 457
  rise of dictators before World War II **W** 284
Mussorgsky (mu-SORG-ski), **Modest,** Russian composer **U** 63
  Boris Godunov, opera **O** 140–41
  opera **O** 136
Mustang, fastback automobile model, picture **A** 535
Mustangs, wild horses of Spanish stock **H** 241

Mustard, vegetable belonging to the same group as the turnip, the cabbage, and the cauliflower. The seeds of several species are the chief source of mustard oil and dressing; these species generally are tall plants with hairy leaves, short pods, and yellow blossoms. The cabbagelike leaves of several other mustard species supply greens for food. Mustards were Old World natives and now are grown everywhere. Picture **S** 381
  what is a spice and what is a condiment **S** 380, 382

Mustelidae (must-E-li-de), family of animals **O** 239
Mutability (mu-ta-BIL-ity), poem by Percy Bysshe Shelley **S** 146
Mutant, cell changed by mutation **C** 95
Mutation theory, in biology **C** 94–95; **E** 346
  cancer research **C** 94–95
  furs, colors of **F** 514
  permanent genetic change **G** 83–84
  viruses **V** 364–65
Mute, term for deaf person who has not been taught to speak **D** 53
Mutemua (mu-tay-MU-a), wife of Thutmose IV, Egyptian ruler **N** 90
Mutesa I (mu-TAY-sa), king of Buganda **U** 7
Mutesa II (Sir Edward Mutesa), former king, then president, of Uganda **U** 7
Mutiny on the Bounty see Bligh, William

ILLUSTRATION CREDITS

The following list credits, by page, the sources of illustrations used in Volume M of THE NEW BOOK OF KNOWLEDGE. Credits are listed illustration by illustration —left to right, top to bottom. Wherever appropriate, the name of the photographer or artist has been listed with the source, the two being separated by a dash. When two or more illustrations appear on one page, their credits are separated by semicolons.

38 Arthur Griffin; Maine Department of Economic Development.
42 Graphic Arts International
43 Eastman Kodak
44 Esther Henderson—Rapho Guillumette; Diversified Map Corp.
49 George Buctel; Paul Hufner—Shostal.
50 Paul Hufner—Shostal
51 George Buctel
53 George Buctel
55 Stockpile—Ewing Krainin; Van Bucker —Photo Researchers.
56 Harrison Forman
57 George Buctel
58 Hector Acebes—Photo Researchers
59 George Buctel
60 George Buctel; Jerry Cooke.
62 Gaetano Di Palma
64 Gaetano Di Palma
65 Gaetano Di Palma
68 Gaetano Di Palma
69 Gaetano Di Palma
70 Alouise Boker—National Audubon Society
71 Gaetano Di Palma
72 Gaetano Di Palma
73 Metropolitan Museum of Art, Gift of Erwin Davis
74 Arabelle Wheatley
75 George Buctel
77 Manitoba Department of Industry and Commerce
78 Diversified Map Corp.
79 Malak
80 Department of Industry and Commerce Manitoba; Department of Industry and Commerce Manitoba; George Hunter—Shostal.
84 Gerald McConnell
87 Gerald McConnell
89 Harry Scott
90 George Buctel
91 Esso Humble Oil & Refining Co.; U.S. Coast & Geodetic Survey, U.S. Department of Commerce; U.S. Geological Survey, U.S. Department of the Interior; George Buctel.
92 Harry Scott; Jeppesen & Co.
94 Harry Scott
95 Gerald McConnell
98 Radio Times—Hulton Picture Library
104 W. S. Tinsen—Republic Observatory, Johannesburg; Miller Pope.
105 U.S. Geological Survey
106 Miller Pope
107 Miller Pope
108 Jet Propulsion Laboratory—NASA
109 © 1969 by New York Times Company, reprinted by permission; NASA.
110 Lowell Observatory Photo; NASA
115 Color Illustration Inc.; Maryland Department of Economic Development; Ron Austing—Photo Researchers; Bob Taylor—FPG.
116 Diversified Map Corp; M. E. Warren.
117 Diversified Map Corp.
118 Diversified Map Corp.
121 M. E. Warren
122 M. E. Warren
125 Graphic Arts International
126 Diversified Map Corp.
127 M. E. Warren
129 M. E. Warren
131 George Bakacs
132 George Bakacs
133 George Bakacs; Graphic Arts International.
134 Color Illustration Inc.; Irving Oakes—Photo Researchers; A. A. Allen; Richard O. Riess.
136 Diversified Map Corp.
137 Diversified Map Corp.

139 Wendler—FPG
140 Thomas Hollyman—Photo Researchers; Fred Sieb—Alpha.
142 Diversified Map Corp.
145 Graphic Arts International
146 Jack Breed—FPG
153 Gerald McConnell
155 Gerald McConnell
156 IBM
157 Harold E. Edgerton
158– Gerald McConnell
160
164 Gerald McConnell
166 Gerald McConnell
167 Gerald McConnell
169 Robert Capa—Magnum
170 Miller Pope
172– Miller Pope
176
178 Miller Pope
179 George Buctel; Marc & Evelyne Bernheim—Rapho Guillumette
181 George Buctel
184 Herman B. Vestal
185 Herman B. Vestal
187 James Cooper
188 Granger Collection
190 Granger Collection
191 W. R. Grace & Co.
193 Ralph Brillhart
194 Ralph Brillhart
196 Birnback
197 Gerald McConnell
199 Chet Reneson
200 Chet Reneson
202 Nes Levotch
205– Bettmann Archive
207
208a Bettmann Archive
208b Elizabeth Wilcox; Bettmann Archive
208c Bettmann Archive; Chas. Pfizer & Co., Inc.
208d–Antony Kokinos
208h
210 Antony Kokinos
212 Thomas Hollyman—Photo Researchers; Ace Williams—Shostal; Ray Manley—Shostal.
214 George Buctel
215 George Buctel
216 Roy Cragnolin
229 American Metals Climax, Inc.; American Metals Climax, Inc.
230 Shostal; Howard Koslow.
231 Howard Koslow; Kaiser Aluminum.
232 British Museum; Lisl Steiner.
234 Douglas P. Wilson; Douglas P. Wilson; Douglas P. Wilson; Hugh Spencer.
235 Hugh Spencer; Hugh Spencer; Hugh Spencer; Arabelle Wheatley.
236 Charles Shapp; Lisl Steiner.
237 D. Jordan-Wilson—Pix
241 George Buctel
243 John Lewis Stage—Photo Researchers
244 Ralph Weiss
245 Marc & Evelyne Bernheim—Rapho Guillumette
246 George Hunter—Shostal
247 Jerry Frank
250 Marc & Evelyne Bernheim—Rapho Guillumette
251 George Buctel
252– Marc & Evelyne Bernheim—Rapho Guillumette
253
254 George Buctel; Miami Metro Dept. of Publicity & Tourism.
255 Scala—Shostal
256 Scala—Shostal
257 Alinari—Art Reference Bureau
259 Color Illustration Inc.; Perry J. Reynolds; William A. Dyer; William A. Dyer.
260 Diversified Map Corp.

261 Shostal
263 Laurence Lowry—Rapho Guillumette
264 Diversified Map Corp.
266 Louis Renault—Photo Researchers
269 Graphic Arts International
270 Diversified Map Corp.
271 Shostal; Shostal; Jerry Cooke—Photo Researchers.
274 Walter Dawn
275 Arabelle Wheatley; Julius Weber.
276 Eric V. Gravé
277 Eric V. Gravé
278 Eric V. Gravé; Walter Dawn.
281 Eric V. Gravé; Roman Vishniac; Arabelle Wheatley.
282 Arabelle Wheatley
284 George Bakacs
285 George Bakacs
286 George Bakacs
287 Julius Weber
288 NASA; RCA.
289 Life Magazine, © Time Inc., all rights reserved
292– Fred Mason
295
297 Compagnie Aérienne Française, Suresnes
298 Herman B. Vestal
299 Herman B. Vestal
301 George Buctel
302 Diane Rawson—Photo Researchers
303 Peter Hufner—Shostal
304 Elmar Schneiwind—Rapho Guillumette; A. Louis Goldman—Rapho Guillumette.
307 Saudi Arabian Information Service; Ormand Gigli—Rapho Guillumette.
308 John Lewis Stage—Photo Researchers; Rene Burri—Magnum.
310 Gerald McConnell
312 George Buctel; Metropolitan Milwaukee Association of Commerce.
315 Gerald McConnell
316– Jerry M. Whiting
318
319 Josef Muench; Jerry M. Whiting; Jerry M. Whiting.
321 George Buctel; A. Louis Goldman—Rapho Guillumette
323 Color Illustration Inc.; Minnesota Museum of Natural History; W. J. Breckenridge; Walter H. Wettschreck—Minnesota Conservation Department.
324 Esther Henderson—Rapho Guillumette
325 Diversified Map Corp.
326 Esther Henderson—Rapho Guillumette
328 Diversified Map Corp.
330 A. Louis Goldman—Rapho Guillumette
332 Graphic Arts International
334 Diversified Map Corp.
335 William Froelich, Jr.
338 U.S. Department of the Treasury, Bureau of the Mint
339 From A Dissertation on the Pageants or Dramatic Mysteries Anciently Performed at Coventry, by Thomas Sharp, 1825—New York Public Library
340 Thomas Hollyman—Photo Researchers
341 U.S. Department of Commerce, Weather Bureau; Nes Levotch.
342 David Linton; Nes Levotch.
343 Wayne Dunham
345 Wayne Dunham
346 Wayne Dunham
348 Deatherage—Monkmeyer
349 Marc & Evelyne Bernheim—Rapho Guillumette
351 Color Illustration Inc.; R. Cornell; Keresztes; National Audubon Society.
352 Jay Leviton—Rapho Guillumette; Diversified Map Corp.
353 Diversified Map Corp.
354 Diversified Map Corp.
357 Robert Yarnall Richie; Shostal

N, 14th letter of the English alphabet **N** 1
  See also Alphabet
NAACP see National Association for the Advancement of
  Colored People
Nabokov (na-BAW-kof), **Vladimir,** Russian-born American
  author **U** 63
Naboth (NAIB-oth), Biblical figure **E** 176

Nabrit, James Madison, Jr. (1900–), American educator and lawyer, Negro, b. Atlanta, Ga. Professor of
law at Howard University, he organized (1938) the first
formal course in Civil Rights Law to be taught at an
American law school. As a lawyer he participated in
almost every civil rights case in the U.S. courts between
1945 and 1960. He was president of Howard University
(1960–68). He served (1966–67) as U.S. Permanent Deputy Representative to the United Nations. Picture **N** 104.

Nachtegall (nock-teg-AL), **Franz,** Danish gymnast **P** 225
Nacre (NAY-ker), or mother-of-pearl **G** 76
  inner surface of oyster shell **O** 271
  pearls made of layers of nacre **P** 113
NAD see National Academy of Design

Nader, Ralph (1934–), American consumer rights
crusader, b. Winsted, Conn. A lawyer and author, he
had advocated greater protection for consumers in areas
such as meat processing and use of gas pipelines. His
Unsafe at Any Speed, which detailed unsafe practices of
car manufacturers, helped lead to the National Traffic
and Motor Vehicle Safety Act of 1966.

Nadir (NADE-ir), astronomical term for the point on the
celestial sphere directly below an observer or place,
straight through the center of the earth. (The celestial
sphere is the imaginary sphere the sky forms around the
earth.) The nadir is at the opposite pole of this sphere
from the zenith—the point in the sky directly above an
observer or place.

Nadir, Moishe, Yiddish author **Y** 351
Nadir Shah (NA-dir shah), king of Persia **I** 133
Naevius (NE-vi-us), **Gnaeus,** Roman epic poet and play-
  wright **L** 77
NAFEC see National Aviation Facilities Experimental Cen-
  ter
Nafis, Ibn al-, Syrian physician **S** 64
Nafud, desert region of Saudi Arabia **S** 46
Nagarjuna, Indian philosopher-poet **O** 220e
Nagasaki (na-ga-SA-ki), Japan **J** 48
  atomic bomb **W** 308
Nagoya (NA-go-ya), Japan **J** 40
Nagrela, Samuel ibn see Ha-nagid, Shmuel
Nagy (NODGE-ya), **Imrè,** Hungarian premier **H** 288
Nahuel Huapi National Park, Argentina, picture **A** 392
Nahum (NAY-hum), book of Bible, Old Testament **B** 155

Naiads (NAY-ads), water nymphs of Greek mythology.
Daughters of Zeus, they presided over streams, rivers,
lakes, and fountains. They were believed to be immortal and to possess the gift of prophecy.
  See also Nymphs

Nails, hardware **N** 2
Nails, of hands and feet
  beauty aids for **B** 110
  care of, for good health **H** 84
  why you can cut them without pain, diagram **B** 270
Nain, Labrador, Canada **N** 143
Nairobi (ny-RO-bi), capital of Kenya **K** 233; picture
  K 228
  Kenya Polytechnic, picture **A** 68

Nairobi National Park, Kenya, picture **T** 294
Naismith, James A., Canadian-born American inventor of
  basketball **B** 82
Nakhman (NOK-mon) **of Braslav** (bra-SLOF), **Rabbi,** Yid-
  dish author **Y** 350
NALC see Negro American Labor Council
NAM see National Association of Manufacturers

Namath, Joe (Joseph William Namath) (1943–),
American football player, b. Beaver Falls, Pa. An All-
American quarterback at the University of Alabama, he
joined the New York Jets in 1965 and was named the
American Football League's Rookie of the Year. In 1969, he
quarterbacked the Jets to victory over the National
League's Baltimore Colts in the Super Bowl, the first win
for an AFL team in the series.

Names N 4–8
  boys' and girls', in French **F** 434
  generic, as for man-made fibers **N** 425
  how naval ships take their names **U** 192
  hurricanes **H** 295
  Japanese **J** 27
  Latin-American family names **L** 56
  longest place name **W** 3
  moon features, how named **M** 449–50
  taxonomy **T** 28–32
  Turks required to select surnames **T** 329
  wildflower names **W** 168, 171
  See also Nicknames
Namgyal (NOM-gol), **Palden Thondup,** ruler of Sikkim
  S 177
Namgyal, Sir Tashi, ruler of Sikkim **S** 177
Namib Desert, South West Africa **S** 336
Namibia, UN name for South West Africa **S** 336
Nanaimo, British Columbia, Canada **B** 406b
Nanchao (non-JOW), former kingdom in China **T** 151
Nanking, China **C** 262, 272
Nanking, Treaty of, 1842 **S** 138
Nanny goats G 244
Nanook of the North, documentary motion picture **M** 476

Nansen, Fridtjof (1861–1930), Norwegian Arctic explorer
and statesman, b. near Christiania (now Oslo). On his
most important Arctic journey he arrived at point (86°
14' N) farther north than any reached by man before
that time (1895). He helped negotiate Norwegian independence from Sweden (1905) and became first minister
to Great Britain (1906–08). He was a member (1910–14)
of North Atlantic expeditions to study the sea. As League
of Nations high commissioner for refugees (1921) he was
awarded Nobel peace prize (1922) for postwar famine
relief work in Russia. His books include *Farthest North.*
  Greenland ice sheet **I** 9

Nansen bottle, to collect water samples, picture **I** 318
Nantes (NANTS), France **F** 406
Nantes, Edict of, 1598 **F** 416
Nanticokes, Indian tribe **D** 92
Nantucket Island, Massachusetts **M** 145
Nantucket sleighride, nickname for whalers' trip through
  the water **W** 152
Nanyang University, Singapore **S** 184

Naomi (nai-O-mi), in Old Testament (Ruth 1–5), wife of
Elimelech of Bethlehem, whose family, because of
famine in Judea, was forced to retreat to Land of Moab.
Following the death of her husband and two sons, she
and daughter-in-law Ruth returned to Judea.

Napalm (NAY-palm), a chemical thickener made of
napthenic and palmitic acids. As an additive to the

Napalm (continued)

gasoline in incendiary bombs, napalm is used in the waging of chemical warfare. Developed by the U.S. Army working with scientists of Harvard University, the chemical was first used during World War II. As an antipersonnel weapon, it increases the effectiveness of flamethrowers and bombs by creating a more highly flammable substance that adheres to everything with which it comes into contact.

NAPBL see National Association of Professional Baseball Leagues

Napier (NAY-pier), **John** (1550–1617), Scottish nobleman and mathematician, b. Merchiston Castle, near Edinburgh. He is best-known for his invention of logarithms. To simplify calculations with his logarithms, he invented a set of calculating rods. Familiarly called **Napier's bones,** these were the ancestors of the slide rule.

Napoleon III (Charles Louis Napoleon Bonaparte) (1808–73), emperor of France (1852–70), b. Paris. A nephew of Napoleon I, he believed his mission in life was to carry on his uncle's dream of greatness for France. After participating in several unsuccessful coups, he was elected president of France in 1848. Four years later he declared himself emperor. Under his leadership France took part in Crimean War (1854–56), fought to help free Italy from Austrian control, and was instrumental in Suez Canal project. But Napoleon's "Mexican empire" fell in 1867, and in 1870 France was crushingly defeated by Prussia. He was exiled and died in England in 1873.

Narcissus (nar-CISS-us), in Greek mythology, beautiful young man, son of river god Cephissus. Although pursued by the nymphs, he scorned them all. One maiden prayed that he might suffer as a rejected lover, and in answer to her prayer Nemesis, goddess of just revenge, caused him to fall in love with his own reflection in a pond. Gazing at his image, he withered away and died. His body disappeared and a flower, called the narcissus, grew up in its place.

Nares Deep, place in the Atlantic Ocean approximately 23,000 ft. deep. It is located northeast of Puerto Rico in the deep-sea Nares Abyssal Plain of the North Atlantic Ocean. The Nares Deep is named after Sir George Strong Nares, British captain of the ocean research vessel the *Challenger* on its expedition to the Antarctic (1872–74).

Narváez (nar-BA-eth), **Panfilo de** (1480?–1528), Spanish soldier and explorer, b. Valladolid. He sailed to America (1498?) and served under Diego de Velázquez in conquest of Cuba (1511). He headed expedition to Mexico (1520) to subdue Cortes but was defeated and imprisoned by Cortes (1522). Given permission to conquer and rule Florida (1526), he led expedition to Florida (1528) but perished with most of his men on return trip to Mexico. Three survivors, led by Alvar Núñez Cabeza de Vaca, arrived in Mexico in 1536.

Nash, Ogden (1902–71), American humorist, b. Rye, N.Y. He was noted for his unconventional use of the English language in writing verses. Among his best-known works are *I'm a Stranger Here Myself, Everyone but Thee and Me, The Untold Adventures of Santa Claus.*

Naskapi (nas-KAP-i), Indians of eastern Canada. Inhabitants of a huge area in northern Quebec province, these Algonkian-speaking bands have no close tribal organization. They live in tipis in family groups and depend for food on the caribou and bear they hunt during the winter. In summer they fish and barter at trading posts. Estimates as to their numbers vary from about 500 3,000.

Indians of North America **I** 164

Nassau, capital of the Bahamas **B** 16
Nasser, Gamal Abdel, president of United Arab Republic (now Arab Republic of Egypt) **N** 15
Egypt, history of **E** 92
Nasser, Lake, Egypt **E** 90e
Sudan, historic sites of **S** 449

Nast, Thomas (1840–1902), American political cartoonist, b. Landau, Germany. He emigrated to United States (1846) and served on staff of *Harper's Weekly* (1862–86). Known for cartoon series on corruption in Tammany Hall in New York, his caricature of Boss Tweed led to recognition and apprehension in Spain of the Tammany leader. He was largely responsible for use of cartoon symbols of the elephant and the donkey.
cartooning, history of **C** 126
pictured Santa Claus **C** 292
Tilden-Hayes election cartoon **H** 80

Nasturtium, one of a group of flowers originally native to South America but now widely cultivated. The many species have shield-shaped leaves and showy flowers of red, yellow, and other colors. The seeds and pods are often pickled for food. The leaves, which have a spicy flavor, are used in salads.

NASW see National Association of Social Workers
Natal, Brazil **B** 373
Natal, South Africa **S** 273
Boer War **B** 299
Zulu huts, picture **A** 303
Natchez Trace, overland trail **O** 255
Mississippi **M** 350
pioneer life **P** 260
Tennessee **T** 79
Natchez Trace National Parkway M 358; **T** 83

Nathan (NATHE-an), Hebrew prophet who served as counselor to David and Solomon of Israel. He reprimanded David for taking Bathsheba, the wife of Uriah. With the priest Zadok he anointed Solomon as king in time to prevent Adonijah, the fourth son of David, from seizing the throne. He persuaded David to delay the erection of a temple at Jerusalem until the rule of Solomon. He recorded the histories of the reigns of David and Solomon.

Nathan, George Jean (1882–1958), American drama critic, editor, and author, b. Fort Wayne, Ind. Noted for sharp critical writing that helped raise standards of American theater. He served as drama critic for various periodicals and newspapers and founded and edited magazines *The American Mercury* (1924–30) and *American Spectator* (1932–37). He was author of *The American Language* (with H. L. Mencken).

Natick (NAY-tick), Massachusetts **M** 149
Nation, Carry, American temperance leader **K** 189

National Academy of Design (NAD), association of painters, architects, sculptors, and other artists founded (1825) to promote design arts in America. The artist Samuel Morse was among its founders. Affiliated with the Metropolitan Museum in New York and Columbia University, it holds exhibits by living artists and publishes an annual Exhibition Catalogue. Its headquarters is in New York, N.Y.

National Aeronautics and Space Administration (NASA), independent U.S. Government agency created by Congress in 1958. Its mission is the peaceful exploration of space by manned and unmanned spacecraft. It also conducts aerodynamics research and the development of advanced aircraft. NASA operates several research and development centers and rocket-launch facilities. Its administrative head is appointed by the president.

National Air and Space Museum, part of the Smithsonian **S** 202; **W** 32
National American Woman Suffrage Association W 212b
National anthems and patriotic songs N 15–27
See also Facts and figures section of country articles
National Archery Association of the United States A 368

National Archives and Record Service, government organization that replaced the independent National Archives establishment in 1949 and is responsible for appraising, preserving, and making available official U.S. records to government and public. Its headquarters is in Washington, D.C., and it publishes *The Territorial Papers of the United States* and reproductions of important historical documents.

National Assembly, France **P** 379
National Association for Stock Car Racing see Stock Car Auto Racing, National Association for
National Association for the Advancement of Colored People (NAACP) **N** 96, 98
Johnson, James Weldon, first Negro secretary of **J** 126
National Association of Amateur Oarsmen, United States **R** 339
National Association of Insurance Commissioners I 296

National Association of Intercollegiate Athletics (NAIA), organization of small 4-year colleges, founded (1940) to develop intercollegiate athletics fully integrated with colleges' educational programs. It sponsors national championships and maintains hall of fame for various sports. Its headquarters is in Kansas City, Mo., and its publications include *NAIA Official Records Book.*

National Association of Manufacturers (NAM), organization of manufacturing firms that promotes interests of industry before government. Founded in 1895, it has headquarters in New York, N.Y. It publishes *NAM News* and bulletins on various topics relating to industry.

National Association of Professional Baseball Leagues (NAPBL), organization founded in 1901 to prevent reorganization of the game. Composed of 18 minor baseball leagues (155 clubs) in United States and Mexico, it is administered by office of president. Headquarters is in Columbus, Ohio.

National Association of Real Estate Boards (NAREB) **R** 113

National Association of Social Workers (NASW), group of professional social workers formed to promote excellence in social-work practices through research, improved professional education, and establishment of high standards. Founded in 1955, it has headquarters in New York, N.Y. It publishes *Social Work, NASW News,* and *Personnel Information.*

National Association of Student Councils (NASC), organization founded (1931) to develop good citizenship, improve student-teacher relationship, establish and direct extracurricular activities, and assist in school management. Headquarters is in Washington, D.C. Publications

National Association of Student Councils (continued) include *Student Life Highlights* and *Student Council Yearbook.*

National Audubon Society *see* Audubon Society, National

National Aviation Facilities Experimental Center (NA-FEC), testing center for research and development projects conducted by Federal Aviation Administration. Programs are designed to improve air-traffic control, navigation systems, airports, aircraft safety, and ability to cope with weather conditions. Established in 1958, it is located at the Atlantic City, N.J., airport.

National banks **B** 46–47, 48
National Baseball Hall of Fame and Museum, Coopers-town, New York **B** 80–81
National Basketball Association, Atlantic, Central, Mid-west, and Pacific divisions **B** 90
National battlefields, parks, and sites, of the United States **N** 52

National Board of Review of Motion Pictures (NBRMP), association of persons concerned with the social conse-quences of films and with technical and artistic aspects of film production. The Committee on Exceptional Films chooses the 10 best movies each year, as well as the best actor, actress, supporting actor, supporting actress, and director. Founded in 1909, it has headquarters in New York, N.Y. It publishes *Films in Review.*

National Book Awards, annual monetary prizes presented to authors of outstanding books in poetry, fiction, and nonfiction. Established (1950) by the American Book Publishers Council, American Booksellers Association, and Book Manufacturers Institute, the awards are distributed through the National Book Committee (since 1960). Books are selected by judges in each of the five categories of poetry, fiction, history and biography, arts and letters, and science, philosophy, and religion.

National Book Committee (NBC), association of persons from business, education, and the arts and sciences. It promotes reading freedom and sponsors programs on reading for children. Founded in 1954, it has headquar-ters in New York, N.Y. It publishes a handbook for parents on children's reading.
   children's book award **B** 310b

National budget, income and expenditures of the U.S. federal government. Income is derived mainly from individual, corporation, sales, and property taxes. Ex-penses include national defense, highway construction, education, and welfare. In most years since World War I federal expenditures have exceeded federal income, resulting in a budget deficit. An annual report is issued by the Bureau of the Budget (established 1921).

National Bureau of Standards *see* Standards, National Bureau of
National Button Society of the United States **B** 479, 480

National Cancer Institute (NCI), oldest of the national institutes of health of the Public Health Service, U.S. Department of Health, Education, and Welfare. It directs research on causes of cancer and methods of prevent-ing, diagnosing, and treating the disease and makes grants available for further research and training. Founded by congressional act in 1937 and supported by Congressional appropriations, it has headquarters in Bethesda, Md. It publishes *Journal of the National Cancer Institute* and issues scientific reports, slides, and films.

National capital parks, of the United States **N** 55
   Maryland **M** 124
   memorials, parks, and shrines in Washington, D.C. **W** 32–33, 35
   Virginia **V** 353, 354

National Catholic Welfare Conference (NCWC) (now U.S. Catholic Conference), voluntary organization of U.S. arch-bishops and bishops who coordinate such activities as social work, compilation of Catholic school statistics, and publicity through the NCWC News Service. Founded in 1919, it has its headquarters in Washington, D.C., and publishes *Social Action for Priests.*

National cemeteries, of the United States **N** 28–31
   National Memorial Cemetery of the Pacific **H** 66–67
   ten that belong to the National Park Service **N** 51
   Tomb of the Unknowns **U** 225
National Center West, for Girl Scouts, Wyoming **G** 219
National Collegiate Athletic Association **F** 356
   college league baseball **B** 78

National Commission on Safety Education (NCSE), organization that advises National Education Association on curriculum for driver and safety education and provides visual teaching aids and guides. Founded in 1943, it has its headquarters in Washington, D.C.

National Committee on Employment of Youth (NCEY), organization that renders aid to high-school-age people seeking and holding jobs. It attempts to further under-standing of youth employment problems through use of mass media. Founded in 1959, it has headquarters in New York, N.Y., and publishes *New Generation.*

National Communism **C** 444
National Conference, National Football League **F** 365

National Conference of Christians and Jews (NCCJ), association of persons from Catholic, Protestant, and Jewish faiths, whose purposes include combined efforts to improve understanding and co-operation among religious groups and to overcome intergroup prejudices. Among activities, they sponsor Brotherhood Week. Founded in 1928, it has headquarters in New York, N.Y., and publishes quarterly *NCCJ Newsletter.*

National Congress of Parents and Teachers *see* Parents and Teachers, National Congress of

National Consumers League (NCL), organization to arouse interest of consumers in production and distribu-tion of goods. It works for consumer protection and advances and supports fair labor standards. Founded in 1899, it has headquarters in Washington, D.C.
   See also Consumer education

National Conventions *see* Conventions, political
National Council for Industrial Safety **S** 7

National Council of Catholic Women (NCCW), association of Catholic women who plan and carry out Catholic action programs, including cultivation of acceptable literature, placement of foreign students in homes, sponsorship of student exchange programs within Ameri-cas, and development of units of study about various areas of the world. Founded in 1920, it has headquarters in Washington, D.C., and publishes *Monthly Message.*

National Council of Negro Women (NCNW), organization of Negro women who are active in civic, business, and church organizations. Founded in 1935, the council has its headquarters in Washington, D.C., and publishes *Telefact,* a monthly.

National Council of Teachers of English (NCTE), association of English teachers in elementary and secondary schools and in colleges. It promotes better instruction in English language and literature. Founded in 1911, it has headquarters in Champaign, Ill. Its publications include the journals *Elementary English, English Journal,* and *College English.* The council also issues films and recordings.

National Council of the Boy Scouts of America B 357

National Council of the Churches of Christ in the United States of America (NCC), association of Protestant and Eastern Orthodox denominations that strives for understanding among religious faiths through the following four main divisions: Christian education, Christian life and work, home missions, and foreign missions. It holds copyright on revised standard edition of Bible. Founded in 1950, it has headquarters in New York, N.Y., and publishes *Interchurch News, International Journal of Religious Education, Yearbook of American Churches.*

National Council on the Arts, Washington, D.C. **T** 161

National debt, debt of central government. It is often incurred when government borrows money, usually by issuing government bonds, to finance public works or to meet emergencies such as wars. National debt plus debts of local governments is called public debt.

National Defense Acts, United States N 43
National Defense Building see Pentagon, The

National Defense Education Act of 1958, measure passed by U.S. Congress containing a program for federal aid to education. It included loan fund for college students, grants to state schools, fellowships for graduate students planning to teach in colleges or universities, and funds for use of educational media.
 financing your college education **T** 44

National Diet Building, Tokyo, Japan **T** 204

National Education Association (NEA) (formerly National Teachers Association), professional organization of educators who work to promote better education through their numerous committees and commissions. Founded in 1857, it has headquarters in Washington, D.C., and publishes *NEA Journal* and *NEA News.*
 American Association of School Librarians, a department of **L** 200

National Farmers Organization (NFO), organization of farmers who bargain collectively, attempting to establish "fair price" (production cost plus reasonable profit) for, and to regulate sale of, their products. Founded 1955, with headquarters, Corning, Iowa, it publishes *NFO Reporter.*

National Federation of Business and Professional Women's Clubs (NFBPWC), organization that offers opportunities to professional and business women through industrial, scientific, and vocational activities. Founded (1919), it has headquarters in Washington, D.C.

National Field Archery Association A 368
National Film Board of Canada C 61

National Football Foundation and Hall of Fame (NFF), organization that honors football's greatest ex-players

and ex-coaches by electing them to its Hall of Fame. It promotes amateur football in schools and colleges. Founded in 1947, it has headquarters in New Brunswick, N.J., and publishes *Football Letter.* It was formerly National Football Shrine and Hall of Fame (until 1949).

National Football League F 365
National Forests, United States **N** 31–37
 forests part of national public lands reserves **P** 507
 Nebraska National Forest, man-made **N** 72, 76
 Roosevelt, Theodore, program of scientific forestry **R** 329
 See also Forests and forestry; National Park System, United States; places of interest section of state articles
National Formulary, book, sets drug standards in United States **D** 322

National Foundation, organization originally for research of polio and the care of polio victims, a purpose broadened after Salk polio vaccine development to include arthritis (until 1964) and birth defects. Supported by March of Dimes campaigns, it was founded in 1938 by Franklin D. Roosevelt. Its headquarters is at White Plains, N.Y.

National Freedom Day H 150
National Gallery, London **N** 38–39
National Gallery of Art, Washington, D.C. **N** 40–41

National Geographic Society (NGS), nonprofit educational and scientific organization that sponsors expeditions and research to increase and spread knowledge in geography and related fields. Founded in 1888, it has headquarters in Washington, D.C., and publishes *National Geographic Magazine, Geographic School Bulletins,* and *National Geographic Atlas of the World.*

National Girls Club Week G 220

National Grange (National Grange of the Patrons of Husbandry), rural fraternal organization founded for improvement of agriculture, strengthening of the farm home, and support of good government. Founded in 1867, it was the first nationally important agricultural society. Headquarters is in Washington, D.C. It publishes *Grange Newsletter* and *Grange.*
 grange movement, history of **M** 337

National Grasslands, United States **N** 31–32
 vegetation in South Dakota **S** 318
National Guard, United States N 42–43
 service to country outside the draft **D** 289
National Guard Armory, New York, N.Y., picture **N** 42
National Health Service, United Kingdom **U** 78
National Highway Traffic Safety Administration D 319
National historical parks, of the United States **N** 52
National historic sites, of the United States **N** 49
 sites of national status but not federally owned **N** 55
National Hockey League (NHL) **I** 35
National holidays around the world H 157

National Honor Society (NHS), association of secondary school students in 10th, 11th, and 12th grades outstanding in scholarship, leadership, and character. It was founded in 1921 and is directed by division of National Education Association, which administers scholarship fund to encourage students to higher education. It has headquarters in Washington, D.C., and publishes *Student Life Highlights.*

National income E 51

National Independent Union Council **L** 7
National Industrial Recovery Act, 1933 **R** 322
  child labor regulation part of the act **C** 235
  Hughes declared act unconstitutional **H** 274
  Supreme Court, U.S., history of **S** 476

National Institute of Arts and Letters (NIAL), association of notable artists, writers, and composers founded
(1898) to foster literature and fine arts in United States.
Its membership is limited to 250 Americans. It awards
grants and maintains a library of books by and about
members.

National Institutes of Health **D** 324

Nationalism, political ideology and sentiment that binds
a person to others who share his language, culture, and
traditions. Though it may stimulate democratic political
change and economic reform, it often results in
excessive loyalty to a state with a tendency to belittle
another nation and can therefore be an obstacle to
international peace and co-operation.

Nationalist China see China, Republic of (Nationalist)
Nationalization see Government ownership
National Labor Relations Act (Wagner Act), 1935
    L 5, 14–15
  Roosevelt, Franklin D. **R** 322
National Labor Relations Board (NLRB) **L** 14–15
National land reserve **P** 507
National Lawn Tennis Hall of Fame and Tennis Museum
    T 99–100
National League, baseball **B** 75, 77
National League for Nursing **N** 413
National Liberation Front (NLF), Vietnam **V** 337
National Maritime Administration **U** 184
National Memorial Cemetery of the Pacific, Hawaii
    N 30
  places of interest in Hawaii **H** 66–67
National memorials, of the United States **N** 49
  See also places of interest section of state articles

National Merit Scholarship Corp. (NMSC), association of
business and philanthropic organizations. It gives financial aid to outstanding students; supervises examinations for high school students, awarding 4-year college
Merit Scholarships to winners; and assists other groups
presenting scholarship awards.

National military parks, of the United States **N** 52
National monuments, of the United States **N** 46
  See also places of interest section of state articles

National Organization for Women (NOW), was founded in
1966 by Betty Friedan, feminist leader and author, who
also served as its first president. The largest of the
women's liberation groups, it has adopted a reformist
rather than a revolutionary philosophy. Members advocate
repeal of abortion laws, equal employment opportunities,
and free child-care centers.

National origins provisions, in immigration
  formula limiting entry, enacted 1924 **I** 100–01
  formula of 1924 eliminated, 1965 **I** 102
National parks, Canada **C** 67
  Banff National Park, Alberta, Canada **B** 42–43
  Jasper National Park, Alberta, Canada **J** 54–55
  See also names of parks; places of interest section of
    province articles
National Park Service, of the United States **N** 51–52, 55
  areas administered by **N** 45
  conservation projects, pictures **C** 486, 487

National Park System, United States **N** 44–55
  Glacier National Park, Montana **G** 221–22
  Grand Canyon National Park **G** 290–92
  regional parks preserve natural scenery **P** 77
  Yellowstone National Park **Y** 345–46
  Yosemite National Park **Y** 352–53
  See also National Forests, United States; names of
    parks; places of interest section of state articles
National parkways, of the United States **N** 55
National Pest Control Association **H** 264
National Radio Astronomy Observatory, Green Bank,
  West Virginia **W** 137; picture **R** 69
National Railroad Passenger Corporation see Amtrak
National Recovery Administration (NRA) **R** 322

National Recreation and Park Association (NRPA), organization comprising recreation leaders and agencies, including park departments. It provides guidelines for the
leadership and organization of recreational activities. It
gives advice and assistance to U.S. armed services, and
to community programs for the aged, the handicapped,
and other special groups. It has headquarters in Washington, D.C. Founded in 1906, it publishes *Parks and Recreation*.

National Research Council, organization established
(1916) at the request of President Wilson under the
National Academy of Sciences to stimulate research and
increase application of mathematical, biological, and
physical sciences. The council has its headquarters in
Washington, D.C., and publishes *Bulletin* and *Annual
Report*.

National resources see Natural resources; articles on
  individual countries
National Rifle Association **R** 233, 235
National Road see Cumberland Road
Nationals, persons loyal to or protected by a nation
  without regard to citizenship **C** 311

National Safety Council (NSC), association of individuals
and organizations from industry, insurance, education,
labor, and government. It compiles statistics on all types
of accidents, publishes materials on cause and prevention of accidents, and maintains the world's most
extensive library on safety. Its headquarters is in
Chicago, Ill. Founded in 1913, it publishes the monthly
National Safety News, quarterly *Family Safety*, and
yearly statistical summary *Accident Facts*.
  driver education **D** 318

National Science Foundation (NSF), independent agency
created by Congress in 1950. NSF supports science
research and education through grants and fellowships
to schools, colleges, and other institutions. It surveys
science research programs in the United States and the
information with other nations. NSF's headquarters is
in Washington, D.C. The president appoints its board and
aid given them. It encourages exchange of scientific
director.

National Science Teachers Association (NSTA), professional organization of classroom science teachers. Its
activities include Future Scientists of America program
and annual Ford Future Scientists Achievement Awards
for Students. Founded in 1895, it has headquarters in
Washington, D.C., and publishes *Science Teacher, Elementary School Science Bulletin,* and *Science and Children.*

National seashores, of the United States **N** 52
  Padre Island National Seashore, Texas **T** 133

Navajo (NAV-a-ho), Indians of North America **I** 192–93
  Arizona **A** 413
  Indian art **I** 156
  New Mexico **N** 186–87
Navajo Indian Reservation **I** 193
Naval Academy, United States see United States Naval
  Academy
Naval Observatory, United States see United States
  Naval Observatory

Naval stores, products such as turpentine, tar, pitch, and
rosin obtained from cone-bearing trees. The term originated because these products were necessary to maintenance of wooden ships.
  Georgia's forests supplied **G** 138
  turpentine and rosin **T** 330

Naval War College, United States, Newport, R.I.
  R 218
Navassa, outlying area of the United States **U** 100
Nave, main part of a church **A** 376
  cathedrals **C** 131
Navel orange **O** 177
Navigation **N** 62–69
  airplane flight instruments **A** 559–62
  animals use built-in clocks and compasses **L** 249–50
  Coast Guard aids to navigation **U** 176
  compass, history of **D** 182, 183
  direction, how to tell **D** 182–83
  fish, how they navigate home **F** 200
  Greenwich Observatory **G** 372
  gyroscope **G** 435–36
  Henry the Navigator directed improvements in **E** 374
  latitude and longitude **L** 81–83
  lighthouses and lightships **L** 275–78
  loran and shoran **R** 38–39
  maps and globes **M** 88–95
  migration of birds **H** 192–93
  nautical measure **W** 115
  ocean liners **O** 18, 22, 23
  radar **R** 36
  rules of the road for boats and for sailing **B** 261–62;
    S 14
  satellites used in navigation **S** 43
  sextants **O** 171
  space navigation **S** 340f–340g
  submarine navigation **S** 443
  transportation needs **T** 261

Navigation Acts, series of laws instituted by British
Parliament (approximately 1650 to 1750) to protect
British trade in its competition with Dutch. They provided that no goods could be imported into or exported from British colonies in America, Asia, or Africa
except in English ships manned by English subjects.
They resulted in British monopoly of trade with colonies.
  events preceding Declaration of Independence **D** 59

Navy, Canadian see Royal Canadian Navy
Navy and Marine Corps (CORE) Medal, American award,
  picture **M** 199
Navy Cross, American award, picture **M** 199
Nazaré (na-za-RAY), Portugal, picture **P** 401
Nazareth, Israel, picture **I** 441
  childhood of Jesus **J** 83
  Mary, Virgin **M** 113
Nazca, ancient Indian civilization of Peru **I** 155; **P** 165
Nazism (NA-tzism) **N** 69–71
  civil and human rights in conflict with idea of
    racial superiority **C** 315–316
  Germany's Third Reich **G** 162–63
  Hitler, Adolf **H** 139–40

Jewish population in Europe **A** 518; **G** 151, 162–63;
  P 358, 362
Nazi-controlled literature **G** 181
persecution of Jews **J** 111
rise of dictators before World War II **W** 284
war crimes trials **W** 9–10
See also Fascism
NBA see National Basketball Association
NBC see National Book Committee
NBRMP see National Board of Review of Motion Pictures
NCC see National Council of Churches of Christ in the
  United States of America
NCCJ see National Conference of Christians and Jews
NCCW see National Council of Catholic Women
NCEY see National Committee on Employment of Youth
NCI see National Cancer Institute
NCL see National Consumers League
NCNW see National Council of Negro Women
NCSE see National Commission on Safety Education
NCTE see National Council of Teachers of English
NCWC see National Catholic Welfare Conference
NDEA see National Defense Education Act
NEA see National Education Association
Neanderthal (ne-AN-der-thall) **man** **P** 443
  evidence of use of fire **F** 139
  head, picture **A** 305
  not direct ancestors of modern man **E** 347
  tools, pictures **P** 444
Neapolitan (ne-a-POL-it-an) **songs,** of Italy **I** 486
Neap tides **T** 183
  surface of the ocean **O** 35
Near East see Middle East
Nearsightedness, eye defect **L** 150, 265
Nebraska **N** 72–87
Nebraska, University of **N** 79
Nebraska National Forest **N** 72, 76
Nebuchadnezzar II (neb-u-cad-NEZ-zar), king of Babylon
  A 241
  Hanging gardens a wonder of the ancient world
    W 214
Nebulae (NEB-u-le), large clouds of gases **U** 196; picture
  U 197
  Rosette nebula, picture **S** 411
  Veil nebula, picture **S** 405
Neches River, Texas, picture **R** 240
Neckar River, Germany, picture **G** 149
Necker (nec-KER), **Jacques,** Swiss-born French statesman
  F 464
Necklaces, jewelry **J** 99, 100; picture **J** 97

Necromancer (NEC-ro-man-cer) (from Greek *necros,*
meaning "dead body," and *manteia,* meaning "divina-
tion"), person who claims to reveal future by communication with dead. The term is applied more generally to
any type of magician.

Necropolis (nec-CROP-olis) ("city of the dead," from
Greek *nekros,* "dead body," and *polis,* "city"), in ancient
Greece and Egypt, term referring to multiple burial
places along the roads near cities. The word is now a
formal term for a cemetery.

Nectar, in Greek mythology, drink of the gods. Nectar
gave youth and immortality to those who drank it.

Nectar, of flowers **F** 278
  bees make nectar into honey **B** 118; **H** 201
  food of butterflies and moths **B** 470

Nectarine, variety of peach having smooth skin and
pulpy flesh. Known for about 2,000 years, it is a mutation of a peach tree grown in the north temperate zones

of both hemispheres. In the United States, nectarines are grown chiefly in California and Oregon.
   stone fruits **P** 106–07

Needfire, to cure diseases of cattle **F** 145
Needle guns **G** 419

Needlepoint, type of embroidery done on canvas, usually in simple, even stitches. Needlepoint includes *petit point,* with about 400 stitches per square inch, and *gros point,* with about 100 stitches per square inch. *Gros point* is generally used for upholstery fabrics.

Needlepoint lace **L** 19
Needles **N** 88–89
   clothing industry **C** 348
   how to magnetize **M** 26
   knitting needles, numbered sizes, American and English **K** 278
   sewing needles **S** 128
Needles, phonograph
   diamond-tipped **D** 155
Needle telegraph **T** 51
Needlework see Embroidery; Sewing
Nefertari, queen of ancient Egypt **N** 90
Nefertiti (nef-er-TI-ti), or **Nefretiri,** queen of ancient Egypt **A** 222; **E** 101
   sculpture of, picture **E** 102
Negative charges, of electricity **E** 123–35
Negative numbers, or those less than zero **N** 384
   algebra **A** 158–59
   arithmetic **A** 398
Negatives, in photography **P** 201
   film pictures **P** 214, 215
Negev (NEG-ev), area of Israel **I** 441, 442, 443
   ancient dams and irrigation systems **D** 16
   housing project, picture **D** 130
Negritos (neg-RI-tos), a people of small stature found in Oceania and Southeast Asia **P** 184
   New Guinea **N** 146
   nomadic life **N** 271
Négritude, African cultural movement **A** 76c
Negro, Río, Uruguay **U** 237

Negro American Labor Council (NACL), organization of Negro trade union members founded in 1960 to fight job discrimination against Negroes and promote equality of employment and apprenticeship opportunities. Chief among its original leaders was labor leader A. Philip Randolph. Its headquarters is in New York, N.Y.
   Negro protest and progress **N** 98

Negroes
   Africa **A** 55; **E** 84
   Africa, early kingdoms of **A** 66–67
   art **A** 70–76; **L** 69; **N** 98, 101
   Brazil **B** 373–74
   civil rights movements **C** 316
   folklore and folk songs **F** 313, 324
   Haiti **H** 9–10
   Jamaica **J** 14–18
   Latin America **L** 51
   Liberia **L** 164–67
   music **A** 77, 78; **J** 57; **L** 74; **N** 101; **U** 126
   Negro history **N** 89–105
   Negro hymns and spirituals **H** 313; **N** 105–07
   races of man, geographical **R** 29–32
   segregation **S** 113–15
   slavery **S** 197–200
   See also Black Americans; names of African countries, Negro leaders and organizations
Negros (NAY-gros) **Island,** Philippines **P** 187

Negro spirituals **N** 105–07
   American folklore and folk songs **F** 313, 324
   hymns **H** 313
   religious folk songs **F** 324
   rock music, development of **R** 262a, 262d
Nehemiah (ne-he-MY-ah), book of the Bible **B** 156
Nehru (NEH-ru), **Jawaharlal,** India's first prime minister **N** 107–08; picture **P** 456a
   India, history of **I** 135
   memorial planned in Delhi **D** 103
   with President Kennedy, picture **K** 210
Neiafu, Tonga **T** 210a
Neisse (NY-se) **River,** Europe **P** 359
Neither snow nor rain nor heat nor gloom of night, etc., motto of the U.S. postal service **P** 405

Nelson, Byron (John Byron Nelson, Jr.) (1912–), American professional golfer, b. near Fort Worth, Tex. He became a professional (1933) and won Professional Golfers' Association championships (1940, 1945), U.S. Golf Association open championship (1939), and Masters (1937, 1942). He set a record by winning 11 consecutive open tournaments and was elected to Hall of Fame (1954).

Nelson, Horatio, Lord, English admiral **N** 108
   monument in Trafalgar Square, London **L** 337
   saved England from invasion by sea **E** 225
Nelson, Ricky, American rock music performer **R** 262c

Nelson, Thomas (1738–1789), American colonial leader, b. Yorktown, Va. He served on His Majesty's Council of Virginia and in the Virgina House of Burgesses (1764). He was a representative to the Continental Congress (1775–77), where he presented resolutions calling for the independence of the colonies. He succeeded Jefferson as governor of Virginia (1781).

Nelson River, Canada **C** 52
   Manitoba **M** 76
Nelson's Column, London, England **L** 337; picture **L** 338

Nelson Trust (The William Rockhill Nelson Trust), funds made available for art purchases and management of the William Rockhill Nelson Gallery of Art in Kansas City, Mo. The gallery sponsors art appreciation programs. Founded in 1926, it has its headquarters in Kansas City, Mo.

Nematode (NEM-a-tode) **worms,** or roundworms **W** 312
   pineapple pests **P** 250
   plant enemies **P** 286; picture **P** 287

Nemean (NE-me-an) **Games,** ancient Greek national celebration held in the city of Nemea. It took place during the second and fourth years of each Greek Olympiad (period of 4 years). It originated as a memorial tribute to a young war hero and was later celebrated to honor Zeus. Winners of athletic and musical competitions were awarded garlands of parsley or celery.

Nemean lion, beast killed by Heracles **G** 363
Nemerov, Howard, American poet
   "Human Things," poem **P** 355
Nemesias (nem-E-sias), flowers, picture **G** 50

Nemesis (NEM-e-sis), in Greek mythology, goddess of righteous revenge who pursues wrongdoers. She is also goddess of retribution, bringing revenge upon those with vast wealth or extreme pride. Romans invoked her aid in war to show that they were fighting for a just cause.

Nemo, Captain, character in Verne's book, *Twenty Thousand Leagues Under the Sea* S 85
Nene (NAY-nay), or Hawaiian goose
    Hawaii's state bird H 56, 61
Nennius, Welsh priest and historian A 445
Nentsi *see* Samoyeds
Neoclassicism (neo-CLASS-i-cism), in art and architecture
    France F 425
    Germany G 170–71
    Italian art I 473
    Latin America L 67
    Prado museum, picture P 429
    sculpture S 101–02
Neoclassicism, in literature E 256
Neoclassicism, in music M 401
    symphonies M 541
Neodymium (ne-o-DIM-ium), element E 155, 162
Neolithic (ne-o-LITH-ic) **Age,** or New Stone Age
    frame building, of houses B 434
    prehistoric man P 445–46
    tools, pictures P 444
    village, picture P 446
Neon, a gaseous element N 109–10
    elements, some facts about E 155, 162
    gases in industry G 62
Neoplasticism (neo-PLAST-i-cism), school of modern painting M 393
    Mondrian, Piet M 408
Neoprene, synthetic rubber R 346
Neorealism
    documentary films M 476–77
Neotropical region, of animal life L 234; diagram L 235
Nepal (nep-ALL) N 111–14
    agriculture, picture A 99
    Everest, Mount E 336–37
    flag F 238
    girl of Indian descent, picture A 459
    hunting safari, picture H 289
    marketplace, picture A 458
    Peace Corps teacher, picture P 102
    veiled woman doll, picture D 267
Nepalese, people of Nepal N 111
    Sikkim S 176
Nephrite (NEPH-rite), gem mineral G 75
    mineral source of jade J 9
Nephritis (neph-RITE-is), kidney disease D 201–02
Nepotism (NEP-o-tism), giving favors to relatives
    church reforms R 293
Neptune, planet P 277–78
    Halley's comet C 418, 419
    mathematical discovery A 475
Neptune, Roman god G 356–57
Neptunium (nep-TU-nium), element E 155, 162
Nereid (NE-re-id), satellite of Neptune P 278

Nereus (NE-re-us), in Greek mythology, gentle, kindly old god of the sea. He was husband of Doris and father of 50 beautiful sea nymph daughters, called Nereids. Like all sea deities, Nereus could change his shape and foretell future.

Nernst, Walther, German schemist and teacher L 35
Nero (NE-ro), Roman emperor N 114; R 304
    persecutions of Christians C 280; R 288
Neruda, Pablo, Chilean poet L 72
Nerves *see* Nervous system

Nervi, Pier Luigi (1891–   ), Italian architect, b. Sondrio. A noted architectural engineer, he pioneered use of prefabricated reinforced concrete. Arches, curves, and weblike ceilings mark his great halls, aerodromes, and sports palaces. Among his well-known works are the UNESCO building, Paris; and the Exhibition Hall, Turin. Little Sports Palace, Rome, Italy, picture A 387
    modern architecture A 386; I 473

Nervous system B 282–83; diagram B 281
    anesthesia A 258
    birds B 203
    brain B 363–65
    dreaming linked with D 307
    drugs act on D 326
    eye B 284
    fishes F 189
    insects I 268–69
    instinctive behavior B 369
    nervous integration theory B 195
    responses characteristic of living things K 255–56
    sleep S 200–01
    synapse, region across which nerve impulse passes, diagram K 255

Nesbit, Edith (1858–1924), English novelist and writer of children's books, b. London. She is best-known for children's stories, in which she rejected popular trend of moralizing and created believable characters in true-to-life situations. Among her stories are *The Treasure Seekers, The Bastable Children, The Would-be Goods.*

Ness, Loch, lake in central Scotland L 32
Nessler, Charles, German hairdresser, created first permanent wave B 111
Nestor, Russian monk and chronicler U 59

Nestorians (nest-OR-ians), followers of Nestorius, patriarch of Constantinople, who separated from the Roman Catholic Church after the Council of Ephesus (431). They believed that Christ was two separate persons—one divine and the other human—rather than the unification of God and man in one person. The belief moved eastward, first to Persia and later (during 6th and 7th centuries) to India and China. Remnants of the movement exist today in Iran, Iraq, Turkey, and India.

Nests
    ants A 323, 326
    birdhouses, how to build B 248–49
    birds B 212–13
    eagles E 2
    extinction of birds by disturbance of nests B 232
    fish F 200–01
    how to build ant observation nest A 330
    identifying birds' nests B 244
    insects I 277–79
    mammals M 67
    penguin, picture P 122
    rabbits and hares R 23
Netherlands N 115–21
    art *see* Dutch art; Flemish art
    cheese market, pictures D 12, F 337
    costumes, traditional Dutch (Volendam), pictures C 349
    dike, picture E 325
    dredging machine invention D 308
    Dutch dolls, picture D 264
    Dutch flag, model for U.S. flag F 244; picture F 240
    early dairy farming D 7
    favorite foods F 341
    gardens, pictures G 43
    invasion by Hitler, 1940 W 288
    music *see* Dutch and Flemish music
    national anthem N 18–19
    natural gas P 512
    Pilgrims' (Separatists') first migration to Leyden A 185–86; P 344

Sinter Klaas (Santa Claus)   **C** 292; picture **C** 293
Surinam, or Dutch Guiana   **G** 396–97

Netherlands Antilles (an-TILL-ese) (Dutch West Indies), island group comprising Leeward Islands of Curaçao, Aruba, and Bonaire off Venezuelan coast and Windward Islands of St. Eustatius, Saba, and part of St. Martin east of Puerto Rico. Governed from Curaçao, the islands were colonized by Dutch in 1634. The group became independent and a member of Kingdom of the Netherlands in 1954. It has internal self-government through the governor and elected legislature. Its revenue is derived chiefly from oil refineries and the growing tourist industry. Languages spoken are Dutch, Spanish, English, and a native mixture, Papiamento.
Caribbean Sea and islands   **C** 116–19
Netherlands, history of   **N** 121

Netherlands East Indies see Indonesia
Nets, for fishing   **F** 218, 224; pictures **F** 219
different ways of using, pictures   **A** 301

Nettle, family of plants closely related to the elms and mulberries. Nettles are common to many parts of the world. Some forms are called stinging nettles because they have tiny stinging hairs on the leaves. The flowers are small and green. Nettles are of little economic value, except for the ramie, which is cultivated for its fiber.
stings, plant defenses   **P** 283

Nettuno, Italy
American cemetery and memorial, picture   **N** 30
Networks, for television   **T** 67, 70b, 70d–71
Networks, in topology   **T** 222

Neuilly (ner-YE), **Treaty of,** pact, following World War I, concluded by the Allied nations with the defeated state of Bulgaria at Neuilly-sur-Seine near Paris (1919). Bulgaria lost territory to Yugoslavia, Greece, and Rumania, and paid heavy reparations for war damages.

Neumann (NOI-monn), **John Nepomucene** (1811–1860), American Roman Catholic bishop, b. Prachatitz, Bohemia. He arrived in the United States in 1836. Appointed bishop of Philadelphia (1852), he stimulated establishment of parochial schools in Philadelphia. He went to Rome (1854) upon invitation from Pius IX to aid in proclaiming doctrine of Immaculate Conception. He was the first U.S. male citizen to be beatified (1963).

Neumes, musical signs   **M** 524
Neurons, nerve cells of brain   **B** 363–64
Neurophysiology (neu-ro-phis-i-OL-ogy), physiology of nervous system
biological studies   **B** 195
Neuroses (neu-RO-sese), forms of mental illness   **M** 224
Neutral, chemical term   **C** 220
Neutrality, nonalignment of nations   **I** 322
Switzerland   **S** 502
War of 1812   **W** 10
Wilson's policies before World War I   **W** 179–80
Neutrinos (neu-TRI-nos), subatomic particles   **A** 486
nuclear energy   **N** 368–69
Neutrons, atomic particles   **A** 486, 487;   **C** 201, 220
cosmic rays   **C** 511, 513
electronics, science of   **E** 143–45
elements   **E** 153–59
modern theories about matter   **P** 232
nuclear energy   **N** 355–56
Neutron stars   Q 8
Nevada   N 122–27
gold discoveries   **G** 251

Nevada, University of   N 130

Nevers, Ernest (1903–   ), American football player, b. Willow River, Minn. Fullback for Stanford University (1923–25), he played for Duluth Eskimos (1926–27) and Chicago Cardinals (1929–31). He was coach of Chicago Cardinals (1929–30, 1931, 1939) and was elected to the National Football Hall of Fame (1951).

Neville, Emily (1919–   ), American author of children's books, b. Manchester, Conn. Her first book, *It's Like This, Cat,* won the Newbery medal (1964).

Nevin, Ethelbert (1862–1901), American pianist and composer, b. Edgeworth, Pa. He studied music in Boston, Mass., and in Europe and made his debut as a concert pianist in Pittsburgh, Pa. (1886). He is best known for his light, pleasant musical compositions for voice and piano. Among the most popular are "Narcissus" (1891) and "The Rosary" (1898).

Nevins (NEV-inz), **Allan** (1890–1971), American writer and historian, b. Camp Point, Ill. As a journalist he worked on newspapers including the New York *Sun* (1924–25) and the New York *World* (1925–27). He was professor of American history at Columbia University (1931–58). Among literary prizes he received were two Pulitzer biography prizes for *Grover Cleveland—A Study in Courage* (1932) and *Hamilton Fish—The Inner History of the Grant Administration* (1937).
American literature, biography and history in   **A** 214

Nevis (NE-vis), one of the Leeward Islands group in the Caribbean, a member of the state of St. Kitts-Nevis-Anguilla of the West Indies Associated States, and self-governing within the Commonwealth of Nations. Chief town is Charlestown, Alexander Hamilton's birthplace. Cotton is its chief product.
Caribbean Sea and islands   **C** 118

Nevski, Alexander see Alexander Nevski
Nevski Prospekt, avenue in Leningrad, U.S.S.R.   **L** 139
New Amsterdam, Dutch settlement in America, now New York City   **A** 190
colony under Peter Minuit   **N** 234
patroon system of settlement   **N** 225
Newark, Delaware   **D** 98
Newark, New Jersey   **N** 177; picture **N** 176

Newberry, Clare (1903–   ), American author and illustrator of children's books, b. Enterprise, Ore. She began as an artist with her first sketchbook, *Herbert the Lion.* She is known for cat stories, including *Mittens* and *Smudge.*

Newbery, John, English publisher   **N** 137
John Newbery Medal, book award   **B** 310, 310b
Little Pretty Pocket-book, picture   **C** 237
published Mother Goose collections   **N** 402
publishing for children   **C** 237
Newbery medal, book award   **B** 310, 310b
origin of   **C** 242
Newbold, Charles, American inventor   **F** 57

New Britain, volcanic island in Pacific, largest in Bismarck Archipelago in Australia's New Guinea trusteeship. The island's largest city and port, Rabaul, was key Japanese naval base during World War II. The principal exports are copra and cocoa.

New Brunswick, Canada   **N** 138–138g
New Brunswick, University of, Canada   **N** 138c
New business, in parliamentary procedure   **P** 80

New Caledonia (cal-e-DO-nia), Pacific island   P 6–7
New Castle, Delaware   D 97, 98
Newcastle, New Brunswick, Canada   N 138c
New Colossus, The, poem by Emma Lazarus, excerpt
    L 168

Newcomb, Simon (1835–1909), American astronomer, b.
Wallace, Nova Scotia. Chief astronomer of his day, he
specialized in calculating orbits in the solar system.

Newcomen (new-COME-en), Thomas, English inventor
    I 237–38
    piston engine   E 209–10
    steam engine   S 419–20; diagram   S 421
New Deal, program of Franklin D. Roosevelt   R 321
    Brandeis, Louis, called father of   B 370
    modifies capitalism   C 104
    policies of political parties   P 381
    recovery from 1929 depression aided by   D 122
New Delhi, capital of India   D 101–03;   I 122
    Birla Temple, picture   I 118
    police, picture   P 374
New England   N 138h–139
    American colonies   A 185–89
    antislavery feeling   S 198
    Boston   B 339–40
    colonial life   C 393–95
    early schools   E 69–70
    farm life in colonial America   C 387
    flowering of American literature   A 201–02
    food specialties, picture   F 338
    local-color writers   A 205
    Smith, John, explorer of   S 201
    witch hunts   W 209
    See also names of states in New England

New England Confederation, defense union of colonies of
Connecticut, Massachusetts Bay, New Haven, and Plymouth. It was formed (1643) as a result of colonies'
unco-ordinated military effort in Indian wars and against
threats of Dutch expansion. It had jurisdiction over
interstate quarrels, fugitives, Indian affairs, and declara-
tions of war. It was replaced by Dominion of New
England, which existed until 1689.
    how our flag got its stripes   F 244

New England Primer (PRIM-er), The, colonial textbook
    T 138
    early education in America   E 69
Newfoundland (NEW-fund-land), Canada   N 140–45
    advection fogs   F 289
    early Canadian history   C 68
    Ericson, Leif   E 275
    landforms of Canada   C 50
    "outports," fishing villages, picture   C 53
    Viking settlements in   E 275;   V 339–40
Newfoundland, dog, picture   D 255
Newfoundland, Memorial University of   N 141, 143
New France, early Canada   C 68–70
    Cartier, Jacques   C 124
    French and Indian War   F 458
    fur trade in the New World   F 520–22
    Saint Lawrence River   S 16
New Freedom, program of Woodrow Wilson   W 179
New Guinea (GHI-ne)   N 146–47
    art of the Pacific islands   P 10
    Australia's dependencies   A 496
    cacao bean workers, picture   C 274
    community house, picture   P 9
    West Irian, formerly West New Guinea   I 220, 222
New Hampshire   N 148–63
    American colonies   A 189

colonial life in America   C 385–99
Founding fathers of the United States   F 395
places of interest in Negro history   N 94
White Mountain National Forest, picture   N 35
New Hampshire, University of   N 157
New Harmony, Indiana   I 143
New Haven, Connecticut   C 467, 477, 480

New Hebrides (HEB-rid-ese), volcanic island group in
southwestern Pacific, east of Australia. Jointly administered by Britain and France, the islands of Espiritu
Santo and Efate were important U.S. military bases
during World War II. The islands are mountainous and
densely forested, but fertile. The chief exports are copra,
cocoa, coffee, and frozen fish.
    islands administered as a condominium   I 435

New Holland, early name of Australia   A 516
Newhouse, S. I., American newspaper publisher   N 200

Ne Win (Maung Shu Maung) (1911–), Burmese statesman and general. He served as minister of defense and
prime minister (1958–60) of Burma. After a bloodless
coup d'etat (1962), in which U Nu was ousted, Ne Win
was made head of the Burmese Government.

New Ireland, volcanic island in Pacific, northeast of New
Guinea, part of Bismarck Archipelago in Australia's New
Guinea Trusteeship. New Ireland's population is primarily Melanesian. The island is mountainous in the south,
with fertile land in the north, where the principal product
is coconuts. The largest city is Kavieng.

New Jersey   N 164–79
    American colonies   A 191
    colonial life in America   C 385–99
    Founding fathers of the United States   F 395
    Wilson, Woodrow, accomplishments as governor
        W 178
New Jersey Plan, for United States Constitution   U 146
Newlands, Francis Griffith, American statesman   N 135
New London, Connecticut   C 473
    United States Coast Guard Academy   U 176

Newman, John Henry, Cardinal (1801–90), English theologian, b. London. A leader of the Oxford Movement in
the Church of England, he later became a Roman Catholic (1845) and was ordained a priest (1847). In 1879 he
was appointed cardinal. He wrote The Idea of a University Defined, and Apologia pro Vita Sua ("History of My
Religious Opinions").
    foremost writer on religion and education in the Vic-
        torian period   E 262;   R 296

Newman, Paul (1925–), American actor, b. Cleveland,
Ohio. Known chiefly as a motion picture actor (Sweet
Bird of Youth, Hud, and Butch Cassidy and the Sundance
Kid), he turned producer and director in 1967 for the film
Rachel, Rachel, which starred his wife, actress Joanne
Woodward (1930–). This film brought him the New York
Film Critics Award as Best Director, and his wife the same
award as Best Actress.

New mathematics   M 161–68
New Mexico   N 180–95
    archeological excavations at Higgins Flat, picture
        A 351
    Carlsbad Caverns   C 152–55
    Compromise of 1850   C 448
    cotton field, picture   C 522
    Taos Pueblo, pictures   A 302;   N 186
New Mexico, University of   N 188

New moon **M** 447
from new moon to new moon **M** 448
New Negro, The, anthology, edited by Alain Locke **N** 98
New Negro Movement N 98
New Netherland, Dutch colony in America **A** 189–91
flag of Dutch colony on Staten Island **F** 228
patroon system of settlement **N** 225
Peter Minuit's purchase from the Indians **N** 234
New Orleans (OR-le-ans), **battle of,** 1815 **J** 4–5
decisive battle of War of 1812 **W** 12
Laffite sides with United States **L** 23
New Orleans, Louisiana **N** 196
American flag raising, 1803, picture **T** 107
cities of Louisiana **L** 360
Civil War **C** 323
fine cookery, picture **F** 338
French Quarter, picture **L** 360
Laffite's smuggling operations **L** 23
Louisiana Purchase **L** 348
Mardi Gras **C** 120; picture **C** 121
New Orleans Jazz J 58
Newport, Christopher, English mariner **A** 183–84
Newport, Oregon
coastline, picture **O** 194
Newport, Rhode Island **R** 223
Bathe at Newport, The, picture by Homer **I** 91
Cliff Walk **R** 222
New Providence Island, Bahamas **B** 16

Newsboys Foundation, for cultural education of newsboys, started by Mr. and Mrs. Harry Burroughs. Founded
in 1928, it has been inactive since 1953. Agassiz Village
in Maine, a camp that was once part of the summer
program of the foundation, continues to function.

News broadcasting J 144
television **T** 70a, 71
New South Wales, Australia **A** 510
paper mill, picture **A** 509
Sydney **S** 503–04
New Spain, now Mexico **M** 248
Costa Rican independence from **C** 518
Newspapers N 197–205
advertising **A** 27, 28
American Indian language newspapers **O** 86
a paper printed on top of a mountain **N** 156
Arkansas Gazette, oldest west of Mississippi **A** 426
cartoons, history of **C** 127, 128
comic strips **C** 422
commercial art technique **C** 426
department store advertising **D** 120
freedom of the press **F** 457
illustration and illustrators **I** 91–92, 94–95
journalism **J** 142–45
mass communication media **C** 440, 441
photography **P** 205
pioneer papers in Indiana **I** 143
printing inks **I** 255
publishing **P** 513
Pulitzer, Joseph, and Pulitzer prizes **P** 524–28
rotary presses for printing **P** 463
Supreme Court ruling on publication of classified
documents **C** 316; **S** 477
See also Communications section of country, province,
and state articles
Newsprint, paper for newspapers **P** 52, 53
Canadian production **C** 56; **N** 143; **Q** 11
Georgia's early use of pine products **G** 133
News services, press associations **N** 200–01
journalism **J** 143, 144–45
TASS **U** 41
voice news services for radio **R** 51

Newsstands, picture **J** 142
New Stone Age, or Neolithic Age
frame building, of houses **B** 434
prehistoric man **P** 445–46
tools, pictures **P** 444
village, picture **P** 446
New Sweden, early American colony on the Delaware
A 190
English acquire control under Penn **P** 144
flag **F** 228
former name of Delaware **D** 99
New Territories, area in Hong Kong **H** 203, 205;
U 79
New Testament, of the Bible **B** 152–53, 159–62
Apostles, The **A** 332–33
Erasmus, scholar of **E** 274
Evangelists, The **E** 335
Paul quoted on women's role **W** 211
Roman Catholic Church **R** 287
See also Christianity
New thing, or free-form jazz **J** 61–62
Newton, Huey, Black Panther leader **N** 105
Newton, Isaac, English scientist **N** 206–07
astronomy becomes an exact science **A** 472–73
calculus created at same time as Leibniz **M** 157
echo and speed of sound study **E** 45
evolution of the theory of relativity **R** 140
forerunner of the scientific revolution **P** 230
laws of motion **M** 469–71
light experiments **L** 268
planetary orbits and gravitation **S** 241–42
reflecting telescope **T** 62
science, advances in **S** 69
signature reproduced **A** 527
universal gravitation theory **G** 320–21
Newtons, units of force **W** 117
New Towns Act, Great Britain, 1946 **U** 234
Newts, land-water animals **F** 476
New Wave movies M 485, 488
New Westminster, British Columbia, Canada **B** 406b
New World
discovery of America **E** 378
What did the early explorers bring back from the New
World? **E** 380
New World monkeys M 420–22
New Year resolutions N 208
New Year's Day N 208–09
bowl games, football **F** 365
how to make a New Year's greeting card **G** 374
January events **J** 22
Japanese celebrations **J** 31
Julian calendar **C** 12
Union of Soviet Socialist Republics **U** 29
New York N 210–26
colonial life in America **C** 385–99
Erie Canal **E** 276–80
Federalist, The, urges ratification of Constitution **F** 78
first state civil service **C** 317
Founding fathers of the United States **F** 395
New York City **N** 227–35
places of interest in Negro history **N** 94
thermal power plant, picture **P** 427
Hudson River **R** 244
New York, State University of N 219
New York Barge Canal see New York State Barge Canal
New York City N 227–35
apartment houses, picture **H** 184
center of jewelry industry **J** 101
cheese shop, picture **D** 12
cities of the world, one of the great, picture **C** 306
Delaware Aqueduct **A** 344
draft riots during Civil War **C** 326; **D** 289

New York City (continued)
  drug problem **D** 330
  effect of the Erie Canal **E** 276–80
  fashion **F** 71
  first paid fire patrols **F** 146
  garment center **C** 354; picture **C** 357
  Hall of Fame **H** 12–14
  harbor, pictures **H** 36, **O** 17
  History of New York, book by Irving **A** 199
  housing project, picture **H** 183
  Liberty, Statue of **L** 168
  Lincoln Center for the Performing Arts **L** 298
  Mayor Fiorello La Guardia **L** 24
  Metropolitan Museum of Art **M** 236–37
  Metropolitan Opera, pictures **O** 130
  National Guard Armory, picture **N** 42
  New Amsterdam renamed **A** 191
  police in early times **P** 373–74
  radar map with map of surrounding area **R** 36
  Revolutionary War **R** 201
  rock music industry **R** 262a–262b
  Seagram building, picture **A** 386
  skyline views **E** 272f, **N** 298
  television industry **T** 70b
  theater **T** 161
  United Nations headquarters, picture **U** 80
  World's Fairs **F** 16, 17
New Yorker, The, magazine
  Thurber, James **T** 174
  White, E. B. **W** 160–61

New York Foundation, privately endowed charitable organization that awards grants for social welfare, health, education, and the arts. Founded in 1909, it has headquarters in New York, N.Y.

New York International Airport see John F. Kennedy International Airport
New York Philharmonic Orchestra, picture **O** 188
New York State Barge Canal **N** 218
  uses, or parallels old Erie Canal route **E** 280
New York State Theater, Lincoln Center for the Performing Arts **L** 298
New York Stock Exchange **S** 430; picture. **S** 429
New York University, New York City, picture **N** 234
  Hall of Fame for Great Americans **H** 12–14
New York World, newspaper **P** 524
New York World's Fair, 1939–40 **F** 16–17
New York World's Fair, 1964–65 **F** 17; picture **F** 16
New Zealand **N** 236–43
  dependencies **C** 428
  electric power plant using hot springs, picture **G** 192
  flag **F** 240
  gold discoveries **G** 253
  national anthem **N** 22
  sheep range, picture **N** 60
  Sutherland waterfall **W** 57
  woman suffrage, first country to allow **W** 213

Next of kin, legal term for one's closest blood relative. The term is often used in legal cases in which an estate is left without a valid will.

Ney (NAY), **Michel** (1769–1815), French general, b. Saarlouis (now Germany). Napoleon I appreciated his bravery and named him Duke of Elchingen and prince of the Moskowa. His greatest feat was the defense of the rear guard of Napoleon's Grand Army in its retreat from Moscow (1812). After Napoleon's abdication Ney was regarded favorably by Louis XVIII, but Ney joined forces with Napoleon at Waterloo. After the defeat, he was arrested by Royalists and shot as a traitor.

Nez Percé (nay per-SAY), Indians of North America **I** 175–77
  Chief Joseph **I** 67
  Indian wars **I** 215
Nezperce (nez-PERCE) **National Forest,** Idaho **I** 64
NFF see National Football Foundation and Hall of Fame
Ngo Dinh Diem (NO DIN Z'YEM), president of Republic of Vietnam (South Vietnam) **V** 334c, 335, 336
Ngo Dinh Nhu, Vietnamese leader **V** 335, 336
Ngoubai, Marien, president of Congo (Brazzaville) **C** 464
Ngugi, James, Kenyan novelist **A** 76c
Nguyen Cao Ky see Ky, Nguyen Cao
Nguyen Khanh, General, Vietnamese leader **V** 336
Nguyen leaders, Vietnam **V** 334c, 334d, 336, 337
Nguyen That Thank see Ho Chi Minh
Nguyen Van Thieu see Thieu, Nguyen Van
NHL see National Hockey League
NHS see National Honor Society
Nhu see Ngo Dinh Nhu
Niacin, a B-complex vitamin **V** 370d
Niagara Escarpment, Ontario, Canada **O** 120a
Niagara Falls **N** 243–44
  Canadian, or Horseshoe Falls, picture **O** 120b
  electric power for New York, picture **N** 221
  rainbow, picture **R** 98
Niagara Peninsula, Canada
  leading agricultural section of Ontario **O** 120a
Niamey (n'ya-MAY), capital of Niger **N** 252; picture **N** 251
Niari River, Congo (Brazzaville) **C** 461
Niaux (ni-O) **Cave,** France **P** 440; picture **P** 439
Nibelungenlied (NE-bel-ung-en-leet) **G** 174
  Norse *Eddas* basis for **N** 277, 280, 281
Nibelungs (NE-bel-ungs), or Niblungs, in Norse mythology **N** 281
Nibelungs, Song of the see Nibelungenlied
Nicaea (ny-CE-a), **Council of,** 325 **C** 283
  Christianity, history of **C** 489
  Easter Sunday established **E** 41
  growth of doctrine in Roman Catholic Church **R** 289
Nicaragua (ni-ca-RA-gua) **N** 245–49
  flag **F** 241
  life in Latin America **L** 47–61
  national anthem **N** 22
  United States Marine Corps action **U** 178
Nicaragua, Lake, Central America **L** 32
Nice (NECE), France **F** 406; picture **F** 404

Nicene (NY-cene) **Creed,** statement of doctrine common to the Roman Catholic, Eastern Orthodox, and many Protestant faiths. Formulated at the first Council of Nicea (A.D. 325) to support doctrine of the Trinity, which was denied by the Arians, the creed was lengthened during the Council of Constantinople (381).

Nicholas I, czar of Russia
  Jews conscripted for military service **J** 110
Nicholas II, czar of Russia
  Jewish persecution **J** 110–11; picture **W** 270

Nicholas, Saint (?–345?), bishop of Myra, Asia Minor, and patron saint of Russia. According to legend, he aided a poverty-stricken nobleman, whose three daughters had no dowry, by throwing a bag of gold in their window on three successive nights so they could marry (origin of filling stockings with gifts on Christmas Eve). The English took the name from the Dutch in New York, changing it to Santa Claus.
  Austria's favorite holiday **A** 520
  "A Visit from St. Nicholas," poem by Clement C. Moore **C** 295
  Christmas customs **C** 292; pictures **C** 293

Nicholas I, Saint (the Great) (800?–867), pope (858–867), b. Rome. Considered one of the great popes of the Middle Ages, he prevented divorce and remarriage of Lothair, King of Lorraine. He defended Ignatius against Photius, who wanted to continue to occupy the see of Constantinople. St. Nicholas' feast day is November 13.

Nicholas, Samuel, American Marine officer **U** 177

Nichols, Mike (Michael Peshkowsky) (1931–), American director, b. Berlin, Germany. His family moved to New York while he was still a child. He gained nationwide fame on television for improvised sketches with Elaine May. He then went on to direct both stage and screen productions. He directed the stage versions of *Barefoot in the Park* and *Plaza Suite.* Among his motion picture credits are *The Graduate,* for which he won the Golden Globe Award as best director (1967), *Catch 22,* and *Carnal Knowledge.*
   motion-picture industry **M** 488c

Nicholson, Ben, English painter **E** 242
Nicholson, Seth, American astronomer **P** 275
Nicholson, William, English scientist **E** 129
Nichrome, chromium alloy **C** 296
Nickel **N** 249–50
   alloys **A** 168, 169
   elements, some facts about **E** 155, 162
   metals, chart of ores, location, properties, uses
      M 227
   mine at Thompson, Manitoba, picture **M** 80
   nickel-producing regions of North America **N** 293
   oil hydrogenation process **O** 77
   Ontario, world's largest source **C** 58
   plating **E** 149–50
   stainless steel sometimes contains **I** 396
Nickelodeons (nick-el-O-de-ons), early motion picture
     theaters **M** 472
Nickel silver **K** 288

Nicklaus, Jack (1940–), American golfer, b. Columbus, Ohio. In 1959 and 1961 he was U.S. Amateur Champion. One of professional golf's most successful players, he became first to win all four major titles at least twice. He won Masters (1963, 1965, 1966), Professional Golf Association championship (1963, 1971), U.S. Open (1962, 1967), and British Open (1966, 1970). Picture **G** 261.

Nicknames **N** 8
   state see state articles
   See also Names
Nicobar (nic-o-BAR) **Islands,** India **I** 435

Nicodemus (nic-o-DE-mus), in New Testament (John), a Pharisee, member of Council of Sanhedrin. He came to Jesus one night to learn about baptism and everlasting life. Later he tried to soften the antagonistic feelings of the Pharisees toward Jesus. After the Crucifixion, Nicodemus came with myrrh and aloes to cover the body of Jesus for burial.

Nicolet (ni-co-LAY), **Jean,** French explorer **N** 250
   discovers Lake Michigan **G** 328
   found Wisconsin, not China **W** 192

Nicollet (ni-coll-AY), **Joseph Nicolas** (1786–1843), French explorer and mathematician, b. Cluses, Savoy. Professor of mathematics at Collège Louis-Le-Grand, he went to United States (1832) and undertook exploration of upper Mississippi River (1836). He was commissioned by the government to survey upper Missouri River (1838, 1839), and he drew up a report, with maps of the upper Mississippi based on surveys.

Nicosia (ni-co-SI-a), capital of Cyprus **C** 557; picture
   C 558
Nicotine, in tobacco
   drugs, abuse of **D** 329
   smoking **S** 203

Niebuhr (NI-boor), **Reinhold** (1892–1971), American theologian, b. Wright City, Mo. Ordained a Protestant minister (1915), he was pastor of Bethel Evangelical Church in Detroit, where he fought for better conditions for auto workers. He was appointed to the staff of Union Theological Seminary (1928) and served as its dean (1950–60). Relatively orthodox in his religious views, he gradually changed his political liberalism for a more conservative approach. Among his many published works are *Moral Man and Immoral Society* (1932).

Niello (ni-ELL-o), engraving technique **G** 303
   method of decorating metals **D** 75

Niemeyer (NI-my-er), **Oscar** (1907–), Brazilian architect, b. Rio de Janeiro. He studied at the National Art School in his native city and became one of Brazil's leading designers. Today he is known throughout the world as an innovator in contemporary architecture. Examples of his style are found in schools, office buildings, hospitals, and residences. He served on the advisory committee for United Nations headquarters in New York and was one of the chief designers of Brasília, his country's new capital.
   modern architecture **A** 387

Niepce (n'YEPS), **Joseph Nicéphore,** French inventor
   P 211
Nietzche (NE-che), **Friedrich,** German philosopher
   G 178
Niger (NY-ger) **N** 251–52
   flag **F** 236
   man from the Niger Republic, picture **A** 54
Nigeria (ni-GE-ria) **N** 253–58
   Boy Scout stamp, picture **S** 399
   college library in Yaba, picture **L** 199
   flag **F** 236
   Ibo proverbs quoted **A** 76a
   indigo dye pits, picture **D** 368
   Lagos, pictures **A** 60, 68
   music **A** 77–78; **N** 253–54
   Nigerian National Democratic Party symbol **P** 380
   sculptured tomb, picture **F** 493
   university theater group, picture **T** 162
   Yoruba metal sculpture, picture **A** 73
Niger River, Africa **R** 245; picture **N** 254
   Mali and Niger **M** 58; **N** 251, 252
   Songhai tribe, picture **A** 59
   third largest in Africa **A** 49
   West Africa **A** 49
Night
   earth's period of rotation **E** 4
   equinoxes and the equator **E** 272h
   length of during the seasons **S** 108
Nightbeauty see Moonflower
Night blindness **V** 370b
Night-blooming cereus, cactus **C** 4
Nighthawks, birds **B** 220
Night Hawks, painting by Hopper **U** 120

Nightingale, brownish bird with white underparts, noted for the beauty of its songs. Although a more active songster at night, the nightingale also sings during the day. It is found in forests and scrublands from northern Eurasia to southeast Asia and South Africa.
   spectrograms of animal sounds, picture **A** 276

Nightingale, Florence, English nurse **N** 259
Nightjar, bird, picture **O** 163
Nightshade, deadly, plant source of belladonna **P** 322
  medicinal in small amounts **P** 314
Nightshade family, of plants **P** 282
  potatoes **P** 411
  tomatoes **T** 209
Night Watch, painting by Rembrandt, detail **R** 156
Night Will Never Stay, The, poem by Eleanor Farjeon
  F 120
Nihombashi (Japan Bridge), Tokyo **T** 205
Nihon (ni-HONE), Japanese name for Japan **J** 42
Niihau (ni-i-HA-oo), one of the Hawaiian Islands **H** 59–60

Nijinska (nij-IN-ska), **Bronislava** (1891–1972), Russian
ballet dancer and choreographer, b. Warsaw (now in
Poland). Noted for introducing new techniques in
classical ballet, she studied ballet at the Imperial School
of St. Petersburg, joined Diaghilev's Ballet Russe in
Paris (1910–14), and started a dance school in Kiev,
Russia (1915?). She returned to Diaghilev's company
(1921) as dancer and choreographer and produced eight
ballets, including *Les Noces, Les Biches,* and a revival of
Sleeping Beauty. She was artistic director of the Polish
Ballet (1937).

Nijinsky (nij-IN-ski), **Vaslav** (1890–1950), Russian ballet
dancer and choreographer, b. Kiev, Russia. He is noted
for revolutionary choreography and dazzling technique
and acting genius. With his sister, Bronislava, he studied
at the Imperial School of Ballet at St. Petersburg.
Closely associated with Serge Diaghilev's Ballet Russe in
Paris, he created notable roles in *Petrouchka* and *La
Spectre de la Rose* and gained recognition for his
choreography of ballets *L'Après-midi d'un Faune* and *Le
Sacre du Printemps.* He was forced to end his career
(1917) because of mental illness.
  ballet, history of **B** 26

Nike (NY-ke), in Greek mythology, esteemed goddess of
victory. Nike was referred to as Victoria by Romans. The
famous statue in the Louvre, known as Nike of Samothrace (306 B.C.), is a representation of this goddess.
Picture **L** 368.

Nike (NY-ke), missile **M** 347

Nikolayev (ni-ko-LA-yef), **Andrian Grigoryevich** (1929–),
Soviet cosmonaut, b. Chorshely, Chuvash. The third
Russian to orbit the earth, he was launched August 11,
1962, in Vostok III and completed 64 orbits before
returning on August 15. There was an apparent effort to
rendezvous with P. R. Popovich, launched on August 12.
Nikolayev married Valentina Tereshkova, the first woman
to fly in space.
  space flight data **S** 344, 345

Nile, battle of the (battle of Aboukir Bay) (August,
1798), naval battle between British fleet, commanded by
Lord Nelson, and Napoleon's French fleet at defense of
Aboukir Bay. British victory ended Napoleon's hope of
establishing French empire in East.
  Lord Nelson's career **N** 108

Nile River, Africa **N** 260–61
  Africa, great rivers of **A** 49
  Aswan High Dam **D** 21
  early agriculture **A** 95
  Egypt **E** 90e
  Egyptian civilization **A** 220–22
  feluccas, picture **R** 240
  flood waters used to good advantage **F** 255

Gezira, irrigated cotton project **S** 448
  source in Lake Victoria **L** 34
  Uganda **U** 5
Niles, Nathaniel, American patriot **N** 23
Nilotic (ni-LOT-ic) **language,** eastern Africa **A** 55

Nilsson, Birgit (Marta Birgit Nilsson) (1918–), Swedish
operatic soprano, b. West Karup. Best-known for roles in
Richard Wagner's operas, she studied at Stockholm
Royal Academy of Music. Her noted roles include that
of Isolde in *Tristan and Isolde,* Brünnhilde in *Die Walküre,*
and Leonore in *Fidelio.*

Nimbo-stratus clouds **C** 360; picture **C** 361

Nimitz, Chester William (1885–1966), American naval
officer, b. Fredericksburg, Tex. Nimitz was assistant
chief (1935–38) and chief (1939–41) of Bureau of
Navigation, Department of the Navy; commander in chief
of U.S. Pacific Fleet (1941–45); and chief of naval
operations (1945–47). He was special assistant to the
Secretary of Navy (1947–66). He led Presidential Committee on Internal Security and Individual Rights (1951).
  World War II in the Pacific **W** 297

Nimrod, in the Old Testament (Genesis), the son of Cush
and great-grandson of Noah. He was reputed to be a
famous hunter and a proud, mighty king who ruled
ancient Babylon and founded Assyrian cities including
Calah and Nineveh. He was the forerunner of Assyrian
kings noted for their love of war and hunting and for
tyrannical rule. The word "nimrod" has become part of
our language, meaning a skilled and daring hunter.

Nimrud, city in ancient Assyria **A** 240
NIMS see Nationwide Improved Mail Service
Niña (NEEN-ya), ship of Christopher Columbus **C** 417;
  E 376; picture **E** 374
Ninepins, a bowling game **B** 348
Nineteenth Amendment, to the United States Constitution
  U 157
  women, role of **W** 212b
Ninety-five theses, of Luther **L** 378; **R** 134
Nineveh (NIN-e-veh), capital of ancient Assyria **A** 226
  a public library of clay tablets **L** 192
  art of the ancient empire **A** 240

Nine Worthies, The, nine heroes selected from ancient
history and legend. They were Joshua, David, and Judas
Maccabaeus from Biblical and Jewish history; Hector,
Alexander the Great, and Julius Caesar from Greek and
Roman tradition and history; and Arthur, Charlemagne,
and Godfrey of Bouillon from medieval legend and
history. They are referred to in *Love's Labour's Lost.*

Niños (NEEN-yos), **Los,** Mexican national heroes **M** 239
Ninth of July Avenue, Buenos Aires, picture **B** 427
Ninth Symphony, of Beethoven **G** 185
  known as Choral Symphony **C** 278

Niobe (NY-o-be), in Greek mythology, wife of Amphion,
King of Thebes. The mother of many beautiful children,
she ridiculed the goddess Leto (Latona), who only had
two children, Apollo and Artemis. To punish Niobe for
her pride and defiance of the gods, Apollo and Artemis
killed all her children. Niobe became a rock, from which
water (tears of grief) flowed.

Niobium (ny-O-bium), element **E** 155, 163
Nipisguit (nip-IS-gwit) **River,** Canada **N** 138a
Nippon, Japanese name for Japan **J** 42
NIRA see National Industrial Recovery Act

Nirvana (nir-VAN a), state of perfect happiness
  Buddhism **B** 423
  Hinduism **H** 131

Nisei (NI-sai) (Japanese for "second generation"), term that refers to children, born and educated in United States, of Japanese parents (issei). Separated from Japanese society by their American citizenship and education, and often subject to racial prejudice of white Americans, they organized Japanese-American Citizens League (1930) to sponsor social activities, combat anti-Oriental prejudice, and during World War II, support nisei enlistment in U.S. armed forces.

Nishinomiya, Japan
  Koshien Stadium, baseball in Japan **B** 78
Niter see Saltpeter
Nitrate (NY-trate)
  Chile, how discovered in **C** 251
  fertilizers **F** 98
Nitrile (NY-tril), synthetic rubber **R** 347
Nitrocellulose (ny-tro-CEL-lu-loce), or gun cotton, explosive **E** 392
  lacquers made from **V** 280
Nitrogen (NY-tro-gen), chemical element **N** 262 ·
  atmosphere contains **A** 479
  bacteria, nitrogen-fixing **B** 12; **M** 280
  elements, some facts about **E** 155, 163
  fertilizers **F** 96, 97
  fertilizers, production of in North America **N** 294–95
  industrial uses and how obtained **G** 59–60
  liquid nitrogen for freezing of food **F** 347
  Mars' atmosphere lacks **M** 108
  raptures of the deep **D** 82; **U** 15
  soils, elements in **S** 232
Nitroglycerin (ny-tro-GLIS-er-in), explosive **E** 390–91, 392
  Nobel, Alfred **N** 264
Nitrous (NY-trous) **oxide,** laughing gas **A** 256–57, 258
  first important discovery of Sir Humphrey Davy **D** 46
Nits, lice eggs **H** 262
Nix Olympica, volcanic mountain on Mars **M** 109
Nixon, Patricia Ryan, wife of Richard M. Nixon **F** 180; **N** 262b
  Nixon family, picture **N** 262d
Nixon, Richard Milhous, 37th president of the United States **N** 262a–262f
  as vice-president, picture **V** 330
  delivering State of the Union Message, picture **G** 273
  television debates with Kennedy **K** 209

Niza (NI-sa), **Marcos de** (also known as Fray Marcos) (?–1558), Italian missionary, b. Nice (duchy of Savoy), now France. Marcos de Niza sailed to America in 1531 and did missionary work in Peru, Guatemala, and Mexico, as well as exploring (1539) present-day Arizona and western New Mexico, which he claimed held great riches. The explorer Coronado, influenced by the reports, got as far as the upper Rio Grande Valley on an expedition (1540) with de Niza. No riches were found, however, and de Niza was in disfavor until his death.
  Arizona, history of **A** 416

Nizhni Novgorod (NEEJ-ni NOV-go-rote), U.S.S.R **F** 11

Nkomo (en-KO-mo), **Joshua** (1917–), nationalist leader in Rhodesia, b. Matebeleland. Secretary of the Rhodesian African Railways Workers' Union (1945–50), he became president-general of the African National Congress (1957). Exiled when the Congress was banned (1959), he was chosen president of Zimbabwe African People's Union (1961), but the party was outlawed (1962). He has been under government arrest since 1964.

Nkrumah (en-KRU-mah), **Kwame,** Ghanaian statesman **N** 262f
  first president of Ghana **G** 198
NKVD see KVD
Noah's Ark, Bible story **B** 163–64
  See also Deucalion, the Greek Noah
Nobel (no-BEL), **Alfred,** Swedish chemist and manufacturer **N** 263, 264
  explosives **E** 391, 392
Nobelium (no-BEL-ium), element **E** 155, 163
Nobel prizes N 264–69
  two-award winner, Marie Curie **C** 553
Nob Hill, San Francisco, picture **S** 31
Nobile, Umberto, Italian explorer **P** 365
Noble gases N 109–10
  chemically inactive, or inert **C** 202
  electric light bulb **I** 334
  electron shells of some inert gases, diagram **C** 203
  gases in industry **G** 62
  inert gases, location of on the periodic table **E** 158
  lighting **L** 285

Noble metals, metals, such as gold, platinum, and silver, that are not easily combined with other elements to form compounds. They do not corrode or tarnish in air or water and are not readily attacked by acids.

Nobunaga Oda (no-bu-NA-ga o-da), Japanese general and statesman **J** 44
Nocake, colonial American corn food **C** 390
Noctule, bat, picture **B** 95
Nocturnal animals
  red light rooms in zoos **Z** 379
Nocturne, in music **M** 537
Nodosaurs (NO-do-saurs), dinosaurs **D** 180
No drama, Japanese plays **J** 32
  dance **D** 33
  Japanese ceremonial drama **D** 292–93
  Japanese theater **T** 164

Noel-Baker, Philip John (Philip John Baker) (1889–   ), British political leader, b. London. He was minister of state (1945–46) and secretary of state for Air (1946–47) and for Commonwealth Relations (1947–50). He won Nobel peace prize (1959) for his contribution to peace and disarmament, and he is author of The Arms Race.

Noëls (no-ELS), French Christmas carols **C** 122
No-fault liability coverage, in automobile insurance **I** 294

Noguchi (no-GU-chi), **Hideyo** (1876–1928), Japanese bacteriologist, b. Fukushima Prefecture, Japan. After graduating from Tokyo Medical College in 1897, he went to the United States where he became known for his work on syphilis and yellow fever. He was the first person to grow pure cultures of the micro-organism that causes syphilis. While working in Accra, Ghana, on the study of the yellow fever virus, he was accidentally infected with that disease and died.

Noguchi, Isamu (1904–), American sculptor, b. Los Angeles, Calif. He won a relief-sculpture competition (1938) at the Associated Press Building, Rockefeller Center, New York, N.Y. His works, influenced by his many trips to Japan, combine traits of Eastern and Western cultures. He experimented with combinations of wood and stone and designed sets for Martha Graham and her dance company (1935–36, 1944–46). His works include sculptures for Yale Library of Precious Books and UNESCO building in Paris.

Noh drama see No drama
Noise N 269–70; S 264
    environment, effect of noise on   E 272c–272d
    insulation and insulating materials   I 292
    white noise, electronic sound   E 142g
Noise anesthesia (an-es-THE-sia), A 259
Nok, early African culture, Nigeria N 256
Nol, Lon see Lon Nol

Nolan, Philip, main character in E. E. Hale's *Man Without a Country,* a story connected with Aaron Burr's treason. Nolan rashly stated a desire never to hear his country's name again, and he was therefore sentenced to live at sea for the rest of his life.

Nolde (NOL-da), **Emil,** German painter **M** 391
Nomads (NO-mads) N 271
    Afghanistan **A** 42; picture **A** 43
    Australian aborigines **A** 499, 501; **D** 127–28
    Bedouins **D** 128; **S** 45
    deserts, people of the **D** 127–28; picture **D** 129
    dress and dwelling in Africa **A** 61
    Gatherers, Indians of North America **I** 172–80
    Genghis Khan unites Mongol tribes **G** 93
    gypsies **G** 434
    helped spread languages **L** 39
    homes of **H** 175–76
    Iran, picture **I** 374
    Kenya's Masai people **K** 230
    Lapland's mountain people **L** 44
    Mauritania **M** 179–80
    Mongolia **M** 413; pictures **A** 302, 458; **N** 271
    Morocco **M** 458
    Plains Indians of North America **I** 156
    Sahara inhabitants **S** 8
    Somalia **S** 253–55
    Tibet **T** 176
Nomberg, H. D., Yiddish author **Y** 351

Nom de plume, French phrase (used in English) meaning "pen name," or pseudonym. A nom de plume is taken by a writer who prefers his real name to remain unknown. For example, O. Henry was the nom de plume of William Sydney Porter.

Nome, Alaska **A** 143

Non-aggression Pact (Nazi-Soviet Pact), treaty (1939) concluded by Joachim von Ribbentrop of Germany and Vyacheslav Molotov of Soviet Union just before World War II. The two powers agreed not to engage in war with each other and to remain neutral in case one of them should be attacked by another state. The pact included an arrangement (secret until 1948) to divide the countries of Eastern Europe between Russian and German spheres of influence.

Non-biodegradable pollutants **W** 59
Noncommissioned officers, United States Army
    U 167
Nonconformists, religious group see Dissenters
Non-Euclidean (non-eu-CLID-e-an), **geometries** **G** 131;
    M 158–59
Non-ferrous alloys **A** 168
Nonfiction **L** 313
    history and biography, creative writing **W** 321
    how classified in libraries **L** 183–84
    Pulitzer prizes **P** 528
Non-flowering plants **P** 290

Nonintercourse Act (1809), act of U.S. Congress permitting international trade with all countries except France

and Britain. It followed Embargo Act of 1807, which prohibited United States international trade. It gave the president authority to resume trade with France and Britain should they cease violating U.S. policy of neutrality on the sea.

Nonintervention, principle
    inter-American treaties under the Good Neighbor Policy
    M 427
    United Nations' policy **U** 81
Nonmetallic minerals **M** 313
    North America, producing regions of **N** 294–95
    properties of **M** 226
Nonpartisan League
    North Dakota **N** 337
Non-Proliferation of Nuclear Weapons Treaty, 1968
    D 185
Nonsense rhymes **N** 272–76
    children's literature **C** 238
    folk music **F** 323
    jabberwocky, a form of humor **H** 279
Nonsporting group, dog breeds **D** 261; pictures **D** 256
Nonthermal radio radiation **R** 75
Nonviolence, or ahimsa, Hindu belief **H** 130
    Martin Luther King's philosophy **K** 248
    Nehru's use of the policy **N** 107
Noodles, food made from wheat **G** 282
Noodle stories **F** 303
Noolbengers, or honey possums, marsupials **K** 175
Noon, midday **T** 188, 189
Noone, Jimmy, American jazz musician **J** 58
Nootka, Indians of North America **I** 180
Nootka Sound, British Columbia
    Vancouver, George **V** 277
NORAD see North American Air Defense Command
Norbeck, Peter, American statesman **S** 325
NOR circuits, of computers **C** 454

Nordenskjöld (NOOR-den-sherld), **Adolf Erik, Baron** (1832–1901), Swedish explorer and geologist, b. Helsinki, Finland. He led expedition to Spitsbergen, a group of islands in Arctic Ocean, and succeeded in reaching highest northern latitude (81° 41') attained by that time (1868). He successfully completed navigation of Northeast Passage aboard the *Vega* (1878–79).

Nordenskjöld, Nils Otto Gustaf (1869–1928), Swedish explorer and geologist, b. Hässleby. He led scientific expeditions to Tierra del Fuego (1895–97), Alaska and Yukon (1898), Antarctic (1901–04), Greenland (1900, 1909), and parts of South America.

Nordhoff, Charles Bernard (1887–1947), American novelist, b. London, England. He is best-known for novels written in collaboration with James Norman Hall about Pitcairn and Norfolk islands in South Pacific. He served (1916–19) as ambulance driver and pilot during World War I. He was commissioned with Hall to write history of Lafayette Flying Corps. Nordhoff journeyed to Tahiti after World War I. Books he wrote with Hall include *Mutiny on the Bounty, Men Against the Sea,* and *Pitcairn's Island.*

Nordic Council, association of representatives from the Nordic countries. It was established by Denmark, Norway, Sweden, and Iceland in 1953 and joined by Finland in 1956. Its purpose is to discuss economic and political co-operation. It is authorized only to submit recommendations to member parliaments. Its achievements include restrictions on tariffs, introduction of common labor market, and elimination of passport controls.

Nordic peoples **S** 482

Nordic skiing S 184b
Nordling, Raoul, Swedish consul P 75
Norfolk, Virginia V 357
  Merrimac-Monitor battle, 1862, Civil War C 323

Norfolk Island, island of volcanic origin, in South Pacific midway between Australia and New Zealand. The island is part of the Commonwealth of Australia. Its fertile soil produces extensive vegetation, including beans and citrus and passion fruit. Norfolk Island is noted for the native Norfolk Island pine tree.

Norfolk Lake, Arkansas, picture A 423
Noria, an undershot waterwheel W 61
Norkey, Tenzing, Sherpa guide and mountain climber
  E 337
  Himalayas H 129
  mountain climbing M 490
Norma, opera by Vincenzo Bellini O 149
Normal curve, or bell-shaped curve, in probability
  P 472
  machine formation, picture P 472
Normal schools
  founded by Horace Mann M 83
Norman Conquest, of England, 1066 E 217
  caused enrichment of the English language W 239–40
  effect on personal and place names N 4
  English architecture, Norman period E 234
  Hastings, battle of, 1066 B 100–01
  Norman rulers of England U 77
  William the Conqueror W 173
Normandie, ocean liner O 17
Normandy, battle and invasion of, 1944, World War II
  B 102; W 299
Norm groups, in testing G 399
Norms, average scores in tests T 116
Norns, Norse maiden goddesses N 277

Norodom Sihanouk (si-han-OOK), Prince (1922–), Cambodian chief of state, b. Oudong. Chosen king by a royal council (1941), he became prime minister (1952) the year before Cambodia received its independence from France. He abdicated the throne (1955) in favor of his father and entered politics. His party, the Popular Socialist Community, won the elections, and he continued as prime minister. He was a neutralist in world affairs. It was at his suggestion that a conference on Laos convened at Geneva (1961). He was deposed in 1970.
  Cambodia, history of C 33

Norris, Frank, American novelist A 206
Norris, George William, American statesman N 85
Norrkoping, Sweden S 485
Norse language and literature see Scandinavian literature
Norsemen, early Scandinavians S 49
  cat revered by C 142
  Ericson, Leif E 275
  Greenland discovered by Eric the Red G 370–71
  Kensington Rune Stone attributed to M 336
  Norse gods and goddesses N 277–81
  Scandinavian literature S 50–53
  See also Vikings
Norse mythology (mith-OL-ogy) N 277–81
  Eddic poetry in Scandanavian literature S 50
  trees T 274
  See also Greek mythology

Norstad, Lauris (1907–), American air force officer, b. Minneapolis, Minn. He was commander of U.S. air forces in central Europe (1951–53) and supreme allied commander of NATO military forces (1956–62). He retired in 1962.

North, Frederick (Lord North), 2nd Earl of Guilford (1732–92), English statesman, b. London. Elected to the House of Commons in 1754, he became chancellor of the exchequer (1767) and later prime minister (1770). As such, he was the agent of George III's coercive policy toward the American colonists, although he did not approve of the policy. He tried to resign several times but his resignation was not accepted until 1782. He then formed a coalition with Charles James Fox, a Whig, opposing the crown's policy. He was active in the opposition until his failing eyesight limited his activities.
  Tea Act, 1773 and the Boston Tea Party R 196

North, Simeon, American inventor M 84
North America N 282–305
  birds of B 225
  defense bases in Canada C 82
  discovery and exploration E 376–78, 382–84
  flags F 241
  French colonial flag F 228
  geographic center near Rugby, North Dakota N 323–24
  Ice Ages, extent of ice sheets, diagrams G 115; I 19
  Indian tribes, location of I 165
  jet stream, path over, diagram J 88
  life in Latin America L 47–61
  mountain peaks, highest in North America M 494–95
  Organization of American States O 210–11
  polar regions P 363, 364–66, 367
  prairies P 430–33
  taiga belt T 10
  time zones T 189
  waterfalls, selected list W 57
  See also Canada; Central America; Mexico; United
    States
North American Air Defense Command (NORAD) C 82;
  U 161, 174
North American Cordillera N 282, 284
  Rocky Mountains R 274
North Asia (Soviet Asia) A 450, 452
North Atlantic Drift, eastward flowing section of the Gulf
  Stream G 411
  Europe's climate moderated by E 309
North Atlantic Treaty Organization (NATO) N 305
  Canadian forces in C 82
  de Gaulle withdraws France D 85
  Eisenhower, first commander of E 110
  flag F 226
  headquarters, Brussels, Belgium B 131; N 305
  Truman's help in shaping T 302
North Battleford, Saskatchewan, Canada S 38g
North Borneo see Sabah
North Carolina N 306–21
  American colonies A 192–93
  colonial life in America C 385–99
  Founding fathers of the United States F 395
North Carolina, University of N 314
North Cascades National Park, Washington W 24, 25
North Dakota N 322–37
  holiday, Discovery Day H 149
  prairie farm, picture P 431
North Dakota, University of N 331

Northeast Passage, Arctic sea route north of Europe and Asia connecting the Atlantic and Pacific oceans. First attempts at navigation were made by the English between 1553 and 1584 and by the Dutch between 1577 and 1624 in search of a short commercial route to the Orient. The first complete navigation was made by a Swedish expedition (1878–79) under Adolf Erik Nordenskjöld. Today the passage is kept open for commercial shipping from June through September by the Soviet Union.
  discovery and exploration of the polar regions P 364

North Equatorial Current G 411
Northern, or Alaskan, fur seals W 6–7
Northern Hemisphere L 81–82
 constellations C 491; chart C 490
 Coriolis force of earth's rotation E 7
 equator divides the hemispheres E 272h
 glaciation during Ice Ages, diagram I 19
 Gulf Stream G 411
 how earth's axis causes summer and winter E 24
 hurricanes, path of H 293–95
 jet streams J 89–90
 month by month see month articles
 ocean currents E 16
 seasons S 110
 taiga, forests T 10–11
 trade winds T 246
 zones Z 372–73
Northern Ireland U 73
 Belfast U 73
 civil and human rights conflicts C 316
 England, history of E 232
 Ireland, history of I 391
Northern lights, or aurora borealis I 353
 IGY studies I 310
Northern Rhodesia (rho-DE-sia), now Zambia Z 367
Northern Territory, Australia A 513
Northern Virginia, Confederate Army of C 323, 324–25
North Korea see Korea, Democratic People's Republic of
North Little Rock, Arkansas A 430
Northmen see Vikings
North Pole P 364
 earth's axis E 4
 Northwest Passage N 338
 Peary, Robert E., first to reach North Pole P 116
 seasonal positions S 108
 shape of the earth E 6
North Saskatchewan River, Canada S 38c
North Sea O 48

North Slope, an area in northern Alaska found in 1969 to be rich in natural gas and oil reserves. It became the center of controversy in the 1970's when conservationists argued that construction of a pipeline to transport oil from the rich North Slope fields to a port in southern Alaska would pose a serious threat to the environment.

North Star, or Polaris C 491
 direction finder D 183
 experiment to show star "trails" E 362
 finding true north for a sundial T 193
 how to find N 63
 variable stars S 408
North Star State, nickname for Minnesota M 323
North Star, The, newspaper published by Frederick Douglass N 94
North temperate zone Z 372
 birds of B 223–225
Northumberland Strait, Canada C 52; N 344b
North Vietnam see Vietnam, Democratic Republic of
Northwest Angle, section of Minnesota M 323–33
 boundary in territorial dispute T 108, 109
North West Company, fur traders F 522–23
 Canada's Nor'Westers C 72; M 82
 Mackenzie's explorations for the company M 5
Northwestern Ice Yachting Association I 29
North West Mounted Police, early name for Royal Canadian Mounted Police C 78
 Alberta, first posts established A 147
 duties of police P 374
Northwest Ordinance, or Ordinance of 1787 W 143
 early history of Ohio O 74

Northwest Passage N 338
 Cartier's search for C 124
 exploration of north polar region P 364
 Hudson, Henry H 272–73
 Mackenzie's search for waterway and fur trade route across North America F 522
 Nicolet dressed to meet a Chinese emperor G 328; N 250
Northwest Rebellion, 1885, Canada C 74, 80
Northwest Territories, Canada Y 360–65
 Manitoba once part of M 82
 Canada's Cordillera C 51
Northwest Territory, in United States history T 47; W 143
 Harrison, William Henry H 50
 Indiana Territory I 150–51
 Northwest Ordinance of 1787 O 74; W 143
 Ohio O 64, 74
Norton, Thomas (1532–1584), English poet, b. London. He translated Calvin's *Institutes* into English and with Thomas Sackville wrote *Tragedy of Gorboduc*, the first English tragedy in blank verse.
 drama, history of D 295

Norway N 339–44; S 49
 agriculture, picture A 97
 codfish drying, picture E 325
 costumes, traditional Hardanger, pictures C 349
 dual monarchy with Sweden S 487
 fairy tales reveal spirit of the people F 22
 favorite foods F 341
 flag F 240
 folk dancers, picture F 297
 Geiranger Fiord, picture E 306
 Grieg, Edvard, Norwegian composer G 376
 holiday, Leif Ericson Day H 149
 Ibsen, Henrik, Norwegian dramatist I 2
 Iceland I 41, 44–45
 invasion by Hitler, 1940 W 288
 Lapland L 44–45
 national anthem N 22
 Scandinavian literature S 50–53
Norway maple, tree
 flower, picture F 276
 leaf, diagram L 114
Norway pine
 state tree of Minnesota M 323
Norway rat H 264; classification K 252
 living things living together K 257
Norwegian (nor-WE-gian) elkhound, dog, picture D 254

Norwegian literature S 50–53
 Ibsen, Henrik I 2
Norwegian music
 Grieg, Edvard G 376
Norwegian Sea O 48
Nose B 286–87
 body's senses on guard B 277
 doctor's examination of the nose M 208g–208h
Nosebleed, first aid for F 158
Noseprints, identification for cats and dogs F 129
No Shop Does the Bird Use, poem by Elizabeth Coatsworth F 120

Nostradamus (nos-tra-DA-mus) (Michel de Nostredame) (1503–56), French astrologer and physician, b. Saint-Remy. He was believed to possess remarkable healing powers and is said to have cured many victims of the plague. His reputation earned him the post of court physician to Charles IX. Nostradamus claimed he could foretell the future, and he recorded alleged prophecies in a verse work entitled *Centuries*.

Notary public, a public official appointed by the executive branch of the state government to verify and certify by signature and seal deeds and copies of documents. Notary publics also administer oaths. They were appointed in the Roman Republic (509–27 B.C.) to compile legal documents. The Frankish Empire had notary publics as early as the 9th century.

Notches, mountain passes **N** 150
Note Hand, system of shorthand **S** 164
Notes, in music **M** 524–25, 529–31
Note-taking, for reports **R** 175
No-Transfer Principle, American foreign policy **M** 427
Notre Dame (no-tr DOM), **Cathedral of,** Paris **P** 73;
  pictures **A** 379, **C** 130
  aerial photograph **G** 266
Nouadhibou, formerly Port Étienne, Mauritania **M** 180
Nouakchott (nu-ock-SHOTT), capital of Mauritania
  M 180
Nougat (NOO-gat), candy **C** 98
Nouns, words that give the names of persons, places,
  or things **P** 90
Nourek Dam, Union of Soviet Socialist Republics **D** 20
Novas, stars **S** 409
  variable stars **A** 476
Nova Scotia (no-va SCO-sha), Canada **N** 344a–344h
  formerly the French colony Acadia **C** 69, 70
  Loyalist settlements in Canada after Revolutionary
    War **C** 71
Nova Sofala (NOV-a so-FA-la), Mozambique **M** 501
Novaya Zemlya, island, U.S.S.R.
  considered part of Europe **E** 307
Novellas (no-VEL-las), stories with compact plots **N** 345
Novelettes (nov-el-ETTS), long stories **S** 165
Novels N 345–49
  African literature in English and French **A** 76b–76d
  American literature **A** 198, 200, 207, 211
  biographical **B** 186
  Chinese literature **O** 220b
  compared to short stories **S** 165
  English literature **E** 259–60, 261
  fiction, types of **F** 110–11
  French "river novel," or *roman fleuve* **F** 442
  German novelists of 20th century **G** 179–80
  historical romances of Dumas *père* **D** 342
  Irish literature, influence of James Joyce **I** 395
  Japanese literature **O** 220b–220d
  Latin-American literature **L** 72
  mystery, detective, and suspense stories **M** 553–56
  novel of manners **E** 261
  place of the novel in literature **L** 314
  science fiction **S** 83–85
  Spain, in the Golden Age **S** 368–69
  writing (authorship) **W** 319–20
November, 11th month of year **N** 350–51
  Thanksgiving Day **T** 152–54
Noverre (nov-ERR), **Jean Georges,** French choreographer
  B 24
  dance, history of the **D** 37
  dance composition **D** 25
Novgorod, Union of Soviet Socialist Republics
  church architecture **U** 52
Novocain (NO-vo-cain), or procaine, synthetic drug
  D 328
  local anesthetic **A** 258

Novotny, Antonin (1904–), president of Czechoslovak National Assembly (1957–68) and First Secretary of the Central Committee of Czechoslovak Communist Party (1953–68), b. Letnany, near Prague. He was representative from Prague to the Seventh Congress of the Communist International, held in Moscow (1935). A leader of the resistance during Nazi occupation of Czechoslovakia, he was imprisoned (1941–45). **C** 564

NOW see National Organization for Women
Nowa Huta (NOV-a HU-ta), Poland **P** 360

Noyes, Alfred (1880–1958), English poet, b. Wolverhampton. He was a professor of English literature (1914–23). His writing style is traditional and conservative. His most famous poems are "The Highwayman" and "The Barrel Organ." His works include books of poetry *The Loom of Years*, *Tales of Mermaid Tavern*, and *The Torch Bearers*, as well as prose works *The Unknown God*, an account of his conversion to Roman Catholicism (1925), and *Two Worlds for Memory*, an autobiography.

N.S., abbreviation for nuclear-powered ships **O** 23
Ntare V, former king of Burundi **B** 464

Nu, U (Thakin Nu) (1907–), Burmese statesman, b. Wakema. Imprisoned by British (1941) for his role in "We Burmans" nationalist society, he was released after Japanese occupation to become foreign minister of Japanese puppet government. After Allied re-occupation he was elected vice-president of the Anti-Fascist People's Freedom League (AFPFL). He helped negotiate the Nu-Atlee treaty (1947) for Burmese independence from Britain. He was the first prime minister (1948–56) of the Burmese Republic but resigned to reorganize AFPFL. He resumed the office of prime minister (1957–58, 1960–62) but was ousted in a bloodless coup by General Ne Win. in 1970 he established a guerrilla presence in Burma.
  Burma, history of **B** 459

Nubian (NU-bian) **language,** eastern Africa **A** 55
Nuclear (NU-cle-ar) **disarmament D** 184, 185
  international law **I** 321
Nuclear energy N 352–71
  atom smashers (nuclear reactors) **A** 489; **N** 363–64
  changes in atomic nuclei **M** 177–78
  chemical discoveries from use of **C** 216
  compared to atomic energy **A** 488, 489
  cosmic rays **C** 511–13
  electromagnets **M** 29
  energy, forms of **E** 199, 203
  fallout from nuclear explosions **F** 35–36
  Fermi's reactor **F** 92
  first chain reaction, Chicago **C** 230
  fluorine used in nuclear work **I** 349
  Nautilus, first nuclear submarine **S** 443
  nuclear fusion **I** 351–52
  physics, the study of matter and energy **P** 237, 239
  power, use of and society, pictures **S** 81
  radioactive elements **R** 68
  rocket power **R** 261–62; **S** 348
  Rutherford's theory of the atom **R** 361
  Savannah, first nuclear-powered commercial ship **O** 23
  solar energy the result of nuclear reactions **S** 235–39
  source of power for thermal power plants **P** 426
  star energy **S** 405–06
  uranium **U** 231
  uranium deposits in North America **N** 295
Nuclear engineering E 206
Nuclear family F 37
Nuclear fission N 360–64
  nuclear changes in matter **M** 177–78
Nuclear force, holding atoms together **N** 365–66
Nuclear fuels F 490
Nuclear fusion N 364–65
  changes in atomic nuclei **M** 178
  plasma and fusion **I** 351–52
  sun's interior **S** 463

Nuclear physics, branch of physics that studies nuclear
    energy **N** 352–71
    engineering **E** 206
    nuclear reactors, atom smashers **A** 489
    physics in the future **P** 238–39
Nuclear power plants **P** 426; picture **P** 427
    electricity, steps in the production of, diagram **N** 363
    environment, problems of **E** 272b, 272g
    public utilities **P** 511
Nuclear reactions, of atomic nuclei **N** 357
Nuclear reactors, atom smashers **A** 489; **N** 363–64
    Antarctic region **P** 371
    inspection of fuel wrappings, picture **E** 206
    model, picture **N** 352
    power plants **P** 426; picture **P** 427
    public utilities **P** 511
    rockets **R** 261; picture **R** 262
    satellites **S** 41
    ships with nuclear power **S** 161
    submarines with nuclear engines **S** 442–43
Nuclear rocket engines **S** 348
Nuclear submarines **S** 442–43
Nuclear test ban *see* Nuclear disarmament
Nuclear weapons
    air and water pollution from fallout **A** 111; **W** 59
    control through disarmament **D** 184, 185
    food contamination from fallout **F** 355
    international law **I** 321
Nucleic (nu-CLE-ic) **acids,** in body chemistry **B** 291, 293
    cancer research **C** 94
    in cell nucleus **C** 161
    viruses **V** 363
Nucleotides (NU-cle-o-tides), nucleic acid chains **B** 291,
    293, 295
Nucleus, of a comet **C** 419
Nucleus (plural nuclei), of the atom **A** 485, 488, 489
    chemistry of the atom **C** 201, 216, 220
    electricity and the makeup of atoms **E** 126
    elements, atomic numbers of **E** 153–59
    modern theories about matter **P** 232
    radioactive elements **R** 67
Nucleus, of the cell **C** 159, 160, 161
    controls growth in human body **B** 267
    protozoans, body plan **M** 277
Nuggets, chunks of solid gold **G** 248, 251
Nuku'alofa, Tonga **T** 210a

Nuku Hiva (NU-ku HE-va), or **Nukuhiva,** volcanic island in
the South Pacific, largest of Marquesas Islands, French
Polynesia. The Taipi (Typee) valley was made famous by
Melville in his book *Typee.*

Nullification (null-if-ic-A-tion)
    Calhoun's theory **C** 13
    Jackson opposes **J** 7
    Ordinance of Nullification, 1832 **S** 311
Numbat, marsupial **K** 174
Number I, painting by Jackson Pollock **M** 396
Number 13, superstition **S** 475
Number games and puzzles **N** 372–77
Number lines, scales to show sets of numbers **N** 384
Number lore **N** 378–83
Numbers, book of Bible, Old Testament **B** 154
Numbers and number systems **N** 384–88
    abacus **A** 2–3
    abbreviations for ordinal numbers **A** 6
    arithmetic, science of numbers **A** 398
    automation uses binary system **A** 530
    decimal fractions **F** 401–02
    flags for the numbers (International Code), pictures
      F 246
    graphs **G** 309–13

    mathematics, the study of numbers **M** 154–61
    number lore **N** 378–83
    numerals and numeration systems **N** 389–401
    Roman numerals **R** 309–10
    some numbers in French, Hebrew, Italian, Spanish
      F 434; **H** 102; **I** 478; **S** 368
    See also Calculators; Computers
Numbers in Color, painting by Jasper Johns **M** 396
Number theory
    branch of mathematics **M** 155
Numerals and numeration systems **N** 389–401
    Braille **B** 253
    early development in mathematics **M** 156
    Roman numerals **R** 309–10
    universal language symbols **U** 195
Numerator (NU-mer-a-tor), of a fraction **F** 398
Numismatics (nu-mis-MAT-ics), coin collecting **C** 374–75
Nuncios (NOON-ci-os), or **Internuncios,** ambassadors of
    the popes **V** 281
    Pius XII, service to Bavaria **P** 266
Nuncupative wills **W** 174
Nuns **M** 294
    Buddhist, picture **B** 424
    Carmelites *see* Theresa, Saint
    Poor Clares *see* Clare, or Clara of Assisi, Saint
    See also Sisters of Charity; Ursulines
Nürburgring, German Grand Prix of automobile racing
    A 538
Nuremberg, Germany **G** 158; picture **G** 156
Nuremberg Trials **W** 9–10

Nureyev (nu-RAY-ev), **Rudolf Hametovich** (1938–   ), Russian ballet dancer, b. near Vladivostok. He is considered
among the greatest dancers. He entered Kirov school in
Leningrad (1955), studying with Alexander Pushkin. He
joined Leningrad Kirov Ballet as soloist (1959), but formed
an independent group with Eric Bruhn, Rosella Hightower,
and Sonia Arora (1961). He joined Britain's Royal Ballet as
permanent guest artist (1962). Picture **B** 25.

Nurmi (NOOR-mi), **Paavo,** Finnish athlete **O** 110, 111
    Finns famous for outdoor activities **F** 131
Nurse midwives **N** 412
Nurseries, for growing of trees and plants
    citrus trees **O** 178
Nursery rhymes **N** 402–08
    candle riddle **J** 132
    nonsense rhymes **N** 272
    part of folklore **F** 304
    Was Mother Goose a real person? **N** 402
Nursery schools **K** 242–47
    classes for deprived children **R** 190
    designed by Le Corbusier, picture **S** 56
Nurses and nursing **N** 409–13
    Barton, Clara **B** 68
    doctors' aids, picture **M** 208d
    first aid **F** 157–63
    giving child care instruction, Nigeria, picture **N** 258
    home nursing **N** 413–15
    hospitals **H** 247–52
    Nightingale, Florence **N** 259
    occupational health and safety **O** 16
    Red Cross **R** 126–27
    social welfare services **W** 121
    See also First aid; Red Cross
Nursing, home **N** 413–15
Nursing aides **N** 412
Nursing homes **O** 99
Nutcracker, ballet, picture **B** 27
    celesta solo for "The Dance of the Sugar Plum Fairy"
      K 240
Nuthatches, birds, picture **B** 242

ILLUSTRATION CREDITS

The following list credits, by page, the sources of illustrations used in Volume N of
THE NEW BOOK OF KNOWLEDGE. Credits are listed illustration by illustration
—left to right, top to bottom. Wherever appropriate, the name of the photographer
or artist has been listed with the source, the two being separated by a dash. When two
or more illustrations appear on one page, their credits are separated by semicolons.

125 Diversified Map Corp.
126 Diversified Map Corp.
129 Ray Atkeson
131 John Ballantine
133 Josef Muench
134 Josef Muench; Chuck Abbott—Rapho Guillumette.
135 Diversified Map Corp.
138a George Hunter; Annan.
138b Photo Researchers; Lyn—Annan.
138d New Brunswick Travel Bureau; D.P.I.
138e Diversified Map Corp.
138f Annan Photo Features
138h E. L. Gockeles—Shostal
139 George Buctel
141 D.P.I.
142 Diversified Map Corp.
144 Richard Harrington; Shostal.
147 George Buctel; Shostal.
149 Color Illustration Inc.; State of New Hampshire, Division of Economic Development; William J. Jakoda—FPG; John H. Gerard.
150 Shostal; R. Bagby—FPG
151 Diversified Map Corp.
152 Diversified Map Corp.
153 Fred H. Ragsdale—FPG
155 Diversified Map Corp.
158 Paul Granger
159 Charles Phelps; Eric M. Sanford; Eric M. Sanford.
160 Diversified Map Corp.
164 Gottscho-Schleisner; Allan D. Cruickshank—National Audubon Society; J. Horace McFarland; Color Illustration Inc.
166 Diversified Map Corp.
167 Pendor Natural Color; Diversified Map Corp.
168 Rutgers, College of Agriculture
170 Diversified Map Corp.
173 The Port of New York Authority; M. Legrov—FPG.
174 Grant Heilman
175 John Ballantine
176 Diversified Map Corp.; John V. Dunigan —DPI.
180 Russ Kinne—Photo Researchers
182 Diversified Map Corp.
184 Diversified Map Corp.
186 Shostal; Clotis Reaves; Shostal; Shostal.
190 John Ballantine
191 Shostal
192 Dick Kent; David Muench; Diversified Map Corp.
196 George Buctel; Jack Zehrt—FPG.
204 New York Times
205 Washington Post
207 George Sottung
210 J. Horace McFarland; Gottscho-Schleisner; David Allen; Color Illustration Inc.
212 Diversified Map Corp.
214 Diversified Map Corp.
215 I. Donald Bowden; E. L. Gockeler— Shostal
216 FPG; International Business Machines.
220 Paul Granger
221 Ray Manley—Shostal; M. Helfer—Shostal.
222 Eastman Kodak Company; Rapho Guillumette.
223 Diversified Map Corp.
227 Charles Shapp
229 George Buctel
230 Suzanne Szasz; from The Face of New York, © 1964 by Andreas Feininger, reprinted by permission of Crown Publishers, Inc.; from New York, © 1964 by Andreas Feininger, reprinted by permission of The Viking Press, Inc.
231 From New York, © 1964 by Andreas Feininger, reprinted by permission of The Viking Press, Inc.
232 Peter Fink from The New York I Love, reprinted by permission of Tudor Publishing Co.; from The Face of New York, © 1964 by Andreas Feininger, reprinted by permission of Crown Publishers, Inc.
233 Charles Shapp; Charles Shapp; Charles Shapp.
234 Robert Isear—Photo Researchers; Shostal.
235 Henry Monroe—United Press International.
237 George Buctel; Allyn Baum—Rapho Guillumette.
238 Allyn Baum—Rapho Guillumette; Shostal.
241 Brian Brake—Magnum
242 Dick Huffman—Monkmeyer
244 Annan
245 George Buctel
247 Charles May
248 Douglas Faulkner
251 George Buctel; Carl Frank—Photo Researchers.
253 Marc & Evelyne Bernheim—Rapho Guillumette
254 George Buctel; Marc & Evelyne Bernheim—Rapho Guillumette.
255 Courtesy of the Consulate General of Nigeria
257 John Moss—Photo Researchers; Stephanie Dinkins—Photo Researchers.
258 Marc & Evelyne Bernheim—Rapho Guillumette
260 John G. Ross—Photo Researchers
261 George Holton—Photo Researchers
262 Gerald McConnell
262a James Cooper
262b Courtesy photo
262c UPI; Parade.
262d Wide World Photos
262e Wide World Photos; United Press International; Wide World Photos.
262f Noel Webster—Toronto Globe Mail
263 Swedish Information Service
271 Harrison Forman
273 Illustration by John Tenniel—Franklin Watts, Inc.
274 From Cautionary Verses by Hilaire Belloc, copyright 1931 by Hilaire Belloc, renewal copyright 1959 by Eleanor Jebb Belloc, Elizabeth Belloc and Hilaire Belloc, illustrations by B.T.B. and Nicholas Bentley, reprinted by permission of Alfred A. Knopf, Inc.
275 Illustration by L. Lesle Brooke from Nonsense Songs by Edward Lear, reproduced with permission of the publisher, Frederick Warne & Company
276 Illustration from Nonsense Omnibus, written and illustrated by Edward Lear, reproduced with permission of Frederick Warne & Company
278 Robin Jacques
280 Robin Jacques
281 Robin Jacques
283 Shostal; A. C. Shelton, Publix Pictorial Service; Shostal; John Lewis Stage— Photo Researchers; George Hunter— Publix Pictorial Service.
284 John Lewis Stage—Photo Researchers; George Hunter—Publix Pictorial Service; David Muench.
286 Jeppesen & Co.
287 Jeppesen & Co.
290 J. Donovan
293 David Muench
294 Shostal
298 Shostal; Constantino Reyes—Shostal.
302 Harry Scott
303 Grant Heilman; George Hunter—Publix Pictorial Service.
304 George Hunter—Publix Pictorial Service
307 Color Illustration Inc.; S. W. Buchanan —North Carolina News Bureau; Charles Clark—North Carolina Department of Conservation and Economic Development; S. W. Buchanan—North Carolina News Bureau.
308 Diversified Map Corp.; Frank J. Miller— FPG.
309 Diversified Map Corp.
310 Lewis P. Watson
312 Diversified Map Corp.
314 Alpha; Shostal.
316 John Ballantine
317 Bruce Roberts—Rapho Guillumette
318 Diversified Map Corp.
319 Frank J. Miller—FPG
323 Color Illustration Inc.; North Dakota Soil Conservation Commission; Greater North Dakota Association; North Dakota Travel Department.
324 Diversified Map Corp.; Bernie Donahue —Publix Pictorial Service.
325 Diversified Map Corp.
327 Wendler—FPG
328 North Dakota State Soil Conservation Commission
330 Diversified Map Corp.
332 Paul Granger
333 Shostal
334 Diversified Map Corp.; George Hunter— Shostal
339 C. A. Peterson—Rapho Guillumette
340 John Lewis Stage—Photo Researchers; Ray Manley—Shostal.
341 George Buctel
344a Annan Photo Features
344c Diversified Map Corp.
344e Annan Photo Features
344f Annan Photo Features
347 George Sottung
348 George Sottung
352 Oak Ridge Institute of Nuclear Studies
353 General Electric Company; U.S. Atomic Energy Commission; Lee J. Ames.
354 Lee J. Ames; Dr. Erwin W. Muller; Lee J. Ames.
355 Lee J. Ames
356 Lee J. Ames
357 Lee J. Ames
359 Lee J. Ames
361 Lee J. Ames
362 Union Carbide Corporation; Lee J. Ames.
363 Lee J. Ames
364 Lee J. Ames
366 University of California, Lawrence Radiation Laboratory (Berkeley); Lee J. Ames.
367 High Voltage Engineering Corporation; Brookhaven National Laboratory.
368 Lee J. Ames
370 University of California (Berkeley)
372- Nes Levotch
374
376 Nes Levotch
377 Nes Levotch
378 Weimer Pursell
380- Weimer Pursell
383
385- Gerald McConnell
397
403 James Caraway
404 Dagmar Wilson
405 Dagmar Wilson
406 Dagmar Wilson
407 Dagmar Wilson
408 Dagmar Wilson
409 Esther Bubley
419 USDA
426 Weimer Pursell
427 Weimar Pursell

O, 15th letter of the English alphabet **O** 1
    See also Alphabet
O. Henry see Henry, O.
O, meaning in names **N** 5
Oahu (o-AH-hu), one of the Hawaiian Islands **H** 59
Oak, poison see Poison oak
Oak, tree
    Acorn Area Indians of North America **I** 174–75
    acorn sprout, picture **T** 279
    bur oak, state tree of Illinois **I** 70
    Charter Oak, Hartford, Conn. **C** 466
    flowers, pictures **F** 276
    leaves, shapes of, pictures **L** 116
    live oak, state tree of Georgia **G** 133
    Iowa, state tree of **I** 357
    oak and redwood compared, picture **G** 200
    red oak, state tree of New Jersey **N** 164
    seed, picture **P** 298
    tanning agent for leather **L** 110
    uses of the wood and its grain, picture **W** 224
    white oak, state tree of Connecticut **C** 466
Oak galls, parasitic insect growths, picture **D** 367
    used for ink in Middle Ages **I** 256
Oak Hill, home of James Monroe **M** 425
Oakland, California **C** 26
Oakley, Annie, American marksman **O** 2
    in Buffalo Bill's Wild West Show **B** 428
Oak Ridge, Tennessee **T** 75
    Y-12 plant, picture **T** 88
OAO see Orbiting astronomical observatories
OAS see Organization of American States
OAS see Secret Army Organization
Oases (o-A-sese), fertile areas in desert lands **O** 2–3
    habitable desert areas **D** 124, 127; picture **D** 125
    Nile delta, picture **N** 261
    Sahara **S** 8
    Saudi Arabia **S** 47

Oates, Titus (1649–1705), English conspirator, b. London.
He and Israel Tonge invented the "Popish Plot" (1678),
a false story about a plan to assassinate King Charles
II, burn London, and forcibly establish Roman Catholicism
in England. Oates was an informer who caused the execution of many Catholics. After accusing the Duke of
York of treason, Oates was convicted of perjury (1685)
and imprisoned, but was later pardoned.

Oath of Hippocrates **M** 208b
Oath of the Horatii (ho-RAY-shi-y), painting by David
    F 424, 425
Oaths, of fealty **F** 101
    receiving knighthood **K** 276
Oaths, or pledges
    Girl Guides and Girl Scouts laws **G** 213, 215
Oaths of office
    presidency of the United States **P** 447
Oatmeal **O** 4
Oats **O** 3–4
    grain and grain products **G** 285
    kinds of grasses **G** 317–18
    seeds, pictures **G** 283
Oats, Peas, Beans, and Barley Grow, folk song **F** 323
OAU see Organization of African Unity
Oaxaca (wa-HA-ca), Mexico **M** 247
Obadiah (o-ba-DY-ah), book of the Bible **B** 155
O'Bannon, Presley, American marine officer **U** 177
Obedience schools, for dogs **D** 259
Obedience trials, in dog shows **D** 261–62
Obelia (o-BE-lia), hydrozoan colony **J** 74–75
Obelisks (OB-el-isks), four-sided pillars tapering to minia-
    ture pyramids at the top **O** 5–6
    Egyptian, one in New York City, one in London **E** 96

Oberammergau (o-ber-OM-mer-gow), Germany **G** 152

Oberlin, Jean Frédéric (1740–1826), Alsatian clergyman,
b. Strasbourg. He became a Protestant minister (1767) in
Ban-de-la-Roche, France, and helped in the agricultural,
industrial, and educational development of his pastorate.
Oberlin College in Ohio was named in his honor.

Oberlin College, Oberlin, Ohio **O** 68
Oberon, king of the fairies in *Midsummer Night's Dream*
    S 136
Oberth (O-bert), **Hermann,** German mathematician and
    pioneer in rocketry **O** 6–7
Obesity see Overweight
Obi (O-bi), sash of Japanese kimono **J** 26
Objective, a set of lenses **L** 144–45
    telescopes **T** 61
Obligation, holy days of, for Roman Catholics **R** 290
Oboe, musical instrument **M** 549; pictures **W** 183
    ancient instrument **A** 245, picture **A** 244
    orchestra seating plan **O** 186

Obote, Milton (1924–), Ugandan political figure, b.
Lango District in Northern Province of Uganda. He
helped establish Kenya African Union (1952) and was
a member of the Uganda Legislative Council in 1958.
He merged the Uganda National Congress with the
Uganda People's Union and founded the Uganda People's
Congress in 1960. Obote was made prime minister of
Uganda in 1962, and president in 1966. He was overthrown
in 1971.
    Uganda, history of **U** 7

Obrecht (O-breckt), **Jacob,** Dutch composer **D** 364; **R** 172

O'Brien, Lawrence F. (1917–), American political figure, b. Springfield, Mass. He is a graduate of Northeastern
University, where he received a law degree in 1942. He
became active in Massachusetts Democratic politics, and
was appointed special assistant to presidents John F.
Kennedy and Lyndon B. Johnson. He was postmaster
general of the United States (1965–68). In 1970 he was
elected National Chairman of the Democratic Party.

Ob (OBE) **River,** Union of Soviet Socialist Republics **R** 245
    flows into the Kara Sea **O** 48
Obscenity, that which is repulsive to the senses, or is
    designed to incite to corruption or evil
    civil liberties **C** 315
Observatories (obs-ERV-a-tories) **O** 8–15
    air pollution checking station, Hawaii **A** 110–11
    Arecibo Observatory, Puerto Rico, picture **R** 73
    balloons **B** 34
    Big Ear, in West Virginia **W** 137
    correct time **T** 192–93
    Greenwich Observatory **G** 372
    Kitt Peak, Arizona **E** 28
    moon or Skylabs ideal **M** 455; **S** 340i, 342–43
    Mount Stromlo, Canberra, Australia **C** 88
    orbiting observatories **E** 29–30; **O** 13–15
    radio and radar astronomy **R** 69, 72, 73
    seismic (earthquake) **E** 31–40
    telescopes **T** 60–64
    tools of the astronomer **A** 473
    See also Planetariums
Obsidian (ob-SID-ian), glass formed in volcanoes
    V 378; picture **V** 379
    formed from lava **R** 264; picture **R** 265
    natural glass **G** 226
Obtuse angles, in geometry **G** 124; diagrams **G** 125
Ocampo (o-COM-po), **Sebastián de,** Spanish explorer in
    Cuba **C** 549

Occupational therapy, creative activities prescribed as
a health aid. These activities are planned and directed
by trained specialists, called **occupational therapists.**
They work with people who are sick, injured, handicapped,
or mentally ill, giving them projects that are pleasant
and constructive. The work may be purely recreational
—painting, weaving, leatherworking, and so on, or it
may be therapeutic—clay modeling or woodworking to
strengthen weak hands. Most therapists work in hospitals,
rehabilitation centers, sanitariums, or nursing homes.

Oceanus (o-CE-an-us), in Greek mythology, a Titan and
the father of the waters. Son of Uranus (sky) and Ge
(earth), Oceanus was often pictured as the river through
which all life flowed.

Ocher (O-ker), or **ochre,** mineral consisting of a mixture
of iron oxides and clay. It has been used for centuries in
making pigment for paints. The color of the pigment
ranges from yellow or yellowish brown to reddish orange.
   paints used by prehistoric man **P** 15, 440–41

Ochs (OCKS), **Adolph Simon** (1858–1935), American
newspaper publisher, b. Cincinnati, Ohio. He became
owner and publisher of the Chattanooga *Times* (1878),
New York *Times* (1896), and Philadelphia *Times* (1901)
and *Public Ledger* (1902). He served as director of
Associated Press (1900–35), and donated funds for
publication of *Dictionary of American Biography.*

O'Connor Basil (1892–   ), American lawyer, b. Taunton, Mass. A law partner with Franklin Delano Roosevelt (1925–33), he has served as president of the American Red Cross (1944–49), president of the National Health Council (1957–58), and president of the National Foundation (since 1938).

O'Connor, Frank, Irish short-story writer **I** 395

O'Connor, Thomas Power (1848–1929), Irish politician and journalist, b. Athlone. He established the newspapers *The Star* (1887) and *The Sun* (1893) and the journal *T. P.'s Weekly* (1902). He was a representative in the House of Commons (1885–1929) and supporter of the Irish home-rule cause. His writing includes *Life of Lord Beaconsfield* and *The Parnell Movement.*

Ocotillo (o-co-Ti-yo), desert shrub, picture **C** 3
Octahedron (oc-ta-HE-dron), eight-sided figure
    crystal form **C** 546
    how to make **G** 128
Octane numbers, gasoline classification **G** 63
Octants, navigation instruments **N** 65
Octave, first eight lines of a sonnet **S** 255
Octaves, in music **M** 527
Octavian or Octavianus see Augustus
October, 10th month of the year **O** 50–51
October Revolutions, revolts against czarist regimes in Russia, 1905, 1917 **U** 50
Octopuses, mollusks **O** 274–75
    adaptability test **A** 286–87
    skin divers in little danger **S** 191
Ocular (OC-u-lar), or eyepiece, a set of lenses of a compound microscope **L** 147

Oculist, physician who is a specialist in eye diseases and defects. He utilizes numerous devices for eye examination, prescribes corrective lenses, and operates on eyes if necessary. He is also called an ophthalmologist.

Oda Nobunaga see Nobunaga

Odd Fellows, Independent Order of (IOOF), men's secret, fraternal, and benevolent society, its main body being the English order, Manchester Unity. Thomas Wildey is said to have founded (1819) the now independent American branch, which has its headquarters in Baltimore, Md.

Odd lots, stocks sold or bought a few at a time **S** 432
Odd-toed mammals F 81–82; **H** 206–07; pictures **H** 211
    horses and their relatives **H** 236–44

O'Dell, Scott (1903–   ), American journalist and author of children's books, b. Los Angeles, Calif. He won the Newbery medal (1961) for *Island of the Blue Dolphins,* his first children's book, written after he had worked as technical director in the film industry, as a journalist, and as a book reviewer.

Odense (O-den-sa), Denmark, birthplace of Hans Christian Andersen **A** 248
Oder River, Europe R 245
    Poland, importance to **P** 359
Odes, forms of lyric poetry **O** 52
    poems of noble sentiment **P** 354
    Schiller's "Ode to Joy", in Beethoven's *Ninth Symphony* **G** 185–86
Odessa, Ukraine, Union of Soviet Socialist Republics **U** 9
Ode to a Nightingale, excerpt **O** 52
Ode to the West Wind, excerpt **O** 52

Odets (o-DETS), **Clifford,** American playwright **A** 216
Odin (O-din), Norse god **N** 278–79
Odoacer (o-do-A-cer), Germanic king **R** 308

Odom, William P. (1920–1949), American aviator, b. Columbus, Ohio. He set a record by flying around the world solo in 73 hours, 5 minutes, in 1947 and established a record for nonstop distance flying in light aircraft (1949). Odom was killed in an air-race crash.

Odometer (o-DOM-et-er), device for measuring distance traveled. An odometer is usually attached to the speedometer of a car and records the total mileage.

O'Donovan, Michael see O'Connor, Frank
Odo (O-do) **of Cheriton** (CHAY-ri-ton), British preacher and fabulist **F** 4
Odontocetes (o-don-to-CE-tese), or toothed whales **W** 147
Odor
    animal communication **A** 278
    different odors of flowers attract different insects **F** 278
    deodorizers act upon **D** 117
    perfumes **P** 154–55
    scents of butterflies and moths **B** 469–70
Odysseus (o-DIS-seus), in Greek mythology **G** 366
    hero of Homer's *Odyssey* **O** 53–54
Odyssey (OD-iss-ey), epic poem by Homer **O** 53–54
    Aeneid compared with **A** 35
    early form of fiction **F** 110
    early Greek literature **G** 350
    Greek mythology **G** 366
    Homer **H** 167
Oedipus (ED-ip-us), king of Thebes in Greek mythology
    riddle of Sphinx solved by **J** 132
Oedipus Rex, play by Sophocles, scene, picture **G** 352
Oehlenschlaeger, Adam, Danish dramatist **S** 51, 52

Oersted (ER-sted), **Hans Christian** (1777–1851), Danish physicist, b. Rudkøbing. In 1819 he discovered that an electric current passing through a wire deflects the needle of a compass placed near the wire, thus showing a relationship between electricity and magnetism. This discovery was the starting point of the science of electromagnetism, which later led to the development of electric motors and generators.
    electric motors, history of **E** 140
    story of the telegraph **T** 51

Oetinger, Frederick, German evangelist
    prayer **P** 435
O'Faoláin (o-fway-LOIN), **Seán,** Irish short-story writer **I** 395
Off-Broadway theaters T 161
Offenbach (OFF-en-bock), **Jacques,** French composer of operettas **O** 55
    French music gives equal importance to words and music **F** 446
    Tales of Hoffmann, The, opera **O** 153–54
Office buildings
    architecture **A** 384–85, 386
    central air conditioning **A** 102
    elevators and escalators **E** 172–74
    Empire State Building, picture **W** 218
    Ghana's Republic House, picture **G** 194
    Guatemala, picture **G** 394
    Sullivan, Louis **S** 457
    See also Skyscrapers
Office machines O 55–58
    bookkeeping and accounting machines, picture **B** 311
    computers **C** 449–57
    typewriters **T** 347–48

Office of, referring to parts of U.S. Government *see* by
name, as Education, United States Office of
Office workers
    labor-management relations **L** 18
    programed instruction **P** 475
    women, role of **W** 212
Offset lithography (lith-OG-raphy), a form of planographic
printing **P** 460–61
    newspapers' use of **N** 204
    plate being fastened to the press, picture **B** 333
Offset plates, for printing **P** 467
Offset printing **P** 460–61
Of Human Bondage, by Maugham **E** 266
O'Flaherty (o-FLA-her-ty), **Liam,** Irish novelist **I** 395

Ogden, Peter Skene (1794–1854), Canadian explorer and
fur trader, b. Quebec. An agent of Hudson's Bay
Company on the Columbia River (1835–54), he was
among the first white men to explore the Great Salt Lake
region. He discovered the Humboldt River in Nevada and
was stationed at Fort Vancouver (1844), where he was
later in command. Ogden, Utah, was named for him.

Ogden, Utah **U** 252
Ogeechee (o-GEE-chee) **River,** Georgia **G** 135
Oglethorpe, James, English founder of Georgia **O** 59
    American colonies, history of **A** 193–94
    Georgia **G** 145
Ogooué (o-GO-way), or **Ogowe, River,** Gabon, central
Africa **G** 3

O'Gorman, Juan (1905–), Mexican architect and artist,
b. Coyoacan. He is noted especially for innovations he
introduced as architect and artist of University of
Mexico's library (1952). The four outside walls of the
library display a mosaic mural 4,700 meters in size,
made of tiny natural colored stones. Other noted murals
of his decorate the Mexico City Airport and the
Pátzcuaro library.
    Latin-American art and architecture **L** 67
    Library of the University of Mexico, picture **M** 253

O'Grady, Standish James, Irish writer **I** 394

O'Hara, John Henry (1905–70), American novelist, b.
Pottsville, Pa. O'Hara was famous for his realistic por-
trayal of American life. Among his best known works are
Butterfield 8, Pal Joey, Appointment in Samarra, and
Ten North Frederick. Several of his books have been
adapted for motion pictures.
    American literature, place in **A** 214

O'Hara, Mary (Mary O'Hara Alsop Sture-Vasa)
(1885–), American author, b. Cape May Point, N.J.
She is remembered for her books about horses on the
western American plains, including *My Friend Flicka,
Thunderhead,* and *Green Grass of Wyoming.* She also
composed music and wrote adaptations for motion
pictures.

O'Hare International Airport, Chicago **C** 230
Oh Christmas Tree, Christmas carol **F** 325
O. Henry *see* Henry, O.
O'Higgins, Bernardo, Chilean statesman and soldier
O 59
    Chile's war for independence **C** 253, 254
Ohio **O** 60–75
    Cleveland **C** 338
    places of interest in Negro history **N** 94
Ohio, University of **O** 68
Ohio and Erie Canal **C** 338; **O** 66
    canal fever in Ohio **O** 74–75

Ohio Company of Associates, group of New England men
under Manasseh Cutler who arranged the purchase of
1,500,000 acres of land in the Ohio River valley from
Congress under terms of 1787 Northwest Ordinance.
    Ohio, history of **O** 64

Ohio Company of Virginia, early (1747) land
company **O** 74
Ohio River, United States **R** 245
    junction of Allegheny and Monongahela, picture **P** 130
    major river and tributaries in Ohio **O** 62
    westward movement into the Ohio Valley **W** 142
Ohio State University, Columbus, Ohio **O** 68
Ohio Wesleyan University, Delaware, Ohio **O** 68

Ohm, Georg Simon (1787–1854), German physicist, b.
Erlangen. He experimented with the flow of electric
current in wires of different lengths and thicknesses and
found that the amount of current was directly proportional to the thickness of the wire and inversely
proportional to its length. In 1827 he announced Ohm's
law, which defines the relationship between current,
voltage, and resistance in any given electrical circuit.
The ohm (unit of electrical resistance) is named for him.
    Ohm's law of electric current **E** 132–33

Ohms, units of measure of electric resistance **E** 133
Ohm's law, in electricity **E** 132–33
O I C, nonsense rhyme **N** 272
Oil *see* Petroleum and petroleum refining
Oil cloth **V** 340
Oil lamps **L** 279
Oil paints **P** 30
Oils **O** 76–79
    citrus peels **O** 179
    coconut **C** 369
    cosmetics made of **C** 509
    detergents and soaps **D** 145, 147
    fire of, how to put out **F** 136, 149
    lighting, forms of **L** 279–82
    liquid fuels **F** 488
    lubrication and lubricants **L** 370–71
    olive oil **O** 101, 102
    perfumes **P** 154–55
    soybeans **S** 337
    whale oil **W** 152
    See also Fats
Oils, essential *see* Essential oils
Oil shale, a slatelike rock **P** 178
Oil tankers, or tankers **S** 161

Ojeda (o-HAI-da), **Alonso de** (1465?–1515), Spanish explorer, b. Cuenca. He accompanied Columbus on his
second voyage (1493) to Hispaniola, explored with Vespucci and Juan de la Cosa the northern coast of South
America (1499–1500). He established a colony on the
Gulf of Darien.

Ojibway (o-JIB-way), or Chippewa, Indians of North
America **I** 178–79
    Hiawatha, setting for the poem **M** 258
    mosaics in Whiteshell Provincial Park, Manitoba **M** 79
Ojukwu, C. O. military leader in Biafra (Eastern Region
Nigeria) **N** 258
OK, American expression **W** 240–41
    Van Buren cartoon, picture **V** 274
Okanagan (o-ka-NA-gan) **Valley,** British Columbia, Canada
B 406a–406b
Okapis (o-KA-pi-s), animals related to giraffes **G** 212
    hoofed mammals **H** 220
Okeechobee (o-kee-CHO-bee), **Lake,** Florida **L** 33
    inland waters of Florida **F** 262

O'Keeffe, Georgia (1887–   ), American painter, b. Sun Prairie, Wis. She is the widow of the photographer Alfred Stieglitz. She is best-known for her symbolic abstracts and New Mexican desert scenes.

Okefenokee (o-ke-fe-NO-kee) **Swamp,** Florida and Georgia F 261; G 132; picture G 143
Okeghem see Ockeghem
Okhotsk (o-KOTSK), **Sea of** O 48
Okhotsk Current, in the Japan Sea O 48
Okigbo, Christopher, Nigerian poet A 76c
Okinawa (o-ki-NA-wa), Ryukyu Islands P 7
  World War II W 305, 308
Oklahoma O 80–95
Oklahoma, University of, picture O 87
Oklahoma City, capital of Oklahoma O 91–92
Oklahoma Run, for the unassigned lands opened for settlement O 80, 95
  end of the frontier P 261
Okmulgee, Oklahoma O 92
Okoume (o-koo-MAY), tree G 2–3

Okra (O-kra), or **gumbo,** vegetable of African origin now also grown in the southern part of the United States and in the West Indies. The plant is cultivated for its green pods, which are used in cooking, especially in soups and stews. V 291

Olaf II (O-laf) (Saint Olaf, or Olaf Haraldsson) (995?–1030), king of Norway (1016–28) and patron saint. After fighting Danes in England, he returned to Norway, where he defeated earls Eric and Sweyn and became king. Having extended his kingdom throughout Norway by harsh rule, he tried to convert the country to Christianity. He was forced to flee when Canute II of Denmark and his followers invaded Norway (1028). He was defeated and killed when he tried to regain his kingdom. Olaf was canonized in 1164.

Olaf V (Alexander Edward Christian Frederick) (1903–   ), king of Norway (since 1957), b. Sandringham, England. He commanded the armed forces when Norway resisted Nazi occupation during World War II, and while in exile (1940–45) organized the Norwegian Forces for Liberation. He assumed monarch's responsibilities when he acted as regent (1955–57) for his ailing father, King Haakon VII. A sports enthusiast, he won a gold medal for yachting in the 1928 Olympics.

Öland (ER-land), Sweden S 484
Olave House, London, center for World Association of Girl Guides and Girl Scouts G 214
Olbers, Heinrich, German astronomer P 273
Old Abe, eagle W 192
Old age O 96–101
  family relationship F 42, 43
  homes designed for needs of H 183–84
  old person makeup, picture P 340
  public-assistance programs W 120–21
  social security S 221–22
  See also Aging
Old age pensions see Social security

Old Catholic Churches, religious group loyal to the customs and doctrines of the Roman Catholic Church but independent since the first Vatican Council (1869–70). Under the leadership of J. J. Dollinger the sect rejected particularly the dogma of papal infallibility and sanctioned marriage of priests, voluntary private confessions, and services in vernacular.

Old Church Slavonic, language U 58

Old Colony see Plymouth Colony
Old Colony State, nickname for Massachusetts M 135

Oldenburg, Claes (1929–   ), American artist, b. Stockholm, Sweden. He began his career as a newspaper reporter in Chicago and did not become interested in art until later in life. His works have the effect of sculptured paintings and are concerned with everyday things—hamburgers, egg beaters, wash basins, ice cream sundaes. In his work he uses a wide range of materials such as vinyl plastic, metal, wood, rubber, and canvas. His subjects are often so exaggerated that they appear grotesque.
  painting in the United States P 31

Old Dominion, nickname for Virginia V 344–45
Old English language see Anglo-Saxon language
Old English literature see Anglo-Saxon (Old English) literature
Old Faithful, geyser, Yellowstone National Park, Wyoming G 192; picture Y 345
Old-fashioned, or English, **gardens** G 26, 46
Old Folks at Home (Swanee River), song by Stephen Foster
  Florida, state song of F 259, 262
Old French F 433
Old Fuss and Feathers, nickname of General Winfield Scott M 239
Old Glory, nickname of flag of United States F 248

Old Guard (in French, *vieille garde*), name given to veteran troops of Napoleon's Imperial Guard (*Garde Impériale*). The Imperial Guard was created in 1804, with its own general staff and commander-in-chief. According to legend, they were so devoted to Napoleon that one division (the Old Guard) refused to surrender to the British at Waterloo. The term "old guard" now describes any loyal old core of a political party or movement.

Old Hickory, nickname given Andrew Jackson J 3
Old Hundredth, hymn H 312
Old Ironsides (*Constitution*), early American naval vessel W 12
Old Ironsides, poem by Oliver Wendell Holmes A 203; H 160
Old King, The, painting by Rouault F 430
Old Kingdom, or Pyramid Age (2780–2250 B.C.), ancient Egypt E 95
Old Lady of Threadneedle Street (Bank of England) B 47
  points of interest in London L 335
Old Line State, nickname for Maryland M 128
Old Man and the Sea, The, novel by Hemingway H 109
Old Man of the Mountain, New Hampshire rock formation N 148; picture N 150
Old Manse, Concord, Mass., home of Emerson and Hawthorne E 190; H 73
Old Millers, primitive Indians of North America I 164
Old mother witch, tag game G 16
Old Norse language and literature S 50–51
Old North State, nickname for North Carolina N 320
Old Northwest see Northwest Territory
Old Orchard Beach, Maine M 35
Old Pretender, James Edward Stuart E 224
Old Rough and Ready, nickname of Zachary Taylor T 36
  Mexican War hero M 238

Olds, Elizabeth (1896–   ), American artist and writer, b. Minneapolis, Minn. She was the first woman to get a Guggenheim fellowship for painting (1925–26) and has

Olds, Elizabeth (continued)
exhibited in many shows and museums. She has written and illustrated children's books, including *The Big Fire, Feather Mountain,* and *Deep Treasure.* Her book *Riding the Rails* was translated into Korean.

Olds, Ransom E., American automobile manufacturer **A** 547

Old Spanish Trail, California **C** 23
  overland trails **O** 259

Old Stone, or Paleolithic, **age**
  art as a record **A** 438, 438b
  prehistoric man **P** 442–44
  tools, pictures **P** 444

Old Sturbridge Village, Massachusetts **M** 145
  museum of colonial life **M** 513–14

Old Testament, of the Bible **B** 152–57, 159
  Abraham **A** 7
  Apocrypha **B** 152, 156–57, 159
  Daniel in the Lion's Den, story **B** 167–68
  David **D** 44
  David and Goliath, story **B** 164–65
  Dead Sea Scrolls **D** 48–49
  Elijah **E** 176
  Ezra **E** 396
  Hebrew literature **H** 101
  idea of equal justice for all **C** 313–14
  Isaac **I** 413
  Isaiah **I** 413
  Jeremiah **J** 77
  Jerome's translation **J** 77
  Jonah, story **B** 166–67
  Joseph **J** 140
  Joshua, leader of Israelites **J** 141
  Judaism, Biblical origins of **J** 102–03
  Moses **M** 468
  Noah's Ark, story **B** 163–64
  Septuagint, Old Testament in Greek **B** 153; **J** 106–07
  Ten Commandments **T** 72–73

Old wives' tales, foolish stories supposedly made up by talkative old women. The term "old wife" was formerly a derogatory reference to an old woman. An example of an old wives' tale is the advice to feed a cold and starve a fever.

Old Woman and the Shoe, The, nursery rhyme **N** 403

Old World monkeys **M** 419–20

Oleander, shrub **P** 321

Olefin (O-lef-in) **fibers,** man-made **N** 425

Oleomargarine (o-le-o-MARGE-ar-in), or margarine, substitute for butter **O** 79

Oleoresin **T** 330

Oleoresinous varnishes **V** 279

Olfactory (ol-FACT-ory) **nerve,** for sense of smell **B** 286–87
  nerve cells in brain of fish **F** 190

Olibanum see Frankincense

Oligarchy (OL-ig-arcky), government by a few and for personal gain **G** 278

Oligocene epoch, of the Cenozoic era, in geology **F** 388

Olingos, animals related to raccoons **R** 27; picture **R** 26

Olive, tree **O** 101–03
  Spain, leading producer **S** 357; picture **S** 353

Olive oil **O** 79
  processing olives **O** 102
  used in castile soap **D** 147

Oliver, Isaac, English painter
  John Donne, portrait **E** 254

Oliver Twist, book by Charles Dickens, excerpt **D** 161–63
  Cruikshank etching from **I** 91

Olives, Mount of (Olivet), chain of four hills approximately 1 mile in length and 2,680 feet in elevation. Situated east of Jerusalem and the narrow Kidron Valley, it is associated with David's flight during the rebellion of his son Absalom (2 Samuel 18) and is noted as a favorite retreat of Jesus. The Garden of Gethsemane lies at its foot, and today it is the site of numerous churches and religious memorials.
  Jerusalem **J** 80
  old olive trees in the Garden of Gethsemane **O** 101

Olivier (o-LIV-i-ay), **Sir Laurence Kerr** (1907–), English actor and director, b. Dorking. He acted with the Birmingham Repertory Theatre (1925–28) and joined the Old Vic Theatre Company as an actor and director in 1944. He produced, directed, and acted in Shakespearean films *Hamlet, Richard III,* and *Henry V* and won an Academy Award (1948). He has directed the National Theatre (since 1962). His other major parts include leading roles in plays of Shaw. In 1970 he became the first actor in the House of Lords when named a peer by Queen Elizabeth II.

Olivines, or peridots, gemstones **G** 76

Olmecs (ol-MECS), ancient peoples of Central America **I** 152

Olmsted, Frederick, American landscape architect, designed Central Park, New York, N.Y. **P** 77

Olympia, capital of Washington **W** 26

Olympia, in ancient Greece
  Olympic Games **O** 104

Olympiad, four-year period of Olympic Games **O** 103
  Olympiad, 1968 **O** 116

Olympic Games **O** 103–16b
  ancient Greek civilization **A** 229
  basketball events **B** 90
  bicycle racing **B** 171, 173
  bobsledding event **B** 265
  boxing **B** 352
  canoeing **C** 101
  diving competition **D** 226, 227, 230–31
  fencing **F** 86
  field hockey meet, 1964, picture **F** 115
  flag **F** 226
  Japan, picture **J** 30
  judo **J** 147
  official stopwatch, picture **W** 49
  physical education in ancient Greece **P** 224–25
  rowing event **R** 339
  rugby **R** 349–50
  skiing **S** 184b
  soccer **S** 218–19
  speed skating **I** 50–53
  swimming **S** 489
  Thorpe, James Francis ("Jim") **T** 169
  Tokyo sports facilities **T** 207
  track and field events **T** 236
  volleyball **V** 387
  water polo **W** 60
  weight lifting **W** 107
  wrestling **W** 314

Olympic Mountains, Washington **W** 16; picture **W** 25
  crevasse, picture **I** 8

Olympic National Park, Washington **W** 24; picture **W** 21
  rain forest, picture **R** 99

Olympic torch **O** 109; picture **O** 106

Olympieum, temple in Athens **G** 348; picture **G** 347

Olympus, Mount, Greece **G** 333
  home of the Greek gods **G** 357

Omaha, Nebraska **N** 84; picture **N** 78

Omaha Beach, Normandy landing, World War II **W** 299

Oman (o-MAN), sultanate, Arabian Peninsula **M** 301
  flag **F** 238

Omar Khayyàm (O-mar ky-YOM) (?–1123?), Persian poet, mathematician, and astronomer, b. Nishapur. He helped develop a new Muslim calendar for the Jalalaean period (beginning 1079). He also wrote a study on algebra, but is best known in the West for his poetic work, *The Rubaiyat*, which was translated into English, paraphrased, and edited by Edward FitzGerald (1859).

Persian writers **I** 373

Ombudsman, public official appointed to receive, investigate, and channel complaints of citizens involving abuses of power by government officials. Although the ombudsman cannot order or reverse administrative action, he can make recommendations for corrective measures. The office originated in Sweden, and the word means "representative."

Omdurman (om-dur-MAN), Sudan **S** 448
Omiéné (o-mi-ay-NAY), a people of Gabon **G** 2

Omnibus Bill, portion of Compromise of 1850 covering organization of territories. Specifically, it provided for admission of California to the union as a free state, establishment of Utah and New Mexico as territories, and determination of Texas' boundaries.

Omnibuses, early vehicles **B** 465
Omnivores, animals that eat both plant and animal food different teeth for different diets **M** 65–66
Omo National Park, Ethiopia **E** 300
Omsk, U.S.S.R., West Siberia **S** 173
Onager (ON-ager), wild horse **H** 244

Onassis, Aristotle (1906–   ), Greek ship owner and financier, b. Smyrna, Turkey. Soon after his family went to Greece as refugees, he emigrated (1923) to Argentina, where he made his fortune in tobacco. His interests shifted to shipping during the 1930's and by the 1960's he was one of the wealthiest men in the world. He married Jacqueline Kennedy, President John F. Kennedy's widow, in 1968.

Onassis, Mrs. Aristotle *see* Kennedy, Jacqueline

Oñate (ohn-YA-tay), **Juan de** (1549?–1624?), Spanish explorer and colonizer in New Mexico, b. Mexico. In 1595 he was sent to colonize the territory on the Rio Grande that is now New Mexico. Founding the capital at San Juan (1598), he was first Spanish governor of New Mexico (1598–1607) and head of expeditions that explored what is now Kansas (1601) and the Gulf of California (1605).

Onchocerciasis (on-co-cer-KY-a-sis), or river blindness, disease **B** 252

O'Neal, Frederick Douglas (1905–   ), American actor, Negro, b. Brooksville, Miss. O'Neal organized Aldridge Players (1927), and first appeared on Broadway (1936) with Civic Repertory Theatre. He helped found American Negro Theatre (1940) and appeared in productions of company; won N.Y. Drama Critics Award for supporting role in *Anna Lucasta* (1944), and also appeared in motion pictures, radio, and television plays. He was elected the first Negro president of Actor's Equity Association (1964–   ), and is the author of *The Negro in American Theatre.*

Onega (o-NE-ga), **Lake,** northwestern Soviet Union **L** 33
One hundred plus ideas, for experiments and projects **E** 356–67
Oneida, Indians of North America **I** 184

Oneida (o-NY-da) **Community** (Perfectionists, or Bible Communists), religious society established by John Humphrey Noyes at Oneida, N.Y. (1848). The community replaced monogamy by a system of complex marriage, which it was forced by public opinion to abandon (1880). It established a joint stock company (1881) noted for manufacture of Community Silver.

O'Neill, Eugene, American playwright **O** 117
American drama **D** 300
place in American literature **A** 215
O'Neill, Hugh, Irish leader **I** 390
O'Neill, William O., American frontier sheriff **A** 416
One small step for a man, one giant leap for mankind, moon landing **E** 368; **S** 340a
Onions **O** 118
bulb sprouting, picture **P** 300
leaves we eat **P** 307; picture **P** 306
vegetable growing **V** 291
Onnes (ON-nes), **Heike Kamerlingh,** Dutch scientist **H** 90
Onomatopoeia (on-o-mat-o-PE-a), use of words with sounds that suggest the subject **P** 353
Onondaga, Indians of North America **I** 184
Ontario (ont-AIR-io), Canada **O** 119–29
Mackenzie, William Lyon **M** 5
Niagara Falls **N** 243–44
Ottawa **O** 237–39
Stratford Festival **C** 62–63; picture **O** 129
Toronto **T** 227–28
Ontario, Lake, one of Great Lakes **G** 328–29
Ontario Northland, Canadian railroad **O** 122
On the Bridge of Avignon (av-ENE-yon), folk song **F** 324
On the Grasshopper and Cricket, poem by Keats **K** 200
On the Road, painting by Otter **T** 106
On the Terrace, painting by Renoir **F** 429
Ontology, the branch of metaphysics that studies the nature of being **P** 192
On Top of Old Smoky, folk song
how to play on the guitar **G** 410
Onyx (ON-ix), quartz **Q** 7
Oolong tea **T** 38–39

Oort (ORT), **Jan Hendrik** (1900–   ), Dutch astronomer, b. Franeker. An authority on the movement of stars, Oort showed that the stars of our galaxy take different periods of time to rotate about its center. He calculated the distance from the sun to the center of our galaxy as 30,000 light-years.

Opacimeters (o-pa-CIM-et-ers), optical instruments **O** 174
Opah, or moon fish, picture **F** 183
Opalescence (o-pal-ES-cence), pearly reflections from inside gemstones **G** 70
Opals, gemstones **G** 70, 75; picture **G** 73
famous opal ring **J** 100
Op art, or optical art **P** 32
modern art after abstract expressionism **M** 398
"Open, Sesame!" (SES-am-e), famous magic words from Arabian Nights' story **A** 346
Open, term used in sports competitions
golf **G** 261
Open and closed shop **L** 15–16

Open city, under international law, city that is demilitarized to avoid attack or bombardment by enemy. The city is usually demilitarized to protect valuable works of art, historic buildings, or hospitals. Paris was declared an open city in World War II.
Paris **P** 75

Open City, motion picture **M** 476
Opencut mining, of coal **C** 365

Open Door Policy, term applied specifically to the U.S. policy toward China that proposed equal and impartial tariff and excise rates within various spheres for all nations in dealings with China. The policy was outlined by Secretary of State John Hay in notes to major European nations and Japan (1899) for the purpose of abolishing monopolies held by individual nations in China.

China and the Open-Door policy in McKinley's administration **M** 189–90

Open-hearth furnace, for turning iron into steel **I** 398; picture **E** 393

Open Housing, the concept that anyone may live where he chooses free of discriminatory restrictions. A number of states and cities have passed open housing laws that forbid discrimination in the sale, rental, or financing of homes and apartments. The U.S. Congress made open housing provisions part of the Civil Rights Act of 1968.

Open-pit mining **M** 317–18; picture **M** 319
largest mine, picture **S** 275
Open Road, magazine **M** 16

Open Season, the portion of any year during which hunting or fishing or specified types of game, fowl, or fish is legal under conservation laws.

Open shop, for labor in industry **L** 15–16
Opera **O** 130–55
baroque period, new form and development **B** 63–64
basic record library **R** 125
Canada **C** 63
Chinese drama **D** 293
classical age **C** 332–33
development of dance music in **D** 36–37
festivals **M** 550
foreign influences on French opera **F** 445
German **G** 187–88
Gershwin's *Porgy and Bess*, picture **G** 190
Gluck, Christoph Willibald **G** 241
Italian music **I** 483–84, 485–86
Italy the home of **I** 448
Metropolitan Opera in Lincoln Center for the Performing Arts **L** 298
Mozart **M** 502
Mussorgsky's *Boris Godunov*, picture **U** 63
Peking Opera school students, picture **D** 293
plots of some well-known operas **O** 139–55
Puccini, Giacomo **P** 515
rock music **R** 262d
romantic age in music **R** 310–11
stories and plots of some famous operas **O** 139–55
Vienna, Austria **A** 520, 521
voices required for **V** 376
Wagner, Richard **W** 2
See also Ballet; Musical comedy; Operetta
Opéra bouffe (BOOF) **M** 542
development during classical period **C** 332
development of comic opera **O** 132
English comic opera of Gilbert and Sullivan **G** 209–11; **M** 542
Opéra comique (co-MEEK) **O** 134
Operant conditioning, psychology **P** 497–98
operant or instrumental conditioning in learning **L** 100–01
Operation Beehive, industrial development, Barbados **B** 53

Operation Bootstrap, Puerto Rican economic improvement program begun in late 1940's under Governor Luis Muñoz Marín. It increased industrial production, expanded the educational system, provided increased employment, and more than doubled per capita income.
Puerto Rico, history of **P** 521

Operation Deep Freeze, Antarctic exploration **P** 370
Operation High Jump, Antarctic exploration **P** 368
Operations, surgical see Surgery
Operation Sea Lion, Hitler's plan to invade England **W** 290
Operation Torch, plan for invasion of French North Africa in World War II **W** 295–96
Operation Windmill, Antarctic exploration **P** 368
Operetta **O** 156–58
compared to musical comedy **M** 542
Gilbert and Sullivan **G** 209–11
Offenbach, Jacques **O** 55
plots of some well-known operettas **O** 157–58
Strauss, Johann, Jr. **S** 437
See also Musical comedy
Ophthalmologist (oph-thal-MOL-o-gist), doctor of medicine, specialist in diseases of the eye **O** 169

Ophthalmology (oph-thal-MOL-ogy), scientific study of structure, function, and diseases of the eye.
instruments to examine the eyes **M** 208g; **O** 169
Ophthalmoscopes (oph-THAL-mo-scopes), optical instruments **M** 208g; **O** 169
Opinion surveys **O** 159–60
audience-measurement for television and radio **T** 70b
research methods **R** 182
Opitz, Martin, German poet **G** 175
Opium, narcotic drug **N** 12
heroin **D** 330
where drugs come from **D** 327
Opium poppy, picture **P** 315

Opium War (1839–42), conflict between China and Britain resulting from China's resistance to British importation of opium into China. It ended with the Treaty of Nanking (1842), ceding the island of Hong Kong to Britain and opening several ports, including Shanghai and Canton, to foreign trade. The treaty also gave Great Britain most-favored-nation status in China.
Hong Kong, history of **H** 205

Opo, porpoise, pet of New Zealand town **D** 278
Oporto (o-POR-to), Portugal **P** 401

Oppenheimer, J. Robert (1904–67), American physicist, b. New York, N.Y. He specialized in nuclear physics and the study of cosmic rays. As director of the Los Alamos Laboratory (1943–45) he was a key person in the development of the atomic bomb. After World War II he argued for international control of nuclear weapons. He was chairman of the General Advisory Committee for the U.S. Atomic Energy Commission from 1947 to 1953, when he was suspended as a security risk. He was also director of the Institute for Advanced Study from 1947 to 1966, when he retired due to ill health. In 1963 he received the Fermi award—the highest granted by the Atomic Energy Commission.

Opossums, marsupials **K** 170–72
animal communication **A** 277
mammals, types of reproduction **M** 70–71
tracks, picture **A** 272
Opposition of Lines: Red and Yellow, painting by Mondrian **M** 392
Opposition party, in a government
prime minister's powers and responsibilities **P** 456
Ops, Roman goddess **G** 356
Optical fibers **O** 168–69
Optical glass **O** 174

Optical illusions O 161–65
 light refraction L 263
 Magnetic Hill, New Brunswick, Canada N 138d
 mirage M 341–42
Optical instruments O 166–75
 contact lenses L 151
 lenses L 141–51, 264–65
 surveyor's transit S 480
 telescopes T 60–64
Optical telescopes O 11; picture O 8
Optician, maker of eyeglasses O 169
Optic nerve, of the eye B 284; M 208g
Optics, study of light
 contributions of Islamic scientists S 64–65
 gases used in research G 62
 Newton, Isaac N 207
Optometrist (op-TOM-et-rist), specialist in fitting glasses
 O 169

Optometry (op-TOM-etry), measurement of strength and
scope of vision, involving eye examination, lens prescrip-
tion, and exercises (not including drugs or surgery).

Oracles, in ancient religions R 146
 Delphi G 338, 361
 prophecies often riddles J 132
Oraibi (o-RY-bi), Hopi Indian community, Arizona A 413
Oral composition C 446
Oral (by way of mouth) **poisoning**
 first aid F 158
Oral reading R 110
Oral schools, for the deaf D 52, 53
Oral surgery, a field of dentistry D 114
Oral tradition, of folklore F 303
 African literature A 76a, 76d
Oral vaccines V 261
 babies, twins, receiving vaccine, picture M 208c
 community programs, picture D 205
Oran (o-RAN), Algeria A 163
Orange O 176–79
 blossom, state flower of Florida F 259
 California, pictures C 18, U 105
 packing, picture F 485
 pollen grains, picture P 297
Orange, House of, Netherlands royal family N 120
Orange Bowl, Miami, Florida, New Year's Day football
 game F 365
Orange Free State, province of South Africa S 273
 Boer War B 298

Orangemen, members of society formed in Northern
Ireland (1795) to protect Protestants from Catholic majority. Named for English king, William III, a prince of Orange,
the society spread to other parts of the British Empire.
 Northern Ireland, history of U 73

Orange pekoe tea T 38
Orange River, Africa R 245
 important river in southern Africa A 49–50
Orangutans (o-RANG-u-tans) M 419
Oratorio (or-a-TOR-io), in music M 537
 choral music C 277–78
 developed in baroque period B 64
 Handel's compositions G 183; H 26
 Italian music I 484
 singing, style for V 376
Oratory (OR-a-tory) O 180–81
 Beecher, Henry Ward B 115
 Bryan, William Jennings B 416
 Greek G 355
 Henry, Patrick H 113–14
 Lewis, John L. L 161

Webster, Daniel W 98–99
 See also Public speaking
Orbital velocity, speed of satellites S 39–40
 launching a spacecraft S 340d
Orbiter I, spacecraft see Lunar Orbiter
Orbiting astronomical observatories (OAO) E 29–30
 unmanned observatories O 14
Orbiting geophysical observatories (OGO) O 14
Orbiting solar observatories (OSO) E 30
 unmanned observatories launched by rockets O 14
Orbiting vehicles see Satellites, man-made
Orbits
 comets C 418–19
 earth's E 4, 22–23
 gravitation and planetary orbits S 241–42
 Mars M 105
 moon's orbit M 446; diagram M 447
 planetary orbits P 269–78; diagram P 274
 satellites S 39–40
 spacecraft S 339, 340d–340e, 340h

Orcagna (or-CON-ya), or **Arcagnolo** (Andrea di Cione)
(1308?–68?), Italian painter, sculptor, and architect, b.
Florence. His main works are the frescoes *The Last
Judgment, Hell,* and *Heaven,* in the Strozzi chapel of
the Church of Santa Maria Novella in Florence. *Coronation of the Virgin,* which belonged to San Pietro Maggiore in Florence, is now in London National Gallery.

Orchards
 apple A 334–35, 337
 best locations for fruitgrowing F 482
 tractors F 57
Orchestra (ORC-hes-tra) O 182–87
 ancient Hebrew music A 246
 baroque period in music B 63, 66
 conducting O 188–91
 classical age in music C 331
 harp for special effects H 43–44
 Indonesian gamelan O 221
 kettledrums, use of D 335
 musical instruments M 544–50
 percussion instruments P 151–53
 piano P 240–42
 records and record collecting R 123–24
 tuning up to avoid interferences of beats of sound
 S 262–63
 Wagner's operas, role in G 188
 wind instruments W 182–83
Orchestra, first floor of a theater T 156
Orchestra conducting O 188–91
 orchestra as an institution with a professional conductor O 186
 seating diagram of an orchestra O 186
 Toscanini, Arturo T 228
Orchestral (orc-EST-ral) **music**
 festivals M 551–52
 romantic compositions R 310–11
Orchestration (orc-hes-TRAY-tion), composing or arranging music for an orchestra O 184
Orchids (ORC-hids) F 281
 aerial roots, picture P 291
 plants that grow in air P 319
 Venezuela's national flower V 298
OR circuits, of computers C 454

Orczy (OR-tsi), **Emmuska,** Baroness (1865–1947), English
novelist, b. Tarnaors, Hungary. She is best known for
her novel *The Scarlet Pimpernel,* which has been adopted
for stage and screen. Her works include other novels in
the Pimpernel series, all set in the French revolutionary
period.

Oriental rugs R 351, 354
Oriente (o-ri-ENT-ay) **Province,** Cuba   C 548, 549, 551
Origami (or-i-GA-mi), art of paper folding   O 222–26
Origin of Species, book by Charles Darwin   E 345–46
   Darwin, Charles Robert   D 41
Orinoco (o-rin-O-co) **River,** South America   R 245
   Amazon and Orinoco river systems, South America
   S 277
   Venezuela   V 297

Orioles, brightly colored land birds found in Europe,
Asia, and Australia. These birds have long wings and
straight bills and are usually yellow, green, or black in
color. Forest-dwellers, orioles feed chiefly on insects.
One of the best-known is the Black-naped oriole. Males
are bright yellow above, pale yellow below, with black
markings on the head, wings, and tail. Females are
duller and usually a different color. Several birds of
a different family found only in the New World are also
called orioles. The well-known Baltimore oriole belongs to
this group of birds. Picture, Baltimore oriole   B 233
   familiar birds and their haunts   B 219–20
   Maryland's state bird   M 115
   nest, picture   B 213

Orion (o-RY-on), constellation   C 491–92
   dust cloud, picture   D 348
   nebula in, diagram   U 197

Orion (o-RY-on), in Greek mythology, huge, powerful
hunter who performed numerous deeds for the king of
Chios to win the hand of his daughter. Blinded by the
king, who never fulfilled his promise of marriage, Orion
regained his eyesight and later went to Crete as
huntsman for Artemis, who eventually killed him. After
his death he was sent to heaven as the brightest
constellation. There he is represented as a hunter with a
belt, sword, and hunting dogs.
   constellations, seasonal   C 491–92
   Dog Star and dog days   D 47

Orion's Belt   C 491–92
Orizaba (o-re-SA-ba), **Mount** (Pico de Orizaba), Mexico
   M 242
Orkney Islands, northeast of Scotland   I 435

Orlando, Vittorio Emanuele (1860–1952), Italian states-
man, b. Palermo. He served as minister of education
(1903–15), minister of justice (1907–09), and prime
minister (1917–19) of Italy. He acted as one of the Big
Four (with Lloyd George, Woodrow Wilson, Georges
Clemenceau) when he headed the Italian delegation at
Paris Peace Conference (1919) following World War I.
Orlando retired from political life after the advent of
Fascism. Picture   W 180.
   Paris Peace Conference, 1919, demands of the Italians
   W 282

Orlando Furioso (fu-ri-O-so), poem by Ariosto   I 478
Orléans (or-lay-ON), **battle of,** 1429   B 101
Orléans, Maid of see Joan of Arc
Orlich, Francisco Bolmarcich, president of
   Costa Rica   C 519
Orlon, man-made fiber   N 424

Ormandy, Eugene (1899–   ), American orchestra conductor, b. Budapest, Hungary. In 1921 he emigrated to
the United States, where he became conductor of the
Minneapolis Symphony Orchestra (1931–36), then associate conductor and director (1936–38) and sole musical
director (since 1941) of the Philadelphia Orchestra.
Picture   O 182.

Ormolu (OR-mo-lu), gilded furniture mountings   D 77;
   picture   D 74
Ornithology see Birds
Ornithopoda (or-nith-OP-o-da), dinosaurs   D 173, 177–78
Ornithopters (OR-nith-op-ters), flapping-wing aircraft
   A 567; picture   A 568
Ornithosis (orn-i-THO-sis), or psittacosis, disease
   I 286
   called parrot fever   B 248
Orogeny (o-ROJ-eny), process of mountain formation
   M 493
Orography (or-OG-raphy), branch of geography dealing
   with mountains
   influence on weather and climate   W 88–89
Oromocto, New Brunswick, Canada   N 138c
Orontes River, Syria   S 507
Orozco (o-RO-sco), **José Clemente,** Mexican painter
   L 67
   Zapatistas, painting   L 66
Orpen, William, English portrait painter   E 242
Orphanages   O 227
   Foundling Hospital, in Florence, Italy   A 438e–
   438f; picture   R 165
   See also Adoption
Orphan Girl at the Cemetery, painting by Eugène
   Delacroix   P 27

Orpheus (OR-phe-us), in Greek mythology, son of Apollo
and Calliope and husband of Eurydice. He was known for
his ability to charm wild beasts with the music of his
lyre. On the *Argo* with Jason, Orpheus soothed and
encouraged the crew by his playing. When his wife died
of a snakebite, he used his lyre to charm the gods of
Hades into releasing her. He agreed, however, not to look
back as they left Hades. He did look back and thus lost
Eurydice forever.

Orr, Bobby (Robert Orr) (1948–   ), Canadian hockey
player, b. Parry Sound, Ontario. An aggressive defenseman always looking for scoring opportunities, he revital-
ized Boston Bruins of National Hockey League after joining
them in 1966. He was named league's best defenseman
(1968–71) and Most Valuable Player (1970–71).

Orrery, small planetarium   P 267
Orsted, Hans Christian see Oersted, Hans Christian
Ortega y Gasset (or-TAY-ga e ga-SET), **José,** Spanish
   philosopher   S 371
Ortelius (or-TE-li-us), **Abraham,** Flemish publisher
   M 93
Orthodontics (ortho-DONT-ics), a field of dentistry
   D 114–15
Orthodox Eastern Churches   O 228–30
   break with Rome   R 291–92
   Bulgarian Church, branch of   B 440
   Byzantine church as origin   B 492
   marriage rites   W 102
   See also Roman Catholic Church
Orthodox Judaism (JU-da-ism)   J 118, 119
Orthographic (or-tho-GRAPH-ic) **projections,** of maps   M 93
Orthography see Spelling

Orthopedics (ortho-PE-dics), field of medicine concerned
with treatment of skeletal deformities.

Ortiz (or-TECE), **Juan,** Spanish adventurer   D 144
Orwell, George, English writer   O 231
   place in English literature   E 267, 292, 293
Oryx (O-rix), hoofed mammal   H 221; picture   H 217
Osaka (o-SA-ka), Japan   O 231–32
   Expo '70   F 18; J 40; picture   F 9
   major cities of Japan   J 40

Osborne, John, English playwright **E** 268

Osborne, Thomas Mott (1859–1926), American prison reformer, b. Auburn, N.Y. When he was appointed chairman of the N.Y.C. Commission for Prison Reform (1913), he disguised himself as an inmate of Auburn Prison to study prison conditions at first hand. He initiated the Mutual Welfare League, which permitted prisoners some self-government and stressed rehabilitation rather than punishment for prisoners. He served as warden of Sing Sing Prison in New York (1914–16); and as commander of the U.S. Naval Prison in Portsmouth, N.H. (1917–20). He was the author of *Within Prison Walls* and *Prisons and Common Sense.*

Oscar, small gold-plated statuette awarded annually (since 1928) by Academy of Motion Picture Arts and Sciences for notable achievements in motion pictures. The name was originated by an executive secretary of the academy, who likened the statuette to her Uncle Oscar.

Osceola (os-ce-O-la), American Indian warrior **O** 232
    grave at Fort Moultrie **S** 304
    Seminoles in Florida **F** 271
Oscillators (OS-cill-ators)
    electronic music produced by **E** 142g, 142h
Osen of Kasamori, woodcut by Suzuki Harunobu **G** 305

Osgood, Samuel (1748–1813), American soldier and political figure, b. Andover, Mass. Osgood served as an American officer in the Revolutionary War. He was a member of the Continental Congress (1781–84), the first commissioner of the U.S. Treasury (1785–89), U.S. Postmaster General (1789–91), and naval officer of the Port of New York (1803–13). He founded the Society for the Establishment of Free Schools for the Education of Poor Children and helped found the American Academy of Fine Arts.
    first U.S. postmaster general **P** 407

Oshima, Nagisa, Japanese motion-picture director
    M 488c
Oshkosh, Wisconsin **W** 205
Osiris (o-SY-ris), in ancient Egyptian religion, king and judge of the dead. According to one tradition, he was a beloved king of Egypt who introduced laws and worship of gods and improved agricultural methods. Killed by his evil and jealous brother, Set, who cut his body into 14 pieces and scattered them about the country, he was restored to life by his wife and sister, Isis, who found the parts and re-assembled them. The legend developed into various cults and laid precedent for mummification.

Osler (o-sler), **Sir William,** Canadian doctor and teacher **O** 233
    famous teacher of medicine **M** 208a
Oslo, capital of Norway **N** 344; picture **N** 340
    Ibsen, Henrik **I** 2

Osman Daar, Aden Abdulla (1908–   ), Somali statesman. He has served as president of Somali Youth League (1954–56, 1958–59) and president of Legislative Assembly (1956–60) and Constituent Assembly (since 1960). As president of Somali Republic (1961–67), he followed a policy of nonalignment.

Osmeña (o-SMANE-ya), **Sergio** (1878–1961), Philippine statesman, b. Cebu. An organizer of the Nationalist Party (1907) and member of the Philippine legislature (1907–35), he served as vice-president of the Commonwealth of the Philippines (1935–44). On the death of Manuel Quezon (1944) he succeeded to the presidency of the Philippine Government, then exiled in the United States because of Japanese occupation of the islands. He returned to Manila (1944) and retired in 1946.
    Philippines, history of **P** 190

Osmium, element **E** 155, 163
    metals, ores, location, properties, uses **M** 227
Osmosis (os-MO-sis), process in which liquids and gases pass through a membrane **O** 233–35
    experiments and demonstrations **E** 367; **O** 235
OSO see Orbiting solar observatories

Osprey, brownish bird with white head, sometimes called a fish hawk. The osprey lives chiefly along seacoasts but also is found near large lakes and rivers. Its chief food is fish, which it catches by diving—feet first—into the water and grasping the prey in long, curved claws. The osprey is found throughout the world, except for the polar regions, New Zealand, and southern South America.
    special adaptations in birds **B** 222

Ossining, New York
    Sing Sing Prison **P** 469
Ostade (o-STA-da), **Adriaen van,** Dutch painter **D** 357

Ostend Manifesto (1854), document issued in Ostend, Belgium, that advocated U.S. purchase of Cuba from Spain and forceful seizure if Spain refused to sell. It was generally motivated by expansionist urges and desire to annex a slave state. Drawn up by U.S. ministers to Great Britain, France, and Spain, it greatly aroused public feeling and was disavowed by U.S. Secretary of State William Marcy.
    efforts to acquire Cuba in the Buchanan and Pierce administrations **B** 419; **P** 247

Osteoarthritis (os-teo-ar-THRY-tis), type of arthritis **D** 193

Osteopathy (os-te-OP-athy), medical practice based on the theory that a normal human body has natural resistance and can remedy its infections if it is in correct adjustment. An osteopath therefore tries to correct adverse body conditions through manipulation of bones and the elimination of conditions of joints, tissues, diet, environment, etc., that disturb the body's natural balance.
    first school of osteopathy in the United States **M** 375

Ostracoderms (OST-ra-co-derms), extinct fishes **F** 182; picture **F** 181
Ostracods, class of small freshwater crustacea **S** 171
Ostrava (o-STRA-va), Czechoslovakia **C** 561, 562
Ostriches, birds
    flightless, due to giant size **G** 204
Ostrogoths see Goths
Ostrovsky (os-TROF-ski), **Alexander,** Russian playwright **U** 60

Osuna, Rafael (1938–69), Mexican tennis player, b. Mexico City. He was the first Mexican to win the United States Nationals (doubles, 1962; singles, 1963). He also won the Wimbledon doubles (1960, 1963). He was a member of the Mexican Davis Cup team for several years and was a winner of the Mexican Nationals.

Oswald, Lee Harvey, American assassin of John F. Kennedy **K** 211
Otello (o-TEL-lo), opera by Giuseppe Verdi **O** 150
Othello, tragedy by Shakespeare **O** 236; **S** 132
    outline of the plot **S** 136

Overpopulation P 396–97
    effect of overcrowding a living space L 253
    environment, problems of E 272b–272c
    poverty P 424a, 424b
Overshot wheel, a kind of waterwheel W 62

Overstreet, Harry Allen (1875–1970), American professor and author, b. San Francisco, Calif. He taught philosophy at University of California, Berkeley (1901–11) and served as chairman of philosophy department at College of the City of New York (1911–39) where he was professor emeritus (1939–70). His best-known work is *The Mature Mind.*

Over the counter, sale of stocks and bonds not listed on an exchange S 433
Over There, song by George M. Cohan N 26
Overtones, or harmonics, of sound S 264–65
    electronic music uses pure tones E 142g
Overture, or sinfonia, to an opera M 537, 540
Overweight, body
    control of P 229
    diets and dieting N 417–19
    heart disorders H 86c
Ovid (AH-vid), Roman poet O 267
    place in Latin literature L 79–80
Oviedo y Valdes (o-vy-A-tho e val-DAS), **Gonzalo Fernandez de,** Spanish soldier-writer L 70
Oviparous (o-VIP-ar-ous), or egg-laying, **animals**
    fishes F 197
Ovules (O-vules), of flowers F 277; picture F 276
    fruits and seeds of plants P 296
Ovum, female reproductive cell E 88
    how genes are passed from parent cells to new individuals G 77
    human ovum, picture E 88
Owen, Richard, English anatomist D 172

Owen, Robert (1771–1850), British industrialist and social reformer, b. Newton, Wales. At his cotton mills in New Lanark, Scotland (1800), he provided his workers with inexpensive housing, schools, and recreational facilities. In 1825 he tried to put his ideas into operation in the United States by founding a model community at New Harmony, Indiana. When this experiment failed, he returned to England where he tried to organize cooperative villages that would combine industrial and agricultural production. His efforts met strong resistance from other manufacturers. Owen supported many labor and educational movements that were far in advance of his time.
    New Harmony, Ind., communistic community I 143
    started infant schools near his mills K 242
    Utopian socialism S 220

Owen, Robert Dale (1801–1877), American writer and politician, b. Glasgow, Scotland. He assisted his father, Robert Owen, in educational work in the co-operative settlements at New Lanark, Scotland, and New Harmony, Indiana. A member of the Indiana legislature (1836–38) and the U.S. Congress (1843–47), he presented the bill that led to establishment of Smithsonian Institution. He became a principal advocate of emancipation (after 1858). His works include *The Wrong of Slavery,* and an autobiography, *Threading My Way.*

Owen, Robert L., American statesman O 93
Owen Falls Dam, Uganda U 5; picture U 7
Owens, Jesse, American athlete N 99; O 111; picture O 112
Owens, Michael Joseph, American inventor and glass manufacturer W 138–39
    bottle making machine B 342

Owensboro, Kentucky K 224
Owl and the Pussycat, The, poem by Edward Lear N 275
Owls, birds B 209; picture B 222
    Audubon painting A 491
    screech owls, birds of the woods B 220; picture B 208
Oxbow lakes M 353; picture N 138a
    Louisiana L 351
Oxcarts, picture H 196
    Costa Rica C 515; picture C 517
Oxen C 147; picture H 196
    Bovidae, cattle family C 147
    hoofed mammals H 208
    India's work animals A 451
Oxford English Dictionary D 165

Oxford Movement, High Church, Anglo-Catholic movement within the Church of England, organized in 1833 at Oxford University to counteract growing indifference and skepticism regarding orthodox doctrine and ceremonies. Its adherents, called Tractarians, included John Henry Newman, John Keble, and Edward Pusey, who published a pamphlet series, Tracts of the Times, to uphold the Catholic theology and ritual of the Anglican Church.
    made better hymns available H 313

Oxford University, England U 67, 206; pictures E 73, G 34
    Bodleian library L 197
    Rhodes scholarships R 227
Oxidation O 268–70
    fire and combustion F 136–37
    metals M 226
    rust, slow oxidation F 137; O 268
    See *also* Oxygen
Oxidizer, liquid oxygen (Lox) F 490
    for rocket fuels R 258

Oxnam, Garfield Bromley (1891–1963), American churchman, b. Sonora, Calif. Noted for his liberalism and his interest in labor, he was Methodist bishop (1930–60), of Boston, then of New York, then of Washington, D.C. He was president of World Council of Churches (1952–60).

Oxus River see Amu Darya
Oxyacetylene (oxy-a-CET-il-ene) **blowtorch** G 60; picture O 270
    welding W 119
Oxygen O 268–70; E 155, 163
    algae, source of A 157
    anaerobic bacteria B 11
    astronauts, life-support systems for M 455; S 340L–341, 349; diagram of space suit S 338
    atmosphere contains A 479
    atomic structure A 485, 486
    bioluminescence B 198
    blood's major task to carry B 255, 275, 277
    body chemistry B 296
    combustion F 136–37
    eutrophication of water sources W 59
    formation of earth's atmosphere E 19
    hyperbaric chambers, medical techniques of M 210
    ice age changes shown by oxygen in fossil shells I 22
    industrial uses and how obtained G 60–61
    Lavoisier's discoveries L 86
    Mars M 111
    photosynthesis P 222–23
    Priestley, Joseph P 455–56
    reaction with a fuel to produce fire F 136
    rocket fuels must have oxidizers R 256
    steelmaking process I 398
    water, structure of W 54–55
    See *also* Nitrogen

Oxygen, liquid (Lox) see Liquid oxygen

Oxygen tent, tentlike enclosure placed over head and shoulders of patient and supplied with flow of oxygen to maintain concentration of about 50 percent oxygen and 50 percent other gases. It is used in treatment of pneumonia and other respiratory illnesses to permit easier breathing. Picture **O** 270.

Oxymorons (oxy-MO-rons), paradoxes **H** 279
Oyo, ancient city, Nigeria **N** 256
   African art **A** 76; picture **A** 73
Oyono, Ferdinand, Cameroonian novelist **A** 76c
Oyster Bay, New York
   Sagamore Hill, home of Theodore Roosevelt
     N 220–21; **R** 330
Oyster drills, gastropods **O** 276

Oysters, mollusks **O** 271–72
   edible in months with R in the word **R** 1
   Japan's cultured pearl industry **J** 38–39
   oyster fishing industry **F** 221
   pearls **P** 113–15
Ozark Mountains, Arkansas **A** 421
   Missouri **M** 367; 368
   origin of name, Ozarks **A** 431
Ozark National Scenic Riverways **M** 366; picture **M** 368
Ozarks, Lake of the, Missouri **M** 369–70; picture **M** 368
Ozocerite (o-zo-CER-ite), a mineral wax **W** 70
Ozone, form of oxygen **O** 269
   layer of the atmosphere **A** 481; **I** 317
   opaque to certain harmful ultraviolet radiation **E** 25
Ozu, Yasujiro, Japanese motion-picture director
    M 487, 488
Ozymandias (oz-i-MAN-di-as), poem by Shelley **S** 146

ILLUSTRATION CREDITS

The following list credits, by page, the sources of illustrations used in Volume O of THE NEW BOOK OF KNOWLEDGE. Credits are listed illustration by illustration —left to right, top to bottom. Wherever appropriate, the name of the photographer or artist has been listed with the source, the two being separated by a dash. When two or more illustrations appear on one page, their credits are separated by semicolons.

P, 16th letter of the English alphabet **P** 1
See also Alphabet

Paca, William (1740–1799), American Revolutionary leader, b. near Abington, Md. A signer of the Declaration of Independence, he was also a member (1774–79) of the Continental Congress, governor of Maryland (1782–85), and U.S. district judge for Maryland (1789–99).

Pace, gait of a horse **H** 234
Pace, measure of distance **W** 109

Pacemaker, a battery-run device implanted in patients with certain heart conditions. The instrument provides electrical stimulation to the heart muscle. **M** 211
heart, problems with rate and rhythm **H** 86c
heart disease **D** 197–98

Pacheco Areco, Jorge, Uruguayan political leader **U** 239
Pachmann, Vladimir de, pianist **R** 123
Pacific, War of the, 1879–83 **P** 166
Chile **C** 255
Pacification teams, in Vietnam War, 1958– **V** 336
Pacific Basin, Canada **C** 52
Pacific Charter, declaration issued by SEATO **S** 335
Pacific coaling stations **T** 114
Pacific Council see Anzus Council
Pacific Fur Company **O** 207
Pacific High, high-pressure center **C** 17–18
Pacific Islands, Trust Territory of the **T** 115
Pacific islands and island groups **P** 2–9
art **P** 9–10
Borneo **B** 336–38
Fiji Islands **F** 121–22
flags **F** 240
funeral customs **F** 494
Hawaii **H** 56–72
Indonesia's major groups **I** 218–20
mountain peaks, highest in this area **M** 495
Nauru **N** 61
New Guinea **N** 146–47
Samoa **S** 23–27
Tonga **T** 210–210a
World War II **W** 293–95
Pacific Mountain System, North America **U** 92
Pacific Northwest, United States **U** 92
Oregon **O** 193–94
Washington **W** 15–16, 20
Pacific Ocean **P** 2–3
Balboa discovered **B** 18
cables, submarine **T** 53, 54
earthquake belt **E** 34–35
international date line avoids land area **T** 192
islands see Pacific Islands and island groups
Magellan, Ferdinand **M** 17
ocean floor explored by geologists **G** 115, 117
Pacific Palisades, California, picture **L** 347
Pacific Rim National Park, British Colombia **B** 406a
Pacifists, people who do not believe in war **P** 105
Doukhobors in Canada's Prairie Provinces **S** 38g
draft exemptions and regulations **D** 289, 290
Packaging
bread and other baked goods **B** 389
commercial art **C** 425
consumer education in unit pricing **C** 494–494a
dried fruits **D** 317
gift wrapping **G** 206–09
meat-packing **M** 195
Packet ships, passenger ships with mail and cargo **S** 159
early ocean liners **O** 23
transportation, history of **T** 261
United States Merchant Marine, history of **U** 183

Packing, how to pack for camping **C** 41
Packing industry see Meat and meat-packing
Pack rats **R** 279
Pact of Paris see Kellogg-Briand Pact, 1928
Paddies, rice fields **R** 232
control of weeds in grain fields **G** 287
Paddlefish, picture **F** 183
Paddles, for canoes **C** 100
Paddle tennis **P** 11
Paddle wheel steamers **O** 23–24
museum of riverboat era in a beached paddle wheel, Winona, Minn. **M** 331
Pademelons, middle sized kangaroos **K** 170

Paderewski (pa-der-EF-ski), **Ignace Jan** (1860–1941), Polish concert pianist, composer, and statesman, b. Kurylowka, Russian Poland. Paderewski was an ardent advocate of Polish independence. When Poland gained independence from Russia after World War I, he became the first premier of the Republic of Poland (1919–20). After Germany invaded Poland during World War II, Paderewski was chosen president of the Polish parliament in exile (1940). In his last years he lived in California. He died in New York City and is buried in Arlington National Cemetery. Among his best known compositions are the six *Humoresques de Concert,* which include the Minuet in G and Concerto in A Minor, and the opera *Manru.*
Poland, history of **P** 362

Padlocks **L** 323; picture **L** 322
Padre Island National Seashore, Texas **T** 133
Padua, University of, Italy, picture **B** 189
Paducah (pa-DU-cah), Kentucky **K** 224
Paez (PA-es), **José Antonio,** Venezuelan soldier and patriot **V** 300

Paganini (pa-ga-NI-ni), **Niccolò** (1782–1840), Italian violinist and composer, b. Genoa. He made his debut in Genoa (1793) and subsequently appeared throughout Europe. Widely acclaimed for his extraordinary virtuosity, he introduced new techniques of violin playing. He was also a guitarist and viola player. Among his compositions are 24 capriccios for unaccompanied violin, two violin concertos, and several sets of variations for violin. A theme from the Capriccio in A minor was used by Brahms, Rachmaninoff, and other composers for variation works.
help from the devil in playing the violin **V** 343
instrumental music in Italy **I** 485

Paganism (PAY-gan-ism)
Christian era begins **C** 280, 281, 282
Christmas customs continued some pagan rituals **C** 289, 291
Elijah's fight against **E** 176
Page, apprentice knight **K** 275–76

Page, Ruth (1903–), American dancer and choreographer, b. Indianapolis, Ind. Leading dancer and ballet director of the Chicago Opera Company (1934–37, 1942–43, 1945), she has appeared in Europe and the Orient. Ballet director of the Chicago Lyric Opera (since 1954), she has also been choreographer and director for the Chicago Opera Ballet since 1956.

Page, Satchel, American baseball player **B** 81
Pageants (PAJ-ents) **P** 12
Frontier Days, Cheyenne, Wyo. **W** 334; picture **W** 328
origin of the word in middle English drama **E** 249
See also annual events section of state articles

Page proof, in printing **P** 479
Pagliacci (pol-YA-chi), I, opera by Leoncavallo **O** 150
Pagodas (pa-GO-das), Buddhist shrines **O** 217; pictures **J** 47, **O** 216
   carved of jade, picture **D** 76
   Rangoon, Burma, pictures **R** 151; **S** 331
   Shwe Dagon Pagoda, picture **B** 457
Pagodas, Land of the (Burma) **B** 454
Pagopago (PAN-go PAN-go), American Samoa **S** 26, 27; picture **S** 24
Pahang River, Malaysia **M** 54
Pahlavi (PAH-la-vi), **Mohammed Riza,** Shah of Iran **I** 377
Pahlavi, Riza Khan, Shah of Iran **I** 377
Pahoehoe (pa-HO-e-ho-e), lava **V** 378; picture **V** 379
Paige, Leroy (Satchel), American baseball player **B** 78, 81
Pain
   anesthesia **A** 256–59
   body's sense of **B** 287
   medical history of a patient **M** 208d–208c
   narcotics **N** 12–14
   painkillers, drugs **D** 326; **N** 12
   What makes a tooth ache? **T** 48

Paine, Robert Treat (1731–1814), American lawyer and statesman, b. Boston, Mass. A signer of the Declaration of Independence, he was also a member (1774–78) of the Continental Congress. Paine served as attorney general of Massachusetts (1777–90) and judge of the Massachusetts Supreme Court (1790–1804).

Paine, Thomas, English-born American writer **P** 12–13
   American literature **A** 198
   how Declaration of Independence was adopted **D** 61
   influence on formation of U.S. government **U** 134
   magazine publisher **M** 14
   Revolutionary War pamphlets **R** 202
Painkillers, drugs **D** 326; **N** 12
Paint see Paints and pigments
Painted Desert, Arizona **A** 404
Painted-lady, butterfly **B** 470; picture **B** 473
   migration **H** 189
Painters, mountain lions **C** 138
Painting **P** 14–32
   Africa, cave and rock paintings **A** 71
   art of the artist **A** 438f–438g
   Audubon's birds **A** 490–491
   Australian aboriginal painters **A** 502
   baroque art **B** 55–62
   Byzantine **B** 489, 490
   Canada **C** 64
   cave paintings, pictures **A** 354, **C** 158, **P** 439–41
   Dutch and Flemish art **D** 349–62; pictures **A** 438a, 438c
   Egyptian art in royal tombs **E** 102; picture **A** 437
   English art **E** 236–41
   Europe, best-known collections in **E** 318
   finger painting **F** 126–28
   folk art **F** 290–96
   French art **F** 421–32; picture **A** 438d
   German art **G** 165–71
   Gothic art **G** 271
   Hermitage Museum collections **H** 120
   Islamic art **I** 421–22
   Italian art **I** 468–69, 470; pictures **A** 438a, 438c
   miniatures of the Rajput school, India **O** 215; picture **O** 213
   modern art **M** 386–98; picture **A** 438d
   oriental art **O** 212–19
   Renaissance art **R** 163–71; pictures **A** 438a
   Roman art **R** 286
   Romanesque art **R** 309

   Spanish painting **S** 361–63
   United States **U** 116–22; picture **A** 438d
   See also Color; names of individual artists, such as Rembrandt, and of specific countries, as Italian art
Painting, industrial **P** 33–34
Painting, religious see Religious art
Paints and pigments **P** 30, 32–34
   effect on art of use of manufactured paints **P** 24, 27
   finger paint, how to make **F** 126
   ivory black **I** 488
   lead **L** 94
   oil paints **P** 30
   pigments of prehistoric paintings **P** 15
   plastics **P** 331
   turpentine as a thinner **T** 330
   See also Lacquers; Varnishes

Paisley, Rev. Ian R. K. (1926–), Irish Protestant minister, member of Parliament and Stormont (parliament of Northern Ireland), b. Northern Ireland. The leader of an extremist Protestant faction, he has conducted a rigid opposition to Ulster's Roman Catholic minority and their struggle for equal treatment.

Paiute (PY-ute), Indians of North America **I** 172–73
Pakistan **P** 35–41
   Afghanistan, relations with **A** 45
   Bangladesh **B** 44–44c; **N** 262f; **P** 41
   children's library at Dacca, picture **L** 199
   civil and human rights conflicts **C** 316
   flag **F** 238
   India, 1947 partition from **I** 134
   Kashmir dispute **K** 198–99
   national anthem **N** 22
   poverty **P** 424a
   reading class, picture **E** 83
Palace of Nations, United Nations, picture **L** 97
Palace of the Inquisition, Cartagena, Colombia, picture **C** 382
Palace of the Governors, Santa Fe, N. M. **N** 189, 191
Palaces
   Islamic architecture **I** 420–21; picture **I** 421
   Italian architecture **A** 381
   King Minos' at Knossus, Crete, picture **A** 355
   Medici Palace, Florence, picture **I** 462
   Minoan architecture **A** 238, 373–74
   museums made from some palaces **M** 512
   Palazzo Vecchio, Florence, Italy **A** 380
   Persian architecture **A** 242, 373
   Royal Palace, Madrid, picture **S** 364
   Versailles **A** 381–82; **B** 62; **P** 74
Palais de Chaillot see Chaillot, Palais de
Palais Royal (pa-LAI rwa-YAL), Paris **P** 74
Palau (pol-OW), Pacific island **P** 7
Palazzeschi, Aldo, Italian author **I** 481
Palazzo Vecchio (pa-LA-tzo VEC-yo), palace in Florence, Italy **A** 380
Paleocene Epoch, of the Cenozoic era, in geology **F** 388
Pale of Settlement, Russian territory restricting Jews **J** 110
Paleolithic (pale-e-o-LITH-ic), or Old Stone, age
   prehistoric man **P** 442–44
   tools, pictures **P** 444
Paleontology (pale-e-on-TOL-ogy), scientific study of past life **F** 380–82
   evolution **E** 342
   relationship to biology **B** 191
   relationship to geology **G** 112
   See also Fossils
Paleozoic Era (pay-le-o-ZO-ic), in geology **F** 383, 384
   prehistoric animals **P** 437; pictures **P** 436
Palermo (pa-LAIR-mo), Sicily, picture **I** 455

Palestine (PAL-es-tine), the Holy Land, now Israel and Jordan **I** 444; **J** 137, 139
    Arab-Israeli war, 1967 **J** 139
    Ben-Gurion, David **B** 140
    Christianity, history of **C** 283
    Crusades in **E** 370
    Jerusalem **J** 81
    Jewish immigration **J** 112
    Jordan River **I** 441–42
    Weizmann, Chaim **W** 118
    World War I **W** 275
    World War II, in the middle East **W** 290
    Zionism **Z** 371
Palestine Arab refugees **J** 139; picture **J** 136
Palestrina (pal-es-TRI-na), Italian composer **P** 41
    hymns **H** 311
    Renaissance music **R** 173–74
    vocal polyphony **I** 483
Palettes, boards or tablets used by artists to lay and mix paints on
    decorated stoneware of ancient Egypt **D** 68
Pali (PA-li), language of sacred Buddhist texts **C** 32
Palindromes (PAL-in-dromes), word games **W** 236
Palisade cells, in plants **P** 294
Palisades, on the Hudson River **N** 166, 176; picture **N** 167
Palk Strait, Ceylon **C** 179
Palladian (pal-LAY-dian) **style,** of architecture **A** 383–84
    English architecture **E** 237
Palladio (pa-LOD-yo), **Andrea,** Italian architect **A** 383, 384
    architecture of Venice **I** 467
    Renaissance architecture **R** 170
    Rotonda, picture **I** 464
Palladium, element **E** 155, 163
    jewelry **J** 92
Pallas, asteroid **P** 273
Pallas Athena see Athena
Pallas cats, or manuls **C** 141

Palliser (PAL-lis-er), **John** (1807–1887), Canadian explorer b. county Waterford, Ireland. He explored the American prairies (1847–48). Commissioned by the British Government to lead an exploratory and scientific expedition to western Canada, he helped define the United States-Canadian boundary from Lake Superior to the Pacific coast (1857–61).

Palm, of the hand **F** 79
Palm, tree
    a monocot, picture **P** 292
    carnauba **B** 378
    coconut palms **C** 368
    dates **D** 41–42
    jungles **J** 154
    leaves, shapes of, pictures **L** 116
    seed, picture **P** 298
    wax obtained from **W** 69
Palma, Ricardo, Peruvian author **P** 166
Palmate (PAL-mate) **veins,** of trees **T** 282
Palm civets, or toddy cats, animals **G** 90–91

Palmer, Alice Elvira Freeman (1855–1902), American educator, b. Colesville, N.Y. She served at Wellesley College as history professor (1879–82) and president (1882–87). She was dean of women at the University of Chicago (1892–95). In 1920 she was elected to the Hall of Fame for Great Americans.

Palmer, Arnold (1929–   ), American golfer, b. Youngstown, Pa. He turned professional in 1954 after winning the National Amateur Championship. He has since won titles in Masters (1958, '60, '62, '64), U.S. Open (1960), and British Open (1961, '62). Picture **G** 261.

Palmer, Nathaniel, American navigator **P** 366
Palmer, William J., American railroad builder **C** 414
Palmer Peninsula, Antarctic region **P** 366
Palmetto (pal-METT-o), tree
    cabbage, or Sabal palmetto, state tree of Florida, South Carolina **F** 259; **S** 296
Palmetto State, nickname for South Carolina **S** 296
Palm Sunday, religious holiday **R** 153
    Easter **E** 41
    Roman Catholic Church, observance of **R** 301
Palmyra (pal-MY-ra), Syria **S** 508
Palo Alto, battle of, 1846 **M** 238
    Taylor's victory in Mexican War **T** 35
Palolo (pa-LO-lo) **worms** **L** 244–45
Palomar (PAL-o-mar), **Mount,** California
    observatory with largest optical telescope **A** 473; **O** 9; picture **O** 8
Palominos (pal-o-MI-nos), horses, picture **H** 235
Paloverde (pa-lo-VAIR-de), state tree of Arizona, picture **A** 402
Palpation, medical examination by touch **M** 208h
Pamela: or Virtue Rewarded, novel by Richardson **F** 111
    first English novels **E** 260
Pamir (pa-MIR), or **Pamirs,** mountains of central Asia
    Afghanistan **A** 43
Pampas, plains of South America **S** 277, 291; picture **G** 314
    Argentina **A** 392–93, 395–96
    Buenos Aires **B** 426
    prairies **P** 430, 431, 432; picture **P** 433
    Puelche Indians **I** 211
Pamphlets
    Paine's *Common Sense* **A** 198

Pan, in Greek mythology, god of woods and shepherds. He is often pictured as half-man and half-goat dancing with nymphs and playing the syrinx (shepherd's flute), a musical instrument made from reeds. It was believed that Pan frightened lonely travelers, and hence the word "panic" now means any sudden or groundless fear. His cult originated in Arcadia and spread throughout Greece. The Romans identified him with their god Faunus.

Panacea (pan-a-CE-a) ("all-healer"), in Greek mythology, goddess of health and daughter of Aesculapius, the god of medicine. With her sister, Hygeia (source of the word "hygiene"), she performed the temple rites and cared for the sacred serpents. The word "panacea" has come to mean a cure-all or single remedy for every disease.

Panama **P** 42–46
    Balboa named it Darien **B** 18
    flag **F** 241
    hunting with blow gun, picture **A** 301
    life in Latin America **L** 47–61
    national anthem **N** 22
    Panama University Library, picture **L** 197
Panama, Isthmus of **P** 42, 46
    a land bridge **L** 237
Panama Canal **P** 46–49
    canal construction **C** 85
    Caribbean Sea made a major waterway **C** 116
    De Lesseps chosen first to head the project **L** 156a
    territorial expansion of the United States **T** 114–15
Panama Canal Zone **P** 47–49
    Roosevelt (Theodore) Corollary to Monroe Doctrine **R** 329
    territorial expansion of the United States **T** 114–15
Panama City, capital of Panama **P** 45; pictures **P** 43

Panama hats **H** 54
Panama-Pacific International Exposition, San Francisco, California, 1915 **S** 31
Pan Am Building, New York City, picture **A** 438g
Pan American Day **H** 150
Pan-American Exhibition, Buffalo, 1901, picture **F** 15
Pan American Highway **P** 50
　famous roads **R** 253
　Thatcher Ferry Bridge, Panama Canal Zone, picture **P** 49
　See also Inter-American Highway
Pan American Sanitary Bureau **P** 502
Pan American Union, Organization of American states
　accomplishment of Harrison's administration **H** 48
　flag **F** 226
Pancake Race, Kansas and English housewives compete **K** 187–88
Pancake Tuesday, religious holiday **R** 153
Panchatantra (pon-cha-TON-tra), fables from India **F** 3

Panchen Lama (PON-chen LA-ma) (1936–), Tibetan prelate and political leader, b. Kumbum, near Sining, China. The Panchen Lama is the second-ranking spiritual and political leader in Tibet and is believed to be the incarnation of the Amitabha Buddha. The present lama was installed in 1941 and appointed chairman of Preparatory Commission (1959) when the Dalai Lama fled to India following a rebellion suppressed by China. He was replaced as chairman in 1965.
　Tibet, history of **T** 175

Pancreas (PAN-cre-as), gland **B** 279
　Banting's findings on insulin extract **B** 52
　cell, picture **C** 163
　digestive function in human body **B** 275
Pandas, animals related to raccoons **R** 28
　giant panda in Peking Zoo, picture **Z** 376
Pandemic (pan-DEM-ic) diseases **D** 188
　worldwide influenza epidemic, 1918 **D** 200
Pandora (pan-DO-ra), Greek goddess **G** 358–59
Panel discussions **D** 55
Panel programs, on television **T** 70d
Panfish, baits and lures **F** 206
Pangolins (pan-GO-lins), mammals **M** 61; picture **M** 69

Panhandle, a geographical term to indicate a long thin strip of land (resembling the handle of a pan). These strips of land usually project from the main part of a territory or state. Some panhandle areas in the United States are found in Texas, West Virginia, Alaska, Idaho, and Oklahoma. The word panhandle is also defined as "to beg, especially in the streets."

Panhandle State, nickname for West Virginia **W** 127
Panhard-Levassor, automobile **A** 543
Panics and depressions see Depressions and recessions
Panizzi (pa-NI-tzi), Sir Anthony, British librarian **L** 198
Pankhurst, Emmeline, British woman suffragist **W** 213
Panmunjom (pan-mun-JOM), South Korea **K** 304
Panning, for gold **G** 251; picture **G** 252
　cassiterite, ore of tin also panned **T** 195
　gravity concentration method **M** 228
Pannonia, area of the Roman Empire, now Austria **A** 524
Panoramas (pan-or-AM-as), curved pictures **D** 2
Panpipes, or syrinxes, ancient musical instruments **O** 209; picture **M** 548
Pansy, flower, picture **G** 44
Panthéon, (PANTH-e-on), Paris
　burial place of heroes of the mind **P** 70, 71
Pantheon, temple in Rome, Italy **R** 313
　Roman civilization **A** 232
　Roman engineers built domes **A** 376

Panthers, black leopards **L** 155
　leopards, kinds of **C** 137
　mountain lions, called pumas **C** 138
Pantomimes, dramatic action without words
　dance **D** 24–25
　dance music **D** 35
　early movies **M** 473, 474
　See also Charades
Pantothenic acid, a B-complex vitamin **V** 370d
Panzer (armored) divisions, in World War II **W** 287
Papacy (PAPE-acy)
　emperors versus popes in Italy **I** 455
　history of Roman Catholic Church **R** 291
　Reformation, a nationalist movement **C** 285–87
　See also Popes, of Roman Catholic Church
Papain (pa-PAI-in), substance from papaya plant **P** 314
　used as a meat tenderizer **M** 74
Papal Inquisition **I** 257
　Roman Catholic Church **R** 292
Papal Line of Demarcation see Line of Demarcation
Papal Schism see Western Schism

Papal States, area of about 15,000 sq. mi., with a population of more than 3,100,000, over which the pope had complete control. Located in central Italy, the papal states were founded in A.D. 754 and declared an independent monarchy in 1201. After 1870 one state after another threw off the papal yoke and joined the kingdom of Italy.
　Italy, history of **I** 456, 457; **R** 291
　papacy ceases to be worldly power **R** 295–96
　Renaissance, growth of city states during **R** 157

Papandreou, George, premier of Greece **G** 339
Papanicolaou ("Pap") test, for cancer of the cervix **C** 95; **M** 201
Papaya (pa-PY-a), or tree melon, a tropical fruit **M** 74
　seeds, picture **P** 298
Paper and paper making **P** 51–57
　bamboo used for making **G** 318
　book matches, how made **M** 153
　communication advanced by invention **C** 432
　Georgia's lumber resources **G** 133
　gift wrapping **G** 206–09
　Japanese houses **H** 171
　Kraft paper **A** 119
　New Hampshire, industry in **N** 154
　origami **O** 222–26
　paper money **M** 411–12
　photographic **P** 201
　Quebec leading producer in Canada **Q** 11
　things to make **I** 223–24
　wax paper, invention of **W** 70
Paperback books **P** 58–58a
　publishing **P** 514
Paper birch, tree, picture **T** 278
　New Hampshire, state tree of **N** 149
Paperboard **P** 53
Paperbound Books in Print, reference book **P** 58a
Paper chromatography **E** 366
Paper mills **P** 51
Paper money **M** 411–12
　bank notes **B** 47
Paper work see Papier mâché
Papier-mâché (paper ma-SHAY) **P** 58b–59
　clay modeling, cast of **C** 337
　early dolls made of **D** 265
Papillae (pa-PILL-e), of mouth and tongue
　birds **B** 202

Papineau (pa-pi-NO), Louis Joseph (1786–1871), French-Canadian liberal political leader, b. Montreal. As member

(1809–37) and speaker (1815–37) of the legislative assembly of Lower Canada, he opposed union of Upper and Lower Canada and was against British rule, sparking the revolt of 1837. Escaping to United States (1837), he failed to gain support for U.S. intervention and went to Paris (1839). In Canada under general amnesty he served in the Lower Canadian legislature (1848–54).

Canada, history of **C** 73

Paprika, spice, picture **S** 381
national spice of Hungary **H** 284; **S** 382
Pap (Papanicolaou) **test,** for cancer **C** 95; **M** 201
Papua (PAP-u-a), **Territory of,** in New Guinea **N** 147
Papuans, a people of New Guinea **I** 220; **N** 146
Papyrus (pa-PY-rus), a plant
invention of the first scrolls **I** 338
"paper," origin of name **P** 51
Phoenicians used as writing paper **A** 170
"paper" rolls for books **B** 318
Par, standard golf score **G** 255
Para-aminosalicylic (para-a-MI-no-sali-sil-ic) **acid, drug** **D** 212

Parable (from Greek *parabole,* meaning "a comparison"), make-believe story that illustrates a moral or religious principle. Parables were told by the early rabbis and included in the Jewish Talmud and Midrash. The form was adopted by Jesus for his teachings.
ministry of Jesus **J** 83

Parabola (pa-RAB-o-la), a type of curve that can be obtained when a cone is cut through by a plane. A thrown ball follows a path that is nearly a parabola. Picture **G** 131.
See also Conic section

Paracas, ancient Indian civilization of Peru **I** 155; **P** 165
Paracelsus (pa-ra-CEL-sus), **Philippus A.,** Swiss doctor **D** 213; **M** 205
beginnings of science of chemistry **C** 208–09
first to name zinc **Z** 370
Renaissance science **R** 160
Parachute Club of America **S** 193
Parachutes **P** 59–61
Garnerin parachutes from balloon **B** 31
law of falling bodies **F** 34
Leonardo da Vinci's design, picture **L** 154
sky-diving **S** 193
spacecraft module lowered **S** 340j; pictures **M** 454, **S** 340c
Parades **P** 61
Easter, origin **E** 42
Labor Day, picture **L** 2
Paradise Glacier, Mt. Rainier, Washington, picture **C** 157
Paradise Lost, poem by John Milton **M** 311
English poetry **E** 255
Paradox, a statement that seems to contradict itself
humor **H** 279

Paraffin, a white, translucent, waxlike, odorless, and tasteless by-product of oil refining, is used in making drugs, cosmetics, food containers, candles, and electrical insulation and for sealing preserves.
matches, use in the manufacture of **M** 152, 153
petroleum waxes **W** 70

Paraguay **P** 62–66
flag **F** 242
life in Latin America **L** 47–61
national anthem **N** 22
school, picture **L** 57

Paraguay River, South America **R** 246
divides Paraguay into two very different regions **P** 63–64
river systems in South America **S** 277
Parakeets, birds **B** 245; picture **B** 247
Carolina parakeets, extinct **B** 232
pets **P** 180–81
"talking" birds **P** 85
Parallax, apparent change in position of a celestial body **S** 410–11
measurement in astronomy **A** 475
Parallel bars, use in gymnastics, pictures **G** 430
Parallel lines, in geometry **G** 124; **M** 159
Parallelograms (par-al-LEL-o-grams), geometric forms **G** 126
Parallels, of latitude **L** 81
Paralympics, sports for the handicapped, picture **H** 29
Paralysis (pa-RAL-i-sis)
drug curare induces **D** 325
physical handicaps, rehabilitation and aids **H** 27–28
polio called "infantile paralysis" **D** 204
Paramaribo (para-MAR-i-bo), capital of Surinam **G** 397
Paramecium (para-ME-cium), micro-organism **M** 276–77; picture **K** 254
freshwater creatures, pictures **L** 257
Paramedical workers, in hospitals **H** 251
Paraná (pa-ra-NA) **River,** South America **R** 246; **S** 277
Argentina **A** 392, 394
Paraguay's rivers **P** 64
Paranoia, mental illness **M** 224
Parapsychology (para-sy-COL-ogy), study of extrasensory perception **E** 394–96
Pará (pa-RA) **River,** Brazil, picture **J** 154
Parasite diseases **D** 186, 188; picture **D** 187
pinworm infection **D** 203
tapeworm **D** 209–10
trichinosis **D** 210–11
Parasites **M** 279
control of parasite diseases **D** 188
flatworms **W** 312
fungi **F** 496, 498
hookworms **W** 312
lampreys **E** 87
leeches **W** 310, 312
parasitic plants **P** 318
pinworms **D** 203
tapeworms **D** 209–10
ticks, carriers of disease to cattle **C** 151
viruses grow only inside cells **V** 361
Parasol ants **A** 326
Parathyroid (para-THY-roid) **glands,** diagram **B** 280
Paratroopers, pictures **P** 60
Parcel post **P** 410
Parchment, writing material **B** 1
books, earliest codex forms **B** 319
illustrated parchment books **I** 89
invention of **I** 338
Pardo Bazán (PAR-do ba-THON), **Emilia,** Spanish writer **S** 371
Pardoning power
presidency of the United States **P** 454
Paré (pa-RAY), **Ambroise,** French surgeon **M** 205
Parent and child
adoption **A** 25–26
baby **B** 2–4
divorce **D** 234–35
family responsibility **F** 37–43
Parentheses (pa-REN-the-sese), punctuation marks **P** 531
Parents and Teachers, National Congress of **P** 67
Parent-teacher associations **P** 66–67
National Congress of Parents and Teachers **P** 67
Parian (PARR-ian) **dolls,** made of bisque china **D** 265

Parícutin (pa-ri-cu-TEEN), **volcano,** Mexico   V 384
  ever-changing earth   E 14
Parini (pa-RI-ni), **Giuseppe,** Italian poet   I 479
Paris, capital of France   P 68–75
  Arch of Triumph   F 432;   P 74; pictures   E 304, P 71
  automobiles and air pollution, picture   E 272c
  Bourse, or stock exchange   S 430
  bridges, picture   B 396
  Daguerre photograph of, picture   D 2
  Eiffel Tower, picture   F 403
  France, places of interest   F 406, 407
  influence on French language   F 433
  Louvre   L 366–68
  Notre Dame cathedral, pictures   A 379,   C 130
  one of the world's great cities, picture   C 307
  Place de la Concorde, pictures   F 420, P 70
  Seine, houseboats on the, picture   H 176
  theater   T 160
Paris, in Greek mythology   G 365;   T 293
  Helen of Troy   H 104
Paris, Treaty of, 1763
  British become masters of Saint Lawrence River
    S 16
  French and Indian Wars   F 462
  French Canada ceded to England   C 70;   Q 16
Paris, Treaty of, 1783   R 208
  Adams, John   A 9
  Franklin's work   F 455
  Revolutionary War settlement   T 105
Paris, Treaty of, 1898   P 190
Paris Bourse (BURSE), or stock exchange   S 430
Parisii (pa-RI-si-I), Gallic tribe   P 73
Paris International Exhibition, 1878, picture   F 14
Parison, conelike mass of glass   G 230
Paris Opera Ballet School   B 24
Paris Opera House, pictures   O 130;   P 72
Paris Peace Conference, 1919   W 281
  between the world wars   W 282–87
Paris peace talks, 1968, Vietnam War   V 334c, 337
Parity, in physics   N 371

Park, Chung Hee (1916–   ), Korean army officer and
politician, b. Kyung Sang Buk Do. After teaching
(1937–40), he served in the Japanese Army (1940–45)
and Korean Army (since 1945). He became chairman of
the Supreme Council for National Reconstruction (1961)
and president of the Republic of Korea (1963).
  Korea, history of   K 302

Park, Mungo (1771–1806), Scottish explorer and surgeon,
b. Selkirk, Scotland. Ascended Gambia and Niger Rivers
in Africa and wrote *Travels in the Interior of Africa.*
  exploration of Africa   A 68;   N 258

Parkas, hooded coats
  Eskimo clothing   E 289
Parker, Al, American illustrator   I 92, 93
Parker, Charlie "Bird," American jazz musician   J 60;
    picture   J 61
Parker, Dorothy, American writer   A 214
Parker, Ely Samuel, Sioux Indian general   I 214
Parker, John, American patriot   R 198
Parker, John Palmer, American cattle rancher   H 64

Parker, Quanah (1845?–1911), American Indian chief, b.
northern Texas (?). A Comanche leader, Quanah terrorized
frontier settlements until his defeat by white buffalo
hunters at Adobe Walls (1874). Quanah then adopted
the white man's ways. He encouraged education and
agriculture, and he increased the Indians' income by
leasing surplus pasture lands. The town of Quanah,
Texas, was named for him.

Parker, Robert A., American astronaut   S 347
Parkes, Australia
  radio-astronomy observatory, picture   O 10
Parking orbit, of a spacecraft   S 340d

Parkinson's disease (parkinsonism or paralysis agitans),
progressive disorder of the central nervous system. The
disease causes tremor of muscles at rest; a stiff,
shuffling walk; and a masklike expression. There is no
known cause or cure, but symptoms are lessened by a
drug called L-dopa and in some cases by brain surgery.
James Parkinson (1755–1824), an English physician, first
described the disease.

Parkman, Francis, American historian   A 202
  kinds of historical writing   H 137
Parks   P 76–77
  mountain parks, parkland regions, grassy plateaus
    N 285;   S 38c
  National Park System, United States   N 44–55
  state parks see state articles
  See *also* Botanical gardens; National parks, Canada;
    National Park System, United States; Zoos; names
    of parks, as Yellowstone; places of interest in
    country, state, and city articles

Parks, Gordon (1912–   ), American photographer,
journalist, and composer, Negro, b. Fort Scott, Kan.
Since 1948 he has served as a photographer for *Life*
magazine, covering such assignments as "Crime in the
U.S.," "Poverty in Brazil," and "Discrimination in the
U.S.," and was named Magazine Photographer of the
Year (1961). He has published *The Learning Tree* (1963)
and an autobiography, *A Choice of Weapons,* 1966. He
is also the composer of numerous works for piano and
wind instruments. Picture   N 104b.

Parley, Peter, American writer for children   C 238
Parliament (PAR-la-ment), British   U 77–78
  Cromwell's Rump Parliament   E 223
  Gladstone's career   G 225
  Houses of Parliament, pictures   L 338, U 70
  impeachment process   I 108
  Long and Short Parliaments   E 223
  official opening by Queen Elizabeth II, picture   G 274
  parliament of the Middle Ages   M 292
  Pitt, William, the Younger, sponsor of Act of Union,
    1801   P 265
  prime minister   P 456
  types of legislative bodies   P 81–82
Parliamentary (par-la-MENT-ary) **procedure**   P 79–80
  debates and discussions   D 54–55
Parliament Building, Quebec City, picture   Q 12
Parliament Hill, Ottawa, Canada   O 237–38
Parliament House, Canberra, Australia   C 87–88
Parliaments   P 81–82
  Canada   C 76–77
  first democratic parliament, Iceland's Althing   I 44
  origin and present make-up of the English Parliament
    E 219;   U 77–78
  parliamentary form of government   G 278
  prime minister   P 456

Parmigianino (par-mi-ja-NI-no), or **Parmigiano, Il** (Girolamo Francesco Maria Mazzuoli, or Mazzola) (1503–40),
Italian painter, b. Parma. Influenced by Correggio, he
was an early mannerist painter, and his style was
refined and elegant. In Rome from 1523 to 1527, he
received commissions from Pope Clement VII. He later
worked in Bologna (1527–31), returning to Parma in
1531. Among his works is *Vision of Saint Jerome.*
  St. Thais, engraving   E 272

Parnassus (par-NAS-sus), a mountain in central Greece, north of the Gulf of Corinth, with an altitude of 8,026 ft. According to the ancient Greeks, Parnassus was sacred to Apollo, Dionysius, and the Muses. It has therefore become a symbol of inspiration for writers and artists.

Parnell (par-NELL), **Charles Stewart,** Irish nationalist leader **I** 391
Paro, former capital of Bhutan **B** 150
Parochial (pa-RO-kial) **schools E** 75
Parody, a form of humor **H** 279–80
  "Song of Milkanwatha" **N** 272
Parole, of prison inmates **P** 470
Parotid glands
  mumps affect **D** 201
Parr, Catherine, sixth wife of Henry VIII of England **H** 109
Parrakeets see Parakeets
Parrington, Vernon Louis, American critic **A** 214

Parrish, Maxfield (1870–1966), American artist and illustrator, b. Philadelphia, Pa. He is noted for the design and color, especially a characteristic shade of blue, of his illustrations. Books he has illustrated include *Arabian Nights Entertainments* and *Mother Goose in Prose.*

Parris Island Marine Base, South Carolina **S** 306
Parrot fever (psittacosis, or ornithosis) **B** 248; **I** 286
  care of feathered pets **P** 181
Parrotfish, picture **F** 192
Parrots P 83–86
  pet birds **B** 246; **P** 180–81
Parry, Edward, English Arctic explorer **N** 338
Parsifal (PAR-si-fol), opera by Richard Wagner **O** 150
Parsis, or **Parsees,** Zoroastrian religious sect **Z** 380
  funeral customs **F** 493
  religions of India **R** 152

Parsley, aromatic herb related to the carrot. It has masses of yellow-green umbrella-shaped blossoms. The leaves are used in salads, as a garnish, and as a seasoning. In ancient times parsley was used as a medicine and was believed to have magical powers. Picture **S** 381.
  herbs and spices **S** 382

Parsnip, hardy plant of the carrot group, native to Europe. Its edible root is long, white, and fleshy and is used as a vegetable or for flavoring stews and soups. The parsnip is planted in the spring and takes several months to mature, making it an ideal winter fodder for cattle, sheep, and poultry.

Parsons, Charles A., English inventor **T** 320

Parsons, James Benton (1911–), American jurist, Negro, b. Kansas City, Mo. He received his M.A. in political science (1946) and his LL.D. (1949) from the University of Chicago. He held various legal posts and taught law until he was appointed (1960) judge of the Superior Court, Cook County, Ill. In 1961 he was appointed a judge of the U.S. District Court in Illinois.

Parthenon, temple in Athens, Greece **A** 228; pictures **C** 306, **E** 322, **G** 335
  architecture **A** 374; picture **A** 375
  Doric style of Greek architecture **G** 346; picture **G** 347
  Pericles **P** 156
Participles, verb forms **P** 91
Particle accelerators, atom-smashing machines **A** 489
  nuclear energy **N** 366–67

Particle boards W 227
Particles, in physics **A** 486
  cloud formation **C** 358–61
  cosmic rays **C** 511–13
  in a solid, a liquid, a gas, diagram **L** 309
  solids **S** 250
  subatomic particles and nuclear energy **N** 354–58
  subatomic particles and nuclear force and behavior **N** 365–71
Parties P 87–89
  Halloween party **H** 15–16
  magic tricks **M** 18–21
  setting for an afternoon tea, picture **T** 39
  sugar-on-snow parties **M** 87
  See also Etiquette; Games
Parties, political see Political parties

Partisan, lightly organized guerilla forces who undermine the enemy, usually in an occupied zone. Although these forces have existed throughout history, the term was popularized during World War II to describe the fighters in German-occupied areas of Europe, especially those in Yugoslavia under leadership of Marshal Tito. Term also refers to the champion of an individual party or cause.
  Revolutionary War, campaigns in South Carolina **R** 208
  Yugoslavia **Y** 358

Partita, a musical form **M** 537
Partnership locks L 326
Parts of a book L 180–81
  how a book is designed **B** 331
  layout **B** 322
  uses of, in study of textbook assignments **S** 441
Parts of speech P 90–92
  grammar **G** 289–92
Party line, official ideology **C** 444
PAS see Para-aminosalicylic acid
Pascal, Blaise, French mathematician and philosopher **H** 301–02
  automation, history of **A** 532
  chance, problems of **P** 471
  experimental method in science **E** 351
  invented adding machine **C** 450; **O** 55–56; picture **C** 451
  place in French literature **F** 438
Pascal's Law, of liquid pressure **H** 302
Pascoli, Giovanni, Italian poet **I** 480
Pashto, language see Pushtu
Pasig River, Philippines **M** 75
Pasolini, Pier Paolo, Italian motion-picture director **M** 488a
Pasqueflower (PASK-flower)
  state flower of South Dakota **S** 313
Passamaquoddy (pass-a-ma-QUOD-dy) **Bay,** Maine, New Brunswick, Canada **M** 37
  trapping sardines, picture **N** 138f
Passenger pigeons, extinct birds **B** 231–32
  Audubon painting **B** 230
Passenger ships O 17
Passenger trains R 80–81
Passing, in football **F** 359–60
Passion, a musical form **M** 537
  choral music **C** 278
  development in baroque period **B** 64
Passion plays, medieval P 12
Passover P 93–94
  Easter **E** 41
Passports P 94–95
  vacations and travel, use in **V** 259
  What is a stateless person? **P** 94
Pastas, Italian styles of dried dough **F** 341

Paste, type of adhesive **G** 242
  collage making **C** 377
Pasteboard
  playing cards **C** 107
Pastels, artist's paints **P** 30
  Degas, Edgar **D** 84
Pasternak (pa-ster-NOK), **Boris,** Russian author **U** 62;
  picture **U** 61
Pasteur (past-UR), **Louis,** French chemist **P** 95–97
  advances in biological sciences **S** 73
  biogenesis, theory of **B** 194
  contributions to medicine **M** 208
  fermentation of wine **F** 89; picture **F** 90
  germ theory of disease developed by **D** 214–15
  signature reproduced **A** 527
Pasteurization (past-u-ri-ZAY-tion) **D** 10
  beer **B** 116
  canning compared to **F** 346
  importance to medicine **M** 208
Pastorales (pas-tor-OLS), plays with music **F** 443
Pastoral nomads, desert people **D** 128
Pastoral poetry, about country life **E** 151, 251
Pastoral prayer **P** 434
Pastrana Borrero, Misael, Colombian president
  C 384
Pasture, The, poem by Robert Frost **F** 480
Pasture grasses **G** 317
Pastures
  grazing lands in U.S. national forests **N** 31–32
  of the sea **L** 231; **O** 37
  pasture grasses **G** 317
  prairies **P** 431
  Taylor Grazing Act of 1934 **C** 486
Patagonia (pat-a-GO-nia), plateau region of South
  America
  Argentina **A** 392, 393
  landforms of South America **S** 276, 280; picture
  S 292
  sheep ranch, picture **P** 433
Patch logging, of timber **L** 373
Patella (kneecap), bone of the leg, diagram **F** 79
Patent lawyers **I** 347
Patent leather **L** 110
Patent Office see United States Patent Office
Patents **P** 97–98
  creation and control of trusts and monopolies **T** 305
  Edison's record number of **E** 60
  first rubber tire patented as a hollow belt **T** 196
  register marks on pottery **A** 320
  some significant inventions and their patent dates
  I 339–45
  technology stimulated by patents **T** 46
  trademarks **T** 244–45
  What is a patent? **I** 347
Pater (PAY-ter), **Walter,** English writer **E** 262
Paterae, circular ornaments on furniture **F** 507; picture
  F 508
Pater Noster see Lord's Prayer
Paterson (PAT-er-son), **Andrew Barton** ("Banjo"), Aus-
  tralian "bush balladist" **A** 501
Paterson, New Jersey **N** 177
Paterson, William, American statesman **N** 177
  proposed New Jersey plan for U.S. constitution **U** 146
Pathetic fallacy, figure of speech **F** 118–19
Pathet Lao, rebel group of Laos **L** 43
Pathfinder, nickname of John Charles Frémont **F** 458
Pathogens, specific causes of diseases **V** 282–83
Pathological (path-o-LOJ-ic-al) **anatomy** **M** 206
Pathology (pa-THOL-ogy), study of the nature of diseases
  medical laboratory tests **M** 201–02
Patient-monitoring system, in hospitals **H** 248; picture
  H 251

Patients, persons who are ill
  nursing care **N** 413–15

Paton (PAY-ton), **Alan Stewart** (1903–), South African
author, educator, and politician, b. Pietermaritzburg. He
wrote *Cry, the Beloved Country* and other works dealing
with social problems of South Africa. He is president of
the anti-racist South African Liberal Party, co-author of
South Africa in Transition, and winner of the Freedom
House award of 1960. He has taught in South Africa and
was principal of Diepkloof Reformatory.
  African literature in English **A** 76b

Patriarchal family **F** 40
  women, role of **W** 212a–212b

Patriarchs (PAY-tri-arks), original rulers of a tribe or
family. The name was used for the ancestral leaders of
the Jewish people. Three ancient Jewish patriarchs were
Abraham, Isaac, and Jacob. The title has been used
since the 7th century for the bishops of the five ancient
sees (official local seat of a bishop) of Jerusalem, Antioch, Alexandria, Constantinople, and Rome. The Pope
of the Roman Catholic Church is also known as the
Patriarch of the West.
  Orthodox Eastern churches **O** 228

Patriarchy see Patriarchal family
Patricians, social class in ancient Rome **P** 378
Patrick, Saint, patron saint of Ireland **P** 98
  Christianity, history of **C** 284
  converted a whole nation (Ireland) **R** 290
  Ireland, history of **I** 390
  Saint Patrick's Day **H** 148
Patriotic holidays **H** 150–52
Patriotic songs see National anthems and patriotic songs
Patriots, colonists critical of British rule **R** 198
  political parties in colonial America **P** 379

Patriot's Day, a holiday celebrated in the states of
Maine and Massachusetts on April 19 of each year. The
holiday commemorates the battles of Lexington and
Concord in the Revolutionary War.

Patroclus (pa-TRO-clus), in Greek mythology, son of Men-
oetius and loyal friend of Achilles. Upon Achilles' refusal
to fight because of a disagreement with Agamemnon,
Patroclus put on Achilles' armor and led the Myrmidons
in routing the Trojans. He was slain by Hector and
avenged by Achilles, who in grief joined the fighting and
took Hector's life.
  Iliad, episodes in **I** 69

Patrolmen, police **P** 375
Patrol system, Girl Scouts form of government **G** 216
Patronage, political **C** 317
  power of U.S. president over appointments and re-
  movals **P** 453, 455
  See also Spoils system
Patronymic (pat-ro-NIM-ic) **method,** of name giving
  N 7
Patroons (pa-TROONS), Dutch landowners in American
  colonies **A** 190
  New York, settlement of **N** 225
Patternmaking
  clothing **C** 353, 354; picture **C** 356
  designs for furniture **F** 505
  dressmaking **D** 311–312
  woodworking **W** 230
Patterson, Floyd, American boxing champion **B** 353
Patterson, Martha Johnson, acting first lady in Andrew
  Johnson's administration **F** 172–73

Patti, Adelina (Adela Juana Maria Patti) (1843–1919), Spanish-Italian coloratura soprano, b. Madrid, Spain. Following her New York debut in 1859, she appeared throughout Europe, playing leading roles in operas of Rossini, Bellini, Donizetti, Gounod, and Verdi. She retired from opera in 1895, subsequently appearing in concerts.

Patton, George Smith, Jr. (1885–1945), American army officer, b. San Gabriel, Calif. He was an aide to General Pershing (1916–17). During World War II he commanded U.S. forces in Morocco (1942) and Sicily (1943). Appointed full general (1945), he led the U.S. occupation forces in Western Europe (1944–45). Known as a colorful, strict commander, he was nicknamed "Old Blood and Guts." He died in Europe of injuries received in an automobile accident.
    World War II **W** 301

Pátzcuaro (POTZ-cua-ro), **Lake,** Mexico **M** 244
Paul III, pope
    Holy Roman and Universal Inquisition **I** 257
Paul VI, pope **P** 99
    reform program **R** 299
Paul, Saint **P** 99
    Apostle of Jesus Christ **A** 333
    Christianity, history of **C** 279–80
    earliest missions **M** 348
    Pauline Epistles **B** 161
    quoted on women's role **W** 211
    Roman Catholic Church **R** 287
    Saint Paul's Day **H** 159
Paulding, James Kirke, American writer **A** 200

Pauli (POW-li), **Wolfgang** (1900–1958), Austrian physicist, b. Vienna. He worked on the theory and study of atomic-particle behavior. Pauli received the 1945 Nobel prize in physics for his development of the Pauli exclusion principle, which states that no two electrons in an atom can have the same quantum number. This principle has proved essential in the solving of problems of atomic structure and behavior. Pauli predicted the existence of neutrinos (detected, 1956).

Pauline Epistles, Bible, New Testament **B** 161

Pauling (PAUL-ing), **Linus Carl** (1901–), American chemist, b. Portland, Ore. He was awarded the Nobel prize in chemistry in 1954 for his work in studying the structure of molecules and the forces holding them together. He was also awarded the 1962 Nobel peace prize for his activities opposing war and the testing of nuclear weapons. He wrote *Nature of the Chemical Bond* and *No More War!* Picture **B** 196.

Paulists, Roman Catholic priests of the Missionary Society of St. Paul the Apostle, established in New York, N.Y., in 1858. The principal purpose of the society is to instruct non-Catholics in the Roman Catholic faith. Although missions have been founded in Toronto and Johannesburg, activities are centered in United States.

Paulo Afonso (POW-loo a-FONE-soo) **Falls,** Brazil **W** 56b
Paul Revere, painting by Copley **U** 118
Paul Revere House, Boston, Massachusetts **U** 123
Paul Revere's Ride, poem by Longfellow, excerpt **R** 192

Pauncefote (PAUNCE-foot), **Sir Julian,** 1st Baron Pauncefote of Preston (1828–1902), English diplomat and lawyer, b. Munich, Germany. He served as attorney general of Hong Kong colony (1865–72) and chief justice of the Leeward Islands (1874) and became the permanent undersecretary of state in the Foreign Office (1882).

As British ambassador to the United States (1893–1902) he greatly improved Anglo-American relations. With United States Secretary of State John Hay he signed the Hay-Pauncefote Treaty (1901), assuring free passage through the Panama Canal to ships of all nations.

Pavane, dance
    Byrd's lighter music **R** 173
Pavements
    mosaics used in **M** 463
Pavers, machines for mixing concrete **R** 252
Pavese, Cesare, Italian novelist **I** 481
Paving machines **B** 448
Pavlov (PA-vlof), **Ivan,** Russian biologist and physiologist
    P 100
    in psychology, methods of studying behavior
    P 496
    learning **L** 99
    theories of reflex action **B** 195

Pavlova (PAV-lo-va), **Anna** (1885–1931), Russian ballet dancer, b. St. Petersburg (now Leningrad). Trained at the Imperial Ballet School, St. Petersburg, she toured Europe and the United States from 1911. With her own company she performed throughout the Americas, Europe, the Orient, Australia, and New Zealand. Her greatest performances included leading roles in *Giselle, The Butterflies, The Dying Swan* (created for her by Michel Fokine).
    ballet, history of **B** 26, 28

Pawn, in chess, picture **C** 221
Pawnbrokers, money lenders, trade sign of three balls
    B 21
Pawnee, Indians of North America **I** 164
Pawtucket (paw-TUCK-et), Rhode Island **R** 223
Pay-as-you-go, income tax provision **I** 111
Payloads
    rockets **R** 257
Payne-Aldrich Act, 1909 **T** 7–8
Paysandú (py-san-DU), Uruguay **U** 238
Pay television **T** 70c
PBS see Public Broadcasting Service
Peabody, Elizabeth, American educator **K** 244
Peabody, George, American merchant and philanthropist
    M 126–27
    set up Peabody Education Fund **F** 390
Peace **P** 104–05
    Addams, Jane **A** 19
    Hammarskjöld, Dag **H** 21
    international law of **I** 321
    international relations **I** 322–25
    Isaiah's call for peace **I** 413
    League of Nations **L** 96–97
    Nobel prizes **N** 267, 268
    United Nations **U** 80–88
    Vietnam negotiations **V** 334c, 337
    What is a pacifist? **P** 105
    See also Disarmament

Peace Bridge, International, steel bridge which joins Canada (at Fort Erie, Ontario) with the United States (at Buffalo, N.Y.). Opened on August 7, 1927, the bridge is 4,400 ft. long.

Peace Conference, Washington, D.C., 1861
    Tyler, John, president of **T** 342
Peace Corps (COR) **P** 101–03
    achievement of the Kennedy administration
    K 211
    anthropology helpful to **A** 309
    class in the Sudan, picture **E** 83
    teachers **T** 43

Peace in our time, Chamberlain's announcement of Munich Pact, 1938 **W** 286
Peace of God **F** 103

Peace pipe, a pipe used by the American Indians as a symbol of peace when smoked during a powwow (conference) between two tribes.
  also called calumet **I** 196
  used by Bison and Wild Rice area Indians **I** 167, 178

Peace River district, Canada **A** 146c; **B** 402, 403
Peach **P** 106–09
  Georgia developed Elberta peach **G** 137
  See also Plum
Peach blossom
  Delaware, state flower of **D** 87
Peacock butterfly, picture **I** 262
Peacocks, birds **B** 212
Peak, Robert, American illustrator **I** 94, 95
Peale, Charles Willson, American painter **M** 126
  Jefferson portrait attributed to, picture **J** 66
  portrait painters of the United States **U** 117

Peale, Norman Vincent (1898–   ), American clergyman, b. Bowersville, Ohio. Ordained in 1922, he has been minister of the Marble Collegiate Reformed Church in New York, N.Y., since 1932. Through his books, sermons, newspaper column "Confident Living," and television program What's Your Trouble, he offers advice on the "art of living" and on relieving tension.

Peale, Rembrandt (1778–1860), American portrait and historical painter, b. near Richboro, Pa. He was commissioned by his father, artist Charles Willson Peale, to do portraits of Thomas Jefferson and government officials (1804). He later went to Paris (1808–10), to paint portraits for his father's collection. Other well-known paintings are portraits of George Washington and Napoleon Bonaparte. He wrote Notes on Italy.

Peale Museum, Baltimore, Maryland **M** 123
Peanut butter **P** 110
Peanut oil **O** 79; **P** 111
Peanuts and peanut products **P** 110–11
  Alabama crop, picture **A** 119
  Carver's work at Tuskegee Institute **C** 128–29
  fruits we eat **P** 308; pictures **P** 309
  Nigeria, largest exporter, picture **N** 257
  peanut oil **O** 79
  Senegal's most important crop **S** 119
Pear **P** 112
  orchard in Oregon, picture **O** 198
  pollen grains, picture **P** 297

Peare, Catherine Owens (1911–71), American author, b. Perth Amboy, N.J. She is noted for her biographies for children. These include Albert Einstein, Mahatma Gandhi, Mark Twain, Jules Verne, and The Helen Keller Story. She wrote the biography William Penn for adults, then published a junior edition of this work.

Pea Ridge National Military Park, Arkansas **A** 427, 432
Pearlfish **F** 204
Pearl Harbor, United States naval base near Honolulu, Hawaii **H** 57, 67; picture **H** 72
  Japan in control of the militarists **J** 48
  World War II **W** 292–93; picture **W** 293
Pearl of the Antilles (an-TILL-ese), Cuba **C** 547–551
Pearl of the Lagoon, Abidjan, Ivory Coast **I** 492
Pearl of the Orient, Ceylon; Manila **C** 177; **M** 75
Pearls and pearl culture **P** 113–15
  early pearl diving methods **U** 13

How are artificial pearls made? **P** 114
Japan's cultured pearl industry **J** 38–39
jewelry **J** 93; picture **J** 96
organic gems **G** 76
oysters **O** 271–72
Pearly nautilus, mollusk **O** 275
  shells and shell collecting **S** 149
Pearse, Pádhraic, Irish patriot **I** 391
Pearson, Hesketh, English biographer **E** 268
Pearson, Lester, prime minister of Canada **P** 115; picture **P** 456a

Peary (PEA-ry), **Josephine Diebisch** (1863–1955), American Arctic traveler and author, b. Washington, D.C. Wife of explorer Robert Edwin Peary (1856–1920), she joined her husband on two Arctic expeditions (1891–92, 1893–94), becoming the first white woman to winter in the Arctic (1891). Her daughter Marie Ahnighito was born farther north than any other white child (1893). Her books include My Arctic Journal and The Snow Baby.

Peary, Robert E., American explorer **P** 116
  polar explorations **P** 364
Peas, vegetable **V** 292
  Mendel crossbred to prove genetic theories **G** 80–81
  pea pods, fruits we eat **P** 308; picture **P** 309
Peasant Dance, painting by Rubens **B** 58
Peasant dances **D** 27
Peasants, farm workers on feudal manors **F** 102; pictures **F** 101. 103
  dolls in peasant costume, picture **D** 264
  Middle Ages, classes of society **M** 292
Peasants' Revolt, 1381, in England **E** 219

Pease, Howard (1894–   ), American author of children's books, b. Stockton, Calif. He is noted for his sea stories, including The Tatooed Man and The Ship Without a Crew. He also wrote Heart of Danger. Numerous other works, including Thunderbolt House, deal with events in San Francisco.

Pease Porridge Hot, nursery rhyme **N** 407
Peat **F** 93
  coal formation **C** 362
  cutting turf, picture **I** 388
  fuel **F** 487; picture **F** 486
  peat moss for mulching **F** 93–94; **G** 42
Peat Bog Soldiers, folk song **F** 327
Peattie, Donald Culross, American writer **A** 214
Pecan (pe-CON), tree
  nuts **N** 422
  Texas, state tree of **T** 123
Peccaries, piglike mammals **P** 249; picture **H** 212
  hoofed mammals **H** 209

Peck, Anne Merriman (1884–   ), American author and illustrator of children's books, b. Piermont-on-Hudson, N.Y. She spent her first earnings from book illustrations on a trip to Europe, which inspired the first book she wrote, Storybook Europe. She has since written books on youth in other countries and histories of Latin-American countries. Her books include Young Mexico.

Peck, Gregory (1916–   ), American actor, b. La Jolla, Calif. He appeared in summer stock and on Broadway during the early 1940's. His first film, Days of Glory (1944), brought him good personal reviews. Some of his motion pictures are Keys of the Kingdom, Gentlemen's Agreement, To Kill a Mockingbird (for which he won the 1962 Oscar for best actor), Marooned, and I Walk the Line.

Pecking orders, among poultry **A** 280

Pecos (PAY-cos) **Bill,** American folk hero story, excerpt F 316–17
Pecos River, New Mexico–Texas N 183; T 125
Pécs (PAICH), Hungary H 286

Pectin, substance found in ripe fruit. It is used mainly in making fruit jams and jellies, as it forms a jelly when sugar and acid are added to it. It is also used in certain medicines.

Pectoral fins, of fishes S 140
Pedestals, used in modern furniture F 510

Pediatrics (pe-di-AT-rics), that part of medical treatment concerned with the care and diseases of babies and children. Specialists in this field are medical doctors called pediatricians.

Pedicabs, tricycle taxis
  Djakarta, Indonesia D 236
  Indonesia's *betjaks,* picture I 216
  Java street, picture A 467
  school bus, Chinese, picture C 258
Pedigree, list of ancestors
  cats C 141
  Herd Book Society of dairy cattle breeders D 8
  stud books, records of thoroughbred horses H 231
Pediment, low gable-like architectural decoration of a building, diagram A 376
Pedipalps, appendages of arachnids S 383

Pedometer, mechanical device, usually attached to the body and shaped like a watch, that records the number of steps taken by a person and the distance walked.

Pedrarias Dávila (pay-DRA-ri-as DA-bi-la), also **Pedro Arias de Ávila,** Spanish colonial governor B 18
  De Soto a protégé of D 144
Pedrell (pay-DRELL), **Felipe,** Spanish composer S 373
Pedro I (PAY-dru), **Dom,** emperor of Brazil B 384
  Portuguese royal family in Brazil P 403
Pedro II, Dom, emperor of Brazil B 384
Peel, Sir Robert, British statesman
  London police organized P 373
Peele, George, English dramatist D 296
Peelites, political followers of Sir Robert Peel G 225

Peerce, Jan (Jacob Pincus Perelmuth) (1904–   ), American tenor, b. New York, N.Y. A singer with Radio City Music Hall (1933–41), he made his Metropolitan Opera debut in 1941 and since has been a leading tenor of Italian opera. He has made numerous concert tours in the Soviet Union, South Africa, Israel, and Australia and throughout the Americas and Europe.

Peer Gynt (PEER GHINT), play by Henrik Ibsen I 2
Pegasus (PEG-a-sus), constellation C 493
Pegasus, winged horse in Greek mythology G 364
Pegasus satellite, picture S 42
Pegmatite dikes, rock masses produce gemstones G 70
Peg-tooth harrows F 58
P.E.I. see Prince Edward Island
Peiping see Peking
Pekin (pe-KIN) **ducks** P 423
Peking (pe-KING), capital of the People's Republic of China P 117–19; pictures C 258, 271
  China, history of C 272
  Communist poster, picture C 445
  kindergarten class, picture A 461
Pekingese (pe-kin-ESE), dog D 259; picture D 256
Peking Man, archeological discovery A 308
  prehistoric man, stages in his development P 442

tools, pictures P 444
  use of fire F 139
Peking Union Medical College P 118
Pelagic (pe-LAJ-ic) **fish**
  eggs F 195
  habitat, feeding habits, uses F 214–15

Pelé (PAY-LAY) (Edson Arantes do Nascimento) (1940–   ), Brazilian soccer player, b. Três Corações. One of the sport's greatest players and its leading scorer, he joined Santos Football Club in 1956 and led it to world club championships. From his inside left position he also starred on Brazil's national team and sparked it to an unprecedented 3 triumphs in World Cup competition (1958, '62, '70). Reputedly world's highest paid athlete, he retired in 1971.

Pelée (pel-AY), **Mount,** Martinique V 377
Pele's hair, volcanic rock, picture V 386
  insulation fibers I 290

Pelias (PE-lias), in Greek mythology, a son of Poseidon and Tyro and half-brother of King Aeson of Iolcus. He seized the throne of Aeson and later was confronted by Jason, his nephew and the son of Aeson, who claimed the kingship. He refused to give up the throne until Jason returned with the Golden Fleece. Jason returned with the sorceress Medea, who persuaded Pelias' daughters to kill their father by falsely promising Pelias that they would raise him to life as a young man.

Pelicans, birds
  state bird of Louisiana L 348
  "The Reason for the Pelican," poem by Ciardi N 274
Pelican State, nickname for Louisiana L 349
Peligot, Eugène, French chemist U 230

Pelion (or Pilion), a mountain in Thessaly, Greece, with an altitude of 5,252 ft. According to an ancient Greek legend, the Aloadae (giants) placed the mountain Pelion on top of Ossa, another mountain, in order to reach Olympus, the home of the gods. Pelion was the home of Chiron, the centaur (half-man and half-horse).

Pellagra (pel-LAG-ra), disease D 216
  niacin, a B-complex vitamin, prevention against pellagra V 370d
Pelléas et Mélisande (pel-lay-AS a may-li-ZOND), opera by Claude Debussy O 150–51
Pellets, ammunition for guns G 424
Peloponnesian (pel-o-pon-NE-sian) **League,** by Greek city-states G 338
Peloponnesian Wars, 431–404 B.C. A 228; G 338
  Pericles P 156
Peloponnesus, peninsula of Greece G 333
Pelota (pe-LO-ta), name of the ball used in playing jai alai J 10; picture J 11
Peltier effect, thermoelectricity principle applied to air conditioning A 103
Pelts, skins of fur-bearing animals F 512–13; picture F 522
Pelvic fins, of fishes S 140
Pemaquid Point, Maine M 37
Pemberton, John, American Civil War general C 325
Pembina, North Dakota N 336–37
Pembroke College, Providence, Rhode Island R 218
Pemmican, dried food F 348
  salmon pemmican, how made I 180
  used by fur traders and Indians F 520; I 166, 196
Penal (PE-nal) **colonies,** of exiled criminals P 468
  Siberia, formerly a Russian penal colony S 173
Penal Laws, imposed on Ireland I 390

Penance, sacrament of Roman Catholic Church **R** 301

Penang, Malaysia **M** 55, 57

Penates see Lares and penates

Pencils **P** 147–48
- graphite used as lead **C** 433
- metal point, early drawing tool **D** 303
- What is the "lead" in a lead pencil? **L** 95

Pendants, jeweled ornaments **J** 94; picture **J** 97
- nose pendant, picture **D** 71

Pendentives (pen-DENT-ives), in architecture **A** 377
- Byzantine, dome support **B** 486

Pendergast, Thomas J., American politician **T** 299

Pendleton Civil Service Act, 1883 **C** 317
- Arthur, Chester Alan, signs into law **A** 441

Pendulum **W** 46
- Galileo discovers laws governing **G** 5
- measures gravity **G** 323; picture **G** 322
- seismometer, for detecting earthquakes **E** 37–38

Penelope (pe-NEL-o-pe), in Greek legend, wife of Odysseus **O** 53, 54
- Homer's tales of heroes of Greek mythology **G** 366

Peneplain (PE-ne-plain), eroded land surface **M** 136

Penfield, Wilder G., Canadian neurosurgeon **Q** 13
- experiments with the memory bank of the brain **B** 288

Penghu, or Pescadores, islands between China and Taiwan **T** 12–13

Penguins **P** 120–26
- adaptation to a habitat **B** 223, 228
- migration **H** 185
- nest building **B** 212, 213
- polar regions, picture **P** 370

Penicillin (pen-i-CILL-in), antibiotic **A** 311, 312; picture **A** 314
- conquest of disease **D** 217
- discovered by Fleming **F** 249
- fermentation process, new use of **F** 90–91
- growing penicillin molds **A** 316
- medicine, history of **M** 208a
- sac fungi produce penicillin **F** 498

Peninsular War, 1808–14 **N** 11

Penitent, The, woodcut by Durer **G** 169

Penitentiaries **P** 468–69

Penknives **P** 146

Penmanship, or handwriting **H** 31–33

Penn, John (1740–88), American Revolutionary leader, b. Caroline County, Va. He was a member of the North Carolina provincial congress (1775) and the Second Continental Congress (1775–80), and a signer of the Declaration of Independence (1776). He was North Carolina's receiver of taxes under the Articles of Confederation (1784).

Penn, William, English Quaker and founder of Pennsylvania **P** 127
- American colonies **A** 191–92
- founding of Philadelphia **P** 182
- peace movements **P** 104
- Pennsylvania **P** 144
- proprietor of Delaware **D** 99–100
- Quaker rule of Pennsylvania **Q** 2

Penney, J. C. (James Cash Penney) (1875–1971), American chain store executive, b. Hamilton, Mo. He began as a clerk and later founded a chain of department stores located throughout the United States. He retired as president of the J. C. Penney Co., Inc., in 1947, and became honorary chairman of the board of directors. His Emmandine Farm will be bequeathed to the University of Missouri in 1996.

Pennine Range, England **E** 212; **U** 69

Penn State Commonwealth Campuses **P** 137

Pennsylvania **P** 128–45
- American colonies **A** 191–92
- colonial life in America **C** 385–99
- Founding fathers of the United States **F** 395
- Penn, William **P** 127
- Philadelphia **P** 182–83
- places of interest in Negro history **N** 94
- poverty in Appalachia **P** 424a–424b
- Susquehanna Valley, picture **N** 283

Pennsylvania, University of **P** 137

Pennsylvania Canal **C** 86

Pennsylvania Dutch, German-speaking American colonists **A** 192
- early settlements in Pennsylvania **P** 128
- folk art, pictures **D** 132, **F** 293

Pennsylvania Magazine **M** 14

Pennsylvania State University **P** 137

Pennsylvania Station, New York **U** 123

Pennsylvania system, of punishment **P** 469

Penny Black, first postage stamp **S** 396

Penny papers, newspapers of 19th century **N** 198

Pennyroyal, area of Kentucky **K** 215

Penny system, of nail lengths **N** 2

Penobscot Bay, Maine **M** 36

Pen-pal letters **L** 159–60

Pens **P** 146–47
- drawing materials **D** 303
- ink types **I** 255
- ruling pens in mechanical drawing **M** 197

Pension, a periodic payment of money to people who have retired from work because of age or disability, for past service, labor, or work. Historically it was a gift from a sovereign or king to an individual for distinguished military service. It was also granted as a reward for an outstanding deed or accomplishment (for socially useful discoveries in the fields of science, literature, and the arts). Modern pension plans are used by governments, corporations, and commercial companies.
- old age, assistance plans **O** 98

Pentadactyl (pen-ta-DAC-til) **limb,** basic pattern of vertebrate feet or hands **F** 79–80

Pentagon, The (also called the National Defense Building), five-sided building in Arlington, Va., separated from Washington, D.C., by the Potomac River. It is the headquarters of the United States Department of Defense, housing the main offices of the Army, Navy, and Air Force. Completed in 1943, it has a total of 150 acres of floor space and can accommodate up to 38,000 persons.
- "The Selling of the Pentagon," documentary television program **T** 71

Pentagon Papers, classified government documents on the Vietnam War **N** 262f

Pentateuch (PEN-ta-teuck), first five books of Bible **B** 154
- Books of Moses **M** 468

Pentathlon (pen-TATH-lon), five contests in Olympic Games **O** 106

Pentatonic (pen-ta-TON-ic) **scale,** in music
- ancient music **A** 245
- used in music of Aztecs, Maya, and Incas **L** 74

Pentecost, or Whitsunday, religious holiday **R** 154, 290

Pentecostal (pen-te-COST-al) **Assemblies of God,** largest pentecostal sect in the United States. Members believe that the holy spirit enters the human body, enabling "speech with other tongues," as a manifestation of Divine presence. Sects are sometimes called holy rollers, for members often fall to the ground in an emotional or trancelike state when speaking. The Pentecostal movement began early in the 20th century, spread to Britain in the 1920's, and now has members all over the world.

Peonage, system of obligatory servitude whereby a debtor labors in payment for his debt. It was adapted from the encomienda system (abolished, 18th century) and existed in South and Central America, Mexico, and the United States, where it developed after the abolition of slavery. Peonage is now illegal in American countries, although all traces have not been erased.

Pepin III, the Short (714?–768), Frankish king (751–68). When his father, Charles Martel, died, Pepin assumed the Frankish throne and founded the Carolingian dynasty (751) after deposing Childeric III, the Merovingian king. He assisted Pope Stephen II by defeating King Aistulf of the Lombards and restoring territories, later incorporated into the Papal States, to the pope. He was the father of Charlemagne.

Peppermint, fragrant herb of the mint family grown primarily for the aromatic oil in its leaves and stems. It is used in flavoring chewing gum, candy, and toothpaste; as a drug; and for scenting perfume. The peppermint plant, native to Europe, is cultivated in temperate zones.

Perch, any one of a large group of small, spiny-finned, freshwater fishes found in temperate parts of Europe, Asia, and North America. The front upper fin is stiff, the rear upper fin is soft. The yellow perch is especially abundant in North America and is popular as a game fish. It reaches a length of 15 inches and a weight of about 4 pounds. Picture **F** 209.

Peri (PAY-ri), **Jacopo** (1561–1633), Italian composer, b. Florence. He was a noted singer and musician of Florentine and Ferrara courts. With poet Ottavio Rinuccini (1562–1621), he wrote *Dafne*—the music of which is lost —generally considered to be the first true opera.

Perigueux, France, picture **M** 297

Perihelion (per-i-HE-li-on), point of a planet's orbit closest to the sun **R** 143–44
  Mars **M** 105
  solar system **S** 241

Periodical indexes see Indexes, periodical

Periodicals see Magazines

Periodic table, of chemical elements **E** 156–59
  atomic numbers **A** 484, 486–87
  history of **C** 213
  importance to physics **P** 231
  Mendeleev's contribution to science **S** 74
  valences and similar properties kept together **C** 201–02, 220

Periods, punctuation marks **P** 530–31

Peripatetics (peri-pa-TET-ics), followers of Aristotle's philosophy **A** 397

Perique tobacco T 201

Periscopes, optical instruments **O** 168
  submarines, picture **S** 444
  use by archeologists, picture **A** 365

Perisphere, symbol of New York World's Fair, 1939, picture **F** 17

Perissodactyla (per-is-so-DAC-til-a), order of odd-toed hoofed mammals **H** 207
  horses and their relatives **H** 236
  mammals, orders of **M** 62, 68

Periwigs H 3

Periwinkle, name of both a plant and a mollusk. The plant is an erect or trailing herb or shrub, grown in the Mediterranean region, the Americas, India, and Madagascar. It is a popular garden or windowbox plant, with white, pink, or blue flowers. The mollusk is a snail with a cone-shaped shell. It is found all over the world. Some species are edible. Periwinkle shell, picture **S** 147.

Perjury, a legal term meaning the act of lying under oath. Perjury committed in a court of law is a felony.

Perkin, William Henry, English chemist **D** 369–70
  first synthetic dyes **C** 214

Perkins, Frances (Mrs. Cauldwell Wilson) (1882–1965), American political figure, b. Boston, Mass. She was appointed New York state industrial commissioner (1929–33) and U.S. secretary of labor (1933–45), becoming the first woman cabinet member. She lectured at Cornell University and wrote several books, including *Women as Employers* and *The Roosevelt I Knew*.
  women, role of **W** 213

Perkins, Jacob, American inventor **R** 136

Permafrost, permanently frozen subsoil **P** 363
  Alaska **A** 132
  soils of Canada **C** 56
  Yukon and Northwest Territories, Canada **Y** 363

Permalloy, alloy **M** 29

Permanent Commission on Human Rights, United Nations **S** 200
  Eleanor Roosevelt, chairman **R** 318

Permanent Court of Arbitration, at The Hague **I** 325

Permanent Court of International Justice L 96

Permanent waves, hairdressing **H** 6
  beauty culture **B** 111

Permeability (per-me-a-BIL-ity), of membranes **O** 234–35

Permian period, in geology **F** 384
  reptiles **D** 174; reconstruction showing **D** 176

Permissibles, explosives **E** 392

Pernicious anemia, disease **V** 370d

Perón (pay-RONE), **Juan**, president of Argentina **A** 396
  Fascism **F** 64

Peroration, conclusion of a speech **O** 180

Pérotin (pare-o-TAN), French organist, composer **C** 277

Perpendiculars (per-pen-DIC-u-lars), in geometry **G** 124

Perpetual-motion machine, hypothetical invention **I** 333

Perrault (perr-O), **Charles**, French poet **F** 20
  Cinderella, or the Little Glass Slipper **F** 305–08
  Mother Goose rhymes **N** 402
  place in French literature **F** 438
  "Sleeping Beauty" **F** 27–29

Perrault, Claude, French architect **L** 368

Perrot (perr-O), **Jules**, French ballet dancer **B** 25
  history of the dance **D** 25–26

Perrot (pair-RO), **Nicholas** (1644?–1718), French explorer and fur trader. A Canadian fur trader and among the first Frenchmen to trade with the Indians, he became mediator between the French and Indians and interpreter for the Algonkin Indians. He influenced the western Indian tribes to join a campaign against the Iroquois (1684), and he discovered the Mississippi lead mines and built forts along the banks of the river (1685–96). He was reduced to poverty when his trading privileges were cancelled (1696). Perrot State Park, Wisc., is named for him.

Perry, a fermented pear juice **P** 112

Perry, Matthew C., American naval commander **P** 156; **R** 225
  Commodore Perry opens Japan's door **J** 46

Perry, Oliver Hazard, American naval officer **P** 157; **R** 225
  monument in Ohio **O** 69
  War of 1812 **W** 12

Perse, Saint-John, French novelist **F** 442

Persecution
  early Christians **C** 281, 282
  witches **W** 209

Perseids (PER-se-ids), meteor shower **C** 420

Persephone (per-SEPH-o-ne), Greek goddess **G** 359–60

Persepolis (per-SEP-o-lis), ancient capital of Persia **A** 152
  ancient world, art of **A** 242, 243
  palace, picture **A** 373

Perseus (PERS-eus), hero in Greek mythology **G** 361, 362

Perseus, statue by Bellini **I** 469

Pershing, John J., American general **P** 157

Persia, now Iran **I** 376–77
  Alexander the Great conquers **A** 151–52
  ancient art **A** 242–43
  ancient civilization **A** 226
  architecture **A** 373
  architecture: dome, meaning of **B** 486
  communication system **C** 435
  cuneiform writing **A** 219, 225
  drugs, early use of **D** 322
  pottery **P** 414
  sculpture **S** 93
  Xerxes **X** 339
  Zoroastrianism **Z** 380
  See also Iran

Persian cats C 142; picture **C** 143

Persian Gulf
  Asia's oil resources **A** 450
  extreme temperatures **A** 451

Persian lamb, fur **F** 518; **S** 336

Persian melons M 216, 217

Persian rugs R 354; picture **R** 353

Persian wars (500–449? B.C.), series of Persian attempts to subdue Greece. The wars, sparked by a revolt of Ionian Greeks, who were supported by Athenians and

Eretrians, began when King Darius I of Persia sent a fleet to Greece in angry revenge (492). The fleet, however, was lost in a storm. A second expedition (490) was defeated at Marathon, and the third saw the heroic Greek defense of Thermopylae, the destruction of Athens, and defeat of the Persian fleet at Salamis (479), marking the end of the Persian offensive. Subsequent fighting freed the Ionian Greeks and equalized Persian-Greek power.

Persian wheel, for irrigation **M** 303

Persimmon (per-SIM-mon), group of trees related to the ebony and growing chiefly in the tropics and the subtropics. They are raised for ornament, food, and timber. Two species, the Japanese and the American, are adapted to living in temperate climates. They yield a large orange-yellow berrylike fruit that can be eaten. The fruit is also used for flavoring and for making preserves.

Personality tests **T** 117–18
Personal names see Names
Personal pronouns **P** 90
Personal property
  disposed of by a testament, or will **W** 174
Personification, figure of speech **F** 118–19
Personnel (per-son-NEL) **management**
  sales personnel **S** 117
Perspective, illusion of depth in drawing **P** 158–59
  ancient Greek art **G** 344
  Brunelleschi, Filippo **R** 163
Perspective maps **M** 93
Perspiration, secretion to rid body of heat energy **E** 201
  deodorizers **D** 117
Perth, capital of Western Australia **A** 512, 514
Peru (pe-RU) **P** 160–66
  ancient tapestry weaving **T** 141
  costume dolls, picture **D** 264
  flag **F** 242
  house in the Amazon Basin, picture **H** 172
  Huascarán Valley citrus groves, picture **S** 290
  Latin-American art and architecture **L** 64
  life in Latin America **L** 47–61
  Machu Picchu ruins, picture **A** 354
  national anthem **N** 22
  Peace Corps teacher, picture **P** 103
  Peruvian Girl Scouts, picture **G** 219
  Pizarro, Francisco **P** 266
  railroad pass in the Andes, picture **G** 102
  San Martín, José de, early fighter for freedom **S** 36
Peru Current, or Humbolt Current **P** 162
  climate of South America affected **S** 279
  earth's rotation and ocean currents **E** 16
  marine life enriched by its salts **L** 232
Peru-Chile Trench **O** 30
Pesaro Madonna see Madonna with Saints and Members of the Pesaro Family
Pescadores (pes-ca-DOR-es), or Penghu, islands between China and Taiwan **T** 12–13
Pestalozzi (pes-la-LOTZ-zi), **Johann Heinrich,** Swiss educational reformer **E** 68
  kindergarten and nursery schools **K** 243
Pesticides
  environment, problems of **E** 272e–272f
  Food and Drug Administration (FDA) inspection **F** 351
  household pest control **H** 260–63
  water pollution **W** 59
Pests
  household pests **H** 260–64
  insects harmful to man **I** 282–83

Pétain (pay-TAN), **Henri Philippe** (1856–1951), French general, b. Cauchy-a-la-Tour. After his successful defense of Verdun (1916) during World War I, he was made commander in chief of French armies (1918) and marshal of France (1918). He later served as minister of war (1934) and ambassador to Spain (1939). In World War II he surrendered to Hitler (1940) and was chosen premier of the pro-fascist Vichy government of France (1940–44). He was sentenced to death for high treason, and imprisoned on the Ile d'Yeu (1945). He was not executed but died in prison 6 years later.
  World Wars I and II in France **F** 419; **W** 277, 289

Petals, of flowers **F** 276
Petate (pe-TA-te), straw mat bed **L** 57
Petén (pay-TAIN), region of Guatemala **G** 392
  Maya ceremonial centers **I** 198, 199
Peter I, czar of Russia see Peter the Great
Peter, M. D., Swiss pioneer in chocolate manufacture **C** 274
Peter, Paul, and Mary, American rock music group **R** 262d
Peter, Saint, one of the 12 Apostles **P** 167
  Apostles, The **A** 332–33
  Christianity, history of **C** 279–80
  "rock" of the Roman Catholic Church **R** 287–88
  Vatican City and St. Peter's Church **V** 280–82
Peter I and II, books of Bible, New Testament **B** 162
Peter and the Wolf, musical composition by Sergei Prokofiev **P** 477
Peterborough, New Hampshire
  first tax-supported library in United States **L** 198, 200; **N** 157; picture **L** 199
Peter Grimes, opera by Benjamin Britten **O** 151
Peter Island, one of Virgin Islands, British **C** 118
  See also Virgin Islands, British

Peterkin, Julia Mood (1880–1961), American writer, b. Laurens County, S.C. She wrote short stories and novels about Negro life on southern plantations. Her works include *Scarlet Sister Mary,* which was awarded the Pulitzer prize (1929), *Green Thursday,* and *Black April.*

Peter of Amiens see Peter the Hermit
Peter Pan, fairy tale in play form, by James M. Barrie, excerpt **P** 167–68
  realism dressed in humor and fantasy **D** 298
Peter Rabbit, Tale of, by Beatrix Potter, picture **C** 241
Peters, Karl, German explorer **T** 19
Petersburg, Virginia
  Civil War battle site **C** 326

Petersham, Miska (Petrezselyem Mihaly) (1889–1960), American author and illustrator, b. near Budapest, Hungary. With his author-illustrator wife, **Maud Petersham** (1890–1971), he wrote and illustrated numerous books for children. Their books include *The Rooster Crows,* which was awarded the Caldecott medal (1946), *The Christ Child,* and *American A.B.C.*

Peterson, Donald H., American astronaut **S** 347

Peterson, Esther Eggertsen (1906–   ), American government official, b. Provo, Utah. A zealous advocate of equal opportunity and benefits for women, she served as director of the labor department's women's bureau (1961). She became the federal government's highest-ranking female as assistant secretary of labor (1961) and was later appointed special assistant to President Johnson for consumer affairs (1964–67). Since 1969 she has been legislative representative of the Amalgamated Clothing Workers of America.

Peter's Pence (Anglo-Saxon *Romefeot*, meaning "Rome-fee"), in the Middle Ages, a yearly tax of a penny per householder paid by peoples of several countries to the Catholic Church in Rome. Originating in England (787) under King Offa of Mercia, it spread to northern European countries in the 10th and 11th centuries. It was nullified in England (1534) under Henry VIII and disregarded in Europe after the Reformation. Presently (since 1860) the term refers to voluntary contributions of Roman Catholics sent by bishoprics to Rome, constituting part of the Vatican's income.

Peter the Great, Russian ruler **P** 168; **U** 49, 59
   Hermitage Museum began with his collections **H** 119
   Leningrad founded by **L** 139–40; **M** 467
   westernization of architecture **U** 53

Peter the Hermit (Peter of Amiens) (1050?–1115), French monk, b. Amiens. An avid supporter of Pope Urban II's call (1096) for a crusade, he aroused popular enthusiasm and led a people's crusade to Asia Minor, where it was destroyed by Turks at Nicea (1096). After joining the First Crusade, which beseiged Antioch (1097–98), he tried to desert but was caught and was subsequently present at Jerusalem's capture (1098).
   aided Pope Victor III to launch first Crusade **C** 538; **R** 292

Petioles (PET-i-oles), of leaves **L** 114

Pétion (pay-ti-ON), **Alexandre Sabès** (1770–1818), Haitian general and politician, b. Port-au-Prince. He fought under Toussaint L'Ouverture and André Rigaud in the slave insurrection (1791–97) and under Jean Jacques Dessalines against the French (1802). After Haitian independence was established (1804), he participated with Christophe in the assassination of Dessalines, who had installed himself as a tyrannical emperor. He became president of the southern republic of Haiti (1807) and carried on a struggle against Christophe in the north (1811–18). Although he was well-loved and democratic, his policies left Haiti divided and impoverished.
   history of Haiti **H** 10

Petipa, Marius, French choreographer **B** 25–26
   history of the dance **D** 26
Petit (PET-ti), or trial, **jury** **J** 159
Petitcodiac (pet-ti-KO-di-ak) **River,** Canada
   tidal bore from Bay of Fundy **T** 184, 185
Petition, freedom of see Freedom of petition
Petitioners, British political party **P** 378

Petition of Right, declaration in constitutional law issued by the English parliament and signed by King Charles I on June 7, 1628. It prohibited exaction of royal tribute without parliamentary approval, billeting of soldiers in private homes, arbitrary imprisonment, and use of martial law in peacetime. It was significant for its acknowledgement of the authority of parliament over that of the throne.

Petitions, asking prayers **P** 435
Petra (PE-tra), Jordan, picture **J** 139
Petrarch (PE-trarck), **Francesco,** Italian poet **I** 476
   described his mountain climbing **M** 489
   Renaissance humanism **R** 159, 160
   sonnets **S** 255

Petrel, any one of a number of small ocean birds found throughout the world. In general, the birds are dark above, and white below. They have long, pointed wings and webbed feet.

Petri (PE-tri) **dishes,** for laboratory cultures, picture **A** 311
Petrified Forest National Park, Arizona **A** 414
Petrified wood **F** 380
   evidence of ancient life **E** 342; picture **E** 341

Petrillo, James Caesar (1892–   ), American labor leader, b. Chicago, Ill. A fighter for musicians' unions, he served as president of the Chicago Federation of Musicians (1922–62) and of AFL-CIO American Federation of Musicians (1940–58).

Petrochemicals (pet-ro-KEM-ic-als), chemicals derived from petroleum or natural gas **P** 176–77
   manufactured in Louisiana **L** 356
Petrograd, Russia see Leningrad, Union of Soviet Socialist Republics
Petroleum and petroleum refining **P** 169–78
   Alaska's Arctic Slope **A** 135, 137
   Asia's resources **A** 450
   Canada's oil deposits and production **C** 56
   desert countries, changes in **D** 127
   distillation process **D** 226
   drilling for oil in the Gulf of Mexico, picture **L** 352
   Europe, oil resources of **E** 311, 315
   gasoline a product of **G** 63
   Iraq's oil resources **I** 380–81
   kerosene derived from **K** 235
   Kuwait's oil reserves **K** 305, 306
   leading industry **I** 247
   liquid fuels **F** 488
   lubricating oils **L** 371
   North Sea deposits of oil and natural gas **U** 70
   ocean pollutant **E** 272e; **W** 59; pictures **C** 487, **E** 272d
   offshore oil won by Texas **T** 137
   oil derricks, Alberta, pictures **A** 146b; **C** 53
   oil refineries, pictures **N** 294, **P** 433
   Oklahoma **O** 84
   petroleum gases as fuels **F** 489
   petroleum-producing regions of North America **N** 295
   seismic prospecting with explosives **E** 394
   Texas, leading oil-producing state **T** 126
   underwater oil well drilling **U** 21
   Union of Soviet Socialist Republics **U** 34
   Venezuela **V** 298
   waxes made from **W** 70
   world distribution **W** 261; diagram **W** 263
Petroleum jelly **W** 70
Petroleum prospecting, oil hunting **P** 170–71
Petrology (pe-TROL-ogy), study of rocks **G** 112
Petronius (pe-TRO-nius), Roman writer **L** 80

Petrosian (pet-rose-YON), **Tigran Vartanovich** (1929–), Soviet chess player, b. Armenia. He was the Soviet (1959–69) and world (1963–69) chess champion. He was a member of the Soviet team that won the 16th chess Olympiad in Tel Aviv, Israel (1964).

Petrouchka, ballet **U** 64
   stage setting, picture **U** 57

Petry, Ann Lane (1912–   ), American author of novels and children's books, Negro, b. Old Saybrook, Conn. She worked as a pharmacist, reporter, and newspaper editor before publishing her first novel, *The Street.* Her books are realistic portrayals of Negroes as sensitive individuals rather than stereotypes. Her other works include *The Narrows* and *Harriet Tubman, Conductor on the Underground Railroad.*

Pets P 179–81
  ants keep pets **A** 325
  birds **B** 245–49
  cats, domestic **C** 141–44
  dogs **D** 252–62
  dolphins and porpoises **D** 278
  ducks **P** 423
  farm birds as pets **B** 248
  guinea pigs **G** 407–08
  hamsters **G** 407–08
  how long they live **A** 83
  lizards and chameleons **L** 318–21
  pigeons **P** 180–81
  tropical fish for aquariums **A** 340–43
  zoos **Z** 374–79
  See also Gerbil
Petty Harbor, Newfoundland, picture **N** 144

Petunia, flowering plant related to the tobacco and potato plants. Originally native to the warmer regions of South America, it has become widely cultivated throughout the world. The blossoms are trumpet shaped, ruffled or doubled, and of almost every color. Pictures **G** 28, 38, 48

Peugeot (poo-JO), automobile **A** 545
Peul *see* Fulani, a people of Africa
Pevsner, Antoine (PEF-sner), Russian sculptor **M** 393; **S** 105
  Developable Column, picture **M** 393
Pewees, birds, picture **B** 242
Pew Memorial Trust, foundation **F** 391

Pewter, soft, silvery-gray metal with dull finish, composed chiefly of tin hardened with copper, antimony, bismuth, or lead. Originally made in ancient Rome and medieval Europe, it was widely used for utensils and housewares in the 17th and 18th centuries in England, the Netherlands, and colonial North America.
  antiques and antique collecting **A** 321
  britannia metal, a similar alloy **K** 288
  knives, forks and spoons **K** 288

Peyote (pay-O-te), hallucinogenic drug **D** 331
  peyote cactus **C** 4
P.G.A. *see* Professional Golfers' Association

Phaedra (PHE-dra), in Greek mythology, the daughter of Minos and Pasiphae and sister of Ariadne. She married Theseus and fell in love with his son Hippolytus. Enraged by his adamant rejection of her, she killed herself, falsely accusing Hippolytus of assaulting her. Believing her, Theseus with Poseidon's aid put his son to death.

Phaethon (PHAY-et-on), in Greek mythology, the son of Helios and Clymene. Exacting permission from Helios to drive the sun's chariot across the sky for a day, he found himself unable to control the horses. To prevent him from setting the world ablaze, Zeus killed him with a thunderbolt, and he plunged into the Eridanus (Po) river. His sisters, the Heliades, inconsolable at his death, were transformed into poplars, their tears perpetually turning into amber.

Phagocytes (PHAG-o-cytes), body cells **I** 104
  white blood cells **B** 256–57
Phagocytosis (phag-o-cy-TO-sis), the feeding process of amoebas **M** 277
Phalangers (pha-LAN-gers), marsupials **K** 174–75
Phalanges (pha-LAN-ges), fingers and toes, bones of the hands and feet, diagrams **F** 79, 80
Phalanx (PHAY-lanx), infantry formation
  used by Alexander the Great **A** 151

Phalarope (PHAL-ar-ope), small wading bird 6 to 9 in. long, with long legs and a slender neck. Phalaropes are excellent swimmers, able to twist and spin rapidly and to float in roughest water. After the eggs are laid, the female flies off, leaving the male to sit on the eggs and to care for the young. Depending on the season, these birds are found around the Arctic Ocean or in northwestern United States and southwestern Canada and along the shores of the Americas.

Pharaohs (PHAIR-ohs), rulers of ancient Egypt **A** 222–23
  Passover **P** 93

Pharisees (PHAR-i-sees) (from Hebrew *perushim,* meaning "separatist"), a Jewish sect active around the 1st century A.D. They were strict followers of traditional oral law in addition to Scriptural written law and taught doctrines of resurrection of the body and existence of spirits and angels. Firm Jewish nationalists, they exerted a strong political influence.

Pharmaceutical (phar-ma-CEU-tic-al), a drug **D** 321
Pharmacology (phar-ma-COL-ogy), science of preparation, uses, and effects of drugs **D** 325
  branch of biochemistry **B** 182
Pharmacy, practice of preparing and selling medicines
  drug industry **D** 321
Pharmacopeia (phar-ma-co-PE-ia), list of drugs and drug formulas **D** 322
  drug industry **D** 321–25
  medicinal plants being sold in 17th century pharmacy, picture **M** 206
Pharos (PHAY-ros), lighthouse of Alexandria, Egypt **L** 275
  one of the seven wonders of the ancient world **W** 216; picture **W** 215
Phascogales (phas-COG-a-lese), marsupials **K** 173
Phase-contrast microscopes M 283
Phases, of celestial bodies
  moon **M** 447
  planets **P** 271
Pheasant, game bird
  ring-necked, state bird of South Dakota **S** 313
Phèdre (PHED-ra), play by Racine **D** 296

Phelps-Stokes Fund, Trustees of the, foundation interested in improving race relations and low-income housing in New York, N.Y. Its research and activities are designed to foster better race relations of North American Indians and of Negroes in the United States and Africa. Incorporated in 1911, it has headquarters in New York, N.Y.

Phenol-formaldehyde (PHE-nol-for-MAL-de-hyde), a plastic **P** 324
Phenolic (phe-NO-lic) **resins**
  varnishes made from **V** 279
Phenylketonuria *see* PKU
Phi Beta Kappa, honor society **V** 352

Phibunsongkhram (te-BOON-sung-kram), **Plaek,** or **Pibul Songgram, Luang** (1897–1964), Thai army officer and politician, b. Bangkok. A participant in a successful bloodless coup to curtail royal power (1932), he became minister of defense (1934). As prime minister (1938–44, 1948, 1950–57), he established an excessively nationalistic military regime, uniting with Japan during World War II. He received political asylum in Cambodia after he finally was ousted by military coup (1957).

Phidias (PHID-i-as), Greek sculptor **G** 345–46
  statue of Zeus **W** 214; picture **W** 215
  things of beauty **A** 228

Philadelphia, (phil-a-DEL-phia), now Amman, Jordan
J 138
Philadelphia, Pennsylvania P 182–83
  Betsy Ross House F 248
  City Hall, picture P 140
  Franklin and the Library Company F 453; L 198
  Independence Hall I 113
  Liberty Bell L 169
  Revolutionary War battle R 203
  signing of Declaration of Independence D 59–61
Philadelphia Light Horse flag, 1775 F 229
Philadelphia Orchestra, pictures O 182, 187
  seating diagram O 186
Philately see Stamps and stamp collecting
Philemon (phil-E-mon), book of Bible, New Testament
  B 161

Philemon (phil-E-mon) and Baucis (BAU-cis), in Greek mythology, an aged couple of Phrygia. Despite their poverty, they offered hospitality to Zeus and Hermes, who, traveling through the country as humans, had been turned away at all other homes. The gods spared them from a deluge that covered the district, transformed their cottage into a temple, and made them priest and priestess. They desired to die together and so were turned into trees at the same moment.

Philharmonic Hall, Lincoln Center for the Performing Arts L 298
Philip II, king of France (Philip Augustus) M 291

Philip IV ("the Fair") (1268–1314), king of France (1285–1314) and son of Philip III, b. Fontainebleau. His dispute with Pope Boniface VIII resulted in the papal bulls Clericis laicos (1296), prohibiting taxation of clergy, and Unam Sanctam (1302), declaring the supremacy of papal authority. He secured election of Pope Clement V, who ruled from Avignon (1305–14). Philip's reign also was marked by centralized administration, curtailment of feudal rights, and persecution of Jews.
  Roman Catholic Church in the Middle Ages M 291;
  R 293

Philip VI, king of France H 281

Philip II (382–336 B.C.), king of Macedon and Greek military commander. After becoming king (359 B.C.), he began invading the borderlands owned by Greek city states. The speeches of Demosthenes, warning Athens against him, were called Philippics—a word still used. By 338 B.C. he had conquered and unified Greece. He was chosen to lead Greek armies against Persia but was murdered before starting. He was succeeded by his son Alexander the Great.
  Philip's pride in Alexander's horsemanship A 151

Philip II, king of Spain E 178–79
  attitude toward the Church R 294
  England and Elizabeth I E 221–22
  establishes court at Madrid M 13

Philip, or Metacomet (?–1676), American Indian chief, son of Massasoit. Called King Philip by the English, he was made chief of the Wampanoags in 1662, and he maintained peaceful relations, despite loss of tribal lands, until charged with conspiracy against the colonists (1671). After the execution of three Wampanoag warriors for slaying an Indian informer, Philip led a violent revolt, known as King Philip's War (1675–76), resulting in the death of thousands of New England colonists and Indians and culminating in his own death.
  Indian wars in Massachusetts I 212; M 149

Philip, prince of the United Kingdom of Great Britain and Northern Ireland, duke of Edinburgh E 179
Philip of Bethsaida, Saint, one of the Twelve Apostles A 333
Philippeville, now Skida, Algeria A 163
Philippians (phil-IP-pi-ans), book of Bible B 161
Philippics (phil-IP-pics), forceful speeches, origin of the term O 180
Philippine mahogany, or lauan, tree
  uses of the wood and its grain, picture W 223
Philippines P 184–90
  abaca prepared for making rope, picture R 332
  American occupation T 114
  dance D 32
  fishing, picture A 301
  flag F 238
  folk dancers, picture F 297
  MacArthur, Douglas M 2
  Manila M 75
  McKinley accepts for the United States M 189
  Mindayan hat, picture H 53
  "miracle rice" F 343
  Moro women weaving mats, picture A 463
  Peace Corps members, picture P 101
  problem of lack of common language E 84
  Quezon, Manuel Q 18
  Spanish-American War S 375
  stilt houses, picture A 303
  Taft, William Howard, governor T 7
  World War II W 293, 304–05
Philippine Sea O 48
Philip the Good, Duke of Burgundy D 363

Philistines (phil-IST-ines), people who came probably from Crete to invade and colonize Canaan on the coast of Palestine in the 12th century B.C. They pushed the Israelites inland and continued warring with them for centuries. Wars reached a peak in the time of Saul, Samson, and David. The Old Testament tale of David and Goliath, a Philistine, dates from this period. They were weakened by David's conquests but not subdued until the 8th century B.C. Their most important cities were Gaza, Ascalon, Ashdod, Gath, and Ekron.
  David and the Philistines D 44; J 103

Phillips, Channing (1928–), American minister and civil rights leader, b. New York, N.Y. He was the first Negro nominated for president by a major political party (1968). Delegation leader from the District of Columbia, he received 67½ votes at the Democratic convention.

Phillips, Wendell, American abolitionist N 94
Phillips Exeter Academy, New Hampshire N 157
Phillips-head screws N 3; picture N 2
  Phillips-head screwdriver, picture T 215
Philo (PHY-lo) Judaeus, Jewish historian D 48
  Jewish concepts fitted into Hellenic (Greek) culture
  J 107
Philosopher's (phil-OS-oph-er's) stone, mythical substance sought by alchemists C 207–08
Philosophy P 191–92
  ancient Greek philosophers A 230
  Aristotle A 396–97
  Chinese literature O 220a
  Confucius C 460
  Descartes, René D 123
  Dewey, John D 151
  education, ideals and aims E 75–76
  Greek literature G 353–55
  Indian literature O 220d–220e
  Kant, Immanuel K 192
  Locke's empiricism L 321

Mill's utilitarian view of human rights **C** 314
Philo Judaeus **D** 48; **J** 107
Plato **P** 332
popular American literature **A** 215
science began with meeting of theory and experiment
S 60
Socrates **S** 228
Spinoza, Baruch **S** 390
Phloem (PHLO-em), plant tissue **P** 293
Phlogiston (phlo-GIST-on), **theory of C** 210
history of science, theories in chemistry **S** 72
Lavoisier's studies **C** 210, 212
Phlox, flowers **G** 46; pictures **G** 28, 50, **W** 169
Phobos (PHO-bos), satellite of Mars **M** 107, 108; **P** 272
named for servant of the god of war **M** 104

Phoebe (PHE-be), in Greek mythology, a Titaness, wife of
Coeus and grandmother of Artemis, goddess of the hunt,
with whom Phoebe is often erroneously identified. In
later writings she is identified with the moon goddess.

Phoebe, satellite of Saturn **P** 276
Phoebes, birds **B** 220; picture **B** 235
banded by Audubon **B** 229
See also Flycatchers
Phoebus Apollo, Greek god **G** 360
Phoenicians (phe-NISH-ans), early people of the eastern
Mediterranean coast
alphabet **A** 170–73; **C** 431
earliest known people in Lebanon **L** 121
sailors and traders **S** 155; **T** 260–61
settlements in Africa **A** 66, 163
Phoenix (PHE-nix), capital of Arizona **A** 411
state fair, picture **C** 121

Phoenix, legendary bird of ancient Egypt, symbol of the
rising and setting sun. A splendid red and gold bird,
it burned itself to death in a pyre of spices after living
about 500 years. It rose, reborn from the ashes, and
flew from its native Arabia to the temple of the sun in
Heliopolis, Egypt. For many religions the phoenix symbolizes rebirth.

Phoenix Islands, a group of eight sparsely populated
coral atolls in the Pacific Ocean south of the equator.
All except Canton and Enderbury belong to the British
Gilbert and Ellice Islands. Canton and Enderbury are
governed jointly by United Kingdom and United States.

Pholidota, order of mammals **M** 61, 62, 69
Phonemes, speech sounds **L** 301
Phonemic (pho-NE-mics) **transcription**, in languages
L 301
Phonics (PHON-ics) **P** 193–96
clues for spelling **S** 378
Japanese phonetic writing **J** 28
phonetics, a branch of linguistics **L** 302
phonetic writing **W** 318
pronunciation **P** 478
reading **R** 108
Phonograms, sets of letters with same pronunciation in
words **P** 194
Phonograph P 196–98
advantages of tape over records **T** 21
communication advanced by **C** 434
Edison, inventor of **E** 59–60
hi-fi and stereo recording **H** 125–27
records and record collecting **R** 123–25
talking books for the blind **B** 252–53
Phonograph records see Records, phonograph
Phonography (pho-NOG-raphy), a kind of shorthand **S** 164
Phony War, 1939–40 **W** 288

Phosphate (PHOS-phate) **rock**
deposits in North America **N** 295
Florida **F** 266
Nauru **N** 61
Phosphates, chemical compounds
detergents, environmental problems **D** 149; **E** 272e
fertilizers **F** 96, 97
water pollution **W** 59
Phosphor bronze, alloy **B** 409
Phosphorescent (phos-phor-ES-cent) **paints P** 34
Phosphors, television **T** 68, 69
Phosphorus, element **E** 155, 163
atomic symbol, picture **D** 15
first element known to be discovered by a particular
man at a particular time **C** 212
tapers, or candles **M** 152

Phosphorus, in Greek mythology, the morning star. The
son of Eos, the goddess of dawn, and Astraeus, he is
often represented as a youth holding a torch. The
morning star is the single bright star in the dawn sky.

Photocells see Photoelectric cells
Photochemical smog E 272g
Photocomposition, in printing **P** 465
Photoconductive cells P 200
Photocopying machines L 174–75, 177
office duplicators **O** 58; picture **O** 56
Photoelectric cells, or photocells **P** 199–200
electron tubes **E** 148
cameras with an electric eye **P** 215; picture
P 202
movie cameras with an electric eye **P** 219
principle of ionization, basis for **I** 350
quantum theory explains **L** 274
Photoelectricity P 199–200
electricity from solar energy **S** 238
Photoelectric tubes see Phototubes
Photoengraving P 458–59
Photo-finish, of a horse race **H** 233
Photoflood lamps, in photography **P** 217
Photogrammetry (pho-to-GRAM-metry), science of measuring by photography **O** 171–72
Photographic (pho-to-GRAPH-ic) **paper P** 201
Photography (pho-TOG-raphy) **P** 201–13
animated cartoons **A** 299
camera hunting **H** 290
camera telescopes **T** 63
commercial art **C** 425
communication advanced by **C** 434
cosmic rays recorded by **C** 512
Daguerre, Louis **D** 2
Eastman, George **E** 44
filming motion pictures **M** 481–82
hobby combined with airplane models **A** 106
hobby photography **P** 214–18
modeling, fashion **M** 384–85
newspapers, important part of **N** 202
observatories, use in **O** 12–13
photocopying machines in libraries and offices
L 174–75, 177; **O** 58
photoengraving **P** 458–59
photogrammetry **O** 171–72
photolithography, or planographic printing **L** 315
photomicrography **P** 205; picture **P** 204
processing color prints, picture **N** 222
Pulitzer prize for news photography **P** 524
separations of color for book illustrations **B** 330
silver compounds **S** 182
Why do motion pictures seem to have motion? **M** 472
See also Blueprints
Photography as a hobby P 214–18

Photolithography (pho-to-lith-OG-raphy), or planographic printing **L** 315

Photometers (pho-TOM-et-ers), instruments for measuring light **O** 12

Photomicrography (pho-to-my-CROG-raphy), photography of microscopic objects **P** 205; picture **P** 204

Photomultipliers, astronomy **O** 11

Photons (PHO-tons), subatomic particles **A** 486
nuclear energy **N** 367
radiant energy **P** 236

Photoperiodism (pho-to-PER-i-od-ism) **P** 295
timing of migration **H** 191–92

Photosphere, of the sun **S** 458
earth and its sun **E** 22

Photosynthesis (pho-to-SIN-the-sis) **P** 221–23
a life process **E** 272a, 272f; **L** 212–13
aquariums benefit by **A** 341
ATP (adenosine triphosphate) **B** 296–97; **P** 222
biochemical research **B** 184
cell building **C** 162–63
energy and life **E** 202–03
energy cycle in body chemistry **B** 296
how sun's energy is used by living things **K** 252–53
leaves, food factories **L** 119; **T** 281–82
life, food chains in **L** 239
oxygen supply renewed by **O** 269
plants, food-producing process for **P** 293–94

Phototropism (pho-TOT-ro-pism), of plants **P** 301
experiment and demonstration **E** 357

Phototubes, a kind of photoelectric cell **P** 200
electron tubes **E** 148

Phrenology, study of the skull shape as indicating mental abilities and character traits. The theory that each bump on the skull indicates a special ability or characteristic was advanced by Franz Gall and Johann Spurzheim about 1810. Although rejected by many scientists the theory became popular in the 19th century, but was largely discredited by the early 1900's.

Phrygia (PHRIJ-ia), ancient country in central Asia Minor (now Turkey) inhabited by Indo-European-speaking people who crossed the Dardanelles from Europe in the 13th century B.C. Conquered by Lydians in the 7th century B.C., they were subsequently ruled by Persia, Greece, and Rome. Phrygian legend and religion greatly influenced Greek mythology. Gordius and Midas were legendary Phrygian kings.

Phrygian cap see Liberty cap

Phrygian mode, seven-note musical scale **A** 247

Phunchhholing, Bhutan **B** 150; picture **B** 151

Phyfe, Duncan, Scotch-born American cabinetmaker **F** 509

Phyla (PHY-la), divisions within the kingdoms of living things **K** 251
taxonomy and biological classification **T** 29

Phylloxera (phil-LOX-er-a), insect, harmful to grapes **G** 297

Physical chemistry **C** 214–16
chemistry overlaps other sciences **C** 205
physics and other sciences **P** 238

Physical dependence, on narcotics **N** 13, 14

Physical education **P** 224–29
gymnastics **G** 428–32
judo **J** 146–47
playground programs **P** 78
running and chasing games **G** 20–22
school "gym" class, picture **H** 83
softball **S** 229
swimming **S** 491–92
See also Games; Sports

Physical examination, by a doctor **M** 208e–208h

Physical features, in geography
names of people derived from **N** 4
See also facts and figures and landform sections of country, province, and state articles

Physical fitness see Physical education

Physical handicaps **H** 27–30

Physical oceanography **O** 31–33
geology and other earth sciences **G** 109

Physical patterns, in geography **G** 99

Physical therapy, or physiotherapy, a form of medical treatment. Physical therapy is employed in the treatment of pain, injury, and certain diseases. It uses physical agents, such as massage, exercise, heat, water, manipulation, and electricity, instead of drugs. It is used extensively in hospitals and rehabilitative institutions.

Physical traits, of people **A** 306–07

Physicians see Doctors

Physics **P** 230–39
atoms **A** 483–89
chemistry and physics compared **C** 196
crystals and crystallography **C** 541–46
Curie, Marie and Pierre **C** 552–53
electricity **E** 123–35
energy **E** 198–203
experiments and projects in physics and chemistry **E** 362–67
Galileo's findings on laws of motion **G** 5
gases **G** 57–59
geophysics **G** 118–21
gravity and gravitation **G** 320–25
heat **H** 86d–95
ions and ionization **I** 350–55
light **L** 260–74
liquids **L** 309–10
magnets and magnetism **M** 24–30
matter, physical changes in **M** 177–78
Newton's laws of motion **M** 469–71
Nobel prizes **N** 268, 268a
physical chemistry **C** 214
radioactive elements **R** 67–68
relativity **R** 139–44
sound and ultrasonics **S** 256–67
See also Nuclear physics

Physiognomy (phys-i-OG-nomy), theory that temperament and character can be judged by outward appearance, particularly facial features. Johann Kaspar Lavater (1741–1801) stimulated European interest in the theory. Criminologist Cesare Lombroso (1836–1909) tried to connect criminal behavior with physical traits. Some physiognomists claim ability to foretell the future from facial structure. The word "physiognomy" also refers to the characteristic expression of the face.

Physiological chemistry see Body chemistry

Physiology (phis-i-OL-ogy), science of the functions of living organisms
body, human **B** 267–83
biochemistry **B** 181–84
body chemistry **B** 289–98
body's senses **B** 283–88
cell and its functions **C** 159–64
child development **C** 231–34
founding of **B** 188, 190
health **H** 82–85
life functions common to all kingdoms of living things **K** 252
Nobel prizes **N** 264–66
nutrition **N** 415–19

reproduction **R** 176–80
sleep and dreaming **D** 305–07; **S** 200–01
voice, apparatus of **V** 375–76
Physiotherapy see Physical therapy
Pi (PY), geometric ratio **G** 127; **M** 154

Piaget (p'ya-JAY), **Jean** (1896–   ), Swiss psychologist, b. Neuchâtel. Widely acclaimed as a leading authority on the thoughts and actions of young children, he is co-director of the Institut J. J. Rousseau in Geneva and professor of psychology at the universities of Geneva and Paris. Among the more than 20 books he has written, many of which have been translated into English and other languages, are *The Language and Thought of the Child* and *Judgment and Reasoning in the Child*.
child development, studies in **C** 234

Piano **P** 240–42
classical age in music **C** 331
Italy develops **I** 484
keyboard instruments **K** 239
Liszt's mastery of **L** 312
orchestra seating plan **O** 186
ragtime **J** 57
recordings **R** 123
romantic age in music **R** 311
Schumann's music **G** 186; **S** 59
types of musical instruments **M** 546
Piano accordion **F** 330
Pianola (pi-an-O-la), or player piano, musical instrument
recordings **R** 123
Piano music
romantic age in music **R** 311
Schumann's suites **G** 186; **S** 59
Piano rolls, recordings **R** 123

Piatigorsky (pi-at-i-GOR-ski), **Gregor** (1903–   ), Russian-born American cellist, b. Yekaterinoslav (now Dnepropetrovsk). First cellist in the Berlin Philharmonic orchestra (1923–28), he has appeared throughout Europe and the Americas in concert and chamber music performances, gaining wide acclaim for his virtuosity.

Piazza di Spagna (pi-YA-tza di SPON-ya), Rome, Italy, picture **R** 312
Piazza Minerva, Rome, Italy **R** 313
Piazza Venezia (ven-AETZ-ia), Rome, Italy **R** 317; picture **R** 316
Piazzi (pi-YA-tzi), **Giuseppe**, Italian astronomer **P** 273
solar system, studies of **S** 243
Pica (PY-ca), a size of type **T** 344
Picadors (PIC-a-dors), in bullfighting **B** 449–51
Picaresque (pic-a-RESK), or rogue, **novels** **N** 346–47
Henry Fielding's *Tom Jones* **E** 260
Spanish literature **S** 369
Picasso (pi-CA-so), **Pablo**, Spanish-born painter of the French school **P** 243
African art influenced **A** 70–71
art of the artist **A** 438g
Demoiselles d'Avignon, Les, painting, **M** 390
drawing, *Deux Pigeons* **D** 304
Girl with a Mandolin, picture **D** 136
Green Still Life, painting **P** 31
Guernica, painting **D** 142
Head of a Woman, sculpture **S** 104
modern art **M** 390
modern Spanish art **S** 365
painting in the 20th century **P** 29–30
Picasso museum in Barcelona, Spain **M** 520
sculpture **S** 104
sculpture in Chicago's Civic Center, picture **C** 229
Still Life, painting **F** 430

use of color **D** 143
worked with Braque **B** 371
Piccadilly Circus, London, England **L** 336–37
Piccard (pi-CAR), **Auguste**, Swiss scientist, inventor, and explorer **P** 244
balloon ascents **B** 32; picture **B** 34
bathyscaphe, for deep-sea study **D** 82; **U** 16–17
oceanography studies **O** 44
Piccard, Jacques, Swiss scientist **P** 244
record descent in bathyscaphe **D** 82
Piccolo, musical instrument **M** 547
Pic du Midi Observatory, France **O** 9
Pick, used in playing a guitar **G** 409
Pick a card, trick **T** 288
Pickerel, fish, picture **F** 209
habitat, feeding habits, uses **F** 216
Picketing, labor union tactic **L** 18; picture **L** 13

Pickett, George Edward (1825–1875), American army officer, b. Richmond, Va. After serving in the Mexican War and in Texas (1849–56), he served on the Northwest frontier (1856–61). Resigning from the Federal Army (1861), he joined the Confederate forces and later was appointed major general in charge of a Virginia division (1862). He led the heroic but futile "Pickett's charge" at Gettysburg against Union forces (1863) and made a valiant stand at Five Forks, Virginia (1865).

Pickford, Mary (Gladys Marie Smith) (1894–   ), American actress and producer, b. Toronto, Canada. Called America's Sweetheart, she made her stage debut at the age of 5 and gained her greatest popularity as a star of silent films, including *Pollyanna*, *Rebecca of Sunny Brook Farm*, and *Poor Little Rich Girl*. She helped found United Artists Corporation (1919). Her books include *My Rendezvous with Life*. Picture **M** 474.
motion pictures, history of **M** 473

Pick guitar **G** 409
Pickling, of food **F** 348
olives **O** 102
Pickling bottle, tool of the marine biologist **O** 36
Pickwick Papers, book by Charles Dickens **D** 158
Picnics **O** 248
ways to avoid food spoilage, picture **F** 353
Pico Turquino (PI-co tur-KI-no), highest peak in Cuba **C** 548
Pictographs **G** 312–13
Picts, early people of Scotland **S** 87
beginnings of English history **E** 215
Picture books **C** 242–43
children's literature, early development of **C** 236, 239
list **C** 245, 247
Picturephone see Video Telephone
Picture tube, of a television set see Cathode-ray tube
Picture writing
alphabet **A** 170
communication method of early man **C** 430–31
development of languages **L** 38
See also individual letters of the alphabet
Piebald, horse marking, picture **H** 238

Pieces of eight, Spanish coins used in the 17th and 18th centuries and circulated in the American colonies, West Indies, and Europe. The coins, made of silver, were stamped with an 8 and valued at 8 *reales* (Spanish monetary unit). The coin is frequently mentioned in pirate stories, such as *Treasure Island*. Picture **M** 410.

Pie charts, or circle graphs **G** 313
Piedmont (PEED-mont) **Region**, eastern United States **N** 285

Piedmont Region (continued)
  farmlands, picture **V** 349
  meaning of the name **G** 134
Pied, or jumbled, **type N** 203

Pied Piper of Hamelin, in German legend, magician who agreed to rid the rat-infested village of Hamelin of its vermin in return for a certain amount of money. Playing his magical pipe, he lured the rats away and into the Weser River, where they drowned. The townspeople, however, would not pay him, so the Pied Piper took up his pipe and enchanted all the children, who followed him and disappeared into Koppenberg hill. Browning's poem "The Pied Piper of Hamelin" tells this story.

Pied Piper of Hamelin, The, poem by Robert Browning, excerpt **B** 413–14
Piepowder Courts, England **F** 10
Pierce, Franklin, 14th President of United States **P** 245–50
  Franklin Pierce Homestead State Historic Site **N** 158
  Hawthorne and Pierce **H** 73
Pierce, Jane Means Appleton, wife of Franklin Pierce **F** 170; **P** 246, 247; picture **F** 171

Pierian (py-ER-ian) **spring,** sacred spring located in the ancient region of Macedonia called Pieria, where the Muses were first worshiped. The spring was believed to be the source of poetic inspiration.

Pierre (PEER), capital of South Dakota **S** 324; picture **S** 325

Pierrot, a character in French pantomime. He is usually dressed as a clown, his face is painted white, and he usually wears a white blouse and pantaloons.

Piers Plowman, English poem **E** 248
Pietà (pi-ae-TA), sculpture by Michelangelo **M** 257
  exhibited at New York World's Fair, 1964–65 **F** 17
Piezoelectricity (py-e-zo-e-lec-TRIS-ity), of quartz crystals **Q** 6
  Curie's research **C** 552
Pigalle (pi-GOLL), **Jean Baptiste,** French sculptor **S** 101
Pigeons, birds **B** 212
  carrier pigeon **C** 435
  carriers of ornithosis, disease **I** 286
  city birds **B** 219
  homing pigeon, picture **H** 193
  learning experiment, picture **L** 103
  passenger pigeons, now extinct **K** 216–17
  patiently pecking pellets **P** 497
  pets **B** 247–48; **P** 180–81
  rock doves **B** 219
  skeleton and interior organs, diagrams **B** 201, 202
  training test, picture **A** 283
  See also Doves
Piggyback, freight hauling service **T** 266; picture **T** 259
  railroads **R** 83
Pig iron I 397
Pig Latin, secret language **C** 371
Pigments see Paints and pigments
Pigmies see Pygmies
Pignotti (pene-YOT-ti), **Lorenzo,** Italian fabulist **F** 4
Pigott diamond, history of D 156
Pigs P 248–49
  hoofed mammals **H** 208–09
  livestock **C** 151
  pig family, pictures **H** 212
  pigskin leather **L** 107
  raising pigs for market **M** 191
  world distribution, diagram **W** 265

Pigs, Bay of, Cuban-invasion disaster **K** 210
Pigskin leather L 107
Pigweed W 106
Pikas, animals of rabbit family **R** 24
  store hay **M** 66
Pike, Albert, American teacher and Indian commissioner **A** 431
Pike, fish **F** 188; pictures **F** 210
  habitat, feeding habits, uses **F** 216
  teeth, picture **F** 187

Pike, Zebulon Montgomery (1779–1813), American soldier, explorer, and discoverer of Pikes Peak in Colorado, b. Lamberton (now a part of Trenton), N.J. At the age of 20 he was commissioned a lieutenant in the U.S. Army. In 1805 he led an expedition to trace the upper course of the Mississippi River. Later, on an expedition to explore the headwaters of the Red and Arkansas rivers and scout Spanish settlements in New Mexico, he discovered Pikes Peak, named in his honor. During the War of 1812 he was promoted to brigadier general. He was killed by a powder-magazine explosion during an attack against the British in Canada.
  exploration of the West **C** 415; **M** 336; **O** 257

Pikes Peak, Colorado **C** 402
  atmospheric pressure, effect of, on boiling point of a liquid **H** 93
  inspired the writing of "America the Beautiful" **N** 25
Pilar, Paraguay **P** 65
Pilasters (PY-las-ters), in architecture **B** 490
Pilate, Pontius, Roman governor of Judea
  Jesus Christ condemned by **J** 84
Pile, of rugs and carpets **R** 351
Pileated woodpeckers, birds
  bill, picture **B** 223
Pile drivers B 448
  bridge construction **B** 401
Piles, of wood **W** 226
Pile weave, of fabrics **T** 144
Pilgrimages
  Chaucer's *Canterbury Tales* **C** 190; **E** 249; picture **E** 248
  Crusades **C** 538–40
  holy places of Hindus **H** 132; picture **H** 128
  Muslims to Mecca **M** 196; **S** 48; picture **S** 44
  ocean liner transport **O** 22
Pilgrim Pope, Paul VI **P** 99
Pilgrims, Separatists from the Church of England **P** 343–46
  American literature **A** 195
  colonial life in America **C** 385–95
  corn, staple food **C** 506
  founders of Plymouth colony **A** 185–87
  Mayflower **M** 184–85
  Mayflower Compact, text **P** 344
  Thanksgiving Day **T** 152–54
Pilgrim's Progress, by John Bunyan **E** 256
  development of the novel **F** 111
Pilion see Pelion
Pillars, in architecture see Columns

Pillars of Hercules, two promontories, or land projections, at the eastern end of the Strait of Gibraltar leading into the Mediterranean. One is the Rock of Gibraltar in Spain, and the other Mount Acho in Africa. They were called Calpe and Abyla, respectively, in ancient times, and various legends offer explanations of their origin. One relates that the two masses were part of one mountain until Hercules broke through to get to the Mediterranean.
  Gibralter **G** 205

Pillboxes, fortifications F 377

Pillory *see* Stocks and pillory

Pilon (pi-LON), **Germain,** French sculptor F 422

Pilotage, airplane navigation A 560

Pilot fishes F 203–04

Pilots, airplane A 559–60

career, requirements for A 566

How do glider pilots get back from their flights? G 239

Pilot snakes *see* Copperheads

Pilot whales, blackfish or potheads W 147; picture
W 148

Pilsen, Bohemia *see* Plzen

Pilsudski (pil-SOOT-ski), **Józef,** Polish statesman P 362

Pima cotton C 524

Pima (PE-ma), Indians of North America A 416; I 189,
190

Pimento, or **pimiento,** the fruit of the Spanish paprika,
a thick-fleshed, sweet red pepper. Pimento is used as
an ingredient in certain dishes, and as a garnish.

Pi mesons, or **pions,** subatomic particles N 368

Pimples D 190

Pinafore (*H.M.S. Pinafore*), operetta by Gilbert and
Sullivan G 210

Pinar del Río, Cuba C 549

Piñata (pin-YA-ta), Latin-American Christmas custom
C 292; picture C 293

Christmas song F 325

street party, picture L 54

Pincers, or claws, of animals
crustacea S 170

Pinchback, Pickney Benton Stewart (1837–1921), American politician, Negro, b. Macon, Ga. He enlisted in the
Union Army when Civil War broke out and organized a
company of Negro volunteers. He entered Louisiana
politics after the war, attending the constitutional
convention (1868) and serving as lieutenant governor
(1871) and acting governor (1872–73). Although elected
to U.S. House of Representatives (1872) and Senate
(1873), he was denied seating in both houses.

Pinchbeck, gold substitute J 92

Pinchot (PIN-cho), **Gifford,** American conservationist
N 34

conservation programs, history of C 485

conservation program with Theodore Roosevelt R 329

controversy with Taft T 8

Pinckney, Charles, American statesman S 308

Pinckney, Charles Cotesworth, American statesman
S 308

Pinckney, Elizabeth Lucas, West Indies-born American
who initiated indigo culture S 308

Pinckney, Thomas, American statesman S 308

Pincushion cacti C 4

Pincushion moss, picture F 94

Pindar, Greek poet G 350

odes, form of lyric poetry O 52

Pindaric odes O 52

Pindling, Lynden Oscar (1930–   ), prime minister of the
Bahamas, Negro, b. Nassau, Bahamas. Educated in the
Bahamas and at the University of London, he received his
law degree in England (1952). Returning to the Bahamas,
he established the Progressive Liberal Party to give
black Bahamians a voice in the economic and political
life of the country. He led the fight for more democratic
election laws and was elected prime minister (1969).

Pine, tree

bristlecone pine, oldest living thing P 317; T 274

conifer forests F 371, 373

eastern white pine, state tree of Maine, Michigan
M 32, 259

leaves, needlelike, picture L 119

Minnesota, state tree of M 323

North Carolina, state tree of N 307

piñon pine, state tree of Nevada and New Mexico
N 123, 180

ponderosa pine, state tree of Montana M 428

shortleaf, state tree of Arkansas, picture A 418

softwoods W 225

turpentine, extracted from T 330

uses of the wood (white and yellow) and its grain, picture W 224

western white pine, state tree of Idaho I 54

wood pulp for paper P 51–52

Pineapple P 249–50

cultivation in South Africa, picture A 98

important crop to Hawaii H 63–64; picture H 62

Pine Barrens, New Jersey N 168

Pine Bluff, Arkansas A 430

Pinel, Philippe, French doctor M 206

Pinero (pi-NE-ro), **Arthur Wing,** English dramatist D 298

Pines and Rocks, painting by Cézanne F 429

Pine Tree flags F 244; pictures F 229

Pine tree shillings, coins M 338

Pine Tree State, Maine M 32

Ping-Pong *see* Table tennis

Pinhole camera E 364

Pinkerton, Allan (1819–84), American detective, b. Glasgow, Scotland. He emigrated to the United States (1842).
In Chicago, Ill., he set up (1850) his own detective agency
(Pinkerton Agency), the first in the United States. He became nationally known when he solved the Adams Express robberies and, during the Civil War, planned
President Lincoln's route to his inauguration (1861). He
organized secret service and counterespionage activities
in Washington, D.C. (1861–62).

Pin money N 88

origin of expression N 209

Pinnate veins, of trees T 282

Pinnipeds, or fin-footed mammals
walruses, sea lions, and seals W 5–7

Pin oak, tree
leaves, shapes of, pictures L 116

Pinocchio (pi-NO-kee-o), a puppet who becomes a living
boy in *The Adventures of Pinocchio,* by Carlo Collodi.
First published as a story in a children's magazine and
then as a book (1883), it has been translated into many
languages. Walt Disney made a motion picture of the
story in 1939.

cover of an Italian edition of the book, showing Pinocchio, picture I 480

Pinocytosis (pin-o-cy-TO-sis), of animal cells C 163

Piñon (PIN-yon), pine tree

Piñon Area Indians of North America I 172–74

state tree of Nevada N 123

state tree of New Mexico N 180

Pins N 88

ancient Greek safety pin, picture A 348

jewelry J 99; picture J 98

Pinschers (PIN-shers), dogs, pictures D 255, 256

Pint, measure of volume W 111, 115

Pinta, ship of Christopher Columbus C 417; E 376;
picture E 374

Pinto, horse marking, picture H 238

Pin tumbler cylinder locks L 324–25

Pinworms, infections caused by D 203

Pinza (PEEN-za), **Ezio** (1892–1957), **American opera singer,** b. Rome, Italy. He was a member of the Metropolitan Opera Company (1926–48), especially well known for singing *Don Giovanni* and *Boris Godunov*. He later had notable roles in *South Pacific* and *Fanny*.

Pinzón (peen-THONE) **family,** three Spanish brothers who accompanied Columbus on his first voyage (1492), b. Palos de la Frontera. **Francisco Martín** (1440?–93?) piloted the *Pinta*, and **Martín Alonso** (1440?–93) commanded it. The third brother, **Vicente Yáñez** (1460?–1524?), commanded the *Niña*. Martín parted from the other ships in November, 1492, and sighted Haiti. Vincente discovered mouth of the Amazon (1500) and explored (with Juan Diaz de Solís) the coast of Yucután (1506).

Pioneer Day, Mormon holiday **S** 22
Pioneer life **C** 399; **P** 251–62
  blab schools **A** 121
  Boone, Daniel **B** 335
  Bowie knife, origin of **B** 344
  Buffalo Bill **B** 428
  Carson, Kit **C** 123
  Conestoga wagon, or prairie schooner **C** 458
  Death Valley, Calif. **D** 131
  education, battle for the common school **E** 70–71
  fur trade in North America **F** 520–24
  gold discoveries **G** 250–53
  guns and ammunition **G** 415–422
  in American literature **A** 208
  Indian attack, picture **B** 9
  Montana **M** 442
  Oklahoma "Sooners" **O** 80
  overland trails **O** 251–67
  Pony Express **P** 392–93
  westward movement **W** 142–46
  Where did pioneer women get cosmetics? **C** 510
Pioneers, Soviet youth organization **U** 30–31
Pioneers, The, by James Fenimore Cooper **A** 200
Pioneer 10, space probe toward Jupiter **O** 15; **S** 349
Pions, or pi mesons, subatomic particles **N** 368
Pipe, musical instrument **F** 329; picture **F** 330
Pipelines **T** 266, 268
  aqueduct in Israel **A** 344
  in deserts of Saudi Arabia, picture **D** 126
  natural gas **N** 56–57
  petroleum products **P** 175
Pipe organ **O** 208–09
Pipes, for conducting liquids, gases, or semisolids
  valves **V** 269–70
Pipes, volcanic lava plugs **D** 153
  diamonds found in **G** 70
Pipes of Pan *see* Panpipes
Pipestone National Monument, in southwestern Minnesota **M** 332–33
Pipils (pip-EELS), Indians of Central America
  El Salvador **E** 184; picture **E** 180

Pippin, Horace (1888–1946), American painter, Negro, b. West Chester, Pa. Though untrained in art, he won wide acclaim as a primitivist painter. His early works, including *The End of the War: Starting Home,* stemmed from his experiences in World War I. Other paintings include *The Holy Mountain* and *John Brown Going to His Hanging.*
  Negro Renaissance **N** 98

Piraeus (py-RE-us), Greece, pictures **G** 337, **M** 212
Pirandello (pi-ron-DEL-lo), **Luigi,** Italian novelist and dramatist **D** 298; **I** 480–81
Piranha (pi-RAN-ya), fish **F** 188; picture **F** 187
  animals' eating habits **A** 266, 274; **P** 64

Pirated books **T** 245
Pirates and piracy **P** 263–64
  Caesar's capture by **C** 5
  Caribbean Sea and islands **C** 119
  Florida's Gasparilla Pirate Invasion **F** 258
  Kidd, Captain William **K** 241
  Laffite, Jean **L** 23
  pirate makeup, picture **P** 340
  See also Vikings
Pirates' House, landmark in Savannah, Georgia, picture **G** 144
Pirates of Penzance, The, operetta by Gilbert and Sullivan **G** 210

Pire (PEER), **Dominique Georges Henri** (1910–1969), Belgian Dominican priest, b. Dinant. Winner of Nobel Peace Prize (1958), he was well-known for his "Europe of the Heart" movement, which helped house Eastern European displaced persons. He received Belgian War Cross with Palms and French Legion of Honor for his help in the fight for liberation in World War II. His "Open Heart to the World" set up a University of Peace in Huy, Belgium (1959). He also established "peace islands" in East Pakistan (1960), and Kalakaddu, India.

Pirogues (pi-ROGUES), dugouts or canoes **C** 99
Pisa (PI-sa), Italy
  cathedral and leaning tower of, pictures **C** 132, **I** 446, **W** 221

Pisano, Giovanni (1245?–1314?), Italian sculptor and architect, b. Pisa. Son of Nicola Pisano, he assisted (1265–68) his father on the pulpit of the Sienese cathedral. He was chief architect of the Cathedral of Siena and Cathedral of Pisa and builder of the Campo Santo in Pisa. His sculpture, which established the Italian Gothic style, includes the pulpits in the Sant' Andrea di Pistoia in Siena and in the Cathedral of Pisa.
  Italian sculpture of the later Middle Ages **I** 463, 464

Pisano, Nicola, or **Niccolo** (1220?–84?), Italian sculptor and architect; b. Pisa. Pisano was an important pre-Renaissance sculptor. His works, in the Romanesque style, include the hexagonal pulpit in the baptistery at Pisa, the *Arca di San Domenico* at Bologna, and the octagonal pulpit in the Cathedral of Siena.
  Italian sculpture of the later Middle Ages **I** 463, 464
  Pisano's pulpit for the Baptistery, Pisa, picture **S** 99

Piscataqua River, New Hampshire **N** 151, 162
Pisces (PI-sez), constellation **C** 490–91; sign of, picture **S** 244
Pi Sheng (BE JUNG), reputed Chinese inventor of printing from movable type **C** 433

Pissarro (pi-SAR-ro), **Camille** (1830–1903), French impressionist painter, b. St. Thomas, West Indies. He moved to Paris in 1855. Inspired by Corot and Manet, he became the leader of the French impressionists, briefly turning to pointillism in the 1880's, and influenced the work of Cézanne. His works, chiefly scenes of Paris and surrounding country, include *Boulevard Montmartre* and *Quais de la Seine.*
  impressionism in modern art **F** 426; **M** 387
  Wheelbarrow, The, painting **F** 428

Pistachio (pis-TA-shi-o) **nuts** **N** 422–23
Pistils, of flowers **F** 276–77
  reproduction of plants **P** 296
Pistols, small guns **G** 416
  decorated, picture **D** 67
  duelists used **D** 340–41

Piston, Walter (1894–   ), American composer, b. Rockland, Maine. He joined the faculty (1926) and became professor of music (1944) at Harvard University. His compositions, noted for classic form, include *Symphonic Piece, Concerto for Orchestra,* the ballet *The Incredible Flutist,* and many symphonies. He received the Pulitzer prize for music (1948).

Piston engines E 209–10
  airplane **A** 557
  hydraulic machinery **H** 301, 303
  internal combustion engines **I** 304
  jet engines compared to **J** 86
  steam engines **S** 419
Piston pumps P 529–30
Piston rings, of internal-combustion engine **I** 304
Pitcairn, John, British commander at battle of Lexington **R** 198

Pitcairn Island, small volcanic island in the South Pacific. It was discovered by Carteret in 1767 but was uninhabited until its occupation (1790) by mutineering British sailors from the *Bounty.* Because of overcrowding, the inhabitants were relocated on Norfolk Island (1856), although some returned later. The island is under the authority of the governor of Fiji.
  See also Bligh, William

Pitch, a dark, sticky substance exuded from certain trees
  natural resin **R** 184
Pitch, in music **M** 534
  African music **A** 79
  electronic music not limited by tuning **E** 142g
  range of the voice **V** 375
Pitch, of sound **S** 258
Pitchblende, ore **U** 230
  Curies' experiments **C** 553
Pitcher, in baseball **B** 73
Pitcher, in softball **S** 229
Pitcher, Molly, American heroine of Revolutionary War **R** 205
  born in New Jersey **N** 177–78
Pitcher plants P 317–18; picture P 316
Pitch pine, tree
  leaves, needlelike, pictures **L** 119
Pith, of trees **W** 222
Pithecanthropus erectus *see* Java man
Pitman, Sir Isaac, English inventor
  shorthand system **S** 164
Pitman, Sir James, English educator and statesman **I** 254
Pitman's Initial teaching alphabet R 109
Pitons, iron spikes used in mountain climbing **M** 490
Pitt, William, earl of Chatham, English statesman P 265
  French and Indian War **F** 461
Pitt, William, the Younger, British statesman P 265–66
  oratory **O** 181
  Pitt's solution to England's trouble with Ireland **E** 228
Pitti Gallery, Florence, Italy **M** 514
Pittsburgh, Pennsylvania P 141; picture P 130
Pituitary (pi-TU-it-ary) **gland** B 280
  relation to the brain **B** 367
Pit vipers, poisonous snakes **I** 284–85; **S** 208; pictures **S** 210
Pius VII (PY-us), pope
  imprisoned by Napoleon **R** 295
Pius X, pope
  canonized **R** 298
  Catholic hymns **H** 313
Pius XI, pope
  Lateran Treaty of 1929 **R** 298

Pius XII, pope **P** 266
  prayer **P** 435
  spiritual renewal and unity for Roman Catholic Church **R** 298

Pixies, small mischievous fairies or elves in the folklore of southwestern England, particularly Cornwall and Devon. It is said that they dance in the moonlight, play tricks on family members, and mislead travelers.

Pixii (peex-EE), **Hippolyte** (i-po-LEET), French instrument maker **E** 140
Pizarro (pi-ZAR-ro), **Francisco,** Spanish conqueror of Peru **P** 266
  conquest of the Incas **I** 207
  Ecuador **E** 57
  exploration of the New World **E** 383, 386
  Peru **P** 165
Pizzas (PE-tzas), Italian pasta **F** 341
Pizzicato (pit-zi-CA-to), plucking the strings of a musical instrument **V** 343
PKU, disease **R** 190
Place de la Concorde *see* Concorde, Place de la
Place des Arts (plos des AR), Montreal, Canada **C** 63
Placeholder, in the new mathematics **M** 165
Place names
  personal names derived from places **N** 4
Placenta, organ attached to uterus **B** 2
Placental (pla-CENT-al) **mammals** M 71
  marsupials compared to **K** 169
Placer mining M 318
  gold **G** 251
Placers, alluvial deposits containing minerals **G** 248–49
  deposits of ores **R** 272–73
Place settings, of knives, forks, and spoons, pictures **K** 286, 287
Places of interest *see* this section of country, province, and state articles
Place value, in numeration systems **N** 392–93, 396
Placoderms (PLAC-o-derms), ancestors of fishes **F** 182
Plagiarism (PLAGE-a-rism), copying original work of another **T** 245
Plague, disease **D** 221
  outbreak in St. Giles slums of London **L** 335
Plaice, fish **H** 189
Plaid, special pattern of cloth **C** 352
Plainclothesmen
  city police **P** 376
Plains, stretches of flat land **P** 430
Plains Indians of North America I 162–69
  Indian Wars in western United States **I** 214
  music **I** 160–61
  skilled in art of painting **I** 156
Plains of Abraham *see* Abraham, Plains of
Plainsong, or plainchant, a musical form **I** 482; **M** 537
  See also Gregorian chants
Plaintiff, in law **C** 527
Plain weave, of fabrics **T** 143
Planarians, worms **W** 312
  maze tests, picture **A** 282
  nervous system, diagram **B** 363
Planck (PLONCK), **Max,** German physicist **L** 274; **P** 236; picture P 237
  science in 20th century **S** 76
Plane, inclined, simple machine **W** 246–47
Plane geometry G 125
Plane mirrors L 261
Planers and shapers, tools **T** 213, 218–19
  preparing wood for furniture-making **F** 502
  woodworking **W** 230
Planes, flat surfaces in design **D** 136
Planes, tools **T** 213

Planetarium (plan-et-AIR-ium) **P** 267–68
  make a carton planetarium **E** 361
  originally museums of astronomy **M** 513
Planetary circulation, of winds **W** 186
Planetary gears **T** 256
Planetesimal (plan-et-ES-i-mal) **theory,** of origin of solar
  system **S** 247
Planetoids (PLAN-et-oids), or asteroids, small planets
  P 273–74
  Mars **M** 107
  origin in the solar system **S** 239–40, 243
Planets **P** 269–78
  astronomy, history of **A** 471–72, 474–75
  comets, orbits of **C** 418–19
  discoveries of planets **A** 474–75
  Do stars have planets circling them? **S** 411
  double planetary system, earth and moon **M** 446–47
  dust-cloud hypothesis of formation **E** 18
  life belt of the sun **E** 22
  Mars **M** 104–111
  planetoids, or asteroids **P** 273–74; **S** 239–40, 243
  radio astronomy studies **R** 75
  solar system, band of the zodiac **S** 243
  space exploration with space probes **S** 348–49
  theories about the sun and planets **S** 240, 247
  "wanderers" among constellations **C** 490; **S** 77, 79
  See also Earth; names of planets
Plankton, drifting mass of small plant and animal life
  P 279–81; picture **L** 230
  algae and environmental pollution **E** 272f
  ocean life **O** 37; picture **O** 39
Planographic printing **P** 460–61
  graphic arts **G** 302
  lithography **L** 315
Plan Overlord, invasion of France, World War II **W** 298
Plan position indicator, or PPI, of radar systems **R** 35–
  36
Plantagenet family, rulers of England **U** 77
Plantain, a bananalike fruit **M** 74
  grown for food and to shade coffee trees **C** 382
Plantain, broad-leafed weed, picture **W** 105
  fibrous roots, picture **P** 291
Plantations
  colonial America **C** 387; pictures **C** 388, 398
  rubber **R** 343–44
  sugarcane plantations, factories in the fields **H** 63–64
  tea plantation in Ceylon, picture **C** 178
Plantation system
  Virginia **V** 348
Plant breeding
  Burbank's contributions to **B** 453
  Mendel, work of **G** 80–82
Plant defenses **P** 282–83
  poisonous plants **P** 321–23
  weeds say "Hands off" **W** 104, 106
Plant diseases
  caused by club fungi **F** 498
  vectors, or carriers of diseases **V** 282–85
  See also Plant enemies and pests; articles on individual plants, as Corn
Planté (plon-TAY), **Gaston,** French scientist **P** 237
Plant enemies and pests **P** 284–87, 288–89
  insecticides used against **I** 258
  plant defenses **P** 282–83
  vectors, or carriers of diseases **V** 284
Planters, machines for sowing seed **F** 58
Plant hormones **E** 352–53
Planting
  chart of times, how and where to plant **G** 51
  gardens and gardening **G** 30, 39–41
  houseplants **H** 265–69
  vegetables **V** 286–94

Plant kingdom **K** 250, 251; **P** 292
Plant pests see Plant enemies and pests
Plant poisoning
  first aid **F** 163
Plant propagation
  apple trees **A** 335, 337
  gardens and gardening **G** 40, 52
  grapes and berries **G** 298
  grasses **G** 316–17
  houseplants **H** 268
Plants **P** 290–304
  algae **A** 155–57
  animals distinguished from plants **L** 212–13
  aquariums **A** 340–41
  atmosphere, formation of **E** 19
  bacteria resemble **B** 10
  bioluminescence **B** 197
  botanical gardens **Z** 379
  botany, study of **B** 340
  bulbs, corms, rhizomes, and tubers **G** 40
  cactus **C** 3–4
  cave life **C** 157
  cell structure **C** 162–63
  climate and vegetation regions **C** 345, 347
  cotton, pictures **C** 520
  desert plants **D** 124
  defenses see Plant defenses
  distribution of see Vegetation
  Does cancer occur in plants? **C** 90
  Do growing plants break up rocks? **S** 231
  dyes, sources of **D** 367
  enemies see Plant enemies and pests
  evolution of **E** 338–47
  experiments, projects in life sciences **E** 356–59
  ferns, mosses, and lichens **F** 92–95
  fertilizer elements, hunger signs for **F** 96
  flowerless **A** 155
  flowers and seeds **F** 276–80
  food see Plants, food
  fossils **F** 378
  fungi **F** 496–500
  garden selection **G** 26, 29–30
  genetics **G** 77–88
  grasses **G** 314–19
  houseplants **H** 265–69
  how the life process differs from animals **L** 212–13
  Humboldt's geographic findings on **G** 98
  insectivorous plants **P** 317; pictures **P** 316
  jungle **J** 154–56
  kingdoms of living things **K** 249–59
  leaves **L** 114–20
  life, adaptations in the world of **L** 214–27
  life, distribution of **L** 227–39
  life, food chain producers **L** 239–43
  life, rhythms and clocks in **L** 248–49
  life, webs of **L** 250–59
  Mars **M** 111
  mechanisms for seed dispersal **F** 282; **T** 284; **W** 106
  medicinal see Plants, medicinal
  Mendel, work of **G** 80–82; **M** 219
  movements, plant responses **P** 301–02
  odd and interesting see Plants, odd and interesting
  osmosis **O** 234
  perfume oils from natural materials, pictures **P** 155
  photosynthesis **P** 221–23
  poisonous see Plants, poisonous
  prairies **P** 430–31
  reproduction, types of **R** 176–80
  seeds, dispersal of **F** 280–82
  spore-bearing **F** 92–95
  symbiosis, or partnership **F** 94–95; **P** 320
  taxonomy **T** 28–32

terrariums **T** 102–04
trees **T** 274–85
vegetables **V** 286–94
waxes, for candles **C** 97
weeds **W** 104–06
wild flowers **W** 168–71
See also Botany, and natural resources section of continent, country, province, and state articles
Plants, food **P** 305–10
dwarf and hybrid varieties of cereal grains **G** 287
oils and fats **O** 76–77, 79
spices, herbs, and condiments **S** 380–83
Plants, medicinal **P** 310–15
disease, conquest of **D** 213–14
drug industry **D** 321–25, 327–28
primitive peoples' use of them **M** 203
Plants, odd and interesting **P** 316–20
giants of nature **G** 199, 200, 202–03
Plants, poisonous **P** 321–23
certain algae **A** 157
leaves **L** 115
mushrooms, poisonous **F** 499; **M** 521; pictures **F** 500
remedial uses **P** 314
used by Indians of South America **I** 209
Plant viruses **V** 365–66
Plasma, blood **B** 255–56
antibodies **I** 107
circulatory system of human body **B** 275–77
medicine, techniques with **M** 210, 211
osmosis process **O** 234–35
transfusion **T** 251
Plasma, fourth state of matter **M** 178
atomic particles **I** 351–52
plasma accelerator engine for spacecraft **S** 348
plasma tongue from a solar flare, diagram **E** 27
sun's interior **S** 463
Plassey (PLA-sey), **battle of,** 1757 **E** 43
British Indian Empire **I** 133

Plaster, mixture of lime, sand, and water. Hair or fiber is often added as a binder. Applied as a soft paste, plaster sets, or hardens, by chemical action. It is used chiefly for coating indoor walls and ceilings.

Plaster of Paris, fine white powder prepared from gypsum (calcium sulfate) that has been strongly heated and ground to powder. When mixed with water, it hardens into a rocklike mass. The powder is used in wall plasters and wallboards and in molds for ceramics.
behaves like thermosetting plastics **P** 328

Plastic, chemical term **C** 220
Plasticine (PLAS-ti-cene), clay **C** 336
Plasticizers, ingredients used in plastics **P** 327
Plastics, man-made materials **P** 324–31
acetylene gas used in making **G** 62
airplane models **A** 104, 105
automobile model kits **A** 536
balloons **B** 32
button manufacturing **B** 478
insulating materials **I** 291–92
jewelry **J** 93
nylon and other man-made fibers **N** 424–28
petrochemicals **P** 176–77
resins used in **R** 185
shoes made of poromerics **S** 163
silicones, synthetic rubber **R** 347
vinyl plastics, floor coverings **V** 341
Plastron, lower part of turtle's shell **T** 331
Plata (PLA-ta), **Río de la,** estuary of the Paraná and Uruguay rivers, South America **R** 247; **A** 388
Buenos Aires **B** 426–28

Montevideo, Uruguay **U** 237
Paraguay-Paraná river system **S** 277
Plateaus (pla-TOS), elevated land areas
Africa, the plateau continent **A** 46
Plate glass **G** 236
Platelets (PLATE-lets), blood corpuscles **B** 256, 257
circulatory system of human body **B** 275–77
Platen (PLATE-en) **presses,** for printing **P** 461
Plateosaurs (PLAT-e-o-saurs), dinosaurs **D** 175–76
Plateresque (PLAT-er-esk) **style,** of architecture **L** 63
Spanish architecture **S** 363
Plates, in printing **P** 465, 467; picture **P** 466
Plates, of the earth crust **E** 11; diagram **E** 11
geology and geophysics **G** 116, 117
Platforms, political **P** 382
Plating, electric see Electroplating
Platinum, element **E** 155, 163
Canada, world's leading producer **C** 56
catalyst **C** 199
jewelry **J** 92
metals, ores, location, properties, uses **M** 227
platinum metals **E** 158
Platinum-iridium bar, formerly standard of measurement
W 111; picture **W** 110
Plato (PLAY-to), Greek philosopher **P** 332
ancient civilizations **A** 230
Aristotle a pupil of Plato **A** 396
importance to Greek literature **G** 353–54
perfect state described in his *Republic* **U** 255
philosophical systems **P** 191–92
Plato's system of studying science **S** 62–63
Platoons, army troop unit **U** 172
Platt Amendment, Cuba–United States pact **C** 550
Platte River, United States **R** 246–47
along the Oregon Trail **O** 261
Colorado **C** 403
Nebraska **N** 74, 86, 87
Platters, American rock music group **R** 262c
Platypuses, or duckbills **P** 333–34
Australian wildlife **A** 504
egg-laying mammals **M** 71; picture **M** 69
Plautus, Titus Maccius, Roman playwright **D** 295
Latin literature **L** 76, 77
quotation **Q** 20
Play
activities of kindergartens and nursery schools
K 245–46
child development **C** 231–34
dolls **D** 263–69
games **G** 10–24
indoor activities for rainy days **I** 223–26
ocean liners, children's playrooms **O** 18; picture **O** 22
playgrounds **P** 77–78
play-party games and folk dancing **D** 28; **F** 299
toys **T** 230–35
See also Games; Hobbies; Sports
Playboy of the Western World, The, play by John Millington Synge **I** 394; scene **I** 393

Player, Gary (1935–), South African golfer, b. Johannesburg. A participant in U.S., African, Australian, and European tournaments, he won his first major title in the British Open in 1959. His other major titles include a 2d British Open win (1968), Masters (1961), Professional Golf Association (1962), and U.S. Open (1965). Picture **G** 261.

Player piano, or pianola, musical instrument **R** 123
Playgrounds **P** 77–78
Holsteinsborg, Greenland, picture **G** 368
housing projects, pictures **H** 183
Playing cards see Card games
Playing 'possum, how the expression originated **K** 171

Play-party games F 299
  dancing D 28
  songs F 323–24
Plays, production of, on the stage P 335–41
  arena stage T 155–56
  miracle plays M 339–40
  posters, pictures A 216
  puppets and marionettes P 537, 539
  theater T 155–64
  See also Drama
Playwrights, or dramatists, writers of plays T 156–57
Playwriting W 320
Plaza de toros (PLA-tha day TO-ros), bullfighting arena
  B 449
Plebes, freshmen at U.S. Naval Academy, picture U 191
Plebians (pleb-E-ans), social class, ancient Rome P 378
  Caesar their favorite C 5

Plebiscite (from the Latin *plebiscitum*, meaning "decree
of the people"). Today a plebiscite usually refers to a
vote by the people of a region or country to determine
who shall rule them and how they should be ruled. In
ancient Rome it denoted a decree decided upon by the
plebs, or common people.

Pledge of Allegiance, pledge to the flag of the United
States. It is thought to have been written by Francis
Bellamy or James B. Upham, staff members of the
magazine *Youth's Companion*, in which the pledge first
appeared (1892). The pledge has been amended several
times and now reads: "I pledge allegiance to the Flag of
the United States of America and to the Republic for
which it stands, one nation under God, indivisible, with
liberty and justice for all."

Pléiades (plai-YOD), French poets F 436

Pleiades (PLE-a-dese), or Seven Sisters (literally, "The
Weepers"), in Greek mythology, the seven daughters of
Atlas and Pleione who, either after death or during the
flight from Orion, were transformed into stars. The
sisters are identified with a group of faint stars in the
constellation Taurus. The barely visible seventh star is
said to represent either Electra, who moved to avoid
seeing the fall of Troy, or Merope, who was ashamed of
her marriage to a mortal. Alcyone, Celeno, Sterope,
Taygeta, and Maia are the names of the five other sisters.

Pleiku (PLAY-KOO), South Vietnam V 336
Pleistocene (PLY-sto-cene) epoch, of the Cenozoic era, in
    geology F 388
  evolution of birds B 209
  Pleistocene Ice Age I 13, 23; stages by name I 21
  prehistoric man P 442–46
Plessy v. Ferguson, Supreme Court ruling sets precedent
    for separate-but-equal facilities N 96
Pliers, tools T 214
Pliny, the Elder, Roman historian
  account of the discovery of glass F 144; G 226
  early geologist G 117
  encyclopedia of arts and sciences E 193
Pliny the Younger, Roman orator and writer L 80
Pliocene epoch, of the Cenozoic era, in geology F 388
  evolution of birds B 209
Plique-a-jour (pli-ka-JOOR), enameling technique E 191
Plots, literary
  novels N 345
Plotter, computer output unit C 452
Plough (PLOW) and the Stars, play by O'Casey, scene
    from D 299

Plover (PLUV-er), any one of several shorebirds with pi-

geonlike bills, large eyes, and long legs. The best known
is the golden plover. This bird breeds in Arctic regions.

Plow-plant, or once-over tillage, for planting corn F 58
Plows F 57
  development of, in agriculture A 96; pictures A 89
  prairies devoloped by cultivation P 431–32
Plowshare F 57
Plucked instruments, in music M 544
Plugs, lures for fishing F 207
Plum P 107–09
  Burbank variety B 453
  seed, picture P 298
  See also Peach
Plumage (PLU-mage), feather coats of birds B 200
Plumbicon, television tube T 65
Plumbing, piping system in a building P 341–43
  bathing, history of B 91
  installing water pipes, picture B 436
  origin of the word E 126; L 94
  system in a house, diagram B 437
Plumb line, tool T 211
Plumules (PLU-mules), of seeds F 283
Plutarch (PLU-tarck), Greek biographer G 355
  biographical essays E 292
  quoted on Alexander the Great A 153
Pluto, cartoon character, picture A 297
Pluto, planet P 278; picture P 269
  astronomy, history of A 475
  space probes of the future S 348–49
  telescope makers, discoveries of T 64
Pluto, Roman god G 357
Plutonic (plu-TON-ic) rocks M 493
Plutonium (plu-TO-nium), element E 155, 163
  metals, chart of ores, location, properties, uses M 227
  Savannah River Plant, near Aiken, S.C. S 300–01

Plutus, in Greek mythology, the personification of wealth.
The son of Iasion and Demeter, he was allegedly blinded
by Zeus so that he might bestow his gifts equally upon
the good and bad. The word "plutocrat," meaning a
person who exerts influence through wealth, is derived
from Plutus' name.

Ply, strands of yarn T 143
Plymouth (PLIM-outh), Massachusetts P 344
  places of interest in Massachusetts M 145
Plymouth Colony, in Massachusetts P 343–46
  American colonies A 186–87; M 148
  colonial life in America C 385
  Mayflower M 185
Plymouth Company, business company to colonize Amer-
    ica A 183, 185
Plymouth Rock, landing spot of Pilgrims P 345
Plywood
  furniture F 503
  need for better adhesives G 243
  wood products W 226–27
Plzeň (PEL-zen-ya), or Pilsen, Czechoslovakia C 562
P.M., postmeridiem, or after noon T 189–90
Pneumatic (neu-MAT-ic) devices P 347–48
  tubes for mail P 406
Pneumatic drills B 447
Pneumatic tires T 196
Pneumatic trailers, for trucks T 297
Pneumonia (neu-MO-nia), infection of lungs D 203–04
Pnompenh (p'nome-PEN-ya), capital of Cambodia C 31,
  33
Po (POO), Fernão do, Portuguese explorer, discovered
    Cameroon C 35
Pocahontas (po-ca-HON-tas), Indian princess J 20, 21
  Smith, John S 201; picture A 183

Pocatello (po-ca-TELL-o), Idaho I 66
Po Chu-i, Chinese poet O 220a
Pocket billiards B 174–76
Pocket gophers, rodents R 277
Pocket mice R 277
Pocket veto see Veto
Pocono Mountains, Pennsylvania P 131
Podiatry see Chiropody
Podzolic soils S 233
    Vermont soils V 310
Poe, Edgar Allan, American writer P 348
    first writer of detective stories M 553
    Fort Moultrie, setting of *The Gold Bug* S 304, 306
    place in American literature A 200–01
    science fiction S 84
    short story, definition of S 166
    types of fiction F 112
Poet laureate (LAUR-e-ate) E 253
    Tennyson, Alfred, Lord T 101
Poetry P 349–55
    Africa's praise poems and epics A 76a
    Arcadian poetry I 479
    ballads B 22–23
    Bible B 154
    children's literature C 241
    Chinese literature O 220–220a, 220b
    creative writing W 320–21
    early Greek literature G 350
    elegies and epitaphs E 151–52
    figures of speech F 118–20
    heroic couplet E 256
    Indian literature O 220e
    Japanese haiku J 28
    Japanese literature O 220b
    limericks N 273, 276
    list of, for children C 247
    nonsense rhymes N 272–76
    nursery rhymes N 402–08
    odes O 52
    Pulitzer prizes P 527–28
    sagas and early Scandinavian poetry S 50, 52
    sonnets S 255–56
    types of literature L 314
    See also literature of each country; names of poems and poets
Poetry: A Magazine of Verse A 209

Poetry Society of America (PSA), organization of professional poets, critics, librarians, educators, and patrons established to aid poets and poetry. It issues awards and maintains a poetry collection at the New York Public Library. Founded in 1910, it has headquarters in New York, N.Y., and publishes *PSA Bulletin*, a monthly.

Poets' Corner, a nickname for Maine M 45
Poets' Corner, Westminster Abbey, London
    Chaucer's burial spot C 190
Pogo, comic strip character
    Okefenokee Swamp, Georgia G 132

Pogrom (from Russian, meaning "destruction"), attacking, killing, and looting of defenseless people, generally with the approval of government officials. The term "pogroms," first incorporated into English usage in 1905 when a series of such attacks were carried out by the reactionary Black Hundreds in Russia, has been applied especially to the massacre of Jews.
    Jews, history of J 110–11

Pogue, William R., American astronaut S 347
Poi (PO-i), staple food of Hawaii H 62
    favorite foods around the world F 340

Poincaré (pawn-ca-RAY) Raymond, French statesman F 419

Poinciana (poin-ci-AN-a), group of small tropical trees and shrubs belonging to the pea family and common to the Eastern and Western hemispheres. The leaves have a featherlike arrangement. The flowers are a brilliant orange or scarlet, and the pods are long and flat. The poinciana is named after an early governor of the French West Indies. It is cultivated in warm regions.

Poinsett, Joel R., American botanist and legislator S 296–97
    flowering plant for Christmas C 291
Poinsettia, plant C 291
Point Barrow, Alaska A 128
Point d'Alençon (PWON d'a-lonce-ON), lace, picture L 19
Pointe du Sable, Jean Baptiste see Du Sable, Jean Baptiste Pointe
Pointe-Noire, Congo (Brazzaville) C 461, 462
Pointer, sporting dog, picture D 253

Point Four Program, U.S. foreign aid program of technical and economic assistance to "free peoples" in underdeveloped countries. The program, introduced as the fourth point in President Truman's inaugural address (1949), was aimed at raising the standard of living through development of the countries' own resources. U.S. foreign aid is presently administered by Agency for International Development (AID), established in 1961.

Point Hope, Alaska
    Eskimo village E 287
Pointillism (PWON-ti-ism), impressionist method of painting F 431
    modern art M 387
Pointing, in sculpture S 91
Point Pleasant, battle of, 1774 V 359
Points, geometric G 124
Point system, of type measurements T 344
Poison, circle game G 15
Poison control centers P 356
Poison hemlock, plant P 314, 321, 322, 323; picture P 315
Poisoning
    by plants, first aid F 163
    by way of mouth (oral), first aid for F 158
    first aid F 158, 163
    preventive measures S 4
Poison ivy P 321
    first aid F 163
    leaves of plants L 115
    plant defenses P 282
Poison oak P 321
    first aid F 163
    leaves of plants L 115
    plant defenses P 282
Poisonous plants see Plants, poisonous
Poisons P 356–57
    animal, as protective devices M 67
    black widow spider I 284
    botulism F 354
    centipedes C 167–68
    food poisoning F 354–55
    gila monsters, lizards L 320
    insecticides I 258
    jellyfishes and other coelenterates J 70–71
    lead L 95
    methyl (wood) alcohol A 147
    millipedes C 168
    poisonous plants P 282, 321–23

Poisons (continued)
  rat control H 264
  remedial uses of poisonous plants P 314
  shrews I 260
  superstitions as to gemstones G 74
  venom of some fishes F 202
Poison sumac P 321–22
  first aid F 163
  leaves of plants L 115
  plant defenses P 282
Poison vetch, plant P 321

Poitier (PWOT-i-ay), **Sidney** (1927–), American actor, Negro, b. Miami, Fla. The star of numerous motion pictures and Broadway plays, he has acted in such films as *Lilies of the Field*, for which he was awarded an Academy Award in 1963, *In the Heat of the Night, Guess Who's Coming to Dinner?* and *They Call Me Mr. Tibbs.* His Broadway credits include roles in *A Raisin in the Sun*, and *Lost in the Stars*. Picture N 102.

Poitiers, battle of, 732 see Tours, battle of
Poitiers (pwot-YAY), **battle of,** 1356 H 282
Poke bonnet, picture H 55
Poland (PO-land) P 358–62
  agriculture, pictures A 97, P 360
  Belorussia B 139
  dancing, picture D 29
  favorite foods F 341
  flag F 240
  invasion by Hitler W 286, 287
  Jewish community J 109
  national anthem N 22
  "national Communism" C 444–45
Polar bears B 108; picture B 107
Polar constellations C 491; charts C 490
Polar explorations P 364–65, 366–71
  Bering, Vitus B 142
  Byrd, Richard B 481
  Northwest Passage N 338
  Peary, Robert E. P 116
Polar ice cap, picture C 344
Polarimeter (po-la-RIM-et-er), how to make E 365
Polaris see North Star
Polaris missile M 347; pictures F 490; M 346
Polarization, of light L 272–73
Polarizing microscopes M 283, 288
Polar-Night Jet Stream J 91
Polar-Night Vortex, of air J 91
Polaroid cameras P 203
Polar regions P 363–71
  animals, pictures A 268
  Byrd, first to fly over both poles B 481
  climate C 346
  Ewing-Donn theory of Ice Ages I 24
  frigid zones Z 372
  glaciers G 223–25
  Hudson, Henry H 272–73
  International Polar Years (IPY-1 and -2) I 310–11
  latitudes of North and South poles L 81, 82
  Mars, polar caps of M 109, 110
  measuring depth of ice and snow I 10–11
Polders, low land reclaimed from a body of water
  Netherlands N 118
Polecats, ferrets, related to weasels O 243
Poles, magnetic M 24–25; E 130
  electricity and magnetism E 130
  electric motors E 136–37
Poles, telephone W 226
Pole vault, field event T 238, 240
Police P 372–77
  Black Panthers and the police N 105

  community's representative in courts C 527
  gendarmes of Paris, picture P 69
  jury trials J 159
  local departments helped by FBI F 77
  motorcycles, use of M 488b–489
  problems of law enforcement L 89
  Royal Canadian Mounted Police C 78; P 374, 375
  special police to handle juvenile delinquency J 164
  traffic control T 247–48
Police dogs D 252
Policewomen P 377
Polichinelle (po-li-shi-NELL), or **Pulcinella,** Italian puppet
  character P 534
Poliomyelitis (po-li-o-my-e-LY-tis), or infantile paralysis,
  virus disease D 204
  polio virus, picture V 361
  Roosevelt, Franklin D., victim of R 321
  Sabin, Albert B. S 2
  Salk, Jonas E., developer of polio vaccine S 18
  vaccination V 260–61
Polish (PO-lish) **Corridor,** created by Treaty of Versailles,
  after World War I G 162
  Poland's outlet to the sea P 362
Polished (POL-ished) **rice** R 232
Polishing see Grinding and polishing
Polish language P 358

Polish National Catholic Church of America, religious organization founded (1897) in Scranton, Pa., by 250 Polish-American families who broke away from the Roman Catholic Church. These people objected to powers given to priests over church members by the Roman Catholic Council of Baltimore (1884). Polish National Catholic clergymen may marry.

Polish Partitions, 1793, 1795 P 362
  Ukraine U 9
Polish Rider, The, painting by Rembrandt van Rijn P 25
Polish United Workers' Party P 361
Politburo, governing body of Soviet Communist Party
  U 42

Politi, Leo (1908–), American author and illustrator, b. Fresno, Calif. He spent much of his childhood in Italy, studying art at the Institute of Monza near Milan. His books include *Song of the Swallows*, which was awarded the Caldecott medal (1950).

Political asylum, refuge granted by a government to a citizen of a foreign country because his political activities have made it dangerous for him to return to his native land.

Political cartoons see Cartoons, political
Political conventions P 382; picture E 112
Political economy see Economics
Political geography G 108
Political parties P 378–82
  beginnings of party system in England E 225, 228, 230
  cartoon symbols C 126
  democratic right to choose D 105
  election of a prime minister P 456
  Electoral College E 116
  government systems determined by G 278
  Jefferson, first president to be a party leader J 68
  national nominating convention originated in Jackson's
    administration J 6
  organization in Congress U 144
  primary elections E 115
  Progressive, or Bull Moose formed by Theodore
    Roosevelt R 330
  solidarity in parliaments P 81

state legislatures do business on party basis **S** 415
U.S. president, his party's leader **P** 455
vice-presidency of the United States **V** 329
women, role of **W** 213
See also government section of country articles; names of parties
Political platforms P 382

Political science, social science concerned with the systematic study of government and the political organization and activities of a state. It includes such areas as political theory, political parties and groups, public opinion, and international relations. Originating in the writings of Plato and Aristotle, it was further developed by the English philosopher Thomas Hobbes (1588–1679), who formulated the social contract theory. Today it deals primarily with the acquisition and use of political power.

Polity, government by the many **G** 274
Poliziano (po-li-tzi-ON-o), Italian poet **I** 477
Polk, James Knox, 11th president of United States **P** 383–87
Mexican War **M** 238
Polk, Sarah Childress, wife of James K. Polk **F** 169–70; **P** 387; pictures **F** 171, **P** 386
Polka, dance **D** 30
Polk Doctrine, American foreign policy **P** 386–87
Pollard, Rebecca, American teacher **P** 194
Pollen and pollination F 277–80
bees **B** 118; **H** 202
corn **C** 506
flowers and seeds of plants **P** 296
fruitgrowing **F** 483
hayfever, cause of **D** 192
plants, odd and interesting **P** 319–20
pollen grains, pictures **F** 276; **P** 297
reproduction **R** 178
trees **T** 283–84
Pollio (POL-li-o), **Marcus Vitruvius,** Roman author **E** 208
Pollock, Jackson, American painter **P** 387; **W** 336
action painting or abstract expressionism in modern art **M** 397; **P** 31
American painting in the 20th century **U** 122
Convergence, picture **D** 135
Number I, painting **M** 396
Polls, public opinion see Public opinion polls

Poll tax, tax of a fixed amount usually levied on every adult male regardless of income or wealth. It is generally not required of women, war veterans, paupers, or the handicapped. The tax was often imposed on subject peoples of ancient Greece and Rome and in some European colonies. In some parts of the United States it has been used as a voting requirement to discourage Negroes from voting, though it was barred by the 24th constitutional amendment (1964) as a voting requirement in federal elections.
qualifications for voting **E** 113; **N** 103
See also Voting Rights Act, 1965, 1970

Pollution and pollutants
air pollution **A** 108–11; **E** 272f–272g
automobiles, search for a low-pollutant engine **A** 552
comic strip that teaches a lesson, picture **C** 422–43
detergents **D** 149; **E** 272d–272e
environment, quality of **E** 272a–272h
fertilizers **E** 272d
fish, contamination of **F** 215, 224
insecticides **E** 272e–272f; **I** 258
noise **E** 272c–272d; **N** 270
population explosion **E** 272b–272c; **P** 396–97
radioactive waste disposal **E** 272b, 272e, 272g

sanitation, sewage, and refuse (solid waste) disposal **E** 272e, 272g; **S** 32–34
water pollution **E** 272d–272e; **W** 58–59
water supply **E** 272e; **W** 68
Pollux, in mythology see Castor and Pollux
Pollux (POLL-ux), star in Gemini constellation **C** 491, 492
Polo, game **P** 388–89
Polo, Marco, Venetian traveler **P** 389–90
China **C** 270, 271
described Oriental cities **C** 307
predecessor of the age of exploration **E** 371
Polonaise (pol-on-AISE), dance of Poland **D** 30
Polonium (po-LO-nium), element **E** 155, 163
discovered by the Curies **C** 553
Polo ponies P 388
Poltava (pol-TA-va), **battle of,** 1709 **B** 101
Peter the Great makes Russia a power **P** 168
Sweden **S** 486

Poltergeist (POLE-ter-gheist) (from German *Polter,* meaning "noise," and *Geist,* meaning "ghost"), destructive spirit or ghost that makes noises and moves objects around the house. In the doctrine of spiritism the term refers to an unseen force assumed to cause rappings and noises that cannot be explained scientifically.

Polyandry, family relationship **F** 41
Polybius, Greek historian **H** 134
Polychaetes (POL-ic-etes), or bristle worms **W** 310
Polyconic grid, of maps **M** 93
Polyester, name for a class of synthetic fibers **N** 424, 425
Polyethylene (poly-ETH-il-ene), a plastic **P** 324
molecule, diagram **P** 327
Polygamy (po-LIG-amy), form of marriage and family organization **F** 41
caused opposition to statehood for Utah **U** 255
Mormons **M** 457
Tibet **T** 176
Polygons, in geometry **G** 125
Polygraph (POL-i-graph), copying machine invented by T. Jefferson, picture **J** 64
Polygyny, family relationship **F** 41
Polyhedrons (poly-HE-drons), geometry **G** 128; **T** 223–24

Polyhymnia (pol-ee-HIM-nia), a goddess in Greek mythology. She and her eight sisters, the daughters of Zeus and Mnemosyne, were the muses, or patrons of the arts and sciences. She presided over oratory and sacred song, and her symbol was the veil.
See also Muses

Polyisoprene, synthetic rubber **R** 347
Polymers and polymerization (po-lim-er-i-ZAY-tion) **P** 324
chemical term defined **C** 220
fibers, synthetic **F** 105, 108; **N** 428
petroleum refining processes **P** 175
synthetic rubber **R** 345–46
Polymorphonuclear cells, of the body **I** 104
Polynesia (poly-NE-sia), Pacific islands **P** 7, 10
Polynesians, Pacific islanders **P** 4
Hawaii **H** 61–62
Maoris of New Zealand **N** 236
Samoa **S** 23
Tonga **T** 210a
Polyoma virus, picture **C** 94
Polypeptides (poly-PEP-tides), germ-killing proteins **I** 104
Polyphemus (poly-PHE-mus), in Greek mythology, one of the Cyclops **O** 53
Polyphony (po-LIPH-ony), in music **I** 482–83
baroque music **B** 63
choral music **C** 276–77
hymns **H** 311

Polyphony (continued)
    Leonin and Perotin, French composers **F** 443
    Middle Ages **M** 299
    religious music **G** 182
Polyps (POL-ips), a form of jellyfish and other coelenterates **J** 71–72, 73, 74–75
    corals **C** 503–04
Polytheism (POL-ith-e-ism), belief in several gods **A** 460; **R** 146
Polytonality (pol-i-to-NAL-ity), in music **M** 400–01
Pomade (po-MADE), a perfumed ointment **P** 155
Pomaks, Bulgarian-speaking Muslims **B** 440
Pomanders, scent boxes **P** 154
    jewelry **J** 94
Pome fruits **P** 112

Pomegranate (POM-e-gran-ate), large round fruit made up of many seeds in juicy, red pulp and having a tough rind. The fruit grows on shrubs or small trees. The pomegranate has been cultivated in Asia, Africa, and southern Europe since ancient times. It is now also grown in many other parts of the world. The plant is a source of food and of chemicals for tanning leather and treating tapeworm infection. Pomegranate juice is the chief ingredient in grenadine syrup. Picture **P** 298.
    Byzantine mosaics with designs of pomegranates **B** 485–86

Pomeranian, dog **D** 259, 261; picture **D** 256
Pomo, Indians of North America **I** 174
    Indian art of basket weaving **I** 156

Pompadour (POM-pa-door), **Marquise de** (Jeanne Antoinette Poisson Lenormand d'Étoiles) (1721–1764), favorite and powerful adviser of Louis XV of France, b. Paris. Introduced to King Louis XV at a ball (1744), she was installed by him at Versailles and given the estate of Pompadour. She then formulated the King's policies—both foreign and domestic. She shifted France's policy toward Austria from one of containment to one of alliance and thus brought on the calamitous Seven Years War (1754–63).

Pomp and Circumstance marches, by Elgar **E** 176, 271
Pompano, fish
    habitats, feeding habits, uses **F** 213
Pompeii (pom-PAY-e), Italy **P** 390; picture **A** 232
    Roman art **P** 17; **R** 286
    ruins, picture **A** 355
Pompey the Great, Roman statesman
    Caesar and Pompey **C** 5–6

Pompidou, Georges Jean Raymond (1911–), French government official, b. Montboudif, France. A former schoolteacher, he filled numerous civil and government posts before he became de Gaulle's premier in 1962. He was replaced as premier in 1968 but was elected president in 1969 after de Gaulle resigned.
    election of 1969 **F** 420

Pompion, colonial American name for pumpkin **C** 390

Ponape (PON-ap-ay) **Island,** volcanic island in western Pacific, one of the Caroline Islands. This forested and fertile land is noted for ruins of a mysterious ancient civilization. During World War II it was used as a Japanese air base, but it is now part of Ponape district in the U.S. Trust Territory of the Pacific Islands.

Ponce (PON-say), **Manuel M.,** Mexican composer **L** 75
Ponce, Puerto Rico **P** 522

Ponce de León (PONE-thay day lay-OHN), **Juan,** Spanish explorer **P** 391
    exploration of the new world **E** 382; picture **A** 81
    Florida **F** 272
    tomb in Cathedral of San Juan Bautista, Puerto Rico **P** 522

Ponchielli (ponc-YEL-li), **Amilcare** (1834–1886), Italian composer, b. near Cremona. His best-known opera and the only one still performed is *La Gioconda*, which contains the popular ballet "Dance of the Hours." The opera was first performed at La Scala, Italy (1876).

Poncho, a cloak or shawl worn in South America **A** 389
    feather poncho, picture **I** 205
Pond, Peter, American fur trader **A** 146h
Ponderosa (pon-der-O-sa) **pine,** tree
    state tree of Montana **M** 428
Ponds, small bodies of water
    a freshwater pond community **L** 255–56; pictures **L** 257
    how they freeze and thaw, diagrams **I** 3, 5
Ponies
    ancient breeds of domestic horses, pictures **H** 237
    Chincoteague ponies **V** 344
    Iceland, picture **I** 45

Pons, Lily (Alice Joséphine Pons) (1904–), French-born American opera singer, b. Cannes. A coloratura soprano, she was noted for her wide vocal range and seemingly effortless artistry. She made her operatic debut (1928) as Lakmé at the Mulhouse Municipal Opera, France, and her U.S. debut as Lucia with the Metropolitan Opera company (1931).

Ponselle (pon-SELL), **Rosa Melba** (Rosa Ponzillo) (1897–), American opera singer, b. Meriden, Conn. A noted soprano with a rich, dramatic voice, she first appeared with the Metropolitan Opera company (1918) as Leonora in *La Forza del Destino*. She made her London debut in *Norma* (1929), gained a reputation for her interpretations of Italian roles, and retired in 1937.

Pontchartrain (PON-char-train), **Lake,** Louisiana **L** 33
    importance to Louisiana and New Orleans **L** 351, 357; **N** 196
Pont du Gard (pon du GAR), near Nîmes, France, picture **B** 395
Ponte Vecchio (PON-tay VEC-yo), bridge, Florence, Italy **B** 396; picture **B** 399
Ponti, Gio, Italian architect **I** 473
Pontiac, chief of the Ottawa Indians **P** 391
    Indian wars in Ohio **O** 74
Pontiac's Rebellion, 1763–66 **P** 391
Pontic Mountains, Turkey **T** 324
Pontil, rod used in shaping glass **A** 318–19
Pontius Pilate see Pilate, Pontius
Pontoon bridges **B** 400
Pony clubs **H** 227, 230
Pony Express, mail service **P** 392–93
    early types of communication **C** 436
    Hollenberg Ranch Station, Kansas **K** 187
    stamp, picture **S** 399
    What is a *mochila*? **P** 392
Pony Express Museum, St. Joseph, Missouri **M** 377
Poodle, dog **D** 261; picture **D** 256
Pool, or pocket billiards **B** 174–76
Poole, Elijah see Elijah Muhammad
Poole, William Frederick, American librarian **L** 188
Pool of London **L** 339
Poor see Poverty
Poor Clares see Clare or Clara, of Assisi, Saint

Poor People's March, protest march on Washington, D.C., by representatives of the U.S. poor (May-June, 1968). First planned by Dr. Martin Luther King, Jr., leadership of the march passed to the Rev. Ralph Abernathy after King's assassination. The marchers were housed in a settlement of huts and tents called Resurrection City, set up near the Lincoln Memorial. On June 19, 50,000 people of all economic levels rallied in support of the poor. The park permit for Resurrection City expired on June 23. The marchers refused to vacate on the grounds that their demands had not been met. On June 24, the leaders of the march were arrested for failure to vacate.

Poor Richard's Almanack, by Benjamin Franklin **A** 197;
    selections **F** 452
  quoted on the importance of a nail **N** 3
Pop art **M** 398
  art of the artist **A** 438g
  reaction against abstract expressionism **P** 31, 32
  United States art movement of the 1960's **U** 122
Popcorn **C** 506
  recipe for popcorn balls **R** 116
Pope, Albert, built first American bicycle **B** 173
Pope, Alexander, English poet **P** 393
  essays in poetry form **E** 292
  place in English literature **E** 258
  quotations from *An Essay on Criticism* **Q** 20
Pope, John, American Union general **C** 323
Pope, John Russell, American architect **N** 40
Popes, of Roman Catholic Church **R** 296–97
  Gregory XIII **G** 375
  Gregory VII, Saint **G** 375
  Holy Roman Empire, emperors and popes **H** 162–64
  infallibility **R** 295
  John XXIII **J** 122
  Leo XIII **L** 152
  papal or Western Schism, Great, two popes **F** 415
  Paul VI **P** 99
  Peter, Saint **P** 167
  Pius XII **P** 266
  power grows in Middle Ages **M** 294
  Ring of the Fisherman, seal ring of the pope **J** 99
  Vatican City **V** 280–82
Popham Beach, Maine **M** 32
Popish Plot, 1678 **P** 378
  against Charles II of England **E** 224
  See *also* Oates, Titus
Poplar, tree
  uses of the wood and its grain, picture **W** 224
Pop music
  rock music **R** 262a–262d
Popocatepetl (po-po-CA-tep-etl), or "Smoking Mountain," Mexico **M** 242; pictures **M** 243, **N** 283

Popovich (pop-O-vich), **Pavel Romanovich** (1930–), Soviet astronaut, b. Uzin, Ukraine. Popovich's spacecraft, Vostok 4, was one of two launched in close parallel orbit on succeeding days. Popovich went up on Aug. 12, 1962; the other craft, piloted by Andrian Nikolayev, was launched Aug. 11. At one point the two craft were estimated to be within 50 miles of each other. The purpose of the twin flight was to gather information on the possibility of a space rendezvous.
  space flight data **S** 344, 345

Poppy, large group of flowering plants. Brightly colored flowers stand on long stems that may be more than 3 feet in height. After a blossom fades, a large capsule containing many small seeds remains. The drug opium is produced from the juice of one species of poppy. Seeds are used in baked goods. Picture **G** 46.
  opium poppy **N** 12; picture **P** 315

Poppy seed **S** 382
Popular sovereignty, or squatter sovereignty
  abolitionist movement **N** 95
  democratic privilege **D** 105
  Douglas proposed **D** 287
  Kansas-Nebraska Act **K** 192
  Lincoln-Douglas debates **L** 294–95, 299
  territory of Kansas **K** 190–91
Popular Front, in France **F** 419
Popular vote, for electors of the Electoral College
  E 116
Population **P** 394–97
  Africa **A** 54–55
  Asia **A** 452–53
  cities, growth of **C** 308
  distribution of world population **W** 263; diagram **W** 262
  environment and population **E** 272b–272c
  Europe's density **E** 315–16
  food and population **F** 343
  genetic distribution **G** 87–88
  How many different censuses are taken? **P** 396
  North America, density in **N** 302
  old age **O** 96–101
  population geography **G** 108
  poverty as result of overpopulation **P** 424a, 424b
  races of man **R** 29–32
  South America **S** 282
  United States, increases in **U** 99
  See *also* facts and figures sections of continent, country, province, state, and city articles
Population density, number of people per square mile **P** 394–95; diagram **P** 396
Population explosion **E** 272b–272c; **P** 396–97
Population geography **G** 108
Populist Party, United States **P** 381
  Harrison's defeat in 1892 **H** 48
Poquelin, Jean Baptiste see Molière
Porcelain (POR-cel-ain) **P** 413, 416–17
  antiques **A** 320
  ceramicwork, development of **C** 172
  coated steels **I** 403
Porcupines, rodents **R** 279–80
  quills, a variety of mammal hair, picture **M** 64
Pore fungi **F** 500
Pores, in the skin **B** 279

Porgy, name of a family of saltwater fishes, including the sheepshead, the jolthead porgy, and the scup, found chiefly in shallow temperate and tropical waters. These fishes have deep, flattened bodies; a single dorsal (upper) fin; pointed pectoral (behind the gill) fins; and stout teeth. The scup (also called porgy), a silvery-brown food fish, is found on the Atlantic coast of the United States from South Carolina to Cape Cod, Mass.
  habitats, feeding habits, uses **F** 214

Porgy and Bess, folk opera by George Gershwin **G** 190
  Negro Renaissance, contributions of the **N** 99
  story of the opera **O** 151
Po River, Italy **R** 247
  main river of Italy **I** 451
Pork, meat of hogs **M** 191; cuts of, picture **M** 193
  tabooed by certain religions **F** 334
  trichinosis from undercooked meat **D** 210–11; **F** 354
Pork-barrel bills, laws to win votes for politicians **A** 441
Poromerics, a type of plastic **S** 163
Porphyry (PORPH-iry), rock **R** 264; picture **R** 265
Porpoises (POR-poses), or dolphins **D** 270–79
  animal intelligence **A** 288
  learning experiments, picture **L** 100
  locomotion **A** 290

Port, left side of a boat or ship **S** 155
  sailing **S** 13
Porta, Giambattista della (Giovanni Battista della Porta), Italian scientist, father of cryptography **C** 369
Portable life-support systems, for astronauts **S** 340a, 340L–341; diagrams **S** 338, 340L
Portage la Prairie, Manitoba **M** 81
Portages, paths connecting sections of a water route around Niagara Falls **N** 243
  Chicago Portage National Historic Site **I** 82
  Grand Portage, Minnesota **M** 332
Portales (por-TA-lace), **Diego,** Chilean statesman **C** 254–55
Port Antonio, Jamaica **J** 17
Port Arthur, Manchuria **O** 49
Portative organ, picture **M** 548
Port-au-Prince (port-o-PRINCE), capital of Haiti **H** 9; picture **H** 11
  "Iron Market" gate, picture **C** 116
Portcullis (port-CULL-is), gate of a castle **F** 375; **H** 178
Port-de-Paix (por d'PAI), Haiti, picture **H** 8
Porter, a type of beer **B** 117
Porter, Cole, American composer **M** 542
Porter, Edwin S., American motion picture producer **M** 472

Porter, Gene Stratton (Geneva Grace Stratton) (1868–1924), American novelist and nature writer, b. Wabash, Ind. She wrote *Homing With the Birds* and other nature books.
  Limberlost State Memorial, Geneva, Ind. **I** 146

Porter, Katherine Anne, American writer **A** 214

Porter, Pleasant (1840–1907), Creek Indian chief, b. near Coweta, Okla. He fought for the Confederacy during the U.S. Civil War and was instrumental in shaping Creek policy when the war was over. He was a member and president of the upper house of the Creek Nation National Council, superintendent of Creek Nation schools, and the last chief of the Creek Nation.

Porter, William Sydney see Henry, O.
Portes Gil (PORT-ace HEEL), **Emilio,** Mexican president **M** 250
Port Étienne, now Nouadhibou, Mauritania **M** 180
Port Gentil (por jon-TI), Gabon, central Africa **G** 3
Port Harcourt, Nigeria **N** 255
Porthos, one of the Three Musketeers **D** 342–43
Portinari (por-ti-NA-ri), **Candido,** Brazilian artist **L** 67
Port La Joie, now Charlottetown, P.E.I., Canada **P** 456h
Portland, Maine **M** 44
Portland, Oregon **P** 398
  Mount Hood in view, picture **O** 198
Portland cement **C** 166
Portland Head Lighthouse, Maine, picture **L** 275
Port Louis, capital of Mauritius **M** 181
Port Moresby, New Guinea **N** 147
Pôrto Alegre (POR-too a-LEG-re), Brazil **B** 380
Porto da Cruz, Madeira Islands, picture **I** 434

Port of call, place for ships to stop and buy necessities, make repairs, and transfer or unload cargoes.

Port of entry, site of a customhouse, where imported goods are checked and aliens may be cleared.

Port of New York Authority
  in interstate commerce **I** 332
  New York Harbor, picture **H** 36
Port of Spain, capital of Trinidad and Tobago **T** 292; picture **T** 290

Porto-Novo, capital of Dahomey **D** 3
Porto Rico see Puerto Rico
Portrait dolls **D** 267–68
Portrait of a Married Couple, painting by Frans Hals **D** 361
Portrait of Charles I Hunting, painting by Anthony van Dyck **D** 359
Portrait painting
  Copley, John Singleton **U** 116–17
  Dutch and Flemish art **D** 357
  early American painters **U** 116–17
  English portrait painting in the age of the Royal Academy **E** 238
  Gainsborough, Thomas **G** 4
  mummy portraits **P** 17
  Peale, Charles Willson **M** 126; **U** 117
  Rembrandt's portraits **R** 155–56; picture **A** 438c
  Reynolds, Sir Joshua **R** 210
  Romney, George **E** 238
  Sargent, John Singer **S** 38
  Stuart, Gilbert **R** 225; **U** 117
  van Dyck, Anthony **V** 277
Portrait sculpture **S** 90, 95
Port Royal, Nova Scotia, Canada **C** 69
Ports see Harbors and ports
Portsmouth, New Hampshire **N** 160
Port Sudan (por su-DAN), Sudan **S** 448
Port Swettenham, Malaysia **M** 55
Port Talbot, Wales, picture **U** 75
Portugal **P** 399–404
  African exploration **A** 67
  Angola **A** 260–61
  beach scene, picture **G** 101
  Brazil **B** 383–84
  bullfighting **B** 450
  exploration and discoveries **E** 374
  flag **F** 240
  Gama, Vasco da, explorer **G** 7
  Henry the Navigator, discoverer of discoverers **E** 374
  Magellan **M** 17
  Mozambique **M** 500
  national anthem **N** 22
  Rio de Janeiro, capital of the empire **R** 237
  slavery in 15th century **S** 197
Portuguese, people of Portugal **P** 399
Portuguese East Africa see Mozambique

Portuguese Guinea (GHIN-e) (pop. 600,000), Portuguese overseas province (13,948 sq. mi.) on western coast of Africa. The province includes the island of Bolama, which is part of the Bijagós archipelago. It is controlled by the Portuguese Ministry of Overseas Provinces through an appointed resident governor. A national liberation movement was begun in 1962 to end Portuguese rule. The capitol is Bissau. Principal agricultural products are peanuts, coconuts, palm oil, and rice.
  Portugal's overseas territories **P** 401–02

Portuguese language
  Brazil **B** 374; **L** 49
Portuguese man-of-war, jellyfish **J** 75; picture **J** 71
Portuguese Timor **P** 402; **S** 328
Portulacas (por-tu-LAC-as), flowers, picture **G** 48
  leaves, special kinds of, pictures **L** 120
Poseidon (po-SY-don), Greek god **G** 356–57
Poseidon missiles **M** 347
  U.S. Navy missiles **U** 193
Positano (pos-i-TA-no), Italy, pictures **C** 343, **M** 212
Positive charges, of electricity **E** 123–35
Positive ions **I** 351
Positive numbers, or those greater than zero **N** 384
  in algebra **A** 158–59

Positrons (POS-i-trons), subatomic particles **A** 486
  nuclear energy **N** 370
Possession is nine points of the law L 93
Possums, marsupials **K** 175

Post, Emily Price (1873–1960), American writer, b. Baltimore, Md. She wrote the book *Etiquette,* which established her as an expert on social manners.

Post, Wiley, American aviator **O** 94
Postage stamps *see* Stamps and stamp collecting
Postal Inspection Service P 410
Postal Reorganization Act, 1970 **P** 408
Postal Service, United States P 408; **U** 111
  Postal Inspection Service **F** 76; **P** 410
Post-and-lintel, architecture **A** 374, 375, 376
Post Boys, 16th-century English mail carriers **P** 406
Post-Dispatch, St. Louis, Missouri newspaper **M** 375
Posters P 404
  commercial art **C** 426; pictures **C** 427
  Communist, pictures **C** 442, 445
  plays, pictures **A** 216
  Toulouse-Lautrec, Henri de **T** 228–29
  uses of silk-screen printing **S** 180
  World War I recruiting poster, picture **W** 273
Posthypnotic (post-hip-NOT-ic) **suggestion H** 315–16
Postimpressionism, in art **F** 431
  modern art **M** 388
  twentieth-century painting **P** 29
  See also the artists by name, as Cézanne, Paul
Posting, in horseback riding, picture **H** 229
Postmarks, on mail **P** 405
Postmaster General, former member of the cabinet of the U.S. **P** 448
Postmasters P 408
Postmaster's Provisionals, stamps **S** 396
Postmen, community helpers **P** 405, 408–09
Post office P 405–10
  canceled stamps in a collection **S** 396–97
  communication advanced by postal service **C** 435–36
  computers sort mail **C** 449
  how to wrap gifts for mailing **G** 209
  interstate commerce under Articles of Confederation **I** 331
  mail cars, post offices on wheels **R** 81
  Pony Express **P** 392–93
  snowmobiles used to deliver mail **S** 215
  United Nations, Universal Postal Union (UPU) **U** 86
Poston (PO-ston), **Charles D.,** American explorer **A** 416
Postriders, early messenger service **C** 435
Postulates (POS-tu-lates), mathematical assumptions **M** 159
  rules in geometry **G** 123
Posture, of the body
  conditioning exercises **P** 226–29
  graceful walkers, picture **G** 198
Potala, seat of the Dalai Lama, Tibet **T** 177; picture **T** 175
Potamogales (pot-a-MOG-al-ese), or otter shrews, animals of insectivore group **I** 261
Potash, potassium fertilizer **F** 97
  Canadian deposits largest in the world **S** 38f
  Congo (Brazzaville) **C** 463
  glass **G** 226
Potassium (po-TASS-ium), element **E** 155, 163
  chemical formulas for compounds **C** 199
  fertilizers **F** 96, 97
  nutrition, use in **N** 417
  producing regions of North America **N** 295
Potassium-40, radioactive element **R** 65
Potassium-argon method, archeological dating process **A** 362

Potassium nitrate (NY-trate), chemical compound
  explosives **E** 390
Potatoes P 411–12
  blight and famine in Ireland **F** 498
  Burbank variety **B** 453
  food plants **P** 307
  fungus blight and famine in Ireland **F** 498; **I** 391
  Idaho's yield **I** 61; picture **I** 58
  Maine, a leading producer **M** 39
  New World crops brought to Europe and Ireland **A** 100; **I** 390
  Prince Edward Island, Canada **P** 456e; picture **P** 456g
  shoots on the tuber, picture **P** 300
  stems we eat **P** 307; picture **P** 306
  vegetable growing **V** 292
  What is the difference between a potato and a sweet potato? **P** 412
Potato famine, in Ireland, 1845–48 **I** 391
Potawatoni, Indians of North America **I** 179

Potemkin (pot-YOM-kin), **Prince Gregori Aleksandrovich** (1739–1791), Russian statesman, b. near Smolensk. A favorite of Empress Catherine II, he participated in the plot against Peter III that placed her on the throne. He was a distinguished fighter against the Turks and a primary influence on Catherine's policy. He was governor of Crimea (1783), built the arsenal of Kherson and the harbor of Sevastopol, ordered the construction of a fleet in the Black Sea, and commanded (1787–91) the Russian Army during the second Turkish War.
  Russian history **U** 49

Potential, electric E 126
Potential energy E 198
Potiphar (POT-i-phar), character in the Bible **J** 140
Potlatch, Indian custom of lavish giving **I** 181
  Indian ceremonials of mythological origin **M** 559–60
Potomac (po-TO-mac), **Army of the,** Civil War **C** 322–26
Potomac River, United States **R** 247
  Maryland **M** 117
  Virginia **V** 347
Potosí (po-to-SE), Bolivia **B** 306
Potsdam, Germany
  Allied Conference, 1945 **W** 308
Pott, Percival, English surgeon **C** 91
Pottawatomie (po-ta-WA-to-me) **Creek,** Kansas, massacre **C** 320
Potter, Beatrix, English artist and writer **C** 241
  Tale of Peter Rabbit, picture **C** 241
Potter's wheel P 413–14
  ceramics **C** 175; picture **C** 173
  uses of the wheel **W** 157
Pottery P 413–19
  ancient Greek art form **G** 343
  antique **A** 320, picture **A** 319
  Arabia brand, of Finland, picture **F** 135
  archeological shards **A** 358, 361
  ceramics **C** 172–76
  fired pottery, man's second great chemical discovery **F** 142
  folk art **F** 295–96
  Greek vase painting **P** 16–17
  Indian art of North and South America **I** 152–57; pictures **I** 184
  Why does an unglazed ceramic jug keep liquids cool? **C** 175
  See also Vases
Potting, of plants **H** 267–68
Pottos, primates **M** 422
Pouched mammals *see* Marsupials
Pouchless marsupials (mar-SU-pials) **K** 169
  numbat, picture **K** 174

Poulenc (poo-LANC), **Francis,** French composer F 448
   French opera O 138

Poulsen (POWL-sen), **Valdemar** (1869–1942), Danish engineer and inventor, b. Copenhagen. In 1898 he invented the wire recorder, which he called the telegraphone. This machine, which recorded sound as magnetic patterns on a steel wire, was the ancestor of today's tape recorder. He also invented (1903) a transmitter used in wireless telegraphy.
   tape and wire recorders, invention of T 20

Poultry (POLT-ry) P 420–23
   animal signals A 276, 277
   chickens as pets P 180
   eggs and embryos E 88–90a
   farm birds as pets B 248
   learning experiment, picture L 103
   marketing for the home M 102
   pecking orders A 280
Poultry seasoning, blend of spices S 382
Poults, young turkeys P 423
Pound, Ezra, American poet A 209
Pound, measure of weight W 112
Pound, Roscoe, American lawyer and educator N 85
Poussin (poo-SAN), **Nicolas,** French painter F 422, 425
   baroque art B 59
   Triumph of Flora, painting F 423

Poutrincourt (poo-tran-COOR), **Jean de Biencourt, sieur de, baron de Saint Just** (1577–1615), French soldier and colonizer in Canada, b. Méry-sur-Seine. He joined a colonizing expedition to Acadia, Nova Scotia, in 1603 and accompanied Champlain on his expedition to the Bay of Fundy, on the eastern coast of Canada, in 1606.

Poverty P 424–424b
   American Indians I 200a–200b
   See also Unemployment; Welfare, Public
POW see Prisoner of War
Powdered milk F 348
Powderly, Terence V., American labor leader L 4
Powder metallurgy M 232
Powders, cosmetics C 509
   beauty culture B 110

Powell, Adam Clayton, Jr. (1908–72), American politician b. New Haven, Conn. He was the first Negro member of the New York City Council (1941), and was elected to the U.S. House of Representatives (1944), where he later became chairman of the Committee on Education and Labor. Excluded from his seat (1967) for alleged improper use of government funds for private use, he was returned (1969) to the House when the U.S. Supreme Court ruled that he had wrongfully been denied his seat. He was defeated in a bid for re-election in the New York primary (1970).

Powell, John (1882–   ), American composer, pedagogue, and pianist, b. Richmond, Va. He was a pupil of composer Theodor Leschetizky in Vienna and made his debut as pianist in Berlin (1907). His compositions include his well-known work *The Negro Rhapsody.*

Powell, John Wesley, American geologist and explorer G 98, 99
   first director of Geological Survey C 485
   Grand Canyon gorge boat trip G 292
Powell, Michael, English motion-picture director M 487
Power, in mechanics W 249–50
   diesel engines power cycle, diagrams D 170
   energy E 198–203

gears for passing along motion and power G 65–66
   internal-combustion engines I 303–08
   new sources for the Industrial Revolution I 235–38
   rocket power R 256–57
   solar power P 427
   sources of, for manufacturing M 83
   uranium resources in North America N 295
   waterpower W 60–63
Power, in optical instruments O 166–67
Power, of government G 273
Powerboats and powerboat racing B 264
Power plants P 425–27
   Canadian water power C 56–57
   coal-burning C 364
   dams D 20, 21
   electric generators E 121–22
   hydroelectric power plant, diagram W 61
   nuclear power plant, picture N 353
   public utilities P 511
   transformers T 249–50
   United States production U 109
Power politics see Balance of Power
Power resources see continent, country, and state articles

Powers, Francis Gary (1930–   ), American pilot. He was shot down in central Soviet Union while piloting a U-2 jet on a military reconnaissance mission (May 1, 1960). In U.S.S.R., Powers was convicted of espionage and sentenced to 10 years' confinement. In 1962, with Frederic Pryor he was exchanged for the Soviet spy Rudolf Abel.

Power shovels B 447
Power tools T 216–19

Powhatan (pow-ha-TAN) (Wahunsonacook) (1550?–1618), American Indian chief, head and founder of group of Algonkin tribes known as the Powhatan confederacy. He ambushed and killed English settlers, but when his daughter Pocahontas married English colonist John Rolfe, a peace was concluded that was kept until Powhatan's death.
   Indian resistance to settlement at Jamestown, Virginia I 212; J 20; V 358

Poznan, Poland P 361
Pozzo (PO-tzo), **Andrea,** Italian painter B 59
PPI see Plan position indicator, of radar systems
Practical nurses N 412
Prades (PROD) **Festival,** France M 551
Prado (PRA-do), museum, Madrid, Spain P 428–29
   great museums of the world M 511
   places of interest in Madrid M 11

Praetorian (pre-TOR-ian) **Guard,** in ancient Rome, bodyguards of the emperor. A military force, it was organized by Augustus. First consisting of nine and then 10 cohorts, it grew so politically powerful that it could make or unmake emperors. The most flagrant of its deeds was the murder of Emperor Pertinax and public auctioning of the empire to Didius Julianus in A.D. 193. The guard was gradually regulated from the end of the 2nd century and was suppressed by Constantine the Great.

Praetorius (prae-TO-rius), **Michael** (1571–1621), German composer, organist, and theorist, b. Kreuzberg, Thuringia. He composed much church music as well as madrigals and instrumental pieces. His chief theoretical work is the *Syntagma Musicum,* which includes an important source of information on medieval and Renaissance musical instruments.

Christmas carols and polyphonic music **C** 122; **G** 182

Pragmatic (prag-MAT-ic) **Sanction,** decree of Austria's Charles VI **A** 525
Pragmatism (PRAG-ma-tism), school of philosophy
Dewey, John **D** 151
James, William **J** 19
Prague (PROG) (Praha), capital of Czechoslovakia **C** 562; pictures **C** 559, 562
Prairie chickens, near-extinct birds **B** 232
Prairie dogs, rodents **R** 276–77
Prairie Dog Town in Mackenzie State Park, Texas **T** 133
"towns" **A** 281
Prairie Hills, South Dakota **S** 314
Prairie Provinces, Canadian provinces of Alberta, Manitoba, Saskatchewan **A** 146a–h–147; **M** 76–82; **S** 38a–38h
interior plains of Canada **C** 51
Winnipeg **W** 190
Prairies **P** 430–33
animals, pictures **A** 269
communities of living things **L** 256, 258
Drift Prairie region of North Dakota **N** 324
in American literature **A** 208
wild flowers **W** 171
Prairie schooners **C** 458
homes on wheels **P** 253–54
wagon trains on overland trails **O** 261–62
Prairie State, nickname for Illinois **I** 71
Prairie wolves see Coyotes
Prakrit (PRA-krit), ancient language of India
dramatic language **D** 293
Prang (PRONG), **Louis,** German-born American lithographer and engraver **G** 373
designed Christmas cards **C** 294
Pranks
American folk humor **F** 313
Praseodymium (prase-e-o-DIM-ium), element **E** 155, 164
Pratolini, Vasco, Italian novelist **I** 481
Pratt, Daniel, American industrial leader **A** 125
Pratt, Edwin John, Canadian author **C** 64
Pravda, Soviet newspaper **U** 41
Prawns, shrimp-like crustaceans **S** 168–71
Praxiteles (prax-IT-el-ese), Greek sculptor **G** 346
Prayer **P** 434–35
forms of in the Roman Catholic Church **R** 301–02
litanies, ritual prayers **O** 229
See also Angelus; Grace

Prayer, Book of Common, official service book of the Church of England and the Episcopal Church in the United States. It was first issued in 1549 under Thomas Cranmer, archbishop of Canterbury, and revised in 1662. It contains prayers, rituals, and a calendar of holy days.
Anglican and Episcopal worship **P** 484
Henry VIII and the Church of England **E** 221
prayers, a selection **P** 434, 435

Prayer, The Lord's see Lord's Prayer, The
Prayer of Manasseh (ma-NASS-eh), apocryphal book of Bible **B** 159

Prayer wheel, device used by Tibetan Buddhists (Lamaists) to aid in prayer. Its usage is allegedly based on a literal interpretation of the scriptures to "turn the wheel of the law." Barrel-shaped, it contains such sacred writings as "The Jewel in the Lotus, Amen," and can be rotated as a substitution for saying the prayers.

Praying mantis, insect see Mantis
Praying Town of Natick, Massachusetts **M** 149
Preakness horse race **H** 232
Pre-Cambrian period, in geology **F** 383
Canadian Shield **C** 50
Precepts, rules of Roman Catholic Church **R** 299
Precession
behavior of a gyroscope **G** 435
Precincts
police districts **P** 375
Precious metals **E** 158
Precious stones
aluminum compounds **A** 176
birthstones **G** 72
carats **J** 92, 93
famous diamonds **D** 156
gemstones **G** 68–76
jewelry **J** 93
Precipitate (pre-CIP-it-ate), in chemistry **C** 220
Precipitation (rain, snow, sleet, and hail) **R** 93–98
climate, types of **C** 343, 346–47
clouds **C** 358–61
descriptive table of kinds of precipitation **W** 76
fog **F** 288
how rivers flow **R** 238–39
hydrologic, or water cycles **W** 52–53
world patterns, diagram **W** 256
world water resources **W** 257
See also climate section of continent, country, province, and state articles

Precipitation probability, phrase used by weather forecasters to describe the chance of rain, snow, or other form of precipitation occurring. For example, "The precipitation probability for tomorrow is 45%."

Precocial (pre-CO-cial) **birds** **B** 215
Predators (PRED-at-ors)
cat family, beasts of prey **C** 134–41
dog family in balance of nature **D** 243
fishes **F** 187
Predestination (pre-des-ti-NATION)
Calvin's doctrine **C** 30
Predicate adjectives **P** 91
Pre-emption laws, for settlers of public lands **P** 506–07
Prefabricated houses **H** 171; picture **H** 174
Prefaces (PREF-a-ces), of books **L** 181
Preferred stocks, those with priority in payment of dividends **S** 428
Prefixes, additions at front of root parts of words **W** 239
Pregnancy **M** 72
women, role of **W** 211
Prehistorian an archeologist **A** 349, 364
Prehistoric animals **P** 436–38
birds, extinct **B** 229–32
dinosaurs **D** 172–81
elephants **E** 170
evolution **E** 338–47
fossils **F** 378–88
marsupials **K** 172
Prehistoric art **P** 439–41
art as a record **A** 438, 438b
cave paintings **C** 158
Lascaux cave paintings, pictures **A** 354, **W** 217
Pacific islands **P** 9–10
painting **P** 14–15
sculpture **S** 92
Prehistoric man **P** 442–46
anthropological studies **A** 306, 308, 309
archeological evidence of **A** 359–61
cave dwellers **C** 157–58
cereal grains **G** 281

Prendergast, Mehitabel Wing (1737?–1812), American heroine, b. Dutchess County, N.Y. At a 1766 trial in Poughkeepsie, N.Y., her husband, William (1727–1811), was sentenced to death by hanging for leading a revolt against landowners. She traveled by horseback to and from New York City in 3 days, getting for him a stay of execution and later a full pardon.

Presidential Medal of Freedom, medal awarded by the president of the United States to honor civilians in peacetime. Given yearly to Americans (since 1963), the medal honors outstanding contributions in such areas as national security, world peace, and the arts.

Presley, Elvis (1935–), American entertainer, b. Tupelo, Miss. His phenomenal career began in 1955 with the recording *Heartbreak Hotel*. Since then, he has made many single records and albums, most of which have sold well over 1,000,000 copies. Presley has appeared in several motion pictures that, although they did not gain critical acclaim, have fared well at the box office. He also continues to be a popular attraction in nightclubs and consistently breaks attendance records wherever he appears. Picture R 262b
  rock music R 262c

Pressure groups, groups that try to promote certain interests. They are minority groups, often political, that wish to sway others to their way of thinking. Some pressure groups employ lobbyists, and some conduct campaigns through the mail and through advertisements.

Prester John ("John the Priest"), legendary Christian king and priest. He supposedly ruled over a fabulous kingdom in either Africa or Asia during the Middle Ages, and many legends sprang up about him. One story claims he had 70 kings as his slaves, and one account of his kingdom tells of ants that mined gold and of a magic herb that did away with demons.

> adventurous explorers hoped to find Prester John's kingdom **E** 373

Prestressed concrete **C** 166
  advantages of, as bridge material **B** 401
  building technology advance **B** 438
Pretoria (pre-TO-ria), administrative capital of South Africa **S** 271
Pretzels, origin of **B** 389
Prevailing winds
  climate and winds **C** 346
  climate control factor **W** 88
Prevention of disease see Disease, prevention of
Preventive medicine **D** 219–22
  doctors **D** 238
  public health **P** 502–06
Prévost, Antoine (Abbé Prévost), French novelist **F** 439
Prez, Josquin des see Josquin des Prez

Priam (PRY-am), in Greek mythology, the king of Troy during the time of the Trojan War. Son of Laomedon and husband of Hecuba, he was the father of more than 60 children—among them Hector, Paris, Troilus, and Cassandra. When the Greeks entered Troy by ruse of the wooden horse, Priam was killed at Zeus's altar.
  Iliad, story of **I** 69

Pribilof (PRIB-i-lof), **Gerasim,** Russian explorer **I** 435
Pribilof Islands, Alaska **I** 435–36
  Alaska **A** 130, 138
  Bering Sea **O** 46
  breeding territory of northern fur seals **W** 6–7
  seals, picture **H** 191

Price, Leontyne (1927–), American soprano, Negro, b. Laurel, Miss. She has sung in most of the leading opera houses of Europe and America. She made her debut at the Metropolitan Opera House as Leonora in *Il Trovatore* (1961). Possessing a rich and perfectly controlled voice of wide range, she has. sung a variety of leading roles. In 1966 she sang Cleopatra (a role written for her) in Samuel Barber's *Antony and Cleopatra,* at opening of new Metropolitan at Lincoln Center. Picture **N** 102.

Prices **E** 50
  depressions and recessions caused by falling prices **D** 121–22
  inflation and deflation of **I** 252–53
  marketing for the home **M** 100
  Nixon's wage-price freeze **N** 262f
Prickly pear, cactus **C** 4; pictures **C** 3, **F** 276, **W** 169
Prides, of lions **C** 135–36

Priestley, J. B. (John Boynton Priestley) (1894–   ), English writer, b. Bradford, Yorkshire. He has written novels (*The Good Companions, Bright Day*) and plays (*Dangerous Corner, An Inspector Calls*) as well as nonfiction (*Literature and Western Man*). In 1946–47 he was the United Kingdom's delegate to the conferences of UNESCO.

Priestley, Joseph, English scientist **P** 455–56
  experiments on oxidation **C** 210; picture **C** 211
  experiments to test ideas **E** 351
  Joseph Priestley House, Northumberland, Penn. **P** 140
Priests **M** 293–94
  women, role of **W** 213
Prima Porta Augustus, statue, picture **R** 286

Primary colors **D** 139
Primary elections **E** 115
Primary products, raw materials **I** 327
Primates (PRIME-ates), order of mammals **M** 417–22
  adaptability tests **A** 287
  adaptations in the world of life **L** 225–26
  hands **F** 83
  mammals, orders of **M** 62, 68
Primaticcio, Francesco, Italian artist **R** 171
Primavera (pri-ma-VER-a) (*Spring*), painting by Botticelli **B** 340b; **P** 20
Prime meridian, or Greenwich meridian **T** 190
  Greenwich observatory **G** 372
  international date line **I** 309–10
  latitude and longitude **L** 83
Prime minister, or premier **P** 456–456a
  Ceylon has first woman prime minister **C** 180
  Commonwealth prime ministers, 1964, picture **E** 232
  Gladstone's career **G** 225
  origin in English history **E** 225
  parliaments **P** 81–82
  United Kingdom **U** 77–78
  women, role of **W** 213; pictures **W** 212b
  See also Political parties
Prime numbers **N** 378–79
  in mathematics **M** 155
Primers, textbooks **T** 138
  basal readers **R** 109
Prime time, in broadcasting
  radio **R** 56
  television **T** 70b, 70d, 71
Priming powder, for guns **G** 415
Primitive art
  art as a record **A** 438, 438b
  folk art **F** 290–96
  Indian art of North and South America **I** 152–57
  sculpture **S** 92
Primitive man
  art as a record **A** 438, 438b
  law enforcement by folkways **L** 88
  North American Indian beginnings **I** 162–64
  religions **R** 145
  superstition **S** 473
Primitive music
  African **A** 77–78
  Indian music of North America **I** 160–61
Primitive religion see Religion, primitive
Primrose, evening, flower
  pollen grains, picture **P** 297

Primrose League, organization of British conservatives founded in 1883. The league was founded to honor Prime Minister Benjamin Disraeli (1804–81).

Primus (PRI-mus), **Pearl** (1921–), American dancer and choreographer, Negro, b. Trinidad, West Indies. Like ·Katherine Dunham, she was a student of anthropology who explored her African heritage in the world of dance. She made her New York concert debut in 1943, opened a school of dance (1947), and was sent to Africa on a Julius Rosenwald Fellowship (1949–51).
  Negro artists **N** 102

Prince, Arthur, English ventriloquist **V** 301
Prince, The, political work by Machiavelli **I** 477–78
Prince Albert, Saskatchewan, Canada **S** 38g
Prince Albert National Park, Saskatchewan, Canada **S** 38f
Prince Charles spaniel, dog, picture **D** 260
Prince Edward Island, Canada **P** 456b–456h
  Canada's "million-acre garden" **C** 50, 58

Prince George, British Columbia, Canada **B** 406d
Prince of Wales, eldest son of the British monarch **W** 4
Prince of Wales College, Charlottetown, P.E.I. **P** 456e
Prince Phillip Prosper of Spain, painting by Diego Veláz-
quez **P** 22, 24
Prince Rupert, British Columbia, Canada **B** 406d
Princes in the Tower, boy prisoners **P** 470
Princess Ida, operetta by Gilbert and Sullivan **G** 210
Princess on the Pea, story by Hans Christian Andersen
F 26
Princeton, New Jersey
Revolutionary War battle **R** 202
Princeton University, Princeton, New Jersey **N** 173
Wilson, Woodrow, as president **W** 178
Princip (PREEN-ceep), **Gavrilo,** Serbian assassin of Arch-
duke Francis Ferdinand **W** 270
Principal focus, of a lens **L** 143–44
refraction of light **L** 263–64
Principality, country ruled by a prince
Liechtenstein **L** 207
Monaco **M** 406–07
Principe, island see São Tomé and Principe

Pring, Martin (1580?–1626?), English explorer, b. Awlis-
combe, Devonshire. He led an expedition to the New World,
becoming the first white man on record to reach New
Hampshire.
New Hampshire, history of **N** 162

Printed circuit, electrical circuit whose parts are connected by metallic conductors that are printed or plated
onto a plastic sheet. (In ordinary circuits the parts are
connected by copper wires soldered from part to part.)
Printed circuits are cheaper to make than soldered
circuits, they save space and weight, and they are more
reliable because there are no wires that can break.
uses of electroplating **E** 150

Printing **P** 457–67
advertising **A** 33, 34
air conditioning effects **A** 102
bookbinding **B** 327–29
book design **B** 323–26
change in education produced by **E** 67
colonial America **C** 394
commercial art **C** 425–26
communication advanced by **C** 433–34
daily cartoons **C** 127
earliest printed books **B** 321; picture **B** 320
electrotyping **E** 150
engraving process **E** 272
etching process **E** 293–95
freedom of the press **F** 457
Gutenberg, Johann **G** 427
How does a printer plan a layout? **P** 464
influenced German language **G** 173
inks **I** 255
invention important to communication **I** 345
lithography **L** 314–15
magnesium used in **M** 23
newspapers **N** 198, 203
paper **P** 51–57
photographic prints **P** 217–18
posters and color lithography **P** 404
presses famous for design **B** 324, 326
proofreading **P** 479
propaganda **P** 481
stamps identified by printer's mark **S** 398
textile dyeing **D** 372
type **T** 343–46
woodcut printing **W** 228–29
Zenger, John Peter **Z** 369

Printing, or manuscript writing **H** 31
language arts **L** 36
Printing presses **P** 461–63
Franklin working at a printing press, picture **F** 451
Leonardo da Vinci's design, picture **L** 154
Prints, copies of a single drawing, how made **G** 302–08
silk-screen printing **S** 180
Printz, Johan, Swedish administrator in America **D** 99
Pripet (PRIP-et) **Marshes,** Ukraine, U.S.S.R. **U** 8
Prisms
lenses in telescopes **L** 147, 265
Prisoner of Chillon, The, poem by Byron, excerpt **B** 482

Prisoner of war, person captured or interned by an
enemy power during wartime. Most prisoners of war are
members of armed forces, although some civilians are
interned as prisoners. Various international agreements
are designed to protect prisoners' rights. "Prisoner of
war" is abbreviated POW.

Prisons **P** 468–70
boy prisoners in the Tower **E** 220; **P** 470
law enforcement **L** 89
Tower of London **L** 334
What is a bridewell? **P** 469
Pritchett, V. S., English critic **E** 268
Private (or free) **enterprise,** economic system
poverty, cures for **P** 424b
women, role of **W** 212a–212b
Privateers, armed private ships, commissioned to fight
the enemy **P** 263–64
War of 1812 **W** 12
Private property see Private (or free) enterprise
Private schools **E** 75

Privy Council, a council originally chosen by the British
monarch to conduct affairs of state. Today it is largely
an honorary body. From the Middle Ages until the 18th
century the Privy Council had considerable power. This
declined after much of the monarch's power passed to
the British Cabinet. Today each cabinet minister is also
a member of the Privy Council.
parliaments, history of **P** 81

Privy Seal, seal first used in conducting British rulers'
private business and later for official business that did
not call for the Great Seal. The Great Seal Act of 1848
simplified the use of the privy seal, and it is now
primarily employed for documents that are later going to
pass the Great Seal. The holder of the office of Lord
Privy Seal is a member of the British Cabinet.

Prix de Rome (pri d' ROM), **Grand,** scholarship given
annually to French architects, engravers, musicians,
painters, or sculptors. Awards are made through the
supervision of Paris' École de Beaux Arts, and winners
study at the French Academy in Rome. The Prix de
Rome dates back to 1666.

Prizefighting, origin of term **B** 353
Prize Song, from *Die Meistersinger,* a few bars **O** 148
Probability, in mathematics **P** 470–74
chance in statistics **S** 418
historical work in classical mathematics **M** 156–57
Probate proceedings, to decide whether a will is genuine
W 175
Probation, in law **C** 530
convicted persons **P** 470
Probes, space see Space probes
Problem box, used for animal trial-and-error studies
A 284–85
Problem solving **P** 499–500

Proboscidea (pro-bos-CID-e-a), order of mammals **M** 62
  elephants **E** 170
Proboscis (pro-BOS-cis), of bees **H** 202
Proboscidea (pro-bos-CID-e-a), order of mammals **M** 62, 68
Proboscis monkeys M 420; pictures **M** 421
Procaine, or Novocain, synthetic drug **D** 328
  local anesthetic **A** 258

Procrustes (pro-CRUST-ese), in Greek mythology, a robber who tied victims to his bed and made them fit it by either cutting off or stretching their limbs. He was killed by Theseus.

Procyon (PRO-ci-on), star **C** 492
Procyonidae (pro-ci-ON-id-e), family of animals **R** 25

Prodigal Son, in New Testament (Luke 15:11—32), the repentant sinner in a parable related by Jesus. The story tells of a young man who leaves his father's house and squanders his inheritance. When he repents his wicked ways and returns home, his father rejoices and prepares a great feast. The phrase is still used to describe a wastrel who reforms.

Prodigal Son, The, engraving by Albrecht Dürer **D** 345
Producers, of plays **T** 157
Product, in multiplication **A** 400
Production, in economics
  consumer education and product testing **C** 494a
  economic factors of **E** 50, 51
  industrial controls **I** 251
  mass production **M** 151
  trusts and monopolies **T** 303—06
  world industrial areas **W** 266—67
  See also industries and products section of country, province, and state articles
Products see facts and figures for country, province, and state articles
Professional football F 365
Professional Golfers' Association (P.G.A.) **G** 262
Professional Placement Center, United States Employment Service **T** 42
Professions see Vocations
Profile Mountain, New Hampshire rock formation **N** 148; picture **N** 150
Profiles in Courage, book by John F. Kennedy **K** 211
  Ross, Edmund, one of the biographees **K** 189
Profit and loss statement, in bookkeeping **B** 312
Profit motive, in economics **E** 50
  motive or aim of capitalism **C** 104—05
  needed in industry **I** 243—44
Programed instruction P 475—477
  materials and methods in education **E** 78
  reading instruction **R** 109
Programing, of computers **C** 452, 457
  automated controls **A** 530
  office machines and computers **O** 58
Program music M 538
  tone poems and romantic music **R** 311
Progressive education E 76
  kindergarten and nursery schools **K** 243—44
Progressive Party, or Bull Moose Party, United States **P** 381
  La Follette, Robert M. **L** 24
  Roosevelt, Theodore **R** 330
  symbol **P** 379
  Truman wins in spite of third parties **T** 301
Wilson wins because of third party **T** 9; **W** 178—79

Prohibition, policy of legally forbidding manufacture, transportation, or sale of alcoholic beverages except for medical or sacramental use. In the United States, prohibition was installed with the passage of the 18th Amendment to the Constitution (1919). Opposition and violation provoked its repeal (21st Amendment, 1933).
  The Roaring 20's of Coolidge's administration **C** 496—97

Prohibition Party, United States **P** 381
Project Head Start, for needy children, picture **E** 76

Project HOPE (Health Opportunity for People Everywhere), program in which a ship, equipped with the latest facilities for medical treatment and training, visits underdeveloped countries that request its aid. Vital medical assistance is rendered, native personnel are trained in up-to-date techniques, and permanent land programs are established. These land projects include an orthopedic rehabilitation center at Saigon, Vietnam, and an internship and residency training program at the University of Trujillo, Peru. Founded in 1960, the project is sponsored by the nonprofit People-to-People Health Foundation Inc. It has its headquarters in Washington, D.C., and publishes the *Hope News.*

Projection, in mechanical drawing **M** 197
Projections, of maps **M** 91—93; pictures **M** 89, 94
Projective geometry, branch of mathematics **M** 157—58
Projectors, in photography
  moviemaking at home **P** 220
Projects, how they differ from experiments **E** 355
  4-H club projects **F** 46, 47
  See also Experiments and projects
Project Stormfury, hurricane control **W** 96
Prokofiev (pro-KO-fi-ef), **Sergei,** Russian composer **P** 477
  opera **O** 138
  Russian music **U** 64
Prometheus (pro-ME-the-us), Greek god **G** 357—58
Promethium (pro-ME-thi-um), element **E** 155, 164
Prominences, flames extending from the sun **S** 461
Promise, poem from *Lyrics of Lowly Life,* by Paul Dunbar **D** 344
Promised Land, or Canaan **M** 468
Promontory, Utah **U** 250
  Golden Spike being driven, picture **A** 204
Prompters, of plays **P** 336
Pronghorn, hoofed mammal **H** 220
  fastest mammal in North America **M** 63
Pronouns, words that stand instead of nouns **P** 90—91
Pronunciation P 478
  alphabet **A** 172, 173
  dialects distinguished by **D** 152
  dictionary, a guide for the speaker **S** 377
  French compared to English **F** 435
  German language, stage pronunciation **G** 173
  how to use the pronunciation guides for this encyclopedia **A** 579—81
  Initial Teaching Alphabet **I** 254
  Latin language **L** 76
  phonics **P** 194
  Sephardic pronunciation of Hebrew **H** 100
  slang imitates sounds **S** 194
  some Greek words in everyday use **G** 349
  some Hawaiian words **H** 63
  speech sounds **S** 377—78
  spelling **S** 378
  vocabulary building, use in **V** 372
  See also individual letters of the alphabet
Proof, amount of alcohol in a beverage **W** 159
Proof, in engraving and printing **E** 272
Proof box, bread-making device **B** 388
Proofreaders' marks P 479

Proofreading P 479
  newspapers N 203
  reports R 176
  spelling S 378
Proof sets, of coins C 375
Propaganda (prop-a-GAN-da) P 480–81
  learning to read critically R 110
Propagation, of plants see Plant propagation
Propane (PRO-pane), gas, used as fuel F 489
Propellants, rocket fuels F 490
  launching of rockets R 258
Propellers
  airplanes A 38–39, 558
  birds have propellers B 204
  ocean liners, history of O 23–24
  screw propellers of ships S 160–61
Proper fractions F 398
Proper nouns P 90
Properties, articles used in plays see Props
Properties, chemical C 196; E 158
Properties, of metals A 168
Properties, of numbers N 387–88
Propertius (pro-PER-shus), Roman poet B 111
Property management, of real estate R 113
Prophets, books of Bible, Old Testament B 154–56
Prophets, Hebrew J 104–05
  Elijah E 176
  Isaiah I 413
  Jeremiah J 77
  Moses M 468
Propmen, of plays P 336
Proportion, in design D 133–34
  ancient Greek vases G 343
  Greek temples A 374
  Italian Renaissance architecture A 381

Proportional Representation (P.R.), voting system designed to give minorities greater representation in governing bodies. Elections are based not on a simple majority but on a ratio of the total number of votes received by each candidate. Some form of the system is used in Norway, France, Italy, and other countries, as well as in a few American cities.

Proprietary (pro-PRY-et-ary) **drugs** D 321
Prop roots, of plants, picture P 291
Props, articles used in plays P 339; pictures P 337, 338
  prop room backstage T 156
Proscenium (pro-CE-nium) **stage** T 155
Prosecutor (PROS-e-cu-ter), in law C 527
  jury trials J 160
Proserpina (pro-SER-pin-a), Roman goddess G 359–60
Prospecting, hunting for minerals M 313–20
  gold G 251
  for uranium with a Geiger counter G 67
Prosperity was just around the corner, slogan H 224

Prosser, Gabriel (1775?–1800), American slave leader, Negro, b. Virginia. He served as coachman in the household of Thomas Prosser (whose last name he adopted). In the summer of 1800 he secretly enlisted hundreds of Negroes in a plot to seize Richmond. The carefully planned night attack failed because of a storm. The participants were betrayed, seized, and punished. Prosser escaped but was captured and hanged.

Prosthesis (pros-THE-sis), mechanical aid for the handicapped H 28
Protactinium (pro-tac-TIN-ium), element E 155, 164
Protected states
  Commonwealth of Nations C 428
Protective coloration L 219–20

butterflies B 470
fishes F 193, 194; pictures F 192
frogs and toads F 477
insects use for protection I 274
molting of birds B 200
tigers T 186
Protective devices, of animals and plants
  aardwolf H 308
  cacti C 3
  coloration and resemblances of butterflies B 470
  eel's body mucus E 85
  electric eels E 86
  frogs, toads, and other amphibians F 477–78
Protective tariff T 25
Protectorates
  Commonwealth of Nations C 428
  United Kingdom U 79
Proteins N 416, 418
  biochemistry, studies in B 183–84
  biosynthesis, making of proteins B 295
  body chemistry B 290, 295–96
  corn and barley yield G 284
  digestion of B 275
  genetics G 84–85
  milk has two kinds M 310–11
  protein deficiency disease, child suffering from picture
    D 189
  research on high-protein crops F 343
  soybeans S 337

Protesilaus (pro-tes-il-A-us), in Greek mythology, the first soldier killed in the Trojan War. According to one legend, Protesilaus knew that the first man to land in Troy would meet this fate and thus knowingly gave his life. His wife, Laodamia, mourned so that the gods, it is said, allowed him to return and visit her for 3 hours.

Protestant churches, major denominations P 486
Protestant Episcopal Church, or Anglican Church
    P 483–84
  United States C 288–89
Protestantism (PROT-est-ant-ism) P 482–86
  Calvin, John C 30
  Christianity, history of C 285–89
  divorce D 234
  English church under Henry VIII and Elizabeth I
    E 220–22, 178
  forms of address for the clergy A 21
  hymns H 310, 311–13
  Luther, Martin, leader of Reformation L 378
  marriage rites W 101
  missions and missionaries M 348–49
  Mormons M 457
  Quakers Q 2–3
  Reformation R 132–35
  Reformation spread standard form of German
    language G 173
  reforms in the Roman Catholic Church R 294

Proteus (PRO-te-us), in Greek mythology, a sea-god who was able to change his shape. If, however, someone caught him and managed to hold him until he assumed his natural shape, Proteus would be forced to answer all questions. It was by this device, according to legend, that Menelaus discovered his way home from Troy.

Prothallus (pro-THAL-lus), of ferns F 92
Protists, third kingdom of living things K 250–51
  microbiology, study of M 276
  plant plankton P 279–80
  separating animals from plants A 265; B 10
Protoceratops (pro-to-CER-a-tops), dinosaurs D 181

Protocol (PRO-to-col), in diplomacy **T** 270
Protons, atomic particles **A** 486, 487; **C** 201, 220
  cosmic rays **C** 511, 513
  electronics, science of **E** 143–45
  elements **E** 153–59
  International Geophysical Year findings **I** 312
  ions and ionization **I** 350–55
  modern theories about matter **P** 232
  nuclear energy **N** 355
  positive (or plus) charges of electricity **E** 123–24, 126
Protoplasm, living matter **B** 193
  cell structure **C** 159, 160
  unique characteristic of living things **K** 252, 254
Prototypes, models
  automobile design **A** 548
Protozoan (pro-to-ZO-an) **diseases** **D** 187
Protozoans, simple one-celled organisms **M** 276–77
  life, webs of **L** 256
Protractor, mechanical drawing tool **M** 197
  drawing geometric figures **G** 130
Proust (PROOST), **Marcel**, French novelist **F** 442
  themes of his novels **N** 348
Provençal (prov-on-SOL), French dialect **F** 433
Proverbs, book of Bible, Old Testament **B** 156
Proverbs, traditional sayings **P** 487
  African literature **A** 76a
  oral tradition of folklore **F** 304
  Poor Richard's Almanack **F** 452
  See also Quotations
Providence, capital of Rhode Island **R** 222–23
  founded by Roger Williams **A** 189; **W** 172
Provincetown, Massachusetts **M** 145
  Pilgrims **P** 344
Provincetown Players, drama group in New York's
    Greenwich Village **O** 117
  theater, history of **T** 161
Provincial government, Canada **C** 77
Provincial Marine, first Canadian naval forces **C** 80–81

Provisional government, an interim ruling administration.
A provisional government takes control when the existing
rule of a country is overthrown. It operates until a new
permanent government can be formed. Provisional
governments were set up at the time of the French
Revolution (1789) and the Russian Revolution (1917).

Provo, Utah **U** 252
Provolone (pro-vo-LO-ne), Italian cheese **D** 13

Provost (PRO-vo), **Etienne** (1782?–1850), Canadian hunter
and guide. He led several expeditions to the Rocky
Mountain region and was for a while connected with the
American Fur Company. In 1843 he accompanied James
Audubon on a western trip. A city, valley, and river in
Utah are named for him.

Prunes **P** 107–09
  dried fruit **D** 317
Pruning, of trees
  apple tree **A** 335
  fruit trees **F** 483
  grape vines **G** 298
Prussia, former German state, now a state of East
    Germany **G** 160
  Berlin, capital of **B** 143
  Bismarck, Otto von **B** 250
Psalms (SALMS), book of Bible, Old Testament **B** 156
  11th-century Psalter, picture **B** 157
  first hymns **H** 309, 312
  religious poems of King David **D** 44
Psalter (SALL-ter), Christian hymnal **H** 309
  11th-century, picture **B** 157

Psaltery, ancient stringed instrument **K** 238
Pseudopods (SEU-do-pods), fingerlike tubes of proto-
    plasm **M** 278; picture **M** 277
Pseudosuchia (seu-do-SU-kia), ancestors of dinosaurs
    D 173
Psilocybin (sil-o-SY-bin), hallucinogenic drug **D** 331
Psittacosis (sit-ta-CO-sis), or ornithosis, disease **I** 286
  pet birds **B** 248; **P** 181

Psoriasis (sor-RY-a-sis), chronic skin disease. It causes
the skin to break out in red patches covered with scales.
Often the scalp, elbows, knees, and back are affected.
The cause is unknown. The condition may be alleviated
by various treatments, but it usually recurs.

Psychiatry (sy-KY-atry)
  first reforms of treatment for mentally ill **M** 206
  hospital services **H** 249
  mental health **M** 220–22
  mental illness **M** 222–25
Psychoanalysis (sy-co-a-NAL-i-sis) **M** 208
  Freud, Sigmund **F** 470
  mental illness **M** 225
Psychological dependence, on narcotics **N** 13, 14
Psychology (sy-COL-ogy) **P** 488–501
  animal behavior, study of **A** 282, 283
  art of misdirection in magic **M** 19
  child development **C** 231–34
  Do you remember everything you perceive? **P** 493
  dreams, need for **D** 307
  extrasensory perception **E** 394–96
  Freud, Sigmund **F** 469–70
  guidance **G** 397–400
  hypnosis **H** 314–16
  importance to American literature **A** 207–08
  learning **L** 98–106
  mental health **M** 220–22
  mental illness **M** 222–25
  motivational research in advertising **A** 33
  Pavlov, Ivan **P** 100
  programed instruction **P** 475–477
  research methods **R** 182
  What is an intelligence test? **P** 489
  What is instinct? **P** 498
  witchcraft beliefs **W** 209
Psychology, applied, in guidance **G** 397–400
Psychoses (sy-CO-sese), forms of mental illness **M** 224
Psychosomatic (sy-co-so-MAT-ic) **diseases** **D** 190
Psychotherapy, treatment for mentally ill **M** 225
  narcotics addicts, treatment of **N** 14
Psychrometers (sy-CROM-et-ers), humidity indicators
    W 81
PT-109, torpedo boat commanded by John F. Kennedy
    K 207
Ptarmigans (TAR-mig-ans), birds **B** 225; picture **B** 224
  willow ptarmigan, state bird of Alaska **A** 129
PTA's see Parent-Teacher associations
Pterosaurs (TER-o-saurs), winged reptiles **L** 215
Ptolemaic (tol-em-MAY-ic) **kings of Egypt** **E** 92
  Egyptian art and architecture of **E** 102–03
Ptolemaic system, of astronomy **A** 471; picture **A** 472

Ptolemy I (TOL-emy) (367?–284? B.C.), founder of the
Ptolemaic dynasty in Egypt, b. Macedonia. After the
death of Alexander the Great (323), Ptolemy won control
of Egypt. He resigned (285) in favor of his son Ptolemy II
after a reign of warfare and intrigue.

Ptolemy, or **Ptolemacus, Claudius**, Alexandrian astrono-
    mer and geographer **G** 98; **S** 79
  astronomy, early history of **A** 471
  history of map making **M** 93

Ptyalin (TY-al-in), digestive enzyme **B** 294
Public assistance *see* Welfare, public
Publication date, birthday of a book **B** 334
Public baths **B** 91
Public broadcasting (educational television) **T** 70b, 70d, 71
Public Broadcasting Service (PBS) **T** 70d, 71
Public domain, of public lands **P** 506–07
Public health **P** 502–06
  air pollution **A** 108–11; **E** 272f–272g
  ancient Rome's sanitation systems **M** 204
  cities, problems of **C** 308b, 309; **U** 232
  community helps in prevention of disease **D** 220–21
  contagious diseases **D** 187
  environment, problems of **E** 272a–272h
  food and drug laws, requirements on labels **M** 100–01
  health, maintaining **H** 82–85
  hospital services **H** 249–50
  medical contributions of the 19th century **M** 207–08
  mental retardation **R** 189–91
  noise pollution and control **E** 272c–272d; **N** 269–70
  nurses and nursing **N** 410
  occupational health and safety **O** 15–16
  Red Cross services **R** 126–27
  sanitation, sewage, and refuse (solid waste) disposal **E** 272e, 272g; **S** 32–34
  smoking, a health hazard **S** 203
  United Nations World Health Organization **U** 85–86
  vaccination required for travel **V** 260–61
  water pollution **E** 272d–272e; **W** 58–59
  water supply **E** 272e; **W** 65–68
Public Health Service, United States **P** 504–05
Publicity, programs of public relations **P** 508
  book publishing **B** 331, 334
Public lands **P** 506–07
  National Forests, United States **N** 31–32
Public libraries *see* Libraries
Public opinion **P** 507–08
  advertising **A** 27–34
  opinion surveys and polls **O** 159–60
  propaganda **P** 480–81
Public opinion polls **O** 160
Public prosecutor, in law **J** 160
Public relations **P** 507–08
  advertising **A** 27–34; **P** 507
  guidance counselors for schools **G** 397–400
  propaganda **P** 480–81
  public opinion polls **O** 159–60
  television production **T** 70b, 70c, 70d–71
Public schools, in England **U** 67
Public schools, in United States **S** 55–58
  battle for tax supported school **E** 70–71
Public services *see* Public utilities
Public speaking **P** 508–10
  ancient schools of rhetoric **E** 64
  formal speech **S** 376–77
  outlines **O** 250–51
  See also Debates and debating; Discussions; Oratory
Public utilities **P** 510–13
  interstate commerce **I** 331–32
  natural monopolies **T** 303–04
  pollution control **W** 59
  See also Water supply
Public welfare *see* Welfare, public
Public Works Administration (PWA) **C** 486
Publishing **P** 513–15
  bookbinding **B** 327–29
  book industry, origin of **B** 321
  books: from author to library **B** 329–34
  comic books **C** 422–23
  commercial art **C** 425
  communication advances **C** 441

copyright **T** 244–45
editors of children's books **C** 241–42
freedom of the press **F** 457
journalism **J** 142–45
librarians' publishers **L** 192
magazines **M** 14–16
newspapers **N** 201
Peking, center of China's book publishing **P** 119
printer-publishers of early books **B** 321–22
Pulitzer, Joseph, and Pulitzer prizes **P** 524–28
reference books **R** 129–31
textbooks **T** 139
See also Book fairs; Copyright; Printing
Puccini (pu-CHI-ni), **Giacomo,** Italian composer **P** 515
  Bohème, La, opera **O** 140
  Madama Butterfly, opera **O** 146
  opera **I** 486; **O** 137–38
  Tosca, opera **O** 154
  Turandot, opera **O** 155
Pucellas (pu-CELL-as), glassmaking instrument **G** 230, 232
Puck, character in Shakespeare's *Midsummer Night's Dream* **M** 309
Puck, used in ice hockey **I** 36–37, 40
Pudus (PU-doos), deer of South America **D** 83; picture **H** 214
  hoofed mammals **H** 219
Puebla (pu-EB-la), Mexico **M** 247
Pueblo, Colorado **C** 413
Pueblo Indians, members of several Indian peoples of Arizona and New Mexico **I** 191, 196
  adobe houses **H** 173–74
  dwellings, pictures **A** 351, 353
  New Mexico **N** 186
Pueblos, Indian settlements **H** 173–74, **I** 196
  adobe, pictures **A** 302, **I** 200
  Hopi settlements **I** 190
Puelche (PUEL-chay), Indians of South America **I** 211
Puerto Cortés (PUER-to COR-tes), Honduras **H** 197
Puerto Montt, Chile **C** 252–53
Puerto Rico **P** 516–23
  Caribbean Sea and islands **C** 116–19
  concrete house, picture **A** 302
  flag **F** 241
  islands of the Caribbean **I** 436
  life in Latin America **L** 47–61
  oceanside hotel, picture **H** 257
  Ponce de León **P** 391
  radio-radar telescope, at Arecibo, picture **R** 73
  taken from Spain, 1898 **T** 114
Puerto Rico, University of **P** 517; picture **P** 519
Puffballs, mushrooms **M** 521
  fungi **F** 500
Puffed cereals **G** 285

Puffer, or blowfish, fresh and saltwater fish found in tropical and subtropical waters. When disturbed, it inflates itself by means of an internal sac, which it fills with air or water.

Puget (PU-jet) **Sound,** Washington **W** 16, 22
Pugilism (PU-jil-ism), or boxing **B** 352
Pugin, Welby Northmore, English architect **E** 241
Pugmill, clay-mixing machine, used in ceramics **C** 174
Pulaski (pu-LAS-ki), **Casimir,** Polish general, volunteer aid to Americans **R** 203
Pulci (POOL-chi), **Luigi,** Italian poet **I** 477
Pulcinella (pool-chi-NEL-la), or **Polichinelle,** Italian puppet character **P** 534
Pulitzer, Joseph, Hungarian-born American newspaper publisher **P** 524–28
  newspapers, history of **N** 198
Pulitzer prizes **P** 524–28

Purgatory (from the Latin *purgare,* meaning "to cleanse"), theologically, a state between heaven and hell for final purification. It is believed that souls of those who die in a state of grace and are destined for heaven remain in purgatory until they have done penance for their last worldly sins. Their stay can be shortened by prayers of the living.

Purvis, Robert (1810–1898), American businessman and abolitionist, b. South Carolina. A free-born Negro, he established a successful business in Philadelphia, Pa., and became one of the leaders of the antislavery movement, as an organizer of the American Anti-Slavery Society and a worker for the Underground Railroad.

Push-ups, in gymnastics **G** 429
Push waves, of earthquakes **E** 33
Pussy willows **T** 283–84
Putnam, Israel, American Revolutionary War officer
  R 199
  Putnam Memorial State Park, Redding, Conn. **C** 478

Putnam, Rufus (1738–1824), American military engineer
and pioneer, b. Sutton, Mass. A self-taught geographer
and mathematician, he served as engineer and rose to
rank of brigadier general in the Continental Army. He
was one of the founders of the Ohio Co. He established a
settlement in Marietta, Ohio (1788), and became judge of
the supreme court of the Northwest Territory (1790–96).
He was U.S. surveyor general (1796–1803).
  Northwest Ordinance, a set of principles of the West-
    ward Movement **W** 143

Putting, in golf, pictures **G** 259
Putting green, of golf course **G** 254–55
Puzzles **T** 289
  lens puzzle **L** 148
  magic square **N** 382, 383
  number puzzles **N** 373–77
  puzzle box in psychology **P** 494–95
  words in a phonemic transcription **L** 301
PWA see Public Works Administration

PX, U.S. Army term for post exchange. This is a store
reserved for Army personnel and their families. It is
run by the Army at a low profit.

Pygmalion (pig-MAY-li-on), in Greek mythology, a sculptor and king of Cyprus who fell in love with the ivory
statue of a beautiful maiden that he himself had carved.
In answer to his request, the goddess Aphrodite gave the
figure, known as Galatea, life, and Pygmalion then
married her. George Bernard Shaw wrote a play called
Pygmalion. A musical adaptation, *My Fair Lady,* played
on Broadway, around the world, and as a movie.

Pygmalion, play by George Bernard Shaw **S** 144
  scene from **D** 292
Pygmies (PIG-mies), a people of Africa **A** 55, 62
  Congo (Brazzaville) **C** 462
  Gabon **G** 2, 3
  nomadic life **N** 271
  people of the rain forest **R** 100
  Zaïre **Z** 366a
Pygmy buffalo, of Philippines **B** 250a
Pygmy hippopotamuses **H** 133

Pyle, Ernie (Ernest Taylor) (1900–1945), American journalist, b. near Dana, Ind. He traveled widely, describing,
in columns for the Scripps-Howard chain and many other
newspapers, the reactions of the man-in-the-street. He
gained his greatest reputation reporting incidents of the
London blitz and Pacific combat areas during World War
II. He was killed near Okinawa, on Ie Island, of the
Ryukyu group. His works include *Here Is Your War* and
Brave Men. **H** 67

Pyle, Howard, American illustrator and author **C** 240;
  D 99
  Book of Pirates, illustration **I** 93
  Merry Adventures of Robin Hood, picture **C** 241

Pyle, Katherine (?–1938), American author and illustrator.
She wrote and adapted a large number of children's
stories, for which she did all her own illustrations.
Among her best-known works are *Careless Jane, The
Counterpane Fairy,* and *Lazy Matilda.*

Pylons, gateway towers **A** 371
Pyongyang (p'YUNG-yong), capital of Democratic People's
  Republic of Korea (North Korea) **K** 301; picture
  K 300
Pyorrhea, an inflamed condition of the gum tissue
  D 115
Pyramids (PIR-a-mids)
  ancient civilizations **A** 217, 220–21
  art as a record **A** 438b
  Egypt, ancient **E** 95–96, 98, 100
  Egyptian architecture **A** 371
  engineering feats **E** 207
  Giza, picture **E** 90b
  Great Pyramid of Cheops **W** 214; picture **W** 215
  Mexico **I** 152
  Pyramid of the Sun, Teotihuacán, Mexico, picture
    A 363
  slave labor, pictures **A** 221; **S** 195

Pyramus (PIR-a-mus) **and Thisbe,** mythological Babylonian lovers. Forbidden by their parents to marry, they
agree to run away and arrange to meet near a white mulberry bush. Thisbe, arriving first, is frightened away by
a lioness. Pyramus finds her abandoned cloak, fears the
lioness has devoured her, and kills himself. Thisbe returns and takes her life with Pyramus' sword. It is said
that their blood colored the mulberries, making them
red forever after. Shakespeare's *A Midsummer Night's
Dream* has a parody of this legend.

Pyre, for funerals **F** 493
Pyrenees (PIR-e-nees), mountains between France and
  Spain
  Andorra, picture **A** 255
  Basques, people **S** 352
  Pic du Midi Observatory **O** 9
Pyrethrum (py-RE-thrum), insecticide **I** 258
Pyrethrum, plant, picture **K** 232
Pyridoxine, vitamin B6 **V** 370d
Pyrite, or "fool's gold" **G** 249; picture **R** 271
Pyroceram, glass ceramic **G** 237
Pyroclastic (py-ro-CLAST-ic) **rocks** **V** 378
Pyrometallurgy (py-ro-MET-al-lurgy), use of heat to treat
  ores **M** 228, 229
Pyrometers (py-ROM-et-ers), optical instruments **O** 174
Pyrometric (py-ro-MET-ric) **cones,** temperature gauge in
  ceramics **C** 175
Pyrope (PY-rope), garnet gemstone **G** 71
Pyrotechnics (py-ro-TEC-nics), fireworks **F** 156
Pyrrha see Deucalion
Pyrrhic (PIR-rhic), or battle, **dance,** of ancient Greece
  D 23

Pyrrhus (PIR-rhus) (318?–272 B.C.), king of Epirus. A
noted military tactician of his day, he went to Taren-
tum's aid against Rome. Although he defeated the
Romans at Heraclea (280) and at Asculum (279), his
losses were heavy and he was unable to effect a
permanent peace. (From his comments on the high price
of victory comes the term "Pyrrhic victory".)

Pythagoras (pi-THAG-or-as), Greek mathematician **A** 471
  amicable numbers **N** 380
  right triangle, theorem of the **G** 125–26
  science, advances in **S** 62
Pythagorean (pith-ag-o-RE-an) **theorem** **G** 126
Pytheas (PITH-e-as), Greek geographer and navigator
  G 98
  Arctic exploration **P** 364
Pythian Apollo see Apollo
Pythias see Damon and Pythias
Pythons, snakes **S** 206

ILLUSTRATION CREDITS

The following list credits, by page, the sources of illustrations used in Volume P of THE NEW BOOK OF KNOWLEDGE. Credits are listed illustration by illustration —left to right, top to bottom. Wherever appropriate, the name of the photographer or artist has been listed with the source, the two being separated by a dash. When two or more illustrations appear on one page, their credits are separated by semicolons.

3 George Buctel
4– Shostal
8
9 Ewing Krainin—Stockpile
10 Ewing Krainin—Stockpile
14 Art Reference Bureau
16 Art Reference Bureau
19 Vatican Library, Rome—Art Reference Bureau; Giraudon—Louvre, Paris; Art Reference Bureau.
20 Art Reference Bureau
21 Louvre, Paris—Art Reference Bureau
22 Metropolitan Museum of Art; Art Reference Bureau; Kunsthistorisches Museum, Vienna—Art Reference Bureau.
25 Frick Collection—New York; Pinacothek, Munich—Art Reference Bureau; Louvre, Paris—Art Reference Bureau.
26 National Gallery, London—Art Reference Bureau; Louvre, Paris—Art Reference Bureau.
27 Real Accademia de Belles Artes de San Fernando, Madrid—Art Reference Bureau; Art Reference Bureau.
28 National Gallery, London—Art Reference Bureau; Louvre, Paris—Art Reference Bureau.
31 Museum of Modern Art, N.Y.; Museum of Modern Art photo—Marlborough-Gerson Gallery, N.Y.; Leo Castelli.
33 The Sherwin-Williams Co.
36 George Buctel
37 Fujihara—Monkmeyer
38 Shostal; Emil Muench—Lenstour
39 Warren Slater—Monkmeyer; Fujihara—Monkmeyer.
40 Stockpile; Fujihara—Monkmeyer
43 Charles Wiley; Lisl Steiner; Charles May.
44 George Buctel
47 George Buctel; Panama Canal Company.
49 ANI
50 Harry Scott
54 International Paper Company; Barney Plotkin; International Paper Company; West Virginia Pulp and Paper Company; West Virginia Pulp and Paper Company; West Virginia Pulp and Paper Company.
55 Barney Plotkin; International Paper Company; West Virginia Paper and Pulp Company.
58 Jonathan Strong—courtesy Paperbacks
58a Gerald McConnell
59 Gerald McConnell
60 Wallace Driver—Pix; U.S. Army; U.S. Army; U.S. Army.
62 Jerry Frank
63 George Buctel
65 Jerry Frank
68 Louis Goldman—Rapho Guillumette
69 Susan McCartney; Susan McCartney.
70 Bernard G. Silberstein—Rapho Guillumette; Susan McCartney.
71 Bernard G. Silberstein—Rapho
72 Serrallier—Rapho Guillumette; Carlé—Centrale Farbbild Agentus.
73 Robert Doisneau—Rapho Guillumette; Louis Goldman—Rapho Guillumette.
74 Ciccione—Rapho Guillumette
75 George Buctel
76 Louis Goldman—Rapho Guillumette

78 Harold Weiner
83 Cy La Tour
84 Nes Levotch
87 George Sottung
89 George Sottung
94 Myles J. Adler
100 Sovfoto
101 Peace Corps, Washington, D.C.
102 Paul Conklin—Pix; Paul Conklin—Peace Corps; ANI.
103 ANI; Paul Conklin—Peace Corps.
106 Gerald McConnell
109 Grant Heilman
110 Gerald McConnell
112 Arabelle Wheatley
113 Cultured Pearl Associations of Japan and America
114 Cultured Pearl Associations of Japan and America
116 Brown Brothers
117 George Buctel
119 Brian Brake—Magnum
120 Philip Smith—National Audubon Society
121 Harry Scott
122 L. G. Richards—Black Starr; U.S. Navy
123 David Linton
124 Alfred Saunders—Annan; U.S. Navy.
125 John Warham
126 Annan; FPG.
129 Color Illustration Inc.; A. A. Allen; M. House; Photo Researchers.
130 Judge Studio
131 Diversified Map Corp.
132 Diversified Map Corp.
135 W. R. Wilson—Alpha; Grant Heilman.
136 Grant Heilman
138 Paul Granger
139 Larry Keighley—Alpha; Zehrt—FPG.
140 J. W. Cella—Photo Researchers; Ellis—Sawyer—FPG.
141 Diversified Map Corp.
146 Gerald McConnell
147 Gerald McConnell
149 Charles McVicker
150 Charles McVicker
152– From Musical Instruments, by A. J.
153 Hipkins and illustrated by William Gibb, published by A. and C. Black, Ltd., London
155 Arabelle Wheatley
158 Gerald McConnell
159 Gerald McConnell
160 Carl Frank
161 George Buctel
163 Ken Heyman—Meridian
164 Carl Frank
165 Jerry Frank
166 Jerry Frank
169 Cornell Capa—Magnum
170 Gerald McConnell
171 Aramco; Gerald McConnell.
172 Gerald McConnell; Standard Oil Company, New Jersey; Standard Oil Company, New Jersey.
173 Standard Oil Company, New Jersey; Aramco.
174 Humble Oil and Refining Co., Houston, Texas
175 Gerald McConnell
179 Martha Shapp
182 George Buctel; Harold M. Lambert—Frederic Lewis.

183 American Airlines
185 George Buctel
186 Shostal
187 United Nations
188 Morton Beebe—Photo Trends
193 George Sottung
197 Brown Brothers; Bob Henriques—Magnum.
199 Miller Pope
200 Miller Pope
201 Nikon
202 Eastman Kodak Co.; Charles McVicker.
203 Ernest Leitz Co.
204 Winton Patnode—Photo Researchers
206 Eastman Kodak Co.
207 California Institute of Technology
208 William Vandivert
209 Russ Kinne—Photo Researchers; National Aeronautics and Space Administration.
210 Culver
211 New York Public Library; Bettmann Archives.
213 Nikon; Weston Master.
214 Russ Kinne—Photo Researchers
215 Russ Kinne—Photo Researchers
216 Jerry Frank
217 Eastman Kodak Co.
218 Russ Kinne—Photo Researchers
219 Eastman Kodak Co.
221 Gaetano Di Palma; Fundamental Photographs; Fundamental Photographs; Fundamental Photographs.
222 Fundamental Photographs
227– Harry Schaare
229
230 George Sottung
232 George Sottung
236 George Sottung
237 George Sottung
238 George Sottung
240 Steinway & Sons; Gerald McConnell.
241 Gerald McConnell
242 Steinway & Sons
244 UPI
245 James Cooper
246 The Granger Collection; The Granger Collection.
248 Grant Heilman
249 Arabelle Wheatley
251– Herman B. Vestal
259
261 Herman B. Vestal
262 Herman B. Vestal
263 Robert Frankenberg
267– Archives, Carl Zeiss, Oberkochen, Württemberg
268
269 Mount Wilson and Palomar Observatories
270 Miller Pope
271 Lowell Observatory
272 NASA
274 Miller Pope
275 © Copyright 1965 by California Institute of Technology and Carnegie Institution of Washington
276 Miller Pope
277 Miller Pope
278 McDonald Observatory, Courtesy of Yerkes Observatory, University of Chicago; McDonald Observatory.
279 Arabelle Wheatley

Q, 17th letter of the English alphabet **Q** 1
See also Alphabet
Qader Fikri, Abdel see Fikri, Abdel Qader
Qamaran Island see Kamaran Island
Qand (GOND), Arabic word for sugar **C** 98
Qatar (KA-tar), sheikhdom in eastern Arabia **M** 301
flag **F** 238

Quackery, practices of one who pretends to have medical skills. "Quack" is a shortened form of "quacksalver" (from Dutch *kwaksalve*), meaning one who quacks, or boasts, of his salves and their healing qualities.

Quadrants, navigation instruments **N** 64
Quadrilaterals (qua-dri-LAT-er-als), geometric forms **G** 126
Quadrille, dance **D** 27
Quadros (QUA-drush), **Jânio,** president of Brazil **B** 384
Quadruple (qua-DRU-ple) **Alliance,** or Grand Alliance, 1815 **I** 324
formed during Congress of Vienna against Napoleon I **I** 324
Quad stereo
tape for **T** 20, 21
Quagga (QUAG-ga), zebra **H** 244
Quahog (QUAW-hog), shellfish **R** 215, 217
Quai d'Orsay (kay d'or-SAY), Paris **P** 70

Quail, several species of small game birds. Quail found in Europe, Africa, and Asia are about 7 in. long, while American quail, such as the bobwhite, are somewhat larger. Quail live on the ground, eat insects and seeds, and travel in flocks called coveys. Picture **B** 233.
birds of the fields **B** 220

Quaison-Sackey, Alexander (1924–), Ghanaian diplomat, b. Winneba. After graduating from Oxford, he returned to Africa and taught school before starting a government career. He was labor attaché (1952–55), attaché in the British Embassy of Brazil (1955–57), head of Chancery and official secretary of the Ghana High Commission (1957–59), and Ghana's permanent representative to the United Nations (1959–65). He was vice-president of the United Nations General Assembly (1961–62) and its president (1964–65). In 1965–66 he served as Ghana's minister of foreign affairs.

Quakers Q 2–3
American colonies **A** 191–92
continuing Reformation in England **R** 135
Penn, William **P** 127
Philadelphia **P** 182–83
prisons, reforms of **P** 468
Underground Railroad **U** 11–12
Quaking aspen, tree, picture **T** 278
Quality control, testing system
automobiles **A** 548
Quanah, Indian chief see Parker, Quanah
Quantitative analysis, in chemistry **C** 218

Quantrill, William Clarke (1837–1865), American Confederate leader, b. Canal Dover, Ohio. He was a schoolteacher and a gambler before the Civil War began in 1861, when he became leader of a guerrilla unit (known as Quantrill's Raiders). He helped capture Independence, Mo. (1862), and received a captaincy in the Confederate Army. He was killed near Taylorsville, Ky.

Quantum theory, in physics **L** 274
Bohr's work basis of **B** 300
radiation **R** 45
science, advances in **S** 76

Quarantine
astronauts returning from the moon **M** 456; **S** 340
disease, prevention of **D** 221
duties of Public Health Service officers **P** 504
flag **F** 246

Quarles, Benjamin (1904–), American historian, Negro, b. Boston, Mass. He has been dean of instruction at Dillard University, New Orleans, La. (1946–53), and head of the history department at Morgan State College, Baltimore, Md. (since 1953). Among his books are *The Negro in the American Revolution* and *Lincoln and the Negro.*

Quarrying Q 4–5
Barre, Vermont **V** 318–19; picture **V** 314
Quarterbacks, in football **F** 362–63
Quarter horses H 232; picture **H** 239
Quartering Act, 1765 **R** 195
Quart, measure of volume **W** 111, 115
different quarts pictured **W** 113
Quartet, a musical form **M** 537
Quartz Q 6–7
abrasive for grinding and polishing **G** 387–88
crystals **C** 541
gemstones **G** 75
gold found in **G** 248
quartz-crystal controlled clocks, the correct time **T** 193
Quartz-iodine lamps L 286
Quartzite, metamorphic rock **R** 269–70; picture **R** 269
Quasars, star-like radio sources **Q** 7–8; **A** 477
radio universe **U** 201
Quasimodo (qua-si-MO-do), **Salvatore,** Italian poet **I** 480–81
Quasimodo, the Hunchback of Notre Dame, picture **F** 112
Quasi-stellar radio sources see Quasars
Quatrain, a poem **P** 353
Quebec (que-BEC), **battle of,** 1759 **F** 461–62
Quebec, Canada **Q** 9–16
Allied Conference, 1943 **W** 297
Champlain, Samuel de **C** 68–69, 187
fish hatchery, picture **C** 486
founding of and early history as part of New France **C** 69–70
Montreal **M** 443–45
Quebec Act of 1774 and British Canada **C** 71
Revolutionary War, American **C** 71; **R** 201
Quebec Act of 1774 C 71
Quebec City, capital of Quebec, Canada **Q** 13, 16–17; pictures **C** 306; **Q** 17
Saint Lawrence River, history of **S** 15
Winter Carnival, picture **C** 121
Quebracho (kay-BRA-cho), tree **A** 393
Quechua (KECH-wa), Indians of South America
Bolivia **B** 302
Peru **P** 160
Quechua, language of the Incas **I** 207

Queen, Ellery, pseudonym of Frederic Dannay (1905–) and Manfred B. Lee (1905–71), American writers, both b. Brooklyn, N.Y. Dannay and Lee (cousins) began their collaboration with *The Roman Hat Mystery* (1929) and made detective-hero Queen world-famous through movies, radio, TV, and about 100 stories (including *Fourth Side of the Triangle, The Finishing Stroke,* and *And on the Eighth Day*). Dannay and Lee co-edited *Ellery Queen's Mystery Magazine* from 1941 and a mystery annual from 1945.

Queen Anne's lace, flowers, picture **W** 168
Queen Anne style, in art and architecture **E** 240
furniture design **F** 507

Queen Anne's War, 1702–13 F 459
Queen ants A 323, 326; picture A 328
Queen bees B 117–18, 121–24
Queen Charlotte Islands, British Columbia, Canada
  B 402
Queen Elizabeth, ocean liner O 17–18
Queen Elizabeth 2, ocean liner O 18; pictures O 20, 20–21
Queen Mary, ocean liner O 17–18
Queen of the May M 182
Queens, borough of New York City N 228
Queen's Birthday, holiday H 150

Queensberry rules, rules of boxing drawn up by the
Scotsman John Sholto Douglas, Marquis of Queensberry
(1844–1900). A sportsman, he sponsored the rules,
drafted by John G. Chambers in 1867, that govern
today's boxing. By 1889 the rules were standardized and
in use in both England and the United States.
  boxing, history of B 353

Queensland, Australia A 510, 512
Queen's Plate, Canadian horse race H 232
Queenstown, New Zealand, picture N 238
Queensware, pottery P 418
Queequeg, character in *Moby Dick* M 217–18

Queirós (kay-ROSH), **Pedro Fernandes de** (1560?–1614),
Portuguese navigator. He sailed (1595) on an expedition
to the Pacific as second in command to Álvaro de
Mendaña de Neyra (1541–95), discoverer of the Marquesas and Solomon islands, and upon the death of his
commander continued the expedition and discovered the
New Hebrides and Tuamotu islands.

Quemoy (ke-MOY), island group, off China's mainland
  C 273
Quenching, of metals M 233

Quercia (QUAIR-cha), **Jacopo della** (1378?–1438), Italian
sculptor, b. Siena. Son of a goldsmith and sculptor, he is
probably most famous for his Gaia fountain in Siena and
the scenes from Genesis and the life of Christ on the
doorway of Bologna's church of San Petronio. Quercia's
work reflects a change from Gothic to Renaissance style
and is said to have influenced Michelangelo.
  Renaissance sculpture S 99

Question and Answer, sculpture, picture M 397
Question marks, punctuation P 531
Questionnaires
  opinion surveys O 159

Quetzal, large Central American bird. It is found in rain
forests from southern Mexico to Costa Rica. The male
quetzal is brilliant green with a bright crimson abdomen
and long feathers above the tail that sometimes grow to
2 feet in length. Females are less brilliantly colored.

Quetzalcoatl (ket-zol-co-OT-el), Aztec god. Some legends
claim that Quetzalcoatl actually existed and was a ruler
of the ancient Toltec civilization of Mexico. The Toltecs
worshiped him as the god of science and the arts and as
the discoverer of maize. The name Quetzalcoatl means
"feathered serpent" in the Nahuatl language, and a
feathered serpent is the symbol of Mexico.
  Cortes and the Spanish conquest of Mexico C 508;
  M 248
  Toltec Indian culture and mythology I 198; M 561–62

Quevedo (kay-VAY-do), **Francisco de,** Spanish poet S 369
Quezon (KAE-zone), **Manuel,** Philippine statesman Q 18
  Philippines, history of P 190

Quezon City, capital of the Philippines P 188–89
Quicksand Q 18–19
Quicksilver see Mercury
Quiet One, The, documentary motion picture M 476
Quileute (quil-e-UTE), Indians of North America
  myths of M 559–60
Quill pens P 146
  steps in the history of writing C 431
Quills, of animals
  porcupine R 280
  protective devices M 67

Quince, fruit of a tree belonging to the rose family. A
small, spicy, acid, hard-fleshed fruit, quince is used for
making marmalade, jelly, and preserves. The quince tree
is native to Central Asia but can be grown in any
temperate climate. The tree, which usually reaches a
maximum height of 12 to 15 feet, grows best on rich,
well-drained soils. Picture G 36.

Quincy, Josiah (1772–1864), American statesman, b.
Braintree (now Quincy), Mass. He was a Massachusetts
state senator (1804–05) and a United States congressman (1805–13), vacating the latter position because he
opposed the War of 1812. He returned to the state senate
(1813–20) and later was mayor of Boston (1823–28),
president of Harvard (1829–45), and an author of
Memoir of the Life of John Quincy Adams.

Quinidine (QUIN-i-dene), drug D 326
Quinine (QUINE-ine), drug made from cinchona bark
  D 213
  plants, medicinal P 311–13
  sources of drugs D 323
Quinterna, musical instrument, picture S 438

Quintero (keen-TER-o), **José** (1924–   ), American theatrical director, b. Panama City, Panama. He trained at
Chicago's Goodman Theater and achieved fame as a
director of off-Broadway revivals of such plays as
Tennessee Williams' *Summer and Smoke* and Eugene
O'Neill's *The Iceman Cometh.* He also directed Broadway
production of O'Neill's *Long Day's Journey into Night.*

Quintilian (quin-TIL-ian), **Marcus Fabius,** Roman
  rhetorician O 181
  Silver Age of Latin literature L 80

Quintuplets (from Latin *quintuplex,* "quint-" meaning
"fifth" and "-plex" meaning "fold"), group of five
children born at one birth. The word "quintuplets"
became widely known in modern times with the birth of
Canada's Dionne quintuplets in 1934.

Quipus, knotted strings, record keeping of Inca Indians
  I 207; picture C 451
Quirinale (QUIR-in-al) **Palace,** Rome, Italy R 313, 315

Quirino (ki-RI-no), **Elpidio** (1890–1956), Philippine statesman, b. Luzon, Vigon province. Entering politics in 1913,
he was a member of the Philippine Senate (1925–35,
1941–45), secretary of finance (1934–36), secretary of
the interior (1936–38), and secretary of foreign affairs
(1946–48). He worked actively for Philippine independence and served as president (1948–53).
  Philippines, history of P 190

Quirós (ke-ROCE), **Cesáreo Bernaldo de** (1879–1968),
Argentine painter, b. Gualeguay. He studied at Buenos
Aires' Academia Nacional de Bellas Artes and specialized in paintings that depict gauchos and their life on
the pampas (treeless plains of Argentina).

Quisling, Vidkun, Norwegian Nazi **W** 288
  underground movement working for Hitler **U** 10
Quito (KI-to), capital of Ecuador **E** 57; pictures **E** 52, 57
  San Francisco Monastery **L** 64
Quiver, case for carrying arrows **A** 367
Quixote, Don see Don Quixote
Quiz shows, on television **T** 70d
Qumram texts see Dead Sea Scrolls
Qumran, community on northwest shore of Dead Sea
  D 48, 49
Quoits
  deck tennis **D** 58

Quonset hut, prefabricated shelter built of corrugated metal, which forms a semicircular arching roof over a base of steel trusses. The huts' name comes from Quonset Point, R.I., where they were first used during World War II for army personnel and for storage.
  Rhode Island's products **R** 213

Quorum, number of the entire body of an organization that must be present in order to conduct business legally. In England "quorum" originally referred to certain justices of the peace who were required to be present at court sessions.
  parliamentary procedure, rules of **P** 79

Quota Act, 1921, limiting immigration **I** 100
Quotas, trade barriers **I** 328
Quotation marks, punctuation **P** 532
Quotations Q 19–20
  excerpts from Lincoln's writings **L** 294
  famous quotes from Shakespeare's plays **S** 133–37
  selections from *Poor Richard's Almanack* **F** 452
  some ironical observations of Mark Twain **H** 281
  use exact words in formal speech **S** 376
  See also Epigram; Proverbs, traditional sayings; sayings by the first word of the quotation
Quotient (QUO-shent), in division **A** 400–401

Quo vadis? (quo VA-dis), Latin for "Where are you going?" *Quo Vadis?* is also the name of a popular historical novel written (1896) by a Pole, Henryk Sienkiewicz, and filmed several times.

Quraish, Arab tribe
  Mohammed's tribe in Mecca **M** 404, 405
Qu'ran (English: Koran), holy book of Islam **K** 294–95

R, 18th letter of the English alphabet **R** 21
See also Alphabet
Ra see Re, Egyptian god
Rabat (ra-BOT), capital of Morocco **M** 461
Rabbinical (rab-BIN-ic-al) ("religious") **literature, Hebrew**
H 101–03
Rabbinic Hebrew language H 100–01
Rabbis (RAB-byes), Jewish religious leaders **J** 120
Talmudists **T** 15
Rabbits R 22–24
Australia overrun with **A** 505–06
Beatrix Potter's *The Tale of Peter Rabbit* **C** 241
man changes distribution of life **L** 238
March Hare in "Alice in Wonderland" **A** 164
pets **P** 179
tracks, picture **A** 271
tularemia **I** 287
What is the difference between a rabbit and a hare?
R 23
White Rabbit and March Hare in "Alice in Wonderland"
A 164
why some small animals hibernate and some do not,
picture **H** 124
Rabbit's foot, a charm **S** 473
Rabéarivelo, Jean-Joseph, Malagasy Republic poet **A** 76c
Rabelais (ra-BLAY), **François,** French poet **F** 436–37
Rabémananjara, Jacques, Malagasy Republic poet **A** 76c

Rabi (RA-bi), **Isidor Isaac** (1898–   ), American physicist, b. Rymanow, Austria-Hungary (now Poland). He was awarded the 1944 Nobel prize in physics for his method of determining the magnetic properties of atomic nuclei. He assisted in the development of radar and of the atomic bomb. He taught (1929–67) in the physics department of Columbia University.

Rabi see Rambi, Pacific Island
Rabies, virus disease **I** 286–87
achievement in the history of medicine **M** 208
foxes spread infection **D** 249
Pasteur, Louis **P** 97
vampire bats as carriers **B** 94
Rabinovich, Solomon J., or **Rabinowitz, Shalom** see
Aleykhem, Sholem
Rabun (RAY-bun) **Gap,** Georgia **G** 132
Raccoon dog D 250
Raccoons R 25–26
animal tests **A** 285; picture **A** 286
furs **F** 519
pets **P** 180
tracks, picture **A** 272
Race, a trough for water **W** 61
Race, Day of the, Latin-American holiday **H** 150
Race music see Rhythm-and-blues music
Races of man R 29–32
Africa **A** 55
Asia **A** 459
Australian aborigines, Australoids **A** 499–500
civil rights conflicts **C** 315–16
Europe, classification of people based on ethnic
groupings and physical characteristics **E** 315–17
language families **L** 38–39
Latin America **L** 50–51; **S** 282
North America, the melting pot **N** 296
prehistoric man **P** 442–46

Rachel (RAY-chel), in Old Testament (Genesis 29–35), daughter of Laban and wife of Jacob. When fleeing from Laban with Jacob, she took household gods and hid them. She bore Jacob two sons, Joseph and Benjamin.

Rachel (ra-SHEL) (stage name of Élisa Félix) (1820–1858),

French actress, b. Mumpf, Switzerland. A street singer in her youth, she studied drama in Paris and achieved her first success (1838) as Camille in *Horace* by Corneille. She subsequently appeared in London, Berlin, St. Petersburg, and the United States. Noted for her parts in plays by Racine and Corneille, she received greatest acclaim in title roles of *Phèdre*, by Racine, and *Adrienne Lecouvreur*, by Eugène Scribe and Gabriel Legouvé.

Rachmaninoff (rock-MA-ni-nof), **Sergey Vassilievitch** (1873–1943), Russian pianist, composer, and conductor, b. Onega, near Novgorod. He conducted opera at Bolshoi Theater (1904–06), made first American tour in 1909 and 1910, and conducted Philharmonic Society in Moscow (1911–13). He left Russia permanently in 1917. His compositions, influenced by Tchaikovsky and other 19th-century Russian composers, include four piano concertos, three symphonies and other orchestral works, three operàs, *Rhapsody on a Theme of Paganini*, many piano pieces, choral works, and songs.
Russian music **U** 64

Racine (ra-CENE), **Jean Baptiste,** French dramatist **R** 32
French literature, place in **F** 438
Greek unities of time, place, action **D** 296
Racine, Wisconsin **W** 204
Racing R 33
air races and long-distance flights **A** 572
automobile racing **A** 538–40
canoeing **C** 101
chariot racing **W** 157
horse racing **H** 231–34
iceboating **I** 29–30
karting **K** 195–96
Korea long-distance marathons **K** 299
model car **A** 537; picture **A** 535
motorcycles **M** 488b–489
Olympic Games **O** 103–16b
pigeons bred for racing **B** 247
powerboat racing **B** 264
regattas **R** 338–39
roller-skating **R** 284
rowing races **R** 339
sailing **S** 14
skiing **S** 184b–187
Soap Box Derby **S** 215
speed skating **I** 50–53
swimming **S** 493
track events **T** 237
Racing shells, boats **R** 339
Rack-and-pinion, devices used for cog railroads **R** 78

Rackham, Arthur (1867–1939), English artist and illustrator, b. London. He contributed artwork to periodicals, including *Punch*, but was best-known for his illustrations of children's books, including Grimm's *Fairy Tales*, Andersen's *Fairy Tales*, *Gulliver's Travels*, and *Peter Pan*.

Rackham illustrations
"Little Red Riding Hood" **C** 248a
"Rumplestiltskin" **I** 93
Radar (RAY-dar) **R** 34–37
astronomy see Radar astronomy
changes in fishing industry **F** 217
electric waves **L** 271
electronic "frog's eye" **F** 478
magnetrons (electron tubes) **E** 148
North American defense bases **C** 82
ocean liners **O** 24
primitive radar of electric fishes **F** 202
signals equal to speed of light **L** 266
tornado detection **H** 299; picture **H** 298

Radio Free Europe (RFE), private organization that broadcasts informative and propaganda programs to Poland, Hungary, Czechoslovakia, Bulgaria, and Rumania. The network, founded in 1950 and supported by Crusade for Freedom Fund, operates more than 30 transmitters.

Radio frequency bands R 58
Radioisotopes see Radioactive isotopes
Radio paging E 142c
Radio programs R 59–61
Radio range stations, airway checkpoints A 560
Radio receivers R 51
Radiosondes (RAY-dio-sonds), instruments to observe weather in upper atmosphere W 84–85
Radio stars, space bodies R 75, 76
  exploration by radio in astronomy A 477; Q 7–8
Radio telegraphy T 54
Radiotelephones R 50; picture E 142a
  new means of communication C 439
  radio telephony T 59
  telephone, descendants of, in electronic communication E 142a–142b
Radio telescopes R 69–72; picture I 314
  electric waves L 271
  Jansky's experiments T 64
  quasars and pulsars Q 7–8
  radio waves of the sun, studies of S 467
Radio transmitters R 53
Radio waves R 54
  ice thickness measured by radio waves I 10
  masers M 131
  quasars and pulsars Q 7–8
  television T 66–67, 68
  transistors T 252–53
  travel through a vacuum V 264
Radishes V 292
  roots we eat P 307; pictures P 291, 306
Radisson (ra-di-SON), Pierre, French explorer O 127
  Hudson's Bay Company, fur traders F 520–21
  Saint Lawrence River S 16
Radium (RAY-dium), element E 155, 164
  atomic structure unstable A 488
  Curies' discovery C 553
  metals, ores, location, properties, uses M 227
  radioctive decay of radium N 358–59
Radius, of a circle G 127
Radome (RAY-dome), for satellites
  located near Andover, Maine M 33
Radon (RAY-don), element E 155, 164
  noble gases N 109
Radula (RAD-ul-a), tongue of snails O 276

Raeburn, Sir Henry (known as the Scottish Reynolds) (1756–1823), Scottish portrait painter, b. Stockbridge, near Edinburgh. Persuaded by Sir Joshua Reynolds to study art in Rome, he returned to Edinburgh in 1787. He painted portraits of leading men of his day, including Sir Walter Scott, James Boswell, and David Hume.
  Royal Academy, Age of E 238

Raffaello, S.S., ocean liner O 19, 23
Raffles, fictional character created by Hornung M 554

Raffles, Sir Thomas Stamford (1781–1826), English colonial administrator, b. at sea near Jamaica. He became assistant to first governor at Malaysian settlement of Penang (1805) and served as lieutenant governor of Java (1811–16) and of Bencoolen, Sumatra (1818–23). He influenced Britain to purchase Singapore from the Netherlands (1819). He compiled historical knowledge of Malaysia and Indonesia in his *History of Java*.
  Malaysia and Singapore, history of M 56; S 184a

Raft of the Medusa, painting by Géricault F 427
Rafts, watercraft T 257
  Amazon River, picture A 179
  ancient ships S 155
  goatskin raft on Tigris River, picture I 380
  water transportation I 337
Rag-Chewers Club, of amateur radio operators R 63
Rag dolls D 266
Raggedy Ann makeup, picture P 340
Raglan sleeve C 352
Ragtime, music rhythm J 57
  introduced into musical comedy M 542
Ragweed, plant, picture W 105
  hayfever, cause of D 192

Rahman (RAH-mon), **Abdul, Prince** (1903–), Malayan statesman, b. Alor Star, Kedah. Elected to Federal Legislative Council (1955), he led delegation (1955) to discuss Malayan independence from Great Britain. He was minister of external affairs (1957–63), and was instrumental in the formation of the Federation of Malaysia. He served as prime minister of Malaysia (1963–70).
  Malaysia, history of M 56

Rail fences P 255
Railroad lantern, picture L 283
Railroads R 77–90
  Africa A 65
  Andes mountain region A 253; picture A 252
  Asia A 466
  broader gauge used as defense by Russians U 40
  canal traffic affected by C 84–85
  Casey Jones, story of T 74
  communication advanced by C 436
  diesel locomotive and train, picture D 168
  first U.S. transcontinental A 204
  first "road of rails" L 329
  Fisherman's Railroad, Alaska A 138
  flanged wheels W 158
  folk songs and stories F 317; T 74
  growth affected U.S. interstate commerce I 331–32
  highest standard gauge in the world P 164
  How did 4 feet 8 inches come to be picked for the width of track? R 86
  locomotives L 327–32
  Midnight Special, The, folk song F 319
  model railroads R 91–92
  monorails, Aerotrains, turbotrains T 267
  narrow-gauge, in operation A 138; C 410; S 324
  postal service P 405, 407
  rails, expansion and contraction of, picture H 94
  Rocky Mountain routes R 274
  South Carolina, early transportation in S 301–02
  transportation, history of T 263
  tunnels T 314
  United States U 110
  viaduct in Switzerland, picture E 328
  Westinghouse's air brake W 125
  yard at Winnipeg, picture M 77
  See *also* Transportation section of country, province, and state articles
Railroads, model R 91–92
Railroad terminals R 83
Railroad ties W 226
Railroad Unemployment Insurance Act, 1938 L 14
Rails, Midway, extinct birds B 231

Railway brotherhoods, five trade unions that represent railroad workers in negotiations with railroad companies. The unions are those of engineers, conductors and brakemen, firemen and enginemen, trainmen, and switchmen.

Railway Labor Act, act passed (1926) to insure quick settlement of disputes between railroad companies and employees. The law provided for a board of mediation and an arbitration board and outlined procedures in case of emergency. An amendment (1934) set up the more effective National Railroad Adjustment Board at Chicago.

Railways see Railroads
Rain and rainfall R 93–95
  cave formation by erosion C 153–54
  climate, effect on C 343–48
  clouds, nimbo-stratus, bring rain C 360; picture C 361
  cloud "seeding" W 67, 91–92
  control of W 91–94
  deserts D 124
  dust particles and liquid droplets D 348
  equatorial climate in the rain forests E 272h
  floods and flood control F 254, 256
  forest growth F 371
  hurricanes and tornadoes H 292–99
  hydrologic, or water cycles W 52
  mountains influence rainfall M 497
  rain forest averages **R 99**
  North America, average precipitation in N 302
  prairies P 430
  rainmaking W 91–94
  South America S 279
  trade winds' influence T 246
  tree rings, record of T 286–87
  water supply W 67
  weather elements W 76, 80
  What is the shape of a falling raindrop? R 93
  world water resources W 257
  See also Clouds; climate section of country, province, and state articles
Rainbow R 98
  a natural prism of color, picture D 138
  effect of atmosphere A 482
  over Victoria Falls, pictures A 47, R 249
  radiation passing through rain R 44
  See also Iris, Greek goddess
Rainbow Bridge National Monument, Utah U 250; picture N 54
Rainbow (42nd) **Division,** United States Army N 43
  MacArthur, Douglas M 2
Rainbow trout, fish, picture F 210
Raindrops, how shaped R 93

Rainey, Joseph Hayne (1832–1887), American politician, b. Georgetown, S.C. He was a member of the executive committee of the newly formed Republican Party of South Carolina (1867) and was elected a delegate to the state constitutional convention (1868) and a state senator (1869–70). He became the first Negro member of the House of Representatives (1870–79).

Rainfall see Rain and rainfall
Rain forest R 99–100; pictures A 47, L 235
  birds of B 225
  Brazil's Amazon Basin B 380–81
  climate, types of C 345
  Congo soil C 462; Z 366b, 366c
  jungles compared to J 154
  layers of habitation L 254
  Olympic National Park, Washington W 24–25
  Puerto Rico, picture N 283
  South America S 280
  tropics T 294
  See also Jungles

Rainier III (ren-YAY) (Louis Henri Maxence Bertrand Rainier de Grimaldi) (1923–   ), b. Monaco. A descendant of the Genoese Grimaldi dynasty that ruled Monaco (968–1731), he became prince of Monaco in 1949. He served in the French Army (1944–45) and founded the Monaco Red Cross (1948). In 1956 he married Grace Kelly.
  Monaco, history of M 407

Rainier (rain-IER), **Mount,** Washington W 14, 16; pictures C 343, F 285
  Seattle, picture S 112

Rain-in-the-Face (named when his war paint streaked in the rain) (1835?–1905), American Sioux Indian chief, b. near forks of Cheyenne River, N.Dak. He fought at battle of Little Bighorn (1876) and fled to Canada with Sitting Bull. He surrendered to American soldiers (1880).

Rainmaking W 91–94
  climate control C 348
Rain shadows, dry areas on leeward sides of mountains M 497
Rainy Lake, Minnesota-Ontario M 325

Raisin, iron- and sugar-rich dried fruit made from grapes of the European *vinifera* variety. Fully ripe grapes are dried in the sun or by artificial heat. Raisin grapes have been grown from ancient times, mainly in Greece, Spain, and the Near East. In the 20th century, raisin-grape production in California and Australia has become important. The major varieties of raisin grapes are Muscat, and Thompson or Sultanina seedless.
  raisin grapes G 297
  Why are dried grapes called raisins? D 317

Raj Path, avenue in New Delhi, picture D 101

Rajputs (ROJ-poots), Hindu people, divided into over 30 clans, residing chiefly in the northwestern Indian state of Rajputana. They claim to be offspring of the ancient warrior caste of the Kshatriyas. Rajputs were at the height of their power as the ruling caste from their historical appearance in the 7th century until the 12th century. Today they are the ruling group of Rajputana and are traditionally of the military profession.
  Rajput school of miniature painting O 215

Raksha Bandhan (rok-SHA bont-ON) **Day,** India H 158

Rale, or **Rasle** (ROL), **Sebastian** (1654?–1724), French Jesuit missionary, b. Pontarlier. After joining the American missions, he spent 2 years among Illinois tribes. Assigned (1693) to serve among the Abnaki Indians, he established a mission at Norridgewock, present-day Maine. He was distrusted by the British for fomenting Indian hostility against English colonists and died in an English attack on Norridgewock (1724). He compiled a dictionary of the Abnaki language, published in 1833.

Raleigh (RALL-e), capital of North Carolina N 318; picture N 319
  Livestock Judging Pavilion, picture A 387
Raleigh, Sir Walter, English soldier, courtier, and poet R 101
  American colonies A 180–81, 182
  poetry of E 251
Ram, constellation see Aries
Rama, hero-god of Hinduism H 132; picture O 220d
Ramadan (ram-a-DON), month of religious fasting for Muslims R 155
  Koran K 295
  observance of the holy month in Morocco M 458–59

Raman (RA-mon), **Sir Chandrasekhara Venkata** (1888–

Raman Sir Chandrasekhara (continued)
1970) Indian physicist, b. Trichinopoly. He was awarded the 1930 Nobel prize in physics for discovering the Raman effect, observed when light is scattered by the molecules of a substance through which it is passed. Some of the light rays lose energy and change in wavelength. By studying this effect, scientists have greatly increased their knowledge of the molecular structure of gases, liquids, and solids.

Ramanuja, Indian philosopher **O** 220e
Ramayana (ra-MA-ya-na), Hindu epic poem **H** 132;
    picture from **O** 220d
  Hindu theater **T** 163
  Indian literature **O** 220d
Ramazzini (ra-ma-TZI-ni), **Bernardino,** Italian doctor
    O 15–16
Rambert, Marie, English ballet director **B** 26

Rambi (ROM-bi), or **Rabi,** volcanic island in South Pacific, in the northern district of Fiji Islands. It has tropical climate and fertile land. Originally owned by Lever Brothers, it was purchased and resettled by Banaban natives of Ocean Island, who raise coconuts.

Rameau (ra-MO), **Jean-Philippe** (1683–1764), French composer and musical theorist, b. Dijon. Following the success of his opera-ballet *Les Indes galantes* and his masterpiece, the opera *Castor et Pollux*, he became the leading composer of operas in France and was named composer of the king's chamber music. He wrote church music and several suites for harpsichord.
  ballet-opera **D** 36; **O** 132
  French music **F** 445
  innovator in handling the orchestra **O** 184

Rameses see Ramses
Ramie, a kind of nettle see Nettle
Ramjet engines **J** 86; diagram **J** 87
  types of engines **E** 211
Rampant, position of lion in heraldry, picture **H** 117
Ramparts, The, peaks in the Rocky Mountains, picture **J** 55
Rams, male sheep **S** 145
Ramsay, Allan, Scottish painter **E** 238
Ramsay, Sir William, British chemist **N** 110
Ramses II (RAM-sese), king of Ancient Egypt **E** 91
  Abu-Simbel temple **E** 100; picture **E** 101
  statues moved from Aswan High Dam site **D** 21
Ramses III, king of ancient Egypt **E** 100

Ramsey, Alexander (1815–1903), American politician, b. near Harrisburg, Pa. He was a member of Congress (1843–47), governor of the territory of Minnesota (1849–53), mayor of Saint Paul (1855), governor of the state of Minnesota (1859–63), U.S. senator (1863–75), and secretary of war (1879–81).
  Minnesota, history of **M** 337

Ram's horn, Hebrew shofar **B** 429
Rana family, of Nepal **N** 114
Ra Nahesi (ra na-HAY-si), Egyptian pharaoh **N** 89
Ranaivo, Flavien, Malagasy Republic poet **A** 76c
Randall, James Ryder, American songwriter **N** 25
Ranch life **R** 102–06
  Australia's sheep industry **A** 498
  desert livestockmen **D** 128
  New Mexico **N** 187
  prairies, land use of **P** 431; picture **P** 433
  roping **R** 333–35
  Uruguay **U** 237; picture **U** 236
  See also Cattle; Livestock

Ranch mink, fur **F** 513–14
Ranch-style homes, picture **H** 168

Rand, Ayn (1905?–), American novelist, b. St. Petersburg, (now Leningrad, U.S.S.R.). She has aroused much controversy with novels that preach supreme individualism. Her novels include *The Fountainhead, We the Living,* and *Atlas Shrugged.* In *For the New Intellectual,* she advocates philosophy of rational egotism.

Rand, South Africa, gold deposit site **G** 253

Randolph, A. Philip (1889–), American labor leader, b. Crescent City, Fla. A noted leader of the Negro labor movement, he organized the Brotherhood of Sleeping Car Porters (1925) and directed March on Washington Movement (1941) to obtain equal job opportunities for Negroes. He helped establish the Fair Employment Practice Committee (1941) and has served as vice-president of the AFL-CIO since 1957. Picture **N** 104.
  continuing struggle in Negro history **N** 104b

Randolph, Martha Jefferson, acting first lady in Jefferson's administration **F** 165–66
  known as Patsy, picture **J** 67

Randolph family, prominent Virginia family whose members held important posts in Virginia and U.S. government. They were descended from **William** (1651–1711), who came to Virginia from England (1673?) and became a leading Virginia planter. **Peyton** (1721–75), grandson of William, served in the House of Burgesses and as president of the Continental Congress (1774–75). **John** (1773–1833), great-grandson of William, served as leader in House of Representatives and Senate and was a leading supporter of Thomas Jefferson's policies until 1805. **Edmund** (1753–1813), nephew of Peyton, proposed Virginia plan at Constitutional Convention (1787) and served as first attorney general (1789–94).
  Edmund Randolph's Virginia Plan **U** 146

Random sampling, in statistics **S** 418
Rangefinders, optical instruments **O** 170–71

Ranger, name of series of U.S. moon probes. Rangers VII through IX, launched in 1964 and 1965, took close-up photographs of the moon's surface, and Ranger IX also sent back live television images. The first six Ranger probes failed to complete their missions. Part of the Apollo manned space program, these probes were designed to gather information about landing conditions on the moon.
  exploring the moon **M** 450, 455; map of landing area sites **M** 449

Rangers, loosely organized body of armed men, usually mounted, who are employed by some constituted authority to defend or protect an area. They helped defend the American frontier against Indians.

Rangoon (ran-GOON), capital of Burma **B** 454
  Shwe Dagon Pagoda, picture **B** 457
Rangoon, University of, Burma, picture
  B 458

Rankin, Jeannette (1880–), American legislator and suffragist, b. near Missoula, Mont. A participant in women's suffrage movements, she was the first woman elected to Congress and served in the House of Representatives (1917–19, 1941–43). She voted against U.S. entry into World War I and was the only member of Congress to oppose war declaration against Japan (1941).

Rankin, Louise Spiker (1897–1951), American author of children's books, b. Baltimore, Md. Her travels through Europe, India, and Burma gave her the background for many of her books, including *Daughters of the Mountain* and *Gentling of Jonathan.*

Ransom, John Crowe, American poet and critic A 211
Ransom, payment for freedom from captivity P 263
   making warfare pay in the Middle Ages K 273

Ransome, Arthur (1884–1967), English author, b. Leeds, Yorkshire. Though best-known as a children's author, he also wrote miscellaneous adult books, including several literary critiques (*Edgar Allan Poe*) and travel books (*Six Weeks in Russia*). His children's stories include *Swallows and Amazons, Swallowdale,* and *Winter Holiday.*

Rape of the Lock, The, by Pope E 258
Raphael (ra-pha-EL), Italian painter R 106
   Head of Youth, drawing R 106
   Italian art in Florence and Rome I 469
   Renaissance art R 162, 167, 169
   Saint George and the Dragon, painting I 471
   School of Athens, The, painting R 168
   style of his paintings of the Madonna and Child
    P 21
Rapid City, South Dakota S 324
Rapids, parts of a river where water rushes over and
   through rocks
   Colorado River, picture G 291
Rapp (ROPP), **George,** German religious leader I 143
Rappel (rap-PEL), descent of a mountain by means of a
   rope M 491
Raptures of the deep, illness attacks deep-sea divers
   D 82
   preventing narcosis U 15–16
Rapunzel (ra-PUNZ-el), fairy tale by Grimm brothers
   G 378–80
Rare-earth elements E 158–59
Rare gases see Noble gases
Raritan River and Bay, New Jersey N 166–67
   radar map compared with map of the area R 36
Rashtrapati Bhavan (RUSH-tra-pa-ti BA-van), president's
   residence in Delhi, India D 103
Rask (ROSK), **Rasmus,** Danish language scholar L 39
Rasle, Sebastian see Rale, Sebastian

Rasmussen (RA-smuss-en), **Knud Johan Victor** (1879–1933), Danish explorer and ethnologist, b. Jacobshavn, Greenland. He led numerous expeditions (from 1902) in Greenland to research his theory that Eskimo and North American Indians can be traced to a common Asian ancestry. He founded the Thule, Greenland, settlement (1910), which became a base for further explorations. He was responsible for discovering and preserving Eskimo folklore. Among his books translated into English are *Greenland by the Polar Sea, Myths and Legends from Greenland,* and *Across Arctic America.*

Raspberries G 298, 301; picture G 299

Rasputin (ra-SPU-tin), **Grigori Efimovich** (1871–1916), Russian holy man, b. Tobolsk province, Siberia. An unlearned peasant who dedicated himself to mysticism (about 1904), he proclaimed himself a holy man, and because he apparently cured the sick crown prince with prayers and mystic rites, he gained complete power over Czarina Alexandra and Czar Nicholas II. An advocate of autocracy, he used his hypnotic power over the Czar and Czarina to rid the court of all liberal ministers, replacing them with his sympathizers. During World War I his control became corrupt, and he was finally assassinated.

Rasses; small civet cats G 90
Ratels (RA-tels), or honey badgers O 246
Ratification, of treaties T 271
Ratings, grades of skills in U.S. Navy U 190
Ratio, in mathematics M 155
   probability P 471
Rational numbers, or quotients of two integers N 385
   new numbers in history of mathematics M 155

Rationing, equal distribution or economical use of a supply, especially during times of disaster, such as war or famine. In the United States during World War II individual allotment of goods including canned foods, meats, gasoline, and fuel oil was controlled by issuance of ration coupons.

Rat kangaroos K 170; picture K 168
Ratline, or clove, **hitch,** knot K 292
Ratoons, pineapples P 249
Rats, rodents R 277–78
   aging experiment, picture A 85
   animal maze tests A 284
   bubonic plague I 287; picture I 286
   disease prevention and rat control D 221
   experiment with living space L 253
   household pests H 264
   how rats are classified K 252
   learning experiments, picture L 102
   pack rats R 279
   tracks, picture A 271
Rattan palm, tree J 154
Rattigan, Terence, English dramatist E 268
Rattlesnake flags F 244; picture F 229
Rattlesnakes S 209; pictures S 210
   animals harmful to man I 284–85
   sensory system of B 366
   timber rattlesnake, picture I 282
Rauschenberg, Robert, American artist P 31
Rauscher viruses, picture C 93
Rauwolfia (ra-WOLF-ia), plant P 313; picture
   P 312

Ravalli, Antonio (1811–1884), Italian missionary, b. Ferrara. He went to Canada (1844) and soon began working among the Indians in what is now Montana. He moved to northern Idaho and was accepted as a leader by the Indians. As white men came west, he became priest and physician to tribesmen and miners.
   Idaho, history of I 68

Ravel (ra-VEL) **Maurice Joseph** (1875–1937), French composer, b. Ciboure, Basses-Pyrénées. His music was controversial and for many years considered too advanced for contemporary tastes. His greatest success was the orchestral work *Boléro* (originally a ballet). Other well-known works include ballets *Daphnis et Chloé* and *La Valse;* an opera, *L'Heure espagnole;* two piano concertos; *Rhapsodie espagnole;* many songs, including the cycle *Shéhérazade;* piano pieces, including *Pavane for a Dead Princess.* Picture F 447.
   chamber music, new C 186
   French music F 447; O 138
   L'Heure espagnole, opera O 145

Raven, constellation see Corvus
Ravenna (ra-VEN-na), Italy
   Byzantine art of B 484
   Sant' Apollinare in Classe church, picture A 370
Ravens, birds P 86
   ravens, of Odin, Norse god N 278
   Sam Houston's Indian name H 271
   symbol of England's royal family H 115

Rawhide
  lariats **R** 333
Rawlings, Marjorie Kinnan, American novelist **A** 213
Raw materials
  forests **F** 371–74
  life, food chains in **L** 239, 242
  mines and mining **M** 313
  primary products in international trade **I** 327
  wood **W** 222–28
  See also agricultural products by name, as Corn
Raw silk **S** 179
Ray, John, English naturalist **B** 191
Ray, Man, American artist **M** 393
  Gift, The (Le Cadeau), dada sculpture, picture **M** 394
Ray, Satyajit, Indian motion-picture director **M** 488
Rayburn, Samuel T., American statesman **T** 135
  helpful to Johnson's early political career **J** 128
Rayleigh (RAY-le), **Lord,** British chemist **N** 110
Rayon, man-made fiber **N** 424
Rays, fishes **S** 140–43
Rays, in geometry **G** 124
Rays, in the new mathematics **M** 168
Rays, on the moon **M** 451
Rays, cosmic *see* Cosmic rays
Razorback hogs **H** 209; picture **H** 212
RCA *see* Radio Corporation of America

Re (RAY), or **Ra,** in ancient Egyptian religion, chief deity and sun god. Re was often compounded with other gods, and from 2000 to 1800 B.C. his name was joined with that of Amon, who later reigned supreme. According to legend, Re created himself from nothingness and then created air, moisture, and eventually mankind. He was considered first king of Egypt, and all succeeding kings took his name. He was symbolized by hawk, scarab, or serpent.

Reaction, force in direction opposite to action **M** 471
  jet propulsion **J** 85
  reaction engines **E** 209, 211
Reaction, in psychology
  response to environment **K** 255–56
Reaction engines **E** 209, 211
Reactions, chemical **C** 196–97, 201
  catalysis **C** 199
Reaction turbines **E** 210

Reade, Charles (1814–1884), English author, b. Oxfordshire. He began his career as a dramatist with the production in 1851 of the comedy *The Ladies' Battle.* He later wrote novels, for which he is chiefly remembered, including his best-known novel, *The Cloister and the Hearth,* depicting early Renaissance life; novels exposing social injustice, such as *It Is Never Too Late to Mend* and *Hard Cash.*

Readers
  easy-to-read, or basal **C** 243
  phonics **P** 194–95
Reader's Digest, The, magazine **M** 15
Readers' Guide to Periodical Literature **R** 130
  indexes to magazines **I** 115
Reading **R** 107–11
  book reports and book reviews **B** 314–17
  Initial Teaching Alphabet **I** 254
  language arts reading program **L** 36
  library reading clubs **L** 170–71
  new and old readers, pictures **E** 77
  nonsense rhymes need to be seen **N** 272
  phonics in teaching reading **P** 193
  vocabulary, how to increase **V** 372
  See also Children's literature

Reading (RED-ing), Pennsylvania **P** 142
Reading readiness **R** 107–08
Ready-made clothing **C** 353

Reagan, Ronald Wilson (1911–), American actor and governor of California, b. Tampico, Ill. His long movie career began in 1937 and included such films as *Brother Rat, King's Row, Voice of the Turtle, The Hasty Heart, John Loves Mary,* and *The Killers.* He has also appeared on TV. He was president of the Screen Actors Guild (1947–62, 1959–60). He was elected governor in 1966, and reelected in 1970.

Real estate **R** 112–13
  disposed of by a will **W** 174
  noise pollution **N** 270
Real images, light pictures **L** 262–63
  lenses **L** 144
Realism, in art
  Dutch and Flemish art **D** 350–51, 352
  French painting **F** 426
  modern art **M** 386–87
Realism, in literature
  American literature **A** 206
  drama **D** 297
  German literature **G** 178
  Italian 20th-century literature **I** 481
  Russian literature **U** 60
  Spanish literature **S** 370
Realistic stories
  list of, for children **C** 247–48
Real numbers, include rational and irrational numbers **N** 385–86
Real property *see* Real estate
Realtors **R** 113
Reaper, harvesting machine **M** 186
  farm machinery **F** 60
Re-apportionment, of government representatives **S** 415
Reason for the Pelican, The, poem by John Ciardi **N** 274
Reasoning *see* Thinking

Réaumur (ray-o-MUR), **René Antoine Ferchault de** (1683–1757), French scientist, b. La Rochelle. His greatest contribution to science is a six-volume work on insect anatomy and behavior. He was first to collect and isolate stomach juices, by recovering sponges swallowed by birds. He showed that food is digested by these juices. He devised a thermometer scale, named for him, that separates boiling and freezing points of water by 80 degrees.
  wood pulp as a source of paper suggested by study of wasp behavior **C** 432; **P** 56–57

Rebec (RE-bec), Arabic musical instrument **V** 342
Rebecca, novel by Daphne du Maurier **M** 556

Rebekah, or **Rebecca,** in the Old Testament (Genesis 24–27), daughter of Bethuel, son of Abraham's brother Nahor. She was escorted from Abraham's birthplace to Negeb to marry Isaac. She bore Isaac two sons, Esau and Jacob, and lived with him in Gerar and Beersheba. She helped Jacob, her favorite son, take Esau's place and receive Isaac's blessing. She was buried next to Sarah, her mother-in-law, in the Cave of Machpelah.
  how a proper wife was found for Isaac **I** 413

Rebellion of 1837, Canada, led by Louis Joseph Papineau **C** 73
Rebellious Stripes, flag **F** 244
Rebuses (RE-bus-es) **W** 236–37
  button collection displayed **B** 480; picture **B** 478
Rebuttal, in a debate **D** 55

Recall see Impeachment; Initiative, referendum, and recall, legislative processes

Récamier (ray-ca-mi-AY), **Madame** (Jeanne Françoise Julie Adélaïde Bernard Récamier) (1777–1849), French society leader, b. Lyons. The wife of Parisian banker Jacques Récamier, she was known as a beautiful and charming hostess who entertained noted people of her day. Her friends included author Madame de Staël and statesman-writer Chateaubriand. Her memoirs were published as *Souvenirs et Correspondance* ("Memories and Letters").

Receptors, specialized nerve cells **B** 365
  body's senses **B** 283
  parts of insects that receive sensation **I** 266
Recessions see Depressions and recessions
Recessive traits, in genetics **G** 80
Recife (ray-CI-fay), capital of Pernambuco, Brazil
  B 378
Recipes (RES-ip-ese) **R** 114–16
  barbecue sauce **O** 247
  Halloween party food and drink **H** 17
  shish kabab **O** 248
Reciprocal (re-CIP-ro-cal) **Trade Agreement Act,** 1934
  I 329
  tariff in international trade **T** 25
Reciprocating engines I 303
Reciprocity (re-ci-PROS-ity) **Treaty,** 1854 **C** 73
Recitals (re-CY-tals), singing **V** 376
Recitatives (res-i-ta-TEVES), sung dialogues or speech-
  songs **M** 537; **O** 131
  musical term, invented during baroque period **B** 63
Reclamation, Bureau of, United States **I** 408
Reclamation Act, 1902 **C** 485; **R** 329
  land under irrigation in Nebraska **N** 87
Recoil mechanism, of artillery **G** 425
Reconstruction Act, 1867, United States **R** 120
  administration of Andrew Johnson **J** 125
Reconstruction Finance Corporation H 224
Reconstruction Period, in United States **R** 117–20
  Hayes' election compromise **H** 79–80
  Johnson, Andrew **J** 125
  Lincoln's plan for **L** 297
  Negro history **N** 95–96
Record (phonograph) **collecting R** 124–25
  basic collection of jazz records **J** 62
Recorder, musical instrument **R** 121–22
  in concert, picture **I** 482
  types of musical instruments **M** 547, 549
Recorders, wire and tape see Tape and wire recorders
Recordings, phonograph see Records, phonograph
Record player, or phonograph **P** 196–98
Records, phonograph P 196–98
  electronic music, outstanding compositions **E** 142h
  hi-fi and stereo recording **H** 125–26
  jazz, outstanding recordings **J** 62
  record collecting and basic record library **R** 123–25
  rock music **R** 262b
  talking books for the blind **B** 252–53
  use of, in libraries, picture **L** 173
Recreation
  family amusement in colonial America **C** 392
  camping **C** 40–47
  mountains, importance of for recreation **M** 498
  national recreation areas **N** 49
  parks and playgrounds **P** 76–78
  parties **P** 87–89
  pioneer life **P** 258
  snowmobiles **S** 215
  television **T** 65–71
  United States **U** 101

  vacations and travel **V** 258–59
  See also Games; Hobbies; Play; Sports
Rectal thermometers M 208f; **N** 414
Rectangles, geometric forms **G** 126
Rectifiers, electric **E** 146
Rectilinear movement, of snakes **S** 211
Recycling, and re-use, of waste materials **S** 34
  environmental problems of solid-waste pollution **E** 272g
  tires a source of carbon black **R** 348
Red, Red Rose, A, poem by Robert Burns **B** 460
Red and the Black, The, novel by Stendhal **N** 348
Red Badge of Courage, The, by Stephen Crane **A** 206
Red-bellied woodpeckers, birds, picture **B** 239
Red blood cells see Red corpuscles
Redbud tree, picture **G** 45
  state tree of Oklahoma **O** 81
Red cabbage
  as an acid-base indicator **C** 217
Red cedar, tree, picture **T** 278
Red China see China, People's Republic of (Communist)

Red Cloud (1822–1909), American Indian chief, b. near Platte River, Nebr. As chief of Oglala Teton Sioux, he opposed U.S. government construction of road from Fort Laramie, Wyo., to gold regions in Montana. After leading Sioux and Cheyenne Indians in fierce battles at Fetterman massacre (1866) and Wagon Box fight (1867), he signed peace treaty (1868) in which the government agreed to abandon construction of the road.

Red clover, plant
  Vermont, state flower of **V** 307
Redcoats, nickname for British soldiers **R** 196
  French and Indian War **F** 460
Red corpuscles (cells), in blood **B** 256
  circulatory system of human body **B** 275–77
  use in medicine **M** 211
Red Crescent Society, Muslim Red Cross **R** 126
  flag **F** 226
Red Cross R 126–27
  Barton, Clara, founder of American branch **B** 68
  flag **F** 226
Red Deer, Alberta, Canada **A** 146g
Red Desert soils S 233
  found in African deserts **A** 52

Redding, Jay Saunders (1906–), American educator and author, Negro, b. Wilmington, Del. For many years he was a professor of literature in various Southern colleges and universities. In 1963 he received his D.Litt. from Brown University. He has won many awards for his books and for his contribution to interracial understanding. His writings include *To Make a Poet Black* (1939), *They Came in Chains* (1950), *On Being Negro in America* (1951), and *The Lonesome Road* (1958).

Red Eagle, Creek Indian leader **A** 112
Red-eyed vireos, birds, picture **B** 239
Red-figure pottery, ancient Greece **P** 414
Red Flag Act, 1865 **A** 542
Red foxes D 248–49; **F** 396

Red Guards, militant Communist Chinese youth organization. It was formed to support, with violence, if necessary, the Cultural Revolution. This is the name given Communist Party Chairman Mao Tse-tung's campaign to impose a more austere form of Communism on China.
  China, history of **C** 273

Red hibiscus (hi-BISC-us), state flower of Hawaii **H** 56

Red Jacket (Sagoyewatha) (1758–1830), American Indian

Red Jacket (continued)
chief, b. Seneca County, N.Y. He was chief of Seneca Indians and was noted particularly for his oratory upholding Indian traditions. He received his popular name from his custom of wearing a red jacket given to him by a British officer. He resisted introduction of white man's institutions, particularly Christianity. In War of 1812 he lent support to the United States.

Red Jungle Fowl, ancestor of chickens **P** 420
Red kangaroos **K** 170; picture **K** 168

Red-letter days, memorable or important days. The term arose from the custom of indicating holy days in red on church calendars.

Red light rooms, in zoos **Z** 379
Red Lion, running and chasing game **G** 21
Red Lion and Sun symbol, Red Cross of Iran **R** 126
  flag **F** 226
Redman, Don, American jazz composer **J** 60
Red Mill, The, operetta by Victor Herbert **O** 158
Red oak, tree
  New Jersey, state tree of **N** 164
Red on yellow, kill a fellow, saying about snakes **S** 209
Red Paint Indians, original inhabitants of Maine **M** 46
Red pepper **S** 382
Red (Norway) pine, tree
  Minnesota, state tree of **M** 323
Red planet, Mars **M** 105
  planets of our solar system **P** 272–73
Red raspberries, picture **G** 299
Red River, of southern United States **O** 83; **T** 125
  Louisiana **L** 351
Red River, southeast Asia **R** 247
  Vietnam **V** 334a
Red River carts, two-wheeled carts of pioneers **N** 329
  early transportation in Minnesota **M** 322
Red River colony, Canada, founded by Lord Selkirk
  C 72, 73
  Manitoba, settlements in **M** 76, 82
Red River of the North
  Manitoba **M** 76
  Minnesota **M** 325
  system in North Dakota **N** 325
Red Rock River, considered as first portion of the Missouri **M** 383
Red Rover, running and chasing game **G** 20
Red Sea **O** 48
  part of a continental drift **E** 20; **G** 116
Red shift, change in galaxy spectrum **U** 201–02
  Doppler effect, law in physics **L** 269
Redshirts, guerrilla band led by Italy's Garibaldi **G** 57
Red Shoes, The, story by Hans Christian Andersen
  A 248
Red snow
  algae **A** 156
  red dust **R** 95
Red spiders, mites **P** 286
Red Square, Moscow **M** 466; picture **U** 27
  anniversary celebration of the Revolution, picture
  U 48
Redstarts, birds, picture **B** 240
Redstone Arsenal, Huntsville, Alabama **A** 113, 124
Red Studio, The, painting by Matisse **M** 389

Red tape, rigid conformity to formal rules of a large organization, hindering or preventing action or decision-making. The term originates from English 17th- and 18th-century procedure of binding documents and official papers with red tape and was popularized in the writings of Thomas Carlyle against official inertia.

Reduction, of metals **M** 226
  direct reduction of iron ore **I** 407
Red wines **W** 188
Red-winged blackbird, pictures **B** 216, 240
Red wolves **W** 210
  dog family **D** 245–46
Redwood, tree **T** 274; picture **G** 104
  California forests **C** 19
  giants of nature **G** 200, 202–03
  leaves, needlelike, pictures **L** 119
  plants, odd and interesting **P** 316
  uses of the wood and its grain, picture **W** 224
  why called sequoias **S** 124
Redwood National Park, California **C** 24
Reed, Walter, American doctor **R** 128
  proved theory of insects as disease carriers **D** 215
  results of Spanish-American War **S** 376
Reed boats, Peruvian craft **S** 155
Reed instruments **W** 182–83
  types of musical instruments **M** 547, 549
Reed organ **O** 208
Reefs, coral **C** 503–04
  underwater life, picture **O** 40
Reelfoot Lake, Tennessee **T** 84; picture **T** 82
Reels, for fishing **F** 206; pictures **F** 207
Re-entry, of spacecraft **S** 340j
Reeve, Tapping, American lawyer and educator **C** 478
Referee (ref-er-EE), in sports
  basketball **B** 83
  boxing **B** 351–52
  football **F** 362
Reference books **R** 129–31
  atlases **M** 93; **R** 129
  Book Review Digest **B** 317
  dictionaries **D** 164–65
  encyclopedias **E** 193–97
  how arranged in libraries **L** 185
  indexes and indexing **I** 114–15
  magazine lists **M** 15
  quotations **Q** 19
  research methods **R** 183
  use in a library research project **L** 187
  word origins, source books **W** 241
  See also Textbooks
Referendum *see* Initiative, referendum, and recall, legislative processes
Referent (re-FER-ent), in semantics, what a word stands for **S** 117
Refining, of fats and oils **O** 77
Refining, of metals **M** 228–29
  aluminum **A** 176–77
  gold **G** 249
Refining, of petroleum **P** 174; picture **P** 175
Reflecting telescopes **T** 61, 62
  lenses **L** 148, 265
Reflection, of light or heat **L** 261–62
  reflective insulation **I** 291
Reflectors, of radio telescopes **R** 72
Reflex action, or reflexes, in psychology **P** 496
  sense of touch and reflex action **B** 287
  spinal cord functions **B** 368
Reforestation **F** 372–74
  Asia **A** 462
  conservation efforts **C** 484–85
Reformation (ref-or-MAY-tion) **R** 132–35
  Calvin, John **C** 30
  Christianity, history of **C** 285–87
  Christmas outlawed in England by Puritans **C** 290
  education in national languages promoted **E** 67–68
  Erasmus' views on the Reformation **E** 274
  Germany's early religious divisions **G** 159–60
  Luther, Martin, leader of Protestant movement **L** 378

monument to Farel, Calvin, Beza, and Knox, pictures
C 287; P 482

Protestantism P 482–86

reforms for Roman Catholic Church R 293–94

Switzerland S 496, 502

Reformatories, for juvenile offenders P 469–70

Reform Bill, 1832, England E 227

Reform Judaism (JU-da-ism) J 118, 119

Reform schools, for juvenile offenders P 470

Refracting telescopes T 61–62

lenses L 147

Refraction, of light L 262–63

lenses L 142–43

optical instruments O 166

Refractive index, of light O 173–74

brilliancy of gemstones G 69

Refractometer (re-frac-TOM-et-er), optical instrument
O 173–74; picture O 169

Refractors, optical instruments O 169

Refreshments, for parties P 89

Refrigerants, substances that do the cooling in refrigerators R 136–37

Refrigeration R 136–38

air conditioning A 103

Bacon's experiment B 7

cool storage of food F 346–47

foods, preservation from spoilage F 355

Refrigerators

electric appliances E 119

food spoilage F 354–55

frozen foods F 346

liquid gases L 308

nitrogen gas used as refrigerant G 60

refrigerator cars, of railroads R 82

trucks T 297

Refugee-Escapee Act, 1957 I 101

Refugee in America, poem by Langston Hughes
H 274

Refugee Relief Act, 1952 I 101

Refugees

Arabs in Jordan J 136

Exodus from East to West Germany G 164

Hong Kong H 205

Jews after World War II J 111

Korean War victims, picture K 303

poverty, victims of P 424a

stateless persons P 94

Refuse (REF-use) **and refuse disposal** S 33–34

community helps in prevention of disease D 220

environment, problems of E 272g

water pollution W 58–59

See also Sewage disposal

Regattas (re-GA-tas)

rowing races R 339; picture R 338

Regelation, refreezing of ice that has melted under pressure. When ice is compressed, it becomes liquid and refreezes at a temperature lower than the normal freezing point of water. Regelation takes place within a snowball when it is packed tightly. Regelation is involved in the movement of glaciers.

Regency, period in a country's history when the monarch is too young, too ill, or otherwise unable to rule and someone else, called a regent (from the Latin word for "ruler"), rules in his place. The term "Regency" now most often refers to the years 1811–20 in England, when the Prince of Wales (later King George IV) was regent for his father, King George III. It is also used to describe the period's styles of architecture, furniture, and dress.

furniture, picture F 506

London of Regency period L 336

Regenerated fibers F 108; N 425, 427

Regeneration, in biology

crustacea replace lost appendages S 171

experiments with amphibians F 478

hydra J 73

starfishes S 403

Regent diamond, history of D 156

Regent's Park, London, England P 77

Regent Street, London, England L 336

Regiment, army troop unit U 172

Regin (RAIG-in), dwarf in Norse Mythology N 280–81

Regina (re-GINE-a), capital of Saskatchewan, Canada
S 38g; picture S 38b

cities of Canada C 67

Regina medal, juvenile literary award founded (1959) by the Catholic Library Association. It is presented annually to an author, illustrator, or editor, regardless of religion or nationality, whose career has been devoted to the advancement of children's literature.

Regional Centre for Education for Community Development, Sirs el Laiyana, U.A.R. T 43

Regional geography G 108

Regional literature, American A 204–05

fiction F 109–10

local-color short stories S 167

novels N 349

Regions, in the new mathematics M 168

Registan, I., Russian poet N 19

Registered mail P 409

Registered nurses N 411

Registration of aliens A 166

Registration of voters, official enrollment of persons qualified to vote. Generally the voter presents his qualifications to the proper officials before an election, and these registration lists serve as check lists at the polls. In periodic registration the process is repeated before each election. In permanent registration lists are made up at longer intervals and kept up to date by a permanent staff.

elections E 112–115

Regs, gravel plains S 8

Regulus (REG-u-lus), star C 492

Rehabilitation, after illness H 248–49; M 208d

Rehabilitation of the handicapped see Handicapped, rehabilitation of the

Rehearsals (re-HER-sals), of plays P 336, 339; pictures
T 157

Rehoboam (re-o-BO-am), in Old Testament (2 Chronicles 9:31–12:10; 1 Kings 11:43–12:24, 14:21–31), son of Solomon and his Ammonite wife, Naamah. He reigned as king of Judah (933?–917 B.C.). His refusal to relieve subjects of oppressive labor and taxes led to the division of Israel into the two-tribe kingdom of Judah under his rule and the 10-tribe kingdom of Israel under Jeroboam. His reign was marked by an Egyptian invasion and general increase of idol worship and immorality.

Reich (RIKE), German word for state

First Reich, founded by Charlemagne G 159

Second Reich, of Germany G 161

Third Reich, of Germany G 162–63

Reichenbach (RIKE-en-bock) **Falls,** Switzerland W 56

Reichstadt, duke of see Napoleon II

Reichstag (RIKE-stoc), national German parliament of elected representatives. Established under the German Empire (1871), it was recreated by the Weimar Constitu-

Reichstag (continued)
tion (1919), which strengthened it with executive power to check actions of chancellor and president, although the president could replace the Reichstag with an emergency cabinet in time of conflict. It surrendered its power by voting for the "enabling act" (1933), which granted legislative power to Chancellor Adolf Hitler and his cabinet. After World War II the Reichstag was replaced by the Bundestag.

Reichstag fire, 1933 **N** 70
 Hitler comes to power **W** 285
Reid (REED), **Samuel,** American naval officer **F** 248
Reign (RAIN) **of Terror,** in French Revolution
 F 467–68
 events in Paris **P** 73
Reilly, Charles, English architect and teacher **E** 241
Reincarnation (re-in-car-NATION), rebirth of the soul in a
 new body **R** 146
 Hinduism **H** 131
Reindeer (RAIN-deer) **D** 83; picture **H** 214
 Asian work animal **A** 451
 cave drawing, picture **D** 303
 hoofed mammals **H** 219
 Lapland **L** 45
Reindeer moss F 95

Reiner (RY-ner), **Fritz** (1888–1963), American conductor, b. Budapest, Hungary. He was music director at Royal Opera House, Dresden, Germany (1914–21). He came to United States (1922) to become music director of the Cincinnati Symphony Orchestra (1922–31) and was director of opera and orchestra departments and conducting teacher at Curtis Institute of Music, Philadelphia (1931–41). He served as conductor of the Pittsburgh Symphony Orchestra (1938–48), the Metropolitan Opera in New York (1948–53), and the Chicago Symphony Orchestra (1953–63).

Reinforced (re-in-FORCED) **concrete C** 166; picture
 C 165
 architectural possibilities **A** 386–87
 building material **B** 431
 homes of **H** 175
 use in Latin America **L** 67
Reinforcement, stimuli procedure in learning **L** 100

Reinhardt (RINE-hart), **Max** (Max Goldmann) (1873–1943), Austrian theatrical producer, b. Baden, near Vienna. He was director at Deutsches Theater, Berlin (1894–1903, 1905–20, 1924–32). Among his renowned productions in Europe were *The Miracle, Everyman,* and *Oedipus Rex.* He came to the United States (1933), at the rise of the Nazis. His stage and screen productions were famous.
 drama, history of **D** 298

Reisen, Abraham, Yiddish author **Y** 351
Rejection of organ transplants see Transplants of body
 organs
Relative humidity W 75–76, 80–81
 wet-and-dry-bulb readings, table **W** 81
Relative pronouns P 91
Relatives, in grammar **G** 289
Relatives, maternal and paternal, in the family
 presidents, U.S., related to other presidents **P** 450
Relativity (rel-a-TIV-ity), a theory in physics **R** 139–44
 Einstein's life, and how he worked out his theories
 E 104–06
 Einstein's new idea of gravitation **G** 325
Relay races, track events **T** 238
 games **G** 18–20
 team racing **R** 33

Relief, in sculpture S 90
 ancient art **A** 233, 238–40, 242–43
 Egypt, ancient **E** 96, 99, 101–02
 Ghiberti's doors **I** 467–68; picture **R** 165
 Romanesque carving **M** 297
Relief, public see Welfare, public
Relief maps M 90
Relief printing G 302
 lithography **L** 315
Religion, primitive R 145
Religions R 145–52
 anthropological studies **A** 304
 art, the meanings of **A** 438
 art as a record **A** 438f
 Asia **A** 460, 468
 Buddha's teachings **B** 423
 Christianity **C** 279–89
 civil rights conflicts **C** 315–16
 colonial America **C** 393–94, 395
 Confucius' teachings **C** 460
 divorce **D** 234–35
 Europe **E** 317–18
 fire worship in primitive religions **F** 144
 folk art **F** 292–93
 folk music **F** 324
 food customs **F** 334
 funeral customs **F** 492–95
 grant money from foundations **F** 393
 Hinduism **H** 130–32
 Indians of North America **I** 171
 Islam **I** 414–16
 Judaism **J** 114–20
 Middle East **M** 305
 mythology **M** 557–64
 Orthodox Eastern Churches **O** 228–30
 pioneer life **P** 259
 prayer **P** 434–35
 primitive rites based on search for food **F** 331–32
 Protestantism **P** 482–86
 Roman Catholic Church **R** 287–302
 wedding customs **W** 100–03
 women, role of **W** 211
 Zoroastrianism **Z** 380
 See *also* facts and figures and people sections of
  continent and country articles
Religious art
 African art **A** 72; pictures **A** 74
 Angelico, Fra **A** 259
 Byzantine **B** 483–90
 Caravaggio **C** 105
 Chagall, Marc **C** 184
 Dutch and Flemish painting **D** 349–58
 illuminated manuscripts **I** 87–88
 Islamic art and architecture **I** 417–22
 Italian **I** 463, 468–70, 472
 Latin America **L** 64
 Middle Ages **M** 296–97
 Raphael **R** 106
 Renaissance **R** 162, 166
 Spanish art and architecture **S** 361–62
Religious drama
 liturgical dramas for modern audiences **F** 443
 Middle English literature **E** 249–50
 miracle, morality, and mystery plays of the Middle
  Ages **D** 295
Religious education E 69
Religious freedom see Freedom of religion
Religious holidays R 153–55
 Christmas **C** 289–95
 December celebrates Christmas and Hanukkah **D** 56
 Easter **E** 41–42
 fasts of the Orthodox Eastern Churches **O** 230

Hanukkah **H** 35
holy days of obligation for Roman Catholics **R** 290
Japanese **J** 31
New Year celebrations around the world **N** 208–09
origin of the trade fair **F** 10
Passover **P** 93–94
Purim **P** 540
toys **T** 233
Religious liberty see Freedom of religion
Religious music
American Indian **I** 160–61
ancient Hebrew **A** 246
Christmas carols **C** 122
Germany **G** 182
hymns **H** 309–13
Negro spirituals **N** 105–07
Renaissance music **R** 172, 173–74
Spain **S** 372
See also Church music
Religious orders
founding of Dominicans and Franciscans **R** 292
Jesuits **R** 294
Loyola, founder of Jesuits **L** 369
missions and missionaries **M** 348
See also Monks and monasticism; Nuns
Remainder, in subtraction **A** 399
Remagen (RAY-mog-en), Germany
battle for the Rhine bridge, 1945 **W** 306
Remarque (rem-ARK), **Erich Maria**, German-born American novelist **G** 180
Rembrandt, Dutch painter **R** 155–56
Abraham's Sacrifice, etching **D** 358
Aristotle Contemplating the Bust of Homer, painting **G** 354
art of the artist **A** 438f
Blindness of Tobit, The, etching **G** 304
Dutch and Flemish art **D** 357–58
etching technique **D** 305–06
Faust in His Study, Watching a Magic Disk, painting **F** 73
Gilder Herman Doomer, The, painting **A** 438c
importance to baroque period **B** 61–62
importance to history of painting **P** 24
Night Watch, The, painting **R** 156
Polish Rider, The, painting **P** 25
signature reproduced **A** 527
Six's Bridge, etching **B** 61
Syndics of the Cloth Guild, The, painting **D** 359
View near Rampoortje, Amsterdam, drawing **D** 302
Windmill, The, etching **E** 294
Remedial (re-ME-di-al), **reading R** 111
Remembering, in psychology **P** 493
learning **L** 105
Remember the Alamo, rallying cry of the Mexican War
H 271; **T** 122
Remember the Maine, Spanish-American war cry **S** 374
Remembrance Day, Canada **H** 152
Remington, Frederic, American painter **U** 121–22
Fight for the Waterhole, painting **U** 119
paintings at Amon Carter Museum of Western Art,
Fort Worth, Texas **T** 131
Remoras, fishes **F** 203–04
curious ways animals move about **A** 266
Remote control mechanical systems
hydraulic machinery **H** 301–02
Remus see Romulus and Remus
Renaissance (ren-ais-SONCE) **R** 157–62
dance and pantomime **D** 24–25
decorative arts **D** 75
drama **D** 295–96
education **E** 67–68
exploration during **E** 373

French music **F** 443–44
historical writings **H** 135
homes **H** 179
Italian literature **I** 476–79
Leonardo da Vinci **L** 152–55
libraries **L** 196–97
medicine **M** 205–06
rebirth of science **S** 66
Reformation a part of the changing world **R** 132
Roman Catholic Church **R** 293–94
upholstery began to be used **U** 226
Renaissance architecture R 163–71
building during the Renaissance **R** 161–62
cathedrals **C** 132–33
England **A** 382–83
Foundling Hospital, in Florence, Italy **A** 438e–438f;
picture **R** 165
France **A** 381–82
Giotto's bell tower, Florence **G** 211
Italy **A** 380–81, picture **A** 384
Michelangelo **M** 257
Renaissance art R 163–71
art, golden age of Renaissance **R** 161–62
art, the meanings of **A** 438
Bellini family **B** 134
Botticelli, Sandro **B** 340b
Donatello **D** 285
Dürer influenced by **D** 345
France **F** 421–22; picture **A** 438a
furniture design **F** 505–06
German painting and sculpture **G** 169
Giotto di Bondone **G** 211
humanism in **A** 438e–438f
Italian art and architecture **I** 464–65
Italian painting **P** 20–21, 23; picture **A** 438a
jewelry making developed **J** 94
Michelangelo **M**.255–57
Raphael **R** 106
sculpture **S** 98–99
tapestries **T** 22–23
Titian **T** 199
Renaissance man R 162
Renaissance music R 172–74
choral music **C** 277
Dutch and Flemish music **D** 364
Italian music **I** 483
Renal dialysis treatment, medicine **M** 211
Rendering, extracting oils and fats from animal tissues
O 76
Rendezvous and docking, in space flights **S** 345
Rennet, or **rennin**, enzyme used for curdling milk
D 13
cheesemaking **F** 333
Reno, Jesse, American inventor **E** 175
Reno, Marcus, American army officer **I** 214
Reno, Nevada **N** 134
Renoir (ren-WA), **Jean**, French motion picture director
M 485
Renoir, Pierre Auguste, French painter **R** 174
Girl with a Watering Can, painting **N** 41
Mother and Child, drawing **D** 304
On the Terrace, painting **F** 429
postimpressionism in French painting **F** 431
use of impressionist techniques **P** 29
Re-odorization, chemicals disguise odors **D** 117
Reorganization Act, 1933 **N** 49
Reparations, payment for damages caused by war
Versailles Treaty, 1919 **W** 281, 282–83
Repartee, humorous speedy dialogue **H** 278
Repeating rifles, guns **G** 422
Repertory theaters T 159
Repletes, liquid-storing ants **A** 327

Reporters and reporting N 201–02
  interviewing Truman, picture T 302
  Pulitzer prizes in journalism P 524
Reports R 175–76
  bibliography B 170
  how to use the library for finding material L 182–88
  how to write up experiments and projects E 355
  opinion surveys O 160
  oral book reports B 315
  outlines O 249–51
  proofreading P 479
  research methods R 183
  scientific reports use taxonomy T 28–29
  See also Compositions
Repoussé (rep-oo-SAY), technique of raising designs by hammering on reverse side D 68
Representative government
  beginnings in America A 185, 188
  democracy D 104–05
  parliaments P 81–82
  problems of local governments M 508
  state governments S 415
Representatives, United States House of
  see United States House of Representatives

Reprieve (from French *reprendre*, meaning "to take back"), in criminal law, the postponement or suspension of the execution of a sentence. It is declared by the court or the pardoning power.

Reproduction R 176–80
  algae A 155
  a life process L 211
  animals: communication and social organization A 278
  baby B 2
  bacteria B 10
  breeding and migration H 188–91
  earthworms W 311
  eggs and embryos E 88–90a
  fishes F 195–96, 200–01
  flowers and seeds F 276–83
  fungi F 497
  genetics and heredity G 77–78
  grasses G 316–17
  jellyfishes and other coelenterates J 73
  mammals M 70–71
  mosses F 93
  process characteristic of all living things K 254–55
  spores F 497
  turtles T 335
  vegetative reproduction P 300
Reptiles R 180–81
  aging process A 83–84
  ancestors of birds B 206, 207
  crocodiles and alligators C 533–35
  desert animals D 124
  dinosaurs D 172–81
  fossils F 383, 387
  giants of nature G 200
  heart, two-chambered M 72
  largest animals in this class A 263
  life, adaptation to surroundings L 214–15
  lizards and chameleons L 318–21
  prehistoric animals, development of P 437, 438
  snakes S 204–14
  turtles T 331–35
Reptiles, Age of M 63
Republic, dialogue by Plato G 353–54
Republican Party, United States P 380–81
  formation in Wisconsin W 207
  Lincoln, Abraham, first elected president L 295

  National Convention, 1968, picture E 112
  Roosevelt, Theodore and the Bull Moose Party R 330
  symbols C 126; P 382
  Willkie, Wendell W 173
Republic House, office building in Ghana, picture G 194
Republics, governments of elected representatives D 104
  United States government U 135
Requiem (RE-qui-em), poem by Robert Louis Stevenson S 424
Requiem mass, a musical form M 537
Resaca de la Palma (ray-SA-ca day la POL-ma), **battle of,** 1846 M 238
  Taylor and the Mexican War T 35
Research R 182–83
  authorship of books B 329–30
  encyclopedia a valuable tool E 197
  indexes, how to use I 114–15
  library research project L 186–88
  recording information sources R 131
  reference books R 129–31
  reports R 175–76
  textbooks T 138–39
Research, scientific S 80–82
  a four-step process R 139–40
  basic and applied C 195; R 182–83
  chemical industry C 194, 195
  cosmic rays, how observed C 512
  Edison's "invention factory" E 60
  experiments in weather control W 94–95
  explaining biological clocks L 249–50
  foundations F 392–93
  International Geophysical Year I 310–20
  libraries L 177–79
  methods of the sociologist S 228
  New Jersey, concentration in N 169, 171
  opinion surveys O 159–60
  Paracelsus, beginnings of scientific method C 208–09
  polar regions P 363–64
  public health P 504
  satellites carry research instruments S 41–42
  science, history of S 60–76
  Smithsonian Institution, Washington, D.C. S 202
  solar energy S 237
  underwater exploration U 13–24
  veterinarians and medical research V 324
Research triangle, of North Carolina N 307, 311, 313
Reserpine (re-SER-pin), drug D 323
  plants, medicinal P 313
  sedatives and tranquilizers D 326
Reserves, of the United States armed forces
  Air Force Reserves and Air National Guard U 165
  Army reserve components U 175
  draft exemptions and regulations D 289
  Marine Corps Reserve U 180
  Naval Reserves U 190–91
  See also National Guard
Reservoirs (RES-erv-wars)
  aqueducts A 344
  artificial lakes L 25
  dams D 16, 19
  flood control F 257
  Tuttle Creek, Kansas, picture K 178
  water supply W 66, 67
Residence, legal E 113
Resident doctors, in hospitals H 250
Residential property R 113
Residual (re-SID-ual) **powers,** in government U 139
Resins R 184–85
  flux in soldering and brazing S 250
  paints and pigments P 32
  plastics P 325, 327
  synthetic adhesives G 243

turpentine **T** 330
   varnishes made from **V** 279
Resistance, in electricity *see* Electric resistance
Resistance arms, of levers **W** 248
Resistance welding **W** 119
Resistance wire, in electric appliances **E** 117
Resist method, of printing textiles **D** 372
Resnais (ren-AY), **Alain,** French director **M** 488a
Resonance (RES-on-ance), in physics
   sound **S** 262
   tides **T** 184
Resource geography **G** 108
Resources, natural *see* Natural resources

Respighi (ray-SPI-ghi), **Ottorino** (1879–1936), Italian
composer, pianist, and conductor, b. Bologna. He studied
with Rimsky-Korsakov and Max Bruch. He is best known
for his symphonic poems, which combined lyric melody
with rich harmony. Among his other works are 10 operas,
including *Re Enzo* and *Semirama.*
   Italian music **I** 486

Respiration, act of breathing **B** 278; **M** 208e
   artificial respiration **F** 159–61
   oxygen and oxidation **O** 269
   plants **P** 294
   vocal organs **V** 375–76
   See also Breathing
Respiratory (RES-pir-a-tory) **system,** of the body,
   diagram **D** 203
   air pollution **A** 111
   breathing system of fishes **F** 186–87
   breath of life **B** 277–78
   of insects **I** 271–72
Responses, in psychology
   characteristic of living things **K** 255–56
   reactions to stimuli **L** 98
Responsible government, retains the vote of confidence
   of the legislative body **P** 82
   Canadian system **C** 77
   concentration of responsibility (British system) **G** 277
   prime minister responsible to parliament **P** 456
Restaurants **R** 186–87
   sanitation **S** 33
   See also Hotels; Motels; Ocean liners
Reston, Virginia, picture **U** 234
Restoration period, in English history **E** 223–24
   drama **E** 256–57
   upsurge in dramatic entertainment **D** 297
Restraining Act, 1775 **R** 197
Rests, in music **M** 530
Resumption Act, 1875 **H** 81
Resurrection, of Jesus Christ **J** 84
Resurrection, The, fresco by Piero della Francesca **E** 41
Resurrection City *see* Poor People's March
Resuscitation *see* Artificial respiration
Retables (RE-tables), altar screens **L** 63
   decorative arts **D** 77
   Spanish art **S** 363
Retailing, selling goods to a consumer **R** 188–89
   consumer education and reliable dealers **C** 494
Retail stores **R** 188–89
   advertising **A** 29
   co-operatives **C** 499–500
   installment buying **I** 288–89
   marketing for the home **M** 100–03
   outlet for industrial products **I** 248
   selling **S** 116–17
   See also Department stores; Mail order; Supermarkets
Retail trade **T** 243

Retainer, act of a client employing a lawyer to ensure

his services and to prevent his working for opposite side.
The term also refers to the fee paid to the attorney.

Retaliation, law of **L** 88
Retardation, mental **R** 189–91
   development of the intelligence test **T** 117
   See also Mental illness
Reticulum, second section of the stomach of a ruminant
   H 208
Retina (RET-in-a), of the eye **B** 284
   eye as an optical instrument **L** 265
   lenses of the eye and vision **L** 149–50
   seen with an opthalmoscope, picture **M** 208g
   sensory system within the brain **B** 365
Retirement **O** 97–101
   social security **S** 221–22
Retirement villages **O** 99–100
Retorts, special containers used in chemistry
   pressure cookers **F** 346
Retrievers, dog breed **D** 259; pictures **D** 253
Retrograde (RET-ro-grade) **motion,** of planets **A** 472
Retrorockets, to reduce speed of satellites **S** 41
   deceleration of spacecraft **S** 340h; picture **S** 340b
Retting, of fibers **F** 106

Reuben (RU-ben), in Old Testament (Genesis), eldest son
of Jacob and Leah. He intervened in the plotted murder of
Joseph by his brothers. He was also the ancestral
patriarch of one of the 12 tribes of Israel that possessed
the land of Trans-Jordan (now Jordan).

Réunion (rai-u-ni-ON) (pop. 430,000), French overseas
department (970 sq. mi.) of volcanic origin, part of
Mascarene Islands group in Indian Ocean. Its capital is
Saint-Denis. Chief export is sugar, trade being mainly
with France. Its status changed from that of a colony to
that of an overseas department in 1946. It is governed
by a French-appointed prefect and an elected council.

Reuters (ROI-ters) **Limited,** common name for Reuter
Agency, an agency that gathers and transmits news. It
was founded by Paul Julius von Reuter as a simple telegraph line between Aachen, Germany, and Verviers,
Belgium (1849). Headquarters were moved to London in
1851, and coverage has become practically worldwide.
   news services **N** 201

Reuther (REU-ther), **Walter P.,** American labor leader
   L 6; **W** 139; picture **L** 7
   labor conference, picture **L** 13
Reveille (REV-ell-e), military bugle call **B** 429
Revelation, book of Bible, New Testament **B** 162

Revels, Hiram Rhoades (1822–1901), American senator
and clergyman, b. Fayetteville, N.C. The first Negro
Congressman, he was chosen to succeed Jefferson Davis
as United States senator from Mississippi (1870). He had
been ordained as African Methodist minister (1845). He
established a school for freedmen in St. Louis (1863).

Reventazón (ray-ven-ta-SONE) **River,** Costa Rica **C** 517
Revenue (REV-en-ue), income from taxation **T** 26–27
Revenue Act, 1862 **I** 110
Revenue Act, 1964 **I** 111
Revenue Cutter Service, and **Revenue Marine,** early
   names of U.S. Coast Guard **U** 175
Reverberation (re-ver-ber-A-tion), of sound **S** 260
Reverberatory (re-VER-ber-a-tory) **furnaces** **M** 228
Revere, Paul, American patriot **R** 192–93
   antique silver, picture **A** 321
   buried in Boston, Mass. **B** 339
   Johnny Tremain accompanies Mr. Revere on the

Revere, Paul (continued)
    Boston Tea Party **R** 209–10
    Patriot's Day (April 19) in Massachusetts honors his
      ride **M** 146
    portrait by Copley **U** 118
    Revolutionary War begins **R** 198
Reverse, now hearts, card game **C** 112
Reversing Falls, New Brunswick, Canada **C** 52; **N** 138d
Revisionists, or Social Democrats **S** 220
Revivalist, art movement **E** 241
Revival of learning see Renaissance
Revivals, in religions feeling **H** 313
Revolutionary Tribunal, in French Revolution **F** 467
Revolutionary War, 1775–81 **R** 194–209
    Adams', Samuel, role in organizing **A** 16–17
    Allen, Ethan, and Green Mountain boys **A** 166–67
    Arnold, Benedict **A** 436
    Attucks, Crispus, first American to die **N** 91; **R** 196
    Burke's speech on conciliation **E** 259
    Canada's role in **C** 71, 79
    "Concord Hymn, The," poem by Emerson **E** 190
    Continental Marines **U** 177
    Declaration of Independence **D** 59–65
    famous spies **S** 388
    first American historical society, outgrowth of **H** 136
    flags carried **F** 244; pictures **F** 229
    Franklin's activities **F** 455
    French aid **F** 416
    Hale, Nathan **H** 12
    Henry, Patrick **H** 113–14
    Independence Hall, a shrine of **I** 113
    Indian allies of the British **I** 212
    Jones, John Paul, naval hero **J** 134–35
    Lafayette, Marquis de **L** 22–23
    Liberty Bell symbol of **L** 169
    Marion, Francis **M** 99
    Negroes who fought in it **N** 91–92
    Paine, Thomas **P** 13
    Pennsylvania **P** 145
    Purple Heart medal established **M** 198
    Revere, Paul **R** 192–93
    Salomon, Haym, helped finance the army **S** 19
    seizure of weapons in New Hampshire, one of first
      events **N** 163
    songs of **N** 23
    underground movements **U** 10
    Washington, George, commander in chief **W** 39–40
    Who was Molly Pitcher? **R** 205
    See also French and Indian War
Revolution of 1910, Mexico **M** 250
    aid to farmers in Mexico **M** 244
Revolutions
    Communism **C** 442–45
    in Latin America **L** 52, 55
    underground movements **U** 10
Revolvers, guns **G** 421–22
Revue, form of musical comedy **M** 542
Rewrite men, on newspapers **N** 202

Rey (RAY), **Hans Augusto** (1898–   ), American author
and illustrator of children's books, b. Hamburg, Germany. After working 12 years for an import firm in
Brazil, he returned to Europe (1936) and began his
writing career. He fled Paris (1940) shortly before the
Nazi invasion and went to the United States. His "Curious George" stories are especially popular.
    picture books for children **C** 243

Reyes, Neftali see Neruda, Pablo
Reykjavik (RAIK-ya-veek), capital of Iceland **I** 43
Reynard (RAY-nard) **the Fox stories,** influence on fable
    writers **F** 4

Reynaud, Paul, French premier **W** 289

Reynolds (REN-olds), **Quentin James** (1902–1965), American journalist and author, b. New York, N.Y. He began as
a sports writer for the New York *Evening World* and
World Telegram and joined (1932) the International News
Service. He was an associate editor for *Collier's*
(1933–45) and a war correspondent during World War II.
His books for children include *The F.B.I. Story* and
Winston Churchill. In a famous law suit he successfully
charged Westbrook Pegler with libel and in 1954 received
the largest amount ($175,001) ever awarded until that
time for damages.

Reynolds, Sir Joshua, English portrait painter **R** 210
    English art **E** 238; **P** 24
    Georgiana Seymour, painting **E** 239
    views on color **D** 143
RFD see Rural Free Delivery

Rhadamanthus (rhad-a-MAN-thus), in Greek mythology,
brother of King Minos of Crete and son of Zeus and
Europa. He was chosen for his integrity and justice to be
judge of the dead in the underworld, along with Aeacus
and Minos.

Rhaetian Alps, Switzerland, picture **S** 495
Rhapsody, a musical form **M** 535, 537
Rhapsody in Blue, by George Gershwin **G** 190
Rhazes, Arab physician
    medical encyclopedias by Arab scientists **S** 64
Rhea (RHE-a), Greek goddess **G** 356

Rhea, large, flightless bird found only in South America.
Brownish with white underparts, the rhea is about 5 ft.
high, with a long neck and long legs. It lives in open
country and travels in small flocks.
    giant birds of the dry tropics **B** 226; **G** 204

Rhea, satellite of Saturn **P** 276

Rhee, Syngman (1875–1965), Korean statesman, b.
Whanghai province. A supporter of Korean independ-
ence, he was head of provisional government at
Shanghai (1919–41). During World War II he served as
head of Korean Commission in Washington, returning to
Korea after fall of Japan (1945) and becoming chairman
of National Assembly (1948). He was president of
Republic of Korea (South Korea) from 1948 to 1960.
    Korea, history of **K** 302

Rheims (RHEEMS) **Cathedral,** France, picture **G** 264
    Gothic architecture, window tracery of **G** 268–69
    statues, pictures **G** 270
Rheims-Douai (RHEEMS-doo-AI) **Version,** of the Bible
    B 153
Rheinfall (RHINE-foll), Switzerland **W** 56b
Rheingold (RHINE-golt), **Das,** opera by Wagner **O** 151–52
Rhenium (RHE-nium), element **E** 155, 164
Rhesus (RHE-sus) **monkeys** **M** 420
    Rh factor in blood named for **B** 258
Rhetoric (RHET-or-ic), study of speaking and writing
    O 180
    schools in ancient Athens **E** 64
Rhetors, early Greek teachers of oratory **O** 180
Rheumatic (rheu-MAT-ic) **fever** **D** 204–05
    heart damaged by **H** 86b–86c
Rheumatoid arthritis (RHEU-ma-toid ar-THRY-tis), type
    of arthritis **D** 193
Rh factor, blood group **B** 258
    possible cause of mental retardation **R** 190
    transfusion, blood **T** 251

Rice (continued)

    seeds, pictures **G** 238

    Southeast Asia's main crop **S** 332, 333

    terraced fields in the Philippines, picture **P** 187

    transplanting, picture **I** 129

    Vietnam, main crop and food **V** 334, 334a

    wedding customs, use in **W** 100–01

    wild rice, or Indian rice **M** 329; **R** 232

    world distribution **W** 264

Rice, Elmer, American playwright **A** 216

Rice, Grantland (1880–1954), American sports journalist, b. Murfreesboro, Tenn. In 1930 he originated a syndicated daily column, "The Sportlight." He did the narration for many of the motion pictures produced by Grantland Rice Sportlight Incorporated. In 1943 he won an Academy Award for a one-reel movie.

Rice University, Houston, Texas **T** 131; **U** 219

Richard I ("the Lion-Hearted"), king of England **F** 443

    Cyprus taken during crusades **C** 558

    led Third Crusade **C** 540

Richard II (1367–1400), king of England (1377–99), b. Bordeaux, France. He succeeded his grandfather Edward II as king in 1377, but until 1389 the government was controlled mainly by his uncle the Duke of Lancaster (John of Gaunt). Lancaster's son, Henry of Bolingbroke, became Richard's rival and was banished by Richard, who took over his Lancastrian estates (1389–99). Richard was finally defeated and captured by Henry of Bolingbroke (later King Henry IV), deposed by Parliament, and probably murdered in prison.

Richard III ("the Crouchback") (1452–1485), king of England (1483–85), b. Fotheringhay. He was made duke of Gloucester (1461) and became protector of Edward V at death of brother Edward IV (1483). The murder of Edward V and his brother Richard, Duke of York, followed Richard's usurpation of throne (1483). He quelled revolt under Duke of Buckingham (1483). Increased opposition to his rule resulted in his death at the hands of Henry Tudor, Earl of Richmond, who succeeded to the throne.

    England, history of **E** 220

Richard II, play by Shakespeare **S** 136

Richard III, play by Shakespeare **S** 136

Richard Roe see John Doe and Richard Roe

Richards, Laura Elizabeth (1850–1943), American author, b. Boston, Mass. Daughter of Samuel Gridley Howe and Julia Ward Howe, she is best-known for her books for children, which include *Captain January, Tirra Lirra,* and the "Hildegarde" books. She also wrote an autobiography, *Stepping Westward,* and biographies of Abigail Adams, Joan of Arc, Samuel Gridley Howe, and (with her sister Maud Howe Elliott) Julia Ward Howe, the last of which received the Pulitzer prize for biography (1917).

    "Eletelephony," nonsense verse **N** 274

Richards Deep, trench in Pacific Ocean **M** 499

Richardson, Henry Hobson, American architect **U** 124

Richardson, Samuel, English novelist **E** 260

    emotionalism of his novels **N** 346

Richard the Lion-Hearted see Richard I

Richelieu (RISH-el-lu), **Cardinal,** French statesman **R** 233

    builder of the Bourbon monarchy in France **F** 415

    Palais-Richelieu now the Palais-Royal in Paris **P** 74

Richmond, capital of Virginia **V** 357; picture **V** 356

    Civil War **C** 323, 326

    Confederate capital **C** 321

Richmond, New York City **N** 229

Richter (RICK-ter), **Conrad Michael** (1890–1968), American author, b. Pine Grove, Pa. His novels are noted for portrayal of American frontier life. His works include *The Sea of Grass,* a trilogy comprised of *The Trees, The Fields,* and *The Town,* which was awarded the Pulitzer prize for fiction (1951), and *The Waters of Kronos,* which received the National Book award (1961).

Richter (RICK-tair), **Svyatoslav Teofilovitch** (1915–), Soviet pianist, b. Zhitomir, Ukraine. He is famous for his vast repertoire, skillfully and imaginatively interpreted. He studied at Moscow Conservatory (1937–47) and introduced the 6th, 7th, and 9th piano sonatas by Prokofiev, with whom he was closely associated. He toured Europe and the United States (1960–61, 1965) and was awarded Stalin prizes.

Rickenbacker (RICK-en-back-er), **Eddie** (Edward Vernon Rickenbacker) (1890–1973), American aviator and airline executive, b. Columbus, Ohio. He won the Medal of Honor as commander of the 94th Aero Pursuit Squadron in World War I and was special representative for the secretary of war during World War II. As an airline executive he became (1938) president, general manager, and director of Eastern Air Lines, Inc. He wrote *Fighting the Flying Circus* and *Seven Came Through.*

    United States Air Force, history of **U** 159

Rickets, a deforming disease that attacks children. It is caused by lack of vitamin D and sunlight. This lack affects proper hardening of the bones and results in deformity. A similar disease in adults is called osteomalacia. The origin of the word "rickets" is unknown, but it may derive from Anglo-Saxon word *wrick,* "to twist."

    nutritional diseases **D** 216

    vitamin D **V** 371

Rickettsias (rick-ETT-si-as), micro-organisms **M** 281–82

Rickover, Hyman G. (1900–), American naval officer, b. Makow, Poland. A graduate of the U.S. Naval Academy at Annapolis (1922), he directed the U.S. Navy project that developed the first atomic-powered submarine, S.S.N. *Nautilus* (1953). He then took charge of the nuclear-propulsion division of the Bureau of Ships and was made chief of the naval-reactors branch of the Atomic Energy Commission. He is author of several books, including *American Education: A National Failure.* In 1965 he won the Enrico Fermi Award for his contribution to atomic science.

Ricotta, Italian cheese **D** 13

Riddles **J** 132–33

    folklore, a section of **F** 304

    word games **W** 236–37

Ride up high, O uncle, tag game **G** 17

Ridge, Major (1771?–1839), American Indian, b. probably Hiwassee County, Tenn. As Cherokee Indian leader with rank of major, he supported Americans in Creek War (1814). Without tribal authority he ceded Cherokee lands east of Mississippi to United States, thus forcing the tribe to move westward. He was killed in revenge for causing westward migration. His son, **John Ridge** (1803–39), was also a tribal leader.

Ridges, oceanic **G** 119–20; **O** 29–30; diagram **G** 121

Ridgway, Matthew Bunker (1895–), American army officer, b. Fort Monroe, Va. Noted for commanding the

82nd Airborne Division, which participated in large-scale operations in Italy, Sicily, and Normandy during World War II, Ridgway was U.S. Army representative to the United Nations Military Staff Committee (1946–48). He succeeded Douglas MacArthur (1951) as supreme commander of Allied forces in Pacific, and he was supreme commander of NATO forces in Europe (1952–53) and army chief of staff (1953–55). He retired in 1955.

Riding see Horseback riding
Riding Mountain National Park, Manitoba **M** 79
   sports and recreation in Canada **C** 67
Riebeeck (RE-bake), **Jan van,** South African statesman **S** 271
   Cape Town, founder of **C** 103

Riel (ri-EL), **Louis** (1844–1885), Canadian rebel leader, b. St. Boniface, Manitoba. He led the métis in resisting (1870, 1885) incorporation of Northwest Territory into Dominion of Canada. Riel established provincial government (1869, 1885) but was captured (1885), tried, and executed for treason.
   Canada, history of **C** 73, 74; **M** 4; **S** 38h

Riffle shuffle, for playing cards **C** 107
Rifle marksmanship R 233–35
   Oakley, Annie **O** 2
Rifles, guns **G** 415, 422, 423; pictures **G** 416, 418, 422, 423
   hunting **H** 291
   rifle marksmanship **R** 233–35
Rifling, of guns **G** 415, 420
Rif Mountains, Morocco **M** 460
Rift Valley, Africa see Great Rift Valley
Riga, capital of Latvia (Latvian Soviet Socialist Republic) **U** 44
Riga, Gulf of, an arm of the Baltic Sea **O** 45
Rigel (RY-ghel), star **C** 491
   brightest stars **S** 407
Riggin, Aileen, American swimmer **O** 110
Rigging, lines and ropes used to work sails
   full-rigged ship, picture-diagram **S** 159
   sailboats **S** 10
Right, political term, origin of **P** 379
Right angles, in geometry **G** 124; diagram **G** 125
Right Bank, of the Seine, Paris **P** 73–74
Right of deposit, in Spanish territories **T** 108
Right of way
   boats **B** 262
Rights, civil see Civil liberties and civil rights
Right to vote see Suffrage
Right to work see Open and closed shop
Right triangle, diagram **G** 125
Right whales W 149; picture **W** 148

Right wing, persons and groups who hold to conservative political doctrine, often advocating compliance with strong governmental authority. The term is derived from certain European legislatures, where conservatives sat to the right, the moderates in the center, and radicals to the left of the presiding officer. It is often applied inaccurately to both moderate conservatives, who resist certain political or economic changes, and to extreme rightists, who would forcibly establish conservative government.

Rigoletto (rig-o-LETT-o), opera by Giuseppe Verdi **O** 151

Riis (REES), **Jacob August** (1849–1914), Danish-American journalist and author, b. Ribe, Denmark. He went to United States in 1870 and became a police reporter for the New York *Tribune* (1877–88) and the New York *Evening Sun* (1888–99). A well-known reformist lecturer and writer, he was author of *How the Other Half Lives,* and *The Children of the Poor.*

Riiser-Larsen (RE-ser-LAR-sen), **Hjalmar** (1890–1965), Norwegian naval officer and polar explorer, b. Oslo. He accompanied the Amundsen-Ellsworth North Pole expedition (1925) and Amundsen-Ellsworth-Nobile transpolar flight (1926). He commanded a Norwegian relief party in search of Nobile's expedition (1928) and two Norwegian expeditions to Antarctica (1929–30, 1930–31). During World War II he was appointed commander in chief of the joint Norwegian Air Forces (1944–46).

Rijksmuseum (RAKES-muse-e-um), Amsterdam, picture **M** 515
Rila Monastery, Bulgaria, picture **B** 441
Riley, James Whitcomb, American poet **I** 149
   children's poetry **C** 241
Rilke, Rainer Maria, Austrian poet **G** 181
Rilles, twisting, valleylike clefts
   Mars **M** 109; **O** 15; **P** 273
   moon **M** 451, 453; picture **M** 452

Rillieux, Norbert (1806–1894), American engineer, b. New Orleans, La. Born a slave, he was educated in France. After returning to Louisiana, he developed a process that cut the production cost and raised the quality of sugar. Although one of the most prominent men in the state, he left Louisiana when, as a Negro, he was required to carry a pass. In Europe he continued to make inventive contributions to the sugar industry and also worked at deciphering hieroglyphics.

Rimbaud (ran-BO), **Arthur,** French poet **F** 440
Rimsky-Korsakov (RIM-ski-KOR-sa-kof), **Nikolay,** Russian composer **U** 63
   influence on Stravinsky **S** 437
   opera **O** 136
   teacher of Prokofiev **P** 477

Rinehart, Mary Roberts (1876–1958), American novelist and mystery story writer, b. Pittsburgh, Pa. Her works include *The Circular Staircase, The Man in Lower Ten,* and numerous stories about Tish.
   mystery and suspense stories **M** 554

Ring des Nibelungen (NI-be-lung-en), **Der,** music dramas by Richard Wagner **O** 151
Ringed seals, animals **W** 8
Ringer, game of marbles **M** 95

Ringling Brothers, seven brothers, five of whom formed Ringling Brothers Classic and Comic Concert Company. They organized a circus (1884) that by 1900 was one of the major ones in the United States. They then enlarged by absorbing Forepaugh-Sells (1906) and Barnum and Bailey (1907) circuses.

Ring-necked pheasant
   South Dakota, state bird of **S** 313
Ring-necked snake, picture **S** 205
Ring of Fire, or Circle of Fire, volcanoes along the Pacific Ocean **M** 499
Ring of the Fisherman, famous religious ring **J** 99
Ring of the Nibelung, in Norse mythology **N** 281
Ringroads, or beltways, around cities
   Baltimore and Washington, D.C. **M** 121
   Boston **M** 141
Rings, jewelry **J** 98, 99
Rings, use in gymnastics, pictures **G** 430
Rings of Saturn P 276–77

Ringtails, animals related to raccoons **R** 26–27
Ringtaw, English game of marbles **M** 95
Ringworm, skin infection **D** 205
Rio de Janeiro (RI-o day jan-AIR-o), Brazil **R** 236–37
  pictures **B** 379, **C** 308a, **L** 47, **R** 236
  central east section of Brazil **B** 378
Rio de la Plata, South America see Plata, Rio de la
Rio Grande (GRAND), river between United States and
  Mexico **R** 247; picture **R** 240
  called Rio Bravo in Mexico **M** 243
  rises in Colorado **C** 403
  Texas **T** 124
Río Muni, province of Equatorial Guinea **E** 273–74;
  S 357
Rio Piedras (pi-A-dras), Puerto Rico, pictures
  P 519, 521

Riparian (ri-PARE-ian) **rights** (from Latin *ripa,* meaning
"bank"), rights of people who own land on the banks of
rivers and streams concerning their use of the water and
ownership of the soil beneath the stream.

Ripley, Elizabeth Blake (1906–), American author and
illustrator of children's books, b. New Haven, Conn. She
has written a number of biographies of artists, including
Leonardo da Vinci, Michelangelo, Rembrandt, and Picasso. She has done the artwork for *Riddle Me This, This
Little Boy Went to Kindergarten,* and other books.

Ripley, Robert Le Roy (1893–1949), American cartoonist
and author, b. Santa Rosa, Calif. His "Believe It or Not"
cartoon series ran in newspapers all over the world and
was also published in book form. Ripley appeared on
radio and TV and in motion pictures in shows based
on his collection of incredible events.

Riposte, counterattack in fencing **F** 85
Ripsaws, tools **T** 212
Ripton, Vermont
  memorial to Robert Frost **F** 480
Rip Van Winkle, story by Washington Irving **S** 166; ex-
  cerpt **I** 411–12
Risen Christ, The, sculpture by Jacob Epstein **E** 242
Risorgimento (ri-sor-gi-MENT-o), Italian literary movement
  I 479

Ritchie, Roland Almon (1910–), Canadian judge, b.
Halifax, Nova Scotia. A member of the bar since 1934, he
was appointed to the Supreme Court in 1959. He is a
member of the board of governors of the University of
Kings College.

Rite of Spring, The, ballet, by Igor Stravinsky **M** 400
Rites and ceremonies
  American Indian dances, pictures **I** 161
  ancient Greek drama **D** 294
  ceremonials of Judaism **J** 116–20
  funeral customs **F** 492–95
  knights and knighthood **K** 272–77
  marriage rites **W** 101–03
  Muslim law **I** 415–16
  sacramentals of the Roman Catholic Church **R** 301
  tea ceremony of Japan **J** 37
  See also Religious holidays; religions by name;
    people section of country articles
Ritscher, Alfred, German explorer **P** 368
Rittenhouse, William, American clergyman, built first paper mill in America **C** 432; **P** 56
Ritter, Johann Wilhelm, German scientist **P** 236

Ritter, Joseph Elmer, Cardinal (1892–1967), American
Roman Catholic clergyman, b. New Albany, Ind. He was
made a cardinal (1961) after serving as bishop (1934–44)
and archbishop (1944–46) of Indianapolis and archbishop of St. Louis, Mo. (1946–67).

Ritter, Karl (1779–1859), German geographer, b. Quedlin-
burg. A founder of modern scientific geography, he
explained how geography effects history and studied
human ecology.
  modern geography, beginnings of **G** 98

Rivals, play by Richard Brinsley Sheridan
  scene with Mrs. Malaprop, picture **E** 257
Rivas (RI-vos), **Duke of,** Spanish writer **S** 369
Rivera (ri-BAY-ra), **Diego,** Mexican painter **L** 67
  Flower Festival, Feast of Santa Anita **L** 65
Rivera, José Adalberto, president of El Salvador **E** 184

Rivera y Orbaneja (ri-BAY-ra e or-ba-NAY-ha), **Miguel
Primo de** (Marqués de Estella) (1870–1930), Spanish
general and dictator, b. Cádiz. During Spanish-American
War he served in Cuba and the Philippines (1898), and
he later served in Morocco (1909–13). In 1923 he seized
power as dictator of Spain. He relinquished some of the
power to the king in 1925 but was forced to retire in
1930.

River blindness, or onchocerciasis, disease **B** 252
River of No Return, nickname for Salmon River, Idaho
  I 54
Rivers **R** 237–49
  Amazon River **A** 178–79
  Atlantic Ocean drainage area **A** 478
  Canada's drainage basins **C** 51
  channels deepened to control floods **F** 256
  conservation and pollution problems **C** 483
  dams **D** 16–21
  erosion caused by **E** 282, 283
  Ganges River, India **G** 25
  harbors and ports **H** 35–37
  how lake basins are formed **L** 25
  Mississippi **M** 364–65
  Missouri River **M** 383
  Nile River **N** 260–61
  systems in Africa **A** 49–50
  systems in Asia **A** 448
  systems in Europe **E** 309
  systems of North America **N** 288
  systems of South America **S** 277–78
  tidal bores **T** 185
  waterfalls **W** 56b
  waterpower **W** 60–63
  See also land section of country, province, and state
    articles; names of rivers
Riverside Church, New York City
  largest carillon in world **B** 137
Riverside Geyser (GUYS-er), Yellowstone Park, Wyoming,
  picture **G** 193
Riverview Gardens, Missouri
  elementary school, picture **S** 56
Rivets, fasteners **N** 3
Riviera (riv-i-AER-a), Mediterranean coastal region of Italy
  and France
  Monaco **M** 406
  Nice, France, picture **F** 404
Riyadh (ri-YODH), capital of Saudi Arabia **S** 48
Rizal, José, Philippine national hero **P** 189
Riza Shah Pahlavi see Pahlavi, Riza Khan, Shah of Iran
R.N. see Registered nurses
RNA (ribonucleic acid) **G** 84; diagrams **B** 292; **G** 85
  cell nucleus **C** 161
  chemical makeup of viruses **V** 363
  function in body chemistry **B** 291, 296

Roaches, insects **H** 262
Roadbeds, under tracks of railroads **R** 78
Road camps, places of short-term imprisonment **P** 468
Road Not Taken, The, poem by Robert Frost **F** 480
Roadrunners or chaparral birds
   New Mexico, state bird of **N** 180
Roads and highways **R** 250–53
   Alaska Highway **A** 138, 143; **C** 61
   automobile design affected by **A** 545
   Brazil, picture **B** 377
   bridges **B** 395–401
   buses and bus travel **B** 465–66
   construction, picture **E** 389
   driver education **D** 318–21
   early travel and trade **T** 258–59
   expressway in Chicago, picture **U** 111
   Going-to-the-Sun Road, in Glacier National Park
     M 436
   interchange in Sweden, picture **E** 328
   Khyber Pass, Asia, picture **A** 467
   log roads in Siberia, picture **S** 173
   longest overwater highway, Lake Pontchartrain,
     Louisiana **L** 33
   Los Angeles freeways, picture **L** 345
   maps, use of symbols **M** 88, 90; picture **M** 91
   national parkways **N** 55
   overland trails **O** 251–67
   paints for highways **P** 34
   Pan American Highway **P** 50
   Pennsylvania Turnpike, picture **P** 136
   plank roads in Louisiana **L** 357
   road-building equipment **B** 448
   road signs, picture **D** 320
   Roman see Roman roads
   stabilization by salt **S** 21
   traffic control **T** 247–48
   Trans-Canada Highway **C** 61
   trucks and trucking **T** 295–97
   tunnels **T** 314
   U.S. interstate commerce **I** 331
   See also transportation section of country, province,
    and state articles
Roaring 20's, or the Jazz Age, United States **C** 496
Roark, Helen Wills see Wills, Helen
Roanoke (RO-an-oke), Virginia **V** 357
Roanoke Island, North Carolina **N** 306
   American colonial settlement **A** 181
Roaring 20's
   Coolidge's administration **C** 496–97
Roasting, of ores **M** 228
Robbia (ROBE-ya), **Luca della,** Florentine sculptor
   S 99–100
   Italian art **I** 468
   Madonna and Angels, sculpture **S** 98
   Madonna and Child, picture **I** 465
   medallions on Brunelleschi's colonnade for Foundling
    Hospital **R** 163; picture **R** 165
   See also Della Robbia family
Robbins, Jerome, American choreographer **B** 28; **M** 543

Robert I (Robert Bruce) (1274–1329), king of Scotland
(1306–29), b. probably Turnberry. He was crowned king
of Scotland (1306) but was defeated by the English army
at Methven (1306) and forced to hide on an island off
the Irish coast. It was there that he is supposed to have
been inspired to return to Scotland (1307) by a spider's
persistence in spinning a web. He eventually defeated
the English, and gained Scotland's independence (1328).
   Scotland, history of **S** 88

Robert, Nicholas Louis, French paper manufacturer **P** 57
Robert, Shaaban, Tanzanian poet **A** 76b

Roberto, Holden Alvaro (Joseph Robert Haldane Gilmore)
(1927–   ), Angolan nationalist leader, b. San Salvador.
He organized the Union of the Peoples of Angola (UPA)
(1954), which has supported northern Angola guerrilla
revolts against Portuguese rule (since 1961). He became
president of the National Liberation Front of Angola
(FNLA) in 1962 and premier of the Revolutionary
Government of Angola in Exile (GRAE) (since 1962),
which has gained recognition from African states,
including the Congo, where it has headquarters.

Roberts, Elizabeth Madox (1886–1941), American novelist
and poet, b. Perrysville, Ky. She began her career as a
poet, winning several prizes, and then published her first
novel, *The Time of Man.* She wrote of the mountain folk
and "poor whites" of Kentucky. Other novels are *My
Heart and My Flesh* and *The Great Meadow.*
   "Firefly," poem and its interpretation **P** 351–52

Roberts, Joseph Jenkins (1809–1876), Liberian statesman, b. Petersburg, Va. He went to Liberia in 1829 and
later became an assistant to the American colonial
governor, Thomas Buchanan. He was the first Negro
governor of Liberia (1842–47) and its first president
when it became a republic (1847). He served as president
of Liberia (1847–55, 1871–76) and as the first president
of the College of Liberia (now called University of
Liberia) (1856–76).
   Liberia, history of **L** 167

Roberts, Kenneth, American novelist **A** 213
Robertson, Alice Mary, American educator and social
   worker **O** 93

Robertson, James (1742–1814), American pioneer, b.
Brunswick County, Va. He led a group of settlers to the
site of present-day Nashville, where he served as
presiding officer of the court, negotiated treaties with
the Indians, and was a trustee of Davidson Academy
(later the University of Nashville) and a delegate to the
North Carolina assembly (1785, 1787) and the Tennessee
senate (1798). In his last years he was Indian agent to
the Chickasaw.

Robert's Rules of Order, for parliamentary procedure
   P 79
Robert the Bruce see Robert I

Roberval (ro-bair-VOL), **Jean François de la Rocque,
Sieur de** (1500?–1560?), French colonizer, b. Carcassonne. He was appointed by King Francis I viceroy and
lieutenant general of New France and leader of first
French colonizing expedition (1541). He reached Newfoundland in 1542 and led an unsuccessful expedition in
search of fabled Saguenay wealth. He returned with
survivors to France in 1543.
   Cartier, Jacques and Roberval **C** 124

Robeson, Paul (1898–   ), American concert baritone
and actor, Negro, b. Princeton, N.J. He won acclaim for
English and American performances in Eugene O'Neill's
Emperor Jones and Shakespeare's *Othello.* He has made
numerous concert tours through United States, Europe,
and Soviet Union (since 1925). His film appearances
include roles in *Showboat, Emperor Jones,* and *Jericho.*
His deep concern over U.S. racial prejudice against
Negroes has led him to uphold Communism. He is
author of the autobiographical *Here I Stand.*
   Negro Renaissance **N** 98, 107

Robespierre (robes-pi-AIR), **Maximilien,** French revolutionary leader **F** 466, 467, 468

Robidou (ro-bi-DO), **Antoine** (1794–1860), American trader and trapper, b. St. Louis, Mo. He was one of the first traders to reach (1822) Taos, N. Mex., and he founded (1832) a major fur-trading post, Fort Uinta (also called Fort Robidou), in northeastern Utah. His brother **Joseph Robidou** (1783–1868) eastablished (1826) a trading post on the site of present-day St. Joseph, Mo. Three other brothers also became well-known as traders and trappers on the Western frontier.

Robin Goodfellow, character in English folklore **M** 309
Robin Hood, legendary English hero and outlaw **R** 253
   duels in literature **D** 341
   king of the May **M** 182
   legends, types of **L** 129
Robins, birds **B** 219, 223; picture **B** 240
   Connecticut, state bird of **C** 466
   feeding signals **A** 276, picture **A** 277
   Michigan, state bird of **M** 259
   tracks, picture **A** 272
   Wisconsin, state bird of **W** 193

Robinson, Bill ("Bojangles") (1878–1949), American tap dancer, Negro, b. Richmond, Va. He danced in nightclubs and in musical comedies (1906–30) and motion pictures, such as *Rebecca of Sunnybrook Farm* and *Little Colonel* with Shirley Temple. He invented many steps, including his widely imitated stair tap—dancing up a flight of stairs. Picture **M** 475.
   Negro Renaissance **N** 98

Robinson, Charles A. (1900–), American author and educator, b. Princeton, N.J. Formerly Professor of Classics at Brown University, he took part in the excavation of ancient Greek cities and was a member of the Commission for Excavation of the Athenian Agora. Among his books for young people are *The First Book of Ancient Bible Lands*, *The First Book of Ancient Egypt*, *The First Book of Ancient Rome*.

Robinson, Edward G., American actor **M** 475
Robinson, Edwin Arlington, American poet **A** 209
   "Dark Hills, The," poem **P** 355
Robinson, Jack Roosevelt ("Jackie"), American baseball player **R** 254
   a player's life in baseball **B** 78
   years of change for the Negro **N** 102

Robinson, James H. (1907–), American religious leader, Negro, b. Knoxville, Tenn. He founded Operation Cross-roads Africa (1957), a private summer work program that starts schools, community centers, clinics, and libraries in Africa. A graduate of the Union Theological Seminary in New York City, he established the Church of the Master in Harlem. He is the author of *Road Without Turning* (1950).

Robinson, John (1576?–1625), English minister, b. Lincolnshire. As pastor of the Separatist Church in Leiden, the Netherlands, he encouraged his followers to migrate to America and helped organize the expedition that, after sailing to England (1620), went to America in the *Mayflower*. Robinson intended to follow the expedition but died in Leiden.

Robinson, Joseph Taylor, American statesman **A** 431
Robinson, Sugar Ray, American boxing champion **B** 353
Robinson Crusoe, by Defoe **E** 259–60
   fiction, development of **F** 111
   novel in down-to-earth style **N** 346
   setting, an island off Chile **C** 251
Robinson Crusoe Islands *see* Juan Fernández Islands

Robles, Marco Aurelio, president of Panama **P** 46

Robot (RO-bot) (from Czech, meaning "work" or "compulsory service"), an automatic machine that can carry out tasks generally performed by human beings. It differs from other machines in its ability to direct own actions. The term was introduced by Czech writer Karel Capek in play *R.U.R.*, depicting a factory with robot workers who ultimately rise up against human masters. Types of robots range from simple thermostat to automatic airplane pilot and digital computers.

Rob Roy (from Gaelic for "Red Robert," derived from his hair color) (Robert MacGregor or Campbell) (1671–1734), Scottish outlaw, b. Buchanan parish. He led the MacGregor clan (after 1693), which was denounced for activities against British Government. Convicted of embezzlement, he became a Highland outlaw, gaining a reputation as one who viciously opposed the wealthy but generously gave to the poor. He was sentenced to exile on Barbados but was pardoned (1727). His life is recounted in Scott's novel *Rob Roy*.

Robson, Mount, British Columbia, Canada **J** 55
Robusti, Jacopo *see* Tintoretto
Roc, giant bird, now extinct **G** 200

Roc, in Arabian folklore, a monstrous bird so large it could carry elephants. It transported Sinbad the Sailor to the Valley of Diamonds in the *Arabian Nights*. The roc is possibly related to other giant birds of Turkish, Egyptian, and Babylonian mythology.

Rochambeau (ro-shom-BO), **Jean Baptiste Donatien de Vimeur,** comte de, French military commander **R** 208
   aided Washington in Revolutionary War **W** 40
Rochdale, England
   co-operative movement, basic principles of **C** 500
Rochester, Minnesota **M** 334
Rochester, New York **N** 223
Rock and roll music *see* Rock music
Rock climbing *see* Mountain climbing
Rock collecting **R** 273
Rock crystal, crystalline quartz **Q** 7
   gemstones **G** 75
Rock doves, or pigeons, birds **B** 219
Rock dusting, in coal mining **C** 367
Rockefeller, John D., American industrialist **R** 254
   founded Standard Oil Company in Cleveland **C** 338
Rockefeller, Nelson Aldrich, American statesman **N** 224
Rockefeller Center, New York City
   Christmas tree **C** 291
   outdoor dining, picture **N** 233
Rockefeller Foundation **F** 391
   "Green revolution" in development of cereals
   F 343

Rockefeller University (formerly Rockefeller Institute for Medical Research), graduate university (since 1954), that promotes medical research through research grants, laboratory study, and clinical observation. It was founded (1901) by John D. Rockefeller. Its headquarters is in New York, N.Y. It publishes *The Journal of Experimental Medicine* and *Journal of General Physiology*.

Rocker, tool used in print making **G** 307
Rocket, early locomotive **L** 330; picture **L** 331
Rocket engines **E** 211; **S** 348
   jet propulsion **J** 86
   supersonic planes, use in **S** 471–72
Rocket planes **A** 574
   space exploration of the future **S** 343, 348

Rockets R 255–62
buzz bombs of World War II **W** 300
Cape Kennedy, picture **F** 266
Echo I, balloon-satellite, launched by **B** 34
engines **E** 211
fuels **F** 490
G-force produced by acceleration **G** 324–25
Goddard, Robert Hutchings, father of American rocketry **G** 244–46; **I** 338
hailstorms, use in taming **W** 95
Huntsville, Ala., space center **A** 113, 124
IGY studies, picture **I** 314
ion-drive **I** 351
jet propulsion **J** 86
liquid gases **L** 308
missiles **M** 343–47
model kits of rockets **A** 106
Oberth, Hermann, pioneer in rocketry **O** 6–7
oxygen gas used for liquid fuel **G** 60
replacing cannons for many uses **G** 426
rocket planes **A** 574; **S** 343, 348
satellite, launching of **S** 40
spacecraft, launching of **S** 339, 340d
space exploration of the future **S** 343, 348
Tsiolkovsky, Konstantin, pioneer rocket scientist **T** 306–07
Rock Falls Colonel, champion English setter dog **D** 261
Rockfish, picture **F** 192
Rockford, Illinois **I** 83
Rock gardens, pictures **G** 35
by a Japanese house, picture **H** 171
Rock Hill, South Carolina **S** 308
Rock music R 262a–262d
electronic amplification of sound **E** 142h
jazz influence **J** 62
rock dancing **D** 28, 37
Rock music festivals R 262d
Rockne, Knute, American football coach **F** 364
Rock of Ages, hymn, words and music **H** 310
Rock of Gibraltar see Gibraltar
Rockport, Massachusetts, picture **M** 140
Rocks R 263–69
Can changes in temperature break up rocks? **S** 230
contain fossils **F** 378, 380
Do growing plants break up rocks? **S** 231
earth's mantle **E** 19
ice ages **I** 18
Idaho's City of Rocks **I** 64–65
Kansas' "Rock City," unusual geological area **K** 187
mines and mining **M** 313
moon (lunar) rocks **M** 451, 453, 456; **S** 340a, 340i, 348
petrology, study of rocks, a branch of geology **G** 112
quarrying **Q** 4–5
radioactive dating **R** 64
rock collecting **R** 273
stone **S** 433
See also Sedimentary rocks; Stone
Rock salt S 20
mine in Columbia **C** 382–83

Rockwell, Norman (1894–   ) American illustrator, b. New York, N.Y. During World War I he painted military portraits for Navy and patriotic pictures for national magazines. He is best-known (since 1916) as cover and story illustrator for *Saturday Evening Post* magazine. His works include the *Four Freedoms.*
most famous of American illustrators **I** 95

Rockwood National Program Center for Girl Scouts, near Washington, D.C. **G** 219
Rock wool, insulation fibers **I** 290–91
Rocky Landscape, painting by Cézanne **M** 389

Rocky Mountain bighorns see Bighorns, or Rocky Mountain sheep
Rocky Mountain Fur Company F 523–24
Rocky Mountain National Park, Colorado **C** 402, 410
Rocky Mountains, North America **R** 274
camping in the Canadian Rockies, picture **G** 104
Canada **C** 51, 55
Colorado **C** 400–03
Denver, trade center **D** 116
Glacier National Park **G** 221–22
gold discoveries **G** 251, 253
Idaho **I** 56
Jasper National Park **J** 54–55
Lewis and Clark Expedition **L** 162–63
Mackenzie, Sir Alexander, early explorer **M** 5
Montana **M** 429–30
mountains and mountain building **M** 499
North American Cordillera **N** 282, 284
United States **U** 91
Utah **U** 243
westward movement **W** 146
Wyoming **W** 325
Rocky Mountain sheep, or Bighorns **H** 221; **S** 145; picture **H** 218
Rocky Mountain spotted fever I 283; **S** 388
wood tick, carrier, picture **S** 387
Rocky Mountain Trench, North America **C** 51
Rococo (ro-CO-co), style of decorative art **D** 77
compared to baroque **B** 62
Fragonard, Jean Honoré **F** 402
France **F** 425
furniture design **F** 508; pictures **F** 509
German music of the period **G** 183
Germany **G** 169–70
Italian art and architecture **I** 473
painting **P** 24
sculpture **S** 101
Rodentia, order of mammals **M** 62; **R** 275
Rodents R 275–80
beavers **B** 112–14
disease carriers **I** 287
guinea pigs **G** 407–08
hamsters **G** 407–08
mammals, orders of **M** 62, 69
pets **P** 179–80
rabbits a separate order **R** 22
teeth for different diets **M** 65–66
See also Hares; Rabbits
Rodeo Cowboys Association (R.C.A.) **R** 281
Rodeos R 281–82
Arizona, picture **A** 413
roping demonstrations **R** 333–35
Rodgers, Richard, American composer **M** 543
Rodin (ro-DAN), **Auguste,** French sculptor **R** 283
Burghers of Calais, sculpture **S** 103
French art of the 20th century **F** 426, 431
modern art **M** 387–88
Monument to Balzac, picture **M** 387
place in the history of sculpture **S** 102–03
The Thinker, statue **F** 426
Rodney, Caesar A., American statesman **D** 99
Rod puppets, or stick puppets **P** 535; picture **P** 534
Rodrigues, island dependency of Mauritius **M** 181
Rodríguez de Francia, José Gaspar see Francia, José Gaspar Rodríguez de
Rods, of retina of the eye **B** 284–85
birds **B** 204
Rods, for fishing **F** 206; pictures **F** 207

Rodzinski (ro-JIN-ski), **Artur** (1894–1958), Polish conductor, b. Spalato, Dalmatia. He assisted conductor Leopold Stokowski of the Philadelphia Orchestra (1926–29) and

Rodzinski, Artur (continued)
later conducted the Los Angeles Philharmonic Orchestra (1929–33), Cleveland Symphony Orchestra (1933–42), New York Philharmonic (1943–47), and Chicago Symphony Orchestra (1947–48).

Roe, Richard see John Doe and Richard Roe

Roebling (ROE-bling), **John Augustus** (1806–1869), American engineer, b. Mühlhausen, Germany. A pioneer in suspension bridges, he performed the "impossible" engineering feat of building (1851–55) a suspension bridge over Niagara Falls, using wire-rope cable he had developed. His most famous bridge is the Brooklyn Bridge, which was finished (1883) by his son, **Washington Augustus Roebling** (1837–1926), when Roebling died in an accident soon after the bridge was begun.
    modern suspension bridges **B** 398, 399

Roemer (RUR-mer), **Olaf**, Danish astronomer **L** 266
Roentgen (RENT-gen), **Wilhelm Konrad**, German scientist **X** 339–40
    discovery of new range of radiation of light **L** 270
    cancer research **C** 92–93
    studies by physicists of radiant energy **P** 237; picture **P** 236
    supplied medicine with a new tool **M** 208
Roentgen rays see X rays
Rogers, Bruce, American book designer **B** 326

Rogers, Joel Augustus (1883–1966), American writer, Negro, b. Jamaica. His research on the Negro has produced many books, including *From Superman to Man*, *The World's Great Men of Color*, and *Africa's Gift to America*. For a number of years he wrote a column on Negro history for the Pittsburgh *Courier*.

Rogers, Will, American actor and humorist **O** 94
    trick and fancy roping **R** 333
    Will Rogers Memorial **O** 88; picture **O** 91

Rogers, William Pierce (1913–   ), American lawyer and government official, b. Norfolk, N. Y. Under Eisenhower he served as attorney general (1957–61). In 1960 he undertook a goodwill tour for the United States to West Africa, later serving on the United Nations South West Africa adhoc committee. In 1969 Rogers brought his foreign affairs experience to President Nixon's cabinet as secretary of state.

Rogers' Rangers, military group in British-American army during 18th-century French and Indian War in America. Led by Major Robert Rogers (1731–95), they were known for their boldness and courage in warfare. Memorable daring encounters include "battle on snowshoes" (1758) at what is now Rogers' Rock, Lake George, N.Y.

Rogerus, first known French architect of Gothic style **G** 266
Roget's Thesaurus (ro-JAY's the-SAUR-us), book of synonyms and antonyms **S** 504
Roggeveen, Jakob, Dutch explorer of Easter Island **I** 429
Rogue elephants **E** 167
Rogue novels see Picaresque novels
Rohde, Ruth Bryan (Owen), American diplomat **N** 85
Rohe, Ludwig Miës van der see Miës van der Rohe, Ludwig

Rojankovsky (ro-jon-KOF-ski), **Feodor** (1891–   ), American illustrator of children's books, b. Mitava, Russia. He left Russia after the revolution and worked in Poland (1920–25) as an art director of a fashion magazine and publishing house. He spent 14 years in Paris and then went to the United States (1941). Works he illustrated include *Great Big Animal Book*, *Rojankovsky's Mother Goose*, and *Little Golden Mother Goose*. He won the Caldecott medal in 1956 for *Frog Went A-Courting*.

Rojas (RO-hos), **Fernando de**, Spanish writer **S** 368
Rojas Pinilla, Gustavo, Colombian president **C** 384
Roland, hero of epic poem **C** 189; **L** 129
    early French literature **F** 435

Roland (ro-LON) **de La Platière, Madame** (Jeanne Manon Phlipon) (1754–1793), French revolutionist, b. Paris. She was the wife of Jean Marie Roland de La Platière, one of the leaders of the Girondists. Her salon in Paris was party headquarters (1791–93). When the Girondists were overthrown by the Jacobins (1793), she was arrested. On her way to the guillotine she cried out to the statue of Liberty in the Place de la Révolution, "O Liberty! What crimes are committed in thy name!" Her *Mémoires*, written in prison, were published in 1795.

Roland and Oliver, legend **L** 130–33

Rolfe, John (1585–1622), English colonist, husband of Pocahontas, b. Norfolk. He went (1609) to Virginia, where he contributed greatly to the colony by introducing a new method of curing tobacco, which became a profitable export crop. His marriage (1614) to the Indian Pocahontas, daughter of Chief Powhatan, forged a peaceful union with the Indians. He was the colony's recorder and secretary (1614–19) and a member of the Council of State (1621–22).
    new type of tobacco as a cash crop introduced at Jamestown, Va. **J** 21; **T** 200; **V** 358–59

Rolland (roll-ON), **Romain**, French novelist **F** 442
Rolled gold plate **G** 248
Rolled oats **G** 285
Roller Derby, sport **R** 284
Roller gin, cotton cleaning machine **C** 523
Roller hockey **R** 284
Rollers, construction machines **B** 447–48
Roller-skating **R** 283–84
Rolling, of metals **M** 231
Rolling mills, for steel shaping **I** 399–400

Rolling Stones, The, an English rock music group. Mick Jagger is the leader of the group, which includes Keith Richard, Charlie Watts, Bill Wyman, and Mick Taylor, who replaced Brian Jones in 1969. "Satisfaction" and "Get Off of My Cloud" are among their best-known songs. Their 1969 United States tour was the subject of the film *Gimme Shelter*. **R** 262c

Rollo, duke of Normandy **V** 339
Rollo books, for children **C** 238
Rölvaag (ROLE-vog), **Ole Edvart**, Norwegian-born American author and educator **M** 335
    American literature, place in **A** 208
Roly poly, running and chasing game **G** 21
Romains (ro-MAN), **Jules**, French novelist **F** 442
Roman, typeface design **T** 345
Roman architecture **R** 285–86
    achievements in engineering and masonry **A** 375–77
    aqueducts **A** 344
    building construction methods **B** 435
    cement and concrete, use of **C** 165
    influence on later architecture **A** 384

Romanticism, movement arising in 18th-century Europe
that influenced literature, philosophy, art, and music.
Characterized by stress on expression of emotion, it is
often said to be in direct contradiction to the rationality
and order of classicism. In art, 19th-century romantic

Romanticism (continued)
painters used dramatic color, form, light, and shadow to arouse the imagination, and stimulate a feeling.

Romany (ROM-any), or Gypsy, **language** **G** 433
Romberg, Sigmund, Hungarian-born American composer **O** 157
   Student Prince, The, operetta **O** 158
Rome, ancient **A** 231–32; **R** 303
   Acta Diurna ("acts of the day"), early newspapers **J** 142
   alphabet **A** 171, 173; **C** 431
   aqueducts **A** 344
   architecture see Roman architecture
   armor **A** 433
   art see Roman art
   beauty culture **B** 110–11
   bookmaking **B** 319
   bread-making industry **B** 386
   bridge building **B** 395
   burning of (A.D. 64) **C** 280
   Caesar's calendar **C** 12
   canal builders **C** 84
   central heating system **H** 98
   ceremonial dancing **D** 23
   Cicero supports the republic **C** 298
   citizenship **C** 311
   concrete, discovery of **B** 393–94
   cork, uses of **C** 505
   cosmetics, use of **C** 510
   decorative arts **D** 70
   drama patterned after Greek plays **D** 295
   education **E** 64–65
   emperors, chart **R** 304
   engineering feats **E** 208
   founding and history of the city **R** 316
   government **P** 378
   highways leading to and from Rome **T** 259
   homes **H** 178
   hospitals, early beginnings **M** 204
   jewelry **J** 94
   Latin language **L** 76–77
   Latin literature **L** 77–80
   libraries **L** 194–95
   Livy's history **L** 317
   locks and keys **L** 322–23
   Merino sheep breeding **C** 145
   mining **M** 320
   mythology **G** 356–66
   New Year's gifts **N** 208
   Olympic Games deteriorated **O** 107
   parades **P** 61
   physical education **P** 224–25
   plan of early cities **U** 232
   postal system **C** 435
   public health measures **M** 204
   Punic Wars **P** 533
   roads **E** 208; **T** 259
   Roman numerals **R** 309–10
   ships and shipbuilding **S** 155, 158
   slavery **S** 196
   standards and flags **F** 225
   tools **T** 211
Rome, capital of Italy **R** 312–17
   architecture of Italian Renaissance **I** 465, 467
   cities of Italy **I** 449
   Little Sports Palace, picture **A** 387
   painting **P** 21
   Renaissance art and architecture **R** 167
   Saint Peter's church, picture **A** 382
   San Carlo alle Quattro Fontane church, picture **A** 383
   Vatican City **V** 280–82

Rome, Georgia **G** 135
Rome, Treaty of, 1957, Common Market agreement **I** 329
Rome-Berlin Axis **F** 64
   World War II **W** 286
Romeo and Juliet, play by William Shakespeare **R** 317–18; **S** 132
   balcony scene, excerpts **R** 317–18
   outline of the plot **S** 137

Rommel, Erwin (1891–1944), German general, b. Heidenheim. A master tactician in tank warfare during World War II, he won distinction (and the nickname "the Desert Fox") as commander of the Afrika Korps. He later (1944) commanded the Army Group in France during the Allied invasion of Normandy.
   World War II **W** 290, 291, 303

Romney, George, English painter **E** 238

Romney, George Wilcken (1907–), American politician b. Chihuahua, Mexico. After serving as a Mormon missionary in Britain, he entered the business world, rising to the position of president of American Motors Corporation. Elected governor of Michigan (1962, 1966), he was named (1969) secretary of housing and urban development. In 1972 he resigned, and the following year became chairman of the National Center for Voluntary Action.

Romulo (ROM-u-lo), **Carlos Pena** (1901–), Filipino statesman, b. Manila. He won (1941) a Pulitzer prize for a series of articles on conditions in Asia and served as press aide to General MacArthur during World War II. He was a member of the Quezon (1943) and Osmeña (1944) cabinets. He has headed the Philippine UN delegation (since 1945) and was elected president of the UN General Assembly (1949). He was appointed ambassador to the United States (1952–53, 1955–61). In 1962 he became president of the University of the Philippines. He was named secretary of foreign affairs in 1969.

Romulus and Remus, in Roman legend, twin sons of Mars and vestal virgin Rhea Silvia, and grandsons of Numitor, King of Alba. When Numitor was deposed by Amulius, the twins were ordered abandoned to die. Suckled by a wolf and taught by shepherds, they later killed Amulius and returned Numitor to throne. They founded Rome, and Romulus allegedly became first king (753–716 B.C.) after killing Remus. According to legend, Romulus was carried off to heaven in the midst of a storm and thereafter was worshipped as Quirinus. **I** 454

Romulus Augustulus, Roman emperor **R** 308
Rondo, a musical form **M** 535
   classical age in music **C** 332
Ronne, Finn, American explorer **P** 368
Ronsard (ron-SAR), **Pierre de,** French poet **F** 436
Roof bolting, of coal mines **C** 367
Roof of the World, Himalaya Mountains **H** 128–29
   Tibet **T** 175
Roofs, of buildings **H** 169; pictures **A** 387
   mansard roof **F** 421–22
Rook, in chess, picture **C** 221
Rookeries, breeding grounds of birds or animals
   penguins **P** 120
Roosa, Stuart A., American astronaut **S** 344, 345, 347
Roosevelt (ROSE-ev-elt), **Anna Eleanor,** wife of Franklin D. Roosevelt **F** 178–79; **R** 320
   crusader for human rights **R** 318
Roosevelt, Edith Kermit Carow, wife of Theodore Roosevelt **F** 175–76; **R** 327; picture **F** 177

Roosevelt, Franklin Delano, 32nd president of United
States **R** 319–24
banking legislation **B** 48
conservation projects in government **C** 486
Franklin D. Roosevelt National Historic Site, Hyde
Park, N. Y. **N** 220
Johnson, Lyndon B. and Roosevelt, picture **J** 129
letter to his mother **L** 156b
modifies capitalism **C** 104
monument in Managua, Nicaragua, picture
N 247
New Deal program **D** 122
presidential leadership **P** 451
quotation from First Inaugural Address **Q** 20
Roosevelt Campobello International Park **M** 43;
N 138d–138e
Supreme Court **S** 476
Teheran Conference, 1943, picture **W** 298

Roosevelt, Kermit (1889–1943), American soldier, explorer, businessman, and writer, b. Oyster Bay, N.Y. A
son of Theodore Roosevelt, he accompanied him on a
hunting trip to Africa (1909–10) and explored regions in
Brazil (1914). He served in both the British and U.S.
armies during World Wars I and II and was president of
the Roosevelt Steamship Co. and vice-president of U.S.
Lines Co. Among his books are *War in the Garden of
Eden* and *The Happy Hunting Grounds.*

Roosevelt, Nicholas J. (1767–1854), American inventor
and engineer, b. New York, N.Y. He built an experimental
steamboat, *Polacca* (1798), which traveled at 3 miles
per hour. He and Robert Fulton first used steamboats on
Western rivers (1809) and built the steamboat *New
Orleans,* which ran from Pittsburgh to New Orleans in 14
days (1811). He was granted a patent for the invention
of vertical paddle wheels (1814).

Roosevelt, Theodore, 26th president of the United States
R 325–30
as Vice-President, picture **V** 329
creates career Foreign Service **F** 370
football rules to make game safer **F** 356
interest in conservation **C** 485
Kipling's correspondence with **K** 261
ranching in North Dakota **N** 322–23
Rough Riders in Spanish-American War **S** 375
Sagamore Hill National Historic Site, Oyster Bay, N.Y.
N 220–21
Taft, feuding with **T** 8–9
Theodore Roosevelt National Memorial Park, North
Dakota **N** 52, 333
"the Trust Buster" **C** 104

Roosevelt, Theodore, Jr. (1887–1944), American government administrator, soldier, and author, b. Oyster Bay,
N.Y. The son of Theodore Roosevelt, 26th president of
the United States, he was elected to the New York State
legislature (1919, 1921) and served as assistant secretary of the Navy (1921–24), governor of Puerto Rico
(1929–32), and governor-general of the Philippine Islands
(1932–33). His works include *Average Americans, All in
the Family,* and *Colonial Policies of the United States.*
An officer in both world wars, he died at the front in
France during World War II.

Roosevelt families
Franklin D. Roosevelt family, picture **R** 320
Theodore Roosevelt family, picture **R** 327
Roosevelt Lake, Washington **D** 19

Roosevelt, Eleanor, Memorial Foundation, organization

established to carry on ideals of Mrs. Roosevelt
(1884–1962). Founded in 1963 by congressional charter,
the organization has headquarters in New York, N.Y. Its
first head was UN ambassador Adlai E. Stevenson. Its
concern is for human rights and the support of the
United Nations as a force for peace. It aids underprivileged children.

Roosevelt River, Brazil (ancient name, River of Doubt)
R 330
Roosters, male chickens **P** 423

Root, Elihu (1845–1937), American statesman and lawyer, b. Clinton, N.Y. While U.S. secretary of war
(1899–1904) he directed administration of Cuba and
Philippine Islands and reorganized the army. As secretary of state (1905–09) he restored good relations with
Latin-American countries. He served as senator from
New York (1909–15). He was prominent in settling the
North Atlantic Fishery dispute (1910) and was a member
of the commission that planned the Permanent Court of
International Justice (1920). He received a Nobel peace
prize (1912).

Root, George F., American composer **N** 25
Rootabaga (root-a-BAY-ga) **Stories,** by Carl Sandburg,
excerpt **S** 29
Root crops **P** 307
potatoes **P** 411–12; **V** 292, 293
Rooters, plowlike machines **B** 447
Root hairs, of trees **T** 280
Root knots, galls caused by round worms **P** 286
Roots, of plants **P** 290; pictures **P** 291
poisonous **P** 322
"root-bound" house plants **H** 267–68
roots we eat **P** 307; picture **P** 306
trees **T** 279–80
weeds **W** 104
Roots, of words **W** 239
Rootstocks, seedlings
orange trees **O** 178
Rope **R** 331–33
games with rope and string, pictures **A** 304
knots **K** 289–92
Rope spinning **R** 333–35
Rope tricks **T** 288–89
Roping **R** 333–35
Roquefort (ROKE-fort), cheese made from sheep's milk
C 192–93
action of molds **F** 498
blue cheese, a dairy product **D** 13
Rorquals, or fin whales **W** 149

Rorschach (ROR-shock), **Hermann** (1884–1922), Swiss
psychiatrist and neurologist, b. Zurich. He devised the
ink-blot test known by his name. The test is widely used
in the diagnosis of psychopathologic conditions. In it the
subject describes what he sees in 10 ink blots of
differing forms and colors. The test is based on the
hypothesis that a person's interpretations of what he
sees project aspects of his personality and emotions.

Rosario (ro-SAR-yo), Argentina **A** 394
Rosary, prayer of Roman Catholic Church **R** 302

Rosas (RO-sos) **Juan Manuel de** (1793–1877), Argentine
dictator, b. Buenos Aires. Though governor only of
Buenos Aires (1829–32, 1835–52), he maintained dictatorial rule over other allied provinces. When his war
against Montevideo (1842–51) was finally brought to
defeat by Brazil, he fled to England (1852–77).
Argentina, history of **A** 395

Rosbaud, Hans (1895–1962), Austrian conductor, b. Graz. He was director of the municipal music school of Mainz (1923–30) and of the Munich Konzertverein (1945–48). As music director of the Baden-Baden radio orchestra (1948–62), he toured widely and introduced the works of many contemporary composers.

Rösch, G. A., German scientist, studies of bees **B** 119
Rose Bowl, Pasadena, California, New Year's Day football game **F** 365
Rose-breasted grosbeaks, birds, picture **B** 240

Rosecrans, William Starke (1819–1898), American soldier, b. Kingston, Ohio. He served as a general in the Union Army during the Civil War and was considered a great strategist. After resigning from the Army (1867), he served as U.S. minister to Mexico (1868–69), representative to Congress from California (1881–85), and register of the treasury (1885–93).
 Civil War, United States, campaigns of **C** 326

Rose Festival, Portland, Oregon **P** 398
Rose garden, picture **G** 31
Rosemary, herb **S** 382; picture **S** 381

Rosenberg, Anna Marie (1902–), American public and industrial consultant, b. Budapest, Hungary. She served with the National Recovery Administration (1934–39) and was regional director of the Social Security Board (1936–43) and of the War Manpower Commission (1942–45). She held the office of assistant secretary of defense (1950-53), highest military post ever attained by a woman. She was assigned by President Roosevelt (1944) and President Truman (1945) to study problems of rehabilitating U.S. soldiers. She was a recipient of the Medal of Freedom (1945) and the first woman recipient of the U.S. Medal for Merit.

Rosenberg, Julius (1918–1953) and **Ethel** (1915–1953), American man and wife convicted of espionage, b. New York, N.Y. Found guilty of delivering (1944–46) secret atomic bomb information to Soviet agents, they were sentenced to death (1951). They were convicted on the testimony of David Greenglass, brother of Ethel employed at a New Mexico atomic research center, who received a 15-year sentence for treason. Their execution (1953) resulted in controversy over the nature of the trial and use of death sentence in peacetime.

Rosenfeld, Morris, Yiddish author **Y** 351
Rosenkavalier (RO-sen-ka-va-lier), **Der,** opera by Richard Strauss **O** 153

Rosenquist, James (1933–), American artist, b. North Dakota. He studied at the Art Students League in New York and early in his career was employed by The General Outdoor Advertising Company as a billboard painter. Considered a super-realist by many, his paintings are in both the realistic and abstract styles.

Rosenwald, Julius, American merchant and philanthropist **I** 85

Rosenwald, Julius, Fund, foundation established (1917) by Julius Rosenwald (1862–1932), American merchant and philanthropist. Originally, its purpose was to build rural schools for underprivileged children, but it was later expanded to include support for projects that would improve opportunities and living conditions for disadvantaged groups, particularly Negroes. It gave assistance to hospitals and health agencies, Negro schools and colleges, and poorly equipped school libraries. The fund aided many promising students, artists, writers, and musicians. A self-limited fund, it was discontinued in 1948.

Rosenwald, Lessing J., American merchant and art collector **N** 41

Rose of Lima (LI-ma), **Saint** (1586–1617), Peruvian Dominican ascetic, b. Lima. She entered the Third Order of St. Dominic (1606) and lived an extremely austere life. Canonized in 1671, she was the first saint born in the New World.

Rose-quartz, gemstone **G** 75; **Q** 7; picture **R** 265
Roses, City of, Portland **P** 398
Roses, flowers **G** 46, 51; pictures **G** 27, 31, 49
 Bulgaria, center of rose-growing industry **B** 441
 New York, state flower of **N** 210
 parts of a flower, diagram **P** 295
 rose designs in furniture, pictures **F** 505, 507
 wild rose, state flower of Iowa, North Dakota **I** 357; **N** 323
Roses, Wars of the, 1455–85 **E** 219–20
Rosetta Stone, first clue to understanding Egyptian hieroglyphics **W** 318; picture **W** 319
 displayed in the British Museum **M** 514
Rosette nebula, picture **S** 411

Rose water, fragrant solution prepared with the scented parts of the rose. It is used as a perfume and, infrequently, in cooking.

Rosé (rose-AY) **wines** **W** 188
Rosewood, tree
 uses of the wood and its grain, pictures **F** 504; **W** 224
Rosh Hashanah (ro-sha-SHO-nah), religious holiday **R** 154
 facts about Judaism **J** 120

Rosicrucianism (rosi-CRU-cian-ism), mystical religious philosophy allegedly established in the early 14th century by Christian Rosenkreutz, who imparted knowledge acquired during his travels in Middle East and Spain to three companions, thus founding the original Society of the Rose and Cross. The cult spread throughout Europe, Britain, and the United States in the 17th century. It emphasizes development of the latent capacity of man to achieve understanding of the spiritual realm, which permeates nature.

Rosin, resin of certain pine trees **R** 184
 by-product from the extraction of turpentine **T** 330
Ross, Betsy, American maker of first stars and stripes flag **R** 335
 flag of 1777 **F** 244; picture **F** 229
Ross, Edmund Gibson, American statesman **K** 189

Ross, George (1730–1779), American jurist, b. New Castle, Del. He was elected to the provincial assembly (1768), serving 7 years, and to the Continental Congress (1774–77), where he signed the Declaration of Independence. He was commissioned a judge of the admiralty court of Pennsylvania (1779).

Ross, Sir James Clark (1800–1862), English polar explorer, b. London. He was a member of Arctic expeditions under Sir William Edward Parry (1819–27). He joined an Arctic expedition (1829–33) under his uncle Sir John Ross and determined the position of the north magnetic pole (1831). He led an Antarctic exploratory voyage (1839–43) that discovered Victoria Land and commanded an Arctic relief expedition in search of Sir John Franklin (1848–49). He was author of *A Voyage of Discovery in the Southern and Antarctic Regions*. Ross Sea, Ross Island, and Ross Ice Shelf in Antarctica are named for him.

Ross, John (Cherokee name Cooweescoowe) (1790–1866), Cherokee chief, b. near Lookout Mountain, Tenn. He served in the War of 1812 under Andrew Jackson. He was president of the national council of Cherokees (1819–26) and chief of eastern Cherokees (1828–39). After an attempt to prevent removal of Cherokees from Georgia, he led movement to present-day Oklahoma (1838–39). He was chief of the united Cherokee nation (1839–66).

Ross, Sir John (1777–1856), Scottish Arctic explorer, b. Inch, Wigtonshire. He led an expedition in search of the Northwest Passage (1818, 1829–33) and explored Boothia peninsula, Gulf of Boothia, and King William Land. He was a consul in Stockholm (1839–46) and headed an expedition in search of Sir John Franklin (1850). He was author of *A Voyage of Discovery* and *Narrative of a Second Voyage in Search of a Northwest Passage*.
    Northwest Passage **N** 338

Ross, Malcolm D., American military balloonist **B** 32, 34
Ross, Nellie Tayloe, American political figure **W** 336
Rossetti (ro-SET-ti), **Christina,** English poet **R** 336
    children's poetry **C** 241
    place in English literature **E** 263
    "Who Has Seen the Wind?," poem **R** 336
Rossetti, Dante Gabriel, English painter and poet **R** 336
    Pre-Raphaelite Brotherhood **E** 241
Rossetti, Gabriele, Italian poet **R** 336
Rossetti, Maria, English writer **R** 336
Rossetti, William, English art critic and essayist **R** 336

Rossini (ro-SI-ni), **Gioacchino Antonio** (1792–1868), Italian composer, b. Pesaro. He was a master of Italian comic opera. Lyric charm and clear texture characterize his nearly 40 works, of which *The Barber of Seville* remains most popular. Other operas include *Tancredi, Otello, La Cenerentola,* and *The Lady of the Lake*. He composed his last opera, *William Tell*, at the age of 37.
    Barber of Seville, The, opera **O** 140
    Cenerentola, La, opera **O** 142
    Italian opera **I** 485; **O** 135

Rosso, Giovanni Battista, Italian artist **R** 171
Ross Sea **O** 48
Ross Shelf, Antarctica **I** 12

Rostand (ros-TON), **Edmond** (1868–1918), French poet and playwright, b. Marseilles. The youngest member ever elected to the French Academy (1901), he is best-known for his romantic drama *Cyrano de Bergerac*. Other works include *La Princesse Lointaine, L'Aiglon,* and *Chantecler*. Several of his plays were written for Sarah Bernhardt.
    drama, history of **D** 298

Roswell, New Mexico **N** 193
    Goddard's experimental rocket station **G** 246
Roszak, Theodore, Polish-born American sculptor **M** 397
Rotary drilling, for petroleum **P** 172
Rotary engines **I** 303
Rotary-hoe cultivators **F** 59

Rotary (RO-tary) **International,** service organization of business and professional men, with clubs located in 145 countries. The first club was founded in 1905, the National Association of Rotary Clubs was formed in 1912, and the International Association was established in 1922. Originally, meetings were held in homes of various members in rotation, and from this system the club derived its name. Headquarters are in Evanston, Ill. Publications are *The Rotarian* and *Revista Rotaria*.

Rotary presses, for printing **P** 462
    newspapers' use of **N** 203; picture **N** 204
Rotary tillers, picture **I** 362
Rotation of crops **A** 93
    vegetable gardening **V** 288
ROTC, Reserve Officers' Training Corps **U** 165, 189
Rotenone (RO-ten-ohn), insecticide **I** 258
Roth, Philip, American writer **A** 214
Rothenburg (RO-ten-burk), West Germany, picture **G** 160
Rotherhithe, etching by Whistler **E** 294
Rothschild, House of, banking enterprises **B** 45
Rothschild, Lionel, English financier and statesman **J** 110
Rothschild, Meyer Amschel, German financier **R** 337
    family banking enterprises **B** 45
Rothschild family **R** 337
Rotifers (RO-ti-fers), or wheelworms, a class of invertebrate animals **P** 281
    nervous system, diagram **B** 363
Rotisseries (ro-TISS-eries), **electric** **E** 120
Rotogravure (ro-to-gra-VURE), printing **P** 460
Rotogravure vinyls, plastics **V** 341
Rotonda, villa designed by Palladio **I** 467; picture **I** 464
Rotors, electromagnets of motors **E** 136–37; picture **E** 141
Rotors, rotating air foils
    autogyros and helicopters **H** 105–06
Rotterdam, ocean liner **O** 19; picture **O** 21
Rotterdam, the Netherlands **N** 118; picture **N** 121
    apartment houses, picture **H** 184
    harbor, picture **H** 36
Rotunda of University of Virginia, picture **A** 384
Rouault (roo-O), **Georges,** French painter **F** 431; **M** 388
    Old King, The, painting **F** 430
Rouge (ROOGE), cosmetic **B** 110; **C** 509
Rouge, polishing powder **O** 174
Rouget de Lisle (roo-JAY d'LEEL), **Claude Joseph,** French officer and composer **N** 17
Roughnecks, men who handle oil drilling equipment **P** 172
Rough Riders, United States Volunteer Cavalry, led by Theodore Roosevelt **R** 327; picture **R** 328
    Spanish-American War **S** 375
    term used by Antoine de Vallambrosa **N** 335
Roumania see Rumania
Round, a musical form **M** 538
    African music **A** 78

Roundheads, Puritans or Parliamentarians, especially the soldiers under Cromwell, during the English Civil War period (1642–49). The term was used by the Cavaliers, or Royalists, who wore long hair, in derogatory reference to the Puritans, who wore short hair.
    Cromwell and the Roundheads **C** 536

Round Table, of King Arthur **A** 442, 444
Roundups, of cattle **C** 146
    ranch life **R** 105
Roundworms, or nematode worms **W** 312
    plant enemies **P** 286; picture **P** 287
Rous, Peyton, American physician **C** 93
Rous sarcoma (rouse sar-CO-ma) **virus** **V** 369

Rousseau (roo-SO), **Henri** (Le Douanier, or "custom-house officer") (1844–1910), French primitive painter, b. Laval. After retiring (1885) from service as a customs official, for which he received his nickname, he concentrated on

Rousseau, Henri (continued)
painting. He exhibited at the Salon des Indépendants (1886–98, 1901–10). His work, often depicting dreams and exotic landscapes, includes *Sleeping Gypsy.*

Rousseau, Jean Jacques, Swiss-born French philosopher and writer **R** 337
  education theories **E** 68
  French Revolution **F** 463
  influence on children's literature **C** 237
  novels **N** 348
  Voltaire and Rousseau **F** 439
Roustabouts, of a circus **C** 303
Rouvroy, Claude Henri de see Saint-Simon, Claude Henri de Rouvroy, comte de
Rover Scouts B 360

Rowan (RO-wan), **Andrew Summers** (1857–1943), American army officer, b. Gap Mills, Va. (now W.Va.). Following the outbreak of Spanish-American War, he entered Cuba to inquire about the state of Cuban forces. After meeting with General Calixto García Iñiguez (1898), he returned to the United States with important information from García. His feat was heralded in an essay by Elbert Hubbard inaccurately titled "A Message to Garcia." Rowan served in Mindanao, Philippines (1905–07), and wrote *The Island of Cuba* and *How I Carried the Message to Garcia.*

Rowan, Carl Thomas (1925–   ), American diplomat and writer, b. Ravenscroft, Tenn. He worked as a copyreader and staff reporter on the Minneapolis *Tribune* (1948–61). After serving in the State Department as deputy assistant secretary of state for public affairs (1961–63), he assumed the post of United States ambassador to Finland (1963–64). He served as director of the United States Information Agency (1964–65), becoming the first Negro to hold a National Security Council post. Since 1965 he has been a columnist for the Chicago Daily News.

Rowan, William, Canadian zoologist **H** 191
Row-crop tractors F 55, 57
Rowing R 338–39
  Olympic race, picture **O** 111

Rowland, Henry Augustus (1848–1901), American physicist, b. Honesdale, Pa. He was the first professor of physics at Johns Hopkins University (1876–1901). His greatest achievement was the invention of the concave diffraction grating—a series of lines scratched on a concave mirror, which then produces a spectrum when it reflects light. Concave gratings are more precise and less costly and cover a wider range of light than the earlier, flat gratings.

Rowlandson, Thomas, English cartoonist **C** 125
  famous illustrator and caricaturist **I** 91
  Sports of a Country Fair, an illustration **I** 90

Rowley, James J. (1908–   ), American secret service agent, b. Bronx, N.Y. A U.S. Secret Service agent since 1938, he was assistant supervising agent (1945–46) and supervising agent (1946–61) of the White House detail. He became chief, U.S. Secret Service (1961–   ).

Rowson, Susanna Haswell, English-born American novelist **A** 198

Roxas y Acuña (RO-hos e a-COON-ya), **Manuel** (1892–1948), Philippine statesman, b. Capiz. He was a member of the house of representatives (1922–34) and national

assembly (1935–38), secretary of finance (1938–41), and president of the Philippines (1946–48).
  Philippines, history of **P** 190

Royal Academy of Arts (Royal Academy), British association of 40 artists elected as royal academicians and approximately 30 associates. Founded in London in 1768 by George III, it promotes the arts of painting, sculpture, and architecture by exhibiting the works of contemporary artists, providing art instruction, and giving financial aid to needy artists.
  English art, age of the Royal Academy **E** 238
  National Gallery (London) **N** 39

Royal Academy of Music, Paris, France **D** 36–37
Royal and Ancient Golf Club (R.A,G.C.), Saint Andrews, Scotland **G** 256
Royal Caledonian Curling Club of Scotland C 555
Royal Canadian Air Force C 82
Royal Canadian Dragoons, picture **C** 79
Royal Canadian Mounted Police P 374, 375; picture **C** 78
  law enforcement in Canada **C** 78
Royal Canadian Mounted Police Museum and Barracks, Regina, Saskatchewan **S** 38f
Royal Canadian Navy C 80–82
  founded by Laurier **C** 75
Royal Gorge, of the Arkansas River, picture **C** 412
Royal Greenwich Observatory see Greenwich Observatory, Royal
Royal Institution of Great Britain T 166
Royal jelly, food of bees **B** 122
Royal Montreal Golf Club, Canada **G** 261
Royal Ontario Museum, Toronto, Canada, picture **M** 520
Royal Shakespeare Theatre, Stratford-on-Avon, England **T** 159
Royal Society of London S 70
  based on principles of Francis Bacon's scientific method **S** 67–68
  Boyle, Robert **B** 354
Royalty, payment to an author or composer **P** 514
  check on royalties if you charge admission to your play **P** 335
  copyright **T** 245

Rozier (roze-YAY), **Jean François Pilâtre de** (1754–1785), French physician and balloonist, b. Metz. He made the first aerial ascent (1783), in a balloon designed by the Montgolfier brothers. With Marquis d'Arlandes, he crossed Paris in first free-balloon flight (1783). He developed and piloted a balloon utilizing hydrogen and hot-air sacs, but he was killed when the hydrogen caught fire and exploded.
  balloons and ballooning, history of **B** 30

R.S.V.P., invitation requiring reply **L** 159
  parties, etiquette of giving **P** 88
Ruanda, former name of Republic of Rwanda **R** 362
Ruanda-Urundi see Burundi; Rwanda
Rubàiyat (RU-by-yot) **of Omar Khayyàm** (O-mar ky-OM), **The E** 263; **I** 373
Rub'al Khali (roob-ol-KA-li), desert region of Saudi Arabia **S** 46; picture **A** 446
Rubarb, plant
  leaf stalks we eat **P** 307; picture **P** 306
Rubato (ru-BA-to), musical term **O** 189
Rubber R 340–48
  a leading industry **I** 246–47
  dolls made of **D** 267
  first rubber balls **B** 20
  Goodyear's vulcanization process **G** 263
  man-made, synthesized by chemists **C** 195

plantation in Malaysia, picture **M** 55
tires **T** 196–98
Rubber tiles, floor covering **V** 341
Rubber trees **R** 342–43; pictures **R** 344
Rubbing alcohol **A** 147; **M** 202
Rubbings, raised textured surfaces **D** 136
Rubella (ru-BELL-a), German measles **D** 196
Rubens, Peter Paul, Flemish painter **R** 348
Adoration of the Magi, painting **D** 356
baroque painting **P** 24
etchings of his paintings **G** 305
Flemish art in 17th century **D** 352
gallery in the Louvre, picture **L** 367
Marie de Medicis, Queen of France, Landing in Marseilles, painting **P** 25
northern baroque art **B** 60
Peasant Dance, painting **B** 58

Rubicon (RU-bic-on), small river in northern Italy that flows into the Adriatic Sea and in ancient Roman times formed the boundary separating Italy and Cisalpine Gaul. It is historically famous as the river Caesar and his army crossed in 49 B.C., precipitating civil war.
Caesar's career **C** 6

Rubidium (ru-BID-ium), element **E** 155, 164
Rubidium-87, radioactive element **R** 65
Rubies, gemstones **G** 69
superstitions about **G** 71

Rubinstein, Anton Grigorievich (1829–1894), Russian composer and pianist, b. Vykhvatinetz. He won wide acclaim as a pianist throughout Europe and the United States. In Russia he became imperial concert director (1858), and he founded St. Petersburg Conservatory of Music (1862), serving as its director (1862–67, 1887–91). His compositions include *Ocean Symphony,* the opera *The Demon,* piano concertos, and solo pieces.
Russian music **U** 63

Rubinstein, Artur (1886–   ), American pianist, b. Lodz, Poland. A widely acclaimed virtuoso, he has made concert tours in numerous countries throughout Europe and South America, and in United States. He is best known for his interpretation of Chopin and Spanish composers, such as Albéniz and Granados. His own compositions include piano pieces and chamber music.

Rublev, Andrei, Russian artist **U** 54
Archangel Michael, icon **U** 55

Ruby, Jack (1911–67), American nightclub owner, b. Chicago, Ill. He killed Lee Harvey Oswald, President Kennedy's assassin.

Rudbeckias (rud-BECK-ias), flowers, picture **G** 28
Rudders, steering devices
airplane **A** 556
ships **I** 337
Rudolf, Lake, eastern Africa **L** 33
Rudolf of Habsburg, ruler of Austria **A** 524

Rudolph, Wilma (1940–   ), American track star, Negro, b. St. Bethlehem, Tenn. In the 1960 Olympics she won three gold medals—for the 100- and 200-meter dashes and as anchor on the women's 400-meter team. Associated Press chose her Female Athlete of the Year (1960).
Olympic stars, pictures **O** 114

Rudolphine tables in astronomy, work of Tycho Brahe **B** 361

Ruffed grouse, bird **B** 208
Pennsylvania, state bird of **P** 129
Rufisque (ru-FEESK), Senegal **S** 120

Rugambwa (ru-GAM-bwa) (means "high renown"), **Laurian, Cardinal** (1912–   ), Tanzanian ecclesiastic, b. Bukongo, Kiyanja. He was ordained a Catholic priest in 1943. He studied in Rome (1948–51) and was appointed bishop of Rutabo (1953). Chosen cardinal by Pope John XXIII (1960), he became the first Negro to hold that office.

Rugby **R** 349–50
See also Football
Rugs and carpets **R** 350–54
Islamic art **I** 422
Kashmir, picture **K** 199
Persian rugs of Iran, picture **I** 373
Samarkand, picture **U** 47
What is the difference between a rug and a carpet? **R** 352
Ruhr district, of Germany **G** 156
Ruidoso, New Mexico
Sierra Blanca ski area, picture **N** 191
Ruins *see* Archeology

Ruisdael (ROIS-dol), or **Ruysdael, Jacob van** (1628?–1682), Dutch landscape painter and etcher, b. Haarlem. After moving to Amsterdam (1657), he traveled through Holland and Germany. He is best known for his landscapes, especially forest and mountain scenes.
Dutch landscape painting **D** 357

Ruiz, José Martínez *see* Martínez Ruiz, José
Ruiz (ru-EETH), **Juan,** Spanish poet **S** 367
Ruiz (RU-ees) **Cortines, Adolfo,** Mexican president **M** 250
Rule, Britannia, patriotic song, words by James Thomson **E** 258
unofficial anthem of the British Empire **N** 27
Rule of Saint Benedict **C** 283, 284
Rulers, measuring tools **T** 215–16
geometry, use in **G** 130
woodworking tools for measuring **W** 230
Rules Committee, United States Congress **U** 141–42
Rules of order *see* Parliamentary procedure
Rules of the road
boats and boating **B** 261–62
sailing **S** 14
Rum, a distilled beverage **W** 159
Rum, Romanism and Rebellion, election campaign catchwords **C** 341
Rumania **R** 355–60
Balkan wars **B** 19
Communism, differences among various countries **C** 444
flag **F** 240
national anthem **N** 22
World War I **W** 275
Rumanian Orthodox Church **R** 355
Rumen, 1st chamber of the stomach of a ruminant **H** 208
Rumford, Count *see* Thompson, Benjamin
Ruminants (RU-min-ants), order of cud-chewing mammals **H** 208
cattle and other livestock **C** 147
Rum Jungle uranium mine, Darwin, Australia, picture **A** 509
Rummy, card game **C** 112–13
canasta **C** 113–14
gin rummy **C** 115
Rumpelstiltskin, folk tale in *Grimm's Fairy Tales*
Rackham illustration **I** 93

Rump Parliament, England **E** 223
Runabouts, small powerboats **B** 260–61
Runaway, The, poem by Robert Frost **P** 355

Runes, characters of the alphabet used in ancient Scandinavian and Teutonic cultures probably after about A.D. 200. The oldest alphabet was comprised of 24 signs, whose simple lines were suited for carving or etching on wood, bone, metal, or stone.

Runge, Philipp Otto, German artist **G** 171
Running
    animals: locomotion **A** 292–94
    mammals, speed of **M** 63
Running, track **T** 237–38
    Bannister, Roger, mile-run champion **B** 51
Running and chasing games **G** 20–22
Running stitches, in sewing **S** 129
Runnymede, meadow near London
    Magna Carta, signing at **M** 22
Runways, of an airport **A** 562; pictures **A** 561, 563

Runyon, Damon (Alfred Damon Runyon) (1880–1946), American journalist and writer, b. Manhattan, Kans. A Hearst war correspondent in Mexico (1912, 1916) and in Europe (1917, 1918), he was a columnist from 1918 for King Features and International News Service. In his short stories about New York underworld, as *Guys and Dolls,* he made use of current slang.

Rupert's Land, Canada **M** 82
    fur trade in Canada **C** 72
Rural Free Delivery (RFD), of mail **P** 409
Rural life see Farm life
Rural poverty **P** 424–424b
Rurik, Russian ruler **M** 466

Rush, Benjamin (1745–1813), American physician and politician, b. Byberry, Pa. Active in state and federal government, he became a member of the Continental Congress (1776) and was a signer of the Declaration of Independence. He was a physician at Pennsylvania Hospital (1783–1813) and treasurer of U.S. Mint (1797–1813). He wrote on medicine and on social reform.

Rush-Bagot Agreement, 1817 **C** 81
Rushlights **L** 279–80; picture **L** 282
    lights before candles **C** 96

Rusk, Dean (1909–   ), American statesman, b. Cherokee County, Ga. He worked for the State Department (1946–52) in various capacities, particularly in the field of foreign relations. From 1952 to 1960 he was president of the Rockefeller Foundation. He served as U. S. secretary of state (1960–69), receiving the Medal of Freedom in 1969. He holds chair in international law at the University of Georgia. Picture **N** 104.

Ruskin, John, English critic and author **E** 262
    criticism of Whistler's painting **W** 160
Russell, Bertrand, English philosopher and writer **R** 360

Russell, Bill (William Felton Russell) (1934–   ), American basketball player, Negro, b. Monroe, La. A noted defensive specialist, 6-foot, 10-inch Russell played on U.S. Olympic basketball team (1956). He joined Boston Celtics of National Basketball Association (NBA) (1956), leading them to record number of championships. He won NBA's Most Valuable Player award 5 times (1958, '61, '62, '63, and '65). He was appointed Celtics' coach in 1966, the first Negro to direct a major professional sports team. He resigned in 1969.

Russell, Charles Marion, American artist **M** 441
    C. M. Russell Gallery, Great Falls, Mont.
      M 437
Russell, George William ("AE"), Irish poet **E** 266

Russell, Lillian (Helen Louise Leonard) (1861–1922), American comic-opera singer, b. Clinton, Iowa. Immensely popular and renowned for her great beauty, she had leads in such Broadway successes as *The Great Mogul, Patience,* and *The Sorcerer.* In 1899 she became part of the Weber and Fields company.

Russell Cave National Monument, Alabama **A** 121
Russell Sage Foundation see Sage, Russell, Foundation
Russia, now Union of Soviet Socialist Republics
    costumes, traditional, pictures **C** 349; **D** 264
    fairs and expositions **F** 11
    flag (until 1917) **F** 227
    history to 1917 **U** 47–50
    origin of name "Russia" **F** 134; **S** 486
    Peter the Great **P** 168
    Vikings **V** 339
    World War I **W** 271–72, 279
    See also Union of Soviet Socialist Republics
Russian America, early name for Alaska **A** 143
Russian architecture **U** 52–54
Russian art **U** 52, 54–58
    ballet **B** 25–26
    Hermitage Museum **H** 119–20
Russian baths **B** 91
Russian Blue cats **C** 142; picture **C** 143
Russian language **U** 58
Russian literature **U** 58–63
    contributions to art of the novel **N** 347–48
    fairy tales **F** 22
    realistic drama **D** 298
    See also names of Russian authors
Russian music **U** 63–64
    bell ringing **B** 135
    opera **O** 136
    See also names of Russian composers
Russian Orthodox Church in America **O** 230
Russian Revolution, and Civil War, 1917–1921
    U 50
    Communism **C** 443
    Lenin made Moscow the capital again **M** 467
    underground movements **U** 10
    World War I **W** 279
Russian Soviet Federal Socialist Republic **U** 43
    half in Soviet Europe **E** 307
    languages **U** 27
    Siberia **S** 173
Russian thistle, weed, picture **W** 105
Russo-Finnish War, 1939 **W** 288
Russo-German Pact, 1939 **W** 287

Russo-Japanese War (1904–05), conflict between Russia and Japan arising from Russian possession of Port Arthur (1898), expansion into Manchuria, and subsequent threat to Japanese dominance in Korea. Japanese forces captured Port Arthur and Mukden and totally defeated the Russian Baltic Fleet in Tsushima Strait (1905). The treaty, concluded at Portsmouth, N.H., acknowledged Japanese supremacy in Korea and provided for simultaneous withdrawal of Russian and Japanese troops from Manchuria. Among the agreements were Japanese acquisition of the following: leased territory in Manchuria; railway between Chanchun and Port Arthur; mines along the railway; southern half of Sakhalin Island; fishery rights along Maritime Province of Siberia. The war established Japan as a major power and contributed to Russian internal disorder (1905).

Russo-Turkish War, 1877–1878
  Bulgaria **B** 444

Russwurm, John Brown (1799–1851), journalist, educator, Negro, b. Port Antonio, Jamaica, B.W.I. He was co-founder of an early Negro newspaper in the United States (1827). Seeking freedom for slaves, he moved to Liberia (1829) where he was active in education, newspaper publishing, and government.
  Negro educators **N** 93, 94

Rust
  phlogiston, theory of **C** 210
  rusting, slow combustion **F** 137
  slow oxidation **O** 268
  See also Corrosion

Rustin, Bayard (1910–), American civil rights leader and lecturer, Negro, b. West Chester, Pa. One of the chief strategists in the Negro struggle for equality in the U.S., he helped to develop the Congress of Racial Equality (CORE) in the 1940's. He was influential in persuading President Franklin D. Roosevelt to ban racial discrimination in industries handling government defense contracts (1941) and President Harry Truman to ban discrimination in the armed forces (1948). His writings resulted in the abolition of chain gangs in North Carolina. Since 1966 he has been director of Philip Randolph Institute.
  continuing struggle in Negro history **N** 104b

Rusts, fungi **F** 498
  diseases of oats **O** 4
Rutgers—The State University, New Brunswick, New Jersey **N** 172–73
Ruth, book of Bible, Old Testament **B** 156
Ruth, George Herman ("Babe"), American baseball player **R** 361
  home run king of baseball **B** 78, 80; picture **B** 81
  signature reproduced **A** 527
  with Harding, picture **H** 40
Ruth, Old Testament heroine **J** 106
Ruthenia, or Carpatho-Ukraine, U.S.S.R. **C** 564
Ruthenium, element **E** 155, 164
Rutherford, Daniel, Scottish chemist **C** 210
Rutherford, Ernest, 1st Baron Rutherford of Nelson, New Zealand-born British physicist **R** 361; picture **C** 215

modern physicists **P** 237; picture **P** 232
  nuclear energy **N** 353
  radio, early history of **R** 52
  work on atomic structure **C** 216
Rutherfordium, radioactive element **E** 155, 164; **R** 68
Rutilated quartz Q 7
Rutland, Vermont **V** 318

Rutledge, Ann (1816–1835), daughter of an innkeeper in New Salem, Ill. Abraham Lincoln lived in her father's inn before going to Springfield and was said to have been engaged to her. She died of malarial fever. Many poems and stories have been written about her and her possible connection with Lincoln.
  Lincoln's early life in Illinois **I** 81; **L** 293

Rutledge, Edward, American official **S** 308
Rutledge, John, American jurist **S** 308
Ruwenzori (ru-wen-ZO-ri) **Mountains,** central Africa **U** 5
  Africa, chief mountain ranges **A** 46
  plantain farm near the mountains, picture **U** 7
Ruysch (ROIS), **Johannes,** Dutch mapmaker **M** 93
Ruysdael, Jacob van, see Ruisdael, Jacob van
Rwanda R 362–63
  flag **F** 236
  See also Burundi
Ryder, Albert Pinkham, American painter **U** 121
  Toilers of the Sea, painting **U** 119
Rye R 364
  cereal grasses **G** 318
  grain and grain products **G** 282, 285
  seeds and ear, pictures **G** 283
  Triticale, species hybrid of wheat and rye **G** 287
Rye-an' injun, colonial American bread **C** 390
Ryerson, Adolphus Egerton, Canadian educator **O** 127
Rymer, Thomas, English critic and writer **O** 236
Rymill, John, English explorer **P** 368
Ryukyu Islands, Pacific Ocean **P** 7
  Okinawa, in World War II **W** 305, 308

Ryun, Jim (James Ronald Ryun) (1947–), American track athlete, b. Wichita, Kan. The first high school athlete to run a mile in less than 4 minutes (1964), he set world records (1967) for the mile (3:51.1), for the 1,500 meters (3:33.1), and one-half mile (1:44.9). He received James E. Sullivan Award as best amateur athlete (1966).

ILLUSTRATION CREDITS

The following list credits, by page, the sources of illustrations used in Volume Q-R of THE NEW BOOK OF KNOWLEDGE. Credits are listed illustration by illustration —left to right, top to bottom. Wherever appropriate, the name of the photographer or artist has been listed with the source, the two being separated by a dash. When two or more illustrations appear on one page, their credits are separated by semicolons.

58 CBS; Gerald McConnell.
59 CBS
60 Gerald McConnell
61 WMCA
62 Van der Meid—Monkmeyer
66 Lee Ames
67 George Bakacs; Grolier Council.
68 Courtesy of R. Veenema and B. Fingerhut, Francis Delafield Hospital, Urological Laboratory, New York City.
69 National Radio Astronomy Observatory
70 Ronan Picture Library; Mount Wilson and Mount Palomar Observatories.
71 Ronan Picture Library; Miller Pope.
72 Stanford University; Courtesy of Bell Telephone Laboratories, Inc.
73 U.S. Army
74 Courtesy of National Research Council, Ottawa, Canada; Yerkes Observatory, University of Chicago.
75 British Information Services, London
76 Mount Wilson and Mount Palomar Observatories; Antonio Petruccelli.
78 Swiss National Tourist Office
79 Charles E. Rotkin—PFI
80 Santa Fe Railway; German Federal Railroad; Union Pacific Railroad.
81 Photo Researchers
85 Charles E. Rotkin—PFI; Charles E. Rotkin—PFI; Shostal.
89 Japanese National Railways
90 The Budd Company
94 Harry Scott
95 U.S. Department of Commerce, Weather Bureau
96 Courtesy of the American Museum of Natural History; Rohidean Studios—U.S. Department of Commerce, Weather Bureau.
97 U.S. Department of Commerce, Weather Bureau; U.S. Department of Commerce, Weather Bureau; Charles C. Williford—U.S. Department of Commerce, Weather Bureau.
98 M. Smith—Annan
99 Brett Weston—Rapho Guillumette
102 George Sottung
104 George Sottung
105 George Sottung
106 Art Reference Bureau
107 Arizona State University Photo Service
108 Suzanne Szasz
109 From *Book 2 Reader,* reprinted by permission of Initial Teaching Alphabet Publications, Inc.
110 Homestead School, Garden City
112 Verne Bowman
118 Culver
119 Culver
120 Fred Mason
121 Gerald McConnell
122 Permission to reproduce "Merrily We Roll Along," "Where Has My Little Dog Gone?" and "Clementine" from *Let's Play the Recorder* by Robert H. Bouchard, © 1962, Bruce Humphries Publishers, Boston, Mass.
127 Esther Bubley
128 George Sottung
130 Gerald McConnell
132 George Sottung
133 George Sottung
137 Gerald McConnell
138 Gerald McConnell
140– Lee Ames
144
146 Werner Bischof—Magnum
147 Verne Bowman
149 Courtesy Swedish Information Service; Courtesy of Government of India, Tourist Office.
150 Marc & Evelyne Bernheim—Rapho Guillumette

151 George Holton—Photo Researchers; John Dominis—© Time Inc., All Rights Reserved.
152 Ron Perkins
156 Art Reference Bureau
158 George Sottung
159 George Sottung
161 George Sottung
164 Art Reference Bureau
165 Scala—Shostal
166 Art Reference Bureau; Art Reference Bureau.
167 Art Reference Bureau
168 Art Reference Bureau
170 Art Reference Bureau; Francis Mayer—Metropolitan Museum of Art, Rogers Fund, 1919.
174 Durand—Ruel, Paris
176 Grant Heilman
177 Gaetano Di Palma
178 Gaetano Di Palma; Wilfred Lee—University of Liverpool; Wilfred Lee—University of Liverpool; Wilfred Lee—University of Liverpool; Wilfred Lee—University of Liverpool.
179 Gaetano Di Palma; Lynwood M. Chace.
181 Leonard Cole
182 Chuck McVicker
183 Chuck McVicker
192 George Sottung
195 Herman B. Vestal
197 Herman B. Vestal
199– Herman B. Vestal
201
203 Herman B. Vestal
206 Herman B. Vestal
211 C. A. W. Guggisberg—Photo Researchers
213 Color Illustration Inc.; M. House; John H. Gerard; J. H. Vondell—Shostal.
214 Diversified Map Corp.
215 Diversified Map Corp.
219 Courtesy of Brown University; Shostal; Russ Kinne—Photo Researchers.
220 Leona Kowal
221 Diversified Map Corp.
222 John Ballantine
223 Devaney Inc.
224 Diversified Map Corp.
228 Carl Frank—Photo Researchers
229 George Buctel
230 H. von Meiss—Photo Researchers; Carl Frank—Photo Researchers.
231 U.S. Department of Agriculture
232 U.S. Department of Agriculture
234 Gerald McConnell
236 George Buctel; Robert Richie
238 Tad Nichols, Tucson
239 IBM
240 D. Edwards—Alpha; Charles E. Rotkin—PFI; Ray Manley—Shostal; Jack Zehrt—Shostal.
243 J. R. Simon—Photo Researchers; Ray Manley—Shostal.
245 Marc & Evelyne Bernheim—Rapho Guillumette
246 Kinkeler—Alpha; Ray Manley—Shostal.
249 *Epoca*—Pictorial Parade; Louis Renault—Photo Researchers; *Paris Match*—Pictorial Parade.
250 George Hunter
255 U.S. Air Force
256 Thiokol Chemical Corp.
257 Esther C. Goddard; Lee Ames.
258 Lee Ames
259 Lee Ames
261 Lee Ames
262 NASA; Aerojet General Corp.
262b Courtesy of RCA Records; Wide World Photos
262c CBS—Columbia Records; Atlantic Records; Zodiac Photographers—Jos. Abels, Sy Friedman
265 Julius Weber—Mrs. Katherine H. Jensen

266– Julius Weber
268
271 Julius Weber
272 Julius Weber
274 Shostal
275 Focht-Rue—Annan; Walther Rohdich—Annan.
277 Ed Cesar—Annan; Karl Maslowski—Photo Researchers; Ken Brate—Photo Researchers; J. R. Simon—Photo Researchers.
278 J. R. Simon—Photo Researchers; Tom McHugh—Photo Researchers; Hans Dommasch—Annan.
279 C. G. Hampson—Annan; C. G. Hampson—Annan.
280 Russ Kinne—Photo Researchers; Russ Kinne—Photo Researchers.
281 Bill Browning—Montana Chamber of Commerce
285 Louis Renault—Photo Researchers
286 Vatican Museum, Rome—Art Reference Bureau
287 Vatican Museum, Rome—Art Reference Bureau
288 George Sottung
299 Life Magazine, © 1965, Time Inc., all rights reserved
300 George Sottung
302 ANI
303 Herman B. Vestal
305 Herman B. Vestal
306 Herman B. Vestal
307 Harry Scott
312 Ray Manley—Shostal; George Holton—Photo Researchers; L. Calnazzo, Milan.
314 Bernard G. Silberstein—Rapho Guillumette; Karl Gullers—Rapho Guillumette.
315 George Buctel
316 Ray Manley—Shostal
319 James Cooper
320 Franklin D. Roosevelt Library, Hyde Park, New York; Underwood & Underwood.
322 Harris & Ewing/Gilloon
324 Franklin D. Roosevelt Library, Hyde Park, New York
325 James Cooper
327 Bettmann Archive
328 Granger Collection; Bettmann Archive.
329 Bettmann Archive
331 ANI
332 Life Magazine, © Time Inc., all rights reserved
334 Harry Schaare
335 Harry Schaare
336 New York Public Library
338 Jerry Cooke
340 Chuck McVicker
342 Harry Scott
343 Firestone Tire & Rubber Co.
344 Inger Abrahamsen—Rapho Guillumette; Jerry Frank; Firestone Tire & Rubber Co.
345 Firestone Tire & Rubber Co.
347 Inger Abrahamsen—Rapho Guillumette
349 Gerald McConnell
351 Gerald McConnell
353 Sandak—property of the Los Angeles County Museum of Art; Metropolitan Museum of Art, Rogers Fund, 1908; Metropolitan Museum of Art, Gift of Samuel H. Kress Foundation, 1946; Metropolitan Museum of Art, The Cloisters Collection, Purchase 1961; Unika-Vaev Corp.; Mohawk Carpet Mills.
355 George Buctel
357 Eastfoto
358 Olga Diamond—Photo Researchers
359 Inge Morath—Magnum; Jerry Cooke.
363 George Buctel; George Holton—Photo Researchers.

Saint George's Cross
symbol of England **F** 227
Saint Gregory the Great, Order of see Gregory the Great, Order of Saint
Saint Helena (ha-LE-na), island in South Atlantic **I** 436
Napoleon's place of exile **N** 12
Saint Jerome in his Study, engraving by Albrecht Dürer **D** 345
Saint Joan, play by George Bernard Shaw **S** 144
Saint John, New Brunswick, Canada **N** 138c; picture **N** 138d
Saint John, Virgin Islands, United States **U** 100
Caribbean Sea and islands **C** 118, 119
territorial expansion of United States **T** 115
Saint John River, between United States and Canada **R** 247
New Brunswick **N** 138a
Saint John's, capital of Newfoundland, Canada **N** 144; picture **N** 141
Saint John's Day, honoring patron saint of Naples **I** 448
Saint-John's-wort, or Klamath weed **W** 106
poisonous plants **P** 323
Saint John the Baptist in the Wilderness, painting by Geertgen tot Sint Jans **D** 354
Saint John the Divine, cathedral, New York City **C** 132

Saint Kitts, or St. Christopher, one of the Leeward Islands in the Caribbean, a member of the state of St. Kitts-Nevis-Anguilla of the West Indies Associated States and self-governing within the Commonwealth of Nations. Basseterre is the capital, largest city, and port. Tourism is a major source of income. Reputedly discovered by Christopher Columbus in 1493, it was here that the British first settled in the West Indies.
Caribbean Sea and islands **C** 118

Saint Laurent (san laur-ON), **Louis Stephen,** Canadian statesman **Q** 13
Saint (SAINT) Lawrence, Gulf of **C** 52
Saint Lawrence Lowland, region of Canada **C** 50
Quebec **Q** 10
Saint Lawrence River **S** 15–17
Atlantic Basin of Canada **C** 51
Cartier, Jacques, discoverer of **C** 124
New France (early Canada) **C** 68
New York **N** 215
Montreal **M** 443–45
Quebec **Q** 12
Saint Lawrence Seaway **S** 16–17
canals, history of **C** 85
Chicago open to ocean-going ships **C** 230
Eisenhower Lock, picture **C** 60
Great Lakes **G** 326–29
Michigan **M** 261
Ontario **O** 122
Quebec **Q** 12
Welland Ship Canal, pictures **C** 83; **O** 123
Saint Leger (LEJ-er), **Barry,** British soldier **R** 202, 204
Saint Louis, Missouri **S** 17–18
Chouteau family, fur dynasty **F** 522–23; **M** 379
cities of Missouri **M** 378
Climatron, The, botanical garden, picture **Z** 378
first public-school kindergarten, 1873 **E** 71
Saint-Louis (san-loo-E), Senegal **S** 120
Saint Louis (saint LOO-i) **Blues,** song by W. C. Handy **H** 34; excerpt **J** 58
blues form of jazz **J** 57–58
Saint Louis (LOU-is) **Post-Dispatch,** newspaper **P** 524

Saint Lucia (sant-LOO-sha), one of the Windward Islands in the Caribbean, a member of the West Indies Associated States, and self-governing within the Commonwealth of Nations. Its capital is Castries. First settled by the French, it came under British possession in 1803.
Caribbean Sea and islands **C** 118

Saint Lusson (san lu-SON), **Simon François Daumont, Sieur de** (?–1674), French explorer. He went to Canada with Commissioner Gaudais-Dupont (1663) and took possession of the territory around the upper Great Lakes for King Louis XIV of France (1671).

Saint (SAINT) Mark's Church, Venice, picture **I** 459
Byzantine style **B** 488
Saint Martin (san mar-TAN), **Alexis,** French-Canadian Indian, served as human laboratory for William Beaumont **B** 109

Saint Martin, one of the Leeward Islands, West Indies, in the northeastern Caribbean Sea. The island was divided in 1648 between France and the Netherlands. The chief French town is Marigot, and the chief Dutch town, Philipsburg. Cotton and salt are produced.
Caribbean Sea and islands **C** 118

Saint Martin (saint MAR-tin) **Dividing his Robe,** painting by Van Dyck **F** 295
Saint Martin's Day (Martinmas) **H** 159; **R** 154–55
Saint Moritz, Switzerland, Toboggan Club **B** 265
Saint Nick, in "A Visit from Saint Nicholas" **C** 295
Saint Nicholas (St. Nicholas), magazine **M** 16
children's literature **C** 240
Saint of the Sword, The, name given to José de San Martín **S** 36
Saint Patrick's Cross, historic flag of Ireland **F** 227
Saint Patrick's Day **H** 148
Saint Paul, capital of Minnesota **M** 321
Saint Paul's Cathedral, London **E** 237–38; pictures **E** 237, **W** 313
Wren's masterpiece **A** 382–83; **W** 313
Saint Paul's Day **H** 159
Saint Peter Port, Guernsey, picture **I** 425
Saint Peter's (basilica), Rome, Italy **A** 381; pictures **A** 382, **R** 314, **V** 281, **W** 218
baroque style **B** 57, 59
basilica plan, diagram **I** 458
Bramante **I** 467
Michelangelo **M** 257
not officially a cathedral **C** 133
obelisk, picture **O** 6
Piazza designed by Bernini, picture **I** 470
Renaissance architecture **R** 167
Vatican Council II, picture **R** 299
Saint Petersburg, Russia see Leningrad, U.S.S.R.
Saint Pierre and Miquelon (MIC-el-on), islands off Newfoundland **I** 436; **N** 143
Saint Rombold, Cathedral of, Mechelen, Belgium
carillon **B** 137; picture **B** 135
Saint Sabina Church, Rome, Italy **I** 458; picture **I** 459
Saint-Saëns (san-SON), **Camille,** French composer **F** 446
Samson et Dalila, opera **O** 153
Saints (SAINTS) and Strangers, Plymouth Colony **P** 344
Saints' days, religious holidays **R** 153
Saint Sebastian, painting by Terbrugghen **D** 359
Saint Sebastian, statue by Berruguete, picture **S** 364
Saint Sebastian, statue by Tilman Riemenschneider, picture **G** 165
Saint-Simon (san-si-MON), **Claude Henri de Rouvroy, Comte de,** French social scientist **S** 220
Saint-Simon, Louis de Rouvroy, Duc de, French social critic **F** 438
Saint Sophia, Byzantine church see Hagia Sophia
Saint Sophia (saint so-PHY-a) **Cathedral,** Kiev, Union of Socialist Republics **U** 52

Saints Peter and Paul, Feast of R 290
Saint Swithin's Day H 159
Saint Thais, engraving E 272
Saint Thomas, Virgin Islands, United States U 100
    Caribbean Sea and islands C 118
    territorial expansion of United States T 115
Saint Valentine's Day H 154

Saint Vincent, one of the Windward Islands in the Caribbean Sea, a member of the West Indies Associated States and self-governing within the Commonwealth of Nations. Its capital is Kingstown, where a new airport and the deep-water harbor have encouraged tourism.
    Caribbean Sea and islands C 118

Saint Vitus's dance see Vitus, Saint

Saipan (sy-PAN), volcanic island in western Pacific, largest of Marianas chain and the first in the chain to be colonized by Japanese. The island was an important Japanese military air base during World War II and was taken in battle by United States (1944). Garapan is the capital of Saipan District in the United States Trust Territory of the Pacific Islands (since 1962).
    World War II, campaigns of W 302

Saïs (SAY-is), ancient Egyptian capital E 102
Sakhalin, island off Siberian coast I 436
Saki see Munro, Hector Hugh
Sakis (SA-kis), monkeys M 422
Sakkara (sa-KA-ra), or **Saqqara**, Egypt, site of Step
    Pyramid E 95, 96

Saladin (SAL-a-din), Yūsuf ibn-Ayyūb (1138–1193), Muslim sultan of Egypt and Syria, b. Tikrit (now part of Iraq). Believing that the Holy Land had been wrongfully seized by the Crusaders, he attacked Palestine (1187) and captured Jerusalem. After the Third Crusade, a peace treaty was signed (1192).
    end of Latin Kingdom of Jerusalem C 540; R 292
    Muslim rulers of Egypt E 92

Salal, Abdullah al- (1917–   ), Yemeni army officer and statesman. He was governor of Hodeida, Yemen (Sana) (1959–62), and chief of staff to Imam Mohammed (1962). In 1962 he led military coup d'etat, establishing republican regime and becoming premier and commander in chief. He was president of the republic (1962–67).

Salamanders, land-water animals F 473–76
    blind, cave dwellers C 157; picture C 158
    locomotion, picture A 291
Salamis, battle of, 480 B.C. X 339
Salamis, island, in Aegean Sea I 436
Salaries, pay for work done, origin of the word F 333
    salt as wages S 20
    salt money M 411
    women's and men's compared W 212a
Salas (SA-los), **Antonio**, Ecuadorian painter L 67
Salazar (sa-la-ZAR), **Antonio de Oliveira**, Portuguese
    premier P 403, 404
Salazar Bridge, Lisbon, Portugal B 398
Salem, capital of Oregon O 204
Salem, Massachusetts M 145

Salem, Peter (1750?–1816), American Revolutionary fighter, Negro. A former slave, he fought at Lexington and Concord. At Bunker Hill, he fired the shot that killed Major John Pitcairn, commander of the British.
    Negro history N 91

Salem Maritime Historic Site, in Massachusetts M 144

Salem Village, Massachusetts
    witch hunt W 209
Salerno (suh-LER-no), Italy
    medical center in the Middle Ages M 204
    World War II W 297
Sales and Marketing Executive International Club J 158
Salesmen S 116–17
    book sales conferences B 334
    consumer education C 494
    See also Selling
Sales personnel (per-son-NEL) S 117
Sales tax T 26

Salic law, rule preventing inheritance of lands and titles through the female line. It was taken from early Germanic law. The French cited the salic law in the 1300's to keep England's Edward III from inheriting the French throne through his mother, Isabella. The French Bourbons and some other European rulers followed this law.

Saline conversion see Water desalting
Saline Water, Office of (O.S.W.) W 56a
Salinger (SAL-in-ger), **J. D.**, American writer A 214
Salinity (sa-LIN-ity), of ocean water O 30–31
Salisbury (SALLS-bury), capital of Rhodesia R 229; picture R 228
Salisbury, England, picture U 72
Salisbury, Maryland M 125
Saliva (sa-LY-va) B 274
Salivary (SAL-iv-ary) **glands** D 201
    of insects I 270
Salk, Jonas E., American doctor S 18–19
    killed-virus vaccines V 260
    polio described D 204
Salk Institute for Biological Studies, La Jolla, Calif. S 19
Sallust (SAL-lust), Roman historian L 79
Salmon (SAM-on), fish F 189, 199–200
    catch in British Columbia, picture B 406b
    eggs, picture E 88
    fish ladders D 20; picture O 197
    habitat, feeding habits, uses F 215
    king salmon, state fish of Alaska A 135
    migration H 189–90
    rhythm in animal life, the salmon run, picture L 244
    Salmon Area Indians of North America I 180
    salmon fishing industry F 220
Salmon River, Idaho I 54
Salmonella, bacteria F 354

Salome (sa-LO-me) (A.D. 14?–62?), daughter of Herod Philip and Herodias. In the New Testament (Mark 6:22–28), Salome, at her mother's urging, danced for Herod Antipas and as a reward demanded the head of John the Baptist. Salome was subject of a poem by Oscar Wilde and an opera by Richard Strauss. Salome was also the name of the mother of the apostles James and John.
    John the Baptist's death J 122

Salome (SAL-o-may), opera by Richard Strauss O 153
Salomon, Haym, Polish-born American financier S 19
Salonika (sal-o-NI-ka), Greece G 331
Salons (sa-LONS), meetings of notable people at the
    home of a prominent person
    French literature F 437
SALT see Strategic Arms Limitation Talks
Salt, common S 19–21
    aluminum damaged by A 177
    Atlantic Ocean content A 478
    body chemistry B 289
    Colombia's Zipaquirá mine C 382
    crystals C 542; picture C 541
    "curing" of meat in brine F 349

diets, low-salt, or salt free **N** 218
dust contains salt crystals **D** 347
Ethiopia **E** 300
food seasoning and preservation **F** 333
Great Salt Flats, Colombia, picture **G** 100
heart disorders **H** 86c
How do we get salt? **S** 20
melting point of ice, effect on **I** 4
money, early form of **M** 410–11
ocean water **E** 16
salt lakes and inland seas **L** 25
salt-producing regions of North America **N** 294
soap-making process **D** 147
superstition about **S** 474–75
table salt, a product of ionization **C** 203
taste, one of the senses of **B** 286
water desalting **W** 56, 56a, 67, 68
world's largest deposit in Dominican Republic **D** 282
Salt-box houses **C** 389
Saltcellar, sculptured by Benvenuto Cellini **D** 77; picture **D** 74
Salt domes, geologic formations **S** 20
landforms of Louisiana **L** 351, 359
oil often found in **P** 170

Salten (ZALT-en), **Felix** (pseudonym of Felix Salzman) (1869–1945), Austrian writer, b. Budapest, Hungary. Although he wrote plays, essays, and criticisms, he is famous for his sensitive book *Bambi,* about a fawn. Among Salten's books are *Bambi's Son* and *Good Comrades.*

Salt Island, Virgin Islands, British **C** 118
See also Virgin Islands, British
Salt Lake City, capital of Utah **S** 22; **U** 251
Mormons **M** 457
Temple Square, picture **U** 253
Young, Brigham **Y** 353
Salt lakes **L** 25
desert regions **D** 124
Salt licks, salt deposits used by animals **S** 21
Salto (SOL-to), Uruguay **U** 238
Salton Sea, salty lake in southern California **L** 33
California's Imperial Valley **C** 17
recreation area near Los Angeles **L** 347
Saltpeter, potassium or sodium nitrate used in making black powder, an explosive **E** 389
iodine source **I** 349
Kentucky deposits **K** 218
Salt River Project, Arizona's conservation plan **A** 407
Salts, chemical compounds **C** 220
iodine and other halogens **I** 349
marine life depends on phosphates and nitrates **L** 232
Salvador (sol-va-DOR) (Bahia), Brazil's first capital **B** 378; picture **B** 381
Salvage, saving or rescuing property
pneumatic devices to raise sunken ships **P** 348
recycling of solid wastes **S** 34
See also Flotsam, jetsam, and lagan
Salvage logging, of lumber **L** 373
Salvarsan, drug **D** 327

Salvation Army, an international charitable and religious organization serving the physical, spiritual, and emotional needs of mankind. Founded in England in 1865 and in the United States in 1880, it has U.S. headquarters in New York, N.Y. Its publications, all weeklies, are: *The War Cry, Young Soldier,* and *Stridsropet* (Swedish).
See also Booth family

Salween (sal-WEEN) **River,** Asia **R** 247
Burma **B** 456

Salzburg (ZALTZ-burk), Austria, picture **A** 519
Salzburg Festival, Germany **M** 550
SAM, surface-to-air anti-aircraft missiles **M** 347

Samaritan, person who helps someone in distress. In New Testament (Luke 10:29–37), Jesus tells the parable of the Good Samaritan who rescues and takes care of a man who has been robbed, beaten, and left on the road to die. Samaritans were a Hebrew religious sect that separated from the mainstream of Judaism about 720 B.C. Their independent existence ended about A.D. 529.

Samarium (sa-MAIR-ium), element **E** 155, 164
Samarkand (sa-mar-KONT), Union of Soviet Socialist Republics
rug sellers and their wares, picture **U** 47
Tomb of Tamerlane, picture **A** 458
Uzbekistan **U** 46
Samba, Brazilian dance music **L** 74
Samoa (sa-MO-a), islands in South Pacific **S** 23–27

Samoset (SAM-o-set) (?–1654?), Indian brave who was a loyal friend of the Pilgrims at Plymouth and helped colonists settle in Maine. Having learned some English from fishermen in the area, he greeted the Pilgrims with the words "Welcome Englishmen." He introduced the Pilgrims to Massasoit, chief of the Wampanoags. Before Samoset's death, he deeded 1,000 acres to Englishmen.
Plymouth Colony, history of **P** 345

Samothrace, Victory of see Winged Victory
Samovars, Russian urns for making tea **T** 37
Samoyeds (sam-o-YEDS), or Nentsi, a people of the Arctic region **P** 365
Samp, corn dish of colonial America **C** 390
Sampans, Chinese boat-homes **H** 203; picture **H** 204
Samplers, embroidery pieces **E** 187
Sampling, a small part for inspection or analysis in statistics **S** 418
population groups chosen as samples for opinion surveys **O** 159
Sampson, William T., American admiral **S** 375

Samson, in Old Testament (Judges 13–16), son of Manoah of the tribe of Dan. The source of his great strength was his long hair. When Delilah cut his hair, the Philistines, the enemies of his people, seized Samson, blinded him, and chained him to the pillars of the temple of Dagon, their god. As Samson's hair grew, his strength returned, and he pulled down the temple with his hands.

Samson et Dalila (son-SON ay da-li-LA), opera by Camille Saint-Saëns **O** 153
Samuel I and II, books of Bible, Old Testament **B** 154
Samuel Book, The, Yiddish poem **Y** 350
Samuel ibn Nagrela see Ha-nagid, Shmuel

Samurai (SA-mu-ry), believed to derive from Japanese verb *saburau,* meaning "to attend the (feudal) lord". The Samurai were the military aristocracy of old Japan. Before the Restoration (1868), they were either men of arms in the service of a feudal lord or guards of the Imperial Palace. Having power of life or death over commoners, they were privileged to wear two swords. On the abolition of the feudal system in 1871, they were allowed to appear without their swords; in 1876 they were forbidden to wear their swords in public.
feudal system in Japanese history **J** 45–46

Samurai doll, Japanese, picture **D** 264
Sana (sa-NA), capital of Yemen (Sana) **Y** 349; picture **Y** 348

San Andreas fault, California   G 117
San Antonio, Texas   T 134
San Carlo alle Quattro Fontane (son CAR-lo ol-lay QUA-tro fon-TA-nay), church in Rome, picture   A 383
San Carlos de Bariloche (CAR-los day ba-ri-LO-chay), resort in Argentina   A 391; picture A 392
Sánchez-Vilella (SAN-chez vil-YAY-la), Roberto, governor of Puerto Rico   P 523
Sancho Panza, character in *Don Quixote*   D 285, 286

Sanctions, international, coercive measures directed against a nation that has violated international law. Usually adopted by several nations together in the hope of forcing the offender to cease, sanctions may include withholding loans, or limiting trade relations.
  economic sanctions against Rhodesia   R 230

Sancy (son-CE) diamond, history of   D 156
Sand   S 231
  ceramics   C 174
  quartz sand   Q 6
  quicksand   Q 18–19
Sand, George, French novelist   F 440–41

Sandalwood, heartwood of a small evergreen tree native to southern Asia. The sweet-scented wood yields a fragrant oil used in perfumes and cosmetics. The wood is also used for ornamental carving and cabinetwork. The sawdust is used in incense.

Sandbars, or tombolos   M 137
Sandburg, Carl, American poet   S 27–29
  American literature   A 209
  poem "Chicago," excerpt   C 227
  poems "Fog" and "Lost"   S 29
  Rootabaga Stories, selection   S 29
Sand casting, of metals   M 230
Sand dollars, echinoderms   S 404
Sand dunes
  fences against erosion, picture   E 281
  national monument areas, pictures   C 411, I 147
Sandglass, or hourglass   W 44–45
Sand Hills area, Nebraska   N 74
Sandhogs, workers in tunnels   T 318
San Diego (di-A-go), California   C 27
Sanding, of wood
  furniture-making   F 503, 504; picture F 502
Sandino, Augusto César, Nicaraguan general   N 249
Sandoz, Mari, American writer   N 85
Sand paintings, Indian art   I 156; picture I 157
Sandpaper, coated abrasive
  grinding and polishing   G 387, 388, 389

Sandpiper, any one of a group of medium-size shore birds. Sandpipers breed in cold regions. In late summer and autumn they migrate in large flocks to warm climates. Picture   B 218.
  birds of the ocean shore   B 221

Sandstone, rock   R 266; pictures R 267
  quartz in building stone   Q 6
  types of stone   S 433
Sandstone Rocks, Bay of Fundy, Canada   N 138d; picture N 138a
Sand verbenas (ver-BE-nas), flowers, picture   W 169

Sandwich, 4th earl of (John Montagu) (1718–1792), English politician, b. London. As first lord of the admiralty (1748, 1763, 1777–82), he led an administration notorious for bribery, corruption, and inefficiency. He is said to have invented the sandwich to save time eating while gambling. The Sandwich Islands (now Hawaiian Islands) were named for him by Captain Cook.
  foods, name origins   F 335

Sandwiches
  Danish *smorrebrod*   F 342
  origin of name   F 335;   N 4
Sandwich glass, first made in Massachusetts   A 319
Sandwich Islands see Hawaii
Saneyev, Viktor, Russian track star, picture   O 116
San Francisco (fran-CIS-co), California   S 30–31
  cities of California   C 26–27
  Fisherman's Wharf, picture   C 24
  gold discoveries   G 250
  rock music   R 262d
  Telegraph Hill, picture   C 27
San Francisco Conference, 1945 see United Nations Conference on International Organization
San Francisco Xavier University, Bolivia   B 303
Sangallo, Antonio, Italian architect   I 467
Sangam, India, center for World Association of Girl Guides and Girl Scouts   G 214
San Giorgio Maggiore Island, Venice, picture   I 426
Sango, language   C 169
Sanhedrin (san-HE-drin), Jewish council   J 110
San Ildefonso (il-de-FON-so), Treaty of, 1800   L 365
Sanitation, a branch of public health   S 32–34
  ancient Rome's water and sewer systems   M 204
  camping   C 45–46
  disease, prevention of   D 220–21
  environment, problems of   E 272g
  restaurants   R 187
  sanitary engineers   E 205
  water pollution   W 58–59
San Jacinto (ja-CIN-to), battle of, 1836   M 238
San Joaquin (wa-KEEN) River, California   C 16, 19
San José (ho-SAY), capital of Costa Rica   C 516

San Juan (son HUAN), capital of Puerto Rico   P 522; pictures   P 516, 518, 519
  hotel, picture   H 257
  Latin America's resort cities, picture   L 60

San Juan Capistrano (san wan ca-pi-STRA-no), Franciscan mission founded (1776) in California by Father Junípero Serra. It was named for St. John of Capistrano, the Crusader. Completed in 1806, it was wrecked by an earthquake 6 years later. Swallows have built nests in the ruins. According to tradition, they leave the mission on St. John's Day (October 23) and return on St. Joseph's Day (March 19). The swallows have been late only once.

San Juan Hill, battle of, 1898   S 375
San Juan National Forest, Colorado, picture   N 37
San Juan River, Utah, picture   R 238
Sankey, Ira D., American gospel song writer   H 313
San Marcos (son MAR-cos), University of, Peru   P 160
  library   L 198
San Marino (san ma-RI-no)   S 35–36
  ancient fortress, picture   F 375
  flag   F 240
San Martín (son mar-TEEN), José de, Argentine general   S 36
  flag   F 227
  O'Higgins and San Martín   O 59
San Men dam, China, foundations, picture   D 18
Sannazaro (sa-na-ZA-ro), Jacopo, Italian writer   I 477
San Pedro Sula, Honduras   H 197
San Pietro (son p'YET-ro) in Montorio (moan-TO-rio), Rome   I 467; picture I 464

San (SON) River, Poland P 359
Sansa, or thumb-piano, African musical instrument
A 79
San Salvador, capital of El Salvador E 183; pictures
E 180, 184
San Salvador, or Watling Island, Bahamas B 16
Sans culottes (son cu-LOTT), French revolutionaries
C 352

Sanskrit, literary language considered to be the parent
of most modern Indic languages. It came from an
unknown old Indic dialect closely related to the language
of the Vedas. Sanskrit was the language of educated
people in India about the 4th century B.C.
Hindu drama uses Sanskrit D 293
Indo-European family of languages L 303
Oriental literature O 220, 220e

Sans serif, without serifs, type T 345
Sansovino, Jacopo (Jacopo Tatti), Italian architect I 467
Santa Ana, El Salvador E 183
Santa Anna, Antonio López de, Mexican general M 238
Santa Barbara Kennel Club D 261
Santa Claus (Saint Nicholas)
Christmas customs C 292; pictures C 293
See also Nicholas, Saint
Santa Cruz (SON-ta CROOZ), Andrés, Bolivian general
and president (1829–39) B 306

Santa Cruz Islands, volcanic group, part of British Solomon Islands Protectorate in southwestern Pacific, administered by Western Pacific High Commission. The
largest island is Ndeni, and the main export is copra.
During World War II the islands were site of important
U. S. naval victory, in battle of Santa Cruz (1942).

Santa Fe (SAN-ta FAY), capital of New Mexico N 192
Santa Fe Trail O 257–59
Arrow Rock Tavern M 377
beginnings in Missouri M 374
New Mexico N 188, 194
Post Office Oak in Council Grove, Kansas K 186
Santa Isabel, capital of Equatorial Guinea E 274
Presidential Palace, picture E 273
Santa Lucia Day, Sweden H 156
Santamaría, Juan, national hero of Costa Rica C 519
Santa Maria, ship of Christopher Columbus C 417;
E 376; picture E 374
Sant'Ambrogio (sant'om-BRO-gio) Church, Milan, picture
I 460

Santana, Manuel (1938–   ), Spanish tennis player, b.
Madrid. He has won a number of European tennis championships and in 1965 became the first Spaniard to win
the men's singles championship of the United States. He
also played on the first Spanish team to reach the
Davis Cup Challenge Round (1965), won by Australia.

Santander (sont-on-DARE), Francisco de Paula, first president of New Granada (now Colombia) C 384
Sant'Apollinare in Classe (sont'a-pol-le-NA-ray een CLA-
say), church in Ravenna, Italy, picture A 370
Santa Sophia see Hagia Sophia

Santayana (son-ta-YA-na), George (1863–1952), American
poet and philosopher, b. Madrid, Spain. He went to the
United States (1872), graduated from Harvard (1886),
and taught philosophy there (1889–1912). His many
books include The Sense of Beauty, The Last Puritan,
The Life of Reason, Three Philosophical Poets, and
Scepticism and Animal Faith.
quoted on human history H 138

Santee (san-TEE), or Sioux, Indians of North America
I 167
Santee River, South Carolina S 298

Santiago (son-ti-OG-o), Spanish name of Saint James the
Great, patron saint of Spain. According to legend, the
apostle preached in Spain for 6 years and was beheaded
by King Herod when he returned to Jerusalem. His
followers carried his body back to Spain and buried it at
the site of the present city of Santiago, Spain.

Santiago, capital of Chile C 253; picture L 54
housing project, picture S 284
National Technical University Library, picture C 251
Santiago de Cuba, Cuba C 548, 549
Sant'Ignazio (sont'een-YOTS-yo) Church, Rome B 59
Santo Domingo (SANT-o do-MIN-go), capital of Domini-
can Republic D 280; picture D 282
Santo Domingo, University of, Dominican Republic
oldest in North America N 297
Santos (SON-tos), Brazil B 379
Santos, Eduardo, president of Colombia C 380
San Vitale (son vi-TA-lay) church, Ravenna, Italy
Byzantine art in, pictures B 484
Sao, ancient people of Chad C 183
São Francisco (sown frun-CI-scu) River, Brazil R 247;
S 276
São Paulo (POW-loo), Brazil S 37–38
central east section of Brazil B 378–79
skyscrapers, picture S 284
waterpower in South America S 281

São Tomé (sahn to-MAY) and Príncipe (PREEN-si-pe)
Islands (pop. 70,000), Portuguese overseas province (372
sq. mi.) of volcanic origin off the western coast of Africa
in Gulf of Guinea. The islands are administered by
Portuguese Ministry of Overseas Provinces through an
appointed resident governor. The capital is São Tomé.
Among important exports are cacao, coffee, and coconuts.
Portuguese overseas territories P 401

Sap, of plants M 86–87; T 280
Sapodilla (sap-o-DIL-la), a tropical fruit M 74
Sapphires (SAPH-ires), gemstones G 71

Sappho (SAPH-o) (612?–565? B.C.), Greek lyric poet, b.
Lesbos. She gathered around her girls who shared her
interest in music and poetry. Many of her poems were
addressed to certain of the girls. First called the 10th
muse by Plato, she is quoted in works of many ancient
authors. Only papyrus fragments of her poems remain.
poets and writers of ancient Greece A 229; G 350
Sapporo, city, Japan
Winter Olympics, 1972 O 116a

Sapwood, of trees T 280
how tree rings are formed T 286
What is wood? W 222–23
woody stems of plants P 290
Saqqara (sa-KA-ra), or Sakkara, Egypt, site of Step Pyramid E 95, 96

Saracens, originally a name given by medieval writers to
the people of the deserts lying between Syria and Arabia.
The word came to be applied to all Arabs. At the time
of the Crusades (in the 11th, 12th, and 13th centuries),
the name "Saracen" included all Muslims.

Sarah, wife of Abraham A 7
Sarah Constant, ship, carried colonists to America A 183
Jamestown colony J 20
Sarajevo (sa-ra-YAY-vo), Yugoslavia Y 357

Saran (sa-RAN), man-made fiber **N** 425

Sarasate (sa-ra-SA-tay), **Pablo de** (Pablo Martín Melitón Sarasate y Navascuez) (1844–1908), Spanish violinist and composer, b. Pamplona. A famous violin virtuoso, he toured widely in Europe and America.

Sarashina, Lady, Japanese diarist **O** 220c
Saratoga (sa-ra-TO-ga), **battle of,** 1777 **B** 101–02; **W** 40
Saratoga, New York
  Revolutionary War **R** 204
Sarawak (sa-RA-wok), a state of Malaysia **M** 53–56
  political makeup of Borneo **B** 336, 338

Sarazen, Gene (1902–), American golf champion, b. Harrison, N.Y. At the age of 20, he won the U.S. Open and the PGA championships. He secured the Open again in 1932 and the PGA in 1922, 1923, and 1933.

Sarcasm, harsh irony **H** 281
Sarcomas (sar-CO-mas), cancers **C** 90
Sarcophagi (sar-COPH-a-guy), burial chests **S** 96
  ancient Crete, picture **A** 227
  Civil War unknowns in Arlington **N** 29
  Italian sculpture **I** 458
Sard, chalcedony quartz **Q** 7
Sardana (sar-DA-na), folk dance **F** 299
Sardines, fish **F** 220
  trapping the young herring, picture **N** 138f
Sardinia (sar-DIN-ia), island, west of Italy **I** 436
  winery, picture **E** 327
Sardonyx (sar-DON-ix), chalcedony quartz **Q** 7
Sardou (sar-DOO), **Victorien,** French dramatist **D** 297
Sargasso (sar-GASS-o) **Sea,** part of Atlantic Ocean **A** 478
  eel spawning grounds **E** 86, 87; **F** 199
  special environment for marine life **L** 229, 231
Sargassum (sar-GASS-um), seaweeds **L** 229
Sargent, John Singer, American painter **S** 38
  United States, art of **U** 121

Sargent, Sir Malcolm (Harold Malcolm Watts-Sargent), (1895–1967), British conductor, b. Stamford, Lincolnshire. Known especially for his concerts of popular music and for his lectures and performances for children, he also conducted the BBC Symphony Orchestra (1950–57) and toured the United States and Canada as conductor of the Royal Philharmonic (1963). Sir Malcolm was associated with most of the major choral societies of England.

Sari, outer garment of Hindu women, picture **D** 264
Sarmiento (sarm-YEN-to), **Domingo F.,** writer and president of Argentina **A** 390, 393, 396
Sarnia, Ontario, Canada **O** 121

Sarnoff, David (1891–1971), American radio and television executive, b. Uzlian, Russia. Starting as a telegraph operator with the Marconi Company (1908), he became RCA general manager (1917), and president (1930–49). He promoted experimental work in television. He was chairman of the board of RCA from 1947 until 1970.

Saro, South American giant otter **O** 241
Sarong (sa-RONG), island dress **C** 351
Saroyan (sa-ROY-an), **William,** American writer **A** 214
Sarrette (sar-RETT), **Bernard,** French bandmaster **B** 39

Sarto, Andrea del (Andrea Domenico d'Agnolo di Francesco) (1486–1531), Italian painter, b. Florence. His paintings reflect international influence: Michelangelo's drawing, Venetian color, Dürer's line quality. Among his most famous works are the frescoes in church of Sant' Annunziata, Florence.

Sartre, Jean-Paul, French author **F** 442
Saskatchewan (sas-KAT-che-wan), Canada **S** 38a–38h
  leading wheat producer **C** 58
  North American landforms, picture **N** 283
Saskatchewan, University of **S** 38d
Saskatchewan River, Canada **R** 247
  Hudson Bay Basin of Canada **C** 52
  Prairie Provinces **M** 76; **S** 38c
Saskatoon (sas-ka-TOON), Saskatchewan, Canada **S** 38g
Sassafras, tree **P** 314; picture **T** 277
  leaves, shapes of, pictures **L** 116
Sassoon, Siegfried, English poet
  "Everyone Sang", poem **F** 120
Satan see Devil

Satellite, in political usage, refers to a nation controlled by, or dependent upon, another nation.

Satellites (SAT-ell-ites) **P** 269
  Mars' satellites **M** 107, 108
  moon **M** 446–56
  planets' satellites **S** 245
Satellites, man-made **S** 39–43
  communication advanced by **C** 440
  communications satellites **T** 59, 60, 67
  Echo I, balloon satellite **B** 34
  IGY studies, picture **I** 314
  Intelsat (International Telecommunications Satellite Consortium) **E** 142e–142f
  meteorological satellites **W** 85–87
  navigation, uses in **N** 68, 69; **O** 18
  orbiting observatories **E** 29–30; **O** 14
  photographic spies **S** 389
  radiation belts, probes **R** 46–47
  rocket engines as launch vehicles **R** 255
  spacecraft, assembling and launching of **S** 342–43
  space stations and Skylab **S** 342–43; picture **G** 325
  Tiros weather satellites **H** 296
Satie (sa-TE), **Erik,** French composer **F** 447–48
Satin stitch, in embroidery **E** 189
Satin weave, of fabrics **T** 143–44
Satire, a form of humor **H** 280
  American literature **A** 196, 208
  Cervantes Saavedra, Miguel de **C** 176
  English literature **E** 256, 257–58, 260, 267
  Gulliver's Travels **E** 258
  Swift, Jonathan **S** 488

Sato, Eisaku (1901–), Japanese statesman, b. Tabuse, Japan. For many years he served as an official in the ministry of transport, becoming chief of its bureau of control in 1941. He was vice minister of transportation from 1947 to 1948, and was elected to parliament (the first of four times) in 1949. In the 1950's and 1960's he served in a series of important cabinet posts, including minister of finance and minister of trade and industry. When Prime Minister Ikeda resigned in 1964, Sato took over the position. Sato's Liberal Democratic Party was returned to power in the national elections of 1967 and 1969. Sato resigned in 1972.

Saturation temperature, or dew point **F** 288
  cloud formation **C** 358
Saturday, origin of name **D** 47
Saturn, planet **P** 276–77
  atmosphere **A** 479
Saturn V, rocket launcher **S** 339, 340d, 340j; pictures **M** 454; **S** 340a
  workshop in space **S** 343
Saturn, Roman god **G** 356

Saud (sa-OOD) (Saud ibn Abdul Aziz ibn Abdul Rahman al

Faisal al Saud) (1902–69), king of Saudi Arabia (1953–64), b. Kuwait. Proving himself to be a competent ruler of several provinces as a prince, he was named successor to the throne (1933). He became king in 1953, and was deposed by his half brother, Faisal, in 1964.

Savage, Augusta Christine (1910–1962), American sculptress, Negro, b. West Palm Beach, Fla. Known for her studies of Negro heads, she was one of four women to do work for the New York World's Fair (1939–40). Her contribution, *Lift Every Voice and Sing,* was a tribute to Negro music. At a one-man show in New York (1939), *The Martyr* and *Woman of Martinique* were displayed. She was the director of the Harlem Community Art Center.

Savang Vatthana (sa-VANG vath-AN-a), **Sri** (1907–   ), king of Laos, b. Luang Prabang. Having gained practical political experience by heading the delegation to the Arbitration Commission (1947) and the Japanese Peace Treaty Conference (1951), he succeeded his father, Sisavang Vong, as king in 1959.

Savonarola (sa-vo-na-RO-la), **Girolamo** (1452–1498), Italian reformer, b. Ferrara. He became a Dominican friar and, in fiery sermons, denounced the corruption of the Church and the government. He went to Florence (1489), where, as prior of San Marco, he became the city's most influential figure. Excommunicated by Pope Alexander VI, he continued to preach until his arrest (1498). After many weeks of torture, he was put to death for heresy.

Sawyer, Ruth (1880–   ), American author, b. Boston, Mass. She took up professional storytelling (1908) and collected folk tales from many countries. *Roller Skates,* a children's book based on her own experience, won the Newbery medal (1937). Other books include *The Way of the Storyteller* and *Year of Jubilo.*

Sayers, Frances Clarke (1897–   ), American librarian and author, b. Topeka, Kans. She served (1941–52) as superintendent of work with children at the New York Public Library. A leading authority in the field of children's literature, she has taught at several library schools and has been in great demand as a writer and speaker. She has published books for children, including *Bluebonnets for Lucinda* and *Tag-Along Tooloo,* and *Summoned by Books: Essays and Speeches.*

Scales, leaves **L** 118
Scales, of animals
    butterflies and moths **B** 468
    fishes **F** 185
    sharks, skates, and rays **S** 142
Scales, sucking insects **P** 289; picture **P** 288
    spread fungi **P** 286
Scallions (SCAL-ions), onions **O** 118
Scallops (SCA-lops), mollusks **O** 273–74
    fishing industry **F** 221
Scan, in poetry, to find where accent falls **P** 353–54
Scandinavia (scan-din-A-via), region in northern Europe
    S 49
    emigration to Minnesota **M** 327
    favorite foods **F** 341
    northwestern uplands of Europe **E** 307–08
    tapestry, art of **T** 24
    welfare programs, pioneers in **W** 121
    See also Denmark; Norway; Sweden
Scandinavian literature S 50–53
    Norse mythology **N** 277–81
Scandium, element **E** 155, 164
Scapa Flow, fleet base on the Orkney Islands **I** 435

Scapegoat, person, group, or thing that receives punishment for a whole group. The term comes from the Old Testament (Leviticus 16), in which Aaron was told to present a goat before the Lord as a scapegoat, putting all the wrongdoings of the children of Israel upon the goat's head and letting it carry them off into the wilderness.

Scarabs, beetles
    Egyptian amulet, picture **J** 95
Scarborough (SCAR-bor-o), Tobago, picture **T** 290
Scarlatina (scar-la-TI-na), disease **D** 205, 207
Scarlatti (scar-LA-ti), **Alessandro,** Italian composer
    B 63, 65; **I** 484
Scarlatti, Domenico, Italian composer and harpsichordist
    B 66
    opera **O** 131
Scarlet fever, disease **D** 205, 207
    causal bacteria, picture **D** 188
Scarlet Letter, The, novel by Nathaniel Hawthorne
    A 201–202
    fiction, development of **F** 111
Scarlet tanagers, birds, picture **B** 240
Scarves
    knitting directions **K** 284
Scauri, Italy
    nuclear power plant, picture **N** 353
Scenery, of plays **P** 339
Scenic designers, of plays **T** 157–58
Scents, of animals
    ants lay scent trails **A** 324
    butterflies and moths **B** 469–70
    skunks **O** 241
Schaefer, Vincent J., American scientist **W** 92
Scheele (SHAY-le), **Karl W.,** Swedish chemist **T** 308
Scheherazade (sheh-hae-ra-ZA-de), heroine of Arabian
    Nights **A** 345
Scheidt, Samuel, German composer **G** 182
Schein, Johann Hermann, German composer **G** 182
Scheldt (SKELDT) **River,** Europe **R** 247
Scherzo (SKERT-so), a musical form **M** 538
    introduced by Beethoven **M** 541
Scheville, W. E. and **Barbara Lawrence,** American scientists **D** 274, 275
Schiaparelli (sc'ya-pa-REL-li), **Giovanni,** Italian astronomer **M** 104

Schick, Bela (1877–1967), American pediatrician, b. Hun-

gary. He came to the United States in 1923. Best-known for the skin test (**Schick test**) he perfected in Vienna (1913) that determines whether or not a person is susceptible to diphtheria, he also did important research in scarlet fever and other diseases.

Schick Gutiérrez, René, Nicaraguan political leader **N** 249

Schiele (SHE-leh), **Egon** (1890–1918), Austrian painter, b. Tulln. Along with Oskar Kokoschka, he was a leader of expressionist art in Vienna. A master of the decorative in art, he did many nature studies and self-portraits. Among his works are *Boy in a Striped Shirt, The Artist's Mother Asleep,* and *Sunflowers.*

Schiller (SHIL-ler), **Johann Christoph Friedrich von,** German poet and dramatist **G** 176
    romanticism in drama **D** 297
Schipperke (SKIP-per-ke), tailless dog **D** 261; picture
    D 260

Schirra, Walter Marty, Jr. (1923–), American astronaut, b. Hackensack, N.J. Schirra, a former Navy fighter pilot, flight instructor, and test pilot, took part in the Mercury 8 (1962), Gemini 6 (1965), and Apollo 7 (1968) space flights. In 1968 he retired from the space program.
    space flight data **S** 344, 345, 347

Schirrmann, Richard, German founder of hosteling
    H 253
Schisms (SIZ-ums), within the church
    Great Schism or Eastern Schism **O** 228
    Western Schism, Great, two popes **F** 415; **R** 293
Schist (SHIST), metamorphic rock **R** 269
Schizophrenia (skitz-o-PHRE-nia), form of mental illness
    M 224
Schizophyta, division of plant kingdom **P** 292
Schleiden, Matthias, German scientist **S** 73
Schlesinger (SLES-in-ger), **Arthur M., Jr.,** American historian **A** 214
Schley (SLY), **Winfield S.,** American commodore
    S 375
Schlieffen (SHLE-fen), **Alfred von,** German general
    W 272–73
Schliemann (SHLE-monn), **Heinrich,** German businessman and archeologist **S** 53–54
    archeological discoveries, picture **A** 350
    excavated site of ancient Troy **T** 293

Schmidt, Augusto Frederico (1906–1965), Brazilian poet and politician, b. Rio de Janeiro. Of great influence in Brazil's progress as well as its intellectual and political life, he founded a publishing house to print the works of new authors in the early 1930's and wrote nationalistic newspaper columns and a book of poems, *Song of the Brazilian.* In 1959, as special presidential representative, he presented a plan for United States aid to South America from which the Alliance for Progress has adopted several ideas.
    Brazilian writers **B** 377

Schmidt, Bernhardt, German astronomer **T** 63
Schmidt telescope T 63
Schmitt, Harrison H., American astronaut **S** 345, 347
Schnauzer (SHNOUT-zer), dog, picture **D** 255
Schnitzler (SHNITZ-ler), **Arthur,** Austrian writer **D** 298
Schoenberg (SHERN-berk), **Arnold,** Austrian-born American composer **S** 55; picture **G** 188
    chamber music **C** 186; **G** 189
    choral music **C** 279
    modern music **M** 400
    opera **O** 138

Scholarships, financial awards given to qualified students to be used for tuition, board, and books. Scholarships are given by schools, colleges, and universities, as well as by public and private institutions and organizations.

Scholastic-aptitude tests T 117–18
  examination for college entrance E 348–49

Schomburg, Arthur A. (1874–1938), American bibliophile, Negro, b. San Juan, Puerto Rico. He began his collection of books on Negro history before he came to the United States (1891). He was curator of the Negro Libraries at Fisk University until 1926, when he left to become curator of his own collection, which the Carnegie Foundation bought and gave to the New York Public Library. The Schomburg Collection of Negro Literature and History in New York is one of the most important centers in the world for the study of the Negro. It is located at 103 West 135th Street, New York, New York.

Schönberg, Arnold see Schoenberg, Arnold
School boards E 74
School books see Textbooks
School buildings S 58; pictures S 56, 57
  materials and methods in education E 79
School buses B 466
Schoolcraft, Henry Rowe, American explorer and specialist in Indian cultures
  discovered source of Mississippi River M 333
  writings provided legends for Longfellow's *Song of Hiawatha* M 258
School districts E 74
  independent unit of municipal government M 504
School for Scandal, The, by Sheridan E 257
Schooling, a form of group behavior
  fishes F 201–02
School libraries L 175–76
  history of the movement L 200
School nurses N 410
School of Athens, The, painting by Raphael R 168
School Partnership Program, project of the Peace Corps P 103
Schools S 55–58
  colleges E 72–73; U 205–24
  colonial America C 392, 394; picture C 391
  education, history of E 61–71
  education in America and around the world E 71–84
  elementary schools E 69–71; S 58
  high schools E 72; S 58
  intermediate, or middle, schools S 58
  junior high schools E 73–74; S 58
  kindergarten and nursery schools K 242–47
  land grants for schools P 506–07
  libraries L 175–76, 200
  parent-teacher associations P 66–67
  parochial schools E 75
  physical education programs P 226
  private schools E 74–75
  programed instruction P 475, 477
  public schools E 70–71; S 55–58
  public schools (independent schools), United Kingdom U 67
  safety measures S 5
  secondary schools E 72; S 58
  teachers T 40–44
  textbooks T 138–39
  vocational schools E 72; S 58
  See also Education; Universities and Colleges; education section of country, province, state, and city articles
Schools, of fish A 280; F 201–02

Schooner, sailboat, picture S 9

Schopenhauer (SHO-pen-how-er), **Arthur** (1788–1860), German philosopher, b. Danzig. His principal work is *The World as Will and Idea.* He was a philosopher of pessimism.

Schubert (SHU-bert), **Franz,** Austrian composer and songwriter S 58
  chamber music C 186
  choral music C 278
  classical age, compositions of C 330, 333
  romantic music G 186
  Symphony in C Major, its heavenly length M 541
Schulmeister, Karl, famous spy S 389
Schulz (SHULTZ), **Charles,** American cartoonist, creator of *Peanuts* C 128
Schulze (SHUL-tza), **Johann Heinrich,** German doctor P 210
Schuman (shu-MON), **Robert,** French statesman E 334
Schumann (SHU-monn), **Clara,** pianist, and wife of Robert Schumann, picture G 186
Schumann, Robert, German composer S 59; picture G 186
  influence on Brahms B 362
  piano miniatures G 186

Schumann-Heink (SHU-man HYNK), **Ernestine** (1861–1936), Austrian-American opera singer (contralto), b. Lieben, near Prague. She made her operatic debut in 1878 at Dresden. Specializing in Wagnerian roles, she made her American debut in Chicago (1898); the following year she became a member of the Metropolitan Opera Company in New York. She sang some 150 roles.

Schurz (SHOORTZ), **Carl** (1829–1906), American statesman and journalist, b. Liblar, Germany. He settled in Wisconsin, where his wife, the former Margarethe Meyer, established the first U.S. kindergarten (1856). He was U.S. minister to Spain (1861–62). An ardent abolitionist, he returned to fight in the Civil War. He served as senator from Missouri (1869–75) and secretary of the interior (1877–81). After 1881 he lived in New York.
  early conservation efforts C 484–85

Schurz, Margarethe, wife of Carl Schurz K 244
Schuss (SHUSS), to ski fast S 187
Schütz (SHURTZ), **Heinrich,** German composer B 64; G 182
  choral music C 278

Schuyler (SKY-ler), **George Samuel** (1895–   ), American writer, Negro, b. Providence, R.I. He joined the editorial staff of the Pittsburgh *Courier* in 1924 and has written for a number of other publications. He is the author of *Black-No-More* and *Slaves Today.*

Schuyler, Philip John (1733–1804), American soldier and statesman, b. Albany, N.Y. Son of a prominent colonial family, he served (1755–60) in the French and Indian War. He was a member of the Continental Congress (1779–80). During the Revolutionary War, he was court-martialed for negligence at the battle of Ticonderoga but was acquitted (1778). He was one of the first two U.S. senators from New York (1789–91, 1797–98).

Schwa, vowel sound P 478
Schwabe (SHVA-ba), **H. S.,** German astronomer A 476
Schwagalp, Switzerland, picture S 501
Schwalbe, Louis, English chemist N 427
Schwann (SHVONN), **Theodor,** German physiologist
  cell theory in biology B 193; S 73

Schwartz, I. I., Yiddish author **Y** 351

Schwarzkopf, Elisabeth (1915–), German soprano, b. Jarocin, near Poznan (now in Poland). She has appeared at La Scala in Milan and Covent Garden in London and has been a member of the Vienna State Opera. She is popular as both an operatic singer and a recitalist.

Schweickert, Russell L., American astronaut **S** 347
Schweitzer (SHVY-tzer), **Albert,** French medical missionary, philosopher, and musician **S** 59
  hospital in Lambaréné, Gabon **G** 3

Schwenkfelders (SHVENK-fel-ters), followers of the German religious reformer Kaspar Schwenkfeld (1489–1561). Persecuted by both Protestants and Catholics, Schwenkfeld's followers fled Silesia (1720). One group emigrated to Philadelphia, Pa. (1734), where they formed a community. Their descendants live in eastern Pennsylvania and maintain their own churches.

Schwitters (SHVITT-ers), **Kurt,** German artist
  M 394
  Merzbild mit Regenbogen, painting **M** 396b
Science
  experiments and projects **E** 350–67
  invention and science **I** 348
  museums **M** 512, 519
  Nobel prizes **N** 264–66, 268–69
  philosophy and science **P** 191–92
  science and society **S** 77–82
  technology and science **T** 45–46
Science, history of **S** 60–76
  astronomy, history of **A** 470–77
  Bacon, Roger, insistence on need for experiment **B** 8
  biology **B** 187–96
  chemistry, history of **C** 205–16
  evolution **E** 338–47
  fire and early science **F** 144
  Galileo **G** 5–7
  geology and geophysics **G** 109–21
  language growth with scientific terms **W** 241
  mathematics **M** 154–68
  Newton's laws of motion **M** 469–71
  nuclear energy, research in **N** 352–71
  Pasteur and the germ theory of disease **P** 95–97
  physics **P** 230–39
  Priestley, Joseph **P** 455–56
  relativity **R** 139–44
  science and society **S** 77–82
  technology **T** 45–46
  See also names of scientists; headings beginning with
    the word Scientific
Science and society **S** 77–82
  technology advances civilization **T** 46

Science Clubs of America, international youth organization founded in 1942 and administered by Science Service, with headquarters in Washington, D.C. The organization sponsors an annual International Science Fair and Science Talent Search. Science Clubs of America seeks to assist young people who are interested in scientific research.

Science fairs **E** 355
Science fiction **S** 83–85
  Verne, Jules **V** 322
  Wells, H. G. **W** 124
Scientific instruments
  inventions **I** 346
Scientific method **S** 79–82
  a four-step process **R** 139–40
  basic research **R** 182–83

  contributions of Bacon **S** 67–68
  experiments and projects **E** 350–67
Scientific research see Research, scientific
Scientific revolution **S** 67–68
Scilly (SILLY) **Islands,** southwest of England **I** 436
Scintillation (sin-til-LATION) **counters,** instruments to
    detect radiation **U** 231
  atomic research **A** 489
Scion (SY-on), tree bud **O** 178
Scipio Africanus (SIP-io af-ri-CAY-nus), the Elder, Roman
    general **P** 533
  spies used in the Punic Wars **S** 388
Scissor-tailed flycatcher, bird
  Oklahoma, state bird of **O** 81
SCLC see Southern Christian Leadership Conference
Scolosaurs, dinosaurs **D** 180
Scoop, type of dredge **D** 308
Scooters, amphibious iceboats **I** 29

Scopes, John (1900–1970), American teacher of biology, b. Paducah, Ky. In 1925 in Dayton, Tenn., he was the defendant in the famous "monkey trial." Scopes was charged with having violated a Tennessee law that prohibited the teaching of evolution because it contradicted the teachings of the Bible. He was defended by Clarence Darrow, a famous attorney, and the trial aroused the interest of the entire nation. Although Scopes was found guilty, the verdict was upset on a technicality.
  Scopes and William Jennings Bryan **B** 416

Score, in music **M** 534
  orchestra conducting **O** 189
Scoria (SCO-ria), lava rock **R** 264
  North Dakota source of clinker rock **N** 326
Scorpion, constellation see Scorpius
Scorpion fishes **F** 202
Scorpions, arachnids **S** 387–88
  compared to insects, picture **I** 263
  harmful to man **I** 284
Scorpius, constellation **C** 493; sign of, picture **S** 245
Scotch Cup Event, world curling championship **C** 555
Scotch drum **D** 335
Scotch pine, tree
  leaves, needlelike, picture **L** 119
Scotland **S** 86–89
  ancient Scottish prayer **P** 435
  Bruce, Robert **B** 414
  costumes, traditional Scottish, pictures **C** 350
  curling, origin of game **C** 554–55
  dances **D** 29
  golf popularized in **G** 254, 260–61
  holidays **H** 147, 156, 159
  kilts **C** 352; picture **C** 350
  tam-o'-shanter, cap, picture **H** 53
  See also United Kingdom of Great Britain and Northern Ireland
Scotland Yard, London **L** 337–38
  military intelligence division **S** 390
  police **P** 373

Scott, Barbara Ann (1928–), Canadian skater, b. Ottawa. She won the North American Figure Skating Championship (1945) and at 19 took the three top titles in her sport—the European, Olympic, and world championships. Her European score was the highest ever awarded, and she and Dick Button were the first skaters from North America to win the European championships. She turned professional in 1948.

Scott, David R., American astronaut **S** 344, 345, 347
Scott, Dred, American slave **D** 310–11
  events leading to the Civil War **C** 320

time **T** 187–94
Why is it hotter in summer than in winter? **S** 109
yearly rhythms in plant and animal life **L** 244
See also Climate; articles on individual months
Sea squirts, sea animals **P** 281

Seat belts, heavy belts buckled around passengers to protect them from being thrown from a moving vehicle. First used in airplanes, they were adopted by automobile industry in 1956. Safety experts recommend them as a means of greatly reducing fatalities and injuries. For extra protection, shoulder harnesses (or belts) are used in combination with seat belts. The U.S. Government requires that all automobiles manufactured after 1967 be equipped with shoulder harnesses as well as seat belts.
National Traffic and Motor Vehicle Safety Act, 1966
A 550

SEATO see Southeast Asia Treaty Organization
Seattle (se-AT-tel), Indian chief **W** 27
Seattle, Washington **S** 112–13
Mount Rainier in the distance, picture **W** 27
Seattle's Century 21 Exposition, 1962 **F** 17
Sea urchins, echinoderms **S** 404; **O** 39
Seawater O 30
common salt **S** 20
magnesium in **M** 23
water desalting **W** 56, 56a
Seaway, or **seastate,** ocean waves caused by wind **O** 34
Seaweeds, marine plants **O** 38; **L** 229
best-known algae **A** 157
Seawolf, United States nuclear submarine **S** 444
Seb see Geb, Egyptian god

Sebastian, Saint, Roman martyr. According to legend, he was an officer in the imperial guard who was shot with arrows (A.D. 286) when he was discovered to be a Christian.

Sebring (SE-bring), Florida, sports-car race, pictures
A 538, 539
SEC see Securities and Exchange Commission
Secession, in United States history
Civil War issue **C** 321, 327
Confederate States **C** 458
Davis, Jefferson **D** 45
Johnson, Andrew opposes **J** 124
Lincoln, Abraham **L** 295
newspaper report, picture **C** 321
states' rights in the 10th amendment to the Constitution **B** 179
Tyler president of Peace Conference, 1861 **T** 342
Second, measure of time **W** 112, 116
Secondary schools see High schools; Schools
Second Republic, France **F** 417
Seconds, in duels **D** 340
Second World War, The, memoirs of Sir Winston Churchill **C** 298

Secord (SE-cord), **Laura Ingersoll** (1775–1868), Canadian loyalist, b. Great Barrington, Mass. She moved to Canada with her parents and later married James Secord. In 1813, when American troops were quartered in her house at Queenston, Canada, she learned of American plans for a surprise attack on Beaver Dams. Making her way through American lines, she walked 20 miles to warn the British at Beaver Dams.

Secretariat (sec-re-TAIR-iat), United Nations **U** 84–85
Secretaries, cabinet officers for the U.S. president
P 447–48
flags **F** 230

Secret Army Organization (OAS), in Algeria **A** 163
Secretary birds B 226; picture **B** 227
Secret ballot E 114–15
Secretions, of the glands **B** 279
Secret police P 374
Secret Service, United States S 390
major federal investigative agencies **F** 76
Secret writing, with codes and ciphers **C** 369–71
shorthand used as **S** 164
Sects, or denominations, in religion
Christianity, history of **C** 288–89
Protestantism **P** 483–85
Securities, certificates, as stocks and bonds **S** 427
Securities and Exchange Commission, United States
F 76
checks on a depression **D** 122
New York Stock Exchange **S** 430
regulating agencies in interstate commerce **I** 332
Security Council, United Nations U 83
UN membership recommendations **U** 82
Sedan (se-DAN), **battle of,** 1870 **B** 102
Sedatives, drugs **D** 326
abuse of **D** 330
Seddon, Richard, New Zealand statesman **N** 243
Seder (SAY-der), of Passover **P** 93
Easter **E** 41

Sedgman, Frank (Francis Arthur Sedgman) (1927–), Australian tennis champion, b. Mont Albert, Victoria. He was the men's singles champion in Australia (1949–50), the United States (1951–52) and England (1952). In 1951, with Kenneth McGregor, he won the Australian, French, English, and American doubles titles, a record for winning all four in 1 year. In 1953 he turned professional.

Sedimentary rocks R 266–68
classification of **R** 263
contrast with glacial till, picture **I** 15
earth's history told in **E** 20–21
evidence of ancient life, fossils **E** 340, 342; **F** 378, 380
geologists' study of earth's changes **G** 117
mountain formation **E** 10, 11; **M** 493
petroleum deposits **P** 169
theory of origin **G** 111
Sedimentation, in geology
formation of rocks **E** 20
water purification **W** 68

Sedition, language or conduct tending to upset the authority of a government or disturb the public order. Sedition, unlike treason, does not aim at direct, open violence or betrayal; but it is considered a step toward treason. Offenses that are regarded as seditious today were originally punishable as treason. Some countries have tried to prevent sedition by law.

Sedition Acts see Alien and Sedition Acts
See, Elliot M., Jr., American astronaut **S** 347
See, seat of a bishop's power **R** 289
See also references, in indexes and catalogs **I** 115
Seebeck (ZAY-beck), **Thomas,** German physicist **P** 426
Seebeck effect, principle of the thermocouple **P** 426–27
Seed drills, machines for sowing seed **F** 58
Seeders, farm machinery **F** 58; picture **F** 56
Seedless grapes G 297
Seed piece, of potatoes **P** 412
Seeds F 280–83; **P** 296–97
adaptations to insects **L** 221
agriculture, planting methods in **A** 96
cotton bolls **C** 519, 524; picture **C** 520
differences in sizes and shapes, pictures **P** 298

Seeds (continued)
   distributed by animal and plant life
      L 233–34
   fig   **F** 117
   garden planting   **G** 30, 39–41
   grapes and berries   **G** 297–301
   grasses   **G** 316–17
   interesting ways of producing seeds   **P** 319–20
   lawn seeding   **L** 90
   Mendel crossbreeds to prove genetic theories   **G** 80–81
   nuts   **N** 419–24
   photosynthesis, role in   **P** 223
   poisonous plants   **P** 322–23
   trees   **T** 279, 284
   weeds   **W** 106
   See also Flowers; Wildflowers

Seeger, Pete (Peter Seeger) (1919–), American folk singer and composer, b. New York, N.Y. Seeger left Harvard in his sophomore year (1938), supporting himself by doing odd jobs. He hitchhiked all over the U.S., picking up songs and banjo techniques. In 1948 Seeger joined the Weavers, a popular singing group, but left them in 1957 to go on his own. Equally popular as a solo performer, Seeger involves his audience in his songs until they all sing along with him. He tours extensively, has made many recordings, and exerts a great influence on younger American folk singers.

Seeing Eye, Inc., school for dog-guides for the blind
      B 253
   working dog breeds   **D** 259
See references, in indexes and library catalogs
      I 114–15
Sefroui, Ahmed, Moroccan writer   **A** 76d
Seggars, or **saggers,** in ceramics   **C** 175
Seghers, Hercules, Dutch artist   **G** 305
Segmented worms   **W** 309
   centipedes and millipedes   **C** 167–68
Sego (SE-go) lilies
   Utah, state flower of   **U** 241

Segovia (se-GO-via), **Andres** (1893–   ), Spanish classical guitarist, b. Linares. He began to play the guitar as a child and gave his first concert (1909) in Granada. A Paris recital (1924) made him world-famous. Segovia established the guitar as an important concert instrument. Composers Manuel Ponce, Turina, and Albert Roussel among others have written music especially for him.
   Spanish music   **S** 373

Segovia, Spain
   The Alcazar, medieval castle, picture   **S** 359

Segrè (SAY-gray), **Emilio Gino** (1905–), American physicist, b. Tivoli, Italy. He played a major part in the discovery of two artificial elements, technetium and astatine. His greatest achievement was in 1955, when with Owen Chamberlain he discovered the antiproton, a particle that has the same mass as a proton but an opposite charge. Segrè and Chamberlain shared the 1959 Nobel prize in physics.

Segregation   **S** 113–15
   education   **E** 82
   Negro struggles against   **N** 100–05
   separate-but-equal precedents set by Supreme Court rulings   **N** 96
Seigneurial (se-NEUR-ial) **system,** in New France, early Canada   **C** 69
Seigneurs, landowners in New France, early Canada
      C 69;   **Q** 9

Seine (SEN) **River,** France   **R** 247; picture   **F** 403
   bridges, picture   **B** 396
   houseboats, picture   **H** 176
   Paris   **P** 69
Seines (SAINS), fishing nets   **F** 217, 218
Sei Shonagon, Lady, Japanese diarist   **O** 220c
Seismic (SIZE-mic) **shooting,** man-made earthquakes
      I 316, 319
Seismic waves, of earthquakes   **E** 32–33
   how scientists learn about the earth's interior   **E** 8
Seismographs (SIZE-mo-graphs), instruments for recording earthquakes   **E** 37–39
   early Chinese earthquake detector, picture   **G** 118
   petroleum prospecting, tool for   **P** 171
   recording vibrations inside the earth   **E** 8
Seismology (size-MOL-ogy), study of earthquakes   **E** 31
   geophysicists picture earth's interior   **G** 119
Seismometers, instruments to detect vibrations   **E** 37
   left on the moon   **M** 451;   **S** 340a, 340i
Seistan (saist-ON), wind, of Asia   **A** 452

Seitz (ZITES), **Frederick** (1911–), American physicist, b. San Francisco, Calif. His major work has been the study of crystals, but he also took part in the development of the atomic bomb. He served on the governing board of the American Institute of Physics (1954–59) and in 1962 became president of the National Academy of Sciences. Since 1968 he has been president of Rockefeller University.

Sekani, Indians of North America   **I** 170
Sekondi-Takoradi, Ghana   **G** 196
Selassie, Sahle, Ethiopian writer   **A** 76b
Selassie, Walda, Ethiopian writer   **A** 76b
Selective cutting, of lumber   **L** 373
Selective Service Act, 1917, draft law   **D** 289
Selective Service System, U.S.   **D** 290
Selectmen, governing body of towns   **M** 504
Selenga (sel-en-GA), river in Mongolia   **M** 414
Selenium (se-LE-nium), element   **E** 155, 164
   glass decolorized by   **G** 226
Seleucids, Hellenistic dynasty of Syria   **J** 81
Self, The, psychology   **M** 220–22
Self-contained underwater breathing apparatus see Scuba diving
Self-defense
   judo   **J** 146–47
   karate   **K** 194

Self-determination, principle that nations have a right to determine their own sovereignty and government. It also involves the right of inhabitants to decide to which of two or more states their territory should belong.
   United Nations policies   **U** 88
   Wilson's policy in the League of Nations   **W** 283

Self-employment   **L** 2, 11
Self-instructional materials see Programed instruction

Self-pollination, process in which the female part of a flower receives pollen produced by the male part of the same plant. The pollen is transferred from the male to the female part mainly by wind, insects, or gravity.
   flowers and seeds   **F** 277

Self Portrait, drawing by Leonardo da Vinci   **L** 153
Self Portrait, painting by Dürer   **R** 170
Self-protection, adaptations for, in biology   **L** 217–20
Self-service markets   **S** 468
Seljuks, Turkish tribes   **T** 328
   Crusades against   **E** 370

Selkirk, Alexander (1676–1721), British sailor, b. Largo,

Scotland. The original Robinson Crusoe, he left his ship (1704) after quarreling with his captain and lived on the uninhabited island of Más a Tierra in the Juan Fernández group. He was rescued (1709) and returned to England (1711). Defoe's *Robinson Crusoe* (1719) is based on his story.

Chile, landforms of **C** 251

Selkirk, Manitoba **M** 81
Selkirk, Thomas Douglas, 5th earl of, Scottish colonizer in Canada **C** 72
  established colony in Manitoba **M** 76, 82
  first settlement in North Dakota **N** 336—37
Selkirk Colony, Manitoba, Canada **M** 76, 82
Selkirk Mountains, Canada **C** 67

Sellers, Peter (Richard Henry Sellers) (1925—), English actor, b. Southsea. Born into a theatrical family, he had a natural talent for mimicry that won him fame on radio and TV and in films. *The Mouse That Roared* brought him popularity in the United States. He received the British Film Academy award (1959) for *I'm All Right, Jack.* His other films include *Dr. Strangelove; or, How I Learned to Stop Worrying and Love the Bomb.*

Selling S 116—17
  advertising **A** 27—34
  commercial art **C** 424—27
  consumer education **C** 494
  jobs in retail stores **R** 189
  Junior Achievement, Inc., student business **J** 157—58
  mail order **M** 31
  women, role of **W** 212
  See also Advertising; Opinion surveys
Selling short, on the stock exchange **S** 432

Selsam, Millicent (1912—), writer of children's books, b. New York City. She has taught biology in New York schools and in Brooklyn College and is well known for her books about nature. Titles include *How to Be a Nature Detective, Greg's Microscope,* and *Tony's Birds.*

Selva, rain forest of Brazil **B** 380—81
Sem, son of Noah *see* Shem
Semantics (se-MAN-tics), science of meanings **S** 117—18

Semaphore, device for sending messages. A semaphore telegraph is a post with two pivoted arms at the top. Letters and numerals are shown by the placement of the arms. Similar semaphores are used as traffic and railroad signals. Two-color semaphore flags, held in different positions, are used by the United States Navy.
  ways of sending messages before radio and telegraph **R** 84—85; **T** 50

Sembene, Ousmane *see* Ousmane, Sembene
Semicolons, punctuation marks **P** 531
Semiconductors, of electricity
  use in transistors to replace electron tubes **E** 148
Semimetals, elements **E** 159
  properties of borderline elements or metalloids **M** 226
Seminole (SEM-in-ole), Indians of North America **F** 259, 273
  Osceola **O** 232
Seminole War, 1835—42 **F** 273
  Indian wars **I** 213
  Osceola **O** 232
  Taylor, Zachary **T** 34
Semiprecious gemstones J 93
Semisynthetic materials
  antibiotics **A** 313
  dyeing of fibers **D** 370

Semites, a people of southwest Asia
  ancient civilizations **A** 218
Semitic (sem-IT-ic) **languages L** 39
  Hebrew **H** 100—01
  in historical linguistics **L** 303
  spoken in Africa **A** 55
  spoken in Asia **A** 460
Semi-trailers T 296—97
Semmelweis (ZEM-mel-vice), **Ignaz,** Hungarian doctor **M** 208
Semolina (sem-o-LI-na), wheat product **W** 156
  grain products **G** 282
Semper Fidelis, Marine Corps motto and march **U** 182
Semple, Letitia, acting first lady in Tyler's administration **F** 169
Senanayake, Dudley, prime minister of Ceylon **C** 180
Senate, Canadian C 76—77
Senate, United States *see* United States Senate
Senate War Investigating Committee (Truman Committee) **T** 299

Sendak, Maurice (1928—), American author and illustrator, b. Brooklyn, N.Y. Marcel Aymé's *Wonderful Farm* was the first children's book he illustrated, and *Kenny's Window* was the first one he wrote and illustrated. *Where the Wild Things Are* won the Caldecott medal (1964), and a number of his books have been runners-up.
  In the Night Kitchen, pictures from **B** 310a

Seneca, Indians of North America **I** 184
Seneca, Lake, New York **L** 28
Seneca, Lucius Annaeus, Roman philosopher **L** 80
Seneca Falls Woman's Rights Convention, 1848 **W** 212b
Seneca Trail W 133
Senefelder (ZANE-ef-el-der), **Aloys,** German inventor of lithography **L** 314
  printing, history of **P** 461
  techniques of the graphic arts **G** 308
Senegal (sen-e-GALL) **S** 119—20
  costume doll, picture **D** 267
  flag **F** 236
  Gambia, The, an enclave of **G** 8
Senegal River, west Africa
  Guinea **G** 404
  Mauritania **M** 179

Senghor (SENG-or), **Léopold Sédar** (1906—), Senegalese writer and politician, b. Joal. Around 1935 he started to write poems and essays about the Africans' longing for their own cultural identification, such as *Chantes d'Ombre.* Elected to the French National Assembly (1946—58) and to the General Council of Senegal (since 1946), he was the leader of the Federal Assembly of the Mali Federation of Senegal and Sudan (1959—60). He has been president of the Republic of Senegal since 1960.
  African literature **A** 76c
  Senegal, history of **S** 120

Senior Girl Scouts G 216, 218; picture **G** 213
Seniority, principle of job security for labor **L** 16—17
Senna (legume), or cassia plant **P** 314
  seeds, picture **P** 298

Sennacherib (sen-NACK-er-ib) (?—681 B.C.), king of Assyria (705—681 B.C.) and son of Sargon II. Most of his reign was spent in military campaigns to enlarge and protect his empire. He exacted tribute from Jerusalem and destroyed many cities, including Babylon (689 B.C.). During his reign, canals and aqueducts were built, and at Nineveh, his capital, he constructed a vast and splendid palace. He was murdered by one of his sons.

Sequoia (se-QUOI-a), giant California evergreen, among the oldest and largest of living things. There are two kinds: redwoods, growing in the coastal fog belt north into Oregon, and Big Trees (giant sequoias), found only in the Sierra Nevada mountains. Redwoods are sometimes over 350 feet tall and provide decay-resistant wood prized by builders. Laws forbid cutting the rarer Big Trees, which may be more than 20 feet thick near the base. Pictures   C 487, T 276.

Seraphim (Hebrew plural of *seraph*), angels who guard the throne of God along with cherubim. The Old Testament (Isaiah 6) describes them as having six wings: one pair to cover their eyes, one pair to cover their feet, and one pair for flying.

Seredy (SHER-edy), **Kate** (1899–   ), American illustrator and author, b. Budapest, Hungary. She served as a war nurse during World War I while studying art in Budapest. After going to the United States (1922), she could find only odd jobs in illustrating. Encouraged to write of her youth in Hungary, she wrote *The Good Master.* She won the Newbery medal (1938) for *The White Stag.*

Serkin, Rudolf (1903–   ), American pianist, b. Eger, Bohemia. He appeared frequently in recital with violinist Adolf Busch. With Busch he made his American debut in Washington, D.C., and has since played with most of the major orchestras in Europe and America. He has given numerous recitals and taught master classes, and is well-known as a chamber music performer.

Service, Robert William (1874–1958), Canadian writer, b. Preston, England. After settling on Vancouver Island (about 1897), he wrote ballads and novels of the Yukon, such as "The Shooting of Dan McGrew."

Service, tennis stroke **T** 95
Service industries and occupations **S** 124–25
  hotels, special features **H** 258
  women, role of **W** 212
  work, the world of **W** 252
Service module (SM), section of Apollo spacecraft **S** 339,
  340a; pictures **M** 454; **S** 340b, 340c
Servomotors (SER-vo-mo-tors), automated devices **A** 530
Sesames (SES-am-ese), herbs **S** 382

Sesame Street, television show produced by Children's
Television Workshop on National Educational Television
network. First presented November 1969, and conceived
for the culturally disadvantaged and inner-city child, it
teaches children about themselves and their world.
  television programs **T** 71; pictures **T** 70c, 70d

Sestet, last six lines of a sonnet **S** 255
Set, Egyptian god **M** 560
Set, in tennis **T** 98
Set designers, of plays **T** 157–58
  Petrouchka set, by Benois, picture **U** 56
  standard sets, pictures **P** 337, 338

Seton (SE-ton), **Mother** (Blessed Elizabeth Ann Bayley
Seton) (1774–1821), American philanthropist, b. New
York, N.Y. She founded (1797) the Society for the Relief
of Poor Widows with Small Children, the first charitable
organization in New York. Founder and first mother superior of the Roman Catholic Sisters of Charity (1809),
she was responsible for the opening in Philadelphia of
the first free parochial school in the United States. She
was beatified on March 17, 1963.

Sets, in mathematics **S** 126–27
  algebra **A** 159
  set theory and the new math **M** 160–61, 163–64
Sets, scenery for plays, pictures **P** 337, 338
Setters, sporting dogs, pictures **D** 253
Setting, of novels **N** 345
Settlement, Act of, 1701, England **E** 225
Setúbal (se-TU-bal), Portugal **P** 401
Seumas Beg, poem by James Stephens **P** 355
Seurat (ser-RA), **Georges,** French painter **F** 431; **M** 387

Seuss (SOOS), **Dr.** (Theodor Seuss Geisel) (1904–),
American author-illustrator, b. Springfield, Mass. Origi-
nator of the Flit cartoons for Standard Oil Co., he pub-
lished his first children's book, *And To Think That I
Saw It on Mulberry Street,* in 1937. He was awarded the
Legion of Merit for his educational films during World
War II and an Academy Award for the films *Design for
Death* (1947) and *Gerald McBoing-Boing* (1951). *The
Cat in the Hat* (1957) started a new trend of books for
beginning readers.
  easy-to-read books for children **C** 243

Sevareid (SEV-are-ide), **Eric** (1912–), American broad-
caster and author, b. Velva, N. Dak. A commentator for
the Columbia Broadcasting System (since 1939), he has
written many articles and books, such as *Not So Wild a
Dream* and *This Is Eric Sevareid.*

Seven, Group of *see* Group of Seven
Seven, outer *see* European Free Trade Association
Seven bridges of Königsberg, topological problem
  T 220–21
Seven Cities of Cibola (CI-bo-la) **I** 192
Seven Days battles, 1862, Civil War **C** 323

Seven deadly sins, seven sins considered by early
Christians to be "deadly," causing the damnation of the

soul. The seven are pride, covetousness, lust, envy,
gluttony, anger, and sloth.

Seven seas, term now applied to the oceans of the
world, formerly to all the waters. In ancient times the
people of the Mediterranean lands knew only of seven
seas. The age of exploration brought knowledge of many
more bodies of water, and the term ceased to be used
for many centuries. But geographers found they were
able to divide the oceans into seven classifications,
which today are: Arctic, Antarctic, North and South
Atlantic, North and South Pacific, and Indian.

Seven Sisters *see* Pleiades
Seventeenth Amendment, to the United States Constitution **U** 143, 157

Seventh-Day Adventists, religious denomination that
observes the 7th day of the week as the Sabbath. The
group set up headquarters in Battle Creek, Mich., during
the 1850's.
  Nigerian clinic run by Seventh-Day Adventists, picture
  M 349

Seventh Day Baptists, Baptist groups that observe
Saturday as the Sabbath. One group of Seventh Day
Baptists is of English origin; the other, German. The
English group (originated 1617) organized a church in
Newport, R.I. (1671). The German Seventh Day Baptist
Church was founded in Ephrata, Pa. (1728).

Seventy, The *see* Septuagint, Bible
Seven wonders of the ancient world **W** 214–16
  See also each of the wonders by name
Seven Years War, 1756–1763 **G** 160
  Canadian history **C** 70, 79
  Frederick the Great **F** 456
  French and Indian War in North America **F** 462
  Pitt, William, Earl of Chatham directed England's war
    against France (French and Indian War) **P** 265
Severn River, United Kingdom **U** 69
  tidal bore **T** 185
Seversky, Alexander Procofieff de *see* De Seversky,
  Alexander Procofieff
Sevier (sev-IER), **John,** American statesman **T** 86

Sévigné (say-veen-YAY), **Marquise** (or Madame) **de** (Marie
de Rabutin-Chantal Sévigné) (1626–1696). French writer
and lady of fashion, b. Paris. Her correspondence with
her daughter, Comtesse de Grignan, who lived in
Provence, is one of the highlights of French literature.
The elegantly written letters tell of daily events in her
life in Paris or at her country estate in Brittany and convey
the inner climate of her age.

Seville (se-VILLE), Spain, picture **S** 358
Sèvres (SEVR) **porcelain** **P** 418; pictures **P** 416
  antiques, picture **A** 318
Sewage disposal
  ancient cities with sewers **A** 223
  ancient Rome's water and sewer systems **M** 204
  bacterial action **B** 13
  community helps in prevention of disease **D** 220
  detergent foam problem **D** 149
  environment, problems of **E** 272e
  fermentation **F** 91
  organic fertilizer **F** 96–97
  plumbing **P** 341–43
  water pollution **W** 58, 59
  See also Refuse and refuse disposal
Sewall, Samuel, American colonial judge **W** 209
  published a diary **A** 196

Seward, William Henry (1801–1872), American statesman, b. Florida, N.Y. Governor (1839–43) and senator (1849–61) from New York and Lincoln's secretary of state (1861–69), he opposed slavery and during the Civil War skillfully handled U.S.-European relations, notably the Trent Affair and the French intervention in Mexico. Seward also served under President Andrew Johnson, supporting reconstructionist policies, and in 1867 made the purchase of Alaska, then called "Seward's Folly."

    Alaska, history of **A** 143
    Lincoln and Seward **E** 186; **L** 295

Seward Peninsula, Alaska **A** 130, 135
Seward's Day, holiday **H** 148
Seward's Folly, purchase of Alaska **A** 143; **T** 112
Sewing **S** 128–29
    bookbinding methods **B** 327
    dressmaking **D** 311–15
    embroidery **E** 187–89
    invention of the sewing needle, key tool for the making of clothing **C** 348
    needles and pins **N** 88–89
    See also Embroidery
Sewing machines **C** 353, 356; picture **C** 357
    dressmaking **D** 311, 313
    Howe, Elias, inventor of **H** 271–72
    industrial design, example of, picture **I** 232
Sex
    adolescent awareness **A** 23
    animal communication between the sexes **A** 278
    reproduction **R** 176–80
Sextants, navigation instruments **N** 65
    optical instruments for navigation **O** 171
Sexual reproduction **R** 178–80
Seychelles (say-SHELLS), island group **I** 436–37
Seymour, Jane, third queen of Henry VIII of England **E** 220; **H** 109
Sfax, Tunisia **T** 310
Sfumato (sfu-MA-to), painting technique **P** 21
Sgraffito (sgraf-FI-to), a kind of decoration on pottery **P** 414
Shaabi, Qahtan al-, president of Yemen (Aden) **Y** 347
Shabuoth (sha-VU-ote), religious holiday **R** 154
Shackleton, Sir Ernest Henry, British explorer **P** 366
Shad, fish **F** 220
    habitat, feeding habits, uses **F** 215
Shade, color **D** 140
Shading, in drawing
    folk art **F** 291
Shadow clocks see Sundials
Shadow puppets **P** 535; picture **P** 534
Shadows
    caused by light traveling in straight lines **L** 260
    eclipses **E** 46–47
    guides to direction **D** 182–83
Shadows, The, plantation house, Louisiana, picture **L** 359
Shafter, William R., American general **S** 375
Shaftesbury, Anthony Ashley Cooper, English statesman **E** 224
Shaft mining, of coal, picture **C** 366
Shafts, in mines **M** 315
Shagbark hickory, tree, picture **T** 278
Shah, title of a ruler of Persia, or Iran **I** 377
Shahaptian, language of Nez Percé Indians of North America **I** 176

Shah Jahan (ja-HON) (1592–1666), Mogul emperor (1628–58). His reign was the high point of Mogul power and the golden age of Muslim architecture in India. He founded the modern city of Delhi (Hindu name, Shahjahanabad) and constructed such famous buildings as the Taj Mahal and the Pearl Mosque in Agra and the palace and Great Mosque in Delhi. A son of Jahangir, he was deposed (1658) by his son Aurangzeb and kept prisoner in the fort at Agra (1658–66). **I** 133

    Taj Mahal **T** 14

Shahn, Ben (1898–1969), American painter, b. Kaunas, Russia. In the 1930's his paintings were dominated by themes of social protest. He worked for the Farm Security Administration (1935–38) and did many murals in public buildings, such as the Social Security Building in Washington, D.C. The Museum of Modern Art selected his work as part of an exhibition to represent contemporary America at the 1954 Italian Biennale Exhibition of International Art.

    Triple Dip, print **G** 306

Shakers, popular name for members of "The United Society of Believers in Christ's Second Appearing." Shakerism began as a branch of the Quakers in the 1700's in England. Its members were called "Shaking Quakers" because they trembled during their worship. Ann Lee (1736–84), a leader of the Shakers, emigrated to New York (1774) and founded a colony (1776) near Albany in Watervliet, N.Y. The number of Shaker communities grew rapidly during the first half of the 19th century. Since then there has been a sharp decline; there are only a handful of members today. Shakers place a high value on celibacy.

Shaker Village, Concord, New Hampshire **N** 158
Shakespeare, William, English poet and dramatist **S** 130–37; picture **E** 252
    dominates Elizabethan drama **D** 296
    duels in literature **D** 341
    England, his description of **E** 212
    English literature, place in **E** 251–52
    Hamlet, tragedy **H** 20–21
    Macbeth, tragedy **M** 2–3
    Midsummer Night's Dream, A, comedy **M** 309
    nonsense verse and prose **N** 276
    Othello, tragedy **O** 236
    plot outlines of his plays **S** 133–37
    quotations from plays **Q** 20
    Romeo and Juliet, tragedy, excerpt **R** 317–18
    signature prized **A** 526; reproduced **A** 527
    sonnets **S** 256
    theater in England **T** 159–60
Shakespeare Memorial theaters
    American Shakespeare Festival Theater, Stratford, Connecticut **C** 477; picture **C** 479
    Royal Shakespeare Theatre, Stratford-on-Avon, England **T** 159
    Stratford Festival, Stratford, Ontario **C** 62–63; picture **O** 129
Shako, military hat, picture **H** 53
Shale, rock **R** 267
    ceramic clay **C** 174
Shallots (shall-OTS), plants of onion family **O** 118
Shalyapin, Feodor see Chaliapin, Feodor
Shamanism (SHA-man-ism), a primitive religion
    Ghost Dance of the North American Indian **I** 169
    Mongolia **M** 413
Shamma, Ethiopian dress **E** 296

Shamrock, cloverleaf symbol of Ireland, chosen because St. Patrick supposedly used it as an illustration of the Holy Trinity mystery. The usual shamrock is the common white clover, though other triple-leafed plants sometimes share the name. Finding a rare four-leafed shamrock is considered good luck.

    St. Patrick, legends about **P** 98

Shang (SHONG), or **Yin, dynasty,** second of the traditional dynasties of China (1523–1028 B.C.). Excavations at the site of the last Shang capital, near Anyang, have produced evidences of an advanced civilization with a highly developed written language. It was followed (1028 B.C.) by the Chou dynasty.

China, history of C 268–69
Oriental sculpture O 216
vase, picture A 360

Shanghai (shang-HY), China S 138–39; picture C 308a
Shangugu, Rwanda see Cyangugu
Shankara, Indian philosopher O 220e

Shankar, Ravi (1920–), Indian sitar-player and composer, b. Banaras. A dancer in his brother's troupe for about 10 years, he then studied the sitar. He was musical director of All-India Radio from 1949 to 1957. He has given concerts all over Europe and in the United States, and has made many records, playing either solo or accompanied by the tambura and tabla. Shankar has played with Yehudi Menuhin and also with the Beatles. In 1967–68 he taught Eastern Music at the City College of New York. Picture O 220d.

rock music R 262d

Shannon Free Airport Industrial Estate, Ireland I 389
Shannon River, Ireland R 247
rivers and lakes in Ireland I 388
Shantung, peninsula of China C 262
SHAPE see Supreme Headquarters, Allied Powers, Europe
Shapers and planers, tools T 218–19
preparing wood for furniture-making F 502
Shapiro (sha-PI-ro), **Karl,** American poet A 211

Shapley (SHAP-ley), **Harlow** (1885–), American astronomer, b. Nashville, Mo. From his study of star clusters and pulsating stars (Cepheid variables), he devised a more accurate method of measuring the distances of stars. Shapley's work demonstrated the vastness of our galaxy and showed that its center was in the constellation Sagittarius.

Shards, pottery bits found at archeological sites A 358

Sharecropper, farm worker who farms someone else's land in return for a share of the crop, often one half. The owner provides the tract of land, tools, stock, and often living quarters. The owner extends credit for fertilizer, processing, and bills for food and supplies. Sharecropping has been common in the American South.
farm life, one kind of F 49
Iraq, way of life in I 378

Sharett, Moshe (1894–1965), Israeli diplomat, b. Kherson, Russia. When he was 12, his family moved to Palestine (Israel). A student of law and economics, he became active in the Zionist movement. During Israel's struggle for independence, he represented his country in negotiations at the UN General Assembly. He was first minister for foreign affairs (1948–56), and he served as prime minister from 1953–55. He was chairman of the Jewish Agency from 1961 until his death.

Shari River see Chari River
Sharks S 140–43
habitat, feeding habits, uses F 214
How do sharks find their prey? S 143
largest fishes A 262–63
ocean scavengers O 38, 40
skin-divers in little danger S 191

Shark suckers, or remoras, fish F 203–04
curious ways animals move about A 266
Sharp, Becky, character in Thackeray's *Vanity Fair* T 145–46
Sharp, Granville, British abolitionist S 175
Sharpsburg (Antietam), **battle of,** 1862 C 324
Sharpshooters, experts at accurate shooting
American frontier riflemen, use of guns G 417
Sharp sign, in musical notation M 528
Shasta, Mount, California, pictures C 17, N 293, V 384
Shasta daisies, flowers, picture G 50
Burbank variety B 453
Shasta dam, California, picture D 17

Shastri (SHA-stri), **Shri Lal Bahadur** (1904–1966), Indian statesman, b. Mughalsarai. Chosen by the Congress Party to succeed Nehru as prime minister (June, 1964), he began his political career as a member of Gandhi's non-co-operation movement and the independence movement of the Indian National Congress. As general secretary (1951) for the Congress Party, he organized the first general election of independent India. He held various posts in the national cabinet (1952–63) and exercised skill in compromise and conciliation when he negotiated a political accord with Pakistani President Ayub Khan on the Kashmir dispute.

Shatalov, Vladimir A., Soviet cosmonaut S 344, 345
Shaw, George Bernard, Irish playwright S 144; picture E 267
leading English-language playwright E 267
realism in drama D 298
Shaw, Henry Wheeler, American humorist A 206
Shaw, T. E. see Lawrence, Thomas Edward (Lawrence of Arabia)
Shawn, musical instrument, picture M 548
Shawn, Ted, American dancer D 33
Shawnees (shaw-NEES), Indians of North America
Tippecanoe, battle of H 50

Shays' Rebellion, series of uprisings in western Massachusetts (1786–87) against the state government. The rebellion was named for Daniel Shays, one of the leaders. Unsettled conditions and economic depression following the Revolutionary War caused outbreaks against the legislature for not acting on the citizens' demands. The insurgents, finally routed by the militia, were pardoned.

Shazar, Zalman (Schneour Zalman Rubashov) (1889–), Israeli statesman and author, b. Mir, Russia. A member of the first, second, and third Knesset (Parliament), he helped establish the Jewish state. An author of articles and books on political, historical, and literary subjects and an editor of *Davar* (1938–48), a daily published by the Labor Zionist Movement, he helped write the declaration of independence of Israel. First minister of education and culture (1949–50), he became the head of the Jewish Agency Executive department of education and culture (1954–63). He was elected president of Israel in 1963 for a 5-year term, and was re-elected in 1968.

Shearer, Hugh Lawson (1923–), prime minister, Jamaica, West Indies, Negro, b. Hanover Parish, Jamaica. He was elected to the Jamaica House of Representatives (1955). His proposal to designate 1968 as Human Rights Year was accepted by the UN General Assembly. He was appointed minister of external affairs (1967) and chosen prime minister (1967).

Shearing, or clipping, fleece of sheep W 234–35

Shearwaters, birds H 188, 192
Sheba (SHE-ba), Queen of, Ethiopian princess E 302
  Solomon, visit to S 252
Sheboygan (she-BOY-gan), Wisconsin W 205
Shedlock, Marie, English lecturer and writer S 435

Sheen, Fulton John, Bishop (1895–   ), American Roman Catholic archbishop, b. El Paso, Ill. While teaching at Catholic University of America (1926–50), he gained a wide audience through his Sunday Catholic Hour broadcasts (1930–52) and his sermons at St. Patrick's Cathedral in New York (1930–52). The author of numerous books, he was named national director of the Society for the Propagation of the Faith (1950–66). He served as bishop of Rochester, N.Y. (1966–69). He is now titular archbishop of Newport, Wales.

Sheep S 145
  Australia's leading agricultural industry A 498, 507; picture A 506
  "follow the leader" social organization A 281
  hoofed mammals H 221
  livestock C 151; picture C 150
  mammal hair, picture M 64
  meat from sheep M 192
  ranching R 105; pictures A 506, P 433
  wild sheep and goats S 145; pictures H 218
  wool W 234–35
  world distribution W 264
Sheepshead, fish
  habitat, feeding habits, uses F 214
Sheepskin, slang word for college diploma C 431
Sheep sorrel, weed, picture W 105
Sheet bends, knots K 291
Sheet music
  rock music R 262a, 262b
Sheet erosion E 281
Sheet-fed gravure, printing P 460
Sheet-fed rotary presses, for printing P 462
Sheet glass G 236
Sheffield plate, silver-clad copper S 182
  antiques A 321
  knives, forks, and spoons K 287

Shehan, Lawrence Joseph, Cardinal (1898–   ), American Roman Catholic prelate, b. Baltimore, Md. The archbishop of Baltimore (since 1961), he was named cardinal by Pope Paul VI (1965). A leader in interfaith relations and racial integration, he was appointed by the Pope to the Vatican Secretariat for the Promotion of Christian Unity.

Sheikhs, leaders of Arabic tribes D 128
Shelby, Isaac, American statesman and soldier K 225
Shellac, a spirit varnish V 279
  lac resins R 184
Shellac wax W 69
Shelley, Mary Wollstonecraft, English writer S 146
  author of *Frankenstein* E 261
Shelley, Percy Bysshe, English poet S 146
  "Mutability," poem S 146
  "Ode to the West Wind," poem, excerpt O 52
  "Ozymandias," poem S 146
  romantic period in English poetry E 261
  "Widow Bird Sate Mourning for Her Love, A," poem S 146
Shellfish F 220–21, 224
  See also Crustacea; Mollusks
Shells, ammunition for guns G 426
Shells, of nuts N 419
Shells and shell collecting S 147–49
  age shown by shells, picture A 86

crustacea S 168–69
  jewelry I 224
  oysters and other mollusks O 271–76
  rhythmic design, picture D 134
  used as money M 411
  Why do you hear a roaring sound in shells? S 265
Shelter see Homes; Housing
Shelterbelts see Windbreaks
Shem, or Sem, son of Noah, ancestor of Semites H 100
Shema (SHE-ma), Judaic prayer J 116; P 434
Shenandoah (shen-and-O-ah) National Park, Virginia V 348, 353; picture V 355
Shenandoah Valley, Virginia V 347
Shenyang (SHUN-yong), or Mukden, China S 150
  borderland cities of China C 265

Shepard, Alan Bartlett, Jr. (1923–   ), American astronaut, b. East Derry, N.H. On May 5, 1961, Shepard made a suborbital flight in his Mercury capsule Freedom 7, becoming the first American to be launched into space. In 1971 he commanded the Apollo 14 mission and was the fifth man to walk on the moon. Before joining the space program, he was a Navy fighter pilot.
  space flight data S 344, 345, 347

Shepard, Ernest H., English illustrator
  drawing from *Winnie-the-Pooh* I 97
Shepherd dog (collie), picture D 255
Shepherd of the Hills Country, Missouri M 368
Sheptoon La-Pha, first king of Bhutan B 151
Sheraton, Thomas, English furniture designer F 507
  antiques A 318
Sherbets, frozen desserts I 34
Sherbrooke, Quebec, Canada Q 13
Sherbrooke, Université de, Quebec Q 10b
Sheridan, Richard Brinsley, English dramatist E 257
  Irish writers who gained fame in England I 393
Sheriffs, county officers P 375
Sherman, James S., vice-president, United States V 331; picture V 329
Sherman, Roger, American stateman C 466
Sherman, William Tecumseh, American general S 151
  Civil War campaigns S 326–27, 460
  march to the sea through Georgia G 147

Sherman Anti-Trust Act (1890), one of the first acts that dealt with the relation of American government to big business. It declared illegal every contract, combination, or conspiracy in restraint of interstate or foreign trade. The act was passed by Congress in reaction to the opposition to the growing number of industrial trusts that were being formed. The act was not successful until 1911, when it dissolved the American Tobacco Company and the Standard Oil Company.
  trust system in capitalism, need for reform, in Harrison's administration C 104; H 47; T 306

Sherman Monument, by Saint-Gaudens, picture U 115
Sherman Silver Purchase Act, 1890 C 342; H 47
Sherpas, a Mongolian people living near Mount Everest, Nepal N 111; picture G 103
  Tenzing Norkey, Sherpa mountain climber E 337
Sherry, wine
  aging casks, picture W 189
  exported from Jerez, Spain S 357
She Stoops to Conquer, play by Oliver Goldsmith, scene from D 296
Shetland Islands, northeast of Scotland I 437
Shickshock Mountains, Gaspé Peninsula, Quebec Q 10
Shields, armor, pictures A 435
  heraldic devices shown on shields H 116
Shield volcanoes V 383

Shigatse (shi-GA-tse), Tibet **T** 177
Shih Huang Ti (SHIR HWANG TI), Chinese emperor
    C 269–70
Shih tzu, dog, picture **D** 260
Shikoku (shi-KO-ku), island of Japan **J** 34
Shiloh (SHY-loh), **battle of,** 1862, Civil War **C** 323
    Grant, Ulysses **G** 295
Shiloh National Military Park T 84
Shinbone see Tibia
Shingles
    roofing a house, picture **B** 436
Shinto, or Shintoism, religion of Japan
    R 148–49
    Asia, chief religions of **A** 460
    gateway to a temple, picture **R** 151
    Japan, religion and way of life **J** 24–25, 31, 37
    marriage rites **W** 102
Shipjack, fish
    habitat, feeding habits, uses **F** 215
Ship models S 151–54
Ships and shipping S 155–61
    Canada **C** 61
    canals **C** 83–86
    capacity measured in tonnage **I** 337
    creation of industrial society in United States **U** 129
    Denmark's fleet **D** 111, 112
    grain loaded into a ship, picture **G** 287
    Greece's merchant navy **G** 337
    harbors and ports **H** 35–37
    icebergs a danger **I** 26–27
    insurance from Lloyd's of London **I** 296
    Japan, world leader in shipbuilding **J** 35
    lanterns **L** 281, picture **L** 282
    lighthouses and light ships **L** 275–78
    navigation **N** 62–69
    ocean liners **O** 17–24
    speed measured in knots **K** 289
    steam turbines **T** 320
    submarines **S** 442–46
    United States Merchant Marine **U** 182–84
    United States Navy, types of ships **U** 192
    Viking ships **V** 338; pictures **E** 275, 368, 369; **S** 152
    whaling ships **W** 152–53
    Why are ships christened with champagne? **S** 160
    Why are the left and right sides of a ship called port
      and starboard? **S** 155
    why boats float **F** 251
Ships of the line, British Navy **W** 11–12
Shipworms, or teredo worms **O** 273
Shipwrecks
    underwater archeology **U** 20–21
Shirazi (shi-RA-zi), original people of Zanzibar
    T 16
Shire horse, picture **H** 240
Shirer (SHY-rer), **William L.,** American writer **A** 214
Shire (SHI-ray) **River,** southeastern Africa
    Maawi **M** 50–51
Shires, or counties, in England **M** 503
Shirley Temple dolls D 268
Shish kebab (SHISH ke-bob), popular food **F** 335
    outdoor cooking and picnics **O** 248
Shmuel Ha-nagid see Ha-nagid, Shmuel
Shock
    electric shock **F** 162
    "playing 'possum," a state of shock **K** 171
    treatment for **F** 161

Shockley, William (1910–), British-American physicist
and inventor, b. London, England. Together with his co-
workers J. Bardeen and W. H. Brattain at the Bell Telephone Laboratories he became interested in the way certain types of crystals transmit electric current. These
investigations led to the invention of the transistor by
the three men in 1948. They shared the 1956 Nobel
prize in physics for this achievement. Picture **E** 147.
    transistors **T** 252

Shocks, of grain **F** 60
Shock waves, in physics
    aerodynamics of compressed air **A** 40
    vibrations of seismic waves of earthquakes **E** 9
    supersonic flight **S** 470

Shoemaker, Willie (William Lee Shoemaker) (1931–),
American jockey, b. near El Paso, Tex. He began riding in
1949 and was a frequent winner of Triple Crown races
(Kentucky Derby, Preakness, and Belmont
Stakes). Four
ft. 11 in. tall and weighing 98 lbs., he holds record for
number of winning races and amount of money won.

Shoemaker and the Elves, The, fairy tale by Grimm
    brothers **G** 377–78
Shoemakers
    at work in their guilds, picture **G** 402
Shoemaker statesman, Roger Sherman **C** 466
Shoes S 162–63
    bowling **B** 346
    leather **L** 107, 111
    Maine's industry began with tannin from hemlock trees
      M 39
    shoemaking industry in New Hampshire **N** 153
    track shoes **T** 236
Shofar (SHO-far), ram's horn **B** 429; **J** 120; picture
    J 117
Shoguns (SHO-guns), early Japanese military governors
    J 43

Sholes, Christopher Latham (1819–1890), American
printer, journalist, and inventor, b. Mooresburg, Pa.
In 1864 Sholes and a friend, Samuel W. Soulé, patented
a paging machine. With a third partner, Carlos Glid-
den, they received a patent for a writing machine,
or typewriter, in 1868. A poor businessman, Sholes
was unable to make a financial success of his latter
invention and in 1873 sold his patent rights to the
Remington Corporation.
    early typewriters **C** 433; **T** 347

Sholokhov (SHOL-o-kof), **Mikhail,** Russian author **U** 62
Shooting
    hunting **H** 289–91
    rifle marksmanship **R** 233–35
    skeet shooting **T** 269
    trapshooting **T** 268–69
Shooting stars, flowers, picture **W** 168
Shooting stars, meteors **C** 418, 419–21
    meteors in the solar system **S** 246
Shopping see Marketing
Shopping center, picture **U** 102
Shoran (SHO-ran), short-range navigation **R** 39
Short circuits, in electricity **E** 133
Shorthair cats C 141
Shorthand, method of rapid writing **S** 164
Shorthorn, breed of beef cattle **C** 147
Shortleaf pine, tree
    Arkansas, state tree of **A** 418
Short Parliament, English E 223
Short sale, of stock not actually owned **S** 432
Short stories S 165–67
    American literature **A** 208–09, 212, 214
    creative writing **W** 320
    fiction, development of **F** 112
    Henry, O. **H** 110–13
    Irish literature **I** 395

Short stories (continued)
Japanese literature **O** 220c
types of literature **L** 314
Short ton, measure of weight **W** 114; picture **W** 113
Short-wave radio **R** 58
See also Radio, amateur
Short-wave radio telephony **T** 59
Shoshone Falls, on the Snake River, Idaho **I** 57
Shostakovich (shost-ak-OV-ich), **Dimitri,** Russian composer
U 64
opera **O** 138
Shotguns, or pellet-firing guns **G** 424
guns for hunting **H** 291
Shot put, field event **T** 241; picture **O** 115
Shotts, or chotts, salt lakes **A** 160; **T** 309
Shoulders, of roads **R** 251
Shoup (SHOOP), **George L.,** American statesman **I** 67
Showboats, steamships with theater and a company of
actors **T** 162
Show Boat, first modern musical comedy **M** 542
Shower baths **B** 91
Show Me State, Missouri **M** 367
Showy lady's slipper, flower
Minnesota, state flower of **M** 323

Shreve, Henry Miller (1785–1851), American steamboat
pioneer, b. Burlington County, N.J. He established the
lead trade down the Mississippi and made steam
navigation practical on the Mississippi and Ohio rivers.
He won the right to navigate the Mississippi in a case
against the Fulton-Livingston interests, who claimed
monopoly. Shreveport, La., is named for him.

Shreveport, Louisiana **L** 360
Shrews, animals of insectivore group **I** 260–61
smallest mammal **A** 265; **M** 61
Shrikes, birds **B** 221
Shrimp Girl, The, painting by Hogarth **E** 239
Shrimps, crustaceans **S** 168–71; picture **L** 230
shrimp boats, South Carolina, picture **S** 301
shrimp fishing industry **F** 221
Shrine of the Book, Jerusalem **J** 81; picture **M** 513
Shrines
Book, Shrine of the, Jerusalem, picture **M** 513
Costa Rica, Our Lady of the Angels in Cartago, picture
C 514
Guadalupe, Virgin of **M** 242
Japan, Shinto shrines, pictures **J** 41, 47
Jerusalem shrines sacred to Jews, Christians and
Muslims **J** 78–81
Shriver, R. Sargent, Jr., American lawyer and government
official **M** 126; **P** 101
Shrouds, coverings to protect satellites **S** 40
Shrouds, wires or ropes on sailboats **S** 10
Shrove Tuesday see Mardi gras
Shrubs, low, usually several-stemmed woody plants
garden selection **G** 29
growth pattern of plants **P** 302
poisonous **P** 323

Shubert (SHU-bert), **Jacob J.** (1880–1964), **Lee** (1875–
1953), and **Sam S.** (1876–1905), American theatrical
managers and producers, b. Syracuse, N.Y. Lee and Sam
became managers (1900) of the Herald Square Theatre,
New York. Eventually the three brothers gained control of
a number of theaters in New York and other cities. They
produced many shows and introduced many stars,
leading the field particularly in the production of revues
and operettas.

Shubin, Fedot, Russian sculptor **U** 54
Shudraka, King, Indian playwright **O** 220e

Shuffle, in card games **C** 107
Shuffleboard, game **S** 172
Shulchan Aruch (shul-CON ar-OOCK), Jewish religious
codes **J** 116, 120

Shultz, George Pratt (1920–   ), American economist, b.
New York, N. Y. He became dean of the Graduate School
of Business in 1962 at the University of Chicago. During
both the Eisenhower and Kennedy administrations, Shultz
acted as a labor consultant. Under Nixon he served as
director of the Office of Management and Budget, secretary of labor (1969–72), and was appointed secretary of
the treasury in 1972. The following year he was also
made a presidential assistant and chairman of the
Council of Economic Advisers.

Shunt motors, electric **E** 138
Shushan, Iran see Susa
Shutters, in cameras **P** 201–02
Shuttle, device of a loom to pass threads **T** 140
invention important to the Industrial Revolution
I 234
Shuttlecock, cork with feathers used in playing bad-
minton **B** 13
Shwe Dagon (SHWAY da-GAWN) **Pagoda,** in Rangoon,
Burma **B** 454, picture **B** 457
Shylock, character in Shakespeare's Merchant of Venice
J 109
Siam see Thailand
Siamese cats **C** 142; picture **C** 144

Siamese twins, two individuals—developed from a single
fertilized egg—whose bodies at birth are joined together
in some way.

Sian (si-ON), China, formerly Changan **C** 270
Sibelius (si-BAY-lius), **Jean,** Finnish composer **S** 172
Finnish contributions to the cultural world **F** 131
song dedicated to Marian Anderson **A** 251
Siberia (sy-BE-ria), Asian section of the U.S.S.R. **S** 173
probable original home of Eskimo **E** 284
white taiga, deciduous forest **T** 11
Siberian tigers **T** 186
Sibley, Henry Hastings, first governor of Minnesota
M 334
Sibling relationships, in the family **B** 4

Sibuyan (si-BU-yon) **Sea,** part of the Pacific Ocean
surrounded by the northern Philippine islands and
connected with Sulu Sea by Tablas Strait. During World
War II it was a scene of action between U.S. and
Japanese naval forces (1944). It contains the Philippine
Visayan Islands.

Sibyls, in ancient mythology, certain women with powers
of prophecy. They appeared in legends in various parts
of the world, including Greece, Egypt, and Italy. The
most famous is the Cumaean sibyl, described by Vergil
in the Aeneid. Michelangelo's five paintings of sibyls
alternate with seven of the prophets on the vault of the
Sistine Chapel in Rome.

Sicily, island, off southwestern tip of Italy **I** 437
Two Sicilies, Kingdom of, Italy's city states
during the Renaissance **R** 157
World War II **W** 297
Sick
first aid **F** 157–63
home nursing **N** 413–15
hospitals **H** 247–52
nurses and nursing **N** 409–13
Sickle, oldest harvesting tool **F** 60

Sickle-cell anemia, disease **G** 85
  crescent-shaped red blood cells, picture **D** 192
Sick Man of Europe, The, name for Turkey in 19th century **T** 328
Siddhartha, Prince, Gautama Buddha *see* Buddha

Siddons, Sarah (1755–1831), English actress, b. Brecon, Wales. She first appeared in London (1775) as Portia in Shakespeare's *The Merchant of Venice* at the Drury Lane Theatre, and with her success in Southerne's *Fatal Marriage* (1782), she became the leading lady of the English theater. Her greatest role was Lady Macbeth, which she first played in 1785. She spent her last years on the stage (1806–12) in her brother's Covent Garden Theatre company.

Side horse, use in gymnastics, pictures **G** 431
Siderite (SID-er-ite), iron ore **I** 404
Sidestroke, swimming **S** 489; picture **S** 491
Side sewing, in bookbinding **B** 327
Sidewalk bank deposit window, picture **B** 49
Sidewalk cafés
  Buenos Aires, picture **B** 427
Sidewalls, of tires **T** 197
Sidewinding, movement of snakes **S** 211

Sidjakov (SID-ja-kof), **Nicolas** (1924–), American illustrator, b. Riga, Latvia. After studying in Paris and working in Europe as a designer and illustrator, he married an American (1954) and went to the United States, where he became a successful advertising artist. He illustrated his first children's book, *The Friendly Beasts,* in 1957 and won the Caldecott medal (1961) for his illustrations for *Baboushka and the Three Kings.*
  picture books for children **C** 243

Sidney, Margaret, pen name of Harriett Mulford Lothrop, American author **C** 240
Sidney, Sir Philip, English poet and statesman **E** 250
Siebe (ZE-ba), **Augustus,** German inventor **D** 79
Siege, warfare strategy
  Alexander the Great, methods of **A** 151
  forts and fortification **F** 375–77
  Jerusalem **J** 81
  Paris **P** 75
  Stalingrad **W** 296
  Troy, Siege of **T** 293–94
Siegfried (SEEG-freed), or **Sigurd,** Norse hero **N** 280–81
Siegfried, opera by Richard Wagner **O** 152

Siegfried (SEEG-freed) **line,** series of trenches built by the Germans in France during World War I. Called the Hindenburg Line by the Germans, it was broken by the Allies during the last offensive of the war. During World War II, a chain of German fortifications running from Switzerland to Holland along the Rhine River was known by the same name. Known as the West Wall by the Germans, it was begun in 1938 and was thought to be impassable. The Allies overran the Siegfried Line (1945).
  forts and fortifications **F** 377

Sieglinde (SEEG-lind), or **Signy,** in Norse mythology **N** 280

Siegmeister, Elie (1909–), American composer, conductor, author, b. New York City. He has composed many orchestral and stage works based on native American themes. His titles include *Invitation to Music, The New Music Lover's Handbook,* and *Work and Sing: A Collection of the Songs That Built America.*

Siegmund (SEEG-mund), or **Sigmund,** Norse hero **N** 280

Siemens (ZE-mens), **Werner von,** German engineer, developed electric elevator **E** 172
Siena (si-EN-a) **Cathedral,** Italy **I** 463; picture **I** 460

Sienkiewicz (shen-ki-EV-ich), **Henryk** (1846–1916), Polish writer, b. Russian Poland. Known for his historical novels written in a romantic manner, he won world-wide fame with *Quo Vadis?* and received the Nobel prize for literature (1905). During World War I he and pianist Ignace Paderewski (1860–1941), both leaders in the cause of Polish independence, organized a committee to aid Polish war victims.

Sierra (except for those listed below) *see* second part of name, as Guadarrama, Sierra de
Sierra Leone (si-AIR-ra le-O-ne) **S** 174–75
  flag **F** 236
Sierra Madre Occidental, mountains, Mexico **M** 242
Sierra Madre Oriental, mountains, Mexico **M** 242
Sierra Maestra (s'YAIR-ra ma-A-stra), mountains in Oriente Province, Cuba **C** 548
Sierra Morena, Spain **S** 352
Sierra Nevada, Spain **S** 352
Sierra Nevada de Mérida (nay-BA-da day MAY-ri-tha), Venezuela **V** 297
Sierra Nevada Mountains, United States **U** 92
  California **C** 16
  Carson range in Nevada **N** 124, 125
Siesta (si-ES-ta), midday rest **L** 61
Sieve (SIV) **of Eratosthenes** (er-a-TOS-the-nese), method of finding prime numbers **N** 379
Sif (SEEF), Norse goddess **N** 279
Sigefroi, founder of Luxembourg **L** 380
Sight B 283–85
  advantages of binocular (two-eyed) vision **P** 490–91
  birds **B** 203–04
  brain, sensory area of **B** 365
  butterflies and moths **B** 469
  color blindness **D** 15, 188
  insects **I** 267; picture **I** 266
  lenses of the eye **L** 149–50
  lighting, rules of good light in practice **L** 288
  optical illusions **O** 161–62
  perception **P** 488
  perspective, how perceived **P** 158
  senses, guards on the alert **B** 280
  stereoscopic vision **P** 490–91
  vitamin A **V** 370b
  See also Eye
Sight reading R 108
Sights, telescopic O 170
Sight switch, developed in space research **S** 349
Sigmund, or **Siegmund,** Norse hero **N** 280
Signal Hill, near St. John's, Newfoundland **N** 143, 144
Signaling radio receivers T 57
Signals and signaling
  African communication by musical instruments **A** 79
  animal communication **A** 275–80
  automobile driving **D** 319–20
  boats: rules of the road **B** 261–62
  communication **C** 437
  distress position of the flag **F** 231
  early ways of sending messages **T** 50
  flags for letters of alphabet in the International Code, pictures **F** 245
  football, code of signals for officials **F** 363
  heliograph **C** 438; **T** 50
  lighthouse fog signals **L** 277
  Morse Code **R** 63
  railroads **R** 84–85
  smoke signals **C** 437; **T** 50
  traffic control, signs and signals **T** 248

Signals and signaling (continued)
warning flags F 246
See also Semaphore
Signatures, or autographs A 526–27; H 31
Signatures, in bookbinding B 327
folding and numbering pages, picture P 464
Signers of Declaration of Independence D 63
Signet (SIG-net) **rings** J 98
Sign language, of the deaf D 52–53
Sign of the Cross R 301
Signs and billboards
folk art, pictures F 290
outdoor advertising A 28–29
posters P 404
traffic signs and signals T 248
See also Billboards; Commercial art
Signs and symbols
chemical elements C 197; E 154–57
communication C 437
currency of some representative countries M 411
doctor's caduceus, picture M 208c
ESP symbol cards used by J. B. Rhine E 395
Evangelists in Book of Kells, picture K 202
flags of the world F 225–48
heraldry H 115–18
maps M 88, 90
musical notation M 524, 525
new mathematics, symbols and terms M 162–63
numerals and numeration systems N 389–401
Olympic Games rings O 109
political P 379–82
sets, in mathematics S 126
some mathematical symbols M 154
universal languages, uses in U 195
use in animal tests A 288
weather symbols W 78
zodiac signs for each month *see* Month articles
Signy, or **Sieglinde,** in Norse mythology N 280
Sigurd, (SI-gurt), or **Siegfried,** Norse hero N 280–81
Sihanouk, Prince Norodom *see* Norodom Sihanouk, Prince
Sihanoukville, now Kompong Som, Cambodia C 32, 33

Sikhs (SEEKS), religious people in the Punjab area of India. Sikhism was founded about 1500 by Nanak, a Hindu ascetic, who was the first guru (teacher); he preached a monotheistic creed and opposed the caste system. Govind Singh, the 10th and last guru, molded the Sikhs into a military community, and they abandoned some of their earlier beliefs. Under Ranjit Singh in the 19th century, the Sikh empire reached its height but was soon conquered by the British (1845, 1848).
hybrid religions in India I 117; R 152

Si Kiang (SI ki-ANG), or West River, China R 247
Si delta on the South China coast C 263
Sikkim, small kingdom, in the Himalayas S 176–77
flag F 238

Sikorsky (sik-OR-ski), **Igor Ivanovich** (1889–1972), Russian-American aeronautical engineer, b. Kiev. In 1913 he built and flew the first multi-engine aircraft. During World War I he built 75 four-engined bombers for the Russian Army. Going to the United States after the war, he was active in the development of new types of aircraft. During the 1930's he developed the first commercial airplanes capable of transoceanic flight. He is known for developing (1939) first practical helicopter.
aviation and helicopters, history of A 574; H 105–06

Silage (SY-lage)
bacteria preserve B 12
Silas (SY-las) **Marner,** novel by George Eliot E 177

Silbermann, Gottfried, German piano builder P 241
Silent Cal, nickname of Calvin Coolidge C 494b
Silent majority, of American voters N 262d
Silent Night, Holy Night, carol C 122
music for the harmonica H 42
Silent pictures, early movies M 472–74

Silhouette (sil-u-ETT), dark image against a lighter background. The word also refers to a portrait, usually black, of the outline of a person's profile. The term has been adopted from the name of a French finance minister, Étienne de Silhouette (1709–67), who introduced economic reforms but received only ridicule and hostility from the nobles. His name was therefore applied to a "mere outline profile drawing" or anything incomplete.

Silhouette, in fashion design F 65
Silhouettes
how to make I 223–24
Silica (SIL-i-ca)
bamboo absorbs from soil G 318
glass G 226
Silicon, element E 155, 164
steel I 396
transistor circuits for computers C 454
Silicon bronze, alloy B 409
Silicon cells, a kind of photoelectric cell P 199
Silicone, synthetic rubber R 347
lubricants L 371
Silicosis (sil-i-CO-sis), disease
mining dust M 317
Silk S 178–80
drying of dyed material, picture D 368
Japanese, picture J 36
natural fibers F 107
Silk-cotton tree or ceiba, yields kapok fibers K 193
Silk routes, trade routes S 178
Silk-screen printing S 180
one of the graphic arts G 308
textiles T 145
Silkworms S 178–79
cats protect cocoons in China and Japan C 142
Pasteur's work on diseases of P 96
Silliman, Benjamin, Jr., American chemist P 177

Sills, Beverly (Belle Silverman) (1929–), American opera singer, b. Brooklyn, N.Y. She began her career as a 3-year-old child star on a weekly radio program. During her teen-age years, she toured with several musical companies. She joined the New York City Opera during the 1955–56 season, but it was not until 1966 and her electrifying performance as Cleopatra in Handel's *Julius Caesar* that she gained worldwide recognition.

Silos, for storing green fodder, or silage, picture I 141
Silt, soil S 231
dams D 18
Silurian period, in geology F 384

Silvanus, in Roman mythology, god of uncultivated fields and woods, often identified with Faunus and Pan. He was the protector of field boundaries and of herds and flocks. Represented as an old man of great strength, a tree in one hand and a pruning hook in the other, he was associated with Hercules and the Lares. It was Silvanus who gave a victory to the Romans by causing panic in the Etruscan camp.

Silver S 181–82
antique A 320–21
compounds used in photography P 210
crystals, picture R 272

dolls made of   D 267
electroplating   E 149
elements, some facts about   E 155, 164
free coinage, Bryan's political issue   B 415–16
Hayes administration, limited coinage restored   H 81
how to clean by electrolysis   I 354
jewelry   J 92
metals, chart of ores, location, properties, uses
   M 227
money   M 411
Nevada mines   N 129
silver-producing regions of North America   N 293
Sherman Silver Purchase Act, 1890   C 342
Why the name "sterling"?   S 182
world distribution   W 261; diagram   W 264
Silver, poem by Walter de la Mare   F 119
Silverfish, insects   H 262; pictures H 263, I 263
Silver iodide
cloud seeding, use in   W 93, 96
Silver-plating, electroplating process   E 149, 150
Silversmithing
Revere, Paul   R 192, 193
Spain   S 364
Silver Springs, Florida   F 262
Silver Star, American award, picture   M 199
Silver State, nickname of Nevada   N 123
Silvertips, grizzly bears   B 107
Silverware
distinctive work of the Mandeans in Iraq   I 379
hallmarks   A 320–21
how to clean by electrolysis   I 354
knives, forks, and spoons   K 285–88
silver   S 182
table settings   T 2–3
Silvester method, of artificial respiration   F 160
Simcoe, John Graves, British colonial governor   O 127
Simeon I (SIM-e-on), czar of Bulgaria   B 444
Simeon II, czar of Bulgaria, in exile   B 444
Simeon Stylites (sty-LY-tese), **Saint,** first of the "stylites"
   or pillar saints   B 487
Simile (SIM-i-le), figure of speech   F 118; P 354
Simms, William Gilmore, American novelist   A 200
Simon (SY-mon), Jewish military leader   D 49
Simon, Robert E. Jr., American city planner   U 234
Simon and Garfunkel, American rock music composers and
   performers   R 262d
Simone di Martino, or Simone Memmi see Martini, Simone
Simon Peter see Peter, Saint
Simons, David G., American military balloonist   B 34

Simont (sim-ONT), **Marc** (1915–   ), American author and
illustrator, b. Paris, France. He moved to the United
States (1927) and studied art in Paris and New York. His
illustrations for *A Tree Is Nice* won the Caldecott medal
(1957). Among the children's books he has written and
illustrated is *The Lovely Summer.*

Simon the Cananaean, Saint, one of the twelve Apostles
   A 333
Simony (SY-mony), sale of sacred things   R 291
Simple-beam bridges   B 397
Simple machines, the lever, the inclined plane, the pul-
   ley   W 246–50
Simplon Pass, through the Alps   A 174

Simpson, Sir George (1792–1860), Canadian administrator, b. Ross, Scotland. In 1820 he arrived in Canada in
the service of the Hudson's Bay Company. The following
year the company merged with the North West Company
and he became governor of the northern department,
later known as Rupert's Land. As governor in chief of all
the company's territories (1826–60), he crossed the

North American continent (1828) and made an overland
journey around the world (1841–42).

Simpson, James, English doctor   A 257

Simpson, O. J. (Orenthal James) (1947–   ), American
football player, Negro, b. San Francisco, Calif. An outstanding running back with the U. of Southern California team, he was awarded the Heisman Trophy
(1968). He agreed to play professionally for Buffalo
Bills of American Football League (1969).

Simpson, Mrs. Wallis see Windsor, Wallis Warfield,
   duchess of
Simulators, machines to imitate certain conditions
   S 341
computer-controlled   C 449
Sinai Peninsula (SY-ny pe-NIN-su-la), Egypt   E 90d
Nasser's nationalistic policies   N 15
Southwest Asia   A 450
wars in   E 92; I 444–45

Sinatra, Frank (1917?–   ), American singer, b. Hoboken,
N.J. Band vocalist for Harry James and Tommy Dorsey,
he went on his own (1942), becoming an idol of teen-
agers and radio's leading male singer of popular songs.
He has played in many films, including *From Here to
Eternity,* for which he won an Academy Award (1953). He
retired in 1971.

Sinbad the Sailor, story from Arabian Nights   A 347

Sinclair, Upton Beall (1878–1968), American author, b.
Baltimore, Md. A crusader for social justice, he brought
about reforms through his writings. He sought public
office unsuccessfully on the Socialist tickets—his most
notable campaign was for the governorship of California
(1934). In 1943 he won the Pulitzer Prize for *Dragon's
Teeth.* His *The Jungle* (1906) led to the passage of the
first Food and Drug Act.
   EPIC (End Poverty in California) program   C 30

Sinews, tendons
Indians use for beadwork   I 158
Sinfonia (sin-fo-NI-a), or overture, to an opera   M 540
Singapore, city, Singapore   S 184a
Singapore, Republic of   S 183–184a; picture   S 331
flag   F 238
port, picture   H 37
skyscraper, picture   A 446
World War II   W 293–94
Singapore, University of, Singapore   S 184

Singer, Isaac Bashevis (1904–   ), Yiddish writer, b. Poland.
He came to the United States in 1935 and settled in New
York City, where he worked as a free-lance writer and
journalist. He writes in Yiddish and assists in the translations. His first great success was *The Family Moskat*
(1950). He has also won acclaim for his children's books,
among which are *Zlateh the Goat and Other Stories* and
*When Schlemiel Went to Warsaw and Other Stories. A
Day of Pleasure: Stories of a Boy Growing Up in Warsaw*
won the 1970 National Book Committee award. His works
have been translated into many languages.   Y 351

Singer, Isaac Merrit (1811–1875), American inventor, b.
Pittstown, N.Y. At the age of 12 he left home and earned
his living at odd jobs. At 19 he became a skilled
machinist. In 1839 he invented a mechanical rock drill.
In 1851 he patented a sewing machine of advanced
design and founded a company to manufacture it. He
later took out 20 patents for improvements.   C 353

Singing V 375–76
  African music **A** 78
  ancient Greek choruses **A** 247
  ancient Hebrew choirs **A** 246
  folk music **F** 318–28
  Indian music of North America **I** 160–61
  See also Choirs; Choral music; Choruses
Singing games F 299, 322
  four familiar games, with the music **G** 11–13
Single-leaf pinyon, or piñon pine
  state tree of Nevada **N** 123
Singleton, Arthur ("Zutty"), American jazz musician **J** 58

Singleton, Benjamin ("Pap") (1809–1892), American Negro slave leader, b. Tennessee. After his escape from slavery, he lived in Canada. After the Emancipation Proclamation (1863) he returned to the South, where he tried to improve the life of the Negroes. Singleton set up three colonies in Kansas, to which he induced thousands of Negroes to migrate. These were some of many westward and northward migrations made by Negroes.

Single-wing formation, in football **F** 363; diagrams **F** 364
Sing Sing Prison, Ossining, New York **P** 469
Singspiel (SING-speel), German half-spoken opera **O** 132
Sinhalese (SING-ha-lese), a people of Ceylon **C** 177, 180
Sinks, or **sinkholes,** in rock formations **F** 261
  caves and caverns **C** 154
Sinkiang (SINK-yang), China **C** 265
  Inner Asia **A** 449
Sinn Fein (shinn FAIN) **party,** of Ireland **I** 391, 392

Sino-Japanese (SY-no-jap-an-ESE) **War** (1894–95), war between China and Japan over Korea. Both Japan and China were trying to dominate Korea (1894) when a revolt there gave them the opportunity to move troops into the disputed area. Japan and China declared war on each other, and the better-trained and -equipped Japanese won easily. According to the terms of the Treaty of Shimonoseki (1895), China recognized Korea's independence, ceded Formosa, the Pescadores Islands, and the Liaotung peninsula to Japan, and paid Japan a large indemnity. Pressure from Western nations later forced Japan to return the Liaotung peninsula to China.
  Taiwan, history of **T** 13

Sino-Japanese War, 1937–45 **C** 227
  Mao Tse-tung **M** 86
  Shanghai **S** 139
Sino-Tibetan (SY-no-ti-BET-an) **languages** **L** 40
  language groups of Asia **A** 460
Sintering, of ores **M** 228
Sinter Klaas, Dutch Santa Claus **C** 292; picture **C** 293
Sioux (SOO), Indians of North America **I** 167–68
  Indian wars **I** 215
  South Dakota **S** 326
  Wyoming uprisings **W** 337
Sioux City, Iowa **I** 369; picture **I** 362
Sioux Falls, South Dakota **S** 324
Sioux State, nickname for North Dakota **N** 323
Siphonophores (sy-PHON-o-phores), tiny luminous sea creatures, picture **B** 198
Siphons (SY-phons), necks of clams **O** 273

Siqueiros (si-KAY-i-roce), **David Alfaro** (1898–), Mexican painter and revolutionist, b. Chihuahua. He joined the revolutionary army of General Venustiano Carranza (1913), led the revolutionary Syndicate of Technical Workers, Artists and Sculptors, which was sponsored by the government, and participated in the Spanish Civil War (1936–39). Through Siqueiros, Mexican painting became an instrument of nationalism and social protest.

His fresco murals in public buildings are noted for the use of Duco paint applied with a spray gun and for their bold and rich depiction of Mexican history.
  modern Latin-American art **L** 67

Sir, British title **K** 277
Sirach, or Wisdom of Jesus (Joshua), Son of Sirach *see* Ecclesiasticus
Sirenia (sy-RE-nia), order of mammals **M** 62, 68
  sea cows **S** 106–07
Sirens, in Greek mythology **O** 54
Sirens, or mud eels, land-water animals **F** 475
Sir George Williams University, Montreal **Q** 10b
Sirimavo Bandaranaike *see* Bandaranaike, Solomon
Sirius, or Dog Star **A** 492
  constellations **C** 492
  dog days **D** 47
  temperature and color of stars **S** 407
Sirloin steak **F** 335
Sirocco (sir-OC-co), a dry wind from the Sahara **M** 213
  Algeria, sandstorms in **A** 161
  erosion, causes of **E** 281

Sisal (SY-sal), spiny-leafed tropical plant of the agave family. The word is also applied to the fiber prepared from it, used for rope, cordage, and sacking. The strong, hard fiber comes from the leaves, which may be up to 6 feet long. The outer leaves are harvested as they mature; new leaves appear at the center of the plant for 6 to 10 years. The plant is native to Mexico.
  rope, kinds of **R** 332
  sisal being loaded in Kenya, picture **A** 63

Sisters of Charity, various groups of Roman Catholic nuns who work in schools, orphanages, clinics, and day nurseries and among the sick and insane. The oldest and largest group in the United States is the Sisters of Charity of St. Vincent de Paul, founded (1809) by Elizabeth Seton, who took as her model the Sisters of Charity, Servants of the Sick Poor, founded (1634) in France by St. Vincent de Paul and Blessed Louise de Marillac.

Sister's Day, in India **H** 158
Sistine Chapel, Vatican, Rome
  Botticelli's wall paintings **B** 340b
  Michelangelo's ceiling decoration **R** 169
  Michelangelo's frescoes for **I** 469
  Michelangelo's paintings **M** 257; pictures **M** 255–56
  Michelangelo's paintings of prophets **B** 158
Sistrum, musical instrument **A** 245

Sisyphus (SIS-iph-us), in Greek mythology, the builder and king of Corinth. Called by Homer "slyest of all men," he was the son of Aeolus, and brother of Athamas. A cunning, greedy man, he was punished in the underworld by having to roll a stone uphill eternally. As he neared the top of the hill, the stone always slipped from his grasp, and he had to start again.

Sitar, Indian musical instrument
  rock music **R** 262d
Sit-down strikes **L** 6
Sites, areas chosen by archeologists for digging **A** 351–58
Sitka, Alaska **A** 141, 143
Sitka National Monument, Sitka, Alaska **A** 141
Sitka spruce, tree
  Alaska, state tree of **A** 129
Sittang River, in Burma **B** 456
Sitting Bull, Sioux Indian leader **S** 325
  drawings made by him **I** 157

Sky-diving, parachuting for fun **S** 193
Skye terrier, dog, picture **D** 260
Skyjacking see Hijacking
Skylab, manned earth-orbiting observatory **O** 15; **S** 343
  crew **S** 345
Skylarks, picture **B** 241

Skyscraper, tall, many-storied building. The term is very flexible: a 12-story apartment house in a small town might be called a skyscraper because it towers over the buildings that surround it. In New York City, however, few buildings under 25 stories are so regarded.

Skyscrapers U 124–25
  architecture today **A** 385–86
  Chicago, pictures **C** 229
  first construction methods **B** 438
  Montreal, pictures **C** 65, **M** 445
  Nebraska's Capitol **N** 83–84
  New York **N** 231; pictures **A** 386, **E** 272f, **N** 227, 298
  Singapore, picture **A** 446
  Sullivan, Louis **A** 457
Skyscraper to the Moon and How the Green Rat with the Rheumatism Ran a Thousand Miles Twice, one of the Rootabaga stories by Carl Sandburg **S** 29
Slag, waste from refining of metals **I** 397
Slalom (SLA-lom), in skiing **S** 185, 187
Slang S 194
  changes in a language **L** 40
  folk speech **F** 310
  See also Figures of speech
Slap Jack, circle game **G** 14
Slapstick, form of humor **H** 278
Slash-and-burn agriculture see Migratory agriculture
Slate, metamorphic rock **R** 269; picture **R** 268
  building stone, fine-grained **S** 433
Slater, Samuel, English-born American manufacturer **I** 240–41; **R** 216–17
  first cotton mills in America **C** 521
  textile industry in the new world **T** 141
  used child labor **C** 235
Slavery S 195–200
  Adams, John Quincy, fights for abolition **A** 15
  American colonies **A** 193; **C** 386, 387
  ancient civilizations **A** 220
  Arthur, Chester Alan, opposed **A** 438h–439
  Brown, John, American abolitionist **B** 411–12
  Civil War issue **C** 318, 320–21, 327–28
  Compromise of 1850 **C** 448
  Confederate States of America **C** 458, 459
  Dred Scott decision **D** 310–11
  Ecuador, first South American country to abolish **E** 58
  Emancipation Proclamation **E** 185–86
  Gold Coast of Africa **G** 197–98
  Kansas-Nebraska Act, 1854 **K** 192
  King Cotton economy in Alabama **A** 127
  Libreville, Gabon **G** 3
  Lincoln-Douglas debates **L** 299
  Lincoln opposes Kansas-Nebraska Act **L** 294–95
  Missouri Compromise **M** 382
  Negro history **N** 91–95
  Pierce supported Kansas-Nebraska Act **P** 247
  rebellion in Haiti **H** 9–10
  Salmon Area Indians of North America **I** 182
  segregation of slaves **S** 114
  serfdom of feudalism **F** 102; **R** 112
  southern Indian tribes involved in the issue **I** 213
  Stowe, Harriet Beecher **S** 436
  Taylor, Zachary opposed compromise **T** 35–36
  Tubman, Harriet **T** 307
  Uncle Tom's Cabin, novel **A** 204; **S** 436
  Underground Railroad **U** 11–12
  Where was slavery abolished first? **S** 199
  Whittier, John Greenleaf, abolitionist **W** 167
  women, role in abolition of **W** 212b
Slavery, among animals
  ants **A** 324–25
Slave trade N 91
  abolished in District of Columbia **C** 448
  Congo slave trade **Z** 366d
  Mozambique **M** 501
  New World use of Negro slaves **S** 197
  Nigeria **N** 258
  Sierra Leone **S** 175
  United States forbids trade, 1808 **C** 318
Slavic (SLAV-ic) **languages**
  Europe **E** 317
  Russian **U** 58
  Union of Soviet Socialist Republics **U** 27
Slavs (SLOVS), a people of eastern Europe
  Bulgaria **B** 439
  Czechs **C** 559–60, 562–63
  Russia, early movement into **U** 46–47
  Yugoslavia **Y** 354
Slayton, Donald K., American astronaut **S** 347
Sled dogs D 259
  Call of the Wild, The **A** 209; picture **A** 208
Sleds, or sleighs
  bobsleds **B** 265
  dogsleds used in mail service **P** 407
  early means of transportation **T** 257
Sleep S 200–01
  amounts needed for health **H** 83
  Do fish sleep? **F** 190
  dolphins and porpoises **D** 273
  dreaming **D** 305–07
  hibernation **H** 121–24
  hypnosis **H** 316
  noise and noise control **N** 269–70
  plants measure time by sleep rhythms **L** 247
Sleepers, rare stamps **S** 397; pictures **S** 399
Sleeping Beauty, story by Charles Perrault **F** 27–29
Sleeping cars, of railroads **R** 81; picture **R** 80

Sleeping sickness, African, disease caused by the presence in the body of trypanosomes, one-celled animals. Trypanosomes are introduced into the body through the bite of an infected tsetse fly, found in Africa. The disease causes swollen lymph glands. In its advanced stages, it affects the brain, causing a deep sleep, coma, and death. There are drugs to prevent and to cure the disease.
  insects harmful to man **I** 283

Sleeping Spinner, painting by Courbet **F** 427
Sleet R 96–97
Sleigh (SLAY) **bells**
  Christmas **C** 290
Sleighs see Sleds, or sleighs
Sleight (SLIGHT) **of hand,** magic tricks **M** 18
Slender lorises, animals related to monkeys **M** 422

Slidell (sly-DELL), **John** (1793–1871), American politician, b. New York, N.Y. He settled in Louisiana in 1819. He was a member of the House of Representatives (1843–45) and the Senate (1853–61). While on the British ship *Trent* as a Confederate representative, with James Mason, to France during Civil War, he was arrested and briefly held prisoner by the Union. This incident created an international uproar and became known as the Trent Affair (1861). Unable to gain recognition of the Confederacy in France, he lived rest of his life abroad.
  Polk and Slidell **P** 386
  Trent Affair and trouble with Britain **C** 322

Slide rule, device for rapid calculation
how to make your own **M** 166–67
Slime molds M 279–80; picture **M** 278
fungi **F** 497–98; picture **F** 496
Slip, a clay mixture used in ceramics **C** 174; **P** 414
Slipware, pottery **A** 320
Sliver (SLY-ver), loose strand of cotton fibers **C** 525

Sloan, John (1871–1951), American painter, b. Lock Haven, Pa. He began his career as a newspaper illustrator and moved to New York in 1904. There he became associated with the so-called ashcan school of painters, who depicted realities of city life. His early New York pictures are regarded as his best-known.
ashcan school of art in the United States **U** 122

Sloane, Sir Hans, British doctor and naturalist **M** 511
Sloan-Kettering Institute for Cancer Research K 236

Slobodkin (slo-BOD-kin), **Louis** (1903–), American illustrator, sculptor, and author, b. Albany, N.Y. He has done sculpture for a number of public and private buildings. His first children's-book illustrations were for *The Moffats*. He won the Caldecott medal (1943) for his illustrations for James Thurber's *Many Moons*. His own books include *The First Book of Drawing, Excuse Me: Certainly!*, and *A Good Place to Hide*.

Sloop, sailboat, picture **S** 9
Slope mining, of coal **C** 365

Sloth, any of a family of tree-dwelling mammals found in Central and South America. Sloths are slow-moving animals. They spend much of their time hanging upside down from tree branches, suspended by their strong, hooked claws. Three-toed sloths have three toes on each front foot and are from 1 to 2 feet long. Two-toed sloths are slightly larger and more active animals and have two toes on each front foot. Picture **E** 341.

Sloth bears B 108
Slot racing, of model cars **A** 537
Slovakia (slo-VA-kia), province of Czechoslovakia
C 559, 560, 563
Slovaks (SLO-voks), Slavic peoples of central Europe
C 559, 563
Slovenia (slo-VE-nia), Yugoslav state **Y** 358
Slugs, gastropods **O** 276
Sluice gates, of canals **C** 84
Slums, of cities
city problems **C** 308–308a
urban renewal **U** 233–34
Slurred notes, or legato, in musical notation **M** 531
Slurries, a group of explosives **E** 392
Slurry, coal suspended in water to be carried through a pipeline **C** 368
ore processing in mining **M** 318
Sluter (SLU-ter), **Claus,** Dutch sculptor **D** 349
Mourning Monk, statue **D** 351
Sluys (SLOYS), **battle of,** 1340 **H** 281
Small arms see Guns
Small craft warning flag F 246
Small-game hunting H 290–91
Small intestine, in digestive function of the body **B** 275
Smallpox, virus disease **D** 207
Jenner conquers with first vaccine **D** 214; **J** 76
Jenner vaccinating a child, picture **M** 207
sores responsible for blindness **B** 251–52
vaccination and inoculation **V** 260

Smalls, Robert (1839–1915), American congressman, former slave, b. Beaufort, S.C. Impressed into service for the Confederacy, he gained national fame (1862) by guiding a Confederate steamer into Union lines. For the rest of the Civil War he served in the U.S. Navy. He was a delegate (1868) to the South Carolina Constitutional Convention and served (1868–74) in the state legislature. He served in the House of Representatives (1875–79, 1882–87), where he worked to provide equal accommodations for Negroes in interstate conveyances.
Negro history **N** 96

Smash, tennis stroke **T** 96
Smaze, composed of smoke and haze
air pollution **A** 109
Smeaton, John, British engineer **L** 275
Smell, sense of B 286
butterflies and moths **B** 469
fishes, smell and taste in **F** 192–93
insects **I** 267
olfactory cell, picture **C** 163
sharks, how they find their prey **S** 143
smelling and tasting work together **B** 281

Smelling salts, a preparation of ammonium carbonate and ammonia water that is sniffed to avoid or relieve faintness or a headache. Often a scent, such as lavender, is added.

Smelt, valuable food fish distantly related to the salmon that lives in the coastal waters of the northern Atlantic and Pacific oceans and also in a number of freshwater lakes in the north central United States, where it was introduced about 1906. These small, slender, silvery-green fish average 7 to 9 inches in length, though a few reach 14 inches. Smelts are among the leading commercial fish in the Great Lakes.

Smelting, of metals **M** 228
Arizona, picture **A** 409
creation of coke **I** 236–37
extracting metals from ores **M** 319
plant in California, picture **C** 18
Smet, Pierre De, see De Smet, Pierre

Smetana (SMET-a-na), **Bedřich** (1824–1884), Czech composer, conductor, and pianist, b. Litomsl. He composed several operas, among which *The Bartered Bride* is still popular. In 1874 he became deaf but continued to compose. His best-known instrumental works include *My Country,* a set of six symphonic poems, and the string quartet *From My Life,* which has an autobiographical program. He is considered the father of Czech music.
Bartered Bride, The, opera **O** 140

Smith, Adam (1723–1790), Scottish political economist, b. Kirkcaldy. While professor of moral philosophy at Glasgow University (1752–64), he published his *Theory of Moral Sentiments* (1759). He traveled to France and became acquainted with the leading thinkers of the day. His *Inquiry into the Nature and Causes of the Wealth of Nations* (1776) laid the foundations of the science of political economy.
principles of taxation **T** 27

Smith, Alfred Emanuel, American statesman **N** 224
presidential election of 1928 won by Hoover **H** 223
Smith, Bessie, American blues singer **J** 58
Smith, David, American sculptor **M** 397
Cubi IX, steel sculpture **S** 105
Question and Answer **M** 397

Smith, Ian Douglas (1919–), Rhodesian political leader, b. Selukwe. An RAF fighter pilot in World War II, he

Smith, Ian Douglas (continued)
served in the Southern Rhodesian Legislative Assembly (1948–53) and the Federal Parliament of the Federation of Rhodesia and Nyasaland (1953–62). He was a founder of the Rhodesian Front party, deputy prime minister, and minister of the treasury (1962–64). He became prime minister of Rhodesia in 1964 and proclaimed its independence from Great Britain (1965).
    Rhodesia, history of **R** 230

Smith, James (1719?–1806), American colonial statesman, b. northern Ireland. Son of an immigrant farmer, he studied law and was admitted to the bar (1745). An ardent patriot, he was a delegate to the provincial conference and a framer of the Pennsylvania constitution. As a member of the Continental Congress (1776–78) he was one of the signers of the Declaration of Independence. After retiring from public life, he practiced law in York, Pa.

Smith, James McCune, American physician **N** 93
Smith, Jedediah, American explorer and trapper
    O 256, 258
    fur traders and mountain men **F** 523–24

Smith, Jessie Willcox (1863–1935), American illustrator, b. Philadelphia, Pa. As a student of author and illustrator Howard Pyle, she was given children's books to illustrate. She went on to create notable illustrations for such books as Robert Louis Stevenson's *Child's Garden of Verses*, Charles Kingsley's *Water Babies*, and George Macdonald's *At the Back of the North Wind*.

Smith, John, English soldier and adventurer **S** 201
    American colonies, settlement of **A** 184, 185, 186
    explored Eastern Shore of Maryland **M** 127
    Jamestown settlement **J** 20–21
    publishes account of Jamestown settlement **A** 195
    visited and named New England **M** 148
Smith, Joseph, American founder of Mormon sect
    M 457; **V** 320
    Brigham Young and Smith **Y** 353
    founded Illinois community **I** 82

Smith, Margaret Chase (1897–   ), American senator, b. Skowhegan, Maine. The circulation manager of a weekly newspaper (1919–28) and later an office manager of a wool mill, she served on the Republican state committee for a number of years (1930–36). Upon the death of her husband, she filled his seat in the United States House of Representatives and served from 1940 to 1949. A senator since 1949, she is the only woman to have been elected for four consecutive terms and has served on the Senate Armed Services, Aeronautical and Space Sciences, and Appropriation committees.
    women, role of **W** 213

Smith, Margaret Court (1942–   ), Australian tennis player. One of the sport's greatest players, she was tennis prodigy as a child. She won 10 Australian singles titles (1960–66, 69–71) and in addition took United States (1962, '65, '69–'70), Wimbledon (British) (1963, '65, '70), and French (1962, '64, '69–'70) singles crowns. In 1970 she was first since 1953 to achieve Grand Slam (all 4 major titles).

Smith, Mary Ellen Spear, English-born Canadian social reformer **B** 404–05
Smith, Monroe and Isobel, founded hosteling in America **H** 254
Smith, Roswell, American publisher **M** 16
Smith, Samuel Francis, American clergyman **N** 24

Smith, Walter Bedell (1895–1961), American army officer and diplomat, b. Indianapolis, Ind. He was chief of staff at Allied Forces Headquarters in North Africa (1942–44) and at SHAEF, European Theater of Operations (1944–45). He served as United States ambassador to the Soviet Union (1946–49), director of the Central Intelligence Agency (1950–53), and undersecretary of state (1953–54).

Smith, William, English geologist **G** 113
    work of surveying led to study of fossils **F** 381–82
Smith, William Alexander see De Cosmos, Amor
Smith, William Jay, American poet **F** 119
Smith–Lever Agricultural Extension Act, 1914 **A** 94
    encouraged research on conservation **C** 485
Smithson, James, English scientist **S** 202
Smithsonian (smith-SO-nian) **Astrophysical Observatory,** Cambridge, Massachusetts **S** 202
Smithsonian Institution, Washington, D.C. **S** 202; **W** 32
    Adams, John Quincy, helped establish **A** 15
    Division of Numismatics **C** 375
    general purpose bequests, early foundations **F** 390
    Goddard's rocket experiments **G** 245
    missile displayed on the grounds, picture **W** 34
    museums of industry and technology **M** 513
    National Gallery of Art (Washington, D.C.) **N** 40–41
Smog, smoke and fog combination **F** 289
    air pollution **A** 109; **E** 272g; picture **E** 272f
Smoke
    air pollution **A** 109
    meat-curing process **F** 349; **M** 192
    smoke candles for search parties **F** 156
    smoke pots used in cloud seeding **W** 93
Smoke-filled room, origin of the term **H** 39
Smokeless powder, used in guns **G** 420
Smoke signals **T** 50
    communication **C** 437
Smokey the Bear, symbol of forest fire prevention
    N 180; picture **A** 34
Smoking, of meat **F** 349; **M** 192
Smoking, of tobacco **S** 203; **T** 200–01
    bronchitis and emphysema **D** 194, 196; **S** 203
    cancer research **C** 91–92
    heart diseases **H** 86c
Smoky quartz, or cairngorm **Q** 7
Smollet, Tobias, Scottish-born English novelist **E** 260
Smoot-Hawley Tariff, 1930 see Hawley-Smoot Tariff, 1930
Smörgåsbord, Swedish meal **F** 341; picture **F** 337
Smudge pots
    protect orchards from cold, picture **F** 483
Smuts, fungi **F** 498
    corn smut **C** 507
    diseases of oats **O** 4

Smuts, Jan Christiaan (1870–1950), South African statesman and soldier, b. Cape Town. A Boer leader during the Boer War, he played a leading role in creating the Union of South Africa (1910). He put down a pro-German rebellion at the start of World War I and represented his country in the Imperial War Cabinet and at the Versailles peace conference (1919). Smuts served as prime minister of South Africa (1919–24, 1939–48).
    South Africa, history of **S** 273

Smyrna see Izmir, Turkey
Smyrna figs **F** 117
Smyth sewing, in bookbinding **B** 327
Snails, mollusks **O** 276
    animal movement on land **A** 265
    aquariums **A** 343
    hibernation **H** 123
    sea snails **O** 276

shells, pictures S 147, 148
  Tyrian purple dye D 367
Snakebites
  first-aid measures I 285
Snake charmers, pictures A 275, 458
Snake River, North America O 195; picture U 106
  Idaho I 57, 59
  Washington W 17
  Wyoming W 326
Snakeroot, plant, source of reserpine drug D 323
Snakeroot, white, poisonous plant P 323
Snakes S 204–14
  adaptations for escaping danger, picture L 218
  animal communication A 275
  Asia's wildlife A 451
  bites, first-aid treatment for I 285
  hibernation of cold-blooded animals H 123
  kinds of reptiles R 181
  largest A 263
  leather made from skins L 107
  locomotion A 294
  mongooses kill and eat G 91–92
  poisonous I 284–85
  serpent a symbol of god of medicine M 208c
  snake charmers, pictures A 275, 458
Snapdragons, flowers, picture G 47

Snapper, name of a large family of saltwater fishes found throughout the world in shallow tropical and subtropical waters. They are usually red in color but may be green, gray, or yellow. They have large heads that are flattened in front. The red snapper is deep red in color and grows to about 30 inches in length. It is found primarily in the Gulf of Mexico.
  habitat, feeding habits, uses F 214

Snap the Whip, painting by Winslow Homer U 119, 121
Snapping turtles T 332; picture T 334
Snare, or side, drum D 333–34; P 151
Snatch, running and chasing game G 22
SNCC see Student National Coordinating Committee

Snead, Sam (Samuel Jackson Snead) (1912–), American golf champion, b. Hot Springs, Va. The winner of over 100 major tournaments, he entered the professional ranks in 1934. He has captured the PGA championship (1942, 1949, 1951), the Masters (1949, 1952, 1954), and the British Open (1946) and has been elected to the Golf Hall of Fame (1953). Picture G 261.

Sneeze, sudden forcing out of air through the nose and mouth. It is a reflex action caused by an irritation to the lining of the nose.

Sneezes, superstitions about S 475

Sneezewort, sturdy flowering plant common in the north temperate zone. It is 1 to 2 ft. high and topped by clusters of white flowers. The pearl and boule-de-neige varieties are favorites with many gardeners. When dried, parts of the plant, especially the root, may cause sneezing.

Snell, Peter, New Zealand athlete, picture O 115

Snelling, Josiah (1782–1828), American soldier, b. Boston, Mass. He fought at Tippecanoe (1811) and for a while was held prisoner by the British. Ordered west, he established Fort Anthony near the present cities of St. Paul and Minneapolis. In his honor the post was renamed Fort Snelling (1825).
  Minnesota, history of M 336

Snipe, any one of a group of long-billed wading birds, closely related to sandpipers. They live in freshwater marshes and wet meadows. The common (or Wilson's) snipe, a game bird found in almost all parts of the world except Australia and the polar regions, is noted for its zigzag flight as it takes off.

Snook, name of a family of fishes recognizable by the black line running from gill to tail and the strong lower jaw that usually juts out beyond the upper jaw. These fishes are found chiefly in saltwater inlets and river mouths. A few species live in fresh water. The largest and most abundant species is a hard-fighting game and food fish found from Florida to Brazil. This fish usually weighs about 4 pounds and reaches 2 feet in length.

Snorkel diving, underwater swimming with tube and
    mouthpiece S 188
Snorkels, breathing tubes
  skin diving S 189
  submarines S 443
Snorri Sturluson, Icelandic poet and historian N 277;
    S 50
Snow R 95–96
  avalanches S 500
  clouds, ice crystal, that bring snow C 359
  floods and flood control F 254
  glaciers G 223
  ice from snow I 6, 11
  igloos, houses of snow H 172–73
  record annual fall in Canada C 55
  "red snow" A 156; R 95
  snowmobiles S 215
  snow observations W 80
  sympathetic vibrations from sound can start snow
    slides S 261–62
  "white killers" of the Alps A 523
Snow, C. P. (Sir Charles Percy), English scientist and
    writer E 267

Snow, Edgar Parks (1905–72), American author, b. Kansas City, Mo. He worked in China during the 1930's and was the first newspaper correspondent to interview Communist leaders during the Chinese civil war. After covering the U.S. Army for the *Saturday Evening Post* (1941), he became the magazine's first world correspondent. His books include *Red Star Over China* and *Journey to the Beginning.* In 1968 he produced and photographed a TV documentary, *One Fourth of Humanity —The China Story.*

Snow, in television T 66

Snowball, or **snowball tree,** tall shrub of European origin now also cultivated in the United States. It is sometimes found growing wild. The leaves are three-lobed. The large, round flower clusters look somewhat like snowballs. The plant is sometimes called the cranberry shrub because its fruit resembles a cranberry.

Snowdrop, small flowering bulb of the amaryllis family. The plant has a single green and white flower hanging at the end of a long stalk; the leaves are long and narrow. Most species bloom early in the spring, sometimes when snow is still on the ground. These hardy plants are usually cultivated for their early blooms.

Snowflakes R 95–96
  crystals C 546
Snow igloos H 172–73
Snow leopard L 155
  cat family C 137–38

Snowmobiles S 215; Y 365

Snow-on-the-mountain, or ghostweed, member of the spurge group. The flowers lack true petals but form large white masses. The many branches are covered with oblong leaves. The higher leaves, nearest the blossoms, have white petal-like margins. Snow-on-the-mountain, a native American plant, is often cultivated but also grows wild, chiefly on the prairies of the midwestern and western United States.

Snowshoe rabbit R 23–24
Snowshoes, picture F 520
Snow Storm, The, painting by J. M. W. Turner P 26
Snowy Mountains Hydroelectric Project, Australian Alps, picture A 509
Soaps D 145–49
   bathing, history of B 91
   not a cosmetic C 509
   oils and fats used O 77, 79
Soap Box Derby, coaster car race, Akron, Ohio S 215
Soap curds, by-product of soap D 145
Soap flakes, manufacturing process D 148
Soap sculpture S 216–17
Soaring see Gliders; Gliding
Sobhuza II, king of Swaziland S 481
Sobrero (so-BRAY-ro), **Ascanio,** Italian chemist, discovered nitroglycerin E 390
Soccer, game S 218–19
   game in Rio de Janeiro, picture S 285
   Guatemalan boys play, picture G 393
   See also Football; Rugby
Social change S 228
Social dancing D 26–28
Social democrats, political group S 220
Social group work S 225
Social growth, or socialization
   child development C 234
Social insurance see Social security; Workmen's compensation
Socialism, an economic theory S 220
   Communism and socialism, differences C 445
   economic system, planned E 51
   poverty, cures for P 424b
   women, role of W 212b
Socialist Labor Party, United States L 8
Socialist Party, United States P 381
Socialization, or social growth
   child development C 234

Socialized medicine, administration of medical and hospital services by an organized group or a state or federal government. The services are made available to a particular group of society or to all members of the population. A form of it is state medicine, which involves control by the national government, is paid for by taxation, and is provided to the whole population.

Social problems S 227
   divorce D 234–35
   world problems W 268
Social security S 221–22
   aid for the blind B 254
   England today E 232
   government regulation of labor L 14
   Medicare I 295; S 222
   New Deal D 122
   old age benefits O 97–98
   Social Security Act, 1935 R 322
   Sweden S 486
   unemployment insurance U 26
   workmen's compensation W 253

Social Security Act, 1935 S 221
   unemployment reforms R 322; U 26
   workers' rights and safety, social legislation for L 14
Social service see Social work
Social settlements
   Hull House, Jane Addams founder A 19
Social studies S 223–24
   economics E 48–51
   geography G 94–108
   history H 134–38
   research R 182–83
   sociology S 226–28
   textbook about Japan, sample pages, picture T 139
Social work S 225–26
   Addams, Jane A 19
   adoption agencies A 25–26
   divorce, problems involving D 235
   foundations, work of F 390–91
   orphanages and foster-family care O 227
   public-assistance programs W 120–21
   public health P 502–06
   See also Peace Corps
Societies
   organization of scientific societies S 69–70
   See also Clubs
Societies, animal
   animal organization A 280–81; M 70
   communities of living things K 257–59
   complex web of life L 253–55
Society and science see Science and society

Society for the Prevention of Cruelty to Animals, American (ASPCA), society seeking to protect animals by enforcement of laws, campaigns for new legislation, and promotion of humane attitudes toward animals. The society maintains a hospital for animal medical and surgical care and shelters for homeless animals. Founded in 1866, it has headquarters in New York, N.Y.

Society for the Prevention of Cruelty to Children (SPCC), organization of persons interested in helping children who are abused or neglected by their parents. The society investigates complaints of neglect and maltreatment and brings cases to family courts and medical authorities. It arranges for placement of children outside the home when necessary. It was founded in 1875 and has headquarters in New York, N.Y.

Society Islands, Pacific Ocean P 8
   fishing, picture P 8
Society of Friends see Quakers
Society of Jesus see Jesuits
Society of Wandering Exhibitions, Russian painters U 55
Sociology S 226–28
   overpopulation, causes of and solutions for P 396–97
   science and society S 82
   urban planning U 232–34
   world social problems W 268
   See also Anthropology; Social studies; Social work
Socket wrenches, tools T 215

Socotra (pop. about 12,000), island (area 1,400 sq. mi.) in the Indian Ocean. Formerly a sultanate under British protection, Socotra became part of Yemen (Aden) in 1967. The economy is based on fishing, pearl-diving, and stock-raising. Dragon's blood, a dark red resin, and frankincense are two famous exports.

Socrates (SOC-ra-tese), Greek philosopher S 228
   ancient civilizations A 230
   dialectical teaching method G 353

educational methods **E** 63–64
first to use analytical method in philosophy **P** 191
Plato recorded teachings of Socrates **P** 332
programed instruction based on similar method **P** 475
Socratic (soc-RAT-ic) **dialogues S** 228
conversations to make people think **E** 63–64
recorded by Plato **P** 332

Soda, common name for several different chemical compounds containing the element sodium. The most familiar of these are baking soda, or sodium bicarbonate; soda ash, or sodium carbonate; and caustic soda, or sodium hydroxide. All are important industrially.
fluxing agent in glassmaking **G** 226

Soda ash, alkali used in soap **D** 146
Sod houses, or soddys, early prairie shelters **N** 72; **P** 254; picture **N** 86
Sodium (SO-dium), element **E** 155, 164
nutrition, use in **N** 417
sodium ion **C** 202–03; picture **C** 204
water desalting **W** 56a
Sodium chloride, common salt **S** 19–21
chlorine obtained from **I** 349
crystals **C** 542, 543–44
Sodium cyanide, solution used to extract gold **G** 249
Sodium fluoride, chemical
prevents tooth decay **F** 283
Sodium hydroxide, or caustic soda in soaps **D** 147
Sodium thiosulfate (thy-o-SUL-fate), or hyposulfite **P** 211
Sodium-vapor lamps N 109

Sodom and Gomorrah (gom-OR-rah), twin cities located near the Dead Sea. They were destroyed by an earthquake about 1900 B.C. In the Old Testament (Genesis 19:24–28) the Lord is said to have destroyed the cities because of the wickedness of the inhabitants.
Abraham and Lot and Lot's wife **A** 7

SOFAR (SOund Fixing And Ranging), method developed by American geophysicist William Maurice Ewing for locating undersea explosions. Shock waves created at certain depths in the sea travel long distances under the surface and are refracted by other layers of sea water. The sounds are picked up by shore stations. Readings from three stations can be used mathematically to locate the explosion. The method can help to find survivors in lifeboats, who drop such charges.

Sofia (SO-fi-a), capital of Bulgaria **B** 442; picture **B** 443
Softball S 229
Soft coal see Bituminous coal
Soft diet N 415
Soft drinks
stain removal **L** 84

Software, a term used in computer technology, referring to any of the written programs or charts that may be used in connection with computer programs. **Software** is in contrast to **hardware,** the electronic or mechanical equipment used in data processing.
See also Hardware

Softwoods, trees
forests **F** 371, 373–74
wood and wood products **W** 225
Soho, district in London, England **L** 337
Soil conservation S 234
erosion **E** 281–83
government conservation programs **C** 486, 488
Soil Conservation Service C 486

Soils S 230–34
alluvial soil, deposited by rivers **M** 365; **R** 238
antibiotics obtained from **A** 312
Can changes in temperature break up rocks? **S** 230
climate and soils **C** 347
conservation of **C** 486, 488
contour plowing, on contour levels **A** 93; pictures **C** 487, **E** 282, **T** 81, **V** 349
Do growing plants break up rocks? **S** 231
dust **D** 347
earthworms **W** 309–11
erosion **E** 281–83, 359
experiment to show temperature variations **E** 360
fertile volcanic soil **V** 384
fertilizers and soil tests **F** 95
flood control **F** 254–57
gardens and gardening **G** 30, 39
grasses beneficial to **G** 319
houseplant potting soil **H** 267
irrigation, problems of **I** 410
land, rules for management of **A** 92–93
lawns **L** 90–91
moon samples **M** 455; **S** 340a, 340i, 348
podzols, acid soils of forest areas **M** 326
prairie soil **I** 360; **P** 430–31
river deltas **M** 365; **R** 238
Why should topsoil be conserved? **S** 233
world distribution of soils **W** 260
See also natural resources section of continent, country, province, and state articles
Sokoto, Nigeria **N** 255
Solar batteries, devices made up of solar cells **S** 238
uses of photoelectricity **P** 200
Solar calendar T 194
Solar cells, devices using sunlight to generate electricity **S** 238
satellites **S** 41
Solar cookers S 237; picture **S** 236
Solar-day rhythms, in plant and animal life **L** 243–44
morning glories, picture **L** 245
Solar days T 187–88
Solar eclipses E 46–47; picture **E** 29
distinguished from eclipses of the moon **M** 448–49
how to watch **E** 46, 361
Solar energy S 235–39
earth and the sun's energy **E** 22
escape of energy from the sun **S** 464
forms of energy **E** 199, 202, 203
solar power **P** 427
Solar-energy collectors S 236–38; pictures **S** 235, 237
Solar flares S 462
earth and its sun **E** 26–27, 28
International Geophysical Year, findings **I** 312–13
radiation belts, how affected **R** 49; **S** 342
Solar heat see Solar energy
Solar heating systems H 99
Solar mass, sun's matter **E** 22
Solar observatories O 9–10
orbiting observatories for modern research **E** 28–29
Solar salt S 20
Solar spectra, pictures **S** 465–66
Solar still, water desalting **W** 56; picture **S** 239
Solar system S 239–49
comets, origin of **C** 419
dust-cloud theory of formation **D** 348; **E** 18
earth's place in the system **E** 3
earth and its sun **E** 22–30
gravity and gravitation **G** 320–25
Mars **M** 104–11
meteors, meteorites, and tektites **C** 419–21
moon **M** 446–56
Newton's findings **A** 473

Solar system (continued)
place of our galaxy in the universe **U** 196–97
planets **P** 269–78
space exploration and travel **S** 343, 348–49
sun **S** 458–67
Solar wind, flow of electrified particles **S** 467
changes the shape of the earth's magnetosphere **R** 48
moon, detection devices placed on **S** 340i
Soldering **S** 249–50
Soldier ants **A** 331
Soldiers
absentee voting **E** 113
Confederate, U.S. Civil War, picture **C** 325
Royal Canadian Dragoons, picture **C** 79
Union, U.S. Civil War, picture **C** 324
United States Army **U** 167
Soldier's Medal, American award, picture **M** 199
Sole, fish, habitats, feeding habits, uses **F** 213
Sole, of the foot **F** 81, 82
Solenodons (so-LE-no-dons), insectivores **I** 261
Solicitors (so-LIS-it-ors), lawyers **L** 93
Are British and American courts different? **C** 529
Solidarity, folk song **F** 320
Solid fuels **F** 490
rockets **R** 258–59
Solid geometry **G** 129; diagrams **G** 128
Solids **S** 250–51
density **F** 250–51
how heat changes matter **H** 91–94
liquids and solids **L** 310; picture **L** 309
matter defined **M** 170
solid solutions **M** 176
states of matter compared **M** 174–75
Solids and planes, in design **D** 136

Solid-state circuit, electronic circuit using semiconductor parts, such as crystals and transistors, instead of electronic tubes. They make it possible to compress a large circuit into a small space. They also require much less electrical power than electron-tube circuits. These circuits are used in transistor radios, spacecraft, and computers, where space and weight must be kept low.

Solid-state physics
properties of crystals **S** 251
welding **W** 119
Solid-waste disposal see Refuse and refuse disposal
Soliloquy (so-LIL-o-quy), a dramatic monologue **H** 20
Hamlet's "To be, or not to be" **H** 21
Solís (so-LECE), **Juan Diaz de,** Spanish explorer **A** 395; **U** 238
Solo man **P** 443
Solomon, king of Israel **S** 252
reign of, in Jewish history **J** 103–04
Sheba **E** 302
Song of Solomon, book of the Bible **B** 156
Solomon ibn Gabirol see Ibn-Gabirol, Solomon
Solomon Islands, Pacific Ocean **P** 8
Solomon R. Guggenheim Museum, New York City **M** 518
Wright's answers to critics **W** 315
Solon (SO-lon), Athenian lawgiver **S** 252; **G** 350
Solresol, universal language **U** 194
Solstice, "stand-still" position of the sun **S** 109
Solution, chemical term **C** 220
mixtures and solutions **M** 175–76
solids dissolved in liquids **L** 310
Solution caves, or caverns **C** 155
Solvent extraction, of fats and oils **O** 77
Solvents
dry-cleaning uses **D** 337
properties of liquids **L** 310
water **W** 54

Solzhenitzyn, Alexander, Russian writer **U** 62
Somalia (so-MA-lia) **S** 253–55
flag **F** 236
Sombrero, Mexican, picture **H** 53
Somers, Sir George, English sea captain **B** 148
Somers Islands (the Bermudas) **B** 146–48
Somme, battles of the, 1916, 1918 **W** 278, 280
Somoza, Anastasio, Nicaraguan political leader **N** 249
Somoza Debayle, Anastasio, president of Nicaragua **N** 249
Somoza Debayle, Luis, Nicaraguan political leader **N** 249
Sonar, sound navigation ranging **R** 37–38
bat's echolocation system compared to sonar **B** 96–97
dolphins and porpoises **D** 275–76
echo **E** 45
submarine navigation **S** 443
United States Navy electronics and weapons **U** 193
uses of ultrasound **S** 265, 267
Sonata (so-NA-ta), in music **M** 538–40
baroque period **B** 66
classical age in music, development of **C** 331–32

Songhai (SONG-hy), African tribe dwelling primarily in the middle valley of the great bend of the Niger river in Mali. Their empire dominated western Sudan during the last half of the 15th and the 16th century, until Moroccan invaders drove them out of Timbuktu (1591) and brought their influence to an end. They are Muslims and earn their living as merchants or by raising livestock and cultivating land. Picture **A** 59.
early kingdoms of western Africa **A** 66–67; **N** 90–91

Song of Germany (Deutschland-Lied), national anthem of Federal Republic of Germany (West Germany) **N** 18
Song of Milkanwatha, nonsense rhyme **N** 272
Song of Solomon, book of Bible, Old Testament **B** 156
Song of the Earth, The, by Mahler **M** 31
Song of the Three Children, apocryphal book of Bible **B** 159
Songs **M** 538
African music **A** 77–78
American Indian music **I** 160–61
ballad, a form of folk song **B** 22–23
carols **C** 122
cowboy songs **F** 304
folklore in song **F** 303
folk music of children's songs and games **F** 322–24
Foster, Stephen **F** 389
German and Austrian music **G** 186
lied, an art song **C** 333
national anthems and patriotic songs **N** 15–27
Negro spirituals **N** 105–07
rock music **R** 262a–262d
Schubert, Franz **S** 58
singing games **G** 11–13
state songs **U** 91–93 and individual state articles
work songs **F** 319
Sonic boom, caused during supersonic flight **S** 470–71
aerodynamics of breaking the sound barrier **A** 40
noise pollution **E** 272c; **N** 270
Sonnets **S** 255–56
English verse forms **E** 250
forms of poetry **P** 353
"How do I love thee?" by Elizabeth Browning **B** 413
Italian poetry **I** 475
Milton, John **M** 311
Shakespeare's published without his consent **S** 131
Sonnets from the Portuguese, by Elizabeth Barrett Browning **B** 412, 413

Sons of Liberty, secret society organized in the American colonies at the time of the Stamp Act controversy (1765). Its members circulated petitions, intimidated British officials, and in general stirred up popular support for colonial self-government. Samuel Adams and Paul Revere were leaders of the Sons of Liberty in New England.

flag, "The Rebellious Stripes" **F** 244

political parties in colonial America **P** 379

Sons and Lovers, novel by D. H. Lawrence **E** 267

Sons of the American Revolution, National Society of (SAR), national patriotic organization for the descendants of men who actively participated in the Revolutionary War. Founded in 1889, SAR has headquarters in Washington, D.C. Its publication is *SAR Magazine.*

Sons of the Revolution (SR), national patriotic organization for descendants, on either parent's side, of veterans of the American forces who served in the Revolution of 1776. Founded in 1890, the SR sponsors essay contests, scholarship awards, and commemorative gatherings. Their headquarters are at Fraunces Tavern on Pearl Street in New York, N.Y., which is where George Washington bade farewell to his officers in 1783.

Soo Canals see Sault Sainte Marie Canals
Sooner State, nickname for Oklahoma **O** 80

Soong family, influential Chinese family. **Soong Mei-ling** (Mme. Chiang Kai-shek) (1898–   ) graduated from Wellesley College in the United States (1917) and assisted her husband in educational and social work in Nationalist China. **Soong Ch'ing-ling** (Mme. Sun Yat-sen) (1890–   ) graduated from Wesleyan College (1913) in the United States and has held high positions in Communist China. **Tsŭ-wên Soong** (T.V. Soong) (1891–1971) graduated from Harvard (1915), and was premier (1944–47) of Nationalist China.

China, history of **C** 227

Soot, black substance in smoke from burning fuels
cancer-causing agent **C** 91
Sophia, Bulgaria, see Sofia
Sophists, teachers of practical philosophy in ancient Greece **E** 63
teachers of oratory **O** 180
Sophocles (SOPH-o-clese), Greek dramatist **D** 294
early forms of fiction **F** 109
Greek civilization **A** 229
Greek literature **G** 351
Soprano (so-PRAN-o) **voice V** 375
choral music **C** 277
Sorata, mountain peak see Illampu
Sorbonne (sor-BONN), a college of the University of Paris **P** 73
Sorcerers, workers of magic or witchcraft **W** 208
prehistoric art **P** 441

Sorensen, Virginia (1912–   ), American author, b. Provo, Utah. Her first children's book was *Curious Missie* (1953). She won the Newbery medal (1957) for *Miracles on Maple Hill.* Other books include *Plain Girl, Lotte's Locket,* and *Where Nothing Is Long Ago.*

Sorghum, a grass **G** 319
grain sorghum **G** 285, 287; picture **O** 87
seeds, pictures **G** 284
Sorgo, or sweet sorghum **S** 453
Sori, spore cases of ferns **F** 92

SOS, international distress call, especially of ships in danger. When radio-telegraph equipment was developed for use on ships, a distress signal easily transmitted in Morse code was needed. SOS translates simply into three short, three long, and three short signals. It was internationally adopted 1912. Any ship hearing SOS must immediately go to the rescue.

Sosigenes (so-SI-ge-nese), Greek mathematician **C** 12
Sostratus (SOS-tra-tus) **of Cnidus** (NY-dus), Greek architect **W** 216
Sotatsu (so-TA-tsu), Japanese painter **O** 218
Sotol (so-TALL) **cactus,** picture **D** 125
Soul food F 342
Soul music see Rhythm-and-blues music
Sound S 256–67
anthropological studies **A** 308
barrier, flying through **A** 40; **S** 470–71
descriptive linguistics **L** 301
Does sound exist with no one to hear it? **S** 265
Doppler effect **L** 269; **S** 263
ear, anatomy of **B** 285
echo **E** 45
electronic music **E** 142g–142h
energy **E** 199, 201
fishes **F** 202
fog horns and signals **L** 277
getting the message from here to there **E** 142c–142f
hi-fi and stereo **H** 125–27
insects' "messages" **I** 268
insulation and insulating materials **I** 292
languages show relationship by matching sounds **L** 39
motion pictures **M** 474
moviemaking at home **P** 220
noise, and noise pollution **E** 272c–272d; **N** 269–70
parrots and other "talking" birds **P** 83–86
phonics **P** 193–96
phonograph **P** 196–98
pictures on tape of animal sounds **A** 275, 276
sonic boom **S** 470–71
spectrograms of animal communication **A** 275, picture **A** 276
tape and wire recorders **T** 20–21
thunder **T** 170
vacuum does not permit sound to travel **V** 264
voice, how produced **V** 375–76
whispering galleries **G** 129
Why do you hear a roaring sound in shells? **S** 265
See also Loran; Radar; Radar astronomy; Shoran; Sonar; Ultrasonics
Sound barrier S 469
aerodynamics of the barrier **A** 40
Sound effects
animated cartoons **A** 299
plays **P** 336
SOund Fixing And Ranging see SOFAR
Sounding, measuring the depth of water **O** 26–27
Sound mind in a sound body, goal of physical education **P** 225
SOund NAvigation Ranging see Sonar
Sound tracks, of movies
phototubes used with, diagram **P** 200
Sound waves, vibrations that hit eardrum **B** 280–81, 285
do not travel through a vacuum **V** 264
getting the message from here to there **E** 142c–142d
musical instruments **M** 544
noise, in decibel units **N** 269–70
thunder **T** 170
Souphannovong (soup-ha-nu-VOHNG), prince of Laos **L** 43
Sour, a sense of taste **B** 286
Souris, P.E.I., Canada **P** 456e
Souris (Mouse) River, Manitoba and North Dakota **N** 325
Sousa (SOO-za), **John Philip,** American bandmaster and composer **B** 40
early cylinder phonograph recordings **R** 123

Southern Christian Leadership Conference, civil rights organization founded (1957) in Atlanta, Ga., and headed (1957–68) by Martin Luther King. A co-ordinating and service agency for local organizations, it works to improve civic, religious, economic, and cultural conditions, particularly in the South, and fosters nonviolent resistance to racial injustice. It publishes the *SCLC Newsletter.*

Southern Education Foundation (SEF), consolidation (1937) of various funds to help southern youth, especially Negroes, receive educational assistance.

Southey, Robert (1775–1843), English poet, b. Bristol. Although he wrote criticism, biography, and history. Southey was in his day considered primarily a poet. One of the Lake poets, he was poet laureate (1813–43).

South Sea Islands *see* Pacific Islands and island groups
South Shore, Quebec, Canada Q 10a
South Temperate zone Z 372
  birds of B 226
South Vietnam *see* Vietnam, Republic of
South West Africa (Namibia) S 336
  South Africa, government of S 272
Southwest Asia *see* Middle East
Souvanna Phouma (soo-VON-na POO-ma), **Prince,**
  Laotian politician L 43
Sovereign equality, principle of the United Nations U 81
Sovereignty (SOV-er-enty)
  popular sovereignty, rule by the people D 105
Soviet (SO-vi-et), a council of workers L 138
Soviet (SO-vi-et) Asia, largest region of Asia A 450;
  E 305, 307
  Soviet Central Asia U 45–46
Soviet Europe E 305, 307
Soviet Far East S 173
Soviet Federal Socialist Republic *see* Russian Soviet
  Federal Socialist Republic
Soviet federation of labor groups L 10
Soviet literature U 62–63
Soviets, local units of government in the Union of Soviet
  Socialist Republics M 508; U 42
Soviet Union *see* Union of Soviet Socialist Republics
Sow bugs, crustaceans S 168; picture S 169
Sows, female pigs H 209; P 248
Soybeans S 337
  Decatur, Ill., soybean capital I 77
  soybean oil O 79
Soyinka, Wole, Nigerian writer A 76c
Soyuz, series of manned Soviet space flights S 344, 345

Spaak (SPOK), **Paul-Henri** (1899–1972), Belgian statesman, b. Brussels. Having served his government as
cabinet member, foreign minister, and premier, he was
the first president of the UN General Assembly (1946),
and a moving force in the establishment of the Common
Market. He served as secretary-general of NATO (1957–
61). He was again Belgian foreign minister (1961–66).

Space
  development of space sense in children C 233
  living organisms need space E 272b; L 252–53
  relativity R 142–43
  shapes, in design D 136–37
  topology, invariant shapes T 220
Space, outer
  aquanauts and astronauts U 24
  astronauts and cosmonauts S 344, 345, 346, 347
  cosmic rays, studies of C 511
  dust D 347
  Echo I, balloon-satellite B 34
  how rockets work in space R 256
  limitation on weapons of mass destruction D 185
  moon landing E 368; M 452–53; S 339–340a, 340g–
    340j
  Outer Space Treaty, 1967 D 185; I 321
  photography in aerospace program P 208
  Piccard's balloon ascents B 32
  radiation belts R 46–49
  radio and radar astronomy R 69–76
  satellites S 39–43
  space exploration and travel S 338–49
  space flights and flight data S 344–45
  terms, selected list defined S 340
  United States Air Force and Navy U 161, 193
  universe and space U 204
  vacuum V 262
Spacebands, in typesetting P 465
Space communications C 440

Spacecraft and spaceships S 339–49
  attitude, or position, of S 340f
  ion-drive I 351
  names of spacecraft and flight data S 344–45
  paths in space, diagram S 340d
  possible communication by lasers, picture M 131
  UFO's mistaken reports on F 285, 287
  See also Satellites, man-made
Space exploration and travel S 338–49
  aerospaceplanes, rocket planes of the future R 262
  economics of S 349
  model kits of spacecraft A 106
  moon landing E 368; M 452–53; S 339–340a, 340g–
    340j
  navigation in space N 68, 69
  new methods of electric power generation P 427
  Oberth's work on astronautics O 6–7
  planetarium can show view from spaceship P 268
  radiation belts R 49
  rockets R 255–62
  satellites of the future S 43
  science teamwork to provide technology S 78
  Tsiolkovsky, pioneer rocket scientist T 306–07
  weightlessness due to lack of gravity G 324–25
Space flights, with flight data S 344–45
Space Needle, symbol of the Seattle World's Fair
  F 17; picture F 16
Space probes S 348–49
  better observations of the sun S 467
  observatory studies O 14
  paths in space, diagram S 340d
Space shapes, in design D 136–37
Spaceships *see* Spacecraft and spaceships
Space shuttles S 343
Space stations S 342–43; picture G 325
  orbiting observatories E 28–29
  paths in space, diagram S 340d
Space suits S 340L; diagram S 338
  armor, new type A 435; picture A 434
  living on the moon and in space M 455; S 340L–341

Spadefish, name of a family of saltwater fishes found
along coasts in tropical and sometimes temperate
climates. The Atlantic spadefish, an important food fish
in the West Indies, is found from Cape Cod, Mass. to
Brazil. It reaches 3 feet in length. It has black and white
vertical stripes on its body.

Spadefoot toads F 477
Spaghetti, food made from wheat G 282

Spahn, **Warren Edward** (1921–), American baseball
player, b. Buffalo, N.Y. An outstanding left-handed pitcher,
he won 20 games 13 times and threw 2 no-hitters. He
joined Boston (later Milwaukee) Braves in 1942 and later
played for New York Mets and San Francisco Giants,
winning 363 games.

Spain S 350–59
  Andorra, between Spain and France A 254–55
  architecture *see* Spanish architecture
  art *see* Spanish art
  bullfighting B 449–51
  costumes, traditional, pictures C 350; D 264
  dance, picture D 30
  favorite foods F 342; picture F 337
  flag F 240
  grape harvest, picture A 98
  language *see* Spanish language
  literature *see* Spanish literature
  Madrid M 11–13
  Moorish-style houses, picture H 180

Spears
  fishing **F** 218
Special agents of Federal Bureau of Investigation F 76
Special Forces, United States Army **U** 173
Specialization, concentration in a certain field **E** 49
  comparative advantage in international trade **I** 326–27
Special libraries L 176–79
Special Libraries Association L 192
Special theory of relativity R 141–42
Specialty stores R 188
Specie (SPE-she) **payment B** 47
Species, divisions of biological classification **T** 29
  classification of living things **K** 252
  differences studied in genetics **G** 77
  evolution **E** 338
Specific (spe-CIF-ic) **gravity,** in physics **M** 172
  floating **F** 253
Specific heat W 53

Specific impulse, measure of the efficiency of a rocket engine. It is measured in terms of the thrust produced by burning a measured quantity of fuel in a specified period of time—for example, pounds of thrust per pound of fuel per second.

Spectacled bears B 108
Spectacles see Eyeglasses
Spectator, The, English journal **E** 258
  magazines, history of **M** 14
Spectrochemical analysis L 269
Spectrograph, optical instrument **O** 173
  a camera attachment for a spectroscope **P** 208
  mass spectograph, cosmic rays studied by **C** 512–13
  observatory instrument **O** 11–12; **S** 464
Spectrography (spec-TROG-raphy), use of spectroscope plus a camera to analyze light **P** 208
Spectroheliograph (spec-tro-HE-lio-graph), combination camera and spectroscope **A** 474
  instrument for analyzing light **E** 28
Spectrohelioscopes (spec-tro-HE-lio-scopes), special kind of spectroscope **S** 466
Spectrophotometer (spec-tro-pho-TOM-et-er), optical instrument **O** 173
Spectroscopes (SPEC-tro-scopes), optical instruments **O** 173
  developments in physical chemistry **C** 215
  instruments that break up light into its various wavelengths **P** 208
  Mars **M** 108
  observing the sun **S** 464
  tools of astronomers **A** 474; **Q** 8
Spectrum (plural: spectra), band of colors formed by light going through a prism **L** 269
  Doppler effect studied through use of spectrum **L** 269
  electromagnetic spectrum, diagrams **L** 270, **R** 43
  first spectroscope **A** 473–74
  Newton's experiments **N** 207
  observing the sun **S** 464–66
  quasars' spectra **Q** 8
  red shift **U** 201
  stars **S** 410
  ultraviolet rays **R** 44; **S** 235
  X rays **L** 270; **X** 339–41
  visible and invisible, of the sun's radiation **E** 24
  white light directed through a prism, diagram **L** 267
Spectrum bomb, antimissile system **M** 347
Speculation, buying and selling involving risk **S** 428–29
Speech S 376–78
  anthropologists study origins **A** 308
  Bell, Alexander G., **B** 132
  communication **C** 430
  deaf, education of the **D** 50–53

dialects **D** 152
  nonsense rhymes **N** 272
  phonics **P** 193–96
  ventriloquism **V** 301–03
  vocal organs **V** 375–76
  See also Language and languages
Speeches
  Bryan's "Cross of Gold" speech **B** 415–16; **O** 181
  Burke's speech "On Conciliation with the Colonies" **E** 259
  how to prepare and give a speech **P** 509–10
  oratory **O** 180–81
  Patrick Henry's "If this be treason" **H** 113–14
  public speaking **P** 508–10
Speed
  animals: locomotion **A** 289–91, 293–94, 295
  automobile racing **A** 540
  controls on electric appliances **E** 119–20
  conversion of mass and energy **M** 173
  iceboating **I** 28, 30
  law of falling bodies **F** 34
  of fishes, related to size **F** 188
  of light **L** 265–66
  relative to pressure **A** 38
  relativity **R** 142
  sound **S** 257
  spacecraft, velocities of **S** 340d
  supersonic flight **S** 469–73
Speed, drug see Methedrine

Speedometer (speed-OM-et-er), instrument that indicates the speed of a car or other vehicle. A dial on the dashboard registers the speed in miles (or kilometers) per hour, the reading being obtained from the rotation of gears in the transmission. The dial is connected to the transmission by a flexible, rotating shaft. The shaft spins a magnet, which in turn causes a spring to move the pointer on the dial. An odometer, which registers total distance traveled, is also part of the speedometer dial.

Speed skating I 50–53
  Olympic event **O** 109
Speedway racing A 539
Speedwell, Pilgrims' ship **P** 344
  abandoned as unseaworthy **A** 186
Speedwriting, abbreviated longhand system **S** 164
Speke, John Hanning, English explorer **L** 34
Speleology (spe-le-OL-ogy) **C** 158
  See also Caves and caverns; Spelunking
Spelling S 378–79
  English language, irregular system **L** 302
  homonyms **H** 194
  Initial Teaching Alphabet **I** 254
  name variations **N** 7
  new and old textbooks, pictures **E** 77
  Webster, Noah, and spelling reform **W** 99

Spellman, Francis Joseph, Cardinal (1889–1967), American Roman Catholic clergyman, b. Whitman, Mass. He became bishop (1932), archbishop of New York (1939), and cardinal (1946). His books include *The Road to Victory* and *Prayers and Poems.*

Spelunking (spe-LUNK-ing), or cave exploring **S** 380
  finding a cave **C** 158
  See also Caves and caverns; Mountain climbing

Spence, Sir Basil Urwin (1907–), British architect, b. India. A graduate of Edinburgh University, Spence began his career designing private homes. After his army service (1939–45), he built churches and other public buildings in England and on the Continent. In 1951 he

SPENCE, SIR BASIL | DICTIONARY INDEX · 549

Spencer, Sir Basil Urwin (continued)
submitted the winning design for a new cathedral for
Coventry, England. (Coventry's 14th-century Cathedral
Church of St. Michael had been destroyed in World War
II air raids.) Among his other buildings are the Air
Terminal in Glasgow and the British Embassy in Rome.
  Coventry Cathedral **E** 241; picture **C** 133

Spence, Thomas, English bookseller and inventor **U** 256

Spence, Wishart Flett (1904–   ), Canadian judge. He has
served as justice of the supreme court of Ontario
(1950–63) and of the supreme court of Canada (since
1963).

Spencer, Herbert (1820–1903), English philosopher, b.
Derby. His 10-volume *System of Synthetic Philosophy*
had an immense influence on scholars throughout the
world during the latter half of the 19th century. The first
to use the phrase "survival of the fittest," Spencer
believed in extreme individualism, as advocated in *Social
Statics,* and the natural development of the intelligence,
as outlined in *Education.*
  sociology, development of **S** 227

Spender, Stephen, English poet **E** 266

Spengler, Oswald (1880–1936), German writer, b. Blankenburg. His most important work on the philosophy of
history, *The Decline of the West,* traced the life and
death of civilizations and predicted the passing of
modern western civilization and the rise of a new Asiatic
civilization.

Spenser, Edmund (1552?–1599), English poet, b. London.
The Shepheardes Calender established him as the
foremost poet of his time. His masterpiece, *The Faerie
Queene,* greatly influenced English poetic literature; the
nine-line stanza he invented for it has since been called
the Spenserian stanza.
  English literature, place in **E** 251

Spenser, Willard, American composer **O** 157
Spenserian (spen-SE-rian) **stanza,** in poetry **P** 353
  English verse forms **E** 251
  sonnets **S** 256
Spermaceti (sperm-a-CET-i) **waxy substance** taken from
  sperm whales **W** 152
  candles made of **C** 97
Spermaceti organs, of sperm whales **W** 147
Sperm cell, male reproductive cell **R** 178
  eggs and embryos **E** 90
  genetics and heredity **G** 77–78
Sperm whales, or cachalots **W** 147; picture **W** 148

Sperry, Armstrong (1897–   ), American author and
illustrator, b. New Haven, Conn. His trips to the South
Pacific gave him material for many of his books for
children. *Call It Courage* won the Newbery medal (1941).

Sperry, Elmer Ambrose (1860–1930), American inventor
and industrialist, b. Cortland, N.Y. A prolific inventor, he
took out 400 patents. His most important invention was
the gyrocompass, developed between 1896 and 1910.
Other inventions include the gyrostabilizer, used in ships
and aircraft, and an electric-arc searchlight.

Spessartite, gem mineral **G** 75
Sphagnum moss **F** 93–94
Sphalerite (SPHAL-er-ite), ore **Z** 370
Sphere, geometric figure **G** 129
  surface tension **L** 310

Spherical aberration, of lenses **L** 148
Sphinx, mythological monster, half lion, half human
  riddle of solved by Oedipus **J** 132
  Great Sphinx of Giza **A** 222; **E** 96; picture **E** 93
  Hittite art **A** 238
Sphinx moths, pictures **I** 277
Sphygmomanometer (sphig-mo-ma-NOM-et-er), instrument
  for measuring blood pressure **M** 208f–208g; picture
  D 199
Spica (SPY-ca), star **C** 492
Spice Islands see Moluccas
Spices and condiments **S** 380–83
  food preservation by pickling **F** 348
  valued as money during Middle Ages **F** 333–34
SPID see Submersible Portable Inflatable Dwelling
Spider crabs, crustaceans, picture **S** 169
Spider monkeys **M** 420, 422; picture **M** 421
  pets **P** 180
Spiders **S** 383–88
  Bruce, Robert, legend **B** 414
  compared to insects, picture **I** 263
  household pests **H** 263
  reproduction **R** 179
  species harmful to man **I** 284; **S** 388
  Why don't spiders get caught in their own webs?
    S 385
Spider webs **S** 385–86
  Charlotte's Web, excerpt **W** 160–61
Spies and spying **S** 388–90
  aerial and infrared photography for military intelligence
    P 206
  FBI investigates spying **F** 77
  kites, man-carrying **K** 267
  Trojan horse **G** 366; **T** 293
  Tubman, Harriet **T** 307
  What are some types of espionage agents? **S** 389
  See also Bugging
Spikes, large nails **N** 2
Spilling salt, superstition **S** 474–75
Spillville, Iowa **I** 367–68
Spillway, surplus water escape passage **D** 18, 20
  control floods **F** 257
Spinach, vegetable **V** 292
  leaves we eat **P** 307; picture **P** 306
Spinal cord, links brain and body, diagram **B** 281
  divisions of the brain and nervous system
    B 366–68
Spindle, part of cell division **C** 164
Spine, or backbone, of animals **K** 251
  animals with and without backbones **A** 264
  birds **B** 201
  body's skeleton **B** 270–271
  snakes have long backbones and short tails **S** 204
Spinel (spin-EL), gem mineral **G** 76
Spines, sharp projections
  hedgehogs **I** 260; picture **I** 261
  porcupines **R** 279–80
  thorns are a special kind of leaf **L** 120
Spinets, keyboard instruments **K** 238; picture **P** 242
  in concert, picture **I** 482

Spingarn medal, gold medal awarded annually by the
National Association for the Advancement of Colored
People (NAACP) to an outstanding American Negro. It
was established (1914) by poet and critic Joel Elias
Spingarn (1875–1939), who served as chairman of
directors (1913–19), treasurer (1919–30), and president
(1930–39) of the NAACP.

Spinnakers, sails **S** 10
Spinneret, a kind of nozzle **N** 426
  organs of spiders that produce silk **S** 385

Spinning, of yarns F 105
  Arkwright's spinning frame I 236, 238; T 140–41
  cotton industry C 520
  handicraft in India, picture I 128
  Hargreave's spinning jenny I 234–35
  Industrial Revolution brought about by inventions in
    spinning I 233–35
  Jacquard's loom A 532; R 352; T 141
  llama wool spinning, picture P 163
  old and new ways, pictures A 533
  textiles industry T 140–41
  wool W 235
  See *also* Weaving
Spinning, fishing F 208
Spinning jenny, machine I 234–35
Spinoza (spin-O-za), **Baruch,** Dutch philosopher S 390
  philosophical systems P 192
Spinster, origin of word I 234
Spiny anteaters, or echidnas P 333–34
  egg-laying mammals M 71–72
Spiracles (SPY-racles), breathing holes of insects I 272
  skates and rays S 142
Spiral, geometric figure, picture G 131
Spiral galaxies U 198; pictures U 197, 199
Spire, in architecture, pictures P484, 485

Spirea (spy-RE-a), common name applied to any flowering shrub of the genus *Spiraea*. Cultivated all over the
world, spireas are anywhere from 6 in. to 12 ft. high.
They have clusters of small white or pink flowers.

Spirillum (spy-RILL-um), a corkscrew-shaped bacteria B 10

Spirit level, instrument for determining if a surface is
level (horizontal to the earth's surface). It consists of a
glass tube filled with a "spirit," or liquid, such as
alcohol. An air bubble remains in the tube, which curves
up slightly at the center. When the tube is perfectly
level, the bubble moves to the center of the tube. The
device, set in a flat bar of metal or wood, is laid on a
surface to determine its levelness.

Spirit of St. Louis, airplane A 573; L 300; picture
  A 569
Spirit of St. Louis, The, autobiography of Charles Lind-
  bergh A 215; L 300
Spirits of turpentine T 330

Spiritualism, the opposite of materialism; the doctrine
that Spirit is the all-pervading reality in the universe. In
spiritism, the more accurate though less popular term, it
is believed that spirits of the dead can communicate
with the living through persons known as mediums.

Spirituals H 313
  See *also* Negro spirituals
Spirit varnishes V 279
Spirit worship R 145
  African art reflects A 72
  China C 260
Spits, or carved sandbars M 137
Spitsbergen see Svalbard Islands
Spittle bugs P 289; pictures I 265, P 288
Spleen, organ of body D 206
Splendid little war, Spanish-American War, 1898
  S 374–76
Splints and slings, for broken bones
  first aid F 162
Split, Yugoslavia, picture Y 354
Split-level houses H 184
Splitrock, or boulder caves C 156–57
Split Rock lighthouse, on Lake Superior, picture M 324

Spock, Benjamin (1903–), American pediatrician,
writer, and university professor, b. New Haven, Conn. His
Common Sense Book of Baby and Child Care (first
published 1946) made him a world-famous, widely
consulted pediatrician. In 1955 he became professor of
child development at Western Reserve University School
of Medicine in Cleveland, Ohio. He retired in June, 1967,
and now lives in New York City. Since his retirement
he has participated in anti-war activities.

Spode, Josiah, II, English porcelain maker P 418
Spoil, mud and silt excavated by dredges D 308, 309
Spoils system, political patronage C 317
  Arthur, Chester Alan A 438h, 439
  Hayes's efforts at reform H 81
  Jackson's administration J 5–6
  Jefferson's efforts to keep judges out of politics J 68
  Van Buren in New York V 273
Spokane, Washington W 26
Spokes, of wheels W 158
Spondees, metrical feet in poetry P 354
Sponges S 391–92
  ancient techniques of sponge divers U 13–14
  Bahamas B 17
  ocean life in shallow waters O 38
  Tarpon Springs, Fla., Sponge Capital of America F 267;
    picture F 266
Spontaneous combustion F 137
Spontaneous generation, biological theory P 96
  Leeuwenhoek helps discredit the theory L 127

Spoonbill, large wading bird found chiefly in tropical and
subtropical regions. Spoonbills range in color from pure
white to pink. The roseate spoonbill, the only American
species, is rose colored with white neck. Spoonbills have
a long, flat bill with a spatula-shaped tip, which they use
to scoop up food from the water. They eat water insects,
frogs, shellfish, and small fish.

Spoonerisms, transposing of initial sounds of words
  H 278–79
Spoon River, Illinois I 73–74
Spoon River Anthology, by Edgar Lee Masters A 209
  a collection of epitaphs in free verse E 151
Spoons K 285–88
  decorative art objects, picture D 66
  origin of "born with a silver spoon in his mouth"
    K 285
  silver-plating of E 149, 150
  table settings T 2–3
Sporangia, spore cases F 497–98
Spore prints, how to make F 499
Spores, reproductive cells of plants R 177–78
  algae A 155
  ferns, mosses, and lichens F 92–95
  fungi F 497
  mushrooms M 521
  photosynthesis, role in P 223

Sport, any individual organism that differs sharply from
its parents, as, for example, a dwarf flower. The term
"mutant" is now more generally used.

Sport, jumping see Sky-diving
Sporting dogs D 252, 259; pictures D 253
Sports
  archery A 366–68
  automobile racing A 538–40
  badminton B 13–15
  ball, various types, pictures B 20, 21
  baseball B 69–81
  basketball B 82–90

Spot, species of saltwater fishes found from Cape Cod to Texas. It is a popular food fish in coastal areas of the southern United States. The upper part of the body is bluish and crossed by diagonal yellow stripes; the underside is silvery. It has very small teeth and scales and a dark spot above the gill.

Spotted Tail (1833?–1881), American Sioux Indian chief, b. near Fort Laramie, Wyo. One of the signers of the treaty (1868) providing for an Indian reservation in the western part of present-day South Dakota, he was known for his friendliness to whites. He helped bring about the surrender (1877) of Crazy Horse, his nephew. Spotted Tail was killed by one of his subchiefs, Crow Dog.

Spring beauty, early spring wild flower belonging to the purslane family. It has a bulblike base, narrow leaves, and loose clusters of white or pink flowers. Spring beauties grow best in shady, moist areas.

Spruce, tree, picture T 276
  Alaska, Sitka spruce, state tree of A 129
  California forest, picture G 94
  leaves, needlelike, picture L 119
  uses of the wood and its grain, picture W 224
  white spruce, state tree of South Dakota S 312
Spuds, beams for supporting dredges D 309
Spumoni, Italian ice cream I 34
Spur gears G 66
Spurges, plants P 322

Sputnik, name given to the first few artificial satellites launched by the Soviet Union. (Sputnik I, put into orbit on October 4, 1957, was the world's first artificial satellite.) "Sputnik" simply means "satellite," and the name no longer is applied to the many Soviet satellites that have been launched since. Names of Soviet series of satellites and space probes include Vostok, Voskhod, Cosmos, Lunik, Zond, and Soyuz.

Spyglass, small telescope
  Galileo devised for use in astronomy G 6

Spyri (SHPE-ri), Johanna (1827–1901), Swiss author, b. Hirzel, near Zurich. The most famous of her children's stories is *Heidi*, set in Switzerland.

Spy stories *see* Mystery, detective, and suspense stories
SQ3R method, of learning L 105
Squabs, young pigeons B 247
Squadron, army troop unit U 172
Squamata (squa-MAY-ta), or scaly reptiles S 204
Squanto, American Indian P 345
Square, geometric figure G 126
Square, or reef, knots K 290
Square dances, or barn dances D 28; pictures D 28, 36
  folk dancing F 299
Square Deal, program of Theodore Roosevelt R 328
Square measure, of area W 115, 111
Square numbers and gnomon numbers in number lore N 383
Square root, of a number N 385
Squares, of numbers
  metric system W 116
  Pythagorean theorem G 126
Square, tool for measuring T 216
  mechanical drawing M 197
  woodworking W 230
Squash, vegetable V 292
Squash bugs P 285
Squash racquets ball, picture B 21
Squatters, settlers on land not legally their own P 260
Squatter sovereignty, or popular sovereignty
  Kansas-Nebraska Act, 1854 K 192
  Lincoln-Douglas debates L 299
  territory of Kansas K 190–91
Squids, mollusks O 275; picture L 230
  animal movement in water A 266, 291
  giants of nature A 265; G 200
  Japanese food, picture J 38
  locomotion A 291; picture A 290
Squinch domes, of mosques I 419
Squire, or shield bearer, knight's apprentice K 276–77
Squirrel-cage electric motor E 139, 141
Squirrel monkeys M 420
Squirrels R 276
  adaptations to life with other organisms L 222
  pets P 180
  tracks, picture A 271
Sri Lanka, Republic of *see* Ceylon
Srinagar (sri-NUG-ar), capital of Kashmir K 197; picture K 199

Sri Ranganatha Temple, Hindu shrine, picture H 131
S.S., abbreviation for steamship O 23
SS, Hitler's official police N 71
  found guilty at war crimes trials W 9
SSM, surface-to-surface missiles M 345–47
SST's (supersonic transport planes) S 472; T 267
St. or Ste., abbreviation for Saint and Sainte *see* names of saints, as Paul, Saint, and Xavier, Francis, Saint. Place names beginning with St. are under Saint, as Saint Louis, Missouri
Stabiae (stay-BI-e), Italy P 390
Stabiles, stationary sculpture of Alexander Calder S 105
Stabilizers, of airplanes
  gyroscopic stabilizers G 436
  tail fins A 554
Stable isotopes (I-so-topes) N 356–57
Staccato (stac-CA-to) notes, in musical notation M 531
Stacking levels, at airports A 564; diagram A 565
Stadacona (sta-DA-co-na), Canada, early Indian village, now Quebec City C 124
  Houston's Astrodome H 270
  original center for the Olympic Games O 105
Staël, Madame de, French writer F 439
Staff, in musical notation M 525
Staff officers, United States Navy U 189
Staff of life, bread B 385

Stafford, Thomas Patten (1930–   ), American astronaut, b. Weatherford, Okla. An Air Force test pilot before joining the space program in 1962, Stafford was co-pilot (with W. M. Schirra as pilot) of the Gemini 6 space capsule. This flight marked the first U.S. rendezvous in space between capsules (with Gemini 7). In 1966 Stafford was command pilot of Gemini 9, and in 1969 he orbited the moon in Apollo 10.
  space flight data S 344, 345, 347

Staffordshire pottery P 418; picture P 416
Stage *see* Plays, production of; Theater
Stagecoaches T 260
  Concord, N. H. coaches N 148
  early form of bus travel B 465
Stage crews, of plays P 336
Stagehands, of a theater T 158
Stage managers, of plays P 336; T 158
Stage scenery and lighting P 339; pictures 337–38
  scenic and lighting designers T 157–58
Stagg, Amos Alonzo, American football coach F 364
Stahl (SHTAHL), Georg E., German chemist, phlogiston theory C 210
Stained-glass windows S 393–95
  Cathedral of Coventry, England, picture C 133
  Chagall, Marc C 184
  Chartres Cathedral, picture G 268
  early European techniques of glassmaking G 230
  Gothic tracery G 268
Stainer (SHTY-ner), Jakob, Austrian violin maker V 342
Stainless steels, alloys A 168; I 396
  chromium alloys C 296
  Faraday produced first stainless steel F 44
  knives, forks, and spoons K 288
  nickel N 250
  salad set, picture D 66
Stain removal L 84
  dyeing and staining D 366
  treatment by spotters in dry cleaning D 338
Stalactites (sta-LAC-tites), cave formations C 154–55
Stalagmites (sta-LAG-mites), cave formations C 154–55
Stalemate, chess term C 225; picture C 224
Stalin, Joseph, Russian premier S 395
  Communist dictatorship of Russia C 443

Standards, National Bureau of, bureau of the Department of Commerce established (1901) to assure the maximum application of physical and engineering sciences to the advancement of technology in industry and commerce. It conducts research and provides services in basic measurement standards, materials research, engineering standards and technology.

Stanfield, Robert Lorne (1914–   ), Canadian lawyer and statesman, b. Truro, Nova Scotia. Formerly premier of Nova Scotia (1956–67), he was chosen leader of Canada's Progressive Conservative Party in 1968, succeeding John Diefenbaker.

Stanford, Leland, American railroad pioneer   **C** 28
Stanford-Binet (STAN-ford-bi-NAY) **Scale,** an intelligence test   **T** 117

Stanhope, Charles, earl of Stanhope (1753–1816), English politician and scientist, b. London. He was a member of Parliament (1780–86), and after becoming the third earl of Stanhope (1786), he entered the House of Lords. When his motion against interfering with the internal affairs of France was defeated (1795) "in a minority of one" (which became his nickname), he temporarily withdrew from Parliament (1795–1800). His many scientific inventions include steam propulsion for ships, a stereotyping process, an iron handpress, two calculating machines, a microscope lens, and fireproof building stucco.

Stanislas of Cracow, Saint (1030–1079), Polish bishop, b. Szczepanowski. Stanislas excommunicated King Boleslav because of the king's cruelty and lust. The king was so angry that he ordered his guards to kill Stanislas. The guards refused, so King Boleslav himself killed Stanislas. Stanislas was canonized (1253) and became the patron saint of Poland and of the city of Cracow.

Stanislavski (sta-nis-LOF-ski), **Konstantin** (Konstantin Sergeevich Alekseev) (1863–1938), Russian actor, director, and teacher, b. Moscow. A co-founder (1898) of the Moscow Art Theatre, he directed and acted in many plays and trained his company by a new method designed to give the illusion of complete reality on stage. He described his acting technique in *My Life in Art* and *An Actor Prepares.* Among Stanislavski's greatest achievements were his productions of Chekhov's plays.

Stanley, Francis Edgar (1849–1918) and **Freelan O.** (1849–1940), American inventors and pioneer automobile makers. They began making steam cars in 1896 after selling a photographic process they had invented to Eastman Kodak. They did not advertise, but gained publicity for their cars by entering them in races. In 1899 they sold their patents to a competitor. The next year they went back into business with a new and superior design. "Stanley Steamers" gained wide fame for their speed and reliability; in 1906 a Stanley Steamer reached 127.6 mph at Daytona, Fla. Identical twins, the brothers always dressed alike.

Stanley, Henry Morton, English explorer   **S** 400
Stanley, Wendell M., American biochemist   **V** 362

Stanley, William (1858–1916), American electrical engineer and inventor, b. Brooklyn, N.Y. In 1886 Stanley designed and set up equipment to light Great Barrington, Mass., by alternating current, which until then had been considered unmanageable. His inventions included alternating-current generators and motors, condensers, and an improved meter for measuring power consumption.

Stanley cup, prize awarded annually to the professional ice hockey champion. Originally awarded to the Canadian championship team, it was first given in 1892 by Lord Stanley, Governor-General of Canada. When, early in the 1900's, professional teams were organized, the Cup became associated with professional ice hockey. Since

1917 the Stanley cup has been in the possession of the National Hockey League.

Stanley Steamer, automobile **A** 542
Stanleyville, Congo (Leopoldville), now Kisangani, Congo (Zaïre) **S** 400
Stannum, Latin name for tin see Tin

Stans, Maurice Hubert (1908–   ), American businessman and government official, b. Shakopee, Minn. Stans was deputy postmaster general (1955–57) and deputy director of the Bureau of the Budget (1958–61). In 1969 Nixon appointed him secretary of commerce.

Stansbury, Howard (1806–1863), American soldier and explorer, b. New York, N.Y. A civil engineer, he entered the Army (1838) and led an expedition (1849) to the Great Salt Lake area. His report on the most practical route was valuable in planning the Union Pacific Railway.

Stanton, Edwin McMasters (1814–1869), American politician, b. Steubenville, Ohio. Appointed secretary of war (1862–68) by President Lincoln, he served ably during the Civil War. Opposing the reconstructionist policies favored by President Andrew Johnson, he intrigued against him and was dismissed (1868) from the Cabinet. Impeachment charges were brought against Johnson because of his dismissal of Stanton.
 Johnson impeachment **J** 125–26

Stanton, Elizabeth Cady (1815–1902), American woman suffragist, b. Johnstown, N.Y. She married Henry Brewster Stanton, a lawyer and abolitionist (1840), and was the mother of 7 children. With Lucretia Mott she helped organize the first woman's rights convention in Seneca Falls, N.Y. (1848). From 1851 she lectured and worked with Susan B. Anthony for woman's suffrage, and was president of the National Woman Suffrage Association (1869–90).
 woman suffrage movement **W** 212b

Stanza, a number of verses of poetry **P** 353
Staphylococcus, bacteria **F** 354
Staple (short) **fibers** **F** 105–06
Staples, fasteners **N** 2
Staple yarns **N** 426
Star, Kansas City, Missouri newspaper **M** 375
Starboard, right side of a boat or ship **S** 155
 sailing **S** 13
Starch **S** 401
 body chemistry of **B** 290
 digestion of **B** 275
 fermentation **F** 88
 grain source of starch **G** 286
 model of its molecule **A** 483
 photosynthesis, starch tests **P** 221; pictures **P** 222
 potatoes **P** 412
Star Chamber, Court of, English history **E** 223
Star charts, of constellations **C** 490, 492–93
Starfishes, echinoderms **S** 402–04
 How does a starfish move? **S** 403
 metamorphosis **M** 234
 nervous system, diagram **B** 363
Starfish House, of Conshelf Station II, pictures **U** 18

Stargazer, name of a family of saltwater fishes found in most parts of the world. The eyes of the stargazer are located on top of the head and look straight up. Stargazers often lie buried in the sand, waiting for small fish or shellfish, which are their prey. The northern stargazer, found from New York to Virginia, reaches 22 inches in length and a weight of about 20 pounds.

Stark, John, American Revolutionary War hero **N** 161; **R** 199, 204
Starlings, birds **B** 219; picture **B** 247
 animal communication **A** 278
 homing and migration **H** 192–93
 "talking birds" **P** 86
Star maps **C** 490, 492–93
Star-nosed moles **I** 259; picture **I** 260
Star of Africa, gem cut from Cullinan diamond **D** 156

Star of Bethlehem, in Old Testament (Matthew 2:2, 7, 9), the star that guided the Wise Men to Bethlehem, where Jesus was born.

Star-of-Bethlehem, small flowering bulb in the lily family, widely cultivated for its clusters of starlike white flowers. The leaves are long and narrow. The bulbs are edible.

Star of David, symbol made of two equilateral triangles joined to form a six-pointed star. In Hebrew it is called Magen (Shield of) David, after King David of Israel. Neither its origin nor its use as a symbol of Judaism has been explained. During World War II Nazis forced Jews to wear the Star of David as a badge. It now appears on flags of the Zionist Organization and of Israel.

Star of South Africa, diamond **S** 273
Starr, J. W., American inventor **I** 334
Star route frauds, post office scandal **A** 440; **G** 55
Star routes, postal service **P** 408, 410
Starry Night, The, painting by Van Gogh **V** 278
Stars **S** 405–11
 colors **E** 22
 constellations **C** 490–93
 cosmic rays and supernovae **C** 513
 direction finders **D** 183
 discoveries and classification in astronomy **A** 475–76, 477
 Do stars have planets circling them? **S** 411
 earth's sun, a stable star **E** 22
 experiment of making a carton planetarium **E** 361
 How many stars can you see at night? **S** 409
 Milky Way, our galaxy **U** 196–98
 navigation by **N** 63
 neutron stars or pulsars **Q** 8
 nuclear fusion **N** 365
 observatories **O** 8–15
 origin of "constellation" in U.S. flag **F** 247
 planetarium **P** 267–68
 Pythagorean theory **A** 471
 quasars and pulsars, radio sources **Q** 7–8
 shooting stars, meteors **C** 418, 419–21
 solar system of our sun **S** 239–49
 star "trails," how to record **E** 362
 sun **S** 458–67
 twinkling, cause of **S** 409
 universe and our galaxy **U** 196–204
 Why can't you see stars during the day? **S** 408
 See also Comets; Meteors and meteorites; Quasars; Tektites
Stars, leading actors and actresses
 motion-picture star system **M** 473, 478
Stars and Bars, Confederate flag **F** 228
Stars and Stripes, flag **F** 247–48; pictures **F** 229
 flag code **F** 231, 234
 See also Pledge of Allegiance
Star-Spangled Banner, The, national anthem of the United States **N** 16
 flag code **F** 231, 234
 flag of 15 stripes for which anthem was written **F** 248; picture **F** 229

Star-Spangled Banner, The (continued)
   Fort McHenry battle inspiration of, picture M 127
   written during War of 1812 W 11
Starved Rock State Park, Illinois I 70; picture I 82
Starving time, in Jamestown A 184; J 21
State, United States Department of
   Foreign Service F 369–70
   Peace Corps P 101–103
State aid, for schools E 74
State banks B 46–47, 48
State fairs, United States
   farm family activities, picture F 50
State governments, United States S 412–15
   Bill of Rights, 10th amendment defines powers left to
      the states B 179–80
   civil service C 317
   conservation program C 488
   elections E 113
   federal-state old-age assistance O 98
   health departments P 503–04
   initiative, referendum, and recall, the Oregon system
      O 205
   municipal and state relations M 506
   National Guard N 42–43
   Nebraska's unicameral legislature N 85
   power of impeachment I 108
   state income tax I 111
   state police P 375
   state libraries L 172
   wills, rights granted for disposition of property W 174
   See also States' rights; government section of state
      articles
State House, in Annapolis, Maryland M 124
Statelessness
   What is a stateless person? P 94
   See also Nolan, Philip, in The Man Without a Country.
State medicine see Socialized medicine
Staten (STAT-en) Island, New York City N 229
State of the Union message P 454
   delivered before Congress G 273
State police, United States P 375
States' rights, in United States history
   Bill of Rights, 10th amendment B 179
   Calhoun, John C. C 13
   Civil War issue C 321, 327
   Federalist, The, interprets the Constitution F 78
   Jefferson Davis' change of viewpoint D 45
   Johnson, Andrew, supports J 125
   Reconstruction Period, 1866–77 R 118–19
   weaknesses of the Articles of Confederation U 145
Static, electrical interference in radio or television R 50
Static electricity E 123
   experiment and demonstration E 364
   experiments of the 18th century S 71
   lightning T 170–71
Stationers, medieval book dealers B 321
Stationery, writing paper P 53
Stations of the Cross R 301
Station wagon, automobile model, picture A 535
Statistical (sta-TIST-ic-al) Abstract of the United States
   P 396
Statistics S 416–18
   census information P 396
   graphs G 309–13
   opinion surveys, sampling techniques O 159–60
   probability P 470–74
   vital statistics, birth and death rates P 394
Stators (STAY-tors), of machines
   electromagnets of motors E 136–37
   in transmissions T 256
Statues see Monuments; Sculpture
Status quo, a policy in international relations I 322

Statute mile, measure of distance W 113, 115
Statutory days, in Canada H 147, 150, 152
Stavanger, Norway N 344
Steady state theory, of the universe U 204
Steaks, meat M 193
   outdoor cooking O 247
Stealing sticks, running and chasing game G 22
Steam, water vapor, a gas H 93
   heating systems H 99
   volcanic steam used for electric power V 384
Steam automobiles A 542
Steam baths B 91
Steamboats T 261–62; picture T 263
   communication advanced by C 436
   early ocean liners O 23–24
   Fulton, Robert F 491
   Howard National Steamboat Museum, Indiana
      I 145
   Mississippi River M 365
   race on the Ohio, picture K 225
   steampower and metal ships S 160
Steam distillation D 225
Steam engines S 419–21
   airplanes, experimental A 567
   automobiles, and the Stanley steamer A 541, 542
   compared to steam turbines T 321
   construction work advanced by B 445–46
   engines, types of E 209–10
   Industrial Revolution I 237–38
   invention introduces a source of energy I 336
   kinetic energy, source of E 202–03
   locomotives L 327–28
   Newcomen's, picture I 236; diagram S 421
   ocean liners O 23
   Stanley steamer, automobile A 542
   Watt, James W 68–69
   Watt's automatic control, the governor A 532
Steam heating H 99
Steam irons E 118
Steam locomotives L 327–28
   railroads, history of R 79
Steam rollers B 448
Steamships S 160
   river steamer, picture O 62
Steam shovel, invention of B 445
Steam turbines T 320–21
   engines, types of E 209–10
   power plants P 425
   turbines, a type of steam engine S 419, 421
Stearic (ste-ARR-ic) acid, candles of C 97
Stearin, paraffin product used in candles L 281
Steel I 396–408
   Alabama has raw materials close together
      A 118
   alloy steels A 167; I 396
   architecture, use in A 385
   armor A 433–35
   Bessemer, Sir Henry B 149
   bridge material B 401
   building material B 430, 438
   buildings of steel construction, pictures B 432, 433
   carbon in steel C 105
   chromium alloys C 296
   Damascus steel T 308
   forgings, picture M 230
   grinding, picture G 388
   industrial importance I 246
   Luxembourg a leading world producer L 380
   magnetic qualities M 26–28
   mill in Canada, picture N 303
   oxygen gas used in purifying G 60
   reinforcing rods in concrete C 166; picture C 165

stainless *see* Stainless steel
steelworks in China, picture **C** 266
United States leading producer **U** 104
welding **W** 118–19
world industry, basis of **W** 266–67
See also Iron
Steele, Sir Richard, English essayist and dramatist
E 258; **I** 393
humorous essays with Addison for *The Tatler* **E** 292
magazine publisher **M** 14

Steele, Wilbur Daniel (1886–1970), American writer, b. Greensboro, N.C. Best-known as a short-story writer, he won a number of O. Henry awards in the 1920's and 30's for such stories as "For They Know Not What They Do.", and "Can't Cross Jordan".

Steel Fish, mobile by Calder **S** 104
Steel industry and trade **I** 396–404
Pittsburgh, Penn. **P** 134–35, 141
Steel King, Andrew Carnegie **C** 119
Steel plates **I** 401
Steel wool, an abrasive **G** 389
Steen (STAIN), **Jan,** Dutch genre painter **D** 357
Steeplechase, horse race **H** 231–32
Steeplechases, track events **T** 238
Steerage, section of ships for passengers paying lowest fares **O** 23
Steering vanes, in rockets **R** 260
Steers **C** 147
Steer wrestling, at rodeos **R** 282
Stefansson, Vilhjalmur, Arctic explorer **P** 364

Steffens, Lincoln (1866–1936), American journalist, b. San Francisco, Calif. A muckraker, one who tries to expose corruption among prominent people or organizations, he wrote magazine and newspaper articles (collected into books such as *The Shame of the Cities*) that awakened people to corruption in politics and big business. He told his life story in *The Autobiography of Lincoln Steffens* and *Lincoln Steffens Speaking.*

Stegosaurs (STEG-o-saurs), dinosaurs **D** 180

Steichen, Edward (1879–1973), American photographer and artist, b. Luxembourg. Realizing the possibilities of photography as an art, Steichen is the creator of photographic murals and has exhibited his photographs and paintings at the leading art centers of Europe and America. He created the Family of Man Exhibition in 1955, received the Presidential Medal of Freedom, and is the author of *A Life in Photography,* published in 1963.

Stein, Clarence, American architect **U** 233
Stein, Gertrude, American writer **A** 211
Hemingway a friend **H** 108–09
Stein, Johann Andreas, Viennese piano builder **P** 241–42
Steinbeck, John, American author **S** 422
American literature, place in **A** 212; **N** 349

Steiner (SHTINE-er), **Rudolf** (1861–1925), Austrian social philosopher, b. Kraljevica, Croatia (now Yugoslavia). The organizer of various movements and institutes, he is best known as the founder of anthroposophy, a doctrine in which life is explained in terms of man's inner nature. A great admirer of Johann von Goethe, he edited Goethe's scientific works.

Steinheim man **P** 443
tools, pictures **P** 444
Steinmetz, Charles Proteus, German-born American engineer **S** 422

Steinway and Sons, piano builders **P** 242
Stela (STE-la), stone pillar or slab used for commemorative purposes
Hammurabi, Code of **A** 236
used by the Maya **I** 198

Stella, Frank (1936–), American artist, b. Walden, Mass. His early training was in the field of commercial art and illustration. Later he experimented with the use of vivid colors as well as with the interrelationship of semicircles with rectangles. The effects often created optical illusions. He was one of the innovators in the use of shaped canvases, a synthesis of painting and sculpture. In 1960 he exhibited at the Museum of Modern Art.
Ctesiphon II, painting **M** 396b
painting **P** 32

Steller, Georg Wilhelm, German naturalist **S** 107
Steller's sea cows **S** 106–07
Steller's sea lions **W** 6
Stellite, chromium alloy **C** 296
Stelvio (STELV-yo) **Pass,** through the Alps **A** 174
Stems, of plants **P** 290; pictures **P** 292, 293
stems we eat, picture **P** 306
Stencils
used in silk-screen printing **S** 180

Stendhal (ston-DAHL) (Marie Henri Beyle) (1783–1842), French writer, b. Grenoble. In Napoleon's army during the Italian, Prussian, and Russian campaigns (1800–02, 1806–14), he later became a consular officer and lived for some years in Italy. His two masterpieces, *The Red and the Black* and *The Charterhouse of Parma*, made him one of the first outstanding French authors of psychological novels.
French novel **F** 441; **N** 348

Stengel, Casey (Charles Dillon Stengel) (1891–), American baseball player and manager, b. Kansas City, Mo. Nicknamed for his birthplace (K.C.), he played with numerous clubs before becoming a manager (1925). As manager of the New York Yankees (1949–60), he won 10 league pennants and seven world championships. He managed the New York Mets (1962–65) before retiring. He was elected to the Baseball Hall of Fame in 1966.

Steno (STAY-no), **Nicaolaus,** Danish scientist and anatomist **G** 112
Stenographers
shorthand and typing **S** 164; **T** 347–48
Stenotype, or machine shorthand **S** 164
Step-down transformers, of electric currents **T** 249–50
electric currents in transformers **E** 135
Stephen, Saint, first king of Hungary **H** 286
Stephen Nemanja, overlord of Serbia **Y** 358

Stephens, Alexander Hamilton (1812–1883), American political figure, b. near Crawfordville, Ga. A lawyer, he was elected to the state legislature (1836) and House of Representatives (1843–59). Chosen vice-president of the Confederacy (1861), he was an emissary to the Hampton Roads peace conference (1865). After the war he was re-elected to the House of Representatives (1873), but he resigned and became governor of Georgia (1883).
secession and the Confederacy **C** 321, 458

Stephens, James, Irish writer **E** 266
"Seumas Beg," poem **P** 355
Stephens, Uriah S., founded Knights of Labor **L** 3–4
Stephenson, George, English inventor **L** 329–30
pioneer of railroading **R** 87
railroad track width **R** 86

Stephenson, Robert (1803–1859), British civil engineer, b. Willington Quay, near Newcastle. Son of the famous locomotive builder George Stephenson, he was an important figure in his own right. In 1829 he assisted his father in designing the famous locomotive "Rocket" and supervised its construction. Later he planned a number of railroads in Britain. He also designed a number of famous bridges, including a high-level bridge at Newcastle, the Britannia tubular-girder bridge across the Menai Straits, and the Victoria Bridge across the St. Lawrence River at Montreal, for years the world's longest.

Steppes, plains regions
    climate **C** 345
    land and climate of U.S.S.R **U** 32–33
    Great Plains of North America **N** 289, 291
    prairies **P** 430–32; picture **P** 433
Step Pyramid, at Sakkara, Egypt **E** 95
Step-roofed houses H 182; picture **H** 170
Steps, running and chasing game **G** 21
Step-up transformers, of electric currents **T** 249–50
    electric currents in transformers **E** 135
Stereo, sound reproduction **H** 126–27
    motion pictures, use of **M** 478
    phonographs **P** 198
    record collecting **R** 124–25
    tape and wire recorders **T** 20, 21
Stereomicroscopes, optical instruments **O** 167
    microscopes **M** 288
Stereophonic reproduction of sound see Stereo

Stereoscope, device for viewing certain photographs to produce the illusion of depth. Two photographs of a scene are taken from slightly different angles, corresponding to the different angles from which a man's two eyes would view the scene. The photos are placed side by side in the stereoscope. When viewed through two eyepieces, the photographs seem to merge into a single, three-dimensional picture.
    perception of space **P** 490–91

Stereoscopic motion pictures M 477
Stereotype plates, for printing, picture **N** 204
Stereotyping, in printing **P** 467
Sterilization
    canning of food **F** 345–46
    early use in medicine **M** 208
    first aid for wounds **F** 158
    making an object germ-free **D** 222
    milk **D** 10

Sterling, standard of purity for silver. Sterling silver is at least 92.5 percent pure.

Sterling silver, a high-quality alloy of silver and copper **S** 181, 182
    jewelry **J** 92
    knives, forks, and spoons **K** 285–88

Stern, Isaac (1920–), American violinist, b. Kremenets, Russia. He made his debut at 11 with the San Francisco Symphony. He has toured extensively, made recordings, and has appeared regularly with leading orchestras.

Sterne, Emma Gelders (1894–), American author, b. Birmingham, Ala. The subjects for her numerous children's books come mostly from the American scene. Among her books are *The Calico Ball, Printers Devil, Mary McLeod Bethune* and *Drums of Monmouth.*

Sterne, Laurence, English theologian and novelist **E** 260
Stern-steerers, iceboats **I** 29

Steroids, lipids in body cells **B** 293

Stethoscope, instrument used by doctors to listen to the sounds made by the heart, lungs, and other organs. Invented about 1819 by René Théophile Hyacinthe Laënnec (1781–1826), a French physician, the early stethoscope was a short wooden tube. The doctor put one end to his ear, the other end to the patient's chest. Today stethoscopes have two ear pieces connected by tubing to a disk or bell placed on the body.
    examining the heart **H** 86b
    medicine, history of **M** 206–07
    medicine, tools of **M** 208e, 208h

Stettin (shtet-EEN), Poland **P** 361
Steuben, Friedrich, Baron von, German general, volunteer aid to Americans **R** 203
Steunenberg, Frank, governor of Idaho **I** 68
Stevens, Albert W., American military balloonist **B** 32
Stevens, Isaac Ingalls, American soldier and first governor of Washington territory **W** 27
Stevens, John, American inventor **L** 330
    built a tiny experimental railroad **R** 87–88
Stevens, Siaka, first president of Sierra Leone **S** 175
Stevens, Thaddeus, American political leader **P** 143
Stevens, Wallace, American poet **A** 210
Stevenson, Adlai E. (1835–1914), vice-president, United States **V** 331; picture **V** 328
Stevenson, Adlai E. (1900–1965), American statesman **S** 423
    quoted on environment **E** 272a
Stevenson, Robert Louis, Scottish author **S** 423–27
    "Bed in Summer," poem **S** 424
    children's literature **C** 241
    Child's Garden of Verses, A, poems from **S** 424
    Kidnapped, excerpt **S** 426–27
    "My Shadow," poem **S** 424
    place in English literature **E** 264–65, 292, 293
    "Requiem," poem **S** 424
    "Swing, The," poem **S** 424
    tomb on Mt. Vaea, Western Samoa **S** 23
    Treasure Island, excerpt **S** 424–26
Stewardesses, airline **A** 566; **S** 125

Stewart, Potter (1915–), American jurist, b. Jackson, Mich. At the time of his appointment in 1958 he was the second youngest justice ever to sit on the United States Supreme Court. A graduate of Yale College and Yale Law School, he practiced law in Cincinnati for several years.

Stewart, William Morris, American lawyer **N** 135
Stickball, picture **B** 21
Sticklebacks, fishes
    animal communication **A** 278; picture **A** 279
    nests **F** 201
Stick puppets, or rod puppets **P** 535; picture **P** 534
Stieber, Wilhelm, German spy **S** 389

Stiegel, Henry William (1729–1785), American glassmaker, b. near Cologne, Germany. Although he settled in Pennsylvania as a young man, he became a British citizen (1760). He made a fortune as an ironmaster. He established the town of Manheim in Lancaster County, Pa., where he built a glass factory (1764). Prized for their beauty and workmanship, examples of Stiegel glass can be found in museums and private collections.
    glassmaking, art of **G** 230

Stigma, top of the pistil of a flower **F** 277; **P** 296; picture **F** 276
Stijl (STILE), de, Dutch art movement
    Mondrian, Piet **M** 408

Stiles, Ezra, American clergyman F 243
Still, Andrew Taylor, American osteopath M 375

Still, William (1821–1902), American Negro leader, b. Shamony, N.J. He was chairman and corresponding secretary of the Philadelphia branch of the Underground Railroad (1851–61) and wrote an account of the system in *The Underground Railroad*. He brought about legislation to end discrimination against Negroes on Philadelphia's streetcars, was a member of the Philadelphia board of trade, and founded the first Negro Y.M.C.A. and a number of welfare establishments.
  Vigilance Committee of the Underground U 12

Still, William (1821–1902), American Negro leader, b. Woodville, Miss. He was the first Negro to conduct a major American orchestra and to compose a symphony, his *Afro-American Symphony* (1931). He sometimes used Negro folk songs in his music. He wrote operas, ballets, chamber and choral works, and many pieces for symphonic band. N 98, 107

Still life, in painting D 357
Still Life, painting by Picasso F 430
Still Life: The Table, painting by Braque B 371
Stills, distilling equipment D 224
  water desalting W 56
  whiskey and other distilled beverages W 159

Stilt, any of a group of wading birds that live in the warmer regions of the world. Stilts average about 13 inches in length. They have very long legs and long necks. Their bills are long and curve upward.

Stilt houses H 168; picture H 169
  Philippines, picture A 303

Stilwell, Joseph Warren ("Vinegar Joe") (1883–1946), American army officer, b. Palatka, Fla. During his many years in China he was military attaché at the United States Embassy in Peking (1932–39) and chief of staff for Generalissimo Chiang Kai-shek (1942–44), commanding Chinese armies in Burma and U.S. forces in China, Burma, and India. After retreating from Burma to India (1942), he built up his forces and returned to Burma to defeat the Japanese.

Stimson, Henry Lewis (1867–1950), American statesman, b. New York, N.Y. An unsuccessful candidate for governor of New York (1910), he served as secretary of war from 1911–13. As secretary of state (1929–33) he denounced Japan's invasion of Manchuria (1931) and in the now famous Stimson Doctrine stated that the United States would not recognize any territory acquired by aggression. During World War II he served as secretary of war (1940–45).
  American reaction to Japan's invasion of Manchuria W 284

Stimson Doctrine, in international relations W 284
  foreign policies of the Hoover administration H 224
  on recognition of treaties T 271
Stimulants, drugs D 326
  abuse of D 330
  caffeine, in coffee C 374
Stimulus and response, in psychology
  characteristic of living things K 255–56
  How do we learn? L 98
Stingrays, fishes S 143
  animals harmful to man I 285
Stings
  first aid F 163

  insects I 276, 282
  plant defenses P 283
Stinkhorns, fungi F 500
Stippler, tool used in texturing a surface
  leathercraft L 113
Stipules, of leaves L 118
Stirrup, bone in the ear, diagram B 285
Stitches, in sewing S 129
Stoae (STO-e), in Greek architecture G 348
Stoats, type of weasels O 242

Stock, flowering garden plant belonging to the mustard family. Stocks are popular among gardeners and florists. The fragrant blossoms grow in large spike-shaped masses, usually in shades of white, purple, or pink.

Stockade, frontier fort. American settlers borrowed from Indians the defense method of surrounding cabins with a fence made of close-set upright logs. Upon attack, settlers fled through the single gate and locked attackers out. Stockades often had blockhouses at the corners, with slits for defenders' rifle fire. In the settlement of Kentucky and Tennessee, such stockades as Boonesborough were vital to survival.
  forts and fortifications F 377

Stock Car Auto Racing, National Association for
  (NASCAR) · A 539
Stock-car racing A 539
Stock cars, of railroads R 82
Stock companies, theater T 162
Stock dams, water storage for livestock D 16
Stock exchanges, places where securities (stocks and bonds) are bought and sold S 431
  old and new ways of preparing reports, pictures A 534
  stock-market crash, 1929 B 48
  Wall Street, New York, N.Y. N 230
Stockhausen, Karlheinz, German composer G 189; picture M 402
  electronic music notation E 142g
Stockholm, capital of Sweden S 484; picture S 487
  highway interchange, picture E 328
Stockholm, ocean liner O 24
Stockinette stitch, in knitting K 280
Stocking dolls D 266
Stock market see Stock exchanges
Stock raising C 145–52
Stocks, certificates representing shares in a company S 427–33
  mass selling causes depressions and recessions D 121
  money invested in industry I 243–44
  See also Dow Jones averages
Stocks and pillory, wooden frames used for punishment P 346

Stockton, Frank Richard (1834–1902), American writer, b. Philadelphia, Pa. His stories for the *Riverside Magazine for Young People* were published as *Ting-a-Ling Tales*. While serving as assistant editor of *St. Nicholas Magazine* (1873–81), he wrote several children's books, including *The Floating Prince and Other Fairy Tales*. Known to adult readers as a humorist, he published short stories and novels, including the popular *Rudder Grange* and *The Casting Away of Mrs. Lecks and Mrs. Aleshine*.
  children's literature, history of C 240

Stockton, Richard (1730–1781), American lawyer and political figure, b. Princeton, N.J. He was a member of the state council (1768–76) and the state Supreme Court (1774–76). Elected to the Continental Congress (1776),

Stockton, Richard (continued)
he was one of the signers of the Declaration of Independence.

Stockton and Darlington Railroad, first open to public
  R 87
Stockyards, pens where animals are kept before being processed into meat
  Omaha, Nebraska, picture **N** 78
  Sioux City, Iowa, picture **I** 362
Stoddert, Benjamin, American merchant
  first secretary of U.S. Navy **U** 185

Stoicism, school of philosophy founded (308 B.C.) in Athens by Zeno of Citium (Cyprus). Stoicism claimed that virtue was the only good and was all that was needed for happiness. The virtuous man remained independent of the society in which he lived but was required to do good to other men. He became more virtuous only by putting his virtue into practice in his relations with other men. By mastering his passions and emotions he could overcome the outside world and find happiness in himself.

Stokes, Carl Burton (1927–), mayor of Cleveland, Ohio, b. Cleveland. Once a high school dropout, Stokes completed his education after his Army service at the end of World War II, graduating from the University of Minnesota. He earned his law degree from Cleveland-Marshall Law School while working as a court probation officer. He served as an assistant city prosecutor and later practiced law in Cleveland. In 1962 he was elected to the Ohio legislature. Stokes's election as mayor of Cleveland, in 1967, made him the first Negro mayor of a major U.S. city. He was re-elected in 1969. Picture **N** 100.
  years of change in Negro history **C** 338; **N** 101

Stokowski (sto-KOF-ski)**, Leopold** (1887–), American conductor, b. London, England. He was conductor of the Cincinnati Orchestra (1909–12) and the Philadelphia Orchestra (1914–36). In 1940 he organized the All-American Youth Orchestra. He has made orchestral transcriptions of Bach's and other composers' works and has appeared in motion pictures. He has also been conductor of the NBC Symphony (1941–44), the New York Philharmonic (1947–50) and the American Symphony Orchestra (since 1963).

Stolons, creeping stems of plants, picture **G** 316
Stomach
  digestive function in human body **B** 275
  of birds **B** 202
  porpoise has three stomachs **D** 272
  research by Beaumont **B** 109
  ruminants, or cud-chewing animals **H** 208
Stomata, of plants
  leaves **L** 120; **P** 294
Stone **S** 433
  ancient Egyptian stonework **B** 435
  building material **B** 430
  gemstones **G** 76
  houses of **H** 175
  quarrying **Q** 4–5
  stone masonry **B** 393, 394

Stone, Edward Durell (1902–), American architect, b. Fayetteville, Ark. His buildings are often designed around a courtyard and have striated, filtered light coming through roofs and ceilings. His works include the U.S. Embassy, New Delhi, India; University of Arkansas Fine Arts Center; American Pavilion, Brussels World's Fair;

and the Huntington Hartford Gallery of Modern Art, New York.

Stone, Lucy (1818–1893), American suffragist and reformer, b. near West Brookfield, Mass. Determined to go to college in spite of family objections, she worked her way through Oberlin College. After graduating (1847), she lectured on behalf of women's rights and the abolition of slavery. She married Henry Brown Blackwell (1855) but continued to use her maiden name. The couple established many women's rights groups and edited the periodical *Woman's Journal.* Married women who continue to use their maiden names are sometimes called "Lucy Stoners."

Stone, measure of weight **W** 112

Stone, Thomas (1743–1787), American political figure, b. Charles County, Md. He studied law at Annapolis and was admitted to the bar (1764). As a delegate to the Continental Congress (1775–78) he helped draw up the Articles of Confederation and was one of the signers of the Declaration of Independence.

Stone age **P** 442
  cave dwellers **C** 157–58; **P** 443
  communication by picture writing **C** 430
  domestication of the horse **H** 236–37
  fire and early man **F** 138–45
  prehistoric art **P** 439–41
  tools **T** 210b
  walls of Jericho, picture **A** 353
Stonefish, picture **F** 192
Stone fruit
  peach, plum and cherry **P** 106–09
Stonehenge, England **E** 214; pictures **E** 215, **W** 219
  beginning of English art and architecture **E** 233
  replica at Maryhill, Washington **W** 23
Stone implements **T** 210b; pictures **T** 210b, **P** 444
  prehistoric man classified by his tools **P** 443–44
Stone martens, animals of the weasel family **O** 244
Stonemasons **B** 393
  Gothic architects **G** 271–72
Stone Mountain, Georgia **G** 134–35, 143
Stone of Denderah, ancient sky map **A** 470
Stones River, Tennessee **C** 325
Stone's sheep **S** 145
Stoneware, pottery **P** 413; pictures **P** 419
  antique containers **A** 320
  Finnish, picture **D** 69
Stoneware clay **C** 174

Stong, Phil (Philip Duffield Stong) (1899–1957), American writer, b. Keosauqua, Iowa. After careers of teaching (1919–23) and journalism (1923–31), he concentrated on writing books for both adults and children. Among his books for young readers are *Young Settler* and *The Hired Man's Elephant,* and his books for adults include *State Fair* (three film versions have been made of this) and *Forty Pounds of Gold.*

Stoolball, English game of Middle Ages **C** 531
Stopes, underground excavations for mining **M** 316
Stoppers, knots **K** 289–90
Stopping by Woods on a Snowy Evening, poem by Robert Frost **F** 480
Stopwatches, or timers **W** 50; picture **W** 49
Storage, of vegetables **V** 293
Storage batteries **B** 99; picture **B** 98
  lead used in **L** 94–95
Stores see Department stores; Marketing; Retail stores; Supermarkets

Stories, told in full
"Ant and the Grasshopper, The," by Aesop **F** 5
"Blind Men and the Elephant, The" (in verse) **F** 7
"Boy Jesus" **B** 168–69
"Daniel in the Lions' Den" **B** 167–68
"David and Goliath" **B** 164–65
"Elephant's Child, The," by Kipling **K** 262–65
"Emperor's New Clothes, The" **A** 249–51
"Enchanted Princess, The" **F** 23–25
"Four Oxen and the Lion, The," by Aesop **F** 5
"Gift of the Magi, The" by O. Henry **H** 110–13
"Hansel and Gretel" **G** 380–86
"Jonah" **B** 166–67
"Legend of the Blue Plate, The" **L** 133
"Legend of the White Deer" **L** 134
"Lion and the Mouse, The," by Aesop **F** 4
"Little Red Riding-Hood" **F** 29–32
"Mallard That Asked Too Much, The," legend **L** 135
"Moth and the Star, The," by Thurber **F** 8
"Noah's Ark" **B** 163–64
"Princess on the Pea" by Hans Andersen **F** 26
"Rapunzel" **G** 378–80
"Roland and Oliver," legend **L** 130–33
Rootabaga Stories, by Carl Sandburg **S** 29
"Shoemaker and the Elves, The" **G** 377–78
"Sleeping Beauty" **F** 27–29
"Tyrant Who Became a Just Ruler, The," by Bidpai **F** 6
See also Children's literature; Fables; Fairy tales; Fiction; Folklore; Greek mythology; Legends; Mystery, detective, and suspense stories; Storytelling, excerpts from longer works by name, as *Oliver Twist,* excerpt

Stork, egret, and heron, group of wading birds inhabiting the shores and flats of lakes, streams, marshes, and seas in many areas of the world. Most of them have long legs and bills, long necks, broad wings, and relatively short tails. They live mainly on fish, shellfish, frogs, reptiles, and insects. Many species migrate long distances with the change in season.

Stormfury, Project **W** 96
Stormont, parliament of Northern Ireland **U** 73
Storms
anvil-topped storm cloud, picture **C** 361
climate and storm centers **C** 347
hail storms **R** 98
how to find out how far away a storm is **T** 173
hurricanes **H** 292–96
thunder and lightning **T** 170–73
tornadoes **H** 296–99
use of the barometer to forecast weather **B** 54
warning flags **F** 246
warning lights and flags for boats **B** 262
weather control **W** 91–96
Storms, Ocean of, moon landing site, map **M** 449
Storm troopers, name for Nazi private army **N** 70
Storting, Norway's national parliament **N** 344

Story, Joseph (1779–1845), American jurist, b. Marblehead, Mass. Through writings such as *Commentaries on the Constitution of the United States* and *The Conflict of Laws* he influenced and molded American legal thought. In addition to writing, he practiced law and was a member of the House of Representatives (1808–09), an associate justice of the U.S. Supreme Court (1811–45), and a professor of law at Harvard (1829–45). In 1900 Story was voted into the American Hall of Fame.

Story boards, in advertising **A** 30
Story boards, scripts for animated cartoons **A** 298

Storytelling **S** 434–36
"Alice in Wonderland," excerpt **A** 164–65
Arabian Nights, The, excerpts **A** 345–47
Arthur, King, legends of, excerpt **A** 442–45
Bible stories **B** 163–69
Charlotte's Web, excerpt **W** 160–61
early form of communication **C** 430
Eskimo children, picture **E** 288
fables **F** 2–8
fairy tales **F** 19
folklore and folklore, American **F** 302–17
Grimm brothers' storyteller, Gammer Grethel **F** 21
Gulliver's Travels, excerpt **G** 412–13
Just So Stories, by Kipling, excerpts **K** 261–65
legends **L** 128–35
library story hour **L** 170
See also excerpts from longer works by name, as *Little Women,* excerpt
Stourbridge Fair, England **F** 10–11
Stourbridge Lion, locomotive **L** 328
Stout, a type of beer **B** 117

Stout, Rex Todhunter (1886–   ), American writer, b. Noblesville, Ind. Noted mainly for his detective fiction, Stout created the detective Nero Wolfe and has written many detective stories, including *How Like a God, Double for Death, Triple Jeopardy,* and *Too Many Clients.* He worked in radio during the early 1940's, was president of the Authors' Guild (1943–45), and was president of the Mystery Writers of America in 1958.

Stoves **H** 97–98
carbon monoxide poisoning **P** 357
electric **E** 118
Stowe, Harriet Beecher, American writer **S** 436
American literature **A** 204
Uncle Tom's Cabin **C** 320
Strabo (STRAY-bo), Greek geographer **G** 355
beginnings of the study of geography **G** 98
Strachey (STRAY-chey), **Lytton,** English biographer **E** 268

Stradivari (stra-di-VA-ri), **Antonio** (1644–1737), Italian violin-maker, b. Cremona. He was apprenticed to violin-maker Nicolò Amati before he founded his own workshop in Cremona. He was assisted by his sons, who carried on his work. He is the most celebrated of violin-makers.
instrumental music of baroque era **B** 66; **I** 483
violin, history of **V** 342

Straight angles, in geometry **G** 124; diagram **G** 125
Straightedges, tools for drawing geometric figures **G** 130
Straightening, of the hair **H** 6
Strait, geographic term see names of straits, as Magellan, Strait of
Strangers and Saints, of the Plymouth Colony **P** 344
Strangler figs, vines **P** 319; picture **P** 318
Straparola (stra-pa-RO-la), **Giovanni,** Italian writer **F** 20
Strasbourg, France **F** 406
Strasbourg Cathedral, France
famous mechanical clock **W** 45
Strata, layers of rock **G** 111
earth's history told in **E** 20
sedimentary rock **R** 266–68
Strategic Air Command, United States **U** 162
Strategic Arms Limitation Talks (SALT) **D** 185; **I** 325
U.S.S.R. **U** 51
Stratford, Connecticut
American Shakespeare Festival Theater, picture **C** 479

Stratford-on-Avon (A-von), England **E** 213, 252
  Shakespeare, William **S** 130–33
  Shakespeare Memorial Theatre **T** 159
Stratford Festival, Stratford, Ontario **C** 62–63; picture
  O 129
Stratigraphy (stra-TIG-raphy), study of the arrangement
  of rock strata **G** 113
  stratigraphic trap, for oil deposits **P** 170
Strato-cumulus clouds C 360; picture **C** 361
Stratosphere, second layer of earth's atmosphere
  A 480–81; **E** 17
  weather **W** 72
Stratus clouds C 360; picture **C** 361

Straus (STROUSE), **Nathan** (1848–1931), American philanthropist, b. Otterberg, Germany. With his family he
migrated to Georgia (1854), and after the Civil War he
settled in New York, N.Y. In 1888 he became a partner in
the R. H. Macy department store. He served as parks
commissioner (1889–93) and as president of the Board
of Health (1898), and was a pioneer in the fight for
pasteurization of milk.

Strauss, Johann (1804–1849), Austrian composer, b.
Vienna. He organized an orchestra (1826) that played his
compositions on concert tours of Europe, and he was
made (1845) the conductor of court balls at Vienna.
Called the father of the waltz, he composed 251 pieces,
of which 152 were waltzes.

Strauss, Johann, Jr., Austrian composer **S** 437
  Bat, The, operetta **O** 156
  Gypsy Baron, The, operetta **O** 158
  operetta **O** 156
Strauss, Richard, German composer **G** 187
  opera **O** 138
  Rosenkavalier, Der, opera **O** 153
  Salome, opera **O** 153
  tone poems **R** 311
Stravinsky (stra-VIN-ski), **Igor,** Russian-born American
  composer **S** 437; picture **M** 401
  ballet music **D** 37
  choral music **C** 279
  modern music **M** 400–01
  opera **O** 138
  Russian music **U** 64
Straw
  brickmaking **B** 391
  hats of **H** 54
  huts of straw, pictures **A** 303
  insulating material **I** 290
Strawberries G 298; picture **G** 299
  Chilean origin **C** 252
  garden fruit **G** 52
  plants sprouting from runners, picture **P** 300
  seeds, picture **P** 298
Strawbery Banke, Portsmouth, New Hampshire **N** 158
Straw votes see Public opinion polls
Streaking, of the hair **H** 6
Streaking, to identify minerals **R** 271
Streamlining
  aerodynamics of **A** 39
  airplane design to reduce drag **A** 559
  car of the future, picture **A** 552
  industrial design **I** 232
  locomotion in animals **A** 289
Stream of consciousness, in literature **E** 266–67
  Joyce's technique of the novel **I** 395
Street, George Edmund, English architect **E** 241
Streetcars and trolleycars T 265
  Branford Trolley Museum, East Haven, Conn. **C** 476
  early trolley cars **B** 465

Street cleaning, picture **S** 32
Street of Silver, Delhi, India **D** 101–02
Streicher (SHTRY-ker), **Johann Andreas,** Viennese piano
  builder **P** 241–42

Streisand, Barbra (1942–), American entertainer, b.
Brooklyn, N.Y. Television appearances, record albums,
and night club engagements followed her first Broadway
role in *I Can Get it for You Wholesale* (1962). She
starred in the movie *Hello, Dolly!* and in the stage and
screen productions of *Funny Girl.*

Strep throats D 207–08
Streptococci (strep-to-COCC-i), bacteria **D** 199
  impetigo **D** 199
  sore throats **D** 207–08
Streptomycin (strept-o-MY-cin), drug **D** 212
  antibiotics **A** 312; picture **A** 314
Stresemann (SHTRAYS-em-onn), **Gustav,** German states-
man **G** 162
Stress, in physics
  airplane design **A** 558
Stride, in walking and running
  animals' speed determined by **A** 293
Strigil, Roman tool used to clean the skin **B** 91
Strike, in baseball **B** 71
Strikebreakers L 12
Strikes and lockouts L 18
  rise of national labor unions **L** 3
  sit-down technique **L** 6
Strindberg, August, Swedish author **S** 51
  realism in drama **D** 297
String beans V 289
Stringed instruments S 438–39
  African music **A** 79
  baroque period **B** 66
  chamber music **C** 184–86
  classical orchestra **C** 331
  folk music instruments **F** 329–30
  guitar **G** 409–10
  harp **H** 43–44
  musical instruments, types of **M** 544–47
  orchestra **O** 182–83; picture **O** 187
  orchestra seating plan **O** 186
  piano **P** 240–42
  violin **V** 342–43
Stringfellow, John, English engineer **A** 567
String orchestra O 182
String quartet, for chamber music **C** 186; **M** 546; picture **C** 185
  classical age in music **C** 331
  German music **G** 184
String telephone, how to make **S** 266
Strip cropping, method of crop planting **A** 93
Strip mining, of coal **C** 365
  West Virginia, erosion problems **W** 141

Stroboscope (STRO-bo-scope), device that emits bright,
rapid flashes of light. Using a stroboscope, a person can
view a rapidly vibrating object as though it were not
moving. The light flashes are timed to correspond to the
vibrations of the object, so that the object is viewed at
the same position during each flash. This produces the
illusion of motionlessness. Stroboscopes are used in
making motion studies and in high-speed photography.

Stroessner (STRESS-ner), **Alfredo,** Paraguayan president
  P 66
Stroganov painters, Russian group **U** 54
Stroke, brain damage **D** 208
Stromlo, Mount, Canberra, Australia
  observatory **C** 88

Strong, Caleb (1745–1819), American political figure, b. Northampton, Mass. After graduating from Harvard College (1764), he studied law and was admitted to the bar (1772). An ardent Federalist, he was a member of the Constitutional Convention (1787) and was a state senator (1789–96) and governor (1800–07, 1812–16).

Strontium, element **E** 155, 164–65
  chemically similar to calcium **E** 156
  food contamination **F** 355
Strontium 90 **E** 165
Strophic form, used in vocal music **M** 535
Strowger, Almon B., American inventor **T** 58
Structural engineering **E** 205
Structural formulas, in chemistry **C** 220
Structural geology **G** 112
Structural materials see Building materials
Structural steel **I** 400

Struve (SHTRU-va), **Otto** (1897–1963), Russian-American astronomer, b. Kharkov, Russia. The descendant of a family of noted astronomers, he is best known for his discovery that hydrogen molecules exist in space. He was director of the National Radio Astronomy Observatory at Green Bank, W. Va. (1959–63).

Strychnine (STRICK-nine), drug **P** 314
Strydom (STRAY-dom), **Gerhardus,** South African statesman **S** 273
Stuart, Gilbert, American portrait painter **R** 225
  George Washington, portrait **U** 118; **W** 37
  United States, art of **U** 117
Stuart, House of, royal family of England **E** 222–25; **U** 77

Stuart, Jeb (James Ewell Brown Stuart) (1833–1864), American army officer, b. Patrick County, Va. Commissioned a second lieutenant by the United States Military Academy at West Point (1854), he was a brilliant scout and cavalry officer. He accompanied Lee in the attack on John Brown at Harpers Ferry (1859). In 1861 he joined the Confederate Army. He took part in many decisive Civil War battles and was promoted to major general. He was mortally wounded at the battle of the Yellow Tavern.

Stucco, type of plaster used to coat the exteriors of buildings. Usually made of cement, sand, and lime, it is applied in a plastic state and dries to form a hard covering. It is also, but less commonly, a fine plaster used in the decoration of interior walls.
  cement mixtures **C** 165

Stud Book, record of thoroughbred horses **H** 231

Studebaker (STU-de-baker), **Clement** (1831–1901), American industrialist, b. Pinetown, Pa. In 1852 he joined his older brother Henry in a blacksmith and wagon-building business. Five years later another brother, John, bought out Henry's share of the business. Their firm became the largest builder of horse-drawn vehicles in the world. In 1897 Clement began experimenting with automobiles. Soon after his death, the company began producing electric and gasoline-powered automobiles.

Student aid, for college education **T** 44
Student and Schoolmate, magazine **M** 16

Student National Coordinating Committee (SNCC) founded (1960) as a civil rights organization, headquarters in Atlanta, Ga. Until 1969 it was called **Student Nonviolent Coordinating Committee.** The Committee now demands

that the black community determine its own needs and solutions to problems, and does not rule out violence.
  Negro history **N** 98, 104

Student Prince, The, operetta by Romberg **O** 158

Students for a Democratic Society (SDS), a radical student movement founded in Michigan (1962) to make the university the stimulus for social and political reform. Over the years, their protests have become increasingly explosive as they sought to spotlight issues which they considered important.

Studios (broadcasting), pictures **R** 59, 60, 61
Study, how to **S** 440–42
  basic types of reference books **R** 129
  college boards, preparing for **E** 349
  how to prepare for tests **T** 120
  how to use your library **L** 180–88
  indexes, how to use **I** 114–15
  outlines **O** 249–51
  reports **R** 175–76
  research **R** 183
  shorthand system, called Note Hand **S** 164
  SQ3R method of learning **L** 105
  spelling **S** 378–79
Stupas (STU-pas), Buddhist monuments **O** 215; picture **O** 213
Sturbridge Village, Old, Massachusetts, museum of colonial life **M** 145, 513–14
Sture-Vasa, Mary see O'Hara, Mary
Sturgeon, fish **F** 216
  long-lived fish **A** 84
  See also Caviar
Sturluson, Snorri see Snorri Sturluson
Stuttgart, Germany **G** 158

Stuyvesant (STY-ves-ant), **Peter** (1592–1672), Dutch official in America, b. West Friesland. While governor of Curaçao, he sustained a bullet wound that resulted in the amputation of his leg. As director general of New Netherland (1647–64) he was a stern ruler, restricting religious freedom and refusing the people a voice in the government. The English captured the colony in 1664 and renamed it New York. Stuyvesant continued to live on his farm until his death.
  Dutch colony in New York **A** 190; **N** 225

Style, in creative writing
  concern of the literary critic **L** 313
Style in dress see Fashion
Styles, parts of flowers **P** 296
Stylus, instrument for writing **B** 319; **C** 432
Stymphalian (stim-PHAY-lian) **birds,** in Greek mythology **G** 363
Styrene, liquid hydrocarbon **R** 346
Styron, William, American novelist **A** 213
Styx (STIX), underworld river in mythology **G** 357
Subatomic particles, of chemical elements **E** 153; chart of some subatomic particles **N** 371
  atoms, structure of **A** 486
  nuclear energy **N** 354–55
Subheadings, of index entries **I** 114
Subjects, of sentences **G** 289

Sublette (SUB-lett), **William** (1799?–1845), American fur trader, b. Lincoln Co., Ky. He trapped beaver in the Rockies, first with William Ashley (1823), then with his own fur company (1826–29). He was among the first to take wagons into the Rockies (1830). He helped build the first Wyoming post, Ft. William, later Ft. Laramie. Part of the Oregon Trail was called Sublette's cutoff.

starch digested as sugar **S** 401
starch sugars from grain **G** 286
world distribution **W** 264
See also Honey
Sugar Act, 1764 **R** 194
Sugar beets S 456–57
field in Colorado, picture **U** 108
Sugar Bowl, New Orleans, Louisiana, New Year's football game **F** 365
Sugarcane S 454–55
sweet grasses **G** 319; picture **G** 318
Cuba, world producer **C** 548; picture **C** 551
Dominican Republic **D** 282
food in ancient times, "sweet sticks of the East"
F 333
important crop to Hawaii **H** 63–64; picture **H** 62
Louisiana **L** 354
Martinique Island crop, picture **C** 117
Sugar gliders, marsupials, picture **K** 174
Sugar maple, tree, picture **T** 277
New York, state tree of **N** 210
Vermont, state tree of **V** 307
West Virginia, state tree of **W** 127
Wisconsin, state tree of **W** 193
Sugar-on-snow parties M 87
Sugar pine, tree, picture **T** 275
Sugar State, nickname for Louisiana **L** 349
Suger (su-JAIR), **Abbé,** French churchman **G** 266
Suggestion, mental *see* Mental suggestion

Suharto (1921–), Indonesian general and political leader, b. Jogjakarta, Java. He was commander of army forces that put down an attempted military coup led by Communist army officers (1965). Appointed army chief of staff, minister for defense, and chairman of the cabinet presidium (1966), he became, in effect, leader of Indonesia. He was named acting president (1967), replacing President Sukarno, and president (1968).
Indonesia, history of **I** 222

Suicide (SU-i-cide), taking one's own life
early studies in sociology **S** 227
Hamlet's "To be, or not to be" **H** 21
Suidae (SU-id-e), swine family **C** 151
Suite (SWEET), in music **M** 538
dance suite **D** 36
Suits, in card games **C** 106
contract bridge **C** 108
Suits, law
courts **C** 526–27

Sukarno (su-KAR-no) (1901–70), Indonesian political leader, b. Surabaya. A revolutionary leader, he proclaimed the independence of Indonesia (formerly the Netherlands East Indies) in 1945 and became its first president (1949). In 1966, after the failure of a Communist coup, he was stripped of all power, but retained title of president. In 1967 he was replaced by General Suharto, who became acting president.
Indonesia, history of **I** 222

Sukhe Bator (SU-kay ba-TOR), Mongolian leader **M** 416
Sukiyaki, Japanese food **J** 27
Sukkertoppen (SU-ker-to-pen), Greenland, picture **G** 368
Sukkoth, or Feast of the Tabernacles, religious holiday **R** 154
Sulawesi *see* Celebes
Suleiman I (su-lai-MON) the Magnificent, sultan of Turkey **T** 328
built wall around Jerusalem **J** 78
Sulfa drugs A 311–12
disease, conquest of **D** 217

drug industry **D** 323
drugs that fight microbes **D** 327
Sulfanilamide (sul-fa-NIL-a-mide), drug **D** 217
antibiotics **A** 311
Sulfate pulping process, of papermaking **P** 52
Sulfides C 196
Sulfite pulping process, of papermaking **P** 52
Sulfur, element **E** 155, 165
air pollution control **A** 110; **E** 272g
atomic symbol, picture **D** 15
Louisiana mines by Frasch process **L** 356
matches made of **M** 152
plant growth, needed for **F** 96
preserves dried fruits **D** 317
rubber ingredient **R** 348
sulfur-producing regions of North America **N** 294
vulcanization process, Goodyear's discovery of **R** 341
Sulfur dioxide, polluting agent **E** 272g
Sulfuric acid
gold treated in refining process **G** 249
Sulkies, carts for harness racing **H** 234
Sulla, Lucius Cornelius, Roman general **C** 5
Sullivan, Anne (Mrs. John A. Macy), teacher of Helen Keller **K** 201
Sullivan, Sir Arthur, English composer **G** 209–11
hymn "Onward Christian Soldiers" **H** 313
Sullivan, John L., American boxing champion **B** 353
Sullivan, Louis, American architect **S** 457
industrial design **I** 231
modern architecture **A** 384–85
United States, architecture of the **U** 124
Wright, Frank Lloyd and Sullivan **W** 315
Sullivans Island, South Carolina
British attack in 1776 **S** 296
Sulphides *see* Sulfides
Sulphur *see* Sulfur
Sultan, title
Morocco **M** 461
Sultan Ahmed (Blue) **Mosque,** Istanbul, picture **T** 323
Sultana grapes G 297
Sultan of Swat, Babe Ruth **R** 361

Sulu Sea (Sea of Mindoro), part of the Pacific Ocean encircled by Borneo and the southern Philippine islands. It contains several small island groups.

Sulzberger, Arthur Hays (1891–1968), American newspaper publisher, b. New York, N.Y. He served as president and director of the New York Times Co. (1935–57), publisher of the New York *Times* (1935–61), and chairman of the *Times* Board (1957–68). Under his direction, the *Times*'s circulation flourished. Its staff became the largest of any newspaper in the world.

Suma, universal language **U** 194
Sumatra (su-MA-tra), island of Indonesia **I** 219
Sumer, Mesopotamia **A** 218–20
Sumerians (su-ME-rians), people of Mesopotamia
ancient civilization **A** 218–20
ancient music **A** 245
art **A** 233–36
building methods **B** 435
Summer, season **S** 108–12
constellations **C** 492–93
Eskimo land **E** 284
flowers for summer bloom **G** 46
See also months by name
Summer camps *see* Camping, organized
Summer Holiday, poem by Robinson Jeffers **P** 355
Summer melons, or muskmelons **M** 216, 217
Summer Palace, Peking **P** 119
Summerside, P.E.I., Canada **P** 456e

Summer snowflake *see* Star-of-Bethlehem
Summer soldier and sunshine patriot, from the words
   of Thomas Paine in *The Crisis*   R 202
Summer theaters   T 162
Summit conferences, between heads of state   I 323
   See also Glassboro

Sumner, Charles (1811–1874), United States senator
(1851–74), b. Boston, Mass. He graduated from Harvard
Law School and for a while lectured there. Elected to the
Senate (1850) with no political background, he became
one of that body's most powerful members. He often was
attacked for his outspoken views on abolition and
equality for freed Negroes. As chairman of the foreign
relations committee (1861–71) he favored an antiwar
policy. He helped organize the Republican Party.

Sumner, James Batcheller (1887–1955), American biochemist, b. Canton, Mass. He specialized in the study of
enzymes and in 1926 was the first to isolate an enzyme.
Tests showed that the enzyme was a protein. Sumner's
discovery opened the way for many important findings
about body chemistry. He shared the 1946 Nobel prize
in chemistry with J. H. Northrop and W. M. Stanley.

Sumner, William G., American sociologist   S 227
Sumo (SU-mo), Japanese wrestling   J 33;   W 314
Sumterville, South Carolina   S 308
Sun   S 458–67
   age of   E 22
   atmosphere reduces radiation   A 481–82
   classified as a star   A 476
   cosmic rays   C 513
   distance from earth   E 3, 22
   earth and sun   E 22–30
   earth's history   E 18
   earth's surface heat, experiment to show   E 6
   eclipses of   E 46–47;   M 448–49
   energy source, in food chain   L 243
   heat   H 86d–95
   ice age theories   I 23
   International Geophysical Year (IGY)   I 310–13
   ions and ionization   I 352–53
   light   L 260
   looking at   E 46, 361;   S 458, 464
   navigation, "shooting the sun"   N 64–65
   nuclear fusion   N 365
   obelisk, sacred Egyptian symbol of   E 96
   one star in one galaxy of the universe   U 198
   orbiting solar observatories   O 14
   radiant energy source of other forms of energy   E 202
   radio astronomy studies   R 74, 75
   seasons   S 108–12
   skin cancer from   C 92
   solar energy   S 235–39
   solar observatories   O 9–10
   solar system   S 239–49
   sunspots and sunspot cycles   A 476
   tides, effect on   T 182–83
   time, the solar day   T 187, 188
Sun, New York newspaper   N 198
Sun, The, sculpture by Richard Lippold, picture   D 135
Sunburn   S 235
Sunda (SOON-da) Islands, Indonesia   I 218, 219
Sun Dance, Plains Indian tribes   I 160;   M 563
Sunday, religious holiday   R 153
   Constantine supported observance of Sunday as
      Christian holy day   C 282, 489
   legal holiday celebrations   H 147
   origin of name   D 47

Sunday, Billy (William Ashley Sunday) (1862–1935),
American evangelist, b. Ames, Iowa. He played professional baseball (1883–91) and did YMCA work (1891–95)
before becoming an evangelist in 1896. Ordained a
Presbyterian minister in 1903, Sunday was noted for his
colorful language and dramatic delivery.

Sundews, plants   P 317; picture   P 316
Sundials   T 192–93; pictures   G 27
   time first measured by shadow clocks   T 188;   W 44
Sundial shell, picture   S 147
Sundiata, king of Mali   N 90

Sundogs, or mock suns, phenomena sometimes seen
near the sun in the sky. Ice clouds 3 to 6 miles high
bend sunlight, producing what look like faint rings and
bands of light around the sun. Two bright spots
commonly appear along one of the bands that runs
parallel to the earth. The spots are called sundogs.
There is one on each side of the sun. Sometimes ice
clouds produce moondogs, a similar effect near the
moon.
   mistaken for flying saucers   F 285

Sunfish
   freshwater creatures, pictures   L 257
Sunflowers
   giants of nature, picture   G 199
   Kansas, state flower of   K 177
   pollen grains, picture   P 297
Sunflowers, painting by Van Gogh   M 389
Sunflower State, nickname for Kansas   K 177
Sungari (sun-ga-RI) River, Asia   R 248

Sung dynasty (960–1279), Chinese dynasty noted for its
great intellectual activity and outstanding achievements
in printing, porcelain, painting, poetry, and historical
and scientific writing. It became the Southern Sung
(1127–1279) after invaders from northern Manchuria
forced it to move southward.
   China, history of   C 270
   Oriental art   O 216

Sun Goddess, Legend of the, myth of origin of Japan
   J 42
Sunken relief, in sculpture   S 90
Sunken treasure *see* Buried treasure
Sun King *see* Louis XIV
Sunlight
   heliograph signaling, with mirror   C 438
   photosynthesis   P 221–23
   vitamin D   V 371
Sunni Ali Ber, ruler of Songhai   N 90
Sunrise service, Easter Sunday   E 41; picture   E 42
Sunscopes, solar observatories   E 28
Sunset
   color through dust   D 348
Sunshine State
   Florida, nickname for   F 259
   South Dakota, nickname for   S 313
Sunshine vitamin, name for vitamin D   V 371
Sunspots and sunspot cycles   A 476;   S 458–60
   earth and its sun   E 25–27
   tree rings, use in study of   T 286
Sunstone, gemstone   G 76
Suntan
   sunlamp   L 288
   ultraviolet light   R 44
Sun Valley, Idaho   I 65; picture   I 64
Sun viewer, for solar eclipse, how to make   E 46
Sun Yat-sen, founder of the Chinese republic   S 467
   birthday a national holiday in China   H 150
   China, history and government   C 262, 272

Suomi see Finland
Suomi College, Hancock, Michigan M 262
Superchargers, in airplane engines A 557
Superconductivity H 90
  extreme cold and pressure, effect of, on matter M 177
  helium used as a cooling agent H 108
  liquid gases L 308
  magnets with strongest fields M 29–30
Supercooled clouds C 359; W 92–93
Supercooling
  clouds C 359; W 92–93
  freezing point of water I 4
  raindrops from ice crystals R 93
Superfluidity, a physical property of matter
  liquid helium, behavior of H 108
Superghosts, a word game W 238
Supergiant stars S 407
Superhighways see Roads and highways
Superior, Lake, one of Great Lakes G 326–27
Superior, Wisconsin W 205
Superior Upland, Wisconsin W 194
Supermarkets S 468
  marketing for the home M 100
  Mexico City, picture M 252
  Tel Aviv, picture I 444
Supernatural, belief in the
  superstition S 473–75
Supernovae (su-per-NO-ve), stars S 409; pictures S 408
  astronomy, history of A 476, 477
  cosmic rays C 513
  quasars and pulsars Q 7–8
Superphosphates, fertilizers F 97, 98
Supersonic flight S 469–73
Superstition S 473–75
  a section of folklore F 305
  black cat C 142
  Christian persecutions C 281
  colonial New England C 394
  gemstones, curious beliefs about G 74
  good luck customs for weddings W 100–01
  Groundhog Day F 74
  Halloween H 15–17
  knots thought to have magical powers K 289
  mistletoe, in Christmas tradition C 291
  number lore N 378
  religions of ancient man R 145
  trials by ordeal and combat M 291
  witchcraft W 208–09
  zodiac, signs of see month articles
  See also Alchemy; Blarney Stone; Magic; Voodoo
Suppawn, or hasty pudding, colonial American dish
  C 390
Suppé (ZU-pay), Franz von, Austrian composer of
  operettas O 156
Supremacy, Act of, 1534 H 109
Suprematism, or constructivism, in art M 393
Supreme Court, Canada C 78
Supreme Court Building, Washington, D.C. W 31; pic-
  ture W 33
Supreme Court of the United States S 476–77
  Bill of Rights, rulings on B 179
  Brandeis, Louis B 370
  busing decision, 1971 N 105
  court of final review C 530
  Dred Scott decision D 310–11
  Holmes, Oliver Wendell, Jr. H 160–61
  Hughes, Charles Evans H 273–74
  Jay, John, first chief justice J 56
  Jefferson's struggle with Federalist justices J 68
  Marshall, John M 112
  re-apportionment of state legislatures S 415
  Roosevelt, Franklin D. R 323

  ruling on confidential Vietnam War documents C 316
  segregation ruling S 115
  Taft, William Howard, as chief justice T 9
  television viewers, decision on rights of T 70d
  Warren, Earl, chief justice W 13
  Who are the Capitol Pages? W 31
  women's role, rulings on W 211

Supreme Headquarters, Allied Powers, Europe (SHAPE),
supreme military headquarters in Europe of the North
Atlantic Treaty Organization (NATO). Located at Rocquen-
court, near Paris, until France withdrew from NATO in
1966, it was moved to Casteau, in southern Belgium.
  North American Treaty Organization N 305

Supreme Soviet, Union of Soviet Socialist Republics U 42
Surati, cheese made from buffalo's milk C 193
Surface tension, of liquids L 310
Surfactants (sur-FAC-tants), cleansing agents of deter-
  gents D 145, 148, 149

Surfbird, species of shore bird found along the Pacific
coasts of North and South America. It resembles the
plovers to which it is related. Average length is 1
foot; bill is short; and color is a mixture of black, brown,
gray, and white. Surfbirds migrate long distances.

Surfboarding see Surfing
Surfboards S 478
Surf casting, fishing F 207
Surfing, sport of riding ocean waves S 478
  surf carnival, Manly Beach, Australia, picture A 496
  Waikiki Beach, picture H 66
Surgeons D 239
Surgeons' needles N 89
Surgery
  anesthesia A 256–59; M 208a; pictures A 256, 257
  appendicitis corrected by D 193
  experiments with hypnosis H 315
  heart surgery, picture D 238
  hospitals H 247; picture H 249
  hyperbaric chambers for oxygen during surgery M 210
  Lister's antiseptics L 311
  medicine, tools and techniques of M 210
  nurses in operating rooms N 410
  spare-parts surgery I 104, 107; M 208c
  surgeons' needles N 89
Suricates (SU-ric-ates), animals related to mongooses
  G 93
Surinam (SU-ri-nam), or Dutch Guiana G 395, 396–97
  Djuka village, picture S 282
  life in Latin America L 47–61
Surnames, family names N 4

Surratt (sur-RATT), Mary E. (1820–1865), American
woman who was allegedly a conspirator in Lincoln's
assassination. She was keeper of the boardinghouse in
Washington, D.C., where John Wilkes Booth and his
associates conspired against Lincoln. Her son and Booth
had become acquainted during the Civil War. She was
hanged for complicity in the assassination on July 7,
1865, although it now seems fairly certain that she took
no part in the plot.

Surrealism, in the arts M 394
  French literary movement F 442
  Klee, Paul K 271
  sculpture S 105
Surveying S 479–80
  aerial photography P 206
  early methods of public land survey and sale P 506
  Mason and Dixon's Line M 133

Surveying (continued)
pioneer life P 260
roads R 251
surveyor's transit, picture O 170
Washington's early career W 36
See also Maps and map making
Surveyors, moon probes S 348
Surveyor 3 M 449, 455; S 348
Survival, in space S 340j–342
Survival of the fittest, Darwinian theory of evolution
E 346
Susa (SU-sa), city of ancient Persia A 242
Susanna, apocryphal book of Bible B 159
Susitna (su-SIT-na) **River,** Alaska A 133
Suspense stories see Mystery, detective, and suspense
stories
Suspension bridges B 398
Brooklyn Bridge B 398; N 230
Europe's longest P 400
Golden Gate Bridge B 398; pictures B 398, S 30,
U 106
Mackinac, picture G 328
Verrazano-Narrows Bridge B 398; picture W 220
Susquehanna (sus-que-HANN-a) **River,** United States
M 117; P 131
Sussex County, Delaware D 93
Susu (SU-su), blind porpoise of Asia A 451
Sutherland, George, English-born American statesman
U 253

Sutherland, Joan (1926–), Australian soprano, b.
Sydney. A coloratura soprano, she made her European
debut at Royal Opera House, Covent Garden, in *The Magic
Flute* (1952). She was given wide acclaim for singing the
difficult role of Lucia in *Lucia di Lammermoor* (1959).
Considered one of the most important singers of her
time, she sings at the Metropolitan Opera, performing
leading roles in *Norma* and *La Sonnambula.* Picture O 147.

Sutherland Falls, New Zealand N 237
famous waterfalls W 56b
Sutter, John Augustus, early California settler C 28
Sutter's Fort, near Sacramento, California G 250
Su Tung-p'o, Chinese poet O 220a
Suva (SU-va), capital of Fiji F 121, 122
police, picture P 374
Suvorov (su-VOR-off), **Aleksander,** Russian general U 49
Suwannee, river in Florida F 262
Suzerainty (SU-zer-inty), overlordship
Andorra's distinctive government A 254
Suzuki, Harunobu see Harunobu, Suzuki, Japanese artist
Svalbard (SVOL-bar) **Islands** (Spitsbergen), Norway I 437
considered part of Europe E 307

Sverdrup (SVAIR-droop), **Otto** (1855–1930), Norwegian
Arctic explorer, b. Bindal. Accompanied the Nansen expedition to Greenland (1888) and to the Arctic (1893–96),
bringing back the *Fram,* a Norwegian ship that had been
imprisoned in the ice for 35 months. He led an
expedition in Greenland (1898–1902) and three in the
Arctic. The latter were in search of lost explorers.

Svoboda (SVO-buh-duh), **Ludvik,** (1895–), president
of Czechoslovakia, b. Hrovnedin, Moravia. He fought in
both World Wars. His 17-year-old son was tortured to
death by the Germans. He served as defense minister
but was imprisoned during the Stalinist period. Released
after Stalin's death, he headed the Czechoslovakian military academy. He was elected president in 1968. He has
over 50 medals, including the American Legion of Merit,
and is one of the few foreigners to hold the title "Hero
of the Soviet Union."

Swahili (swa-HE-li), a special Bantu language of Africa
A 56
African literature A 76b

Swallow, any one of a group of small, long-winged birds
found in many parts of the world and noted for their
swift, graceful flight. The long wings, when closed,
extend to or beyond the forked tail. The feet are small,
adapted chiefly to perching. Swallows fly in large flocks,
usually during the day. Some forms, such as the cliff
and barn swallows, have come to inhabit houses and
barns. Pictures B 218, 244.
adaptations to a habitat B 221
See also San Juan Capistrano

Swallow, John C., English oceanographer O 33
Swallow float, detects deep ocean currents O 33; picture O 34
Swallowtail butterflies
chrysalis, picture I 265
larva showing false eye spots, picture, I 275

Swammerdam (SWAH-mer-dahm), **Jan** (1637–80), Dutch
naturalist, b. Amsterdam. Although educated for the
ministry, he turned to medicine. A pioneer in the use
of the microscope, he did important studies on insects
and the human anatomy, and may have been the first to
detect red corpuscles (1658). His chief collection of
descriptions and finely executed drawings was published
in the original Dutch accompanied by a Latin translation
(2 vols., 1737–38) and appeared in English as the *Bible
of Nature* (1758).
biology, advances in B 190

Swamp Fox, name for Francis Marion, American Revo-
lutionary War officer M 99; R 207
Swamps
cranberry bogs, picture G 300
Dismal Swamp, Virginia V 346
Florida, picture F 260
formed from lakes L 25
muskegs of Canada's taiga region T 111
Swamp white oak, tree
leaves, shapes of, pictures L 116
Swan, constellation see Cygnus
Swan, Sir Joseph, English scientist F 108
electric light bulb, experiments on I 334
first regenerated fibers N 427
Swan dive D 230
Swanee River (Old Folks at Home), song by Stephen
Foster
Florida, state song of F 259, 262
Swan Islands, outlying areas of the United States U 100
Swan Lake, ballet, picture B 25
Swans, birds A 265, 294; picture A 295
flight feathers B 200
Swarming, of bees B 121
Swaziland (SWA-zi-land) S 481
flag F 236
Sweat glands
regulate body temperature B 279; diagram B 278
Sweathouses, for bathing
Nez Percé Indians I 175–76, 197
Sweatshops, early system in the clothing industry
C 353–54
Sweden S 482–87
apartment development near Göteborg, picture H 182
favorite foods F 341
flag F 240
holidays H 156, 158
Lapland L 44–45
national anthem N 22

old-age pension plans **O** 98
postman, picture **P** 407
Scandinavia, meaning of the name **S** 49
Scandinavian literature **S** 50–53
taiga, picture **T** 10
women, role of **W** 213

Swedenborg, Emanuel (1688–1772), Swedish theologian and scientist, b. Stockholm. A brilliant mathematician and geologist, he was a visionary and mystic best-known for his philosophical and religious writings. After his death his followers established the Church of the New Jerusalem, partly based on his teachings. Among his works are *Principia*, and *Divine Love and Wisdom*.

Swedes in America A 190
early settlers in Delaware **D** 86, 89, 99
Swedish language S 482
Swedish literature S 50–53
Swedish Museum, Skansen, Sweden **M** 513
Swedish Nightingale, singer Jenny Lind **L** 300
Sweelinck (SWAY-linck), **Jan Pieters,** Dutch composer and organist **D** 365
baroque music **B** 65
Sweeney, Thomas, American glassmaker **W** 126
Sweepers, in game of curling **C** 554
Sweep rowing R 338
Sweet, a sense of taste **B** 286
Sweet Afton, poem by Robert Burns **B** 460
Sweet alyssum, flowers, pictures **G** 27, 28
Sweet corn C 506
Sweet flag, or calamus root, plant
plant remedy **P** 314; picture **P** 315
Sweet grasses C 319
Sweet gum, tree
shapes of leaves, picture **L** 116

Sweet pea, vinelike plant of the pea (legume) family. Thousands of varieties have been known and many are still cultivated in gardens the world over. Sweet peas may grow to a height of 6 feet; the leaves are oval, the flowers of many colors, and the pods long. The plant's oil may be used in perfume. Picture **G** 47.

Sweet potatoes P 412; **V** 293
roots we eat **P** 307; picture **P** 306
Sweet Singer of Israel D 44
Sweet William see Phlox
Swells, of the ocean **O** 34
Sweyn (SWAIN), **Forkbeard,** king of the Danes
V 340

Swift, Gustavus Franklin (1839–1903), American cattle dealer and meat packer, b. near Sandwich, Mass. As a boy he worked in his brother's butcher shop before opening the first of his own stores (1859). He settled in Chicago, where he founded Swift & Co. He was a pioneer in introducing such innovations as the shipping of dressed beef in refrigerated trains, the profitable use of by-products, and the establishment of foreign markets.

Swift, Jonathan, English author **S** 488
children's literature **C** 236
Gulliver's Travels, excerpt **G** 412–13
place in Irish literature **I** 393
quoted on Africa **A** 46
satire and political writings **E** 257–58; **H** 280
Swiftcurrent Lake, Glacier National Park, Montana, picture **G** 221
Swifties, word parodies **H** 280

Swifts, birds resembling swallows but actually related to the goatsuckers and hummingbirds. The bill is small, the wings are very long, and the feet small and weak. Swifts are found in many parts of the world. They spend most of their time on the wing, catching and eating insects. The chimney swift has adapted to nesting in man-made dwellings. Picture **B** 218.
where birds live **B** 220

Swigert, John L., Jr., American astronaut **S** 344, 345, 347
Swim bladder, of a fish **F** 202–03
Swim fins, or flippers, for skin diving **S** 189
Swimmerets, small appendages of animals
crustacea **S** 171
Swimming S 488–94
Ederle, Gertrude **E** 58
fishes **F** 189; diagram **F** 188
from boats **B** 263
locomotion of fishes **A** 289–91
Olympic event, picture **O** 113
safety measures **S** 6
safety rules for campers **C** 46
skin diving **S** 188–91
speed of dolphins and porpoises **D** 272–73
water polo **W** 60
See also Diving
Swimming pools
Tokyo, picture **J** 32
Swinburne, Algernon Charles, English poet **E** 263
Swine see Pigs
Swing, The, poem by Robert Louis Stevenson **S** 424
Swing-span bridges B 400
Swiss Alps
hostelers, picture **H** 253
Swiss cheese D 13
Swiss Guards, of Vatican City **V** 281–82
fame of Swiss warriors **S** 502
Swiss lake dwellers, a prehistoric people
homes **H** 177
See also Lake dwellers
Switchboards
telegraph **T** 54
telephone **T** 57–58
Switches, electric see Electric switchgear

Swithin, or **Swithun, Saint** (?–862), English churchman, b. near Winchester. Bishop of Winchester (852?–862), he requested burial outside the Winchester Cathedral. On July 15, 971, when monks sought to honor him by reburying him within the church, it rained for 40 days—supposedly Saint Swithin's protest at being moved and the origin of the legend that rain on July 15 (Saint Swithin's day) means 40 days of rain will follow.

Swithin, Saint, Feast of H 159
Switzerland S 495–502
camps, organized **C** 47
costumes, traditional Appenzell, picture **C** 350
flag **F** 240
glacier with lateral moraine, picture **I** 18
Langweiser Viaduct, picture **E** 328
mealtime for skiers, picture **F** 336
mountain slopes, picture **G** 102
national anthem **N** 22
Reformation **C** 286
Rhone Glacier, picture **G** 225
Swiss and German literature **G** 178, 179
watch and clock industry **W** 50
watchmakers, picture **E** 327
Zermatt, picture **E** 305
Sword dance, picture **D** 29
Swordfish, habitats, feeding habits, uses **F** 215

Swords
  King Arthur legends **A** 443, 444
  knights' swords **K** 273
Sycamore (SIC-a-more), tree, picture **T** 277
  seed, picture **P** 298
  uses of the wood and its grain **W** 224
Sydenham (SID-en-am), **Thomas,** English doctor **M** 206
Sydney (SID-ney), capital of New South Wales, Australia
    S 503–04; pictures **A** 513, 515, **C** 310, **S** 503
Sydney, Nova Scotia, Canada **N** 344d
Sydney Harbour Bridge, Australia, picture **B** 399, **S** 503
Syllables, speech sounds pronounced as a unit **P** 478
Sylphide (seel-PHEDE), **La,** ballet **B** 25
Sylvis, William H., American labor union leader **L** 3
Symbiosis (sim-by-O-sis), co-operative living arrangement
    between unlike plants or animals
  clown fish and sea anemone **F** 203–04
  lichens **F** 94–95
  yucca and the moth **P** 320
Symbolic logic **M** 161
Symbolic triad, Japanese flower arranging **J** 49–50
Symbolism, in art
  Dutch and Flemish art **D** 351
  in color **D** 140
Symbolism, in literature
  French poets **F** 440
  in poetry **A** 210
  Russian literature **U** 61
Symbols see Signs and symbols
Symbols, chemical see Chemical symbols
Symmetry, in physics **N** 371
  body plan of man and certain other animals **B** 269
Sympathetic nerves, controlling involuntary muscles
    and glands, diagram **B** 281
Sympathetic vibrations, of sound **S** 261–62
Symphonic (sim-PHON-ic) **poem,** in music **M** 538
  developed by Franz Liszt **L** 312
  German music **G** 187
  Romantic age in music **R** 311
Symphony (SIM-pho-ni), in music **M** 540–41
  basic record library **R** 125
  Beethoven **B** 124–25
  Brahms's First **O** 189
  festivals **M** 551
  Haydn's works **G** 184
  Mozart **M** 502
  See also names of composers, as Brahms, Johannes
Symphony No. 5, of Beethoven, first page **O** 185
Symphony orchestra **O** 182–84
Symposium, by Xenophon, describes dancing **D** 35
Synagogues (SIN-a-gogs), congregations of Jews
    J 104, 115
  choral music **C** 276
  New York City, picture **R** 152
  Touro Synagogue, Newport, Rhode Island **R** 212;
    picture **R** 220
Synanon, organization for non-medical treatment of
    narcotics addicts **N** 14
Synapse (SIN-aps), diagram **K** 255
Synchronizing pulse, television **T** 66, 68
Synchronous (SINC-ro-nous) **motors,** electric **E** 138–39
Synchrotrons, "atom-smashing" machines **M** 29–30
Syncopation (sin-co-PATION), in music
  folk music **F** 328
  jazz developments of new ideas of rhythm **J** 62
Syndics of the Cloth Guild, The, painting by Rembrandt
    D 359
Synge (SING), **John Millington,** Irish playwright **I** 394
  Abbey Theatre contributions to drama **D** 298
  Irish Renaissance in English literature **E** 266
Synodic (sin-OD-ic) **month**
  life rhythms of animals affected by **L** 244

Synonyms and antonyms **S** 504
Synoptic maps, in meteorology **W** 77
Syntax, grammatical word order **L** 302
  Biblical Hebrew language parallelisms **H** 100
  English language word order **E** 244
  grammar **G** 288–90
Synthesis, in chemistry **C** 220
Synthesis gas **G** 61
Synthesizer see Electronic synthesizer
Synthetic materials **M** 85
  adhesives using synthetic resins **G** 243
  antibiotics **A** 313
  chemical industry **C** 194, 195
  clothes today **C** 352
  detergents **D** 145, 148, 149
  drugs **D** 323, 328
  dry-cleaning solvents **D** 337
  dyes **D** 369–71
  dyes, first produced by Perkin **C** 214
  elements, man-made **E** 159
  fashion **F** 65–66
  fibers **F** 108; **N** 425
  fishing industry equipment **F** 217
  furniture **F** 510
  gases **G** 59, 61
  gemstones **G** 70–71
  grain liquid furfural **G** 281
  How are man-made fibers named? **N** 425
  industrial importance **I** 250
  insecticides **I** 258
  ivory substitutes **I** 488
  jewelry made of imitation stones **J** 93
  manufactured diamonds **D** 155
  modern textiles **T** 141–42
  nitrate fertilizers **F** 98
  nylon and other man-made fibers **N** 424–28
  pearls, artificial **P** 114
  plastics **P** 324–31; chart of properties, uses **P** 328–29
  resins **R** 184–85
  resins for varnishes and lacquers **V** 279–80
  rope **R** 332–33
  rubber, synthetic **R** 345–46
  rugs and carpets **R** 354
  saccharin **S** 455
  synthetic rubber **R** 345–46
Synthetic method, of philosophy **P** 191–92
Syphilis, venereal disease **D** 208–09
  Ehrlich's 606, treatment for **D** 216
Syracuse, battle of, 413 B.C. **B** 100
Syracuse, New York **N** 223

Syr Darya, one of the main rivers of Central Asia. It
originates in the Tien Shan mountain range.

Syria (SI-ria) **S** 505–08
  flag **F** 238
  UAR (United Arab Republic) withdrawal from **N** 15
Syrian bear, picture **B** 108
Syringa (si-RING-a), flowering shrub
  Idaho's state flower **I** 54
Syrinxes, or panpipes, ancient musical instruments
    O 209; picture **M** 548
Syrups, made from sugar **S** 453
  maple **M** 86–87
Systole, action of the heart **H** 86
Systolic pressure, of blood **D** 199; **M** 208f, 208g
Szczecin see Stettin, Poland
Szechwan (SECH-wan) **Basin,** region of China **C** 262;
    picture **C** 263
Szeged, Hungary **H** 286

Szell (SELL), **George** (1897–1970), American conductor

b. Budapest, Hungary. He conducted in various German opera houses before going to the United States, where he conducted at the Metropolitan Opera House (1942–45). He became permanent conductor of the Cleveland Orchestra in 1946 and raised that orchestra to a rank among the world's best. He was also a composer and pianist.

Szilard, Leo (1898–1964), American physicist, b. Budapest, Hungary. He emigrated to the United States in 1937 and became an American citizen. He was one of the nuclear physicists responsible for developing the atomic bomb. With Enrico Fermi at Columbia University he conducted experiments that resulted in the first controlled chain reaction from an atomic pile.

Szold (ZOLD), **Henrietta** (1860–1945), American Jewish leader, b. Baltimore, Md. Daughter of a rabbi, she was a teacher, editor, and translator. A trip to Palestine convinced her of the necessity of improving the lot of its inhabitants. With a small group, she organized (1912) Hadassah, the Women's Zionist Organization of America. She spent most of her life working in Palestine. During World War II she directed the rescue and resettlement of European refugee children.

See also Hadassah

ILLUSTRATION CREDITS

The following list credits, by page, the sources of illustrations used in Volume S of THE NEW BOOK OF KNOWLEDGE. Credits are listed illustration by illustration—left to right, top to bottom. Wherever appropriate, the name of the photographer or artist has been listed with the source, the two being separated by a dash. When two or more illustrations appear on one page, their credits are separated by semicolons.

T, 20th letter of the English alphabet **T** 1
  See *also* Alphabet
Tabasco, Mexico **M** 247
Tabernacles (TAB-er-nacles), **Feast of the,** or Sukkoth, religious holiday **R** 154
Tabitha *see* Dorcas
Tabito, Okura, Japanese poet **O** 220b
Table manners
  table settings, how arranged **T** 2–3
Table of contents, of a book **L** 181
Tables, statistical **S** 416–18
  graphs **G** 309–13
Table salt *see* Sodium chloride
Table settings **T** 2–3
  knives, forks, and spoons, pictures **K** 286, 287
Table sugar *see* Sucrose
Table tennis, or Ping-Pong **T** 4–5
  China trip by U.S. team **C** 273
  United States team at the Great Wall of China, picture **N** 262f
Tabloids, small-size newspapers, containing many illustrations **N** 198
Taboos (ta-BOOS), system of setting things apart as forbidden
  food taboos **F** 334–35

Tabor (TAY-bor), **Horace Austin Warner** (1830–1899), American silver prospector, b. Holland, Vt. He amassed a fortune mining silver in Colorado. He served as lieutenant governor of Colorado (1879–93) and filled an incompleted term in U.S. Senate (1883). He lost his wealth after 1893 and was appointed postmaster in Denver (1898).
  Denver, history of **D** 116

Tabor, small drum **F** 329; picture **F** 330
Tabora, Tanzania **T** 19
Tabriz (ta-BREEZ), Iran **I** 376

Tachometer (ta-COM-et-er), device used to measure speed of rotation of a shaft. The speed is shown on a dial by a pointer, which is moved by a mechanism connected with the rotating shaft. Tachometers are used in speedometers and airplane engines.

Tacitus (TAS-it-us), **Cornelius,** Roman historian **L** 80
Tacking, in sailing **S** 12–13
Tackle, for fishing **F** 206; pictures **F** 207
Tackling, in football, picture **F** 359
Tacks, small nails **N** 2
Tacoma (ta-CO-ma), Washington **W** 26
  Tacoma v. Rainier as name for the mountain **W** 14
Taconic (ta-CON-ic) **Mountains,** eastern United States **N** 214
  Connecticut **C** 469, 470
  Massachusetts **M** 136
  Vermont **V** 308
Taconite (TAC-on-ite), rock containing iron ore **I** 404
TACtical Airborne Navigation (TACAN), radio navigation system **A** 562
Tadjikistan, capital of Tadzhikistan (Tadzhik Soviet Socialist Republic) **U** 46
Tadoussac (ta-doos-SOC), Quebec, Canada **C** 68
Tadpoles, larvae of frogs **F** 470, 472–73
  freshwater creatures, pictures **L** 257
  frogs' eggs **E** 89
  metamorphosis of the frog **M** 234; picture **M** 235
  pond life, pictures **L** 257
Tadzhiks (ta-JEEKS), or Tajiks, people of
  Afghanistan **A** 42
  Tadzhikistan **U** 46

Tadzhik Soviet Socialist Republic (Tadzhikistan) **U** 46; picture **U** 36
  languages **U** 28

Tael, in eastern Asia, a unit of weight of approximately 1⅓ oz., with some variation according to region of country. "Tael" also refers to a Chinese monetary unit based upon the weight of a tael of silver.

Taft, Helen Herron, wife of William Howard Taft **F** 176; pictures **F** 177, **T** 7

Taft, Robert Alphonso (1889–1953), American lawyer and politician, b. Cincinnati, Ohio. He was a son of President William Howard Taft. He served in Ohio State Legislature (1921–26, 1931–32) and unsuccessfully attempted to secure Republican presidential nomination (1940, 1944, 1948, 1952). A co-sponsor of Taft-Hartley Labor Act (1947), he was a leading moderate conservative Republican spokesman in the Senate (1939–53). Picture **T** 9.

Taft, William Howard, 27th president of United States **T** 6–9
  William Howard Taft National Historic Site, Ohio **O** 69

Taft, William Howard III (1915–), American government official, b. Bar Harbor, Maine. Following a teaching career (1940–48) he entered government service and served with the Central Intelligence Agency (1952–53) and as ambassador to Ireland (1953–57) before joining the Department of State in 1962.

Taft-Hartley Act *see* Labor-management relations Act
Tagalog (ta-GA-log), a language of the Philippines **P** 184
Tag games **G** 16–18

Tagliavini (tol-ya-VI-ni), **Ferruccio** (1913–), Italian tenor, b. Reggio Emilia. He made his operatic debut in Florence in 1939 and at the Metropolitan Opera Company in New York in 1946. He has also sung in South America and is chiefly noted for lyric tenor roles in operas.

Taglioni (tal-YO-ni), **Marie,** Italian ballerina **B** 25

Tagore (ta-GORE), **Sir Rabindranath** (1861–1941), Indian poet, writer, and artist, b. Calcutta. He founded (in Bengal) an international university, Visva-Bharati, and used money from his 1913 Nobel prize for literature to help support the school. Tagore painted and composed music in addition to writing volumes of poetry, collections of stories (*Mashi*), the play *Sacrifice*, novels, such as *The Home and the World*, and nonfiction. Picture **O** 220e.
  Indian literature **O** 220e

Tagus (TAY-gus) **River,** Spain and Portugal **R** 248
  at Toledo, Spain **S** 356
  divides Portugal into quite different halves **P** 400
Taharka (ta-HAR-ka), Ethiopian king of Egypt **N** 90
Tahiti (ta-HE-ti), Pacific island **P** 8
  Gauguin's paintings of **G** 64
Tahoe (TA-hoe), **Lake,** between California and Nevada **L** 33; picture **N** 134
Tahoua (tah-OO-ah), Niger **N** 252
Taichung, Taiwan **T** 13
Taiga (ty-GA), forests of northern regions **T** 10–11
  Alaska, picture **C** 343
  Finland **F** 132
  high-latitude climates **C** 346
  North Asia **A** 450

Taiga (continued)
polar continental climate of North America **N** 289
vegetation belts in Europe **E** 310
Tailorbirds **B** 213
Tailoring **C** 353
See also Dressmaking
Tainan, Taiwan **T** 13
Tainter, Charles S., American inventor **P** 197
Taipei (TY-pai), capital of Taiwan **T** 13; pictures **C** 257, **T** 12
nationalist China **C** 265, 273

T'ai-P'ing (TY-ping) **rebellion** (1850–64), revolutionary movement in China. Hung Hsiu-ch'üan (1812–64), told by visions to lead a rebellion against the Manchu dynasty, declared himself emperor of the T'ai-P'ing (Great Peace) Kingdom. The revolutionary movement spread, had some military success, and brought about some social reforms before it was put down.

Tais, or **Thais,** people of Thailand **T** 147

T'ai Tsung (TY JOONG) (597–649), Chinese emperor. Emperor of the T'ang Dynasty (627–649), he was a strong ruler who extended Chinese influence and trade to Persia and India, improved the army, and supported education and the arts.

Taiwan (TY-wan), or Formosa **T** 12–13
agriculture, picture **A** 99
Chiang Kai-shek **C** 227
China, Republic of (Nationalist) **C** 257, 265, 272–73
Chinese children, picture **A** 459
Chinese farmers, picture **A** 464
Taiz (ta-IZ), Yemen (Sana) **Y** 349
Tajiks (ta-JEEKS), or Tadzhiks, people of Afghanistan **A** 42
Taj Mahal (TOJ ma-HOL), tomb in India **T** 14; pictures **I** 130; **T** 14
India's cities **I** 122
Islamic architecture **I** 420
structure of the Mogul period in India **O** 215
Tajumulco (ta-hu-MOOL-co), inactive volcano of Guatemala
highest peak in Central America **C** 171
Takai Kito see Kito

Takamine (ta-KA-mi-nay), **Jokichi** (1854–1922), Japanese chemist and industrialist, b. Takaoka. Chemist of Japanese department of agriculture (1883–88), he established first chemical fertilizer plant in Japan (1886). He lived in United States from 1890. His discovery of adrenalin in 1901 made him the first to isolate a pure hormone.

Talbot, Thomas (1771–1853), Canadian colonist, b. Malahide Castle, Ireland. Sent to Canada (1790), he served (1792–94) on staff of John Simcoe, lieutenant governor of Upper Canada. After living in England (1794–1802), he returned to Canada (1802) and founded Port Talbot (1802) on northern shore of Lake Erie. He settled numerous townships and governed settlers for nearly 50 years.

Talbot, William Henry Fox, English scientist **P** 212

Talc, gray, white, or greenish mineral. It has a soapy feel, can be scratched with a knife, and is easily crushed. Talc is used in talcum powder and as a cleaning powder called French chalk. Impure talc, called steatite or soapstone, is harder than pure talc and is used for electrical insulation.

Tale of a Tub, A, by Jonathan Swift **S** 488

Tale of Genji, The, by Lady Murasaki **J** 43; picture from **O** 220c
Japanese literature **O** 220b–220c
Tale of the Heike, Japanese novel **O** 220c
Tales of Hoffmann, The, opera by Offenbach **O** 153–54
Tales of Tsutsuni Chunagon, The, Japanese short stories **O** 220c
Taliesin (ta-li-ES-in) **Fellowship,** school for architects **W** 315
Taliesin West, Arizona home of Frank Lloyd Wright, picture **W** 315
Talisman, a charm
gemstones **G** 74
Talking books, recorded books for the blind **B** 252–53
Talking pictures, or talkies **M** 474
Tallahassee (tal-la-HASS-ee), capital of Florida **F** 270
Tallapoosa (tal-la-POO-sa) **River,** Alabama **A** 115
Tallchief, Maria, American ballerina, picture **B** 27

Talleyrand-Perigord (TAL-ley-rand-PAY-ri-gor), **Charles Maurice de** (1754–1838), French statesman, b. Paris. He became a priest (1775) and was made bishop of Autun (1789). As member of the National Assembly (1789), he proposed nationalization of church properties and was excommunicated by the pope (1791). After serving as minister of foreign affairs (1797–1807) under Napoleon I, he helped restore Bourbons to throne and became minister of foreign affairs (1814) under Louis XVIII. He was ambassador to Great Britain (1830–34) and assisted in the establishment of Quadruple Alliance (1834).
Adams and the XYZ Affair **A** 9

Tallinn, capital of Estonia (Estonian Soviet Socialist Republic) **U** 43
Tallis (TAL-lis), **Thomas,** English composer **E** 269
choral music **C** 277
Tallmadge, James, American statesman **M** 382
Tallow, fat from cattle and sheep **O** 79
candles made of **C** 96, 97, 399
lighting, history of **L** 280
Tall tales **F** 303
Davy Crockett's hunting story **C** 533
exaggerations in account of Jamestown **A** 195
folklore, American **F** 110
folk music **F** 323
Tally marks, for counting **N** 389
Talmud (TAL-mud), authoritative body of Jewish tradition **T** 15; **J** 116
attacks against, in Middle Ages **J** 108
created by Jews in the Babylon period **J** 107
guide to customs and ceremonials of Jewish life **J** 116
Mishnaic Hebrew language **H** 101
Talon (ta-LON), **Jean,** French intendent in Canada **C** 69
Talons (TAL-ons), claws
eagles **E** 2
Tamarind, a tropical fruit **M** 74
Tamarins, monkeys **M** 420; picture **M** 421
Tamatave (ta-ma-TOV), Malagasy Republic **M** 49

Tamayo (ta-MA-yo), **Rufino** (1899–   ), Mexican painter, b. Oaxaca. His work is marked by brilliant color and a style in which modern techniques often are used to depict Mexican folk themes. His paintings hang in leading museums (such as New York's Museum of Modern Art), and his murals decorate several buildings, UNESCO's Paris building among them.

Tambora, or conga drum **D** 336
Tambour, device for ringing bells **B** 136
Tambourine (tam-bour-ENE), drum **D** 335
ancient music **A** 245, 246
percussion instruments **P** 152

Tamerlane, or **Timur,** or **Timur-Lenk** (meaning "Timur the Lame") (1336?–1405), Tatar conqueror b. near Samarkand, central Asia. Succeeding to the chieftancy of a Turkish tribe (1360) and Turkestan (1370), he proceeded to conquer most of central Asia. His armies conquered Persia, central Asia, and had penetrated as far as Russia (1381). He then invaded India (1398), Egypt, and Syria. After defeating the Ottoman Turks (1402), he died while preparing to invade China.
Islamic painting **I** 421
tomb in Samarkand **I** 420; picture **A** 458
Soviet Central Asia **U** 46

Tamil Nadu, formerly Madras state, India **M** 10
Tamils, a people of Ceylon and Madras **C** 177, 180; **M** 10
Taming of the Shrew, The, play by Shakespeare **S** 137

Tammany, or **Tamanen,** Delaware Indian chief. One of the signers of land deed to William Penn (1683), he was by legend endowed with all possible noble characteristics. During Revolutionary War he became a symbol of colonial protest against British. After the war he became patron saint of many political organizations, or "Tammany Societies," most well-known being Sons of King Tammany (later, Sons of Saint Tammany) (1772) and Society of Tammany of New York, N.Y. (1786).

Tammany Hall, Democratic political organization that was begun in New York City as a charitable society (1789). The most influential Tammany leader, William M. Tweed (1865–71), made the party a dominant force in city and state politics before discovery of graft led to his imprisonment. The organization retained dominance, notably corrupt, until investigation (1930–31) forced resignation of the Tammany-backed New York City mayor, James Walker (1932).

Tammany Tiger, political symbol, picture **C** 126
Tam-o'-shanter, Scottish hat, pictures **H** 53
Tampa, Florida **F** 270
Tampere, Finland **F** 133
Tampico (tam-PI-co), Mexico **M** 247
Tam'si, Tchicaya U, Congolese poet **A** 76c
Tana (TA-na), Lake, largest lake in Ethiopia **E** 299

Tanager, one of a group of birds related to finches. Though most species are found in tropical forests of Central and South America, a few are found in the woods of the United States and Canada, the best-known of these being the scarlet tanager. The male scarlet tanager is bright red with black wings and tail. The female is a dull green.

Tanaka, Kakuei (1918–), Japanese statesman, b. Nishiyama, Niigata Prefecture, Japan. A wealthy businessman, he was elected to Parliament in 1947. He served in various government posts, including deputy minister of justice, minister of postal services, and minister of finance. In 1965 he became secretary-general of the Liberal-Democratic Party, the majority party. He was serving as minister of international trade and development when, in 1972, he succeeded Eisaku Sato as prime minister.

Tananarive (ta-na-na-REVE), capital of Malagasy Republic **M** 49
Tandjung Priok (tand-jung pri-OK), seaport of Djakarta **D** 236
Taney, Roger Brooke, American jurist **M** 126
chief justice of United States **C** 320
Dred Scott decision **D** 310–11
Tanga, Tanzania **T** 19

Tanganyika (tan-gan-YI-ka), former republic, now part of Tanzania **T** 16
Tanganyika, Lake, east central Africa **L** 33
Tanzania **T** 17
T'ang (TONG) **dynasty,** ancient China **C** 270; **O** 217
Chinese literature **O** 220a

Tangelo (TAN-gel-o), citrus fruit obtained by crossing grapefruit and tangerine. It is pear-shaped, acid, and thin-skinned, and its color varies from lemon yellow to deep orange. Picture **O** 176.
citrus fruit, kinds of **O** 179

Tangents, of circles **G** 127
Tangerine (tan-ger-ENE), a citrus fruit **O** 179; pictures **A** 90, **O** 176
Tangier, Morocco **M** 461
Tanglewood, near Lenox, Mass. see Berkshire Music Festival
Tanglewood Tales, by Hawthorne, excerpt **H** 74–76
Tango, Latin-American dance **L** 69–70
Latin-American music **L** 74
Tanguy, Yves, French artist **M** 395
Tanka, Japanese verse form **O** 220b
Tank cars, of railroad **R** 83
Tankers, or **oil tankers,** ships **S** 161; **U** 184
transportation of petroleum **P** 175
Tanks, armored
World War I **W** 278; picture **W** 277
Tank trucks, picture **T** 296

Tanner, Henry Ossawa (1859–1937), American painter, Negro, b. Pittsburgh, Pa. Tanner studied at Pennsylvania Academy of Fine Arts under American painter Thomas Eakins and then moved to Paris in 1891. He painted primarily religious subjects, including *The Annunciation, Raising of Lazarus,* and *Daniel in the Lions' Den.*
Negro Renaissance **N** 98

Tannhäuser, opera by Richard Wagner **O** 154
Tannin, or **tannic acid,** vegetable compound
avoid bitter taste of, in making tea **T** 38
bark extract used in leather tanning **L** 107
Maine's hemlock trees provided tannin **M** 39
Tanning, of leather **L** 107–10
leathering of furs **F** 515
Tantalum, element **E** 155, 165

Tantalus (TAN-ta-lus), in Greek mythology, according to most traditions, king of Lydia, son of Zeus, and father of Niobe and Pelops. Tantalus was condemned to stand in a pool of water up to his chin beneath a fruit-laden tree, and although he suffered eternal hunger and thirst, he was unable to partake of either fruit or water. Reasons for his punishment vary, but his crimes included serving his son Pelops as food to the gods and stealing food of the gods (ambrosia and nectar) to give to man.

Tanzania (tanz-a-NI-a) **T** 16–19
flag **F** 236
Peace Corps doctor, picture **P** 102
Taoism (TA-o-ism), a religion of China **R** 148
Asia, chief religions of **A** 460
Chinese literature **O** 220a
religions in China **C** 260–61
Taos (TA-os), New Mexico
Taos Pueblo, pictures **A** 302, **I** 200, **N** 186
Taoudéni (tow-DEN-i), Mali **M** 59
T'ao Yüan-ming, Chinese poet **O** 220a
Tapa (TA-pa), cloth made from bark **S** 24
Tape and wire recorders **T** 20–21
communication advanced by **C** 434

Tape and Wire Recorders (continued)
dictation machines **O** 57
electronic music **E** 142g–142h; **M** 532
hi-fi and stereo **H** 125
library use for information storage and retrieval
L 174
spectrograms of animal sounds **A** 275; picture **A** 276
teaching machines **P** 477
Tapestry (TAP-estry), handwoven textiles, usually for
hangings **T** 22–24
Bayeux tapestry **E** 187
Peru's ancient weaving skills **T** 141
Tapeworms **W** 312
infections caused by **D** 209–10
Tàpies, Antonio, Spanish artist **S** 365

Tapioca, a starchy granular substance obtained from the
thick fleshy roots of cassava plant (*Manihot esculenta*).
It is cultivated in tropical climates and used in making
bread, puddings, and soups.
manioc processed and exported as tapioca **B** 376

Tapirs (TAY-pirs), hoofed mammals **H** 207; picture
H 211
Taproots, of trees **T** 279; pictures **P** 291

Taps (from Dutch *tap toe*, meaning "bar is closed"),
signal usually played in soldiers' and sailors' quarters,
originally by drum but more commonly by bugle, to turn
out lights at night. Taps is also used at military funerals.
notes of the call **B** 429

Tar, thick, sticky, dark-colored liquid with a strong odor,
obtained by the destructive distillation of coal, wood,
petroleum, and other organic materials. Tar is often
further distilled to yield pitch (used in making roofing
paper, in road construction, and in waterproofing
underground pipes) and a number of chemicals used in
making dyes, plastics, drugs, and rubber products.

Tara, Ireland **I** 390
Tarantella (tarr-an-TEL-la), dance **D** 29
Tarantelle, engraving by Hayter **G** 306
Tarantulas (ta-RAN-tu-las), spiders **S** 386; picture
S 387
poisonous and harmful **I** 284

Tarawa (ta-RA-wa), atoll comprised of nine major and
several small islets in the central western Pacific, capital
of British Gilbert and Ellice Islands. Tarawa is a port of
entry and large commercial center. The principal export
is copra. Formerly occupied by Japan (1941), the island
was site of a World War II battle (1943).
World War II in the Pacific **W** 297

Tarbela Dam, Pakistan **D** 21
Targets
archery **A** 368
rifle markmanship **R** 234–35

Targum, Aramaic translation and interpretation of the
Hebrew Scriptures. It originated when Aramaic was sub-
stituted for Hebrew as the spoken language of the Jews,
and Hebrew Scriptures read in the synagogues were
orally explained and translated into Aramaic. Developing into permanent written texts by the 5th century,
noted targums include the literal translation of Onkelos
and freer translation of Jonathan ben Uzziel.

Tarheel State, nickname for North Carolina **N** 306
Tariff of Abominations
Calhoun's protest **C** 13

Tariffs **T** 25
Abominations, Tariff of, 1828 **C** 13
agriculture **A** 94
Arthur, Chester Alan, efforts to lower **A** 441
Clay's compromises **C** 335
European Economic Community **E** 334–35
free ports **I** 330
GATT (General Agreement on Tariffs and Trade)
I 329; **T** 25
international trade **I** 328–30
McKinley Tariff, 1890 **M** 187–88
Payne-Aldrich Act, 1909 **T** 7–8
regulatory taxation **T** 26
Wilson, Woodrow, reforms of **W** 179
Tarkington, Booth, American novelist **A** 207–08
Tarlton's Jests, early English joke book **J** 133
Taro (TAR-o), plants **P** 283; picture **H** 61
Tarok (ta-ROK), European card game **C** 106
Tarots (ta-ROSE), early Italian playing cards
C 106

Tarpeian (tar-PE-an) **Rock,** name given to peak of Capi-
toline Hill in Rome where criminals and traitors were
cast to their death. It was named after a Roman woman,
Tarpeia, who allegedly betrayed Rome to the Sabine
invaders for their gold armbands but was crushed to
death by the Sabine shields.
sculptured record to warn of traitor's fate **R** 286

Tarpon, fish **F** 189; pictures **F** 189, **L** 215
Alabama, state fish of **A** 118
Tarpon Springs, Florida
sponge fisherman, picture **F** 266
Tarragon, herb **S** 382; picture **S** 381
Tar sands, varieties of sandstone containing petroleum
particles **P** 178
Alberta, Canada, deposits in **A** 146c, 146d
Tarsiers (TAR-si-ays), primates **M** 422
have four hands **F** 83
Tartan see Plaid

Tartar, or **argol,** reddish crusty deposit of potassium
bitartrate formed in wine fermentation. It is purified to
produce cream of tartar, used in baking powders,
candies, and electroplating. It also yields Rochelle salt,
used in silvering mirrors; tartaric acid, used in soft
drinks, jelly candies, textile printing, and certain photographic processes; and tartar emetic.

Tartaric acid crystals, diagram **L** 274
Tartars see Tatars

Tartini (tar-TI-ni), **Giuseppe** (1692–1770), Italian composer and violinist, b. Pirano (now in Yugoslavia). The
most famous violinist of his day, Tartini was responsible for changing the shape of the bow and the
technique of bowing.
famous violin virtuosos and composers **V** 343

Tascalusa (ta-sca-LU-sa), or **Tuscaluca** ("Black Warrior," from the Indian *taska,* meaning "warrior" and
lusa, meaning "black"), Indian chief, probably of the
Alibamu tribe. He led his tribesmen against the Spaniards of De Soto's army in 1540 in the fierce and bloody
battle of Mabila. His fate remains unknown. Black
Warrior River and the town of Tuscaloosa, Alabama, are
named for him.

Taschereau (tash-RO), **Robert B.** (1896–   ), Canadian
jurist, b. Quebec City. Professor of criminal law at
Laval University (1929–40), he was also a member of
Quebec Provincial House (1930–36) and judge of Su-

preme Court of Canada (1940–63). He was Chief Justice of Supreme Court (1963–67).

Taylor, Edward, American poet A 196

Taylor, Elizabeth (1932–   ), American actress, b. London, England. Her first movies, *Lassie Come Home* (1943) and *National Velvet* (1944) brought her to the attention of the movie-going public. She became one of Hollywood's most famous child stars. Her films, which made her one of the highest paid actresses in the motion picture industry, include *A Place in the Sun*, *Cat on a Hot Tin Roof*, *Cleopatra*, and *The Only Game in Town*. She won an Academy Award (1960) as best actress for *Butterfield 8*, and again (1966) for *Who's Afraid of Virginia Woolf?* in which she appeared with her husband, Richard Burton. Picture M 477.

Taylor, George (1716–1781), American ironmaster, b. Ireland. He arrived in America around 1736 and became an ironmaster in Bucks County, Pa. He served in the Continental Congress (1776–77) and was a signer of the Declaration of Independence.

Taylor, Jane and Ann, English poets C 237

Taylor, Jeremy (1613–1667), English clergyman and writer, b. Cambridge. In a rich, poetic prose he wrote on various phases of religion and was an outstanding theologian, Anglican preacher, and chaplain to Charles I.

Taylor, Lee, American speed boat racing champion B 264
Taylor, Margaret Mackall Smith, wife of Zachary Taylor F 170

Taylor, Maxwell Davenport (1901–   ), American Army officer and diplomat, b. Keytesville, Mo. He taught French and Spanish at U.S. Military Academy at West Point (1927–32). Taylor took part in major campaigns in Italy, Sicily, and northwestern Europe during World War II and was superintendent of U.S. Military Academy at West Point (1945–49). Since serving in Germany, Korea, and Far East (1949–55), he has been chief of staff of U.S. Army (1955–59), chairman of Joint Chiefs of Staff (1962–64), and ambassador to South Vietnam (1964–65). He was chairman of the Foreign Intelligence Advisory Board (1965–70).

Taylor, Richard (1826–1879), American Confederate Army officer, b. New Orleans, La. Son of President Zachary Taylor, he was a Louisiana planter before the Civil War. He fought under Stonewall Jackson. Later he commanded Confederate forces of East Louisiana, Mississippi, and Alabama until May, 1865.

Taylor, Zachary, 12th president of United States T 33–36
  Jefferson Davis and Taylor D 45
  Mexican War M 238
  Polk's policies in the Mexican War P 386
Taylor Grazing Act of 1934 C 486
Taymur, Muhammad and Mahmud (brothers), Egyptian writers A 76d
Tay-Sachs disease G 85
Tchaikovsky (tchy-KOF-ski), Peter Ilyitch, Russian composer T 36
  Eugene Onegin, opera O 143
  opera O 136
  Russian music U 63–64
  symphonic poems R 311
Tea T 37–40
  Boston Tea Party R 196, 209–10
  Ceylon, plantation in, picture C 178
  How do tea-drinking customs differ throughout the world? T 37

How is tea made? T 38
  Japanese tea ceremony J 37
  maté, or yerba maté A 393
  world distribution, diagram W 266
Tea bags T 39
Teach, Edward see Blackbeard, British pirate
Teachers and teaching T 40–44
  Aristotle A 396–97
  blind, education of the B 252–53
  Confucius' way to an orderly world C 460
  deaf, teachers of the D 53
  education, history of E 61–84
  guidance G 397–400
  Jesus Christ J 82–84
  kindergarten and nursery schools K 242–47
  Osler, Sir William, teacher of medicine O 233
  parent-teacher associations P 66–67
  Peace Corps P 101–03
  retarded, education for the educable R 191
  school librarians L 175
  schools S 55–58
  Socratic dialogue, teaching method E 63–64; S 228
  team teaching E 78–79
  test scores and teachers' marks T 119–20
  women, role of W 212, 212a
  See also Carnegie Foundation for the Advancement of Teaching; National Education Association
Teacher's Day, Confucius' birthday celebrated in China C 260
Teachers of Righteousness (RIGHT-eus-ness), Jewish priests D 49
Teaching machines P 475, 477

Teak, tall tree used for timber. Its sturdy yellowish-brown wood resists warping and is used in shipbuilding, in furniture manufacture, and for flooring. Native to the East Indies, it is now cultivated in West Africa and in tropical America.
  uses of the wood and its grain, picture W 224

Teal, wild ducks
  story of the boy trapper K 259
Team sports
  Olympic events O 109
  physical education programs P 226
  See also Sports
Teamsters Union see International Brotherhood of Teamsters
Team teaching E 78–79
Teapot Dome oil scandal C 496
  Harding's administration H 41
  Wyoming's Naval oil reserve involved W 330
Teardrop, shape
  car of the future, picture A 552
Teasdale, Sara, American poet A 210

Tebaldi (teb-OL-di), Renata (1922–   ), Italian opera singer, b. Pesaro. She made her professional debut at Rovigo, Italy (1944). Her first appearance with New York Metropolitan Opera was in 1955. She is a lyric soprano. Her most celebrated roles include Aïda and Tosca.

Technetium (tec-NE-shum), element E 155, 165
Technical assistance
  foreign aid F 368
  Peace Corps P 101–03
  Truman, Harry S and his Point Four program T 302
Technicolor process, in photography P 204
Technological (tec-no-LOJ-ic-al) unemployment U 25
  poverty caused by P 424a, 424b
Technology (tec-NOL-ogy) T 45–46
  applied science I 348

art, the meanings of **A** 438
automation **A** 528–34
man's influence on natural resources **N** 60
mass production **M** 151
museums **M** 513
science and technology **S** 80–81
technological unemployment **P** 424a, 424b
work methods, changes in **W** 251
See also Engineering; Inventions; Manufacturing
Tecumseh (te-CUM-seh), Shawnee Indian leader **T** 47
defeated at Battle of Tippecanoe **I** 213
Indian resistance in Indiana **I** 151
Tecumseh threatens Harrison **H** 50; picture **H** 51
Tee, of golf course **G** 254
Teen-agers, and adolescence **A** 22–24
junior volunteer movement in hospitals **H** 251;
picture **H** 249
los niños, Mexican national heroes **M** 239
smoking **S** 203
travel opportunities **V** 259
young adult library services **L** 171
See also Clubs; Youth organizations
Teeth **T** 47–49
birds, fossil **B** 209
care of **H** 85
cats **C** 134
crystal formation **C** 541
dentistry **D** 114
dinosaurs **D** 175, 178
elephants' molars **E** 169
fangs, of animals **S** 207, 383; picture **L** 218
fishes' teeth tell what they eat **F** 187
fluoridation **F** 283–84
horses **H** 243
ivory **I** 487
mammals **M** 66; pictures **M** 65
rodents, gnawing mammals **R** 275
saber-toothed tiger **C** 135; picture **C** 136
seal tooth, with growth ridges, picture **A** 86
sharks, skates, and rays **S** 142
What makes a tooth ache? **T** 48
See also Orthodontics
Tegucigalpa (teg-u-ci-GAL-pa), capital of Honduras
H 197; pictures **H** 197, **L** 48
Teheran (ter-ON), capital of Iran **T** 49–50
pictures **I** 377, **M** 308
Allied Conference, 1943 **W** 297
major cities of Iran **I** 376
Teheran, University of **T** 50
Tehuantepec (tuh-WAHN-tuh-pek) **Isthmus of,** Mexico
M 243
Tehuelche (teh-WEL-cheh), Indians of South America
I 211

Tejas (TE-jas), or **Teja** (?–553), last of the Ostrogoth
(East Goth) kings. He succeeded Totila (552), conqueror
of Italy. Defeated by forces of Emperor Justinian, he was
killed near Vesuvius at Mount Lactarius, present-day
Monte Lattere.

Tektite I and II, underwater habitats **U** 20
Tektites **C** 421; picture **C** 420
Tel Aviv, Israel **I** 443–44, picture **I** 445
apartment houses, picture **A** 468
beach, picture **M** 304
Telecommunication, distant communication
developments in radio **R** 53
electronic communication **E** 142–142f
first experimental telecast, picture **E** 147
Teledu (TEL-e-du), badger **O** 242
Telegraph **T** 50–55
and its descendants in electronic communication

E 142–142a
communication advanced by **C** 438
first transatlantic message from Signal Hill,
Newfoundland **N** 143
International Morse Code **R** 63
Morse, Samuel, inventor **M** 462
railroads' use of **R** 84–85
Telegraph lines *see* Electric lines
Telegraphy
telegraph and its descendants in electronic com-
munication **E** 142–142a
wireless telegraphy, Marconi's invention **M** 98
Tel el Amarna (a-MAR-na), ancient Egyptian capital **E** 101
Telemachus (te-LEM-ac-hus), in Greek legend, son of
Odysseus **O** 53, 54

Telemetry (tel-EM-etry), branch of technology concerned
with the development of electric and electronic systems
that can make measurements and observations and
then relay the data obtained over long distances to be
recorded. Telemetry is important, for example, in designing artificial satellites, which may measure such
things as the radiations and temperatures they en-
counter in space.
space flights, use in **S** 340g

Teleosts (TEL-e-osts), ray-finned fishes **F** 183

Telepathy (tel-EP-athy), thought transference, or the communication of thoughts from one mind to another without the use of the senses. The term was originally used
(1882) by English philosopher Frederic William Henry
Myers, a founder of the Society of Psychical Research.
Although telepathy is a popular subject for psychical
research, the results of experiments are controversial.

Telephone **T** 55–60
and its descendants in electronic communication
E 142a–142b
Bell, Alexander Graham, inventor of **B** 132–33
communication advanced by **C** 438–39
first telephone call, picture **B** 133
getting the message from here to there **E** 142c–142d
"hot line," direct communication between governments
D 185
lineman at work, picture **I** 248
one-piece telephones, pictures **I** 229
public utility **P** 512–13
special service in Vienna, Austria, for tuning musical
instruments **A** 524
See also Telegraph
Telephone lines *see* Electric lines
Telephoto lenses, for cameras **P** 203; picture **P** 213
Teleprinter, or teletypewriter **T** 53; picture **E** 142a
electronic communication, history of **E** 142a
Telescopes **T** 60–64
balloon gondolas used for holding **B** 34
Galileo's spyglass **G** 6
lenses **L** 147–48, 265
modern astronomy begins **A** 472–73; **G** 6
observatories, how mounted in **O** 8, 11
optical instruments **O** 167
radio and radar telescopes **R** 70–74
surveyor's transit **S** 480
tools of astronomers **A** 473
Telescopic gunsights **O** 170
Teletype
teaching machines **P** 477
Teletypesetter system, for use with newspapers **N** 204
Teletypewriter (tel-e-TYPE-writer) **T** 53; picture
E 142a
communications systems **C** 438

Tell, William, legendary 14th-century Swiss patriot. When he refused to acknowledge imposed Austrian authority, he was ordered to shoot an apple off his son's head with a bow and arrow. Though successful, he was arrested, but he escaped en route to prison. He shot Gessler, the local governor, allegedly leading to a revolt giving the Swiss states independence. The opera *William Tell* by Rossini is based on the legend. Picture **G** 177.

Teller, Edward (1908–   ), Hungarian-American physicist, b. Budapest, Hungary. Fleeing Europe because of the Nazis, he went to the United States in 1935. During World War II he helped develop the atomic bomb. Convinced that an even more powerful nuclear weapon based on the fusion of hydrogen nuclei could be made, Teller persuaded the Atomic Energy Commission to develop such a weapon and took a leading part in the actual development of the hydrogen bomb. He won the Enrico Fermi Award in 1962.

Temperance, organized movement to encourage abstinence from alcoholic beverages. It gained national influence as a social movement with the founding of the American Society for Promotion of Temperance (1826). It became a national political movement (about 1815). Prominent leaders, Women's Christian Temperance Union (1874), and Anti-Saloon League (1893) all avidly supported the Prohibition Party and were influential in obtaining Federal Prohibition (1919–33).

Temperature-humidity index (THI), or **comfort index**, part of many daily weather reports during warm seasons. It is a number on a simple numerical scale derived by arithmetic from humidity and temperature readings. Most people feel comfortable at a THI of 70 and uncomfortable at a THI of 80 or more.

Buddhist Temple of the Dawn, Thailand, picture **T** 147
Diana of Ephesus **W** 214; picture **W** 215
Egypt, ancient **E** 93–95, 100; pictures **A** 363; **E** 91
Egyptian architecture **A** 371–72
Greek temples in three orders **G** 346–47
Hindu temples, pictures **I** 118, 130
Jain temple, Calcutta, picture **C** 10
Jewish Temple, Jerusalem **J** 79, 81
Peking, Temple of Heaven **P** 119
pre-Aztec temple pyramid, picture **A** 354
Sumerian architecture **A** 235
Temple of Bacchus, Lebanon, picture **L** 124
ziggurats **A** 218, 240; picture **A** 350
See also Cathedrals; Mosques; Pagodas
Tempo, musical term **M** 531
orchestra conducting **O** 188–89, 190
Temptation of Saint Anthony, painting by Hieronymus
Bosch **D** 355
Temuco (tay-MU-co), Chile **C** 249
Tenant farmers **F** 49
Chile **C** 250
English migration to America **A** 182
See also Sharecroppers
Ten Commandments, or Decalogue **T** 72–73
Christianity **C** 281
E, letter, in legend puzzle **E** 1
first ten commandments of Buddhism similar **L** 41
Hebraic faith, foundation of **J** 102
Moses **M** 468
Ten Commandments The, motion picture **M** 474
Tenderfoot, a rank in the Boy Scouts **B** 359, 360
Tenders, of locomotives **L** 327
Tendons, cords joining muscles to bones **B** 273
Tendrils, of plants **P** 295
Tenebrism (TEN-e-brism), style in art **S** 362
Tenerife (TEN-e-rif), Spain **I** 428

Teniers (ten-IERS), **David** (Teniers the Younger) (1610–
1690), Flemish painter, b. Antwerp, Belgium. The son of
Flemish painter Teniers the Elder (1582–1649), he received
many commissions from the Netherlands Government and
Philip IV of Spain. His subject matter was chiefly genre,
landscapes, and portraits. Among his numerous works
are *The Denial of Saint Peter* and *The Prodigal Son*.

Tenkamenin, ruler of Ghana **N** 90
Tennessee (tenn-es-SEE) **T** 74–89
Civil War **C** 323, 326
places of interest in Negro history **N** 94
Tennessee, University of **T** 82
Tennessee River, United States **R** 248; **T** 77; picture
T 82
Alabama **A** 115, 120
Kentucky Dam and Lake, picture **K** 214
TVA dam system **D** 19
Tennessee Valley Authority (TVA) **C** 486; **T** 77, 89
Land Between the Lakes, recreation area **T** 84
Roosevelt, Franklin D., achievement of his administra-
tion **R** 321
system of dams **D** 18–19
Tennessee Walking Horse **T** 74
Tenniel (TENN-yel), **Sir John**, English illustrator of "Alice
in Wonderland" **A** 165
Tennis **T** 90–100
court tennis **T** 100
deck tennis **D** 58
Gibson, Althea **G** 206
paddle tennis **P** 11
table tennis **T** 4–5
Tennis Court Oath, in French Revolution **F** 464
Tennyson, Alfred, Lord, English poet **T** 100–01
"Eagle, The" **T** 101

English literature of the Victorian period **E** 262–63
"Flower in the Crannied Wall" **T** 101
"Lady of Shalott," part I **T** 101
Tenochtitlán (tay-nock-ti-TLON) (now Mexico City), capi-
tal of Aztec empire **M** 251
Aztec civilization, center of **I** 155, 197; picture **I** 194
Cortes **C** 508
famous ancient cities **C** 307
Spanish conquest of **M** 248
Texcoco, Lake, Aztec farmland **I** 195
Tenoners, machine tools
preparing wood for furniture-making **F** 502
Tenor, male voice **C** 277
voice training and singing **V** 375
Tenor drum **D** 334
Tenpins, for bowling **B** 345, 348
Tenrecs, animals of insectivore group **I** 261
Tense, of verbs **P** 91
Tentacles
coral polyps **C** 503; picture **C** 504
Tent catepillars, picture **I** 278
Tenth Amendment, to United States Constitution **S** 412

Ten Tribes, Hebrew tribes of the ancient northern
kingdom of Palestine who were exiled as a result of the
Assyrian invasion around 721 B.C. Since their fate was
not certain, they came to be called the "ten lost tribes."
Claims of descendancy have been made among various
races, such as the American Indians. It is believed that
they were absorbed by the peoples with whom they
lived and finally disappeared as a separate group.

Tents
camping **C** 42
circus tent, the Big Top **C** 302
houses that move **H** 175–76
Indian tipis and wickiups **I** 166, 197, pictures
I 167, 193
Mongolian nomads, picture **A** 302
Tenure of Office Act, 1867
Johnson, Andrew, impeached for violating **J** 125–26
Tenure of teachers **T** 44

Ten Years War (1868–78), Cuban revolt for independence from Spain. It was caused by dissatisfaction with
Spain's rigid tax and trade control and monopoly of
government offices. Ruthless guerrilla fighting ended
with Treaty of Zanjon (1878), in which Spain guaranteed
reform. Though seemingly fruitless, it foreshadowed the
Cuban rebellion against Spanish rule (1895) that led to
Spanish-American War (1898).

Tenzing, Norkey see Norkey, Tenzing
Teotihuacán (tay-o-ti-hua-CON), Mexico **M** 253
Indian art **I** 152
Pyramid of the Sun, picture **A** 363
Tepees, tent dwellings of North American Indians **H** 175
tipis and wickiups **I** 166, 197; pictures **I** 167, 193
Tepe (TEP-ay) **Sarab**, Iran
archeological trench, picture **A** 357
Terbium, element **E** 155, 165

Terborch (tair-BORK), or **Ter Borch**, or **Terburg, Gerard**
(1617–1681), Dutch painter, b. Zwolle. A student of the
genre painter Pieter de Molyn, he painted chiefly genre
scenes and portraits characterized by close attention to
detail. His works include *Peace Congress of Munster*.
Dutch and Flemish art **D** 357

Terbrugghen (ter-BRU-ghen), **Hendrick**, Dutch artist
D 357
Saint Sebastian, painting **D** 359

Teredo (ter-E-do), or shipworms **O** 273
Terence, Roman playwright **D** 295
   Latin literature **L** 77

Tereshkova (ter-esh-KO-va), **Valentina Vladimirovna** (1937–), Soviet astronaut, b. Maslennikovo. On June 16, 1963, she became the first woman to pilot a spacecraft. Her craft, Vostok 6, remained aloft 2 days 22 hours 50 minutes, completing 48 orbits. Hers was the world's second twin-orbit flight—the other craft, Vostok 5, was piloted by Valery Bykovsky. During the flight both astronauts were seen on television in various eastern European countries. Tereshkova married a fellow astronaut, Andrian Nikolayev, on November 3, 1964. They have one daughter.
   space flight data **S** 344, 345

Terhune, Albert Payson (1872–1942), American journalist and novelist, b. Newark, N.J. He is remembered for novels and short stories about dogs. He served on staff of New York *Evening World* (1894–1916) and raised prize-winning collies in Sunnybank Kennels, N.J. His books include *Syria from the Saddle*, and *Lad: a Dog*.

Term, or temporary, **insurance** **I** 294–95
Terminal moraines, ridges formed by glacial deposits **I** 19; **M** 136; picture **I** 18
Terminals, of computers **C** 452, 454–55
Terminal velocity, maximum speed of a falling body **G** 322–23
   Galileo's law **F** 34
Termites, insects **I** 270; picture **I** 271
   benefited by a flagellate parasite **M** 279
   household pests **H** 261–62; pictures **H** 263
   termite-proof house, picture **A** 302
Terms, of fractions **F** 398
Ternary form, design for writing music **M** 535
Terns, birds **B** 226; picture **B** 235
   birdbanding of arctic terns **B** 229

Terpsichore (terp-SIK-o-ree), goddess in Greek mythology. She and her eight sisters, the daughters of Zeus and Mnemosyne, were the muses, or patrons of the arts and sciences. She was the muse of dancing, which she was supposed to have invented. Her symbol was a crown of laurels, and she carried cymbals or a lyre.
   See also Muses

Terracing, of fields
   Philippine rice fields, picture **E** 282

Terra-cotta (from Italian, meaning "baked earth"), fired, usually unglazed clay, ranging from pink to reddish-brown and used for sculpture and architectural decoration. Noted examples include vases and figurines from pre-dynastic Egypt, architectural ornaments from ancient Greece and sculpture of Italian Renaissance.
   early Greek art on terra-cotta **G** 343
   early plumbing systems **P** 342–43

Terramycin (terr-a-MY-cin), antibiotic **A** 312, 316;
   chart of production **A** 313
Terre Haute, Indiana **I** 149
Terramycin (terr-a-MY-cin), antibiotic **A** 312; chart of production **A** 313
Terrapins, turtles **T** 332
Terrariums (ter-RAR-iums), gardens under glass **T** 102–04
   mosses **F** 94
Terrazzo (te-RA-tzo), concrete flooring **C** 166

Terrell, Mary Church (1863–1954), American civil rights worker, Negro, b. Memphis, Tenn. Pioneer in the fight

for integration, she was the first president of the National Association of Colored Women.

Terrestrial telescopes **O** 167
Terriers, dog breed **D** 259, 261; picture **D** 255
Territorial expansion of the United States **T** 105–15
   Alaska purchase **A** 143
   American Samoa **S** 27
   Arizona **A** 417
   flags, historic **F** 228
   Florida becomes a state **F** 273
   Hawaii **H** 71
   industrial expansion **U** 129–30
   Louisiana Purchase **L** 364–65
   Manifest Destiny concept **M** 238; **P** 385
   Mexican War **M** 238–39
   Northwest Ordinance, 1787 **W** 143
   outlying areas of the United States **U** 100
   overland trails **O** 251–67
   Panama Canal zone **P** 47–49
   public lands **P** 506–07
   Puerto Rico **P** 522–23
   Texas, annexation of **P** 384–85; **T** 137, 341–42
   westward movement **W** 142–46
Territory songs, of birds **A** 278; picture **A** 279

Terry, Bill (William Harold Terry) (1898–), American baseball player and manager, b. Atlanta, Ga. In 1930 he was named the Most Valuable Player after hitting .401 for the New York Giants, a batting average which no National Leaguer has reached since. He had an average of 156 hits every season for 14 years. He also showed great skill as a first baseman and later as Giants manager (1932–41). He was elected to Hall of Fame in 1954.

Terry, Ellen Alicia, or **Alice** (1847–1928), English actress, b. Coventry. She made her professional debut in 1863 as a member of the Haymarket Theatre company. She became Sir Henry Irving's leading lady (1878–1902) and gained fame for such Shakespearean roles as Portia in *The Merchant of Venice* and Lady Macbeth in *Macbeth*, as well as for roles in plays by Wills. She received the title of Dame in 1925.

Tertiary (TER-shi-ary) **period,** of Age of Mammals, geologic period· **F** 389
   Nebraska fossil beds **N** 73
Tertullian (ter-TUL-lian), Christian writer of Carthage **C** 281
Teshekpuk Lake, Alaska **A** 133

Tesla, Nikola (1856–1943), American physicist and electrical engineer, b. Croatia, now part of Yugoslavia. He arrived in United States in 1884 and was for a while a colleague of Thomas Edison. He is famous for having developed transformers and motors that made alternating current practical.
   how radar began **R** 34
   squirrel cage electric motor, invention of **E** 141

Tesserae (TESS-er-e), pieces used in mosaics **M** 463
   Byzantine art form **B** 484–85
Testator, of a will **W** 174
Test bans, for nuclear weapon testing **D** 185
Testimony, in law courts **C** 529
Test pits, for archeological excavations **A** 356; picture **A** 357
Tests and testing **T** 116–21
   animal intelligence and behavior **A** 283–88
   examinations for college entrance **E** 348–49
   guidance **G** 399

In psychology P 492
Peace Corps placement tests P 101
points on test-taking E 349
What is an intelligence test? P 489
Why are tests important? T 119
word games W 237
Tetanus (lockjaw), disease D 200–01
booster shots V 261
Tetherball, picture B 21
Tet offensive, 1968, in Vietnam War V 337
Teton (TE-ton) Range, Rocky Mountains W 325; picture
W 327
Teton Sioux, Indians of North America I 168
Tetracycline (tet-ra-CY-clene), antibiotic A 313
Tetrahedron (tet-ra-HE-dron), geometric form, how to
make G 128
Tetrahydrocannabinol, active chemical in marijuana
and hashish D 331
Teutoburg (TOIT-o-burk) Forest, battle of, A.D. 9 B 100

Teutons (TEU-tons), a Germanic tribe of unkown origin
that lived in vicinity of Jutland (2nd century B.C.). After migrating into Gaul (110? B.C.), they subdued Roman armies
(109–105 B.C.) but suffered harsh defeat at the hands of
Roman commander Gaius Marius at present-day Aix (102
B.C.). The name also refers to those speaking a Germanic
language of the Indo-European language group.
The Roman Empire and the German tribes M 289–90

Teutonic, or Germanic languages L 39
Tewa (TE-wa), Indians of North America A 302
Texas T 122–37
annexation, a policy of Polk and Tyler P 384–85;
T 341–42
cattle raising C 146–47
Compromise of 1850 C 448
Dallas D 14
flag of the Texas Navy, 1836 F 228
goat raising C 152
Houston, Samuel H 270–71
lunch hour, "noon in," picture F 338
Mexican War M 238–39; P 386
oil refinery and tanks, pictures P 174, U 97
State Fair at Dallas D 14
territorial expansion of the United States T 109–10
Texas, Republic of T 137
Texas, University of T 131
Texas A&M University T 131; U 222
Texas bluebonnets, flowers, picture W 170
Texas longhorns see Longhorn cattle
Texcoco (tes-CO-co), Lake, Mexico I 195
Texoma (tex-O-ma), Lake, Oklahoma, picture O 82
Textbooks T 138–39
early books for children C 236
first in biology B 188
programed textbooks P 477
publishing P 514
study, uses in S 441
the new and the old, pictures E 77–78
Textiles T 140–45
cotton, history of C 519–25
dyes and dyeing D 370–72; pictures D 368, 372
fibers F 104–08
folk art F 296
Industrial Revolution creates factories I 239
Lahore, Pakistan, dyed fabric, picture A 463
mill in Georgia, picture G 137
nylon and other man-made fibers N 424–28
rugs and carpets R 350–54
silks S 178–80
South Carolina, textile industry in S 300
tapestry T 22–24

"textile highway," South Carolina S 308
weaving W 97–98
wool W 234–35
See also Clothing
Texture, in design D 135–36
Teyte, Dame Maggie, English singer V 376
T formation, in football F 362–63; diagram F 364
Thackeray, William Makepeace, English novelist
T 145–46
English literature of the Victorian period E 263–64
satirical novelist N 346
self-portrait E 264
Vanity Fair, excerpt T 145–46
Thaddaeus see Jude, Saint
Thailand (TY-land) T 147–51
Buddhist monks, picture A 447
dance D 31
dyed silk drying, picture D 368
flag F 238
funeral procession, picture F 495
percussion instruments, picture P 153
Siam in the history of Southeast Asia S 334–35
village industry, umbrellas, picture A 463
Thais, people T 147
Thalamus (THAL-am-us), part of the brain B 367
Thales (THALE-ese), Greek philosopher and scientist
G 95, 98; P 191
discovered static electricity E 123
earth theory C 206
science, advances in S 61

Thalia (tha-LY-a), goddess in Greek mythology. She and
her eight sisters, the daughters of Zeus and Mnemosyne,
were the muses, or patrons of the arts and sciences.
Thalia was the muse of comedy. Her symbol was the
comic mask. She carried a shepherd's staff and wore
the thin-soled shoe, or "sock," of the comic actors in
plays of ancient times.
See also Muses

Thallium (THAL-lium), element E 155, 165
Thallophyta, division of the plant kingdom P 292
Thames (TEMS), battle of the, 1813, Canada W 12
Tecumseh killed and Indians defeated T 47
Thames River, Canada
London, Ontario situated on it O 125
Tecumseh's last stand T 47
Thames River, Connecticut C 470
Thames River, England R 248; U 69
London, places of interest L 339; picture L 338
London Bridge B 396
Tower Bridge, pictures B 400; R 246
Thanatopsis (than-a-TOP-sis), poem by Bryant B 416

Thanatos, Greek figure representing death who appeared
more in folklore and poetical works than in mythology.
He has been referred to as the twin brother of Sleep. At
first, he was pictured with a fierce face. Later, he was
described as a quiet youth who removed pain.

Thanes, name for Anglo-Saxon warriors E 216
Thanksgiving Day T 152–54; picture H 147
beginning of traditional American dishes F 342
first celebrated by Pilgrims A 187
holiday turkey P 422–23
Martinmas, Thanksgiving Day of the Middle Ages
R 154–55
Plymouth Colony P 345
Thanksgiving prayer P 434
Thant (THONT), U, secretary-general of United Nations
T 154
Thatch, Edward see Blackbird, British pirate

Thatch, roofs of **B** 435
   thatched houses **H** 169–70; pictures **A** 302, 303
Thatcher, Becky, in Mark Twain's *Adventures of Tom Sawyer* **T** 337–38
Thatcher Ferry Bridge, Panama Canal Zone, picture **P** 49
"That's one small step for a man, one giant leap for mankind," first words spoken on moon **E** 368; **S** 340a
Thayendanegea (tha-yen-da-NAIG-e-a), Indian name of Mohawk chief Joseph Brant **B** 371
THC *see* Tetrahydrocannabinol
Theater **T** 155–64
   Barrymore family **B** 67–68
   Canada **C** 62–63
   Little Theater movement **D** 300
   miracle plays **M** 339–40
   motion picture industry **M** 472–88
   musical comedy **M** 542–43
   "Off-Broadway" drama **D** 300
   opera **O** 130–55
   pageants **P** 12
   puppets and marionettes **P** 534–39
   putting on a play **P** 335–41
   Shakespeare, William **S** 130–33
   See also Drama; Motion-picture industry
Theater in the round, or arena stage **T** 155–56
Theater of the Nations, festival in Paris **T** 159
Theaters of the world **T** 158–64
   ancient Roman, Leptis Magna, Libya, picture **L** 204
   Elizabethan playhouses **D** 295–96
   Epidaurus, Greece, picture **G** 335
   Lincoln Center for the Performing Arts **L** 298
   showboats **T** 162
   Stratford Shakespearean Theater, Stratford, Ontario **C** 62–63; picture **O** 129

Theatre Guild, association of theater artists formed in New York (1919) by Washington Square Players for presentation of outstanding plays. Establishing its name with a production of *Heartbreak House,* by George Bernard Shaw (1920), it continued to present new and unusual plays, one of the most famous being *Oklahoma!*

Thebes, Egypt
   Egyptian art of royal tombs **E** 98, 100, 102
Theme and variation, musical form **C** 332
Themes, compositions **C** 446–47
Themes, of literary works
   novels **N** 345
   short stories **S** 166, 167

Thénard (tay-NAR), **Baron Louis Jacques** (1777–1857), French chemist, b. La Louptière-Thénard. With Joseph Gay-Lussac, Thénard improved method of analyzing organic (carbon-containing) compounds and of preparing alkali metals and also discovered the element boron. (Humphry Davy, working separately, discovered boron at about the same time.) Thénard discovered hydrogen peroxide and Thénard's blue, a dye.

Theocracy (the-OC-racy), government or political rule guided directly by God or through his representatives such as the clergy, having civil as well as spiritual power.

Theocritus (the-OC-rit-us) (3rd century B.C.), Greek poet, b. Syracuse. Regarded as the creator of pastoral poetry, which he called *Idylls,* he wrote about shepherds who sang of their feelings. Among his existing works are 30 idylls and more than 20 epigrams. His work is distinguished for its combination of realism and romanticism.
   the first pastoral elegies **E** 151; **G** 355

Theodolites (the-OD-ol-ites), surveyors' instruments **S** 480
Theodora (the-o-DO-ra), Byzantine empress **B** 484
Theodore, Archbishop of Tarsus **C** 284
Theodore Roosevelt National Memorial Park, North Dakota **N** 52, 333
Theodoric (the-OD-o-ric) **the Goth** **L** 130

Theodosius I (theo-DO-sius) (Flavius Theodosius) ("the Great") (346?–395), Roman general and emperor, b. Spain. Summoned by Emperor Gratian to share in the rule of the empire, he was appointed Augustus of the East (379). In a few years he succeeded in making peace with the Goths. After the death of Gratian he defeated Maximus, who had invaded Italy, and thus Theodosius soon became sole emperor of the Roman world. Before his death, he divided his empire into the East and West between his two sons.
   Christianity made the state religion **C** 282

Theology, body of religious teaching
   Christianity, history of **C** 283
   Roman Catholic Church **R** 289
Theophanes (the-OPH-a-nese), **the Greek,** painter **U** 54
Theorem, in geometry **G** 123
Theoretical probability **P** 473

Theosophy (the-OS-ophy), combination of philosophical, religious, and scientific doctrines, especially those of ancient Indian and Buddhist religions. It claims insight into nature of God through study and contemplation. Theosophical Society was formed in Russia in 1874 by Elena Petrovna Blavatsky.

Theotocopoulos, Kyriakos *see* Greco, El
The Pas, Manitoba, Canada **M** 81

Therapy (from Greek *therapeia,* meaning "medical treatment"), treatment of disease. The word is often used in compound form, as in hydrotherapy, the scientific use of water in the treatment of disease, and in radiotherapy, the use of radiation in treatment of disease.
   medicine, tools and techniques of **M** 208d–211
   occupational and physical therapists **H** 28, 248–49
   See also Physical therapy

Theravada (ther-a-VA-da), teachings of Buddha **B** 423

Theremin (THERE-em-in) (Etherophone), electronic musical instrument, invented by a Russian, Leon Thérémin (1924), that converts electrical waves into musical notes. It is played by moving right hand over projecting metal rod to create variations in pitch. The instrument was improved by addition of a fingerboard, permitting greater control in determination of pitch.

Theresa, Saint (of Avila) (1515–1582), Spanish nun and writer, b. Avila. Joining the Carmelite order (1534), she established the reform order of Discalced Carmelite Nuns (1562). She was noted for her mysticism and spiritual experiences. She was canonized (1622) and named a "Doctor of the Church" in 1970.
   Spain's mystic literature **S** 368

Thérèse de Lisieux (tay-REZ d'lese-Y-ER), **Saint** (Marie Françoise Thérèse Martin), "The Little Flower" (1873–1897), French nun, b. Alençon. Noted for simplicity and perfection in daily tasks, she joined the Carmelite order in Lisieux (1888) and became mistress of novices (1895). An account of her life is found in *Letters and Spiritual Counsels.* She was canonized in 1925.

Thermal pollution E 272g
  water pollution W 59
Thermal power plants P 425; picture P 427
Thermal radio radiation R 75
Thermal upcurrents, of air G 238
Thermionic generators P 427
Thermocouples, to measure temperature P 427
  a solar-energy collector S 237
Thermodynamics, study of energy in all its forms
      E 200–01
  laws of, in the study of heat H 90
Thermoelectricity
  possible use in air-conditioning systems A 103
  power generation, a new method of P 426–27
Thermometer (ther-MOM-et-er), a device to measure heat
      or cold T 165
  comparison and conversions of Fahrenheit and Celsius
      scales H 89; W 116
  how a nurse takes a temperature N 414
  how oceanographers measure ocean temperature
      O 31; picture O 32
  how to change a Fahrenheit reading to a Celsius or
      reverse the process H 89; W 116
  invention and development of thermometers H 88–89
  thermostats A 103, 528
  weather thermometers W 79–81
  Why must a fever thermometer be shaken? M 208f
Thermonuclear fusion see Nuclear fusion
Thermonuclear (hydrogen) **weapons**
  disarmament D 184
Thermoplastics P 328

Thermopylae (ther-MOP-il-e) (Greek for "hot gates"), in
ancient Greece, a narrow pass located in east central
Greece between Mount Oeta and swamp along Gulf of
Lamia. It was a famous battleground where a large
Persian army under King Xerxes met heroic resistance of
300 Spartans, commanded by Leonidas, and 700 Thes-
pians (480 B.C.). The pass was also the scene of Greek
defeat by the Gauls (279 B.C.) and a Roman victory over
Antiochus III of Syria (191 B.C.).
  Xerxes, exploits of X 339

Thermos bottles see Vacuum bottles
Thermosetting plastics P 328–29
  molecule diagram P 327
Thermostats, temperature control devices A 103
  automation A 528; picture A 529
  electric appliances E 118
Theropoda (the-ROP-o-da), dinosaurs D 173
Thesaurus (the-SAUR-us), book of synonyms and
      antonyms S 504
Theseus (THE-seus), hero in Greek mythology G 365
  story retold in Hawthorne's *Tanglewood Tales,* excerpt
      H 74–76
Thesis, a research paper to present and defend an idea
      E 67
Thespis (THESP-is), Greek poet G 351
Thessalonians (thess-al-O-nians) **I and II,** books of
      Bible, New Testament B 161
Thetis (THE-tis), in Greek legend I 69
THI see Temperature-Humidity Index
Thiamine, or vitamin B$_1$ V 370c–370d
Thief ants A 324

Thieu, Nguyen Van (TYOO nwin-vahn) (1923–   ), President of South Vietnam, b. Phanrang. A graduate of the
Vietnamese Military Academy (1949), he fought against
the Viet Minh in the early 1950's. In 1963, as a general
and division commander, he played an important part in
the overthrow of President Ngo Dinh Diem. When a military junta took power in 1965, Thieu became chief of
state. He was elected president in 1967.
  Vietnam, history of V 334c

Thimbleberries, raspberries G 301
Thimbles, for sewing S 128
Thimbu, capital of Bhutan B 150
Thingvellir (THEENG-vet-lir), ancient assembly place of
      Iceland's parliament I 44
Thinker, The, statue by Rodin R 283; picture F 426
Thinking P 499–500
  Can computers reason? C 455
  development of, in children C 234
  dictionary definition of "to think" D 165
  learning L 98–106
  scientific method S 79–82
  study, how to S 440–42
Thinking Day Fund, promotes guiding and girl scouting
      G 214
Thinners, paint P 32

Third degree, method of attempting to force confessions
from suspects prior to court trial by mental or physical
torture. The term was introduced by Richard Sylvester,
then president of the International Association of Chiefs
of Police, to denote police questioning. It violates the
Fifth, Sixth, and Fourteenth Constitutional amendments.
Evidence extracted by such methods is generally inad-
missible in court.

Third Estate, class of people, France F 462, 464
  rise of political parties in France P 379

Third International (Communist International, or Comintern), association of Communist parties established by
Lenin and Soviet leaders (1919) to succeed Second
International (1889–1914). Its purpose was to further the
cause of world peace through world revolution and to
unite Communist countries. It was dissolved (1943) to
appease Russian allies during World War II but was
revived (1947) with the formation of the Cominform
(Communist Information Bureau).

Third parties, United States P 381–82
Third Reich (RIKE), of Germany G 162–63
Third Republic, France F 418
Thirteen, superstition about S 475
Thirteen colonies see American colonies
Thirteenth Amendment, to U.S. Constitution U 156
  Nevada speeds statehood to pass the amendment
      N 136
  ratified after Lincoln's death L 296
  slavery abolished in the United States N 95

Thirty Years War, European religious and political
conflict fought mainly in Germany (1618–48). It began
when Protestant Czechs of Bohemia revolted against
attempts of Habsburgs of Austria to restore Roman
Catholic Church. Spain allied with Catholics, while
Denmark, Sweden, and France supported Protestants in
hope of winning land from defeat of Habsburgs. The war
ended with signing of Treaty of Westphalia (1648).
  Austria, history of A 524
  religious toleration, struggle for C 287; G 160

Thisbe see Pyramus and Thisbe
This is the place, Brigham Young's words about Great
      Salt Lake valley M 457; Y 353
  Salt Lake City S 22

Thomas (to-MA), **Ambroise** (Charles Louis Ambroise
Thomas) (1811–1896), French composer, b. Metz. He
served as director of the Paris Conservatory (1871–96).

Thomas, Ambroise (continued)
The composer of numerous operas and choral works, he is remembered for the light opera *Mignon*, based on Goethe's *Wilhelm Meister*. His other works include *Hamlet* and *Françoise de Rimini*.

Thomas (TOM-as), **Dylan,** Welsh poet   E 266;   W 3

Thomas, George Henry (1816–1870), American Union Army officer, b. Southampton County, Va. He served in Seminole and Mexican Wars and during Civil War was a commander at battle of Chattanooga (1863) and in Sherman's Atlanta campaign (1864). He later commanded the military division of the Pacific (1869–70).
   Civil War, United States, campaigns of   C 326, 327

Thomas, Jesse Burgess, American statesman   M 382

Thomas, Lowell Jackson (1892–   ), American author, lecturer, and news commentator, b. Woodington, Ohio. He first won fame as a world traveler and lecturer. For over 25 years (beginning 1930) he was one of radio's outstanding personalities, broadcasting news five times a week. Thomas wrote many articles in addition to more than 40 books, many of them about travel and adventure, such as *With Lawrence in Arabia*.

Thomas, Norman Mattoon (1884–1968), American Socialist leader, humanitarian, pacifist, b. Marion, Ohio. A Princeton graduate (1905), he also earned a divinity degree from Union Theological Seminary (1911). He joined the Socialist Party (1918) becoming its recognized leader in 1928. A six-time Socialist candidate for the U.S. presidency, he lived to see many of his recommendations for social reforms—among them unemployment insurance, minimum wages, old-age pensions and health insurance—become laws of the land. His advanced social thinking in the mid-1920's caused him to be branded a dangerous radical, but his unwavering dedication to the rights of the individual slowly won him the public's respect. He wrote many pamphlets and articles in addition to 20 books, which include *The Great Dissenter, The Prerequisites for Peace,* and *A Socialist's Faith*.
   third parties in the United States   P 381

Thomas, Saint, one of the 12 Apostles   A 333
Thomas, Theodore, American conductor
   May Music Festival   M 551
Thomas, William I., American sociologist   S 227
Thomas à Becket see Becket, Saint Thomas à
Thomas A. Edison, U.S. nuclear submarine, diagram
   S 443
Thomas à Kempis see Kempis, Thomas à
Thomas Aquinas, Saint see Aquinas, Saint Thomas
Thompson, Benjamin, American-born British scientist
   T 166
   experiments with heat   H 86d–87
   fireplaces   H 97

Thompson, David (1770–1857), Canadian explorer, geographer, and fur trader, b. London, England. He was with Hudson's Bay Company (1784–97) and then joined Northwest Company (1797), exploring much of western Canada. He was the first white man to survey the Columbia River. From charts of explorations he produced a map of western Canada that became a model for all later maps. He was head of British commission to survey Canadian-American boundary (1816–26).
   exploration and fur trading in the West   C 72;   I 67

Thompson, Dorothy (1894–1961), American journalist and political commentator, b. Lancaster, N.Y. She was internationally known for her brilliant mind and uncompromising opinions. She had been a social worker (1917–20), foreign correspondent (1920–28) in Vienna and Berlin, and in 1936 started her newspaper column On the Record for the New York *Herald Tribune*.

Thompson, Francis Joseph (1859–1907), English poet and essayist, b. Preston. A life of poverty and ill health led him to drug addiction. His poems were first published (1888) in *Merry England*, edited by Wilfred Meynell, and he was cared for by the Meynells for the rest of his life. His works include *Poems* (including "The Hound of Heaven"), *Sister Songs*, and *Essay on Shelley*.
   English literature, place in   E 263

Thompson, Sir John Sparrow David (1844?–1894), Canadian statesman, b. Halifax, Nova Scotia. Serving briefly as prime minister (1882), he became judge of Supreme Court of Nova Scotia (1882–85). He was Dominion minister of justice and was elected to House of Commons (1885). He was prime minister of Canada (1892–94) and Great Britain's representative on Bering Sea arbitration.

Thompson, Manitoba, Canada   M 81
Thompson, Polly, American educator, companion of Helen
   Keller, picture   K 201
Thompson seedless grapes   G 297
Thomson, Charles, American Revolutionary War patriot
   G 329
Thomson, James, English poet   E 258
Thomson, J. J., English scientist, atomic structure theory
   C 216; picture C 215
Thomson, Robert William, British inventor   T 196
Thomson, Tom, Canadian painter   C 64
Thomson, Virgil, American composer   U 127
   opera   O 139
Thomson, William see Kelvin, William Thomson, 1st Baron
Thor, Norse god   N 279
Thorax, chest cavity of animals
   crustacea   S 168
   insects   I 262, 263
Thoreau (tho-RO), **Henry,** American writer   T 167–69
   American literature   A 201
   Walden, excerpts   T 167–69
Thorium (THOR-ium), element   E 155, 165
   atomic structure unstable   A 488
   radioactive dating   R 64
   radioactive elements   R 67
Thorndike, Edward L., American psychologist   P 494–95
Thornhill, Sir James, English painter   E 238
Thorns, on plants
   weeds   W 104

Thornton, Matthew (1714?–1803), American physician and patriot, b. Ireland. He practiced medicine in New Hampshire (from 1740) and was a member of the Continental Congress (1776) and a signer of the Declaration of Independence.

Thornton, William E., American astronaut   S 347
Thoroughbred horses   H 231; picture H 239
Thoroughbred racing see Horse racing
Thorpe, James Francis ("Jim"), American athlete   T 169
   first president of National Football League   F 365
   Olympiad, 1912   O 110
   professional football   F 365

Thorvaldsen, (TOR-vol-sen) or **Thorwaldsen, Bertel** (1768–1844), Danish sculptor, b. Copenhagen. He designed figures of classical mythology and was regarded as a leader in the classical revival. His best-known work is a colossal statue of a lion at Lucerne, Switzerland.

Thorvaldsson, Eric see Eric the Red
Thoth, Egyptian god **W** 317
Thousand Islands, in St. Lawrence River, Canada **O** 120
Thoughts of Mao Tse-tung, poems **M** 86
Thrace, region, Greece and European Turkey **G** 333; **T** 324–25

Thrash, Dox (1892–   ), American artist, Negro, b. Griffin, Ga. A specialist in prints and lithography, he is co-inventor of a carborundum process for printmaking. He has taught at the Chicago Art Institute, and his work has been exhibited at the Corcoran Gallery, Carnegie Institute, and other important galleries.

Thrasher, any of several songbirds. About 8–12 inches long, thrashers have long tails. They are grayish-brown above and white streaked with brown below. They build open, cuplike nests in low brush or in trees.

Thread, for sewing **S** 128
Three Brownie B's, Girl Scouts program **G** 217
Three-cushion billiards B 176
Three-dimensional design D 136–37
Three-dimensional motion pictures M 477
Three Musketeers, The, by Dumas père, excerpt **D** 342–43
Threepenny Opera, The, by Bertolt Brecht **G** 179
    modern version of Gay's *The Beggar's Opera* **E** 257
Three-phase electric current E 139
Three-toed sloth see Sloth
Three-wheelers, automobiles **A** 544
Three Wise Men see Magi
Threshing, of grain **F** 60
    Afghanistan, picture **A** 44
Threshing machines W 155
Threshold of hearing S 259–60
Thrips, insects **P** 289; picture **P** 288
Throat and nose examination M 208g–208h
Through the Looking-Glass, book by Lewis Carroll **C** 123; excerpt **A** 165
    humorous play upon words in "Jabberwocky" **H** 279
    Humpty Dumpty defines some words in "Jabberwocky" **N** 273
Thrushes, birds **B** 236
    spectrogram of animal sounds, pictures **A** 276
Thrust, force created to oppose drag
    aerodynamics theory **A** 38
    aviation **A** 553, 557
    rockets **R** 255
Thrusters, rocket engines for spacecraft **S** 340e, 340f
Thucydides (thu-CID-i-dese), Greek statesman and historian **G** 351; **H** 134
Thule (THU-le), Greenland **G** 367
Thulium (THU-lium), element **E** 155, 165
Thumb, of the hand
    opposable in man **F** 83
Thumb-piano, or sansa, African musical instrument **A** 79
Thumbtacks N 3
Thunder T 170–73
Thunder Bay, Ontario, Canada **O** 124
Thunderclouds T 171–72
Thunderstorms T 170–73
    IGY studies **I** 317
    tornadoes **H** 297
Thurber, James, American writer **T** 174
    American literature **A** 215
    Great Quillow, The, excerpt **T** 174
    humorous drawings with his stories **H** 280
    modern fables **F** 4
    "Moth and the Star, The" **F** 8
    nonsense literature **N** 276
Thurmond J. Strom, American political leader **T** 301
    third parties in the United States **P** 381

Thursday, origin of name **D** 47
    Ear of Wheat Thursday, religious holiday **R** 153–54, 290
Thurston, Howard, American magician **M** 18
Thutmose III (THUT-mose), king of ancient Egypt **A** 222–23
Thylacine, or Tasmanian wolf, marsupial **K** 173
    dog family **D** 248
Thyme, herb **S** 382; picture **S** 381
Thymus gland, of the body **I** 107
Thyroid gland B 279, 280
    controls metamorphosis in frogs **M** 234–35
Tiahuanaco (t'ya-hua-NA-co), ancient Indian civilization of Bolivia **I** 155
    art, picture **I** 204
    Bolivia, history of **B** 306
Tiamat (TI-am-at), Babylonian goddess **M** 557
Tiberias, Lake see Kinneret, Lake

Tiberius (ty-BE-rius), **Claudius Nero Caesar** (42 B.C.–A.D 37), Roman emperor (A.D. 14–37). He married Julia, daughter of Augustus (A.D. 4) and joined campaigns in Armenia and Germany. Adopted as heir by Augustus, he became emperor (14), ruling from Capri after 26. He promoted financial stability through reduced spending, which increased his unpopularity.

Tiber (TY-ber) **River,** Italy **R** 248; picture **R** 249
    rivers of Italy **I** 452
    sights of Rome **R** 313
Tibet (tib-ET) **T** 175–78
    Buddhism **B** 425
    China's borderland **C** 265, 273
    Everest, Mount **E** 336–37
    refugees in Sikkim **S** 176
Tibetan Buddhism see Lamaism
Tibia (TIB-i-a), also called shinbone, the inner and larger bone of the leg below the knee, diagram **B** 271

Ticker, telegraphic machine that mechanically prints news or stock prices on a paper strip called ticker tape. The first model was invented (1856) by David Edward Hughes. Ticker tape is often tossed from office windows during celebrations or parades.
    stock market, operations of **S** 431

Tickling, a sense of touch **B** 287
Ticks, arachnids **S** 388; picture **S** 387
    harmful to man **I** 283–84
    household pests **H** 263
Ticonderoga (ti-con-der-O-ga), **battle of,** 1758 **F** 461
Tidal bores T 185
Tidal mills W 62
Tidal theory, of origin of solar system **S** 248–49
Tidal waves see Tsunamis, sea waves
Tides T 179–85
    Canada's Bay of Fundy, world's highest tides **C** 52
    first tidal-power station **F** 411
    gravity, strength of **G** 321
    hurricanes cause higher than usual tides **H** 296
    IGY studies of tidal drag **I** 318–19
    moon's gravitational pull **M** 449
    rhythms in plant and animal life affected by **L** 244–45
    surface of the ocean **O** 35
Tidewater, coastal region of United States
    Maryland's Eastern Shore **M** 116, 117
    North Carolina **N** 308
    Virginia **V** 346
Tied notes, in musical notation **M** 531

Tie-dyeing, a technique for dyeing cloth to form a design. Sections of the cloth are bunched together and tied into

Tie-dyeing (continued)
tight knots. When the cloth is dyed, the knotted portions do not take the dye, and a design is formed.

Tiefencastel (tee-fen-CA-stel), Switzerland, picture S 495
Tientsin (ti-EN-tsin), China T 185
  north China, port of C 262
  seaport of Peking P 117

Tiepolo (ti-EP-o-lo), **Giovanni Battista** (1696–1770), Italian decorative painter, b. Venice. A master of the Venetian school, he was influenced by Paolo Veronese and painted works of a religious or allegorical nature. His frescoes adorn numerous churches and palaces in Italy and Spain.
  Italian art I 473; P 24

Tierra del Fuego (ti-AIR-ra del fu-AY-go), archipelago off the southern tip of South America. It is a bleak, desolate region with much rainfall and high winds, best suited to sheep and cattle grazing. It was discovered (1520) by Magellan and is separated from the mainland by the Strait of Magellan. Control is divided between Chile and Argentina. Picture S 275.
  Argentina's control of the east section A 388, 392
  "Land of Fire," why so named C 253
  marginal tribes of Indians I 210–11

Tiffany, Louis, American artist and glassmaker S 395
Tiffany glass, picture G 233
Tiger, The, Georges Clemenceau C 337
Tiger, The, poem by William Blake B 250b
Tigers T 186
  cat family C 136–37
  circus act, picture C 300
  saber-toothed cats C 135; picture C 136
  Tammany symbol, picture C 126
Tiger salamanders, land-water animals F 475; pictures F 473, 474
  fresh water creatures, picture L 257
Tiger's eye, gemstone G 75
Tignish (tig-NISH), P.E.I., Canada P 456e
Tigris-Euphrates (TY-gris-eu-PHRATE-ese) **valley,** southwest Asia A 466
Tigris River, Asia R 248
  Iraq I 379; picture I 380
Tiki, Polynesian stone figure, picture P 10

Tilden, Samuel Jones (1814–1886), American politician, b. New Lebanon, N.Y. He practiced law in New York and became a leader in the Democratic Party. He was active in the Free-Soil movement (from 1848) and played a part in the destruction of the Tweed Ring (1868–72). He was governor of New York (1875–76). As a candidate for the presidency (1876), he had more popular votes but lost to Rutherford B. Hayes by one electoral vote.
  Hayes and Tilden H 79–80; N 226

Tilden, Sir William, English chemist R 346
Tiles see Asphalt tiles; Ceramics; Cork tiles; Vinyl tiles
Till, soil deposited by glaciers S 234
  action of glaciers during Ice Ages I 14–15
Tillage, of the soil F 57
  vegetable gardening V 288
Tillers, steering devices on boats S 13
Till Eulenspiegel see Eulenspiegel, Till
Tilley, Sir Samuel L., Canadian statesman N 138g

Tillich (TILL-ick), **Paul Johannes** (1886–1965), American Protestant theologian and scholar, b. Guben, Germany. Because of his opposition to the Nazi regime, he lost his professorship in philosophy at the University of Frankfurt (1933). Arriving in the United States, he served on the faculty of Union Theological Seminary in New York (1933–54) and later at Harvard University Divinity School, Cambridge, Mass. A distinguished scholar, he wrote about 25 books, including *The Courage to Be.*

Tillman, Benjamin Ryan ("Pitchfork Ben"), American politician S 311
Tilting at windmills, expression coming from an episode in *Don Quixote* D 285
Timbales, drums D 336
Timber see Forests and forestry; Lumber and lumbering; Trees; Wood
Timber dams, temporary structures D 18

Timberline, altitude level above which trees cannot grow. The level reaches higher altitudes in tropical latitudes and on mountainsides that are sunny or protected from strong winds. The area is characterized by scrub growth and bushes. The upper limit of timberline is the snowline, the level of perennial snow.
  where trees grow F 371; M 497–98; Z 373

Timber rattlesnake, picture I 282
Timber wolves, or gray wolves W 210
  dog family D 243–44
Timbuktu (tim-buk-TU), Mali M 59
Time T 187–94
  calendars C 11–13
  changes with speeds near speed of light R 142
  dreaming periods D 306
  Galileo invents timing device G 5
  Greenwich standard time G 372
  idea of time in children C 233
  international date line I 309–10
  living things measure time L 246–50
  longitude determined by time differences L 83
  measures of W 112, 115
  motors that tell time E 120
  observatories supply time signals O 8
  sense of, in birds H 192–93
  sun dials T 192–93; W 44
  watches and clocks W 44–50
Time, magazine M 15
Time deposits, banking B 48
Time line, chart
  used to illustrate book reports B 316
Time locks L 326
Timepieces see Clocks; Watches
Time reversal, law of N 371
Timers, or stopwatches W 50; picture W 49
Time scales, in geology F 383, 384, 387, 388
Time-sharing, of computers C 454–55
Time signature, in musical notation M 531–32
Times Square, New York City, picture M 486
Times that try men's souls, from the words of Thomas Paine in *The Crisis* P 13
  winter of 1776, Revolutionary War R 202
Time zones, geographical areas within which the same standard time is used T 189–91
  international date line I 309–10
  railroads responsible for establishing R 90
Timing, management of time or speed of an event
  bowling B 347

Timon (TY-mon) **of Athens,** tragedy by Shakespeare. It tells of Timon, a wealthy Athenian, whose friends are constantly by him while he is lavish with his wealth but who desert him when, ruined, he turns to them for help. Timon lives in a cave, even after uncovering a treasure of gold, refusing to return and help the city.

Timor (TI-mor), island in Malay Archipelago, Southeast Asia **P** 402; **S** 328

Timor Sea (ti-MOR), part of the Indian Ocean between the northern coast of Australia and Timor Island. It joins the Arafura Sea in the northeast.

Timothy I and II, books of Bible **B** 161, 162
Timpani, or kettledrum **D** 335–36
  orchestra seating plan **O** 186
  percussion instruments **M** 549, 550; **P** 151–52; picture **M** 548
Timrod, Henry, American poet **A** 204
Timur the Lame see Tamerlane
Tin, metal **T** 195
  alloys **A** 168
  antiques **A** 321
  bronze **B** 408–09
  Catavi mine, Bolivia, picture **S** 278
  coated steel **I** 403
  elements, some facts about **E** 155, 165
  japanned tin coffee pot, picture **A** 318
  metals, ores, location, properties, uses **M** 227
Tin cans, containers **T** 195
  coated steels and electrolytic tin-plating **I** 403, 406
  invention of **F** 345–46
Tinctoris (tinc-TO-ris), **Johannes,** Flemish musician and musical theorist **D** 364
Tinder, for fires **F** 140
Tinderbox, for holding firemaking materials **M** 152
Tin-enamel glaze, on pottery **P** 414
Tingi (TIN-ghi) **Hills,** Sierra Leone **S** 174
Tin Lizzie, the Model T Ford automobile **F** 367
Tintern Abbey, Wales **U** 72
Tintoretto (tint-o-RETT-o), Italian painter **T** 196
  follower of Titian **I** 470
  Last Supper, painting **I** 470, 471
  techniques seem very modern **P** 23
Tintypes or ferrotypes, kind of photograph **P** 212
Tipis see Tepees
Tippecanoe (TIP-pe-ca-noo), **battle of,** 1811 **H** 50
  Indian wars **I** 213
Tippecanoe and Tyler, too, campaign slogan for Harrison **H** 51
  battles in War of 1812 make presidents **W** 12
Tippett, Michael, English composer **N** 107
Tipping, origin of the word **R** 186
Tipplers, pigeons **P** 180
Tiptoe, manner of walking **F** 81
Tirana (ti-RA-na), capital of Albania **A** 144; pictures **A** 146
Tires **T** 196–98
  production in Akron, Ohio, picture **O** 65
  rubber **R** 346, 348
Tirol see Tyrol
Tiros (Television Infrared Observation Satellite), weather satellite **W** 85–87; picture **S** 42
  results of IGY research **I** 320
Tirso de Molina (TEER-so day mo-LI-na), Spanish writer **S** 369
Tishri, Hebrew month of the New Year **R** 153
Tissue cultures
  virus studies **V** 367, 369
Tissue paper **P** 53
Tissues, animal
  body, human **B** 269; diagram **B** 268
Titan (TY-tan), satellite of Saturn **P** 276
Titan II, missile **M** 345–46
Titan, The, documentary motion picture **M** 476
Titania (tit-A-nia), queen of the fairies, in Shakespeare's *Midsummer Night's Dream* **M** 309; **S** 136
Titania, satellite of Uranus **P** 277

Titanic (ty-TAN-ic), British steamship, largest and fastest of its time, that sank on first voyage after colliding with an iceberg (1912). Of 2,208 passengers and crew, 1,503 perished. Later investigation revealed that warnings to reduce speed had not been heeded, too few lifeboats were aboard, and nearby ships did not react immediately to flares for help. The tragedy helped dispel over-confidence and led to adoption of sea safety rules.
  iceberg accidents to ocean liners **I** 27; **O** 24

Titanium (ty-TAY-nium), element **E** 155, 165
  supersonic planes have skins of **S** 471
Titano (ti-TA-no), **Mount,** San Marino **S** 35
Titans (TY-tans), in mythology **G** 356

Tithe, contribution or tax amounting to a tenth of one's income. In Biblical Israel a tenth of one's produce and flocks was given to the sanctuary for offerings, to priests and levites for their support, and to the poor. In Europe, until the 20th century, the term referred to rent paid in produce by a tenant to a landowner. Today a tithe is donated by some people to their religious affiliations.

Tithonus (ti-THO-nus), in Greek mythology **A** 84
Titian (TISH-an), Venetian painter **T** 199
  Girl With a Bowl of Fruit (Lavinia), painting **I** 471 ·
  golden age in the arts **R** 162
  Greco, El, a pupil of Titian **G** 330
  Madonna with Saints and Members of the Pesaro Family, painting **P** 22, 23
  master of oil technique **P** 23
  Renaissance art **R** 169
  Venetian painting during the Renaissance **I** 469–70
Titicaca (ti-ti-CA-ca), **Lake,** between Peru and Bolivia **L** 33; pictures **A** 252, **B** 304, **L** 30, 50
  ancient Indian civilization developed at the lake **B** 302, 306; **P** 162–63
  Andes have highest large lake in the world **A** 253
  lakes in South America **S** 278
Title page, of a book **B** 331
Titles, forms of address used in speaking and writing **A** 19–21
Titles, of books
  how counted, in publishing **P** 515
Title search, of land ownership **R** 113

Titmice, group of small birds, gray to brown in color, with head crest and long tail. There are several species, including tufted titmouse, plain titmouse, and bridled titmouse. They live in much of the United States and northern Mexico. They nest in abandoned tree holes or in hollow stumps. Titmice feed on insects, seeds, and fruit. The birds often hang upside down while seeking food. Picture **B** 241.

Tito (TI-to), Yugoslav political leader **T** 199
  Communism **C** 444
  Yugoslavian government and history **Y** 357, 358–59

Titov, Herman Stepanovich (1935–), Soviet astronaut, b. Verkhneye Zhilino, Siberia. He was the second person to complete successfully a flight into space and the first to complete more than one orbit. His craft, Vostok 2, was launched August 6, 1961. He remained aloft 25 hours and completed 17 orbits.
  space flight data **S** 344, 345

Tittle, Y. A. (Yelberton Abraham Tittle) (1926–), American professional football player, b. Marshall, Tex. During his 14 years in the National Football League, he threw the greatest number of passes in the League's history.

Tittle, Y. A. (continued)
Traded to the New York Giants in 1961, he led the team to three successive Eastern Division championships. He retired from football in 1964.

Titus (TY-tus), book of Bible, New Testament **B** 161, 162

Titus (TY-tus), **Flavius Sabinus Vespasianus** (40?–81), Roman emperor, eldest son of emperor Vespasian. He commanded Roman forces in war against the Jews, terminating in destruction of Jerusalem (70). Ruling with his father (after 71) and as sole ruler (after 79), he bestowed gifts freely on subjects, completed construction of Colosseum, and erected Baths of Titus. His brother and successor, Domitian, built the Arch of Titus in memory of the victory at Jerusalem.

Titus Andronicus (an-DRON-ic-us), a drama in verse dating from the last decade of the 16th century and attributed to Shakespeare. The infrequently played tragedy is a bloody horror tale of a Roman general's revenge for the crimes of Tamora, queen of the Goths.

Tivoli, amusement park in Copenhagen, Denmark
　　D 106, 107
　　children's playground, picture **P** 78
TKO, technical knockout in boxing **B** 352
Tlaloc (tlah-LOKE), Aztec rain god **M** 251
Tlingit, or **Tlinkit,** Indians of North America **I** 180
　　Alaska **A** 136, 141
TNT, explosive **E** 392
　　weight compared to weight of atomic bomb, diagram
　　N 354
Toads **F** 471–73, 477–78; pictures **F** 470, 478
　　animal communication **A** 278
　　Can a person get warts from handling a toad?
　　F 473
　　freshwater area creatures, pictures **L** 257
Toadstools, mushrooms **F** 500; **M** 521
　　bioluminescence, picture **B** 197
Toasters, electric **E** 118
　　"Toaster, The," poem by William Jay Smith **F** 119
To a T, saying **T** 1
To Autumn, poem by John Keats **K** 200
Tobacco **T** 200–01
　　cancer research **C** 91–92
　　Cuba **C** 549
　　Jamestown crop saved colony **J** 21
　　"money crop" for Virginia colony **A** 185
　　smoking **S** 203
Tobacco mosaic virus **V** 362; pictures **P** 287, **V** 361;
　　model **V** 362
Tobago see Trinidad and Tobago
To be, or not to be, soliloquy from *Hamlet* **H** 21

Tobias (to-BY-as), **Channing Heggie** (1882–1961), American social worker, Negro, b. Augusta, Ga. An ordained minister, Tobias was professor of Biblical literature at Paine College in Augusta before joining (1911) the Y.M.C.A. For many years he was a secretary of its National Council and toured and lectured throughout the world. He was chairman of the board of directors (1954–59) of the NAACP, trustee of many educational and philanthropic institutions, and a member of the President's Commission on Civil Rights (1946). He was the recipient of the Spingarn medal (1948).

Tobit (TO-bit), apocryphal book of Bible **B** 157
Toboggans, bobsleds developed from **B** 265
Tobruk (to-BROOK), Libya
　　World War II **W** 290
Toccata, a musical form **M** 538

Toch (TOCK), **Ernst** (1887–1964), Austrian-American composer, b. Vienna, Austria. He won various musical awards, including Mozart stipend (1909), Mendelssohn stipend (1910), and Austrian State prize. He was professor of composition at University of Southern California (1940). His compositions include operas, symphonies, choral works, and chamber music. Awarded Pulitzer prize (1956) for his Third Symphony, he also wrote musical scores for films.

Tocopherol, or vitamin E **V** 371
Toddy cats, or palm civets, animals **G** 90–91
Toes, of the feet **F** 81–82
　　hoofed mammals **H** 206
　　primates **M** 417
Toffee, candy **C** 98
TOFS see Troops on Foreign Soil
Toga, Roman dress **C** 351
Toggle bolts, fasteners, picture **N** 2
Togo **T** 202–03
　　flag **F** 236
　　relations with Ghana **G** 198
Toilers of the Sea, painting by Ryder **U** 119, 121
Toilet water, a perfumed liquid **P** 154

Tojo (TO-jo), **Hideki** (Eiki Tojo) (1884–1948), Japanese army officer and statesman, b. Tokyo. Minister of war in Konoye Cabinet (1940–41), premier of Japan (1941–44) and leader of the military circle, he declared war on United States and Britain after Japanese attack on Pearl Harbor. After unsuccessfully attempting suicide (1945), he was found guilty of war crimes and sentenced to death by International Military Tribunal.
　　Japan, history of **J** 48

Tokaido (to-KY-do), Eastern Sea Road linking Kyoto and
　　Tokyo, Japan **J** 45
Tokay, dessert wine **W** 189
Tokyo (TO-kio), capital of Japan **T** 204–08
　　cities of the world, pictures **C** 305
　　International Airport, picture **A** 467
　　Japan's major city **J** 39–40, 45, 46
　　major city of Asia **A** 453
　　"Movie House Street," picture **M** 486
　　Olympic Games, picture **O** 103
　　Tokaido Express train, picture **R** 89
Tokyo Tower, Tokyo, Japan **T** 204; picture **W** 221
Tokyo University **T** 205
Toledo (to-LAY-tho), **Francisco de,** Spanish viceroy **P** 165
Toledo, Montes de, Spain **S** 354
Toledo (to-LE-do), Ohio **O** 71–72
Toledo, Spain **S** 356
Toledo swords **I** 405
Toledo War, between Ohio and Michigan territory **O** 75
Tolerance, for drugs **D** 328, 330; **N** 13
Tolerance, Edict of, 1781, granted religious freedom to
　　Austria **A** 525
Toleration Act, 1649, guaranteed religious liberty in Maryland **A** 192; **M** 128
Toleration Act, 1689, landmark of Glorious Revolution in
　　England **E** 224
　　Quakers **Q** 2

Tolkien, John R. R. (1892–1973), British author and professor, b. Bloemfontein, South Africa. He was a professor of Anglo-Saxon, and English Language and Literature. Many of his stories are similar to fairy tales, dealing with an imaginary world of elves, dragons, "hobbits," and other creatures. His fantasy trilogy, *Lord of the Rings,* and its prelude, *The Hobbit,* became very popular.

Toller, Ernst, German poet and playwright **D** 298

Toll roads see Turnpikes
Tollund man, prehistoric man, picture **A** 362
Tolstoi (tol-STOI), **Leo,** Russian writer **T** 208
  Russian literature **U** 61
  themes of his novels **N** 348
Toltecs, Indians of North America **I** 198
  colossal sculptures, picture **I** 153
  mythology **M** 561–62
Toluca (to-LU-ca), Mexico, picture **M** 245
Tomahawk, axe used by the American Indians **I** 196
Tomarctus, ancestor of dog family **D** 243
Tomatoes **T** 209; **V** 293
  grown in New Jersey, picture **N** 168
  love apples, so called, win acceptance **F** 335
  paste **F** 348
  seeds and fruit, pictures **P** 298, 309
Tombaugh (TOM-bau), **Clyde W.,** American astronomer **A** 475
  an ATM (amateur telescope maker) became an astronomer **T** 64
  discovered Pluto **P** 278
Tombigbee River, Alabama-Mississippi **A** 115, 120; **M** 352–53
Tomb of Countess Maria Christina, sculpture by Canova **S** 102
Tomb of the Unknowns **U** 225
  Washington, D.C., places of interest **W** 32–33
Tombolos (TOME-bo-los), or sandbars **M** 137
Tombs
  ancient Egyptian religious customs **A** 220–21, 371
  archeological findings, pictures **A** 352, 361, 365
  Egyptian art and architecture **E** 95–102
  Italian sculpture **I** 458
  Mausoleum at Halicarnassus **W** 216; picture **W** 215
  Taj Mahal **T** 14
  Tomb of Tamerlane, picture **A** 458
  Tomb-Mosque of Sultan Hasan **I** 419–20; picture **I** 417
  Treasury of Atreus, at Mycenne, ancient Greece **G** 341
  tunnel systems **T** 314
  Unknown Soldier **U** 225
  See also Catacombs
Tom Jones, novel by Fielding **F** 111
  development of the novel **N** 346
  18th-century English literature **E** 260
Tommy, rock opera **R** 262d
Tommy Atkins see Atkins, Tommy
Tommy guns **G** 424
Tommy Tiddler's ground, tag game **G** 17

Tomochichi (Bocachee, Tomochaichi, Thamachaychee) (1650?–1739), Creek Indian chief, b. probably Alabama. He settled near what is now Savannah, Ga., after he was outlawed by his people. He helped negotiate treaty of alliance between Lower Creek Indians and Georgia Colony of James Oglethorpe (1733).

Tompkins, **Daniel D.,** vice-president, United States **V** 331; picture **V** 325
Tom Sawyer, The Adventures of, book by Mark Twain, excerpt **T** 336–38
  place of Mark Twain in American literature **A** 205

Tom Thumb, **General** (Charles Sherwood Stratton) (1838–83), American midget, b. Bridgeport, Conn. Though born of normal-sized parents, Stratton never grew taller than 3 feet 4 inches and never weighed more than 70 pounds. He was "discovered" in 1842 by showman P. T. Barnum, who gave Stratton his stage name. Under Barnum's direction he toured throughout the world. Stratton's marriage in 1863 to Lavinia Warren, a dwarf, brought tremendous publicity.

Tom Thumb, locomotive built by Peter Cooper **C** 498
  early locomotives **L** 330
Tom turkey, picture **P** 422
Ton, measure of weight **W** 114
  short and long ton compared, picture **W** 113
Tone, a musical sound **M** 534
Tone, **Theobald Wolfe,** Irish patriot **I** 391
Tone poem, or symphonic poem, in music **G** 187; **M** 538
  developed by Franz Liszt **L** 312
  Gershwin's *An American in Paris* **G** 190
  romantic age in music **R** 311
Tonga **T** 210–210a
  flag **F** 240
  islands in the South Pacific **P** 8
Tongass National Forest, Alaska **A** 140

Tongatapu (TONG-a-ta-pu), group of coral islands in South Pacific. Nukualofa, the chief port and capital of Tonga is on Tongatapu, the largest island in the group. During World War II the islands were a base for New Zealand and United States troops.
  Tonga **T** 210

Tongue **B** 286; **M** 208h
  senses, guards on the alert **B** 281
Tongue depresser **M** 208h

Tongue twister, group of words or phrases difficult to say quickly and accurately because of similarity of successive consonants, such as "Miss Smith's fish-sauce shop." Examples **F** 304; **N** 276.

Tonkin, northern region of Vietnam **V** 334d, 336
Tonkin, Gulf of, Vietnam **V** 334c, 336
Tonkin Resolution, 1964 **V** 336
Tonle Sap, lake and river, Cambodia **C** 32, 33
Tonquin Valley, Jasper National Park, Canada, picture **J** 55
Tonsillitis (ton-sil-LY-tis), bacterial disease **D** 210
Tonsillectomy (ton-sil-LECT-omy), surgical removal of tonsils **D** 210
Tonti (ton-TE), **Henri de,** French explorer **A** 431; **I** 85
Tonto National Forest, Arizona **A** 414

Tony (Antoinette Perry Memorial) **Award,** given annually since 1947 to those who have made outstanding contributions to the theater. It is presented by the American Theater Wing, an organization composed of persons in the entertainment field. Awards are given for achievements such as best play, best musical, best stars.

Tooling, of leather **L** 112–13
Tools **T** 210b–19
  abrasives for grinding and polishing **G** 389
  archeologists use for digging **A** 356–57; picture **A** 358
  Bronze Age **B** 408–09
  camping **C** 43–44
  deep-sea diving equipment **D** 81
  diamonds used as tools **D** 153, 155
  dies and molds **D** 166–67
  garden equipment **G** 30
  hydraulic machinery **H** 303–04
  inventions **I** 348
  medicine, tools and techniques of **M** 208d–211
  pneumatic devices **P** 347–48
  prehistoric man **P** 443; pictures **P** 444
  sculptors' tools **S** 91
  sewing tools **S** 128
  simple machines, inclined plane, lever **W** 243–50
  use in intelligence tests for animals **A** 287–88
  woodworking **W** 229–34
Toothed wood ferns, picture **F** 93

Tourmalines, gemstones **G** 69, 75–76
Tournaments
  armor, pictures **A** 434
  duels of the Middle Ages **D** 339–40
  golf **G** 262
  King Arthur's court **A** 444–45
  tourneys, sport of knights **K** 274; picture **K** 273
Tourniquets (TOUR-ni-kets), how used in first aid
  F 157–58
Touro Synagogue, Newport, Rhode Island **R** 212; picture
  R 220
Tours, battle of, 732 **B** 100; **F** 415
  Muslim threat to church removed **R** 290–91
  See also Charles Martel
Toussaint L'Ouverture (too-SAN l'oo-vair-TURE), liberator
  of Haiti **T** 229
  history of Haiti **H** 10; **N** 93
Tower Bridge, London, pictures **B** 400, **E** 305,
  R 246
Tower of Babel see Babel, Tower of
Tower of London **L** 334
  boy prisoners in the tower **E** 220; **P** 470
Towers, in architecture
  bell towers, campaniles **I** 460
  Eiffel Tower, Paris **P** 70; picture **F** 403
  Leaning Tower of Pisa, picture **C** 132
  minarets, pictures **I** 415, 416
  Norman tower on Canterbury Cathedral, picture
  E 234
  Tower of London **L** 334
  ziggurats **A** 218, 240; picture **A** 350
Towhees (to-HEES), or chewinks, birds **B** 220; picture
  B 236
Townes, Charles H., American scientist
  maser developed by **M** 131

Town meeting, legal assembly of town inhabitants
qualified to vote, who meet to discuss town matters and
transact public business. It originated in New England,
where it continues to exercise power in small towns and
villages. Picture **C** 395.

Towns
  in local and municipal government **M** 504
  in New England, political units of the state **C** 475;
  N 139
  town meetings in American colonies **A** 188; **C** 394;
  picture **C** 395

Townsend, Francis Everett (1867–1960), American physician, b. Fairbury, Ill. In 1934 he originated the Townsend
Recovery Plan, or Old Age Revolving Pension, calling for
monthly payments of $200 to U.S. citizens over 60 years
of age. The funds were to be provided by a 2 percent
business transaction tax. The plan attracted millions of
supporters, for it offered means of stimulating business
during depression years. Bills presenting the plan were
continually defeated in Congress, but they paved the
way for passage of Social Security Act in 1935.
  California, economic plans for **C** 30

Townshend Acts, 1767 **R** 196
Townshend (TOWNS-hend), **Charles "Turnip,"** English
  statesman and agriculturalist **A** 100

Township, territorial unit approximately 6 miles square,
divided into 36 sections as defined in U.S. public land
ordinance of 1785. In northeast and north central United
States, it is regarded as a unit of local government, with
powers to administer schools, dispense relief, and
maintain roads.
  municipal government **M** 504

Toxins, poisons **D** 206, 219
  vaccination and inoculation **V** 260
Toxoid, substance that opposes toxin **D** 206
  treatment of disease **D** 219
  vaccination **V** 260

Toy group, dog breeds **D** 259; pictures **D** 256
Toynbee, Arnold, English historian **E** 268
Toynbee Hall, English settlement house
  served as example for Hull House **A** 19
Toyotomi (to-yo-TO-mi), **Hideyoshi,** Japanese warrior
  and statesman **J** 44–45
Toy poodle, dog **D** 261
Toys **T** 230–35
  ancient toys from Indus Valley, picture **A** 224
  automobile models **A** 535
  Child Protection and Toy Safety Acts, 1966,
  1969 **F** 352
  colonial hobbyhorse, picture **C** 389
  dolls **D** 263–69
  folk art, pictures **F** 291, 292
  gyroscope **G** 435–36
  kaleidoscope **K** 166
  kites **K** 266–71
  modelmaking **M** 385
  tops **T** 226
  weather forecasters **W** 82

Trace elements, chemical elements found in living
organisms in tiny amounts but essential to their life.
Scientists are not certain in all cases how the trace
elements are used, however. Cobalt, magnesium, iodine,
and copper are among the trace elements found in the
human body.
  chemical oceanographers study trace elements **O** 34

Tracers, radioactive elements, picture **R** 68
Tracery, ornamental pattern work, a typical Gothic form
  G 268–69
  decorative arts **D** 75
  traceried iron gate, picture **G** 267
Tracheids, cells, of woody stems, picture **P** 293
Tracheotomy, operation on the windpipe **D** 195
Trachoma (tra-CO-ma), eye disease causing blindness
  B 251
Trachymyrmex, fungus-growing ants **A** 325
Track and field, sports **T** 236–41
  historic race of Roger Bannister **B** 51
  Olympic events, pictures **O** 114, 115
  Zaharias, Mildred "Babe" Didrikson **Z** 366
  See also names of athletes
Tracking and data acquisition stations, for satellites
  S 41, 340g
Tracklayer tractors **F** 55
Tracks, for railroads **R** 86; **T** 264
Tracks, of animals, pictures **A** 271, 272
Tractarians see Oxford Movement
Traction elevators **E** 173
Tractors **B** 446–47
  "cat" train, picture **M** 80
  farm tractors **F** 55–57
  on an Irish farm, picture **A** 97
  plowing a rice paddy, picture **B** 456
Tractor shovels **B** 447
Tractor-trailers **T** 296–97

Tracy, Spencer (1900–67), American actor, b. Milwaukee,
Wis. He began acting at the age of 18 in stock companies and eventually moved to the Broadway stage. He
entered films in 1930, and won Academy Awards for best
actor in 1937 for *Captains Courageous,* and again the
following year for *Boys Town.* Other films that were well-

Transfusion, blood T 251
  blood types **B** 258
  medicine, techniques of **M** 210–11
Transhumance (trans-HU-mance), a grazing practice
  N 187
  seasonal migration of livestock and herders **H** 129
Transistors, electronic devices **T** 252–54
  computer circuits **C** 454
  properties of crystals **S** 251
  semiconductors in electronics **E** 148
  telephone, uses in **T** 60
  television **T** 70

Transit, in astronomy, the passing of one heavenly
object in front of another and larger object, as seen from
the earth. Venus sometimes is seen to pass directly
across the sun's disk as it moves between the sun and
the earth. This is called a transit of Venus. Mercury, too,
is seen in transit. The term also refers to the passing of
heavenly object across a telescope's field of view.
  eclipses, kinds of **E** 47

Transitive verbs **P** 91
  grammar **G** 289
Transits, surveying instruments **S** 480
  optical instruments for measuring angles **O** 170
Transjordan, former name of Jordan **J** 136, 139
Trans-Lunar Injection (TLI), spacecraft maneuver **S** 340e
Transmarine Council, Portuguese colonial rule of Latin
  America **L** 52
Transmigration of the soul see Reincarnation
Transmissions, in motor vehicles **T** 255–56
  automobiles **A** 543
  gear ratios of trucks **T** 296
Transmitter, of a telephone **T** 55
Transparent materials **L** 262–63
Transpiration, of plants **P** 294
Transplanting, in gardening **G** 40

Transplants of body organs, a surgical procedure in which
a living person's diseased organ is removed and replaced
by a healthy organ taken from a person recently dead.
Among organs transplanted have been the heart, kidneys,
lungs, pancreas, and eye corneas. The first heart transplant was performed by Dr. Christiaan N. Barnard in
Capetown, South Africa (1968).
  rejection, causes of **I** 104, 107; **M** 211
  transplants of organs and tissues **M** 211
  See also Barnard, Christiaan

Transportation **T** 257–68; **E** 50
  automobiles, economic impact of **A** 551–52
  aviation **A** 566
  bicycles, history of **B** 171, 173
  buses **B** 465–66
  camels, trial use of, in United States **A** 402
  caravans, picture **S** 8
  Chicago, railroad center **C** 230
  cities and suburbs, traffic problems and suggested
    solutions **C** 308b
  Conestoga wagon **C** 458
  discrimination and segregation in travel **N** 103
  elevators and escalators **E** 172–75
  environment, effect on **E** 272c
  fruit, shipping of **F** 485
  helicopters, uses of **H** 106
  industrial importance **I** 246
  Industrial Revolution in America **I** 241
  inventions in **I** 336–38
  Mississippi River **M** 365
  motorcycles **M** 488b–489
  New York City **N** 229–30

  noise control **N** 270
  ocean liners **O** 17–24
  petroleum products for transportation **P** 175–76
  pioneer life **P** 260
  Pony Express **P** 392–93
  postal service **P** 407
  railroads **R** 79–90
  refrigeration **R** 138
  river commerce and trade **R** 241
  ships and shipbuilding **S** 155–61
  trade and commerce **T** 242–43
  traffic control **T** 247–48
  transportation engineers **E** 205
  trucks and trucking **T** 295–97
  United States interstate commerce **I** 331
  vegetable shipping **V** 294
  wheels **W** 157–58
  world pattern of transportation **W** 267–68
  See also Bridges; Canals; Communication; Harbors and
    ports; Navigation; Roads and highways; Subways;
    Trade routes; Tunnels; transportation section of
    country, province, and state articles
Transportation, United States Department of **P** 448
  Johnson urged its creation **J** 131
  See also Volpe, John
Transport planes, pictures **S** 472
Transposition ciphers, in secret writing **C** 370
Trans-Siberian Railroad **S** 173; **U** 40
  Asia's east-west link **A** 466
Transuranium (trans-u-RAY-nium) **elements** **E** 159
Transvaal (trans-VOL), South Africa **S** 270, 273
  Boer War **B** 298
Transylvania (tran-sil-VAY-nia), Rumania **R** 355–56
Transylvania College, Lexington, Kentucky **K** 219–20
Transylvania Land Company, Kentucky **K** 212
Transylvanian Alps, southeastern Europe **R** 356
Trapdoor spiders **S** 387; picture **S** 386
Trapezoids (TRAP-ez-oids), geometric forms **G** 126
Trappers, fur traders **F** 520–24
Trapping, for furs **F** 512
  story of the boy trapper **K** 259
  See also Hunting

Trappists, monks of the Roman Catholic order of
Reformed Cistercians, noted for austere life. Reforms
making Cistercian monastic rules more stringent were
introduced by Armand de Rancé (1664?) of La Trappe
Abbey, France. Trappists' activities include observance
of church rites, manual labor, religious study, and
prayer. Recreation, conversation, and eating of meat,
fish, and eggs (except for the sick) are forbidden. The
order was united (1892) under the abbot-general of
Citeaux.

Traprock, or trap, igneous rock **M** 136
  a form of basalt rock **R** 264
  building stone **S** 433
  New Jersey deposits **N** 172
Traps, bends in pipes **P** 341–42
Trapshooting **T** 268–69
Travel **V** 258–59
  camping **C** 40–46
  health inspection, picture **D** 220
  hostels and hosteling **H** 253–56
  hotels and motels **H** 256–59
  ocean liners, floating hotels **O** 17–24
  Public Health Service, inspection by **P** 504
  passports and visas **P** 94–95
  Polo, Marco **P** 389–90
  vaccination **V** 261
  See also Tourist industry; places of interest section of
    country, province, state, and city articles

Travel agencies V 258–59

Travelers Aid Association of America, chain of social service agencies helping people who have problems connected with being away from home. Often whole families are displaced in the search for employment. Travelers Aid provides help with immediate and underlying problems. Founded in 1917, the organization has 82 affiliates in the United States and Canada, and more than 800 co-operating representatives. Headquarters are at 44 East 23rd Street, New York, N.Y. 10010.

Traveler's checks V 259
Traveling libraries see Bookmobiles
Travers (TRAV-ers), Morris William, British chemist N 110

Travers, Pamela (1906–), British author and actress, b. North Queensland, Australia. She moved to England (1923) and became an actress, playing mainly Shakespearean roles. She left theater (1936) to turn attention to writing. Her books include Mary Poppins, Moscow Excursion, and I Go by Sea, I Go by Land.

Travers, race for 3-year-old horses at Saratoga, N.Y. H 232
Traverse City, Michigan M 270
Travertine (TRAV-er-tene), a kind of limestone S 433
Traviata (trov-YA-ta), La, opera by Verdi O 154–55
Travis, William B., American lawyer and soldier, hero of the Alamo T 135
Travois (tra-VOI), American Indian vehicle I 166, 197; pictures I 168, 213
Trawlers, fishing boats F 223
Trawlnet, for catching fish O 36
Tread, of tires T 197–98

Trease, Geoffrey (1909–), English author, b. Nottingham. Trease is the author of over 60 books, most of them for young readers, including The Seven Queens of England and The Young Traveler in Greece.

Treason, act of betraying one's country
  Arnold, Benedict A 436
  Burr's arrest for treason B 462
  famous speech of Patrick Henry, "If this be treason" H 113–14
Treasure Island, by Robert Louis Stevenson, excerpt S 424–26
Treasure State, nickname for Montana M 434
Treasure trove see Buried treasure
Treasury, U.S. Department of the P 448
  federal investigative agencies F 76
  Internal Revenue Service, United States I 110
Treat, Lawrence, author of detective stories M 556
Treaties, written agreements between nations T 270–73
  fishing industry F 224
  inter-American, based on Monroe Doctrine M 427
  international law I 320–21
  international relations I 322–25
  presidency of the United States, treaty-making powers of P 454
  radio, amateur, only hobby regulated by international treaty R 62
  See also names of treaties, as Paris, Treaty of, 1783
Treatises, long written articles
  essay compared with E 292
Trebizond, Turkey, picture T 325
Treble clef, or G clef, in musical notation M 525
Tree dwellers
  mammals M 63–64
  monkeys, apes, and other primates M 417–18

Tree farming M 355
Tree frogs F 477; picture F 471
Tree Grows in Naples, A, painting by De Kooning M 396
Tree kangaroos K 170; picture K 168
Tree melon, or papaya, a tropical fruit M 74
Tree rings T 286–87
Trees T 274–85
  Arbor Day, "tree-planting" day H 152–53
  cork bark C 505
  felled by beavers, picture B 112
  fruitgrowing F 481–85
  giants of nature G 200, 202–03
  how to fertilize, picture F 97
  kinds of, in forests F 371
  "Land of the little sticks" in the Yukon Y 360
  leaves L 114–20
  marked trees for the British Navy L 372
  Mississippi a leading tree-farm state M 355
  nut trees N 419–24
  papermaking P 51–57
  petrified, picture E 341
  pollination of flowers of trees F 277
  ring counting method of archeological dating A 361
  seedlings for reforestation, picture N 33
  state U 90–93; for pictures see state articles
  wood W 222–28
  See also Forests and forestry; Lumber and lumbering; names of trees
Tree shrews, primates M 422
Trefoil (TRE-foil), three-leafed clover, emblem of Girl Guides and Girl Scouts G 214
Trejos Fernández, José Joaquim, Costa Rican leader C 519
Trellis ciphers C 369
Tremblant (trom-BLON), Mont, Canada C 67
Trench mouth, bacterial disease D 210
Trenches, field fortifications F 377
  World War I W 274
Trent, Council of, 1545–63 C 287
  Gregory XIII, legal advisor to papal delegates G 375
  Roman Catholic reforms R 294

Trent Affair (1861), dispute between Great Britain and United States. The American captain Charles Wilkes seized two Confederate diplomats, James Mason and John Slidell, en route to England aboard British steamer Trent. The North was elated with the seizure, but the British, outraged by the action, threatened war and declared embargo on war supplies. Confederates were released, since Wilkes should have taken Trent into port for judicial hearing instead of seizing the men from a neutral ship, violating freedom of the seas.
  Civil War, and trouble with Britain C 322
  See also Wilkes, Charles

Trenton, battle of, 1776 W 39–40
Trenton, capital of New Jersey N 176
  Revolutionary War R 202
Trésaguet, Pierre-Marie, French road builder R 250–51
Tressini, Domenico, Italian architect U 53

Trevino, Lee Buck (1939–), Mexican-American professional golfer, b. Dallas, Tex. He emerged from obscurity to win U.S. Open (1968) and became a colorful and popular performer. In 1971 he took British, Canadian, and U.S. Open titles.

Trevithick, Richard, English inventor A 541
  locomotives L 329
  steam engines S 421
  transportation, history of T 263
Triad (TRY-ad), musical chord M 529
Trial, or petit, jury J 159

Trial and error, psychology **P** 495
  animal learning, "fumble and find" **A** 283–85
Trial by Jury, operetta by Gilbert and Sullivan
  G 209
Trials, law
  courts **C** 528–29
  jury **J** 159–60
  Magna Carta guaranteed jury trials **M** 22
  ordeal and combat in the Middle Ages **M** 291
  steps in law enforcement **L** 88, 89
  war crimes trials **W** 9–10
Triangle, Japanese flower-arranging basic form **J** 49–50
Triangle, musical instrument **M** 550; picture **M** 548
  percussion instruments **P** 152
Triangle numbers **N** 380–81
Triangles, in geometry **G** 125
Triangular (try-AN-gu-lar) **trade,** New England, West
  Indies, Africa **S** 198
Triangulation (try-an-gu-LA-tion), in surveying **S** 480
  optical instruments **O** 170
Triassic (try-AS-sic) period, in geology **F** 387
  dinosaurs **D** 172, 173, 174; picture **D** 177
Tribal Trust Lands, Rhodesia **R** 228
Tribes and tribal life
  Africa **A** 58; pictures **A** 59, 60
  African art **A** 72–76
  African music **A** 77–78
  dance celebrations **D** 22–23
  early traditional local government **M** 508
  Germanic or Teutonic **M** 289–90
  Gypsies **G** 433–34
  Indian tribes of North and South America **I** 162–211
  jungle life **J** 154–56
  See also Celts
Tributaries (TRIB-u-taries), of rivers **R** 237–38
Tribute, payment by one ruler or nation to another **A** 254
  pirates **P** 263
Tribute Money, The, fresco by Masaccio **P** 20
Triceratops (try-CER-a-tops), dinosaur **D** 181
Trichinosis (tric-i-NO-sis), infection of the muscles
  D 210–11
  undercooked pork, source of **F** 354
Trick or treat, Halloween custom **H** 17
Tricks **T** 288–89
  animal learning **A** 282
  circus acts **C** 304
  rope tricks **R** 333–35
  tricks taught to animals by operant conditioning
  P 498
Trickster tales
  American Indian folktales **F** 313
Tricolor (TRY-color), French flag **F** 243; picture **F** 239
Tricorne, three-cornered hat, picture **H** 55
Tricycle, airplane landing gear **A** 557

Trieste (tri-EST) (Yugoslav **Trst**), Italian seaport (pop.
280,017) on Gulf of Trieste at head of Adriatic Sea, east-
northeast of Venice. Colonized by the Romans, Trieste
came under Austrian control in 1382. Made a free port
(1718), it became the leading port of Central Europe.
In 1919 it was annexed by Italy. The Free Territory of
Trieste (including the port and surrounding territory)
was established in 1947 under United Nations control. In
1954 it was divided between Italy (which received the
port as a free port) and Yugoslavia.
  Yugoslavia, history of **Y** 359

Trieste, underwater craft, picture **O** 43
Triglycerides (try-GLIS-er-ides), fats and oils **O** 76
Trigonometry (trig-on-OM-etry), branch of mathematics
  M 155
  relation to geometry **G** 126

Trillium, or **wake-robin,** or **birthroot,** plants of the lily
family, native to both the Eastern Hemisphere and the
Western Hemisphere. The plants have thickened roots,
long stems, a trio of leaves on each stalk, and large
three-petaled flowers of various colors. They are quite
hardy and bloom early, growing wild or cultivated in
gardens. Picture **W** 168.

Trilobite (TRY-lo-bite), any one of several extinct sea-
dwelling creatures with a flattened, oval-shaped body
divided into three lobes. Once worldwide in distribution,
they became extinct about 230,000,000 years ago. Trilo-
bites are often used as index fossils to help determine
the age of rocks in which they are found.

Trinidad and Tobago **T** 290–92
  Caribbean Sea and islands **C** 116–19
  flag **F** 242
  life in Latin America **L** 47–61
  Tobago, Caribbean island, picture **C** 118
Trinità dei Monti Church, Rome, Italy, picture **R** 312
Trinitrotoluene (try-ny-tro-TOL-u-ene), or TNT, explosive
  E 392

Trinity, Christian doctrine that conceives of God as three
co-equal divine persons—God the Father, God the Son,
and God the Holy Ghost—not divisible but together,
forming one eternal God. The first clear definition of the
Trinity was made in the 4th-century Nicene Creed, which
has since been dogma of Christian churches.

Trinity College, or University of Dublin, Ireland **I** 386
Trinity Sunday, religious holiday **R** 154
Triodes (TRY-odes), electron tubes **E** 146
Triple Alliance, Germany, Austria-Hungary, Italy **W** 270
Triple Dip, silk screen print by Shahn **G** 306
Triple Entente, France, England, and Russia 1907 **F** 418
  background to World War I **W** 270–71
Tripoli, Lebanon **L** 122
Tripoli, Libya, dual capital with Benghazi **L** 203–04;
  picture **M** 212
Tripolitan (trip-OL-it-an) **War,** 1801 **U** 185
Triptych (TRIP-tick), picture in three parts
  Departure, painting by Beckmann **G** 168
Triremes (TRY-remes), ships **T** 261; picture **S** 198
Tristan da Cunha (TRIS-tan da COON-ya) **Islands,** in
  South Atlantic **I** 437
Tristan und Isolde (TRIS-ton unt i-ZOL-da), opera by
  Richard Wagner **O** 155
  romance by Gottfried von Strassburg **G** 174
Tristram, knight of King Arthur's court **A** 442
  French literature, legend of Tristan and Isolde **F** 436
Tristram Shandy, by Sterne **E** 260
Triticale (trid-a-KA-lee), new species hybrid of
  wheat and rye **G** 287
Tritium (TRIT-ium), isotope, model **A** 487; **E** 153
  half life of, diagram **N** 357
  nuclear energy **N** 356

Triton (TRY-ton), in Greek mythology, a sea god, son of
Poseidon (Neptune) and Amphitrite. Triton is pictured as
half man and half fish and is usually shown carrying a
large sea shell as a trumpet. In the story of the Argonauts he aids the Greek travelers by calming the seas.

Triton, atomic submarine, picture **C** 473
Triton, satellite of Neptune **P** 278
Triumph, ceremonial entrance of a victorious general
  into a city **P** 61
  Julius Caesar entering Rome, picture **C** 5
Triumph of Flora, painting by Poussin **F** 422; picture
  F 423

Trochaic pentameter (tro-CAY-ic pen-TAM-et-er), a meter in poetry P 354
Trochees (TRO-kees), metrical feet in poetry P 354
Troika, dance by threes F 299

Troilus, in Greek mythology, son of Priam and Hecuba who was killed by Achilles in Trojan War. The tragic story of his love for Cressida has been told by many writers, including Shakespeare and Chaucer.

Troilus and Cressida, play by Shakespeare S 137
Troilus and Criseyde, by Geoffrey Chaucer C 190
Trois Frères (trwa FRAIR), Les, cave, France P 441
Trois Rivières (reve-YARE), Quebec, Canada Q 13
Trojan horse, in Greek mythology G 366; T 293
Trojan War T 293–94
  Greek mythology G 365–66
  Helen of Troy H 104
  Homer's version of the story H 167
  Iliad I 69
  See also Aeneid
Trolleycars and streetcars T 265
  Branford Trolley Museum, East Haven, Conn. C 476
  early trolley cars B 465
Trollope, Anthony, English novelist E 264

Trolls, in Scandinavian mythology, originally thought to be mighty but dull-witted giants who inhabited caves and frequented dark forests. More recently people have imagined them to be wily dwarflike men, particularly skilled in crafts, who live in caves and are hostile toward man.

Trombone, musical instrument M 549; picture M 547
  orchestra seating plan O 186
Trondheim, Norway N 344
Troodos (TRO-o-thos) **Mountains,** Cyprus C 557

Trooping the Colour, annual British military spectacle at Horse Guards in London in which troops are reviewed by sovereign on his or her official birthday in early June. Representatives from infantry and cavalry of British Army, in ceremonial dress, participate in elaborate parade, culminating in salute to sovereign's color (banner) to beating of drums. It has been an annual event since 1820.

Troops on Foreign Soil (TOFS), Girl Scouts organization G 215
Troop units, United States Army U 171
Tropical fishes
  aquariums A 343
  colors, purpose of F 193
Tropical fruits M 74
  fruitgrowing F 481
  pineapple P 249–50
Tropic of Cancer, line of latitude T 294
Tropic of Capricorn, line of latitude T 294
Tropics, or torrid zone T 294–95; Z 372–73
  birds of B 225–26
  climates C 345
  jungles J 154–56
  rain forests R 99–100
  tropical woods W 224
Tropopause (TRO-po-pause), atmospheric boundary A 480
  jet streams J 89
  weather W 72
Troposphere, bottom layer of earth's atmosphere A 479–80; E 17
  weather W 72
Trot, gait of a horse H 234; picture H 229

Trotsky, Leon (Leib Davydovich Bronstein) (1877–1940), Russian revolutionist, b. Yanovka, Ukraine. Exiled to Siberia (1900 and 1905) for preaching Marxist doctrines and participating in Russian revolutionary movements, he escaped both times to Europe. With Lenin he helped organize the successful October Revolution of Bolsheviks (1917) and was commissar for foreign affairs (1917) and commissar of war (1918). He began to lose power (after 1919) when he opposed Lenin's policies. With Stalin's rise to power (1924) he was banished from the Soviet Union (1929). As an exile in Turkey, France, Norway, and Mexico he continued to criticize Stalin's dictatorial rule. He was assassinated in Mexico (1940). His books include *History of the Russian Revolution, Stalin,* and *Diary in Exile.*

Trotter, W. Monroe, American journalist N 96
Trotting races see Harness racing
Troubadours (TROO-ba-doors) **and trouvères** (troo-VERES), French poet musicians F 443
  early French literature F 436
  Middle Ages, music of the M 298
Trough, low part of a wave O 34
Trout, fish, pictures F 210
  baits and lures F 206
  cutthroat trout, state fish of New Mexico N 185
  fish hatchery, Quebec, Canada, picture C 486
  locomotion A 290
  Murray Spillway, P. E. I., Canada, picture P 456f
  reproduction (spawning) R 179; picture R 178
Trouvères see Troubadours and trouvères
Trovatore (tro-va-TO-ray), Il, opera by Verdi O 155

Trowbridge, Alexander B. (1930–   ), American political figure, b. Englewood, N.J. Mr. Trowbridge was engaged in the international petroleum business until his appointment as assistant secretary for Domestic and International Business (1965) in the Department of Commerce. He served as secretary of Commerce (1967–68), and has been president of the American Management Association.

Troy, ancient city of Asia Minor, in present-day Turkey T 293
  archeological excavation, picture A 350
  Greek mythology G 365
  Ilion of Homer's Iliad H 167; I 69
  Schliemann, Heinrich, discoverer of the ruins S 53–54
Troyes, Chrétien de see Chrétien de Troyes
Troy pound, measure of weight W 113, 115
  origin of name F 10
Truce, flag of F 246
Truce of God F 103
Trucial States (Trucial Oman), now United Arab Emirates, sheikdom states in eastern Arabia M 301
  flag F 238
Truckee River, California, Nevada N 124, 134; O 264
Truck farming, growing vegetables V 288
Trucks and trucking T 295–97
  automobiles adapted to carry heavy loads A 541, 551
  dispatcher with two-way radio, picture R 55
  freight carriers T 265–66
  fuel oil truck, picture F 489
  ore truck, picture M 318
  right-hand drive for mail carriers P 408

Trudeau (TRUDE-o), **Edward Livingstone** (1848–1915), American physician and pioneer in tuberculosis treatment, b. New York, N.Y. Tuberculosis forced him to give up his medical practice, and he retired to the Adirondack Mountains of New York in 1873. His health improved, and he resumed his medical career in 1880, concentrating on the study of tuberculosis, about which little was known at the time. He opened the first open-air sanitarium in the United States (later known as the Trudeau Sanitarium).

Trudeau (tru-DO), **Pierre Elliott,** prime minister of
  Canada   **Q** 13–14
Trudgen, John, English athlete   **S** 489–90
Trudgen, swimming stroke   **S** 489–90
True Cross
  symbol of Crusades, picture   **C** 540
Truffaut, François, French motion-picture director   **M** 488
Truffles, fungi   **F** 498

Trujillo Molina (tru-HEEL-yo mo-LI-na), **Rafael Leonidas** (1891–1961), Dominican army officer and politician, b. San Cristóbal. He was commander in chief of armed forces under presidency of Vasquez and president (1930–38 and 1942–52). He exercised dictatorial powers even when not president. As generalissimo of republic (1932–61), he achieved notable economic progress in his country but used terrorism in suppressing opposition. Trujillo was responsible for the massacre of nearly 15,000 Haitians in 1937. He was assassinated.
  Dominican Republic, history of   **D** 283

Truk, Pacific islands   **P** 8
Truly, Richard H., American astronaut   **S** 347
Truman, Bess Wallace, wife of Harry S Truman   **F** 179;
  picture   **F** 178
Truman, Harry S, 33rd president of United States
  T 298–303
  as Vice-President, picture   **V** 330
  atomic attack on Japan   **J** 48
  containment policy in international relations   **I** 325
  Harry S Truman Library, Independence, Mo.   **M** 376
Truman Doctrine, foreign policy   **T** 302
  containment policy in international relations   **I** 325
  Marshall helped form   **M** 111

Trumbull, John (1756–1843), American painter, b. Lebanon, Conn. After fighting in the American Revolution, he studied under Benjamin West in London, where he began his historical painting. He painted portraits of George Washington and Thomas Jefferson and was commissioned to paint four pictures for the Rotunda of the Capitol, Washington, D.C.—*Declaration of Independence, Surrender of General Burgoyne, Surrender of Cornwallis,* and *Washington Resigning His Commission.*

Trumbull, Jonathan (1710–1785), American political leader and Revolutionary War patriot, b. Lebanon, Conn. After graduating from Harvard College (1727), Trumbull put aside a career as a minister to go into business. He became active in politics, serving in the Connecticut Assembly (from 1733), as deputy governor and chief justice of the superior court (1766–69), and as governor of Connecticut (1769–84). An early supporter of the rights of the colonists, he was the only colonial governor to take the patriot side during the Revolution and aided Washington's army with men and supplies.

Trumpet, musical instrument   **M** 549; picture   **M** 547
  ancient music   **A** 246
  orchestra seating plan   **O** 186
Trumpeter swans, birds   **B** 232; picture   **B** 230
Trumpet shell, picture   **S** 148
Trumps, in contract bridge   **C** 110
Trunk, of the elephant   **E** 168–69
Trunkfish   **F** 189; picture   **F** 183
Trunks, of trees   **T** 280
  woody stems of plants   **P** 290–91
Trunnions, gun barrel supports   **G** 425

Truss, in architecture   **A** 375; picture   **A** 376
Truss bridges   **B** 397; picture   **B** 399
Trust departments, at banks   **B** 49
Trustees, of corporations   **T** 305–06
Trusteeship Council, United Nations   **U** 84

Trusteeship system, method of administering non-self-governing territories placed under United Nations supervision. It replaced mandate system of League of Nations. By this system, territories are placed under administration of an authorized U.N. member, which exercises full legislative and judicial control in preparing territory for self-government and independence. Except in the case of strategic area trusts, which are under the Security Council, the Trusteeship Council supervises by evaluating progress in territory and making recommendations to administering country.

Trusts and monopolies   **T** 303–06
  capitalism   **C** 104
  charitable trusts, foundations   **F** 390
  Theodore Roosevelt, "trustbuster"   **R** 328
Trust territories
  Commonwealth of Nations   **C** 428
  United Nations   **U** 84
  United States   **T** 115; **U** 100, 103
Truth, Sojourner, American antislavery speaker   **N** 94
Trylon, symbol of New York World's Fair, 1939, picture
  F 17
Try square, measuring tool   **T** 216
  mechanical drawing   **M** 197
  woodworking   **W** 230
Ts'ao Hsueh-ch'in, Chinese novelist   **O** 220b
Tsar see Czar
Tsaratanana (tsa-ra-ta-NA-na), **Mount,** in Malagasy Republic   **M** 49
Tschaikovsky, Peter Ilyitch see Tchaikovsky, Peter Ilyitch

Tsetse (TSET-se) **fly,** any one of a number of bloodsucking flies, many of which carry human sleeping sickness and nagana, a cattle disease. Tsetse flies look much like houseflies but are larger and browner. The flies are found only in Africa.

Tshombe (CHOME-bay), **Moïse-Kapenda** (1919–69), African political leader, b. Katanga province, Belgian Congo. He was a member of Katanga Advisory Provincial Council (1951–54) and was made president of the Republic of Katanga (1960). He declared the secession of Katanga province shortly after the Republic of Congo gained independence (1960) but lost control to United Nations (1962). He served as premier of Central Congolese Government (1965) but was expelled (1966) and went into exile. He was being held in preventive detention in Algiers when he died.
  Zaïre, history of   **Z** 366d

Tsientang Kiang tidal bore, China   **T** 185
Tsimshian, Indians of North America   **I** 180
  Alaska   **A** 136
Tsiolkovsky (tsi-ol-KOV-ski), **Konstantin,** Russian scientist
  T 306–07

Tsiranana (seer-a-NA-na), **Philibert** (1912–   ), president of Malagasy Republic, b. Amborikorono, Madagascar. A former deputy from Madagascar to the French National Assembly, Tsiranana was elected (1958) first president of the Malagasy Republic.

T square, a ruler with a crosspiece at one end
  M 197
Tsu Hsi see Tzu Hsi

Tsunamis (tsu-NA-mis), sea waves caused by earth
    movements   **T** 185
    earthquakes   **E** 36
    hurricanes   **H** 296
    surface of the ocean   **O** 35
    volcanoes   **V** 382
Tsurayuki, Ki no, Japanese poet   **O** 220b, 220c
Tuamotu (tu-a-MO-tu) **Islands,** Pacific Ocean   **P** 8
Tuaregs, a people of North Africa
    Mali   **M** 58
    Niger   **N** 251
Tuataras (tu-a-TAR-as), reptiles   **R** 181
    New Zealand, native to   **N** 240
Tuba, musical instrument   **M** 549; picture **M** 547
    orchestra seating plan   **O** 186
Tube feet, of echinoderms
    starfishes   **S** 403
Tuberculosis (tu-berc-u-LO-sis), disease   **D** 211–12
    control of, for cattle   **C** 149
Tuberous begonia centerpiece, picture   **J** 51
Tuberous roots   **G** 41
Tubers, underground stems   **G** 41
    garden selection   **G** 29
    potatoes   **P** 411
    propagation of plants   **P** 300
Tubes, electron see Electron tubes
Tubes, pneumatic   **P** 347–48
    mail service, use in   **P** 406
Tubman, Harriet, Abolitionist leader   **T** 307
    Negro history   **N** 94
    Underground Railroad   **U** 12

Tubman, William Vacanarat Shadrach (1895–1971), president of Liberia, b. Harper. The son of an American-born
mother and a Liberian father, Tubman practiced law
before being elected in 1923 to the Liberian Senate. In
1937 he was appointed associate justice of the Liberian
Supreme Court. He was first elected president of Liberia in 1943 and was re-elected several times. Under
his administration Liberian women were given the right
to vote.
    Liberia, history of   **L** 167

Tubuai Islands see Austral Islands
Tubulidentata, order of mammals   **M** 62, 69

Tucker, Richard (1914–), American opera singer, b.
Brooklyn, N.Y. He was an established cantor before
making his debut with the Metropolitan Opera Association (1945), where he has since become one of the
leading tenors. He has appeared on radio and television,
is a recording star, and has given many concert tours.

Tucson (TU-son), Arizona   **A** 411; picture **A** 410
Tudor, Antony, English choreographer   **B** 26
Tudor, House of, English royal family   **E** 220; **U** 77
    Henry VIII   **H** 109

Tudor, Tasha (1915–), American illustrator and author
of children's books, b. Boston, Mass. The daughter of the
portrait painter Rosamond Tudor, she has written and
illustrated such books as *The White Goose* and *Thistly
B.* She has also illustrated the *Mother Goose Rhymes*
and the *Fairy Tales* by Hans Christian Andersen.

Tudor style, in English architecture   **E** 235–36
    Bramhall, in Cheshire, picture   **E** 233
    furniture design   **F** 506
    Stratford-on-Avon, picture   **S** 130
Tuesday, origin of name   **D** 47
    Mardi Gras, fat Tuesday   **C** 120
Tuff, a rock   **V** 380

Tufted titmice, birds, picture   **B** 241
    See also Titmice
Tufting, carpet weaving process   **R** 353
Tu Fu, Chinese poet   **O** 220a
Tugela (tu-GAY-la) **Falls,** South Africa   **W** 56b
Tugwell, Rexford Guy, American public official   **P** 523
Tuileries (TWE-ler-is) **Gardens,** Paris   **P** 70
Tukulor (TU-ku-lor), a people of Africa
    Senegal   **S** 119
Tulane University, New Orleans, Louisiana   **L** 357; **N** 196
Tularemia (tu-la-RE-mia), disease   **I** 287
Tule (TU-le) **Lake Waterfowl Refuge,** California, picture
    B 211
Tulips, flowers   **G** 42; pictures **G** 36, 43
    Netherlands' national flower   **N** 116; picture **N** 117
Tulip tree, or tulip poplar (also yellow poplar), tree
    Indiana, state tree of   **I** 136
    Kentucky, state tree of   **K** 213
    shapes of leaves, picture   **L** 116
Tull, Jethro, English agriculturalist   **A** 100
    first farm machinery   **F** 55
Tulsa, Oklahoma   **O** 92
Tumblers, drinking glasses, pictures   **G** 228
Tumblers, parts of a lock   **L** 322, 324–25
Tumblers, pigeons   **P** 180
Tumbleweeds   **W** 106
Tumbling, gymnastics   **G** 428–29
Tumeric, a resin to color and season food   **R** 184
Tumors, masses of tissue of "wild" cells in human
    body   **D** 194
    cancer   **C** 89
    plants   **C** 90
    tumor viruses   **V** 369
Tumpline, a sling for carrying heavy loads, picture   **T** 258
Tuna, fish   **F** 220
    day aboard a tuna boat   **F** 221–22
    habitat, feeding habits, uses   **F** 215
Tundra, arctic and subarctic plains   **P** 364
    Alaska   **A** 133, 135; picture **C** 344
    Canada   **C** 56; **Y** 363
    climate   **C** 346
    desert grasses   **D** 124
    Europe   **E** 310
    soils   **S** 233
    subpolar climate, North America   **N** 289
Tung oil   **O** 79
    varnish made from   **V** 279
Tungsten, a metallic element   **T** 308
    China's deposits   **A** 450
    electric light filament   **I** 334
    elements, some facts about   **E** 155, 165
    lighting bulbs   **L** 286
    metals, chart of ores, location, properties, uses   **M** 227
    needle tip showing pattern of atoms   **N** 354
    pattern of atoms, picture   **A** 484
    steel   **I** 396
    tungsten-producing regions of North America   **N** 294
Tungsten carbide   **T** 308
Tungting (DUNG-ting), **Lake,** central China   **L** 33
Tung trees
    grown in Mississippi   **M** 351
    oil   **O** 79
Tunicates (TU-ni-cates), marine animals   **P** 281
Tuning fork   **S** 261–62, 264
    demonstration   **S** 266
    electronic watches   **W** 49
Tunis (TU-nis), capital of Tunisia   **T** 311
Tunis, University of, picture   **T** 310
Tunisia (tu-NE-zha)   **T** 309–12
    El Djem, picture   **A** 66
    flag   **F** 236
    Roman amphitheater, picture   **A** 66

Tunnel race, game G 20
Tunnels T 313–18
  Alps tunnels, railroad and highway A 174
  Chesapeake Bay Bridge-Tunnel B 399
  How are tunnels built? T 315
  Mont Blanc Tunnel, picture W 221
  New York City N 230
  See also Subways

Tunney, Gene (James Joseph Tunney) (1897–   ), American boxer, b. New York City. After World War I he won light-heavyweight title and in 1926 defeated Jack Dempsey for heavyweight crown. He outboxed Dempsey in rematch in 1927, benefiting from "long count" after Dempsey had knocked him down, and retired undefeated in 1928. His son, **John V. Tunney** (1934–   ), b. New York City, served California in House of Representatives (1965–71) and is now serving in the Senate (1971–   ).

Tuns, water casks I 337

Tupelo (TU-pel-o), family of trees and shrubs related to the dogwoods and native to Asia and North America. The two American species grow mostly in swamps of eastern and central North America. One of them, the black, or sour, gum is a tree that grows up to 50 feet tall. It has long, oval leaves and small purplish fruit. The other, the tupelo gum, or cotton gum, has larger leaves and a swollen trunk base. The wood is used for handles, containers, and furniture.

Tupi, Indians of South America I 209, 210

Tupper, Sir Charles (1821–1915), Canadian statesman, b. Amherst, Nova Scotia. A prominent figure in the movement for Canadian confederation, he held various posts in cabinets of Sir John A. Macdonald. As minister of railways and canals, Tupper helped bring about completion of Canadian-Pacific Railway. He was high commissioner for Canada in London (1883–96). He was elected Canadian prime minister (1896), but he failed to restore power of Conservative Party.

Turandot (tu-ron-DORT), opera by Puccini O 155
Turban, head covering, picture H 53
Turbidity current, of Atlantic Ocean O 29
Turbines, engines T 319–22
  automobiles, search for a low-pollutant engine A 552
  engines, types of E 209–11
  hydraulic machinery H 301
  internal-combustion engines I 308
  jet engines in airplanes A 557
  jet propulsion J 85–86
  ocean liners powered by steam and electricity O 23
  turbines a type of steam engine S 419, 421
  waterpower furnished by W 62
Turbofan engines J 86; diagram J 87
  airplanes A 557
Turbojet engines J 85–86
  airplanes, power and propulsion A 557
  turbines T 322
  types of engines E 211
Turboprop engines J 86; diagram J 87
  airplanes A 557
Turbotrain, new development in transportation T 267
Turbulence, disturbance of air A 39
Turgenev (tour-GAIN-yef), **Ivan,** Russian author U 60
  development of the novel N 347
  first psychological drama in Russian theater D 298
  short stories S 166
Turgot (tur-GO), **Anne Robert Jacques,** baron de l'Aulne, French statesman F 464

Turin (TU-rin), Italy I 450
  aircraft production line, picture E 327
Turkey T 323–29
  Albanian conquest A 146
  Armenia U 44
  Balkan wars B 19
  bands introduce new percussion instruments B 39; P 152
  Bulgaria B 444
  costumes, traditional, picture C 350
  Cyprus C 556–58
  flag F 238
  Galata Bridge, Istanbul, picture E 319
  Hungary, conquest of H 287–88
  import delivery, picture I 329
  Jewish settlement J 109
  national anthem N 22
  Red Crescent Society R 126
  World War I W 274
Turkey Girl, the Cinderella of the Zuni Indian folktale F 302
Turkeys, poultry P 422–23
Turkey vultures, birds, picture A 295
Turkic languages
  Afghanistan A 42
  Union of Soviet Socialist Republics U 28
Turkish baths B 91
Turkish crescent, percussion instrument P 152
Turkish Ottoman Empire see Ottoman Empire
Turkmen Soviet Socialist Republic (Turkmenistan) U 46
  languages of central Asia U 28
Turkomans, people of Afghanistan A 42
Turks, people of Asia A 459
  Byzantine Empire conquered by B 490, 492
  Crusades against C 538–40
Turksib Railroad U 40
Turku, former capital of Finland F 133, 134
Turmeric, a spice product S 382
Turner, Frederick Jackson, American historian W 206
Turner, Ike and Tina, American rock music performers R 262d
Turner, Joseph Mallord William, English artist T 329
  Dutch Fishing Boats, painting E 239
  English landscape painting E 240; P 27
  modern art M 387
  Steamer in a Snowstorm, painting P 26

Turner, Nat (1800–1831), American preacher and slave leader, Negro, b. Southampton County, Va. He claimed to be commissioned by "divine will" to liberate the slaves. He organized a fanatical revolt, resulting in death of over 50 whites (1831), and was brought to trial and hanged. His insurrection increased antagonism of South toward the emancipation cause.
  Negro history N 93

Turnip Rock, in Lake Huron, picture M 261
Turnips V 293
  roots we eat, picture P 306
  wonder crop in agriculture A 96
Turnpikes, toll roads R 251

Turnverein (TOORN-fer-ine), organization that stresses athletic training along with social and political education. It originated in Germany (1811) through work of Friedrich Ludwig Jahn, and its purpose was to combat German disunity and French dominance and to encourage political liberalism. The movement, organized by German immigrants, grew in other countries. The national American Turners grew out of the Turnverein formed in the United States as the Cincinnati Turngemeinde (1850).

Turpentine T 330
  distilled from resin of certain pine trees **R** 184
  dry cleaning's early use of **D** 337
Turquoises, gemstones **G** 69, 76
Turret shell, picture **S** 147
Tursiops, bottlenose dolphin **D** 270–73, 274, 276
Turtle, early American submarine **S** 445
Turtles and tortoises (TOR-toses) **T** 331–35
  aging process **A** 84, 87
  eggs, picture **E** 88
  freshwater creatures, pictures **L** 257
  Galápagos Islands, Ecuador **E** 56
  How do turtles move, keep warm, and defend themselves? **T** 332, 334
  pets **P** 181
  reptiles **R** 181
Tuscaloosa (tus-ca-LOO-sa), Alabama **A** 124, 127
Tuscaluca see Tascalusa
Tuscan dialect, of Italy **D** 152
Tuscan Sea see Tyrrhenian Sea
Tuscany, Italy
  Etruscan art **R** 285
Tuscarora, Indians of North America **I** 184
Tusitala (tu-si-TA-la), or teller of tales, nickname of Robert Louis Stevenson **S** 423
Tuskegee (tus-KEEG-e) **Institute,** Alabama **A** 121
  Carver, George Washington **C** 128–29
  Negro history **N** 96
  Negro spirituals popularized **N** 107
  Washington, Booker T. **W** 29
Tusks, of animals **D** 83
  elephants **E** 169
  ivory **I** 487–88
  walruses **W** 7
Tusk shells, mollusks **S** 149

Tussaud (tu-SO), **Marie** ("Madame Tussaud") (1760–1850), Swiss sculptor in wax, b. Bern. She modeled the heads of some of the leading figures in the French Revolution. Settling in London (1802), she established a museum (1833) of her wax models, which she displayed in conjunction with a "chamber of horrors," containing possessions of criminals and implements for torture.

Tutankhamen (tu-ton-KA-men) (original name Tutankhaton), Egyptian Pharaoh of 18th Dynasty (flourished about 1358 B.C.). He was one of successors of Ikhnaton. Increased influence of priests of Amen (local deity of Thebes) led him to re-establish capital at Thebes, restore Amen's name to monuments, change his name to Tutankhamen, and gradually abandon worship of Aton. His tomb, a valuable archeological find, was discovered in 1922. Picture of the tomb **E** 96.

Tutsi, a people of Africa
  African music **A** 77, 78
  Burundi **B** 463
  races of Africa **A** 55
  Rwanda **R** 362
  Watusi headdress, picture **H** 53
Tuttle Creek Reservoir, Kansas **K** 179; picture **K** 178
Tutuila (tu-tu-E-la), island of American Samoa **S** 25
Tutuola, Amos, Nigerian novelist **A** 76c
Tutwiler, Julia Strudwick, American educator **A** 125
Tuyeres, in a Bessemer process furnace **I** 398
TVA see Tennessee Valley Authority
Twa, a people of Rwanda **R** 362
Twain, Mark (Samuel Langhorne Clemens), American writer **T** 336–38
  American literature **A** 205–06
  children's literature **C** 240
  development of the novel **N** 349

early use of the typewriter **T** 347
house in Hannibal where he lived, picture **M** 380
humorous observations, quoted **H** 281
quoted **Q** 20
signature reproduced **A** 527
Tom Sawyer, The Adventures of, excerpt **T** 336–38
'Twas the night before Christmas, first line of "A Visit from St. Nicholas" **C** 295

Tweed, William Marcy ("Boss Tweed") (1823–1878), American political boss, b. New York, N.Y. He was a member of the United States House of Representatives (1853–55) and New York State senator (1867–71). A grand sachem of Tammany Hall (1868), he headed the political machine ("The Tweed Ring") that embezzled an estimated $30,000,000 to $200,000,000 from city funds and dictated Democratic nominations for mayor of New York City and governor of the state. Tweed was tried and convicted in both criminal and civil suits. In 1875 he escaped from detention and fled to Spain. Arrested and returned by Spanish officials (1876), he was recommitted to jail, where he died.
  first use of the Tammany tiger symbol in a political cartoon **C** 126

Twelfth Amendment, to the United States Constitution **U** 156
  12th and 25th deal with vice-presidents **V** 329, 330
Twelfth Night see Epiphany
Twelfth Night, or What You Will, play by Shakespeare **S** 137
Twelve Apostles see Apostles, The
Twelve labors of Heracles, in Greek mythology **G** 363

Twelve Tables, ancient Roman law code inscribed on bronze (450? B.C.). Compiled from Greek law and Roman oral law and tradition, they resulted from public demand for clearly defined laws available to common people.

Twelve-tone, or serial, **technique,** in music **M** 400, 402
  Schoenberg, Arnold **S** 55
Twentieth Amendment, U.S. Constitution **U** 157
Twenty-fifth Amendment, U.S. Constitution **U** 148, 158
  presidential disability **P** 453
  vice-presidential vacancy **V** 330
Twenty-first Amendment, U.S. Constitution **U** 158
Twenty-fourth Amendment, U.S. Constitution, **U** 158
  abolished poll tax **N** 103
Twenty questions, guessing game **I** 226
Twenty-second Amendment, U.S. Constitution **U** 158
  limits term of U.S. president **P** 455
Twenty-sixth Amendment, U.S. Constitution **U** 148, 158
  voting qualifications for elections **E** 113
Twenty-third Amendment, U.S. Constitution **U** 158
Twenty-third Psalm, Bible **P** 435
Twenty Thousand Leagues Under the Sea, by Jules Verne, excerpt **S** 85; scene from **F** 440
Twenty Years at Hull House, by Jane Addams **A** 19
Twilight **M** 453
Twilight of the Gods, The, opera by Wagner **O** 152–53
Twill weave, of fabrics **T** 143
Twin Cities, Minneapolis–Saint Paul, Minnesota **M** 321
Twine **R** 331

Twining, Nathan Farragut (1897–), American air force officer, b. Monroe, Wis. He served in South Pacific and Italy during World War II, rising to rank of general of U.S. Air Force (1950). He was vice-chief of staff (1950–53) and chief of staff (1953–57) of U.S. Air Force, and he was chairman of Joint Chiefs of Staff (1957–60) until his retirement.

ILLUSTRATION CREDITS

The following list credits, by page, the sources of illustrations used in Volume T of
THE NEW BOOK OF KNOWLEDGE. Credits are listed illustration by illustration
—left to right, top to bottom. Wherever appropriate, the name of the photographer
or artist has been listed with the source, the two being separated by a dash. When two
or more illustrations appear on one page, their credits are separated by semicolons.

49 George Buctel; Vahidi—Monkmeyer.
53 Wayne Dunham
56 American Telephone & Telegraph Co.
58 Wesley B. McKeown—American Telephone & Telegraph Company
59 Wesley B. McKeown
61 Miller Pope
62 Mount Wilson and Mount Palomar Observatories; Yerkes Observatory.
63 Courtesy of Bell Telephone Laboratories
64 Mount Wilson and Mount Palomar Observatories
67– Miller Pope
70
70c Children's Television Workshop
70e Children's Television Workshop
75 Color Illustration Inc.; Tennessee State Information & Tourist Office; Sam Grimes; Photo Researchers.
76 Diversified Map Corp.; S. J. Ovenshire—FPG.
77 Diversified Map Corp.
80 Diversified Map Corp.
81 Tennessee Valley Authority, Knoxville; Hollyman—Photo Researchers.
82 Shostal; Billy Davis; Ellis-Sawyer—FPG.
84 Paul Granger
85 Diversified Map Corp.
87 Shostal
88 Courtesy of Public Information Office, Oak Ridge Operations
92 Ed Vebell
93 Ed Vebell
94 Ed Vebell
96 Ed Vebell
101 United Press International
102 Roche Photography
103 Arabelle Wheatley
106 Nelson Gallery and Atkins Museum, Nelson Fund, Kansas City, Missouri; George F. Mobley—National Geographic (Courtesy of U.S. Capital Historical Society).
107 Bettmann Archive; Granger Collection; Leslie's Weekly, Sept. 15, 1898.
110– Harry Scott
113
115 Harry Scott
118 Copyright 1954 by Harcourt, Brace & World, New York; Copyright 1965, Houghton Mifflin Company.
119 Copyright 1953, California Test Bureau
123 Color Illustration Inc.; Hal H. Harrison, Camera Clix; Texas Highway Department; Texas Highway Department.
124 Diversified Map Corp.; Ray Manley—Shostal.
125 Diversified Map Corp.
128 Diversified Map Corp.
130 Ray Manley—Shostal
132 Paul Granger
134 Diversified Map Corp.
135 Shostal
139 From Japan: Home of the Sun by Jennie T. Dearmin & Helen E. Peck, © 1963, reprinted by permission of The Harr Weigner Publishing Company.
141 Bradley Smith—Photo Researchers
142 Hedrick Blessing—Alpha; M. Lowenstein & Sons, Inc.
143 Gerald McConnell
144 Gerald McConnell
147 David Muench; Ace Williams—Shostal.
148 David Muench; David Muench; Ray Manley—Shostal.
149 George Buctel
150 Ernst Haas—Magnum
152 Gerald McConnell
153 Nes Levotch
155 Minnesota Theater Company
156 Friedman-Abeles
157 Max Waldman; Werner J. Kuhn; Werner J. Kuhn; Werner J. Kuhn.

158 Ming Cho Lee
162 Marc & Evelyne Bernheim—Rapho
164 Consulate General of Japan, New York City
165 Gerald McConnell
166 The Royal Institution of Great Britain
168 Culver
169 Culver
170 Noel M. Kleim—U.S. Department of Commerce, Weather Bureau
171 Nes Levotch
172 The General Electric Company; U.S. Department of Commerce, Weather Bureau; The General Electric Company.
173 The Westinghouse Electric Corporation
174 Copyright 1932, 1960, James Thurber, from The Seal in the Bedroom, published by Harper and Row.
175 George Buctel; Ju Shui-chu, China Photo Service—Eastfoto.
176 Harrison Forman
178 Harrison Forman
179 M. Woodbridge Williams
180– Alex Ebel
183
184 New Brunswick Travel Bureau
185 George Buctel
186 Robert Van Nostrand—National Audubon Society; Erik Parbst—Black Star.
189– Wesley B. McKeown
193
195 Corocraft, Ltd.
196 The Firestone Tire & Rubber Co.
197 George Bakacs
198 The Firestone Tire & Rubber Co.
200 Bernard G. Silberstein—Rapho
202 Marc & Evelyne Bernheim—Rapho
203 George Buctel
204 George Buctel
205 Sampei Hosoi
206 Ray Manley—Shostal; Max Tatch—Shostal.
207 Consulate General of Japan, New York City; Japan National Tourist Association; Marc Riboud, Magnum.
210 John Lewis Stage—Photo Researchers
210b–Harry Schaare
216
218 Harry Schaare
220– Gerald McConnell
225
227 George Buctel; Canadian Government Travel Bureau.
229 Museum of Modern Art, New York, Gift of Mrs. John D. Rockefeller, Jr., 1946
230 Verne Bowman
232 Courtesy of Ideal Toy Corp.; Courtesy of Remco Industries.
233 Courtesy of A. C. Gilbert
234 Marshall Hartman—Courtesy of Brooklyn Children's Museum; Courtesy of Brooklyn Museum.
235 Ron Perkins—Courtesy of Cepelia Corporation; Ron Perkins—Courtesy of Sona, The Golden One; Courtesy of Reeves International; Ron Perkins—Courtesy of Azuma.
237 Ed Vebell
239– Ed Vebell
241
245 Courtesy of Kimberly-Clark Corp.; Courtesy of General Foods Co.; Courtesy of Eastman Kodak Co.
246 Graphic Arts International
247 John V. Dunigan—Design Photographers International
249 The General Electric Company
250 Lee Ames
252– Miller Pope
254
255 Ted Henke
256 Ted Henke
258 George Sottung

259 George Sottung
262 George Sottung
263 George Sottung
265 George Sottung
269 Gerald McConnell
274 Arabelle Wheatley
275 Arthur W. Ambler—National Audubon Society; John H. Gerard; John H. Gerard; Arabelle Wheatley; V. R. Johnston—Photo Researchers; Russ Kinne—Photo Researchers; Paul W. Nesbit—National Audubon Society.
276 Stephen Collins—Photo Researchers; FPG; Franklin R. Schmidt—Courtesy of A. Polonsky Estate; David Muench; Arabelle Wheatley; McIntyre—Annan; Josef Muench; Josef Muench.
277 Irvin L. Oakes—Photo Researchers; Stephen Collins—Photo Researchers; Chuck Abbott—Rapho Guillumette; John H. Gerard; Arabelle Wheatley; A. C. Shelton—A. Devaney, Inc., Clarence D. Cook—National Audubon Society; William M. Harlow—National Audubon Society.
278 Irvin L. Oakes—Photo Researchers; Stephen Collins—Photo Researchers; California Academy of Sciences, Charles Webber Collection; David Muench; Arabelle Wheatley; Russ Kinne—Photo Researchers; David Muench; Stephen Collins—Photo Researchers.
279 Lynwood M. Chace; S. I. Gale—National Audubon Society; Arabelle Wheatley.
280 Arabelle Wheatley
282 Arabelle Wheatley
283 Arabelle Wheatley
285 Arabelle Wheatley
286 Charles W. Herbert—Western Ways
287 Charles W. Herbert—Western Ways
289 Gerald McConnell
290 Dana Brown—Alpha; Hans Hannau—Rapho Guillumette.
291 George Buctel
293 Herman B. Vestal
294 Marc & Evelyne Bernheim
296 Pacific Intermountain Express
297 Pacific Intermountain Express; Arrow Equipment Co., Inc.; Great Dane Trailers, Inc.
298 James Cooper
299– Wide World Photos
301
302 UPI
306 Granger Collection
309 George Buctel
310 Carl Frank—Photo Researchers
311 Pat Morin—Monkmeyer
312 Inge Morath—Monkmeyer
313 Birnback
315 Australian News & Information Bureau
316 Carew—Monkmeyer
317 Gerald McConnell
319– Gerald McConnell
322
323 Bernard Silberstein—Rapho Guillumette
324 George Buctel
325 Marc Riboud—Magnum
327 Jerry Cooke; Ray Manley—Shostal.
328 Marc Riboud—Magnum
330 R. R. Leahey—Shostal
331 Russ Kinne—Photo Researchers
333 Jane Burton-Photo Researchers; R. Van Nostrand–National Audubon Society.
334 Lynwood M. Chace—National Audubon Society; Russ Kinne—Photo Researchers.
337 Morse Collection, Yale University
338 George Sottung
339 James Cooper
340 Three Lions
344 Gerald McConnell
347 The Lighthouse of the New York Association for the Blind; IBM; IBM.
348 IBM

U, 21st letter of the English alphabet **U** 1
See also Alphabet
Uakaris (ua-KA-ris), monkeys **M** 420; picture **M** 421
UAW see United Automobile Workers
Ubangi (oo-BONG-i) **River,** tributary of Congo, central Africa **C** 169, 170
Ubangi-Chari see Central African Republic
Ubastet, cat-headed Egyptian goddess **C** 142

U-boat (from German *U-boot,* for *Unterseeboot,* meaning "undersea boat"), term usually applied to German submarines of World Wars I and II. They were first constructed for German Navy by Krupp Shipbuilding Works (1904). The German U-boat fleet was virtually destroyed by Allied vessels during World War II.
submarines in World Wars I and II **S** 446; **W** 276, 291–92

Uccello (oo-CHEL-lo), **Paolo,** Italian painter **R** 166

Uchida, Yoshiko (1921–), American writer of children's books, b. Alameda, California. After attending the University of California and Smith College, she won a 2-year scholarship in Japan. Her experiences there provided her with the background for her stories of Japanese life. Titles include *Full Circle, Dancing Kettle and Other Japanese Folk Tales,* and *Mik and the Prowler.*

Udaipur (oo-DY-pure), India, picture **I** 123

Udall, Nicholas (Nicholas Uvedale) (1505–1556), English dramatist and educator, b. Hampshire. Headmaster of Eton (1534–41) and Westminister School (1554–56), he wrote the play *Ralph Roister Doister,* considered the earliest English comedy.
Renaissance drama **D** 295

Udall, Stewart Lee (1920–), American political leader, b. St. Johns, Ariz. A former lawyer in Tucson, Udall served in the U.S. House of Representatives (1955–1960) and under Kennedy and Johnson as secretary of the interior (1960–69). In 1969 he helped organize a firm to seek ways to solve man's environmental problems.

Udder, or mammary gland **M** 310
Uffizi (oof-FI-tzi) **Gallery,** Florence, Italy **U** 2–3
great museums of the world **M** 511
UFO's see Unidentified flying objects
Uganda (u-GAN-da) **U** 4–7; pictures **A** 59, 60
flag **F** 236
veld, picture **G** 315
Ugly Duckling, The, story by Hans Christian Andersen **A** 247, 248
UHF, frequency **T** 66–67
Uinta (u-IN-ta) **Basin,** Utah **U** 242
Uinta Mountains, Utah **U** 243
Ukiyoe (oo-ki-YO-ye), Japanese style of making prints **G** 303
oriental art **O** 217
Ukraine (U-kraine), Union of Soviet Socialist Republics **U** 8–9, 37
flag **F** 240
folk dancing, done only by boys **F** 299
national dance **D** 30
Soviet Union **U** 27, 29, 36
Ukulele (u-ke-LAY-le), instrument related to the guitar **F** 329
Ulan Bator (OO-lon BA-tor), capital of Mongolia **M** 415; picture **M** 416

Ulanova (oo-LA-no-va), **Galina Sergeyevna** (1910–), Russian dancer. Considered one of greatest Soviet ballet dancers, she revived classical tradition in Russian ballet. She has been soloist of Leningrad Theater Ballet (1928–44) and of Bolshoi Theater (since 1944). Noted for performances in *Romeo and Juliet, Giselle,* and *Swan Lake,* she was named National Artist of Soviet Union (1940). She starred in the film *The Ballet of Romeo and Juliet,* awarded first prize at Cannes Film Festival (1955).

Ulate (oo-LA-tay), **Otilio,** president of Costa Rica **C** 519

Ulbricht (OOL-brickt), **Walter** (1893–1973), East German political leader, b. Leipzig. He helped found German Communist Party (1919) and was deputy in Reichstag (1928–33). A member of National Committee for Free Germany, he helped merge Social Democratic Party (SPD) and Communist Party (KPD) into Social Unity Party (SED) (1945), and he was elected to central secretariat of SED (1946). Virtual head of East Germany until 1971, he is known for planning the Berlin Wall (1961) that sealed off his Communist country from the West.

Ulcers, open sores **D** 202–03

Ulloa (ool-YO-a), **Francisco de,** Spanish explorer who lived during first half of 16th century. Sent from Mexico by Cortes to explore Gulf of California (1539), he established that Lower California is a peninsula.

Ulster, Northern Ireland and Ireland **U** 73
Ulster Cycle, group of Irish tales **I** 392
Ultracentrifuge, machine **V** 365
Ultrahigh frequency, of sound waves **S** 265, 267

Ultramarine, blue pigment, originally made from powdered lapis lazuli, an ornamental stone found in Afghanistan, Russia, and China. It is now produced artificially and more cheaply by chemical process and is used chiefly in paints, printing inks, and laundry bluing.

Ultramicroscopes (ul-tra-MY-cro-scopes)
dust particles revealed by **D** 347
Ultrasonics (ul-tra-SON-ics), very high-frequency sound **S** 265–67
dolphins and porpoises, sonar abilities **D** 274–76
experiments with bats **B** 96–97
Ultrasonoscope, an aid in medical diagnosis **M** 209
Ultraviolet microscopes **M** 283
Ultraviolet radiation **R** 44
food preservation **F** 349
light rays **L** 270
skin cancer from **C** 92
mercury and fluorescent lamps **L** 287–88
ozone layer in the stratosphere absorbs **A** 481; **E** 17
quartz-glass tubes of sun lamps permit passage of rays **Q** 6
solar energy **S** 235
vitamin D in sunlight **V** 371
Ulyanov, Vladimir Ilich see Lenin, Vladimir I.
Ulysses, Greek hero see Odysseus
Ulysses (u-LISS-ese), novel by James Joyce **I** 395
stream of consciousness novel **E** 266–67
Umanak Fjord (OO-ma-nok F'YORD), Greenland, pictures **G** 367, 368
Umatilla, Indians of North America **I** 175

Umber, earth pigment containing iron and manganese oxides, found chiefly in Italy and Cyprus. It is used either as raw umber, which has a greenish-brown color, or as burnt umber, which has a rich dark-brown color.

Umbra, complete shadow region in eclipses **E** 46–47

Umbrella bird, South and Central American bird that resembles a crow in size and color, the male being glossy black. The bird gets its name because of the crest on the head of the male, which expands into the shape of an umbrella.

See also Cotingas

Umbrella tree, small tree in the magnolia family. It has large, broad leaves over 1 ft. long, which grow in bunches at the tips of its branches and make it look like an umbrella. The tree bears reddish fruit and large white cup-shaped flowers, which smell unpleasant. The umbrella tree is native to America.

Un-American Activities, House Committee on, committee organized to investigate subversive activity in United States and to make recommendations for corrective legislation. McCarran Act of 1950 came about largely because of the committee's findings. Originally a special committee of the House of Representatives (1938–45), it was made into a standing committee (1945). In 1969 it became the House Internal Security Committee.

Unamuno (oo-na-MOON-o) **y Jugo, Miguel de** (1864–1936), Spanish philosopher, essayist, and educator, b. Bilbao in Basque area. He advocated individualism and was strongly antimaterialistic. Works include *The Tragic Sense of Life in Men and in Peoples.*

Uncas (1588?–1683?), American Indian chief. He was born into Pequot tribe but was banished after rebelling against its chief. He became chief of Mohegan tribe and sided with English in Pequot War (1637). Later he fought the Narraganset tribe and surrendered their chief to the English. His name appears in James Fenimore Cooper's *Last of the Mohicans.*

Uniats (U-ni-ats), those Eastern churches in communion with Rome who accept the authority of the Pope but who have their own liturgy and organization. In general, they differ from Roman Catholics by allowing marriage of clergy and practicing baptism by immersion. Uniats include Alexandrians, Antiochenes, Armenians, Chaldeans, Copts, Rumanians, and Ukrainians.

Unicameral (u-ni-CAM-er-al), or one-house **legislature**

UNICO National (UNICO), organization of business and professional men, Italian by birth or married to a person of Italian descent. Founded in 1922, the organization absorbed National Civic League (1947). It publishes *UNICO Bulletin.*

Unicorn (U-ni-corn) (from the Latin *unum cornum,* meaning "one horn"), mythical animal with head and body of a horse and a single horn in the middle of its forehead. The unicorn represented chastity and purity in the Middle Ages, and it was often depicted on tapestries. According to medieval belief, it was the only animal that dared attack an elephant. The earliest description of it was by Ctesias (400 B.C.).

Uniforms C 353; pictures C 355
  Boy Scouts and Cub Scouts, picture **B** 358
  Civil War, U.S., pictures **C** 324, 325
  Girl Scouts **G** 216
  mailmen's uniforms **P** 409
  medals, how to wear **M** 200
  school smocks in Argentina **A** 390
  United States Air Force insignia, pictures
    U 163–64
  United States Army insignia, pictures **U** 169–70
  United States Marine Corps insignia, pictures **U** 181
  United States Navy insignia **U** 187–88
Union, of a flag **F** 234
Union, Acts of see Acts of Union
Union Cycliste Internationale (U.C.I.) **B** 171
Union Jack, English flag **F** 243; picture **F** 227
Union Now, peace movement **P** 105
Union of Soviet Socialist Republics **U** 27–51
  Balkans **B** 19
  Belorussian Soviet Socialist Republic **B** 138–39
  Communism **C** 442–45
  Communist China, differences with **C** 445
  Council for Mutual Economic Aid **E** 330
  differences with Communist China **C** 445
  education **E** 82
  Europe, seven Soviet republics **E** 307
  flag **F** 240
  Hitler's invasion under Plan Barbarossa **W** 290–91
  holidays **H** 148, 153
  Khrushchev, Nikita **K** 240–41
  kindergarten and nurseries **K** 247
  Lapland **L** 44–45
  Lenin **L** 138
  Leningrad **L** 139–40
  marriage rites **W** 103
  Mongolia **M** 416
  Moscow **M** 464–67
  municipal government system **M** 508
  music after the Revolution **U** 64
  national anthem **N** 19
  old-age pension plans **O** 98
  purpose painting **U** 55–56
  Russian art and architecture **U** 51–57
  Russian family, picture **F** 42
  Russian foods **F** 341
  Russian Jewry under communism **J** 111–12
  Russian language and literature **U** 57–62
  Russian music **U** 62–64
  Siberia **S** 173
  Soviet architecture **U** 53
  Soviet literature **U** 61–62
  space exploration **M** 447, 455; **S** 344, 345, 348
  Stalin, Joseph **S** 395
  steppes, picture **P** 433
  supersonic transport planes **S** 472; **T** 267
  theater **T** 161
  Ukraine **U** 8–9
  women, role of **W** 212, 213
  World War II **W** 306; picture **W** 304
  See also names of republics
Union Pacific Railroads
  largest steam locomotives **L** 332
Unions, labor see Labor unions
Union shop **L** 15–16

Union Veterans of the Civil War, Sons of (SUVCW),
organization of male descendants of veterans of the
Union Army of the Civil War, founded in 1881 with
headquarters in Gettysburg, Pa. Their aims include the
proper observance of national holidays, supervision of
Civil War memorials, keeping informed of subversive
activities, and enlightening public opinion.

Unisphere, symbol of the New York World's Fair,
    1964–65 **F** 17; picture **F** 16
Unitarian Church, New Hampshire, picture **P** 484

Unitarianism, religious denomination in Christian tradition that rejects doctrine of trinity, believing instead that
God exists only in one person. It originated during
Protestant Reformation with establishment of communities in Poland, Hungary, and England. It became a less
doctrinal, more tolerant religion in middle of 19th century. American Unitarian Association was established in
1825. It merged with Universalist Church in 1961.

Unitarian-Universalist Association, consolidation of two
religious bodies, American Unitarian Association and
Universalist Church of America, in 1962.

Unitas, John (1933–), American professional football
player, b. Pittsburgh, Pa. Since joining the Baltimore
Colts as a quarterback in 1956, he has built an outstanding passing record and has twice been named most
valuable player in the National Football League. He has
the highest career total of completed passes and touchdown passes in professional football.

United Arab Emirates (formerly Trucial States) **M** 301
United Arab Republic see Egypt (The Arab Republic of
    Egypt)

United Automobile Workers (UAW) (International Union,
United Automobile, Aerospace, and Agricultural Imple-
ment Workers of America), labor union of workers
employed in production of motor vehicles and aircraft
and in aerospace and metal industries. Formed (1935)
under charter of American Federation of Labor (AFL), it
later withdrew from AFL and joined Congress of Industrial Organization (CIO) (1936). The union won its first
major strike victory in 1937. It operated under the
merger of AFL and CIO (1955), but became disaffiliated
(1968), for having joined the Alliance for Labor Action.
  U.S. labor organizations **L** 6–7

United Church of Canada see Canada, United Church of
United Church of Christ **P** 484
United Empire Loyalists, term used for Loyalists who
    settled in Canada **N** 138c, 138g; **O** 128
  Canada during the Revolutionary War **C** 71
United Fruit Company **H** 196
United Fund see Community chest
United Kingdom of Great Britain and Northern Ireland
    U 65–79
  Commonweath of Nations **C** 428
  courts, of law **C** 529
  dependencies, list **U** 78
  East India Company, trade empire of **E** 43
  Elizabeth II **E** 179
  England, geography of **E** 212–14
  England, history of **E** 214–32
  English art and architecture **E** 233–42
  English literature **E** 245–68
  English music **E** 268–71
  flag **F** 243; picture **F** 240
  Gibraltar, a crown colony **G** 205
  government, British system of **G** 277
  government, municipal, British system of **M** 508
  holidays **H** 148–49, 152, 159
  Honduras, British **H** 199–200
  Hong Kong **H** 203–05
  immigration **I** 103
  Jewish establishment in Palestine **J** 112–13
  London **L** 333–40
  Middle East interests **M** 301

United Kingdom (continued)
  national anthem and patriotic song **N** 16–17, 27
  old-age benefits **O** 98
  parliament **P** 81–82
  police and police system **P** 372–73, 374
  political parties, English **P** 378–79
  prime minister **P** 456
  rulers of England, Great Britain, and United Kingdom, chart **U** 77
  Scotland **S** 86–89
  typical English meals **F** 339; picture **F** 336
  Wales **W** 3–4
  World War I **W** 272–81
  World War II **W** 289–90, 299–300, 303
  See also Commonwealth of Nations; England; England, history of; Ireland; Ireland, Northern; Scotland; Wales
United Mine Workers of America, labor union **C** 367; **L** 7
  Lewis, John L. **L** 161
United Nations **U** 80–88
  agencies aiding the blind **B** 254
  Bunche, Ralph **B** 452
  Canadian troops in Emergency Force **C** 82
  Cartographic Office **M** 88
  Commonwealth of Nations **C** 428
  Dag Hammarskjöld Library, picture **L** 178
  dates of admission of member countries *see* chart of countries in continent articles
  Declaration of Human Rights **G** 278
  European headquarters, the Palace of Nations, on Lake Geneva, picture **L** 97
  family planning activities **F** 343
  flag **F** 226
  food additives, control of **F** 352
  foreign-aid programs **F** 368
  Forestry Division **F** 374
  genocide outlawed **C** 316
  Hammarskjöld, Dag **H** 21
  Indonesia's withdrawal **I** 222
  international law **I** 321
  International Organization of Consumers Unions, as consultant to UN agencies **C** 494a
  Korean War **K** 303–04
  League of Nations preceded **L** 97
  Lie, Trygve, first secretary-general **L** 205
  newly independent nations and human rights **C** 315
  partition of Palestine and admission of Israel **J** 113
  peace movements **P** 104, 105
  Pearson awarded Nobel prize for creation of UN Emergency Force **P** 115
  poverty, efforts to combat **P** 424a, 424b
  regional peace organizations **I** 322
  similarities with government under Articles of Confederation **U** 135
  slavery, actions on **S** 199–200
  Stevenson, Adlai E., United States ambassador **S** 423
  Suez Canal, intervention, 1956 **N** 15
  Swedish troops in cause of world peace **S** 487
  Thant, U **T** 154
  treaties, problems of maintaining **T** 273
  United States hopes for collective security **U** 138–39
  Universal Declaration of Human Rights **B** 180; **C** 314–15; **U** 84, 88
United Nations Charter, preamble **U** 82
United Nations Commission on Human Rights
  permanent commission to outlaw slavery **S** 200
  Eleanor Roosevelt, chairman **F** 178; **R** 318
United Nations Conference on International Organization, 1945 **U** 80
United Nations Day **H** 154
United Nations Educational, Scientific and Cultural Organization (UNESCO) **U** 85

  teacher-training centers **T** 43
  earthquake studies **E** 36
United Nations Industrial Development Organization **A** 520; **U** 81
United Nations International Children's Emergency Fund (UNICEF) **U** 88
  child care for orphans **O** 227
  Halloween trick or treat collections for **H** 17
  milk supplied to children, picture **U** 87
United Nations Relief and Works Agency for Palestine Refugees (UNRWA) **J** 136
United Nations War Crimes Commission **W** 9
United Press, news service **N** 200–01
United Press International, news service **N** 201
United Provinces of Central America **C** 171

United Service Organizations (USO), federation of six welfare organizations providing facilities for the social and spiritual needs of U.S. Armed Forces servicemen. Founded in 1941, USO has headquarters in New York.

United Society of Believers in Christ's Second Appearing *see* Shakers
United States **U** 89–114
  American agriculture **A** 88–92, 93–95, 100; **U** 104–05, 108
  American family, picture **F** 39
  American Jewish community **J** 113
  architecture *see* United States, architecture of the
  art *see* United States, art of the
  automobiles per capita **A** 551
  Canada, military co-operation with **C** 82
  census, how taken **P** 397
  cities *see* principal cities by name
  civil and human rights conflicts **C** 316
  climate types **W** 89–90
  consumer protection agencies **C** 494a
  education, cost of and growth rate **E** 79–80
  education, history of **E** 69–80
  flag and flag code **F** 229, 231, 234, 241
  food habits **F** 342
  geographical center, Kansas **K** 176
  government *see* United States, government of the
  Great Seal of the United States **G** 329–30
  history *see* United States, history of the
  holidays **H** 147–59
  interstate commerce **I** 331–32
  music *see* United States, music of the
  national anthems and patriotic songs **N** 15–16, 22–26
  national cemeteries **N** 28–31
  national emblem, the bald eagle **E** 2
  national forests and grasslands, map **N** 32
  National Park System **N** 44–55
  naturalization **N** 58
  police organization **P** 375–77
  Postal service **P** 408–10
  poverty **P** 424a–424b
  public lands **P** 506–07
  road and traffic signs, pictures **D** 320
  segregation and civil rights movement **S** 115
  standard of living **P** 424a; **U** 100–01
  theater **T** 161
  universities and colleges **U** 208–24
  Washington, D.C., capital **W** 30–35
  women, role of **W** 212–213
  See also names of states, territories, and principal cities
United States, American frigate **S** 159
United States, architecture of the **U** 122–25; picture **A** 438g
  colonial and modern **A** 383–85; **C** 388–89
  Jefferson, Thomas, aids classic revival **J** 66

United States, art of the U 115–22
  interest in all forms of art U 103
  modern art M 395, 397; pictures A 438d, 438e
  painting P 30, 31–32
United States, government of the U 139–42
  Articles of Confederation, first government U 134–35
  Bill of Rights B 177–80
  Cabinet of the United States P 447–48
  citizenship C 312–13
  civil service C 317
  elections E 112–15
  Electoral College E 116
  Federal Bureau of Investigation F 76–77
  Federal Reserve System, government banks B 50
  flags F 230
  Foreign Service F 369–70
  freedom of the press C 316
  Interstate Commerce Commission I 332
  naturalization N 58
  political parties P 379–82
  presidency P 447–55
  separation of powers G 277
  state governments S 412–15
  Supreme Court S 476–77
  United States Congress U 142–45
  United States Constitution U 145–58
  vice-presidency of the United States V 325–32
  woman suffrage W 212b–213; picture W 212
  See also departments by name
United States, history of the U 128–39
  American colonies A 180–94
  Civil War, United States C 318–28
  Confederate States C 458–60
  colonial life in America C 385–99
  Cuba C 550, 551
  Declaration of Independence D 59–65
  Emancipation Proclamation E 185–86
  Federalist, The F 78
  Founding fathers of the United States F 393–96
  in American literature A 202, 214
  Korean War K 303–04
  Louisiana Purchase L 364–65
  Mexican War M 238–39
  Monroe Doctrine M 425, 426–27
  National Guard N 42–43
  Negro history in the United States N 91–105
  Northwest Ordinance, or Ordinance of 1787 W 143
  overland trails O 251–67
  pioneer life P 251–62
  political parties P 379–82
  Reconstruction Period R 117–20
  Revolutionary War R 194–209
  slavery issue develops S 197–98
  Spanish-American War S 374–76
  Supreme Court S 476–77
  territorial expansion of the United States T 105–15
  United States Constitution U 145–58
  U.S.S.R. relations U 51
  War of 1812 W 10–12
  westward movement W 142–46
  World War I W 279–81
  World War II W 292–308
  See also names of presidents; state articles
United States, literature of the see American literature
United States, music of the U 125–27, 103
  folk music F 327–28
  jazz J 57–62
  musical comedy M 542–43
  opera O 138–39
  operetta O 157
  See also names of composers and musicians
United States, S.S., ocean liner O 17

United States Air Force U 159–66
  Arctic flights P 365
  "Army Air Corps Song" N 26
  flag F 230
  Joint chiefs of Staff U 173
  medals and decorations M 199–200
  UFO's, investigation of F 285, 287
  uniform, picture C 355
  YF-12A fighter plane, picture S 473
  See also Civil Air Patrol (CAP)
United States Air Force Academy U 166; pictures
    C 412; U 159
United States Armed Forces
  burial in national cemeteries N 28
  draft or conscription with classifications D 289–90
  military powers of the president P 455
  military training camps in Panama Canal Zone P 47
  National Guard N 42–43
  segregation ended in N 100–01
  uniforms, pictures C 355
  What are the Special Forces? U 173
  Who are the Joint Chiefs of Staff? U 173
  See also United States Air Force; United States Army;
    United States Coast Guard; United States Marine
    Corps; United States Navy
United States Arms Control and Disarmament Agency
  D 186
United States Army U 166–75
  automatic weapons G 423
  "Caisson Song" N 25–26
  Engineers Corps promotes interstate commerce
    I 332
  flag F 230
  Grant, Ulysses S., first full general after Washington
    G 295
  medals and decorations M 199–200
  Pershing, John J. P 157
  uniform, picture C 355
  What are the Special Forces? U 173
  "What Do You Do in the Infantry," song N 26
  Who are the Joint Chiefs of Staff? U 173
United States Army Reserve U 175
United States Bureau of the Census P 396
  automation used for data A 532
  formula for number of representatives in Congress
    U 142–43
United States Bureau of Mines E 392
United States Catholic Conference see National Catholic
    Welfare Conference
United States Chess Federation (USCF) C 222
United States Civil Service
  beginnings under Arthur's administration A 441
  civil service C 317
United States Coast and Geodetic Survey
  Division of Seismology E 34
United States Coast Guard U 175–76
  flag F 230
  ice patrol, picture I 27
  lighthouses L 278
  Marine Inspection Office pamphlets on piloting rules
    B 262
  medals and decorations M 199–200
United States Coast Guard Academy, New London, Conn.
  U 176

United States Coast Guard Women's Reserve (SPARS),
organization created (1942) to release Coast Guardsmen
for combat duty. SPAR comes from the first letters of
the Latin Coast Guard motto and its English translation:
Semper Paratus—Always Ready.

United States Congress U 142–45; picture G 273

individual committees, including Alpine Certified Officials, Cross Country, Hall of Fame, and Intercollegiate Skiing. It was founded in 1904, has its headquarters in Denver, Colo., and publishes *United States Ski News.*

United States Steel Foundation, Inc., philanthropic organization that supports nationwide charitable, educational, and scientific programs. Its activities include contributions to social welfare and distribution of research and study grants. Founded in 1953, the organization has its headquarters in New York, N.Y.

United States Supreme Court *see* Supreme Court of the United States

United States Table Tennis Association (USTTA), organization that authorizes table tennis tournaments, establishes and changes game rules, and sends U.S. players to biennial world championships. Founded in 1933, the organization has its headquarters in Detroit, Mich., and distributes instructional pamphlets and films.

United States Volleyball Association (USVBA), organization that authorizes volleyball tournaments, develops game rules, and certifies officials. The organization was founded in 1928, has its headquarters in Encino, Calif., and publishes *Official Guide and Rule Book.*

United States Water Quality Improvement Act, 1970 **W** 59

United Steelworkers of America (USA), industrial union. Founded in 1936, it has headquarters in Pittsburgh, Pa., and publishes *Steel Labor.*

Universalists, Christian religious group that preaches universal salvation and existence of one God, as opposed to Trinity. They have no official doctrine or Bible interpretation, believing rather in individual approach to religion. The movement began in England in middle 1700's, and by late 1700's Universalist Church of America was founded. Its most important early leader was Hosea Ballou, who wrote on Universalist philosophy: *Treatise of the Atonement* (1805). It was consolidated with American Unitarian Association (1961) and is now the Unitarian Universalist Association.

Untermeyer (UN-ter-my-er), **Louis** (1885–   ), American anthologist and author, b. New York, N.Y. He compiled numerous poetry anthologies, including *Modern American Poetry, The Book of Living Verse,* and *This Singing World* (for children). He is author of many works and translator of works by Heine and Horace. He was poetry editor of *The American Mercury* (1934–37) and English-poetry consultant for Library of Congress (1961–63).

Unwin, Nora Spicer (1907–), American author and illustrator of books for children, b. Surrey, England. Her engravings have been exhibited internationally. She illustrated several works by Elizabeth Yates as well as her own books, which include *Poquito: the Little Mexican Duck, Doughnuts for Lin,* and *Proud Pumpkin.*

Upper Volta   U 228–29; pictures   A 54, 59
  flag   F 236
Uppsala (UPP-sa-la), **University of**   S 482
Upshur, Abel P., American statesman   T 341
Ur, ancient city of Mesopotamia
  ruins and ziggurat, now points of interest in Iraq
    I 382
  Sumerian art, picture   A 233
  ziggurat, picture   A 350
Ural-Altaic (U-ral-al-TAY-ic) **languages**   L 40
  language groups of Asia   A 460
Ural Mountains, Union of Soviet Socialist Republics
    E 309
Ural River, Union of Soviet Socialist Republics   R 248

Urania (u-RAY-ni-a), goddess in Greek mythology. She and
her eight sisters, the daughters of Zeus and Mnemosyne,
were the muses, or patrons of the arts and sciences.
Urania was the muse of astronomy.
  See also Muses

Uranium (u-RAY-ni-um)   U 230–31
  atomic structure   A 488
  Australian mine, picture   A 509
  Canada, world's largest reserves   C 56, 58;   O 121
  Curie, Marie and Pierre, research of   C 553
  elements, some facts about   E 155, 165
  energy, new sources of   E 203
  Geiger counter   G 67–68
  metals, chart of ores, location, properties, uses   M 227
  mine in Saskatchewan, picture   S 38b
  New Mexico deposits   N 185, 187
  nuclear energy, use of, and society, pictures   S 81
  nuclear energy from uranium fission   N 360–64
  radioactive dating   R 64
  radioactive elements   R 67
  Utah, production in   U 247

Uranus (U-ran-us) (from Greek word meaning "heaven"),
in Greek mythology, god of the sky; son and husband of
Gaea (earth); and father of Titans, Cyclopes, and
Hecatoncheires. Fearing his children's rebellion, he imprisoned them, angering Gaea. She aroused Cronus, a
Titan, to overthrow him. At Uranus' death, the Giants
and Erinyes arose from his blood that fell on the earth,
while the goddess Aphrodite arose from the foam produced when his blood hit the sea. Uranus is the name of
the seventh planet in our solar system.

Uranus, planet   P 277; picture   P 278
  Herschel discovered   A 475
Urban, Sylvanus see Cave, Edward
Urban II, pope
  preached First Crusade   C 538
Urban IV, pope   C 284
Urban geography   G 108
Urbanization (ur-ban-i-ZAY-tion), growth of cities
  re-apportionment of state legislatures   S 415
  shift of population from rural to city life   P 397
Urban League, National   N 96, 98
Urban planning   U 232–34
  air pollution   A 111;   E 272g
  Canberra, Australia   C 88
  city planners, engineers   E 205
  city problems   C 308–10
  environment, problems of   E 272a–272h
  housing developments   H 183–84
  local government, problems of   M 508
  Metro, union of Toronto and suburbs   T 227
  New Delhi   D 101
  parks and playgrounds   P 76–78
  re-apportionment of state legislatures   S 415

  shift of population from rural to city life   P 397
  traffic control   T 247–48
  See also Federal cities
Urban Renewal Administration   U 234
Urban renewal programs
  Constitution Plaza, Hartford, Conn., pictures   C 481,
    U 233
  government housing projects   H 183
Urdu, official language of Pakistan   I 119
  Indian literature   O 220e
Urea (u-RE-a), organic substance
  Wöhler's biochemical discoveries   B 182;   C 214
Urethra, canal by which urine leaves the body, diagram
    B 278
Urial (OO-ri-al), a kind of wild sheep   S 145
Urinalysis (u-rin-AL-i-sis)   M 201, 209
Urinary (U-rin-ary) **system**
  waste disposal of human body   B 278–79
Urine (U-rin), excretion of the kidneys   B 278–79;   D 326
  spacecraft waste disposal   S 341
  urinalysis, an essential part of a medical examination
    M 209

Uris, Leon Marcus (1924–   ), American novelist, b.
Baltimore, Md. He is noted for novels about modern
Israel and the Jewish people, including *Mila 18,
Armageddon,* and *Exodus.* He also wrote *Battle Cry,*
about Marines in World War II, and various screenplays.

Ursa Major (Great Bear), polar constellation   C 491
Ursa Minor (Little Bear), polar constellation   C 491

Ursuline (UR-su-lin), first authorized Roman Catholic
teaching order for women. It was founded in 1535 by
Saint Angela Merici at Brescia, Italy, for the education of
young women. The order established convents, especially
in France, Canada, and United States.

Uruguay (U-ru-guay)   U 235–39
  flag   F 242
  life in Latin America   L 47–61
  national anthem   N 22
Uruguay River, South America   R 248;   U 237
Urville, Jules Sébastian César Dumont d' see Dumont
    d'Urville, J.S.C.
Urzig, Germany, picture   G 153
Usage (U-sage), in grammar   G 290
  linguistics not a study of the "correct" forms of
    speech   L 302
USIA see United States Information Agency
Usman dan Fodio, Fulani religious leader   N 256
USO see United Service Organization
U.S.S.R. see Union of Soviet Socialist Republics

Ustinov, Peter Alexander (1921–   ), British actor, playwright, and producer, b. London. He is noted for
performances in motion pictures *Quo Vadis, Hot Millions,*
and *Viva Max* and was awarded the Academy Award as
best supporting actor for both *Spartacus* and *Topkapi.* He
produced, directed, and starred in *Billy Budd.* His plays
include *House of Regrets* and *Photo Finish.*

Utah (U-tah)   U 240–55
  Compromise of 1850   C 448
  Mormons   M 457
  Rainbow Bridge National Monument, picture   N 54
  rock formation, erosion, picture   E 12
  Salt Lake City   S 22
  San Juan River, picture   R 238
  Young, Brigham   Y 353
  Zion National Park, picture   N 53
Utah, University of   U 248

Utah Beach, Normandy invasion landing, World War II
   W 299–300
Utah juniper, tree, picture **T** 275
Utamaro (oo-TA-ma-ro), **Kitagawa,** Japanese artist **O** 218
   Two Women, picture **O** 218
Ute, Indians of North America
   Colorado **C** 407, 415
Ute Black Hawk War, 1865–68 **U** 255
Uterus, female organ **B** 2
U Thant see Thant, U
Uther (U-ther), king of Britain **A** 443
Utility gliders **G** 240
Utopia (u-TO-pia), by Sir Thomas More **E** 250; **M** 456
Utopias, imaginary perfect societies **U** 255–56
   American literature **A** 206
   More's *Utopia* **M** 456
   New Harmony, Indiana **I** 143
   Utopian socialism **S** 220

Utrecht (u-treckt), the Netherlands **N** 118
Utrecht, Treaty of, 1713 **E** 224; **F** 459
   French losses in Canada **C** 70
Utrecht school, Dutch group of painters **D** 357
Utrillo (oot-REEL-yo), **Maurice,** French artist
   U 256
Uvedale, Nicholas see Udall, Nicholas

Uzbek (ooz-BEK), or **Uzbeg,** ethnic and linguistic group of Turkic people in parts of Soviet Union, China, and Afghanistan. They engage primarily in agricultural pursuits. Descended from a mixture of Turks, Mongols, and Iranians, they were converted to Islam in 14th century.
   Soviet Central Asia **U** 46

Uzbek Soviet Socialist Republic (Uzbekistan) **U** 46
   languages of Soviet Union **U** 28

V, 22nd letter of the English alphabet **V** 257
   See also Alphabet
V-2, or Vengeance Weapon II, German rocket **M** 343
Vaca, Alvar Núñez Cabeza de see Cabeza de Vaca
Vacations **V** 258–59
   camping **C** 40–46
   camping, organized **C** 47
   hostels and hosteling **H** 253–56
   hotels and motels **H** 256–59
   ocean liners **O** 17–24
Vaccination (vac-cin-NAY-tion) **and inoculation**
      (in-oc-u-LAY-tion) **V** 260–61
   antibodies and antigens **A** 317
   disease, prevention of **D** 219–22
   Jenner, Edward **J** 76
   medical techniques of **M** 209–10
   medicine, history of **M** 207, 208
   Pasteur, Louis **P** 96–97
   rabies **I** 287
   "shots" for dogs **D** 257
   smallpox **D** 207, 214
Vaccines (vac-CENES) **V** 260–61
   active immunity **I** 105; **M** 209, 210
   animal sources of drugs **D** 323
   first vaccine **D** 214
   origin of word **A** 317
   polio, oral program, picture **D** 205
   polio vaccine **S** 2, 18
   prevention of virus diseases, study of **V** 370–70a
   Sabin, Albert B. **S** 2
   Salk, Jonas E. **S** 18
   toxoid **D** 206
   See also Vaccination and inoculation
Vaclav I (VOTS-lof), **Saint,** ruler of Bohemia **C** 563
Vacuoles (VAC-u-oles), holes or bubbles in cells **M** 276
   plant cells **C** 163
Vacuum (VAC-u-um), space containing very little matter
      V 262–65
   matter displaced **M** 171
   sound carried by a medium **S** 257
   space, survival in **S** 340j–340L, 343
Vacuum bottles **V** 265
Vacuum cleaners **E** 119
Vacuum distillation **D** 225
Vacuum melting, for producing alloy steels **I** 399
Vacuum tubes see Electron tubes
Vaduz (fa-DOOTS), capital of Liechtenstein **L** 206, 207
Vagabond King, The, operetta by Rudolf Friml **O** 158

Vail, Alfred (1807–1859), American telegraph pioneer, b.
Morristown, N.J. He helped finance Samuel Morse in final
development of telegraph (1837–38) and solved many
mechanical problems. He also helped Morse demonstrate
and promote the invention, but withdrew about 1848.
   Morse and Vail **T** 51

Vaiont Dam, Italy **D** 21
Vaishyas (va-ISH-yas), a caste in Hindu society **H** 130
Valadon (va-la-DON), **Suzanne,** French artist **U** 256
Valdivia, Pedro de, Spanish soldier **C** 253, 254

Valedictorian (val-e-dic-TOR-ian) (from Latin *valedicere,*
meaning "to say farewell"), highest-ranking student in a
graduating class. The valedictorian gives the valedictory,
or farewell, speech at commencement exercises.

Valence (VALE-ence), in chemistry **C** 199–200, 214, 220
   periodic table **C** 201–02
Valencia, Spain **S** 357
Valencia orange **O** 177; picture **O** 176
Valenciennes (va-lance-YENN), France
   lace, picture **L** 19

Valenti, Jack Joseph (1921–), American government
official and businessman, b. Houston, Tex. He headed
advertising and public relations firms, took part in
Texas politics, and served as a presidential aide (1963–
66) to Lyndon B. Johnson. In April, 1966, he was elected
president of the Motion Picture Association of America.

Valentines **V** 266–68
   early greeting cards **G** 373
   Valentine's Day **H** 154
Valentine's Day **V** 266
   festivals and frolics **H** 154

Valentino (val-en-TI-no), **Rudolph** (Rodolpho d'Antongu-
olla), (1895–1926), American film star, b. Castellaneta,
Italy. He went to United States (1913), where he performed as dancer. His first important film role was in
The Four Horsemen of the Apocalypse. He portrayed a
romantic lover in such films as *Blood and Sand* and
The Sheik. Picture **M** 474.
   motion pictures, history of **M** 473

Vale of Kashmir **K** 197, 198
Valera (va-LAY-ra), **Juan,** Spanish writer **S** 370
Valéry, Paul, French poet **F** 441
Valhalla (val-HAL-la), feast hall of Norse gods **N** 278
Valjean (vol-JON), **Jean,** hero of *Les Misérables*
      H 275–77
Valkyries (val-KIR-ies), **The,** opera by Wagner **O** 152
Valkyries, warrior maidens in Norse mythology **N** 278
Vallambrosa, Antoine de, Marquis de Mores, Frenchman,
   early resident of North Dakota **N** 335

Vallee, Rudy (Herbert Prior Vallée) (1901–), American
entertainer, b. Island Pond, Vt. He organized a band, the
Connecticut Yankees (1928). "My Time is Your Time"
became his theme song on Fleischmann Hour radio show
(1929–39). A movie idol of the 1930's and 1940's, he also
appeared on the Broadway stage in *How to Succeed in
Business Without Really Trying* (1961).

Valle-Inclán (VOL-lay-een-CLON), **Ramón del,** Spanish
   writer **S** 371
Vallejo (vol-YAY-ho), **Antonio Buero,** Spanish writer
      S 372

Vallejo (va-YEH-o), **Mariano Guadalupe** (1808–1890),
American soldier and pioneer, b. Monterey, Calif. He
supported California rebellion against Mexican rule (1832)
and aided his nephew Juan Alvarado, who headed the
California revolt (1836). He helped gain California's
admission to United States, and he became a senator
in California's first legislature.

Valletta (val-LET-ta), capital of Malta, picture **M** 60
Valley Forge, Pennsylvania
   Valley Forge State Park **P** 140; picture **P** 139
   Washington's winter camp **R** 203
Valley glaciers see Alpine glaciers
Valley quail, bird
   California state bird, picture **C** 14

Vallisneria (val-lis-NER-ia) (also called tape grass or eat-
grass), freshwater plant with ribbonlike leaves. Female
flowers of the plant grow on long, coiling stalks that
reach the water's surface, and male flowers grow on
short stalks that remain submerged. Vallisneria often are
used in aquariums.

Valmy, battle of, 1792 **B** 102
Valparaíso (val-pa-RISE-o), Chile **C** 253
Value, of color in art **D** 143

Value added by manufacture G 97
Valves, devices to regulate flow of liquids or gases
   V 269–70
   air brakes R 88
   ballooning B 30–31
   pumps, pictures P 529
Valves, of the heart H 86, 86b
   heart disease D 197, 198
Vamba see Bertelli, Luigi
Vamp, of a shoe, diagram S 162

Vampire, in legends, a corpse that cannot rest in its grave and spends the night searching for a victim in order to drink its blood. Anyone bitten by a vampire is supposed to become a vampire at death. Vampires appear most often in the mythologies of Slavic countries.

Vampires, tropical bats B 94; picture B 95
   teeth of mammals M 66
Vamps, acting roles in motion pictures M 473
Vanadium (va-NAY-di-um), element E 155, 165
   alloys A 168
   metals, ores, location, properties, uses M 227
   vanadium-producing regions of North America N 294
Van Allen, James A., American scientist R 46
   earth's magnetic field traps radiation E 27
   International Geophysical Year I 310–11
Van Allen belts, of radiation S 342
   discovery of R 46

Vanbrugh (VAN-bru), **Sir John** (1664–1726), English dramatist and architect, b. London. After being imprisoned (1690–92) in France under suspicion of being an English spy, he returned to England and wrote for stage. His plays, characterized by lively, farcical humor, include *The Relapse* and *The Provok'd Wife.* He was commissioned as architect for Blenheim Palace, Castle Howard, and The Queen's Theatre.

Van Buren, Martin, 8th president of United States
   V 271–75
   as Vice-president, picture V 326
Van Buren, Sarah Angelica Singleton, acting first lady in
   Van Buren's administration F 169; picture F 168
Vance, Zebulon B., American statesman N 319
Vancouver (van-COO-ver), British Columbia, Canada
   V 276; pictures B 403, C 65, V 276
   major cities of Canada B 406b, C 64
Vancouver, George, English navigator V 277
   British Columbia B 405
   Washington W 28
Vancouver Foundation F 392
Vancouver Island, British Columbia, Canada B 402;
   C 55
Vandalia (van-DAY-lia), former capital of Illinois I 71

Vandals, ancient Germanic tribe that migrated through Gaul, Spain, and North Africa in early 5th century. They gained strength under leadership of King Gaiseric and by middle of 5th century A.D. controlled Carthage and Mediterranean islands. Vandals sacked Rome (455), causing great destruction (thus the term "vandalism"). They vanished as nation with capture of Carthage by Romans (533).
   Christianity accepted C 283

Van de Graaff (van 'dGRAF) **generator,** picture N 367
Vandenberg, Arthur Hendrick, United States senator
   M 272
Vandenberg Air Force Base, California C 22

Vanderbilt, Cornelius ("Commodore" Vanderbilt) (1794–1877), American financier and railroad magnate, b. Staten Island, N.Y. He was engaged in trade on Long Island Sound and Hudson River with his own steamboats (1829–59), and he opened a shipping line between New York and San Francisco via Nicaragua (1850) after discovery of gold in California. He acquired control of Hudson River and New York Central Railroad by 1867, and unsuccessfully attempted to gain control of Erie Railroad. He expanded New York Central Railroad through questionable manipulation and amassed a fortune valued at $100,000,000 at his death.

Vandegrift (VAN-de-grift), **Alexander Archer** (1887–   ), American Marine Corps officer, b. Charlottesville, Va. Commissioned into the Marine Corps in 1909, he served in Nicaragua, Mexico, Haiti, and China. He commanded the Marines in the World War II landing and operations on Guadalcanal (1942) and Bougainville (1943). In 1945 he became the first marine to attain the rank of general. He retired 4 years later.

Van Diemen's (van DE-men's) **Land,** former name of
   Tasmania, Australia A 516

Van Doren, Carl Clinton (1885–1950), American editor and historian, b. Hope, Ill. He taught English at Columbia University (1911–30). Literary editor of *The Nation* (1919–22), *Century Magazine* (1922–25), and Literary Guild (1926–34), he was awarded Pulitzer prize (1939) for biography *Benjamin Franklin.* His other books include *Many Minds, The Ninth Wave, Secret History of the American Revolution.*
   American literature A 215

Van Doren, Mark Albert (1894–1972), American poet, critic, and editor, b. Hope, Ill. Brother of editor Carl Van Doren, he was a faculty member of English department at Columbia University (1920–59). Literary editor (1924–28) and motion picture critic of *The Nation* (1935–38), he was awarded Pulitzer prize (1940) for *Collected Poems.* Other works of his include the critical studies *Henry David Thoreau* and *The Poetry of John Dryden* and the novels *The Transients* and *Windless Cabins.*

Van Druten, John William (1901–1957), English dramatist, b. London. He became an American citizen in 1944. His plays include *The Voice of the Turtle, I Remember Mama, Bell, Book and Candle,* and *I Am a Camera.*

Van Dyck, Anthony, Flemish painter V 277
   baroque art B 60
   English art, outstanding figure in E 237
   etchings G 305
   Flemish artist and pupil of Rubens D 352, 357
   Portrait of Charles I Hunting, painting D 359
   Saint Martin Dividing His Robe, painting F 295
Van Eyck (van-IKE), **Jan and Hubert,** Flemish painters
   D 349–51; P 18, 20
   Madonna with the Chancellor Rolin, painting D 350
   Renaissance art R 162, 171
Van Gogh (van GOH), **Vincent,** Dutch painter V 278
   Dutch and Flemish art D 362
   Field of Yellow Corn, painting P 28
   modern art M 388
   reaction against realism of the impressionists P 29
   Starry Night, The, painting V 278
   Sunflowers, painting M 389
   Vincent's Room at Arles, painting D 362
Van Hoevenberg, Mount, bobrun near Lake Placid
   B 265–66
Van Horne, William Cornelius, builder of Canadian
   Pacific Railway C 74

Van Houten (HOW-ten), C. J., Dutch pioneer in chocolate manufacture C 274
Vanier, Georges Philias, Canadian statesman Q 14

Vanilla, tropical plant of the orchid family, grown chiefly for its seedpod, which yields a flavoring extract. It is native to Mexico but is cultivated in the East Indies and the West Indies. Vanilla flavoring is used in ice cream, baked goods, and other confections. The plant was introduced into Europe by the Spanish explorer Hernando Cortes, who was served a beverage of chocolate and vanilla at the Aztec court in Mexico.

Vanishing point, in perspective P 158
Vanity Fair, novel by Thackeray N 346; excerpt
    T 145–46
Vanity presses, publishing P 514
Van Loon, Hendrik Willem, American historian A 214

Vann, Robert Lee (1879?–1940), American editor and publisher, Negro, b. Ahoskie, N.C. He was editor of the Pittsburgh *Courier* (1912–40), which had a wide circulation among Negroes. He also practiced law until 1936, when he decided to give all his time to the paper.

Van Paassen (van PA-sen), Pierre (Pieter Antonie Laurusse Van Paassen) (1895–1968), American journalist and clergyman, b. Gorcum, the Netherlands. As foreign correspondent and columnist for the New York *Evening World* and North American Newspaper Alliance (1924–31) and for the Toronto *Star* (1932–35), he covered political affairs in Europe, the Middle East, North Africa, and Russia. A Unitarian minister (from 1946), he was ardent advocate of Zionism and democracy. Among his works are *Days of Our Years, Earth Could be Fair,* and *Jerusalem Calling.*

Van Rensselaer (van REN-sel-er), Kiliaen (1595–1644), Dutch diamond and pearl merchant, b. Amsterdam. He was a founder of Dutch West India Company (chartered 1621). By proxy, he bought land from American Indians. The land constituted a patroonship, today comprising counties of Albany, Columbia, and Rensselaer, N.Y.

Van Rensselaer, Stephen (1764–1839), American soldier and politician, b. New York, N.Y. A descendant of Kiliaen Van Rensselaer, he was lieutenant governor of New York (1795–1801). As member of first and second canal commissions and president of second commission (1825–39), he promoted construction of Erie Canal. He was a congressman (1822–29) and the founder of Rensselaer Polytechnic Institute (1824).

Van't Hoff (vont HOFF), Jacobus H., Dutch chemist
    C 214
Vanua Levu (va-NU-a LEV-u), one of the Fiji Islands
    F 122

Van Vechten (van VECK-ten), Carl (1880–1965), American author, b. Cedar Rapids, Iowa. He was a music critic for the New York *Times* (1906–13) and also wrote novels —including *The Tattooed Countess*—and became an expert photographer. Long interested in Negro art and literature, he gave a large collection by and about Negroes to Yale University.

Vapor, gas formed from a substance that is usually a liquid or a solid
    drug abuse by inhaling vapors D 331
    evaporation H 93
    water vapor in clouds C 358–59
Vapor lamps, mercury L 287

Varangians (va-RAN-gi-ans), Vikings who settled in Russia V 339
    early Scandinavians in what is now Union of Soviet Socialist Republics U 47
Vardhamana see Mahavira

Vardon, Harry (1870–1937), English golfer, b. Jersey. He was six-time winner of British Open (between 1896 and 1914) and winner of American (1900) and German (1911) Open championships. He is credited with introducing the overlapping grip. The Vardon trophy, named for him, is awarded annually to top American and British golfers.

Vare, Glenna Collett, American golfer, picture G 261
Vargas, Getúlio, president of Brazil B 384
Vargas, Manuela, Spanish flamenco dancer, picture
    S 373
Variable image reflector, or imagemaker, a criminal identification tool P 376
Variables, in mathematics M 156
Variable stars S 408
    earth's sun contrasted with E 22
    research at observatories O 13
Variation, in biology see Mutation theory, in biology
Variety stores R 188
Varifocal (VARE-i-fO-cal) objectives, lenses L 145
Varnishes V 279–80
    resins used in R 184
    turpentine as a thinner T 330
Varro, Marcus Terentius, Roman scholar, encyclopedist
    E 193
Varves, glacial sediment I 22
Varying hares R 23–24

Vasari (va-ZA-ri), Giorgio (1511–1574), Italian architect, painter, and writer, b. Arezzo. He was one of the first art historians, and his *Lives of the Most Excellent Italian Architects, Painters, and Sculptors* is a valuable source book on Italian Renaissance artists.
    designed the Uffizi Palace U 3

Vasco da Gama see Gama, Vasco da
Vascular bundles, of plant tissues P 293
Vases, pictures G 227, 233
    ancient amphoras recovered by scuba divers, pictures
        A 364, U 14
    ancient Greek vases G 343; P 16–17; pictures
        A 228, 230, G 342
    Greece, ancient decorative arts D 69
    how to make for flower arranging J 50, 53
    Nazca Indian, picture I 154
    porcelain, pictures P 415, 416
Vásquez (VA-scase), Horacio, president of Dominican Republic D 283
Vasquez de Coronado Francisco see Coronado, Francisco, Vasquez de
Vassa, Gustavus, American seafarer N 93
Vassals, holders of fiefs under a feudal king F 100
    land management and allotment R 112

Vassar, Matthew (1792–1868), American philanthropist and brewer, b. Norfolk, England. Vassar ran a brewery in Poughkeepsie, N.Y. He also founded a women's college (1861), later called Vassar College, which helped advance the idea of higher education for women.

Vasteras, Sweden S 485
Vat dyes D 371
Vatican City, sovereign state ruled by the Pope V 280–82
    flag F 240
    Italian art and architecture I 469
    Roman Catholic Church, history of R 296

Vatican Council II R 298–99
Vatican Library, Rome L 197; picture L 177
Vau, Calvert, American landscape architect P 77
Vauban (vo-BON), Sebastien de, French engineer and
    soldier F 377
Vaudeville (VAUD-e-ville), entertainment consisting of a
    variety of acts
    compared with musical comedy M 542
    ventriloquism V 301
Vaughan Williams, Ralph, English composer E 271
    choral music C 279
Vaults, in architecture A 376, 378, 379
    Gothic ribbed A 378; G 265
    Middle Ages, architecture of the M 296
Vaults, in banks, picture B 50
Vauquelin (vo-kul-AN), Louis, French chemist, discovered
    chromium C 296
Veal, meat of calves M 192
    raising cattle for market C 149
    cuts of veal, picture M 194
Vecelli, Tiziano see Titian
Vectors, disease carriers V 282–85
    conquest of disease aided by discovery of D 215
    insecticides I 258
    typhoid fever D 212
Vectors, in mathematics M 159–60
Vedas (VAY-das), source books of Hinduism H 130, 132
    Indian literature O 220d–220e
    literatures of Asia A 461
    religions of Asia A 461
Vega, Garcilaso de la see Garcilaso de la Vega
Vega (VE-ga), star C 492
Vega Carpio (BAY-ga CARP-yo), Lope Félix de, Spanish
    dramatist and poet D 296
    Spanish literature, place in S 369
Vegetable, or kitchen, gardens G 26, 51–52; picture
    G 28
Vegetables V 286–94
    cooking hints R 114
    Did you know that many vegetables are related?
        V 286
    fruits thought of as vegetables F 481
    kitchen gardens G 26, 51–52; picture G 28
    leaves and flowers we eat P 307
    marketing for the home M 102, 103
    nutrition, use in N 417
    oils and fats obtained from O 76–77
    onions O 118
    roots we eat P 307
    tomatoes T 209
Vegetable tanning, leather process L 108–09
Vegetation
    deserts D 123–31
    forests F 371–74
    how shown on maps, picture M 92
    jungles J 154–56
    where birds live B 224
    prairies P 430–33
    rain forests R 99–100
    taiga and tundra T 11
    world patterns W 254; diagram W 262
    See also natural resources section of continent,
        country, province, and state articles
Vehicle, or medium, for artist's paints P 30
Vehicle Assembly Building, Florida, picture W 220
Veil nebula, picture S 405
Veils, for Muslim women I 415; M 459; picture M 458
Veins, blood vessels B 277
    heart, function of H 86–86a
Veins, of leaves L 116
Velasco (vay-LA-sco), José María, Mexican painter L 67
Velasco Alvarado, Juan, president of Peru P 166

Velasco Ibarra, José María, president of Ecuador E 58
Velásquez (vay-LA-sketh), Diego, Spanish soldier C 549
    Cortes and Velásquez C 508
Velázquez, Diego, Spanish painter V 294
    baroque art B 60
    court painter to Philip IV of Spain P 23–24
    Don Baltasar Carlos in Hunting Costume, painting
        S 361
    Equestrian Portrait of Prince Balthasar Carlos V 294
    Meninas, Las, painting P 428
    Prince Phillip Prosper of Spain, painting P 22, 24
    Prado, paintings in P 428–29
    Spanish art, place in S 362
Velde (VEL-de), Henry van de, Belgian artist D 78
Velde, William van de, Dutch painter D 357
Velds, open grassland P 430, 432; S 270
    in Uganda, picture G 315
Vellum, calfskin, early writing material B 319
Velocipede (ve-LOS-i-pede), bicycle B 173
Vence (VONCE), France, Matisse chapel M 169
Vending machines
    animals trained to operate A 288
    dry cleaning D 338
Vendôme (von-DOME) Column, Paris, picture P 74
Veneer (ve-NEER), a thin covering
    brick veneer or facing B 393
    furniture F 503–04
    plywood veneer W 226–27
    used by Romans F 505
Venera 4, or Venus 4, Soviet space probe O 14; P 271
Venera 7, Soviet space probe P 271
Venerable Bede, The see Bede, The Venerable
Venereal (ven-E-re-al) diseases
    gonorrhea D 196
    syphilis D 208–09
Venetian (ven-NE-tian) glass G 229; picture G 227
Venetian lace L 19
Venezuela (ven-ez-WAY-la) V 295–300
    drilling for oil in Gulf of Paria, picture G 100
    flag F 242
    holiday, Simón Bolívar's Birthday H 149
    life in Latin America L 47–61
    national anthem N 22
    oil derricks in Lake Maracaibo, picture P 169
    origin of the name "Little Venice" L 32; V 295
Vengeance Weapon II, or V-2, German rocket M 343
Veni, vidi, vici, Caesar's victory message C 6
Venice, Italy I 450; picture C 308b
    arts center I 448
    bottles of Venetian glass B 341–42
    Church of Santa Maria della Salute, picture B 55
    Grand Canal, pictures E 304, H 179, I 456
    Italian art and architecture I 467, 469–70
    opera's beginning O 131
    painting P 21, 23–24
    Renaissance, growth of city states R 157
    Renaissance art and architecture R 169
    rowing regatta, picture R 338
    Saint Mark's church B 488
    San Giorgio Maggiore, island, picture I 426
    Venetian Traders flag F 227

Venizelos (ven-i-ZEL-os), Eleutherios (1864–1936), Greek
statesman, b. Crete. He was a leader in efforts to free
Crete from Turkish rule and in the insurrection that led
to the Greco-Turkish War (1897). He served as Greece's
premier most of the time from 1910 to 1933, taking
Greece into World War I on the Allied side and participating in the peace conference. After organizing armed
uprisings to keep the royalists from restoring the monarchy, he was forced to flee to Paris. He died in exile.
    Greece in World War I G 339; W 275

Venn diagrams, in set theory S 126
Venom, poison I 285
    fishes F 202
    snakes S 207
Ventilation
    air conditioning A 101–03
    fans F 43
    safety in mines M 316–17
    tunnels T 317
Ventricles, chambers of the heart B 276; D 197;
    diagrams B 276, D 198
    heart, its function and action H 86
Ventriloquism (ven-TRIL-o-quism), changing or seeming
    to throw the voice V 301–03
    puppets and marionettes P 535
Venture Scouts B 360
Venturi (vain-TU-ri), Giovanni, Italian scientist A 37
Venturi tube, in air pressure experiments A 37–38
Venus (VE-nus), planet P 270–72
    both "morning" and "evening" star S 244–45
    Galileo's discoveries G 6
    radar astronomy A 476, 477
    space probes O 14; S 348
Venus, Roman goddess G 361
Venus 4, or Venera 4, Soviet space probe O 14; P 271
Venus de Milo (VE-nus de MY-lo), Greek statue L 368
Venus's Flower Basket, a sponge S 392; picture S 391
Venus's-flytraps, plants P 317; picture P 316
Venus shell, picture S 147
Veracruz (ver-a-CROOZ), Mexico M 247; picture N 283
    Indian folk dance L 69
    Cortes, founder C 508
Verazzano see Verrazano, Giovanni da
Verbal learning L 101

Verbena (ver-BE-na) (also called vervains), any of a group
of flowering plants found chiefly in tropical or subtropical parts of the New World. Many species exist, both
wild and cultivated. The small fragrant flowers are of all
shades from white and pink to purple.

Verbs, words that express action or being P 91
    English sentence patterns G 289
Verdelot (ver-de-LO), Philippe, Flemish composer
    R 173
Verdi (VAIR-di), Giuseppe, Italian composer V 304
    Aïda, opera O 139
    choral music C 279
    Don Carlos, opera O 143
    Falstaff, opera O 144
    Forza del Destino, La, opera O 144–45
    Italian operatic masterpieces I 486
    Masked Ball, The, opera O 148–49
    opera O 135
    Otello, opera O 150
    Rigoletto, opera O 151
    Traviata, La, opera O 154–55
    Trovatore, Il, opera O 155
Verdict, in law C 530
    jury trials J 159, 160

Verdigris (VER-di-gri), grayish-green to bluish-green
poisonous substance obtained from action of acetic acid
on copper.

Verdun (ver-DUN), battle of, 1916 W 277–78
Verdun, Quebec, Canada Q 13
Verdun, Treaty of, 843 G 159
Verga (VAIR-ga), Giovanni, Italian writer I 480
Vergil, Latin poet V 304–05
    Aeneid A 35
    place in Latin literature L 79

Verigin, Peter, Russian-born leader of Doukhobors in
    Canada B 405
Verismo (vay-RI-smo), Italian operatic form I 486

Veríssimo (ver-RI-si-mu), Erico (1905–   ), Brazilian novelist, b. Cruz Alta. His novels, such as Crossroads, describe
life in modern Brazil.

Verkhoyansk (ver-ho-YONSK), Siberia
    extreme temperatures A 451
Verlaine, Paul, French poet F 440
Vermeer (ver-MARE), Jan, Dutch painter V 305
    Artist in His Studio, painting D 360
    baroque art B 60–61
    Dutch art D 357
    Head of a Young Girl, painting B 58
    painted humble scenes of daily life P 24
Vermiculite, mineral
    Montana largest supplier M 436

Vermilion, bright orange-red pigment composed of mercury and sulfur. Formerly obtained by grinding the
mineral cinnabar, it is now produced synthetically.

Vermont V 306–21
    Allen, Ethan, led fight for statehood A 166–67
    village in winter, picture U 107
Vernacular (ver-NAC-u-lar), everyday language
    national literature during the Renaissance R 159–60
Vernal equinox (E-qui-nox), start of spring
    April A 338
    Easter E 41
    March M 96
Vernal Falls, Yosemite National Park, picture Y 352
Verne, Jules, French writer V 322
    science fiction S 84
    Twenty Thousand Leagues Under the Sea, excerpt
        S 85
    types of fiction F 441
Veronese (vair-o-NAY-zay), Paolo, Italian painter
    I 469, 470
    Feast in the House of Levi, painting J 82

Veronica, Saint, in Christian legends, a woman from
Jerusalem who wiped the face of Jesus with a veil as he
carried the cross to his crucifixion at Calvary. Christ's
face was ·miraculously imprinted upon the veil, which
was reputedly preserved in Rome and venerated.

Verónicas (ve-RON-ic-as), passes in bullfighting B 450
Verrazano (ver-ra-TSA-no), Giovanni da, Florentine navi-
    gator V 323
    exploration of the new world E 383
Verrazano-Narrows Bridge, New York B 398; V 323
    modern wonder of the world, picture W 220

Verrocchio (vair-RO-kio), Andrea del (Andrea di Michele
Cione) (1435–1488), Italian sculptor, b. Florence. He took
his name from Giuliano dei Verrocchio, a goldsmith to
whom he was apprenticed before becoming the pupil of
Donatello. His best-known works are a statue of David
in Florence and the equestrian statue of General
Bartolommeo Colleoni in Venice.

Versailles (ver-SY), Palace of, near Paris P 74
    architecture A 381–82
    baroque style B 62
    French Revolution F 465
    gardens, picture G 33
    mirrors made of blown plate glass G 230
Versailles, Treaty of, 1919 W 281
    a hard peace for Germany G 162

disarmament, hope for **D** 184
France received Alsace and Lorraine and reparations for damages suffered in World War I **F** 418–19
map of Europe redrawn **W** 282–83
Poland **P** 362
Wilson, Woodrow **W** 181
Verse, a line of poetry **P** 353
nonsense rhymes **N** 272–74
Vertebrae (VER-te-bre), bones of the spinal column
birds **B** 200–01
Vertebrates, animals with backbones **K** 251
aging **A** 84
animal kingdom **A** 264
animals: locomotion **A** 291–94
birds **B** 206
feet and legs **F** 80–81
feet of flying vertebrates **F** 84
fishes outnumber other vertebrates **F** 181
learning ability **L** 104
mammals **M** 61–73
prehistoric animals **P** 437
reptiles **R** 180–81
Vertex of an angle, in geometry **G** 124
Vertical files
use in libraries **L** 187; picture **L** 175
Vertical life zones **Z** 372–73
Yosemite National Park **Y** 353
Vertical Take Off and Landing (VTOL) aircraft **A** 41, 574

Verwoerd (fair-VOORT), **Hendrik Frensch** (1901–66), South African political leader, b. Amsterdam, the Netherlands. He was professor of psychology and sociology at the University of Stellenbosch (1927–37), editor of the Johannesburg National Party paper, *Die Transvaler* (1938–48), and member of Parliament (1948–58). As minister of Native Affairs (1950–58), he was principal designer of apartheid policy. He was prime minister of Union of South Africa (1958–61) and of independent Republic (from 1961). He was assassinated on September 6, 1966.
South Africa, history of **S** 273

Very-high-frequency Omnidirectional Range (VOR), radio navigation system **A** 561, 562
Very pistol **F** 156
Vesalius (ve-SAY-lius), **Andreas,** Belgian anatomist **M** 204
anatomy, advance in the science of **S** 67
Renaissance discoveries and science **R** 160
Vesey, Denmark, American leader of slave revolt **N** 93
Vespasian (vesp-A-sian), Roman emperor **R** 304
Colosseum was begun in his reign, picture **W** 217
Vesper see Hesper, or Hesperus
Vespers, evening service **C** 278
Vespucci (ves-PU-chi), **Amerigo,** Italian navigator **V** 323
exploration of the New World **E** 378
Vesta, asteroid **P** 274
Vesta, Roman goddess **G** 357

Vestal virgins, Roman priestesses bound by vows of religion and chastity to serve Vesta, goddess of the hearth. The priestesses, chosen from prominent families and trained from youth, served for a period of 30 years at the shrine of Vesta in Roman Forum, keeping alive the sacred perpetual fire that burned there.
fire in primitive religions **F** 144

Vestris, Gaetan, French ballet dancer **B** 24
Vesuvius, volcano, Italy **V** 382; picture **V** 377
earth's crust of moving plates **G** 117
Pompeii **P** 390
Veterans
civil service **C** 317

Dependent Pension Act, 1890 **H** 47
national cemeteries, who may be buried in **N** 28

Veterans Administration (VA), United States bureau created (1930) to combine government agencies concerned with providing benefits for veterans and their dependents. It administers laws governing such benefits as pension, education, and insurance, and it maintains homes and hospitals.

Veterans' Day **H** 152

Veterans of Foreign Wars of the United States (VFW), organization, founded 1899, of overseas veterans of World Wars I and II and the Korean War.

Veterinarians (vet-er-in-AIR-ians), doctors who specialize in animal health **V** 324
inoculate against cat flu **C** 141
"shots" for dogs **D** 257
treating animals in zoos **Z** 377
Veterinary medicine see Veterinarians
Vetiver (VET-iv-er), a grasslike plant **L** 356

Veto (from the Latin, meaning "I forbid"), the power of an executive officer to prohibit the passage of a bill. In the United States Government, the veto is the President's constitutional right (Article I, Section 7). The President vetoes a bill by returning it to Congress within 10 days, without his signature. He must also submit his reasons in writing. Congress may re-pass the bill by a two-thirds majority of both houses. The bill then becomes a law without the President's signature. Sometimes the President objects to a bill, but for political reasons prefers not to veto it. If Congress adjourns before the 10-day waiting period expires, the bill is considered defeated. This stratagem, known as the **pocket veto,** has been popularly used since first applied by President Madison.
powers of the U.S. president **P** 454; **U** 140

Veto power, in international agreements **D** 184
Veuster (veust-AIR), **Joseph Damien de,** Belgian priest, missionary to Hawaiian leper colony **H** 70
Vexillum (vex-IL-lum), Roman cavalry flag **F** 225
VFR see Visual Flight Rules
VFW see Veterans of Foreign Wars of the United States
VHF, frequency **T** 66
Via Appia see Appian Way, Roman road
Via Dolorosa (VY-a dol-o-RO-sa), Jerusalem **J** 80
Vibrations, source of sounds **S** 256, 260–62
inside the ear, body's hearing organ **B** 285
noise and noise pollution **N** 269–70
Vicar of Wakefield, by Goldsmith **E** 257
Vicente (vi-SAIN-te), **Gil,** Spanish writer **S** 367
Vicenza (vi-CHEN-tza) Italy
Villa Capra, picture **A** 384
Vice-presidency of the United States **V** 325–32
Adams, John, first in office **A** 9
Electoral College **E** 116
flag **F** 230
Indiana called "Mother of Vice-Presidents" **I** 150
Jefferson's election **J** 67
presidential disability **P** 453
Tyler, first to become president **T** 339–42
Viceroy butterfly, picture **I** 275
Vichy (VI-she) **Government,** in France **F** 419
government under German occupation **W** 289
Vietnam **V** 334c, 334d
World War II, Operation Torch **W** 295–96
Vicksburg, Mississippi **M** 363
Civil War battle site **C** 325
Grant's victory over Confederates **G** 295; **C** 460

Vicksburg National Military Park, Mississippi **M** 359
Vico (VI-co), **Giambattista,** Italian writer **I** 479

Victor Emmanuel II (1820–1878), king of Italy (1861–78), b. Turin. He became king of Sardinia upon abdication of his father (1849). He appointed Cavour as political counselor (1852) and pursued a goal of unification of Italy by annexing Lombardy (1859), Tuscany, Parma, Modena, Romagna, Two Sicilies, the Marches, and Umbria (1860). He took title of first "King of Italy" (1861). He was succeeded by his son Humbert I.
 Italy, history of **I** 457

Victor Emmanuel III (1869–1947), king of Italy (1900–46), b. Naples. He became king after assassination of his father, Humbert I (1900). He joined (1915) Allied powers in World War I, in violation of Triple Alliance agreement. He accepted Fascist leadership and requested Mussolini to organize government (1922). He became emperor of Ethiopia (1936) and king of Albania (1939). In 1943 he replaced Mussolini with General Badoglio. His long support of Mussolini resulted in popular disfavor and his abdication (1946). He was succeeded by son Humbert II and was exiled in Egypt until his death.

Victor Emmanuel Monument, Rome, Italy, picture **R** 316
 Italy's tomb of an unknown soldier **U** 225
Victoria, Australia **A** 510
 Melbourne, capital **M** 215
 Yallourn Coal Mine, picture **A** 509
Victoria, capital of British Columbia, Canada **B** 406b; **C** 64; picture **B** 403
Victoria, capital of Hong Kong **H** 203
Victoria, Guadalupe, Mexican president **M** 249
Victoria, Lake, east central Africa **L** 34
 Africa, lakes of **A** 50
 Uganda **U** 5
Victoria, queen of Great Britain **V** 332; pictures **E** 230, 262
 Victorian era **E** 226–27
 Disraeli, Benjamin **D** 223
 Victoria Day, holiday **H** 150
Victoria and Albert Museum, London **M** 514
Victoria Cross, British award, picture **M** 200
Victoria Day **H** 150
Victoria Falls, Africa **A** 50; **W** 56b; pictures **A** 47, **R** 230, 249
Victoria Island, Northwest Territories, Canada **Y** 363
Victoria Memorial, in Calcutta **C** 11
Victorian Gothic, style in architecture **E** 241
Victorian period **E** 226–27
 English literature **E** 262–64
 furniture design **F** 509
 parlor, picture **H** 181
Victor Talking Machine Company **P** 197
Victory of Samothrace see Winged Victory
Vicuñas (vi-COON-yas), hoofed mammals **H** 210; picture **H** 213
 native to the Andes **A** 253
Video cassettes, or cartridge television **T** 70c, 71
Video signal, television **T** 66
Video tape **T** 70a
 used by doctors, picture **M** 208b
Video Telephone, telephonic device by which persons can see each other **E** 142b
Vidyapati, Indian poet **O** 220e
Viehmännin, Frau see Gammer Grethel
Vielle (v'YELL), musical instrument **V** 342
Vienna (vi-EN-na), capital of Austria **A** 520
 classical composers of **C** 333
 Staatsoper (State Opera), picture **A** 519
 Viennese operetta **O** 156–57

Vienna, Congress of, a conference of European nations held in Vienna in 1814–15. Its purpose was to restore the balance of power in Europe after the overthrow of Napoleon I (1814). The leading figures at the Congress were Viscount Castlereagh of Great Britain, Prince von Metternich of Austria, Czar Alexander I and Count Nesselrode of Russia, Prince von Hardenberg of Prussia, and the French minister Talleyrand. During the deliberations Napoleon escaped from exile and returned to power briefly, before his final defeat at Waterloo (1815). The results of the Congress were wide in scope. The monarchies toppled by Napoleon were restored. A kingdom of the Netherlands (comprising present-day Belgium and the Netherlands) was created, and a confederation of German states (replacing the old Holy Roman Empire) was formed. An independent, neutral Switzerland was re-established. Part of Poland (the former Grand Duchy of Warsaw) became a kingdom under the rule of the Russian czar; other Polish territory went to Prussia and Austria. Prussia received much of Saxony and other German land, and Austria acquired northern Italy. Norway, formerly part of Denmark, was given to Sweden.
 Foreign Service begun **F** 369
 Germany made a confederation of states **G** 161
 international organizations **I** 324
 Switzerland's neutrality and borders established **S** 502

Vientiane (vi-ent-YEN), administrative capital of Laos **L** 41
Vietcong (vi-ET CONG), Communist guerillas **V** 334c, 336

Viète (vi-ET), **François** (Franciscus Vieta) (1540–1603), French mathematician and lawyer, b. Fontenay-le-Comte, Vendée. Called father of modern algebra, he was one of the first to use letters in algebraic equations. He served in Privy Council of Henry IV and deciphered the secret code that King Philip II of Spain was using to send messages during war with France.

Viet Minh (vi-ET MIN), faction, Indochina **V** 334c, 334d
Vietnam (VYET-NOM), **Democratic Republic of** (North Vietnam) **V** 333–334c
 flag **F** 238
Vietnam, Republic of (South Vietnam) **V** 333–334c
 flag **F** 238
Vietnamization, of Vietnam War **V** 337
Vietnam War, 1958– **V** 334d–37
 Johnson's decision to accelerate **J** 131
 peace movements **P** 105
 U.S. Supreme Court ruling on confidential documents **C** 316
 Vietnam, history of **V** 334c
 war crimes trials **W** 10
Vieux Carré (vieu car-RAY) (Old Square), New Orleans **N** 196
Viewfinders, on cameras **P** 215–16
View Near Rampoortje, Amsterdam, drawing by Rembrandt **D** 302
View of Harbor, painting by Claude Lorrain **F** 423
View of Toledo (to-LE-do), painting by El Greco **P** 22
Vigano (vi-GA-no), **Salvatore,** Italian choreographer
 choreodrama dance form **D** 37
Vigilantes (vi-gi-LANT-ese), pioneer government and law **P** 260
 Montana **M** 442
Vigny, Alfred de, French poet **F** 440
Vigo, Jean, French motion-picture director **M** 484–85
Vihuela, musical instrument **S** 372
Viking, a Mars probe **M** 111
Vikings **V** 338–40
 Alfred the Great fought and defeated **A** 154–55
 England invaded by **E** 216–17

Ericson, Leif **E** 275
exploration and discovery **E** 369
flag **F** 228
Greenland and Eric the Red **G** 370–71
how to make a model viking ship **S** 152–54
Iceland settled by **I** 41, 44
Ireland invaded by **I** 390
Norway's Viking Age **N** 344
ornaments, picture **D** 71
ships, clinker-built **S** 158
Sweden **S** 485, 486
Swedish Vikings in Finland **F** 134
See also Norsemen
Vilakazi, Benedict, South African poet and novelist
  A 76b
Villa (VEEL-ya), **Pancho,** Mexican bandit and soldier
  M 250
New Mexico, raids into **N** 195
Pershing, John J. **P** 157
Villa Capra, Vicenza, Italy, picture **A** 384
Villa Cisneros (VEEL-ya cees-NAY-rose), Spanish
  Sahara **S** 356
Villa d'Este gardens, Lake Como, Italy, picture **G** 33
Village Blacksmith, The, poem by Longfellow **L** 342–43
Village greens or commons **P** 77
Lebanon Green, Lebanon, Conn. **C** 478
New England, picture **N** 138h
Villa-Lobos (VIL-la-LO-bos), **Heitor,** Brazilian composer
  L 75
the arts in Brazil **B** 377
Villanueva (veel-yon-WAY-ba), **Juan de,** Spanish architect
  P 429

Villas, elegant, spacious country estates built in Roman
times but abandoned from Middle Ages until the Renaissance, when ancient Roman villas were often used as
models for nobles' country estates. In 16th and 17th
centuries, garden and landscape designs of villas were
highly developed, as in the Villa d'Este at Tivoli in Italy
and the Rotonda, near Vicenza, Italy. Picture **I** 464.
country homes near Venice **I** 467

Villasur, Pedro de, Spanish soldier **N** 86
Villeda Morales, Ramón, president of Honduras **H** 199
Villi, threadlike projections in intestine **B** 275
Villon (vi-YON), **François,** French poet **F** 436
Vilna, capital of Lithuania (Lithuanian Soviet Social-
  ist Republic) **U** 44
Viña del Mar, Chile **C** 254
Vinca see Periwinkle

Vincennes (van-CEN), **François Marie Bissot, Sieur de**
(1700–1736), French soldier, b. Montreal. A member of
the French colonial army, he built a fort near Lafayette,
Ind., and another on the site of present-day Vincennes,
Ind. (1731 or 1732). During a war with the Chickasaw
Indians he was taken to their village on the Tombigbee
River and burned at the stake.

Vincennes, Indiana
capture by Clark, 1779 **I** 150
Revolutionary War **R** 205

Vincent de Paul, Saint (1581?–1660), French priest, b.
Pouy, Gascony. Ordained in 1600, he devoted his life to
charitable deeds. He founded Congregation of the Priests
of the Mission (called Lazarists or Vincentians) and
Daughters of Charity. He was canonized in 1737. Society
of St. Vincent de Paul continues his work.

Vincent of Beauvais (bo-VAI), French scholar and encyclopedist **E** 193

Vincent's Room at Arles, painting by Van Gogh **D** 362
Vinci, Leonardo da see Leonardo da Vinci
Vindobona, Roman camp, now Vienna, Austria **A** 524
Vinegar **F** 348
apple **A** 337
Vines, climbing plants
grapes **G** 297–98
Vineyards (VIN-yards), grape-growing area, pictures
  G 300, **S** 497
Vinifera (vy-NIF-er-a) **family,** of grapes **W** 188

Vining, Mrs. Elizabeth Gray (1902–   ), American author of
children's books, b. Philadelphia, Pa. Mrs. Vining won
Newbery medal (1943) for *Adam of the Road.* In *Windows for the Crown Prince* she wrote about experiences
tutoring Japanese prince Akihito. She wrote biographies
Young Walter Scott and *Penn.*
Japan, history of **J** 48

Vinland, or **Wineland,** Viking name for America **V** 339
Ericson's voyages and discoveries **E** 275

Vinson, Fred M. (Frederick Moore Vinson) (1890–1953),
American lawyer, government official, and 13th chief
justice of the United States, b. Louisa, Ky. He was a
member of Congress (1923–29, 1931–38). He became
associate justice of the U.S. Court of Appeals, District of
Columbia (1938–43), and was chosen by President
Truman to become secretary of treasury (1945–46). He
was appointed chief justice in 1946.

Vinyl (VY-nil) **plastics** **V** 341
coated steels **I** 403
Vinyl resins
varnishes made from **V** 279
Vinyl tiles, floor covering **V** 341
Viol (VY-ol), musical instrument **M** 545–46
chamber music **C** 185
English music **E** 270
Viola (vi-O-la), a musical instrument, picture **M** 545
orchestra seating plan **O** 186
Viola da gamba (vi-O-la da GOM-ba), or bass viol, musical
  instrument, picture **S** 439
in concert, picture **I** 482
Viola d'amore (d'am-O-re), musical instrument, picture
  S 439
Violets, flowers, picture **W** 169
a dicot, picture **P** 292
Illinois, state flower of **I** 70
New Jersey, state flower of **N** 164
Rhode Island, state flower of **R** 213
Wisconsin, state flower of **W** 193
Violin **V** 342–43
development in baroque period **B** 66
sections in an orchestra **O** 182–83, 186
types of musical instruments **M** 545–46
Viotti (v'YOT-ti), **Giovanni Battista,** Italian-born French
  violinist and composer **V** 343
Vipers, snakes **S** 208; pictures **S** 209
Virchow (FEER-co), **Rudolf,** German pathologist **B** 193
Vireos (VIR-e-os), birds, picture **B** 239
Virgil see Vergil
Virgin, constellation see Virgo
Virgin, Jesus and St. Anne, The, painting by Leonardo da
  Vinci **I** 466, 469
Virginal, keyboard instrument **K** 238; picture **S** 439
English composers for **E** 269
instrumental music in the Renaissance **R** 173
Virgin and Child with St. Anne and the Infant St. John,
  by Leonardo da Vinci **L** 153
Virginia **V** 344–60
Civil War **C** 322–23, 326

Virginia (continued)
   colonial life in America C 385–99
   first successful American colony A 183–85
   Founding fathers of the United States F 395
   Lee chooses his state L 125
   places of interest in Negro history N 94
   poverty in Appalachia P 424a–424b
Virginia, Army of C 323
Virginia, ironclad warship see Merrimac
Virginia, University of
   Jefferson, Thomas, founder J 69
   Rotunda, picture A 384
Virginia bluebells, flowers, picture W 170
Virginia City, Montana M 439
Virginia City, Nevada N 132
Virginia Company, Second (Plymouth), P 344
Virginia Company of London V 344

Virginia creeper (also called woodbine), vine of the grape
family. It can grow to a height of 50 to 75 ft. The leaves
become bright red in autumn. The plant has tiny white
flowers that develop into small blue berries. The Virginia
creeper grows wild from southeastern Canada to Florida
and is found as far west as Texas and Mexico.

Virginia Falls, Canada Y 361
Virginia plan, for United States Constitution U 146
Virginia reels D 28
   origin in contra dance, Sir Roger de Coverley F 299

Virgin Islands, British, group of islands in the Caribbean
Sea, east of Puerto Rico. Acquired by Great Britain in
1666, they were part of the Leeward Islands colony until
1958. The major islands are Tortola, Virgin Gorda, and
Anegada. Road Town, the capital, is on Tortola. The
islands' economy depends on farming (mainly tobacco),
fishing, and the raising of livestock.
   Caribbean Sea and islands C 116–19

Virgin Islands, United States T 115
   Caribbean Sea and islands C 116–19
   outlying areas of the United States U 100
Virgin Islands National Park, Virgin Islands, picture N 48

Virginius Affair (1873), international incident that occurred during Cuban revolt (1868–78). Spanish captured
Virginius, a ship illegally represented as American, carrying arms to Cuban rebels. The captain and 36 crew
members (some American) were shot as pirates. The incident violated an international law forbidding seizure
on high seas and massacre of men. U.S. Secretary of
State Hamilton Fish negotiated for return of ship, and
indemnity was paid by Spain.

Virgin Mary see Mary, Virgin
Virgo, constellation C 492; sign of, picture S 245
Virologists (vy-ROL-o-gists), scientists who study viruses
   V 363
Virtual image, formed by lenses L 145–46
   lamp-lens-card experiment with light through a
      diverging lens L 264
Virtues, cardinal see Cardinal virtues
Virtuosos (virt-u-O-sos)
   piano P 242
   violin V 342–43
Virunga (vi-ROON-ga) Mountains, central Africa U 5
Virus diseases D 187; V 370
   chicken pox D 194
   common cold D 194–95
   German measles D 196
   hepatitis D 198
   influenza D 200

measles D 201
   mumps D 201
   pneumonia D 204
   poliomyelitis D 204
   smallpox D 207
   warts F 473
Viruses V 361–70a
   antibiotics A 316
   biochemistry deals with study of viruses B 184
   cancer research C 93–94
   life process, viruses lack certain features L 211
   microbiology, studies in M 281–82
   heredity, mechanism of, new studies B 196
   plant enemies, mosaic viruses P 286–87
   possible fourth kingdom of living things K 251
   preventive measures against virus diseases D 218
   vectors carry viruses V 282–83
   What diseases are caused by viruses? V 370
Visakha Puja, religious holiday R 154
Visa, painting by Stuart Davis U 120
Visas, approval by authorities on passports P 94
   vacations and travel V 259
Viscose rayon, man-made fiber N 424
Viscosity (vis-COS-ity), or fluid friction L 370
Visible light spectrum R 43
Visigoths, or West Goths, Germanic tribe M 289–90
   acceptance of Christianity C 283
   church architecture S 360
   Spain S 351, 356
   Spanish language, additions to S 366
Vision see Sight
Vision of Saint Theresa, sculpture by Bernini, picture
   B 56
Visit From St. Nicholas, A, poem by Clement Moore
   C 295
VISTA see Volunteers in Service to America
Vista-dome cars, of railroads R 81
Vistula River, Poland R 248
   rivers of Poland P 359
Visual aids, for education E 78
   graphs G 309–13
   maps and globes M 88–95
Visual Flight Rules (VFR), of airplanes A 564
Visual telephones T 57
Vital statistics, population birth and death rates P 394
   insurance actuarial tables I 297
   See also population figures with each country,
      province, and state article
Vitamin A V 370b–370c
   blindness caused by deficiency B 251
Vitamin B complex V 370c–370d
Vitamin C, or Ascorbic Acid V 370d
Vitamin D V 370d–371
Vitamin deficiency diseases V 370b–371
Vitamin E, or Tocopherol V 371
Vitamin K V 371
Vitamins V 370a–371
   B_1 crystals, diagram L 274
   bacterial fermentation produces F 91
   bark of almeda tree, a source of P 310
   body chemistry B 294
   conquest of deficiency diseases D 216
   deficiency diseases D 189–90
   dried fruits D 317
   drugs supply to body D 326
   enriched bread B 387
   fish-liver oils O 79
   milk fortified with, and homogenized D 11; M 310
   nutrition N 417, 418
Viti Levu (VI-ti LEV-u), one of the Fiji Islands F 122
Vitruvius Pollio (vit-RU-vi-us POLL-io), Roman architect
   G 272

Vittorino da Feltre (vi-to-RI-no da FEL-tray), Italian scholar P 225

Vitus (VY-tus), **Saint,** child martyr under Diocletian in the late 3rd century. The nerve disease chorea is also known as Saint Vitus's dance.

Vivaldi (vi-VOL-di), **Antonio,** Italian composer I 485

Viverridae (vy-VER-rid-e), animal family of genets, civets, and mongooses G 89–93

Vivian Beaumont Theater, Lincoln Center for the Performing Arts L 298

Viviparous (vy-VIP-ar-ous) **animals,** those that give birth to living young
fishes F 197

Vivisection, the practice of dissecting or operating on living animals for purposes of medical research. The term is also used in a broader sense to include any form of medical experimentation using animals.

Vizcaíno (vi-ska-E-no), **Sebastián** (1550?–1615), Spanish explorer, b. Huelva. He led expeditions from Acapulco to what is now San Diego, Calif. (1596–97). Later (1602–03) he explored the California coast, anchoring (1603) at Point Reyes. He commanded an expedition (1611–14) to Japan and tried to effect trade with that country.

Vizier (vi-ZIER), assistant to an Egyptian king A 220

Vladimir (vlod-YI-mir), Union of Soviet Socialist Republics church architecture U 52

Vladivostok (vla-div-os-TOK), Siberia, U.S.S.R. S 173

Vlaminck (vla-MANK), **Maurice de** (1876–1958), French painter, b. Paris. Influenced by works of Derain, Matisse, and Van Gogh, he was known (by 1905) as one of the prominent fauvist painters, a group characterized by use of bright color and free form. Later, influenced by Cézanne, he used a more realistic style to paint some of the landscapes and flowers for which he is best-known. His works include *Village Square, Village Street, Thatched Cottages,* and *The Storm.*
Fauvism in modern art M 388, 390

Vltava (VUL-ta-va) **River,** Czechoslovakia C 562

Vocabulary V 371–72
controlled, for easy-to-read books C 243
English language E 244
German influenced by other languages G 173
Hebrew word roots H 100
linguistics L 302
slang S 194
using new words in oral book reports B 316
word games W 236–38
word origins W 241

Vocal cords, in the speaking mechanism S 377
voice training and singing V 375–76

Vocal music
baroque period B 63–65
early use of plainsong in Italy I 482
English E 269–71

Vocal organs, in the speaking mechanism S 377
sounds produced by, in languages L 37
sound-wave fundamentals and overtones
S 264–65
voice training V 375

Vocational education E 75; S 58; picture E 74
Egypt E 90d
farm clubs for vocational agriculture F 45
home economics H 165–66
job retraining P 424a, 424b
Peace Corps programs P 101–03
prisons and reformatories P 469–70

Vocational Education Act (1963), comprehensive legislation providing for permanent federal assistance, amounting to $225,000,000 per year, for programs preparing people for employment in any occupation not requiring a college degree. Money allocated to states must be matched on a 50-50 basis. A new Act was passed in 1969 (to cover 1969–72). It provides $3.1 billion for the four-year period.

Vocational guidance and counseling V 373–74
blind, employment of B 254
changes in kinds of work W 252
deaf, employment of D 53
handicapped, rehabilitation of the H 27–30
industrial arts I 227–28
See also Vocations; names of careers, jobs, occupations, and professions

Vocational rehabilitation, under workmen's compensation W 253

Vocational schools *see* Vocational education

Vocations
accounting and bookkeeping B 313–14
advertising as a career A 33
anthropology A 305, 309
archeology A 362, 364–65
astronomy O 12–13
aviation A 566
book design B 323–24, 326
bookkeeping and accounting B 313–14
buyer for stores F 70
cartoonists C 128
civil service C 317
clothing industry C 356
colonial America C 387–88
conservation service C 489
dentistry D 115
doctors, medical D 240–41
drug industry careers D 325
engineering E 206–07
fashion designer F 66, 70
FBI agents F 76–77
firemen F 150, 152–53
Foreign Service F 370
foresters F 374
Forest Rangers, United States N 32
geographers G 107
geologists G 114; M 313
geophysicist G 120
guidance counseling G 398
home economics H 165–66
hospital careers H 251
hotel operation H 258–59
illuminating engineering L 289
industrial arts I 227–28
industrial designer I 231
insurance I 297
interior decorators I 303
jewelers J 101
journalism J 145
lawyers L 92–93
librarianship L 190
merchant marine U 182–84
mining engineers M 313
models, fashion M 385
museum workers M 520
newspaper work N 205
nursing N 409–13
paleontology, study of fossils F 380–82
plumbers P 343
police department careers P 376–77
professional singers V 376
public health nursing N 410

Volunteer fire companies F 146

Volunteers in Service to America (VISTA), U.S. federal antipoverty organization founded by the Economic Opportunity Act (1964) to carry out educational, health, agricultural, and community programs in poverty-stricken areas. Volunteers, who are at least 18 years of age and permanent residents of the United States or its dependencies, work in urban and rural areas, migrant-worker camps, hospitals, and schools and institutions for the mentally retarded.

Volunteers of America, religious social welfare organization founded (1896) by Ballington Booth (1859–1940) after he broke away from the Salvation Army, founded by his father, General William Booth. Volunteers of America aid prisoners and support day-care centers and mission churches. Headquarters are in New York, N.Y.

Volunteer State, nickname for Tennessee T 75, 89
Volvox, a colony of flagellate microorganisms M 279
Volynov, Boris, Soviet cosmonaut S 344, 345
Von, in proper names see under last part of name except for those below

Von Braun, Wernher Magnus Maximillian (1912–), German-American rocket engineer, b. Wirsitz, Germany. During World War II he headed the group that developed the first V-2 missiles. He went to United States in 1945. As head of missile development program at Redstone Arsenal, Huntsville, Ala. (1950–60), he directed the group that sent the first American satellite into orbit (1958). He was director of the Space Flight Center of the National Aeronautics and Space Administration (1960–70), and in 1970 was appointed NASA's deputy associate administrator for planning.

Vo Nguyen Giap, Vietnamese leader V 334d
Vonnegut, Bernard, American scientist W 93

Vonnegut, Kurt, Jr. (1922–), American writer, b. Indianapolis, Ind. He began working as a newspaper reporter (1946) then turned to free-lance writing (1950–65) and teaching (1965–). His reflections on life, using satire, fantasy, and humor, are popular with American youth. Among his works are *Sirens of Titan* and *Cat's Cradle*.

Von Neumann (fon NOI-monn), **John** (1903–1957), American mathematician, b. Budapest, Hungary. He taught at Institute for Advanced Study, Princeton, N.J., from 1933 to 1955, when he joined Atomic Energy Commission. He is known for work in quantum mechanics, as well as for his development of "game theory" principles, used to calculate strategies in games and rivalries. With Oskar Morgenstern he wrote *Theory of Games and Economic Behavior*. He received the Fermi award (1956).

Von Saltza, Chris, American athlete O 113
Vontsiras, civets G 93
Voodoo, folk religion H 9
    cults and dances L 69
VOR see Very-high-frequency Omnidirectional Range
Voronoff, Serge, Russian-born French surgeon A 87
Vorster, Balthazar J., South African leader S 273
Voskhod, series of manned Soviet space flights S 344, 345
Vostok, series of manned Soviet space flights S 344, 345
Vote of confidence
    prime minister dependent on P 456
Voting
    Canada C 77
    dyeing the voter's thumb D 366

elections and voting qualifications E 112–15
Electoral College E 116
initiative, referendum, and recall O 205
parliamentary procedure for voting on motions
    P 80
qualifications E 113, and government fact boxes of
    state and province articles
Twenty-fourth amendment abolished poll tax N 103
Twenty-sixth Amendment, U.S. Constitution, vote
    granted to young people U 158
votes of vice-presidents in the Senate V 327
Voting Rights Act, 1965 E 115; N 103
wagon trains, selecting a captain for O 261
woman suffrage W 212b–213; picture W 212
Voting machines, picture E 114

Voting Rights Act (1965, 1970), legislation suspending use of literacy or other qualifications, authorizing appointment of federal voting examiners for Negro registration in areas not meeting certain voter-participation requirements, and providing for federal initiation of court suits to bar discriminatory poll taxes.
    Negro history N 103
    qualifications for voting E 113

Voussoirs (voos-WARS), wedge-shaped parts of arches
    A 376
Vowels, speech sounds A 1
    alphabet A 170, 173
    evolution of letters I and J into vowel and consonant
    I 1; J 1
    Latin language L 76
    pronunciation P 478
    speech S 377–78
Voyageurs (vwa-ya-JERS), French-Canadian "travelers," guides for fur traders F 520
Voyageurs National Park, Minnesota M 332

Voznesensky, Andrei A. (1933–), Russian poet, b. Moscow. He graduated from Moscow Institute of Architecture, but became one of Russia's most popular and controversial young poets. He had been criticized by the Soviet Government for his outspoken dissatisfaction with the Soviet system. He has made three U.S. poetry-reading tours. In 1967, however, his New York recital was cancelled by the Soviet Writers Union because of "pro-American misdeeds." He wrote a protest letter, was censured by the Writers Union, but later was reconciled to the Soviet literary establishment. His poetry collections include *An Achilles' Heart* and *Selected Poems*.

Vredefort (FRE-def-oort) **Ring,** crater in South Africa
    C 421
Vrubel, Mikhail, Russian artist U 56
VTOL aircraft see Vertical TakeOff and Landing

Vuillard (vwe-YAR), **Jean Édouard** (1868–1940), French painter, b. Cuiseaux. Closely associated with Pierre Bonnard, he was influenced by the use of color in impressionist works and by Japanese prints. His works are characterized by decorative and colorful interior scenes, as *Child in Room* and *La Toilette*.

Vulcan, Roman god G 358
Vulcanization, rubber hardening process R 341–42
    Goodyear invented process G 263
    tires T 198
Vulgate, St. Jerome's Latin version of Bible B 153;
    J 77
    Roman Catholic Church R 289
Vultures, large soaring birds related to eagles, hawks, and falcons B 205

The following list credits, by page, the sources of illustrations used in Volume U-V of THE NEW BOOK OF KNOWLEDGE. Credits are listed illustration by illustration —left to right, top to bottom. Wherever appropriate, the name of the photographer or artist has been listed with the source, the two being separated by a dash. When two or more illustrations appear on one page, their credits are separated by semicolons.

2 Gaetano Barone; Uffizzi Gallery, Florence—Art Reference Bureau.
3 Gaetano Barone
4 Marc & Evelyne Bernheim—Rapho Guillumette
5 George Buctel
7 Shostal; Marc & Evelyne Bernheim—Rapho Guillumette.
8 Shostal
9 George Buctel
14 John Cochran
16 New York Zoological Society; General Dynamics Corp.
17 Ron Church—Rapho Guillumette
18 Jacques Yves Cousteau, "World Without Sun," Columbia Pictures
19 U.S. Rubber Co.
20 U.S. Navy; U.S. Navy; U.S. Navy; Les Requins Associes.
22 U.S. Navy
23 Peter David
24 Theodore Martin
27 Harold Wiener
28 Jere Donovan
30 Sovfoto
31 Jerry Cooke
33 Jerry Cooke
34 Ed Drews—Photo Researchers
35 Sovfoto
36 Sovfoto
39 George Buctel
40– Jerry Cooke
42
47 S.-E. Hedin—Ostman
48 Luba Paz
49 Fred M. Hublitz—Courtesy of Mrs. Merriweather Post Collection, Hillwood, Washington, D.C.
50 Mary Ann Joulwan
54 Jerry Cooke
55 George Holton—Photo Researchers; William Froelich, Jr.
56 Fred M. Hublitz—Courtesy of Mrs. Merriweather Post Collection, Hillwood, Washington, D.C.; William Froelich, Jr.; U.S.S.R. Magazine—Sovfoto.
57 Life Magazine, © 1950, Time, Inc., all rights reserved; Collection, Museum of Modern Art, New York, acquired through the Lillie P. Bliss Bequest.
58 Birnback; George Holton-Photo Researchers; Birnback; Ray Manley-Shostal.
60 George Buctel.
61 Jerry Cooke
62 Rizzoli—Pix
63 FPG; Gerald McConnell
66 George Buctel
67 Ray Manley—Shostal
68 A. Williams—Shostal
69 Louis H. Frohman—Rapho Guillumette
70 Ray Manley—Shostal
72 Shostal; Tom Hollyman—Photo Researchers.
73 Slim Aarons—Photo Researchers
74 Ray Manley—Shostal
75 Paris Match, from Pictorial Parade, Inc.
78 Pictorial Parade, Inc.
79 Shostal
80 United Nations
82 United Nations
87 Marc & Evelyne Bernheim—UNICEF
89 Harry Scott

95 Harry Scott
97 Ray Manley—Shostal; William G. Froelich, Jr.
99 Harry Scott
101 E. L. Gockeler—Shostal; Frank Muth—Shostal; Shostal; Shostal.
102 Max Tatch—Shostal; Charles May—Photo Researchers.
105 Upitis—FPG; Shostal; Fred Bond—Publix Pictorial Service; Grant Heilman.
106 David Muench; Grant Heilman; John Titcher—Publix Pictorial Service; Shostal; David Muench.
107 Jack Zehrt—Shostal; Shostal; Publix Pictorial Service; William Froelich, Jr.
108 Ray Atkeson; Grant Heilman; Art D'Arazien—Shostal.
110 Harry Scott
111 Shostal; Ron Perkins.
112 Jeppesen & Co.
113 Jeppesen & Co.
115 Massachusetts Department of Commerce; Peter Stibane—Photo Researchers.
116 Collection, Museum of Modern Art, New York
117 John Launois—Black Star; National Gallery of Art, Index of American Design.
118 Courtesy of Museum of Fine Arts, Boston, gift of Joseph W. Revere, William B. Revere and Edward H. R. Revere; Pennsylvania Academy of the Fine Arts; National Audubon Society; Collection of Museum of Art, Carnegie Institute, Pittsburgh.
119 Butler Institute of American Art; Courtesy of Smithsonian Institution, National Collection of Fine Arts; Hogg Brothers Collection of the Museum of Fine Arts, Houston; Collection, Museum of Modern Art, New York, purchase fund and gift of Wolfgang Schwabacher; Addison Gallery of American Art, Phillips Academy, Andover, Massachusetts.
120 Art Institute of Chicago; Collection, Museum of Modern Art, New York, Larry Aldrich Foundation Fund; Collection, Museum of Modern Art, New York, gift of Mrs. Gertrud A. Mellon.
122 Wayne Andrews
124 Wayne Andrews; Sandak.
125 Emil Romano—CBS
128– Herman B. Vestal
137
140 Herman B. Vestal
141 Gerald McConnell
143 Herman B. Vestal
146 Herman B. Vestal
147 Herman B. Vestal
159 W. R. Wilson—Alpha
163 Ron Perkins
164 Ron Perkins
167 U.S. Army
169 Ron Perkins
170 Ron Perkins
181 Ron Perkins—Courtesy Hilborn-Hamburger, Military Equipment, New York
185 U.S. Navy
187 Ron Perkins—Courtesy Hilborn-Hamburger, Military Equipment, New York
188 Ron Perkins—Courtesy Hilborn-Hamburger, Military Equipment, New York

191 U.S. Navy
196 Lund Observatory, Sweden
197 Alex Ebel
198 Alex Ebel
199 Mount Wilson & Mount Palomar Observatories; Lick Observatory; Yerkes Observatory, University of Chicago, Williams Bay, Wisconsin.
200 Alex Ebel; U.S. Navy.
201– Alex Ebel
203
225 D. Jordan Wilson—Pix
226 Bruce Roberts—Rapho Guillumette
227 Jane Latta; U.S. Department of the Interior—National Park Services.
228 Shostal
229 George Buctel
233 The Travelers Insurance Co.
234 George Tames—New York Times
235 George Buctel; Charles Wiley.
236 Charles Wiley; J. Allan Cash—Rapho Guillumette.
241 Color Illustration Inc.; H. B. Hawkes; Ward Roylance; A. A. Allen.
242 Diversified Map Corp.; Shostal.
243 Diversified Map Corp.
246 Diversified Map Corp.
248 Shostal; Josef Muench.
251 Paul Granger
252 Diversified Map Corp.
253 Josef Muench
258 Van Bucher—Photo Researchers
262– Wayne Dunham
265
266– Ken Longtemps
268
269 George Bakacs
270 George Bakacs
271 James Cooper
272 Art Commission of City of New York
273 Library of Congress
274 Library of Congress
276 George Buctel; Rapho Guillumette.
277 National Gallery, London—Art Reference Bureau
278 Collection, Museum of Modern Art, New York, acquired through the Lillie P. Bliss Bequest
280 George Buctel
281 (©) 1962 by Charles E. Rotkin from Europe: An Aerial Close-up, Lippincott
283– Lee Ames
285
286 Grant Heilman
289– Ann Brewster
293
294 Art Reference Bureau
295 George Buctel
297 Lee Boltin
298 Charles Wiley
301 Wide World
307 Color Illustration Inc.; Robert Holland; Hal Harrison—Camera Clix; Gottscho-Schleisner.
308 Diversified Map Corp.; FPG.
309 Diversified Map Corp.
310 Esther Henderson—Rapho Guillumette; Jon Allen—Photo Researchers.
312 Diversified Map Corp.
314 Carlos Elmer—Shostal; Rock of Ages Quarry, Barre, Vermont; FPG.
317 Warren Miller

W, 23rd letter of the English alphabet **W** 1
  See also Alphabet
Wabash (WAU-bash) **River,** Indiana **I** 136, 138
WAC *see* Women's Army Corps
Wace, Anglo-Norman poet **A** 445
Wade, John Francis, English composer of carols **C** 122
Wadi, dry riverbed **R** 239
  Algeria **A** 161
  Nile River **N** 260
Wading birds B 223
  See also Stork, egret, and heron
WAF *see* Women in the Air Force
Wages
  depressions and recessions **D** 122
  effect of labor union contracts **L** 18
  laboring class (wage earners) created by Industrial
    Revolution **L** 2–3
  Nixon's wage-price freeze **N** 262f
  women's and men's compared **W** 212a
  See also Salaries
Wagner, Honus, American baseball player, picture
  B 81
Wagner (VOG-ner), **Richard,** German composer **W** 2;
  picture **G** 187
  Bayreuth Festival **M** 550
  Fliegende Holländer, Der, opera **O** 144
  Götterdämmerung, Die, opera **O** 152–53
  Lohengrin, opera **O** 145
  Meistersinger von Nürnberg, Die, opera **O** 149
  music dramas **G** 187
  opera **O** 135–36
  orchestra conducting **O** 188
  Parsifal, opera **O** 150
  Rheingold, Das, opera **O** 151–52
  Ring des Nibelungen, Der, music dramas **O** 151
  Ring of the *Niebelung,* German and Norse names for
    characters **N** 280
  romanticism in German drama **D** 297
  Siegfried, opera **O** 152
  Tannhäuser, opera **O** 154
  Tristan und Isolde, opera **O** 155
  Walküre, Die, opera **O** 152

Wagner (WAG-ner), **Robert F., Jr.** (1910–), American politician, b. New York, N.Y. Following the political career of
his father, he was a member of the N.Y. State Assembly
(1938–41). He was appointed city tax commissioner
(1946) and (later that year) commissioner of housing and
buildings, which post he left to become chairman of the
city planning commission. He was elected president of
the Borough of Manhattan (1950–53) and then mayor of
New York City (1954–65). In 1968–69 he was U.S. Ambassador to Spain.

Wagner, Siegfried, German composer and conductor
  W 2
Wagner Act *see* National Labor Relations Act, 1935
Wagon Box Victory, 1867 **W** 337
Wagons, carriages, and carts **T** 260
  Conestoga wagon **C** 458
  Costa Rica's decorative oxcarts **C** 515;
    picture **C** 517
  early wheeled vehicles **W** 157–58
Wagon trains C 458
  famous train to Oregon, 1843 **O** 197
  overland trails **O** 257–63
  pioneers' homes on wheels **P** 253–54
  westward movement, picture **W** 145
Wahhabism (wah-HA-bism), reform movement of Islam
  Saudi Arabia **S** 44, 49
Waikiki (wy-ki-KI) **Beach,** Honolulu, Hawaii **H** 69; pic-
  tures **H** 66, **U** 106

Wailing Wall, now Western Wall, Jerusalem **J** 79, 138
Wailuku (WYLOO-koo), Hawaii **H** 69
Wainwright, Jonathan M., American army officer
  W 293
Waitangi (wy-TONG-i), **Treaty of,** 1840 **N** 242
Wakefield, Edward Gibbon, British politician **N** 242
Wake Island, Pacific Ocean **P** 8–9
  Pacific coaling stations **T** 114

Waksman, Selman Abraham (1888–1973), American biochemist, specialist in soil microbiology, b. Priluka, Kiev,
Russia. Dr. Waksman joined the staff of Rutgers
University in 1918. He was director of the Institute of
Microbiology (1949–58). In 1952 he was awarded the
Nobel prize in physiology and medicine for his discovery
of streptomycin, the first antibiotic found effective in
treatment of tuberculosis. In 1954 he wrote his autobiography, *My Life with the Microbes.* Picture **A** 315.

Walachia (wa-LAY-kia), former principality, now a region
  of Rumania **R** 355
Walcott, Jersey Joe, American boxer **B** 353

Wald, Lillian D. (1867–1940), American social worker, b.
Cincinnati, Ohio. She became active in every phase of
social work. She pioneered in establishing public health
nursing and in 1893 founded the Henry Street Settlement
in New York. She encouraged establishment of the
Federal Children's Bureau, created by Congress in 1908.
She was elected first president of National Organization
for Public Health Nursing in 1912. Miss Wald wrote *The
House on Henry Street* and *Windows on Henry Street.*

Walden, book by Thoreau **A** 201; excerpts **T** 167–69
Walden Pond, near Concord, Massachusetts **T** 167
Waldensian Protestants I 448
Wales W 3–4
  See also United Kingdom of Great Britain and North-
    ern Ireland

Walker, Madame C. J. (1869–1919), Negro, American
manufacturer of cosmetics for Negroes, b. Delta, La. She
was one of the first American women to become a million-
aire by her own efforts.

Walker, David Harry, Canadian novelist **C** 64

Walker, Ewell Doak (1927–), American football player,
b. Dallas, Tex. He was a quarterback for Southern
Methodist University (1947–49) and played for Detroit
Lions (1950–55). A winner of the Heisman trophy (1948),
he was named All-American (1947–49) and is a member
of the National Football Hall of Fame.

Walker, Jimmy (James John Walker) (1881–1946), American politician, b. New York, N.Y. Admitted to the New
York bar (1912), he soon entered politics as a member of
the state Senate (1915). Elected mayor of New York City
(1925–32), he resigned after investigation of his government by the state legislature. He became an arbitrator
for the New York Cloak & Dress Industry.

Walker, John, English druggist
  invention of matches **M** 152

Walker, Joseph A. (1921–66), American test pilot, b.
Washington, Pa. He went on his first flights, while a
physics major in college, with the Civilian Pilot Training
Program. In 1942 he enlisted in the Air Corps and 3
years later went to work for the National Aeronautics
and Space Administration, first as a physicist and finally
as the chief research pilot. In 1962 he flew the X-15 at

Walker, Joseph A. (continued)
4,105 miles per hour, a record speed for manned winged aircraft. He was killed in an airplane collision.

Walker, Joseph Reddeford (1798–1876), American trapper and guide, b. Virginia. He joined Benjamin Bonneville's expedition to trap and explore in western region from Salt Lake to the Pacific (1832–34) and is thought to have been the first white man to see Yosemite Valley. Walker acted as guide to J. C. Frémont's third expedition to California (1845–46) and was among the first "Forty-niners" to reach California (1849).

Walker, Mickey (Edward Patrick Walker) (1901–   ), American boxer, b. Elizabeth, N.J. Welterweight boxing champion (1922–26) and middleweight champion (1926–31), he was elected to boxing Hall of Fame (1955).

Walker, Thomas (1715–1794), American army officer and explorer, b. King and Queen County, Va. He made large speculations in frontier land, helping to settle southwestern Virginia. As chief agent of Loyal Land Company, he explored westward regions (1750) and surveyed 800,000 acres of land granted to the company. Walker was a member of the Virginia House of Burgesses (1752, 1756–61), the Virginia Committee of Safety (1776), and the Virginia executive council (1776–81).
Kentucky, history of **K** 226

Walker, William, American adventurer **N** 248
Costa Rica National holiday celebrates Walker's defeat **C** 518–19

Walker Cup, trophy awarded the winning team in an amateur golf competition between United States and Great Britain, held biennially in alternate countries. First awarded in 1922, it was donated by George H. Walker, president of U.S. Golf Association (USGA).

Walker-McKay Tariff, 1846 **P** 385
Walkie-talkies, two-way radios **R** 50
Citizens Band Radio **E** 142c
Walking
adaptations of mammals **M** 63
animals: locomotion **A** 291–92
child development **C** 232
See *also* Hiking
Walking fern **F** 93
Walking horse see Tennessee walking horse
Walkingstick, insect, picture **I** 275
camouflage for self-protection, picture **L** 218
Walking under a ladder, superstition **S** 474
Walk the plank, to be forced to walk over the side of the ship **P** 263
Walküre (VOL-kur-e), **Die,** opera by Richard Wagner **O** 152
Wallabies (WA-la-bies), or **wallaroos,** kangaroos **K** 170; picture **K** 168
Australia's wildlife **A** 505
Wallace, Alfred Russel, English naturalist **D** 41
theory of natural selection in evolution **E** 345; **S** 73

Wallace, George Corley (1919–   ), American politician, b. Clio, Ala. After serving in the Alabama House of Representatives (1950–54) and as an Alabama circuit court judge (1954–62), Wallace was elected governor of Alabama. Prevented by Alabama law from serving more than one term as governor, in 1967 Wallace was succeeded in office by his wife, **Lurleen** (1926–68). In 1968, Wallace ran for president as a third-party candidate. He was re-elected governor in 1970. In 1972, while campaigning for president again, he was shot and critically injured.

Wallace, Henry Agard, American statesman **I** 369; **V** 331; picture **V** 330
Progressive Party candidate for president, 1948 **P** 381–82; **T** 301
Wallace, Idaho, picture **I** 58
Wallace, Lewis ("Lew"), American author **I** 149
Ben Hur, popular novel **A** 206

Wallace, Sir William (1272?–1305), Scottish patriot. He led a Scottish uprising for independence from England and successfully defeated English at battle of Stirling Bridge (1297). Acting as guardian of Scotland, he was defeated by King Edward I of England at Falkirk (1298). He subsequently sought aid for Scotland, but he was betrayed to England (1305), condemned as a traitor, and hanged, drawn, and quartered.
Scotland, history of **S** 88

Wallboard
insulating slabs or boards **I** 291

Wallenstein (WAL-len-stine), **Alfred Franz** (1898–   ), American cellist and conductor, b. Chicago, Ill. He was first cellist of the New York Philharmonic (1929–36) and organizer of a radio broadcast, the Wallenstein Sinfonietta (1933). He has been conductor and musical director of the Los Angeles Philharmonic Orchestra (1943–56) and guest conductor with leading symphonic orchestras.

Waller, Edmund (1606–1687) English poet, b. Coleshill. He became a member of the House of Commons (1621) but was expelled (1643) for his part in "Waller's Plot," a conspiracy against Parliament. Fined and exiled (1644), he returned to England when sentence was revoked (1651) and again served as member of Parliament (1661–87). His works include the Sacharissa poems, *A Panegyric to My Lord Protector,* and *To the King Upon His Majesty's Happy Return.*

Waller, Thomas ("Fats") (1904–1943) American jazz pianist, singer, and composer, Negro, b. New York, N.Y. An accomplished organist and conductor, he made numerous successful tours in Europe (1932, 1938, 1939) and gave a solo recital at Carnegie Hall (1942). His works include scores for musical revues *Keep Shufflin'* and *Hot Chocolates* and songs "Ain't Misbehavin'," "Honeysuckle Rose," and "I've Got a Feelin' I'm Fallin'."

Wall of Shame, Berlin **B** 144
Wall of the Sun, The, painting by Miró **S** 362
Walloons, French-speaking people of Belgium **B** 126
early settlements in New York state **N** 225
Walloping Window-blind, The, poem by Charles E. Carryl **N** 275
Wall painting see Mural painting
Walls
archeological discoveries **A** 353, 356–57
Berlin Wall **B** 144
brick masonry **B** 391–93
building construction **B** 430–38
Byzantine, texture of **B** 487
coverings for **I** 300
early fortifications **F** 375
Great Wall of China **C** 270; pictures **C** 256, **W** 219
Nebuchadnezzar's palace ruins, Iraq, picture **B** 394
Wailing, now Western, Wall, Jerusalem **J** 79, 138
Wall Street, New York City **N** 230
Wall Street Journal **N** 200
Walnut, tree
uses of the wood and its grain, picture **W** 224
Walnuts **N** 423–24
Walpole, Horace, 4th earl of Orford, English writer **E** 260

Walpole, Sir Robert, 1st earl of Orford (1676–1745), English statesman, b. Houghton, Norfolk. He entered Parliament (1701) and was secretary at war (1708–10) and treasurer of the navy (1710–11). A leader of the Whigs, he supported the succession of King George I (1714). Walpole was prime minister, and first lord of the treasury and chancellor of the exchequer (1715–17; 1721–42). He is usually considered England's first prime minister. Picture **P** 456a.

Walpole Island, uninhabited coral island in South Pacific. A dependency of New Caledonia, it is administered by France.

Walruses W 7; picture **W** 5
Walsh-Healey Public Contracts Act, 1936 **C** 235

Walter (VOL-ter), **Bruno** (Bruno Walter Schlesinger) (1876–1962), American conductor and composer, b. Berlin, Germany. He was director of Vienna State Opera (1936–38) and went to the United States (1939), where he was guest conductor for leading symphonic orchestras. Walter was conductor of New York Philharmonic (1947–49), and conducted many performances of Metropolitan Opera. He wrote an autobiography, *Theme and Variations.*

Walter, Thomas U., American architect **U** 123
Walter Reed Society D 324
Walters, William Thompson, American businessman and art collector **M** 127
Walters Art Gallery, Baltimore, Maryland **M** 123
Walther von der Vogelweide (VOL-ter fon der FO-ghel-vy-da), German minnesinger **G** 181
German poetry **G** 174

Walton, George (1741–1804), American lawyer and patriot, b. near Farmville, Va. Interrupting his law practice in Georgia, he became a member of the Continental Congress (1776–81) and a signer of the Declaration of Independence and the Articles of Confederation. Governor of Georgia (1779–80, 1789), he also was the state chief justice (1783–89) and later a United States senator (1795–96).

Walton, Izaak (1593–1683), English author and ironmonger, b. Stafford. Called the father of angling, he is famous for *The Compleat Angler, or the Contemplative Man's Recreation,* a discourse on the pleasures of fishing written as a conversation between a fisherman, a hunter, and a falconer. He also wrote biographies of John Donne, Richard Hooker, and others.

Walt Whitman House, Camden, New Jersey **N** 175
Waltz, dance **D** 27
operetta **O** 156
Strauss, Johann, Jr. **S** 437
Waltzing Matilda, song of Australia **A** 501
Walvis Bay, South West Africa **S** 336
Wampum, beads made of shells **C** 374; **I** 197
used as money **M** 411
Wamsutta see Alexander, Chief

Wanamaker, John (1838–1922), American merchant, b. Philadelphia, Pa. He formed a men's clothing firm (1861) with his brother-in-law, Nathan Brown. The firm expanded into a department store (1877), called John Wanamaker and Co. He was postmaster general (1889–93).

Waneta (wan-ET-a) (1795?–1848), American Sioux Indian chief, b. S. Dak. He fought for English during War of 1812. He was promoted to captain and was awarded a

trip to England after the war. But he sided with Americans after 1820 and signed a trade treaty at Ft. Pierre (1825) and a Sioux border treaty (1825).

Wang Wei, Chinese poet **O** 220a
Waning and waxing, of the moon **M** 447
Wankel engine I 303, 308, 309
automobiles, search for a low-pollutant engine **A** 552
Wapiti (WA-pi-ti), or American elk **H** 219
War
anthropological studies **A** 303
armor **A** 433–35
battles important in world history **B** 100–02
Cold War **I** 325
draft or conscription **D** 289–90
elephants, use of **E** 171
Fascism and war **F** 64
feudal lords make warfare pay **F** 103
folk music **F** 327
forts and fortification **F** 375–77
guerrilla warfare **U** 10, 173
guns and ammunition **G** 414–26
international law of **I** 320–21
international relations **I** 323–24
Nazism and war **N** 69–71
neutrality, problems of **I** 322
pirates and piracy **P** 263–64
propaganda **P** 480–81
underground movements **U** 10
See also Disarmament; Peace; names of wars and battles
War and Peace, novel by Tolstoi **N** 348
War Between the States see Civil War, United States
Warblers, birds, picture **B** 214
War bonnet, American Indian, picture **H** 53
War crimes trials W 9–10

Ward, Aaron Montgomery (1843–1913), American merchant, b. Chatham, N.J. After much experience as a traveling salesman in the Middle West he started a business (1872) with George R. Thorne and made a variety of goods available at low rates to people in rural areas. This led to the large mail-order house of Montgomery Ward & Company.

Ward, Artemas (1727–1800), American Revolutionary officer and politician, b. Shrewsbury, Mass. He assumed command of Massachusetts troops at siege of Boston (1775). With the arrival of Washington (1775) he ranked second in command in Continental Army. He served in the Continental Congress (1780–81), and in the United States House of Representatives (1791–95).
Revolutionary War, campaigns of **R** 198

Ward, Artemus, see Browne, Charles Farrar

Ward, Lynd (1905–), American illustrator and author, b. Chicago, Ill. Awarded Caldecott medal (1953) as illustrator and author of *The Biggest Bear,* he frequently illustrates children's books written with his wife, **May McNeer,** including *Prince Bantam, Stop Tim, Waif Maid,* and *Golden Flash.* Ward is also author of novels illustrated with woodcuts, such as *Madman's Drum.*

Ward, Nathaniel, American writer and satirist **A** 196
Ward, Nathaniel B., English physician **T** 102

Ward, Rodger (1921–), American auto racer, b. Indianapolis, Ind. A two-time winner of the "Indianapolis 500" (1959, 1962), he also finished second in 1960 and 1964.

Wardian cases see Terrariums

Wardrobe mistress, theater, picture **T** 157
Wards, in locks **L** 323

Warfield, William (1920–), American baritone, Negro, b. Helena, Ark. Beginning his stage career (1946) with the traveling company of *Call Me Mister*, he made his concert debut at the New York Town Hall (1950) and received wide praise. On tours abroad, he sang the role of Porgy in *Porgy and Bess.*
   Negro artists and singers **N** 101

War Hawks, of 1812 **W** 11
   Clay, Henry **C** 335
Warheads, of missiles **M** 343, 344, 347
Warhol, Andy, American artist **P** 31
   Green Coca Cola Bottles, painting **P** 31
Warka (war-KA), site of ziggurat in Babylon **A** 235, 237
Warlocks, or wizards **W** 208
Warm-air heating systems H 98
Warm-blooded animals B 259
   hibernation **H** 123
Warm front, in meteorology **W** 76; diagram **W** 77
Warm Springs, Georgia **G** 192
   The Little White House, where Franklin D. Roosevelt died **G** 142
Warner, Glenn ("Pop"), American football coach **F** 364

Warner, Seth (1743–1784), American Revolutionary soldier, b. Roxbury, Conn. With Ethan Allen and Benedict Arnold he helped capture Fort Ticonderoga (1775). As lieutenant colonel of the regiment of Green Mountain Boys, he served in Canada and Vermont. He fought British at Hubbardton (1775), retreated to Manchester, Vt., and attacked General Burgoyne's expedition near Bennington, Vt. (1775). Warner was appointed brigadier general in 1778.

War of 1812 W 10–13
   Americans attempt invasion of Canada **C** 72, 80, 81
   Calhoun, leader of war hawks **C** 13
   cause of economic changes in United States **U** 129–30
   Clay and the War Hawks **C** 335
   Jackson, Andrew, hero of **J** 4–5
   Madison, James **M** 8–9
   Napoleon's Continental System **N** 11
   Perry, Oliver Hazard **P** 157
   Perry's victory on Lake Erie **M** 273
   rockets used in **M** 343
   United States Navy **U** 186
War of the Austrian Succession *see* Austrian Succession, War of
War of the Reform, 1857–1861, Mexico **M** 249
War of the Roses *see* Roses, War of the
War of the Spanish Succession *see* Spanish Succession, War of the
Warp, lengthwise strands on a loom **T** 140
   Industrial Revolution inventions in weaving of cloth **I** 234
Warping, of wood
   furniture-making techniques to prevent **F** 501–03
Warrant Officers
   United States Army **U** 167
   United States Navy **U** 190
Warren, Earl, American statesman and jurist **W** 13
   inaugural of Kennedy, picture **K** 208
Warren, Francis Emory, American statesman **W** 335
Warren, John C., American doctor **A** 257

Warren, Joseph (1741–1775), American Revolutionary officer and physician, b. Roxbury, Mass. He delivered notable speeches at anniversaries (1772, 1775) of Boston Massacre, and he drafted Suffolk Resolves, which protested British coercion. Warren despatched Paul Revere and William Dawes to Lexington to warn Hancock and Adams of their personal danger. He was killed at battle of Bunker Hill.
   Revolutionary War, campaigns of **R** 198, 200

Warren, Leonard (1911–1960), American opera singer, b. New York, N.Y. Accepted by Metropolitan Opera Company and sent to Milan, Italy, for study (1938), he made numerous tours throughout North and South America. He founded Leonard Warren Scholarship Fund to give aid to promising singers (1952). His repertoire included principal baritone roles in *Rigoletto, Falstaff, Aida, The Barber of Seville, Pagliacci,* and *Il Trovatore.*

Warren, Robert Penn, American writer and poet **A** 211

Warren Report, detailed account and investigation of assassination of President John F. Kennedy (Nov. 22, 1963). It was prepared by a seven-member commission created by President Johnson (1963) to evaluate facts and circumstances surrounding assassination of the president and the killing of his alleged assassin, Lee Harvey Oswald. Published in 1964, the report concluded that Lee Oswald, who assassinated President Kennedy, and Jack Ruby, who shot and killed Oswald, had both acted independently and were not involved in any conspiracy.
   Warren, Earl and the Warren report **W** 13

Warsaw, capital of Poland **P** 360; picture **P** 361

Warsaw Pact (Eastern European Mutual Assistance Treaty), military alliance signed by representatives of Albania, Bulgaria, Hungary, East Germany, Poland, Rumania, Czechoslovakia, and Soviet Union in Warsaw, Poland (1955). Pledged to unify military forces and to assist any participant country in event of attack, the pact was drawn up to counterbalance North Atlantic Treaty Organization (NATO) between United States and Western European countries. It is also known as the Warsaw Treaty Organization.

Warships S 155, 159
   submarines **S** 442–46
   United States Navy organization **U** 191
   World Wars I and II **W** 276, 291, 293, 302
Wars of the Roses *see* Roses, Wars of, 1455–85

Wart, horny projection of varying appearance, color, and size on the skin, caused by a virus. They may appear at any age, but are frequent in children and not often seen in the aged. They often develop in an area exposed to constant irritation. Some disappear without treatment.
   Can a person get warts from handling a toad? **F** 473

Warthogs, wild pigs **H** 209; **P** 248–49; picture **H** 212
   in Kenya, picture **T** 294
War to end war, World War I **W** 181
Warwick, Rhode Island **R** 223
Wasatch (WAU-satch) **Range,** Utah **U** 243; picture **U** 248
   Salt Lake City **S** 22
Wascana Lake, Saskatchewan, picture **S** 38b
Wasco-Wishram, Indians of North America **I** 180

Washakie (wa-SHA-kie) (1804–1900), American Indian chief, b. probably Montana. He was noted for friendship and close co-operation with white men. As chief of Eastern Band of Shoshone in Wyoming, he led exploits against Blackfoot and Crow Indians. He aided hunters and trappers of American and Hudson's Bay fur companies and served as scout in military operations against hostile Indian tribes (1869). He was buried with military honors at Fort Washakie, Wyo.

Wash-and-wear clothing, of cotton **C** 525
Washburn, Cephas, American missionary to Cherokee Indians in Arkansas **A** 426
Wash drawings **D** 303
Washers, for faucets
 how to change a washer **P** 342
Washing machines
 bottle-washing machines **B** 342
 dry cleaning machines similar **D** 337
 laundry **L** 84
Washington **W** 14–29
 Gifford Pinchot National Forest, picture **N** 37
 lumbering, picture **L** 375
 Mount Rainier National Park, picture **N** 48
 Seattle **S** 112–13
Washington, Booker T., American educator **W** 29
 Alabama school founded by **A** 121, 125
 Booker T. Washington National Monument **V** 353
 Tuskegee Institute educational program **N** 96
Washington, D.C., capital of the United States **W** 30–35
 Jefferson Memorial, picture **J** 69
 National Parks **N** 52
 Smithsonian Institution **S** 202
 War of 1812, burning of **W** 11
 White House **W** 162–65
Washington, Dinah, American singer **R** 262c
Washington, George, 1st president of United States **W** 36–43
 agriculture, interest in **A** 100
 cherry tree, legend of the **L** 130
 codes used during American Revolution **C** 369, 371
 commander of Continental Army, picture **A** 11
 flag design **F** 243
 French and Indian War, Washington's part in **F** 460
 George Washington Birthplace National Monument **V** 354
 holiday on his birthday **H** 147–48
 Houdon's *George Washington,* statue **S** 101
 Lafayette's son named for Washington **L** 23
 letter to Jewish congregation in Rhode Island **R** 212
 portrait by Gilbert Stuart **U** 118; **W** 37
 Purple Heart medal established and awarded **M** 198
 Revolutionary War **R** 200–09
 Thanksgiving Day proclamation **T** 153–54
 Who were the Founding fathers of the United States? **F** 393–94
Washington, Lake, west central Washington **L** 34
Washington, Lawrence, half-brother of George Washington **W** 36
Washington, Martha Dandridge Custis, wife of George Washington **F** 164–65; **W** 37
Washington, Mount, New Hampshire **N** 150
Washington, University of **W** 23

Washington, Walter E. (1915–   ), American political official, b. Dawson, Ga. Great-grandson of a slave, he graduated from Howard University and Howard University Law School. After 20 years in federal service, in the housing field, he became first Negro head of the National Capital Housing Authority. He was appointed (1966) chairman of the New York City Housing Authority, and resigned (1967) when he was appointed by President Johnson the first commissioner of the District of Columbia, heading the newly reorganized government of Washington, D.C.

Washington Armament Conference, 1920–21 **W** 283

Washington College, now Washington and Lee University, Lexington, Virginia
 Lee accepts presidency of **L** 126
Washington Crossing State Park, New Jersey, Pennsylvania **N** 175; **P** 140–41
Washington Five-Power Naval Treaty, 1922 **U** 186

Washington Island, small, barren coral atoll in central Pacific, one of Line Islands and part of British Gilbert and Ellice Islands. Owned by Fanning Island Plantations, Ltd., it has no native population, and Gilbertese labor is imported to produce copra.

Washington Monument, Washington, D.C. **W** 32; pictures **W** 34, 218
Washington's Birthday, holiday **H** 147–48
 calendar, old and new style **C** 13
Washington's Cruisers flag, 1775 **F** 229
Washington University, St. Louis, Missouri **M** 375
Wasps, insects **I** 279; pictures **I** 278
 cocoons of the braconid wasp, picture **I** 269
 enemies of butterflies **B** 470
 help pollinate figs **F** 117
 household pests **H** 261
Wassail, drink **N** 209
Wassail Song, English carol **C** 122

Wasserman (WOSS-er-man), **August von** (1866–1925), German bacteriologist, b. Bamberg. He did research in germ diseases at Robert Koch Institute (1890) and became director of the Kaiser Wilhelm institute in Berlin-Dahlem (1913). He developed the Wasserman test for the detection of syphilis (1906). This test is based on the detection of antibodies in blood indicating the presence in the body of the spirochete causing syphilis.

Wassermann, Jakob, German writer **G** 179
Waste disposal see Refuse and refuse disposal
Waste Land, The, poem by T. S. Eliot **E** 177
Wastes
 disposal wells **W** 124
 environment, problems of **E** 272d–272e; **S** 33–34
 refuse and refuse disposal **S** 33–34
Waste water **E** 272e; **W** 58, 59, 124; picture **E** 272d
Watauga (wa-TO-ga) **Association,** early government in Tennessee **T** 88
Watch and ward system, early police **P** 372
Watches **W** 44–50
 correct time **T** 192–93
 finding direction by **D** 183
 Switzerland **S** 500–01
Watches, periods of duty for sailors and crew **U** 192

Watchful Waiting, President Wilson's policy of nonrecognition of the Huerta government in Mexico (1913), a government in power as a result of military takeover.

Watchmen, police officers **P** 372
Water **W** 51–55
 affects all forms of life **L** 250–51
 air conditioning **A** 101, 103
 ancient "element," theories of early scientists **C** 206
 aquariums require conditioned water **A** 340
 atmosphere contains water vapor **A** 479
 Bernoulli's principle **A** 36; diagram **A** 40
 body chemistry **B** 289
 calculating water pressure, easy rule for **U** 16
 capillary action **L** 310
 caves, making of **C** 153–56
 chemical formula and molecule **C** 198
 climate and bodies of water **C** 346
 cloud formation and water vapor **C** 358–59

Water bug, name applied to various insects, but usually refers to the giant water bugs—a family of insects that live in fresh water among dense plant life.

Watergate investigations, name given to public hearings on presidential campaign practices. The investigations were conducted in 1973 by a committee of seven U.S. senators headed by Chairman Sam J. Ervin, Jr. (Dem.), and Howard H. Baker, Jr. (Rep.). The hearings got their name from the June 1972 attempt to burglarize Democratic National Committee headquarters located in a group of buildings in Washington, D.C., called Watergate.

Waterloo, battle of (1815), final defeat of Napoleon by British and allied forces under Duke of Wellington, near Belgian village of Waterloo. Arrival of General Blücher and his troops helped decide the outcome. The defeat ended Napoleon's hopes of regaining his position as French emperor after his return from exile in Elba.
    battles important in world history   B 102
    Wellington, Duke of   W 122

Water plants (hydrophytes), plants that grow entirely or partly under water or in mud. The group includes such plants as cattails, papyrus, and water lilies.
    wild flowers   W 171

Waters, Ethel (1900–), American singer and actress, Negro, b. Chester, Pa. Her autobiography (1951) is titled *His Eye Is on the Sparrow.* N 98

Water sports
 canoeing C 99–101
 diving D 226–33
 from boats B 263
 Olympic aquatic events O 109
 rowing R 338–39
 sailing S 9–15
 skin diving S 188–91
 surfing S 478
 swimming S 488–94
 water polo W 60
 water-skiing W 63–65
Waterspouts, tornadoes at sea H 299
Water supply W 65–68
 aqueducts A 344
 canals C 85
 community helps in prevention of disease D 220–21
 dams D 16–21
 distillation plant, Kuwait, world's largest K 305
 environment, problems of E 272e
 fluoridation F 283–84
 forests, importance of F 371
 irrigation I 408–10
 metered service to homes P 512
 North America, factors affecting use N 295–96
 plumbing P 341–43
 public utility waterworks P 512
 pumps P 528–30
 purity and safety, methods for ensuring S 32–33
 reservoirs control floods F 257
 salt used in softening S 21
 water desalting W 56, 56a
 water pollution W 58–59
 wells W 122–24
 See *also* natural resources section of continent,
  country, province, and state articles
Water table, top layer of water-soaked earth W 122
Waterton-Glacier International Peace Park, United States
  and Canada C 67; G 222
Waterton Lakes National Park, Alberta, Canada A 146d
Water transportation T 260–62
 ships and shipping S 155–61
 See *also* Canals; Waterways; transportation section of
  country and state articles
Water-tube boilers S 421
Water turbines T 319–20
Water vapor W 51
 condensation to form rain R 93
 how a fog is formed F 288
Waterways
 dredges used for maintaining D 308
 Great Lakes, North America G 326–29
 interstate commerce I 331
 Intracoastal Waterway, U.S. N 313–14
 Louisiana transportation L 356
 Mississippi River M 364–65
 North America, systems in N 304
 Saint Lawrence River and Seaway S 15–17
 United States U 110
 United States Army Engineer Waterways Experiment
  Station M 359–60
 See *also* Canals; Inland waterways; transportation sec-
  tion of country, provinces, and state articles
Waterwheels W 61–62; I 335
Waterworks P 512

Watie (WA-tie), **Stand** (1806–1871), Cherokee Indian
leader and planter, b. near present-day Rome, Ga. He
signed New Echota treaty (1835), through which Cherokees yielded their land in Georgia and moved to
Oklahoma. Opposed by majority, he headed a small
party in support of the treaty. During the Civil War, he
was commissioned as colonel of Cherokee Mounted
Rifles (1861) and as brigadier general (1864) by
Confederate government.
 Cherokee Indians in Oklahoma I 214; O 95

Watkins Glen, New York, United States Grand Prix auto-
  mobile racing A 538
Watling Island, or San Salvador, one of the Bahamas
  B 16
Watson, Dr., fictional character created by Arthur Conan
  Doyle D 288; M 554
Watson, Elkanah, father of American fairs F 12

Watson, Helen Orr (1892–   ), American author, b.
Pipestone, Minn. She is author of animal stories for
children, including *Chanco, U.S. Homing Pigeon; Topkick,
U.S. Army Horse;* and *Beano, Circus Dog.*

Watson, James Dewey (1928–   ), American biochemist.
He shared the 1960 Nobel prize in medicine and
physiology with F. H. C. Crick and M. H. F. Wilkins for his
part in determining the structure of DNA—the molecule
that carries the instructions for the development of a
new organism. From their knowledge of DNA's structure,
Watson and Crick correctly predicted how chromosomes
duplicate themselves and how genetic information is
coded on the molecule. Watson wrote *The Double Helix*
(1968) about the discovery of DNA's structure.

Watson, John B., American psychologist L 100
Watson, Thomas A., American engineer T 56
 "Mr. Watson, come here," famous words in the history
  of communication C 438
 worked with Alexander Graham Bell B 132–33
Watt, James, Scottish inventor W 68–69
 contribution to Industrial Revolution I 239
 invented automated governor A 532
 Newcomen engine, improvement on E 210
 steam engine S 420
 unit of electric power named for E 134
Watteau (wa-TO), **Jean Antoine,** French painter F 425
 Embarkation for Cythera, painting P 25
 Mezzetin, painting F 424
 rococo style P 24
Wattle and daub, building method B 434
 houses H 173
Watts, Isaac, English clergyman and hymn writer H 312
 carols C 122
Watts, units of electric power T 250
 named for James Watt E 134
Watusi, or Watutsi see Tutsi
Waugh (WAU), **Evelyn,** English novelist E 267
Waveguide, of a radio telescope R 72
Waves
 earthquake (seismic) E 32–33
 erosion by waves E 283
 interferometers, length-measuring instruments O 172
 light L 268
 masers and lasers M 132–33
 ocean waves O 34–35
 radiation R 41–42
 sound waves S 258–59
 tsunami, seismic sea waves E 36
 X rays X 341
Waves and wave lengths
 amplitude modulation R 57
 Doppler effect L 269; S 263
 spectrum colors determined by wave lengths, diagrams
  L 268
WAVES see Women's Reserve of the United States
  Naval Reserve
Wawasee (wa-wa-SEE), **Lake,** Indiana I 138

Wawel Castle, Cracow, Poland   P 361
Wax dolls   D 265
Waxes   W 69–70
    candles, history and manufacture of   C 96–97, 399
Waxing and waning, of the moon   M 447
Wax myrtles, shrubs see Bayberry
Wax paper   W 70

Waxwing, bird about 8 in. long, generally brown with a yellow or red band on the tail tip and crested head feathers. They are gentle and sociable birds, except at breeding time, when they separate into pairs to nest in treetops. Waxwings are found mainly in northern Europe, Asia, and in North America.

Waxy corn   C 506
Waybills, records of freight shipments   R 83
Wayne, Anthony ("Mad Anthony"), American patriot and
    army officer P 143
    Indian wars, Battle of Fallen Timbers, 1794   I 213
    Revolutionary War campaigns   R 206
    Wayne County, Michigan named for him   M 272

Wayne, John (Marion Michael Morrison), (1907–   ), American actor, b. Winterset, Iowa. Wayne started as a prop boy at Fox studios. He rose to stardom in such films as Stagecoach, Red River, Sands of Iwo Jima, True Grit, and Big Jake. He won an Academy Award as Best Actor of 1969 for his performance in True Grit.

Way of All Flesh, The, by Samuel Butler   E 264
Way of the Cross, Jerusalem   J 80
WCTU see Woman's Christian Temperance Union,
    National
Wealth of Nations, The, book by Adam Smith   T 27
Weapons
    ancient arms and armor   A 433–35
    atomic bomb   N 362–63; picture N 353
    bows and arrows   A 366–68; I 335
    Bronze Age   B 409; P 446
    duelists allowed choice of   D 340
    guns and ammunition   G 414–26
    missiles   M 343–47
    prehistoric man, tools and weapons   P 443–46
    rifles   R 233–35
    Shang dynasty, China, bronze weapons of   C 268–69
Weasels   O 242–43; pictures L 218
Weather   W 71–90
    air pollution may affect heat and rainfall   A 110
    atmosphere   A 480
    climates, types of   C 343–48
    control of the weather   W 91–96
    cyclones   H 293; W 74, 187
    drought conditions   W 75
    dust, effects of   D 348
    fog and smog   F 288–89
    freak conditions cause reports of flying saucers
        F 287
    Groundhog Day, and others   H 159
    hail   R 97–98
    hurricanes   H 292–96
    IGY studies   I 316–17
    jet streams   J 88–91
    rain   R 93–95
    satellites in weather research   S 43
    sleet   R 96–97
    snow   R 95–96
    solar energy its main cause   S 235
    thunder and lightning   T 170–73
    tornadoes   H 296–99
    tree rings, use in study of   T 286–87
    warning flags   F 246

winds and weather   W 184–87
    See also Barometer; Climate; Clouds
Weather control   W 91–96
Weatherford, William see Red Eagle
Weather forecasting   W 77–79
    clouds, weather-in-the-making   C 360; pictures C 361
    computers   C 457
Weathering
    formation of gumbotil, glacial deposits   I 20
    See also Erosion
Weather instruments   W 79–84
Weather maps   W 77–79
Weather stations   W 77
Weather vane, picture   F 293
Weaver, Pauline, American scout and prospector   A 416

Weaver, Robert Clifton (1907–   ), American government official and educator, b. Washington, D.C. He has served as specialist and adviser to various government agencies concerned with Negro labor, housing, and education. His posts have included those of New York State rent commissioner (1955–59) and administrator of the Housing and Home Finance Agency (1961). As secretary of the Department of Housing and Urban Development (1966–68) he was the first Negro cabinet member. He was president of Bernard M. Baruch College of the City University of New York (1968–70). Picture   N 101.
    years of change in Negro history   N 100, 101

Weaver ants   A 323; picture A 324
Weaving   W 97–98
    automated loom   A 532
    fabrics from various fibers, pictures   F 107
    how to weave a place mat   I 224
    Indian beadwork   I 158
    Industrial Revolution   I 233–35
    Mexican handloom, picture   T 141
    rugs and carpets   R 350–54
    tapestry   T 22–24
    weave types of textiles   T 143–44, 140
Webb, Sim, American railroad fireman   T 74

Weber (VAY-ber), Carl Maria (Friedrich Ernst) von (1786–1826), German composer, conductor, and pianist, b. Eutin. Considered founder of German romantic opera, he was conductor of German Opera at Prague (1813–17) and director of German Opera Theater at Dresden (1817). His works include operas Der Freischutz, Euryanthe, Oberon, symphonies, concertos, masses, songs, chamber works, and piano pieces.
    opera in the classical age   C 332–33; G 187; O 134

Weber (WEB-er), Max (1881–1961), American painter, b. Bialystok, Russia. A leader in the introduction of modern European art to United States, he was influenced by the Fauves' use of color and by cubism. His paintings based on New York scenes and Jewish life include Chinese Restaurant, Geranium, and The Rabbi.

Weber (VAY-ber), Max, German sociologist   S 227

Webern (VAY-bern), Anton von (1883–1945), Austrian composer, b. Vienna. An orchestral conductor in Vienna, Prague, and Germany (1908–14), after World War I he devoted himself to writing and teaching composition. He was a principal conductor of the Vienna Workers' Symphony Concerts (1922–24). Associated with Schoenberg, he adopted the 12-tone system and has been called an extreme modernist. His works include Five Orchestral Pieces and Six Bagatelles for string quartet.
    chamber music composers of the 20th century   C 186;
        G 189; M 402

Web-perfecting rotary presses, for printing   P 462–63
Webster, Daniel, American statesman and orator
  W 98–99
  Daniel Webster Birthplace State Historic Site
    N 158
  New Hampshire, famous people from   **N** 161
  Seventh of March speech supporting Compromise of
    1850   **C** 448

Webster, John (1580?–1625), English dramatist. He collaborated on plays written for theater manager Philip Henslowe. With Thomas Dekker he wrote *Northward Hoe* and *Westward Hoe*. Noted for his tragedies, particularly *The White Devil* and *The Duchess of Malfi,* he wrote other plays, including *Devil's Law Case* and *Appius and Virginia.*
  drama, history of   **D** 296

Webster, Noah, American author and compiler of a
  dictionary   **W** 99
  Connecticut, famous people from   **C** 478
  copyright laws passed in some states   **T** 244
  early textbooks   **T** 138
  his was first in series of dictionaries   **D** 164
  introduced phonics with his Blue-Backed spellers
    P 193–94
  spelling words from Blue-Backed Speller   **S** 379
Webster-Ashburton Treaty, 1842   **T** 108
  Maine's boundary and "Bloodless Aroostook War"
    settled   **M** 47; **N** 138g
  Tyler and Webster negotiated the treaty   **T** 339
Weddell Sea   **O** 49
Wedding customs   **W** 100–03
  bridal rings   **J** 98
  Burmese bride and groom, picture   **F** 41
  folk music   **F** 326
  1951 he left the service to enter private business.
  Japan   **J** 26; **W** 102
  knives as gifts   **K** 286
  Korea   **K** 298
  Latin America   **L** 56
  wedding in Greek Orthodox Church, picture   **O** 228
Wedding Dance, The, painting by Brueghel   **B** 415
Wedding rings   **W** 100
  bridal rings, jewelry   **J** 98

Wedemeyer (WED-e-my-er), **Albert Coady** (1897–   ), American general, b. Omaha, Neb. He was made the commander of the U.S. Army forces in the China theater of war (1944–46). Regarded as an expert in war plans, he returned to China (1947) on a presidential mission to make a survey of the country's situation. The following year he became deputy chief of staff of the Army and commanding general of the Sixth Army (1949–51). In 1951 he retired from the Army.

Wedgwood (WEDGE-wood), or Wedgwood ware   **P** 418–19;
  picture   **A** 319

Wedgwood, Josiah (1730–1795), English ceramicist, b. Burslem. Born into a family of ceramicists, he began experimenting with new techniques at an early age. His cream-colored earthenware, called queen's ware after his patron, Queen Charlotte, found a world-wide market. When Thomas Bentley, a Liverpool merchant, became his partner (1768), he began manufacturing ornamental wares, for which he built (1769) a factory, called Etruria, near Hanley. Wedgwood's researches into materials, his efforts to improve communications, and his advanced labor concepts and business organization made him one of the leaders of the Industrial Revolution.
  pottery, history of   **P** 418–19

Wedgwood, Thomas, English inventor   **P** 210
Wednesday, origin of name   **D** 47
  Ash Wednesday   **R** 153, 301
Weed-killers
  water pollution   **W** 58, 59
Weeds   **W** 104–06
  August, weed-month   **A** 492
  cotton crops, weed control   **C** 524
  how long seeds stay alive   **P** 299
  lawn care   **L** 90–91
  plant poisoning of animals   **P** 323
  weeding gardens   **G** 42
Week
  origin of, for the calendar   **C** 11–12
Weeks, Feast of, or Pentecost, religious holidays   **R** 154
Weeks Law, 1911   **N** 34
Weelkes, Thomas, English composer   **E** 269–70

Weems, Mason Locke (1759–1825), American clergyman and author, b. Anne Arundel County, Md. He served as a pastor in Maryland (1784–92), and then became a traveling book agent. Weems wrote numerous moral tracts, as well as biographies of George Washington, Benjamin Franklin, and William Penn. His *Life and Memorable Actions of George Washington* was responsible for the popular story of Washington chopping down the cherry tree.

Weeping willow, tree, picture   **T** 276
  shapes of leaves, picture   **L** 116

Weevil, one of a group of small plant-eating beetles whose heads extend downward into a beak or snout with sharp jaws at the end. Some species, such as the cotton boll weevil, cause great damage by destroying crops. Weevils are found throughout the world. Picture   **P** 288.
  boll weevil   **C** 523
  plant enemies and pests   **P** 285, 289

Weft, or filling, crosswise strands on a loom   **T** 140
  called woof threads on the loom   **I** 234
Wegener (VAIG-en-er), **Alfred,** German geophysicist   **G** 117
We have met the enemy and they are ours, words of
  Commander Perry after battle of Lake Erie   **P** 157

Weidman (WIDE-man), **Charles Edward** (1901–   ), American dancer and choreographer, b. Lincoln, Nebr. He developed a style of modern dance derived from pantomime. With Doris Humphrey he founded a school and dance group in New York (1927), for which he created the dramatic composition *Lynchtown* and a comic routine, *Flickers.* He founded his own group, Theatre Dance Company (1948), and adapted James Thurber's *Fables of Our Times* for the dance.
  modern dance groups   **D** 34

Weight, pull of gravity on matter
  air has weight   **A** 479; demonstration **A** 481
  density   **F** 250–51
  gravity affects weight   **G** 324
Weight, atomic *see* Atomic weight
Weight, body *see* Overweight
Weightlessness, zero gravity   **S** 340k–340L
  lack of gravitational pull   **G** 324
Weight lifting   **W** 107
  Olympic Games, gymnastic sports   **O** 109
Weights and measures   **W** 108–17
  African gold weights, art objects   **A** 72
  areas and volumes, geometric rules for   **G** 129
  barometer   **B** 54
  British thermal unit   **H** 91
  calories and kilocalories   **H** 91

Weights and measures (continued)
  carat, unit for measuring gemstones **J** 92
  heat units **E** 199
  how to convert degrees of latitude into miles **L** 82–83
  international trade problems **I** 328
  karat, unit for measuring gold **J** 92
  thermometer **T** 165
  tonnage of ships **I** 337

Weil, Lisl (1910–), American illustrator and author of children's books, b. Vienna, Austria. She has had her own program, Children's Sketch Book, on TV and has illustrated music in pictures at concerts of the Little Orchestra Society in New York, N.Y. Her books include *The Busiest Boy in Holland*, and *I Wish, I Wish*.
  picture books for children **C** 243

Weimar (VY-mar), Germany **G** 157
Weimaraner (vy-ma-RA-ner), sporting dog, picture **D** 253
Weimar (VY-mar) **Republic**, of Germany **G** 162
Weir, Robert Stanley, Canadian lawyer and poet **N** 27
Weirs, brush fences for trapping fish **F** 217

Weisgard (WICE-gard), **Leonard Joseph** (1916–), American author and illustrator, b. New Haven, Conn. He has written and illustrated books for children, including *Just Like Me, Treasures to See*, and *Who Dreams of Cheese?* He received Caldecott medal (1947) for his illustrations for Margaret Wise Brown's *The Little Island*.

Weiss, Ehrich, see Houdini, Harry
Weissenberg, I. M., Yiddish author **Y** 351

Weissmuller, Johnny (1904–) American swimmer and movie actor, b. Chicago, Ill. He won the Olympic gold medal at Paris (1924) in 100- and 400-meter freestyle races and at Amsterdam (1928) in the 100-meter freestyle race and as anchorman in the 800-meter relay race. He retired from swimming (1929) and became known as film star, playing role of Tarzan in the movie *Tarzan, The Ape Man* and a series of Jungle Jim films.

Weitz, Paul J., American astronaut **S** 345, 347
Weizäcker, Carl von, German astronomer **S** 249
Weizmann (VITES-monn), **Chaim,** Russian-born president of Israel **W** 118
  improves Pasteur's method of producing acetone **F** 90
  Jewish homeland **J** 112
Welding W 118–19
  helium used in **N** 109
  nitrogen gas **N** 262
  oxyhydrogen welding torches **G** 61
  soldering and brazing **S** 249–50
  See also Brazing; Soldering

Welensky, Sir Roy (Roland Welensky) (1907–), Rhodesian political leader, b. Salisbury, Southern Rhodesia. Formerly a railroad worker and union leader, he began his political career as an elected member of Legislative Council (1938) and Executive Council (1940) of Northern Rhodesia. He played a major part in formation of the Federation of Rhodesia and Nyasaland (now Rhodesia, Malawi, and Zambia) in 1953. He served as Federation prime minister, minister of External Affairs, and president of United Federal Party (1956–63).

Welfare, public W 120–21
  adoption agencies **A** 25–26
  changes proposed under Nixon administration **N** 262d
  grant money from foundations **F** 390–92
  Kuwait, à welfare state **K** 305

  mental retardation **R** 189–91
  orphanages and foster-family care **O** 227
  public assistance, or relief **S** 221
  social security **S** 221–22
  social work **S** 225–26
  Sweden's "Middle Way" **S** 486
Welland Ship Canal, Great Lakes **G** 328; **O** 121–22
  pictures **C** 83, **O** 123

Welles, Orson (George Orson Welles) (1915–), American producer, director, and actor, b. Kenosha, Wis. He began his acting career with the Gate Theatre, Dublin, Ireland (1931–32), later establishing the Mercury Theater (1937). He has acted in and directed radio drama *War of the Worlds* (so realistic it created panic among listeners), the movie *Citizen Kane*, and plays *King Lear, Julius Caesar*, and *Dr. Faustus*. He has appeared in numerous films including *Moby Dick, Compulsion, A Man for All Seasons, Catch 22*, and *The Kremlin Letter*. He is author of *Mr. Arkadin* and editor, with Roger Hill, of *Mercury Shakespeare*.
  Citizen Kane, motion picture **M** 485

Welles (WELLS), **Sumner** (1892–1961), American diplomat, b. New York, N.Y. Secretary to the American Embassy in Tokyo (1915–17) and Buenos Aires (1917–19), he soon laid the foundation for the Good Neighbor Policy in the Dominican Republic and in Honduras. He was United States ambassador to Cuba (1933) and United States delegate to the Pan-American Congress (1936). Undersecretary of state (1937–43) and president of Freedom House (1952–61), he is the author of *We Need Not Fail*.

Wellesley, Arthur see Wellington, Duke of
Wellington, capital of New Zealand **N** 241; picture **N** 242
Wellington, Duke of, British general **W** 122
  England's victory over Napoleon **E** 225
  Waterloo **N** 12
Wells W 122–24
  Cyprus well, picture **C** 556
  famous wells of history **W** 66
  oases **O** 2–3
  oil wells, "Christmas trees" **P** 173–74
  pumps **P** 528–30
  water pollution **W** 58
  water supply from wells **W** 66
Wells, H. G., English writer **W** 124
  Modern Utopia, A **U** 256
  science fiction **S** 84
Wells, Horace, American dentist **A** 257
  introduced "laughing gas" as an anesthetic **M** 208a

Wells, Fargo and Company, express company founded in 1852 by Henry Wells and William Fargo. It carried mail, gold, and silver to and from California and the West—by sea through the Panama Canal and overland by coach, railroad, and briefly by Pony Express. The company expanded service to the United States Atlantic coast, Canada, Alaska, Mexico, Central America, and the Caribbean. It combined with the American Railway Express Company (1918) but retained railroad service in Mexico and Cuba as a separate company.

Well-tempered Clavichord (CLAV-i-cord), **The,** by Bach **B** 5
Welsh corgis (CORG-is), dogs, picture **D** 254
Welsh language W 3
Welterweight, in boxing **B** 352
Welty, Eudora, American novelist **A** 213
  short stories **S** 167

Wenceslaus (WEN-ces-laus), king of Bohemia   **C** 563
Wentle trap, mollusk
   shell, picture   **S** 147
Werfel, Franz, German writer   **G** 179
Werner (VAIR-ner), **Abraham,** German geologist   **G** 111
Wesak, religious holiday   **R** 154
Weser (VASE-er) **River,** Germany   **R** 248; picture   **G** 154
Wesley, Charles, English Methodist preacher   **C** 288
   carols   **C** 122
   hymn writer   **H** 312

Wesley, Charles Harris (1892–   ), American educator and historian, Negro, b. Louisville, Ky. He was professor of history and chairman of the department at Howard University (1921–42) and president of Wilberforce University in Ohio (1942–47). He was president of Central State College, Wilberforce, Ohio, from 1947 to 1965. He is co-author of *The Negro in Our History.*

Wesley, John, English founder of Methodism   **W** 125
   Christianity, history of   **C** 288
   oratory   **O** 181
   Protestantism   **P** 482–86
   Reformation in England   **R** 135
Wesleyan Free Church of Tonga   **T** 210a

West, Benjamin (1738–1820), American painter, b. near Springfield, Pa. He painted, principally portraits, in Philadelphia, New York, and Italy until he settled in London (1763). Favored by King George III, who appointed him court historical painter (1772) and made him charter member of Royal Academy (1768), he is best-known for historical paintings, including *Death of Wolfe* and *Penn's Treaty with the Indians.*

West, James E., first Chief Scout Executive of Boy Scouts of America   **B** 357
West, Jessamyn, American novelist   **H** 278
West, Nathanael, American novelist   **A** 213
West, The, of United States
   Buffalo Bill   **B** 428
   Carson, Kit   **C** 123
   cattle wars   **W** 337
   cowboys   **C** 146–47;   **R** 102–03
   Denver, "western capital"   **D** 116
   Frémont, John Charles   **F** 458
   Indian Wars   **I** 212–15
   James, Jesse   **J** 19
   Lewis and Clark expedition   **L** 162–63
   overland trails   **O** 251–67
   pioneer life   **P** 251–62
   Pony Express   **P** 392–93
   ranch life   **R** 102–06
   rodeos   **R** 281–82
   westward movement   **W** 142–46
West, Thomas see Delaware, Lord
West bank, Jordan River   **J** 139
West Berlin, Germany   **B** 144–45
   Hansa quarter, picture   **E** 332
West End, London, England   **L** 336
Westerlies, winds   **W** 186–87
Western Australia   **A** 512
Western Development Museum, Saskatchewan   **S** 38f
Western Dvina (dvi-NA) **River,** U.S.S.R.   **R** 248
Western Hemisphere
   highest and lowest points   **N** 285
   Monroe Doctrine   **M** 425, 426–29
   Organization of American States   **O** 210–11
Western hemlock, tree
   state tree of Washington   **W** 15
Western meadowlarks, birds
   Kansas, state bird of   **K** 177

   Montana, state bird of   **M** 428
   Nebraska, state bird of   **N** 72
   North Dakota, state bird of   **N** 323
   Oregon, state bird of   **O** 193
   Wyoming, state bird of   **W** 322
Western Penitentiary, Allegheny, Pennsylvania
   P 468
Western Reserve, Connecticut's land in Ohio Territory
   O 64
Western Reserve University, now Case Western Reserve University, Cleveland, Ohio   **C** 338
Western Roman Empire   **R** 308, 317
   Middle Ages, beginnings of   **M** 289–90
Western saddle, picture   **H** 227
Western Samoa   **S** 23–25
   Apia River, picture   **P** 7
   flag   **F** 240
Western Schism, Great (1378–1431), within the Roman Catholic Church   **R** 293
   two popes   **F** 415
Western Union Telegraph Company   **T** 52
Western Wall, Jerusalem   **J** 79, 138
Western white pine
   Idaho's state tree   **I** 54
West Germany see Germany, Federal Republic of
West Goths see Visigoths
West Highland white terrier, dog, picture   **D** 255

West Indies, archipelago in the Caribbean Sea stretching in an arc from Florida to the coast of Venezuela. The islands were discovered (1492) and named by Christopher Columbus, who thought he had reached India. They are usually separated into three groups: the Bahamas, the Greater Antilles (including Cuba, the Dominican Republic, Haiti, Puerto Rico, Jamaica), and the Lesser Antilles.
   Caribbean Sea and Islands   **C** 116–19

West Indies Associated States, island states in the Caribbean, each of whom has self government within the Commonwealth of Nations. The United Kingdom has retained responsibility for defense and foreign affairs. Established in 1967, the group includes the states of Antigua, St. Kitts-Nevis-Anguilla, Dominica, St. Lucia, Grenada, and St. Vincent. Anguilla attempted to secede from the St. Kitts-Nevis-Anguilla associate state and from the Commonwealth (1969), but later agreed to postpone action.
   Caribbean Sea and islands   **C** 118, 119

West Indies Federation   **J** 18
Westinghouse, George, American inventor   **W** 125
   invention of the air brake   **R** 88
West Irian (ir-i-ON), Indonesia   **I** 220, 222;   **N** 147
Westminster, borough of London, England   **L** 335
Westminster, Palace of, official name of British Houses of Parliament, pictures   **L** 338, **U** 70
Westminster Abbey, London, England   **L** 335; pictures   **P** 483,   **U** 67
   Britain's tomb of an unknown soldier   **U** 225
   Poets' Corner, Chaucer's burial spot   **C** 190
   tracery pattern work in   **G** 269
Westminster Kennel Club   **D** 261
Westmoreland, William C., American general   **V** 336
West New Guinea (GHIN-e), now West Irian   **I** 220, 222; **N** 417
West Pakistan see Pakistan
Westphalia (west-PHAIL-ia), **Peace of,** 1648   **C** 287
   paved way for religious toleration in Germany   **G** 160
   Swiss independence   **S** 502
West Point, New York
   United States Military Academy   **U** 168

West Quoddy Head, Maine, easternmost point in the United States **M** 32, 43
West Troy, New York
   locks of the Erie Canal, picture **E** 276
West Virginia **W** 126–41
   Monongahela National Forest, picture **N** 37
   places of interest in Negro history **N** 94
   poverty in Appalachia **P** 424a–424b
   Virginia counties against secession **V** 360
West Virginia University **W** 134
Westward movement, United States **W** 142–46
   Boone and the Wilderness Road **B** 335; **O** 255
   fur trade in North America **F** 520–24
   gold discoveries **G** 250–53
   Indian Wars **I** 212–15
   Jefferson anticipates Northwest Ordinance **J** 65
   Lewis and Clark expedition **L** 162–63
   Louisiana Purchase **L** 364–65
   migration to Oregon **O** 193, 197, 207
   Missouri River **M** 383
   Oregon Trail **O** 260–63
   overland trails **O** 251–67
   pioneer life **P** 251–62
   public lands **P** 506–07
   territorial expansion of the United States **T** 106–10
   What was the Northwest Ordinance? **W** 143
Westward the Course of Empire Takes Its Way, painting by Lentze **T** 106
Wet suits see Cold-water suits for skin diving

Weyden (VY-den), **Rogier van der** (Roger de la Pasture) (1399?–1464) Flemish painter, b. Tournai, Belgium. He followed Van Eyck as leader in Flemish school. He became city painter in Brussels (1436) and painted for churches and other public buildings, as well as for private patrons. Known for religious paintings, he gained fame with the painting *Descent from the Cross.* His other works include *Last Judgment* and *Christ Appearing to His Mother.*
   Descent from the Cross, painting **D** 353
   Dutch and Flemish art **D** 351

Weygand (vay-GON), **Maxime** (1867–1965), French general, b. Brussels, Belgium. As chief of staff under Marshal Foch (1914–23) he helped the Poles resist a Russian invasion of Warsaw (1920). During World War II he took over command in France (1940) but was unable to prevent a German victory. Under the Vichy regime he was military commander in North Africa (1940) and governor-general of Algeria. (1941). He was arrested by the Germans in 1942. After the liberation (1945), he was cleared of charges of collaborating with them.

Weyler y Nicolau (WAY-ler e ni-co-LA-u), **Valeriano,** Spanish general **S** 374

Weymouth (WAY-muth), or **Waymouth, George,** English navigator and explorer, b. Devonshire. Commissioned by the East India Company to find a northwestern passage to India, Weymouth reached Hudson Strait (1602) but was forced to turn back because of mutiny. On his second voyage (1605) he explored the coast of present-day Maine.

Whalebone, or baleen **W** 147
   whale products **W** 152
Whale oil **W** 152
Whales **W** 147–51
   aging **A** 84, 86
   Are whales fish? **O** 39
   blue whale, largest mammal **M** 61
   dolphins **D** 270
   evolution of **E** 346

   giants of nature **G** 200, 202, 204
   growth, rate of **G** 202
   "Jonah and the Whale," Bible story **B** 166–67
   largest animals **A** 262
   locomotion **A** 290
   migration **H** 191
   ocean dwellers **O** 39
   porpoises **D** 270
   short food chain **L** 241
   spermaceti wax, candles of **C** 97
   whaling **W** 152–53
   See also Dolphins; Porpoises
Whaling **W** 152–53
   early Massachusetts industry **M** 140–41
   lighting by whale oil caused growth of the industry **L** 279
   protecting whales **W** 151
   whaling ships, "factories" **S** 159
Whangpoo River, China
   Shanghai **S** 138–39

Wharton, Clifton R. (1899–   ), American diplomat, Negro, b. Baltimore, Md. Leaving his law practice in Boston (1920–24), he became a foreign service officer the following year and served as a consul to the Canary Islands (1930–41) and consul general to Lisbon (1950–53). He continued with the service as envoy to Rumania (1958–60) and ambassador extraordinary to Norway (1961–64).

Wharton, Edith, American novelist **A** 208
   themes of her novels **N** 349

Wharton, William H. (1802–1839), American lawyer and leader in Texas revolt, b. Albemarle County, Va. He was president of the San Felipe Convention (1832), which met to protest a decree by Mexico prohibiting further American settlement of Texas. He advocated Texan independence from Mexico. In 1836 he negotiated American annexation of Texas.

What Do You Do in the Infantry?, song, by Loesser **N** 26
What hath God wrought! first telegraph message **T** 51
   Morse, Samuel **M** 462
Wheat **W** 154–56
   Australian wheat farm, picture **A** 506
   Canada's wheat belt **C** 58; **S** 38f; pictures **A** 146b; **C** 59; **S** 38b
   cereal grasses **G** 317
   dwarf strains **G** 88
   fields of the Great Plains, pictures **A** 90–91; **K** 178
   flour and flour milling **F** 274–75
   grain and grain products **G** 282, 287
   improved varieties, dwarfed or hybridized **G** 287
   prairie crops of spring and winter wheat **P** 432
   rust, life cycle **F** 498; diagram **F** 499
   rye compared to **R** 364
   seeds and ear, pictures **G** 283
   Triticale, species hybrid, wheat and rye **G** 287
   Turkey Red strain brought to Kansas **K** 181
   world distribution, diagram **W** 265
Wheatland, near Lancaster, Pa., home of James Buchanan **B** 419
Wheatley, Phillis, Senegal-born American poet **W** 156
   Negro history **N** 93
Wheat state, nickname for Kansas **K** 177

Wheatstone, Sir Charles (1802–1875), English physicist and inventor, b. Gloucester. He was noted for his studies in sound, electricity, and vision. His inventions include an electric telegraph, for which he and W. F. Cooke took out a patent in 1837, and a dynamo. His name has been given to the Wheatstone bridge, a device for measuring resistance in an electric circuit. He drew attention to the device, but its inventor was S. H. Christie.

the needle telegraph, invention of **T** 51

Wheelbarrow, painting by Pissarro **F** 428
Wheelchairs H 28; pictures **H** 29, 30
Wheel ditchers, machines **B** 448
Wheeler, Burton Kendall, American statesman **M** 441
Wheeler, Joseph, American general **S** 375
Wheeler, Schuyler Skaats, American inventor **F** 43
Wheeler, William A., vice-president, United States **V** 331; picture **V** 328
Wheeling, West Virginia **W** 138; picture **W** 139
Wheel locks, early guns **G** 415—16
Wheels W 157—58
abrasive wheels for grinding **T** 219
automobiles **A** 544
grinding and polishing **G** 389; picture **G** 388
importance to transportation **T** 257
invention harnesses energy for men's use **I** 335, 337
tires **T** 196—98
turbines **T** 319—22
See also Tires; Turbines
Wheelworms, or rotifers, a class of invertebrate animals **P** 281
Welks, mollusks **O** 276
When all the world is young, lad, first line of Kingsley's poem **P** 351
Whey (WHAY), of milk **D** 12—13
what milk contains **M** 311
Which, magazine for Consumers' Association of Great Britain **C** 494a
Whiddy Island, near Bantry, Ireland **I** 389
Whig Party, United States **P** 380
Fillmore, last Whig president **F** 123—25
symbol **P** 379
Tyler, John **T** 339—41
Whigs, British political party **P** 378—79
Gladstone's career **G** 225

Whip, member of a legislative body appointed by his political party to act as an assistant floor leader. Among his duties are enforcing party discipline, requesting the attendance of members at important sessions, and keeping the leaders informed of the attitudes of members toward public questions.

organization of Congress **U** 144

Whipping posts, punishment
Delaware **D** 98

Whipple, William (1730—1785), American Revolutionary War leader, b. Kittery, Maine. A merchant at Portsmouth, N.H., he became a member of the provincial congress of the state (1775) and of the Continental Congress (1776—79). As such, he was a signer of the Declaration of Independence. He served as a militia commander in two campaigns and as an associate justice of the New Hampshire superior court (1782—85).

Whippoorwill, brownish bird with rounded wings, rounded tail tip, and bristles around its bill. The whippoorwill is active chiefly at night. The bird is named for its call, which it repeats over and over—hundreds of times in a single night. The whippoorwill is found from southern Canada to Central America.

Whip with Six Strings, legislative act of Henry VIII **C** 286
Whirling dervish see Dervish

Whirlpool, liquid spinning around a lower central area.

As water empties from a tub down a drain it forms a small whirlpool. Tiny whirlpools are seen in moving water where currents from different directions meet. Large whirlpools in the sea or in river channels are caused by similar forces. Winds, rocks, tides, even the shape of a shore, may cause a whirlpool. Some can be dangerous to ships during storms.

Whiskers, of cats **C** 134
Whiskey, a distilled beverage **W** 159
malt extracts of various grains **G** 286
rye mash **R** 364

Whiskey Rebellion, or **Whiskey Insurrection,** uprising, stemming from general grievances against the government, of farmers from the backwoods of western Pennsylvania against the excise tax put on whiskey. Although the tax was lowered in 1792 and 1794, the people wanted it repealed. Federal troops put down the rebellion (1794).

Hamilton and Washington enforced federal authority **H** 19; **W** 43

Whispering galleries, ellipse-shaped domes **G** 129
Whist, card game **C** 107
Whistler, James Abbott McNeill, American painter **W** 160
Rotherhithe, etching **E** 294
United States, art of the **U** 121
White, a combination of all colors **D** 139

White, Byron R. ("Whizzer") (1917—), American justice, b. Fort Collins, Colo. To help pay his way through law school, he was a professional football player with the Detroit Lions and was named to the National Football Hall of Fame in 1954. He practiced corporation law in Denver (1947—60) and was named deputy attorney general (1961—62). He has been an associate justice of the Supreme Court since 1962.

persons connected with football **F** 356

White, Clarence Cameron (1880—1960), American violinist and composer, Negro, b. Clarksville, Tenn. Noted for compositions based on Negro and Haitian themes, he composed the opera *Ouanga, a Negro Rhapsody.*

White, E. B., American writer **W** 160—61
American literature **A** 214
Charlotte's Web, excerpt **W** 160—61
White, Edward Douglass, American jurist **L** 361

White, Edward Higgins II (1930—67), American astronaut, b. San Antonio, Texas. On June 3—7, 1965, White and James Alton McDivitt made a 62-orbit flight in Gemini 4. During the flight, White left the capsule for 21 minutes and maneuvered freely in space, while remaining attached to Gemini 4 by a long cord. He was the first astronaut to do so. White, and astronauts Virgil Grissom and Roger Chaffee, died during test runthrough of Apollo launching.

space flight data **S** 344, 345, 347
walk in space, picture **S** 340e

White, George Henry (1852—1918), American politician, Negro, b. Rosindale, N.C. After earning his law and Ph.D. degrees, he rose rapidly in North Carolina politics, serving in the state house (1880) and senate (1884). He was elected to 2 terms in Congress (1896—1900) on the Republican ticket. Born a slave, he fought for Negro equality and was first congressman to introduce an anti-lynching bill.

White, Israel Charles, American geologist **W** 138
White, Jim, New Mexican cowboy **C** 152—53

White, John (16th century), artist and colonial governor, b. probably England. In 1585 he was sent by Sir Walter Raleigh to his colony of Roanoke Island, N.C., to paint native life in America in the hope of interesting people in the New World. It is probable that he returned in 1587 as governor. Later that year he went to England for supplies, not to return for 3 years, after which time he could not find any trace of the colony. Among his works were a series of watercolor drawings, one of the best records of life in the early days of settlement.
the "Lost Colony" **A** 181

White, Josh (1908–69), American folk singer, Negro, b. Greenville, S.C. Through his recordings of Negro spirituals, he became popular as the Singing Christian, and through blues songs, as Pinewood Tom. He sang in clubs and cafés and made numerous concert appearances, accompanying himself on the guitar.

White, Peregrine, first white child born in New England
M 185

White, Robert M. (1924–), American test pilot, b. New York, N.Y. He was a fighter pilot during World War II. A test pilot at Edwards Air Force Base since 1955, he set a world airplane altitude record of 314,750 feet in the X-15 (1962). The same year he became the first to receive the Air Force astronaut rating in a winged aircraft.

White, Stanford, American architect
designed Hall of Fame for Great Americans **H** 12
White, T. H., English author **E** 248

White, Walter Francis (1893–1955) American novelist and sociologist, Negro, b. Atlanta, Ga. Secretary of the National Association for the Advancement of Colored People (1931–55), he was a member of the Advisory Council for the Government of the Virgin Islands (1934). His first novel, *Fire in the Flint,* on lynching in a small Southern town, was reprinted in many European countries. A later work, *A Man Called White,* is autobiographical.

White, William Allen, American author and journalist
K 190
White ants see Termites
White ash, tree, picture **T** 277
leaf, diagram **L** 114
White blood cells **B** 256–57
circulatory system of human body **B** 275–77
role in immunity **I** 104

White cedar, name for various trees in the pine family, especially some cedars, junipers, and cypresses. The northern white cedar, or arbor vitae, has tiny, flat scalelike needles and small oblong cones. It grows to a height of 50 feet in the swamps of northeastern and north central North America.

White cliffs of Dover, England **E** 213
White-collar workers **L** 8
White Deer, Legend of the **L** 134
White dwarfs, stars **S** 407–08

White elephant, term for some object no longer of value to the owner, the expense or responsibility in owning it often being more than it is worth. According to one story, the King of Siam (Thailand) gave a white elephant to a courtier he disliked, and the cost of feeding the animal brought the courtier to financial ruin. There is in fact a rare albino Indian elephant, worshiped by some people in India, Ceylon, Thailand, and Burma.

White fir, evergreen tree in the pine family. It is also called the Colorado fir. It may grow to a height of 200 feet. It has long needles, fairly long cones, and furrowed bark. The white fir is found on the mountain slopes of western North America, from the Columbia River to northern Mexico, at elevations of from 4,000 feet to 10,000 feet. Its timber is used commercially.

Whitefish
habitat, feeding habits, uses **F** 216
White foxes **D** 249–50
White gold **G** 248
Whitehall, London street leading to the Houses of Parliament **L** 335

Whitehead, Sir Edgar Cuthbert Fremantle (1905–), Rhodesian political leader, b. Berlin, Germany. Went to Southern Rhodesia in 1928 and served as acting high commissioner for Southern Rhodesia in London (1945–46). He served also as minister of finance and as minister of posts and telegraphs in Southern Rhodesia (1946–53), and as a member of the parliament of Southern Rhodesia (now Rhodesia) (since 1953). He was prime minister (1958–62) and was leader of the opposition (1962–65).

Whitehorse, capital of Yukon Territory, Canada **Y** 365
White Horse, The, painting by Gauguin **G** 64
White House, Washington, D.C. **W** 162–65
Adams, Abigail, first first lady to live there **F** 165
Adams, John, 1st president to occupy **A** 9
Arthur, Chester Alan, redecorated **A** 441
belongs to National Park System **N** 55
Christmas tree ceremony **C** 291
Cleveland's wedding **C** 341
first ladies **F** 164–80
Jefferson's occupancy **J** 68
points of interest in Washington, D.C. **W** 33
shown in 1800 drawing **A** 10
White House office staff **P** 447
White Leghorn, chickens **P** 422; picture **P** 421
White light **L** 267–68
White magic, used for good purposes **W** 208

Whiteman, Paul (1891–1967), American dance band leader, b. Denver, Colo. He organized his first band (1919) and became known in United States and Europe for his "symphonic jazz" music. He commissioned George Gershwin's *Rhapsody in Blue* and introduced Grofé's *Grand Canyon* Suite. He founded the Museum of American Music at Williams College (1936).

White matter, of the nervous system **B** 367
White Mountain National Forest, New Hampshire-Maine **N** 157; **M** 41; picture **N** 35
White Mountains, part of the Appalachians **N** 150
Maine **M** 36
White Nile River, Africa **N** 260
White noise, electronic sound **E** 142g
White oak, tree, picture **T** 277
leaves, shapes of, pictures **L** 116
state tree of Connecticut **C** 466
White on White, painting by Malevich **M** 392

White paper, detailed report issued by a government or private organization. It may be a statement of policy or an informative record of action already taken. White-paper reports of international importance include the British White Paper (1939), which outlined policy regarding Jewish settlement in Palestine, and U.S. White Paper (1965), defining U.S. involvement in South Vietnam.

White pine, tree, picture **T** 275
  leaves, needlelike, picture **L** 119
White Plymouth Rock, chickens **P** 421
White potatoes, or Irish potatoes **P** 411–12
White Rajahs of Sarawak M 56, 57
White River, Ontario, picture **G** 327
White Russia (Belorussia) **B** 138–39
White Sands Missile Range, New Mexico, picture **N** 186
  first test of the atomic bomb **W** 308
White Sea O 49
White sharks S 140
White snakeroot, poisonous plant **P** 323
White spirituals, gospel songs and hymns **H** 313; **N** 106
White spruce
  leaves, needlelike, pictures **L** 119
  state tree of South Dakota **S** 313
White Sulphur Springs, West Virginia **W** 137
White-tailed deer H 219; picture **H** 215
White-water canoeing C 101
White whales, or belugas **W** 147
White wines W 188
Whitfield House, Guilford, Conn. **C** 476; picture **C** 479
Whiting, fish
  habitats, feeding habits, uses **F** 213

Whitley, William (1749–1813), American Indian fighter, b. Amherst County, Va. His house became the center of the religious, political, and social life in the Transylvania region of Kentucky. Although ranked as a colonel, he enlisted as a private when the War of 1812 began and was killed in battle.

Whitman, Marcus, American doctor-missionary **W** 27
  Oregon Trail **O** 260
Whitman, Narcissa, American missionary **O** 260
Whitman, Walt, American poet **W** 165–66
  American literature **A** 203–04
  "O Captain! My Captain!" **W** 165–66
  Walt Whitman House, Camden, N.J. **N** 175
Whitman College, Walla Walla, Washington **W** 23
Whitney, Eli, American inventor **W** 166
  cotton gin **C** 523; picture **C** 521
  gun factory in New Haven, Conn. **C** 473
  introduced cotton gin to Georgia **G** 132
  introduced interchangeable parts to manufacturing **M** 84
Whitney, Mount, California **C** 16
  highest point in conterminous United States **N** 285
Whitney Museum of American Art, New York City **N** 219
  concrete, use of in modern architecture **A** 386
Whitsunday, or Pentecost, religious holiday **R** 154, 290
Whittaker, James W., American mountain climber **E** 337
Whittier, John Greenleaf, American poet **W** 167
  American literature **A** 202–03

Whittington, Dick (Richard Whittington) (1358?–1423), English merchant and philanthropist. A destitute orphan in London, legend says that he gained his fortune by sending his only possession, a cat, on a ship bound for Morocco. The King of Morocco, who was troubled with mice, bought Whittington's cat for a fabulous sum. Whittington was a member of the common council of London (1385, 1387) and served as sheriff (1393–94). He was the lord mayor of London (1397–98, 1406–07, 1419–20).

Whittle, Sir Frank (1907–   ), British officer and inventor, b. Coventry. One of the ablest pilots in the Royal Air Force, Whittle began experimenting with jet propulsion in 1929. By 1937 he had produced the world's first successful jet-propulsion engine. The British Government ordered the first jet-propelled airplane in 1939. For his work, Whittle was knighted in 1948.
  jet engines for airplanes, history of **A** 573; **J** 86

WHO see World Health Organization
Who Has Seen the Wind?, poem by Christina Rossetti **R** 336
Whole numbers, in arithmetic **A** 398
Wholesale selling S 116–17
Wholesale trade T 243
Whole steps, or tones, or major seconds, in music **M** 527
Whole wheat flour W 156
  does not need to be enriched **F** 275
Whooping cough, disease **D** 212
Whooping cranes, near-extinct birds **B** 232; picture **B** 230
  genetic change slow in members of single populations **G** 88
Why England Slept, book by John F. Kennedy **K** 206
Wichita, Kansas K 188
Wichita State University K 183
Wickersham, James, American statesman **A** 142
Wickets
  in cricket **C** 531
  in croquet **C** 536
Wickham, Sir Henry, English pioneer in rubber plantations **R** 342
Wickiups, Indian dwellings **I** 172, 174, 197; picture **I** 173
Wicks, of candles **C** 96
Wide-angle lenses, for cameras **P** 203
Widener, P. A. B., American businessman and art patron **N** 40
Widow Bird Sate Mourning for Her Love, A, poem by Percy Bysshe Shelley **S** 146
Widow's walk, origin of the term **F** 212, 217
  shown on house in Portsmouth, picture **H** 181
Wieland, Christoph, German writer **G** 176
Wieprecht, Wilhelm, German bandmaster **B** 39

Wiese (VE-sa)**, Kurt** (1887–   ), American author and illustrator of children's books, b. Minden, Germany. He began writing and drawing (1919) in Germany, later living and traveling in Brazil, where he continued writing for children before going to United States. He wrote and illustrated *The Cunning Turtle, Fish in the Air, Groundhog and His Shadow,* and *You Can Write Chinese.*

Wiggin, Kate Douglas (1856–1923), American writer and educator, b. Philadelphia, Pa. In 1878 she opened in San Francisco the first free kindergarten on the western coast. Two years later, Kate and her sister, Nora Archibald Smith, started the California Kindergarten Training School. She was also a writer of children's books, and her works include *The Birds' Christmas Carol* and *Rebecca of Sunnybrook Farm.*
  children's literature, history of **C** 240

Wigglesworth, Michael, American poet **A** 196
Wight, Isle of, in English Channel **I** 437
Wightman Cup, one of the high honors for female tennis players **T** 99

Wigner, Eugene Paul (1902–   ), American physicist, b. Budapest, Hungary. He was awarded the 1963 Nobel prize in physics, with M. Mayer and J. Jensen, for his research on the structure and behavior of the atomic nucleus. He has contributed significantly to many aspects of particle physics. For example, his prediction of certain effects of neutrons upon graphite atoms proved to be of importance in the design of nuclear reactors. He was a member of the general advisory

Wigner, Eugene Paul (continued)
committee to the United States Atomic Energy Commission (1952–57, 1959–64).

Wigs
beauty aids **B** 111
periwigs **H** 3
Wigwams, Indian dwellings **I** 171, 178, 197
Wilbur, Richard, American poet **A** 211
Wilbye (WIL-be), **John,** English composer **E** 269–70
Wild boars, pigs **H** 209; **P** 248; picture **H** 212
Wild cards, in games **C** 113
Wildcat banks **B** 47
Wildcat oil wells **P** 171
Wildcats, pictures **C** 134–41
Wild dogs **D** 242–51
Wild Duck, The, play by Henrik Ibsen **I** 2
Wilde, Oscar, Irish author **W** 167
a "well-made play" romanticist of the drama
D 298
Lady Windemere's Fan, quotation **Q** 20
place in English literature **E** 264
Wildebeest see Gnu

Wilder, Laura Ingalls (1867–1957) American author of children's books, b. Pepin, Wis. She wrote about a pioneer family in northwest, taking subject matter directly from her own childhood experiences on the prairie. Her books include *The Little House in the Big Woods, Farmer Boy,* and *On The Banks of Plum Creek.*

Wilder, Laura Ingalls, book award **B** 310b
Wilder, Thornton Niven, American writer **W** 206
American drama of the 20th century **A** 216; **D** 300
Wilderness, battle of the, 1864, Civil War **C** 326
Wilderness areas
Allagash Wilderness Waterway, Maine **M** 41
National Forests, United States **N** 34
Wilderness Road, pioneer trail **T** 79
overland trail pioneered by Boone **O** 255
Wild flowers **W** 168–71
make a woodland terrarium **T** 102–04
weeds, wildflowers out of place **W** 104–06
Wild horses **H** 241
Wildlife
Africa **A** 50–52
Andes **A** 253
Australia's unusual wildlife **A** 504–06
conservation of **C** 482, 486; pictures **C** 488
jungle **J** 155
life in the forest **F** 371–72
South America **S** 281
See *also* natural resources section of country articles
Wildlife refuges
bird sanctuaries and refuges **B** 211, 230
Moosehorn National Wildlife Refuge, Maine **M** 41
Panama Canal Zone, refuge at Barro, Colorado **P** 44
Wildlife Restoration Act, 1937 **C** 486
Wild rice, or Indian rice **M** 329; **R** 232
Wild Rice Area Indians of North America **I** 177–80
Wild roses, parts of the flower, diagram **P** 295
Iowa, state flower of **I** 357
North Dakota, state flower of **N** 323
Wildsmith, Brian, English illustrator
Brian Wildsmith's ABC, picture from **B** 210b
Wild Turkey, painting by Audubon **U** 118
Wild West shows, produced by Buffalo Bill **B** 428
Wiley, Harvey Washington, American chemist **I** 149
food regulations and laws **F** 350
Wilhelm I (VIL-helm) see William I, king of Prussia
Wilhelm II, German kaiser **W** 271, 281; picture **W** 270
dismissed Bismarck **G** 161

Wilhelmina (wil-hel-MI-na) (Wilhelmina Helena Pauline Maria) (1880–1962), Queen of the Netherlands (1890–1948), b. The Hague. She became queen at the age of 10, her mother acting as regent until 1898. After the conquest of the Netherlands (1940) in World War II, she went to London to lead the Dutch government-in-exile. She gave up the throne in 1948, her daughter Juliana becoming queen.

Wilhelm Meister (VIL-helm MY-ster), novel by Goethe
G 246

Wilkes (WILKS), **Charles** (1798–1877), American naval officer and explorer, b. New York, N.Y. He led an exploratory expedition to the Pacific islands, the coast of Antarctica, and the American northwestern coast (1838–42). During the Civil War, as commander of the *San Jacinto,* he seized Confederate diplomats James Mason and John Slidell from the British steamer *Trent,* sparking the "Trent Affair." Wilkes Land in Antarctica is named for him.

Wilkes-Barre, Pennsylvania **P** 142

Wilkins, Roy (1901–), American civil rights leader, Negro, b. St. Louis, Mo. He was managing editor of *The Call* in Kansas City (1923–31) before joining the National Association for the Advancement of Colored People (NAACP) and serving as editor (1934–49) of its official magazine, *Crisis,* and as administrator for internal affairs (1950–55). He became executive secretary of the NAACP in 1955, and executive director in 1964. Picture **N** 104.
continuing struggle in Negro history **N** 104b

Wilkins, Sir Hubert, Australian explorer **P** 368
Wilkinson, James, American Revolutionary War general
denounced Aaron Burr **B** 462
Willaert (WILL-art), **Adrian,** Flemish musician **D** 365
Willamette Valley, Oregon **O** 194, 199
Willapa Hills, Washington **W** 16
Willard, Emma, American educator **W** 172
pioneered education for women **E** 72
schools and colleges in Vermont **V** 316

Willard, Frances Elizabeth Caroline (1839–1898), American reformer, b. Churchville, N.Y. A teacher at various institutions, she was president of the Evanston College for Ladies (1871–74). Elected president of the Chicago Woman's Christian Temperance Union (1874), she held the same office in the National W.C.T.U (1879) and the World's WCTU (1891). In 1882 she helped organize the Prohibition Party. She was elected to the Hall of Fame for Great Americans (1910).

Willard, Jess (1883–1968), American professional boxer, b. Pottawatomie county, Kans. He was world heavyweight boxing champion (1915–19). He won the title from Jack Johnson and lost it to Jack Dempsey.

Willemstad (VILL-em-stot), capital of Curaçao, picture
C 116

Willet, large shore bird with a thick bill. A brownish-gray bird, it shows a white patch in the wings when in flight. The willet breeds in southern Canada and in the eastern and western parts of the United States.

Willett, Marinus, American officer **R** 205
William I, king of England see William the Conqueror

William III (1650–1702), king of England (1689–1702), b. The Hague, Netherlands. He was proclaimed *stadholder* (viceroy) in the Netherlands (1672–1702) and captain general at the same time for the campaign against Louis XIV of France. In 1677 he married Mary, daughter of the future James II of England, and 12 years later, at the request of Parliament, he accepted the Declaration of Rights and became joint ruler of England with Mary, deposing her father. While in power, he accepted the Act of Toleration (1689). He formed the Grand Alliance and tried to preserve the balance of power in Europe.

England and the Netherlands, history of E 224;
  N 120

William I (Wilhelm Friedrich Ludwig) (1797–1888), king of Prussia (1861–88) and German emperor (1871–88), b. Berlin, Germany. He received title prince of Prussia (1840) when his brother Friedrich Wilhelm IV became king of Prussia. When his brother was declared insane, William I ruled as regent (1858–61) and then as king. Under the leadership of Otto von Bismarck, minister-president of Prussia, William made war on Denmark (1864) and Austria (1866), and defeated France in the Franco-Prussian War (1870–71), which led to the unification of Germany. He was proclaimed German emperor at Versailles in 1871.

Bismarck, Otto von B 250
Germany, history of G 161

William I, prince of Orange see William the Silent
William and Mary, College of, Williamsburg, Va. V 352
  colonial education C 397
William and Mary, of England see Mary II, queen of England; William III, king of England
William and Mary style
  furniture design F 507
William F. Cody Memorial Museum, for Buffalo Bill B 428
William Henry Seward's Day, holiday H 148
William Morris Word Games W 237
William of Nassau, Netherlands national anthem
  N 18–19
William Penn Charter School P 137

Williams, Bert (Egbert Austin Williams) (1876?–1922), American minstrel entertainer, Negro, b. Antigua, West Indies. He and George Walker appeared in hit musicals, and as singing-dancing comedians they performed before the English royal family with the show *In Dahomey.* Williams later joined the Ziegfeld Follies.

Williams, Bill (William Sherley) (?–1849), American trapper and guide, b. probably Kentucky. After being a member of the Santa Fe Trail surveying party (1825–26), he trapped in the Gila country and lived among the Hopi Indians. He joined the Walker California expedition (1833–34) and lived in the West among the Ute until he became active as a guide to various parties, including the fourth Frémont expedition (1848).

Williams, Charles Grenville, English chemist R 345
Williams, Clifton C., Jr., American astronaut S 347

Williams, Daniel Hale (1858–1931), American surgeon, b. Hollidaysburg, Pa. He founded the Provident Hospital in Chicago, Ill. (1891), to supplement lack of training schools for Negro interns and nurses. He was a charter member of the American College of Surgeons, the only Negro to be so honored. He was a member of the Illinois state board of health (1887–91) and a founder of the National Medical Association.

Negro scholars and scientists N 98

Williams, Eric, prime minister of Trinidad and Tobago
  T 292

Williams, Garth Montgomery (1912–), American illustrator of children's books, b. New York, N.Y. He was awarded the Prix de Rome for sculpture (1936). The books he illustrated include *Stuart Little, Charlotte's Web,* and *Sailor Dog.* He also wrote and illustrated *The Rabbits' Wedding.*

Williams, Ralph Vaughan see Vaughan Williams, Ralph
Williams, Roger, English founder of Rhode Island W 172
  American colonies, history of A 188–89
  Rhode Island, history of R 224, 226
  writings against religious intolerance A 196

Williams, Spencer (1889–1965), American composer, Negro, b. New Orleans, La. Among his best-known songs are *I Ain't Got Nobody, Basin Street Blues,* and *Everybody Loves My Baby.*

Williams, Tennessee, American playwright A 216
  characteristically American plays D 300

Williams, Ted (Theodore Samuel Williams) (1918–), American baseball player, b. San Diego, Cal. A natural hitter who batted .406 in 1941, Williams played with the Boston Red Sox (1939–59), except during World War II and the Korean War, when he was a pilot. He won six batting championships and was voted Most Valuable Player in the American League (1946, 1949). In 1966 he was elected to Baseball Hall of Fame. He became manager of the Washington Senators (1969).

Williams, William (1731–1811), American merchant and politician, b. Lebanon, Conn. He provided financial aid for the troops during the Revolutionary War. He later was a member of the Continental Congress (1776–78, 1783–84) and a signer of the Declaration of Independence. He was a member of the state legislature for 21 years and the governor's council for 19 years.

Williams, William Carlos (1883–1963), American writer and physician, b. Rutherford, N.J. He began his medical practice and had his first book, *Poems,* published in the same year (1909). His works included more than 40 volumes of novels, essays, short stories, plays, and poems. Among them are *Paterson,* and *Pictures from Breughel,* which won a Pulitzer prize in poetry (1963).

American literature, place in A 210

Williamsburg, Virginia V 354; picture A 193
  colonial architecture U 123
  Colonial Williamsburg restoration, a history museum
  M 514

Williamson, Hugh (1735–1819), American statesman and physician, b. West Nottingham, Pa. He witnessed the Boston Tea Party and carried the news to England, becoming involved in delivering various dispatches. During the Revolutionary War he was the surgeon general of the North Carolina troops (1779–82). A member of the North Carolina House of Commons (1782, 1785) and the Continental Congress (1782–85, 1787–89), he signed the Constitution and was elected to the first and second sessions of Congress (1789–93).

William the Conqueror, king of England W 173
  Hastings, battle of B 100–01; W 173
  jury system J 159
  kings and lords of the Middle Ages M 291–92
  Norman Conquest of England E 217
William the Silent N 120
Willis, Richard S., American composer of carols C 122
Williston Basin, North Dakota N 326

climate and winds C 346
climate control factor W 88
convection currents, circulation of heat H 95
cyclones H 293; W 74, 187
erosion by E 281
foehn A 523; S 500
fog and smog F 288–89
hurricanes H 292–96; W 95–96
jet streams J 88–91
khamsin E 90e; J 137; S 507
kinetic energy, source of E 202
Mars M 108
monsoon A 452; C 346
moon has none M 454
ocean currents, started by winds E 16
ocean waves result from O 34
pollination of flowers F 277
seed dispersal F 280–81; T 284
solar winds S 467
tornadoes H 296–99
trade winds and the horse latitudes T 246; W 185
weather observations W 83–84
What makes atmosphere move? W 73
williwaws of Alaska A 134
windless regions (horse latitudes) T 246; W 185
Wind sock, at airports A 562

Windsor, Duke of (Edward VIII) (1894–1972), king of Great Britain (Jan.–Dec., 1936), b. Richmond, England. Made Prince of Wales and Earl of Chester (1911), he became King Edward VIII in January, 1936. His decision to marry Mrs. Wallis Simpson, an American divorcee, aroused intense opposition, and in December he abdicated. He later served as governor of the Bahama islands (1940–45). He and the Duchess of Windsor lived outside England. He was buried at Windsor Castle.
Elizabeth II E 179
England, history of E 231–32

Windsor, House of, English royal family E 227; U 77
Windsor, Ontario O 125
Windsor, Wallis Warfield, Duchess of E 232
Windsor Castle, England, picture U 79
Wind tunnels, in aviation A 559
air pollution research A 111
testing airplane design A 559; picture A 39
tests showing shock waves S 470
Windward, on the side toward the wind S 13
Windward Islands, Caribbean island group C 118
Windward Islands, of the Society Islands group, Pacific Ocean P 8
Windy City, Chicago C 227–30
Wine W 188–89
Pasteur, Louis P 96
varieties of grapes G 297
Wineland, or **Vinland,** Viking name for America V 339
Ericson's voyages and discoveries E 275
Winfrid, English missionary see Boniface, Saint
Wing chairs U 226
Winged Horse, constellation see Pegasus, constellation
Winged Victory of Samothrace, or Nike of Samothrace, Greek statue L 368
Wings, airplane A 554; pictures A 39, 40, 41
variable sweep wings for supersonic flight S 471; picture S 470
Wings, of animals
bats B 92
birds B 199, 204–05, 221
butterflies and moths, wings of B 468
first birds, fossil records B 206
flying reptiles, related to dinosaurs D 173; F 387–88
insects I 272–73

locomotion in air A 294–96
pentadactyl hand pattern changed for flying F 8
queen ant, picture A 328
Winnie-the-Pooh, book by A. A. Milne
Shepard illustration I 97
Winnipeg, capital of Manitoba, Canada W 190; pictures C 65; M 77, 79; W 190
cities of Canada C 64
urban and rail center of Manitoba M 81
Winnipeg, Lake, Manitoba, Canada L 34; M 76, 79, 81
Winnipeg, University of M 79
Winnipeg Foundation F 392
Winnipegosis, Lake, Canada M 76
Winnipeg River, Canada M 76
Winnipesaukee (win-ni-pe-SAU-kee) **Lake,** New Hampshire N 151
Winston-Salem, North Carolina N 318
Salem originally established by the Moravians N 317
Winter, season S 108–12
birds in winter B 217
constellations C 491–92
Eskimo land E 284
farm life in winter F 53–54; picture F 48
hibernation H 121–24
origin of in Norse mythology N 279
See also months by name

Wintergreen, name of various plants in different groups. One kind (also called checkerberry) is found in eastern North America. It is an evergreen, about 5 in. high, with a creeping stem and red berries. Its shiny dark-green leaves yield an oil used to flavor soft drinks, candy, chewing gum, and toothpaste.

Winter Olympic Games O 108, 109
speed skating I 50–53
Winter Palace, Leningrad
Hermitage Museum H 119–20
Winter sports
bobsledding B 264–66
curling C 554–55
iceboating I 28–31
ice hockey I 35–40
ice skating I 46–53
on the farm, picture F 48
skiing S 184b–187
Winter's Tale, The, play by Shakespeare S 137
Winterthur, Switzerland S 499
Winterthur Museum, Delaware D 96
Winter wheat W 154
Winthrop, John, governor of Massachusetts Bay Colony A 188
Puritan writings in American literature A 195
Winthrop, John, Jr., colonial governor of Connecticut C 480
Wire W 190a
barbed wire, use of in World War I W 274
cables T 52, 59–60
copper C 502
dies used for making D 167
electric appliances, heating element E 117
electricity, wire for conducting E 128
jewelry, how to make J 100
metal drawing process M 231–32
nails N 2
needles and pins, how made N 88, 89
rope R 333
safety precautions with electricity E 135
steel I 401
wire saws used in quarrying Q 5
Wire and tape recorders T 20–21
Wireless, first term for radio R 53

Wireless telegraphy (tel-EG-raphy), Marconi's invention
M 98
early history of radio **R** 52
See also Radio
Wirephoto, news service **N** 200
Wire saws, for quarrying **Q** 5
Wire sculpture, art **W** 190b, 191
Wire services see News services
Wire tapping see Bugging
Wireworms **P** 285, 289; picture **P** 288

Wirtz, William Willard (1912–), American labor expert, b. De Kalb, Ill. He served on the Board of Economic Warfare (1942), the War Labor Board (1943–45), and the National Wage Stabilization Board (1946). He was secretary of labor under Presidents Kennedy and Johnson. Trained as a labor-law professor, he has won fame as a mediator in labor disputes and planner of labor policies.

Wisconsin **W** 192–208
holiday, Landing Day **H** 149
La Follette, Robert M. and Robert, Jr. **L** 24
Milwaukee **M** 312
Nicolet, Jean **N** 250
places of interest in Negro history **N** 94
Wisconsin, University of **W** 201; picture **W** 203
Wisconsin Dells, Wisconsin **W** 203; picture **W** 194
Wisdom literature, of the Bible **B** 157, 159
Wisdom of Solomon, apocryphal book of Bible
B 157, 159
Wisdom teeth **T** 47

Wise, Stephen Samuel (1874–1949), American rabbi, b. Budapest, Hungary. He founded the Free Synagogue in New York (1907), which he headed the rest of his life. He also founded the Zionist Organization of America (1898) and the Jewish Institute of Religion (1922). He was a member of the American Jewish Congress delegation to the Paris Peace Conference (1918). His many books include *How to See Life.*

Wishbone, of birds **B** 201
superstition about **S** 475

Wisteria, or **wistaria,** shrubby or treelike flowering vine in the pea family. Species are native to Asia and North America. The plant's bell-shaped flowers, which hang in long, drooping clusters, are white, pink, purple, or blue. The pods are long and flat; the stems are thick and woody. Picture **G** 45; **P** 298

Wit and humor see Humor
Witchcraft **W** 208–09
colonial America **C** 394
Halloween, costumes and decoration **H** 15
supernatural forces in Macbeth **M** 2–3
the Old One in *Hansel and Gretel,* pictures **G** 384, 385
trial of Joan of Arc **J** 121
See also Magic; Superstition; Voodoo
Witch doctors see Medicine men
Witches' Sabbaths, assemblies of witches, devils for celebration of rites, ceremonies **W** 208
Faust and the witches, picture **G** 176
Witchhazel, shrub
seeds, picture **P** 298
Witch makeup, picture **P** 340
Withering, William, English doctor **D** 214

Witherspoon, John (1723–1794), Scottish-American churchman and patriot, b. Yester, Scotland. He left his Scottish pastorate to be president of the College of New Jersey, later Princeton University (1768–94). Member of the Continental Congress (1776–82), he signed the Declaration of Independence. He was a leader of the Presbyterian Church, a state legislator, and the coiner of the term "Americanism."

Withholding, income tax provision **I** 111
With malice toward none, speech of Abraham Lincoln, excerpt **L** 294
Witnesses, in law courts **C** 528–29
jury trials **J** 159, 160
Wittenberg, East Germany **G** 157
Luther, Martin **L** 378
site of the event that brought the Reformation to Germany **C** 285–86
Witwatersrand, near Johannesburg, South Africa **P** 432
Witwatersrand, University of, South Africa **S** 271
Wizard of Menlo Park, nickname of Thomas A. Edison
E 60
Wizard of Oz, The, motion picture **M** 475
Wizard of Schenectady (ske-NEC-tady), nickname of Charles Steinmetz **S** 422
Wizards, or warlocks **W** 208
magic tricks **M** 18
WMO see World Meteorological Organization
Woad, herb, source of dyestuff **D** 367
Wobblies, nickname for Industrial Workers of the World
L 6

Wodehouse (WOOD-house), **P. G.** (Pelham Grenville Wodehouse) (1881–), American writer, b. Guilford, England. Most popular for humorous novels of English life, he wrote over 70 novels, many starring the valet Jeeves. He adapted *Blandings Castle* and *Leave it to Psmith* for the stage. He became an American citizen in 1955.
musical comedy form, advancement of **M** 542

Woden, House of, Anglo-Saxon royal family **H** 115
Woden, Norse god see Odin
Wöhler (VER-ler), **Friedrich,** German chemist **B** 182
discovery of urea **C** 214; **S** 74
isolated aluminum **A** 176

Wojciechowska (vy-chec-OFF-ska), **Maia** (1927–), American writer, b. Warsaw, Poland. She went to the United States in 1942 and won the Newbery medal (1965) for *Shadow of a Bull.* Other books for children include *Kingdom in a Horse* and *A Single Light.*

Wolcott (WOOL-cott), **Oliver** (1760–1833), American politician, b. Litchfield, Conn. A protegé of Hamilton, he was United States auditor (1789–91), comptroller (1791–95), and Hamilton's successor as secretary of the treasury (1795–1800). He helped start the Bank of America (1812) and served as governor of Connecticut (1817–1827).

Wolf see Wolves

Wolf (VOLF), **Hugo** (1860–1903), Austrian composer, b. Windischgraz. His songs, widely performed in Austria and Germany during his lifetime, rank him as one of the greatest composers of the modern art song. He wrote about 300 before he died at age of 42.
traditions of song writing **G** 188

Wolf Cub Scout program **B** 360
Wolfe, James, English general **F** 461
Seven Years War in Canada **C** 70
Wolfe, Thomas Clayton, American writer **N** 319–20
American literature, place in **A** 212
Carolina Playmakers dramatic group at Chapel Hill, N.C. **N** 315

Wolf-Ferrari (volf-fer-RA-ri), **Ermanno** (1876–1948), Italian composer, b. Venice. He is especially noted for his lyrical comic operas. His works include opera *Il Segreto de Susanna* (*The Secret of Susanne*) and choral and chamber music.

Wolffish, any one of several marine fishes found in deep waters of the North Atlantic and North Pacific. About 5 or 6 ft. long, a wolffish has sharp front teeth and large back teeth that it uses for crushing the shells of animals on which it feeds.

Wolfram see Tungsten
Wolf spiders **S** 386; picture **S** 384
Wolofs (WO-lofs), a people of Africa **S** 119

Wolsey (WOOL-sey), **Thomas, Cardinal** (1475?–1530), English statesman and clergyman, b. Ipswich. He rose to great power under King Henry VIII, becoming archbishop of York (1514), cardinal (1515), and lord chancellor (1515), and directing much of the King's foreign policy. He lost Henry's favor when he failed to arrange his divorce from Catherine of Aragon. He was stripped of most of his offices (1529), charged with treason, and died soon after. Wolsey founded Christ Church College at Oxford (1525).
    Henry VIII and Wolsey **H** 109

Wolverines (wool-ver-ENES), animals **O** 244, 246
Wolverine State, nickname for Michigan **M** 262
Wolves **W** 210
    animal communication **A** 277
    dog family **D** 243–46
    spectrogram of a wolf howl, picture **A** 276
Woman suffrage **W** 212b–213; picture **W** 212
    Addams, Jane **A** 19
    civil liberties and civil rights **C** 315
    federal suffrage in Switzerland **S** 501
    Wyoming called the Equality State **W** 335
Woman with a Parrot, painting by Manet **M** 73

Woman's Christian Temperance Union, National (WCTU), organization founded (1874) in Cleveland, Ohio, to work for abolition of the use, manufacture and sale of alcoholic drinks. The WCTU sponsors educational projects, has two affiliated youth groups, and publishes *Young Crusader* and *Union Signal.* Headquarters is in Evanston, Ill. World's Woman's Christian Temperance Union, an international group, was started in 1883.

Woman's International Bowling Congress (WIBC), federation of bowling associations, which provides regulations for local leagues and supports championship competitions. Founded 1916, it has headquarters in Columbus, Ohio. It publishes *Woman Bowler.*

Womb, female organ see Uterus
Wombats, marsupials **K** 175
Women
    Amazon warriors **A** 179
    divorce **D** 234–35
    draft for military service, Israel **D** 289
    executive jobs in retail stores **R** 189
    family **F** 37–43
    labor movement in 1900's, picture **L** 8
    life span greater than men **A** 81
    old age, problems of **O** 97
    policewomen **P** 377
    proportion of, in populations **P** 397
    Quaker meetings, right of speaking, picture **Q** 3
    status among Muslims **I** 415–16
    underwater exploration **U** 20

WAC, Women's Army Corps **U** 168
WAF, women in the U.S. Air Force **U** 165–66
WAVES, women in the U.S. Navy **U** 190
women Marines **U** 180
    See also United States Coast Guard Women's Reserve (SPARS); Women's Royal Naval Service (WRENS)
Women, education of see Education of women
Women, role of **W** 211–13
    See also Friedan, Betty; Millett, Kate; National Organization for Women (NOW); Women's Liberation

Women in the Air Force (WAF), part of the United States Air Force, established 1948, and made up of all women in the Air Force except those in Nurse Corps and Medical Specialist Corps. Members are volunteers over 18.
    Air Force personnel **U** 165–66

Women's Army Corps (WAC), branch of United States Army established (1943) to replace the Women's Army Auxiliary Corps (WAAC). Members are volunteers 18 and over. All women in the Army except those in the Army Nurse Corps and the Army Medical Specialist Corps are in the WAC.
    Army personnel **U** 168

Women's International League for Peace and Freedom, organization founded (1915) to work for achievement of freedom from fear of war, want, and discrimination. Its activities include work for universal disarmament, civil liberties, and integration and the publication of *Four Lights* and *Washington Newsletter.* U. S. headquarters are in Philadelphia, the international in Geneva, Switzerland.

Women's Liberation, a movement in the United States led by a coalition of women from all age groups and all walks of life. Many women's organizations as well as individual women have joined together in an effort to gain equal rights for women in such areas as wages, job opportunities, education, government, and civil rights. First major demonstration was held Aug. 26, 1970, 50th anniversary of 19th (woman suffrage) amendment.
    civil liberties and civil rights **C** 315
    rally in New York City, picture **W** 212a
    women, role of **W** 213
    See also Friedan, Betty; Millett, Kate; National Organization for Women (NOW)

Women's Reserve of the United States Naval Reserve, organization established in 1942 and made up of Women Accepted for Volunteer Emergency Service, or WAVES, who served at shore stations to release men for combat duty. In 1948 the WAVES were integrated into the regular Navy and the Naval Reserve.

Women's rights see Women, role of

Women's Royal Naval Service (WRENS), part of the Royal Navy, first established in Great Britain in 1917 as W.R.N.S., disbanded in 1919, and re-established in 1939. Members serve throughout the world.

Wonder drugs, antibiotics and sulfa drugs **D** 217
Wonders of the world **W** 214–21
    See also objects and structures by name as Colosseum
Wondrychoun, large fishing net **F** 217
Wood **W** 222–28
    bamboo **G** 318–19
    building material **B** 430
    chemical energy, source of **E** 202
    drying of lumber **L** 376; picture **L** 373
    fuel **F** 487

Wood (continued)
   furniture-making **F** 501–04
   "green gold" of Finland **F** 133
   houses of **H** 171
   matches **M** 152–53
   paper from **C** 432
   pencils, how made **P** 147
   petrified wood **F** 380
   woody stems of plants **P** 290–91
   See also Forests and forestry; Lumber and lumbering;
      names of trees
Wood, Gar, American boat racer **B** 264
Wood, Grant, American painter **W** 221
Wood, Leonard, American officer
   Spanish-American War **S** 375
Wood alcohol **A** 147
   structural formula, diagram **C** 200
Woodbine *see* Virginia creeper
Wood-block printing *see* Woodcut printing
Wood Buffalo National Park, Alberta, Canada **A** 146d
   wildlife of Canada **C** 57
Wood carving **W** 228
   African sculpture **A** 70, 75, 76
   art of the Pacific islands **P** 9
   cigar-store Indian, picture **U** 117
   early American carving **U** 115
Wood charcoal **C** 105; **F** 487
   Japan produces **J** 35
Wood chisel, tool, picture **T** 213
Woodchucks, or ground hogs, rodents **R** 276; pictures
      R 275, 277
   body changes in hibernation **H** 123

Woodcock, plump, brownish bird found in woodlands of
temperate regions. About 14 inches long, the woodcock
has a long, straight bill and eyes placed high on its
head. In swampy areas it probes for worms by pushing
its sensitive bill straight down into the earth. It can open
the end of its bill to grasp its catch. Picture **B** 218.
   birds of the woods and fields **B** 221

Woodcut printing **W** 228–29
   bookmaking, medieval origin **B** 321
   China ancient **C** 433; picture **C** 432
   Dürer, Albrecht **D** 345
   German art **G** 169
   graphic arts, techniques and uses of **G** 302–03
   illustrations in early printed books **I** 90; picture **I** 89
   Japanese art **A** 438f
   This is the Cock that Crowed, by Frasconi **D** 132
   Two Women, by Japan's Utamaro, picture **O** 218
Wood engraving **W** 229
   engraving, types of **E** 272
   graphic arts, history and techniques of **G** 305
Woodpeckers, birds **B** 222; picture **B** 238
Wood pewees, birds, picture **B** 242
Wood pulp **W** 227
   paper making **P** 51–52
   Quebec leading producer in Canada **Q** 13
Wood rasp, tool, picture **T** 213

Woods, Granville T. (1856–1910), American inventor,
Negro, b. Columbus, Ohio. Among his more than 35
patents is the one he obtained for the synchronous
multiplex railway telegraph. This device averts accidents
by alerting each train to the whereabouts of the one
ahead of or behind it.

Woods, Lake of *see* Lake of the Woods

Woodson, Carter Godwin (1875–1950), American educator, editor, and author, Negro, b. New Canton, Va.

Woodson was dean at Howard University (1919–20) and
West Virginia Collegiate Institute (1920–22). He was a
founder of the Association for the Study of Negro Life
and History (1915) and editor of its *Journal of Negro
History* (1916–50). In 1921 he formed Associated Publish-
ers to print Negro literature. His numerous books include
The Negro in Our History, The Rural Negro, and *The
Negro Professional and the Community.* He received the
Spingarn medal in 1926.
   Negro scholars and scientists **N** 98

Woodstock, motion picture **M** 488c; picture **M** 488b
Woodstock, New Brunswick, Canada **N** 138c
Woodstock, New York
   rock music festival **R** 262d
Wood thrush, bird
   spectrograms of animal sounds, pictures **A** 276
Woodwind instruments **W** 182–83
   clarinet **C** 329
   orchestra, woodwind section **O** 183, 186; picture **O** 187
   types of musical instruments **M** 547, 549; pictures
      M 546
Woodworking **W** 229–34
   nails, screws, and rivets **N** 2–3
   school woodshop, picture **I** 228
Woof *see* Weft
Wool **W** 234–35
   How is wool obtained? **W** 234
   rugs and carpets made of **R** 354
   sheep raising **C** 151
   textile industry **T** 140–43
   wool fibers **F** 107

Woollcott, Alexander (1887–1943), American critic and
writer, b. Phalanx, N.J. He was drama critic for the New
York *Times* and New York *World* (1925–28). He exerted
considerable influence on public literary opinion as a
radio critic (1929–40) and through his column for *The
New Yorker* magazine. His books include *Mrs. Fiske, Enchanted Aisles,* and *While Rome Burns.* With George S.
Kaufman he wrote the plays *The Dark Tower* and *Channel
Road.*

Woolf, Virginia, English writer **E** 267
Woolman, John, American writer **A** 198
Wool wax *see* Lanolin

Woolworth, Frank Winfield (1852–1919), American merchant, b. Rodman, N.Y. He opened a successful "5 and
10 cent store" at Lancaster, Pa., in 1879. His rapidly
spreading, successful chain of shops established the
"dime store" idea. A multimillionaire, he put up the 792-
foot Woolworth Building in New York (1913).

Woonsocket, Rhode Island **R** 224
Worcester (WOO-ster), Massachusetts **M** 147
Worcester, Noah, American theologian **P** 104
Worden, Alfred M., American astronaut **S** 344, 345, 347
Word games **W** 236–38
Word origins **W** 238–41
   changes in languages **L** 40
   tracing word origins helps build vocabulary **V** 372
   See also Names; Nicknames
Words
   antonyms and synonyms **S** 504
   English language **E** 243
   grammar **G** 288–90
   homonyms **H** 194
   languages show relationship by key words **L** 39
   learning experiment in sense and nonsense words
      L 103
   origins of words **W** 238–41

parts of speech P 90–92
phonics P 193–96
poetry P 350
pronunciation P 478
semantics S 117–18
slang S 194
some Australian words and phrases A 502
some French words in everyday use F 434
some German words in everyday use G 172
some Greek (classical and modern) in everyday use
  G 349
some Hawaiian words H 63
some Hebrew words H 102
some Italian words in everyday use I 478
some Spanish words in everyday use S 368
spelling S 378–79
synonyms and antonyms S 504
thinking, use in P 500
vocabulary V 371–72
See also Alphabet; Language and languages
Wordsworth, William, English poet W 242
"Composed Upon Westminster Bridge" S 255
"Daffodils" W 242
"My Heart Leaps Up When I Behold" W 242
odes O 52
romantic period in English literature E 260
sonnets S 255
Work, Henry Clay, American songwriter and printer N 25
Work, in mechanics W 243–46
energy, meaning of E 198
hydraulic systems H 303

Work, John Wesley (1901–67), American composer,
Negro, b. Tullahoma, Tenn. His music, based mostly on
American themes, includes such well-known songs as
"Steal Away to Jesus." *Appalachia,* for piano, *From the
Deep South,* for orchestra, and *The Singers,* for orchestra
and chorus, are among his longer works.
Negro spirituals N 107

Work, world of W 251–53
automation effects A 534
capitalism C 104–05
child labor C 235
clothing industry C 353–54
engineering E 204–08
petroleum workers P 175–76
retarded, opportunities for R 191
vocational guidance and counseling V 373–74
women, role of W 212–212a
workmen's compensation W 253
See also Labor; Labor and management; Vocations
Worker ants A 322–23; picture A 331
Worker bees H 202
Workhorses, breeds, pictures H 240
Workhouses, or houses of correction P 468
Working dogs D 252, 259; pictures D 254, 255
Working Men's Institute Library, New Harmony, Ind. I 143
Workingmen's Party, first U.S. labor party L 7
Workmen's compensation W 253
government regulation of labor L 14
occupational health and safety O 15–16
organizing for safety S 7
social security S 221
Work songs F 319
African A 78
American F 310–11
Negro spirituals N 105–06
of occupations in folklore F 304
Works Progress Administration (WPA) R 322
Work-study activities and programs
part of a reading program R 111

World W 254–69
agriculture around the world A 88–100; W 263–64
anthropological studies of people A 306–08
art museums, partial list M 516–17
cereal grains, new varieties G 287
climatic zones, diagram Z 373
coal centers and resources C 363
continents joined by land bridges to form the world
  continent L 237
currency units for representative countries M 411
earthquake belts E 35
environment, problems of E 272h
flags of the world F 225–48
food around the world F 335–43
forest regions F 373
freshwater areas and ocean currents, diagram L 232
geography G 94–108
history museums, partial list M 518
languages L 37–40; U 194–95
maps and globes, projections M 91–93; pictures
  M 89, 94
mountain peaks, highest M 494–95
national anthems and patriotic songs N 20–22
natural resources N 60
newspapers of the world, by continent N 199
ocean depths, map-diagram O 29
oceans and seas, locator map-diagrams O 46–47
population P 394; diagram P 396
prairie land distribution P 430
races of man R 29–32
rainfall R 94
regions according to distribution of life L 234–35
religions of the world R 145–52
rubber producing areas, map-diagram R 342
science museums, partial list M 519
soils, distribution of S 232
telephone cable routes, chart C 439
time meridians and International Date Line T 190–92
universities of the world, selected list U 206–08
volcanic regions of the world V 385
waterfalls, selected list W 57
wonders of the world W 214–21
zones Z 372–73
See also Earth
World Association of Girl Guides and Girl Scouts
  G 213, 214
World Bank see International Bank for Reconstruction
  and Development
World Boxing Association B 352
World Bureau, Boy Scouts B 357

World Council of Churches (WCC), association of 235
Christian churches in 90 countries and territories. The
churches represent the Eastern Orthodox, Protestant, Anglican, and Old Catholic traditions. Organized at Amsterdam in 1948 to promote Christian unity, the council
sponsors work camps, a school in Switzerland, and aid to
refugees. Publications include the *Ecumenical Courier* and
the *Ecumenical Review.* Headquarters is in Geneva.
ecumenical movement P 486

World Court see International Court of Justice
World Data Centers, for International Geophysical Year
  I 311
World Federation of Trade Unions (W.F.T.U.) (Soviet Union)
  L 10
World Health Organization (WHO) U 85–86
narcotics control N 14
public health P 502, 505
role in disease prevention D 221
travel health rules V 261
World Hockey Association I 35

Wright, Frank Lloyd, American architect **W** 315
  Guggenheim Museum **M** 518; **W** 315
  houses **A** 385
  Sullivan, Louis **S** 457
  United States, architecture of the **U** 124–25
  Wisconsin his native state **W** 206

Wright, Jane C. (1919–   ), physician, b. New York, N.Y.
A leading researcher in cancer chemotherapy, she was
appointed associate dean and professor of surgery at
New York Medical College, N.Y. (1967).

Wright, Richard, American novelist **W** 316
  American literature of the 20th century **A** 213;
    N 102
Wright, Wilbur and Orville W 316–17
  aviation history **A** 568, 572
  glider experiments **G** 240
  signature of Orville Wright reproduced **A** 527
Wristbones (carpals), of the arm, diagram **F** 79
Wristwatches W 47
Writing W 317–21
  African literature **A** 76a
  alphabet **A** 170, 172, 173
  ancient civilizations **A** 219, 225, 227
  Braille, for the blind **B** 252–53
  Chinese **C** 258–59, 269
  codes and ciphers **C** 369–71
  communication advanced by **C** 430–33
  fractur style in folk art **F** 293
  handwriting **H** 31–33
  Hebrew **H** 100
  inks for different pens **I** 255
  invention of writing **I** 338
  Japanese **J** 27–29
  origin and development of languages **L** 38
  paper **P** 51–57
  pens and pencils **P** 146–48
  punctuation **P** 530–33
  Sequoya developed Cherokee Indian writing **S** 124
  shorthand **S** 164
  spelling **S** 378–79
  systems studied by linguists **L** 302
  See also individual letters of the alphabet
Writing (authorship) **W** 318–21
  biography, autobiography, and biographical novel
    B 185–86
  books: from author to library **B** 329–34
  compositions **C** 446–47
  copyright **T** 244–45
  drama **D** 292–300
  essays **E** 292–93
  figures of speech **F** 118–20
  grammar **G** 288–90
  journalism **J** 145
  language arts writing program **L** 36
  letter writing **L** 157–60
  library research project **L** 186–88
  literary criticism **L** 312–13
  novels **N** 345–49
  outlines **O** 249–51
  parts of speech **P** 90–92
  poetry, influence of **P** 352–53
  reports **R** 175–76
  research **R** 182–83
  short stories **S** 165–67
Writs of assistance, warrants used against American
    colonists **R** 196
  Otis argues against **O** 237
Wroclaw (VRAWTS-lov), Poland **P** 361

Wrought iron I 405
  building material **B** 438
Wu Cheng-en, Chinese novelist **O** 220b
Wuhan (WU-hon), China **C** 262
Wuthering Heights, novel by Emily Brontë **B** 408

Wu Ti (WU DI) (157–87 B.C.) Chinese emperor of the Han
dynasty. His long reign (140–87 B.C.) was noted for
imperial expansion. He strengthened government through
central regulation of commerce, coinage, and public
works and introduced new crops from the West, including
alfalfa and grapes. The first of the famous imperial histories was written during his reign.
  development of Confucianism in China **A** 468

Wyandotte, now Kansas City, Kansas **K** 188, 191

Wyatt, Sir Thomas (1503?–1542), English poet, b. Kent.
He served as a courtier of Henry VIII, contributed poems
to *Tottel's Miscellany,* and with translations from
Petrarch's sonnets, helped introduce the Italian sonnet
form to England.
  sonnets **S** 255–56

Wycherly (WICH-erly), **William** (1640?–1716), English dramatist, b. Shrewsbury. His Restoration dramas are noted for
their biting wit, coarseness, and satire. *The Country Wife*
and *The Plain Dealer* are revived often.
  Restoration drama **D** 297

Wycliffe (WIC-liff), **John,** English religious reformer **R** 132
Wye oak, tree
  Maryland's state tree **M** 114

Wyeth, Andrew Newell (1917–   ), American artist, b.
Chadds Ford, Pa. He was trained by his illustrator father,
Newell Convers Wyeth. Using tempera paints, he often
places solitary figures in expansive landscape of muted
colors. His paintings include *Christina's World, A Crow
Flew By, Young America,* and *Her Room.* In 1970 his works
were exhibited in a one-man show at the White House.

Wyeth, Nathaniel, American pioneer **I** 67
  Oregon Trail **O** 260

Wyeth, Newell Convers (1882–1945), American artist, b.
Needham, Mass. His murals are in many public and
private buildings, including the Missouri State Capitol,
the Hubbard Memorial Building of the National Geographic Society in Washington, D.C., and the Metropolitan Life Insurance Building in New York. He also
illustrated 20 classics of children's literature. The artist
Andrew Wyeth is his son.
  illustration from *The Yearling* **C** 248

Wylie, Elinor, American poet **A** 210
Wynken, Blynken, and Nod, from "A Dutch Lullaby" by
    Eugene Field **F** 114
Wyoming W 322–37
  Grand Teton National Park, picture **N** 47
  Yellowstone National Park **Y** 345–46
Wyoming, University of W 331

Wythe (WITH), **George** (1726–1806), American jurist, b.
Elizabeth City Co., Va. As a member of the Continental
Congress (1775–76) he signed the Declaration of
Independence. Later he helped revise Virginia's laws and
became America's first law professor, at William and
Mary College and then with his own law school. He was
chancellor of Virginia (1778–1801).

X, 24th letter of the English alphabet **X** 338
  See *also* Alphabet
X-1, rocket-powered airplane, picture **S** 469
X-15, rocket-powered airplane for hypersonic flight, with speeds above Mach 4 or 5 **S** 472–73; pictures **R** 262, **S** 471

Xanadu, place referred to as the site of the "stately pleasure dome" in the poem "Kubla Khan" by Samuel Taylor Coleridge. The name was taken from a passage in an old travel book describing the palace of Kublai Khan, a ruler of the Mongol dynasty of China. Coleridge fell asleep while reading this passage and dreamed the fantasy scene described in his poem.
  Coleridge, his place in English literature **E** 260

Xanthippe (zan-TIP-pe), wife of Socrates **S** 228

Xavier (ZAV-i-er), **Saint Francis** ("Apostle of the Indies") (1506–1552), Spanish missionary, b. near Pamplona. A founding member of the Jesuit order (1534), he was ordained a priest at Venice (1537) and served in Rome until 1540. He was sent as a missionary to the Portuguese colony of Goa (1542), and from there he traveled to southern India, Malacca, various islands of the East Indies, and Japan and China. He died on his way back from China and was canonized in 1622.
  Japan, history of **J** 44
  missions and missionaries **M** 348

Xavier University, Ohio **U** 224
Xavier University of Louisiana **U** 224

Xenocrates (ze-NOC-ra-tese) (396–314 B.C.), Greek philosopher, b. Chalcedon. A follower of Plato, he presided (339–314 B.C.) over the Academy, founded by Plato. He supported the Pythagorean doctrine of numbers.

Xenon (ZE-non), element **E** 155, 165
  rarest of the noble gases **N** 109–10
  use of noble gases in industry **G** 62

Xenophanes (ze-NOPH-an-ese) (570?–480? B.C.), Greek philosopher, b. Colophon, Asia Minor. About 536 B.C. he settled in Elea, Italy, and founded the so-called Eleatic school of philosophy, which held that a supreme deity, or intelligence, was identical with the world. Portions of elegies by Xenophanes and a long poem on nature have been preserved.
  quoted on the value of fire to man **F** 144

Xenophon (ZEN-o-phon), Greek historian and essayist **G** 354–55
  description of ancient dancing entertainment **D** 35
Xerophthalmia, disease **V** 370c
Xerxes (ZERX-ese), king of Persia **X** 339
  King Ahasuerus and Queen Esther **P** 540
Ximenez de Quesada, Gonzalo see Jiménez de Quesada, Gonzalo
Xochimilco (so-chi-MEEL-co), **Lake,** near Mexico City **L** 34; picture **L** 30
  floating gardens an attraction of Mexico City **M** 253
X-ray microscopes **M** 288
X rays **X** 339–41
  cancer caused by prolonged exposure **C** 92–93
  cancer treatment **C** 90, 95
  chest X rays for tuberculosis **D** 212
  doctors studying X rays, picture **H** 249
  energy, types of **E** 199
  gastro-intestinal examinations by doctors **M** 208h
  lead shields **L** 94
  light rays **L** 270
  medicine, uses in **M** 208, 208h
  mutation of genes caused by **G** 83–84
  mutations **C** 95
  new techniques learned in space research **S** 349
  observatories, x rays detected and measured **O** 14
  photography **P** 206
  radiation, short-wave spectrum of **R** 44
  solar radiation **S** 235
Xylem (ZY-lem), plant tissue **P** 291
Xylophone (ZY-lo-phone), musical instrument **M** 550
  African music **A** 78, 79
  make a test-tube xylophone **S** 266
  percussion instruments **P** 153
XYZ Affair, incident during John Adams' presidency **A** 9–10
  See *also* Gerry, Elbridge

Y, 25th letter of the English alphabet   **Y** 342
   See also Alphabet
Yachts (YOTS)
   basins in British Columbia, picture   **B** 404
   See also America's Cup
Yacine, Kateb, Algerian novelist   **A** 76d

Yadin, Yigael (formerly Rav-Aloof Yigael, Sukenik), (1917–
   ), Israeli archeologist and soldier, b. Jerusalem. Israel's
youngest general and a hero of its war of independence
(1948), Dr. Yadin is a member of the faculty of the
Hebrew University, Jerusalem. His excavations at Hazor,
Masada, and along the west shore of the Dead Sea have
uncovered cities and manuscripts dating back to Biblical
times. His books about them include *The Message of the
Scrolls* (1957), *The Art of Warfare in Biblical Lands in
the Light of Archaeological Study* (1963), and *Masada*
(1966).

Yahgan, Indians of South America   **I** 211
Yahweh *see* Jehovah
Yahya Khan, General, Pakistani leader   **B** 44c;   **P** 41
Yakamochi, Otomo, Japanese poet   **O** 220b
Yaks, animals of the Himalayas   **H** 129; picture
   H 216
   "The Yak," poem by Hilaire Belloc   **N** 274
   Tibet's most important animal   **T** 176, 177

Yale, Elihu (1649–1721), English merchant and philanthropist, b. Boston, Mass. He grew up in England and in
1671 was employed by East India Company. He also
made a large fortune through private trading. In
1699 he returned to England and became a director of
the company. In 1718 he gave a large donation of
books and merchandise to the Collegiate School in
Saybrook, Conn., which was renamed Yale College in
his honor.

Yale, Linus, American locksmith   **L** 324
Yale locks   **L** 324–25
Yale University, at New Haven, Conn.   **C** 475
Yallourn Coal Mine, Victoria, Australia, picture   **A** 509
Yalta, Union of Soviet Socialist Republics, picture   **U** 33
Yalta Conference, 1945
   Churchill, Roosevelt, Stalin, picture   **R** 324
   plans for a United Nations organization   **U** 80
   Poland   **P** 362
Yalu (YA-lu) **River,** Asia   **R** 248
   boundary between Manchuria and Korea   **K** 299

Yam, common name of family of plants grown in warmer
regions of Eastern and Western Hemispheres. There are
hundreds of different species—some edible, others decorative. The tuberous roots of yams grown for food can
be 6 to 8 feet long, weighing as much as 100 pounds.
They are a staple food in tropical climates. True yams
are botanically different from sweet potatoes; the moist,
deep-orange-colored variety of sweet potatoes are often
incorrectly called yams in the United States.

Yamamoto (ya-ma-MO-to), **Isoroku** (1884–1943), Japanese
naval officer, b. Niigata Prefecture. As admiral in
command of Japan's combined fleet (1941) during World
War II, he planned the attack on Pearl Harbor and
Japan's war strategy in the Pacific. He was reported shot
down in an air ambush in the southwestern Pacific.

Yamasaki, Minoru (1912–   ), American architect, b.
Seattle, Wash. Working mainly in precast concrete,
which he says gives him more freedom, he has designed
a number of award-winning buildings, including the St.
Louis Municipal Airport Terminal Building.

Yamashita (ya-MA-shi-ta), **Tomobumi** (1885–1946), Japanese general, b. Kochi Prefecture. He commanded the
Japanese Army in Malaya and Singapore (1941–42) and
the Philippines (1944). In the war crimes trials following
World War II he was convicted and executed.

Yamato, imperial line of Japan   **J** 42–43
Yamato-e, Japanese art   **O** 217

Yang, Chen-Ning (1922–   ), Chinese-American physicist,
b. Hofei, China. He studied under Enrico Fermi at the
University of Chicago and specialized in nuclear physics.
Together with Tsung-Dao Lee he disproved the concept
of the conservation of parity, thus opening new pathways
for the study of subatomic particles. For this achievement he shared the 1957 Nobel prize in physics with Lee.

Yangtze River, China   **Y** 343
   junks on the river, picture   **R** 249
   lands in China along the Yangtze   **C** 262; pictures
   C 263, 266
   Shanghai   **S** 138–39

Yankee, probably the diminutive of the Dutch name Jan,
or John. Time of origin is unknown, but Dutch colonists
in the New World may have called Englishmen Jan or Janke
(Yankee) for the John of John Bull, symbol of the
English. During the Civil War, Southerners called Northerners Yankees. Later the term came to be used for all
Americans by people of other countries.

Yankee clippers, or clipper ships, sailing ships
   S 159–60
Yankee Doodle, folk song   **F** 327
   origins of national anthems and patriotic songs
   N 23
Yankee peddlers   **C** 467
Yaoundé (ya-OON-day), capital of Cameroon   **C** 35;
   picture   **C** 36
Yap, Pacific island   **P** 9
Yapocks (ya-POCKS), or water opossums   **K** 172
Yard, measure of length   **W** 110, 115
Yardsticks   **W** 110
Yarns, of fibers   **F** 105
   dyed yarn, picture   **D** 368
   embroidery   **E** 187–89
   knitting   **K** 277–81, 284
   rope   **R** 331–32
   wool   **W** 235

Yashima, Taro (1908–   ), Japanese author and artist, b.
Kyushu island. Studying art in the United States at the
outbreak of World War II, he joined the American
intelligence department (Office of Strategic Services).
After the war he wrote and illustrated children's books,
including *The Village Tree, Crow Boy,* and *Umbrella.* He
has had one-man art shows in both the United States
and Japan.

Yasilikaya, holy shrine of Hittites   **A** 238–39

Yastrzemski, Carl Michael ("Yaz") (1939–   ), American
baseball player, b. Southhampton, N.Y. He joined Boston
Red Sox as an outfielder in 1961 and won American
League batting title in 1963, '67, '68. In 1967 he was
named league's Most Valuable Player after winning
Triple Crown (batting average, home runs, and runs
batted in).

Yates, Elizabeth (1905–   ), American author, b. Buffalo,
N.Y. Although she has written adult books (*Beloved
Bondage*), she is known chiefly for children's books,

Yates, Elizabeth (continued)
such as *Amos Fortune: Free Man*, which won the Newbery award for 1951. Her fondness for animals and the countryside has been reflected in such stories as "Rainbow 'Round the World" and "Mountain Born."

Yates, Robert (1738–1801), American jurist, b. Schenectady, N.Y. He was appointed (1777) a justice of the New York Supreme Court and served as chief justice from 1790 to 1798. A leader of the Antifederalists, he opposed the writing of a federal constitution at the Philadelphia Convention (1787), wrote a series of antifederalist letters, and voted against ratification of the Constitution.

Yawarai Street, Bangkok, Thailand, picture **T** 147
Yawl, sailboat, picture **S** 9

Yaws, chronic tropical disease caused by a germ similar to syphilis germ. The germs enter the body through a cut in the skin, causing sores and lumpy growths on the skin. The disease is spread by contact with pus from sores and possibly by insects. It affects mainly children and can be cured by penicillin. Yaws is found chiefly in Africa, southern Asia, and Central and South America.

Yazoo Fraud, controversy created by the Georgia legislature when it granted 35,000,000 acres in the present states of Alabama and Mississippi to four land companies for $500,000. The fraud got its name from the Yazoo River, which ran through part of the grant. Because both Georgia and the federal government claimed the land and because most of the supporters of the grant had been bribed, the grant was repealed in 1796. The land companies denied the right of Georgia to repeal the grant and were upheld by Supreme Court on 1810. The claimants were paid several million dollars in 1814.

Yazoo-Tallahatchie river system, Mississippi **M** 352
Yeager, Charles E., American Air Force officer **S** 469
Year
   annual rhythms: plant and animal life **L** 244
   calendar **C** 11–13
   earth's period of revolution **E** 4
   Martian year **M** 105
   New Year's Day around the world **N** 208–09
   seasons **S** 108–12
   solar year **T** 194
   See also months by name
Yearbooks, books of information and statistics published
    annually **R** 130–31
   encyclopedias **E** 197
   use in research **R** 183
Yeast **F** 88; pictures **F** 89
   beer and brewing **B** 116–17
   bread and baking **B** 385
   considered sac fungi **F** 496, 498
   food spoilage **F** 352
Yeats (YATES), **William Butler,** Irish poet and dramatist
    Y 344; **I** 394
   Abbey Theatre connection **D** 298
   Irish Renaissance in English literature **E** 266
   "Lake Isle of Innisfree, The" **Y** 344
   "Under Ben Bulben," excerpt **Y** 344
Yedo see Tokyo

Yegorov, Boris Borisovich (1937–), Soviet astronaut, b. Moscow. With Vladimir Komarov and Konstantin Feoktistov, he took part in the flight of Voskhod 1 on Oct. 12 and 13, 1964, the world's first multimanned space flight. Yegorov, a doctor, was the first medical man to take active part in a space flight.
   space flight data **S** 344, 345

Yeibichai, night chant and dance of the Navajo Indians **I** 160; picture **I** 161
Yeliseyev, Alexei S., Soviet cosmonaut **S** 344, 345
Yellow, color
   sun's color **E** 22
Yellow dogtooth violets, flowers, picture **W** 168

Yellow fever, disease caused by a virus. It is passed to man through the bite of an infected *Aedes aegypti* mosquito. The disease affects the liver, causing jaundice (a condition in which the skin is yellow) and vomiting of blood. Yellow fever occurs in tropical parts of Africa and South America. Vaccination and mosquito control are the methods used to prevent large-scale outbreaks.
   insects harmful to man **I** 283
   Reed, Walter and control of the disease **R** 128
   viruses **V** 282–85

Yellowfin, fish
   habitat, feeding habits, uses **F** 215
Yellowhammers, or flickers, birds, pictures **B** 208, 242
   state bird of Alabama **A** 113
Yellowhammer State, nickname for Alabama **A** 113
Yellow jackets, wasps **I** 282
Yellow jasmine, flower
   state flower of South Carolina **S** 296
Yellowknife, capital of Northwest Territories, Canada **Y** 365
Yellow Knife, Indians of North America **I** 164, 170
Yellow perch, fish, picture **L** 257
Yellow poplar, or tulip poplar, tree
   state tree of Kentucky **K** 213
   state tree of Tennessee **T** 75
Yellow River, or Hwang Ho, in northern China **C** 262
   San Men dam foundations, picture **D** 18
Yellow Sea **O** 49
Yellowstone Falls, picture **Y** 345
Yellowstone National Park, Wyoming **Y** 345–46
   regional and national parks, purpose and use **P** 77
   canyons, picture **E** 12
   Colter, John, first white man to see it **W** 335
   first national park **N** 44, 46
   geysers and hot springs **G** 192; picture **G** 193
Yellowstone River, United States **M** 431

Yellowthroat, a small bird of the wood warbler family. About 5 inches long, the yellowthroat has a greenish back, yellow throat, and whitish underparts. The males have a black face mask. The yellowthroat usually is found in marshes from Alaska to the West Indies.

Yemen (Aden) **Y** 347
   flag **F** 238
   Middle East, Arabian Peninsula **M** 301; picture **M** 303
Yemen (Sana) **Y** 348–49
   countries of the Middle East **M** 301
   flag **F** 238
   Jewish communities of exile **J** 107
   Middle East, countries of the **M** 301
Yenisei (yen-i-SAI) **River,** Union of Soviet Socialist Republics **R** 248
   flows into Kara Sea **O** 48

Yeomen of the Guard, or **Beefeaters,** since 1485, bodyguard for the king of England. The Yeomen usually wear a red tunic uniform and were nicknamed Beefeaters about 1643 because of their large daily ration of beef. Today's Beefeaters are veterans elected for distinguished conduct.

Yerba maté see Maté, tea

Yerty, Frank Garvin (1916–   ), American author, Negro b. Augusta, Ga. He is known for his historical romances, often about the South of the Civil War era. Such novels as *The Foxes of Harrow*, *Pride's Castle*, and *Griffin's Way* have been best sellers, and several of his books have been made into movies. He received an O. Henry Memorial award in 1944 for his short story "Health Card."

Yerkes (YER-kese), **Robert Mearns** (1876–1956), American psychologist, b. Breadysville, Pa. He is best-known for his studies of intelligence in animals, especially chimpanzees and gorillas. He organized and directed the Yale Laboratories of Primate Biology (renamed Yerkes Laboratories in 1942) in Orange Park, Florida (1929–1941). The first intelligence test for U.S. Army draftees was devised in 1917 under his direction.

Yerkes Observatory, Wisconsin
    largest refracting telescope **A** 473
    refracting telescopes, types of **T** 61–62
Yeshaq, governor of Aksum, Ethiopia
    The Glory of Kings, epic poem **A** 76b
Yeti see Abominable Snowman
Yevtushenko (yev-tu-SHAIN-ko), **Yevgeny,** Russian author **U** 62

Yews, evergreen shrubs that are cultivated for their valuable wood or for ornamental landscape planting. poisonous shrubs **P** 323

Yezidis see Devil worshipers
Yggdrasil (IGG-dra-sil), mythological tree **N** 277
Yiddish language and literature **Y** 350–51
    See also Hebrew language; Hebrew literature
Yin dynasty see Shang dynasty
YMCA see Young Men's Christian Association, National Council of
YMHA see Young Men's and Young Women's Hebrew Association

Yoga, system of Hindu philosophy formulated by Patanjali about A.D. 300. It aims at complete union with the supreme spirit, attained through mental and physical discipline, peace of mind, and a deeper insight into the nature of reality. The ways of achieving its aim include moral preparation, control of the breath and the senses, special postures, mental concentration, and meditation. Picture **H** 132.

Yogurt, or **yoghurt,** Turkish name for a milk product made by adding a culture of certain bacteria to fresh milk. The bacteria cause fermentation, or the formation of acids that prevent the growth of harmful bacteria. Yogurt originated in the Middle East, where fermentation was a valuable means of preserving milk. Yogurt is popular as a nutritious, low-calorie food.

Yoho National Park, British Columbia **B** 406a; picture **B** 406d
Yoknapatawpha (yok-na-pa-TAW-pha), Faulkner's imaginary Mississippi county **F** 71
Yokohama (yo-ko-HA-ma), Japan **J** 40; picture **J** 41
Yolk, egg **E** 88
Yom Kippur, Jewish holy day **J** 120
    religious holidays **R** 154
Yonge (YUNG), **Charlotte Mary,** English novelist **C** 238
Yoritomo Minamoto (yo-ri-TO-mo mi-na-MO-to), first Japanese shogun **J** 43

York, Duke of, English title first held by Edmund of Langley (1341–1402). His grandson, Richard Plantagenet

(1411–60), third duke of York, began the War of the Roses (1455) between the House of York (white rose) and the House of Lancaster (red rose). Since the time of Edward IV (1442–83), who created his younger son duke of York (1474), the title has frequently been given to the second son of the English sovereign.

York, Pennsylvania **P** 142

York, Sergeant (Alvin C. York) (1887–1964), American soldier, b. Fentress County, Tenn. In the battle of the Argonne during World War I he killed 20 Germans, forced the surrender of 132 more, and captured 35 machine guns during one engagement. For this action, which Marshal Foch called the greatest thing accomplished by any noncommissioned soldier in all the armies of Europe, he was awarded the Medal of Honor and the Croix de Guerre. After the war he was given a farm bought by public contributions, and an educational foundation was established in his name.
    famous people from Tennessee **T** 87

York, House of, English royal family **U** 77
    War of the Roses **E** 220
York Factory, trading post, Hudson Bay **M** 82
Yorktown, Virginia
    Revolutionary War ends **R** 208
    Washington receives British surrender **W** 40
Yoruba (YO-ru-ba), a people of Africa
    African art **A** 76; picture **A** 73
    Dahomey **D** 3, 4
    empire of Oyo **N** 256
    Nigeria **N** 253
    poetry **A** 76a
Yosemite (yo-SEM-i-te) **Falls,** California **W** 56b; picture **C** 24
Yosemite National Park **Y** 352–53
    places of interest in California **C** 24
Yoshimasa, Japanese shogun **J** 43–44

Yost, Charles W. (1907–   ), American diplomat, b. Watertown, N.Y. He entered foreign service (1930), and rose to the rank of ambassador. He was U.S. deputy representative to United Nations (1961–66), and was appointed U.S. ambassador to the United Nations (1969).

Yost, Fielding Harris ("Hurry Up") (1871–1946), American athletics director, b. Fairview, W. Va. As director of physical education at the University of Michigan (1901–27), he coached Michigan's "point-a-minute" football teams, winning 164 games, losing 29, tieing 10. He also served as director of athletics at Michigan (1921–41).

Youlou, Fulbert (1917–   ), Congolese politician, b. Moumboulo, French Equatorial Africa. A former Roman Catholic parish priest who was suspended from his priestly functions (1956), he founded a new political party (1956), was elected mayor of Brazzaville (1956), and served as premier and president of the Republic of the Congo (Brazzaville) (1959–63) until forced to resign by labor and military leaders opposed to his policies.

You may fire, when you are ready, Gridley, words of Dewey at battle of Manila Bay, 1898 **S** 375
Young, Brigham, Mormon leader **Y** 353
    Mormons, history of **M** 457
    Mormon Trail **O** 265
    Salt Lake City **S** 22
    Utah, history of **U** 252, 254

Young, Charles (1864–1922), American soldier, b. Mays-

Young, Charles (continued)
lick, Ky. Appointed (1884) to West Point, he•reached the highest rank (colonel) of any Negro in the U.S. Army up to that time. He was in charge of a Negro regiment sent to Cuba during the Spanish-American War and is given credit for coming to the aid of Theodore Roosevelt in the battle of San Juan Hill. His last service was as a military attaché in Liberia, reorganizing the Liberian Army.

Young, "Cy" (Denton True) (1867–1965), American baseball player, b. Gilmore, Ohio. The first man in modern baseball to pitch a perfect game, he pitched 906 games in 22 years, winning 511 (more than any other pitcher). He played for National League teams in Cleveland (1890–98), St. Louis (1899–1900), and Boston (1911) and American League teams in Boston (1901–08) and Cleveland (1909–11). He was elected to the Baseball Hall of Fame in 1937. Baseball's annual pitching awards are named after him.

Young, James, Scottish chemist **K** 235
early use of petroleum **P** 177

Young, John Watts (1930–), American astronaut, b. San Francisco, Calif. A former Navy pilot, Young joined the space program in 1962. He participated in the Gemini 3 (1965), Gemini 10 (1966), and Apollo 10 (1969) flights.
space flight data **S** 344, 345, 347

Young, John Wesley (1879–1932), American mathematician and educator, b. Columbus, Ohio. Young taught at the University of Kansas and at Dartmouth College (1910–32). He was editor of the *Bulletin* of the American Mathematical Society (1907–25) and a founder of the Mathematical Association of America.

Young, Lester, American jazz musician **J** 60
Young, Mahonri, American sculptor **U** 240

Young, Owen D. (1874–1962), American industrialist, b. Van Hornesville, N.Y. He served on the international committees that formed the Dawes Plan and the Young Plan for German reparations and rehabilitation after World War I and on many U.S. Government committees concerned with industrial and economic problems. At the government's request, he created the Radio Corporation of America and became its first chairman (1919–33). He was also chairman of the board of General Electric Co. (1922–39, 1942–44).

Young, Stark (1881–1963), American author, b. Como, Miss. Known especially for his theater reviews, he was on the editorial staff of the *New Republic* (1921–24, 1925–47), associate editor of *Theatre Arts Monthly* (1921–40), and drama critic for the New York *Times* (1924–25). He also wrote poems, plays, and novels.

Young, Thomas (1773–1829), English scientist, b. Milverton. The founder of physiological optics, he discovered the law of the interference of light (contributing to the wave theory of light) and suggested a theory of color sensation that was later developed by Helmholtz (the Young-Helmholtz theory). His work on hieroglyphics helped to decipher the Rosetta stone.
theories about the nature of light **S** 75

Young, Whitney M., Jr. (1921–71), American social-work administrator, Negro, b. Lincoln Ridge, Ky. After working with the St. Paul Urban League (1947–50) and the Omaha Urban League (1950–53), he moved south and became dean of the School of Social Work at Atlanta University (1954–60). As executive director of the National Urban League (1961–71), he was concerned with providing equal opportunity for Negroes. Picture **N** 104.

Young adults see Young people
Youngberries G 301

Young Canada's Book Week, annual event founded (1949) by the Canadian Association of Children's Librarians to interest Canadians in the best reading for young people.

Young Communist League, Soviet youth organization **U** 30–31
Young Hickory, nickname of Franklin Pierce **P** 245
Younghusband, Sir Francis E., English officer **T** 178

Young Life Campaign (YLC) organization, founded in 1941, with headquarters in Colorado Springs, Colo., to present the Christian faith to high-school-age groups. It encourages students' participation in local churches, sponsors the Young Life Institute to prepare youth-work leaders, operates resorts for teen-agers in the western United States and Canada, and publishes *Focus Magazine.*

Young Men's and Young Women's Hebrew Association (YM-YWHA), the Jewish community centers providing social, cultural, and recreational programs. They offer classes in a variety of the arts and sponsor concert hall events in addition to a scholarship program for students, two summer day camps, and other activities. The YMHA and YWHA were founded as separate organizations in 1874 and merged in 1945. Publication is the *Y Bulletin.*

Young Men's Christian Association, National Council of the (YMCA), worldwide fellowship concerned with improving the spiritual, social, recreational, and physical life of young people. The YMCA sponsors sports programs and offers adult education classes and cultural events. Founded in 1851, it has headquarters in New York, N.Y. The YMCA publishes the *National Council Bulletin.*
world headquarters in Jerusalem **J** 80

Young Octobrists, Soviet youth organization **U** 30–31
Young people
adolescence **A** 22–24
drug abuse **D** 329, 331, 332
fashion **F** 71
junior volunteers in hospitals **H** 251; picture **H** 249
paperback books **P** 58a
poverty, chance to break cycle of **P** 424b
rock music **R** 262b, 262c, 262d
service in libraries **L** 171
smoking **S** 203
Twenty-sixth Amendment, U.S. Constitution, vote granted **U** 158
voting for 18 year olds by the 26th amendment **E** 113
See also Clubs; Youth organizations
Young Person's Guide to the Orchestra, The, by Benjamin Britten **E** 271
Youngstown, Ohio O 72
Young Turks, political party **T** 329

Young Women's Christian Association of the United States of America (YWCA), organization of women and girls over 12 that offers recreation programs, clubs, and classes of all kinds. Founded in 1855, it has headquarters in New York, N.Y. It publishes *YWCA Magazine.*

Young Women's Hebrew Association see Young Men's and Young Women's Hebrew Association
Youth hostels H 253–56

Youth organizations
    Boys' Clubs of America **B** 355
    Boy Scout Explorer Posts and Sea Explorer Ships **B** 360
    Camp Fire Girls **C** 37–39
    Exploring division of Scouting for young men and women **B** 360
    farm clubs **F** 45–47
    Future Farmers of America **F** 45, 46
    Future Teachers of America **T** 41–42
    Girl Guides and Girl Scouts **G** 213–19
    Junior Achievement, Inc. **J** 157–58
    parliamentary procedure **P** 79–80
    See *also* Future Homemakers of America; New Farmers of America
Youth's Companion, magazine **M** 16
Ypres (E-pr), **battle of,** 1914 **W** 274
Yriarte (e-ri-AR-tay), **Tomas de,** Spanish fabulist **F** 4
Ytterbium (it-TER-bi-um), element **E** 155, 165
Yttrium, element **E** 155, 165

Yüan dynasty (1260–1368), rule of the Mongols in China. Founded by Kublai Khan, the Yüan dynasty made China part of a huge Mongol empire. The dynasty had 11 rulers and was followed by the Ming dynasty.

Yuan Shih-k'ai (yer-ON sher-KY), Chinese military leader **S** 467
Yucatán (yu-ca-TAN) **Peninsula,** Mexico **M** 243
    ruins of ancient city, Chichén Itzá, picture **I** 153
Yucca plants, picture **W** 169
    method of pollination **P** 320
    state flower of New Mexico **N** 180

Yugoslavia (yu-go-SLA-via) **Y** 354–59
    Balkan wars **B** 19
    flag **F** 240
    folk dancing **F** 299
    "national Communism" **C** 444
    Nixon's visit, picture **N** 262e
    Tito **T** 199
Yukawa (yu-KA-wa), **Hideki,** Japanese scientist **N** 367
Yukon (YU-kon) **River,** North America **R** 248–49
    Alaska **A** 132, 133
    Canada **C** 52; **Y** 361; picture **Y** 362
Yukon Territory, Canada **Y** 360–65
    Canada's Cordillera **C** 51
Yule, William Truman, English chemist **D** 316
Yule log, Christmas custom from Norse mythology **N** 277
Yulee, David Levy, American statesman **F** 271
Yuma, Arizona **A** 412

Yung Lo (1359–1424), third emperor (1403–24) of the Ming dynasty in China. His rule is noted for the naval expeditions sent to countries south of China and the transfer (1421) of the capital from Nanking to Peking.

Yuri Dolgoruki (dol-go-RU-ki), Russian prince **M** 466
Yurok, Indians of North America **I** 180
Yurts, tents **D** 128; pictures **A** 458, **M** 415, **N** 271
    homes that move about **H** 175–76
    Mongolia's nomads **M** 413
YWCA *see* Young Women's Christian Association of the United States of America
YWHA *see* Young Men's and Young Women's Hebrew Association

Z, 26th letter of the English alphabet **Z** 366
See also Alphabet
Zacharias (zack-a-RY-as), father of John the Baptist
J 122
Zadkine (zod-KENE), **Ossip,** Russian-French sculptor
statue in Rotterdam **N** 121

Zafrullah (za-frull-AH) **Khan, Chaudhri Sir Muhammad**
(1893–   ), Pakistani statesman, b. Sialkot, West
Pakistan. Since 1926 he has been active in government
affairs, first for the local Punjab district, then for India,
and after the division of India and Pakistan, for
Pakistan. From 1947 to 1954 he was minister of foreign
affairs and commonwealth relations for Pakistan and
leader of Pakistan's delegation to the United Nations. In
1962 he was elected president of the United Nations
General Assembly and in 1964 was appointed to the
International Court of Justice.

Zagreb (ZA-greb), Yugoslavia **Y** 357; picture **Y** 356
Zagros Mountains, Iran and Iraq **I** 374, 379
Zaharias (za-HARR-i-as), **Mildred "Babe" Didrikson,**
American athlete **Z** 366
a one-girl track team at the 1932 Olympiad **O** 111
first popular woman professional golfer **G** 262
Zahir, Mohammed see Mohammed Zahir Shah

Zaibatsu, group of powerful financial families in Japan,
composed mainly of the Mitsui, the Mitsubishi, the
Sumitomo, and the Yasuda families. After World War I
these families were encouraged by the government to
invest in business and by the 1930's they controlled
most of the industry, commerce, and banking in Japan.
Closely allied with the government, *zaibatsu* families
held many important posts. After World War II, by
authority of General MacArthur, no member of the
zaibatsu could hold office or a high position in business.
But the *zaibatsu* families are still very influential.

Zaïre, Republic of **Z** 366a–366d
flag **F** 235
independence from Belgium **B** 131
village, picture **A** 60
Zalofs, nonsense figures **P** 501
Zambezi (zom-BE-zi) **River,** east central Africa **R** 249
Africa, rivers of **A** 50
Kariba dam construction, picture **D** 17
Mozambique **M** 500–01
Rhodesia **R** 229
Zambia **Z** 367–68
Zambia **Z** 367–68
flag **F** 236

Zambo, Spanish-American word for people of mixed
Negro and Indian origin. During the 17th century, the
Spanish brought slaves into the Caribbean area to work
the plantations. Many of the slaves escaped into the
jungles, and eventually a mixed Indian and Negro
population grew up.

Zamboanga, Philippines, picture **F** 297
Zamenhof (ZOM-yen-hof), **Ludwig Lazarus,** Russian inventor of Esperanto **U** 194; **L** 40

Zane, Ebenezer (1747–1812), American pioneer, b. near
what is now Moorefield, W. Va. In 1770 he settled with his
family at the mouth of Wheeling Creek in the northern
panhandle of West Virginia. Zane's tiny fort marked the
end of settled land, and pioneers moving West stopped
there before crossing the Ohio River. During the
Revolutionary War, Zane defended the fort against the
Indians and the British. Zane and his brother Jonathan

explored most of Ohio and guided surveying expeditions
through the unknown territory. The Zane family founded
the town of Zanesville, Ohio, in 1799 and the town of
Lancaster in 1800.

Zane's Trace, early trail **O** 66
pioneer life **P** 260

Zangwill, Israel (1864–1926), English novelist and playwright, b. London. He wrote historical studies of the
achievements of the Jewish people, such as *Dreamers of
the Ghetto, Children of the Ghetto,* and *The Melting Pot.*
He also wrote general fiction, including *Merely Mary Ann,*
a humorous story about a servant girl. Like many of his
other works, this novel was also made into a play.
Zangwill was an extremely outspoken man, and he
defended unpopular issues.

Zanuck, Darryl Francis (1902–   ), American film producer, b. Wahoo, Neb. He was with Warner Brothers
(1924–33), helped found the company that became 20th-
Century Fox, and made government films during World
War II. He started with Fox in 1945 and except for 6 years
(1956–62), when he was an independent producer, he continued to run the studio until he relinquished the chairmanship in 1971. Zanuck was partly responsible for the
introduction of talking pictures (1927), and in 1953 he
produced the first cinemascope film (*The Robe*). His
other films include *The Grapes of Wrath, All About Eve,*
and *The Longest Day.*

Zanzibar, former republic, now part of Tanzania **T** 16
Zanzibar Town, Tanzania **T** 19; picture **T** 18
Zapata (sa-PA-ta), **Emiliano,** Mexican soldier **M** 250
Zapatistas, painting by Orozco **L** 66
Zappa, Frank, American rock music composer and
performer **R** 262d
Zarathustra (zar-a-THU-stra), or **Zoroaster,** founder of the
religion of ancient Persia **Z** 380
civilization of ancient Persia **A** 226
religions of the world **R** 152
Zaruma (sa-RU-ma), Ecuador **E** 55
Zealand, island on which Copenhagen is built **D** 106
Zebedee, father of Apostles James and John **A** 333
Zebra fish, picture **F** 202
Zebras **H** 244; picture **H** 211
in Africa, pictures **A** 47, **T** 294
Zebu (say-BO), or humped cattle **H** 221; picture **H** 216
livestock of Nepal **N** 113

Zebulun (ZEB-u-lun), or **Zabulon,** in the Old Testament,
the 10th son of Jacob. The name also refers to the one of
the 12 tribes of Israel descended from him. "Zebulun" is
said to mean "dwelling," and the land where the tribe of
Zebulun lived was supposedly very fertile, with good harbors nearby.

Zebulun Valley, Israel **I** 441

Zechariah (zeck-a-RY-ah), in the Old Testament (Zechariah
1–8), 11th minor prophet, son of Berechiah. He lived
during the second half of the 6th century B.C., in the
period of the return of the Jews to Palestine from
Babylonian exile. His major aims were the rebuilding of
the Temple and the revival of ritual.
Michelangelo's painting of **B** 158

Zechariah, book of Bible, Old Testament **B** 155, 156

Zedekiah (zed-e-KY-ah), son of Josiah and last king of
Judah (597–586 B.C.). He was a weak ruler, placed on the
throne by the Babylonian conqueror Nebuchadnezzar.

When Zedekiah joined the Egyptian rebellion against the Babylonians, Nebuchadnezzar besieged Jerusalem. As famine spread in the city, the frightened Zedekiah called in the prophet Jeremiah, who warned the king that all would be lost unless he made peace with the Babylonians. Zedekiah refused to listen, and Jeremiah's prophecies came true. Zedekiah's sons were put to death, and he was taken in captivity to Babylon.

Zeeman (ZAY-mon), **Pieter** (1865–1943), Dutch physicist, b. Zonnemaire. He is best known for his discovery in 1896 of the Zeeman effect: the spectral lines of a source of light surrounded by a very strong magnetic field are split up. This effect confirmed the theories of Zeeman's former teacher, H. A. Lorentz, who collaborated with Zeeman in the experiment. The two men shared the 1902 Nobel prize in physics for this discovery.

Zeno (ZE-no) **of Citium** (lived during late 4th and early 3rd century B.C.), Greek philosopher, native of Citium, Cyprus. Zeno founded the Stoic philosophy, which professed the belief that the world was regulated by natural laws that no one could change; but man, by mastering his own emotions and understanding his actions, could live a virtuous and happy life independent of all that went on around him. Zeno founded a school called the Painted Porch (Stoa Poecilē), where he taught this philosophy.

Zeno of Elea (5th century B.C.), Greek philosopher, native of Elea, a Greek colony in Lucania, Italy. Zeno defended the philosophy of Parmenides, who believed that what was true never changed, while other philosophers held that the universe was built around orderly changes.

Zeppelin (ZEPP-lin), **Count Ferdinand von,** (1838–1917) German soldier, designer of the first really successful airship, or dirigible, b. Constance, on the German-Swiss border. Zeppelin, a retired army officer, began work on power-driven lighter-than-air craft in the 1890's; his first airship was completed in 1900. The cigar-shaped craft reached a height of over 1,000 feet and reportedly stayed aloft for 17 minutes, until mechanical failure forced it down into Lake Constance. Zeppelin improved the performance of subsequent airships until by 1913 a regular passenger service was possible.

Zhukov (ZHU-kof), **Georgi Konstantinovich** (1894–), Soviet general, b. Staelkova. During World War II he was victorious against the Germans at Moscow (1941) and Stalingrad (1942) and was promoted to marshal of the Soviet Union (1943). Relegated to a minor post by Stalin after the war, he was later reinstated (1953). He was appointed minister of defense (1955) and made a member of the Presidium (1956). His military prestige helped Khrushchev overcome attempted coup by Malenkov in 1957, but soon after that Zhukov himself was removed from power. He wrote *The Memoirs of Marshal Zhukov.*

Ziegfeld (ZIG-feld), **Florenz** (1867–1932), American theater manager, b. Chicago, Ill. In 1907 Ziegfeld presented a spectacular musical revue based on Paris' Folies Bergères, the first of the revues that came to be known as the Ziegfeld Follies. He also produced other shows, such as Noel Coward's *Bitter Sweet* and Jerome Kern and Oscar Hammerstein's *Show Boat.*

Zimbalist, Efrem (1889–), Russian-American violinist, b. Rostov, Russia. He studied under Leopold Auer, and in 1907 he made his European debut in Berlin and toured Europe. He went to the United States (1911) and in 1914 married singer Alma Gluck. Since 1941 Zimbalist has been director of the Curtis Institute of Music in Philadelphia, Pa. He has written many works for violin, piano, voice, and orchestra.

Zinnia, summer- and autumn-flowering plant native to Mexico and Central America. Zinnias were first planted in gardens in North America and Europe around 1860. The round, button-shaped zinnia flower is made up of many rows of closely packed petals. Zinnias are very colorful. They are hardy and easily grown from seed. Pictures **G** 38, 48.

Zinzendorf (TZIN-tzen-dorf), **Nikolaus Ludwig, Count von** (1700–1760), German religious reformer, b. Dresden. Zin-

Zinzendorf, Nikolaus Ludwig, Count von (continued) zendorf turned his country estate, Herrnhut, into a refuge for persecuted Moravians and developed the small Protestant sect into a large, strongly-united missionary group. His zeal led to his exile in 1736. In 1741 he went to America where he established Moravian congregations, mainly in Pennsylvania. He returned to Germany in 1748.

Zip code, numerical system to speed up mail delivery. Each zip code is made up of five numbers. The first number stands for geographical areas designated 1 through 10. The second and third numbers stand for an area in the states. Thus the first three numbers grouped together pinpoint the specific area to which the mail is addressed. The fourth and fifth numbers together are the former zone number. The zip-code system was started in 1961 by the United States Post Office to service the 50 states, Puerto Rico, and the Virgin Islands.

Zipper, slide fastener for clothing, briefcases, and other objects, first developed in the 1890's. Most zippers have two sets of interlocking teeth, which are joined by pulling a catch along the teeth. Zippers are made of many materials, including brass, steel, aluminum, nickel, silver, and nylon. In 1950 a tongue-and-groove zipper was introduced. These zippers are made of plastic.

Zipporah (zip-PO-rah), in Old Testament (Exodus 2:21, 4:24, 18:3), wife of Moses. Moses came to the defense of the seven daughters of the Midian priest Jethro, who were being chased away from a well by shepherds. In gratitude Jethro gave Moses his daughter Zipporah in marriage. Zipporah bore two sons.

Zircon, mineral composed of zirconium silicate ($ZrSiO_4$). Found in igneous rocks, it usually occurs as tetragonal crystals. Its color may be brown, gray, green, reddish, or violet. Clear crystals are used as gems. Zircons are used industrially as catalysts, ceramics, electrical insulators, and heat-resisting materials. Zircon is also useful as an ore of the metal zirconium.

Zombi, or **zombie,** Voodoo term for the so-called walking dead. Members of the Voodoo cult believe a zombi to be a dead person whose soul has been stolen by a sorcerer. The zombi walks about, but has no will of his own and must do all that the owner of his soul demands. Some authorities believe that the myth about zombis grew up because practitioners of voodoo sometimes drugged their victims so that they moved in a deathlike trance.

Zorach (ZO-rock), **William** (1887–1966), American sculptor and painter, b. Eurburg, Lithuania. Zorach's stone and wood carvings are in museums throughout the United States. Four of his paintings were shown at the famous 1912 Salon d'Automne show in Paris. His work was also in the 1913 New York Armory Show, the first major exhibition of modern art in America. He taught sculpture at the Art Students League until 1960. His sculptures include *Floating Figure* and *Reclining Cat.*

Zorn (SORN), **Anders** (1860–1920), Swedish artist, b. Mora. A sculptor, painter, and etcher, he was particularly popular as a portraitist. He traveled widely, painting portraits of Theodore Roosevelt and William Howard Taft, among others, during a visit to the United States. His other paintings are mainly genre scenes of Swedish peasant life and female nudes.

South Africa **S** 268
Zulu girl, picture **A** 54
Zuni (ZOON-yi), Indians of North America **I** 191–92

Zuppke, Robert Carl (1879–1957), American football coach, b. Berlin, Germany. A resident of the United States since 1881, he made his name as head football coach at the University of Illinois (1913–41). A believer in surprise maneuvers and a training system based on rhythm, he coached national champion teams in 1914, 1919, 1923, and 1927. He was elected to the National Football Hall of Fame (1951).

Zurbarán (thoor-ba-RON), **Francisco de,** Spanish painter **B** 60
Zurich, Switzerland **S** 498; picture **S** 499

Zweig (TZVIKE), **Stefan,** Austrian writer **G** 181

Zwingli (TZVING-li), **Huldreich** (1484–1531), Swiss religious leader, b. Wildhaus. Starting the Protestant Reformation in Switzerland, he believed in the ultimate authority of Scriptures and the subordination of Church administration to the state government. He was excommunicated from the Roman Catholic Church, whose ritual and papal politics he criticized severely, but he gained support of the people of Zurich. In 1531 Zwingli and his followers fought the papal forces, and Zwingli was killed in the battle of Kappel.
Protestantism in the history of Christianity **C** 286

Zworykin (ZWOR-i-kin), **Vladimir,** Russian-born American television specialist, picture **E** 147

ILLUSTRATION CREDITS

The following list credits, by page, the sources of illustrations used in volume W-X-Y-Z of THE NEW BOOK OF KNOWLEDGE. Credits are listed illustration by illustration—left to right, top to bottom. Wherever appropriate, the name of the photographer or artist has been listed with the source, the two being separated by a dash. When two or more illustrations appear on one page, their credits are separated by semicolons.

3 George Buctel
4 British Travel Association
5 U.S. Department of the Interior, Fish and Wildlife Service; Marineland of the Pacific, Los Angeles.
7 Marineland of the Pacific, Los Angeles; U.S. Department of the Interior, Fish and Wildlife Service.
8 Ylla—Rapho Guillumette
12 Granger Collection
15 Color Illustration Inc.; Rutherford Platt; Bob & Elsie Boggs; Bob & Ira Spring.
16 Ed Drews—Photo Researchers; Diversified Map Corp.
17 Diversified Map Corp.
18 Diversified Map Corp.
21 Washington Department of Commerce and Economic Development; David Muench; David Muench.
24 Paul Granger
25 National Park Service
26 Diversified Map Corp.
27 Ray Atkeson; Ellis-Sawyer—FPG.
31 George Buctel
33 K. B. Roche—Monkmeyer; K. B. Roche—Monkmeyer; K. B. Roche—Monkmeyer.
34 Sidney Bernstein—Photo Researchers; G. Tames—Globe; Tom Hollyman—Photo Researchers; K. B. Roche—Monkmeyer.
36 James Cooper
37 Pennsylvania Academy of the Fine Arts
38 *American Heritage*—Mellon Collection, National Gallery of Art
41 *American Heritage*—Henry Francis Du-Pont Winterthur Museum, Wilmington
42 Bradley Smith—Photo Researchers
44 American Clock and Watch Museum, Bristol, Connecticut; Courtesy of Metropolitan Museum of Art, Gift of the Estate of James Hayen Hyde, 1959.
45 Bettmann Archive
47 Russ Kinne—Photo Researchers; ZFA.
48 Russ Kinne—Photo Researchers; Lisl Steiner; Russ Kinne—Photo Researchers; Russ Kinne—Photo Researchers; Russ Kinne—Photo Researchers.
49 Omega Watch Co.
50 Bulova Watch Co.; Le Coultre Watch Co.
51 Florida State News Bureau

52- Lee J. Ames
54
55 George Bakacs
56a Publishers Graphics
58 U.S. Public Health Service
61 George Bakacs
64 Fred Mason
67 George Bakacs
69 George Sottung
73- Wayne Dunham
75
77- Wayne Dunham
79
81- Wayne Dunham
83
84 U.S. Department of Commerce, Weather Bureau; Wayne Dunham.
85 Wayne Dunham
86 Wayne Dunham
88- Wayne Dunham
90
91 U.S. Department of Commerce, Weather Bureau
92 Research Information Services, General Electric Research Laboratories, The General Electric Company
93 U.S. Department of Agriculture
94 United Air Lines
96 U.S. Department of Commerce, Weather Bureau
97 Ron Perkins—Basketry, courtesy of Azuma, New York City, material, courtesy of America House, New York City, tapestry, "Easterwood," courtesy of America House, pillow, "Auvil," courtesy of America House; Gerald McConnell.
98 Gerald McConnell
100 H. B. Vestal
102 H. B. Vestal
103 H. B. Vestal
105 Arabelle Wheatley
107 Edward Vebell
108 Lee J. Ames
109 Lee J. Ames
110 U.S. Department of Commerce, National Bureau of Standards
112 Lee J. Ames
113 Lee J. Ames
123 Lee J. Ames
127 Color Illustration Inc.; Stephen Collins—Photo Researchers; Stephen Collins—

Photo Researchers; West Virginia Department of Commerce.
128 Schaefer & Seawell; Diversified Map Corp.
129 Diversified Map Corp.
130 Diversified Map Corp.
133 Schaefer & Seawell
134 Ragsdale—FPG
136 Warren Miller
137 Diversified Map Corp.
139 Shostal; Zehrt—FPG.
145 George Sottung
146 George Sottung
148 Chet Reneson
149 Chet Reneson
151 Chet Reneson
153 D. Richard Statile—DPI
155 James Curran
157 Jack Hearne
163 White House Historical Association
164 White House Historical Association
168 Chet Reneson
169 Publix Pictorial Service; Fred H. Ragsdale—Publix Pictorial Service; Josef Muench; Franklin Photo Agency; Robert Lee Behme—Photo Researchers; Jane Kinne—Photo Researchers; Franklin Photo Agency; Shostal.
170 Franklin Photo Agency; Josef Muench; Irvin L. Oakes—Photo Researchers; Louis Quitt—Photo Researchers; Irvin L. Oakes—Photo Researchers; Josef Muench; Ken Brote—Photo Researchers.
171 Chet Reneson
176 James Cooper
177 Granger Collection
178 Underwood & Underwood
180 Brown Brothers; Granger Collection; Granger Collection.
182- From *Musical Instruments* by A. J.
183 Hipkins, illustrated by William Gibb, published by A. & C. Black, Ltd., London
184 Harry Schaare
185 UPI
186 Harry Schaare
187 Harry Schaare
189 Tom Hollyman—Photo Researchers
190 George Buctel; National Film Board of Canada, Ottawa, Courtesy of Information Office, Canadian Consulate General, New York.

190b Reprinted by permission of Van Nostrand Reinhold Company from *Building with Wire* by John Lidstone, photographs by Roger Kerkham.

191 Reprinted by permission of Van Nostrand Reinhold Company from *Building with Wire* by John Lidstone, photographs by Roger Kerkham.

193 Color Illustration Inc.; Robert Holland; Russ Kinne—Photo Researchers; L. L. Steimley.

194 Diversified Map Corp.; FPG.

195 Diversified Map Corp.

198 Diversified Map Corp.

200 Kraft Foods, Division of National Dairy Products Corp.; C. W. Sorensen.

202 Warren Miller

203 University of Wisconsin, News and Publications Service

204 Ewing Galloway

205 Diversified Map Corp.

209 Ken Longtemps

210 Tom McHugh—Photo Researchers; James R. Simon—Photo Researchers (England).

211 Bettmann Archive

212a Leonard Freed—Magnum Photos

212b Marilyn Silverstone—Magnum Photos; Burt Glinn—Magnum Photos—UPI.

215 George Sottung

217 Art Reference Bureau; Shostal; Shostal; Louis Renault—Photo Researchers.

218 Shostal; Shostal; Laurence Lowry—Rapho Guillumette; Tatch—Shostal.

219 Gullers—Rapho; Baum—Rapho; Riboud—Magnum; Silberstein—Rapho.

220 Laurence Lowry—Rapho Guillumette; NASA; Government of India Tourist Office; Marc & Evelyne Bernheim—Rapho Guillumette; Sovfoto.

221 Harrison Forman; Serrillier—Rapho Guillumette; Ray Manley—Shostal.

223 Ron Perkins—United States Plywood Corp.; Ron Perkins—Dykes Lumber Company; Ron Perkins—Albert Constantine & Son, Inc.; Ron Perkins—Dykes Lumber Company; Ron Perkins—Dykes Lumber Company; Ron Perkins—United States Plywood Corp.; Ron Perkins—Albert Constantine & Son, Inc.; Ron Perkins—Albert Constantine & Son, Inc.; Ron Perkins—Dykes Lumber Company; Ron Perkins—Albert Constantine & Son, Inc.; Ron Perkins—Albert Constantine & Son, Inc.; Ron Perkins—Dykes Lumber Company.

224 Ron Perkins—Dykes Lumber Company; Ron Perkins—Dykes Lumber Company; Ron Perkins—Dykes Lumber Company; Ron Perkins—Albert Constantine & Son, Inc.; Ron Perkins—Dykes Lumber Company; Ron Perkins—Dykes Lumber Company; Ron Perkins—Dykes Lumber Company; Ron Perkins—Albert Constantine & Son, Inc.; Ron Perkins—Dykes Lumber Company; Ron Perkins—United States Plywood Corp.; Ron Perkins—Dykes Lumber Company; Ron Perkins—Albert Constantine & Son, Inc.

229 Museum of Modern Art, New York, Gift of Victor S. Riesenfeld

231 Gerald McConnell

232 Gerald McConnell

233 Gerald McConnell

234 Jerry Cooke—Photo Researchers

244— Miller Pope

250

252 Chuck McVicker

255 NASA photograph, courtesy, Hasselblad

256 Wesley B. McKeown

258 Harry Scott

259 Harry Scott

260— Wesley B. McKeown

267

270 Brown Brothers; Brown Brothers; Granger Collection; Granger Collection; Granger Collection; Brown Brothers; Brown Brothers.

271 © 1914 by The New York Times Company, reprinted by permission

272 Wide World Photos

273 Musée de la Guerre, Paris; J. M. Flagg—West Point Museum.

275 L'Illustration; Radio Times Hulton Picture Library.

276 © 1915 by The New York Times Company, reprinted by permission

277 Imperial War Museum, London; Pictorial Parade; Camera Press-Pix; Imperial War Museum, London.

278 Wesley B. McKeown

279 Wesley B. McKeown

280 Brown Brothers

286 Wide World Photos

287 UPI

289 Keystone Press Agency

292 Harry Scott

293 U.S. Navy

294 Harry Scott

295 British Information Services

296 Harry Scott

298 UPI

299 UPI

300 Harry Scott

301 U.S. Army

304 UPI

307 Wide World Photos

309 Walter Dawn

310 Douglas Faulkner; R. C. Hermes—National Audubon Society; Russ Kinne—Photo Researchers.

311 Don Miller

312 Russ Kinne—Photo Researchers; Hugh Spencer

313 Tom Hollyman—Photo Researchers

315 Ezra Stoller—E. Stoller Associates

319 British Museum

320 Maryland Diocesan Manuscripts on deposit in the Peabody Institute Library, Baltimore, Maryland; Ross Collection, Museum of Fine Arts, Boston.

321 Pierpont Morgan Library

322 James R. Simon; Bernt L. Wills; James R. Simon; Color Illustration Inc.

324 Diversified Map Corp.

326 Diversified Map Corp.

327 Tuffin—Photo Trends

328 C. W. Sorensen

332 Warren Miller

333 Grant Heilman; Esther Henderson—Rapho Guillumette.

334 Shostal; Diversified Map Corp.

340 Eastman Kodak Company; Lee J. Ames.

341 Lee J. Ames; Eastman Kodak Company.

343 Ho Shikyao, China Photo Service—Eastfoto; Caio Mario Garrubba—Ralpho Guillumette.

344 Yu Chen Chien, China Photo Service—Eastfoto; Hsiao Chua, China Photo Service—Eastfoto.

346 Shostal; David Muench; Esther Henderson—Rapho Guillumette.

348 Arab Information Center

349 George Buctel

352 Shostal; David Muench.

354 Shostal

355 George Buctel

356 Carl Frank—Photo Researchers

359 Fritz Henle—Photo Researchers; Jerry Cooke—Photo Researchers.

360 Annan

362 Josef Muench

363 George Buctel

364 National Film Board of Canada

366a George Buctel

366c W. D. Friedman—PIP

366d Cyr Agency

367 George Buctel

368 Editorial Photocolor Archives

373 Graphic Arts International

375 Jerry Cooke; Gottscho-Schleisner.

376 Marc Riboud—Magnum

377 Shostal; Jerry Cooke.

378 W. H. Hodge; J. Zehrt—FPG.